McDougal Littell
CLASSZONE

Visit **classzone.com** and get connected.

ClassZone resources provide instruction, planning and assessment support for teachers.

State-Specific Resources

- Select your state and access state-specific resources

Literature and Reading Center

- Selection-specific content includes vocabulary practice, research links, and extension activities for writing and critical thinking
- Author Online provides information about each author, as well as in-depth author studies on selected writers
- English Learner support for a variety of languages includes audio summaries of selections and a Multi-Language Academic Glossary

Vocabulary Center

- Vocabulary practice and games reinforce skills
- Multi-Language Academic Glossary provides definitions in many languages

Writing and Grammar Center

- Quick-Fix Editing Machine provides grammar help in a student-friendly format
- Writing Templates and graphic organizers promote clear, orderly communication

Media Center

- Media Analysis Guides encourage critical thinking skills
- Project Ideas, Storyboards, and Production Templates inspire creative media projects

You have immediate access to the the online version of the textbook and *ClassZone* resources at **www.classzone.com**

M C D K L M L H L P I H U

Use this code to create your own user name and password.

McDougal Littell
Where Great Lessons Begin

McDougal Littell
LITERATURE

Essential Course of Study

Table of Contents

Student Guide

Embedded Standards Support

Full Standards Correlation

McDougal Littell
EVANSTON, ILLINOIS • BOSTON • DALLAS

SENIOR PROGRAM CONSULTANTS

JANET ALLEN
Reading and Literacy Specialist, Lecturer, Consultant, and Author; creator of the "It's Never Too Late for Literacy" institutes

JUDITH A. LANGER
Distinguished Professor at the University at Albany, State University of New York; Director of the Center on English Learning and Achievement; Director of the Albany Institute for Research in Education

ARTHUR N. APPLEBEE
Leading Professor, School of Education at the University at Albany, State University of New York; Director of the Center on English Learning and Achievement

ROBERT J. MARZANO
Senior Scholar at Mid-Continent Research for Education and Learning (McREL); Associate Professor at Cardinal Stritch University in Milwaukee, Wisconsin; President of Marzano & Associates

JIM BURKE
Lecturer and Author; Teacher of English at Burlingame High School, Burlingame, California

DONNA M. OGLE
Professor of Reading and Language at National-Louis University in Chicago, Illinois

DOUGLAS CARNINE
Professor of Education at the University of Oregon; Director of the Western Region Reading First Technical Assistance Center

CAROL BOOTH OLSON
Senior Lecturer in the Department of Education at the University of California, Irvine; Director of the UCI site of the National Writing Project

YVETTE JACKSON
Executive Director of the National Urban Alliance for Effective Education

CAROL ANN TOMLINSON
Professor of Educational Research, Foundations, and Policy at the University of Virginia; Co-Director of the University's Institutes on Academic Diversity

ROBERT T. JIMÉNEZ
Professor of Language, Literacy, and Culture at Vanderbilt University

ENGLISH LEARNER SPECIALISTS

MARY LOU McCLOSKEY
Director of Teacher Development
and Curriculum Design for Educo
in Atlanta, Georgia

LYDIA STACK
International ESL consultant

CURRICULUM SPECIALIST

WILLIAM L. McBRIDE
Curriculum Specialist,
Lecturer and Author

MEDIA SPECIALISTS

DAVID M. CONSIDINE
Professor of Instructional
Technology and Media Studies
at Appalachian State University
in North Carolina

LARKIN PAULUZZI
Teacher and Media Specialist;
trainer for the New Jersey
Writing Project

LISA K. SCHEFFLER
Teacher and Media Specialist

McDougal Littell
LITERATURE

Where Great Lessons Begin

Great Lessons Begin with You.

You teach. You inspire. We help.

We help you with support for every standard, every selection, and every student.

WriteSmart CD-ROM
An interactive writing instruction tool, resource bank, and rubric generator.

Resource Manager
Provides all-in-one support for true differentiation.

Standards Lesson File
Gives you a fast, organized approach to teaching every standard.

CONSULTANT'S CORNER

Bob Marzano
McDougal Littell provides maximum support to teachers in terms of instructional strategies and addressing national and state standards. Used well, this literature series can dramatically enhance student achievement while maximizing teacher creativity.

Great Lessons Begin with
Your Students.

They wonder. They question. We help.

We help your students become active readers, writers, and thinkers.

The **Student's Edition** helps engage and motivate students with a vibrant mix of selections.

Media Smart DVD-ROM
Helps promote critical thinking through analysis of a variety of media.

CONSULTANT'S CORNER

Janet Allen
In choosing to work on writing a literature program, I found a home with McDougal Littell because all our decisions could be based on students' needs and teachers' expertise. It was a perfect match for my interests and experience.

Carol Ann Tomlinson
Students come to us as a mixed set. They don't learn in the same ways, aren't motivated by the same things, and don't function at the same pace or depth. What I've always cared about is how teachers can help diverse learners succeed by teaching flexibly......that flexibility is built into this program.

Great Lessons Begin with
McDougal Littell

Teacher Resources

Time-saving, easy-to-use teacher resources make
lesson planning and preparation simple.

Electronic Resources

Core Teacher Resources include:

Teacher's Edition

Easy Planner DVD-ROM

Resource Manager

MediaSmart
Helps promote critical
thinking through analysis
of a variety of media.

WriteSmart
An interactive writing
instruction tool, resource
bank, and rubric generator.

Power Presentations
A collection of dynamic classroom
presentation materials including
leveled discussion questions,
graphic organizers, and interactive
vocabulary practice.

McDougal Littell Assessment System
Test Generator

Assessment File
Provides comprehensive opportunities
to assess student progress with an array
of tests including placement, selection,
unit, and benchmark.

Best Practices Toolkit
Motivate students with engaging
activities, over 200 graphic
organizer transparencies, and
research-based strategies from
our program consultants.

Standards Lesson File
Stand-alone lessons ensure
standards mastery.

Literature.

Student Resources

A complete program of technology and print resources provides support for differentiated student learning.

Core Student Resources include:

Student's Edition

eEdition online and DVD-ROM

InterActive Reader & Writer
- **Strategic Reading Support**
- **Critical Analysis**

Both versions of the InterActive Reader & Writer include leveled readings, additional nonfiction, and test preparation.

Audio Anthology
Enables students to hear pronunciation, phrasing, and interpretations as they follow along in their textbook.

Multi-Language Academic Glossary Online
Facilitates comprehension of academic vocabulary with key terms and definitions in 10 languages.

ClassZone.com
Provides a wealth of interactive resources for literature, reading, writing, grammar, vocabulary, spelling, and assessment.

Novels
Over 700 novels, works of nonfiction, and plays promote independent learning and reading.

Grammar for Writing

Grammar for Writing Workbook
Supports systematic, student-friendly instruction in all aspects of grammar, usage, and mechanics.

Great Lessons Begin with
Assessment that Informs Your Daily Instruction

Ongoing, integrated test practice and assessment give you the power, flexibility and feedback to prepare all your students for success. McDougal Littell also provides tools for reteaching and remediation that ensure skills mastery for all students.

- **Assessment File** Everything you need to structure an assessment plan that both evaluates student success and informs instruction. In addition to Selection Tests, Quizzes, and Daily Skills Practice, you will also have Benchmark Tests to track your students' accomplishments.

- **Grammar for Writing** A comprehensive handbook that provides instruction and practice for all aspects of grammar, usage, and mechanics and facilitates preparation for standardized tests.

McDougal Littell
LITERATURE

- **WriteSmart** A rich presentation tool for writing instruction that includes Ideas for Writing, InterActive Student Models for guided and independent analysis, InterActive Graphic Organizers, InterActive Revision Lessons, and a Rubric Generator.

- **Test Generator** This CD-ROM helps you assess both skills and comprehension with leveled, customizable test questions.

Available at **CLASSZONE.COM.**

The **McDougal Littell Assessment System (MLAS)** is a flexible, web-based program that allows you to use assessment as a teaching tool. This seamless testing and remediation system gives you a fast and easy way to:

TEST Unique testing is custom-built to your standards.

SCORE Automatic scoring gives you results in minutes.

REPORT Diagnostic reports show you what standards were missed.

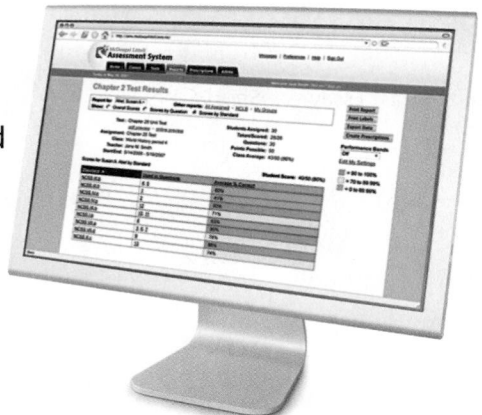

RETEACH Personalized remediation helps you target reteaching.

Introducing

The Essential Course of Study

So much to read and test with so little time! McDougal Littell helps you choose the lessons your students need to master critical skills that appear on all types of assessments.

The Essential Course of Study on the pages that follow indicates which selections and workshops you should teach in order to cover the main skills needed in the language arts curriculum. ▶

Essential Course of Study

	UNIT 1 Narrative Structure	UNIT 2 Characterization and Point of View	UNIT 3 Setting, Mood, and Imagery	UNIT 4 Theme and Symbol
LITERATURE	Literary Analysis Workshop: Plot and Conflict *A Sound of Thunder* *The Most Dangerous Game* *Daughter of Invention* *The Gift of the Magi* • Plot stages • Conflict • Sequence • Foreshadowing • Irony • Predict • Inferences	Literary Analysis Workshop: Character and Point of View *Pancakes* *The Necklace* *Hamadi* • Point of view • Conclusions • Inferences • Monitor • Character motivation	Literary Analysis Workshop: Setting, Mood, and Imagery *A Christmas Memory* *Through the Tunnel* *The Cask of Amontillado* • Setting • Setting as symbol • Mood • Imagery • Paraphrase • Details	Literary Analysis Workshop: Theme and Symbol *Marigolds* *The Scarlet Ibis* *Poem on Returning to Dwell in the Country/ My Heart Leaps Up/* *The Sun* • Theme • Universal theme • Symbol • Inferences • Conclusions
NONFICTION AND INFORMATIONAL MATERIAL	*Seabiscuit* *Four Good Legs Between Us/ Seabiscuit/ Races on the Radio* • Sequence • Author's purpose • Synthesize • Conclusions		*A Walk in the Woods* *Wilderness Letter* • Setting amd mood • Author's perspective • Primary sources • Cite evidence	Math and After Math • Implied main idea • Sequence
WRITING	Personal Narrative	Comparison-contrast Essay	Short Story	
SPEAKING, LISTENING, AND MEDIA	Informal Speech			

UNIT 5 Author's Purpose	UNIT 6 Argument and Persuasion	UNIT 7 Poetry	UNIT 8 Style and Voice	UNIT History, Culture, and the Author
	Primal Screen / The Pedestrian • Message across genres	Literary Analysis Workshop: The Language of Poetry *My Papa's Waltz/ I ask My Mother to Sing/ Grape Sherbet* *For Poets / Ode to My Socks /egg horror poem* *O What Is That Sound* • Structure and form • Figurative language • Sound devices • Imagery • Inferences • Speaker	Literary Analysis Workshop: Author's Style and Voice *Where Have You Gone, Charming Billy* *A narrow Fellow in the Grass/ "Hope" is the thing with feathers* *Luxury/ Kidnap Poem* • Style • Word choice • Sentence structure • Sequence	Literary Analysis Workshop: History, Culture, and the Author *Angela's Ashes* *American History* *Haiku/ Haiku/ Honku* • Author's background • Historical context • Cultural context • Allusions
Critical Reading Workshop: Author's Purpose *Island Morning* *Who Killed the Ice Man? / Skeletal Sculptures* *The Lost Boys* *The House on Mango Street* • Author's perspective • Author's purpose • Patterns of organization • Text features • Note taking • Graphic aids • Inferences	Critical Reading Workshop: Argument and Persuasion *I Have a Dream* *Testimony Before the Senate* *How Private Is Your Private Life? /* *Privacy Debate* • Argument • Persuasive techniques • Rhetorical devices • Fact and opinion • Summarize • Bias		*A Few Words* • Tone • Paraphrase	*President Dead/ A White House Diary/ Special Report/ Lincoln Weeping* • Summarize multiple sources • Synthesize
Problem-solution Essay	Persuasive Speech		Response to Literature	Persuasive Essay
Media Study • News formats	Persuasive Speech Media Study • Persuasive techniques		Media Studies • Visual elements in media	Debate

	UNIT 10 Romeo and Juliet	UNIT 11 The Odyssey	UNIT 12 Research Workshops	Student Resource Bank
LITERATURE	Literary Analysis Workshop: Shakespearean Drama *The Tragedy of Romeo and Juliet* • Characteristics of Shakespearean tragedy • Character foils • Language of Shakespeare			Literary Texts
NONFICTION AND INFORMATIONAL MATERIAL			Research Strategies Workshop • Research plan • Internet • Media center • Evaluate information	Informational Texts • Text features • Patterns of organization • Forms
WRITING			Research Paper • Research questions • Sources • Plagiarism • Note-taking • Documentation	Workplace and Technical Writing
SPEAKING, LISTENING, AND MEDIA	Media Study • Shakespearean drama in movies			

McDougal Littell
LITERATURE

Life is full of questions.
LITERATURE *helps you answer them.*

What's worth **FIGHTING** *for?*

When is **STRENGTH** more than muscle?

How important is **STATUS?**

What if life had a **RESET** *button?*

What does it take to be a **SURVIVOR?**

Can a **DREAM** *change the world?*

ACKNOWLEDGMENTS

INTRODUCTORY UNIT

Simon & Schuster: Excerpt from *The Old Man and the Sea* by Ernest Hemingway. Copyright © 1952 by Ernest Hemingway, copyright renewed 1980 by Mary Hemingway. Reprinted with permission of Scribner, an imprint of Simon & Schuster Adult Publishing Group.

Arte Público Press: "Los Ancianos," from *My Own True Name* by Pat Mora. Copyright © 2000 by Pat Mora. Reprinted by permission of Arte Público Press, University of Houston.

Flora Roberts Inc.: Excerpt from *The Miracle Worker* by William Gibson. Copyright © 1956, 1957 by William Gibson, copyright 1959, 1960 by Tamarack Productions, Ltd., and George S. Klein and Leo Garel as trustees under three separate deeds of trust, copyright renewed 1977 by William Gibson. Used by permission of Flora Roberts, Inc.

Little, Brown and Company: Excerpt from *Nisei Daughter* by Monica Sone. Copyright © 1953 by Monica Sone, copyright renewed 1981 by Monica Sone. Used by permission of Little, Brown and Co., Inc.

New York Times: Excerpt from "Japan Wars on U.S. and Britain; Makes Sudden Attack on Hawaii; Heavy Fighting At Sea Reported," by Frank L. Kluckhohn from the *New York Times,* December 8, 1941. Copyright © 1941 by The New York Times. Reprinted by permission of The New York Times.

Barbara Hogenson Agency: Excerpt from "The Secret Life of Walter Mitty," from *My World—And Welcome To It* by James Thurber. Copyright © 1942 by James Thurber, copyright renewed 1970 by Rosemary A. Thurber. Reprinted by arrangement with Rosemary A. Thurber and The Barbara Hogenson Agency. All rights reserved.

Continued on page R155

ART CREDITS

COVER, TITLE PAGE

Untitled (2002), Jerry N. Uelsmann. © Jerry N. Uelsmann.

Continued on page R161

ISBN 13: 978-0-618-21586-7   ISBN 10: 0-618-21586-7

Printed in the United States of America.

1 2 3 4 5 6 7 8 9—DWO—12 11 10 09 08 07

McDougal Littell
LITERATURE

Janet Allen

Arthur N. Applebee

Jim Burke

Douglas Carnine

Yvette Jackson

Robert T. Jiménez

Judith A. Langer

Robert J. Marzano

Mary Lou McCloskey

Donna M. Ogle

Carol Booth Olson

Lydia Stack

Carol Ann Tomlinson

McDougal Littell
EVANSTON, ILLINOIS • BOSTON • DALLAS

SENIOR PROGRAM CONSULTANTS

 **JANET ALLEN** Reading and Literacy Specialist; creator of the popular "It's Never Too Late"/"Reading for Life" Institutes. Dr. Allen is an internationally known consultant who specializes in literacy work with at-risk students. Her publications include *Tools for Content Literacy; It's Never Too Late: Leading Adolescents to Lifelong Learning; Yellow Brick Roads: Shared and Guided Paths to Independent Reading; Words, Words, Words: Teaching Vocabulary in Grades 4–12;* and *Testing 1, 2, 3 . . . Bridging Best Practice and High-Stakes Assessments.* Dr. Allen was a high school reading and English teacher for more than 20 years and has taught courses in both subjects at the University of Central Florida. She directed the Central Florida Writing Project and received the Milken Foundation National Educator Award.

 **ARTHUR N. APPLEBEE** Leading Professor, School of Education at the University at Albany, State University of New York; Director of the Center on English Learning and Achievement. During his varied career, Dr. Applebee has been both a researcher and a teacher, working in institutional settings with children with severe learning problems, in public schools, as a staff member of the National Council of Teachers of English, and in professional education. Among his many books are *Curriculum as Conversation: Transforming Traditions of Teaching and Learning; Literature in the Secondary School: Studies of Curriculum and Instruction in the United States;* and *Tradition and Reform in the Teaching of English: A History.* He was elected to the International Reading Hall of Fame and has received, among other honors, the David H. Russell Award for Distinguished Research in the Teaching of English.

 **JIM BURKE** Lecturer and Author; Teacher of English at Burlingame High School, Burlingame, California. Mr. Burke is a popular presenter at educational conferences across the country and is the author of numerous books for teachers, including *School Smarts: The Four Cs of Academic Success; The English Teacher's Companion; Reading Reminders; Writing Reminders;* and *ACCESSing School: Teaching Struggling Readers to Achieve Academic and Personal Success.* He is the recipient of NCTE's Exemplary English Leadership Award and was inducted into the California Reading Association's Hall of Fame.

 **DOUGLAS CARNINE** Professor of Education at the University of Oregon; Director of the Western Region Reading First Technical Assistance Center. Dr. Carnine is nationally known for his focus on research-based practices in education, especially curriculum designs that prepare instructors of K-12 students. He has received the Lifetime Achievement Award from the Council for Exceptional Children and the Ersted Award for outstanding teaching at the University of Oregon. Dr. Carnine frequently consults on educational policy with government groups, businesses, communities, and teacher unions.

 **YVETTE JACKSON** Executive Director of the National Urban Alliance for Effective Education. Nationally recognized for her work in assessing the learning potential of underachieving urban students, Dr. Jackson is also a presenter for the Harvard Principal Center and is a member of the Differentiation Faculty of the Association for Supervision and Curriculum Development. Dr. Jackson's research focuses on literacy, gifted education, and cognitive mediation theory. She designed the Comprehensive Education Plan for the New York City Public Schools and has served as their Director of Gifted Programs and Executive Director of Instruction and Professional Development.

 **ROBERT T. JIMÉNEZ** Professor of Language, Literacy, and Culture at Vanderbilt University. Dr. Jiménez's research focuses on the language and literacy practices of Latino students. A former bilingual education teacher, he is now conducting research on how written language is thought about and used in contemporary Mexico. Dr. Jiménez has received several research and teaching honors, including two Fulbright awards from the Council for the International Exchange of Scholars and the Albert J. Harris Award from the International Reading Association. His published work has appeared in the *American Educational Research Journal, Reading Research Quarterly, The Reading Teacher, Journal of Adolescent and Adult Literacy,* and *Lectura y Vida.*

JUDITH A. LANGER Distinguished Professor at the University at Albany, State University of New York; Director of the Center on English Learning and Achievement; Director of the Albany Institute for Research in Education. An internationally known scholar in English language arts education, Dr. Langer specializes in developing teaching approaches that can enrich and improve what gets done on a daily basis in classrooms. Her publications include *Getting to Excellent: How to Create Better Schools* and *Effective Literacy Instruction: Building Successful Reading and Writing Programs.* She was inducted into the International Reading Hall of Fame and has received many other notable awards, including an honorary doctorate from the University of Uppsala, Sweden, for her research on literacy education.

ROBERT J. MARZANO Senior Scholar at Mid-Continent Research for Education and Learning (McREL); Associate Professor at Cardinal Stritch University in Milwaukee, Wisconsin; President of Marzano & Associates. An internationally known researcher, trainer, and speaker, Dr. Marzano has developed programs that translate research and theory into practical tools for K-12 teachers and administrators. He has written extensively on such topics as reading and writing instruction, thinking skills, school effectiveness, assessment, and standards implementation. His books include *Building Background Knowledge for Academic Achievement; Classroom Management That Works: Research-Based Strategies for Every Teacher;* and *What Works in Schools: Translating Research Into Action.*

DONNA M. OGLE Professor of Reading and Language at National-Louis University in Chicago, Illinois; Past President of the International Reading Association. Creator of the well-known KWL strategy, Dr. Ogle has directed many staff development projects translating theory and research into school practice in middle and secondary schools throughout the United States and has served as a consultant on literacy projects worldwide. Her extensive international experience includes coordinating the Reading and Writing for Critical Thinking Project in Eastern Europe, developing integrated curriculum for a USAID Afghan Education Project, and speaking and consulting on projects in several Latin American countries and in Asia. Her books include *Coming Together as Readers; Reading Comprehension: Strategies for Independent Learners; All Children Read;* and *Literacy for a Democratic Society.*

CAROL BOOTH OLSON Senior Lecturer in the Department of Education at the University of California, Irvine; Director of the UCI site of the National Writing Project. Dr. Olson writes and lectures extensively on the reading/writing connection, critical thinking through writing, interactive strategies for teaching writing, and the use of multicultural literature with students of culturally diverse backgrounds. She has received many awards, including the California Association of Teachers of English Award of Merit, the Outstanding California Education Research Award, and the UC Irvine Excellence in Teaching Award. Dr. Olson's books include *Reading, Thinking, and Writing About Multicultural Literature* and *The Reading/Writing Connection: Strategies for Teaching and Learning in the Secondary Classroom.*

CAROL ANN TOMLINSON Professor of Educational Research, Foundations, and Policy at the University of Virginia; Co-Director of the University's Institutes on Academic Diversity. An internationally known expert on differentiated instruction, Dr. Tomlinson helps teachers and administrators develop effective methods of teaching academically diverse learners. She was a teacher of middle and high school English for 22 years prior to teaching at the University of Virginia. Her books on differentiated instruction have been translated into eight languages. Among her many publications are *How to Differentiate Instruction in Mixed-Ability Classrooms* and *The Differentiated Classroom: Responding to the Needs of All Learners.*

ENGLISH LEARNER SPECIALISTS

MARY LOU McCLOSKEY Past President of Teachers of English to Speakers of Other Languages (TESOL); Director of Teacher Development and Curriculum Design for Educo in Atlanta, Georgia. Dr. McCloskey is a former teacher in multilingual and multicultural classrooms. She has worked with teachers, teacher educators, and departments of education around the world on teaching English as a second and foreign language. She is author of *On Our Way to English, Voices in Literature, Integrating English,* and *Visions: Language, Literature, Content.* Her awards include the Le Moyne College Ignatian Award for Professional Achievement and the TESOL D. Scott Enright Service Award.

LYDIA STACK International ESL consultant. Her areas of expertise are English language teaching strategies, ESL standards for students and teachers, and curriculum writing. Her teaching experience includes 25 years as an elementary and high school ESL teacher. She is a past president of TESOL. Her awards include the James E. Alatis Award for Service to TESOL (2003) and the San Francisco STAR Teacher Award (1989). Her publications include *On Our Way to English; Wordways: Games for Language Learning;* and *Visions: Language, Literature, Content.*

CURRICULUM SPECIALIST

WILLIAM L. McBRIDE Curriculum Specialist. Dr. McBride is a nationally known speaker, educator, and author who now trains teachers in instructional methodologies. A former reading specialist, English teacher, and social studies teacher, he holds a Masters in Reading and a Ph.D. in Curriculum and Instruction from the University of North Carolina at Chapel Hill. Dr. McBride has contributed to the development of textbook series in language arts, social studies, science, and vocabulary. He is also known for his novel *Entertaining an Elephant,* which tells the story of a burned-out teacher who becomes re-inspired with both his profession and his life.

MEDIA SPECIALISTS

DAVID M. CONSIDINE Professor of Instructional Technology and Media Studies at Appalachian State University in North Carolina. Dr. Considine has served as a media literacy consultant to the U.S. government and to the media industry, including Discovery Communications and Cable in the Classroom. He has also conducted media literacy workshops and training for county and state health departments across the United States. Among his many publications are *Visual Messages: Integrating Imagery into Instruction,* and *Imagine That: Developing Critical Viewing and Thinking Through Children's Literature.*

LARKIN PAULUZZI Teacher and Media Specialist; trainer for the New Jersey Writing Project. Ms. Pauluzzi puts her extensive classroom experience to use in developing teacher-friendly curriculum materials and workshops in many different areas, including media literacy. She has led media literacy training workshops in several districts throughout Texas, guiding teachers in the meaningful and practical uses of media in the classroom. Ms. Pauluzzi has taught students at all levels, from Title I Reading to AP English IV. She also spearheads a technology club at her school, working with students to produce media and technology to serve both the school and the community.

LISA K. SCHEFFLER Teacher and Media Specialist. Ms. Scheffler has designed and taught media literacy and video production curriculum, in addition to teaching language arts and speech. Using her knowledge of mass communication theory, coupled with real classroom experience, she has developed ready-to-use materials that help teachers incorporate media literacy into their curricula. She has taught film and television studies at the University of North Texas and has served as a contributing writer for the Texas Education Agency's statewide viewing and representing curriculum.

TEACHER ADVISORS

These are some of the many educators from across the country who played a crucial role in the development of the tables of contents, the lesson design, and other key components of this program:

Virginia L. Alford, MacArthur High School, San Antonio, Texas

Yvonne L. Allen, Shaker Heights High School, Shaker Heights, Ohio

Dave T. Anderson, Hinsdale South High School, Darien, Illinois

Kacy Colleen Anglim, Portland Public Schools District, Portland, Oregon

Beverly Scott Bass, Arlington Heights High School, Fort Worth, Texas

Jordana Benone, North High School, Torrance, California

Patricia Blood, Howell High School, Farmingdale, New Jersey

Marjorie Bloom, Eau Gallie High School, Melbourne, Florida

Edward J. Blotzer, Wilkinsburg Junior/Senior High School, Wilkinsburg, Pennsylvania

Stephen D. Bournes, Evanston Township High School, Evanston, Illinois

Barbara M. Bowling, Mt. Tabor High School, Winston-Salem, North Carolina

Kiala Boykin-Givehand, Duval County Public Schools, Jacksonville, Florida

Laura L. Brown, Adlai Stevenson High School, Lincolnshire, Illinois

Cynthia Burke, Yavneh Academy, Dallas, Texas

Hoppy Chandler, San Diego City Schools, San Diego, California

Gary Chmielewski, St. Benedict High School, Chicago, Illinois

Delorse Cole-Stewart, Milwaukee Public Schools, Milwaukee, Wisconsin

L. Calvin Dillon, Gaither High School, Tampa, Florida

Dori Dolata, Rufus King High School, Milwaukee, Wisconsin

Jon Epstein, Marietta High School, Marietta, Georgia

Helen Ervin, Fort Bend Independent School District, Sugarland, Texas

Sue Friedman, Buffalo Grove High School, Buffalo Grove, Illinois

Chris Gee, Bel Air High School, El Paso, Texas

Paula Grasel, The Horizon Center, Gainesville, Georgia

Christopher Guarraia, Centreville High School, Clifton, Virginia

Rochelle L. Greene-Brady, Kenwood Academy, Chicago, Illinois

Michele M. Hettinger, Niles West High School, Skokie, Illinois

Elizabeth Holcomb, Forest Hill High School, Jackson, Mississippi

Jim Horan, Hinsdale Central High School, Hinsdale, Illinois

James Paul Hunter, Oak Park-River Forest High School, Oak Park, Illinois

Susan P. Kelly, Director of Curriculum, Island Trees School District, Levittown, New York

Beverley A. Lanier, Varina High School, Richmond, Virginia

Pat Laws, Charlotte-Mecklenburg Schools, Charlotte, North Carolina

Diana R. Martinez, Treviño School of Communications & Fine Arts, Laredo, Texas

Natalie Martinez, Stephen F. Austin High School, Houston, Texas

Elizabeth Matarazzo, Ysleta High School, El Paso, Texas

Carol M. McDonald, J. Frank Dobie High School, Houston, Texas

Amy Millikan, Consultant, Chicago, Illinois

Terri Morgan, Caprock High School, Amarillo, Texas

Eileen Murphy, Walter Payton Preparatory High School, Chicago, Illinois

Lisa Omark, New Haven Public Schools, New Haven, Connecticut

Kaine Osburn, Wheeling High School, Wheeling, Illinois

Andrea J. Phillips, Terry Sanford High School, Fayetteville, North Carolina

Cathy Reilly, Sayreville Public Schools, Sayreville, New Jersey

Mark D. Simon, Neuqua Valley High School, Naperville, Illinois

Scott Snow, Sequin High School, Arlington, Texas

Jane W. Speidel, Brevard County Schools, Viera, Florida

Cheryl E. Sullivan, Lisle Community School District, Lisle, Illinois

Anita Usmiani, Hamilton Township Public Schools, Hamilton Square, New Jersey

Linda Valdez, Oxnard Union High School District, Oxnard, California

Nancy Walker, Longview High School, Longview, Texas

Kurt Weiler, New Trier High School, Winnetka, Illinois

Elizabeth Whittaker, Larkin High School, Elgin, Illinois

Linda S. Williams, Woodlawn High School, Baltimore, Maryland

John R. Williamson, Fort Thomas Independent Schools, Fort Thomas, Kentucky

Anna N. Winters, Simeon High School, Chicago, Illinois

Tonora D. Wyckoff, North Shore Senior High School, Houston, Texas

Karen Zajac, Glenbard South High School, Glen Ellyn, Illinois

Cynthia Zimmerman, Mose Vines Preparatory High School, Chicago, Illinois

Lynda Zimmerman, El Camino High School, South San Francisco, California

Ruth E. Zurich, Brown Deer High School, Brown Deer, Wisconsin

MCDOUGAL LITTELL LITERATURE
CONTENTS IN BRIEF

INTRODUCTORY UNIT

The Power of Ideas

LITERARY GENRES WORKSHOP
- Fiction
- Poetry
- Drama
- Literary and Informational Nonfiction
- Types of Media

READING STRATEGIES WORKSHOP
- Preview
- Set a Purpose
- Connect
- Use Prior Knowledge
- Predict
- Visualize
- Monitor
- Make Inferences

WRITING PROCESS WORKSHOP
- Writing Process Review
- Key Traits

PART 1: LITERARY ELEMENTS

THE PLOT THICKENS
UNIT 1 **Narrative Structure**
LITERARY WORKSHOP: Plot, Conflict, Sequence
WRITING WORKSHOP: Personal Narrative

PEOPLE WATCHING
UNIT 2 **Characterization and Point of View**
LITERARY WORKSHOP: Narrator, Point of View, Characterization, Motivation
WRITING WORKSHOP: Comparison-Contrast Essay

A SENSE OF PLACE
UNIT 3 **Setting, Mood, and Imagery**
LITERARY WORKSHOP: Setting, Mood, Imagery
WRITING WORKSHOP: Short Story

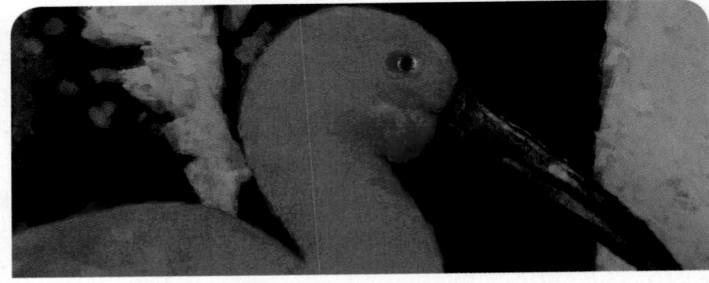

PART 2: A WORLD OF IDEAS

GETTING THE MESSAGE
UNIT 4 **Theme and Symbol**
LITERARY WORKSHOP: Theme, Symbol
WRITING WORKSHOP: Literary Analysis

IDEAS MADE VISIBLE
UNIT 5 **Author's Purpose**
CRITICAL READING WORKSHOP: Purpose, Perspective, Tone, Organization, Format
WRITING WORKSHOP: Problem-Solution Essay

TAKING SIDES
UNIT 6 **Argument and Persuasion**
CRITICAL READING WORKSHOP: Elements of an Argument, Persuasive Techniques, Rhetorical Devices
WRITING WORKSHOP: Persuasive Speech

PART 3: THE AUTHOR'S CRAFT

SPECIAL EFFECTS
UNIT 7 The Language of Poetry
LITERARY WORKSHOP: Form, Rhyme, Sound Devices, Rhythm and Meter, Figurative Language
WRITING WORKSHOP: Personal Response to a Poem

A WAY WITH WORDS
UNIT 8 Author's Style and Voice
LITERARY WORKSHOP: Elements of Style, Voice
WRITING WORKSHOP: Analysis of an Author's Style

PUTTING IT IN CONTEXT
UNIT 9 History, Culture, and the Author
LITERARY WORKSHOP: Understanding Historical and Cultural Context, Writer's Background
WRITING WORKSHOP: Persuasive Essay

PART 4: THE CLASSIC TRADITION

SHAKESPEAREAN DRAMA
UNIT 10 The Tragedy of Romeo and Juliet
LITERARY WORKSHOP: Shakespearean Tragedy, Shakespeare's Language, Reading Shakespeare
WRITING WORKSHOP: Comparing a Play and a Film

EPIC POETRY
UNIT 11 The Odyssey
LITERARY WORKSHOP: Characteristics of the Epic, The Language of Homer, Reading the Epic
WRITING WORKSHOP: Subject Analysis

INVESTIGATION AND DISCOVERY
UNIT 12 The Power of Research

Online LITERATURE CLASSZONE.COM

LITERATURE AND READING CENTER
- Author Biographies
- Additional Selection Background
- Literary Analysis Frames
- Power Thinking Activities

WRITING AND GRAMMAR CENTER
- Writing Templates and Graphic Organizers
- Publishing Options
- Quick-Fix Editing Machine

VOCABULARY CENTER
- Vocabulary Strategies and Practice
- Multi-Language Academic Vocabulary Glossary
- Vocabulary Flash Cards

MEDIA CENTER
- Production Templates
- Analysis Guides

RESEARCH CENTER
- Web Research Guide
- Citation Guide

ASSESSMENT CENTER
- Assessment Practice and Test-Taking Tips
- SAT/ACT Practice and Tips

MORE TECHNOLOGY

eEdition
- Interactive Selections
- Audio Summaries

WriteSmart
- Writing Prompts and Templates
- Interactive Student Models
- Interactive Graphic Organizers
- Interactive Revision Lessons
- Rubric Generator

MediaSmart DVD
- Media Lessons
- Interactive Media Studies

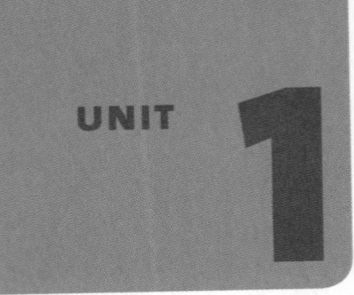

UNIT 1

The Plot Thickens
NARRATIVE STRUCTURE

• IN FICTION • IN MEDIA • IN NONFICTION • IN POETRY • IN DRAMA

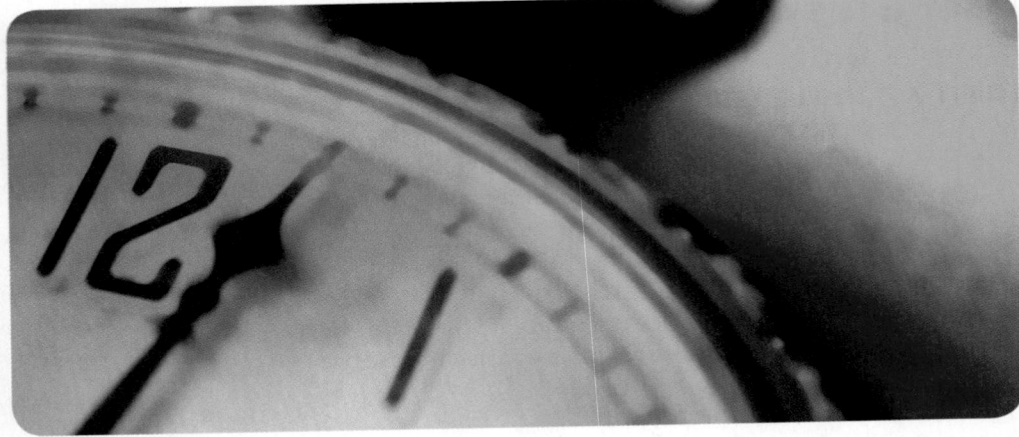

Skills and Standards
Plot Stages and Conflict,
Sequence and Time, Flashback,
Foreshadowing

LITERARY ANALYSIS WORKSHOP: PLOT AND CONFLICT   **24**

SHORT STORY
Checkouts   Cynthia Rylant   **28**

FICTION

Foreshadowing,
Analyze Sequence

SHORT STORY
A Sound of Thunder   Ray Bradbury   **32**

Reading for Information
From Here to There: The Physics of Time Travel MAGAZINE ARTICLE   **51**

Conflict, Visualize

SHORT STORY
The Most Dangerous Game   Richard Connell   **52**

Plot and Character,
Make Inferences

SHORT STORY
Daughter of Invention   Julia Alvarez   **78**

Irony, Predict

SHORT STORY
The Gift of the Magi   O. Henry   **94**

MEDIA

Suspense in Movies

FILM CLIP
from **The Lord of the Rings:**   Peter Jackson   **106**
The Fellowship of the Ring

MEDIA SMART DVD

• *The Most Dangerous Game*

InterActive
READER & WRITER

- Integrated Test Practice
- Related Nonfiction Readings

McDougal Littell LITERATURE

Skills and Standards			

NONFICTION

AUTOBIOGRAPHY

Autobiography, Identify Cause and Effect

● **The Rights to the Streets of Memphis** — Richard Wright — **110**
from **Black Boy**

BIOGRAPHY

Suspense in Biography, Identify Author's Purpose

from **Seabiscuit: An American Legend** — Laura Hillenbrand — **120**

Reading for Information

Synthesize, Draw Conclusions

from **Four Good Legs Between Us** MAGAZINE ARTICLE — **133**
Seabiscuit TIMELINE — **134**
Races on the Radio: Santa Anita Handicap RADIO TRANSCRIPT — **135**

POETRY

NARRATIVE POEM

Narrative Poetry, Strategies for Reading Poetry

The Raven — Edgar Allan Poe — **138**

NARRATIVE POEM

Incident in a Rose Garden — Donald Justice — **145**

DRAMA

TELEPLAY

Plot in Drama, Strategies for Reading a Teleplay

Sorry, Right Number — Stephen King — **148**

Reading for Information

from **On Writing** MEMOIR — **165**

Narrative Techniques

WRITING WORKSHOP: PERSONAL NARRATIVE — **168**

SPEAKING AND LISTENING: INFORMAL SPEECH — **175**

Plot Stages, Conflict, Sequence, Predicting, Cause and Effect

ASSESSMENT PRACTICE: NARRATIVE STRUCTURE — **176**

PERSONAL NARRATIVE
Fish Cheeks — Amy Tan

ESSAY
from **Piedra** — Gary Soto

GREAT READS: IDEAS FOR INDEPENDENT READING — **182**

VOCABULARY STRATEGIES

Latin roots: *mal, p. 49*
Denotation and connotation, *p. 76*
Latin prefixes: *in-, p. 92*

Greek roots: *chron, p. 104*
Synonyms and antonyms, *p. 118*
Word families: *aud, p. 131*

InterActive
READER & WRITER

• Integrated Test Practice
• Related Nonfiction Readings

McDougal Littell LITERATURE

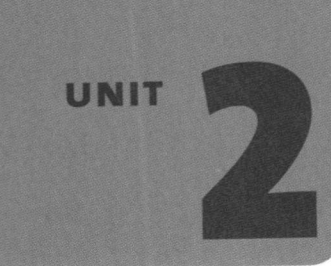

UNIT 2

People Watching
CHARACTERIZATION AND POINT OF VIEW

• IN FICTION • IN NONFICTION • IN POETRY • ACROSS GENRES

• The Necklace

InterActive
READER
& WRITER

• Integrated Test Practice
• Related Nonfiction Readings

McDougal Littell LITERATURE

Skills and Standards

Point of View,
Character Traits and Motivation

LITERARY ANALYSIS WORKSHOP:
CHARACTER AND POINT OF VIEW

186

FICTION

First-Person Point of View,
Draw Conclusions

SHORT STORY
Pancakes — Joan Bauer — **192**

Character Motivation,
Make Inferences

SHORT STORY
• **The Necklace** — Guy de Maupassant — **206**

Reading for Information
Spending Spree MAGAZINE ARTICLE — **221**

Third-Person Limited
Point of View, Monitor

SHORT STORY
Hamadi — Naomi Shihab Nye — **222**

NONFICTION

Characterization in
Autobiography,
Analyze Perspectives

AUTOBIOGRAPHY
from **I Know Why the Caged Bird Sings** — Maya Angelou — **236**

Connect
Caged Bird POEM — Maya Angelou — **246**

xii

xii

Skills and Standards

Character Study,
Interpret Graphic Aids

MAGAZINE ARTICLE
Blind to Failure   Karl Taro Greenfeld   **250**

Reading for Information
A Different Level of Competition NEWSPAPER ARTICLE   **264**

Identify Main Ideas,
Make Generalizations

POETRY

Speaker, Strategies for
Reading Poetry

POEM
A Voice   Pat Mora   **268**

POEM
My Father's Song   Simon J. Ortíz   **272**

COMPARING ACROSS GENRES

Characterization Across Genres,
Set a Purpose for Reading

BIOGRAPHY
from **Rosa Parks**   Douglas Brinkley   **274**

POEM
Rosa   Rita Dove   **280**

Organization,
Use Transitions

WRITING WORKSHOP: COMPARISON-CONTRAST ESSAY   **284**

PUBLISHING WITH TECHNOLOGY: POWER PRESENTATION   **291**

Character Traits,
Character Motivation,
Point of View

ASSESSMENT PRACTICE: CHARACTERIZATION   **292**
AND POINT OF VIEW

SHORT STORY
from **Powder**   Tobias Wolff

PROSE POEM
from **Maud Martha**   Gwendolyn Brooks

GREAT READS: IDEAS FOR INDEPENDENT READING   **298**

VOCABULARY STRATEGIES

Latin roots: *bene, p. 204*   Multiple-meaning words, *p. 248*
Latin roots: *spec, p. 219*   Specialized vocabulary, *p. 263*
Words from Greek culture, *p. 234*   Etymologies, *p. 282*

InterActive
READER & WRITER

• *The Cask of Amontillado*

• Integrated Test Practice
• Related Nonfiction Readings

McDougal Littell **LITERATURE**

Skills and Standards
Setting and Characters, Setting and Conflict, Imagery, Mood

LITERARY ANALYSIS WORKSHOP:
SETTING, MOOD, AND IMAGERY   **302**

FICTION

Details of Setting,
Analyze Imagery

SHORT STORY
A Christmas Memory   Truman Capote   **308**

Setting as Symbol,
Analyze Details

SHORT STORY
Through the Tunnel   Doris Lessing   **326**

Mood, Paraphrase

SHORT STORY
The Cask of Amontillado   Edgar Allan Poe   **342**

Reading for Information
The Story Behind "The Cask of Amontillado" BOOK EXCERPT   **352**

MEDIA

Setting and Mood in Movies

FILM CLIP
from **The Cask of Amontillado**    MEDIA SMART DVD   Joyce Chopra   **356**

xiv

Skills and Standards

NONFICTION

TRAVEL NARRATIVE

Setting and Mood, Identify Author's Perspective

from **A Walk in the Woods**   Bill Bryson   **360**

Reading for Information

Reading Primary Sources, Cite Evidence

Wilderness Letter LETTER   Wallace Stegner   **372**

POETRY

POEM

Imagery and Mood, Connect

The Sharks   Denise Levertov   **378**

POEM

The Peace of Wild Things   Wendell Berry   **382**

Narrative Techniques

WRITING WORKSHOP: SHORT STORY   **384**

PUBLISHING WITH TECHNOLOGY: VIDEO PRESENTATION   **391**

Setting, Mood, Imagery

ASSESSMENT PRACTICE: SETTING, MOOD, AND IMAGERY   **392**

FICTION

from **The Hobbit**   J.R.R. Tolkien

GREAT READS: IDEAS FOR INDEPENDENT READING   **398**

VOCABULARY STRATEGIES

Connotation and denotation, *p. 324*

Latin roots: *quest, quer,* and *quisit, p. 340*

Word families: *clud, p. 354*

Context clues, *p. 371*

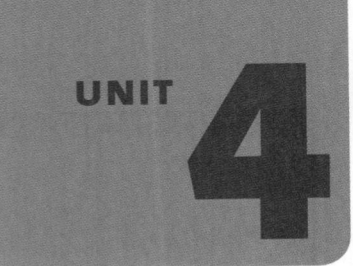

UNIT **4**

Getting the Message
THEME AND SYMBOL

• **IN FICTION** • **IN NONFICTION** • **IN POETRY** • **ACROSS GENRES**

Skills and Standards
Universal Themes,
Identify Themes, Symbol

LITERARY ANALYSIS WORKSHOP: THEME AND SYMBOL   **402**

SHORT STORY
The Sniper   Liam O'Flaherty   **405**

FICTION

Theme and Setting,
Draw Conclusions

SHORT STORY
Marigolds   Eugenia Collier   **408**

Outline, Analyze Ideas

Reading for Information
Sowing Change NEWSPAPER ARTICLE   **422**

Symbol, Make Inferences
About Characters

SHORT STORY
• **The Scarlet Ibis**   James Hurst   **426**

Connect
Woman with Flower POEM   Naomi Long Madgett   **442**

NONFICTION

Implied Main Idea, Analyze
Sequence of Events

ESSAY
Math and After Math   Lensey Namioka   **446**

Author's Perspective, Monitor

ESSAY
The Future in My Arms   Edwidge Danticat   **458**

• *The Scarlet Ibis*

InterActive
READER
& WRITER

• Integrated Test Practice
• Related Nonfiction Readings

McDougal Littell LITERATURE

Skills and Standards	**POETRY**		
	POEM		
Universal Theme, *Reading Poetry for Theme*	**Poem on Returning to Dwell in the Country**	T'ao Ch'ien	**466**
	POEM		
	My Heart Leaps Up	William Wordsworth	**469**
	POEM		
	The Sun	Mary Oliver	**470**

COMPARING ACROSS GENRES

	SHORT STORY		
Theme Across Genres, Set a *Purpose for Reading*	**Two Kinds**	Amy Tan	**472**
	POEM		
	Rice and Rose Bowl Blues	Diane Mei Lin Mark	**486**

Responding to Literature	**WRITING WORKSHOP: LITERARY ANALYSIS**	**490**
	SPEAKING AND LISTENING: PANEL DISCUSSION	**497**
Theme, Symbol	**ASSESSMENT PRACTICE: THEME**	**498**
	SHORT STORY	
	The Apple-Tree Katherine Mansfield	
	GREAT READS: IDEAS FOR INDEPENDENT READING	**504**

VOCABULARY STRATEGIES

Suffixes: *-or, p. 421*   Using context clues, *p. 457*
Connotation, *p. 444*   Word origins, *p. 488*

UNIT 5

Ideas Made Visible
AUTHOR'S PURPOSE

• IN NONFICTION • IN MEDIA • IN FICTION

Skills and Standards
Author's Purpose and
Perspective, Organization
and Format

CRITICAL READING WORKSHOP: AUTHOR'S PURPOSE   **508**

NONFICTION

Diction, Analyze Patterns
of Organization

DESCRIPTIVE ESSAY
Island Morning   Jamaica Kincaid   **514**

Tone, Identify Implied
Main Ideas

BIOGRAPHICAL ESSAY
Georgia O'Keeffe   Joan Didion   **524**

Text Features, Take Notes

MAGAZINE ARTICLE
Who Killed the Iceman?   *National Geographic* **534**

PROCESS DESCRIPTION
Skeletal Sculptures   Donna M. Jackson   **540**

Author's Purpose,
Interpret Graphic Aids

MAGAZINE ARTICLE
The Lost Boys   Sara Corbett   **546**

• *The Lost Boys*

InterActive
READER
& WRITER

• *Integrated Test Practice*
• *Related Nonfiction Readings*

McDougal Littell **LITERATURE**

Skills and Standards

MEDIA

News Formats

TV NEWSCAST CLIP
Nine Coal Miners Brought Up Safely   MEDIA SMART DVD   NBC News   **556**

WEB NEWS REPORT
All Nine Pulled Alive from Mine   MEDIA SMART DVD   CNN.com   **556**

FICTION

Tone and Author's Purpose, Predict

SHORT STORY
The Open Window   Saki   **560**

Author's Perspective, Make Inferences About Character

NOVEL EXCERPT
from **The House on Mango Street**   Sandra Cisneros   **568**

Persuasive Techniques

WRITING WORKSHOP: PROBLEM-SOLUTION ESSAY   **576**

SPEAKING AND LISTENING: VIDEO DOCUMENTARY   **583**

Author's Perspective, Author's Purpose, Patterns of Organization, Text Features

ASSESSMENT PRACTICE: AUTHOR'S PURPOSE   **584**

ESSAY
His Name Was Pete   William Faulkner

ONLINE ARTICLE
Dog Proves As Smart As Average Toddler   Margaret Munro

GREAT READS: IDEAS FOR INDEPENDENT READING   **590**

VOCABULARY STRATEGIES

Word roots: *gen*, p. 532   Latin roots: *fract*, p. 555
Specialized fields: *"ologies,"* p. 545

• from *The House on Mango Street*

InterActive
READER & WRITER

• Integrated Test Practice
• Related Nonfiction Readings
McDougal Littell LITERATURE

Taking Sides
ARGUMENT AND PERSUASION

- IN NONFICTION • IN MEDIA • ACROSS GENRES

Skills and Standards
Elements of Argument,
Persuasive Techniques,
Rhetorical Devices

CRITICAL READING WORKSHOP:
ARGUMENT AND PERSUASION   **594**

• *I Have a Dream*

NONFICTION

Argument, Understand
Rhetorical Devices

SPEECH
• **I Have a Dream**   Dr. Martin Luther King Jr.   **600**

Persuasive Techniques,
Summarize

SPEECH
Testimony Before the Senate   Michael J. Fox   **610**

Fact and Opinion, Recognize Bias

MAGAZINE ARTICLE
How Private Is Your Private Life?   Andrea Rock   **620**

NEWSPAPER EDITORIAL
The Privacy Debate: Arthur M. Ahalt   **628**
One Size Doesn't Fit All

Skills and Standards

MEDIA

PUBLIC SERVICE ANNOUNCEMENT

Persuasive Techniques   **"Billy Thomas"**   MEDIA SMART DVD   Boys and Girls Clubs of America   **634**

PUBLIC SERVICE ANNOUNCEMENT

"Life Is Calling"   MEDIA SMART DVD   Peace Corps   **634**

COMPARING ACROSS GENRES

ESSAY

Writer's Message Across Genres, Set a Purpose for Reading   **Primal Screen**   Ellen Goodman   **638**

SHORT STORY

The Pedestrian   Ray Bradbury   **642**

Persuasive Techniques   **WRITING WORKSHOP: PERSUASIVE SPEECH**   **650**

SPEAKING AND LISTENING: PRESENTING A PERSUASIVE SPEECH   **657**

Elements of Argument, Persuasive Techniques, Rhetorical Devices, Fact and Opinion   **ASSESSMENT PRACTICE: ARGUMENT AND PERSUASION**   **658**

ESSAY

Appearances Are Destructive   Mark Mathabane

GREAT READS: IDEAS FOR INDEPENDENT READING   **664**

VOCABULARY STRATEGIES

Political words, *p. 609*   Internet words, *p. 632*
Using a dictionary, *p. 618*

Special Effects
THE LANGUAGE OF POETRY

Skills and Standards
Form, Poetic Elements, Sound Devices, Imagery, Figurative Language

LITERARY ANALYSIS WORKSHOP: THE LANGUAGE OF POETRY   **668**

POEM
Not In A Silver Casket . . .   Edna St. Vincent Millay   **674**

POEM
I Am Offering This Poem   Jimmy Santiago Baca   **675**

POEMS ABOUT FAMILY

Lyric Poetry, Imagery, Make Inferences

• **My Papa's Waltz**   Theodore Roethke   **676**

• **I Ask My Mother to Sing**   Li-Young Lee   **680**

• **Grape Sherbet**   Rita Dove   **681**

POEMS ABOUT NATURE

Elegy, Diction, Paraphrase

Spring is like a perhaps hand   E. E. Cummings   **684**

Elegy for the Giant Tortoises   Margaret Atwood   **688**

Today   Billy Collins   **689**

Reading for Information
U. S. Poet Laureates: Getting the Word Out   MAGAZINE ARTICLE   **690**

• *My Papa's Waltz*
• *I Ask My Mother to Sing*
• *Grape Sherbet*

InterActive
READER & WRITER

• Integrated Test Practice
• Related Nonfiction Readings

McDougal Littell LITERATURE

Skills and Standards			

POEMS ABOUT COMPETITION

Concrete Poetry, Form, Connect	**400-Meter Free Style**	Maxine Kumin	692
	Bodybuilders' Contest	Wislawa Szymborska	696
Synthesize, Support an Opinion	Reading for Information **The Night Poetry Rocked the House** MAGAZINE ARTICLE		698

POEMS ABOUT IMAGINATION

Ode, Figurative Language, Visualize	**For Poets**	Al Young	702
	Ode to My Socks	Pablo Neruda	706
	egg horror poem	Laurel Winter	710

POEM ABOUT WAR

Ballad, Sound Devices, Analyze Speakers	**O What Is That Sound**	W. H. Auden	714

POEMS ABOUT LIFE'S JOURNEY

Dramatic Monologue, Meter, Analyze Ideas in Poetry	**The Seven Ages of Man**	William Shakespeare	720
	The Road Not Taken	Robert Frost	724

Responding to Literature	**WRITING WORKSHOP: PERSONAL RESPONSE TO A POEM**	726
	PUBLISHING WITH TECHNOLOGY: MULTIMEDIA PRESENTATION	733
Poetic Structure, Form, Sound Devices, Figurative Language, Imagery	**ASSESSMENT PRACTICE: THE LANGUAGE OF POETRY**	734

	The Sower	Victor Hugo
	To Be of Use	Marge Piercy

GREAT READS: IDEAS FOR INDEPENDENT READING	740

• *The Seven Ages of Man*
• *The Road Not Taken*

InterActive
READER & WRITER

• *Integrated Test Practice*
• *Related Nonfiction Readings*

McDougal Littell LITERATURE

UNIT 8

A Way with Words
AUTHOR'S STYLE AND VOICE

• IN FICTION • IN MEDIA • IN NONFICTION • IN POETRY • IN DRAMA

Skills and Standards
Style, Voice, Word Choice,
Sentence Structure, Tone

LITERARY ANALYSIS WORKSHOP: AUTHOR'S STYLE AND VOICE 744

FICTION

Realism, Analyze Sequence •
SHORT STORY
Where Have You Gone, Charming Billy? Tim O'Brien **750**

Reading for Information
Tim O'Brien: The Naked Soldier INTERVIEW **760**

Parody, Predict
FABLE
The Princess and the Tin Box James Thurber **764**

MEDIA

Style in Movies
FILM CLIP
from **The Birds** MEDIA SMART DVD Alfred Hitchcock **770**

NONFICTION

Humor, Summarize
ESSAY
Going to Japan Barbara Kingsolver **774**

Tone, Paraphrase
ESSAY
A Few Words Mary Oliver **782**

• *Where Have You Gone, Charming Billy?*

InterActive
READER & WRITER

• Integrated Test Practice
• Related Nonfiction Readings

McDougal Littell LITERATURE

Skills and Standards

POETRY

Dickinson's Style, Strategies for Reading Poetry

POEM
A narrow Fellow in the Grass   Emily Dickinson   **790**

POEM
"Hope" is the thing with feathers   Emily Dickinson   **793**

Reading for Information
Unraveling the Mystery of Emily Dickinson JOURNAL ARTICLE   **794**

Giovanni's Style, Interpret Ideas in Poetry

POEM
Luxury   Nikki Giovanni   **796**

POEM
Kidnap Poem   Nikki Giovanni   **800**

DRAMA

Farce, Visualize

DRAMA
The Sneeze   Neil Simon   **802**
from **The Good Doctor**   Based on a story
                                                        by Anton Chekhov

Responding to Literature

WRITING WORKSHOP: ANALYSIS OF AN AUTHOR'S STYLE   **812**

SPEAKING AND LISTENING: ORAL INTERPRETATION   **819**

Style, Word Choice, Sentences, Tone

ASSESSMENT PRACTICE: AUTHOR'S STYLE AND VOICE   **820**

NOVEL EXCERPT
from **The Sea Wolf**   Jack London

ESSAY
from **Pilgrim at Tinker Creek**   Annie Dillard

GREAT READS: IDEAS FOR INDEPENDENT READING   **826**

VOCABULARY STRATEGIES

Prefixes: *in-* , *p. 762*   Homonyms, *p. 788*
Appropriate word choice, *p. 781*

Putting It in Context
HISTORY, CULTURE, AND THE AUTHOR
• IN NONFICTION • IN FICTION • IN POETRY

Skills and Standards
Historical and Cultural Context,
Author's Background

LITERARY ANALYSIS WORKSHOP:
HISTORY, CULTURE, AND THE AUTHOR   **830**

POEM
The Vietnam Wall   Alberto Ríos   **834**

NONFICTION

MEMOIR
Memoir, Use Allusions   *from* **Angela's Ashes**   Frank McCourt   **836**
to Make Inferences
    Reading for Information
    The Education of Frank McCourt MAGAZINE ARTICLE   **848**

ESSAY
Cultural Symbol, Monitor   **Revisiting Sacred Ground**   N. Scott Momaday   **852**

FICTION

SHORT STORY
Voice and Dialect, • **Blues Ain't No Mockin Bird**   Toni Cade Bambara   **862**
Draw Conclusions

SHORT STORY
Influence of Author's   **American History**   Judith Ortiz Cofer   **874**
Background, Connect

Skills and Standards

Synthesize, Summarize Information from Multiple Sources

Reading for Information

President Dead: Connally Also Hit by Sniper NEWSPAPER ARTICLE 888

A White House Diary DIARY ENTRY 890

Special Report MAGAZINE ARTICLE 891

Lincoln Weeping POLITICAL CARTOON 892

POETRY

Harlem Renaissance Literature, Strategies for Reading Poetry

POEM
The Tropics in New York Claude McKay 894

POEM
Theme for English B Langston Hughes 898

Reading for Information

The Harlem Renaissance: A Cultural Explosion MAGAZINE ARTICLE 900

Haiku, Historical and Cultural Context, Interpret Imagery

POEMS
Haiku Matsuo Bashō 902

POEMS
Haiku Richard Wright 905

POEMS
Honku Aaron Naparstek 906

Persuasive Techniques **WRITING WORKSHOP: PERSUASIVE ESSAY** 908

SPEAKING AND LISTENING: DEBATING AN ISSUE 915

Author's Background, Historical and Cultural Context, Multiple Sources

ASSESSMENT PRACTICE: HISTORY, CULTURE, AND THE AUTHOR 916

NOVEL EXCERPT
from **All Quiet on the Western Front** Erich Maria Remarque

GREAT READS: IDEAS FOR INDEPENDENT READING 922

VOCABULARY STRATEGIES

Latin roots: *fid, p. 850*   Idioms, *p. 887*
Greek words: *cosmo, p. 861*

UNIT 10

Shakespearean Drama
THE TRAGEDY OF ROMEO AND JULIET
• IN DRAMA • IN MEDIA • IN POETRY

Shakespeare's World	**926**
LITERARY ANALYSIS WORKSHOP: SHAKESPEAREAN DRAMA	**930**

Skills and Standards
Characteristics of Shakespearean Tragedy, The Language of Shakespeare, Reading Shakespearean Drama

Tragedy, Soliloquy, Aside, Allusion, Comic Relief, Blank Verse

DRAMA

The Tragedy of Romeo and Juliet	William Shakespeare	**938**
Prologue		**941**
Act One		**942**
Act Two		**968**
Act Three		**992**
Act Four		**1018**
Act Five		**1034**

Skills and Standards

MEDIA

FILM CLIP

Shakespearean Drama in Movies

from **Romeo and Juliet**   MEDIA SMART DVD   Franco Zeffirelli   **1052**

Reading for Information

Analyze a Critical Review,
Compare and Contrast

Great Movies: Romeo and Juliet CRITICAL REVIEW   **1056**

POETRY

MYTH

Myth, Analyze Sequence

Pyramus and Thisbe   Ovid   **1062**
from the **Metamorphoses**

Compare and Contrast

WRITING WORKSHOP: COMPARING A PLAY AND A FILM   **1070**

SPEAKING AND LISTENING: STAGING A SCENE   **1077**

Tragedy, Character Motivation,
Tragic Hero, Blank Verse

ASSESSMENT PRACTICE: SHAKESPEAREAN DRAMA   **1078**

DRAMA

from **The Tragedy of Romeo and Juliet**   William Shakespeare

GREAT READS: IDEAS FOR INDEPENDENT READING   **1084**

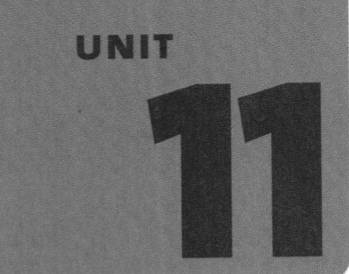

Homer's World   1088

Skills and Standards
Characteristics of the Epic,
The Language of Homer,
Reading an Epic Poem

LITERARY ANALYSIS WORKSHOP: THE EPIC   1094

EPIC
───

from the **Odyssey**   Homer   1102
                                                Translated by
                                                Robert Fitzgerald

Epic Hero, Archetypal Character,   **Part One: The Wanderings of Odysseus**   1102
Imagery, Figurative Language
                                      Book 1   A Goddess Intervenes   1104

                                      Book 5   Calypso, the Sweet Nymph   1106

                                      Book 9   New Coasts and Poseidon's Son   1110
                                                   "I Am Laertes' Son"   1110
                                                   The Lotus Eaters   1112
                                                   The Cyclops   1112

                                      Book 10 Circe, the Grace of the Witch   1124

                                      Book 11 The Land of the Dead   1126

                                      Book 12 The Sirens; Scylla and Charybdis   1130

Skills and Standards
Plot, Setting, Theme,
Archetypes, Summarize

Part Two: The Homecoming   **1140**

   Book 16   Father and Son   **1142**

   Book 17   The Beggar at the Manor   **1148**

   Book 21   The Test of the Bow   **1150**

   Book 22   Death in the Great Hall   **1156**

   Book 23   The Trunk of the Olive Tree   **1162**

Connect
Penelope POEM   Dorothy Parker   **1166**

Expository Techniques

WRITING WORKSHOP: SUBJECT ANALYSIS   **1170**

SPEAKING AND LISTENING: DELIVERING AN ORAL REPORT   **1177**

Epic, Setting, Conflict,
Theme, Epic Hero

ASSESSMENT PRACTICE: EPIC POETRY   **1178**
EPIC
from the **Odyssey, Book 9**   Homer

GREAT READS: IDEAS FOR INDEPENDENT READING   **1184**

VOCABULARY STRATEGIES

Prefixes: *fore-, p. 1139*   Latin roots: *solus, p. 1168*

Investigation and Discovery
THE POWER OF RESEARCH

Skills and Standards
Use Reference Materials and Technology, Evaluate Sources

RESEARCH STRATEGIES WORKSHOP	**1188**
Planning Your Research	**1189**
Using the Internet	**1191**
Using the Library or Media Center	**1194**
Evaluating Information	**1201**
Collecting Your Own Data	**1206**
Research Tips and Strategies	**1208**

Research, Synthesis

WRITING WORKSHOP: RESEARCH PAPER	**1210**
Developing Research Questions	**1217**
Finding and Evaluating Sources	**1218**
Avoiding Plagiarism	**1221**
Documenting Your Sources	**1224**
Reviewing MLA Citation Guidelines	**1228**

PUBLISHING WITH TECHNOLOGY: CREATING A WEB SITE	**1231**

Student Resource Bank

Reading Handbook — R2
Reading Literary Texts — R2
Reading Informational Texts: Text Features — R3
Reading Informational Texts: Patterns of Organization — R8
Reading Informational Texts: Forms — R14
Reading Persuasive Texts — R21
Adjusting Reading Rate — R27

Writing Handbook — R28
The Writing Process — R28
Building Blocks of Good Writing — R30
Descriptive Writing — R34
Narrative Writing — R36
Expository Writing — R37
Persuasive Writing — R40
Workplace and Technical Writing — R42

Grammar Handbook — R46
Quick Reference: Parts of Speech — R46
Quick Reference: The Sentence and Its Parts — R48
Quick Reference: Punctuation — R49
Quick Reference: Capitalization — R51
Nouns — R52
Pronouns — R52
Verbs — R55
Modifiers — R57
The Sentence and Its Parts — R59
Phrases — R60
Verbals and Verbal Phrases — R60
Clauses — R62
The Structure of Sentences — R63
Writing Complete Sentences — R64
Subject-Verb Agreement — R65

Vocabulary and Spelling Handbook — R68
Using Context Clues — R68
Analyzing Word Structure — R69
Understanding Word Origins — R70
Synonyms and Antonyms — R70
Denotation and Connotation — R71
Analogies — R71
Homonyms and Homophones — R71
Words with Multiple Meanings — R72
Specialized Vocabulary — R72
Using Reference Sources — R72
Spelling Rules — R72
Commonly Confused Words — R75

Speaking and Listening Handbook — R76
Speech — R76
Different Types of Oral Presentations — R78
Other Types of Communication — R81
Active Listening — R82

Media Handbook — R84
Five Core Concepts in Media Literacy — R84
Media Basics — R85
Film and TV — R86
News — R88
Advertising — R90
Elements of Design — R91
Evaluating Media Messages — R92

Test-Taking Handbook — R93
General Test-Taking Strategies — R93
Critical Reading — R94
Writing — R99
Essay — R101

Glossary of Literary Terms — R102

Glossary of Reading & Informational Terms — R115

Glossary of Vocabulary in English & Spanish — R121

Pronunciation Key — R130

Index of Fine Art — R131

Index of Skills — R133

Index of Titles and Authors — R153

Acknowledgments — R155

Art Credits — R161

Selections by Genre

FICTION

SHORT STORIES

American History Judith Ortiz Cofer 874

The Apple-Tree Katherine Mansfield 498

Blues Ain't No Mockin Bird Toni Cade Bambara 862

The Cask of Amontillado Edgar Allan Poe 342

Checkouts Cynthia Rylant 28

A Christmas Memory Truman Capote 308

Daughter of Invention Julia Alvarez 78

The Gift of the Magi O. Henry 94

Hamadi Naomi Shihab Nye 222

Marigolds Eugenia Collier 408

The Most Dangerous Game Richard Connell 52

The Necklace Guy de Maupassant 206

The Open Window Saki 560

Pancakes Joan Bauer 192

The Pedestrian Ray Bradbury 642

Powder Tobias Wolff 292

The Princess and the Tin Box James Thurber 764

The Scarlet Ibis James Hurst 426

The Sniper Liam O'Flaherty 405

A Sound of Thunder Ray Bradbury 32

Through the Tunnel Doris Lessing 326

Two Kinds Amy Tan 472

Where Have You Gone, Charming Billy?
Tim O'Brien 750

NOVELS

from **All Quiet on the Western Front**
Erich Maria Remarque 916

from **The Hobbit** J.R.R. Tolkien 392

from **The House on Mango Street** Sandra Cisneros 568

from **The Sea Wolf** Jack London 820

EPIC

The Odyssey Homer 1102

NONFICTION

AUTOBIOGRAPHY/MEMOIR

Angela's Ashes Frank McCourt 836

Fish Cheeks Amy Tan 176

I Know Why the Caged Bird Sings Maya Angelou 236

On Writing Stephen King 165

Rights to the Streets of Memphis *from* **Black Boy**
Richard Wright 110

A White House Diary 890

BIOGRAPHY

from **Rosa Parks** Douglas Brinkley 274

Seabiscuit: An American Legend Laura Hillenbrand 120

ESSAYS

A Few Words Mary Oliver 782

Appearances Are Destructive Mark Mathabane 658

The Future in My Arms Edwidge Danticat 458

Georgia O'Keeffe Joan Didion 524

Going to Japan Barbara Kingsolver 774

Great Movies: Romeo and Juliet *Critical Review* 1056

His Name Was Pete William Faulkner 584

I Have a Dream Dr. Martin Luther King Jr. 600

Island Morning Jamaica Kincaid 514

Math and After Math Lensey Namioka 446

Piedra Gary Soto 177

Pilgrim at Tinker Creek Annie Dillard 821

Primal Screen Ellen Goodman 638

Revisiting Sacred Ground N. Scott Momaday 852

A Walk in the Woods Bill Bryson 360

INFORMATIONAL NONFICTION

Blind to Failure Karl Taro Greenfeld *Magazine Article* . . . 250

A Different Level of Competition *Newspaper Article* 264

Dog Proves As Smart As Average Toddler
Margaret Munro *Online Article* 585

The Education of Frank McCourt *Magazine Article* 848

Four Good Legs Between Us *Magazine Article* 133

From Here to There: The Physics of Time Travel
Magazine Article 51

The Harlem Renaissance: A Cultural Explosion
Magazine Article 900

How Private Is Your Private Life? Andrea Rock
Magazine Article 620

Lincoln Weeping *Political Cartoon* 892

The Lost Boys Sara Corbett *Magazine Article* 546

The Night Poetry Rocked the House *Magazine Article* . . . 698

President Dead: Connally Also Hit by Sniper
Newspaper Article 888

The Privacy Debate: One Size Doesn't Fit All Arthur M. Ahalt
Newspaper Editorial 628

Races on the Radio: Santa Anita Handicap
Radio Transcript 135

Seabiscuit *Timeline* 134

Skeletal Sculptures Donna M. Jackson
Process Description 540

The Story Behind "The Cask of Amontillado"
Book Excerpt 352

Sowing Change *Newspaper Article* 422

Special Report *Magazine Article* 891

Spending Spree *Magazine Article* 221

Testimony Before the Senate Michael J. Fox *Speech* 610

Tim O'Brien: The Naked Soldier *Interview* 760

U. S. Poet Laureates: Getting the Word Out
Magazine Article 690

Unraveling the Mystery of Emily Dickinson
Journal Article 794

Who Killed the Iceman? *National Geographic*
Magazine Article 534

Wilderness Letter Wallace Stegner *Letter* 372

Bodybuilders' Contest Wislawa Szymborska 696

POETRY

Caged Bird Maya Angelou 246

egg horror poem Laurel Winter 710

Elegy for the Giant Tortoises Margaret Atwood 688

For Poets Al Young 702

400-Meter Free Style Maxine Kumin 692

Grape Sherbet Rita Dove 681

Haiku Matsuo Bashō, Richard Wright 902

Honku Aaron Naparstek 906

"Hope" is the thing with feathers Emily Dickinson 793

I Am Offering This Poem Jimmy Santiago Baca 675

I Ask My Mother to Sing Li-Young Lee 680

Incident in a Rose Garden Donald Justice 145

Kidnap Poem Nikki Giovanni 800

Luxury Nikki Giovanni 796

Maud Martha Gwendolyn Brooks 292

My Father's Song Simon J. Ortíz 272

My Heart Leaps Up William Wordsworth 469

My Papa's Waltz Theodore Roethke 676

A narrow Fellow in the Grass Emily Dickinson 790

Not in a Silver Casket . . . Edna St. Vincent Millay 674

O What Is That Sound W. H. Auden 714

Ode to My Socks Pablo Neruda 706

The Peace of Wild Things Wendell Berry 382

Penelope Dorothy Parker 1166

Poem on Returning to Dwell in the Country T'ao Ch'ien . . 466

Pyramus and Thisbe Ovid 1062

The Raven Edgar Allan Poe 138

Rice and Rose Bowl Blues Diane Mei Lin Mark 486

The Road Not Taken Robert Frost 724

Rosa Rita Dove 280

The Seven Ages of Man William Shakespeare 720

The Sharks Denise Levertov 378

The Sower Victor Hugo 734

Spring is like a perhaps hand E. E. Cummings 684

The Sun Mary Oliver 470

Theme for English B Langston Hughes 898

To Be of Use Marge Piercy 735

Today Billy Collins 689

The Tropics in New York Claude McKay 894

The Vietnam Wall Alberto Ríos 834

A Voice Pat Mora 268

Woman with Flower Naomi Long Madgett 442

DRAMA

The Sneeze *from* **The Good Doctor** Neil Simon 802

Sorry, Right Number Stephen King 148

The Tragedy of Romeo and Juliet
William Shakespeare 938

Features

READING AND LITERATURE WORKSHOPS

Plot and Conflict 24

Character and Point of View 186

Setting, Mood, and Imagery 302

Theme and Symbol 402

Author's Purpose 508

Argument and Persuasion 594

The Language of Poetry 668

Author's Style and Voice 744

History, Culture, and the Author 830

Shakespearean Drama 930

The Epic 1094

 LITERATURE CENTER at ClassZone.com

WRITING WORKSHOPS

Personal Narrative 168

Comparison-Contrast Essay 284

Short Story 384

Literary Analysis 490

Problem-Solution Essay 576

Persuasive Speech 650

Personal Response to a Poem 726

Analysis of an Author's Style 812

Persuasive Essay 908

Comparing a Play and a Film 1070

Subject Analysis 1170

Research Paper 1210

 WriteSmart

VOCABULARY STRATEGIES

pages 49, 76, 92, 104, 118, 131, 204, 219, 234, 248, 263, 282, 324, 340, 354, 371, 421, 444, 457, 488, 532, 545, 555, 609, 618, 632, 762, 781, 788, 850, 861, 887, 1139, 1168

GRAMMAR AND STYLE

pages 50, 77, 93, 105, 119, 167, 205, 220, 235, 249, 325, 341, 355, 445, 465, 523, 533, 567, 619, 633, 683, 713, 763, 789, 851, 873, 1051, 1169

SPEAKING, LISTENING, AND VIEWING

Informal Speech 175

Power Presentation 291

Video Presentation 391

Panel Discussion 497

Video Documentary 583

Persuasive Speech 657

Multimedia Presentation 733

Oral Interpretation 819

Debating an Issue 915

Staging a Scene 1077

Delivering an Oral Report 1177

Creating a Web Site 1231

 MEDIA CENTER at **ClassZone.com**

MEDIA STUDY

The Lord of the Rings: The Fellowship of the Ring
Peter Jackson *Film Clip* 106

The Cask of Amontillado Joyce Chopra *Film Clip* 356

Nine Coal Miners Brought Up Safely
TV Newscast Clip 556

All Nine Pulled Alive from Mine
Web News Report 556

"Billy Thomas" *Public Service Announcement* 634

"Life Is Calling" *Public Service Announcement* 634

The Birds Alfred Hitchcock *Film Clip* 770

Romeo and Juliet Franco Zeffirelli *Film Clip* 1052

MediaSmart DVD

The Power of Ideas

For help using this Introductory Unit, see

 RESOURCE MANAGER—Introductory Unit
p. 1

INTRODUCING THE ESSENTIALS

- Literary Genres Workshop
- Reading Strategies Workshop
- Writing Process Workshop

About the Art *(Clockwise, from bottom left)*

In 2000, Christopher Myers published the flying boy image in his book *Wings*. See Unit 7, page 704 for more information.

The production still, also shown on page 773 of Unit 8, captures a scene from Alfred Hitchcock's *North by Northwest* (1959).

Daniel Nevins painted *Healing* (bottom right, also appearing on page 228) in 1996, which also appears on page 228. For more information about Nevins, see page 224.

1

What Are Life's Big Questions?

The introductory unit provides an overview of the ways in which the anthology engages students in the processes of reading and writing. This unit introduces students to regularly appearing features, such as **Key Ideas, Big Questions,** and **Close Reads.** Students will preview skills and strategies that they will study in greater depth in later units. Pay attention to side column and bottom channel notes provided to support all students in your classroom.

These two pages will help you introduce students to the concepts of **Big Questions** and **Key Ideas** and how readers can use both to explore literature. Begin by having students respond to "The Power of Ideas," the title on this page. Ask:

- How would you define the word *idea?* ***Possible answer:*** *a thought, concept, or theme*

- How can ideas have power? ***Possible answer:*** *Ideas can expand people's thinking and motivate them to take action.*

Challenge students to think of ideas that have had an impact on history, on society, and on their own lives.

Next, have students read and discuss the introductory paragraph, which presents the idea that literature is a way to explore life's **Big Questions** and **Key Ideas.** Read through the examples of **Big Questions** on pages 2 and 3, and discuss with students their first thoughts about and reactions to each one. Point out that the **Big Questions** on these pages span cultures and time periods.

The Power of Ideas

What Are Life's Big Questions?

Love and hate, freedom and responsibility, growing up and growing old—these emotions and experiences touch us all, and they are at the heart of the big questions that we ask about the world. This book is all about big questions like the ones shown here. Even though they are challenging to answer, such questions prompt us to think about key ideas that affect our lives. Through reading, discussing, and writing about literature, we can unlock the power of these ideas and come closer to understanding ourselves and the world.

How powerful is LOVE?

In the name of love, Romeo and Juliet risk everything to be together. Similarly, love drives a young wife in O. Henry's "The Gift of the Magi" to chop off her hair. Love is a powerful force, but is it strong enough to overcome all obstacles? You will read works by such writers as William Shakespeare, O. Henry, and Julia Alvarez that explore this age-old question.

What makes a HERO?

In Homer's epic the *Odyssey,* the hero bravely battles dangerous monsters. In 1955, Rosa Parks refused to give up her bus seat to a white passenger. As a young girl, Maya Angelou admired a more personal hero—the neighborhood woman who introduced her to the power of literature. We can find heroes in ancient stories, recent history, today's movies, and our own lives. What extraordinary qualities set heroes apart?

Introductory Unit Resources

* Resources for Differentiation

Does good always TRIUMPH?

In Hollywood movies like *The Lord of the Rings,* we expect satisfying endings—ones in which good characters prevail and evil forces are defeated. Literature, like real life, does not always have happily-ever-after endings. Read Edgar Allan Poe's classic spine tingler "The Cask of Amontillado" or Liam O'Flaherty's eye-opening story "The Sniper." Then ask yourself: Does good always triumph?

What is FAMILY?

Family can mean different things to different people. Relatives, friends, neighbors, and people who share similar cultural and religious backgrounds all can be considered family. You'll explore this idea further in Naomi Shihab Nye's "Hamadi" and in the ripped-from-the-headlines article "The Lost Boys."

Then have students generate other **Big Questions.** Explain that every lesson in this anthology will begin with a Big Question like the ones shown on these pages. Each Big Question will allow students to explore important ideas in depth and to make connections between the literature and their own lives.

OBJECTIVES

- understand the types and characteristics of different literary genres
- become familiar with the academic vocabulary used to write about and discuss literature

The Genres

Determine Readiness Ask students for possible definitions of each genre listed on the page. Then review the genres, pointing out the definition provided for each one.

Discuss and Review Ask students to cite specific examples of each genre that they are familiar with, such as a short story, a lyric poem, a comic play, a news article, and a motion picture.

- Drawing on student examples, point out that different genres allow writers and readers to explore ideas through a variety of approaches and from different perspectives.
- Point out that some literary works can combine genre characteristics. For example, a narrative poem might share some characteristics with a work of fiction. Similarly, a drama usually incorporates elements of fiction, but some dramas include long passages that would be considered nonfiction speeches if they stood apart from the dramatic context. Invite student questions or comments before moving on to the more detailed genre studies on pages 5–10.

Exploring Ideas in Literature

At some point in your life, you have probably considered big questions and ideas like the ones on the preceding pages. For thousands of years, writers have also asked these questions, trying to make sense of the world around them. Many have left a written record of their lives and ideas: literature. Literature is writing that is worth reading, considering, and remembering, for both its ideas and the forms those ideas take.

The Genres

Literature encompasses a wide range of genres. Some are meant to be read; others are meant to be performed by actors on a stage. Media such as feature films are not technically literature, but they are similarly important to learn about today. Regardless of the genre, good literature allows readers to grapple with timeless questions and connect to other times and cultures.

In this book, you will explore questions and ideas in many genres. An ancient story, a news article, and a poem—despite their differences in form—can all help you explore a key idea, such as love or heroism. Before delving into the ideas in literature, familiarize yourself with the genres.

GENRES AT A GLANCE

FICTION
Fiction is narrative writing that springs from an author's imagination.
- short stories
- novels
- novellas

POETRY
Poetry is the most compact form of literature. Words are chosen and arranged to create powerful effects.
- haiku
- sonnets
- narrative poems
- lyric poems

DRAMA
Drama is meant to be performed. Characters and conflicts are developed through dialogue and action.
- comedies
- tragedies
- farces

NONFICTION
Nonfiction is prose writing that deals with real people, events, and places.
- essays
- autobiographies
- news articles
- speeches
- biographies
- feature articles

TYPES OF MEDIA

Media are forms of communication that reach large numbers of people. They include many subgenres, each with its own forms and characteristics.
- feature films
- advertising
- Web sites

4 THE POWER OF IDEAS

DIFFERENTIATED INSTRUCTION

FOR LESS–PROFICIENT READERS

Note Taking For students who need help with note taking, hand out the note-taking copy master before discussing the genres. Have students read the introductory paragraph silently. As you discuss the main points in the Literary Genres Workshop, have students record them on the copy master.

R RESOURCE MANAGER—Copy Master
Note Taking p. 2

FOR ENGLISH LEARNERS

Vocabulary: Cognates Many of the genres and examples of genres have names that share linguistic roots with Spanish. Students whose first language is Spanish can use these examples to clarify their understanding:

- English: *fiction* / Spanish: *ficción*
- English: *novel* / Spanish: *novela*
- English: *poetry* / Spanish: *poesía*
- English: *tragedy* / Spanish: *tragedia*
- English: *media* / Spanish: *medios*

FICTION

At the heart of fiction is **narrative,** the telling of a story. Although fiction can be inspired by real events and people, it is mainly the product of a writer's imagination. A fiction writer shapes his or her narrative to capture and hold readers' interest, often creating memorable settings and characters who face challenging conflicts. Fictional stories can take any of a wide variety of forms, including science fiction, mystery, romance, and historical fiction. Regardless of the form, a work of fiction usually is one of three types.

- A **short story** often focuses on a single event or incident and usually can be read in one sitting.
- A **novel** is an extended work of fiction. Because it is much longer than a short story, a novel gives a writer space to develop a wider range of characters and a more complex plot.
- A **novella** is longer than a short story but shorter than a novel. Most novellas focus on a limited number of characters and a short time span.

Read the Model This excerpt is taken from a novella about an old Cuban fisherman named Santiago. After more than three months at sea, Santiago finally hooks a giant marlin. Can the old man muster enough strength to reel in the fish as it circles his boat? As you read, notice the elements of fiction that the author uses to hook readers and to explore the **key idea** of strength.

> *from*
> # THE *Old Man*
> ## AND THE *Sea*
>
> #### Novella by **Ernest Hemingway**
>
> The fish was coming in on his circle now calm and beautiful looking and only his great tail moving. The old man pulled on him all that he could to bring him closer. For just a moment the fish turned a little on his side. Then he straightened himself and began another circle.
> 5 "I moved him," the old man said. "I moved him then."
> He felt faint again now but he held on the great fish all the strain that he could. I moved him, he thought. Maybe this time I can get him over. Pull, hands, he thought. Hold up, legs. Last for me, head. Last for me. You never went. This time I'll pull him over.
> 10 But when he put all of his effort on, starting it well out before the fish came alongside and pulling with all his strength, the fish pulled part way over and then righted himself and swam away.
> "Fish," the old man said. "Fish, you are going to have to die anyway. Do you have to kill me too?"

ACADEMIC VOCABULARY FOR FICTION
- plot
- conflict
- character
- setting
- theme
- narrator
- point of view

Close Read

1. Using terms from the Academic Vocabulary list, describe what is happening in this work of fiction.

2. **Key Idea: Strength** The old man's strength comes from his relentless will to catch the fish. In your opinion, what gives someone **strength?**

FICTION

Begin by asking students to read the introductory paragraph while you write the **Academic Vocabulary for Fiction** on the board. Then ask students to identify favorite works of fiction and to explain why they found each work memorable. As you write their examples on the board, encourage students to use **Academic Vocabulary for Fiction,** such as *plot, character,* and *setting,* in their explanations.

Close Read

Introduce the model by pointing out that it is taken from a novella by Ernest Hemingway, a famous American author noted for the strength of his spare prose. Ask a volunteer to read the model. Then have students answer the **Close Read** questions.

Possible answers:

1. *This part of the novella's plot focuses on the conflict between two characters: an old fisherman (Santiago) and a large fish (a giant marlin). With a setting on the sea, and told from the point of view of a narrator who is not a part of the story, this scene suggests a theme of perseverance as it shows the old man's determination to catch a fish that seems determined not to be caught.*

2. *Strength—inner strength, which may manifest itself as physical strength—comes from the belief that one's goals and motivations are meaningful and worthwhile.*

CHECK UNDERSTANDING Ask for volunteers to explain the difference between a short story and a novella.

FOR LESS–PROFICIENT READERS
Concept Support Have students adapt a Story Map by using these terms from the **Academic Vocabulary for Fiction:** *plot, conflict, character, setting, theme, narrator.* Then help students complete their story map by identifying these elements for a story they have read.

BEST PRACTICES TOOLKIT—Transparency
Story Map p. D14

FOR ENGLISH LEARNERS
Language: Punctuation and Print Clues In this passage, Hemingway shows what Santiago says and thinks. Point out that the quotation marks in lines 5 and 13–14 indicate when Santiago speaks aloud (to himself and to the fish). Then direct students to lines 7–9, in which Santiago's thoughts appear as silent dialogue without quotation marks. Note, too, the use of the tags "old man said" (lines 5 and 13) to indicate speech and "he thought" (lines 7 and 8) to indicate thoughts.

POETRY

Direct students to read the first three paragraphs while you write the **Academic Vocabulary for Poetry** and then this poem on the board:

> My mother told me, "Come and see
> Your newborn baby brother Jack."
> I looked at him, she smiled at me
> Till I said, "Give him back."

Have students explain how the poem illustrates terms from the **Academic Vocabulary for Poetry,** such as *line, stanza, speaker, rhyme, rhythm,* and *meter.*

Close Read

Read the model, pausing as indicated by the punctuation in the poem. Invite volunteers to read stanzas of their choice. If time permits, also have students listen to the poem on the *Audio Anthology CD.* Then direct students to answer the **Close Read** questions.

Possible answers:

1. *The poem consists of three stanzas. The poem has no regular rhythm or rhyme; however, it uses sound devices (such as the /s/ sounds in lines 2 and 4), imagery (such as the description of the couple's clothing in lines 5–7), and figurative language (the comparison of love to dried flowers in lines 16–17) to convey meaning and emotion.*

   If students need help . . . Explain that although many poems have a regular rhythm and rhyme, others do not. Urge students to think about the mental pictures and feelings that "Los ancianos" suggests and the words that Pat Mora uses to express them.

2. *Other qualities of love include patience, respect, compassion, thoughtfulness, and a romantic nature.*

CHECK UNDERSTANDING Ask students to identify the line where the first stanza ends.

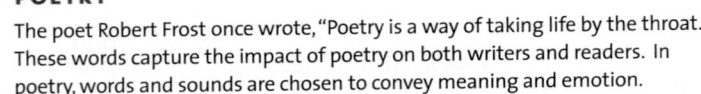

POETRY

The poet Robert Frost once wrote, "Poetry is a way of taking life by the throat." These words capture the impact of poetry on both writers and readers. In poetry, words and sounds are chosen to convey meaning and emotion.

What you'll most likely notice first about a poem is its **form,** or arrangement on the page. Usually, poems are divided into **lines,** which are arranged into groups called **stanzas.** While some poets follow fixed rules of form, others break with convention and invent unique forms to echo their subjects.

If you have ever read a poem aloud, you know that its impact depends on more than its form. The way a poem sounds—its brash **rhythms** or its predictable **rhymes,** for example—is part of its effect. Language delivers other powerful effects. **Imagery,** which consists of language that recreates sensory experiences, helps readers see, hear, and feel what a poem describes.

Read the Model Here, the love of an older couple—*los ancianos,* in Spanish—is described in striking detail. As you read, notice the poetic elements that help to paint a moving portrait of the couple. Also, consider what the poet is saying about the **key idea** of love.

ACADEMIC VOCABULARY FOR POETRY

- form
- line
- stanza
- speaker
- rhyme
- rhythm
- meter
- sound devices
- figurative language
- imagery

Los ancianos

Poem by **Pat Mora**

> They hold hands
> as they walk with slow steps.
> Careful together they cross the plaza
> both slightly stooped, bodies returning to the land,
> 5 he in faded khaki and straw hat,
> she wrapped in soft clothes, black
> *rebozo*[1] round her head and shoulders.
>
> Tourists in halter tops and shorts
> pose by flame trees and fountains,
> 10 but the old couple walks step by step
> on the edge.
> Even in the heat, only their wrinkled
> hands and faces show. They know
> of moving through a crowd at their own pace.
>
> 15 I watch him help her
> off the curb and I smell love
> like dried flowers, old love
> of holding hands with one man for fifty years.

---

1. *rebozo* (rĭ-bō′sō) *Spanish:* shawl.

6   THE POWER OF IDEAS

Close Read

1. What characteristics immediately signal that this is a poem? Cite specific details.

2. **Key Idea: Love** The couple in this poem seem compatible and comfortable with each other. What other qualities of a relationship are essential for **love** to last over the years?

DIFFERENTIATED INSTRUCTION

FOR LESS–PROFICIENT READERS

Analysis Support: Poetry To help students apply the **Academic Vocabulary for Poetry** to "Los ancianos" or another poem of your choice, have them work in a group to complete the Core Analysis Frame: Poetry. Monitor their progress, offering assistance as requested or needed.

 BEST PRACTICES TOOLKIT—Transparency
Core Analysis Frame: Poetry pp. D21, D34

FOR ENGLISH LEARNERS

Language: Skill Words Write these lines on the board, and have students discuss them using one or more terms from the **Academic Vocabulary for Poetry:**

- I adore / That town on the shore. (*rhyme, line, speaker, rhythm*)

- A smile like a sunny summer day / Lit up her face and found my heart. (*sound devices, line, speaker, rhythm, meter, figurative language, imagery*)

DRAMA

Characters in conflict are at the heart of drama, just as they are in fiction. But since drama is meant to be performed for an audience rather than read, the plot is carried by **dialogue** and **action**—what the characters say and do. Dramas are usually divided into **scenes,** with each scene set in a different time or place. In long plays, scenes are grouped into **acts.**

With their heroes, villains, and sets, dramas have been captivating audiences since ancient times. However, dramas also make good reading. To help yourself visualize a drama, you need to consider not only the dialogue but also the **stage directions**—the writer's instructions for the actors, the director, and the other people working on the play. Often printed in italic type, stage directions describe everything from the setting and the props to the characters' movements.

Read the Model *The Miracle Worker* dramatizes Helen Keller's relationship with Annie Sullivan, the teacher who taught Helen to use sign language and communicate with others. At this point in the drama, Helen has learned the mechanics of sign language, but she still does not understand the meanings behind the words. Here, Annie expresses her frustration to Helen's mother, Kate. How does Annie's attitude help you understand the **key idea** of determination?

ACADEMIC VOCABULARY FOR DRAMA
• plot
• character
• act
• scene
• stage directions
• monologue
• dialogue
• dialect

---

from

The Miracle Worker

Drama by **William Gibson**

from **Act Three**

Annie. . . . We're born to use words, like wings, it has to come.

Kate. How?

Annie (*another pause, wearily*). All right. I don't know how. (*She pushes up her glasses to rub her eyes.*)

5 I've done everything I could think of. Whatever she's learned here—keeping herself clean, knitting, stringing beads, meals, setting-up exercises each morning, we climb trees, hunt eggs, yesterday a chick was born in her hands—all of it I spell, everything we do, we never stop spelling. I go to bed with—writer's cramp from talking so much!

10 **Kate.** I worry about you, Miss Annie. You must rest.

Annie. Now? She spells back in her *sleep,* her fingers make letters when she doesn't know! In her bones those five fingers know, that hand aches to—speak out, and something in her mind is asleep, how do I—nudge that awake? That's the one question.

Close Read

1. How do you know that Annie is exhausted? Cite specific details that reveal her state of mind.

2. **Key Idea: Determination** How do you think Annie's **determination** will eventually play out? Explain whether you think people can accomplish anything if they are determined enough.

DRAMA

Ask students to read the first two paragraphs to themselves and note the boldfaced words while you list the **Academic Vocabulary for Drama** on the board. Discuss elements that readers might find in both fiction and drama, such as *plot, character, dialogue,* and *dialect.*

Close Read

Introduce the model by reading the third paragraph aloud. Ask students to read the model silently. Then assign roles to students and ask them to read the model again, this time aloud. Afterward, have students answer the **Close Read** questions.

Possible answers:

1. *The stage directions—Annie's weary pause and rubbing of her eyes (lines 3 and 4)—show that she is exhausted, as do the breaks in her words to Kate (indicated by dashes). Kate's comment, "I worry about you, Miss Annie. You must rest" (line 10), indicates that Annie's exhaustion is apparent to others.*

2. *Given time and her determination to teach Helen to understand and learn sign language, Annie probably will succeed. Determination may help people reach some goals, but other goals require more than determination (for example, special skills, education, or funding), and some goals are too unrealistic ever to be reached.*

CHECK UNDERSTANDING Have students identify details in the passage that demonstrate Annie's determination.

FOR LESS-PROFICIENT READERS

Analysis Support: Dramatic Character Have students reread lines 1–4 of the model and identify characters, stage directions, and dialogue. Ask them to use a chart to record lines where these elements appear.

	Line Numbers
Characters	Annie (lines 1, 3) Kate (line 2)
Stage Directions	Lines 3, 4
Dialogue	Lines 1–3

NONFICTION AND INFORMATIONAL TEXT

Read the introductory paragraph and point out the terms *literary nonfiction* and *informational texts*. To clarify the distinction, show students a copy or give the title of several specific works of literary nonfiction, such as Bill Bryson's *A Walk in the Woods*. Similarly, show specific examples of informational texts, such as an autobiography. Invite students to suggest additional examples for each category. Discuss the characteristics of each type of nonfiction listed on the page. Then point out that the **Academic Vocabulary for Nonfiction** refers to terms students will encounter and use in their study of nonfiction.

NONFICTION AND INFORMATIONAL TEXT

When you see the word *nonfiction*—especially in a literature book— you probably expect to find what is considered **literary nonfiction,** such as biographies, speeches, and essays. Nonfiction also includes **informational texts,** such as news articles and train schedules, which provide factual information. Because you encounter informational texts all the time, you should know what to expect from them.

ACADEMIC VOCABULARY FOR NONFICTION
- purpose
- patterns of organization
- argument
- persuasion

TYPE OF NONFICTION	CHARACTERISTICS	
AUTOBIOGRAPHY/ BIOGRAPHY The true story of a person's life, told by that person (autobiography) or by another person (biography)	• Provides details that give readers insights into a person's life • Is told from the first-person point of view (autobiography) or from the third-person point of view (biography) • Presents the person's own thoughts about his or her life experiences (autobiography) or information from a variety of sources (biography)	
ESSAY A short work that focuses on a single subject. Common types include personal essays and persuasive essays.	• May have the following purposes: to express feelings, to inform, to entertain, to persuade • May be **formal,** with an organized structure and an impersonal style • May be **informal,** with a conversational style	
SPEECH An oral presentation of the ideas, beliefs, or proposals of a speaker	• May have the following purposes: to express feelings, to inform, to entertain, to persuade • Achieves its power through effective language and a compelling delivery	
NEWS/FEATURE ARTICLES Informative writing in newspapers and magazines. A news article reports on recent events. A feature article focuses on human-interest topics.	• Are primarily intended to inform or entertain • May use statistics, quotations from sources, examples, and graphic aids to convey information • Usually are objective and balanced	
FUNCTIONAL DOCUMENTS Writing that serves a practical purpose. Types include consumer documents, such as instruction manuals, and workplace documents, such as memos and résumés.	• Are written for a specific audience (for example, the user of a product or a potential employer) • May present information in charts or other easy-to-navigate formats • Often include specialized jargon	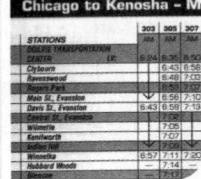

DIFFERENTIATED INSTRUCTION

FOR LESS–PROFICIENT READERS
Language: Skill Words Discuss the meanings of these terms from the chart:

- *point of view:* the perspective from which a text is narrated
- *conversational:* like casual, everyday speech
- *statistics:* numerical facts
- *graphic aids:* charts, diagrams, or other drawings
- *jargon:* specialized words used in a certain profession

Comprehension: Nonfiction Have students identify these types of nonfiction:

- An attempt to get readers to support a change of the school mascot (*essay*)
- The story of your life (*autobiography*)
- Details about the city council meeting (*news article*)
- A political leader talking to a group of local voters (*speech*)

MODEL 1: AUTOBIOGRAPHY

This excerpt is from an autobiography by Monica Sone, a Japanese-American woman who grew up in Seattle during World War II. Here, Sone remembers the moment when she and her brother Henry found out from a classmate about Japan's attack on Pearl Harbor. Notice how Sone describes her feelings, and think about the **key idea** of identity as you read this text.

from

 **Nisei** Daughter

Autobiography by **Monica Sone**

With that, Chuck swept out of the room, a swirl of young men following in his wake. Henry was one of them. The rest of us stayed, rooted to our places like a row of marionettes. I felt as if a fist had smashed my pleasant little existence, breaking it into jigsaw puzzle pieces. An old wound opened up again,
5 and I found myself shrinking inwardly from my Japanese blood, the blood of an enemy. I knew instinctively that the fact that I was an American by birthright was not going to help me escape the consequences of this unhappy war.

Close Read

1. How does Sone react to the news about the attack on Pearl Harbor? Cite details that reveal her feelings.

2. **Key Idea: Identity** Sone feels torn between her American upbringing and her Japanese blood. In your opinion, what forces shape a person's **identity?**

MODEL 2: NEWS ARTICLE

This article can help you explore the **key idea** of war. It was published in the *New York Times* on December 8, 1941, one day after the attack on Pearl Harbor.

DECEMBER 8, 1941

JAPAN MAKES SUDDEN ATTACK

NEWS ARTICLE BY **Frank L. Kluckhohn**

WASHINGTON, Monday, Dec. 8—Sudden and unexpected attacks on Pearl Harbor, Honolulu, and other United States possessions in the
5 Pacific early yesterday by the Japanese air force and navy plunged the United States and Japan into active war.

The initial attack in Hawaii, apparently launched by torpedo-
10 carrying bombers and submarines, caused widespread damage and death.

It was quickly followed by others. There were unconfirmed reports that German raiders participated in the attacks.
15 Guam was assaulted from the air, as were Davao, on the island of Mindanao, and Camp John Hay, in Northern Luzom, both in the Philippines. Lieut. Gen. Douglas MacArthur, commanding
20 the United States Army of the Far East, reported there was little damage, however.

Close Read

1. How do the details in this article differ from those in Sone's account? Cite evidence from both texts to support your answer.

2. **Key Idea: War** Consider other wars you've studied or read about. For what reasons do countries go to **war?**

9

Read the models aloud, explaining that they provide different types of information about the same historical event. Then have students answer the **Close Read** questions.

MODEL 1: AUTOBIOGRAPHY
Close Read

Possible answers:

1. *Sone reacts with shock and fear. She is stunned by the news (lines 3–4), and she worries about what the future will bring her as a Japanese American (lines 4–7).*

2. *The forces that shape a person's identity include his or her heritage, the community in which he or she has grown up, family traditions and values, education, and occupations.*

MODEL 2: NEWS ARTICLE
Close Read

Possible answers:

1. *Sone's account is a first-person, emotional reflection; she says more about her feelings than about the attack. The article, however, focuses on facts as it gives a third-person, objective account of the attack. Accept all relevant details.*

   If students need help . . . Ask them to think about the difference between a fact and an opinion. Which passage has more facts (names, dates, places)? How would a reader describe the content of the other passage?

2. *Countries sometimes go to war to settle land disputes or political or religious differences, to defend themselves from enemy attacks, or to support allies.*

CHECK UNDERSTANDING Have students explain how the purposes of the two nonfiction models differ.

FOR LESS–PROFICIENT READERS

Analysis Support: Nonfiction Model the use of Reporter's Questions as a means of gathering information from and comparing these two nonfiction passages. Answer a few of the questions for the excerpt from *Nisei Daughter;* then have students answer the rest as a group. Allow them to answer the questions about the news article on their own.

Who attacked Pearl Harbor?	Japan
What happened?	Bombers and submarines attacked with torpedoes, causing damage and deaths
When was the attack?	December 7, 1941

BEST PRACTICES TOOLKIT—Transparency
Reporter's Questions p. C9

TYPES OF MEDIA

Have students read over the introductory paragraph while you write the **Academic Vocabulary for Media** on the board. Then discuss why it is important to develop media literacy. Point out the types of media listed on the page, as well as characteristics particular to each type. Then have students compare the purpose and effects of the various types of media. Finally, briefly explain how the **Academic Vocabulary for Media** applies to the types of media listed on the page.

CHECK UNDERSTANDING Ask students where examples of news media can be found.

TYPES OF MEDIA

You may not think of media as literature, but learning how to "read" the media is a key part of being literate in today's world. From screaming headlines at the checkout counter to in-your-face advertising, all media messages have been constructed for a purpose—to grab your attention, entertain you, or influence your decisions. Becoming **media literate** starts with knowing the basics and thinking critically about *all* messages in this media-saturated age.

ACADEMIC VOCABULARY FOR MEDIA
- medium
- message
- purpose
- target audience

TYPE OF MEDIA	CHARACTERISTICS	
FEATURE FILMS Motion pictures that use narrative elements to tell a story	• Are intended to entertain and make money • Use camera shots, sound effects, music, actors, and sets to tell compelling stories • Are at least 60 minutes in length	
NEWS MEDIA Accounts of current events as presented on TV, in newspapers and magazines, on the radio, and on the Web	• Are intended to inform and entertain • Have varying degrees of accuracy and credibility • Medium (TV, radio, print) affects the presentation and delivery of information	
TV SHOWS Programs broadcast on television, including dramas, sitcoms, and reality shows	• Are usually intended to inform or entertain • Are financed by sponsors who pay to air ads during the programs • Use visuals and sounds to create programming that will engage viewers • Are typically 30–60 minutes in length	
ADVERTISING A sponsor's paid use of media to promote products, services, or ideas	• Is intended to persuade a target audience to buy a product or service or to adopt an idea • Uses persuasive techniques, visuals, and sounds to appeal to an audience • Is strategically printed or aired where a target audience is likely to encounter it	
WEB SITES Collections of "pages" on the World Wide Web. From a home page, users can explore other pages on a Web site by clicking hyperlinks or menus.	• Can be accessed at any time by anyone with a computer and an Internet connection • Are not always a reliable source of information (because anyone can publish on the Web) • Present content through text, graphics, video, sound, and interactive features	

DIFFERENTIATED INSTRUCTION

FOR LESS–PROFICIENT READERS

Note Taking Suggest that students use a Three-Column Journal to record key facts from this page. Instruct students to focus on medium, purpose, and methods. (Point out that the messages and target audiences for each medium are practically infinite.) Model the example at right.

 BEST PRACTICES TOOLKIT—Transparency Three-Column Journal p. B10

Medium	Purpose	Methods
feature films	entertain (and make money)	camera shots, sound effects, music, actors, sets

FOR ENGLISH LEARNERS

Language: Skill Words Have students identify the **Academic Vocabulary for Media** term that each statement illustrates.

- "Wow—that movie really made me think!" (*message*)
- "A new TV series will be based on that movie." (*medium*)
- "Teens will love this show." (*target audience*)
- "Do we merely want to entertain them, or to teach them?" (*purpose*)

Strategies That Work: Literature

❶ Ask the Right Questions

An important part of analyzing literature is knowing what questions to ask as you read. What should you be looking for when you are reading a drama? a news article? a classic novel? The following features will help you develop your own instincts for asking the right questions.

Where to Look	What You'll Find
Literary Analysis Workshops (at the beginning of every unit) ▶	Interactive practice models and **Close Read** questions
Side notes and discussion questions ▶	Questions (throughout and following each selection) that focus on the analysis of literary elements and key ideas
Analysis Frames (Literature Center at ClassZone.com) ▶	Guided questions for analyzing different genres of literature

❷ Make Connections

"I can relate to the main character because...," "This writer's view of love is different from..."—connections like these are what make the ideas in literature meaningful. Here are some ways to tap into the selections in this book:

- **Big Questions and Key Ideas** Life and literature are both about exploring big questions and key ideas. Look for opportunities to connect what you read with experiences in your own life.
- **Discussion/Journaling** Share your insights with others or jot them down. Consider questions such as:
  - What does this mean to me?
  - Who or what does this remind me of?

❸ Record Your Reactions

Writing down your ideas in a **Reader's Notebook** can help you both remember and sort through your reactions and observations. Try a variety of formats.

GRAPHIC ORGANIZER

Set up a graphic organizer, such as a cluster diagram.

TWO-COLUMN NOTES

Divide each page into two columns, one for quotations and information from the text, and the other for your responses.

"Los ancianos"	My Impressions
"I watch him help her off the curb and I smell love" (lines 15–16)	Shows the power of the couple's love; also conveys how moved the speaker is by this sight

---

Strategies That Work: Literature

Point out that practically any activity that students may enjoy—sports, art, music, or drama—involves strategies, or ways of helping them become better at that particular activity. Elicit that such activities become more exciting as students' personal involvement with them grows. As you discuss **Strategies That Work,** emphasize that these strategies can help make reading literature engaging and exciting.

1. **Ask the Right Questions**
   Point out to students that throughout the anthology they will be guided in asking questions that they will need to analyze the selections. As you discuss the features listed under "Where to Look" and "What You'll Find," explain that students will find these features throughout the anthology.

2. **Make Connections**
   Reinforce for students the importance of connecting to literature on a personal level. Explain that their ideas and reactions are valid as long as they can support them with examples from the text. As you discuss the explanations of **Big Questions** and **Key Ideas** and **Discussion/Journaling,** encourage students to use these opportunities to connect and respond to the selections in the anthology.

3. **Record Your Reactions**
   Emphasize to students the importance of creating a **Reader's Notebook** to record their reactions to what they are reading. Encourage them to use the kinds of graphic formats suggested by the text, as well as the questions, reactions, and connections that might occur to them as they read.

FOR LESS–PROFICIENT READERS

Concept Support Use these activities to reinforce the teaching in the text:

1. Have students turn to pages 24–31 to see a Literary Analysis Workshop. Point out its models and **Close Read** questions. Similarly, have students skim through some of the side notes and discussion questions in "A Sound of Thunder," the first selection in Unit 1. If you have a classroom computer, go to **ClassZone.com** and show students an example of an analysis frame.

2. Use "A Sound of Thunder" to illustrate **Big Questions** and **Key Ideas.** Then call on volunteers to share positive experiences that they have had with discussion groups and journaling.

3. Have students read the Cluster Diagram and the Two-Column Notes against the text of "Los ancianos" (p. 6). Ask students to suggest how the format could be used to record their reactions to the excerpt from *The Old Man and the Sea* (p. 5).

OBJECTIVES

- become familiar with the skills and strategies needed for active reading
- practice reading skills and strategies, such as **visualize, monitor, make inferences,** and **connect**

Explain to students that, like explorers discovering new worlds, active readers use a variety of skills and strategies to learn what they need to know in a text until they have thoroughly explored its contents. Even when they have finished, active readers will continue to share and explore new ideas.

After students have read through the explanation at the top of the page, ask them what strategies they used while exploring this material. For example, did they set a purpose for reading? Did they develop questions to ensure that they understand the material? Encourage students to examine the **SKILLS AND STRATEGIES FOR ACTIVE READING** and to cite those that might also have been useful.

Becoming an Active Reader

To really explore ideas in literature, you need to open your mind to ideas that might be different from anything you've ever imagined. Learning how to be an active reader can help you do just that. The tools you need to be an active reader are already within your grasp. In fact, you use them when you are watching TV, surfing the Web, or curled up with a suspenseful page-turner. The skills and strategies shown here are ones that you will apply throughout this book.

SKILLS AND STRATEGIES FOR ACTIVE READING

Preview
Get a sense of a text before you start to read.
- Look for clues in the title, graphics, and subheadings.
- Skim the opening paragraphs.

Set a Purpose
Decide *why* you are reading a particular text.
- Ask: Am I reading to be entertained, to get information, or for another reason?
- Consider how your purpose might affect the way you approach a text. Take notes or just enjoy?

Connect
Relate personally to what you are reading.
- Think about whether you've encountered people or situations like the ones described.
- Ask: If I were in this situation, how would I react?

Use Prior Knowledge
Call to mind what you already know about a topic.
- Before reading, jot down what you already know.
- As you read, connect what you know to what you are learning.

Predict
Try to guess what will happen next.
- Note details about plot or characters that hint at where the story is heading.
- Keep reading to find out how accurate your prediction was.

Visualize
Form a mental picture of what is being described.
- Look for descriptive details about characters, settings, and events.
- Use this information to conjure up a vivid scene in your mind's eye.

Monitor
Check your own comprehension as you read.
- **Question** what is happening and why.
- **Clarify** your understanding by rereading difficult parts or asking for help.
- **Evaluate** how well you are understanding the text.

Make Inferences
Make logical guesses, using evidence in the text and what you know from experience.
- Record details about characters and events.
- Ask: How can common sense and my own experiences help me understand this character or situation?

Details in "Walter Mitty"	What I Know	My Inference
Mitty daydreams a lot that he's a hero.	Daydreams are a way to escape real life.	Mitty is probably not content with his real life.

DIFFERENTIATED INSTRUCTION

FOR LESS–PROFICIENT READERS
Note Taking For those students who need help, hand out the note-taking copy master for the Reading Strategies Workshop. Read and discuss the introductory paragraph on this page. As students examine the **SKILLS AND STRATEGIES FOR ACTIVE READING,** assist them in completing the copy master as needed.

R RESOURCE MANAGER—Copy Master
Note Taking p. 3

Concept Support Remind students that they already use many of the skills and strategies used by active readers. Ask students to recall a movie or TV program they have recently seen. Have them explain and give examples of how they used the **SKILLS AND STRATEGIES FOR ACTIVE READING** when viewing this material.

In this excerpt from James Thurber's classic story, exhilirating daydreams help save Walter Mitty from his own dull existence. As you move between Mitty's imaginary adventures and his ordinary routines, use the **Close Read** questions to practice active reading skills and strategies.

from

The Secret Life of Walter Mitty

Short story by **James Thurber**

"We're going through!" The Commander's voice was like thin ice breaking. He wore his full-dress uniform, with the heavily braided white cap pulled down rakishly[1] over one cold gray eye. "We can't make it, sir. It's spoiling for a hurricane, if you ask me." "I'm not asking you, Lieutenant Berg,"
5 said the Commander. "Throw on the power lights! Rev her up to 8,500! We're going through!" The pounding of the cylinders increased: ta-pocketa-pocketa-pocketa-*pocketa-pocketa*. The Commander stared at the ice forming on the pilot window. He walked over and twisted a row of complicated dials. "Switch on No. 8 auxilary!" he shouted. "Switch on No. 8 auxilary!" repeated
10 Lieutenant Berg. "Full strength in No. 3 turret!" shouted the Commander. "Full strength in No. 3 turret!" The crew, bending to their various tasks in the huge, hurtling eight-engined Navy hydroplane, looked at each other and grinned. "The Old Man'll get us through," they said to one another. "The Old Man ain't afraid of Hell!" . . .

15 "Not so fast! You're driving too fast!" said Mrs. Mitty. "What are you driving so fast for?"

"Hmm?" said Walter Mitty. He looked at his wife, in the seat behind him, with shocked astonishment. She seemed grossly unfamiliar, like a strange woman who had yelled at him in a crowd. "You were up to fifty-five," she said.
20 "You know I don't like to go more than forty. You were up to fifty-five." Walter Mitty drove on toward Waterbury in silence, the roaring of the SN202 through the worst storm in twenty years of Navy flying fading in the remote, intimate airways of his mind. "You're tensed up again," said Mrs. Mitty. "It's one of your days. I wish you'd let Dr. Renshaw look you over."

25 Walter Mitty stopped the car in front of the building where his wife went to have her hair done. "Remember to get those overshoes while I'm having my hair done," she said. "I don't need overshoes," said Mitty. She put her mirror back into her bag. "We've been all through that," she said, getting out of the car. "You're not a young man any longer." He raced the engine a little. "Why

1. **rakishly:** with a confident, carefree, and dashing look.

Close Read

1. **Visualize** Which details in lines 1–14 help you picture the excitement of the scene? Cite details about the setting and the conflict.

2. **Monitor** In the boxed text, the story shifts scenes, from a thrilling adventure to an uneventful car ride. Clarify your understanding by summarizing what is happening.

DIFFERENTIATED INSTRUCTION

FOR ENGLISH LEARNERS

Vocabulary: Idioms and Sayings Discuss these idioms and sayings, which appear in the Mittys' conversation (some real, some imagined):

- *going through* (line 1), "proceeding"
- *can't make it* (line 3), "won't succeed"
- *It's spoiling for a hurricane* (lines 3–4), "looks like a hurricane is approaching"
- *Throw on* (line 5) and *Switch on* (line 9), "Put into operation"

- *Rev her up* (line 5), "Increase the speed"
- *What are you driving so fast for?* (lines 15–16), "Why are you driving so fast?"
- *You were up to fifty-five* (line 19), "You increased the speed to fifty-five miles per hour"
- *tensed up* (line 23), "stressed"
- *look you over* (line 24), "examine you"

Explain to students that reading the model will provide them with the opportunity to practice the **SKILLS AND STRATEGIES FOR ACTIVE READING.** Ask students to pay attention to the ways in which each strategy provides different information about and insights into the passage.

MODEL: SHORT STORY

Close Read

Call on a volunteer to read aloud the introductory paragraph. Point out that students will have to decide which parts of the story present daydreams and which parts present real life. As time permits, also have students listen to the complete story on the *Audio Anthology CD.* Then direct them to answer the **Close Read** questions.

Possible answers:

1. *Details that convey excitement include the references to bad weather (lines 3–4 and 7–8), the sound of the engines (lines 6–7), and the many shouted commands. The setting is aboard a "huge, hurtling eight-engined Navy hydroplane" (line 12). The main conflict is between the plane's crew (especially the Commander) and a potentially deadly storm; there also is a brief conflict between the Commander and Lieutenant Berg.*

2. *Mitty has been daydreaming about commanding a Navy hydroplane in a storm when he is snapped back to reality by his wife's command to drive more slowly. As he realizes where he is, the daydream fades, and his wife says that he should see Dr. Renshaw because he is tense.*

If students need help . . . Use the Read Aloud/Think Aloud strategy to model a summary of lines 11–14. Then help students summarize the rest of the boxed text.

 BEST PRACTICES TOOLKIT—Transparency Read Aloud/Think Aloud p. A34

Possible answers:

3. *Unlike the take-charge hero of his day-dreams, the real-life Mitty quietly does what his wife demands of him, even though he seems to want to rebel against her (as evidenced in his racing the engine [line 29] and taking off his gloves as soon as she is out of sight [lines 31–33]). The fact that Mitty's wife dominates the conversation in a very critical way suggests that the Mittys do not have an entirely happy relationship.*

4. *If this daydream is like the previous one, it will be cut short, just before reaching its climax, by words spoken to Mitty in real life.*

   If students need help . . . Review what happened in Mitty's previous daydream. In particular, have students reread lines 11–16, noting that (1) Mitty's daydream is interrupted before its story ends and (2) the interruption comes in the form of critical words from Mrs. Mitty.

5. *Accept all reasonable responses. Students may suggest that people dream that they are stars because they want to escape the dullness of their everyday lives or because they admire the wealth, power, attractiveness, confidence, or adoration that they think stars enjoy.*

CHECK UNDERSTANDING Ask students how using various reading strategies increased their understanding and enjoyment of Thurber's story.

---

30 don't you wear your gloves? Have you lost your gloves?" Walter Mitty reached in a pocket and brought out the gloves. He put them on, but after she had turned and gone into the building and he had driven on to a red light, he took them off again. "Pick it up, brother!" snapped a cop as the light changed, and Mitty hastily pulled on his gloves and lurched ahead. He drove around the
35 streets aimlessly for a time, and then he drove past the hospital on his way to the parking lot.

     ". . . It's the millionaire banker, Wellington McMillan," said the pretty nurse. "Yes?" said Walter Mitty, removing his glasses slowly. "Who has the case?" "Dr. Renshaw and Dr. Benbow, but there are two
40 specialists here, Dr. Remington from New York and Mr. Pritchard-Mitford from London. He flew over." A door opened down a long, cool corridor and Dr. Renshaw came out. He looked distraught and haggard. "Hello, Mitty," he said. "We're having the devil's own time with McMillan, the millionaire banker and close personal friend of Roosevelt. Obstreosis of the ductal tract.[2] Tertiary.
45 Wish you'd take a look at him." "Glad to," said Mitty.
     In the operating room there were whispered introductions: "Dr. Remington, Dr. Mitty. Mr. Pritchard-Mitford, Dr. Mitty." "I've read your book on streptothricosis," said Pritchard-Mitford, shaking hands. "A brilliant performance, sir." "Thank you," said Walter Mitty. "Didn't know you were
50 in the States, Mitty," grumbled Remington. "Coals to Newcastle,[3] bringing Mitford and me up here for tertiary." "You are very kind," said Mitty. A huge, complicated machine, connected to the operating table, with many tubes and wires, began at this moment to go pocketa-pocketa-pocketa. "The new anesthetizer is giving way!" shouted an intern. "There is no one in the East
55 who knows how to fix it!" "Quiet, man!" said Mitty, in a low, cool voice. He sprang to the machine, which was now going pocketa-pocketa-queep-pocketa-queep. He began fingering delicately a row of glistening dials. "Give me a fountain pen!" he snapped. Someone handed him a fountain pen. He pulled a faulty piston out of the machine and inserted a pen in its place. "That will
60 hold for ten minutes," he said. "Get on with the operation." A nurse hurried over and whispered to Renshaw, and Mitty saw the man turn pale. "Coreopsis has set in," said Renshaw nervously. "If you would take over, Mitty?" Mitty looked at him and at the craven figure of Benbow, who drank, and at the grave, uncertain faces of the two great specialists. "If you wish," he said. They
65 slipped a white gown on him; he adjusted a mask and drew on thin gloves; nurses handed him shining . . .
     "Back it up, Mac! Look out for that Buick!" Walter Mitty jammed on the brakes. "Wrong lane, Mac," said the parking-lot attendant, looking at Mitty closely. "Gee. Yeh," muttered Mitty. . . .

---

2. **Obstreosis of the ductal tract:** Thurber made up this and other terms to sound like—and poke fun at—medical jargon.

3. **Coals to Newcastle:** an unnecessary task. This expression refers to Newcastle, England, which was a major coal-producing city.

3. **Make Inferences** Given Mitty's actions in lines 29–34, what can you infer about his personality and his relationship with his wife?

4. **Predict** Now Mitty pictures himself in an operating room with an important patient. What do you imagine will happen?

5. **Connect** Have you ever been the hero in your own dreams? Explain why you think many people have dreams in which they are stars.

DIFFERENTIATED INSTRUCTION

FOR LESS–PROFICIENT READERS

Check Comprehension Ask pairs of students to create five sentences about events in the story, leaving out key details, as in these examples:

- In Mitty's first daydream, he calls himself " _____ ," and his crew admiringly calls him " _____ ." (*the Commander; the Old Man*)

- In real life, his wife criticizes him for _____ and urges him to see _____ . (*driving too fast; Dr. Renshaw*)

- As "Dr. Mitty," he is called upon to fix _____ and to operate on _____ , who is a _____ . (*a failing anesthetizer machine; McMillan; wealthy banker and good friend of Roosevelt*)

Have each pair exchange its sentences for those created by another pair and complete the sentences that they receive.

Strategies That Work: Reading

❶ Read Independently
The best way to become a better reader is to read as much as you can, every chance you get.

What Should I Read?	Where Should I Look?
Novels 	▶ Experiment with different authors and genres. Also, consult the **Great Reads** feature (at the end of every unit) for suggested novels tied to key ideas.
Magazines Newspapers Web sites 	▶ Every time you check your favorite Web site or leaf through the daily newspaper, you are reading. Pick up whatever interests you, and keep reading.

❷ Use Graphic Organizers
Graphic organizers can help you track the action in a work of literature, recognize relationships, and understand what is happening. Look for suggested graphic organizers in each lesson.

Real Mitty	Fantasy Mitty
henpecked husband	commander, surgeon
boring life	series of adventures
meek, confused	courageous, confident
often yelled at or admonished	highly respected by many

❸ Build Your Vocabulary
Creating a personal word list can help you better understand not only a specific selection but also other readings throughout your life. Use these tips to get started:

- **List difficult words.** Consider listing vocabulary words from the selections, as well as other challenging terms you encounter.
- **Go beyond the definitions.** To help you remember each word and its meaning, list synonyms and antonyms, or write a sentence using the word.
- **Get some practice.** Visit the **Vocabulary Center** at **ClassZone.com** for interactive practice.
- **Try them out.** Using new words in your writing and discussions is one of the best ways to build your vocabulary.

Word	Meaning
haggard adj. "The Secret Life of Walter Mitty," line 42	**Definition:** having a worn appearance **Synonyms:** gaunt, worn **Antonyms:** lively, energetic Months of fierce battle had taken a toll on the haggard soldier.

Strategies That Work: Reading

Discuss **Strategies That Work: Reading.** Ask students if they ever have tried any of the strategies listed; invite comments. Explain that these and other features contained in the anthology will help them to develop these strategies and become more engaged, informed, and active readers.

1. Read Independently
Point out that reading independently allows readers to practice reading strategies, increase their reading fluency, and improve their vocabulary. Invite students to share titles and passages from favorite readings, where appropriate, in class.

2. Use Graphic Organizers
Encourage students to use graphic organizers to record their thoughts and reactions while reading as well as to organize questions or useful information. Urge students to record graphic organizers in their **Reader's Notebooks.**

3. Build Your Vocabulary
Challenge students to record their personal word lists in their **Reader's Notebooks.** Emphasize that a strong vocabulary will help them to read and communicate more effectively. If you have a classroom computer, demonstrate how to access **ClassZone.com: Vocabulary Center.**

FOR LESS–PROFICIENT READERS

Concept Support Use these activities to reinforce the teaching in the text:

1. Have students create a list of fiction and nonfiction readings that they have enjoyed and would recommend to others. Encourage students to try some of the readings during the school year.

2. Point out that graphic organizers have various purposes. For example, the Two-Column Chart is an effective way to record the contrasts in Walter Mitty's world, but if there were also similarities between Mitty's daydreams and his real life, a Venn diagram would be more appropriate.

3. Invite students to share tips about learning and using new words. Also explain that each unit in the anthology opens with a feature that includes academic vocabulary—terms relating to the skills and strategies appearing in that unit's lessons. Encourage students to use those terms in writing and discussions, as well.

OBJECTIVES

- understand the relationship between purpose, audience, and format
- become familiar with the stages of the writing process
- become familiar with the key traits of effective writing
- understand how rubrics can be used to evaluate writing

Consider Your Options

Draw a triangle on the board and label its corners Purpose, Audience, and Format.

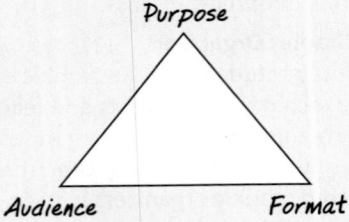

Read the questions that appear beneath these terms in the text, as well as the answers provided. Illustrate how these writing variables affect each other. For example, an explanatory piece on penguins might be presented in these ways:

- in the format of a short story if the audience consists of children
- in the format of a research paper if the audience consists of a teacher
- in the format of a magazine article if the audience consists of adults

Invite students to suggest similar examples.

Writing Process Workshop

Expressing Ideas in Writing

Writing is a way of reaching people—of telling them something they didn't know, stirring their emotions, or even persuading them to stand up for a cause. Whether you're writing for the millions (an entry in a blog) or one in a million (a love letter), the act of putting words on paper can have remarkable power.

Consider Your Options

Maybe you want to write a review of a movie, advising other viewers to avoid it at all costs. Maybe you've decided to write an essay on a character in literature whose conflict seems familiar to you. Maybe you're drafting a letter to apply for a job. All kinds of writing start as ideas long before they are transformed into words on a page. Whether you are responding to a prompt or writing in your journal, start by considering **purpose**, **audience**, and **format**.

PURPOSE	AUDIENCE	FORMAT
Why am I writing? • to entertain • to inform or explain • to persuade • to describe • to express thoughts and feelings • to inspire	**Who are my readers?** • classmates • teachers • friends • community members • potential employers • Web users	**Which format will best suit my purpose and audience?** • essay • speech • letter • research paper • poem • short story • review • journal entry • script • Web site • power presentation

DIFFERENTIATED INSTRUCTION

FOR LESS–PROFICIENT READERS

Note Taking An understanding of the writing process will help students communicate effectively—both in class and throughout their lives. If students need help, hand out the note-taking copy master for the Writing Process Workshop. As you discuss the main points on these four pages, have students record them on the copy master.

R RESOURCE MANAGER—Copy Master
Note Taking p. 4

FOR ENGLISH LEARNERS

Language: Skill Words Have students identify the term—*purpose, audience,* or *format*—that each of these statements illustrates:

- "I'm writing for the members of the school's Science Club." (*audience*)
- "Should I present a written report, or a speech?" (*format*)
- "I want to share some information about tornadoes." (*purpose*)

Continue with the Process

Every writer has a different process, and many use different processes at different times. But it's a rare writer who sits down with no plan in mind and types a final draft for publication. The **Writing Workshops** in this book are designed to help you develop and refine your own process for writing. Familiarize yourself with the basic process before you decide what works for you.

THE WRITING PROCESS

What Should I Do?	What Does It Look Like?
PREWRITING Explore your ideas and determine what you want to write about. In addition to considering the questions on the preceding page, try some of these brainstorming strategies: **freewriting, clustering, listing.**	**CLUSTER DIAGRAM** 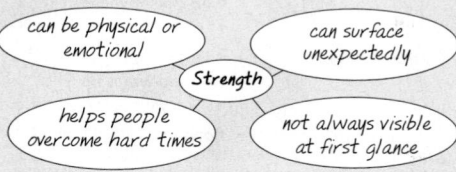
DRAFTING Turn your prewriting ideas into a first draft without worrying about errors. If you are writing a formal essay, you might **draft from an outline,** such as the one shown. Another option is **drafting to discover**—writing with no set plan, letting the ideas develop as you go.	**OUTLINE** 1. Emotional strength comes from a will to succeed in difficult circumstances. 　A. _The Old Man and the Sea_ (The old man doesn't let fatigue/age stop him) 　B. _The Miracle Worker_ (Annie Sullivan perseveres in the face of failure)
REVISING AND EDITING Review your draft, making changes to content, structure, and style. • Check your writing against a **rubric** (page 18). • Get suggestions from a **peer reader.** • Proofread for errors in grammar, usage, and mechanics.	**PEER SUGGESTIONS** In Ernest Hemingway's _The Old Man and the Sea_ and William Gibson's _The Miracle Worker_, the main characters display emotional strenth. ⌃g **Suggestion:** May want to begin with a more creative statement. Try: "Strength is much more than muscle for the main characters in . . ."
PUBLISHING Let your idea loose on the world. Where you publish, of course, depends on your **purpose, audience,** and **format.**	**PUBLISHING OPTIONS**  

Continue with the Process

Review the stages of the writing process listed under "What Should I Do?"

Determine Readiness Assess students' familiarity with this material by asking them about their experience with each stage. For example, you might ask how students prewrite and draft, what they have gained from working with peer readers, and whether they have ever published their work (and, if so, how). Explain that students will learn much more about these stages and ways to apply them to specific kinds of writing in the **Writing Workshops** found throughout the anthology.

FOR LESS–PROFICIENT READERS

Concept Support Draw a flow chart on the board to help students envision the writing process by writing the name of each stage, circling it, and connecting it with an arrow to the next stage. Explain that the arrows indicate the natural progression from one stage to the next. Also point out (adding more arrows, if you wish) that the process is recursive; for example, when a writer is revising, he or she may go back and do some prewriting to rework a difficult passage.

FOR ENGLISH LEARNERS

Academic Vocabulary Analysis Help students grasp the stages of the writing process by discussing these prefixes and roots:

• _prewriting:_ Pre- means "before," so _prewriting_ refers to tasks you do before the main writing.

• _drafting:_ This word comes from a Middle English word that means "to draw or pull." _Drafting_ refers to drawing out your writing ideas.

• _revising:_ Re- means "again," and -vis- means "to see," so _revising_ refers to looking again at what you have written.

• _publishing:_ This word comes from a Middle English word that means "to make known publicly." _Publishing_ refers to taking your finished writing to the public.

Do a Self-Check

Briefly discuss the Key Traits Rubric, explaining that the rubric is a means by which students can evaluate their writing. (The word *rubric* refers to categorizing—here, categorizing a piece of writing according to its strengths.) Make certain that students understand the meaning and purpose of each of the Key Traits:

- *Ideas:* Make sure that ideas are clear, focused, and supported with relevant details.
- *Organization:* Arrange ideas in a logical order to help the reader move easily through the text.
- *Voice:* Express ideas in a way that shows an individual style and personality.
- *Word Choice:* Use language that is precise, powerful, and engaging.
- *Sentence Fluency:* Create an interesting rhythm and flow by using varied sentence lengths and structures.
- *Conventions:* Use correct grammar, spelling, and punctuation.

Remind students that the Key Traits will appear in every Writing Workshop.

CHECK UNDERSTANDING Have students identify the point in the writing process at which a writer uses the Key Traits Rubric.

Do a Self-Check

Whether you're analyzing a short story or urging others to support a cause, being aware of the key traits of effective writing will help you stay on track. Use this rubric to evaluate how far you've come with your idea, and how far you have to go.

KEY TRAITS RUBRIC

	Strong	Average	Weak
Ideas	• centers around a clear, focused topic • is supported by vivid, well-chosen details	• has a topic, but it needs to be developed more • contains general statements with some details	• has no clear topic • lacks details or has unclear details
Organization	• opens in an engaging way and wraps up with a satisfying conclusion • flows in a logical manner	• has both an introduction and a conclusion, but they are uninteresting • lacks some transitions	• has no real introduction or conclusion • contains a confusing jumble of ideas
Voice	• conveys a strong sense of individual style • uses a tone that is well suited to the purpose and audience	• sounds "flat" in some places • lapses into an inappropriate tone at times	• has little or no "life" • employs a completely inappropriate tone for the intended purpose and audience
Word Choice	• uses words that are precise and colorful • conveys meaning in a powerful yet natural-sounding manner	• uses words that are correct, but ordinary • gets meaning across, but is not memorable	• uses words that are vague or incorrect • fails to convey meaning clearly
Sentence Fluency	• includes sentences of varied lengths and structures • creates a pleasing flow from one idea to the next	• has some sentence variety but not enough • lacks flow in some places	• includes mostly short or rambling sentences • is awkward or repetitious
Conventions	• shows a strong grasp of grammar and usage • has few problems with mechanics (spelling, capitalization, and punctuation)	• has minor grammar and usage problems • contains some mechanical errors	• has such poor grammar and usage that meaning is unclear • contains so many mechanical errors that the writing is hard to read

---

DIFFERENTIATED INSTRUCTION

FOR ENGLISH LEARNERS

Language Support Have pairs of students look up and share the meanings of skill words such as *topic, transition, style, tone, fluency,* and *usage.* Also discuss the contextual meanings of these adjectives in the rubric:

- *focused:* specific
- *general:* lacking detail; not specific
- *vivid:* able to create mental images for the reader; lively

- *engaging:* capturing and holding the reader's interest and attention; attractive
- *individual:* written in a way that shows the writer's distinct, personal touch
- *flat:* lacking a sense of the writer's distinct, personal touch; dull
- *colorful:* lively and interesting
- *vague:* lacking a precise meaning; unclear

Strategies That Work: Writing

❶ Use Prewriting Strategies

Deciding on a topic and developing ideas can seem like the hardest parts of the process. Try these approaches to jumpstart your process:

- **Freewrite.** Write down anything that comes into your head.
- **Go graphic.** Use cluster diagrams, charts, and other graphic organizers to capture your thoughts.
- **Keep a journal.** Collect quotes, observations, song lyrics, photographs, freewrites, and other possible sources of inspiration.
- **Talk it out.** Brainstorm topics or supporting details with classmates.
- **Write from a prompt.** Consider the prompts in the **Writing Workshops.**

❷ Get Feedback from Peers

Other writers can help you at any stage of the process, from brainstorming ideas with you to proofreading your final draft. Consider these tips:

When You're the Writer	When You're the Reader
• Tell your readers what kind of feedback you are looking for. Should they focus on content, structure, or both?	• Be honest but kind. Offer positive reactions first.
• Listen to their comments without arguing or explaining.	• Be specific. Don't say, "That character was unbelievable" without giving specific details to support your opinion.
• Let their suggestions sink in before you decide how you want to proceed.	• Let the writer make the final decisions.

❸ Read, Read, Read

Reading other people's writing is one of the best ways to develop your own individual style. Consult these sources:

LITERATURE
For inspiration, look to the fiction, drama, poetry, and nonfiction in this book, as well as novels and periodicals that match your interests.

WRITING COMMUNITY
If you're serious about writing, form a writing group with others to share your efforts.

ONLINE RESOURCES
Consult the world of writing resources on the Web. Check out blogs, student publication sites, and the **Writing Center at ClassZone.com.**

Strategies That Work: Writing

Share with students that **Strategies That Work: Writing** can open up exciting possibilities for them as writers. Encourage students to make constant use of the strategies to help them with their writing, both in and outside of class.

1. **Use Prewriting Strategies**
   Discuss the examples of prewriting strategies. Ask students if they are familiar with these strategies and, if so, which ones they have found helpful and why.

2. **Get Feedback from Peers**
   Discuss with students their experiences with peer feedback, both positive and negative. Whatever their experiences have been, remind them that peer feedback, if done responsibly, can be invaluable in learning about themselves and each other as readers and writers. Note that whether they are the writer or the reader in a peer review, they should be as specific as possible. Point out the tips listed for peer readers and writers, emphasizing that readers and writers owe each other respect, sensitivity, and patience.

3. **Read, Read, Read**
   Finally, point out that reading a variety of material can be instructive and inspiring. Once again, encourage students to share what they read outside of class, particularly if it inspired a topic, style, or other helpful information for writing. Offer to help students form writing groups. If you have a classroom computer, go to **ClassZone.com** and show students some of the writing resources.

FOR LESS–PROFICIENT READERS

Concept Support Use these activities to reinforce the teaching in the text:

1. Show students what a prompt is by looking with them at the prompt in the first Writing Workshop (page 168). Tell students that as they read various prompts, they will learn how to analyze a prompt for clues about the type of writing being asked for and the audience for whom it is intended.

2. Emphasize that working with peers is not limited to peer readers during the revising and editing stage; peers can help students narrow topics and clarify their plans for a piece of writing.

3. As students read the selections in this anthology, urge them to make notes about topics, style points, and other elements that they would like to attempt in their own writing. Encourage them to experiment with these elements as they develop their individual writing style.

UNIT
The Plot Thickens

NARRATIVE STRUCTURE

- In Fiction
- In Media
- In Nonfiction
- In Poetry
- In Drama

21

About the Art Julio Larraz (b. 1944) painted *Casanova*. For more information, see page 65.

For help in planning this unit, see

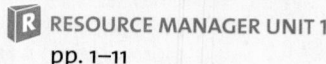 RESOURCE MANAGER UNIT 1
pp. 1–11

INTRODUCE THE UNIT

When a gravy or sauce thickens, it usually becomes richer, more intense in flavor, and more satisfying. The plot of a piece of writing is said to thicken when surprises and other complications occur and tension rises. Most readers find that such moments make the writing richer, more intense, and more satisfying.

Invite students to consider how the pictures on this page suggest the thickening of a plot. To elicit ideas, ask:

- As you look at each picture, what kind of story do you imagine?
- How might each picture suggest danger? surprise? suspense?
- Which picture does a better job of suggesting that the plot is thickening? Why?

Tell students that as they read the selections in this unit, they will see how a thickening plot fits into the narrative structure of a work. Explain that **narrative structure** includes the elements found on a story map, such as character, setting, events, climax, and resolution. It also includes elements related to plot, such as conflict, complications, rising action, suspense, and foreshadowing. In this unit, students will discover how the elements combine to thicken a plot and enrich a story.

SKILLS STRAND	Literary Analysis Workshop: Plot and Conflict pp. 24–31	A Sound of Thunder pp. 32–51 Short Story *Level: Average*	The Most Dangerous Game pp. 52–77 Short Story *Level: Average*	Daughter of Invention pp. 78–93 Short Story *Level: Average*	The Gift of the Magi pp. 94–105 Short Story *Level: Challenging*	Media Study: *from* The Lord of the Rings pp. 106–109 Film Clip
Literary Analysis	Plot Stages and Conflict pp. 24–25, 28–31 Chronological Order, Foreshadowing, Flashback pp. 26–27, 30	Foreshadowing pp. 33, 34, 36, 37, 48 Review: Plot pp. 36	Conflict pp. 53, 54, 57, 62, 68, 70, 72, 75	Plot and Character pp. 79, 82, 86, 89, 91	Irony pp. 95, 98, 102, 103	
Reading and Informational Texts	Analyze the Literature pp. 25, 27–31 Analyze Sequence pp. 26–27, 30	Analyze Sequence pp. 33, 40, 42, 48 Read a Magazine Article p. 51 Review: Make Inferences pp. 37, 41, 47, 48 Review: Predict p. 44	Visualize pp. 53, 56, 57, 58, 63, 74, 75 Review: Predict pp. 56, 58, 63, 66, 70, 72	Make Inferences pp. 79, 80, 84, 87, 88, 90, 91 Review: Clarify p. 86	Predict pp. 95, 99, 100, 101, 103	
Vocabulary	Academic Vocabulary pp. 24, 26	Word Acquisition pp. 33, T33, 49 Context Clues p. T33 Latin Roots (*mal*) p. 49	Word Acquisition pp. 53, T53, 76 Context Clues p. T53 Denotation and Connotation p. 76	Word Acquisition pp. 79, T79, 92 CLOZE Practice p. T79 Latin Prefixes (*in-*) p. 92	Word Acquisition pp. 95, T95, 104 Context Clues p. T95 Greek Roots (*chron*) p. 104	Academic Vocabulary (Film) p. 107
Writing, Grammar, and Style		Realistic Dialogue pp. 40, 50 Sentence Fragments and Contractions pp. 40, 50	Descriptive Details pp. 69, 75, 77 Prepositional Phrases pp. 69, 77	Descriptive Details pp. 82, 93 Modifiers pp. 82, 93	Word Choice pp. 102, 105 Precise Verbs pp. 102, 105	
Speaking, Listening, Viewing, and Media	Discuss pp. T24–T27	Discuss pp. 32, T34–T47, 48, T51 Analyze Visuals pp. 34, T38, 43, T46	Discuss pp. 52, T54–T74, 75 Analyze Visuals pp. 54, T59, T60, 65, T67, T68, T71, T73	Discuss pp. 78, T80–T90, 91 Analyze Visuals pp. 80, T85, T87, 89	Discuss pp. 94, T96–T102, 103 Analyze Visuals pp. 96, T98, T101	Discuss pp. 106, 109 Analyze and Evaluate Film Elements pp. 107–109 Create a Storyboard p. 109

Assessment-Based Planning: Skills in red are assessed on the Unit 1 Test. **T** = Teacher's Edition page

The Rights to the Streets of Memphis pp. 110–119 Autobiography *Level: Average*	*Linked selections* from **Seabiscuit** pp. 120–131 Biography *Level: Average*	**Horse of the Century** pp. 132–137 Magazine Article, Timeline, Radio Transcript *Level: Challenging*	The Raven/Incident in a Rose Garden pp. 138–147 Narrative Poems *Level: Challenging*	Sorry, Right Number pp. 148–167 Teleplay *Level: Easy*	Writing Workshop: Personal Narrative pp. 168–175
Autobiography pp. 111, 114, 115, 117	Suspense in Biography pp. 121, 124, 127, 129, 130		Narrative Poetry pp. 139, 140, 142, 144, 145, 146, 147	Plot in Drama pp. 149, T154, T159, 166	
Identify Cause and Effect pp. 111, 112, 116, 117	Identify Author's Purpose pp. 121, 122, 126, 130 Review: Predict p. 124	Synthesize pp. 132, 133, 134, 135, 136, 137 Draw Conclusions p. 137	Strategies for Reading Poetry pp. 139, 142, 143, 144, 146, 147	Strategies for Reading a Teleplay pp. 149, 152, T157, T161, 166 Read a Memoir p. 165	Analyze a Personal Narrative pp. 169–170, 174
Word Acquisition pp. 111, T111, 118 Context Clues p. T111 Synonyms and Antonyms p. 118	Word Acquisition pp. 121, T121, 131 Context Clues p. T121 Latin Roots (*aud*) p. 131				
Word Choice pp. 115, 119 Strong Verbs in a Series pp. 115, 119				Dialogue p. 167 Informal Language (Slang) p. 167	Write a Personal Narrative pp. 168–175 Precise Words p. 170, 172, 173 Punctuate Dialogue p. 174
Discuss pp. 110, T112–T116, 117 Analyze Visuals pp. 112, T114	Discuss pp. 120, T122–T129, 130 Analyze Visuals pp. 122, T124, 127, 128	Discuss pp. 132, T133–T136, 137	Discuss pp. 138, T140–T146, 147 Analyze Visuals pp. 140, T144, T145	Discuss pp. 148, T150–T165, 166 Analyze Visuals pp. T151, T153, T154, T157, T161, T163	Discuss pp. 168–170 Present an Informal Speech p. 175

Skills Assessed on the Unit 1 Test:

Literary Analysis
- Analyze stages of plot and plot development
- Analyze conflict and its complications
- Analyze irony

Reading and Informational Texts
- Predict
- Make inferences
- Analyze sequence of events
- Identify cause-and-effect relationships

Vocabulary
- Use synonyms and antonyms to determine word meaning
- Understand and use Latin and Greek word roots

Writing, Grammar, and Style
- Write a personal narrative
- Create realistic characters
- Use realistic dialogue
- Add descriptive details
- Use prepositional phrases
- Use modifiers
- Use precise verbs
- Use strong verbs in a series
- Additional writing and grammar skills

For additional lesson planning help, see **Easy Planner DVD.**

OBJECTIVES

- establish prior knowledge about **great stories**
- discuss story events and elements in the context of **great stories**

What makes a GREAT STORY?

Read and discuss the introductory paragraph. Point out that the greatness of a story lies partly in what it is about but even more in how it is told. To illustrate, present these sentences:

> Roberto sped toward the finish line, the roar of the crowd numbing his ears.

> "That's the car for me," Emily said, "and I'm buying it right now!"

Ask students which sentence they think would be part of a great story. Elicit that the first sentence captures readers' interest more quickly and evokes more curiosity about the outcome. Note, however, that either sentence has the potential to become part of a great story.

ACTIVITY Encourage students to think the story through before summarizing it. When discussing the questions, students should share specific examples. Guide students to conclude that a **great story** appeals to readers' interests and emotions and has a memorable style.

CHECK UNDERSTANDING Have students use their conclusions to create an original definition of the term **great story.**

Unit Resources

What makes a GREAT STORY?

Whether you are riveted by the latest comedy at the local movie theater, caught up in the pages of your favorite novel, or transfixed by your grandparents' tales of growing up, what these **great stories** have in common is that each is told by someone who can capture your interest, hold your attention, and make you want to know how the story will end.

ACTIVITY Think of a story you have read or heard. It can be a favorite piece of fiction or a powerful true story, such as the saga of tragic events in *The Perfect Storm*. With a partner, share a summary of the story you chose. Then discuss the following questions:

- What made the story interesting?
- What emotions did the story evoke in you?
- Was the story told in any unusual ways?
- Did the story remind you of any other stories?

After answering these questions, think about what great stories have in common.

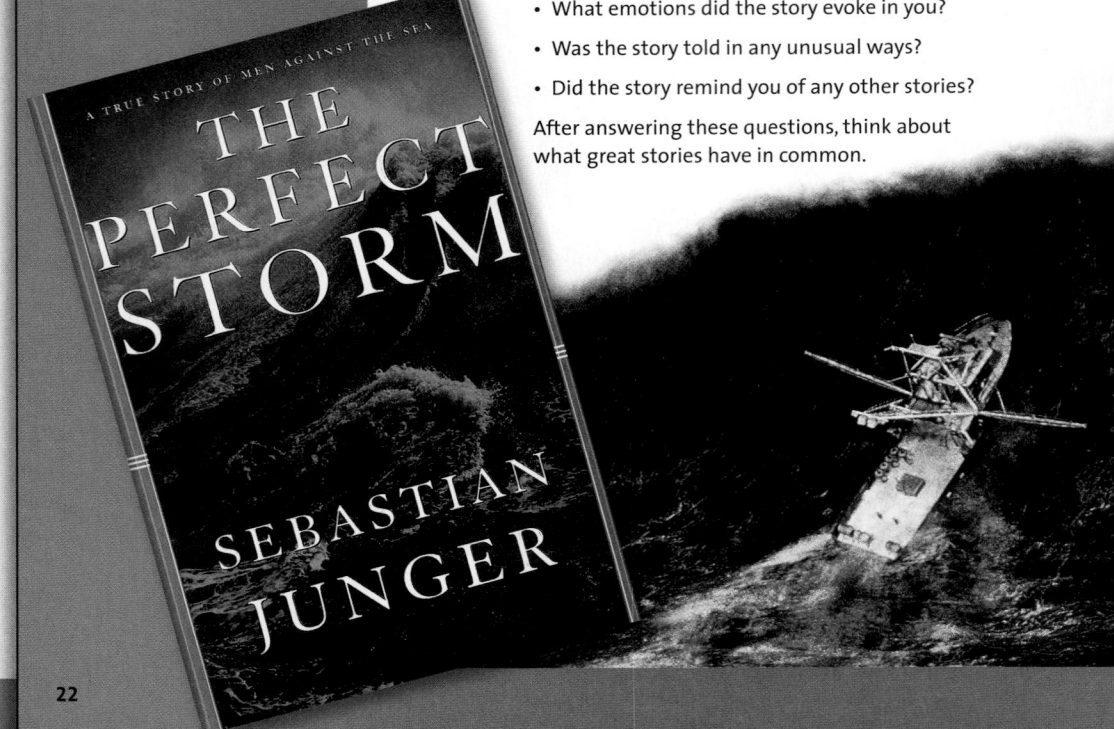

22

R RESOURCE MANAGER UNIT 1	Easy Planner DVD-ROM	eEdition DVD-ROM & Online
BEST PRACTICES TOOLKIT	WriteSmart CD-ROM	McDougal Littell Assessment System
S STANDARDS LESSON FILE	ClassZone.com	Test Generator CD
	Audio Anthology CD	MediaSmart DVD-ROM
	Multi-Language Academic Vocabulary Online	

 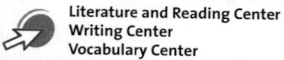
Preview Unit Goals

LITERARY ANALYSIS	• Analyze stages of plot and plot development • Identify and analyze conflict and its complications • Analyze narrative techniques, including foreshadowing, irony, and suspense • Identify narrative elements in poetry and drama
READING	• Use reading strategies, including predicting and visualizing • Recognize sequence and cause-and-effect relationships • Make inferences and draw conclusions • Synthesize information from multiple texts
WRITING AND GRAMMAR	• Write a personal narrative • Use realistic dialogue, descriptive details, and realistic characters to achieve a purpose • Use precise verbs and modifiers
SPEAKING, LISTENING, AND VIEWING	• Identify the aesthetic qualities of film and evaluate the techniques used to create them • Use a variety of media techniques to convey a cohesive story
VOCABULARY	• Use word roots to help unlock meaning • Use synonyms and antonyms to understand meanings of words
ACADEMIC VOCABULARY	• complications • plot • conflict • suspense • foreshadowing • synthesis • irony

23

DIFFERENTIATED INSTRUCTION

FOR ENGLISH LEARNERS

Academic Vocabulary Use the copy master to help students learn the Academic Vocabulary.

1. Read aloud each term. Have students find it on their copy master.

2. Discuss the meaning or example shown, and complete the chart as a class.

3. Have students work in small groups to complete the remaining activities.

Additional Academic Vocabulary Use the copy master to help students learn academic words they will use in subsequent lessons and on the Assessment Practice. Follow the same procedure as for the Academic Vocabulary copy master.

R RESOURCE MANAGER—Copy Masters
Academic Vocabulary p. 9
Additional Academic Vocabulary p. 10

Preview Unit Goals

This page presents an overview of the skills and strategies covered in this unit. Explain to students that they can get more from their reading by previewing. Then ask them to skim the page to preview the skills that they will learn. Note that each strand or category of skill is color-coded on this page and throughout the unit.

Model the strategy of copying the Academic Vocabulary and writing a preliminary definition for each term. Suggest that students use their journals for this purpose. Encourage them to use the terms in discussions and in writing. Also urge students to revisit each term throughout the unit and to refine its meaning.

ADDITIONAL UNIT GOALS

These skills will be taught in this unit but are not the major focus of the unit:

Literary Analysis
• Analyze plot and character
• Genre study: short story, autobiography, biography, poetry, teleplay, magazine and newspaper articles, timeline, radio transcript

Reading
• Identify an author's purpose

Writing and Grammar
• Describe a scene
• Make effective word choices
• Emphasize action
• Use sentence fragments, contractions, and slang for effect
• Use prepositional phrases correctly
• Punctuate dialogue correctly

Speaking, Listening, and Viewing
• Present an informal speech, considering audience and purpose

Vocabulary
• Use prefixes to help unlock meaning
• Understand word origins
• Understand connotative and denotative meanings of words

23

Focus and Motivate

OBJECTIVES

- identify and analyze stages of plot
- identify and analyze conflict
- identify and analyze chronological order, flashback, and foreshadowing

Teach

Part 1: Plot Stages and Conflict

Conflict Explain to students that a story may contain several conflicts, but the main conflict is the one that most clearly drives the key events. Use this activity to reinforce the idea of the main conflict driving the key events:

- Brainstorm a list of well-known stories from literature or from the movies.
- For each story, identify one or more struggles that take place between characters, within a character's mind, or between one or more characters and some other force.
- List these conflicts in a chart, labeling each as *internal* or *external*. Once students have completed the exercise, ask them to identify the conflict that is most critical in each story. Be sure to have them defend their choices with specific examples.

Story Title

What is the conflict?	Internal	External

Stages of Plot Point out to students that few stories have plots that neatly match the five stages shown in the plot diagram. Many stories, for example, don't reach their climax until just before the end. Other stories end with a climax. (To illustrate this, you might want to talk about horror or suspense movies that end at the moment of highest tension.) Almost every story, though, begins with an exposition that introduces the characters, setting, and main conflict. In addition, every story has a rising action that introduces events that intensify or complicate the conflict.

 **BEST PRACTICES TOOLKIT—Transparency**
Analysis Frame: Plot pp. D21, D28

Plot and Conflict

Every good story is fueled by conflict. Can the hero survive the dangerous journey? Will the star-crossed lovers end up together, despite their feuding families? When a story grabs your interest, it's usually because the conflict is exciting and dramatic. Looking closely at how conflicts develop throughout the stages of a plot is a key part of analyzing a story and understanding *why* it hooks you.

Part 1: Plot Stages and Conflict

The series of events in a narrative is called **plot.** At the heart of any plot is a **conflict,** or struggle, between opposing forces. A conflict is internal or external.

- An **internal conflict** is a struggle within a character's mind. The struggle usually centers on a choice or decision the character must make. Should she tell the truth? Can he overcome his jealousy?
- An **external conflict** is a clash between a character and an outside force, such as another character, society, or a force of nature. Will the athlete defeat her bitter rival? Can the soldiers endure the war?

Whether internal or external, a conflict is usually introduced at the beginning of a narrative. As the characters attempt to resolve the conflict, "the plot thickens" at each stage. Will the characters succeed? You keep turning the pages to find out the answer to this question.

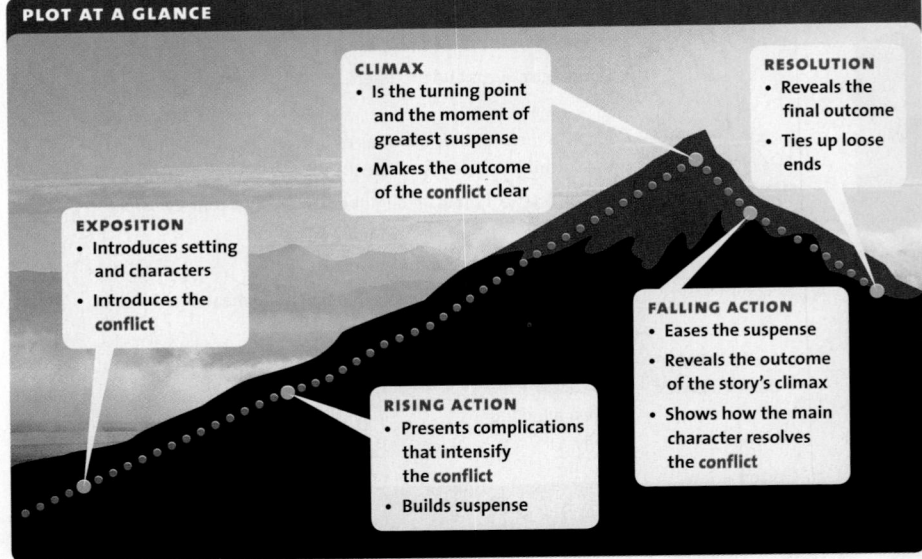

PLOT AT A GLANCE

EXPOSITION
- Introduces setting and characters
- Introduces the conflict

RISING ACTION
- Presents complications that intensify the conflict
- Builds suspense

CLIMAX
- Is the turning point and the moment of greatest suspense
- Makes the outcome of the conflict clear

FALLING ACTION
- Eases the suspense
- Reveals the outcome of the story's climax
- Shows how the main character resolves the conflict

RESOLUTION
- Reveals the final outcome
- Ties up loose ends

DIFFERENTIATED INSTRUCTION

For general guidelines on differentiating instruction, see

 **BEST PRACTICES TOOLKIT**
Differentiated Instruction pp. 31–38

FOR LESS–PROFICIENT READERS

Note Taking For students who need help with note taking, hand out the note-taking copy master before discussing the paragraph. Then have students read the first paragraph silently. As you discuss the

main points of the paragraph, have students record them on the copy master.

Illustrate Conflict Have students work in small groups to sketch the scene in Model 1 on page 25. They may use stick figures, lines, dots, X's, or other markings. Have each group write a caption for its illustration.

RESOURCE MANAGER—Copy Master
Note Taking p. 15

MODEL 1: CONFLICT IN EXPOSITION

In the exposition of this story, a young warrior named Temas is about to face a crucial test of adulthood in Masai culture—killing a lion. What conflicts emerge as Temas prepares for this pivotal moment?

from
BROTHERS ARE THE SAME
Short story by **Beryl Markham**

Yet in his mind Temas now trembled. Fear of battle was a nonexistent thing—but fear of failure could be real, and was. It was real and living—and kept alive by the nearness of an enemy more formidable than any lion— an enemy with the hated name Medoto.

5   He thought of Medoto—of that Medoto who lay not far away in the deep grass watching the same ravine. Of that Medoto who, out of hate and jealousy over a mere girl, now hoped in his heart that Temas would flinch at the moment of his trial. . . .

Close Read

1. Review the boxed detail. What does it tell you about the building conflict between Temas and Medoto?

2. In addition to his conflict with Medoto, what internal conflict is plaguing Temas?

MODEL 2: CONFLICT AT CLIMAX

Later, Temas learns that his rival is actually a friend. Find out how the conflict between Temas and Medoto changes at the story's climax.

During the test, Temas feels relieved when the lion attacks another hunter. Then Medoto throws a stone, causing the lion to charge Temas. Without hesitation, Temas kills the lion. Later, Medoto explains himself to Temas.

"If, until now, I have seemed your enemy, it was because I feared you would be braver than I, for when I fought my lion my knees trembled and my heart was white—until that charge was made. No one knew that, and I am called Medoto, the unflinching, but I flinched. I trembled."

5   He stepped closer to Temas. He smiled. "It is no good to lie," he said. "I wanted you to fail, but when I saw you hesitate I could not bear it because I remembered my own hour of fear. It was then I threw the stone—not to shame you, but to save you from shame—for I saw that your fear was not fear of death, but fear of failure—and this I understood. You are a greater warrior than

10   I—than any—for who but the bravest would do what you have done?" Medoto paused and watched a light of wonderment kindle in Temas's eye. The hand of Temas slipped from his sword, his muscles relaxed. Yet, for a moment, he did not speak, and as he looked at Medoto, it was clear to both that the identical thought, the identical vision, had come to each of them. It was the vision that

15   must and always will come to young men everywhere, the vision of a girl.

Now this vision stood between them, and nothing else. But it stood like a barrier, the last barrier.

Close Read

1. How has the conflict between Temas and Medoto changed? Support your answer with evidence.

2. What aspect of Medoto's and Temas's conflict still remains unresolved? Explain.

MODEL 1: CONFLICT IN EXPOSITION
Close Read

1. ***Possible answer:*** *Medoto and Temas are in conflict over the love of a girl. Temas is afraid of failing in his battle with the lion, since his rival would relish such defeat. Since Medoto is jealous, Temas is probably the preferred suitor but could lose this advantage if he fails.*

2. ***Possible answer:*** *Temas is also in conflict over issues related to bravery and manhood. He considers his most frightening enemy to be Medoto (line 3) and not the lion. His defeat would prove Medoto to be the greater warrior and thus more worthy of the girl.*

MODEL 2: CONFLICT AT CLIMAX
Close Read

1. ***Possible answer:*** *By this point in the story, Medoto and Temas are no longer in conflict over issues related to bravery and manhood. Medoto acknowledges Temas's greater bravery by saying, in lines 9–10, "'You are a greater warrior than I.'" Temas learns that he can trust Medoto as a man and a warrior. Temas shows this trust when he takes his hand off his sword.*

2. ***Possible answer:*** *Medoto and Temas remain in conflict over the girl, shown by lines 14–17: "the identical thought, the identical vision, had come to each of them.... the vision of a girl. Now this vision stood between them ...."*

FOR LESS–PROFICIENT READERS
Concept Support

1. Draw two word webs. Label one *External Conflicts* and the other *Internal Conflicts*. Write *main character against* in the center circle of each web.

2. List these terms on the board, clarifying as necessary: *sea, earthquake, brother, friend, personal history, school rules,* and *own values.*

3. Have volunteers write the terms in surrounding circles in the appropriate webs.

FOR ADVANCED LEARNERS/PRE–AP*
Analyze Plot Stages Have students read the workshop independently. Direct students to identify the plot stages in favorite stories or novels by summarizing and labeling the events.

* Pre-AP is a registered trademark of the College Entrance Examination Board. Use of the trademark does not constitute production participation, sponsorship, or endorsement by the College Board.

Teach

Part 2: Sequence and Time

Flashback After students read the chart, challenge them to develop examples of sentences or phrases that would signal different kinds of flashbacks, such as these:

- I stared at the tattered posters, suddenly remembering my first trip to the circus.
- As Marcus strode into the ballpark for his first major-league game, he thought about the first time his dad had pressed a baseball into his hand.
- Looking at Charla, no one could have imagined the gangly, awkward girl she had once been.

After students generate the sample sentences, have them brainstorm other clue words that might signal flashbacks. (*in the past, when I was ___ years old, the previous winter, years before*)

Foreshadowing After students read the chart, explain that the hints or clues of what is to come may be subtle, often appearing in ordinary conversation. In addition to the tips in the chart, suggest that students watch for these clues:

- unusual statements that make a reader wonder, "Why did he or she say that?"
- an ominous or uncertain mood or tone
- warnings that are stated directly or are subtly implied
- heightened suspense
- suggestions that something always or never happens—often a signal that the pattern is about to change
- an unusual setting that seems tailor-made

You may also wish to elicit from students examples of events or dialogue that foreshadow later developments in favorite movies.

CHECK UNDERSTANDING

Have students write definitions of *foreshadowing* and *flashback* in their own words.

Part 2: Sequence and Time

From fairy tales, with their "once upon a time" beginnings and "happily ever after" endings, to modern classics, many great stories feature **chronological order.** The events follow a linear structure—that is, they take place one after the other.

Sometimes, however, a writer plays with time by interrupting the chronological order of events. He or she may suddenly focus on an event from the past or hint at future events. A writer may manipulate time for a variety of reasons—for example, to give you a deeper sense of the characters and conflicts or to keep you wondering what will happen next.

Flashback and **foreshadowing** are two common devices that writers use to introduce past and future events. By recognizing these devices, you can follow a story more closely and better understand your reactions to characters and events.

FLASHBACK	FORESHADOWING
What is it? An account of a conversation, episode, or event that happened before the beginning of the story, or at an earlier point	**What is it?** A writer's use of hints or clues in early scenes to suggest events that will occur later

▼	▼
What does it do? • Interrupts the main action to describe earlier events • Shows how past events led up to the present situation • Provides background information about a character or event	**What does it do?** • Prepares readers for events that come later—often in the climax or the resolution • Creates suspense • Makes readers eager to keep reading
▼	▼
How can I recognize it? • Look for possible clue words and phrases, such as "that summer," "as a young boy," or "her earliest memories." • Keep track of the chronological order of events so that you will be aware of events that interrupt this order.	**How can I recognize it?** • Pay attention to repeated or emphasized ideas and descriptions. • Notice when characters make important statements or behave in unusual ways.

DIFFERENTIATED INSTRUCTION

FOR LESS–PROFICIENT READERS

Note Taking For those students who need help, hand out the note-taking copy master for this page. Read and discuss the top of the page. Assist students in completing their note-taking copy master as needed.

 RESOURCE MANAGER—Copy Master
Note Taking p. 16

FOR ENGLISH LEARNERS

Language: Skill Words On the board, list the academic vocabulary shown in italics. Then give the examples in random order for students to classify.

- *chronological order:* After the game, they gathered in the cafeteria.
- *flashback:* As his sister gets off the train, he remembers the summer she was six.
- *foreshadowing:* The tranquil kitten would not stay that way for long.

Flash-
back

MODEL: FLASHBACK

Moments after meeting the narrator in this story, you are transported to an earlier time in his life. As you read, notice what this flashback reveals about the narrator and his family.

from # Sweet Potato Pie

Short story by **Eugenia Collier**

From up here on the fourteenth floor, my brother Charley looks like an insect scurrying among other insects. A deep feeling of love surges through me. . . .

Because I see Charley so seldom, my thoughts hover over him like hummingbirds. The cheerful, impersonal tidiness of this room is a world away
5 from Charley's walk-up flat in Harlem and a hundred worlds from the bare, noisy shanty where he and the rest of us spent what there was of childhood. I close my eyes, and side by side I see the Charley of my boyhood and the Charley of this afternoon, as clearly as if I were looking at a split TV screen. Another surge of love, seasoned with gratitude, wells up in me.
10 As far as I know, Charley never had any childhood at all. The oldest children of sharecroppers never do. Mama and Pa were shadowy figures whose voices I heard vaguely in the morning when sleep was shallow and whom I glimpsed as they left for the field before I was fully awake or as they trudged wearily into the house at night when my lids were irresistibly heavy.
15 They came into sharp focus only on special occasions. One such occasion was the day when the crops were in and the sharecroppers were paid. In our cabin there was so much excitement in the air that even I, the "baby," responded to it. For weeks we had been running out of things that we could neither grow nor get on credit. On the evening of that day we waited anxiously for our
20 parents' return. Then we would cluster around the rough wooden table—I on Lil's lap or clinging to Charley's neck, little Alberta nervously tugging her plait, Jamie crouched at Mama's elbow, like a panther about to spring, and all seven of us silent for once, waiting. Pa would place the money on the table—gently, for it was made from the sweat of their bodies and from their children's tears.
25 Mama would count it out in little piles, her dark face stern and, I think now, beautiful. Not with the hollow beauty of well-modeled features but with the strong radiance of one who has suffered and never yielded.

"This for store bill," she would mutter, making a little pile. "This for c'llection. This for piece o'gingham . . ." and so on, stretching the money as
30 tight over our collective needs as Jamie's outgrown pants were stretched over my bottom. "Well, that's the crop." She would look up at Pa at last. "It'll do." Pa's face would relax, and a general grin flitted from child to child. We would survive, at least for the present.

Close Read

1. Explain what happens before the flashback.

2. At what point does the flashback begin? Explain the words or phrases that helped you identify it.

3. Find three details that describe the narrator's and Charley's family. One has been boxed. What do these details tell you about their childhood?

4. How does the flashback help you understand the narrator's feelings about Charley?

MODEL: FLASHBACK

BACKGROUND

After the Civil War, former slaves had no land, tools, or places to live and few choices for earning a living. Many of them survived by becoming sharecroppers, farmers who lived and worked on the land of large landowners. In return for the use of the land, the share-croppers gave a large share of their crops to the landowners. This resulted in a lot of hard work and a meager, often desperate existence.

Close Read

1. ***Possible answer:*** *The narrator looks lovingly down on Charley from a tidy room on the fourteenth floor.*

2. ***Possible answer:*** *The flashback begins with the reference to something "a hundred worlds" away (line 5). A more concrete clue follows: "I close my eyes, and . . . I see. . . ." A final clue is the reference to the split TV screen (line 8).*

   If students need help . . . Draw a split screen and discuss how it shows two images at once. Help students by labeling the two sides of the split screen "present" and "past," or "Charley now" and "the Charley of my boyhood."

3. ***Possible answer:*** *There were five children: the narrator was the youngest and Charley was the oldest (lines 10–11, 17, 20–23); the mother and father were weary from long days of work in the fields (lines 13–14); payday was an exciting time for the family because they desperately needed the money for necessities (lines 15–17, 28–31). These details indicate a childhood of love and closeness as well as poverty.*

4. ***Possible answer:*** *Because the narrator and Charley survived tough times together, they have a bond. With the parents away so much, Charley may also have played a nurturing or protective role, for the narrator sometimes clung to his brother's neck.*

DIFFERENTIATED INSTRUCTION

FOR LESS–PROFICIENT READERS

Comprehension: Story Elements Write these story elements on the board and have students identify them by analyzing the first sentence:

Narrator: *Charley's brother*
Main character: *Charley*
Setting: *fourteenth-floor window*

Analysis Support: Flashback Do a choral reading of the second paragraph. Have students snap their fingers when they read phrases that refer to the flashback (*"a world away from," "a hundred worlds from," "I see the Charley of my boyhood"*).

Practice and Apply

Part 3: Analyze the Literature

Close Read

1. **Possible answer:** *The setting is Cincinnati. The narrator has just moved there against her will.*

2. **Possible answer:** *The conflict may involve problems relating to the girl falling in love with a bag boy.*

3. **Possible answer:** *The girl is melodramatic (lines 4–5); she finds it hard to leave the past behind (lines 9–11); she likes solitary pursuits (lines 9–11, 16–17); she looks inward (lines 16–17).*

   If students need help . . . Ask students to describe what grocery shopping is like for the girl by deciding which term in each of these pairs of opposites describes feelings about shopping: *solitary* or *social, easy* or *challenging, relaxing* or *anxiety provoking.*

Part 3: Analyze the Literature

It seems like a familiar story. Girl meets and falls in love with boy. Boy falls in love with girl. After overcoming a few problems, they live happily ever after. Right? Wrong. This story traces a conflict, but that conflict is not resolved in a predictable way. As you read, use what you've learned about plot, conflict, and sequence to analyze the story.

Checkouts

Short story by **Cynthia Rylant**

    Her parents had moved her to Cincinnati, to a large house with beveled glass[1] windows and several porches and the *history* her mother liked to emphasize. You'll love the house, they said. You'll be lonely at first, they admitted, but you're so nice you'll make friends fast. And as an impulse tore at her to lie on the floor,
5 to hold to their ankles and tell them she felt she was dying, to offer anything, anything at all, so they might allow her to finish growing up in the town of her childhood, they firmed their mouths and spoke from their chests and they said, It's decided.
    They moved her to Cincinnati, where for a month she spent the greater
10 part of every day in a room full of beveled glass windows, sifting through photographs of the life she'd lived and left behind. But it is difficult work, suffering, and in its own way a kind of art, and finally she didn't have the energy for it anymore, so she emerged from the beautiful house and fell in love with a bag boy at the supermarket. Of course, this didn't happen all at once,
15 just like that, but in the sequence of things that's exactly the way it happened.
    She liked to grocery shop. She loved it in the way some people love to drive long country roads, because doing it she could think and relax and wander. Her parents wrote up the list and handed it to her and off she went without

---

1. **beveled glass:** glass whose edges are cut at an angle.

Close Read

1. What do you learn about the setting and the main character's situation in the exposition of this story?

2. Reread lines 11–15, which set the stage for the main conflict. What do you think the conflict will be about?

3. Review the boxed details about the girl. What do they reveal about her personality?

DIFFERENTIATED INSTRUCTION

FOR LESS–PROFICIENT READERS

Vocabulary Support Introduce these words from "Checkouts." Have students read the context for each word and suggest a synonym to replace it.

- *emerged* (line 13), "came out of"
- *sacrifice* (line 19), "giving up"
- *lapse* (line 25), "fall"
- *reverie* (line 25), "daydream"
- *bland* (line 44), "mild," "plain"
- *brazen* (line 44), "bold"
- *deftly* (line 54), "skillfully"
- *tattered* (line 57), "shabby"

complaint to perform what they regarded as a great sacrifice of her time and a
20 sign that she was indeed a very nice girl. She had never told them how much
she loved grocery shopping, only that she was "willing" to do it. She had an
intuition which told her that her parents were not safe for sharing such strong,
important facts about herself. Let them think they knew her.

Once inside the supermarket, her hands firmly around the handle of the
25 cart, she would lapse into a kind of reverie and wheel toward the produce.
Like a Tibetan monk[2] in solitary meditation, she calmed to a point of deep,
deep happiness; this feeling came to her, reliably, if strangely, only in the
supermarket.

*T*hen one day the bag boy dropped her jar of mayonnaise and that is how
30 she fell in love.

He was nervous—first day on the job—and along had come this fascinating
girl, standing in the checkout line with the unfocused stare one often sees in
young children, her face turned enough away that he might take several full
looks at her as he packed sturdy bags full of food and the goods of modern life.
35 She interested him because her hair was red and thick, and in it she had placed
a huge orange bow, nearly the size of a small hat. That was enough to distract
him, and when finally it was her groceries he was packing, she looked at him
and smiled and he could respond only by busting her jar of mayonnaise on the
floor, shards of glass and oozing cream decorating the area around his feet.
40 She loved him at exactly that moment, and if he'd known this perhaps he
wouldn't have fallen into the brown depression he fell into, which lasted the
rest of his shift. He believed he must have looked a fool in her eyes, and he
envied the sureness of everyone around him: the cocky cashier at the register,
the grim and harried store manager, the bland butcher, and the brazen bag
45 boys who smoked in the warehouse on their breaks. He wanted a second
chance. Another chance to be confident and say witty things to her as he threw
tin cans into her bags, persuading her to allow him to help her to her car so
he might learn just a little about her, check out the floor of the car for signs of
hobbies or fetishes and the bumpers for clues as to beliefs and loyalties.
50 But he busted her jar of mayonnaise and nothing else worked out for the
rest of the day.

---

2. **Tibetan monk:** a member of a Buddhist sect in central Asia that practices meditation.

Close Read

4. What event on this page sets the rising action in motion?

5. How would you describe the conflict faced by the girl and the bag boy? How does this conflict make the story more interesting?

Close Read

4. ***Possible answer:*** *The bag boy drops a jar of mayonnaise (line 29).*

5. ***Possible answer:*** *Each feels attracted to the other, but neither is able to show it (lines 31–42). This builds some suspense. The reader wants to know what will happen next.*

FOR LESS–PROFICIENT READERS

Analysis Support: Plot

1. Have learners copy the graphic and headings from the plot diagram on page 24.

2. Provide these line numbers as clues to the opening plot elements in "Checkouts": lines 9–14 (setting, characters); lines 40–42 (conflict).

3. Have students work in pairs to fill in the details for each plot element.

6. Possible answer: *After the boy drops the jar, the girl falls in love. The boy becomes depressed and wishes for a second chance to be confident and talk to the girl. As four weeks pass, they look for each other but do not meet. Suspense develops from understanding the characters' feelings and wondering what will happen when they meet again.*

7. Possible answer: *Details include words and phrases like "reason enough to be alive," "hope," "anticipation," and "possibilities of mystery and romance" (lines 70–71, 77).*

If students need help . . . Explain that the word *ecstasy* in line 69 suggests excitement and joy. Have students look for other words and phrases in the paragraph that convey positive emotions.

Strange, how attractive clumsiness can be. She left the supermarket with stars in her eyes, for she had loved the way his long nervous fingers moved from the conveyor belt to the bags, how deftly (until the mayonnaise) they
55 had picked up her items and placed them into her bags. She had loved the way the hair kept falling into his eyes as he leaned over to grab a box or a tin. And the tattered brown shoes he wore with no socks. And the left side of his collar turned in rather than out.

The bag boy seemed a wonderful contrast to the perfectly beautiful house
60 she had been forced to accept as her home, to the *history* she hated, to the loneliness she had become used to, and she couldn't wait to come back for more of his awkwardness and dishevelment.

Incredibly, it was another four weeks before they saw each other again. As fate would have it, her visits to the supermarket never coincided with
65 his schedule to bag. Each time she went to the store, her eyes scanned the checkouts at once, her heart in her mouth. And each hour he worked, the bag boy kept one eye on the door, watching for the red-haired girl with the big orange bow.

Yet in their disappointment these weeks there was a kind of ecstasy. It is
70 reason enough to be alive, the hope you may see again some face which has meant something to you. The anticipation of meeting the bag boy eased the girl's painful transition into her new and jarring life in Cincinnati. It provided for her an anchor amid all that was impersonal and unfamiliar, and she spent less time on thoughts of what she had left behind as she concentrated on what
75 might lie ahead. And for the boy, the long and often tedious hours at the supermarket which provided no challenge other than that of showing up the following workday . . . these hours became possibilities of mystery and romance for him as he watched the electric doors for the girl in the orange bow.

And when finally they did meet up again, neither offered a clue to the other
80 that he, or she, had been the object of obsessive thought for weeks. She spotted him as soon as she came into the store, but she kept her eyes strictly in front of her as she pulled out a cart and wheeled it toward the produce. And he, too, knew the instant she came through the door—though the orange bow was gone, replaced by a small but bright yellow flower instead—and he never

---

6. Review lines 29–68. Summarize the sequence of events that begins with the boy's dropping the jar. How do these events build suspense about what will happen?

7. What details in lines 69–78 tell you that the girl and the boy are enjoying the excitement of the building conflict? One has been boxed.

DIFFERENTIATED INSTRUCTION

FOR LESS–PROFICIENT READERS

Analysis Support: Plot

Have student pairs complete their plot diagrams. Provide these line numbers as clues to the closing plot elements in the story:

Rising Action: lines 63–78
Climax: lines 79–86
Falling Action: lines 87–101
Resolution: lines 102–111

FOR ENGLISH LEARNERS

Vocabulary: Idioms Help students use context clues to determine the meanings of these idioms in the story: *check out* (line 48), "to examine something"; *stars in her eyes* (line 53), "dazzled by happy dreams"; *As fate would have it* (line 64), "as events of life unfolded"; *heart in her mouth* (line 66), "a feeling of nearly choking from a strong emotion, such as shyness." Then ask volunteers to act out or mime the meanings.

85 once turned his head in her direction but watched her from the corner of his
vision as he tried to swallow back the fear in his throat.

It is odd how we sometimes deny ourselves the very pleasure we have longed
for and which is finally within our reach. For some perverse reason she would
not have been able to articulate, the girl did not bring her cart up to the bag
90 boy's checkout when her shopping was done. And the bag boy let her leave the
store, pretending no notice of her.

This is often the way of children, when they truly want a thing, to pretend
that they don't. And then they grow angry when no one tries harder to give
them this thing they so casually rejected, and they soon find themselves in a
95 rage simply because they cannot say yes when they mean yes. Humans are very
complicated. (And perhaps cats, who have been known to react in the same
way, though the resulting rage can only be guessed at.)

The girl hated herself for not checking out at the boy's line, and the
boy hated himself for not catching her eye and saying hello, and they most
100 sincerely hated each other without having ever exchanged even two minutes
of conversation.

Eventually—in fact, within the week—a kind and intelligent boy who lived
very near her beautiful house asked the girl to a movie and she gave up
her fancy for the bag boy at the supermarket. And the bag boy himself grew
105 so bored with his job that he made a desperate search for something better
and ended up in a bookstore where scores of fascinating girls lingered like
honeybees about a hive. Some months later the bag boy and the girl with the
orange bow again crossed paths, standing in line with their dates at a movie
theater, and, glancing toward the other, each smiled slightly, then looked away,
110 as strangers on public buses often do, when one is moving off the bus and the
other is moving on.

Close Read

8. Reread lines 79–86, which mark the story's climax. How do the characters resolve the main conflict?

9. In the falling action stage, lines 87–101, the characters reflect on their actions. Are they happy with the way they've handled the conflict? Explain.

10. Reread the resolution in lines 102–111. What are the results of the conflict for each character?

Close Read

8. *Possible answer: The characters resolve the conflict by pretending not to notice each other.*

9. *Possible answer: The characters hate themselves and each other for the way they've handled the situation: "The girl hated herself ... and the boy hated himself ... and they most sincerely hated each other...."* (lines 98–100).

If students need help ... Write lines 98–101 on the board. Underline the verb *hated* each time it appears. Ask volunteers to identify the object of hatred in each case. Circle their correct answers.

10. *Possible answer: Each character moves on and finds someone new. In addition, the bag boy gets a better job, and the girl seems to be adjusting to her new home.*

Assess and Reteach

Assess
Have students summarize "Checkouts" by identifying the exposition, rising action, climax, falling action, and resolution.

Reteach
For students who are unable to apply the workshop skills to "Checkouts," select from these reteaching options:

1. Review with them the note-taking copy masters for this lesson. Have students
- read aloud the information recorded about each skill
- explain one skill to a small group, with each person in the group taking a turn to explain another skill
- review the note-taking copy master for homework

2. Refer students to a story the class has read recently. Have students name the events associated with the plot, and list them on the board. Briefly define each plot event as you write the events in story order. Help students locate the plot event in the story. Annotate the list on the board to help students make an association between the terms and the events in the selection.

FOR ENGLISH LEARNERS
Vocabulary: Multiple-Meaning Words
- Explain that the word *very* is most often used to mean "extremely," as in "very long," or "truly," as in "very nice." In line 87, however, *very* means "exact" or "precise."
- Discuss various meanings of *checkout* and *check out*. Have students tell which meanings the author had in mind when she

titled the story. *Possible answer: to examine someone or something for suitability; an area in a store where goods are paid for*

Focus and Motivate

OBJECTIVES

Literary Analysis
- explore the key idea of **consequences**
- analyze foreshadowing
- read a short story and a magazine article

Reading
- analyze sequence of events

Vocabulary
- build vocabulary for reading and writing
- use the Latin word root *mal* to help unlock meaning *(also an EL language objective)*

Grammar and Writing
- use sentence fragments and contractions in realistic dialogue
- use writing to analyze literature

SUMMARY

"A Sound of Thunder" describes a safari back to the time of dinosaurs. Eckels, a hunter intent upon shooting a *Tyrannosaurus rex,* is warned not to disturb the jungle, because doing so could change the future. When Eckels sees the dinosaur, however, he panics and disobeys. His actions result in a future dictatorial government—and in his own death.

Would you visit the PAST *if you could?*

Discuss the question with students. To lead into the *KEY IDEA,* ask students for examples of stories that involve time travel. Were the **consequences,** or results, of the time travel positive or negative? Extend the discussion by having students complete the *QUICKWRITE.*

Selection Resources

A Sound of Thunder
Short Story by Ray Bradbury

Would you visit the PAST *if you could?*

KEY IDEA Imagine that you could board a time machine and travel into the past. In "A Sound of Thunder," the main character does just that. His journey, however, has unexpected **consequences.**

QUICKWRITE If time travel were possible, what era would you most like to visit? Imagine one or two things you might do during your adventure. How would your actions affect the future? Create a cause-and-effect chart describing your actions and their possible consequences.

Era: Prehistoric Times
What I'd Do → Result

32

R RESOURCE MANAGER UNIT 1

Plan and Teach pp. 17–24

Literary Analysis
Summary pp. 25†*, 26‡*
Foreshadowing pp. 27, 28†*
Question Support p. 35*

Reading
Analyze Sequence pp. 29, 30†*
Reading Check p. 34
Reading Fluency p. 37

Vocabulary
Study p. 31*
Practice p. 32
Strategy p. 33

Grammar and Writing
Use Realistic Dialogue p. 36

Assessment
Selection Tests A, B/C pp. 39*, 41*
Test Generator CD

BEST PRACTICES TOOLKIT

Differentiated Instruction
pp. 31–38*

Scaffolding Instruction
pp. 43–46*

Graphic Organizers/Strategies
Two-Column Chart • Word Squares • Jigsaw Reading • Comparison Matrix • Timeline • New Word Analysis • Predicting

Reading Support
Audio Anthology CD*

Technology
Literature and Vocabulary Centers at **ClassZone.com**
WriteSmart CD

* Resources for Differentiation   † Also in Spanish   ‡ In Haitian Creole and Vietnamese

LITERARY ANALYSIS: FORESHADOWING

Foreshadowing is a writer's use of hints or clues to suggest events that will happen later in a story. By using this technique, Bradbury creates **suspense**, which in turn makes his readers want to know what will happen next. Foreshadowing often occurs when a character makes an unusual statement or issues a strong warning, as in the following example:

"So be careful. Stay on the Path. Never step off!"

Watch for other examples of foreshadowing as you read Bradbury's story.

Review: **Plot**

READING SKILL: ANALYZE SEQUENCE

A story about time travel presents some interesting challenges. If you were to create a timeline to track the characters' travels, it would go backward and then forward again. Yet the events in the story are presented in the order in which they happen to the characters. As you read the story, keep track of the **sequence** of events by creating a chart like the one shown. Record important events before, during, and after the time safari.

Before	During	After
Eckels prepares to travel back in time to hunt dinosaurs.		

Review: **Make Inferences, Predict**

▲ VOCABULARY IN CONTEXT

Bradbury builds an intensity in this story by using the following words. See which ones you already know. Place each word in the appropriate column. Then write a brief definition of each word you're familiar with.

WORD LIST		
annihilate	malfunctioning	subliminal
correlate	paradox	undulate
expendable	resilient	
infinitesimally	stagnating	

Know Well	Think I Know	Don't Know

Author Online

Ray Bradbury
born 1920

Social Critic for the Future
A major writer in the genres of science fiction and fantasy, Ray Bradbury explores the future, outer space—and the human heart. Over his long career, he has lived to see much science fiction become science fact. His most chilling stories comment on the human consequences of progress and often reflect the ironies of life.

A Library Education Bradbury fervently believes in the importance of reading. "I didn't go to college, but when I graduated from high school I went down to the local library," he has said. For ten years Bradbury spent two or three days each week reading in the local public library in Los Angeles, California.

Not Quite a Technophobe This master of science fiction writes his stories on a typewriter rather than a computer, scorns the Internet, and has never even driven a car. Still, Bradbury is a strong advocate of space travel because he views it as "life-enhancing."

 MORE ABOUT THE AUTHOR
For more on Ray Bradbury, visit the **Literature Center** at ClassZone.com.

Background

The Fourth Dimension Time travel has been a popular idea in science fiction ever since the British author H. G. Wells wrote his short novel *The Time Machine* in 1895. In the novel, Wells suggested that in addition to the three dimensions of length, height, and width, there was a fourth dimension of duration, or time. Wells speculated that if a machine could be invented to move along the fourth dimension, travel backward and forward in time would be possible.

Teach

STANDARDS FOCUS

LITERARY ANALYSIS

● FORESHADOWING

For instructional support, read aloud this example:

"People say the shortcut is cursed and that using it will bring serious consequences," Carlos chuckled. "But I don't believe them."

Have students explain how Carlos's comments might foreshadow future events. **Possible answer:** *Carlos's description of the curse suggests that his decision to take the shortcut will have "serious consequences."*

CHECK UNDERSTANDING Elicit other examples of foreshadowing from stories or movies.

READING SKILL

■ ANALYZE SEQUENCE

Help students see that sequence can indicate how one event leads to another.

Point out that an author may present events chronologically, moving forward in time (historical novel), or may first describe an occurrence and then show the events that led up to it (detective story).

CHECK UNDERSTANDING Ask students what sequence of events they might see in a story about travel to the past.

 RESOURCE MANAGER—Copy Master
Analyze Sequence p. 29 (for student use while reading the selection)

VOCABULARY SKILL

▲ VOCABULARY IN CONTEXT

DIAGNOSE WORD KNOWLEDGE To determine preteaching needs, have all students complete Vocabulary in Context. Check students' definitions against those on the selection pages: *annihilate* (p. 38), *correlate* (p. 39), *expendable* (p. 39), *infinitesimally* (p. 39), *malfunctioning* (p. 44), *paradox* (p. 40), *resilient* (p. 41), *stagnating* (p. 44), *subliminal* (p. 45), *undulate* (p. 41).

PRETEACH VOCABULARY Use the Vocabulary Study copy master to help students predict meanings for each boldfaced word in the copy master.

1. Read item 1 aloud, emphasizing *annihilate*.
2. Point out the phrase "with a stamp of your foot" and the word "dead." Elicit possible meanings for *annihilate*, such as "to kill."
3. Have students record their predictions.
4. Repeat the procedure for items 2–10.

 RESOURCE MANAGER—Copy Master
Vocabulary Study p. 31

For general guidelines on differentiating vocabulary instruction and for alternative vocabulary activities for students not needing vocabulary preteaching, see

BEST PRACTICES TOOLKIT
Scaffolding Vocabulary Instruction pp. 43–46

ⓘ Vocabulary Center at ClassZone.com

ANALYZE VISUALS

Possible answer: The lush growth suggests an exotic world, filled with plant and animal life. The abundant growth suggests that the climate is temperate or warm with plenty of sunshine. Since there is no sign of human activity, the region is undeveloped and possibly unexplored.

About the Art Austrian artist Joseph Selleny (1824–1875) is known for his landscape paintings and lithographs. After studying at the Viennese Academy, Selleny traveled by boat around the world and returned with exotic studies that he later turned into paintings, such as the one on page 35.

LITERARY ANALYSIS

Ⓐ FORESHADOWING

Possible answer: The warning foreshadows the possibility of dangerous events during the safari (for there is no guarantee that Eckels will "come back alive"). The mention of a penalty also foreshadows the possibility that someone may "disobey instructions."

If students need help . . . Explore the sense of danger by working together to complete a Two-Column Chart like this one:

When I read . . .	I wonder . . .
"We guarantee nothing"	Why can't you offer a guarantee?
"If he says no shooting"	
"If you disobey"	

 BEST PRACTICES TOOLKIT—Transparency
Two-Column Chart p. A25

A SOUND OF THUNDER

RAY BRADBURY

The sign on the wall seemed to quaver under a film of sliding warm water. Eckels felt his eyelids blink over his stare, and the sign burned in this momentary darkness:

> TIME SAFARI, INC.
> SAFARIS TO ANY YEAR IN THE PAST.
> YOU NAME THE ANIMAL.
> WE TAKE YOU THERE.
> YOU SHOOT IT.

A warm phlegm gathered in Eckels's throat; he swallowed and pushed it
10 down. The muscles around his mouth formed a smile as he put his hand slowly out upon the air, and in that hand waved a check for ten thousand dollars to the man behind the desk.

"Does this safari guarantee I come back alive?"

"We guarantee nothing," said the official, "except the dinosaurs." He turned. "This is Mr. Travis, your Safari Guide in the Past. He'll tell you what and where to shoot. If he says no shooting, no shooting. If you disobey instructions, there's a stiff penalty of another ten thousand dollars, plus possible government action, on your return." Ⓐ

ANALYZE VISUALS
Examine this picture. What information can you **infer** about the world it portrays?

❶ **Targeted Passage**

Ⓐ **FORESHADOWING**
Reread lines 13–18. What might the man's warning to Eckels foreshadow?

DIFFERENTIATED INSTRUCTION

FOR ALL STUDENTS

Expert Groups Allow students to become experts or members of expert groups by researching and choosing a way to share information about one of these topics:

- Cretaceous period
- the interdependence of organisms
- the "domino effect" in various contexts
- time travel in literature and in movies

FOR LESS–PROFICIENT READERS

In combination with the *Audio Anthology CD*, use one or more Targeted Passages (pp. 34, 36, 39, 42, 47) to ensure that students focus on key story events, concepts, and skills. Targeted Passages are also good for English learners.

❶ **Targeted Passage [Lines 4–14]**

This passage introduces the main character, Eckels; the futuristic setting; and the elements of time travel and danger.

BACKGROUND

Tyrannosaurus rex This safari will take Eckels back in time so that he can shoot a *Tyrannosaurus rex,* "the most incredible monster in history" (lines 46–47). This 40-foot-long, meat-eating dinosaur (whose name literally means "tyrant lizard king") is believed to have lived at least 65 million years ago. Adults could reach a height of about 18 feet and weigh more than 6 tons. These dinosaurs used their powerful jaws, long claws, and 6-inch-long, serrated teeth to tear apart their prey and devour the remains.

- What does the Time Safari ad promise?
- Why does Eckels pay $10,000?
- Does the story open in the past, present, or future?
- What clue can you find to the dangers of the trip?

FOR ENGLISH LEARNERS

Key Academic Vocabulary Use Word Squares to teach these words: *guarantee* (line 13), *reverse* (line 25), *decade* (line 60), *survive* (line 113), *eventually* (line 115).

 BEST PRACTICES TOOLKIT—Transparency
Word Squares p. E10

Prereading For prereading instruction for English learners, see

 BEST PRACTICES TOOLKIT
Scaffolding Reading Instruction pp. 43–46

FOR ADVANCED LEARNERS/PRE–AP

Pre-AP Exercises in the bottom channel provide additional challenge for students. Use these suggestions for small groups or individuals.

ADDITIONAL GUIDELINES

For more help with differentiation and tips for classroom management, see

 BEST PRACTICES TOOLKIT
Differentiated Instruction pp. 31–38

LITERARY ANALYSIS

Ⓑ FORESHADOWING

Possible answer: The conversation might foreshadow the frightening possibility that under different circumstances, Deutscher, not Keith, would be the next president. The man's comments (especially the prefix anti- in several of his words) suggest that Deutscher would make the "worst kind" of president.

LITERARY ANALYSIS: *Review*

Ⓒ PLOT

Possible answer: Eckels, a hunter who has signed up to go on a safari back to the time of dinosaurs, meets with an official of Time Safari, Inc., to firm up the plans. After introducing Mr. Travis, who will be the safari guide, the official warns of the great danger in encountering "the most incredible monster in history." He wants to screen out anyone who might panic and jeopardize the safety of others and the success of the trip. Eckels is determined to go, despite his apparent nervousness.

Eckels glanced across the vast office at a mass and tangle, a snaking and
20 humming of wires and steel boxes, at an aurora[1] that flickered now orange,
now silver, now blue. There was a sound like a gigantic bonfire burning all of
Time, all the years and all the parchment calendars, all the hours piled high
and set aflame.

A touch of the hand and this burning would, on the instant, beautifully
reverse itself. Eckels remembered the wording in the advertisements to the
letter. Out of chars and ashes, out of dust and coals, like golden salamanders,
the old years, the green years, might leap; roses sweeten the air, white hair turn
Irish-black, wrinkles vanish; all, everything fly back to seed, flee death, rush
down to their beginnings, suns rise in western skies and set in glorious easts,
30 moons eat themselves opposite to the custom, all and everything cupping one
in another like Chinese boxes,[2] rabbits into hats, all and everything returning
to the fresh death, the seed death, the green death, to the time before the
beginning. A touch of a hand might do it, the merest touch of a hand.

"Unbelievable." Eckels breathed, the light of the Machine on his thin face.
"A real Time Machine." He shook his head. "Makes you think. If the election
had gone badly yesterday, I might be here now running away from the results.
Thank God Keith won. He'll make a fine President of the United States."

"Yes," said the man behind the desk. "We're lucky. If Deutscher[3] had gotten
in, we'd have the worst kind of dictatorship. There's an anti-everything man
40 for you, a militarist, anti-Christ, anti-human, anti-intellectual. People called us
up, you know, joking but not joking. Said if Deutscher became President they
wanted to go live in 1492. Of course it's not our business to conduct Escapes,
but to form Safaris. Anyway, Keith's President now. All you got to worry
about is— Ⓑ

"Shooting my dinosaur," Eckels finished it for him.

"A *Tyrannosaurus rex*. The Tyrant Lizard, the most incredible monster in
history. Sign this release. Anything happens to you, we're not responsible.
Those dinosaurs are hungry."

Eckels flushed angrily. "Trying to scare me!"

50 "Frankly, yes. We don't want anyone going who'll panic at the first shot. Six
Safari leaders were killed last year, and a dozen hunters. We're here to give you
the severest thrill a real hunter ever asked for. Traveling you back sixty million
years to bag the biggest game in all of Time. Your personal check's still there.
Tear it up."

Mr. Eckels looked at the check. His fingers twitched. Ⓒ

"Good luck," said the man behind the desk. "Mr. Travis, he's all yours."

They moved silently across the room, taking their guns with them, toward
the Machine, toward the silver metal and the roaring light.

Ⓩ **Targeted Passage**

Ⓑ **FORESHADOWING**
What might the conversation about the election results foreshadow?

Ⓒ **PLOT**
What have you learned about the characters' situation in the **exposition**?

---

1. **aurora** (ə-rôr′ə): a shifting, streaming display of light, like those sometimes seen in the sky in the northern and southern regions of the earth.
2. **Chinese boxes:** a set of boxes, each of which fits neatly inside the next larger one.
3. **Deutscher** (doi′chər).

DIFFERENTIATED INSTRUCTION

FOR LESS–PROFICIENT READERS

Ⓩ **Targeted Passage [Lines 34–45]**

This passage sets up a crucial story concept: that Keith just defeated the evil Deutscher for the presidency.

- Who just won the election? Who lost?
- How do Eckels and the man behind the desk feel about the election results?
- The prefix *anti-* means "against." What kinds of things is Deutscher against?

FOR ENGLISH LEARNERS

Language: Conversational Patterns Explain that in line 49 the words *are you* are left out but understood in the dialogue "Trying to scare me!" Have mixed language-ability Jigsaw groups study the dialogue in the rest of the story. Ask each group to fill in missing words in their assigned passages and report back to the class.

 **BEST PRACTICES TOOLKIT**
Jigsaw Reading p. A1

F irst a day and then a night and then a day and then a night, then it was
60 day-night-day-night-day. A week, a month, a year, a decade! A.D. 2055.
A.D. 2019. 1999! 1957! Gone! The Machine roared.

They put on their oxygen helmets and tested the intercoms.

Eckels swayed on the padded seat, his face pale, his jaw stiff. He felt the
trembling in his arms, and he looked down and found his hands tight on the
new rifle. There were four other men in the Machine. Travis, the Safari Leader;
his assistant, Lesperance;[4] and two other hunters, Billings and Kramer. They
sat looking at each other, and the years blazed around them. **D**

"Can these guns get a dinosaur cold?" Eckels felt his mouth saying.

"If you hit them right," said Travis on the helmet radio. "Some dinosaurs
70 have two brains, one in the head, another far down the spinal column. We stay
away from those. That's stretching luck. Put your first two shots into the eyes,
if you can, blind them, and go back into the brain."

The Machine howled. Time was a film run backward. Suns fled, and ten
million moons fled after them. "Think," said Eckels. "Every hunter that ever
lived would envy us today. This makes Africa seem like Illinois."

The Machine slowed; its scream fell to a murmur. The Machine stopped.
The sun stopped in the sky.

The fog that had enveloped the Machine blew away, and they were in an
old time, a very old time indeed, three hunters and two Safari Heads with their
80 blue metal guns across their knees.

"Christ isn't born yet," said Travis. "Moses has not gone to the mountain to
talk with God.[5] The Pyramids are still in the earth, waiting to be cut out and
put up. *Remember* that. Alexander, Caesar, Napoleon, Hitler—none of them
exists."

The man nodded.

"That"—Mr. Travis pointed—"is the jungle of sixty million two thousand
and fifty-five years before President Keith."

He indicated a metal path that struck off into green wilderness, over
streaming swamp, among giant ferns and palms.

90 "And that," he said, "is the Path, laid by Time Safari for your use. It floats
six inches above the earth. Doesn't touch so much as one grass blade, flower,
or tree. It's an antigravity metal.[6] Its purpose is to keep you from touching this
world of the past in any way. Stay on the Path. Don't go off it. I repeat. *Don't
go off.* For *any* reason! If you fall off, there's a penalty. And don't shoot any
animal we don't okay." **E**

"Why?" asked Eckels.

They sat in the ancient wilderness. Far birds' cries blew on a wind, and the
smell of tar and an old salt sea, moist grasses, and flowers the color of blood.

---

4. **Lesperance** (lĕs'pər-äns).
5. **Moses ... talk with God:** According to the Old Testament, God spoke directly to Moses several times
   in mountainous locations, as when Moses received the Ten Commandments on Mount Sinai.
6. **antigravity metal:** a metal that counteracts the pull of gravity.

D MAKE INFERENCES
On the basis of details
presented so far, what
kind of person is Eckels?

E FORESHADOWING
What might Travis's
warning to the hunters
foreshadow? How
does his warning create
suspense?

A SOUND OF THUNDER **37**

READING SKILL: *Review*

D MAKE INFERENCES

*Possible answer: Eckels appears to be
a high-strung person. He's excited but
nervous about the safari. He's concerned
about coming back alive (line 13), and he
reacts with quick anger when challenged
(line 49). Details such as "face pale ... jaw
stiff. ... trembling in his arms ... hands
tight on the new rifle" (lines 63–65) also
suggest his tension.*

If students need help ...

- Have students read lines 63–65. Discuss
  why a person might look the way that
  Eckels does at this moment.
- Have students read lines 46–49. Talk
  about what Eckels's strong reaction
  suggests about his personality.

LITERARY ANALYSIS

E FORESHADOWING

*Possible answer: Travis's warning fore-
shadows that someone probably will go
off the Path. The warning creates suspense
because the reader wonders who will do so,
why, and what the consequences will be.*

Extend the Discussion How does the Path
help safari leaders control the hunters?

FOR ADVANCED LEARNERS/PRE–AP

Analyze Allusions [small-group option] Use a
Comparison Matrix with students to discuss
and compare the figures mentioned in lines
81–84. Then discuss the significance
of these allusions:

- *Christ* and *Moses:* Both are central to a major
  world religion. The names hint at the use of
  B.C. and A.D. in tracing the passage of time.
- *Alexander* and *Caesar:* Both were conquerors and rulers in the ancient world.

- *Napoleon* and *Hitler:* Both belong to a more
  modern era, but like Alexander and Caesar,
  they were powerful conquerors and rulers.

After reading the story, have students
discuss why Bradbury may have included
the last four figures. In what way might
they foreshadow the election of Deutscher?

BEST PRACTICES TOOLKIT—Transparency
Comparison Matrix p. A24

REINFORCE *KEY IDEA:* CONSEQUENCES

Discuss Why does Travis say, "We don't belong here in the Past"? *Possible answer: He understands that altering the past may have undesirable consequences in the future. He also knows that the government disapproves of the company and allows it to operate only because it pays "big graft."*

ANALYZE VISUALS

Activity Ask students how the jungle scene in this painting helps them visualize the setting of the story. *Possible answer: The painting depicts a variety of creatures in a dense jungle, which is similar to the prehistoric jungle setting of the story.*

About the Art *Orinoco Jungle Life* is one of many pieces of art from German painter and zoologist Anton Goering (1836–1905). Sponsored by the Zoological Society of London, Goering traveled in Venezuela between 1866 and 1874, detailing its landscapes and collecting specimens of birds. His work made a faraway land—a land that might have seemed as exotic as the prehistoric world seemed to the hunters in Bradbury's story—accessible to many Europeans.

"We don't want to change the Future. We don't belong here in the Past. 100 The government doesn't *like* us here. We have to pay big graft to keep our franchise.[7] A Time Machine is finicky business. Not knowing it, we might kill an important animal, a small bird, a roach, a flower even, thus destroying an important link in a growing species."

"That's not clear," said Eckels.

"All right," Travis continued, "say we accidentally kill one mouse here. That means all the future families of this one particular mouse are destroyed, right?"

"Right."

"And all the families of the families of the families of that one mouse! With a stamp of your foot, you **annihilate** first one, then a dozen, then a thousand, 110 a million, a *billion* possible mice!"

"So they're dead," said Eckels. "So what?"

"So what?" Travis snorted quietly. "Well, what about the foxes that'll need those mice to survive? For want of ten mice, a fox dies. For want of ten foxes, a lion starves. For want of a lion, all manner of insects, vultures, infinite billions of life forms are thrown into chaos and destruction. Eventually it all boils down to this: fifty-nine million years later, a caveman, one of a dozen on the

annihilate
(ə-nī′ə-lāt′) *v.* to destroy completely

---

7. **pay big graft to keep our franchise:** pay large bribes to officials in return for their approval of the business.

DIFFERENTIATED INSTRUCTION

FOR LESS–PROFICIENT READERS

Concept Support After students read lines 112–148, discuss how a very small change can lead to a large change—for example, how one's day can be totally changed by being one minute late for a bus. Help them connect this concept with the evolutionary chain assumed in the story.

FOR ENGLISH LEARNERS

Comprehension: Sequence Use a Timeline to help students understand that the story opens in 2055 and that the characters are now back in the time of dinosaurs.

 BEST PRACTICES TOOLKIT—Transparency Timeline p. B23

entire world, goes hunting wild boar or saber-toothed tiger[8] for food. But you, friend, have *stepped* on all the tigers in that region. By stepping on one single mouse. So the caveman starves. And the caveman, please note, is not just *any*
120 **expendable** man, no! He is an *entire future nation.* From his loins would have sprung ten sons. From *their* loins one hundred sons, and thus onward to a civilization. Destroy this one man, and you destroy a race, a people, an entire history of life. It is comparable to slaying some of Adam's grandchildren. The stomp of your foot, on one mouse, could start an earthquake, the effects of which could shake our earth and destinies down through Time, to their very foundations. With the death of that one caveman, a billion others yet unborn are throttled in the womb. Perhaps Rome never rises on its seven hills. Perhaps Europe is forever a dark forest, and only Asia waxes healthy and teeming. Step on a mouse, and you crush the Pyramids. Step on a mouse, and you leave your
130 print, like a Grand Canyon, across Eternity. Queen Elizabeth might never be born; Washington might not cross the Delaware; there might never be a United States at all. So be careful. Stay on the Path. *Never* step off!"

"I see," said Eckels. "Then it wouldn't pay for us even to touch the *grass?*"

"Correct. Crushing certain plants could add up **infinitesimally.** A little error here would multiply in sixty million years, all out of proportion. Of course maybe our theory is wrong. Maybe Time *can't* be changed by us. Or maybe it can be changed only in little subtle ways. A dead mouse here makes an insect imbalance there, a population disproportion later, a bad harvest further on, a depression, mass starvation, and, finally, a change in *social*
140 temperament in far-flung countries. Something much more subtle, like that. Perhaps only a soft breath, a whisper, a hair, pollen on the air, such a slight, slight change that unless you looked close you wouldn't see it. Who knows? Who really can say he knows? We don't know. We're guessing. But until we do know for certain whether our messing around in Time *can* make a big roar or a little rustle in history, we're being careful. This Machine, this Path, your clothing and bodies, were sterilized, as you know, before the journey. We wear these oxygen helmets so we can't introduce our bacteria into an ancient atmosphere."

"How do we know which animals to shoot?"
150 "They're marked with red paint," said Travis. "Today, before our journey, we sent Lesperance here back with the Machine. He came to this particular era and followed certain animals."

"Studying them?"

"Right," said Lesperance. "I track them through their entire existence, noting which of them lives longest. Very few. How many times they mate. Not often. Life's short. When I find one that's going to die when a tree falls on him, or one that drowns in a tar pit, I note the exact hour, minute, and second. I shoot a paint bomb. It leaves a red patch on his side. We can't miss it. Then I **correlate** our arrival in the Past so that we meet the Monster not more than

---

8. **saber-toothed tiger:** a type of extinct wild cat that lived about 40 million years ago.

expendable
(ĭk-spĕn′də-bəl)
adj. not worth keeping; not essential

infinitesimally
(ĭn′fĭn-ĭ-tĕs′ə-mə-lē)
adv. in amounts so small as to be barely measurable

❸ **Targeted Passage**

correlate (kôr′ə-lāt′)
v. to figure out or create a relationship between two items or events

Lines 105–148
DISCUSSION PROMPTS
Use these prompts to help students understand the dangers of altering the past:

Connect Would Travis's explanation of his theory worry you? Why or why not? *Many students will suggest that there is good reason to worry if the theory is correct.*

Analyze What might be the effects of introducing the visitors' bacteria into the ancient atmosphere? *Possible answer: No living thing in the ancient time would be immune to the visitors' bacteria. The result might be widespread death and destruction of birds, animals, and plant life.*

Synthesize How might the possible "change in *social* temperament" that Travis refers to in lines 139–140 be reflected in a country? *Possible answers: A change in historical circumstances might reshape society's values or its attitudes toward certain groups of people in the society. A change in economic conditions might influence how people feel and think, which in turn affects their choice of leaders and government.*

FOR LESS—PROFICIENT READERS

❸ **Targeted Passage [Lines 132–148]**

This passage sets up the key cause-effect conflict: If a Safari traveler changes anything in the past, the future may be changed.

• Why is it so important for Safari travelers to stay on the Path?

• How might you paraphrase this sentence: "A little error here would multiply in sixty million years, all out of proportion"?

FOR ADVANCED LEARNERS/PRE—AP

Evaluate Have students work in pairs to discuss whether Time Safari, Inc., is taking sufficient precautions to protect history. Challenge students to make a list of at least five additional precautions the company might take.

160 two minutes before he would have died anyway. This way, we kill only animals with no future, that are never going to mate again. You see how *careful* we are?"

"But if you came back this morning in Time," said Eckels eagerly, "you must've bumped into *us*, our Safari! How did it turn out? Was it successful? Did all of us get through—alive?"

Travis and Lesperance gave each other a look.

"That'd be a **paradox**," said the latter. "Time doesn't permit that sort of mess—a man meeting himself. When such occasions threaten, Time steps aside. Like an airplane hitting an air pocket. You felt the Machine jump just before we stopped? That was us passing ourselves on the way back to
170 the Future. We saw nothing. There's no way of telling *if* this expedition was a success, *if we* got our monster, or whether all of us—meaning *you*, Mr. Eckels —got out alive."

Eckels smiled palely.

"Cut that," said Travis sharply. "Everyone on his feet!" **F**

They were ready to leave the Machine.

The jungle was high and the jungle was broad and the jungle was the entire world forever and forever. Sounds like music and sounds like flying tents filled the sky, and those were pterodactyls[9] soaring with cavernous gray wings, gigantic bats of delirium and night fever. Eckels, balanced on the narrow Path,
180 aimed his rifle playfully.

"Stop that!" said Travis. "Don't even aim for fun, blast you! If your guns should go off—"

Eckels flushed. "Where's our *Tyrannosaurus?*"

Lesperance checked his wristwatch. "Up ahead. We'll bisect his trail in sixty seconds. Look for the red paint! Don't shoot till we give the word. Stay on the Path. *Stay on the Path!*"

They moved forward in the wind of morning.

"Strange," murmured Eckels. "Up ahead, sixty million years, Election Day over. Keith made President. Everyone celebrating. And here we are, a million
190 years lost, and they don't exist. The things we worried about for months, a lifetime, not even born or thought of yet."

"Safety catches off, everyone!" ordered Travis. "You, first shot, Eckels. Second, Billings. Third, Kramer."

"I've hunted tiger, wild boar, buffalo, elephant, but now, this is it," said Eckels. "I'm shaking like a kid." **G**

"Ah," said Travis.

Everyone stopped.

Travis raised his hand. "Ahead," he whispered. "In the mist. There he is. There's His Royal Majesty now."
200 The jungle was wide and full of twitterings, rustlings, murmurs, and sighs. Suddenly it all ceased, as if someone had shut a door.

Silence.

A sound of thunder.

---

9. **pterodactyls** (tĕr′ə-dăk′təlz): extinct flying reptiles.

40 UNIT 1: NARRATIVE STRUCTURE

paradox (păr′ə-dŏks′) *n.* a statement or an event that sounds impossible but seems to be true

F **ANALYZE SEQUENCE**
Up until now, the men have spent most of their time talking and arguing. Now, however, the action begins to pick up. As you read the next sequence of events, pay attention to what happens.

G **GRAMMAR AND STYLE**
Reread lines 188–195. Notice how Bradbury uses **sentence fragments** and **contractions** to create realistic dialogue.

READING SKILL

F **ANALYZE SEQUENCE**

As Eckels moves through the prehistoric jungle, he is recalling events that occurred in the future (lines 188–191). How is this sequence different from the usual order in a story? *Possible answer: More typically, a character in the present recalls events that occurred in the past.*

G **GRAMMAR AND STYLE**

Analyze Dialogue Spoken language differs from more formal written language in many ways. For example, when people converse, they often use sentence fragments and contractions. To create realistic dialogue, therefore, authors have their characters do the same. Ask students to identify the fragments and contractions in lines 188–195. Then have them find other places in the text where Bradbury's dialogue "breaks the rules" in order to imitate spoken language.

DIFFERENTIATED INSTRUCTION

FOR ENGLISH LEARNERS

Language: Idioms Use New Word Analysis to teach these idioms from the story: *to the letter* (lines 25–26), "exactly"; *so what* (line 111), "it's not that important"; *boils down to* (lines 115–116), "in summary"; *cut that* (line 174), "stop doing that"; *give the word* (line 185), "express permission"; *take it easy* (line 322), "stay relaxed."

 BEST PRACTICES TOOLKIT—Transparency
New Word Analysis p. E8

FOR ADVANCED LEARNERS/PRE–AP

Paradox Have students discuss the time paradox presented in lines 162–172 and determine whether they think Bradbury has plausibly addressed the paradox. Then challenge students to name other paradoxes related to time travel or space.

Out of the mist, one hundred yards away, came *Tyrannosaurus rex.*

"It," whispered Eckels. "It . . ."

"Sh!"

It came on great oiled, **resilient,** striding legs. It towered thirty feet above half of the trees, a great evil god, folding its delicate watchmaker's claws close to its oily reptilian chest. Each lower leg was a piston, a thousand pounds of
210 white bone, sunk in thick ropes of muscle, sheathed over in a gleam of pebbled skin like the mail of a terrible warrior. Each thigh was a ton of meat, ivory, and steel mesh. And from the great breathing cage of the upper body those two delicate arms dangled out front, arms with hands which might pick up and examine men like toys, while the snake neck coiled. And the head itself, a ton of sculptured stone, lifted easily upon the sky. Its mouth gaped, exposing a fence of teeth like daggers. Its eyes rolled, ostrich eggs, empty of all expression save hunger. It closed its mouth in a death grin. It ran, its pelvic bones crushing aside trees and bushes, its taloned feet clawing damp earth, leaving prints six inches deep wherever it settled its weight. It ran with a gliding ballet
220 step, far too poised and balanced for its ten tons. It moved into a sunlit arena warily, its beautifully reptilian hands feeling the air.

"Why, why," Eckels twitched his mouth. "It could reach up and grab the moon."

"Sh!" Travis jerked angrily. "He hasn't seen us yet."

"It can't be killed." Eckels pronounced this verdict quietly, as if there could be no argument. He had weighed the evidence, and this was his considered opinion. The rifle in his hands seemed a cap gun. "We were fools to come. This is impossible."

"Shut up!" hissed Travis. **H**

230 "Nightmare."

"Turn around," commanded Travis. "Walk quietly to the Machine. We'll remit one-half your fee."

"I didn't realize it would be this *big,*" said Eckels. "I miscalculated, that's all. And now I want out."

"It *sees* us!"

"There's the red paint on its chest!"

The Tyrant Lizard raised itself. Its armored flesh glittered like a thousand green coins. The coins, crusted with slime, steamed. In the slime, tiny insects wriggled, so that the entire body seemed to twitch and **undulate,** even while
240 the monster itself did not move. It exhaled. The stink of raw flesh blew down the wilderness.

"Get me out of here," said Eckels. "It was never like this before. I was always sure I'd come through alive. I had good guides, good safaris, and safety. This time, I figured wrong. I've met my match and admit it. This is too much for me to get hold of."

"Don't run," said Lesperance. "Turn around. Hide in the Machine."

"Yes." Eckels seemed to be numb. He looked at his feet as if trying to make them move. He gave a grunt of helplessness.

resilient (rĭ-zĭl'yənt)
adj. strong but flexible; able to withstand stress without injury

H MAKE INFERENCES
Why do you think Travis is annoyed with Eckels?

undulate (ŭn'jə-lāt')
v. to move in waves or in a smooth, wavelike motion

A SOUND OF THUNDER   **41**

FOR ENGLISH LEARNERS

Culture: Clarify Read aloud "Sh!" (line 224), and demonstrate the finger-to-lips gesture that often accompanies this sound. Explain the intensity and urgency of Travis's hissing "Shut up!" (line 229)

Vocabulary: Word Associations Have pairs of students study lines 213–219 and identify body parts and movements of the dinosaur ("*arms dangled,*" "*hands . . . pick up,*" "*neck coiled,*" "*mouth gaped,*" "*eyes rolled,*" "*feet clawing*").

FOR ADVANCED LEARNERS/PRE–AP

Figurative Language To convey the dinosaur's size from Eckels's viewpoint, in lines 222–223, Bradbury writes, "It could reach up and grab the moon." Have students mimic the author's style by writing two original similes or metaphors that would similarly convey Eckels's thoughts about the dinosaur. Suggest that students use the illustration on pages 42–43 for inspiration.

H MAKE INFERENCES

Possible answer: *Travis is annoyed because Eckels will not be quiet. The dinosaur is not yet aware of the hunters' presence—"He hasn't seen us yet" (line 224)—but the sound of Eckels's voice is likely to draw the dinosaur's attention and give away their position.*

If students need help . . .

- Have them discuss the significance of line 224.
- Point out that Travis already has told Eckels twice to be quiet (lines 206, 224).

Extend the Discussion Why do you think Eckels continues to speak despite Travis's warnings to remain silent?

Lines 207–245
DISCUSSION PROMPTS

Use these prompts to help students understand Eckels's reaction:

Connect Eckels realizes he has made a mistake and wants out of what he knows is a dangerous situation. What advice would you give Eckels at this point in the story? *Responses should reflect an understanding of the situation.*

Analyze Eckels says, "It was never like this before" (line 242). What does he mean? Why does he make this statement? ***Possible answer:*** *Never before has Eckels encountered a creature as fearsome as the* Tyrannosaurus rex *(lines 207–221 and 237–241). On previous safaris, he has felt safe, protected, and in control. Now he is terrified and fears for his life (lines 242–245).*

Synthesize What kind of a person is Eckels? Explain your thinking. ***Possible answer:*** *Eckels is compulsive and not particularly thoughtful. He should have known how dangerous it would be to hunt dinosaurs. Also, he was warned at the outset and given the chance to opt out of the trip (lines 46–54).*

A SOUND OF THUNDER   **41**

Lines 257–266
DISCUSSION PROMPTS

Use these prompts to help students understand the dangerous situation:

Connect Have you or anyone you know ever panicked to the degree that, even for a moment, you didn't realize what you were doing? Explain. *Accept all reasonable responses.*

Analyze How does Bradbury characterize the dinosaur? Cite evidence. ***Possible answer:*** *Bradbury characterizes the dinosaur as awesome in its power. He describes how "trees exploded" (line 261) when the dinosaur swung its tail. He refers to the dinosaur's intent "to twist [the men] in half, to crush them like berries" (line 263).*

Evaluate Faced with the charging *Tyrannosaurus*, Eckels, "not knowing it" (line 257), steps off the Path. Should he be held responsible for his actions? *Answers may vary.*

READING SKILL

❶ ANALYZE SEQUENCE

Possible answer: Eckels steps off the Path, which he has been warned repeatedly not to do. Leaving the Path and coming into physical contact with the prehistoric jungle could affect the future in unforeseen ways. He may have killed a species of plant or animal, thus changing the balance of nature.

"Eckels!"

250 He took a few steps, blinking, shuffling.

"Not *that* way!"

The Monster, at the first motion, lunged forward with a terrible scream. It covered one hundred yards in six seconds. The rifles jerked up and blazed fire. A windstorm from the beast's mouth engulfed them in the stench of slime and old blood. The Monster roared, teeth glittering with sun.

④ **Targeted Passage**

Eckels, not looking back, walked blindly to the edge of the Path, his gun limp in his arms, stepped off the Path, and walked, not knowing it, in the jungle. His feet sank into green moss. His legs moved him, and he felt alone and remote from the events behind. ❶

260 The rifles cracked again. Their sound was lost in shriek and lizard thunder. The great level of the reptile's tail swung up, lashed sideways. Trees exploded in clouds of leaf and branch. The Monster twitched its jeweler's hands down to fondle at the men, to twist them in half, to crush them like berries, to cram them into its teeth and its screaming throat. Its boulder-stone eyes leveled with the men. They saw themselves mirrored. They fired at the metallic eyelids and the blazing black iris.

❶ **ANALYZE SEQUENCE** Reread lines 252–259. What important event occurs in these lines? What do you think might happen as a result of this event?

42 UNIT 1: NARRATIVE STRUCTURE

DIFFERENTIATED INSTRUCTION

FOR LESS-PROFICIENT READERS

④ **Targeted Passage [Lines 250–259]**

This passage presents the moment that changes everything: Eckels steps off the Path! The dangers in his action were foreshadowed in the warning in the Targeted Passage on page 39.

• Why does Eckels step off the Path?

• Why do Eckels's actions pose a danger for this moment in the past? What might they mean to the future?

• What warning foreshadows this moment earlier in the story?

ANALYZE VISUALS
What qualities of *Tyrannosaurus rex* are emphasized in this illustration? Explain.

Like a stone idol, like a mountain avalanche, *Tyrannosaurus* fell. Thundering, it clutched trees, pulled them with it. It wrenched and tore the metal Path. The men flung themselves back and away. The body hit, ten
270 tons of cold flesh and stone. The guns fired. The Monster lashed its armored tail, twitched its snake jaws, and lay still. A fount of blood spurted from its throat. Somewhere inside, a sac of fluids burst. Sickening gushes drenched the hunters. They stood, red and glistening.

The thunder faded.

The jungle was silent. After the avalanche, a green peace. After the nightmare, morning.

Billings and Kramer sat on the pathway and threw up. Travis and Lesperance stood with smoking rifles, cursing steadily.

In the Time Machine, on his face, Eckels lay shivering. He had found his
280 way back to the Path, climbed into the Machine.

Travis came walking, glanced at Eckels, took cotton gauze from a metal box, and returned to the others, who were sitting on the Path.

"Clean up."

ANALYZE VISUALS
Possible answer: The illustration emphasizes the massive size and fearsome appearance of the dinosaur.

Lines 267–273
REINFORCE *KEY IDEA:* CONSEQUENCES
Discuss When the dinosaur unexpectedly charged, the hunters had to fire to keep from being killed. What were the **consequences** of their action? *Possible answer: The falling body of the dinosaur pulled down trees and "wrenched and tore the metal Path," flinging the men backward. The hunters were closer to the animal than they intended to be and were splattered with its blood and body fluids.*

FOR ENGLISH LEARNERS
Vocabulary: Phrasal Verbs Explain that *"Clean up"* (line 283) is an order to clean, whereas *clean out* can mean "use up someone's money." Assign pairs of students one or two of these phrasal verbs to look up in a dictionary, and have them share their definitions: *put on* (line 62), *go off* (line 182), *pick up* (line 213), *turn around* (line 231), *threw up* (line 277), *gave up* (line 303), *get up* (line 311), *go out* (line 313).

FOR ADVANCED LEARNERS/PRE–AP
Analyze Absence of Dialogue Remind students that although Billings and Kramer are present on the safari, their characters have no dialogue in the story. Have students write a brief essay explaining why Bradbury might have included these silent characters.

DISCUSSION PROMPTS

Use these prompts to help students understand Travis's reaction to Eckels's behavior:

Connect Think about a time when you had to talk to someone who severely disappointed you or ruined your plans. How does that experience help you understand Travis's feelings toward Eckels? *Answers should demonstrate an understanding of the anger and perhaps the fear involved in the confrontation.*

Analyze Why does Travis react as he does? *Possible answer: Travis had repeatedly warned Eckels about his behavior (lines 132, 181–182, 206, 224, 229). By disregarding these warnings, Eckels nearly got all of them killed, may have cost the company its license, and may have altered history.*

Evaluate Which is Travis more justified in being concerned about—the government's penalties or the possible effects on time and history? Give reasons. *Students may answer either way, but their responses should address Travis's grasp of the issues involved.*

READING STRATEGY: *Review*

PREDICT

Possible answer: The future may be altered—perhaps in a minor way but possibly in a major way.

If students need help . . . Review lines 105–148 with students and help them use the Predicting chart to speculate about what damage Eckels might have caused by leaving the Path.

 BEST PRACTICES TOOLKIT—Transparency
Predicting p. A10

They wiped the blood from their helmets. They began to curse too. The Monster lay, a hill of solid flesh. Within, you could hear the sighs and murmurs as the furthest chambers of it died, the organs **malfunctioning**, liquids running a final instant from pocket to sac to spleen, everything shutting off, closing up forever. It was like standing by a wrecked locomotive or a steam shovel at quitting time, all valves being released or
290 levered tight. Bones cracked; the tonnage of its own flesh, off balance, dead weight, snapped the delicate forearms, caught underneath. The meat settled, quivering.

Another cracking sound. Overhead, a gigantic tree branch broke from its heavy mooring, fell. It crashed upon the dead beast with finality.

"There." Lesperance checked his watch. "Right on time. That's the giant tree that was scheduled to fall and kill this animal originally." He glanced at the two hunters. "You want the trophy picture?"

"What?"

"We can't take a trophy back to the Future. The body has to stay right here
300 where it would have died originally, so the insects, birds, and bacteria can get at it, as they were intended to. Everything in balance. The body stays. But we *can* take a picture of you standing near it."

The two men tried to think, but gave up, shaking their heads.

They let themselves be led along the metal Path. They sank wearily into the Machine cushions. They gazed back at the ruined Monster, the **stagnating** mound, where already strange reptilian birds and golden insects were busy at the steaming armor.

A sound on the floor of the Time Machine stiffened them. Eckels sat there, shivering.
310 "I'm sorry," he said at last.

"Get up!" cried Travis.

Eckels got up.

"Go out on that Path alone," said Travis. He had his rifle pointed. "You're not coming back in the Machine. We're leaving you here!"

Lesperance seized Travis's arm. "Wait—"

"Stay out of this!" Travis shook his hand away. "This fool nearly killed us. But it isn't *that* so much, no. It's his *shoes!* Look at them! He ran off the Path. That *ruins* us! We'll forfeit! Thousands of dollars of insurance! We guarantee no one leaves the Path. He left it. Oh, the fool! I'll have to report to the
320 government. They might revoke our license to travel. Who knows *what* he's done to Time, to History!"

"Take it easy; all he did was kick up some dirt."

"How do we *know?*" cried Travis. "We don't know anything! It's all a mystery! Get out there, Eckels!"

Eckels fumbled his shirt. "I'll pay anything. A hundred thousand dollars!"

Travis glared at Eckels's checkbook and spat. "Go out there. The Monster's next to the Path. Stick your arms up to your elbows in his mouth. Then you can come back with us."

malfunctioning
(măl-fŭngk′shə-nĭng) *adj.* not working or operating properly **malfunction** *v.*

stagnating (stăg′nā′tĭng) *adj.* becoming foul or rotten from lack of movement **stagnate** *v.*

PREDICT
What do you predict might be the consequences of Eckels's action?

DIFFERENTIATED INSTRUCTION

FOR ENGLISH LEARNERS

Language: Pronoun Referents Explain the referents for the pronouns, shown in italics, from line 316: "'Stay out of *this [the disagreement]!*' Travis shook *his [Lesperance's]* hand away." Then have learners work in mixed-language groups to identify referents for the remaining pronouns in Travis's angry speech (lines 316–318).

FOR ADVANCED LEARNERS/PRE–AP

Evaluate Have students work in small groups to discuss what they think is a reasonable punishment for Eckels. When groups are finished, list their ideas on the board. Have the class vote for the punishment they would choose.

"That's unreasonable!"

330 "The Monster's dead, you idiot. The bullets! The bullets can't be left behind. They don't belong in the Past; they might change anything. Here's my knife. Dig them out!"

The jungle was alive again, full of the old tremorings and bird cries. Eckels turned slowly to regard the primeval garbage dump, that hill of nightmares and terror. After a long time, like a sleepwalker he shuffled out along the Path.

He returned, shuddering, five minutes later, his arms soaked and red to the elbows. He held out his hands. Each held a number of steel bullets. Then he fell. He lay where he fell, not moving.

"You didn't have to make him do that," said Lesperance.

340 "Didn't I? It's too early to tell." Travis nudged the still body. "He'll live. Next time he won't go hunting game like this. Okay." He jerked his thumb wearily at Lesperance. "Switch on. Let's go home."

1492. 1776. 1812.

They cleaned their hands and faces. They changed their caking shirts and pants. Eckels was up and around again, not speaking. Travis glared at him for a full ten minutes.

"Don't look at me," cried Eckels. "I haven't done anything."

"Who can tell?"

"Just ran off the Path, that's all, a little mud on my shoes—what do you
350 want me to do—get down and pray?"

"We might need it. I'm warning you, Eckels, I might kill you yet. I've got my gun ready."

"I'm innocent. I've done nothing!"

1999. 2000. 2055.

The Machine stopped.

"Get out," said Travis.

The room was there as they had left it. But not the same as they had left it. The same man sat behind the same desk. But the same man did not quite sit behind the same desk.

360 Travis looked around swiftly. "Everything okay here?" he snapped.

"Fine. Welcome home!"

Travis did not relax. He seemed to be looking at the very atoms of the air itself, at the way the sun poured through the one high window.

"Okay, Eckels, get out. Don't ever come back."

Eckels could not move.

"You heard me," said Travis. "What're you *staring* at?"

Eckels stood smelling of the air, and there was a thing to the air, a chemical taint so subtle, so slight, that only a faint cry of his **subliminal** senses warned him it was there. The colors, white, gray, blue, orange, in the wall, in the
370 furniture, in the sky beyond the window, were . . . were . . . And there was a *feel*. His flesh twitched. His hands twitched. He stood drinking the oddness with the pores of his body. Somewhere, someone must have been screaming one of those whistles that only a dog can hear. His body screamed silence in return.

subliminal
(sŭb-lĭm′ə-nəl) *adj.* below the level of consciousness

Lines 330–332
REINFORCE *KEY IDEA*: CONSEQUENCES

Discuss Why does Travis want Eckels to return to the dinosaur? Is this task really necessary? *Possible answer: Travis wants Eckels to retrieve the bullets because they do not belong in the past. Changing the past in any way might have severe **consequences** in the future. Most students will agree that it was necessary to retrieve the bullets.*

Lines 339–352
DISCUSSION PROMPTS

Use these prompts to help students compare the viewpoints of Eckels and Travis:

Connect With which character do you identify more—Eckels or Travis? Why? *Students' answers should demonstrate an understanding of the characters' personalities and motives.*

Analyze How does Eckels's reaction to what he has done differ from Travis's reaction? *Possible answer: Eckels feels defensive about what happened (line 347) and tries to downplay the whole episode (lines 349–350). He says that he is "innocent" (line 353), and he tries to insist that his actions will have no negative consequences. Travis, on the other hand, is worried about the consequences (lines 340 and 348). Travis remains furious at Eckels and even suggests that he might kill him (lines 351–352).*

Evaluate Do you think that Eckels understands the seriousness of the situation? Do you think that Travis is overreacting? Explain your answers. *Students should support their opinions with solid reasons, including details from the story.*

FOR ENGLISH LEARNERS

Comprehension: Transitions Point out that each of the sentences beginning with "But" (lines 357–358) connects to the previous sentence by telling ways it is no longer true.

Language: Prefixes Point out the words *subtle* and *subliminal* in line 368, and explain that their common prefix *sub-* means "under" or "below." Discuss how these words are story clues showing that something *under* the surface is not right.

Activity Ask students how this painting highlights the conclusion of the story. *Possible answer: The painting relates directly to lines 390–397. It focuses our attention on a single beautiful butterfly, the death of which was enough to alter the future dramatically.*

About the Art In his first several years as a painter, Pennsylvania-born artist Martin Johnson Heade (1819–1904) produced rather stiff portraits. When he took an interest in landscapes and still lifes, however, his style matured. On trips to South America, Heade focused on small paintings of the flowers he saw there as well as the animals that could be found in their company. Heade's interest in intimate views of nature and his love for the rainforest setting are both evident in *Blue Morpho Butterfly*.

Blue Morpho Butterfly (1864–1865), Martin Johnson Heade. Oil on canvas, 12¼″ × 10″. © Manoogian Collection.

Beyond this room, beyond this wall, beyond this man who was not quite the same man seated at this desk that was not quite the same desk . . . lay an entire world of streets and people. What sort of world it was now, there was no telling. He could feel them moving there, beyond the walls, almost, like so many chess pieces blown in a dry wind. . . .

But the immediate thing was the sign painted on the office wall, the same
380 sign he had read earlier today on first entering.

Somehow, the sign had changed:

TYME SEFARI INC.

SEFARIS TU ANY YEER EN THE PAST.

YU NAIM THE ANIMALL.

WEE TAEKYUTHAIR.

YU SHOOT ITT.

Eckels felt himself fall into a chair. He fumbled crazily at the thick slime on his boots. He held up a clod of dirt, trembling, "No, it *can't* be. Not a *little* thing like that. No!"

390 Embedded in the mud, glistening green and gold and black, was a butterfly, very beautiful and very dead.

"Not a little thing like *that!* Not a butterfly!" cried Eckels. **K**

It fell to the floor, an exquisite thing, a small thing that could upset balances and knock down a line of small dominoes and then big dominoes and then gigantic dominoes, all down the years across Time. Eckels's mind whirled. It *couldn't* change things. Killing one butterfly couldn't be *that* important! Could it?

His face was cold. His mouth trembled, asking: "Who—who won the presidential election yesterday?"

400 The man behind the desk laughed. "You joking? You know very well. Deutscher, of course! Who else? Not that fool weakling Keith. We got an iron man now, a man with guts!" The official stopped. "What's wrong?"

Eckels moaned. He dropped to his knees. He scrabbled at the golden butterfly with shaking fingers. "Can't we," he pleaded to the world, to himself, to the officials, to the Machine, "can't we take it *back;* can't we *make* it alive again? Can't we start over? Can't we—"

He did not move. Eyes shut, he waited, shivering. He heard Travis breathe loud in the room; he heard Travis shift his rifle, click the safety catch, and raise the weapon.

410 There was a sound of thunder. ✎

K **MAKE INFERENCES**
What important discovery does Eckels make? Why do you think it horrifies him so?

⑤ Targeted Passage

K **MAKE INFERENCES**

Possible answer: Eckels discovers that he unknowingly stepped on and killed a butterfly. His actions in the past apparently set in motion a chain of events that may have significantly changed the future.

If students need help . . . Ask these questions to help students speculate about the possible **consequences** of killing a butterfly:

- If one butterfly is killed, what happens to that butterfly's future families?

- If the butterfly's future families are eliminated, what might be the effect on the animals that would have eaten them? on the flowers they might have pollinated?

- What effects might these changes have on humans and civilization?

SELECTION WRAP-UP

REFLECT Have students think about the various changes Eckels finds upon his return to the present. Are these changes major or minor? subtle or obvious? positive or negative? Ask students how they would characterize the consequences of Eckels's actions overall.

⭐ **CRITIQUE** Have students evaluate the ending of the story and explain why they think it is or is not effective. Ask students to suggest other ways in which Bradbury might have ended the story.

READING FLUENCY

Distribute the copy masters and have students work in pairs or groups to practice fluency.

R RESOURCE MANAGER—Copy Masters
Reading Fluency p. 37

DIFFERENTIATED INSTRUCTION

FOR LESS-PROFICIENT READERS

⑤ Targeted Passage [Lines 379–410]

This passage concludes the story with the consequences of Eckels's action: Deutscher becomes president and Travis shoots Eckels.

- How did the ad on page 34 change? Why is the change significant?

- How did Eckels change the past and the future by stepping off the Path?

- What finally happens to Eckels? Why?

FOR ADVANCED LEARNERS/PRE-AP

Synthesize Tell students to reread lines 400–402 and then go back to read lines 38–44. Have them explain the change in social temperament that results from Eckels's careless actions.

Practice and Apply

After Reading

For additional support of post-reading questions, use these copy masters:

 RESOURCE MANAGER—Copy Masters

Reading Check p. 34 (to check understanding of the selection)

Foreshadowing p. 27 (for practice of literary analysis standards focus)

Question Support p. 35 (After Reading questions adapted for English learners and less-proficient readers)

For additional questions, see page 21.

To challenge students further, see
ⓘ Bob Marzano's Power Thinking Activities at **ClassZone.com**

ANSWERS

Comprehension

1. *He steps off the Path and kills a butterfly.*

2. *He thinks that there is a different "feel" to this world. The language on the company's sign has changed, and Deutscher, not Keith, has won the presidential election.*

3. *Travis shooting Eckels.*

Literary Analysis

Possible answers:

4. *Its practices are corrupt; it bribes government officials in order to operate.*

5. *He blames Eckels for altering the future.*

6. ■ **STANDARDS FOCUS** *Analyze Sequence* *Before the safari, Eckels had a chance to back out (lines 50–55). During the safari, Eckels could have returned quietly to the Time Machine, as Travis ordered him to do (lines 231–232). Also, Travis could have had someone escort Eckels back to the ship to avoid any problems.*

7. ● **STANDARDS FOCUS** *Foreshadowing* *Foreshadowing: "We're lucky. If Deutscher had gotten in, we'd have the worst kind of dictatorship" (lines 38–39). Outcome: Deutscher wins.*

   Foreshadowing: "A little error here would multiply in sixty million years, all out of proportion" (lines 134–135). Outcome: Killing a butterfly changes the future.

   Foreshadowing: "I'm warning you, Eckels, I might kill you yet" (line 351). Outcome: Travis shoots Eckels.

Comprehension

1. **Recall** What does Eckels do in the past that has far-reaching **consequences?**

2. **Summarize** When Eckels returns from the world of dinosaurs, what is different about the present?

3. **Clarify** What is the "sound of thunder" at the end of the story?

Literary Analysis

4. **Make Inferences** How would you characterize the business practices of Time Safari, Inc.?

5. **Draw Conclusions** Why does Travis kill Eckels? Explain your answer.

6. **Understand Sequence** Look again at the chart you filled out as you read. Determine two points in the story where a character could have taken an action that might have prevented changing the future.

7. **Interpret Foreshadowing** Note three or four examples of foreshadowing in the story and the outcome of each example. Make a chart like the one below to record your results. An example has been filled in for you.

Foreshadowing	Outcome
"If you disobey instructions . . ."	Eckels steps off the Path.

8. **Analyze Theme** What theme, or message, is Bradbury conveying through this story? Cite evidence to support your answer.

9. **Evaluate Author** "A Sound of Thunder" is a work of science fiction, yet there are realistic aspects to the story. In your opinion, has Bradbury created a believable story? Cite specific examples to support your opinion.

Literary Criticism

10. **Critical Interpretations** In a review of *Dinosaur Tales*, a collection of Bradbury stories that contains "A Sound of Thunder," the critic Andrew Andrews remarked that Bradbury "gets to you—in simple ways he shows you how to marvel over these awesome, startling creatures." Reread Bradbury's description of *Tyrannosaurus rex*. What words and phrases convey its terrifying force?

---

8. *Every action has consequences, and people need to take responsibility for their actions. Both the company's actions and Eckels's actions have disastrous consequences. Neither Travis nor Eckels gave sufficient consideration to what could happen.*

9. *Believable: Such "scientific" details as the construction of the antigravity Path and the careful marking of specific dinosaurs with red paint add to the believability. **Not believable:** The paradoxes of time travel (for example, lines 162–172) make the basic premise less believable. Also, the idea that nothing was disturbed on previous safaris is hard to believe.*

Literary Criticism

Possible answer:

10. *"Each lower leg was a piston . . . thick ropes of muscle. . . . steel mesh. . . . teeth like daggers. . . . pelvic bones crushing aside trees" (lines 209–218).*

Vocabulary in Context

VOCABULARY PRACTICE

Answer the questions to show your understanding of the vocabulary words.

1. Which is more **expendable** in a jungle, a book or bug repellent?
2. Which is probably **stagnating**, a weed-filled pond or a flowing stream?
3. If I **correlate** information, do I throw it out or see how it fits together?
4. Would a **malfunctioning** phone never ring or have two choices of ring?
5. If a change happens **infinitesimally**, is it easy or difficult to detect?
6. What makes a person's body more **resilient**, exercising or reading?
7. Which might **annihilate** a bird species, a severe virus or a tasty plant?
8. Is a **subliminal** response an unconscious memory or a prepared speech?
9. Would ocean waves or broken glass be more likely to **undulate?**
10. Which is a **paradox,** a rose's blooming in snow or a tree's budding in spring?

WORD LIST

annihilate
correlate
expendable
infinitesimally
malfunctioning
paradox
resilient
stagnating
subliminal
undulate

VOCABULARY IN WRITING

Use at least three vocabulary words in a short paragraph that describes Eckels's thoughts when he steps off the path. You might start like this.

> **EXAMPLE SENTENCE**
>
> *Eckels was sure that the huge dinosaur would **annihilate** him.*

VOCABULARY STRATEGY: THE LATIN WORD ROOT *mal*

The vocabulary word *malfunctioning* contains the Latin root *mal*, meaning "bad" or "wrongly." When *mal* is used as a prefix with English base words, as in *malfunction* and *maltreat*, you can easily figure out meanings. To understand other words containing *mal*, you may need to use context clues as well as your knowledge of the root.

PRACTICE Use the meaning of the root, along with context clues, to figure out the meanings of the underlined words.

1. In his speech, the candidate <u>maligned</u> his opponents.
2. She was grateful that the tumor on her spine was not <u>malignant</u>.
3. Anyone who complains as much as he must be a <u>malcontent</u>.
4. Lincoln wanted to begin his second term as president "with <u>malice</u> toward none, with charity for all."
5. We now know that <u>malaria</u> is spread by mosquitoes, not through the air.

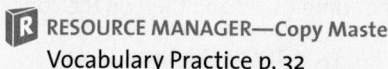

VOCABULARY PRACTICE
For more practice, go to the **Vocabulary Center** at **ClassZone.com**.

A SOUND OF THUNDER **49**

DIFFERENTIATED INSTRUCTION

FOR ENGLISH LEARNERS

Vocabulary: Cognates Point out that the Spanish cognate *función* is similar to the English word *function* in the vocabulary word *malfunctioning*. Encourage students who speak Latin-based languages to search for and explain five words in the story similar to those in their language. Have the students compare the similarities in their languages.

FOR ADVANCED LEARNERS/PRE–AP

Vocabulary in Writing Have students use at least three vocabulary words in a paragraph written in the first person from the point of view of one of the characters.

ANSWERS

Vocabulary in Context

VOCABULARY PRACTICE

1. *a book*
2. *a weed-filled pond*
3. *see how it fits together*
4. *never ring*
5. *difficult to detect*
6. *exercising*
7. *a severe virus*
8. *an unconscious memory*
9. *ocean waves*
10. *a rose's blooming in snow*

R RESOURCE MANAGER—Copy Master
Vocabulary Practice p. 32

VOCABULARY IN WRITING

Tell students to put themselves in Eckels's place and to consider both their senses and their emotions. For example, what do they see, hear, and smell when they step off the Path? What are their thoughts and feelings?

VOCABULARY STRATEGY: THE LATIN WORD ROOT *mal* (also an EL language objective)

- For each item, help students use their knowledge of the root and context clues to determine word meaning.
- Point out that in item 3, *mal* is used as a prefix, just as it is in *malfunction* and *maltreat*. Students will more easily be able to figure out the meaning of the word.

Possible answers:

1. *said bad things about; a candidate might say bad things about an opponent.*
2. *harmful; a person would be grateful that a tumor was not harmful.*
3. *an unhappy person; someone who complains a lot is not happy.*
4. *ill will; the opposite of charity is ill will.*
5. *a disease; some diseases are spread through the air and others through insect bites.*

R RESOURCE MANAGER—Copy Master
Vocabulary Strategy p. 33

i Vocabulary Center at ClassZone.com
Additional Vocabulary Activities

Reading-Writing Connection

WRITING PROMPTS

- For Prompt A, encourage students to reread lines 400–402 to get a feel for the attitude of the man behind the desk. Point out that the other two hunters are also present, though Bradbury has not developed them.

- For Prompt B, have students use the Two-Column Chart to list pros and cons of time travel, based on details from the selection. As students write, have them focus first on the pros of time travel and then on the cons.

BEST PRACTICES TOOLKIT—Transparency
Two-Column Chart p. A25

For an extended writing activity, see
i Carol Booth Olson's Reading-Writing Lesson Plans at **ClassZone.com**

REVISION: GRAMMAR AND STYLE

- After students examine the student model, list common contractions on the board.

- Write this dialogue on the board. Have students suggest revisions to make the dialogue sound more natural.

"I ~~cannot~~ can't believe ~~that~~ you did that," cried the man behind the desk. "~~I think that you have~~ You've lost your mind!"

"~~Do not~~ Don't tell anyone what happened," Travis said.

"~~There is no possible way~~ It's impossible to keep something like this quiet. ~~You have~~ You've crossed a line here, Travis."

RESOURCE MANAGER—Copy Master
Use Realistic Dialogue p. 36

Assess and Reteach

Assess

R RESOURCE MANAGER—Copy Masters
Selection Test A pp. 39–40
Selection Test B/C pp. 41–42

Test Generator CD

Reteach

S STANDARDS LESSON FILE
Literature Lesson 8: Foreshadowing and Flashback
Reading Lesson 6: Recognize Sequence and Chronological Order
Vocabulary Lessons 7–8: Latin Roots

Reading-Writing Connection

Broaden your understanding of "A Sound of Thunder" by responding to these prompts. Then use **Revision: Grammar and Style** to improve your writing.

WRITING PROMPTS	SELF-CHECK
A. Short Response: Write Dialogue What might the characters say to one another after the shooting of Eckels? Using Bradbury's style of dialogue as a model, write **one-half page** of dialogue to show how the characters react to the main incident in the story and its **consequences**.	*A successful dialogue will . . .* • use informal, conversational language • show an understanding of how the characters are likely to respond
B. Extended Response: Write Across Texts What are the advantages and risks of time travel? Use "A Sound of Thunder" and "From Here to There: The Physics of Time Travel" on the next page to write a **three-to-five-paragraph response**.	*A strong analysis will . . .* • state the pros and cons of time travel • provide examples from the story and the article

REVISION: GRAMMAR AND STYLE

USE REALISTIC DIALOGUE Review the **Grammar and Style** note on page 40. Bradbury successfully crafts his dialogue by using the following techniques:

1. **Sentence fragments** Although seldom used in formal writing, sentence fragments are common in everyday conversation.

2. **Contractions** Using contractions, like *I've, we'll, hasn't,* and *don't,* makes dialogue sound less formal and more natural. Here is an example from the story:

   "A Tyrannosaurus rex. The Tyrant Lizard, the most incredible monster in history. Sign this release. Anything happens to you, we're not responsible. Those dinosaurs are hungry."

   Eckels flushed angrily. "Trying to scare me!" (lines 46–49)

Notice how the revisions in red make this dialogue sound realistic. Revise your response to Prompt A by using similar techniques.

> **STUDENT MODEL**
>
> "Why did you do that? Have you lost your mind?" Lesperance cried.
>
> "He was a simpering idiot. He ruined it for all of us. The world is better off without him," Travis shot back.

WRITING TOOLS
For prewriting, revision, and editing tools, visit the **Writing Center** at ClassZone.com.

DIFFERENTIATED INSTRUCTION

FOR LESS-PROFICIENT WRITERS

For Prompt A:

- List the characters that might speak.

- Help students write one sentence in which Travis explains why he shot Eckels.

- Help students write one sentence that would require Travis to make that statement and one sentence that someone would say in response to that statement.

- Suggest that students organize their dialogue in this way:

Beginning: Everyone expresses shock and demands an explanation.

Middle: Travis defends his action.

Close: The others decide what they will do.

For Prompt B:

- Limit the length of the assignment to no more than two paragraphs.

- Help students generate two pros and two cons before continuing on their own.

- Have students work in small groups to brainstorm a list of pro and cons.

MAGAZINE ARTICLE Will it ever be possible to vacation in the past? And if so, would the fate of a prehistoric butterfly really determine the course of a civilization? Questions like this have been the subject of debate among physicists.

From Here to There:
The Physics of TIME TRAVEL
Brad Stone

TIME TRAVEL—it's the dream of every science-fiction hack who's ever picked up a pen, and the fantasy of many of the rest of us, too. How wonderful to go back and right the wrongs of the past! But time travel could also let you go back and cause an accident that kills your great-great-grandfather, negating your own existence and provoking a potentially universe-ending paradox. At least that's what armchair temporal theorists worry about. But not Paul Nahin. He's a professor of electrical engineering at the University of New Hampshire and the author of *Time Machines: Time Travel in Physics, Metaphysics, and Science Fiction.* And he's able to translate into plain English an ongoing, esoteric debate between some of the smartest minds in physics over whether time travel is actually possible. "The laws of physics as we know them now don't disallow time travel," explains the 57-year-old Nahin. "Anything that physics doesn't forbid must be considered."

Scientific consideration of time travel has its roots, with much of modern physics, in the genius of Albert Einstein, who married space and time in his theory of relativity. Doing further work on relativity in 1948, mathematician Kurt Gödel declared that it would actually be possible to travel through time under the right conditions. Serious scientists didn't give the matter much thought until the mid-'80s, when Carl Sagan's novel *Contact* sent its heroine on a journey through space-time via a wormhole (a theoretical hyperspace tunnel connecting two points of the universe). That intrigued researchers at Caltech, who three years later released a groundbreaking report on the plausibility of traveling through wormholes.

British physicist Stephen Hawking has been the most prominent skeptic, hypothesizing that any attempt at time travel would lead to a "back reaction," a massive buildup of energy that would rip space apart. His theory is called the Chronology Protection Conjecture, since it would make history safe from explorers who might meddle in important historical events. The best evidence against time travel, according to Hawking's writings, is that "we have not been invaded by hordes of tourists from the future."

Other physicists, hoping to prove that time travel is theoretically possible, have devised on paper four different ways to do it. But all require unrealistic quantities of energy under hugely improbable conditions.

Each proposal has supporters and detractors. But the one thing that physicists don't waste much time on is the paradoxes—like altering the present by killing someone in the past. Nahin says time-travel paradoxes are "manifestations of imperfect understanding." So whatever the resolution of the time-travel debate, rest assured that your great-great-grandpa is safe.

CONNECT
Use this selection either as support for Writing Prompt B on page 50 or as a mini-lesson on reading for information.

READING FOR INFORMATION
Point out that "From Here to There: The Physics of Time Travel" is a magazine article.

- Ask students how magazine and newspaper articles are alike and how they differ. *Possible answer: Both kinds of articles provide facts, but magazine articles are written to entertain as well as to inform. In addition, most newspaper articles are meant to provide the key facts about immediate events, whereas many magazine articles go into greater depth or have a slower pace.*

- After students have read the article, discuss how they can tell that it is more of a "popular science" article than a "hard science" article. *Possible answer: It is not overly technical; it explains the topic so that a wide range of readers can understand it.*

DISCUSSION PROMPTS
Use these prompts to help students consider the feasibility of time travel:

Connect How did reading this article affect your appreciation of "A Sound of Thunder"? *Accept all reasonable answers.*

Analyze According to this article, what has been the ultimate contribution (so far) to the idea that time travel is possible? Explain. *Possible answer: So far, the greatest contribution has been the theory of wormholes; if the theory about them is correct, wormholes could provide "tunnels" through which people could travel through time.*

Synthesize Suppose that Professor Nahin proved to be correct and that time travel posed no danger of altering events. To what extent would a company such as Time Safari, Inc., benefit from safe time travel? *Possible answer: Time travel probably would become wildly popular, and such a company would be much in demand. However, competing companies also would spring up as time travel became big business.*

Focus and Motivate

OBJECTIVES

Literary Analysis
- explore the key idea of **survival**
- analyze conflict and its complications
- read a short story

Reading
- visualize setting, characters, and events

Vocabulary
- build vocabulary for reading and writing
- understand and use denotative and connotative meanings of words *(also an EL language objective)*

Grammar and Writing
- use prepositional phrases to add descriptive details
- use writing to analyze literature

SUMMARY

In this harrowing tale, hunter Sanger Rainsford becomes stranded on a remote island where he seeks help at the château of General Zaroff. Zaroff, also a hunter, seems cultured at first but then forces Rainsford to become his quarry in a hunt to the death. Zaroff seems destined to win, but Rainsford outwits Zaroff and kills him.

What does it take to be a SURVIVOR?

Introduce the question and discuss the words *survivor* and *survival*. To lead into the **KEY IDEA,** ask whether mental or physical strength contributes more to **survival.** Why? After students complete the **DISCUSS** activity, have them compare their lists and rankings.

Selection Resources

The Most Dangerous Game
Short Story by Richard Connell

What does it take to be a SURVIVOR?

KEY IDEA In a test of **survival,** what traits enable a person to succeed? That's the question posed in "The Most Dangerous Game," an adventure story that has thrilled readers since it was first published.

DISCUSS Brainstorm in a group to identify a situation that could be a test of survival. This could be as dramatic as a raging flood or as personal as losing a parent. Discuss the qualities and abilities that a person would need to meet the test, and provide reasons for each choice. Then list all the traits you generated and rank the top four, placing them in a diagram like the one shown.

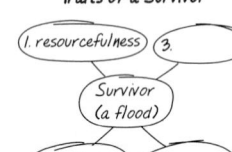

Traits of a Survivor
- 1. resourcefulness
- 2. intelligence
- 3.
- 4.
- Survivor (a flood)

LITERARY ANALYSIS: CONFLICT

In the **rising action** of a story, a writer generally introduces one or more **conflicts** that the main character faces. As the rising action unfolds, complications arise that intensify the conflicts and add to the reader's sense of suspense. In "The Most Dangerous Game," Richard Connell expertly builds suspense as the main character encounters one conflict after another. As you read, identify the conflicts and note any complications that arise.

READING STRATEGY: VISUALIZE

Good readers constantly **visualize,** or use details to form a mental picture of the settings, characters, and events of a story. In this story, Connell includes details that help create an image of a dangerous island where strange things happen. As you read, practice the strategy of visualizing. Allow it to help you gain insight into the setting, characters, and events that surround this adventure. Use a chart like the one shown to record story details that form mental images for you.

Details from Story	What I Visualize
Dank tropical night ... thick warm blackness	The dark, heavy air is almost like a blanket.

Review: **Predict**

▲ VOCABULARY IN CONTEXT

Use the context to help you figure out the meaning of each boldfaced word below.

1. real and **tangible**
2. the hunter's **quarry**
3. put at ease by his **disarming** smile
4. a charming, **cultivated** woman
5. a cruise ship offering every **amenity**
6. **condone** rather than condemn
7. a **droll,** self-mocking grin
8. felt no **scruples** about breaking traffic laws
9. asked **solicitously** about my health
10. recommended but not **imperative**
11. **zealous** support of the mayor's program
12. an **uncanny** coincidence

Author On|ine

Richard Connell
1893–1949

A Writing Life
Even as a young boy, Richard Connell loved to write. When he was only 10 years old, he covered baseball games for his father's daily newspaper in Poughkeepsie, New York. By 16, Connell was city editor for the same newspaper. After graduating from Harvard and serving in World War I, Connell wrote more than 300 short stories, as well as novels and screenplays. Many of his short stories became successful films. Connell's success enabled him to travel the world and then settle comfortably in Beverly Hills, California, on the opposite side of the country from his previous hometown of Poughkeepsie.

One-Story Legacy Although Connell became a prosperous writer during his lifetime, only one of his stories—"The Most Dangerous Game"—is widely read today. It won the O. Henry Memorial Prize in 1924. Because of its action-packed and suspenseful plot, it remains a popular and frequently anthologized work.

Background

Big-Game Hunting Hunting for big game, such as lions, rhinos, and leopards, was a popular sport among wealthy people in the early 20th century. These people had time and money to spend on travel and on satisfying their thirst for conquest, danger, and excitement. The two main characters in "The Most Dangerous Game" are experienced hunters in search of a greater challenge.

MORE ABOUT THE AUTHOR AND BACKGROUND
To learn more about Richard Connell and big-game hunting, visit the **Literature Center** at **ClassZone.com.**

THE MOST DANGEROUS GAME   **53**

Teach

STANDARDS FOCUS

LITERARY ANALYSIS

● CONFLICT

To support student learning, read aloud this example:

> The refugee could get on the boat, or she could return to a life of hiding at home. Some people who had taken boats before had been lost at sea.

Have students identify the **conflict** and the complication that the refugee faces. *Possible answer: Her conflict is between taking the boat or returning to hiding; the complication is that she might die if she goes to sea, but she will not have freedom if she stays.*

CHECK UNDERSTANDING Ask students to name conflicts in a story or movie.

READING STRATEGY

◼ VISUALIZE

Ask students to close their eyes and picture a dangerous tropical island. Have students sketch and describe what they imagine.

CHECK UNDERSTANDING Have students use *Background* details to **visualize** a scene with wealthy hunters in the early 20th century.

Ⓡ RESOURCE MANAGER—Copy Master
Visualize p. 55 (for student use while reading the selection)

VOCABULARY SKILL

▲ VOCABULARY IN CONTEXT

DIAGNOSE WORD KNOWLEDGE To determine preteaching needs, have all students complete Vocabulary in Context. *Possible answers:*
1. *touchable;* 2. *prey;* 3. *intended to relax or comfort;* 4. *refined;* 5. *comfort, luxury;* 6. *allow, accept;* 7. *amusing;* 8. *sense of right and wrong;* 9. *in a concerned way;* 10. *absolutely necessary;* 11. *enthusiastic;* 12. *strange, mysterious*

PRETEACH VOCABULARY Use the Vocabulary Study copy master to help students predict meanings for each boldfaced word in the copy master.

1. Read the passage aloud. Then reread the first sentence, emphasizing *disarming.*
2. Point out the phrase "that charmed everyone." Elicit possible meanings for *disarming,* such as "charming."
3. Repeat for the remaining words.

Ⓡ RESOURCE MANAGER—Copy Master
Vocabulary Study p. 57

For general guidelines on differentiating vocabulary instruction and for alternative vocabulary activities for students not needing vocabulary preteaching, see

BEST PRACTICES TOOLKIT
Scaffolding Vocabulary Instruction pp. 43–46
ⓘ Vocabulary Center at **ClassZone.com**

ANALYZE VISUALS

Possible answer: Despite the blue sky and the greenery, the island does not seem welcoming. The jagged mountains seem inhospitable to human life, the shore seems too small to permit a safe landing, and a deep shadow falls across much of the island. These details combine to create a rather forbidding mood that contrasts with the calm blue sea and the puffy white clouds.

LITERARY ANALYSIS

Ⓐ CONFLICT

Possible answer: Rainsford's unfeeling remarks about wildlife reveal his uncaring and arrogant attitude.

If students need help . . . Have two volunteers read the dialogue aloud, with expression. Then ask these questions:

- How does Rainsford refer to what Whitney has said? *Possible answer: He calls it "rot" (line 18) and says, "Bah!" (line 21).*
- What tone do you hear in Rainsford's voice? *Possible answer: arrogance*
- How sure is Rainsford about his opinions? *Possible answer: quite confident*

Extend the Discussion Do you agree with Rainsford that an animal has no feelings or understanding? Explain.

The Most Dangerous Game

Richard Connell

"Off there to the right—somewhere—is a large island," said Whitney. "It's rather a mystery—"

"What island is it?" Rainsford asked.

"The old charts call it 'Ship-Trap Island,'" Whitney replied. "A suggestive name, isn't it? Sailors have a curious dread of the place. I don't know why. Some superstition—"

"Can't see it," remarked Rainsford, trying to peer through the dank tropical night that was palpable as it pressed its thick warm blackness in upon the yacht.

"You've good eyes," said Whitney, with a laugh, "and I've seen you pick off a
10 moose moving in the brown fall bush at four hundred yards, but even you can't see four miles or so through a moonless Caribbean night."

"Nor four yards," admitted Rainsford. "Ugh! It's like moist black velvet."

"It will be light enough in Rio,"[1] promised Whitney. "We should make it in a few days. I hope the jaguar guns have come from Purdey's. We should have some good hunting up the Amazon. Great sport, hunting."

"The best sport in the world," agreed Rainsford.

"For the hunter," amended Whitney. "Not for the jaguar."

"Don't talk rot, Whitney," said Rainsford. "You're a big-game hunter, not a philosopher. Who cares how a jaguar feels?"

20 "Perhaps the jaguar does," observed Whitney.

"Bah! They've no understanding." Ⓐ

ANALYZE VISUALS
What **mood** does the photo stir in you? Decide which details work to evoke this feeling.

❶ Targeted Passage

Ⓐ CONFLICT
Reread lines 16–21. What can you conclude about Rainsford from his conflict with Whitney?

---

1. **Rio:** Rio de Janeiro (rē′ō dā zhə-nâr′ō), a city on the coast of Brazil.

DIFFERENTIATED INSTRUCTION

FOR ALL STUDENTS

Journal As they read, ask students to keep a journal noting questions, observations, and reflections about characters and situations. Ask students to refer to their notes when completing other activities that accompany the selection.

FOR LESS–PROFICIENT READERS

In combination with the *Audio Anthology CD*, use one or more Targeted Passages (pp. 54, 57, 62, 68, 71, 74) to ensure that students focus on key story events, concepts, and skills. Targeted Passages are also good for English learners.

❶ Targeted Passage [Lines 3–21]

This passage introduces several expository details relating to characters, setting,

BACKGROUND

Big-Game Hunting In the early years of the 20th century, big-game hunting was a popular sport among the upper classes. Those who could afford the expense traveled to exotic climes such as Burma (now called Myanmar), Malaysia, India, and various parts of North and South America. Notice how on page 62, an avid hunter lists a series of particularly popular "trophy" animals—the Cape buffalo, an Amazonian jaguar, an Indian crocodile, an American grizzly bear and an African rhinoceros. These animals were killed for their coats or skins, or to have their heads preserved as trophies of the hunt. All of the species mentioned on that page are now endangered, some to near extinction.

Lines 15–20
REINFORCE *KEY IDEA:* SURVIVAL

Discuss At what point does this conversation introduce the idea of **survival?** *Possible answer: When the conversation turns to jaguar hunting, the idea of survival is introduced. For the hunter, it is a great sport; for the jaguar, it is a matter of life or death.*

and atmosphere.

- Which characters are speaking?
- Where are they as they talk?
- What do sailors call the nearby island? How do they feel about it?
- What is the conflict between the two characters?

FOR ENGLISH LEARNERS

Options for Reading Have students preview the pictures and make predictions about what the story will be about. Then cover the story in sections, asking a question about a half-page or more of text and then having pairs of students scan the section for the answer.

Prereading For prereading instruction for English learners, see

 BEST PRACTICES TOOLKIT
Scaffolding Reading Instruction pp. 43–46

FOR ADVANCED LEARNERS/PRE–AP

Pre-AP Exercises in the bottom channel provide additional challenge for students. Use these suggestions for small groups or individuals.

ADDITIONAL GUIDELINES
For more help with differentiation and tips for classroom management, see

 BEST PRACTICES TOOLKIT
Differentiated Instruction pp. 31–38

B PREDICT

Possible answer: Someone or something on the island will put a visitor in a life-or-death situation.

If students need help . . . Use the Predicting chart to help students list details that create a feeling of evil, such as these:

- the sailors' "curious dread" over a superstition (lines 5)
- the comments about fear, death, and "the hunters and the huntees" (lines 22–26)
- the "Godforsaken" place (line 32)
- the "poisonous" air (line 40)

Work with students to make at least one prediction, based on these details.

Extend the Discussion How may Rainsford's skepticism make him more vulnerable to the island's "vibrations of evil" (line 50)?

 BEST PRACTICES TOOLKIT—Transparency Predicting p. A10

READING STRATEGY

C VISUALIZE

Possible answer: Rainsford's nonchalant mood is reflected in the description of him reclining in a steamer chair and puffing indolently on a pipe. Rainsford is not at all frightened by the possible threat from the nearby island. Instead, he is very relaxed—perhaps too much so for someone who prides himself on his quick hunter's reflexes.

"Even so, I rather think they understand one thing—fear. The fear of pain and the fear of death."

"Nonsense," laughed Rainsford. "This hot weather is making you soft, Whitney. Be a realist. The world is made up of two classes—the hunters and the huntees. Luckily, you and I are hunters. Do you think we've passed that island yet?"

"I can't tell in the dark. I hope so."

"Why?" asked Rainsford.

30 "The place has a reputation—a bad one."

"Cannibals?" suggested Rainsford.

"Hardly. Even cannibals wouldn't live in such a Godforsaken place. But it's gotten into sailor lore, somehow. Didn't you notice that the crew's nerves seemed a bit jumpy today?"

"They were a bit strange, now you mention it. Even Captain Nielsen—"

"Yes, even that tough-minded old Swede, who'd go up to the devil himself and ask him for a light. Those fishy blue eyes held a look I never saw there before. All I could get out of him was: 'This place has an evil name among seafaring men, sir.' Then he said to me, very gravely: 'Don't you feel

40 anything?'—as if the air about us was actually poisonous. Now, you mustn't laugh when I tell you this—I did feel something like a sudden chill. **B**

"There was no breeze. The sea was as flat as a plate-glass window. We were drawing near the island then. What I felt was a—a mental chill; a sort of sudden dread."

"Pure imagination," said Rainsford. "One superstitious sailor can taint the whole ship's company with his fear."

"Maybe. But sometimes I think sailors have an extra sense that tells them when they are in danger. Sometimes I think evil is a **tangible** thing—with wavelengths, just as sound and light have. An evil place can, so to speak,

50 broadcast vibrations of evil. Anyhow, I'm glad we're getting out of this zone. Well, I think I'll turn in now, Rainsford."

"I'm not sleepy," said Rainsford. "I'm going to smoke another pipe up on the afterdeck."

"Good night, then, Rainsford. See you at breakfast."

"Right. Good night, Whitney."

There was no sound in the night as Rainsford sat there but the muffled throb of the engine that drove the yacht swiftly through the darkness, and the swish and ripple of the wash of the propeller.

Rainsford, reclining in a steamer chair, indolently puffed on his favorite

60 brier.[2] The sensuous drowsiness of the night was on him. "It's so dark," he thought, "that I could sleep without closing my eyes; the night would be my eyelids—" **C**

---

2. **brier** (brī'ər): a tobacco pipe.

B PREDICT
Reread lines 30–41. Notice that even a hard-boiled sailor is fearful of the island. What do you predict might happen on the island?

tangible (tăn'jə-bəl) *adj.* capable of being touched or felt; having actual form and substance

C VISUALIZE
Reread lines 59–62, trying to visualize Rainsford. What does the author's description tell you about Rainsford's mood?

DIFFERENTIATED INSTRUCTION

FOR ADVANCED LEARNERS/PRE–AP

Evaluate Author's Choices At line 54, Whitney leaves the story. After students have finished reading the selection, ask them to think about the impact of his brief appearance. Then have them debate this question in small groups: Did Connell need to include Whitney in this story? In their responses, students should demonstrate an understanding of Whitney's personality and attitudes and how they influence the story's plot and ideas (particularly in regard to the nature of the island and the ethics of hunting).

An abrupt sound startled him. Off to the right he heard it, and his ears, expert in such matters, could not be mistaken. Again he heard the sound, and again. Somewhere, off in the blackness, someone had fired a gun three times.

Rainsford sprang up and moved quickly to the rail, mystified. He strained his eyes in the direction from which the reports had come, but it was like trying to see through a blanket. He leaped upon the rail and balanced himself there, to get greater elevation; his pipe, striking a rope, was knocked from his
70 mouth. He lunged for it; a short, hoarse cry came from his lips as he realized he had reached too far and had lost his balance. The cry was pinched off short as the blood-warm waters of the Caribbean Sea closed over his head.

He struggled up to the surface and tried to cry out, but the wash from the speeding yacht slapped him in the face, and the salt water in his open mouth made him gag and strangle. Desperately he struck out with strong strokes after the receding lights of the yacht, but he stopped before he had swum fifty feet. A certain cool-headedness had come to him; it was not the first time he had been in a tight place. There was a chance that his cries could be heard by someone aboard the yacht, but that chance was slender and grew more slender
80 as the yacht raced on. He wrestled himself out of his clothes and shouted with all his power. The lights of the yacht became faint and ever-vanishing fireflies; then they were blotted out entirely by the night. **D**

Rainsford remembered the shots. They had come from the right, and doggedly he swam in that direction, swimming with slow, deliberate strokes, conserving his strength. For a seemingly endless time he fought the sea. He began to count his strokes; he could do possibly a hundred more and then—

Rainsford heard a sound. It came out of the darkness, a high, screaming sound, the sound of an animal in an extremity of anguish and terror.

He did not recognize the animal that made the sound; he did not try to;
90 with fresh vitality he swam toward the sound. He heard it again; then it was cut short by another noise, crisp, staccato.

"Pistol shot," muttered Rainsford, swimming on.

Ten minutes of determined effort brought another sound to his ears—the most welcome he had ever heard—the muttering and growling of the sea breaking on a rocky shore. He was almost on the rocks before he saw them; on a night less calm he would have been shattered against them. With his remaining strength he dragged himself from the swirling waters. Jagged crags appeared to jut up into the opaqueness; he forced himself upward, hand over hand. Gasping, his hands raw, he reached a flat place at the top. Dense jungle
100 came down to the very edge of the cliffs. What perils that tangle of trees and underbrush might hold for him did not concern Rainsford just then. All he knew was that he was safe from his enemy, the sea, and that utter weariness was on him. He flung himself down at the jungle edge and tumbled headlong into the deepest sleep of his life. **E**

2 Targeted Passage

D CONFLICT
Here the author builds **suspense** by introducing a complication. What do you think will happen next?

E VISUALIZE
Reread lines 93–104. Which details in this passage help you visualize the scene?

THE MOST DANGEROUS GAME **57**

LITERARY ANALYSIS

D CONFLICT

Possible answer: Rainsford will swim to shore.

If students need help . . . After students reread lines 77–81, ask what words or phrases suggest that Rainsford is determined to survive and come out the winner in this conflict. *Possible answers: "cool-headedness," "not the first time he had been in a tight place," "all his power"*

READING STRATEGY

E VISUALIZE

Possible answer: The "rocky shore" (line 95) and "swirling waters" (line 97) create an overall visual impression of the scene. The "opaqueness" (line 98) conveys the darkness of the night, while the "jagged crags" (line 97), "dense jungle" (line 99), and "tangle of trees and underbrush" (lines 100–101) present a clear picture of the dangerous terrain.

If students need help . . . Ask them what they knew about the setting before they read these lines. *Possible answer: It is night, on the sea, near an island.* Then, focusing on each line, have pairs of students describe what they see as if they were Rainsford.

Extend the Discussion How do the details help you realize that even though Rainsford has escaped the sea, he is far from safe?

FOR LESS-PROFICIENT READERS

2 Targeted Passage [Lines 63–85]

This passage presents a pivotal event: an accident that throws the self-assured Rainsford into danger and begins the rising action.

- What sound does Rainsford hear? What might this suggest about the island?

- How does Rainsford fall overboard?

- How does Rainsford react to his situation? What does this tell you about him?

THE MOST DANGEROUS GAME **57**

F PREDICT

Possible answer: The men will be as forbidding as the island and as "snarled" and "ragged" as its jungle; in short, they will be evil.

If students need help . . . Have them work in pairs to isolate story details from lines 108–110 (in particular, the pistol shots and the characteristics of the land along the shore). Have students consider what they know about story grammar (plot) and their own knowledge to make predictions. Discuss the predictions as a class.

Lines 111–128
REINFORCE *KEY IDEA:* SURVIVAL

Discuss In these lines, how does Rainsford demonstrate that he has **survival** skills?
Possible answer: He finds evidence, examines it, makes hypotheses, and successfully finds and follows a trail.

G VISUALIZE

Possible answer: The château is not welcoming. It seems like a set in a horror movie—positioned high on steep cliffs with pointed towers and a "spiked iron gate." It is imposing and frightening.

If students need help . . .

- Work with them to list specific details from these lines, such as "lofty structure . . . pointed towers . . . gloom. . . . palatial château. . . . spiked iron gate. . . . stone steps . . . massive door . . . leering gargoyle for a door-knocker."

- Ask them to categorize each detail as warm and inviting, neutral, or cold and off-putting.

Extend the Discussion If you were in Rainsford's position, would you knock on this door? Consider your options.

When he opened his eyes, he knew from the position of the sun that it was late in the afternoon. Sleep had given him new vigor; a sharp hunger was picking at him. He looked about him, almost cheerfully.

"Where there are pistol shots, there are men. Where there are men, there is food," he thought. But what kind of men, he wondered, in so forbidding a
110 place? An unbroken front of snarled and ragged jungle fringed the shore. **F**

He saw no sign of a trail through the closely knit web of weeds and trees; it was easier to go along the shore, and Rainsford floundered along by the water. Not far from where he had landed, he stopped.

Some wounded thing, by the evidence a large animal, had thrashed about in the underbrush; the jungle weeds were crushed down, and the moss was lacerated; one patch of weeds was stained crimson. A small, glittering object not far away caught Rainsford's eye, and he picked it up. It was an empty cartridge.

"A twenty-two," he remarked. "That's odd. It must have been a fairly large
120 animal, too. The hunter had his nerve with him to tackle it with a light gun. It's clear that the brute put up a fight. I suppose the first three shots I heard was when the hunter flushed his **quarry** and wounded it. The last shot was when he trailed it here and finished it."

He examined the ground closely and found what he had hoped to find—the print of hunting boots. They pointed along the cliff in the direction he had been going. Eagerly he hurried along, now slipping on a rotten log or a loose stone, but making headway; night was beginning to settle down on the island.

Bleak darkness was blacking out the sea and jungle when Rainsford sighted
130 the lights. He came upon them as he turned a crook in the coastline, and his first thought was that he had come upon a village, for there were many lights. But as he forged along, he saw to his great astonishment that all the lights were in one enormous building—a lofty structure with pointed towers plunging upward into the gloom. His eyes made out the shadowy outlines of a palatial château; it was set on a high bluff, and on three sides of it cliffs dived down to where the sea licked greedy lips in the shadows.

"Mirage," thought Rainsford. But it was no mirage, he found, when he opened the tall spiked iron gate. The stone steps were real enough; the massive door with a leering gargoyle for a knocker was real enough; yet about it all
140 hung an air of unreality. **G**

He lifted the knocker, and it creaked up stiffly as if it had never before been used. He let it fall, and it startled him with its booming loudness. He thought he heard steps within; the door remained closed. Again Rainsford lifted the heavy knocker and let it fall. The door opened then, opened as suddenly as if it were on a spring, and Rainsford stood blinking in the river of glaring gold light that poured out. The first thing Rainsford's eyes discerned was the largest man

F PREDICT
Answer Rainsford's question. What kind of men do you think Rainsford will encounter on the island?

quarry (kwôr′ē) *n.* the object of a hunt; prey

G VISUALIZE
Reread lines 129–140. Describe your mental image of the chateau. Does it seem like a warm and welcoming place? Explain.

DIFFERENTIATED INSTRUCTION

FOR ENGLISH LEARNERS
Vocabulary: Phrasal Verbs Use Definition Mapping to teach the meanings of these phrasal verbs from the story:

- *pick off* (line 9), "shoot and kill"
- *pinched off* (line 71), "stopped"
- *picking at* (line 107), "bothering"
- *put up* (line 121), "engaged in [an activity]"
- *get about* (lines 463–464), "move"
- *pressed on* (line 615), "continued"

🧰 BEST PRACTICES TOOLKIT—Transparency
Definition Mapping p. E6

Castle at Noon, William Low. © William Low.

Rainsford had ever seen—a gigantic creature, solidly made and black-bearded to the waist. In his hand the man held a long-barreled revolver, and he was pointing it straight at Rainsford's heart.

150   Out of the snarl of beard two small eyes regarded Rainsford.

"Don't be alarmed," said Rainsford, with a smile which he hoped was **disarming.** "I'm no robber. I fell off a yacht. My name is Sanger Rainsford of New York City."

The menacing look in the eyes did not change. The revolver pointed as rigidly as if the giant were a statue. He gave no sign that he understood Rainsford's words, or that he had even heard them. He was dressed in uniform, a black uniform trimmed with gray astrakhan.[3]

"I'm Sanger Rainsford of New York," Rainsford began again. "I fell off a yacht. I am hungry."

160   The man's only answer was to raise with his thumb the hammer of his revolver. Then Rainsford saw the man's free hand go to his forehead in a military salute, and he saw him click his heels together and stand at attention. Another man was coming down the broad marble steps, an erect, slender man in evening clothes. He advanced to Rainsford and held out his hand.

In a **cultivated** voice marked by a slight accent that gave it added precision and deliberateness, he said: "It is a very great pleasure and honor to welcome Mr. Sanger Rainsford, the celebrated hunter, to my home."

disarming (dĭs-är′mĭng) *adj.* removing or overcoming suspicion; inspiring confidence

cultivated (kŭl′tə-vā′tĭd) *adj.* refined or cultured in manner

---

3. **astrakhan** (ăs′trə-kăn′): a fur made from the curly, wavy wool of young lambs from Astrakhan (a city of southwest Russia).

THE MOST DANGEROUS GAME   **59**

FOR LESS-PROFICIENT READERS
Practice Visualizing Have students sketch Ivan and make inferences based on the details. Suggest that students complete a Making Inferences chart.

 BEST PRACTICES TOOLKIT—Transparency
Making Inferences p. A13

FOR ENGLISH LEARNERS
Key Academic Vocabulary Use Definition Mapping to teach these words: *uniform* (line 156), *military* (line 162), *ceased* (line 253), *trace* (line 378), *invariably* (line 400), *inevitable* (line 652).

 BEST PRACTICES TOOLKIT—Transparency
Definition Mapping p. E6

ANALYZE VISUALS

Activity Ask students to compare and contrast the castle in this painting with the "palatial château" that Rainsford first spies in lines 129–140. *Possible answer: Both the château in the story and the castle in the painting are lofty and immense, with pointed towers (line 133). However, the château is depicted at night, with "many lights" (line 131) illuminating it in the darkness, while the castle is dark inside and illuminated by sunlight. Another contrast is that the château is depicted as threatening, with a "spiked iron gate" and a "leering gargoyle" as a door knocker (lines 138–139), while the castle seems mysterious but not ominous.*

About the Art In *Castle at Noon*, contemporary painter William Low (b. 1959) shows the eerily amputated midsection of the building. The odd presentation suggests that the viewer does not know the castle's entire story, just as Rainsford does not yet know the entire story of the château where he seeks refuge.

Lines 150–167
DISCUSSION PROMPTS

Use these prompts to help students understand how Connell uses the initial events to develop character and build toward the story's central conflict:

Connect Have you or someone you know ever had to "think on your feet" under adverse circumstances? How does that experience help you to understand Rainsford's predicament in this scene? *Possible answer: It can be very difficult to stay cool and calm. Rainsford must have nerves of steel, confidence, and great self-control.*

Analyze What initial impression does the "slender man in evening clothes" present? *Possible answer: He presents the impression of being in control, polished, and commanding.*

Synthesize What is the purpose of this scene? *Possible answer: It creates suspense (lines 160–161), reminds readers that Rainsford is cool and collected under stress (lines 151–153 and 158–159), and shows similarities between Rainsford and the man in evening clothes (lines 165–167).*

THE MOST DANGEROUS GAME   **59**

ANALYZE VISUALS

Activity This photograph, called *Mounted Animals in a Taxidermy Show Room*, presents a variety of hunting prizes that have been preserved for display. Ask students what they think of such a display; for example, does it reflect pride, accomplishment, wealth, cruelty, love of sport, decorating sense, or other values? *Answers will vary, but students should be able to present a reasonable defense of their view.* What does General Zaroff's similar display tell the reader about him? *Possible answers: He enjoys hunting; he is proud of his skill as a hunter; he is obsessed with killing.*

Lines 193–201
REINFORCE *KEY IDEA*: SURVIVAL

Discuss Zaroff calls Ivan "a bit of a savage" (lines 197–198) and a "Cossack" (line 200). But then Zaroff refers to himself as a Cossack. How does this new information about Ivan and Zaroff raise the question of Rainsford's **survival** and build suspense? *Possible answer: It suggests that, despite his refined manners, Zaroff, too, may be "a bit of a savage." Rainsford's survival may require confronting people with savage tendencies, adopting savage tendencies, or both. The fact that Zaroff may not be as civilized as he first appeared increases suspense as to what might happen.*

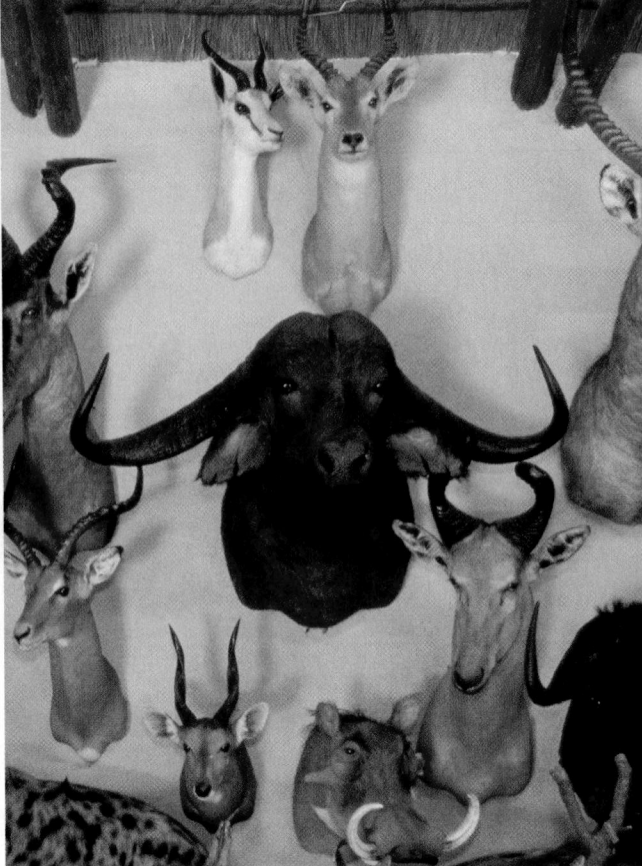

Automatically Rainsford shook the man's hand.

170 "I've read your book about hunting snow leopards in Tibet,[4] you see," explained the man. "I am General Zaroff."

Rainsford's first impression was that the man was singularly handsome; his second was that there was an original, almost bizarre quality about the general's face. He was a tall man past middle age, 180 for his hair was a vivid white; but his thick eyebrows and pointed military moustache were as black as the night from which Rainsford had come. His eyes, too, were black and very bright. He had high cheekbones, a sharp-cut nose, a spare, dark face, the face of a man used to giving orders, the face of an aristocrat. Turning to the giant 190 in uniform, the general made a sign. The giant put away his pistol, saluted, withdrew.

"Ivan is an incredibly strong fellow," remarked the general, "but he has the misfortune to be deaf and dumb. A simple fellow, but, I'm afraid, like all his race, a bit of a savage."

"Is he Russian?"

200 "He is a Cossack,"[5] said the general, and his smile showed red lips and pointed teeth. "So am I.

"Come," he said, "we shouldn't be chatting here. We can talk later. Now you want clothes, food, rest. You shall have them. This is a most restful spot."

Ivan had reappeared, and the general spoke to him with lips that moved but gave forth no sound.

"Follow Ivan, if you please, Mr. Rainsford," said the general. "I was about to have my dinner when you came. I'll wait for you. You'll find that my clothes will fit you, I think."

4. **Tibet** (tə-bĕt′): a region in central Asia.

5. **Cossack** (kŏs′ăk): a member of a southern Russian people, many of whom served as fierce cavalrymen under the Russian tsars.

DIFFERENTIATED INSTRUCTION

FOR ENGLISH LEARNERS

Vocabulary: Cognates Point out that the Spanish word *original* is spelled exactly like the English word *original* (line 177) but that it has a slightly different pronunciation. (Call on Spanish-speaking students to help you demonstrate the difference.) Ask pairs of students who speak the same home language to look for five other English words in the story that are similar to words in their home language. Have students share their findings.

It was to a huge, beam-ceilinged bedroom with a canopied bed big enough
210 for six men that Rainsford followed the silent giant. Ivan laid out an evening
suit, and Rainsford, as he put it on, noticed that it came from a London tailor
who ordinarily cut and sewed for none below the rank of duke.

The dining room to which Ivan conducted him was in many ways
remarkable. There was a medieval magnificence about it; it suggested a
baronial hall of feudal times with its oaken panels, its high ceiling, its vast
refectory table where two score men could sit down to eat. About the hall were
the mounted heads of many animals—lions, tigers, elephants, moose, bears;
larger or more perfect specimens Rainsford had never seen. At the great table
the general was sitting, alone.
220 "You'll have a cocktail, Mr. Rainsford," he suggested. The cocktail was
surpassingly good; and, Rainsford noted, the table appointments were of the
finest—the linen, the crystal, the silver, the china.

They were eating *borsch*, the rich red soup with whipped cream so dear to
Russian palates. Half apologetically General Zaroff said: "We do our best to
preserve the **amenities** of civilization here. Please forgive any lapses. We are
well off the beaten track, you know. Do you think the champagne has suffered
from its long ocean trip?"

"Not in the least," declared Rainsford. He was finding the general a most
thoughtful and affable host, a true cosmopolite.[6] But there was one small trait
230 of the general's that made Rainsford uncomfortable. Whenever he looked up
from his plate, he found the general studying him, appraising him narrowly.

"Perhaps," said General Zaroff, "you were surprised that I recognized your
name. You see, I read all books on hunting published in English, French, and
Russian. I have but one passion in my life, Mr. Rainsford, and it is the hunt."

"You have some wonderful heads here," said Rainsford as he ate a
particularly well cooked filet mignon. "That Cape buffalo is the largest I
ever saw."

"Oh, that fellow. Yes, he was a monster."

"Did he charge you?"
240 "Hurled me against a tree," said the general. "Fractured my skull. But I got
the brute."

"I've always thought," said Rainsford, "that the Cape buffalo is the most
dangerous of all big game."

For a moment the general did not reply; he was smiling his curious red-
lipped smile. Then he said slowly: "No. You are wrong, sir. The Cape buffalo is
not the most dangerous big game." He sipped his wine. "Here in my preserve
on this island," he said, in the same slow tone, "I hunt more dangerous game."

Rainsford expressed his surprise. "Is there big game on this island?"

The general nodded. "The biggest."
250 "Really?"

"Oh, it isn't here naturally, of course. I have to stock the island."

---

6. **cosmopolite** (kŏz-mŏp'ə-līt'): a sophisticated person who can handle any situation well.

---

amenity (ə-mĕn'ĭ-tē)
n. something that adds
to one's comfort or
convenience

Lines 209–237
DISCUSSION PROMPTS
Use these prompts to help students see that
Zaroff and Rainsford are well-matched oppo-
nents for playing the "most dangerous game":

Connect Have you or someone you know
ever dined in a highly formal setting? How
comfortable would you feel dining with
Zaroff? *Possible answer: I would feel intimidated by his sophistication and uncomfortable
with his finery.*

Analyze In what ways are Zaroff and Rainsford alike, based on details in the passage?
*Possible answer: Both men are sophisticated;
both lead privileged lives in which they are
able to assess the quality of upscale things
like silver and champagne.*

Evaluate Why does Connell make these two
characters so alike in some ways? *Possible
answers: He is matching them for the contest
or game that lies ahead; he is making a
statement about hunters or about privileged
people who can afford to play games; the
fact that they are alike makes the contest
more exciting.*

FOR ADVANCED LEARNERS/PRE-AP

Defend an Interpretation Offer this statement to students: *Zaroff and Rainsford are
essentially the same, but they wear different
cultural clothing.* Challenge students to find
evidence from the story so far that proves
or disproves this interpretation of these two
characters. Ask them to write one or two
paragraphs supporting or challenging this
interpretation. Let the two sides take turns
sharing their writing with the class.

CONFLICT

Possible answer: *The clues—especially Zaroff's comments about being bored by traditional big game—suggest that Zaroff and Rainsford will become involved in an extremely dangerous hunt for a bizarre type of quarry.*

If students need help . . . Use the Making Inferences chart to help students think about details that may signal future events. You might start with these examples:

Details from Story	+	What I Know from Reading or Experience	=	My Inference
"No thrill left in tigers" (line 254)	+	Tigers' only enemies may be people.	=	He might be thinking of hunting people.
"I live for danger" (line 255)	+	Danger-seekers take greater and greater risks.	=	He might involve Rainsford in a weird activity.

Extend the Discussion By now, you probably suspect the nature of the upcoming conflict. Why doesn't Rainsford seem to get it?

🧰 BEST PRACTICES TOOLKIT—Transparency Making Inferences p. A13

BACKGROUND

Zaroff again refers to his Cossack heritage in lines 274–275. The Cossacks, a privileged class, often were called upon for the toughest jobs in the Russian military. They became known for the daring exploits that mark a warrior culture.

"What have you imported, General?" Rainsford asked. "Tigers?"

The general smiled. "No," he said. "Hunting tigers ceased to interest me some years ago. I exhausted their possibilities, you see. No thrill left in tigers, no real danger. I live for danger, Mr. Rainsford."

The general took from his pocket a gold cigarette case and offered his guest a long black cigarette with a silver tip; it was perfumed and gave off a smell like incense.

260 "We will have some capital hunting, you and I," said the general. "I shall be most glad to have your society."

"But what game—" began Rainsford.

"I'll tell you," said the general. "You will be amused, I know. I think I may say, in all modesty, that I have done a rare thing. I have invented a new sensation. May I pour you another glass of port, Mr. Rainsford?"

"Thank you, General." 🅗

The general filled both glasses and said: "God makes some men poets. Some he makes kings, some beggars. Me he made a hunter. My hand was made for the trigger, my father said. He was a very rich man with a quarter of a million acres in the Crimea, and he was an ardent sportsman. When I was only five 270 years old, he gave me a little gun, specially made in Moscow for me, to shoot sparrows with. When I shot some of his prize turkeys with it, he did not punish me; he complimented me on my marksmanship. I killed my first bear in the Caucasus[7] when I was ten. My whole life has been one prolonged hunt. I went into the army—it was expected of noblemen's sons—and for a time commanded a division of Cossack cavalry, but my real interest was always the hunt. I have hunted every kind of game in every land. It would be impossible for me to tell you how many animals I have killed."

The general puffed at his cigarette.

"After the debacle in Russia I left the country, for it was imprudent for 280 an officer of the Tsar[8] to stay there. Many noble Russians lost everything. I, luckily, had invested heavily in American securities, so I shall never have to open a tearoom in Monte Carlo or drive a taxi in Paris. Naturally, I continued to hunt—grizzlies in your Rockies, crocodiles in the Ganges,[9] rhinoceroses in East Africa. It was in Africa that the Cape buffalo hit me and laid me up for six months. As soon as I recovered, I started for the Amazon to hunt jaguars, for I had heard they were unusually cunning. They weren't." The Cossack sighed. "They were no match at all for a hunter with his wits about him, and a high-powered rifle. I was bitterly disappointed. I was lying in my tent with a splitting headache one night when a terrible thought pushed its way into my

---

7. **Crimea** (krī-mē'ə) . . . **Caucasus** (kô'kə-səs): regions in the southern part of the former Russian Empire, near the Black Sea.

8. **debacle in Russia . . . Tsar** (zär): a reference to the 1917 Russian Revolution, in which the emperor, Tsar Nicholas II, was violently overthrown.

9. **Ganges** (găn'jēz'): a river in northern India.

🅗 CONFLICT
Reread lines 228–265. The conversation between Rainsford and Zaroff hints at further plot **complications.** Use clues to predict future events.

③ Targeted Passage

DIFFERENTIATED INSTRUCTION

FOR LESS–PROFICIENT READERS
③ Targeted Passage [Lines 266–277]

By describing Zaroff's background—in Zaroff's words—this passage offers insights into his character and helps set up the conflict that will drive the most important part of the story.

• How old was Zaroff when he was given his first gun? What did he do with it, and what was the result?

• What happened when Zaroff was ten years old? What does this reveal about him?

• What does this passage tell you about how Zaroff views himself?

• What need does hunting fulfill for Zaroff?

290 mind. Hunting was beginning to bore me! And hunting, remember, had been my life. I have heard that in America businessmen often go to pieces when they give up the business that has been their life."

"Yes, that's so," said Rainsford. **I**

The general smiled. "I had no wish to go to pieces," he said. "I must do something. Now, mine is an analytical mind, Mr. Rainsford. Doubtless that is why I enjoy the problems of the chase."

"No doubt, General Zaroff."

"So," continued the general, "I asked myself why the hunt no longer fascinated me. You are much younger than I am, Mr. Rainsford, and have not
300 hunted as much, but you perhaps can guess the answer."

"What was it?"

"Simply this: hunting had ceased to be what you call 'a sporting proposition.' It had become too easy. I always got my quarry. Always. There is no greater bore than perfection."

The general lit a fresh cigarette.

"No animal had a chance with me any more. That is no boast; it is a mathematical certainty. The animal had nothing but his legs and his instinct. Instinct is no match for reason. When I thought of this, it was a tragic moment for me, I can tell you."

310 Rainsford leaned across the table, absorbed in what his host was saying.

"It came to me as an inspiration what I must do," the general went on.

"And that was?"

The general smiled the quiet smile of one who has faced an obstacle and surmounted it with success. "I had to invent a new animal to hunt," he said. **J**

"A new animal? You're joking."

"Not at all," said the general. "I never joke about hunting. I needed a new animal. I found one. So I bought this island, built this house, and here I do my hunting. The island is perfect for my purposes—there are jungles with a maze of trails in them, hills, swamps—"

320 "But the animal, General Zaroff?"

"Oh," said the general, "it supplies me with the most exciting hunting in the world. No other hunting compares with it for an instant. Every day I hunt, and I never grow bored now, for I have a quarry with which I can match my wits."

Rainsford's bewilderment showed in his face.

"I wanted the ideal animal to hunt," explained the general. "So I said: 'What are the attributes of an ideal quarry?' And the answer was, of course: 'It must have courage, cunning, and, above all, it must be able to reason.'"

"But no animal can reason," objected Rainsford.

330 "My dear fellow," said the general, "there is one that can."

"But you can't mean—" gasped Rainsford.

"And why not?"

"I can't believe you are serious, General Zaroff. This is a grisly joke."

I VISUALIZE

As you read the rest of this page, visualize the expression on Rainsford's face as he listens to General Zaroff. How does his expression change over the course of the conversation?

J PREDICT

What "new animal" do you think General Zaroff likes to hunt? Support your answer with evidence.

READING STRATEGY

I VISUALIZE

Possible answer: At this point, Rainsford probably has a polite look of agreement on his face. This look becomes less friendly as Zaroff continues. By mid-page, when the general mentions his "new animal" (line 314), Rainsford's expression may be neutral or slightly puzzled. By line 325, Rainsford looks confused; by line 331, shocked or outraged.

If students need help . . . Have them read the conversation aloud. Talk about how each character's tone of voice changes or stays the same as the conversation progresses.

Extend the Discussion Why does General Zaroff lead up so slowly to the information that he is probably most eager to share?

READING STRATEGY: *Review*

J PREDICT

Possible answer: It is human beings. Zaroff wants a quarry that acts on reason, not just instinct (lines 306–308), and only human beings have the ability to reason.

Extend the Discussion How will Rainsford react to Zaroff's solution to his boredom?

FOR LESS–PROFICIENT WRITERS

Comprehension Support (lines 315–324) To make sure students understand this key passage, ask why this sophisticated man came to live on such an island. Have students cite details from the passage.

FOR ENGLISH LEARNERS

Vocabulary: Idioms Use New Word Analysis to teach these story idioms: *tight place* (line 78), "difficult situation"; *making headway* (line 127), "progressing"; *go to pieces*

(line 291), "lose self-control"; *held his tongue in check* (line 390), "kept quiet"; *give you my word* (line 494), "promise"; *got a grip on himself* (line 522), "took control of his feelings"; *taking stock of* (line 523), "judging."

BEST PRACTICES TOOLKIT—Transparency
New Word Analysis p. E8

"Why should I not be serious? I am speaking of hunting."

"Hunting? Good God, General Zaroff, what you speak of is murder."

The general laughed with entire good nature. He regarded Rainsford
quizzically. "I refuse to believe that so modern and civilized a young man as
you seem to be harbors romantic ideas about the value of human life. Surely
your experiences in the war—"

340   "Did not make me **condone** cold-blooded murder," finished Rainsford,
stiffly.

Laughter shook the general. "How extraordinarily **droll** you are!" he said.
"One does not expect nowadays to find a young man of the educated class,
even in America, with such a naïve, and, if I may say so, mid-Victorian point
of view. It's like finding a snuffbox in a limousine. Ah, well, doubtless you had
Puritan ancestors. So many Americans appear to have had. I'll wager you'll
forget your notions when you go hunting with me. You've a genuine new thrill
in store for you, Mr. Rainsford."

"Thank you, I'm a hunter, not a murderer."

350   "Dear me," said the general, quite unruffled, "again that unpleasant word.
But I think I can show you that your **scruples** are quite ill-founded."

"Yes?"

"Life is for the strong, to be lived by the strong, and, if needs be, taken by
the strong. The weak of the world were put here to give the strong pleasure.
I am strong. Why should I not use my gift? If I wish to hunt, why should I
not? I hunt the scum of the earth—sailors from tramp ships—lascars,[10] blacks,
Chinese, whites, mongrels—a thoroughbred horse or hound is worth more
than a score of them."

"But they are men," said Rainsford, hotly.

360   "Precisely," said the general. "That is why I use them. It gives me pleasure.
They can reason, after a fashion. So they are dangerous."

"But where do you get them?"

The general's left eyelid fluttered down in a wink. "This island is called Ship
Trap," he answered. "Sometimes an angry god of the high seas sends them to
me. Sometimes, when Providence is not so kind, I help Providence a bit. Come
to the window with me."

Rainsford went to the window and looked out toward the sea.

"Watch! Out there!" exclaimed the general, pointing into the night.
Rainsford's eyes saw only blackness, and then, as the general pressed a button,
370 far out to sea Rainsford saw the flash of lights.

The general chuckled. "They indicate a channel," he said, "where there's
none: giant rocks with razor edges crouch like a sea monster with wide-open
jaws. They can crush a ship as easily as I crush this nut." He dropped a walnut
on the hardwood floor and brought his heel grinding down on it. "Oh, yes,"
he said, casually, as if in answer to a question, "I have electricity. We try to be
civilized here."

condone (kən-dōn')
v. to forgive or overlook

droll (drōl) *adj.* amusingly
odd or comical

scruple (skrōō'pəl)
n. a feeling of uneasiness
that keeps a person from
doing something

---

10. **lascars** (lăs'kərz): sailors from India.

Detail of *Downtime*, Dale Kennington © Dale Kennington/Superstock.

Lines 375–388
DISCUSSION PROMPTS

Use these prompts to help students follow the story's mounting tension:

Connect How do you react to Zaroff's statement "We try to be civilized here"? *Possible answer: Zaroff's comment seems ridiculous in view of his hunting game, but I'd be afraid to voice strong objections.*

Analyze Why does Rainsford's comment anger Zaroff? *Possible answer: Rainsford is saying that Zaroff is uncivilized, and Zaroff obviously disagrees.*

Synthesize What comments does Zaroff make to prove that Rainsford is wrong and that he, Zaroff, is civilized? *Possible answer: He tells Rainsford that he treats his "visitors" well (lines 381–383).* What does Zaroff tell Rainsford to contradict his own argument? *Possible answer: He imprisons his "visitors" in the cellar (lines 385–386).*

"Civilized? And you shoot down men?"

A trace of anger was in the general's black eyes, but it was there for but a second, and he said, in his most pleasant manner: "Dear me, what a righteous
380 young man you are! I assure you I do not do the thing you suggest. That would be barbarous. I treat these visitors with every consideration. They get plenty of good food and exercise. They get into splendid physical condition. You shall see for yourself tomorrow."

"What do you mean?"

"We'll visit my training school," smiled the general. "It's in the cellar. I have about a dozen pupils down there now. They're from the Spanish bark *Sanlúcar* that had the bad luck to go on the rocks out there. A very inferior lot, I regret to say. Poor specimens and more accustomed to the deck than to the jungle."

He raised his hand, and Ivan, who served as waiter, brought thick Turkish
390 coffee. Rainsford, with an effort, held his tongue in check.

"It's a game, you see," pursued the general, blandly. "I suggest to one of them that we go hunting. I give him a supply of food and an excellent hunting

knife. I give him three hours' start. I am to follow, armed only with a pistol of the smallest caliber and range. If my quarry eludes me for three whole days, he wins the game. If I find him"—the general smiled—"he loses."

"Suppose he refuses to be hunted?"

"Oh," said the general, "I give him his option, of course. He need not play that game if he doesn't wish to. If he does not wish to hunt, I turn him over to Ivan. Ivan once had the honor of serving as official knouter[11] to the Great
400 White Tsar, and he has his own ideas of sport. Invariably, Mr. Rainsford, invariably they choose the hunt."

"And if they win?"

The smile on the general's face widened.

"To date I have not lost," he said.

Then he added, hastily: "I don't wish you to think me a braggart, Mr. Rainsford. Many of them afford only the most elementary sort of problem. Occasionally I strike a tartar.[12] One almost did win. I eventually had to use the dogs."

"The dogs?"

410 "This way, please. I'll show you."

The general steered Rainsford to a window. The lights from the windows sent a flickering illumination that made grotesque patterns on the courtyard below, and Rainsford could see moving about there a dozen or so huge black shapes; as they turned toward him, their eyes glittered greenly.

"A rather good lot, I think," observed the general. "They are let out at seven every night. If anyone should try to get into my house—or out of it— something extremely regrettable would occur to him." He hummed a snatch of song from the Folies Bergère.[13]

"And now," said the general, "I want to show you my new collection of
420 heads. Will you come with me to the library?"

"I hope," said Rainsford, "that you will excuse me tonight, General Zaroff. I'm really not feeling at all well."

"Ah, indeed?" the general inquired, **solicitously.** "Well, I suppose that's only natural, after your long swim. You need a good, restful night's sleep. Tomorrow you'll feel like a new man, I'll wager. Then we'll hunt, eh? I've one rather promising prospect—"

Rainsford was hurrying from the room.

"Sorry you can't go with me tonight," called the general. "I expect rather fair sport—a big, strong black. He looks resourceful— Well, good night,
430 Mr. Rainsford; I hope you have a good night's rest."

The bed was good, and the pajamas of the softest silk, and he was tired in every fiber of his being, but nevertheless Rainsford could not quiet his brain with the opiate of sleep. He lay, eyes wide open. Once he thought he heard stealthy steps in the corridor outside his room. He sought to throw open the

---

11. **knouter** (nou'tər): a person who whipped criminals in Russia.

12. **strike a tartar:** encounter a fierce opponent.

13. **Folies Bergère** (fô-lē' bĕr-zhěr'): a music hall in Paris, famous for its variety shows.

66   UNIT 1: NARRATIVE STRUCTURE

door; it would not open. He went to the window and looked out. His room was high up in one of the towers. The lights of the château were out now, and it was dark and
440 silent, but there was a fragment of sallow moon, and by its wan light he could see, dimly, the courtyard; there, weaving in and out in the pattern of shadow, were black, noiseless forms; the hounds heard him at the window and looked up, expectantly, with their green eyes. Rainsford went back to the bed and lay down. By many methods
450 he tried to put himself to sleep. He had achieved a doze when, just as morning began to come, he heard, far off in the jungle, the faint report of a pistol.

General Zaroff did not appear until luncheon. He was dressed faultlessly in the tweeds of a country squire. He was solicitous about the state of Rainsford's health.

"As for me," sighed the general, "I do not feel so well. I am worried, Mr. Rainsford. Last night I detected traces of my old complaint."

To Rainsford's questioning glance the general said: "Ennui. Boredom."

460 Then, taking a second helping of crêpes suzettes, the general explained: "The hunting was not good last night. The fellow lost his head. He made a straight trail that offered no problems at all. That's the trouble with these sailors; they have dull brains to begin with, and they do not know how to get about in the woods. They do excessively stupid and obvious things. It's most annoying. Will you have another glass of Chablis,[14] Mr. Rainsford?"

"General," said Rainsford, firmly, "I wish to leave this island at once."

The general raised his thickets of eyebrows; he seemed hurt. "But, my dear fellow," the general protested, "you've only just come. You've had no hunting—"

470 "I wish to go today," said Rainsford. He saw the dead black eyes of the general on him, studying him. General Zaroff's face suddenly brightened.

He filled Rainsford's glass with venerable Chablis from a dusty bottle.

"Tonight," said the general, "we will hunt—you and I."

Rainsford shook his head. "No, General," he said. "I will not hunt."

The general shrugged his shoulders and delicately ate a hothouse grape. "As you wish, my friend," he said. "The choice rests entirely with you. But may I not venture to suggest that you will find my idea of sport more diverting than Ivan's?"

---

14. **Chablis** (shă-blē'): a type of white French wine.

ANALYZE VISUALS

Activity The title of this photograph is *Dog Running on the Beach.* Ask students to compare the details and overall impression conveyed by this image with the description of the dogs in lines 411–414. *Possible answer: The dog in the photograph is similar to the description of the dogs in lines 411–414 because it looks scary, even though its features are indistinct, and because it, too, is large and dark. The main difference is that the dog in the picture does not have the glittering green eyes of Zaroff's dogs (line 414).*

Lines 466–478
REINFORCE *KEY IDEA:* SURVIVAL

Discuss Why might you call what Rainsford does at lunch with General Zaroff an attempt at **survival**? How does his attempt backfire, making survival a greater issue than before? *Possible answer: Departing from the atmosphere of gentility, Rainsford demands to be taken away from the island. The attempt backfires because when he insists upon leaving without hunting, Zaroff decides to make him the next quarry in his hunt.*

FOR ENGLISH LEARNERS

Reading: Predict Use Reciprocal Teaching to show students how to make predictions at these points in the story: line 333, lines 476–478, lines 569–570, lines 680–681. After students make each prediction, work together with them to confirm or adjust it.

🧰 BEST PRACTICES TOOLKIT—Transparency
Reciprocal Teaching p. A35

L CONFLICT

Possible answer: *The main conflict is be-tween Rainsford and Zaroff—the hunted against the hunter. Rainsford will now have to fight for his life in a battle of brains, skill, strength, and stamina; in other words, "outdoor chess," as Zaroff puts it.*

Extend the Discussion What does the expression "worthy of my steel" mean, and how does that term add to the conflict between the main characters?

ANALYZE VISUALS

Activity The title of this photograph is *Person Running at Night.* Ask students how well it fits with the way they visualize Rainsford at this point in the story. *Possible answer: The photograph shows a figure running through the woods, as if being chased by someone or something. Up to this point, Rainsford has been a strong and fearless character, but Zaroff has just challenged him to a hunt. Rainsford now has a vision—perhaps a vision like that in this image—of what the next few days (and, per-haps, the last few days) of his life will be like.*

He nodded toward the corner to where the giant stood, scowling, his thick
480 arms crossed on his hogshead of chest.
"You don't mean—" cried Rainsford.
"My dear fellow," said the general, "have I not told you I always mean what I say about hunting? This is really an inspiration. I drink to a foeman worthy of my steel—at last." **L**
The general raised his glass, but Rainsford sat staring at him.
"You'll find this game worth playing," the general said, enthusiastically. "Your brain against mine. Your woodcraft against mine. Your strength and stamina against mine. Outdoor chess! And the stake is not without value, eh?"
"And if I win—" began Rainsford, huskily.
490 "I'll cheerfully acknowledge myself defeated if I do not find you by midnight of the third day," said General Zaroff. "My sloop will place you on the mainland near a town."
The general read what Rainsford was thinking.
"Oh, you can trust me," said the Cossack. "I will give you my word as a gentleman and a sportsman. Of course, you, in turn, must agree to say nothing of your visit here."
"I'll agree to nothing of the kind," said Rainsford.

L CONFLICT
The main conflict in the story has now become clear. What is it?

④ Targeted Passage

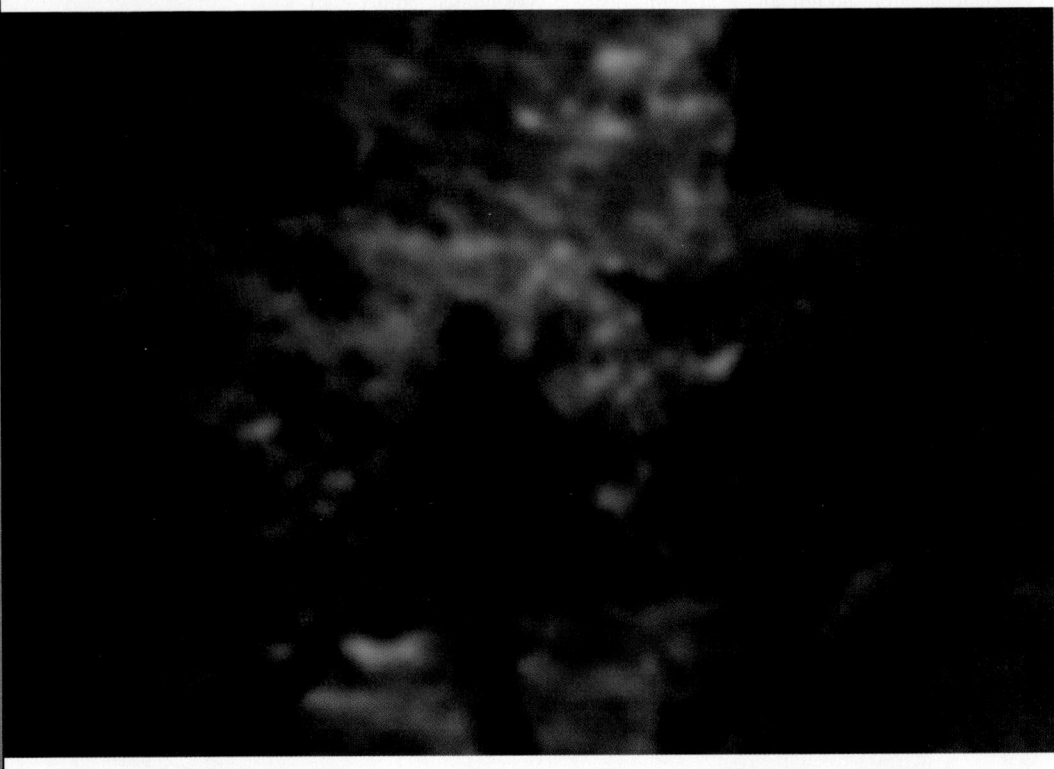

DIFFERENTIATED INSTRUCTION

FOR LESS–PROFICIENT READERS

④ Targeted Passage [Lines 482–497]

This passage brings the conflict between Rainsford and Zaroff into full focus.

- How is Zaroff feeling about his contest with Rainsford?
- How is their contest like "outdoor chess" (line 488)?
- What happens if Rainsford wins the contest? if he loses?

- What agreement does Zaroff try to make with Rainsford? How does Rainsford re-spond?

FOR ENGLISH LEARNERS

Language: Punctuation and Print Clues Sever-al dashes (—) appear in the dialogue on these pages; indeed, they have been part of the story since line 1. To help students understand the purpose of this usage, read aloud lines 479–492 to show that the dashes indicate both a pause and the suggestion that something sinister or dangerous is about to happen.

"Oh," said the general, "in that case— But why discuss that now? Three days hence we can discuss it over a bottle of Veuve Clicquot,[15] unless—"

500   The general sipped his wine.

    Then a businesslike air animated him. "Ivan," he said to Rainsford, "will supply you with hunting clothes, food, a knife. I suggest you wear moccasins; they leave a poorer trail. I suggest, too, that you avoid the big swamp in the southeast corner of the island. We call it Death Swamp. There's quicksand there. One foolish fellow tried it. The deplorable part of it was that Lazarus followed him. You can imagine my feelings, Mr. Rainsford. I loved Lazarus; he was the finest hound in my pack. Well, I must beg you to excuse me now. I always take a siesta after lunch. You'll hardly have time for a nap, I fear. You'll want to start, no doubt. I shall not follow till dusk. Hunting at night is so

510 much more exciting than by day, don't you think? Au revoir,[16] Mr. Rainsford, au revoir."

    General Zaroff, with a deep, courtly bow, strolled from the room.

    From another door came Ivan. Under one arm he carried khaki hunting clothes, a haversack of food, a leather sheath containing a long-bladed hunting knife; his right hand rested on a cocked revolver thrust in the crimson sash about his waist. . . . Ⓜ

    Rainsford had fought his way through the bush for two hours. "I must keep my nerve. I must keep my nerve," he said, through tight teeth.

    He had not been entirely clear-headed when the château gates snapped shut

520 behind him. His whole idea at first was to put distance between himself and General Zaroff, and, to this end, he had plunged along, spurred on by the sharp rowels of something very like panic. Now he had got a grip on himself, had stopped, and was taking stock of himself and the situation.

    He saw that straight flight was futile; inevitably it would bring him face to face with the sea. He was in a picture with a frame of water, and his operations, clearly, must take place within that frame.

    "I'll give him a trail to follow," muttered Rainsford, and he struck off from the rude path he had been following into the trackless wilderness. He executed a series of intricate loops; he doubled on his trail again and again, recalling all

530 the lore of the fox hunt, and all the dodges of the fox. Night found him leg-weary, with hands and face lashed by the branches, on a thickly wooded ridge. He knew it would be insane to blunder on through the dark, even if he had the strength. His need for rest was **imperative,** and he thought, "I have played the fox; now I must play the cat of the fable."[17] A big tree with a thick trunk and outspread branches was nearby, and, taking care to leave not the slightest mark, he climbed up into the crotch and, stretching out on one of the broad limbs, after a fashion, rested. Rest brought him new confidence and almost a feeling of security. Even so **zealous** a hunter as General Zaroff could not trace him

---

15. **Veuve Clicquot** (vœv′ klĭ-kō′): a French champagne.

16. **au revoir** (ō′ rə-vwär′): goodbye; farewell till we meet again.

17. **I have played the fox . . . fable:** In Aesop's fable "The Cat and the Fox," the fox brags of knowing many ways to escape an enemy. The cat knows only one, but is successful with it.

Ⓜ **GRAMMAR AND STYLE**
Reread lines 513–516. Notice how Connell uses multiple **prepositional phrases**—such as "on a cocked revolver" and "in the crimson sash"—to add descriptive details.

imperative (ĭm-pĕr′ə-tĭv) *adj.* absolutely necessary

zealous (zĕl′əs) *adj.* intensely enthusiastic

Ⓜ **GRAMMAR AND STYLE**

Analyze Descriptive Details After students read the lines, point out that the descriptive details answer questions (such as "How does Zaroff bid Rainsford farewell?" and "Where is the revolver?"). Ask students how the descriptive details add drama and interest. *Possible answer: The first detail ("with a deep, courtly bow") is a reminder of Zaroff's attempt to appear civilized. The other details help the reader visualize Ivan. In particular, "in the crimson sash" makes Ivan seem even more exotic, for few people in the United States would wear such an item; furthermore, it is the color of blood.* Have students find other prepositional phrases that enliven this part of the story and/or that lend insight into the characters or their conflict.

FOR ADVANCED LEARNERS/PRE–AP
Analyze Options [paired-activity option]
Have students come up with options for Rainsford, such as these:

- Go to the swamp, where it would be dangerous for Zaroff and his dogs to follow.

- Turn and fight Zaroff as soon as possible.

- Find a hiding place, and wait for rescue from a passing ship.

- Surrender and accept Zaroff's original offer.

Ask students to choose the best option and explain their reasoning.

there, he told himself; only the devil himself could follow that complicated
540 trail through the jungle after dark. But perhaps the general was a devil—

An apprehensive night crawled slowly by like a wounded snake, and sleep did not visit Rainsford, although the silence of a dead world was on the jungle. Toward morning, when a dingy gray was varnishing the sky, the cry of some startled bird focused Rainsford's attention in that direction. Something was coming through the bush, coming slowly, carefully, coming by the same winding way Rainsford had come. He flattened himself down on the limb, and through a screen of leaves almost as thick as tapestry, he watched. The thing that was approaching was a man.

It was General Zaroff. He made his way along with his eyes fixed in utmost
550 concentration on the ground before him. He paused, almost beneath the tree, dropped to his knees, and studied the ground. Rainsford's impulse was to hurl himself down like a panther, but he saw that the general's right hand held something metallic—a small automatic pistol. **N**

The hunter shook his head several times, as if he were puzzled. Then he straightened up and took from his case one of his black cigarettes; its pungent, incenselike smoke floated up to Rainsford's nostrils.

Rainsford held his breath. The general's eyes had left the ground and were traveling inch by inch up the tree. Rainsford froze there, every muscle tensed for a spring. But the sharp eyes of the hunter stopped before they reached the
560 limb where Rainsford lay; a smile spread over his brown face. Very deliberately he blew a smoke ring into the air; then he turned his back on the tree and walked carelessly away, back along the trail he had come. The swish of the underbrush against his hunting boots grew fainter and fainter.

The pent-up air burst hotly from Rainsford's lungs. His first thought made him feel sick and numb. The general could follow a trail through the woods at night; he could follow an extremely difficult trail; he must have **uncanny** powers; only by the merest chance had the Cossack failed to see his quarry.

Rainsford's second thought was even more terrible. It sent a shudder of cold horror through his whole being. Why had the general smiled? Why had he
570 turned back?

Rainsford did not want to believe what his reason told him was true, but the truth was as evident as the sun that had by now pushed through the morning mists. The general was playing with him! The general was saving him for another day's sport! The Cossack was the cat; he was the mouse. Then it was that Rainsford knew the full meaning of terror. **O**

"I will not lose my nerve. I will not."

He slid down from the tree and struck off again into the woods. His face was set, and he forced the machinery of his mind to function. Three hundred yards from his hiding place he stopped where a huge dead tree leaned
580 precariously on a smaller, living one. Throwing off his sack of food, Rainsford took his knife from its sheath and began to work with all his energy.

70 UNIT 1: NARRATIVE STRUCTURE

N PREDICT This is one of the most **suspenseful** moments in the story. What do you think General Zaroff will do to Rainsford? Why?

uncanny (ŭn-kăn′ē) *adj.* so remarkable as to seem supernatural

O CONFLICT What **complication** is introduced to intensify the conflict and build **suspense**?

READING STRATEGY: *Review*

N PREDICT

Possible answer: Zaroff may try to kill Rainsford, since that is the point of the hunt.

Extend the Discussion What does Zaroff's ability to find Rainsford's location show about Zaroff? What does it show about Rainsford? How does this detail help you make predictions about the rest of the story?

LITERARY ANALYSIS

O CONFLICT

Possible answer: Rainsford realizes that Zaroff knew exactly where he was. Zaroff could have killed him then but chose not to do so. Instead, the general prefers to continue his "fun" (and Rainsford's distress). This knowledge adds another layer of tension to Rainsford's already stressful situation.

DIFFERENTIATED INSTRUCTION

FOR ADVANCED LEARNERS/PRE-AP
Evaluate Have students discuss Connell's effectiveness in building suspense. To what extent does his success depend upon plot, character, or setting? How does foreshadowing contribute to the suspense?

The job was finished at last, and he threw himself down behind a fallen log a hundred feet away. He did not have to wait long. The cat was coming again to play with the mouse.

Following the trail with the sureness of a bloodhound came General Zaroff. Nothing escaped those searching black eyes, no crushed blade of grass, no bent twig, no mark, no matter
590 how faint, in the moss. So intent was the Cossack on his stalking that he was upon the thing Rainsford had made before he saw it. His foot touched the protruding bough[18] that was the trigger. Even as he touched it, the general sensed his danger and leaped back with the agility of an ape. But he was not quite quick enough; the dead tree, delicately adjusted to rest on the cut living one, crashed down and struck the general a glancing blow on the shoulder as it fell; but for his
600 alertness, he must have been smashed beneath it. He staggered, but he did not fall; nor did he drop his revolver. He stood there, rubbing his injured shoulder, and Rainsford, with fear again gripping his heart, heard the general's mocking laugh ring through the jungle.

"Rainsford," called the general, "if you are within sound of my voice, as I suppose you are, let me congratulate you. Not many men know how to make a Malay man-catcher. Luckily for me I,
610 too, have hunted in Malacca.[19] You are proving interesting, Mr. Rainsford. I am going now to have my wound dressed; it's only a slight one. But I shall be back. I shall be back." ⑤ **Targeted Passage**

When the general, nursing his bruised shoulder, had gone, Rainsford took up his flight again. It was flight now, a desperate, hopeless flight, that carried him on for some hours. Dusk came, then darkness, and still he pressed on. The ground grew softer under his moccasins; the vegetation grew ranker, denser; insects bit him savagely. Then, as he stepped forward, his foot sank into the ooze. He tried to wrench it back, but the muck sucked viciously at his foot as if it were a giant leech. With a violent effort he tore his foot loose. He knew
620 where he was now. Death Swamp and its quicksand.

His hands were tight closed as if his nerve were something tangible that someone in the darkness was trying to tear from his grip. The softness of the

---

18. **protruding bough** (bou): a tree branch that extends or juts out.

19. **Malay** (mə-lā′) ... **Malacca** (mə-lăk′ə): The Malays are a people of southeast Asia. Malacca is a region they inhabit, just south of Thailand.

Tree Circle (1992), Peter Schroth. Oil on paper, 7½″ × 8½″.
© Peter Schroth.

ANALYZE VISUALS

Activity Call students' attention to how the trees in this landscape painting enclose the foreground with their shadows falling like prison bars across the ground. Then have students locate images of imprisonment or entrapment in the story, including details that suggest prison bars (like the shadows in the painting).

About the Art This oil painting, *Tree Circle*, by contemporary American landscape painter Peter Schroth does not depict the story's jungle setting, but offers a vision of entrapment that suggests Rainsford's situation.

Lines 586–612
DISCUSSION PROMPTS

Use these prompts to help students understand Zaroff's strength as an adversary:

Connect How do you feel about Zaroff at this point in the story? *Accept all reasonable answers.*

Analyze Zaroff knows that Rainsford is nearby. Why does Zaroff choose to end the day's hunt, rather than try to finish off Rainsford as soon as possible? *Possible answer: He knows that it is smarter to conserve his own strength and wear Rainsford down. And, he may enjoy Rainsford's torment.*

Synthesize How does Zaroff's personality add suspense to the scene? *Possible answer: Zaroff is both cool and cruel. He is a focused predator who understands that his prey can be worn down psychologically as well as physically. The reader is left in suspense about what he will do when he comes back.*

FOR LESS–PROFICIENT READERS
⑤ **Targeted Passage [Lines 586–612]**

This passage, which describes how one of Rainsford's traps goes off but fails to kill Zaroff, vividly captures the story's tensions and the deadly seriousness of the hunt.

• What has Rainsford set up?

• What happens to Zaroff when he encounters the trap?

• What does Zaroff promise Rainsford?

P PREDICT

Possible answer: No. The trap apparently is at the edge of the quicksand, and Zaroff has already spoken of the importance of staying away from that area. Furthermore, Zaroff has proven himself to be aware of traps (and now, having been slightly wounded, he is likely to be even more alert). In addition, given Zaroff's years of hunting around the world, it is likely that he is familiar with all manner of exotic traps.

If students need help . . . Encourage them to make a chart in which they record story details related to the question. Then they can examine those details and add their own prior knowledge to them to make predictions. Remind students that their predictions should be based on story details.

LITERARY ANALYSIS

Q CONFLICT

Possible answer: The only escape route at this point seems to be the sea, where the dogs cannot follow.

If students need help . . . Discuss these questions with students to help them understand why the dogs are a problem for Rainsford:

- What would the dogs do if they found Rainsford?

- Why can't Rainsford just stay near the swamp?

- Could the dogs follow his scent if he hid somewhere in the jungle?

- Could they follow his scent if he ran off?

- Could they follow his scent in the sea?

---

earth had given him an idea. He stepped back from the quicksand a dozen feet or so, and like some huge prehistoric beaver, he began to dig.

Rainsford had dug himself in in France when a second's delay meant death. That had been a placid pastime compared to his digging now. The pit grew deeper; when it was above his shoulders, he climbed out and from some hard saplings cut stakes and sharpened them to a fine point. These stakes he planted in the bottom of the pit with the points sticking up. With flying fingers he
630 wove a rough carpet of weeds and branches, and with it he covered the mouth of the pit. Then, wet with sweat and aching with tiredness, he crouched behind the stump of a lightning-charred tree. **P**

He knew his pursuer was coming; he heard the padding sound of feet on the soft earth, and the night breeze brought him the perfume of the general's cigarette. It seemed to Rainsford that the general was coming with unusual swiftness; he was not feeling his way along, foot by foot. Rainsford, crouching there, could not see the general, nor could he see the pit. He lived a year in a minute. Then he felt an impulse to cry aloud with joy, for he heard the sharp crackle of the breaking branches as the cover of the pit gave way; he heard the
640 sharp scream of pain as the pointed stakes found their mark. He leaped up from his place of concealment. Then he cowered back. Three feet from the pit a man was standing, with an electric torch in his hand.

"You've done well, Rainsford," the voice of the general called. "Your Burmese tiger pit[20] has claimed one of my best dogs. Again you score. I think, Mr. Rainsford, I'll see what you can do against my whole pack. I'm going home for a rest now. Thank you for a most amusing evening."

At daybreak Rainsford, lying near the swamp, was awakened by a sound that made him know that he had new things to learn about fear. It was a distant sound, faint and wavering, but he knew it. It was the baying of a
650 pack of hounds. **Q**

Rainsford knew he could do one of two things. He could stay where he was and wait. That was suicide. He could flee. That was postponing the inevitable. For a moment he stood there, thinking. An idea that held a wild chance came to him, and, tightening his belt, he headed away from the swamp.

The baying of the hounds grew nearer, then still nearer, nearer, ever nearer. On a ridge Rainsford climbed a tree. Down a watercourse, not a quarter of a mile away, he could see the bush moving. Straining his eyes, he saw the lean figure of General Zaroff; just ahead of him, Rainsford made out another figure whose wide shoulders surged through the tall jungle weeds; it was the giant
660 Ivan, and he seemed pulled forward by some unseen force; Rainsford knew that Ivan must be holding the pack in leash.

They would be on him any minute now. His mind worked frantically. He thought of a native trick he had learned in Uganda.[21] He slid down the tree.

---

20. **Burmese** (bər-mēz') **tiger pit:** a trap used for catching tigers in Myanmar, a country in Southeast Asia formerly called Burma.

21. **Uganda** (yōō-găn'də): a country in central Africa.

P PREDICT
Will the trap ensnare the general? Give reasons for your prediction.

Q CONFLICT
The introduction of the pack of hounds poses a new complication. What recourse does Rainsford have?

DIFFERENTIATED INSTRUCTION

FOR LESS–PROFICIENT READERS

Concept Building: World War I Explain that Rainsford's having "dug himself in in France" (line 625) is a reference to military service in Europe during World War I (1914–1918). The Germans' early attempt to sweep westward across France was met by the resistance of Allied forces, and both sides "dug in," creating a system of opposing trenches from which most of the war was fought, with high casualties and little movement. More than any other war, before or after, World War I was known for its trench warfare, and the dismal conditions in the trenches (including rats and lice, disease, and constant concern about enemy shellfire and snipers) probably toughened Rainsford's survival skills.

Activity This photograph of crashing waves (called *Wakes on Sea*) presents the sea as a forbidding place. Have students suggest why an image of the sea appears at this point in the story. *Possible answer: This image may be a reminder that the sea is how Rainsford got to this island and put him into a life-threatening position; it also may be a foreshadowing of an escape route.*

Lines 662–669
REINFORCE *KEY IDEA:* SURVIVAL

Discuss How has Rainsford changed since the beginning of the story, when he talked with Whitney about hunting? *Possible answer: Rainsford seemed arrogant and insensitive when he spoke with Whitney about hunting; now he understands what it is to be vulnerable and how a hunted animal must feel.* Discuss how circumstances have tested Rainsford's survival skills in ways he could not have predicted or trained for.

He caught hold of a springy young sapling, and to it he fastened his hunting knife, with the blade pointing down the trail; with a bit of wild grapevine he tied back the sapling. Then he ran for his life. The hounds raised their voices as they hit the fresh scent. Rainsford knew now how an animal at bay feels.

He had to stop to get his breath. The baying of the hounds stopped abruptly, and Rainsford's heart stopped, too. They must have reached the knife.

670 He shinned excitedly up a tree and looked back. His pursuers had stopped. But the hope that was in Rainsford's brain when he climbed died, for he saw in the shallow valley that General Zaroff was still on his feet. But Ivan was not. The knife, driven by the recoil of the springing tree, had not wholly failed.

R VISUALIZE

Possible answer: The contrast between the desperate Rainsford and the nonchalant Zaroff makes a dramatic impact: It reminds readers that although these characters seemed at first to be kindred spirits, they differ in one important value—and, at this point, readers do not yet know whose value will triumph.

If students need help . . . Have them work in small groups to complete this chart:

	Zaroff	Rainsford
Physical State		
Mental State		

SELECTION WRAP-UP

REFLECT After eliciting comments about the overall appeal of "The Most Dangerous Game," ask students whether they think that Connell's story is making serious comments on topics like wealth, hunting, or class differences, or whether students see it as just a powerful adventure tale. Have them explain their responses.

★ CRITIQUE Have students tell what they think are the most believable and unbelievable parts of this story.

READING FLUENCY

Distribute the copy master and have students work in pairs or groups to practice fluency.

R RESOURCE MANAGER—Copy Master
Reading Fluency p. 63

Rainsford had hardly tumbled to the ground when the pack took up the cry again.

"Nerve, nerve, nerve!" he panted, as he dashed along. A blue gap showed between the trees dead ahead. Ever nearer drew the hounds. Rainsford forced himself on toward that gap. He reached it. It was the shore of the sea. Across a cove he could see the gloomy gray stone of the château. Twenty feet below him
680 the sea rumbled and hissed. Rainsford hesitated. He heard the hounds. Then he leaped far out into the sea. . . .

When the general and his pack reached the place by the sea, the Cossack stopped. For some minutes he stood regarding the blue-green expanse of water. He shrugged his shoulders. Then he sat down, took a drink of brandy from a silver flask, lit a perfumed cigarette, and hummed a bit from *Madama Butterfly*.[22] **R**

General Zaroff had an exceedingly good dinner in his great paneled dining hall that evening. With it he had a bottle of Pol Roger and half a bottle of Chambertin.[23] Two slight annoyances kept him from perfect enjoyment. One
690 was the thought that it would be difficult to replace Ivan; the other was that his quarry had escaped him; of course the American hadn't played the game—so thought the general as he tasted his after-dinner liqueur. In his library he read, to soothe himself, from the works of Marcus Aurelius.[24] At ten he went up to his bedroom. He was deliciously tired, he said to himself, as he locked himself in. There was a little moonlight, so before turning on his light he went to the window and looked down at the courtyard. He could see the great hounds, and he called "Better luck another time" to them. Then he switched on the light.

A man, who had been hiding in the curtains of the bed, was standing there.
700 "Rainsford!" screamed the general. "How in God's name did you get here?"

"Swam," said Rainsford. "I found it quicker than walking through the jungle."

The general sucked in his breath and smiled. "I congratulate you," he said. "You have won the game."

Rainsford did not smile. "I am still a beast at bay," he said, in a low, hoarse voice. "Get ready, General Zaroff."

The general made one of his deepest bows.

"I see," he said. "Splendid! One of us is to furnish a repast[25] for the hounds. The other will sleep in this very excellent bed. On guard, Rainsford. . . ."

710 He had never slept in a better bed, Rainsford decided. ❧

R VISUALIZE
Picture in your mind the contrasting images of Rainsford's dramatic escape and Zaroff's "civilized" actions at the edge of the water. What is the impact of this contrast?

G Targeted Passage

22. *Madama Butterfly:* a famous opera by the Italian composer Giacomo Puccini.
23. **Pol Roger** (pôl′ rô-zhä′) . . . **Chambertin** (shăm-bĕr-tăɴ′): Pol Roger is a French champagne. Chambertin is a red French wine.
24. **Marcus Aurelius** (mär′kəs ô-rē′lē-əs): an ancient Roman emperor and philosopher.
25. **furnish a repast:** serve as a meal.

DIFFERENTIATED INSTRUCTION

FOR LESS-PROFICIENT READERS

G Targeted Passage [Lines 694–710]

This passage concludes the story with a plot twist: Rainsford wins the "most dangerous game" by confronting Zaroff in the general's own bedroom.

- How did Rainsford get to the château?
- How does Rainsford respond when Zaroff congratulates him?
- Who sleeps in Zaroff's bed that night?

Comprehension Support Explain that the phrase "a beast at bay" (line 705) means "an animal that is unable to retreat and forced to face danger," and that an animal "at bay" is extremely dangerous. Point out that Rainsford calls himself "a beast of bay"; then ask

- How has Rainsford changed? Has he become an animal?
- Was he always an animal?

Students can discuss their ideas in small groups and present their answers to the class.

Comprehension

1. **Recall** Before arriving at the island, what is Rainsford's position on hunting?

2. **Recall** Why has Zaroff begun hunting human "game"?

3. **Clarify** What happens at the end of the story?

Literary Analysis

4. **Draw Conclusions** In your opinion, why does Rainsford choose to confront Zaroff in the end, rather than simply ambush him? What does this reveal about his personality? Cite evidence.

5. **Compare and Contrast Characters** Use a Venn diagram to compare and contrast Rainsford and Zaroff. Start by listing each man's **character traits** in the appropriate circle. Then note their similarities where the circles overlap.

Rainsford *Zaroff*

6. **Analyze Conflict** Reread lines 473–484. Connell does not reveal the main conflict until a good deal of the story has passed. Why? Support your answer.

7. **Examine Foreshadowing** Connell makes use of foreshadowing to help readers predict future events in the story. Find at least three examples of foreshadowing in the story. How does this technique add to the **suspense** of this story? Cite evidence.

8. **Visualize Description** Look back at the descriptive details you recorded as you read. Choose at least two details that evoked the most striking pictures in your mind. Which particular words helped make each of these images so vivid?

9. **Make Judgments** At the end of the story, do you think Rainsford has changed his mind about hunting? Support your opinion.

Literary Criticism

10. **Critical Interpretations** One critic has remarked that "ironically, Zaroff's belief in his invincibility as a hunter weakens him and causes his defeat." Cite evidence from the story to support or challenge this statement.

foreshadows a strange type of quarry; the fortress-like appearance of Zaroff's residence (lines 132–140) suggests a place where secret or evil things occur. This technique causes readers to read on, and it makes them somewhat fearful for Rainsford.

8. ● **STANDARDS FOCUS** *Visualize* The dining room with its oaken panels, high ceiling, and huge table is described in vivid detail (lines 213–219). So is Rainsford's approach to the Death Swamp (lines 615–620) through rank, dense vegetation, savage insects, muck, and ooze.

9. *Rainsford might not have changed, considering how well he slept after killing Zaroff. He might have changed, considering his new understanding of how an "animal at bay" feels (line 667).*

Literary Criticism
Possible answer:

10. *Before retiring, Zaroff ate well, drank, and read without worry, underestimating Rainsford by assuming that his quarry had drowned (lines 687–698).*

After Reading
For additional support of post-reading questions, use these copy masters:

R RESOURCE MANAGER—Copy Masters
Reading Check p. 60 (to check understanding of the selection)
Conflict p. 53 (for practice of literary analysis standards focus)
Question Support p. 61 (After Reading questions adapted for English learners and less-proficient readers)

For additional questions, see page 47.

For additional exercises to challenge students, see

ⓘ Power Thinking at **ClassZone.com**

ANSWERS

Comprehension
1. *He calls it "the best sport in the world."*
2. *Zaroff has come to the conclusion that it is too easy to catch animals; he wants the challenge of a quarry that can reason.*
3. *Rainsford eludes Zaroff and returns to the château. He hides in the general's bedroom, where he surprises and kills Zaroff.*

Literary Analysis
Possible answers:

4. *Rainsford plays by the rules. Earlier in the story he called Zaroff's game "murder" (line 335), so he will not kill Zaroff in cold blood; rather, he will fight Zaroff face to face. Rainsford's insistence on playing by the rules, telling the general to "get ready" (line 706), reveals that he is honorable.*

5. *Rainsford:* American, plays by the rules
   Zaroff: Russian, lives on island, breaks rules
   Both: great hunters, high social status, wealthy, both become the hunted

6. ● **STANDARDS FOCUS** *Conflict* Throughout the first part of the story, Connell is busy establishing character and setting and building suspense. He does this to intensify the surprise and underscore the horror of the main conflict when it is revealed.

7. *Whitney's comments about their location and sailor's lore (lines 1–5, 30–51) foreshadow the yachting accident; Rainsford's finding the spent cartridge (lines 116–120)*

ANSWERS

Vocabulary in Context

VOCABULARY PRACTICE

1. *tangible*
2. *disarming*
3. *imperative*
4. *cultivated*
5. *amenity*
6. *solicitously*
7. *scruples*
8. *quarry*
9. *droll*
10. *condone*
11. *zealous*
12. *uncanny*

 **RESOURCE MANAGER—Copy Master**
Vocabulary Practice p. 58

VOCABULARY IN WRITING

Remind students that they can prewrite for this activity just as they can prewrite for any type of writing. For example, suggest that they create a cluster graphic with *Rainsford* or *Zaroff* at the center and then note four vocabulary words related to the character's personality and/or behavior. Students can use their completed cluster as an idea base for writing their paragraph.

VOCABULARY STRATEGY: DENOTATION AND CONNOTATION *(also an EL language objective)*

- For additional instruction on connotation and denotation, focus on the word *syrupy*. Explain that the denotation, or meaning, of *syrupy* is "sweet," but the word has the negative connotation of "overly sweet," as in *Nancy did not trust the girl's* syrupy *compliments*.

- Explain that *solicitous* also can signal a behavior that is a bit too concerned or overdone, as in *That morning, I tried to avoid running into my ever-smiling, solicitous neighbor.*

- Ask students to imagine the tone of voice in which each sentence is spoken. Have volunteers read the sentences aloud in these different tones and describe the different connotative values of *solicitous* and *solicitously*.

Possible answers:

1. *reckless*
2. *reactionary*
3. *tightfisted*
4. *bizarre*
5. *impudent*
6. *notorious*

Sentences will vary but should demonstrate an understanding of the words' negative connotations.

RESOURCE MANAGER—Copy Master
Vocabulary Strategy p. 59

Vocabulary Center at ClassZone.com
Additional Vocabulary Activities

Vocabulary in Context

VOCABULARY PRACTICE

Choose the word from the list that best completes each sentence.

1. As Rainsford swam ashore, the air was so humid it was almost _____.
2. He spoke in a(n) _____ way in order to try not to anger Zaroff's guard.
3. For his own safety, Rainsford felt it _____ not to come across as an intruder.
4. Zaroff's love of fine food and wine made him seem a(n) _____ person.
5. His house offered every _____ that could make a guest comfortable.
6. In the morning, Zaroff inquired _____ whether Rainsford had slept well.
7. But Zaroff lacked the _____ that moral people have.
8. He saw nothing wrong with hunting a human _____.
9. In fact, with an odd, or a(n) _____, smile he stalked his prisoners.
10. Rainsford strongly disagreed with Zaroff and refused to _____ his hunting.
11. Zaroff was _____ in tracking down his victims.
12. Rainsford soon found that Zaroff had a(n) _____ ability to follow difficult trails.

WORD LIST

amenity
condone
cultivated
disarming
droll
imperative
quarry
scruple
solicitously
tangible
uncanny
zealous

VOCABULARY IN WRITING

Using at least four vocabulary words, write a paragraph characterizing either Rainsford or Zaroff. Here is a sample opening sentence.

> **EXAMPLE SENTENCE**
> *Rainsford loved to hunt big **quarry**.*

VOCABULARY STRATEGY: DENOTATION AND CONNOTATION

A word's **denotation** is its basic dictionary meaning; its **connotations** are the overtones of meaning that it may take on. For example, the vocabulary word *cultivated* means "cultured"; so does *highbrow*. However, *cultivated* has mostly positive overtones; *highbrow* has negative connotations of snobbishness.

PRACTICE Choose the word you would use to convey negative connotations. Then use the word appropriately in a sentence.

1. bold/reckless
2. conservative/reactionary
3. tightfisted/thrifty
4. unique/bizarre
5. outspoken/impudent
6. famous/notorious

VOCABULARY PRACTICE
For more practice, go to the **Vocabulary Center** at **ClassZone.com**.

DIFFERENTIATED INSTRUCTION

FOR ENGLISH LEARNERS

Vocabulary: Multiple-Meaning Words Before students complete Vocabulary practice, use Word Squares to help them understand the meanings of these multiple-meaning words:

- *quarry* (line 122)
- *disarming* (line 152)
- *cultivated* (line 165)
- *imperative* (line 533)

BEST PRACTICES TOOLKIT—Transparency
Word Squares p. E10

FOR ADVANCED LEARNERS/PRE–AP

Rank Connotations Have students use a thesaurus to locate three synonyms for a vocabulary word of their choice. Ask students to rank the synonyms on a continuum in order from negative to positive connotations or to put them in a chart according to their connotations. *Example for* zealous: rabid *(negative);* enthusiastic *(neutral);* ardent *(positive)*. Encourage students to share and explain their work.

Reading-Writing Connection

Explore the themes of "The Most Dangerous Game" by responding to these prompts. Then use **Revision: Grammar and Style** to improve your writing.

WRITING PROMPTS	SELF-CHECK
A. Short Response: Write a Diary Entry In the dialogue at the beginning of the story, Whitney empathizes with hunted animals. What does Rainsford learn about the feelings of hunted animals from his experience of being hunted? Write **one or two paragraphs** of a diary entry that Rainsford might write on this subject after his experience.	*A successful diary entry will ...* • accurately reflect Rainsford's personality • describe Rainsford's feelings during the experience • tell what Rainsford learned from his experience
B. Extended Response: Evaluate a Statement Early in the story Rainsford says to Whitney, "The world is made up of two classes—the hunters and the huntees." Decide whether you agree or disagree, and write **two to three paragraphs** expressing your opinion. Support your position with evidence from your own experiences.	*A strong evaluation will ...* • explain what the statement means • clearly state an opinion • provide at least two examples from real life to support the opinion

REVISION: GRAMMAR AND STYLE

ADD DESCRIPTIVE DETAILS Review the **Grammar and Style** note on page 69. Writers often use **prepositional phrases** to add descriptive details that show what events are taking place and where, when, and how they are taking place. Here is an example from the story:

> *He executed a series of intricate loops; he doubled on his trail again and again, recalling all the lore of the fox hunt, and all the dodges of the fox. Night found him leg-weary, with hands and face lashed by the branches, on a thickly wooded ridge.* (lines 528–531)

Notice how the revisions in red add descriptive details that show how, when, and where in this diary entry. Revise your responses to the prompts by using the same techniques.

STUDENT MODEL

in a cold sweat in the middle of the night,

Even though it's been several weeks, I still wake up, trembling

like a chill in my veins

with fear. The feeling of panic is ~~intense~~, and I can't move.

> **WRITING TOOLS**
> For prewriting, revision, and editing tools, visit the **Writing Center** at **ClassZone.com.**

FOR LESS-PROFICIENT WRITERS

For Prompt A:

• Have partners brainstorm a list of words that describe the feelings that Rainsford experienced when he became Zaroff's quarry (lines 519–681).

• Have students reread the paragraph where Rainsford comes to an understanding of how an animal at bay feels (lines 662–667).

For Prompt B:

• Help students develop a position statement.

• Help students find evidence.

• Suggest this organization for their writing:

Paragraph 1: introduction to topic; position statement

Paragraph 2 (optional): evidence for position

Paragraph 3: most compelling evidence for position; conclusion/restatement of position

---

Reading-Writing Connection

Reading-Writing Connection

WRITING PROMPTS

• For Prompt A, suggest that students brainstorm or freewrite to recapture the feeling of being hunted.

• For Prompt B, ask students to think about competitive situations in which the statement might apply, such as in sports or in a job. Suggest that they think about who would be the "hunter" and who would be the "huntee" in each situation. Then have them write opinions in support of or in opposition to the statement.

 BEST PRACTICES TOOLKIT—Transparency
Main Idea and Details p. B6

For an extended writing activity, see
ℹ️ Carol Booth Olson's Reading-Writing Lesson Plans at **ClassZone.com**

REVISION: GRAMMAR AND STYLE

• Discuss the revisions to the student model, eliciting the kind of information that each added phrase provides. For more on prepositional phrases, see **Grammar Handbook,** page R60.

• Have students add prepositional phrases to this sentence:

> When Rainsford returns, he hides. ***Possible answer:*** *When Rainsford returns* <u>to the château</u>*, he hides* <u>in Zaroff's bedroom</u> *until* <u>the general's return</u>*.*

 RESOURCE MANAGER—Copy Master
Add Descriptive Details p. 62

Assess and Reteach

Assess

 RESOURCE MANAGER—Copy Masters
Selection Test A pp. 65–66
Selection Test B/C pp. 67–68

💿 Test Generator CD

Reteach

📄 STANDARDS LESSON FILE
Literature Lesson 6: Conflict and Suspense
Literature Lesson 9: Setting and Its Roles
Vocabulary Lesson 17: Denotation and Connotation

OBJECTIVES

Literary Analysis
- explore the key idea of **parent-child conflicts**
- analyze plot and character
- read a short story

Reading
- make inferences about characters

Vocabulary
- build vocabulary for reading and writing
- use the prefix *in-* to help unlock meaning *(also an EL language objective)*

Grammar and Writing
- use precise modifiers to describe a scene
- use writing to analyze literature

SUMMARY

The narrator, a recent immigrant from the Dominican Republic, is chosen to write a speech for school. After finding inspiration in the lines of a famous poem, she shares her draft with her parents. The girl's father finds the speech disrespectful to teachers and tears it up. The narrator's mother writes an alternate speech that the daughter finds bland but that pleases the teachers—and her father.

What is a GENERATION GAP?

Direct students to the question. Together, discuss differences between students' generation and the ones that preceded it. To lead into the *KEY IDEA,* ask students how a generation gap contributes to **parent-child conflicts.** Continue the exploration by having students complete and discuss the *ROLE-PLAY.*

Daughter of Invention
Short Story by Julia Alvarez

What is a GENERATION GAP?

KEY IDEA What causes **parent-child conflicts?** Is it inevitable that parents and teenagers disagree? In "Daughter of Invention," a father and his teenage daughter confront this issue head-on.

ROLE-PLAY With a small group of classmates, develop a list of subjects that may trigger disagreements between parents and teenagers. With a partner, role-play a dialogue between a parent and a teenager on one of these subjects. Then switch roles and have the conversation again. What insights do you gain?

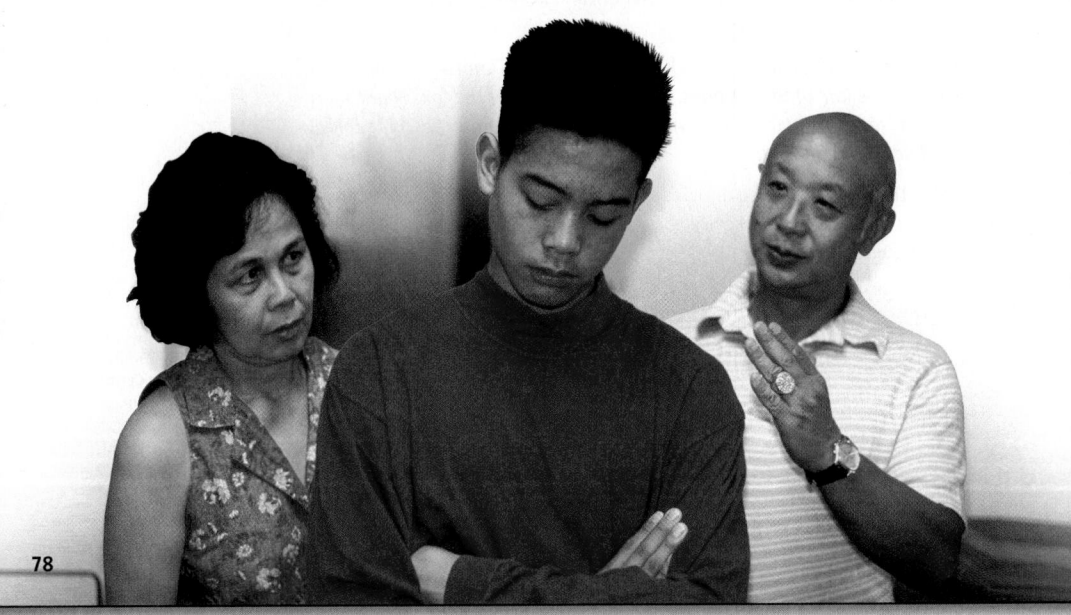

78

R **RESOURCE MANAGER UNIT 1**

Plan and Teach pp. 69–76

Literary Analysis
Summary pp. 77†*, 78‡
Plot and Character pp. 79, 80†*
Question Support p. 87*

Reading
Make Inferences pp. 81, 82†*
Reading Check p. 86

Vocabulary
Study p. 83*
Practice p. 84
Strategy p. 85

Grammar and Writing
Set the Scene p. 89

Assessment
Selection Tests A, B/C pp. 91*, 93*
 Test Generator CD

BEST PRACTICES TOOLKIT

Differentiated Instruction
pp. 31–38*

Scaffolding Instruction
pp. 43–46*

Graphic Organizers/Strategies
Making Inferences • Word Questioning • Two-Column Chart • Sequence Chain • Word Squares

Technology
ⓘ Literature and Vocabulary Centers at **ClassZone.com**
⊘ Write*Smart* CD

---

* Resources for Differentiation   † Also in Spanish   ‡ In Haitian Creole and Vietnamese

LITERARY ANALYSIS: PLOT AND CHARACTER

The plot of a story is shaped by the problems, or **conflicts,** that the main character faces. As the main character responds to the conflict—by making decisions, taking actions, and interacting with other characters—the plot moves forward and engages the reader.

The poet's words shocked and thrilled me.... That night, at last, I started to write, recklessly, three, five pages, looking up only once....

As you read "Daughter of Invention," notice how the narrator's actions and interactions influence the plot.

READING SKILL: MAKE INFERENCES

Often a writer will not tell you everything that is going on in a character's mind. Instead, you may need to **make inferences,** or logical guesses, about what the character thinks and feels. To do this, you need to combine story details with what you know from your own experiences.

As you read, look for clues to how the narrator and her parents feel about living in the United States. For each character, use a chart like the one shown to record your observations and inferences.

Mother		
Details	My Own Experience	Inference
• She begins inventing in the U.S.	New surroundings could lead to a fresh perspective.	
•		
•		

Review: Clarify

▲ VOCABULARY IN CONTEXT

The following words all have negative connotations. Try writing definitions for as many of these words as you can.

1. disclaimer
2. inhospitable
3. insubordinate
4. misnomer
5. noncommittal
6. plagiarized

Immigrant Experience Like the narrator in "Daughter of Invention," Julia Alvarez emigrated with her family from the Dominican Republic to the United States. As a ten-year-old in New York City, she felt out of place and was sometimes subjected to name-calling. It was at this

Julia Alvarez born 1950

time that Alvarez began to write, finding comfort in recording memories of her old life in the Dominican Republic. "I found myself turning more and more to writing as the one place where I felt I belonged," Alvarez has said.

Literary Success Alvarez has won many awards for her writing, which includes novels and poetry as well as short stories. Her fiction often centers on the grim political history of the Dominican Republic, as well as the experiences of Hispanic immigrants in New York City. Her poetry and short stories have appeared in numerous magazines and anthologies.

> **MORE ABOUT THE AUTHOR**
> For more on Julia Alvarez, visit the **Literature Center** at ClassZone.com.

Background

The Dominican Republic Under Trujillo In 1960, Alvarez's family fled the Dominican Republic after the discovery of her father's involvement in a plot to overthrow Rafael Trujillo (rä-fä-ĕl′ trōō-hē′ō). Trujillo, a brutal dictator, ruled the Dominican Republic from 1930 to 1961, staying in power by suppressing all political opposition. Those who criticized him simply "disappeared"—often after the black Volkswagens of the SIM, Trujillo's secret police, drove up to their homes.

Teach

STANDARDS FOCUS

LITERARY ANALYSIS

● PLOT AND CHARACTER

For instructional support, read aloud this example:

> Carl works all weekend, trying to prove to his doubting parents that he can follow through on something he starts.

Ask students what action the main character in this example takes in response to his conflict. *Possible answer: Carl responds to his conflict with his parents by working hard to disprove their doubts.*

CHECK UNDERSTANDING Ask students to predict what actions Carl's parents might take in response to his efforts to prove himself.

READING SKILL

■ MAKE INFERENCES

Use the text under *Background* to model how to make inferences.

- I know from my own experience that people in the United States can express political views without "disappearing."
- I can infer that the author's family fled the Dominican Republic because they were afraid the father might "disappear."

CHECK UNDERSTANDING Ask students to infer what really happened to those who "disappeared."

> **RESOURCE MANAGER—Copy Master**
> Make Inferences p. 81 (for student use while reading the selection)

VOCABULARY SKILL

▲ VOCABULARY IN CONTEXT

DIAGNOSE WORD KNOWLEDGE To determine preteaching needs, have all students complete Vocabulary in Context. *Possible answers:* **1.** *excuse that removes responsibility for a statement or action,* **2.** *unfriendly,* **3.** *disobedient,* **4.** *an incorrect name,* **5.** *not willing to take a side,* **6.** *copied*

PRETEACH VOCABULARY Use the Vocabulary Study copy master to help students determine the meaning of each boldfaced word, using context clues.

1. Read the first item aloud, emphasizing *disclaimer.*
2. Point out the word *denied* in the first sentence and the phrase "is not responsible" in the second sentence. Discuss possible meanings for *disclaimer,* such as "denial."
3. Repeat the procedure for items b–f.

> **RESOURCE MANAGER—Copy Master**
> Vocabulary Study p. 83

For general guidelines on differentiating vocabulary instruction and for alternative vocabulary activities for students not needing vocabulary preteaching, see

> **BEST PRACTICES TOOLKIT**
> Scaffolding Vocabulary Instruction pp. 43–46
> **ⓘ** Vocabulary Center at **ClassZone.com**

ANALYZE VISUALS

Possible answer: The woman's facial expression and posture reflect her absorption in the book and suggest her intellectual curiosity.

About the Art In this painting, French Fauve artist Henri Charles Manguin (1874–1949) uses color to present the subject as the focal point of the portrait. The dark shades of paint on the wall and table contrast with the lighter tints of the woman's shawl to create an intimate and cozy world where she sits calmly reading. Similarly, the mother in the story absorbs herself in solitary and creative activity.

Ⓐ MAKE INFERENCES

Possible answer: Story details suggest that the mother is at home attending to the house and children during the day, while the father goes to work, doing what "was for men to do." Therefore, when it is night-time, and she finally has time for herself, the mother wants to engage her mind and creative talents.

If students need help . . . Have them reread the first and last sentences of paragraph 2. Ask them why the mother might wait to invent until after "settling her house down."

Daughter of Invention

JULIA ALVAREZ

She wanted to invent something, my mother. There was a period after we arrived in this country, until five or so years later, when my mother was inventing. They were never pressing, global needs she was addressing with her pencil and pad. She would have said that was for men to do, rockets and engines that ran on gasoline and turned the wheels of the world. She was just fussing with little house things, don't mind her.

She always invented at night, after settling her house down. On his side of the bed my father would be conked out for an hour already, his Spanish newspaper draped over his chest, his glasses, propped up on his bedside table,
10 looking out eerily at the darkened room like a disembodied guard. But in her lighted corner, like some devoted scholar burning the midnight oil, my mother was inventing, sheets pulled to her lap, pillows propped up behind her, her reading glasses riding the bridge of her nose like a schoolmarm's. On her lap lay one of those innumerable pads of paper my father always brought home from his office, compliments of some pharmaceutical company, advertising tranquilizers or antibiotics or skin cream; in her other hand, my mother held a pencil that looked like a pen with a little cylinder of lead inside. She would work on a sketch of something familiar, but drawn at such close range so she could attach a special nozzle or handier handle, the thing looked peculiar.
20 Once, I mistook the spiral of a corkscrew for a nautilus shell, but it could just as well have been a galaxy forming. Ⓐ

ANALYZE VISUALS
Examine the portrait. What details help you **draw conclusions** about the woman's personality?

❶ Targeted Passage

Ⓐ MAKE INFERENCES
Why might the mother spend her evenings sketching inventions?

Reader with Green Hat (1909), Henri Charles Manguin. Musée d'Art Moderne de la Ville de Paris, Paris. © Giraudon/Art Resource, New York/2007 Artists Rights Society (ARS), New York/ADAGP, Paris.

80 UNIT 1: NARRATIVE STRUCTURE

DIFFERENTIATED INSTRUCTION

FOR ALL STUDENTS

Expert Groups Allow students to become experts or members of expert groups by researching and choosing a way to share information about one of these topics:

- life in the Dominican Republic under Rafael Trujillo and just afterward
- the patent process
- women inventors

FOR LESS–PROFICIENT READERS

Use one or more Targeted Passages (pp. 80, 82, 85, 87, 90) to ensure that students focus on key story events, concepts, and skills. Targeted Passages are also good for English learners.

❶ Targeted Passage [Lines 1–7]

This passage provides significant information about the mother in the story and her drive to invent.

BACKGROUND

Family Structure In 1960, Dominican Republic society held strong expectations for women to stay at home and for men to work, typically in the fields or in construction. Starting in the 1960s in the United States, however, the role of women began to change and expand, a change that has profound effects on the family described in "Daughter of Invention."

Cultural Connection Historically, fixed division of labor between men and women was found in other agrarian societies, including Ireland, Mexico, and China. Have students discuss division of labor in contemporary society.

- Who is the narrator in relation to the mother?
- What do you learn about the mother?
- What connection can you make between this passage and the title of the story?

FOR ENGLISH LEARNERS

Options for Reading Have students read pages 80–88 together. Then have them write four questions related to the reading. Students can discuss the answers with a partner. Finally, have students read the rest of the story together.

Prereading For prereading instruction for English learners, see

 BEST PRACTICES TOOLKIT
Scaffolding Reading Instruction pp. 43–46

FOR ADVANCED LEARNERS/PRE–AP

Pre-AP Exercises in the bottom channel provide additional challenge for students. Use these suggestions for small groups or individuals.

ADDITIONAL GUIDELINES

For more help with differentiation and tips for classroom management, see

 BEST PRACTICES TOOLKIT
Differentiated Instruction pp. 31–38

It was the only time all day we'd catch her sitting down, for she herself was living proof of the *perpetuum mobile*[1] machine so many inventors had sought over the ages. My sisters and I would seek her out now when she seemed to have a moment to talk to us: We were having trouble at school or we wanted her to persuade my father to give us permission to go into the city or to a shopping mall or a movie—in broad daylight! My mother would wave us out of her room. "The problem with you girls . . ." I can tell you right now what the problem always boiled down to: We wanted to become Americans and my

30 father—and my mother, at first—would have none of it.

"You girls are going to drive me crazy!" She always threatened if we kept nagging. "When I end up in Bellevue,[2] you'll be safely sorry!"

She spoke in English when she argued with us, even though, in a matter of months, her daughters were the fluent ones. Her English was much better than my father's, but it was still a mishmash of mixed-up idioms and sayings that showed she was "green behind the ears," as she called it.

If my sisters and I tried to get her to talk in Spanish, she'd snap, "When in Rome, do unto the Romans . . ."

I had become the spokesman for my sisters, and I would stand my ground

40 in that bedroom. "We're not going to that school anymore, Mami!"

"You have to." Her eyes would widen with worry. "In this country, it is against the law not to go to school. You want us to get thrown out?"

"You want us to get killed? Those kids were throwing stones today!"

"Sticks and stones don't break bones . . ." she chanted. I could tell, though, by the look on her face, it was as if one of those stones the kids had aimed at us had hit her. But she always pretended we were at fault. "What did you do to provoke them? It takes two to tangle, you know."

"Thanks, thanks a lot, Mom!" I'd storm out of that room and into mine. I never called her *Mom* except when I wanted her to feel how much she had

50 failed us in this country. She was a good enough Mami, fussing and scolding and giving advice, but a terrible girlfriend parent, a real failure of a Mom. **B**

Back she'd go to her pencil and pad, scribbling and tsking and tearing off paper, finally giving up, and taking up her *New York Times*. Some nights, though, she'd get a good idea, and she'd rush into my room, a flushed look on her face, her tablet of paper in her hand, a cursory knock on the door she'd just thrown open: "Do I have something to show you, Cukita!"

This was my time to myself, after I'd finished my homework, while my sisters were still downstairs watching TV in the basement. Hunched over my small desk, the overhead light turned off, my lamp shining poignantly on

60 my paper, the rest of the room in warm, soft, uncreated darkness, I wrote my secret poems in my new language. **C**

---

1. *perpetuum mobile* (pĕr-pĕt'ōō-əm mō'bĭ-lĕ) *Latin:* perpetual motion (operating continuously without a sustained input of energy).

2. **Bellevue** (bĕl'vyōō'): a large hospital in New York City, with a well-known psychiatric ward.

---

2 Targeted Passage

B PLOT AND CHARACTER
Why was the narrator disappointed in her mother?

C GRAMMAR AND STYLE
Reread lines 57–61. Alvarez uses **modifiers** such as *poignantly, warm, soft,* and *secret* to convey the special atmosphere that surrounds the narrator as she writes.

LITERARY ANALYSIS

B PLOT AND CHARACTER

Possible answer: The narrator feels that her mother is not living up to her image of an American mom. The narrator feels that such a mother would be sympathetic to her daughters' concerns and try to solve them.

If students need help . . . Read aloud lines 48–51, beginning with the words "Thanks, thanks a lot, Mom!" Help students use a Two-Column Chart to show the narrator's two perceptions of her mother—one as a Mami and one as a Mom.

 BEST PRACTICES TOOLKIT—Transparency Two-Column Chart p. A25

C GRAMMAR AND STYLE

Analyze the Use of Modifiers Good writers use modifiers, which include adjectives and adverbs, to make their writing more descriptive and therefore more interesting. To highlight the impact of the modifiers used by the author in lines 57–61, invite a volunteer to read aloud the passage, omitting the adjectives and adverb. Then discuss the difference in the passage with and without modifiers. Have students look for other modifiers in the selection and notice how they add to the descriptions of characters, settings, and events.

DIFFERENTIATED INSTRUCTION

FOR LESS–PROFICIENT READERS
2 Targeted Passage [Lines 39–51]
This passage sets up the conflict between the daughters and their mother.

- What problem do the children face at school?

- How do you think the mother's reaction to the problem makes the narrator feel? What clues in the passage help you know this?

FOR ENGLISH LEARNERS
Reading: Background Explain that in the United States, inventors can register their ideas with the Patent Office to prevent someone from stealing them.

"You're going to ruin your eyes!" My mother would storm into my room, turning on the overly bright overhead light, scaring off whatever shy passion I had just begun coaxing out of a labyrinth of feelings with the blue thread of my writing.

"Oh Mami!" I'd cry out, my eyes blinking up at her. "I'm writing."

"Ay, Cukita." That was her communal pet name for whoever was in her favor. "Cukita, when I make a million, I'll buy you your very own typewriter." (I'd been nagging my mother for one just like the one father had bought her
70 to do his order forms at home.) "Gravy on the turkey" was what she called it when someone was buttering her up. She'd butter and pour. "I'll hire you your very own typist."

Down she'd plop on my bed and hold out her pad to me. "Take a guess, Cukita?" I'd study her rough sketch a moment: soap sprayed from the nozzle head of a shower when you turned the knob a certain way? Coffee with creamer already mixed in? Time-released water capsules for your plants when you were away? A key chain with a timer that would go off when your parking meter was about to expire? (The ticking would help you find your keys easily if you mislaid them.) The famous one, famous only in hindsight, was the stick
80 person dragging a square by a rope—a suitcase with wheels? "Oh, of course," we'd humor her. "What every household needs: a shower like a car wash, keys ticking like a bomb, luggage on a leash!" By now, as you can see, it'd become something of a family joke, our Thomas Edison Mami, our Benjamin Franklin Mom.[3]

Her face would fall. "Come on now! Use your head." One more wrong guess, and she'd tell me, pressing with her pencil point the different highlights of this incredible new wonder. "Remember that time we took the car to Bear Mountain,[4] and we re-ah-lized that we had forgotten to pack an opener with our pick-a-nick?" (We kept correcting her, but she insisted this is how
90 it should be said.) "When we were ready to eat we didn't have any way to open the refreshments cans?" (This before fliptop lids, which she claimed had crossed her mind.) "You know what this is now?" A shake of my head. "Is a car bumper, but see this part is a removable can opener. So simple and yet so necessary, no?"

"Yeah, Mami. You should patent it." I'd shrug. She'd tear off the scratch paper and fold it, carefully, corner to corner, as if she were going to save it. But then, she'd toss it in the wastebasket on her way out of the room and give a little laugh like a **disclaimer**. "It's half of one or two dozen of another . . ."

I suppose none of her daughters was very encouraging. We resented her
100 spending time on those dumb inventions. Here, we were trying to fit in America among Americans; we needed help figuring out who we were, why these Irish kids whose grandparents were micks two generations ago, why they

disclaimer
(dĭs-klā′mər) n. a denial of responsibility or knowledge

---

3. **Thomas Edison Mami ... Benjamin Franklin Mom:** Edison and Franklin were celebrated inventors.
4. **Bear Mountain:** a state park not far from New York City.

Lines 73–94
DISCUSSION PROMPTS

Use these prompts to help students understand the irony of the mother's inventive ideas:

Connect Which of the mother's inventive ideas have you seen either in person or in an advertisement? *Students should cite evidence from their lives (lines 74–80, 87–94).*

Analyze What is the narrator's intent in comparing her mother to Thomas Edison and Benjamin Franklin? Cite evidence. *Possible answer: Her mother is so passionate about her ideas for inventions that the family jokingly compares her to two historically significant inventors (lines 82–84).*

Synthesize What is ironic about the way the narrator perceives her mother's ideas for inventions and the destinies of those same concepts? *Possible answer: Many of the invention ideas the mother conceived and later disregarded were eventually patented and produced by other people. Many of these products are sold today.*

Lines 99–107
REINFORCE *KEY IDEA:* PARENT-CHILD CONFLICTS

Discuss How does limited understanding of a situation or of another's perspective contribute to the **parent-child conflicts** in this story? *The daughters have no understanding of their mother's need to invent (lines 99–100); the mother doesn't have enough understanding of American culture to know how to help her daughters fit in (lines 104–107).*

FOR LESS-PROFICIENT READERS

Comprehension Support Direct students to lines 99–103. Point out how this passage gives insight into the conflicts between the daughters and their mother. The daughters are upset that the mother devotes so much attention and time to her inventions. They feel she should be helping them figure out how to fit in.

D MAKE INFERENCES

Possible answer: Although Papi is successful in America, he continues to struggle with memories of his terrifying past. He dreams about it (line 118) and secretly fears the Dominican authorities will come after him and his family (line 120).

If students need help . . . Have students list the story details in lines 112–116 that tell about life in the Dominican Republic.

Lines 110–120
ADDITIONAL TEACHING OPPORTUNITY

Flashback Recall that a flashback is usually an account of a conversation, an episode, or an event that happened before the beginning of the story, one that often shows how past events led up to the present situation. How does this flashback about Papi's experiences in the Dominican Republic help you understand his behavior in this scene?

Lines 108–143
DISCUSSION PROMPTS

Use these prompts to help students understand the narrator's mother:

Connect How do you feel about the mother? Explain. *Accept all reasonable responses.*

Analyze What are the mother's personality traits? Cite evidence. *Possible answers: The way she calls out at night while her husband is sleeping shows that she is lively and emotional (line 110). She is creative and invents things (lines 125–127). She is a hard worker (lines 140–143).*

Evaluate How does the author bring the mother's personality to life? *Possible answer: The author effectively shows that the mother is excitable through her lively language with all of its mixed-up American sayings (lines 125–132, 136–137).*

were calling us spics.[5] Why had we come to the country in the first place? Important, crucial, final things, you see, and here was our own mother, who didn't have a second to help us puzzle any of this out, inventing gadgets to make life easier for American moms. Why, it seemed as if she were arming our own enemy against us!

One time, she did have a moment of triumph. Every night, she liked to read *The New York Times* in bed before turning off her light, to see what the
110 Americans were up to. One night, she let out a yelp to wake up my father beside her, bolt upright, reaching for his glasses which, in his haste, he knocked across the room. "*Que pasa? Que pasa?*" What is wrong? There was terror in his voice, fear she'd seen in his eyes in the Dominican Republic before we left. We were being watched there; he was being followed; he and mother had often exchanged those looks. They could not talk, of course, though they must have whispered to each other in fear at night in the dark bed. Now in America, he was safe, a success even; his Centro Medico[6] in Brooklyn was thronged with the sick and the homesick. But in dreams, he went back to those awful days and long nights, and my mother's screams confirmed his secret fear: we had
120 not gotten away after all; they had come for us at last. **D**

"Ay, Papi, I'm sorry. Go back to sleep, Cukito. It's nothing, nothing really." My mother held up the *Times* for him to squint at the small print, back page headline, one hand tapping all over the top of the bedside table for his glasses, the other rubbing his eyes to wakefulness.

"Remember, remember how I showed you that suitcase with little wheels so we would not have to carry those heavy bags when we traveled? Someone stole my idea and made a million!" She shook the paper in his face. She shook the paper in all our faces that night. "See! See! This man was no *bobo!* He didn't put all his pokers on a back burner. I kept telling you, one of these days
130 my ship would pass me by in the night!" She wagged her finger at my sisters and my father and me, laughing all the while, one of those eerie laughs crazy people in movies laugh. We had congregated in her room to hear the good news she'd been yelling down the stairs, and now we eyed her and each other. I suppose we were all thinking the same thing: Wouldn't it be weird and sad if Mami did end up in Bellevue as she'd always threatened she might?

"*Ya, ya!* Enough!" She waved us out of her room at last. "There is no use trying to drink spilt milk, that's for sure."

It was the suitcase rollers that stopped my mother's hand; she had weather vaned a minor brainstorm. She would have to start taking herself seriously.
140 That blocked the free play of her ingenuity. Besides, she had also begun working at my father's office, and at night, she was too tired and busy filling in columns with how much money they had made that day to be fooling with gadgets!

D MAKE INFERENCES
What **internal conflict** does the narrator's father struggle with? Use details to support your answer.

---

5. **micks . . . spics:** derogatory terms for people of Irish descent and people of Hispanic descent, respectively.

6. **Centro Medico** (sĕn′trô mĕ′dē-kô): medical center.

DIFFERENTIATED INSTRUCTION

FOR ENGLISH LEARNERS

Key Academic Vocabulary Use Word Questioning to teach these words: *crucial* (line 104), *assembly* (line 149), *relax* (line 189), *appropriate* (line 210), *draft* (line 216), *required* (line 230).

🧰 BEST PRACTICES TOOLKIT—Transparency
Word Questioning p. E9

FOR ADVANCED LEARNERS/PRE–AP

Research Activity Have students research the adjustment process of recent immigrants to the United States, especially those from repressive dictatorships. Ask students to compare the experiences of these families with the experience of the family described in "Daughter of Invention," especially with regard to recent immigration policies, educational opportunities, and how families grapple with redefining traditional roles of authority.

She did take up her pencil and pad one last time to help me out. In ninth grade, I was chosen by my English teacher, Sister Mary Joseph, to deliver the teacher's day address at the school assembly.

③ **Targeted Passage**

150 Back in the Dominican Republic, I was a terrible student. No one could ever get me to sit down to a book. But in New York, I needed to settle somewhere, and the natives were unfriendly, the country **inhospitable,** so I took root in the language. By high school, the nuns were reading my stories and compositions out loud

160 to my classmates as examples of imagination at work.

This time my imagination jammed. At first I didn't want and then I couldn't seem to write that speech. I suppose I should have thought of it as a "great honor," as my father called it. But I was mortified. I still had a pronounced lilt to my accent, and I did not like

170 to speak in public, subjecting myself to my classmates' ridicule. Recently, they had begun to warm toward my sisters and me, and it took no great figuring to see that to deliver a eulogy for a convent full of crazy, old overweight nuns was no way to endear myself to the members of my class.

But I didn't know how to get out of it. Week after week, I'd sit down, hoping to polish off some quick, **noncommittal** little speech. I couldn't get

180 anything down.

The weekend before our Monday morning assembly I went into a panic. My mother would just have to call in and say I was in the hospital, in a coma. I was in the Dominican Republic. Yeah, that was it! Recently, my father had been talking about going back home to live.

La Mère de l'artiste ["The artist's mother"] (1889), Paul Gauguin. Oil on canvas. Staatsgalerie, Stuttgart. © Staatsgalerie, Stuttgart. Photo © akg-images, London

inhospitable
(ĭn-hŏs′pĭ-tə-bəl) *adj.* not welcoming; hostile

noncommittal
(nŏn′kə-mĭt′l) *adj.* not committing oneself; not revealing what one thinks

E CLARIFY

Help students understand the meaning of the quotation "Necessity is the mother of invention." Discuss why the author may have chosen to have the mother misquote this saying when she states, "Necessity is the daughter of invention." **Possible answer:** *Throughout the story, the mother mixes up familiar phrases, a behavior the daughters might find endearingly humorous. Because the mother has many ideas for inventing gadgets that are "necessities," it makes sense that the narrator is thought of as a daughter of invention.*

LITERARY ANALYSIS

F PLOT AND CHARACTER

Possible answer: The quotation from Whitman shows that the poet "sings" about himself. In other words, he writes about himself in his own words. He learns to "destroy the teacher"; that is, he does not look to others to find out what he should say. Whitman seems more real to the narrator than other poets she has read.

My mother tried to calm me down. "Just remember how Mister Lincoln couldn't think of anything to say at the Gettysburg, but then, Bang! 'Four score and once upon a time ago,'"[7] she began reciting. Her version of history was half invention and half truths and whatever else she needed to prove a point. "Something is going to come if you just relax. You'll see, like the Americans
190 say, 'Necessity is the daughter of invention.' I'll help you." **E**

All weekend, she kept coming into my room with help. "Please, Mami, just leave me alone, please," I pleaded with her. But I'd get rid of the goose only to have to contend with the gander. My father kept poking his head in the door just to see if I had "fulfilled my obligations," a phrase he'd used when we were a little younger, and he'd check to see whether we had gone to the bathroom before a car trip. Several times that weekend around the supper table, he'd recite his valedictorian speech from when he graduated from high school. He'd give me pointers on delivery, on the great orators and their tricks. (Humbleness and praise and falling silent with great emotion were his favorites.)
200 My mother sat across the table, the only one who seemed to be listening to him. My sisters and I were forgetting a lot of our Spanish, and my father's formal, florid diction was even harder to understand. But my mother smiled softly to herself, and turned the Lazy Susan at the center of the table around and around as if it were the prime mover, the first gear of attention.

That Sunday evening, I was reading some poetry to get myself inspired: Whitman in an old book with an engraved cover my father had picked up in a thrift shop next to his office a few weeks back. "I celebrate myself and sing myself . . ." "He most honors my style who learns under it to destroy the teacher."[8] The poet's words shocked and thrilled me. I had gotten used to the
210 nuns, a literature of appropriate sentiments, poems with a message, expurgated texts. But here was a flesh and blood man, belching and laughing and sweating in poems. "Who touches this book touches a man."

That night, at last, I started to write, recklessly, three, five pages, looking up once only to see my father passing by the hall on tiptoe. When I was done, I read over my words, and my eyes filled. I finally sounded like myself in English! **F**

As soon as I had finished that first draft, I called my mother to my room. She listened attentively, as she had to my father's speech, and in the end, her eyes were glistening too. Her face was soft and warm and proud. "That is a beautiful, beautiful speech, Cukita. I want for your father to hear it before he
220 goes to sleep. Then I will type it for you, all right?"

Down the hall we went, the two of us, faces flushed with accomplishment. Into the master bedroom where my father was propped up on his pillows, still awake, reading the Dominican papers, already days old. He had become interested in his country's fate again. The dictatorship had been toppled. The

E CLARIFY
Reread lines 185–190. The correct proverb is "Necessity is the mother of invention." Note that the title of the story is taken from the mother's misquotation.

F PLOT AND CHARACTER
Why do you think the experience of reading Whitman finally freed the narrator to write her speech?

---

7. **"Four score and once upon a time ago"**: Mami is misquoting President Abraham Lincoln's Gettysburg Address, which begins "Four score and seven years ago,..."

8. **"I celebrate . . . destroy the teacher"**: lines from the long poem "Song of Myself," by the American poet Walt Whitman (1819–1892).

DIFFERENTIATED INSTRUCTION

FOR ENGLISH LEARNERS

Vocabulary: Idioms and Sayings Explain that throughout this story, Mami misuses or misstates common English sayings. For each example, introduce the correct form or saying, and explain its meaning.

Examples:

- *Green behind the ears* (line 36), combines "green" and "wet behind the ears." Meaning: new at something; a novice

- *When in Rome, do unto the Romans* (lines 37–38), combines "When in Rome, do as the Romans do" and "Do unto others as you would have others do unto you." Meaning: adjust your behavior to match the place where you are.

- *It takes two to tangle* (line 47), original saying: "It takes two to tango." Meaning: it takes two to create an argument.

- *It's half of one or two dozen of another* (line 98), original saying: "Six of one, half

a dozen of the other." Meaning: it doesn't matter which choice you make, both are equal.

- *Necessity is the daughter of invention* (line 190), original saying: "Necessity is the mother of invention." Meaning: our needs cause us to invent devices.

interim government was going to hold the first free elections in thirty years. There was still some question in his mind whether or not we might want to move back. History was in the making, freedom and hope were in the air again! But my mother had gotten used to the life here. She did not want to go back to the old country where she was only a wife and a mother (and a failed one at that, since she had never had the required son). She did not come straight out and disagree with my father's plans. Instead, she fussed with him about reading the papers in bed, soiling those sheets with those poorly printed, foreign tabloids. "*The Times* is not that bad!" she'd claim if my father tried to humor her by saying they shared the same dirty habit. **G**

The minute my father saw my mother and me, filing in, he put his paper down, and his face brightened as if at long last his wife had delivered a son, and that was the news we were bringing him. His teeth were already grinning from the glass of water next to his bedside lamp, so he lisped when he said, "Eh-speech, eh-speech!"

"It is so beautiful, Papi," my mother previewed him, turning the sound off on his TV. She sat down at the foot of the bed. I stood before both of them, blocking their view of the soldiers in helicopters landing amid silenced gun reports and explosions. A few weeks ago it had been the shores of the Dominican Republic. Now it was the jungles of Southeast Asia they were saving. My mother gave me the nod to begin reading.

> I didn't need much encouragement. I put my nose to the fire, as my mother would have said, and read from start to finish without looking up. When I was done, I was a little embarrassed at my pride in my own words. I pretended to quibble with a phrase or two I was sure I'd be talked out of changing. I looked questioningly to my mother. Her face was radiant. She turned to share her pride with my father.
>
> But the expression on his face shocked us both. His toothless mouth had collapsed into a dark zero. His eyes glared at me, then shifted to my mother, accusingly. In barely audible Spanish, as if secret microphones or informers were all about, he whispered, "You will permit her to read *that?*"

④ Targeted Passage

G MAKE INFERENCES
How has the mother changed since coming to the United States? Cite evidence.

Pedro Mañach (1901), Pablo Picasso. Oil on linen, 41¹/₂″ × 27″; framed: 53″ × 38⁷/₈″ × 4″. National Gallery of Art, Washington, D.C., Chester Dale Collection. © 2004 Board of Trustees of the National Gallery of Art/2007 Estate of Pablo Picasso/Artists Rights Society (ARS), New York (1963.10.53).

Lines 265–268

REINFORCE *KEY IDEA:* PARENT-CHILD CONFLICTS

Discuss What aspect of the parents' history widens the generation gap in the story and contributes to the family's conflicts? *Possible answer:* The narrator's parents lived most of their lives in a country where questioning authority was frowned upon and where inter-actions between parent and child were more formal than in the United States. These cultural values are what the parents are used to and what adds to the gap between them and their children.

READING SKILL

Ⓗ MAKE INFERENCES

Possible answer: One emotion is fear, stemming from the father's anxiety about the Dominican Republic authorities' cruelty. He also wants to teach his daughter the value of being respectful in her new country. He may even be worried that his own authority is being threatened by a house full of independent women.

If students need help . . . Have students reread lines 286–288, beginning with "By now, my father . . . ." A Making Inferences chart or a chart like this will help them answer the question:

Details: What I Know from Reading		
The Story	My Experience	My Inference
mother joining forces with daughters	father feeling out-numbered	conflict building between females in family and father

🧰 **BEST PRACTICES TOOLKIT—Transparency**
Making Inferences p. A13

My mother's eyebrows shot up, her mouth fell open. In the old country, any whisper of a challenge to authority could bring the secret police in their black V.W.'s. But this was America. People could say what they thought. "What is wrong with her speech?" my mother questioned him.

"What ees wrrrong with her eh-speech?" My father wagged his head at
270 her. His anger was always more frightening in his broken English. As if he had mutilated the language in his fury—and now there was nothing to stand between us and his raw, dumb anger. "What is wrong? I will tell you what is wrong. It shows no gratitude. It is boastful. 'I celebrate myself'? 'The best student learns to destroy the teacher'?" He mocked my **plagiarized** words. "That is **insubordinate.** It is improper. It is disrespecting of her teachers—" In his anger he had forgotten his fear of lurking spies: Each wrong he voiced was a decibel higher than the last outrage. Finally, he was yelling at me, "As your father, I forbid you to say that eh-speech!"

My mother leapt to her feet, a sign always that she was about to make a
280 speech or deliver an ultimatum. She was a small woman, and she spoke all her pronouncements standing up, either for more protection or as a carry-over from her girlhood in convent schools where one asked for, and literally took, the floor in order to speak. She stood by my side, shoulder to shoulder; we looked down at my father. "That is no tone of voice, Eduardo—" she began.

By now, my father was truly furious. I suppose it was bad enough I was rebelling, but here was my mother joining forces with me. Soon he would be surrounded by a house full of independent American women. He too leapt from his bed, throwing off his covers. The Spanish newspapers flew across the
290 room. He snatched my speech out of my hands, held it before my panicked eyes, a vengeful, mad look in his own, and then once, twice, three, four, countless times, he tore my prize into shreds. Ⓗ

"Are you crazy?" My mother lunged at him. "Have you gone mad? That is her speech for tomorrow you have torn up!"

"Have *you* gone mad?" He shook her away. "You were going to let her read that . . . that insult to her teachers?"

"Insult to her teachers!" My mother's face had crumpled up like a piece of paper. On it was written a love note to my father. Ever since they had come to this country, their life together was a constant war. "This is America, Papi,
300 America!" she reminded him now. "You are not in a savage country any more!"

I was on my knees, weeping wildly, collecting all the little pieces of my speech, hoping that I could put it back together before the assembly tomorrow morning. But not even a sibyl[9] could have made sense of all those scattered pieces of paper. All hope was lost. "He broke it, he broke it," I moaned as I picked up a handful of pieces.

---

9. **sibyl** (sĭb′əl): a female prophet. (According to the Roman poet Virgil, the sibyl of Cumae recorded the words of her prophecies on tree leaves, which she arranged on the floor of her cave. If the wind scattered the leaves, the prophecies became unintelligible.)

88 UNIT 1: NARRATIVE STRUCTURE

plagiarized
(plā′jə-rīzd′) *adj.* copied from someone else's writings **plagiarize** *v.*

insubordinate
(ĭn′sə-bôr′dn-ĭt)
adj. disobedient to a superior

Ⓗ **MAKE INFERENCES**
Reread lines 269–292. What emotions besides anger might be behind the father's action?

DIFFERENTIATED INSTRUCTION

FOR ADVANCED LEARNERS/PRE–AP
External or Internal Conflict Have students list the various conflicts in the story, identify them as external or internal, and explain the reasoning behind their choices. For example:

- *Mother versus daughters:* The mother says the girls will drive her crazy. (external)

- *Father versus daughter:* He disapproves of the first draft of the narrator's speech. (external)

- *Mother versus Father:* The mother disagrees with Papi's reaction to the narrator's speech. (external)

- *Father's past versus father's present:* Papi is still haunted by his experiences in the Dominican Republic. (internal)

- *Daughter versus father:* She weeps as she gathers up the shreds of her speech. (external)

- *Daughter versus writing speech:* At first she is mortified to write her speech. (internal)

88 UNIT 1: NARRATIVE STRUCTURE

Probably, if I had thought a moment about it, I would not have done what I did next. I would have realized my father had lost brothers and comrades to the dictator Trujillo. For the rest of his life, he would be haunted by blood in the streets and late night disappearances. Even after he had been in the 310 states for years, he jumped if a black Volkswagen passed him on the street. He feared anyone in uniform: the meter maid giving out parking tickets, a museum guard approaching to tell him not to touch his favorite Goya[10] at the Metropolitan.

I took a handful of the scraps I had gathered, stood up, and hurled them in his face. "Chapita!" I said in a low, ugly whisper. "You're just another Chapita!"

It took my father only a moment 320 to register the hated nickname of our dictator, and he was after me. Down the halls we raced, but I was quicker than he and made it to my room just in time to lock the door as my father threw his weight against it. He called down curses on my head, ordered me on his authority as my father to open that door this very instant! He throttled 330 that doorknob, but all to no avail. My mother's love of gadgets saved my hide that night. She had hired a locksmith to install good locks on all the bedroom doors after our house had been broken into while we were away the previous summer. In case burglars broke in again, and we were in the house, they'd have a second round of locks to contend with before they got to us. ❶

"Eduardo," she tried to calm him down. "Don't you ruin my new locks."

He finally did calm down, his anger spent. I heard their footsteps retreating 340 down the hall. I heard their door close, the clicking of their lock. Then, muffled voices, my mother's peaking in anger, in persuasion, my father's deep murmurs of explanation and of self-defense. At last, the house fell silent, before I heard, far off, the gun blasts and explosions, the serious, self-important voices of newscasters reporting their TV war.

A little while later, there was a quiet knock at my door, followed by a tentative attempt at the doorknob. "Cukita?" my mother whispered. "Open up, Cukita."

"Go away," I wailed, but we both knew I was glad she was there, and I needed only a moment's protest to save face before opening that door.

---

10. **Goya** (goiʹə): a painting by the Spanish artist Francisco de Goya y Lucientes (1746–1828).

DAUGHTER OF INVENTION   89

ANALYZE VISUALS
This painting depicts the execution of a group of Spaniards by Napoleon's occupying army. Why do you think a painting like this might appeal to someone like Papi? Explain.

The Third of May, 1808 (1814), Francisco de Goya y Lucientes. Oil on canvas, 266 cm × 345 cm. Museo del Prado, Madrid. Photo © Erich Lessing/Art Resource, New York.

❶ **PLOT AND CHARACTER**
Why does the narrator's father become enraged at her?

ANALYZE VISUALS

Possible answer: Papi would probably relate to the painting's strong depiction of violence and tyranny. Having lived through political terror in the Dominican Republic, Papi may have witnessed such scenes (lines 308–309). His fear of anyone in uniform is so great it carries over to his early years in the United States (lines 311–313).

About the Art Spanish painter Francisco de Goya y Lucientes (1746–1828) depicts the horror of political tyranny in this painting called *The Third of May, 1808*.

LITERARY ANALYSIS

❶ **PLOT AND CHARACTER**

Possible answer: The speech itself threatens the father's view of authority. He doesn't want his daughter to be disrespectful to her teachers, and he feels that her speech does just that (lines 272–275). The fact that his daughter calls him "Chapita" reminds him of his life in the Dominican Republic. There, he fought against a dictator (nicknamed "Chapita") who was cruel and brutal to citizens. Hearing his daughter compare him to the dictator is very hurtful and insulting (lines 316–321).

FOR ENGLISH LEARNERS

Comprehension: Transitions Reread lines 339–347. Point out the signal words that help readers keep track of the sequence of events: *finally, then, at last, later, followed by.* Have students use a Sequence Chain to list these events in the order they occurred, using the signal words.

 BEST PRACTICES TOOLKIT—Transparency
   Sequence Chain p. B21

READING SKILL

J MAKE INFERENCES

Possible answer: The mother helps her daughter with the speech because the narrator is "too upset" to do it herself (line 354). Also, the mother liked her daughter's original speech and didn't agree with her husband's reaction to it. She wants to support her daughter in their new country where people are free to speak openly (lines 299–300) yet respect her husband's wishes at the same time. That's why the speech is made up of "stale compliments and the polite commonplaces on teachers" (lines 351–352).

If students need help . . . Direct students to the phrase in lines 354–355 where the narrator tells why her mother helped write the speech. Ask students if they think their parents would have done the same thing. If not, how do they think their parents would have handled the situation differently?

SELECTION WRAP–UP

REFLECT Ask students to think about the parent-child conflicts in the story and how they are resolved. What does the narrator learn as a result of these conflicts? What do her parents learn?

★ **CRITIQUE** Have students evaluate the story by rating it from 1 (not an accurate portrayal of parent-child conflicts in the United States) to 5 (an accurate portrayal of parent-child conflicts in the United States). Then have students indicate the parts they support or do not support and tell why.

350　What we ended up doing that night was putting together a speech at the last moment. Two brief pages of stale compliments and the polite commonplaces on teachers, wrought by necessity without much invention by mother for daughter late into the night in the basement on the pad of paper and with the same pencil she had once used for her own inventions, for I was too upset to compose the speech myself. After it was drafted, she typed it up while I stood by, correcting her **misnomers** and mis-sayings. **J**

　　She was so very proud of herself when I came home the next day with the success story of the assembly. The nuns had been flattered, the audience had stood up and given "our devoted teachers a standing ovation," what my
360　mother had suggested they do at the end of my speech.

　　She clapped her hands together as I recreated the moment for her. "I stole that from your father's speech, remember? Remember how he put that in at the end?" She quoted him in Spanish, then translated for me into English.

　　That night, I watched him from the upstairs hall window where I'd retreated the minute I heard his car pull up in front of our house. Slowly, my father came up the driveway, a grim expression on his face as he grappled with a large, heavy cardboard box. At the front door, he set the package down carefully and patted all his pockets for his house keys—precisely why my mother had invented her ticking key chain. I heard the snapping open of the
370　locks downstairs. Heard as he struggled to maneuver the box through the narrow doorway. Then, he called my name several times. But I would not answer him.

　　"My daughter, your father, he love you very much," he explained from the bottom of the stairs. "He just want to protect you." Finally, my mother came up and pleaded with me to go down and reconcile with him. "Your father did not mean to harm. You must pardon him. Always it is better to let bygones be forgotten, no?"

　　I guess she was right. Downstairs, I found him setting up a brand new electric typewriter on the kitchen table. It was even better than the one I'd
380　been begging to get like my mother's. My father had outdone himself with all the extra features: a plastic carrying case with my initials, in decals, below the handle, a brace to lift the paper upright while I typed, an erase cartridge, an automatic margin tab, a plastic hood like a toaster cover to keep the dust away. Not even my mother, I think, could have invented such a machine!

　　But her inventing days were over just as mine were starting up with my schoolwide success. That's why I've always thought of that speech my mother wrote for me as her last invention rather than the suitcase rollers everyone else in the family remembers. It was as if she had passed on to me her pencil and pad and said, "Okay, Cukita, here's the buck. You give it a shot." ∿

misnomer
(mĭs-nō′mər) *n.* an inaccurate or incorrect name

J MAKE INFERENCES
Why does the narrator's mother write the speech for her?

5 Targeted Passage

DIFFERENTIATED INSTRUCTION

FOR LESS–PROFICIENT READERS

5 Targeted Passage [Lines 350–384]

This passage depicts the resolution in conflict between the narrator and her parents.

- How does the mother show that she is proud of her daughter? How does the father show his pride?

- How do you think the narrator's view of her parents changes at the end of the story? How do you think this new view will affect the relationship between them?

FOR ENGLISH LEARNERS

Culture: Clarify Call students' attention to the pronouns used by the father in lines 373 and 374. Point out that when he says, "he love you very much" and "He just want to protect you," he means, "I love you very much" and "I just want to protect you."

Comprehension

1. **Recall** How do the daughters respond to their mother's inventions?

2. **Recall** What difficulties do the daughters face in their new country?

3. **Clarify** How does the narrator's father react to his daughter's speech?

4. **Represent** Create a timeline showing key events in the order they occur. Circle the event that represents the **climax** of the story.

Literary Analysis

5. **Make Inferences** Review the inference chart you created for each character. How do the cultural differences between the Dominican Republic and the United States contribute to the **parent-child conflicts** between the narrator and her father? Cite evidence to support your answer.

6. **Plot and Character** What do you learn about the narrator from the way she resolves the conflict with her father? If she had acted differently, how might the conflict have been resolved?

7. **Make Judgments** Does the mother do the right thing by composing a flattering speech for her daughter to give? Explore this question in a chart like the one shown.

Pros	Cons
No one's feelings are hurt.	

8. **Compare and Contrast Characters** Compare the narrator's qualities with her mother's. Are mother and daughter more alike or more different? Support your interpretation with evidence from the story.

9. **Draw Conclusions** Reread lines 385–389. In what ways might the narrator's future be different from her past?

10. **Synthesize** Reread lines 378–384. A **symbol** is a person, place, object, or activity that stands for something beyond itself. What does the typewriter represent in this story?

Literary Criticism

11. **Critical Interpretations** One critic has said that at the end of this story, the reader is left with the impression that the narrator "is living in a new world where even the old obstacles of culture can be overcome." Do you agree with this interpretation? Support your answer.

DAUGHTER OF INVENTION 91

the women do not stand up for what is meaningful to them.

8. *They are more alike. Although the mother invents and the daughter writes, both like a quiet time alone at night (lines 7, 57–58). Both are generally strong and determined, but they accept Papi's will about the speech.*

9. *In the future, the narrator will be writing more. She may be better accepted at school.*

10. *It symbolizes Papi's love for his daughter and his desire to see her succeed. It also symbolizes the narrator's potential as a writer.*

Literary Criticism
Possible answers:

11. **Agree:** *The end of the story points to the narrator's social acceptance and success in writing in the English language. Earlier, she found her own voice in English.*

Disagree: *The narrator will always be influenced by her own memories and by her parents, whose ties to their homeland remain strong.*

After Reading

For additional support of post-reading questions, use these copy masters:

R RESOURCE MANAGER—Copy Masters
Reading Check p. 86 (to check understanding of the selection)
Plot and Character p. 79 (for practice of literary analysis standards focus)
Question Support p. 87 (After Reading questions adapted for English learners and less-proficient readers)

For additional questions, see page 73.

ANSWERS

Comprehension

1. *The girls gently mock or criticize her when discussing the inventions (lines 80–84).*

2. *Other students call the girls names (lines 100–103). Some throw stones (line 43).*

3. *The father is greatly upset and he forbids her to read it (lines 259–264, 275–278). He tears it up into tiny pieces (lines 290–292).*

4. **Possible answer:** *First, narrator is asked to write speech (lines 146–149); next, she finds inspiration (lines 205–214); next, she reads speech to father (lines 250–252); next, father rips up speech (climax) (lines 290–292); next, narrator and mother write a new speech (lines 350–356); next, narrator delivers speech (lines 357–360); last, father apologizes and buys her a typewriter (lines 373–374, 378–379).*

Literary Analysis
Possible answers:

5. ■ **STANDARDS FOCUS** *Make Inferences The mother and father experienced great terror in the Dominican Republic that affects their lives in the United States. In the Dominican Republic, people who questioned authority "disappeared." Papi still "feared anyone in uniform: the meter maid giving out parking tickets" (lines 308–311). He did not want his daughter showing disrespect to her teachers in her speech.*

6. *By calling her father "Chapita," the nickname of the hated dictator, the narrator reveals that she is angry and hurt. Had she tried to reason with her father, he might have understood her better.*

7. **Pros:** *The speech gets done on time and is a success.* **Cons:** *The narrator does not do her own work or express her own thoughts;*

ANSWERS

Vocabulary in Context

VOCABULARY PRACTICE

1. *c*   4. *b*

2. *b*   5. *b*

3. *a*   6. *c*

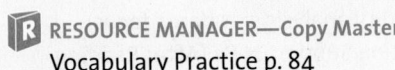 **RESOURCE MANAGER—Copy Master**
Vocabulary Practice p. 84

VOCABULARY IN WRITING

Suggest to students that they put themselves in the narrator's place as they write the speech. Remind them to consider the narrator's family history and the generation gap that often causes conflict between the daughter and her parents.

VOCABULARY STRATEGY: THE LATIN PREFIX *in-* *(also an EL language objective)*

- Model for students how the prefix *in-* changes form depending on the word it precedes.

- Ask students to predict what form the prefix *in-* takes when added to these words: *possible* (im), *mature* (im), *respective* (ir), *legible* (il).

Possible answers:

1. *informal—"not formal, casual"*
   inedible—"not fit to be eaten"

2. *illegible—"not readable"*
   illegal—"not legal"

3. *immobile—"not moveable"*
   improbable—"not likely to occur"

4. *irregular—"not following a usual procedure"*
   irresistible—"impossible to resist"

5. *incapable—"not able"*
   insufferable—"not to be endured or tolerated"

6. *imbalance—"without balance"*
   immature—"lacking maturity or growth"

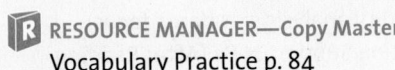 **RESOURCE MANAGER—Copy Master**
Vocabulary Strategy p. 85

ⓘ Vocabulary Center at **ClassZone.com**
Additional Vocabulary Activities

Vocabulary in Context

VOCABULARY PRACTICE

Write the word with a meaning closest to that of each boldfaced vocabulary word.

1. **inhospitable:** (a) inoperable, (b) unnecessary, (c) unwelcoming
2. **misnomer:** (a) mission, (b) misidentification, (c) misspent
3. **plagiarized:** (a) copied, (b) returned, (c) postmarked
4. **disclaimer:** (a) importance, (b) denial, (c) theory
5. **noncommittal:** (a) loyal, (b) cautious, (c) nonsensical
6. **insubordinate:** (a) inaccurate, (b) buried, (c) defiant

WORD LIST
disclaimer
inhospitable
insubordinate
misnomer
noncommittal
plagiarized

VOCABULARY IN WRITING

Write the opening paragraph of a speech that the narrator of this story might give in her school assembly. Use three or more vocabulary words. Here is a sample opening for such a speech.

> **EXAMPLE SENTENCE**
>
> *When I first came to this school, it felt like an **inhospitable** jungle.*

VOCABULARY STRATEGY: THE LATIN PREFIX *in-*

In- at the beginning of a word may be a prefix meaning "not," as in the vocabulary words *inhospitable* and *insubordinate*. If you can identify a root or a base word in words like these, you can easily figure out their meanings. (When the prefix *in-* precedes certain letters, it is spelled *il-, im-,* or *ir-.*)

PRACTICE Use a dictionary to help you find two words in each group that contain a prefix meaning "not." Then write a short definition of each word.

1. informal, internal, inedible
2. illegible, illegal, illness
3. imperial, immobile, improbable
4. irritate, irregular, irresistible
5. intellect, incapable, insufferable
6. imbalance, imagine, immature

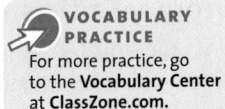 **VOCABULARY PRACTICE**
For more practice, go to the **Vocabulary Center** at **ClassZone.com.**

DIFFERENTIATED INSTRUCTION

FOR ENGLISH LEARNERS

Task Support: Reteach Use Word Squares to reteach the vocabulary words before students begin the Vocabulary in Context activities.

 BEST PRACTICES TOOLKIT—Transparency
Word Squares p. E10

FOR ADVANCED LEARNERS/PRE–AP

Vocabulary in Writing Have students write a closing paragraph of a speech that the narrator of this story might give in her school assembly, using as many vocabulary words as possible. *Example: Although my words may have seemed insubordinate to my father, I indeed have a sincere respect for him and my teachers.*

Reading-Writing Connection

Increase your understanding of "Daughter of Invention" by responding to these prompts. Then use **Revision: Grammar and Style** to improve your writing.

WRITING PROMPTS	SELF-CHECK
A. Short Response: Evaluate Characters Early in the story, the narrator describes her mother as "a real failure of a Mom." Would the narrator evaluate her differently at the end of the story? Write **one or two paragraphs** expressing your opinion.	*A strong response will . . .* • clearly state an opinion • include at least two examples from the text to support the opinion
B. Extended Response: Write a Scene It's a year later, and the narrator has been asked to write another speech for school. Will the **parent-child conflicts** resume? Write **three to five paragraphs** describing the scene.	*A successful scene will . . .* • present events that are logical outcomes of the story • effectively use modifiers

REVISION: GRAMMAR AND STYLE

SET THE SCENE Review the **Grammar and Style** note on page 82. Alvarez has carefully chosen **modifiers** that describe not only the physical details but also the atmosphere of the room.

Modifiers, which include **adjectives** and **adverbs,** are words and phrases that give information about other words. When describing a scene, incorporate modifiers that will paint a vivid picture for your audience. Here is another example of Alvarez's effective use of modifiers to enhance a scene:

> . . . *My father would be conked out for an hour already, his Spanish newspaper draped over his chest, his glasses, propped up on his bedside table, looking out eerily at the darkened room like a disembodied guard. But in her lighted corner, like some devoted scholar burning the midnight oil, my mother was inventing . . .*
> (lines 8–12)

Now study this model. Notice how the revisions in red help to make the images more vivid. Use similar techniques to revise your response to Prompt B.

STUDENT MODEL

As I sat down at the table, I slid my *trembling* fingers over the *black* typewriter keys. What was I going to write? Would my *well-meaning* father insist on reading every word again? I loaded a piece of *smooth, cream-colored* paper into the typewriter and stared *longingly* at its emptiness.

WRITING TOOLS
For prewriting, revision, and editing tools, visit the **Writing Center** at ClassZone.com.

Reading-Writing Connection

WRITING PROMPTS

• For Prompt A, have students list details from the end of the story that support their opinions.

• For Prompt B, distribute a Sequence Chain for use in planning or mapping the scene.

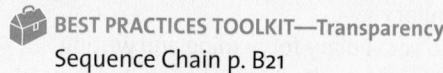 BEST PRACTICES TOOLKIT—Transparency
Sequence Chain p. B21

For writing support, see

ℹ️ Writing Center at **ClassZone.com**

REVISION: GRAMMAR AND STYLE

• After students examine the student model, list the modifiers in red on the board. Point out that the modifier *longingly* is an adverb because it tells about the verb *stared.* Then point out that the modifier *trembling* is an adjective because it describes the noun *fingers.*

• Have students say whether each word listed on the board is used to modify a noun or a verb.

• Have students replace the modifiers in red in the student model with a new set of modifiers. Discuss whether or not the new modifiers changed the feel of the student model.

🄡 RESOURCE MANAGER—Copy Master
Set the Scene p. 89

Assess and Reteach

Assess

🄡 RESOURCE MANAGER—Copy Masters
Selection Test A pp. 91–92
Selection Test B/C pp. 93–94

💿 Test Generator CD

Reteach

🄢 STANDARDS LESSON FILE
Literature Lesson 6: Conflict and Suspense
Reading Lesson 8: Making Inferences
Vocabulary Lesson 2: Prefixes

FOR LESS–PROFICIENT WRITERS

For Prompt A:

• Topic sentence states position.

• Body cites specific evidence.

• Topic sentence relates to or restates the position statement, evidence, explanation of evidence.

For Prompt B:

• Introductory paragraph describes the scene.

• Second paragraph gives examples of parent-child relationship.

• Third paragraph (a) compares old parent-child relationship with new and (b) reaffirms opinion.

Focus and Motivate

OBJECTIVES

Literary Analysis
- explore the key idea of **sacrifice**
- analyze and evaluate irony
- read a short story

Reading
- make predictions about events and ideas

Vocabulary
- build vocabulary for reading and writing
- use the Greek word root *chron* to help unlock meaning (*also an EL language objective*)

Grammar and Writing
- use precise verbs to make effective word choices
- use writing to analyze literature

SUMMARY

"The Gift of the Magi" recounts the sacrifices a young couple make for each other. Each sells a prized possession to buy the other a Christmas gift—but ironically, each sells the very thing that makes the other's gift special. Della sells her beautiful hair to buy a chain for Jim's watch, while Jim sells his beloved watch to buy combs for his wife's hair. When they exchange gifts, they discover the strength of their love.

What are you willing to SACRIFICE?

Explore the question and *KEY IDEA* by asking students to describe **sacrifices** they have made for others, as well as sacrifices others have made for them. Extend the discussion by having students complete the *DISCUSS* activity.

Selection Resources

The Gift of the Magi

Short Story by O. Henry

What are you willing to SACRIFICE?

KEY IDEA Have you ever made a **sacrifice** in order to help others or make someone happy? In "The Gift of the Magi," a young couple have to decide what each is willing to do to show love for the other.

DISCUSS With a small group, list examples of sacrifices that people make for those they love. Consider examples in real life as well as those in books, movies, and television shows. Do all the sacrifices involve material items? Which are the hardest ones to make? Which sacrifice shows the greatest love?

Sacrifices for
Someone You Love
1. Spending a week's allowance to buy a gift
2.
3.
4.
5.

For Flood Victims

94

RESOURCE MANAGER UNIT 1

Plan and Teach pp. 95–102

Literary Analysis
Summary pp. 103†*, 104‡*
Irony pp. 105, 106†*
Question Support p. 113*

Reading
Predict pp. 107, 108†*
Reading Check p. 112
Reading Fluency p. 115

Vocabulary
Study p. 109*
Practice p. 110
Strategy p. 111

Grammar and Writing
Make Effective Word Choices
p. 114

Assessment
Selection Tests A, B/C pp. 117*, 119*
Test Generator CD

BEST PRACTICES TOOLKIT

Differentiated Instruction
pp. 31–38*

Scaffolding Instruction
pp. 43–46*

Graphic Organizers/Strategies
Read Aloud/Think Aloud
- Definition Mapping • Predicting
- T Chart

Reading Support
Audio Anthology CD*

Technology
Literature and Vocabulary Centers at **ClassZone.com**

WriteSmart CD

---

* Resources for Differentiation   † Also in Spanish   ‡ In Haitian Creole and Vietnamese

● LITERARY ANALYSIS: IRONY

Irony is a contrast between what is expected to happen and what actually occurs. There are three types of irony commonly used in literature:

- **Situational irony:** when a character or the reader expects one thing to happen but something else happens instead
- **Verbal irony:** when what is said is the opposite of what is meant
- **Dramatic irony:** when what a character knows contrasts with what the audience knows

O. Henry is well-known for writing stories in which situational irony results in surprising plot twists. As you read "The Gift of the Magi," be ready for the unexpected.

● READING STRATEGY: PREDICT

If a story is well written, it will keep you wondering what happens next. You may ask yourself questions and find yourself **predicting** possible answers. In this story, for example, what can you predict from the title?

As you read "The Gift of the Magi," jot down two or three predictions. Then see whether you were right—or whether O. Henry managed to surprise you.

▲ VOCABULARY IN CONTEXT

The following words are key to understanding this story of love and sacrifice. To see how many words you already know, substitute a different word or phrase for each boldfaced term.

1. **instigate** a rebellion
2. a package in the **vestibule**
3. as **agile** as a gymnast
4. **falter** in his determination
5. **ransack** the entire house
6. show **prudence** in her decisions
7. a face marked by the **ravage** of time
8. an **assertion** that can't be proved
9. win the **coveted** prize
10. a **chronicle** of the year's events

Author Online

O. Henry
1862–1910

A Life Like His Fiction Using the pen name O. Henry, William Sydney Porter wrote hundreds of short stories. In some ways, his own life reflected the twists and turns of his stories. Born in Greensboro, North Carolina, and raised by his grandmother and aunt after his mother's death, Porter left school at age 15 to work in a drugstore. At age 20, he moved to Texas and worked on a ranch. After he married and had a child, he went to work as a bank clerk. Then, after leaving this position, he was accused of having embezzled bank funds. Porter fled to Central America to avoid trial. When he returned to visit his dying wife, he was arrested, convicted, and imprisoned for three years. He always maintained his innocence.

From Prison to Fame Porter refined his short story style while serving time in prison. By the time of his release, he was already selling stories to magazines. Today the most renowned annual collection of new American short stories bears his pen name—the O. Henry Awards.

 MORE ABOUT THE AUTHOR
For more on O. Henry, visit the **Literature Center** at ClassZone.com.

Background

Bearers of Gifts In this story, O. Henry makes an **allusion,** or reference, to the Magi. According to Christian tradition, the Magi were three wise men or kings who traveled to Bethlehem, guided by a miraculous star, to present gifts of gold, frankincense, and myrrh to the infant Jesus. These gifts were prized possessions, having monetary, medicinal, and ceremonial value.

THE GIFT OF THE MAGI **95**

Teach

STANDARDS FOCUS

● IRONY

To support instruction, read this example:

Ana didn't see Emilio anywhere in the station. She was sure that he had left, as he had said he would if she was late. Sadly, Ana started home. When Emilio ran in seconds later, his fear about being late turned to anger. "I meant what I said," he thought, and he boarded the train.

Discuss the irony in the situation. ***Possible answer:*** *Thinking she was too late, Ana didn't wait for Emilio, but it was really he who was late.*

CHECK UNDERSTANDING Ask students to identify ironic twists in their experiences or in stories they have read.

● PREDICT

Model making predictions, using the story title.

- The title offers clues about the story.
- I can predict that a gift may be a focus in the story and that the story takes place around Christmas because of the magi.

CHECK UNDERSTANDING After students read ***Background,*** ask what prediction they can make about the nature of a gift or gifts in the story.

 RESOURCE MANAGER—Copy Master
Predict p. 107 (for student use while reading the selection)

VOCABULARY SKILL

▲ VOCABULARY IN CONTEXT

DIAGNOSE WORD KNOWLEDGE To determine preteaching needs, have all students complete Vocabulary in Context. ***Possible answers:***
1. *start,* 2. *lobby,* 3. *nimble,* 4. *hesitate,*
5. *search,* 6. *caution,* 7. *ruin,* 8. *declaration,*
9. *desirable,* 10. *record*

PRETEACH VOCABULARY Use the Vocabulary Study copy master to help students predict meanings of each boldfaced word, using context clues.

1. Read aloud item 1. Ask
   —From the context, what do you think the boldfaced word means? Why?
   —What words in the sentence provide clues to the word's meaning?
2. Repeat these questions for item 2. Then have students complete Exercise B.

 RESOURCE MANAGER—Copy Master
Vocabulary Study p. 109

For general guidelines on differentiating vocabulary instruction and for alternative vocabulary activities for students not needing vocabulary study, see

📋 **BEST PRACTICES TOOLKIT**
Scaffolding Vocabulary Instruction pp. 43–46
ⓘ Vocabulary Center at **ClassZone.com**

ANALYZE VISUALS

Possible answer: The characters in the story are deeply in love. They treat each other with affection and tenderness.

About the Art Édouard Vuillard (1868–1940) was a French painter and lithographer. He is known especially for his scenes of Montmartre in Paris and of intimate home life, as exemplified by *The Kiss*. Vuillard was a member of the Nabis, a group of artists active in the 1890s. These artists were strongly influenced by Paul Gauguin. They developed a style that features boldly outlined surface patterns and the adventuresome use of bright color.

The Gift of the Magi

O. Henry

One dollar and eighty-seven cents. That was all. And 60 cents of it was in pennies. Pennies saved one and two at a time by bulldozing the grocer and the vegetable man and the butcher until one's cheeks burned with the silent imputation of parsimony[1] that such close dealing implied. Three times Della counted it. One dollar and eighty-seven cents. And the next day would be Christmas.

There was clearly nothing to do but flop down on the shabby little couch and howl. So Della did it. Which **instigates** the moral reflection that life is made up of sobs, sniffles, and smiles, with sniffles predominating.

10 While the mistress of the home is gradually subsiding from the first stage to the second, take a look at the home. A furnished flat at $8 per week. It did not exactly beggar description, but it certainly had that word on the lookout for the mendicancy squad.[2]

ANALYZE VISUALS
From this painting, what can you **infer** about the characters in this story?

1 Targeted Passage

instigate (ĭn'stĭ-gāt')
v. to stir up; provoke

---

1. **imputation** (ĭm'pyŏŏ-tā'shən) **of parsimony** (pär'sə-mō'nē): suggestion of stinginess.
2. **mendicancy** (mĕn'dĭ-kən-sē) **squad:** a police unit assigned to arrest beggars.

The Kiss (1891), Édouard Vuillard. Philadelphia Museum of Art, The Louis E. Stern Collection, 1963. © 2007 Artists Rights Society (ARS), New York/ADAGP, Paris (1963-181-76).

DIFFERENTIATED INSTRUCTION

FOR ALL STUDENTS

Anchor Activities Provide independent learning opportunities for students to research daily life in New York City at the turn of the 20th century. Challenge students to provide helpful graphics and illustrations. Encourage them to wear period costumes and provide background music from the early 1900s. To help students, see

R RESOURCE MANAGER
Ideas For Extension pp. 100–101

FOR LESS–PROFICIENT READERS

In combination with the *Audio Anthology CD*, use one or more Targeted Passages (pp. 96, 99, 100, 102) to ensure that students focus on key story events, concepts, and skills. Targeted Passages are also good for English learners.

1 Targeted Passage [Lines 1–8]

This passage introduces conflict in the plot: Della has no money at Christmas time.

• How has Della managed to save $1.87?

BACKGROUND

Christmas Gifts The custom of gift giving on Christmas goes back to the pre-Christian, Roman festivals of Saturnalia and Kalends. The very first gifts were simple items such as twigs from a sacred grove that were believed to bring good luck. Soon, items such as food, small pieces of jewelry and candles were considered appropriate gifts.

To the early Christians, gift giving at Christmas was a pagan holdover and was therefore frowned upon. However, people would not part with the practice. The Church found some justification in the gift giving of the magi, the three wise men. By the Middle Ages, Christians accepted gift giving at Christmas, although it was more common to exchange gifts on New Year's Day or Twelfth Night.

Cultural Connection Countries around the world have different holiday gift-giving traditions. In Brazil and Spain, children put their shoes beside the window or outside the door on Epiphany, or Three Kings Day (January 6). They find them the next day filled with small treats. In Italy, "La Befana" brings gifts to the children on January 6. Today in Russia, many families put up a decorated tree for New Year's, and gifts are exchanged at that time. Invite students to share their families' gift-giving traditions or what they know about gift-giving traditions in other cultures.

- How does she feel about how she saved the money?
- Why does Della burst into tears?

FOR ENGLISH LEARNERS

Options for Reading Use Read Aloud/Think Aloud to introduce the story. Then have learners listen to the *Audio Anthology CD* as they read along.

 BEST PRACTICES TOOLKIT—Transparency
  Read Aloud/Think Aloud p. A34

Prereading For prereading instruction for English learners, see

 BEST PRACTICES TOOLKIT
  Scaffolding Reading Instruction pp. 43–46

FOR ADVANCED LEARNERS/PRE–AP

Pre-AP Exercises in the bottom channel provide additional challenge for students. Use these suggestions for small groups or individuals.

ADDITIONAL GUIDELINES

For more help with differentiation and tips for classroom management, see

 BEST PRACTICES TOOLKIT
  Differentiated Instruction pp. 31–38

ANALYZE VISUALS

Activity Ask students to discuss how Degas's image visually echoes O. Henry's description of Della in lines 50–52. **Possible answer:** *The woman's flowing hair in the painting corresponds to O. Henry's description of Della's hair.*

About the Art French painter and sculptor Edgar Degas (1834–1917) is celebrated for the way he combined traditional styles of painting with a more relaxed style known as impressionism.

Woman Combing Her Hair, Edgar Degas. Charcoal and pastel. © The Fine Art Society, London/Bridgeman Art Library.

In the **vestibule** below belonged to this flat a letterbox into which no letter would go and an electric button from which no mortal finger could coax a ring. Also appertaining thereunto was a card bearing the name "Mr. James Dillingham Young."

The "Dillingham" had been flung to the breeze during a former period of prosperity when its possessor was being paid $30 per week. Now, when
20 the income was shrunk to $20, the letters of "Dillingham" looked blurred, as though they were thinking seriously of contracting to a modest and unassuming D. But whenever Mr. James Dillingham Young came home and reached his flat above, he was called "Jim" and greatly hugged by Mrs. James Dillingham Young, already introduced to you as Della. Which is all very good.

Della finished her cry and attended to her cheeks with the powder rag. She stood by the window and looked out dully at a gray cat walking a gray fence in a gray backyard. Tomorrow would be Christmas Day, and she had only $1.87

vestibule (vĕs′tə-byōōl′) *n.* a small entryway within a building

Ⓐ **IRONY**
You might expect someone named Mr. James Dillingham Young to be rich. Is he?

98 UNIT 1: NARRATIVE STRUCTURE

DIFFERENTIATED INSTRUCTION

FOR LESS-PROFICIENT READERS

Language Support Explain that throughout this story the author uses formal language to create a comic effect. Identify and discuss the example of this in line 16: "Also appertaining there unto was a card . . ." (meaning: "Also belonging to this flat was a card . . ."). Discuss similar hard-to-understand language patterns, such as those in lines 44–49 and lines 92–95.

FOR ENGLISH LEARNERS

Key Academic Vocabulary Use Definition Mapping to teach these words: *period* (line 18), *income* (line 20), *obtain* (line 36), *accurate* (line 37), *conception* (line 37), *task* (line 83).

 BEST PRACTICES TOOLKIT—Transparency
Definition Mapping p. E6

FOR ADVANCED LEARNERS/PRE-AP

Personification To convey the extent to which the Youngs' financial status has recently dwindled, in lines 19–22, O. Henry humorously paints a picture with words— literally—in the description of the letters in *Dillingham* on the mailbox. Have students sketch the mailbox, showing the Dillingham name as it might have appeared after Jim's cut in salary.

with which to buy Jim a present. She had been saving every penny she could
for months, with this result. Twenty dollars a week doesn't go far. Expenses
30 had been greater than she had calculated. They always are. Only $1.87 to buy
a present for Jim. Her Jim. Many a happy hour she had spent planning for
something nice for him. Something fine and rare and sterling—something just
a little bit near to being worthy of the honor of being owned by Jim.

There was a pier glass[3] between the windows of the room. Perhaps you
have seen a pier glass in an $8 flat. A very thin and very **agile** person may, by
observing his reflection in a rapid sequence of longitudinal strips, obtain a
fairly accurate conception of his looks. Della, being slender, had mastered
the art.

Suddenly she whirled from the window and stood before the glass. Her eyes
40 were shining brilliantly, but her face had lost its color within twenty seconds.
Rapidly she pulled down her hair and let it fall to its full length.

Now, there were two possessions of the James Dillingham Youngs in which
they both took a mighty pride. One was Jim's gold watch that had been his
father's and his grandfather's. The other was Della's hair. Had the Queen of
Sheba[4] lived in the flat across the air shaft, Della would have let her hair hang
out the window some day to dry and mocked at Her Majesty's jewels and gifts.
Had King Solomon[5] been the janitor, with all his treasures piled up in the
basement, Jim would have pulled out his watch every time he passed, just to
see him pluck at his beard from envy. **B**

50 So now Della's beautiful hair fell about her, rippling and shining like a
cascade of brown waters. It reached below her knee and made itself almost a
garment for her. And then she did it up again nervously and quickly. Once she
faltered for a minute and stood still while a tear or two splashed on the worn
red carpet.

On went her old brown jacket; on went her old brown hat. With a whirl of
skirts and with the brilliant sparkle still in her eyes, she fluttered out the door
and down the stairs to the street.

Where she stopped, the sign read "Mme. Sofronie. Hair Goods of All
Kinds." One flight up Della ran and collected herself, panting, before
60 Madame, large, too white, chilly, and hardly looking the "Sofronie."

"Will you buy my hair?" asked Della.

"I buy hair," said Madame. "Take yer hat off and let's have a sight at the
looks of it."

Down rippled the brown cascade.

"Twenty dollars," said Madame, lifting the mass with a practiced hand.

"Give it to me quick," said Della.

Oh, and the next two hours tripped by on rosy wings. Forget the hashed
metaphor. She was **ransacking** the stores for Jim's present.

---

3. **pier glass:** a large mirror set in a wall section between windows.

4. **Queen of Sheba:** in the Bible, a rich Arabian queen.

5. **King Solomon:** a Biblical king of Israel, known for his wisdom and wealth.

---

agile (ăj′əl) *adj.* able to move quickly and easily

② **Targeted Passage**

B PREDICT
What events might occur involving these prized possessions?

falter (fôl′tər) *v.* to hesitate from lack of courage or confidence

ransack (răn′săk′) *v.* to search or examine vigorously

READING STRATEGY

B PREDICT

Possible answer: *Because it is Christmas time and Della wants to buy a gift, it is possible that the prized possessions will be sold to raise money.*

If students need help . . . Have students use a Predicting chart, or a chart like this one, to help them make predictions about story events:

Predicting Chart		
Clues	Inference(s)	Predictions
Della did up her hair again nervously.	She is anxious because she might trade it for money.	She will probably explore such a trade.

BEST PRACTICES TOOLKIT—Transparency
Predicting p. A10

Lines 67–68
REINFORCE *KEY IDEA:* SACRIFICE

Discuss Why do you think O. Henry portrays Della as happy right after she makes the **sacrifice** of selling her hair? ***Possible answer:*** *Della's sacrifice has made her most important goal possible: the purchase of a special gift to show her love for Jim.*

FOR LESS–PROFICIENT READERS

② **Targeted Passage [Lines 42–57]**

This passage marks a significant event in the plot: Della cuts her hair to buy a present for Jim.

- What has Della decided to do?

- Why do you think Della made that decision?

- Why do you think Della faltered for a minute, stood still, and cried?

FOR ENGLISH LEARNERS

Language: Pronoun Referents Explain the referent for the pronoun *it* in line 63: "Take yer hat off and let's have a sight at the looks of it." (*It* refers to Della's hair.) Then have learners work in mixed-language groups to identify referents for the pronouns in lines 69–79.

She found it at last. It surely had been made for Jim and no one else.
There was none other like it in any of the stores, and she had turned all of them inside out. It was a platinum fob chain[6] simple and chaste in design, properly proclaiming its value by substance alone and not by meretricious ornamentation[7]—as all good things should do. It was even worthy of The Watch. As soon as she saw it, she knew that it must be Jim's. It was like him. Quietness and value—the description applied to both. Twenty-one dollars they took from her for it, and she hurried home with the 87 cents. With that chain on his watch Jim might be properly anxious about the time in any company. Grand as the watch was, he sometimes looked at it on the sly on account of the old leather strap that he used in place of a chain.

When Della reached home, her intoxication gave way a little to **prudence** and reason. She got out her curling irons and lighted the gas and went to work repairing the **ravages** made by generosity added to love. Which is always a tremendous task, dear friends—a mammoth task.

Within forty minutes her head was covered with tiny, close-lying curls that made her look wonderfully like a truant schoolboy. She looked at her reflection in the mirror long, carefully, and critically.

"If Jim doesn't kill me," she said to herself, "before he takes a second look at me, he'll say I look like a Coney Island[8] chorus girl. But what could I do—oh, what could I do with a dollar and eighty-seven cents!"

At 7 o'clock the coffee was made, and the frying pan was on the back of the stove hot and ready to cook the chops.

Jim was never late. Della doubled the fob chain in her hand and sat on the corner of the table near the door that he always entered. Then she heard his step on the stair away down on the first flight, and she turned white for just a moment. She had a habit of saying little silent prayers about the simplest everyday things, and now she whispered: "Please, God, make him think I am still pretty."

The door opened, and Jim stepped in and closed it. He looked thin and very serious. Poor fellow, he was only twenty-two—and to be burdened with a family! He needed a new overcoat, and he was without gloves.

Jim stopped inside the door, as immovable as a setter at the scent of a quail. His eyes were fixed upon Della, and there was an expression in them that she could not read, and it terrified her. It was not anger, nor surprise, nor disapproval, nor horror, nor any of the sentiments that she had been prepared for. He simply stared at her fixedly with that peculiar expression on his face.

Della wriggled off the table and went for him.

"Jim, darling," she cried, "don't look at me that way. I had my hair cut off and sold it because I couldn't have lived through Christmas without giving you a present. It'll grow again—you won't mind, will you? I just had to do it. My

G **Targeted Passage**

G **PREDICT**
What will Jim say about Della's hair?

prudence (pro͞od′ns) n. the use of good judgment and common sense

ravage (răv′ĭj) n. serious damage

---

6. **fob chain:** a short chain for a pocket watch.
7. **meretricious** (mĕr′ĭ-trĭsh′əs) **ornamentation:** cheap, gaudy decoration.
8. **Coney Island:** a resort district of Brooklyn, New York, famous for its amusement park.

G PREDICT

Possible answer: *He will express his confusion, but he will not criticize Della, because of his deep love for her.*

If students need help . . . Read aloud lines 103–105, beginning with the words "It was not anger . . .". Help students see that Jim will not express anger or disapproval, because of his respect for Della's decisions.

Lines 98–100
REINFORCE *KEY IDEA:* SACRIFICE

Discuss How do these details hint that Jim, as well as Della, is capable of **sacrifice?** *Possible answer: Rather than spend money on himself, Jim sacrifices by going without a much-needed new overcoat and gloves.*

DIFFERENTIATED INSTRUCTION

FOR LESS–PROFICIENT READERS

G Targeted Passage [Lines 92–105]

This passage sets up new tension in the plot, through an event that Della does not predict: Jim says nothing about her hair.

• Why does Della whisper a prayer?

• Why is Della terrified?

FOR ADVANCED LEARNERS/PRE–AP

Analyze Author's Technique Point out the author's direct address to the reader in lines 82–83. Have students find other examples.

1. Ask students to explain the effect of this technique in each context.

2. Discuss what these comments show about the author and his purpose.

3. Have students write a paragraph about how this device may produce a story that is similar to a parable or morality tale.

hair grows awfully fast. Say 'Merry
Christmas!' Jim, and let's be happy.
You don't know what a nice—what
a beautiful, nice gift I've got for
you."

"You've cut off your hair?" asked
Jim, laboriously, as if he had not
arrived at that patent fact yet even
after the hardest mental labor.

"Cut it off and sold it," said
Della. "Don't you like me just as
well, anyhow? I'm me without my
hair, ain't I?"

Jim looked about the room
curiously.

"You say your hair is gone?" he
said, with an air almost of idiocy.

"You needn't look for it," said
Della. "It's sold, I tell you—sold
and gone too. It's Christmas Eve,
boy. Be good to me, for it went for
you. Maybe the hairs of my head
were numbered," she went on with
a sudden serious sweetness, "but
nobody could ever count my love
for you. Shall I put the chops on,
Jim?"

Out of his trance Jim seemed
to quickly wake. He enfolded
his Della. For ten seconds let us
regard with discreet scrutiny[9] some
inconsequential object in the other
direction. Eight dollars a week
or a million a year—what is the
difference? A mathematician or
a wit would give you the wrong
answer. The magi brought valuable gifts, but that was not among them. This
dark **assertion** will be illuminated later on.

Jim drew a package from his overcoat pocket and threw it upon the table.

"Don't make any mistake, Dell," he said, "about me. I don't think there's
anything in the way of a haircut or a shave or a shampoo that could make me
like my girl any less. But if you'll unwrap that package, you may see why you
had me going awhile at first."

---

9. **discreet scrutiny:** cautious observation.

assertion (ə-sûr'shən)
n. a statement

D PREDICT
What do you predict Jim's
gift will be? Explain.

ANALYZE VISUALS

Activity Ask students, "How does this image
of a pocket watch seem appropriate to show
at this point in the story?" *Possible answer: We
know that Della has sold her hair to buy a chain
for Jim's watch. The watch is shown very large,
which gives it great importance. It is also somewhat blurred, which gives it an air of mystery.
The watch will likely figure in an important, but
as yet unclear, way in the rest of the story.*

Lines 115–136
DISCUSSION PROMPTS
Use these prompts to help students understand
how the author builds tension in this passage:

Connect What is your most treasured
possession? Would you ever sell it?
Responses will vary.

Analyze What is Della feeling at this point?
*Possible answer: She is eager to know Jim's
reactions and is anxious to enjoy Christmas
Eve with the person she loves.*

Evaluate How does suspense contribute to
the success of this short story? *Possible
answer: It heightens and maintains the
reader's interest in the actions of Jim and
Della.*

READING STRATEGY

D PREDICT

*Possible answer: Jim's gift will have some-
thing to do with Della's hair. Jim has mentioned her hair several times by this point.*

If students need help . . .

- Have students reread Jim's speech,
  lines 149–152.

- Ask students to think about the cause-
  and-effect relationship between the
  emphasis on Della's new hairstyle and
  the confusion Jim experienced after he
  entered the flat.

- Remind students that Jim's presentation
  of the gift in his overcoat pocket will
  show Della, and us, the reason that he
  reacted as he did (lines 151–152).

Extend the Discussion How do you think
that Jim, whose salary has decreased, has
managed to buy Della a special gift?

White fingers and nimble tore at the string and paper. And then an ecstatic scream of joy, and then, alas! a quick feminine change to hysterical tears and wails, necessitating the immediate employment of all the comforting powers of the lord of the flat.

For there lay The Combs—the set of combs, side and back, that Della had worshiped for long in a Broadway window. Beautiful combs, pure tortoise shell, with jeweled rims—just the shade to wear in the beautiful vanished hair.

160 They were expensive combs, she knew, and her heart had simply craved and yearned over them without the least hope of possession. And now, they were hers, but the tresses that should have adorned the **coveted** adornments were gone. **E**

But she hugged them to her bosom, and at length she was able to look up with dim eyes and a smile and say, "My hair grows so fast, Jim!"

And then Della leaped up like a little singed cat and cried, "Oh, oh!"

Jim had not yet seen his beautiful present. She held it out to him eagerly upon her open palm. The dull, precious metal seemed to flash with a reflection of her bright and ardent spirit.

170 "Isn't it a dandy, Jim? I hunted all over town to find it. You'll have to look at the time a hundred times a day now. Give me your watch. I want to see how it looks on it."

Instead of obeying, Jim tumbled down on the couch and put his hands under the back of his head and smiled.

"Dell," said he, "let's put our Christmas presents away and keep 'em a while. They're too nice to use just at present. I sold the watch to get the money to buy your combs. And now suppose you put the chops on." **F**

The magi, as you know, were wise men—wonderfully wise men—who brought gifts to the Babe in the manger. They invented the art of giving

180 Christmas gifts. Being wise, their gifts were no doubt wise ones, possibly bearing the privilege of exchange in case of duplication. And here I have lamely related to you the uneventful **chronicle** of two foolish children in a flat who most unwisely sacrificed for each other the greatest treasures of their house. But in a last word to the wise of these days let it be said that of all who give gifts these two were of the wisest. Of all who give and receive gifts, such as they are the wisest. Everywhere they are the wisest. They are the magi. ❧

coveted (kŭv′ĭ-tĭd)
adj. greedily desired or wished for **covet** *v.*

E GRAMMAR AND STYLE
Reread lines 160–163. O. Henry uses the **precise verbs** *craved* and *yearned* to show Della's great desire for the combs.

4 Targeted Passage

F IRONY
Reread lines 175–177. What is ironic about the resolution of the plot?

chronicle (krŏn′ĭ-kəl)
n. a record of events

Analyze Precise Verbs After students read the sentence containing the verbs *craved* and *yearned* (lines 160–161), discuss how these verbs are more specific than alternatives such as *wanted* or *longed for*. Encourage students to find other examples of precise verbs in the selection.

LITERARY ANALYSIS

F IRONY

Possible answer: The gifts for which Jim and Della made such sacrifices are now useless because Jim has sold his watch and Della has sold her hair.

SELECTION WRAP–UP

REFLECT Have students think about and suggest other possible titles for the story. Ask students to state what key idea their title addresses?

★ CRITIQUE Ask students what lasting impressions they will take away from this story. Ask them to share favorite images or passages with the class.

READING FLUENCY

Distribute the copy master and have students work in pairs or groups to practice fluency.

R RESOURCE MANAGER—Copy Master
Reading Fluency p. 115

DIFFERENTIATED INSTRUCTION

FOR LESS–PROFICIENT READERS

4 Targeted Passage [Lines 167–186]

This passage concludes the story with a plot twist and reveals the irony: the two characters have sacrificed their most prized possessions to buy now useless gifts for each other.

• What is ironic about the gifts Jim and Della have bought?

• What is O. Henry's opinion of the actions of Jim and Della?

FOR ADVANCED LEARNERS/PRE–AP

Evaluate Have students evaluate the tone of the story by rating it on a scale of 1 (not sentimental) to 5 (overly sentimental). Ask students to cite evidence from the story to support their opinions.

Comprehension

1. **Recall** Why is Della unhappy when the story begins?

2. **Recall** What two possessions do Della and Jim treasure?

3. **Summarize** What **sacrifices** do the Youngs make to buy each other gifts?

Literary Analysis

4. **Predict** Reexamine the predictions you made as you read the story. Were you able to predict the outcome of the story, or were you surprised? Go back through the story to find passages that hint at the surprise ending.

5. **Analyze Irony** This story contains **situational irony**, in which characters, or the reader, expect one thing to happen but something entirely different occurs. To explore the situational irony in this story, make a chart like the one shown.

What Della Plans:	What Actually Happens:
What Jim Plans:	What Actually Happens:

For each character, identify what is expected to happen and what actually does happen. There is a double irony here. How are the two ironies related?

6. **Draw Conclusions About the Narrator** Reread lines 22–24. In this and many other passages, the narrator speaks directly to the reader. How would you describe the narrator's personality? Cite evidence.

7. **Make Judgments** Reread lines 178–186. Here the narrator uses an **allusion**, or indirect reference to a person, place, event, or literary work. Why does the narrator compare Della and Jim to the Magi? What does this imply about the characters and the events in this story?

8. **Synthesize** What does this story seem to be saying about material possessions? Cite evidence to support your answer.

Literary Criticism

9. **Critical Interpretations** For several years in the early 1900s, O. Henry was one of the most widely read short story writers in the United States. Even today, some of his stories are considered classics. What elements in "The Gift of the Magi" might account for his continued popularity?

6. ▇ **STANDARDS FOCUS** *Draw Conclusions About the Narrator* *The narrator's personality is affectionate (lines 22–24), amused (lines 44–49), and a bit moralizing (lines 82–83). Students should cite evidence to support their descriptions.*

7. *He compares them to the magi because their sacrifices demonstrated both wisdom and love. The comparison implies that Jim and Della were not foolish but profoundly wise and caring.*

8. *The story implies that material possessions are far less important than love and sacrifice. The author reinforces this implication in the closing paragraph, in which he calls the Youngs "the wisest" and "the magi" (line 186).*

Literary Criticism

Possible answer:

9. *O. Henry's appeal might be based on the vivid setting, appealing characters, surprise ending, use of irony, and clear theme or message in "The Gift of the Magi."*

Practice and Apply

After Reading

For additional support of post-reading questions, use these copy masters:

R RESOURCE MANAGER—Copy Masters

Reading Check p. 112 (to check understanding of the selection)

Irony p. 105 (for practice of literary analysis standards focus)

Question Support p. 113 (After Reading questions adapted for English learners and less-proficient readers)

For additional questions, see page 99.

To challenge students further, see
ℹ Bob Marzano's Power Thinking Activities at **ClassZone.com**

ANSWERS

Comprehension

1. *She has only $1.87 to buy Jim a present.*

2. *Della treasures her hair, Jim his watch.*

3. *Della sells her hair and Jim sells his watch.*

Literary Analysis

Possible answers:

4. *Students' responses about their predictions will vary. The following passages may provide hints about the surprise ending:*

   - *"But what could I do—oh, what could I do with a dollar and eighty-seven cents!" (lines 88–89)*

   - *"It was not anger, nor surprise, nor disapproval, nor horror, nor any of the sentiments that she had been prepared for." (lines 103–105)*

   - *"The magi brought valuable gifts, but that was not among them. This dark assertion will be illuminated later on." (lines 146–147)*

5. ● **STANDARDS FOCUS** *Irony*
   What Della Plans: to sell her hair and use the money to buy a chain for Jim's watch; What Actually Happens: Jim has sold his watch, which makes the chain a useless gift. What Jim Plans: to sell his watch and use the money to buy combs for Della's hair; What Actually Happens: Della has sold her hair, which makes the combs a useless gift. The double irony is that the couple is still poor but no longer has their prized possessions. With their useless gifts, they are worse off than before.

ANSWERS

Vocabulary in Context

VOCABULARY PRACTICE

1. *d*	6. *c*
2. *a*	7. *b*
3. *d*	8. *c*
4. *a*	9. *d*
5. *b*	10. *a*

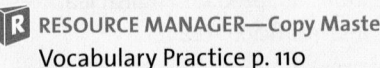 RESOURCE MANAGER—Copy Master
Vocabulary Practice p. 110

VOCABULARY IN WRITING

Point out to students that many of the words in the Vocabulary Practice are associated with specific parts of the story: for example, *ransack* (line 68) describes Della's shopping for the watch chain. Which other words do students associate with specific story events?

VOCABULARY STRATEGY: THE GREEK WORD ROOT *chron* (also an EL language objective)

- To help students understand word roots, focus on the vocabulary words *chronometer* and *synchronize*.
- Model for students how the word *chronometer* contains two roots (*chron* and *meter*) and that *synchronize* contains a prefix and a root (*syn* and *chron*).

Possible answers:

1. *chronic*
2. *chronological*
3. *chronicle*
4. *synchronize*
5. *chronometer*

RESOURCE MANAGER—Copy Master
Vocabulary Strategy p. 111

ℹ️ Vocabulary Center at **ClassZone.com**
Additional Vocabulary Activities

Vocabulary in Context

VOCABULARY PRACTICE

Write the letter of the word that is most different in meaning from the others.

1. (a) destruction, (b) ravage, (c) ruin, (d) creation
2. (a) stop, (b) stir, (c) urge, (d) instigate
3. (a) desired, (b) coveted, (c) craved, (d) unwanted
4. (a) cellar, (b) vestibule, (c) foyer, (d) entryway
5. (a) waver, (b) proceed, (c) falter, (d) hesitate
6. (a) assertion, (b) declaration, (c) denial, (d) statement
7. (a) limber, (b) clumsy, (c) flexible, (d) agile
8. (a) loot, (b) plunder, (c) organize, (d) ransack
9. (a) history, (b) record, (c) chronicle, (d) prediction
10. (a) carelessness, (b) caution, (c) prudence, (d) wisdom

WORD LIST

agile
assertion
chronicle
coveted
falter
instigate
prudence
ransack
ravage
vestibule

VOCABULARY IN WRITING

How might Della or Jim describe the events in this story? Assume the role of one of them and briefly retell the story as that character. Use three or more vocabulary words. Here is an example of an opening:

> **EXAMPLE SENTENCE**
>
> Here is my sad **_chronicle_** of the Christmas that almost wasn't.

VOCABULARY STRATEGY: THE GREEK WORD ROOT *chron*

The vocabulary word *chronicle* contains the Greek root *chron*, which means "time." This root is found in a number of English words. To understand the meaning of words with *chron*, use context clues as well as your knowledge of the root.

PRACTICE Write the word from the word web that best completes each sentence. Use context clues to help you or, if necessary, consult a dictionary.

1. A _____ illness is one that lasts a long time.
2. In a personal narrative, events are usually presented in _____ order.
3. The mayor kept a _____ to record events of his years in office.
4. If we _____ our watches, we'll be sure to meet at exactly noon.
5. A _____ in a ship is an aid in determining longitude.

🔍 **VOCABULARY PRACTICE**
For more practice, go to the **Vocabulary Center** at ClassZone.com.

chronicle   chronological
chron
chronic   chronometer
synchronize

DIFFERENTIATED INSTRUCTION

FOR ENGLISH LEARNERS

Vocabulary: Cognates Remind Spanish speakers that in Spanish, the equivalent of *chron* (as in *chronicle*) is *cron*, and that the *h* is silent in the English root.

FOR ADVANCED LEARNERS/PRE–AP

Vocabulary as Character Clues Have students take the characters' personalities into account in their retellings. *Example: Della, who is impulsive and emotional, might use words with strong connotations, such as ransack, coveted, and ravages.* Ask students to take notes about strong words used by Della or Jim and summarize their findings in a paragraph.

Reading-Writing Connection

Demonstrate your understanding of "The Gift of the Magi" by responding to these prompts. Then use **Revision: Grammar and Style** to improve your writing.

WRITING PROMPTS	SELF-CHECK
A. Short Response: Understand Theme "The Gift of the Magi" isn't simply a story about giving presents. O. Henry's main message concerns love and **sacrifice.** Write **one or two paragraphs** in which you discuss the theme of this story.	*A strong response will . . .* • state the story's message about love and sacrifice • cite specific details to explain the message
B. Extended Response: Write a Description What do you imagine Jim's shopping trip was like? Write **three to five paragraphs** describing Jim's actions and thoughts as he sells his watch and buys the combs for Della.	*A successful description will . . .* • explain what Jim does and thinks as he shops for the gift • include precise verbs that accurately reflect Jim's thoughts and actions

REVISION: GRAMMAR AND STYLE

MAKE EFFECTIVE WORD CHOICES Review the **Grammar and Style** note on page 102. Throughout the story, O. Henry uses **precise verbs** to descriptively convey the thoughts, feelings, and actions of his characters. By incorporating precise verbs into your own writing, you can give readers a greater and more accurate sense of your characters and their behavior.

In the following excerpts, notice how O. Henry uses verbs that help create vivid images for the reader:

With a whirl of skirts and with the brilliant sparkle still in her eyes, she fluttered out the door and down the stairs to the street. (lines 55–57)

Instead of obeying, Jim tumbled down on the couch. . . . (line 173)

Now study this model. Notice how the revisions in red help you to better visualize Jim's trip to the shop. Use similar methods to revise your responses to the prompts.

> **STUDENT MODEL**
>
>
> Jim walked to the shop; the store would close in just an hour. He reached into his right pocket, took out the watch, and held it in his hands.

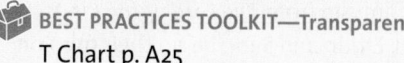
WRITING TOOLS
For prewriting, revision, and editing tools, visit the **Writing Center** at **ClassZone.com**.

THE GIFT OF THE MAGI **105**

Reading-Writing Connection

WRITING PROMPTS

• For Prompt A, ask students to reread lines 178–186. Have them think about a personal experience that illustrates a sacrifice made for love.

• For Prompt B, ask students to list strong, precise action verbs and sensory details. Have them orally present their paragraphs as they demonstrate the speaker's point of view and relationship with the subject.

BEST PRACTICES TOOLKIT—Transparency
   T Chart p. A25

For writing support, see

Writing Center at **ClassZone.com**

REVISION: GRAMMAR AND STYLE

• After students study the student model, list these words on the board: *scurried, ambled, scuttled, fluttered, tumbled, sprang, hustled, burst into, pounded.*

• Write this passage on the board. Have students suggest more precise verbs to replace the underlined verbs. (For more information on using language effectively, see pages R34–35 of the **Student Resource Book.**)

> *Jim 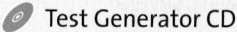 out of the pawnshop and headed to the store. As he , his heart beat quickly.*

Possible answers: *ambled, burst in, fluttered*

RESOURCE MANAGER—Copy Master
   Make Effective Word Choices p. 114

Assess and Reteach

Assess

RESOURCE MANAGER—Copy Masters
   Selection Test A pp. 117–118
   Selection Test B/C pp. 119–120

Test Generator CD

Reteach

STANDARDS LESSON FILE
   Literature Lesson 37: Situational Irony
   Literature Lesson 38: Verbal and Dramatic Irony
   Reading Lesson 1: Predicting
   Vocabulary Lesson 6: Word Parts: Anglo-Saxon and Greek

FOR LESS–PROFICIENT WRITERS

For Prompt A:

• The topic sentence states the story's theme about love and sacrifice.

• The body cites supporting details, including examples for each character.

• The last sentence restates the theme.

For Prompt B:

• The introductory paragraph presents Jim's decision to purchase a gift for Della.

• The body describes Jim's sale of the watch and purchase of the combs.

• The last paragraph gives Jim's thoughts as he travels home with the gift.

THE GIFT OF THE MAGI **105**

Focus and Motivate

OBJECTIVES

Media Literacy

- explore the key idea of **suspense**
- view a film clip to understand how visual, sound, and editing techniques are used to build suspense
- create a storyboard to demonstrate understanding of shot selection and shot types

SUMMARY

In this film clip from *The Lord of the Rings*, two hobbits, Frodo and Sam, begin their mission to take a mysterious and powerful ring to a safer location. As they travel through a forest, they encounter two other hobbits, Merry and Pippin. Suddenly, an ominous wind blows, and Frodo senses an approaching threat. A Black Rider—a shadowy, deadly being who is pursuing the ring—stops to search the area. The hobbits run and hide, eventually escaping the Black Rider by raft.

What keeps you in SUSPENSE?

To help students explore the *KEY IDEA,* ask them to talk about any **suspense**-filled movies they've seen recently. What filmmaking techniques helped make the movies suspenseful? Did they include music, fast-paced action, or the slow, agonizing way in which directors prolong tense situations?

BACKGROUND

The Lord of the Rings, by J. R. R. Tolkien, is an epic fantasy that was first published in 1954. Although it is one long story, it was originally published in three volumes: *The Fellowship of the Ring, The Two Towers,* and *The Return of the King.* Together, the books tell the story of a hobbit, Frodo Baggins. As part of a fellowship that includes an elf, a dwarf, several humans, and other hobbits, Frodo goes on a quest to destroy the One Ring that could ensure the victory of the powers of evil. The book became wildly popular in the 1960s, inspiring a whole genre of fantasy books that dealt with imaginary lands and mythical races of creatures. It also inspired several movies, of which director Peter Jackson's are the most famous.

Media Study

from The Lord of the Rings

Film Clip on ⊙ **MediaSmart** DVD

What keeps you in SUSPENSE?

KEY IDEA Have you ever been thrust into a situation that made your heart pound and your palms sweat? In this scene, Frodo Baggins, a young hobbit, has hardly started on a mission when he senses something ominous. Notice how the director builds **suspense** as danger reveals itself.

Background

Imagining Tolkien's World In 1999 the director Peter Jackson began to transform J. R. R. Tolkien's fantasy epic *The Lord of the Rings* into one of the most critically acclaimed movies of all time. As one reviewer stated, "This astounding movie accomplishes what no other fantasy film has been able to do: transport viewers to an entirely different reality, immerse them in it, and maroon them there...."

In the first installment, *The Fellowship of the Ring,* Frodo Baggins inherits a ring that has the power to destroy civilization. Frodo accepts the challenge of taking the ring to Rivendell, a place where a council will decide the ring's fate. He is joined on this mission by his loyal friend Sam and two other hobbits.

106

Media Study Resources

R RESOURCE MANAGER UNIT 1

Plan and Teach pp. 121–124

Media Analysis

Summary pp. 125†*, 126‡*

Viewing Guide p. 127

Close Viewing p. 128

Viewing Activity p. 129

Produce Your Own Media p. 130

S STANDARDS LESSON FILE

Media Lesson 1: Active Viewing

Media Lesson 4: Analyze Visuals

Media Lesson 5: Analyze Sound

Media Lesson 6: Analyze Editing

ℹ Media Center at **ClassZone.com**

MEDIA VIEWING

⊘ Media*Smart* DVD

* Resources for Differentiation   † Also in Spanish   ‡ In Haitian Creole and Vietnamese

Media Literacy: Suspense in Movies

Suspense is a feeling of growing tension and excitement. Writers build suspense by making readers feel uncertain about what will happen next. Like writers, directors have the ability to make viewers feel excited or nervous as events unfold from one scene to the next. A skillful director can use basic filmmaking techniques, such as **camera shots, editing,** and **sound,** to create suspense and draw viewers into the action.

FILM TECHNIQUES	STRATEGIES FOR VIEWING	
A **shot** is a single, continuous view filmed by a camera. A director sets up shots that will advance a story's plot and tell the story in a compelling way.	• Pay attention to **point-of-view shots;** they show what characters see. In suspenseful scenes, they can make viewers sympathize with the characters and feel as if they are in danger themselves. • Notice how **high-angle shots,** in which the camera looks down on objects or persons, can make characters seem helpless. **Low-angle shots,** with the camera looking up, can make characters seem powerful or threatening.	
Editing is the process of selecting and arranging shots in a sequence. Editors and directors build tension by increasing the pace from one shot to the next.	Be aware of **pace,** which is influenced by the length of time each shot stays on the screen. As suspense increases, the length of shots gets shorter. **Quick cuts,** which may last no longer than a second, perhaps even less, are used to create excitement and build viewers' anticipation.	
Sound consists of the **music, sound effects,** and **dialogue** used in a scene. Sounds can be manipulated to increase viewers' emotional response to the scene.	• Listen for the use of **music.** Shrill tones or quick, steady beats often signal danger. • In particular, notice how any prolonged **absence of sound** affects you. Silence can heighten a tense moment.	

Teach

Media Literacy

Review with students the definition of *suspense* and ask them to recall particularly suspenseful moments from movies they have seen. Ask what made those episodes so gripping. On the board, list any answers students might generate, such as *eerie music, sound effects,* and *lighting.* Make sure *camera shots, editing,* and *sound* are included on the list. Then discuss the chart on page 107.

- **Camera Shots** To reinforce the importance of camera shots and angles, present a common situation, such as an encounter with an angry dog. Ask students, How would the scene be presented from the point of view of an outsider? of the person encountering the dog? of the dog? Would the dog look more or less menacing if seen head on or from above?

- **Editing** Mention to students that in an action scene, shots and camera angles can change several times in just a few moments. Challenge them to actually count the changes the next time they watch this kind of scene.

- **Sound** Have students think about the range of sound effects they've been exposed to through video games, TV, and movies. Speculate with them about the kinds of sounds or music they might expect to hear in a fantasy that involves intense action and a variety of strange creatures. List the sound effects for students to revisit once they've viewed the clip.

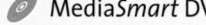 Media*Smart* DVD

MEDIA STUDY: TEACHING OPTIONS

Teaching Option 1: The Basics (1–2 Days)
1. Begin the Media Study using the material provided on pages 106–107.
2. Show the Introduction on Media*Smart.* Then show the First Viewing. As they watch, have students use the Viewing Guide on page 108, along with the corresponding copy master on page 127 of the Resource Manager. Discuss their responses.
3. Return to the pupil book for the extension activities on page 109.

Teaching Option 2: In-Depth Study (2–3 Days)
1. Begin the Media Study using pages 106–107.
2. Show the Introduction and First Viewing from Media*Smart.* Then continue on Media*Smart* with the Media Lessons, using the teacher notes available in the Resources section.
3. Show the Guided Analysis presentation. Have students record their observations on the Student Viewing Guide available in the Resources section from Media*Smart.*
4. Return to the pupil book, page 109.

Practice and Apply

VIEWING GUIDE

1. As students prepare to view the clip, tell them that they will be asked to identify techniques used to build suspense and help the viewer identify with the hobbits. Encourage them to watch and listen for these elements:

    - the types of **shots** that make it clear that Frodo is the main character, at the center of the action

    - **editing** that shows how the hobbits are reacting to the unexpected danger

    - **sound effects** and **music** that reflect the mysterious nature of what the hobbits confront and that guide the audience's expectations

2. Some students may have difficulty ignoring the narrative to focus on the technical aspects of this scene. To help students analyze the visuals, have them watch the clip without sound. To help them pay attention to the music and sound effects, suggest they listen to the scene without viewing the action.

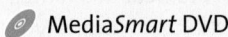 RESOURCE MANAGER—Copy Masters
    Viewing Guide p. 127
    Close Viewing p. 128
    Viewing Activity p. 129

Use this resource with the Viewing Guide:

💿 Media*Smart* DVD

ANSWERS

FIRST VIEWING: Comprehension

1. *The hobbits hide and then run, finally making their way to Buckleberry Ferry and escaping on a raft.*

2. *At the start of the scene, it is daytime, and the setting looks peaceful. By the end of the scene, it is presumably nighttime, and the setting appears threatening.*

CLOSE VIEWING: Media Literacy

Possible answers:

3. *Sound: howling wind; loud, eerie choral music; screeching horse; low, rumbling horns*

    Editing and shots: quick cuts, high-angle shots, close-up shots

---

💿 **Media*Smart* DVD**
- **Film Clip:** *The Lord of the Rings*
- **Director:** Peter Jackson
- **Rating:** PG-13
- **Genre:** Fantasy
- **Running Time:** 4 minutes

108

Viewing Guide for
The Lord of the Rings

In this scene Frodo and the other hobbits take a peaceful break from their journey only to discover that a Black Rider is pursuing them.

As you watch this clip, pay attention to particular moments that draw you into the action and create suspense. Plan on watching the scene several times. To help you analyze suspense, refer to the questions that follow.

NOW VIEW

FIRST VIEWING: Comprehension

1. **Recall** How do the hobbits escape the Black Rider?

2. **Summarize** How does the setting change as the scene progresses?

CLOSE VIEWING: Media Literacy

3. **Make Inferences** What techniques does the director use to lead you to believe that the Black Rider is evil?

4. **Analyze Sound** How does the director use sound to increase tension in the scene? Think about sound effects, music, changes in volume, and absence of sound.

5. **Analyze Camera Shots** How does the director use **point-of-view shots** and **high-angle** and **low-angle shots** to influence viewers' perception of the events? Think about the following shots:

    - Frodo's view of the road
    - Frodo's view of the horse's mouth and bit and hoof
    - the shot of the Black Rider standing directly above the hobbits' hiding place

6. **Evaluate Editing** Toward the end of the scene, the Black Rider is closing in on Frodo and the other hobbits. What effect do the **pace** and the use of **quick cuts** have on viewers?

---

4. *At key moments, the director uses the absence of sound to build suspense. Music and sound effects are used to signal the presence of danger; the volume of the music increases as the situation worsens.*

5. *Point-of-view shots show what the characters see. Frodo's view of the road indicates that something is coming. Low-angle shots convey that the Black Rider is powerful or menacing. High-angle shots convey helplessness and danger.*

6. *The pace and quick cuts increase the suspense. Viewers probably become anxious about Frodo's fate as the hobbit nearly comes within reach of the Black Rider.*

Write or Discuss

Evaluate Suspense A director's ultimate goal when filming a suspenseful scene is to make viewers feel the tension and anxiety that the characters feel. Evaluate the effectiveness of the director's portrayal of a suspenseful situation in the scene you viewed. Think about the following:

- the film techniques the director uses to create suspense
- specific emotions and reactions you think the director is trying to evoke
- your reactions to the clip

Produce Your Own Media

Create a Storyboard A **storyboard** is a device used to plan the shooting of a film and to help the director envision what the finished product will look like. Create a storyboard revisiting the beginning of the *Fellowship of the Ring* scene. Your storyboard should emphasize the Black Rider's point of view and should include between eight and ten shots.

HERE'S HOW Think of your storyboard as a set of rough sketches that includes descriptions of each shot. Here are some tips to get you started:

- Break down the incident shot by shot, in chronological order.
- Consider using a variety of shots and angles, including close-ups, high-angle and low-angle shots, and point-of-view shots.
- Once you establish the scene, use point-of-view shots to show what the Black Rider sees.
- Think about the sounds you want to accompany each shot.

> **MEDIA TOOLS**
> For help with creating a storyboard, visit the **Media Center** at **ClassZone.com**.

STUDENT MODEL

Shot type: LS (long shot)
Action: Black Rider races dangerously fast.
Audio: Horse screeches. Silence.

Shot type: MS (medium shot)
Action: Camera zooms in to show image of Black Rider. Audio: Music plays to indicate danger.

Production Tip
Use abbreviations of shot types in your storyboard.

POV = point-of-view shot
LS = long shot
MS = medium shot
CU = close-up shot
ELS = extreme long shot

Write or Discuss

Evaluate Suspense In their evaluations, students should address film techniques the director uses: *camera shots, such as high-angle and low-angle shots; editing; and sound.* Make sure students understand how camera shots are used to create suspense. For example, a low-angle shot can make one character appear powerful while another appears weak and helpless. In addition, students should include their own personal reactions to the clip and cite evidence to support their responses.

ADDITIONAL TEACHING OPPORTUNITY

Compare Evaluations: Ask students to compare their written evaluations with a published review of *The Lord of the Rings: The Fellowship of the Ring* found in

ℹ Media Center at **ClassZone.com**.

MEDIA STUDY WRAP–UP

Have students summarize what they have learned about visual, sound, and editing techniques that filmmakers use to create suspense. Encourage students to use terms such as *high-angle shots* and *quick cuts* in their explanations.

RETEACH

ⓢ STANDARDS LESSON FILE
Media Lesson 1: Active Viewing Strategies
Media Lesson 4: Analyze Visuals in Film and TV
Media Lesson 5: Analyze Sound in Film and TV
Media Lesson 6: Analyze Editing in Film and TV

Produce Your Own Media

Rubric: Create a Storyboard A strong storyboard should have

- an establishing shot, such as a long shot or an extreme long shot
- a variety of shots that show events in chronological order
- point-of-view shots to reflect what the Black Rider sees
- an accurate description of the action
- appropriate sounds to match each shot when necessary
- properly labeled shot types

 **RESOURCE MANAGER**—Copy Master
Produce Your Own Media p. 130

Focus and Motivate

OBJECTIVES

Literary Analysis
- explore the key idea of **convictions**
- read an excerpt from an autobiography

Reading
- identify cause and effect

Vocabulary
- build vocabulary for reading and writing
- use synonyms and antonyms to determine the meaning of unfamiliar words *(also an EL language objective)*

Grammar and Writing
- use strong verbs in a series
- use writing to analyze literature

SUMMARY

In this excerpt from his autobiography, *Black Boy*, Richard Wright recalls a turning point in his childhood. Sent to buy groceries, Wright is twice robbed by a gang of boys. His mother gives him a heavy stick and orders him to stand up for himself. Though terrified, Wright fends off the gang and returns home with the groceries—and a new sense of self-respect.

What is worth FIGHTING FOR?

Discuss the question with students. Then lead into the **KEY IDEA** by discussing the meaning of **convictions** ("strong beliefs"). After students complete the **DISCUSS** activity, have them compare their lists. Were there any recurring issues?

Selection Resources

The Rights to the Streets of Memphis
Autobiography by Richard Wright

What is worth FIGHTING FOR?

KEY IDEA An important part of becoming an adult is learning to stand up for yourself and maintain your **convictions**. In "The Rights to the Streets of Memphis," Richard Wright recalls an episode from his early childhood when he was threatened by a neighborhood gang.

DISCUSS What would draw you to a rally or make you speak out in a crowd? With a small group, generate a list of issues or values that you would defend at any cost. Why is each one so important to you? Choose a spokesperson to present the one your group cares about the most.

What I Would
Fight For
1. Freedom
2. Equal pay
3.
4.
5.

110

 RESOURCE MANAGER UNIT 1

Plan and Teach pp. 131–138

Literary Analysis
Summary pp. 139†*, 140‡*
Autobiography pp. 141, 142†*
Question Support p. 149*

Reading
Identify Cause and Effect
    pp. 143, 144†*
Reading Check p. 148
Reading Fluency p. 151

Vocabulary
Study p. 145*
Practice p. 146
Strategy p. 147

Grammar and Writing
Emphasize Action p. 150

Assessment
Selection Tests A, B/C pp. 153*, 155*
 Test Generator CD

 BEST PRACTICES TOOLKIT

Differentiated Instruction
  pp. 31–38*

Scaffolding Instruction
  pp. 43–46*

Graphic Organizers/Strategies
Word Questioning • New Word Analysis • Two-Column Chart • Cause and Effect Graphics

Technology
ⓘ Literature and Vocabulary Centers at **ClassZone.com**

⊘ Write*Smart* CD

Reading Support
⊘ Audio Anthology CD*

InterActive
READER & WRITER

• Integrated Test Practice
• Related Nonfiction Readings

McDougal Littell LITERATURE

---

* Resources for Differentiation   † Also in Spanish   ‡ In Haitian Creole and Vietnamese

LITERARY ANALYSIS: AUTOBIOGRAPHY

An **autobiography** is the story of a person's life, written by that person. Writers of autobiographies generally use the same narrative techniques that are found in fiction. This makes the events they relate come to life for the reader. As you read "The Rights to the Streets of Memphis," notice how Richard Wright employs these and other narrative techniques:

- describes the **conflict** he faced
- builds **suspense** as events reach a **climax**
- uses realistic **dialogue** to reveal events and personalities

READING SKILL: IDENTIFY CAUSE AND EFFECT

Writers of autobiographies often explain the **causes** and **effects** of important events in their lives in order to help readers understand the full significance of their experiences. For example, to describe the magnitude of his hunger, Wright explains:

The hunger I had known before this . . . had made me beg constantly for bread. . . . But this new hunger baffled me, scared me . . .

As you read Wright's autobiography, jot down the cause-and-effect relationships he points out.

Cause	Effect
Father leaves.	Family is without food.

VOCABULARY IN CONTEXT

Use an appropriate vocabulary word to complete each phrase.

WORD LIST			
clamor	flay	stark
dispirited	retaliate	

1. _____, absolute fear
2. a loud _____
3. _____ with a whip
4. _____, or get even
5. depressed and _____

Author Online

A Hard Beginning
The son of a sharecropper and a teacher, Richard Wright grew up in poverty in the South. Because his family moved often and his mother became ill, Wright attended school irregularly. He dropped out of high school after only a few weeks and then traveled the country, working at odd jobs. Brilliant but troubled, he read widely. He also wrote powerful stories that earned him respect and recognition.

Richard Wright
1908–1960

French Citizenship After establishing himself as a writer with the success of his novel *Native Son*, Wright moved to France in 1947 to get away from the racism he had experienced in the United States. He settled in Paris and became a French citizen, continuing to write until his death.

> **MORE ABOUT THE AUTHOR**
> For more on Richard Wright, visit the **Literature Center** at ClassZone.com.

Background

Memphis in the Early 1900s This excerpt from Wright's autobiography *Black Boy* deals with a time when Wright was living in a tenement in Memphis, Tennessee. In the early 1900s, African Americans experienced harsh economic conditions in Memphis and other cities throughout the South. Federal welfare efforts, such as subsidized housing, food stamps, and aid to dependent children, did not exist. Most of the jobs available to black men and women paid very low wages. Like Wright's mother, many black women worked as poorly paid domestic servants.

111

Teach

STANDARDS FOCUS

● AUTOBIOGRAPHY

For instructional support, read this passage aloud, and have students discuss what the dialogue reveals about the father:

> "If you believe in something," Dad told me, "you have to speak out." When I shared my terror of making people angry, he replied, "Maybe so, Maria. But what is important is being true to yourself."

Possible answer: *The father believes in speaking out and being true to oneself.*

CHECK UNDERSTANDING Ask students what the passage reveals about the writer.

■ IDENTIFY CAUSE AND EFFECT

Use **A Hard Beginning** to model cause and effect.

- **Cause:** Wright's family moved often, and his mother became ill.
- **Effect:** Wright attended school irregularly.
- The word *because* in the passage signals a cause-effect relationship.

CHECK UNDERSTANDING After students read **French Citizenship,** ask what caused Wright to move to France.

> ℝ **RESOURCE MANAGER—Copy Master**
> Identify Cause and Effect p. 143
> (for student use while reading the selection)

VOCABULARY SKILL

▲ VOCABULARY IN CONTEXT

DIAGNOSE WORD KNOWLEDGE To determine preteaching needs, have all students complete Vocabulary in Context. *Answers:* **1.** *stark,* **2.** *clamor,* **3.** *flay,* **4.** *retaliate,* **5.** *dispirited*

PRETEACH VOCABULARY Use the Vocabulary Study copy master to help students predict the meaning of each boldfaced word in the copy master.

1. Read aloud item 1, emphasizing *clamor.*
2. Point out the phrase "loud enough for everyone to hear." Elicit possible meanings for *clamor,* such as "a loud noise."
3. Repeat the procedure for items 2–5.

> ℝ **RESOURCE MANAGER—Copy Master**
> Vocabulary Study p. 145

For general guidelines on differentiating vocabulary instruction and for alternative vocabulary activities for students not needing vocabulary preteaching, see

> 🧰 **BEST PRACTICES TOOLKIT**
> Scaffolding Vocabulary Instruction pp. 43–46
> ⓘ Vocabulary Center at **ClassZone.com**

ANALYZE VISUALS

Possible answer: The angles and shadows, together with the dominant grayness of the scene, convey a sense of hardship for those living in the tenement. Most of the people in the painting are shown with downcast heads. This posture suggests boredom, weariness, and discontent.

About the Art Jacob Lawrence (1917–2000) was an American painter best known for his series of paintings that deal with African-American people and subjects. Lawrence's art was influenced by the abstract elements of cubism and by his personal experiences living in New York City's Harlem, where he witnessed scenes of tenement life such as the one shown in *Alley*.

READING SKILL

A CAUSE AND EFFECT

Possible answer: Wright began to recognize that the new, more frightening kind of hunger was causing him to feel different. He was becoming less active and wasn't thinking clearly.

If students need help . . . Have students reread lines 6–10. Ask them to describe the "new" hunger that Wright is experiencing. Then have students reread lines 11–13 and describe the effect that the "new" hunger has on Wright.

Extend the Discussion What does Wright mean when he writes that the hunger he had known before had not been a stranger? What does this tell you about his life?

THE Rights TO THE Streets OF Memphis

Richard Wright

Hunger stole upon me so slowly that at first I was not aware of what hunger really meant. Hunger had always been more or less at my elbow when I played, but now I began to wake up at night to find hunger standing at my bedside, staring at me gauntly. The hunger I had known before this had been no grim, hostile stranger; it had been a normal hunger that had made me beg constantly for bread, and when I ate a crust or two I was satisfied. But this new hunger baffled me, scared me, made me angry and insistent. Whenever I begged for food now my mother would pour me a cup of tea which would still the **clamor** in my stomach for a moment or two; but a little later I would feel
10 hunger nudging my ribs, twisting my empty guts until they ached. I would grow dizzy and my vision would dim. I became less active in my play, and for the first time in my life I had to pause and think of what was happening to me. **A**

"Mama, I'm hungry," I complained one afternoon.
"Jump up and catch a kungry," she said, trying to make me laugh and forget.
"What's a *kungry*?"
"It's what little boys eat when they get hungry," she said.
"What does it taste like?"
20 "I don't know."
"Then why do you tell me to catch one?"
"Because you said that you were hungry," she said, smiling.
I sensed that she was teasing me, and it made me angry.
"But I'm hungry. I want to eat."

ANALYZE VISUALS

What impressions of tenement life does the painting on page 113 convey?

① **Targeted Passage**

clamor (klăm′ər) *n.* a noisy outburst; outcry

A CAUSE AND EFFECT

What cause-and-effect relationship did Wright begin to recognize?

Alley (1942), Jacob Lawrence. Courtesy of Clark Atlanta University Art Galleries. © 2007 Gwendolyn Knight Lawrence/ Artists Rights Society (ARS), New York.

112 UNIT 1: NARRATIVE STRUCTURE

DIFFERENTIATED INSTRUCTION

FOR ALL STUDENTS

Expert Groups Allow students to become experts or members of expert groups by researching and choosing a way to share information about one of these topics:

- tenement life
- 1901 Tenement House Act
- Memphis, Tennessee (history)

FOR LESS–PROFICIENT READERS

In combination with the *Audio Anthology CD*, use one or more Targeted Passages (pp. 112, 114, 115, 116) to ensure that students focus on key story events, concepts, and skills. Targeted Passages are also good for English learners.

① **Targeted Passage [Lines 1–13]**

This passage establishes one of the difficult circumstances of Wright's young life.

BACKGROUND

Tenement Housing In the late 19th and early 20th centuries, many of the thousands of immigrants who came to America lived in tenements such as the one shown in the painting on this page. Tenement landlords were more concerned with making a profit than with providing comfortable living conditions. As a result, urban tenements were typically run-down, dirty, crowded buildings, with no electricity, heat, or indoor plumbing. Living conditions gradually improved with the passage of tenement housing laws in the early 1900s.

- What hardship is the author describing? What might this suggest about the kind of childhood Wright experienced?
- In what way is this hardship greater now than ever before?

FOR ENGLISH LEARNERS

Key Academic Vocabulary Use Word Questioning to teach these words: *aware* (line 1), *constantly* (line 5), *vision* (line 11), *restrictions* (line 45), *image* (line 57).

 BEST PRACTICES TOOLKIT—Transparency Word Questioning p. E9

Prereading For prereading instruction for English learners, see

 BEST PRACTICES TOOLKIT Scaffolding Reading Instruction pp. 43–46

FOR ADVANCED LEARNERS/PRE–AP

Pre-AP Exercises in the bottom channel provide additional challenge for students. Use these suggestions for small groups or individuals.

ADDITIONAL GUIDELINES

For more help with differentiation and tips for classroom management, see

 BEST PRACTICES TOOLKIT Differentiated Instruction pp. 31–38

Activity After students read the selection, ask them to compare and contrast the woman in the portrait with the author's mother. *Possible answer: The woman in the portrait appears to have endured hardship, as did Wright's mother. While the expression on the woman's face seems weary and a bit sad, she, like Wright's mother, also projects strength.*

About the Art Charles White (1918–1979) was an American painter and graphic artist known for his paintings of African Americans, such as *Woman Worker*, shown here.

LITERARY ANALYSIS

B AUTOBIOGRAPHY

Possible answer: The dialogue reveals that Wright's father has apparently abandoned the family.

Lines 139–159
DISCUSSION PROMPTS

Use these discussion prompts to help students understand the narrator's character development:

Connect Have you or anyone you know ever counted on someone for something only to be left to fend for yourself? Explain. *Accept all reasonable responses.*

Analyze What kind of child do you think the narrator was before his father's departure? *Possible answer: He seems to have been high-spirited but repressed from the "restrictions" (line 45) that his father shouted at him.*

Synthesize How does the narrator's attitude about his father's departure change from line 40 to line 59? *Possible answer: Initially, he was relieved and enjoyed the freedom to make as much noise as he wanted to. But that soon turned to a "deep, biological bitterness" (lines 58–59) when he became hungry and realized that his father wasn't coming home to provide food.*

"You'll have to wait."

"But I want to eat now."

"But there's nothing to eat," she told me.

"Why?"

"Just because there's none," she explained.

30 "But I want to eat," I said, beginning to cry.

"You'll just have to wait," she said again.

"But why?"

"For God to send some food."

"When is He going to send it?"

"I don't know."

"But I'm hungry!"

She was ironing, and she paused and looked at me with tears in her eyes.

"Where's your father?" she asked me.

40 I stared in bewilderment. Yes, it was true that my father had not come home to sleep for many days now and I could make as much noise as I wanted. Though I had not known why he was absent, I had been glad that he was not there to shout his restrictions at me. But it had never occurred to me that his absence would mean that there would be no food.

"I don't know," I said.

"Who brings food into the house?" my mother

50 asked me.

"Papa," I said. "He always brought food."

"Well, your father isn't here now," she said.

"Where is he?"

"I don't know," she said.

"But I'm hungry," I whimpered, stomping my feet.

"You'll have to wait until I get a job and buy food," she said. **B**

As the days slid past the image of my father became associated with my pangs of hunger, and whenever I felt hunger I thought of him with a deep biological bitterness.[1]

60 My mother finally went to work as a cook and left me and my brother alone in the flat each day with a loaf of bread and a pot of tea. When she returned at evening she would be tired and **dispirited** and would cry a lot. Sometimes, when she was in despair, she would call us to her and talk to us for hours, telling us that we now had no father, that our lives would be different from those of other children, that we must learn as soon as possible to take care of ourselves, to dress ourselves, to prepare our own food; that we must take upon ourselves the responsibility of the flat while she worked. Half frightened, we

Woman Worker (1951), Charles White. © 1951 The Charles White Archive.

B AUTOBIOGRAPHY
Reread lines 39–56. What life-changing event does Wright reveal through **dialogue?**

dispirited (dĭ-spĭr′ĭ-tĭd) *adj.* dejected

② **Targeted Passage**

---

1. **deep, biological bitterness:** bitterness caused by the pangs of hunger.

DIFFERENTIATED INSTRUCTION

FOR LESS–PROFICIENT READERS

② **Targeted Passage [Lines 60–67]**

This passage continues to paint a picture in the reader's mind of the hardships faced by the author as a result of being abandoned by his father.

• Why are the author and his brother left alone in the flat each day? How do you think the mother feels about this?

• How are the boys' lives now "different from those of other children"?

FOR ENGLISH LEARNERS

Culture: Clarify Help students use context clues to figure out the meaning of the word *flat* in line 61. Ask, Where did the mother leave the boy and his brother when she went to work each day? Explain that *flat* is another word for "small apartment." Have students work in pairs to use context clues to figure out the meaning of these other words with which they might not be familiar: *pavement* (line 75), *presently* (line 103), *baffled* (line 107).

would promise solemnly. We did not understand what had happened between our father and our mother and the most that these long talks did to us was to
70 make us feel a vague dread. Whenever we asked why father had left, she would tell us that we were too young to know.

One evening my mother told me that thereafter I would have to do the shopping for food. She took me to the corner store to show me the way. I was proud; I felt like a grownup. The next afternoon I looped the basket over my arm and went down the pavement toward the store. When I reached the corner, a gang of boys grabbed me, knocked me down, snatched the basket, took the money, and sent me running home in panic. That evening I told my mother what had happened, but she made no comment; she sat down at once, wrote another note, gave me more money, and sent me out to the grocery
80 again. I crept down the steps and saw the same gang of boys playing down the street. I ran back into the house. **C**

"What's the matter?" my mother asked.

"It's those same boys," I said. "They'll beat me."

"You've got to get over that," she said. "Now, go on."

"I'm scared," I said.

"Go on and don't pay any attention to them," she said.

I went out of the door and walked briskly down the sidewalk, praying that the gang would not molest me. But when I came abreast of them someone shouted.

90 "There he is!"

> They came toward me and I broke into a wild run toward home. They overtook me and flung me to the pavement. I yelled, pleaded, kicked, but they wrenched the money out of my hand. They yanked me to my feet, gave me a few slaps, and sent me home sobbing. My mother met me at the door. **D**
>
> "They b-beat m-me," I gasped. "They t-t-took the m-money."
>
> I started up the steps, seeking the shelter of the house.
>
> "Don't you come in here," my mother warned me.
>
> I froze in my tracks and stared at her.
>
> "But they're coming after me," I said.
>
> 100 "You just stay right where you are," she said in a deadly tone. "I'm going to teach you this night to stand up and fight for yourself."
>
> She went into the house and I waited, terrified, wondering what she was about. Presently she returned with more money and another note; she also had a long heavy stick.
>
> "Take this money, this note, and this stick," she said. "Go to the store and buy those groceries. If those boys bother you, then fight."

I was baffled. My mother was telling me to fight, a thing that she had never done before.

"But I'm scared," I said.

110 "Don't you come into this house until you've gotten those groceries," she said.

C AUTOBIOGRAPHY
Why do you suppose Wright includes such specific details about this experience?

D GRAMMAR AND STYLE
Reread lines 91–94. Wright uses **strong verbs in a series**—like *yelled, pleaded,* and *kicked*—to help readers visualize the attack.

3 Targeted Passage

C AUTOBIOGRAPHY

Possible answer: Wright most likely includes the details so that the reader can vividly "see" the events he describes. The details also help build suspense and set the scene for Wright's next encounter with the gang of boys.

Extend the Discussion Why do you think the author is able to recall these events in such detail many years after they occurred?

D GRAMMAR AND STYLE

Verbs in a Series Authors often use a series of verbs or verb phrases to emphasize action, create drama, and give life to their writing. The verbs usually convey a rapid sequence of actions and sometimes also indicate increasing intensity. After students reread the lines, discuss how Wright's use of language creates a vivid impression of events. Encourage students to find other places in the selection where Wright uses strong verbs in a series to make an impression.

Lines 100–101
REINFORCE KEY IDEA: CONVICTIONS

Discuss What do these lines suggest about the **convictions** of Wright's mother? *Possible answer: She believes that people should stand up for themselves and even use physical force if necessary.*

FOR LESS–PROFICIENT READERS

3 Targeted Passage [Lines 91–106]

This passage shows how Wright's mother makes him stand up for himself against the boys who are chasing him.

- What is Wright hoping will happen when he climbs the steps to his home?
- Why is the reaction of Wright's mother surprising?
- What does Mrs. Wright hope to accomplish by giving Wright the stick?

FOR ENGLISH LEARNERS

Vocabulary: Idioms Use New Word Analysis to teach these idioms from the story: *froze in my tracks* (line 98), "stopped suddenly and did not move"; *let up* (line 132), "stopped"; *egging them on* (lines 137–138), "urging them to do"; *tore out* (line 139), ran away quickly.

 BEST PRACTICES TOOLKIT—Transparency
New Word Analysis p. E8

E CAUSE AND EFFECT

Possible answer: *The fighting has made Wright stronger. It has given him confidence and self-respect by showing him that he can stand up to bullies and defend himself.*

If students need help . . . Help students compare Wright's feelings and actions before and after the climactic encounter by completing a Two-Column Chart.

Before	After
Feels terrified	*Feels frightened but determined*
Pleads, cries	*Fights off his attackers*
Runs away	*Taunts attackers*
Fails to accomplish task	*Accomplishes his task*

 BEST PRACTICES TOOLKIT—Transparency
Two-Column Chart p. A25

SELECTION WRAP–UP

SUMMARIZE Ask students to summarize the important lessons Wright learns as a result of the childhood experience he recounts in this selection.

★ **CRITIQUE** Have students discuss and evaluate the message that Richard Wright seems to be conveying in this selection. Is it a valid message? Does it apply to everyone?

READING FLUENCY

Distribute the copy master and have students work in pairs or groups to practice fluency.

RESOURCE MANAGER—Copy Master
Reading Fluency p. 151

"They'll beat me; they'll beat me," I said.

"Then stay in the streets; don't come back here!"

I ran up the steps and tried to force my way past her into the house. A stinging slap came on my jaw. I stood on the sidewalk, crying.

"Please, let me wait until tomorrow," I begged.

"No," she said. "Go now! If you come back into this house without those groceries, I'll whip you!"

She slammed the door and I heard the key turn in the lock. I shook with
120 fright. I was alone upon the dark, hostile streets and gangs were after me. I had the choice of being beaten at home or away from home. I clutched the stick, crying, trying to reason. If I were beaten at home, there was absolutely nothing that I could do about it; but if I were beaten in the streets, I had a chance to fight and defend myself. I walked slowly down the sidewalk, coming closer to the gang of boys, holding the stick tightly. I was so full of fear that I could scarcely breathe. I was almost upon them now.

"There he is again!" the cry went up.

They surrounded me quickly and began to grab for my hand.

"I'll kill you!" I threatened.

130 They closed in. In blind fear I let the stick fly, feeling it crack against a boy's skull. I swung again, lamming another skull, then another. Realizing that they would **retaliate** if I let up for but a second, I fought to lay them low, to knock them cold, to kill them so that they could not strike back at me. I **flayed** with tears in my eyes, teeth clenched, **stark** fear making me throw every ounce of my strength behind each blow. I hit again and again, dropping the money and the grocery list. The boys scattered, yelling, nursing their heads, staring at me in utter disbelief. They had never seen such frenzy. I stood panting, egging them on, taunting them to come on and fight. When they refused, I ran after them and they tore out for their homes, screaming. The parents of the
140 boys rushed into the streets and threatened me, and for the first time in my life I shouted at grownups, telling them that I would give them the same if they bothered me. I finally found my grocery list and the money and went to the store. On my way back I kept my stick poised for instant use, but there was not a single boy in sight. That night I won the right to the streets of Memphis. ✎ **E**

④ Targeted Passage

retaliate (rĭ-tăl′ē-āt′) *v.* to pay back an injury in kind

flay (flā) *v.* to whip or lash

stark (stärk) *adj.* complete or utter; extreme

E CAUSE AND EFFECT
What effect did the fighting have on Wright's personality?

DIFFERENTIATED INSTRUCTION

FOR LESS–PROFICIENT READERS

④ **Targeted Passage [Lines 127–145]**

This passage concludes the excerpt with the author's momentous experience: he defends himself.

- What happens when the gang starts to attack Wright again?

- What do Wright's actions suggest about how he's changed?

- How do you think Wright feels after the encounter?

FOR ADVANCED LEARNERS/PRE–AP

Synthesize Have students reread *About the Author* (p. 111). Then ask them to speculate about how the incident described in this autobiography and Wright's later success as a writer might be connected.

Comprehension

1. **Recall** Why does Richard's mother have no food for him?

2. **Recall** What choice does Richard have to make?

3. **Clarify** What does the **title** refer to?

Literary Analysis

4. **Identify Cause and Effect** Review the cause-and-effect relationships you listed as you read. What are the main causes of Richard's predicament?

5. **Examine Language** Reread lines 1–10 and note the words and phrases that Wright uses to make hunger seem human. What effect does this **personification** have on the reader?

6. **Analyze Dialogue** Wright not only narrates events but also uses dialogue to bring a sense of reality to his narrative. Review the conversations between Wright and his mother. What does it suggest about their relationship and the way it changes?

7. **Predict** Reread the last paragraph of the selection. Will Richard be different after fighting the street gang? Cite evidence to support your prediction.

8. **Interpret Autobiography** In an autobiography, the writer must choose which life experiences to include and which to leave out. In your opinion, why did Wright choose to share this particular episode in his life? Support your opinion.

9. **Evaluate Narrative Techniques** Find examples of each narrative technique listed in the graphic shown. Which narrative techniques does Wright make the best use of in this autobiography? Explain your evaluation.

Techniques	Examples
• Describes conflict	
• Uses believable dialogue	
• Builds suspense	
• Develops personalities	

Literary Criticism

10. **Critical Interpretations** When this autobiography was published in 1945, a critic wrote, "It is not easy for those who have had happier childhoods, with little restraint or fear in them, to face up to the truth of this childhood of Richard Wright." Do you agree with this statement? Explain why or why not.

THE RIGHTS TO THE STREETS OF MEMPHIS   **117**

8. **● STANDARDS FOCUS Autobiography** This episode marks the point at which Wright overcomes his fear and stands up for himself. Vivid detail and the dramatic way the episode is portrayed show how important the episode was to Wright.

9. **Describes conflict:** lines 72–81, 91–94, 130–142. **Uses believable dialogue:** lines 14–56, 82–118. **Builds suspense:** lines 100–108, 119–130. **Develops personalities:** lines 1–13, 60–71, 100–118. Students may choose any of these techniques, but should provide reasons for their choices.

Literary Criticism
Possible answers:

10. **Agree:** If a person had been fortunate enough to have had a happy childhood, it may be difficult to relate to and understand the hardship that Wright suffered during his childhood. **Disagree:** People who have not suffered the kinds of hardships faced by Wright might still be able to feel sympathy for him and his situation. Most people have had to face some kind of difficulties in their own lives.

Practice and Apply

After Reading

For additional support of post-reading questions, use these copy masters:

R RESOURCE MANAGER—Copy Masters
Reading Check p. 148 (to check understanding of the selection)
Autobiography p. 141 (for practice of literary analysis standards focus)
Question Support p. 149 (After Reading questions adapted for English learners and less-proficient readers)

For additional questions, see page 135.

To challenge students further, see
ℹ Bob Marzano's Power Thinking Activities at **ClassZone.com**

ANSWERS

Comprehension

1. *Richard's father had provided the food, but he abandoned the family.*

2. *Richard must choose between standing up for himself against bullies or getting punished by his mother.*

3. *The title refers to Richard's having earned the right to walk safely on the streets of his neighborhood.*

Literary Analysis
Possible answers:

4. **● STANDARDS FOCUS Identify Cause and Effect** *The main causes are his father's abandonment of the family, the gang's assaults on him, and his mother's conviction that Richard has to learn to fight for himself.*

5. *Personifying hunger by describing it as if it were a living creature makes the hunger and its effects seem more vivid to the reader.*

6. *The early dialogue suggests that the two have a comfortable relationship. The son feels free to ask for what he wants and the mother teases her son in a good-natured way. The later dialogue reveals that the mother exerts strong control when an important issue is at stake, which forces the son to change.*

7. *It is likely that Richard will now be more self-confident and less fearful. He has become aware of his own power (lines 136–142) and recognizes the victory that it has brought him (lines 144–145).*

ANSWERS

Vocabulary in Context

VOCABULARY PRACTICE

1. *dispirited*

2. *stark*

3. *clamor*

4. *retaliate*

5. *flay*

R RESOURCE MANAGER—Copy Master
Vocabulary Practice p. 146

VOCABULARY IN WRITING

Encourage students to include specific details in their descriptions and to use sensory language to make their writing come alive. Remind them to consider not only what they would see as observers but also what they would hear.

VOCABULARY STRATEGY: SYNONYMS AND ANTONYMS *(also an EL language objective)*

- Point out that words such as *and* in the example phrase "tired and dispirited" offer clues as to whether an unknown word could be a synonym or antonym of another word in the sentence.

- After students complete the practice, discuss the clue words in each sentence.

Possible answers:

1. *containing plenty*

2. *surprised*

3. *rich*

4. *lying*

5. *unwillingness to compromise*

R RESOURCE MANAGER—Copy Master
Vocabulary Strategy p. 147

ℹ Vocabulary Center at **ClassZone.com**
Additional Vocabulary Activities

Vocabulary in Context

VOCABULARY PRACTICE

Write the word from the list that best completes each sentence.

clamor
dispirited
flay
retaliate
stark

1. Alone and hungry, Richard felt _____ as he walked the streets.

2. He knew it would be hard to rise above his family's _____ poverty.

3. He tried to concentrate amid the _____ as several older boys shouted at him.

4. If they tried to harm him, he intended to _____ immediately.

5. He would _____ them with his stick if necessary.

VOCABULARY IN WRITING

Suppose you had been a neighbor of Richard's, watching the events in the street. How would you describe the encounter with the other boys? Write three sentences about what you saw, using three vocabulary words. Here is an example.

> **EXAMPLE SENTENCE**
>
> *I saw a look of **stark** horror on Richard's face.*

VOCABULARY STRATEGY: SYNONYMS AND ANTONYMS

Synonyms are words with the same, or almost the same, meaning. **Antonyms** are words with opposite meanings. Recognizing synonyms and antonyms can help you figure out the meanings of unknown words. For example, Wright says his mother felt "tired and dispirited." Though *tired* is not an exact synonym of *dispirited*, it is close enough in meaning to help you figure out what *dispirited* means.

PRACTICE In each sentence, the boldfaced word is either a synonym or an antonym of the underlined word. Use the boldfaced word to help you figure out the meaning of the underlined word. Then write a definition of the underlined word.

1. The table was **overflowing** with <u>bountiful</u> platters of food.

2. Though Alice was <u>nonplused</u> by his remarks, I was **unsurprised.**

3. The <u>affluent</u> Henleys were sometimes shunned by their **poorer** neighbors.

4. She wasn't **deceiving** anyone with her <u>prevaricating</u>.

5. <u>Intransigence</u> and **stubbornness** won't help us overcome this problem.

🔊 VOCABULARY PRACTICE
For more practice, go to the **Vocabulary Center** at **ClassZone.com.**

DIFFERENTIATED INSTRUCTION

FOR ENGLISH LEARNERS

Vocabulary: Cognates For speakers of Romance languages, point out that the word *encounter* in the **Vocabulary in Writing** directions is a cognate.

FOR ADVANCED LEARNERS/PRE–AP

Vocabulary in Writing Have students use at least three vocabulary words in a paragraph written from the point of view of one of the boys in the gang.

Reading-Writing Connection

Demonstrate your understanding of the characters in "The Rights to the Streets of Memphis" by responding to these prompts. Then use **Revision: Grammar and Style** to improve your writing.

WRITING PROMPTS	SELF-CHECK
A. Short Response: Write a Different Conclusion How might things have been different if Richard had not been victorious? Imagine that Richard lost the fight and the grocery money despite his strong **convictions.** Then write **one or two paragraphs** about his defeat and its consequences.	*A strong conclusion will . . .* • provide details about how Richard lost the fight • describe his and his mother's reactions to the loss
B. Extended Response: Interpret Motives Mrs. Wright left her two young sons alone during the day. She ordered Richard to bring home groceries even if he must fight a gang to do so. Why did she act as she did? Write a **three-to-five-paragraph response,** describing her actions and explaining her motives.	*A successful response will . . .* • describe Mrs. Wright's actions • explain the reasons for her actions

REVISION: GRAMMAR AND STYLE

EMPHASIZE ACTION Review the **Grammar and Style** note on page 115. There, Wright uses **strong verbs in a series** to emphasize the actions taking place. By incorporating similar techniques into your own writing, you can help readers to easily visualize events, as Wright does.

Here is another example from the story:

> *When I reached the corner, a gang of boys grabbed me, knocked me down, snatched the basket, took the money, and sent me running home in panic.* (lines 75–77)

Now study this model. Notice how the revisions in red make the sentence much stronger, yet still concise. Revise your responses to the prompts by using the same techniques.

STUDENT MODEL

To help her son survive, Mrs. Wright ~~used several tactics to make~~ *urged, commanded, and finally compelled* him *to* face his deepest fears.

 **WRITING TOOLS**
For prewriting, revision, and editing tools, visit the **Writing Center** at ClassZone.com.

THE RIGHTS TO THE STREETS OF MEMPHIS **119**

FOR LESS—PROFICIENT WRITERS

For Prompt A:
- Help students visualize the sequence of events.
- Help students express each step in a separate sentence. For example: *Richard swung the stick and hit one boy. Then another boy grabbed the stick.*
- Encourage students to continue the sequence of action through the point when Richard ultimately returns home.

For Prompt B:
- Limit the length of the assignment to no more than two paragraphs.
- Help students analyze Mrs. Wright's actions in terms of cause and effect.

Reading-Writing Connection

WRITING PROMPTS

- For Prompt A, encourage students to consider what Richard might have learned about himself even if he lost the fight. Then have them think about whether Mrs. Wright would have softened her convictions if her son had lost the fight.

- For Prompt B, have students use a Cause and Effect Diagram to reflect on these questions: Why is Mrs. Wright's life difficult? Why does she want her son to stand up for himself? Why doesn't she accompany him to the store? Are her expectations of her son unfair?

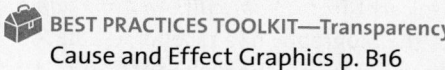 **BEST PRACTICES TOOLKIT**—Transparency
Cause and Effect Graphics p. B16

For writing support, see

Writing Center at **ClassZone.com**

REVISION: GRAMMAR AND STYLE

After students examine the revisions in the student model, write this sentence on the board. Have students suggest similar changes to emphasize the action. Remind students to follow each verb or verb phrase in a series with a comma.

> *The fans ~~expressed great joy~~ leapt, shouted, and sang when their soccer team scored in the final minute of play.*

 **RESOURCE MANAGER**—Copy Master
Emphasize Action p. 150

Assess and Reteach

Assess

RESOURCE MANAGER—Copy Masters
Selection Test A pp. 153–154
Selection Test B/C pp. 155–156

Test Generator CD

Reteach

STANDARDS LESSON FILE
Literature Lesson 6: Conflict and Suspense
Literature Lesson 43: Dialogue and Dialect
Reading Lesson 7: Recognizing Cause-and-Effect: Single and Multiple
Vocabulary Lesson 18: Synonyms and Antonyms

THE RIGHTS TO THE STREETS OF MEMPHIS **119**

Focus and Motivate

OBJECTIVES

Literary Analysis
- explore the key idea of what makes a **winner**
- analyze suspense
- read a biography

Reading
- identify author's purpose

Vocabulary
- build vocabulary for reading and writing
- understand and use the Latin word root *aud* (also an EL language objective)

SUMMARY

In this excerpt from *Seabiscuit: An American Legend,* the biography of a racehorse, Laura Hillenbrand recounts the 1937 Santa Anita Handicap. Rivals Seabiscuit and Rosemont compete in a hard-fought race, but Seabiscuit falters at the end and loses. Hillenbrand suggests that the loss may have been due to jockey Red Pollard's partial blindness, which he had kept secret.

What makes a WINNER?

Lead into a discussion of the **KEY IDEA** by posing the question. Have students identify qualities that characterize a **winner**. Extend the discussion by asking how a person might be a "winner" even without participating in a competition. Then have students complete the **PRESENT** activity.

Selection Resources

from Seabiscuit: An American Legend
Biography by Laura Hillenbrand

What makes a WINNER?

KEY IDEA In the heat of competition, what separates a **winner** from a loser? That's the question explored in *Seabiscuit,* the story of the legendary racehorse that won the hearts of millions of Americans.

PRESENT With a partner, choose someone you consider to be a winner. Create a "portrait" of the person in words and images, labeling the qualities that you feel led to his or her success. Share your portrait with the rest of the class.

RESOURCE MANAGER UNIT 1

Plan and Teach pp. 157–164
Literary Analysis
Summary pp. 165†*, 166‡*
Suspense in Biography pp. 167, 168†*
Question Support p. 176*

Reading
Identify Author's Purpose
  pp. 169, 170†*
Reading Check p. 175
Reading Fluency p. 177

Vocabulary
Study p. 171*
Practice p. 172
Strategy p. 173
Assessment
Selection Tests A, B/C pp. 179*, 181*
Test Generator CD

BEST PRACTICES TOOLKIT

Differentiated Instruction
  pp. 31–38*

Scaffolding Instruction
  pp. 43–46*

Graphic Organizers/Strategies
New Word Analysis • Predicting
• Word Sorts

Reading Support
Audio Anthology CD*

Technology
Literature and Vocabulary
  Centers at **ClassZone.com**
Write*Smart* CD

* Resources for Differentiation   † Also in Spanish   ‡ In Haitian Creole and Vietnamese

LITERARY ANALYSIS: SUSPENSE IN BIOGRAPHY

A **biography** is a true account of someone's life. The biography you are about to read is unusual in that the author has chosen to make not a person but a famous horse the focus of her work.

Though biographers must research and report facts accurately, a good biographer is also a storyteller who engages readers. Through the use of **foreshadowing,** for example, the biographer can build **suspense** in the same way that a fiction writer does. Notice how the first sentence sets up a feeling of tension and concern about future events:

Quiet trepidation settled over the Howard barn in the week before the Santa Anita Handicap.

As you read this selection from *Seabiscuit,* pay attention to the various ways Laura Hillenbrand creates suspense.

READING SKILL: IDENTIFY AUTHOR'S PURPOSE

An **author's purpose** is the reasons the author has for writing a particular work. An author typically has one or more of these basic purposes in mind:

- to inform or explain
- to express thoughts or feelings
- to persuade
- to entertain

Understanding an author's purpose for writing can provide insight into the message, or theme, of a work. It can also help you decide *how* to read. For example, if you realize that an author is trying to inform or explain by including detailed information, you might decide to take notes as you read in order to revisit important content later on.

As you read this selection, try to decide Hillenbrand's purpose. Consider whether she might have had more than one purpose in mind. Record your findings, and be ready to discuss them.

Review: **Predict**

VOCABULARY IN CONTEXT

Try to figure out the meaning of each boldfaced word.

1. felt **trepidation** waiting
2. mumbled **inaudibly**
3. looking for the **optimal** solution
4. tiny **increment** of speed
5. a slow, steady **cadence**
6. clumsy and **inept**
7. **inexplicably** dropped out of the race
8. finally reached an **unequivocal** decision

Author Online

Laura Hillenbrand born 1967

The Will to Overcome At the age of 19, Laura Hillenbrand's life changed forever. Up until then, she had been physically active, swimming competitively, riding horses, and playing tennis. Suddenly, she was stricken with chronic fatigue syndrome, an illness that sometimes made her too weak even to feed herself. To find purpose in her life and "a way to endure the suffering," Hillenbrand started writing. As she wrote *Seabiscuit,* she found a link between herself and her subject—a horse who had the will to overcome obstacles.

A Thorough Researcher Although her illness sometimes left her bedridden, Hillenbrand meticulously researched the life of Seabiscuit. She placed ads in horseracing magazines, interviewed aging jockeys by phone, and sought information from the Library of Congress. Her research paid off in a best-selling biography filled with suspenseful events and memorable details.

 MORE ABOUT THE AUTHOR For more on Laura Hillenbrand, visit the **Literature Center** at **ClassZone.com.**

Background

Horseracing Known as the sport of kings, horseracing is one of the oldest of all spectator sports. A popular type of horserace is the handicap, a race in which the horses carry different amounts of weight based on factors such as age and past performances. Faster horses carry more weight; slower horses carry less. The goal is to give all the horses an equal chance of winning. To ride a racehorse, a jockey needs balance, coordination, strength, and quick reflexes. According to Hillenbrand, "The extraordinary athleticism of the jockey is unparalleled."

Teach

STANDARDS FOCUS

● SUSPENSE IN BIOGRAPHY

For instructional support, read aloud this example:

> Maria has trained hard for months, yet everyone insists she has no chance. She is older than all the other runners and has not competed since her injury.

Ask students how this example creates suspense. ***Possible answer:*** *Although the odds are stacked against Maria, she has been training hard to win. The suspense lies in the question of whether she can beat the odds and prove the naysayers wrong.*

CHECK UNDERSTANDING Ask students to describe suspenseful moments in stories.

READING SKILL

■ IDENTIFY AUTHOR'S PURPOSE

After students read the page, have them identify possible purposes for writing a nonfiction book about track stars. ***Possible answer:*** *to inform, to entertain, to express admiration or enthusiasm*

CHECK UNDERSTANDING Ask students to identify possible purposes for writing a science-fiction novel about horses with superpowers, including an ability to fly.

R **RESOURCE MANAGER—Copy Master**
Identify Author's Purpose p. 169 (for student use while reading the selection)

VOCABULARY SKILL

▲ VOCABULARY IN CONTEXT

DIAGNOSE WORD KNOWLEDGE To determine preteaching needs, have all students complete Vocabulary in Context. Check students' definitions against those on the selection pages. *Possible answers:* **1.** *fear,* **2.** *too quietly to be heard,* **3.** *best,* **4.** *increase,* **5.** *rhythm,* **6.** *incompetent,* **7.** *without explanation,* **8.** *without doubt*

PRETEACH VOCABULARY Use the Vocabulary Study copy master to help students predict meanings for each boldfaced word in the copy master.

1. Read the first item aloud, emphasizing *trepidation.*
2. Point out the phrase "anxiously waited for the horse race to begin." Elicit possible meanings for *trepidation,* such as "nervousness."
3. Repeat the procedure for the other items.

 RESOURCE MANAGER—Copy Master
Vocabulary Study p. 171

For general guidelines on differentiating vocabulary instruction and for alternative vocabulary activities for students not needing vocabulary preteaching, see

 BEST PRACTICES TOOLKIT
Scaffolding Vocabulary Instruction pp. 43–46
 Vocabulary Center at **ClassZone.com**

Possible answer: Seabiscuit's muscular body and powerful legs, as he surges forward, convey his strength and will to win. He appears totally focused, ears alert and forward. In addition, the angle of the photograph suggests that Seabiscuit is leading the race.

READING SKILL

Ⓐ AUTHOR'S PURPOSE

Possible answer: The detailed account in the opening of the biography shows that the author's main purpose is to inform readers about the rivalry between Seabiscuit and Rosemont. Her style of writing and choice of engaging details suggests that she also intends to entertain her readers with a fascinating, true story.

If students need help . . .

• Have students identify factual information that the author presents in the first three paragraphs. Also note the author's explanation of how the racetrack is prepared (lines 3–4). Remind students about the extensive research that was required to unearth so many details.

• Call attention to the author's vivid phrases, such as "licking flames" (line 4), "scorched the track" (line 5), and "Rumors swirled" (lines 7– 8), as well as the literary features she uses (characterization, dialogue, and setting). Discuss how lines 13–22 build excitement.

Extend the Discussion *Seabiscuit* was the basis for a popular movie. How can you tell, even at the beginning of the selection, that Hillenbrand's account might make an exciting film?

Seabiscuit:
AN AMERICAN LEGEND

Laura Hillenbrand

Quiet **trepidation** settled over the Howard barn in the week before the Santa Anita Handicap.[1] Late in the week, a long, soaking shower doused the racing oval. When the rain stopped, asphalt-baking machines droned over the course, licking flames over the surface to dry the soil. Rosemont emerged from the barn three days before the race and scorched the track in his final workout. Reporters waited for Smith[2] to give his horse a similar workout, but they never saw Seabiscuit doing anything more than stretching his legs. Rumors swirled around the track that Seabiscuit was lame. Rosemont's stock rose; Seabiscuit's dropped.

10   Smith had fooled them. At three o'clock one morning shortly before the race, he led Seabiscuit out to the track and gave him one last workout in peace and isolation. The horse ran beautifully.

On February 27, 1937, Charles and Marcela Howard[3] arrived at Santa Anita to watch their pride and joy go for the hundred-grander. They were giddy with anticipation. "If Seabiscuit loses," mused a friend, "Mrs. Howard is going to be so heartbroken that I'll have to carry her out. If he wins, Charley'll be so excited that I'll have to carry him." Howard couldn't keep still. He trotted up to the press box and made the wildly popular announcement that if his horse won, he'd send up a barrel of champagne for the reporters. He went down 20 to the betting area, and seeing that the line was too long to wait, he grabbed a bettor and jammed five $1,000 bills into his hand. "Put it all on Seabiscuit's nose,[4] please," he told the bewildered wagerer before trotting off again. Ⓐ

---

1. **Santa Anita Handicap:** a race at the Santa Anita track in California, with a prize of $100,000.
2. **Smith:** Tom Smith, Seabiscuit's trainer.
3. **Charles and Marcela Howard:** Seabiscuit's owners.
4. **"put it . . . nose":** bet all the money on Seabiscuit's coming in first.

trepidation
(trĕp'ĭ-dā'shən)
n. nervous fear

ANALYZE VISUALS
Examine the photograph of Seabiscuit. What details convey his strength and will to win?

❶ Targeted Passage

Ⓐ AUTHOR'S PURPOSE
From what you have read so far, what do you think is the author's main purpose for writing?

DIFFERENTIATED INSTRUCTION

FOR ALL STUDENTS
Learning Center In your classroom or school library, create a Learning Center devoted to the life and career of Seabiscuit. Provide books, print, and online articles as well as photos that cover key events. Assign groups to research these key events, and allow time for students to present their findings.

FOR LESS–PROFICIENT READERS
In combination with the *Audio Anthology CD,* use one or more Targeted Passages (pp. 122, 125, 127, 129) to ensure that students focus on key story events, concepts, and skills. Targeted Passages are also good for English learners.

❶ Targeted Passage [Lines 1–14]
This passage establishes the conflict and the setting and introduces several key characters, including the two rival horses.

ANALYZE VISUALS

Activity Ask students what physical attributes of a successful jockey the photograph highlights. What other traits might a trainer look for in a jockey? *Possible answer: A successful jockey needs to be small-framed and lightweight. Other traits that a trainer might look for are physical strength and endurance, determination, and the ability to communicate with horses.*

BACKGROUND

Point out that jockeys tend to have small builds and to weigh less than 115 pounds. Every additional two or three pounds a horse carries can slow it down by a length in a mile-long race, successful jockeys must be small and light.

°LITERARY ANALYSIS

ⓑ SUSPENSE IN BIOGRAPHY

Possible answer: The writer builds tension by spotlighting the two main competitors, describing the particular challenges that each horse and each rider must face, and emphasizing their rivalry.

If students need help . . . Focus on the obstacles that concerned each jockey.

- Why was Seabiscuit's jockey worried? (*lines 32–40*)
- What problem did Rosemont's jockey face? (*lines 40–47*)
- Why does Hillenbrand concentrate on the concerns of the two main competitors? (*lines 48–50*)

READING STRATEGY: *Review*

ⓒ PREDICT

Possible answer: Seabiscuit seems likely to win, based on his good start in the race, Pollard's confidence, and the horse's present lead on Rosemont. Also, the passage implies that the "speed horses" won't be able to maintain their pace.

If students need help . . . Review lines 52–63 with students, and help them use Predicting to predict the winner.

 BEST PRACTICES TOOLKIT—Transparency Predicting p. A10

124 UNIT 1: NARRATIVE STRUCTURE

At a little past 4:00 P.M. Pollard[5] and Seabiscuit parted from Smith at the paddock gate and walked out onto the track for the Santa Anita Handicap. A record crowd of sixty thousand fans had come to see eighteen horses try for the richest
30 purse in the world. Millions more listened on radio.

As Pollard felt Seabiscuit's hooves sink into the russet soil, he had reason to worry. The baking machines had not completely dried the surface. Rain and dirt had blended into a heavy goo along the rail; breaking from the three post,[6] Seabiscuit would be right
40 down in it. Far behind him in the post parade, jockey Harry Richards was contemplating a different set of obstacles for Rosemont. He had drawn the seventeenth post position. He was going to have the luxury of a hard, fast track, but his problem would be traffic. As a late runner, Rosemont would have to pick his way through the cluttered field.

The two jockeys virtually bookended the field as they moved to the post. Pollard feared nothing but Richards and Rosemont. Richards feared nothing
50 but Pollard and Seabiscuit. The two horses stood motionless while the field was loaded around them. ⓑ

At the sound of the bell, Seabiscuit bounded forward. To his outside, a crowd of horses rushed inward to gain **optimal** position. The field doubled over on itself, and the hinge was Seabiscuit, who was pinched back to ninth. In a cloud of horses, Pollard spotted daylight five feet or so off the rail. He banked Seabiscuit out into it, holding him out of the deep part of the track. He slipped up to fourth position, just off of front-running Special Agent. On the first turn Seabiscuit was crowded back down to the rail. As the field straightened into the backstretch, Pollard found another avenue and eased him
60 outward again, to firmer ground. Ahead, Special Agent was setting a suicidal pace, but Pollard sensed how fast it was and was not going to be lured into it. He sat back and waited. Behind him, Rosemont was tugging along toward the back of the field, waiting for the speed horses to crumble. ⓒ

Seabiscuit owner C. S. Howard, jockey Red Pollard, and trainer Tom Smith.

ⓑ SUSPENSE IN BIOGRAPHY
Reread lines 32–51. What technique does the writer use to build suspense?

optimal (ŏp′tə-məl) *adj.* most favorable; best

ⓒ PREDICT
Which horse do you predict will win the race? Why do you think so?

---

5. **Pollard:** Red Pollard, Seabiscuit's jockey.

6. **the three post:** in the starting gate, the third position out from the railing.

124 UNIT 1: NARRATIVE STRUCTURE

DIFFERENTIATED INSTRUCTION

FOR ENGLISH LEARNERS

Vocabulary: Multiple-Meaning Words
Remind students that a word can have two different meanings with the same spelling. Use New Word Analysis to teach these multiple-meaning words from the selection: *purse* (line 30), *post* (line 48), *field* (line 53), *banked* (line 56), *track* (line 56), *avenue* (line 59), *move* (line 65), *fold* (line 72), *rump* (line 74), *wire* (line 79), *rest* (line 87), *toy* (line 97), *rail* (line 101).

 BEST PRACTICES TOOLKIT—Transparency New Word Analysis p. E8

With a half mile to go, Pollard positioned Seabiscuit in the clear and readied for his move. Behind him, Richards sensed that the moment had come to shoot for Seabiscuit. He began threading Rosemont through the field, cutting in and out, picking off horses one by one, talking in his horse's ear as clumps of dirt cracked into his face. His luck was holding; every hole toward which he guided his horse held open just long enough for him to gallop through. On
70 the far turn he reached Seabiscuit's heels and began looking for a way around him. Ahead of him, Pollard crouched and watched Special Agent's churning hindquarters, waiting for him to fold.

② Targeted Passage

At the top of the stretch Special Agent faltered. Pollard pulled Seabiscuit's nose to the outside and slapped him on the rump. Seabiscuit pounced. Richards saw him go and gunned Rosemont through the hole after him, but Seabiscuit had stolen a three-length advantage. Special Agent gave way grudgingly along the inside as Indian Broom rallied up the outside, not quite quick enough to keep up.

Lengthening stride for the long run to the wire, Seabiscuit was alone on the
80 lead in the dry, hard center of the track. Pollard had delivered a masterpiece of reinsmanship, avoiding the traps and saving ground while minimizing his run along the boggy rail. He had won the tactical battle with Richards. He was coming into the homestretch of the richest race in the world with a strong horse beneath him. Behind them were seventeen of the best horses in the nation. To the left and right, sixty thousand voices roared. Ahead was nothing but a long strip of red soil.

The rest of the field peeled away, scattered across thirty-two lengths of track behind them. It was down to Rosemont and Seabiscuit.

Seabiscuit was moving fastest. He charged down the stretch in front with
90 Pollard up over his neck, moving with him, driving him on. Rosemont was obscured behind him. He was gaining only by **increments.** Seabiscuit sailed through midstretch a full length ahead of Rosemont. Up in the stands, the Howards and Smith were thinking the same thing: Rosemont is too far behind. Seabiscuit is going to win.

Without warning, horse and rider lost focus. Abruptly, **inexplicably,** Pollard wavered. He lay his whip down on Seabiscuit's shoulder and left it there.

Seabiscuit paused. Perhaps he slowed in hopes of finding an opponent to toy with. Or maybe he sensed Pollard's hesitation. His composure, which Smith had patiently schooled into him over six months, began to unravel. Seabiscuit
100 suddenly took a sharp left turn, veering ten feet across the track and back down into the deep going, straightening himself out just before hitting the rail. He had given away several feet of his lead. The **cadence** of his stride dropped. What had been a seamless union was now only a man and a horse, jangling against each other.

increment (ĭn'krə-mənt) *n.* a small, slight growth or increase

inexplicably (ĭn-ĕk'splĭ-kə-blē) *adv.* in a way that is difficult or impossible to explain

cadence (kād'ns) *n.* a balanced, rhythmic flow

SEABISCUIT **125**

Lines 105–112
REINFORCE *KEY IDEA:* WINNER

Discuss Does the Richards-Rosemont combination have the characteristics of a **winner?** Explain. *Possible answer: The Richards-Rosemont combination does, indeed. Richards is a skilled jockey ready to take advantage of any weakness in the competition, and Rosemont is a fast horse that responds well to the jockey.*

READING SKILL

D AUTHOR'S PURPOSE

Possible answer: The author layers an astonishing amount of detail to describe a few seconds of the race. Specific numbers help readers to visualize the action ("fifteen strides," "ten feet," "six feet"), as does mention of "half-moon blinker cups" that limit Seabiscuit's vision. Hillenbrand also describes "the roar from the grandstand" (lines 119–120) and the shrieking crowd (line 123). This detailed, sensory account is both informative and entertaining.

If students need help . . . Work with students to brainstorm details that appeal to sight and to sound. Record their ideas, using concept webs.

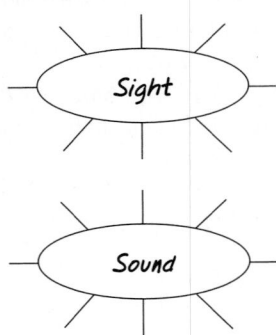

Extend the Discussion How do the short, clipped sentences in lines 121–123 help to build the excitement?

From between Rosemont's ears, Richards saw Seabiscuit's form disintegrate. He looked toward the wire. It seemed close enough to touch, but Rosemont still wasn't past Seabiscuit's saddlecloth. He had been riding on instinct, reflex, but now his heart caught in his throat: *I am too late.* Desperate, he flung himself over Rosemont's neck, booting and whipping and screaming,
110 "Faster, baby, faster!" Striding high in the center of the track, Rosemont was suddenly animated by Richards's raging desire. He dropped his head and dug in. Seabiscuit's lead, stride by stride, slipped away.

For a few seconds at the most critical moment of their careers, Pollard and Seabiscuit faltered. For fifteen strides, more than the length of a football field, Pollard remained virtually motionless. Rosemont was some ten feet to his outside, leaving plenty of room for Pollard to swing Seabiscuit out of the rail-path's slow going, but Pollard didn't take the opportunity. From behind his half-moon blinker cups,[7] Seabiscuit could see nothing but an empty track ahead of him, nor is it likely that he could hear Rosemont over the roar from
120 the grandstand. Or perhaps he was waiting for him. His left ear swung around lazily, as if he were paying attention to something in the infield. His stride slowed. His mind seemed scattered. The lead was vanishing. A length. Six feet. A neck. The wire was rushing at them. The crowd was shrieking. **D**

D AUTHOR'S PURPOSE
Reread lines 113–123. What details make this passage not only informative but entertaining?

---

7. **blinker cups:** flaps put over a horse's eyes to keep it from seeing sideways.

DIFFERENTIATED INSTRUCTION

FOR LESS-PROFICIENT READERS
Language Support Elicit or provide the meaning of the idiomatic phrase *his heart caught in his throat* (line 108), "felt intense, momentary worry or despair." Ask volunteers to share examples of experiences that caused their hearts to catch in their throats.

FOR ADVANCED LEARNERS/PRE-AP
Analyze Style Hillenbrand uses literary techniques to convey information while simultaneously creating an exciting account of the neck-and-neck race. Have students work in small groups to identify and discuss examples of characterization, point of view, and dialogue. How do these techniques help the author to accomplish both purposes?

Rosemont edges out Seabiscuit to win the Santa Anita Handicap by a nose.

ANALYZE VISUALS
What elements of the dramatic finish are captured by this photograph? What does the photo add to your understanding of the story? Be specific.

With just a few yards to go, Pollard broke out of his limbo. He burst into frenzied motion. Seabiscuit's ears snapped back and he dived forward. But Rosemont had momentum. The lead shrank to nothing. Rosemont caught Seabiscuit, then took a lead of inches. Seabiscuit was accelerating, his rhythm building, his mind narrowed down to his task at the urgent call of his rider. But Richards was driving harder, scratching and yelling and pleading for
130 Rosemont to run. Seabiscuit cut the advantage away. They drew even again.
Rosemont and Seabiscuit flew under the wire together. **E**

Up in their box, the Howards leapt up. Charles ran to the Turf Club bar, calling for champagne for everyone. Voices sang out and corks popped and a wild celebration began.

Gradually, the revelers went silent. The crowd had stopped cheering. The stewards posted no winner. They were waiting for the photo. The exhausted horses returned to be unsaddled, and the fans sat in agonized anticipation. Two minutes passed. In the hush, a sibilant sound attended the finish photo as it slid down to the stewards. There was a terrible pause. The numbers blinked up
140 on the board.

Rosemont had won.

E SUSPENSE IN BIOGRAPHY
Reread lines 124–131. What words does the writer use to build excitement in this passage?

3 Targeted Passage

FOR LESS–PROFICIENT READERS

3 Targeted Passage [Lines 131–141]

This passage presents the climax of the race: a photo finish victory for Rosemont.

- Which two horses cross the finish line at the same time?
- Why were the fans sitting "in agonized anticipation" (line 137)?
- What does the photo finish show?

ANALYZE VISUALS

Possible answer: The photograph shows just how close Rosemont and Seabiscuit are and how far ahead of the pack these two lead horses are. The photo highlights the intensity, speed, and demands of the race in the horses' strained efforts and the jockeys' athletic contortions. It contributes to the viewer's understanding of the astonishing skill required to win such a race.

LITERARY ANALYSIS

E **SUSPENSE IN BIOGRAPHY**

Possible answer: The writer uses action words and phrases to build excitement, such as broke out, burst into frenzied motion, snapped back, dived forward, accelerating, urgent call, driving harder, scratching and yelling and pleading, and flew under the wire.

Extend the Discussion What effect does line 131 have on the reader?

BACKGROUND

Photo Finish A photograph taken at the moment that the horses cross the finish line must be examined before officials announce the winner of a close race. As in the 1937 Santa Anita Handicap, a horse may win by such a small margin that the winner can be determined only by studying the photograph taken at the wire, literally making the race a "photo finish." The term is also used informally to describe any very close contest.

REINFORCE *KEY IDEA:* WINNER

Discuss It has been said that true **winners** must also know how to lose. How might this saying apply to Charles and Marcela's behavior after the race? How might it apply to Pollard?
Possible answers: True winners are gracious in defeat. Charles and Marcela smile bravely and continue passing out champagne. Pollard goes directly to Richards and congratulates him on his victory.

ANALYZE VISUALS

Possible answer: Pollard's smile shows his fondness for Seabiscuit. That he appears to be putting a blanket on the horse suggests that he takes good care of the animal. Seabiscuit seems calm and content. The photograph reflects their strong, close bond and the communication generated by this connection.

A howl went up from the grandstand. Thousands of spectators were certain that the stewards had it wrong, that Seabiscuit had been robbed. But the photo was <u>**unequivocal**</u>: Rosemont's long bay muzzle hung there in the picture, just a wink ahead of Seabiscuit's. "Dame Fortune," wrote announcer Joe Hernandez, "made a mistake and kissed the wrong horse—Rosemont—in the glorious end of the Santa Anita Handicap."

Charles and Marcela collected themselves. The length of Rosemont's nose had cost them $70,700. They continued passing out the champagne, brave 150 smiles on their faces.

Pollard didn't need to look at the tote board. He knew he had lost from the instant the noses hit the line. Wrung to exhaustion and deathly pale, he slid from Seabiscuit's back. He walked over to Richards, who was being smothered in kisses by his tearful wife. Pollard's face was blank, his voice barely above a whisper. All around him, people regarded him with expressions of cool accusation.

unequivocal
(ŭn′ĭ-kwĭv′ə-kəl)
adj. allowing no doubt or misunderstanding

ANALYZE VISUALS
What does this photo of Seabiscuit and Red Pollard show you about their relationship? Be specific.

128   UNIT 1: NARRATIVE STRUCTURE

DIFFERENTIATED INSTRUCTION

FOR LESS–PROFICIENT READERS
Language Support Elicit or provide the meaning of the phrase *Dame Fortune . . . kissed the wrong horse* (lines 145–146)—"the less talented horse (that is, Rosemont) had better luck." Explain that this kind of figure of speech is called *personification,* attributing human characteristics to animals, objects, places, or forces of nature. Ask students to suggest other examples.

FOR ENGLISH LEARNERS
Vocabulary: Cognates Remind students that the prefix *un-* means "not." Then call attention to the vocabulary word *unequivocal* (line 144). Point out that the Spanish cognate *equivocar* means "to mistake," so *unequivocal* means "no mistaking" (or "unmistakable"). Have students who speak Latin-based languages identify other words similar to those in their language and share their findings.

"Congratulations, Harry, you rode a swell race," Pollard said.

"Thanks," said Richards, his face covered in lipstick and his voice breaking; he had shouted it away urging Rosemont on. "But it was very close."

160 "Close, yes," said Pollard almost **inaudibly**, "but you won."

Pollard saw Howard hovering nearby, waiting for him. The jockey went to him.

"What happened?" Howard asked gently. Ashen and spent, Pollard said that the rail had been slow, and that he had been unable to get outside without fouling Rosemont. If he and Rosemont had switched positions, he was sure Seabiscuit would have won.

It was a thin excuse. Pollard must have known that to save his professional standing, he would have to offer more that than, say something that would explain how he had allowed Rosemont to come to him without fighting back 170 until the last moment. Already, harsh words were being hung on him: *arrogant,* **inept**, *overconfident.* He could not have mistaken the reproach on the faces of those around him. His reputation was tumbling. But Pollard gave the public nothing to make them reconsider.

Perhaps he couldn't. He had a secret to keep, a gamble he had made years earlier and remade with each race. But he could no longer think that its risks affected only himself.

Perhaps Pollard didn't see Rosemont coming because of the blindness of his right eye. **ⓕ**

It is unlikely that he could have heard Rosemont over the din from the 180 crowd. Rosemont's surge, unexpected and sudden, may have eluded Pollard until very late in the race. Pollard did not begin urging Seabiscuit in earnest until Rosemont was alongside him, just forward enough for Pollard to see him with his left eye, upon turning his head. One good eye offers little depth perception, so he may not have been able to judge whether Rosemont was far enough to his right to allow Seabiscuit to move outward.

If this explanation is correct, then Pollard was trapped. He was publicly accused of inexcusable failure in the most important race of his career, but he could not defend himself. Had he let on that he was blind in one eye, his career would have been over. Like most jockeys in the 1930s, he had nowhere 190 else to go, nothing else to live on, nothing else he loved. For Red Pollard, there was no road back to Edmonton. If his blindness was the cause of the loss, his frustration and guilt must have been consuming.

Howard accepted Pollard's explanation without criticism. Neither he nor Smith blamed him.

Almost everyone else did. ∾

inaudibly (ĭn-ô′də-blē) *adv.* in a way that is impossible to hear

inept (ĭn-ĕpt′) *adj.* generally incompetent

ⓕ SUSPENSE IN BIOGRAPHY
Notice that the writer withholds this important piece of information from the reader until after the race is over. If the writer had revealed this information before describing the race, would the suspense have been greater or less? Explain.

④ Targeted Passage

LITERARY ANALYSIS

ⓕ SUSPENSE IN BIOGRAPHY

Possible answers: The suspense would have been **less:** *Readers might have expected something would go wrong as a result of Pollard's partial blindness.* **The suspense would have been** **greater:** *The possibility of the partially blind jockey missing important visual information would have created tension. Readers would have wondered if Pollard could overcome his limitation.*

SELECTION WRAP—UP

REFLECT Have students consider to what extent this excerpt is about Seabiscuit and to what extent it is about Red Pollard. Would the story be more interesting or less interesting if the author had omitted details about Pollard? Why?

⭐ **CRITIQUE** Ask students: What did you admire most about Seabiscuit? about Pollard? Ask them to give reasons that support their answers.

READING FLUENCY

Distribute the copy master, and have students work in pairs or groups to practice fluency.

📋 **RESOURCE MANAGER—Copy Master** Reading Fluency p. 177

FOR LESS—PROFICIENT READERS

④ Targeted Passage [Lines 170–195]

This passage reveals Pollard's secret: his partial blindness, which may have cost him the race.

• Who does the public blame for Seabiscuit's loss?

• Why doesn't Pollard say more in his own defense?

• What secret has Pollard been hiding?

• Why has he been hiding it?

• What consequence may this secret have had?

FOR ADVANCED LEARNERS/PRE—AP

Make Judgments Have students work in small groups to debate whether or not Pollard was justified in concealing his partial blindness. Encourage students to consider what they might have done in his situation.

Practice and Apply

After Reading

For additional support of post-reading questions, use these copy masters:

R RESOURCE MANAGER—Copy Masters

Reading Check p. 175 (to check understanding of the selection)

Suspense in Biography p. 167 (for practice of literary analysis standards focus)

Question Support p. 176 (After Reading questions adapted for English learners and less-proficient readers)

For additional questions, see page 161.

ANSWERS

Comprehension

1. *Rosemont was Seabiscuit's main challenger in the race.*

2. *The stewards studied a photograph of the horses crossing the finish line.*

3. *If Pollard's secret got out, his career would be over, because no one would hire a jockey who was blind in one eye.*

Literary Analysis

Possible answers:

4. ■ **STANDARDS FOCUS** *Identify Author's Purpose* *Hillenbrand's main purpose was to inform—that is, to tell Seabiscuit's story. To do this, she provided researched facts and explanations. However, the author also hoped to entertain, as evidenced by her lively narrative style, vivid language, and use of suspense and other literary techniques.*

5. ● **STANDARDS FOCUS** *Analyze Suspense in Biography*

Raising questions in reader's minds: *"Rumors swirled . . . that Seabiscuit was lame" (lines 7–8).* **Foreshadowing:** *"Rain and dirt had blended into a heavy goo along the rail . . . Seabiscuit would be right down in it. . . . [Rosemont's] problem would be traffic" (lines 36–46).* **Withholding certain information:** *"Perhaps Pollard didn't see Rosemont coming because of the blindness of his right eye" (lines 180–181).*

6. *In desperation, Richards intensified his efforts as they approached the finish line, and Rosemont was "animated" by Richardson's "raging desire" (line 111) to win. In contrast, Pollard "inexplicably . . . wavered" and "lay his whip down" (lines 95–96); Seabiscuit*

Comprehension

1. **Recall** Which horse was Seabiscuit's main challenger in the race?

2. **Recall** How did the stewards determine which horse had won the race?

3. **Clarify** Why did Pollard keep the blindness in his right eye a secret?

Literary Analysis

4. **Identify Author's Purpose** Review your notes. What do you think Hillenbrand's main purpose was in writing this **biography?** What other purposes might she have had? Support your answer with evidence.

5. **Analyze Suspense in Biography** How does the author create suspense in this biography? In a chart like the one shown, give examples of each of her narrative techniques.

Narrative Technique	Example
Raising questions in reader's mind	• Rosemont's stock rose
Foreshadowing	
Withholding certain information	

6. **Compare and Contrast** Compare Seabiscuit and Pollard with Rosemont and Richards. What qualities made the difference between the **winner** and the loser of the Santa Anita Handicap?

7. **Make Judgments** Reread lines 186–195. Was it fair to blame Pollard for losing the race? Support your answer with reasons and evidence.

8. **Evaluate** Though not a short story, this selection reads like one. Identify the events that comprise the **falling action** and the **resolution** of the plot. How does the revelation about Pollard's blindness in his right eye affect your evaluation of Seabiscuit as a racing horse?

Literary Criticism

9. **Historical Context** Commenting on her biography of Seabiscuit, Hillenbrand said, "The subjects that I've written about—the men and the horse—were radically different individuals, but the one thread that pulls through all of their lives and through the events that they lived through together is this struggle between overwhelming hardship and the will to overcome it." When Seabiscuit was making racing history, the United States was reeling from the Great Depression, a catastrophic economic collapse that began in 1929 and continued through the 1930s. What might Seabiscuit have represented to the country at that time?

---

then lost his composure.

7. *It probably was fair to blame him because the partially blind jockey "did not begin urging Seabiscuit in earnest until Rosemont was alongside him, just forward enough for Pollard to see him with his left eye . . ." (lines 184–186).*

8. *The falling action follows the announcement of the winner: Pollard congratulates Richards, then converses with Howard. The resolution is Hillenbrand's commentary about how Pollard's partial blindness may have caused Seabiscuit's loss. Revealing*

Pollard's blindness makes the reader wonder if Seabiscuit could have performed better with a different jockey.

Literary Criticism

Possible answer:

9. *Seabiscuit may have represented hope for the country—that a combination of hard work, perseverance, and luck would ultimately enable people to overcome the hardships they faced.*

Vocabulary in Context

VOCABULARY PRACTICE

Write *true* or *false* for each statement.

1. A person who speaks **inaudibly** can easily be heard.
2. The **optimal** time to spot Mars is on a cloudy night.
3. To honor your ancestors, you might build an **increment.**
4. An **inept** person is not a good choice to manage a project.
5. If you have **trepidation** about heights, you may not like skydiving.
6. Troops might march to the **cadence** of a band.
7. If an event occurs **inexplicably,** it is hard to understand why it happens.
8. An **unequivocal** "no" answer indicates that you have not made up your mind.

WORD LIST

cadence
inaudibly
increment
inept
inexplicably
optimal
trepidation
unequivocal

VOCABULARY IN WRITING

Use three or more vocabulary words in a paragraph describing the last few seconds of the race. Here is an example of a sentence you might use.

> **EXAMPLE SENTENCE**
>
> The __cadence__ of the two horses grew faster and faster.

VOCABULARY STRATEGY: THE *aud* WORD FAMILY

The word *inaudibly* can be traced back to the Latin root *aud,* which means "to hear." Many other words belong to the same word family as *inaudibly.* If you can recognize the root in these words, you can understand how they are related in meaning.

PRACTICE Use each word below in a sentence that shows its connection in meaning to *inaudibly.* If necessary, consult a dictionary.

1. audit
2. audiology
3. audience
4. audio-visual
5. auditorium
6. audition

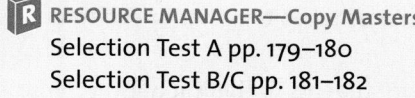

VOCABULARY PRACTICE
For more practice, go to the **Vocabulary Center** at **ClassZone.com.**

ANSWERS

Vocabulary in Context

VOCABULARY PRACTICE

1. *false*   5. *true*
2. *false*   6. *true*
3. *false*   7. *true*
4. *true*   8. *false*

 RESOURCE MANAGER—Copy Master
Vocabulary Practice p. 172

VOCABULARY IN WRITING

Tell students to imagine the sights and sounds of the race as they write. Encourage them to include details that capture the excitement.

VOCABULARY STRATEGY: THE *aud* WORD FAMILY *(also an EL language objective)*

- To help students with the **PRACTICE** activity, work with them on the first item: *audit.* Begin by eliciting or explaining its meaning ("a careful examination of financial records").
- Ask how *audit* might relate to the meaning of *aud.* Model the thinking process with this example: A tax examiner conducting an *audit* of a business would want to *hear* an explanation of the records.

 RESOURCE MANAGER—Copy Master
Vocabulary Strategy p. 173

ⓘ Vocabulary Center at **ClassZone.com**
Additional Vocabulary Activities

Assess and Reteach

Assess

R **RESOURCE MANAGER**—Copy Masters
Selection Test A pp. 179–180
Selection Test B/C pp. 181–182

Test Generator CD

Reteach

S **STANDARDS LESSON FILE**
Literature Lesson 6: Conflict and Suspense
Reading Lesson 3: Determining Author's Purpose
Vocabulary Lesson 7: Latin Roots

DIFFERENTIATED INSTRUCTION

FOR ENGLISH LEARNERS

Vocabulary: Prefixes Have students use Word Sorts to sort vocabulary words in these two categories: those that *do* have a prefix that means "not," and those that *don't* have a prefix that means "not." Explain to students that the *in* in *increment* is not a prefix.

 **BEST PRACTICES TOOLKIT**—Transparency
Word Sorts p. E5

FOR ADVANCED LEARNERS/PRE–AP

Vocabulary in Writing Challenge students to use as many vocabulary words as they can in a brief news story recounting the Santa Anita Handicap. Remind them that news writing attempts to address the Reporter's Questions: *who, what, where, when, why,* and *how.*

Focus and Motivate

OBJECTIVES

Reading for Information
- synthesize information
- draw conclusions
- read a magazine article
- read a timeline
- read a radio transcript

SUMMARY

"Horse of the Century" consists of three brief pieces about Seabiscuit: a magazine article excerpt describing the horse's amazing popularity; a timeline tracing Seabiscuit's racing career; and a radio transcript of the exciting 1937 Santa Anita Handicap, which was the focus of the previous excerpt from *Seabiscuit: An American Legend.*

What's the Connection?

Use a KWL chart to prepare students for the three brief selections. For the first column, have students recall what they already know about Seabiscuit. In the second column, have them write questions about what they want to know. After reading, have students write what they have learned.

 BEST PRACTICES TOOLKIT—Transparency
KWL p. A21

Teach

Skill Focus: Synthesize

- Explain that synthesizing information from different sources is a little like assembling a puzzle. Each source presents different pieces, and the pieces taken together form a total picture.

- Encourage students to think about the genre of each piece before they read it. Have them consider what kind of information they can expect to find. For example, a magazine article is likely to provide interesting details, while a timeline will give dates of significant events.

 RESOURCE MANAGER—Copy Master
Synthesize p. 191

Horse of the Century
- Magazine Article, page 133
- Timeline, page 134
- Radio Transcript, page 135

Use with *Seabiscuit: An American Legend,* page 122.

What's the Connection?

In the selection from *Seabiscuit: An American Legend,* you read about one of the most famous horseraces of the 20th century. The following selections will help you get a sense of what it was like to actually be at that race and why many Americans practically held their breath as they listened to it on the radio.

Skill Focus: Synthesize

When you read different texts on the same topic, you **synthesize** information—that is, you put together the facts, ideas, and details you get from each of them. As a result, you gain a fuller understanding of the topic than you would from reading only one text.

Here's how you can synthesize the ideas and information in the pieces about Seabiscuit:

- Summarize the main ideas and details in each piece.
- Jot down any questions that come to you as you learn new information.
- When information in one source conflicts with information in another, jot down these conflicts as questions, too.
- Reread each piece to answer your questions and fill in gaps in your understanding.

For more help synthesizing, complete a chart like the one started here as you read the following selections.

Source	Main Ideas	New Information & Questions
From *Seabiscuit: An American Legend*	Jockey, owner, and fans were surprised by his defeat in the Santa Anita Handicap.	Why was this horse so popular?
From "Four Good Legs Between Us"	Even though Seabiscuit lost this race, he was fast becoming a celebrity.	Howard made him popular by racing him all over the country. What was going on in Europe?

Selection Resources

 RESOURCE MANAGER UNIT 1

Plan and Teach pp. 183–187

Reading
Summary pp. 189†*, 190‡*
Synthesize pp. 191, 193†*
Reading Check p. 195
Draw Conclusions pp. 192, 194†*
Question Support p. 197*

Assessment
Selection Tests A, B/C pp. 199*, 201*

 Test Generator CD

Reading Support
Audio Anthology CD*

BEST PRACTICES TOOLKIT
KWL • New Word Analysis • Venn Diagram

* Resources for Differentiation   † Also in Spanish   ‡In Haitian Creole and Vietnamese

from
Four Good Legs Between Us
Laura Hillenbrand

Though Seabiscuit had lost [the Santa Anita Handicap], he was rapidly becoming a phenomenal celebrity. Two factors converged to create and nourish this. The first was Charles Howard. A born adman, Howard courted the nation on behalf of his horse much as he had hawked his first Buicks, undertaking exhaustive promotion that presaged the modern marketing of athletes. Crafting daring, unprecedented coast-to-coast racing campaigns, he shipped Seabiscuit over fifty thousand railroad miles to showcase his talent at eighteen tracks in seven states and Mexico. The second factor was timing. The nation was sliding from economic ruin into the whirling eddy of Europe's cataclysm. Seabiscuit, Howard, Pollard, and Smith, whose fortunes
10 swung in epic parabolas, would have resonated in any age, but in cruel years the peculiar union among the four transcended the racetrack. **A**

The result was stupendous popularity. In one year Seabiscuit garnered more newspaper column inches than Roosevelt, Hitler, or Mussolini. *Life* even ran a pictorial on his facial expressions. Cities had to route special trains to accommodate the invariably record-shattering crowds that came to see him run. Smith, fearing Seabiscuit wouldn't get any rest, hoodwinked the press by trotting out a look-alike. Such fame fueled the immediate, immense success of Howard's Santa Anita and California's new racing industry, today a four-billion-dollar business.

A SYNTHESIZE
Summarize the two causes of Seabiscuit's popularity.

INFORMATIONAL ANALYSIS

A SYNTHESIZE

Possible answer: Charles Howard was an outstanding promoter who built Seabiscuit's popularity by showcasing the horse "at eighteen tracks in seven states and Mexico" (line 7). In addition, during difficult economic and political times, people found inspiration in the team of Seabiscuit, Howard, Pollard, and Smith.

If students need help . . .
Draw a chart like this one on the board and fill it in together:

Seabiscuit's Popularity	
Summary 1	Summary 2
_____	_____
_____	_____
_____	_____
_____	_____
_____	_____

DIFFERENTIATED INSTRUCTION

FOR LESS-PROFICIENT READERS

Vocabulary Support Have students work in small groups to define difficult words in the article, such as *presaged* (line 5), *eddy, cataclysm, parabolas, resonated,* and *transcended* (lines 9–11), and *hoodwinked* (line 16). Have students paraphrase difficult sentences.

FOR ENGLISH LEARNERS

Build Background Review key facts that students learned in *Seabiscuit: An American Legend,* such as Seabiscuit's loss to Rosemont in the Santa Anita Handicap.

Options for Reading Read the first two sentences of the first paragraph, making sure students understand their meaning. Explain that these sentences state the paragraph's main idea. Call on volunteers to read the supporting sentences. Repeat this procedure with the second paragraph, pointing out that the first sentence states the paragraph's main idea.

DISCUSSION PROMPTS

Use these prompts to help students reflect on information displayed in the timeline:

Connect Which event shown on the timeline did you read about in *Seabiscuit: An American Legend* (pp. 122–129)? *Possible answer: The timeline shows Seabiscuit's loss to Rosemont in the Santa Anita Handicap of 1937.*

Apply Which horse other than Rosemont does the timeline imply was a major rival of Seabiscuit? *Possible answer: War Admiral was also a major rival.*

Evaluate Who was Seabiscuit's jockey in 1940? Does this surprise you in light of the events you read about in *Seabiscuit: An American Legend*? Give reasons for your answer. *Possible answer: Red Pollard was the jockey. Students should support their answers with thoughtful reasoning.*

INFORMATIONAL ANALYSIS

B SYNTHESIZE

Answers may vary, but students may point to new information related to the selection they read from Seabiscuit: An American Legend; *Seabiscuit beat Rosemont in the Brooklyn Handicap on June 26, 1937, four months after losing to him in the Santa Anita Handicap; Seabiscuit won his third try at the Santa Anita Handicap, on March 2, 1940.*

Extend the Discussion How can a timeline help you to synthesize information from several sources?

Timeline: Seabiscuit

1937 *February 27:* In his first try at the Santa Anita Handicap, Seabiscuit loses to Rosemont by a nose, in a photo finish.

March 6: Seabiscuit draws a crowd of 45,000 excited fans and wins the San Juan Capistrano Handicap by seven lengths, smashing the track record.

May 6: The German airship *Hindenburg* bursts into flames as it is about to land in Lakehurst, New Jersey.

June 5: War Admiral captures the Triple Crown after a win at the Belmont Stakes.

June 26: Seabiscuit runs in the Brooklyn Handicap, beating rival Rosemont and local horse Aneroid.

July: Seabiscuit wins the Butler Handicap and the Yonkers Handicap easily, despite carrying far more weight than his competitors in both races.

September 11: At the Narragansett Special in Rhode Island, Seabiscuit finishes third due to muddy track conditions.

October 12: Seabiscuit wins the Continental Handicap in New York, gaining the top spot in the 1937 winnings race with $152,780 earned, $8,000 ahead of War Admiral.

October 30: Seabiscuit and War Admiral are slated to meet on the track, but Seabiscuit is scratched from the Washington Handicap due to muddy track conditions, allowing an easy victory for his rival.

December 7: War Admiral is named horse of the year by *Turf and Sport Digest*.

1938 *October 30:* Orson Welles's radio broadcast of *The War of the Worlds*, the tale of a Martian invasion on Earth, creates panic among listeners who mistake it for news.

November 1: With 40 million listeners tuned in across the country, Seabiscuit beats War Admiral by four lengths in just over a minute fifty-six for the mile and three-sixteenths, a new Pimlico record.

1939 *February 14:* Seabiscuit injures his suspensory ligament in a prep race for Santa Anita.

September 3: Britain and France declare war on Germany.

1940 *March 2:* Seabiscuit wins in his third try at the $100,000 Santa Anita Handicap. He clocks the fastest mile and a quarter in Santa Anita's history, the second fastest ever run in the United States. The most people ever to attend an American horse race—75,000—watch as Pollard leads Seabiscuit from behind to victory.

April 10: Seabiscuit retires to Charles Howard's Ridgewood Ranch. **B**

B SYNTHESIZE
Identify one or two new ideas or pieces of information that this timeline provides about Seabiscuit.

DIFFERENTIATED INSTRUCTION

FOR ENGLISH LEARNERS
Vocabulary: Idioms Use New Word Analysis to teach the meanings of the idioms in the timeline: *slated to* (October 30, 1937), "scheduled to"; *is scratched* (October 30, 1937), "dropped from or taken out"; *tuned in* (November 1, 1938), "listened to the broadcast."

BEST PRACTICES TOOLKIT—Transparency
New Word Analysis p. E8

FOR ADVANCED LEARNERS/PRE–AP
Expand Timeline Challenge students to identify other notable national or international events that occurred between February 27, 1937, and April 10, 1940, and add them to the timeline. Discuss which events were the most significant and why.

Races on the Radio
Santa Anita Handicap (1937)
with Clem McCarthy and Buddy Twist

CLEM McCARTHY:

Eddy Thomas won't take the start until he's on his toes and the jockey is ready. Then he'll push that button, the bell will ring, and they'll be on their way. We don't have any starting barriers now, as you know. Here they go. And they're on their way down the stretch. The break was good; every horse got a chance just as they left there. **C**

As they come down here to the eighth pole, it is Time Supply and Special Agent. Special Agent is trying to force his way to the front and he's going to do a good job of it as they pass the stands. Here on the outside comes Rosemont in a good position. And as they go by me it is

10 Special Agent on the lead by one length. Special Agent has the lead and then comes Time Supply in second place right along beside him. Going to the first turn is Special Agent by a length. Time Supply is second and on the outside of him is Accolade. And Boxthorn is close up. Far back in the crowd, on the inside, in about twelfth place is Red Rain. Up there close is Rosemont in about sixth place.

They're going into the stretch; they've gone half a mile. And the time for the first quarter over this track was 22 and two fifths seconds, the half in 45 and four. They're turning into the backstretch with Special Agent on the lead. Special Agent has a lead now of one length

20 and a half. Right behind him comes Time Supply. And in there, slipping through on the inside is . . . Indian Broom is going up on the inside now in a good position. Around that far turn, there's still no change in the positions. Rosemont is having a hard time working his way through, he's now in sixth position going around on the inside, he's saving ground, he's got plenty left. If he's enough horse, he may get home.

C SYNTHESIZE
Read all or part of this transcript aloud, using the tone and style of a sports announcer. Where do you speed up the pace?

INFORMATIONAL ANALYSIS

C SYNTHESIZE

Possible answer: Readers will speed up the pace when something exciting or unexpected occurs, as in lines 21–22, lines 28–29, and lines 30–38. In a close race such as this one, an announcer would naturally tend to pick up the pace as the horses approach the finish line.

Extend the Discussion In what ways is listening to a radio broadcast of a horse race different from reading about the event in a newspaper?

FOR LESS–PROFICIENT READERS
Vocabulary Support Have students point out racing-related terms: *stretch* (line 4), *pole* (line 6), *length* (line 10), and *backstretch* (line 18). Ask them to define these terms using context, and check their responses in a dictionary.

Lines 26-38
DISCUSSION PROMPTS

Use these prompts to help students understand how announcers bring horse races to life:

Connect Have you ever listened to a radio broadcast of a sporting event? Describe it. *Students' answers will vary.*

Analyze How does McCarthy build the excitement? *Possible answer: He describes the rapidly changing positions of the horses as they maneuver for position. He also uses exciting phrases, such as "challenging head-and-head" (line 30), "challenging boldly" (line 35), and "the battle is on" (lines 35–36).*

Synthesize Did reading this transcript help you to understand the information you read about in the excerpt from *Seabiscuit* in a new way? Explain. *Students may respond that the transcript provided a sense of what it was like to actually witness the race and experience the confusion many must have felt in trying to determine who won.*

INFORMATIONAL ANALYSIS

D SYNTHESIZE

Possible answer: The transcript reveals the time of the race (2:02 and four-fifths) and the fact that the track was about the same as two years earlier. The transcript also describes news photographers waiting to learn the winner and people cheering.

And on the outside, here comes the other one, Indian Broom. And Goldeneye is moving up from the rear. Here comes Accolade in second position. And Seabiscuit is now moving up and is challenging as they turn for home.

30   It's Special Agent and Seabiscuit challenging head-and-head as they swing into the stretch. And they've only got a quarter of a mile to come. They've stepped the first mile in 1:36 and four-fifths—and that shows you what this pace is. He can't live at it. Seabiscuit has got the lead half way down the stretch. But here comes one of the Baroni entries challenging on the outside, challenging boldly. And the battle is on. Indian Broom is coming fast and here comes Rosemont between horses. And Rosemont may take it all. It's gonna be a photograph finish. And it's anybody's race right to the end.

    I think Rosemont got the money. I think Rosemont was first. It
40 was an eyebrow finish. And Seabiscuit was the second horse. Seabiscuit was second and one of the Taylor entries; I think Indian Broom, was third. It was very close. That was an eyelash finish. Rosemont was closing strong, but Seabiscuit hung on. The time of the race was 2:02 and four-fifths, which makes the track almost identically like the track of two years ago . . .

BUDDY TWIST:

Oh boy, one of the most thrilling finishes I think that I've ever seen in a horse race in my life, Clem. The crowd down here has gone completely mad. The photographers are outside the charm circle, which is a white circle here, where the winner will come up in just a moment. Newsreel
50 photographers are setting up on every hand. The horses are just coming back now. And everybody, depending on who was their favorite, was shouting "Rosemont," "Seabiscuit"—one would call Rosemont, one Seabiscuit. There were half-a-dozen here who were just as sure Rosemont won as Seabiscuit, they don't know what to think of it. One of the most beautiful driving finishes I think I've ever seen.

CLEM McCARTHY:

Here's the photograph finish. Hold it now. Get ready for it. Just a few seconds and we'll know the winner of this race. I think Rosemont won it, but that's only my guess from where I stand. The photograph will tell us the actual winner. The naked eye is not as good as the photograph,
60 we'll have it in a second. They're looking at it down there. I know it was an eyelash finish. Either horse won by a whisker and that's all. Just about a quarter of an inch, I can't see any more between them. I really shouldn't express an opinion on a finish that close. And they're still waiting. That shows you what a difficult . . . There it is, Rosemont is the winner. Rosemont by a nose. Seabiscuit is second. Just a minute Buddy until I get it. Rosemont is the winner—I want you to get that jockey if you got him—Seabiscuit is second. And the Taylor entry finished third and fourth. They haven't put up the distinguishing numbers and they finished very close together. **D**

D SYNTHESIZE
What does this transcript reveal about the end of the race that was not included in the other texts?

DIFFERENTIATED INSTRUCTION

FOR ENGLISH LEARNERS

Language: Contractions Remind students that speakers often use contractions in informal oral language. Identify these contractions the first time they appear in the radio transcript, and explain their meanings: *won't* (line 1), "will not"; *he's* (line 1), "he is"; *don't* (line 3), "do not"; *It's* (line 30), "it is"; *Here's* (line 56), "here is"; *that's* (line 58), "that is"; *shouldn't* (line 63), "should not"; *haven't* (line 68), "have not."

FOR ADVANCED LEARNERS/PRE-AP

Compare and Contrast Use a Venn Diagram with students to help them compare Hillenbrand's account of the Santa Anita Handicap in *Seabiscuit: An American Legend* with the radio transcript. Then have students write a brief essay summarizing similarities and differences and share their essays with the class.

🗄 BEST PRACTICES TOOLKIT—Transparency
Venn Diagram p. A26

Comprehension

1. **Recall** Which horse won the Santa Anita Handicap in 1937? What kind of a finish was it?

2. **Recall** How many times did Seabiscuit enter the Santa Anita Handicap before winning?

3. **Summarize** What major world events took place during Seabiscuit's rise to fame?

Critical Analysis

4. **Analyze Mood and Tone** What elements of the radio transcript contribute to the sense of excitement? Be specific.

5. **Synthesize** Review the ideas and information you noted in your chart. How did the world events of the day contribute to Seabiscuit's popularity? Use evidence from the texts to support your answer.

Read for Information: Draw Conclusions

WRITING PROMPT

In a paragraph, state and support your conclusions about one of the following topics:

- horseracing as a spectator sport
- Seabiscuit's popularity
- jockeys

To answer this prompt, you will need to pick your topic and follow these steps:

1. Gather information about your topic from the three selections, as well as from Hillenbrand's biography of Seabiscuit.

2. Consider the main ideas and information you have collected. Ask yourself what conclusion(s) you can draw from them.

3. State your conclusion(s) in a topic sentence. Then, support those conclusions with ideas and information from the texts.

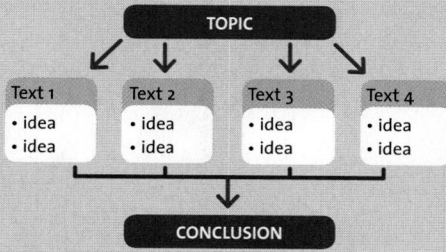

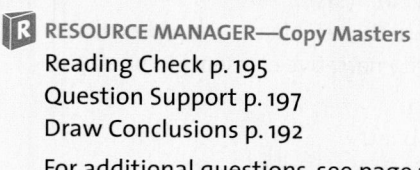

Practice and Apply

For additional support of post-reading questions, use these copy masters:

R RESOURCE MANAGER—Copy Masters
Reading Check p. 195
Question Support p. 197
Draw Conclusions p. 192

For additional questions, see page 185.

ANSWERS

Comprehension

1. *Rosemont won the race in a photo finish.*

2. *Seabiscuit won on his third try.*

3. *The Great Depression occurred; the* Hindenburg *burst into flames; Britain and France declared war on Germany.*

Critical Analysis

Possible answers:

4. *McCarthy details how the horses compete for position as they race. He uses strong verbs, such as* challenge, *and Twist includes comments such as "one of the most thrilling finishes ... I've ever seen ... in my life."*

5. ■ **STANDARDS FOCUS** *Synthesize People found inspiration and escape in Seabiscuit's races during the "cruel years," when the "nation was sliding from economic ruin" (page 133, lines 8–11).*

Read for Information: Draw Conclusions

Writing Prompt *Responses will vary, but students should state their conclusions in a topic sentence and support them.*

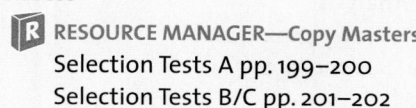

Assess and Reteach

Assess

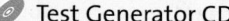 **R RESOURCE MANAGER—Copy Masters**
Selection Tests A pp. 199–200
Selection Tests B/C pp. 201–202

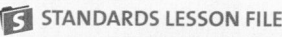 Test Generator CD

Reteach

S STANDARDS LESSON FILE
Reading Lesson 14: Synthesize Information
Reading Lesson 9: Drawing Conclusions

FOR LESS–PROFICIENT WRITERS

Read for Information

- Direct students to narrow their topic. For example, if they choose "jockeys," they should think in terms of a complete statement, such as "The life of a jockey is exciting but difficult."

- Encourage students to begin by writing their conclusions in a topic sentence. Explain that they can revise their sentences later, but starting with a conclusion will help them stay focused.

FOR ADVANCED LEARNERS/PRE–AP

Author's Purpose Challenge students to write two separate paragraphs accomplishing different main purposes: to inform or explain, to express their thoughts or feelings, to persuade, or to entertain. Have them share their paragraphs with a partner.

Focus and Motivate

OBJECTIVES

Literary Analysis
- explore the key idea of the **unknown**
- identify narrative elements in poetry

Reading
- read poetry

SUMMARIES

"The Raven" The speaker in Edgar Allan Poe's classic poem is a man grieving over the death of his beloved Lenore. A raven mysteriously flies into his study late one dreary night and responds with the word "Nevermore" to each of the man's questions, adding to his torment. In the end, the man demands that the raven leave, but the bird remains.

"Incident in a Rose Garden" In Donald Justice's ironic poem, a man discovers that Death has come not for his gardener, but for him.

Why are we fascinated by the UNKNOWN?

Begin the discussion of the *KEY IDEA* by asking the question. Elicit examples of different kinds of the **unknown,** such as speculation about life on other planets and questions about the existence of ghosts. Extend the exploration by having students complete the *DISCUSS* activity. Then ask volunteers to share their favorite stories with the class.

Selection Resources

The Raven
Poem by Edgar Allan Poe

Incident in a Rose Garden
Poem by Donald Justice

Why are we fascinated by the UNKNOWN?

KEY IDEA Have you ever skimmed the strange headlines of a tabloid newspaper when standing in line at the supermarket? Do you channel-surf for television shows about strange phenomena? Our fascination with weird or unexplained events makes us part of a long tradition of writers and readers who enjoy speculating on the **unknown** or the unexplainable. The writers of the two poems you are about to read relied on that universal fascination when they introduced us to two strange, and perhaps imaginary, visitors.

DISCUSS With a partner, share the story of a movie, television show, or urban legend that you find fascinating or unbelievable.

138

R RESOURCE MANAGER UNIT 1

Plan and Teach pp. 203–210

Literary Analysis
Narrative Poetry pp. 211, 212†*
Question Support p. 215*

Reading
Reading Poetry pp. 213, 214†*
Reading Fluency p. 216

Assessment
Selection Tests A, B/C pp. 217*, 219*
Test Generator CD

 BEST PRACTICES TOOLKIT

Differentiated Instruction
pp. 31–38*

Scaffolding Instruction
pp. 43–46*

Graphic Organizers/Strategies
Comparison Matrix

Reading Support
Audio Anthology CD*

Technology
Literature and Vocabulary Centers at **ClassZone.com**
Write*Smart* CD

LITERARY ANALYSIS: NARRATIVE POETRY

Like fiction, a **narrative poem** contains the elements of plot, conflict, character, and setting that combine to create a story. Because of the nature of poetry, these elements are often condensed into images and compact descriptions. For example, notice that this line contains information about setting, plot, and character:

Once upon a midnight dreary, while I pondered, weak and weary

In each of the following narrative poems, the **speaker,** or voice that talks to the reader, is also the main character in the story. As you read, note what events each speaker describes and how these create a compelling story in verse form.

READING SKILL: READING POETRY

When you read a narrative poem, certain reading strategies will help you understand the poem's story and meaning.

- First, read the poem silently to grasp the basic story line.
- Then read it aloud several times, and listen to how it sounds. Pay attention to sound devices, such as **rhyme, rhythm,** and **repetition.** Does the poem include **alliteration,** the repetition of consonant sounds at the beginning of words? How do these sound devices add to the effect of the poem? (To review the definitions of these sound-device terms, see the **Glossary of Literary Terms,** page R102.)
- Look for clues that reveal something about the **speaker.** What does the speaker feel about the poem's characters and events?

As you read each poem, record the most striking examples of sound devices in a chart similar to the following:

Sound Device	"The Raven"	"Incident in a Rose Garden"
alliteration	"nodded, nearly napping"	

Author Online

Edgar Allan Poe 1809–1849

Edgar Allan Poe: A Life of Tragedy One of America's literary giants, Edgar Allan Poe has fascinated generations of readers with his haunting poetry and tales of horror. (See "The Cask of Amontillado" on page 344.) Poe suffered many tragic losses in his short life. He was orphaned at the age of 2 and taken in by foster parents, but never formally adopted. Poe later quarreled bitterly with his foster father. At the age of 27, Poe married a 13-year-old cousin, Virginia Clemm. She died about ten years later, after an agonizing battle with tuberculosis.

Death-Haunted Poetry Poe's poetry often deals with the subject of death. According to Poe, the "death then of a beautiful woman is, unquestionably, the most poetical topic in the world."

Donald Justice 1925–2004

Donald Justice: From Music to Poetry Donald Justice originally intended to become a composer and studied for a degree in music before deciding to become a writer. He then earned a doctorate in creative writing, participating in the Iowa Writers' Workshop. A Pulitzer Prize–winning poet, Justice taught English at a number of universities.

   MORE ABOUT THE AUTHOR
For more on Edgar Allan Poe and Donald Justice, visit the **Literature Center** at ClassZone.com.

139

Teach

STANDARDS FOCUS

LITERARY ANALYSIS

● NARRATIVE POETRY

To support instruction, write these lines of poetry on the board and read them aloud:

> Down, and away from the sun's warming rays,
> Down, past the fishes' incredulous gaze,
> I dove down deep to the shadowy wreck
> And wondered what lay 'neath the hole in the deck.

Ask students to explain what these lines convey about the speaker, setting, and plot of the story the poem is about to tell. *Possible answer: The speaker is a diver who is about to explore the wreck of a sunken ship. The setting is undersea, near and within the wreck. The plot will reveal what is now unknown about the ship.*

CHECK UNDERSTANDING Elicit examples of songs and poems that tell a story.

READING SKILL

■ READING POETRY

Use the lines written on the board for the **LITERARY ANALYSIS** activity to reinforce students' understanding of these sound devices:

- **Rhyme** is the repetition of sounds at the ends of words. Ask students to identify the rhymes in these lines (rays/gaze *and* wreck/deck).
- Have students identify the **alliteration**—the repetition of initial consonant sounds (<u>D</u>own, <u>d</u>ove, <u>d</u>eep, *and* <u>d</u>eck).
- Ask students to identify examples of **repetition** (down *is used three times*).
- Help students identify the poem's **rhythm**—its pattern of accented and unaccented syllables—by marking the stressed syllables with a ´ and the unstressed syllables with a ˘.

CHECK UNDERSTANDING Have students create examples of each sound device.

 RESOURCE MANAGER—Copy Master
Reading Poetry p. 213 (for student use while reading the selection)

DIFFERENTIATED INSTRUCTION

FOR LESS–PROFICIENT READERS
Comprehension Support Write on the board the boldfaced terms used on page 139, and have students review the meaning of each one: *narrative poem, speaker, rhyme, rhythm, repetition,* and *alliteration.* Elicit examples of sound devices in popular songs and familiar poems. Discuss how these devices contribute to the overall mood or feeling.

Concept Support Explain that a *narrative* is a story. Then create a simple word web linking this word to related terms: *narrative poem, narrate, narration,* and *narrator.* Elicit or provide the meaning of each term, and have students use the terms in sentences that illustrate this meaning.

narrative

ANALYZE VISUALS

Possible answer: The smudges and indistinct features of the drawing almost seem to vibrate, creating a mood of agitation and even menace.

About the Art Contemporary painter Jim Dine (b. 1935) uses charcoal to create a deep, dense blackness with smudges and seemingly random marks.

LITERARY ANALYSIS

A NARRATIVE POETRY

Possible answer: The speaker's internal conflict is that he is trying, without success, to get over the grief he feels for his "lost Lenore" (line 10), who has died.

Lines 1–18
DISCUSSION PROMPTS

Use these prompts to help students explore the speaker's changing state of mind:

Connect Have you ever had an experience in which familiar surroundings suddenly seemed unfamiliar or even frightening? Explain. *Students may mention returning to their old house, neighborhood, or school, and feeling that the once-familiar place looked different.*

Analyze Why do the speaker's surroundings suddenly seem strange to him? *Possible answer: It is a cold night. The fire is dying, but the room seems strangely alive with "sad, uncertain rustling" curtains (line 13) and a strange tapping noise.*

Synthesize How does the speaker's state of mind change during the first three stanzas of the poem? Cite details to support your answer. *Possible answer: At the beginning of the poem, the speaker is sorrowful, weak, and weary (lines 1 and 10), but he is not nervous or scared. By the third stanza, however, his state of mind has changed, and he is now frightened and agitated because of the tapping on his door. He is filled with "fantastic terrors never felt before" (line 14), and his heart is beating heavily (line 15). The familiar setting of his chamber has become a source of terror; even the rustling of the curtains scares him (lines 13–14).*

The Raven
EDGAR ALLAN POE

Once upon a midnight dreary, while I pondered, weak and weary,
Over many a quaint and curious volume of forgotten lore—
While I nodded, nearly napping, suddenly there came a tapping,
As of someone gently rapping, rapping at my chamber door.
5 "'Tis some visitor," I muttered, "tapping at my chamber door—
　　Only this and nothing more."

Ah, distinctly I remember it was in the bleak December;
And each separate dying ember wrought its ghost upon the floor.
Eagerly I wished the morrow;—vainly I had sought to borrow
10 From my books surcease of sorrow[1]—sorrow for the lost Lenore—
For the rare and radiant maiden whom the angels name Lenore—
　　Nameless *here* forevermore. **A**

And the silken, sad, uncertain rustling of each purple curtain
Thrilled me—filled me with fantastic terrors never felt before;
15 So that now, to still the beating of my heart, I stood repeating
"'Tis some visitor entreating entrance at my chamber door;—
Some late visitor entreating entrance at my chamber door;—
　　That it is and nothing more."

Presently my soul grew stronger; hesitating then no longer,
20 "Sir," said I, "or Madam, truly your forgiveness I implore;
But the fact is I was napping, and so gently you came rapping,
And so faintly you came tapping, tapping at my chamber door,
That I scarce was sure I heard you"—here I opened wide the door;—
　　Darkness there and nothing more.

1. **from my books surcease of sorrow:** from reading, an end to sorrow.

ANALYZE VISUALS
What **mood** is conveyed by the style of the drawing?

A NARRATIVE POETRY
With what **internal conflict** does the speaker struggle?

Raven (1994), Jim Dine. Charcoal on wall, 128″ × 98¹/₂″. Kunstverein Ludwigsburg, Germany, destroyed. © 2007 Jim Dine/Artists Rights Society (ARS), New York.

DIFFERENTIATED INSTRUCTION

For general guidelines on differentiating instruction, see

 BEST PRACTICES TOOLKIT
Differentiated Instruction pp. 31–38

FOR LESS—PROFICIENT READERS

Options for Reading Read "The Raven" aloud as the class follows along. Emphasize the dramatic narrative elements, building the mood as you read. Because "The Raven" is a long poem, students may benefit from your pausing every few stanzas to make a comment or ask a question. However, their primary purpose for this first reading should be listening to the sound and rhythm of the poem and its haunting, melancholy quality.

BACKGROUND

The Raven In Western culture, the raven has a symbolic association with evil omens, mystery, and death. Poe initially considered using a parrot or an owl in the poem, but he chose the raven instead because of the bird's cultural associations. In addition, the raven seemed a more suitable choice for the dark and melancholy mood of the poem.

Lines 13–24
REINFORCE *KEY IDEA:* UNKNOWN

Discuss How does Poe build suspense about the **unknown** source of the tapping on the door? *Possible answer: He builds suspense by creating tension between the speaker's increasingly uneasy mental state and the origin of strange sounds he hears outside his door. The speaker is filled with "fantastic terrors" (line 14) and is aware of "the beating of [his] heart" (line 15) as he tries to reassure himself that the tapping is nothing more than "some visitor" (line 16). When at last he opens the door, he finds "Darkness there and nothing more" (line 24). The speaker—and the reader— is left in suspense about who or what is tapping on the door.*

25 Deep into that darkness peering, long I stood there wondering, fearing,
Doubting, dreaming dreams no mortal ever dared to dream before;
But the silence was unbroken, and the stillness gave no token,
And the only word there spoken was the whispered word, "Lenore!"
This I whispered, and an echo murmured back the word "Lenore!"
30   Merely this and nothing more. **B**

Back into the chamber turning, all my soul within me burning,
Soon again I heard a tapping somewhat louder than before.
"Surely," said I, "surely that is something at my window lattice;
Let me see, then, what thereat is, and this mystery explore—
35 Let my heart be still a moment and this mystery explore;—
       'Tis the wind and nothing more!"

Open here I flung the shutter, when, with many a flirt and flutter,
In there stepped a stately Raven of the saintly days of yore.[2]
Not the least obeisance made he;[3] not a minute stopped or stayed he;
40 But, with mien of lord or lady,[4] perched above my chamber door—
Perched upon a bust of Pallas[5] just above my chamber door—
       Perched, and sat, and nothing more.

Then this ebony bird beguiling[6] my sad fancy into smiling,
By the grave and stern decorum of the countenance[7] it wore,
45 "Though thy crest be shorn and shaven, thou," I said, "art sure no craven,[8]
Ghastly grim and ancient Raven wandering from the Nightly shore—
Tell me what thy lordly name is on the Night's Plutonian[9] shore!"
       Quoth the Raven, "Nevermore." **C**

Much I marveled this ungainly fowl to hear discourse so plainly,
50 Though its answer little meaning—little relevancy bore;
For we cannot help agreeing that no living human being
Ever yet was blessed with seeing bird above his chamber door—
Bird or beast upon the sculptured bust above his chamber door,
       With such name as "Nevermore."

---

2. **saintly days of yore:** sacred days of the past.
3. **not the least obeisance** (ō-bā'səns) **made he:** he did not bow or make any other gesture of respect.
4. **with mien of lord or lady:** with the appearance of a noble person.
5. **bust of Pallas:** statue of the head and shoulders of Athena, Greek goddess of war and wisdom.
6. **this ebony bird beguiling** (bĭ-gī'lĭng): this black bird that is charming or delighting.
7. **grave and stern decorum ... countenance** (koun'tə-nəns): serious and dignified expression on the face.
8. **art sure no craven:** are surely not cowardly.
9. **Plutonian:** having to do with Pluto, Roman god of the dead and ruler of the underworld.

142 UNIT 1: NARRATIVE STRUCTURE

READING SKILL

B READING POETRY

Possible answer: *Alliteration occurs in line 25—"Deep into that darkness"—but line 26 provides a better example: "Doubting, dreaming dreams . . . dared to dream . . . ." Poe uses alliteration throughout the poem (for example: "weak and weary" [line 1], "lost Lenore" [line 10], "flirt and flutter" [line 37], "shorn and shaven" [line 45]) to create a rhythmic, almost hypnotic, effect; an atmosphere of melancholy; and a feeling of inevitability.*

LITERARY ANALYSIS

C NARRATIVE POETRY

Possible answer: *The speaker reacts to the raven's entrance with a smile, finding the raven "beguiling" (line 43), and asks the bird his name (line 47). He seems to welcome this visitor as a source of relief from his "sad fancy" (line 43). We can conclude from this reaction that the speaker feels lonely and is grateful for a distraction from his low spirits.*

B READING POETRY
Reread lines 25–30. Identify examples of **alliteration**, the repetition of consonant sounds at the beginning of words. Notice how often this **sound device** occurs in this narrative poem. What is the effect?

C NARRATIVE POETRY
What can you conclude about the **speaker** from the way he reacts to the raven's entrance?

DIFFERENTIATED INSTRUCTION

FOR LESS–PROFICIENT READERS
Vocabulary Support
Line 34: *thereat*—poetic expression for "at that place"
Lines 49, 71: *ungainly*—"awkward-looking"

Concept Support To build understanding of alliteration, give students an opportunity to create their own alliterative phrases. Have them begin by pairing up adjectives or making adjective-noun combinations, as in "beautiful blue butterfly" or "delicious dinner."

FOR ENGLISH LEARNERS
Language: Modifiers Explain that poets often do not follow customary language patterns. For example, adjectives usually precede the word they modify, as in "bleak December" (line 7) and "purple curtain" (line 13), but Poe reverses the order in "midnight dreary" (line 1) and "land enchanted" (line 87). Explore how Poe departs from the usual word order in such lines as 37–38, 49, and 57. Have small groups find other examples of unusual word order in the poem and share them with the class.

55 But the Raven, sitting lonely on the placid bust, spoke only
   That one word, as if his soul in that one word he did outpour.
   Nothing farther then he uttered—not a feather then he fluttered—
   Till I scarcely more than muttered, "Other friends have flown before—
   On the morrow *he* will leave me, as my hopes have flown before."
60   Then the bird said, "Nevermore."

   Startled at the stillness broken by reply so aptly spoken,
   "Doubtless," said I, "what it utters is its only stock and store
   Caught from some unhappy master whom unmerciful Disaster 🅓
   Followed fast and followed faster till his songs one burden bore—
65 Till the dirges of his Hope[10] that melancholy burden bore
         Of 'Never—nevermore.'"

   But the Raven still beguiling all my fancy into smiling,
   Straight I wheeled a cushioned seat in front of bird and bust and door;
   Then, upon the velvet sinking, I betook myself to linking
70 Fancy unto fancy, thinking what this ominous bird of yore—
   What this grim, ungainly, ghastly, gaunt, and ominous bird of yore
         Meant in croaking, "Nevermore."

   This I sat engaged in guessing, but no syllable expressing
   To the fowl whose fiery eyes now burned into my bosom's core;
75 This and more I sat divining,[11] with my head at ease reclining
   On the cushion's velvet lining that the lamp-light gloated o'er,
   But whose velvet violet lining with the lamp-light gloating o'er,
         She shall press, ah, nevermore!

   Then, methought, the air grew denser, perfumed from an unseen censer
80 Swung by Seraphim[12] whose foot-falls tinkled on the tufted floor.
   "Wretch," I cried, "thy God hath lent thee—by these angels he hath sent thee
   Respite—respite and nepenthe[13] from thy memories of Lenore;
   Quaff, oh quaff this kind nepenthe[14] and forget this lost Lenore!"
         Quoth the Raven, "Nevermore."

---

10. **dirges** (dûr'jĭz) **of his Hope:** funeral hymns mourning the loss of hope.

11. **divining** (dĭ-vī'nĭng): guessing or speculating.

12. **censer swung by Seraphim** (sĕr'ə-fĭm): container of burning incense swung by angels of the highest rank.

13. **he hath sent thee respite** (rĕs'pĭt) **...nepenthe** (nĭ-pĕn'thē): God has sent you relief and forgetfulness of sorrow.

14. **quaff, oh quaff this kind nepenthe:** drink this beverage that eases pain.

THE RAVEN   **143**

🅓 **READING POETRY**
Reread line 63. Notice the **internal rhyme**—similar or identical sounds within a line—of the words *master* and *disaster.* Find examples of internal rhyme in other stanzas, and notice how they help emphasize certain words.

READING SKILL

🅓 **READING POETRY**

Possible answer: Poe uses internal rhyme to enhance the melodic and rhythmic quality of the poem and draw attention to certain words. Examples of internal rhyme include peering, fearing *(line 25);* unbroken, token *(line 27);* turning, burning *(line 31);* shutter, flutter *(line 37);* beguiling, smiling *(line 43);* shaven, craven *(line 45);* ungainly, plainly *(line 49);* uttered, fluttered *(line 57);* broken, spoken *(line 61).*

Lines 37–102
REINFORCE *KEY IDEA:* **UNKNOWN**

Discuss How does Poe use the raven to make the **unknown** seem increasingly frightening? *Possible answer:* He uses the raven to emphasize the speaker's deteriorating mental state. When the mysterious raven first appears, the bird seems harmless to the speaker. He welcomes the raven with a smile and talks with the bird as though he were a friend. However, the raven's repeated single-word response of "Nevermore" frustrates the speaker and turns his initial calm into torment. Poe emphasizes the speaker's fear and agitation by using alarming adjectives to describe the raven, as in line 71: "grim, ungainly, ghastly, gaunt, and ominous."

FOR LESS–PROFICIENT READERS

Comprehension Support Discuss how lines 71, 74, and 85 show the speaker's increasing displeasure with the raven. Also have students compare "whose fiery eyes now burned into my bosom's core" (line 74) with "Take thy beak from out my heart" (line 101). Explore whether the speaker's distress is actually caused by the raven or results mainly from the speaker's own inner torment.

FOR ADVANCED LEARNERS/PRE-AP

Compare and Contrast Have students work in small groups to analyze the speaker's changing reactions to the raven, from the time the bird first appears until the end of the poem. Ask students to use a Comparison Matrix to compare how the speaker feels at the end of each stanza and explain both how and why his feelings change as the poem progresses.

🧰 **BEST PRACTICES TOOLKIT—Transparency**
Comparison Matrix p. A24

THE RAVEN   **143**

ANALYZE VISUALS

Activity After students finish reading the poem, ask them to explain which of the two art pieces seems to better match the mood of the selection—the charcoal drawing of the raven on page 141 or this cardboard relief which pictures both a raven and a heart. *Students' responses should reflect an understanding of the poem's mysterious and melancholy mood.*

About the Art Jim Dine (b. 1935) is known for his emotional style and recurrent subjects—hearts, birds, robes, flowers, and portraits. After receiving a B.F.A. at the University of Ohio, Athens, Dine moved to New York City where he began his career as a Pop artist. During his prolific career, Dine has worked as a painter, sculptor, print-maker, and photographer.

Red Passion (1996), Jim Dine. Cardboard relief intaglio. Image size 33 1/8" × 59". Paper size 39 1/2" × 63 7/8". Published by Pace Editions, Inc. Edition of 12 © 2007 Jime Dine/Artists Rights Society (ARS), New York.

85   "Prophet!" said I, "thing of evil!—prophet still, if bird or devil!—
      Whether Tempter sent, or whether tempest tossed[15] thee here ashore,
      Desolate yet all undaunted,[16] on this desert land enchanted—
      On this home by Horror haunted—tell me truly, I implore—
      Is there—*is* there balm in Gilead?[17]—tell me—tell me, I implore!" **E**
90   Quoth the Raven, "Nevermore."

      "Prophet!" said I, "thing of evil!—prophet still, if bird or devil!
      By that Heaven that bends above us—by that God we both adore—
      Tell this soul with sorrow laden if, within the distant Aidenn,[18]
      It shall clasp a sainted maiden whom the angels name Lenore—
95   Clasp a rare and radiant maiden whom the angels name Lenore."
          Quoth the Raven, "Nevermore."

      "Be that word our sign of parting, bird or fiend!" I shrieked, upstarting—
      "Get thee back into the tempest and the Night's Plutonian shore!
      Leave no black plume as a token of that lie thy soul hath spoken!
100 Leave my loneliness unbroken!—quit the bust above my door!
      Take thy beak from out my heart, and take thy form from off my door!"
          Quoth the Raven, "Nevermore."

      And the Raven, never flitting, still is sitting, *still* is sitting
      On the pallid bust of Pallas just above my chamber door;
105 And his eyes have all the seeming of a demon's that is dreaming,
      And the lamp-light o'er him streaming throws his shadow on the floor;
      And my soul from out that shadow that lies floating on the floor
          Shall be lifted—nevermore! **F**

---

15. **whether Tempter sent . . . tempest tossed:** whether the devil sent or a violent storm carried.
16. **desolate yet all undaunted:** alone and yet unafraid.
17. **balm in Gilead** (gĭl'ē-əd): relief from suffering.
18. **Aidenn** (ād'n): heaven.

144   UNIT 1: NARRATIVE STRUCTURE

DIFFERENTIATED INSTRUCTION

FOR LESS–PROFICIENT READERS

Comprehension Support To make sure students understand lines 97–108, ask what the speaker demands that the raven do in lines 97–101 and whether the raven does as the speaker asks. Have students cite specific lines and phrases to support their responses. To extend the discussion, ask students to paraphrase one or both stanzas.

FOR ADVANCED LEARNERS/PRE–AP

Analyze Explain that "The Raven" is open to various interpretations. For example, some readers think that the poem is not meant to be taken too literally—that its meaning is mainly symbolic. Others believe that the poem is a study in madness—that the raven exists only in the grief-stricken speaker's mind. Have students write a brief essay giving their own interpretations, with supporting details from the poem. Have volunteers share their essays with the class.

Incident *in a* Rose Garden

DONALD JUSTICE

The Back of a Man with a Rose, René Magritte.
Private Collection Bloch, Santa Monica, CA. © 2007
C. Herscovici, Brussels/Artists Rights Society (ARS),
New York. Photo © Superstock, Inc.

The gardener came running,
An old man, out of breath.
Fear had given him legs.
    Sir, I encountered Death
5   *Just now among the roses.*
    Thin as a scythe he stood there.
    I knew him by his pictures.
    He had his black coat on,
    Black gloves, a broad black hat.
10   *I think he would have spoken,*
    Seeing his mouth stood open.
    Big it was, with white teeth.
    As soon as he beckoned, I ran.
    I ran until I found you.
15   *Sir, I am quitting my job.*
    I want to see my sons
    Once more before I die.
    I want to see California. **G**
We shook hands; he was off.

G NARRATIVE POETRY
In lines 4–18, the gardener
(whose words are
italicized) describes
Death as a **character.**
What do these lines
suggest the **conflict** of
this poem will be?

FOR LESS–PROFICIENT READERS

Options for Reading Read "Incident in a Rose Garden" aloud. Use your tone of voice to emphasize the differences among the three characters in the poem—the gardener, the speaker, and Death—and to help demonstrate the ominous atmosphere of the poem. Then have students listen to the poem on the *Audio Anthology CD* as they read along.

Comprehension Support To make sure that students understand the poet's technique, ask what the italic type represents (someone speaking). As students read the second and third stanzas, elicit or explain that the italic type continues to serve the same purpose, but the speaker changes. Have students identify the three speakers.

ANALYZE VISUALS

Activity After students read the poem, have them compare Justice's representation of Death with the "man with a rose" in this painting. How are the two alike? How do they differ? *Possible answer: Both wear a black coat and hat, although the hat in the poem is described as "broad," unlike the one shown in the painting. Both figures hold a rose.*

About the Art The paintings of surrealist artist René Magritte (1898–1967) are misleading in their apparent simplicity. Like so much of Magritte's work, *The Back of a Man with a Rose* raises many questions in the viewer's mind but provides few answers. Magritte once remarked that his paintings "evoke mystery and, indeed, when one sees one of my pictures, one asks oneself this simple question 'What does that mean?' It does not mean anything, because mystery means nothing either, it is unknowable."

LITERARY ANALYSIS

G NARRATIVE POETRY

Possible answer: By describing Death as a character, these lines suggest that the conflict will be between the character of Death and another character who does not want to die.

Extend the Discussion What specific details in these lines personify Death as a character?

Lines 1–18
REINFORCE *KEY IDEA:* UNKNOWN

Discuss How does the gardener react to his encounter with the **unknown,** represented by the figure of Death? *Possible answer: Frightened, the gardener runs away and quits his job, hoping to "see [his] sons once more before I [he dies.]"*

H READING POETRY

Possible answer: *The rhythm adds emphasis to the slow and deliberate actions of Death as he pinches off one bloom after another, apparently enjoying—like a "connoisseur" (line 28).*

Extend the Discussion Why do you think the poet tells us that Death holds the blooms to his nose before discarding them?

I NARRATIVE POETRY

Possible answer: *While there are no out-right words or phrases that would give away the surprise ending—that Death has come not for the gardener but for his employer—is not specifically hinted at, the careful reader can discover the clues the poet includes. The gardener flees before giving Death a chance to speak (line 13), perhaps suggesting that Death's purpose may prove to be other than expected. In addition, when the gardener runs off, Death does not pursue him, but instead waits patiently (lines 20–25), perhaps suggest-ing that he has other business to attend to. Finally, referring to Death's hand as a "cage of bone" (line 42) suggests that the hand may capture the person who shakes it.*

SELECTION WRAP–UP

SYNTHESIZE Have students compare and contrast how Poe and Justice create an eerie, ominous atmosphere in their poems.

⭐ **CRITIQUE** Ask students to explain which poem's ending they found more satisfying, and why.

READING FLUENCY

Distribute the copy master and have students work in pairs or groups to practice fluency.

R **RESOURCE MANAGER—Copy Master**
Reading Fluency p. 216

20 And there stood Death in the garden,
   Dressed like a Spanish waiter.
   He had the air of someone
   Who because he likes arriving
   At all appointments early
25 Learns to think himself patient.
   I watched him pinch one bloom off
   And hold it to his nose—
   A connoisseur of roses—
   One bloom and then another. **H**
30 They strewed the earth around him.
      Sir, you must be that stranger
      Who threatened my gardener.
      This is my property, sir.
      I welcome only friends here.

35 Death grinned, and his eyes lit up
   With the pale glow of those lanterns
   That workmen carry sometimes
   To light their way through the dusk.
   Now with great care he slid
40 The glove from his right hand
   And held that out in greeting,
   A little cage of bone.
      Sir, I knew your father,
      And we were friends at the end.
45   *As for your gardener,*
      I did not threaten him.
      Old men mistake my gestures.
      I only meant to ask him
      To show me to his master.
50   *I take it you are he?* **I**

for Mark Strand

H READING POETRY
Read aloud lines 26–29, and note the **rhythm** created by the words. What effect does this add to the image presented?

I NARRATIVE POETRY
For most readers, this poem has a **surprise ending.** Did any clues hint at this outcome?

DIFFERENTIATED INSTRUCTION

FOR LESS–PROFICIENT READERS

Comprehension Support Elicit or explain that Justice uses personification in his poem—representing death as a character. Direct students' attention to lines 6–13, 20–30, and 35–50, and have them identify details that the poet uses to portray death in human form.

FOR ADVANCED LEARNERS/PRE–AP

Imagery [small-group option] Have students discuss how the descriptive images in lines 6–9, 22–30, and 35–42 give a sinister air to Death. Ask which image seems most menacing, and why. Extend the discussion by asking whether Death's politeness in the third stanza makes him seem more or less sinister.

After Reading

Comprehension

1. **Recall** What is the **setting** of each poem?

2. **Recall** In "The Raven," what loss is the speaker trying to recover from?

3. **Recall** In "Incident in a Rose Garden," for whom has Death really come?

4. **Clarify** What happens at the end of each poem?

Literary Analysis

5. **Analyze** Reread lines 7–12 of "The Raven." The **speaker** has tried to forget his sadness and loss. What is his mental state at the end of the poem? Do you think the raven is real or just a figment of his imagination? Support your views with details from the poem.

6. **Identify Irony** Explain the ironies, or unexpected twists, in "Incident in a Rose Garden."

7. **Interpret Narrative Poetry** Use a chart to identify the narrative elements found in these poems. In each poem, which element plays the largest role? Support your answer.

Narrative Element	"The Raven"	"Incident in a Rose Garden"
Characters		
Setting		
Conflict		
Resolution (How does it end?)		

8. **Reading Poetry** Review the chart you filled in as you read the poems. Which poet depends more heavily on **sound devices** to help convey mood and meaning? Cite evidence.

Literary Criticism

9. **Critical Interpretations** With the publication of "The Raven" in 1845, Poe became famous overnight. More than 160 years later, the poem is still considered a classic. What accounts for its continued appeal? Be specific in your answer.

Practice and Apply

After Reading

For additional support of post-reading questions, use these copy masters:

R RESOURCE MANAGER—Copy Masters
Narrative Poetry p. 211 (for practice of literary analysis standards focus)
Question Support p. 215 (After Reading questions adapted for English learners and less-proficient readers)

For additional questions, see page 207.

ANSWERS

Comprehension

1. *"The Raven": the speaker's "chamber," on "a midnight dreary" in "bleak December"; "Incident in a Rose Garden": a rose garden*

2. *the death of his beloved Lenore*

3. *the speaker*

4. *"The Raven": The raven remains in the speaker's chamber, casting his shadow forever over the speaker's soul. "Incident in a Rose Garden": Death reveals that he has come not for the gardener but for "his master."*

Literary Analysis
Possible answers:

5. *The speaker is in a state of utter despair at the end. Whether students respond that the raven is real or imaginary, they should support their opinions with evidence.*

6. *The central irony is that Death has come not for the gardener, who fears him, but for the speaker, who bravely orders Death to leave. It is also ironic to call Death a "connoisseur of roses," because Death's enjoyment of roses involves killing them.*

7. ● **STANDARDS FOCUS** *Narrative Poetry After students have used the chart to identify the different narrative elements in the poems, they may choose these elements as the most important: "The Raven": the characters, because their interaction creates the poem's conflict and sustains its eerie mood; "Incident in a Rose Garden": the resolution, because the surprise ending provides the poem's central irony and meaning*

8. ■ **STANDARDS FOCUS** *Reading Poetry Poe uses sound devices—rhyme, rhythm,* repetition, alliteration—much more than Justice to convey mood and meaning.

Literary Criticism
Possible answer:

9. *Poe's poem deals with significant and timeless themes, such as love and loss. In addition, its sound devices and eeriness make it an entertaining and memorable poem. Finally, its ambiguity (is the raven real or imaginary?) teases the reader and encourages discussion.*

Assess and Reteach

Assess

R RESOURCE MANAGER—Copy Masters
Selection Test A pp. 217–218
Selection Test B/C pp. 219–220

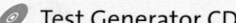 Test Generator CD

Reteach

S STANDARDS LESSON FILE
Literature Lesson 20: Speaker
Literature Lesson 21: Rhyme

Focus and Motivate

OBJECTIVES

Literary Analysis
- explore the key idea of the **supernatural**
- analyze and evaluate plot in drama
- read a teleplay and an excerpt from the author's memoir

Reading
- read a teleplay

Grammar and Writing
- use realistic dialogue to create realistic characters
- use writing to analyze literature

SUMMARY

"Sorry, Right Number" is the suspenseful tale of a woman who receives an alarming phone call from an unidentified, though somehow familiar, caller. Katie Weiderman and her husband, Bill, try without success to identify the caller. Five years after her husband's fatal heart attack, Katie learns that the message was a warning from the future, and that she herself was the caller.

What sends a CHILL *down your spine?*

Discuss the question with students. Encourage them to think about the *KEY IDEA* by asking them about books and movies that they find scary. Discuss how suspense, the **supernatural,** and sudden surprises affect the "chill factor." Have students complete the *QUICKWRITE.* Follow up by asking why an unknown or unseen force can be more frightening or suspenseful than a known one.

Selection Resources

Sorry, Right Number
Teleplay by Stephen King

What sends a CHILL *down your spine?*

KEY IDEA Not all horror stories give readers a fright by portraying gory scenes. Some present ordinary people doing ordinary things—until something creepy, or even **supernatural,** happens. In *Sorry, Right Number,* a family is puzzled by a mysterious phone caller pleading for help.

QUICKWRITE Supernatural events play a part in many stories of fantasy, mystery, and horror. Work with a group to generate a list of supernatural occurrences in stories, movies, and TV programs. Arrange them in a "chill factor" chart according to how powerfully they affect you.

Chill Factor
10. (Terrifying)
9.
8.
7. (Nail biter)
6.
5.
4.
3. (Tame)
2.
1.

148

 **RESOURCE MANAGER UNIT 1**

Plan and Teach pp. 221–228

Literary Analysis
Summary pp. 229†*, 230‡*
Plot in Drama pp. 231, 232†*
Question Support p. 236*

Reading
Reading a Teleplay pp. 233, 234†*
Reading Check p. 235
Reading Fluency p. 238

Grammar and Writing
Create Realistic Characters p. 237

Assessment
Selection Tests A, B/C
pp. 239*, 241*
 Test Generator CD

BEST PRACTICES TOOLKIT

Differentiated Instruction
pp. 31–38*

Scaffolding Instruction
pp. 43–46*

Graphic Organizers/Strategies
Readers' Theater • Knowledge Rating • New Word Analysis • Storyboard • Two-Column Chart

Reading Support
Audio Anthology CD*

Technology
Literature and Vocabulary Centers at **ClassZone.com**
WriteSmart CD

---

* Resources for Differentiation   † Also in Spanish   ‡ In Haitian Creole and Vietnamese

LITERARY ANALYSIS: PLOT IN DRAMA

As you probably know, a **drama** is basically a story told in dialogue form. Like a work of fiction, drama establishes a setting, presents a series of **plot** events, and centers around one or more **conflicts** that the characters must cope with. Because a drama does not use a narrator to describe what happens, the plot unfolds through the characters' words and actions. As you read this drama, note what the dialogue and camera directions reveal about the setting, the conflict, and the unusual events that surround the cast of characters. Also, be ready for Stephen King's special brand of suspense.

READING SKILL: READING A TELEPLAY

Reading a teleplay is different from reading a script for a stage play. Your mind's eye will be challenged to **visualize** what the camera is focusing on. For example, in *Sorry, Right Number*, when a camera direction calls for an extreme close-up and then takes you inside a telephone receiver, you have to imagine not only how this looks but also what effect it creates. In addition, in a teleplay, you don't have to wait for formal scene changes to have changes in setting, as you do with a regular stage play. You can be instantly thrown from one setting to the next, even from one time period to another, by a camera direction that reads "slam cut to."

Before you read, study Stephen King's note at the beginning of the teleplay to familiarize yourself with common teleplay terms. As you read, use your experience watching TV and movies to help you visualize what the camera wants you to see.

Author Online

From the Trash Can to the Bestseller List Stephen King nearly threw away his writing career before it began. He dumped the manuscript of his first horror novel, *Carrie*, into the trash, but his wife retrieved it and urged him to continue working on it. Later, after *Carrie* became a hit movie,

Stephen King
born 1947

King went on to have six titles on the *New York Times* bestseller list at the same time. Credited with reviving the market for both horror fiction and horror films, King has been called a "one-man entertainment industry."

From Brain to Screen King has written that the idea for *Sorry, Right Number* came to him "one night on my way home from buying a pair of shoes." He wrote the script in two sittings and about a week later submitted it to a friend who produced a TV series called *Tales from the Darkside*. The friend bought the teleplay the day he read it and had it in production a week or two later; and it was broadcast a month after that—"one of the fastest turns from in-the-head to on-the-screen that I've ever heard of," King commented.

 MORE ABOUT THE AUTHOR
For more on Stephen King, visit the **Literature Center** at **ClassZone.com.**

Background

Writing for Television Mixed in with the camera directions in *Sorry, Right Number* are passages in King's own voice. King acts as both author and "narrator" of the play, frequently addressing the reader. He explains abbreviations, points out things he wants the reader to know, and comments on situations.

SORRY, RIGHT NUMBER **149**

DIFFERENTIATED INSTRUCTION

FOR ENGLISH LEARNERS

Language: Skill Words Make sure students understand the meanings of these words related to plot in drama:

- *drama:* a literary form in which dialogue— the words the characters say—tells the story
- *characters:* the people who take part in the story
- *plot:* the sequence of events in the story
- *conflicts:* the struggles that the characters face

Teach

STANDARDS FOCUS

LITERARY ANALYSIS

● PLOT IN DRAMA

Narrative prose and dialogue can convey similar information, but in different ways. For instructional suppport, have students compare these examples:

> The creature moved toward the two girls. They wanted to run, but the door was locked.

> "The creature's moving toward us, Amy!"
> "Run!"
> "It's no use. The door is locked."

Discuss whether the narrative prose or the dialogue is more effective, and why. ***Possible answer:*** *Dialogue, because it conveys the emotions of the characters and intensifies the suspense.*

CHECK UNDERSTANDING Ask which approach—narrative prose or dialogue— reveals plot mainly through characters' words.

READING SKILL

■ READING A TELEPLAY

Tell students to imagine having to "watch" a scary movie or TV show with their eyes closed. Ask them how the experience would affect their enjoyment and their understanding of the plot. Tell students that because a teleplay is written to be performed on television, it is important for readers to think visually when reading one. Readers must "keep their eyes opened" to see the events that are unfolding on the page.

CHECK UNDERSTANDING Ask students which they think would be scarier, and why: watching a scary movie without the sound or listening to it without the picture.

 RESOURCE MANAGER—Copy Master
Reading a Teleplay p. 233 (for student use while reading the selection)

Lines 1–20
DISCUSSION PROMPTS

Use these prompts to help students understand the characters who have been introduced thus far, and the format of the teleplay:

Connect Think of your favorite television programs. How are the stories typically set up at the beginning? *Possible answer: They usually begin by establishing where the action is going to take place and who one or more of the main characters are, and hint at what the conflict will be that will drive the action.* Students may give examples.

Analyze What can you tell about Bill from Katie's conversation? *Possible answer: It seems as if Bill is a writer. He is prone to chronic worry and complaints about his health.*

Evaluate How do setting and character work in this scene to point toward future conflicts? *Possible answer: The setting suggests that the Weidermans are well off; they have a comfortable home with modern conveniences. The dialogue suggests that potential problems may lie ahead for the Weidermans, possibly with regard to Bill's health.*

SORRY, RIGHT NUMBER

Stephen King

CAST OF CHARACTERS

Katie Weiderman

Jeff Weiderman

Connie Weiderman

Dennis Weiderman

Bill Weiderman

Polly Weiderman

Operator

Dawn

Minister

Groundskeeper

Hank

Author's note: Screenplay abbreviations are simple and exist, in this author's opinion, mostly to make those who write screenplays feel like lodge brothers.[1] In any case, you should be aware that *CU* means *close-up; ECU* means *extreme close-up; INT.* means *interior; EXT.* means *exterior; B.G.* means *background; POV* means *point of view.* Probably most of you knew all that stuff to begin with, right?

Act I

Targeted Passage ①

(*Fade in on* Katie Weiderman's *mouth, ECU*)

(*She's speaking into the telephone. Pretty mouth; in a few seconds we'll see that the rest of her is just as pretty.*)

Katie. Bill? Oh, he says he doesn't feel very well, but he's always like that between books . . . can't

sleep, thinks every headache is the first symptom of a brain tumor . . . once he gets going on something new, he'll be fine.

10 (*Sound, B.G.: the television*)

(*The camera draws back.* Katie *is sitting in the kitchen phone nook, having a good gab with her sister while she idles through some catalogues. We should notice one not-quite-ordinary thing about the phone she's on: it's the sort with two lines. There are lighted buttons to show which ones are engaged. Right now only one—Katie's—is. As* Katie *continues her conversation, the camera swings away from her, tracks across the kitchen, and through the arched*
20 *doorway that leads into the family room.*)

Katie (*voice, fading*). Oh, I saw Janie Charlton today . . . yes! Big as a *house!* . . .

---

1. **lodge brothers:** members of the same men's social organization. Lodges sometimes have special rituals or vocabularies.

DIFFERENTIATED INSTRUCTION

FOR ALL STUDENTS

Anchor Activity Provide independent learning opportunities for students to research horror and fantasy television programs of the 1970s and 80s. Assign groups to research programs and allow time for group presentations. After reading the selection, ask students to compare "Sorry, Right Number" with the programs they researched. To help students, see

R RESOURCE MANAGER
Ideas For Extension, pp. 226–227

FOR LESS–PROFICIENT READERS

In combination with the *Audio Anthology CD,* use one or more Targeted Passages (pp. 150, 153, 161, 163, 164) to ensure that students focus on key story events, concepts, and skills. Targeted Passages are also good for English learners.

① **Targeted Passage [Lines 1–22]**

This passage sets the scene of the teleplay. It introduces one of the main characters

BACKGROUND

Television in the 1980s "Sorry, Right Number" was written in 1987, a time when network television achieved new levels of realism in its prime-time progams. Even comedies like *Cheers* and *Wings* (mentioned on p. 152) focused on relationships between family and friends and gave a more accurate portrayal of American life than did the more idealized comedies of the 1950s and early 1960s. "Sorry, Right Number" portrays a family held together by strong relationships, but those bonds are about to be tested in some dramatic, even extraordinary ways.

ANALYZE VISUALS

Activity Ask students how the photograph relates to both the title and the opening scene of the teleplay. *Possible answer: The photograph shows a woman on the telephone; the teleplay opens with Katie Weiderman on the phone. The title is a play on the familiar phrase "sorry, wrong number," which a caller might say after dialing incorrectly.*

---

and gives readers an important piece of information.

- What "not-quite-ordinary" thing does the author want readers to take note of?
- What significance do you think this detail might have for the rest of the story?

FOR ENGLISH LEARNERS

Reading: Background Tell students that they will be reading a teleplay, a play written for television. Have students share any experiences they have had watching a stage play.

Options for Reading Use the Readers Theater strategy to introduce the play. Assign the roles to groups of students.

 BEST PRACTICES TOOLKIT
Readers' Theater p. A1

Prereading For prereading instruction for English learners, see

 BEST PRACTICES TOOLKIT
Scaffolding Reading Instruction pp. 43–46

FOR ADVANCED LEARNERS/PRE–AP

Pre-AP Exercises in the bottom channel provide additional challenge for students. Use these suggestions for small groups or individuals.

ADDITIONAL GUIDELINES

For more help with differentiation and tips for classroom management, see

 BEST PRACTICES TOOLKIT
Differentiated Instruction pp. 31–38

Lines 28–80
DISCUSSION PROMPTS

Use these prompts to help students understand the interrelationships of the Weiderman family members:

Connect Based on your experience, do the relationships among the Weiderman children seem realistic? *Students will probably answer yes.*

Analyze Based on the dialogue among the children, what do you learn about the Weidermans as a family? *Possible answer: They are creatures of habit—they watch the same TV programs every week—but they are also thoughtful and close-knit.*

Evaluate What kind of mother is Katie? *Possible answer: She is caring and concerned, attentive even to the tone of her family's voices.*

READING SKILL

▶ READING A TELEPLAY

Notice how King calls for two close-up (CU) shots on this page. What are they, and how do they add suspense to the scene?

Possible answer: The two close-ups are of the Dracula poster on Bill's study door (line 87), and the photographs of Katie and the Weiderman children (line 88). Taken together, the reader may wonder if there is any connection between the eerie caption coming out of Dracula's mouth ("'Listen! My children of the night!'") and what might lie ahead for the Weidermans.

(*She fades. The TV gets louder. There are three kids: Jeff,* eight, *Connie,* ten, *and Dennis,* thirteen. *Wheel of Fortune is on, but they're not watching. Instead they're engaged in that great pastime, Fighting About What Comes On Later.*)

Jeff. Come onnn! It was his first *book!*

Connie. His first *gross* book.

30 **Dennis.** We're gonna watch *Cheers* and *Wings,*[2] just like we do every week, Jeff.

(*Dennis speaks with the utter finality only a big brother can manage. "Wanna talk about it some more and see how much pain I can inflict on your scrawny body, Jeff?" his face says.*)

Jeff. Could we at least tape it?

Connie. We're taping CNN[3] for Mom. She said she might be on the phone with Aunt Lois for quite a while.

40 **Jeff.** How can you tape CNN, for God's sake? It *never* stops!

Dennis. That's what she likes about it.

Connie. And don't say God's sake, Jeffie—you're not old enough to talk about God except in church.

Jeff. Then don't call me Jeffie.

Connie. Jeffie, Jeffie, Jeffie.

(*Jeff gets up, walks to the window, and looks out into the dark. He's really upset. Dennis and Connie, in*
50 *the grand tradition of older brothers and sisters, are delighted to see it.*)

Dennis. Poor Jeffie.

Connie. I think he's gonna commit suicide.

Jeff (*turns to them*). It was his *first* book! Don't you guys even *care?*

Connie. Rent it down at the Video Stop tomorrow, if you want to see it so bad.

Jeff. They don't rent R-rated pictures to little kids and you know it!

60 **Connie** (*dreamily*). Shut up, it's Vanna! I *love* Vanna!

Jeff. Dennis—

Dennis. Go ask Dad to tape it on the VCR in his office and quit being such a totally annoying little booger.

(*Jeff crosses the room, poking his tongue out at Vanna White as he goes. The camera follows as he goes into the kitchen.*)

Katie. . . . so when he asked me if *Polly* had tested strep positive,[4] I had to remind him she's away at
70 prep school[5] . . . Lois, I miss her . . .

(*Jeff is just passing through, on his way to the stairs.*)

Katie. Will you kids *please* be quiet?

Jeff (*glum*). They'll be quiet. *Now.*

(*He goes up the stairs, a little dejected. Katie looks after him for a moment, loving and worried.*)

Katie. They're squabbling again. Polly used to keep them in line, but now that she's away at school . . . I don't know . . . maybe sending her to Bolton wasn't such a hot idea. Sometimes when
80 she calls home she sounds so *unhappy* . . .

(*INT. Bela Lugosi[6] as Dracula, CU*)

(*Drac's standing at the door of his Transylvanian castle. Someone has pasted a comic-balloon coming out of his mouth which reads: "Listen! My children of the night! What music they make!" The poster is on a door but we only see this as Jeff opens it and goes into his father's study.*)

(*INT. a photograph of Katie, CU*)

(*The camera holds, then pans slowly right. We pass*
90 *another photo, this one of Polly, the daughter away at school. She's a lovely girl of sixteen or so. Past Polly is Dennis . . . then Connie . . . then Jeff.*)

---

2. **Cheers and Wings:** popular television sitcoms of the 1980s and 1990s.

3. **CNN:** the Cable News Network.

4. **had tested strep positive:** had strep throat, an infection caused by bacteria called streptococci.

5. **prep school:** a private high school that prepares students for college.

6. **Bela Lugosi:** a Hungarian-born actor (1882–1956) best known for his roles in U.S. horror films of the 1930s and 1940s.

152   UNIT 1: NARRATIVE STRUCTURE

DIFFERENTIATED INSTRUCTION

FOR ENGLISH LEARNERS

Key Academic Vocabulary Use Knowledge Rating to teach these words: *tape* (p. 152, line 36), *tradition* (p. 152, line 50), *positive* (p. 152, line 69), *residence* (p. 153, line 133), *network* (p. 159, line 116), *area* (p. 163, line 314).

 BEST PRACTICES TOOLKIT—Transparency Knowledge Rating p. E3

FOR ENGLISH LEARNERS

Culture: Connect Explain to students that *residence* means "home." Then point out that Katie's phone greeting, "Hello, Weiderman residence," is a common way to answer the phone in the United States. Have volunteers share phone greetings used in their own culture. Then have them repeat the phone greeting used by Katie Weiderman, replacing *Weiderman* with their own surnames.

(*The camera continues to pan and also widens out so we can see* Bill Weiderman, *a man of about forty-four. He looks tired. He's peering into the word-processor on his desk, but his mental crystal ball must be taking the night off, because the screen is blank. On the walls we see framed book-covers. All of them are spooky. One of the titles is* Ghost Kiss.)

100 (Jeff *comes up quietly behind his dad. The carpet muffles his feet.* Bill *sighs and shuts off the word-cruncher. A moment later* Jeff *claps his hands on his father's shoulders.*)

Jeff. BOOGA-BOOGA!

Bill. Hi, Jeffie.

(*He turns in his chair to look at his son, who is disappointed.*)

Jeff. How come you didn't get scared?

Bill. Scaring is my business. I'm case-hardened.
110 Something wrong?

Jeff. Daddy, can I watch the first hour of *Ghost Kiss* and you tape the rest? Dennis and Connie are hogging *everything*.

(Bill *swivels to look at the book-jacket, bemused.*)

Bill. You sure you want to watch *that*, champ? It's pretty—

Jeff. *Yes!*

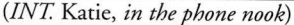 Targeted Passage ②

(*INT.* Katie, *in the phone nook*)

(*In this shot, we clearly see the stairs leading to her*
120 *husband's study behind her.*)

Katie. I *really* think Jeff needs the orthodontic work but you know Bill—

(*The other line rings. The other light stutters.*)

Katie. That's just the other line, Bill will—

(*But now we see* Bill *and* Jeff *coming downstairs behind her.*)

Bill. Honey, where're the blank videotapes? I can't find any in the study and—

Katie. (*to* Bill). *Wait!*
130 (*to* Lois). Gonna put you on hold a sec, Lo.

(*She does. Now both lines are blinking. She pushes the top one, where the new call has just come in.*)

Katie. Hello, Weiderman residence.

(*Sound: desperate sobbing*)

Sobbing voice (*filter*). Take . . . please take . . . t-t-

Katie. Polly? Is that you? What's wrong?

(*Sound: sobbing. It's awful, heartbreaking.*)

Sobbing voice (*filter*). *Please—quick—*

(*Sound: sobbing . . . Then, click! A broken*
140 *connection.*)

Katie. Polly, calm down! Whatever it is can't be that b—

(*hum of an open line*)

(Jeff *has wandered toward the TV room, hoping to find a blank tape.*)

Activity Ask students how the doorway in the photograph functions as a transitional tool. *Possible answer: The door helps guide the reader from one scene to another.*

Lines 133–143
**REINFORCE *KEY IDEA:*
THE SUPERNATURAL**

Discuss Up until the time Katie answers the other line, the events described have been ordinary. What is it about the phone call that changes the mood of the story? *Possible answer: The voice on the phone is accompanied by "desperate sobbing," described as "awful, heartbreaking," and the connection is suddenly lost. The mood is now disturbing and unsettling.*

FOR LESS-PROFICIENT READERS
② **Targeted Passage [Lines 118–143]**

This passage brings readers back to the two-line telephone that was introduced on page 150. It marks a turning point in the plot as Katie puts a caller on hold to take another call.

- Why does Katie put her call on hold?

- Whose voice does Katie think she hears on the other line?

- Why does the call end abruptly?

- What effect does this call have on the teleplay's level of suspense?

Bill. Who was that?

(*Without looking at her husband or answering him,* Katie *slams the lower button in again.*)

Katie. Lois? Listen, I'll call you back. That was
150 Polly, and she sounded very upset. No . . . she
hung up. Yes. I will. Thanks.

(*She hangs up.*)

Bill (*concerned*). It was Polly?

Katie. Crying her head off. It sounded like she was trying to say "Please take me home" . . . I knew that school was bumming her out . . . Why I ever let you talk me into it . . .

(*She's rummaging frantically on her little phone desk. Catalogues go slithering to the floor around*
160 *her stool.*)

Katie. *Connie did you take my address book?*

Connie (*voice*). No, Mom.

(Bill *pulls a battered book out of his back pocket and pages through it.*)

Bill. I got it. Except—

Katie. I know, dorm phone is always busy. Give it to me.

Bill. Honey, calm down.

Katie. I'll calm down after I talk to her. She is
170 sixteen, Bill. Sixteen-year-old girls are prone to depressive interludes. Sometimes they even k . . . just give me the number!

Bill. 617-555-8641.

(*As she punches the numbers, the camera slides in to CU.*)

Katie. Come on, come on . . . don't be busy . . . just this once . . .

(*Sound: clicks. A pause. Then . . . the phone starts ringing.*)

180 **Katie** (*eyes closed*). Thank You, God.

Voice (*filter*). Hartshorn Hall, this is Frieda.

Katie. Could you call Polly to the phone? Polly Weiderman? This is Kate Weiderman. Her mother.

Voice (*filter*). hang on, please, Mrs. Weiderman.

(*Sound: the phone clunks down.*)

Voice (*filter, and very faint*). Polly? Pol? . . . Phone call! . . . It's your mother!

(*INT. a wider angle on the phone nook, with* Bill)

190 **Bill.** Well?

Katie. Somebody's getting her. I hope.

(Jeff *comes back in with a tape.*)

Jeff. I found one, Dad. Dennis hid em. As usual.

Bill. In a minute, Jeff. Go watch the tube.

Jeff. But—

Bill. I won't forget. Now go *on.*

(Jeff *goes.*)

Katie. Come on, come on, come on . . .

Bill. Calm down, Katie.

200 **Katie** (*snaps*). If you'd heard her, you wouldn't tell me to calm down! She sounded—

Polly (*filter, cheery voice*). Hi, mom!

Katie. Pol? Honey? Are you all right?

Polly (*happy, bubbling voice*). Am I *all right?* I aced my bio exam, got a B on my French Conversational Essay, and Ronnie Hansen asked me to the Harvest Ball. I'm so all right that if one more good thing happens to me today, I'll probably blow up like the *Hindenburg*.[7]

210 **Katie.** You didn't just call me up, crying your head off?

(*We see by* Katie's *face that she already knows the answer to this question.*)

Polly (*filter*). Heck no!

Katie. I'm glad about your test and your date, honey. I guess it was someone else. I'll call you back, okay?

Polly (*filter*). 'Kay. Say hi to Dad!

Katie. I will.

220 (*INT. the phone nook, wider*)

Bill. She okay?

Katie. Fine. I could have *sworn* it was Polly, but . . . *she's* walking on air.

Bill. So it was a prank. Or someone who was crying so hard she dialed a wrong number . . . "through a shimmering film of tears," as we veteran hacks like to say.

Katie. It was not a prank and it was not a wrong number! It was someone in *my family!*

230 **Bill.** Honey, you can't know that.

Katie. No? If Jeffie called up, just crying, would you know it was him?

Bill (*struck by this*). Yeah, maybe. I guess I might.

(*She's not listening. She's punching numbers, fast.*)

Bill. Who you calling?

(*She doesn't answer him. Sound: phone rings twice. Then:*)

Older Female Voice (*filter*). Hello?

Katie. Mom? Are you . . . (*She pauses.*) Did you 240 call just a few seconds ago?

Voice (*filter*). No, dear . . . why?

Katie. Oh . . . you know these phones. I was talking to Lois and I lost the other call.

Voice (*filter*). Well, it wasn't me. Kate, I saw the *prettiest* dress in La Boutique today, and—

Katie. We'll talk about it later, Mom, okay?

Voice (*filter*). Kate, are you all right?

Katie. I have . . . Mom, I think maybe I've got diarrhea. I have to go. 'Bye.

250 (*She hangs up.* Bill *hangs on until she does; then he bursts into wild donkey-brays of laughter.*)

Bill. Oh boy . . . diarrhea . . . I gotta remember that the next time my agent calls . . . oh Katie, that was so cool—

Katie (*almost screaming*). *This is not funny!*

(Bill *stops laughing.*)

(*INT. the TV room*)

(Jeff *and* Dennis *have been tussling. They stop. All three kids look toward the kitchen.*)

260 (*INT. the phone nook, with* Bill *and* Katie)

Katie. *I tell you it was someone in my family and she sounded*—oh, you don't understand. I *knew* that voice.

Bill. But if Polly's okay and your mom's okay . . .

Katie (*positive*). It's Dawn.

Bill. Come on, hon, a minute ago you were sure it was Polly.

Katie. It *had* to be Dawn. I was on the phone with Lois and Mom's okay, so Dawn's the only other 270 one it *could* have been. She's the youngest . . . I could have mistaken her for Polly . . . and she's out there in that farmhouse alone with the baby!

Bill (*startled*). What do you mean, alone?

Katie. Jerry's in Burlington! It's Dawn! *Something's happened to Dawn!*

(Connie *comes into the kitchen, worried.*)

Connie. Mom? Is Aunt Dawn okay?

Bill. So far as we know, she's fine. Take it easy, doll. Bad to buy trouble before you know it's on sale.

---

7. *Hindenburg:* an airship that exploded, crashed, and burned spectacularly in 1937.

Use these prompts to help students understand the author's technique for building suspense:

Connect After Katie speaks with Polly, Bill concludes that the sobbing phone call was either "a prank" or "someone who . . . dialed a wrong number." Katie, however, strongly disagrees. Do you agree with Bill or with Katie? Why? *Responses should reflect an understanding of the situation.*

Analyze How does the author maintain the tension level after Katie talks to Polly? *Possible answer: Katie insists that the call "was not a prank and it was not a wrong number! It was someone in my family!" Then she concludes that something must have happened to Dawn, her younger sister.*

Evaluate How does the difference in the way that Katie and Bill react to the phone call add to the suspense? *Possible answer: The contrast between Bill's relative calmness and Katie's apprehension heightens the suspense. The reader isn't sure who more accurately grasps what's going on, Bill or Katie.*

FOR ADVANCED LEARNERS/PRE–AP
Draw Conclusions About Characterization
[paired-activity option] Bill tells Katie, "Bad to buy trouble before you know it's on sale." Discuss with students whether they think this is an appropriate comment. Use a Storyboard to help pairs of students write and perform an extended dialogue between Bill and Katie on this topic.

 BEST PRACTICES TOOLKIT—Transparency
Storyboard p. C11

DISCUSSION PROMPTS

Use these prompts to help students understand how the author builds suspense through a progression of events and attitudes:

Connect Do you feel that the operator acted appropriately in this scene? Explain. *Responses should reflect an understanding of the situation and what it might mean.*

Analyze How is Bill's attitude changing? What is the effect of this change on the level of tension? *Possible answer: Previously, Bill seemed relatively unconcerned. He no longer seems quite as confident that nothing is wrong, which makes readers wonder whether Katie's fears may be well-founded.*

Evaluate Why do you think King includes the operator's personal comments about Bill's books? *Possible answer: The operator's chatty conversation—broken off when Bill abruptly hangs up—contrasts sharply with the stress that Katie and Bill are feeling, which helps heighten the suspense.*

Lines 323–329
REINFORCE *KEY IDEA:* THE SUPERNATURAL

Discuss A supernatural event is an event that could not happen naturally in our world under any circumstances. What natural and supernatural reasons might account for the phone at the farmhouse being off the hook? *Possible answers: Natural—someone took the phone off the hook because he or she didn't want to be disturbed; the phone was knocked off the hook during a struggle; an intruder cut the phone wires so no one could call for help. Supernatural—some type of energy from space or another dimension is interfering with the phone lines.*

---

280 (*Katie punches numbers and listens. Sound: the dah-dah-dah of a busy signal. Katie hangs up. Bill looks a question at her with raised eyebrows.*)

Katie. Busy.

Bill. Katie, are you sure—

Katie. She's the only one left—it had to be her. Bill, I'm scared. Will you drive me out there?

(*Bill takes the phone from her.*)

Bill. What's her number?

Katie. 555-6169.

290 (*Bill dials. Gets a busy. Hangs up and punches 0.*)

Operator (*filter*). Operator.

Bill. I'm trying to reach my sister-in-law, operator. The line is busy. I suspect there may be a problem. Can you break into the call, please?

(*INT. the door to the TV room*)

(*All three kids are standing there, silent and worried.*)

(*INT. the phone nook, with* Bill *and* Katie)

Operator (*filter*). What is your name, sir?

Bill. William Weiderman. My number is—

300 **Operator** (*filter*). Not the William Weiderman that wrote *Spider Doom?!*

Bill. Yes, that was mine. If—

Operator (*filter*). Oh, I just *loved* that book! I love *all* your books! I—

Bill. I'm delighted you do. But right now my wife is very worried about her sister. If it's possible for you to—

Operator (*filter*). Yes, I can do that. Please give me your number, Mr. Weiderman, for the records.

310 (*She giggles.*) I *promise* not to give it out.

Bill. It's 555-4408.

Operator (*filter*). And the call number?

Bill (*looks at* Katie). Uh . . .

Katie. 555-6169.

Bill. 555-6169.

Operator (*filter*). Just a moment, Mr. Weiderman . . . *Night of the Beast* was also great, by the way. Hold on.

(*Sound: telephonic clicks and clacks*)

---

320 **Katie.** Is she—

Bill. Yes. Just . . .

(*There's one final click.*)

Operator (*filter*). I'm sorry, Mr. Weiderman, but that line is not busy. It's off the hook. I wonder if I sent you my copy of *Spider Doom*—

(*Bill hangs up the phone.*)

Katie. Why did you hang up?

Bill. She can't break in. Phone's not busy. It's off the hook.

330 (*They stare at each other bleakly.*)

(*EXT. A low-slung sports car passes the camera. Night.*)

(*INT. the car, with* Katie *and* Bill)

(*Katie's scared. Bill, at the wheel, doesn't look exactly calm.*)

Katie. Hey, Bill—tell me she's all right.

Bill. She's all right.

Katie. Now tell me what you really think.

Bill. Jeff snuck up behind me tonight and put the old booga-booga on me. He was disappointed as hell when I didn't jump. I told him I was case-hardened. (*pause*) I lied.

Katie. Why did Jerry have to move out there when he's gone half the time? Just her and that little tiny baby? *Why?*

Bill. Shh, Kate. We're almost there.

Katie. Go faster.

(*EXT. the car*)

(*He does. That car is smokin.*)

350 (*INT. the Weiderman TV room*)

(*The tube's still on and the kids are still there, but the horsing around has stopped.*)

Connie. Dennis, do you think Aunt Dawn's okay?

Dennis (*thinks she's dead, decapitated by a maniac*). Yeah. Sure she is.

(*INT. the phone, POV from the TV room*)

(*just sitting there on the wall in the phone nook, lights dark, looking like a snake ready to strike*)

(*Fade out.*)

DIFFERENTIATED INSTRUCTION

FOR ENGLISH LEARNERS

Culture: Clarify Explain that the words *booga-booga* are common children's language for magic spells and scary things in general. Point out other uniquely American references and explain their meanings. For example:

- *R-rated pictures* (p. 152, line 58): films meant for adult audiences. *R* stands for "restricted."
- *Harvest Ball* (p. 155, line 207): a school dance that takes place in the fall

- *Huey Lewis and the News* (p. 158, line 62): a musical group popular in the 1980s
- *It's network* (p. 159, line 116): The program is on a channel that is available to all. *boogeyman* (p. 159, line 135): an imaginary monster

Act II

(*EXT. an isolated farmhouse*)

(*A long driveway leads up to it. There's one light on in the living room. Car lights sweep up the driveway. The Weiderman car pulls up close to the garage and stops.*)

(*INT. the car, with* Bill *and* Katie)

Katie. I'm scared.

(Bill *bends down, reaches under his seat, and brings out a pistol.*)

10 **Bill** (*solemnly*). Booga-booga.

Katie (*total surprise*). How long have you had that?

Bill. Since last year. I didn't want to scare you or the kids. I've got a license to carry. Come on.

(*EXT.* Bill *and* Katie)

(*They get out.* Katie *stands by the front of the car while* Bill *goes to the garage and peers in.*)

Bill. Her car's here.

(*The camera tracks with them to the front door. Now we can hear the TV, playing loud.* Bill *pushes the*

ANALYZE VISUALS

Activity Ask students how the photograph relates to the atmosphere of the story.
Possible answer: The photograph shows how isolated and vulnerable the house is, visually suggesting that the occupants may be in danger.

READING SKILL

■ READING A TELEPLAY

How do the first two camera directions at the beginning of Act II build suspense?
Possible answer: The first two camera directions at the beginning of Act II connect an exterior shot of Dawn's isolated farmhouse with an interior shot in which Katie says how scared she is (line 1–7). Given what the reader now knows about the location of the farmhouse, Katie's fear may be justified.

FOR ENGLISH LEARNERS

Vocabulary: Word Associations and Phrasal Verbs As students read, help them identify and understand words that typically occur together in the English language, such as these:

- *right now* (p. 150, line 17): "at the present time"
- *hot idea* (p. 152, line 79): "great suggestion"
- *calm down* (pp. 153, 154, lines 141, 168): "relax"
- *take it easy* (p. 155, line 278): "relax"
- *come on* (p. 157, line 13): "follow me"
- *heart attack* (p. 161, lines 264–265): a sudden blockage of blood flow to the heart

- *learning process* (p. 165): the method or steps involved in learning something

FOR ADVANCED LEARNERS/PRE–AP

Apply Similar Similes [paired-activity option] At the end of Act I, King compares the phone to "a snake ready to strike." Discuss what King is trying to communicate with this simile. Have students write two original similes or metaphors that would convey a similar feeling.

DISCUSSION PROMPTS

Use these prompts to help students understand plot structure and development:

Connect Have you or someone you know ever encountered something unusually suspicious or out of the ordinary? Did your encounter turn out to be easily explained or did it remain a mystery? *Accept all answers.*

Analyze What chain of events has intensified the suspense at this point in the plot? *Possible answers: King increases the suspense through a sequence of events: Bill takes out a gun; there is no answer to the doorbell; the lock has been tampered with; as Bill enters the house, he tells the "terrified" Katie to "be ready to run."*

Evaluate How have the roles of Bill and Katie changed as a result of plot development at this point? *Possible answer: Earlier, it was mainly Katie who set plot events into motion. Now it is Bill who is controlling the action.*

---

20 *doorbell. We hear it inside. They wait.* Katie *pushes it. Still no answer. She pushes it again and doesn't take her finger off.* Bill *looks down at:)*

(EXT. the lock, Bill's *POV)*

(big scratches on it)

(EXT. Bill *and* Katie*)*

Bill *(low).* The lock's been tampered with.

*(*Katie *looks, and whimpers.* Bill *tries the door. It opens. The TV is louder.)*

Bill. Stay behind me. Be ready to run if something
30 happens. I wish I'd left you home, Kate.

(He starts in. Katie *comes after him, terrified, near tears.)*

(INT. Dawn *and* Jerry's *living room)*

(From this angle we see only a small section of the room. The TV is much louder. Bill *enters the room, gun up. He looks to the right . . . and suddenly all the tension goes out of him. He lowers the gun.)*

Katie *(draws up beside him).* Bill . . . what . . .

(He points.)

40 *(INT. the living room, wide,* Bill *and* Katie's *POV)*

(The place looks like a cyclone hit it . . . but it wasn't robbery and murder that caused this mess; only a healthy eighteen-month-old baby. After a strenuous day of trashing the living room, Baby got tired and Mommy got tired and they fell asleep on the couch together. The baby is in Dawn's *lap. There is a pair of Walkman earphones on her head. There are toys— tough plastic Sesame Street and PlaySkool stuff, for the most part—scattered hell to breakfast. The baby
50 has also pulled most of the books out of the bookcase. Had a good munch on one of them, too, by the look.* Bill *goes over and picks it up. It is* Ghost Kiss.*)*

Bill. I've had people say they just eat my books up, but this is ridiculous.

(He's amused. Katie *isn't. She walks over to her sister, ready to be mad . . . but she sees how really exhausted* Dawn *looks and softens.)*

(INT. Dawn *and the baby,* Katie's *POV)*

*(Fast asleep and breathing easily, like a Raphael
60 painting of Madonna and Child.[8] The camera pans down to: the Walkman. We can hear the faint strains of Huey Lewis and the News. The camera pans a bit further to a Princess telephone[9] on the table by the chair. It's off the cradle. Not much; just enough to break the connection and scare people to death.)*

(INT. Katie*)*

(She sighs, bends down, and replaces the phone. Then she pushes the stop button on the Walkman.)

(INT. Dawn, Bill, *and* Katie*)*

70 *(*Dawn *wakes up when the music stops. Looks at* Bill *and* Katie, *puzzled.)*

Dawn *(fuzzed out).* Well . . . hi.

(She realizes she's got the Walkman phones on and removes them.)

Bill. Hi, Dawn.

Dawn *(still half asleep).* Shoulda called, guys. Place is a mess.

(She smiles. She's radiant when she smiles.)

Katie. We *tried.* The operator told Bill the phone
80 was off the hook. I thought something was wrong. How can you sleep with that music blasting?

Dawn. It's restful. *(Sees the gnawed book* Bill's *holding)* Oh Bill, I'm sorry! Justin's teething and—

Bill. There are critics who'd say he picked just the right thing to teethe on. I don't want to scare you, beautiful, but somebody's been at your front door lock with a screwdriver or something. Whoever it was forced it.

Dawn. Gosh, no! That was Jerry, last week. I
90 locked us out by mistake and he didn't have his key and the spare wasn't over the door like it's supposed to be. He was mad because he had to take a whiz real bad and so he took the screwdriver to it. It didn't work, either—that's one tough lock. *(pause)* By the time I found my key he'd already gone in the bushes.

---

8. **Raphael . . . Madonna and Child:** Raphael (1483–1520) was a well-known painter of mostly religious subjects in the period known as the Renaissance.

9. **Princess telephone:** an early type of compact telephone, popular in the 1960s.

DIFFERENTIATED INSTRUCTION

FOR ADVANCED LEARNERS/PRE–AP

First-Person Narrative Ask students to write a first-person narrative from Dawn's point of view describing Bill and Katie's entrance. Use details from the narrator's commentary as well as what you have learned about the characters to develop the scene. Then have students read their narratives aloud.

Bill. If it wasn't forced, how come I could just open the door and walk in?

Dawn (*guiltily*). Well . . . sometimes I forget to
100 lock it.

Katie. You didn't call me tonight, Dawn?

Dawn. Gee, no! I didn't call *anyone!* I was too busy chasing Justin around! He kept wanting to eat the fabric softener! Then he got sleepy and I sat down here and thought I'd listen to some tunes while I waited for your movie to come on, Bill, and I fell asleep—

(*At the mention of the movie* Bill *starts visibly and looks at the book. Then he glances at his watch.*)

110 **Bill.** I promised to tape it for Jeff. Come on, Katie, we've got time to get back.

Katie. Just a second.

(*She picks up the phone and dials.*)

Dawn. Gee, Bill, do you think Jeffie's old enough to watch something like that?

Bill. It's network. They take out the blood-bags.

Dawn (*confused but amiable*). Oh. That's good.

(*INT.* Katie, *CU*)

Dennis (*filter*). Hello?

120 **Katie.** Just thought you'd like to know your Aunt Dawn's fine.

Dennis (*filter*). Oh! Cool. Thanks, Mom.

(*INT.* the phone nook, with Dennis *and the others*)

(*He looks very relieved.*)

Dennis. Aunt Dawn's okay.

(*INT.* the car, with Bill *and* Katie)

(*They drive in silence for awhile.*)

Katie. You think I'm a hysterical idiot, don't you?

Bill (*genuinely surprised*). No! I was scared, too.

130 **Katie.** You sure you're not mad?

Bill. I'm too relieved. (*laughs*) She's sort of a scatterbrain, old Dawn, but I love her.

Katie (*leans over and kisses him*). I love *you.* You're a sweet man.

Bill. I'm the *boogeyman!*

Katie. I am not fooled, sweetheart.

(*EXT.* the car)

(*Passes the camera and we dissolve to:*)

(*INT.* Jeff, *in bed*)

140 (*His room is dark. The covers are pulled up to his chin.*)

Jeff. You *promise* to tape the rest?

(*Camera widens out so we can see* Bill, *sitting on the bed.*)

Bill. I promise.

Jeff. I especially liked the part where the dead guy ripped off the punk rocker's head.

Bill. Well . . . they *used* to take out all the blood-bags.

150 **Jeff.** What, Dad?

Bill. Nothing. I love you, Jeffie.

Jeff. I love you, too. So does Rambo.

(*Jeff* holds up a stuffed dragon of decidedly unmilitant aspect.[10] Bill *kisses the dragon, then* Jeff.)

Bill. 'Night.

Jeff. 'Night. (*as* Bill *reaches his door*) Glad Aunt Dawn was okay.

Bill. Me too.

(*He goes out.*)

160 (*INT. TV, CU*)

(*A guy who looks like he died in a car crash about two weeks prior to filming [and has since been subjected to a lot of hot weather] is staggering out of a crypt. The camera widens to show* Bill, *releasing the VCR pause button.*)

Katie (*voice*). Booga-booga.

(*Bill* looks around companionably. The camera widens out more to show* Katie, *wearing a nightgown.*)

170 **Bill.** Same to you. I missed the first forty seconds or so after the break. I had to kiss Rambo.

Katie. You sure you're not mad at me, Bill?

---

10. **unmilitant aspect:** unaggressive appearance.

SORRY, RIGHT NUMBER **159**

LITERARY ANALYSIS

● **PLOT IN DRAMA**

King has ruled out characters who could have been responsible for the mysterious call—Polly, Katie's mother, and Dawn. How does he use dialogue to maintain suspense? *Possible answer: The reader's attention has been drawn more and more to the character of Bill. The reader learned (p. 150, line 5) that Bill has had health problems (p. 157, line 132) and that he has secretly obtained a permit to carry a gun (p. 159, lines 140–145). Now, on page 159, Bill is going to be alone in his study.*

Extend the Discussion How do repeated references to the horror movie based on Bill's book add suspense?

FOR ADVANCED LEARNERS/PRE–AP

Analyze Plot Devices King structures the plot to sustain the mood and keep readers involved.

1. Have students discuss how King uses patterns of rising and falling action that result in alternating periods of tension and relaxation.

2. Have pairs of students make a Two-Column Chart listing excerpts that demonstrate tension or relaxation.

 **BEST PRACTICES TOOLKIT—Transparency** Two-Column Chart p. A25

(*He goes to her and kisses her.*)

Bill. Not even a smidge.

Katie. It's just that I could have sworn it was one of mine. You know what I mean? One of mine?

Bill. Yes.

Katie. I can still hear those sobs. So lost . . . so heartbroken.

180 **Bill.** Kate, have you ever thought you recognized someone on the street, and called her, and when she finally turned around it was a total stranger?

Katie. Yes, once. In Seattle. I was in a mall and I thought I saw my old roommate. I . . . oh. I see what you're saying.

Bill. Sure. There are sound-alikes as well as look-alikes.

Katie. But . . . *you know your own.* At least I thought so until tonight.

190 (*She puts her cheek on his shoulder, looking troubled.*)

Katie. I was so *positive* it was Polly . . .

Bill. Because you've been worried about her getting her feet under her at the new school . . . but judging from the stuff she told you tonight, I'd say she's doing just fine in that department. Wouldn't you?

Katie. Yes . . . I guess I would.

Bill. Let it go, hon.

200 **Katie** (*looks at him closely*). I hate to see you looking so tired. Hurry up and have an idea, you.

Bill. Well, I'm trying.

Katie. You coming to bed?

Bill. Soon as I finish taping this for Jeff.

Katie (*amused*). Bill, that machine was made by Japanese technicians who think of near everything. It'll run on its own.

Bill. Yeah, but it's been a long time since I've seen this one, and . . .

210 **Katie.** Okay. Enjoy. I think I'll be awake for a little while.

(*She starts out, then turns in the doorway as something else strikes her.*)

Katie. If they show the part where the punk's head gets—

Bill (*guiltily*). I'll edit it.

Katie. 'Night. And thanks again. For everything.

(*She leaves.* Bill *sits in his chair.*)

(*INT. TV, CU*)

220 (*A couple is necking in a car. Suddenly the passenger door is ripped open by the dead guy and we dissolve to:*)

(*INT.* Katie, *in bed*)

(*It's dark. She's asleep. She wakes up . . . sort of.*)

Katie (*sleepy*). Hey, big guy—

(*She feels for him, but his side of the bed is empty, the coverlet still pulled up. She sits up. Looks at:*)

(*INT. a clock on the night-table,* Katie's *POV*)

(*It says 2:03 A.M. Then it flashes to 2:04.*)

(*INT.* Katie)

230 (*Fully awake now. And concerned. She gets up, puts on her robe, and leaves the bedroom.*)

(*INT. the TV screen, CU*)

(*snow*)

Katie (*voice, approaching*). Bill? Honey? You okay? Bill? Bi—

(*INT.* Katie, *in Bill's study*)

(*She's frozen, wide-eyed with horror.*)

(*INT.* Bill, *in his chair*)

(*He's slumped to one side, eyes closed, hand inside his*
240 *shirt. Dawn was sleeping.* Bill *is not.*)

(*EXT. a coffin, being lowered into a grave*)

Minister (*voice*). And so we commit the earthly remains of William Weiderman to the ground, confident of his spirit and soul. "Be ye not cast down, brethren . . ."

(*EXT. graveside*)

DIFFERENTIATED INSTRUCTION

FOR ADVANCED LEARNERS/PRE—AP

Research Activity: The Undead Throughout the teleplay, King has included references to horror stories and movies, such as *Ghost Kiss*, written by the character Bill and *Dracula*. Have students research classic horror stories and legends about the undead and present their findings to the class.

(*All the Weidermans are ranged here.* Katie *and* Polly *wear identical black dresses and veils.* Connie *wears a black skirt and white blouse.* Dennis *and* 250 Jeff *wear black suits.* Jeff *is crying. He has Rambo the Dragon under his arm for a little extra comfort.*)

(*Camera moves in on* Katie. *Tears course slowly down her cheeks. She bends and gets a handful of earth. Tosses it into the grave.*)

Katie. Love you, big guy.

(*EXT.* Jeff)

Targeted Passage ③

(*weeping*)

(*EXT. looking down into the grave*)

(*scattered earth on top of the coffin*)

260 (*Dissolve to:*)

(*EXT. the grave*)

(*A* Groundskeeper *pats the last sod into place.*)

Groundskeeper. My wife says she wishes you'd written a couple more before you had your heart attack, mister. (*pause*) I like Westerns, m'self.

(*The* Groundskeeper *walks away, whistling.*)

(*Dissolve to:*)

(*EXT. A church. Day.*)

(*Title card: Five Years Later*)

270 (*The Wedding March is playing.* Polly, *older and radiant with joy, emerges into a pelting shower of rice. She's in a wedding gown, her new husband by her side.*)

(*Celebrants throwing rice line either side of the path. From behind the bride and groom come others. Among them are* Katie, Dennis, Connie, *and* Jeff . . . *all five years older. With* Katie *is another man. This is* Hank. *In the interim,* Katie *has also taken a husband.*)

■ **READING A TELEPLAY**

Like other narratives, teleplays need to condense the passage of time but not leave out important events. What devices does King use on page 161 to disclose important events that happen to the Weidermans over a period of time? *Possible answer: King links a series of exterior shots with a brief monologue and narrator's commentary to move from Bill's death to Polly's wedding. The first three shots disclose Bill's death by building from the shot of Katie using the nickname "big guy," an affectionate term she had for her husband, to a shot of Jeff crying, to a shot of a coffin in a grave. The fourth exterior shot, accompanied by a short monologue by a groundskeeper, discloses that Bill died from a heart attack. The fifth exterior shot of the church shows Polly emerging in a wedding gown and the title card tells us that it is five years later.*

FOR LESS–PROFICIENT READERS

③ **Targeted Passage [Lines 263–279]**

This brief section explains the passage of time and describes very important events that have occurred in the interim.

• To whom is the groundskeeper speaking?

• How much time passes between the funeral and Polly's wedding? How do you think this passage of time has changed the Weiderman family?

DISCUSSION PROMPTS

Use these prompts to help students understand the relationship between Polly and Hank:

Connect Do you feel that the Weidermans are depicted as behaving in a realistic manner following Bill's death? *Accept thoughtful answers.*

Analyze What might have caused problems between Polly and Hank in the past?
Possible answer: Judging from Hank's comment to Polly, it is likely that Polly missed her natural father and resented Hank because he took the father's place in the household.

Evaluate How does the reference to the tension between Hank and Polly contribute to the plot? *Possible answer: The tension indicates that Bill is very much missed and his death is still unresolved for the family.*

280 (Polly *turns and her mother is there.*)

Polly. Thank you, Mom.

Katie (*crying*). Oh doll, you're so welcome.

(*They embrace. After a moment* Polly *draws away and looks at* Hank. *There is a brief moment of tension, and then* Polly *embraces* Hank, *too.*)

Polly. Thank you too, Hank. I'm sorry I was such a creep for so long . . .

Hank (*easily*). You were never a creep, Pol. A girl only has one father.

290 **Connie.** Throw it! Throw it!

(*After a moment,* Polly *throws her bouquet.*)

(*EXT. the bouquet, CU, slow motion*)

(*turning and turning through the air*)

(*dissolves to:*)

(*INT. The study, with* Katie. *Night.*)

(*The word-processor has been replaced by a wide lamp looming over a stack of blueprints. The book jackets have been replaced by photos of buildings.*)

DIFFERENTIATED INSTRUCTION

FOR ADVANCED LEARNERS/PRE–AP

Create a Monologue Write a monologue in Polly's voice that might be used as a voice-over for the shot of her tossing the bouquet. The monologue should include questions she might have about past events as well as concerns she might have about the future. Have students perform their monologues for the class.

Ones that have first been built in Hank's mind, presumably.)

(Katie *is looking at the desk, thoughtful and a little sad.*)

Hank (*voice*). Coming to bed, Kate?

(*She turns and the camera widens out to give us Hank. He's wearing a robe over pajamas. She comes to him and gives him a little hug, smiling. Maybe we notice a few streaks of gray in her hair; her pretty pony has done its fair share of running since Bill died.*)

310 **Katie.** In a little while. A woman doesn't see her first one get married every day, you know.

Hank. I know.

(*The camera follows as they walk from the work area of the study to the more informal area. This is much the same as it was in the old days, with a coffee table, stereo, TV, couch, and Bill's old easy-chair. She looks at this.*)

Hank. You still miss him, don't you?

Katie. Some days more than others. You didn't
320 know, and Polly didn't remember.

Hank (*gently*). Remember what, doll?

Katie. Polly got married on the five-year anniversary of Bill's death.

Hank (*hugs her*). Come on to bed, why don't you?

Katie. In a little while.

Hank. Okay. Maybe I'll still be awake.

(*He kisses her, then leaves, closing the door behind him. Katie sits in Bill's old chair. Close by, on the coffee table, is a remote control for the TV and an
330 extension phone. Katie looks at the blank TV, and the camera moves in on her face. One tear rims one eye, sparkling like a sapphire.*)

Katie. I *do* still miss you, big guy. Lots and lots. Every day. And you know what? It hurts.

(*The tear falls. She picks up the TV remote and pushes the on button.*)

(*INT. TV, Katie's POV*)

(*An ad for Ginsu Knives comes to an end and is replaced by a star logo.*)

④
Targeted Passage

340 **Announcer** (*voice*). Now back to Channel 63's Thursday night Star Time Movie . . . *Ghost Kiss.*

(*The logo dissolves into a guy who looks like he died in a car crash about two weeks ago and has since been subjected to a lot of hot weather. He comes staggering out of the same old crypt.*)

(*INT. Katie*)

(*Terribly startled—almost horrified. She hits the off button on the remote control. The TV blinks off.*)

(*Katie's face begins to work. She struggles against the
350 impending emotional storm, but the coincidence of the movie is just one thing too many on what must have already been one of the most emotionally trying days of her life. The dam breaks and she begins to sob . . . terrible, heartbroken sobs. She reaches out for the little table by the chair, meaning to put the remote control on it, and knocks the phone onto the floor.*)

(*Sound: the hum of an open line*)

(*Her tear-stained face grows suddenly still as she looks at the telephone. Something begins to fill it
360 . . . an idea? an intuition? Hard to tell. And maybe it doesn't matter.*)

(*INT. the telephone, Katie's POV*)

(*The camera moves in to ECU . . . moves in until the dots in the off-the-hook receiver look like chasms.*)

(*sound of open-line buzz up to loud*)

(*We go into the black . . . and hear:*)

Bill (*voice*). Who are you calling? Who do you *want* to call? Who *would* you call, if it wasn't too late?

370 (*INT. Katie*)

(*There is now a strange hypnotized look on her face. She reaches down, scoops the telephone up, and punches in numbers, seemingly at random.*)

(*Sound: ringing phone*)

(*Katie continues to look hypnotized. The look holds until the phone is answered . . . and she hears herself on the other end of the line.*)

Katie (*voice; filter*). Hello, Weiderman residence.

(*Katie—our present-day Katie with the streaks of gray
380 in her hair—goes on sobbing, yet an expression of*

REINFORCE *KEY IDEA:* THE SUPERNATURAL

What does Katie realize that is pivotal to the plot? *Possible answer: The mysterious phone call turns out to be Katie from the future trying to warn herself in the past about Bill's imminent heart attack.*

SELECTION WRAP–UP

REFLECT Remind students that some stories are meant to communicate an author's point of view or convey a particular message while others are written purely for the purpose of entertaining readers. Why do you think King wrote "Sorry, Right Number"?

⭐ **CRITIQUE** Ask students to evaluate King's story for believability. Have them identify specific places where the author either gains or loses credibility. Encourage students to share and compare their reactions regarding the "surprise" ending.

READING FLUENCY

Distribute the copy master and have students work in pairs or groups to practice fluency.

🅡 RESOURCE MANAGER—Copy Master
   Reading Fluency p. 238

---

desperate hope is trying to be born on her face. On some level she understands that the depth of her grief has allowed a kind of telephonic time-travel. She's trying to talk, to force the words out.)

Katie *(sobbing).* Take . . . please take . . . t-t-

(INT. Katie, in the phone nook, reprise)

(It's five years ago, Bill *is standing beside her, looking concerned.* Jeff *is wandering off to look for a blank tape in the other room.)*

390 **Katie.** Polly? What's wrong?

(INT. Katie, in the study)

Katie *(sobbing). Please—quick—*

(Sound: click of a broken connection)

Katie *(screaming). Take him to the hospital! If you want him to live, take him to the hospital! He's going to have a heart attack! He—*

(Sound: hum of an open line)

(Slowly, very slowly, Katie *hangs up the telephone. Then, after a moment, she picks it up again. She*
400 *speaks aloud with no self-consciousness whatever. Probably doesn't even know she's doing it.)*

Katie. I dialed the old number. I dialed—

(Slam cut to:)

(INT. Bill, *in the phone nook with* Katie *beside him)*

(He's just taken the phone from Katie *and is speaking to the operator.)*

Operator *(filter, giggles). I promise* not to give it out.

410 **Bill.** It's 555-

(Slam cut to:)

(INT. Katie, *in Bill's old chair, CU)*

Katie *(finishes).* -4408.

(INT. the phone, CU)

(Katie's trembling finger carefully picks out the number, and we hear the corresponding tones: 555-4408.)

(INT. Katie, *in Bill's old chair, CU)*

(She closes her eyes as the phone begins to ring. Her
420 *face is filled with an agonizing mixture of hope and fear. If only she can have one more chance to pass the vital message on, it says . . . just one more chance.)*

Katie *(low).* Please . . . please . . .

Recorded voice *(filter).* You have reached a non-working number. Please hang up and dial again. If you need assistance—

(Katie hangs up again. Tears stream down her cheeks. The camera pans away and down to the telephone.)

430 *(INT. the phone nook, with* Katie *and* Bill, *reprise)*

Bill. So it was a prank. Or someone who was crying so hard she dialed a wrong number . . . "through a shimmering film of tears," as we veteran hacks like to say.

Katie. It was not a prank and it was not a wrong number! It was someone in *my family!*

(INT. Katie *[present day] in Bill's study)*

Katie. Yes. Someone in *my family.* Someone very close. *(pause)* Me.

440 *(She suddenly throws the phone across the room. Then she begins to sob again and puts her hands over her face. The camera holds on her for a moment, then dollies across to:)*

(INT. the phone)

(It lies on the carpet, looking both bland and somehow ominous. Camera moves in to ECU—the holes in the receiver once more look like huge dark chasms. We hold, then:)

(Fade to black.)

⑤
Targeted Passage

DIFFERENTIATED INSTRUCTION

FOR LESS–PROFICIENT READERS

⑤ **Targeted Passage [Lines 385–439]**

This passage marks a crucial turning point in the plot and concludes the story: Katie realizes it was her own voice in the initial call.

• Who was the mysterious caller?

• What was the purpose of the call?

• When Katie tries to call the second time, why is her face "filled with . . . hope and fear"?

MEMOIR Stephen King wrote a memoir of his life as a writer. Here are a few words of advice from the book.

from

On Writing

Stephen King

If you want to be a writer, you must do two things above all others: read a lot and write a lot. There's no way around these two things that I'm aware of, no shortcut.

I'm a slow reader, but I usually get through seventy or eighty books a year, mostly fiction. I don't read in order to study the craft; I read because I like to read. It's what I do at night, kicked back in my blue chair. Similarly, I don't read fiction to study the art of fiction, but simply because I like stories. Yet there is a learning process going on. Every book you pick up has its own lesson or lessons, and quite often the bad books have more to teach than the good ones.

Good writing, on the other hand, teaches the learning writer about style, graceful narration, plot development, the creation of believable characters, and truth-telling. A novel like *The Grapes of Wrath* may fill a new writer with feelings of despair and good old-fashioned jealousy— "I'll never be able to write anything that good, not if I live to be a thousand"—but such feelings can also serve as a spur, goading the writer to work harder and aim higher. Being swept away by a combination of great story and great writing—of being flattened, in fact—is part of every writer's necessary formation. You cannot hope to sweep someone else away by the force of your writing until it has been done to you.

DISCUSSION PROMPTS

Use these prompts to help students understand how the author's views on writing had an impact on "Sorry, Right Number":

Connect How has reading some of King's thoughts on writing helped you appreciate the author's creation of "Sorry, Right Number"? *Possible answer: King is clearly enthusiastic about reading and writing fiction, and he views each book that he reads as part of a never-ending learning process. His enjoyment of writing and his broad background in fiction are reflected in his teleplay.*

Analyze King refers to the importance of "plot development" and "believable characters." How are these two aspects of good writing linked in "Sorry, Right Number"? *Possible answer: For the teleplay to succeed, the story must unfold in a logical and suspenseful manner. At the same time, the characters who move the plot must be credible in action and speech in order for readers to get caught up in the events.*

Evaluate Do you think that King was equally successful in plot development and character creation in the teleplay? Give reasons for your answer. *Answers will vary, but students should provide thoughtful reasons as support.*

Practice and Apply

After Reading

For additional support of post-reading questions, use these copy masters:

R RESOURCE MANAGER—Copy Masters

Reading Check p. 235 (to check understanding of the selection)

Plot in Drama p. 231 (for practice of literary analysis standards focus)

Question Support p. 236 (After Reading questions adapted for English learners and less-proficient readers)

For additional questions, see page 225.

ANSWERS

Comprehension

1. *She thinks the caller is her daughter Polly.*

2. *He has a fatal heart attack.*

3. *Polly gets married; an emotionally overwrought Katie subsequently experiences "a kind of telephonic time travel" during which she telephones herself in the past in a futile effort to warn of Bill's coming heart attack.*

4. *The sobbing caller is Katie herself.*

Literary Analysis

Possible answers:

5. ■ **STANDARDS FOCUS** *Reading a Teleplay Page 163: "The camera moves in to ECU . . . until the dots in the off-the-hook receiver look like chasms." Page 164: The phone looks "somehow ominous. Camera moves in to ECU—the holes in the receiver once more look like huge dark chasms."*

6. ● **STANDARDS FOCUS** *Analyze Plot in Drama Exposition: Family members interact; **Rising Action:** Katie gets upsetting phone call; Katie and Bill try to identify caller without success; Bill has fatal heart attack; Katie has emotional breakdown after Polly's wedding; **Climax:** Katie makes emotional phone call; **Falling Action:** Katie tries in vain to call again; **Resolution:** Katie realizes that she herself had been the sobbing caller.*

7. *Foreshadowing: Page 150: Katie says that Bill "doesn't feel very well." Outcome: On pages 153 and 160, Bill is described as looking "tired"; he subsequently has a heart attack. Foreshadowing: Page 156: King compares the phone to "a snake ready to strike." Outcome: The phone does in a sense "strike" during the climax.*

Comprehension

1. **Recall** At first, whom does Katie believe the sobbing caller to be?

2. **Recall** Why doesn't Bill return to bed after watching the movie?

3. **Summarize** What happens on the fifth anniversary of Bill's death?

4. **Clarify** Who is the sobbing caller?

Literary Analysis

5. **Reading a Teleplay** Look back through the play. What clues do the camera directions give you for interpreting the play's **supernatural** occurrences?

6. **Analyze Plot in Drama** Create a plot diagram like the one shown. Then place the events of *Sorry, Right Number* in their correct positions on the diagram. More than one event may be placed in each position.

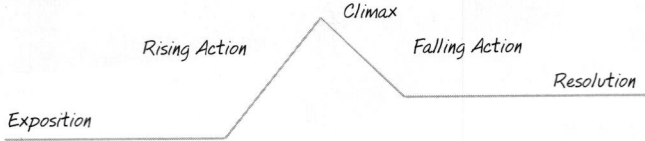

7. **Analyze Foreshadowing** In drama as in other fiction, foreshadowing can deepen a mood of suspense by hinting at future events. Go back through the teleplay and find examples of foreshadowing. For each example, provide a description of what eventually happens.

8. **Interpret** How would you explain the vague understanding—the "desperate hope . . . trying to be born"—that comes to Katie after she hears her own voice on the phone? Support your answer.

9. **Make Judgments** Could Katie be in any way responsible for her husband's death?

10. **Evaluate** Revisit the "chill factor" chart you created before reading the play. Where would you place *Sorry, Right Number* on a scale of 1 to 10? Support your answer.

Literary Criticism

11. **Author's Style** In the excerpt from *On Writing* (page 165), Stephen King lists what he considers the qualities of good writing: "style, graceful narration, plot development, the creation of believable characters, and truth-telling." Which of these qualities does this teleplay best exemplify? Cite details, including lines of dialogue and examples of camera directions, to support your opinion.

---

8. *The realization that she is connecting with the past is dawning on her, along with the idea of warning about the heart attack.*

9. *Responsible: Her near-hysteria about the phone call certainly raised Bill's stress level. Not Responsible: Bill "doesn't feel very well" (p. 150) from the start; also, Bill was fated to have the heart attack—otherwise there would have been no call from the future!*

10. *Students should support their opinions with clear reasons.*

Literary Criticism

Possible answer:

11. *The teleplay probably best exemplifies "plot development" and "creation of believable characters." Students may or may not agree, but in any case they should support their opinions with specific and relevant details.*

Reading-Writing Connection

Increase your understanding of *Sorry, Right Number* by responding to these prompts. Then use **Revision: Grammar and Style** to improve your writng.

WRITING PROMPTS

SELF-CHECK

A. Short Response: Create Dialogue
Imagine that Katie tries to explain to her family what occurred with the phone call. What does she say? How does her family react? Write **one-half page** of the dialogue that you imagine would occur.

▶ *A strong dialogue will . . .*
- consist of informal, conversational language
- reflect how the characters probably would respond

B. Extended Response: Write a Review
Imagine that you are reviewing *Sorry, Right Number* for your school newspaper. Write a **three-to-five-paragraph review** in which you summarize the plot and explain your reaction to the teleplay. Do not give away the surprise ending in your review.

▶ *A successful review will . . .*
- summarize the plot with correct use of grammar
- contain details that support a reaction to the teleplay

REVISION: GRAMMAR AND STYLE

CREATE REALISTIC CHARACTERS At various points, King uses **slang** to suggest the youth of a character. In writing dialogue, it is important to choose language that accurately reflects the characteristics of the people who are speaking; otherwise, your audience will find it difficult to believe what they are reading. Here is an example of King's use of slang in *Sorry, Right Number:*

> **Katie.** *Just thought you'd like to know your Aunt Dawn's fine.*
>
> **Dennis** (filter). *Oh! Cool. Thanks, Mom.* (Act II, lines 120–122)

Notice how the revisions in red make the following dialogue more accurately reflect the ages of the speakers. Revise your response to Prompt A by making the same kinds of revisions.

STUDENT MODEL

Katie. Now, I know you're going to think this couldn't have happened.

But five years ago, on the day Bill died, I got a call from myself.

Polly. ~~That sounds really odd.~~ *Whatever, Mom.*

Dennis. Mom, ~~that's a strange thing to say.~~ *you're freaking out!*

Hank. You're wrong, Katie. Let's talk about this.

WRITING TOOLS
For prewriting, revision, and editing tools, visit the **Writing Center** at ClassZone.com.

DIFFERENTIATED INSTRUCTION

FOR LESS–PROFICIENT WRITERS

For Prompt A:

1. First speaker, Katie, summarizes what has happened.
2. Body of dialogue expresses disbelief.
3. Next speaker also expresses disbelief of Katie's claims.

For Prompt B:

1. Help students recall the major plot events:

- the telephone call that Katie receives and her reaction to it

- the understanding that the call didn't come from Polly or Dawn
- Bill's death while watching *Ghost Kiss*
- Polly's wedding on the fifth anniversary of Bill's death
- the phone call that brings Katie to the realization of who the caller was five years ago

2. Help students articulate whether or not they liked the teleplay, and why.

Reading-Writing Connection

WRITING PROMPTS

- For Prompt A, encourage students to imagine themselves as each individual character in order to create realistic dialogue. Point out that the children are five years older than they were at the beginning of the teleplay, so their dialogue should sound more mature. Have students use their dialogue to write a scene for the teleplay. Remind them to include stage directions. Invite students to perform their scenes for the class.

- For Prompt B, have students read examples of reviews before beginning work on their own.

For writing support, see

ℹ️ Writing Center at **ClassZone.com**

REVISION: GRAMMAR AND STYLE

- After students examine the student model, remind them that the children are now five years older, and their language, thinking, and manner of interacting should all reflect the passage of time. Jeff is now 13, Connie, 15, Dennis, 18, and Polly, 21.

- Point out that adults, such as Katie and Hank, might also use slang, but it's likely to differ from the slang used by younger people.

R RESOURCE MANAGER—Copy Master
Create Realistic Characters p. 237

Assess and Reteach

Assess

R RESOURCE MANAGER—Copy Masters
Selection Test A pp. 239–240
Selection Test B/C pp. 241–242

💿 Test Generator CD

Reteach

S STANDARDS LESSON FILE
Literature Lesson 25: Elements of Drama
Writing Lesson 44: Writing Dialogue

Focus and Motivate

OBJECTIVES

- analyze a student model that reflects the key traits of personal narratives
- use the writing process to produce a personal narrative
- revise and edit, using a rubric for personal narratives
- create and present an informal speech, considering audience and purpose

WRITER'S ROAD MAP

WRITING PROMPTS 1 AND 2

To help students choose a prompt that will result in a good story, point out that the incident they write about should have personal significance and be dramatic. For example, they might write about a conflict they had with someone, a time when someone helped them, or a setback they had to overcome.

ADDITIONAL PROMPTS

Use these prompts for practice with business writing and writing in the humanities:

WRITING PROMPT 3

Writing for a Job Write a letter to a prospective employer describing how a personal experience makes you well suited for the job.

WRITING PROMPT 4

Writing Inspired by Fine Art In an online museum or a book, find a work of art that reminds you of a significant experience you had. As you write about your experience, include descriptive details to create a vivid picture of the setting, characters, and action.

Art That Might Inspire

- scenes of people on mountaintops, alone in diners, or with others in a café
- moments that capture feelings of jealousy, doubt, or victory
- dramatic scenes showing people in conflict with others or with nature

For additional writing prompts, see

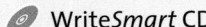 WriteSmart CD

Writing Center at **ClassZone.com**

KEY TRAITS

Review the six **KEY TRAITS** with students, focusing on ideas and organization. Compare the list of traits with the rubric on page 174.

Personal Narrative

Your life is a series of stories, all of them uniquely yours. Each reveals something about you and the people and events that shape your life. When you write about yourself, you can begin to gain a deeper understanding of why certain experiences were important to you. In this workshop, you will write a personal narrative, a story that describes a memorable event from your past. Begin by studying the **Writer's Road Map.**

WRITER'S ROAD MAP

Personal Narrative

WRITING PROMPT 1

Writing from Your Life Write a personal narrative describing a meaningful experience in your life. Your narrative should explain the significance of the experience and include details that help the reader visualize the characters and unfolding events.

Experiences to Explore
- a memorable incident from your childhood
- a challenging experience that taught you a lesson
- an accomplishment you are proud of

WRITING PROMPT 2

Writing from Literature Incidents and conflicts that characters face can remind us of similar experiences in our own lives. Choose a character whose story you can relate to. Write a personal narrative describing the real-life incident or conflict you are reminded of.

Characters to Relate To
- the narrator in "Daughter of Invention"
- Richard Wright in "The Rights to the Streets of Memphis"

 WRITING TOOLS
For prewriting, revision, and editing tools, visit the **Writing Center** at **ClassZone.com.**

KEY TRAITS

1. IDEAS
- Focuses on an interesting, well-defined **experience**
- Re-creates the experience, using vivid and relevant **details**
- Uses **dialogue** and gestures to develop characters

2. ORGANIZATION
- Hooks the reader with an intriguing **introduction**
- Clearly shows the **order** in which events occurred
- Concludes by summarizing the **significance** of the experience

3. VOICE
- Uses a **tone** appropriate for the audience and purpose
- Reflects the writer's **personality and style**

4. WORD CHOICE
- Uses **precise words** to help the reader visualize the characters and action

5. SENTENCE FLUENCY
- Varies **sentence structures** to create a pleasing rhythm and flow

6. CONVENTIONS
- Employs **correct grammar and usage**

Writing Workshop Resources

 RESOURCE MANAGER UNIT 1

Plan and Teach pp. 243–246
Prewriting–Editing pp. 247–251
Writing Rubric p. 252
Speaking and Listening p. 253
Writing Support p. 254*

 STANDARDS LESSON FILE

Writing Lesson 31: Personal Narrative
Writing Lesson 44: Writing Dialogue

 BEST PRACTICES TOOLKIT

Scaffolding Writing Instruction pp. 43–46*
Open Mind • Reporter's Questions
• Storyboard • Story Frames • Writing
Template: Personal Narrative

TECHNOLOGY

 Easy Planner DVD
Writing Center at **ClassZone.com**
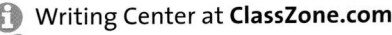 WriteSmart CD

* Resources for Differentiation

Part 1: Analyze a Student Model

Rich Rosario
Franklin High School

Facing My Fear: Riding the River

"A rafting trip through the Grand Canyon? For a week? Really?" I said, a grin pasted on my face. "That's a great idea, Dad." I felt a knot forming in my stomach.

My two brothers high-fived each other. "This is gonna be awesome!"
5 they hollered. My mother grinned her approval.

I'm not the best athlete at Franklin High, but I work hard, and I enjoy competition. However, I used to avoid rafting, sailing, kayaking, and similar sports. Here's why: When I was ten, I climbed a railing, slipped, and fell into the Dungeness River. My uncle jumped in
10 immediately and fished me out. I came up coughing and spluttering, with a brand-new fear of drowning. Rushing, churning water filled my nightmares.

The night my father told us about the vacation, I looked through the expedition catalog from Western Adventures, and my worst fears
15 were confirmed. On the cover was a photograph of a huge orange raft vanishing into a giant rapid. The vacationers clung to the sides, tiny and powerless. Now, I'm an OK swimmer. But as I looked at the catalog, I wondered why anyone, even a champion swimmer, would want to go whitewater rafting. Does anyone really think that the guides can control
20 everything that happens during the journey? I asked myself.

I didn't say anything, of course, and in August we headed off for our adventure in Arizona. We joined our raftmates, four other families, at the point where the Colorado slices its way through the canyon.

"If you fall in, relax and go with the flow," one of the lean,
25 sunburned tour guides said. "We'll pull you out!" he added.

KEY TRAITS IN ACTION

Opens with an intriguing **introduction** that focuses on a clearly defined **experience.** This essay has a conversational **tone.**

Uses **dialogue** and gestures to develop characters.

Voice reflects the writer's **personality and style.** Varied **sentence structures** create a pleasing rhythm.

Uses relevant **details** to explain the experience. The writer describes his thoughts and feelings. The question is an example of interior monologue (words the writer says to himself or herself).

Part 1: Analyze a Student Model

Have students read the student model and **KEY TRAITS IN ACTION.** Then discuss the model with the class, noting specific examples of each trait and building on what students have already noted. You may also wish to incorporate these activities:

- **Dialogue and Gestures** Point out the description of gestures and physical actions, and the use of dialogue in the first two paragraphs. Discuss how these elements convey the reactions of the narrator and other family members to the idea of the trip. Have students identify text evidence of each character's feelings about the rafting trip.

- **Voice** Tell students that *voice* is the unique way a writer or narrator expresses himself or herself. Voice gives readers insight into the writer's or narrator's feelings, personality, and attitude. Various elements, such as sentence structure, **dialogue,** and word choice, contribute to a writer's voice.

Discuss the elements that add to the narrator's voice in the student model. *Possible answers: Paragraph 1: The writer's word choices create vivid images and contribute to the narrator's voice. (grin pasted on face; knot forming in stomach); Paragraph 4: The writer uses a variety of sentence structures that contribute to a conversational tone. The narrator states his concerns in a believable way that shows readers a vulnerable side to his personality.*

DIFFERENTIATED INSTRUCTION

For general guidelines on differentiating writing instruction, see

 BEST PRACTICES TOOLKIT
Scaffolding Writing Instruction
pp. 43–46

FOR ENGLISH LEARNERS

Language: Skill Words Write these terms on the board and review them with students:

- *tone:* expression of writer's attitude toward the subject, the reader, or both—for example, conversational, humorous, sarcastic, formal

- *dialogue:* conversation between characters—for example, line 1 of the student model

- *gestures:* movements of the head, limbs, or body and facial expressions that convey

attitudes, feelings, or information—for example, the high-five in line 4

- *sensory details:* details that describe what something feels, tastes, looks, sounds, or smells like—for example, the whooshing sound made by the river rapids

- *sequence of events:* order in which things happen—for example, first, next, and last

- **Precise Words** Write this imprecise sentence on the board:

  > Then the front of the raft was out of the water again.

  Ask students to compare the imprecise sentence with the sentence in lines 40–41 of the student model. **Possible answer:** *The sentence on the board doesn't help readers visualize the scene, because there are no precise nouns, verbs, or modifiers. The sentence in lines 40–41 uses more precise and vivid language. For example, the verb "shot" creates a more vivid image than the verb "was"; the phrase "seconds later" is more precise than the word "then"; and the modifier "like a cannonball" adds precision and visual interest to the narrative.*

- **Order** Explain the importance of writing a personal narrative in which the order of events is clear and well organized. As an example of how words and phrases can signal order, point out the phrase "Within a few minutes" in line 28 of the student model.

  Ask students to identify other words and phrases on page 170 of the student model that signal the order in which events occurred. **Possible answers:** *"Seconds later" (line 40), "And then suddenly" (line 41), "in the next five days" (lines 44–45), "During that vacation" (line 46), "By the end of the week" (lines 49–50).*

For interactive student models, see

🖸 Write*Smart* CD

ⓘ Writing Center at **ClassZone.com**

As our raft drifted down the river, the knot in my stomach grew larger and tighter. I could feel every bump and sway, and I could hear the whoosh of the river all around me. Within a few minutes, the whooshing sound began to seem more like a thunderstorm. Our guides ordered us to
30 grab the ropes and brace ourselves. The sound ahead resembled the roar of a jet engine. My heart thudded in my chest.

Up ahead, the waters of the Colorado appeared to be boiling, bubbling up into the air and crashing back down. In the center was a trough that looked to be 30 or 40 yards long—and we were headed
35 right for it. I held on to the ropes until my fingers felt raw. The raft held 20 people, but the raging river tossed it around like a rubber toy in a bathtub. We flew up out of the water and crashed back down. The front of the raft was submerged in icy water. There was no doubt in my mind: I was going to drown.

40 Seconds later, the front of the raft shot out of the water like a cannonball. And then, suddenly, it was all over. We had made it.

The rafters erupted in wild shouts, all of us laughing about how we were soaking wet and what a thrill the ride had been. The knot in my stomach eased a bit. We encountered many more rapids in the next five
45 days, but my fear was never again as knife-sharp.

During that vacation, I faced my worst fear not just once, but dozens of times. I learned that worrying about an experience can be worse than the experience itself. I realized that I am tougher than I thought. I found out that it's all right to express fear—even to scream if I need to. By the
50 end of the week, I had a real smile on my face, not a pasted-on grin. And the knot in my stomach was long gone.

Re-creates the experience for the reader with vivid sensory **details.** Describing the knot in his stomach is more effective than writing "I was scared."

Uses **precise nouns** (*trough*), **verbs** (*flew, crashed*), and **modifiers** (*raw, raging*) that enable the reader to picture what is being described.

Includes words and phrases throughout the essay that signal the **order** in which events occurred.

Strong concluding paragraph summarizes the **significance** of the experience. By using some of the same details as in the introduction, the writer gives his essay unity and coherence.

2

DIFFERENTIATED INSTRUCTION

FOR ENGLISH LEARNERS

Comprehension: Transitions List sequence words and phrases that are often used in narratives, such as *first, next, then, later, finally, at last, before, during, meanwhile, today, yesterday, last year,* and *eventually.*

1. Write, say, and act out a simple sequence of events, such as

   clear the table

   put the dishes in sink

   wash the dishes

   dry the dishes

   put the dishes away

2. Work with students to add transitional words and phrases from the list provided. Have students read and then act out the edited sequence in order.

To provide English learners with additional writing support, see

🅡 RESOURCE MANAGER—Copy Master
Writing Support p. 254

Part 2: Apply the Writing Process

PREWRITING

What Should I Do?	What Does It Look Like?

1. Analyze the prompt.
Study the prompt you chose on page 168. Circle the phrase that tells you what to write. Underline important details about the assignment.

▶ **WRITING PROMPT** Write a (personal narrative) describing a meaningful experience in your life. Your narrative should explain the significance of the experience and include details that help readers visualize the characters and unfolding events.

This should be about an event that's important to me. I have to include lots of vivid details and explain why I think the event is important.

2. Choose a story to tell.
Think back over your life, recalling memorable, challenging **experiences.** Create a timeline of peaks and valleys in your life. Include the great experiences and the ones that involved real challenges. Circle the experience that you want to write about.

▶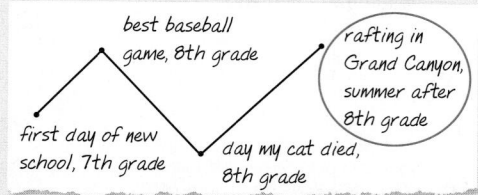

best baseball game, 8th grade

rafting in Grand Canyon, summer after 8th grade

first day of new school, 7th grade

day my cat died, 8th grade

3. Consider your audience and purpose.
Bring your narrative into focus. Make a chart that shows who your audience is and what particular information they might need to understand your story. Add a **statement of purpose** to your chart. This statement will help you explain why the experience is important.

▶

Audience	Information	Purpose
• Teacher • Classmates • Readers of an "outdoor" magazine?	• Why I was scared—the experience when I was ten • Details about rafting	I'll show that fears seem real but they can be faced and sometimes conquered.

4. List the details of your experience.
Think about the story you want to tell. Your narrative is like a short story, so think about ways to engage your reader, such as using **sensory details.**

▶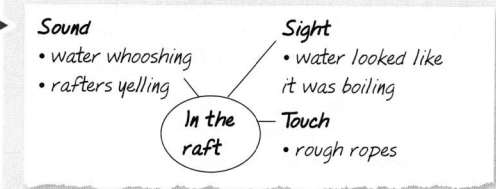

Sound
• water whooshing
• rafters yelling

Sight
• water looked like it was boiling

In the raft

Touch
• rough ropes

FOR LESS–PROFICIENT WRITERS
List Details Help students use Reporter's Questions to gather information about their stories. Encourage them to include sensory details within each category.

 BEST PRACTICES TOOLKIT—Transparency
Reporter's Questions p. C9

FOR ENGLISH LEARNERS
Consider Audience and Purpose As an alternative to the chart, have students complete these statements:

• **Audience:** I am writing this for _____.
• **Information:** The experience I am writing about is _____. I will include details about _____.
• **Purpose:** This was important because _____. I will show that _____.

Practice and Apply

To support students during the writing process, use these copy masters:

R RESOURCE MANAGER—Copy Masters
Prewriting–Editing pp. 247–251
Writing Rubric p. 252
Writing Support p. 254 (for English learners)

Part 2: Apply the Writing Process

PREWRITING

1. Analyze the prompt. After students mark the important elements in their prompt, have them restate it in their own words. Then have students restate the kinds of vivid details they can include—for example, sensory details and precise nouns.

2. Choose a story to tell. As an alternative to the timeline, students may list categories that might act as memory triggers, such as summer camp, middle school, or a specific sport. Then students can list specific memorable events under each category. The first part of this activity lends itself to paired or grouped brainstorming about shared **experiences.**

3. Consider your audience and purpose. Note the two main purposes of a personal narrative: to tell your story in a clear and engaging way and to convey why the event is significant to you. Have students complete this sentence to fill in the *Purpose* column of the chart: *This memory is significant to me because* _____.

4. List the details of your experience. Before students identify specific **sensory details,** they might use the Open Mind organizer to record their thoughts and feelings during the event they will retell.

 BEST PRACTICES TOOLKIT—Transparency
Open Mind p. D9

For interactive graphic organizers, see

🖉 Write*Smart* CD

ℹ Writing Center at **ClassZone.com**

DRAFTING

1. **Prepare a story map.** Stress the importance of this stage of the process. Students should have a clear idea of what will happen in their narratives before they begin their drafts. Remind students that the ending they write in their map can be the final event of the narrative or a statement about the significance of the experience, as in the student model. Encourage students to experiment with different types of story maps to help them plan their narratives.

    BEST PRACTICES TOOLKIT—Transparencies
   Story Frames p. C10
   Storyboard p. C11

2. **Write an interesting beginning.** Suggest other ways to grab the reader's attention, such as beginning with a statement of surprise, a well-known saying, or a vivid detail about the event. Encourage students to experiment with a few different beginnings and choose the one they think will have the greatest effect on the reader.

3. **Include vivid details.** Help students analyze the improvement from prewriting notes to draft. Ask them to identify vivid modifiers, such as *boiling, bubbling,* and *crashing.* Point out that the prepositional phrases "up into the air" and "in the center" add spatial information.

For a personal narrative writing template, see

   BEST PRACTICES TOOLKIT—Transparency
   Writing Template: Personal Narrative
   pp. C16, C18

   *Write*Smart CD

   Writing Center at **ClassZone.com**

DRAFTING

What Should I Do?

1. **Prepare a story map.**
   Preparing a story map will help you make sure that your narrative includes all important details and events. The map will also help you put events in the proper order.

   Most narratives use **chronological order,** also called time order—the sequence in which events happened. You may describe events in a different order, as long as you use transition words or other clues that help your reader understand the sequence.

2. **Write an interesting beginning.**
   Grab your reader's attention with a strong start. You might use a question, a description, or some dialogue. Sometimes plunging right into the story will make your reader hungry for more.

3. **Include vivid details.**
   Create vivid pictures for your reader as you write. What details can you add that will help a reader see what you saw, hear what you heard, and feel what you felt?

   TIP Before revising, consult the key traits on page 168 and the rubric and peer-reader questions on page 174.

What Does It Look Like?

STORY MAP

> **Title:** *Facing My Fear: Riding the River*
>
> **Characters:** *me, Mom, Dad, Frank, Dave*   **Setting:** *home, Dungeness River, Colorado River*
>
> **Problem:** *My family is going whitewater rafting, but I am scared of drowning.*
>
> **Event 1:** *Dad tells us we're going rafting.*
> **Event 2:** *I remember the time I almost drowned.*
> **Event 3:** *I look at the rafting catalog and get nervous.*
> **Event 4:** *We get through the first rapid.*
>
> **Solution or Ending:** *I learned that I can face my worst fear.*

A question
Have you ever stared fear in the face and lived to laugh about it? I have.

A bit of dialogue
"A rafting trip through the Grand Canyon? For a week? Really?" I said, a grin pasted on my face.

From prewriting notes . . .
The rapids turned out to be fierce and challenging.

. . . to draft
Up ahead, the waters of the Colorado appeared to be boiling, bubbling up into the air and crashing back down. In the center was a trough that looked to be 30 or 40 yards long—and we were headed right for it.

172 UNIT 1: NARRATIVE STRUCTURE

DIFFERENTIATED INSTRUCTION

FOR ENGLISH LEARNERS

Prepare a Story Map Because of cultural differences, students might need extra guidance in organizing time order for their maps. Suggest that they write each event they will include in their narratives on an index card. Then have them organize content by arranging the cards in order, from what happened first to what happened last.

FOR ADVANCED LEARNERS/PRE–AP

Incorporate Foreshadowing and Flashback As students revise their narratives, have them look for places to incorporate foreshadowing and flashback. Remind students to use transitions or other clues to help readers understand the sequence.

REVISING AND EDITING

What Should I Do?	What Does It Look Like?
1. Show, don't tell. Instead of telling your reader "I was scared" or "She looked happy," show your characters' emotions and reactions. <u>Underline</u> any statements in your essay that sound like these examples. Consider adding dialogue, or information about tone of voice, expressions, or gestures or other movements.	~~All of us were glad the scary part was over. I started to feel somewhat less nervous.~~ The rafters erupted in wild shouts, all of us laughing about how we were soaking wet and what a thrill the ride had been. The knot in my stomach eased a bit.
2. Consider your tone. Is your narrative funny? bittersweet? scary? Highlight words and details that give the narrative its tone. If you have few highlights, or if you don't like the tone in certain places, ask a peer reader for help.	~~Are these idiots crazy or what? I asked myself. What are they thinking, anyway?~~ Does anyone really think that the guides can control everything that happens during the journey?
3. Include sensory images. • (Circle) places where sensory images—words and phrases that appeal to sight, sound, taste, smell, and touch—seem to be missing. • Add specific nouns, powerful verbs, and vivid adjectives and adverbs. Consider using figurative language, such as similes and metaphors. **See page 672:** Figurative Language	(The ride was starting to get really bumpy and noisy.) I could feel every bump and sway, and I could hear the whoosh of the river all around me. Within a few minutes, the whooshing sound began to seem more like a thunderstorm. Our guides ordered us to grab the ropes and brace ourselves. The sound ahead resembled the roar of a jet engine.
4. Don't forget the significance. • Ask a peer reader to tell you why the experience was important. • If he or she can't tell you, add information about the event's significance to the conclusion and at other points, if appropriate. **See page 174:** Ask a Peer Reader	~~I'm glad we took that trip. It turned out to be a really good vacation after all.~~ During that vacation, I faced my worst fear not just once, but dozens of times. I learned that worrying about an experience can be worse than the experience itself. I realized that I am tougher than I thought.

WRITING WORKSHOP **173**

REVISING AND EDITING

1. **Show, don't tell.** Write this "telling" sentence on the board:

   The tour guide said not to be scared.

   Then ask a student to read aloud lines 24–25 from the student model (p. 169). Have students identify the specific ways this sentence "shows" rather than "tells," compared to the sentence on the board. *Possible answers The student model uses dialogue and descriptive details. These elements bring the event to life. The reader can visualize the narrator's reaction to the guide's comment about falling in.*

2. **Consider your tone.** Explain to students that *tone* refers to feelings and attitudes an author has toward a subject that are revealed through his or her word choice. Remind students to keep the tone of their narratives consistent. Students should avoid academic-sounding language, overly complicated sentences, and passive voice.

3. **Include sensory images.** Have readers exchange drafts and answer these questions: What can I see, hear, smell, taste, or touch? What can the writer do to make the narrative more vivid?

4. **Don't forget the significance.** Remind students to use precise and strong verbs, such as *faced, learned, realized, survived,* and *overcame,* to show change. Offer some sequence or cause-and-effect phrases to help students link their experiences to the final result: *In the end . . . ; As a result of . . . ; Because of. . . .*

For interactive revision tools, see

⊘ Write*Smart* CD

ⓘ Writing Center at **ClassZone.com**

Review the GRAMMAR AND STYLE note on page 82. Remind students that using modifiers helps readers more clearly imagine and feel the significance of the event they are writing about in their narratives.

FOR ENGLISH LEARNERS

Ask a Peer Reader For clarity, restate the points below **Ask a Peer Reader** on page 174 as questions. Write them on the board for students to use:

• What problem did I face? What happened to me?

• Where do I need to tell more about what happened?

• What did I learn from this experience?

Write these sentence starters on the board for students to use when answering the questions:

• My problem was _____. In the beginning, I _____. Next, I _____. Finally, I _____.

• I need to tell more about _____.

• I learned _____.

Preparing to Publish

Support for meeting the goals in the writing rubric is supplied throughout the Writing Workshop on pages 171–173.

For Rubric Bank, see

 WriteSmart CD

Writing Center at **ClassZone.com**

Assess and Reteach

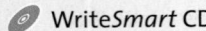 **STANDARDS LESSON FILE**

Writing Lesson 31: Personal Narrative
Writing Lesson 44: Writing Dialogue

Apply the Rubric

A strong personal narrative . . .

☑ captures the reader's interest with an intriguing beginning

☑ focuses on a clear, well-defined experience

☑ uses dialogue to develop characters and add realism

☑ includes words and phrases that signal chronological order

☑ creates vivid descriptions through the use of precise language and strong sensory details

☑ maintains a consistent tone

☑ shows the writer's style

☑ uses a variety of sentence structures

☑ concludes by explaining why the experience mattered to the writer

Ask a Peer Reader

- What is the main incident or conflict in my narrative?

- How would you explain in your own words the significance of the experience to me?

Check Your Grammar

- When writing dialogue, enclose each speaker's actual words in quotation marks. Begin a new paragraph whenever the speaker changes.

> "A rafting trip through the Grand Canyon? For a week? Really?" I said, a grin pasted on my face. "That's a great idea, Dad." I felt a knot forming in my stomach.
>
> My two brothers high-fived each other. "This is gonna be awesome!" they hollered.

- Unless the speaker's words are a question or an exclamation, use a comma to separate the speaker's words from the phrase identifying the speaker. Place the comma inside the closing quotation mark.

> "If you fall in, relax and go with the flow," one of the lean, sunburned tour guides said.

- If the speaker's words are a question or an exclamation, use a question mark or exclamation point in place of a comma. Place the punctuation mark inside the closing quotation mark.

> "We'll pull you out!" he added.

See page R50: Quick Reference: Punctuation

Writing Online

 PUBLISHING OPTIONS
For publishing options, visit the **Writing Center** at **ClassZone.com**.

ASSESSMENT PREPARATION
For writing and grammar assessment practice, go to the **Assessment Center** at **ClassZone.com**.

Presenting an Informal Speech

Captivate your classmates with a **narrative presentation**—a retelling of the incident you described in your personal narrative.

Planning the Presentation

Adapt what you wrote. Here's how to turn your writing into an effective speech:

- Use shorter sentences.
- Eliminate minor characters and unnecessary dialogue.
- Be sure the sequence of events is clear.
- Focus on the descriptive details related to setting and characters. This will help your audience "live" the experience and understand its importance.
- If you are using notes, mark your text to show where you will use a different voice, a certain facial expression, a gesture, or sound effects. Notice how Rich Rosario adapted parts of his personal narrative.

Written Narrative	Informal Speech
"A rafting trip through the Grand Canyon? For a week? Really?" I said, a grin pasted on my face. "That's a great idea, Dad." I felt a knot forming in my stomach.	[grin] You should have seen the grin on my face when my dad told me about our next family vacation! [pause] It was a _fake_ grin. We were going on a rafting trip through the Grand Canyon. [frown] Yuck!
My two brothers high-fived each other. "This is gonna be awesome!" they hollered. My mother grinned her approval.	My two brothers high-fived each other. "This is gonna be awesome!" they hollered. My mother grinned her approval.

Delivering the Presentation

1. **Use a conversational tone.** Use some of the same inflections and gestures you use when you share an important event with a friend. You might speak at a faster pace to describe exciting events and at a slower pace to create suspense or drama.

2. **Find out your time limit, if any.** Pace your delivery so that you finish on time. (You might have a friend time you as you practice.)

See page R79: Evaluate a Narrative Speech

SPEAKING AND LISTENING

Ask students to read this page to get an overview of how to plan, present, and deliver an informal speech. Students who choose this option should familiarize themselves with the features of a speech and with tools, such as a tape recorder, that might help them prepare.

Before students begin working, review this rubric with them so that they understand their goals:

Rubric A strong informal speech

- has a clear sequence of events
- focuses on the key ideas and exciting moments of the narrative
- includes descriptive details to help the audience picture the experience and understand its significance
- avoids unnecessary details and long, complex sentences
- is presented effectively using gestures, facial expressions, and sound effects to help convey the content and emotions of the story
- is delivered using a conversational tone
- is completed in the allotted time

When students begin listening to the presentations, have them use the rubric to evaluate the effectiveness of their classmates' speeches.

R RESOURCE MANAGER—Copy Master
Speaking and Listening p. 253

S STANDARDS LESSON FILE
Speaking and Listening Lesson 2: Informal Speeches

Assessment Practice

CHECK READINESS

Read aloud the paragraph under **ASSESS** and stress to students that this is not the full Unit Test, but a way for them to check their readiness for it. Then have students examine the skills listed under **REVIEW** and look back in the unit or in the **Student Resource Bank** for any skills they need to review.

READ THE SELECTIONS

Remind students to keep unit goals in mind as they read each passage, paying particular attention to these literary and reading skills:

- plot stages
- conflict
- sequence
- predict
- cause and effect

To help students focus on conflict while reading, encourage them to ask questions such as

- What concerns the narrator in "Fish Cheeks"? What worries her the most?
- How is the boy's daydream in "Piedra" different from his reality?

ANSWER THE QUESTIONS

Direct students to pages R93–R101 of the **Handbook** to review test-taking strategies.

- Remind students not to choose the first alternative that seems to fit when answering a multiple-choice question. Instead, they should read through all the choices, eliminate any that are clearly wrong, and then choose the *best* answer—the one that is most accurate and complete.

- Also remind students to read each set of directions carefully, looking for key words. After students complete the first item, they may want to reread the directions to ensure that they understand what is being asked.

Assessment Practice

ASSESS

The practice test items on the next few pages match skills listed on the Unit Goals page (page 23) and addressed throughout this unit. Taking this practice test will help you assess your knowledge of these skills and determine your readiness for the Unit Test.

REVIEW

After you take the practice test, your teacher can help you identify any skills you need to review.

- Plot Stages
- Conflict
- Sequence
- Predict
- Cause and Effect
- Synonyms and Antonyms
- Latin Word Roots
- Modifiers
- Precise and Strong Verbs

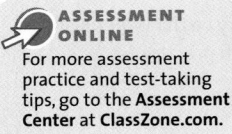

ASSESSMENT ONLINE
For more assessment practice and test-taking tips, go to the **Assessment Center at ClassZone.com.**

Reading Comprehension

DIRECTIONS *Read the following selections and then answer the questions.*

Fish Cheeks

Amy Tan

I fell in love with the minister's son the winter I turned fourteen. He was not Chinese, but as white as Mary in the manger. For Christmas I prayed for this blond-haired boy, Robert, and a slim new American nose.

When I found out that my parents had invited the minister's family over for Christmas Eve dinner, I cried. What would Robert think of our shabby *Chinese* Christmas? What would he think of our noisy *Chinese* relatives who lacked proper American manners? What terrible disappointment would he feel upon seeing not a roasted turkey and sweet potatoes but *Chinese* food?

On Christmas Eve I saw that my mother had outdone herself in creating a
10 strange menu. She was pulling black veins out of the backs of fleshy prawns. The kitchen was littered with appalling mounds of raw food: A slimy rock cod with bulging fish eyes that pleaded not to be thrown into a pan of hot oil. Tofu, which looked like stacked wedges of rubbery white sponges. A bowl soaking dried fungus back to life. A plate of squid, their backs crisscrossed with knife markings so they resembled bicycle tires.

And then they arrived—the minister's family and all my relatives in a clamor of doorbells and rumpled Christmas packages. Robert grunted hello, and I pretended he was not worthy of existence.

Dinner threw me deeper into despair. My relatives licked the ends of their
20 chopsticks and reached across the table, dipping them into the dozen or so plates of food. Robert and his family waited patiently for platters to be passed to them. My relatives murmured with pleasure when my mother brought out the whole steamed fish. Robert grimaced. Then my father poked his chopsticks just below the fish eye and plucked out the soft meat. "Amy, your favorite," he said, offering me the tender fish cheek. I wanted to disappear.

At the end of the meal my father leaned back and belched loudly, thanking my mother for her fine cooking. "It's a polite Chinese custom to show you are satisfied," explained my father to our astonished guests. Robert was looking down at his plate with a reddened face. The minister managed to muster up a
30 quiet burp. I was stunned into silence for the rest of the night.

After everyone had gone, my mother said to me, "You want to be the same as American girls on the outside." She handed me an early gift. It was a miniskirt in beige tweed. "But inside you must always be Chinese. You must be proud you are different. Your only shame is to have shame."

DIFFERENTIATED INSTRUCTION

FOR ENGLISH LEARNERS
Assessment Practice: Work Backward

Prepare students by having them read the questions *before* reading the passages. Have pairs find unfamiliar words in test directions and questions and follow these steps:

1. Write each word on an index card.
2. Look up the meaning in a dictionary and write it on the back of the card.
3. Use the cards to practice the words with your partner and to teach them to others.

Culture: Clarify Read aloud the first paragraph on page 176. Explain that "Mary in the manger" (line 2) refers to the mother of Jesus. In religious artworks, Mary is often shown near a manger, a trough that holds feed for livestock, in a barn where she is said to have given birth to her son. In some of these paintings, Mary's complexion is very light, much like the blond-haired Robert.

And even though I didn't agree with her then, I knew that she understood how much I had suffered during the evening's dinner. It wasn't until many years later—long after I had gotten over my crush on Robert—that I was able to fully appreciate her lesson and the true purpose behind our particular menu. For Christmas Eve that year, she had chosen all my favorite foods.

from Piedra

Gary Soto

Piedra. River of rock, place where our family went for a Saturday picnic. It was a fifteen-mile drive past plum and almond orchards, dairies, the town with its green sign, Minkler—Population 35, *Mexicanos* pruning orange trees on ladders, and our mother's talk that if our grades didn't improve we would be like *those* people. Past cows with grassy jaws, past fallen fences, groceries, tractors itching with rust, the Griffin ranch with its mowed pasture and white fence that proclaimed he was a gentleman farmer. We gawked at his ranch, and counted his cows, which seemed cleaner, better looking than the fly-specked ones we had passed earlier.

10   I dreamed about Griffin's daughters. I imagined that their hair was tied in ponytails and bounced crazily when they rode horses in knee-high grass near the river. They were the stuff of romance novels, sad and lonely girls who were in love with a stable boy, who was also sad and lonely but too poor for the father's liking, because he himself had once been poor but now was rich and liked to whip horses, cuss, and chase gasping foxes at daybreak.

My dreaming stopped when the road narrowed, gravel ticked under a fender, and we began our climb through the foot-hills.

ITEM ANALYSIS

COMPREHENSION AND WRITTEN RESPONSE	ITEMS	UNIT PAGES
Plot Stages	3, 4, 6, 7, 9, 10, 16	24–31
Exposition	3, 9	24–31
Rising Action	4, 10	24–31
Climax	16	24–31
Resolution	6, 7	24–31
Conflict	1, 2, 4, 12, 15	24–31, 53
Sequence	3, 6, 10, 11	24–31, 33
Predict	5, 14	95
Cause and Effect	2, 4, 8, 15, 16	111

VOCABULARY	ITEMS	UNIT PAGES
Synonyms and Antonyms	1, 2, 3	118
Latin Word Roots	4, 5, 6, 7	49

WRITING AND GRAMMAR	ITEMS	UNIT PAGES
Modifiers	1, 2, 3	93
Precise and Strong Verbs	4, 5, 6	105, 119

Comprehension

Model a thinking process for answering multiple-choice questions.

1. **A is correct.** *The narrator's concerns, expressed in lines 5–8, show that she is worried about Robert's reaction to a Chinese Christmas in her home. B is incorrect because even though the narrator wishes for a slim nose, this is not a main conflict. C is incorrect because it is contradicted in line 39. D is not supported by any information in the selection.*

2. **B is correct.** *In lines 10–15, the narrator calls the menu "strange" and describes the foods in unappetizing ways. A is incorrect, as shown by line 39. C and D are untrue.*

3. **A is correct.** *The narrator describes the food in lines 10–15, in the early part of the story in which the setting, tone, and other elements are being presented. The rising action (B), climax (C), and falling action (D) do not occur until line 16 and beyond. Therefore, B, C, and D are incorrect.*

4. **D is correct.** *The offer of the fish cheeks complicates the conflict by further humiliating the narrator, as expressed in line 25. The actions expressed in A and C are true, but they do not complicate the conflict. B is incorrect because it is an event that occurs before the rising action.*

5. **C is correct.** *This prediction is based on the narrator's behavior as described in lines 17–18 and on the events during the meal at her house. A and D are incorrect because the narrator's humiliation would not lead her to be friendly. B is incorrect because the narrator has no reason to be rude to Robert.*

6. **D is correct.** *The narrator explains in lines 35–39 that the conflict is resolved "many years later," presumably when the narrator is an adult. A is incorrect because the belch is part of the climax. B is incorrect because the skirt did not resolve the plot. C is incorrect because it is part of the exposition.*

7. **C is correct.** *This answer is implied in line 38, when the narrator acknowledges the "true purpose behind our [Chinese] menu." A is untrue. B is true, but it is not part of the resolution. D is incorrect because the conflict does not involve the narrator's preference for Chinese food.*

Comprehension

DIRECTIONS *Answer these questions about "Fish Cheeks."*

1. What is the narrator's main conflict?
   A She is afraid that Robert won't like her when he sees how her family celebrates Christmas.
   B She wishes she had a slim nose like those of the American girls.
   C She doesn't like any of the foods that her mother is preparing for Christmas Eve dinner.
   D She doesn't want to spend Christmas Eve with people that she hardly knows.

2. Why is the narrator worried about her mother's Christmas Eve dinner menu?
   A She doesn't like any of the foods on the menu.
   B She thinks the food will seem strange to the guests.
   C She worries that her mother doesn't know how to prepare all the unusual dishes.
   D She wishes that the food choices were healthier.

3. In what part of the plot does the narrator describe the unusual food that awaits the minister's family?
   A exposition
   B rising action
   C climax
   D falling action

4. In the rising action, which of these events complicates the conflict?
   A The narrator ignores the minister's son.
   B The narrator cries about Christmas Eve dinner.
   C The narrator's relatives murmur with pleasure.
   D The narrator's father offers her the fish cheeks.

5. Which of the following would the narrator probably do when she sees Robert at school after Christmas?
   A wave at him and shout hello
   B say something rude to him
   C try to avoid meeting his eyes
   D invite him back to her house

6. The resolution of the plot occurs when
   A the narrator's father belches
   B the narrator's mother gives her a miniskirt
   C the narrator is in love with Robert
   D the narrator is an adult

7. In the resolution of the story, the narrator realizes that
   A she never agreed with her mother
   B her mother was a superb cook
   C she should be proud to be Chinese
   D she preferred Chinese food after all

DIRECTIONS *Answer these questions about the excerpt from "Piedra."*

8. Why does the mother tell her children to get better grades?
   A She wants them to do as well as the tree pruners they saw.
   B She wants them to have better-paying jobs than pruning trees.
   C She wants them to be smarter than their friends.
   D She wants them to learn how to run a ranch.

8. **B is correct.** *In lines 3–5, the mother implies that her children will have low-paying jobs like the pruners if their grades don't improve. A is incorrect because it is the opposite of what the mother is saying. C and D are not supported by information in the selection.*

9. **B is correct.** *He "gawks" at Griffin's ranch and counts its clean cows (lines 6–9). There is no evidence to support A, C, or D.*

9. What do you learn about the main character in this excerpt?

   A He would like to get good grades.

   B He admires the Griffin ranch.

   C He and his family live in a city.

   D He wants to be a farmer.

10. The rising action of the plot begins when

    A they go through Minkler

    B they drive past Griffin's ranch

    C the narrator daydreams about girls

    D they climb through the foothills

11. What prompts the narrator to begin daydreaming?

    A seeing the green Minkler sign

    B passing the people who prune trees for a living

    C seeing a ranch that is better than all the others

    D feeling the car start its climb through the foothills

DIRECTIONS *Answer these questions about both selections.*

12. Which issue seems more important to the mother in "Fish Cheeks" than to the mother in "Piedra"?

    A money

    B tradition

    C school

    D friendship

13. In what way are the narrators of both selections alike?

    A Both narrators are parents who care about their children.

    B They are both students who want to get better grades.

    C Both narrators are children who disobey their parents.

    D They both long for something they do not have.

Written Response

SHORT RESPONSE
Write three or four sentences to answer each question.

14. How would the narrator of "Fish Cheeks" probably react if her parents invited the minister's family to dinner for the next holiday? Give evidence from the selection to back up your answer.

15. In "Fish Cheeks," how can you tell that the guests were embarrassed at the end of the meal? Give three pieces of evidence from the story.

EXTENDED RESPONSE
Write two to three paragraphs to answer this question.

16. In "Fish Cheeks," what does the narrator's mother mean when she says, "Your only shame is to have shame"? How does she want her daughter to feel? What does she do to change her daughter's feelings?

GO ON

---

10. **D is correct.** This excerpt contains no rising action: it is all exposition. Readers must assume that the action begins when the narrator says that his dreaming stops (lines 16–17). A, B, and C are incorrect because they are part of the exposition.

11. **C is correct.** Seeing the ranch inspires the daydreaming. A and B are incorrect because these events occur before the car passes the Griffin ranch. D is incorrect because this is when the daydreaming stops.

12. **B is correct.** Lines 31–34 show that the mother values her heritage and traditions. A, C, and D are incorrect because the mother in "Fish Cheeks" does not show concern for these things.

13. **D is correct.** The narrator in "Fish Cheeks" wants to be more American than Chinese; the narrator in "Piedra" wants to be part of a prosperous ranch. A is incorrect because the narrators are telling about childhood events. B is incorrect because the narrators themselves do not say they want to get better grades. C is incorrect because neither child disobeys the parents.

Written Response

Possible short responses:

14. *The narrator would probably protest another invitation, since to her, the first dinner was a disaster, and she would likely worry about her relatives' behavior and the "strange menu" (lines 6–8, 10).*

15. *Lines 28–30 reveal the guests' embarrassment. The guests react to the burp with astonishment (line 28). Then Robert looks at his plate with "a reddened face" (lines 28–29). The minister musters up a "quiet burp" (lines 29–30).*

Possible extended response:

16. *The narrator's mother wants her daughter to be unashamed of her heritage. The mother wants the daughter to feel the same pride she feels about being Chinese. In fact, as the narrator later realizes, the mother was teaching the daughter a lesson about pride in heritage by cooking the daughter's favorite Chinese foods.*

DIFFERENTIATED INSTRUCTION

FOR ENGLISH LEARNERS

Assessment Vocabulary To help students understand the Comprehension questions, teach or review these key vocabulary words:

- Item 4: *complicates*—"makes more complex or difficult"; "makes the conflict deeper or harder to resolve"
- Item 9: *excerpt*—"part of a story"; "passage"
- Item 11: *prompts*—"causes"

Vocabulary

1. **C** *is correct.* C is the best answer, since the word doorbells *suggests sound. A crowd (A) makes a loud sound, but the word* crowd *usually does not refer to doorbells.* B *and* D *are incorrect, since they do not suggest sound.*

2. **C** *is correct. The minister needed to produce a burp in order to appear polite. Because he did not* hide *or* excuse *his burp,* A *and* D *are incorrect. To* echo *the father's burp, the minister would have had to produce a loud, rather than quiet, burp, so* B *is incorrect.*

3. **B** *is correct.* B *is the best answer, since both words indicate soundless reactions, but* grimacing *is negative, while* smiling *is positive. Although* laughing *(A), in contrast to* grimacing, *shows positive feelings, it does involve sound.* C *and* D *are incorrect since the words* growled *and* gasped, *like* grimaced, *show negative reactions.*

4. **B** *is correct.* B *is the best choice because it is the closest match to the root* pall. *An* appalling *scene or event could cause someone to turn pale.* A, C, *and* D *contain some of the same letters as the root* pall, *but none of their meanings suggest shock, surprise, or other emotions that might make a person turn pale.*

5. **A** *is correct.* Resembled *probably means "appeared alike."* Like *is a synonym for* alike; *it is also the closest match to* simil. B, C, *and* D *do not share similarities with* resembled *or the root* simil, *either in meaning or spelling.*

6. **B** *is correct.* Polished *is the closest match to* polit. *When a person is polite, his or her behavior might be called* polished *or* refined. A, C, *and* D *do not share similarities with the word* polite *or the root* polit, *either in meaning or spelling.*

7. **D** *is correct.* Proclaimed *means "announced," which suggests a kind of crying out; the base word* claim *also closely resembles the root* clam. A, B, *and* C *do not share similarities with the root* clam, *either in meaning or in spelling.*

Vocabulary

DIRECTIONS *Use your knowledge of synonyms to answer the following questions.*

1. Choose the word that is a synonym of the underlined word in the following sentence from "Fish Cheeks."

   And then they arrived—the minister's family and all my relatives in a <u>clamor</u> of doorbells and rumpled Christmas packages.

   A crowd
   B shabbiness
   C noise
   D offering

2. Choose the word that is a synonym of the underlined phrase in the following sentence from "Fish Cheeks."

   The minister managed to <u>muster up</u> a quiet burp.

   A hide
   B echo
   C produce
   D excuse

DIRECTIONS *Use your knowledge of antonyms to answer question 3.*

3. Choose the word that is an antonym of the underlined word in the following passage from "Fish Cheeks."

   Dinner threw me deeper into despair. My relatives licked the ends of their chopsticks and reached across the table, dipping them into the dozen or so plates of food. Robert and his family waited patiently for platters to be passed to them. My relatives murmured with pleasure when my mother brought out the whole steamed fish. Robert <u>grimaced</u>.

   A laughed   **C** growled
   B smiled   **D** gasped

DIRECTIONS *Use your knowledge of vocabulary and the Latin word roots given to answer the following questions.*

4. The root *pall* means "pale." Which word in "Fish Cheeks" may have something to do with making a person turn pale and probably comes from the Latin root *pall?*

   A disappear
   B appalling
   C polite
   D pleaded

5. The word *resembled* in line 15 of "Fish Cheeks" comes from the Latin root *simil.* What does this root probably mean?

   A like
   B inflated
   C tread
   D shame

6. The word *polite* in line 27 of "Fish Cheeks" comes from the Latin root *polit.* What does this root probably mean?

   A pretend
   B polish
   C pluck
   D platter

7. The Latin root *clam* means "cry out." Which word in "Piedra" likely comes from the root *clam?*

   A counted
   B gawked
   C climb
   D proclaimed

DIFFERENTIATED INSTRUCTION

FOR ENGLISH LEARNERS
Review Academic Vocabulary On the board, list the academic vocabulary shown in italics. Then give the examples in random order and have students classify them. Elicit additional examples from students.

- *conflict:* Brothers are fighting against each other.
- *rising action:* Lila discovers she is lost on the mountain. Then she loses her water bottle.
- *resolution:* The money is found, and Jamal returns to his home and job.

Writing & Grammar

DIRECTIONS *Read this passage and answer the questions that follow.*

(1) Schools are adding outdoor learning experiences. (2) This is happening nationwide. (3) Kids can work in an edible garden. (4) They grow lettuce, tomatoes, and peas. (5) The students at one school built an oven. (6) They used clay, straw, and water to build it. (7) They mixed the materials together. (8) Kids also dig in the dirt, pull weeds, and remove pests from their plants. (9) Butterflies and bees fly around the plants. (10) Tomatoes hang over the garden wall.

1. Choose the best way to rewrite sentences 1 and 2, using a prepositional phrase.

   A Schools are adding outdoor learning experiences, and these schools are nationwide.

   B Schools across the nation are adding outdoor learning experiences.

   C The nation's schools are adding outdoor learning experiences.

   D Schools are adding outdoor learning experiences nationwide.

2. Choose the best way to add details to sentence 4, using modifiers.

   A They grow fresh lettuce, tomatoes, and peas.

   B They grow crunchy lettuce, juicy tomatoes, and green peas.

   C They grow crisp lettuce, tomatoes, and peas.

   D Lettuce, tomatoes, and peas grow well.

3. Which prepositional phrase would add details to sentence 5 that describe the oven the students built?

   A out of natural materials

   B with enthusiasm

   C in the sky

   D underneath the garden

4. Choose the best way to rewrite sentence 8, using strong verbs in a series. Choose D if no change is needed.

   A Kids also heave the dirt, yank out weeds, and exterminate pests from their plants.

   B Kids also hoe in the dirt and remove weeds and pests from their plants.

   C Kids also dig in the dirt, weed, nurture their plants, and remove pests.

   D No change is needed.

5. Choose the best way to rewrite sentence 9, using a precise verb or verbs. Choose D if no change is needed.

   A Butterflies and bees move around the plants.

   B There are butterflies and bees around the plants.

   C Butterfies flit and bees hover around the plants.

   D No change is needed.

6. Choose the best way to rewrite sentence 10, using a precise verb. Choose D if no change is needed.

   A Tomatoes lie on the garden wall.

   B Tomatoes are on the garden wall.

   C Tomatoes cascade over the garden wall.

   D No change is needed.

STOP

181

ANSWERS

Writing & Grammar

1. B is correct. Only B contains a prepositional phrase—"across the nation." In A, the original sentences have been combined using a coordinating conjunction. In C, modifiers from sentence 2 have been incorporated into sentence 1. In D, a direct object—"outdoor learning experiences"—has been added.

2. B is correct. B is the best answer, since an adjective modifies each noun. A and C contain only one adjective. D contains only an adverb.

3. C is correct. Only C gives details about the oven. A, B, and D do not refer to the oven.

4. A is correct. A is the best answer, since it contains a series of strong, vivid verbs, and the elements in the series are parallel in form. B is incorrect, since it contains a compound predicate, and not a series. In C, the verbs are not strong, and the elements are not parallel. In the original sentence (D), the elements are parallel, but the verbs are not strong.

5. C is correct. C is the best answer, since *flit* and *hover* are precise verbs. A is incorrect because *move* is too vague. In B, the verb *are* does not describe the movement of the bees and butterflies. In the original sentence (D), the verb *fly* does not precisely describe the movements of the butterflies and bees.

6. C is correct. C is the best answer, since *cascade* is both precise and accurate. A is incorrect because *lie* is not accurate. B uses a weak state-of-being verb. The original sentence (D) contains a less precise and vivid verb than does C.

Assessment Support: Prepositional Phrases and Modifiers

- Review with students that adjectives modify nouns and pronouns and that adverbs modify verbs, adjectives, or other adverbs.

- Have students identify the modifiers in lines 10–15 of "Piedra."

- Remind students that a prepositional phrase is a modifier made up of a preposition and an object of a preposition. Also clarify the difference between an infinitive phrase and a prepositional phrase in lines 26–30 of "Fish Cheeks."

INTRODUCE *GREAT READS*

In Unit 1, students have discussed a number of big questions. Invite students to tell which question they found most intriguing and why, and then focus attention on the three that appear on this page. Discuss the recommended books and their summaries, pointing out how each connects to the related question. Encourage students to choose one or more of these "great reads" to read independently.

ⓘ ClassZone.com

To find additional books that match students' interests and ability levels, visit the Literature Center at **ClassZone.com**.

Ideas for Independent Reading

Which of the questions in Unit 1 intrigued you the most? Continue exploring them through independent reading.

What does it take to be a survivor?

The Autobiography of Miss Jane Pittman
by Ernest J. Gaines

This unusual novel is written as an autobiography. A 110-year-old woman tells the story of her life, from her childhood as a slave in Louisiana to the civil rights era of the 1960s.

And Then There Were None
by Agatha Christie

At certain points, this mystery novel might bring to mind the sizzling plot elements of "The Most Dangerous Game." Ten strangers are lured to an island from which there is no escape.

In These Girls, Hope Is a Muscle
by Madeleine Blais

This true account goes behind the scenes as a basketball team tries to survive the state playoffs.

What is worth fighting for?

Shoeless Joe
by W. P. Kinsella

Against everyone's advice, Ray Kinsella builds a baseball diamond in a cornfield to give Shoeless Joe Jackson, a legendary outfielder done in by scandal and now dead, a chance to play.

All Quiet on the Western Front
by Erich Maria Remarque

This fictional antiwar classic follows Paul Baumer into the German army during World War I. While fighting the human enemy, Paul also fights a more deadly enemy—the hate that leads men into war.

The Pact: Three Young Men Make a Promise and Fulfill a Dream
by Dr. Sampson Davis, et al.

Three young men from the wrong side of the tracks in Newark, New Jersey, made a pact: they would all become doctors and they would do it together. Over-coming numerous obstacles, they all achieved their goal.

What makes a winner?

Bad Boy: A Memoir
by Walter Dean Myers

The author of many novels about black characters remembers his own childhood in Harlem. Surrounded by poverty and drugs, he seeks escape and adventure in books and succeeds in becoming a writer.

The Natural
by Bernard Malamud

Roy Hobbs, a talented athlete whose promising career is cut short by his own misdeeds, makes a comeback in middle age. He struggles to be a great player and to fulfill his dream.

The Miracle Worker
by William Gibson

This play tells the true story of the dedicated Annie Sullivan's struggle to free Helen Keller from the prison of her dark and silent world. Convinced that she can give Helen the gift of language, Annie applies herself with fanatical dedication.

UNIT 2

People Watching

CHARACTERIZATION AND POINT OF VIEW

- In Fiction
- In Nonfiction
- In Poetry
- Across Genres

183

About the Art Marie Louise Élisabeth Vigée-LeBrun (1755–1842) painted *Louise Augusta, Queen of Prussia* in 1801. For more information, see page 208 of the teacher's edition.

For help in planning this unit, see

 RESOURCE MANAGER UNIT 2 pp. 1–11

INTRODUCE THE UNIT

In a park, at the beach, or at the mall, observing the clothing, facial expressions, and body language of passersby is a great way to learn about people of all cultures, ages, and genders. Ask volunteers to tell about some of the interesting people they have observed. Question them about what they learned from their observations.

Invite students to use their people-watching skills to discuss the pictures on this page. To elicit ideas, ask:

- When might each person have lived?
- How would you describe each person's manner of dress? What can you learn from it?
- How might you describe each person's attitude?
- What might each person be thinking and feeling?
- If you wrote a story about each of them, what might be the title?

Discuss with students which of their ideas are facts and which are speculation. Point out that we can learn only so much from observing people in a portrait or book illustration or even in real life. In this unit, students will explore how **characterization, point of view,** and the other techniques an author uses to develop a character allow readers to get below the surface and truly know the character.

183

UNIT 2

Skills Trace

SKILLS STRAND	Literary Analysis Workshop: Character and Point of View pp. 186–191	Pancakes pp. 192–205 Short Story *Level: Easy*	The Necklace pp. 206–221 Short Story *Level: Challenging*	Hamadi pp. 222–235 Short Story *Level: Easy*	*from* I Know Why the Caged Bird Sings pp. 236–249 Autobiography *Level: Average*
Literary Analysis	Character Traits and Motivation pp. 188–190, 191 Point of View pp. 186–187, 191	First-Person Point of View pp. 193, 197, 201, 203 Review: Character Traits pp. 196, 200, 203	Character Motivation pp. 207, 212, 215, 217, 218 Review: Point of View pp. 214, 218	Third-Person Limited Point of View pp. 223, 226, 227, 229, 233	Characterization in Autobiography pp. 237, 238, 242, 243, 245, 247
Reading and Informational Texts	Analyze the Literature pp. 187, 189–190, 191 Academic Vocabulary pp. 186, 188, 190	Draw Conclusions pp. 193, 194, 198, 199, 203 Review: Predict pp. 199, 202	Make Inferences pp. 207, 208, 210, 218 Review: Predict p. 217 Preview and Read a Magazine Article p. 221	Monitor pp. 223, 224, 227, 230, 231, 233 Review: Make Inferences pp. 229, 231	Analyze Perspectives pp. 237, 240, 245, 247 Analyze a Poem p. 246 Review: Make Inferences p. 240
Vocabulary		Word Acquisition pp. 193, T193, 204 Word Map p. T193 Latin Roots (*ben*) p. 204	Word Acquisition pp. 207, T207, 219 Context Clues p. T207 Latin Roots (*spec*) p. 219	Word Acquisition pp. 223, T223, 234 Context Clues p. T223 Words from Greek Culture p. 234	Word Acquisition pp. 237, T237, 248 Context Clues p. T237 Multiple-Meaning Words p. 248
Writing, Grammar, and Style		Supporting Details pp. 196, 205 Precise Adjectives pp. 196, 205	Variety in Sentence Beginnings pp. 214, 220	Repetition for Emphasis pp. 232, 235	Descriptive Details pp. 243, 249 Adjective Clauses, Relative Adverbs pp. 243, 249
Speaking, Listening, Viewing, and Media	Discuss pp. T186–T190	Discuss pp. 192, T194–T202, 203 Analyze Visuals pp. 194, 198	Discuss pp. 206, T208–T217, 218, 221 Analyze Visuals pp. 208, T211, 213, 216	Discuss pp. 222, T224–T232, 233 Analyze Visuals pp. 224, 228	Discuss pp. 236, T238–T246, 247 Analyze Visuals pp. 238, 241, T244

Assessment-Based Planning: Skills in red are assessed on the Unit 2 Test. **T** = Teacher's Edition page

Blind to Failure pp. 250–263	*Linked selections* A Different Level of Competition pp. 264–267	A Voice/My Father's Song pp. 268–273	*from* Rosa Parks/Rosa pp. 274–283	Writing Workshop: Comparison-Contrast Essay pp. 284–291
Magazine Article *Level: Average*	Newspaper Article *Level: Easy*	Poems *Level: Easy*	Biography/Poem *Level: Average*	
Character Study pp. 251, 252, 254, 256, 258, 262		Speaker pp. 269, 270, 271, 272, 273	Characterization Across Genres pp. 275, 278, 279, 280, 281	
Interpret Graphic Aids pp. 251, 255, 260, 262 Review: Connect p. 257 Review: Draw Conclusions pp. 261, 262	Identify Main Ideas pp. 264, 265, 266, 267 Make Generalizations p. 267 Review: Predict p. 265	Strategies for Reading Poetry pp. 269, 270, 273	Set a Purpose for Reading p. 275 Compare Characterization Across Genres p. 281	Analyze a Comparison-Contrast Essay pp. 285–286, 290
Word Acquisition pp. 251, T251, 263 Context Clues p. T251 Specialized Vocabulary p. 263			Word Acquisition pp. 275, T275, 282 Context Clues p. T275 Etymologies p. 282	
			Write for Assessment p. 283	Write a Comparison-Contrast Essay pp. 284–291 Transitions pp. 286, 288, 290 Commas and Quotation Marks p. 290
Discuss pp. 250, T252–T261, 262 Analyze Visuals pp. 252, 259	Discuss pp. 264, 267	Discuss pp. 268, T270–T272, 273 Analyze Visuals pp. 271, T272	Discuss pp. 274, T276–T280, 281 Analyze Visuals p. 276	Discuss pp. T284–T286 Create and Present a Power Presentation p. 291

Skills Assessed on the Unit 2 Test:

Literary Analysis
- Analyze point of view
- Analyze methods of characterization
- Analyze character traits, motivation

Reading and Informational Texts
- Draw conclusions
- Make inferences
- Monitor understanding
- Recognize main ideas and support
- Interpret graphic aids

Vocabulary
- Use knowledge of word origins to understand words
- Determine the correct usage of words with multiple meanings

Writing, Grammar, and Style
- Write a comparison-contrast essay
- Vary sentence beginnings
- Add supporting and descriptive details
- Use repetition to add emphasis
- Use precise adjectives
- Use adjective clauses, relative pronouns, and relative adverbs
- Additional writing and grammar skills

For additional lesson planning help, see **Easy Planner DVD.**

OBJECTIVES

- establish prior knowledge about **character** and characterization
- discuss memorable characters

What makes a CHARACTER memorable?

To introduce the page, invite students to describe memorable characters from books or from TV shows, plays, or movies they have seen. Call on volunteers to describe or demonstrate how the character walked, spoke, gestured, or used facial expressions. As you proceed, discuss how these details help communicate the character's personality.

ACTIVITY Encourage students to be specific when responding to the questions. Guide students to conclude that a writer needs to have a strong sense of the character's physical appearance, manner of speaking and acting, personality, and even a sense of the character's past.

CHECK UNDERSTANDING Have students sum up what they have learned about **characters.**

What makes a CHARACTER memorable

Any skilled actor knows that it takes more than costumes and makeup to create a memorable **character.** Everything from the voice to the walk to the simplest of gestures and facial expressions must be considered and carefully chosen.

ACTIVITY With a group of classmates, think of several strong characters that you remember from TV shows, books, or movies. Describe each one, including details about both looks and personality. Then consider the following questions:

- On what details did you base your first impression of each character?

- How did your impression change as you got to know the character better? What details led to this change?

- Considering your discussion, what would you imagine a writer needs to keep in mind when creating a character?

Unit Resources

- **RESOURCE MANAGER UNIT 2**
- **BEST PRACTICES TOOLKIT**
- **STANDARDS LESSON FILE**

- Easy Planner DVD-ROM
- Write*Smart* CD-ROM
- ClassZone.com
- Audio Anthology CD
- Multi-Language Academic Vocabulary Online

- eEdition DVD-ROM & Online
- McDougal Littell Assessment System
- Test Generator CD
- Media*Smart* DVD-ROM

 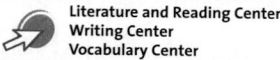
LITERARY ANALYSIS	• Identify and analyze point of view
	• Analyze character traits and motivation
	• Identify different types of characters
	• Understand the methods writers use to develop characters
	• Analyze and compare characterization in a variety of texts
READING	• Make inferences and draw conclusions
	• Make generalizations
	• Monitor strategies while reading
	• Recognize main ideas and supporting details
	• Interpret graphic aids
WRITING AND GRAMMAR	• Write a compare-and-contrast essay; cite evidence
	• Use supporting and descriptive details; use precise adjectives
	• Vary sentence beginnings by using phrases and clauses
SPEAKING, LISTENING, AND VIEWING	• Create and present a power presentation
VOCABULARY	• Use knowledge of word origins to help unlock meaning
	• Determine correct usage and meaning of multiple-meaning words and specialized vocabulary
ACADEMIC VOCABULARY	• character motives • first-person point of view
	• character traits • third-person point of view (omniscient or limited)

185

Preview Unit Goals

This page provides the big picture of the skills and strategies covered in this unit. Point out that each skill strand is a different color and that throughout the unit, the skills taught within a strand match the color of that strand. Encourage students to think about their ability to use each skill or strategy as they read the page.

Suggest that students copy the Academic Vocabulary terms in their journals and define them in their own words as they work through the unit. Encourage students to use these words in their discussion of the selections and in their writing.

ADDITIONAL UNIT GOALS

These skills will be taught in this unit but are not the major focus of the unit:

Literary Analysis
• Analyze speaker
• Genre study: short story, autobiography, magazine article, newspaper article, poetry, biography

Reading
• Set a purpose for reading
• Use strategies for reading poetry
• Analyze the speaker in a poem
• Analyze perspectives
• Compare and contrast

Writing and Grammar
• Use pronouns and articles correctly
• Use repetition to add emphasis

Vocabulary
• Understand specialized vocabulary
• Understand the etymology of a word in a dictionary entry

DIFFERENTIATED INSTRUCTION

FOR ENGLISH LEARNERS

Academic Vocabulary Use the copy master to help students learn the Academic Vocabulary listed on this page.

1. Read aloud each term. Have students find it on their copy master.

2. Discuss the meanings or examples shown, and complete the chart as a class.

3. Have students work in small groups to complete the remaining activities.

Additional Academic Vocabulary Use the copy master to help students learn academic words they will use in subsequent lessons and on the Assessment Practice. Follow the same procedure as for the Academic Vocabulary copy master.

 RESOURCE MANAGER—Copy Masters
   Academic Vocabulary p. 9
   Additional Academic Vocabulary p. 10

Focus and Motivate

OBJECTIVES

- identify and analyze character traits
- identify and analyze point of view
- analyze character motivation

Teach

Part 1: Point of View

Point of View Explain that point of view influences how a story is told. Have students imagine that a bank robbery has taken place in their town. Then discuss how each of these participants or onlookers might retell the event:

- the robber
- the driver of the getaway car
- a bank employee who faced the robber
- a customer who witnessed the robbery
- a police officer who pursued the robber
- a local newspaper reporter

Point out that details of the story would vary according to the point of view of the narrator. Ask students which persons might be expected to know the most and the least about the robbery. Then discuss whose point of view might be more emotional or biased and whose might be more objective.

 BEST PRACTICES TOOLKIT—Transparency
Analysis Frame: Character pp. D21, D26

Character and Point of View

When you read a book or watch a movie, you become involved on an emotional level with the characters. Like real people, characters can win your sympathy, make your blood boil with anger, get on your nerves, or give you insights into human nature. By asking some pointed questions, you can better understand why you are reacting the way you are. For example, through whose eyes are you experiencing events? Which details are shaping your impression of each character?

Part 1: Point of View

The perspective from which a story is told is called **point of view.** Think of point of view as the lens that a writer chooses for his or her readers to look through. Point of view determines what you learn about the characters and may influence how you feel about them. It also affects the choice of the **narrator**—the voice that tells the story. Knowing a story's point of view can help you evaluate the details you receive about characters and events.

FIRST-PERSON POINT OF VIEW	THIRD-PERSON POINT OF VIEW
The Narrator 	**The Narrator**
• is a main or minor character in the story	• is not a character in the story
• refers to himself or herself as *I* or *me*	• may not be an identifiable person but merely a voice that tells the story
• presents his or her own thoughts and feelings	• is called **omniscient** if he or she knows the thoughts and feelings of all the characters
• does not have direct access to the thoughts and feelings of other characters	• is called **limited** if he or she focuses on the thoughts and feelings of one character
▼	▼
Impact on the Reader	**Impact on the Reader**
• Your understanding of characters and events is limited to what this narrator reveals about them.	• You are likely to learn more about characters and events than if the story were told by a first-person narrator.
• You can't necessarily trust the narrator's interpretation of events.	• You might not feel as connected to the characters because the story is told in a less personal way.
• The story seems real, almost as if the narrator were talking to you.	

DIFFERENTIATED INSTRUCTION

For general guidelines on differentiating instruction, see

 BEST PRACTICES TOOLKIT
Differentiated Instruction pp. 31–38

FOR LESS–PROFICIENT READERS

Note Taking For students who need help with note taking, hand out the note-taking copy master before discussing the page. Have students read the first paragraph under

Part 1. As you discuss the paragraph, model finding and recording the first answer.

Illustrate Scene To understand the perceptions of the narrator in Model 1, have students work in pairs to illustrate the room and label its contents. Then have students list the narrator's perceptions in order, using the pronoun *I.*

 RESOURCE MANAGER—Copy Master
Note Taking p. 15

MODEL 1: FIRST-PERSON POINT OF VIEW

A first-person narrator allows you to experience events from his or her perspective. Even though you are getting only one view of the action, you often feel as though you are right at the scene. As you read this excerpt, consider how the boy's thoughts affect the way you picture the room.

from
GREAT EXPECTATIONS
Novel by **Charles Dickens**

. . . I was half afraid. However, the only thing to be done being to knock at the door, I knocked, and was told from within to enter. I entered, therefore, and found myself in a pretty large room, well lighted with wax candles. No glimpse of daylight was to be seen in it. It was a dressing-room, as I supposed
5 from the furniture, though much of it was of forms and uses then quite unknown to me. But prominent in it was a draped table with a gilded looking-glass, and that I made out at first to be a fine lady's dressing-table.
Whether I should have made out this object so soon, if there had been no fine lady sitting at it, I cannot say. In an arm-chair, with an elbow resting on
10 the table and her head leaning on that hand, sat the strangest lady I have ever seen, or shall ever see.

Close Read

1. How does the first-person point of view influence the way you visualize this scene?

2. How do you think this scene would be different if the lady were the narrator?

MODEL 2: THIRD-PERSON POINT OF VIEW

In a story told from the third-person point of view, an outside narrator tells you about the story's characters and events. As you read this excerpt, think about whether the character would describe himself in the same way the third-person narrator does.

from
The Chocolate War
Novel by **Robert Cormier**

The Goober was beautiful when he ran. His long arms and legs moved flowingly and flawlessly, his body floating as if his feet weren't touching the ground. When he ran, he forgot about his acne and his awkwardness and the shyness that paralyzed him when a girl looked his way. Even his thoughts
5 became sharper, and things were simple and uncomplicated—he could solve math problems when he ran or memorize football play patterns. Often he rose early in the morning, before anyone else, and poured himself liquid through the sunrise streets, and everything seemed beautiful, everything in its proper orbit, nothing impossible, the entire world attainable.

Close Read

1. Find an example of a direct comment about the Goober. Then find an example in which the narrator allows you to "see" his thoughts. An example of each has been boxed.

2. Identify a sentence that the Goober probably would not have used to describe himself and his running.

LITERARY ANALYSIS WORKSHOP **187**

MODEL 1: FIRST-PERSON POINT OF VIEW

Close Read

1. *Possible answer: You are seeing everything through the boy's eyes and experiencing the eerie scene as he is experiencing it. His fear (line 1) probably influences his perception and description of the scene.*

2. *Possible answer: If you were seeing the scene through the woman's eyes, you might learn her thoughts and feelings about being interrupted by a strange boy at the door. Also, since the woman is in familiar surroundings, she would probably not describe its details as strange or eerie.*

MODEL 2: THIRD-PERSON POINT OF VIEW

Close Read

1. *Possible answer: Direct comment: "His long arms and legs moved flowingly and flawlessly" (lines 1–2). Narrator allows you to see Goober's thoughts: "He could solve math problems when he ran" (lines 5–6).*

   If students need help . . . Have students compare the two boxed examples. Note that the first boxed example is a comment, and the second uses the verb *forgot* to signal inner thoughts and feelings.

2. *Possible answer: The Goober probably wouldn't have written the first sentence to describe himself: "The Goober was beautiful when he ran."*

FOR LESS–PROFICIENT READERS

Comprehension: Story Elements Write these story elements on the board and have students identify them by analyzing the first three sentences of the excerpt from *Great Expectations:*

Narrator: *a boy*
Main Character: *the narrator*
Setting: *large, candle-lit room*
Other Characters: *a woman in the room*

FOR ADVANCED LEARNERS/PRE–AP

Analyze Point of View Have students read the workshop independently. Assign previously read selections to individuals. Direct students to identify and describe the points of view of the narrators in their assigned selections and to tell how these points of view affect what the reader learns.

Teach

Part 2: Character Traits and Motivation

Character Traits Before reading the page, write the word *traits* on the board and record students' ideas about possible meanings. Then ask students to recall memorable characters from selections they have read and to describe the characters' traits—what the characters were like.

Explain that an author may directly identify a character's traits but that most characterization is indirect. The author reveals characters through methods, such as appearance, words, thoughts, actions, and other characters' thoughts and actions.

Methods of Characterization After discussing the chart with students, read each example and have students identify the method.

- She arrived in a crisp white T-shirt and pressed jeans. *physical appearance*
- Alberto spoke in a booming voice accompanied by dramatic gestures. *speech, thoughts, and actions*
- Jenny had a multitude of friends in her orbit, all of them vying for her time. *other characters*

Invite volunteers to generate their own sample sentences or phrases, and have the class identify the method.

CHECK UNDERSTANDING

Have students name three or more character traits.

Part 2: Character Traits and Motivation

As a story develops, you might wonder why the characters act the way they do, question their choices, and feel satisfied when they learn from their mistakes. By analyzing characters' traits and motivations, you can develop a complete picture of the characters you meet and understand your reactions to them.

CHARACTER TRAITS

You have probably encountered characters who are athletic, shy, arrogant, or wise—words you might also use to describe people in your life. These words are descriptions of **character traits,** or qualities shown by characters. Sometimes a narrator directly identifies a character's traits, but more often, traits are revealed through indirect methods of characterization. This means that a writer *shows* you a character without telling you what kind of person he or she is. Using the clues in the text, you must form your own impression.

METHODS OF CHARACTERIZATION	EXAMPLES
1. PHYSICAL APPEARANCE Descriptions of the character's • clothing • physical characteristics • body language and facial expressions • gestures or mannerisms	• A character who usually wears unmatched socks and stained shirts might be described as **slovenly.** • If a character is always smiling and making eye contact with others, you might infer that she is **warm** or **friendly.**
2. SPEECH, THOUGHTS, AND ACTIONS  Presentation of the character's • speech patterns • habits • tastes • talents and abilities • interaction with others	• A character who speaks so quietly that others can't hear might be described as **timid.** • You might infer that a character who repeatedly misses softball practice without telling the coach is **irresponsible** or **unreliable.**
3. OTHER CHARACTERS Presentation of other characters' • reactions to the character • relationships with the character • impression of the character's reputation	• If a character's girlfriend describes him as a "no-good lying jerk," you might infer that he is **insensitive** and **dishonest.** • If people often confide their troubles to a character, you might conclude that she is **trustworthy.**

DIFFERENTIATED INSTRUCTION

FOR LESS-PROFICIENT READERS

Note Taking For those students who need help, hand out the note-taking copy master for page 188. Read this page. Assist students in completing the copy master as needed.

 RESOURCE MANAGER—Copy Master
Note Taking p. 16

FOR ENGLISH LEARNERS

Classification Chart Use a Classification Chart to show the difference between direct and indirect characterization. Label the first column *Direct* and the second column *Indirect*. In the first column, write "tells traits." In the second column, list "appearances"; "speech, thoughts, and actions"; and "other characters." Have students summarize the diagram.

 BEST PRACTICES TOOLKIT—Transparency
Classification Chart p. B17

MODEL 1: PHYSICAL APPEARANCE

Whether it is accurate or not, your first impression of a character may be based solely on his or her appearance. As you read this excerpt, consider how the narrator's description of her unique wardrobe affects your impression of her. How would you describe the narrator to others?

from Life Without **Go-Go** Boots

Personal essay by **Barbara Kingsolver**

. . . In fifth grade, when girls were wearing straight shifts with buttons down the front, I wore pastel shirtwaists with cap sleeves and a multitude of built-in petticoats. My black lace-up oxfords, which my parents perceived to have orthopedic value, carried their own weight in the spectacle. I suspected people
5 noticed, and I knew it for sure on the day Billy Stamps announced to the lunch line: "Make way for the Bride of Frankenstein."

Close Read

1. What do you learn about the narrator's traits from her own description of how she dresses? Find two details that reveal these traits.

2. Identify one trait that is revealed through Billy Stamps's reaction to the narrator.

MODEL 2: SPEECH, THOUGHTS, AND ACTIONS

In this excerpt from the novel *To Kill a Mockingbird,* the writer creates a distinct portrait of Miss Maudie by showing her in action. As you read, think about how the writer reveals Miss Maudie's personality.

from To Kill a Mockingbird

Novel by **Harper Lee**

Miss Maudie hated her house: time spent indoors was time wasted. She was a widow, a chameleon lady who worked in her flower beds in an old straw hat and men's coveralls, but after her five o'clock bath she would appear on the porch and reign over the street in magisterial beauty.
5 She loved everything that grew in God's earth, even the weeds. With one exception. If she found a blade of nut grass in her yard it was like the Second Battle of the Marne: she swooped down upon it with a tin tub and subjected it to blasts from beneath with a poisonous substance she said was so powerful it'd kill us all if we didn't stand out of the way.

Close Read

1. What do you learn about Miss Maudie in this excerpt? Describe her as completely as you can.

2. Miss Maudie is both elegant and energetic. Which details in the text reveal these traits? One has been boxed.

MODEL 1: PHYSICAL APPEARANCE

BACKGROUND

Go-go boots were popular in the 1960s, the time period described in Kingsolver's essay. These white, tight-fitting, calf-high boots were worn by dancers on afternoon discotheque shows on television and were quickly adopted by teenagers. These boots are in stark contrast to the black lace-up oxfords worn by the narrator.

Close Read

1. *Possible answer: The narrator was probably unpopular and embarrassed by her wardrobe, which was very different from that of the other girls. Details that reveal these traits: "when girls were wearing . . . I wore . . . ." Her self-conciousness and embarrassment are conveyed when she says that her oxfords "carried their own weight in the spectacle."*

2. *Possible answer: Billy Stamps's reaction to the narrator confirms that the narrator was considered strange by the other students and subject to their ridicule.*

MODEL 2: SPEECH, THOUGHTS, AND ACTIONS

Close Read

1. *Possible answer: Miss Maudie hates the indoors. She has two sides: the rumpled gardener (lines 2–3) and the regal lady of the neighborhood (line 4). She loves all growing things except nut grass, which she exterminates mercilessly (lines 5–8).*

2. *Possible answer: Details that reveal her elegance: "magisterial beauty" (line 4); details that reveal her energy: "time spent indoors was time wasted" (line 1); "she swooped down upon it" (line 7).*

FOR LESS–PROFICIENT READERS

Draw the Contrast To help students comprehend the passage in Model 1, have them work in pairs to illustrate what girls wore and what the narrator wore. You may need to explain terms such as *shifts, shirtwaists, cap sleeves,* and *petticoats.* Have them point out the differences between the two styles.

CHARACTER MOTIVATION

Character Motivation Use a three-column chart such as the one below to explore character motivation in a selection that students have previously read.

Action	Motivation	Clues
Scout fights at school.	A boy insults her father.	She is devoted to her father.

Close Read

1. *Possible answer: The narrator's birth filled the parents with ambition and a desire to get ahead in the world.*

2. *Possible answer: The mother was motivated by stories of historical figures who rose from poverty to greatness. She thinks that her child will have more opportunities as the son of a businessman rather than as the son of a farmer (lines 9–10).*

CHECK UNDERSTANDING

Have students think of a character in a book or film they have read or seen recently and describe the character's motivation.

Why does a character move across the country, steal money from a friend, go to war, or live alone on a mountaintop? Figuring out a character's **motivation**—the reasons behind his or her actions—is a key part of understanding the character. Love, hate, vengeance, ambition, and desperation are some of the emotions that drive characters' behavior. Sometimes a writer will directly tell you about a character's motivation, but more often you must look for details in the story that reveal the motivation. As you read any story, consider the following clues:

- the narrator's direct comments about a character's motivation

- the character's actions, thoughts, feelings, values, and interactions with other characters

- your own insights into human behavior

In the following excerpt, why does the mother persuade her husband to make some changes? As you read, use the clues in the text to uncover the mother's motivation.

from # THE EGG

Short story by **Sherwood Anderson**

It was in the spring of his thirty-fifth year that father married my mother, then a country school-teacher, and in the following spring I came wriggling and crying into the world. Something happened to the two people. They became ambitious. The American passion for getting up in the world took possession of

5 them.

It may have been that mother was responsible. Being a school-teacher she had no doubt read books and magazines. She had, I presume, read of how Garfield, Lincoln, and other Americans rose from poverty to fame and greatness, and as I lay beside her . . . she may have dreamed that I would some day rule men and

10 cities. At any rate she induced father to give up his place as a farmhand, sell his horse, and embark on an independent enterprise of his own. . . . For herself she wanted nothing. For father and myself she was incurably ambitious.

Close Read

1. How does the narrator's birth change his parents?

2. Reread the boxed text. What does it tell you about the mother's motivation for convincing her husband to give up farming?

DIFFERENTIATED INSTRUCTION

FOR LESS–PROFICIENT READERS

Vocabulary Support Introduce these terms from "The Egg." Have students read the context for each word and suggest a synonym to replace it:

- *presume* (line 7), "assume," "guess"
- *induced* (line 10), "caused"
- *embark on* (line 11), "begin," "start"
- *enterprise* (line 11), "business," "undertaking"
- *incurably* (line 12), "hopelessly"

Concept Support To help students gain familiarity with the terms *motivate* and *motivation,* list the following emotions and situations on the board:

- greed
- love of family
- being fired from a job
- peer pressure

Explain that each emotion or situation might motivate or cause a character to say or do

something. Have students suggest an action or word for each motivation.

Part 3: Analyze the Literature

Use what you've just learned about point of view, character traits, and motivation to analyze this excerpt from a novel about Hana, a Japanese woman who comes to the United States in the early 20th century. In the excerpt, some neighbors visit the new home of Hana and her husband, Taro. As you read, notice how the writer reveals Hana's and Taro's personalities. How does the choice of the narrator affect your understanding of the scene?

from Picture *Bride*
Novel by **Yoshiko Uchida**

The men glanced around the living room which Hana had taken great pains to decorate properly. A new flowered rug lay on the floor, and fresh white curtains that Kiku had helped Hana sew hung at the windows. The first tight buds of the flowering peach in their yard had begun to swell, and knowing
5 there would be callers, Hana had arranged a spray on the mantel.

"We'll come right to the point," a tall red-headed man said without bothering to sit down. "There've been some complaints from the neighborhood about having Japanese on this block."

Taro caught his breath. "I see. Can you tell me who it was that
10 complained?"

"Just some of the neighbors."

"What is it we have done to offend them?"

"Well, nothing specific."

Taro looked at each of the men in turn and tried to keep his voice steady.
15 "Gentlemen," he began. "My wife and I looked many, many months to find a home where we might raise our daughter. When the owner said there would be no objection to our moving in here, we trusted him. It was a dream come true for us. We have already spent much time and money to make this house our home. And now, you would ask us to leave?"
20 Taro dared not stop before he finished all he wanted to say. "I should like to meet those neighbors who object to us," he said. "Is it any of you gentlemen?"

The men looked uncomfortable. "We're just here to represent them."

"Then please invite them to come talk to me. If they can tell me why we aren't desirable or why we do not deserve their respect, I shall consider their
25 request. I am the proprietor of Takeda Dry Goods and Grocers on Seventh Street and I would be happy to have them visit my shop as well."

The men glanced uneasily at one another and had nothing more to say.

Close Read

1. From which point of view is this story told? Explain how you know.

2. What do you learn about Hana's traits from the description of the room in lines 1–5?

3. What kind of people are the men in Taro's and Hana's home? Find two details that reveal their traits. An example has been boxed.

4. Reread lines 14–19 and 23–26. What is Taro's motivation for bravely speaking his mind? Explain what his words tell you about his character.

5. How would the story be different if Taro were the narrator?

Practice and Apply

Part 3: Analyze the Literature
Close Read

1. **Possible answer:** *The story is told from the third-person omniscient point of view: the narrator is not a character in the story; the reader knows the thoughts of Taro, Hana, and, arguably, the men.*

2. **Possible answer:** *Hana is meticulous, enjoys decorating her home, takes pride in it, and is eager to impress visitors.*

3. **Possible answer:** *The men are rude, disrespectful, abrupt, prejudiced, possibly unable to be direct about their own issues, and unprepared for a confrontation. Supporting details: lines 6–8, 22, and 27.*

4. **Possible answer:** *Taro is motivated by the wish to stay in his home and by pride. Also, he was assured that he would have no problems moving into this neighborhood. He is proud, straightforward, hardworking, and frustrated by the situation.*

5. **Possible answer:** *If Taro were the narrator, readers might learn more about his inner reactions to the men's entering his house and gain insight into his thoughts and feelings about the men's request.*

Assess and Reteach

Assess

Have students identify what motivates the main characters in *Picture Bride*. Also have them identify the narrator and reflect on what he or she knows about the characters, their thoughts, and their motivations.

Reteach

For students who are unable to apply the workshop skills to the excerpt from *Picture Bride*, select from these reteaching options.

- Review the note-taking copy masters for this lesson. Have students choose one skill and explain it to a partner.

- Name a story the class has read recently. Have students identify the narrator, the point of view, and details that show the main character's traits and motivation.

FOR LESS-PROFICIENT READERS
Analysis Support: Character Traits

1. Draw a three-column chart with the heads *Taro, Hana,* and *The Men.* Write these sideheads: *Words, Actions.*

2. Have students work in pairs to list the characters' words and actions and the traits they reveal.

3. Discuss what students know about the main characters in this excerpt. Ask from whose point of view the story is told.

FOR ENGLISH LEARNERS

Vocabulary: Idioms Help students use context clues to determine the meanings of these idioms in the story:

- *great pains* (line 1), "a lot of effort"
- *come right to the point* (line 6), "speak directly"
- *caught his breath* (line 9), "stopped breathing for a second"

Focus and Motivate

OBJECTIVES

Literary Analysis
- explore the key idea of being a **perfectionist**
- analyze first-person point of view
- read a short story

Reading
- draw conclusions

Vocabulary
- build vocabulary for reading and writing
- use knowledge of the Latin word root *ben* (also an EL language objective)

Grammar and Writing
- add supporting details by using precise adjectives
- use writing to analyze literature

SUMMARY

"Pancakes" is Joan Bauer's comic account of a teenager's obsession with perfection. Jill is proud of having a system for everything and is critical of others' shortcomings. When she faces a mob of hungry customers as the sole waitress in a pancake restaurant, however, she is nearly overcome. At a critical moment, her ex-boyfriend and his parents arrive. Their offer of help teaches Jill a lesson about her priorities.

Are you a PERFECTIONIST?

Lead into the *KEY IDEA* by asking the question. After the students read the paragraph and take the quiz, have them give examples of being a **perfectionist.** Encourage them to use those examples in the *DISCUSS* activity.

Selection Resources

Pancakes
Short Story by Joan Bauer

Are you a PERFECTIONIST?

KEY IDEA The main character in "Pancakes" is a **perfectionist**—she needs everything to be perfect in order to be happy. Would you describe yourself this way? Take this true-false quiz to find out. If you answer "true" to three or more statements, you are flirting with perfectionism.

DISCUSS After you take the quiz, form a small group with two to four of your classmates to discuss the pros and cons of perfectionism. Is striving for perfection ever helpful or necessary? When might it be difficult to cope with this trait?

quiz ⊙⊙ HOW PERFECT IS TOO PERFECT?
Answer the following questions to discover if a perfectionist lurks within you.

1. I won't even attempt to do something unless I know that I will be able to do it without a mistake.
   ☐ TRUE   ○ FALSE

2. I am so competitive that my best friends won't play sports with me.
   ☐ TRUE   ○ FALSE

3. I know what I will be wearing every day for the next week.
   ☐ TRUE   ○ FALSE

4. I won't eat food unless it's prepared exactly the way I like it.
   ☐ TRUE   ○ FALSE

5. I can't sleep unless my CDs are correctly categorized and in alphabetical order.
   ☐ TRUE   ○ FALSE

192

RESOURCE MANAGER UNIT 2

Plan and Teach pp. 17–24

Literary Analysis
Summary pp. 25†*, 26‡*
First-Person Point of View
    pp. 27, 28†*
Question Support p. 35*

Reading
Draw Conclusions pp. 29, 30†*
Reading Check p. 34

Vocabulary
Study p. 31*
Practice p. 32
Strategy p. 33

Grammar and Writing
Add Supporting Details p. 37

Assessment
Selection Tests A, B/C pp. 39*, 41*
    Test Generator CD

BEST PRACTICES TOOLKIT

Differentiated Instruction
    pp. 31–38*

Scaffolding Instruction
    pp. 43–46*

Graphic Organizers/Strategies
Definition Mapping • Two-Column Chart • Analysis Frame: Character • New Word Analysis • Problem and Solution Charts • Character Traits Web • Open Mind

Reading Support
    Audio Anthology CD*

Technology
    Literature and Vocabulary Centers at **ClassZone.com**
    Write*Smart* CD

---

* Resources for Differentiation   † Also in Spanish   ‡ In Haitian Creole and Vietnamese

LITERARY ANALYSIS: FIRST-PERSON POINT OF VIEW

"Pancakes" is told from a **first-person point of view.** Jill, the narrator, is a character in the story, and she describes events as she herself experiences them. You will see the other characters and the actions in the story through Jill's eyes and learn exactly what she thinks and how she feels. As you read "Pancakes," look for comments that reveal Jill's feelings about her life and help explain the causes of her perfectionism.

Review: **Character Traits**

READING SKILL: DRAW CONCLUSIONS

After reading a story, you often add up the details you've read about and develop your own ideas about what they mean. This process is called **drawing conclusions.** A conclusion is a logical judgment that a reader makes. In order to be logical, a conclusion must be based on

- evidence from the text
- your own experience and knowledge

As you read "Pancakes," use a chart like the one shown to record important details about Jill's thoughts, actions, and relationships. Include your own ideas of what these details reveal about Jill.

Details About Jill	My Thoughts
She refers to her mother as "Ms. Subtlety" after her mother tapes an article on perfectionism to Jill's mirror.	Jill is being sarcastic. She might feel her mother is picking on her.

After reading, you can use the information you've gathered to draw conclusions about Jill's perfectionism.

Review: **Predict**

▲ VOCABULARY IN CONTEXT

Joan Bauer makes use of the following boldfaced words to tell this amusing story. Try to figure out the meaning of each word from the context of the phrase given.

1. mustard and other **condiments**
2. a **degenerate** with no morals
3. the **benign** climate of Hawaii
4. ill-behaved and **crass**
5. **steel** yourself against insults
6. **rabid** with anger

Author Online

Joan Bauer
born 1951

Comic Relief From a very young age, Joan Bauer knew she wanted to have a career making people laugh. She remembers having an early fascination with things that were funny—especially the stories told to her by her grandmother, whom she calls her greatest creative influence. Bauer often crafts characters who share the same anxieties she felt as a teenager—apprehension about her parents' divorce, worry about her appearance—and chronicles the relief and inspiration that humor can bring to adverse situations. Describing her motivation to write, Bauer says, "I want to create stories that link life's struggles with laughter."

Accidents and Accolades Bauer's first novel, *Squashed,* began as a screenplay. When she suffered severe injuries in a car accident, however, she found herself unable to meet the tight schedule the film industry demanded. During her long recovery, she turned her screenplay into a prize-winning novel. "The humor in that story kept me going," Bauer explains.

> **MORE ABOUT THE AUTHOR**
> For more on Joan Bauer, visit the **Literature Center at ClassZone.com.**

Background

Writing from Experience Like Jill in "Pancakes," Bauer, as a teenager, waited tables in a pancake restaurant. She vividly remembers the Sunday morning when she was the only waitress on duty, frantically trying to attend to all her customers. The memory still haunts her: "I remember the sheer terror of dozens of hungry people looking to me and me alone for breakfast. To this day, whenever I walk into a pancake house, I hyperventilate."

Teach

STANDARDS FOCUS

LITERARY ANALYSIS

● FIRST-PERSON POINT OF VIEW

To support instruction, read aloud this passage:

> I sat at my desk, surrounded by my new classmates, and smiled. I knew that everyone would like me.

Ask students what this passage reveals about the narrator's feelings. *Possible answer: She is confident that she will make new friends.*

CHECK UNDERSTANDING Ask students to name stories that they have read with a first-person point of view and to tell what they recall about the narrator.

READING SKILL

◙ DRAW CONCLUSIONS

Use the text under **Comic Relief** to model drawing conclusions.

1. The author wants to make people laugh.
2. From experience, I know that humor often helps people cope with problems.
3. I conclude that the humor in "Pancakes" helps students see problems in perspective.

CHECK UNDERSTANDING After students read **Accidents and Accolades,** ask what conclusion they can draw about Bauer's need to use humor in her stories.

> **RESOURCE MANAGER—Copy Master**
> Draw Conclusions p. 29 (for student use while reading the selection)

VOCABULARY SKILL

▲ VOCABULARY IN CONTEXT

DIAGNOSE WORD KNOWLEDGE To determine preteaching needs, have all students complete Vocabulary in Context. *Possible answers:*
1. *substances that add flavor to food;* 2. *person having an evil, unwholesome character;*
3. *favorable, mild;* 4. *crude or unruly;*
5. *to make strong like steel;* 6. *furious, raging*

PRETEACH VOCABULARY Use the Vocabulary Study copy master to help students create a word map for each boldfaced word in the copy master.

1. Read the first phrase in Part A aloud.
2. Guide students in creating a word map like the one shown. Use the sidenotes in the pupil edition as the source for definitions.
3. Repeat the procedure for each of the other five phrases.

 RESOURCE MANAGER—Copy Master
Vocabulary Study p. 31

For general guidelines on differentiating vocabulary instruction and for alternative vocabulary activities for students not needing vocabulary preteaching, see

 BEST PRACTICES TOOLKIT
Scaffolding Vocabulary Instruction pp. 43–46
 Vocabulary Center at **ClassZone.com**

Practice and Apply

ANALYZE VISUALS

Possible answer: The blurry background of a restaurant and the fuzzy image of a waitress carrying a loaded food tray convey a feeling of urgency, characterized by quick movements and a hectic pace.

About the Art The photographer titled this composition *Speedy Service at Diner.* Focusing on the waitress in the foreground while using a slow shutter speed makes the background blurry and gives the photograph a feeling of rapid movement. The mood of the photograph matches the narrator's upcoming description of a busy pancake restaurant (starting at line 105).

READING SKILL

A DRAW CONCLUSIONS

Possible answer: Jill is self-confident and has a strong self-image. She boasts that she looks spectacular in the shirt because its color complements her hair and eyes (lines 23–25).

If students need help . . . Have students add their thoughts about these prior details to the chart that they began on page 193:

- comments about Allen (lines 6–8)
- interaction with the mirror (lines 8–11)

Discuss how their responses establish a strong self-image for Jill from the start.

Extend the Discussion Find some examples on this page of Jill's tendency to exaggerate. How do the exaggerations add to your impression of her self-image?

Pancakes

JOAN BAUER

> The last thing I wanted to see taped to my bathroom mirror at five-thirty in the morning was a newspaper article entitled "Are You a Perfectionist?" But there it was, courtesy of my mother, Ms. Subtlety herself. I was instantly irritated because Allen Feinman had accused me of perfectionism when he broke up with me last month. The term he used was "**rabid** perfectionism," which I felt was a bit much—but then Allen Feinman had no grip on reality whatsoever. He was rabidly unaware, if the truth be known, like a **benign** space creature visiting Earth with no interest in going native. I tore the article off the mirror; this left tape smudges. Dirty mirrors drove me crazy. I grabbed
> 10 the bottle of Windex from the closet and cleaned off the gook until the mirror shined, freed of yellow journalism.[1]

I glowered at the six telltale perfectionist signs in the now crumpled article.

1. Do you have a driving need to control your environment?
2. Do you have a driving need to control the environment of others?
3. Are you miserable when things are out of place?
4. Are your expectations of yourself and others rarely met?
5. Do you believe if something is to be done right, only you are the one to do it?
6. Do you often worry about your performance when it is less
20 than perfect?

Number six had particular sting, for it was that very thing that Allen Feinman had accused me of the day he asked for his green and black lumberjack shirt back, a truly spectacular shirt that looked a lot more spectacular on me than it did on him because it brought out the intensity of my short black hair and my mysterious brown eyes. He had accused me **A** of numbers one through five as well, but on this last fateful day he said, "The problem with you, Jill, is that if the least little thing goes wrong, you

---

1. **yellow journalism:** journalism that exploits or exaggerates the news to create sensations and attract readers.

194 UNIT 2: CHARACTERIZATION AND POINT OF VIEW

① Targeted Passage
ANALYZE VISUALS
What qualities of this photograph convey the fast-paced atmosphere of a busy restaurant? Explain how these qualities work together to convey a specific **mood**, or feeling.

rabid (răb′ĭd) *adj.* uncontrollable; fanatical

benign (bĭ-nīn′) *adj.* good; kindly

A DRAW CONCLUSIONS
Reread lines 21–25 to draw a conclusion about the narrator's sense of self. Do you think Jill has a strong or a weak self-image? Record your answer in your chart.

DIFFERENTIATED INSTRUCTION

FOR ALL STUDENTS
Journal As they read, ask students to keep a journal noting questions, observations, and reflections about characters and situations. Ask students to refer to their notes when completing other activities that accompany the selection.

FOR LESS–PROFICIENT READERS
In combination with the *Audio Anthology CD,* use one or more Targeted Passages (pp. 194, 196, 201, 202) to ensure that students focus on key story events, concepts, and skills. Targeted Passages are also good for English learners.

① Targeted Passage [Lines 1–11]
This passage introduces Jill, the first-person narrator of the story, and reveals her strongest personality trait: her perfectionism.

BACKGROUND

Teens at Work According to U.S. Department of Labor Statistics, youth employment in America is booming. An estimated 5.9 million young people between the ages of 16 and 19 have jobs. Today, two-thirds of American high school students have jobs. The percentage of youths who work increases with age, and the type of work changes—from freelance work such as mowing lawns and babysitting for 13- and 14-year-olds to retail trade and service jobs for 15- to 17-year-olds. Some 62 percent of youths in that older group are employed during the school months in the retail trade industry. Older male and female youths are equally likely to work in the restaurant trade, with boys employed primarily as cooks and busboys and girls as waitresses and cashiers. In "Pancakes," Jill opens the restaurant on weekends—an unusual responsibility for someone so young.

Cultural Connection Various forms of pancakes, a batter cake fried with oil or butter, are found in cultures around the world. Examples include French *crêpes,* Ethiopian *injire,* Egyptian *katief,* and the Russian *blintz.* In Britain, "Pancake Races" are held in which participants must toss pancakes in a frying pan while they run. Invite students to share examples of pancakes they are familiar with.

- What does Jill find taped to her mirror? Why is she displeased about it?
- What does she call her mother?
- Who is Allen? Why is Jill irritated with him?
- What does she do to the mirror? Why?

FOR ENGLISH LEARNERS

Key Academic Vocabulary Use Definition Mapping to teach these words: *environment* (line 13), *consumed* (line 66), *anticipate* (line 93), *challenge* (line 143), *ultimate* (line 303).

 BEST PRACTICES TOOLKIT—Transparency
Definition Mapping p. E6

Prereading For prereading instruction for English learners, see

 BEST PRACTICES TOOLKIT
Scaffolding Reading Instruction pp. 43–46

FOR ADVANCED LEARNERS/PRE–AP

Pre-AP Exercises in the bottom channel provide additional challenge for students. Use these suggestions for small groups or individuals.

ADDITIONAL GUIDELINES

For more help with differentiation and tips for classroom management, see

 BEST PRACTICES TOOLKIT
Differentiated Instruction pp. 31–38

B CHARACTER TRAITS

Possible answer: *Her irritation with anything out of place, having and using a spot remover kit, and her expectation that Allen would have appreciated her planning and organization illustrate her obsession with perfection.*

If students need help . . . Have students use a chart to match Jill's actions in lines 38–45 with the "telltale perfectionist signs" in lines 13–20.

Jill's Actions	Perfectionist Signs
uses spot remover kit	miserable with disorder
fluffs pillows; removes spot, plucks dead leaf	needs to control environment
offered to organize Allen's CD collection	needs to control others

 BEST PRACTICES TOOLKIT—Transparency
Two-Column Chart p. A25

C GRAMMAR AND STYLE

Analyze Supporting Details Discuss how *short clipped* hair (line 56) and *just-manicured* nail (line 57) suggest Jill's obsession for meticulous detail. Then ask students to read Mr. Halloran's statement in lines 55–56 and comment on what the precise adjectives *organized* and *competent* suggest about his view of Jill's personality. Encourage students to find other examples of precise adjectives in the story and discuss their effectiveness.

---

can't handle it. Everything has to follow this impossible path to perfection. Someone, and I hope it's soon for your sake, you're going to have to settle for
30 sub-par performance and realize that you're imperfect like the rest of us." He stormed off like an angry prophet who had just delivered a curse, muttering that if I was like this at seventeen, imagine what I would be like at thirty.

"Good riddance," I shouted. "I hope you find a messy, inconsiderate girlfriend who can never find her purse or her car keys, who has no sense of time, no aptitude for *planning*, and that you spend the rest of your adolescent years on your hands and knees looking for your contacts!"

I padded down the hall to my bedroom. It was Sunday morning. I was due at my waitress job at the Ye Olde Pancake House in forty-five minutes. I sat on my white down quilt, saw the chocolate smudge, quick got up and brushed the
40 smudge with my spot remover kit that I kept in my top dresser drawer, being careful to brush the nap against the grain. I put the kit back in the drawer, refluffed my two white pillows, plucked a dead leaf off my philodendron plant, and remembered my second to last fight with Allen when he went completely ballistic at my selfless offer to alphabetize his CD collection with a color-coded cross-reference guide by subject, title, and artist. **B**

Males.

I put on my Ye Olde Pancake House waitress uniform that I had ironed and starched the night before: blue, long-sleeved ankle-length dress, white apron, white-and-blue flowered bonnet. I could have done without the bonnet, but
50 when you're going for the ye olde look, you have to sacrifice style. I was lucky to have this job. I got it one week after my parents and I moved to town, got hired *because* I am a person of order who knows there is a right way and a wrong way to do things. I replaced a waitress who was a complete disorganized slob. As Howard Halloran, the owner of the Ye Olde Pancake House, said to me, "Jill, if you're half as organized and competent as you look, I will die happy." I smoothed back my short clipped hair, flicked a sesame seed off my just-manicured nail, and told him that I was. **C**

"I have a system for everything," I assured him. "Menu first, bring water when you come back to take the order, call it in, bring coffee immediately to
60 follow. Don't ever let customers wait." Then I mentioned my keen knack for alphabetizing **condiments,** which was always a bonus, particularly when things got busy, and how a restaurant storage closet should be properly organized to take full advantage of the space.

"You're hired," Howard Halloran said reverently, and put me in charge of opening and setting up the restaurant on Saturday and Sunday mornings, which is when nine-tenths of all pancakes in the universe are consumed and you don't want some systemless person at the helm. You want a waitress of grit with a strategic battle plan that never wavers. Sunday morning in a pancake house is war.

I tied my white apron in a perfect bow across my back, tiptoed past my
70 parents' bedroom, taking care not to wake them, even though my mother had taken an insensitive potshot at me without provocation.

It's not like my life had been all that perfect.

196 UNIT 2: CHARACTERIZATION AND POINT OF VIEW

B CHARACTER TRAITS Both the narrator's mother and her former boyfriend have accused her of perfectionism. In what ways do Jill's own actions and emotions illustrate this character trait?

2 Targeted Passage

C GRAMMAR AND STYLE Reread lines 47–57. Bauer's use of the **precise adjectives** *short, clipped,* and *just-manicured* provide insight into Jill's personality.

condiment (kŏn′də-mənt) *n.* a sauce, relish, or spice used to season food

---

DIFFERENTIATED INSTRUCTION

FOR LESS—PROFICIENT READERS

2 Targeted Passage [Lines 50–68]

This passage not only shows how Jill got the job of which she is so proud but also underscores her perfectionism.

- What does Jill say about the person who used to have her job?
- What does Jill tell Mr. Halloran about her abilities and skills?
- What special task does he give her? How does she feel about this responsibility?

FOR ADVANCED LEARNERS/PRE–AP

In-Depth Textual Analysis [small-group option] Have students use the Analyzing Character part of the Analysis Frame to explore the way in which Jill responds to and is changed by her challenge in "Pancakes." Urge students to note relevant story details and to use those details as they discuss the story.

 BEST PRACTICES TOOLKIT—Transparency
Analysis Frame: Character pp. D21, D26

Did I ask to move three times in eighteen months because my father kept getting transferred? Did I ask to attend three high schools since sophomore year? Did I complain about being unfairly uprooted?

Well . . . I did complain a little. . . .

Didn't I figure out a way to handle the pressure? When my very roots were being yanked from familiar soil, I became orderly and organized. I did things in the new towns so that people would like me and want to hire me, would
80 want to be my friends. I baked world-class cookies for high school bake sales, even if it meant staying up till three A.M.; I joined clubs and volunteered for the grunge jobs that no one wanted; I always turned in a spectacular performance and people counted on me to do it. I made everything look easy. People looked up to me, or down, depending—I'm five four. And I sure didn't feel like defending all that success before dawn! **D**

I tiptoed out the back door to my white car (ancient, yet spotless) and headed for work.

Syrup, I tried explaining to Hugo, the busboy, must be poured slowly from the huge cans into the plastic pourers on the tables because if you pour it fast, you
90 can't control the flow and you get syrup everywhere, which never really cleans up. It leaves a sticky residue that always comes back to haunt you. Syrup, I told him, is our enemy, but like Allen Feinman, Hugo was a male without vision. He couldn't anticipate disaster, couldn't cope with forethought and prevention; he let life rule him rather than the other way around, which was why *I* personally filled the syrup containers on Sunday mornings—maple, strawberry, boysenberry, and pecan. **E**

I had just filled the last containers and was putting them on the tables in horizontal rows. I had lined up the juice glasses and coffee mugs for optimal efficiency, which some people who shall remain nameless would call
100 perfectionism, but when the place gets busy, trust me, you want everything at your fingertips or you'll lose control. I never lose control. Hugo had set the back tables and I followed him, straightening the silverware. You'd think he'd been born in a barn. Andy Pappas, the cook, was making the special hash browns with onion and green pepper that people loved.

I **steeled** myself for the hungry Sunday morning mob that would descend in two hours. I always mentally prepared for situations that I knew were going to be stressful—it helped me handle them right. I could see me, Shirl, and Lucy, the other waitresses, serving the crowd, handling the cash register. Usually Howard Halloran took the money, but he was taking a long-needed
110 weekend off since his wife said if he didn't she would sell the place out from under him. I could see myself watching my station like a hawk, keeping the coffee brewing, getting the pancakes delivered hot to the tables. Do it fast, do it right—that was my specialty.

It was seven o'clock. Shirl and Lucy were late, but I knew that Lucy's baby was sick and Shirl was picking her up, so I didn't worry. They'd been late before. I myself was never late. I unlocked the front door, and a few customers

PANCAKES **197**

D POINT OF VIEW
Reread lines 72–85. How, if at all, do the thoughts and feelings of the **narrator** change your perception of her? Explain your answer.

E POINT OF VIEW
Reread lines 88–96. Think about the way Jill's point of view affects your impression of Hugo. How might this passage be different if Hugo were the narrator?

steel (stēl) *v.* to make hard or strong

D POINT OF VIEW

Possible answer: Jill's comments about trying to handle pressure and have people like her make her a more sympathetic character.

If students need help . . . Use these questions to help them better understand Jill:

- What does Jill say she does in new situations? *Possible answer:* She becomes very active, very quickly.

- What does Jill's admission in lines 78–80 suggest about her? *Possible answers:* Jill keeps busy to cover her insecurity; she has a poor view of what true friendship is all about.

Extend the Discussion Do you think that other people understand Jill's motivation? What leads you to that opinion?

E POINT OF VIEW

Possible answer: Since Jill sees Hugo as incompetent, readers may also. If Hugo were the narrator, he might explain how well he tries to do his job and what he thinks of Jill's attempts to improve him.

Extend the Discussion How do you think Hugo feels about Jill's explanations (lines 88–93)—grateful? annoyed? angry? Explain your answer.

FOR ENGLISH LEARNERS
Vocabulary: Idioms Use New Word Analysis to teach these idioms from the story: *went completely ballistic* (lines 43–44), "became extremely angry"; *world-class* (line 80), "excellent"; *dug in* (line 133), "began to eat"; *as good as dead* (lines 158–159), "certain to fail"; *on her way* (line 192), "coming"; *fall guy* (line 265), "person receiving the blame."

 BEST PRACTICES TOOLKIT—Transparency
New Word Analysis p. E8

FOR ADVANCED LEARNERS/PRE–AP
Hypothesize About Plot Jill is so proud of her efficiency that readers can guess that she is about to have it challenged in some way. Have students write a paragraph, supported by details on pages 196–197, in which they discuss specific hypotheses about (1) what that challenge will be and (2) how Jill will respond to it. Ask students to share their paragraphs with a partner.

F DRAW CONCLUSIONS

Possible answer: *Jill admires Andy for his organizational and planning skills, as she comments that "the man had total focus" (line 123).*

If students need help . . . Have students reread the paragraph. Model how to tell the difference between the facts in the paragraph (what Andy cooks and how he does it) and the one opinion that it contains (Jill's comment about Andy's "total focus").

Extend the Discussion How did Jill compliment Andy when she first spoke about him (lines 103–104)? Do you think that she sees Andy as a kindred soul—or just as a person who is somewhat less incompetent than most of the people around her?

ANALYZE VISUALS

Possible answer: *The huge numerals on the clock face and the sweeping second hand reinforce a feeling of time pressure and of time speeding by.*

Lines 153–159
REINFORCE *KEY IDEA:* PERFECTIONIST

Discuss Why does such a **perfectionist** as Jill feel threatened by the arrival of a tour bus? **Possible answers:** *She realizes that this group will push her system of organization to the limit; she knows that even with her system, she can't serve all these people by herself, and the other waitresses have not come in yet.*

---

came straggling in with their Sunday newspapers, settling into the booths. Nothing I couldn't handle. Things didn't start getting crazy until around eight-thirty. I had my system.

120   I took orders, walked quickly to the kitchen window. "Four over easy on eight with sausage," I said crisply. "Side of cakes." That was restaurant-speak for four plates of two eggs over easy with sausage and pancakes on the side. Andy tossed his spatula in the air, went to work. The man had total focus. He could have two dozen eggs cooking in front of him and he knew when to flip each one. **F**

A young family came in with three small children; gave them the big table by the window. Got them kid seats, took their order.

"Number three."

That was my waitress number. Andy called the number over the loudspeaker when my order was ready and I went and picked it up. A nice time-efficient

130   system. I walked quickly to the counter (running made the customers nervous), grabbed the eggs, sausage, and pancakes, carried them four up on my left arm to table six, smiled professionally. Everything all right here, folks? Everyone nodded happily and dug in. Everything was always merry and pleasant at the Ye Olde Pancake House. That's why people came. Merry people left big tips.

I checked the ye old wall clock. Seven forty-seven. Still no Shirl or Lucy. They'd never been this late. Allen Feinman had been more than an hour late plenty of times. Allen Feinman didn't care about time—his or anyone else's. I didn't understand the grave problems he had at first; I was so caught up in him—this cute, brainy, funny guy who really seemed to want a shot

140   of discipline. I put in my usual extra effort into the relationship—baked his favorite cookies (cappuccino chip), packed romantic picnics (French bread, brie,[2] and strawberries), thought about unusual things to do in Coldwater, Michigan, which was quite a challenge, but I went to the library and came up with a list of ten possible side trips around town that we could do for free.

"You're just so *organized*," he would say, which I thought was a true compliment. Later on, I realized, coming from him, it was the darkest insult.

Andy was flipping pancakes on the grill. I scanned my customers to make sure everyone was cared for, turned to dash into

150   the bathroom quickly when a screech of tires sounded in the parking lot. I looked out the window. A lump caught in my throat.

A large tour bus pulled to a grinding halt. I watched in horror as an army of round, middle-aged women stepped from the bus and headed toward the restaurant like hungry lionesses stalking prey.

It was natural selection—I was as good as dead.

160   "Number three."

2. **brie** (brē): a soft French cheese.

198   UNIT 2: CHARACTERIZATION AND POINT OF VIEW

F DRAW CONCLUSIONS
Think about Jill's description of Andy. Does he seem like someone Jill would admire? Cite evidence to support your conclusion.

ANALYZE VISUALS
As you examine the photograph below, think about why the photographer chose to take such an extreme close-up of the clock. What effect does this create?

DIFFERENTIATED INSTRUCTION

FOR ENGLISH LEARNERS

Vocabulary: Idioms and Sayings Point out these sayings and explain their meanings: *people who shall remain nameless* (line 99), "people whose names I will not reveal"; *he'd been born in a barn* (line 103), "he never had learned proper manners"; *watching . . . like a hawk* (line 111), "watching very carefully"; *A lump caught in my throat* (line 152), "I was frightened and upset."

FOR ADVANCED LEARNERS/PRE–AP

Evaluate Author's Choices In lines 136–146, in the middle of describing a busy Sunday morning, Jill interrupts herself to recall how she had tried to give Allen some discipline. Have pairs of students debate whether this interruption weakens the story, each student taking either the *pro* or the *con* side. Students also should discuss why they think Bauer included this interruption.

I looked at Andy, who raised his face to heaven.

"Call them," I shrieked. "Call Shirl and Lucy! Tell them to get here!"

Andy reached for the phone.

I turned to the front door as the tour bus women poured in. They were all wearing sweatshirts that read MICHIGAN WOMEN FOR A CLEANER ENVIRONMENT. "A table for sixty-six," said a woman, laughing.

My lungs collapsed. Sixty-six hungry environmentalists. I pointed to a stack of menus, remembering my personal Waitress Rule Number One: Never let a customer know you're out of control.

170   "Sit anywhere," I cooed. "I'll be right with you." **G**

"If you wrote the menu on a blackboard you wouldn't waste paper," one said.

"Number three." I raced back to the kitchen. Pancakes for table eight. I layered the plates on my left arm, plopped butter balls from the ye olde butter urn on the pancakes. Andy said he'd tried Shirl and Lucy and no one answered. At least they were on their way. I raced to table eight. The little girl took one look at her chocolate chip pancakes and burst into tears.

"They're not the little ones," she sobbed.

"Oh, now, precious," said her father, "I'm sure this nice young lady doesn't

180   want you to be disappointed."

I looked at the environmentalists who needed coffee. Life is tough, kid.

"Tell the waitress what you want, precious."

Precious looked at me, loving the control. She scrunched up her dimples, dabbed her tears, and said, "I want the teeny weeny ones, pwease."

"Teeny weeny ones coming up," I chirped, and raced to Andy. "Chocolate silver dollars for the brat on eight," I snarled. "Make them perfect, or someone dies."

"You're very attractive when you get busy," Andy said laughing.

"Shut up."

190   The phone rang. I lunged for it. It was Lucy calling from the hospital. Her baby had a bronchial infection,[3] needed medicine. She couldn't come in, but Shirl was on her way, she should be pulling onto the interstate now.

"Are you all right there, Jill?"

"Of course," I lied. "Take care of that baby. That's the most important thing."

"You're terrific," she said, and hung up.

I'm terrific, I told myself. I can handle this because, as a terrific person, I have an organized system that always works. I grabbed two coffee pots and raced to the tour group, smiling. Always smile. Poured coffee. They'd only get

200   water if they asked. We're so glad you came to see us this morning. Yes, we have many tours pass through, usually we have more waitresses, though. It's a safe bet that any restaurant on this earth has more waitresses than the Ye Olde Pancake House does at this moment. **H**

---

3. **bronchial infection:** an infection of the bronchial tubes—the tubes that connect the windpipe to the lungs.

G **DRAW CONCLUSIONS**
Consider the difference between what Jill is thinking and what she actually says. What does this indicate about her character? Explain how you came to this conclusion.

H **PREDICT**
Will Jill be able to handle the crisis at the pancake house? Make a prediction about what will happen as Jill struggles to cope with the teeming crowd of hungry customers.

G **DRAW CONCLUSIONS**

Possible answer: Jill wants people to like her and depend upon her, so she doesn't always tell the truth or say what she really thinks. You can make this conclusion based on the fact that Jill tries to do things perfectly so that people will like her (lines 78–84). We also know that she believes that a waitress must always appear to her customers to be in control (lines 168–169), and so she would never say anything that would suggest that she is feeling panicky.

If students need help . . . Call their attention to lines 133–134, where Jill describes Ye Old Pancake House as always being "merry and pleasant." Point out that this statement reveals that Jill considers it her responsibility to maintain that cheerful atmosphere, even if it means not always telling the truth.

H **PREDICT**

Possible answers: She will fail because she is overwhelmed and needs help but tries to manage on her own; she will succeed because someone (perhaps Shirl) will come to help her.

FOR LESS–PROFICIENT READERS

Solve Problems Jill has just learned that she has a problem: She must serve the early-morning breakfast crowd alone. What should she do? Using the Problem and Solution Charts, help students speculate about possible solutions to Jill's problem.

BEST PRACTICES TOOLKIT—Transparency
Problem and Solution Charts p. B20

I took their orders like a shotgunner shooting clay pigeons.
Pull!
Pigs in a blanket.
Steak and fried eggs.
Buttermilk pancakes.
Betsy Ross (buttermilks with strawberry and blueberry compote).
210   Colonial Corn Cakes (Allen Feinman's favorite).
A round-faced woman looked at me, grinning. "Everything looks so good."
She sighed. "What do you recommend?"

I recommend that you eat someplace else, ma'am, because I do not have time for this. I looked toward the front of the restaurant; six large men were waiting to be seated. Hugo was pouring syrup quickly into pourers to torture me, sloshing it everywhere. I said, "Everything's great here, ma'am. I'll give you a few seconds to decide." I turned to the woman in the next booth. The round-faced woman grabbed my arm. I don't like being touched by customers.

220   "Just a minute. Well . . . it all looks so good."
"Number three." I glared in Andy's direction. "And number three again."
A cook can make or break you.

The round-faced woman decided on buttermilk pancakes, a daring choice. I ran to the kitchen window. "Hit me," Andy said.

"I'd love to. You're only getting this once. Buttermilks on twelve. Pigs on four, Betsy's on three. Colonials on seven." I threw the rest of the orders at him.

"You have very small handwriting," he said. "That's often the sign of low self-esteem."

230   I put my hand down in one of Hugo's syrup spills, pushed back my bangs with it; felt syrup soak my scalp.

Andy said, "You're only one person, Jill."

I scanned the restaurant—juice glasses askew, hungry people waiting at dirty tables. I could do anything if I worked hard enough. Shirl would be here any minute.

"Waitress, we're out of syrup!" A man held his empty syrup container up. I looked under the counter for the extra maple syrup containers I had cleverly filled, started toward the man, tripped over an environmentalist's foot, which sent the syrup container flying, caught midair, but upside down by a
240   trucker who watched dumbly as syrup oozed onto the floor in a great, sticky glop. I lunged for the syrup container, slid on the spill, felt sugared muck coat my exposed flesh.

"Hugo!" I screamed, pointing at the disaster. "Hot water!"
"Number three."

I moved in a daze as more and more people came. Got the tour bus groups fed and out. Had they mentioned separate checks, one woman asked?
Noooooooooo . . .

---

❶ CHARACTER TRAITS
Think about Andy's character traits and what he says to Jill in line 232. Would you describe Andy as a perfectionist? Why or why not?

---

❶ CHARACTER TRAITS

Possible answer: Andy may try to do things well, but he is a realist rather than a perfectionist. His advice to Jill shows that he understands that Jill cannot handle every crisis or make everyone happy.

If students need help . . . Use the Character Traits Web to help them note Andy's skill at remembering orders, his sense of humor, and his ability to get along with people. Discuss which traits do not fit Jill.

Extend the Discussion How is the tone of Andy's comment here different from the tone of his comment to Jill in lines 228–229? Why do you think his tone has changed?

🧰 BEST PRACTICES TOOLKIT—Transparency
Character Traits Web p. D7

Lines 220–244
DISCUSSION PROMPTS

Use these prompts to help students understand Jill's increasing frustration:

Connect Have you ever felt overwhelmed by a job or task? How does that help you to understand Jill's situation? *Accept all reasonable responses.*

Analyze How do the details show that Jill is beginning to lose control? *Possible answer: Jill throws orders at Andy (lines 226–227), trips over a customer's foot (line 238), and screams at Hugo (line 243).*

Evaluate Does the humor here overshadow the ideas that Bauer is trying to communicate? Defend your answer. *Possible answer: The humor is strong, but Bauer uses it to create a situation in which the reader feels sympathy for Jill and her predicament.*

DIFFERENTIATED INSTRUCTION

FOR ENGLISH LEARNERS
Vocabulary: Multiple-Meaning Words Have groups use a dictionary and context clues to determine the correct meaning for each of these words: *driving* (line 13), *grit* (line 67), *counter* (line 130), *felt* (line 241), *coat* (line 241), *dead* (line 268), *grounds* (line 301), *missed* (line 333).

FOR LESS–PROFICIENT READERS
Support Ideas Help students locate evidence from this page that helps them realize that Jill is trying to maintain a positive attitude over the chaos in the restaurant. *Possible answer: She announces that "everything's great here" (line 216), despite the problems swirling around her.*

Made coffee. More coffee. Told
everyone I was the only waitress here,
250 if they were in a hurry, they might
want to go someplace else. But no
one left. They just kept coming,
storming through the restaurant like
Cossacks.[4] People were grabbing my
arm as I ran by.

"What's your name, babe?" asked
a lecherous man.

"*Miss*," I snarled.

"Number three."

260 "I had a life when I woke up this
morning! Everything was in place!"

Buckwheats on table three.
The man looked at them. . . . He
said, "You call these buckwheats?
Buckwheats are supposed to be enormous and hearty." I'm the fall guy for
everything that happens in the restaurant. It's my tip that's floating down the
river waving bye-bye. I embraced my personal Waitress Rule Number Two: The
customer is always right, even if they're dead wrong. I said, "That's the way we
do them here, sir," and he said he can't eat them, he can't look at them, he'll have
270 the buttermilks, not knowing the trouble he's caused me. Andy gets sensitive if
someone sends the food back—he's an artist, can't handle criticism. You have to
lie to him or he slows down. I raced back to the kitchen.

"The man's a **degenerate**," I said to Andy. "He wouldn't know a world-class
buckwheat if it jumped in his lap. He doesn't deserve to be in the presence
of your cooking."

The phone rang. I lunged for it. It's Shirl calling from someone's car phone on
the interstate with impossible news. A trailer truck had jackknifed, spilling soda
cans everywhere. There was a five-mile backup. She'd be hours getting to work.

"Are you all right?" Shirl asked.

280 I looked at the line of cars pulling into the parking lot, the tables bulging with
hungry customers, the coffee cups raised in anticipation of being filled, the line at
the cash register. I heard a woman say how the restaurant had gone downhill, and
the people were looking at me like I was their breakfast savior, like I had all the
power and knowing, like I could single-handedly make sure they were happy and
fed. And I was ashamed that I couldn't do it, but no one could. **J**

Not even me!

I tore off my ye olde bonnet. "I'm trapped in a pancake house!" I shrieked
into the phone, and, like in all sci-fi stories, the connection went dead.

"Number three."

290 I limped toward him, a shadow of my former self.

"We're out of sausage," Andy said solemnly.

---

4. **Cossacks:** a people of southern Russia, known as fierce cavalrymen.

degenerate (dĭ-jĕn'ər-ĭt)
n. a corrupt or vicious
person

J POINT OF VIEW
Reread lines 280–285.
Consider how learning
Jill's thoughts contributes
to your understanding
of her character. How
would your reaction to
Jill be different if you
didn't know what Jill was
thinking and feeling?

③ Targeted Passage

Lines 287–290
REINFORCE *KEY IDEA*:
PERFECTIONIST

Discuss How does the image of Jill tearing
off her bonnet, shrieking into the telephone,
and limping toward Andy suggest a change in
her **perfectionist** self-image? *Possible answer:*
*The image is a dramatic outward sign that she
is losing control—that her "system" has been
overwhelmed and is failing her.*

LITERARY ANALYSIS

J POINT OF VIEW

*Possible answer: Up to this moment, Jill
appears outwardly self-assured and in a
measure of control. Only her thoughts
reveal her insecurity and vulnerability.
If we did not know what she was thinking
and feeling, we might react the way that
the customers are reacting—with annoyance at her confident, sometimes insensitive, attitude toward others.*

Extend the Discussion The customers see
Jill's behavior, but they don't know her
thoughts. What do you make of the fact
that none of them seems to care that Jill is
overburdened?

FOR LESS–PROFICIENT READERS

③ Targeted Passage [Lines 276–288]

This passage shows how circumstances are
pushing Jill toward her moment of greatest
frustration.

• Who calls the restaurant, and why?

• What do the things that Jill looks at during
the conversation have in common?

• What does she hear a customer say?

• How does Jill describe herself in line 285?
in line 287?

"Good. It's one less thing to carry." I stood on the counter, put my head back, and screamed, "We're out of sausage and it's not my fault!"

A man at a back table hollered that he needed ketchup for his eggs. I reached down in the K section under the counter. Nothing under K. I got on my knees, hands shaking, rifling through jams, jellies, lingonberries. *Hugo!* I shrieked.

He ran up to me.

"Ketchup, Hugo! Wake up! The sky is falling!"

He pointed to the C section. "Catsup," he said meekly.

300 I was falling down a dark, disorderly tunnel. There was no end in sight. Coffee grounds were in my eyebrows, my hands smelled like used tea bags. I was exhausted, syrup encrusted, I'd had to go to the bathroom for three hours. People were going to get their own coffee—the ultimate defeat for any waitress. I looked at my haggard reflection in the coffee urn. The only consolation was that I wouldn't live till noon.

"Waitress!"

I raced down the aisle to table twelve, seeing the hunted look in my customer's eyes. I wanted to be perfect for every one of you. I wanted you all to like me. I'm sorry I'm not better, not faster. Please don't hate me, I'm only one

310 person, not even a particularly tall person.

"I'm sorry," I said to a table of eight, "but I simply can't do everything!"

I felt a ripple of **crass** laughter in the air. I turned. Allen Feinman had walked in with his parents. 🅚

No. . . . Anything but this.

Our eyes met. I could hear the taunts at school, the never-ending retelling of this, my ultimate nightmare.

"Can I help, Jill?" He rolled up his shirtsleeves. Allen Feinman was offering to help.

I grabbed his arm. "Can you work the register?"

320 "Of course." Allen organized the people into a line, made change, smiled. He had such a nice smile. Thanked everyone for their patience, got names on lists.

Mrs. Feinman took off her jacket and asked, "Can I make coffee, dear?"

"Mrs. Feinman, you don't have to—"

"We've always been so fond of you, Jill."

I slapped a bag of decaf in her sainted hands. Mr. Feinman poured himself a cup of coffee and went back to wait in the car.

We whipped that place into shape. All I needed was a little backup. My pockets were bulging with tips, and when Shirl raced in at eleven forty-five, I pushed a little girl aside who'd been waiting patiently by the bathroom door

330 and I lunged toward the toilet stall. Life is tough, kid.

By one-thirty the crowds had cleared. Lucy called—her baby was home and doing better. Allen Feinman and I were sitting at a back table eating pancakes. He said he'd missed me. I said I'd missed him, too. Hugo was speed-pouring boysenberry syrup, spilling everywhere—but somehow it didn't matter anymore. It was good enough.

And that, I realized happily, was fine by me. ∾

crass (krăs) *adj.* crude; unrefined

🅚 **PREDICT**
Predict what might happen with the arrival of Allen. Give reasons for your prediction.

④ **Targeted Passage**

🅚 PREDICT

Possible answers: Allen might laugh at Jill, too, for he still may be upset about her criticism of him; he might surprise Jill by helping her with the customers, even though earlier she had been critical of him.

If students need help . . . Have them review Allen's prediction in lines 29–30. Discuss how Jill has seen the prediction begin to come true this morning. Also have students speculate about why Allen might want the prediction to come true.

Extend the Discussion Why do you think Allen offered to help Jill?

SELECTION WRAP-UP

REFLECT Students may know someone like Jill and even may see some of Jill's personality in themselves. Have students note what they have learned from this story about (1) how much they should expect of themselves and other people and (2) what it takes to get along with people whose personalities are different from their own.

⭐ **CRITIQUE** Have students evaluate the author's use of humor in the story by rating it from 1 (did not care for it at all) to 5 (liked it a lot). Then ask them to indicate their favorite passage and explain why they liked it.

DIFFERENTIATED INSTRUCTION

FOR LESS-PROFICIENT READERS

④ **Targeted Passage** [Lines 317–336]

In this concluding passage, Allen and his mother come to the rescue—and Jill decides that "good enough" is just fine.

- Who offers to help Jill, and how? Why does she accept their offers?

- How does Jill react to Hugo's mess? What is the significance of her response?

FOR ADVANCED LEARNERS/PRE-AP

Analyze Character Development [paired activity option] Ask students to consider (1) how and why Jill's attitude toward Allen has changed and (2) how and why Allen's attitude toward Jill has changed. Have students create a diagram that illustrates and explains these characters' changed attitudes toward each other. Encourage students to cite details from the story to support their explanations.

Comprehension

1. **Recall** List two reasons why Jill is upset at the beginning of the story.

2. **Summarize** What crisis does Jill face in this story, and how is her crisis resolved?

3. **Clarify** What does Jill fear will happen when Allen Feinman shows up at the restaurant? Why does Allen's behavior surprise her?

Literary Analysis

4. **Draw Conclusions** Review the chart you made as you read. What drives Jill to constantly strive for perfection? Cite evidence to support your conclusion.

5. **Analyze Character** A **static character** is a character who changes very little, if at all, during the course of a story. A **dynamic character** is a character who changes significantly as a result of his

Jill's Traits at Beginning of Story	Jill's Traits at End of Story
1. Critical of others	
2. Meticulous	

or her experiences. In a chart like the one shown, list the character traits Jill exhibits at the beginning of the story and those she shows signs of as the story ends. Would you describe Jill as a static character or a dynamic character? Cite evidence from the text to support your answer.

6. **Analyze Point of View** With a **first-person narrator,** you see the story unfold through one character's eyes. Would a **third-person omniscient narrator—** a narrator who sees into the minds of all the characters in a story—have presented a more accurate picture of the events? Support your opinion.

7. **Evaluate Character Traits** "Pancakes" clearly points out the downside of **perfectionism,** but it suggests that this trait can be a positive force as well. Citing evidence from the story, decide whether perfectionism is an asset or a fault. Then compare your answer with the ideas you had about perfectionism before you read the story.

Literary Criticism

8. **Author's Style** In an essay titled "Humor, Seriously," Joan Bauer explains that her technique for creating humorous characters involves "layering nutty traits over serious personalities and situations." How effective is Bauer at developing a quirky character who confronts real-life problems in a humorous way? Cite specific dialogue and descriptions from "Pancakes" to explain your opinion.

Literary Criticism

Possible answer:

8. Students probably find Bauer quite effective in her character development. Support may include the following: "A large tour bus pulled to a grinding halt. I watched in horror as an army of round, middle-aged women stepped from the bus and headed toward the restaurant like hungry lionesses stalking prey" (lines 153–157); "'What do you recommend?' I recommend that you eat someplace else, ma'am . . .'" (lines 212–213); "'Hit me,' Andy said. 'I'd love to. You're only getting this once'" (lines 224–225); "I was falling down a dark, disorderly tunnel. There was no end in sight. Coffee grounds were in my eyebrows, my hands smelled like used tea bags" (lines 300–301).

Practice and Apply

After Reading

For additional support of post-reading questions, use these copy masters:

R **RESOURCE MANAGER—Copy Masters**
 Reading Check p. 34 (to check understanding of the selection)
 First-Person Point of View p. 27 (for practice of literary analysis standards focus)
 Question Support p. 35 (After Reading questions adapted for English learners and less-proficient readers)

For additional questions, see page 21.

ANSWERS

Comprehension

1. *She resents her mother's implication that she is a perfectionist. She is irritated at being called a "rabid perfectionist" by Allen.*

2. *She is left to wait on an unusually large crowd at the restaurant by herself. The crisis is resolved when Allen and his parents arrive and Allen and his mother offer to help Jill.*

3. *She believes that Allen will humiliate her at school by telling people about her loss of control. Instead, he offers to help.*

Literary Analysis

Possible answers:

4. ◼ **STANDARDS FOCUS** *Draw Conclusions*
 Jill wants people to like her and look up to her. Evidence may vary.

5. *Jill is a dynamic character. At first, she demands perfection from herself and others. She is meticulous, controlling, and critical. However, when Jill gives up some control by accepting help and realizes that people like her for herself, being perfect no longer seems as important.*

6. ● **STANDARDS FOCUS** *Point of View*
 A third-person omniscient narrator would have explained how other characters saw events and each other. Because the story is meant to focus on Jill, such an in-depth picture may be unnecessary.

7. *Answers will vary, but students should note that Jill's perfectionism helped her get a job and handle special responsibility.*

ANSWERS

Vocabulary in Context

VOCABULARY PRACTICE

1. *degenerate*
2. *rabid*
3. *steel*
4. *crass*
5. *condiment*
6. *benign*

R RESOURCE MANAGER—Copy Master
Vocabulary Practice p. 32

VOCABULARY IN WRITING

Have students relate each of the vocabulary words to something with which they are already familiar. Suggest that they explain how the term is related to the story, or have them make a connection to their personal experiences.

VOCABULARY STRATEGY: THE LATIN WORD ROOT *ben* (also an EL language objective)

- Point out that the words in the word web all begin with *ben* but are different parts of speech. *Benign* and *benevolent* are adjectives; *benediction, beneficiary,* and *benefactor* are nouns; *benefit* can be a noun or a verb.

- Using a dictionary, model for students how some of the words use *ben* to help make meaning.

  benediction = a "good" speaking; a blessing

  benefactor = one who does "well"; a helper or protector

  benevolent = wishing "good" for others; having a kindly character

Possible answers:

1. *benefit*
2. *benediction*
3. *benign*
4. *beneficiary*
5. *benefactor*
6. *benevolent*

R RESOURCE MANAGER—Copy Master
Vocabulary Strategy p. 33

ⓘ Vocabulary Center at **ClassZone.com**
Additional Vocabulary Activities

Vocabulary in Context

VOCABULARY PRACTICE

Write the word from the list that best completes each sentence.

1. Allen Feinman may have been critical of Jill's attitude, but that did not make him a _____.
2. He did not have a _____ temper, nor was he outrageous in other ways.
3. Jill had to _____ herself against panic when she saw Allen walking into the restaurant.
4. Perhaps it was a bit _____ when he snickered at her plight.
5. Seeing each _____ lined up precisely would have made him laugh.
6. Still, the way he and his mother helped Jill out of a jam was quite _____.

WORD LIST
benign
condiment
crass
degenerate
rabid
steel

VOCABULARY IN WRITING

Pretend you are Allen, and write a paragraph giving reasons why Jill should not hate you. Use at least three vocabulary words. Here is one way you might start.

> **EXAMPLE SENTENCE**
>
> *I can't understand why Jill has such **rabid**, negative feelings about me.*

VOCABULARY STRATEGY: THE LATIN WORD ROOT *ben*

The vocabulary word *benign* contains the Latin root *ben*, which means "well." This root and the related form *bene* are found in a number of English words. To understand the meaning of words with *ben*, use context clues as well as your knowledge of the root.

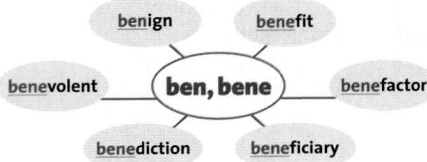

PRACTICE Write the word from the word web that best completes each sentence. Use context clues to help you or, if necessary, consult a dictionary.

1. One _____ of a good night's sleep is feeling rested in the morning.
2. The minister offered a _____ at the end of the prayer service.
3. He assured us that his intentions were entirely _____.
4. There was only one _____ listed in Grandma's will.
5. Jennifer's _____ offered to pay her way through college.
6. Most charities involve themselves in _____ works.

➤ VOCABULARY PRACTICE
For more practice, go to the **Vocabulary Center** at **ClassZone.com**.

DIFFERENTIATED INSTRUCTION

FOR ENGLISH LEARNERS

Vocabulary: Cognates Before completing the Vocabulary Strategy section, ask Spanish speakers what common words in their language have this same Latin root. ***Possible answers:*** benévolo *(benevolent),* bien *(good, well),* bienvenido *(welcome),* bueno/buena *(good).*

FOR ADVANCED LEARNERS/PRE–AP

Vocabulary in Writing Have students create an advertisement for Ye Olde Pancake House that uses as many vocabulary words as reasonably possible. For example, students might promote the restaurant as "a place that caters to *rabid* breakfast appetites" or promise that "no one will call you *crass* if you ask for refills on our out-of-this-world coffee."

Reading-Writing Connection

Demonstrate your understanding of the characters in "Pancakes" by responding to these prompts. Then use **Revision: Grammar and Style** to improve your writing.

WRITING PROMPTS	SELF-CHECK
A. Short Response: Write a Description Imagine what Allen Feinman thought when he walked into the Ye Olde Pancake House and saw Jill, usually in control, surrounded by chaos. Write **one or two paragraphs** describing the scene from Allen's point of view.	*An effective description will . . .* • relate in clear detail what Allen sees • convey what Allen thinks about Jill's situation
B. Extended Response: Compare Attitudes Referring to details in the story, write **three to five paragraphs** comparing Jill's and Andy's attitudes toward their work at the restaurant. Make sure to include examples of Jill's **perfectionism**.	*A strong comparison will . . .* • compare three aspects of Jill's and Andy's attitudes • include explicit examples

REVISION: GRAMMAR AND STYLE

ADD SUPPORTING DETAILS Review the **Grammar and Style** note on page 196. Here, Joan Bauer uses **precise adjectives** to convey important physical details that support her characterization of Jill's personality. Revise your responses to the prompts by using similar techniques.

1. **Replace vague adjectives with more precise ones.** Some adjectives, such as *nice,* are too general. Instead, use adjectives that say exactly what you mean.

2. **Avoid using too many adjectives.** Too many adjectives can result in overwriting. Choose adjectives carefully, and you will need only a few.

Here are some additional examples of Bauer's use of precise adjectives:

> . . . *He went completely ballistic at my selfless offer to alphabetize his CD collection with a color-coded cross-reference guide.* . . . (lines 43–45)

> *I was exhausted, syrup-encrusted.* . . . (line 302)

Notice how the revisions in red improve the precision of this first draft.

STUDENT MODEL

Jill and Andy both have ~~good~~ *excellent* attitudes toward their jobs. They are both ~~hard~~ *diligent*, ~~fast~~ *careful* workers. Jill makes preparations for Sunday's crowd by arranging all of the condiments neatly in *alphabetical* order. Andy fries his hash browns ahead of time, so that when customers walk in, they are greeted with ~~a nice~~ *an enticing* aroma.

WRITING TOOLS
For prewriting, revision, and editing tools, visit the **Writing Center** at ClassZone.com.

PANCAKES **205**

FOR LESS–PROFICIENT WRITERS

For Prompt A:

- To get students started, list a few details that show the chaos in the restaurant.

- Help students write one sentence that describes a specific scene in the restaurant. Then write a sentence that focuses on Jill and her appearance.

- Suggest that students organize their details in this way:

Detail about the restaurant: *A long line of unhappy customers waits for a table.*

Detail about Jill: *The front of Jill's hair is covered with sticky pancake syrup.*

For Prompt B:

- Limit the assignment to only two paragraphs.

- Help students recall three details about Jill and three details about Andy before organizing the information into paragraphs.

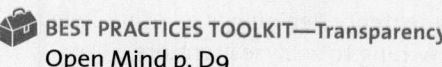

Reading-Writing Connection

WRITING PROMPTS

- For Prompt A, suggest that students reread lines 301–306 to get a mental image of the chaos in the restaurant. Explain that good descriptions appeal to many senses—for example, smell and hearing as well as sight.

- For Prompt B, have students use Open Mind to explore Jill's and Andy's attitudes before comparing them. Students may find it easier to focus first on Jill's and then on Andy's attitude. Remind students to support their ideas with details from the story.

BEST PRACTICES TOOLKIT—Transparency
Open Mind p. D9

For writing support, see

ℹ️ Writing Center at **ClassZone.com**

REVISION: GRAMMAR AND STYLE

- Identify *many, great,* and *weird* as other examples of vague adjectives. Have students use each one in a sentence and then replace it with a more precise adjective.

- As you discuss the Student Model, invite suggestions about other precise adjectives that might have been used.

R RESOURCE MANAGER—Copy Masters
Add Supporting Details p. 37

Assess and Reteach

Assess

R RESOURCE MANAGER—Copy Masters
Selection Test A pp. 39–40
Selection Test B/C pp. 41–42

💿 Test Generator CD

Reteach

S STANDARDS LESSON FILE
Literature Lesson 10: Narrator and First-Person Points of View
Reading Lesson 9: Drawing Conclusions
Vocabulary Lesson 8: Latin Roots: Human Body and Spirit

Focus and Motivate

OBJECTIVES

Literary Analysis
- explore the key idea of **status**
- analyze character motivation
- read a short story and a magazine article

Reading
- make inferences about characters

Vocabulary
- build vocabulary for reading and writing
- use knowledge of the Latin word roots *spec*, *dict*, and *grat* to unlock meaning (also an EL language objective)

Grammar and Writing
- vary sentence beginnings to refine style
- use writing to analyze literature

SUMMARY

Written by Guy de Maupassant in 1884, "The Necklace" tells the story of a young woman's tragic pursuit of status. Madame Loisel, the wife of a clerk, borrows a diamond necklace to wear to an elegant party but then loses it. The Loisels replace the necklace, thus acquiring ten hard years of debt, only to learn later that the original necklace was a fake.

How important is STATUS?

Direct students to the question. Be sure they understand the meaning of *status*. To help students explore the **KEY IDEA,** ask who has **status** in our society and how they achieved it. Continue the exploration by having students complete and discuss the **QUICKWRITE.**

Selection Resources

The Necklace
Short Story by Guy de Maupassant

How important is STATUS?

KEY IDEA What happens to people who place too much importance on **status,** or the standing they have in a group? In "The Necklace," you'll meet Madame Loisel, an unforgettable character whose pursuit of status costs her more than she could ever have imagined.

QUICKWRITE With a group, generate a list of factors that determine a person's status at your school. Add to or delete from the list that is shown. Then write a short paragraph explaining whether you think status should be determined by these factors.

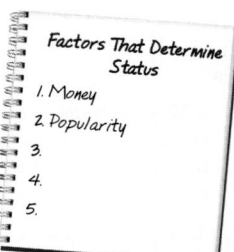

Factors That Determine Status
1. Money
2. Popularity
3.
4.
5.

206

LITERARY ANALYSIS: CHARACTER MOTIVATION

Motivation is the reason behind a character's behavior; it's what drives a character to think and act in a certain way. For example, a character might want the lead in a school play or perhaps to fit in with popular students. What the character says and does would reflect that desire. As you read "The Necklace," consider how Madame Loisel's words and actions reflect her motivation.

Review: **Point of View**

READING SKILL: MAKE INFERENCES

Instead of directly telling readers what a character is like, a writer often includes details that turn out to be clues to the character's personality. Readers can use these details, along with their own knowledge, to **make inferences,** or logical guesses, about the character's traits, values, and feelings.

In a chart like the one shown, record your inferences as you read, along with the details and experiences that helped you make them.

Details About Characters	Personal Experience	My Inference
Madame Loisel married her husband because she had no other prospects.	People are usually frustrated when they do something simply because they feel they have no choice.	She didn't really choose to marry her husband and probably feels frustrated.

Review: **Predict**

▲ VOCABULARY IN CONTEXT

Restate each phrase, using a different word or words for the boldfaced term.

1. few **prospects** for success
2. talked **incessantly** all day
3. **vexation** about their argument
4. a desperate **pauper**
5. **adulation** from her fans
6. **disconsolate** after losing his dog
7. **aghast** at her rude remarks
8. run the **gamut** of possibilities
9. a prisoner's **privation**
10. messy, with his tie all **askew**

Author Online

Master Storyteller
Guy de Maupassant (gē′ də mō-pä-säɴ′) is considered by many to be the greatest French short story writer. He created his characters with remarkable precision, focusing on the exact gesture, feeling, or word that defined each character. As a result, his stories seem to be, in his words, "pieces of human existence torn from reality."

**Guy de Maupassant
1850–1893**

Reversal of Fortune Although Maupassant was born into an upper-middle-class family in France, the family fortune ran out early. He was forced to work for a time as a government clerk, the position that the main character's husband holds in "The Necklace." Eventually, though, Maupassant turned to writing and managed to achieve some wealth and fame through his hundreds of stories. Sadly, his success was short-lived. After suffering from mental illness, Maupassant died in a Paris asylum at age 42.

 MORE ABOUT THE AUTHOR
For more on Guy de Maupassant, visit the **Literature Center** at **ClassZone.com.**

Background
Status for Sale This story takes place in Paris in the second half of the 19th century. At the time Maupassant wrote "The Necklace," European societies were divided into upper, middle, and lower classes. Birth usually determined a person's class. Sometimes a man could buy his way into a higher class by acquiring wealth. A woman could improve her status by marrying into a higher class. One obstacle for women was the tradition of the dowry—money or property that a bride's family was expected to give her new husband, but that poorer families could not provide.

THE NECKLACE **207**

Teach

STANDARDS FOCUS

● CHARACTER MOTIVATION

For instructional support, read aloud this example:

Invited to a party given by the most popular girl at school, Lily used all her savings to buy designer jeans.

Have students identify the motivation for Lily's action. *Possible answer: She wanted to fit in with more popular girls.*

CHECK UNDERSTANDING Name some actions of familiar characters. Ask students to suggest the characters' motivations.

READING SKILL

■ MAKE INFERENCES

Use the text in **Master Storyteller** to have students practice making an inference.

Point out that the traits Maupassant gave his characters were very realistic. Ask students what they can infer about the author from his ability to craft such precisely described characters. *Possible answer: He was very observant and attentive to detail.*

CHECK UNDERSTANDING Have students use **Reversal of Fortune** to infer themes found in Maupassant's writing.

R RESOURCE MANAGER—Copy Master
Make Inferences p. 55 (for student use while reading the selection)

VOCABULARY SKILL

▲ VOCABULARY IN CONTEXT

DIAGNOSE WORD KNOWLEDGE To determine preteaching needs, have all students complete **Vocabulary in Context.** *Possible answers:*
1. *possibilities;* 2. *without stopping;*
3. *frustration;* 4. *very poor person;* 5. *flattery, compliments;* 6. *heartbroken, disappointed;*
7. *shocked;* 8. *range;* 9. *hardship, poverty;*
10. *crooked, out of place*

PRETEACH VOCABULARY Use the Vocabulary Study copy master to help students predict meanings for each boldfaced word in the copy master.

1. Read item 1 aloud, emphasizing *prospects*.
2. Point out the phrase *for the future*. Discuss possible meanings for *prospects*, such as "things that lie ahead" or "future chances."
3. Repeat the procedure for items 2–10.

 RESOURCE MANAGER—Copy Master
Vocabulary Study p. 57

For general guidelines on differentiating vocabulary instruction and for alternative vocabulary activities for students not needing vocabulary preteaching, see

 BEST PRACTICES TOOLKIT
Scaffolding Vocabulary Instruction pp. 43–46

ⓘ Vocabulary Center at **ClassZone.com**

ANALYZE VISUALS

Possible answer: The woman's attractive hair-style, elegant pearls, stylish dress, and smooth skin suggest that she is a member of the middle class or perhaps even the upper class.

About the Art *Louise Augusta, Queen of Prussia* was one of many portraits of prominent Europeans and Russians that French neoclassical artist Marie Louise Élisabeth Vigée LeBrun (1755–1842) painted between 1770 and 1835. One of the most in-demand portrait artists of her time, she completed more than 900 paintings, including 700 portraits, during her career.

READING SKILL

A MAKE INFERENCES

Possible answer: Madame Loisel grieves over her shabby apartment and furnishings (lines 11–14), feels enraged by her middle-class existence (lines 14–17), and dreams of a life of wealth and luxury (lines 17–20). These feelings stem from her belief that she was born for such a life.

If students need help . . . Call their attention to the sentence in lines 11–12. Help students understand that Madame Loisel expected more out of life. She believed that she deserved more than she had, and felt cheated.

Extend the Discussion How have you felt when you haven't gotten something you expected or thought you deserved?

THE
Necklace
Guy de Maupassant

She was one of those pretty and charming girls, born, as if by an accident of fate, into a family of clerks. With no dowry, no **prospects,** no way of any kind of being met, understood, loved, and married by a man both prosperous and famous, she was finally married to a minor clerk in the Ministry of Education.

She dressed plainly because she could not afford fine clothes, but was as unhappy as a woman who has come down in the world; for women have no family rank or social class. With them, beauty, grace, and charm take the place of birth and breeding. Their natural poise, their instinctive good taste, and their mental cleverness are the sole guiding principles which make daughters
10 of the common people the equals of ladies in high society.

She grieved **incessantly,** feeling that she had been born for all the little niceties and luxuries of living. She grieved over the shabbiness of her apartment, the dinginess of the walls, the worn-out appearance of the chairs, the ugliness of the draperies. All these things, which another woman of her class would not even have noticed, gnawed at her and made her furious. The sight of the little Breton[1] girl who did her humble housework roused in her disconsolate regrets and wild daydreams. She would dream of silent chambers, draped with Oriental tapestries and lighted by tall bronze floor lamps, and of two handsome butlers in knee breeches, who, drowsy from the heavy warmth
20 cast by the central stove, dozed in large overstuffed armchairs. **A**

ANALYZE VISUALS
Examine the portrait on page 209. What social class do you think the woman belongs to? Identify the details that helped you draw this **inference.**

prospects (prŏs'pěkts') *n.* chances or possibilities, especially for financial success

incessantly (ĭn-sĕs'ənt-lē) *adv.* without interruption; continuously

A MAKE INFERENCES
Consider what you learn about Madame Loisel's situation in lines 11–20. Why do you think she feels the way she does?

① Targeted Passage

---

1. **Breton** (brĕt'n): from Brittany, a region in northwestern France.

Louise Augusta, Queen of Prussia (1801), Marie Louise Élisabeth Vigée LeBrun. Pastel, 51 cm × 41 cm. Stiftung Preussische Schlösser und Gärten Berlin-Brandenburg. Photo by J. P. Anders.

DIFFERENTIATED INSTRUCTION

FOR ALL STUDENTS

Anchor Activity Provide independent learning opportunities for students to explore alternate endings to the story. Assign groups to alter key events in the plot. Ask students to take on roles of key characters and act out the groups' plot changes for the class. For details, see

R RESOURCE MANAGER
Ideas for Extension pp. 48–49

FOR LESS–PROFICIENT READERS

In combination with the *Audio Anthology CD,* use one or more Targeted Passages (pp. 208, 210, 212, 217) to ensure that students focus on key story events, concepts, and skills. Targeted Passages are also good for English learners.

① Targeted Passage [Lines 11–20]

This passage introduces Madame Loisel's frustration with her life, a frustration that will drive the rest of the story.

• What is Madame Loisel's home like?

B MAKE INFERENCES

Possible answer: Her dreams of dinner parties, fine foods, fancy dresses and jewelry, and the admiration of the wealthy (lines 21–25, 29–34, 36–37) suggest that she values status over substance and the admiration of powerful friends over a close relationship with her husband.

If students need help . . . Read aloud lines 29–37, beginning with the words "she would dream of." As students identify Madame Loisel's desires, list them in a Making Inferences or Two-Column Chart. Then, together, use the list to make inferences about her values.

Dreams and Desires	Values
butlers	status
fancy dinner parties	admiration
delicious dinners	wealth

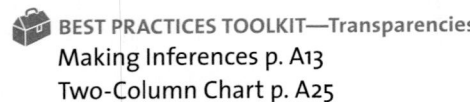 **BEST PRACTICES TOOLKIT—Transparencies**
Making Inferences p. A13
Two-Column Chart p. A25

Lines 38–41
REINFORCE *KEY IDEA:* STATUS

Discuss How does Madame Loisel's refusal to visit her well-to-do friend show her obsession with **status**? *Possible answer: Madame Loisel probably refuses to visit the friend because seeing her reminds Madame Loisel of all that she herself must do without. She weeps with jealousy over the friend's status and grieves because her own status is not similarly high (and perhaps never will be).*

She would dream of great reception halls hung with old silks, of fine furniture filled with priceless curios, and of small, stylish, scented sitting rooms just right for the four o'clock chat with intimate friends, with distinguished and sought-after men whose attention every woman envies and longs to attract.

hen dining at the round table, covered for the third day with the same cloth, opposite her husband, who would raise the cover of the soup tureen, declaring delightedly, "Ah! A good stew! There's nothing I like better . . ." she would dream of fashionable dinner parties, of gleaming silverware, of tapestries making the walls
30 alive with characters out of history and strange birds in a fairyland forest; she would dream of delicious dishes served on wonderful china, of gallant compliments whispered and listened to with a sphinxlike[2] smile as one eats the rosy flesh of a trout or nibbles at the wings of a grouse.

She had no evening clothes, no jewels, nothing. But those were the things she wanted; she felt that was the kind of life for her. She so much longed to please, be envied, be fascinating and sought after. **B**

She had a well-to-do friend, a classmate of convent-school days whom she would no longer go to see, simply because she would feel so distressed on
40 returning home. And she would weep for days on end from **vexation**, regret, despair, and anguish.

Then one evening, her husband came home proudly holding out a large envelope.

"Look," he said, "I've got something for you."

She excitedly tore open the envelope and pulled out a printed card bearing these words:

"The Minister of Education and Mme. Georges Ramponneau[3] beg M. and Mme. Loisel[4] to do them the honor of attending an evening reception at the Ministerial Mansion on Friday, January 18."
50   Instead of being delighted, as her husband had hoped, she scornfully tossed the invitation on the table, murmuring, "What good is that to me?"

"But, my dear, I thought you'd be thrilled to death. You never get a chance to go out, and this is a real affair, a wonderful one! I had an awful time getting a card. Everybody wants one; it's much sought after, and not many clerks have a chance at one. You'll see all the most important people there."

B MAKE INFERENCES
Think about Madame Loisel's dreams and desires up to this point. What can you infer about her values?

vexation (věk-sā′shən) *n.* irritation; annoyance

② **Targeted Passage**

2. **sphinxlike:** mysterious (from the Greek myth of the sphinx, a winged creature that killed those who could not answer its riddle).

3. **Mme. Georges Ramponneau** (zhôrzh′ răN-pô-nō′): *Mme.* is an abbreviation for *Madame* (mə-däm′), a title of courtesy for a French married woman.

4. **M. and Mme. Loisel** (lwä-zĕl′): *M.* is an abbreviation for *Monsieur* (mə-syœ′), a title of courtesy for a Frenchman.

210   UNIT 2: CHARACTERIZATION AND POINT OF VIEW

DIFFERENTIATED INSTRUCTION

FOR LESS–PROFICIENT READERS
② **Targeted Passage [Lines 42–51]**

By introducing an upcoming elegant party, this passage spotlights a contrast between Madame and Monsieur Loisel and introduces a situation that will shape the rest of the story.

- How does Monsieur Loisel feel about the invitation? Why?

- How does Madame Loisel react? Why might she react that way?

FOR ENGLISH LEARNERS

Culture: Connect According to line 35, Madame Loisel "had no evening clothes." Explain that in this time and place, the expression *evening clothes* means fancy, formal clothing such as ball gowns and tuxedos. Have students compare that kind of clothing to what they would describe as "evening clothes" for young adults today.

A Paris Street, Rain (1877), Gustave Caillebotte. Oil on canvas. The Art Institute of Chicago.
© Erich Lessing/Art Resource, New York.

She gave him an irritated glance and burst out impatiently, "What do you think I have to go in?"

He hadn't given that a thought. He stammered, "Why, the dress you wear when we go to the theater. That looks quite nice, I think."

60 He stopped talking, dazed and distracted to see his wife burst out weeping. Two large tears slowly rolled from the corners of her eyes to the corners of her mouth; he gasped, "Why, what's the matter? What's the trouble?"

By sheer will power she overcame her outburst and answered in a calm voice while wiping the tears from her wet cheeks:

"Oh, nothing. Only I don't have an evening dress and therefore I can't go to that affair. Give the card to some friend at the office whose wife can dress better than I can."

He was stunned. He resumed. "Let's see, Mathilde.[5] How much would a suitable outfit cost—one you could wear for other affairs too—something 70 very simple?"

She thought it over for several seconds, going over her allowance and thinking also of the amount she could ask for without bringing an immediate refusal and an exclamation of dismay from the thrifty clerk.

Finally, she answered hesitatingly, "I'm not sure exactly, but I think with four hundred francs[6] I could manage it."

---

5. **Mathilde** (mä-tēld').

6. **francs** (frăngks): The franc was the basic monetary unit of France.

Activity Point out that the couple in the foreground is middle class, like the Loisels. Ask students if this information surprises them or affects their opinion of Madame Loisel.

About the Art This famous painting by French Impressionist Gustave Caillebotte (1848–1894) provides a glimpse of Paris during the time frame of "The Necklace." Like other Impressionistic works, this street scene captures a single moment in everyday life.

Lines 42–67
DISCUSSION PROMPTS

Use these prompts to help students understand the relationship between the Loisels:

Connect For whom do you feel more sympathy, Madame Loisel or her husband? Why? *Students may choose either character as long as their reasons accurately reflect story details about that character and his or her situation.*

Analyze How do these two characters react differently to the invitation? *Possible answer: He is proud and happy (lines 42–44, 52–55), but she is negative (lines 50–51, 56–57, 60–67).*

Evaluate Do both characters have valid reactions or feelings? Explain. *Students may cite evidence from their lives or from the text to support their evaluations.*

FOR LESS–PROFICIENT READERS

Review the Loisels' Argument (lines 56–80) Help students see how Madame Loisel gets what she wants point by point. Paraphrase her husband's proposals and discuss her response to each:

- "Wear your theater dress." (lines 58–59)
- "Buy a simple dress that you can wear on other occasions, as well." (lines 68–70)
- "How little money will be enough?" (line 68)
- "I'll give you four hundred francs." (line 79)

FOR ADVANCED LEARNERS/PRE-AP

Examine Perspectives [small-group option] Guy de Maupassant has been called a misogynist (a hater of women) by some contemporary scholars. Have students look for evidence in the story that supports or contradicts that view and then present their findings in a class discussion.

C CHARACTER MOTIVATION

Possible answers: He wants to please his wife; he fears that she will be bitter and hard to live with if he doesn't give her the money.

Extend the Discussion Maupassant does not include Madame Loisel's reaction to her husband's offer. Do you think that she was grateful? overjoyed? indifferent? Explain.

Lines 88–91
REINFORCE *KEY IDEA:* STATUS

Discuss Madame Loisel rejects the idea of wearing flowers rather than jewels. How does this response relate to her desire for **status**? *Possible answers: Madame Loisel thinks that flowers are too simple or affordable; she prefers to wear something that is a symbol of wealth.*

D CHARACTER MOTIVATION

Possible answer: Madame Loisel's motivation for choosing an expensive and glittering diamond necklace comes from her desire to appear wealthy and to be noticed and admired by others.

If students need help . . . Revisit the chart on page 210 that lists Madame Loisel's dreams, desires, and values. Review with students that Madame Loisel valued the status that she believed would be hers if she wore the diamond necklace.

He turned a bit pale, for he had set aside just that amount to buy a rifle so that, the following summer, he could join some friends who were getting up a group to shoot larks on the plain near Nanterre.[7]

However, he said, "All right. I'll give you four hundred francs. But try to get
80 a nice dress." **C**

As the day of the party approached, Mme. Loisel seemed sad, moody, and ill at ease. Her outfit was ready, however. Her husband said to her one evening, "What's the matter? You've been all out of sorts for three days."

And she answered, "It's embarrassing not to have a jewel or a gem—nothing to wear on my dress. I'll look like a **pauper:** I'd almost rather not go to that party."

He answered, "Why not wear some flowers? They're very fashionable this season. For ten francs you can get two or three gorgeous roses."

90 She wasn't at all convinced. "No. . . . There's nothing more humiliating than to look poor among a lot of rich women."

But her husband exclaimed, "My, but you're silly! Go see your friend Mme. Forestier[8] and ask her to lend you some jewelry. You and she know each other well enough for you to do that."

She gave a cry of joy, "Why, that's so! I hadn't thought of it."

The next day she paid her friend a visit and told her of her predicament.

Mme. Forestier went toward a large closet with mirrored doors, took out a large jewel box, brought it over, opened it, and said to Mme. Loisel, "Pick something out, my dear."

100 At first her eyes noted some bracelets, then a pearl necklace, then a Venetian cross, gold and gems, of marvelous workmanship. She tried on these adornments in front of the mirror, but hesitated, unable to decide which to part with and put back. She kept on asking, "Haven't you something else?"

"Oh, yes, keep on looking. I don't know just what you'd like."

All at once she found, in a black satin box, a superb diamond necklace; and her pulse beat faster with longing. Her hands trembled as she took it up. Clasping it around her throat, outside her high-necked dress, she stood in ecstasy looking at her reflection.

Then she asked, hesitatingly, pleading, "Could I borrow that, just that and
110 nothing else?"

"Why, of course."

She threw her arms around her friend, kissed her warmly, and fled with her treasure. **D**

The day of the party arrived. Mme. Loisel was a sensation. She was the prettiest one there, fashionable, gracious, smiling, and wild with joy. All the

---

C CHARACTER MOTIVATION
What do you think is Monsieur Loisel's motivation for giving the money to his wife? Explain your answer.

pauper (pô′pər) *n.* a poor person, especially one who depends on public charity

3 Targeted Passage

D CHARACTER MOTIVATION
Why does Madame Loisel choose the diamond necklace? Explain her motivation.

---

7. **Nanterre** (näN-tĕr′): a city of north central France.
8. **Forestier** (fô-rĕs-tyā′).

DIFFERENTIATED INSTRUCTION

FOR LESS-PROFICIENT READERS
3 Targeted Passage [Lines 92–113]

This passage introduces the object that gives the story its title.

- Why does Madame Loisel visit Madame Forestier?
- What does Madame Forestier say when Madame Loisel explains her situation?
- Name two things that Madame Loisel looks at but then discards.
- What does she finally borrow?

men turned to look at her, asked who she was, begged to be introduced. All the Cabinet officials wanted to waltz with her. The minister took notice of her.

120 She danced madly, wildly, drunk with pleasure, giving no thought to anything in the triumph of her beauty, the pride of her success, in a kind of happy cloud composed of all the **adulation,** of all the admiring glances, of all the awakened longings, of a sense of complete victory that is so sweet to a woman's heart.

She left around four o'clock in the morning. Her husband, since midnight, had been dozing in a small empty sitting room with three other gentlemen whose wives were having too good a time.

He threw over her shoulders the wraps he had brought for going home, modest garments of everyday life whose shabbiness clashed with the stylishness of her evening clothes. She felt this and longed to escape, unseen by the other women who were draped in expensive furs.

adulation (ăj´ə-lā´shən) *n.* excessive praise or flattery

ANALYZE VISUALS
In your opinion, how well does this painting reflect the **setting** of the party? Describe the details that influenced your opinion.

The Ball, Victor Gabriel Gilbert. © Christie's Images/Corbis.

THE NECKLACE   213

E POINT OF VIEW

***Possible answer:** Telling the two characters' thoughts allows readers to learn about their different reactions and personalities and to emphasize how superficial Madame Loisel is.*

If students need help . . . Ask them what Madame Loisel's life will be like the next day. Ask whether going to the party changed her life in any lasting way. Help students understand that after the elegant party, Madame Loisel might be more disappointed than ever with her dreary life.

F GRAMMAR AND STYLE

Analyze Sentence Beginnings Many good writers, such as Maupassant, vary their sentence beginnings to make their writing more interesting and lively. After students read the sentences beginning with *Before the mirror* (line 142) and *Suddenly* (line 143), discuss how the author's choices add rhythm and drama to the sentences. Encourage students to find other sentences in the selection that begin in interesting and dramatic ways and to tell how those sentences affect them as readers.

---

130   Loisel held her back.

"Hold on! You'll catch cold outside. I'll call a cab."

But she wouldn't listen to him and went rapidly down the stairs. When they were on the street, they didn't find a carriage; and they set out to hunt for one, hailing drivers whom they saw going by at a distance.

They walked toward the Seine,[9] **disconsolate** and shivering. Finally on the docks they found one of those carriages that one sees in Paris only after nightfall, as if they were ashamed to show their drabness during daylight hours.

It dropped them at their door in the Rue des Martyrs,[10] and they climbed 140 wearily up to their apartment. For her, it was all over. For him, there was the thought that he would have to be at the Ministry at ten o'clock. **E**

Before the mirror, she let the wraps fall from her shoulders to see herself once again in all her glory. Suddenly she gave a cry. The necklace was gone. **F**

Her husband, already half-undressed, said, "What's the trouble?"

She turned toward him despairingly, "I . . . I . . . I don't have Mme. Forestier's necklace."

"What! You can't mean it! It's impossible!"

They hunted everywhere, through the folds of the dress, through the folds of the coat, in the pockets. They found nothing.

150   He asked, "Are you sure you had it when leaving the dance?"

"Yes, I felt it when I was in the hall of the Ministry."

"But if you had lost it on the street, we'd have heard it drop. It must be in the cab."

"Yes. Quite likely. Did you get its number?"

"No. Didn't you notice it either?"

"No."

They looked at each other **aghast**. Finally Loisel got dressed again.

"I'll retrace our steps on foot," he said, "to see if I can find it."

And he went out. She remained in her evening clothes, without the strength 160 to go to bed, slumped in a chair in the unheated room, her mind a blank.

Her husband came in about seven o'clock. He had had no luck.

He went to the police station, to the newspapers to post a reward, to the cab companies, everywhere the slightest hope drove him.

That evening Loisel returned, pale, his face lined; still he had learned nothing.

"We'll have to write your friend," he said, "to tell her you have broken the catch and are having it repaired. That will give us a little time to turn around."

She wrote to his dictation.

disconsolate (dĭs-kŏn′sə-lĭt) *adj.* extremely depressed or dejected

E POINT OF VIEW
What is the impact of having the narrator explain what Madame Loisel and her husband each think?

F GRAMMAR AND STYLE
Reread lines 142–143. Notice how Maupassant varies his sentence beginnings by using words and phrases such as *before the mirror* and *suddenly.*

aghast (ə-găst′) *adj.* filled with shock or horror

---

9. **Seine** (sĕn): the principal river of Paris.

10. **Rue des Martyrs** (rü′ dā mär-tēr′): a street in Paris.

DIFFERENTIATED INSTRUCTION

FOR ENGLISH LEARNERS
Language: Punctuation and Print Clues
Remind students that authors often use punctuation in ways that help their readers understand how the characters are speaking. Point out the ellipses and exclamation points in lines 145–147. Have volunteers read the words aloud in the way they think the characters said them.

FOR ADVANCED LEARNERS/PRE–AP
Contrast Characters Have students write a paragraph in response to this question: *What details in the story thus far support the view that Madame Loisel is a romantic and Monsieur Loisel is a realist?* Invite students to compare their responses.

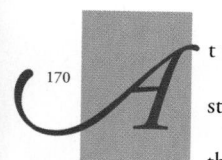

t the end of a week, they had given up all hope.

170   And Loisel, looking five years older, declared, "We must take steps to replace that piece of jewelry."

The next day they took the case to the jeweler whose name they found inside. He consulted his records. "I didn't sell that necklace, madame," he said. "I only supplied the case."

Then they went from one jeweler to another hunting for a similar necklace, going over their recollections, both sick with despair and anxiety.

They found, in a shop in Palais Royal, a string of diamonds which seemed exactly like the one they were seeking. It was priced at forty thousand francs. They could get it for thirty-six.

180   They asked the jeweler to hold it for them for three days. And they reached an agreement that he would take it back for thirty-four thousand if the lost one was found before the end of February.

Loisel had eighteen thousand francs he had inherited from his father. He would borrow the rest.

He went about raising the money, asking a thousand francs from one, four hundred from another, a hundred here, sixty there. He signed notes, made ruinous deals, did business with loan sharks, ran the whole **gamut** of moneylenders. He compromised the rest of his life, risked his signature without knowing if he'd be able to honor it, and then, terrified by the outlook
190 for the future, by the blackness of despair about to close around him, by the prospect of all the **privations** of the body and tortures of the spirit, he went to claim the new necklace with the thirty-six thousand francs which he placed on the counter of the shopkeeper. **G**

When Mme. Loisel took the necklace back, Mme. Forestier said to her frostily, "You should have brought it back sooner; I might have needed it."

She didn't open the case, an action her friend was afraid of. If she had noticed the substitution, what would she have thought? What would she have said? Would she have thought her a thief?

Mme. Loisel experienced the horrible life the needy live. She played her
200 part, however, with sudden heroism. That frightful debt had to be paid. She would pay it. She dismissed her maid; they rented a garret under the eaves.

She learned to do the heavy housework, to perform the hateful duties of cooking. She washed dishes, wearing down her shell-pink nails scouring the grease from pots and pans; she scrubbed dirty linen, shirts, and cleaning rags which she hung on a line to dry; she took the garbage down to the street each morning and brought up water, stopping on each landing to get her breath. And, clad like a peasant woman, basket on arm, guarding sou[11] by sou her scanty allowance, she bargained with the fruit dealers, the grocer, the butcher, and was insulted by them.

gamut (găm'ət) *n.* an entire range or series

privation (prī-vā'shən) *n.* the lack of a basic necessity or a comfort of life

G CHARACTER MOTIVATION
Consider why the Loisels don't tell Mathilde's friend the truth. What motivates them to go into such debt?

---

11. **sou** (soo): a French coin of small value.

LITERARY ANALYSIS

G CHARACTER MOTIVATION

Possible answer: The Loisels are ashamed of their carelessness, and they fear Madame Forestier's reaction. By replacing the necklace secretly, they hope to maintain their honor and dignity.

If students need help... Ask students how they would feel if they lost something of great value that belonged to someone else. Have them name some of the thoughts that might go through their heads while they pondered what to do. *Thoughts and feelings probably would include embarrassment, regret, shame, worry, or even panic, and fear of consequences.*

Extend the Discussion Discuss whether the Loisels made the right decision.

Lines 199–209
DISCUSSION PROMPTS

Use these prompts to help students understand what happens to Madame Loisel because of the decision that she and her husband have made:

Connect What is your opinion of Madame Loisel at this point? *Students should cite evidence to support their opinions.*

Analyze How has Madame Loisel's attitude changed since the beginning of the story? Why has it changed? *Possible answer: She has changed from feeling sorry for herself and angry because of the lack of luxuries in her life (lines 11–17), to being resigned to a life of poverty and hard work (lines 202–206). These changes were brought about by the need to replace the necklace, which she lost.*

Evaluate Do you think that Maupassant has made Madame Loisel a more admirable character than she was at the beginning of the story? Explain. *Students should defend their responses.*

FOR LESS–PROFICIENT READERS
Monitor Understanding Ask students to check their understanding by having small groups prepare two lists, using details from this page:

- a list of ways in which Monsieur Loisel raises the money to buy the diamond necklace (lines 180–193)
- a list of ways in which Madame Loisel changes her life in order to set aside money to repay that amount (lines 201–209)

FOR ADVANCED LEARNERS/PRE–AP
Analyze Plot Elements [paired-activity option] A *contrivance* is an illogical or unlikely action or event in a plot. Upon reading it, the reader might exclaim, "That's ridiculous!" or "That never would happen in real life." Have students prepare a statement that considers (1) whether or not Madame Forestier's failure to open the jewelry case is a contrivance and (2) if there are other contrivances in this story.

ANALYZE VISUALS

Possible answer: The elegant hairdo, pearls, apparent leisure, and beautiful gown in the portrait on page 209 show a woman living a privileged life—the kind of life that Madame Loisel had dreamed of having. The messy hair, lack of jewelry, menial task, rough clothing, and weary appearance in the portrait on page 216 convey a life of drudgery—the kind of life that Madame Loisel lives now. Similarly, the contrast between the smooth brushstrokes of the earlier portrait and the rough style of this artwork suggests how Madame Loisel has changed from a relatively well-off, middle-class homemaker to a common worker.

About the Art Edgar Degas (1834–1917) is well known for artwork that shows people in daily activities such as bathing, combing their hair, and working in laundries. A French Impressionist, Degas often showed his subjects in natural, spontaneous poses.

ANALYZE VISUALS
Compare this artwork with the one shown on page 209. How do the details and styles of each reflect the changes that Madame Loisel endures?

The Laundress (1869), Edgar Degas. Pastel, white crayon, and charcoal. Musée d'Orsay, Paris. Photo © Jean Schormans/Réunion des Musées Nationaux/Art Resource, New York.

210 Each month notes had to be paid, and others renewed to give more time.
    Her husband labored evenings to balance a tradesman's accounts, and at night, often, he copied documents at five sous a page.
    And this went on for ten years.
    Finally, all was paid back, everything including the exorbitant rates of the loan sharks and accumulated compound interest.

DIFFERENTIATED INSTRUCTION

FOR ENGLISH LEARNERS
Vocabulary: Multiple-Meaning Words
Point out that some English words have more than one meaning. Have students use context clues and prior knowledge to determine how each of these words is used in the story:

- *raising* (line 185)
- *sharks* (line 187)
- *notes* (line 210)
- *compound* (line 215)
- *common* (line 233)
- *mean* (line 239)

Mme. Loisel appeared an old woman, now. She became heavy, rough, harsh, like one of the poor. Her hair untended, her skirts **askew,** her hands red, her voice shrill, she even slopped water on her floors and scrubbed them herself. But, sometimes, while her husband was at work, she would sit near the
220 window and think of that long-ago evening when, at the dance, she had been so beautiful and admired.

What would have happened if she had not lost that necklace? Who knows? Who can say? How strange and unpredictable life is! How little there is between happiness and misery!

Then one Sunday when she had gone for a walk on the Champs Élysées[12] to relax a bit from the week's labors, she suddenly noticed a woman strolling with a child. It was Mme. Forestier, still young-looking; still beautiful, still charming. **H**

Mme. Loisel felt a rush of emotion. Should she speak to her? Of course. And
230 now that everything was paid off, she would tell her the whole story. Why not?

She went toward her. "Hello, Jeanne."

The other, not recognizing her, showed astonishment at being spoken to so familiarly by this common person. She stammered. "But . . . madame . . . I don't recognize . . . You must be mistaken."

"No, I'm Mathilde Loisel."

Her friend gave a cry, "Oh, my poor Mathilde, how you've changed!"

"Yes, I've had a hard time since last seeing you. And plenty of misfortunes— and all on account of you!" **I**

"Of me . . . How do you mean?"

240 "Do you remember that diamond necklace you loaned me to wear to the dance at the Ministry?"

"Yes, but what about it?"

"Well, I lost it."

"You lost it! But you returned it."

"I brought you another just like it. And we've been paying for it for ten years now. You can imagine that wasn't easy for us who had nothing. Well, it's over now, and I am glad of it."

Mme. Forestier stopped short, "You mean to say you bought a diamond necklace to replace mine?"

250 "Yes. You never noticed, then? They were quite alike."

And she smiled with proud and simple joy.

Mme. Forestier, quite overcome, clasped her by the hands. "Oh, my poor Mathilde. But mine was only paste.[13] Why, at most it was worth only five hundred francs!" ❧

---

12. **Champs Élysées** (shän zā-lē-zā′): a famous wide street in Paris.
13. **paste:** a hard, glassy material used in making imitation gems.

askew (ə-skyōō′) *adj.* crooked; to one side

H PREDICT

Do you think Madame Loisel will tell her friend the truth? Why or why not?

I CHARACTER MOTIVATION

Think about what motivates Madame Loisel to approach her friend. Does this action surprise you, given Madame Loisel's earlier thoughts and actions? Explain your response.

④ Targeted Passage

H PREDICT

Possible answer: *She has kept the secret for ten years, to avoid shame; she is likely to keep it now.*

If students need help . . . Review lines 196–198 and discuss Madame Loisel's fear of losing status in Madame Forestier's eyes.

LITERARY ANALYSIS

I CHARACTER MOTIVATION

Possible answers: *Yes, it is surprising that Madame Loisel has decided to reveal her fall in status; No, it is not surprising that she would want to confront Madame Forestier, whom she blames (at least in part) for the reversal that she has suffered.*

SELECTION WRAP-UP

REFLECT Have students suggest what might happen next if the story were to continue. Based on what Madame Loisel learns, what might the characters say and do?

★ CRITIQUE Have students evaluate the story by rating it from 1 (did not like) to 5 (liked a lot) and then indicate which parts they liked or disliked and tell why. Have students revisit their evaluations after discussing the story to see if their original opinions change.

READING FLUENCY

Distribute the copy master and have students work in small groups or with partners to practice fluency.

R RESOURCE MANAGER—Copy Master
Reading Fluency p. 63

FOR LESS-PROFICIENT READERS

④ Targeted Passage [Lines 240–254]

As the story ends, this passage reveals a surprise: the true value of the necklace.

- What confession does Madame Loisel make? How does she feel as she does so?
- How does Madame Forestier react?
- How much was the lost necklace worth? Why was it worth so little?

FOR ADVANCED LEARNERS/PRE-AP

Analyze Theme Madame Loisel borrowed the necklace to look like the upper-class people she envied. Had she not lost the necklace, or felt the need to borrow it in the first place, the Loisels' life would have been much better. What lesson might the author be trying to convey about an excessive concern for status? What other lessons might readers learn from this story?

Practice and Apply

After Reading

For additional support of post-reading questions, use these copy masters:

R RESOURCE MANAGER—Copy Masters
Reading Check p. 60 (to check understanding of the selection)
Character Motivation p. 53 (for practice of literary analysis standards focus)
Question Support p. 61 (After Reading questions adapted for English learners and less-proficient readers)

For additional questions, see page 47.

For additional exercises to challenge students, see

ℹ Power Thinking at **ClassZone.com**

ANSWERS

Comprehension

1. *She dreams of a life of wealth and elegance, rather than her ordinary, middle-class life.*

2. *Madame Loisel loses the necklace.*

3. *Madame Loisel learns that the necklace was fake and was worth very little.*

Literary Analysis

Possible answers:

4. ■ **STANDARDS FOCUS** *Make Inferences Madame Loisel has changed a great deal. At the start, she feels she was born for riches and hates her middle-class life (lines 11–20). She is also too proud to attend the ball in the dress she owns (lines 65–67). By the end of the story, she is able to admit to having "nothing" (line 246) and to have labored for ten years.*

5. *Madame Loisel, who had wanted a life of having much more, finds that it was unnecessary for her to have spent ten years getting by with so much less.*

6. *He does not seem as desperate. He thinks that the dress that his wife wears to the theater "looks quite nice" (line 59); he is not worried about attire or jewelry for the reception (lines 58–62, 88–89).*

7. ● **STANDARDS FOCUS**
Character Motivation

Motivation #1: She feels that she has no suitable dress and so cannot attend the ball.

Motivation #2: She wants to appear wealthy.

Comprehension

1. **Recall** Why is Madame Loisel discontented at the beginning of the story?

2. **Recall** What causes the change in the Loisels' financial situation?

3. **Summarize** What twist occurs at the end of the story?

Literary Analysis

4. **Make Inferences** Review the inferences you wrote down during reading. How much do you think Madame Loisel has changed by the time the story ends? Explain your answer.

5. **Analyze Irony** The most common kind of irony is **situational irony,** which occurs when a character—or the reader—expects one thing to happen but something entirely different occurs. What is ironic about the ending of "The Necklace"?

6. **Compare and Contrast Characters** Does Monsieur Loisel long for **status** as desperately as his wife does? Cite evidence to support your opinions.

7. **Interpret Motivation** Consider what you know about the characters' feelings and goals. For each action described in the chart shown, decide on the character's motivation.

Action	Motivation
Mme. Loisel weeps when she receives the invitation. (line 60)	
Mme. Loisel borrows jewelry rather than wear flowers. (line 109)	
Monsieur Loisel advises his wife not to tell her friend about the lost necklace. (line 166–167)	

8. **Analyze Point of View** For most of "The Necklace," the narrator focuses on Madame Loisel's thoughts and feelings. However, since this story is told from the **third-person omniscient point of view,** the narrator also relays the thoughts of Monsieur Loisel. Did knowing Monsieur Loisel's inner thoughts affect your opinion of Madame Loisel? Explain your answer.

9. **Evaluate** Reread lines 199–201. Do you agree that Madame Loisel shows heroism in paying off her debt? Find examples to support your opinion.

Literary Criticism

10. **Critical Interpretations** The literary critic Edward D. Sullivan declared that "The Necklace" is not just a story pointing to a moral, such as "Honesty is the best policy," but a story showing that in people's lives "blind chance rules." Do you agree or disagree with Sullivan's argument? Cite evidence to support your opinion.

Motivation #3: He is ashamed of the loss; he needs to stall for time to figure out how to repay the debt.

8. *Knowing that Monsieur Loisel also becomes "sick with despair and anxiety" over the lost necklace (line 176) makes Madame Loisel's foolish need for it seem all the worse.*

9. *Heroic: She does the housework herself, bargains with tradespeople, and sacrifices her refinement. Not heroic: The Loisels' problem is mostly her fault, so she should carry part of the burden.*

Literary Criticism

Possible answers:

10. *Agree: Chance is to blame, as seen in Madame Loisel's position at birth and the accidental loss of the necklace. Disagree: Dishonesty is to blame, as seen in Madame Loisel's pretense of wealth and the Loisels' cover-up of the item's loss.*

Vocabulary in Context

VOCABULARY PRACTICE

For each item, choose the word from the list that relates in meaning.

1. dejected, miserable, low
2. irritation, displeasure, anger
3. opportunities, possibilities, chances
4. range, extent, scope
5. praise, worship, adoration
6. horrified, dismayed, appalled
7. loss, damage, hardship
8. slanting, sideways, crooked
9. beggar, debtor, have-not
10. steadily, ceaselessly, perpetually

WORD LIST
adulation
aghast
askew
disconsolate
gamut
incessantly
pauper
privation
prospects
vexation

VOCABULARY IN WRITING

Use each vocabulary word in a sentence of your own to describe one of the characters in "The Necklace." Here is an example.

> **EXAMPLE SENTENCE**
>
> Madame Loisel ignores compliments from her husband, but she seeks **adulation** from wealthy acquaintances.

VOCABULARY STRATEGY: THE LATIN WORD ROOT *spec*

The word *prospect* contains the Latin root *spec* or *spect,* which means "look" or "see." How is the root reflected in the meanings of the other words in the word family shown on the right?

PRACTICE This chart lists two additional roots and example words from "The Necklace." Use the roots and context clues to figure out the meanings of the underlined words.

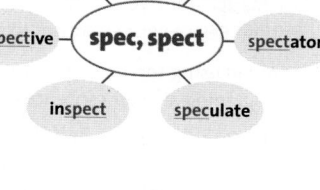

Root	Meaning	Example
dict = speak	dictation (line 168)
grat = thanks	gracious (line 115)

1. The courtroom was silent as the judge announced the <u>verdict</u>.
2. The actress expressed <u>gratitude</u> in her acceptance speech.
3. The confused defendant <u>contradicted</u> his earlier testimony.
4. What an <u>ingrate</u>! Sam didn't acknowledge our gift.
5. The subjects were afraid to defy the king's <u>edict</u>.

VOCABULARY PRACTICE
For more practice, go to the **Vocabulary Center** at ClassZone.com.

DIFFERENTIATED INSTRUCTION

FOR ENGLISH LEARNERS

Writing: Task Support Encourage students to use the Character Traits and Textual Evidence chart to plan their sentences for the Vocabulary in Writing activity.

BEST PRACTICES TOOLKIT—Transparency
Character Traits and Textual Evidence p. D6

FOR ADVANCED LEARNERS/PRE–AP

Vocabulary in Writing [small-group option] Have students create headlines that reflect the plot of "The Necklace," using as many vocabulary words as possible. *Example: Loisels Disconsolate over Ruinous Debts*

ANSWERS

Vocabulary in Context
VOCABULARY PRACTICE

1. *disconsolate*
2. *vexation*
3. *prospects*
4. *gamut*
5. *adulation*
6. *aghast*
7. *privation*
8. *askew*
9. *pauper*
10. *incessantly*

 RESOURCE MANAGER—Copy Master
Vocabulary Practice p. 58

VOCABULARY IN WRITING

Point out to students that each set of words in the Vocabulary Practice offers familiar synonyms for the vocabulary words. Reviewing these synonyms can help students think of ideas for the sentence-writing activity.

VOCABULARY STRATEGY: LATIN WORD ROOT *spec* (also an EL language objective)

- To help students understand word roots, focus on the vocabulary word *disconsolate*.
- Model for students how the prefix *dis-* and the suffix *-ate* combine with the root *console* to form the word *disconsolate* and its meaning:

  dis- (not) + *console* (to make feel better [from *com* = with; *solari* = sun]) + *-ate* (able to be) = *disconsolate* (not able to be made to feel better)

- Point out that *disconsolate* has the same root as *consoler* in French and *desconsolado* in Spanish. Ask students who speak these or other romance languages to share other non-English words related to the roots on the page.

Possible answers:

1. *a speaking about guilt or innocence*
2. *thankfulness*
3. *spoke against*
4. *a person who is not thankful*
5. *a speaking out, or announcement*

RESOURCE MANAGER—Copy Master
Vocabulary Strategy p. 59

Vocabulary Center at **ClassZone.com**
Additional Vocabulary Activities

Reading-Writing Connection

WRITING PROMPTS

- For Prompt A, have students use a Two-Column Chart to organize the examples of characteristics of the relationship and the details that support their conclusions.

- For Prompt B, remind students that a "yes" or "no" response is not sufficient; students must defend their opinions.

🧰 BEST PRACTICES TOOLKIT—Transparency
Two-Column Chart p. A25

For an extended writing activity, see
ℹ️ Carol Booth Olson's Reading-Writing Lesson Plans at **ClassZone.com**

REVISION: GRAMMAR AND STYLE

- Point out the words *when, where,* and *how.* Have students brainstorm for words, phrases, and clauses that might answer these questions in a sentence.

- After discussing the student model, write this paragraph (in black) on the board and have students suggest revisions (in red) to vary the sentence beginnings.

On returning home from the ball, ~~Tthe~~ *Loisels discover that the borrowed necklace is missing. They search frantically but to no avail. After a few days,* ~~Tthey~~ *are forced to give up. Without telling Madame Forestier what has happened,* ~~Tthey~~ *purchase a new necklace. ~~without telling Madame Forestier what has happened.~~*

ℝ RESOURCE MANAGER—Copy Master
Sentence Beginnings p. 62

Assess and Reteach

Assess

ℝ RESOURCE MANAGER—Copy Masters
Selection Test A pp. 65–66
Selection Test B/C pp. 67–68

💿 Test Generator CD

Reteach

🅂 STANDARDS LESSON FILE
Literature Lesson 2: Character Motivation
Reading Lesson 8: Making Inferences
Vocabulary Lesson 7: Latin Roots

Reading-Writing Connection

Increase your understanding of "The Necklace" by responding to these prompts.
Then use **Revision: Grammar and Style** to improve your writing.

WRITING PROMPTS	SELF-CHECK
A. Short Response: Analyze Characters How would you characterize the relationship between Monsieur and Madame Loisel at the beginning of the story? Using examples from the text, write **one or two paragraphs** to describe their marriage. Include details that show how they treat each other.	*A strong description will . . .* • list three characteristics of their relationship • cite specific details that support the conclusions
B. Extended Response: Write Across Texts Is it possible for a **status**-conscious person today to fall into the same financial situation as the Loisels? Use "The Necklace" and "Spending Spree" on page 221 to write a **three-to-five-paragraph response.**	*A successful response will . . .* • clearly state an opinion in the introduction • provide examples from the story, the article, and real life to support the opinion

REVISION: GRAMMAR AND STYLE

VARY SENTENCE BEGINNINGS Review the **Grammar and Style** note on page 214.
Like Maupassant, you can vary your sentence beginnings to add interest to your
writing. Revise your responses to the prompts by employing these techniques:

1. **Avoid using too many pronouns and articles.** Don't fall into the trap of beginning all your sentences with the words *he, she, it,* and *the.*

2. **Use words, phrases, and clauses that let readers know when, where, or how.** By using a variety of words, phrases, and clauses, Maupassant added descriptive details and avoided repetitive beginnings. Here are two examples:

   Finally, she answered hesitatingly . . . (line 74)

   As the day of the party approached, Mme. Loisel seemed sad. . . . (line 81)

Notice how the revisions in red improve the rhythm and flow of this first draft.

> **STUDENT MODEL**
> *Before the necklace is lost,*
> ∧The Loisels do not have a good marriage. Madame Loisel treats her husband
>   *Without a care for his feelings, At the party,*
> poorly. ∧She frequently snaps at him. ∧She ignores him☉ ~~at the party.~~
> *However,*   *Sensitive to her needs,*
> ∧He seems to always dote on her. ∧He does everything she wants.

🖊️ **WRITING TOOLS**
For prewriting, revision, and editing tools, visit the **Writing Center** at ClassZone.com.

DIFFERENTIATED INSTRUCTION

FOR LESS-PROFICIENT WRITERS
Possible Organization for Prompt A:
1. The topic sentence describes the Loisels' marriage.
2. The body cites specific characteristics of that relationship and at least one detail that illustrates each characteristic.
3. The final sentence reviews and/or remarks on that relationship.

Possible Organization for Prompt B:
1. The introductory paragraph states an opinion about the topic.
2. The second paragraph compares the Loisels' borrowing of money with teens' use of credit cards.
3. The third paragraph (a) compares attitudes toward possessions then with attitudes today and (b) reaffirms the opinion stated at the start.

MAGAZINE ARTICLE In "The Necklace," the Loisels borrow and buy their way into years of debt. Unfortunately, in their desire to achieve status, some teens today are falling into this same cycle.

$pending $pree

Been shopping lately? No matter which income bracket teens fall into, their general attitude stays the same: spend, don't save. On average, teens spend $100 a week on entertainment, clothing, and food. Perhaps this is why they're becoming the new target group of credit card marketers.

Pay or Play

While many teens might find the lure of a credit card to be irresistible, spending comes with a price. More and more often, young people are joining the ranks of those in debt.

What's the cause for this? Teens are often pressured to wear the same clothes, buy the same CDs, and own the same products. The credit card industry feeds off of this need to consume by offering credit cards to those who are barely out of high school.

Since most 18-year-olds are still unfamiliar with handling their personal finances, many don't pay their credit card bills on time, if at all. The result is a rapid build-up of debt.

Incentives for $aving

To help curb this financial downward spiral, one city has even established a "financial literacy" program. The Private Industry Council of Milwaukee County launched the pilot program, aimed at central-city teens. The training that teens receive through the program encourages them to save and instructs them in how to open a bank account.

Payoff

Learning to handle money responsibly early on can reap great rewards down the line. Not only does it contribute to a person's peace of mind to know that he or she is financially secure, but it also helps to establish a good credit record. So count your pennies, and avoid becoming one of the many Americans who are currently in debt.

Convenient or Costly? The chart shows how credit card charges can accumulate, assuming you miss three monthly payments.

CD PLAYER	$40.00
CLOTHES	$100.00
DVDs	$28.00
Original total due:	$168.00
Credit card late fees and finance charges:	**+** $83.00
Credit card total due:	**=** $251.00

DIFFERENTIATED INSTRUCTION

FOR ENGLISH LEARNERS

Language: Word Roots Point out that the word *credit* includes the Latin root *cred*, which means "trust" or "believe." Explain that credit allows you to buy something now in the trust or belief that you will pay for it in the future.

Culture: Clarify Explain that credit card companies, banks, and stores make money by penalizing people who make late payments. People pay fees, called "interest" or "finance charges," which can be very costly. With a "revolving charge," for example, you make payments that are only part of what you owe. Thus, you end up paying interest on the interest. In addition, many companies charge a yearly fee for their credit cards.

CONNECT

Use this selection either as support for Writing Prompt B on page 220 or as a mini-lesson on reading for information.

READING FOR INFORMATION

Point out that "Spending Spree" is a magazine article. Have students preview the article, noting the title, photo, subheadings, and chart. Then ask:

- What information do the text features and graphic aids provide? *Possible answer: The title and photo suggest the topic. The blue subheadings introduce the key ideas, while the chart and the caption make clear how interest can accumulate and lead to increased debt.*

- What effect might the playful tone and style of the subheadings have on readers? *Possible answer: They add interest, make the text less intimidating, and focus attention on key ideas.*

- What is the main idea of this article? *Possible answer: Teens are becoming the new target of credit card marketers (lines 5–6).*

DISCUSSION PROMPTS

Use the questions below to help students understand the issue of spiraling teen credit card debt:

Evaluate Based on this article, do you think that financial literacy programs are the answer to solving the problem of spiraling teen credit card debt? Explain your answer. *Possible answer: While financial literacy is one way to make teens aware of the dangers in taking on debt, teens also need to be taught ways to avoid taking on huge amounts of debt.*

Synthesize How might Madame Loisel's life have been different had she lived today and had easy credit available? *Possible answers: She would have been better off because she could have paid off her debt over time; her life would be no better because she still would have to pay back a huge debt plus the compounding interest.*

Focus and Motivate

OBJECTIVES

Literary Analysis
- explore the key idea of being **remarkable**
- analyze third-person limited point of view
- read a short story

Reading
- monitor comprehension

Vocabulary
- build vocabulary for reading and writing
- use word origins to understand words
  (also an EL language objective)

Grammar and Writing
- add emphasis by using repetition
- use writing to analyze literature

SUMMARY

In Naomi Shihab Nye's "Hamadi," high school freshman Susan is fond of her family's courtly, elderly friend Saleh Hamadi. She considers him a surrogate grandparent, and she invites him to go Christmas caroling with her English Club. He strikes the carolers as odd and amusing. During the caroling, Susan's friend Tracy realizes that Eddie, a classmate she loves, is not interested in her. When she cries and turns to Hamadi for comfort, he gently urges her to "go on."

What makes someone REMARKABLE?

Ask the question. As students read the *KEY IDEA*, explain that **remarkable** conveys the idea of being worth admiration. After students have completed the *PRESENT* activity, point out that this oral activity demonstrates the essence of *remarkable*.

Selection Resources

Hamadi
Short Story by Naomi Shihab Nye

What makes someone REMARKABLE?

KEY IDEA Whether it's an outrageous sense of humor or an aura of quiet confidence, some people have qualities that are hard not to notice. Susan, the main character in the short story "Hamadi," has a friend with a unique way of looking at the world. Susan finds Hamadi **remarkable;** she notices him because of his extraordinary personality.

PRESENT What makes individuals stand out to you? What traits give them striking personalities? Pick one remarkable person and list his or her traits. Then "introduce" this person to a classmate in a way that makes it clear why the individual is so extraordinary.

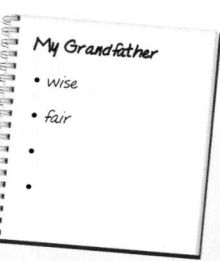

My Grandfather
- wise
- fair
-
-

222

RESOURCE MANAGER UNIT 2

Plan and Teach pp. 69–76

Literary Analysis
Summary pp. 77†*, 78*‡
Third-Person Limited Point of
   View pp. 79, 80†*
Question Support p. 87*

Reading
Monitor pp. 81, 82†*
Reading Check p. 86

Vocabulary
Study p. 83*
Practice p. 84
Strategy p. 85

Grammar and Writing
Add Emphasis p. 89

Assessment
Selection Tests A, B/C pp. 91*, 93*
Test Generator CD

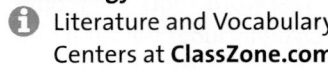 **BEST PRACTICES TOOLKIT**

Differentiated Instruction
   pp. 31–38*

Scaffolding Instruction
   pp. 43–46*

Graphic Organizers/Strategies
Readers Theater • Word Question-
ing • Analysis Frame: Character
• Venn Diagram • New Word
Analysis • Character Traits and
Textual Evidence

Reading Support
   Audio Anthology CD*

Technology
   Literature and Vocabulary
   Centers at **ClassZone.com**
   WriteSmart CD

---

* Resources for Differentiation   † Also in Spanish   ‡ In Haitian Creole and Vietnamese

LITERARY ANALYSIS: THIRD-PERSON LIMITED POINT OF VIEW

"Hamadi" is told from a **third-person limited point of view.** The narrator is an outside voice that tells what only one character thinks, feels, and observes. The narrator of "Hamadi" zeroes in on the thoughts and feelings of a high school freshman named Susan. As you read "Hamadi," pay attention to what the narrator reveals about Susan, and consider how this affects your perception of her.

READING STRATEGY: MONITOR

When you read, pause every few minutes to check, or **monitor,** how well you are understanding the story.

- **Visualize:** Picture characters, events, and settings.
- **Clarify:** Stop now and then to review what you understand.
- **Question:** Ask questions about the events and characters.
- **Predict:** Look for hints of what might happen next.
- **Connect:** Compare events with your own experiences.

As you read "Hamadi," use the "Monitor" annotations to help you gain insight into the characters.

Review: **Make Inferences**

▲ VOCABULARY IN CONTEXT

Which of the following words might be used to describe

1. an ornate piece of furniture?
2. an ancient language?
3. an empty room?
4. a subtle joke?
5. a meal after a long journey?

WORD LIST	anthem	lavish	sustenance
	archaic	spartan	wry
	expansive	surrogate	

Author Online

More Than One Way to See
Naomi Shihab Nye was born in St. Louis, Missouri. Like Susan, the main character in "Hamadi," Nye grew up in an Arab-American family. In 1966 her family moved to the Middle East, and Nye spent her freshman year at a high school in East Jerusalem, then a part of Jordan. Nye says her year in the Middle East changed her irrevocably. "This is one of the best things about growing up in a mixed family or community," she says. "You never think only one way of doing or seeing anything is right."

**Naomi Shihab Nye
born 1952**

A Writer of Vision Best known as a poet, Nye is also a short story writer, essayist, children's book author, novelist, and songwriter. In all of her work, Nye honors diverse viewpoints and celebrates the mixing of cultures. Literature, she believes, gives us "insight into all the secret territories of the human spirit."

 MORE ABOUT THE AUTHOR
For more on Naomi Shihab Nye, visit the **Literature Center** at **ClassZone.com.**

Background

Seeking Refuge In this story, both the main character's father and her friend Hamadi come from a region torn by conflict. Hamadi is from Lebanon, a country devastated by a 16-year civil war. Susan's father is Palestinian. In 1947, the United Nations proposed a plan to partition what was then Palestine to create the state of Israel, a homeland for the Jewish people. More than 50 years later, the conflict between Israelis and Palestinians is still unresolved and often marked by violence. These situations have created millions of refugees—people who have fled their native lands in search of shelter and protection.

Teach

STANDARDS FOCUS

LITERARY ANALYSIS

● THIRD-PERSON LIMITED POINT OF VIEW

For instructional support, read aloud this passage:

> Ten years went by, and Harris no longer remembered. He felt agitated when he saw Mrs. Coombs, but could not say why he felt this way. As to what Mrs. Coombs felt, one could not possibly know.

Have students explain why the passage is an example of the third-person limited point of view. *Possible answer: The narrator is not a character in the story and tells what only one character is thinking and feeling.*

CHECK UNDERSTANDING Which character in the passage does the narrator zero in on?

READING STRATEGY

● MONITOR

Discuss the monitoring strategies described on the page. Then model using the suggestions to monitor your understanding of *About the Author.* For example, clarify that Nye lived in the Middle East and the United States, and predict that Susan will be similar in some ways to Nye.

CHECK UNDERSTANDING Have students repeat the process you modeled, using the *Background* text.

 RESOURCE MANAGER—Copy Master
Monitor p. 81 (for student use while reading the selection)

VOCABULARY SKILL

▲ VOCABULARY IN CONTEXT

DIAGNOSE WORD KNOWLEDGE To determine preteaching needs, have all students complete Vocabulary in Context. *Possible answers:*
1. *lavish* 2. *archaic* 3. *spartan* 4. *wry*
5. *sustenance*

PRETEACH VOCABULARY Use the Vocabulary Study copy master to introduce students to the boldfaced words in the copy master.

1. Read the first sentence on the worksheet, emphasizing *anthem.*
2. Have students mark on the worksheet whether they have heard the word before.
3. Have students write their own sentence and a possible meaning.
4. Repeat the procedure for items 2–8.

 RESOURCE MANAGER—Copy Master
Vocabulary Study p. 83

For general guidelines on differentiating vocabulary instruction and for alternative vocabulary activities for students not needing vocabulary preteaching, see

 BEST PRACTICES TOOLKIT
Scaffolding Vocabulary Instruction pp. 43–46
ℹ️ Vocabulary Center at **ClassZone.com**

ANALYZE VISUALS

Possible answer: *The dreamlike quality is created by the man's floating and his distracted look and sleepy eyes. The swirling pattern in his clothing and the stylized clouds add to this mood.*

About the Art Contemporary artist and New Jersey native Daniel Nevins earned a graphic arts degree from the University of Florida in 1985 and worked as a designer until he turned to painting. The dreamlike quality of *Inspiration* is apparent in many of his paintings.

READING STRATEGY

A MONITOR

Possible answer: *Susan's grandmother is calm, wise, slightly mysterious, steadfast, hardworking, and unhurried. She also may be religious.*

If students need help . . .

- Display a photograph of the Sphinx, and elicit adjectives to describe it, such as *quiet, calm, wise, secretive,* and *mysterious.*

- Then read aloud lines 11–20, and ask students to visualize the grandmother. Note any different words students might use.

HAMADI

Naomi Shihab Nye

"It takes two of us to discover truth:
one to utter it and one to understand it."

KAHLIL GIBRAN, *Sand and Foam*

Susan didn't really feel interested in Saleh Hamadi[1] until she was a freshman in high school carrying a thousand questions around. Why this way? Why not another way? Who said so and why can't I say something else? Those brittle women at school in the counselor's office treated the world as if it were a yardstick and they had a tight hold of both ends.

Sometimes Susan felt polite with them, sorting attendance cards during her free period, listening to them gab about fingernail polish and television. And other times she felt she could run out of the building yelling. That's when she daydreamed about Saleh Hamadi, who had nothing to do with any of

10 it. Maybe she thought of him as escape, the way she used to think about the Sphinx at Giza[2] when she was younger. She would picture the golden Sphinx sitting quietly in the desert with sand blowing around its face, never changing its expression. She would think of its **wry,** slightly crooked mouth and how her grandmother looked a little like that as she waited for her bread to bake in the old village north of Jerusalem.[3] Susan's family had lived in Jerusalem for three years before she was ten and drove out to see her grandmother every weekend. They would find her patting fresh dough between her hands, or pressing cakes of dough onto the black rocks in the *taboon,* the rounded old oven outdoors. Sometimes she moved her lips as she worked. Was she praying? Singing a secret

20 song? Susan had never seen her grandmother rushing. **A**

Now that she was fourteen, she took long walks in America with her father down by the drainage ditch at the end of their street. Pecan trees shaded the

---

1. **Saleh Hamadi** (sä'lĕкн hä-mä'dē).
2. **Sphinx at Giza** (gē'zə): a huge ancient statue with a man's head and a lion's body, near the city of Giza in northern Egypt.
3. **Jerusalem:** the capital of Israel and a holy city for Jews, Christians, and Muslims.

224 UNIT 2: CHARACTERIZATION AND POINT OF VIEW

ANALYZE VISUALS
Susan daydreams about Saleh Hamadi to escape from the everyday. What aspects of this painting have a dreamlike quality?

① **Targeted Passage**

wry (rī) *adj.* dryly humorous, often with a bit of irony

A MONITOR
Reread lines 8–20. As you read, **visualize** the scene Susan remembers. Describe Susan's grandmother's **traits.**

Inspiration (1994), Daniel Nevins. Oil, acrylic, and collage on wood, 6.6″ × 9.0″. Private collection. © Daniel Nevins/SuperStock.

DIFFERENTIATED INSTRUCTION

FOR ALL STUDENTS
Enhancing Learning Styles Provide these independent projects for various learning preferences:

- **Visual** Design "remarkable" stamps.
- **Linguistic** Write riddles like Hamadi.
- **Spatial** Provide captions for a map.

For further details on these projects, see

R RESOURCE MANAGER
Ideas for Extension pp. 74–75

FOR LESS–PROFICIENT READERS
In combination with the *Audio Anthology CD,* use one or more Targeted Passages (pp. 224, 226, 229, 232) to ensure that students focus on key story events, concepts, and skills. Targeted Passages are also good for English learners.

① Targeted Passage [Lines 1–10]

This passage introduces Susan and Hamadi, the story's two main characters.

BACKGROUND

Names The name *Hamadi* means "praised" or "one who praises," and it comes from the same root as the name *Muhammad.* As students will see, Hamadi is a person who praises—or, at least, encourages—others. The name *Saleh* means "good" or "right"; as the story unfolds, this quality becomes clear in the gracious way that Saleh Hamadi treats the people around him. If students know the meaning of their own names, invite them to share that information.

Lines 8–20
REINFORCE *KEY IDEA:* REMARKABLE

Discuss Think about what you have just read about Hamadi. What, if anything, might lead you to think of him as **remarkable?** *Possible answer: Nye is just setting up the story; it may be too early for her to show us why Hamadi is special. All we know so far is that Susan identifies him with her grandmother (lines 13–15) and that she considers him worth thinking about (which is the basis for her talking about him—the essence of the word* remarkable*).*

- When does Susan begin to take an interest in Saleh Hamadi?
- What questions does Susan ask about the world?
- What does she think about the women in the school counselor's office?
- When does she daydream about Hamadi?

FOR ENGLISH LEARNERS

Options for Reading Use Readers Theater to help students read this story. Assign a narrator to read non-highlighted text and individual students to read each character's part.

 BEST PRACTICES TOOLKIT
Readers Theater p. A1

Prereading For prereading instruction for English learners, see

 BEST PRACTICES TOOLKIT
Scaffolding Reading Instruction pp. 43–46

FOR ADVANCED LEARNERS/PRE–AP

Pre-AP Exercises in the bottom channel provide additional challenge for students. Use these suggestions for small groups or individuals.

ADDITIONAL GUIDELINES

For more help with differentiation and tips for classroom management, see

BEST PRACTICES TOOLKIT
Differentiated Instruction pp. 31–38

B POINT OF VIEW

Possible answer: *Susan cares about her heritage; she is helpful, selfless, thoughtful, and generous.*

If students need help . . . Have students complete this chart to make inferences about Susan's personality:

Lines	Detail	Character Trait(s)
23	childhood stories	interested in her heritage
24–26	helps her mother	selfless and uncomplaining
28	wants to visit Hamadi	thoughtful and generous

Lines 32–57
DISCUSSION PROMPTS

Use these prompts to help students see how details reveal Hamadi's appearance and personality:

Connect Think of someone you know who is unusual but admirable. How would you make those traits clear to someone who had never met that person? *Possible answer: by using precise and vivid language to describe the traits that seem the most distinctive or remarkable*

Analyze In lines 32–34, Susan compares Hamadi's jacket to the "earth's surface just above the treeline—thin, somehow purified." What does this detail tell us about Hamadi? about Susan? *Possible answer: Hamadi is a rare individual who values the purity of simple surroundings while embracing the wider world of books and people of many nations. Susan is sensitive and observant; someone else might simply think of Hamadi as impoverished and old.*

Synthesize How does this description of Hamadi's outlook on life make him seem **remarkable?** *Possible answer: Hamadi has endured loneliness and poverty while maintaining a life of dignity and thoughtfulness.*

---

path. She tried to get him to tell stories about his childhood in Palestine.[4] She didn't want him to forget anything. She helped her American mother complete tedious kitchen tasks without complaining—rolling grape leaves around their lemony rice stuffing, scrubbing carrots for the roaring juicer. Some evenings when the soft Texas twilight pulled them all outside, she thought of her faraway grandmother and said, "Let's go see Saleh Hamadi. Wouldn't he like some of that cheese pie Mom made?" And they would wrap a slice of pie and
30 drive downtown. Somehow he felt like a good substitute for a grandmother, even though he was a man. **B**

Usually Hamadi was wearing a white shirt, shiny black tie, and a jacket that reminded Susan of the earth's surface just above the treeline on a mountain— thin, somehow purified. He would raise his hands high before giving advice.

"It is good to drink a tall glass of water every morning upon arising!" If anyone doubted this, he would shake his head. "Oh Susan, Susan, Susan," he would say.

He did not like to sit down, but he wanted everyone else to sit down. He made Susan sit on the wobbly chair beside the desk and he made her father or
40 mother sit in the saggy center of the bed. He told them people should eat six small meals a day.

They visited him on the sixth floor of the Traveler's Hotel, where he had lived so long nobody could remember him ever traveling. Susan's father used to remind him of the apartments available over the Victory Cleaners, next to the park with the fizzy pink fountain, but Hamadi would shake his head, pinching kisses at his **spartan** room. "A white handkerchief spread across a tabletop, my two extra shoes lined by the wall, this spells 'home' to me, this says 'mi casa.' What more do I need?"

Hamadi liked to use Spanish words. They made him feel **expansive,** worldly.
50 He'd learned them when he worked at the fruits and vegetables warehouse on Zarzamora[5] Street, marking off crates of apples and avocados on a long white pad. Occasionally he would speak Arabic, his own first language, with Susan's father and uncles, but he said it made him feel too sad, as if his mother might step into the room at any minute, her arms laden with fresh mint leaves.

He had come to the United States on a boat when he was eighteen years old and he had never been married. "I married books," he said. "I married the wide horizon."

"What is he to us?" Susan used to ask her father. "He's not a relative, right? How did we meet him to begin with?"
60 Susan's father couldn't remember. "I think we just drifted together. Maybe we met at your uncle Hani's house. Maybe that old Maronite priest[6] who used to cry after every service introduced us. The priest once shared an apartment

---

4. **Palestine:** a historical region at the east end of the Mediterranean Sea.

5. **Zarzamora** (zär′zə-môr′ə).

6. **Maronite priest:** The Maronites are a Christian group allied with the Roman Catholic Church. They live primarily in Lebanon, the country to the north of Israel.

226 UNIT 2: CHARACTERIZATION AND POINT OF VIEW

B POINT OF VIEW
Reread lines 21–31. What important **character traits** of Susan's does the narrator reveal in this paragraph?

2 Targeted Passage

spartan (spär′tn) *adj.* simple, plain, and frugal

expansive (ĭk-spăn′sĭv) *adj.* outgoing; showing feelings openly and freely

---

DIFFERENTIATED INSTRUCTION

FOR LESS–PROFICIENT READERS
2 Targeted Passage [Lines 32–54]

In this passage, Hamadi himself enters the story, and many details about his life and personality are revealed.

- What clothing does Hamadi usually wear?

- How do his words and actions show that he cares about people?

- How does Hamadi furnish his room?

- Why does Hamadi feel sad when he speaks Arabic?

FOR ENGLISH LEARNERS
Key Academic Vocabulary Use Word Questioning to teach these words: *substitute* (line 30), *distinctions* (line 79), *responded* (line 152), *significant* (line 237), *preliminary* (line 237), *immigrants* (line 244).

 BEST PRACTICES TOOLKIT—Transparency Word Questioning p. E9

with Kahlil Gibran[7] in New York—so he said. And Saleh always says he stayed with Gibran when he first got off the boat. I'll bet that popular guy Gibran has had a lot of roommates he doesn't even know about."

Susan said, "Dad, he's dead."

"I know, I know," her father said.

Later Susan said, "Mr. Hamadi, did you really meet Kahlil Gibran? He's one of my favorite writers." Hamadi walked slowly to the window of his room and
70 stared out. There wasn't much to look at down on the street—a bedraggled flower shop, a boarded-up tavern with a hand-lettered sign tacked to the front, GONE TO FIND JESUS. Susan's father said the owners had really gone to Alabama.

Hamadi spoke patiently. "Yes, I met brother Gibran. And I meet him in my heart every day. When I was a young man—shocked by all the visions of the new world—the tall buildings—the wild traffic—the young people without shame—the proud mailboxes in their blue uniforms—I met him. And he has stayed with me every day of my life."

"But did you really meet him, like in person, or just in a book?"

He turned dramatically. "Make no such distinctions, my friend. Or your life
80 will be a pod with only dried-up beans inside. Believe anything can happen."

Susan's father looked irritated, but Susan smiled. "I do," she said. "I believe that. I want fat beans. If I imagine something, it's true, too. Just a different kind of true." **C**

Susan's father was twiddling with the knobs on the old-fashioned sink. "Don't they even give you hot water here? You don't mean to tell me you've been living without hot water?"

On Hamadi's rickety desk lay a row of different "Love" stamps issued by the post office.

"You must write a lot of letters," Susan said.

90 "No, no, I'm just focusing on that word," Hamadi said. "I particularly like the globe in the shape of a heart," he added.

"Why don't you take a trip back to your village in Lebanon?" Susan's father asked. "Maybe you still have relatives living there."

Hamadi looked pained. "'Remembrance is a form of meeting,' my brother Gibran says, and I do believe I meet with my cousins every day."

"But aren't you curious? You've been gone so long! Wouldn't you like to find out what has happened to everybody and everything you knew as a boy?" Susan's father traveled back to Jerusalem once each year to see his family.

"I would not. In fact, I already know. It is there and it is not there. Would
100 you like to share an orange with me?" **D**

His long fingers, tenderly peeling. Once when Susan was younger, he'd given her a **lavish** ribbon off a holiday fruit basket and expected her to wear it on her head. In the car, Susan's father said, "Riddles. He talks in riddles. I don't know why I have patience with him." Susan stared at the people talking and laughing in the next car. She did not even exist in their world.

---

7. **Kahlil Gibran** (kə-lēl' jə-brän'): a Lebanese-American philosopher and mystic poet whose best known work is *The Prophet*.

C MONITOR
Reread lines 68–83. As you read, **question** whether Hamadi actually met Gibran in person. What does Hamadi's own answer to this question reveal about his character?

D POINT OF VIEW
Reread lines 87–100. Although the **narrator** does not directly convey Hamadi's thoughts, the narrator does give the reader clues about how Hamadi thinks and feels. What are these clues, and what do they tell you about Hamadi?

lavish (lăv'ĭsh) *adj.* extravagant; more than is needed

C MONITOR

Possible answer: There seems to be no way to know for sure if Hamadi ever met Gibran. Hamadi certainly shares the imaginative and spiritual qualities that characterize Gibran's writings.

If students need help . . .

- Review lines 63–65. Elicit that Susan's father doubts Hamadi's claim.
- Review lines 73–74. Note that although Gibran is dead (line 66), Hamadi still meets him each day, in his heart.
- Review lines 68–69 and line 78. Elicit that Susan knows that one can meet a person through his or her writings.

Extend the Discussion What do Hamadi's words to Susan in lines 79–80 mean?

D POINT OF VIEW

Possible answer: The "Love" stamps and Hamadi's unwillingness to travel suggest that he wants to view the world optimistically. He ignores unpleasant change; instead, he remembers people and events through fond memories.

If students need help . . . Ask:

- According to lines 87–91, why does Hamadi buy so many stamps? *Possible answer: He likes the sentiment of the "Love" stamps.*
- Based on lines 94–100, why do you think he does not want to return to Lebanon? *Possible answer: He does not want to see how things have changed.*

Extend the Discussion Who can deal better with life: a realist (like Susan's father) or a romantic (like Hamadi)? Explain.

FOR ENGLISH LEARNERS
Culture: Connect Multiple references to Middle Eastern foods appear in this story. List these references on the board and have students add to the list as they read the story: grape leaves with rice stuffing (lines 25–26); cheese pies (lines 28–30); fresh mint leaves (line 54). Invite students to compare these foods with foods of their own culture and to describe some of the similarities and differences to the class.

FOR ADVANCED LEARNERS/PRE–AP
Evaluate Ideas In line 80, Hamadi offers this advice: "Believe anything can happen." Does that idea make sense? Is it practical—or even possible? Ask students to write a short essay in which they apply that advice to a real-life situation, evaluating how positive thinking either brings success on its own or must be balanced by other factors. Have students share their essays with the class.

Possible answer: *The mood in* Healing *is more peaceful than the mood in the painting on page 225. The female figure here appears relaxed, as indicated by her gentle smile, calm eyes, curving limbs, gentle gestures, wavy lines, and heart cradled within her chest. The male figure in* Inspiration *seems tense by comparison, with his unsmiling mouth, sad or wistful eyes, angular arms, and heart above his head.* Healing *has a soothing blue background with a smooth texture;* Inspiration *has a dreary greenish-blue background and a rough texture.*

ANALYZE VISUALS
Compare the mood of this painting with the mood of the painting on page 225. Consider the colors, lines, and textures in each painting, as well as each figure's facial expression and gestures.

Healing (1996), Daniel Nevins. Oil on wood, 7.4″ × 9.0″. © Daniel Nevins/SuperStock.

S usan carried *The Prophet* around on top of her English textbook and her Texas history. She and her friend Tracy read it out loud to one another at lunch. Tracy was a junior—they'd met at the literary magazine meeting where Susan, the only freshman on the staff, got assigned to do
110 proofreading. They never ate in the cafeteria; they sat outside at picnic tables with sack lunches, whole wheat crackers and fresh peaches. Both of them had given up meat.

228   UNIT 2: CHARACTERIZATION AND POINT OF VIEW

DIFFERENTIATED INSTRUCTION

FOR ENGLISH LEARNERS

Reading: Background Supplement the footnote on page 227 by explaining that Kahlil Gibran (1883–1931) was a writer and artist. Born in Lebanon, he and most of his family immigrated to Boston in 1895. His first published work was a newspaper article in 1904. *The Prophet* (1923) was not Gibran's first book, but it is his most famous. In it, a visionary named Almustafa offers spiritual insights on a range of subjects, including love, friendship, pain, work, and freedom.

FOR ADVANCED LEARNERS/PRE–AP

In-depth Textual Analysis Have students use the Character Analysis Frame to explore this story and, in particular, the characters of Hamadi and Susan. Students may refer to the Analysis Frame as they discuss "Hamadi" in class or write about it after reading.

🧰 BEST PRACTICES TOOLKIT—Transparency
Analysis Frame: Character pp. D21, D26

Tracy's eyes looked steamy. "You know that place where Gibran says, 'Hate is a dead thing. Who of you would be a tomb?'"

Susan nodded. Tracy continued. "Well, I hate someone. I'm trying not to, but I can't help it. I hate Debbie for liking Eddie and it's driving me nuts."

"Why shouldn't Debbie like Eddie?" Susan said. "*You* do."

Tracy put her head down on her arms. A gang of cheerleaders walked by giggling. One of them flicked her finger in greeting.

120 "In fact, we *all* like Eddie," Susan said. "Remember, here in this book—wait and I'll find it—where Gibran says that loving teaches us the secrets of our hearts and that's the way we connect to all of Life's heart? You're not talking about liking or loving, you're talking about owning."

Tracy looked glum. "Sometimes you remind me of a minister." **E**

Susan said, "Well, just talk to me someday when *I'm* depressed."

Susan didn't want a boyfriend. Everyone who had boyfriends or girlfriends seemed to have troubles. Susan told people she had a boyfriend far away, on a farm in Missouri, but the truth was, boys still seemed like cousins to her. Or brothers. Or even girls.

130 A squirrel sat in the crook of a tree, eyeing their sandwiches. When the end-of-lunch bell blared, Susan and Tracy jumped—it always seemed too soon. Squirrels were lucky; they didn't have to go to school.

Susan's father said her idea was ridiculous: to invite Saleh Hamadi to go Christmas caroling with the English Club. "His English is **archaic,** for one thing, and he won't know *any* of the songs."

"How could you live in America for years and not know 'Joy to the World' or 'Away in a Manger'?"

"Listen, I grew up right down the road from 'Oh Little Town of Bethlehem' and I still don't know a single verse."

140 "I want him. We need him. It's boring being with the same bunch of people all the time." **F**

So they called Saleh and he said he would come—"thrilled" was the word he used. He wanted to ride the bus to their house, he didn't want anyone to pick him up. Her father muttered, "He'll probably forget to get off." Saleh thought "caroling" meant they were going out with a woman named Carol. He said, "Holiday spirit—I was just reading about it in the newspaper."

Susan said, "Dress warm."

Saleh replied, "Friend, my heart is warmed simply to hear your voice."

All that evening Susan felt light and bouncy. She decorated the coffee can 150 they would use to collect donations to be sent to the children's hospital in Bethlehem. She had started doing this last year in middle school, when a singing group collected $100 and the hospital responded on exotic onion-skin stationery[8] that they were "eternally grateful."

---

8. **onion-skin stationery:** a thin, strong typing paper.

E MAKE INFERENCES
Consider what you know about Susan so far. Why does Tracy compare her to a minister? Explain your answer.

3 Targeted Passage

archaic (är-kā'ĭk) *adj.* very old or unfashionable

F POINT OF VIEW
Why does Susan find Hamadi so interesting? Decide whether you would be able to answer this question if Susan were not the point-of-view character.

E MAKE INFERENCES

Possible answer: *Like a minister, Susan offers spiritual counsel. Tracy also may feel that Susan is telling her something that she knows is true but does not want to hear. People often say that they have been "preached at" in such situations.*

If students need help . . . Have them reread lines 120–124. Ask:

- How do ministers try to help troubled people? **Possible answers:** *They offer support and comfort. They may give advice to troubled people about improving their lives.*

- Why is Tracy glum after hearing Susan's words? **Possible answer:** *She wishes that Susan had taken her side and been more supportive.*

LITERARY ANALYSIS

F POINT OF VIEW

Possible answer: *Hamadi is different from the people Susan knows. Readers could not answer the question if another character were the point of view character because readers would not know Susan's thoughts and feelings.*

If students need help . . . Use a Venn diagram to help them compare Hamadi to Susan's friends.

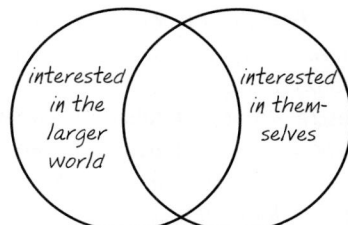

Hamadi   Susan's Friends

interested in the larger world / interested in them-selves

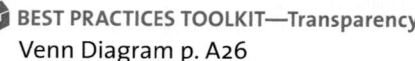

BEST PRACTICES TOOLKIT—Transparency Venn Diagram p. A26

FOR ENGLISH LEARNERS
Culture: Clarify Explain the tradition of Christmas caroling (line 134). Have groups of students list ten Christmas carols and then see which of the carols named in the story appear on their list: "Joy to the World" (lines 136–137); "Away in a Manger" (line 137); "Oh Little Town of Bethlehem" (line 138); "We Wish You a Merry Christmas" (lines 191–192); "What Child Is This?" (lines 225–226); "The Friendly Beasts" (line 226).

FOR LESS–PROFICIENT READERS
3 Targeted Passage [Lines 116–143]

This passage introduces a conflict: Tracy's competition with Debbie for Eddie's attention. It also develops the contrast between Hamadi and Susan's family and friends.

- What does Tracy say about Debbie? Why?

- What idea does Susan's father ridicule?

- How do Susan and Hamadi both feel about going Christmas caroling?

G MONITOR

Possible answer: Hamadi offers Susan intellectual and emotional support, as a grandmother would. Like Susan's grandmother, Hamadi is an enigmatic, interesting person, who makes Susan pause, think, and ask questions.

If students need help... Suggest that they read on to line 163 and focus on the statement "We have a connection." Invite students to freewrite about the "connection," as they see it, and then compare responses with partners or in small groups.

Lines 173–179
DISCUSSION PROMPTS

Use these prompts to help students understand the relationship between Susan's ideas about holidays and her character:

Connect Do you ever have the feeling about holidays described in lines 175–176? Explain. *Various attitudes are acceptable. Responses may address the idea of not feeling "ready" for holidays, for example.*

Analyze Why does Susan mention a woman who celebrates fresh asparagus (lines 177–178)? What does the reference suggest about Susan's character? *Possible answer: Susan cites the woman in order to illustrate the idea of making up one's own holidays. The reference suggests that Susan is imaginative and positive.*

Synthesize What generalization can you make about Susan's character, based on her attitude toward holidays? *Possible answer: She looks at life in a unique, even remarkable, way.*

Her father shook his head. "You get something into your mind and it really takes over," he said. "Why do you like Hamadi so much all of a sudden? You could show half as much interest in your own uncles."

Susan laughed. Her uncles were dull. Her uncles shopped at the mall and watched TV. "Anyone who watches TV more than twelve minutes a week is uninteresting," she said.

160   Her father lifted an eyebrow.

"He's my **surrogate** grandmother," she said. "He says interesting things. **G** He makes me think. Remember when I was little and he called me The Thinker? We have a connection." She added, "Listen, do you want to go too? It's not a big deal. And Mom has a *great* voice. Why don't you both come?"

A minute later her mother was digging in the closet for neck scarves, and her father was digging in the drawer for flashlight batteries.

Saleh Hamadi arrived precisely on time, with flushed red cheeks and a sack of dates stuffed in his pocket. "We may need **sustenance** on our journey." Susan thought the older people seemed quite giddy as they drove down to the
170   high school to meet the rest of the carolers. Strands of winking lights wrapped around their neighbors' drainpipes and trees. A giant Santa tipped his hat on Dr. Garcia's roof.

Her friends stood gathered in front of the school. Some were smoothing out song sheets that had been crammed in a drawer or cabinet for a whole year. Susan thought holidays were strange; they came, and you were supposed to feel ready for them. What if you could make up your own holidays as you went along? She had read about a woman who used to have parties to celebrate the arrival of fresh asparagus in the local market. Susan's friends might make holidays called Eddie Looked at Me Today and Smiled.

180   Two people were alleluia-ing in harmony. Saleh Hamadi went around the group formally introducing himself to each person and shaking hands. A few people laughed silently when his back was turned. He had stepped out of a painting, or a newscast, with his outdated long overcoat, his clunky old man's shoes and elegant manners.

Susan spoke more loudly than usual. "I'm honored to introduce you to one of my best friends, Mr. Hamadi."

"Good evening to you," he pronounced musically, bowing a bit from the waist.

What could you say back but "Good evening, sir." His old-fashioned
190   manners were contagious.

They sang at three houses that never opened their doors. They sang "We Wish You a Merry Christmas" each time they moved on. Lisa had a fine, clear soprano. Tracy could find the alto harmony to any line. Cameron and Elliot had more enthusiasm than accuracy. Lily, Rita, and Jeannette laughed every time they said a wrong word and fumbled to find their places again. Susan

surrogate (sûr′ə-gĭt) *adj.* serving as a substitute

G MONITOR
After you read line 161, stop to **clarify.** Why does Susan call Hamadi her "surrogate grandmother"?

sustenance (sŭs′tə-nəns) *n.* food or provisions that sustain life

DIFFERENTIATED INSTRUCTION

FOR ENGLISH LEARNERS

Vocabulary: Idioms Use New Word Analysis to teach these idioms from the story: *takes over* (line 155), "assumes control"; *a big deal* (line 164), "important"; *fell into step* (line 222), "walked together at the same pace"; *get booked up* (line 234), "have all of its reservations taken (by other people)"

🧰 **BEST PRACTICES TOOLKIT—Transparency**
New Word Analysis p. E8

FOR ADVANCED LEARNERS/PRE–AP

Synthesize [small-group option] Challenge students to prepare a statement about how the Christmastime setting serves to reinforce ideas in this story. Then ask students to imagine that "Hamadi" was set during another religious or patriotic holiday. Have students discuss the new setting and prepare a statement about how the story might change.

loved to see how her mother knew every word of every verse without looking at the paper, and how her father kept his hands in his pockets and seemed more interested in examining people's mailboxes or yard displays than in trying to sing. And Saleh Hamadi—what language was he singing in? He didn't even 200 seem to be pronouncing words, but humming deeply from his throat. Was he saying, "Om"?[9] Speaking Arabic? Once he caught her looking and whispered, "That was an Aramaic[10] word that just drifted into my mouth—the true language of the Bible, you know, the language Jesus Christ himself spoke."

By the fourth block their voices felt tuned up and friendly people came outside to listen. Trays of cookies were passed around and dollar bills stuffed into the little can. Thank you, thank you. Out of the dark from down the block, Susan noticed Eddie sprinting toward them with his coat flapping, unbuttoned. She shot a glance at Tracy, who pretended not to notice. "Hey guys!" shouted Eddie. "The first time in my life I'm late and everyone else is 210 on time! You could at least have left a note about which way you were going." Someone slapped him on the back. Saleh Hamadi, whom he had never seen before, was the only one who managed a reply. "Welcome, welcome to our cheery group!"

Eddie looked mystified. "Who is this guy?"

Susan whispered, "My friend." **H**

Eddie approached Tracy, who read her song sheet intently just then, and stuck his face over her shoulder to whisper, "Hi." Tracy stared straight ahead into the air and whispered "Hi" vaguely, glumly. Susan shook her head. Couldn't Tracy act more cheerful at least?

220 They were walking again. They passed a string of blinking reindeer and a wooden snowman holding a painted candle.

Eddie fell into step beside Tracy, murmuring so Susan couldn't hear him anymore. Saleh Hamadi was flinging his arms up high as he strode. Was he power walking?[11] Did he even know what power walking was? Between houses, Susan's mother hummed obscure songs people hardly remembered: "What Child Is This?" and "The Friendly Beasts."

Lisa moved over to Eddie's other side. "I'm *so excited* about you and Debbie!" she said loudly. "Why didn't she come tonight?"

Eddie said, "She has a sore throat."

230 Tracy shrank up inside her coat. **I**

Lisa chattered on. "James said we should make our reservations *now* for dinner at the Tower after the Sweetheart Dance, can you believe it? In December, making a reservation for February? But otherwise it might get booked up!"

H MAKE INFERENCES
Compare how Susan answers Eddie's question in line 215 with how she introduces Hamadi in lines 185–186. Why does her attitude change?

I MONITOR
Think about how Tracy is feeling and why she acts the way she does. Can you **connect** her behavior to anything you've experienced?

---

9. **om:** a sacred syllable in certain Eastern religions, repeated to aid one's concentration while meditating.
10. **Aramaic** (ăr′ə-mā′ĭk).
11. **power walking:** fast walking with rhythmic swinging of the arms, done as a form of exercise.

FOR LESS–PROFICIENT READERS

Recognize Dialogue The mix of dialogue and text on this page, especially the "Thank you, thank you" comment in line 206, may challenge some readers. Remind them that authors usually enclose a speaker's words in quotation marks; point out several examples. Then have small groups of students read lines 199–230 aloud, each student taking the role of one character and one student serving as a narrator.

H MAKE INFERENCES

Possible answer: Susan is embarrassed to realize how formal and odd Hamadi seems compared to the popular Eddie and his casual ways.

If students need help . . . Have them review lines 178–179. Ask:

- How do the girls feel about Eddie? *Possible answer: They all like him a great deal.*

- Why might they change their behavior around him? *Possible answer: They want him to notice and think well of them, so they probably wouldn't do anything to create an unfavorable impression.*

- Compare these lines with lines 158–162. Why is the idea that Hamadi is "interesting" now a shortcoming? *Possible answer: Eddie seems to have a poor first impression of him, and Susan does not want it to reflect poorly on her.*

READING STRATEGY

I MONITOR

Possible answer: Students might have acted like Tracy in front of someone they had a crush on, respected very much, or admired greatly (such as a famous public figure).

Lines 199–226
REINFORCE *KEY IDEA:* REMARKABLE

Discuss What is remarkable about Hamadi as he attempts to participate in the caroling? *Possible answer: Hamadi brings an exotic flair and a thoughtful presence to the group. He sings in Aramaic, the actual spoken language of Jesus Christ. He is friendly and welcoming, perhaps more so than many other members of the group.*

SELECTION WRAP-UP

REFLECT Have students reread Hamadi's anthem-like statement in lines 259–261. Then encourage students to make some notes about what these words mean to them.

★ **CRITIQUE** Point out that the story ends with only a few of the carolers realizing what Hamadi has done for Tracy and Susan. Have students explain whether or not they would have preferred to have all of the characters come to see Hamadi in a new way.

Saleh Hamadi tuned into this conversation with interest; the Tower was downtown, in his neighborhood. He said, "This sounds like significant preliminary planning! Maybe you can be an international advisor someday." Susan's mother bellowed, "Joy to the World!" and voices followed her, stretching for notes. Susan's father was gazing off into the sky. Maybe he 240 thought about all the refugees in camps in Palestine far from doorbells and shutters. Maybe he thought about the horizon beyond Jerusalem when he was a boy, how it seemed to be inviting him, "Come over, come over." Well, he'd come all the way to the other side of the world, and now he was doomed to live in two places at once. To Susan, immigrants seemed bigger than other people, and always slightly melancholy. They also seemed doubly interesting. Maybe someday Susan would meet one her own age. ♦

Two thin streams of tears rolled down Tracy's face. Eddie had drifted to the other side of the group and was clowning with Cameron, doing a tap dance shuffle. "While fields and floods, rocks, hills and plains, repeat the sounding 250 joy, repeat the sounding joy . . ." Susan and Saleh Hamadi noticed her. Hamadi peered into Tracy's face, inquiring, "Why? Is it pain? Is it gratitude? We are such mysterious creatures, human beings!"

Tracy turned to him, pressing her face against the old wool of his coat, and wailed. The song ended. All eyes were on Tracy and this tall, courteous stranger who would never in a thousand years have felt comfortable stroking her hair. But he let her stand there, crying, as Susan stepped up firmly on the other side of Tracy, putting her arms around her friend. And Hamadi said something Susan would remember years later, whenever she was sad herself, even after college, a creaky **anthem** sneaking back into her ear, "We go on. On and on. 260 We don't stop where it hurts. We turn a corner. It is the reason why we are living. To turn a corner. Come, let's move."

Above them, in the heavens, stars lived out their lonely lives. People whispered, "What happened? What's wrong?" Half of them were already walking down the street. ❧

♦ GRAMMAR AND STYLE
Reread lines 235–246. Nye repeats the phrase "Maybe he thought about" to add emphasis to her writing.

④ **Targeted Passage**

anthem (ăn′thəm) *n.* an uplifting song or hymn

Detail of *Inspiration* (1994), Daniel Nevins.   Detail of *Healing* (1996), Daniel Nevins.

232   UNIT 2: CHARACTERIZATION AND POINT OF VIEW

DIFFERENTIATED INSTRUCTION

FOR LESS-PROFICIENT READERS
④ **Targeted Passage [Lines 247–264]**

This concluding passage shows Hamadi and Susan at their most noble moment: joining forces to comfort Susan's friend Tracy.

• Why does Tracy start crying?

• To whom does Tracy turn for comfort?

• What does Susan then do?

• What does Hamadi say?

Comprehension

1. **Recall** Why does Susan begin to feel interested in Hamadi?

2. **Recall** What does Susan invite Hamadi to do?

3. **Clarify** What happens to Tracy at the end of the story?

Literary Analysis

4. **Evaluate Monitoring Strategies** Review the monitoring strategies listed on page 223. Which strategy did you find most helpful as you read the story? Cite examples.

5. **Analyze Point of View** Think about how "Hamadi" might be different if it were told from a **first-person point of view,** with Hamadi himself as the narrator. How might your perception of Hamadi change?

6. **Draw Conclusions** Reread lines 257–261. Why do you think Hamadi's words have such a profound effect on Susan? Citing evidence from the text, explain why you think she finds Hamadi's words so meaningful.

7. **Analyze Characters** A **round character** is one who is complex and highly developed, displaying a variety of different traits in his or her personality. A **flat character** is not highly developed. He or she usually has one outstanding trait or role and exists mainly to advance the plot of a story. Identify one round character and one flat character in the story. Then explain how each fits the criteria above.

8. **Compare Literary Works** Compare Susan with Jill, the narrator of "Pancakes" on pages 194–202. Use a Venn diagram like the one shown to record Susan's and Jill's **traits.** Which character has the more **remarkable** personality?

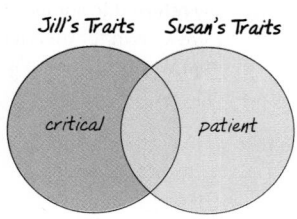

Jill's Traits — critical
Susan's Traits — patient

Literary Criticism

9. **Critical Interpretations** In reviewing *Habibi,* Nye's first novel, the critic Karen Leggett observed, "Adolescence magnifies the joys and anxieties of growing up even as it radically simplifies the complexities of the adult world. . . . Nye is meticulously sensitive to this rainbow of emotion. . . ." Paraphrase this quotation. Then explain whether you think Leggett's comment applies to "Hamadi."

7. *Susan is a round character because she comes to a realization about life. Tracy is a flat character because she serves only to show the travails of unrequited teenage love.*

8. *Susan: interested in life and people, compassionate, unusual point of view, self-confident; Jill: judgmental, sarcastic, self-absorbed, perfectionist, insecure; Both: responsible, straightforward. Opinions will vary as to who is more remarkable, but students may have more positive feelings toward Susan.*

Literary Criticism
Possible answer:

9. *Teenagers experience love and worry very intensely. They extend this black-and-white view to the adult world, oversimplifying the challenges they will face. The comment applies to Tracy, who reacts very emotionally to Eddie's indifference. Susan, on the other hand, seems very aware of the hardships that Hamadi endures.*

Practice and Apply

After Reading

For additional support of post-reading questions, use these copy masters:

R RESOURCE MANAGER—Copy Masters
  Reading Check p. 86 (to check understanding of the selection)
  Third-Person Limited Point of View p. 79 (for practice of literary analysis standards focus)
  Question Support p. 87 (After Reading questions adapted for English learners and less-proficient readers)

  For additional questions, see page 73.

ANSWERS

Comprehension

1. *Hamadi is so different from the other people she knows that she sees him as an escape from her everyday life.*

2. *She invites him to go Christmas caroling with her friends from the English Club.*

3. *Tracy cries because Eddie does not return her affections. She turns to Hamadi for comfort, and he and Susan comfort her.*

Literary Analysis
Possible answers:

4. ■ **STANDARDS FOCUS** **Monitor**
Choices and examples will vary, but these strategies might be included.

Visualize Imagining Hamadi's appearance or the Christmas caroling scene makes the story easier for students to understand.

Question Students might respond to Susan's own questions in the story.

Connect Students might grasp the story's situation better by remembering an unusual family friend or relative.

5. ● **STANDARDS FOCUS** **Point of View**
It might change quite a bit. Hamadi probably would not realize that other people think of him as odd. He also might not seem as remarkable because his actions and appearance would not be filtered through Susan's perception of him.

6. *Hamadi's endurance, love, and optimism help answer Susan's questions about life (lines 1–20, 78–83).*

ANSWERS

Vocabulary in Context

VOCABULARY PRACTICE

1. *true*	5. *true*
2. *false*	6. *true*
3. *false*	7. *true*
4. *true*	8. *false*

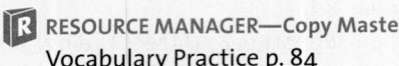 **RESOURCE MANAGER**—Copy Master
Vocabulary Practice p. 84

VOCABULARY IN WRITING

To help students use the words correctly, label each word with its part of speech, as used in the story (nouns: *anthem, sustenance*; adjectives: *archaic, expansive, lavish, spartan, surrogate, wry*). In addition, discuss each word's positive or negative connotation before having students write.

VOCABULARY STRATEGY: WORDS FROM GREEK CULTURE *(also an EL language objective)*

To help students understand how these words are used, construct and discuss a chart like this:

Word	Part of Speech	Meaning
Hercules Herculean	noun adjective	Greek hero very difficult
Colossus of Rhodes colossal	noun adjective	statue enormous
Narcissus narcissistic	noun adjective	Greek figure self-absorbed
Titans titanic	noun adjective	Greek gods huge

Possible answers:

1. *the Empire State Building; a cruise ship*
2. *himself or herself*
3. *earning a medical degree; building a house by oneself*
4. *that the ship was huge*

 RESOURCE MANAGER—Copy Master
Vocabulary Strategy p. 85

ⓘ Vocabulary Center at **ClassZone.com**
Additional Vocabulary Activities

Vocabulary in Context

VOCABULARY PRACTICE

Indicate whether each statement is true or false.

1. It can be hard to tell when someone with a **wry** sense of humor is kidding.
2. **Spartan** hotel rooms are very elaborately furnished.
3. Someone with an **expansive** personality is usually rather shy.
4. Six courses and two desserts would constitute a **lavish** meal.
5. A poem filled with **archaic** words might be hard to understand.
6. Your **surrogate** grandmother would not necessarily be related to you.
7. Seeds and berries provide **sustenance** for many birds.
8. An **anthem** is a song written for an old person's funeral.

> **WORD LIST**
> anthem
> archaic
> expansive
> lavish
> spartan
> surrogate
> sustenance
> wry

VOCABULARY IN WRITING

Use at least four vocabulary words to write descriptive sentences about Saleh Hamadi. Describe his appearance or his personality or both. Here is an example.

> **EXAMPLE SENTENCE**
> Hamadi is usually **expansive** in his talk, even with strangers.

VOCABULARY STRATEGY: WORDS FROM GREEK CULTURE

The vocabulary word *spartan* originally referred to someone from the Greek city-state of Sparta, whose citizens were known for their rejection of luxury and comfort. Knowing the histories of other words related to ancient Greece can help you to understand their meanings.

PRACTICE Read the chart and then answer the questions.

Character/Item	Description
Hercules	a mythological hero whose strength helped him perform almost impossible tasks
Colossus of Rhodes	an enormous statue of the Greek sun god
Narcissus	a mythological youth who fell in love with his own reflection
Titans	a race of mighty gods who preceded Zeus and his family

1. What is a modern-day example of something **colossal**?
2. What would a **narcissistic** person most likely talk about?
3. What might be an example of a **herculean** task?
4. By calling their ship *Titanic*, what were the ship owners suggesting?

> **VOCABULARY PRACTICE**
> For more practice, go to the **Vocabulary Center** at **ClassZone.com.**

DIFFERENTIATED INSTRUCTION

FOR ENGLISH LEARNERS

Writing: Task Support Encourage students to use the Character Traits and Textual Evidence chart to plan their sentences for the Vocabulary in Writing activity.

🧰 **BEST PRACTICES TOOLKIT**—Transparency
Character Traits and Textual Evidence p. D6

FOR ADVANCED LEARNERS/PRE–AP

Analyze Antonyms Have students identify antonyms (opposites) for as many of the vocabulary words as possible. Allow them to check their responses in a dictionary or thesaurus. Then have students write three sentences, showing in each one a word and its opposite in a way that makes the difference clear. Offer this example: *Uncle David has an _expansive_ personality, but Aunt Maria is rather _unsociable_.*

Reading-Writing Connection

Increase your understanding of "Hamadi" by responding to these prompts. Then use **Revision: Grammar and Style** to improve your writing.

WRITING PROMPTS

A. Short Response: Interpret the Quotation
Reread the quotation from Kahlil Gibran at the beginning of "Hamadi." How does the quotation apply to the story? Which character utters the truth? Which one understands it? What is that truth and why is it important? Write **one or two paragraphs** that discuss the relationship between the quotation and the story.

B. Extended Response: Analyze Characterization
Analyze how Nye creates the character of Susan. In **three to five paragraphs,** identify the traits Susan exhibits, as well as the methods of characterization Nye uses to show the reader these traits.

SELF-CHECK

A good interpretation will . . .
- explain the meaning of the quotation
- show how the characters and the story itself illustrate the quotation

A strong analysis will . . .
- discuss Susan's important traits
- identify at least three methods of characterization used to reveal these traits
- provide evidence from the text to support the analysis

REVISION: GRAMMAR AND STYLE

ADD EMPHASIS Review the **Grammar and Style** note on page 232. Throughout the story, Nye uses **repetition** to impress upon the reader the thoughts and actions of her characters. Use repetition in your own writing when you want to add emphasis.

Here are some examples from the story. Note that Nye repeats the same pronouns, nouns, and verbs:

Her uncles were dull. Her uncles shopped at the mall and watched TV. (lines 157–158)

A minute later her mother was digging in the closet for neck scarves, and her father was digging in the drawer for flashlight batteries. (lines 165–166)

Notice how the revision in red adds emphasis to this first draft. Use similar techniques to revise your responses to the prompts.

> **WRITING TOOLS**
> For prewriting, revision, and editing tools, visit the **Writing Center** at ClassZone.com.

> STUDENT MODEL
>
> —*remarkable because*
> Susan is a remarkable person. She is observant and kind and curious about life.

HAMADI **235**

FOR LESS–PROFICIENT WRITERS

Possible Organization for Prompt A:

Topic sentence: Explain how Hamadi is the one who utters the truth about "going on" and how Susan is the one who understands it best.

Body sentences: Give examples showing how Hamadi overcomes his loneliness and pain and how Susan comes to appreciate him.

Conclusion: Connect Hamadi's "truth" to his status as Susan's "surrogate grandmother."

Possible Organization for Prompt B:

Introductory Paragraph: Make a statement about the impact of Susan's character.

Intermediate Paragraph(s): Cite examples of Susan's curiosity, wisdom, generosity, and kindness. Refer to Susan's thoughts and actions and other characters' reactions to her.

Concluding Paragraph: Connect Susan's chief traits to the word *remarkable*.

Reading-Writing Connection

WRITING PROMPTS

- For Prompt A, have students paraphrase the quotation in at least two ways. Then pair students to discuss how the quotation applies to the story's plot, conflict, characters, and main ideas. Remind students to proofread their writing (or their partner's writing) for misspellings and other types of errors.

- For Prompt B, have students list the character traits that first come to mind when they think about Susan.

For writing support, see

ℹ Writing Center at **ClassZone.com**

REVISION: GRAMMAR AND STYLE

- Have students locate the repetition in the examples *(her uncles* and *was digging).* Elicit that in both examples, Nye repeats a key phrase to stress the characters' identity and actions and help readers visualize the scenes.

- Invite students to use repetition to add emphasis to this passage.

  Susan's heart ached with Tracy's pain. ~~Susan knew~~ *It ached with the disappointment and embarrassment that Tracy felt.*

R RESOURCE MANAGER—Copy Master
Add Emphasis p. 89

Assess and Reteach

Assess

R RESOURCE MANAGER—Copy Masters
Selection Test A pp. 91–92
Selection Test B/C pp. 93–94

⊘ Test Generator CD

Reteach

S STANDARDS LESSON FILE
Literature Lesson 11: Narrator and Third-Person Points of View
Reading Lesson 2: Monitoring
Vocabulary Lesson 6: Word Parts: Anglo-Saxon and Greek

Focus and Motivate

OBJECTIVES

Literary Analysis
- explore the key idea of being a **mentor**
- analyze characterization
- read an autobiography and a poem

Reading
- analyze perspectives

Vocabulary
- build vocabulary for reading and writing
- define and use multiple-meaning words correctly *(also an EL language objective)*

Grammar and Writing
- use adjective clauses, relative pronouns, and relative adverbs to add descriptive details
- use writing to analyze literature

SUMMARY

In this excerpt from her 1970 autobiography, Angelou recalls the day that the sophisticated Mrs. Flowers took her home for lemonade, cookies, and "a little talking to." Mrs. Flowers gave the young, withdrawn Angelou reading assignments, lessons in living, and a sense of being liked that lasted a lifetime.

What is a TEACHER?

Ask the question and elicit answers. After students have read the *KEY IDEA*, have them freewrite about a **mentor** they have known. They can use the results to complete the *DISCUSS* activity.

---

from **I Know Why the Caged Bird Sings**

Autobiography by Maya Angelou

What is a TEACHER?

KEY IDEA Your teachers at school are dedicated to helping you acquire knowledge, but are there individuals outside the classroom who teach you important things as well? In this selection, you'll meet Mrs. Flowers, a woman who acted as a **mentor**—a wise and trusted counselor or teacher—to a young Maya Angelou.

DISCUSS Think of people who have shared wisdom with you, helped you to see things in new ways, or pushed you when you needed encouragement. With a small group of classmates, discuss the impact a mentor can have, and then generate a word web detailing the most important traits of a mentor.

patience

Qualities of a Mentor

generosity

236

Selection Resources

R RESOURCE MANAGER UNIT 2

Plan and Teach pp. 95–102

Literary Analysis
Summary pp. 103†*, 104‡*
Characterization in Autobiography
   pp. 105, 106†*
Question Support p. 113*

Reading
Analyze Perspectives
   pp. 107, 108†*
Reading Check p. 112
Reading Fluency p. 115

Vocabulary
Study p. 109*
Practice p. 110
Strategy p. 111

Grammar and Writing
Add Descriptive Details p. 114

Assessment
Selection Tests A, B/C pp. 117*, 119*
   Test Generator CD

BEST PRACTICES TOOLKIT

Differentiated Instruction
   pp. 31–38*

Scaffolding Instruction
   pp. 43–46*

Graphic Organizers/Strategies
Predicting • Knowledge Rating
• New Word Analysis • Two-
Column Chart • Word Squares
• Venn Diagram

Reading Support
   Audio Anthology CD*

Technology
   Literature and Vocabulary
   Centers at **ClassZone.com**
   Write*Smart* CD

* Resources for Differentiation   † Also in Spanish   ‡ In Haitian Creole and Vietnamese

● LITERARY ANALYSIS: CHARACTERIZATION IN AUTOBIOGRAPHY

When describing important individuals they have known, writers of **autobiography** often make use of the same methods of **characterization** that fiction writers do. These include

- description of a person's physical appearance
- examples of the person's speech, thoughts, or feelings
- the speech, thoughts, or feelings of other people
- the narrator's comments about the person

As you read, look for details that reveal Mrs. Flowers's personality **traits** and ways she influenced the young Angelou.

● READING SKILL: ANALYZE PERSPECTIVES

Though autobiographies are written in first-person point of view, they often reflect two different **perspectives:**

- that of the writer at the time he or she experienced certain events
- that of the writer looking back on these events years later

As you read this selection, use a chart like the one shown to record Angelou's thoughts and observations about Mrs. Flowers from both her childhood and adult perspectives.

Child's Viewpoint	Adult's Viewpoint
"Why on earth did she insist on calling her Sister Flowers? Shame made me want to hide my face." (lines 25–26)	"She was one of the few gentle-women I have ever known, and has remained throughout my life the measure of what a human being can be." (lines 18–19)

Review: Make Inferences

▲ VOCABULARY IN CONTEXT

Make a chart like the one shown, placing each word in the column where it fits. Write brief definitions for the words in the first two columns.

WORD LIST	cascade	illiteracy	sacrilegious
	clarity	infuse	taut
	homely	leer	

Know Well	Think I Know	Don't Know

Author Online

Marguerite Moves South
Maya Angelou was born Marguerite Johnson in St. Louis, Missouri. The name Maya was originally given to her by her older brother, Bailey, who called her "mya sister" as a child. When their parents divorced, Marguerite and Bailey were sent to live with

Maya Angelou born 1928

their grandmother in the small, rigidly segregated town of Stamps, Arkansas. Their grandmother, whom they called Momma, ran the only African American–owned store in her community, in a part of town referred to as Black Stamps.

Childhood Trauma After being abused by a family friend when she was eight, Angelou withdrew into herself and spoke to no one but Bailey for five years. It is at this point in her life that this selection takes place.

Never Defeated Angelou has come a long way since her early struggles. In 1993, when she read her poem "On the Pulse of Morning" to commemorate Bill Clinton's swearing in as president, she became only the second poet to speak at an inauguration. She served as a coordinator of Martin Luther King Jr.'s Southern Christian Leadership Conference and has taught in Africa and the United States. Her writings have achieved tremendous popularity, inspiring millions of people around the world. When asked what advice she'd like to pass on to her readers, Angelou replied, "You may encounter many defeats, but you must not be defeated."

MORE ABOUT THE AUTHOR For more on Maya Angelou, visit the **Literature Center** at ClassZone.com.

I KNOW WHY THE CAGED BIRD SINGS **237**

Teach

STANDARDS FOCUS

LITERARY ANALYSIS

● CHARACTERIZATION IN AUTOBIOGRAPHY

For instructional support, have students identify methods of characterization in this sentence:

> She was young and had a childlike face; but people said that when she spoke, she seemed old and wise.

Possible answer: *physical description, thoughts of others, narrator's comments*

CHECK UNDERSTANDING Ask what method of characterization students would use in their own autobiography, and why.

READING SKILL

■ ANALYZE PERSPECTIVES

Discuss this chart. Elicit that the child's perspective is self-centered and limited and that the adult's perspective reflects greater life experience and a sense of "looking back."

Child's Viewpoint	Adult's Viewpoint
I didn't care if my lollipop was lying on the floor. I wanted it!	My dad never gave in to my tantrums.

CHECK UNDERSTANDING Discuss how Angelou's comment at the end of **Never Defeated** is an adult's viewpoint.

RESOURCE MANAGER—Copy Master Analyze Perspectives p. 107 (for student use while reading the selection)

VOCABULARY SKILL

▲ VOCABULARY IN CONTEXT

DIAGNOSE WORD KNOWLEDGE To determine preteaching needs, have all students complete **Vocabulary in Context.** *Possible answers: cascade,* "fall in waves"; *clarity,* "clearness"; *homely,* "plain, ugly"; *illiteracy,* "inability to read or write"; *infuse,* "to spread throughout"; *leer,* "to look at with evil interest"; *sacrilegious,* "involving an insult against a religion"; *taut,* "tight"

PRETEACH VOCABULARY Use the Vocabulary Study copy master to help students predict meanings for each boldfaced word in the copy master.

1. Read item 1 aloud, emphasizing *cascade.*
2. Point out the words *flowing* and *down.* Discuss possible meanings for *cascade,* such as "to flow or fall like water."
3. Repeat the procedure for items 2–8.

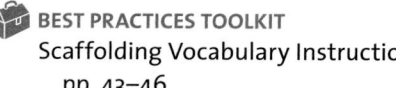
RESOURCE MANAGER—Copy Master Vocabulary Study p. 109

For general guidelines on differentiating vocabulary instruction and for alternative vocabulary activities for students not needing vocabulary preteaching, see

BEST PRACTICES TOOLKIT Scaffolding Vocabulary Instruction pp. 43–46
ⓘ Vocabulary Center at **ClassZone.com**

Practice and Apply

ANALYZE VISUALS

Possible answer: *Like Mrs. Flowers, the woman in the painting is "thin without the taut look of wiry people" (line 7) and has skin that is "a rich black" (line 10). She also wears a hat (line 8) and seems to have an aristocratic air (line 4). Unlike Mrs. Flowers, she carries an umbrella, does not wear gloves, and probably is not wearing a voile dress.*

About the Art In *Woman with Umbrella*, Connecticut-born Bill Farnsworth (born 1958) creates an image of a woman set apart by her elegance and by the umbrella that forms the shadow in which she walks. Farnsworth explains, "Using light, color, and texture, I try to bring the viewer into the painting, so they too can feel the moment in time.... My goal is to tell the story 'without words.'"

LITERARY ANALYSIS

Ⓐ CHARACTERIZATION

Possible answer: *Mrs. Flowers seems unaffected by weather conditions, and her clothing matches her alone. She stays apart from others and, unlike them, wears gloves.*

If students need help ... Have them identify the information in these lines:

- lines 4–6: her resistance to weather conditions
- lines 7–8: her "perfect" clothing
- lines 11–12: her distance from others
- lines 12–13: her lack of familiarity and her gloves

238   UNIT 2

I KNOW WHY THE *Caged Bird* SINGS

MAYA ANGELOU

For nearly a year, I sopped around the house, the Store, the school and the church, like an old biscuit, dirty and inedible. Then I met, or rather got to know, the lady who threw me my first life line.

Mrs. Bertha Flowers was the aristocrat of Black Stamps. She had the grace of control to appear warm in the coldest weather, and on the Arkansas summer days it seemed she had a private breeze which swirled around, cooling her. She was thin without the **taut** look of wiry people, and her printed voile dresses and flowered hats were as right for her as denim overalls for a farmer. She was our side's answer to the richest white woman in town.

10   Her skin was a rich black that would have peeled like a plum if snagged, but then no one would have thought of getting close enough to Mrs. Flowers to ruffle her dress, let alone snag her skin. She didn't encourage familiarity. She wore gloves too. Ⓐ

I don't think I ever saw Mrs. Flowers laugh, but she smiled often. A slow widening of her thin black lips to show even, small white teeth, then the slow, effortless closing. When she chose to smile on me, I always wanted to thank her. The action was so graceful and inclusively benign.

She was one of the few gentlewomen I have ever known, and has remained throughout my life the measure of what a human being can be.

20   Momma had a strange relationship with her. Most often when she passed on the road in front of the Store, she spoke to Momma in that soft yet carrying voice, "Good day, Mrs. Henderson." Momma responded with "How you, Sister Flowers?"

ANALYZE VISUALS
Examine this portrait. How does it compare with Angelou's description of Mrs. Flowers? Cite details from the painting and the text to support your answer.

taut (tôt) *adj.* pulled or drawn tight

Ⓐ CHARACTERIZATION
Reread lines 4–13. What is distinctive about Mrs. Flowers's appearance and demeanor?

① Targeted Passage

238   UNIT 2: CHARACTERIZATION AND POINT OF VIEW

Woman with Umbrella,
Bill Farnsworth.
© Images.com/Corbis.

DIFFERENTIATED INSTRUCTION

FOR ALL STUDENTS
Enhancing Learning Styles Provide these independent projects for various learning preferences:

- **Tactile** Create a caged bird.
- **Verbal** Write a diary entry.
- **Musical** Compose a song.

For further details on these projects, see

R RESOURCE MANAGER
Ideas for Extension pp. 100–101

FOR LESS–PROFICIENT READERS
In combination with the *Audio Anthology CD*, use one or more Targeted Passages (pp. 238, 243, 245) to ensure that students focus on key story events, concepts, and skills. Targeted Passages are also good for English learners.

① Targeted Passage [Lines 12–23]

This passage clarifies the fact that although Mrs. Flowers seems aristocratic, she is gracious and kind.

- What does Mrs. Flowers not encourage?

BACKGROUND

Southern Stratification This excerpt from Angelou's autobiography highlights the class distinctions that existed within the African-American community in the South during the 1930s. Point out that the refined Mrs. Flowers belongs to a higher social class than Marguerite's family and most other African Americans in Stamps, Arkansas. Yet within that community, even the most genteel and educated African Americans were looked down upon by the white lower class, whose members were often sharecroppers or subsistence farmers. Explain that "powhitefolks" (line 56) is a phonetic spelling of "poor white folks." Marguerite is troubled by the idea that poor whites would address Mrs. Flowers disrespectfully as "Bertha"—just as she is embarrassed that her grandmother addresses her too familiarly as "Sister Flowers."

Lines 18–19
REINFORCE *KEY IDEA:* MENTOR

Discuss Think about what it means to be a **mentor.** Based on what Angelou says here, what did she learn from Mrs. Flowers?
Possible answer: *She learned the meaning of being a gentlewoman, and she learned the standard of what it means to be a human being, in the richest sense.*

- How does she smile? How does Angelou remember feeling when Mrs. Flowers smiled at her?

- What kind of "measure" is Mrs. Flowers?

- How does she greet Momma?

FOR ENGLISH LEARNERS

Options for Reading Have students listen to the entire selection on the *Audio Anthology CD.* Then divide the selection among student pairs. Have students look up unfamiliar words not explained in the text and then paraphrase and share their sections with the class.

Prereading For prereading instruction for English learners, see

 BEST PRACTICES TOOLKIT
Scaffolding Reading Instruction pp. 43–46

FOR ADVANCED LEARNERS/PRE–AP

Pre-AP Exercises in the bottom channel provide additional challenge for students. Use these suggestions for small groups or individuals.

ADDITIONAL GUIDELINES
For more help with differentiation and tips for classroom management, see

 BEST PRACTICES TOOLKIT
Differentiated Instruction pp. 31–38

I KNOW WHY THE CAGED BIRD SINGS **239**

Mrs. Flowers didn't belong to our church, nor was she Momma's familiar.[1] Why on earth did she insist on calling her Sister Flowers? Shame made me want to hide my face. Mrs. Flowers deserved better than to be called Sister. Then, Momma left out the verb. Why not ask, "How *are* you, *Mrs.* Flowers?" With the unbalanced passion of the young, I hated her for showing her ignorance to Mrs. Flowers. It didn't occur to me for many years that they
30 were as alike as sisters, separated only by formal education.

Although I was upset, neither of the women was in the least shaken by what I thought an unceremonious greeting. Mrs. Flowers would continue her easy gait up the hill to her little bungalow, and Momma kept on shelling peas or doing whatever had brought her to the front porch.

Occasionally, though, Mrs. Flowers would drift off the road and down to the Store and Momma would say to me, "Sister, you go on and play." As I left I would hear the beginning of an intimate conversation, Momma persistently using the wrong verb, or none at all.

"Brother and Sister Wilcox is sho'ly the meanest—" "Is," Momma? "Is"?
40 Oh, please, not "is," Momma, for two or more. But they talked, and from the side of the building where I waited for the ground to open up and swallow me, I heard the soft-voiced Mrs. Flowers and the textured voice of my grandmother merging and melting. They were interrupted from time to time by giggles that must have come from Mrs. Flowers (Momma never giggled in her life). Then she was gone. **B**

She appealed to me because she was like people I had never met personally. Like women in English novels who walked the moors[2] (whatever they were) with their loyal dogs racing at a respectful distance. Like the women who sat in front of roaring fireplaces, drinking tea incessantly from silver trays full
50 of scones and crumpets.[3] Women who walked over the "heath"[4] and read morocco-bound[5] books and had two last names divided by a hyphen. It would be safe to say that she made me proud to be Negro, just by being herself.

She acted just as refined as whitefolks in the movies and books and she was more beautiful, for none of them could have come near that warm color without looking gray by comparison.

It was fortunate that I never saw her in the company of powhitefolks. For since they tend to think of their whiteness as an evenizer, I'm certain that I would have had to hear her spoken to commonly as Bertha, and my image of her would have been shattered like the unmendable Humpty-Dumpty. **C**
60 One summer afternoon, sweet-milk fresh in my memory, she stopped at the Store to buy provisions. Another Negro woman of her health and age would have been expected to carry the paper sacks home in one hand, but Momma said, "Sister Flowers, I'll send Bailey up to your house with these things."

---

1. **familiar:** a close friend or associate.
2. **moors:** broad open areas of countryside with marshes and patches of low shrubs.
3. **scones** (skōnz) **and crumpets** (krŭm'pĭts): Scones are small, biscuitlike pastries; crumpets are rolls similar to English muffins.
4. **heath** (hēth): another word for a moor.
5. **morocco-bound:** Morocco is a soft leather sometimes used for expensive book covers.

240 UNIT 2: CHARACTERIZATION AND POINT OF VIEW

B ANALYZE PERSPECTIVES
Reread lines 39–45. Which parts of this passage are written from a child's perspective? Which are written from the viewpoint of an adult reflecting on the experience? Record your answers in your chart.

C MAKE INFERENCES
In lines 56–59, what can you infer about race relations in Stamps, Arkansas, in the 1930s? Consider whether you would be able to make these inferences if Angelou did not comment on her childhood experiences from her adult viewpoint.

Possible answer: The embarrassment over Momma's grammatical errors (lines 39–41) reflects a child's viewpoint. The comment that "Momma never giggled in her life" (line 44) reflects an adult's viewpoint.

Possible answer: The reader can infer that race relations were strained and that segregation and discrimination were common. The lines suggest that "powhitefolks" would not have used a title of respect such as "Mrs. Flowers"; rather, they would have thought themselves to be superior to her merely because their skin was white. They would have "spoken to [her] commonly as Bertha." The reader would probably not be able to make such inferences if Angelou had not provided her adult perspective on what she felt as a child. Marguerite probably realized that poor whites would have felt superior to Mrs. Flowers because of their skin color, but she would not have been able to articulate the idea so clearly.

If students need help . . . Have students consider what might happen if they called the school principal by his or her first name. What kind of attitude would that action convey?

DIFFERENTIATED INSTRUCTION

FOR LESS-PROFICIENT READERS

Predict Plot This narrative's action does not really begin until line 60. As students near that point, use Predicting to list key details from the exposition and predict why Mrs. Flowers might be important as the selection continues.

 BEST PRACTICES TOOLKIT—Transparency
Predicting p. A10

FOR ENGLISH LEARNERS

Key Academic Vocabulary Use Knowledge Rating to teach these words: *occur* (line 29), *persistently* (line 37), *refined* (line 53), *equivalent* (line 73), *generations* (line 165), *conclusions* (line 194).

BEST PRACTICES TOOLKIT—Transparency
Knowledge Rating p. E3

She smiled that slow dragging smile, "Thank you, Mrs. Henderson. I'd prefer Marguerite, though." My name was beautiful when she said it. "I've been meaning to talk to her, anyway." They gave each other age-group looks.

Momma said, "Well, that's all right then. Sister, go and change your dress. You going to Sister Flowers's."

ANALYZE VISUALS
Does the girl in this painting look similar to how you envision Marguerite? Describe the **details** that influenced your answer.

Ancilla with an Orange (1956), Dod Procter. Oil on canvas. Royal West of England Academy, Bristol, UK. © The Bridgeman Art Library.

I KNOW WHY THE CAGED BIRD SINGS **241**

ANALYZE VISUALS

Possible answer: The girls are somewhat similar. Marguerite is about to change into a nice dress, perhaps like the one in the picture. Also, in Mrs. Flowers's presence, Marguerite might look as pensive as the painting's subject.

About the Art Inspired by impressionist and post-impressionist painters, British artist Dod Procter (1892–1972) created a light-filled canvas showing a young girl with an orange. As in many paintings by the impressionist master Renoir, her subject is a girl placed against a colorful background.

Lines 39–68
DISCUSSION PROMPTS

Use these prompts to help students understand the role of Momma in this account:

Recall How does Momma treat Mrs. Flowers in the store? *Possible answer: Momma pays special attention to Mrs. Flowers, sending someone to deliver her groceries.*

Analyze How does Momma's attitude toward Mrs. Flowers seem to have influenced Marguerite? *Possible answer: Marguerite appears to be in awe of Mrs. Flowers, just as Momma is.*

Synthesize What does Momma probably think when Mrs. Flowers asks to have Marguerite carry her groceries home? Explain. *Possible answer: Momma may be proud that such a fine woman is paying attention to Marguerite. Also, since they now exchange "age-group looks" (line 66), Momma may be glad to see that something that she and Mrs. Flowers have planned is about to occur.*

FOR ENGLISH LEARNERS

Vocabulary: Idioms and Sayings Use New Word Analysis to teach the meanings of these idioms and sayings as you come across them in the reading:

- *sweet-milk fresh* (line 60), "vivid and pleasant"
- *what on earth* (line 69), "what (among all possible choices)"
- *handed out* (line 82), "given"

- *it would be fitting* (line 105), "It would be right for the situation"
- *bear in mind* (lines 118–119), "remember"
- *tried her hand at* (lines 150–151), "attempted"
- *pay me a visit* (line 182), "visit me"

 **BEST PRACTICES TOOLKIT—Transparency** New Word Analysis p. E8

D CHARACTERIZATION

Possible answer: Marguerite is extremely shy and modest, and she is obedient (lines 88, 100–103). She is perceptive of other people's feelings and attitudes, as well as sensitive about how others view her (lines 100–103). She also hides inside a rich interior life of unspoken thoughts and imagination (lines 104–106).

If students need help . . . Use a Two-Column Chart to help students locate details in the text that reveal Marguerite's character and then note how these details suggest specific character traits:

Text Detail	Character Trait
turns around when Momma tells her to (lines 85–86)	obedient
terrified when Momma tells her to take off her dress (lines 87–91)	modest, shy
can't look at Momma or Mrs. Flowers (lines 100–101)	modest, shy
realizes Mrs. Flowers had known she would be embarrassed, while Momma had not (lines 102–103)	perceptive, sensitive
hopes she drops dead from sunstroke (lines 104–106)	vivid imagination, dramatic

 BEST PRACTICES TOOLKIT—Transparency Two-Column Chart p. A25

Extend the Discussion What does Marguerite think, say, or do in this scene that reveals who she really is despite how she acts?

The chifforobe[6] was a maze. What on earth did one put on to go to
70 Mrs. Flowers's house? I knew I shouldn't put on a Sunday dress. It might be
sacrilegious. Certainly not a house dress, since I was already wearing a fresh one. I chose a school dress, naturally. It was formal without suggesting that going to Mrs. Flowers's house was equivalent to attending church.

I trusted myself back into the Store.

"Now, don't you look nice." I had chosen the right thing, for once.

"Mrs. Henderson, you make most of the children's clothes, don't you?"

"Yes, ma'am. Sure do. Store-bought clothes ain't hardly worth the thread it take to stitch them."

"I'll say you do a lovely job, though, so neat. That dress looks professional."

80 Momma was enjoying the seldom-received compliments. Since everyone we knew (except Mrs. Flowers, of course) could sew competently, praise was rarely handed out for the commonly practiced craft.

"I try, with the help of the Lord, Sister Flowers, to finish the inside just like I does the outside. Come here, Sister."

I had buttoned up the collar and tied the belt, apronlike, in back. Momma told me to turn around. With one hand she pulled the strings and the belt fell free at both sides of my waist. Then her large hands were at my neck, opening the button loops. I was terrified. What was happening?

"Take it off, Sister." She had her hands on the hem of the dress.

90 "I don't need to see the inside, Mrs. Henderson, I can tell . . ." But the dress was over my head and my arms were stuck in the sleeves. Momma said, "That'll do. See here, Sister Flowers, I French-seams[7] around the armholes." Through the cloth film, I saw the shadow approach. "That makes it last longer. Children these days would bust out of sheet-metal clothes. They so rough."

"That is a very good job, Mrs. Henderson. You should be proud. You can put your dress back on, Marguerite."

"No ma'am. Pride is a sin. And 'cording to the Good Book, it goeth before a fall."

"That's right. So the Bible says. It's a good thing to keep in mind."

100 I wouldn't look at either of them. Momma hadn't thought that taking off my dress in front of Mrs. Flowers would kill me stone dead. If I had refused, she would have thought I was trying to be "womanish" and might have remembered St. Louis. Mrs. Flowers had known that I would be embarrassed and that was even worse. I picked up the groceries and went out to wait in the hot sunshine. It would be fitting if I got a sunstroke and died before they came outside. Just dropped dead on the slanting porch. **D**

There was a little path beside the rocky road, and Mrs. Flowers walked in front swinging her arms and picking her way over the stones.

---

6. **chifforobe** (shĭf′ə-rōb′): a chest of drawers combined with a small closet for hanging clothes.

7. **French-seams:** sew seams that are turned in and stitched on the wrong side so that the unfinished edges of the cloth are not visible.

sacrilegious (săk′rə-lĭj′əs) *adj.* disrespectful toward a sacred person, place, or thing

D CHARACTERIZATION
In addition to describing her mentor in a compelling way, Angelou also presents a vivid portrait of herself as a child. List three **traits** Marguerite exhibits.

DIFFERENTIATED INSTRUCTION

FOR ENGLISH LEARNERS

Vocabulary: Multiple-Meaning Words Have students work in groups to identify the correct meaning and part of speech for each of these words as used in the story: *even* (line 15), *carrying* (line 22), *warm* (line 54), *meaning* (line 66), *trusted* (line 74), *film* (line 93), *fall* (line 98), *picking* (line 108), *shades* (line 124), *diet* (line 155), *country* (line 164), *lined* (line 173), *sense* (line 191).

FOR ADVANCED LEARNERS/PRE–AP

Compare and Contrast Allusions [small-group option] This scene contains several allusions to belief in the Bible; indeed, it provides a reference for much of what Momma says. Later, Mrs. Flowers and Angelou allude to secular literature. After students have read the selection, ask them to compare and contrast these allusions and draw conclusions about what the allusions indicate about the account's main characters.

She said, without turning her head, to me, "I hear you're doing very good school work, Marguerite, but that it's all written. The teachers report that they have trouble getting you to talk in class." We passed the triangular farm on our left and the path widened to allow us to walk together. I hung back in the separate unasked and unanswerable questions.

"Come and walk along with me, Marguerite." I couldn't have refused even if I wanted to. She pronounced my name so nicely. Or more correctly, she spoke each word with such **clarity** that I was certain a foreigner who didn't understand English could have understood her.

"Now no one is going to make you talk—possibly no one can. But bear in mind, language is man's way of communicating with his fellow man and it is language alone which separates him from the lower animals." That was a totally new idea to me, and I would need time to think about it.

"Your grandmother says you read a lot. Every chance you get. That's good, but not good enough. Words mean more than what is set down on paper. It takes the human voice to **infuse** them with the shades of deeper meaning." **E**

I memorized the part about the human voice infusing words. It seemed so valid and poetic.

She said she was going to give me some books and that I not only must read them, I must read them aloud. She suggested that I try to make a sentence sound in as many different ways as possible.

"I'll accept no excuse if you return a book to me that has been badly handled." My imagination boggled at the punishment I would deserve if in fact I did abuse a book of Mrs. Flowers'. Death would be too kind and brief.

The odors in the house surprised me. Somehow I had never connected Mrs. Flowers with food or eating or any other common experience of common people. There must have been an outhouse, too, but my mind never recorded it.

The sweet scent of vanilla had met us as she opened the door.

"I made tea cookies this morning. You see, I had planned to invite you for cookies and lemonade so we could have this little chat. The lemonade is in the icebox."

It followed that Mrs. Flowers would have ice on an ordinary day, when most families in our town bought ice late on Saturdays only a few times during the summer to be used in the wooden ice-cream freezers.

She took the bags from me and disappeared through the kitchen door. I looked around the room that I had never in my wildest fantasies imagined I would see. Browned photographs **leered** or threatened from the walls and the white, freshly done curtains pushed against themselves and against the wind. I wanted to gobble up the room entire and take it to Bailey, who would help me analyze and enjoy it. **F**

"Have a seat, Marguerite. Over there by the table." She carried a platter covered with a tea towel. Although she warned that she hadn't tried her hand at baking sweets for some time, I was certain that like everything else about her the cookies would be perfect.

Line numbers: 110, 120, 130, 140, 150

I KNOW WHY THE CAGED BIRD SINGS **243**

---

clarity (klăr′ĭ-tē)
n. clearness

② **Targeted Passage**

infuse (ĭn-fyōōz′) *v.* to fill, as if by pouring

E **CHARACTERIZATION**
Reread lines 109–124. What does this passage reveal about the **conflict** developing in this selection? Summarize what you already know about Marguerite's conflict.

leer (lîr) *v.* to give a sly, evil glance

F **GRAMMAR AND STYLE**
Reread lines 143–148. Angelou uses the **adjective clause** "that I had never in my wildest fantasies imagined I would see" to convey with precision Marguerite's excitement.

LITERARY ANALYSIS

E **CHARACTERIZATION**

Possible answer: The passage reveals that Marguerite has a great deal to say but has a hard time saying it. In this passage, she is impressed by Mrs. Flowers's speaking ability, but she must overcome her own hesitancy to speak up as Mrs. Flowers wants her to. In the opening paragraph of the selection, Marguerite says that she "sopped around the house . . . like an old biscuit," suggesting that she has been unhappy and troubled. Her unhappiness may have something to do with her reticence.

Lines 130–131
REINFORCE KEY IDEA: MENTOR

Discuss As a **mentor,** Mrs. Flowers has Marguerite's interests at heart. What does this warning show about her as a **mentor?** *Possible answer: She has firm expectations for Marguerite and will hold her to high standards.*

F **GRAMMAR AND STYLE**

Add Descriptive Details Explain that adjective clauses modify nouns or pronouns, telling *what kind* or *which one*. In this sentence, the adjective clause modifies the noun *room*, but Angelou's phrasing captures Marguerite's excitement. Have students find other sentences in the selection that contain adjective clauses and explain how the clauses add descriptive details. To help students locate clauses, explain that adjective clauses often begin with *that, which, who,* or *whom* and immediately follow the noun or pronoun that they modify. Examples of adjective clauses include *who didn't understand English* (lines 116–117); *which separates him from the lower animals* (line 120); *who would help me analyze and enjoy it* (lines 147–148); and *that I could take home to my brother* (line 157).

FOR LESS–PROFICIENT READERS

② **Targeted Passage [Lines 109–129]**

This passage reveals Mrs. Flowers's reason for inviting Marguerite to her home.

- According to Mrs. Flowers, what is Marguerite doing right at school? What problem is she having?
- What "totally new idea" does she present to Marguerite?
- What does she want Marguerite to do with the books that she borrows?

FOR ENGLISH LEARNERS

Vocabulary: Phrasal Verbs Point out that some English verbs often "go together" with other words (words that otherwise may be prepositions or adverbs) to form phrasal verbs with unique meanings. Guide students to define some of the phrasal verbs on these pages: *put on* (line 70); *turn around* (line 86); *take off* (line 89); *picked up* (line 104); *hung back* (line 113); *set down* (line 123); *gobble up* (line 147).

About the Art Contemporary painter Michele Hausman (born 1952) represents nature in landscapes, florals, and still lifes. She believes that "seeing is the greatest joy of existence" and uses her paintings to express that joy.

Activity Marguerite regards her snack with Mrs. Flowers as a perfect interlude on a hot summer day. How does the painting suggest that perfection? ***Possible answer:*** *Its mood and colors are cool and refreshing.*

Lines 153–159
DISCUSSION PROMPTS

Use these prompts to discuss how Angelou characterizes herself as a girl:

Connect Have you or someone you know ever been a guest in a fancy setting? What details stood out? Explain. *Encourage students to be as specific as possible in their descriptions.*

Analyze Why are the details about the cookies important? What do they show about Marguerite? ***Possible answer:*** *The details reveal her feelings at that moment— in particular, her delight in the special treatment that Mrs. Flowers gives her.*

Evaluate What is the value of such small details in an autobiography? ***Possible answers:*** *They show Marguerite's inner thoughts; they show how a child's mind might work; they give the reader a chance to visualize; they may help readers identify with Marguerite.*

Lemonade (2002), Michele Hausman. © Michele Hausman.

They were flat round wafers, slightly browned on the edges and butter-yellow in the center. With the cold lemonade they were sufficient for childhood's lifelong diet. Remembering my manners, I took nice little lady like bites off the edges. She said she had made them expressly for me and that she had a few in the kitchen that I could take home to my brother. So I jammed one whole cake in my mouth and the rough crumbs scratched the insides of my jaws, and if I hadn't had to swallow, it would have been a dream come true.

160   As I ate she began the first of what we later called "my lessons in living." She said that I must always be intolerant of ignorance but understanding of **illiteracy.** That some people, unable to go to school, were more educated and even more intelligent than college professors. She encouraged me to listen carefully to what country people called mother wit. That in those **homely** sayings was couched the collective wisdom of generations.

   When I finished the cookies she brushed off the table and brought a thick, small book from the bookcase. I had read *A Tale of Two Cities*[8] and found it up to my standards as a romantic novel. She opened the first page and I heard poetry for the first time in my life.

illiteracy (ĭ-lĭt′ər-ə-sē) *n.* a lack of ability to read and write

homely (hōm′lē) *adj.* characteristic of home life; simple; everyday

---

8. ***A Tale of Two Cities:*** a novel by Charles Dickens, set in Paris and London during the French Revolution (1789–1799).

DIFFERENTIATED INSTRUCTION

FOR ADVANCED LEARNERS/PRE–AP
Make Judgments Have students reread the "lessons in living" discussed in lines 160–165. Is this the counsel that Marguerite most needs to hear? Is it practical? Ask students to respond to these questions by writing a paragraph that expresses a judgment about the quality of Mrs. Flowers's "lessons."

170 "It was the best of times and the worst of times . . ."[9] Her voice slid in and curved down through and over the words. She was nearly singing. I wanted to look at the pages. Were they the same that I had read? Or were there notes, music, lined on the pages, as in a hymn book? Her sounds began **cascading** gently. I knew from listening to a thousand preachers that she was nearing the end of her reading, and I hadn't really heard, heard to understand, a single word.

"How do you like that?"

It occurred to me that she expected a response. The sweet vanilla flavor was still on my tongue and her reading was a wonder in my ears. I had to speak.

180 I said, "Yes, ma'am." It was the least I could do, but it was the most also. **G**

"There's one more thing. Take this book of poems and memorize one for me. Next time you pay me a visit, I want you to recite."

> I have tried often to search behind the sophistication of years for the enchantment I so easily found in those gifts. The essence escapes but its aura remains.[10] To be allowed, no, invited, into the private lives of strangers, and to share their joys and fears, was a chance to exchange the Southern bitter wormwood for a cup of mead with Beowulf or a hot cup of tea and milk with Oliver Twist.[11] When I said aloud, "It is a far, far better thing that I do, than I have ever done . . ."[12] tears of love filled my eyes at my selflessness.
>
> 190 On that first day, I ran down the hill and into the road (few cars ever came along it) and had the good sense to stop running before I reached the Store.
>
> I was liked, and what a difference it made. I was respected not as Mrs. Henderson's grandchild or Bailey's sister but for just being Marguerite Johnson.
>
> Childhood's logic never asks to be proved (all conclusions are absolute). I didn't question why Mrs. Flowers had singled me out for attention, nor did it occur to me that Momma might have asked her to give me a little talking to. All I cared about was that she had made tea cookies for *me* and read to *me* from her favorite book. It was enough to prove that she liked me. ∾ **H**

cascade (kă-skād') *v.* to fall or flow like a waterfall

G CHARACTERIZATION
What does Angelou mean when she says that speaking was both the least and the most she could do?

3 Targeted Passage

H ANALYZE PERSPECTIVES
Reread lines 183–198. In which lines is Angelou directly narrating her actions and experiences as a child? In which lines is she sharing insights she learned later, as she grew up? Explain your answers.

---

9. **"It was . . . the worst of times . . .":** the famous opening sentence of *A Tale of Two Cities*.

10. **The essence . . . remains:** The basic quality of a thing or event escapes, but the feelings or atmosphere that it creates remains.

11. **a chance to exchange . . . with Oliver Twist:** Angelou compares her existence as a black child in the bigoted South to wormwood, a bitter herb. Mead (a liquor made from honey) and tea with milk were common drinks in the respective eras of Beowulf and Oliver Twist, two characters from English literature. Angelou suggests that reading about such characters provided an escape from her racist Southern surroundings.

12. **"It is a far . . . than I have ever done . . .":** the final line of *A Tale of Two Cities*, spoken by a man who sacrifices his own life to save that of another.

FOR LESS–PROFICIENT READERS

3 Targeted Passage [Lines 183–198]

In this concluding passage, Angelou reflects upon what Mrs. Flowers did for her.

- In line 184, what does Angelou call the things that Mrs. Flowers did for her?

- According to line 192, what now makes a difference to her?

- According to lines 197–198, what did she care about on that day? Why?

FOR ENGLISH LEARNERS

Comprehension: Transitions Explain that the word *but* in a sentence usually signals contrasting ideas. Have students discuss how the ideas within these sentences are different:

- *"That's good, but not good enough."* (lines 122–123)

- *It was the least I could do, but it was the most also.* (line 180)

- *The essence escapes but its aura remains.* (lines 184–185)

LITERARY ANALYSIS

G CHARACTERIZATION

Possible answer: *Because Marguerite is so quiet, just saying "Yes, ma'am" is hard for her—perhaps the most she can do. The statement also refers to the respect that she owes: Mrs. Flowers has done so much for her, and she has been so moved by hearing Mrs. Flowers read, that answering is the least she can do in return.*

Extend the Discussion What is Marguerite feeling when she says, "Yes, ma'am"?

READING SKILL

H ANALYZE PERSPECTIVES

Possible answer: *Angelou narrates actions and experiences as a child in lines 190–193 and 197–198; Angelou shares adult insights in lines 183–189 and 194–197.*

SELECTION WRAP–UP

SUMMARIZE Have students summarize the development of the character of Marguerite.

⭐ **CRITIQUE** Ask students to recall what passages from the selection they found particularly moving and to explain why.

READING FLUENCY

Distribute the copy master and have students work in pairs or groups to practice fluency.

R RESOURCE MANAGER—Copy Master
Reading Fluency p. 115

DISCUSSION PROMPTS

Use these prompts to help students explore the symbol of the "caged bird" and connect Angelou's poem to the autobiography:

Connect What connotations do you associate with the image of a caged bird? Explain. *Some students will say that the image has negative connotations because a cage suggests confinement and lack of freedom.*

Analyze What is the purpose of including the "free bird" in the poem (lines 1, 23)? How does it help to understand the function of the caged bird? Explain. **Possible answer:** *The free bird sets up a contrast with the caged bird. The free bird can experience nature such as the wind (line 2) and makes the sky its own (lines 7, 26). The caged bird sings out of frustration and longing.*

Evaluate Ask students to tell which selection they prefer and then to explain how effectively it portrays what it is like to be caged. *Students who prefer the excerpt from the autobiography may say that it vividly portrays a child who is trapped within herself and is unable to escape her torment without help. Students who prefer the poem may argue that it uses dramatic images and figures of speech to describe the rage, frustration, and pain of feeling trapped but, in doing so, shows us the power of the caged bird who expresses feelings in song.*

Caged Bird Maya Angelou

A free bird leaps
on the back of the wind
and floats downstream
till the current ends
5 and dips his wing
in the orange sun rays
and dares to claim the sky.

But a bird that stalks
down his narrow cage
10 can seldom see through
his bars of rage
his wings are clipped and
his feet are tied
so he opens his throat to sing.

15 The caged bird sings
with a fearful trill
of things unknown
but longed for still
and his tune is heard
20 on the distant hill
for the caged bird
sings of freedom.

The free bird thinks of another breeze
and the trade winds soft through the sighing trees
25 and the fat worms waiting on a dawn-bright lawn
and he names the sky his own

But a caged bird stands on the grave of dreams
his shadow shouts on a nightmare scream
his wings are clipped and his feet are tied
30 so he opens his throat to sing.

The caged bird sings
with a fearful trill
of things unknown
but longed for still
35 and his tune is heard
on the distant hill
for the caged bird
sings of freedom.

Comprehension

1. **Recall** What is Mrs. Flowers's feeling about language?

2. **Summarize** What kinds of assignments does Mrs. Flowers give Marguerite?

3. **Clarify** What does Mrs. Flowers mean when she tells Marguerite that some people, though lacking formal schooling, are "more educated and even more intelligent than college professors"?

Literary Analysis

4. **Understand Motives** What motivates Mrs. Flowers to help Marguerite?

5. **Analyze Perspectives** Review the chart that you filled in while reading. How does Angelou's adult perspective help you to understand the long-range effect that Mrs. Flowers had on her life? Cite evidence.

6. **Evaluate Characterization in Autobiography** Skim the selection and find examples of the various methods of characterization used by Angelou in her autobiography. Which would you say is the most powerful method used to characterize Mrs. Flowers? Use the list shown to help you with your response.

> **Methods of Characterization**
>
> • description of a person's physical appearance
>
> • examples of the person's speech, thoughts, or feelings
>
> • the speech, thoughts, or feelings of other people
>
> • the narrator's comments about the person

7. **Compare Literary Works** Reread the poem "Caged Bird" on page 246. Does Mrs. Flowers teach the young Marguerite to "sing"? If so, in what way?

Literary Criticism

8. **Biographical Context** The title *I Know Why the Caged Bird Sings* is an allusion to the poem "Sympathy" by Paul Laurence Dunbar. The last stanza reads:

> I know why the caged bird sings, ah me,
>   When his wing is bruised and his bosom sore,—
> When he beats his bars and he would be free;
> It is not a carol of joy or glee,
>   But a prayer that he sends from his heart's deep core,
> But a plea, that upward to Heaven he flings—
> I know why the caged bird sings!

Why do you think Angelou refers to this poem in the title of her autobiography?

may be Angelou's own poetic comments. Students should cite evidence.

7. *Yes; Mrs. Flowers requires Marguerite to participate in the power of the spoken word in literature. It is implied that doing so will draw Marguerite out of her silence and will foster her ability to free herself through writing.*

Literary Criticism

Possible answer:

8. *As a young victim of abuse, Angelou also was "bruised." She was not singing any "carol of joy or glee"; rather, she was trapped in an isolating silence. Despite being "caged" by abuse and by segregation, Angelou does, indeed, learn to sing.*

Practice and Apply

After Reading

For additional support of post-reading questions, use these copy masters:

R RESOURCE MANAGER—Copy Masters

> Reading Check p. 112 (to check understanding of the selection)
>
> Characterization in Autobiography p. 105 (for practice of literary analysis standards focus)
>
> Question Support p. 113 (After Reading questions adapted for English learners and less-proficient readers)

For additional questions, see page 99.

For additional exercises to challenge students, see

ⓘ Power Thinking at ClassZone.com

ANSWERS

Comprehension

1. *Mrs. Flowers says that language separates people from animals (line 120) and that the human voice gives meaning to words (line 124).*

2. *Marguerite is to read books aloud and to make each sentence sound in as many different ways as possible (lines 127–129). Marguerite also must memorize a poem to recite (lines 181–182).*

3. *She probably means that wisdom does not depend upon formal education.*

Literary Analysis

Possible answers:

4. *Momma probably asked Mrs. Flowers to help Marguerite (lines 196–197). Teachers' concerns are mentioned (lines 110–111), as well.*

5. ● STANDARDS FOCUS **Analyze Perspectives** *Angelou recalls that Mrs. Flowers enabled her to hear "poetry for the first time in my life" (lines 168–169). She also remarks on the "enchantment I . . . found in those gifts" (line 184) and how it remains with her. She summarizes Mrs. Flowers's effect in lines 18–19.*

6. ● STANDARDS FOCUS **Characterization in Autobiography** *Angelou describes Mrs. Flowers's physical appearance, gives examples of her speech, and offers her own comments. The most powerful method*

ANSWERS
Vocabulary in Context
VOCABULARY PRACTICE

1. *cascade*   5. *sacrilegious*
2. *leer*   6. *clarity*
3. *illiteracy*   7. *taut*
4. *homely*   8. *infuse*

 RESOURCE MANAGER—Copy Master
Vocabulary Practice p. 110

VOCABULARY IN WRITING

Before students draft their sentences, review the words' parts of speech. Help students distinguish among action words, naming words, and words that describe.

VOCABULARY STRATEGY: MULTIPLE-MEANING WORDS *(also an EL language objective)*

Explain that context clues are the best tool for distinguishing multiple meanings. Give this illustration.

> I sing in the choir.
> The poet sings of freedom.
> If she thinks she can avoid going to jail, the woman who helped with the crime might sing.

Have students use context clues to determine the meaning of *sing* in each sentence.

Possible answers:

1. *b*   3. *c*
2. *a*   4. *c*

 RESOURCE MANAGER—Copy Master
Vocabulary Strategy p. 111

ℹ️ **Vocabulary Center at ClassZone.com**
Additional Vocabulary Activities

Vocabulary in Context

VOCABULARY PRACTICE

Determine the relationship between the first pair of words in each analogy. Then write the word that best completes the second pair.

1. *Drift* is to *snow* as _____ is to *water*.
2. *Smile* is to *sweetness* as _____ is to *wickedness*.
3. *Disease* is to *medicine* as _____ is to *education*.
4. *Fancy* is to *special* as _____ is to *everyday*.
5. *Toxic* is to *environment* as _____ is to *religion*.
6. *Bewilderment* is to *confusion* as *understanding* is to _____.
7. *Untied* is to *tied* as *loose* is to _____.
8. *Help* is to *assist* as _____ is to *inject*.

WORD LIST
cascade
clarity
homely
illiteracy
infuse
leer
sacrilegious
taut

VOCABULARY IN WRITING

What are some beliefs that Marguerite learned from Mrs. Flowers? Write three to four sentences about her beliefs, using at least five vocabulary words.

> **EXAMPLE SENTENCE**
> *Marguerite learned that **clarity** in speaking is essential.*

VOCABULARY STRATEGY: MULTIPLE-MEANING WORDS

Sometimes words, such as the vocabulary word *homely* in this selection, do not have the meanings you expect. Many English words have a number of meanings, and to understand what you are reading, you must decide which of these meanings the writer intends.

PRACTICE Write the letter of the best definition for each boldfaced word.

1. She **distinguished** herself from her friends by wearing all black.
   (a) successful or commanding great respect, (b) set oneself apart,
   (c) recognized differences among several choices
2. **Channel** your energies into some worthwhile project.
   (a) direct into a particular course of action, (b) body of water connecting two larger bodies of water, (c) band of radio or television frequencies
3. The store sold **notions** as well as yarn and knitting needles.
   (a) beliefs about something, (b) vague understandings of something,
   (c) needles, buttons, and other sewing materials
4. Amassing **capital** was his primary goal.
   (a) city where government is located, (b) punishable by death, (c) money

VOCABULARY PRACTICE
For more practice, go to the **Vocabulary Center** at **ClassZone.com.**

DIFFERENTIATED INSTRUCTION

FOR ENGLISH LEARNERS
Task Support: Reteach Use Word Squares to reteach the vocabulary words before students begin the Vocabulary in Context activities.

 BEST PRACTICES TOOLKIT—Transparency
Word Squares p. E10

FOR ADVANCED LEARNERS/PRE–AP
Vocabulary Strategy Have students determine the meaning of each of these words as it is used in the selection from *I Know Why the Caged Bird Sings* and then use a dictionary to find at least one additional meaning for each word: *measure* (line 19), *refined* (line 53), *provisions* (line 61), *finish* (line 83), *pronounced* (line 115), and *novel* (line 168).

Reading-Writing Connection

Broaden your understanding of this selection by responding to these prompts. Then use **Revision: Grammar and Style** to improve your writing.

A. Short Response: Compare Forms

An autobiography is the story of a person's life written by that person; a biography is the story of a person's life written by someone else. What advantages and disadvantages might an autobiography have as opposed to a biography? Use examples from this selection to write **one or two paragraphs** comparing these forms.

An effective comparison will . . .

- discuss at least two advantages and two disadvantages an autobiography might have compared with a biography
- use evidence from the selection to support your points

B. Extended Response: Analyze Traits

Think about the most important character traits Mrs. Flowers exhibits. Then review the word web you created detailing the qualities a **mentor** should possess. Write **three to five paragraphs** describing Mrs. Flowers's traits and analyzing how these traits compare with the qualities you listed.

A strong analysis will . . .

- list at least three of Mrs. Flowers's traits, supported by evidence from the text
- compare the traits Mrs. Flowers exhibits with the qualities you discussed before reading

REVISION: GRAMMAR AND STYLE

ADD DESCRIPTIVE DETAILS Review the **Grammar and Style** note on page 243. In her writing, Angelou uses **adjective clauses** to add interesting, vivid details about her characters and their emotions. Adjective clauses are subordinate clauses that, like adjectives, modify nouns and pronouns. They are introduced by **relative pronouns** such as *who, whom, whose, that,* and *which* and **relative adverbs** such as *when, where,* and *why.* Here are some examples from the selection:

> . . . *It seemed she had a private breeze which swirled around.* . . . (line 6)
> . . . *From the side of the building where I waited for the ground to open up and swallow me, I heard the soft-voiced Mrs. Flowers.* . . . (lines 40–42)

Notice how the revisions in red make this first draft more descriptive. Use similar methods to revise your responses to the prompts.

STUDENT MODEL

who goes out of her way to make Marguerite feel at ease

Mrs. Flowers is a generous person. She invites Marguerite over to
, where she serves cookies and lemonade
her house and reads out loud from a book, that captivates the girl.

WRITING TOOLS
For prewriting, revision, and editing tools, visit the **Writing Center** at **ClassZone.com.**

FOR LESS–PROFICIENT WRITERS

For Prompt A:

To help students explore the differences between each form, ask:

- Which author knows the subject better?
- Which author is more objective?
- Which author is more likely to take advice and input from others?
- Which author would be more worried about revealing personal information?

Possible Organization for Prompt B:

First paragraph: Introduction and thesis

Middle paragraph(s): One or more of Mrs. Flowers's traits (named in at least one topic sentence) and explanation of the comparison

Final paragraph: Summary and conclusion

Reading-Writing Connection

- For Prompt A, suggest students begin by exploring the terms *biography* and *autobiography* in a Venn diagram.
- A Venn diagram is also useful for Prompt B. The circles should be labeled *Mrs. Flowers's Traits* and *Traits of a Mentor.*

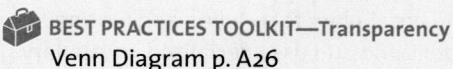 **BEST PRACTICES TOOLKIT—Transparency**
Venn Diagram p. A26

For an extended writing activity, see
ⓘ Carol Booth Olson's Reading-Writing Lesson Plans at **ClassZone.com**

REVISION: GRAMMAR AND STYLE

1. Discuss the revisions to the student model. Note how the added adjective clauses elaborate on the original sentences.
2. List nouns and have students add adjective clauses to expand them. Here are some examples.
   - the Store *Possible answer: that Momma runs*
   - the lemonade *Possible answer: which is deliciously cool on a hot summer day*
   - Marguerite *Possible answer: who doesn't speak*

R RESOURCE MANAGER—Copy Master
Add Descriptive Details p. 114

Assess and Reteach

Assess

R RESOURCE MANAGER—Copy Masters
Selection Test A pp. 117–118
Selection Test B/C pp. 119–120

 Test Generator CD

Reteach

S STANDARDS LESSON FILE
Literature Lesson 3: Characterization
Literature Lesson 47: Author's Perspective
Vocabulary Lesson 19: Multiple-Meaning Words

Focus and Motivate

OBJECTIVES

Elements of Nonfiction
- explore the key idea of **bravery**
- analyze characterization
- read a magazine article

Reading
- interpret graphic aids

Vocabulary
- build vocabulary for reading and writing
- understand and use specialized vocabulary *(also an EL language objective)*

SUMMARY

"Blind to Failure" is Karl Taro Greenfeld's report on blind mountaineer Erik Weihenmayer's remarkable climb to the summit of Mount Everest. Weihenmayer's courage and determination helped him overcome other people's doubts, as well as his own, and to triumph over the physical challenges and extreme dangers of the world's highest peak.

When is STRENGTH *more than muscle?*

Introduce the question and have students read the *KEY IDEA.* Then together discuss what kinds of strength are required for **bravery.** Continue the exploration by having students complete the *QUICKWRITE* and compare their charts.

Blind to Failure
Magazine Article by Karl Taro Greenfeld

When is STRENGTH *more than muscle?*

KEY IDEA It's easy to think of people who are strong in body. Many famous athletes have tremendous physical strength. But some people are extremely strong in mind and spirit as well. In "Blind to Failure," you'll meet one such individual, Erik Weihenmayer, who was the first blind mountaineer to reach the top of Mount Everest. In scaling the world's highest peak, Weihenmayer became an inspiring portrait of **bravery** and determination.

QUICKWRITE Think of different types of strength—physical, emotional, spiritual, and so forth. Think of people who exemplify each type of strength and put them in categories in a chart like the one shown. Do any of the people belong in more than one category?

Physical Strength	Emotional Strength	Spiritual Strength
•	•	•
•	•	•
•	•	•

250

Selection Resources

 **RESOURCE MANAGER UNIT 2**

Plan and Teach pp. 121–128

Elements of Nonfiction
Summary pp. 129†*, 130‡*
Character Study pp. 131, 132†*
Question Support p. 140*

Reading
Interpret Graphic Aids pp. 133, 134†*
Reading Check p. 139
Reading Fluency p. 141

Vocabulary
Study p. 135*
Practice p. 136
Strategy p. 137

Assessment
Selection Tests A, B/C pp. 143*, 145*
 Test Generator CD

BEST PRACTICES TOOLKIT

Differentiated Instruction
pp. 31–38*

Scaffolding Instruction
pp. 43–46*

Graphic Organizers/Strategies
Character Analysis Chart • Word Squares • Y Chart • New Word Analysis

Reading Support
Audio Anthology CD*

Technology
Literature and Vocabulary Centers at **ClassZone.com**
WriteSmart CD

---

* Resources for Differentiation   † Also in Spanish   ‡ In Haitian Creole and Vietnamese

● ELEMENTS OF NONFICTION: CHARACTER STUDY

Some nonfiction writers provide insight into the personalities of individuals by writing **character studies.** A character study usually includes extensive details about its subject's appearance, speech, and actions. As you read "Blind to Failure," look for the following types of details about Erik Weihenmayer:

- actions that have made him newsworthy or famous and his own comments about those actions
- descriptions of his physical traits and facial expressions
- others' reactions to his accomplishments

● READING SKILL: INTERPRET GRAPHIC AIDS

Magazine articles like "Blind to Failure" often include **graphic aids**—charts, graphs, and maps—that present important information in visual form. This article features a **diagram,** a drawing in which lines, symbols, and words are used to help the reader picture a process, an event, or the way something works. As you read "Blind to Failure," turn back and forth between the text and the diagram to better understand the difficulties of the climb and to follow the climbers' progress. Use a chart to record the information you learn from the diagram.

Camp or Location	Elevation	Related Events/ Details of Climb	Other Information
Base Camp	17,600 feet	Below Khumbu Icefall	

Review: **Connect, Draw Conclusions**

▲ VOCABULARY IN CONTEXT

Which of these words do you already know? Write a sentence for each of the words. Then check your understanding after you've read the selection.

WORD LIST			
	acclimatization	crevasse	insurmountable
	aplomb	demeanor	paramount
	arduous	inevitability	transcend
	banal		

Author On|ine

Striking Stories

Karl Taro Greenfeld was born in Kobe, Japan, and grew up in Los Angeles, California. As a journalist, he has made his home in Hong Kong, China, investigating everything from entertainment fads to economic disasters. In June of 2001, Greenfeld set out for Nepal to interview members of the Everest expedition that included Erik Weihenmayer, the climber you will read about.

Karl Taro Greenfeld born 1965

Background

Reaching for the Peak At 29,035 feet, Mount Everest is the highest peak on earth. To reach the summit, mountaineers establish a series of camps at intervals up the mountain and then make numerous trips between them, carrying supplies from the base camp to the highest camp. When the highest camp is well stocked and the weather is favorable, the climbers make a push for the summit.

The Perils of Everest Climbing Mount Everest is incredibly dangerous, even for the most experienced climbers. Extreme cold makes frostbite common. Sunshine reflected off the snow can cause temporary blindness and fatal falls. Climbers often suffer dizziness and confusion due to lack of oxygen. The region above 26,000 feet is called the Death Zone. At that altitude, blood thickens, the heart speeds up, and the brain can swell, with serious injury or death a possible result. Ninety percent of climbers attempting to scale Mount Everest fail to reach the summit.

 BUILDING BACKGROUND To learn more about Mount Everest, visit the **Literature Center** at **ClassZone.com.**

Teach

STANDARDS FOCUS

ELEMENTS OF NONFICTION

● CHARACTER STUDY

For instructional support, read aloud this passage:

> Thompson raised the trophy triumphantly, his muscles bulging. "I am the best!" he roared, pumping his fist in the air. Spectators frowned at the new champion's boast.

Have students identify details that help provide a character study of Thompson. *Possible answer: his bulging muscles, his bragging statement and gestures, the spectators' unfavorable reaction*

CHECK UNDERSTANDING Have students identify similarly revealing details in previous selections from this text.

READING SKILL

■ INTERPRET GRAPHIC AIDS

After reading the page, ask students what kinds of graphic aids they have seen or used. *Examples may include various types of maps, illustrated user manuals, and scientific diagrams.*

CHECK UNDERSTANDING Brainstorm for ideas about graphic aids that students might expect to find in an article about a mountain climber.

 RESOURCE MANAGER—Copy Master Interpret Graphic Aids p. 133 (for student use while reading the selection)

VOCABULARY SKILL

▲ VOCABULARY IN CONTEXT

DIAGNOSE WORD KNOWLEDGE To determine preteaching needs, have all students complete **Vocabulary in Context.** Check students' definitions against those on the selection pages: *acclimatization* (p. 254), *aplomb* (p. 256), *arduous* (p. 257), *banal* (p. 254), *crevasse* (p. 252), *demeanor* (p. 256), *inevitability* (p. 257), *insurmountable* (p. 259), *paramount* (p. 258), *transcend* (p. 257).

PRETEACH VOCABULARY Use the Vocabulary Study copy master to help students predict the meaning of each boldfaced word in the copy master, using context clues.

1. Read item 1, emphasizing *acclimatization.*
2. Point out the phrase "to get used to the mountain climate." Elicit possible meanings for *acclimatization,* such as "to adjust to."
3. Have students record their predictions.
4. Repeat the procedure for items 2–10.

RESOURCE MANAGER—Copy Master Vocabulary Study p. 135

For general guidelines on differentiating vocabulary instruction and for alternative vocabulary activities for students not needing vocabulary preteaching, see

BEST PRACTICES TOOLKIT Scaffolding Vocabulary Instruction pp. 43–46

Vocabulary Center at **ClassZone.com**

ANALYZE VISUALS

Based upon his stance and appearance, Weihennmayer seems to exhibit determination, preparedness, and confidence.

ELEMENTS OF NONFICTION

Ⓐ CHARACTER STUDY

Possible answer: *Such a person may be in good physical condition. He also is either very brave or very foolhardy.*

If students need help . . . Have students use a Character Analysis Chart or expand upon a chart like this to help them make inferences about Weihenmayer.

Information from Article	My Knowledge and Experience	My Inferences
Erik planned to climb Mount Everest.	Few people have reached this goal.	Erik is daring and brave.
Erik had difficulty reaching Camp 1.	More difficult parts of the climb are to come.	Perhaps Erik is taking on too great a challenge.

BEST PRACTICES TOOLKIT—Transparency
Character Analysis Chart p. D5

BLIND *to* FAILURE

Karl Taro Greenfeld

When he saw Erik Weihenmayer arrive that afternoon, Pasquale Scaturro[1] began to have misgivings about the expedition he was leading. Here they were on the first floor of Mount Everest, and Erik—the reason for the whole trip—was stumbling into Camp 1 bloody, sick, and dehydrated. "He was literally green," says fellow climber and teammate Michael O'Donnell. "He looked like George Foreman[2] had beaten him for two hours." The beating had actually been administered by Erik's climbing partner, Luis Benitez.[3] Erik had slipped into a **crevasse,** and as Benitez reached down to catch him, his climbing pole raked Erik across the nose and chin. Wounds heal slowly at that altitude
10 because of the thin air.

As Erik passed out in his tent, the rest of the team gathered in a worried huddle. "I was thinking maybe this is not a good idea," says Scaturro. "Two years of planning, a documentary movie, and this blind guy barely makes it to Camp 1?"

This blind guy. Erik Weihenmayer, thirty-three, wasn't just another yuppie trekker who'd lost a few rounds to the mountain. Blind since he was thirteen, the victim of a rare hereditary disease of the retina, he began attacking mountains in his early twenties. Ⓐ

But he had been having the same doubts as the rest of the team. On that
20 arduous climb to camp through the Khumbu Icefall,[4] Erik wondered for the first time if his attempt to become the first sightless person to summit Mount Everest was a colossal mistake, an act of Daedalian hubris[5] for which he would be punished. There are so many ways to die on that mountain, spanning

---

1. **Erik Weihenmayer** (wī′ən-mā′ər) . . . **Pasquale Scaturro** (päs-kwä′lā skä-tōō′rō).
2. **George Foreman:** a former heavyweight boxing champion.
3. **Luis Benitez** (lōō-ēs′ bĕ-nē′tĕs).
4. **Khumbu** (kōōm′bōō) **Icefall:** a stretch of glacier beginning at about 18,000 feet and extending to the area of Camp 1 at 20,000 feet.
5. **Daedalian hubris** (dǐ-dā′lē-ən hyōō′brĭs): excessive pride like that of Daedalus, a master craftsman in Greek mythology. When Daedalus fashioned wings for himself and his son from feathers and wax, his son flew too near the sun, the wax in his wings melted, and he fell into the sea and drowned.

252 UNIT 2: CHARACTERIZATION AND POINT OF VIEW

ANALYZE VISUALS
Examine the photograph of Weihenmayer. Identify three character **traits** you would attribute to him solely on the basis of this picture.

crevasse (krĭ-văs′) *n.* a deep crack or split in a glacier

① Targeted Passage

Ⓐ CHARACTER STUDY
Think about the endeavor Weihenmayer undertook and his fellow climbers' descriptions of the expedition to this point. What **inferences** can you make about someone who would attempt such a feat?

DIFFERENTIATED INSTRUCTION

FOR ALL STUDENTS

Expert Groups Allow students to become experts or members of expert groups by researching and choosing a way to share additional information about one of these topics:

- geographical facts about the Himalayas
- attempts to conquer Mount Everest
- facilities and activities for the blind in your community

FOR LESS–PROFICIENT READERS

In combination with the *Audio Anthology CD*, use one or more Targeted Passages (pp. 252, 254, 259, 261) to ensure that students focus on key events, concepts, and skills. Targeted Passages are also good for English learners.

① Targeted Passage [Lines 1–14]

This passage introduces Erik and reveals the almost insurmountable physical challenge that he faces.

Climbing Mount Everest Until the early 20th century, people living near Mount Everest considered the Himalayas sacred, and no climbers ascended the mountains. Starting in the 1920s, however, foreign expeditions ventured into the Himalayas, assisted by people of the hardy Sherpa ethnic group. In 1953, Edmund Hillary of New Zealand and Sherpa Tenzing Norgay of Nepal were the first to reach the top of Mount Everest. The first woman to climb to the summit was Junko Tabei of Japan, in 1975.

Lines 19–23
REINFORCE *KEY IDEA:* BRAVERY

Discuss Do Eric's doubts show a lapse of bravery? Explain. *Student responses may vary but many may answer that bravery is often necessary for honestly facing the facts of a difficult situation.*

- In what condition is Erik Weihenmayer when he first arrives at Camp 1? Why?
- How do the other climbers react when they first see Erik?
- How does the group's leader feel about Erik being on the expedition?

FOR ENGLISH LEARNERS

Key Academic Vocabulary Use Word Squares to teach these words: *teammate* (line 5), *partner* (line 7), *rely* (line 40), *achievement* (line 114), *capable* (line 157), *primarily* (line 244).

 BEST PRACTICES TOOLKIT—Transparency
Word Squares p. E10

Prereading For prereading instruction for English learners, see

🧰 BEST PRACTICES TOOLKIT
Scaffolding Reading Instruction pp. 43–46

FOR ADVANCED LEARNERS/PRE–AP

Pre-AP Exercises in the bottom channel provide additional challenge for students. Use these suggestions for small groups or individuals.

ADDITIONAL GUIDELINES
For more help with differentiation and tips for classroom management, see

🧰 BEST PRACTICES TOOLKIT
Differentiated Instruction pp. 31–38

Use these prompts to help students understand the challenges that a blind climber faces:

Connect Have you ever felt that you were out of your "comfort zone"? How does that memory help you understand Erik in these paragraphs? *Responses should reflect an understanding of Erik's uncertainty.*

Analyze What evidence does Greenfeld give to explain why the icefall terrain is so much more dangerous for Weihenmayer than for a sighted person? *Possible answer: "The blind thrive on patterns . . ." (lines 37–40), but "the trail through the Himalayan glacier is patternless . . ." (lines 41–49).*

Evaluate What is your opinion of Erik Weihenmayer up to this point? Defend your answer. *Opinions will vary but should be supported with solid reasons and information from the article.*

ELEMENTS OF NONFICTION

B CHARACTER STUDY

Possible answer: Weihenmayer is tough and determined. He insists upon carrying his own weight rather than letting the rest of the team shoulder his load. He also cuts his time down to five hours (line 64) from the initial thirteen (line 53).

Extend the Discussion Why is the comparison of being "carried to the top and spiked like a football" (line 62) an effective way to show Weihenmayer's reaction?

---

the spectacular (fall through an ice shelf into a crevasse, get waylaid by an avalanche, develop cerebral edema[6] from lack of oxygen and have your brain literally swell out of your skull) and the **banal** (become disoriented because of oxygen deprivation and decide you'll take a little nap, right here, in the snow, which becomes a forever nap).

30   Erik, as he stumbled through the icefall, was so far out of his comfort zone that he began to speculate on which of those fates might await him. For a moment he flashed on all those clichés about what blind people are supposed to do—become piano tuners or pencil salesmen—and thought maybe they were stereotypes for good reason. Blind people certainly shouldn't be out here, wandering through an ever changing ice field, measuring the distance over a 1,000-foot-deep crevasse with climbing poles and then leaping, literally, over and into the unknown.

   The blind thrive on patterns: stairs are all the same height, city blocks roughly the same length, curbs approximately the same depth. They learn to identify the patterns in their environment much more than the sighted
40 population do, and to rely on them to plot their way through the world.

   But in the Khumbu Icefall, the trail through the Himalayan glacier is patternless, a diabolically cruel obstacle course for a blind person. It changes every year as the river of ice shifts, but it's always made up of treacherously crumbly stretches of ice, ladders roped together over wide crevasses, slightly narrower crevasses that must be jumped, huge seracs,[7] avalanches, and—most frustrating for a blind person, who naturally seeks to identify patterns in his terrain—a totally random icescape.

   In the icefall there is no system, no repetition, no rhyme or reason to the lay of the frozen land. On the other hand, "it is so specific in terms of where
50 you can step," Erik recalls. "Sometimes you're walking along and then boom, a crevasse is right there, and three more steps and another one, and then a snow bridge. And vertical up, then a ladder and then a jumbly section." It took Erik thirteen hours to make it from Base Camp through the icefall to Camp 1, at 20,000 feet. Scaturro had allotted seven.

   A typical assault on Everest requires each climber to do as many as ten traverses through the icefall, both for **acclimatization** purposes and to help carry the immense amount of equipment required for an ascent. After Erik's accident, the rest of the National Federation of the Blind (NFB) team discussed letting him stay up in Camp 1, equipped with videotapes and food, while the rest of the team and
60 the Sherpas[8] did his carries for him. No way, said Erik. No way was he going to do this climb without being a fully integrated and useful member of the team. "I wasn't going to be carried to the top and spiked like a football," he says. The next day he forced himself to head back down through the icefall. He would eventually make ten passes through the Khumbu, cutting his time to five hours. **B**

banal (bə-năl′) *adj.* commonplace; trite

② Targeted Passage

acclimatization (ə-klī′mə-tĭ-zā′shən) *n.* the act of getting accustomed to a new climate or environment

B CHARACTER STUDY Reread lines 55–64. What do you learn about Weihenmayer from his reaction to his teammates' idea?

---

6. **cerebral edema** (sĕr′ə-brəl ĭ-dē′mə).
7. **seracs** (sə-răks′): large, pointed masses of ice isolated by intersecting crevasses.
8. **Sherpas:** a Himalayan people who live around the Nepal-Tibet border and often assist climbers of Everest.

DIFFERENTIATED INSTRUCTION

FOR LESS–PROFICIENT READERS

② Targeted Passage [Lines 41–64]

This largely descriptive passage reveals some dangerous climbing conditions—and Erik's refusal of special treatment.

- What makes the Khumbu Icefall dangerous?
- Why are icefalls especially difficult for a blind person?
- What offer do his teammates make? Why does Erik turn them down?

FOR ENGLISH LEARNERS

Vocabulary: Word Associations Explain these word associations, or "word chunks," as you come across them in the reading:

- *get waylaid* (line 24), "be stopped"
- *diabolically cruel* (line 42), "extremely difficult"
- *circus-freak variety* (line 111), "very strange type"

MOUNT EVEREST: THE ROUTE TO THE SUMMIT C

Mount Everest
29,035 ft.
(8,850 m)

Hillary Step
South Summit

Camp 4
26,000 ft.
(7,925 m)

Camp 3
24,000 ft.
(7,315 m)

Camp 2
21,300 ft.
(6,492 m)

South Face

Camp 1
20,000 ft.
(6,100 m)

Khumbu Icefall

Base Camp
17,600 ft.
(5,364 m)

C INTERPRET GRAPHIC AIDS
What information about Camp 1 do you learn from this **diagram**? Record the information in your chart.

Sometimes, when Erik is giving a motivational speech for one of his corporate clients . . . a fat, balding, middle-aged middle manager will approach him and say, "Even I wouldn't do that stuff." Erik calls it the Even I Syndrome. And he has to resist an impulse to say, "You're fat, out of shape, and you smoke. Why would you even think of doing any of this stuff? Just because you 70 can see?" Erik is not impatient or smug, but he tires of people assuming that sight will trump all other attributes and senses combined.

By all accounts, Erik is gifted with strong lungs, a refined sense of balance, a disproportionately powerful upper body, rubbery legs, and flexible ankles. His conditioning is exemplary and his heart rate low. He is stockier than most mountaineers, who tend toward lanky, long muscles. But he possesses an

---

READING SKILL

C INTERPRET GRAPHIC AIDS

Possible answer: *Camp 1 is located on the South Face of Mount Everest, above the Khumbu Icefall. The elevation of Camp 1 is 20,000 feet, placing it more than 2,000 feet above Base Camp. The ascent to Camp 2 (1,300 feet higher) is indirect.*

If students need help . . . Model for students how to record this information on the chart that they began on page 251.

Camp or Location: Camp 1

Elevation: 20,000 feet

Related Events/Details of Climb: Ascent from Camp 1 to Camp 2 is indirect.

Other Information: On the South Face, above Khumbu Icefall; 2,400 feet above Base Camp; 1,300 feet below Camp 2

Lines 65–71
REINFORCE *KEY IDEA:* BRAVERY

Discuss How does Erik's encounter with someone who has the "Even I Syndrome" help show what **bravery** is—and is not? ***Possible answer:*** *It is a reminder that bravery is not just a matter of physical vision; although there is a physical factor, attitude plays a major role.*

FOR ENGLISH LEARNERS
Comprehension: Sequence Urge students to use transitions to help them understand the sequence of events. Ask them to reread lines 65–71, noting the phrase *Sometimes, when . . .* Elicit that the article has focused on past events up to this point but that *Sometimes, when . . .* signals a flash-forward to Erik's life in the present.

FOR ADVANCED LEARNERS/PRE–AP
Evaluate Assumptions [small-group option] Greenfeld writes that Weihenmayer "tires of people assuming that sight will trump all other attributes and senses combined" (lines 70–71).

Ask students what other assumptions they think able-bodied people make about people with physical disabilities. Have them prepare a response and then present and defend it in class.

abundance of the one indispensable characteristic of a great mountaineer: mental toughness, the ability to withstand tremendous amounts of cold, discomfort, physical pain, boredom, bad food, insomnia, and tedious conversation when you're snowed into a pup tent for a week on a three-foot-
80 wide ice shelf at 20,000 feet. (That happened to Erik on Alaska's Denali.[9])
On Everest, toughness is perhaps the most important trait a climber can have. "Erik is mentally one of the strongest guys you will ever meet," says fellow climber Chris Morris.

Everybody gets sick on Everest. It's called the Khumbu Krud, brought on by a combination of high altitude, dirty food, fetid water, intestinal parasites, and an utterly alien ecosystem. On Erik's team, at any given moment, half the climbers were running fevers, the others were nauseated, and they all suffered from one form or another of dysentery, an awkward ailment when there's a driving snowstorm and it's thirty below outside the tent. . . .

90 Scaling Everest requires the enthusiasm and boosterism of a physical-education teacher combined with the survival instinct of a Green Beret.[10] You have to want that summit. And if you whine . . . your teammates might discard you before you get there. Erik, beneath his beard and quiet **demeanor,** was both booster and killer. "He was the heart and soul of our team," says Eric Alexander. "The guy's spirit won't let you quit." **D**

E rik walks through these Kathmandu[11] streets with remarkable ease, his red-tipped cane searching out ahead of him, measuring distance, pitch, and angle. You give him little hints as he goes—"There's a doorway. Okay, now a right—no, left, sorry"—and he follows, his stride confident but easily arrested
100 when he bumps into an old lady selling shawls, and then into the wheel of a scooter. The physical confidence that he projects has to do with having an athlete's awareness of how his body moves through space. Plenty of sighted people walk through life with less poise and grace than Erik, unsure of their steps, second-guessing every move. And certainly most of the blind don't maneuver with Erik's **aplomb.** As he takes a seat in a crowded restaurant, ordering pizza, spaghetti, ice cream . . . —you work up an appetite climbing Everest—he smiles and nods as other diners ask, "Hey, aren't you the blind guy . . . ?"

With his Germanic, sculpted features and light brown hair, Erik looks a bit like a shaggy, youthful Kirk Douglas. He is a celebrity now: strangers ask for
110 his autograph, reporters call constantly, restaurants give him free meals. But is his celebrity the circus-freak variety—of a type with the Dogboy and the two-headed snake?

At its worst, Erik fears, it is. Casual observers don't understand what an achievement his Everest climb was, or they assume that if a blind guy can do it, anyone can. And indeed, improved gear has made Everest, at least in some

---

9. **Denali** (də-nä′lē): the highest peak in North America, also known as Mount McKinley.
10. **Green Beret:** a member of the U.S. Army Special Forces.
11. **Kathmandu** (kăt′măn-dōō′): the capital of Nepal.

256 UNIT 2: CHARACTERIZATION AND POINT OF VIEW

demeanor (dĭ-mē′nər) *n.* a way of behaving; manner

D **CHARACTER STUDY**
Think about how your perception of Weihenmayer would be different if his teammates' descriptions of him were omitted.

aplomb (ə-plŏm′) *n.* poise; self-assurance

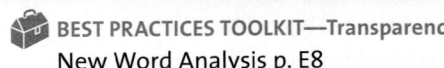

people's minds, a bit smaller. In the climbing season there's a conga line[12] to the top, or so it seems, and the trail is a junkyard of discarded oxygen tanks and other debris. But Everest eats the unready and the unlucky. Almost 90 percent of Everest climbers fail to reach the summit. Many—at least 165 since 120 1953—never come home at all, their bodies lying uncollected where they fell. Four died in May. "People think because I'm blind, I don't have as much to be afraid of, like if I can't see a 2,000-foot drop-off I won't be scared," Erik says. "That's insane. Look, death is death, if I can see or not."

Everest expeditions break down into two types: those like Erik's, which are sponsored and united by a common goal, and those like the one described by Jon Krakauer in *Into Thin Air*,[13] in which gangs of climbers pay $65,000 each for the opportunity to stand on top of the world. But as conditions become more **arduous,** these commercial teams start squabbling, blaming weaker members for slowing them down and sometimes even refusing to help 130 teammates in distress.

Many pros wouldn't go near Erik's team, fearing they might have to haul the blind guy down. "Everyone was saying Erik was gonna have an epic," says Charley Mace, a member of the film crew. ("Epic" is Everest slang for disaster.) Another climber planned to stay close, boasting that he would "get the first picture of the dead blind guy."

For Erik, who knew almost as soon as he could speak that he would lose his vision in his early teens, excelling as an athlete was the result of accepting his disability rather than denying it. Growing up with two brothers in Hong Kong and then Weston, Connecticut, he was always an athletic kid, a tough gamer 140 who developed a bump-and-grind one-on-one basketball game that allowed him to work his way close to the hoop. He was, his father Ed says, "a pretty normal kid. While bike riding, he might have run into a few more parked cars than other kids, but we didn't dwell on his going blind."

His blindness was a medical **inevitability,** like a court date with a hanging judge.[14] "I saw blindness like this disease," he explains. "Like AIDS or something that was going to consume me." Think about that—being a kid, ten, eleven years old, and knowing that at some point in the near future your world is going to go dark. Certainly it builds character—that mental toughness his fellow climbers marvel at—but in a child, the natural psychological defense 150 would be denial. **E**

When he lost his vision, Erik at first refused to use a cane or learn Braille, insisting he could somehow muddle on as normal. "I was so afraid I would seem like a freak," he recalls. But after a few embarrassing stumbles—he couldn't even find the school rest rooms anymore—he admitted he needed help. For Erik, the key was acceptance—not to fight his disability but to learn to work within it; not to **transcend** it but to understand fully what he was

---

12. **conga line:** The conga is a Latin American dance in which the dancers form a long, winding line.
13. *Into Thin Air:* a best-selling book about the 1996 climbing season at Mount Everest, during which eight climbers died.
14. **hanging judge:** a judge who always hands out very harsh sentences.

BLIND TO FAILURE **257**

---

arduous (är′jōō-əs) *adj.* requiring much effort; difficult

inevitability (ĭn-ĕv′ĭ-tə-bĭl′ĭ-tē) *n.* something that is certain to happen

E **CONNECT**
Reread lines 136–150. Do you agree that denial would be the natural response to a situation like Weihenmayer's? Explain.

transcend (trăn-sĕnd′) *v.* to pass beyond the limits of

Lines 113–123
DISCUSSION PROMPTS
Use these prompts to help students appreciate the problem of underestimating Everest:

Connect Conquering Everest would make you a celebrity. Would that motivate you to climb? *Answers will vary but should recognize the difficulties involved in the attempt.*

Apply How might the statement that "Everest eats the unready and the unlucky" (line 118) affect a potential climber? *Possible answer: It might give him or her second thoughts.*

Evaluate How would you evaluate Erik's perceptions of the dangers involved in climbing Mount Everest? *Possible answer: Erik's statement that "death is death" (line 123) shows a realistic grasp of the dangers of the situation.*

READING STRATEGY: *Review*

E **CONNECT**

Possible answer: Agree: Because he lived for several years as a sighted person, young Erik probably felt some denial regarding his eventual loss of vision. Disagree: Some people may live in fear or prepare for the worst, knowing they will eventually lose their sight.

Extend the Discussion Weihenmayer calls blindness "something that was going to consume [him]" (line 146). Do you think that he truly believed this as a child, or do these words express an adult's perspective?

FOR ADVANCED LEARNERS/PRE–AP

Compare and Contrast Lines 124–130 describe two types of Everest expeditions: those that are "united by a common goal" and those that are "commercial teams." Ask students to write an essay in which they contrast the two types of teams, making note of how words and details in the article (1) support the image of Erik's group as a unified team and (2) imply Greenfeld's disapproval of commercial teams.

BLIND TO FAILURE **257**

Lines 151–167
REINFORCE *KEY IDEA:* BRAVERY

Discuss How did Weihenmayer show **bravery** in adjusting to his loss of vision? Cite evidence to support your answer. ***Possible answer:*** *He found the inner strength to accept his situation and to explore alternate avenues of achievement (lines 155–158). For example, he found that wrestling was a sport "where feel and touch mattered more than sight" (lines 163–164), and he was able to excel in it.*

ELEMENTS OF NONFICTION

Ⓕ CHARACTER STUDY

Possible answer: *Weihenmayer's words show that he's basically "just like most guys" (line 175). Some students may suggest that Weihenmayer's comments about using his blindness to meet women (line 171) and devising a secret handshake to alert him to attractive women (lines 173–174) lower their opinion of him.*

capable of achieving within it; not to pretend he had sight but to build systems that allowed him to excel without it. "It's tragic—I know blind people who like to pass themselves off as being able to see," Erik says. "What's the point of that?"

He would never play basketball or catch a football again. But then he discovered wrestling. "I realized I could take sighted people and slam them into the mat," he says. Grappling was a sport where feel and touch mattered more than sight: if he could sense where his opponent had his weight or how to shift his own body to gain better leverage, he could excel using his natural upper-body strength. As a high school senior he went all the way to the National Junior Freestyle Wrestling Championship in Iowa.

Wrestling gave him the confidence to reenter the teenage social fray. He began dating when he was seventeen; his first girlfriend was a sighted woman three years older than he. Erik jokes that he is not shy about using his blindness to pick up women. "They really go for the guide dog," he explains. "You go into a bar, put the guide dog out there, and the girls just come up to you." He and his friends devised a secret handshake to let Erik know if the girl he was talking to was attractive. "Just because you're blind doesn't make you any more selfless or deep or anything. You're just like most guys, but you look for different things," Erik says. . . . And the voice becomes **paramount.** "My wife has the most beautiful voice in the world," Erik says. Married in 1997, he and his wife Ellie have a one-year-old daughter, Emma. Ⓕ

paramount (păr'ə-mount') *adj.* of highest importance

Ⓕ **CHARACTER STUDY**
Reread lines 168–178, and think about Weihenmayer's **traits.** How do his own words affect your opinion of him?

Erik first went hiking with his father when he was thirteen, trying to tap his way into the wild with a white cane and quickly becoming frustrated stubbing his toes on rocks and roots and bumping into branches and trunks. But when he tried rock climbing, at sixteen while at a camp for the disabled in New Hampshire, he was hooked. Like wrestling, it was a sport in which being blind didn't have to work against him. He took to it quickly, and through climbing gradually found his way to formal mountaineering.

Watching Erik scramble up a rock face is a little like watching a spider make its way up a wall. His hands are like antennae, gathering information as they flick outward, surveying the rock for cracks, grooves, bowls, nubbins, knobs, edges, and ledges, converting all of it into a road map etched into his mind. "It's like instead of wrestling with a person, I am moving and working with a rock," he explains. "It's a beautiful process of solving a puzzle." He is an accomplished rock climber, rated 5.10 (5.14 being the highest), and has led teams up sections of Yosemite's notorious El Capitan.[15] On ice, where one wrong strike with an ice ax can bring down an avalanche, Erik has learned to listen to the ice as he pings it gently with his ax. If it clinks, he avoids it. If it makes a thunk like a spoon hitting butter, he knows it's solid ice.

15. **Yosemite's** (yō-sĕm'ĭ-tēz) **notorious El Capitan:** a 3,604-foot granite peak with a sheer cliff face, in Yosemite National Park, California.

DIFFERENTIATED INSTRUCTION

FOR ADVANCED LEARNERS/PRE–AP

Evaluate Figurative Language [paired-activity option] Have students reread the last paragraph on page 258, identify as many similes and metaphors in the paragraph as they can, and express an opinion about which are the most effective and least effective. Invite students to compare their responses.

Despite being an accomplished mountaineer—summiting Denali, Kilimanjaro in Africa, and Aconcagua[16] in Argentina, among other peaks, and, in the words of his friends, "running up 14ers" (14,000-foot peaks)—Erik viewed Everest as
200 **insurmountable** until he ran into Scaturro at a sportswear trade show in Salt Lake City, Utah. Scaturro, who had already summited Everest, had heard of the blind climber, and when they met the two struck an easy rapport. A geophysicist who often put together energy-company expeditions to remote areas in search of petroleum, Scaturro began wondering if he could put together a team that could help Erik get to the summit of Everest.

"Dude," Scaturro asked, "have you ever climbed Everest?"

"No."

"Dude, you wanna?"

C limbing with Erik isn't that different from climbing with a sighted
210 mountaineer. You wear a bell on your pack, and he follows the sound, scuttling along using his custom-made climbing poles to feel his way along the trail. His climbing partners shout out helpful descriptions: "Death fall two feet to your right!" "Emergency helicopter-evacuation pad to your left!" He is fast, often running up the back of less experienced climbers. His partners all have scars from being jabbed by Erik's climbing poles when they slowed down.

For the Everest climb, Scaturro and Erik assembled a team that combined veteran Everest climbers and trusted friends of Erik's. Scaturro wrote up a Braille proposal for the Everest attempt and submitted it to Marc Maurer, president of
220 the National Federation of the Blind. Maurer immediately pledged $250,000 to sponsor the climb. . . . For Erik, who already had numerous gear and clothing sponsors, this was the greatest challenge of his life. If he failed, he would be letting down not just himself but all the blind, confirming that certain activities remained the preserve of the sighted.

He argued to anyone who would listen that he was an experienced mountaineer and that if he failed, it would be because of his heart or lungs or brain rather than his eyes. He wasn't afraid of physical danger—he had made dozens
230 of skydives and scaled some of the most dangerous cliff faces in the world—but he was frightened of how the world would perceive him. "But I knew that if I went and failed, that would feel better than if I didn't go at all," Erik says. "It could be like [the wrestling] Junior Nationals all over again. I went out to Iowa, and I got killed. But I needed to go to understand what my limits were."

---

16. **Kilimanjaro** (kĭl′ə-mən-jär′ō) . . . **Aconcagua** (äk′ən-kä′gwə): the highest peaks in Africa and South America, respectively.

insurmountable
(ĭn′sər-moun′tə-bəl) *adj.* impossible to overcome

ANALYZE VISUALS
How does this photograph, which shows Weihenmayer and his teammates clambering over one of Everest's many crevasses, contribute to your understanding of Weihenmayer?

❸ **Targeted Passage**

G INTERPRET GRAPHIC AIDS

Possible answer: Camp 4; perhaps Camp 3 as well

If students need help . . . Have them reread lines 239–241 and then review the diagram to determine which camps are above or close to 25,000 feet.

H INTERPRET GRAPHIC AIDS

Possible answer: We know that the unlabeled features must be above Camp 4 (line 251) but below the summit. We also know that they are reached via the South Face (line 264) and that the Southeast Ridge begins at 27,500 feet (line 264), whereas the diagram shows the summit to be at 29,035 feet. We know, too, that the Southeast Ridge leads up to the South Summit (lines 271–273).

Lines 242–245
REINFORCE *KEY IDEA*: BRAVERY

Discuss What does the statement "At that altitude, Erik could rely on no one but himself" say about Erik's **bravery**? Explain. *Possible answer: It says that he must be very brave. He has undertaken the ascent even though he knows that his teammates will not always be able to help him.*

Oxygen deprivation does strange things to the human body. Heart rates go haywire, brain function decreases, blood thickens, intestines shut down. Bad ideas inexplicably pop into your head, especially above 25,000 feet, where, as Krakauer famously wrote in *Into Thin Air*, climbers have the "mind of a reptile." **G**

At that altitude, Erik could rely on no one but himself. His teammates would have to guide him, to keep ringing the bell and making sure Erik stayed on the trail, but they would be primarily concerned about their own survival in some of the worst conditions on earth. Ironically, Erik had some advantages as they closed in on the peak. For one thing, at that altitude all the climbers wore goggles and oxygen masks, restricting their vision so severely that they could not see their own feet—a condition Erik was used to. Also, the final push for the summit began in the early evening, so most of the climb was in pitch darkness; the only illumination was from miner's lamps.

When Erik and the team began the final ascent from Camp 4—the camp he describes as Dante's Inferno with ice and wind[17]—they had been on the mountain for two months, climbing up and down and then up from Base Camp to Camps 1, 2, and 3, getting used to the altitude and socking away enough equipment—especially oxygen canisters—to make a summit push. They had tried for the summit once but had turned back because of weather. At 29,000 feet, the Everest peak is in the jet stream, which means that winds can exceed one hundred miles per hour and that what looks from sea level like a cottony wisp of cloud is actually a killer storm at the summit. Bad weather played a fatal role in the 1996 climbing season documented in *Into Thin Air*.

On May 24, with only seven days left in the climbing season, most of the NFB expedition members knew this was their last shot at the peak. That's why when Erik and Chris Morris reached the Balcony,[18] the beginning of the Southeast Ridge, at 27,500 feet, after a hard slog up the South Face,[19] they were terribly disappointed when the sky lit up with lightning, driving snow, and fierce winds. "We thought we were done," Erik says. "We would have been spanked if we made a push in those conditions." A few teammates gambled and went for it, and Jeff Evans and Brad Bull heroically pulled out fixed guidelines that had been frozen in the ice. By the time Base Camp radioed that the storm was passing, Erik and the entire team were coated in two inches of snow. Inspired by the possibility of a break in the weather, the team pushed on up the exposed Southeast Ridge, an additional 1,200 vertical feet to the South Summit.[20] At that point the climbers looked like astronauts walking on some kind of Arctic moon. They moved slowly because of fatigue from their huge, puffy down suits, backpacks with oxygen canisters and regulators, and goggles.

---

17. **Camp 4 . . . ice and wind:** Camp 4, at 26,000 feet, is compared to the hell described in the *Inferno*, the first part of Dante Alighieri's long poem *The Divine Comedy*.
18. **Balcony:** a natural platform where climbers often stop to rest.
19. **South Face:** the whole side of Everest on which Erik's group climbed to get to the summit.
20. **South Summit:** a peak several hundred feet below the true summit of Everest.

G INTERPRET GRAPHIC AIDS
Turn back to the **diagram** on page 255. In which camp or camps would the climbers have been subject to oxygen deprivation if they had run out of supplemental oxygen?

H INTERPRET GRAPHIC AIDS
As you read about the group's push for the summit, use the **diagram** on page 255 to follow the climbers' progress after they left Camp 4. How can you **infer** the locations of unlabeled features, such as the Balcony and the Southeast Ridge?

With a 10,000-foot vertical fall into Tibet on one side and a 7,000-foot fall into Nepal on the other, the South Summit, at 28,750 feet, is where many climbers finally turn back. The 656-foot-long knife-edge ridge leading to the Hillary Step[21] consists of ice, snow, and fragmented shale, and the only way to 280 cross it is to take baby steps and anchor your way with an ice ax. "You can feel the rock chip off," says Erik. "And you can hear it falling down into the void."

The weather was finally clearing as they reached the Hillary Step, the 39-foot rock face that is the last major obstacle before the true summit. Erik clambered up the cliff, belly-flopping over the top. "I celebrated with the dry heaves," he jokes. And then it was forty-five minutes of walking up a sharply angled snow slope to the summit.

"Look around, dude," Evans told the blind man when they were standing on top of the world. "Just take a second and look around."

290 t could be called the most successful Everest expedition ever, and not just because of Erik's participation. A record nineteen climbers from the NFB team summited, including the oldest man ever to climb Everest—sixty-four-year-old Sherman Bull—and the second father-and-son team ever to do so—Bull and his son Brad.

What Erik achieved is hard for a sighted person to comprehend. What do we compare it with? How do we relate to it? Do we put on a blindfold and go hiking? That's silly, Erik maintains, because when a sighted person loses his vision, he is terrified and disoriented. And Erik is clearly neither of those things. Perhaps the point is really that there is no way to put what Erik has done in perspective because no one has ever done anything like it. It is a unique achievement, one 300 that in the truest sense pushed the limits of what man is capable of. Maurer of the NFB compares Erik to Helen Keller. "Erik can be a contemporary symbol for blindness," he explains. "Helen Keller lived one hundred years ago. She should not be our most potent symbol for blindness today." ∎

Erik, sitting in the Kathmandu international airport, waiting for the flight out of Nepal that will eventually return him to Golden, Colorado, is surrounded by his teammates and the expedition's seventy-five pieces of luggage. Success has made the group jubilant. This airport lounge has become the mountaineering equivalent of a winning Super Bowl locker room. . . .

In between posing for photos and signing other passengers' boarding passes, 310 Erik talks about how eager he is to get back home. He says summiting Everest was great, probably the greatest experience of his life. But then he thinks about a moment a few months ago, before Everest, when he was walking down the street in Colorado with daughter Emma in a front pack. They were on their way to buy some banana bread for his wife, and Emma was pulling on his hand, her little fingers curled around his index finger. That was a summit, too, he says. There are summits everywhere. You just have to know where to look. ❧

∎ **DRAW CONCLUSIONS**
What value might Maurer's idea have?

④ **Targeted Passage**

---

21. **Hillary Step:** a spur named for Sir Edmund Hillary, who, with the Sherpa Tenzing Norgay, was the first successful climber of Everest.

DIFFERENTIATED INSTRUCTION

FOR LESS–PROFICIENT READERS

④ **Targeted Passage [Lines 297–316]**

This concluding passage celebrates Erik's achievement and puts it in the context of his everyday life.

- To whom does Marc Maurer compare Erik Weihenmayer, and why?

- Why does Greenfeld compare the climbers to Super Bowl winners?

- What happened to Erik at home, before Everest? Why is that scene important?

FOR ENGLISH LEARNERS

Culture: Clarify Some students may not have heard of Helen Keller (lines 301–303) or be familiar with the Super Bowl (line 308). Explain that Helen Keller (1880–1968) was a famous writer and public speaker who had become blind and deaf in early childhood and that the Super Bowl is the National Football League's championship game.

∎ DRAW CONCLUSIONS

Possible answer: Erik, like Helen Keller, would show the world that blind people can take part in activities that sighted people enjoy. However, he would make the point for today's world, not just the world of a century ago.

SELECTION WRAP–UP

REFLECT Greenfeld notes that Weihenmayer "is a celebrity now" (line 109). Do students think that Weihenmayer has earned celebrity status? Do they think that he wants to be treated as a celebrity? Have students share their thoughts in a paragraph or two.

⭐ **CRITIQUE** On a scale of 1 to 5, how did you enjoy reading this story? What advantages, if any, does a nonfiction article like this have over fiction?

READING FLUENCY

Distribute the copy master and have students work in pairs or groups to practice fluency.

🅡 RESOURCE MANAGER—Copy Master
Reading Fluency p. 141

Practice and Apply

After Reading

For additional support of post-reading questions, use these copy masters:

R RESOURCE MANAGER—Copy Masters

Reading Check p. 139 (to check understanding of the selection)

Character Study p. 131 (for practice of literary analysis standards focus)

Question Support p. 140 (After Reading questions adapted for English learners and less-proficient readers)

For additional questions, see page 125.

ANSWERS

Comprehension

1. *He wanted to be the first blind person to climb Mount Everest and show that such a feat is not restricted to sighted people.*

2. *He did accomplish his goal, for he reached the summit of Mount Everest despite the difficulties of the climb.*

3. **Advantages:** *not hampered by lack of visibility, highly sensitive to sound;* **Disadvantages:** *unable to see terrain or gauge distance*

Literary Analysis

Possible answers:

4. ● **STANDARDS FOCUS** *Character Study* **Courage:** *lines 229–231, 242–245;* **Determination:** *lines 60–64, 276–286;* **Inner strength:** *lines 75–80, 90–95*

5. *Textual evidence can support either view.* **Internal struggle:** *lines 29–36, 223–225, 229–233;* **External struggle:** *lines 19–28, 41–47, 199–200*

6. *His presence may have inspired the others. In the words of one teammate, he was "the heart and soul" of the team (line 94).*

7. ■ **STANDARDS FOCUS** *Interpret Graphic Aids In conjunction with the chart, the diagram helps readers visualize the challenge and the danger in the ascent. It might have been even more helpful if it had included callouts indicating how long the climbers took to advance from point to point.*

Comprehension

1. **Recall** What was Erik Weihenmayer's goal, and why did he take on that challenge?

2. **Recall** Did Weihenmayer reach his goal? Explain your response.

3. **Summarize** What were Weihenmayer's advantages and disadvantages in comparison with the sighted members of his expedition?

Literary Analysis

4. **Analyze a Character Study** The purpose of a character study is to provide insight into the personality of an individual. In a chart, list Weihenmayer's three most outstanding traits. For each, cite examples from the text.

Outstanding Traits	Examples from Text
1.	
2.	
3.	

5. **Draw Conclusions** Think about the **conflicts** that Weihenmayer faced in "Blind to Failure." Which do you view as the main conflict—his internal struggle with his disability or his external struggle with the mountain? Support your conclusion with evidence from the text.

6. **Analyze Cause and Effect** How might Weihenmayer's presence have contributed to the great success of the expedition, with 19 climbers reaching the summit? Cite evidence from the selection.

7. **Evaluate Information from Graphic Aids** Review the chart you made as you read. How did the **diagram** help you understand this article? What other kinds of information, if any, would it have been useful to include in the graphic aid?

Literary Criticism

8. **Different Perspectives** Helen Keller once proclaimed, "No pessimist ever discovered the secret of the stars, or sailed to an uncharted land, or opened a new doorway for the human spirit." What might Keller say about Weihenmayer's **bravery** if she were alive today? Explain your answer.

Literary Criticism

Possible answer:

8. *She probably would have praised him for having the courage to attempt what no other blind person had done before.*

Vocabulary in Context

VOCABULARY PRACTICE

Identify the words in each pair as synonyms or antonyms.

1. acclimatization/adaptation
2. demeanor/appearance
3. inevitability/certainty
4. banal/unusual
5. paramount/insignificant
6. arduous/simple
7. transcend/exceed
8. insurmountable/impossible
9. aplomb/awkwardness
10. crevasse/summit

WORD LIST

acclimatization
aplomb
arduous
banal
crevasse
demeanor
inevitability
insurmountable
paramount
transcend

VOCABULARY IN WRITING

Create five questions that you would want to ask Erik Weihenmayer in an interview. Use at least five vocabulary words. Here is a sample question.

EXAMPLE SENTENCE

What was the hardest part of your __acclimatization__ to Everest?

VOCABULARY STRATEGY: SPECIALIZED VOCABULARY

Sports like mountaineering, as well as many occupations, have their own **specialized vocabularies.** A specialized vocabulary often includes words (like *crevasse*) that are used primarily within the particular field, as well as familiar words (like *face*) that are used with special meanings in the field. When familiar words have special meanings, it is often possible to figure out those meanings from the context. Otherwise, check a dictionary, looking for labels, such as *Mountaineering*, that may precede definitions giving special meanings of words.

PRACTICE Write the mountaineering term that matches each definition. If you need to, check a dictionary.

ascenders	chimney	crampons	face	saddle

1. devices attached to a rope to help one climb it
2. spiked iron plates on shoes to prevent slipping on ice
3. the sloping side of a mountain
4. a wide vertical crack into which the body of a climber can fit
5. a flat ridge connecting two higher elevations

 VOCABULARY PRACTICE
For more practice, go to the **Vocabulary Center** at ClassZone.com.

BLIND TO FAILURE 263

DIFFERENTIATED INSTRUCTION

FOR ENGLISH LEARNERS

Culture: Connect To extend the Vocabulary Strategy discussion, invite students to share specialized vocabulary from their home language. For example, students might name terms relating to clothing, cuisine, arts and crafts, and sports. Interested students might create a bulletin board display on the basis of this discussion.

FOR ADVANCED LEARNERS/PRE–AP

Vocabulary in Writing Have students write answers to their five questions, as though Erik Weihenmayer were responding, and then write up the questions and answers to simulate an interview transcript. Students should use the vocabulary words in their answers.

ANSWERS

Vocabulary in Context

VOCABULARY PRACTICE

1. *synonyms*   6. *antonyms*
2. *synonyms*   7. *synonyms*
3. *synonyms*   8. *synonyms*
4. *antonyms*   9. *antonyms*
5. *antonyms*   10. *antonyms*

R RESOURCE MANAGER—Copy Master
Vocabulary Practice p. 136

VOCABULARY IN WRITING

Suggest that students use the "5 W's + H"— *who, what, where, when, why,* and *how*—to help them formulate questions.

VOCABULARY STRATEGY: SPECIALIZED VOCABULARY *(also an EL language objective)*

- Invite students to explain specialized vocabulary terms in areas of interest, such as sports, music, and computers.
- Encourage students to use context clues, prior knowledge, and logic to determine the meaning of the Practice words.

Answers:

1. *ascenders*   4. *chimney*
2. *crampons*   5. *saddle*
3. *face*

R RESOURCE MANAGER—Copy Master
Vocabulary Strategy p. 137

i Vocabulary Center at **ClassZone.com**
Additional Vocabulary Activities

Assess and Reteach

Assess

R RESOURCE MANAGER—Copy Masters
Selection Test A pp. 143–144
Selection Test B/C pp. 145–146

⌀ Test Generator CD

Reteach

S STANDARDS LESSON FILE
Literature Lessons 1–3: Character
Informational Text Lesson 24: Diagrams

BLIND TO FAILURE 263

Focus and Motivate

OBJECTIVES

Reading for Information

- recognize main idea and support
- make generalizations
- read a newspaper article

SUMMARY

This article focuses on athletes with disabilities who compete in a variety of team sports. It makes the point that these athletes are not any different from athletes without disabilities.

What's the Connection?

Use an Anticipation Guide to prepare students for the selection. Write these statements on the transparency. Have students respond to each one before and after reading.

- Many athletes with disabilities play team sports.
- Athletes with disabilities always rely on athletes without disabilities.
- Athletes with disabilities are less intense than athletes without disabilities.
- Athletes with disabilities can participate in most sports.

 BEST PRACTICES TOOLKIT—Transparency
Anticipation Guide p. A14

Teach

Skill Focus: Identify Main Ideas

Guide students through the process of looking for key ideas. Explain that one clue to the key idea of a section, and ultimately to the main idea of the selection, is information that is repeated or illustrated by examples. Use questions to guide students to the key ideas.

- What words identify the topic and tell what this section is about?
- What idea about athletes with disabilities is most important? What examples support it?
- What point are these athletes making? How has playing sports influenced their lives?
- Is there one sentence that sums up the information in this section?

R RESOURCE MANAGER—Copy Master
Identify Main Ideas p. 155

A Different Level of Competition
Newspaper Article

Use with
"Blind to Failure," page 252.

What's the Connection?

In "Blind to Failure" you read about Erik Weihenmayer, a mountaineer who successfully climbed Mount Everest despite having lost his vision as a teenager. Now, in "A Different Level of Competition," you will read about other intensely driven athletes who are taking the sports world by storm—despite their disabilities.

Skill Focus: Identify Main Ideas

The **main idea** of a nonfiction selection is the most important idea the selection expresses about its topic. It may be stated explicitly in a sentence in the text, or it may be implied. The main idea is often suggested by smaller key ideas, each developed in a paragraph or a longer section of the work. These ideas, too, may be stated or implied.

In the following article, various key ideas are developed one at a time over the course of several paragraphs. Use a chart like the one shown to note these key ideas.

Section	Key Idea
Title	"A Different Level of Competition"
Lead-in	Sports help people with disabilities.
Section 1 (paragraphs 1–5)	
Section 2 (paragraphs 6–9)	
Section 3 (paragraphs 10–16)	
Section 4 (paragraphs 17–20)	
Section 5 (paragraphs 21–24)	

Review: Predict

Selection Resources

 RESOURCE MANAGER UNIT 2

Plan and Teach pp. 147–151

Reading
Summary pp. 153†*, 154‡*
Identify Main Ideas pp. 155, 157†*
Reading Check p. 159
Make Generalizations pp. 156, 158†*
Question Support p. 161*

Assessment
Selection Tests A, B/C pp. 163*, 165*

 Test Generator CD

Reading Support
 Audio Anthology CD*

 BEST PRACTICES TOOLKIT
Anticipation Guide • New Word Analysis

* Resources for Differentiation   † Also in Spanish   ‡ In Haitian Creole and Vietnamese

A Different Level of Competition

by Anne Stein

Sports for people with disabilities offer chances to build body and spirit Ⓐ

Here's a secret about young guys with disabilities who play team sports: They talk trash. And depending on the sport, they throw punches and crash into each other so hard that games can look like gladiator competitions.

In other words, a competitive athlete with a disability isn't any less intense than a competitive athlete without a
10 disability. Ⓑ

Take sled hockey, for example. A player balances on two ice-skating blades mounted beneath a molded plastic sled/seat. Sitting just inches above the ice, the athlete holds two small hockey sticks with metal teeth on one end to whip his body and sled around the rink; the other end is used for puck-handling. The stick is rotated to hit the puck.

20 "There are games that are rougher than others, but our team tries to focus more on the puck than the body," said Sylvester Flis, 27, a member of the 2002 U.S. Paralympic sled hockey team. Flis, who was born with spina bifida, lives in Chicago and practices with the RIC Blackhawks, sponsored by the Chicago Blackhawks and the Rehabilitation Institute of Chicago.

30 "We don't have big fights often, but there's lots of pushing and shoving. You've got to be very strong and athletic. You have to be in top shape to perform at the national level," Flis said.

Champion skier Sandy Dukat's lower leg was amputated when she was four.

But fighting and body checking aren't what draw people with disabilities to sports and competition. Besides the social aspects, there is an attitude of encouragement often lacking in able-
40 bodied athletics.

Matt Coppens, 30, of Richton Park lost both legs when a teenage driver ran into his car as Coppens set up roadside traffic cones.

Coppens wasn't much of an athlete before the accident. Now he trains full time and will join Flis on the sled hockey team. He also represented the United States at the 2000 Sydney Paralympics
50 in volleyball.

"There's so much camaraderie here," he said. "No matter what team you're on, you can't help but feel a closeness." Ⓒ

Whether it's competitive or recreational, sports serve an important role for people with disabilities, just as it does for the able-bodied.

"The benefits of participating in team sports have been studied a lot over the
60 years, especially in terms of what it does for youth and people without disabilities. [Team sports] does all the same things, and more, for people with disabilities,"

Ⓐ **PREDICT**
From the title and the lead-in, what do you think will be the main idea of this article?

Ⓑ **MAIN IDEA**
What key idea does Stein convey in her introduction?

Ⓒ **MAIN IDEA**
Identify the key idea introduced in this paragraph. How is the anecdote about Matt Coppens related to this idea?

READING STRATEGY: *Review*

Ⓐ PREDICT

Possible answer: The main idea of this article probably will be that people with disabilities participate in competitive sports.

INFORMATIONAL ANALYSIS

Ⓑ MAIN IDEA

Possible answer: Athletes with disabilities compete as intensely as non-disabled athletes.

INFORMATIONAL ANALYSIS

Ⓒ MAIN IDEA

Possible answer: Camaraderie is important among athletes with disabilities. Athletes with disabilities grow very close to their teammates, as Coppens learned while training for the sled hockey team.

If students need help . . . Clarify that an anecdote is a brief story and *camaraderie* means "friendly fellowship." Then have students identify the anecdote and tell how Coppens felt about sports before and after his accident. *Possible answer: The anecdote in lines 41–53 shows Coppens's disinterest before the accident and his full involvement afterward due to the camaraderie.*

Extend the Discussion Discuss why being a member of an elite sports team might be so important to a handicapped athlete.

BACKGROUND

Sports Events for People with Disabilities
Like the more well-known Special Olympics, Paralympics are local, state, national, and international athletic competitions. While the Special Olympics are for athletes with a cognitive disability who have varying athletic abilities, Paralympic events are for athletes with any type of permanent physical disability. The Paralympic Games, which are held shortly after the Olympic Games, are international events in which only the highest level, or elite, athletes are chosen to compete.

said Jeff Jones, director of the Galvin Center for Health and Fitness at the Rehabilitation Institute of Chicago.

"Team sports teaches cooperation, sportsmanship, socialization and how to win and lose," Jones said. "It also 70 teaches people with disabilities to challenge themselves. There's a phrase that's kicked around a lot among people with disabilities: 'If I can do this, I can do anything.'"

Jones said sled hockey players are some of the most conditioned, fit people he knows. They just happen to have a disability.

"They get what everyone gets out of 80 team sports: a sense of accomplishment, enjoyment, satisfaction, conditioning and better health. And that makes everyday activities easier, just like it does for someone without a disability. They just don't happen to have as many opportunities as people without disabilities have to participate in sports," Jones said. "Our athletes are much more appreciative of the opportunities than 90 those without disabilities. They can't just quit one team and go to another. The opportunities are few and far between."

Jerri Voda, who was born with cerebral palsy, races sailboats each summer through the Chicago-based Judd Goldman Adaptive Sailing Program.

"It's absolutely boosted my self-esteem," she said. "It's truly exhilarating for anyone with physical disabilities to 100 participate in an activity that an able-bodied person can participate in. And the feeling of being out on the water driving a boat has totally heightened my independence and made me feel capable of achieving more in the future." **D**

Nearly every sport, recreational or competitive, can be adapted to the physical capabilities of participants.

Among the hundreds of sports available 110 are wheelchair basketball, football and tennis; quadriplegic rugby; water and snow-skiing for the blind and visually impaired; and chair-based aerobics.

There are track and field and swimming events for every category of amputee, as well as blind softball and competitions for people with cerebral palsy and head injury. There is even a fledgling soccer league worldwide played 120 by amputees on crutches.

Chicagoan Sandy Dukat, 29, is a member of the U.S. disabled ski team. Born without a femur, her leg was amputated at the knee at age 4, but the disability never stopped her from being a jock. Dukat competed against able-bodied kids in baseball, basketball and high jump, where she used one leg to clear a very competitive 4 feet, 11 inches.

130 Now Dukat's sport is alpine skiing, where she reaches speeds up to 50 m.p.h. perched on one ski and two poles with tiny ski-like attachments called outriggers. She didn't ski growing up in Ohio, but her fearlessness and speed caught the eye of coaches who encouraged her to train.

Though Dukat loves the thrill of sport, she would like to be seen as an elite athlete, not an athlete with a disability. 140 She also would like people to stop clapping when she runs or skates along the lakefront path.

"People with disabilities are very capable," Dukat said. "We can work, have a family, a job, we can balance things."

She said someday people won't be shocked by the sight of her jogging with a prosthetic leg.

"It should be the norm. I don't look 150 at someone with two legs and say, 'That's so cool.' It shouldn't be a surprise to see someone with disabilities doing this." **E**

D MAIN IDEA
What key idea is developed by the details in this section? Identify the sentence that states this idea.

E MAIN IDEA
What last point does the author make?

INFORMATIONAL ANALYSIS

D MAIN IDEA

Possible answer: The key idea is that participating in team sports does the same things and more for people with disabilities as it does for participants without disabilities. Lines 54–57 and lines 98–101 state this idea.

INFORMATIONAL ANALYSIS

E MAIN IDEA

Possible answer: People should not be surprised that disabled people can be athletes. Rather, it should be accepted as common knowledge.

DIFFERENTIATED INSTRUCTION

FOR LESS–PROFICIENT READERS

Vocabulary Support Explain that an *elite* athlete (line 138) would be one of the best or most-skilled players in his or her sport. Ask students to name some athletes they would consider to be among the elite players of their favorite sport.

FOR ENGLISH LEARNERS

Vocabulary: Idioms Use New Word Analysis to teach these idioms from the story: *kicked around* (line 72), "discussed"; *jock* (line 126), "athlete"; *caught the eye* (line 135), "attracted the attention"; *balance things* (line 145), "keep a harmonious mix of elements in one's life"; *That's so cool* (lines 150–151), "That is very impressive."

🧰 **BEST PRACTICES TOOLKIT—Transparency** New Word Analysis p. E8

Comprehension

1. **Recall** Name three sports that have been adapted for disabled athletes.

2. **Summarize** How are athletes with disabilities similar to other athletes?

Critical Analysis

3. **Identify Main Idea** Review the key ideas you recorded in your chart. On the basis of these ideas, what would you say is the entire article's main idea? Explain your answer.

4. **Compare and Contrast** What do the athletes described in this article have in common with Erik Weihenmayer? Are they different from him in any way? Give examples to support your comparison.

Read for Information: Make Generalizations

WRITING PROMPT

What do people with disabilities gain from participating in rigorous sports and undertaking other physical challenges? Use information from "Blind to Failure" and "A Different Level of Competition" to support your response.

To respond to this prompt, you will have to make a generalization. A **generalization** is a broad statement about a category, based on a study of some members of that category. To make a generalization, follow these steps:

1. Gather evidence—anecdotes and direct statements—about what people with disabilities gain from playing sports.

2. Look for key ideas suggested by this evidence.

3. Make a general statement based on these key ideas.

Review your evidence to make sure your generalization is true and fair; revise your generalization if necessary.

Evidence → Evidence → Evidence → Evidence

Key Idea   Key Idea

Generalization

DIFFERENTIATED INSTRUCTION

FOR LESS-PROFICIENT WRITERS
Read for Information

- Remind students to record evidence on index cards, one anecdote or direct statement per card, and then organize their cards according to the key idea each card supports.

- If students write an answer to the prompt, advise them to begin with their generalization, state the key ideas that led to the generalization, and support each idea with evidence from the article.

FOR ADVANCED LEARNERS/PRE-AP
Read for Information Encourage students to incorporate evidence from at least one additional source in their written response to the writing prompt.

Practice and Apply

For additional support of post-reading questions, use these copy masters:

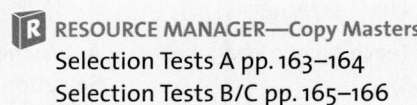 **RESOURCE MANAGER—Copy Masters**
Reading Check p. 159
Question Support p. 161
Make Generalizations p. 156

For additional questions, see page 150.

ANSWERS

Comprehension

1. *Possible answers:* basketball, football, tennis, sled hockey, sailboat racing

2. *They are competitive, fit, and interested in challenge. They receive the same benefits from sports.*

Critical Analysis
Possible answers:

3. ■ **STANDARDS FOCUS** *Main Idea*
Athletes with disabilities compete on an elite level for the same reason that people without disabilities do, but they appreciate the opportunities even more.

4. *Compare and Contrast The athletes do not share Eric's disability or sport. However, like Eric, they are resolute and seek challenges.*

Read for Information: Make Generalizations

Writing Prompt *Possible answer: Athletes with disabilities reap the same benefits as do other athletes, but they especially value the way physical challenge develops self-confidence.*

Assess and Reteach

Assess

 **RESOURCE MANAGER—Copy Masters**
Selection Tests A pp. 163–164
Selection Tests B/C pp. 165–166

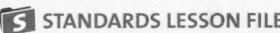 **Test Generator CD**

Reteach

S **STANDARDS LESSON FILE**
Reading Lesson 4: Recognizing Main Idea and Details
Reading Lesson 10: Making Generalizations

Focus and Motivate

OBJECTIVES

Literary Analysis
- explore the key idea of **memories**
- analyze the speaker
- read poetry

Reading
- read poetry for understanding

SUMMARIES

"A Voice" In this poem, the speaker describes her admiration for her Mexican-born mother, who overcame challenges to become a fluent speaker and writer of English. The speaker recalls her mother's story of having gone onstage at the state capitol but being unable to speak when she saw the audience of strangers.

"My Father's Song" In this poem about a son's love and longing for his father, the speaker recounts a tender memory that epitomizes his father's gentle character. While planting corn together, father and son discover a nest of baby mice that they move to a safe place.

What makes a MEMORY?

Direct students' attention to the question. To introduce the *KEY IDEA,* ask, "Think about your favorite or most vivid **memory**. What makes it stand out in your mind?" Extend the discussion by having students complete the *QUICKWRITE.*

A Voice
Poem by Pat Mora

My Father's Song
Poem by Simon J. Ortiz

What makes a MEMORY?

KEY IDEA Whether they're once-in-a-lifetime occurrences or everyday experiences, some things remain imprinted on your mind long after they happen. In "A Voice" and "My Father's Song," two poets write about old **memories** that remain vivid many years later.

QUICKWRITE Think of a memory that remains very clear to you. Write a paragraph describing the memory in as much detail as you can. In a small group, try to generalize about the kinds of memories that retain their sharpness. Do memories of extraordinary events remain more vibrant than those of ordinary events? Do positive memories stand out more than negative ones?

268

Selection Resources

 **RESOURCE MANAGER UNIT 2**

Plan and Teach pp. 167–174

Literary Analysis
Speaker pp. 175*, 176†*
Question Support p. 179*

Reading
Reading Poetry pp. 177, 178†*
Reading Fluency p. 180

Assessment
Selection Tests A, B/C pp. 181*, 183*
⊘ Test Generator CD

 BEST PRACTICES TOOLKIT

Differentiated Instruction
pp. 31–38*

Graphic Organizers/Strategies
Read Aloud/Think Aloud

Reading Support
⊘ Audio Anthology CD*

Technology
ℹ️ Literature Center at **ClassZone.com**
⊘ Write*Smart* CD

---

* Resources for Differentiation   † Also in Spanish

LITERARY ANALYSIS: SPEAKER

The **speaker** in a poem is the voice that "talks" to the reader. Like the narrator in a work of fiction, the speaker relates the ideas or the story of the poem from a specific **point of view.** The speaker can be detached from or intensely involved with the experience or ideas expressed in the poem. It is important to keep in mind that the speaker is not necessarily the poet, even when he or she uses the pronouns *I* and *me.* As you read "A Voice" and "My Father's Song," ask yourself these questions about each speaker:

* Whom is the speaker addressing?
* What is the speaker's relationship to the subject of the poem?
* How would I characterize the speaker's attitude toward the person being described?

READING SKILL: READING POETRY

There are two ways to read lines of poetry:

* Read the lines continuously—paying attention to entire sentences, regardless of line breaks or stanzas.
* Read each line in isolation—noting the ideas and images in it, regardless of sentence structure.

Try both approaches with the following passage from "A Voice":

The family story says your voice is the voice of an aunt in Mexico, spunky as a peacock.

When the lines are read together, they read like a regular sentence. When they are read with a pause at the end of each line, what gets emphasized?

Read "A Voice" and "My Father's Song" aloud using the first method, then silently using the second. Note how the line breaks help bring emphasis to certain words and ideas.

Author On|ine

Pat Mora: The Power of Words

Pat Mora began writing poems while in elementary school in El Paso, Texas, where she was born and raised. Her mother, who dreamed of becoming a writer, won several speech contests while in school but was unable to continue her education when

Pat Mora
born 1942

the Great Depression hit. She passed on her ambition and her love of language to her daughter—gifts that have played an integral part in Mora's career. Discussing her motives for writing, the poet, essayist, and short story writer explains, "I am fascinated by the pleasure and power of words."

Simon J. Ortiz: A Voice of Inspiration

Simon J. Ortiz, an Acoma Pueblo Indian, was born in Albuquerque, New Mexico, and raised in the Acoma Pueblo homeland about 65 miles outside the city. He attributes his love of words to his father, who sang and talked to his son while working. Another

Simon J. Ortiz
born 1941

source of inspiration for Ortiz is his Native American heritage. His poems, short stories, and essays often center on themes of Native American history and culture. But they also explore more universal, personal subjects like identity and loneliness. Of his poetry, Ortiz says, "I tell you about me and my world so you may be able to see yourself."

 MORE ABOUT THE AUTHOR
For more on these poets, visit the **Literature Center** at ClassZone.com.

A VOICE / MY FATHER'S SONG   **269**

Teach

STANDARDS FOCUS

LITERARY ANALYSIS

● **SPEAKER**

After students read the page, read aloud these lines for instructional support:

> Grandmother's hugs were
> two parts furniture polish
> four parts curry powder
> One part damp garden dirt.

Ask students who the speaker in this poem is. *Possible answer: The speaker is a grandson or granddaughter who is describing his or her grandmother.*

CHECK UNDERSTANDING Does the speaker sound detached or involved with the subject of the poem?

READING SKILL

■ **READING POETRY**

Tell students that long, obvious pauses at the ends of lines can make a poem sound choppy and can interrupt the flow of ideas. Explain that pausing slightly, particularly if a line ends with a punctuation mark, gives the poem a more natural rhythm.

CHECK UNDERSTANDING Have partners take turns reading aloud stanzas from their favorite poems, trying to hear how different ways of pausing at the ends of lines can change the emphasis of certain words or images.

 RESOURCE MANAGER—Copy Master
Reading Poetry p. 177 (for student use while reading the selection)

LITERARY ANALYSIS

Ⓐ SPEAKER

*Possible answer: Readers can **infer** that the speaker knows the person she describes very well. The speaker gives readers intimate details about the person.*

If students need help . . . Have students read lines 6–7. Ask them how well you need to know someone to describe what her or his home smells like.

READING SKILL

Ⓑ READING POETRY

Possible answer: The line break emphasizes the importance of speaking "about patriotism and democracy" for the person the speaker is addressing.

If students need help . . . Read aloud lines 17–18. Pause at the end of line 17 before reading line 18. Ask students to discuss how the phrasing affects the meaning of the words.

ADDITIONAL TEACHING OPPORTUNITY

Appreciate Oral Poetry: Point out that the impact of poetry changes when it is heard rather than read silently. Choose students to read the poems in this lesson aloud. Tell students to listen for enjoyment during a first reading, and then listen for and note examples of rhyme, vivid imagery, and characterization. Invite students to comment on how their perceptions changed when the poems were read aloud. (To learn more about appreciating oral poetry, see **Reading Handbook,** page R2.)

A Voice
Pat Mora

Even the lights on the stage unrelenting
as the desert sun couldn't hide the other
students, their eyes also unrelenting,
students who spoke English every night

5 as they ate their meat, potatoes, gravy.
Not you. In your house that smelled like
rose powder, you spoke Spanish formal
as your father, the judge without a courtroom

in the country he floated to in the dark
10 on a flatbed truck. He walked slow Ⓐ
as a hot river down the narrow hall
of your house. You never dared to race past him,

to say, "Please move," in the language
you learned effortlessly, as you learned to run,
15 the language forbidden at home, though your mother
said you learned it to fight with the neighbors.

You liked winning with words. You liked Ⓑ
writing speeches about patriotism and democracy.
You liked all the faces looking at you, all those eyes.
20 "How did I do it?" you ask me now. "How did I do it

when my parents didn't understand?"
The family story says your voice is the voice
of an aunt in Mexico, spunky as a peacock.
Family stories sing of what lives in the blood.

Ⓐ SPEAKER
What can you **infer** about the speaker's relationship with the person she describes?

Ⓑ READING POETRY
By breaking the line after "you liked," what idea does the poet emphasize?

DIFFERENTIATED INSTRUCTION

For general guidelines on differentiating instruction, see

 BEST PRACTICES TOOLKIT
   Differentiated Instruction pp. 31–38

FOR LESS–PROFICIENT READERS
Options for Reading Read aloud "A Voice" to students. Clarify that the speaker is addressing her mother, whose family came from Mexico. Tell students to pay attention to the mood of the poem as well as to what effect your pauses have on the story told in the poem. Then have students listen to the selection on the *Audio Anthology CD* (also recommended for English learners) as they read along.

BEST PRACTICES TOOLKIT—Transparency
   Read Aloud/Think Aloud p. A34

25 You told me only once about the time you went
   to the state capitol, your family proud as if
   you'd been named governor. But when you looked
   around, the only Mexican in the auditorium,
   you wanted to hide from those strange faces.
30 Their eyes were pinpricks, and you faked
   hoarseness. You, who are never at a loss
   for words, felt your breath stick in your throat

   like an ice-cube. "I can't," you whispered.
   "I can't." Yet you did. Not that day but years later.
35 You taught the four of us to speak up.
   This is America, Mom. The undo-able is done **C**

   in the next generation. Your breath moves
   through the family like the wind
   moves through the trees.

C SPEAKER
What is revealed in lines 35–36 about the speaker's relationship to the person she is addressing?

ANALYZE VISUALS
What do the sizes and positions of the two women in the painting suggest?

Girls from Guadalupita, New Mexico, Miguel Martinez. Oil pastel on paper, 30″ × 40″. Contemporary Southwest Galleries, Sante Fe, New Mexico.

A VOICE   **271**

BACKGROUND

Between 1900 and 1929, more than one million Mexicans migrated to the United States. Many found jobs as unskilled workers here. They also found discrimination. Mexicans were blamed for increases in crime and violence; they were the victims of physical and verbal attacks; and they were often regarded as inferior. It was the crushing weight of these stereotypes that the speaker's mother felt when she could not speak at the state capitol.

LITERARY ANALYSIS

C SPEAKER

Possible answer: The lines reveal that the you *addressed by the speaker is her mother.*

If students need help . . . Reread line 36. Note that the speaker uses the word *Mom.*

Extend the Discussion What is the significance of the speaker using the English *Mom* instead of the Spanish *mama?*

ANALYZE VISUALS

Possible answer: The larger size and foreground placement of the figure on the left suggest that she is stronger and more dominant than the figure on the right. Her attitude also seems protective. The figure on the left is the focus of the painting, as the mother in the poem is the focus of the family.

About the Art For contemporary painter Miguel Martinez (born 1951), this work is typical: large, expressive faces of women fill the canvas.

Lines 25–34
REINFORCE *KEY IDEA:* MEMORIES

Discuss Why is the memory of the trip to the state capitol an important one for the *you* of the poem? Why is it important for the speaker? *Possible answer: For the* you *of the poem, it is a painful memory of a rare moment of failure (lines 31–32), one that, years later, she overcame (line 34). For the speaker, that strength becomes a source of inspiration.*

FOR LESS–PROFICIENT STUDENTS

Comprehension Support Ask students to explain in their own words what happened at the state capitol. Help them understand the meaning of these phrases:

• *their eyes were pinpricks* (line 30), "their stares were painful"
• *never at a loss for words* (lines 31–32), "always has a comment; always has something to say"
• *to speak up* (line 35), "to say something; to make a comment"

FOR ADVANCED LEARNERS/PRE–AP

Imagery Have students find examples of imagery in the poem, such as eyes like "pinpricks" in line 30 and breath that moves "like the wind moves through the trees" in lines 38–39. Ask students to discuss whether the poet's use of imagery helps the reader get a better picture of, or more insight into, the character and explain how.

Prereading for this poem is found on page 268.

LITERARY ANALYSIS

❶ SPEAKER

Possible answer: *The speaker's attitude is one of love and longing for his father. He misses him, wishes he could speak to him (lines 1–2), and recalls endearing details about him (lines 3–5).*

Extend the Discussion Why do you think the poet refers to his father's speaking as a "song" (line 7)?

ANALYZE VISUALS

Activity After students finish reading the poem, ask them which details in this painting relate to the poem and which do not.

About the Art Contemporary Navajo artist Shonto Begay (born 1954) plays on the two meanings of *plant.* In the foreground, he paints a traditional Navajo man planting in the desert. In the background, a nuclear or other power plant is shown. The powerful relationship of the Navajo man to the earth is in sharp contrast to the ominous stacks creating power on the horizon.

SELECTION WRAP–UP

SYNTHESIZE Ask students to state each poem's central message or meaning. Then invite students to name other works of art or popular culture that express similar themes. *Students' statements of theme and examples of works should relate to the importance of memory, family stories, or a parent's love.*

⭐ **CRITIQUE** Have students discuss which poem they found more memorable and why.

READING FLUENCY

Distribute the copy master and have students work in pairs or groups to practice fluency.

📘 RESOURCE MANAGER—Copy Master
Reading Fluency p. 180

Wanting to say things,
I miss my father tonight.
His voice, the slight catch,
the depth from his thin chest,
5 the tremble of emotion
in something he has just said
to his son, his song: ❶

    We planted corn one Spring at Acu[1]—
    we planted several times
10   but this one particular time
    I remember the soft damp sand
    in my hand.

    My father had stopped at one point
    to show me an overturned furrow;[2]
15   the plowshare had unearthed
    the burrow nest of a mouse
    in the soft moist sand.

    Very gently, he scooped tiny pink animals
    into the palm of his hand
20   and told me to touch them.
    We took them to the edge
    of the field and put them in the shade
    of a sand moist clod.

    I remember the very softness
25   of cool and warm sand and tiny alive mice
    and my father saying things.

❶ SPEAKER
From the description in this first stanza, what can you tell about the speaker's attitude toward the father?

Navajo Power Plant (1990), Shonto Begay. © Shonto Begay.

---

1. **Acu** (ä′kōō): the Acoma people's name for the Acoma Pueblo.
2. **furrow** (fûr′ō): a long, shallow trench made in the ground by a plow.

272   UNIT 2: CHARACTERIZATION AND POINT OF VIEW

DIFFERENTIATED INSTRUCTION

FOR LESS–PROFICIENT READERS
Options for Reading Read aloud "My Father's Song" to students. Ask students to pay attention to the way the speaker describes his father and to the mood the memory of his father creates. Then have students listen to the *Audio Anthology CD* as they read along chorally.

FOR ADVANCED LEARNERS/PRE–AP
Analyze Content and Meaning [small-group option] Ask students what they think this particular memory of the son shows about his father's character. Have them present their ideas in one or two paragraphs.

Comprehension

1. **Recall** Describe the incident related in "My Father's Song."

2. **Recall** What happens to the speaker's mother in "A Voice"?

3. **Clarify** In "A Voice," what is the speaker's mother referring to in line 20 when she asks, "How did I do it?"

Literary Analysis

4. **Compare Speakers** Review the questions listed on page 269. Then use a chart like this one to compare the two poems. What characteristics do they share?

	"A Voice"	"My Father's Song"
Person Being Addressed		
Relationship to Subject		
Attitude Displayed		

5. **Reading Poetry** Phrasing in poetry helps bring emphasis to certain words and ideas. It can also affect the interpretation of a poem. Why did Pat Mora choose to split certain sentences between lines or stanzas in "A Voice"? What does this call attention to? Cite specific examples.

6. **Interpret Imagery** Poets often make use of images that appeal to the five senses: sight, sound, touch, smell, and taste. In "My Father's Song," which of these senses does the poet evoke? What is the effect of using such images? Support your answer.

7. **Evaluate** In your opinion, which poem does a better job of characterizing the person being **remembered?** Support your opinion with details.

Literary Criticism

8. **Biographical Context** Both Mora and Ortiz are known for their efforts to preserve the cultures from which they come. To what extent does each of these poems fulfill that mission? Support your opinion.

6. *Touch is foremost: the speaker recalls the soft damp sand, the shade of a moist sand clod, and the tiny, living mice he touched. Other sensory images are of sound—the father's voice with its tremble of emotion— and sight, as the poet describes the scene in vivid detail.*

7. *Students' opinions will vary.* **"A Voice"** *gives more details about the mother by explaining the home she grew up in, her conflict with her father, and the incident at the state capitol.* **"My Father's Song"** *evokes the gentle essence of the father's character and his love of all living things through his concern about the mice.*

Literary Criticism

Possible answer:

8. *Mora expresses admiration and gratitude toward her elders for the bravery they exhibited to overcome the challenges they faced as immigrants. Ortiz shows the gentle spirit of his father, who was connected to the land and nature through his cultural heritage.*

Practice and Apply

After Reading

For additional support of post-reading questions, use these copy masters:

R RESOURCE MANAGER—Copy Masters
Speaker p. 175 (for practice of literary analysis standards focus)
Question Support p. 179 (After Reading questions adapted for English learners and less–proficient readers)

For additional questions, see page 171.

ANSWERS

Comprehension

1. *The speaker recalls a time when, while planting corn, his father unearthed a nest of mice and had the speaker touch them.*

2. *The mother goes to the state capitol and becomes too frightened to speak to the large, strange audience.*

3. *She is referring to learning to speak English when the language was forbidden in her home, and also standing out as she spoke it.*

Literary Analysis

Possible answers:

4. ● **STANDARDS FOCUS** *Compare Speakers* **"A Voice":** *addresses the speaker's mother; secondhand relationship to subject; attitude of respect, honor, pride.* **"My Father's Song":** *addresses the reader; firsthand experience; attitude of admiration.*

5. ■ **STANDARDS FOCUS** *Reading Poetry* *The breaks in the sentences slow down the reader and tend to put emphasis on the word at the end of the line, such as* faked *at the end of line 30 and* done *in line 36.*

Assess and Reteach

Assess

R RESOURCE MANAGER—Copy Masters
Selection Test A pp. 181–182
Selection Test B/C pp. 183–184

● Test Generator CD

Reteach

S STANDARDS LESSON FILE
Literature Lesson 20: Speaker

Focus and Motivate

OBJECTIVES

Literary Analysis
- explore the key idea of **dignity**
- analyze and compare characterizations
- read biography and poetry

Reading
- set a purpose for reading

Vocabulary
- build vocabulary for reading and writing
- understand etymology in a dictionary entry
  (also an EL language objective)

SUMMARY

"Rosa Parks" This selection from Douglas Brinkley's biography *Rosa Parks* chronicles the day in 1955 on which Rosa Parks, an African-American seamstress, refused to give up her seat to a white passenger on a segregated bus in Montgomery, Alabama. As he notes, Parks's courage and quiet dignity served as an inspiration in the civil rights movement.

"Rosa" In this brief poem, Rita Dove presents impressions of Rosa Parks on the same historic day. She emphasizes Parks's dignity, everyday sensibilities, and symbolic importance.

What is DIGNITY?

Introduce the **KEY IDEA** by asking the question and having students read the paragraph. After students generate the list for the **DISCUSS** activity, ask them to identify the qualities that individuals with **dignity** have in common.

Selection Resources

---

from **Rosa Parks**
Biography by Douglas Brinkley

Rosa
Poem by Rita Dove

What is DIGNITY?

KEY IDEA Some people have it—quiet strength and an air of personal **dignity.** One such person was Rosa Parks. You are about to read two selections about Rosa Parks—a biography and a poem. Both pieces portray her dignity and courage and the important role she played in the civil rights movement.

DISCUSS With a small group, generate a list of real people, living or dead, as well as characters in books, movies, or TV shows, whom you consider to have dignity. Then discuss whether dignity comes mainly from within or from the approval of others.

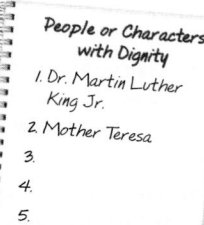

People or Characters with Dignity
1. Dr. Martin Luther King Jr.
2. Mother Teresa
3.
4.
5.

LITERARY ANALYSIS: CHARACTERIZATION ACROSS GENRES

As you know, fiction writers use methods of **characterization** to develop the made-up characters that populate their work. However, when writers of nonfiction and poetry portray real people, they cannot make up facts and details. Instead, writers in these **genres** shape readers' impressions of particular people by combining factual information with techniques unique to the genres in which they are working. The biography and the poem that follow both tell about Rosa Parks. The chart below shows the genre techniques each writer uses to characterize her.

Techniques Used in the Biography	Techniques Used in the Poem
• facts and details about Rosa Parks's actions, thoughts, and appearance	• word choice to describe Rosa Parks's actions and appearance
• quotations from Rosa Parks	• images to depict Rosa Parks's traits
• quotations from others who knew Rosa Parks	

As you read, notice the techniques each writer uses to portray this historic figure.

READING STRATEGY: SET A PURPOSE FOR READING

When you **set a purpose** for reading, you choose specific reasons for reading a work. In this lesson, you will read a biography and a poem in order to compare and contrast the ways they portray Rosa Parks. As you read, think about your impressions of Rosa Parks. After you read, you will use the **Points of Comparison** chart on page 281 to compare and contrast the two pieces.

▲ VOCABULARY IN CONTEXT

Restate each phrase, using a different word or words for each boldfaced term.

1. cheering **frenetically** during the final seconds of the game
2. a **protégé** of the company president
3. letting the mind wander in a pleasant **reverie**
4. an **exhortation** to try harder to win
5. as **serene** as a calm summer day
6. **retrieve** a lost scarf

Author Online

Douglas Brinkley: Historian and Educator Douglas Brinkley has written award-winning books about Henry Ford, Franklin Delano Roosevelt, and Jimmy Carter, among others. In 1993 Brinkley published *The Majic Bus: An American Odyssey*. In this first-person account, he described a class he taught aboard a cross-country bus. Visiting 30 states, his students attended lectures, read widely, listened to American music, toured historical sites, and met celebrated authors.

Douglas Brinkley born 1961

Rita Dove: Honored Poet According to Rita Dove, "Poetry is language at its most distilled and most powerful." In 1993 she became the poet laureate of the United States—the youngest person and the first African American so honored.

Rita Dove born 1952

 MORE ABOUT THE AUTHOR For more on the authors, visit the **Literature Center at ClassZone.com.**

Background

Civil Rights Southern states once had laws that enforced racial segregation. Among other injustices, African Americans were forced to sit in separate sections of buses. In 1955, Rosa Parks's refusal to give up her seat on a bus triggered a 382-day bus boycott by African Americans in Montgomery, Alabama. The boycott brought Rosa Parks, Dr. Martin Luther King Jr., and their cause to national prominence. In 1956, the Supreme Court ruled that segregation on buses and other transportation was unconstitutional.

ROSA PARKS / ROSA **275**

Teach

STANDARDS FOCUS

● CHARACTERIZATION ACROSS GENRES

For instructional support, read aloud these examples:

> The players' dignity moved us all;
> Despite defeat, they all stood tall.

> "They're an impressive group," the coach said. "The players stayed positive, even after a 20-point loss."

Have students compare how the writers shape our impressions. ***Possible answer: The poet creates an image to show the players' acceptance. The prose writer uses a quotation to identify the players' attitude.***

CHECK UNDERSTANDING Ask students which example they preferred, and why.

 RESOURCE MANAGER—Copy Master
Characterization Across Genres
pp. 195–196 (for student use while reading the selections)

■ SET A PURPOSE FOR READING

Elicit that setting a purpose is a good reading strategy because it helps readers focus on what is important to them.

CHECK UNDERSTANDING Discuss purposes for reading a biography.

▲ VOCABULARY IN CONTEXT

DIAGNOSE WORD KNOWLEDGE To determine preteaching needs, have all students complete **Vocabulary in Context.** *Possible answers:*
1. *madly;* 2. *person guided and supported by;*
3. *daydream;* 4. *appeal;*
5. *peaceful;* 6. *recover*

PRETEACH VOCABULARY Use the Vocabulary Study copy master to help students predict the meaning of each boldfaced word in the copy master, using context clues.

1. Read item 1 aloud, emphasizing *frenetically*.
2. Point out the phrases *busy season* and *to keep up with*. Elicit possible meanings for *frenetically,* such as "in an extremely excited manner."
3. Repeat the procedure for items 2–6.

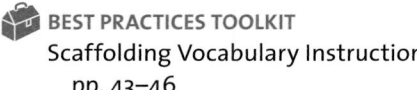 RESOURCE MANAGER—Copy Master
Vocabulary Study p. 200

For general guidelines on differentiating vocabulary instruction and for alternative vocabulary activities for students not needing vocabulary preteaching, see

BEST PRACTICES TOOLKIT
Scaffolding Vocabulary Instruction pp. 43–46
Vocabulary Center at **ClassZone.com**

Practice and Apply

ANALYZE VISUALS

Possible answer: The photograph conveys her seriousness, reserve, and perhaps determination.

About the Photo No camera recorded Rosa Parks's historic bus ride. This famous picture was taken by United Press International a little more than a year later, when the Montgomery bus boycott finally brought about the integration of the city's public transportation system (symbolized by the fact that a white man is seated behind Parks). Even then, Rosa Parks's importance was being recognized.

Lines 13–21
DISCUSSION PROMPTS

Use these prompts to help students gain insight into Rosa Parks's attitudes and values:

Connect Have you ever felt conflicted about being in one place but wanting to be in another? How did you cope? *Answers will vary.*

Analyze How does Parks put her coffee-break time to good use? *Possible answer: She calls the university president to reserve a classroom for the workshop that she is organizing.*

Synthesize What does the fact that Parks can focus on NAACP activities despite the bustle at work tell you about her? *Possible answer: The work of the NAACP is very important to her, and she takes it seriously.*

Rosa Parks headed to work on December 1, 1955, on the Cleveland Avenue bus to Court Square. It was a typical prewinter morning in the Alabama capital, chilly and raw, topcoat weather. Outside the Montgomery Fair Department Store a Salvation Army Santa rang his bell for coins in front of window displays of toy trains and mannequins modeling reindeer sweaters. Every afternoon when school let out, hordes of children would invade the store to gawk at the giant Christmas tree draped with blinking lights, a mid-1950s electrical marvel. But Rosa Parks saw little of the holiday glitter down in the small tailor shop in the basement next to the huge steam presses, where the
10 only hint of Yuletide cheer came from a sagging, water-stained banner reading "Merry Christmas and a Happy New Year."

Not that many of Montgomery Fair's lower-level employees had the time to let the faded decoration make them sad. The department store rang up nearly half of its sales between Thanksgiving and New Year's Day, which turned the tailor shop into a beehive of activity every December. But even on days spent **frenetically** hemming, ironing, and steam-pressing, Parks's mind was more with the NAACP[1] than her workday duties. She was in the midst of organizing a workshop to be held at Alabama State University on December 3–4 and spent the morning during her coffee break telephoning H. Council Trenholm,
20 president of the university, applying enough quiet persuasion to be granted the use of a classroom over the weekend. "I was also getting the notices in the mail

ANALYZE VISUALS
What qualities of Rosa Parks does the photograph convey?

① **Targeted Passage**

frenetically
(frə-nĕt′ĭk-lē) *adv.* in a frenzied or frantic way

---

1. **NAACP:** a civil rights organization. The initials stand for National Association for the Advancement of Colored People.

276 UNIT 2: CHARACTERIZATION AND POINT OF VIEW

DIFFERENTIATED INSTRUCTION

FOR ALL STUDENTS
Anchor Activity Provide independent learning opportunities for students to research the history of segregation in the United States. Assign groups and allow time for presentations. Challenge students to provide helpful graphics and illustrations. For details, see

R RESOURCE MANAGER
Ideas for Extension pp. 190–191

FOR LESS–PROFICIENT READERS
In combination with the *Audio Anthology CD*, use one or more Targeted Passages (pp. 276, 278, 279) to ensure that students focus on key events, concepts, and skills. Targeted Passages are also good for English learners.

① Targeted Passage [Lines 13–21]

This passage sets up the contrast between Rosa Parks's busy job and her participation in civil rights activities.

BACKGROUND

Transportation Discrimination African Americans suffered many humiliations in Montgomery, Alabama, even though they made up at least two-thirds of bus ridership and paid the same fare as whites. Under Montgomery's segregation laws, bus drivers could make black passengers pay the fare and then step off and board through the rear door, so as not to walk past white riders. At times, a bus driver would drive away before these passengers reached the rear door. Some other rules are mentioned in this selection. Black riders who violated these rules could be removed from the bus, arrested, and fined.

Cultural Connection When Rosa Parks made her momentous decision not to surrender her seat on the bus in Montgomery, Alabama, she joined a tradition of nonviolent resistance that spans many cultures. In the 1940s, Mohandas Karamchand Gandhi (1869–1948) used nonviolent fasts and protests to lead the people of India to independence from British rule. The Indian people called Gandhi "Mahatma," meaning Great Soul. In the 1980s, Lech Walesa (born 1943) led a strike that forced Poland's Communist government to legally recognize the polish workers' union, Solidarity. Later, Walesa became president of Poland and won the Nobel Peace Prize. Invite students to share knowledge of figures from their cultures who contributed to the cause of freedom.

- Why is the department store's tailor shop described as a "beehive"?
- To what organization does Rosa Parks belong? What is its purpose?
- Who is Parks trying to impress? Why?

FOR ENGLISH LEARNERS

Options for Reading Ask a question about a set of paragraphs or range of numbered lines; then have pairs of students scan the designated text to find the answer.

Prereading For prereading instruction for English learners, see

 BEST PRACTICES TOOLKIT
Scaffolding Reading Instruction pp. 43–46

FOR ADVANCED LEARNERS/PRE–AP

Pre-AP Exercises in the bottom channel provide additional challenge for students. Use these suggestions for small groups or individuals.

ADDITIONAL GUIDELINES

For more help with differentiation and tips for classroom management, see

 BEST PRACTICES TOOLKIT
Differentiated Instruction pp. 31–38

Ⓐ CHARACTERIZATION

Possible answer: *At the store, Parks worked as a seamstress (lines 15–16), but her NAACP tasks called upon her organizational and communication skills (lines 17–25). Brinkley probably wanted to show that Parks had a strong commitment to both types of work.*

If students need help . . . Have them reread the previous paragraph. Use a Classification Chart to help them distinguish Parks's job from her NAACP duties.

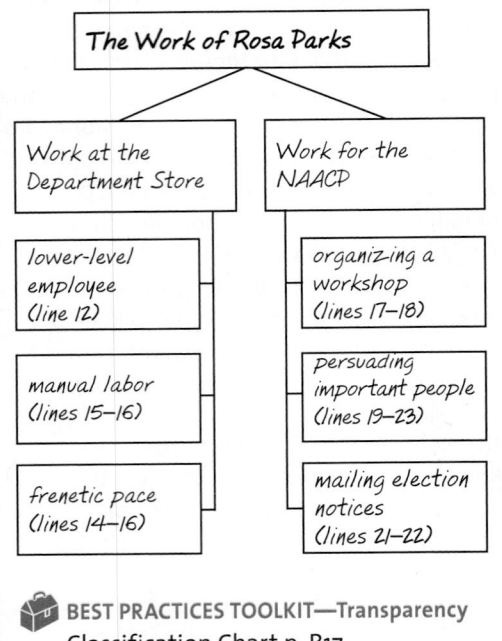

The Work of Rosa Parks

Work at the Department Store
- lower-level employee (line 12)
- manual labor (lines 15–16)
- frenetic pace (lines 14–16)

Work for the NAACP
- organizing a workshop (lines 17–18)
- persuading important people (lines 19–23)
- mailing election notices (lines 21–22)

🧰 **BEST PRACTICES TOOLKIT—Transparency**
Classification Chart p. B17

Ⓑ CHARACTERIZATION

Possible answer: *She is practical and makes productive use of her time. She is also thoughtful and generous.*

---

for the election of officers of the senior branch of the NAACP, which would be [the] next week," Parks recalled. That afternoon, she lunched with Fred Gray, the lawyer who defended Claudette Colvin and was serving as Clifford Durr's[2] **protégé** at his law office above the Sears Auto Tire Store.

"When 1:00 P.M. came and the lunch hour ended, Mrs. Parks went back to her work as a seamstress," Gray would write in his civil rights memoir, *Bus Ride to Justice*. "I continued my work and left the office in the early afternoon for an out-of-town engagement." Ⓐ

30 Shortly after 5:00 P.M., Rosa Parks clocked out of work and walked the block to Court Square to wait for her bus home. It had been a hard day, and her body ached, from her feet swollen from the constant standing to her shoulders throbbing from the strain and her chronic bursitis. But the bus stand was packed, so Parks, disinclined to jockey for a rush-hour seat, crossed Dexter Avenue to do a little shopping at Lee's Cut-Rate Drug. She had decided to treat herself to a heating pad but found them too pricey. Instead, she bought some Christmas gifts, along with aspirin, toothpaste, and a few other sundries, and headed back to the bus stop wondering how her husband's day had been at the Maxwell Air Force Base Barber Shop and thinking about what her mother would cook for dinner. Ⓑ

40 It was in this late-day **reverie** that Rosa Parks dropped her dime in the box and boarded the yellow-olive city bus. She took an aisle seat in the racially neutral middle section,[3] behind the movable sign which read "colored." She was not expecting any problems, as there were several empty spaces at the whites-only front of the bus. A black man was sitting next to her on her right and staring out the window; across the aisle sat two black women deep in conversation. At the next two stops enough white passengers got on to nearly fill up the front section. At the third stop, in front of the Empire Theater, a famous shrine to country-music fans as the stage where the legendary Hank Williams got his start, the last front seats were taken, with one man left standing.

50 The bus driver twisted around and locked his eyes on Rosa Parks. Her heart almost stopped when she saw it was James F. Blake, the bully who had put her off his bus twelve years earlier. She didn't know his name, but since that incident in 1943, she had never boarded a bus that Blake was driving. This day, however, she had absentmindedly stepped in. "Move y'all, I want those two seats," the driver barked on behalf of Jim Crow,[4] which dictated that all four blacks in that row of the middle section would have to surrender their seats to accommodate a single white man, as no "colored" could be allowed to sit parallel with him. A stony silence fell over the bus as nobody moved. "Y'all

protégé (prō′tə-zhā′) *n.* a person who is guided or supported by an older or more influential person

Ⓐ CHARACTERIZATION
How did Parks's work for the NAACP differ from her job at the store? Why do you think Brinkley chose to highlight these differences?

Ⓑ CHARACTERIZATION
Reread lines 30–39. What do Rosa Parks's thoughts and actions reveal about her?

reverie (rĕv′ə-rē) *n.* a state of daydreaming

② Targeted Passage

---

2. **Claudette Colvin . . . Clifford Durr's:** Claudette Colvin was an African-American teenager who had refused to give up her seat on a Montgomery city bus earlier in 1955. Clifford Durr was a white lawyer who worked for civil rights.

3. **racially neutral middle section:** a section of the bus where African Americans could sit, as long as no whites needed or wanted seats there.

4. **Jim Crow:** a term referring to the segregation of African Americans.

DIFFERENTIATED INSTRUCTION

FOR LESS–PROFICIENT READERS
② Targeted Passage [Lines 40–58]

This pivotal passage introduces this account's conflict: an irritated bus driver whose demand is about to change history.

- Where does Rosa Parks sit? Why?
- What happens at the front of the bus?
- What does Blake, the driver, want Parks and three other passengers to do?
- In the past, how did Parks come into conflict with Blake?

FOR ENGLISH LEARNERS
Key Academic Vocabulary Use Word Questioning to teach these words: *civil* (line 27), *section* (line 42), *incident* (line 53), *accommodate* (line 57), *obviously* (line 83), *liberating* (line 85).

 BEST PRACTICES TOOLKIT—Transparency
Word Questioning p. E9

better make it light on yourselves and let me have those seats," Blake sputtered,
60   more impatiently than before. Quietly and in unison, the two black women
sitting across from Parks rose and moved to the back. Her seatmate quickly
followed suit, and she swung her legs to the side to let him out. Then Parks slid
over to the window and gazed out at the Empire Theater marquee promoting
A Man Alone, a new Western starring Ray Milland. **C**

The next ten seconds seemed like an eternity to Rosa Parks. As Blake
made his way toward her, all she could think about were her forebears, who,
Maya Angelou would put it, took the lash, the branding iron, and untold
humiliations while only praying that their children would someday "flesh out"
the dream of equality. But unlike the poet, it was not Africa in the days of the
70   slave trade that Parks was thinking about; it was racist Alabama in the here and
now. She shuddered with the memory of her grandfather back in Pine Level
keeping watch for the KKK[5] every night with a loaded shotgun in his lap,
echoing abolitionist John Brown's[6] **exhortation:** "Talk! Talk! Talk! That didn't
free the slaves. . . . What is needed is action! Action!" So when Parks looked up
at Blake, his hard, thoughtless scowl filled her with pity. She felt fearless, bold,
and **serene.** "Are you going to stand up?" the driver demanded. Rosa Parks
looked straight at him and said: "No." Flustered and not quite sure what to do,
Blake retorted, "Well, I'm going to have you arrested." And Parks, still sitting
next to the window, replied softly, "You may do that."
80   Her majestic use of "may" rather than "can" put Parks on the high ground,
establishing her as a protester, not a victim. "When I made that decision,"
Parks stated later, "I knew I had the strength of my ancestors with me," and
obviously their dignity as well. And her formal dignified "No," uttered on a
suppertime bus in the cradle of the Confederacy as darkness fell, ignited the
collective "no" of black history in America, a defiance as liberating as John
Brown's on the gallows in Harpers Ferry. ∾ **D**

C **CHARACTERIZATION**
Reread lines 50–64. What
do you learn about Rosa
Parks from the way she
reacted to the bus driver's
commands?

3 **Targeted Passage**

exhortation
(ĕg'zôr-tā'shən) *n.* a
communication strongly
urging that something
be done

serene (sə-rēn') *adj.*
calm; peaceful

D **CHARACTERIZATION**
How does Brinkley convey
Rosa Parks's dignity and
strength?

---

5.   **back in Pine Level . . . KKK:** Pine Level is a town about 100 miles southeast of Birmingham. The KKK was
the Ku Klux Klan, an extremist secret society that often violently terrorized blacks in the South.

6.   **abolitionist John Brown's:** Brown, a white militant, performed radical acts to force the abolition of
slavery, including a failed attempt to steal guns from the U.S. arsenal at Harpers Ferry, Virginia.

ROSA PARKS   **279**

LITERARY ANALYSIS

C **CHARACTERIZATION**

Possible answer: *Parks is resolute and firm
but not aggressive. She makes her feelings
known through silent disobedience—that
is, passive resistance.*

Lines 75–80
REINFORCE *KEY IDEA:* DIGNITY

Discuss How does Parks's manner toward
Blake demonstrate her **dignity**? *Possible answer: Rather than be loudly defiant, she simply
meets his gaze and speaks just a few soft words
that are to the point.*

LITERARY ANALYSIS

D **CHARACTERIZATION**

Possible answer: *He describes Parks's feelings of courage and calmness, quotes her
later comments about the source of her
strength, and connects her action to the
larger story of "black history in America."*

If students need help . . . Ask:

- What words does Brinkley use in lines
75–76 to describe Parks? *Possible answer:
He calls her "fearless, bold, and serene."*

- In line 82, what does Parks say about her
strength? *Possible answer: It was "the
strength of [her] ancestors."*

Extend the Discussion In line 80, Brinkley
says that Parks took "the high ground."
Do you agree? Explain.

FOR LESS–PROFICIENT READERS
3 **Targeted Passage** [Lines 65–86]

In this concluding passage, Brinkley reveals the
climax and resolution of Parks's clash with the
driver. He also offers his thoughts about the
implications of that moment.

- As Blake approaches, what does Parks think
about?

- What two things does she tell him?

- Why does Brinkley compare Parks to John
Brown?

FOR ADVANCED LEARNERS/PRE–AP

Analyze Irony [paired-activity option] Have
students prepare and share a statement
about the irony in the title of the movie playing at the Empire Theater (*A Man Alone,* line
64). If time permits, expand the activity by
having students discuss any other details in
the account that they find ironic.

Prereading for this poem is found on page 274.

LITERARY ANALYSIS

Ⓔ CHARACTERIZATION

Possible answer: *Images in lines 4–6 ("trim name with its dream of a bench to rest on" and "sensible coat") suggest a modest, unextravagant person. Images in lines 1–3 ("How she sat there...") and 7–9 ("Doing nothing..." and "clean flame of her gaze") suggest a strong, serious individual.*

If students need help . . . Guide students through the poem, stanza by stanza. Categorize each detail as either "modest and unextravagant" or "strong and serious."

- *stanza 1:* The image of Parks sitting on the bus (doing nothing else) suggests her quiet but serious strength/determination.
- *stanza 2:* "That trim name" and "sensible coat" suggest practicality and seriousness.
- *stanza 3:* "The clean flame of her gaze" suggests Parks's strength.
- *stanza 4:* The image of Parks responding with courtesy to an act of kindness suggests the strength of her graciousness.

SELECTION WRAP–UP

SYNTHESIZE Ask students how reading the excerpt from the biography helped them understand the poem. **Possible answer:** *The excerpt describes Parks's refusal to give up her seat on a bus. Knowing that history makes it easier to understand what the poem refers to.*

⭐ **CRITIQUE** Have students evaluate and compare their reactions to these two works. In particular, have them explain which work made them think more, and why.

READING FLUENCY

Distribute the copy master and have students work in pairs or groups to practice fluency.

🅡 RESOURCE MANAGER—Copy Master
Reading Fluency p. 205

Rosa
Rita Dove

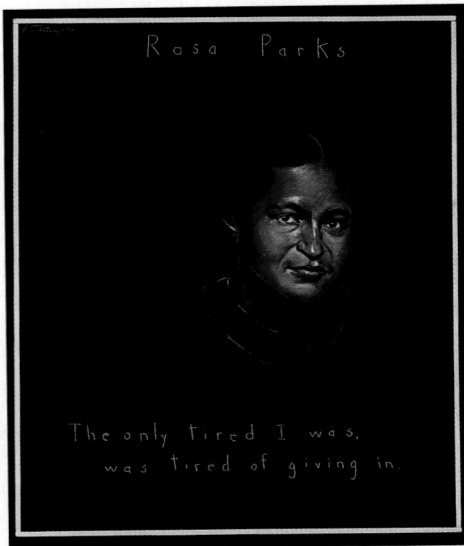

From *Americans Who Tell the Truth*, Robert Shetterly. Used by permission of Dutton Children's Books, a division of Penguin Young Readers Group, a member of Penguin Group, Inc. © Robert Shetterly.

How she sat there,
the time right inside a place
so wrong it was ready.

That trim name with
5 its dream of a bench
to rest on. Her sensible coat.

Doing nothing was the doing:
the clean flame of her gaze
carved by a camera flash.

10 How she stood up
when they bent down to **retrieve**
her purse. That courtesy. Ⓔ

retrieve (rĭ-trēv′) *v.* to find and return safely

Ⓔ **CHARACTERIZATION**
Which **images** portray Rosa Parks as a modest, unextravagant person? Which portray her as strong and serious?

DIFFERENTIATED INSTRUCTION

FOR ENGLISH LEARNERS
Options for Reading Have students listen to the entire poem on the *Audio Anthology CD* (also good for English learners) as they read along. Then use Jigsaw Reading to divide the poem among student pairs, each becoming experts on one stanza in their own words and sharing their paraphrases with the class.

 BEST PRACTICES TOOLKIT
Jigsaw Reading p. A1

FOR ADVANCED LEARNERS/PRE–AP
Analyze Imagery Ask students to contrast the "clean flame" of Parks's gaze in line 8 with the camera flash in line 9. While both images relate to light, how do differences between them suggest a contrast between Parks and the society she is trying to reform? **Possible answer:** *The flame suggests Parks's constancy, strength, and purposefulness. The camera flash suggests the transitory nature of society, as well as its artificiality, invasiveness, and perhaps even destructiveness.*

Comprehension

1. **Recall** Where did Rosa Parks sit after boarding the bus in the evening?

2. **Recall** Why did the bus driver order her to move?

3. **Summarize** What decision did Rosa Parks make?

Literary Analysis

4. **Draw Conclusions** Rosa Parks, an ordinary person, helped launch the civil rights movement. Why was she able to wield such enormous influence?

5. **Analyze Characterization** In both the biography and the poem, what words and actions convey Rosa Parks's **dignity?**

6. **Make Inferences** A **paradox** is a statement that seems contradictory but is still true. Reread line 7 of the poem. In what way does this line express a paradox? Explain your thinking.

Comparing Across Genres

Now that you've read both selections about Rosa Parks, think about the similarities and differences you found in the ways Rosa Parks is portrayed. Create a **Points of Comparison** chart like the one shown, and respond in your own words to the questions. If a point of comparison is not covered in one of the selections, leave the box blank.

Points of Comparison	In the Biography	In the Poem
What did you learn about Rosa Parks's appearance?		
What did you learn about her daily life?		
What did you learn about her personality, thoughts, and feelings?		
What did you learn about her values and the things she thought were important?		
What genre techniques did the writer use to portray Rosa Parks?		

Practice and Apply

After Reading

For additional support of post-reading questions, use these copy masters:

R **RESOURCE MANAGER**—Copy Masters

Reading Check p. 203 (to check understanding of the selection)

Characterization Across Genres pp. 195–197 (for practice of literary analysis standards focus)

Question Support p. 204 (After Reading questions adapted for English learners and less-proficient readers)

For additional questions, see page 189.

ANSWERS

Comprehension

1. *She sat in "the racially neutral middle section," where blacks were allowed unless seats were needed for whites.*

2. *The front of the bus filled up, leaving one white man standing. All four black riders in Parks's row were supposed to move so that the white man could sit there.*

3. *She decided not to move, even if her refusal led to her arrest.*

Literary Analysis

Possible answers:

4. *The time had finally come for collective action, and Parks's refusal to move served as the igniting spark.*

5. ● **STANDARDS FOCUS** *Characterization Across Genres* *"Rosa Parks looked straight at him and said: 'No'" (lines 76–77) and "You may do that" (line 79). "How she sat there" (line 1); "Her sensible coat" (line 6) and "the clean flame of her gaze" (line 8).*

6. *"Doing nothing" usually means taking no action. In this case, however, doing nothing represented taking an action— an action of quiet defiance.*

Comparing Across Genres

Possible answers:

(appearance)

Biography: *(implied), appears tired*

Poem: *sensible coat*

(daily life)

Biography: *works as seamstress; commutes by bus*

Poem: *[not covered]*

(personality, thoughts, feelings)

Biography: *determined, brave, sincere, serious*

Poem: *modest, unextravagant (implied)*

(values/what was important)

Biography: *taking a stand against segregation*

Poem: *not moving from her seat ("doing nothing")*

(genre techniques)

Biography: *facts, details, quotations*

Poem: *word choice, imagery, metaphor*

Vocabulary in Context

Vocabulary in Context

VOCABULARY PRACTICE

1. *reverie*	4. *exhortation*
2. *frenetically*	5. *serene*
3. *protégé*	6. *retrieve*

R RESOURCE MANAGER—Copy Master
Vocabulary Practice p. 201

VOCABULARY IN WRITING

Encourage students to make some notes about the situation before beginning to write. Remind them that Rosa Parks's refusal was a startling act and an arrestable offense. Suggest that students recall a time when they observed someone break a rule—especially a rule that they themselves considered improper—and consider how that action made them feel.

VOCABULARY STRATEGY: ETYMOLOGIES
(also an EL language objective)

Explain that etymologies vary somewhat from dictionary to dictionary. Most etymologies, however, show word history in reverse chronological order, tracing the word back, step by step, to its origins.

Possible answers:

1. Middle English, Anglo-French, Latin, Greek
2. "to dream"
3. *exhortari*, from *ex-*, meaning "out," + *hortari*, meaning "to urge or incite"
4. French

R RESOURCE MANAGER—Copy Master
Vocabulary Strategy p. 202

ℹ Vocabulary Center at **ClassZone.com**
Additional Vocabulary Activities

Vocabulary in Context

VOCABULARY PRACTICE

Write the word that best completes each sentence.

1. Boarding the bus, Rosa Parks was lost in a private _____ of memories and wishes.
2. She had been working _____ all day because it was the busy Christmas season.
3. She lunched with a lawyer who was a _____ of a famous civil rights lawyer.
4. She recalled her grandfather's _____ to act.
5. Her belief in the rightness of her refusal made her calm and _____.
6. She knew that if she lost her self-respect now, she might never _____ it.

> **WORD LIST**
> exhortation
> frenetically
> protégé
> retrieve
> reverie
> serene

VOCABULARY IN WRITING

Imagine you are one of the other African-American passengers on the bus with Rosa Parks. Write a paragraph describing your reaction when she refuses to give up her seat. Use two or more vocabulary words in your paragraph. You might start like this.

> **EXAMPLE SENTENCE**
> *Rosa calmly refused to obey the driver, but I was feeling far from **serene**.*

VOCABULARY STRATEGY: ETYMOLOGIES

Researching a word's **etymology**—that is, its history and origin—can give you insight into the word's meaning. One easy way to learn a word's etymology is to look the word up in a dictionary. Information about the word's origin will appear near the beginning or end of the dictionary entry.

> **se•rene** (sə-rēn′) *adj.* **1.** Unaffected by disturbance; calm and unruffled. See synonyms at **calm. 2.** Unclouded; fair: *serene skies and a bright blue sea.* **3.** often **Serene** Used as a title and form of address for certain members of royalty: *Her Serene Highness; His Serene Highness.* [Middle English, from Latin *serenus*, serene, clear.] —**se•rene′ly** *adv.* —**se•rene′ness** *n.*

PRACTICE Use a dictionary to answer these questions.

1. Through what languages can the history of *frenetic* be traced?
2. Does the Old French verb that gave rise to *reverie* mean "to be happy" or "to dream"?
3. From what Latin word does *exhort* derive, and what does it mean?
4. What language is the source of *protégé*?

⟳ VOCABULARY PRACTICE
For more practice, go to the **Vocabulary Center** at **ClassZone.com**.

DIFFERENTIATED INSTRUCTION

FOR ENGLISH LEARNERS

Vocabulary Strategy: Etymologies To provide more instruction with etymologies, help students use a dictionary to find the etymologies of the word signature. Discuss how knowing the etymology can help students understand the meaning of the word. (Signature *comes from Latin* signum, *which means "sign" and is related to* signare, *'to mark." To put one's signature on something is to mark it with one's name, or to leave a sign of oneself.)*

FOR ADVANCED LEARNERS/PRE–AP

Vocabulary in Writing Have students use at least two vocabulary words in a paragraph written in the first person from the point of view of a white passenger on the bus.

Writing for Assessment

1. READ THE PROMPT

In writing assessments, you will often be asked to compare and contrast how two writers treat the same subject. You are now going to practice writing an essay that requires this type of focus.

> **PROMPT**
>
> Like many people, Douglas Brinkley and Rita Dove seem fascinated by Rosa Parks and the courage she displayed when she defied racist laws and refused to give up her bus seat. In a four- or five-paragraph essay, compare and contrast the portrayals of Rosa Parks. Do they create the same impression of her? In what ways do they differ? Give evidence to support your response.

◀ **STRATEGIES IN ACTION**

1. I need to write an essay that shows **similarities and differences** between the two works on Rosa Parks.

2. I have to consider how each writer **reveals Parks's traits** and personality.

3. I need to **include examples or quotations** from the two works.

2. PLAN YOUR WRITING

- Review the **Points of Comparison** chart you created on page 281.
- Using your chart, find examples to use as evidence for the points you will develop in your essay. If necessary, review the selections to identify more examples.
- Create an outline to organize your main points. You might base this outline on the categories used in the chart.

3. DRAFT YOUR RESPONSE

Introduction Introduce the topic, Rosa Parks, and then explain that you will be comparing portrayals of her in a biography and a poem. Be sure to include the title and author of each work.

Body Use the topics in your comparison-and-contrast chart as a guide to the key points of your comparison. In one paragraph, for example, you might compare and contrast how each writer describes her appearance. Within each paragraph you write, give specific details to back up your points.

Conclusion Wrap up your essay with a restatement of your main idea and a brief summary of your main points.

Revision Check your use of transitional words and phrases to connect your ideas. Words and phrases such as *likewise, both,* and *in the same way* signal similarities. *On the other hand, instead, nevertheless,* and *however* signal differences.

FOR LESS–PROFICIENT WRITERS

Reinforce Outlining Demonstrate different approaches to outlining, urging students to use the method that works best for them. For example, present an Outline and ask students to consider whether it meets their needs. Be sure to explain that each main point with its supporting information becomes a paragraph.

 **BEST PRACTICES TOOLKIT—Transparency**
Outline p. B19

Writing for Assessment

1. READ THE PROMPT

- Remind students that comparing and contrasting means discussing both similarities and differences.
- Encourage students to read the prompt carefully, making sure they know exactly what they are being asked to discuss.

2. PLAN YOUR WRITING

- Explain that an outline helps writers gather and organize ideas and supporting details.
- Emphasize that ideas about this topic must be supported by examples (such as quotations or vivid details) from each work.

3. DRAFT YOUR RESPONSE

- Explain that students should choose the method that they feel best showcases the points they wish to make. For example, they might focus on the biography in one paragraph and the poem in the next paragraph. Alternatively, they might focus on similarities between the two works in one paragraph and differences in another.
- Point out that the use of transitional words and phrases is only one thing that students should check as they revise. They also should review the clarity of their main points, the accuracy of supporting details, and so on.

Assess and Reteach

Assess

RESOURCE MANAGER—Copy Masters
Selection Test A pp. 207–208
Selection Test B/C pp. 209–210

Test Generator CD

Reteach

STANDARDS LESSON FILE
Literature Lesson 3: Characterization
Vocabulary Lessons 25: Etymologies

Focus and Motivate

OBJECTIVES

- analyze a student model that reflects the key traits of comparison-contrast writing
- use the writing process to produce a comparison-contrast essay
- revise and edit, using a rubric for comparison-contrast writing
- create and present a power presentation

WRITER'S ROAD MAP

WRITING PROMPTS 1 AND 2

Help students choose a prompt by reviewing characters from the unit or by brainstorming pairs of people from the real world who might make interesting subjects. Point out that characters should be similar enough to compare but different enough to make the comparison interesting.

ADDITIONAL PROMPTS

Use these prompts for practice with business writing and writing in the humanities.

WRITING PROMPT 3

Writing from Your Life Write a short article for a consumer Web site that compares two products that buyers might need help evaluating.

Possible Subjects

- two fast-food restaurants
- two brands of athletic shoes
- two movies or television shows

WRITING PROMPT 4

Writing About Songs Examine the lyrics of two songs from different periods in history. Write an essay that compares and contrasts the two eras, using the songs as a base. Your essay should include quotations from both songs and draw conclusions about the songs' meanings and messages.

For additional writing prompts, see

- WriteSmart CD
- Writing Center at **ClassZone.com**

KEY TRAITS

Review the six **KEY TRAITS** with students, focusing primarily on ideas and organization. Compare the list of traits with the rubric on page 290.

Writing Workshop

Comparison-Contrast Essay

How does high school differ from middle school? Which video game should you buy? Why should you support one political candidate over another? You compare and contrast all the time in life—often to answer questions like these. In this workshop, you will write an essay comparing and/or contrasting two characters. Begin by consulting the **Writer's Road Map.**

WRITER'S ROAD MAP

Comparison-Contrast Essay

WRITING PROMPT 1

Writing from Literature Write an essay comparing and/or contrasting two characters from literature. Your essay should provide your reader with new insights into those characters.

Characters to Consider
- Madame Loisel and her husband in "The Necklace"
- Jill and Andy, the cook, in "Pancakes"
- Mami and Papi in "Daughter of Invention"

WRITING PROMPT 2

Writing from the Real World Write an essay about two people who exemplify strong contrasts within their profession.

People to Consider
- two athletes with different playing styles
- two musicians known for their distinctive sounds
- two comedians with unique approaches to their craft

 WRITING TOOLS
For prewriting, revision, and editing tools, visit the **Writing Center** at ClassZone.com.

KEY TRAITS

1. IDEAS
- Clearly states the **subjects** being compared and/or contrasted
- Presents a **thesis statement** that identifies similarities and/or differences
- Uses specific **examples** to support key ideas

2. ORGANIZATION
- Includes an engaging **introduction** and a satisfying **conclusion**
- Follows a consistent **organizational pattern**
- Uses **transitional words and phrases**

3. VOICE
- Uses language appropriate for the **audience and purpose**

4. WORD CHOICE
- Uses **precise adjectives** to convey similarities and differences

5. SENTENCE FLUENCY
- Varies **sentence beginnings** for good pacing and variety

6. CONVENTIONS
- Employs **correct grammar and usage**

284   UNIT 2: CHARACTERIZATION AND POINT OF VIEW

Writing Workshop Resources

 RESOURCE MANAGER UNIT 2

Plan and Teach pp. 211–214
Prewriting–Editing pp. 215–219
Writing Rubric p. 220
Publishing with Technology p. 221
Writing Support p. 222*

 **STANDARDS LESSON FILE**

Writing Lesson 24: Comparison-Contrast Essay
Grammar Lesson 21: Commas

 BEST PRACTICES TOOLKIT

Scaffolding Writing Instruction pp. 43–46*
Venn Diagram • Y Chart • T Notes • Analysis Frame: Character • Writing Template: Compare-Contrast

TECHNOLOGY
- Easy Planner DVD
- Writing Center at **ClassZone.com**
- WriteSmart CD

* Resources for Differentiation

Part 1: Analyze a Student Model

Eve Zimmerman
Randolph High School

Madame Loisel and Della: Different Values

What do you value in life? Madame Loisel in Guy de Maupassant's "The Necklace" and Della in O. Henry's "The Gift of the Magi" would answer this question differently. Madame Loisel dreams of living a life of luxury. Della wants to give her husband the perfect Christmas gift,
5 but she lacks enough money. Both women long for things they cannot afford, but their similarities end there. Their thoughts, treatment of their husbands, and responses to difficult situations reveal the differences in their values. While Madame Loisel equates happiness with her social status, Della looks to her husband and her quiet life for contentment.

10 Madame Loisel's and Della's thoughts reveal a great deal about their values. Both women spend time reflecting on their situations. Madame Loisel's thoughts convey her selfish side. At the beginning of the story, readers learn that "she grieved incessantly, feeling that she had been born for all the little niceties and luxuries of living." Constantly fantasizing
15 about a life of wealth and attention, Madame Loisel is the star of her daydreams, and her husband does not even play a supporting role. Like Madame Loisel, Della grieves about her situation, but only as it relates to her husband. Della spends "many a happy hour" coming up with the perfect gift for Jim. Her thoughts show that Jim's happiness means more
20 to her than her own.

Madame Loisel's and Della's values are also evident in the ways they interact with their husbands. Madame Loisel acts as if her husband is a nuisance to her. She is unappreciative and hot tempered when he brings home the invitation to the party. When her husband finally agrees to

KEY TRAITS IN ACTION

Identifies the **characters** being compared and contrasted.

Introduction includes a focused **thesis statement** that presents the points that will be contrasted.

This writer uses point-by-point **organization**. This paragraph elaborates on the first point—the characters' thoughts. Varied **sentence beginnings** add sophistication.

Begins to examine the second point—the characters' treatment of their husbands. The formal tone is appropriate for the **audience and purpose.**

Part 1: Analyze a Student Model

Have students read the student model and **KEY TRAITS IN ACTION.** Then discuss the model with the class, pointing out specific examples of each trait and building on what students have already noted. You may also wish to incorporate these activities:

- **Thesis Statement** Write this weak thesis statement on the board.

  Madame Loisel in "The Necklace" and Della in "The Gift of the Magi" are similar in some ways but different in others.

  Ask a student to read this statement and lines 5–9 of the student model aloud. Ask students to compare the two. ***Possible answers:** The thesis statement on the board provides little information about what will be covered in the essay. The thesis statement in the model lists three specific differences between the two characters. The statements that precede and follow it elaborate on the idea.*

- **Organization** To illustrate the clarity of the point-by-point organization of the model, ask students to identify the topic of each body paragraph. ***Possible answers: Paragraph 2:** the thoughts of the two characters;* ***Paragraph 3:** the ways the characters treat their husbands;* ***Paragraph 4:** their responses to difficult situations*

DIFFERENTIATED INSTRUCTION

For general guidelines on differentiating writing instruction, see

 BEST PRACTICES TOOLKIT
Scaffolding Writing Instruction pp. 43–46

FOR ENGLISH LEARNERS
Language: Skill Words Write these terms on the board and review them with students.

- *subject:* a person or thing being discussed or written about; for example, two songs may be the subjects of a comparison.

- *point of comparison:* a feature that is being compared—for example, the melody of two songs.

- *thesis statement:* one or two sentences stating the main idea of an essay. In a comparison-contrast essay, the thesis statement names the subjects and points of comparison. Share this example:

  The husbands in "The Necklace" and "The Gift of the Magi" both make sacrifices to please their wives, but their actions have very different results.

- **Transitional Phrases** Remind students that they can find a list of transitions useful for comparison-contrast writing on page 290. Point out that words like *on the other hand, similarly,* and *in contrast* help readers understand relationships between ideas.

  Point out the words highlighted in line 27. Then ask students to find additional transitions that signal comparisons. ***Possible answers:*** *"art" (line 6), "Like Madame Loisel" (lines 16–17), "However" (lines 36), "Unlike Madame Loisel" (lines 39–40)*

- **Examples** Throughout this essay, the writer cites evidence from the literature to support the points she makes about the characters. Have students look through the essay to find at least three examples of statements supported by quotations or examples.

For interactive student models, see

📀 Write*Smart* CD

ℹ️ Writing Center at **ClassZone.com**

---

25 give her money to buy a dress, she does not even thank him. Later, she ignores him at the party and feels embarrassed by him when they finally leave together. Della, on the other hand, showers her husband with attention and love. After sacrificing her best feature, she does not spend time reflecting on her hair. Instead, she encourages Jim to look on the

30 bright side, saying, "My hair grows awfully fast. Say 'Merry Christmas!' Jim, and let's be happy." For Della, happiness is about Jim and their love for each other.

In addition to their thoughts and treatment of their husbands, Madame Loisel and Della reveal their values through their responses to

35 difficult situations. To her credit, Madame Loisel repays her debt "with sudden heroism" and takes pride in her hard work. However, her values do not change. Even after everything she has been through, Madame Loisel often thinks back to the time "she had been so beautiful and admired." This response shows that she is still selfish and vain. Unlike

40 Madame Loisel, Della does not seem to mind the unfortunate situation she and her husband are in. At the end of the story, she and Jim do not dwell on their losses. They respond to the situation by saving their presents for a later time and enjoying each other's company over dinner.

Madame Loisel's and Della's thoughts, relationships, and responses

45 to their circumstances show just how different they are. To Madame Loisel, happiness means wearing the best clothes, being admired, and living a privileged life. To Della, however, happiness means loving and being loved by her husband. Both women find themselves in similar situations, but their values—like most people's—have more to do with

50 their personalities than their situations in life.

*Uses a **transitional phrase** to signal one difference.*

Introduces the third point—the characters' responses to difficult situations.

*Includes **examples** and **precise adjectives** that show the differences between the characters.*

Conclusion *summarizes similarities and differences and offers an observation about values.*

2

DIFFERENTIATED INSTRUCTION

FOR ENGLISH LEARNERS

Comprehension: Transitions Check to make sure students understand the different signal words and phrases. If students are not familiar with the terms, use this activity to illustrate the concepts of likeness and similarity.

1. Hold up pictures of two dogs.

2. Using the words and phrases in the chart on page 290, provide a series of model sentences that compare and contrast the dogs:

One dog is large, **but** the other is small. *(difference)*

While this dog is quite large, it is not frightening. *(difference)*

The other dog is small, **but** its bark is very loud. *(difference)*

Both dogs are friendly. *(similarity)*

They are **similarly** colored. *(similarity)*

The length of the large dog's fur is **like** that of the small dog. *(similarity)*

3. Now hold up two new pictures and repeat the exercise, this time asking students to provide the sentences.

To provide English learners with additional writing support, see

 **RESOURCE MANAGER—Copy Master** Writing Support p. 222

Part 2: Apply the Writing Process

PREWRITING

What Should I Do?	What Does It Look Like?

1. Analyze the prompt.
Look again at the prompt you chose on page 284. Find words that state the **topics** you should compare and your **audience, purpose,** and **format.** If the prompt is not specific, then the choice is up to you.

> **TIP** Avoid choosing subjects that are too similar. Make sure there is a compelling reason to compare or contrast them.

▶ **WRITING PROMPT** Write an (essay) comparing and/or contrasting (two characters from) (literature.) Your essay should provide your reader with new insights into those characters.

> *Audience isn't stated, but I know that I'm writing for my teacher and classmates. My purpose is to analyze two characters and help readers understand them.*

2. Brainstorm similarities and differences.
Use a Venn diagram, a chart, or another graphic organizer to record all the similarities and differences you can think of. Note the characters' looks, personalities, values, and relationships.

▶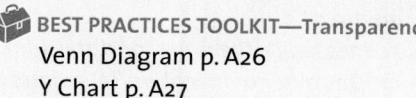
Madame Loisel
* Values status
* Always thinks of herself
* Treats husband terribly

Both
* Want things they can't afford

Della
* Values her husband
* Thinks only about Jim
* Makes best of situation

3. Decide on a focus and write a thesis.
What are the most striking similarities or differences you noted? What conclusions can you draw about the characters? Using your answers to these questions, determine your focus and write a **thesis statement** that conveys your main idea. Then identify the points that will help you prove your thesis.

▶ **Working Thesis:** *Madame Loisel and Della both want things they can't afford, but they have different values.*

> **Points:** 1. Thoughts
> 2. Treatment of husbands
> 3. Responses to hard times

4. Collect evidence.
Use a chart to collect **examples** and **quotations** that relate to each point you identified.

▶

Point	Madame Loisel	Della
1. Thoughts	grieves "incessantly" about her financial situation	thinks only about Jim's gift

---

FOR ENGLISH LEARNERS
Writing: Thesis Statement Have students use these sentence starters to help them state their thesis and develop their support.

* My subjects are _____ and _____.
* My thesis is _____.
* The points I will compare are _____.
* For my first point, my evidence is _____.

FOR ADVANCED LEARNERS/PRE–AP
Have students use the Analysis Frame: Character to help them explore their subjects in depth or to provide ideas for more challenging thesis statements.

 BEST PRACTICES TOOLKIT—Transparency
    Analysis Frame: Character pp. D21, D26

Practice and Apply

To support students during the writing process, use these copy masters:

 **RESOURCE MANAGER**—Copy Masters
    Prewriting–Editing pp. 215–219
    Writing Rubric p. 220
    Writing Support p. 222 (for English learners)

Part 2: Apply the Writing Process

PREWRITING

1. Analyze the prompt. Be sure that students understand what their chosen prompt is asking of them. Have them circle key words, as in the model. Then have students who have chosen the same prompt brainstorm topic ideas as a group, making sure they have noted the **TIP** in the first step.

2. Brainstorm similarities and differences. This activity is excellent for paired and small-group work. Encourage groups to experiment with different graphic organizers to help them generate ideas.

    BEST PRACTICES TOOLKIT—Transparencies
    Venn Diagram p. A26
    Y Chart p. A27
    T Chart p. A25

3. Decide on a focus and write a thesis. Have students develop a working thesis and supporting points, as in the model. Do a quick check of their plans, making sure each student has a valid outline before beginning to write.

4. Collect evidence. Suggest that students review lines 10–20 of the student model one more time before they begin collecting evidence. Point out how quotations, restatements, and interpretations may all be used to support a point.

For interactive graphic organizers, see

    WriteSmart CD
    Writing Center at **ClassZone.com**

DRAFTING

1. **Choose an organization.** Before students begin their drafts, discuss the advantages and challenges of each type of organization. (*With subject-by-subject organization, the writer can focus on one subject at a time. However, the comparisons and contrasts may be harder for the reader to track. Point-by-point organization keeps the focus on the comparison.*)

2. **Use transitions.** Remind students of the importance of transitional words in keeping their readers on track. Direct them once again to the list of transitions on page 290.

3. **Incorporate supporting details.** Warn students not to simply drop in a quotation with no introductory sentence or phrase. Also encourage them to incorporate their own thoughts and analyses. Point to lines 11–14 and 29–32 of the student model for excellent examples. Display models of wording students might use to cite evidence, and discuss the correct use of quotation marks, commas, and periods.

   - *Madame Loisel often thinks back to the time "she had been so beautiful and admired."*
   - *In lines 31–33, the narrator states that . . .*
   - *In "Daughter of Invention," the narrator describes her father as "haunted" and filled with "secret fear."*

For a comparison-contrast essay writing template, see

🧰 BEST PRACTICES TOOLKIT—Transparency
    Writing Template: Compare-Contrast
      (by subject) pp. C16, C24
✏️ Write*Smart* CD
ℹ️ Writing Center at **ClassZone.com**

DRAFTING

What Should I Do?

1. **Choose an organization.**
   Two ways to organize the body of a comparison-contrast essay are shown here. You may want to try out both before selecting the one that works best for your purpose.

   - **Subject-by-Subject Organization**
     Discusses all the points relating to the first subject before moving on to the second subject
   - **Point-by-Point Organization**
     Compares or contrasts both subjects, one point at a time

2. **Use transitions.**
   Transitional words and phrases, such as *like, also, similarly, but,* and *unlike,* are cues that signal similarities or differences.

   See page 290: Check Your Grammar

3. **Incorporate supporting details.**
   Show, don't tell, readers about the characters' similarities and differences. Use the evidence you collected earlier to help you prove your point.

   TIP Before revising, consult the key traits on page 284 and the rubric and peer-reader questions on page 290.

What Does It Look Like?

SUBJECT-BY-SUBJECT ORGANIZATION	POINT-BY-POINT ORGANIZATION

Subject A: Madame Loisel
  Point 1: Thoughts
  Point 2: Treatment of husband
  Point 3: Response to hard times
Subject B: Della
  Point 1: Thoughts
  Point 2: Treatment of husband
  Point 3: Response to hard times
	Point 1: Thoughts
	  Subject A: Madame Loisel
	  Subject B: Della
	Point 2: Treatment of husband
	  Subject A: Madame Loisel
	  Subject B: Della
	Point 3: Response to hard times
	  Subject A: Madame Loisel
	  Subject B: Della

Like Madame Loisel, Della grieves about her situation, but only as it relates to her husband. Her thoughts show that Jim's happiness means more to her than her own.

Madame Loisel's and Della's values are also evident in the ways they interact with their husbands.

Madame Loisel's values do not change. —Key point
Even after everything she has been through, she often thinks back to the time "she had been so beautiful and admired." This response shows that —Support
she is still vain. Unlike Madame Loisel, Della does not seem to mind the unfortunate situation that she is in. —Key point
At the end of the story, she and Jim decide to enjoy each other's company and forget about —Support
the gifts.

DIFFERENTIATED INSTRUCTION

FOR LESS–PROFICIENT WRITERS

Choose an Organization To help students with point-by-point organization, provide this frame and explain that it represents the organization in the student model. Have students follow this model to plan their essays.

Beginning Paragraph
- Name the two subjects.
- State your thesis. Use the questions on page 287, number 3, for help with determining the focus and writing the thesis statement.

Middle Paragraphs—Point of Comparison (number will vary)
- Present the first subject.
  —Provide evidence from the text.
  —Provide an explanation.
- Present the second subject.
  —Provide evidence from the text.
  —Provide an explanation.

End Paragraph
- Restate the subjects and the points of comparison.
- Bring your essay to a satisfying close by offering an observation and stating your conclusion.

REVISING AND EDITING

What Should I Do?	What Does It Look Like?

1. Improve your introduction.
- Put [brackets] around the first one or two sentences of your introduction.
- Review the bracketed text. If you are simply stating the obvious, try adding an interesting detail, such as a question or quotation, to hook readers.

▶

What do you value in life?
[*Madame Loisel in Guy de Maupassant's "The Necklace" and Della in O. Henry's "The Gift of the Magi," ~~are very different people.~~*]
would answer this question differently.

2. Make sure you have included enough support.
- Underline the examples and quotations that you have used.
- If your essay lacks underlines, add examples and quotations to help readers understand the characters.

▶

Madame Loisel's thoughts convey her selfish side. She constantly dreams of a life of wealth and attention.
At the beginning of the story, readers learn that "she grieved incessantly, feeling that she had been born for all the little niceties and luxuries of living."

3. Monitor your tone.
- If you are writing an essay for class, use a formal tone. Read your draft aloud and highlight words and phrases that are too conversational.
- Replace words with ones more appropriate to your audience and purpose.

▶

acts as if her husband is a nuisance to her.
Madame Loisel ~~is ridiculous. What's the deal with how she treats her husband? She gives him major attitude~~ when he brings home the invitation to the party.
is unappreciative and hot tempered

4. Check that your ideas flow smoothly.
- Draw boxes around the transitional words and phrases that signal the characters' similarities or differences.
- If your essay lacks boxes, add transitions where it makes sense to cue readers.

See page 290: Add Transition Words

▶

Madame Loisel treats her husband badly. She ignores him at the party and feels embarrassed by him when they finally leave together. Della showers her husband with attention.   , on the other hand,

---

1. Improve your introduction. Remind students of these useful techniques for engaging the reader:
- Begin with a question (as in the student model).
- Begin with a quotation.
- Make a provocative statement.
- Connect to something the reader is familiar with.

2. Make sure you have included enough support. Students who are writing about literature should check to see that they have cited evidence from the text whenever appropriate. Students writing about other topics should be reminded that they can use facts and statistics, sensory details, anecdotes, and specific examples to support their points. Also suggest that students use the questions for peer readers on page 290 to ensure they have included enough support.

3. Monitor your tone. Remind students that formal language
- does not contain slang or too many contractions
- contains more complex vocabulary and sentence structures than informal language

4. Check that your ideas flow smoothly. If some students feel they need to add transitions, caution them not to sprinkle transitions in their papers without considering whether they make sense.

For interactive revision tools, see

⊘ Write*Smart* CD

ℹ Writing Center at **ClassZone.com**

Review the **GRAMMAR AND STYLE** note on page 214. Remind students that varying sentence beginnings creates smoother, more rhythmic, and infinitely more interesting writing.

FOR ENGLISH LEARNERS

Writing: Transitions Provide sentence frames such as these to help students use transitions in their writing:

- Both [subject A] and [subject B] _____.
- While [subject A] _____, [subject B] _____.
- Unlike [subject A], [subject B] _____.
- However, they both _____.
- [Subject A] _____; however, [subject B] _____.
- Although [subject A] _____, [subject B] _____.

Preparing to Publish

Support for meeting the goals in the writing rubric is supplied throughout the Writing Workshop on pages 284–289.

For Rubric Bank, see

 Write*Smart* CD

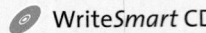 Writing Center at **ClassZone.com**

Assess and Reteach

S STANDARDS LESSON FILE

Writing Lesson 24: Comparison-Contrast Essay

Grammar Lesson 21: Missing or Misplaced Commas

Preparing to Publish **Comparison-Contrast Essay**

Apply the Rubric

A strong comparison-contrast essay . . .

☑ opens with an engaging introduction that presents the subjects being compared and/or contrasted

☑ has a focused thesis statement

☑ supports the thesis with examples

☑ follows a consistent organization

☑ includes precise adjectives and varied sentence beginnings

☑ uses transitional words and phrases

☑ uses an appropriate tone

☑ summarizes the comparison and/or contrast in a satisfying conclusion

Ask a Peer Reader

- How would you summarize the similarities and differences between the characters I wrote about?

- Which examples are strong? Which are weak?

- Where do I need to include more supporting details?

Add Transition Words

For Comparing	For Contrasting
also	but
and	however
another	in contrast
both	instead
in addition to	on the other hand
like	unlike
too	yet

Check Your Grammar

- Use a comma to set an introductory transitional phrase off from the rest of the sentence.

  Like Madame Loisel , Della grieves about her situation.

- Use quotation marks around exact words cited from a story. Periods and commas should always go inside quotation marks.

  Madame Loisel repays her debt " with sudden heroism."

See pages R49–R50: Quick Reference: Punctuation

Writing On**l**ine

 PUBLISHING OPTIONS
For publishing options, visit the **Writing Center** at **ClassZone.com**.

ASSESSMENT PREPARATION
For writing and grammar assessment practice, go to the **Assessment Center** at **ClassZone.com**.

Creating and Presenting a Power Presentation

Most computers come equipped with software that lets users create slide presentations. Adapting your comparison-contrast essay to this format lets you express your ideas with extra style.

Preparing the Presentation

1. **Focus on the big ideas.** Your introduction and conclusion, as well as the main points, should get at least one slide apiece. Each slide should have one headline and three to five short bullet points.

2. **Choose a template.** If you have a flair for design, choose your own fonts and colors. If not, use one of the prefabricated templates provided in the software program.

3. **Use effects to complement your message.** Consider adding visuals or music. Avoid fancy effects and animations, as these detract from your main points. Each slide should be easy to read from the back of the room.

4. **Practice the presentation.** If you can, practice in the room you will present in, with the equipment you will use. Otherwise, print out your presentation and practice it in front of friends or family. Double-check that each point is logical, that any quotations you included are accurate, and that your spelling is correct.

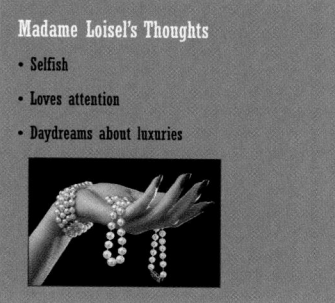

Madame Loisel's Thoughts
- Selfish
- Loves attention
- Daydreams about luxuries

Delivering the Presentation

1. **Present to audience members—don't read to them.** Using each point as a reminder, elaborate on your topic so that your audience truly understands your opinions and evidence.

2. **Be respectful of other presenters.** Show them the same attention and consideration that you want them to give you.

3. **Find out how you did.** When you have finished, distribute a questionnaire to audience members. Ask for feedback about the content and style of your presentation.

WRITING WORKSHOP **291**

PUBLISHING WITH TECHNOLOGY

Ask students to read this page to get an overview of how to create a power presentation. Students who choose this option should then familiarize themselves with the particular software program they will use by taking advantage of the tutorial option that is usually included.

Before students begin working, review this rubric with them so that they understand their goals:

Rubric A strong power presentation

- contains accurate information
- is clearly presented, with one headline and three to five short bullet points per slide
- has a sensible organization
- includes coherent introductory and concluding slides
- is attractively designed, with easy-to-read type
- is presented rather than read to the audience, by a presenter who understands the subject and who speaks loudly enough, clearly, and calmly

R RESOURCE MANAGER—Copy Master
Publishing with Technology p. 221

S STANDARDS LESSON FILE
Media Lesson 22: Creating a Power Presentation

Assessment Practice

CHECK READINESS

Read aloud the paragraph under **ASSESS** and stress to students that this is not the full Unit Test, but a way for them to check their readiness for it. Then have students examine the skills listed under **REVIEW** and look back in the unit or in the **Student Resource Bank** for any skills they need to review.

READ THE SELECTIONS

Remind students to keep unit goals in mind as they read each passage, paying particular attention to these literary and reading skills:

- character traits and motivation
- point of view
- draw conclusions
- make inferences
- monitor understanding

To help students focus on the characters while reading, encourage them to ask questions such as

- What are the father and the son like in "Powder"? What do I learn about them from their actions and words?

- What is Maud Martha like? What does she wish for? What is her sister like?

ANSWER THE QUESTIONS

Direct students to pages R93–R101 of the **Handbook** to review test-taking strategies.

- Remind students not to choose the first alternative that seems to fit when answering a multiple-choice question. Instead, they should read through all the choices, eliminate any that are clearly wrong, and then choose the *best* answer—the one that is most accurate and complete.

- Point out that students should not go back and change an answer unless they are sure that it is incorrect.

BACKGROUND

Thelonious Monk, a renowned jazz pianist, became famous in the late 1950s.

Reading Comprehension

ASSESS
The practice test items on the next few pages match skills listed on the Unit Goals page (page 185) and addressed throughout this unit. Taking this practice test will help you assess your knowledge of these skills and determine your readiness for the Unit Test.

REVIEW
After you take the practice test, your teacher can help you identify any skills you need to review.

- Character Traits
- Character Motivation
- Point of View
- Draw Conclusions
- Make Inferences
- Monitor
- Multiple-Meaning Words
- Word Origins
- Supporting and Descriptive Details
- Words, Phrases, Clauses

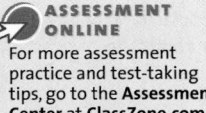

ASSESSMENT ONLINE
For more assessment practice and test-taking tips, go to the **Assessment Center** at **ClassZone.com**.

DIRECTIONS *Read the following selections and then answer the questions.*

from Powder
Tobias Wolff

Just before Christmas my father took me skiing at Mount Baker. He'd had to fight for the privilege of my company, because my mother was still angry with him for sneaking me into a nightclub during his last visit, to see Thelonious Monk.

He wouldn't give up. He promised, hand on heart, to take good care of me and have me home for dinner on Christmas Eve, and she relented. But as we were checking out of the lodge that morning it began to snow, and in this snow he observed some rare quality that made it necessary for us to get in one last run. We got in several last runs. He was indifferent to my fretting. Snow
10 whirled around us in bitter, blinding squalls, hissing like sand, and still we skied. As the lift bore us to the peak yet again, my father looked at his watch and said, "Criminy. This'll have to be a fast one."

By now I couldn't see the trail. There was no point in trying. I stuck to him like white on rice and did what he did and somehow made it to the bottom without sailing off a cliff. We returned our skis and my father put chains on the Austin-Healey while I swayed from foot to foot, clapping my mittens and wishing I was home. I could see everything. The green tablecloth, the plates with the holly pattern, the red candles waiting to be lit.

We passed a diner on our way out. "You want some soup?" my father asked.
20 I shook my head. "Buck up," he said. "I'll get you there. Right, doctor?"

I was supposed to say, "Right, doctor," but I didn't say anything.

A state trooper waved us down outside the resort. A pair of sawhorses were blocking the road. The trooper came up to our car and bent down to my father's window. His face was bleached by the cold. Snowflakes clung to his eyebrows and to the fur trim of his jacket and cap.

"Don't tell me," my father said.

The trooper told him. The road was closed. It might get cleared, it might not. Storm took everyone by surprise. So much, so fast. Hard to get people moving. Christmas Eve. What can you do.
30 My father said, "Look. We're talking about five, six inches. I've taken this car through more than that."

The trooper straightened up. His face was out of sight but I could hear him. "The road is closed."

DIFFERENTIATED INSTRUCTION

FOR ENGLISH LEARNERS
Assessment Practice: Work Backward
Prepare students by having them read the questions *before* reading the passages. Have pairs find unfamiliar words in test directions and questions and follow these steps.

1. Write each word on an index card.
2. Look up the meaning in a dictionary and write it on the back of the card.
3. Use the cards to practice the words with a partner and to teach them to others.

Culture: Clarify Read aloud lines 5–6 and explain or elicit the significance of Christmas Eve. Ask volunteers to suggest how families celebrate Christmas in the United States. Then read aloud these words from lines 17–18: "The green tablecloth, the plates with the holly pattern, the red candles waiting to be lit." Call on volunteers to describe the meaning of each Christmas symbol or ritual.

My father sat with both hands on the wheel, rubbing the wood with his thumbs. He looked at the barricade for a long time. He seemed to be trying to master the idea of it. Then he thanked the trooper, and with a weird, old-maidy show of caution turned the car around. "Your mother will never forgive me for this," he said.

"We should have left before," I said. "Doctor."

40 He didn't speak to me again until we were in a booth at the diner, waiting for our burgers. "She won't forgive me," he said. "Do you understand? Never."

"I guess," I said, but no guesswork was required; she wouldn't forgive him.

"I can't let that happen." He bent toward me. "I'll tell you what I want. I want us all to be together again. Is that what you want?"

"Yes, sir."

He bumped my chin with his knuckles. "That's all I needed to hear."

When we finished eating he went to the pay phone in the back of the diner, then joined me in the booth again. I figured he'd called my mother, but he didn't give a report. He sipped at his coffee and stared out the window at the
50 empty road. "Come on, come on," he said, though not to me. A little while later he said it again. When the trooper's car went past, lights flashing, he got up and dropped some money on the check. "Okay. Vamanos."

The wind had died. The snow was falling straight down, less of it now and lighter. We drove away from the resort, right up to the barricade. "Move it," my father told me. When I looked at him he said, "What are you waiting for?" I got out and dragged one of the sawhorses aside, then put it back after he drove through. He pushed the door open for me. "Now you're an accomplice," he said. "We go down together." He put the car into gear and gave me a look. "Joke, son."

Description of
Maud Martha

Gwendolyn Brooks

What she liked was candy buttons, and books, and painted music (deep blue, or delicate silver) and the west sky, so altering, viewed from the steps of the back porch; and dandelions.

She would have liked a lotus, or China asters or the Japanese Iris, or meadow lilies—yes, she would have liked meadow lilies, because the very word

 **GO ON**

ITEM ANALYSIS

COMPREHENSION AND WRITTEN RESPONSE	ITEMS	UNIT PAGES
Character Traits	6, 8, 9, 10, 11, 14	186–191, 237, 251, 275
Character Motivation	3, 4, 5, 13	188–191, 207
Point of View	1, 2, 7	186–191, 193, 223
Draw Conclusions	6, 8, 10, 14	193
Make Inferences	3, 5, 9, 11, 13	207
Monitor	4, 12	223

VOCABULARY	ITEMS	UNIT PAGES
Multiple-Meaning Words	1, 2, 3, 4	248
Word Origins	5, 6, 7	204, 219, 234, 282

WRITING AND GRAMMAR	ITEMS	UNIT PAGES
Supporting and Descriptive Details	1, 3, 4	205, 249
Words, Phrases, Clauses	1, 2, 3, 4	218, 220

FOR LESS-PROFICIENT READERS

Assessment Support Consider these options for completing the Assessment Practice.

- Have students "work backward" to review the test questions *before* reading the passages.
- Select random questions in the Assessment, and have students demonstrate how and where to look for the answers.
- Ask students to locate unfamiliar vocabulary words in the Assessment. Elicit their meanings from the class.
- Have students record useful testing words and definitions in their journals for later reference.
- Read the selections or parts of them aloud to aid in student comprehension.

McDougal Littell
Assessment System

After checking student readiness with this Assessment Practice, you may administer the complete Unit 2 Test in order to more thoroughly evaluate student mastery of unit goals.

ANSWERS

Comprehension

Model a thinking process for answering multiple-choice questions.

1. **A is correct.** B would be true if the story were told by an omniscient narrator. C and D would be true if the story were told by any third-person narrator.

2. **A is correct.** A third-person point of view could include the thoughts and feelings of both characters, thus providing a more objective picture of the father. B is incorrect because the size of a character's role would not be affected by point of view. C is incorrect because the narrator already includes details and dialogue. D is incorrect because a third-person point of view could include the son's feelings.

3. **A is correct.** The son refuses to joke out of anger over his father's decision to ski—and then keep skiing—despite the boy's desire to get home. The son is not flattered, as in B, or happy as in C. The boy wants to be home to be part of the Christmas celebration and not because he misses his mother, so D is incorrect.

4. **A is correct.** The father wants the trooper to think he agrees with him about the danger. B is incorrect because he does not look at the trooper as he turns the car. C is incorrect, as shown by lines 30–31. D is partly true, as he plans to get around the barricade, but this desire does not motivate his show of caution.

5. **C is correct.** His words in lines 43–44 show his motivation. He does prove his skill, as in A, and challenge authority, as in D, but these are not his reasons. B is incorrect because he needs no practice.

6. **C is correct.** The father appears humorous when he jokes with the boy and rebellious when he drives around the barricade illegally. A is only partly true, as he is concerned only when he thinks he will be late. B and D are completely untrue.

7. **D is correct.** We know the story is told in the third person because Maud Martha is not the narrator of the story, as in A, and because she is referred to as "she." B could be true for either point of view and is therefore incorrect.

---

meadow made her breathe more deeply, and either fling her arms or want to fling her arms, depending on who was by, rapturously up to whatever was watching in the sky. But dandelions were what she chiefly saw. Yellow jewels for everyday, studding the patched green dress of her back yard. She liked their demure prettiness second to their everydayness; for in that latter
10 quality she thought she saw a picture of herself, and it was comforting to find that what was common could also be a flower.

And could be cherished! To be cherished was the dearest wish of the heart of Maud Martha Brown, and sometimes when she was not looking at dandelions (for one would not be looking at them all the time, often there were chairs and tables to dust or tomatoes to slice or beds to make or grocery stores to be gone to, and in the colder months there were no dandelions at all), it was hard to believe that a thing of only ordinary allurements—if the allurements of any flower could be said to be ordinary—was as easy to love as a thing of heart-catching beauty.

Such as her sister Helen! who was only two years past her own age of seven, and was almost her own height and weight and thickness. But oh, the long lashes, the grace, the little ways with
20 the hands and feet.

Comprehension

DIRECTIONS *Answer these questions about the excerpt from "Powder."*

1. You can tell the story is told from the first-person point of view because the narrator
   A is a character in the story
   B knows all the characters' thoughts
   C doesn't take part in the story's action
   D is a voice outside the story

2. How would the story be different if it were told from the third-person point of view?
   A The story would give a more objective picture of the father.
   B The mother would play a bigger role in the story.
   C The story would have more descriptive details and more dialogue.
   D It would be harder to understand the son's feelings.

3. What can you infer about the son's motivation for refusing to say "Right, doctor" in line 21?
   A He is angry at his father.
   B He is flattered that his father jokes with him.
   C He is happy to be on a trip with his father.
   D He misses his mother.

4. Reread lines 27–38 and monitor your understanding. Why does the father turn around with a "show of caution"?
   A He wants the trooper to see how carefully he drives.
   B He wants to see what the trooper is doing at all times.
   C He doesn't want to damage his car.
   D He wants to get around the barricades.

294

---

8. **B is correct.** Maud Martha seems sensitive to nature and beauty and sincere about what she loves and wants. The chores show that she is not lazy, as in A. The things she likes show that she is not harsh and uncaring, as in C. Her love of the ordinary dandelion flower shows that she is not exotic, as in D.

9. **B is correct.** Maud Martha's chores show that she works hard. A is incorrect because she loves dandelions, which she does not consider beautiful. C is incorrect because she does not consider gazing at flowers to be a waste of time. D is incorrect because she considers herself as possessing ordinary allurements.

5. The father's motivation for driving on the closed road is to

   A prove he's an excellent driver

   B practice driving in the snow

   C keep his promise to get his son home

   D challenge the trooper's authority

6. Which pair of adjectives best describes the father's character traits?

   A concerned and thoughtful

   B awkward and unsure

   C humorous and rebellious

   D serious and cautious

DIRECTIONS *Answer these questions about "Maud Martha."*

7. How do you know the selection is told from the third-person point of view?

   A Maud Martha is the narrator.

   B Maud Martha is the only character.

   C Maud Martha is referred to as "I."

   D Maud Martha is referred to as "she."

8. According to what the narrator reveals about Maud Martha, which adjectives best describe her character traits?

   A lazy and conceited

   B sensitive and sincere

   C harsh and uncaring

   D graceful and exotic

9. What can you infer about Maud Martha from lines 12–17?

   A She loves only beautiful things.

   B She works hard for a child.

   C She wastes time on flowers.

   D She feels like a special person.

10. What conclusion can you draw about Maud Martha's feelings for Helen?

   A She sees Helen as a dandelion.

   B She feels sorry for Helen.

   C She admires Helen's beauty.

   D She wishes Helen were prettier.

DIRECTIONS *Answer this question about both selections.*

11. How is Maud Martha like the son in "Powder"?

   A Both show a sense of responsibility.

   B Both act carefree most of the time.

   C Both have sisters they admire.

   D Both disagree with their parents' actions.

Written Response

SHORT RESPONSE
Write three or four sentences to answer each question.

12. Which character do you picture more clearly, the son in "Powder" or Maud Martha? Use the monitoring skill of visualizing to help you answer this question. Give examples of descriptive details in the text that help you visualize the character.

13. What is the father's motivation for calling his son an accomplice in line 57? What can you tell about the father from his words?

EXTENDED RESPONSE
Write two to three paragraphs to answer this question.

14. How are the father and son in "Powder" different? Are there any ways in which they are similar? Use story details to support your ideas.

 GO ON

10. C is correct. *A is incorrect because Helen's beauty is not ordinary like a dandelion. B is incorrect because Maud Martha does not pity Helen but rather envies her for the beauty that makes her so easy to love. D is incorrect because Maud Martha finds Helen very beautiful.*

11. A is correct. *Maud Martha does many chores, and the boy in "Powder" is concerned about getting home in time for dinner. B is incorrect because neither one is carefree most of the time. C is incorrect because the boy in "Powder" does not mention a sister. D can be eliminated because the narrator does not mention Maud Martha's parents or any disagreement with them.*

Written Response

Possible short responses:

12. *I get a clearer picture of Maud Martha. I picture her as plain or "common" but pleasing to look at, since she compares herself to an "everyday" dandelion, which she considers pretty in a "demure" way (lines 9–11). She is not graceful like her sister (lines 18–20).*

13. *The father wants to make his son feel that they are both working toward the same goal, that of getting through the snow to keep a promise to the mother. His words show both an awareness of his rebellious side and his desire to be close to his son.*

Possible extended response:

14. *The response should contrast the boy's caution, sense of responsibility, and tendency to think ahead with the father's risk taking, breaking of rules, and inclination to follow his whims. Similarities might include a mutual interest in skiing, a pleasure in joking with each other, and a strong desire to please the mother and be a family. Answers should include examples, such as dialogue, actions, thoughts, feelings, and the narrator's direct comments.*

DIFFERENTIATED INSTRUCTION

FOR ENGLISH LEARNERS

Test-Taking Strategies: Understanding Instructions Read aloud the eight sets of test instructions on pages 294–297.

- Explain words such as *excerpt* ("part of a story") and *passage* ("text").
- Have students locate the passages and text referred to in each set of instructions.
- For the longer sets, model answering one question, and then have students demonstrate answering a second question.

Vocabulary

1. **C is correct.** *Because the context involves skiing, which is a sport,* gear *must mean "equipment for a sport."* A, B, *and* D *have nothing to do with skiing.*

2. **A is correct.** *Skiing down a snowy hill, the boy could possibly see the track of an animal, as in B, or something that hangs loosely, as in C. However, A is the best answer because the boy would be more concerned with seeing the course or path. The word* see *in the sentence helps to eliminate* D, *because a chain of consequences cannot be seen.*

3. **A is correct.** *The word* her *suggests that the arms are Maud Martha's own limbs, not those of an animal, as in B, or of a large mass, as in C. The word* fling *helps to eliminate* D *because power or authority cannot be physically moved.*

4. **B is correct.** *Although hands and feet are aspects of Helen (D), the meaning of* ways *relates more to the actions of the hands and feet. The words* lashes, grace, hands, *and* feet *help to eliminate* A *and* C *because they do not refer to a road or specific directions.*

5. **A is correct.** Iris *is the best answer. As goddess of the rainbow,* Iris *is, by definition, colorful. We can eliminate* B *and* D *because* aster *and* Narcissus *have no connection to the eye, and* C *because* Lotus-eater *has no connection to a flower or the eye.*

6. **D is correct.** *Love of self is mentioned in relation to Narcissus. We can eliminate* A *because love of bright colors relates to Iris;* B, *because astronomy relates to the word* aster; *and* C, *because excessive love of food relates to none of the terms.*

7. **B is correct.** *Since* dis- *means "the opposite of" and* aster *is a word for a star, the word* disastrous *must mean something like "under an unlucky star."*

Vocabulary

DIRECTIONS *Use your knowledge of multiple-meaning words to answer the questions below.*

1. Which meaning of the word *gear* is used in the sentence below?

   The skiers gathered up their <u>gear</u> after the last ski run.
   A the harness for a horse
   B part of a car's transmission
   C equipment for a sport
   D a sailor's personal effects

2. Which meaning of *trail* is used in the sentence below from "Powder"?

   By now I couldn't see the <u>trail</u>.
   A a course or path
   B a scent or track of an animal
   C something that hangs loosely
   D a chain of consequences

3. Which meaning of *arm* is used in the part of a sentence below from "Maud Martha"?

   . . . and either fling her <u>arms</u> or want to fling her <u>arms</u> . . .
   A an upper limb of the human body
   B a forelimb of an animal
   C something branching out from a large mass
   D power or authority

4. Which meaning of *ways* is used in the sentence below from "Maud Martha"?

   But oh, the long lashes, the grace, the little <u>ways</u> with the hands and feet.
   A roads or paths
   B courses of action
   C specific directions
   D aspects or features

DIRECTIONS *Use the following Greek terms to help you answer the questions below.*

Item	Description
Iris	the Greek goddess of the rainbow
aster	a flower named after the Greek word for a star
Lotus-eaters	characters in the *Odyssey* who lost their memories when they ate lotus plants
Narcissus	a mythological person who fell in love with his reflection and turned into a flower

5. Which term is used for both a colorful flower and the colored part of the eye?
   A iris
   B aster
   C Lotus-eater
   D Narcissus

6. Narcissism is
   A a love of bright colors
   B a love of astronomy
   C an excessive love of food
   D an excessive love of oneself

7. Since the Latin prefix *dis-* can mean "the opposite of," what might *disastrous* mean?
   A colorless
   B under an unlucky star
   C having an excellent memory
   D hating one's reflection

DIFFERENTIATED INSTRUCTION

FOR ENGLISH LEARNERS

Review Academic Vocabulary On the board, list the academic vocabulary shown in italics. Then give the examples in random order and have students classify them. Elicit additional examples from students.

- *first-person point of view:* "My name is Manuel but everyone calls me The Man. I like that."
- *third-person point of view:* "Chin wondered why her friend wasn't invited."
- *character traits:* sweet; witty; mean; sneaky; brave
- *narrator:* the person telling a story

Writing & Grammar

DIRECTIONS *Read the following passage and then answer the questions.*

(1) Mary Kingsley was an Englishwoman born in 1862. (2) She spent years traveling in Africa. (3) Her family expected her to stay home to care for her mother and younger brother. (4) Her mother was sick at the time. (5) Her parents died in 1892. (6) After their deaths, she went to West Africa. (7) Kingsley hacked through jungles in the heat. (8) Even then, she dressed like a proper English matron. (9) She always wore a dress made out of thick fabric. (10) She also wore boots and a hat. (11) Once she fell onto the spikes of an animal trap. (12) "It is at these moments you realize the blessings of a good thick skirt," she wrote later.

1. Choose the best way to rewrite sentences 1 and 2, using an adjective clause. Choose D if no change is needed.

   A Mary Kingsley, an Englishwoman, was born in 1862 and spent years traveling in Africa.

   B Born in 1862, Mary Kingsley was an Englishwoman who spent years traveling in Africa.

   C Mary Kingsley was an Englishwoman. Born in 1862, she spent years traveling in Africa.

   D No change is needed.

2. Choose the best way to vary the beginnings of sentences 3–5. Choose D if no change is needed.

   A Kingsley's family expected her to stay home to care for her mother and younger brother. Kingsley's mother was sick at the time. Kingsley's parents died in 1892.

   B Kingsley's family expected her to stay home to care for her mother and younger brother. Her mother was sick at the time. In 1892, her parents died.

   C Her family expected her to stay home to care for her mother and younger brother. Mary's mother was sick at the time. Mary's parents died in 1892.

   D No change is needed.

3. Choose the best way to rewrite sentences 6 and 7, using an adjective clause. Choose D if no change is needed.

   A After their deaths, Kingsley went to West Africa, where she hacked through jungles in the heat.

   B After their deaths, she went to West Africa. There, Kingsley hacked through jungles in the heat.

   C After their deaths, she went to West Africa and hacked through jungles in the heat.

   D No change is needed.

4. Choose the best way to rewrite sentences 9–10, using precise adjectives. Choose D if no change is needed.

   A She always wore a flowing black dress made out of thick fabric. She also wore buttoned black boots and a wool hat.

   B She always wore a long dress made out of thick fabric. She also wore black boots and a hat.

   C She always dressed all in black: long skirt, boots, and a hat.

   D No change is needed.

STOP

297

ANSWERS

Writing & Grammar

1. **B is correct.** *The words "who spent years traveling in Africa" are an adjective clause. A contains an appositive and two verbs. C contains a participial phrase. The original sentences (D) contain participial phrases.*

2. **B is correct.** *B is the best answer because the three sentences begin with different words. In A, all three sentences begin with the same word,* Kingsley's. *In C, two sentences begin with* Mary's. *In the original (D), all three sentences begin with* Her.

3. **A is correct.** *The words "where she hacked through jungles in the heat" are an adjective clause. Neither B nor C includes a clause that is not independent. The original sentences (D) contain only independent clauses.*

4. **A is correct.** *A is the best answer because it includes the precise adjectives* flowing black, thick, buttoned black, *and* wool. *B and C do not include the adjectives* flowing, buttoned, *and* wool. *The original sentences (D) contain only one adjective,* thick.

FOR ENGLISH LEARNERS

Assessment Support: Adjectives and Adjective Clauses

- Remind students that adjectives modify nouns and pronouns. An adjective clause is a subordinate clause that functions as an adjective. It is introduced by a word such as *who, whom, which,* or *that.*

- Have students identify the adjectives in lines 9–11 of "Powder" and the nouns they modify.

- Then write this sentence on the board, and have students identify the adjective clause: *The father appeared to listen to the trooper* <u>*who had stopped the car.*</u>

INTRODUCE *GREAT READS*

In Unit 2, students have discussed a number of big questions. Invite students to tell which question they found most intriguing and why, and then focus attention on the three that appear on this page. Discuss the recommended books and their summaries, pointing out how each connects to the related question. Encourage students to choose one or more of these "great reads" to read independently.

ⓘ ClassZone.com

To find additional books that match students' interests and ability levels, visit the Literature Center at **ClassZone.com.**

Ideas for Independent Reading

What makes a character grow and change? How many ways can you define strength? Find out by reading these additional works.

Are you a perfectionist?

Into the Wild
by Jon Krakauer

This true account of an idealistic young man tells of his wish to give up the trappings of wealth and privilege. He leaves a comfortable life to live a simple one in the wilderness. And he almost makes it.

The Chosen
by Chaim Potok

Two neighbor boys live with different sets of parental expectations. Reuven, the narrator, slowly comes to understand the weight of responsibility that rests on his best friend Danny's shoulders.

Pride and Prejudice
by Jane Austen

The mother of five daughters Mrs. Bennet wants to find the perfect husband for each of them. As you read this Jane Austen novel, see if Mrs. Bennet and her daughters need to compromise their rather unrealistic standards.

How important is status?

The Outsiders
by S. E. Hinton

In this classic young-adult novel, the "greasers" are the poor kids' gang and the "socs" are a gang of rich kids. Tragedy forces Ponyboy, a greaser, to change the way he lives.

A Connecticut Yankee in King Arthur's Court
by Mark Twain

Hank Morgan lives in 19th-century Connecticut. After a head injury he wakes up in the England of King Arthur, where he is definitely not one of the privileged. Twain's social satire is still relevant to today's world.

Kaffir Boy
by Mark Mathabane

This is the true story of a black youth's coming of age under the apartheid policy in South Africa.

When is strength more than muscle?

Finding Fish
by Antwone Fisher

Fisher's autobiography tells of his life in a foster home, where he was humiliated and abused. Fisher escaped, first into the navy and then into a life of writing, where his talent flourished. His award-winning screenplay *Antwone Fisher* became a feature film.

Coming of Age in Mississippi
by Anne Moody

Moody's autobiographical classic describes her childhood in the Mississippi of the 1950s. She was unwilling to accept the racist world of that time and challenged it through her work in the civil rights movement.

O Pioneers!
by Willa Cather

After her father dies, Alexandra inherits the family farm—over the protests of her brothers. She struggles to overcome tragedy and hardship while keeping her family together and forging a living on the hard Nebraska prairie.

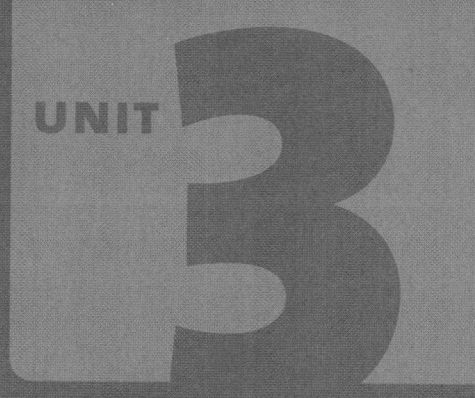

UNIT 3

A Sense of Place

SETTING, MOOD, AND IMAGERY

- In Fiction
- In Media
- In Nonfiction
- In Poetry

299

About the Art This photograph depicts the Catacomb of Saint Callisto, Rome, Italy. See also page 349.

For help in planning this unit, see

 RESOURCE MANAGER UNIT 3
pp. 1–11

INTRODUCE THE UNIT

A hospital emergency room, a school basketball court, a colony of humans on Mars—these are places where we can imagine stories happening. Ask students to share a few impressions of these places. Then have them focus on the places pictured on this page. Ask

- How would you describe each place?
- What detail or element in each picture catches your attention the most? Why?
- What emotions do you feel as you look at each place? Why?
- What events can you imagine happening in each place?

Explain that students have just been thinking about **setting, mood,** and **imagery**—three elements that they will explore as they read the selections in this unit. Students will learn how these elements combine to create vivid, believable worlds in both factual writing and fiction.

Skills Trace

SKILLS STRAND	Literary Analysis Workshop: Setting, Mood, and Imagery pp. 302–307	A Christmas Memory pp. 308–325 Short Story *Level: Average*	Through the Tunnel pp. 326–341 Short Story *Level: Average*	The Cask of Amontillado pp. 342–355 Short Story *Level: Challenging*	Media Study: *from* The Cask of Amontillado pp. 356–359 Film Clip
Literary Analysis	Setting pp. 302–303, 306–307 Imagery and Mood pp. 304–305, 306–307	Details of Setting pp. 309, 310, 314, 319, 321, 323	Setting as Symbol pp. 327, 330, 335, 339	Mood pp. 343, 346, 348, 351, 353	
Reading and Informational Texts	Analyze the Literature pp. 303, 305, 306–307	Analyze Imagery pp. 309, 313, 314, 317, 323 Review: Make Inferences pp. 312, 314, 317, 319, 322	Analyze Details pp. 327, 328, 330, 332, 335, 339 Review: Draw Conclusions pp. 332, 334	Paraphrase pp. 343, 344, 351, 353 Review: Make Inferences pp. 347, 353 Read a Book Excerpt p. 352	
Vocabulary	Academic Vocabulary pp. 302, 304	Word Acquisition pp. 309, T309, 324 Context Clues p. T309 Connotation and Denotation p. 324	Word Acquisition pp. 327, T327, 340 Context Clues p. T327 Latin Roots (*quest, quer, quisit*) p. 340	Word Acquisition pp. 343, T343, 354 Context Clues p. T343 Latin Roots (*clud*) p. 354	Academic Vocabulary (Film) p. 357
Writing, Grammar, and Style		Word Choice pp. 316, 325 Verb Tense pp. 316, 325	Conciseness pp. 331, 341 Compound Predicates pp. 331, 341	Formal Language pp. 348, 355	
Speaking, Listening, Viewing, and Media	Discuss pp. 302–305	Discuss pp. 308, T310–T322, 323 Analyze Visuals pp. 310, T312, T315, 316, T318, T321	Discuss pp. 326, T328–T338, 339 Analyze Visuals pp. 328, 332, T336	Discuss pp. 342, T344–T352, 353 Analyze Visuals pp. 344, 349, T350	Discuss pp. 356, 359 Evaluate Film Techniques Used to Create Setting and Mood pp. 357–359 Compare Film and Written Versions of a Story p. 359 Create a Production Design Board p. 359

Assessment-Based Planning: Skills in red are assessed on the Unit 3 Test. **T** = Teacher's Edition page

from **A Walk in the Woods** pp. 360–371	**Wilderness Letter** pp. 372–377	**The Sharks/The Peace of Wild Things** pp. 378–383	**Writing Workshop: Short Story** pp. 384–391	Skills Assessed on the Unit 3 Test:
Travel Narrative *Level: Average*	Letter *Level: Average*	Poems *Level: Average*		**Literary Analysis** • Identify details of setting • Analyze setting and its impact on conflict • Identify and analyze imagery • Identify mood and analyze ways writers convey mood • Understand setting as symbol
Setting and Mood pp. 361, 362, 364, 368, 370		Imagery and Mood pp. 379, 380, 383		
Identify Author's Perspective pp. 361, 362, 366, 370 Review: Cause and Effect p. 364 Review: Make Inferences p. 369	Read and Analyze a Primary Source pp. 372–377 Cite Evidence p. 377	Connect pp. 379, 382, 383	Analyze a Short Story pp. 385–386, 390	**Reading and Informational Texts** • Analyze details • Paraphrase • Identify author's perspective • Cite evidence
Word Acquisition pp. 361, T361, 371 Context Clues pp. T361, 371				**Vocabulary** • Understand and use connotative and denotative meanings of words • Use context clues to unlock word meaning
			Write a Short Story pp. 387–390 Descriptive Details pp. 384, 385, 390 Prepositional Phrases p. 390	**Writing, Grammar, and Style** • Write a short story • Use dialogue to develop characters' personalities • Write in the present tense for effect • Use compound predicates to write concisely • Use descriptive details • Use prepositional phrases to add important details • Additional writing and grammar skills
Discuss pp. 360, T362–T369, 370 Analyze Visuals pp. 362, T365, T369	Discuss pp. 372, T373–T376, 377	Discuss pp. 378, T380–T382, 383 Analyze Visuals pp. 380, T382	Discuss pp. 384–386, 390 Create a Video Presentation p. 391	

Linked selections

For additional lesson planning help, see **Easy Planner DVD.**

OBJECTIVES

- establish prior knowledge about **settings**
- discuss ways to travel without leaving home

How can you TRAVEL without leaving home?

To introduce the page, ask the question and have students read the paragraph. Then have them think of two settings: a familiar one in which they probably would feel very comfortable (for example, their best friend's home) and an unfamiliar one in which they might feel very uncomfortable (for example, a concert hall for a performance of music that they dislike). Ask students to make some notes about sights, sounds, and other sensory details that they associate with each setting.

ACTIVITY Call on volunteers to share their responses. Discuss which details and images provided them with an especially strong sense of place. Help students draw the conclusion that in a well-presented setting, vivid images and accurate details work together to create a believable world—even if the setting is imaginary—and a specific mood.

CHECK UNDERSTANDING Have students define the term **setting** and explain how setting is related to imagery and mood.

How can you TRAVEL without leaving home?

We can experience the sights and sounds of a war-torn country long ago or a bustling city in the modern day. We can visit any place in the world—past, present, or future—because talented writers transport us to **settings** we have never seen and can only imagine.

ACTIVITY Recall a story you have read or a film you have viewed that you felt transported you to another place or time period. Concentrate on the setting of the story and think about all the ways in which the writer or director brought the setting to life. Then answer the following questions:

- How was the time period suggested?
- What details were used to portray the location?
- What information made the setting vivid and engaging?
- If the setting was completely imaginary, how was it made believable?

Unit Resources

- **R** RESOURCE MANAGER UNIT 3
- **B** BEST PRACTICES TOOLKIT
- **S** STANDARDS LESSON FILE

- *@* Easy Planner DVD-ROM
- *@* Write*Smart* CD-ROM
- *i* ClassZone.com
- *@* Audio Anthology CD
- *i* Multi-Language Academic Vocabulary Online

- *@* eEdition DVD-ROM & Online
- *i* McDougal Littell Assessment System
- *@* Test Generator CD
- *@* Media*Smart* DVD-ROM

 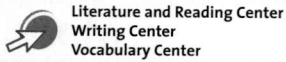
Preview Unit Goals

LITERARY ANALYSIS	• Identify and analyze setting and its impact on conflict and character
	• Identify and analyze imagery
	• Identify mood and analyze ways in which writers convey mood
READING	• Analyze details
	• Paraphrase
	• Make inferences
	• Identify author's perspective
	• Distinguish between primary and secondary sources
WRITING AND GRAMMAR	• Write a short story
	• Bring immediacy to writing by choosing an effective verb tense
	• Write concisely by using compound predicates
SPEAKING, LISTENING, AND VIEWING	• Create a video presentation
	• View and interpret a film production
	• Analyze how film and design techniques convey meaning
VOCABULARY	• Use context clues to unlock meaning
	• Understand and use connotative and denotative meanings of words
ACADEMIC VOCABULARY	• connotation and denotation • primary and secondary sources
	• imagery • setting
	• mood • symbol
	• paraphrase

301

Preview Unit Goals

This page introduces the major skills and strategies that this unit will cover. Have students preview the categories and skills, making note of the color-coding that identifies each strand throughout the unit.

Remind students to copy the Academic Vocabulary into their journals. Throughout the unit, model using the vocabulary. Have students use it in discussions and in writing, as well. By the end of the unit, students should have developed a clear, accurate, and useful definition of each term.

ADDITIONAL UNIT GOALS

These skills will be taught in this unit but are not the major focus of the unit:

Literary Analysis
- Analyze setting as symbol
- Genre study: short story, travel narrative, poetry, primary source, letter

Reading
- Connect to personal experience
- Cite evidence

Writing and Grammar
- Use formal language appropriately
- Maintain a consistent point of view
- Use active voice
- Use dialogue to reveal characters
- Use descriptive details and prepositional phrases that add important details

Speaking, Listening, and Viewing
- Analyze visuals

Vocabulary
- Use word roots to help unlock meaning
- Understand and use word families

DIFFERENTIATED INSTRUCTION

FOR ENGLISH LEARNERS

Academic Vocabulary Use the copy master to help students learn the Academic Vocabulary listed on this page.

1. Read aloud each term. Have students find it on their copy master.

2. Discuss the meanings or examples shown, and complete the chart as a class.

3. Have students work in small groups to complete the remaining activities.

Additional Academic Vocabulary Use the copy master to help students learn academic words they will use in subsequent lessons and on the Assessment Practice. Follow the same procedure as for the Academic Vocabulary copy master.

 RESOURCE MANAGER—Copy Masters
Academic Vocabulary p. 9
Additional Academic Vocabulary p. 10

OBJECTIVES

- identify and analyze setting and its effect on characters, conflict, and mood
- identify and analyze setting as symbol
- identify and analyze imagery and its effect on mood
- identify and analyze mood

Teach

Part 1: Setting

Setting To introduce the topic of setting, ask students to list details identifying the time and place of a well-known book or movie. Remind students that setting includes when a story takes place as well as *where* it takes place. For example, the characters and events in a story set in the Great Plains in the late 19th century will be different from characters and events in a story set in the Great Plains today. Next, focus on ideas associated with seasons, certain times of day, historical periods, and places by having students complete a chart such as the one shown here.

Time, Place	Association
fall	harvest, increasing darkness
dawn	fresh starts, the beginning
1849 Gold Rush	adventure, hope, trust
Los Angeles	creativity, urban sprawl

Role of Setting Review how setting can

- influence character: Ask students how being in a war might affect one's character.
- create conflicts: Ask students what conflicts occur in their lives that did not occur in the lives of students in the early 1900s.
- serve as a symbol: Have students tell what these settings might represent—a jungle, a tower, a futuristic laboratory.

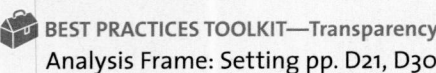 **BEST PRACTICES TOOLKIT—Transparency** Analysis Frame: Setting pp. D21, D30

Setting, Mood, and Imagery

A good story is much more than the events that happen or the conflicts between characters. When and where a story takes place also affects your reading experience. Consider, for example, a story about two lost hikers who are fighting for survival. It's the setting details—the towering trees, the stark winter sky, and the approaching snowstorm—that make you care about the conflict. By creating an unforgettable setting, a writer seizes your imagination and whisks you into the world of a story.

Part 1: Setting

You know that the **setting** of a story is the time and place in which the action occurs. The time could be a particular year, a specific season, a time of day, or a historical period. The place could be anywhere—from a bustling ancient city to a deserted tropical island.

In addition to describing the time and location of a story, setting details often reveal information about the characters' lives, their occupations, and their beliefs. Setting may also play a more active role by creating conflicts for the characters or by influencing their decisions and lifestyles.

ROLE OF SETTING	EXAMPLE SETTING
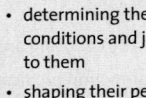 **Setting can influence characters by** • determining the living conditions and jobs available to them • shaping their personalities, their dreams, and their values	**A poor, drought-stricken Midwestern farm town in the 1930s** Despite months of grueling work, Joe's crops are failing again. Realizing that his life may never improve, he becomes bitter and angry.
 **Setting can create conflicts by** • exposing the characters to dangerous weather, such as a storm or a drought • making characters endure a difficult time period, such as the Great Depression	The drought has lasted seven years, and most of the farms are failing. People have begun to sell their most prized possessions because they need money. Recently, Mrs. Wilkes sold her wedding band to buy shoes for her daughter.
 **Setting can serve as a symbol by** • representing an important idea • representing a character's hopes, future, or predicament	Some people have planted a small flower garden in the town square. The garden is a symbol of their hope that their community can still thrive.

DIFFERENTIATED INSTRUCTION

For general guidelines on differentiating instruction, see

 BEST PRACTICES TOOLKIT Differentiated Instruction pp. 31–38

FOR LESS–PROFICIENT READERS

Note Taking For students who need help with note taking, hand out the note-taking copy master before discussing the page. Then have students read silently the first paragraph under "Part 1: Setting." As you discuss the main points on this page, have students record them on the copy master.

 RESOURCE MANAGER—Copy Master Note Taking p. 15

MODEL 1: SETTING AND CHARACTERS

Nervous Conditions takes place in a British colony in Africa during the 1960s. Nhamo has left his village to attend school at a mission. How has this opportunity affected him?

from Nervous **Conditions**

Novel by **Tsitsi Dangarembga**

. . . Nhamo was forced once a year to return to his squalid homestead, where he washed in cold water in an enamel basin or a flowing river, not in a bathtub with taps gushing hot water and cold; where he ate *sadza* regularly with his fingers and meat hardly at all, never with a knife or fork; where there was no
5 light beyond the flickering yellow of candles and homemade paraffin lamps to enable him to escape into his books when the rest of us had gone to bed.

All this poverty began to offend him, or at the very least to embarrass him after he went to the mission, in a way that it had not done before.

Close Read

1. Identify two details that help you understand Nhamo's life in both settings—the mission and the homestead. An example has been boxed.

2. How has Nhamo's experience at the mission influenced his perception of life on the homestead?

MODEL 2: SETTING AND CONFLICT

In George Orwell's novel *1984*, the country is run by a government that monitors citizens' every move and demands loyalty to its leader—Big Brother. As you read this excerpt, pay attention to the description of this society. How might the setting create conflicts for the characters?

from **1984**

Novel by **George Orwell**

Outside, even through the shut window pane, the world looked cold. Down in the street little eddies of wind were whirling dust and torn paper into spirals, and though the sun was shining and the sky a harsh blue, there seemed to be no color in anything except the posters that were plastered everywhere.
5 The black-mustachio'd face gazed down from every commanding corner. There was one on the house front immediately opposite. BIG BROTHER IS WATCHING YOU, the caption said, while the dark eyes looked deep into Winston's own. Down at street level another poster, torn at one corner, flapped fitfully in the wind. . . . In the far distance a helicopter skimmed down between
10 the roofs, hovered for an instant like a blue-bottle, and darted away again with a curving flight. It was the Police Patrol, snooping into people's windows. The patrols did not matter, however. Only the Thought Police mattered.

Close Read

1. In what kind of world does this story take place? Identify four details that help you visualize the setting. One has been boxed.

2. What conflicts might this society create for Winston and other citizens? Explain your answer.

MODEL 1: SETTING AND CHARACTERS

Close Read

1. *Possible answer: Two details that help readers understand Nhamo's life in both settings are: "where he ate sadza regularly with his fingers [home], never with a knife and fork" [as he does at school] and "where there was no light beyond the flickering yellow of candles and homemade paraffin lamps [home] to enable him to escape into his books" [as he does at school, with ample light].*

2. *Possible answer: Readers learn that Nhamo is now offended and embarrassed by the "squalid" conditions of his family's homestead. Students may say that living in better conditions at the mission probably opened Nhamo's eyes to "all this poverty" at home.*

MODEL 2: SETTING AND CONFLICT

Close Read

1. *Possible answer: The story takes place in an eerie and unsettling world. Four of the details that help readers visualize the setting are "eddies of wind were whirling dust and torn paper into spirals" (lines 2–3); "though the sun was shining and the sky a harsh blue, there seemed to be no color in anything" (lines 3–4); "the dark eyes looked deep into Winston's own" (lines 7–8); "snooping into people's windows" (line 11).*

2. *Possible answer: People are probably unable to live freely and do what they want. They have to operate as if their every move is being watched and monitored. This could create major conflicts. People must choose between following the rules and doing what they want at the risk of getting caught.*

FOR LESS-PROFICIENT READERS

Illustrate Setting Have students quickly sketch the scene or part of the scene from the *1984* excerpt. Then ask them to imagine themselves in the scene and to discuss how the setting might affect them. Guide them to focus on conflicts that they might feel.

FOR ENGLISH LEARNERS

Language: Skill Words On the board, list the academic vocabulary shown in italics. Then give the examples in random order for students to classify.

- *setting*: mountaintop; beach; classroom
- *conflict*: fight between friends; desire to leave home and to please parents
- *symbol*: flag; sword; heart

Teach

Part 2: Imagery and Mood
IMAGERY

Sensory Details Tell students that sensory details help a reader create images, or pictures, in his or her mind. The more precise a writer's details, the better a reader is able to form mental images of story characters, settings, and events. As students read the models on pages 303–307, have them look for details that appeal to the senses and record them in a chart like this.

Sense	Detail
Sight	
Hearing	
Smell	
Taste	
Touch	

MOOD

Mood Point out that imagery and setting combine to create the mood in the picture. For additional practice, display another image—such as a forest in spring, an abandoned city street, or a lavish, busy dining room—and elicit the sensory details that combine to create a single mood, such as hope, despair, or festivity.

CHECK UNDERSTANDING

Have partners write a short description of a scene at school using sensory details that create a mood.

Part 2: Imagery and Mood

To create a setting that stays with you long after a story ends, a writer paints pictures with words. With the right choice of details and language, a writer can transport you to any scene and affect how you feel about a story.

IMAGERY

Imagery consists of words and phrases that recreate sensory experiences for readers. Rather than describing every aspect of a setting, a writer may use **sensory details**—words and phrases that appeal to the senses of sight, hearing, smell, taste, and touch—to help you visualize a scene. For example, in the *1984* excerpt on the previous page, Orwell uses phrases like these to appeal to the senses of sight and hearing:

- *"eddies of wind were whirling dust"*
- *"another poster . . . flapped fitfully in the wind"*

Armed with these details, your imagination fills in the rest of the scene. While Orwell does not mention anxious people and wailing sirens, you can picture these details as part of the setting.

MOOD

A writer also uses imagery and setting details to create the **mood,** or atmosphere, of a story. Whether it is lighthearted, hopeful, or mysterious, a story's mood can affect your emotional reaction to the characters and events. For example, the bleak, eerie mood established in *1984* might prompt you to sympathize with the characters as you are drawn into their unsettling world.

How do the sensory details in the graphic convey a mood of terror and fear?

SIGHT: "Flashes of lightning illuminated the ink-black sky."

TOUCH: "Another cobweb stuck to her cold, clammy skin."

TASTE: "She could not get the metallic taste of fear out of her mouth."

SOUND: "Her heart thumped wildly when she heard an ominous scratching on the door."

SMELL: "The foul smell of dead mice hung in the air."

304

MODEL 1: IMAGERY

This excerpt is from a chilling story by H. P. Lovecraft, a master of horror and suspense. As you read, pay attention to the sensory details he uses to describe an unusual street.

from

The Music *of* Erich Zann

Short story by **H. P. Lovecraft**

The Rue d'Auseil lay across a dark river bordered by precipitous brick blear-windowed warehouses and spanned by a ponderous bridge of dark stone. It was always shadowy along that river, as if the smoke of neighboring factories shut out the sun perpetually. The river was also odorous with evil stenches
5 which I have never smelled elsewhere. . . . Beyond that bridge were narrow cobbled streets with rails; and then came the ascent, at first gradual, but incredibly steep as the Rue d'Auseil was reached.
I have never seen another street as narrow and steep as the Rue d'Auseil. It was almost a cliff, closed to vehicles, consisting in several places of flights
10 of steps, and ending at the top in a lofty ivied wall. Its paving was irregular, sometimes stone slabs, sometimes cobblestones, and sometimes bare earth with struggling greenish-grey vegetation. The houses were tall, peaked-roofed, incredibly old, and crazily leaning backward, forward, and sidewise.

Close Read

1. The boxed detail appeals to the sense of smell. Find three more details and identify the sense each one appeals to.

2. What mood does this setting create? Point out specific examples of imagery that contributes directly to the mood.

MODEL 2: MOOD

The imagery in this excerpt evokes a very different atmosphere. Notice the specific sensory details that contribute to the mood.

from

Their Eyes Were Watching God

Novel by **Zora Neale Hurston**

It was a spring afternoon in West Florida. Janie had spent most of the day under a blossoming pear tree in the back-yard. She had been spending every minute that she could steal from her chores under that tree for the last three days. That was to say, ever since the first tiny bloom had opened. It had called her to
5 come and gaze on a mystery. From barren brown stems to glistening leaf-buds; from the leaf-buds to snowy virginity of bloom. It stirred her tremendously.

Close Read

1. How would you describe the mood of this excerpt?

2. Find four details that help to convey the mood. One has been boxed.

MODEL 1: IMAGERY
Close Read

1. ***Possible answer:*** *Sight: "a dark river bordered by precipitous brick blear-windowed warehouses" (lines 1–2); sight and smell: "shadowy along that river, as if the smoke of neighboring factories shut out the sun perpetually" (lines 3–4); sight: "the houses were tall, peaked-roofed . . . crazily leaning backward, forward, and sidewise" (lines 12–13).*

2. ***Possible answer:*** *The mood created by the setting is eerie and ominous. Examples of imagery contributing to this mood: "odorous with evil stenches" (line 4); "sometimes bare earth with struggling greenish-grey vegetation" (lines 11–12); and "the houses were tall, peaked-roofed . . . crazily leaning backward, forward, and sidewise" (lines 12–13).*

If students need help . . . To reinforce that every detail has meaning, examine choices made by the writer:

- "precipitous . . . warehouses" instead of small, cozy houses on gently rolling hills
- a "lofty ivied wall" instead of a fragrant garden path
- "struggling greenish-grey vegetation" instead of delicate pink flowers

MODEL 2: MOOD
Close Read

1. ***Possible answer:*** *The mood might be described as wondrous, uplifting, or hopeful.*

2. ***Possible answer:*** *Four details that convey mood are "spring afternoon", (line 1), "first tiny bloom", (line 2), "from barren brown stems to glistening leaf-buds", (line 5), and "it stirred her tremendously", (line 6).*

DIFFERENTIATED INSTRUCTION

FOR ENGLISH LEARNERS

Comprehension: Analysis To help students comprehend Model 1, explain that the prepositions *across, along,* and *beyond* tell *where* and enable readers to visualize the setting. Draw a wavy line, label it "dark river," and draw the Rue d'Auseil *across* it. Then have students point out the location of shadows or smoke *along* the river (line 3) and the narrow cobbled streets *beyond* it (lines 5–6).

Practice and Apply

Part 1: Analyze the Literature
Close Read

1. **Possible answer:** *The introduction says that the setting is in the mountains of New Mexico. Details reveal that the setting is near ranches and a cowboy camp, during the late afternoon in summer when the temperature is fairly hot. The narrator is a cowboy or ranch hand who spends his evenings with other cowboys after a hard day of work.*

2. **Possible answer:** *Images include "the forests were fresh, green, and gay" (line 8); "the cattle moved slowly, fat and sleek in the August sun and shadow" (lines 8–9); "the sun was setting behind me in a riot of streaks and colors" (lines 13–14); "deep, harmonious silence" (line 14). These details create a mood of laziness and calm.*

3. **Possible answer:** *The mood changes from calm to intense excitement and even mystery. Words or phrases conveying this change include "a deafening quiet" (line 16), "comes to a standstill" (line 16), and "sun flares hotly" (line 17).*

   If students need help . . . Reread lines 8–14. Have students find details that point to the relaxed or sleepy mood, including words like *drowsy, lethargy,* and *dozing.* Then ask how "a deafening quiet" is different from a sleepy feeling.

4. **Possible answer:** *Exclamation points let the reader know that the narrator is excited to see the horse and that spotting the Wonder Horse is a rare occurrence. Details such as "pride, prestige, and art incarnate in animal flesh" and "an ideal" show that the narrator is enthralled by the beauty and intrigue of the horse. The words* statue *and* engraving *emphasize the narrator's perception of the horse as a work of art.*

Part 3: Analyze the Literature

Using what you've learned in this workshop, analyze setting, mood, and imagery in these two short story excerpts.

The first excerpt is from a story that takes place in the mountains of New Mexico, where people tell tales about a legendary white horse that roams the wild. As you read, notice the details that the writer uses to describe the setting and create a distinct mood.

from

My Wonder Horse

Short story by **Sabine R. Ulibarrí**

I was fifteen years old. Although I had never seen the Wonder Horse, he filled my imagination and fired my ambition. I used to listen open-mouthed as my father and the ranch hands talked about the phantom horse who turned into mist and air and nothingness when he was trapped. I joined in the universal obsession—like the hope of winning the lottery—of putting my lasso on him some day, of capturing him and showing him off on Sunday afternoons when the girls of the town strolled through the streets.

It was high summer. The forests were fresh, green, and gay. The cattle moved slowly, fat and sleek in the August sun and shadow. Listless and drowsy in the lethargy of late afternoon, I was dozing on my horse. It was time to round up the herd and go back to the good bread of the cowboy camp. Already my comrades would be sitting around the campfire, playing the guitar, telling stories of past or present, or surrendering to the languor of the late afternoon. The sun was setting behind me in a riot of streaks and colors. Deep, harmonious silence.

I sit drowsily still, forgetting the cattle in the glade. Suddenly the forest falls silent, a deafening quiet. The afternoon comes to a standstill. The breeze stops blowing, but it vibrates. The sun flares hotly. The planet, life, and time itself have stopped in an inexplicable way. For a moment, I don't understand what is happening.

Then my eyes focus. There he is! The Wonder Horse! At the end of the glade, on high ground surrounded by summer green. He is a statue. He is an engraving. Line and form and white stain on a green background. Pride, prestige, and art incarnate in animal flesh. A picture of burning beauty and virile freedom. An ideal, pure and invincible, rising from the eternal dreams of humanity. Even today my being thrills when I remember him.

Close Read

1. Describe the setting in this excerpt. Find details that reveal the season, the weather, and the narrator's lifestyle.

2. Find four examples of imagery in lines 8–14. One has been boxed. What mood do these details create?

3. How does the mood change in lines 15–19? Find three words or phrases that convey this change.

4. Which details in lines 20–25 help you understand how the narrator feels about the horse? Explain.

DIFFERENTIATED INSTRUCTION

FOR LESS—PROFICIENT READERS
Analysis Support: Setting and Mood

1. Have students reread lines 8–10, one sentence at a time. As they read the sentences, write on the board the words that provide clues to the time of the setting: *summer, August,* and *late afternoon.*

2. Have partners complete a Two-Column Chart with words and phrases that demonstrate the change in mood. Have them label the headings of their chart

Before and *After.* Refer them to lines 8–14 for the beginning mood and lines 20–25 for the ending mood.

 BEST PRACTICES TOOLKIT—Transparency Two-Column Chart p. A25

Now read this excerpt, taken from a story that is based on an experience from the writer's life. In 1897, Crane was a passenger on a ship that sank off the coast of Florida. He and three other men rowed back to shore in a flimsy lifeboat. How does Crane's use of imagery help convey a different setting and mood?

from
The
OPEN
BOAT

Short story by **Stephen Crane**

None of them knew the color of the sky. Their eyes glanced level, and were fastened upon the waves that swept toward them. These waves were of the hue of slate, save for the tops, which were of foaming white, and all of the men knew the colors of the sea. The horizon narrowed and
5 widened, and dipped and rose, and at all times its edge was jagged with waves that seemed thrust up in points like rocks.
  Many a man ought to have a bathtub larger than the boat which here rode upon the sea. These waves were most wrongfully and barbarously abrupt and tall, and each froth-top was a problem in small-boat navigation. The cook
10 squatted in the bottom, and looked with both eyes at the six inches of gunwale which separated him from the ocean. His sleeves were rolled over his fat forearms, and the two flaps of his unbuttoned vest dangled as he bent to bail out the boat. Often he said, "That was a narrow clip." As he remarked it he invariably gazed eastward over the broken sea.
15   The oiler, steering with one of the two oars in the boat, sometimes raised himself suddenly to keep clear of water that swirled in over the stern. It was a thin little oar, and it seemed often ready to snap. The correspondent, pulling at the other oar, watched the waves and wondered why he was there.
  The injured captain, lying in the bow, was at this time buried in that
20 profound dejection and indifference which comes, temporarily at least, to even the bravest and most enduring when, willy-nilly, the firm fails, the army loses, the ship goes down.

Close Read

1. Using details from the text, describe the setting as completely as you can.

2. Identify five sensory details. One has been boxed. What senses do they appeal to?

3. How would you describe the mood of this excerpt? Explain how the sensory details you found help to create this mood.

4. In which excerpt does setting play a more important role? Support your opinion with specific details.

Close Read

1. *Possible answer: The setting is a small boat in the ocean during rough weather. The smallness of the boat is shown by the sentence "Many a man ought to have a bathtub larger than the boat" (line 7). The rough water is shown by the phrases "jagged with waves" (line 5) and "barbarously abrupt and tall" (lines 8–9).*

2. *Possible answer: Sight: waves "barbarously abrupt and tall" (lines 8–9) and "sleeves were rolled over his fat forearms" (lines 11–12); sight and touch: "foaming white" (line 3) and "jagged with waves" (line 5); sight and sound: "water that swirled in over the stern" (line 16).*

3. *Possible answer: The mood is one of danger and excitement. Details listed for question 2 emphasize the rough waters and the dangerous situation. Details about the passengers, such as "raised himself suddenly" (lines 15–16), convey a readiness for action.*

4. *Possible answer: The setting plays a more important role in "The Open Boat," because the rough weather causes a life-or-death conflict for the passengers.*

Assess and Reteach

Assess

Have students describe the setting and mood of "My Wonder Horse" and "The Open Boat."

Reteach

For students who are unable to apply the workshop skills to the stories, select from these reteaching options:

- Have students review the information on the note-taking copy masters and choose one skill to describe using a cluster.

- Have students identify the setting and mood of a scene from a recently read story.

FOR LESS–PROFICIENT READERS

Vocabulary Support Introduce these terms from "The Open Boat." Have students use context or structural clues to suggest synonyms.

- *hue* (line 3), "color"
- *thrust* (line 6), "pushed"
- *invariably* (line 14), "always"
- *dejection* (line 20), "hopelessness"

FOR ENGLISH LEARNERS

Vocabulary: Idioms and Sayings Help students use context clues to determine the meanings of these phrases:

- *save for* (line 3), "except"
- *many a man* (line 7), "many men"
- *a narrow clip* (line 13), "an accident that almost happens"
- *keep clear of* (line 16), "stay away from"

Focus and Motivate

OBJECTIVES

Literary Analysis
- explore the key idea of **friendship**
- analyze details of setting
- read a short story

Reading
- analyze imagery

Vocabulary
- build vocabulary for reading and writing
- identify and use connotative meanings of words (also an EL language objective)

Grammar and Writing
- choose effective present or past verb tense
- use writing to analyze literature

SUMMARY

The adult narrator recalls the days leading up to Christmas when he was seven years old and his best friend was an elderly but childlike cousin. As they do every year, Buddy and his friend gather ingredients and bake fruitcakes, cut down a Christmas tree, and make ornaments and gifts. On Christmas Day, they fly the kites they have made for each other. It would be their last Christmas together: Buddy is sent to military school, and his friend dies a few years later.

What do you look for in a FRIEND?

After students have read the cartoon, ask the question and record responses. Then have students read the *KEY IDEA* and discuss how difficult situations can lead to or strengthen **friendships.** Finally, have students complete the *QUICKWRITE* and discuss their insights.

Selection Resources

A Christmas Memory
Short Story by Truman Capote

What do you look for in a FRIEND?

KEY IDEA Think about your current friends as well as friends from the past. What draws you to someone and creates that special bond of **friendship?** Does a friend have to be your age? Do you always share the same interests and values? "A Christmas Memory" shows how important friendship can be to two very different individuals.

QUICKWRITE With a partner, write a "top ten" list of the key qualities you look for in a friend. Then compare your list with those of your classmates. Does everyone list similar qualities? Are physical traits and intellectual or emotional factors equally important?

Top 10 Qualities of a Good Friend
1. Sense of humor
2. Similar interests
3.
4.
5.

PEANUTS.

Peanuts: © United Feature Syndicate, Inc.

308

RESOURCE MANAGER UNIT 3

Plan and Teach pp. 17–24

Literary Analysis
Summary pp. 25†*, 26‡*
Details of Setting pp. 27, 28†*
Question Support p. 35*

Reading
Analyze Imagery pp. 29, 30†*
Reading Check p. 34
Reading Fluency p. 37

Vocabulary
Study p. 31*
Practice p. 32
Strategy p. 33

Grammar and Writing
Choose Effective Verb Tense p. 36

Assessment
Selection Tests A, B/C pp. 39*, 41*
Test Generator CD

BEST PRACTICES TOOLKIT

Differentiated Instruction
pp. 31–38*

Scaffolding Instruction
pp. 43–46*

Graphic Organizers/Strategies
Definition Mapping • Observation Chart • New Word Analysis • Open Mind • Making Inferences • Whip Around • Word Sorts • Sensory Notes

Reading Support
Audio Anthology CD*

Technology
Literature and Vocabulary Centers at **ClassZone.com**
*Write*Smart CD

* Resources for Differentiation   † Also in Spanish   ‡ In Haitian Creole and Vietnamese

LITERARY ANALYSIS: DETAILS OF SETTING

In "A Christmas Memory," the adult narrator focuses on describing a particular period in his childhood. In fact, the narrator seems more interested in recreating the **setting** of this period than in telling about events. Through the use of **details,** the narrator describes not only the time and place of his childhood but also the historical era—the buildings, people, customs, and rituals that existed. The richness of the details makes the setting seem real and helps readers understand its importance to the narrator. Notice the vivid details used to describe walking through the woods:

Always, the path unwinds through lemony sun pools and pitch-black vine tunnels.

As you read, look for details that reveal the setting.

● READING SKILL: ANALYZE IMAGERY

Good descriptive writing is usually filled with **imagery**—words and phrases that appeal to the senses. Capote gives readers a lasting impression of a holiday memory by creating descriptions that appeal to one or more senses. For example, note how this phrase appeals to your sense of hearing:

Lovely dimes, the liveliest coin, the one that really jingles.

As you read, use a chart like the one below to jot down words and phrases that you find especially striking. Check off the senses that are appealed to in each case.

Description	Sight	Smell	Hearing	Taste	Touch
Cracking open the pecans	✓		✓	✓	

Review: Make Inferences

▲ VOCABULARY IN CONTEXT

To see how many words you know, restate each phrase, using a different word or words for the boldfaced word.

1. to **inaugurate** a project
2. a day that **exhilarates**
3. party **paraphernalia**
4. **squander** your money
5. ordinary, **prosaic** ideas
6. **suffuse** with perfume
7. a **potent** medicine
8. **goad** her to action
9. **cavort** in the park
10. **sever** all contact

Author Online

Early Ambitions Raised by elderly relatives in a small Alabama town, Capote started writing to fill the loneliness. He began publishing his short stories in his teens. As he later explained, "I always knew that I wanted to be a writer and that I wanted to be rich and famous." By the time his first novel, *Other Voices, Other Rooms,* was published in 1948, he was on his way to achieving these goals.

Truman Capote
1924–1984

The Nonfiction Novel Capote enjoyed the celebrity that followed other successful publications, including the novel *Breakfast at Tiffany's* (1958). Then his career took a dramatic turn when he began what he called a nonfiction novel, a factual story written in the form of a novel. The result, *In Cold Blood* (1965), was an instant bestseller and made him a multimillionaire. Still, the six years he spent on this book took a toll on him.

Personal Decline Capote's life ultimately descended into a haze of addiction, illness, and writer's block. Although some critics contend he threw away his talent in the pursuit of celebrity, most acknowledge his talent as a storyteller.

> **MORE ABOUT THE AUTHOR**
> For more on Truman Capote, visit the **Literature Center at ClassZone.com.**

Background

The Facts Behind the Fiction This story is based on Capote's childhood during the Great Depression of the 1930s. His friend was a much older cousin named Sook Faulk. Writing in the voice of an adult, Capote condenses years of experiences with his cousin into one memorable Christmas.

Teach

LITERARY ANALYSIS

● DETAILS OF SETTING

For instructional support, have students identify descriptive details in this sentence:

> That ancient six-by-six tree house, with its creaking, moldy boards and leaking roof, was our secret hideaway.

Possible answer: ancient; six-by-six; creaking, moldy boards; and leaking roof

CHECK UNDERSTANDING Have students list and discuss stories and novels that have vivid settings.

READING SKILL

■ ANALYZE IMAGERY

Point out that not all images are mental pictures. Ripples of thunder or fluttering wings are images; so, too, is a rose's aroma or the prick of its thorn. Discuss the various types of images in this passage:

> *Plunk!* The second after Jenna dropped her keys, the jets of water whooshed them away in a jangling whirl of silver.

CHECK UNDERSTANDING Ask students what senses they associate with Christmas or another holiday and why.

> **RESOURCE MANAGER—Copy Master**
> Analyze Imagery p. 29 (for student use while reading the selection)

VOCABULARY SKILL

▲ VOCABULARY IN CONTEXT

DIAGNOSE WORD KNOWLEDGE To determine preteaching needs, have all students complete Vocabulary in Context. *Possible answers:*
1. *begin;* 2. *energizes;* 3. *equipment;*
4. *waste;* 5. *dull;* 6. *fill;* 7. *powerful;* 8. *urge;*
9. *frolic;* 10. *cut off*

PRETEACH VOCABULARY Use the Vocabulary Study copy master to help students predict meanings for each boldfaced word in the copy master.

1. Read item 1 aloud, emphasizing *cavort.*
2. Point out the words *lively, laughing,* and *happily.* Discuss possible meanings for *cavort,* such as "play happily."
3. Have students record their predictions.
4. Repeat the procedure for items 2–10.

> **RESOURCE MANAGER—Copy Master**
> Vocabulary Study p. 31

For general guidelines on differentiating vocabulary instruction and for alternative vocabulary activities for students not needing vocabulary preteaching, see

> **BEST PRACTICES TOOLKIT**
> Scaffolding Vocabulary Instruction pp. 43–46
> Vocabulary Center at **ClassZone.com**

Practice and Apply

A Christmas Memory
Truman Capote

Imagine a morning in late November. A coming of winter morning more than twenty years ago. Consider the kitchen of a spreading old house in a country town. A great black stove is its main feature; but there is also a big round table and a fireplace with two rocking chairs placed in front of it. Just today the fireplace commenced its seasonal roar.

A woman with shorn white hair is standing at the kitchen window. She is wearing tennis shoes and a shapeless gray sweater over a summery calico dress. She is small and sprightly, like a bantam hen; but, due to a long youthful illness, her shoulders are pitifully hunched. Her face is remarkable—not

10 unlike Lincoln's, craggy like that, and tinted by sun and wind; but it is delicate too, finely boned, and her eyes are sherry-colored and timid. "Oh my," she exclaims, her breath smoking the windowpane, "it's fruitcake weather!"

The person to whom she is speaking is myself. I am seven; she is sixty-something. We are cousins, very distant ones, and we have lived together— well, as long as I can remember. Other people inhabit the house, relatives; and though they have power over us, and frequently make us cry, we are not, on the whole, too much aware of them. We are each other's best friend. She calls me Buddy, in memory of a boy who was formerly her best friend. The other Buddy died in the 1880's, when she was still a child. She is still a child.

20 "I knew it before I got out of bed," she says, turning away from the window with a purposeful excitement in her eyes. "The courthouse bell sounded so cold and clear. And there were no birds singing; they've gone to warmer country, yes indeed. Oh, Buddy, stop stuffing biscuit and fetch our buggy. Help me find my hat. We've thirty cakes to bake."

It's always the same: a morning arrives in November, and my friend, as though officially **inaugurating** the Christmas time of year that **exhilarates** her imagination and fuels the blaze of her heart, announces: "It's fruitcake weather! Fetch our buggy. Help me find my hat." Ⓐ

Anna Kuerner (1971), Andrew Wyeth. Tempera on panel. © Andrew Wyeth.

DIFFERENTIATED INSTRUCTION

FOR ALL STUDENTS
Anchor Activity Provide independent learning opportunities for students to analyze imagery by collecting objects crucial to key scenes from the story. Then explain their significance to the class.

Ⓡ RESOURCE MANAGER
Ideas for Extension pp. 22–23

FOR LESS–PROFICIENT READERS
In combination with the *Audio Anthology CD*, use one or more Targeted Passages (pp. 310, 314, 318–319, 322) to ensure that students focus on key story events, concepts, and skills. Targeted Passages are also good for English learners.

Ⓞ Targeted Passage [Lines 13–19]

This passage introduces the theme of friendship, as seen in Buddy's description

BACKGROUND

Rural America and the Great Depression
Although many segments of the U.S. population had prospered in the years just before the Great Depression, farmers had not. Their economic difficulties increased beginning in late 1929. The stock market crash, bank failures, deflating prices, and rising unemployment had a ripple effect, threatening the living conditions not only in cities but also across rural America. The early years of the depression in particular were a bleak time for farmers. New Deal programs such as the Agricultural Adjustment Administration were established to provide relief by regulating farm production and raising prices for agricultural products. Undoubtedly, however, many rural families felt the economic hardships of the depression very strongly during the holiday season, as touched upon in this story.

Cultural Connection Fruitcake is one of the culinary traditions of Christmas. Other traditional Christmas desserts and sweets include Christmas puddings or plum puddings in Australia; the *bûche de Noël*, or yule log cake, in France; the *panettone* cake of Italy; and, among the Christians of Tanzania, *kashata*, or coconut candy. Call on volunteers to tell about foods or treats that are a part of their various holiday traditions.

of his older cousin and friend.

- What is the age difference between Buddy and his friend? Does the difference seem to matter to them?

- Who else lives in the house? How do Buddy and his friend feel about them?

- How strong is the friendship between Buddy and his cousin? How can you tell?

FOR ENGLISH LEARNERS

Key Academic Vocabulary Use Definition Mapping to teach these words: *commenced* (line 5), *contracted* (line 107), *lectured* (line 167), *locate* (line 288), *succession* (line 355).

 BEST PRACTICES TOOLKIT—Transparency
Definition Mapping p. E6

Prereading For prereading instruction for English learners, see

 BEST PRACTICES TOOLKIT
Scaffolding Reading Instruction pp. 43–46

FOR ADVANCED LEARNERS/PRE–AP

Pre-AP Exercises in the bottom channel provide additional challenge for students. Use these suggestions for small groups or individuals.

ADDITIONAL GUIDELINES
For more help with differentiation and tips for classroom management, see

 BEST PRACTICES TOOLKIT
Differentiated Instruction pp. 31–38

The hat is found, a straw cartwheel corsaged with velvet roses out-of-doors
30 has faded: it once belonged to a more fashionable relative. Together, we guide
our buggy, a dilapidated baby carriage, out to the garden and into a grove of
pecan trees. The buggy is mine; that is, it was bought for me when I was born.
It is made of wicker, rather unraveled, and the wheels wobble like a drunkard's
legs. But it is a faithful object; springtimes, we take it to the woods and fill
it with flowers, herbs, wild fern for our porch pots; in the summer, we pile it
with picnic **paraphernalia** and sugar-cane fishing poles and roll it down to the
edge of a creek; it has its winter uses, too: as a truck for hauling firewood from
the yard to the kitchen, as a warm bed for Queenie, our tough little orange and
white rat terrier who has survived distemper and two rattlesnake bites. Queenie
40 is trotting beside it now. **B**

Three hours later we are back in the kitchen hulling a heaping buggyload of
windfall pecans. Our backs hurt from gathering them: how hard they were to
find (the main crop having been shaken off the trees and sold by the orchard's
owners, who are not us) among the concealing leaves, the frosted, deceiving
grass. Caarackle! A cheery crunch, scraps of miniature thunder sound as the
shells collapse and the golden mound of sweet oily ivory meat mounts in the
milk-glass bowl. Queenie begs to taste, and now and again my friend sneaks
her a mite, though insisting we deprive ourselves. "We mustn't, Buddy. If
we start, we won't stop. And there's scarcely enough as there is. For thirty
50 cakes." The kitchen is growing dark. Dusk turns the window into a mirror:
our reflections mingle with the rising moon as we work by the fireside in the
firelight. At last, when the moon is quite high, we toss the final hull into the

paraphernalia
(păr´ə-fər-nāl´yə) *n.*
the articles needed
for a particular event
or activity

B MAKE INFERENCES
Reread lines 30–40. What
do you learn about Buddy
and his friend from their
activities with the buggy?

Wild Dog Mushroom (1974), Bob Timberlake. © Bob Timberlake.

Lines 31–40
REINFORCE *KEY IDEA:* FRIENDSHIP

Discuss Buddy speaks of the older woman
as if they were equals. What obstacle or
obstacles might they have had to overcome to
establish their **friendship?** Explain. *Possible*
*answer: Their age difference might have been
the main obstacle. However, since the older
woman had a childlike personality, age was
not the issue that it might have been for other
people.*

ANALYZE VISUALS

Activity Ask students how well they think
this painting resembles the setting where
Buddy and his friend gather pecans for the
fruitcakes. *Answers will vary, but students may
note Capote's reference to "concealing leaves"
(line 44).*

About the Art Contemporary artist Bob
Timberlake (born 1933) paints realistic rural
landscapes, including wooded lots and rolling
hills, of his native North Carolina. In *Wild
Dog Mushroom* he conveys not only the look
but the texture of the leaf-covered ground in
autumn.

DIFFERENTIATED INSTRUCTION

FOR ENGLISH LEARNERS
Vocabulary: Multiple-Meaning Words
Explain that some words in English have
more than one meaning and even can be
used as more than one part of speech.
Discuss how each of these words is used in
the selection: *object* (line 34), *hard* (line 42),
leaves (line 44), *bowl* (line 47), *jam* (line 55),
kind (line 56), *prize* (line 66), *slide* (line 73).

FOR ADVANCED LEARNERS/PRE–AP
Research Activity Have students research
famous friendships in literature, such as that
of Huck and Jim in *The Adventures of Huckle-
berry Finn*. After they have finished reading
"A Christmas Memory," ask them to compare
the friendship between Buddy and his friend
with the friendship they researched.

fire and, with joined sighs, watch it catch flame. The buggy is empty, the bowl is brimful. **C**

We eat our supper (cold biscuits, bacon, blackberry jam) and discuss tomorrow. Tomorrow the kind of work I like best begins: buying. Cherries and citron, ginger and vanilla and canned Hawaiian pineapple, rinds and raisins and walnuts and whiskey and oh, so much flour, butter, so many eggs, spices, flavorings: why, we'll need a pony to pull the buggy home.

60   But before these purchases can be made, there is the question of money. Neither of us has any. Except for skinflint sums persons in the house occasionally provide (a dime is considered very big money); or what we earn ourselves from various activities: holding rummage sales, selling buckets of hand-picked blackberries, jars of homemade jam and apple jelly and peach preserves, rounding up flowers for funerals and weddings. Once we won seventy-ninth prize, five dollars, in a national football contest. Not that we know a fool thing about football. It's just that we enter any contest we hear about: at the moment our hopes are centered on the fifty-thousand-dollar Grand Prize being offered to name a new brand of coffee (we suggested "A.M.";
70   and, after some hesitation, for my friend thought it perhaps sacrilegious, the slogan "A.M.! Amen!"). To tell the truth, our only *really* profitable enterprise was the Fun and Freak Museum we conducted in a back-yard woodshed two summers ago. The Fun was a stereopticon[1] with slide views of Washington and New York lent us by a relative who had been to those places (she was furious when she discovered why we'd borrowed it); the Freak was a three-legged biddy chicken hatched by one of our own hens. Everybody hereabouts wanted to see that biddy: we charged grownups a nickel, kids two cents. And took in a good twenty dollars before the museum shut down due to the decease of the main attraction.
80   But one way and another we do each year accumulate Christmas savings, a Fruitcake Fund. These moneys we keep hidden in an ancient bead purse under a loose board under the floor under a chamber pot under my friend's bed. The purse is seldom removed from this safe location except to make a deposit or, as happens every Saturday, a withdrawal; for on Saturdays I am allowed ten cents to go to the picture show. My friend has never been to a picture show, nor does she intend to: "I'd rather hear you tell the story, Buddy. That way I can imagine it more. Besides, a person my age shouldn't **squander** their eyes. When the Lord comes, let me see him clear." In addition to never having seen a movie, she has never: eaten in a restaurant, traveled more than five miles
90   from home, received or sent a telegram, read anything except funny papers and the Bible, worn cosmetics, cursed, wished someone harm, told a lie on purpose, let a hungry dog go hungry. Here are a few things she has done, does do: killed with a hoe the biggest rattlesnake ever seen in this county (sixteen rattles), dip snuff[2] (secretly), tame hummingbirds (just try it) till they balance

---

1. **stereopticon** (stĕr′ē-ŏp′tĭ-kŏn′): an early slide projector that could merge two images of the same scene on a screen, resulting in a 3-D effect.

2. **dip snuff:** to place a small amount of finely ground tobacco (snuff) in one's mouth.

A CHRISTMAS MEMORY   **313**

C ANALYZE IMAGERY
What words and phrases in this passage appeal to the senses and help you imagine the characters shelling pecans?

squander (skwŏn′dər) v. to spend or use wastefully

A CHRISTMAS MEMORY   **313**

D MAKE INFERENCES

Possible answer: *She has religious faith and has led a sheltered life (lines 88–91); she is gentle and kind (lines 91–92); she is tough and well versed in country ways (lines 92–98); she is willing to work to achieve her goals (lines 80–83).*

If students need help . . . Ask

- How far has Buddy's friend traveled?
- What unusual things has she done?
- What are her beliefs?
- How does she treat other people?

E ANALYZE IMAGERY

If students need help . . . Discuss why Capote compares the dollar bills to May buds. **Possible answer:** *Both represent the promise of something pleasant to come—the dollar bills will result in the baking of fruitcakes, even as the May buds will yield flowers.*

Extend the Discussion Which money imagery do you find the most interesting, creative, or effective? Explain.

F DETAILS OF SETTING

Possible answer: *dancing (line 121); Mrs. Haha's "brassy peroxided hair" (line 124); grisly murders (lines 131–132); the wailing Victrola (line 134); the garish, naked light bulbs (line 128); and the shabby, deserted appearance of Haha's in the daytime (line 134)*

on her finger, tell ghost stories (we both believe in ghosts) so tingling they chill you in July, talk to herself, take walks in the rain, grow the prettiest japonicas in town, know the recipe for every sort of old-time Indian cure, including a magical wart remover. **D**

100 Now, with supper finished, we retire to the room in a faraway part of the house where my friend sleeps in a scrap-quilt-covered iron bed painted rose pink, her favorite color. Silently, wallowing in the pleasures of conspiracy, we take the bead purse from its secret place and spill its contents on the scrap quilt. Dollar bills, tightly rolled and green as May buds. Somber fifty-cent pieces, heavy enough to weight a dead man's eyes.[3] Lovely dimes, the liveliest coin, the one that really jingles. Nickels and quarters, worn smooth as creek pebbles. But mostly a hateful heap of bitter-odored pennies. Last summer others in the house contracted to pay us a penny for every twenty-five flies we killed. Oh, the carnage of August: the flies that flew to heaven! Yet it was not work in which we took pride. And, as we sit counting pennies, it is as though

110 we were back tabulating dead flies. Neither of us has a head for figures; we count slowly, lose track, start again. According to her calculations, we have $12.73. According to mine, exactly $13. "I do hope you're wrong, Buddy. We can't mess around with thirteen. The cakes will fall. Or put somebody in the cemetery. Why, I wouldn't dream of getting out of bed on the thirteenth." This is true: she always spends thirteenths in bed. So, to be on the safe side, we subtract a penny and toss it out the window. **E**

Of the ingredients that go into our fruitcakes, whiskey is the most expensive, as well as the hardest to obtain: State laws forbid its sale. But everybody knows you can buy a bottle from Mr. Haha Jones. And the next

120 day, having completed our more **prosaic** shopping, we set out for Mr. Haha's business address, a "sinful" (to quote public opinion) fish-fry and dancing café down by the river. We've been there before, and on the same errand; but in previous years our dealings have been with Haha's wife, an iodine-dark Indian woman with brassy peroxided hair and a dead-tired disposition. Actually, we've never laid eyes on her husband, though we've heard that he's an Indian too. A giant with razor scars across his cheeks. They call him Haha because he's so gloomy, a man who never laughs. As we approach his café (a large log cabin festooned inside and out with chains of garish-gay naked light bulbs and standing by the river's muddy edge under the shade of river trees where moss

130 drifts through the branches like gray mist) our steps slow down. Even Queenie stops prancing and sticks close by. People have been murdered in Haha's café. Cut to pieces. Hit on the head. There's a case coming up in court next month.

Naturally these goings-on happen at night when the colored lights cast crazy patterns and the Victrola[4] wails. In the daytime Haha's is shabby and deserted. I knock at the door, Queenie barks, my friend calls: "Mrs. Haha, ma'am? Anyone to home?" **F**

---

3. **heavy enough to weight a dead man's eyes:** from the custom of putting coins on the closed eyes of corpses to keep the eyelids from opening.

4. **Victrola:** a trademark for a brand of old record player.

DIFFERENTIATED INSTRUCTION

FOR LESS–PROFICIENT READERS

2 Targeted Passage [Lines 99–116]

By focusing on a shared activity, this descriptive passage underscores the bond between Buddy and his friend.

- Where do the friends go after dinner?
- What have they hidden? What do they plan to do with it?
- What job did they share to earn money?
- When their totals differ, what do the friends agree to do?

FOR ENGLISH LEARNERS

Culture: Connect In most Latin American and European countries, the number 13 implies bad luck. Some cultures also consider certain days of the week unlucky. In Latin America, for example, Tuesday is felt to be an unlucky day. Ask students if they know of other days, numbers, or actions that are considered bad luck in their home cultures.

Footsteps. The door opens. Our hearts overturn. It's Mr. Haha Jones
himself! And he *is* a giant; he *does* have scars; he *doesn't* smile. No, he glowers
at us through Satan-tilted eyes and demands to know: "What you want
140 with Haha?"

For a moment we are too paralyzed to tell. Presently my friend half-finds her
voice, a whispery voice at best: "If you please, Mr. Haha, we'd like a quart of
your finest whiskey."

His eyes tilt more. Would you believe it? Haha is smiling! Laughing, too.
"Which one of you is a drinkin' man?"

"It's for making fruitcakes, Mr. Haha. Cooking."

This sobers him. He frowns. "That's no way to waste good whiskey."
Nevertheless, he retreats into the shadowed café and seconds later appears
carrying a bottle of daisy-yellow unlabeled liquor. He demonstrates its sparkle
150 in the sunlight and says: "Two dollars."

We pay him with nickels and dimes and pennies. Suddenly, as he jangles
the coins in his hand like a fistful of dice, his face softens. "Tell you what," he
proposes, pouring the money back into our bead purse, "just send me one of
them fruitcakes instead."

"Well," my friend remarks on our way home, "there's a lovely man. We'll
put an extra cup of raisins in *his* cake."

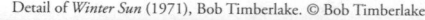

Detail of *Winter Sun* (1971), Bob Timberlake. © Bob Timberlake.

A CHRISTMAS MEMORY **315**

Lines 127–156
DISCUSSION PROMPTS

Use these prompts to help students understand the scene at Haha's:

Connect Have you ever misjudged anyone
because of his or her physical appearance?
Explain. *Answers will vary.*

Analyze Why doesn't Mr. Haha take the
money for the whiskey? *Possible answers:
He is amused by these visitors; he is touched
to think that his whiskey will be used in fruitcakes that will bring people Christmas cheer.*

Synthesize What does this scene show
about Buddy's friend? *Possible answer: She
is capable of charming someone as fearsome
as Haha. But she also has poor judgment.
She takes a seven-year-old to visit a bootlegger, and she thinks that a man who may be a
criminal is "lovely" because he gives her the
bottle of whiskey for free.*

ANALYZE VISUALS

Activity Ask students whether what they
learn about Buddy is, like this painting, illuminated in some ways but dark and closed off in
others. Have students explain their answers.

About the Art In addition to painting the rural
landscapes of North Carolina, Bob Timberlake
(see page 312) also paints its rural structures,
such as log cabins and porches. This experiment
in the use of light presents the side of the house
in clear detail, but its entrance is obscured in
shadow.

FOR LESS-PROFICIENT READERS
Monitor Comprehension If students seem
to be having trouble tracking the plot, urge
them to think of it as a series of key scenes.
For each scene (perhaps corresponding with
the Targeted Passages), have them fill in an
Open Mind chart. They should record the key
details of the scene and any comments that
they wish to make about the scene.

BEST PRACTICES TOOLKIT—Transparency
Open Mind p. D9

FOR ENGLISH LEARNERS
Language: Conversational English Patterns
Explain that *We hear* is left out but under-
stood in the sentence in line 137: *Footsteps.*
Discuss these unusual language patterns in
the rest of the story:

- *send me one of them fruitcakes*
  (lines 153–154)
- *giveya two-bits cash for that ol tree*
  (line 254)
- *out it goes* (line 312)

Possible answer: *The black stove (line 157) is the most obvious detail. The many pots on the stove suggest a flurry of cooking activity, as described in the paragraph. The stack of wood suggests that this stove, like the stove in the story, was stoked with firewood.*

About the Art In *Mrs. Dorsett's Kitchen,* North Carolina artist Bob Timberlake (see pages 312 and 315) focuses on a country kitchen, where a large cast-iron stove takes the viewer back to a former way of life. The setting is complete with cooking pots that also recall an earlier era. The scene suggests an old farmhouse, with its pine floors and old-time shelves in lieu of cabinets and counters.

Mrs. Dorsett's Kitchen (1973), Bob Timberlake. © Bob Timberlake.

ANALYZE VISUALS
What **details** in this painting evoke the scene described in lines 157–162?

The black stove, stoked with coal and firewood, glows like a lighted pumpkin. Eggbeaters whirl, spoons spin round in bowls of butter and sugar, vanilla sweetens the air, ginger spices it; melting, nose-tingling odors saturate
160 the kitchen, **suffuse** the house, drift out to the world on puffs of chimney smoke. In four days our work is done. Thirty-one cakes, dampened with whiskey, bask on windowsills and shelves.

Who are they for?

Friends. Not necessarily neighbor friends: indeed, the larger share is intended for persons we've met maybe once, perhaps not at all. People who've struck our fancy. Like President Roosevelt. Like the Reverend and Mrs. J. C. Lucey, Baptist missionaries to Borneo[5] who lectured here last winter. Or the little knife grinder who comes through town twice a year. Or Abner Packer, the driver of the six o'clock bus from Mobile, who exchanges waves with
170 us every day as he passes in a dust-cloud whoosh. Or the young Wistons, a

suffuse (sə-fyōōz′) *v.* to gradually spread through or over

GRAMMAR AND STYLE
Notice how Capote makes use of the **present tense** even though the memory is part of the narrator's past. This creates a sense of immediacy for the reader.

5. **Borneo** (bôr′nē-o′): a large island in the South China Sea, southwest of the Philippines.

316 UNIT 3: SETTING, MOOD, AND IMAGERY

GRAMMAR AND STYLE

Choose Effective Verb Tense Point out that present-tense verbs dominate "A Christmas Memory" but that present tense is not the traditional tense used to narrate past events. The traditional tense is past tense. To illustrate, have one or more students read aloud lines 157–162, changing the present-tense verbs to past-tense verbs. Discuss how the paragraph now resembles a traditional story—interesting, but not quite as immediate as it sounded with present-tense verbs. For an extra challenge, have students change the present-tense verbs to future-tense verbs; then discuss how the paragraph now conveys a sense of anticipation.

DIFFERENTIATED INSTRUCTION

FOR ADVANCED LEARNERS/PRE–AP

Analyze Style [small-group option] Have students analyze Capote's **style** in "A Christmas Memory"—his particular way of writing and communicating ideas. Suggest that they begin by examining pages 316–317 and then draw from other passages in the story to develop and support their analysis. Have students consider these stylistic elements and record their ideas in a journal or two-column chart:

- diction (word choice)
- active vs. passive verbs
- sentence length and structure
- imagery and figurative language
- sound devices (such as alliteration)
- tone
- use of dialogue

To conclude the activity, ask students to deliver a brief class presentation that summarizes their analysis of Capote's style.

California couple whose car one afternoon broke down outside the house and who spent a pleasant hour chatting with us on the porch (young Mr. Wiston snapped our picture, the only one we've ever had taken). Is it because my friend is shy with everyone *except* strangers that these strangers, and merest acquaintances, seem to us our truest friends? I think yes. Also, the scrapbooks we keep of thank-you's on White House stationery, time-to-time communications from California and Borneo, the knife grinder's penny post cards, make us feel connected to eventful worlds beyond the kitchen with its view of a sky that stops. **H**

180 Now a nude December fig branch grates against the window. The kitchen is empty, the cakes are gone; yesterday we carted the last of them to the post office, where the cost of stamps turned our purse inside out. We're broke. That rather depresses me, but my friend insists on celebrating—with two inches of whiskey left in Haha's bottle. Queenie has a spoonful in a bowl of coffee (she likes her coffee chicory-flavored and strong). The rest we divide between a pair of jelly glasses. We're both quite awed at the prospect of drinking straight whiskey; the taste of it brings screwed-up expressions and sour shudders. But by and by we begin to sing, the two of us singing different songs simultaneously. I don't know the words to mine, just: *Come on along,*
190 *come on along, to the dark-town strutters' ball.* But I can dance: that's what I mean to be, a tap dancer in the movies. My dancing shadow rollicks on the walls; our voices rock the chinaware; we giggle: as if unseen hands were tickling us. Queenie rolls on her back, her paws plow the air, something like a grin stretches her black lips. Inside myself, I feel warm and sparky as those crumbling logs, carefree as the wind in the chimney. My friend waltzes round the stove, the hem of her poor calico skirt pinched between her fingers as though it were a party dress: *Show me the way to go home,* she sings, her tennis shoes squeaking on the floor. *Show me the way to go home.* **I**

Enter: two relatives. Very angry. **Potent** with eyes that scold, tongues that
200 scald. Listen to what they have to say, the words tumbling together into a wrathful tune: "A child of seven! whiskey on his breath! are you out of your mind! feeding a child of seven! must be loony! road to ruination! remember Cousin Kate? Uncle Charlie? Uncle Charlie's brother-in-law? shame! scandal! humiliation! kneel, pray, beg the Lord!"

Queenie sneaks under the stove. My friend gazes at her shoes, her chin quivers, she lifts her skirt and blows her nose and runs to her room. **J**

Long after the town has gone to sleep and the house is silent except for the chimings of clocks and the sputter of fading fires, she is weeping into a pillow already as wet as a widow's handkerchief.
210 "Don't cry," I say, sitting at the bottom of her bed and shivering despite my flannel nightgown that smells of last winter's cough syrup, "don't cry," I beg, teasing her toes, tickling her feet, "you're too old for that."

"It's because," she hiccups, "I *am* too old. Old and funny."

H MAKE INFERENCES
Why do you think Buddy and his friend send their fruitcakes to strangers?

I ANALYZE IMAGERY
In lines 187–198, Capote appeals to four out of the five senses. Identify as many of these sensory details as you can.

potent (pōt′nt) *adj.* powerful

J MAKE INFERENCES
Reread lines 199–206. What impression do you get of the relatives?

READING SKILL: Review

H MAKE INFERENCES

Possible answer: They probably have few friends of their own. They live an isolated life and mainly have only each other.

If students need help . . . Ask them to list other characters they have met so far (the other people in the house; Mr. Haha). Have them make a statement gauging how emotionally close each one is to Buddy and his friend.

Extend the Discussion Does it seem more pathetic or more charming that Buddy and his friend send their fruitcakes to strangers? How does the narrator feel about it as a child? as an adult looking back?

READING SKILL

I ANALYZE IMAGERY

Possible answer: Sight: rollicking shadow, paws "plowing" the air; Hearing: singing, rocking voices and giggling, the wind in the chimney, squeaking shoes; Taste: whiskey; Touch: tickling and "sparky" warmth, "pinched" calico skirt

READING SKILL: Review

J MAKE INFERENCES

Possible answer: They are angry and judgmental; they appear to notice only problems and mistakes.

Extend the Discussion Do you think this description of the relatives is formed more from accurate recall or from the one-sided impressions of a seven-year-old? Explain.

FOR LESS-PROFICIENT READERS

Make Inferences For help with making inferences, such as those presented in the lettered questions on this page, help students use an inference chart or other graphic organizer that requires them to analyze details in a step-by-step fashion.

BEST PRACTICES TOOLKIT—Transparency
Making Inferences p. A13

FOR ENGLISH LEARNERS

Culture: Clarify Explain Buddy's reference to tap dancing in lines 190–191. Point out that tap dancing, singing, and chorus lines were popular features in movies of the 1930s because they helped distract people's minds from the worries of the Great Depression. Indeed, many people, like Buddy, came to equate tap dancing with fame and fortune.

ANALYZE VISUALS

Activity When students have finished reading, ask them if this painting accurately reflects their ideas about the setting. Urge them to support their answers with story details.

About the Art This painting by Bob Timberlake (see pages 312, 315, and 316) underscores rural isolation. It presents the viewer with a foreground that is empty and a wooded background that seems a natural barrier to human contact. Note how dull or muted the light is and how little variation there is in color.

Lines 210–221
REINFORCE *KEY IDEA:* FRIENDSHIP

Discuss One reason that Buddy can turn his cousin's sadness and self-pity into eager anticipation is that both of them understand **friendship.** Review your *QUICKWRITE* list, "Top 10 Qualities of a Good Friend" (page 308). What qualities on that list are reflected in this turnaround? *Answers will vary from list to list but may include qualities such as these: no fear of displaying personal thoughts and feelings; understanding me better than just about anyone else; wanting me to be happy or optimistic.*

Detail of *Another World* (1974), Bob Timberlake. © Bob Timberlake.

"Not funny. Fun. More fun than anybody. Listen. If you don't stop crying you'll be so tired tomorrow we can't go cut a tree."

She straightens up. Queenie jumps on the bed (where Queenie is not allowed) to lick her cheeks. "I know where we'll find real pretty trees, Buddy. And holly, too. With berries big as your eyes. It's way off in the woods. Farther than we've ever been. Papa used to bring us Christmas trees from there:
220 carry them on his shoulder. That's fifty years ago. Well, now: I can't wait for morning."

Morning. Frozen rime⁶ lusters the grass; the sun, round as an orange and orange as hot-weather moons, balances on the horizon, burnishes the silvered winter woods. A wild turkey calls. A renegade hog grunts in the undergrowth. Soon, by the edge of knee-deep, rapid-running water, we have to abandon the buggy. Queenie wades the stream first, paddles across barking complaints at the swiftness of the current, the pneumonia-making coldness of it. We follow, holding our shoes and equipment (a hatchet, a burlap sack) above our heads. A mile more: of chastising thorns, burrs and briers that catch at

❸ Targeted Passage

---

6. **rime:** a white frost.

318   UNIT 3: SETTING, MOOD, AND IMAGERY

DIFFERENTIATED INSTRUCTION

FOR ENGLISH LEARNERS
Language: Punctuation and Print Clues Point out Capote's unusual use of the colon to emphasize a pause. Read aloud lines 219–221 and model the pauses that the colons suggest. Then ask students to look for similar uses of the colon (for example, in lines 229–231, 233–235, 241–242, 259–260, 261–264, 264–266, and 267–268) and to read the sentences aloud, using appropriate pauses.

FOR ADVANCED LEARNERS/PRE–AP
Apply Style Ask students to create and share sentences that place the underlined words in these unusual descriptions in a new context.
- "a renegade hog" (line 224)
- "chastising thorns" (line 229)
- "an ecstasy of shrillings" (line 231)
- "a disturbed armada of speckled trout" (lines 233–234)
- "frogs the size of plates" (line 234)

230 our clothes; of rusty pine needles brilliant with gaudy fungus and molted
feathers. Here, there, a flash, a flutter, an ecstasy of shrillings remind us that
not all the birds have flown south. Always, the path unwinds through lemony
sun pools and pitch-black vine tunnels. Another creek to cross: a disturbed
armada of speckled trout froths the water round us, and frogs the size of plates
practice belly flops; beaver workmen are building a dam. On the farther shore,
Queenie shakes herself and trembles. My friend shivers, too: not with cold but
enthusiasm. One of her hat's ragged roses sheds a petal as she lifts her head and
inhales the pine-heavy air. "We're almost there; can you smell it, Buddy?" she
says, as though we were approaching an ocean. **K**

240   And, indeed, it is a kind of ocean. Scented acres of holiday trees, prickly-
leafed holly. Red berries shiny as Chinese bells: black crows swoop upon
them screaming. Having stuffed our burlap sacks with enough greenery and
crimson to garland a dozen windows, we set about choosing a tree. "It should
be," muses my friend, "twice as tall as a boy. So a boy can't steal the star." The
one we pick is twice as tall as me. A brave handsome brute that survives thirty
hatchet strokes before it keels with a creaking rending cry. Lugging it like a
kill, we commence the long trek out. Every few yards we abandon the struggle,
sit down and pant. But we have the strength of triumphant huntsmen; that
and the tree's virile, icy perfume revive us, **goad** us on. Many compliments
250 accompany our sunset return along the red clay road to town; but my friend
is sly and noncommittal when passers-by praise the treasure perched in our
buggy: what a fine tree, and where did it come from? "Yonderways," she
murmurs vaguely. Once a car stops, and the rich mill owner's lazy wife leans
out and whines: "Giveya two-bits[7] cash for that ol tree." Ordinarily my friend
is afraid of saying no; but on this occasion she promptly shakes her head: "We
wouldn't take a dollar." The mill owner's wife persists. "A dollar, my foot! Fifty
cents. That's my last offer. Goodness, woman, you can get another one." In
answer, my friend gently reflects: "I doubt it. There's never two of anything." **L**

Home: Queenie slumps by the fire and sleeps till tomorrow, snoring loud
260 as a human.

    A trunk in the attic contains: a shoebox of ermine tails (off the opera cape
of a curious lady who once rented a room in the house), coils of frazzled tinsel
gone gold with age, one silver star, a brief rope of dilapidated, undoubtedly
dangerous candylike light bulbs. Excellent decorations, as far as they go, which
isn't far enough: my friend wants our tree to blaze "like a Baptist window,"
droop with weighty snows of ornament. But we can't afford the made-in-Japan
splendors at the five-and-dime. So we do what we've always done: sit for days
at the kitchen table with scissors and crayons and stacks of colored paper. I
make sketches and my friend cuts them out: lots of cats, fish too (because
270 they're easy to draw), some apples, some watermelons, a few winged angels
devised from saved-up sheets of Hershey-bar tin foil. We use safety pins to
attach these creations to the tree; as a final touch, we sprinkle the branches

---

7. **two-bits:** 25 cents.

③ Targeted Passage
continued

K DETAILS OF SETTING
Reread lines 222–239.
What is the effect of
including such vivid
details of this natural
setting?

goad (gōd) v. to drive
or urge

L MAKE INFERENCES
Reread lines 253–258.
What do you learn about
Buddy's friend from her
response to the mill
owner's wife?

LITERARY ANALYSIS

K DETAILS OF SETTING

*Possible answer: The vivid, imaginative
details combine to make getting the tree
sound like a wonderful adventure in a
beautiful, isolated, and almost magical
place. Words like* silvered *(line 223) and*
lemony *(line 232) help create a wondrous
setting; details about speckled trout and
frogs (line 234) celebrate undisturbed
nature. The "pine-heavy air" (line 238)
helps convey the beauty, the peace, and
the delightfulness of the woodsy setting.*

If students need help . . . Use one of the
charts suggested on page 313 to remind
students of the senses that details such
as these address:

- "lemony sun pools" (lines 232–233)
  Possible answer: sight, smell, taste
- "froths the water" (line 234)
  Possible answer: sight, hearing
- "pine-heavy air" (line 238)
  Possible answer: smell, touch

READING SKILL: *Review*

L MAKE INFERENCES

*Possible answer: She is proud; she thinks
little of people whom she sees as lazy; she
appreciates the value of hard work.*

If students need help . . . Recall the
description in lines 210–221 of how the
promise of cutting down a tree with Buddy
cheered up his friend. What can you
infer from that scene as well as from this
one about how much the tree means to
Buddy's friend?

Extend the Discussion What might the
mill owner's wife be thinking as she
drives off?

FOR LESS–PROFICIENT READERS

③ Targeted Passage [Lines 222–249]

By recounting the search for a Christmas tree,
this passage prepares readers for the friends'
last Christmas Day together.

- Where do the friends go to find a tree?
  What kind of day is it?
- Why does Buddy's friend shiver?
- What kind of tree do they finally choose?
- Why do they go on, even though the hard
  work has tired them?

FOR ENGLISH LEARNERS

Culture: Clarify Explain that what Buddy refers
to as "Hershey-bar tin foil" (line 271) is the shiny
foil paper in which candy makers used to wrap
chocolate candy. (Some chocolates are still
wrapped in foil.) Point out that Hershey is a
chocolate-manufacturing company located in
Pennsylvania. Its mass-production techniques
made chocolate candy affordable for almost all
Americans, even during the Great Depression.

DISCUSSION PROMPTS

Use these prompts to explore how this scene illuminates the character of Buddy's friend:

Connect What do you think is important in choosing a gift for someone? *Answers will vary.*

Analyze What does the comment made by Buddy's friend about what "gets [her] goat" (line 286) show about her? *Possible answer: She has a generous, selfless nature. She is frustrated that she cannot do as much as she would like to do for Buddy.*

Evaluate How well does Capote present a child's perspective by describing the presents that Buddy and his friend give to each other? Defend your answer. *Possible answer: He presents it rather well. By showing someone who seems almost too good to be true, Capote captures a child's limited understanding and tendency to idolize or simplify.*

Lines 306–311

REINFORCE *KEY IDEA:* FRIENDSHIP

Discuss How is the bond between these two stronger than mere **friendship?** Defend your answer. *Possible answer: They are quite comfortable with one another. They love each other, and Buddy's friend seems as if she would do anything for Buddy. In some ways, they are more like a mother and son, or a grandmother and grandchild, than friends.*

---

with shredded cotton (picked in August for this purpose). My friend, surveying the effect, clasps her hands together. "Now honest, Buddy. Doesn't it look good enough to eat?" Queenie tries to eat an angel.

After weaving and ribboning holly wreaths for all the front windows, our next project is the fashioning of family gifts. Tie-dye scarves for the ladies, for the men a home-brewed lemon and licorice and aspirin syrup to be taken "at the first Symptoms of a Cold and after Hunting." But when it comes time for

280 making each other's gift, my friend and I separate to work secretly. I would like to buy her a pearl-handled knife, a radio, a whole pound of chocolate-covered cherries (we tasted some once, and she always swears: "I could live on them, Buddy, Lord yes I could—and that's not taking his name in vain"). Instead, I am building her a kite. She would like to give me a bicycle (she's said so on several million occasions: "If only I could, Buddy. It's bad enough in life to do without something *you* want; but confound it, what gets my goat is not being able to give somebody something you want *them* to have. Only one of these days I will, Buddy. Locate you a bike. Don't ask how. Steal it, maybe"). Instead, I'm fairly certain that she is building me a kite—the same as last year

290 and the year before: the year before that we exchanged slingshots. All of which is fine by me. For we are champion kite fliers who study the wind like sailors; my friend, more accomplished than I, can get a kite aloft when there isn't enough breeze to carry clouds.

Christmas Eve afternoon we scrape together a nickel and go to the butcher's to buy Queenie's traditional gift, a good gnawable beef bone. The bone, wrapped in funny paper, is placed high in the tree near the silver star. Queenie knows it's there. She squats at the foot of the tree staring up in a trance of greed: when bedtime arrives she refuses to budge. Her excitement is equaled by my own. I kick the covers and turn my pillow as though it were a

300 scorching summer's night. Somewhere a rooster crows: falsely, for the sun is still on the other side of the world.

"Buddy, are you awake?" It is my friend, calling from her room, which is next to mine; and an instant later she is sitting on my bed holding a candle. "Well, I can't sleep a hoot," she declares. "My mind's jumping like a jack rabbit. Buddy, do you think Mrs. Roosevelt will serve our cake at dinner?" We huddle in the bed, and she squeezes my hand I-love-you. "Seems like your hand used to be so much smaller. I guess I hate to see you grow up. When you're grown up, will we still be friends?" I say always. "But I feel so bad, Buddy. I wanted so bad to give you a bike. I tried to sell my cameo Papa gave

310 me. Buddy"—she hesitates, as though embarrassed—"I made you another kite." Then I confess that I made her one, too; and we laugh. The candle burns too short to hold. Out it goes, exposing the starlight, the stars spinning at the window like a visible caroling that slowly, slowly daybreak silences. Possibly we doze; but the beginnings of dawn splash us like cold water: we're up, wide-eyed and wandering while we wait for others to waken. Quite deliberately my friend drops a kettle on the kitchen floor. I tap dance in front of closed doors. One

---

DIFFERENTIATED INSTRUCTION

FOR ADVANCED LEARNERS/PRE–AP

Evaluate Have students discuss which they found more effective, Capote's depiction of characters or his depiction of setting. Have students list details that describe (1) Buddy's friend and (2) the story's setting. Ask them to analyze their lists and draw a conclusion based on the textual evidence they have collected. Then have students compare their conclusions and defend their opinions if classmates have reached a different conclusion.

Christmas Orange (1975), Bob Timberlake. © Bob Timberlake.

by one the household emerges, looking as though they'd like to kill us both; but it's Christmas, so they can't. First, a gorgeous breakfast: just everything you can imagine—from flapjacks and fried squirrel to hominy grits and honey-in-
320 the-comb. Which puts everyone in a good humor except my friend and me. Frankly, we're so impatient to get at the presents we can't eat a mouthful.

Well, I'm disappointed. Who wouldn't be? With socks, a Sunday school shirt, some handkerchiefs, a hand-me-down sweater, and a year's subscription to a religious magazine for children. *The Little Shepherd*. It makes me boil. It really does.

My friend has a better haul. A sack of satsumas,[8] that's her best present. She is proudest, however, of a white wool shawl knitted by her married sister. But she *says* her favorite gift is the kite I built her. And it *is* very beautiful; though not as beautiful as the one she made me, which is blue and scattered with gold
330 and green Good Conduct stars;[9] moreover, my name is painted on it, "Buddy."

"Buddy, the wind is blowing."

The wind is blowing, and nothing will do till we've run to a pasture below the house where Queenie has scooted to bury her bone (and where, a winter hence, Queenie will be buried, too). There, plunging through the healthy waist-high grass, we unreel our kites, feel them twitching at the string like sky

---

8. **satsumas** (săt-sōō′məz): fruit similar to tangerines.
9. **Good Conduct stars:** small, shiny, glued paper stars often awarded to children for good behavior or perfect attendance in school.

Ⓜ DETAILS OF SETTING
What do the gifts received by Buddy and his friend tell you about the economic circumstances of the household?

ANALYZE VISUALS

Activity Have students locate story details that relate to the key elements of this painting. *Possible answer: Lines 240–243 describe bags filled with holly; line 326 reveals that Buddy's friend receives a sack of satsumas as a Christmas gift.* Students also might comment on whether or not they consider the painting's overall effect to be merry and on how well its mood relates to the mood of the Christmas in Capote's story.

About the Art Here contemporary American painter Bob Timberlake (see pages 312, 315, 316, and 318) presents the viewer with some traditional images of Christmas. Oranges were common gifts or stocking stuffers when times were harder and citrus less commonly available. Holly with red berries is a typical example of Christmas greenery.

LITERARY ANALYSIS

Ⓜ DETAILS OF SETTING

Possible answer: The family is struggling. The most obvious example of this may be the hand-me-down sweater presented as a gift (line 323).

If students need help . . . Use a Whip Around activity to generate immediate responses to the gifts. Discuss how responses such as "boring," "practical," and "cheap" relate to what students already know of the household's limited resources.

🧰 **BEST PRACTICES TOOLKIT**
Whip Around p. B1

FOR ENGLISH LEARNERS

Culture: Connect Point out the elements of what Buddy calls "a gorgeous breakfast" (line 318) in that past era and rural locale. Have students compare and contrast the meal with the supper described in line 55. Then encourage students to describe foods they enjoy for breakfast, supper, or special occasions in their home cultures.

fish as they swim into the wind. Satisfied, sun-warmed, we sprawl in the grass and peel satsumas and watch our kites **cavort**. Soon I forget the socks and hand-me-down sweater. I'm as happy as if we'd already won the fifty-thousand-dollar Grand Prize in that coffee-naming contest.

340 "My, how foolish I am!" my friend cries, suddenly alert, like a woman remembering too late she has biscuits in the oven. "You know what I've always thought?" she asks in a tone of discovery and not smiling at me but a point beyond. "I've always thought a body would have to be sick and dying before they saw the Lord. And I imagined that when he came it would be like looking at the Baptist window: pretty as colored glass with the sun pouring through, such a shine you don't know it's getting dark. And it's been a comfort: to think of that shine taking away all the spooky feeling. But I'll wager it never happens. I'll wager at the very end a body realizes the Lord has already shown himself. That things as they are"—her hand circles in a gesture that gathers

350 clouds and kites and grass and Queenie pawing earth over her bone—"just what they've always seen, was seeing him. As for me, I could leave the world with today in my eyes."

This is our last Christmas together.

Life separates us. Those who Know Best decide that I belong in a military school. And so follows a miserable succession of bugle-blowing prisons, grim reveille-ridden[10] summer camps. I have a new home too. But it doesn't count. Home is where my friend is, and there I never go. **N**

And there she remains, puttering around the kitchen. Alone with Queenie.
360 Then alone. ("Buddy dear," she writes in her wild hard-to-read script, "yesterday Jim Macy's horse kicked Queenie bad. Be thankful she didn't feel much. I wrapped her in a Fine Linen sheet and rode her in the buggy down to Simpson's pasture where she can be with all her Bones . . ."). For a few Novembers she continues to bake her fruitcakes single-handed; not as many, but some: and, of course, she always sends me "the best of the batch." Also, in every letter she encloses a dime wadded in toilet paper: "See a picture show and write me the story." But gradually in her letters she tends to confuse me with her other friend, the Buddy who died in the 1880's; more and more, thirteenths are not the only days she stays in bed: a morning arrives in November, a leafless birdless coming of winter morning, when she cannot
370 rouse herself to exclaim: "Oh my, it's fruitcake weather!"

And when that happens, I know it. A message saying so merely confirms a piece of news some secret vein had already received, **severing** from me an irreplaceable part of myself, letting it loose like a kite on a broken string. That is why, walking across a school campus on this particular December morning, I keep searching the sky. As if I expected to see, rather like hearts, a lost pair of kites hurrying toward heaven. ❧

---

10. **reveille-ridden** (rĕv′ə-lē-rĭd′n): dominated by an early-morning signal, as on a bugle, to wake soldiers or campers.

cavort (kə-vôrt′) v. to leap or romp about

N MAKE INFERENCES
Who are "Those who Know Best"?

④ **Targeted Passage**

sever (sĕv′ər) v. to cut off

N MAKE INFERENCES

Possible answer: "Those who Know Best" are probably the other relatives, the people who stepped in to scold when Buddy's friend gave him the whiskey.

Extend the Discussion Why do you think Buddy does not tell us specifically who these people are?

ADDITIONAL TEACHING OPPORTUNITY

Evaluate Theme: Ask students to identify the story's theme—its underlying message about life or human nature. Then have students evaluate that theme—decide whether they think it is valid. Tell students to use these questions as their evaluation criteria:

- Does the theme express a broad insight into life or human nature, or simply an idea that applies only to a few people?
- Does the theme offer a meaningful insight, or is it too obvious or clichéd?
- Is the theme a realistic observation, or is it too optimistic, cynical, or narrow-minded?

Point out to students that a theme may be valid even if they do not personally agree with it. (To learn more about evaluating theme, see **Reading Handbook**, page R2.)

SELECTION WRAP–UP

REFLECT Point out that some stories transport us to another time and place. Ask students if "A Christmas Memory" affected them in that way and to explain why or why not.

★ CRITIQUE Ask students to respond to the story as a whole. Have them point out what they liked best and least, providing examples to support and clarify their responses.

READING FLUENCY

Distribute the copy masters and have students work independently to practice fluency.

R RESOURCE MANAGER—Copy Master
Reading Fluency p. 37

DIFFERENTIATED INSTRUCTION

FOR LESS–PROFICIENT READERS

④ **Targeted Passage [Lines 353–376]**

This bittersweet passage reveals what has happened to Buddy and his friend since the time of the narrative.

- Where did Buddy go for the next several years after this Christmas?
- What happened to Queenie?
- Why did the friend's letters change?
- How does Buddy learn about his friend's death? How does he react?

Comprehension

1. **Clarify** How is Buddy's friend different from most people her age?

2. **Recall** What makes Christmas with his friend so memorable for Buddy?

3. **Summarize** What happens to the two friends after this particular Christmas?

Literary Analysis

4. **Examine Character** Think about your impression of Buddy's friend. What **details** helped create this character portrait?

5. **Draw Conclusions About Characters** Buddy is 7; his friend is over 60. Why are they such good **friends?** Give examples from the story to support your answer.

6. **Interpret Symbols** A symbol is a person, place, or object that represents something beyond itself. What might the kites at the end of the story represent, or symbolize? Give reasons for your interpretation.

7. **Evaluate Imagery** Look over the examples of imagery that you noted in your chart. Which example seemed the most vivid? What sense or senses did it appeal to? Explain your choice.

8. **Examine Details of Setting** Locate two passages in which the description of setting helps you understand something about the **historical era,** or time period, in which the story takes place. Then explain what the details tell you about the historical era.

9. **Analyze Influence of Setting** Think about the impact of setting on the events and characters in this story. What might change if the story were set in a city instead of the country or in contemporary times instead of the past? Choose one detail of time or place from the story and explain how the story would be different if this detail were altered.

10. **Make Judgments** In your opinion, is this story merely a vivid portrayal of a memory, or does it also convey a **theme,** or message?

Literary Criticism

11. **Biographical Context** Since its publication, "A Christmas Memory" has stirred debate among readers and critics. If it is based to a large degree on actual people and events, why is it called fiction? Explain why Capote might have chosen to call this work fiction as opposed to autobiography.

Practice and Apply

After Reading

For additional support of post-reading questions, use these copy masters:

R RESOURCE MANAGER—Copy Masters

Reading Check p. 34 (to check understanding of the selection)

Details of Setting p. 27 (for practice of literary analysis standards focus)

Question Support p. 35 (After Reading questions adapted for English learners and less-proficient readers)

For additional questions, see page 21.

ANSWERS

Comprehension

1. *Although she is in her sixties, the woman is childlike in her attitudes and some of her actions.*

2. *It is a time—the last time—that he shares pleasant, familiar tasks and the spirit of Christmas with the only person to whom he seems deeply connected.*

3. *They are separated soon afterward, and they never see each other again.*

Literary Analysis

Possible answers:

4. *She is childlike and enjoys children's pastimes, like flying kites; she is generous (for though money is tight, she gives Buddy a dime every Saturday for the movies); she thinks the best of people (as seen in her calling bootlegger Mr. Haha "a lovely man").*

5. *They are friends because they enjoy each other's company and like the same activities. They also appear to be isolated from the rest of the family and thus have no one else.*

6. *Buddy himself compares the kites to hearts. They may represent the hearts or souls of Buddy and his friend, rising toward heaven, where they would be reunited forever. Buddy's wish is to be once more with his friend, who was so important to him, as she leaves this earth.*

---

7. ■ **STANDARDS FOCUS** *Analyze Imagery*
The image of counting out the money seemed most vivid. One can "see" the rolled bills, feel the weight of the half-dollars, and smell the bitter odor of the pennies.

8. ● **STANDARDS FOCUS** *Details of Setting*
In lines 266–267, Buddy refers to the "made-in-Japan splendors at the five-and-dime." This was the era when Japan had begun to produce and export cheap consumer goods. The thank-you notes (line 176) point to the Franklin Roosevelt administration.

9. *In a city, Buddy and his friend would not chop down a Christmas tree for free.*

10. *The story portrays how deeply a caring person and simple activities can affect a child. It also expresses themes about acceptance, imagination, and the power of friendship.*

Literary Criticism

Possible answer:

11. *Calling the work fiction enabled Capote to embellish it for literary or dramatic effect.*

ANSWERS

Vocabulary in Context

VOCABULARY PRACTICE

1. *d*   6. *c*
2. *c*   7. *a*
3. *b*   8. *c*
4. *b*   9. *d*
5. *a*   10. *c*

R RESOURCE MANAGER—Copy Master
Vocabulary Practice p. 32

VOCABULARY IN WRITING

Suggest that *The others think that Buddy and his friend* _____ is a good sentence starter for using *cavort* and *squander*, but note that students are asked to expand upon that example sentence. Invite students to compare their sentences in small groups.

VOCABULARY STRATEGY: CONNOTATION AND DENOTATION (*also an EL language objective*)

Ask students to explain the connotations of the underlined words in these sentences:

I was tired after basketball practice, but I knew that a shower and fresh clothes would <u>exhilarate</u> me.

The odor in the old house was so <u>potent</u> that my eyes began to water.

As you review the Practice items, have students explain each choice in terms of its connotation as well as its denotation.

Possible answers:

1. *spent*
2. *foolhardy*
3. *unassuming*
4. *fraud*
5. *thin*

R RESOURCE MANAGER—Copy Master
Vocabulary Strategy p. 33

ℹ Vocabulary Center at **ClassZone.com**
Additional Vocabulary Activities

Vocabulary in Context

VOCABULARY PRACTICE

Identify the word that is not related in meaning to the other words in the set.

1. (a) gear, (b) paraphernalia, (c) materials, (d) notice
2. (a) vigorous, (b) robust, (c) prosaic, (d) forceful
3. (a) start, (b) finish, (c) begin, (d) inaugurate
4. (a) destroy, (b) suffuse, (c) demolish, (d) consume
5. (a) depress, (b) invigorate, (c) energize, (d) exhilarate
6. (a) squander, (b) waste, (c) conserve, (d) misuse
7. (a) retreat, (b) urge, (c) spur, (d) goad
8. (a) potent, (b) mighty, (c) possible, (d) strong
9. (a) cavort, (b) prance, (c) frolic, (d) fight
10. (a) cut, (b) separate, (c) join, (d) sever

> **WORD LIST**
> cavort
> exhilarate
> goad
> inaugurate
> paraphernalia
> potent
> prosaic
> sever
> squander
> suffuse

VOCABULARY IN WRITING

Write several sentences about how others in the household seem to regard the two friends. Use three or more vocabulary words in your sentences. Here is a sample.

> **EXAMPLE SENTENCE**
>
> *The others think that Buddy and his friend collect a lot of useless* **paraphernalia***.*

VOCABULARY STRATEGY: CONNOTATION AND DENOTATION

A word's **denotation** is its basic dictionary meaning; its **connotations** are the overtones of meaning that it may take on. For example, the vocabulary word *goad* means "to urge," but it has connotations of physically forcing or bullying that *urge* does not have. When you choose words in writing, be sure to consider whether their connotations fit the context.

PRACTICE Choose the word that works best in each sentence.

1. Though the Smiths (spent, squandered) a lot of money, they thought putting their son through college was worth it.
2. It was (brave, foolhardy) of Karen not to study before final exams.
3. Al has a modest, (unassuming, groveling) manner that puts people at ease.
4. Anyone treating patients without a medical degree is a (fraud, pretender).
5. The haircut framed her (thin, emaciated) face quite nicely.

 VOCABULARY PRACTICE For more practice, go to the **Vocabulary Center** at **ClassZone.com**.

DIFFERENTIATED INSTRUCTION

FOR ENGLISH LEARNERS

Task Support: Reinforce Use Word Sorts to reinforce understanding of the Word List before students begin the **Vocabulary Practice** activity.

BEST PRACTICES TOOLKIT—Transparency
Word Sorts p. E5

FOR ADVANCED LEARNERS/PRE–AP

Multiple Connotations Elicit from students that some words can have more than one connotation, depending on the context of the sentence. For example, the word *paraphernalia* is often used to describe paperwork, or it can describe a random collection of things. Ask students what kinds of connotations those two meanings bring to mind. Then, lead a similar discussion using the rest of the words.

Reading-Writing Connection

Increase your understanding of "A Christmas Memory" by responding to these prompts. Then use **Revision: Grammar and Style** to improve your writing.

WRITING PROMPTS	SELF-CHECK
A. Short Response: Rewrite a Scene Imitation is a good way to learn from a master stylist like Truman Capote. Pick your favorite scene from the story and create a **one- or two-paragraph description** of it, using your own images.	*A strong description will . . .* • clearly evoke the time and place • include sensory details
B. Extended Response: Analyze a Character Consider what you learn in this story about Buddy's **friend** and her values. Write a **three-to-five-paragraph response** in which you describe the kind of person she is, using quotations from the story to illustrate your analysis.	*A successful response will . . .* • give a detailed description of the person's values • include examples and quotations as support

REVISION: GRAMMAR AND STYLE

CHOOSE EFFECTIVE VERB TENSE Review the **Grammar and Style** note on page 316. By choosing to tell his story in the **present tense,** Capote invites the reader to relive the memory along with the narrator. Here is an example from the story:

> *Long after the town has gone to sleep and the house is silent except for the chimings of clocks and the sputter of fading fires, she is weeping into a pillow . . .* (lines 207–208)

Notice how the revisions in red, changing past to present tense, bring an immediacy to the writing, as though the events were occurring now. Try using a similar technique as you revise your draft of Prompt A.

> **STUDENT MODEL**
>
> My friend jammed her hat down on her head and recklessly navigated the
> baby buggy across the frosty grass. The pecans we sought were hiding under
> rotting leaves and twigs.

> **WRITING TOOLS**
>
> For prewriting, revision, and editing tools, visit the **Writing Center** at **ClassZone.com.**

A CHRISTMAS MEMORY 325

FOR LESS—PROFICIENT WRITERS

For Prompt A:

• Urge students to generate their own details rather than reusing Capote's.
• Remind students that even though their writing is descriptive, it still needs a topic sentence for each paragraph and a main idea that unifies the details.

For Prompt B:

• Limit the length of the assignment to no more than three paragraphs.
• Have students review their responses to the lettered questions throughout the story to make inferences about the values that Buddy's friend holds.
• Point out that students are asked to quote from the story, not just to refer to its details indirectly. Tell students to include at least one quotation for each major point.

Reading-Writing Connection

WRITING PROMPTS

• For Prompt A, have students visualize the scene that they have chosen, using Sensory Notes to record details and images. Urge students to capture ways in which the details appeal to various senses.
• For Prompt B, review some of the things that students learned about characterization in Unit 2—for example, character motivation and various methods of characterization that writers employ.

 BEST PRACTICES TOOLKIT—Transparency
Sensory Notes p. B9

For an extended writing activity, see
ℹ️ Carol Booth Olson's Reading-Writing Lesson Plans at **ClassZone.com**

REVISION: GRAMMAR AND STYLE

Discuss the revisions to the student model. In particular, point out the spelling changes. (For information on present-tense verbs, see **Grammar Handbook**, page R55.)

• *Jammed* drops the doubling of a letter to become *jams*.
• *Navigated* changes its last letter but not its stem to become *navigates*.
• *Sought* and *were* change form completely to become *seek* and *are*.

If necessary, refer students to a chart of irregular verbs as they revise Prompt A.

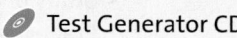 RESOURCE MANAGER—Copy Master
Choose Effective Verb Tense p. 36

Assess and Reteach

Assess

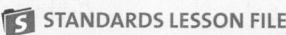 RESOURCE MANAGER—Copy Masters
Selection Test A pp. 39–40
Selection Test B/C pp. 41–42
💿 Test Generator CD

Reteach

🅢 STANDARDS LESSON FILE
Literature Lesson 9: Setting and Its Roles
Literature Lesson 28: Imagery
Vocabulary Lesson 17: Denotation and Connotation
Grammar Lesson 16: Basic Verb Tenses

Focus and Motivate

OBJECTIVES

Literary Analysis
- explore the key idea of **risks**
- analyze setting as symbol
- read a short story

Reading
- analyze descriptive details

Vocabulary
- build vocabulary for reading and writing
- understand Latin word roots *quest, quer, quist* (*also an EL language objective*)

Grammar and Writing
- use compound predicates to write concisely
- use writing to analyze literature

SUMMARY

While vacationing with his mother at a beach resort, 11-year-old Jerry explores a wild-looking bay and admires some older local boys as they swim through a treacherous underwater tunnel. Jerry decides that he, too, must swim through the tunnel and trains himself to hold his breath for longer and longer periods of time. He finally makes the dangerous swim yet keeps his accomplishment a secret from his mother.

When is a RISK *worth taking?*

After you ask the question, invite students to define the **KEY IDEA** of **risks.** Have them read the paragraph and suggest examples of various kinds of risks. Wrap up by having students complete the **DISCUSS** and compare the resulting balance scales.

Selection Resources

Through the Tunnel
Short Story by Doris Lessing

When is a **RISK** *worth taking?*

KEY IDEA In "Through the Tunnel," Jerry risks his personal safety. Sometimes people take such **risks** to prove something to themselves or others. The risks can be physical, emotional, or social. But when is an action too risky to attempt? More importantly, how do you calculate risk?

DISCUSS Think about a time when you or someone you know took a risk to prove something. Create a balance scale like the one shown to weigh that risk. In the base of the scale, write down the dangerous or risky activity. Jot down the risks in one box and the possible benefits in the other. Share your balance scale with your classmates, and discuss with them whether the possible benefits outweighed the risks of the behavior.

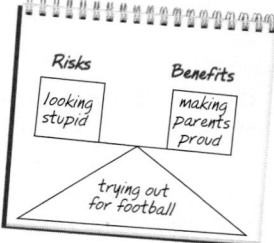

Risks — looking stupid

Benefits — making parents proud

trying out for football

326

RESOURCE MANAGER UNIT 3

Plan and Teach pp. 43–50

Literary Analysis
Summary pp. 51†*, 52‡*
Setting as Symbol pp. 53, 54†*
Question Support p. 62*

Reading
Analyze Details pp. 55, 56†*
Reading Check p. 61
Reading Fluency p. 64

Vocabulary
Study p. 57*
Practice p. 58
Strategy p. 59

Grammar and Writing
Write Concisely p. 63

Assessment
Selection Tests A, B/C pp. 65*, 67*
Test Generator CD

BEST PRACTICES TOOLKIT

Differentiated Instruction
pp. 31–38*

Scaffolding Instruction
pp. 43–46*

Graphic Organizers/Strategies
Two-Column Chart • Word Questioning • New Word Analysis • Jigsaw Reading • Comparison Matrix• Think Aloud • Summary Frame: Narrative

Reading Support
Audio Anthology CD*

Technology
Literature and Vocabulary Centers at **ClassZone.com**

WriteSmart CD

---

* Resources for Differentiation   † Also in Spanish   ‡ In Haitian Creole and Vietnamese

LITERARY ANALYSIS: SETTING AS SYMBOL

A **symbol** is a person, place, object, or activity that stands for something beyond itself. For example, a star often symbolizes hope or excellence. A handshake communicates goodwill.

In "Through the Tunnel," various **settings** symbolize important ideas. As you read, think about what the beach, the bay, the tunnel, and the events that take place in each location might symbolize to Jerry.

● READING SKILL: ANALYZE DETAILS

In order to understand the symbolic significance of each setting in "Through the Tunnel," you must analyze the **descriptive details** and pay attention to the larger meanings they imply. For example, the big beach is a familiar place where Jerry's mother goes. What might this represent to Jerry? As you read, keep track of words and phrases that describe each setting by using a chart similar to the one shown.

Beach	Bay	Tunnel
crowded	wild and rocky	
familiar		

Review: **Draw Conclusions**

▲ VOCABULARY IN CONTEXT

Lessing uses the numbered words in her story about coming of age. Try to match each word with a synonym.

1. contrition   a. cliff
2. incredulous   b. perseverance
3. inquisitive   c. regret
4. persistence   d. request
5. promontory   e. questioning
6. supplication   f. unbelieving

Author Online

Distinguished Writer
Doris Lessing has been celebrated as one of the 20th century's "most powerful and compelling novelists." In sheer size and variety, her body of work is impressive: over 45 books ranging from novels and short story collections to essays, a thus far two-volume autobiography, and a book about cats.

**Doris Lessing
born 1919**

Crossing Boundaries Born in Persia (now Iran), Lessing grew up on a farm in Southern Rhodesia (now Zimbabwe) with her British parents. As part of the small community of white settlers in Africa, she saw firsthand the injustices of white minority rule and racial segregation. In 1949, Lessing left Rhodesia for London to start a new life as a writer. Her first novel, *The Grass Is Singing* (1950), and many of her other early works are set in Rhodesia and deal critically with the colonial society she had known. Her best-known novel is *The Golden Notebook* (1962), a story about a woman writer in London struggling to come to terms with her life and times.

Child of Africa Lessing insists, "Whatever I am, I have been made so by central Africa." Her self-confidence, strength, and independence can be traced to her youth in the rough, unforgiving country of the African bush. There she could roam freely but, like other African children, had to deal at an early age with dangerous thunderstorms, droughts, snakes, scorpions, and insects. Survival—emotional, intellectual, and physical—is at the heart of her life and work.

 MORE ABOUT THE AUTHOR
For more on Doris Lessing, visit the **Literature Center at ClassZone.com.**

THROUGH THE TUNNEL **327**

Teach

STANDARDS FOCUS

LITERARY ANALYSIS

● SETTING AS SYMBOL

For instructional support, have students explain what each of these scenes represents:

- a soldier waving a white flag on a battlefield *Possible answer: surrender*
- a courtroom statue of a blindfolded woman holding a scale *Possible answer: equal treatment under the law*

CHECK UNDERSTANDING Elicit other examples of symbolic settings from fiction, movies, or students' personal experiences.

READING SKILL

■ ANALYZE DETAILS

Point out that there can be more than one larger meaning to a given detail or group of details. Illustrate by asking students what a lush garden filled with blooming flowers suggests to them. *Possible answers: peace; beauty; romance; extravagance*

CHECK UNDERSTANDING Ask students what a dark forest or a sunny beach suggests to them.

 RESOURCE MANAGER—Copy Master
Analyze Details p. 55 (for student use while reading the selection)

VOCABULARY SKILL

▲ VOCABULARY IN CONTEXT

DIAGNOSE WORD KNOWLEDGE To determine preteaching needs, have all students complete Vocabulary in Context. *Possible answers:* **1.** *c;* **2.** *f;* **3.** *e;* **4.** *b;* **5.** *a;* **6.** *d*

PRETEACH VOCABULARY Use the Vocabulary Study copy master to help students predict the meaning of each boldfaced word in the copy master.

1. Read aloud the first sentence in Part A, emphasizing *contrition*.

2. Point out the phrase "did not mean to hurt her feelings." Elicit possible meanings for *contrition,* such as "apology."

3. Repeat the procedure for the other words.

 **RESOURCE MANAGER—Copy Master**
Vocabulary Study p. 57

For general guidelines on differentiating vocabulary instruction and for alternative vocabulary activities for students not needing vocabulary preteaching, see

BEST PRACTICES TOOLKIT
Scaffolding Vocabulary Instruction pp. 43–46
ⓘ Vocabulary Center at **ClassZone.com**

Practice and Apply

ANALYZE VISUALS

Possible answer: The painting emphasizes the contrast between the power and mystery of nature and the confined safety of the beach. Nature is alluring, represented by the soft blues of the water, but it is also mysterious, possibly dangerous, represented by the black, irregularly shaped cave in the upper right. The beach is narrow and bright, backed by the boxlike building behind the bathers.

About the Art As the subject matter and style of *La Jolla Cove* demonstrate, Alson Skinner Clark (1876–1949) was an American Impressionist.

READING SKILL

A ANALYZE DETAILS

***Possible answer:** The beach is safe and crowded; the bay is wild and dangerous.*

If students need help . . . Explore the larger meaning of the details by helping students complete a Two-Column Chart. Model the thinking by which you reach the first two responses; then help students add to the chart.

Detail	Larger Meaning
"wild and rocky bay" (line 2)	dangers of adult life; lack of protection from mother
"crowded beach" (line 3)	safety of childhood

 BEST PRACTICES TOOLKIT—Transparency Two-Column Chart p. A25

THROUGH THE
Tunnel

Doris Lessing

Going to the shore on the first morning of the vacation, the young English boy stopped at a turning of the path and looked down at a wild and rocky bay, and then over to the crowded beach he knew so well from other years. His mother walked on in front of him, carrying a bright striped bag in one hand. Her other arm, swinging loose, was very white in the sun. The boy watched that white, naked arm, and turned his eyes, which had a frown behind them, toward the bay and back again to his mother. When she felt he was not with her, she swung around. "Oh, there you are, Jerry!" she said. She looked impatient, then smiled. "Why, darling, would you rather not come with
10 me? Would you rather—" She frowned, conscientiously worrying over what amusements he might secretly be longing for, which she had been too busy or too careless to imagine. He was very familiar with that anxious, apologetic smile. **Contrition** sent him running after her. And yet, as he ran, he looked back over his shoulder at the wild bay; and all morning, as he played on the safe beach, he was thinking of it. **A**

Next morning, when it was time for the routine of swimming and sunbathing, his mother said, "Are you tired of the usual beach, Jerry? Would you like to go somewhere else?"

ANALYZE VISUALS
What elements of this painting are emphasized by its **composition**—the sizes, shapes, and arrangement of its parts?

1 Targeted Passage

contrition (kən-trĭsh′ən) *n.* a feeling of regret for doing wrong

A ANALYZE DETAILS
From what you've learned so far, what contrast exists between the beach and the bay?

328 UNIT 3: SETTING, MOOD, AND IMAGERY

DIFFERENTIATED INSTRUCTION

FOR ALL STUDENTS
Journal As they read, ask students to keep a journal noting questions, observations, and reflections about characters and situations. Ask students to refer to their notes when completing other activities that accompany the selection.

FOR LESS–PROFICIENT READERS
In combination with the *Audio Anthology CD*, use one or more Targeted Passages (pp. 328, 331, 334, 335, 338) to ensure that students focus on key story events, concepts, and skills. Targeted Passages are also good for English learners.

1 Targeted Passage [Lines 1–15]
This passage introduces the setting of the rocky bay and the attraction that it has for Jerry, the main character.

BACKGROUND

Dangers in Diving While diving (introduced in line 65) is an age-old activity, it poses real dangers. Later, Jerry will break the primary rule of diving: Never dive alone. Also, since Jerry does not grasp the dangers of diving, he will not react appropriately when he experiences "shallow water blackout," a potentially fatal condition that results in loss of consciuosness due to low oxygen levels in the blood stream.

Cultural Connection "Through the Tunnel" describes how Jerry becomes more mature by reaching a difficult goal. Jerry's maturation is informal, but many cultures have formal celebrations of maturity. In Judaism, for example, children become adult members of the congregation upon their thirteenth birthday. The ceremony for a boy is called a *bar mitzvah*; for a girl, a *bat mitzvah* or *bas mitzvah*. Similarly, traditional Apaches often celebrate *Na'ii'ees*—"the Sunrise Dance"—for girls of about the same age. Its eight phases symbolize the passage from childhood to adulthood. At its conclusion, participants are considered mature members of the community. Invite students to share what they may know about other coming-of-age ceremonies.

- Where are Jerry and his mother? What are they doing there?
- What does Jerry keep looking at?
- Why does his mother frown?
- What does Jerry think about all morning?

FOR ENGLISH LEARNERS

Options for Reading Ask a question about a set of paragraphs or range of numbered lines. Have pairs of students scan the designated text to find the answer.

Prereading For prereading instruction for English learners, see

 BEST PRACTICES TOOLKIT
Scaffolding Reading Instruction pp. 43–46

FOR ADVANCED LEARNERS/PRE–AP

Pre-AP Exercises in the bottom channel provide additional challenge for students. Use these suggestions for small groups or individuals.

ADDITIONAL GUIDELINES

For more help with differentiation and tips for classroom management, see

 BEST PRACTICES TOOLKIT
Differentiated Instruction pp. 31–38

B SETTING AS SYMBOL

Possible answer: *The beach might symbolize the safety of childhood; the bay, the excitement and dangers of adulthood.*

If students need help . . . Guide them through specific lines in the passage.

- At line 21, elicit that Jerry wants to see the rocks, which can stand for danger.

- At line 22, elicit that the bay's wildness is in the mother's thinking, not Jerry's.

- Reread lines 23–30. Discuss why the mother urges Jerry to go to the bay. Help them connect her thinking to the symbolism of the bay and the beach. ***Possible answer:*** *She urges him to go because she fears that she has been overprotective, trying to keep him from growing up. Thus, the beach can stand for childhood; the bay, for adulthood.*

C ANALYZE DETAILS

Possible answer: *The cold, deep water that "shocked his limbs" (lines 45–46) suggests this is the real sea, not the sheltered cove. Furthermore, Jerry crossed "a middle region," with monsterlike rocks, to reach it (lines 43–45).*

---

20 "Oh, no!" he said quickly, smiling at her out of that unfailing impulse of contrition—a sort of chivalry. Yet, walking down the path with her, he blurted out, "I'd like to go and have a look at those rocks down there."

She gave the idea her attention. It was a wild-looking place, and there was no one there; but she said, "Of course, Jerry. When you've had enough, come to the big beach. Or just go straight back to the villa, if you like." She walked away, that bare arm, now slightly reddened from yesterday's sun, swinging. And he almost ran after her again, feeling it unbearable that she should go by herself, but he did not.

She was thinking, Of course he's old enough to be safe without me. Have I been keeping him too close? He mustn't feel he ought to be with me. I must be 30 careful. **B**

He was an only child, eleven years old. She was a widow. She was determined to be neither possessive nor lacking in devotion. She went worrying off to her beach.

As for Jerry, once he saw that his mother had gained her beach, he began the steep descent to the bay. From where he was, high up among red-brown rocks, it was a scoop of moving bluish green fringed with white. As he went lower, he saw that it spread among small **promontories** and inlets of rough, sharp rock, and the crisping, lapping surface showed stains of purple and darker blue. Finally, as he ran sliding and scraping down the last few yards, 40 he saw an edge of white surf and the shallow, luminous movement of water over white sand, and, beyond that, a solid, heavy blue.

He ran straight into the water and began swimming. He was a good swimmer. He went out fast over the gleaming sand, over a middle region where rocks lay like discolored monsters under the surface, and then he was in the real sea—a warm sea where irregular cold currents from the deep water shocked his limbs. **C**

When he was so far out that he could look back not only on the little bay but past the promontory that was between it and the big beach, he floated on the buoyant surface and looked for his mother. There she was, a speck of 50 yellow under an umbrella that looked like a slice of orange peel. He swam back to shore, relieved at being sure she was there, but all at once very lonely.

On the edge of a small cape that marked the side of the bay away from the promontory was a loose scatter of rocks. Above them, some boys were stripping off their clothes. They came running, naked, down to the rocks. The English boy swam toward them, but kept his distance at a stone's throw. They were of that coast; all of them were burned smooth dark brown and speaking a language he did not understand. To be with them, of them, was a craving that filled his whole body. He swam a little closer; they turned and watched him with narrowed, alert dark eyes. Then one smiled and waved. It was enough. In 60 a minute, he had swum in and was on the rocks beside them, smiling with a

---

B SETTING AS SYMBOL
Reread lines 21–30. What might the beach symbolize? The bay?

promontory
(prŏm′ən-tôr′ē) *n.*
a high ridge of land or rock jutting out into a body of water

C ANALYZE DETAILS
Reread lines 42–46. Why might Jerry consider this area "the real sea"?

DIFFERENTIATED INSTRUCTION

FOR ENGLISH LEARNERS
Key Academic Vocabulary Use Word Questioning to provide instruction and practice for these Key Academic Vocabulary words: *region* (line 43), *proceeded* (line 63), *visible* (line 82), *inspection* (line 93), *impact* (line 133), *brief* (line 262).

BEST PRACTICES TOOLKIT—Transparency
Word Questioning p. E9

FOR ADVANCED LEANERS/PRE–AP
Analyze Setting [paired activity option] Ask students to sketch the setting described in lines 34–51 from the perspective of either Jerry or his mother. Include only those details each would see from his or her perspective, including each as seen by the other. Then ask each student to explain his or her choices of representation.

desperate, nervous **supplication.** They shouted cheerful greetings at him; and then, as he preserved his nervous, uncomprehending smile, they understood that he was a foreigner strayed from his own beach, and they proceeded to forget him. But he was happy. He was with them.

They began diving again and again from a high point into a well of blue sea between rough, pointed rocks. After they had dived and come up, they swam around, hauled themselves up, and waited their turn to dive again. They were big boys—men, to Jerry. He dived, and they watched him; and when he swam around to take his place, they made way for him. He felt he was accepted and
70 he dived again, carefully, proud of himself.

Soon the biggest of the boys poised himself, shot down into the water, and did not come up. The others stood about, watching. Jerry, after waiting for the sleek brown head to appear, let out a yell of warning; they looked at him idly and turned their eyes back toward the water. After a long time, the boy came up on the other side of a big dark rock, letting the air out of his lungs in a sputtering gasp and a shout of triumph. Immediately the rest of them dived in. One moment, the morning seemed full of chattering boys; the next, the air and the surface of the water were empty. But through the heavy blue, dark shapes could be seen moving and groping.
80 Jerry dived, shot past the school of underwater swimmers, saw a black wall of rock looming at him, touched it, and bobbed up at once to the surface, where the wall was a low barrier he could see across. There was no one visible; under him, in the water, the dim shapes of the swimmers had disappeared. Then one, and then another of the boys came up on the far side of the barrier of rock, and he understood that they had swum through some gap or hole in it. He plunged down again. He could see nothing through the stinging salt water but the blank rock. When he came up the boys were all on the diving rock, preparing to attempt the feat again. And now, in a panic of failure, he yelled up, in English, "Look at me! Look!" and he began splashing and kicking
90 in the water like a foolish dog.

They looked down gravely, frowning. He knew the frown. At moments of failure, when he clowned to claim his mother's attention, it was with just this grave, embarrassed inspection that she rewarded him. Through his hot shame, feeling the pleading grin on his face like a scar that he could never remove, he looked up at the group of big brown boys on the rock and shouted, *"Bonjour! Merci! Au revoir! Monsieur, monsieur!"*[1] while he hooked his fingers round his ears and waggled them.

Water surged into his mouth; he choked, sank, came up. The rock, lately weighted with boys, seemed to rear up out of the water as their weight was
100 removed. They were flying down past him, now, into the water; the air was full of falling bodies. Then the rock was empty in the hot sunlight. He counted one, two, three. . . .

---

1. *Bonjour! Merci! Au revoir! Monsieur, monsieur!* (bôn-zhōor′ měr-sē′ ō′rə-vwär′ mə-syœ′ mə-syœ′)
   French: Good day! Thank you! Goodbye! Sir, sir!

---

② Targeted Passage

Ⓓ GRAMMAR AND STYLE
Reread lines 80–81. Notice how Lessing uses a **compound predicate** to concisely describe several actions taking place.

Ⓓ GRAMMAR AND STYLE

Write Concisely Have students incorporate each part of the compound predicate into its own distinct sentence. (*Jerry dived. He shot past the school of underwater swimmers. He saw . . .*) Discuss how the original is more concise. Point out that the concise style helps create the story's suspense and flow.

Then challenge students to find a few other sentences in the text in which Lessing uses compound predicates (for example, line 98: " . . . he choked, sank, came up").

Lines 65–88
DISCUSSION PROMPTS
Use these prompts to help students understand the significance of the local boys to the story:

Summarize What happens in these lines? What is Jerry trying to achieve? *Possible answers: Jerry watches and tries to imitate a group of boys who are diving. Jerry concludes that they are swimming through an underwater tunnel and he tries unsuccessfully to follow them. He calls to the boys, who ignore him. Jerry is trying to be noticed and accepted.*

Analyze What does swimming to "the far side of the barrier" (line 84) represent to Jerry? *Possible answers: A seemingly impossible challenge; something that he must do to regain or maintain his self-respect.*

Evaluate What does the lack of spoken response from the older boys in line 91 contribute to the story? *Possible answer: The lack of response makes it all the more important to Jerry that he get the boys to notice him.*

FOR LESS–PROFICIENT READERS
② Targeted Passage [Lines 68–93]

By introducing the diving challenge, this passage sets up the conflict that will drive the rest of the story.

- How do the local boys treat Jerry at first?
- What does the biggest boy then do? How do the other local boys react?
- What does Jerry do to get their attention? How does he feel about it afterward?

FOR ENGLISH LEARNERS
Vocabulary: Idioms Use New Word Analysis to teach these idioms from the story:

- *made way* (line 69), "moved aside"
- *was off* (line 131), "left"
- *caught a glimpse . . . of* (line 167), "viewed briefly and incompletely"
- *overdo it* (line 298), "do too much"

  BEST PRACTICES TOOLKIT—Transparency
New Word Analysis p. E8

At fifty, he was terrified. They must all be drowning beneath him, in the watery caves of the rock! At a hundred, he stared around him at the empty hillside, wondering if he should yell for help. He counted faster, faster, to hurry them up, to bring them to the surface quickly, to drown them quickly—anything rather than the terror of counting on and on into the blue emptiness of the morning. And then, at a hundred and sixty, the water beyond the rock was full of boys blowing like brown whales. They swam back to the shore
110   without a look at him.

He climbed back to the diving rock and sat down, feeling the hot roughness of it under his thighs. The boys were gathering up their bits of clothing and running off along the shore to another promontory. They were leaving to get away from him. He cried openly, fists in his eyes. There was no one to see him, and he cried himself out. **E**

It seemed to him that a long time had passed, and he swam out to where he could see his mother. Yes, she was still there, a yellow spot under an orange umbrella. He swam back to the big rock, climbed up, and dived into the blue pool among the fanged and angry boulders. Down he went, until he
120   touched the wall of rock again. But the salt was so painful in his eyes that he could not see. **F**

He came to the surface, swam to shore, and went back to the villa to wait for his mother. Soon she walked slowly up the path, swinging her striped bag, the flushed, naked arm dangling beside her. "I want some swimming goggles," he panted, defiant and beseeching.

She gave him a patient, **inquisitive** look as she said casually, "Well, of course, darling."

F ANALYZE DETAILS
What does the description of the boulders in line 119 suggest about the tunnel?

inquisitive (ĭn-kwĭz′ĭ-tĭv) *adj.* curious; inquiring

But now, now, now! He must have them this minute, and no other time. He nagged and pestered until she went with him to a shop. As soon as she had
130   bought the goggles, he grabbed them from her hand as if she were going to claim them for herself, and was off, running down the steep path to the bay.

Jerry swam out to the big barrier rock, adjusted the goggles, and dived. The impact of the water broke the rubber-enclosed vacuum, and the goggles came loose. He understood that he must swim down to the base of the rock from the surface of the water. He fixed the goggles tight and firm, filled his lungs, and floated, face down, on the water. Now, he could see. It was as if he had eyes of a different kind—fish eyes that showed everything clear and delicate and wavering in the bright water.

Under him, six or seven feet down, was a floor of perfectly clean, shining
140   white sand, rippled firm and hard by the tides. Two grayish shapes steered there, like long, rounded pieces of wood or slate. They were fish. He saw them nose toward each other, poise motionless, make a dart forward, swerve off, and come around again. It was like a water dance. A few inches above them the water sparkled as if sequins were dropping through it. Fish again—myriads of

Reflections (1970), Ken Danby. Original egg tempera, 38″ × 52″. © Ken Danby/Gallery Moos, Toronto, Canada.

READING SKILL: *Review*

E DRAW CONCLUSIONS
Possible answer: Jerry is upset because he feels that the boys are deliberately abandoning him (lines 113–114).

READING SKILL

F ANALYZE DETAILS
Possible answer: The reference to "fanged and angry boulders" suggests that the tunnel is treacherous, like a wild, predatory animal.

If students need help . . . Have students draw the boulders, based on the description in line 119. Discuss how the pictures look like dangerous animals.

Extend the Discussion The expression "fanged and angry boulders" implies that the boulders are alive. Is this type of language an effective way to describe something that is not alive? Defend your answer.

ANALYZE VISUALS
Possible answer: The monotone brown palette, the boy's contemplative stance, and the craggy overhanging rocks create a quiet, thoughtful mood. (The fact that the name of the painting is Reflections *reinforces this interpretation.)*

About the Art *Reflections* is typical of the work of contemporary Canadian painter Ken Danby because of its realistic style and naturalistic setting.

DIFFERENTIATED INSTRUCTION

FOR ENGLISH LEARNERS

Vocabulary: Suffixes Have students explain the meaning of *grayish* in line 140. Point out that the suffix *-ish* often means "like." Then ask Jigsaw Reading groups to list five other adjectives with the *-ish* suffix that they think fit the story (for example, *childish, foolish, doggish, feverish,* and *nightmarish*). Instruct groups to look up and discuss their words. Then ask group representatives to tell the class what the words mean and how they relate to "Through the Tunnel." Repeat this activity for the word *motionless* (line 142) and the suffix *-less*, meaning "without."

BEST PRACTICES TOOLKIT
Jigsaw Reading p. A1

Lines 118–121

REINFORCE *KEY IDEA:* RISKS

Discuss The boulders are "fanged and angry." The salt stings Jerry's eyes so badly that he cannot see. However, Jerry keeps diving, trying to find the tunnel. Why does Jerry take this painful, dangerous **risk?** *Possible answer: He feels compelled to prove his maturity because he senses that the older boys have rejected him.*

FOR ADVANCED LEARNERS/PRE–AP

Research Activity Have students research rituals that use water as a symbol of rebirth, such as the Christian rite of baptism or the Hindu practice of bathing in the sacred waters of the Ganges River. Note how, for many of these rituals, a symbolic death is a key element of the rite of transformation.

minute fish, the length of his fingernail, were drifting through the water, and in a moment he could feel the innumerable tiny touches of them against his limbs. It was like swimming in flaked silver. The great rock the big boys had swum through rose sheer out of the white sand—black, tufted lightly with greenish weed. He could see no gap in it. He swam down to its base.

150   Again and again he rose, took a big chestful of air, and went down. Again and again he groped over the surface of the rock, feeling it, almost hugging it in the desperate need to find the entrance. And then, once, while he was clinging to the black wall, his knees came up and he shot his feet out forward and they met no obstacle. He had found the hole.

    He gained the surface, clambered about the stones that littered the barrier rock until he found a big one, and, with this in his arms, let himself down over the side of the rock. He dropped, with the weight, straight to the sandy floor. Clinging tight to the anchor of stone, he lay on his side and looked in under the dark shelf at the place where his feet had gone. He could see the hole.

160 It was an irregular, dark gap; but he could not see deep into it. He let go of his anchor, clung with his hands to the edges of the hole, and tried to push himself in.

    He got his head in, found his shoulders jammed, moved them in sidewise, and was inside as far as his waist. He could see nothing ahead. Something soft and clammy touched his mouth; he saw a dark frond moving against the grayish rock, and panic filled him. He thought of octopuses, of clinging weed. He pushed himself out backward and caught a glimpse, as he retreated, of a harmless tentacle of seaweed drifting in the mouth of the tunnel. But it was enough. He reached the sunlight, swam to shore, and lay on the diving rock.

170 He looked down into the blue well of water. He knew he must find his way through that cave, or hole, or tunnel, and out the other side. **G**

    First, he thought, he must learn to control his breathing. He let himself down into the water with another big stone in his arms, so that he could lie effortlessly on the bottom of the sea. He counted. One, two, three. He counted steadily. He could hear the movement of blood in his chest. Fifty-one, fifty-two. . . . His chest was hurting. He let go of the rock and went up into the air. He saw that the sun was low. He rushed to the villa and found his mother at her supper. She said only "Did you enjoy yourself?" and he said "Yes."

    All night the boy dreamed of the water-filled cave in the rock, and as soon

180 as breakfast was over he went to the bay.

    That night, his nose bled badly. For hours he had been underwater, learning to hold his breath, and now he felt weak and dizzy. His mother said, "I shouldn't overdo things, darling, if I were you."

    That day and the next, Jerry exercised his lungs as if everything, the whole of his life, all that he would become, depended upon it. Again his nose bled at night, and his mother insisted on his coming with her the next day. It was

G DRAW CONCLUSIONS
Reread lines 155–171. How does Jerry's perception of the tunnel change? What does this tell you about him?

❸ Targeted Passage

G DRAW CONCLUSIONS

Possible answer: *Initially, Jerry feels panic over imagined danger. When he sees the tunnel for what it is, he becomes more determined than ever to find a way through. This change in perception suggests Jerry's growing maturity.*

If students need help . . . Use the Comparison Matrix to help them draw conclusions about the change in Jerry.

 BEST PRACTICES TOOLKIT—Transparency
Comparison Matrix p. A24

Lines 163–171
DISCUSSION PROMPTS

Use these prompts to explore Jerry's first attempt to swim the tunnel:

Connect Do you know of any scary passageways, like a cave or a tunnel? What details stand out in your mind? ***Possible answers:*** *Students may draw from personal experience or from television or movies.*

Analyze How might the tunnel be symbolic of the passage from childhood to adulthood? ***Possible answer:*** *It is mysterious and scary.*

Synthesize How does this symbolism reflect the idea that Jerry is changing? ***Possible answer:*** *Jerry decides to be more grown up. If he can pass through the tunnel, perhaps he will be grown up, like the older boys he saw earlier.*

DIFFERENTIATED INSTRUCTION

FOR LESS–PROFICIENT READERS
❸ Targeted Passage [Lines 169–185]

This passage reveals the challenges involved in preparing for a swim through the tunnel.

- As he looks into the water, what goal does Jerry set for himself?

- How does he learn to control his breathing?

- Why does he start getting nosebleeds?

- What advice does his mother give him?

FOR ENGLISH LEARNERS
Vocabulary: Multiple-Meaning Words

Have students work in groups to identify the correct meaning and part of speech for each of these words as used in the story: *rose* (line 148), *down* (line 150), *lie* (line 173), *safe* (line 189), *count* (line 192), *strain* (line 203), *open* (line 222), *clear* (line 234), *crack* (line 253), *sink* (line 269).

a torment to him to waste a day of his careful self-training, but he stayed with her on that other beach, which now seemed a place for small children, a place where his mother might lie safe in the sun. It was not his beach. **H**

190   He did not ask for permission, on the following day, to go to his beach. He went, before his mother could consider the complicated rights and wrongs of the matter. A day's rest, he discovered, had improved his count by ten. The big boys had made the passage while he counted a hundred and sixty. He had been counting fast, in his fright. Probably now, if he tried, he could get through that long tunnel, but he was not going to try yet. A curious, most unchildlike **persistence**, a controlled impatience, made him wait. In the meantime, he lay underwater on the white sand, littered now by stones he had brought down from the upper air, and studied the entrance to the tunnel. He knew every jut and corner of it, as far as it was possible to see. It was as if he
200 already felt its sharpness about his shoulders.

    He sat by the clock in the villa, when his mother was not near, and checked his time. He was **incredulous** and then proud to find he could hold his breath without strain for two minutes. The words "two minutes," authorized by the clock, brought close the adventure that was so necessary to him.

In another four days, his mother said casually one morning, they must go home. On the day before they left, he would do it. He would do it if it killed him, he said defiantly to himself. But two days before they were to leave—a day of triumph when he increased his count by fifteen—his nose bled so badly that he turned dizzy and had to lie limply over the big rock like
210 a bit of seaweed, watching the thick red blood flow on to the rock and trickle slowly down to the sea. He was frightened. Supposing he turned dizzy in the tunnel? Supposing he died there, trapped? Supposing—his head went around, in the hot sun, and he almost gave up. He thought he would return to the house and lie down, and next summer, perhaps, when he had another year's growth in him—*then* he would go through the hole.

    But even after he had made the decision, or thought he had, he found himself sitting up on the rock and looking down into the water; and he knew that now, this moment, when his nose had only just stopped bleeding, when his head was still sore and throbbing—this was the moment when he would
220 try. If he did not do it now, he never would. He was trembling with fear that he would not go; and he was trembling with horror at that long, long tunnel under the rock, under the sea. Even in the open sunlight, the barrier rock seemed very wide and very heavy; tons of rock pressed down on where he would go. If he died there, he would lie until one day—perhaps not before next year—those big boys would swim into it and find it blocked. **I**

    He put on his goggles, fitted them tight, tested the vacuum. His hands were shaking. Then he chose the biggest stone he could carry and slipped over the

H SETTING AS SYMBOL
What does the big beach symbolize to Jerry now? Cite details in this paragraph that support your interpretation.

persistence (pər-sĭs′təns) *n.* the act of refusing to stop or be changed

incredulous (ĭn-krĕj′ə-ləs) *adj.* doubtful; disbelieving

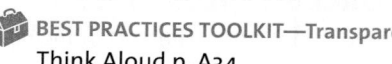
4 Targeted Passage

I ANALYZE DETAILS
Reread lines 205–225. How dangerous is the tunnel? Point out details that reveal this.

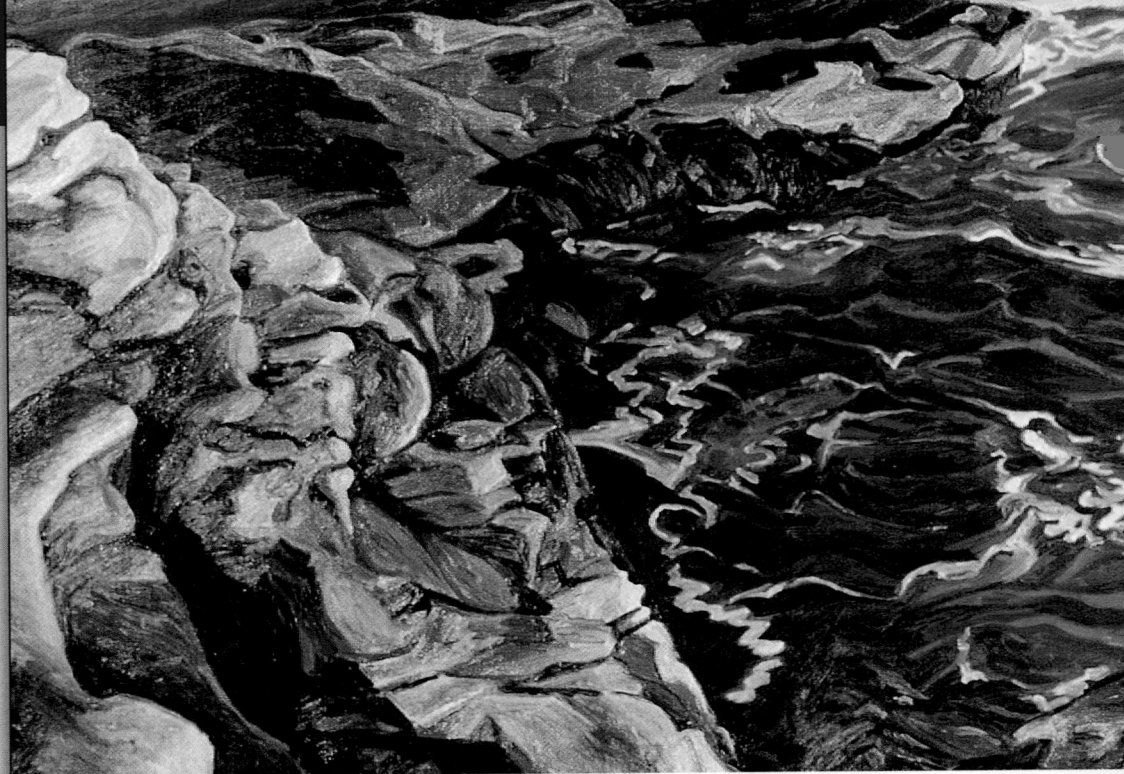

Ice Blue (1981), Susan Shatter. Oil on canvas, 40″ × 90″. Private collection. Courtesy of the Fischback Gallery, New York.

ANALYZE VISUALS

Activity As a class, discuss what specific details in this painting reinforce the sense of danger and risk that Jerry experiences at this point in the story. ***Possible answer:*** *The turbulence of the water, the absence of people in the scene, the rocky ledges and outcroppings, and the overhead vantage point reflect the sense of danger and risk.*

About the Art Artist Susan Shatter (born 1943) paints in both oils and watercolors. Educated at New York's Pratt Institute and at Boston University, Shatter uses art to express emotional responses to nature. *Ice Blue* is typical of her work because it shows her ability to capture what she calls the flow of water.

Lines 234–242
REINFORCE *KEY IDEA:* RISKS

Discuss What hints does the author include in these two paragraphs to suggest the danger in the **risk** that Jerry has taken? ***Possible answer:*** *"a sharp pain dizzied him" (lines 237–238); "water seemed to press upon him with the weight of rock" (line 239); "his head was pulsing" (line 241)*

edge of the rock until half of him was in the cool, enclosing water and half in the hot sun. He looked up once at the empty sky, filled his lungs once, twice,
230 and then sank fast to the bottom with the stone. He let it go and began to count. He took the edges of the hole in his hands and drew himself into it, wriggling his shoulders in sidewise as he remembered he must, kicking himself along with his feet.

Soon he was clear inside. He was in a small rock-bound hole filled with yellowish-gray water. The water was pushing him up against the roof. The roof was sharp and pained his back. He pulled himself along with his hands—fast, fast—and used his legs as levers. His head knocked against something; a sharp pain dizzied him. Fifty, fifty-one, fifty-two. . . . He was without light, and the water seemed to press upon him with the weight of rock. Seventy-one, seventy-
240 two. . . . There was no strain on his lungs. He felt like an inflated balloon, his lungs were so light and easy, but his head was pulsing.

He was being continually pressed against the sharp roof, which felt slimy as well as sharp. Again he thought of octopuses, and wondered if the tunnel might be filled with weed that could tangle him. He gave himself a panicky,

336 UNIT 3: SETTING, MOOD, AND IMAGERY

DIFFERENTIATED INSTRUCTION

FOR ENGLISH LEARNERS

Language: Punctuation and Print Clues Point out Lessing's use of dashes and ellipses and her insertion of numbers on these two pages. Explain that although these elements make the passage a little harder to read, they are purposeful stylistic choices. Read aloud lines 236–240 and 249–252 so that students can hear how these features build tension and reflect Jerry's breathlessness.

convulsive kick forward, ducked his head, and swam. His feet and hands moved freely, as if in open water. The hole must have widened out. He thought he must be swimming fast, and he was frightened of banging his head if the tunnel narrowed.

A hundred, a hundred and one. . . . The water paled. Victory filled him.
250 His lungs were beginning to hurt. A few more strokes and he would be out. He was counting wildly; he said a hundred and fifteen, and then, a long time later, a hundred and fifteen again. The water was a clear jewel-green all around him. Then he saw, above his head, a crack running up through the rock. Sunlight was falling through it, showing the clean, dark rock of the tunnel, a single mussel shell, and darkness ahead.

He was at the end of what he could do. He looked up at the crack as if it were filled with air and not water, as if he could put his mouth to it to draw in air. A hundred and fifteen, he heard himself say inside his head—but he had said that long ago. He must go on into the blackness ahead, or he would
260 drown. His head was swelling, his lungs cracking. A hundred and fifteen, a hundred and fifteen pounded through his head, and he feebly clutched at rocks

Lines 249–267
DISCUSSION PROMPTS
Use these prompts to focus on the suspense in the story's climax:

Connect Can you think of a time when you or someone you know was pushed to the limit and yet had to keep going? *Answers will vary, but students should recognize the struggle between determination and panic that a person would probably feel in such a situation.*

Apply How does your answer to the previous question help you understand that this passage is the climax of "Through the Tunnel"? *Possible answer: Jerry feels the same kind of struggle. This passage represents the climax of the story because it is the moment of greatest emotional intensity and suspense about the outcome of Jerry's struggle: he will either swim through the tunnel or die inside it.*

Evaluate Does Lessing's language here effectively emphasize the tension in the plot? Explain. *Possible answer: Her language is effective. She creates tension with vivid modifiers ("water paled," "counting wildly," "lungs cracking") and repetition ("he said a hundred and fifteen, and then, a long time later, a hundred and fifteen again. . . . A hundred and fifteen, he heard himself say inside his head . . . a hundred and fifteen pounded through his head").*

FOR ADVANCED LEARNERS/PRE–AP
Analyze Details Ask students to recall the research that they gathered for the activity on page 333. Then ask them in what ways Jerry symbolically dies and is reborn in the story. Make sure students notice details such as images of darkness and light.

Evaluate Theme: Ask students to identify the story's **theme**—its underlying message about life or human nature. Then have students evaluate that theme—decide whether they think it is valid. Tell students to use these questions as their evaluation criteria:

- Does the theme express a broad insight into life or human nature, or simply an idea that applies only to a few people?
- Does the theme offer a meaningful insight, or is it too obvious or clichéd?
- Is the theme a realistic observation, or is it too optimistic, cynical, or narrow-minded?

Point out to students that a theme may be valid even if they do not personally agree with it. (To learn more about evaluating theme, see **Reading Handbook**, page R2.)

SELECTION WRAP–UP

REFLECT Have students think about Jerry's determination to swim through the tunnel. What does achieving this goal mean to him, and why?

⭐ **CRITIQUE** Ask students to consider how Jerry changes during the story, and whether they think the change is realistic. Have students defend their evaluations.

READING FLUENCY

Distribute the copy master and have students work independently to practice fluency.

[R] RESOURCE MANAGER—Copy Master
Reading Fluency p. 64

---

in the dark, pulling himself forward, leaving the brief space of sunlit water behind. He felt he was dying. He was no longer quite conscious. He struggled on in the darkness between lapses into unconsciousness. An immense, swelling pain filled his head, and then the darkness cracked with an explosion of green light. His hands, groping forward, met nothing; and his feet, kicking back, propelled him out into the open sea.

He drifted to the surface, his face turned up to the air. He was gasping like a fish. He felt he would sink now and drown; he could not swim the few feet
270 back to the rock. Then he was clutching it and pulling himself up onto it. He lay face down, gasping. He could see nothing but a red-veined, clotted dark. His eyes must have burst, he thought; they were full of blood. He tore off his goggles and a gout of blood went into the sea. His nose was bleeding, and the blood had filled the goggles.

He scooped up handfuls of water from the cool, salty sea, to splash on his face, and did not know whether it was blood or salt water he tasted. After a time, his heart quieted, his eyes cleared, and he sat up. He could see the local boys diving and playing half a mile away. He did not want them. He wanted nothing but to get back home and lie down.

280   In a short while, Jerry swam to shore and climbed slowly up the path to the villa. He flung himself on his bed and slept, waking at the sound of feet on the path outside. His mother was coming back. He rushed to the bathroom, thinking she must not see his face with bloodstains, or tearstains, on it. He came out of the bathroom and met her as she walked into the villa, smiling, her eyes lighting up.

"Have a nice morning?" she asked, laying her hand on his warm brown shoulder a moment.

"Oh, yes, thank you," he said.

"You look a bit pale." And then, sharp and anxious, "How did you bang
290 your head?"

"Oh, just banged it," he told her.

She looked at him closely. He was strained; his eyes were glazed-looking. She was worried. And then she said to herself, Oh, don't fuss! Nothing can happen. He can swim like a fish.

They sat down to lunch together.

"Mummy," he said, "I can stay under water for two minutes—three minutes, at least." It came bursting out of him.

"Can you, darling?" she said. "Well, I shouldn't overdo it. I don't think you ought to swim any more today."

300   She was ready for a battle of wills, but he gave in at once. It was no longer of the least importance to go to the bay. ❧

⑤ Targeted Passage

DIFFERENTIATED INSTRUCTION

FOR LESS–PROFICIENT READERS
⑤ **Targeted Passage [Lines 280–301]**

This passage presents the falling action of the story and hints that Jerry's accomplishment has changed him profoundly.

- What does Jerry do when he hears his mother coming? Why?

- What kinds of answers does he give to her questions?

- When she advises him not to do any more swimming that day, why does he give in?

Comprehension

1. **Recall** Describe Jerry's age and family situation.

2. **Summarize** What happens between Jerry and the older boys?

3. **Clarify** Why is it so important for Jerry to swim through the tunnel? Explain what he is trying to prove.

Literary Analysis

4. **Identify Conflicts** Identify the external and internal conflicts Jerry faces in the story. How are these conflicts resolved?

5. **Analyze Suspense** Reread lines 234–267. How does Lessing build suspense in this passage? What other techniques does she use to build suspense in this story? Give examples to support your answers.

6. **Analyze Relationships** Explain Jerry's relationship with his mother. How has their relationship changed by the end of the story?

7. **Analyze Details** Look over the chart you made as you read. What are the major differences between the big beach and the bay? What does each place **symbolize** to Jerry?

8. **Interpret Setting as Symbol** What does Jerry's swim through the tunnel symbolize? Cite descriptions of the tunnel, its connection to the older boys, and Jerry's feelings about the tunnel to support your interpretation.

9. **Make Judgments About Motive** Does Jerry accomplish what he wants by swimming through the tunnel? To help you decide, create a two-column chart, briefly describing Jerry before and after his swim.

Before, Jerry is . . .	After, Jerry is . . .
anxious to please his mother lonely	

10. **Evaluate** Do the benefits of Jerry's accomplishment outweigh the **risks?** Base your decision on evidence from the story, such as Jerry's preparation, as well as on your own knowledge and experience.

Literary Criticism

11. **Critical Interpretations** The critic Martha Duffy once praised Lessing for the "unsparing clarity and frankness" of her writing. What evidence do you find in "Through the Tunnel" to support this assessment of Lessing's work?

8. ● **STANDARDS FOCUS** *Setting as Symbol*
It symbolizes rebirth, a journey, and a passage to adulthood that the older boys have had. The descriptions in lines 234–235, 245–246, and 254 suggest the birth process. Jerry's mix of fear and determination suggests that he must undergo this journey to mature.

9. *Jerry accomplished what he wanted. He still agrees to his mother's request, but now he does so for his own reason (lines 300–301). Similarly, he still may be alone,* but he no longer feels the need for the companionship of the older boys.

10. *Students who felt the risk was worth it may argue that Jerry has matured because of the experience. Students who disagree may argue that he might have died.*

Literary Criticism
Possible answer:

11. *The description of Jerry's trip through the tunnel (lines 226–267) is just one example that supports the assessment.*

Practice and Apply

After Reading

For additional support of post-reading questions, use these copy masters:

R RESOURCE MANAGER—Copy Masters
Reading Check p. 61 (to check understanding of the selection)
Setting as Symbol p. 53 (for practice of literary analysis standards focus)
Question Support p. 62 (After Reading questions adapted for English learners and less-proficient readers)

For additional questions, see page 47.

To challenge students further, see
ⓘ Bob Marzano's Power Thinking Activities at **ClassZone.com**

ANSWERS

Comprehension

1. *Jerry is an 11-year-old English boy being raised by his widowed mother.*

2. *At first, the boys are friendly, allowing him to dive with them. When Jerry immaturely clowns around, they ignore him and then leave him.*

3. *Jerry wants to prove that he belongs with the older boys and is worthy of their friendship and admiration.*

Literary Analysis
Possible answers:

4. *Jerry's internal conflict against his physical and psychological limitations is resolved when he swims through the tunnel. His external conflicts with the older boys, his mother, and the tunnel also are resolved at that point (lines 278–279 and 300–301).*

5. *Lessing traces Jerry's injuries, pain (lines 237–242, 261–266), and fear (lines 244–248). Vivid modifiers (as in lines 242–245) make the scene more terrifying.*

6. *At first, Jerry and his mother are emotionally attached. By the end, Jerry asserts his independence, and his mother begins to accept his assertion.*

7. ■ **STANDARDS FOCUS** *Analyze Details*
The big beach is crowded and safe; the bay is desolate and dangerous. The beach symbolizes childhood and dependency; the bay, adulthood and independence.

Vocabulary in Context

VOCABULARY PRACTICE

1. *false*
2. *true*
3. *false*
4. *true*
5. *true*
6. *true*

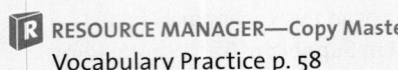 **RESOURCE MANAGER**—Copy Master
Vocabulary Practice p. 58

VOCABULARY IN WRITING

Point out that the older boys each also had a "first swim" though the tunnel. How would that experience affect their perspective on Jerry and his accomplishment? Would they accept him now as an equal? Invite students to compare their paragraphs in small groups.

VOCABULARY STRATEGY: THE LATIN ROOTS *quest, quer,* AND *quisit* (also an EL language objective)

Help students pronounce each word, especially *conquistador* and *query*.

As you discuss each word to be defined, guide students to use what they know of these Latin roots and other roots to determine word meaning. For example, *conquistador* is a Spanish word that contains the root for *conquer*.

Possible answers:

acquire, "to gain"; *requisite,* "necessary"; *inquisition,* "official investigation"; *query,* "question"; *conquistador,* "one of the 16th-century Spanish conquerors of the Americas"; *inquest,* "legal or judicial inquiry" *Sentences will vary but should present the words accurately.*

RESOURCE MANAGER—Copy Master
Vocabulary Strategy p. 59

ℹ️ Vocabulary Center at **ClassZone.com**
Additional Vocabulary Activities

Vocabulary in Context

VOCABULARY PRACTICE

Drawing on your understanding of the words, write *true* or *false* for each item.

1. If you feel **contrition** for something you did, you feel proud of your actions.
2. You should not live on a **promontory** if you are afraid of heights.
3. An **inquisitive** child will rarely ask why.
4. You might hear a **supplication** at a prayer service.
5. A person shows **persistence** by repeating a job until she gets it right.
6. If you are **incredulous** about a friend's advice, you likely will ignore it.

WORD LIST
contrition
incredulous
inquisitive
persistence
promontory
supplication

VOCABULARY IN WRITING

Using four vocabulary words, write a paragraph describing how one of the older boys might have reacted to Jerry's swim. Here is a sample opening.

> **EXAMPLE SENTENCE**
> The young English boy's **_persistence_** was amazing . . .

VOCABULARY STRATEGY: THE LATIN ROOTS *quest, quer,* AND *quisit*

The word *inquisitive* contains the root of the Latin word *quaerere*, meaning "to seek." Common forms of this root include *quest, quer,* and *quisit.* When the Latin prefix *in-* ("into") and the suffix *-ive* ("tending toward a specific action") are added to *quisit,* they make the word *inquisitive,* which literally means "inclining to seek into." Remembering the meaning of *quest, quer,* and *quisit* will help you understand words in this family.

PRACTICE Try your hand at writing a definition for each of these words in the *quest, quer,* and *quisit* family. Use a dictionary to confirm your definitions. Then, for each word, write a sentence that shows its meaning.

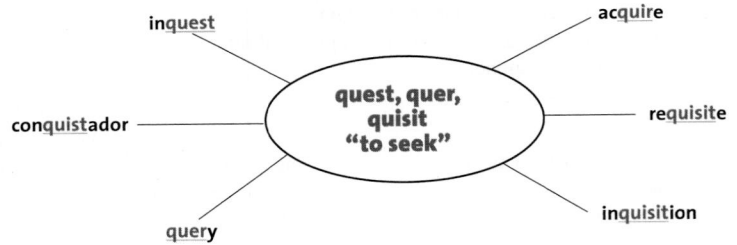

inquest · acquire · conquistador · requisite · query · inquisition

quest, quer, quisit "to seek"

 **VOCABULARY PRACTICE**
For more practice, go to the **Vocabulary Center** at **ClassZone.com**.

DIFFERENTIATED INSTRUCTION

OR ENGLISH LEARNERS

Vocabulary: Prefixes Before completing the Vocabulary Strategy section, explain that the prefix *in-* in the word *inquisitive* means "into" but that *in-* sometimes means "not." Provide these additional examples:

in- = **"into"**: inspect, inform, intelligent
in- = **"not"**: incredulous, inept, inadequate

OR ADVANCED LEARNERS/PRE AP

Vocabulary in Writing Ask students to use at least three vocabulary words in a journal entry. Have them write as a diver who is concerned about the dangers for the boys who have been seen swimming through the tunnel.

Reading-Writing Connection

Further explore the characters in "Through the Tunnel" by responding to these prompts. Then use **Revision: Grammar and Style** to improve your writing.

WRITING PROMPTS	SELF-CHECK

A. Short Response: Analyze a Character's Actions
Do you think Jerry's mother is right to trust him by himself? Consider the **risks** Jerry takes, as well as his success, and then write a **one- or two-paragraph response** that explains your answer.

A strong response will . . .
- clearly state your opinion
- include details and examples from the story to support your point

B. Extended Response: Create a Dialogue
Imagine a time when Jerry might tell his mother about his swim through the tunnel. How old would he be? What would he say? Using what you know about the characters, write a **one-page dialogue** in which Jerry tells his mother about his experience.

An effective dialogue will . . .
- show how each character thinks and feels
- include reactions and speech consistent with each character

REVISON: GRAMMAR AND STYLE

WRITE CONCISELY Review the **Grammar and Style** note on page 331. Like Lessing, you can use **compound predicates** to make your writing more concise and improve the flow of your sentences.

A predicate indicates what a subject is or does or what happens to the subject. By combining predicates, you can avoid writing a series of short, choppy sentences that begin with the same noun or pronoun.

Here is an example of how Lessing uses this technique:

He looked up once at the empty sky, filled his lungs once, twice, and then sank fast to the bottom with the stone. He let it go and began to count.
(lines 229–231)

Notice how the revisions in red improve sentence flow.

STUDENT MODEL

I think Jerry's mom is a responsible parent. She pays attention to Jerry. ~~She~~ tries to figure out what he wants. *and* ~~He wants her to~~ give him more freedom. *when he asks for it* She knows he is a good swimmer. *and* ~~She~~ decides to let him go to the bay.

WRITING TOOLS
For prewriting, revision, and editing tools, visit the **Writing Center** at ClassZone.com.

THROUGH THE TUNNEL **341**

Reading-Writing Connection

WRITING PROMPTS

- For Prompt A, encourage students to reread lines 296–301 to assess Jerry's level of maturity. Suggest that students spend five minutes or so freewriting about Jerry and his swim.

- For Prompt B, have students use a Summary Frame to trace Jerry's journey through the tunnel and the reasons behind it. Remind students to set off each speaker's words with quotation marks and to begin a new paragraph each time the speaker changes.

 BEST PRACTICES TOOLKIT—Transparency
Summary Frame: Narrative p. B13

For an extended writing activity, see
ℹ Carol Booth Olson's Reading-Writing Lesson Plans at **ClassZone.com**

REVISION: GRAMMAR AND STYLE

- Model the finding of predicates in "Through the Tunnel." Then, as you discuss the student model, call on volunteers to isolate each part of the compound predicate.

- Write these sentences on the board. Have students suggest ways to use compound predicates to revise the short sentences.

Jerry swam a little closer to the older boys, . ~~Then he turned quickly,~~ . ~~Next, he waved to them eagerly,~~ and . ~~In addition, he watched them closely.~~

 RESOURCE MANAGER—Copy Master
Write Concisely p. 63

Assess and Reteach

Assess
Ⓡ RESOURCE MANAGER—Copy Masters
Selection Test A pp. 65–66
Selection Test B/C pp. 67–68
⊘ Test Generator CD

Reteach
Ⓢ STANDARDS LESSON FILE
Literature Lessons 9, 31: Setting and Its Roles; Symbols and Symbolism
Vocabulary Lesson 7: Latin Roots

FOR LESS–PROFICIENT WRITERS

For Prompt A:
Help students make a jotted outline.
I. Topic Sentence: Jerry's mother is wise to trust her son.
II. Reason #1: The risks are minor.
  A. Lines 84–88: The other boys succeed easily.
  B. Lines 269–279: Jerry recovers quickly from his swim.

III. Reason #2: Jerry's achievement is great.
  A. Lines 278–279: Jerry no longer needs to impress the local boys.
  B. Lines 300–301: Jerry has matured, so he no longer needs to fight with his mother.

For Prompt B:
Help students generate ideas by working in pairs to role-play this scene, with one student taking the part of Jerry's mother and the other taking the part of Jerry. Students might record this improvisation for use as they write.

THROUGH THE TUNNEL **341**

Focus and Motivate

OBJECTIVES

Literary Analysis
- explore the key idea of **revenge**
- analyze mood
- read a short story

Reading
- paraphrase

Vocabulary
- build vocabulary for reading and writing
- understand and use the Latin word family *clud* (*also an EL language objective*)

Grammar and Writing
- use formal language appropriately
- use writing to analyze literature

SUMMARY

"The Cask of Amontillado" is Edgar Allan Poe's classic tale of revenge. Montresor, the narrator of this dark short story, tricks Fortunato into accompanying him to the burial vaults beneath his palace, where Montresor stores his wine. Once there, Montresor leads the inebriated Fortunato deep into the catacombs and then walls him up inside a crypt, leaving him there to die.

Is REVENGE
ever justified?

Introduce the question and have students read the **KEY IDEA**. Then discuss different opinions students may have on the subject. Have students complete the **PRESENT** activity. Extend the discussion by asking them to suggest alternatives to taking **revenge**.

Selection Resources

The Cask of Amontillado
Short Story by Edgar Allan Poe

Is REVENGE
ever justified?

KEY IDEA Montresor, the narrator of "The Cask of Amontillado," feels that **revenge** is necessary to right a wrong. Some would argue that two wrongs never make a right and that revenge leads only to more wrongdoing. Do acts of revenge ever resolve conflicts?

PRESENT An act of revenge often causes a chain reaction, and the repercussions can go on for months or years. With a group, think of one act of revenge and chart out the possible chain of effects. Share your chain of events with the rest of the class.

Event
Girl makes fun of boy.

↓

Act of Revenge
Boy spills ink on her uniform.

↓

Effects
• Uniform is ruined.
• Girl's parents have to buy a new one.

342

Selection Resources

RESOURCE MANAGER UNIT 3

Plan and Teach pp. 69–76

Literary Analysis
Summary pp. 77†*, 78‡*
Mood pp. 79, 80†*
Question Support p. 87*

Reading
Paraphrase pp. 81, 82†*
Reading Check p. 86
Reading Fluency p. 90

Vocabulary
Study p. 83*
Practice p. 84
Strategy p. 85

Grammar and Writing
Use Appropriate Language p. 89

Assessment
Selection Tests A, B/C pp. 91*, 93*
Test Generator CD

BEST PRACTICES TOOLKIT

Differentiated Instruction
pp. 31–38*

Scaffolding Instruction
pp. 43–46*

Graphic Organizers/Strategies
Word Questioning • Jigsaw Reading

Technology
Literature and Vocabulary Centers at **ClassZone.com**
Write*Smart* CD

Reading Support
Audio Anthology CD*

InterActive
READER & WRITER
• Integrated Test Practice
• Related Nonfiction Readings
McDougal Littell LITERATURE

---

* Resources for Differentiation   † Also in Spanish   ‡ In Haitian Creole and Vietnamese

LITERARY ANALYSIS: MOOD

In "The Cask of Amontillado," Edgar Allan Poe creates an unforgettable **mood** of suspense and horror. From the beginning, the narrator's talk of injuries borne, unforgivable insults, and threatened revenge conveys a sinister feeling. Poe develops this mood by means of

- the sensory details and imagery used to convey the setting
- the repetition of words and the rhythm of the language
- words describing thoughts, feelings, and actions

As you read, notice how Poe's descriptions of the setting and his use of language combine to create a memorably dark tale.

READING STRATEGY: PARAPHRASE

Poe often uses long, complex sentences that are especially challenging to modern readers. To make sure that you understand the events in this story, try paraphrasing. To **paraphrase** is to restate information in one's own words. A paraphrase is about the same length as the original text. It includes all the details of the original but is written in simpler language. As you read this story, take time to paraphrase difficult passages. Here is an example.

Text	Paraphrase
"It must be understood, that neither by word nor deed had I given Fortunato cause to doubt my good-will." (lines 9–10)	You must understand that I said and did nothing to make Fortunato mistrust me.

Review: Make Inferences

▲ VOCABULARY IN CONTEXT

The boldfaced words help create a mood of horror. Use context clues to figure out the meaning of each word. Then use each word in a sentence. After reading the selection, check to see whether you used the words correctly.

1. to **preclude** pain
2. to lie with **impunity**
3. **immolation** of an enemy
4. **abscond** with money
5. everlasting **repose**
6. **termination** of a job
7. to help anger to **subside**
8. to close off an **aperture**

Author Online

Edgar Allan Poe
1809–1849

The Genius of Poe
Edgar Allan Poe started out as a poet but turned to writing short fiction to earn a living. His career in fiction officially began in 1833, with a $50 prize for his story "MS. Found in a Bottle." At the time he was living in poverty with his beloved aunt Maria Clemm and her daughter, Virginia. With the prize money came recognition and a job offer from a literary magazine. By 1838, Poe had married Virginia and moved the family to Philadelphia, where he worked for several leading literary magazines.

Master of the Macabre Poe may have started writing horror fiction because that's what the reading public wanted. Gothic tales were popular at the time, and newspapers regularly printed sensational reports of bizarre murders. Poe adapted elements of Gothic fiction, took a few story ideas from news headlines, added his psychological insights into the mix, and soon became the undisputed master of the genre.

 MORE ABOUT THE AUTHOR
For more on Edgar Allan Poe, visit the **Literature Center** at **ClassZone.com**.

Background

A Different Burial Ground Although this story begins during a time of carnival festivities, the setting soon shifts to the dark, cool burial vaults under the narrator's palace, where he also stores his wine. In such underground cemeteries, called catacombs, bodies were placed in carved recesses along the walls of burial chambers. The largest and most famous are those of Rome, in which early Christians were entombed.

THE CASK OF AMONTILLADO **343**

Teach

LITERARY ANALYSIS

● MOOD

For instructional support, read aloud this example:

> A cold wind sliced across the silent and empty graveyard. Stanton shivered and glanced up at the moon, a pale sliver behind dark clouds. He heard footsteps, then more footsteps, and his stomach knotted. *Shouldn't have come,* he thought.

Ask what mood this paragraph conveys, and how. ***Possible answer:*** *It conveys fear and mystery through sensory details and imagery ("pale sliver," "stomach knotted"), repetition ("footsteps"), and thoughts ("Shouldn't have come").*

CHECK UNDERSTANDING Elicit from students other examples of writing that creates a strong mood.

READING STRATEGY

■ PARAPHRASE

Explain that paraphrasing is a way to reword information so that it is easier to understand yet retains the original meaning.

CHECK UNDERSTANDING Provide several examples of formal language for students to paraphrase.

 **RESOURCE MANAGER—Copy Master**
Paraphrase p. 81 (for student use while reading the selection)

VOCABULARY SKILL

▲ VOCABULARY IN CONTEXT

DIAGNOSE WORD KNOWLEDGE To determine preteaching needs, have all students complete Vocabulary in Context. Students' use of the words should be consistent with the definitions on selection pages: **1.** *preclude* (p. 344), **2.** *impunity* (p. 344), **3.** *immolation* (p. 344), **4.** *abscond* (p. 346), **5.** *repose* (p. 347), **6.** *termination* (p. 349), **7.** *subside* (p. 350), **8.** *aperture* (p. 351).

PRETEACH VOCABULARY Use the Vocabulary Study copy master to help students predict meanings of each boldfaced word on the copy master.

1. Read item 1 aloud, emphasizing *abscond*.
2. Point out the phrase "even though he told them not to leave the house." Elicit possible meanings for *abscond*, such as "to leave."
3. Have students record their predictions.
4. Repeat the procedure for items 2–8.

 RESOURCE MANAGER—Copy Master
Vocabulary Study p. 83

For general guidelines on differentiating vocabulary instruction and for alternative vocabulary activities for students not needing vocabulary preteaching, see

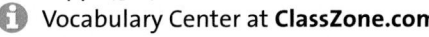 **BEST PRACTICES TOOLKIT**
Scaffolding Vocabulary Instruction pp. 43–46
ⓘ Vocabulary Center at **ClassZone.com**

ANALYZE VISUALS

Possible answer: Though the mask and colorful costume may suggest a festive event, the photo's overall mood is sinister. The mask is unsmiling, with a disquieting contrast between the bright white face and black eye sockets. The dark background adds to the sinister mood, as does the angle of the tower behind the subject.

READING STRATEGY

A PARAPHRASE

Possible answer: I had put up with Fortunato's abuse as well as I could, but when he insulted me, I was determined to get even. However, I did not threaten him or give him any reason to worry. I would get my revenge, all right, but in due time and without risk to myself. Getting even is not worth it if the person getting even is punished for what he has done. It is also not worth it unless the target of the revenge understands that the person he has wronged is paying him back for what he did.

The narrator vows revenge because Fortunato has insulted him. He considers revenge to be successful if the "avenger" escapes punishment and if the victim knows that he has been paid back for a wrong he committed.

If students need help . . . Encourage students to reread the paragraph. Then have them paraphrase it one or two sentences at a time.

Extend the Discussion What might the "thousand injuries" (line 1) refer to?

The Cask of Amontillado

EDGAR ALLAN POE

The thousand injuries of Fortunato I had borne as I best could; but when he ventured upon insult, I vowed revenge. You, who so well know the nature of my soul, will not suppose, however, that I gave utterance to a threat. *At length* I would be avenged; this was a point definitively settled—but the very definitiveness with which it was resolved, **precluded** the idea of risk. I must not only punish, but punish with **impunity.** A wrong is unredressed when retribution overtakes its redresser. It is equally unredressed when the avenger fails to make himself felt as such to him who has done the wrong. A

10 It must be understood, that neither by word nor deed had I given Fortunato cause to doubt my good-will. I continued, as was my wont, to smile in his face, and he did not perceive that my smile *now* was at the thought of his **immolation.**

He had a weak point—this Fortunato—although in other regards he was a man to be respected and even feared. He prided himself on his connoisseurship[1] in wine. Few Italians have the true virtuoso spirit. For the most part their enthusiasm is adopted to suit the time and opportunity—to practice imposture upon the British and Austrian *millionaires*. In painting and gemmary[2] Fortunato, like his countrymen, was a quack—but in the matter of old wines he was sincere. In this respect I did not differ from him materially; I 20 was skillful in the Italian vintages myself, and bought largely whenever I could.

It was about dusk, one evening during the supreme madness of the carnival[3] season, that I encountered my friend. He accosted me with excessive warmth, for he had been drinking much. The man wore motley.[4] He had on a tight-fitting parti-striped dress, and his head was surmounted by the conical cap and bells. I was so pleased to see him, that I thought I should never have done wringing his hand.

---

1. **connoisseurship** (kŏn'ə-sûr'shĭp): expertise or authority, especially in the fine arts or in matters of taste.
2. **gemmary** (jĕm'ə-rē): knowledge of precious gems.
3. **carnival:** a festival before the fasting period of Lent, characterized by fanciful costumes, masquerades, and feasts.
4. **motley:** the costume of a court jester.

344 UNIT 3: SETTING, MOOD, AND IMAGERY

---

1 Targeted Passage

ANALYZE VISUALS
Would you describe the mood of this photograph as festive or sinister? Explain.

preclude (prĭ-klōōd') *v.* to make impossible, especially by taking action in advance

impunity (ĭm-pyōō'nĭ-tē) *n.* freedom from penalty or harm

A PARAPHRASE
Paraphrase the opening paragraph. Why does the narrator vow revenge? What does he consider a successful revenge?

immolation (ĭm'ə-lā'shən) *n.* death or destruction

DIFFERENTIATED INSTRUCTION

FOR ALL STUDENTS

Enhancing Learning Styles Provide these independent projects for various learning preferences:

- **Visual** Create a poster.
- **Verbal** Write a prelude to the story.
- **Musical** Compose background music.

For further details on these projects, see

R RESOURCE MANAGER
Ideas for Extension pp. 74–75

FOR LESS–PROFICIENT READERS

In combination with the *Audio Anthology CD*, use one or more Targeted Passages (pp. 344, 347, 350, 351) to ensure that students focus on key story events, concepts, and skills. Targeted Passages are also good for English learners.

1 Targeted Passage [Lines 1–12]

This passage establishes the narrator's feelings and intentions toward Fortunato.

- Why does the narrator, Montresor, want revenge against Fortunato?

Carnival Season The "supreme madness of the carnival season" (lines 21–22) is a time of merrymaking, feasting, costumes, and parades celebrated just before Lent. Festive carnival traditions remain popular today in many parts of the world, from New Orleans, Louisiana (Mardi Gras), to Rio de Janeiro, Brazil. In "The Cask of Amontillado," the narrator's choice of this time of year to exact his revenge was probably deliberate, not only because people would be distracted but also because Fortunato would likely have been drinking and celebrating and therefore unlikely to suspect any foul play.

- What does the narrator mean when he says that he "must not only punish, but punish with impunity" (lines 5–6)?

- How does the narrator feel about Fortunato? How does he act toward him? What does this contrast suggest?

FOR ENGLISH LEARNERS

Key Academic Vocabulary Use Word Questioning to teach these words: *resolved* (line 5), *impose* (line 47), *explicit* (line 61), *sufficient* (line 62), *indication* (line 175).

 BEST PRACTICES TOOLKIT—Transparency Word Questioning p. E9

Prereading For prereading instruction for English learners, see

 BEST PRACTICES TOOLKIT Scaffolding Reading Instruction pp. 43–46

FOR ADVANCED LEARNERS/PRE–AP

Pre-AP Exercises in the bottom channel provide additional challenge for students. Use these suggestions for small groups or individuals.

ADDITIONAL GUIDELINES

For more help with differentiation and tips for classroom management, see

 BEST PRACTICES TOOLKIT Differentiated Instruction pp. 31–38

I said to him: "My dear Fortunato, you are luckily met. How remarkably well you are looking to-day! But I have received a pipe of what passes for Amontillado,[5] and I have my doubts."

30 "How?" said he. "Amontillado? A pipe? Impossible! And in the middle of the carnival!"

"I have my doubts," I replied; "and I was silly enough to pay the full Amontillado price without consulting you in the matter. You were not to be found, and I was fearful of losing a bargain."

"Amontillado!"

"I have my doubts."

"Amontillado!"

"And I must satisfy them."

"Amontillado!"

40 "As you are engaged, I am on my way to Luchesi.[6] If anyone has a critical turn, it is he. He will tell me—"

"Luchesi cannot tell Amontillado from Sherry."

"And yet some fools will have it that his taste is a match for your own."

"Come, let us go."

"Whither?"

"To your vaults."

"My friend, no; I will not impose upon your good nature. I perceive you have an engagement. Luchesi—"

"I have no engagement;—come."

50 "My friend, no. It is not the engagement, but the severe cold with which I perceive you are afflicted. The vaults are insufferably damp. They are encrusted with niter."[7]

"Let us go, nevertheless. The cold is merely nothing. Amontillado! You have been imposed upon. And as for Luchesi, he cannot distinguish Sherry from Amontillado." **B**

Thus speaking, Fortunato possessed himself of my arm. Putting on a mask of black silk, and drawing a *roquelaure*[8] closely about my person, I suffered him to hurry me to my palazzo.[9]

There were no attendants at home; they had **absconded** to make merry in 60 honor of the time. I had told them that I should not return until the morning, and had given them explicit orders not to stir from the house. These orders were sufficient, I well knew, to insure their immediate disappearance, one and all, as soon as my back was turned.

B MOOD
Reread lines 27–55. How does Poe build a mood of suspense in this conversation between the narrator and Fortunato?

abscond (ăb-skŏnd')
v. to go away suddenly and secretly

---

5. **a pipe . . . Amontillado** (ə-mŏn'tl-ä'dō): a barrel of a wine that is supposed to be a type of pale, dry sherry, named for a town in southern Spain.

6. **Luchesi** (lōō-kā'sē).

7. **niter:** a white, gray, or colorless mineral, consisting of potassium nitrate.

8. *roquelaure* (rŏk-lōr') *French:* a man's knee-length cloak, popular during the 18th century.

9. **palazzo** (pə-lät'sō): a palace or mansion.

B MOOD

Possible answer: Readers know that the narrator intends revenge by getting Fortunato to his mansion, but Fortunato does not. Suspense is built in this conversation by the narrator's manipulation of Fortunato with his false concern about Fortunato's health and his need to be elsewhere, the repetition of the word friend, *and the narrator's appeal to Fortunato's vanity by his mention of Luchesi several times. In the end, the reader still does not know what the narrator plans to do at his palazzo.*

Lines 56–63
REINFORCE *KEY IDEA:* REVENGE

Discuss The narrator puts on a mask and wraps himself in a cloak. He also explains that he was able "to insure" there would be "no attendants at home." What do these actions suggest about his plan for **revenge**? *Possible answer: The narrator has carefully laid the groundwork for whatever he is planning. These actions will most likely prevent anyone from identifying him or witnessing his crime. They will allow him to go unpunished, an important factor for him, as he gets his revenge.*

DIFFERENTIATED INSTRUCTION

FOR ENGLISH LEARNERS
Language: Conversational Patterns Help students understand the formal and antiquated language used in the story by explaining such sentences as these:

- "I was skillful in the Italian vintages myself, and bought largely whenever I could" (lines 19–20): "I knew about Italian wines and bought many of them whenever I could."

- "'My dear Fortunato, you are luckily met'" (line 27): "How fortunate we are to meet."

FOR ADVANCED LEARNERS/PRE–AP
Analyze Dialogue After reading the story, have students reread lines 27–55. Have them explain exactly how Montresor uses psychology to manipulate Fortunato into doing what he wants him to do.

I took from their sconces two flambeaux,[10] and giving one to Fortunato, bowed him through several suites of rooms to the archway that led into the vaults. I passed down a long and winding staircase, requesting him to be cautious as he followed. We came at length to the foot of the descent and stood together on the damp ground of the catacombs of the Montresors.

The gait of my friend was unsteady, and the bells upon his cap jingled as
70 he strode.

"The pipe?" said he.

"It is farther on," said I; "but observe the white web-work which gleams from these cavern walls."

He turned toward me, and looked into my eyes with two filmy orbs that distilled the rheum of intoxication.[11]

"Niter?" he asked, at length.

"Niter," I replied. "How long have you had that cough?"

"Ugh! ugh! ugh!—ugh! ugh! ugh!—ugh! ugh! ugh!—ugh! ugh! ugh!—ugh! ugh! ugh!"

80 My poor friend found it impossible to reply for many minutes.

"It is nothing," he said, at last.

"Come," I said, with decision, "we will go back; your health is precious. You are rich, respected, admired, beloved; you are happy, as once I was. You are a man to be missed. For me it is no matter. We will go back; you will be ill, and I cannot be responsible. Besides, there is Luchesi—"

"Enough," he said; "the cough is a mere nothing; it will not kill me. I shall not die of a cough."

"True—true," I replied; "and, indeed, I had no intention of alarming you unnecessarily; but you should use all proper caution. A draft of this Medoc[12]
90 will defend us from the damps."

Here I knocked off the neck of a bottle that I drew from a long row of its fellows that lay upon the mold. **C**

"Drink," I said, presenting him the wine.

He raised it to his lips with a leer. He paused and nodded to me familiarly, while his bells jingled.

"I drink," he said, "to the buried that **repose** around us."

"And I to your long life."

He again took my arm, and we proceeded.

"These vaults," he said, "are extensive."

100 "The Montresors," I replied, "were a great and numerous family."

"I forget your arms."

"A huge human foot d'or,[13] in a field azure; the foot crushes a serpent rampant whose fangs are imbedded in the heel."

---

10. **from their sconces two flambeaux** (flăm'bōz'): from their wall brackets two lighted torches.
11. **filmy . . . intoxication**: eyes clouded and glazed over from drunkenness.
12. **Medoc** (mā-dôk'): a red wine from the Bordeaux region of France.
13. **d'or** (dôr) *French*: colored gold. (Montresor is describing his coat of arms, the distinctive emblem of his family.)

THE CASK OF AMONTILLADO **347**

C MAKE INFERENCES
Reread lines 74–92. What is **ironic** about this conversation?

repose (rĭ-pōz') *v.*
to lie dead or at rest

C MAKE INFERENCES

Possible answer: The conversation is ironic in three ways. First, the narrator expresses great concern for the welfare of his "poor friend" (line 80), when in reality he means him only harm. Second, Fortunato says that he "shall not die of a cough" (lines 86–87), and the narrator agrees. However, the two men have very different reasons for believing that it won't be a cough that kills Fortunato. Third, the narrator urges Fortunato to be careful, as he carefully lures him into the catacombs.

Lines 64–99
DISCUSSION PROMPTS

Use these prompts to help students understand how setting and character help to create the dark mood of the short story:

Connect Based on the narrator's words, would you trust him? *Possible answer: Responses may vary, but students should recognize that the narrator is treacherous and wily and has done little, if anything, to arouse Fortunato's suspicions.*

Analyze How does the change in setting contribute to the mood of the story? *Possible answer: The catacombs, underground burial vaults, are dark, damp, and isolated. This setting is in sharp contrast to the crowded, merry carnival setting at the beginning of the story.*

Evaluate Do you think the narrator has made Fortunato a more sympathetic figure in this passage? Explain how. *Possible answer: Responses may vary but could include such details as "the bells upon his cap jingled" (line 69), "Ugh! ugh! ugh! . . ." (lines 78–79), "He . . . nodded to me familiarly, while his bells jingled" (lines 94–95), and "'I drink,' he said, "'to the buried that repose around us'" (line 96).*

FOR LESS–PROFICIENT READERS
2 Targeted Passage [Lines 64–70]

This passage introduces a change of setting and sets up the events that follow.

- Where does the narrator lead Fortunato?
- Why does the narrator feel the need to take with them "two flambeaux" (line 64)?
- Why is Fortunato's "gait . . . unsteady" (line 69)?

Vocabulary: Multiple-Meaning Words Help students use their prior knowledge in combination with context clues to determine the meaning of these words as they are used in the story: *accosted* (line 22), "greeted"; *warmth* (line 22), "friendliness"; *engaged* (line 40), "busy"; *imposed upon* (line 54), "deceived"; *possessed* (line 56), "took"; *suffered* (line 57), "allowed"; *arms* (line 101), "family symbol"; *extremity* (line 155), "farthest point"; *arrested* (line 155), "stopped"; *depended* (line 158), "hung."

THE CASK OF AMONTILLADO **347**

"And the motto?"

"Nemo me impune lacessit." [14]

"Good!" he said.

The wine sparkled in his eyes and the bells jingled. My own fancy grew warm with the Medoc. We had passed through walls of piled bones, with casks and puncheons[15] intermingling, into the inmost recesses of the catacombs. I

110 paused again, and this time I made bold to seize Fortunato by an arm above the elbow.

"The niter!" I said; "see, it increases. It hangs like moss upon the vaults. We are below the river's bed. The drops of moisture trickle among the bones. Come, we will go back ere it is too late. Your cough—" **D**

"It is nothing," he said; "let us go on. But first, another draft of the Medoc."

I broke and reached him a flagon of De Grâve.[16] He emptied it at a breath. His eyes flashed with a fierce light. He laughed and threw the bottle upward with a gesticulation I did not understand.

I looked at him in surprise. He repeated the movement—a grotesque one.

120 "You do not comprehend?" he said.

"Not I," I replied.

"Then you are not of the brotherhood."

"How?"

"You are not of the masons."[17]

"Yes, yes," I said; "yes, yes."

"You? Impossible! A mason?"

"A mason," I replied.

"A sign," he said.

"It is this," I answered, producing a trowel[18] from beneath the folds of my

130 *roquelaure.*

"You jest," he exclaimed, recoiling a few paces. "But let us proceed to the Amontillado."

"Be it so," I said, replacing the tool beneath the cloak, and again offering him my arm. He leaned upon it heavily. We continued our route in search of the Amontillado. We passed through a range of low arches, descended, passed on, and descending again, arrived at a deep crypt, in which the foulness of the air caused our flambeaux rather to glow than flame.

At the most remote end of the crypt there appeared another less spacious. Its walls had been lined with human remains, piled to the vault overhead,

140 in the fashion of the great catacombs of Paris. Three sides of this interior **E**

---

14. ***Nemo me impune lacessit*** (nä′mō mä ĭm-pōō′nĕ lä-kĕs′ĭt) *Latin:* No one injures me with impunity.

15. **casks and puncheons:** large storage containers for wine.

16. **De Grâve** (də gräv′): a red wine from the Bordeaux region of France.

17. **of the masons:** a Freemason, a member of a social organization with secret rituals and signs.

18. **producing a trowel:** Montresor is playing on another meaning of *mason*—"one who builds with stone or brick."

LITERARY ANALYSIS

D MOOD

Possible answer: *Poe's use of sensory details—"walls of piled bones," "inmost recesses of the catacombs," "'hangs like moss,'" "'drops of moisture trickle among the bones'"—helps the reader visualize the setting and creates a dark and sinister mood.*

Extend the Discussion What irony may there be in the narrator's suggestion to Fortunato that they "go back ere it is too late" (line 114)?

E GRAMMAR AND STYLE

Formal Language Poe's use of formal language gives an air of seriousness to the story—for example, "Then you are not of the brotherhood" (line 122). This formal style is appropriate for the manner in which Montresor and Fortunato interact. Have students write a one-paragraph response to this question: If Montresor and Fortunato were truly close friends, would formal language be as effective in the telling of the story? Why or why not?

Possible answer: *Responses may vary but should include a basis for their opinions.*

D MOOD

In lines 108–114, note the sensory details and imagery that help you visualize the setting. What mood do they create?

E GRAMMAR AND STYLE

Notice Poe's use of **formal language,** including complex sentence structures.

DIFFERENTIATED INSTRUCTION

FOR LESS–PROFICIENT READERS

Vocabulary Support Encourage students to use context clues to unlock the meaning of these words: *flagon* (line 116), "a container for liquids"; *gesticulation* (line 118), "a gesture or movement"; *grotesque* (line 119), "strange"; *trowel* (line 129), "a tool used for spreading mortar"; *crypt* (line 136), "an underground room or vault."

FOR ENGLISH LEARNERS

Language: Punctuation and Print Clues Explain to students how conversation and dialogue can be identified by the use of opening and closing quotation marks and, often, the identification of the speaker. Point out lines 120–129 as examples. Have students identify the punctuation marks and the speaker in the dialogue.

ANALYZE VISUALS
What qualities of the catacomb are emphasized by the two arches? Explain.

crypt were still ornamented in this manner. From the fourth the bones had been thrown down, and lay promiscuously upon the earth, forming at one point a mound of some size. Within the wall thus exposed by the displacing of the bones, we perceived a still interior recess, in depth about four feet, in width three, in height six or seven. It seemed to have been constructed for no especial use within itself, but formed merely the interval between two of the colossal supports of the roof of the catacombs, and was backed by one of their circumscribing walls of solid granite.

150　　It was in vain that Fortunato, uplifting his dull torch, endeavored to pry into the depth of the recess. Its **termination** the feeble light did not enable us to see.

"Proceed," I said; "herein is the Amontillado. As for Luchesi—"

"He is an ignoramus," interrupted my friend, as he stepped unsteadily forward, while I followed immediately at his heels. In an instant he had

termination
(tûr′mə-nā′shən) *n.* an end, limit, or edge

ANALYZE VISUALS
Possible answer: The arches emphasize that the catacomb is deep underground and that within it there are chambers within chambers. These qualities are described in the text in lines 135–148.

Lines 149–154
REINFORCE *KEY IDEA:* REVENGE

Discuss What **revenge** do you predict Montresor has in mind? *Possible answer: He plans to trap Fortunato in the recess.*

FOR ENGLISH LEARNERS
Vocabulary: Idioms and Sayings Explain that these phrases are idioms, expressions that have a different meaning from the individual words. Have students use context clues to determine the meaning of these idioms or sayings.

- *at his heels* (line 154), "behind him"
- *in a great measure* (line 174), "mostly"
- *worn off* (line 174), "gone away"

Have students work in pairs to create sentences with each idiom.

FOR ADVANCED LEARNERS/PRE–AP
Analyze Ask students to reread lines 117–131. Have them work in pairs to discuss why Poe included this exchange between Montresor and Fortunato about the brotherhood of Freemasons. What do these lines add to our understanding of the characters? How does the exchange add to the suspense of the story?

Activity Ask students how the image supports the events described. *Possible answer: The massiveness of the chain and handcuffs underscore the seriousness of Fortunato's situation, suggesting that escape will be impossible.*

ADDITIONAL TEACHING OPPORTUNITY

Evaluate Theme: Ask students to identify the story's **theme**—its underlying message about life or human nature. Then have students evaluate that theme—decide whether they think it is valid. Tell students to use these questions as their evaluation criteria.

- Does the theme express a broad insight into life or human nature, or simply an idea that applies only to a few people?

- Does the theme offer a meaningful insight, or is it too obvious or clichéd?

- Is the theme a realistic observation, or is it too optimistic, cynical, or narrow-minded?

Point out to students that a theme may be valid even if they do not personally agree with it. (To learn more about evaluating theme, see **Reading Handbook,** page R2.)

---

reached the extremity of the niche, and finding his progress arrested by the rock, stood stupidly bewildered. A moment more and I had fettered him to the granite. In its surface were two iron staples, distant from each other about two feet, horizontally. From one of these depended a short chain, from the other a padlock. Throwing the links about his waist, it was but the work of a few
160 seconds to secure it. He was too much astounded to resist. Withdrawing the key I stepped back from the recess.

"Pass your hand," I said, "over the wall; you cannot help feeling the niter. Indeed it is *very* damp. Once more let me *implore* you to return. No? Then I must positively leave you. But I must first render you all the little attentions in my power."

"The Amontillado!" ejaculated my friend, not yet recovered from his astonishment.

"True," I replied; "the Amontillado."

As I said these words I busied myself among the pile of bones of which I
170 have before spoken. Throwing them aside, I soon uncovered a quantity of building stone and mortar. With these materials and with the aid of my trowel, I began vigorously to wall up the entrance of the niche.

I had scarcely laid the first tier of the masonry when I discovered that the intoxication of Fortunato had in a great measure worn off. The earliest indication I had of this was a low moaning cry from the depth of the recess. It was not the cry of a drunken man. There was then a long and obstinate silence. I laid the second tier, and the third, and the fourth; and then I heard the furious vibrations of the chain. The noise lasted for several minutes, during which, that I might hearken to it with the more satisfaction, I ceased
180 my labors and sat down upon the bones. When at last the clanking **subsided,**

❸ Targeted Passage

subside (səb-sīd′) *v.* to decrease in amount or intensity; settle down

DIFFERENTIATED INSTRUCTION

FOR LESS—PROFICIENT READERS

❸ Targeted Passage [Lines 156–172]

This passage reveals Montresor's planned revenge and underscores his cruel nature.

- What does Montresor do to Fortunato when they reach the end of the niche?

- When Montresor says, "let me *implore* you to return," what does his request tell you about his nature?

- What revenge does Montresor appear to be taking against Fortunato?

FOR ENGLISH LEARNERS

Comprehension: Transitions Discuss the use of *but* to signal contrasting ideas in these sentences: "I must not only punish, but . . ." (lines 5–6); "I had no intention of alarming you unnecessarily; but . . ." (lines 88–89); "Then I must positively leave you. But . . ." (lines 163–164). Have Jigsaw Reading groups paraphrase the sentences and share their paraphrases with the class.

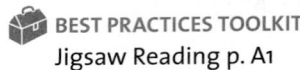 **BEST PRACTICES TOOLKIT**
Jigsaw Reading p. A1

I resumed the trowel, and finished without interruption the fifth, the sixth, and the seventh tier. The wall was now nearly upon a level with my breast. I again paused, and holding the flambeaux over the mason-work, threw a few feeble rays upon the figure within. **F**

A succession of loud and shrill screams, bursting suddenly from the throat of the chained form, seemed to thrust me violently back. For a brief moment I hesitated—I trembled. Unsheathing my rapier,[19] I began to grope with it about the recess; but the thought of an instant reassured me. I placed my hand upon the solid fabric of the catacombs, and felt satisfied. I reapproached the wall. I
190 replied to the yells of him who clamored. I re-echoed—I aided—I surpassed them in volume and in strength. I did this, and the clamorer grew still. **G**

It was now midnight, and my task was drawing to a close. I had completed the eighth, the ninth, and the tenth tier. I had finished a portion of the last and the eleventh; there remained but a single stone to be fitted and plastered in. I struggled with its weight; I placed it partially in its destined position. But now there came from out the niche a low laugh that erected the hairs upon my head. It was succeeded by a sad voice, which I had difficulty in recognizing as that of the noble Fortunato. The voice said—

"Ha! ha! ha!—he! he!—a very good joke indeed—an excellent jest. We will
200 have many a rich laugh about it at the palazzo—he! he! he! —over our wine—he! he! he!"

"The Amontillado!" I said.

"He! he! he!—he! he! he!—yes, the Amontillado. But is it not getting late? Will not they be awaiting us at the palazzo, the Lady Fortunato and the rest? Let us be gone."

"Yes," I said, "let us be gone."

"For the love of God, Montresor!"

"Yes," I said, "for the love of God!" **H**

But to these words I hearkened in vain for a reply. I grew impatient. I called
210 aloud,

"Fortunato!"

No answer. I called again,

"Fortunato!"

No answer still. I thrust a torch through the remaining **aperture** and let it fall within. There came forth in return only a jingling of the bells. My heart grew sick—on account of the dampness of the catacombs. I hastened to make an end of my labor. I forced the last stone into its position; I plastered it up. Against the new masonry I re-erected the old rampart of bones. For the half of a century no mortal has disturbed them. *In pace requiescat!*[20] ∿

④ **Targeted Passage**

19. **rapier** (rā′pē-ər): a long, slender sword.

20. **In pace requiescat** (ĭn pä′kĕ rĕ-kwē-ĕs′kät) *Latin:* May he rest in peace.

F MOOD
Reread this paragraph. What **details** make this description especially horrifying?

G PARAPHRASE
Restate what happens in lines 185–191. What emotions does Montresor experience at this point in the story?

H MOOD
Reread lines 192–208. Point out **images** and other **details** that convey the mood of the scene.

aperture (ăp′ər-chər) *n.* an opening, such as a hole or a gap

---

LITERARY ANALYSIS

F MOOD
Possible answer: *"low moaning cry" (line 174), "furious vibrations of the chain" (line 178), "that I might hearken to it with the more satisfaction, I ceased my labors and sat down upon the bones" (lines 179–180), "threw a few feeble rays upon the figure within" (lines 183–184).*

READING STRATEGY

G PARAPHRASE
Possible answer: *Fortunato begins to scream, which briefly unnerves Montresor, and he reaches for his rapier. But then Montresor realizes that Fortunato is trapped and yells back at him until he is silent. A feeling of triumph has replaced Montresor's moment of doubt.*

LITERARY ANALYSIS

H MOOD
Possible answer: *"It was now midnight" (line 192), "there remained but a single stone to be fitted and plastered in" (lines 194–195), "there came from out the niche a low laugh that erected the hairs upon my head" (lines 196–197), "'For the love of God, Montresor!'" (line 207).*

SELECTION WRAP–UP

REFLECT Have students consider what the planning and preparation Montresor must have done to carry out his revenge suggests about his character.

★ **CRITIQUE** Have students evaluate the story and tell why they think it is or is not realistic.

READING FLUENCY

Distribute the copy master and have students work in teams to practice fluency.

R RESOURCE MANAGER—Copy Master
Reading Fluency p. 90

FOR LESS–PROFICIENT READERS

④ Targeted Passage [Lines 214–219]

This passage concludes the story, hinting at Montresor's momentary remorse.

• What revenge does Montresor carry out against Fortunato?

• Why does Montresor claim that his "heart grew sick" (lines 215–216)? Do you accept his explanation? Why or why not?

• Does Montresor get away with his crime? How do you know?

FOR ENGLISH LEARNERS

Language: Pronoun Referents Ask students whom the phrases "him who clamored" (line 190) and "the clamorer" (line 191) refer to. (*Both refer to Fortunato.*) Then have students read lines 203–205. Have pairs discuss and share their ideas about whom or what each of these pronouns refers to: in line 203, *it* (*the time*); in line 204, *they* ("the *Lady Fortunato and the rest*"); in line 205, *us* (*Fortunato and Montresor*).

DISCUSSION PROMPTS

Use these prompts to help students understand the connection between "The Cask of Amontillado" and the murder that may have inspired Poe to create his short story:

Connect How has "The Story Behind 'The Cask of Amontillado'" affected your appreciation of Poe's story? ***Possible answer:*** *Poe was inspired by real-life events, just as many writers are today. This does not diminish his talent as a writer or storyteller. Rather, it highlights his ability to explore the darker side of human behavior.*

Analyze What details does Edward Rowe Snow use to make his narrative read like a horror story? Be specific. ***Possible answer:*** *Snow uses details like "moonless night," "ancient dungeons," "subterranean casemate," and "heavy iron handcuffs and footcuffs" to evoke a scary setting and atmosphere.*

Evaluate In what ways does "The Story Behind 'The Cask of Amontillado'" stand out as distinct from "The Cask of Amontillado"? ***Possible answer:*** *"The Story Behind 'The Cask of Amontillado'" has more details. While the reader never learns what Fortunato's mysterious "insult" actually was, Snow reveals specifically why the officers sought revenge on Captain Green—he killed Lieutenant Massie, a beloved fellow officer. Captain Green was also a livelier character than Fortunato. Student answers may vary about which narrative they like best.*

THE STORY BEHIND
The CASK *of Amontillado*
EDWARD ROWE SNOW

While at Fort Independence, Poe [who was a private there in 1827] became fascinated with the inscriptions on a gravestone on a small monument outside the walls of the fort. . . .

Beneath this stone are deposited the remains of Lieut. ROBERT F. MASSIE, of the U. S. Regt. of Light Artillery. . . .

During the summer of 1817, Poe learned, twenty-year-old Lieutenant Robert F. Massie of Virginia had arrived at Fort Independence as a newly appointed officer. Most of the men at the post came to enjoy Massie's friendship, but one officer, Captain Green, took a violent dislike to him. Green was known at the fort as a bully and a dangerous swordsman.

When Christmas vacations were allotted, few of the officers were allowed to leave the fort, and Christmas Eve found them up in the old barracks hall, playing cards. Just before midnight, at the height of the card game, Captain Green sprang to his feet, reached across the table and slapped Lieutenant Massie squarely in the face. "You're a cheat," he roared, "and I demand immediate satisfaction!" . . .

The duel began. Captain Green, an expert swordsman, soon had Massie at a disadvantage and ran him through. Fatally wounded, the young Virginian was carried back to the fort, where he died that afternoon. His many friends mourned the passing of a gallant officer. . . .

Feeling against Captain Green ran high for many weeks, and then suddenly he completely vanished. Years went by without a sign of him, and Green was written off the army records as a deserter.

According to the story which Poe finally gathered together, Captain Green had been so detested by his fellow officers at the fort that they decided to take a terrible revenge on him for Massie's death. . . .

Visiting Captain Green one moonless night, they pretended to be friendly and plied him with wine until he was helplessly intoxicated. Then, carrying the captain down to one of the ancient dungeons, the officers forced his body through a tiny opening which led into the subterranean casemate.[1] . . .

His captors began to shackle him to the floor, using the heavy iron handcuffs and footcuffs fastened into the stone. Then they all left the dungeon and proceeded to seal the captain up alive inside the windowless casemate, using bricks and mortar. . . .

Captain Green shrieked in terror and begged for mercy, but his cries fell on deaf ears. The last brick was finally inserted, mortar applied, and the room sealed up, the officers believed, forever. . . .

[In 1905, workmen repairing the fort found a skeleton inside, shackled to the floor with a few fragments of an old army uniform clinging to the bones.]

1. **subterranean casemate** (sŭb′tə-rā′nē-ən kās′māt′): a fortified underground or partly underground room.

Comprehension

1. **Recall** Why does Montresor, the narrator, want **revenge?**

2. **Recall** How does Montresor trick Fortunato into joining him?

3. **Summarize** What does Montresor do to ensure the success of his plan?

4. **Summarize** What happens to Fortunato?

Literary Analysis

5. **Make Inferences About Character** What kind of man is Montresor? Think of four or five character traits that you can infer from Montresor's words and actions. Record your answers in a chart like the one shown.

Montresor's Character Traits	Words/Actions
1. shrewdness	He knows how to take advantage of Fortunato's pride.
2.	

6. **Analyze Mood** What is the overall mood, or atmosphere, of this story? In your opinion, what contributes most to the mood—the setting, the sound and rhythm of the language, or the descriptions of Montresor's thoughts, feelings, and actions? Provide details from the story to support your opinion.

7. **Make Judgments** Review your **paraphrase** of lines 1–8. Does Montresor achieve the kind of revenge he wants? Cite details to support your answer.

8. **Evaluate Narrator** Consider whether Montresor is a **reliable** or an **unreliable narrator.** Is the reader to believe, as Montresor does, that his revenge is justified? Give evidence from the story.

9. **Evaluate Dramatic Irony** A situation in which the reader knows something that a character does not is an example of dramatic irony. The first paragraph of the story prepares the way for dramatic ironies by giving the reader information that Fortunato does not have. Identify three examples of dramatic irony. What is the effect of the irony on your experience as a reader?

10. **Compare and Contrast** Poe often drew inspiration for his tales of horror from the real world. Compare the details of "The Story Behind 'The Cask of Amontillado'" on page 352 with the story of Montresor and Fortunato. How similar are these accounts?

Literary Criticism

11. **Critical Interpretations** In defining the short story as a literary form, Poe emphasized that every word should contribute to a "unity of effect or impression." He believed that a writer should first choose a "unique or single effect" to convey, then invent events "as may best aid him in establishing this preconceived effect." How well does Poe achieve a "unity of effect" in this story? Give examples from the text to support your answer.

THE CASK OF AMONTILLADO **353**

8. *Unreliable: Montresor never explains the "thousand injuries" or "insult," so we can't judge whether his revenge is justified—if murder is every justified.*

9. *When Montresor urges his "friend" to turn back because his "health is precious" (lines 80–82), the reader suspects he is really luring his enemy to the vaults to kill him, and that Fortunato will "not die of a cough" (line 87). When Fortunato approves of the Montresor family motto (lines 105–106), the reader understands its true, murderous*

meaning. These dramatic ironies heighten the reader's anticipation of the murder.

10. *In both accounts a man is given wine, chained, walled in, and left to die while he pleads for mercy. The stories differ in setting, and in Poe's story the revenge is carried out by one person, not a group.*

Literary Criticism

11. *Students should support their responses with relevant examples.*

Practice and Apply

After Reading

For additional support of post-reading questions, use these copy masters:

R RESOURCE MANAGER—Copy Masters
Reading Check p. 86 (to check understanding of the selection)
Mood p. 79 (for practice of literary analysis standards focus)
Question Support p. 87 (After Reading questions adapted for English learners and less-proficient readers)

For additional questions, see page 73.

For additional exercises to challenge students, see
ⓘ Power Thinking at **ClassZone.com**

ANSWERS

Comprehension

1. *Montresor wants revenge because he feels that Fortunato has insulted him.*

2. *Montresor plays on Fortunato's pride and vanity, pretending to need his expertise to judge some Amontillado he has purchased.*

3. *Montresor pretends to be Fortunato's friend. He carries out his plan when there are "no attendants at home." He gives Fortunato wine to drink.*

4. *Montresor lures Fortunato deep into the catacombs in his mansion, then chains him up, walls him in, and leaves him there to die.*

Literary Analysis

Possible answers:

5. *Trait (T): vengeful, Words/Actions (W/A): lines 1–8; T: calculating, W/A: carefully plans revenge; T: devious, W/A: manipulates Fortunato through flattery; T: heartless, W/A: lines 178–180.*

6. ● **STANDARDS FOCUS Mood** *The overall mood is sinister, created mainly by Montresor's diabolical thoughts, feelings, and actions. For example, he carries out his revenge while pretending to be Fortunato's friend; he taunts Fortunato (lines 162–165) and enjoys his suffering (lines 177–191).*

7. ■ **STANDARDS FOCUS Paraphrase** *Yes. He kills Fortunato without getting caught. His victim dies knowing who killed him, but perhaps not why.*

ANSWERS

Vocabulary in Context

VOCABULARY PRACTICE

1. *a*	**5.** *a*
2. *b*	**6.** *b*
3. *a*	**7.** *a*
4. *b*	**8.** *a*

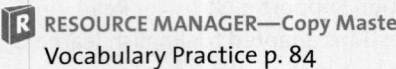 **RESOURCE MANAGER—Copy Master**
Vocabulary Practice p. 84

VOCABULARY IN WRITING

Tell students to imagine being in Montresor's place. What mixture of emotions would they experience? Would it include satisfaction? regret? fear? What thoughts would they have about Fortunato?

VOCABULARY STRATEGY: THE *clud* WORD FAMILY (*also an EL language objective*)

- To help students with the **PRACTICE** activity, work with them on the first item: *include.* Begin by eliciting or providing its meaning ("to take in or contain as part of a whole or group").

- Ask how *include* might relate to the meaning of *clud.* Model the thinking process with this example: A book that *includes* names and dates would contain useful information.

- Additional words in the *clud* family: *exclude, disclose, enclosure.*

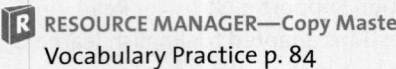 **RESOURCE MANAGER—Copy Master**
Vocabulary Strategy p. 85

ⓘ Vocabulary Center at **ClassZone.com**
Additional Vocabulary Activities

Vocabulary in Context

VOCABULARY PRACTICE

Choose the situation that most closely relates to each vocabulary word.

1. **aperture:** (a) a crack in a building's foundation, (b) a large stack of lumber
2. **subside:** (a) two cars racing through traffic, (b) a heavy wind lessening in force
3. **impunity:** (a) getting away with a personal foul in football, (b) a tiny hole in a shirt
4. **termination:** (a) someone starting a new job, (b) someone being fired
5. **repose:** (a) lying on a deserted beach, (b) carrying a heavy load of books
6. **abscond:** (a) making a public announcement, (b) sneaking out of a meeting
7. **immolation:** (a) fatalities in a train accident, (b) cartons of spoiled produce
8. **preclude:** (a) getting vaccinated against polio, (b) planting bulbs in fall

WORD LIST
abscond
aperture
immolation
impunity
preclude
repose
subside
termination

VOCABULARY IN WRITING

How do you think Montresor feels after sealing up the wall? Using three or more vocabulary words, write a paragraph describing his feelings. You might begin as shown below.

> **EXAMPLE SENTENCE**
>
> *Montresor felt strange as he closed the final **aperture**.*

VOCABULARY STRATEGY: THE *clud* WORD FAMILY

The root of the word *preclude* can be traced back to a Latin word meaning "to close." This root—the spellings of which include *clud, clos, clus,* and *claus*—has given rise to a large word family. *Preclude,* in which the root is combined with the prefix *pre-*, literally means "to close before." If you can recognize the root in the family of words, you can understand how they are related in meaning.

PRACTICE Use each word in a sentence that shows the connection between its meaning and that of *preclude*. Then, using a dictionary, identify three additional words in the *clud* family.

1. include	**5.** closet
2. recluse	**6.** clause
3. foreclosure	**7.** seclusion
4. exclusive	**8.** conclude

VOCABULARY PRACTICE
For more practice, go to the **Vocabulary Center** at **ClassZone.com**.

DIFFERENTIATED INSTRUCTION

FOR ENGLISH LEARNERS

Vocabulary: Prefixes Encourage students to use their knowledge of the prefixes *im-* (meaning "not") and *sub-* (meaning "under" or "below") to help them remember the definitions of *impunity* and *subside.*

FOR ADVANCED LEARNERS/PRE–AP

Practice Vocabulary Challenge students to write a coherent paragraph using as many of the vocabulary words as they can. Have volunteers share their paragraphs with the class.

Reading-Writing Connection

Expand your understanding of "The Cask of Amontillado" by responding to these prompts. Then use **Revision: Grammar and Style** to improve your writing.

WRITING PROMPTS	SELF-CHECK
A. Short Response: Interpret Ending Montresor ends his story with a Latin sentence meaning "May he rest in peace." Does he mean these words in the usual sense? If not, what does he mean? Write a **one- or two-paragraph response** that explains your interpretation of his meaning.	*A successful response will . . .* • clearly state an opinion about the meaning of Montresor's words • include details from the story to support that opinion
B. Extended Response: Create a Monologue What do you think goes through Fortunato's mind after he realizes what has happened to him? Why doesn't he try to reason with Montresor? Use what you know about Fortunato to write a **three-to-five-paragraph monologue,** retelling the last part of the story from his point of view.	*An effective monologue will . . .* • maintain a consistent point of view • be consistent with Fortunato's character as revealed in the story • clearly show Fortunato's feelings

REVISION: GRAMMAR AND STYLE

USE APPROPRIATE LANGUAGE Review the **Grammar and Style** note on page 348. Poe uses **formal language** to tell his suspenseful tale. This style of language contains challenging vocabulary, includes complex sentence structures and standard punctuation, and avoids contractions. Use formal language when you want your writing to have a serious quality. Here is an example from the story:

> I continued, as was my wont, to smile in his face, and he did not perceive that my smile now was at the thought of his immolation. (lines 10–12)

Notice how the revisions in red make use of formal language that better reflects Poe's style. Use similar methods to revise your response to prompt B.

STUDENT MODEL

I soon realized, to my horror, was ~ing
It hadn't occurred to me that Montresor would actually wall up the entrance
    Surely this was merely a jest. After all, how could
to the niche. Where'd he think he was going? I couldn't believe he would
wretched, cavernous enclosure?
leave me in this damp place!

WRITING TOOLS
For prewriting, revision, and editing tools, visit the **Writing Center** at ClassZone.com.

THE CASK OF AMONTILLADO **355**

FOR LESS–PROFICIENT WRITERS

For Prompt A:

• Elicit or provide the usual sense of the expression "May he rest in peace."

• Help students understand the significance of the sentence "For the half of a century no mortal has disturbed them."

• Help students write a topic sentence.

For Prompt B:

• Limit the length of the monologue to no more than three paragraphs.

• Encourage students to imagine themselves in Fortunato's situation. Have pairs or small groups of students share their thoughts and feelings orally before committing them to paper.

Reading-Writing Connection

WRITING PROMPTS

• For Prompt A, encourage students to reread the last paragraph of the story, paying special attention to lines 218–219. Elicit or explain that Fortunato has been "resting in peace" for 50 years, undisturbed—and undiscovered—by anyone.

• For Prompt B, have students reread lines 173–215 and reflect on Fortunato's reactions to what has happened to him. Suggest that students consider at what point Fortunato finally realizes Montresor's intent to kill him.

For an extended writing activity, see
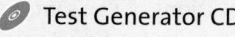 Carol Booth Olson's Reading-Writing Lesson Plans at **ClassZone.com**

REVISION: GRAMMAR AND STYLE

After students examine the student model, write these sentences on the board, and have students suggest revisions. (For information on formal language, see **Grammar Handbook,** page R46.)

> What had I done to make Montresor so mad? I couldn't remember a thing. Besides, nothing I might have said or done would have deserved this!

Possible answer: *What wrong had I committed to provoke such anger in Montresor? No injustice or insult of any sort occurred to me. Moreover, no word or deed merited such punishment.*

 RESOURCE MANAGER—Copy Master
Use Appropriate Language p. 89

Assess and Reteach

Assess

R RESOURCE MANAGER—Copy Masters
Selection Test A pp. 91–92
Selection Test B/C pp. 93–94

Test Generator CD

Reteach

S STANDARDS LESSON FILE
Literature Lesson 44: Mood
Vocabulary Lesson 10: Word Families and Derivatives

Focus and Motivate

OBJECTIVES

Media Literacy

- explore the key idea of **sinister** setting and mood
- view a film clip to understand how elements of set design, costuming, props, music, sound effects, and acting create a sinister setting and mood
- create a production design board to demonstrate understanding of set elements such as scenery, costumes, and props

SUMMARY

In this film clip from *The Cask of Amontillado,* Montresor and the "friend," Fortunato, on whom he has vowed revenge, descend into the catacombs beneath Montresor's palazzo. Montresor lures the drunken Fortunato, a wine connoisseur, with the promise of tasting a rare sherry. Finally, Montresor lures his "friend" into a tiny niche where the cask of sherry supposedly lies. There Montresor shackles the dumbfounded Fortunato to the wall and takes his revenge by walling him into the niche.

What makes a setting SINISTER?

To help students explore the **KEY IDEA,** ask them what the word **sinister** means. Invite them to share moments from film or TV that felt sinister. Have them describe elements of the lighting, music, and setting that created the sinister mood. For example, perhaps the lighting was shadowy, the music was ominous, or the setting included sinister places, such as dark attics. Ask how these elements contributed to the sinister mood.

BACKGROUND

This version of "The Cask of Amontillado" is one of many TV and film adaptations of Poe's works. Horror filmmaker Roger Corman produced versions of Poe's stories "The Fall of the House of Usher," "The Pit and the Pendulum," and "The Masque of the Red Death." Poe's works have also been used in satires, as in the popular TV series *The Simpsons.* One Halloween episode was based on Poe's poem "The Raven," and an episode titled "The Tell-Tale Head" was loosely based on Poe's "The Tell-Tale Heart."

Media Study

from **The Cask of Amontillado**

Film Clip on **MediaSmart** DVD

What makes a setting SINISTER?

KEY IDEA In his writings, Edgar Allan Poe drafted a blueprint for spine-tingling effects that countless creative artists have followed. View a film adaptation of "The Cask of Amontillado" to explore how a team of filmmakers, guided by Poe's descriptions, evoked a time and place and a consistently **sinister** mood.

Background

Tale from the Crypt One could argue that had Poe been born in the 20th century, he might have enjoyed page-to-film success similar to that of the modern writer Stephen King. Beginning in the silent-film era of the 1920s, filmmakers saw potential in Poe's shadowy characters and in his haunting settings. Over time, Hollywood adapted a few of his horror classics into movies.

This version of "Cask" is part of a program called "Edgar Allan Poe: Terror of the Soul" that was first broadcast in 1995. The set design was based on actual 18th-century Italian catacombs. According to the production designer, David Wasco, "The descent into the catacombs was supposed to get spookier and spookier."

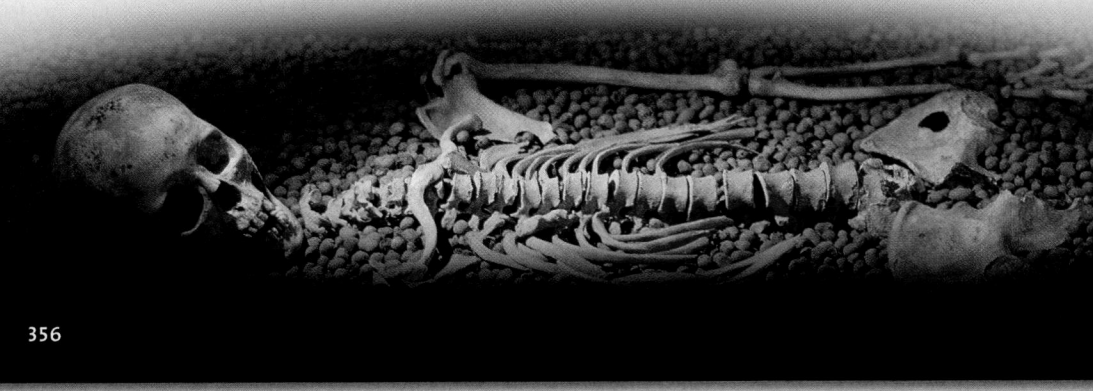

356

Media Study Resources

 **RESOURCE MANAGER UNIT 3**

Plan and Teach pp. 95–98

Media Analysis
Summary pp. 99†*, 100‡*
Viewing Guide p. 101
Close Viewing p. 102
Viewing Activity p. 103
Produce Your Own Media p. 104

STANDARDS LESSON FILE

Media Lesson 4: Analyzing Visuals in Film and TV

Media Lesson 7: Evaluating Films and TV Shows

ℹ️ Media Center at **ClassZone.com**

MEDIA VIEWING
🔘 Media*Smart* DVD

* Resources for Differentiation   † Also in Spanish   ‡ In Haitian Creole and Vietnamese

Media Literacy: Setting and Mood in Movies

To recreate settings of the past onscreen, filmmakers focus on representing the time and place of the story and the class, culture, and customs of the characters. After researching these areas, filmmakers select visual and sound elements that will accurately represent the period. These elements include **set design, costuming, props, music,** and **acting.**

When adapting a written work into a film, the director collaborates with other members of the filmmaking team. The art director, the production (or set) designer, the costume designer, the cinematographer, and the music composer all contribute ideas on how to make a setting vivid and how to convey the appropriate mood.

FROM PAGE TO FILM	STRATEGIES FOR VIEWING	
Creating Setting **Writers** reveal details of settings through description and dialogue. **Filmmakers** design specific sets and enhance them.	• Focus on the details of the **set design.** Are the **props**—the objects in the scene—appropriate to the time and place? • Look for distinctive details in the **costumes.** For example, an 18th-century character of high status would probably wear rich fabrics of velvet and silk.	
Creating Mood **Writers** often rely on word choice to describe vivid **details**—factual or sensory—that create atmosphere. **Filmmakers** create atmosphere primarily through visual and sound techniques.	• Be aware of the overall effect—lighthearted, gloomy, or mysterious—that **lighting** creates in scenes. • Notice how the **music** varies in tone. • Listen for **sound effects.** Creaking floorboards or hollow echoes can enhance an atmosphere established by the visual elements.	
Creating Dramatic Irony **Writers** reveal to readers details that some characters don't know through **narration** and **dialogue.** **Filmmakers** use visual and sound techniques to reveal details.	• Look for clues in the **compositions.** A character might be placed deliberately in the foreground to suggest weakness or vulnerability. • Pay attention to **close-ups** that show characters' facial expressions revealing what other characters don't know. • Notice the tone of voice an actor might use in a line of **dialogue** to convey more than one meaning.	

MEDIA STUDY: TEACHING OPTIONS

Teaching Option 1: The Basics (1–2 Days)
1. Begin the Media Study using the material provided on pages 356–357.
2. Show the Introduction on Media*Smart*. Then show the First Viewing. As they watch, have students use the Viewing Guide on page 358, along with the corresponding copy master on page 101 of the Resource Manager. Discuss their responses.
3. Return to the pupil book for the extension activities on page 359.

Teaching Option 2: In-Depth Study (2–3 Days)
1. Begin the Media Study using pages 356–357.
2. Show the Introduction and First Viewing from Media*Smart*. Then continue on Media*Smart* with the Media Lessons, using the teacher notes available in the Resources section.
3. Show the Guided Analysis presentation. Have students record their observations on the Student Viewing Guide available in the Resources section from Media*Smart*.
4. Return to the pupil book, page 359.

Teach

Media Literacy

Review with students the elements that filmmakers use to create story setting and mood. Ask the class to recall scenes from a familiar movie set in either the distant past or the future. On the board, list "Set Design and Props," "Costumes," "Lighting," "Music and Sound Effects," "Acting." List students' descriptions of each aspect of the film. Link the listed features to the overall mood in the film. Then discuss the chart on page 357.

- **Creating Setting** To emphasize the impact of set design, have students imagine a male and female actor in front of a blank blue screen. The actors are fleeing from something. Then ask students to add (1) these different backgrounds: first an army of giant ants in a desert, then a battalion of Roman warriors; (2) these costumes: first sleek silver futuristic flight suits, then loose togas; and (3) these props: first X-ray weapons, then swords. Ask how each change of background, costumes, and props changes the viewer's experience.

- **Creating Mood** Ask students to recall kinds of music and sound effects that make a movie viewer uneasy or frightened. List these ideas on the board. Revisit the list after students view the clip, and allow time to add new ideas.

- **Creating Dramatic Irony** Point out that film shots may position characters near objects, such as an ax hanging on the wall, that predict something to the audience but not to the character. Ask students for additional examples of this technique. Have students explore the impact of tone of voice. Ask volunteers to say these words, first as if having an ordinary conversation and then as if hinting at something unspoken: "This will be an interesting day."

📀 Media*Smart* DVD

Practice and Apply

VIEWING GUIDE

1. Before students view the clip, tell them that they will be asked to identify techniques used to convey a sinister setting and mood. Encourage them to watch and listen for these elements:

   - **set design** and **props** and the way they combine to create a sense of impending doom for Fortunato

   - **costumes** and how they provide information about the time period in which Fortunato and Montresor live

   - **lighting** in the catacombs and how it creates a somber mood

   - **music** and **sound effects** that add to the gloomy atmosphere in the catacombs

   - **composition, close-ups,** and **dialogue** that show Montresor's sinister intentions and Fortunato's ultimate terror

2. Some students may have difficulty isolating the elements that go into creating the clip's sinister mood. Before they view the clip, you might encourage them to make a chart with these headings: "Set Design and Props," "Costumes," "Lighting," "Music and Sound Effects," "Composition," "Close-Ups," "Dialogue." Urge students to take notes during the viewing.

RESOURCE MANAGER—Copy Masters

Viewing Guide p. 101
Close Viewing p. 102
Viewing Activity p. 103

Use this resource with the Viewing Guide:

*Media*Smart DVD

ANSWERS

FIRST VIEWING: Comprehension

1. *Stone and brick walls, dim lighting, exposed skeletons in crypts, narrow passages, descending stairways, the niter seeping through cracks*

2. *A close-up shot of Fortunato's face lit by the dim, flickering flame of a torch*

---

*Media*Smart DVD
- **Film Clip:** *The Cask of Amontillado*
- **Director:** Joyce Chopra
- **Production Designer:** David Wasco
- **Genre:** Horror
- **Running Time:** 10.5 minutes

358

Viewing Guide for
The Cask of Amontillado

This film excerpt from "The Cask of Amontillado" begins with the search for the Amontillado. You already know how this tale of revenge ends. So, as you watch the adaptation, focus on how film techniques create a sinister atmosphere and evoke a particular mood.

Watch the excerpt several times. To help you focus on elements of setting and mood, refer to the questions that follow.

NOW VIEW

FIRST VIEWING: Comprehension

1. **Recall** What did you see in the set design of the movie that made it clear that the characters are in the catacombs?

2. **Clarify** What type of shot do you see at the moment that Fortunato realizes he's caught in a trap?

CLOSE VIEWING: Media Literacy

3. **Analyze Setting and Mood** How does the director convey the sinister and claustrophobic setting of the catacombs? Think about the following:

   - the atmosphere of the **set design**
   - the use of **composition** and **lighting**
   - the **music** as the characters descend lower and lower

4. **Analyze Costumes** How does each character's **costume** reflect the role he plays in this cat-and-mouse tale?

5. **Analyze Dramatic Irony** To Fortunato, Montresor disguises his intentions. To viewers, he reveals them. How is the truth revealed? As you cite specific shots to support your response, think about

   - the use of **composition** and **close-ups**
   - the actors' facial expressions and behavior

CLOSE VIEWING: Media Literacy

Possible answers:

3. **Set design:** *conveys the cramped space of the catacombs, with the low ceiling often visible;* **composition:** *shows close proximity of characters;* **lighting:** *dim throughout the story;* **music:** *more foreboding as the characters descend*

4. *Fortunato wears a silk jester's costume, suggesting both wealth and buffoonery. Montresor's black cloak suggests foreboding; it is the dress of a criminal and an executioner.*

5. *As Montresor follows Fortunato deeper into the catacombs, close-up shots reveal Montresor's anger and distaste toward Fortunato. As the men near the end of the catacombs, Montresor appears increasingly anxious.*

Write or Discuss

Compare Film and Written Versions Edgar Allan Poe was a master at using words to create eerie and frightening story settings. In your opinion, does the film adaptation of "The Cask of Amontillado" effectively portray the story's sinister setting? To compare the film and written versions, note the following:

- Poe's description of the catacombs versus the visual presentation
- the sequence of events in the catacombs
- the film techniques used to enhance the scenes, including sound, lighting, and camera shots

Produce Your Own Media

Create a Production Design Board Imagine that you're part of a production team assigned to design sets for an adaptation of "The Cask of Amontillado." You'll use a production design board to present ideas for creating a sinister setting. A production design board visually represents different elements of a set, such as scenery, costumes, and props. The board displays small parts or drawings of these elements.

HERE'S HOW Work with a partner to review the short story and decide what scene (or scenes) to depict and how to present it. Consider these suggestions:

- Keep the presentation simple. Use labels to identify key elements.
- Using foam board as the background, apply photos or sketches of design elements and fabric samples (or magazine clippings of patterns).
- Attach quotations from the tale that inspired your selections.

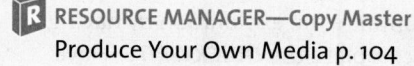

MEDIA TOOLS
For help with creating a production design board, visit the **Media Center** at **ClassZone.com.**

STUDENT MODEL

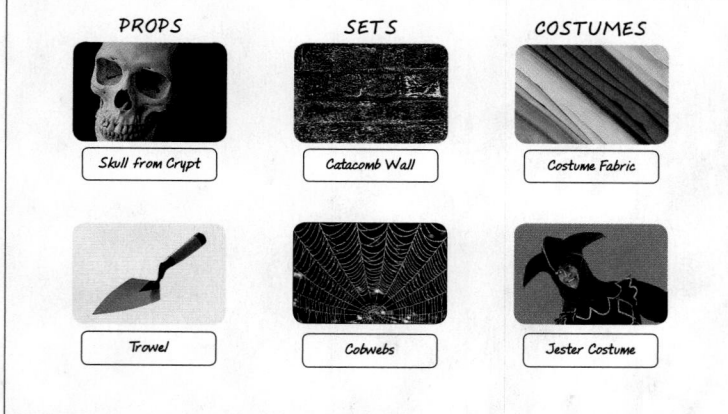

PROPS — Skull from Crypt — Trowel
SETS — Catacomb Wall — Cobwebs
COSTUMES — Costume Fabric — Jester Costume

Tech Tip
Use a clip-art program as a source of images of props and other elements of a set's design.

Write or Discuss

Compare Film and Written Versions In their evaluations, students should address techniques used by set, costume, sound, and lighting designers as well as film techniques such as camera shots. Make sure students recognize the impact that elements of setting and film technique have on mood. For example, students might compare Poe's description of human remains lining the walls of the crypt with the set designer's use of skulls and skeletons to create a sinister setting. In addition, encourage students to include their own personal reactions to the written story versus the filmed version.

Produce Your Own Media

Rubric: Create a Production Design Board
A strong production design board should have

- a label for each key element
- a variety of set elements, such as props and costumes
- a variety of design elements, such as sketches, fabric samples, magazine clippings, and pieces of clip art
- quotations from the story that relate to the design elements
- a clear identification of the scene or scenes
- a strong focus on the particular scene or scenes
- a simple and easy-to-understand format

R RESOURCE MANAGER—Copy Master
Produce Your Own Media p. 104

MEDIA STUDY WRAP–UP

Have students summarize what they have learned about set, costume, sound, and lighting design for film and how these elements contribute to mood. Encourage students to use such terms as *set design, props, costuming, lighting, music, sound effects, composition, close-up,* and *dialogue* in their explanations.

RETEACH

S STANDARDS LESSON FILE
Media Lesson 4: Analyzing Visuals in Film and TV
Media Lesson 7: Evaluating Films and TV Shows

Focus and Motivate

OBJECTIVES

Literary Analysis
- explore the key idea of **adventure**
- analyze details of setting
- analyze mood
- analyze effect of setting on mood
- read a travel narrative

Reading
- analyze descriptive details
- identify author's perspective

Vocabulary
- build vocabulary for reading and writing
- use context clues (general, comparison, example) to determine the meaning of unfamiliar words (*also an EL language objective*)

SUMMARY

In this excerpt from *A Walk in the Woods*, travel writer Bill Bryson presents a harrowing account of his encounter with a furious snowstorm while hiking the Appalachian Trail. Caught between an insurmountable mountain and a treacherous ledge, Bryson and his companion, Stephen Katz, manage to survive, while learning the importance of being well prepared.

Where do you find ADVENTURE?

Pose the question, and then explore the *KEY IDEA* by having students share and compare their concepts of **adventure**. Ask whether they think adventure must entail an element of risk. Continue the exploration by having students complete the *QUICKWRITE*. Have volunteers describe their adventures.

Selection Resources

---

from **A Walk in the Woods**
Travel Narrative by Bill Bryson

Where do you find ADVENTURE?

KEY IDEA Do you find **adventure** in physically risky activities, such as rock climbing and skateboarding, or in everyday pursuits? In this selection, you'll read about the adventures of Bill Bryson, a well-known travel writer whose hike along the Appalachian Trail took some unexpected turns.

QUICKWRITE With a small group, generate a list of adventures you've had or would like to have. Then select one adventure and write a short paragraph explaining how you would prepare for it.

RESOURCE MANAGER UNIT 3

Plan and Teach pp. 105–112

Literary Analysis
Summary pp. 113†*, 114‡*
Setting and Mood pp. 115, 116†*
Question Support p. 123*

Reading
Identify Author's Perspective
   pp. 117, 118†*
Reading Check p. 122
Reading Fluency p. 125

Vocabulary
Study p. 119*
Practice p. 120
Strategy p. 121

Assessment
Selection Tests A, B/C pp. 127*, 129*
   Test Generator CD

BEST PRACTICES TOOLKIT

Differentiated Instruction
   pp. 31–38*

Scaffolding Instruction
   pp. 43–46*

Graphic Organizers/Strategies
Definition Mapping • Two-Column Chart • New Word Analysis • Jigsaw Reading

Reading Support
   Audio Anthology CD*

Technology
   Literature and Vocabulary Centers at **ClassZone.com**

   Write*Smart* CD

---

* Resources for Differentiation   † Also in Spanish   ‡ In Haitian Creole and Vietnamese

● LITERARY ANALYSIS: SETTING AND MOOD

Setting can play an important role in creating a **mood**. In this selection, Bill Bryson describes the Appalachian Trail by using sensory details and precise verbs. These, in turn, convey a mood to the reader and help bring Bryson's experience to life. As you read, think about how the mood influences your impressions of the Appalachian Trail and those who travel it.

■ READING SKILL: IDENTIFY AUTHOR'S PERSPECTIVE

People often look at a subject from different perspectives. For example, a person living in Florida may react negatively to a 30-degree day, while a person raised in northern Minnesota might view such weather as a blessing. The combination of beliefs, values, and feelings that influence how a writer looks at a subject is called the **author's perspective.** In order to figure out an author's perspective, it's important to pay attention to

- statements of opinion
- details the writer chooses to include
- the writer's tone, or attitude (such as a humorous or serious tone)

As you read Bill Bryson's account of hiking the Appalachian Trail, try to figure out his perspective by completing a chart like the one shown.

Statement, Detail, or Tone	What It Reveals About Bryson
"Life takes on a neat simplicity...." (line 6)	He values a lack of complication.

Review: **Cause and Effect, Make Inferences**

▲ VOCABULARY IN CONTEXT

Put each vocabulary word in the appropriate column, and then write a brief definition of each word you're familiar with.

WORD LIST		
abysmal	reconnoiter	unnerving
buffeted	singularity	veneer
daunted	superannuated	

Know Well	Think I Know	Don't Know At All

Author Online

Bill Bryson
born 1951

Native Son
Bill Bryson (brī'sən) is a popular travel writer whose hiking stories combine humor and human interest with a sense of adventure. Bryson spent more than 20 years of his adult life in England, touring the countryside and writing best-selling books. In 1995 Bryson returned to the United States and settled in New Hampshire near a branch of the famous Appalachian Trail. Soon after, he became inspired to hike the length of the trail, hoping to improve his fitness and become better acquainted with his homeland. *A Walk in the Woods* records Bryson's adventures with his friend Stephen Katz as they traveled the trail.

A Challenging Trip When he and Katz began their trip, Bryson was used to casual walks through the English countryside. He knew little about the rugged conditions to be found in the U.S. wilderness. As a result, Bryson and Katz were ill prepared for the many challenges they faced, including carrying 40-pound packs, making their own meals, and sleeping outdoors. Much of the humor and suspense in *A Walk in the Woods* stems from their lack of preparation.

 MORE ABOUT THE AUTHOR For more on Bill Bryson, visit the **Literature Center** at ClassZone.com.

Background
A Path for the People The Appalachian Trail is a footpath that spans more than 2,100 miles from Mount Katahdin in Maine to Springer Mountain in Georgia. It passes through 14 states. The idea for the trail began in 1921 with a proposal by conservationist Benton MacKaye. On August 14, 1937, the trail was completed.

A WALK IN THE WOODS **361**

Teach

STANDARDS FOCUS

● SETTING AND MOOD

For instructional support, read aloud this example:

> The crumbling tombstones cast long shadows in the pale dawn light. An icy wind slashed across the graveyard as a piercing scream shattered the silence.

Have students identify sensory details and precise verbs that convey setting and mood. ***Possible answer:*** *"crumbling tombstones," "long shadows in the pale dawn light," "icy wind slashed across the graveyard," "piercing scream shattered"*

CHECK UNDERSTANDING Elicit other details and verbs that could convey a similar setting and mood.

READING SKILL

■ IDENTIFY AUTHOR'S PERSPECTIVE

Have students write several sentences telling why they do or do not enjoy outdoor activities. Then explore with them how their statements of opinion, supporting details, and tone reveal their perspective.

CHECK UNDERSTANDING Elicit details and statements that would reveal a perspective different from the student's own.

R RESOURCE MANAGER—Copy Master
Identify Author's Perspective p. 117 (for student use while reading the selection)

VOCABULARY SKILL

▲ VOCABULARY IN CONTEXT

DIAGNOSE WORD KNOWLEDGE To determine preteaching needs, have all students complete Vocabulary in Context. Check students' definitions against those on the selection pages: *abysmal* (p. 365), *buffeted* (p. 366), *daunted* (p. 367), *reconnoiter* (p. 368), *singularity* (p. 362), *superannuated* (p. 369), *unnerving* (p. 364), *veneer* (p. 364).

PRETEACH VOCABULARY Use the Vocabulary Study copy master to help students predict meanings for each boldfaced word in the copy master.

1. Read aloud the first two sentences in Part A, emphasizing *unnerving*.

2. Point out "courage" and "sense of adventure" in contrast to *unnerving*. Elicit possible meanings for *unnerving,* such as "scary."

3. Repeat the process for remaining words.

R RESOURCE MANAGER—Copy Master
Vocabulary Study p. 119

For general guidelines on differentiating vocabulary instruction and for alternative vocabulary activities for students not needing vocabulary preteaching, see

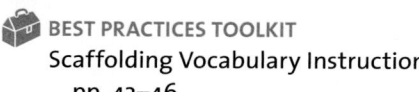 **BEST PRACTICES TOOLKIT**
Scaffolding Vocabulary Instruction pp. 43–46
ⓘ Vocabulary Center at **ClassZone.com**

A Walk in the Woods

BILL BRYSON

Distance changes utterly when you take the world on foot. A mile becomes a long way, two miles literally considerable, ten miles whopping, fifty miles at the very limits of conception. The world, you realize, is enormous in a way that only you and a small community of fellow hikers know. Planetary scale is your little secret.

Life takes on a neat simplicity, too. Time ceases to have any meaning. When it is dark, you go to bed, and when it is light again you get up, and everything in between is just in between. It's quite wonderful, really.

You have no engagements, commitments, obligations, or duties; no special
10 ambitions and only the smallest, least complicated of wants; you exist in a tranquil tedium,[1] serenely beyond the reach of exasperation, "far removed from the seats of strife," as the early explorer and botanist William Bartram[2] put it. All that is required of you is a willingness to trudge.

There is no point in hurrying because you are not actually going anywhere. However far or long you plod, you are always in the same place: in the woods. It's where you were yesterday, where you will be tomorrow. The woods is one boundless **singularity**. Every bend in the path presents a prospect indistinguishable from every other, every glimpse into the trees the same tangled mass. For all you know, your route could describe a very large,
20 pointless circle. In a way, it would hardly matter. Ⓐ

At times, you become almost certain that you slabbed this hillside three days ago, crossed this stream yesterday, clambered over this fallen tree at least twice today already. But most of the time you don't think. No point. Instead, you exist in a kind of mobile Zen mode,[3] your brain like a balloon tethered with string, accompanying but not actually part of the body below. Walking for hours and miles becomes as automatic, as unremarkable, as breathing. At the end of the day you don't think, "Hey, I did sixteen miles today," any more than you think, "Hey, I took eight-thousand breaths today." It's just what you do. Ⓑ

ANALYZE VISUALS
How does the angle of this photograph affect the **mood** conveyed?

① Targeted Passage

singularity
(sĭng′gyə-lăr′ĭ-tē) *n.*
something peculiar or unique

Ⓐ SETTING AND MOOD
Reread lines 14–20. What mood is created by Bryson's description of the woods?

Ⓑ AUTHOR'S PERSPECTIVE
What was Bryson's attitude about hiking at this point? Cite details that helped you draw your **conclusion**.

1. **tranquil tedium:** calm and peaceful boredom.
2. **William Bartram** (bär′trəm): one of the first explorers of the Appalachian Mountains, who wrote about his experiences in a book published in 1791.
3. **mobile Zen mode:** walking, perfectly in tune with one's environment to the point of feeling at one with the surroundings.

362 UNIT 3: SETTING, MOOD, AND IMAGERY

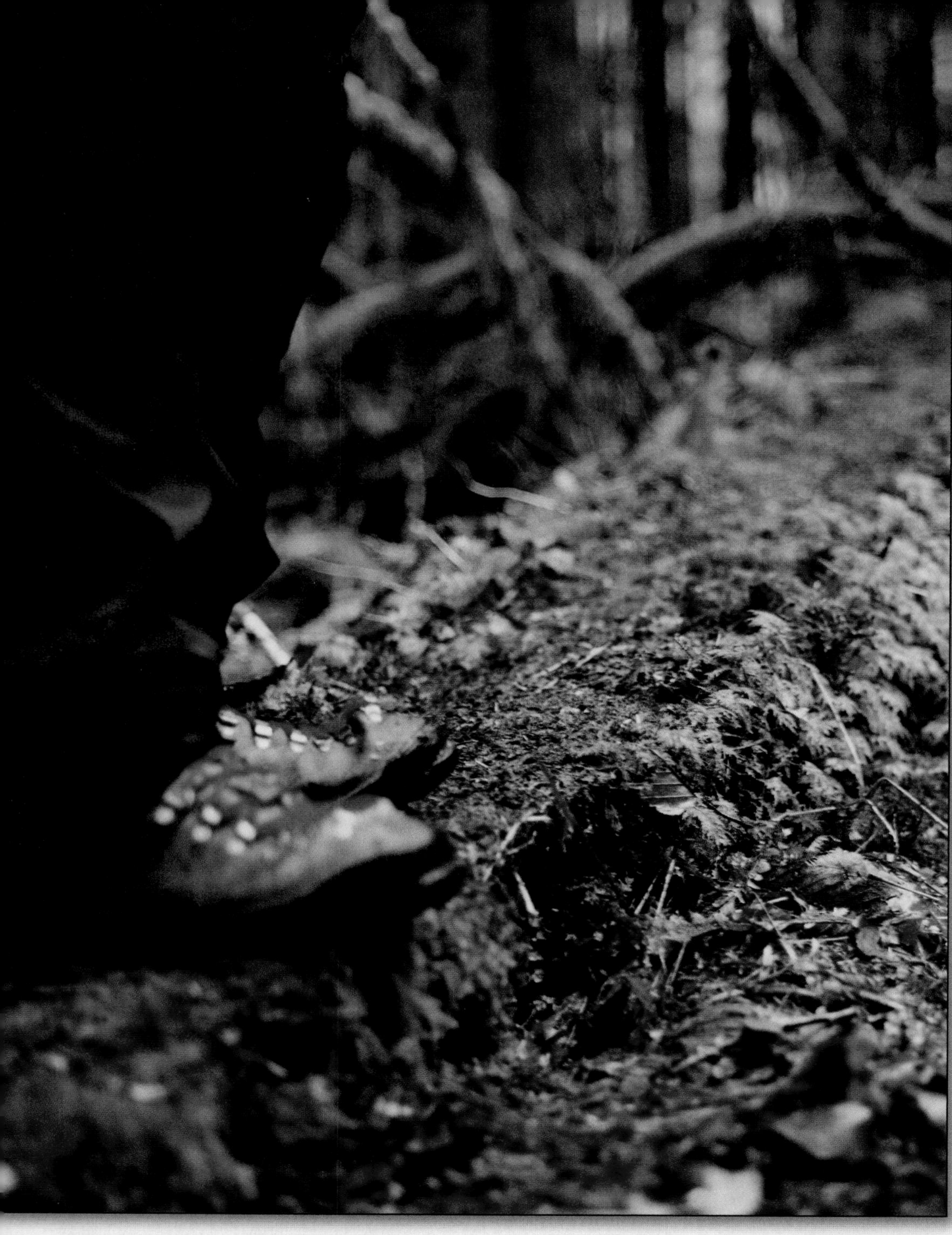

BACKGROUND

The Appalachian National Scenic Trail This trail is part of America's national park system. However, unlike most national parks, the AT, as hikers call it, is not located in one state. Instead, it is in 14 different states, passing through some 60 different parks and forests. Hiking the entire length of the AT usually takes five to seven months. While the national parks are patrolled and maintained by paid government workers, numerous volunteers devote their time to preserving the AT through "trail maintenance clubs" throughout the Appalachian Mountains.

- What is the setting of this narrative?
- How is the author traveling? What does this suggest about the author?
- What clues help you identify the author's attitude about hiking in the woods?

FOR ENGLISH LEARNERS

Key Academic Vocabulary Use Definition Mapping to teach these words: *route* (line 19), *accompanying* (line 25), *accumulating* (line 59), *vary* (line 76), *intensely* (line 215).

BEST PRACTICES TOOLKIT—Transparency
Definition Mapping p. E6

Prereading For prereading instruction for English learners, see

BEST PRACTICES TOOLKIT
Scaffolding Reading Instruction pp. 43–46

FOR ADVANCED LEARNERS/PRE–AP

Pre-AP Exercises in the bottom channel provide additional challenge for students. Use these suggestions for small groups or individuals.

ADDITIONAL GUIDELINES

For more help with differentiation and tips for classroom management, see

BEST PRACTICES TOOLKIT
Differentiated Instruction pp. 31–38

And so we walked, hour upon hour, over rollercoaster hills, along knife-edge
30 ridges and over grassy balds, through depthless ranks of oak, ash, chinkapin,
and pine. The skies grew sullen and the air chillier, but it wasn't until the third
day that the snow came. It began in the morning as thinly scattered flecks,
hardly noticeable. But then the wind rose, then rose again, until it was blowing
with an end-of-the-world fury that seemed to have even the trees in a panic,
and with it came snow, great flying masses of it. By midday we found ourselves
plodding into a stinging, cold, hard-blowing storm. Soon after, we came to a
narrow ledge of path along a wall of rock. **C**

Even in ideal circumstances this path would have required delicacy and care.
It was like a window ledge on a skyscraper, no more than fourteen or sixteen
40 inches wide, and crumbling in places, with a sharp drop on one side of perhaps
eighty feet, and long, looming stretches of vertical granite on the other. Once
or twice I nudged foot-sized rocks over the side and watched with faint horror
as they crashed and tumbled to improbably remote resting places. The trail
was cobbled with rocks and threaded with wandering tree roots against which
we constantly stubbed and stumbled, and **veneered** everywhere with polished
ice under a thin layer of powdery snow. At exasperatingly frequent intervals,
the path was broken by steep, thickly bouldered streams, frozen solid and
ribbed with blue ice, which could only be negotiated in a crablike crouch. And
all the time, as we crept along on this absurdly narrow, dangerous perch, we
50 were half-blinded by flying snow and jostled by gusts of wind, which roared
through the dancing trees and shook us by our packs. This wasn't a blizzard; it
was a tempest. We proceeded with painstaking deliberativeness, placing each
foot solidly before lifting the one behind. Even so, twice Katz made horrified,
heartfelt, comic-book noises ("AIEEEEE!" and "EEEARGH!") as his footing
went, and I turned to find him hugging a tree, feet skating, his expression bug-
eyed and fearful. **D**

It was deeply **unnerving**. It took us over two hours to cover six-tenths of
a mile of trail. By the time we reached solid ground at a place called Bearpen
Gap, the snow was four or five inches deep and accumulating fast. The whole
60 world was white, filled with dime-sized snowflakes that fell at a slant before

C CAUSE AND EFFECT
Reread lines 29–37
and note the changes in
setting. How did these
changes affect Bryson
and his friend Katz?

veneer (və-nîr') v. to
cover with a thin layer
of material

D SETTING AND MOOD
Reread lines 38–56. How
does Bryson's description
of the setting and of Katz
influence the mood in this
paragraph? Cite details to
support your answer.

unnerving (ŭn-nûr'vǐng)
adj. causing loss of
courage **unnerve** v.

DIFFERENTIATED INSTRUCTION

FOR ADVANCED LEARNERS/PRE–AP
Author's Perspective In lines 53–56, the
author uses humorous language in his
description of Katz: "comic-book noises
('AIEEEEE!' and 'EEEARGH!')"; "bugeyes."
Have students discuss how this touch
of humor affects the suspense of the
narrative, even though the situation is
filled with danger.

being caught by the wind and hurled in a variety of directions. We couldn't see more than fifteen or twenty feet ahead, often not even that.

> The trail crossed a logging road, then led straight up Albert Mountain,[4] a bouldered summit 5,250 feet above sea level, where the winds were so wild and angry that they hit the mountain with an actual wallop sound and forced us to shout to hear each other. We started up and hastily retreated. Hiking packs leave you with no recognizable center of gravity at the best of times; here we were literally being blown over. Confounded, we stood at the bottom of the summit and looked at each other. This was really quite grave. We were caught
> 70 between a mountain we couldn't climb and a ledge we had no intention of trying to renegotiate. Our only apparent option was to pitch our tents—if we could in this wind—crawl in, and hope for the best. I don't wish to reach for melodrama, but people have died in less trying circumstances.

② Targeted Passage

I dumped my pack and searched through it for my trail map. Appalachian Trail maps are so monumentally useless that I had long since given up using them. They vary somewhat, but most are on an **abysmal** scale of 1:100,000, which ludicrously compresses every kilometer of real world into a mere centimeter of map. Imagine a square kilometer of physical landscape and all that it might contain—logging roads, streams, a mountaintop or two, perhaps
80 a fire tower, a knob or grassy bald, the wandering AT,[5] and maybe a pair of important side trails—and imagine trying to convey all that information on an area the size of the nail on your little finger. That's an AT map.

Actually, it's far, far worse than that because AT maps—for reasons that bewilder me beyond speculation—provide less detail than even their meager scale allows. For any ten miles of trail, the maps will name and identify perhaps only three of the dozen or more peaks you cross. Valleys, lakes, gaps, creeks, and other important, possibly vital, topographical features are routinely left unnamed. Forest Service roads are often not included, and, if included, they're inconsistently identified. Even side trails are frequently left

abysmal (ə-bĭz′məl) *adj.* very bad

---

4. **Albert Mountain:** a peak in western North Carolina.

5. **AT:** Appalachian Trail.

off. There are no coordinates, no way of directing rescuers to a particular place, no pointers to towns just off the map's edge. These are, in short, seriously inadequate maps. **E**

E AUTHOR'S PERSPECTIVE
What is Bryson's opinion of AT maps?

In normal circumstances, this is merely irksome. Now, in a blizzard, it seemed closer to negligence. I dragged the map from the pack and fought the wind to look at it. It showed the trail as a red line. Nearby was a heavy, wandering black line, which I presumed to be the Forest Service road we stood beside, though there was no actual telling. According to the map, the road (if a road is what it was) started in the middle of nowhere and finished half a dozen miles later equally in the middle of nowhere, which clearly made no sense—
100 indeed, wasn't even possible. (You can't start a road in the middle of forest; earth-moving equipment can't spontaneously appear among the trees. Anyway, even if you could build a road that didn't go anywhere, why would you?) There was, obviously, something deeply and infuriatingly wrong with this map.

"Cost me eleven bucks," I said to Katz a little wildly, shaking the map at him and then crumpling it into an approximately flat shape and jabbing it into my pocket.

"So what're we going to do?" he said.

I sighed, unsure, then yanked the map out and examined it again. I looked from it to the logging road and back. "Well, it looks as if this logging road
110 curves around the mountain and comes back near the trail on the other side. If it does and we can find it, then there's a shelter we can get to. If we can't get through, I don't know, I guess we take the road back downhill to lower ground and see if we can find a place out of the wind to camp." I shrugged a little helplessly. "I don't know. What do you think?"

He issued a single bitter guffaw and returned to the hysterical snow. I hoisted my pack and followed.

We plodded up the road, bent steeply, **buffeted** by winds. Where it settled, the snow was wet and heavy and getting deep enough that soon it would be impassable and we would have to take shelter whether we wanted to or not.
120 There was no place to pitch a tent here, I noted uneasily—only steep, wooded slope going up on one side and down on the other. For quite a distance—far longer than it seemed it ought to—the road stayed straight. Even if, farther on, it did curve back near the trail, there was no certainty (or even perhaps much likelihood) that we would spot it. In these trees and this snow you could be ten feet from the trail and not see it. It would be madness to leave the logging road and try to find it. Then again, it was probably madness to be following a logging road to higher ground in a blizzard.

Gradually, and then more decidedly, the trail began to hook around behind the mountain. After about an hour of dragging sluggishly through ever-
130 deepening snow, we came to a high, windy, level spot where the trail—or at least *a* trail—emerged down the back of Albert Mountain and continued on into level woods. I regarded my map with bewildered exasperation. It didn't give any indication of this whatever, but Katz spotted a white blaze twenty yards into the woods, and we whooped with joy. We had refound the AT.

buffeted (bŭf′ĭ-tĭd) *adj.* knocked about or struck **buffet** *v.*

③ Targeted Passage

Sidebar (left column)

READING SKILL

E AUTHOR'S PERSPECTIVE

Possible answer: Bryson finds AT maps "monumentally useless" (line 75) and "seriously inadequate" (lines 91–92).

Extend the Discussion Summarize the reasons for Bryson's opinion of AT maps. Do you think his feelings are justified? Why or why not?

Lines 93–127
DISCUSSION PROMPTS

Use these prompts to help students understand the perilous situation Bryson and Katz find themselves in:

Summarize What options are available to Bryson and Katz at this moment in their journey? What is your opinion of those options? *Possible answer: They can either follow the Forest Service road, which might lead to a shelter, or they can go back downhill and try to camp. Either journey would be difficult in a blizzard.*

Analyze How does Bryson reach a decision about what to do? *Possible answer: To reach a decision, Bryson evaluates the alternatives and then asks Katz for his opinion (lines 108–114). Katz, apparently agreeing with Bryson's logic, continues walking along the logging road, and Bryson follows (lines 115–116).*

Evaluate How well do you think Bryson and Katz work as a team? Explain. *Possible answer: Bryson and Katz don't seem to work well as a team. Katz doesn't appear to be of much help. He seems to rely on Bryson (line 107) and doesn't offer any suggestions of his own (line 115). Meanwhile, Bryson himself is uncertain of what to do (line 108), having only a poor map to consult.*

DIFFERENTIATED INSTRUCTION

FOR LESS–PROFICIENT READERS

③ Targeted Passage [Lines 108–134]

In this passage, Bryson decides how to progress: They will take the logging road to get around the mountain.

- What causes Bryson to feel uneasy as they follow the logging road?
- At what point does Bryson know he has made the right decision?
- What insight into hiking does Bryson and Katz's dangerous predicament give you?

FOR ENGLISH LEARNERS

Vocabulary: Multiple-Meaning Words Have students use context clues and prior knowledge to figure out the meanings of these multiple-meaning words from the selection:

- *trying* (line 73), "difficult"
- *scale* (line 85), "size"
- *bitter* (line 115), "unhappy"
- *affair* (line 140), "object"

A shelter was only a few hundred yards farther on. It looked as if we would live to hike another day.

The snow was nearly knee deep now, and we were tired, but we all but pranced through it, and Katz whooped again when we reached an arrowed sign on a low limb that pointed down a side trail and said "BIG SPRING SHELTER."
140 The shelter, a simple wooden affair, open on one side, stood in a snowy glade—a little winter wonderland—150 yards or so off the main trail. Even from a distance we could see that the open side faced into the wind and that the drifting snow was nearly up to the lip of the sleeping platform. Still, if nothing else, it offered at least a sense of refuge.

We crossed the clearing, heaved our packs onto the platform, and in the same instant discovered that there were two people there already—a man and a boy of about fourteen. They were Jim and Heath, father and son, from Chattanooga,[6] and they were cheerful, friendly, and not remotely **daunted** by the weather. They had come hiking for the weekend, they told us (I hadn't
150 even realized it was a weekend), and knew the weather was likely to be bad, though not perhaps quite this bad, and so were well prepared. Jim had brought a big clear plastic sheet, of the sort decorators use to cover floors, and was trying to rig it across the open front of the shelter. Katz, uncharacteristically, leapt to his assistance. The plastic sheet didn't quite reach, but we found that with one of our groundcloths lashed alongside it we could cover the entire front. The wind walloped ferociously against the plastic and from time to time tore part of it loose, where it fluttered and snapped, with a retort like gunshot, until one of us leaped up and fought it back into place. The whole shelter was, in any case, incredibly leaky of air—the plank walls and floors were full
160 of cracks through which icy wind and occasional blasts of snow shot—but we were infinitely snugger than we would have been outside.

So we made a little home of it for ourselves, spread out our sleeping pads and bags, put on all the extra clothes we could find, and fixed dinner from a reclining position. Darkness fell quickly and heavily, which made the wildness outside seem even more severe. Jim and Heath had some chocolate cake, which they shared with us (a treat beyond heaven), and then the four of us settled down to a long, cold night on hard wood, listening to a banshee[7] wind and the tossing of angry branches.

When I awoke, all was stillness—the sort of stillness that makes you sit up
170 and take your bearings. The plastic sheet before me was peeled back a foot or so and weak light filled the space beyond. Snow was over the top of the platform and lying an inch deep over the foot of my sleeping bag. I shooed it off with a toss of my legs. Jim and Heath were already stirring to life. Katz slumbered heavily on, an arm flung over his forehead, his mouth a great open hole. It was not quite six.

daunted (dôn'tĭd) *adj.* discouraged **daunt** *v.*

---

6. **Chattanooga** (chăt'ə-nōō'gə): a city in southeastern Tennessee.

7. **banshee** (băn'shē): in Gaelic folklore, a female spirit who wails as a sign that death is coming.

Lines 145–161
DISCUSSION PROMPTS

Use these prompts to help students compare Bryson and Katz with Jim and his son:

Connect Can you think of an experience when you or someone you know was surprised by unexpected support during a tense situation? How does that help you understand Bryson and Katz's reaction to Jim and Heath? *Accept all reasonable responses.*

Compare How does Jim and Heath's state of mind differ from Bryson's? *Possible answer: Jim and Heath are "cheerful . . . and not remotely daunted by the weather" (lines 148–149), while Bryson is no doubt physically and emotionally drained by the situation.*

Evaluate Why have Jim and his son apparently fared better than Bryson and Katz? *Possible answer: Jim and Heath are better prepared and perhaps more experienced hikers. For example, they anticipated the weather (line 150) and had packed a plastic sheet (lines 151–152).*

REINFORCE *KEY IDEA:* ADVENTURE

Discuss What lesson might Bryson have learned from his **adventure** thus far? *Possible answer: Bryson has probably learned that he needs to be better prepared when hiking the AT and that he has to expect the unexpected.*

FOR ENGLISH LEARNERS

Vocabulary: Word Associations Have students work in groups to figure out the meanings of these common word groups, using context clues: *all but* (line 137), "nearly"; *make a move* (line 199), "begin moving"; *as well as* (line 220), "in addition to"; *set off* (line 236), "went."

FOR ADVANCED LEARNERS/PRE–AP

Characterization On this page (lines 153–154, 173–175), as in a number of other places in the narrative, Bryson depicts his friend Stephen Katz in an unflattering way. Ask students to consider why the author may have made this choice. Does it add humor or does it detract from the narrative? Ask students to explain their responses in a short paragraph.

reconnoiter (rē'kə-noi'tər)
v. to make a preliminary
inspection

I decided to go out to **reconnoiter** and see how stranded we might be. I hesitated at the platform's edge, then jumped out into the drift—it came up over my waist and made my eyes fly open where it slipped under my clothes and found bare skin—and pushed through it into the clearing,

180 where it was slightly (but only slightly) shallower. Even in sheltered areas, under an umbrella of conifers, the snow was nearly knee deep and tedious to churn through. But everywhere it was stunning. Every tree wore a thick cloak of white, every stump and boulder a jaunty snowy cap, and there was that perfect, immense stillness that you get nowhere else but in a big woods after a heavy snowfall. Here and there clumps of snow fell from the branches, but otherwise there was no sound or movement. I followed the side trail up and under heavily bowed limbs to where it rejoined the AT. The AT was a plumped blanket of snow, round and bluish, in a long, dim tunnel of overbent rhododendrons. It looked deep and hard going. I walked a few yards as a test.

190 It was deep and hard going. **F**

When I returned to the shelter, Katz was up, moving slowly and going through his morning groans, and Jim was studying his maps, which were vastly better than mine. I crouched beside him and he made room to let me look with him. It was 6.1 miles to Wallace Gap and a paved road, old U.S. 64. A mile down the road from there was Rainbow Springs Campground, a private campsite with showers and a store. I didn't know how hard it would be to walk seven miles through deep snow and had no confidence that the campground would be open this early in the year. Still, it was obvious this snow wasn't going to melt for days and we would have to make a move sometime; it might as well

200 be now, when at least it was pretty and calm. Who knew when another storm might blow in and really strand us?

Jim had decided that he and Heath would accompany us for the first couple of hours, then turn off on a side trail called Long Branch, which descended steeply through a ravine for 2.3 miles and emerged near a parking lot where they had left their car. He had hiked the Long Branch trail many times and knew what to expect. Even so, I didn't like the sound of it and asked him hesitantly if he thought it was a good idea to go off on a little-used side trail, into goodness knows what conditions, where no one would come across him and his son if they got in trouble. Katz, to my relief, agreed with me. "At least

210 there's always other people on the AT," he said. "You don't know what might happen to you on a side trail." Jim considered the matter and said they would turn back if it looked bad.

Katz and I treated ourselves to two cups of coffee, for warmth, and Jim and Heath shared with us some of their oatmeal, which made Katz intensely happy. Then we all set off together. It was cold and hard going. The tunnels of boughed rhododendrons, which often ran on for great distances, were exceedingly pretty, but when our packs brushed against them they dumped volumes of snow onto our heads and down the backs of our necks. The three adults took it in turns to walk in front because the lead person always received

220 the heaviest dumping, as well as having all the hard work of dibbing holes in the snow.

LITERARY ANALYSIS

F SETTING AND MOOD

Possible answer: The mood is mixed. On the one hand, it's more relaxed now that the immediate danger has passed. There is a feeling of appreciation for the beautiful surroundings (lines 182–185). On the other hand, the mood reflects Bryson's uneasiness about moving on (lines 181–182, 189–190).

If students need help . . . Have students use the information in lines 176–190 to complete a Two-Column Chart.

Setting Details	Effect on Mood
• snow is more than waist deep (lines 177–178)	• surprising and worrisome
•	•

 BEST PRACTICES TOOLKIT—Transparency
Two-Column Chart p. A25

Lines 215–221
REINFORCE *KEY IDEA:* ADVENTURE

Discuss How do these lines highlight both positive and negative aspects of Bryson's hiking **adventure?** *Possible answer: While the hikers experience the beauty of the woods (lines 216–217), they must also cope with difficulties caused by the snow (lines 217–221).*

F SETTING AND MOOD
Reread lines 176–190. Describe the mood in this paragraph. What details of the setting contribute to the mood?

DIFFERENTIATED INSTRUCTION

FOR LESS–PROFICIENT READERS
Figurative Language Remind students that a metaphor is a figure of speech that makes a comparison between two unlike things without using *like* or *as*. Have students identify the metaphors in lines 182–183 and 187–188. Model the process of determining the comparison in lines 182–183 by asking: If the trees are described as wearing a cloak and a cap, what are they being compared to?

FOR ADVANCED LEARNERS/PRE-AP
Author's Perspective [small-group option] Bryson describes his harrowing experience with a light touch. Ask students if they think the tone of his narrative accurately reflects his feelings at the time. Have them write their thoughts, supported with evidence from the text.

The Long Branch trail, when we reached it, descended steeply through bowed pines—too steeply, it seemed to me, to come back up if the trail proved impassable, and it looked as if it might. Katz and I urged Jim and Heath to reconsider, but Jim said it was all downhill and well-marked, and he was sure it would be all right. "Hey, you know what day it is?" said Jim suddenly and, seeing our blank faces, supplied the answer. "March twenty-first."

Our faces stayed blank.

"First day of spring," he said.

230   We smiled at the pathetic irony of it, shook hands all around, wished each other luck, and parted. **G**

Katz and I walked for three hours more, silently and slowly through the cold, white forest, taking it in turns to break snow. At about one o'clock we came at last to old 64, a lonesome, **superannuated** two-lane road through the mountains. It hadn't been cleared, and there were no tire tracks through it. It was starting to snow again, steadily, prettily. We set off down the road for the campground and had walked about a quarter of a mile when from behind there was the crunching sound of a motorized vehicle proceeding cautiously through snow. We turned to see a big jeep-type car rolling up beside us. The

240   driver's window hummed down. It was Jim and Heath. They had come to let us know they had made it, and to make sure we had likewise. "Thought you might like a lift to the campground," Jim said. ❧

G MAKE INFERENCES
What does Bryson mean by "the pathetic irony" of its being the first day of spring?

superannuated
(sōō'pər-ăn'yōō-ā'tĭd) *adj.* obsolete with age

④ Targeted Passage

A WALK IN THE WOODS   **369**

ANALYZE VISUALS

Activity Ask students how the scene in the photo might compare to the setting of the selection. *Possible answer: The snowy trail in the photo is beautiful, but it probably does not reflect the much snowier terrain on the AT. Here, the sun is out and the path is clear. In the text, we read that the road was not plowed and that it started snowing again.*

READING SKILL: *Review*

G MAKE INFERENCES

Possible answer: *Spring usually brings with it warmer temperatures, but the hikers find themselves in a wintry, snow-covered world.*

SELECTION WRAP–UP

SUMMARIZE Ask students to recall in order the steps Bryson and Katz took to survive the storm and make it to the highway. How much of their survival was skill and how much was luck?

⭐ **CRITIQUE** In his narrative, Bryson uses several writing techniques normally associated with fiction, such as dialogue and figurative language. Have students evaluate the author's writing style and explain why it does or does not make the narrative more effective.

READING FLUENCY

Distribute the copy master and have students work in pairs to practice fluency.

R RESOURCE MANAGER—Copy Master
Reading Fluency p. 125

FOR LESS–PROFICIENT READERS

④ Targeted Passage [Lines 232–242]

This passage concludes the excerpt. Everyone appears to have made it through the adventure safely.

- How do you think Bryson and Katz felt when they made it to the road and found that it hadn't been cleared?

- Do you think they took the ride to the campground? Explain your answer.

FOR ENGLISH LEARNERS

Vocabulary: Idioms Use New Word Analysis to teach students the following idioms:

- *here and there* (line 185), "in a few places"
- *hard going* (line 190), "difficult"
- *ran on* (line 216), "extended"
- *made it* (line 241), "succeeded"
- *a lift* (line 242), "a ride"

 **BEST PRACTICES TOOLKIT—Transparency**
New Word Analysis p. E8

Practice and Apply

After Reading

For additional support of post-reading
questions, use these copy masters:

R RESOURCE MANAGER—Copy Masters

Reading Check p. 122 (to check understanding of the selection)

Setting and Mood p. 115 (for practice of
literary analysis standards focus)

Question Support p. 123 (After Reading
questions adapted for English learners
and less-proficient readers)

For additional questions, see page 109.

ANSWERS

Comprehension

1. *They have set out to hike the length of the Appalachian Trail.*

2. *They encounter a fierce snowstorm.*

3. *They follow a logging road around the mountain, which leads them to a shelter.*

Literary Analysis

Possible answers:

4. ● **STANDARDS FOCUS** *Analyze Setting and Mood The details about the woods (lines 14–20), the terrain (lines 29–31, 38–56), and the snow and wind (lines 32–37, 58–62, 117–127) contribute to the mood in the selection.*

5. ■ **STANDARDS FOCUS** *Identify Author's Perspective Bryson found it peaceful, relaxing, and beautiful (lines 6–13, 23–25, 182–185). However, through this experience, Bryson also realized that hiking can be dangerous (lines 72–73) and that it's important to be prepared (lines 149–152, 192–193).*

6. *Unlike Jim's maps—"vastly better than mine" (lines 192–193)—Bryson's maps were "monumentally useless" (line 75) and "seriously inadequate" (lines 91–92). As a result, readers aren't sure if he can find his way to the shelter.*

7. *Bryson seems uncertain and unprepared for the circumstances he encounters. Katz is not much help. He relies on Bryson and seems to offer no suggestions of his own (lines 68–69, 107–108, 115). Together, they do not build confidence in the reader that they are a winning combination.*

After Reading

Comprehension

1. **Recall** What have Bill Bryson and Stephen Katz set out to do?

2. **Recall** What stands in their way?

3. **Summarize** How do they survive the ordeal?

Literary Analysis

4. **Analyze Setting and Mood** What elements of setting most strongly contribute to the mood in this selection? Consider the time of day, the season, the weather, and the natural landscape. Cite details from the text to support your answer.

5. **Identify Author's Perspective** Review the chart you completed as you read. In a sentence or two, summarize Bryson's perspective on walking the Appalachian Trail. Explain whether you think his perspective changes in any way as the episode unfolds. Support your ideas with evidence from the text.

6. **Interpret Suspense** How do Bryson's poor preparations for his adventure contribute to the suspense of this selection? Explain.

7. **Evaluate Personality Traits** In what way do Bryson and Katz make unlikely heroes in this **adventure** story? Cite examples from the text.

8. **Make Judgments** In *A Walk in the Woods,* as in many outdoor adventure stories, nature is the **antagonist**—that is, the force that the central figure, or **protagonist,** struggles against. To what degree is nature really responsible for the troubles Bryson and Katz face? Use a graphic like this one in your evaluation.

Problem or Conflict	Caused by Nature	Caused by Hikers
Bryson and Katz are caught in a snowstorm.	✓	

Literary Criticism

9. **Critical Interpretations** Bill Bryson has been described by one critic as a writer "who could wring humor from a clammy sleeping bag." Judging by this selection, do you agree or disagree with that statement? Cite details from the selection to support your opinion.

---

8. *Students should recognize that while the snowstorm and the rugged terrain are natural obstacles, the troubles that Bryson and Katz face are aggravated by their lack of experience and preparation. For example, they brought poor maps, apparently did not check the weather forecast, and did not bring emergency items, such as the plastic sheet that Jim had with him.*

Literary Criticism

Possible answer:

9. *While not all students will find Bryson especially amusing, he does write with a dry sense of humor, even when describing a dangerous situation (lines 51–56, 72–73, 104–106, 166, 177–179).*

Vocabulary in Context

VOCABULARY PRACTICE

Decide whether the words in each pair are synonyms or antonyms.

1. buffeted/battered
2. veneer/uncover
3. reconnoiter/inspect
4. superannuated/rejuvenated
5. daunted/inspired
6. unnerving/encouraging
7. abysmal/wonderful
8. singularity/commonality

WORD LIST
abysmal
buffeted
daunted
reconnoiter
singularity
superannuated
unnerving
veneer

VOCABULARY IN WRITING

What do you think was the worst thing about the situation Bryson found himself in? Write a paragraph explaining your opinion, using at least four vocabulary words. You might start like this.

EXAMPLE SENTENCE
What made Bryson's situation **unnerving** was that the snow wouldn't stop.

VOCABULARY STRATEGY: CONTEXT CLUES

Often you can figure out the meaning of an unfamiliar word by examining the words and sentences that surround it. Three types of context clues that can help you determine the meanings of unfamiliar words in *A Walk in the Woods* are

- **general context clues,** which allow you to infer the meaning of an unfamiliar word by reading information in the sentences that surround it
- **comparison clues,** in which the unknown word is likened to something known
- **example clues,** in which one or more examples are included in the text to suggest the meaning of the unfamiliar word

PRACTICE Use context clues to figure out the meaning of each word that follows. First identify the type of context clue that helps you determine the meaning of the word. Then write a definition of the word.

slabbed (line 21)
renegotiate (line 71)
topographical (line 87)
retort (line 157)

 VOCABULARY PRACTICE
For more practice, go to the **Vocabulary Center** at ClassZone.com.

DIFFERENTIATED INSTRUCTION

FOR ENGLISH LEARNERS

Task Support: Simplify Use Jigsaw Reading to divide among student pairs or groups the words listed in **VOCABULARY STRATEGY: CONTEXT CLUES.** Have each pair or group identify the context clues that help them figure out the meaning of each word. Then have students share their word meanings with the class.

 BEST PRACTICES TOOLKIT
Jigsaw Reading p. A1

FOR ADVANCED LEARNERS/PRE–AP

Vocabulary in Writing Have students use at least two vocabulary words in a paragraph written in the first person from Jim's viewpoint to describe his first meeting with Bryson and Katz (page 367).

ANSWERS

Vocabulary in Context

VOCABULARY PRACTICE

1. *synonyms*
2. *antonyms*
3. *synonyms*
4. *antonyms*
5. *antonyms*
6. *antonyms*
7. *antonyms*
8. *antonyms*

R RESOURCE MANAGER—Copy Master
Vocabulary Practice p. 120

VOCABULARY IN WRITING

Tell students to imagine themselves in Bryson's situation. How might they feel?

VOCABULARY STRATEGY: CONTEXT CLUES
(*also an EL language objective*)

To model using context clues, focus on the vocabulary word *reconnoiter* (line 176). Point out to students how information in lines 169–170 and 177–190 can help them infer the meaning of the word.

Possible answers:

slabbed—"crossed"

renegotiate—"cross again"

topographical—"having to do with physical features of land"

retort—"a reply"

R RESOURCE MANAGER—Copy Master
Vocabulary Strategy p. 121

i Vocabulary Center at **ClassZone.com**
Additional Vocabulary Activities

Assess and Reteach

Assess

R RESOURCE MANAGER—Copy Masters
Selection Test A pp. 127–128
Selection Test B/C pp. 129–130

Test Generator CD

Reteach

S STANDARDS LESSON FILE
Literature Lesson 9: Setting and Its Roles
Literature Lesson 44: Mood
Literature Lesson 47: Author's Perspective
Vocabulary Lessons 11–16: Context Clues

Focus and Motivate

OBJECTIVES

Reading for Information

- read and analyze a primary source (letter)
- cite evidence

SUMMARY

This selection is a letter in which the writer argues for the preservation of wilderness, not for its recreational uses but on the basis of its historic significance and its value for people's spiritual health.

What's the Connection?

Use a KWL chart to prepare students for the selection. For the first column, help students brainstorm a list of things they already know about the wilderness. In the second column, have them write questions about what they want to know about the wilderness. After reading, have students write what they have learned about the wilderness.

 BEST PRACTICES TOOLKIT—Transparency
KWL p. A21

Teach

Skill Focus: Read Primary Sources

Guide students in their analysis of Wallace Stegner's letter. Explain that Stegner's distinctive writing style is such that students may need to reread some parts of the letter to fully grasp his meaning. To help them complete the chart as they read, encourage students to pay attention to details. Use these questions to get students started:

- To whom did Stegner write the letter?
- In what year did Stegner write the letter?
- What is Stegner's purpose for writing?

 RESOURCE MANAGER—Copy Master
Read Primary Sources p. 139

Wilderness Letter

Use with *A Walk in the Woods,* page 362.

What's the Connection?

In *A Walk in the Woods,* you read about some of the pleasures and perils of hiking the Appalachian Trail in a government-protected wilderness area. Now, in a letter from Wallace Stegner, you will read one of many arguments that have been made in favor of preserving such wilderness areas.

Skill Focus: Read Primary Sources

Primary sources are materials written by people who witnessed the events portrayed. These sources can give us unique insights into a subject. Letters, speeches, interviews, public documents, and other texts—whether published, archived, or only saved in someone's attic—are all types of primary sources. To get the most out of a primary source, consider

- the form and purpose of the text
- where and when it was written
- the intended audience
- the author's position in his or her family, society, or profession

To further analyze a primary source, complete a chart such as the one here. Try doing this as you read Wallace Stegner's letter.

What is the form and purpose of this document?	
What, if anything, do I already know about the author and his times?	
What seems to be the relationship between the author and his audience?	
What does the document tell me about life at the time it was written?	

Selection Resources

 RESOURCE MANAGER UNIT 3

Plan and Teach pp. 131–135

Reading
Summary pp. 137†*, 138‡*
Read Primary Sources pp. 139, 141†*
Reading Check p. 143
Cite Evidence pp. 140, 142†*
Question Support p. 145*

Assessment
Selection Tests A, B/C pp. 147*, 149*
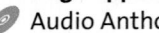 Test Generator CD

Reading Support
 Audio Anthology CD*

 BEST PRACTICES TOOLKIT
KWL

* Resources for Differentiation   † Also in Spanish   ‡ In Haitian Creole and Vietnamese

Wilderness Letter
Wallace Stegner

Los Altos, Calif.
Dec. 3, 1960

David E. Pesonen
Wildland Research Center
Agricultural Experiment Station
243 Mulford Hall
University of California
Berkeley 4, Calif.

Dear Mr. Pesonen:

I believe that you are working on the wilderness portion of the Outdoor Recreation Resources Review Commission's report. If I may, I should like to urge some arguments for wilderness preservation that involve recreation, as it is ordinarily conceived, hardly at all. Hunting, fishing, hiking, mountain-climbing, camping, photography, and the enjoyment of natural scenery will all, surely, figure in your report. So will the wilderness as a genetic reserve, a scientific yardstick by which we may measure
10 the world in its natural balance against the world in its man-made imbalance. What I want to speak for is not so much the wilderness uses, valuable as those are, but the wilderness idea, which is a resource in itself. Being an intangible and spiritual resource, it will seem mystical to the practical-minded—but then anything that cannot be moved by a bulldozer is likely to seem mystical to them.

I want to speak for the wilderness idea as something that has helped form our character and that has certainly shaped our history as a people. . . . **A**

A PRIMARY SOURCES
What does the beginning of this letter suggest about Stegner's purpose for writing?

READING FOR INFORMATION **373**

AUTHOR BIOGRAPHY

Although not all of his stories are set in the West, Wallace Stegner (1909–1993) is called the dean of Western writers. A passionate environmentalist, Stegner not only wrote about the importance of preserving the West, he fought for it. In 1960, Stegner wrote *Wilderness Letter*. In his letter, he stated that wild places were in need of federal protection. Four years later, *Wilderness Letter* was influential in the passage of the Wilderness Act.

Lines 1–15 [first paragraph]
DISCUSSION PROMPTS

Use these prompts to help students understand Stegner's viewpoint:

Connect What is your experience of the wilderness? Cite memorable examples from movies, television, or your own life. *Responses will vary.*

Compare and Contrast What does Stegner mean when he refers to measuring "the world in its natural balance against the world in its man-made imbalance" (lines 9–10)? *Possible answer: The untouched wilderness represents a natural balance of living things; the rest of the world is imbalanced because people have altered the natural state.*

Evaluate How does Stegner's tone suggest the direction his letter is taking? Cite evidence to support your answer. *Possible answer: Stegner's tone suggests that he disapproves of some people's view of the environment. For example, he remarks, "anything that cannot be moved by a bulldozer is likely to seem mystical" to people who are "practical-minded."*

INFORMATIONAL ANAYSIS

A PRIMARY SOURCES

Possible answer: Stegner is writing to argue in favor of wilderness preservation. However, he is basing his arguments on "not so much the wilderness uses . . . but the wilderness idea, which is a resource in itself" (lines 10–12).

DIFFERENTIATED INSTRUCTION

FOR LESS–PROFICIENT READERS
Build Comprehension Explain that Stegner's style includes challenging sentence structures. Encourage students to reread sentences that seem confusing.

- Discuss how the words *hardly at all* at the end of the second sentence alter the sentence's meaning. Help students rewrite the sentence in their own words.

- Discuss what the pronoun *it* in line 13 refers to.

FOR ENGLISH LEARNERS
Reading: Background Explain that U.S. citizens often tell government leaders about changes they want to see. Point out that this is a letter from a citizen who wanted the government to preserve the wilderness.

Options for Reading Read aloud selected sections to students. After discussing the sections, have students listen to the rest of the selection in the *Audio Anthology CD*.

READING FOR INFORMATION **373**

Something will have gone out of us as a people if we ever let
20 the remaining wilderness be destroyed; if we permit the last
virgin forests to be turned into comic books and plastic cigarette
cases; if we drive the few remaining members of the wild species
into zoos or to extinction; if we pollute the last clear air and
dirty the last clean streams and push our paved roads through
the last of the silence, so that never again will Americans be free
in their own country from the noise, the exhausts, the stinks of
human and automotive waste. And so that never again can we
have the chance to see ourselves single, separate, vertical and
individual in the world, part of the environment of trees and
30 rocks and soil, brother to the other animals, part of the natural
world and competent to belong in it. Without any remaining
wilderness we are committed wholly, without chance for even
momentary reflection and rest, to a headlong drive into our
technological termite-life, the Brave New World[1] of a completely
man-controlled environment. We need wilderness preserved—as
much of it as is still left, and as many kinds—because it was the
challenge against which our character as a people was formed.
The reminder and the reassurance that it is still there is good for
our spiritual health even if we never once in ten years set foot
40 in it. It is good for us when we are young, because of the
incomparable sanity it can bring briefly, as vacation and rest, into
our insane lives. It is important to us when we are old simply
because it is there—important, that is, simply as idea. **B**

We are a wild species. . . . Nobody ever tamed or domesticated
or scientifically bred us. But for at least three millennia we have
been engaged in a cumulative and ambitious race to modify and
gain control of our environment, and in the process we have
come close to domesticating ourselves. Not many people are
likely, any more, to look upon what we call "progress" as an
50 unmixed blessing. Just as surely as it has brought us increased
comfort and more material goods, it has brought us spiritual
losses, and it threatens now to become the Frankenstein that will
destroy us. One means of sanity is to retain a hold on the
natural world, to remain, insofar as we can, good animals.
Americans still have that chance, more than many peoples; for
while we were demonstrating ourselves the most efficient and
ruthless environment-busters in history, and slashing and
burning and cutting our way through a wilderness continent, the
wilderness was working on us. It remains in us as surely as
60 Indian names remain on the land. If the abstract dream of
human liberty and human dignity became, in America, something

---

1. **Brave New World:** a reference to Aldous Huxley's 1932 science fiction novel,
   Brave New World, depicting a society in which happiness and the most basic
   natural life functions are controlled by technology.

B PRIMARY SOURCES
What does Stegner's
description suggest about
life in the United States at
the time he wrote this?

INFORMATIONAL ANALYSIS

B PRIMARY SOURCES

Possible answer: Stegner's description suggests that litter, pollution, and highway construction are destroying the wilderness, while people are rushing toward a world dominated by technology.

Extend the Discussion What do you think Stegner means when he writes: "Without any remaining wilderness we are committed . . . to a headlong drive into our technological termite-life . . ." (lines 31–34)?

DIFFERENTIATED INSTRUCTION

FOR ENGLISH LEARNERS
Language: Punctuation and Print Clues
Read aloud the first sentence (lines 19–27), phrase by phrase. Point out how each phrase is parallel and separated by a semicolon. Have students restate each phrase. Tell them to look for other places in the story where punctuation helps to simplify a longer sentence by breaking it up into understandable parts.

FOR ADVANCED LEARNERS/PRE–AP
Evaluate [paired-activity option] Stegner suggests that progress may "become the Frankenstein that will destroy us" (lines 52–53). What do you think he means by this dramatic statement?

more than an abstract dream, mark it down at least partially to the fact that we were in subtle ways subdued by what we conquered. . . . **C**

The American experience has been the confrontation by old peoples and cultures of a world as new as if it had just risen from the sea. That gave us our hope and our excitement, and the hope and excitement can be passed on to newer Americans, Americans who never saw any phase of the frontier. But only so
70 long as we keep the remainder of our wild as a reserve and a promise—a sort of wilderness bank. . . .

We need to demonstrate our acceptance of the natural world, including ourselves; we need the spiritual refreshment that being natural can produce. And one of the best places for us to get that is in the wilderness where the fun houses, the bulldozers, and the pavements of our civilization are shut out.

Sherwood Anderson, in a letter to Waldo Frank in the 1920's, said it better than I can. "Is it not likely that when the country was new and men were often alone in the fields and the forest
80 they got a sense of bigness outside themselves that has now in some way been lost . . . Mystery whispered in the grass, played in the branches of trees overhead, was caught up and blown across the American line in clouds of dust at evening on the prairies . . . I am old enough to remember tales that strengthen my belief in a deep semi-religious influence that was formerly at work among our people. The flavor of it hangs over the best work of Mark Twain . . . I can remember old fellows in my home town speaking feelingly of an evening spent on the big empty plains. It had taken the shrillness out of them. They had learned the trick
90 of quiet . . ."

We could learn it too, even yet; even our children and grand-children could learn it. But only if we save, for just such absolutely non-recreational, impractical, and mystical uses as this, all the wild that still remains to us. . . .

For myself, I grew up on the empty plains of Saskatchewan and Montana and in the mountains of Utah, and I put a very high valuation on what those places gave me. And if I had not been able periodically to renew myself in the mountains and deserts of western America I would be very near bughouse. Even
100 when I can't get to the back country, the thought of the colored deserts of southern Utah, or the reassurance that there are still stretches of prairie where the world can be instantaneously perceived as disk and bowl, and where the little but intensely important human being is exposed to the five directions and the thirty-six winds, is a positive consolation. The idea alone can

C PRIMARY SOURCES
What does Stegner say is one potential cost of "progress"?

INFORMATIONAL ANALYSIS

C PRIMARY SOURCES

Possible answer: Stegner writes that progress has caused us "spiritual losses" (lines 51–52), taking us farther and farther away from the natural world.

If students need help . . .

- Have students read lines 48–60.
- Ask: What are the positive aspects of progress? *(lines 50–51)* What are the negative aspects? *(lines 51–53)*
- Ask: What represents "sanity" for Stegner? *(lines 53–54)*

DISCUSSION PROMPTS

Use these prompts to help students understand Stegner's view of the value of nature:

Connect What effect does the experience of a peaceful natural environment—such as a forest or a seashore—have on your emotions? *Accept all thoughtful responses.*

Analyze Why does Stegner believe that preservation of the existing wilderness is so important? *Possible answer: The existing wilderness is all that remains of the wild that was. We need to preserve what's left of the natural world so that we can pass it on to future generations.*

Synthesize Do you think Stegner approves of national parks? Why or why not? *Possible answers: Yes—They protect the environment while allowing people to enjoy nature in a relatively unspoiled state. No—By allowing cars, concession stands, and the like, we are reducing nature to a poor imitation of the wild.*

DIFFERENTIATED INSTRUCTION

FOR ENGLISH LEARNERS

Language: Conversational English Patterns Help students understand some of the unusual word groups used by the author. Explain that the phrase *speaking feelingly* means "speaking with feeling" (line 88) and the phrase *as good a place as any* means "this place is as good as any other place" (line 134).

D PRIMARY SOURCES

Possible answer: Stegner explains how the natural beauty of the plains and mountains where he grew up allowed him to renew his spirit whenever the need arose. He explains that even now, when he can't return to the places he so fondly pictures in his mind, his memories of them console him.

E PRIMARY SOURCES

Possible answer: Stegner concludes by stating that we need to preserve the wilderness because it offers us a way to get back in touch with the unspoiled natural world and renew our spirit.

---

sustain me. But as the wilderness areas are progressively exploited or "improved," as the jeeps and bulldozers of uranium prospectors scar up the deserts and the roads are cut into the alpine timberlands, and as the remnants of the unspoiled and 110 natural world are progressively eroded, every such loss is a little death in me. In us. . . . D

Let me say something on the subject of the kinds of wilderness worth preserving. Most of those areas contemplated are in the national forests and in high mountain country. For all the usual recreational purposes, the alpine and forest wildernesses are obviously the most important, both as genetic banks and as beauty spots. But for the spiritual renewal, the recognition of identity, the birth of awe, other kinds will serve every bit as well. Perhaps, because they are less friendly to life, more abstractly 120 nonhuman, they will serve even better. On our Saskatchewan prairie, the nearest neighbor was four miles away, and at night we saw only two lights on all the dark rounding earth. The earth was full of animals—field mice, ground squirrels, weasels, ferrets, badgers, coyotes, burrowing owls, snakes. I knew them as my little brothers, as fellow creatures, and I have never been able to look upon animals in any other way since. The sky in that country came clear down to the ground on every side, and it was full of great weathers, and clouds, and winds, and hawks. I hope I learned something from knowing intimately the creatures of the 130 earth; I hope I learned something from looking a long way, from looking up, from being much alone. A prairie like that, one big enough to carry the eye clear to the sinking, rounding horizon, can be as lonely and grand and simple in its forms as the sea. It is as good a place as any for the wilderness experience to happen; the vanishing prairie is as worth preserving for the wilderness idea as the alpine forests.

So are great reaches of our western deserts, scarred somewhat by prospectors but otherwise open, beautiful, waiting. . . .

These are some of the things wilderness can do for us. That is 140 the reason we need to put into effect, for its preservation, some other principle than the principles of exploitation or "usefulness" or even recreation. We simply need that wild country available to us, even if we never do more than drive to its edge and look in. For it can be a means of reassuring ourselves of our sanity as creatures, a part of the geography of hope. E

Very sincerely yours,

Wallace Stegner

Wallace Stegner

D PRIMARY SOURCES
Reread this paragraph. **Paraphrase** what Stegner is saying about the benefits of wilderness to his own life.

E PRIMARY SOURCES
Reread Stegner's closing paragraph. In a sentence, **summarize** his conclusion.

DIFFERENTIATED INSTRUCTION

FOR LESS–PROFICIENT READERS

Vocabulary Support Point out the words *exploited* (line 107) and *exploitation* (line 141). Explain that the base word *exploit* means "to make productive use of." Next, point out the words *improved* and *usefulness,* which follow *exploited* and *exploitation.* Explain that the author places quotation marks around these words to show that while others may believe that the tearing down of our wilderness has improved the usefulness of space, he doesn't.

Comprehension

1. **Summarize** In Stegner's view, what is the danger for humans in losing touch with nature?

Critical Analysis

2. **Identify Author's Purpose** What does Stegner want Pesonen to understand?

3. **Analyze Primary Source** Review the chart you developed as you read Stegner's letter. What was being done to wilderness areas at that time? Explain.

4. **Evaluate Author's Message** Stegner makes a point of distinguishing between the recreational value of the wilderness and its value as a source of spiritual renewal. Do you agree that this is an important difference? Include specific references to the text in your answer.

Read for Information: Cite Evidence

WRITING PROMPT

Bill Bryson and Wallace Stegner, each in his own way, have written in favor of wilderness areas. How are the pieces similar in this regard? How are they different? Support your response with specific quotations, ideas, and facts from Stegner's letter and Bryson's account.

The following steps will help you respond to the prompt:

1. Reread Bryson's narrative and Stegner's letter, looking for direct statements, facts, and anecdotes about wilderness areas.

2. Record direct quotations and summarize longer passages that seem relevant to your comparison. Note the author, source, and page numbers.

3. Review your notes and evaluate each item's usefulness in writing your comparison.

4. As you write your comparison, support your statements with direct quotations and citations of facts or anecdotes from these two sources. Always credit your sources and be sure to use quotation marks around direct quotations.

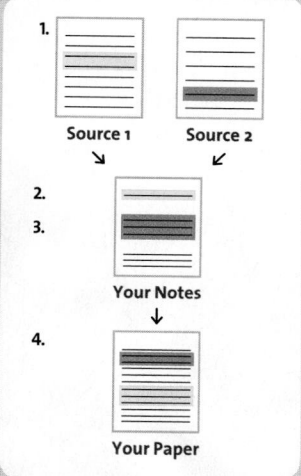

DIFFERENTIATED INSTRUCTION

FOR LESS–PROFICIENT WRITERS

Read for Information

- Suggest that students first summarize similarities between the two pieces. Then have students explain the differences.

- Remind students to use quotation marks for direct quotations—that is, when they quote a person's exact words.

Practice and Apply

For additional support of post-reading questions, use these copy masters:

R RESOURCE MANAGER—Copy Masters
Reading Check p. 143
Question Support p. 145
Cite Evidence p. 140

For additional questions, see page 133.

ANSWERS

Comprehension

1. *Possible answer: Stegner fears that people will not be able to connect with their history.*

Critical Analysis

Possible answers:

2. **Identify Author's Purpose** *The wilderness is a precious spiritual resource and has intrinsic value beyond practical uses.*

3. ■ **STANDARDS FOCUS** *Analyze Primary Sources Technological "progress" was causing the destruction of wilderness areas. For example, trees were being cut so paved roads could be built through wooded areas.*

4. *Evaluate Author's Message Students may agree or disagree but should develop their answers using specific textual references.*

Read for Information: Cite Evidence

Writing Prompt *Students should support their comparisons with evidence from both texts.*

Assess and Reteach

Assess

R RESOURCE MANAGER—Copy Masters
Selection Test A, pp. 147–148
Selection Tests B/C, pp. 149–150

🔘 Test Generator CD

Reteach

S STANDARDS LESSON FILE
Research Lesson 5: Using Primary and Secondary Sources

Research Lesson 10: Documentation

Focus and Motivate

OBJECTIVES

Literary Analysis
- explore the key idea of the **faces of nature**
- read poetry
- identify imagery and mood

Reading
- connect

SUMMARIES

"The Sharks" The speaker of this poem by Denise Levertov dares to swim into deep water on her last day at the ocean. At sundown, the ocean fills with sharks, evoking fear and worry.

"The Peace of Wild Things" In this lyric poem by Wendell Berry, the speaker awakens, troubled by the state of the world. Lying down by a lake, he finds peace in proximity to nature's "wild things" that do not despair about the future.

What are the different faces of NATURE?

Introduce the question and ask students to respond to the *KEY IDEA.* Invite them to identify and describe different natural settings that display the different **faces of nature** before going on to complete the *DISCUSS* activity. Students can arrange their list of elements on a continuum from extremely soothing to terrifying.

The Sharks
Poem by Denise Levertov

The Peace of Wild Things
Poem by Wendell Berry

What are the different faces of NATURE?

KEY IDEA What do you think of when you hear the word *nature*? Storms? Flowers? Insects? Nature can have a variety of associations, such as peace, beauty, danger, and destruction. In the poems "The Sharks" and "The Peace of Wild Things," two poets describe sharply different **faces of nature.**

DISCUSS List eight elements of nature, four that you view as unsettling or frightening and four that you view as peaceful or soothing. After you have completed your list, get together with one or two classmates and compare notes.

378

Selection Resources

 **RESOURCE MANAGER UNIT 3**

Plan and Teach pp. 151–158

Literary Analysis
Imagery and Mood pp. 159, 160†*
Question Support p. 163*

Reading
Connect pp. 161, 162†*
Reading Fluency p. 164

Assessment
Selection Tests A, B/C pp. 165*, 167*
Test Generator CD

 BEST PRACTICES TOOLKIT

Differentiated Instruction
pp. 31–38*

Scaffolding Instruction
pp. 43–46*

Reading Support
Audio Anthology CD*

Technology
Literature and Vocabulary Centers at **ClassZone.com**

Write*Smart* CD

---

* Resources for Differentiation   † Also in Spanish   ‡ In Haitian Creole and Vietnamese

LITERARY ANALYSIS: IMAGERY AND MOOD

To create **mood** in poetry, writers rely on **imagery**—words and phrases that appeal to the reader's senses.

*Dark fins appear, innocent
as if in fair warning.*

In the above example from "The Sharks," note how the visual image of "dark fins" helps establish a mood of sinister foreboding.

As you read each poem in this lesson, use a chart to keep track of words and phrases that evoke a particular mood.

Imagery	Mood Created
"Dark fins appear, innocent as if in fair warning."	foreboding, threatening

READING STRATEGY: CONNECT

Reading poetry can be a meaningful experience when you **connect** your own experiences and knowledge with the thoughts and feelings expressed in a poem. For example, you might have enjoyed the peaceful surroundings of a park or lake, like the speaker in "The Peace of Wild Things."

By allowing yourself to connect with the experience revealed in a poem, you enhance your understanding of the speaker and the ideas conveyed. As you read, make use of the "connect" strategy whenever appropriate.

Author Online

Denise Levertov: Destined for Poetry

Born in England, Denise Levertov (lĕv'ər-tôv') grew up in a home full of books, reading, and lively conversation. She began writing when she was five, and once said that she knew "from an early age—perhaps by 7 . . . that I was an

Denise Levertov
1923–1997

artist-person and had a destiny." She wrote all of her life, publishing more than 30 volumes of poetry and prose. In commenting on her work, she emphasized the need for "precision in poetry." Levertov immigrated to the United States in 1948 and, in addition to her writing, was passionately committed to causes of peace and social justice.

Wendell Berry: A Love for the Land

A novelist, essayist, and poet, Wendell Berry grew up on a farm in Kentucky. After starting a promising career as a writer and college professor in California and then New York City, Berry chose to return to Kentucky. There

Wendell Berry
born 1934

he has combined farming and writing in a life committed to conserving the land and preserving the values of small farms and communities. Berry's novels, essays, and poems reflect his love of nature, the richness of farm and family life, and his concerns about the world and its problems. He writes in a direct style that evokes the rural world he knows so well.

 MORE ABOUT THE AUTHOR
For more on these poets, visit the **Literature Center at ClassZone.com.**

379

Teach

STANDARDS FOCUS

LITERARY ANALYSIS

● IMAGERY AND MOOD

For instructional support, read aloud this example:

A feathery fog settled upon the valley like a lazy lapdog. At high noon, it slipped away, searching for shade.

Ask students to identify words or images that appeal to the senses. What mood do they elicit?

Possible answer: *"feathery fog settled," "like a lazy lapdog"; the mood is light-hearted.*

CHECK UNDERSTANDING Ask students to suggest how to change the image to create a malevolent mood; they might start with "black choking smoke" instead of "feathery fog."

 RESOURCE MANAGER—Copy Master
Imagery and Mood p. 159 (for student use while reading the selection)

READING SKILL

■ CONNECT

Encourage students to respond to the photograph of the lightning storm on page 378. How does the picture make them feel? Does it remind them of times they were out in a storm?

CHECK UNDERSTANDING Have students cover up the lightning in the photograph. What reaction do they have to the picture now? Are their feelings about the photograph different with the lightning covered up? Why or why not?

DIFFERENTIATED INSTRUCTION

FOR LESS–PROFICIENT READERS

Imagery and Mood Have students close their eyes and imagine walking in a meadow on a sunny summer afternoon. What images do they see, hear, and smell? How does this scene make them feel? Ask them to be as specific as possible. Continue this activity by having students picture the changes that a sudden storm would create.

THE
SHARKS

Denise Levertov

Well then, the last day the sharks appeared.
Dark fins appear, innocent
as if in fair warning. The sea becomes
sinister, are they everywhere? **A**
5 I tell you, they break six feet of water.[1]
Isn't it the same sea, and won't we
play in it any more?
I liked it clear and not
too calm, enough waves
10 to fly in on. For the first time
I dared to swim out of my depth.
It was sundown when they came, the time
when a sheen of copper stills the sea,
not dark enough for moonlight, clear enough
15 to see them easily. Dark
the sharp lift of the fins.

LITERARY ANALYSIS

A IMAGERY AND MOOD

Possible answer: *The image of dark fins (line 2) and the words* warning *and* sinister *help to establish the ominous mood.*

If students need help . . . Remind students that mood is the feeling the author creates through images and specific words. Discuss the meaning of *warning* in line 3 ("an alert") and *sinister* in line 4 ("evil or threatening") before asking how these words and the image of dark fins in line 2 make them feel.

ANALYZE VISUALS

Possible answer: *The large, menacing black fin slicing through the clear blue water and the shadows around it capture the poem's frightening mood.*

A IMAGERY AND MOOD
Reread lines 1–4. What is the mood at the beginning of this poem? Which words and images help establish this mood?

ANALYZE VISUALS
How does the photograph reflect the mood of the poem?

1. **they break . . . water:** Sharks often show their dorsal fin if water is shallow enough.

DIFFERENTIATED INSTRUCTION

For general guidelines on differentiating instruction, see

BEST PRACTICES TOOLKIT
Differentiated Instruction pp. 31–38

FOR LESS–PROFICIENT READERS

Options for Reading Read aloud each poem, emphasizing the dark, sinister mood of "Sharks" and the transcendent, mystical feeling of "The Peace of Wild Things."

DISCUSSION PROMPTS

Use these prompts to focus on how the speaker's actions reveal the poem's theme:

Connect Have you ever seen the ocean? If not, what do you imagine that it looks like? Describe. *Students may describe personal experiences as well as what they know from movies or television.*

Analyze What kind of person likes "enough waves / to fly in on" (lines 9–10)? ***Possible answer:*** *These lines describe a somewhat timid person who seems to long for adventure (for a sea that is "not / too calm") but takes only moderate risk, maintaining safe parameters.*

Evaluate How do the speaker's actions and attitude help us infer the poem's theme? ***Possible answer:*** *The speaker is like many people who take measured risks: when she ventures too far, she confronts real or imagined danger. The poem's theme, taking risks (and venturing beyond one's comfort zone), means confronting dangerous situations and our fears of them.*

REINFORCE *KEY IDEA:* FACES OF NATURE

Discuss What **faces of nature** does Levertov portray in "The Sharks"? ***Possible answer:*** *She portrays nature as unpredictable and frightening.*

FOR LESS–PROFICIENT READERS

Characterization To help students understand the speaker's apprehension, ask: Would a fearless person swim close to shore? What kind of water would a fearless person want to swim in? Why did the speaker wait until the last day to dare to swim out of her depth (lines 10–11)?

FOR ADVANCED LEARNERS/PRE–AP

Symbolism Discuss how the sharks symbolize the speaker's fears about becoming an adult and accepting the responsibilities, as well as the independence, of adulthood. Which time words in the poem reinforce the idea that the speaker is on the verge of a change or major transition in her life? Invite students to speculate about why the speaker asks, "won't we / play in it [the sea] any more?" (lines 6–7)

Prereading for this poem is found on page 378.

B CONNECT

Possible answer: Students are likely to share the speaker's feeling that nature is a comfort and refuge from everyday life.

Extend the Discussion How do the images in lines 8–10 convey the poem's peaceful and comforting mood?

REINFORCE *KEY IDEA:* FACES OF NATURE

Discuss What aspects of nature give the speaker the greatest comfort? ***Possible answer:** The speaker finds comfort lying near a marsh or lake with the stars shining overhead.*

ANALYZE VISUALS

Activity How does this photo reflect the poem's mood? ***Possible answer:** It shows a wild duck afloat in still water that reflects an extraordinary light. The mood is peaceful and soothing.*

SELECTION WRAP–UP

SYNTHESIZE How do both poems convey the power of nature over the individual?

⭐ **CRITIQUE** Nature is the setting for both poems. How effectively does each poem use this setting to develop its theme?

READING FLUENCY

Distribute the copy master and have students work in pairs to practice fluency.

R RESOURCE MANAGER—Copy Master
Reading Fluency p. 164

The Peace of Wild Things

Wendell Berry

When despair for the world grows in me
and I wake in the night at the least sound
in fear of what my life and my children's lives may be,
I go and lie down where the wood drake[1]
5 rests in his beauty on the water, and the great heron feeds.
I come into the peace of wild things
who do not tax their lives with forethought
of grief. I come into the presence of still water.
And I feel above me the day-blind stars
10 waiting with their light. For a time
I rest in the grace of the world, and am free. **B**

---

1. **wood drake:** a type of male duck.

B CONNECT
Think about how you feel when you walk in the woods, alongside a lake, or through a scenic park. In what ways does your experience connect with the speaker's ideas?

DIFFERENTIATED INSTRUCTION

FOR ADVANCED LEARNERS/PRE-AP
Analyze Language Ask students to consider the last sentence of the poem. Ask them to write a short paragraph in which they explain their understanding of what the author means by "the grace of the world" and why and how it provides rest and freedom for him.

Comprehension

1. **Recall** What situation is presented in "The Sharks"?

2. **Summarize** What problem does the speaker in "The Peace of Wild Things" experience, and what does he do about it?

Literary Analysis

3. **Connect** As you read the poems, what connections were you able to make? Which of these had the strongest impact? Explain why.

4. **Identify Speaker** In "The Sharks," whom do you imagine the speaker to be? Consider the evidence in the poem about the speaker's age and situation. Remember that the speaker and the poet are not necessarily the same person.

5. **Analyze Speaker** Reread line 1 of "The Peace of Wild Things." Considering the speaker's "despair for the world," how would you describe the speaker?

6. **Compare and Contrast** Describe the **faces of nature** presented in each poem. What differences do you see in the comfort level each speaker has with his or her natural surroundings? Are there any similarities in their attitudes toward nature? Support your conclusions.

7. **Evaluate Mood** Review the charts you filled in as you read the poems. What overall mood is created by each poem? How effective are the **images** in creating each mood? Explain your opinion.

8. **Compare Literary Works** Reread Wallace Stegner's "Wilderness Letter" on pages 373–376. Which of Stegner's ideas does "The Peace of Wild Things" support?

Literary Criticism

9. **Historical Perspective** Reread "The Peace of Wild Things." Is Berry's perspective strictly a modern one? Might a person living 200 years ago, for example, have felt this same "despair for the world"? Give reasons for your opinions.

Practice and Apply

After Reading

For additional support of post-reading questions, use these copy masters:

R RESOURCE MANAGER—Copy Masters
Imagery and Mood p. 159 (for practice of literary analysis standards focus)
Question Support p. 163 (After Reading questions adapted for English learners and less-proficient readers)

For additional questions, see page 155.

ANSWERS

Comprehension

1. *The speaker has ventured too far into the ocean and is surrounded by sharks.*

2. *Unable to sleep because of his despair over the state of the contemporary world, the speaker eases his distress by going into nature.*

Literary Analysis

Possible answers:

3. ■ **STANDARDS FOCUS** *Connect Answers and explanations will vary, but students may connect with fear in the first poem, peace in the second.*

4. *The speaker in "The Sharks" is likely a timid person on the verge of maturity, at the end of a vacation (lines 1, 6–7, 11).*

5. *The speaker is a parent who worries about the world that he and his generation are bequeathing to their heirs (lines 1–3).*

6. *"The Sharks" presents nature's terrifying face; "The Peace of Wild Things," nature's soothing face. The first speaker's fears keep*

her from venturing far from shore. The second speaker's ease in nature enables him to find solace near a marsh. Both speakers acknowledge nature's power and influence on their feelings (lines 3–5 of the first poem and lines 8–11 of the second).

7. ● **STANDARDS FOCUS** *Imagery and Mood The frightening mood of the first poem is created by alarming images of "Dark fins" and "a sheen of copper" stilling the sea at sundown. The calm, comforting mood of the second poem is created by the peaceful images of a wood drake resting* on water and a great heron feeding, and by the consoling image of "the day-blind stars / waiting with their light."

8. *According to both selections, nature is important for spiritual well-being.*

Literary Criticism

Possible answer:

9. *People 200 years ago may have felt a similar despair because the Industrial Revolution was disrupting lives.*

Assess and Reteach

Assess

R RESOURCE MANAGER—Copy Masters
Selection Test A pp. 165–166
Selection Test B/C pp. 167–168

◉ Test Generator CD

Reteach

S STANDARDS LESSON FILE
Literature Lesson 28: Imagery
Literature Lesson 44: Mood

Focus and Motivate

OBJECTIVES

- analyze a student model that reflects the key traits of a short story
- use the writing process to produce a short story
- revise and edit, using a rubric for short story writing
- create and present a video presentation

WRITER'S ROAD MAP

WRITING PROMPTS 1 AND 2

Help students choose a prompt by brainstorming a list of people and events in the news. Point out that a good story idea often springs from combining several factors, for example, a particular type of person facing a certain kind of conflict. Remind students to use varied sentences, with appropriate punctuation.

ADDITIONAL PROMPTS

Use these prompts for practice with business writing and writing in the humanities:

WRITING PROMPT 3

Writing for the Real World Write an advertisement in which a product speaks and tells a story illustrating one of its features.

Possible Products
- a car that can call 9-1-1
- a backpack with a tracking device

WRITING PROMPT 4

Writing About Fine Art Find artwork that tells a story or suggests a story to you. Create a story revolving around one of the characters, the setting, or the situation depicted.

Possible Subjects
- two people engaged in conversation or quietly enjoying a moment
- people in transit—on a train, or walking
- a rite of passage or milestone, such as a wedding

For additional writing prompts, see

- WriteSmart CD
- Writing Center at **ClassZone.com**

KEY TRAITS

Review the six **KEY TRAITS** with students, focusing on ideas, organization, and word choice. Compare the list of traits with the rubric on page 390.

Writing Workshop

Short Story

The power of storytelling is evident in the literature you have read in this unit and in the stories you encounter in everyday life. Now you have a chance to invent a story of your own. The story you write can entertain, teach a lesson, or express your observations and feelings. To begin creating your fictional world, consult the **Writer's Road Map.**

WRITER'S ROAD MAP

Short Story

WRITING PROMPT 1

Writing from the Real World You have probably read many stories that were inspired by real-world events, issues, or people. Write your own short story based on a conflict, person, or setting that you find intriguing.

Places to Find Ideas
- news articles on events, scientific discoveries, or weather disasters
- magazine features that profile interesting people
- situations that you have seen or experienced, such as a conflict between siblings

WRITING PROMPT 2

Writing from Literature The best stories are often the ones that spring from life's big questions. From this unit, choose a prereading question that intrigues you. Then write a short story inspired by that question.

Questions to Inspire You
- When is a risk worth taking? ("Through the Tunnel")
- Is revenge ever justified? ("The Cask of Amontillado")
- Where do you find adventure? (*A Walk in the Woods*)

 WRITING TOOLS
For prewriting, revision, and editing tools, visit the **Writing Center** at ClassZone.com.

KEY TRAITS

1. IDEAS
- Focuses on a well-developed **plot** and compelling **characters**
- Introduces, develops, and resolves a **central conflict**
- Includes **descriptive details** that reveal the setting and characters
- Uses **dialogue** to show characters' personalities

2. ORGANIZATION
- Sets the stage by **introducing** the characters, setting, or action
- Presents a clear and engaging **sequence of events**
- Resolves the conflict in a convincing **conclusion**

3. VOICE
- Maintains a consistent **point of view**

4. WORD CHOICE
- Uses **sensory language** to help readers imagine the fictional world

5. SENTENCE FLUENCY
- Uses the **active voice**

6. CONVENTIONS
- Employs **correct grammar and usage**

Writing Workshop Resources

 RESOURCE MANAGER UNIT 3

Plan and Teach pp. 169–172
Prewriting–Editing pp. 173–177
Writing Rubric p. 178
Publishing with Technology p. 179
Writing Support p. 180*

 **STANDARDS LESSON FILE**

Writing Lessons 10, 23, 34, 44
Media Lessons 20

 BEST PRACTICES TOOLKIT

Scaffolding Writing Instruction pp. 43–46*
Story Map • Sequence Chain • Analysis Frame: Author's Craft • Writing Template: Short Story • Storyboard

TECHNOLOGY
- Easy Planner DVD
- Writing Center at **ClassZone.com**
- WriteSmart CD

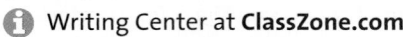

* Resources for Differentiation

Part 1: Analyze a Student Model

Sarah Yovovich
Evanston Township High School

Like a Flower

"Just lend me ten bucks, John," Jessica begged. "Come on!"

"I'm sure the shirt is very cute and pink and perfect, Sis, but I don't have the ten. Now move—I gotta mow the lawn."

"In this heat?" she asked, fanning herself with manicured nails.

5 "You know, Mom and Dad pay me ten bucks to mow," John said.

"Oh! So you can lend it to me after you finish?"

He snorted. "Yeah, right. I'll let you mow the lawn, though."

"No way! That mower's heavy!" Jessica said, her mouth open.

"You know, a little physical labor wouldn't kill you."

10 "It *might*," she insisted.

"Okay, fine, wear something else." He paused. "What's that I hear? Oh—it's the sound of a thousand cute tops crying!"

"Shut up and show me how the thing works," she snapped. They went to the garage, and John pulled out the mower for her.

15 "So I just pull this cord?" She pulled tentatively, and the mower let out a brief, disgruntled growl. Jessica jumped back and let out an "Eep!"

"It's fine, Jess. Pull as hard as you can," John said. Jessica braced herself and pulled. The mower roared to life. She looked at John with terror.

20 "Good job!" he hollered. "Go to it!"

"Wait!" she squeaked, but he was gone. She took a deep breath and nudged the mower forward a few inches. It made a hideous *crrrunch* as it chewed up some twigs and spat out their remains. She shrieked, thinking of how *not* cute she would look with missing toes. The mower

25 kept roaring, and she realized that she didn't know how to turn it off.

KEY TRAITS IN ACTION

Uses **dialogue** and **descriptive details** (manicured nails) to reveal the characters' personalities.

Maintains a consistent third-person **point of view.**

Lively **sensory language** shows the reader how it felt to mow the lawn. The writer uses the **active voice.**

Teach

Part 1: Analyze a Student Model

Have students read the student model and **KEY TRAITS IN ACTION.** Then discuss the model with the class, pointing out specific examples of each trait and building on what students have already noted. You may also wish to incorporate these activities:

- **Dialogue** Write this line of dialogue on the board:

  "I am only asking for a loan of ten dollars, John," Jessica begged. "Please reconsider my request."

  Ask a student to read the dialogue aloud. Discuss why it does not sound as lifelike as the dialogue in the student model. ***Possible answer: The dialogue on the board uses complete sentences and formal language. It does not sound like a typical teenager. The dialogue throughout the model uses informal language and incomplete sentences. When read aloud, it sounds the way a teen would sound.***

- **Sensory Language** Review with students that sensory language appeals to the five senses. Invite students to name these senses (*sight, smell, touch, taste,* and *hearing*) and to identify examples in the text. Discuss how this language helps readers feel, see, and hear along with the character.

Point out that prepositional phrases are important for adding detail and variety. Review the GRAMMAR AND STYLE note on page 390.

- **Point of View** Remind students that a third-person narrator can use shifting perspectives to reveal several characters' thoughts, feelings, and attitudes toward another character or event.

- **Plot** Point out that a good plot has a series of events that arise from the story's central conflict—in this case, Jessica versus the lawn mower. The actions that the character takes to resolve the conflict build toward a climax, or turning point. In this story, Jessica takes several actions that lead to a change in her attitude.

Ask students to identify the actions that leave Jessica no longer afraid of the mower.

Possible answers:

Lines 26–27: "She nudged the evil machine forward"

Line 33: "pushed down on the handle"

Line 35: "she turned, then pushed forward"

Lines 36–37: "she had perfected her turning technique"

- **Resolution** Explain that the resolution of a story shows the final outcome. This story has a somewhat surprising ending. Discuss with students what has changed about Jessica's attitude. Have them find evidence that shows she has changed.

For interactive student models, see

🖉 Write*Smart* CD

ℹ Writing Center at **ClassZone.com**

"John!" she shouted, but there was no way he could hear her. She nudged the evil machine forward and watched grass spew out the side. It was kind of cool. Terrifying, but cool.

She kept pushing, all the way to the other side of the lawn. The
30 mower was heavy, but she was strong enough. Turning around was another issue. She'd seen John tilt the machine and turn it a hundred and eighty degrees, but he was a foot taller and two years older. Still, she was tough, even if she liked pink. She pushed down on the handle, and the mower tilted up surprisingly easily. The sound was much louder,
35 but she didn't flinch. Slowly, she turned, then pushed forward to mow the next strip of grass. By the time she got to the end of the lawn, she had perfected her turning technique so that it was one fluid motion— push-swivel-drop-mow! The grass cringed at her approach, and she left no survivors.

40 No longer afraid of the mower, she moved her sweaty face closer to examine the controls. She found the off switch and cut the engine.

John emerged from inside and surveyed the lawn. "Nice job, Jess."

"Thank you. Excuse me, but I have money to collect, a shower to take, and a top to buy," she said as she walked past him.

45 That night she looked amazing in her new silk top. Her friend Alice said, "You look beautiful! Like a flower or something!"

"Thank you!" Jessica replied, thinking about how much fun it would be to mow right through a field of flowers, petals flying everywhere.

> Develops a **plot** and a **central conflict** (Jessica versus the lawn mower) that make the piece a story, not just a description.

> **Sequence of events** is clear. The writer **resolves** the conflict in a believable way.

> Lighthearted **conclusion** shows how Jessica's attitude has changed.

2

DIFFERENTIATED INSTRUCTION

FOR ENGLISH LEARNERS

Comprehension: Transitions Make sure that students recognize signal words and phrases that show sequence. Explain that many stories are told in the order in which they happened. Authors use signal words and phrases to make the order of events clear.

1. Draw attention to these signal words and phrases in the student model.

   Line 35: "Slowly, she turned, then pushed"

Line 36: "By the time she got to the end"

Line 44: "she said as she walked past him"

Line 45: "That night she looked amazing"

2. Provide additional oral examples.

   At first, Jessica was afraid of the mower.

   Later, she lost her fear.

   She imagined mowing flowers some day.

3. Number the examples 1–3 and point out that they are in chronological order.

4. Display an illustration of a sequence, such as a seed sprouting or a child growing older. Ask students to tell what is happening and to use signal words and phrases that make the order clear.

To provide English learners with additional writing support, see

📋 RESOURCE MANAGER—Copy Master
   Writing Support p. 180

Part 2: Apply the Writing Process

PREWRITING

What Should I Do?

1. Think of a story you want to tell.
Brainstorm ideas for **plots, characters, settings,** or **themes** you want to get across. Use a graphic organizer to keep track of the possibilities. Highlight the idea that seems most promising.

TIP Can't think of anything? Choose a picture, a print advertisement, or another visual and start writing about the person or place shown.

2. Flesh out your characters.
What do they look like? How do they speak and act? How do other characters treat them? What **conflicts** do they face? Create a chart to help you keep track of your characters and to make each of them distinct.

3. Map your story.
Create a story graph, story map, list, or flow chart showing what happens to your characters. Ask yourself "what if" questions about problems or experiences they might have.

TIP Think about the rising action, climax, and falling action of your story, as shown in this story graph.

See page 172 for an example of a story map.

What Does It Look Like?

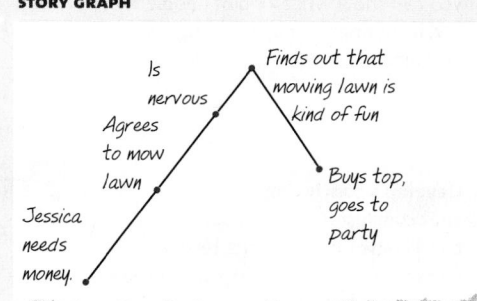

Kid gets revenge on brother who ignores him.

Girl finds out she's tougher than she thought.

Plots

Pet dog saves kid from drowning.

Songwriter gets rich, can't write songs anymore.

Characters	Details
Jessica	has manicure, likes to look good, favorite color is pink, goes to lots of parties, doesn't like to be seen as weak
John	older, teases his sister but thinks she's OK, is willing to help her

STORY GRAPH

Is nervous

Finds out that mowing lawn is kind of fun

Agrees to mow lawn

Buys top, goes to party

Jessica needs money.

FOR ENGLISH LEARNERS

Writing: Story Map Have students use sentence starters to help them create a story map.

- My characters are _____.
- The story takes place _____.
- The main conflict is _____.
- The major events will be _____.
- The story ends with _____.

FOR ADVANCED LEARNERS/PRE–AP

In-Depth Analysis Have students use the Analysis Frame to analyze a favorite author's style. Challenge them to create a story in the style of that author.

 BEST PRACTICES TOOLKIT—Transparency
   Analysis Frame: Author's Craft
      pp. D21, D24

Practice and Apply

To support students during the writing process, use these copy masters:

R **RESOURCE MANAGER**—Copy Masters
   Prewriting–Editing pp. 173–177
   Writing Rubric p. 178
   Writing Support p. 180 (for English learners)

Part 2: Apply the Writing Process

PREWRITING

1. Think of a story you want to tell.
Tell students that another way to brainstorm ideas for a story is to recall familiar plots from fables or books and change important elements, such as characters or setting. For example, the fable of the tortoise and the hare could be told with humans racing to a distant star. Have pairs of students brainstorm familiar stories and various ways they could be changed.

2. Flesh out your characters. This activity provides practice in noting important or revealing details. List several people who are familiar to the entire class: musical artists, school staff, or local personalities. Have students take turns describing an unnamed person so that others will be able to guess who it is.

3. Map your story. Urge students to look at a variety of graphic organizers, including Story Frames and Sequence Chains, before choosing one. Point out that they can begin to fill in the graphic anywhere—starting with a character, the setting, or an event. Their starting point can help them decide which graphic organizer will be most helpful.

 BEST PRACTICES TOOLKIT—Transparencies
   Story Map p. D14
   Sequence Chain p. B21

For interactive graphic organizers, see

🖉 Write*Smart* CD

ℹ️ Writing Center at **ClassZone.com**

DRAFTING

1. **Start out strong.** Discuss additional ways to begin stories—for example, with a sound effect, an exclamation or a shout, a suspenseful moment, a description of a strong emotion felt by the narrator, or a detail from the end of the story.

2. **Choose a point of view.** Remind students that point of view is shown not only by the choice of pronouns but also by the events that are described. If students use a first-person narrator, then the events should be limited to those that the narrator took part in, witnessed, or heard about. This point of view is often used to build suspense.

3. **Use dialogue to reveal characters' personalities.** Encourage students to visualize their characters clearly before creating dialogue. Suggest that they picture a real person—perhaps an actor—who fits the role, then use the image in their mind as a starting point for determining the character's age, education, and manner of speech.

4. **Develop a conclusion.** Explain that even though a conclusion may be surprising, it should not introduce ideas that are totally new. Direct students to lines 28 and 37–38 in the student model, and have them find clues that hinted at the story's conclusion.

Have students trade first drafts with a partner. Students should evaluate their partner's papers according to the key traits listed at the beginning of the workshop.

For a short story writing template, see

📋 **BEST PRACTICES TOOLKIT**—Transparency
Writing Template: Short Story
pp. C16, C39

💿 Write*Smart* CD

ℹ️ Writing Center at **ClassZone.com**

What Should I Do?	*What Does It Look Like?*
1. Start out strong. Consider beginning with some **dialogue** or a description of the scene or of a character. ▶ **TIP** If you can't come up with a great beginning right away, just start writing. You can revise later.	**Dialogue** *"Just lend me ten bucks, John," Jessica begged.* **Sensory language/descriptive details** *The spiky, overgrown grass wilted in the blazing heat.*
2. Choose a point of view. Decide who will tell your story. Use a **first-person narrator** if your main goal is to draw readers into the story; use a **third-person narrator** to give a broad view of characters and events. ▶	**First-person point of view** *We went to the garage, and John pulled out the mower for me.* **Third-person point of view** *They went to the garage, and John pulled out the mower for her.*
3. Use dialogue to reveal characters' personalities. By carefully choosing characters' words, you can show what kind of people they are, including their ages, thoughts, and feelings. ▶	*"You know, a little physical labor wouldn't kill you."* *"It might," she insisted.* *"Okay, fine, wear something else." He paused. "What's that I hear? Oh—it's the sound of a thousand cute tops crying!"* *"Shut up and show me how the thing works," she snapped.*
4. Develop a conclusion. Your conclusion might resolve the conflict, tie up loose ends, reveal something surprising, or give your reader something to think about. ▶ **TIP** Some writers decide how they want a story to end and work backwards from there.	*That night she looked amazing in her new silk top. Her friend Alice said, "You look beautiful! Like a flower or something!"* *"Thank you!" Jessica replied, thinking about how much fun it would be to mow right through a field of flowers, petals flying everywhere.*

DIFFERENTIATED INSTRUCTION

FOR LESS–PROFICIENT WRITERS

Use Dialogue To help students create lively dialogue, suggest that they follow these tips:

- Have them begin by writing only the characters' words. When they are satisfied with the words, they can go back to insert punctuation and speaker tags.
- Encourage students to use precise words in speaker tags and to vary their placement. Call attention to the dialogue in the student model. Discuss the different placement of speaker tags in lines 1, 4, and 7. Then point out the use of precise verbs in the speaker tags, such as *begged* (line 1), *insisted* (line 10), *snapped* (line 13), *hollered* (line 20), and *squeaked* (line 21).

REVISING AND EDITING

What Should I Do?

1. Evaluate how you start.
- Ask a peer reader to read the first two or three paragraphs.
- Discuss whether your beginning is clear or confusing, tired or attention grabbing.

See page 390: Ask a Peer Reader

2. Make dialogue believable.
- Read aloud any dialogue in your story. <u>Underline</u> parts that seem phony or unnatural.
- Revise your dialogue to include contractions, slang, pauses, jargon, or exclamations that match the characters' ages and personalities.

3. Use active voice.
- The passive voice can make writing dull and lifeless. When the subject performs the action, the verb is in the active voice: *Jessica mowed the lawn.* In the passive voice, the subject is acted upon: *The lawn was mowed by Jessica.*
- Circle passive-voice verbs and change them to the active voice.

4. Brainstorm a title that fits.
Jot down titles that are appropriate for your story and that might capture a reader's interest. You might use a character's name or a bit of dialogue. This writer chose a title that refers to the conclusion of her story.

What Does It Look Like?

Reviewer's question: Are Jessica and John related?

"I'm sure the shirt is very cute and pink and perfect, but I don't have the ten." Sis,

~~"I will let you mow the lawn," he said.~~
~~"I do not want to. The lawnmower is very heavy."~~
He snorted. "Yeah, right. I'll let you mow the lawn, though."
"No way! That mower's heavy!"

Passive voice
The mower was pulled out of the garage by John.
Active voice
John pulled the mower out of the garage.

~~Mowing the Lawn~~
~~Jessica, John, and the Lawnmower~~
~~The Party's Tonight~~
Like a Flower *

REVISING AND EDITING

1. **Evaluate how you start.** Some writers may begin somewhat stiffly and then develop a voice as they write. Suggest that students decide whether the tone of their lead matches the tone of the rest of their story. They might want to ask themselves: Would this beginning grab or bore a reader? Tell students that beginning a story with dialogue can set up a situation quickly and make a story livelier.

2. **Make dialogue believable.** Students may find it easier to evaluate their dialogue after hearing another student read it aloud.

3. **Use active voice.** Note that passive verbs include a form of the verb *be.* Have students identify passive verbs in these examples and restate the ideas in the active voice:
   - The grass was thrown everywhere by the mower.
   - The entire student body was moved by Kyle's speech.
   - The silk top was finally bought by Jess.

   Review the GRAMMAR AND STYLE note on page 316. Remind students that it is also important to avoid shifting tenses unnecessarily in their writing.

4. **Brainstorm a title that fits.** Encourage students to be playful as they brainstorm. Students might consider trying one of the following for their titles: a new twist on an old saying; a phrase that makes sense only after the story has been read; a catchy phrase that rhymes or repeats an initial letter; a title that identifies the genre, such as "The Mystery of . . ."; or a one-word title.

   For interactive revision tools, see

   WriteSmart CD

   Writing Center at **ClassZone.com**

FOR ENGLISH LEARNERS
Revising: Sensory Language Help students develop a vocabulary of precise sensory language to use for revising. Name the five senses, then list words that describe sights, sounds, tastes, feelings, and smells.

sights: orange, crooked, curved
sounds: shrill, muffled, thumping
tastes: acid, tart, salty
feelings: bumpy, sticky, slippery
smells: burnt, smoky, perfumed

To help generate more words for the list, display pictures for students to describe. Encourage them to add precise sensory words such as these to their drafts.

Preparing to Publish

Support for meeting the goals in the writing rubric is supplied throughout the Writing Workshop on pages 384–389.

For Rubric Bank, see

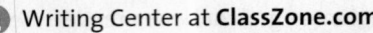 WriteSmart CD

 Writing Center at ClassZone.com

Assess and Reteach

S STANDARDS LESSON FILE

Writing Lesson 10: Using Active and Passive Voice

Writing Lesson 23: Short Story

Writing Lesson 34: Elaborate with Sensory Details

Writing Lesson 44: Writing Dialogue

Preparing to Publish Short Story

Apply the Rubric

A strong short story . . .

☑ begins in a way that will interest the reader

☑ has a well-developed plot and intriguing characters

☑ develops an interesting and clearly presented central conflict

☑ includes descriptive details, sensory language, and dialogue

☑ makes the sequence of events clear and engaging

☑ maintains a consistent point of view

☑ uses the active voice

☑ resolves the conflict in a convincing conclusion

Ask a Peer Reader

• What could I do to make the beginning of my story clearer or more interesting?

• How would you describe the central conflict in my story?

• Which characters or actions would you like to know more about?

Use Descriptive Details

Use words like these to help your reader see and hear the action.

Sensory Verbs	Sensory Adjectives
flinch	delicate
holler	glittery
nudge	heavy
roar	pink
shiver	rough
snort	silky
squeak	sour

Check Your Grammar

• Use prepositional phrases to add important details to your story.

> She shrieked, thinking of how _not_ cute she would look with missing toes.
>
> She pushed down on the handle.
>
> The grass cringed at her approach.

See page R48: The Sentence and Its Parts

 Writing Online

PUBLISHING OPTIONS
For publishing options, visit the **Writing Center** at **ClassZone.com.**

ASSESSMENT PREPARATION
For writing and grammar assessment practice, go to the **Assessment Center** at **ClassZone.com.**

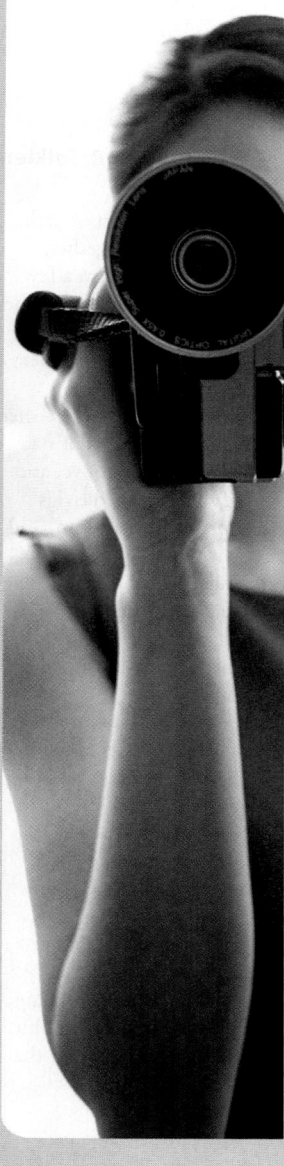

Creating a Video Presentation

Have you ever wanted to direct a movie? Videotaping a scene from your short story can bring its characters, setting, and action to life.

Planning the Video

1. **Focus on a scene.** Think about the action you want to portray. Choose a scene that makes sense without extra explanation.
2. **Cast the characters and settle on a setting.** Ask classmates to take on the roles of your characters. Find a location that matches the setting. If you have set your story in another country or time period, you may need to use painted backdrops.
3. **Create a script.** Map out dialogue and action in a **rough script.** In addition to the characters' own words, consider using **voice-overs,** an offscreen person's descriptions of characters or actions. Include notes on **visual effects** and **sound effects** if applicable.
4. **Storyboard your scene.** Use sketches to show what shots you will need. Include a variety of perspectives, such as **establishing shots, medium shots,** and **close-ups.**

(Close-up) John: Good job! Go to it!   *(Medium shot) Jessica: Wait!*

Producing the Video

1. **Roll camera!** Follow your script and storyboard in shooting your video. You may want to have a classmate help you.
2. **Edit your masterpiece.** Use an editing software program to assemble your best footage. Then record voice-overs if needed, add music if you wish, and create a title screen and credits.

WRITING WORKSHOP **391**

PUBLISHING WITH TECHNOLOGY

Ask students to read this page to get an overview of one way to create a video presentation. Students who choose this option should learn how to operate a video camera either by watching a demonstration or by reading a manual. Suggest that students learn how to avoid camera jiggle, how to pan smoothly, and how to frame scenes correctly. Additional guidance may be found in these components:

 BEST PRACTICES TOOLKIT—Transparency
Storyboard p. C11

Before students begin working, review this rubric with them so that they have clear goals:

Rubric A strong video presentation . . .

- shows evidence of rehearsal and planning
- presents events in a clear sequence
- includes clear, focused images that vary in perspective and that show establishing shots, medium shots, and close-ups
- switches between shots smoothly
- incorporates a sound track that coordinates with the images
- contains a title and credits

R **RESOURCE MANAGER—Copy Master**
Publishing with Technology p. 179

S **STANDARDS LESSON FILE**
Media Lesson 20: Producing a Video

Assessment Practice

CHECK READINESS

Read aloud the paragraph under **ASSESS** and stress to students that this is not the full Unit Test, but a way for them to check their readiness for it. Then have students examine the skills listed under **REVIEW** and look back in the unit or in the **Student Resource Bank** for any they need to review.

READ THE SELECTION

Remind students to keep unit goals in mind as they read the passage, paying particular attention to these literary and reading skills:

- setting
- imagery
- mood
- analyze details
- make inferences
- paraphrase

To help students focus on setting and mood, encourage them to ask questions such as

- What details help me picture the setting? What mood do these details create?
- How dangerous is the characters' situation? How do I know?

ANSWER THE QUESTIONS

Direct students to pages R93–R101 of the **Handbook** to review test-taking strategies.

- Remind students not to choose the first alternative that seems to fit when answering a multiple-choice question. Instead, they should read through all the choices, eliminate any that are clearly wrong, and then choose the *best* answer—the one that is most accurate and complete.
- Suggest that students look over the entire test before they begin and think about how to divide up their time for each section. This will help them avoid unpleasant surprises, such as discovering that a test is four pages instead of two.

Assessment Practice

ASSESS
The practice test items on the next few pages match skills listed on the Unit Goals page (page 301) and addressed throughout this unit. Taking this practice test will help you assess your knowledge of these skills and determine your readiness for the Unit Test.

REVIEW
After you take the practice test, your teacher can help you identify any skills you need to review.

- Setting
- Mood
- Imagery
- Analyze Details
- Make Inferences
- Paraphrase
- Connotation and Denotation
- Context Clues
- Present Tense
- Compound Predicates

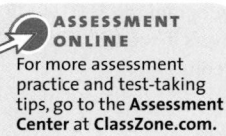

ASSESSMENT ONLINE
For more assessment practice and test-taking tips, go to the **Assessment Center** at ClassZone.com.

Reading Comprehension

DIRECTIONS *Read the following selection and then answer the questions.*

from The Hobbit
Chapter VIII: Flies and Spiders
J. R. R. Tolkien

They walked in single file. The entrance to the path was like a sort of arch leading into a gloomy tunnel made by two great trees that leaned together, too old and strangled with ivy and hung with lichen to bear more than a few blackened leaves. The path itself was narrow and wound in and out among the trunks. Soon the light at the gate was like a little bright hole far behind, and the quiet was so deep that their feet seemed to thump along while all the trees leaned over them and listened.

As their eyes became used to the dimness they could see a little way to either side in a sort of darkened green glimmer. Occasionally a slender beam of sun
10 that had the luck to slip in through some opening in the leaves far above, and still more luck in not being caught in the tangled boughs and matted twigs beneath, stabbed down thin and bright before them. But this was seldom, and it soon ceased altogether.

There were black squirrels in the wood. As Bilbo's sharp inquisitive eyes got used to seeing things he could catch glimpses of them whisking off the path and scuttling behind tree-trunks. There were queer noises too, grunts, scufflings, and hurryings in the undergrowth, and among the leaves that lay piled endlessly thick in places on the forest-floor; but what made the noises he could not see. The nastiest things they saw were the cobwebs: dark dense
20 cobwebs with threads extraordinarily thick, often stretched from tree to tree, or tangled in the lower branches on either side of them. There were none stretched across the path, but whether because some magic kept it clear, or for what other reason they could not guess.

It was not long before they grew to hate the forest as heartily as they had hated the tunnels of the goblins, and it seemed to offer even less hope of any ending. But they had to go on and on, long after they were sick for a sight of the sun and of the sky, and longed for the feel of wind on their faces. There was no movement of air down under the forest-roof, and it was everlastingly still and dark and stuffy. Even the dwarves felt it, who were used to tunneling,
30 and lived at times for long whiles without the light of the sun; but the hobbit, who liked holes to make a house in but not to spend summer days in, felt that he was being slowly suffocated.

DIFFERENTIATED INSTRUCTION

FOR ENGLISH LEARNERS
Assessment Practice: Work Backward
Suggest that students "work backward" by reading the questions *before* they read the test passages. Then have pairs of students follow these directions:

1. Find unfamiliar words in the test directions and questions and write each one on an index card.

2. Look up the meanings in a dictionary or in the pupil edition and write them on the appropriate cards.

3. Use the word cards to practice learning the meanings of the words.

The nights were the worst. It then became pitch-dark—not what you call pitch-dark, but really pitch: so black that you really could see nothing. Bilbo tried flapping his hand in front of his nose, but he could not see it at all. Well, perhaps it is not true to say that they could see nothing: they could see eyes. They slept all closely huddled together, and took it in turns to watch; and when it was Bilbo's turn he would see gleams in the darkness round them, and sometimes pairs of yellow or red or green eyes would stare at him from a little
40 distance, and then slowly fade and disappear and slowly shine out again in another place. And sometimes they would gleam down from the branches just above him; and that was most terrifying. But the eyes that he liked the least were horrible pale bulbous sort of eyes. "Insect eyes," he thought, "not animal eyes, only they are much too big."

Although it was not yet very cold, they tried lighting watch-fires at night, but they soon gave that up. It seemed to bring hundreds and hundreds of eyes all round them, though the creatures, whatever they were, were careful never to let their bodies show in the little flicker of the flames. Worse still it brought thousands of dark-grey and black moths, some nearly as big as your hand,
50 flapping and whirring round their ears. They could not stand that, nor the huge bats, black as a top-hat, either; so they gave up fires and sat at night and dozed in the enormous uncanny darkness.

All this went on for what seemed to the hobbit ages upon ages; and he was always hungry, for they were extremely careful with their provisions. Even so, as days followed days, and still the forests seemed just the same, they began to get anxious. The food would not last for ever: it was in fact already beginning to get low. They tried shooting at the squirrels, and they wasted many arrows before they managed to bring one down on the path. But when they roasted it, it proved horrible to taste, and they shot no more squirrels.
60 They were thirsty too, for they had none too much water, and in all the time they had seen neither spring nor stream. This was their state when one day they found their path blocked by a running water. It flowed fast and strong but not very wide right across the way, and it was black, or looked it in the gloom. It was well that Beorn had warned them against it, or they would have drunk from it, whatever its color, and filled some of their emptied skins at its bank.

 GO ON

ITEM ANALYSIS

COMPREHENSION AND WRITTEN RESPONSE	ITEMS	UNIT PAGES
Setting	1, 4, 14, 15	302–305, 309, 327, 361
Mood	2, 5, 9	302–305, 343, 361, 379
Imagery	2, 3, 7, 9, 10, 11	302–305, 309, 379
Analyze Details	5, 9, 10, 13, 14, 15	327
Make Inferences	3, 4, 7, 15	309, 343, 361
Paraphrase	6, 8, 12	343

VOCABULARY	ITEMS	UNIT PAGES
Connotation and Denotation	1, 2, 3, 4	324
Context Clues	5, 6, 7, 8	371

WRITING AND GRAMMAR	ITEMS	UNIT PAGES
Present Tense	1, 3, 5	325
Compound Predicates	2, 4, 6	341

FOR LESS–PROFICIENT READERS

Assessment Support Consider these options for completing the Assessment Practice:

- Have students "work backward" by reviewing the test questions *before* reading the passage.
- Select random questions in the Assessment, and have students demonstrate how and where to look for the answers.
- Ask students to locate unfamiliar vocabulary words in the Assessment. Elicit their meanings from the class.
- Have students record useful testing words and definitions in their journals for later reference.
- Read the selection or parts of it aloud to aid in student comprehension.

McDougal Littell
Assessment System

After checking student readiness with this Assessment Practice, you may administer the complete Unit 3 Test in order to more thoroughly evaluate student mastery of unit goals.

Comprehension

Model a thinking process for answering multiple-choice questions.

1. **B** *is correct. Line 18 identifies the setting as a forest floor. A may appear to be correct because a tunnel is mentioned in line 2, but it is a tunnel created by trees in the forest. C and D are incorrect because no details refer to a park or a desert.*

2. **A** *is correct. Besides "strangled" and "blackened," which do suggest dead things, the phrase "darkened green glimmer" in line 9 is also creepy. B is untrue because the passage is one of gloom, not joy. C may seem logical at first, but there are many small noises. D is partially accurate; the path is narrow. Yet the impression is one of eeriness rather than crowding.*

3. **D** *is correct. Because the beams of sunlight "soon ceased altogether," they are "defeated." A is incorrect because the sun does more than just slip through the leaves: it also ceases to slip through. B and C are incorrect because no details show the travelers as "lucky" or "threatening."*

4. **D** *is correct. The travelers grew "to hate the forest," felt they were being "slowly suffocated," and huddled in the "pitch-dark." These details convey their reactions against the forest's "dark stuffiness." The characters do not have positive feelings like the excitement in A, confidence in B, or comfort in C.*

5. **D** *is correct. Grunts are sounds. Scuffling and hurrying are actions that can be heard. Such sounds cannot be seen as in A, smelled as in B, or touched as in C.*

6. **C** *is correct. Bilbo heard "grunts, scufflings, and hurryings" in the leaves and undergrowth, but he couldn't see where the noises came from. A is incorrect because it fails to reflect the information in lines 18 and 19. B and D are incorrect because they leave out Bilbo and his perceptions.*

7. **B** *is correct. The description of cobwebs "stretched from tree to tree" and tangled in the branches on either side of the travelers suggests a trap. A is not correct because the cobwebs are not hanging. C and D are incorrect because there is no suggestion of weaving or artistry.*

Comprehension

DIRECTIONS *Answer these questions about the excerpt from* The Hobbit.

1. Which of the following is the setting of "Flies and Spiders"?
   - **A** a gloomy tunnel
   - **B** a large, dense forest
   - **C** a squirrel-filled park
   - **D** a waterless desert

2. In lines 1–13 imagery is used to describe the path. What kind of mood does that imagery create?
   - **A** The mood is creepy because "strangled" and "blackened" suggest dead things.
   - **B** The mood is happy because the travelers are going for a walk.
   - **C** The mood is quiet because the leaves muffle footsteps.
   - **D** The mood makes the travelers feel crowded because the path is so narrow.

3. How does the description of the sunlight in lines 9–13 reflect the travelers' conflict?
   - **A** The sun shows sneakiness by slipping through the leaves.
   - **B** The sun is lucky to reach the ground, just as the travelers are lucky.
   - **C** The sun seems as threatening as the travelers when it stabs down through the leaves.
   - **D** The sun is soon defeated by the darkness, which hints at what will happen to the travelers.

4. From the way the characters react to the setting, you can tell that they are
   - **A** excited by the prospect of an adventure
   - **B** confident that they will get through the forest
   - **C** comfortable with the closeness of their surroundings
   - **D** disturbed by the dark stuffiness of the forest

5. The phrase "grunts, scufflings, and hurryings" appeals to which sense?
   - **A** sight
   - **B** smell
   - **C** touch
   - **D** hearing

6. Which is the best way to paraphrase the sentence that starts in line 16 and ends in line 19?
   - **A** Bilbo heard the scuffling noises the squirrels made.
   - **B** The leaves were piled so thick that they muffled all sounds.
   - **C** Bilbo heard strange noises but couldn't see what made them.
   - **D** Strange animals rushed through the undergrowth, grunting and scuffling.

7. The image of cobwebs in lines 19–21 suggests
   - **A** ropes hanging from trees
   - **B** a trap about to spring
   - **C** woven fabric
   - **D** a work of art

---

8. **A** *is correct. A is the best answer, since it describes how the characters slept and states that Bilbo saw the eyes on his turn to watch. B is incorrect because the action seems to occur while Bilbo is sleeping in the group. C omits that the characters slept crowded together. D is incorrect because it suggests that the pairs of yellow or green eyes belong to those who were sleeping.*

9. **D** *is correct. The eyes are creepy. They are described in line 42 as "terrifying" and in line 43 as "horrible" and "bulbous." These negative adjectives cancel out the possibility of the positive moods described in A, B, and C.*

8. Which is the best way to paraphrase the sentence that starts in line 37 and ends in line 41?

   A They slept crowded together, and when it was Bilbo's turn to watch, he could see pairs of yellow or red or green eyes staring at him.

   B They slept crowded together, and yellow or red or green eyes stared at Bilbo, then faded and shone out again elsewhere.

   C When it was Bilbo's turn, pairs of yellow or red or green eyes stared at him.

   D When they slept crowded together, pairs of yellow or red or green eyes stared at Bilbo.

9. The image of the eyes in lines 38–44 creates a mood of

   A eager expectation

   B admiration for their beauty

   C curiosity and interest

   D fear and anxiety

10. From the details about strange noises, extraordinarily thick cobwebs, and watching eyes, you can infer that

    A the travelers are looking for trouble

    B other travelers are lost in the forest

    C strange creatures are watching the travelers

    D the forest is a very noisy place

11. Which image in lines 45–52 best describes the bats?

    A dark-grey and black

    B flapping and whirring

    C black as a top-hat

    D as big as your hand

12. Which is the best way to paraphrase lines 60–63?

    A When they were nearly out of drinking water, their path was blocked by a stream that looked black.

    B A stream that flowed fast and looked dark reminded the travelers of how thirsty they were.

    C Fast-running water blocked their path when they were nearly out of drinking water.

    D The thirsty travelers were nearly out of water when a fast-running black stream blocked their path.

Written Response

SHORT RESPONSE
Write three or four sentences to answer each question.

13. Identify four sensory details in lines 45–59 and tell what sense each appeals to.

14. Why was night the most difficult time for the travelers? Support your response with details from the story.

EXTENDED RESPONSE
Write two to three paragraphs to answer the following question.

15. Describe some problems the characters face in this passage. Explain how the setting causes each problem.

 **GO ON**

---

10. **C is correct.** *The eyes suggest witnesses; the noises suggest another presence; the cobwebs suggest activity by others.* A *is incorrect because the travelers seem only to hide, listen, and fear rather than to take action themselves.* B *is incorrect because details and clues do not suggest other travelers.* D *is incorrect because the noises are little, furtive noises of sneaking about rather than loud noises.*

11. **C is correct.** *These words follow* bats *in line 51 and modify the word.* A, B, *and* D *are incorrect because these words describe the moths in line 49.*

12. **D is correct.** D *is the best answer, since it includes the concepts of thirst, lack of water, and the black stream.* A *is incorrect because it omits the thirst;* B *is incorrect because it omits the lack of water and the blackness of the stream;* C *is incorrect because it omits the thirst and the blackness of the stream.*

Written Response

Possible short responses:

13. *Watch-fires appeal to the senses of sight and touch (due to heat they generate). The description of "hundreds of eyes" appeals to the sense of sight; of "flapping and whirring" moths, to the senses of sight and sound; and of squirrels "horrible to taste," to the sense of taste.*

14. *The night is so dark that the characters cannot see anything but frightening eyes. They also cannot make a fire, because it would attract creatures such as moths and bats.*

Possible extended response:

15. *The characters run short of food and water because the forest is vast and it takes them a long time to get through it. They are hungry, but they cannot eat the horrible-tasting squirrels. They are thirsty, but they have been warned not to drink from the stream. They feel threatened at all times by creatures they cannot see but whose eyes shine from the darkness.*

DIFFERENTIATED INSTRUCTION

FOR ENGLISH LEARNERS
Test-Taking Strategies: Use Active Reading Strategies

• Remind students to make notes as they read the passage.

• Because they are working backwards, students know they will be asked questions about setting, mood, conflict, and imagery. They can pay special attention to, question, and record these elements of the passage as they read.

• Model an active strategy you would use while reading the passage, such as asking yourself: Where are the characters now? What is this place like?

• Remind students that active reading strategies should also be applied to items. Model asking yourself: Do I know what this question asks? Also model mentally underscoring a word like *conflict* or *image*.

Vocabulary

1. **B is correct.** *The connotation is one of sneakiness because the creatures are barely glimpsed. The creatures are too furtive to be joyful, so we can eliminate A and C. D can be eliminated because the travelers, not the creatures, are threatened.*

2. **B is correct.** *The sense conveyed is one of unusually thick threads, the opposite of A. We can eliminate C because, while the threads may be useful, the context emphasizes thickness, and D because the context contains no clues to hopefulness.*

3. **C is correct.** *The paragraph begins with "The nights were the worst." This makes the reason for huddling in fear very clear. We can eliminate A and D because they have positive connotations and B because the travelers are being watched.*

4. **B is correct.** *The word* enormous *appears just before "uncanny darkness," suggesting an insurmountable largeness. We can eliminate A and D because the darkness is worse than just irritating or ordinary and C because the darkness is characterized as negative and terrifying.*

5. **A is correct.** *Bilbo obviously wants to see what is in the forest. The word* guess *in line 23 is also a clue. We can eliminate B because Bilbo is doing more than seeing and C because there are no context clues to support it. Bilbo is more curious than fearful, so D is also incorrect.*

6. **D is correct.** *The word* big *in line 44 is the best clue. A may appear to make sense, but it is not supported by the context. We can eliminate B and C because they are nouns, while* bulbous *is an adjective.*

7. **A is correct.** *Line 54 relates hunger with* provisions; *line 56 restates the term* provisions *as "food." We can eliminate B and C because line 54 describes provisions as something to be careful with. D relates to hunting, not eating.*

8. **C is correct.** *The skins can be emptied and filled, so they are containers. We can eliminate A, B, and D because, although they may hold water for a moment, they cannot be filled.*

Vocabulary

DIRECTIONS *Use your knowledge of connotation and denotation to answer the following questions. The line numbers will help you find the words in the excerpt from* The Hobbit.

1. The denotation of *scuttling* in line 16 is "running hastily." Which word below best describes its connotation?

   A jumping with joy

   B sneaking

   C celebrating

   D escaping

2. What connotation does *extraordinarily* have in line 20?

   A typically

   B surprisingly

   C usefully

   D hopefully

3. The author used the word *huddled* in line 37 with a connotation of

   A coziness

   B privacy

   C fear

   D warmth

4. What connotation does *enormous* have in line 52?

   A irritating

   B overwhelming

   C generous

   D ordinary

DIRECTIONS *Use context clues to answer the following questions. The line numbers will help you find the words in the excerpt from* The Hobbit.

5. Use context clues in lines 14–23 to decide what *inquisitive* means.

   A curious

   B far-seeing

   C pale

   D fearful

6. Which words give you a clue to the meaning of *bulbous* in line 43?

   A horrible pale

   B insect eyes

   C animal eyes

   D much too big

7. Which context clues help you figure out the meaning of *provisions* in line 54?

   A hungry, food

   B ages, days

   C always, same

   D shooting, arrows

8. Use context clues to figure out the meaning of *skins* in line 65.

   A fur coats

   B hands

   C containers

   D membranes

DIFFERENTIATED INSTRUCTION

FOR ENGLISH LEARNERS

Review Academic Vocabulary Write the academic vocabulary listed in italics below. Give examples or definitions in random order, and have students match them with the correct term. Have students supply additional examples.

- *setting:* an empty classroom at dawn
- *imagery:* the soft crunch of dead brown leaves underfoot
- *conflict:* people battling against a fierce storm
- *mood:* an atmosphere of joy and celebration
- *paraphrase:* replacing "All this went on for what seemed to the hobbit to be ages and ages" with "It went on for a long time."

Writing & Grammar

DIRECTIONS *Read the passage and answer the questions that follow.*

> (1) It was crowded at the 54th Street park. (2) Many different activities were in progress. (3) People are racing models. (4) People are playing chess. (5) People are jogging. (6) A group was playing bocce, a game brought over from Italy many years ago. (7) Grace brings her collie, Jake, to the park. (8) She throws sticks for him to fetch. (9) The dog ran circles around Grace. (10) Jake runs over to the bocce game. (11) He grabs the ball in his mouth. (12) He takes off.

1. To change sentences 1 and 2 to the present tense, which words need to be replaced?

   A crowded, activities

   B It, were

   C was, were

   D park, activities

2. Choose the correct way to rewrite sentences 3–5, using a compound predicate.

   A People are racing models. They are playing chess. People are jogging.

   B People are racing models. People are playing chess. Some are jogging.

   C People are racing models, playing chess, and jogging.

   D People are racing models; people are playing chess; people are jogging.

3. How would you change sentence 6 to the present tense?

   A Change "was" to "is."

   B Change "was playing" to "played."

   C Change "brought" to "that was brought."

   D Change "many years ago" to "recently."

4. Choose the correct way to rewrite sentences 7 and 8, using a compound predicate.

   A Grace brings her collie, Jake, to the park; she throws sticks for him to fetch.

   B Grace brings her collie, Jake, to the park and throws sticks for him to fetch.

   C Grace brings her collie, Jake, to the park, where she throws sticks for him to fetch.

   D Grace brings her collie, Jake, to throw sticks for him to fetch.

5. Choose the correct way to write sentence 9 in the present tense.

   A The dog has run circles around Grace.

   B The dog runs circles around Grace.

   C The dog will run circles around Grace.

   D The dog was running circles around Grace.

6. Choose the correct way to rewrite sentences 10–12, using a compound predicate.

   A Jake runs over to the bocce game. Jake grabs the ball in his mouth. He takes off.

   B Jake runs over to the bocce game, grabs the ball in his mouth, and takes off.

   C Jake runs over to the bocce game. Grabbing the ball in his mouth, he takes off.

   D Jake runs over to the bocce game. He grabs the ball in his mouth before taking off.

STOP

ANSWERS

Writing & Grammar

1. C is correct. *Replacing the past-tense verbs* was *and* were *will change the sentence to the present tense.* A *is incorrect since* crowded *is an adjective, and* kinds *is a noun.* B *is incorrect since* it *is a pronoun.* D *is incorrect since both words are nouns.*

2. C is correct. *The compound predicate is "racing models, playing chess, and jogging."* A *and* B *contain only simple predicates.* D *is a compound sentence.*

3. A is correct. *Replacing the past-tense verb* was *with the present-tense verb* is *will change the sentence to the present tense.* B, C, *and* D *are incorrect since the tense of the sentence will not change.*

4. B is correct. B *contains the compound predicate "brings her collie . . . and throws sticks."* A, C, *and* D *are incorrect since none of these contains a compound predicate.*

5. B is correct. *Only* B *is written in the present tense.* A *uses the present perfect tense;* C *uses the future tense; and* D *uses the progressive form of the past tense.*

6. B is correct. B *contains the compound predicate "runs over to the bocce game, grabs the ball . . . , and takes off."* A, B, *and* D *are incorrect since none of the sentences contains a compound predicate.*

FOR ENGLISH LEARNERS

Assessment Support: Present Tense and Compound Predicates Review grammatical terms and provide practice.

- Have students change the past-tense verbs in these sentences to the present tense:
  Our heroes walked in single file. (*walk*)
  Creatures were in the woods. (*are*)

- Have students identify the compound predicate in each of these sentences:
  The small creatures watched and waited. (*watched and waited*)
  They stirred the fires, told scary stories; then dozed in the darkness. (*stirred the fires, told scary stories, then dozed in the darkness*)

INTRODUCE *GREAT READS*

In Unit 3, students have discussed a number of big questions. Invite students to tell which question they found most intriguing and why, and then focus attention on the three that appear on this page. Discuss the recommended books and their summaries, pointing out how each connects to the related question. Encourage students to choose one or more of these "great reads" to read independently.

ⓘ ClassZone.com

To find additional books that match students' interest and ability levels, visit the Literature Center at **ClassZone.com.**

Ideas for Independent Reading

Are there different kinds of adventure? Does seeking revenge lead to justice? Consider these questions when you read these works.

What do you look for in a friend?

The Moves Make the Man
by Bruce Brooks

"Jayfox," the only black student in his school, loves basketball. Bix, a white student, worships baseball. The two meet in a home ec class where each is learning to cook because his mother is ill.

The Friends
by Rosa Guy

When Phyllisia arrives in New York City from the West Indies, her classmates ridicule her. Only Edith tries to befriend her, but Phyllisia is not interested. Eventually, tragedies in her family change Phyllisia's mind about the meaning of friendship.

Sula
by Toni Morrison

Sula and Nel, both black and poor, meet as young girls in an Ohio town. For years they share everything, until life separates them. They meet years later to renew their friendship and heal old wounds.

Is revenge ever justified?

In the Middle of the Night
by Robert Cormier

Denny's father was the usher when a theater tragedy killed many children. His family endures hate mail and threats. When Denny answers the phone one night, a survivor initiates a plot for revenge, using Denny himself.

Hamlet
by William Shakespeare

Shakespeare's dramatic classic describes the agony of Hamlet, the prince of Denmark, as he determines how best to revenge his father's murder at the hands of his uncle.

One Flew over the Cuckoo's Nest
by Ken Kesey

McMurphy never intends to end up in a mental health ward. Once there, he organizes the inmates to resist the cruel Nurse Ratched. His plan for revenge against her humiliations has tragic consequences.

Where do you find adventure?

The Call of the Wild
by Jack London

London's classic novel tells the story of Buck, a domesticated dog stolen from his home and made to work as a sled dog during the Alaskan gold rush.

The Last Unicorn
by Peter Beagle

Beagle's classic fantasy tells of a lonely unicorn who searches for more of her own kind. She's aided in her thrilling and dangerous adventure by the totally incompetent magician Schmendrick, along with Molly Grue, a human girl.

The Birthday Boys
by Beryl Bainbridge

This historical novel is based on the diaries of five explorers, led by Robert Falcon Scott, who tried to be the first to reach the South Pole. They were beaten to the pole, and bad weather and poor planning led to the deaths on their way back to base camp.

Getting the Message

THEME AND SYMBOL

- In Fiction
- In Nonfiction
- In Poetry
- Across Genres

399

For help in planning this unit, see

 RESOURCE MANAGER UNIT 4
pp. 1–11

INTRODUCE THE UNIT

If you want to share a message, you might make a speech, whisper a few words, or send a note by e-mail. Ask students to name some messages that might be conveyed in these ways. Point out that artists share messages, too, through the visual images that they create.

Invite students to consider how the painting and the photograph on this page convey a similar message. To elicit ideas, ask:

- How are the figures in the painting and the photograph similar?
- How are the mother figures different?
- What message do you get when you look at each image separately?
- How does the message change when you look at the images together?

Point out that looking for a message in an image is similar to looking for a message in a story, poem, or other piece of writing. A reader notices an overall effect and then reads carefully for details. Tell students that the overriding message of a piece of writing is called a **theme.** In this unit, students will consider the theme of each selection by looking for details and synthesizing the overall idea of each selection. The better they understand a theme, the more they will appreciate the writing that expresses it.

About the Art April Harrison's *Mama's Cradle* focuses on the warmth and comfort of family love. For more information on Harrison and her work, see page 460.

Dorothea Lange's 1936 photograph, known as "Migrant Mother," shows a destitute mother of seven children in California.

UNIT 4

Skills Trace

SKILLS STRAND	Literary Analysis Workshop: Theme and Symbol pp. 402–407	Linked selections		The Scarlet Ibis pp. 426–445	Math and After Math pp. 446–457
		Marigolds pp. 408–421 — Short Story Level: Average	Sowing Change pp. 422–425 — Newspaper Article Level: Easy	Short Story Level: Average	Essay Level: Average
Literary Analysis	Theme, Universal Themes, and Symbol pp. 402–407	Theme and Setting pp. 409, 410, 414, 415, 417, 418, 420		Symbol pp. 427, 430, 439, 440, 443 Review: Mood pp. 428, 443 Review: Theme pp. 432, 443	
Reading and Informational Texts	Analyze the Literature pp. 403, 405–407	Draw Conclusions pp. 409, 412, 413, 416, 417, 419, 420 Review: Paraphrase p. 419	Outline pp. 422, 423, 424, 425 Analyze Ideas p. 425	Make Inferences About Characters pp. 427, 428, 430, 432, 433, 434, 437, 441, 443 Read a Poem p. 442	Implied Main Idea pp. 447, 451, 452, 454, 455, 456 Analyze a Sequence of Events pp. 447, 450, 452, 456
Vocabulary	Academic Vocabulary p. 402	Word Acquisition pp. 409, T409, 421 Context Clues p. T409 Suffixes (-or) p. 421		Word Acquisition pp. 427, T427, 444 Context Clues p. T427 Connotation p. 444	Word Acquisition pp. 447, T447, 457 Word Maps p. T447 Context Clues p. 457
Writing, Grammar, and Style				Variety in Sentence Structures pp. 434, 445 Independent and Subordinate Clauses pp. 434, 445	
Speaking, Listening, Viewing, and Media	Discuss pp. T402–T404	Discuss pp. 408, T410–T419, 420 Analyze Visuals pp. 410, 415, T418	Discuss pp. 422, 425	Discuss pp. 426, T428–T442, 443 Analyze Visuals pp. 428, T431, T435, 436, T438, T442	Discuss pp. 446, T451–T455, 456 Analyze Visuals pp. 448, T450, T453

Assessment-Based Planning: Skills in red are assessed on the Unit 4 Test. **T** = Teacher's Edition page

The Future in My Arms pp. 458–465 Essay *Level: Average*	Poem On Returning to Dwell in the Country/My Heart Leaps Up/The Sun pp. 466–471 Poems *Level: Challenging*	Two Kinds/Rice and Rose Bowl Blues pp. 472–489 Short Story/Poem *Level: Average*	Writing Workshop: Literary Analysis pp. 490–497
Author's Perspective pp. 459, 460, 462, 464	Universal Theme pp. 467, 469, 470, 471	Theme Across Genres pp. 473, 474, 476, 477, 478, 480, 481, 483, 486, 487	
Monitor pp. 459, 460, 462, 464	Strategies for Reading Poetry for Theme pp. 467, 468, 470, 471	Set a Purpose for Reading p. 473 Compare Theme Across Genres pp. 487, 489 Review: Draw Conclusions pp. 480, 485	Analyze a Literary Analysis pp. 491–492, 496
		Word Acquisition pp. 473, T473, 488 Context Clues p. T473 Word Origins (Eponyms) p. 488	
Rhetorical Questions pp. 462, 465		Write for Assessment p. 489	Write a Literary Analysis pp. 490–497 Variety in Sentence Structures pp. 492, 495 Punctuation of Quotations p. 496
Discuss pp. 458, T460–T463, 464 Analyze Visuals pp. 460, T463	Discuss pp. 466, T468–T470, 471 Analyze Visuals pp. T468, T469	Discuss pp. 472, T479, T482, T484, 487 Analyze Visuals pp. 474, T478, T481, T484, T486	Discuss pp. T490–T492 Participate in a Panel Discussion p. 497

Skills Assessed on the Unit 4 Test:

Literary Analysis
- Identify and analyze theme
- Analyze theme across genre
- Identify and interpret a symbol
- Analyze how symbols convey meaning and develop theme

Reading and Informational Texts
- Identify an implied main idea
- Identify and analyze a sequence of events
- Outline a text
- Analyze ideas

Vocabulary
- Use context clues to unlock word meaning
- Use knowledge of suffixes to understand words

Writing, Grammar, and Style
- Write a literary analysis
- Add rhetorical questions for effect
- Vary sentence structure
- Use correct grammar and usage
- Additional writing and grammar skills

For additional lesson planning help, see **Easy Planner DVD.**

OBJECTIVES

- establish prior knowledge about timeless messages and **themes**
- discuss the **themes** of familiar stories

What MESSAGES *are timeless?*

Introduce the page by reading the first paragraph. Explain that a theme is expressed most accurately as a sentence rather than as a single word such as *loyalty* or *patriotism*. To extend discussion of timeless messages, have students look carefully at the image of the eagle and the flag. Offer this example of the message, or theme of this image:

> Being like the eagle—proud, alert, and fiercely determined—will help a person handle any situation.

Discuss students' responses to this theme and suggestions for alternate themes.

ACTIVITY Suggest that students name books and movies that will be familiar to other students. As students compare their lists, ask them to name a **theme** or message that they noticed in their selections. Explain that time-less themes may occur in very different stories.

CHECK UNDERSTANDING After compiling the group list, ask volunteers to identify **themes** that they feel are timeless.

Unit Resources

What MESSAGES *are timeless?*

"Beauty is in the eye of the beholder." "Love conquers all." These statements may have been communicated to you by family, friends, teachers, or others who wanted to send you messages about life and human nature. Those messages, called **themes** when they appear in works of fiction or movies, are often expressed in similar ways by writers across different cultures or time periods.

ACTIVITY Think about three or four of your favorite books or movies. For each, write down the theme that you think the author or director was trying to express. Consider the following questions:

- Does the book or movie have something to say about the way people behave under particular circumstances?
- Does the book or movie teach something about an abstract concept, such as war, love, or friendship?
- Does the book or movie try to convince you to act in a specific way?

Get together with your classmates to see how many of your listed items have similar themes. Make a group list of titles that are good examples of a particular theme.

400

R RESOURCE MANAGER UNIT 4	Easy Planner DVD	eEdition CD & Online	
BEST PRACTICES TOOLKIT	WriteSmart CD	McDougal Littell Assessment System	
S STANDARDS LESSON FILE	ClassZone.com	Test Generator CD	
	Audio Anthology CD	MediaSmart DVD	
	Multi-Language Academic Vocabulary Online		

400

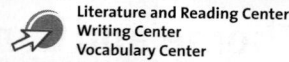

Preview Unit Goals

LITERARY ANALYSIS	• Identify and analyze a theme; analyze a theme across genres
	• Compare and contrast universal themes
	• Identify and interpret a symbol and how it conveys meaning
	• Identify an author's perspective
READING	• Use reading strategies, including monitoring
	• Make inferences and draw conclusions
	• Identify an implied main idea
	• Outline a text and analyze key ideas
WRITING AND GRAMMAR	• Write a literary analysis
	• Develop ideas logically and support them with evidence
	• Use rhetorical questions for effect
	• Use independent clauses and subordinate clauses
SPEAKING, LISTENING, AND VIEWING	• Participate in a panel discussion
VOCABULARY	• Use context clues to unlock meaning
	• Use suffixes to understand the meanings of words
	• Understand and use the connotative meanings of words
ACADEMIC VOCABULARY	• context clues • symbol
	• compare and contrast • theme
	• outline and analyze ideas

Preview Unit Goals

The goals on this page highlight the main concepts that will be covered in the unit. Encourage students to skim the list as they prepare for the unit. Remind students that the color-coded skill strand will be repeated throughout the unit.

Have students record the Academic Vocabulary terms in their journals, with a preliminary definition for each term. Urge students to confirm and perhaps refine the definitions as they read and discuss or write about the selections in the unit.

ADDITIONAL UNIT GOALS

These skills will be taught in this unit but are not the major focus of the unit:

Literary Analysis
• Identify and analyze setting
• Genre study: short story, poetry, newspaper article, nonfiction text

Reading
• Set a purpose for reading
• Identify and analyze sequence of events
• Analyze ideas
• Skim and scan a text

Writing and Grammar
• Vary sentence structure

401

DIFFERENTIATED INSTRUCTION

FOR ENGLISH LEARNERS

Academic Vocabulary Use the copy master to help students learn the Academic Vocabulary listed on this page.

1. Read aloud each term. Have students find it on their copy master.

2. Discuss the meanings or examples shown, and complete the chart as a class.

3. Have students work in small groups to complete the remaining activities.

Additional Academic Vocabulary Use the copy master to help students learn academic words they will use in subsequent lessons and on the Assessment Practice. Follow the same procedure as for the Academic Vocabulary copy master.

 RESOURCE MANAGER—Copy Masters
Academic Vocabulary p. 9
Additional Academic Vocabulary p. 10

Focus and Motivate

OBJECTIVES

- identify and analyze theme
- identify and interpret symbol
- analyze how symbols develop theme

Teach

Part 1: Big Ideas in Literature

Universal Themes Explain to students that universal themes are based on experiences and feelings that everyone goes through. Ask them to name some feelings, such as love, hate, happiness, sadness, and loss, that everyone understands. Use the following activity to reinforce the concept of universal themes:

1. Have small groups choose one of the universal themes in the box on page 402 or identify a new one.

2. Ask each group to list at least two stories or movies that share the theme.

3. Have each group write its theme in the center circle of a web and examples in adjoining circles.

4. Guide a discussion of the groups' webs.

Symbols Explain that objects, places, and events in stories are often used as symbols to stand for something else. However, students should be careful not to over-interpret such details. For example, a rainstorm may symbolize sadness, or it may simply be a rainstorm. Have small groups revisit the universal themes they placed in their word webs. Ask each group to identify a color, an object, and an event that might be used as symbols to convey their themes.

 BEST PRACTICES TOOLKIT—Transparency
Analysis Frame: Theme pp. D21, D32

Theme and Symbol

A dramatic plot, heart-pounding action, intriguing characters—one or all of these elements may play a part in capturing, and holding, your interest in a story. Often, though, stories resonate most when they provide insights into life or human nature. The meaning behind a story is the **theme,** the underlying message or big idea that the writer wants you to remember. Understanding this message and the writer's view of the world is the payoff you'll earn for reading carefully.

Part 1: Big Ideas in Literature

Many themes deal with emotions and experiences that are common across virtually all time periods and cultures. These **universal themes** show up again and again in literature—from ancient stories to today's bestsellers.

EXAMPLES OF UNIVERSAL THEMES

- People can learn from the mistakes and triumphs of past generations.
- Family can be a source of strength in challenging times.
- When it comes to war, there are no winners.
- Difficult choices are part of growing up.
- Revenge doesn't pay.
- Love binds people together.

A writer can use virtually every element of a story—characters, plot, and setting—to develop a theme. To convey a theme about the challenges of growing up, for example, a writer might craft a story about an insecure teenager who is plagued by difficult choices. As the character struggles to resolve the conflicts, he or she may learn a lesson about life.

A writer may also reinforce theme through the use of symbols. A **symbol** is a person, place, object, or activity that stands for something beyond itself. In the same story about the doubt-ridden teenager, a writer may use the following symbols to communicate the theme without having to directly state it:

- a fork in the road (an important decision)
- the color red (a character's anger at the world)
- a torrential rainstorm (an emotional upheaval)

DIFFERENTIATED INSTRUCTION

For general guidelines on differentiating instruction, see

 BEST PRACTICES TOOLKIT
Differentiated Instruction pp. 31–38

FOR LESS–PROFICIENT READERS

Note Taking For students who need help with note taking, hand out the note-taking copy master before reading the first paragraphs. Then read them aloud. As you discuss theme, have students record a definition for *theme* on the copy master. Continue with the rest of the page, giving students time to record definitions and examples.

 RESOURCE MANAGER—Copy Master
Note Taking p. 15

MODEL: THEME AND SYMBOL

Some symbols, like the ivy leaf in this story, are hard *not* to notice. The story is about Johnsy and Sue, two artists who become friends while living in New York City. When Johnsy becomes sick with pneumonia, she sinks into a deep depression. How does the symbol help you to understand Johnsy's emotions?

> # from The Last Leaf
> ### Short story by **O. Henry**
>
> "Couldn't you draw in the other room?" asked Johnsy, coldly.
>
> "I'd rather be here by you," said Sue. "Besides, I don't want you to keep looking at those silly ivy leaves."
>
> "Tell me as soon as you have finished," said Johnsy, closing her eyes, and
> 5 lying white and still as a fallen statue, "because I want to see the last one fall. I'm tired of waiting. I'm tired of thinking. I want to turn loose my hold on everything, and go sailing down, down, just like one of those poor, tired leaves." . . .
>
> When Sue awoke from an hour's sleep the next morning she found Johnsy
> 10 with dull, wide-open eyes staring at the drawn green shade.
>
> "Pull it up; I want to see," she ordered, in a whisper.
>
> Wearily Sue obeyed.
>
> But, lo! after the beating rain and fierce gusts of wind that had endured through the livelong night, there yet stood out against the brick wall one ivy
> 15 leaf. It was the last on the vine. Still dark green near its stem, but with its serrated edges tinted with the yellow of dissolution and decay, it hung bravely from a branch some twenty feet above the ground.
>
> "It is the last one," said Johnsy. "I thought it would surely fall during the night. I heard the wind. It will fall to-day, and I shall die at the same time." . . .
>
> 20 The day wore away, and even through the twilight they could see the lone ivy leaf clinging to its stem against the wall. And then, with the coming of the night the north wind was again loosed, while the rain still beat against the windows and pattered down from the low Dutch eaves.
>
> When it was light enough Johnsy, the merciless, commanded that the shade
> 25 be raised.
>
> The ivy leaf was still there.
>
> Johnsy lay for a long time looking at it. And then she called to Sue, who was stirring her chicken broth over the gas stove.
>
> "I've been a bad girl, Sudie," said Johnsy. "Something has made that last leaf
> 30 stay there to show me how wicked I was. It is a sin to want to die."

Close Read

1. Reread lines 4–8. How do the ivy leaves symbolize Johnsy and her feelings about life?

2. Examine the boxed description of the last leaf. Which words or phrases might also be used to describe Johnsy? Explain.

3. The theme is revealed in lines 29–30. Explain what the writer is saying about how people should view life. How does the symbol help to convey the theme?

MODEL: THEME AND SYMBOL
Close Read

1. *Possible answer:* Johnsy is waiting to die, and she sees herself as a "tired" leaf ready to fall down.

2. *Possible answer:* "Yellow of dissolution and decay" (line 16) might apply to Johnsy because she is sick. Also, the last leaf is "still dark green near its stem" (line 15), which is evidence of some life. Johnsy also has some life left in her, despite her wanting to die. And, "it hung bravely" (line 16) might also apply to Johnsy, who seems as if she is hanging on to life by a thread.

3. *Possible answer:* The theme of the story is that people should never give up on life. According to Johnsy, it is a sin to want to die. The last leaf, symbolizing life (no matter how fragile), helps to show Johnsy the error of her ways and helps to communicate the theme as well.

FOR LESS-PROFICIENT READERS

Language Support: Vocabulary Use Word Squares to provide instruction and practice for these words: "serrated" (line 16), "dissolution" (line 16), "twilight" (line 20), and "merciless" (line 24).

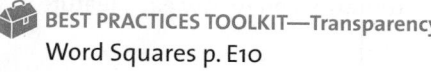 **BEST PRACTICES TOOLKIT—Transparency**
Word Squares p. E10

FOR ADVANCED LEARNERS/PRE-AP

Analyze Symbols Have students reread lines 13–17. Ask them what the "beating rain" and "fierce gusts of wind" might stand for (*life's hardships*). Ask students to suggest other symbols for the hardships of life.

Part 2: Identify Theme

Theme Point out that the theme of a story is like a lesson that the author is trying to teach. Show students how to use a story's topic to determine and evaluate its theme. To find the topic, students should answer in a word or phrase, "What is the story about?" (You might provide an example of a topic such as "growing up.") After determining the topic of the story, students should ask, "What is the writer trying to teach about the topic?" The answer to this question is often the story's theme. ("Learning to take responsibility for one's actions is part of growing up.") To evaluate the theme, students can ask, "How was the author successful in addressing the theme?"

Clues to Theme Students can use story elements as clues to figure out theme. They can also use story elements to evaluate their preliminary ideas about theme. They might assess whether an idea about theme is on target by answering these questions:

- How does the title relate to this theme?
- How do the story conflicts support it?
- How do the characters' actions or statements hint at the theme?
- How does the setting support it?
- Which symbols support the theme?

CHECK UNDERSTANDING

Have students explain **theme** in their own words.

Part 2: Identify Theme

Writers rarely state a story's theme directly. More often, the theme is implied. You have to analyze the layers of clues—for example, the characters and the conflicts—to see what they reveal about the theme. As you try to uncover the theme of a story, keep these guidelines in mind:

- The theme is not the subject of a story; it is what a story means. Love is a subject or topic. A theme is the writer's insight or idea about love, such as "Love may come when you least expect it."
- You can summarize a story's message by writing a theme statement. Use one or two complete sentences, not single words or phrases.
- Some works of literature have more than one theme, but in short stories, usually one theme stands out.

CLUES TO THEME

TITLE
The title may reflect a story's subject or a significant idea. Ask
- What in the story does the title refer to?
- Does the title have more than one meaning?
- What ideas does the title highlight?

CHARACTERS
Characters can reflect theme by what they do or say. Ask
- What do the main character's thoughts and actions reveal about him or her?
- How does the main character change?
- What lessons does the character learn?

PLOT AND CONFLICT
A story revolves around conflicts that are central to the theme. Ask
- What conflicts do the characters face?
- How are the conflicts resolved?
- Is the resolution portrayed positively or negatively?

SETTING
Setting can convey theme because of what it means to the characters and readers. Ask
- How does the setting affect the characters and the plot?
- What might the setting represent?

IMPORTANT STATEMENTS
The narrator or the characters may make statements that hint at the theme. Ask
- What key statements are made by the characters or the narrator?
- What ideas do these statements emphasize?

SYMBOLS
Characters, conflicts, and settings can serve as symbols that support the theme. Ask
- What might the characters, conflicts, and setting represent?
- What ideas do these symbols communicate?

DIFFERENTIATED INSTRUCTION

FOR ENGLISH LEARNERS
Language: Skill Words On the board, list the academic vocabulary shown in italics. Then give the examples in random order for students to classify.

- *conflict:* The two students glared at each other with hate in their eyes.
- *setting:* The beach stretched for miles under a cloudless sky.
- *characters:* Alison nervously whistled her favorite song as she walked to her first job interview.

FOR LESS-PROFICIENT READERS
Note Taking Provide the note-taking copy master to students who experience difficulty with note taking. Read and discuss the top of the page. Then review the "Clues to Theme" section. Ask students to fill in the copy masters after you review each feature.

 RESOURCE MANAGER—Copy Master
Note Taking p. 16

Part 3: Analyze the Literature

This story takes place in Dublin, Ireland, during a civil war that erupted in 1922. Hidden by darkness, a sniper waits for his next target. As you read, track the clues to the theme. What message about war is the writer communicating?

The Sniper
Short story
by **Liam O'Flaherty**

The long June twilight faded into night. Dublin lay enveloped in darkness, but for the dim light of the moon, that shone through fleecy clouds, casting a pale light as of approaching dawn over the streets and the dark waters of the Liffey. Around the beleaguered Four Courts the heavy guns roared. Here and
5 there through the city machine guns and rifles broke the silence of the night, spasmodically, like dogs barking on lone farms. Republicans and Free Staters[1] were waging civil war.

On a roof-top near O'Connel Bridge, a Republican sniper lay watching. Beside him lay his rifle and over his shoulders were slung a pair of field-glasses.
10 His face was the face of a student—thin and ascetic, but his eyes had the cold gleam of the fanatic. They were deep and thoughtful, the eyes of a man who is used to looking at death.

He was eating a sandwich hungrily. He had eaten nothing since morning. He had been too excited to eat. He finished the sandwich, and taking a flask
15 of whiskey from his pocket, he took a short draught. Then he returned the flask to his pocket. He paused for a moment, considering whether he should risk a smoke. It was dangerous. The flash might be seen in the darkness and there were enemies watching. He decided to take the risk. Placing a cigarette between his lips, he struck a match, inhaled the smoke hurriedly and put out
20 the light. Almost immediately, a bullet flattened itself against the parapet[2] of the roof. The sniper took another whiff and put out the cigarette. Then he swore softly and crawled away to the left.

Cautiously he raised himself and peered over the parapet. There was a flash and a bullet whizzed over his head. He dropped immediately. He had
25 seen the flash. It came from the opposite side of the street.

He rolled over the roof to a chimney stack in the rear, and slowly drew himself up behind it, until his eyes were level with the top of the parapet. There was nothing to be seen—just the dim outline of the opposite housetop against the blue sky. His enemy was under cover.
30 Just then an armored car came across the bridge and advanced slowly up the street. It stopped on the opposite side of the street fifty yards ahead. The sniper could hear the dull panting of the motor. His heart beat faster. It was an enemy car. He wanted to fire, but he knew it was useless. His bullets would never pierce the steel that covered the grey monster.

---

1. **Republicans and Free Staters:** The Irish Republican Army (Republicans) wanted complete independence from England. The Irish Free Staters wanted Ireland to govern itself but still remain part of the British Empire.

2. **parapet:** a low wall along the edge of a roof or balcony.

Close Read

1. Which setting details in the first paragraph help convey a grim, dangerous picture of war? One detail has been boxed.

2. Reread the description of the sniper in lines 8–18. Through the character of the sniper, what might the writer be saying about soldiers who fight in wars?

Part 3: Analyze the Literature
Close Read

1. *Possible answer:* Details include "lay enveloped in darkness" (line 1), "dark waters of the Liffey" (lines 3–4), "beleaguered Four Courts" (line 4), "rifles broke the silence of the night" (line 5), and "like dogs barking on lone farms" (line 6). All these details show how war is disrupting a once-peaceful city.

2. *Possible answer:* O'Flaherty characterizes the sniper as being indifferent to death. As a risk-taker, he gets an adrenaline rush from the dangerous situations he often finds himself in. The writer describes the sniper as a "fanatic," hardly a favorable impression of soldiers who fight in wars. The writer is probably trying to emphasize the cold-blooded, indifferent nature of soldiers who have been programmed to kill.

ADDITIONAL TEACHING OPPORTUNITY

Evaluate Theme: Ask students to identify the story's **theme**—its underlying message about life or human nature. Then have students evaluate that theme and decide whether they think it is valid. Tell students to use these questions as their evaluation criteria:

- Does the theme express a broad insight into life or human nature, or simply an idea that applies only to a few people?

- Does the theme offer a meaningful insight, or is it too obvious or clichéd?

- Is the theme a realistic observation, or is it too optimistic, cynical, or narrow-minded?

Point out to students that a theme may be valid even if they do not personally agree with it. (To learn more about evaluating theme, see **Reading Handbook,** page R2.)

DIFFERENTIATED INSTRUCTION

FOR ADVANCED LEARNERS/PRE–AP

Analyze Title Have students discuss what ideas the title highlights. Why doesn't the author use the sniper's name in the story?

Close Read

3. *Possible answer: The sniper thinks the woman is an informer—someone who told the man in the car about the sniper's location. The sniper thought that the man was preparing to shoot him, so the sniper acted first.*

4. *Possible answer: The enemy shoots the sniper in the arm, and the sniper feels immense pain. He has to bandage his wound and continue to be discreet so that his cover is not blown.*

5. *Possible answer: By thinking about the other sniper as only "the enemy," the sniper dehumanizes his target. As a soldier, it's probably best not to think of your target as a human being.*

35   Then round the corner of a side street came an old woman, her head covered by a tattered shawl. She began to talk to the man in the turret of the car. She was pointing to the roof where the sniper lay. An informer.

The turret opened. A man's head and shoulders appeared, looking towards the sniper. The sniper raised his rifle and fired. The head fell heavily on the
40   turret wall. The woman darted toward the side street. The sniper fired again. The woman whirled round and fell with a shriek into the gutter.

Suddenly from the opposite roof a shot rang out and the sniper dropped his rifle with a curse. The rifle clattered to the roof. The sniper thought the noise would wake the dead. He stopped to pick the rifle up. He couldn't lift it. His
45   forearm was dead. . . . He muttered, "I'm hit."

Dropping flat on to the roof, he crawled back to the parapet. With his left hand he felt the injured right forearm. The blood was oozing through the sleeve of his coat. There was no pain—just a deadened sensation, as if the arm had been cut off.
50   Quickly he drew his knife from his pocket, opened it on the breastwork of the parapet and ripped open the sleeve. There was a small hole where the bullet had entered. On the other side there was no hole. The bullet had lodged in the bone. It must have fractured it. He bent the arm below the wound. The arm bent back easily. He ground his teeth to overcome the pain.
55   Then, taking out his field dressing, he ripped open the packet with his knife. He broke the neck of the iodine bottle and let the bitter fluid drip into the wound. A paroxysm of pain swept through him. He placed the cotton wadding over the wound and wrapped the dressing over it. He tied the end with his teeth.
60   Then he lay still against the parapet, and closing his eyes, he made an effort of will to overcome the pain.

In the street beneath all was still. The armored car had retired speedily over the bridge, with the machine gunner's head hanging lifeless over the turret. The woman's corpse lay still in the gutter.
65   The sniper lay for a long time nursing his wounded arm and planning escape. Morning must not find him wounded on the roof. The enemy on the opposite roof covered his escape. He must kill that enemy and he could not use his rifle. He had only a revolver to do it. Then he thought of a plan.

Taking off his cap, he placed it over the muzzle of his rifle. Then he pushed
70   the rifle slowly upwards over the parapet, until the cap was visible from the opposite side of the street. Almost immediately there was a report, and a bullet pierced the center of the cap. The sniper slanted the rifle forward. The cap slipped down into the street. Then, catching the rifle in the middle, the sniper dropped his left hand over the roof and let it hang, lifelessly. After a few
75   moments he let the rifle drop to the street. Then he sank to the roof, dragging his hand with him.

Crawling quickly to the left, he peered up at the corner of the roof. His ruse had succeeded. The other sniper seeing the cap and rifle fall, thought that

Close Read

3. Why does the sniper shoot the man in the armored car and the woman? Explain how you think the writer wants you to feel about the sniper's actions.

4. What conflicts are created by the presence of the enemy sniper?

5. Notice how the sniper refers to the other sniper only as "the enemy" in lines 65–68. In what ways might this help the sniper be effective in war?

DIFFERENTIATED INSTRUCTION

FOR LESS–PROFICIENT READERS
Concept Support To help students understand how the sniper depersonalized his enemy, ask them to suppose the sniper knew his enemy's name. Guide a discussion of their responses to the following questions:

- Would he be more likely or less likely to hate the other sniper?

- Would he be more likely or less likely to want to hurt the other sniper?

- Would he be more likely or less likely to want to kill the other sniper?

FOR ADVANCED LEARNERS/PRE–AP
Analyzing Symbols Ask students what the woman symbolizes. *Possible answer: She symbolizes all the faceless victims of war, innocent people who die simply because they are in the wrong place at the wrong time.*

he had killed his man. He was now standing before a row of chimney pots,
80 looking across, with his head clearly silhouetted against the western sky.

The Republican sniper smiled and lifted his revolver above the edge of the
parapet. The distance was about fifty yards—a hard shot in the dim light, and
his right arm was paining him. . . . He took a steady aim. His hand trembled
with eagerness. Pressing his lips together, he took a deep breath through his
85 nostrils and fired. He was almost deafened with the report and his arm shook
with the recoil.

Then, when the smoke cleared, he peered across and uttered a cry of joy.
His enemy had been hit. He was reeling over the parapet in his death
agony. He struggled to keep his feet, but he was slowly falling forward,
90 as if in a dream. The rifle fell from his grasp, hit the parapet, fell over, bounded
off the pole of a barber's shop beneath and then clattered on to the pavement.

Then the dying man on the roof crumpled up and fell forward. The body
turned over and over in space and hit the ground with a dull thud. Then it
lay still.
95 The sniper looked at his enemy falling and he shuddered. The lust of battle
died in him. He became bitten by remorse. The sweat stood out in beads on
his forehead. Weakened by his wound and the long summer day of fasting and
watching on the roof, he revolted from the sight of the shattered mass of his
dead enemy. His teeth chattered. He began to gibber to himself, cursing the
100 war, cursing himself, cursing everybody.

He looked at the smoking revolver in his hand and with an oath he hurled
it to the roof at his feet. The revolver went off with the concussion, and the
bullet whizzed past the sniper's head. He was frightened back to his senses by
the shock. His nerves steadied. The cloud of fear scattered from his mind and
105 he laughed.

Taking the whiskey flask from his pocket, he emptied it at a draught.
He felt reckless under the influence of the spirits. He decided to leave the roof
and look for his company commander to report. Everywhere around was quiet.
There was not much danger in going through the streets. He picked up his
110 revolver and put it in his pocket. Then he crawled down through the sky-light
to the house underneath.

When the sniper reached the laneway on the street level, he felt a sudden
curiosity as to the identity of the enemy sniper whom he had killed. He
decided that he was a good shot whoever he was. He wondered if he knew
115 him. Perhaps he had been in his own company before the split in the army.
He decided to risk going over to have a look at him. He peered around the
corner into O'Connell Street. In the upper part of the street there was heavy
firing, but around here all was quiet.

The sniper darted across the street. A machine gun tore up the
120 ground around him with a hail of bullets, but he escaped. He threw
himself face downwards beside the corpse. The machine gun stopped.

Then the sniper turned over the dead body and looked into his
brother's face.

Close Read

6. How does the Republican sniper resolve his conflict with the second sniper?

7. Reread the boxed text. How does the sniper change after seeing his enemy fall?

8. Which details in lines 112–116 tell you that the sniper starts to realize his fallen enemy is a human being? Explain.

9. Consider the last line of the story and the clues you noticed while reading. What is the writer saying about war? State the theme and cite details that helped you understand it.

FOR LESS–PROFICIENT READERS

Language Support: Vocabulary Have partners find and define two unfamiliar verbs from "The Sniper." Make sure they find descriptive, vivid verbs. Ask students to quickly draw a sketch showing the action of each verb. Then have them share their sketches and definitions with another pair.

Close Read

6. Possible answer: *The sniper tricks his enemy by sticking his cap on the top of his rifle. Seeing the cap and thinking it is the sniper himself, the enemy shoots his target. The sniper lets the cap fall and dangles his arm so that it looks like he's been shot. Thinking the sniper is now dead, the enemy comes out of hiding. The sniper takes aim and successfully kills his enemy.*

7. Possible answer: *After the sniper kills his enemy, he starts to develop a conscience. He is no longer interested in the rush he gets from battles and killing. Partly due to his wound and his hunger, he briefly questions the point of the war. Also, he is disgusted by the sight of the dead enemy.*

8. Possible answer: *Details revealing that the sniper sees his enemy as a human being include "sudden curiosity as to the identity," "he was a good shot," and "wondered if he knew him." These details contrast with the sniper's earlier thoughts about the "enemy." For the first time, the sniper starts thinking of his enemy as "he" and "him"—another human being.*

9. Possible answer: *War is pointless and brutal; it literally pits brother against brother. Details that help to convey this theme: the change in the sniper's character, the powerful last line, the details about the dangerous setting.*

Assess and Reteach

Assess

Have students explain how the theme of "The Sniper" is revealed through the conflicts, characters, and setting.

Reteach

Select from these reteaching options to help students who experienced difficulty applying the workshop skills to "The Sniper":

1. Review the note-taking copy masters. Have students define terms and explain how each story feature gives clues to the theme.

2. Ask students to name a familiar story and to suggest ideas for its theme. Have them discuss how the story's conflicts, characters, setting, and symbols support the theme they suggested.

Focus and Motivate

OBJECTIVES

Literary Analysis
- explore the key idea of **regret**
- identify and analyze theme and setting
- read a short story

Reading
- draw conclusions

Vocabulary
- build vocabulary for reading and writing
- use knowledge of the suffix *-or* to help unlock meaning *(also an EL language objective)*

SUMMARY

In "Marigolds," Eugenia Collier tells of a summertime incident through which 14-year-old Lizabeth begins to think like an adult. Lizabeth lives in an impoverished Maryland town during the Depression. Her family's difficulties frustrate and frighten her. Ultimately, Lizabeth vents her stress by destroying elderly Miss Lottie's cherished marigold garden. Years later, Lizabeth still regrets the act; through it, however, she has learned a life lesson about compassion.

What if life had a RESET *button?*

Ask the question and have students read the **KEY IDEA** paragraph. Explore the **KEY IDEA** by asking students what kinds of words and behaviors people often **regret**. Invite students to incorporate their answers into the **QUICK-WRITE,** but allow them to keep their responses private.

Selection Resources

Marigolds
Short Story by Eugenia Collier

What if life had a RESET *button?*

KEY IDEA It's a terrible thing to drop your grandmother's prized china vase on the kitchen floor or to put your foot in your mouth in front of the cute new girl or boy in your class. And did you really have to be so mean to your little brother yesterday? At one time or another, we've all done or said something that makes us cringe with **regret.** We wish we could turn back the clock by a minute or a day and just do the whole thing over.

QUICKWRITE Think of something you wish you'd said or done differently. Write a paragraph describing the event and explain what you'd do if you were given the chance to try again.

408

RESOURCE MANAGER UNIT 4

Plan and Teach pp. 17–24

Literary Analysis
Summary pp. 25†*, 26‡*
Theme and Setting pp. 27, 28†*
Question Support p. 35*

Reading
Draw Conclusions pp. 29, 30†*
Reading Check p. 34
Reading Fluency p. 36

Vocabulary
Study p. 31*
Practice p. 32
Strategy p. 33

Assessment
Selection Tests A, B/C pp. 39*, 41*
Test Generator CD

BEST PRACTICES TOOLKIT

Differentiated Instruction
pp. 31–38*

Scaffolding Instruction
pp. 43–46*

Graphic Organizers/Strategies
Word Squares • Open Mind
• Cause-and-Effect Graphics

Reading Support
Audio Anthology CD*

Technology
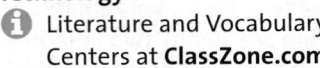 Literature and Vocabulary Centers at **ClassZone.com**
WriteSmart CD

---

* Resources for Differentiation   † Also in Spanish   ‡ In Haitian Creole and Vietnamese

LITERARY ANALYSIS: THEME AND SETTING

"Marigolds" takes place in a rural African-American community during the 1930s—a time of racial segregation, poverty, and limited opportunity. This **setting** offers important clues to the story's **theme,** or underlying message about life and human nature. For example, the description of the setting as "arid" and "sterile" hints at the hopelessness of the narrator's situation. As you read "Marigolds," think about how the details of the setting contribute to the story's meaning. How does the setting influence the narrator's childhood experiences and the conflicts she faces? What message do those experiences teach us about life?

READING SKILL: DRAW CONCLUSIONS

You remember that a **conclusion** is a logical judgment based on information in the text and on your own experience and prior knowledge. As you read "Marigolds," create a graphic organizer like the one shown. Include information from the text and your thoughts about the information. Then record your conclusions.

Text Information	+ Prior Knowledge	= Conclusion
All the narrator remembers about her hometown is the dust.	+ Most people recall pleasant memories of their past.	= She must not have many pleasant memories, or she would have remembered them.

Review: Paraphrase

▲ VOCABULARY IN CONTEXT

Collier creates a story based on her heritage with the help of the following words. See which ones you already know. Place each word in the appropriate column. Then write a brief definition of each word you are familiar with.

WORD LIST		
bravado	impotent	poignantly
degradation	nostalgia	retribution
exuberance	ostensibly	squalor
futile	perverse	stoicism

Know Well	Think I Know	Don't Know

Author Online

Respect for Education
Eugenia Collier grew up in the segregated part of Baltimore, Maryland, the city where she still lives today. From her parents, a doctor and a teacher, Collier learned the value of education at a young age. This led her to graduate with high honors from Howard University. She then received a master of arts from Columbia University.

Eugenia Collier born 1928

Award-Winning Teacher and Writer
After working for five years as a caseworker for the Baltimore Department of Public Welfare, Collier became a college professor and started her writing career. She credits her African-American heritage as her inspiration. "The fact of my blackness is the core and center of my creativity." "Marigolds," one of her first stories, won the Gwendolyn Brooks Award for fiction in 1969. Since then, her stories, poems, and essays have appeared in many anthologies and magazines. She was selected as an outstanding educator from 1972–75 and won a Distinguished Writers Award in 1984.

 MORE ABOUT THE AUTHOR For more on Eugenia Collier, visit the **Literature Center** at **ClassZone.com.**

Background
Hard Times During the Great Depression of the 1930s, millions of Americans suffered from unemployment. Government programs, such as the unemployment insurance available today, did not yet exist to help people get through the tough times. Although many Americans suffered, African Americans were particularly hard hit. In an age of racial segregation and prejudice, black people generally had fewer job opportunities and experienced higher unemployment rates.

MARIGOLDS **409**

Teach

LITERARY ANALYSIS

● THEME AND SETTING

For instructional support, read aloud this example:

> Lakeside was a town of mansions and luxury cars. Its residents spoke of wealth but never of wisdom or regret.

Discuss how the setting might be connected to a theme. ***Possible answer:*** *The setting suggests rich residents; the theme might be their materialism or arrogance.*

CHECK UNDERSTANDING Have students name settings and themes from other stories that they have read or viewed.

READING SKILL

■ DRAW CONCLUSIONS

Use **Respect for Education** and *Background* to model drawing conclusions.

- The Depression affected African Americans quite severely.
- Collier's parents were a doctor and a teacher. Doctors and teachers are less likely to be unemployed than other workers.
- Collier probably did not suffer as much as other African-American children did.

CHECK UNDERSTANDING Discuss how the **About the Author** subheads express conclusions about the text.

R RESOURCE MANAGER—Copy Master Draw Conclusions p. 29 (for student use while reading the selection)

VOCABULARY SKILL

▲ VOCABULARY IN CONTEXT

DIAGNOSE WORD KNOWLEDGE To determine preteaching needs, have all students complete Vocabulary in Context. Check students' definitions against those on the selection pages. *bravado* (p. 414), *degradation* (p. 418), *exuberance* (p. 416), *futile* (p. 410), *impotent* (p. 416), *nostalgia* (p. 410), *ostensibly* (p. 413), *perverse* (p. 414), *poignantly* (p. 412), *retribution* (p. 413), *squalor* (p. 419), *stoicism* (p. 414).

PRETEACH VOCABULARY Use the Vocabulary Study copy master to help students predict the meaning of each boldfaced word in the copy master, using context clues.

1. Read the first sentence in Part A aloud, emphasizing *bravado.*
2. Point out the word "outer" and the phrase "masked the fear." Elicit possible meanings for *bravado,* such as "false courage."
3. Have students record their ideas.
4. Repeat the procedure for items 2–12.

 **RESOURCE MANAGER—Copy Master** Vocabulary Study p. 31

For general guidelines on differentiating vocabulary instruction and for alternative vocabulary activities for students not needing vocabulary preteaching, see

BEST PRACTICES TOOLKIT Scaffolding Vocabulary Instruction pp. 43–46
ⓘ Vocabulary Center at **ClassZone.com**

ANALYZE VISUALS

Possible answer: The bright colors of the flowers create a cheerful mood. The fact that a spittoon is used as a flowerpot for the blooms also adds to the upbeat feeling.

About the Art If students have read "A Christmas Memory" in Unit 3, they already have met North Carolina artist Bob Timberlake (born 1933). Known for his realistic style, Timberlake has painted many scenes of the rural South. The bright marigolds in this painting help students envision this story's title and the description of Miss Lottie's marigolds as "a brilliant splash of sunny yellow" (lines 10–11).

LITERARY ANALYSIS

Ⓐ THEME AND SETTING

Possible answer: The author helps readers visualize the setting by describing in detail the late-summer dust (lines 1–4) and summing up the setting as "the dry September of the dirt roads and grassless yards of the shanty-town" (lines 8–9). She contrasts this setting with her town's lush lawns and shade trees (lines 5–6), which she knows must have existed but which she does not remember. She also contrasts the "arid, sterile dust" (line 2) that she does remember with the marigolds' "brilliant splash of sunny yellow" (lines 10–11).

Marigolds

Eugenia Collier

When I think of the home town of my youth, all that I seem to remember is dust—the brown, crumbly dust of late summer—arid, sterile dust that gets into the eyes and makes them water, gets into the throat and between the toes of bare brown feet. I don't know why I should remember only the dust. Surely there must have been lush green lawns and paved streets under leafy shade trees somewhere in town; but memory is an abstract painting—it does not present things as they are, but rather as they *feel*. And so, when I think of that time and that place, I remember only the dry September of the dirt roads and grassless yards of the shanty-town where I lived. And one other thing I
10 remember, another incongruency of memory—a brilliant splash of sunny yellow against the dust—Miss Lottie's marigolds. Ⓐ

Whenever the memory of those marigolds flashes across my mind, a strange **nostalgia** comes with it and remains long after the picture has faded. I feel again the chaotic emotions of adolescence, illusive as smoke, yet as real as the potted geranium before me now. Joy and rage and wild animal gladness and shame become tangled together in the multicolored skein of 14-going-on-15 as I recall that devastating moment when I was suddenly more woman than child, years ago in Miss Lottie's yard. I think of those marigolds at the strangest times; I remember them vividly now as I desperately pass away the time
20 waiting for you, who will not come.

I suppose that **futile** waiting was the sorrowful background music of our impoverished little community when I was young. The Depression that gripped the nation was no new thing to us, for the black workers of rural Maryland had always been depressed. I don't know what it was that we were waiting for; certainly not for the prosperity that was "just around the corner," for those were white folks' words, which we never believed. Nor did we wait for hard work and thrift to pay off in shining success as the American Dream[1] promised, for we knew better than that, too. Perhaps we waited for a miracle,

ANALYZE VISUALS
How would you describe the **mood** created by this painting?

❶ Targeted Passage

Ⓐ THEME AND SETTING
Identify details that help you **visualize** the setting. What contrasts are presented?

nostalgia (nŏ-stăl′jə) *n.* bittersweet longing for things from the past

futile (fyōōt′l) *adj.* having no useful result

---

1. **American Dream:** the belief that through hard work one will achieve a comfortable and prosperous life.

Full Spittoon (1974), Bob Timberlake. Watercolor. Private Collection. © Bob Timberlake.

410 UNIT 4: THEME AND SYMBOL

DIFFERENTIATED INSTRUCTION

FOR ALL STUDENTS
Journal As they read, ask students to keep a journal noting questions, observations, and reflections about characters and situations. Ask students to refer to their notes when completing other activities that accompany the selection.

FOR LESS–PROFICIENT READERS
In combination with the *Audio Anthology CD*, use one or more Targeted Passages (pp. 410, 416, 417, 419) to ensure that students focus on key story events, concepts, and skills. Targeted Passages are also good for English learners.

❶ Targeted Passage [Lines 8–24]
This passage establishes "Marigolds" as a recollection of events from the narrator's

REINFORCE *KEY IDEA:* REGRET

Discuss Which words and phrases in this paragraph suggest that the narrator feels some **regret** about the past? *Possible answer: The narrator's reference to her nostalgia as "strange" (lines 12–13) may hint at regret. The negative terms "chaotic emotions" (line 14) and "rage" (line 15) are stronger, and they lead to the most telling word: "shame" (line 16). The connection between shame and the "devastating moment" that she recalls (line 17) suggests a strong sense of regret about the past—specifically, about some past action.*

troubled adolescence.

- What time in her life is the narrator recalling? How can you tell?
- Why was her life difficult at that time?
- What details suggest that Miss Lottie and her marigolds will be important in the story that the narrator is about to tell?

FOR ENGLISH LEARNERS

Key Academic Vocabulary Use Word Squares to teach these words: *community* (line 22), *Depression* (line 22), *strategy* (line 92), *reinforce* (line 92), *exploits* (line 123), *ignorant* (line 307).

 BEST PRACTICES TOOLKIT—Transparency
Word Squares p. E10

Prereading For prereading instruction for English learners, see

BEST PRACTICES TOOLKIT
Scaffolding Reading Instruction pp. 43–46

FOR ADVANCED LEARNERS/PRE–AP

Pre-AP Exercises in the bottom channel provide additional challenge for students. Use these suggestions for small groups or individuals.

ADDITIONAL GUIDELINES

For more help with differentiation and tips for classroom management, see

 BEST PRACTICES TOOLKIT
Differentiated Instruction pp. 31–38

amorphous in concept but necessary if one were to have the grit to rise before
30 dawn each day and labor in the white man's vineyard until after dark, or to
wander about in the September dust, offering one's sweat in return for some
meager share of bread. But God was chary[2] with miracles in those days, and so
we waited—and waited.

We children, of course, were only vaguely aware of the extent of our poverty.
Having no radios, few newspapers, and no magazines, we were somewhat
unaware of the world outside our community. Nowadays we would be called
"culturally deprived" and people would write books and hold conferences
about us. In those days everybody we knew was just as hungry and ill-clad as
we were. Poverty was the cage in which we all were trapped, and our hatred
40 of it was still the vague, undirected restlessness of the zoo-bred flamingo who
knows that nature created him to fly free. **B**

As I think of those days I feel most **poignantly** the tag-end of summer, the
bright dry times when we began to have a sense of shortening days and the
imminence of the cold.

By the time I was 14 my brother Joey and I were the only children left at our
house, the older ones having left home for early marriage or the lure of the city,
and the two babies having been sent to relatives who might care for them better
than we. Joey was three years younger than I, and a boy, and therefore vastly
inferior. Each morning our mother and father trudged wearily down the dirt
50 road and around the bend, she to her domestic job, he to his daily unsuccessful
quest for work. After our few chores around the tumbledown shanty, Joey and I
were free to run wild in the sun with other children similarly situated.

For the most part, those days are ill-defined in my memory, running
together and combining like a fresh water-color painting left out in the rain.
I remember squatting in the road drawing a picture in the dust, a picture that
Joey gleefully erased with one sweep of his dirty foot. I remember fishing for
minnows in a muddy creek and watching sadly as they eluded my cupped
hands, while Joey laughed uproariously. And I remember, that year, a strange
restlessness of body and of spirit, a feeling that something old and familiar was
60 ending, and something unknown and therefore terrifying was beginning. **C**

One day returns to me with special clarity for some reason, perhaps because
it was the beginning of the experience that in some inexplicable way marked
the end of innocence. I was loafing under the great oak tree in our yard, deep
in some reverie which I have now forgotten except that it involved some secret,
secret thoughts of one of the Harris boys across the yard. Joey and a bunch of
kids were bored now with the old tire suspended from an oak limb which had
kept them entertained for a while.

"Hey, Lizabeth," Joey yelled. He never talked when he could yell. "Hey,
Lizabeth, let's us go somewhere."

---

2. **chary** (châr'ē): sparing or stingy.

B DRAW CONCLUSIONS

Possible answer: The narrator is poor, as suggested in references to the shanty-town (line 9) and to being hungry and ill-clad (line 38). Her family has suffered financially for some time, for "The Depression . . . was no new thing to us . . ." (lines 22–23). The comment that "God was chary with miracles" (line 32) and the comparison of poverty to a cage (line 39) indicate that the narrator does not expect her life to improve.

Extend the Discussion Why do you think the narrator compares her life to that of a "zoo-bred flamingo" (line 40)?

C DRAW CONCLUSIONS

Possible answer: The changes are that Lizabeth feels restless and worried that familiar things in her life are being replaced with things that are unknown and frightening. In short, Lizabeth is moving toward young adulthood.

If students need help . . . Have them reread lines 13–18 and 58–60. Model adding this information to the chart from page 409:

Text Information: Lizabeth, who is almost 15, is restless. She feels that part of her life is ending and another part is beginning.

Prior Knowledge: At 14 and 15, people are no longer children, but they are not yet adults. It can be an unsettling time.

Conclusion: Lizabeth senses that she is moving toward adulthood.

B DRAW CONCLUSIONS
Based on what you've read so far, what conclusions can you draw about the narrator's life? Cite details to support your answer.

poignantly
(poin'yənt-lē) *adv.*
in a profoundly moving manner

C DRAW CONCLUSIONS
Reread lines 58–60. Lizabeth, the narrator, is almost 15 at this point in the story. What changes are taking place in her life?

DIFFERENTIATED INSTRUCTION

FOR ENGLISH LEARNERS
Language: Pronoun Referents Explain the usage of *one* in lines 28–32. There, *one* is the formal equivalent of the informal *you* or the impersonal *someone*. Reinforce the concept by discussing the use of *one* and *one's* in lines 307–308.

FOR ADVANCED LEARNERS/PRE–AP
Analyze Figurative Language [paired-activity option] Eugenia Collier uses two linked metaphors in this statement: "Poverty was the cage in which we all were trapped, and our hatred of it was still the vague, undirected restlessness of the zoo-bred flamingo who knows that nature created him to fly free" (lines 39–41). Have students analyze the metaphors and explain why the metaphors are effective.

70　I came reluctantly from my private world. "Where you want to go? What you want to do?"

　　The truth was that we were becoming tired of the formlessness of our summer days. The idleness whose prospect had seemed so beautiful during the busy days of spring now had degenerated to an almost desperate effort to fill up the empty midday hours.

　　"Let's go see can we find some locusts on the hill," someone suggested.

　　Joey was scornful. "Ain't no more locusts there. Y'all got 'em all while they was still green."

　　The argument that followed was brief and not really worth the effort.

80　Hunting locust trees wasn't fun any more by now.

　　"Tell you what," said Joey finally, his eyes sparkling. "Let's go over to Miss Lottie's."

　　The idea caught on at once, for annoying Miss Lottie was always fun. I was still child enough to scamper along with the group over rickety fences and through bushes that tore our already raggedy clothes, back to where Miss Lottie lived. I think now that we must have made a tragicomic spectacle, five or six kids of different ages, each of us clad in only one garment—the girls in faded dresses that were too long or too short, the boys in patchy pants, their sweaty brown chests gleaming in the hot sun. A little cloud of dust followed

90　our thin legs and bare feet as we tramped over the barren land.

　　When Miss Lottie's house came into view we stopped, **ostensibly** to plan our strategy, but actually to reinforce our courage. Miss Lottie's house was the most ramshackle of all our ramshackle homes. The sun and rain had long since faded its rickety frame siding from white to a sullen gray. The boards themselves seemed to remain upright not from being nailed together but rather from leaning together like a house that a child might have constructed from cards. A brisk wind might have blown it down, and the fact that it was still standing implied a kind of enchantment that was stronger than the elements. There it stood, and as far as I know is standing yet—a gray rotting thing with

100　no porch, no shutters, no steps, set on a cramped lot with no grass, not even any weeds—a monument to decay. **D**

　　In front of the house in a squeaky rocking chair sat Miss Lottie's son, John Burke, completing the impression of decay. John Burke was what was known as "queer-headed." Black and ageless, he sat, rocking day in and day out in a mindless stupor, lulled by the monotonous squeak-squawk of the chair. A battered hat atop his shaggy head shaded him from the sun. Usually John Burke was totally unaware of everything outside his quiet dream world. But if you disturbed him, if you intruded upon his fantasies, he would become enraged, strike out at you, and curse at you in some strange enchanted

110　language which only he could understand. We children made a game of thinking of ways to disturb John Burke and then to elude his violent **retribution.**

ostensibly (ŏ-stĕn′sə-blē) *adv.* seemingly; to all outward appearances

D DRAW CONCLUSIONS
Reread lines 91–101. What does this description of Miss Lottie's home add to your understanding of her and her social and financial standing?

retribution
(rĕt′rə-byōō′shən) *n.* something given in repayment, usually as a punishment

---

DISCUSSION PROMPTS
Use these prompts to help students explore the children's attitudes:

Connect Have you ever had too much free time on your hands? Describe how you felt. *Answers should show an understanding of the children's boredom.*

Analyze Lizabeth is almost 15 years old. Why, then, does she go along with the younger kids' idea of annoying Miss Lottie? *Possible answer: Lizabeth is still a child at heart and feels as bored as the others. She describes herself as "child enough to scamper along with the group" (line 84).*

Synthesize The narrator notes that "we must have made a tragicomic spectacle" (line 86). What does she mean? Do you think that she felt this way when she was 14? *Possible answer: The group is tragicomic in that the children's ragtag appearance is funny to behold, but sad in that it reflects their poverty. At 14, Lizabeth might not have had the maturity to make this observation.*

READING SKILL

D DRAW CONCLUSIONS
Possible answer: The narrator says that Miss Lottie's decaying house was "the most ramshackle of all our ramshackle homes" (line 93). Its ill repair may indicate that Miss Lottie cannot afford to pay anyone to help her. As the owner of the worst-looking house in an impoverished community, Miss Lottie probably has a very low social and financial standing.

FOR LESS–PROFICIENT READERS
Comprehension Support Make sure that students understand the moment in lines 70–83 that sets the rising action of the plot into motion. Ask students to explain why the children decide to annoy Miss Lottie, even though they probably know that it is not nice to do.

FOR ENGLISH LEARNERS
Vocabulary: Phrasal Verbs Explain that *caught on* (line 83) means "became popular" (with the other children, in this case). Ask pairs of students to look up the meanings of these other phrasal verbs in the story and to share their findings: "blown . . . down" (line 97), "made up" (line 122), "come on" (line 249).

Discuss Lizabeth does not gather pebbles. Might she sense that she will **regret** participating? If so, why does she change her mind?

Possible answer: The more adult part of Lizabeth realizes the silliness of the activity (line 152) and may sense that she will regret participating. She changes her mind because she doesn't want the younger children to think that she is scared (lines 153–154).

LITERARY ANALYSIS

Ⓔ THEME AND SETTING

Possible answers: To Miss Lottie, the marigolds represent beauty in her difficult life. They may also represent one of the few things in her life that she can control. To the children, the marigolds represent the beauty that is absent from their lives. As a result, the children hate the flowers, without understanding why (lines 136–143).

If students need help . . . Ask them to work in small groups to discuss the characters' actual or probable thoughts about the marigolds. Have groups use the results to complete and then compare two Open Mind diagrams—one to represent Miss Lottie, the other to represent the children.

 BEST PRACTICES TOOLKIT—Transparency Open Mind p. D9

But our real fun and our real fear lay in Miss Lottie herself. Miss Lottie seemed to be at least a hundred years old. Her big frame still held traces of the tall, powerful woman she must have been in youth, although it was now bent and drawn. Her smooth skin was a dark reddish-brown, and her face had Indian-like features and the stern **stoicism** that one associates with Indian faces. Miss Lottie didn't like intruders either, especially children. She never left her yard, and nobody ever visited her. We never knew how she managed those
120 necessities that depend on human interaction—how she ate, for example, or even whether she ate. When we were tiny children, we thought Miss Lottie was a witch and we made up tales, that we half believed ourselves, about her exploits. We were far too sophisticated now, of course, to believe the witch-nonsense. But old fears have a way of clinging like cobwebs, and so when we sighted the tumble-down shack, we had to stop to reinforce our nerves.

"Look, there she is," I whispered, forgetting that Miss Lottie could not possibly have heard me from that distance. "She's fooling with them crazy flowers."

"Yeh, look at 'er."

Miss Lottie's marigolds were perhaps the strangest part of the picture.
130 Certainly they did not fit in with the crumbling decay of the rest of her yard. Beyond the dusty brown yard, in front of the sorry gray house, rose suddenly and shockingly a dazzling strip of bright blossoms, clumped together in enormous mounds, warm and passionate and sun-golden. The old black witch-woman worked on them all summer, every summer, down on her creaky knees, weeding and cultivating and arranging, while the house crumbled and John Burke rocked. For some **perverse** reason, we children hated those marigolds. They interfered with the perfect ugliness of the place; they were too beautiful; they said too much that we could not understand; they did not make sense. There was something in the vigor with which the old woman destroyed
140 the weeds that intimidated us. It should have been a comical sight—the old woman with the man's hat on her cropped white head, leaning over the bright mounds, her big backside in the air—but it wasn't comical, it was something we could not name. We had to annoy her by whizzing a pebble into her flowers or by yelling a dirty word, then dancing away from her rage, reveling in our youth and mocking her age. Actually, I think it was the flowers we wanted to destroy, but nobody had the nerve to try it, not even Joey, who was usually fool enough to try anything. Ⓔ

"Y'all git some stones," commanded Joey now, and was met with instant giggling obedience as everyone except me began to gather pebbles from the
150 dusty ground. "Come on, Lizabeth."

I just stood there peering through the bushes, torn between wanting to join the fun and feeling that it was all a bit silly.

"You scared, Lizabeth?"

I cursed and spat on the ground—my favorite gesture of phony **bravado.** "Y'all children get the stones; I'll show you how to use 'em."

stoicism (stō′ĭ-sĭz′əm) *n.* indifference to pleasure or pain; a lack of visible emotion

perverse (pər-vûrs′) *adj.* stubbornly contrary; wrong; harmful

Ⓔ THEME AND SETTING What do the marigolds represent to Miss Lottie? to the children?

bravado (brə-vä′dō) *n.* a false show of courage or defiance

DIFFERENTIATED INSTRUCTION

FOR ENGLISH LEARNERS

Language: Conversational English Patterns Explain that some contractions in the story, such as "'er" (line 128), "y'all" (line 148), "'em" (line 155), and "gonna" (line 215), are regional and/or nonstandard contractions. They are found most often in writing that imitates casual conversation. Encourage students to identify other examples of nonstandard contractions in the story.

FOR ADVANCED LEARNERS/PRE–AP

Analyze Syntax Have students reread the sentence in lines 131–133. Challenge them to explain why the author uses such an unusual sentence structure—placing the subject (*strip*) in the middle of the sentence, after two prepositional phrases and the verb (*rose*). Then ask students to identify the adjectives and adverbs in the sentence and to explain their significance.

Field of Hope, Charly Palmer. Mixed media collage on canvas, 24″ × 18″. © Charly Palmer.

ANALYZE VISUALS
How does this image compare with the narrator's description of the setting and Miss Lottie?

I said before that we children were not consciously aware of how thick were the bars of our cage. I wonder now, though, whether we were not more aware of it than I thought. Perhaps we had some dim notion of what we were, and how little chance we had of being anything else. Otherwise, why would we
160 have been so preoccupied with destruction? Anyway, the pebbles were collected quickly, and everybody looked at me to begin the fun. **F**

"Come on, y'all."

We crept to the edge of the bushes that bordered the narrow road in front of Miss Lottie's place. She was working placidly, kneeling over the flowers, her

F **THEME AND SETTING**
What connection is made between poverty and destruction in lines 156–161?

REINFORCE *KEY IDEA:* REGRET

Discuss What role does **regret** play in Lizabeth's bad mood that afternoon?

Possible answer: Lizabeth is in a bad mood because she regrets her part in the attack on Miss Lottie (lines 189–190) and feels ashamed of herself (line 188).

READING SKILL

G DRAW CONCLUSIONS

Possible answer: The childish part of Lizabeth sees fun in such wild behavior. Lizabeth is torn, however, because the more adult part of her realizes that she has maliciously attacked an elderly woman without provocation.

If students need help . . . Direct them to the conjunction *but* in line 189. Point out that *but* signals a contrast and that conflicting feelings are a type of contrast. After students reread the sentence in lines 188–190, elicit that it provides the best information for answering the question.

Extend the Discussion Why do you think Lizabeth's conflicting feelings led her to argue with Joey (lines 194–195)?

---

dark hand plunged into the golden mound. Suddenly "zing"—an expertly-aimed stone cut the head off one of the blossoms.

"Who out there?" Miss Lottie's backside came down and her head came up as her sharp eyes searched the bushes. "You better git!"

170 We had crouched down out of sight in the bushes, where we stifled the giggles that insisted on coming. Miss Lottie gazed warily across the road for a moment, then cautiously returned to her weeding. "Zing"—Joey sent a pebble into the blooms, and another marigold was beheaded.

Miss Lottie was enraged now. She began struggling to her feet, leaning on a rickety cane and shouting, "Y'all git! Go on home!" Then the rest of the kids let loose with their pebbles, storming the flowers and laughing wildly and senselessly at Miss Lottie's **impotent** rage. She shook her stick at us and started shakily toward the road crying, "Git 'long! John Burke! John Burke, come help!"

Then I lost my head entirely, mad with the power of inciting such rage,
180 and ran out of the bushes in the storm of pebbles, straight toward Miss Lottie chanting madly, "Old witch, fell in a ditch, picked up a penny and thought she was rich!" The children screamed with delight, dropped their pebbles and joined the crazy dance, swarming around Miss Lottie like bees and chanting, "Old lady witch!" while she screamed curses at us. The madness lasted only a moment, for John Burke, startled at last, lurched out of his chair, and we dashed for the bushes just as Miss Lottie's cane went whizzing at my head.

I did not join the merriment when the kids gathered again under the oak in our bare yard. Suddenly I was ashamed, and I did not like being ashamed. The child in me sulked and said it was all in fun, but the woman in me flinched
190 at the thought of the malicious attack that I had led. The mood lasted all afternoon. When we ate the beans and rice that was supper that night, I did not notice my father's silence, for he was always silent these days, nor did I notice my mother's absence, for she always worked until well into evening. Joey and I had a particularly bitter argument after supper; his **exuberance** got on my nerves. Finally I stretched out upon the palette in the room we shared and fell into a fitful doze. **G**

When I awoke, somewhere in the middle of the night, my mother had returned, and I vaguely listened to the conversation that was audible through the thin walls that separated our rooms. At first I heard no words, only voices.
200 My mother's voice was like a cool, dark room in summer—peaceful, soothing, quiet. I loved to listen to it; it made things seem all right somehow. But my father's voice cut through hers, shattering the peace.

"Twenty-two years, Maybelle, twenty-two years," he was saying, "and I got nothing for you, nothing, nothing."

"It's all right, honey, you'll get something. Everybody's out of work now, you know that."

"It ain't right. Ain't no man ought to eat his woman's food year in and year out, and see his children running wild. Ain't nothing right about that."

impotent (ĭm′pə-tənt) *adj.* powerless; lacking strength or vigor

2 Targeted Passage

exuberance (ĭg-zōō′bər-əns) *n.* condition of unrestrained joy

G DRAW CONCLUSIONS
Reread lines 187–196. Why is the narrator torn between conflicting feelings?

DIFFERENTIATED INSTRUCTION

FOR LESS–PROFICIENT READERS

2 Targeted Passage [Lines 179–190]

This passage targets the adolescent child-adult conflict with which Lizabeth struggles.

- How does Lizabeth feel while she and the other children are taunting Miss Lottie?

- How are her feelings different afterward?

- In line 189, what two people does she say are "in me"? What does she mean?

"Honey, you took good care of us when you had it. Ain't nobody got
210 nothing nowadays."

"I ain't talking about nobody else, I'm talking about me. God knows I try."
My mother said something I could not hear, and my father cried out louder,
"What must a man do, tell me that?" **H**

"Look, we ain't starving. I git paid every week, and Mrs. Ellis is real nice
about giving me things. She gonna let me have Mr. Ellis' old coat for you
this winter—"

"Damn Mr. Ellis' coat! And damn his money! You think I want white folks'
leavings? Damn, Maybelle"—and suddenly he sobbed, loudly and painfully,
and cried helplessly and hopelessly in the dark night. I had never heard a man
220 cry before. I did not know men ever cried. I covered my ears with my hands
but could not cut off the sound of my father's harsh, painful, despairing sobs.
My father was a strong man who would whisk a child upon his shoulders and
go singing through the house. My father whittled toys for us and laughed so
loud that the great oak seemed to laugh with him, and taught us how to fish
and hunt rabbits. How could it be that my father was crying? But the sobs
went on, unstifled, finally quieting until I could hear my mother's voice, deep
and rich, humming softly as she used to hum to a frightened child.

The world had lost its boundary lines. My mother, who was small and soft,
was now the strength of the family; my father, who was the rock on which
230 the family had been built, was sobbing like the tiniest child. Everything
was suddenly out of tune, like a broken accordion. Where did I fit into this
crazy picture? I do not now remember my thoughts, only a feeling of great
bewilderment and fear. **I**

Long after the sobbing and the humming had stopped, I lay on the palette,
still as stone with my hands over my ears, wishing that I too could cry and
be comforted. The night was silent now except for the sound of the crickets
and of Joey's soft breathing. But the room was too crowded with fear to allow
me to sleep, and finally, feeling the terrible aloneness of 4 A.M., I decided to
awaken Joey.

240 "Ouch! What's the matter with you? What you want?" he demanded
disagreeably when I had pinched and slapped him awake.

"Come on, wake up."

"What for? Go 'way."

I was lost for a reasonable reply. I could not say, "I'm scared, and I don't want
to be alone," so I merely said, "I'm going out. If you want to come, come on."

The promise of adventure awoke him. "Going out now? Where to,
Lizabeth? What you going to do?"

I was pulling my dress over my head. Until now I had not thought of going
out. "Just come on," I replied tersely.

250 I was out the window and halfway down the road before Joey caught
up with me.

H DRAW CONCLUSIONS
From the dialogue in lines
203–213, what can you
conclude is bothering
Lizabeth's father?

3 Targeted Passage

I THEME AND SETTING
How does the
conversation between
Lizabeth's parents affect
her? Cite details to
support your answer.

H DRAW CONCLUSIONS

Possible answer: *The father's grieving
outcries show that he wants to take care of
his family but is frustrated that he cannot
find a job.*

Extend the Discussion Why does the
mother's attempt at comforting her
husband (lines 209–210) fail?

I THEME AND SETTING

Possible answers: *The conversation confuses and frightens Lizabeth, for it suggests
that her parents have switched their traditional roles. Her mother, the breadwinner,
now seems stronger than her unemployed
father, whom the mother now comforts like
a little child (lines 228–230).*

If students need help . . . Have them use
Cause-and-Effect Graphics to explore details like these and their effect on Lizabeth.

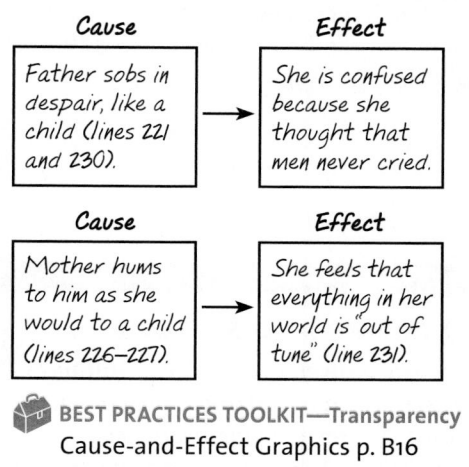

Cause		Effect
Father sobs in despair, like a child (lines 221 and 230).	→	She is confused because she thought that men never cried.

Cause		Effect
Mother hums to him as she would to a child (lines 226–227).	→	She feels that everything in her world is "out of tune" (line 231).

BEST PRACTICES TOOLKIT—Transparency
Cause-and-Effect Graphics p. B16

FOR LESS–PROFICIENT READERS
3 Targeted Passage [Lines 218–245]

This passage establishes Lizabeth's
emotional state, which will lead her to
take an important action.

- In what ways has Lizabeth's world "lost its
boundary lines" (line 228)?

- What does she wish for (lines 235–236)?

- Why does Lizabeth awaken Joey?

FOR ENGLISH LEARNERS
Vocabulary: Multiple-Meaning Words Point
out that certain words have more than one
meaning and that students must determine
the appropriate definition in a given use.
Help students use context clues to figure out
the meaning of "madly" (line 181); "thin" (line
199); "cried" (line 212); "whisk" (line 222); "rich"
(line 227); and "soft" (lines 228 and 237, with
different meanings).

ANALYZE VISUALS

Activity Invite students to study the girl in the foreground of *New Dreams* and to describe her mood. Then ask them to scan the story "Marigolds" up to this point. Which passage(s) could best be illustrated by the picture? Encourage students to keep the image in mind as they read the rest of the story. **Possible answer:** The girl appears to be deep in thought, creating a serious, quiet, and reflective mood. The picture could illustrate the narrator's reflections in lines 189–190 as the "woman in her" considered guiltily the "malicious attack" that she had led.

About the Art Once described as a "visual storyteller," Ernest Crichlow (1914–2005) first attained national distinction in the 1930s. He was born in Brooklyn to immigrants from Barbados, and the immigrant experience was often a subject in his art. Over his long and acclaimed career, Crichlow integrated personal feelings with social commentary in his art.

Lines 256–259
REINFORCE *KEY IDEA:* REGRET

Discuss How does **regret** influence the way that Lizabeth sees Miss Lottie's house? **Possible answer:** *She sees the house as she sees her life "foul and crumbling, a grotesque caricature" (lines 257–258). The house looked haunted, Lizabeth says, "because I was haunted too" (lines 258–259).*

New Dreams (2002), Ernest Crichlow. Litograph (Edition 150), 24¾″ × 16¾″. Photo by Maureen Turci, Mojo Portfolio. Courtesy of the Ernest Crichlow Estate.

"Wait, Lizabeth, where you going?"

I was running as if the Furies[3] were after me, as perhaps they were—running silently and furiously until I came to where I had half-known I was headed: to Miss Lottie's yard.

The half-dawn light was more eerie than complete darkness, and in it the old house was like the ruin that my world had become—foul and crumbling, a grotesque caricature.[4] It looked haunted, but I was not afraid because I was haunted too.

260 "Lizabeth, you lost your mind?" panted Joey.

I had indeed lost my mind, for all the smoldering emotions of that summer swelled in me and burst—the great need for my mother who was never there, the hopelessness of our poverty and **degradation,** the bewilderment of being neither child nor woman and yet both at once, the fear unleashed by my father's tears. And these feelings combined in one great impulse toward destruction. **J**

degradation
(dĕg'rə-dā'shən) *n.* condition of being brought to a lower level; humiliation

J THEME AND SETTING
Reread lines 261–265. Why do the narrator's emotions produce an urge to destroy?

---

3. **Furies:** In Greek and Roman mythology, the Furies were three goddesses of vengeance, or revenge.

4. **a grotesque caricature** (grō-tĕsk' kăr'ĭ-kə-chŏŏr'): a bizarre and absurdly exaggerated representation of something.

418 UNIT 4: THEME AND SYMBOL

LITERARY ANALYSIS

J THEME AND SETTING

Possible answer: *Lizabeth's circumstances utterly frustrate and confuse her (lines 261–262). Her emotions overwhelm her, too (lines 261–265). Needing a way to vent these feelings, Lizabeth feels compelled to destroy the beautiful flowers that stand in contrast to the ugliness of her life.*

DIFFERENTIATED INSTRUCTION

FOR ADVANCED LEARNERS/PRE–AP

Analyze Allusions Use the reference to the Furies in line 253 as the springboard for a mini-lesson about allusions. Have a small group of students work together to prepare a presentation in which they define the term, analyze the power of the allusion in terms of the theme of the selection, and discuss a few examples of allusions from other works that they have read.

"Lizabeth!"

I leaped furiously into the mounds of marigolds and pulled madly, trampling and pulling and destroying the perfect yellow blooms. The fresh smell of early morning and of dew-soaked marigolds spurred me on as I went
270 tearing and mangling and sobbing while Joey tugged my dress or my waist crying, "Lizabeth stop, please stop!"

And then I was sitting in the ruined little garden among the uprooted and ruined flowers, crying and crying, and it was too late to undo what I had done. Joey was sitting beside me, silent and frightened, not knowing what to say. Then, "Lizabeth, look."

I opened my swollen eyes and saw in front of me a pair of large calloused feet; my gaze lifted to the swollen legs, the age-distorted body clad in a tight cotton night dress, and then the shadowed Indian face surrounded by stubby white hair. And there was no rage in the face now, now that the garden was
280 destroyed and there was nothing any longer to be protected.

"M-miss Lottie!" I scrambled to my feet and just stood there and stared at her, and that was the moment when childhood faded and womanhood began. That violent, crazy act was the last act of childhood. For as I gazed at the immobile face with the sad, weary eyes, I gazed upon a kind of reality that is hidden to childhood. The witch was no longer a witch but only a broken old woman who had dared to create beauty in the midst of ugliness and sterility. She had been born in **squalor** and lived in it all her life. Now at the end of that life she had nothing except a falling-down hut, a wrecked body, and John Burke, the mindless son of her passion. Whatever verve there was left in her,
290 whatever was of love and beauty and joy that had not been squeezed out by life, had been there in the marigolds she had so tenderly cared for. **K**

Of course I could not express the things that I knew about Miss Lottie as I stood there awkward and ashamed. The years have put words to the things I knew in that moment, and as I look back upon it, I know that that moment marked the end of innocence. People think of the loss of innocence as meaning the loss of virginity, but this is far from true. Innocence involves an unseeing acceptance of things at face value, an ignorance of the area below the surface. In that humiliating moment I looked beyond myself and into the depths of another person. This was the beginning of compassion, and one cannot have
300 both compassion and innocence. **L**

The years have taken me worlds away from that time and that place, from the dust and squalor of our lives and from the bright thing that I destroyed in a blind childish striking out at God-knows-what. Miss Lottie died long ago and many years have passed since I last saw her hut, completely barren at last, for despite my wild contrition she never planted marigolds again. Yet, there are times when the image of those passionate yellow mounds returns with a painful poignancy. For one does not have to be ignorant and poor to find that one's life is barren as the dusty yards of one's town. And I too have planted marigolds. ❧

④ Targeted Passage

squalor (skwŏl′ər) *n.* a filthy, shabby, and wretched condition, as from poverty

K DRAW CONCLUSIONS
A change has taken place in Lizabeth. Why is she suddenly able to see Miss Lottie as she really is?

L PARAPHRASE
Paraphrase the narrator's thoughts about innocence and compassion in lines 295–300.

MARIGOLDS **419**

Practice and Apply

After Reading

or additional support of post-reading
uestions, use these copy masters

R RESOURCE MANAGER—Copy Masters

Reading Check p. 3 (to check understanding of the selection)

Theme and Setting p. 2 (for practice of
literary analysis standards focus)

Question Support p. 3 (fter Reading
uestions adapted for nglish learners
and less-proficient readers)

or additional uestions, see page 2 .

ANSWERS

Comprehension

1. *The narrator is 14, almost 15 (line 16).*

2. *They do not fit in with their environment—
Miss Lottie's ugly, decaying property.*

3. *She destroys Miss Lottie's marigolds.*

Literary Analysis

Possible answers:

4. *The story takes place in an impoverished
rural black community during the
Depression. The dreary setting shapes
the narrator's hopeless outlook.*

5. ■ **STANDARDS FOCUS** *Draw Conclusions
Lizabeth's act results from frustration at
feeling trapped in poverty (lines 39–41 and
136–139). It also comes from the emotional
pressure of seeing her parents struggling
with financial problems (lines 228–233).*

6. *The climax occurs when Lizabeth destroys
the marigolds, only to come face to face
with Miss Lottie (lines 267–291). For
Lizabeth, this is "the moment when
childhood faded and womanhood began"
(line 282). For Miss Lottie, it is the
end of the last spark of beauty in her life
(lines 289–291 and 305).*

7. *Charts will vary. Associating details like
the "brilliant splash of sunny yellow"
(lines 10–11) with the sun's energy suggests
that the marigolds symbolize beauty that
has life-affirming power.*

Comprehension

1. **Recall** How old is the narrator in the story?

2. **Recall** What is unusual about Miss Lottie's marigolds?

3. **Summarize** What does the narrator do that she later **regrets?**

Literary Analysis

4. **Understand the Influence of Setting** Note the most prominent features of the
story's setting. How do they affect the narrator's outlook on life?

5. **Draw Conclusions** Review the chart you made as you read. What leads the
young Lizabeth to destroy Miss Lottie's marigolds? Support your conclusions
with evidence from the story.

6. **Analyze Climax** Identify the climax of the story. What change does this
turning point initiate in the narrator? in Miss Lottie? Cite evidence to support
your answers.

7. **Analyze Symbolism** Miss Lottie's marigolds are central to the story. What do
they symbolize? To help you interpret their meaning, create a chart like the
one shown to record descriptions of the marigolds and the ideas you associate
with them.

Description of Marigolds	Associations
"a brilliant splash of sunny yellow" (lines 10–11)	"sunny yellow," like the sun, gives energy and life

8. **Interpret Theme and Setting** The narrator and Miss Lottie respond to their
impoverished surroundings in very different ways. What message does the
story convey about the impact of poverty on people's lives? What other
themes does the story impart?

9. **Evaluate Ideas** Reread the next-to-last paragraph (lines 292–300). Do
you agree with what the narrator says about innocence and compassion?
Use evidence from the story as well as your own experiences to explore
your answer.

Literary Criticism

10. **Social Context** Can "Marigolds" be considered social commentary on racial
segregation? Cite evidence to support your opinion.

8. ● **STANDARDS FOCUS** *Theme and Setting
The story suggests that poverty limits
people's lives and deprives them of much
of life's beauty. It also suggests that a
barren life can take different forms but
that people can find ways to create beauty
and counteract such barrenness.*

9. *Students may agree or disagree but should
support their responses with thoughtful,
well-supported reasons.*

Literary Criticism

Possible answer:

10. *Students should recognize that the strongest indication of segregation lies in the
parents' job situations. Opinions will vary
but should be clearly stated and reasonably defended.*

Vocabulary in Context

VOCABULARY PRACTICE

Decide whether the words in each pair are similar or different in meaning.

1. perverse/agreeable
2. squalor/splendor
3. exuberance/enthusiasm
4. retribution/retaliation
5. nostalgia/homesickness
6. futile/effective
7. poignantly/indifferently
8. bravado/timidity
9. degradation/humiliation
10. ostensibly/apparently
11. impotent/powerless
12. stoicism/emotionalism

> **WORD LIST**
> bravado
> degradation
> exuberance
> futile
> impotent
> nostalgia
> ostensibly
> perverse
> poignantly
> retribution
> squalor
> stoicism

VOCABULARY IN WRITING

Pretend you are Lizabeth's 12-year-old brother Joey, and write a paragraph describing your feelings about your childhood and the events in this story. Use four or more vocabulary words. You might start this way.

> **EXAMPLE SENTENCE**
> When I think of my childhood, I feel no **nostalgia**.

VOCABULARY STRATEGY: THE SUFFIX -or

Many words have endings called **suffixes** that can help you determine a word's meaning. For example, the word *squalor* ends with *-or,* a noun suffix meaning "state or condition of." You may recognize it as similar to the word *squalid,* meaning "very dirty or filthy." These two insights can help you conclude that *squalor* means "a filthy condition." Recognizing this suffix in other unfamiliar words can provide clues to the meanings of those words.

PRACTICE Use each numbered word in a sentence. Then use your knowledge of the suffix *-or* to figure out the meaning of each word. Use a dictionary to check your work.

1. terror
2. furor
3. candor
4. stupor
5. fervor
6. pallor

 VOCABULARY PRACTICE
For more practice, go to the **Vocabulary Center** at **ClassZone.com**.

MARIGOLDS   **421**

DIFFERENTIATED INSTRUCTION

FOR ENGLISH LEARNERS
Vocabulary: Prefixes and Suffixes Have students work in small groups to review the Word List. Group members should teach each other the prefixes and suffixes whose meanings they know, using a dictionary for confirmation. They should then use the dictionary to explore the meanings of word parts that are unfamiliar to them.

FOR ADVANCED LEARNERS/PRE–AP
Vocabulary Practice Ask students to use five pairs of words in sentences that compare or contrast people, places, or events. Have students compare the uses that they found for these words.

ANSWERS

Vocabulary in Context

VOCABULARY PRACTICE

1. *different*
2. *different*
3. *similar*
4. *similar*
5. *similar*
6. *different*
7. *different*
8. *different*
9. *similar*
10. *similar*
11. *similar*
12. *different*

R RESOURCE MANAGER—Copy Master
Vocabulary Practice p. 32

VOCABULARY IN WRITING

Urge students to skim the story, locating words and actions that might be clues about Joey's feelings.

VOCABULARY STRATEGY: THE SUFFIX *-or*
(also an EL language objective)

Encourage students to use context in combination with suffix clues to figure out the meaning of unfamiliar words.

Possible definitions:

1. *condition of great fear*
2. *furious state or condition*
3. *candid condition or expression*
4. *condition of dulled sense*
5. *state of intense feeling*
6. *pale condition*

R RESOURCE MANAGER—Copy Master
Vocabulary Strategy p. 33

i Vocabulary Center at **ClassZone.com**
Additional Vocabulary Activities

Assess and Reteach

Assess

R RESOURCE MANAGER—Copy Masters
Selection Test A pp. 39–40
Selection Test B/C pp. 41–42

o Test Generator CD

Reteach

S STANDARDS LESSON FILE
Literature Lesson 9: Setting and Its Roles
Literature Lesson 12: Theme
Reading Lesson 9: Drawing Conclusions

MARIGOLDS   **421**

Focus and Motivate

OBJECTIVES

Reading for Information
- outline a text
- skim and scan text
- analyze ideas
- read a newspaper article

SUMMARY

Donna Freedman's article explains how members of a Chicago neighborhood worked together to turn a barren lot into a garden that beautifies the community and celebrates African-American heritage.

What's the Connection?

Use a Comparison Matrix to prepare students for the selection. Have students note these aspects of Miss Lottie's garden: who created it, who maintained it, what it looked like, what plants it contained, and what it meant to people. Then have them fill in details about the African Heritage Garden as they read. Discuss comparisons and contrasts.

Items to Compare	Who Created the Garden
Miss Lottie's garden	Miss Lottie
African Heritage Garden	North Lawndale neighborhood

 BEST PRACTICES TOOLKIT—Transparency
Comparison Matrix p. A24

Teach

Skills Focus: Outline

Guide students through the process of outlining "Sowing Change." Explain that a main idea and its supporting details may span more than one paragraph. Point out that some main ideas are stated directly, while others are implied.

 RESOURCE MANAGER—Copy Master
Outline p. 51

Reading for Information

Sowing Change
Newspaper Article

Use with "Marigolds," page 410.

What's the Connection?

In "Marigolds," Miss Lottie's garden is the only bright spot in her difficult life. In the North Lawndale neighborhood of Chicago, Illinois, a garden has also become a bright spot for residents. To find out more about this garden and its impact on the community, read "Sowing Change."

Skill Focus: Outline

When you need to thoroughly understand and absorb a great many ideas and facts, outlining can help. An **outline** is a way of organizing a text's main ideas and supporting details according to their levels of importance. Since the main ideas and supporting details are written in the form of brief phrases, an outline can be considered a text's skeleton. You can take notes in outline form by following these steps:

- Skim the text to figure out its main topic, subtopics, and pattern of organization.
- Draft a basic outline by recording the main topics (numbered with Roman numerals) and the subtopics (lettered with capital letters) in the order presented by the writer. Use sentences or phrases as outline headings.
- Then, as you read the text closely, find and add supporting details to your outline at the appropriate levels of importance. Use Arabic numerals and lower-case letters to show further levels of detail.

Follow the steps above to take notes on "Sowing Change" in outline form. You can use the outline begun here as your starting point or create a new one. (For more information on outlining, see the **Reading Handbook,** page R4.)

> **The African Heritage Garden in North Lawndale**
> I. What the Garden Looks Like
>   A. Covers a large corner lot
>   B. Contains many plants and special features
>   1.
>   a.
>   b.
>   2.
> II. What It Took to Create the Garden

Selection Resources

 RESOURCE MANAGER UNIT 4

Plan and Teach pp. 43–47

Reading
Summary pp. 49†*, 50‡*
Outline pp. 51, 53†*
Analyze Ideas pp. 52, 54†*
Reading Check p. 55
Question Support p. 57

Assessment
Selection Tests A, B/C pp. 59*, 61*
 Test Generator CD

Reading Support
 Audio Anthology CD*

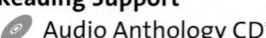 **BEST PRACTICES TOOLKIT**
Comparison Matrix • Cause-Effect
Graphics • New Word Analysis

* Resources for Differentiation † Also in Spanish ‡ In Haitian Creole and Vietnamese

Sowing Change

DONNA FREEDMAN

Many hands join to transform a barren city lot into a thriving green space for plants—and people in North Lawndale **A**

The 20-by-32-foot bed of marigolds is not just a sea of orange blooms, but a Rorschach blot. Back up a few feet, look again and the shape of the African continent emerges on a North Lawndale street corner.

A pair of doorway-like arbors invite passersby off the sidewalk and into a garden where raised beds are a glory of
10 lilies, daisies, hibiscus, nicotiana, shrub roses and other plants. In some places, flowers fight for space among broccoli, sweet potatoes and purple kale that are almost treelike in their vigor.

Three low, bark-covered mounds, plus a limestone-terraced hill at the rear of the site, give a sense of terrain. Shrubs, ornamental grasses and young hackberry, black locust, crab apple and magnolia trees
20 also provide vertical uplift on this city lot.

"This is what we need: open space, a place to sit and talk, to think a while," says North Lawndale resident Gerald Earles, sitting in the garden at 12th Place and Central Park Avenue. The 130-by-100-foot garden seemed to spring up in a single day in late April. **B**

In reality, it took more than two years, about 400 volunteers and $200,000 in
30 donated materials and expertise to create the African Heritage Garden.

"I've always known that the community [was] capable of a project of this magnitude. We just needed a focus," says Valerie Leonard, executive director of the non-profit North Lawndale Small Grants Human Development Corp.

The corporation's attempts to garden on the site withered and died due to lack
40 of water. But things finally came together this year after the Chicago Botanic Garden NeighborSpace, a non-profit land trust, and The Enterprise Companies, a residential real estate development firm, provided financial and design support.

About 200 people, including about 25 people from the community, attended a design session in March to determine

A OUTLINE
Before you begin taking notes, **skim** the entire article to see what its main topics and subtopics are.

B OUTLINE
What important information in this paragraph is not covered in the draft outline on page 422? Add it to your own outline.

A OUTLINE

Possible answer: The main topics are what the garden looks like, how it was created, how it continues to be cared for, and what it means to the community today. Subtopics will vary but may include the plants and features of the garden, the kinds of people who contributed and still contribute labor and materials, and neighbors' comments about the finished garden.

If students need help . . . Review what *skimming* means: Instead of reading every word, they should read quickly through the paragraphs, looking for ideas that stand out but skipping over minor details.

B OUTLINE

Possible answer: This paragraph gives the dimensions of the garden (lines 25–26). The paragraph also tells exactly where the garden is located (lines 24–25), though this information is of less importance. In addition, the paragraph gives an impression of the garden: "'open space, a place to sit and talk, to think a while'" (lines 21–22).

Extend the Discussion How do Gerald Earles's words help readers understand the value of the garden?

DIFFERENTIATED INSTRUCTION

FOR LESS–PROFICIENT READERS

Build Comprehension Have students use Cause-and-Effect Graphics to analyze lines 38–45. Discuss these questions.

- Why did the corporation's early efforts to establish a garden fail?
- What actions led to the project's eventual success?

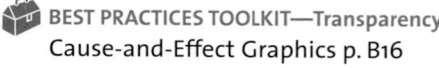 BEST PRACTICES TOOLKIT—Transparency
Cause-and-Effect Graphics p. B16

FOR ENGLISH LEARNERS

Culture: Clarify Explain the terms *Rorschach blot* (line 3), *Grants* (line 37), *Botanic Garden* (lines 41–42), and *trust* (line 43). Also be prepared to show pictures or otherwise describe some of the varieties of flowers, trees, and other vegetation named in lines 10–19.

C OUTLINE

Possible answer: *The comparison to Unity Park suggests that one purpose of the African Heritage Garden is to improve the quality of the neighborhood by discouraging the presence of criminals.*

If students need help . . . Focus on Gladys Woodson's comment in lines 63–65. Discuss her background and how her words apply to the African Heritage Garden.

D OUTLINE

Possible answer: *The community continues to care for the garden.*

C OUTLINE
What do lines 63–67 add to your understanding of the purpose of this garden?

D OUTLINE
What new topic is introduced in lines 95–98?

what the garden would become. All
50 agreed that the site should have a bed shaped like the African continent and incorporate a number of plants that grow in Africa. Both ideas were part of Leonard's original plan, which was inspired by Unity Park, another Lawndale project.

That park was created five years ago by residents fed up with crime near 19th Street and Kostner Avenue. Gladys Woodson, who spearheaded that project,
60 says that once the site became a well-used and neatly maintained park, the criminal element left.

"If you get enough good people to come out, the bad people are going to leave," Woodson says. She and other Unity Park organizers are helping at the African Heritage Garden as well. **C**

In fact, the heritage garden is thriving under the care and nurturing of a variety
70 of groups, including the North Lawndale Greening Committee, the Combined Block Club, and Slumbusters. Neighbor-Space, which purchased the land from the city and leases it to North Lawndale,
also paid to install a water hookup.

The plants and landscape materials, design, and onsite supervision were paid for by a grant from the Chicago Botanic Garden's Neighborhood Gardens
80 program. Each year, the Chicago Botanic Garden awards money to community groups interested in greening their neighborhoods.

It all came together on April 26 when about five dozen volunteers of varying ages, mostly neighborhood residents, planted hundreds of flowers and vegetable seedlings under the supervision of the Chicago Botanic Garden's Community
90 Gardens division. The Safer Foundation, which helps men make the transition from prison to the outside world, sent clients to build arbors and a half-dozen large raised beds.

With regular watering, the garden has thrived—as have the weeds. Scheduled work parties and neighborhood residents keep the weeds at bay. **D**

In late June, the Chicago Botanic
100 Garden brought more trees and flowers, which were planted by about 30 volunteers, including 9-year-old Nikky Pierce. Nikky, who lives down the street from the garden, is pleased with the results.

"Before, it was just dirty and trashy," she says. "It looks pretty when there are flowers in it."

Elder plantswoman and neighborhood resident Annie Lott lends a hand as well as
110 her expertise. At 92, she is an avid gardener who grows numerous flowers and 16 kinds of vegetables. It was her suggestion to put "some food, something that's healthy" in the flower beds.

"I love this garden because it brings back memories of how I was raised," says Lott, who is from Mississippi. "I was raised on a farm and our father taught us to do things for others and share."
120 The African Heritage Garden is a work in progress. Areas among the beds and mounds still need to be covered with stones. A shelter symbolizing a tribal hut, made with thatch and other materials from Africa, is in the works. Park benches also are likely.

But the progress has been huge, says Leonard, even though some of the volunteers had no gardening experience.
130 "They were involved, and now they're asking, 'When can we do it again?'

"That's music to my ears," Leonard says. "When you see how it was being used before and how it's being used now, that's an awesome feeling. It belongs to the community now."

DIFFERENTIATED INSTRUCTION

FOR LESS–PROFICIENT READERS

Vocabulary Support Explain that *expertise* (lines 30 and 110) means "special skill or knowledge." Discuss what kinds of expertise would be needed to create a community garden. Then invite students to identify areas in which they think that they have expertise (for example, in a sport or hobby).

FOR ENGLISH LEARNERS

Vocabulary: Idioms Use New Word Analysis to teach these idioms from the article:

- *withered and died* (line 39), "failed"
- *spearheaded* (line 59), "led"
- *at bay* (line 98), "under control"
- *music to my ears* (line 132), "something that I am happy to hear"

 BEST PRACTICES TOOLKIT—Transparency
New Word Analysis p. E8

Comprehension

1. **Summarize** How has the African Heritage Garden changed the North Lawndale community?

Critical Analysis

2. **Analyze Your Outline** Review the outline you created as you read. What main ideas did you identify?

3. **Make Inferences** What are some of the values held by the North Lawndale community? How does the garden represent these values? Cite details from the article to support your answer.

4. **Make Judgments** Consider what you know about crime as well as what the article tells you about this particular community garden. Why would something as simple as a garden reduce crime in an area?

Read for Information: Analyze Ideas

> **WRITING PROMPT**
> Both "Marigolds" and "Sowing Change" feature gardeners and their work. Write a brief analysis of the benefits of gardens. Use details from the short story and the article to support your ideas.

Writing an **analysis** involves identifying and explaining the parts of a subject and, finally, arriving at a conclusion. For help, follow these steps:

1. To analyze the benefits of gardens, review the benefits and consider how you might break them down. For example, the benefits might split naturally into "benefits to gardeners" and "benefits to the community."

2. Reread the selections to take notes on the particular benefits you want to address.

3. Review your notes. Identify any conclusions you can draw about gardening and its benefits.

As you write your analysis, be systematic. Introduce each main idea, identify its parts, and then elaborate on those parts before arriving at your conclusion.

Introduce Subject → **Examine Part of Subject** → **Draw a Conclusion**

Practice and Apply

For additional support of post-reading questions, use these copy masters:

 **RESOURCE MANAGER**—Copy Masters
  Reading Check p. 55
  Question Support p. 57
  Analyze Ideas p. 52

  For additional questions, see page 46.

ANSWERS

Comprehension

1. *Possible answer:* The garden has provided residents with an attractive, peaceful space in place of a barren lot.

Critical Analysis

Possible answers:

2. ■ **STANDARDS FOCUS** *Analyze Your Outline Possible answer: What the Garden Looks Like, What It Took to Create the Garden, How the Garden Continues to Be Cared For, What the Garden Means to the Community Today*

3. *Make Inferences The North Lawndale community values safety and beauty. The garden represents these values by providing an attractive place for residents (lines 21–22 and 105–107) that may also discourage the presence of criminals (lines 63–65).*

4. *Make Judgments Criminals tend to plan and act in secrecy. A beautiful public space that residents frequent would probably become a place where secretive activity would be difficult to conduct.*

Read for Information: Analyze Ideas

Writing Prompt *Possible answer: Gardens provide beauty and tranquility. Gardens also provide the people who tend them with a satisfying activity. In "Marigolds," Miss Lottie's garden was an island of beauty in her bleak life. In "Sowing Changes," a garden transformed a barren lot and refreshed the community's spirit.*

Assess and Reteach

Assess

RESOURCE MANAGER—Copy Masters
  Selection Tests A, B/C pp. 59–60, 61–62

  Test Generator CD

Reteach

STANDARDS LESSON FILE
  Study Skills Lesson 15: Outlining Your Reading

  Writing Lesson 27: Analysis Essay

Focus and Motivate

OBJECTIVES

Literary Analysis
- explore the key idea of **mixed emotions**
- identify and interpret symbols
- read a short story and a poem

Reading
- make inferences about characters

Vocabulary
- build vocabulary for reading and writing
- identify and use connotative meanings of words (also an EL language objective)

Grammar and Writing
- use compound, complex, and compound-complex sentences to vary sentence structure
- use writing to analyze literature

SUMMARY

The narrator of "The Scarlet Ibis" recounts major events in the short life of Doodle, his disabled younger brother. To avoid being embarrassed by Doodle, he teaches Doodle to walk, but while he is leading him—sometimes heartlessly so—to further accomplishments, Doodle dies in a thunderstorm.

Why do we HURT the ones we LOVE?

Write the term *mixed emotions* on the board, and elicit students' ideas about its meaning. Discuss reasons for **mixed emotions** in real-life situations. Then ask and discuss the *KEY IDEA* question. Conclude by having students complete the *DISCUSS* activity, perhaps with a focus on sibling relationships.

Selection Resources

The Scarlet Ibis
Short Story by James Hurst

Why do we HURT the ones we LOVE?

KEY IDEA Cruelty can intrude on the most loving relationship, often in moments of anger or disappointment. How do you deal with **mixed emotions** like these? Adults usually control such urges, but children are more likely to act on their immediate feelings. What harm can come from a thoughtless word or action?

DISCUSS Sometimes we are harder on loved ones than on anyone else. Why do you think this is? Discuss this question with a small group of your classmates.

FOXTROT © 1997 Bill Amend. Reprinted with permission of UNIVERSAL PRESS SYNDICATE. All rights reserved.

426

R RESOURCE MANAGER UNIT 4

Plan and Teach pp. 63–70

Literary Analysis
Summary pp. 71†*, 72‡*
Symbol pp. 73, 74†*
Question Support p. 81*

Reading
Make Inferences About
    Characters pp. 75, 76†*
Reading Check p. 80
Reading Fluency p. 84

Vocabulary
Study p. 77*
Practice p. 78
Strategy p. 79

Grammar and Writing
Vary Sentence Structure
    p. 83

Assessment
Selection Tests A, B/C pp. 85*, 87*
Test Generator CD

BEST PRACTICES TOOLKIT

Differentiated Instruction
    pp. 31–38*

Scaffolding Instruction
    pp. 43–46*

Graphic Organizers/Strategies
Word Squares • New Word Analysis • Cause-and-Effect Graphics • Cluster Diagram • Two-Column Chart • Plot Diagram • Reporter's Questions • Character Traits Web

Technology
i Literature and Vocabulary Centers at **ClassZone.com**
WriteSmart CD

Reading Support
Audio Anthology CD*

InterActive
READER & WRITER
• Integrated Test Practice
• Related Nonfiction Readings
McDougal Littell LITERATURE

---

* Resources for Differentiation   † Also in Spanish   ‡ In Haitian Creole and Vietnamese

● LITERARY ANALYSIS: SYMBOL

A **symbol** is a person, animal, place, object, or activity that stands for something beyond itself. A dove, for instance, often serves as a symbol for peace. Writers use symbols to emphasize important ideas in a story, which can act as clues to the theme. In "The Scarlet Ibis," for example, a swamp comes to symbolize the love between two brothers. To identify other symbols in this story, use these strategies as you read:

• Look for ideas that the writer emphasizes.

• Note striking images and character descriptions.

• Ask yourself what associations each one brings to mind.

Review: Mood, Theme

◼ READING SKILL: MAKE INFERENCES ABOUT CHARACTERS

When you make an **inference,** you make a logical guess based on observations or information in a text and on your own knowledge and experience. Sometimes called "reading between the lines," making inferences is an essential step in understanding the characters and, ultimately, the story itself. As you read, use a chart like the one shown to record inferences about the relationship between the narrator and his brother.

Quotations	Inferences About Relationship
"Doodle ... was a nice crazy, like someone you meet in your dreams".	Narrator basically liked his brother, but thought he was odd.

▲ VOCABULARY IN CONTEXT

The following boldfaced words are important to understanding this story of two brothers. To see how many of these words you already know, restate each phrase, using a different word for the boldfaced word.

1. **exotic** flowers from the tropics
2. **reiterate** your idea for emphasis
3. **evanesce,** like smoke into thin air
4. in **imminent** danger of falling
5. claimed **infallibility** in his deeply-held beliefs
6. worked hard and with **doggedness**
7. balanced **precariously** on the edge
8. dangerous beliefs that bordered on **heresy**

Author Online

A Man of Many Talents
James Hurst lives near the North Carolina coast, not far from the farm where he was born. After attending college and serving in the U.S. Army during World War II, he studied singing at New York's famous Juilliard School. Hoping for an operatic career, he also studied in Rome, Italy, but soon gave up on this goal. Then, in 1951, he settled into a long career at a large New York bank.

James Hurst
born 1922

A Tribute to the Human Spirit During his early years at the bank, Hurst published short stories and a play. "The Scarlet Ibis" received national attention after appearing in the *Atlantic Monthly* in July 1960 and winning the Atlantic First award that same year. When asked about the meaning of the story, Hurst once replied, "I hesitate to respond, since authors often do not understand what they write. That is why we have critics. I venture to say, however, that it comments on the tenacity and the splendor of the human spirit."

 MORE ABOUT THE AUTHOR
For more on James Hurst, visit the
Literature Center at ClassZone.com.

Background

Drawn from Nature "The Scarlet Ibis" takes its title from a tropical bird rarely found in coastal North Carolina, where the story takes place. The lush natural environment of this setting is prominent in the story. In addition to the ibis, Hurst uses the local names of plants for the power of their symbolic associations. For example, the exotic ibis lands in a "bleeding tree," a type of pine that oozes a white sap when cut. "Graveyard flowers" are fragrant white gardenias often planted in cemeteries because they bloom year after year.

Teach

STANDARDS FOCUS

LITERARY ANALYSIS

● SYMBOL

To help students understand symbols, write this sentence on the board:

James Hurst fought for his flag during World War II.

Ask students to explain what the flag symbolized for Hurst. *Possible answer: his country, the United States*

CHECK UNDERSTANDING Have students name symbols that could represent love, greed, war, and a love of writing.

READING SKILL

◼ MAKE INFERENCES ABOUT CHARACTERS

Have students imagine a teenage child's parent who is raging with anger at one moment and then hugging his or her child the next. Have students make an inference about the relationship or events. *Possible answer: The parent loves the child, but the child has misbehaved, undermining the parent's authority. The parent is experiencing mixed emotions.*

CHECK UNDERSTANDING Invite students to make inferences about the characters in the *FoxTrot* comic strip on page 426.

R **RESOURCE MANAGER**—Copy Master
Make Inferences About Characters
p. 75 (for student use while reading the selection)

VOCABULARY SKILL

▲ VOCABULARY IN CONTEXT

DIAGNOSE WORD KNOWLEDGE To determine preteaching needs, have all students complete Vocabulary in Context. *Possible answers:*
1. *foreign;* 2. *repeat;* 3. *disappear;* 4. *immediate;* 5. *inability to make a mistake;* 6. *determination;* 7. *dangerously;* 8. *the opposite of accepted beliefs*

PRETEACH VOCABULARY Use the Vocabulary Study copy master to help students predict the meaning of each boldfaced word in the copy master, using context clues.

1. Read item 1 aloud, emphasizing *doggedness.*
2. Point out the phrase "did not give up." Elicit possible meanings for *doggedness,* such as "persistence."
3. Repeat the procedure for items 2–8.

R **RESOURCE MANAGER**—Copy Master
Vocabulary Study p. 77

For general guidelines on differentiating vocabulary instruction and for alternative vocabulary activities for students not needing vocabulary preteaching, see

 BEST PRACTICES TOOLKIT
Scaffolding Vocabulary Instruction
pp. 43–46
ⓘ Vocabulary Center at **ClassZone.com**

LITERARY ANALYSIS: *Review*

A MOOD

Possible answer: the description that "summer was dead but autumn had not yet been born"; words like "stained," "rotting," and "rank" (lines 2–3); details of the "empty cradle" (line 5) of the nest and the graveyard flowers whose scent was "speaking softly the names of our dead" (line 7)

If students need help . . . Model for students how to find some of the details that relate to things that are dying, disappearing, or missing.

ANALYZE VISUALS

Possible answer: With his seated position, large eyes and ears, delicate features, and closed mouth, the boy appears more of an observer and thinker than a doer. The roughness of the lines and the lack of detail in the solid-colored clothing give the impression that the boy is not quite realized.

About the Art American portrait artist Alice Neel (1900–1984) created this oil painting.

READING SKILL

B MAKE INFERENCES

Possible answer: We can infer that Doodle was born with some illness or disability. We can make this inference based on these text details: he "seemed all head, with a tiny body which was red and shriveled" (lines 20–21); everybody thought he would die (line 21).

The
Scarlet Ibis
James Hurst

It was in the clove of seasons,[1] summer was dead but autumn had not yet been born, that the ibis lit in the bleeding tree. The flower garden was stained with rotting brown magnolia petals and ironweeds grew rank amid the purple phlox. The five o'clocks by the chimney still marked time, but the oriole nest in the elm was untenanted and rocked back and forth like an empty cradle. The last graveyard flowers were blooming, and their smell drifted across the cotton field and through every room of our house, speaking softly the names of our dead. **A**

It's strange that all this is still so clear to me, now that that summer has long since fled and time has had its way. A grindstone stands where the bleeding 10 tree stood, just outside the kitchen door, and now if an oriole sings in the elm, its song seems to die up in the leaves, a silvery dust. The flower garden is prim, the house a gleaming white, and the pale fence across the yard stands straight and spruce. But sometimes (like right now), as I sit in the cool, green-draped parlor, the grindstone begins to turn, and time with all its changes is ground away—and I remember Doodle.

Doodle was just about the craziest brother a boy ever had. Of course, he wasn't a crazy crazy like old Miss Leedie, who was in love with President Wilson and wrote him a letter every day, but was a nice crazy, like someone you meet in your dreams. He was born when I was six and was, from the 20 outset, a disappointment. He seemed all head, with a tiny body which was red and shriveled like an old man's. Everybody thought he was going to die— everybody except Aunt Nicey, who had delivered him. She said he would live because he was born in a caul,[2] and cauls were made from Jesus' nightgown. Daddy had Mr. Heath, the carpenter, build a little mahogany coffin for him. But he didn't die, and when he was three months old, Mama and Daddy decided they might as well name him. They named him William Armstrong, which was like tying a big tail on a small kite. Such a name sounds good only on a tombstone. **B**

---

1. **the clove of seasons:** a time between two seasons, in this case, summer and autumn.
2. **born in a caul:** born with a thin membrane covering the head.

428 UNIT 4: THEME AND SYMBOL

A MOOD
What words or images contribute to the mood of sadness and longing in lines 1–7?

1 Targeted Passage

ANALYZE VISUALS
What qualities does the boy in the painting seem to have? Point to details of color, line, shape, and texture to support your answer.

B MAKE INFERENCES
What inferences can you make about Doodle from the **details** offered in this paragraph? Explain your thought process.

Richard at Age Five (1944), Alice Neel. Oil on canvas, 26″ × 14″. © Estate of Alice Neel. Courtesy Robert Miller Gallery, New York.

DIFFERENTIATED INSTRUCTION

FOR ALL STUDENTS

Anchor Activity Provide independent learning opportunities for students to analyze nature symbolism. Ask students to find examples of exotic wildlife that can be found in coastal North Carolina and then explain how each example could be used symbolically in the story. See

R RESOURCE MANAGER
Ideas for Extension pp. 94–95

FOR LESS–PROFICIENT READERS

In combination with the *Audio Anthology CD*, use one or more Targeted Passages (pp. 428, 433, 435, 439, 441) to ensure that students focus on key story events, concepts, and skills. Targeted Passages are also good for English learners.

1 Targeted Passage [Lines 8–16]

This passage helps to establish the setting and narrator of the story.

BACKGROUND

The Summer of 1918 The climax of "The Scarlet Ibis" is set in July and August of 1918, a time crucial to American involvement in World War I. During those months, American forces played a key role in the Second Battle of the Marne, a series of battles involving German, British, French, and American forces. Hundreds of thousands of soldiers were killed or wounded. The battle defeated the last major German offensive of the war, resulting in the German surrender the following November. Although the war is never specifically referred to in "The Scarlet Ibis," in many respects, the destruction and senseless tragedy that mark the end of the story parallel events occurring in Europe at that time. Many would have agreed with the narrator's comment "That summer, the summer of 1918, was blighted" (line 226).

Lines 16–20
REINFORCE *KEY IDEA:* MIXED EMOTIONS

Discuss How do these lines show that the narrator had **mixed emotions** about Doodle from the boy's birth? *Possible answer: He says that Doodle was both "a nice crazy" (line 18) and "from the outset, a disappointment" (lines 19–20).*

- Who is telling the story? How can you tell?
- What do you learn about the narrator from these sentences? In particular, who is Doodle?
- When did the events that the narrator is about to retell take place?

FOR ENGLISH LEARNERS

Options for Reading Read the first Targeted Passage aloud and explain that "The Scarlet Ibis" is a personal and emotional journey back into childhood. Then have learners listen to the *Audio Anthology CD* as they read along.

Prereading For prereading instruction for English learners, see

 BEST PRACTICES TOOLKIT
Scaffolding Reading Instruction pp. 43–46

FOR ADVANCED LEARNERS/PRE–AP

Pre-AP Exercises in the bottom channel provide additional challenge for students. Use these suggestions for small groups or individuals.

ADDITIONAL GUIDELINES
For more help with differentiation and tips for classroom management, see

 BEST PRACTICES TOOLKIT
Differentiated Instruction pp. 31–38

I thought myself pretty smart at many things, like holding my breath,
30 running, jumping, or climbing the vines in Old Woman Swamp, and I wanted
more than anything else someone to race to Horsehead Landing, someone to
box with, and someone to perch with in the top fork of the great pine behind
the barn, where across the fields and swamps you could see the sea. I wanted a
brother. But Mama, crying, told me that even if William Armstrong lived, he
would never do these things with me. He might not, she sobbed, even be "all
there." He might, as long as he lived, lie on the rubber sheet in the center of
the bed in the front bedroom where the white marquisette curtains billowed
out in the afternoon sea breeze, rustling like palmetto fronds.[3]

It was bad enough having an invalid brother, but having one who possibly
40 was not all there was unbearable, so I began to make plans to kill him by
smothering him with a pillow. However, one afternoon as I watched him, my
head poked between the iron posts of the foot of the bed, he looked straight
at me and grinned. I skipped through the rooms, down the echoing halls,
shouting, "Mama, he smiled. He's all there! He's all there!" and he was. **C**

When he was two, if you laid him on his stomach, he began to move
himself, straining terribly. The doctor said that with his weak heart this strain
would probably kill him, but it didn't. Trembling, he'd push himself up,
turning first red, then a soft purple, and finally collapse back onto the bed
like an old worn-out doll. I can still see Mama watching him, her hand
50 pressed tight across her mouth, her eyes wide and unblinking. But he learned
to crawl (it was his third winter), and we brought him out of the front
bedroom, putting him on the rug before the fireplace. For the first time he
became one of us.

As long as he lay all the time in bed, we called him William Armstrong,
even though it was formal and sounded as if we were referring to one of our
ancestors, but with his creeping around on the deerskin rug and beginning to
talk, something had to be done about his name. It was I who renamed him.
When he crawled, he crawled backward, as if he were in reverse and couldn't
change gears. If you called him, he'd turn around as if he were going in the
60 other direction, then he'd back right up to you to be picked up. Crawling
backward made him look like a doodlebug, so I began to call him Doodle, and
in time even Mama and Daddy thought it was a better name than William
Armstrong. Only Aunt Nicey disagreed. She said caul babies should be treated
with special respect since they might turn out to be saints. Renaming my
brother was perhaps the kindest thing I ever did for him, because nobody
expects much from someone called Doodle. **D**

Although Doodle learned to crawl, he showed no signs of walking, but he
wasn't idle. He talked so much that we all quit listening to what he said. It was
about this time that Daddy built him a go-cart and I had to pull him around.

---

3. **palmetto fronds:** the fanlike leaves of a kind of palm tree.

430 UNIT 4: THEME AND SYMBOL

READING SKILL

C MAKE INFERENCES

Possible answer: The narrator's initial response is to want to kill Doodle; his response to Doodle's grin shows joy and hopefulness. The narrator probably sees some chance for a relationship with the "all there" Doodle.

If students need help . . . Have students re-read the previous paragraph, name the plans that the narrator had had for a brother, and then contrast those plans with his reaction to Doodle's grin. Ask students to consider what the narrator has inferred about his brother based on his smile, and why.

LITERARY ANALYSIS

D SYMBOL

Possible answer: Compared with William Armstrong, *a dignified name,* Doodle *seems like a name for a toy or a pet. It suggests something inconsequential or amusing and indicates that the family has few or low expectations for Doodle.*

C MAKE INFERENCES
Compare the narrator's initial reaction to Doodle with his response to Doodle's grin. What can you infer about the change in the narrator's attitude?

D SYMBOL
Reread lines 60–66. A nickname can sometimes be a kind of symbol. What does Doodle's nickname tell you about the feelings and expectations others have for him?

DIFFERENTIATED INSTRUCTION

FOR ENGLISH LEARNERS

Key Academic Vocabulary Use Word Squares to teach these words: *reverse* (line 58), *reveal* (line 164), *surveying* (line 235), *schedule* (line 247), *contrarily* (line 275), *parallel* (line 378).

 BEST PRACTICES TOOLKIT—Transparency Word Squares p. E10

Language: Conversational Patterns Adapt the New Word Analysis strategy to teach these conversational phrases:

- *be "all there"* (lines 35–36), "be capable of normal mental functioning"
- *might turn out to be* (line 64), "someday might become"
- *if I so much as* (line 72), "if I even"
- *when the going got rough* (line 81), "when challenges arose"

- *he was a sight* (line 82), "he looked ridiculous"
- *barring rain* (line 161), "if it didn't rain"
- *don't you dare* (line 320), "do not do what you are thinking about doing"
- *there's no telling* (line 320), "there is no way to predict or explain"

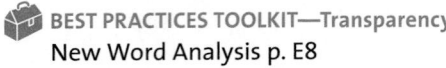 **BEST PRACTICES TOOLKIT—Transparency** New Word Analysis p. E8

Cypress Swamp, Texas (1940), Florence McClung. Oil on masonite, 24″ × 30″. Gift of the Roger H. Ogden Collection. The Ogden Museum of Southern Art.

70 At first I just paraded him up and down the piazza, but then he started crying to be taken out into the yard, and it ended up by my having to lug him wherever I went. If I so much as picked up my cap, he'd start crying to go with me, and Mama would call from wherever she was, "Take Doodle with you."

He was a burden in many ways. The doctor had said that he mustn't get too excited, too hot, too cold, or too tired and that he must always be treated gently. A long list of don'ts went with him, all of which I ignored once we got out of the house. To discourage his coming with me, I'd run with him across the ends of the cotton rows and careen him around corners on two wheels. Sometimes I accidentally turned him over, but he never told Mama. His skin

80 was very sensitive, and he had to wear a big straw hat whenever he went out. When the going got rough and he had to cling to the sides of the go-cart, the hat slipped all the way down over his ears. He was a sight. Finally, I could see I was licked. Doodle was my brother and he was going to cling to me forever, no matter what I did, so I dragged him across the burning cotton field to share with him the only beauty I knew, Old Woman Swamp. I pulled the go-cart through the sawtooth fern, down into the green dimness where the palmetto

THE SCARLET IBIS **431**

Lines 74–85

DISCUSSION PROMPTS

Use these prompts to help students understand the narrator's attitude toward Doodle:

Connect How would you feel about having a younger sibling who wanted to go everywhere you went? *Students might mention the responsibilities and stresses that such a situation would create.*

Analyze How does the narrator respond to his role as a caretaker? *Possible answer: He sees his brother as a burden (line 74) and mistreats him sometimes (lines 76–79), but eventually he shares what he loves with Doodle (lines 82–85).*

Synthesize How does the point of view help to tone down the mistreatment and resentment expressed in these lines? *Possible answer: The first-person point of view reveals a narrator whose resentments seem understandable for a child of his age. Nevertheless, there is a cruelty in turning over the helpless Doodle and in making him "cling" to the sides of the go-cart.*

ANALYZE VISUALS

Activity Ask students how this scene helps them visualize Old Woman Swamp. *Possible answer: The painting shows huge trees and standing water; it shows exotic-looking vegetation. Yet, there is a house in sight, so while the swamp seems unspoiled, like Old Woman Swamp, it is not entirely separated from human life.*

About the Art American painter Florence McClung (1894–1992) is known for her regional paintings. Like many of her other works, *Cypress Swamp, Texas* documents an environment for which she felt affection. The huge cypress trees, standing in water and hung with mosses, suggest a world that is strange yet wonderful—much like the world of Old Woman Swamp in this story.

FOR ADVANCED LEARNERS/PRE–AP

Analyze Style [paired-activity option] Have students mine pages 430–431 for characteristics of Hurst's style, including the way he varies sentence lengths, places lists within sentences, uses poetic language, and creates a unique voice through the use of rhetorical devices and through the tone of the narrator. Have students share their findings and look for additional examples as they continue reading.

Possible answer: *The brothers find ways to enjoy their shared time. One reason may be that they have only each other; they must adapt. Another reason may be that Doodle lets his brother lead.*

LITERARY ANALYSIS: *Review*

F THEME

Possible answer: *Inside me (and inside others, too), some cruelty mixes with love, just as life always contains the possibility of death, and sometimes I was cruel to Doodle.*

If students need help . . . Have students ignore the parenthetical material at first. Note that *borne* means "carried."

Lines 100–118
REINFORCE *KEY IDEA:*
MIXED EMOTIONS

Discuss What **mixed emotions** do you see in the brothers' relationship when the narrator shows Doodle the coffin? ***Possible answer:*** *The narrator is cruel when he shows Doodle his own coffin and when he threatens to leave his brother alone with it in the barn, but he is also caring when he carries Doodle outside. Doodle is defiant in resisting his brother's demand to touch the coffin, but dependent in his pleading not to be left alone.*

---

fronds whispered by the stream. I lifted him out and set him down in the soft rubber grass beside a tall pine. His eyes were round with wonder as he gazed about him, and his little hands began to stroke the rubber grass. Then he
90 began to cry.

"For heaven's sake, what's the matter?" I asked, annoyed.

"It's so pretty," he said. "So pretty, pretty, pretty."

After that day Doodle and I often went down into Old Woman Swamp. I would gather wildflowers, wild violets, honeysuckle, yellow jasmine, snakeflowers, and water lilies, and with wire grass we'd weave them into necklaces and crowns. We'd bedeck ourselves with our handiwork and loll about thus beautified, beyond the touch of the everyday world. Then when the slanted rays of the sun burned orange in the tops of the pines, we'd drop our jewels into the stream and watch them float away toward the sea. **E**

100 There is within me (and with sadness I have watched it in others) a knot of cruelty borne by the stream of love, much as our blood sometimes bears the seed of our destruction, and at times I was mean to Doodle. One day I took **F** him up to the barn loft and showed him his casket, telling him how we all had believed he would die. It was covered with a film of Paris green[4] sprinkled to kill the rats, and screech owls had built a nest inside it.

Doodle studied the mahogany box for a long time, then said, "It's not mine."

"It is," I said. "And before I'll help you down from the loft, you're going to have to touch it."

"I won't touch it," he said sullenly.

110 "Then I'll leave you here by yourself," I threatened, and made as if I were going down.

Doodle was frightened of being left. "Don't go leave me, Brother," he cried, and he leaned toward the coffin. His hand, trembling, reached out, and when he touched the casket he screamed. A screech owl flapped out of the box into our faces, scaring us and covering us with Paris green. Doodle was paralyzed, so I put him on my shoulder and carried him down the ladder, and even when we were outside in the bright sunshine, he clung to me, crying, "Don't leave me. Don't leave me."

When Doodle was five years old, I was embarrassed at having a brother of
120 that age who couldn't walk, so I set out to teach him. We were down in Old Woman Swamp and it was spring and the sick-sweet smell of bay flowers hung everywhere like a mournful song. "I'm going to teach you to walk, Doodle," I said.

He was sitting comfortably on the soft grass, leaning back against the pine. "Why?" he asked.

I hadn't expected such an answer. "So I won't have to haul you around all the time."

"I can't walk, Brother," he said.

---

4. **Paris green:** a poisonous green powder used to kill pests.

E MAKE INFERENCES
Describe the relationship that develops between the brothers. What do you think is the reason that Doodle wins the narrator over?

F THEME
In lines 100–102, the narrator makes a direct statement that offers clues to the theme. Paraphrase the message he expresses.

DIFFERENTIATED INSTRUCTION

FOR LESS–PROFICIENT READERS
Concept Support As you review lines 119–128, discuss the idea that teaching Doodle to walk seems noble—until we understand the narrator's reason for doing so (a reason that he both thinks to himself and says to Doodle). Point out this mix of the narrator's positive action and negative motivation as students read on.

FOR ENGLISH LEARNERS
Vocabulary: Phrasal Verbs Explain that *set out* (line 120) can mean "begin" (as with a literal or figurative journey) but it also can mean "to put" or "to place," as in "to set out the dinner plates." Have students find one or more definitions for the phrasal verbs "give up" (line 141), "took up" (line 188), "work out" (line 208), and "broke into" (line 225) and determine which meaning is used in context.

"Who says so?" I demanded.

130 "Mama, the doctor—everybody."

"Oh, you can walk," I said, and I took him by the arms and stood him up. He collapsed onto the grass like a half-empty flour sack. It was as if he had no bones in his little legs.

"Don't hurt me, Brother," he warned.

"Shut up. I'm not going to hurt you. I'm going to teach you to walk." I heaved him up again, and again he collapsed.

This time he did not lift his face up out of the rubber grass. "I just can't do it. Let's make honeysuckle wreaths."

"Oh yes you can, Doodle," I said. "All you got to do is try. Now come on,"

140 and I hauled him up once more.

It seemed so hopeless from the beginning that it's a miracle I didn't give up. But all of us must have something or someone to be proud of, and Doodle had become mine. I did not know then that pride is a wonderful, terrible thing, a seed that bears two vines, life and death. Every day that summer we went to the pine beside the stream of Old Woman Swamp, and I put him on his feet at least a hundred times each afternoon. Occasionally I too became discouraged because it didn't seem as if he was trying, and I would say, "Doodle, don't you *want* to learn to walk?" **G**

He'd nod his head, and I'd say, "Well, if you don't keep trying, you'll never 150 learn." Then I'd paint for him a picture of us as old men, white-haired, him with a long white beard and me still pulling him around in the go-cart. This never failed to make him try again.

Finally one day, after many weeks of practicing, he stood alone for a few seconds. When he fell, I grabbed him in my arms and hugged him, our laughter pealing through the swamp like a ringing bell. Now we knew it could be done. Hope no longer hid in the dark palmetto thicket but perched like a cardinal in the lacy toothbrush tree, brilliantly visible.

"Yes, yes," I cried, and he cried it too, and the grass beneath us was soft and the smell of the swamp was sweet.

160 With success so **imminent**, we decided not to tell anyone until he could actually walk. Each day, barring rain, we sneaked into Old Woman Swamp, and by cotton-picking time Doodle was ready to show what he could do. He still wasn't able to walk far, but we could wait no longer. Keeping a nice secret is very hard to do, like holding your breath. We chose to reveal all on October eighth, Doodle's sixth birthday, and for weeks ahead we mooned around the house, promising everybody a most spectacular surprise. Aunt Nicey said that, after so much talk, if we produced anything less tremendous than the Resurrection,[5] she was going to be disappointed.

At breakfast on our chosen day, when Mama, Daddy, and Aunt Nicey were 170 in the dining room, I brought Doodle to the door in the go-cart just as usual and had them turn their backs, making them cross their hearts and hope to

---

5. **the Resurrection:** the rising of Jesus Christ from the dead after his burial.

THE SCARLET IBIS **433**

G MAKE INFERENCES
Why does the narrator try so hard to teach Doodle to walk? Point out statements in lines 141–148 that support your answer.

② Targeted Passage

imminent (ĭm′ə-nənt) *adj.* about to occur

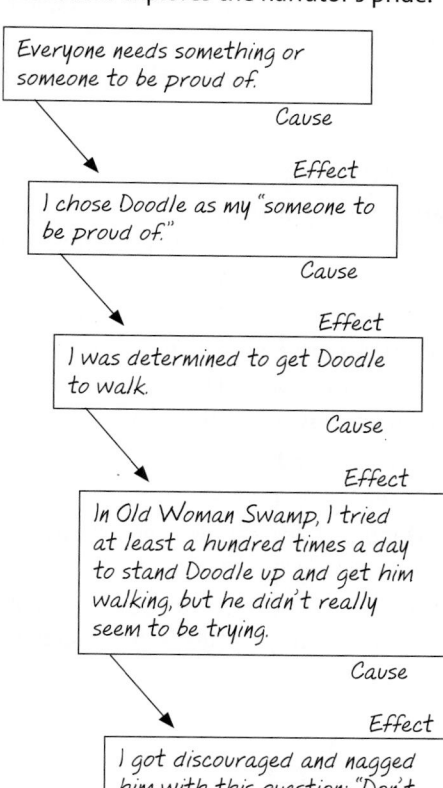
FOR LESS–PROFICIENT READERS

② Targeted Passage [Lines 149–159]

This passage presents a pivotal moment in the story—the moment when Doodle and the narrator know that Doodle will walk.

- What mental image never fails to get Doodle to try to walk one more time?

- What accomplishment occurs? How does the narrator respond?

- What does he say that they know? What does he say that he feels?

FOR ENGLISH LEARNERS

Vocabulary: Idioms and Sayings Adapt the New Word Analysis strategy to teach these idioms and sayings:

- *mooned around* (line 165), "daydreamed or acted as if lost in a daydream"

- *cross their hearts and hope to die* (lines 171–172), "make a gesture that signifies a promise"

BEST PRACTICES TOOLKIT—Transparency
New Word Analysis p. E8

die if they peeked. I helped Doodle up, and when he was standing alone I let them look. There wasn't a sound as Doodle walked slowly across the room and sat down at his place at the table. Then Mama began to cry and ran over to him, hugging him and kissing him. Daddy hugged him too, so I went to Aunt Nicey, who was thanks praying in the doorway, and began to waltz her around. We danced together quite well until she came down on my big toe with her brogans,[6] hurting me so badly I thought I was crippled for life.

Doodle told them it was I who had taught him to walk, so everyone wanted
180 to hug me, and I began to cry.

"What are you crying for?" asked Daddy, but I couldn't answer. They did not know that I did it for myself; that pride, whose slave I was, spoke to me louder than all their voices, and that Doodle walked only because I was ashamed of having a crippled brother. **H**

Within a few months Doodle had learned to walk well and his go-cart was put up in the barn loft (it's still there) beside his little mahogany coffin. Now, when we roamed off together, resting often, we never turned back until our destination had been reached, and to help pass the time, we took up lying. From the beginning Doodle was a terrible liar and he got me in the habit. Had
190 anyone stopped to listen to us, we would have been sent off to Dix Hill.[7]

My lies were scary, involved, and usually pointless, but Doodle's were twice as crazy. People in his stories all had wings and flew wherever they wanted to go. His favorite lie was about a boy named Peter who had a pet peacock with a ten-foot tail. Peter wore a golden robe that glittered so brightly that when he walked through the sunflowers they turned away from the sun to face him. When Peter was ready to go to sleep, the peacock spread his magnificent tail, enfolding the boy gently like a closing go-to-sleep flower, burying him in the gloriously iridescent, rustling vortex.[8] Yes, I must admit it. Doodle could beat me lying. **I**

200 Doodle and I spent lots of time thinking about our future. We decided that when we were grown we'd live in Old Woman Swamp and pick dog-tongue for a living. Beside the stream, he planned, we'd build us a house of whispering leaves and the swamp birds would be our chickens. All day long (when we weren't gathering dog-tongue) we'd swing through the cypresses on the rope vines, and if it rained we'd huddle beneath an umbrella tree and play stickfrog. Mama and Daddy could come and live with us if they wanted to. He even came up with the idea that he could marry Mama and I could marry Daddy. Of course, I was old enough to know this wouldn't work out, but the picture he painted was so beautiful and serene that all I could do was whisper Yes, yes.

---

6. **brogans** (brō'gənz): heavy, ankle-high work shoes.
7. **Dix Hill:** common name for a mental hospital in Raleigh, North Carolina.
8. **iridescent rustling vortex:** the shimmering, rainbow-colored peacock feathers are in a funnel shape, like a whirlpool or whirlwind (vortex).

434 UNIT 4: THEME AND SYMBOL

H MAKE INFERENCES
Reread lines 181–184. Why is the narrator ashamed of himself?

◆ GRAMMAR AND STYLE
Reread lines 194–199. Hurst uses a variety of sentence structures, containing **independent** and **subordinate clauses**, to add rhythm and interest to his writing.

READING SKILL

H MAKE INFERENCES

Possible answer: The others assume there is a selfless motivation for his teaching Doodle to walk; they think that he did it out of love or concern for Doodle. The narrator knows that he did it for himself, "because I was ashamed of having a crippled brother" (lines 183–184).

Extend the Discussion Suppose that the narrator were to admit his true motivation to his parents at this moment. How do you think that they would react? Would they punish him, or try to counsel him? Explain your answer.

◆ GRAMMAR AND STYLE

Vary Sentence Structure Check students' understanding by having them categorize these clauses in lines 196–199:

- "When Peter was ready to go to sleep" *Possible answer: subordinate clause*
- "the peacock spread his magnificent tail" *Possible answer: independent clause*
- "Yes, I must admit it" *Possible answer: independent clause*
- "Doodle could beat me lying" *Possible answer: independent clause*

Have students identify other examples of varied sentence structure in the selection.

DIFFERENTIATED INSTRUCTION

FOR ENGLISH LEARNERS

Vocabulary: Multiple-Meaning Words Have pairs of students use a dictionary and a Cluster Diagram to find and present multiple meanings of these story words: "licked" (line 83), "living" (line 202), "drive" (line 249), "rail" (line 347), and "rustling" (line 359). Discuss how context determines the story meaning in each instance of use.

🧰 BEST PRACTICES TOOLKIT—Transparency
Cluster Diagram p. B18

FOR ADVANCED LEARNERS/PRE–AP

Hypothesize About Setting [small-group option] Would the relationships and conflicts that we see in this story have developed if there had been no swamp (which, as is pointed out in lines 200–209, shapes the brothers' dreams about the future as well as their present lives) or if the events had taken place in a city of that time or in today's world? Have students gather story evidence to argue their case.

Activity Ask students to explain how this painting compares to and contrasts with story events. *Possible answer: Contrast: There are five rather than two children; the setting appears to be a quarry, not a swamp; all of the children appear equally capable. Comparison: One boy seems to be the leader; the situation could be one in which timid children are encouraged or pressured to act beyond their comfort zone.* Ask students why the painting is appropriate, even if its details do not match the story exactly. *Possible answer: It is a scene that the narrator and Doodle may imagine being a part of if Doodle's progress continues.*

About the Art In this painting, Canadian artist Vincent McIndoe shows five children at a swimming hole, one of whom is the focus of activity at the moment. Though the scene is one of natural beauty, the setting is not entirely inviting, with its steep rocks and unsupervised, somewhat risky diving activity.

210   Once I had succeeded in teaching Doodle to walk, I began to believe in my own **infallibility,** and I prepared a terrific development program for him, unknown to Mama and Daddy, of course. I would teach him to run, to swim, to climb trees, and to fight. He, too, now believed in my infallibility, so we set the deadline for these accomplishments less than a year away, when, it had been decided, Doodle could start to school.

     That winter we didn't make much progress, for I was in school and Doodle suffered from one bad cold after another. But when spring came, rich and warm, we raised our sights again. Success lay at the end of summer like a pot of gold, and our campaign got off to a good start. On hot days, Doodle

220 and I went down to Horsehead Landing, and I gave him swimming lessons or showed him how to row a boat. Sometimes we descended into the cool greenness of Old Woman Swamp and climbed the rope vines or boxed

infallibility
(ĭn-făl′ə-bĭl′ĭ-tē) *n.* an inability to make errors

❸ Targeted Passage

Lines 210–219
REINFORCE *KEY IDEA:* MIXED EMOTIONS

Discuss What **mixed emotions** does the narrator seem to feel as he prepares his development program for Doodle? Explain. *Possible answer: He is pleased enough with the program to call it "terrific" (line 211) but concerned enough to leave it "unknown to Mama and Daddy" (line 212). In addition, he may be glad that it might do Doodle some good—but he already has admitted that pride is his motivation, and here he proudly speaks of his "infallibility" (line 211).*

THE SCARLET IBIS   **435**

FOR LESS—PROFICIENT READERS

❸ Targeted Passage [Lines 210–219]

This passage sets up increased tension, as the narrator pushes Doodle toward a specific goal.

- What four things does the narrator plan to teach Doodle to do?

- From whom does he keep this plan a secret? Why?

- At the end of this passage, about how close are they to their deadline?

FOR ENGLISH LEARNERS

Comprehension: Comparisons Have small groups find what is being compared in these similes and record their comparisons in a Two-Column Chart: "like a closing go-to-sleep flower" (line 197); "like a pot of gold" (lines 218–219); "like a hawk at the entrails of a chicken" (line 231); "like a broken vase of red flowers" (line 305).

BEST PRACTICES TOOLKIT—Transparency Two-Column Chart p. A25

Possible answer: *The dull browns and greens combine with the images of dying plants and falling leaves to create a mood of loss or sorrow. The brushstrokes that depict decaying plant matter are quick and fleeting, like the decomposing life itself.*

About the Art The influential American landscape artist Charles Burchfield (1893–1967) blended the feelings and atmosphere of a landscape with the spiritual qualities of the objects within them.

Lines 226–241
DISCUSSION PROMPTS

Use these prompts to help students understand how details of this scene foreshadow disaster:

Connect Have you ever experienced nature in a particularly destructive way? Describe. *Students may mention hurricanes, tornadoes, thunderstorms, floods, or even earthquakes.*

Analyze How would you describe the roles of the brothers in this scene? ***Possible answer:*** *The brothers are figures of innocence and perhaps unfounded optimism, giggling and having fun, "knowing that everything would be all right" (lines 240–241), despite the signs of blight and sorrow around them.*

Synthesize What function does this passage serve for the story? Explain your answer. ***Possible answer:*** *It shifts the mood. The previous pages have been full of the joy of Doodle's learning to walk and the narrator's confidence in his own infallibility. In this passage, death and destruction enter in, uninvited and invincible. Their presence foretells of their power in scenes to come.*

Autumn Embers (Frosted Scarlet Sage) (1944), Charles Burchfield. © Kennedy Galleries, New York.

scientifically beneath the pine where he had learned to walk. Promise hung about us like the leaves, and wherever we looked, ferns unfurled and birds broke into song.

That summer, the summer of 1918, was blighted. In May and June there was no rain and the crops withered, curled up, then died under the thirsty sun. One morning in July a hurricane came out of the east, tipping over the oaks in the yard and splitting the limbs of the elm trees. That afternoon it roared
230 back out of the west, blew the fallen oaks around, snapping their roots and tearing them out of the earth like a hawk at the entrails of a chicken. Cotton bolls were wrenched from the stalks and lay like green walnuts in the valleys between the rows, while the cornfield leaned over uniformly so that the tassels touched the ground. Doodle and I followed Daddy out into the cotton field, where he stood, shoulders sagging, surveying the ruin. When his chin sank down onto his chest, we were frightened, and Doodle slipped his hand into mine. Suddenly Daddy straightened his shoulders, raised a giant knuckly fist, and with a voice that seemed to rumble out of the earth itself began cursing heaven, hell, the weather, and the Republican Party.[9] Doodle and I, prodding
240 each other and giggling, went back to the house, knowing that everything would be all right.

---

9. **Republican Party:** In 1918, most Southerners were Democrats.

DIFFERENTIATED INSTRUCTION

FOR ADVANCED LEARNERS/PRE–AP
Analyze Metaphor Have students write a paragraph or two explaining *blight* as a metaphor in "The Scarlet Ibis." Encourage them to analyze the wider context of the story, including the war in Europe, as well as the more narrow world of the characters. Also ask students to reflect on how the concept of blight does or does not fit in with some of the other seasonal and natural imagery in the story.

And during that summer, strange names were heard through the house: Château-Thierry, Amiens, Soissons, and in her blessing at the supper table, Mama once said, "And bless the Pearsons, whose boy Joe was lost at Belleau Wood."[10]

So we came to that clove of seasons. School was only a few weeks away, and Doodle was far behind schedule. He could barely clear the ground when climbing up the rope vines, and his swimming was certainly not passable. We decided to double our efforts, to make that last drive and reach our pot of
250 gold. I made him swim until he turned blue and row until he couldn't lift an oar. Wherever we went, I purposely walked fast, and although he kept up, his face turned red and his eyes became glazed. Once, he could go no further, so he collapsed on the ground and began to cry.

"Aw, come on, Doodle," I urged. "You can do it. Do you want to be different from everybody else when you start school?"

"Does it make any difference?"

"It certainly does," I said. "Now, come on," and I helped him up.

As we slipped through dog days,[11] Doodle began to look feverish, and Mama felt his forehead, asking him if he felt ill. At night he didn't sleep well,
260 and sometimes he had nightmares, crying out until I touched him and said, "Wake up, Doodle. Wake up." **J**

It was Saturday noon, just a few days before school was to start. I should have already admitted defeat, but my pride wouldn't let me. The excitement of our program had now been gone for weeks, but still we kept on with a tired **doggedness.** It was too late to turn back, for we had both wandered too far into a net of expectations and had left no crumbs behind.

Daddy, Mama, Doodle, and I were seated at the dining-room table having lunch. It was a hot day, with all the windows and doors open in case a breeze should come. In the kitchen Aunt Nicey was humming softly. After a long
270 silence, Daddy spoke. "It's so calm, I wouldn't be surprised if we had a storm this afternoon."

"I haven't heard a rain frog," said Mama, who believed in signs, as she served the bread around the table.

"I did," declared Doodle. "Down in the swamp."

"He didn't," I said contrarily.

"You did, eh?" said Daddy, ignoring my denial.

"I certainly did," Doodle **reiterated,** scowling at me over the top of his iced-tea glass, and we were quiet again.

Suddenly, from out in the yard, came a strange croaking noise. Doodle
280 stopped eating, with a piece of bread poised ready for his mouth, his eyes popped round like two blue buttons. "What's that?" he whispered.

---

10. **Château-Thierry** (shā-tō-tyĕ-rē′), **Amiens** (ä-myăN′), **Soissons** (swä-sôN′), . . . **Belleau** (bel′ō) **Wood:** places in France where famous battles were fought near the end of World War I (1914–1918).

11. **dog days:** the hot, uncomfortable days between early July and early September (named after the Dog Star, Sirius, which rises and sets with the sun at this time).

J MAKE INFERENCES
What is happening to Doodle?

doggedness
(dô′gĭd-nĭs)
n. persistence; stubbornness

reiterate (rē-ĭt′ə-rāt′)
v. to repeat

THE SCARLET IBIS **437**

READING SKILL

J MAKE INFERENCES

Possible answer: Doodle may be getting ill. He appears to be showing signs of exhaustion from the demanding schedule that his brother has set. There even is a small chance that Doodle, who has been associated with death since his birth, and whose coffin (though now too small) seems to await him in the barn, is dying.

Lines 246–266
REINFORCE *KEY IDEA:* MIXED EMOTIONS

Discuss Why do you think the narrator presses Doodle so hard with his program of physical exercise? *Possible answer: After his success at teaching Doodle to walk, the narrator truly believes that he can teach his brother to run, swim, and do other physical activities so that he will not be "different from everybody else" when he starts school. But the narrator has **mixed emotions:** he is motivated by selfishness as well as love. He is ashamed of Doodle's disability and wants him to be like everybody else so that his brother won't embarrass him—not because fitting in is that important for Doodle's own happiness or development.*

FOR ENGLISH LEARNERS

Comprehension: Contrast Have students locate the contrasts signaled by "different from" (line 255) and by "but" (lines 263 and 264) and explain what is being contrasted. *Possible answer: line 255: Doodle and everyone else; line 263: defeat and pride; line 264: doggedness and lack of excitement*

FOR ADVANCED LEARNERS/PRE–AP

Evaluate Pacing Effective pacing means that as a story progresses to a climax, it must engage readers in the conflict, expose characters and theme, and build rising action. How well is "The Scarlet Ibis" paced? Have small groups of students use a Plot Diagram to map the story before discussing the question.

 **BEST PRACTICES TOOLKIT—Transparency**
Plot Diagram p. D10

ANALYZE VISUALS

Activity Invite comments about this dramatic image; in particular, ask students what makes the bird seem both wonderful and terrible. Have them consider the three main colors (red, green, and black), as well as the foreground and background. ***Possible answer:*** *The bird is both beautiful and dramatic because of its bright red color, its curved neck, and its long beak. The background against which it is set, however, is far more somber: The bird is framed by a black, perhaps menacing, tree trunk and a blurred sea of muted green. This background is just as large as, if not larger than the foreground image.*

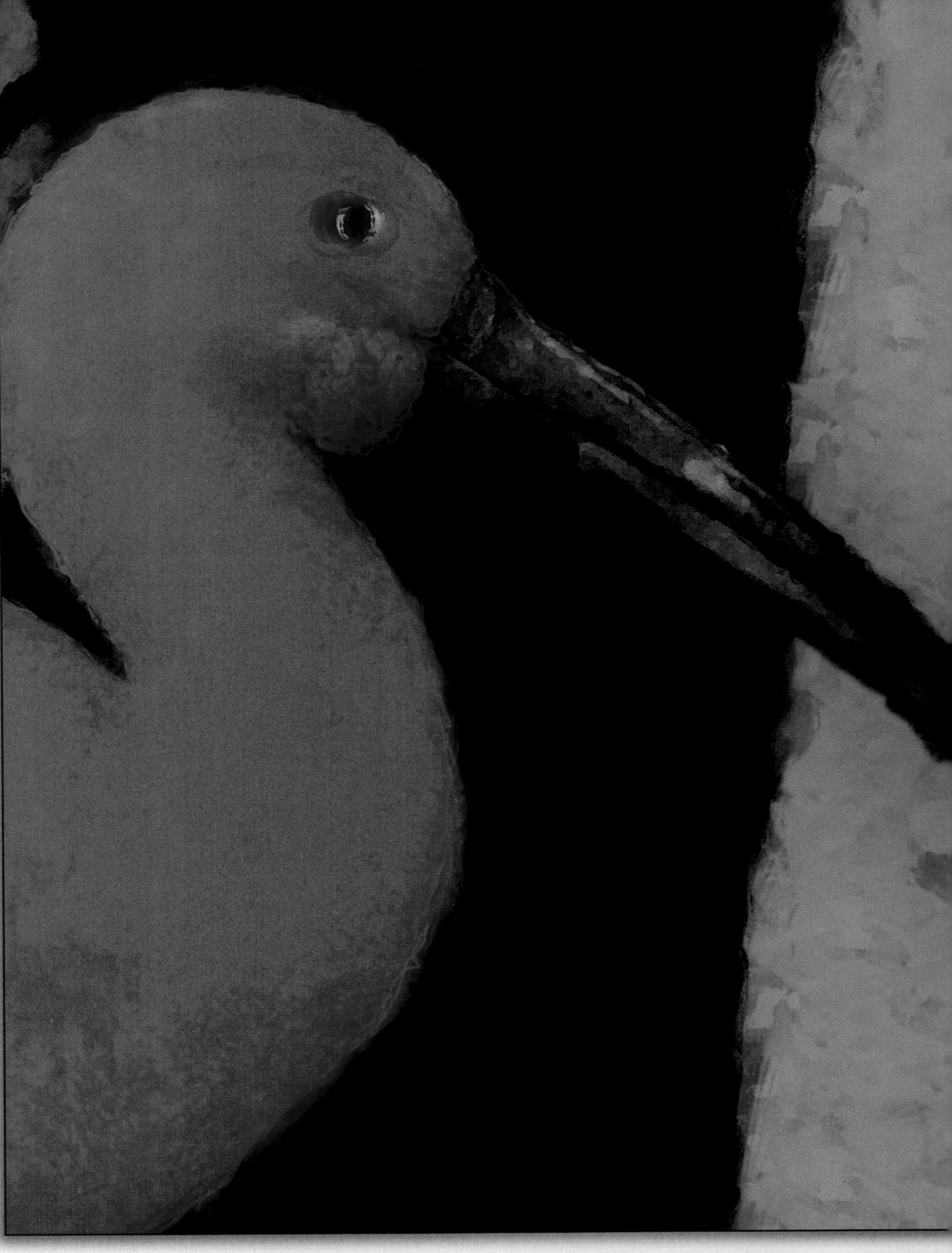

DIFFERENTIATED INSTRUCTION

FOR LESS—PROFICIENT READERS

Identify Key Facts The arrival of the scarlet ibis is an important moment in this story. Help students check their comprehension of the scene by answering a set of Reporter's Questions about it.

- *Who* are the people in this scene? ***Possible answer:*** *the narrator, Doodle, Daddy, and Mama*
- *When* does the scene take place? ***Possible answer:*** *lunchtime*
- *What* unexpected event happens? ***Possible answer:*** *A scarlet ibis comes to their yard.*
- *Where* does the scarlet ibis land? ***Possible answer:*** *at the top of the bleeding tree*
- *Why* does it fall to the ground? ***Possible answer:*** *It is dying.*
- *How* does Doodle react to what has happened? ***Possible answer:*** *He wants to bury it, and Mama reluctantly agrees.*

BEST PRACTICES TOOLKIT—Transparency Reporter's Questions p. C9

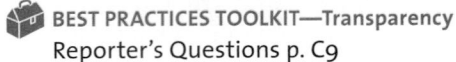

I jumped up, knocking over my chair, and had reached the door when Mama called, "Pick up the chair, sit down again, and say excuse me."

By the time I had done this, Doodle had excused himself and had slipped out into the yard. He was looking up into the bleeding tree. "It's a great big red bird!" he called. **K**

The bird croaked loudly again, and Mama and Daddy came out into the yard. We shaded our eyes with our hands against the hazy glare of the sun and peered up through the still leaves. On the topmost branch a bird the size
290 of a chicken, with scarlet feathers and long legs, was perched **precariously.** Its wings hung down loosely, and as we watched, a feather dropped away and floated slowly down through the green leaves.

"It's not even frightened of us," Mama said.

"It looks tired," Daddy added. "Or maybe sick."

Doodle's hands were clasped at his throat, and I had never seen him stand still so long. "What is it?" he asked.

Daddy shook his head. "I don't know, maybe it's—"

At that moment the bird began to flutter, but the wings were uncoordinated, and amid much flapping and a spray of flying feathers, it
300 tumbled down, bumping through the limbs of the bleeding tree and landing at our feet with a thud. Its long, graceful neck jerked twice into an S, then straightened out, and the bird was still. A white veil came over the eyes and the long white beak unhinged. Its legs were crossed and its clawlike feet were delicately curved at rest. Even death did not mar its grace, for it lay on the earth like a broken vase of red flowers, and we stood around it, awed by its **exotic** beauty. **L**

"It's dead," Mama said.

"What is it?" Doodle repeated.

"Go bring me the bird book," said Daddy.
310 I ran into the house and brought back the bird book. As we watched, Daddy thumbed through its pages. "It's a scarlet ibis," he said, pointing to a picture. "It lives in the tropics—South America to Florida. A storm must have brought it here."

Sadly, we all looked back at the bird. A scarlet ibis! How many miles it had traveled to die like this, in *our* yard, beneath the bleeding tree.

"Let's finish lunch," Mama said, nudging us back toward the dining room.

"I'm not hungry," said Doodle, and he knelt down beside the ibis.

"We've got peach cobbler for dessert," Mama tempted from the doorway.

Doodle remained kneeling. "I'm going to bury him."

4 **Targeted Passage**

320 "Don't you dare touch him," Mama warned. "There's no telling what disease he might have had."

"All right," said Doodle. "I won't."

Daddy, Mama, and I went back to the dining-room table, but we watched Doodle through the open door. He took out a piece of string from his pocket

K SYMBOL
What clues suggest that the appearance of the bird might be important?

precariously
(prĭ-kâr′ē-əs-lē) *adv.* insecurely; in a dangerous or unstable way

exotic (ĭg-zŏt′ĭk) *adj.* excitingly strange

L SYMBOL
What characteristics of the scarlet ibis are emphasized in lines 298–306?

LITERARY ANALYSIS

K SYMBOL

Possible answer: The appearance of the bird is important because it is unexpected and startling. It causes the narrator to jump up, knock over his chair, and run for the door. Doodle, too, is amazed by the bird; he acts on his own to see it and speaks up about it, both of which are uncharacteristic of him. In addition, the story's title is "The Scarlet Ibis," so the first appearance of the title character is probably important.

If students need help . . . Have them list the actions in lines 279–286. Discuss how these actions compare with ordinary responses that they might have to seeing a bird land in a tree.

LITERARY ANALYSIS

L SYMBOL

Possible answer: The lines mention the bird's lack of coordination (line 299), its collapse to the ground (lines 299–301), the jerking of its graceful neck (line 301), the filming over of its eyes (line 302), the opening of its beak (line 303), its crossed legs (line 303), its delicate feet (lines 303–304), and its exotic, flower-like quality (lines 304–306). Taken together, the details emphasize the bird's graceful beauty—and the fact that it has died.

FOR LESS–PROFICIENT READERS

4 Targeted Passage [Lines 314–319]

This passage sets up a connection between Doodle and the ibis that has just died.

- When Mama says, "Let's finish lunch," what does Doodle say and do?

- How does Mama try to get Doodle's mind off the ibis?

- What does Doodle announce that he is going to do?

FOR ENGLISH LEARNERS

Comprehension: Transitions Explain that some words and phrases signal time; they tell *when* or in *what order.* Have students find these and other sequence words in the selection: "at first . . . but then" (line 70); "as" (line 258); "by the time" (line 284); "at that moment" (line 298); "after" (line 350). Discuss how each word or phrase signals time or time order.

and, without touching the ibis, looped one end around its neck. Slowly, while singing softly "Shall We Gather at the River," he carried the bird around to the front yard and dug a hole in the flower garden, next to the petunia bed. Now we were watching him through the front window, but he didn't know it. His awkwardness at digging the hole with a shovel whose handle was twice as long
330 as he was made us laugh, and we covered our mouths with our hands so he wouldn't hear.

When Doodle came into the dining room, he found us seriously eating our cobbler. He was pale and lingered just inside the screen door. "Did you get the scarlet ibis buried?" asked Daddy.

Doodle didn't speak but nodded his head.

"Go wash your hands, and then you can have some peach cobbler," said Mama.

"I'm not hungry," he said.

"Dead birds is bad luck," said Aunt Nicey, poking her head from the
340 kitchen door. "Specially *red* dead birds!" Ⓜ

As soon as I had finished eating, Doodle and I hurried off to Horsehead Landing. Time was short, and Doodle still had a long way to go if he was going to keep up with the other boys when he started school. The sun, gilded with the yellow cast of autumn, still burned fiercely, but the dark green woods through which we passed were shady and cool. When we reached the landing, Doodle said he was too tired to swim, so we got into a skiff and floated down the creek with the tide. Far off in the marsh a rail was scolding, and over on the beach locusts were singing in the myrtle trees. Doodle did not speak and kept his head turned away, letting one hand trail limply in the water.
350 After we had drifted a long way, I put the oars in place and made Doodle row back against the tide. Black clouds began to gather in the southwest, and he kept watching them, trying to pull the oars a little faster. When we reached Horsehead Landing, lightning was playing across half the sky and thunder roared out, hiding even the sound of the sea. The sun disappeared and darkness descended, almost like night. Flocks of marsh crows flew by, heading inland to their roosting trees; and two egrets, squawking, arose from the oyster-rock shallows and careened away.

Doodle was both tired and frightened, and when he stepped from the skiff he collapsed onto the mud, sending an armada of fiddler crabs rustling off into
360 the marsh grass. I helped him up, and as he wiped the mud off his trousers, he smiled at me ashamedly. He had failed and we both knew it, so we started back home, racing the storm. We never spoke (What are the words that can solder[12] cracked pride?), but I knew he was watching me, watching for a sign of mercy. The lightning was near now, and from fear he walked so close behind me he kept stepping on my heels. The faster I walked, the faster he walked, so

---

12. **solder** (sŏd′ər): to join or bond together.

Ⓜ SYMBOL
What is the connection between Doodle and the scarlet ibis?

Ⓜ **SYMBOL**

Possible answer: *Both are exotic creatures that have landed in a time or place that is not entirely hospitable to them. Both are delicate, frail, unusual beauties with short lives and tragic deaths.*

Lines 358–370
DISCUSSION PROMPTS

Use these prompts to help students understand details that will lead to the climax and resolution of the story:

Connect Think about a time when you let someone down. How does that experience help you understand what Doodle feels at this moment? *Answers may address emotions such as guilt, dependence, and despair.*

Analyze What makes this scene so challenging for Doodle? ***Possible answer:*** *The thunder and lightning would frighten anyone near or in water. Doodle is also extremely exhausted; feels shame at having let his brother down; and still has a terrible need for his brother, as evidenced by his cries of "Don't leave me!" (line 370)*

Evaluate Why is Hurst's reference to a "sign of mercy" (lines 363–364) effective? ***Possible answer:*** *It reminds readers how cruel the narrator has been—pushing Doodle mercilessly for weeks and now working him into such a state of exhaustion that he has collapsed onto the mud.*

DIFFERENTIATED INSTRUCTION

FOR ENGLISH LEARNERS

Comprehension: Prepositions Explain that some prepositions signal place. Invite students to use simple drawings to explain the concepts of place signaled by "across the burning cotton field" (line 84); "down into the green dimness where the palmetto fronds whispered by the stream" (lines 86–87); "far off . . . and over on the beach" (lines 347–348); "was playing across half the sky" (line 353).

FOR ADVANCED LEARNERS/PRE–AP

Make Judgments It is unlikely that a storm could have brought a scarlet ibis to North Carolina. In fact, the comment that the bird ranges as far north as Florida (line 312) is inaccurate. Does this create a serious flaw in this story? To make their judgments, students should build a case for what the story might have lost or gained had there been no scarlet ibis or had it been replaced by some other creature.

I began to run. The rain was coming, roaring through the pines, and then, like a bursting Roman candle, a gum tree ahead of us was shattered by a bolt of lightning. When the deafening peal of thunder had died, and in the moment before the rain arrived, I heard Doodle, who had fallen behind, cry out,

370 "Brother, Brother, don't leave me! Don't leave me!"

The knowledge that Doodle's and my plans had come to naught[13] was bitter, and that streak of cruelty within me awakened. I ran as fast as I could, leaving him far behind with a wall of rain dividing us. The drops stung my face like nettles, and the wind flared the wet glistening leaves of the bordering trees. Soon I could hear his voice no more. **N**

I hadn't run too far before I became tired, and the flood of childish spite **evanesced** as well. I stopped and waited for Doodle. The sound of rain was everywhere, but the wind had died and it fell straight down in parallel paths like ropes hanging from the sky. As I waited, I peered through the downpour, but no

380 one came. Finally I went back and found him huddled beneath a red nightshade bush beside the road. He was sitting on the ground, his face buried in his arms, which were resting on his drawn-up knees. "Let's go, Doodle," I said.

He didn't answer, so I placed my hand on his forehead and lifted his head. Limply, he fell backward onto the earth. He had been bleeding from the mouth, and his neck and the front of his shirt were stained a brilliant red.

"Doodle! Doodle!" I cried, shaking him, but there was no answer but the ropy rain. He lay very awkwardly, with his head thrown far back, making his vermilion[14] neck appear unusually long and slim. His little legs, bent sharply at the knees, had never before seemed so fragile, so thin.

390 I began to weep, and the tear-blurred vision in red before me looked very familiar. "Doodle!" I screamed above the pounding storm and threw my body to the earth above his. For a long long time, it seemed forever, I lay there crying, sheltering my fallen scarlet ibis from the **heresy** of rain. ∾

N MAKE INFERENCES
Why does the narrator continue to run when he knows Doodle has fallen behind him?

evanesce (ĕv'ə-nĕs') v. to disappear; vanish

⑤ Targeted Passage

heresy (hĕr'ĭ-sē) n. an action or opinion contrary to what is generally thought of as right

---

13. **had come to naught:** had resulted in nothing.
14. **vermilion** (vər-mĭl'yən): bright red to reddish orange.

THE SCARLET IBIS **441**

FOR LESS–PROFICIENT READERS

⑤ Targeted Passage [Lines 380–393]

This passage presents the story's resolution and clarifies its title.

- Where does the narrator find Doodle?

- What happens when he tries to get Doodle up? Why does Doodle not respond?

- How does the narrator describe Doodle's neck and legs? Why is the description familiar?

- In the final line, what does he call Doodle?

N MAKE INFERENCES

Possible answer: *The narrator is frustrated or irritated with Doodle, and running away seems to be his way of punishing him. Also, the reference to "cracked pride" (line 363) suggests that the narrator has given up on helping Doodle out of a sense of pride.*

ADDITIONAL TEACHING OPPORTUNITY

Evaluate Theme: Ask students to identify the story's **theme**—its underlying message about life or human nature. Then have students evaluate that theme and decide whether they think it is valid. Tell students to use these questions as their evaluation criteria:

- Does the theme express a broad insight into life or human nature, or simply an idea that applies only to a few people?

- Does the theme offer a meaningful insight, or is it too obvious or clichéd?

- Is the theme a realistic observation, or is it too optimistic, cynical, or narrow-minded?

Point out to students that a theme may be valid even if they do not personally agree with it. (To learn more about evaluating theme, see **Reading Handbook,** page R2.)

SELECTION WRAP–UP

REFLECT In what ways is "The Scarlet Ibis" a realistic story about childhood? In what ways is it more like a fantasy?

⭐ **CRITIQUE** "The Scarlet Ibis" is stuffed with symbols and loaded with imagery. Ask students whether they find the dense details and multiple symbols effective and interesting or over the top. Encourage them to cite details that support their answers.

READING FLUENCY

Distribute the copy master and have students work in pairs or groups to practice fluency.

RESOURCE MANAGER—Copy Master
Reading Fluency p. 84

ANALYZE VISUALS

Activity Ask students how well this image matches the instructions for plant care given in the poem. *Possible answer: The flower does seem to have been left alone or even abandoned, for it sits by an icy window in relative darkness. Still, the bloom is not seeking "the sunlight for itself"; instead, it has been turned to face the viewer.*

DISCUSSION PROMPTS

Use these prompts to help students make thematic and symbolic connections between "The Scarlet Ibis" and "Woman with Flower":

Connect How do you react to the concluding statement, "The things we love we have to learn to leave alone"? *Students may discuss the virtues of, or problems with, noninterference. They may argue that people are not plants.*

Apply Do the terms "careful prodding" (line 7) and "eager tenderness" (line 8) apply to events and characters in "The Scarlet Ibis"? Explain. *Possible answers: Yes, there was careful prodding as the narrator helped Doodle walk and then eagerly goaded him on to the possibility of greater accomplishments; No, the prodding was not careful or tender but arose from the narrator's pride and self-interest and was often cruel.*

Synthesize How do you think Doodle, the narrator, and their parents would react to the idea that the "leaf's inclined to find its own direction; / Give it a chance to seek the sunlight for itself"? Why? *Possible answer: All but the narrator might have agreed with this statement. They were content to let Doodle be who and what he would be; they did not have ambitions for him. Only the narrator saw things differently.*

WOMAN
with Flower

Naomi Long Madgett

I wouldn't coax the plant if I were you.
Such watchful nurturing may do it harm.
Let the soil rest from so much digging
And wait until it's dry before you water it.
5 The leaf's inclined to find its own direction;
Give it a chance to seek the sunlight for itself.

Much growth is stunted by too careful prodding,
Too eager tenderness.
The things we love we have to learn to leave alone.

442 UNIT 4: THEME AND SYMBOL

Comprehension

1. **Clarify** How is Doodle different from other children?

2. **Recall** What are the narrator's motives for teaching Doodle?

3. **Summarize** What happens to Doodle, and why?

Literary Analysis

4. **Make Inferences** Look back at the chart you made as you read. Review the inferences you made about the relationship between Doodle and the narrator. How would you describe their relationship over the course of the story?

5. **Analyze Character** The narrator has **mixed emotions** about Doodle. How might he answer the big question on page 426?

6. **Interpret Symbol** The narrator sees Doodle as the scarlet ibis at the end, but Doodle identifies with the exotic bird immediately. To explore this symbolic connection, identify as many similarities between the ibis and Doodle as you can. Record your comparison in a chart like the one shown.

Scarlet Ibis and Doodle
Both are unusual and don't fit in their surroundings.

7. **Analyze Theme and Symbol** Which of the following themes does the **symbolism** of the ibis support? Find details to support your answer.

   a. Selfish pride generally causes more harm than good.

   b. Delicate creatures need to be protected and cared for.

   c. Spiteful cruelty toward a loved one often stems from wounded pride.

8. **Examine Foreshadowing and Mood** Reread lines 298–306. The dramatic death of the ibis foreshadows Doodle's death. Find at least three other examples of such foreshadowing. What mood do they create?

9. **Compare Literary Works** What advice does the speaker in "Woman with Flower" seem to offer the narrator of "The Scarlet Ibis"? In what ways are the themes of these works similar? In what ways are they different?

Literary Criticism

10. **Author's Style** "The Scarlet Ibis" can be viewed as an example of Southern literature, which is characterized in part by its emphasis on details of time and place, the importance of family and community, an exploration of the past, and a sense of moral dilemma. How are these characteristics evident in this story? Cite details from the story to support your answer.

THE SCARLET IBIS 443

---

8. *Doodle's touching the coffin and his cry of "Don't leave me" immediately afterward are foreshadowing, as is the narrator's early comment that Doodle's real name, William Armstrong, "sounds good only on a tombstone." These details, all related to death and loss, create a mood of impending tragedy.*

9. *The speaker's advice is not to coax but to "learn to leave alone" the things we love. The narrator coaxed too eagerly, which, given the outcome of the story, suggests that too much interference is a bad thing.*

Nevertheless, the story presents mixed results of noninterference, whereas the poem suggests only its virtues.

Literary Criticism

Possible answer:

10. *Time and place: lines 1–3, 85–99; family and community: lines 16–22, 169–180; the past: lines 5–15; moral dilemma: lines 74–85, 100–118*

Practice and Apply

After Reading

For additional support of post-reading questions, use these copy masters:

R RESOURCE MANAGER—Copy Masters
  Reading Check p. 80 (to check understanding of the selection)
  Symbol p. 73 (for practice of literary analysis standards focus)
  Question Support p. 81 (After Reading questions adapted for English learners and less-proficient readers)

For additional questions, see page 67.

For additional exercises to challenge students, see:

ℹ Power Thinking at **ClassZone.com**

ANSWERS

Comprehension

1. *He is physically weaker than other children.*

2. *The narrator is motivated by embarrassment about his brother and by pride and self-interest.*

3. *Doodle dies in a storm. He tried to keep up with his brother, who ran from him, but the effort was too much for his frail body.*

Literary Analysis

Possible answers:

4. ■ **STANDARDS FOCUS** *Make Inferences They love each other, but Doodle is more innocent and needy, while the narrator is full of pride and self-interest. In many ways, their relationship is somewhat normal for children.*

5. *The narrator might say that we hurt the ones we love because we have the power to do so or because we may not be thinking about anyone but ourselves.*

6. ● **STANDARDS FOCUS** *Symbol Both are exotic. Both are out of place. Both are victims of storms; both die. Both are associated with red (Doodle is red with blood when he dies).*

7. *All three fit the story, but the symbolism of the ibis specifically supports theme b because both the ibis and Doodle are delicate creatures. For evidence, see lines 45–53, 250–253, and 287–306.*

ANSWERS

Vocabulary in Context

VOCABULARY PRACTICE

1. *b*	5. *b*
2. *d*	6. *b*
3. *b*	7. *b*
4. *c*	8. *d*

R RESOURCE MANAGER—Copy Master
Vocabulary Practice p. 78

VOCABULARY IN WRITING

To help students get started, ask questions such as these:

- What words or actions might Doodle *reiterate*?
- How did Brother's *doggedness* affect Doodle?

VOCABULARY STRATEGY: CONNOTATION
(also an EL language objective)

Begin by defining any words that students may not know, such as *simper*. Students may have an easier time placing the words if they first associate each word with a tone of voice, facial expression, or other indicator of attitude. For example, for the first item, they might think about the tone of voice and volume that might be used to talk, vent, or articulate and relate that to positive or negative feelings.

Possible answers:

1. *highly negative: vent; neutral: talk, articulate*

2. *neutral: new; positive: fresh, original*

3. *negative: finicky; negative to neutral: choosy; positive: particular*

4. *negative: smirk; positive: grin, smile*

5. *neutral: responsibility, obligation; neutral to positive: duty*

R RESOURCE MANAGER—Copy Master
Vocabulary Strategy p. 79

i Vocabulary Center at **ClassZone.com**
Additional Vocabulary Activities

Vocabulary in Context

VOCABULARY PRACTICE

Identify the word that is not related in meaning to the other words in the set.

1. (a) exotic, (b) ordinary, (c) unusual, (d) foreign
2. (a) impending, (b) imminent, (c) approaching, (d) remote
3. (a) fidelity, (b) heresy, (c) conformity, (d) compliance
4. (a) echo, (b) repeat, (c) originate, (d) reiterate
5. (a) errancy, (b) infallibility, (c) inaccuracy, (d) imperfection
6. (a) insecurely, (b) cleverly, (c) precariously, (d) dangerously
7. (a) disappear, (b) float, (c) vanish, (d) evanesce
8. (a) doggedness, (b) perseverance, (c) tenacity, (d) casualness

> **WORD LIST**
> doggedness
> evanesce
> exotic
> heresy
> imminent
> infallibility
> precariously
> reiterate

VOCABULARY IN WRITING

Use at least four vocabulary words in a paragraph that describes Doodle. Make sure that your paragraph creates a vivid image of him. Here is an example.

> **EXAMPLE SENTENCE**
>
> *From the very beginning, Doodle was like an* **exotic** *bird, staring at everyone with his arms flapping about.*

VOCABULARY STRATEGY: CONNOTATION

The term **connotation** refers to the attitudes or feelings associated with a word. For example, *doggedness* and *stubbornness* could both be defined as "the quality of not giving in readily," but Hurst's choice of the word *doggedness* to describe Doodle's efforts conveys positive connotations not associated with *stubbornness*. Writers use connotation to communicate certain feelings and to evoke a mood. Being aware of these connotations can enrich your understanding of what you read.

PRACTICE Place the words in each group on a continuum like the one shown to show the positive or negative associations each word connotes. Then compare your answers with those of a classmate.

highly negative ←——————————————→ *highly positive*

1. talk, vent, articulate
2. new, fresh, original
3. choosy, finicky, particular
4. smile, smirk, grin
5. responsibility, obligation, duty

> **VOCABULARY PRACTICE**
> For more practice, go to the **Vocabulary Center** at **ClassZone.com.**

DIFFERENTIATED INSTRUCTION

FOR ENGLISH LEARNERS

Vocabulary: Modifiers To review words that describe verbs, ask students to identify which words in the Vocabulary Practice describe verbs. *Possible answer: all the words in item 6* Ask students how they know this; if needed, review *-ly* endings for many words that describe verbs.

FOR ADVANCED LEARNERS/PRE–AP

Vocabulary in Writing Have students use some or most of the vocabulary words in two ways: one in a sentence that James Hurst might have written and the other in a sentence that another writer whose work they have read (such as Ray Bradbury in "A Sound of Thunder" [Unit 1]) might have written.

Reading-Writing Connection

Add to your understanding of "The Scarlet Ibis" by responding to these prompts. Then use **Revision: Grammar and Style** to improve your writing.

WRITING PROMPTS	SELF-CHECK

A. Short Response: Analyze Character
What is your opinion of Doodle's character? Write a **one- or two-paragraph response** that discusses his strengths and weaknesses, his fears, his imagination, and his relationship with his brother.

▶ *A successful explanation will . . .*
- identify at least one strength and one weakness
- include details or examples that support your opinion

B. Extended Response: Analyze Actions
Do you blame the narrator for what happens to Doodle? Consider his age, his **mixed emotions,** and what he says about himself. Write a **three-to-five-paragraph response** analyzing his role in Doodle's death.

▶ *A strong analysis will . . .*
- explain your judgment of the narrator's actions
- provide examples and quotations from the story

REVISION: GRAMMAR AND STYLE

VARY SENTENCE STRUCTURE Review the **Grammar and Style** note on page 434. Hurst uses a variety of sentence structures in his writing. Using only one type of sentence can make your writing sound dull.

All complete sentences contain at least one **independent clause,** which can stand on its own (*Doodle went to sleep.*) Some combine the independent clause or clauses with one or more **subordinate clauses,** which cannot stand alone. (*Doodle went to sleep <u>while the family ate dinner.</u>*) This kind of variety, as found in this passage from Hurst's story, makes for better-sounding prose:

> *I lifted him out and set him down in the soft rubber grass beside a tall pine. His eyes were round with wonder as he gazed about him, and his little hands began to stroke the rubber grass.* (lines 87–89)

Notice how the revisions in red improve the rhythm of this first draft. Revise your responses to the prompts by incorporating a variety of sentence structures.

> **STUDENT MODEL**
>
> The narrator sometimes shows he cares for Doodle. He also seems to enjoy making his brother feel trapped and alone. He treats Doodle like an animal. In reality, Doodle is just a child. He does his best to overcome a serious illness.

WRITING TOOLS
For prewriting, revision, and editing tools, visit the **Writing Center** at **ClassZone.com.**

DIFFERENTIATED INSTRUCTION

FOR LESS–PROFICIENT WRITERS

For Prompt A:

1. Provide a sentence starter such as *I think that Doodle is _____.* Ask for ways to complete it and choose one.
2. Write the completed sentence and add the word *because.*
3. Elicit reasons that support the opinion.

For Prompt B:

1. Have pairs discuss the issue and take notes.
2. Ask them to list quotations from the text that support their discussion points.
3. Have them refer to their notes as they write.

Reading-Writing Connection

WRITING PROMPTS

- For Prompt A, adapt the Character Traits Web copy master as a prewriting tool. Remind students to find textual evidence and details during the prewriting stage.

- For Prompt B, urge students to state their opinions and give three reasons for their opinons before they begin to write out their response.

For an extended writing activity, see
ⓘ Carol Booth Olson's Reading-Writing Lesson Plans at **ClassZone.com**

🧰 **BEST PRACTICES TOOLKIT—Transparency**
Character Traits Web p. D7

REVISION: GRAMMAR AND STYLE

1. Point out that the first sentence in the sample passage is a simple sentence, even though it has a compound predicate. The second sentence is compound-complex because it contains two independent clauses and a subordinate clause. (To learn more about clauses, see **Grammar Handbook,** page R62.)

2. Discuss how dull the student model is as a series of short sentences. Note that the first new sentence is compound-complex and that the second is complex.

3. Invite students to suggest other ways of revising the student model.

📕 **RESOURCE MANAGER—Copy Master**
Vary Sentence Structure p. 83

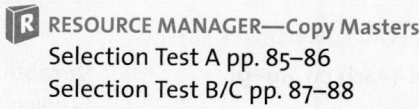
Assess and Reteach

Assess

📕 **RESOURCE MANAGER—Copy Masters**
Selection Test A pp. 85–86
Selection Test B/C pp. 87–88

💿 Test Generator CD

Reteach

 STANDARDS LESSON FILE
Literature Lesson 31: Symbols and Symbolism
Reading Lesson 8: Making Inferences
Vocabulary Lesson 17: Denotation and Connotation

Focus and Motivate

OBJECTIVES

Literary Analysis
- explore the key idea of **talent**
- analyze implied main idea
- read an essay

Reading
- analyze sequence of events

Vocabulary
- build vocabulary for reading and writing
- use context clues to help unlock the meaning of words in dialect

SUMMARY

In "Math and After Math," Lensey Namioka describes how she finally discovered her true talent. After a shaky start learning the abacus in China, Namioka immigrated to the United States and excelled in math, despite American gender prejudices. Over time, however, she came to realize that writing, rather than math, inspired her.

What are you really GOOD *at?*

Read and discuss the question with students. To lead into the **KEY IDEA,** ask students why they enjoy certain activities more than others. Have students link their enjoyment or success to a **talent.** Continue the dialogue by having partners complete the **DISCUSS** activity.

Math and After Math

Essay by Lensey Namioka

What are you really GOOD *at?*

KEY IDEA Knowing what you're good at can take you a long way toward finding work and activities that you enjoy. In "Math and After Math," Lensey Namioka describes how she first embarked on one career path and then later discovered her true **talent.**

DISCUSS Make a list of activities you particularly enjoy. For each one, list the skills that help you succeed at the activity. With a partner, brainstorm career possibilities that could make use of those skills.

Cooking
- ability to follow recipes
- knack for combining ingredients

446

Selection Resources

R RESOURCE MANAGER UNIT 4

Plan and Teach pp. 89–96

Literary Analysis
Summary pp. 97†*, 98‡*
Implied Main Idea pp. 99, 100†*
Question Support p. 109*

Reading
Analyze Sequence of Events
pp. 101, 102†*
Reading Check p. 107

Vocabulary
Study p. 103*
Practice p. 104
Strategy p. 105

Assessment
Selection Tests A, B/C pp. 111*, 113*
Test Generator CD

BEST PRACTICES TOOLKIT

Differentiated Instruction
pp. 31–38*

Scaffolding Instruction
pp. 43–46*

Graphic Organizers/Strategies
Jigsaw Reading • Sequence Chain
• Word Squares • New Word
Analysis

Reading Support
Audio Anthology CD*

Technology
Literature and Vocabulary Centers at **ClassZone.com**
WriteSmart CD

---

* Resources for Differentiation   † Also in Spanish   ‡ In Haitian Creole and Vietnamese

● ELEMENTS OF NONFICTION: IMPLIED MAIN IDEA

In nonfiction, the writer's central idea or message is called the **main idea**. The main idea may be stated directly, or it may be implied or suggested through details or anecdotes.

In "Math and After Math," Lensey Namioka develops the main idea primarily through a series of anecdotes. To identify the implied main idea as you read, ask yourself, What important idea is conveyed by the anecdotes? How does this idea relate to the author's conclusion?

■ READING SKILL: ANALYZE SEQUENCE OF EVENTS

The events in a memoir are not always described in the same sequence in which they occurred. When relating events, a writer may move back and forth in time to make a point. This skipping around in time can be confusing, however, so it's important for the reader to keep track of the real **sequence of events**. Signal words, such as *when, by the time,* or *for years,* help to clarify this sequence.

As you read "Math and After Math," use a chart to jot down the important events in each stage of Namioka's life. Then number them in the order they occurred in time.

Stage in Life	Order	Event
Second grade		Namioka suffers "abacus anxiety."
Years later		Family emigrates to America. Math is best subject.

▲ VOCABULARY IN CONTEXT

Lensey Namioka uses the following boldfaced words to tell her tale of personal discovery. Use context clues to determine the meaning of each one.

1. The speaker's **dialect** revealed that he was not a native of the area.
2. The movie's **scenario** included no plot twists or surprises.
3. Her ability to act is **intuitive**; she has never had a lesson.
4. The detective's **analytic** approach to solving problems led him to the killer.
5. Your **hypothesis** will not stand up to further testing.

Author Online

Lensey Namioka born 1929

Always an Outsider Lensey Namioka was born in China and moved to the United States when she was nine years old. She has lived in many places and, consequently, has felt herself to be something of an outsider wherever she has lived. It's not surprising, then, that the protagonists in her stories for young adults are usually outsiders too.

Multicultural Author Namioka's writing draws on both her Chinese heritage and her husband's Japanese heritage. She has written humorous novels about young Chinese immigrants in America, as well as a series of adventure-mystery books about two 16th-century Japanese samurai.

 MORE ABOUT THE AUTHOR
For more on Lensey Namioka, visit the **Literature Center** at **ClassZone.com**.

Background

Girls and Math In "Math and After Math," Namioka describes how she stood out in her American classrooms as a girl who was good at math. Researchers have long sought to determine whether the differences in math performance between girls and boys stem from biology or culture. In elementary school, girls tend to outperform boys in many subjects, including math. In high school, however, the situation changes. Statistics show that, as a group, boys score slightly higher than girls on math aptitude tests. Also, boys tend to choose math-related college majors and careers more often than girls do, although this is changing. Researchers continue to debate various hypotheses that explain these gender differences.

Teach

STANDARDS FOCUS

ELEMENTS OF NONFICTION

● IMPLIED MAIN IDEA

To support instruction, read aloud this anecdote, and ask what it implies about the character's musical interest and talent:

> Every afternoon, Dave listened to the jazz station on the radio. After he got a keyboard for his birthday, he spent every free minute learning his favorite pieces. Soon he was jamming with a band.

***Possible answer:** It implies that Dave's interest and talent in jazz are serious and may lead to continued involvement.*

CHECK UNDERSTANDING Ask what the *Background* implies about the current status of the biology–culture debate.

READING SKILL

■ ANALYZE SEQUENCE OF EVENTS

Stress the usefulness of signal words for tracking the sequence of events. For instructional support, ask students what the phrase *the other day* might signal: a recent event, or something that happened long ago. (*a recent event*)

CHECK UNDERSTANDING Ask students what each of these terms might signal: *now, a few years ago, on a recent outing.*

 **RESOURCE MANAGER—Copy Master**
Analyze Sequence of Events p. 101 (for student use while reading the selection)

VOCABULARY SKILL

▲ VOCABULARY IN CONTEXT

DIAGNOSE WORD KNOWLEDGE To determine preteaching needs, have all students complete Vocabulary in Context. *Possible answers:*
1. *regional or ethnic way of speaking,* 2. *plot summary,* 3. *instinctive,* 4. *logical,* 5. *theory*

PRETEACH VOCABULARY Use the Vocabulary Study copy master to help students explore meaning, using a word map, for each boldfaced word in the copy master.

1. Read the phrases with boldfaced vocabulary words.
2. Help students fill out a word map for *hypothesis,* using the chart on the copy master.
3. Have them create word maps for the other vocabulary words.

 **RESOURCE MANAGER—Copy Master**
Vocabulary Study p. 103

For general guidelines on differentiating vocabulary instruction and for alternative vocabulary activities for students not needing vocabulary preteaching, see

 BEST PRACTICES TOOLKIT
Scaffolding Vocabulary Instruction pp. 43–46
i Vocabulary Center at **ClassZone.com**

Practice and Apply

ANALYZE VISUALS

Possible answer: The girl in the photograph is poised to complete the problem on the blackboard, but her fingers have yet to write the answer. Perhaps, like the writer, she is stalled by anxiety. An abacus, like the one the writer describes in line 5, is in the upper right corner.

Lines 6–11
REINFORCE *KEY IDEA:* TALENT

Discuss How might the circumstances Namioka describes affect her mathematical **talent?**

Possible answer: *Moving to a strange part of the country under traumatic circumstances, as well as trying to adjust to an unfamiliar dialect, have created "abacus anxiety," a kind of nervous reaction that undercuts her ability to perform well in class.*

Math
and After Math

LENSEY NAMIOKA

"Seven!" shouted the teacher.

Or did he shout "Four"?

I shrank down in my seat. Math class was an absolute nightmare. The teacher scared me so much that my hands got sweaty, and my fingers slipped on the abacus[1] beads.

I was in the second grade when I discovered that I suffered from abacus anxiety. The trouble was that I was going to a school where the teacher spoke a different **dialect.** I grew up with Mandarin, the dialect spoken by the majority of the Chinese. When the eastern part of China was occupied by the Japanese, 10 our family moved inland, to a region where I could barely understand the local dialect.

Writing was pretty much the same in any dialect, so in language and history classes I didn't have trouble with what was on the blackboard. My problems started in the math class, where we had to learn the abacus. Before the days of the calculator, the abacus was the main tool for adding and multiplying. It still is, in many parts of China (as well as in countries like Japan and Russia).

The abacus teacher would shout out the numbers he wanted us to add or multiply. My ears didn't always understand what he said, so *seven,* for instance, sounded a lot like *four.*

ANALYZE VISUALS
What elements of the photograph reflect the writer's attitude toward math?

① Targeted Passage

dialect (dĭ'ə-lĕkt') *n.* a variety of a standard language unique to a certain region or social group

---

1. **abacus** (ăb'ə-kəs): a manual computing device consisting of rods hung within a frame and strung with movable counters.

DIFFERENTIATED INSTRUCTION

FOR ALL STUDENTS

Expert Groups Allow students to become experts or members of expert groups by researching and choosing a way to share information about one of these topics:

- the Japanese occupation of China
- U.S. immigration patterns since World War II
- the Cultural Revolution

FOR LESS–PROFICIENT READERS

In combination with the *Audio Anthology CD,* use one or more Targeted Passages (pp. 448, 451, 454, 455) to ensure that students focus on key events, concepts, and skills. Targeted Passages are also good for English learners.

① Targeted Passage [Lines 1–7]

This passage establishes the topic of Namioka's essay—the causes of girls' success or failure in math.

The Abacus This calculating device may have originated in ancient Babylon more than 2,000 years ago. Originally it was probably a board or slab with sand spread on top for tracing letters. The abacus developed into a board marked with lines and equipped with counters. The positions of the counters indicated numerical values, such as ones, tens, and hundreds. Today, the counters of an abacus are usually strung on wires. Experts possess the skill to compete on the abacus with modern mechanical calculators.

- Where does the opening anecdote take place?
- What grade was Namioka in at the time?
- Why did she suffer from anxiety in math class?

FOR ENGLISH LEARNERS

Options for Reading Have students use a Jigsaw Reading strategy to read sections of the essay and then come together to share what they have learned.

 BEST PRACTICES TOOLKIT
Jigsaw Reading p. A1

Prereading For prereading instruction for English learners, see

 BEST PRACTICES TOOLKIT
Scaffolding Reading Instruction pp. 43–46

FOR ADVANCED LEARNERS/PRE–AP

Pre-AP Exercises in the bottom channel provide additional challenge for students. Use these suggestions for small groups or individuals.

ADDITIONAL GUIDELINES

For more help with differentiation and tips for classroom management, see

 BEST PRACTICES TOOLKIT
Differentiated Instruction pp. 31–38

Ⓐ SEQUENCE OF EVENTS

Possible answer: *"Until," "Years later," "when," "forever"*

If students need help . . . To clarify how the signal words in this passage help establish a time sequence, complete a short Sequence Chain together.

> *until that class (math had been one of her better subjects)*
> **1.**

↓

> *during that class (begins to have trouble in math class)*
> **2.**

↓

> *years later (when her family has emigrated to America)*
> **3.**

 **BEST PRACTICES TOOLKIT—Transparency**
Sequence Chain p. B21

---

20   Until that class, math was one of my better subjects, especially when it came to multiplication. Years later, when we emigrated to America, I was astounded to hear one of my American friends recite the multiplication table:

"Two times one is two. Two times two is four. Two times three is six . . ." It seemed to take forever. Ⓐ

The multiplication table is much shorter in Chinese. One reason is that the Chinese names for numbers are all one-syllable. We don't have numbers like *seven*.

Also, we omit words like *times* and *equals* while reciting. Instead of "Seven times two equals fourteen," we say, *Er qi shi si,* or literally, *two seven fourteen.* So we do it in four syllables instead of eight.

30   The best trick is that we memorize only half as many entries, because we know that seven times two is the same as two times seven. (I learned later this was called the Commutative Law.)

This meant I could rattle off the multiplication table about three times faster than my American classmates. But I learned the table even faster than my *Chinese* classmates. The reason was that I sang it.

"You can remember a tune better than a string of numbers," my father told me. "So I want you to sing the multiplication table."

The standard way to teach musical notation in Chinese schools was to give numbers to the diatonic scale:[2] *do* was one (not a female deer), *re* was two (not

40   a ray of sunshine), *mi* was three, and so on. When I had to remember that two times seven was fourteen, my father told me to hum the little tune *re ti do fa.* This was not a pretty tune, but it certainly stuck in my mind.

---

2. **diatonic** (dī'ə-tŏn'ĭk) **scale:** the standard musical scale of seven tones, often referred to as *do, re, mi, fa, sol, la,* and *ti.*

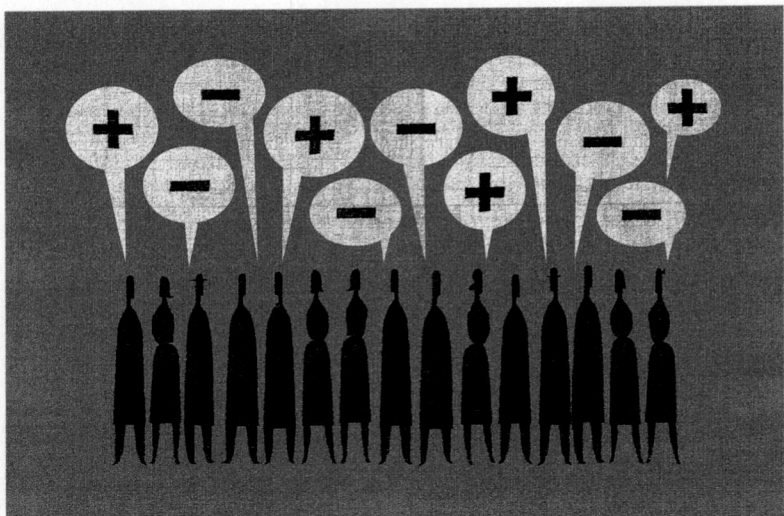

© Images.com/Corbis

Ⓐ **SEQUENCE OF EVENTS**
Reread lines 20–24. Which words indicate the passage of time?

DIFFERENTIATED INSTRUCTION

FOR ENGLISH LEARNERS

Multiple-Meaning Words Explain that *string* (line 36) refers here to a "series" or "sequence." As a noun, *string* can also mean "a thin piece of twisted fiber." Have mixed-language-ability Jigsaw Reading groups investigate these other multiple-meaning words and report their findings: "top" (line 72), "slip" (line 100), "addressed" (line 104), "argument" (line 108), "manage" (line 133), "crept" (line 136), and "squeeze" (line 202).

 BEST PRACTICES TOOLKIT
Jigsaw Reading p. A1

Following Father's suggestion, I learned the multiplication table very quickly, and even now I still hum. The other day, when I was in the store buying candy bars, I noticed another customer staring at me. I was trying to figure out if my fistful of change was enough for four candy bars, and I must have been humming as I multiplied.

When I entered American schools, my best subject was math. I didn't need to know much English to manage the Arabic numbers,[3] and my Chinese
50 school had been a year ahead of American schools in math (because of shorter multiplication tables, maybe). **B**

After a while I realized that my classmates found me weird. During our early years in America, my family lived in towns where there weren't too many Asians, and I looked different from everybody else in class. It turned out that my weirdness wasn't just because I looked different, or because I hummed funny tunes.

"How come you're so good at math?" asked one of my classmates.

"Why shouldn't I be?" I asked.

"You're a girl!"

60 In America, apparently, it was unusual for a girl to be good at math. It was different in China, where women were good at figures. They regularly kept the household accounts and managed the family budget.

A few years ago, I saw a movie about Chinese-Americans called *Dim Sum.*[4] A Chinese man who ran a restaurant in Chinatown brought his receipts to a woman friend, who figured out his accounts for him.

My American friends found the situation strange. "It's not unusual at all," I told them. "In my family, for instance, my mother made the major financial decisions."

In fact, my mother made a financial killing when we were living in Berkeley,
70 California. A neighbor took her to a land auction. A piece of land near our house was offered for sale, and Mother thought it would be fun to bid on it. Someone was bound to top her bid, she thought.

She was stunned when nobody else made a bid, and Mother found herself the owner of a large plot of land.

As she and her friend prepared to leave the auction room, a man rushed up to them. He was a realtor who had planned to bid for the land, but had arrived at the auction too late.

"I'll give you whatever you paid, plus something extra!" he told Mother.

"No, thank you," said Mother. "I'm quite happy with the purchase."

80 The realtor raised his offer, but Mother still turned him down. He became frantic. "Look, I'll go as high as two thousand dollars above your bid!"

This just made Mother more stubborn. "No, I want to keep the land."

The realtor obtained our address and phone number, and immediately called our house.

---

3. **Arabic numbers:** the numerical symbols *1, 2, 3, 4, 5, 6, 7, 8, 9,* and *0.*

4. **Dim Sum:** the movie title refers to a Chinese cuisine in which small portions of a variety of foods, including an assortment of dumplings, are served.

MATH AND AFTER MATH **451**

B IMPLIED MAIN IDEA
Consider Namioka's childhood success with math. What is she implying about Chinese math education?

2 Targeted Passage

ELEMENTS OF NONFICTION

B IMPLIED MAIN IDEA

Possible answer: Namioka implies that Chinese math education is more efficient, interesting, and fun.

If students need help . . . Have them find evidence in lines 48–51 that shows Namioka had a strong background in math when she came to the United States. Did her Chinese school build her confidence in math? Did it build her skills in math?

Lines 69–82
REINFORCE *KEY IDEA*: TALENT

Discuss What does this anecdote by Namioka suggest about her mother's **talent**? *Possible answer: The anecdote suggests that Namioka's mother had a talent for spotting a profitable real estate investment.*

FOR LESS–PROFICIENT READERS

2 Targeted Passage [Lines 52–59]

This passage introduces the conflicts generated by cultural differences and gender stereotypes.

- In what ways did Namioka's classmates find her "weird"?

- What was distinctive about the towns Namioka lived in at that time?

- What did Namioka's classmates say about her talent for math?

FOR ENGLISH LEARNERS

Key Academic Vocabulary Use Word Squares to teach these words: *financial* (line 68), *purchase* (line 79), *investment* (line 89), *assigned* (line 132), *debate* (line 155).

BEST PRACTICES TOOLKIT—Transparency Word Squares p. E10

C IMPLIED MAIN IDEA

Possible answer: The main idea is that Namioka's mother, with her husband's support and trust, made shrewd financial decisions.

If students need help . . .

- Have students read lines 78–81. What did the realtor offer Namioka's mother?
- Have students read line 82. Why did her mother become "more stubborn"?
- Have students read lines 85–88. How was Father's attitude different from the realtor's?

D SEQUENCE OF EVENTS

Possible answer: She is able to reveal the connection she felt between mathematical "story problems" and writing, especially in the areas of fiction and romance. In contrast, the American students seem to have found story problems difficult and unappealing.

Extend the Discussion What does this passage show about the writer's imagination?

When Father answered the phone, the realtor shouted, "Do you know what your wife just did? She threw away a chance to make two thousand dollars!"

"I'm sure she had her reasons," Father answered calmly. Nothing that the realtor said could disturb him.

The land turned out to be an excellent investment, and helped to provide a 90 tidy nest egg for my parents in their old age. **C**

In many other Asian countries, too, the housewife is the one who manages money. It's normal for the husband to hand over his paycheck to his wife, and out of it she gives him an allowance. Perhaps it's the result of Confucius's teaching[5] that a gentleman is above money, so it's the woman's duty to be concerned with such petty matters.

Things were very different in America. An American husband would hit the roof if his wife did what my mother had done. Women here were supposed to be hopeless when it came to money matters and figures.

Many girls got good math grades in elementary school, but their grades 100 began to slip when they entered middle school. By then they were getting interested in boys, and they didn't want the boys to think they were weird.

I was weird in elementary and middle school because I was a real whiz at multiplication. In high school, I continued to be a whiz in my geometry and algebra classes. I was lucky to have a geometry teacher who addressed us by last name and didn't care whether you were a boy or a girl, as long as you agreed with Euclid.[6]

My high school geometry class was also the first place where the word *argument* meant something good. My parents complained that I was always arguing. In geometry class, making an argument meant presenting something 110 in an orderly, logical manner.

I also liked the story or word problems in my algebra class. Years later, when I was teaching math, I couldn't understand why many students complained bitterly about them. To me, story problems meant fiction, romance. The most **D** exciting one involved an army column marching forward at a certain speed. A messenger at the head of the column was sent back to the rear. If the column was so many miles long, would he be able to deliver his message in time? I pictured the following **scenario:**

"We expect to engage the enemy in half an hour," the commander told the messenger. "You have to get word to the men in the rear of the column!"

120 The mud-splashed rider desperately lashed his horse, while arrows fell on him from ambushers. How fast did he have to ride so that he would reach the rear guard in time to deliver his message?

Attacking these story problems with relish, I was usually one of the first in the class to finish, and I was often sent to the board to write out the solution.

---

5. **Confucius's** (kən-fyōō'shəs-ĭz) **teaching:** the Chinese philosopher Confucius (551–479 B.C.) taught ideas about practical moral values that are still widely followed in China today.

6. **Euclid** (yōō'klĭd): a third-century-B.C. Greek mathematician upon whose ideas much of the study of geometry in schools is based.

C IMPLIED MAIN IDEA
Reread Namioka's anecdote about her mother's real estate purchase. What is the main idea of this anecdote?

D SEQUENCE OF EVENTS
In this paragraph Namioka flashes forward to her adulthood. What is she able to reveal by doing this?

scenario (sĭ-når'ē-ō') *n.* a description of a possible course of action or events

---

DIFFERENTIATED INSTRUCTION

FOR ENGLISH LEARNERS

Vocabulary: Idioms and Sayings Use New Word Analysis to teach these idioms and expressions from the essay: *nest egg* (line 90), "money put aside as a reserve fund"; *hit the roof* (lines 96–97), "become very angry"; *whiz* (line 102), "expert."

 BEST PRACTICES TOOLKIT—Transparency
New Word Analysis p. E8

FOR ADVANCED LEARNERS/PRE–AP

Allusions [small-group option] Point out that writers use allusions, or references to famous people, events, literature, or ideas, to add interest, voice, or tone. Have students review Namioka's allusions to Confucius (lines 93–95) and Euclid (lines 104–106). Ask them to explain how each allusion adds an amusing note to Namioka's style.

A math lecture in a university lecture hall

By the time I started college, I began to realize that it was unusual, unnatural—maybe even unhealthy—for girls to be good at math. I entered Radcliffe College, which was connected with Harvard. Some of my laboratory courses were taken together with the Harvard students, but classes such as English and math were taught separately on the small Radcliffe campus.

130   The English classes usually had around twenty students, but my beginning calculus class had only five of us. According to rumor, new instructors at Harvard were assigned to teach Radcliffe math classes as a test.

"If they manage to get through the year without breaking down, they're allowed to go on to higher things," we heard.

On the first day of our math class, the instructor (who later became a famous mathematician) crept into the room without looking at us, and spent the whole period mumbling into the blackboard. In fact, he spent the whole year mumbling into the blackboard.

"He's awfully shy, isn't he?" I remarked to a friend.

140 "Maybe he's just scared of girls who study math," she said.

Things got better when I entered the University of California, which was co-ed. The math classes were larger, and five girls in a class of forty boys weren't enough to scare the instructors.

By this time I knew that in America a girl who was good at math was not only unusual, unnatural, unhealthy, but—worst of all—unattractive.

"Boys don't date you if you're a math whiz," I was told. **E**

The situation was different for me. First of all, racial cross-dating was still rare when I was in college, so I dated only Chinese-American boys, who were hardened to the sight of their mothers or sisters doing math.

150 I got very good grades in math throughout my school years and majored in mathematics in college. I had a head start in the multiplication table, and I loved arguing and proving things. By the time I learned that I wasn't supposed to do well in math, it was too late.

A hot topic when I was in graduate school was the right-brain, left-brain debate. Scientists decided that men tended to use their left brain, which was the reasoning part, while women used their right brain, the **intuitive** part.

"That's why we're good at hard sciences and math," the boys in my classes assured us. "You girls should stick with poetry, history, art, and things like that. It's a matter of genes or hormones."

160 Then, later studies showed that the Japanese listened to insect sounds with their left (**analytic**) brain, while Westerners listened to insects with their right brain. Still other studies showed that professional musicians (both male and female) listened to music with the analytic side of their brain, while the general public listened with their intuitive side.

It began to seem that training and social pressure, not genes and hormones, influenced which side of the brain was used. I eagerly followed the debate and could hardly wait for the day when it was okay for women to study science and math in America. **F**

Today, attitudes are finally beginning to change. My daughters tell me that
170 girls in high school math classes are less afraid to do well, and many women go into science and math in college. (One of my daughters is a computer scientist, and the other is an engineer.)

> For years, I seemed to be doing well in math because of my Chinese background, because I wasn't afraid to get good math grades in school. I did all the assigned problems without much trouble. But it wasn't enough to do all the problems assigned by the teacher. To be a creative mathematician, you also have to make up problems. I finally learned that I would never do really original work in mathematics.
>
> I found that, for math at least, I lacked what the Chinese call *huo qi,*[7]
180 literally "fiery breath," in other words, ambition and drive. In English the

3 Targeted Passage

---

7. ***huo qi*** (hwō chē).

Sidebar (left column)

ELEMENTS OF NONFICTION

E IMPLIED MAIN IDEA

Possible answer: The anecdotes suggest that American girls do poorly in math because of prejudice, narrow-mindedness, and gender stereotypes that equate success in math to unattractiveness.

ELEMENTS OF NONFICTION

F IMPLIED MAIN IDEA

Possible answer: The studies referred to in these lines support Namioka's main idea that talent and success are not "built-in" or "hard-wired" features in an individual. Instead, to a large degree, they are products of training and social expectations.

Lines 169–172
REINFORCE *KEY IDEA*: TALENT

Discuss Why does Namioka believe attitudes today are changing, and that girls and women are less afraid to show their **talent** in math and science? *Possible answer: Namioka believes what her daughters tell her: Girls do well in high school math classes and then pursue careers in science and math. Her daughters' own careers are proof. One daughter is a computer scientist, and the other is an engineer.*

Sidebar (right column)

E IMPLIED MAIN IDEA
What do Namioka's anecdotes about college suggest is the main reason that American girls do poorly in math?

intuitive (ĭn-tōō′ĭ-tĭv) *adj.* based on what seems to be true without conscious reasoning; instinctive

analytic (ăn′ə-lĭt′ĭk) *adj.* using logical reasoning or analysis

F IMPLIED MAIN IDEA
Reread lines 160–168. How do these later studies on the brain support Namioka's main idea?

DIFFERENTIATED INSTRUCTION

FOR LESS-PROFICIENT READERS

3 Targeted Passage [Lines 173–180]

This passage introduces the last section of the essay, where Namioka's focus shifts from prejudice and social pressure to her honest evaluation of her true talents.

- Why was Namioka not afraid to do well in math in school?
- What do you need in order to become a creative mathematician?
- What did Namioka find she lacked in the field of mathematics?

FOR ENGLISH LEARNERS

Vocabulary: Phrasal Verbs Explain that *threw away* (line 86) means "wasted." Assign students these phrasal verbs to look up in a dictionary and have them share definitions: "make up" (line 177), "dried up" (line 189), "thrown in" (line 206), "worked out" (line 207).

expression "fire in the belly" comes close. I didn't think I was creative enough in mathematics to do good research, nor did I have the drive. **G**

My immediate excuse for getting out of math was the difficulty of arranging for childcare. To be completely honest, I have to admit that I left mathematics because I wasn't all that good, despite my early impressive grades.

I made the transition from mathematics to freelance writing through translation work. For a brief period, I translated mathematical papers from Chinese into English.

190 My work dried up, however, when the Cultural Revolution[8] swept over China. Mathematicians, like other scholars, were ordered to stop research and write papers confessing their political shortcomings. (These were the lucky ones. The unlucky ones spent their time cleaning latrines.) With no mathematical papers to translate, I eventually took up freelance writing.

My parents reproached me. "How can you give up a beautiful subject like mathematics?"

"We can admire beautiful pictures or music," I told them. "But we don't all have the gift to paint or compose."

"You spent so many years studying math," some people say. "Does it help you at all in your writing?"

200 Math has taught me the useful lesson of thrift. I've met hundreds of mathematicians, and not one of them was a spendthrift. In math you're taught to squeeze the strongest possible result out of the weakest possible **hypothesis**—in other words, you try to get the most value for your money.

This thrifty habit stayed with me after I became a writer. When I put people or events into a book, I squeeze the most out of them. Very few things are thrown in and then forgotten later. As a result my plots seem to be carefully worked out in advance, instead of being made up as I go along.

Years ago, I enjoyed story problems because the stories fired my imagination. In fact, writing fiction was where I finally found my "fiery breath." Instead

210 of story problems, I can write problem stories. And that's what I'm still doing today. ❧

---

8. **Cultural Revolution:** a political upheaval in China in the 1960s that resulted in many attacks on intellectuals.

G IMPLIED MAIN IDEA
What does Namioka suggest is needed in order for a person to express a true talent?

④ Targeted Passage

hypothesis (hī-pŏth′ĭ-sĭs) *n.* an assumption made in order to test its possible consequences

---

ELEMENTS OF NONFICTION

G IMPLIED MAIN IDEA

Possible response: Namioka suggests that a person needs ambition and drive, or "fire in the belly," to express a true talent.

SELECTION WRAP-UP

SUMMARIZE Have students sum up what Namioka learned about the effects of society and culture on an individual's intellectual development.

⭐ **CRITIQUE** Have students evaluate Namioka's ideas about talent and ability. Ask them to explain whether they agree with her and to give reasons.

FOR LESS-PROFICIENT READERS
④ Targeted Passage [Lines 200–211]

This passage concludes the essay by drawing a parallel between Namioka's enjoyment of math and her discovery of her true talent: writing stories.

• What does Namioka mean by "thrift"?

• How does Namioka's "thrifty habit" help her with developing characters and plots?

• When did Namioka finally find her "fiery breath"?

FOR ADVANCED LEARNERS/PRE-AP

Apply [small-group option] Have students consider how Namioka's essay might apply to other fields or careers besides math. Ask them how stereotypes contribute to lower expectations and prevent people from developing their true talents. Ask them to write a small paragraph expressing their responses.

Practice and Apply

After Reading

For additional support of post-reading questions, use these copy masters:

R **RESOURCE MANAGER—Copy Masters**

Reading Check p. 107 (to check understanding of the selection)

Implied Main Idea p. 99 (for practice of elements of nonfiction standards focus)

Question Support p. 109 (After Reading questions adapted for English learners and less-proficient readers)

For additional questions, see page 93.

ANSWERS

Comprehension

1. *She learned math under the easier Chinese system, where expectations were high for girls' performance in math.*

2. *They regarded her talent as unusual, even weird, because, in America, girls were not expected to do well in math.*

3. *The Chinese typically assume that girls and women have an aptitude for math, and so they exhibit a relaxed and evenhanded attitude toward them.*

4. *She realized that she lacked the creativity needed for research and the ambition and drive necessary for high achievement.*

Critical Analysis

Possible answers:

5. *The main cultural difference is in the different expectations of girl's learning math. In China, girls are expected to perform well in math. Namioka's experiences at school and college in America, as well as her story about her mother's financial dealing, illustrate this difference.*

6. *The internal conflict concerns Namioka's self-image as a member of an ethnic minority and as a talented student of math—an unusual strength for girls in America. The external conflict revolves around the expectations of Namioka's peers and of her parents.*

7. ● **STANDARDS FOCUS** *Implied Main Idea The main idea is that gender stereotypes lead to poor performance, which in turn contributes to low expectations for success. This damaging cycle has little to*

Comprehension

1. **Recall** Why did Namioka do so well in math as a young child?

2. **Recall** In the United States, how did Namioka's classmates regard her talent for math? Why?

3. **Summarize** According to Namioka, what is the typical Chinese attitude about girls' and women's abilities in the area of math?

4. **Clarify** Why did Namioka finally give up her work in mathematics?

Critical Analysis

5. **Compare and Contrast Cultures** What is the main cultural difference discussed in this selection? Support your answer with details from the selection.

6. **Analyze Conflict** In this essay, Namioka traces her struggle to determine her true **talent**. What part of this conflict is **internal?** What part is **external?** Give reasons for your responses.

7. **Identify Implied Main Idea** In your own words, state the main idea of this selection. Cite evidence from the selection to support your answer.

8. **Evaluate Sequence** On your sequence chart, review the parts of the essay where Namioka describes events out of chronological order. In each case, evaluate the effect of this change of sequence. Do you think this is a good technique? Cite evidence to explain your opinion.

9. **Make Judgments** How do contemporary views on women's talent in math compare with those discussed in this selection? Cite evidence to support your claim.

456 UNIT 4: THEME AND SYMBOL

---

do with true talent or ability. Most of the anecdotes in the essay support this idea.

8. ■ **STANDARDS FOCUS** *Analyze Sequence Students may cite anecdotes such as Namioka's surprise about the recital of the multiplication table when she first emigrated to America (lines 21–24), or the reference to the Chinese movie (lines 63–65). In each case, the departure from chronological sequence helps Namioka elaborate or flesh out the main idea.*

9. *Contemporary views about girls and women in math are more tolerant and relaxed than they used to be. As evidence, Namioka cites her daughters' experiences and the fact that one is a computer scientist, and the other is an engineer (lines 169–172).*

Vocabulary in Context

VOCABULARY PRACTICE

Decide whether these statements are true or false.

1. If you have an **intuitive** understanding of a procedure, you will probably check each step as you go.
2. Spanish is a **dialect** of English.
3. A student asking for more homework is an unlikely **scenario.**
4. A **hypothesis** is often the first step in an investigation.
5. A person with an **analytic** mind could probably be a successful mathematician.

> **WORD LIST**
> analytic
> dialect
> hypothesis
> intuitive
> scenario

VOCABULARY IN WRITING

Write a summary of this memoir using at least three of the vocabulary words. Here is a sample opening.

> **EXAMPLE SENTENCE**
> The teacher's **dialect** confused young Namioka and stopped her from doing her best in math.

VOCABULARY STRATEGY: USING CONTEXT CLUES

Dialect refers to a variety of speech that differs from the standard speech patterns of a given culture. Vocabulary is one element of dialect. For example, a person might refer to a sweet, carbonated beverage as a soda, a pop, or a soft drink, depending on where he or she lives in the United States. You can often infer the meaning of a word in dialect by noting **context clues** in the sentences and paragraphs that surround the word.

PRACTICE Identify the meaning of the underlined term in each sentence. Use context clues and your own knowledge to determine its meaning. Work with other students to try to identify where or by whom the term is mostly used.

1. Put a <u>schmeer</u> of cream cheese on that bagel.
2. The <u>gumbands</u> holding the papers together were old and frayed.
3. You can pack your lunch in that little <u>poke</u>.
4. My grandparents lived on the top floor of the <u>two-flat</u> where I grew up.
5. That <u>plug</u> ought to be put out to pasture.
6. After drinking the chocolate <u>frappé</u>, he wasn't hungry for dinner.
7. Leon is getting together with his <u>homeboys</u>.
8. You can get some water from the <u>bubbler</u> in the hallway.

> **VOCABULARY PRACTICE**
> For more practice, go to the **Vocabulary Center** at **ClassZone.com.**

ANSWERS

Vocabulary in Context

VOCABULARY PRACTICE

1. *false*	3. *true*	5. *true*
2. *false*	4. *true*	

 RESOURCE MANAGER—Copy Master
Vocabulary Practice p. 104

VOCABULARY IN WRITING

Suggest that students begin by listing the major anecdotes Namioka uses to support the main idea of her essay.

VOCABULARY STRATEGY: USING CONTEXT CLUES *(also an EL language objective)*

Have students work with a partner during this activity, taking turns substituting a meaning for each underlined word.

Possible answers:

1. small portion (Yiddish)
2. rubber bands (Pennsylvania)
3. sack; carrying bag (Southern)
4. two-story (Chicago)
5. old horse (Western)
6. partly iced drink; milk shake (Eastern)
7. close friends; buddies (urban)
8. water cooler (Wisconsin, Australia)

RESOURCE MANAGER—Copy Master
Vocabulary Strategy p. 105

Vocabulary Center at **ClassZone.com**
Additional Vocabulary Activities

Assess and Reteach

Assess

RESOURCE MANAGER—Copy Masters
Selection Test A pp. 111–112
Selection Test B/C pp. 113–114

Test Generator CD

Reteach

STANDARDS LESSON FILE
Literature Lesson 12: Theme
Reading Lesson 6: Recognizing Sequence and Chronological Order
Vocabulary Lesson 15: Context Clues

Focus and Motivate

OBJECTIVES

Literary Analysis
- explore the key idea of **responsibility**
- analyze author's perspective
- read an essay

Reading
- monitor comprehension

Grammar and Writing
- add rhetorical questions for effect
- use writing to analyze literature

SUMMARY

In her essay "The Future in My Arms," Haitian-born writer Edwidge Danticat recalls becoming an aunt at the age of thirty. Holding her new-born niece, Danticat feels both protective and humbled as she reflects on the responsibility of adults to provide a *repozwa*—a sacred place of refuge—for their community's children.

What does a community OWE *its* CHILDREN?

Read and discuss the question with students. Explore the *KEY IDEA* by asking students to paraphrase the African proverb and suggest the kinds of **responsibility** involved in raising a child. Then use the proverb to introduce the *QUICKWRITE*, in which students think about the "village" that has raised them. Suggest that students jot down some notes about the person they choose before they start writing. Invite students to share their paragraphs or to give a copy to the person about whom they have written.

Selection Resources

The Future in My Arms
Essay by Edwidge Danticat

What does a community OWE *its* CHILDREN?

KEY IDEA Parents, of course, have a huge commitment to their children. But what is the **responsibility** of a community to its young? A familiar African proverb states, "It takes a village to raise a child." Do you agree?

QUICKWRITE In a small group, discuss how people in your community have influenced your life. Did someone teach you to play soccer or baseball? What about the person who always made a point of asking how you were doing? Create a concept web, as shown, with people who have helped you. Then choose one person and write a paragraph describing how he or she has made a difference in your life.

People Who Helped Me

Basketball Coach

taught me to be a team player

458

R RESOURCE MANAGER UNIT 4

Plan and Teach pp. 115–122

Literary Analysis
Summary pp. 123†*, 124‡*
Author's Perspective pp. 125, 126†*
Question Support p. 130*

Reading
Monitor pp. 127, 128†*
Reading Check p. 129

Grammar and Writing
Add Rhetorical Questions p. 131

Assessment
Selection Tests A, B/C pp. 133*, 135*
Test Generator CD

BEST PRACTICES TOOLKIT

Differentiated Instruction
pp. 31–38*

Scaffolding Instruction
pp. 43–46*

Graphic Organizers/Strategies
Word Squares • Two-Column Chart

Reading Support
Audio Anthology CD*

Technology
Literature and Vocabulary Centers at **ClassZone.com**
Write*Smart* CD

---

* Resources for Differentiation   † Also in Spanish   ‡ In Haitian Creole and Vietnamese

LITERARY ANALYSIS: AUTHOR'S PERSPECTIVE

An **author's perspective** is the lens through which a writer views a subject. This lens is made up of the writer's ideas, values, feelings, and beliefs—products of the writer's life experiences and cultural upbringing. For example, in "Math and After Math" (page 448), Lensey Namioka writes from the perspective of a Chinese–American female who has a talent for math and was raised to believe that it is "not unusual at all" for a woman to excel at mathematics. Readers learn her perspective from direct statements as well as anecdotes that illustrate her views.

As you read "The Future in My Arms," determine Edwidge Danticat's perspective by examining the following:

- statements of opinion
- tone, or attitude
- diction, or word choice
- repeated words or ideas
- the descriptions of cultural customs
- the portrayal of her niece

READING STRATEGY: MONITOR

Monitoring is the strategy of checking your comprehension as you read and intentionally using other strategies to improve it. For example, if as you read you realize that you are not understanding the text very well, you might decide you need to slow down your reading pace, reread, or skim the next section before reading it. With "The Future in My Arms," the following strategies may be especially helpful:

- **Predict** what will happen later in the selection.
- **Question** the events described and their significance.
- **Reread** passages that you find confusing.

As you read, keep track of your thoughts, ideas, and questions by jotting them down.

Author Online

An Early Start
When Edwidge Danticat came to the United States from Haiti at the age of 12, she had a hard time fitting in at school. She sought refuge in writing and began a story that would develop into her first novel, *Breath, Eyes, Memory.* She published the novel in 1994, when she was in her mid-20s, after earning a Master of Fine Arts degree in creative writing from Brown University. Other major works include *Krik? Krak!*, *The Farming of Bones*, and *The Dew Breaker*.

Edwidge Danticat born 1969

One Voice in a Million Critics have acclaimed Danticat as "the voice of Haitian Americans," but she resists the title. Danticat says, "There are millions and millions of Haitian voices. Mine is only one. My greatest hope is that mine becomes one voice in a giant chorus that is trying to understand and express artistically what it's like to be a Haitian immigrant in the United States."

 MORE ABOUT THE AUTHOR
For more on Edwidge Danticat, visit the **Literature Center** at ClassZone.com.

Background

The Haitian Diaspora Danticat's transition into a new country and culture was eased by the support of her family and of the Haitian community in Brooklyn, New York. Many Haitians emigrate to the United States and other countries to escape the extreme poverty and political instability of their native country. This emigration of hundreds of thousands of Haitians to other countries has been called the Haitian Diaspora.

Teach

STANDARDS FOCUS

LITERARY ANALYSIS

● AUTHOR'S PERSPECTIVE

For instructional support, discuss what the quotation in **One Voice in a Million** suggests about Danticat's perspective. *Possible answer: The quotation suggests that Danticat is proud of her Haitian heritage and is eager to share her experiences as an immigrant. Discuss what students might expect the essay to be like, based on that perspective. Possible answer: The essay might present Haitian culture in a way that is appealing and that shows Danticat's pride in her people and their traditions.*

CHECK UNDERSTANDING Have students choose two passages from this essay and discuss the author's perspective in each one.

READING STRATEGY

■ MONITOR

Model using the strategies to monitor understanding of the *Background* text. For example, predict that the essay will give a sense of what the Haitian community is like, question the events that led Haitians to leave their homeland, and reread the final sentence to clarify the meaning of *Haitian Diaspora*.

CHECK UNDERSTANDING Have students repeat the process you modeled, using **An Early Start.**

 RESOURCE MANAGER—Copy Master
Monitor p. 127 (for student use while reading the selection)

DIFFERENTIATED INSTRUCTION

FOR ENGLISH LEARNERS
Culture: Connect The references on this page to Edwidge Danticat's immigrant experience will resonate with many students who are learning English. Invite students who were born (or whose parents were born) outside the United States to add their special insights to class discussions of "The Future in My Arms."

FOR ADVANCED LEARNERS/PRE–AP
Evaluate a Quotation When students have finished reading "The Future in My Arms," have them return to this page and reread the Danticat quotation in **One Voice in a Million.** Ask them if they think that this essay has fulfilled what Danticat calls her "greatest hope" by sharing her experiences in an artistic but clear manner. Urge students to cite textual details that support their views.

Ⓐ MONITOR

Possible answer: The title's reference to the future and the painting's image of the little child suggest that the essay may focus on adults' responsibility to care for children.

Ⓑ AUTHOR'S PERSPECTIVE

Possible answer: These lines show Danticat to be sensitive, observant, and tenderly appreciative of children. Supporting details include her waiting intensely for the birth of her niece (line 5) and her lifelong dream of having a sister (line 9).

ANALYZE VISUALS

Possible answer: The repozwa *concepts of "sacred place," "shelter," and "a place where a child can rest her head," are suggested by the peaceful embrace of the woman and the quiet sleep of the child on her shoulder.*

About the Art April Harrison's art features an intricate mix of layered artistic materials, including paints and powders. She is well-known for her tapestry of vibrant, rich colors. A self-taught artist, Harrison often focuses her work on the warmth, strength, and comfort of bonded relationships, especially of motherly love. She lives and works in Greenville, South Carolina.

THE FUTURE in My Arms Ⓐ
Edwidge Danticat

I had never held any living thing so tiny in my hands. Six pounds and one ounce, lighter than my smallest dumbbell was my newborn niece, her face bright pink, her eyes tightly shut, her body coiled around itself in a fetal position, still defiantly resisting the world into which she'd just been thrust. I had been awaiting her birth with feverish anticipation; I was going away for the summer, and I didn't want to leave before she was born, only to come back eight weeks later and find that she had grown accustomed to most things in the world except her only auntie on her father's side, the sole woman child in a family of men, who all her life had dreamed of having a sister. Ⓑ

10 She arrived the day before I was to leave. I was at the Brooklyn Public Library researching an article when I called to check my messages. In a breathless voice, my brother Andre announced, "You are now the proud aunt of Nadira Amahs Danticat.[1] Her name means, 'She whom God has chosen.'"

I ran out of the library and headed toward a flower shop on Flatbush Avenue. As I approached, I heard someone call out my name. It was my brother Karl and Mia, who were expecting their own child in a few months. They, too, were heading to the hospital to see Nadira.

On the way there, I remembered a message that a girlfriend of mine, a new mother, had sent me for my thirtieth birthday a few months before. "May 20 your arms always be a repozwa, a place where a child can rest her head," it said. I had told her that two of my brothers were becoming fathers, and she wanted me to share those words with them. But I'd decided to wait until both my niece and nephew were born to share this with their parents—that we had each become a *repozwa*,[2] the Haitian Creole[3] term for "sacred place," in whose shelter children would now seek rest.

---

1. **Nadira Amahs Danticat** (nä-dîr'ä ä-mäs' dăn-tĭ-kä').
2. *repozwa* (rā-pōz-wä').
3. **Haitian Creole:** the French-based language spoken in Haiti.

Ⓐ **MONITOR**
Based on the essay title and the painting, what do you **predict** this essay will be about?

Ⓑ **AUTHOR'S PERSPECTIVE**
What do lines 1–9 reveal about Danticat's attitude toward children, especially her niece? Cite details.

① **Targeted Passage**

ANALYZE VISUALS
What elements of this painting suggest the idea of *repozwa* mentioned and defined in lines 22–25?

Mama's Cradle, April Harrison. Mixed media collage on canvas board, 14" × 18". © April Harrison.

DIFFERENTIATED INSTRUCTION

FOR ALL STUDENTS

Enhancing Learning Styles Provide these independent projects for various learning preferences:

- **Verbal** Write a dialogue.
- **Musical** Compose a lullaby.
- **Visual** Create an illustration.

For further details, see

R RESOURCE MANAGER
Ideas for Extension pp. 120–121

FOR LESS–PROFICIENT READERS

In combination with the *Audio Anthology CD*, use one or more Targeted Passages (pp. 460, 462, 463) to ensure that students focus on key events, concepts, and skills. Targeted Passages are also good for English learners.

① Targeted Passage [Lines 18–25]

This passage introduces the term *repozwa*, which embodies the essay's theme.

- What birthday message had Danticat received from one of her friends?

THE FUTURE IN MY ARMS **461**

Possible answer: The lines might signify that older family or community members share a common destiny—traveling through life's journey—with children.

If students need help . . . Note the title of the poem and remind students that Danticat herself is thirty years old (line 19). Call on a volunteer to read the lines of poetry aloud. Ask students to describe the speaker and guess who "you" might be in the lines "i want to tell / you about me . . . / here is my hand."

LITERARY ANALYSIS

D AUTHOR'S PERSPECTIVE

Possible answer: Danticat's promises indicate a belief that adults have a responsibility to love, protect, and shelter the children in their community.

Extend the Discussion Does this idea conflict with the belief that adults should help children learn to become responsible adults? Why or why not?

E GRAMMAR AND STYLE

Rhetorical Questions Explain that readers are expected to think about rather than answer rhetorical questions. Also note that a series of rhetorical questions can increase a writer's emotional impact. Have students identify the list of items in each question and discuss their importance.

By the time we got to the hospital, my sister-in-law, Carol, had already had a few visitors. She appeared exhausted but in good spirits as she and Andre took us down the corridor to the maternity-ward window. Which one was Nadira? Andrew wanted us to guess, to pick her out of the rows of infants like a long-lost relative in a crowd of strangers. We were aided in our task by the small pink name tag glued to her bassinet. Carol asked if we wanted to have a closer look. We went back to the room and waited for the nurse to bring her in.

We all stood up when she was carried in. I knew I was getting ahead of myself, but this made me think of a wedding where everyone immediately— and almost instinctively—rises to greet the bride. She was passed from loving hand to loving hand, but I kept her longer. I would soon have to leave, so I wanted to hold her, to cradle her in my arms, let her tiny head rest in the crook of my elbow. I wanted to watch her ever so slightly open her eyes and tighten her mouth as she battled to make sense of all the new sounds around her, all the laughter, the wild comparisons with relatives living and gone, all so very present in her face. I wanted to read her lines from Sonia Sanchez's "Poem at Thirty": "i am here waiting / remembering that / once as a child / i walked two / miles in my sleep. / did i know / then where i / was going? / traveling. i'm always traveling. / i want to tell / you about me . . . / here is my hand." **C**

Nadira's presence had already transformed the room. Her opening her eyes was like a Hollywood press conference, with all the video and picture cameras going off, trying to capture something that perhaps none of us knew how to express, that we had suddenly been allowed a closer view of one of life's great wonders, and by being there, were an extension of a miracle that happened every second of every day in every part of the world, but had generously now granted us a turn.

That day, when we lined up for a glance, a touch, a picture, and tried to imagine a life for Nadira in a new country, we each made our own silent promises not to let her face that new world alone. We were telling her and her parents that we were her village with our offers of baby-sitting favors, our giant teddy bears, our handfuls of flowers, and the crooks of our arms and necks and laps, which we hoped that she would run to if she ever needed a refuge. **D**

Looking back on my own thirty years, having crossed many borders, loved and lost many family and friends, young and old, to time, migrations, illnesses, I couldn't help but worry for Nadira, and for my nephew yet to be born. Are there ahead for them wars, a depression, a holocaust, a new civil-rights struggle as there were for those children born at the dawn of the last century? Will they have to face the colonization of new planets, genetic cloning, new forms of slavery, and other nightmares we have yet to imagine? Will we, their tiny village, give them enough love and assurance to help them survive, thrive, and even want to challenge those things? **E**

Before handing Nadira back to her parents, I felt torn between wanting her to grow up quickly so that her body might match the wits she'd need to face her future and at the same time wanting her to stay small so that she might be

C MONITOR
Reread lines 42–45. What significance might these lines of poetry have for Danticat?

2 Targeted Passage

D AUTHOR'S PERSPECTIVE
What do Danticat's promises suggest about her beliefs concerning the responsibility adults have toward children?

E GRAMMAR AND STYLE
Reread lines 62–67. Notice how Danticat poses a series of **rhetorical questions** about the future to prompt readers to share her concern.

DIFFERENTIATED INSTRUCTION

FOR LESS—PROFICIENT READERS

2 Targeted Passage [Lines 46–52]

This passage focuses on Danticat's love for her infant niece.

- Why does Danticat compare the scene at the hospital to a Hollywood press conference?

- What effect does Nadira have on the hospital room?

- What "miracle" is happening all the time, everywhere? Why, then, is it so special to Danticat?

FOR ENGLISH LEARNERS

Comprehension: Transitions Point out that events that occur simultaneously or nearly at the same time can be sequenced by using signal words and phrases such as "when" (lines 11 and 34), "as" (line 15), "on the way there" (line 18), "until" (line 22), "when . . . and" (line 53), "before" (line 68), and "at the same time" (line 70).

Circle of Joy, Keith Mallett. © Keith Mallett Studio, Inc./www.keithmallett.com.

easier to shield and carry along the length of our elbows to the reach of our palms. I wanted to tell her parents that though I had never held any living thing so tiny in my hands, I had never held anything so grand either, a bundle so elaborately complex and yet fragile, encompassing both our past and our future.

Though Nadira and my soon-to-arrive nephew were not created specifically with me in mind, I felt as though they were the most magical gifts that could ever have blessed my thirtieth year of life. Humbled by my responsibility to them, I silently promised their parents that for the next thirty years and the

80 thirty after that, my heart and soul would be their children's repozwa, a sacred place where they would always find rest. ◌

Activity Ask students how the image highlights Danticat's overall theme of adult responsibility toward children. *Possible answer: The three women (who may be the child's mother, grandmother, and great-grandmother) tenderly cradle the infant in their arms. The image conveys a sense that multigenerational family members are creating a strong safety net for the child. The image relates well to Danticat's concluding promise to be Nadira's repozwa at all times (lines 78–81).*

About the Art The subject matter of American artist Keith Mallet (b. 1948) ranges from figurative to still life and abstracts.

SELECTION WRAP–UP

SUMMARIZE In what ways does the family of Nadira Amahs Danticat promise to be a *repozwa* for her?

⭐ **CRITIQUE** Ask students to state whether they felt that Danticat made a compelling argument. Do students feel that it is realistic to ask adults to help care for other people's children? What are some benefits and advantages that adults derive from mentoring youngsters?

FOR LESS–PROFICIENT READERS

③ Targeted Passage [Lines 76–81]

As the essay concludes, this passage sets a tone of loving determination.

• What kind of "gifts" does Danticat call her niece and nephew?

• Why does she say that she is blessed? Why does she say that she is humbled?

• What promise does she make? If she keeps that promise, what can her niece and nephew expect of her in the future?

FOR ADVANCED LEARNERS/PRE–AP

Analyze Structure [paired-activity option] Have students reread and compare the paragraphs in lines 18–25 and lines 76–81. Ask students why Danticat might have chosen to return to the idea of *repozwa* at the end of the essay, thus creating a circular structure in her writing.

Practice and Apply

After Reading

For additional support of post-reading questions, use these copy masters:

R RESOURCE MANAGER—Copy Masters

Reading Check p. 129 (to check understanding of the selection)

Author's Perspective p. 125 (for practice of literary analysis standards focus)

Question Support p. 130 (After Reading questions adapted for English learners and less-proficient readers)

For additional questions, see page 119.

ANSWERS

Comprehension

1. *Danticat is the baby's aunt.*

2. *Danticat regards the baby as "one of life's great wonders" (lines 49–50) and as one of "the most magical gifts" that she could receive (line 77).*

3. *Besides the author, the baby is the only female child in a family of men.*

4. *She hopes to be a* repozwa, *a place where the girl always can find safety and rest.*

Literary Analysis

Possible answers:

5. ■ **STANDARDS FOCUS** *Main Idea Adults in a community have a responsibility to protect and care for the community's children, even if these children are not their own.*

6. ● **STANDARDS FOCUS** *Author's Perspective Danticat believes that adults must give children "love and assurance to help them . . . thrive" (line 66). Adults also must convey a sense of identity and cohesiveness to the community's children by accepting the responsibility of care and concern (lines 55–58).*

7. *Origin: Haitian Creole*
Literal Meaning: "sacred place"
Connotations: shelter, refuge, love, concern, protection, spirituality
Significance in Essay: sums up writer's thesis or main idea

8. *Nadira encompasses the past because she is the descendant of relatives, both living and dead (line 41). She encompasses the future because she will confront challenges that*

After Reading

Comprehension

1. **Recall** What is Danticat's relationship to the baby she holds?

2. **Recall** How does Danticat regard the baby and her birth?

3. **Clarify** Why is the baby so special to her?

4. **Summarize** What role does she hope to play in the baby's life?

Literary Analysis

5. **Identify Main Idea** Review the questions, thoughts, and ideas you noted as you **monitored** your reading. Then, using this information as a guide, state the main idea, or **thesis**, of "The Future in My Arms."

6. **Make Inferences About Author's Perspective** What can you infer about Danticat's values, feelings, and beliefs concerning the role of adults in children's lives? Support your inferences with details from the text.

7. **Analyze Concept** Complete a concept chart like the one shown for the word *repozwa*. What is the significance of the word in this essay? Give evidence to support your answer.

Repozwa
Origin:
Literal Meaning:
Connotations:
Significance in Essay:

8. **Interpret Text** Reread lines 72–75. What does Danticat mean when she states that the baby Nadira encompasses "both our past and our future"? Support your answer with details from the essay.

Literary Criticism

9. **Social Context** How do your community's views on the **responsibility** of adults toward children compare with those in this selection? Consider the role of institutions such as parks, schools, daycare facilities, and neighborhood-watch programs in your area. What role do neighbors and extended families have in the care of children? Cite evidence to support your evaluation.

464 UNIT 4: THEME AND SYMBOL

---

present-day adults may not even imagine (lines 62–65).

Literary Criticism

9. *Accept any response that is adequately supported by specific details and that makes a reasonable comparison.*

Reading-Writing Connection

Increase your understanding of "The Future in My Arms" by responding to these prompts. Then use **Revision: Grammar and Style** to improve your writing.

WRITING PROMPTS

A. Short Response: Analyze a Text
Danticat has many concerns about the world her niece and nephew will encounter. Are her fears valid, or is she overreacting? Write a **one- or two-paragraph response** explaining your thoughts.

SELF-CHECK

A strong analysis will . . .
- state an opinion and give reasons to support it
- provide examples from the text as support

B. Extended Response: Write a Letter
How might Danticat encourage a community to become a *repozwa* for its children? Drawing on ideas in her essay, write a **three-to-five-paragraph letter** that Danticat might send to a local newspaper encouraging that community to examine its **responsibilities** to its children.

A successful response will . . .
- clearly state the writer's views
- include rhetorical questions to motivate readers

REVISION: GRAMMAR AND STYLE

ADD RHETORICAL QUESTIONS Review the **Grammar and Style** note on page 462. Here, the author uses **interrogative sentences** to ask rhetorical questions that not only express her own concerns but also prompt similar concerns in her readers. Unlike other questions, **rhetorical questions** do not require answers; they are used for effect. For example, notice how the following rhetorical questions make this paragraph more powerful than it would be with only declarative statements:

A community is only as strong as its members. Our community needs to reach out to all children who live in our town. What are their needs? What will help them grow strong? How can we help them become responsible citizens who will, in turn, make this a better community?

Now study the following model. Notice how the revisions in red make this first draft more powerful and effective.

STUDENT MODEL

What is my responsibility to this child? What is our responsibility to all children in the community?

Recently, I became an aunt to a beautiful baby girl. This joyous occasion caused me to reflect upon my role in her life. ~~I started to consider my responsibilities to her and the other children in our community.~~

> **WRITING TOOLS**
> For prewriting, revision, and editing tools, visit the **Writing Center** at ClassZone.com.

THE FUTURE IN MY ARMS **465**

DIFFERENTIATED INSTRUCTION

FOR LESS–PROFICIENT WRITERS

For Prompt A:
- Encourage students to jot notes or do some freewriting to explore their thoughts about the various fears that Danticat mentions.
- Work with students to write a sentence that states their opinion clearly.
- Encourage peer reviews in which students can evaluate and strengthen their explanation.

For Prompt B:
- Suggest that students limit their response to two or three paragraphs.
- Help students generate persuasive arguments relating to two civic or community organizations or programs.
- Have students brainstorm in small groups to develop arguments that relate to the specific needs of their community.

Reading-Writing Connection

WRITING PROMPTS
- For Prompt A, have students reread the specific details that Danticat mentions in lines 62–65. Encourage them to use a Two-Column Chart to list her fears and their response to each one.
- For Prompt B, suggest that students look for ideas about community responsibility in their answer to question 9 on page 464. Students can use lines 62–67 as a model for their rhetorical questions.

 BEST PRACTICES TOOLKIT—Transparency
Two-Column Chart p. A25

For writing support, see

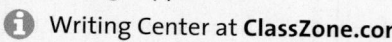 Writing Center at **ClassZone.com**

REVISION: GRAMMAR AND STYLE
After students examine the paragraph and the student model, have them rewrite the rhetorical questions in the paragraph as declarative sentences. When students compare the two versions, they probably will agree that the rhetorical questions strengthen the persuasive appeal of the paragraph.

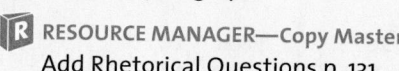 **RESOURCE MANAGER**—Copy Master
Add Rhetorical Questions p. 131

Assess and Reteach

Assess

RESOURCE MANAGER—Copy Masters
Selection Test A pp. 133–134
Selection Test B/C pp. 135–136

Test Generator CD

Reteach

STANDARDS LESSON FILE
Literature Lesson 47: Author's Perspective
Reading Lesson 2: Monitoring

THE FUTURE IN MY ARMS **465**

Focus and Motivate

OBJECTIVES

Literary Analysis
- explore the key idea of **nature**
- compare and contrast universal themes
- read poetry

Reading
- read poetry for theme

SUMMARIES

"Poem on Returning to Dwell in the Country"
The speaker explains that he was once ambitious and materialistic, but has now given up such entrapments. He will return to the mountains and hills that he loved as a child and will live simply in a cottage.

"My Heart Leaps Up" The speaker shares his lifelong joy at seeing rainbows and declares that he would prefer death to losing his ability to feel joy in nature.

"The Sun" The speaker describes the pleasure the sun gives to those who are open to its beauty. She asks if the reader understands—or is, instead, crazily pursuing power and material objects.

Where do you go to GET AWAY *from it all?*

Read the question and discuss the paragraph. Ask students to name aspects of **nature** that many people enjoy (such as mountains, beaches, and sunsets). After students complete the *QUICKWRITE,* invite volunteers to share their paragraphs.

Selection Resources

Poem on Returning to Dwell in the Country
Poem by T'ao Ch'ien

My Heart Leaps Up
Poem by William Wordsworth

The Sun
Poem by Mary Oliver

Where do you go to GET AWAY *from it all?*

KEY IDEA What does **nature** do for you? Whether it's staring at a fishbowl, escaping to the mountains, or simply taking a walk in the park, many people look to nature for beauty, serenity, or rejuvenation. The poems that follow reflect on the experience of basking in the natural world.

QUICKWRITE Make a concept web like the one shown, identifying a part of nature you enjoy and how it makes you feel. Then write a paragraph explaining your thoughts.

Requires patience; slows me down

Going Fishing

Makes me feel self-sufficient *Quiet is soothing*

466

RESOURCE MANAGER UNIT 4

Plan and Teach pp. 137–144

Literary Analysis
Universal Theme pp. 145, 146†*
Question Support p. 149*

Reading
Reading Poetry for Theme
    pp. 147, 148†*
Reading Fluency p. 150

Assessment
Selection Tests A, B/C pp. 151*, 153*
⊘ Test Generator CD

BEST PRACTICES TOOLKIT

Differentiated Instruction
    pp. 31–38*

Graphic Organizers/Strategies
Y Chart

Reading Support
⊘ Audio Anthology CD*

Technology
ℹ Literature and Vocabulary Centers at **ClassZone.com**
⊘ Write*Smart* CD

LITERARY ANALYSIS: UNIVERSAL THEME

Some poems have a **universal theme;** they express ideas that people from many cultures and times have found to be true. The poems you are about to read all describe a love of nature. Although written by poets who lived centuries apart and in very different cultures, all three poems touch upon the same universal theme. As you read each poem, use these strategies to identify their shared message:

- Think about the idea each poem is expressing about nature. What theme does each poem convey?
- Examine each poet's approach to the subject and look for similarities and differences.

READING STRATEGY: READING POETRY FOR THEME

The words in a poem are carefully chosen and arranged to convey the poet's message. As a result, to understand **theme** in poetry, you need to look at details differently than you would when reading prose. The strategies that follow can help you discover the theme in each poem in this lesson:

- Identify the **speaker,** or voice, that "talks" to the reader. What attitude does the speaker have toward the subject of the poem?
- Notice key **images** and think about their meanings.
- Identify words and phrases that are emphasized or repeated or that strike you as important. Consider what ideas and feelings the words and phrases convey.

As you read, keep a list of significant words, images, and phrases from each poem.

"Poem on Returning to Dwell in the Country"

"For my nature always/loved the hills and mountains." (lines 3–4)

Author Online

T'ao Ch'ien: Grandfather of Chinese Wilderness Poetry T'ao Ch'ien worked for the government before he returned to his family farm to live as a farmer—a radical decision at the time. His poetry reflects Taoist philosophy, which emphasizes living simply and close to nature. Both his life and his natural, conversational style of poetry inspired many later Chinese writers.

T'ao Ch'ien
365–427

William Wordsworth: England's Poet of Nature William Wordsworth grew up in the Lake District of northern England. As a boy, he loved being outdoors and appreciated the natural beauty of the region; this love of nature never left him. His poetry introduced a new view of the relationship between people and nature. Wordsworth became one of the leaders of the Romantic movement in English literature.

William Wordsworth
1770–1850

Mary Oliver: American Celebrant of Nature Mary Oliver became a distinguished poet and professor without ever having finished college. Her poetry, which links the worlds of people, animals, and plants, has won the Pulitzer Prize and the National Book Award.

Mary Oliver
born 1935

 MORE ABOUT THE AUTHOR
For more on these poets, visit the **Literature Center** at ClassZone.com.

467

Teach

STANDARDS FOCUS

LITERARY ANALYSIS

● UNIVERSAL THEME

To help students learn, write these lines on the board:

> Filled with excitement and yet with fear,
> I drop my toys and approach the door.
> Stepping through, I face a year
> Of change, of growth, of wonders in store!

Elicit that this stanza suggests **universal themes** related to growing up and/or facing the future.

CHECK UNDERSTANDING Ask students to name other themes that they would consider universal.

READING STRATEGY

■ READING POETRY FOR THEME

Apply the strategies in the text to the stanza in the **Literary Analysis** teaching activity. Ask students what feelings are suggested by *fear* and *change* and by *excitement, growth,* and *wonders.* Then discuss why certain words stand out and why the image of stepping through an open doorway is effective.

CHECK UNDERSTANDING Have students work with partners to present a **theme** from the same stanza in their own words, following the strategies in the text.

R RESOURCE MANAGER—Copy Master
Reading Poetry for Theme p. 147
(for student use while reading the selections)

DIFFERENTIATED INSTRUCTION

FOR LESS–PROFICIENT READERS
Clarify Concepts As the text notes, part of determining a poem's theme involves examining the poet's approach to his or her subject. Make sure that students understand what is meant by an "approach."

- Define *approach* as "the methods that an author uses to accomplish his or her purpose." If writing is meant to persuade, for example, then *approach* refers to the ways

in which the author tries to get readers to agree with him or her.

- Explain that many poems are meant to describe. In this case, *approach* refers to the ways in which the poet tries to help readers experience sensory impressions.
- Explain that poets use various methods to achieve their purposes. Vivid images, precise word choices, repetition, and unusual comparisons are just a few methods in a poet's approach.

Practice and Apply

ANALYZE VISUALS

Activity Ask students to describe how the painting captures the key idea of **nature**.

Possible answer: *The painting presents a beautiful natural landscape, but it also emphasizes the appreciation of nature by portraying a person who is admiring that landscape.*

About the Art *Plum Blossoms by Moonlight* by Chinese artist Ma Yuan (c. A.D. 1190–c. A.D. 1225) shows a scholar contemplating the moon beyond a plum tree.

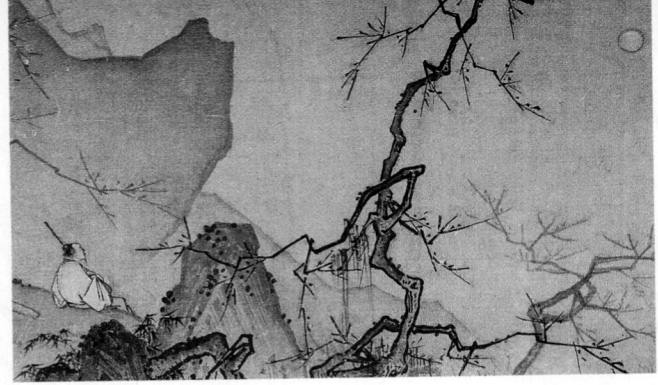

Plum Blossoms by Moonlight, Ma Yuan, Southern Sung. John M. Crawford, Jr. Collection. Photo © Wan-go H. C. Weng/Metropolitan Museum of Art, New York.

Poem on Returning to Dwell in the Country

T'ao Ch'ien

In youth I had nothing
    that matched the vulgar tone,[1]
For my nature always
    loved the hills and mountains.
5 Inadvertently I fell
    into the Dusty Net,[2]
Once having gone
    it was more than thirteen years.
The tame bird
10 longs for his old forest—
The fish in the house-pond
    thinks of his ancient pool. Ⓐ
I too will break the soil
    at the edge of the southern moor,
15 I will guard simplicity
    and return to my fields and garden.
My land and house—
    a little more than ten acres,
In the thatched cottage—
20 only eight or nine rooms.
Elms and willows
    shade the back verandah,
Peach and plum trees
    in rows before the hall.

Ⓐ **READING POETRY**
Consider the **images** in lines 9–12. Why does the speaker mention the tame bird and the fish in the house-pond?

---

1. **matched the vulgar tone:** The speaker is saying that he was never coarse or raucous in his youth.

2. **Dusty Net:** a term that refers to being caught up in professional ambition and materialism.

468   UNIT 4: THEME AND SYMBOL

DIFFERENTIATED INSTRUCTION

For general guidelines on differentiating instruction, see

 BEST PRACTICES TOOLKIT
Differentiated Instruction pp. 31–38

FOR LESS–PROFICIENT READERS

Options for Reading Before helping students analyze each of the poems in this lesson, read each poem aloud. Encourage students to enjoy the images, sounds, and ideas that each poet expresses. After students have examined the poems, allow individuals to give a dramatic reading of one of the poems or have small groups plan and present a choral reading.

25 Hazy and dimly seen
        a village in the distance,
    Close in the foreground
        the smoke of neighbors' houses.
    A dog barks
30   amidst the deep lanes,
    A cock is crowing
        atop a mulberry tree.
    No dust and confusion
        within my doors and courtyard;
35 In the empty rooms
        more than sufficient leisure.
    Too long I was held
        within the barred cage.
    Now I am able
40   to return again to Nature. **B**

            Translated by William Acker

B UNIVERSAL THEME
Reread the last four lines.
What is the "barred cage"?

My Heart Leaps Up

WILLIAM WORDSWORTH

My heart leaps up when I behold
    A rainbow in the sky:
So was it when my life began;
So is it now I am a man;
5 So be it when I shall grow old,
    Or let me die! **C**
The Child is father of the Man;
And I could wish my days to be
Bound each to each by natural piety.[1]

C UNIVERSAL THEME
Paraphrase what the
speaker reveals in lines
1–6 about his feelings
toward nature.

---

1. **piety** (pī'ĭ-tē): the quality of showing devotion or
   being reverent.

FOR ENGLISH LEARNERS
Comprehension: Transitions Understanding
these terms that signal spatial relationships
in T'ao Ch'ien's poem will help students
appreciate the scope and vividness of its
description of nature: "at the edge of" (line
14), "in" (lines 19, 24, 26, 27, and 35), "before"
(line 24), "amidst" (line 30), "atop" (line 32),
"within" (lines 34 and 38).

FOR ADVANCED LEARNERS/PRE–AP
Synthesize Wordsworth ends "My Heart
Leaps Up" with a statement that includes
the expression "natural piety" (line 9). After
students have read all three poems in this
lesson, come back to this statement. Ask
students to write an extended definition
of *natural piety* based on details in the
three poems. Have students compare their
definitions in small groups.

Lines 21–32
REINFORCE *KEY IDEA:* NATURE
Discuss Review the details about the speaker's
new setting. What generalization can you
make about why he will enjoy returning to
nature? *Possible answer: The natural setting
will be beautiful and serene.*

LITERARY ANALYSIS

B UNIVERSAL THEME

*Possible answer: The "barred cage" is
the way of life that the speaker is giving
up—his life of being trapped in the "Dusty
Net" (line 6) of ambition and materialism,
far removed from nature.*

**Prereading for "My Heart Leaps Up" is found
on page 466.**

LITERARY ANALYSIS

C UNIVERSAL THEME

*Possible answer: I feel joy when I see a
rainbow. It is a feeling I have had since
childhood, and it continues today. I will
feel the same pleasure in rainbows when I
am old; if I cannot, I don't want to live!*

ANALYZE VISUALS

Activity This contemporary photograph by
Bill Binzen is titled *The Heart of Trees.* Ask
students how the image whimsically captures
Wordsworth's attitude toward nature.
*Answers will vary, but students should point
out the connection between the heart-shaped
cutout in the tree and Wordsworth's image.
The heart in the photograph provides a literal
window into nature, while the speaker's heart
leaps up in response to nature.*

Prereading for this poem is found on page 466.

SELECTION WRAP–UP

SYNTHESIZE Have students explain how all of the poems encourage them to view **nature**.

⭐ **CRITIQUE** Have students choose one element of each poet's technique and evaluate its effectiveness.

READING FLUENCY

Distribute the copy master and have students work in pairs or groups to practice fluency.

RESOURCE MANAGER—Copy Master
Reading Fluency p. 150

The SUN
Mary Oliver

Have you ever seen
anything
in your life
more wonderful

5 than the way the sun,
every evening,
relaxed and easy,
floats toward the horizon

and into the clouds or the hills,
10 or the rumpled sea,
and is gone—
and how it slides again

out of the blackness,
every morning,
15 on the other side of the world,
like a red flower

streaming upward on its heavenly oils,
say, on a morning in early summer,
at its perfect imperial distance—
20 and have you ever felt for anything **D**

such wild love—
do you think there is anywhere, in any language,
a word billowing enough
for the pleasure

25 that fills you,
as the sun
reaches out,
as it warms you

as you stand there,
30 empty-handed—
or have you too
turned from this world—

or have you too
gone crazy
35 for power,
for things? **E**

D READING POETRY
Note the **imagery** in lines 5–20. What can you **infer** about the speaker's attitude toward nature from this description of the sun?

E UNIVERSAL THEME
Notice that the speaker asks several questions in this poem. What clues do these questions give you for identifying the theme?

DIFFERENTIATED INSTRUCTION

FOR LESS–PROFICIENT READERS
Clarify Structure Mary Oliver presents "The Sun" as a single long sentence. Help students break the poem into the five questions that form its true structure. Have them locate the occurrences of "have you"—the words that introduce questions in lines 1, 20, 31, and 33. Then point out "do you," which signals the question in line 22. Note, too, that the first four questions end with a dash instead of a question mark.

FOR ADVANCED LEARNERS/PRE-AP
Analyze Style [small-group option] Point out that "The Sun" is an example of free verse. Since the poem lacks rhyme, meter, and a fixed form such as that of a sonnet, the poet must unify ideas using various other methods. Challenge students to analyze how Oliver uses repetition, the sounds of words, and other literary elements to unify ideas in this poem.

Comprehension

1. **Recall** In "Poem on Returning to Dwell in the Country," what change does the speaker make in his life?

2. **Recall** In "My Heart Leaps Up," what does the speaker wish for?

3. **Summarize** In "The Sun," what does the speaker regard as the most wonderful thing in life?

Literary Analysis

4. **Compare and Contrast** In "Poem on Returning to Dwell in the Country," contrast the speaker's feelings about his former life in the city and his new life in the country. Why does the speaker prefer the country life? Provide evidence from the poem to support your answer.

5. **Interpret Meaning** "My Heart Leaps Up" includes the famous line "The Child is father of the Man." Think about how childhood experiences influence the person one becomes as an adult. What do you think the speaker means?

6. **Make Inferences** In "The Sun," who is the **speaker** addressing? Pay particular attention to the last stanza of the poem.

7. **Analyze Universal Theme** Use a chart like the one shown to record the theme reflected in each poem. Then come up with a single universal theme that all three poems share.

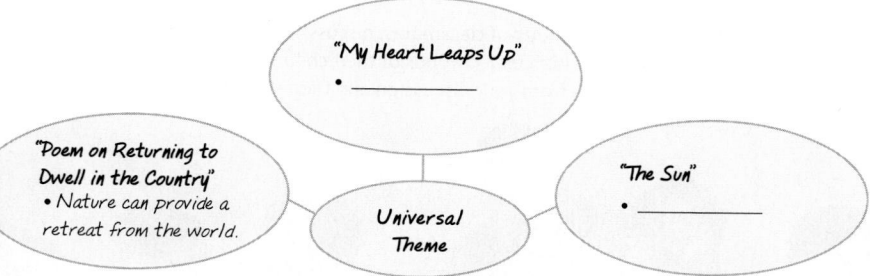

8. **Evaluate** In your opinion, which poem makes the strongest statement about the power of **nature?** Cite evidence to support your choice.

Literary Criticism

9. **Historical Context** England's Romantic poets had a deep reverence for nature. Their work shows an emphasis on imagination, the expression of emotions, and wonder at the world around them. How does Wordsworth's poem reflect this tradition? To what extent do these traits appear in T'ao Ch'ien's and Mary Oliver's poems? Cite evidence to support your answer.

---

7. ● **STANDARDS FOCUS** *Universal Theme* **"My Heart Leaps Up":** *rainbow sparks joy; can't live without nature.* **"The Sun":** *delight in sunrises and sunsets; nature better than power and things.* **UNIVERSAL THEME:** *Nature, unlike power and materialism, brings enduring comfort.*

8. *Students may choose "My Heart Leaps Up" because the speaker would rather die than live untouched by nature.*

Literary Criticism
Possible answer:

9. *Wordsworth's poem typifies romanticism by expressing the speaker's love of nature and wonder in its power to move him (lines 1–6). Similarly, T'ao Ch'ien's poem shows the speaker's love of nature, especially in lines 21–32. Oliver's poem also expresses the speaker's deep emotional connection to nature, notably in lines 20–30.*

Practice and Apply

After Reading
For additional support of post-reading questions, use these copy masters:

R RESOURCE MANAGER—Copy Masters
Universal Theme p. 145 (for practice of literary analysis standards focus)
Question Support p. 149 (After Reading questions adapted for English learners and less-proficient readers)
For additional questions, see page 141.

ANSWERS

Comprehension

1. *The speaker leaves his materialistic lifestyle and moves to the country.*

2. *The speaker wishes that he will always rejoice in rainbows and that his days will be linked by devotion to nature.*

3. *The speaker regards the sun, especially sunrises and sunsets, as the most wonderful thing in life.*

Literary Analysis
Possible answers:

4. *The speaker prefers country life for its simplicity (line 15), beauty (lines 21–32), lack of dust and confusion (lines 33–34), leisure (lines 35–36), and freedom (lines 37–40).*

5. *Our childhood experiences and attitudes shape (or should shape) our adulthood.*

6. *The word "too" (lines 31 and 33) implies that the speaker once turned away from nature to pursue power and "things" (lines 35–36). We can infer that the speaker is talking to someone who may have made the same choice.*

Assess and Reteach

Assess

R RESOURCE MANAGER—Copy Masters
Selection Test A pp. 151–152
Selection Test B/C pp. 153–154

💿 Test Generator CD

Reteach

S STANDARDS LESSON FILE
Literature Lesson 12: Theme
Literature Lesson 20: Speaker

Focus and Motivate

OBJECTIVES

Literary Analysis
- explore the key idea of **expectations**
- identify and analyze theme across genres
- read a short story and a poem

Reading
- set a purpose for reading

Vocabulary
- build vocabulary for reading and writing
- use word origins to help unlock word meaning (*also an EL language objective*)

SUMMARIES

"Two Kinds" In this story, the narrator's mother pushes her to become a prodigy. At first, the narrator tries to excel, but then she rebels by sabotaging her piano lessons and humiliating her mother at a talent show. Years later, the narrator accepts the family piano as a gift—and as a sign of her mother's love and forgiveness.

"Rice and Rose Bowl Blues" The speaker in this poem is a girl who wants to play football but whose mother wants her to learn to cook.

How do EXPECTATIONS *affect performance?*

Explore the question and *KEY IDEA* with students by asking whether they think high **expectations** are more likely to lead to disappointment or great achievement. Then have small groups complete the *DISCUSS* activity.

Selection Resources

Comparing Across Genres

Two Kinds
Short Story by Amy Tan

Rice and Rose Bowl Blues
Poem by Diane Mei Lin Mark

How do EXPECTATIONS *affect performance?*

KEY IDEA Think of a time when someone in authority set a very high goal for you. Perhaps a coach expected you to be the team's top scorer, or a parent expected you to get straight A's. How did you respond to these **expectations?** Were you motivated to work harder? Did you inwardly rebel?

DISCUSS With a small group of classmates, discuss why parents in particular might have high expectations of their children. Record three or more reasons from your discussion and then share them with other groups.

472

RESOURCE MANAGER UNIT 4

Plan and Teach pp. 155–162

Literary Analysis
Summary pp. 163†*, 164‡*
Theme Across Genres
   pp. 165, 168†*
Question Support p. 174*

Reading
Reading Check p. 173
Reading Fluency p. 175

Vocabulary
Study p. 170*
Practice p. 171
Strategy p. 172

Assessment
Selection Tests A, B/C pp. 177*, 179*
   Test Generator CD

BEST PRACTICES TOOLKIT

Differentiated Instruction
  pp. 31–38*

Scaffolding Instruction
  pp. 43–46*

Graphic Organizers/Strategies
Word Squares • Two-Column Chart • Comparison Matrix • New Word Analysis • Timeline

Reading Support
   Audio Anthology CD*

Technology
   Literature and Vocabulary Centers at **ClassZone.com**
   Write*Smart* CD

---

* Resources for Differentiation   † Also in Spanish   ‡ In Haitian Creole and Vietnamese

● LITERARY ANALYSIS: THEME ACROSS GENRES

The short story and the poem you are about to read are literary works about young people struggling to be themselves in the face of parental expectations. Each has a specific **theme**, or message, about that topic. The fiction writer and the poet use different techniques to express the theme of the work. The chart shows the techniques each writer uses.

As you read, try to identify the theme of each work by paying attention to the following.

In the Short Story	In the Poem
• details about the main character's traits, motivations, and values	• words and phrases describing the speaker's thoughts and feelings
• details about how the characters change and the lessons they learn	• key images
• the major internal and external conflicts	• stanzas and lines that present an idea or compare images
• information about the setting	• sound devices, such as alliteration and repetition, that may emphasize an idea
• the story's title	• the poem's title

● READING STRATEGY: SET A PURPOSE FOR READING

When you **set a purpose for reading**, you establish specific reasons to read a work. For example, your purpose for reading "Two Kinds" and "Rice and Rose Bowl Blues" is to identify the theme of each so that you can compare and contrast them. As you read, think about the important struggles each main character faces. After you read, you will use the **Points of Comparison** chart on page 487 to help you analyze and compare the two selections.

Review: **Draw Conclusions**

▲ VOCABULARY IN CONTEXT

Decide whether each word in the list has a positive or a negative connotation.

WORD LIST			
	debut	fiasco	prodigy
	discordant	lament	reproach
	encore	mesmerizing	

Author Online

Amy Tan
born 1952

Amy Tan: Late Bloomer
Like the narrator in "Two Kinds," Amy Tan is the daughter of Chinese immigrants. Raised in the San Francisco Bay area, she spent most of her high school years traveling through Europe with her family after the death of her father and brother. Although she had studied literature and worked as a business writer, Tan did not turn to fiction writing until age 33 when her analyst fell asleep during a session for the third time. At that point, she abandoned therapy in favor of fiction.

Overnight Success After publishing a handful of short stories, Tan came out with *The Joy Luck Club*, a collection of related short stories about four Chinese women friends and their daughters. Critically acclaimed, the book became a bestseller and was made into a movie. Her work has been translated into more than 20 languages, including Chinese.

Diane Mei Lin Mark: Maker of Images:
A fifth-generation Chinese American, Diane Mark is a successful writer and filmmaker. She co-produced the film *Picture Bride*, a lyrical depiction of Hawaii's plantation culture in the early 20th century. The film won the Audience Award for Best Dramatic Film at the 1995 Sundance Film Festival.

Diane Mei Lin Mark

 MORE ABOUT THE AUTHOR
For more on Amy Tan and Diane Mei Lin Mark, visit the **Literature Center** at **ClassZone.com.**

473

Teach

Two Kinds

Amy Tan

My mother believed you could be anything you wanted to be in America. You could open a restaurant. You could work for the government and get good retirement. You could buy a house with almost no money down. You could become rich. You could become instantly famous.

"Of course you can be **prodigy**, too," my mother told me when I was nine. "You can be best anything. What does Auntie Lindo know? Her daughter, she is only best tricky."

America was where all my mother's hopes lay. She had come here in 1949 after losing everything in China: her mother and father, her family home, her
10 first husband, and two daughters, twin baby girls. But she never looked back with regret. There were so many ways for things to get better. **A**

We didn't immediately pick the right kind of prodigy. At first my mother thought I could be a Chinese Shirley Temple.[1] We'd watch Shirley's old movies on TV as though they were training films. My mother would poke my arm and say, "*Ni kan*"—You watch. And I would see Shirley tapping her feet, or singing a sailor song, or pursing her lips into a very round O while saying, "Oh my goodness."

"*Ni kan*," said my mother as Shirley's eyes flooded with tears. "You already know how. Don't need talent for crying!"

20 Soon after my mother got this idea about Shirley Temple, she took me to a beauty training school in the Mission district[2] and put me in the hands of a student who could barely hold the scissors without shaking. Instead of getting big fat curls, I emerged with an uneven mass of crinkly black fuzz. My mother dragged me off to the bathroom and tried to wet down my hair.

"You look like Negro Chinese," she lamented, as if I had done this on purpose.

The instructor of the beauty training school had to lop off these soggy clumps to make my hair even again. "Peter Pan is very popular these days,"

---

1. **Shirley Temple:** a popular child movie star of the 1930s.
2. **Mission district:** a residential neighborhood in San Francisco.

474   UNIT 4: THEME AND SYMBOL

prodigy (prŏd′ə-jē) *n.* a person who is exceptionally talented or intelligent

① Targeted Passage

A THEME
Reread lines 1–11. What does the narrator's mother want for her daughter? Consider what this suggests about the mother's **character.**

ANALYZE VISUALS
What do the posture, facial expressions, dress, and printed background suggest about the mother and daughter in this picture? Explain.

A THEME

Possible answer: The narrator's mother wants wealth and success for her daughter (lines 3–4). Her aspirations suggest that she is optimistic as well as ambitious.

If students need help . . . Ask them to find evidence in the story's first paragraph that reveals the mother's longings.

ANALYZE VISUALS

Possible answer: The pose and clothing are both traditional, with the daughter standing dutifully by her mother. Both have calm, mysterious expressions. However, there is a hint of mischief and longing in the girl's demeanor, which is neither as stiff nor as formal as her mother's.

DIFFERENTIATED INSTRUCTION

FOR ALL STUDENTS

Enhancing Learning Styles Provide these independent projects for various learning preferences:

- **Spatial** Create a cause and effect chain.
- **Tactile** Make a thematic collage.
- **Linguistic** Write a dialogue.

For further detail on these projects, see

R RESOURCE MANAGER
Ideas for Extension pp. 160–161

FOR LESS–PROFICIENT READERS

In combination with the *Audio Anthology CD*, use one or more Targeted Passages (pp. 474, 479, 483, 485) to ensure that students focus on key story events, concepts, and skills. Targeted Passages are also good for English learners.

① Targeted Passage [Lines 5–14]

This passage establishes the major story elements: the main characters, setting, conflicts, and theme.

BACKGROUND

Confucius's Influence The primacy of the parent-child relationship has been deeply embedded in Chinese thinking for 2,500 years. In Confucian philosophy, children are duty-bound to care for their parents and, more important, to love and revere them. According to Confucius, filial piety is the most primary of all virtues. Confucianism spread throughout China after Confucius's death in 479 B.C., and has remained linked with the Chinese way of life ever since. In "Two Kinds," Amy Tan explores the relationship between a mother and daughter in the context of Chinese-American culture.

Lines 1–11
REINFORCE *KEY IDEA:* EXPECTATIONS

How might the mother's ambitions affect her **expectations** for her daughter? *Possible answer: Her mother believes that you can be "anything you wanted to be in America" (line 1), and therefore she has high expectations for her daughter. The mother also seems to want to live through her daughter's achievements.*

- What does the mother want for her daughter?

- When did the mother come to America?

- What do you learn about the mother's past?

- What do mother and daughter watch on TV together? Why is that important?

FOR ENGLISH LEARNERS

Key Academic Vocabulary Use Word Squares to teach these words: *instructor* (line 27), *quoted* (line 55), *predicting* (line 65), *conduct* (line 165), *layered* (line 239), *assumed* (line 289).

 BEST PRACTICES TOOLKIT—Transparency
Word Squares p. E10

Prereading For prereading instruction for English learners, see

 BEST PRACTICES TOOLKIT
Scaffolding Reading Instruction pp. 43–46

FOR ADVANCED LEARNERS/PRE–AP

Pre-AP Exercises in the bottom channel provide additional challenge for students. Use these suggestions for small groups or individuals.

ADDITIONAL GUIDELINES

For more help with differentiation and tips for classroom management, see

 BEST PRACTICES TOOLKIT
Differentiated Instruction pp. 31–38

TWO KINDS **475**

the instructor assured my mother. I now had hair the length of a boy's, with
30   straight-across bangs that hung at a slant two inches above my eyebrows. I
liked the haircut, and it made me actually look forward to my future fame.

    In fact, in the beginning, I was just as excited as my mother, maybe even
more so. I pictured this prodigy part of me as many different images, trying
each one on for size. I was a dainty ballerina girl standing by the curtains,
waiting to hear the right music that would send me floating on my tiptoes.
I was like the Christ child lifted out of the straw manger, crying with holy
indignity. I was Cinderella stepping from her pumpkin carriage with sparkly
cartoon music filling the air.

    In all of my imaginings, I was filled with a sense that I would soon become
40   *perfect.* My mother and father would adore me. I would be beyond **reproach.** I
would never feel the need to sulk for anything.

    But sometimes the prodigy in me became impatient. "If you don't hurry
up and get me out of here, I'm disappearing for good," it warned. "And then
you'll always be nothing." **B**

    Every night after dinner, my mother and I would sit at the Formica[3]
kitchen table. She would present new tests, taking her examples from stories
of amazing children she had read in *Ripley's Believe It or Not,* or *Good
Housekeeping, Reader's Digest,* and a dozen other magazines she kept in a pile
in our bathroom. My mother got these magazines from people whose houses
50   she cleaned. And since she cleaned many houses each week, we had a great
assortment. She would look through them all, searching for stories about
remarkable children.

    The first night she brought out a story about a three-year-old boy who knew
the capitals of all the states and even most of the European countries. A teacher
was quoted as saying the little boy could also pronounce the names of the
foreign cities correctly.

    "What's the capital of Finland?" my mother asked me, looking at the
magazine story.

    All I knew was the capital of California, because Sacramento was the name
60   of the street we lived on in Chinatown. "Nairobi!"[4] I guessed, saying the most
foreign word I could think of. She checked to see if that was possibly one way
to pronounce "Helsinki" before showing me the answer.

    The tests got harder—multiplying numbers in my head, finding the queen
of hearts in a deck of cards, trying to stand on my head without using my
hands, predicting the daily temperatures in Los Angeles, New York, and
London.

    One night I had to look at a page from the Bible for three minutes and then
report everything I could remember. "Now Jehoshaphat[5] had riches and honor
in abundance and . . . that's all I remember, Ma," I said. **C**

---

3. **Formica** (fôr-mī'kə): a heat-resistant material used on kitchen counters, table tops, and similar surfaces.
4. **Nairobi** (nī-rō'bē): the capital of the African nation of Kenya.
5. **Jehoshaphat** (jə-hŏsh'ə-făt'): a king of the ancient Biblical land of Judah in the ninth century B.C.

  UNIT 4: THEME AND SYMBOL

reproach (rĭ-prōch') *n.*
blame; criticism

B THEME
Reread lines 32–44.
What are the narrator's
conflicting feelings about
being a prodigy?

C THEME
Reread lines 45–69.
How successfully does
the narrator perform
the tests given by her
mother?

LITERARY ANALYSIS

B THEME

*Possible answer: Although the narrator
yearns for her mother's approval and is
excited by what her future might hold,
she is impatient and insecure about the
likelihood of success.*

LITERARY ANALYSIS

C THEME

*Possible answer: The narrator fails one
impossible test after another (lines 57–58,
63–69). Given her mother's unrealistic
expectations, the narrator seems doomed
for failure.*

If students need help . . . Analyze the
tests that the mother has set up for the
narrator by working together to complete
a Two-Column Chart. Continue it throughout the story.

Test	Why It Is Unrealistic
national capitals	hasn't studied them
finding queen	need to know trick

 **BEST PRACTICES TOOLKIT—Transparency**
Two-Column Chart p. A25

DIFFERENTIATED INSTRUCTION

FOR LESS–PROFICIENT READERS

Comprehension Support Make a list of the
words that the narrator uses to describe
herself at different times. Depending on
her mood, she felt "sad," "ugly," and "crazed"
(lines 74–75), or "angry," "powerful," and
"willful" (lines 79–80).

FOR ENGLISH LEARNERS

Culture: Clarify Point out that the magazines
mentioned in lines 47–48 were all popular at
the time of the story and some still are today.
Also, explain that the "Chinese Shirley Temple"
was a real child who performed regularly on
the *Ed Sullivan Show* in the 1950s.

70   And after seeing my mother's disappointed face once again, something inside of me began to die. I hated the tests, the raised hopes and failed expectations. Before going to bed that night, I looked in the mirror above the bathroom sink and when I saw only my face staring back—and that it would always be this ordinary face—I began to cry. Such a sad, ugly girl! I made high-pitched noises like a crazed animal, trying to scratch out the face in the mirror.

   And then I saw what seemed to be the prodigy side of me—because I had never seen that face before. I looked at my reflection, blinking so I could see more clearly. The girl staring back at me was angry, powerful. This girl and I
80 were the same. I had new thoughts, willful thoughts, or rather thoughts filled with lots of won'ts. I won't let her change me, I promised myself. I won't be what I'm not. **D**

   So now on nights when my mother presented her tests, I performed listlessly, my head propped on one arm. I pretended to be bored. And I was. I got so bored I started counting the bellows of the foghorns out on the bay while my mother drilled me in other areas. The sound was comforting and reminded me of the cow jumping over the moon. And the next day, I played a game with myself, seeing if my mother would give up on me before eight bellows. After a while I usually counted only one, maybe two bellows at most.
90 At last she was beginning to give up hope.

   Two or three months had gone by without any mention of my being a prodigy again. And then one day my mother was watching The *Ed Sullivan Show*[6] on TV. The TV was old and the sound kept shorting out. Every time my mother got halfway up from the sofa to adjust the set, the sound would go back on and Ed would be talking. As soon as she sat down, Ed would go silent again. She got up, the TV broke into loud piano music. She sat down. Silence. Up and down, back and forth, quiet and loud. It was like a stiff, embraceless dance between her and the TV set. Finally she stood by the set with her hand on the sound dial.

100   She seemed entranced by the music, a little frenzied piano piece with this **mesmerizing** quality, sort of quick passages and then teasing lilting ones before it returned to the quick playful parts.

   "*Ni kan,*" my mother said, calling me over with hurried hand gestures, "Look here."

   I could see why my mother was fascinated by the music. It was being pounded out by a little Chinese girl, about nine years old, with a Peter Pan haircut. The girl had the sauciness of a Shirley Temple. She was proudly modest like a proper Chinese child. And she also did this fancy sweep of a curtsy, so that the fluffy skirt of her white dress cascaded slowly to the floor
110 like the petals of a large carnation.

D THEME
Reread lines 70–82. What causes the narrator to rebel against her mother? Point out statements that reveal her new insights and provide clues to the theme.

mesmerizing
(měz′mə-rīz′ĭng) *adj.* holding one's attention in an almost hypnotic manner **mesmerize** *v.*

---

6. **The *Ed Sullivan Show*:** a popular television variety show in the 1950s and 1960s.

TWO KINDS   **477**

LITERARY ANALYSIS

D THEME

Possible answer: *After being set up for failure, the narrator moves from self-hatred ("Such a sad, ugly girl!," line 74) to rebellion ("The girl staring back at me was angry, powerful. This girl and I were the same. I had new thoughts, willful thoughts, or rather thoughts filled with lots of won'ts," lines 79–81).*

Lines 100–110
REINFORCE *KEY IDEA:* EXPECTATIONS
Why might the child on the *Ed Sullivan Show* appeal to the mother's **expectations** for her daughter? ***Possible answer:*** *Unlike Shirley Temple, this child star is Chinese, and so the mother's expectations for her daughter seem more realistic.*

FOR ADVANCED LEARNERS/PRE–AP
Analyze Figurative Language [small-group option] Use the Comparison Matrix with students to analyze the similes on page 477. Encourage students to discuss how each simile contributes to characterization and to the story's emotional texture.

- "like a crazed animal" (line 75)
- "like a stiff, embraceless dance between her and the TV set" (lines 97–98)
- "like the petals of a large carnation" (line 110)

After discussing the similes, direct students to the metaphor in lines 70–82, and ask what the two faces in the mirror stand for. How do the two faces connect to the title and the theme?

 BEST PRACTICES TOOLKIT—Transparency Comparison Matrix p. A24

Activity Ask students how the photograph helps to establish the story's setting. *Possible answer: The TV set helps to date the setting in the 1950s, when most sets showed only black-and-white images and needed attached antennae for reception. The image on the screen is Ed Sullivan himself, striking a typical pose.*

In spite of these warning signs, I wasn't worried. Our family had no piano and we couldn't afford to buy one, let alone reams of sheet music and piano lessons. So I could be generous in my comments when my mother bad-mouthed the little girl on TV.

120   "Play note right, but doesn't sound good! No singing sound," complained my mother.

"What are you picking on her for?" I said carelessly. "She's pretty good. Maybe she's not the best, but she's trying hard." I knew almost immediately I would be sorry I said that.

"Just like you," she said. "Not the best. Because you not trying."
130 She gave a little huff as she let go of the sound dial and sat down on the sofa.

The little Chinese girl sat down also to play an **encore** of "Anitra's Dance" by Grieg.[7] I remember the song, because later on I had to learn how to play it.

Three days after watching *The Ed Sullivan Show,* my mother told me what my schedule would be for piano lessons and piano practice. She had talked to Mr. Chong, who lived on the first floor of our apartment building. Mr. Chong
140 was a retired piano teacher and my mother had traded housecleaning services for weekly lessons and a piano for me to practice on every day, two hours a day, from four until six.

When my mother told me this, I felt as though I had been sent to hell. I whined and then kicked my foot a little when I couldn't stand it anymore.

"Why don't you like me the way I am? I'm *not* a genius! I can't play the piano. And even if I could, I wouldn't go on TV if you paid me a million dollars!" I cried.

My mother slapped me. "Who ask you be genius?" she shouted. "Only ask you be your best. For you sake. You think I want you be genius? Hnnh! What
150 for! Who ask you!"

"So ungrateful," I heard her mutter in Chinese. "If she had as much talent as she has temper, she would be famous now." **E**

encore (ŏn'kōr') *n.* a repeated or additional performance

---

7. **Grieg** (grēg): Norwegian composer Edvard Grieg (1843–1907).

Mr. Chong, whom I secretly nicknamed Old Chong, was very strange, always tapping his fingers to the silent music of an invisible orchestra. He looked ancient in my eyes. He had lost most of the hair on top of his head and he wore thick glasses and had eyes that always looked tired and sleepy. But he must have been younger than I thought, since he lived with his mother and was not yet married.

160   I met Old Lady Chong once and that was enough. She had this peculiar smell like a baby that had done something in its pants. And her fingers felt like a dead person's, like an old peach I once found in the back of the refrigerator; the skin just slid off the meat when I picked it up.

    I soon found out why Old Chong had retired from teaching piano. He was deaf. "Like Beethoven!" he shouted to me. "We're both listening only in our head!"[8] And he would start to conduct his frantic silent sonatas.

    Our lessons went like this. He would open the book and point to different things, explaining their purpose: "Key! Treble! Bass! No sharps or flats! So this is C major! Listen now and play after me!"

    And then he would play the C scale a few times, a simple chord, and then, 170 as if inspired by an old, unreachable itch, he gradually added more notes and running trills and a pounding bass until the music was really something quite grand.

    I would play after him, the simple scale, the simple chord, and then I just played some nonsense that sounded like a cat running up and down on top of garbage cans. Old Chong smiled and applauded and then said, "Very good! But now you must learn to keep time!"

    So that's how I discovered that Old Chong's eyes were too slow to keep up with the wrong notes I was playing. He went through the motions in half-time. To help me keep rhythm, he stood behind me, pushing down on my 180 right shoulder for every beat. He balanced pennies on top of my wrists so I would keep them still as I slowly played scales and arpeggios.[9] He had me curve my hand around an apple and keep that shape when playing chords. He marched stiffly to show me how to make each finger dance up and down, staccato[10] like an obedient little soldier.

    He taught me all these things, and that was how I also learned I could be lazy and get away with mistakes, lots of mistakes. If I hit the wrong notes because I hadn't practiced enough, I never corrected myself. I just kept playing in rhythm. And Old Chong kept conducting his own private reverie.

    So maybe I never really gave myself a fair chance. I did pick up the basics 190 pretty quickly, and I might have become a good pianist at that young age.

2 **Targeted Passage**

---

8. **Beethoven . . . in our head!** (bā'tō'vən): Ludwig van Beethoven (1770–1827) continued to compose great music even after becoming totally deaf during the last years of his life.

9. **arpeggios** (är-pĕj'ē-ōz'): chords in which the notes are played separately in quick sequence rather than at the same time.

10. **staccato** (stə-kä'tō): producing distinct, abrupt breaks between successive tones.

TWO KINDS   **479**

Lines 163–184
DISCUSSION PROMPTS
Use these prompts to help students understand the narrator's dilemma:

Connect How would you feel if your parents forced you to take unwanted lessons and to practice two hours each day in your free time? What would you do? *Responses should reflect an understanding of the conflicts that such a situation would likely engender.*

Analyze The narrator nicknames her piano teacher "Old Chong." What does this nickname suggest about the narrator's attitude? *Possible answer: The nickname suggests that she is not respectful toward her teacher or serious about her lessons.*

Evaluate What is your opinion of the narrator's actions? Does she have any alternatives? *Possible answer: The narrator's mother leaves little room for compromise, making rebellion or capitulation her only alternatives.*

FOR LESS–PROFICIENT READERS
2 **Targeted Passage** [Lines 185–190]
This passage reflects the narrator's inner conflict: her mixed feelings about fooling Old Chong.

- What does the narrator do when she hits the wrong notes?
- What is Old Chong's reaction to the narrator's mistakes?
- What does the narrator say she might have become?

FOR ADVANCED LEARNERS/PRE–AP
Evaluate Allusions [small-group options]
Discuss the composers mentioned on pages 478–480: Grieg (line 135), Beethoven (lines 164–165), and Schumann (line 218). Encourage volunteers to research one of these composers and share what they discover about the composer and his music. After they finish the story, have students discuss how Amy Tan uses music history to enrich the story and develop her characters.

Over the next year, I practiced like this, dutifully in my own way. And then
one day I heard my mother and her friend Lindo Jong both talking in a loud,
bragging tone of voice so others could hear. It was after church, and
I was leaning against the brick wall wearing a dress with stiff white petticoats.
Auntie Lindo's daughter, Waverly, who was about my age, was standing farther
down the wall about five feet away. We had grown up together and shared all
the closeness of two sisters squabbling over crayons and dolls. In other words,
200 for the most part, we hated each other. I thought she was snotty. Waverly Jong
had gained a certain amount of fame as "Chinatown's Littlest Chinese
Chess Champion."

"She bring home too many trophy," **lamented** Auntie Lindo that Sunday.
"All day she play chess. All day I have no time do nothing but dust off her
winnings." She threw a scolding look at Waverly, who pretended not to
see her.

"You lucky you don't have this problem," said Auntie Lindo with a sigh to
my mother.

And my mother squared her shoulders and bragged: "Our problem worser
210 than yours. If we ask Jing-mei[12] wash dish, she hear nothing but music. It's like
you can't stop this natural talent."

And right then, I was determined to put a stop to her foolish pride. **G**

A few weeks later, Old Chong and my mother conspired to have me play
in a talent show which would be held in the church hall. By then, my parents
had saved up enough to buy me a secondhand piano, a black Wurlitzer spinet[13]
with a scarred bench. It was the showpiece of our living room.

For the talent show, I was to play a piece called "Pleading Child" from
Schumann's[14] *Scenes from Childhood*. It was a simple, moody piece that
sounded more difficult than it was. I was supposed to memorize the whole
220 thing, playing the repeat parts twice to make the piece sound longer. But I
dawdled over it, playing a few bars and then cheating, looking up to see what
notes followed. I never really listened to what I was playing. I daydreamed
about being somewhere else, about being someone else.

The part I liked to practice best was the fancy curtsy: right foot out, touch
the rose on the carpet with a pointed foot, sweep to the side, left leg bends,
look up and smile.

---

11. **preludes** (prĕl'yōōdz'): short piano compositions, each usually based on a single musical theme.
12. **Jing-mei** (jĭng'mā').
13. **Wurlitzer spinet:** Wurlitzer was a well-known manuracturer of organs and pianos, including the small upright piano known as a spinet.
14. **Schumann's** (shōō'mänz'): composed by Robert Schumann (1810–1856), a German composer famous for his piano works.

LITERARY ANALYSIS

F THEME

Possible answer: Because her mother's expectations are so high and her demands so unreasonable, the narrator feels helpless and angry, and she rebels by performing poorly at her piano lessons. The narrator's disrespectful treatment of her teacher is a way of getting back at her mother.

Extend the Discussion Why does the narrator say that she practiced "dutifully in my own way" (line 193)?

READING STRATEGY: *Review*

G DRAW CONCLUSIONS

Possible answer: Foolish pride may be one motivation: her mother wants the narrator to outshine Waverly. However, her ambition, optimism, and love also drive her.

F THEME
Why does the narrator intentionally do poorly in her piano lessons?

discordant (dĭ-skôr'dnt) *adj.* having a disagreeable or clashing sound

lament (lə-mĕnt') *v.* to express grief or deep regret

G DRAW CONCLUSIONS
After overhearing her mother's conversation with Auntie Lindo in lines 203–211, the narrator concludes that "foolish pride" motivates her mother. Based on what you know about the mother so far, do you agree? Explain your answer.

DIFFERENTIATED INSTRUCTION

FOR LESS–PROFICIENT READERS

Concept Support Help students to understand how the narrator is feeling when she decides to put a stop to her mother's "foolish pride."

Have students reread the dialogue leading up to her decision (lines 203–212) before asking these questions:

- How does the narrator feel about her piano lessons?

- What does her mother say that is probably untrue?
- How does this untruth make the narrator feel?
- What might the narrator be planning?

ANALYZE VISUALS

Activity This photograph shows San Francisco's Chinatown, the setting of the story. Ask students what aspects of that setting the photograph highlights. ***Possible answer:*** *The photograph shows that the story takes place in a lively, urban setting with lots of restaurants.*

My parents invited all the couples from the Joy Luck Club[15] to witness my **debut.** Auntie Lindo and Uncle Tin were there. Waverly and her two older brothers had also come. The first two rows were filled with children both

230 younger and older than I was. The littlest ones got to go first. They recited simple nursery rhymes, squawked out tunes on miniature violins, twirled Hula-Hoops,[16] pranced in pink ballet tutus, and when they bowed or curtsied, the audience would sigh in unison, "Awww," and then clap enthusiastically.

When my turn came, I was very confident. I remember my childish excitement. It was as if I knew, without a doubt, that the prodigy side of me really did exist. I had no fear whatsoever, no nervousness. I remember thinking to myself, This is it! This is it! I looked out over the audience, at my mother's blank face, my father's yawn, Auntie Lindo's stiff-lipped smile, Waverly's sulky expression. I had on a white dress layered with sheets of lace, and a pink bow

240 in my Peter Pan haircut. As I sat down I envisioned people jumping to their feet and Ed Sullivan rushing up to introduce me to everyone on TV. **H**

And I started to play. It was so beautiful. I was so caught up in how lovely I looked that at first I didn't worry how I would sound. So it was a surprise to me when I hit the first wrong note and I realized something didn't sound quite right. And then I hit another and another followed that. A chill started at the top of my head and began to trickle down. Yet I couldn't stop playing, as though my hands were bewitched. I kept thinking my fingers would adjust themselves back, like a train switching to the right track. I played this strange jumble through two repeats, the sour notes staying with me all the way

250 to the end.

---

15. **Joy Luck Club:** the social group to which the family in this story belongs.

16. **Hula-Hoops:** plastic hoops that are whirled around the body by means of hip movements.

debut (dā-byōo′) *n.* first public performance or showing

H THEME
Reread lines 234–241. What **internal conflict** is revealed by the narrator's expectations of her own performance?

LITERARY ANALYSIS

H THEME

Possible answer: *These lines reveal the narrator's internal conflict about being a prodigy: Though she resents her mother's pushing, she longs for the adulation and approval that extraordinary talent would bring her.*

TWO KINDS **481**

FOR ENGLISH LEARNERS

Language: Multiple-Meaning Words Remind students that two words can have the same spelling but different meanings. Use New Word Analysis to teach these multiple-meaning words from the story: *bars* (line 221), *sweep* (line 225), *hit* (line 244), *sour* (line 249).

 BEST PRACTICES TOOLKIT—Transparency New Word Analysis p. E8

FOR ADVANCED LEARNERS/PRE–AP

Analyze Irony The narrator was determined to put an end to her mother's foolish pride. How is this determination ironic in light of the narrator's surprise during her terrible performance (lines 234–250)? Ask students to write a paragraph explaining their responses.

Lines 251–288
DISCUSSION PROMPTS

Use these prompts to help students understand the shame that the narrator caused herself and her parents:

Connect Think about a time when you were embarrassed or when you observed someone else's embarrassment. How does that experience help you understand the narrator's feelings after her terrible performance? *Answers should demonstrate an understanding of her shame, guilt, and disappointment.*

Analyze Why did the narrator suddenly realize how many people were in the audience? *Possible answer: The jolt of shame shook her out of her daydream, so she noticed the other people around her (lines 260–262).*

Evaluate The narrator reports that her mother gave her "a quiet, blank look that said she had lost everything. I felt the same way" (lines 279–280). What does she mean? *Possible answer: She was identifying with her mother's sense of loss and shame.*

When I stood up, I discovered my legs were shaking. Maybe I had just been nervous and the audience, like Old Chong, had seen me go through the right motions and had not heard anything wrong at all. I swept my right foot out, went down on my knee, looked up and smiled. The room was quiet, except for Old Chong, who was beaming and shouting, "Bravo! Bravo! Well done!" But then I saw my mother's face, her stricken face. The audience clapped weakly, and as I walked back to my chair, with my whole face quivering as I tried not to cry, I heard a little boy whisper loudly to his mother, "That was awful," and the mother whispered back, "Well, she certainly tried."

260   And now I realized how many people were in the audience, the whole world it seemed. I was aware of eyes burning into my back. I felt the shame of my mother and father as they sat stiffly throughout the rest of the show.

We could have escaped during intermission. Pride and some strange sense of honor must have anchored my parents to their chairs. And so we watched it all: the eighteen-year-old boy with a fake mustache who did a magic show and juggled flaming hoops while riding a unicycle. The breasted girl with white makeup who sang from *Madama Butterfly*[17] and got honorable mention. And the eleven-year-old boy who won first prize playing a tricky violin song that sounded like a busy bee.

270   After the show, the Hsus,[18] the Jongs, and the St. Clairs from the Joy Luck Club came up to my mother and father.

"Lots of talented kids," Auntie Lindo said vaguely, smiling broadly.

"That was somethin' else," said my father, and I wondered if he was referring to me in a humorous way, or whether he even remembered what I had done.

Waverly looked at me and shrugged her shoulders. "You aren't a genius like me," she said matter-of-factly. And if I hadn't felt so bad, I would have pulled her braids and punched her stomach.

But my mother's expression was what devastated me: a quiet, blank look

280   that said she had lost everything. I felt the same way, and it seemed as if everybody were now coming up, like gawkers at the scene of an accident, to see what parts were actually missing. When we got on the bus to go home, my father was humming the busy-bee tune and my mother was silent. I kept thinking she wanted to wait until we got home before shouting at me. But when my father unlocked the door to our apartment, my mother walked in and then went to the back, into the bedroom. No accusations. No blame. And in a way, I felt disappointed. I had been waiting for her to start shouting, so I could shout back and cry and blame her for all my misery.

I assumed my talent-show **fiasco** meant I never had to play the piano again.

290   But two days later, after school, my mother came out of the kitchen and saw me watching TV.

fiasco (fē-ăs′kō) *n.* a complete failure

17. ***Madama Butterfly:*** a famous opera by the Italian composer Giacomo Puccini.
18. **Hsus** (shüz).

DIFFERENTIATED INSTRUCTION

FOR ENGLISH LEARNERS
Vocabulary: Word Associations Have pairs of students identify the feelings associated with the verb in each phrase: *eyes burning into my back* (line 261), "people were looking at me, and I was feeling so embarrassed it felt like their eyes were burning my back"; *honor must have anchored my parents to their chairs* (line 264), "my parents stayed in their seats, and it seemed as if their pride kept them fastened or tied there."

FOR ADVANCED LEARNERS/PRE–AP
Evaluate Dialogue Many characters make comments about the narrator's piano performance, but only a little boy (line 258) speaks with complete honesty, and only her mother, who is usually talkative, says nothing. Have students discuss how Amy Tan uses dialogue in this scene to develop character, irony, and humor.

"Four clock," she reminded me as if it were any other day. I was stunned, as though she were asking me to go through the talent-show torture again. I wedged myself more tightly in front of the TV.

"Turn off TV," she called from the kitchen five minutes later.

I didn't budge. And then I decided. I didn't have to do what my mother said anymore. I wasn't her slave. This wasn't China. I had listened to her before and look what happened. She was the stupid one.

300 She came out from the kitchen and stood in the arched entryway of the living room. "Four clock," she said once again, louder.

"I'm not going to play anymore," I said nonchalantly. "Why should I? I'm not a genius."

She walked over and stood in front of the TV. I saw her chest was heaving up and down in an angry way.

"No!" I said, and I now felt stronger, as if my true self had finally emerged. So this was what had been inside me all along.

"No! I won't!" I screamed.

She yanked me by the arm, pulled me off the floor, snapped off the TV. She was frighteningly strong, half pulling, half carrying me toward the piano 310 as I kicked the throw rugs under my feet. She lifted me up and onto the hard bench. I was sobbing by now, looking at her bitterly. Her chest was heaving even more and her mouth was open, smiling crazily as if she were pleased I was crying.

"You want me to be someone that I'm not!" I sobbed. "I'll never be the kind of daughter you want me to be!"

"Only two kinds of daughters," she shouted in Chinese. "Those who are obedient and those who follow their own mind! Only one kind of daughter can live in this house. Obedient daughter!" ❶

"Then I wish I wasn't your daughter. I wish you weren't my mother," I 320 shouted. As I said these things I got scared. It felt like worms and toads and slimy things crawling out of my chest, but it also felt good, as if this awful side of me had surfaced, at last.

"Too late change this," said my mother shrilly.

And I could sense her anger rising to its breaking point. I wanted to see it spill over. And that's when I remembered the babies she had lost in China, the ones we never talked about. "Then I wish I'd never been born!" I shouted. "I wish I were dead! Like them."

It was as if I had said the magic words. Alakazam!—and her face went blank, her mouth closed, her arms went slack, and she backed out of the 330 room, stunned, as if she were blowing away like a small brown leaf, thin, brittle, lifeless.

❶ **THEME**
The **title** of a story is often a clue to its theme. The title of this story comes from the exchange between mother and daughter in lines 314–318. How do the narrator's values differ from her mother's? Cite examples in your answer.

❸ **Targeted Passage**

LITERARY ANALYSIS

❶ THEME

Possible answer: The title suggests their conflict in values: The narrator is the kind of daughter who follows her own mind, while her mother expects the other kind, an obedient daughter. This conflict derives in part from cultural differences, as the mother embodies traditional Chinese values that demand reverence for parents, while the daughter has been inculcated with American pride in the individual. At every turn, the narrator's strong will clashes with her mother's demands for obedience.

Extend the Discussion The daughter was born and raised in America, while the mother grew up in China. To what extent are cultural differences responsible for their conflicts?

FOR LESS–PROFICIENT READERS

❸ **Targeted Passage [Lines 324–331]**

This passage reflects the climax of the narrator's conflict with her mother.

- Why does the narrator mention the babies her mother had lost? What does the narrator wish for herself?

- How does the mother react to her daughter's words?

FOR ENGLISH LEARNERS

Culture: Connect Read aloud the word *Alakazam* (line 328), and explain that it is a nonsense word, like *abracadabra*, sometimes used by magicians in fairy tales. Ask volunteers to name similar words in their home languages.

Lines 316–318
REINFORCE *KEY IDEA:* EXPECTATIONS

Discuss The narrator's mother tells her that there are only two kinds of daughters. What does this statement reveal about the mother's **expectations**? *Possible answer: The statement reveals the fact that the mother is rigid in her expectations; she expects them to be shared and fulfilled without question.*

ANALYZE VISUALS

Activity The photograph shows an immigrant with portraits of her parents. Ask students what it suggests about how people integrate their past history with their current lives.
Possible answer: The photograph suggests that for many immigrants their hearts and memories are with their home country and its culture. Despite her American clothing, the woman remains connected with the culture of China, where ancestors are honored.

Lines 332–337
DISCUSSION PROMPTS

Use these prompts to help students understand the narrator's relationship with her mother toward the end of the story:

Connect How do you feel about the narrator's mother by this point in the story? Does she still exert a strong influence over her daughter? Should she? Explain. *Accept all reasonable responses.*

Analyze What does the narrator mean when she says in lines 336–337, "I did not believe I could be anything I wanted to be. I could only be me"? *Possible answer: The narrator means that she no longer believes she can achieve whatever her mother expects from her simply by trying hard, regardless of her own natural abilities or interests.*

Synthesize Why do you think that the narrator falls short of her mother's expectations for her in high school and college? *Possible answer: The narrator rebels against her mother's unrealistic expectations for her as a way of "asserting [her] own will" (line 333). She may also have been trying to punish her mother by deliberately achieving less than she was capable of or by pursuing interests that did not meet her mother's ideas of success.*

It was not the only disappointment my mother felt in me. In the years that followed, I failed her so many times, each time asserting my own will, my right to fall short of expectations. I didn't get straight A's. I didn't become class president. I didn't get into Stanford. I dropped out of college.

For unlike my mother, I did not believe I could be anything I wanted to be. I could only be me.

And for all those years, we never talked about the disaster at the recital or my terrible accusations afterward at the piano bench. All that remained
340 unchecked, like a betrayal that was now unspeakable. So I never found a way to ask her why she had hoped for something so large that failure was inevitable.

And even worse, I never asked her what frightened me the most: Why had she given up hope?

484 UNIT 4: THEME AND SYMBOL

DIFFERENTIATED INSTRUCTION

FOR ENGLISH LEARNERS

Comprehension: Sequence Use a Timeline to review key events in the story. Make sure students understand that the narrator's conflicts with her mother (lines 332–341) continue for years after her piano fiasco.

 BEST PRACTICES TOOLKIT—Transparency
   Timeline p. B23

FOR ADVANCED LEARNERS/PRE–AP

Compare Characters Throughout the story, the narrator stresses the differences between herself and her mother. Have students work in small groups to discuss how they are alike.

For after our struggle at the piano, she never mentioned my playing again. The lessons stopped. The lid to the piano was closed, shutting out the dust, my misery, and her dreams.

So she surprised me. A few years ago, she offered to give me the piano, for my thirtieth birthday. I had not played in all those years. I saw the offer as a sign of forgiveness, a tremendous burden removed.

350 "Are you sure?" I asked shyly. "I mean, won't you and Dad miss it?"

"No, this your piano," she said firmly. "Always your piano. You only one can play."

"Well, I probably can't play anymore," I said. "It's been years."

"You pick up fast," said my mother, as if she knew this was certain. "You have natural talent. You could been genius if you want to."

"No I couldn't."

"You just not trying," said my mother. And she was neither angry nor sad. She said it as if to announce a fact that could never be disproved. "Take it," she said. **J**

360 But I didn't at first. It was enough that she had offered it to me. And after that, every time I saw it in my parents' living room, standing in front of the bay windows, it made me feel proud, as if it were a shiny trophy I had won back.

Last week I sent a tuner over to my parents' apartment and had the piano reconditioned, for purely sentimental reasons. My mother had died a few months before and I had been getting things in order for my father, a little bit at a time. I put the jewelry in special silk pouches. The sweaters she had knitted in yellow, pink, bright orange—all the colors I hated—I put those in mothproof boxes. I found some old Chinese silk dresses, the kind with little

370 slits up the sides. I rubbed the old silk against my skin, then wrapped them in tissue and decided to take them home with me.

After I had the piano tuned, I opened the lid and touched the keys. It sounded even richer than I remembered. Really, it was a very good piano. Inside the bench were the same exercise notes with handwritten scales, the same secondhand music books with their covers held together with yellow tape.

I opened up the Schumann book to the dark little piece I had played at the recital. It was on the left-hand side of the page, "Pleading Child." It looked more difficult than I remembered. I played a few bars, surprised at how easily

380 the notes came back to me.

And for the first time, or so it seemed, I noticed the piece on the right-hand side. It was called "Perfectly Contented." I tried to play this one as well. It had a lighter melody but the same flowing rhythm and turned out to be quite easy. "Pleading Child" was shorter but slower; "Perfectly Contented" was longer, but faster. And after I played them both a few times, I realized they were two halves of the same song. ❧

J DRAW CONCLUSIONS
Reread lines 354–359. Has the mother changed during the course of the story or not? Explain your answer.

④ Targeted Passage

TWO KINDS **485**

READING STRATEGY: *Review*

J DRAW CONCLUSIONS

Possible answer: The mother's attitude toward her daughter hasn't changed, as she still insists that her daughter could have been a genius, if only she had tried (lines 355–357). In offering her daughter the piano, however, she seems to have come to some level of acceptance. This gesture also reflects her enduring love and affection for her child.

Lines 377–386
REINFORCE *KEY IDEA:* **EXPECTATIONS**

How do these two song titles show how the narrator has changed in her response to her mother's **expectations?** *Possible answer: At the beginning of the story, the narrator is pleading for her mother's love and acceptance by attempting to meet her expectations. Later in the story, the narrator rebels against those expectations yet is still pleading for her mother to love her for who she is. At the end of the story, the narrator is perfectly contented because her mother's gift of the piano is a peace offering that signals that she does love her for who she is, even though she still believes that her daughter could have met her high expectations if she had tried harder.*

FOR LESS–PROFICIENT READERS

④ Targeted Passage [Lines 377–386]

This passage concludes the story with a discovery of two important piano pieces.

- What is the first piece the narrator plays? What does she remember about it?

- What is the second piece? What does she notice about it?

- What does the narrator conclude after she plays both piano pieces a few times?

FOR ADVANCED LEARNERS/PRE–AP

Evaluate Symbols Have students discuss the symbolic meaning of the Schumann piano pieces.

- How are the two piano pieces like the two kinds of daughters?

- How do the two pieces symbolize the narrator and her conflict with her mother?

- What symbolic resolution do the two pieces provide?

Prereading for this poem is found on page 473.

ANALYZE VISUALS

Activity This photograph shows a rice bowl and chopsticks. Ask students what image they might select to illustrate a poem about their own cultural or family traditions. *Students may mention images of specific types of food, clothing, or ceremonial objects.*

Lines 6–8
REINFORCE *KEY IDEA:* EXPECTATIONS

Discuss What is the significance of Mama's expectation that her daughter learn to wash rice? *Possible answer: Learning to wash rice, a woman's job, signals a coming of age that will usher in new roles and new duties.*

LITERARY ANALYSIS

Ⓚ THEME

Possible answer: The text in parentheses reveals that the speaker's heart is still with the players on the football field. The parentheses underscore her need for secretiveness about her true feelings.

LITERARY ANALYSIS

Ⓛ THEME

Possible answer: The speaker's reaction to Roland shows that she feels rebellious and angry about the changes in her life.

SELECTION WRAP–UP

SYNTHESIZE Ask students to consider what the narrator in "Two Kinds" and the speaker in "Rice and Rose Bowl Blues" have in common.

★ CRITIQUE Have students evaluate whether the mother in the story and Mama in the poem have unfair expectations for their daughters.

READING FLUENCY

Distribute the copy master and have students work in pairs or groups to practice fluency.

Ⓡ RESOURCE MANAGER—Copy Master
    Reading Fluency p. 175

R I C E
and
R O S E
B O W L
B L U E S

Diane Mei Lin Mark

I remember the day
Mama called me in from
the football game with brothers
and neighbor boys
5 in our front yard

said it was time
I learned to
wash rice for dinner

glancing out the window
10 I watched a pass interception
setting the other team up
on our 20
        Pour some water
        into the pot,
15   she said pleasantly,
        turning on the tap
        Rub the rice
        between your hands,
        pour out the clouds,
20   *fill it again*
        (I secretly traced
        an end run through
        the grains in
        between pourings) **Ⓚ**
25 with the rice
    settled into a simmer
    I started out the door
    but was called back

    the next day
30 Roland from across the street
    sneeringly said he heard
    I couldn't play football
    anymore

    I laughed loudly,
35 asking him
    where
    he'd heard
    such a thing **Ⓛ**

Ⓚ THEME
Reread lines 21–24. What does the text in parentheses tell you about the speaker's feelings and interests? Why do you think the poet used parentheses here?

Ⓛ THEME
What can you tell about the speaker's feelings from her reaction to Roland?

DIFFERENTIATED INSTRUCTION

FOR LESS–PROFICIENT READERS
Comprehension Support Because there are no periods and only minimal capitalization in the poem, students may need help understanding its structure. Read the poem aloud, emphasizing the flow of ideas. Then work with students to divide the poem into sentences by deciding where complete thoughts end and where they continue into the next line or stanza. If necessary, have students "edit" the poem by suggesting where to add periods and capitalization.

FOR ENGLISH LEARNERS
Culture: Clarify Point out that the Rose Bowl is a famous college football championship played in California on New Year's Day. Also explain the football terminology *pass interception* (line 10), "a throw that is caught by the other team"; *on our 20* (line 12), "20 yards from our goal."

Comprehension

1. **Recall** In "Two Kinds," what does the narrator's mother want her to become?

2. **Recall** What does the narrator's mother offer her on her 30th birthday?

3. **Recall** How does the narrator feel after the talent show?

4. **Summarize** What can you tell about the character of the speaker in "Rice and Rose Bowl Blues"?

Literary Analysis

5. **Analyze Conflict** In "Two Kinds," why does the narrator's conflict with her mother last so long and become so bitter? Is it ever resolved? Cite evidence from the story to support your answer.

6. **Make Judgments** The narrator in "Two Kinds" insists that her mother wants to change her. Is it possible that her mother only wants to help her discover who she really is? Support your opinion with evidence.

7. **Interpret Text** The story ends with the narrator at the piano, playing with enjoyment for the first time and at peace with the music and herself. What might the narrator mean by saying that "Pleading Child" and "Perfectly Contented" are "two halves of the same song"?

8. **Analyze Gender Roles** In "Rice and Rose Bowl Blues," how does gender play a role in the tension between the speaker and her mother? Use evidence from the poem to support your answer.

Comparing Across Genres

Now that you have read both selections about parental **expectations,** you are ready to identify each writer's **theme,** or message. The **Points of Comparison** chart will help you get started.

Points of Comparison	In the Short Story	In the Poem
How would you describe the main conflict?		
What lesson does the narrator or the speaker learn?		
What images strike you as important?		
What idea does the title emphasize?		
Write a sentence stating the theme as you interpret it.		
Which techniques are important in conveying the theme?		

Comparing Across Genres

● **STANDARDS FOCUS** *Theme Across Genres*
Possible answers:

Main Conflict: Short Story *The mother's expectations conflict with the daughter's desire to be herself.* **Poem** *The mother's expectations conflict with the daughter's wish for freedom.*

Lesson: Short Story *The narrator learns that her mother loves her despite disappointments.* **Poem** *The speaker learns that she can find ways to claim her freedom.*

Images: Short Story *things that come in twos: twin babies, faces in the mirror, piano songs* **Poem** *rice washing, football playing*

Title: Short Story *It emphasizes the conflicts between the obedient daughter and the willful daughter.* **Poem** *It emphasizes the conflict between traditional female roles and the freedom of childhood.*

Theme: Short Story *Unrealistic expectations create bitterness.* **Poem** *Expectations can't always stifle treasured freedoms.*

Techniques: Short Story *figurative language, humor, contrasts* **Poem** *alliteration, metaphor*

Practice and Apply

After Reading

For additional support of post-reading questions, use these copy masters:

🅡 RESOURCE MANAGER—Copy Masters
  Reading Check p. 173 (to check understanding of the selection)
  Theme Across Genres p. 167 (for practice of literary analysis standards focus)
  Question Support p. 174 (After Reading questions adapted for English learners and less-proficient readers)

For additional questions, see page 159.

ANSWERS

Comprehension

1. *The narrator's mother wants her to be "the best"—in other words, a prodigy or a genius.*

2. *The narrator's mother offers her the family piano on her 30th birthday.*

3. *The narrator feels overwhelmed by shame and disappointment.*

4. *The speaker is a self-assured tomboy and a reluctantly obedient daughter.*

Literary Analysis

Possible answers:

5. *The mother's unrealistically high expectations make failure likely, and her unwillingness to compromise gives the daughter reason to feel bitter. Even after the piano fiasco, the conflict continues as mother and daughter fight this same battle through high school and college (lines 332–335). A resolution comes with the gift of the piano, which represents the mother's love, the only kind of acceptance she can offer.*

6. *Although unaware of her desire to change her daughter, the narrator's mother pushes her in a way that suggests that this is her motive, insisting to the very end that the daughter only needed to try harder (lines 354–357).*

7. *The narrator means that she has made peace with herself over failing to meet her mother's expectations and wanting to be herself as is indicated by the song titles.*

8. *The speaker's mother has gender-specific expectations that clash with the speaker's interests and create tension between the two of them. When forced to stop playing football for a cooking lesson, the speaker's heart is still with her football team.*

ANSWERS

Vocabulary in Context

VOCABULARY PRACTICE

1. *no; an early bloomer*

2. *your dog's death*

3. *knocking over a bookcase*

4. *feel bad*

5. *a rerun*

6. *blaring car horns*

7. *a shiny toy*

8. *excited*

VOCABULARY IN WRITING

Remind students that a reviewer would consider only the performance itself and would know nothing personal about the narrator. Suggest that they reread the narrator's description of her playing and the audience reaction (lines 242–259).

VOCABULARY STRATEGY: WORD ORIGINS
(also an EL language objective)

1. *Adolphe Sax (1814–1894) invented the saxophone.*

2. *Charles C. Boycott (1832–1897) was an English land agent in Ireland who was shunned because he refused to lower his rents.*

3. *Joel R. Poinsett (1799–1851) discovered this tropical American flower.*

4. *Frankfurt, Germany, is a city known for smoked sausage.*

5. *Bedlam Hospital of St. Mary of Bethlehem, London, was an infamous insane asylum.*

6. *General Henry Shrapnel (1761–1842) invented artillery shells that contained metal balls.*

7. *Tangier, Morocco, in North Africa produces this orange citrus fruit.*

8. *George W. G. Ferris (1859–1896) invented this amusement park ride.*

R RESOURCE MANAGER—Copy Master
Vocabulary Strategy p. 172

ⓘ Vocabulary Center at **ClassZone.com**
Additional Vocabulary Activities

Vocabulary in Context

VOCABULARY PRACTICE

Answer the questions to show your understanding of the vocabulary words.

1. Is a **prodigy** considered a late bloomer?

2. Which would you be more likely to **lament**—your dog's death or an A on a test?

3. Which might be a **fiasco**—enjoying a vacation or knocking over a bookcase?

4. Would a **reproach** cause someone to rejoice or feel bad?

5. If a television show is an **encore** presentation, is it a new program or a rerun?

6. Which are **discordant** sounds—blaring car horns or softly rippling waves?

7. Which might be **mesmerizing** to a child—a newspaper or a shiny toy?

8. If someone is making a **debut,** is he or she likely to be excited or bored?

WORD LIST
debut
discordant
encore
fiasco
lament
mesmerizing
prodigy
reproach

VOCABULARY IN WRITING

Write a short review of the narrator's piano performance for a local newspaper. Use four or more vocabulary words. You might begin like this.

> **EXAMPLE SENTENCE**
>
> *Usually we like to say kind things about a young performer's **debut**.*

VOCABULARY STRATEGY: WORD ORIGINS

Words that derive from the names of people or places are called **eponyms.** For example, the vocabulary word *mesmerizing* (the present participle of *mesmerize*) comes from the name Franz Mesmer, an Austrian doctor who popularized hypnotism. The etymology in the dictionary entry of an eponym will help you understand the term's origin.

> **mes•mer•ize** (mĕz′mə-rīz′) *tr.v.* **-ized, -iz•ing, -iz•es 1.** To spellbind; enthrall. **2.** To hypnotize. [After Franz Mesmer, Austrian physician, 1734–1815.]

PRACTICE Use an unabridged dictionary to identify the person or place from which each word derives. Then write a brief explanation of the connection.

1. saxophone
2. boycott
3. poinsettia
4. frankfurter
5. bedlam
6. shrapnel
7. tangerine
8. Ferris wheel

VOCABULARY PRACTICE
For more practice, go to the **Vocabulary Center** at **ClassZone.com**.

DIFFERENTIATED INSTRUCTION

FOR ENGLISH LEARNERS
Vocabulary: Word Origins Invite students to share eponyms from their languages and to explain the origins of each word.

FOR ADVANCED LEARNERS/PRE–AP
Vocabulary Research Have students further investigate one of the eponyms. Ask them to report their findings to the class.

Writing for Assessment

1. READ THE PROMPT

In writing assessments, you will often be asked to **compare and contrast** two works of literature that contain a similar conflict. You are now going to practice writing an essay that requires this type of focus.

PROMPT

The conflict between parents and children is an age-old problem, explored here by Amy Tan and Diane Mei Lin Mark. In Tan's story "Two Kinds," what is the theme expressed by the mother-daughter struggle? What is the theme of Mark's poem "Rice and Rose Bowl Blues"? In a three- or four-paragraph essay, explore how their messages are similar or different. Do you think the similarities have anything to do with culture? Support your analysis with evidence.

◀ **STRATEGIES IN ACTION**

1. I have to state the **theme** of each work.
2. I need to **compare and contrast** the themes.
3. I need to include **details and quotations** from each work.

2. PLAN YOUR WRITING

- Review the **Points of Comparison** chart you created on page 487.
- Decide whether the themes are basically similar or markedly different.
- Using your chart, find examples to use as evidence for the points you develop in your essay. If necessary, review the selections again to identify more examples.
- Create an outline to organize your ideas. You may want to discuss each selection separately and then compare them, or you may choose to discuss each point of comparison in its own paragraph.

I. Conflict
A. Tan piece
B. Mark piece

II. Lesson learned
A. Tan piece
B. Mark piece

3. DRAFT YOUR RESPONSE

Introduction Introduce the topic—parental expectations—and then explain that you will discuss what the two works say about it. Include the titles and authors of the selections.

Body State and explain Amy Tan's theme in the second paragraph and Diane Mei Lin Mark's in the third. In a fourth paragraph, compare the two themes.

Conclusion Wrap up your essay with a final thought about parental expectations.

Revision Check your use of transitional words and phrases to connect ideas within and between paragraphs. Words and phrases such as *likewise, both,* and *in the same way* signal similarities. *On the other hand, however, in contrast,* and *nevertheless* signal differences.

TWO KINDS / *RICE AND ROSE BOWL BLUES* **489**

FOR LESS-PROFICIENT WRITERS

- Help students find two quotations that give clues to the theme from each selection.
- Suggest that students highlight the introduction, body, and conclusion in their outlines.
- Review students' statements of theme from their **Points of Comparison** charts.
- Limit the length of the assignment to no more than four paragraphs.

Writing for Assessment

1. *READ THE PROMPT*

Review with students how different features of a story or poem give clues to its theme. Remind them that characters, conflict, and symbols support the theme. Suggest that they review the Literary Analysis Workshop (pages 402–407) before they begin writing.

2. *PLAN YOUR WRITING*

- After students have reviewed the Points of Comparison chart on page 487, ask them to write a statement or two that compares and contrasts the themes in the two selections.
- Have students look at the outline on page 489. Remind them that one way to organize an essay is to use a point-by-point organization that compares and contrasts the two selections. Alternatively, they can organize their essay by comparing and contrasting the selections in separate paragraphs, using a subject-by-subject organization.
- Ask students to determine which organization suits their purpose and have them create an outline for their essay.

3. *DRAFT YOUR RESPONSE*

Ask students to check their outlines to make sure they allow for an introduction, body, and conclusion. Point out that they can identify in their outlines where they will plug in quotes from each work.

Assess and Reteach

Assess

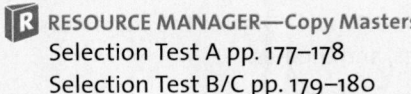
RESOURCE MANAGER—Copy Masters
Selection Test A pp. 177–178
Selection Test B/C pp. 179–180

Test Generator CD

Reteach

STANDARDS LESSON FILE
Literature Lesson 12: Theme
Reading Lesson 3: Determining Author's Purpose

Focus and Motivate

OBJECTIVES

- analyze a student model that reflects the key traits of a literary analysis
- use the writing process to produce a literary analysis
- revise and edit, using a rubric for literary analysis writing
- plan and present a panel discussion

WRITER'S ROAD MAP

WRITING PROMPTS 1 AND 2

Review the terms *theme* and *graphic novel*. Clarify that a theme conveys a literary work's underlying message about life or human nature; theme can often be inferred from the experiences, actions, and feelings of the characters. A graphic novel tells a story through images and words. Help students choose a prompt for a literary element or story source they find interesting.

ADDITIONAL PROMPTS

Use these prompts for practice with real-world writing and writing in the humanities:

WRITING PROMPT 3

Writing for the Real World Write a critical literary analysis of a song for readers of an online or print music magazine.

Possible Subjects

- a song that reflects an element of U.S. culture
- a song that expresses political or social ideas
- a song that sticks in your head

WRITING PROMPT 4

Writing from Media/Fine Art Write an analysis of a visual image such as a painting or a television ad. Discuss the characters, settings, and themes.

Possible Subjects

- an illustration for a selection in this book
- a Norman Rockwell cover illustration
- a television, online, or print ad or cartoon

For ideas for writing, see

- WriteSmart CD
- Writing Center at **ClassZone.com**

KEY TRAITS

Review the six *KEY TRAITS* with students, focusing mainly on ideas, organization, and word choice. Compare the list of traits with the rubric on page 496.

Writing Workshop

Literary Analysis

The selections in this unit and other works of literature can surprise you, enlighten you, or even change your life. A good way to enhance your understanding of a story and to share what you have learned from it is to write a literary analysis. Begin your writing process by carefully examining the **Writer's Road Map**.

WRITER'S ROAD MAP

Literary Analysis

WRITING PROMPT 1

Writing from Literature Write an essay analyzing the meaning of a literary work. Your essay should focus on one or more literary elements and explain how they contribute to the work's meaning.

Literary Elements to Analyze

- symbols and character in "The Scarlet Ibis"
- setting and theme in "Marigolds"
- character and dialogue in "Two Kinds"

WRITING PROMPT 2

Writing from the Real World Stories are everywhere— not just in your literature anthology. Write an analysis of a memorable story you recently viewed or read. Make sure you go beyond a summary of the story to analyze the elements that make it meaningful and interesting.

Sources of Stories

- television shows that use conflict, suspense, or surprise endings
- movies that have compelling main characters
- graphic novels with a strong sense of setting and mood

WRITING TOOLS
For prewriting, revision, and editing tools, visit the **Writing Center** at ClassZone.com.

KEY TRAITS

1. IDEAS
- Presents a **thesis statement** that clearly identifies key points of the discussion
- Uses **evidence** from the text to support each key point

2. ORGANIZATION
- Has an engaging **introduction** that identifies the literary work being analyzed
- Includes a clear **organizational pattern**
- Summarizes ideas and makes broader judgments about the work in a strong **conclusion**

3. VOICE
- Uses a **tone** that is appropriate for the audience and purpose

4. WORD CHOICE
- Uses precise **adjectives** and **adverbs** to convey ideas clearly

5. SENTENCE FLUENCY
- Varies **sentence structures**

6. CONVENTIONS
- Employs **correct grammar and usage**

Writing Workshop Resources

 RESOURCE MANAGER UNIT 4

Plan and Teach pp. 181–184
Prewriting–Editing pp. 185–189
Writing Rubric p. 190
Speaking and Listening p. 191
Writing Support p. 192*

STANDARDS LESSON FILE

Writing Lesson 27: Analysis Essay
Writing Lesson 36: Elaborate

BEST PRACTICES TOOLKIT

Scaffolding Writing Instruction pp. 43–46*
Analysis Frames • List-Group-Label
• Writing Template: Literary Analysis

TECHNOLOGY

- Easy Planner DVD
- Writing Center at **ClassZone.com**
- WriteSmart CD

* Resources for Differentiation

Part 1: Analyze a Student Model

Jason Bernales
Escalante High School

"The Scarlet Ibis" and the Theme of Pride

"All of us must have something or someone to be proud of, and Doodle had become mine. I did not know then that pride is a wonderful, terrible thing, a seed that bears two vines, life and death."
In these words from "The Scarlet Ibis," James Hurst states one of the
5   story's main themes: that pride is both wonderful and terrible. Because of his feelings of pride, the narrator forces his brother Doodle to become stronger. He also rejects Doodle for showing signs of weakness.

As a child, the narrator is full of pride: "I thought myself pretty smart at many things, like holding my breath, running, jumping, or
10   climbing." When he is six, his mother gives birth to a baby who is disabled, physically and perhaps mentally. "It was bad enough having an invalid brother, but having one who possibly was not all there was unbearable," the narrator explains. Shockingly, he plans to kill his brother—until the baby smiles at him.
15   The child, nicknamed Doodle, learns to crawl but not to walk. The narrator is too proud to allow such an unusual situation to continue: "When Doodle was five years old, I was embarrassed at having a brother of that age who couldn't walk, so I set out to teach him."

Doodle is content to accept what his mother and the doctor have
20   told him—that he will never walk. But the narrator is determined. He and Doodle spend weeks practicing, the narrator hauling Doodle to a standing position again and again. When Doodle does learn to walk, the family is delighted. "Everyone wanted to hug me," says the narrator, "and I began to cry. . . . They did not know that I did it for myself; that

KEY TRAITS IN ACTION

Introduction captures reader's attention with a powerful quotation, identifies the literary work being analyzed, and makes a strong **thesis statement**.

Follows a clear **organizational pattern,** concentrating on one element (theme) and proceeding chronologically. Uses precise **adjectives** (*unusual*) and **adverbs** (*shockingly*).

Includes quotations and other **evidence** from "The Scarlet Ibis" to support the thesis.

Teach

Part 1: Analyze a Student Model

Have students read the student model and **KEY TRAITS IN ACTION.** Then discuss the model with the class, pointing out specific examples of each trait and building on what students have already noted. You may also wish to incorporate these activities:

- **Thesis Statement** Explain that a good thesis statement provides a roadmap to a literary analysis. The complete statement may include several sentences. Ask students what two ideas are stated in lines 6–7. *Possible answer: The narrator forces his brother to become stronger; he rejects Doodle.*

  Note that these sentences add detail to the thesis stated in lines 4–5. Readers now expect to read examples and details that support these statements.

- **Evidence** Point out that writers can choose from many different types of evidence:

  - **examples,** which are specific instances from the text that prove a statement
  - **sensory details** that tell how things look, sound, smell, taste, and feel
  - **anecdotes,** or brief stories, that reveal character or make some point
  - **facts,** or statements that can be proved true
  - **statistics,** or facts that are expressed in numbers

  Discuss the types of claims that different types of evidence could be used to support. For example, if a writer claimed that a character was stubborn, evidence might include examples, anecdotes, and statistics that showed how many times the character refused to do something.

DIFFERENTIATED INSTRUCTION

For general guidelines on differentiating writing instruction, see

 BEST PRACTICES TOOLKIT
Scaffolding Writing Instruction pp. 43–46

FOR ENGLISH LEARNERS
Language: Skill Words Write these terms on the board and review them with students:

- *quotation:* words, phrases, or sentences that are taken directly from the literary work
- *thesis statement:* one or two sentences stating the main idea of an essay. The thesis statement of a literary analysis should include the title and the author's name.

- *organizational pattern:* how ideas are arranged and presented in an essay. Writers can organize ideas in different ways:

  time order: The writer discusses ideas in the order in which they appear in the work.

  main idea and details: The writer discusses details that support one main idea and then details that discuss another main idea. The main ideas may be arranged in order of importance or interest.

- **Tone** Be sure that students understand that tone is an expression of the writer's attitude toward a subject. The tone of a work might be playful, serious, or humorous. Tone is communicated in two ways: by word choice and by the choice of details. To help students distinguish tone, write these sentences on the board:

  Doodle is actually OK with how he is, but his brother tries to whip him into shape before school starts. This training pushes the kid over the edge.

Ask a student to read these sentences and lines 30–32 of the student model. Ask students to compare the tone of the two. *Possible answer: The lines on the board sound like someone talking to a friend. They use informal English and slang. The lines in the student model use standard English and no slang. The words are precise and sound like someone speaking to a teacher or other adult.*

- **Varied Sentence Structure** To illustrate the varied sentences that the writer uses, ask students to find

  - a sentence that begins with the subject
  - a compound sentence, made up of two or more independent clauses joined by *and, but,* or *or*
  - a sentence that begins with descriptive words or a dependent clause
  - a short sentence
  - a long sentence

For interactive student models, see

- WriteSmart CD
- Writing Center at **ClassZone.com**

---

25 pride, whose slave I was, spoke to me louder than all their voices, and that Doodle walked only because I was ashamed of having a crippled brother."

Success makes the narrator's pride even stronger: "I began to believe in my own infallibility, and I prepared a terrific development program
30 for him." Doodle doesn't see why being different is bad, but his brother stubbornly expects him to run, swim, climb, and fight by the time school starts. The training leaves Doodle weak and feverish. "I should have already admitted defeat, but my pride wouldn't let me," the narrator explains.

35 Days before school begins, a scarlet ibis dies in the family's yard. The bird was weak and unsure of itself, much like Doodle. That day the narrator makes his brother practice rowing, but Doodle is tired and sad after burying the ibis. The boys are far from home when a storm begins: "We never spoke (What are the words that can solder cracked pride?),
40 but I knew he was watching me . . . for a sign of mercy." Instead, the narrator runs too fast for Doodle, leaving him to collapse and die.

Devastated and heartbroken, the narrator weeps. He loved his brother but also resented and punished him, feelings that he describes as "a knot of cruelty borne by the stream of love." The narrator's pride leads to a
45 wonderful event, Doodle's learning to walk. It also leads to a terrible event, Doodle's death. The contrast between these two types of pride is a powerful theme that makes "The Scarlet Ibis" a compelling story.

Serious, sincere **tone** is formal enough for its audience (a teacher and perhaps classmates) and purpose (to analyze literature).

Conclusion goes beyond summary to explain why the theme of pride is crucial to the story. Writer varies **sentence structures** to make the essay more interesting and sophisticated.

2

DIFFERENTIATED INSTRUCTION

FOR ENGLISH LEARNERS

Comprehension: Transitions Help students identify words and phrases in the model that show shifts in time. Draw their attention to verb tenses, explaining that the student author uses the present tense to analyze theme. The story's narrator, however, speaks in the past tense. Clarify that present tense refers to actions or events happening *now*, while past tense refers to actions or events that happened in the *past*.

Make two columns on the board, labeled *Present* and *Past*. Identify and list several verbs from the first paragraph for each category.

Present: "states" (line 4), "forces" (line 6), "rejects" (line 7)

Past: "had become," "did not know" (line 2)

Have students look at the next paragraph and add verbs to each column. Help them use verb tense to distinguish quotations from the main text.

To provide English learners with additional writing support, see

RESOURCE MANAGER—Writing Support
Writing Support p. 192

Part 2: Apply the Writing Process

PREWRITING

What Should I Do?	What Does It Look Like?

1. Explore the elements of the story.
Use a graphic organizer to list observations or questions you have about story elements such as characters, plot, symbols, and theme. (Circle) the element or elements that intrigue you most.

Characters	Doodle, narrator, ibis (?)
Plot	Narrator teaches Doodle to walk. Narrator makes Doodle do too much, helps cause his death.
Symbols	What does ibis stand for— Doodle, death?
Theme	*Narrator's pride helps and hurts his brother.*

2. Choose a focus for your analysis.
Decide which story element you want to write about. Then jot down a **working thesis statement** that identifies the literary element you've chosen and lists the key points you want to make about it.

Working Thesis Statement:

The theme of "The Scarlet Ibis" is that "pride is a wonderful, terrible thing." Because of his pride, the narrator helps his brother Doodle to become stronger. However, the narrator rejects Doodle for showing signs of weakness.

3. Collect evidence from the story.
Read through the story again carefully. List quotations, details, and ideas that support the key points you noted in your **working thesis statement.**

Evidence	What It Means
"I was embarrassed at having a brother … who couldn't walk"	Narrator decides to teach brother to walk
Narrator cries when Doodle learns to walk	Narrator is proud of what he did but ashamed of why he did it.
"My pride wouldn't let me" stop training Doodle.	Narrator wants Doodle to be like other kids, no matter what.

WRITING WORKSHOP **493**

FOR ENGLISH LEARNERS

Writing: Thesis Statement Have students use sentence starters to help them explore the story elements and choose a focus.

- The characters in the story are _____.
- The theme of the story is _____.
- The setting of the story is _____.
- My working thesis is _____.
- The key points I want to make are _____ and _____.

FOR ADVANCED LEARNERS/PRE–AP

Analyzing Style [small-group option] Have students analyze how the author's style conveys a viewpoint, or set of attitudes about the world. Explain that *style* is how a work is written. It is not what is said but how it is said. Elements of style include word choice, tone, sentence structure and length, dialogue, figurative language, and point of view.

 BEST PRACTICES TOOLKIT—Transparency
Analysis Frame: Author's Craft pp. D21, D24

Practice and Apply

To support students during the writing process, use these copy masters:

 RESOURCE MANAGER—Copy Masters
Prewriting–Editing pp. 185–189
Writing Rubric p. 190
Speaking and Listening p. 191
Writing Support p. 192

Part 2: Apply the Writing Process

PREWRITING

1. **Explore the elements of the story.** This activity lends itself to paired or small-group work. Encourage students to consider and experiment with several graphic organizers, which can help them explore story elements in different ways:

    BEST PRACTICES TOOLKIT—Transparency
   Core Analysis Frame: Fiction
   pp. D21, D22
   Analysis Frame: Plot pp. D21, D28
   Analysis Frame: Character pp. D21, D26
   Analysis Frame: Setting pp. D21, D30
   Analysis Frame: Theme pp. D21, D32

   For interactive graphic organizers, see

   WriteSmart CD

   Writing Center at **ClassZone.com**

2. **Choose a focus for your analysis.** Look through a selection to identify and assess ambiguities and think about their impact on the story. Point out that students may wish to write about those parts of the story that they found difficult to understand instead of those that they understand fully. For example, they may wish to focus on symbolism and theme, which are more abstract and require inference, rather than on clearer elements such as setting. This approach can lead to more in-depth analysis as students work to understand the elements.

3. **Collect evidence from the story.** Review the discussion about different kinds of evidence from page 491. Tell students to list more support than they think they will use. When they draft their essays, they can choose the evidence that works best with the flow of their ideas.

WRITING WORKSHOP **493**

DRAFTING

1. **Organize your ideas.** Help students consider additional organizational methods for their analyses:

   order of importance Main points are arranged in order either from least important to most important, or from most to least.

   structure Main points are organized according to the structure of the work, such as by chapter, episode, or setting.

   cause and effect A cause-and-effect relationship between literary elements is shown.

2. **Support each key point with details from the text.** To emphasize the importance of providing textual support, suggest that students imagine themselves writing for someone who constantly says, "Prove it!" or asks, "But why?"

3. **Create a satisfying and memorable conclusion.** A satisfying conclusion ties together all the ideas that students presented. It also lets readers know that the essay is finished. A memorable conclusion sticks in readers' minds even after they have finished reading.

   Offer two additional techniques for writing conclusions:

   Ask and answer a question. For example, How does an author capture that special relationship between brothers? *James Hurst just tells their story, with all its beauty and horror.*

   Tell why the work has universal appeal. For example, *Every pair of siblings is tied together by bonds that are a complex mix of love, self-interest, and competition. Hurst's story exposes this complexity in a powerful way.*

   For a literary analysis writing template, see

   🧰 BEST PRACTICES TOOLKIT—Transparency
       Writing Template: Literary Analysis
         pp. C16, C30

   💿 Write*Smart* CD

   ℹ️ Writing Center at **ClassZone.com**

DRAFTING

What Should I Do?

1. **Organize your ideas.**
   Consider different ways of presenting your material. Do you want to start with your most important, complex, or interesting idea—or end with it? This writer developed ideas in the order they're discussed in the story (Pattern 1).

   > Review your key points to be sure that each one directly relates to your thesis statement.

2. **Support each key point with details from the text.**
   Every statement that you make should be backed up with evidence from the story. You also should explain how and why each detail supports your ideas.

3. **Create a satisfying and memorable conclusion.**
   Summarize your key ideas and give your reader something new to think about. This could be an overall statement about the literary work or its effect on readers.

   TIP Before revising, consult the **key traits** on page 490 and the **rubric and peer-reader questions** on page 496.

What Does It Look Like?

PATTERN 1

Introduction and Thesis
1. *Doodle is born.*
2. *Doodle crawls.*
3. *Doodle learns to walk.*
4. *Narrator trains Doodle harder.*
5. *Narrator abandons Doodle.*
Conclusion

PATTERN 2

Introduction and Thesis
A. *Pride is wonderful.*
   1. Narrator teaches Doodle to walk.
B. *Pride is terrible.*
   1. Narrator plans to kill Doodle.
   2. Narrator is ashamed of Doodle.
   3. Narrator abandons Doodle.
Conclusion

As a child, the narrator is full of pride: — Key point

"I thought myself pretty smart at many things, like holding my breath, running, jumping, or climbing."   — Support

The narrator's pride leads to a wonderful event, Doodle's learning to walk. It also leads to a terrible event, Doodle's death.   — Summary

The contrast between these two types of pride is a powerful theme that makes "The Scarlet Ibis" a compelling story.   — Why it matters

---

DIFFERENTIATED INSTRUCTION

FOR LESS–PROFICIENT WRITERS
Supporting Key Points To help students organize their support, provide a four-column chart with these heads: *Key Point, Quotations, Summary Statements, Story Details.*

Have students begin by listing the key points that they want to make. Then have them reread the work, looking for support. Encourage them to find at least one of each type of support.

Have students return to the student model to see how the writer links the key points with support. Discuss words and phrases that students can use in their own papers.

- For example, the character . . .
- Such details show . . .
- After [event], [describe change] . . .
- The setting is [adjective]: [quotation] . . .

REVISING AND EDITING

What Should I Do?

1. Strengthen your introduction.
- Draw a box around the first two or three sentences of your essay.
- Ask yourself: Would this beginning capture my attention?
- Consider starting with a powerful quotation, a question, or an unexpected idea.

2. Tune your tone.
- Ask a peer reader to [bracket] vocabulary that is too slangy or casual.
- Revise your essay so that it is formal throughout.

See page 496: Ask a Peer Reader

3. Choose adjectives and adverbs carefully and wisely.
- Circle adjectives and adverbs in your essay.
- If you don't have many circles, think of modifiers to add.
- Ask yourself: Could I use sharper modifiers to express myself more accurately?

4. Vary the types and structures of your sentences.
- Read your essay aloud. Highlight repeated sentence types or structures.
- Rewrite some of these sentences to give your writing fluency and a pleasing rhythm.

What Does It Look Like?

An unexpected idea
Pride can motivate us to do great things, but it can also cause us to hurt the people we love.

A quotation
"All of us must have something or someone to be proud of, and Doodle had become mine. I did not know then that pride is a wonderful, terrible thing, a seed that bears two vines, life and death."

The narrator is disgusting. He's ready to kill his own little brother just for not being perfect. But then the kid smiles at him and he changes his mind.
Shockingly, he plans to kill his brother—until the baby smiles at him.

Doodle doesn't see why being different is bad, but his brother stubbornly expects him to run, swim, climb, and fight by the time school starts. The training leaves Doodle tired, weak and feverish.

The narrator weeps. He loved his brother. He also resented and punished him.
Devastated and heartbroken, the narrator weeps. He loved his brother but also resented and punished him.

REVISING AND EDITING

1. Strengthen your introduction. This activity is excellent for paired and small-group work. Encourage students to work together to evaluate their present introductions and to brainstorm other possibilities using the techniques listed: a **powerful quotation,** a **question,** and an **unexpected idea.**

2. Tune your tone. Remind students that **formal** language
- contains no slang and few contractions
- uses precise language that shows an understanding of the connotations of words, as well as the denotations
- avoids overused expressions and catch phrases
- uses complex vocabulary and sentence structure
- does not use the personal pronouns *I* or *me* to refer to the student writing

3. Choose adjectives and adverbs carefully and wisely. Part of choosing **modifiers** wisely is not overusing them. Although some students will circle only a few adjectives and adverbs, others may circle many. Suggest that these students eliminate such overload by using more precise nouns and verbs, such as *shouted* instead of "spoke loudly."

4. Vary the types and structures of your sentences. Review with students various types of sentences, including simple statements and questions. Point out that one way to vary sentence structure is by adding independent and subordinate clauses. Point out that the last sentence of the revision is two independent clauses connected by a coordinating conjunction (*but*). Also, review the GRAMMAR AND STYLE note on page 434 and the sentences to which it refers. Remind students that varying sentence types and structures creates more interesting writing.

For interactive revision tools, see

- WriteSmart CD
- Writing Center at **ClassZone.com**

FOR ENGLISH LEARNERS

Recognizing Tone Students may need help categorizing idioms, sayings, and phrasal verbs as formal and informal, or slangy. Use a List-Group-Label activity with students. Have them list words and phrases that they used in their analyses. Discuss the category each belongs in—*formal* or *informal*. Then have students select language that they are unsure about. Work together to classify terms as *formal* or *informal.*

BEST PRACTICES TOOLKIT—Transparency
List-Group-Label p. A15

Preparing to Publish

Support for meeting the goals in the writing rubric is supplied throughout the Writing Workshop on pages 493–495.

For Rubric Bank, see

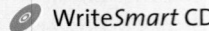 Write*Smart* CD

 Writing Center at **ClassZone.com**

Assess and Reteach

S STANDARDS LESSON FILE
Writing Lesson 27: Analysis Essay
Writing Lesson 36: Elaborate with Incidents, Examples, and Quotations

---

Preparing to Publish **Literary Analysis**

Apply the Rubric

A strong literary analysis . . .

☑ opens by identifying the author and the literary work

☑ includes a strong, clear thesis statement

☑ develops ideas in a logical organizational scheme

☑ supports ideas with specific evidence from the text

☑ has a tone appropriate to the audience and purpose

☑ maintains interest with strong modifiers and varied sentence structures

☑ concludes with a statement addressing the work or its effect as a whole

Ask a Peer Reader

• How would you restate my thesis in your own words?

• Is the tone right for a literary analysis, or should some parts be more formal?

• Which parts of my analysis do you most strongly agree or disagree with? Why?

Check Your Grammar

• A literary analysis contains many quotations. Make sure that you punctuate them correctly. Periods and commas go inside quotation marks.

> "I should have already admitted defeat, but, my pride wouldn't let me," the narrator explains.

• If you choose to omit words from within a quotation, use ellipses (three spaced periods).

> "I knew he was watching me . . . for a sign of mercy."

• If you quote a word or phrase within a sentence of your own, do not capitalize the first letter of the word or phrase.

> He loved his brother but also resented and punished him, feelings he described as "a knot of cruelty borne by the steam of love."

• You can use a colon to introduce a long quotation.

> Success makes the narrator's pride even stronger: "I began to believe in my own infallibility, and I prepared a terrific development program for him."

See pages R49–R51: Quick Reference: Punctuation and Capitalization

Writing On|ine

 PUBLISHING OPTIONS
For publishing options, visit the **Writing Center** at **ClassZone.com**.

ASSESSMENT PREPARATION
For writing and grammar assessment practice, go to the **Assessment Center** at **ClassZone.com**.

Participating in a Panel Discussion

Taking part in a panel discussion can deepen your understanding of a literary work, improve your public-speaking skills, and give you practice in "thinking on your feet."

Planning the Discussion

1. **Identify panel members.** The teacher may choose participants, or students interested in a specific story may form a panel.

2. **Appoint a moderator.** Panel members should ask for a volunteer or appoint one student to moderate the discussion.

3. **Agree on rules for the discussion.** Participants should agree to speak clearly and concisely, listen respectfully without interrupting, and ask thoughtful questions.

4. **Review the story and your thoughts about it.** Reread both the literary work and your written analysis of it. Jot down your main thoughts about the story.

Holding the Discussion

1. **Get started.** The moderator should identify the story, introduce the panelists, and ask a question such as, "What literary element contributes most to the meaning of this story?"

2. **State your ideas.** Respond to the question posed by the moderator. Make any related points that support your answer.

3. **Give others a chance to respond.** Listen while another speaker summarizes your ideas and adds his or her own thoughts.

> "So you're saying that the setting of "The Scarlet Ibis" is the most important literary element in the story? I agree that it is a sad place filled with death and that this contributes to the story's mood and theme. But I think the dialogue in the story is more important. Here's why."

4. **Be respectful.** Give everyone a chance to talk.

5. **Wrap it up.** The moderator should summarize the ideas and thank the panelists for participating.

SPEAKING AND LISTENING

Ask students to read this page to get an overview of how to create a panel discussion. Spend some time reviewing each of the rules and guidelines for discussion, making sure students understand the reasoning behind them. Ask questions, such as "What does it mean to be concise, and why would this matter?"

Remind students that literary analysis may require several readings. First, students should read for the story's literary qualities. Next, they can review the story for evidence that supports ideas. Allow time for students to review the literary work they will discuss with the panel. In addition, provide time for students to take notes, and encourage them to organize their notes or label them for easy scanning during the discussion.

Before students begin work, review this rubric with them so that they have clear goals:

Rubric A strong panel discussion

- follows agreed-upon rules for discussion
- demonstrates that participants have carefully read and considered the literary work
- includes opinions and ideas that are supported by the text or by logical reasons
- has participants who listen quietly while others speak
- discusses questions that show thought and an understanding of the ideas of others
- consists of participants who speak clearly at an appropriate rate

R RESOURCE MANAGER—Copy Master
Speaking and Listening p. 191

S STANDARDS LESSON FILE
Speaking and Listening Lesson 3: Group Discussions

Assessment Practice

CHECK READINESS

Read aloud the paragraph under **ASSESS** and stress to students that this is not the full Unit Test but a way for them to check their readiness for it. Then have students examine the skills listed under **REVIEW** and look back in the unit or in the **Student Resource Bank** for any skills they need to review.

READ THE SELECTION

Remind students to keep unit goals in mind as they read the passage, paying particular attention to these literary and reading skills:

- theme
- symbol
- make inferences
- draw conclusions

To help students focus on what the apple tree might represent, encourage them to ask questions such as

- What is the title of the selection? How can it help me recognize an important story element?
- What makes this tree important to the narrator? What makes it important to other characters?

ANSWER THE QUESTIONS

Direct students to pages R93–R101 of the **Handbook** to review test-taking strategies.

- Remind students not to choose the first alternative that seems to fit when answering a multiple-choice question. Instead, they should read through all the choices, eliminate any that are clearly wrong, and then choose the *best* answer—the one that is most accurate and complete.
- Tell students that sometimes an answer may not be obvious. In that case, they should be ready to refer back to the selection as needed. Often, rereading a few sentences will help them identify the correct answer.

Assessment Practice

ASSESS
The practice test items on the next few pages match skills listed on the Unit Goals page (page 401) and addressed throughout this unit. Taking this practice test will help you assess your knowledge of these skills and determine your readiness for the Unit Test.

REVIEW
After you take the practice test, your teacher can help you identify any skills you need to review.

- Theme
- Symbol
- Make Inferences
- Draw Conclusions
- Context Clues
- Suffixes
- Independent and Subordinate Clauses

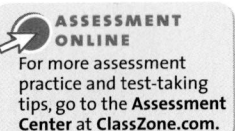

ASSESSMENT ONLINE
For more assessment practice and test-taking tips, go to the **Assessment Center** at ClassZone.com.

Reading Comprehension

DIRECTIONS *Read the following selection and answer the questions.*

The Apple-Tree
Katherine Mansfield

There were two orchards belonging to the old house. One, that we called the "wild" orchard, lay beyond the vegetable garden; it was planted with bitter cherries and damsons and transparent yellow plums. For some reason it lay under a cloud; we never played there, we did not even trouble to pick up the fallen fruit; and there, every Monday morning, to the round open space in the middle, the servant girl and the washerwoman carried the wet linen—Grandmother's nightdresses, Father's striped shirts, the hired man's cotton trousers and the servant girl's "dreadfully vulgar" salmon-pink flannelette drawers jigged and slapped in horrid familiarity.

10 But the other orchard, far away and hidden from the house, lay at the foot of a little hill and stretched right over to the edge of the paddocks—to the clumps of wattles bobbing yellow in the bright sun and the blue gums with their streaming sickle-shaped leaves. There, under the fruit trees, the grass grew so thick and coarse that it tangled and knotted in your shoes as you walked, and even on the hottest day it was damp to touch when you stopped and parted it this way and that, looking for windfalls—the apples marked with a bird's beak, the big bruised pears, the quinces, so good to eat with a pinch of salt, but so delicious to smell that you could not bite for sniffing. . . .

One year the orchard had its Forbidden Tree. It was an apple-tree discovered 20 by Father and a friend during an after-dinner prowl one Sunday afternoon.

"Great Scott!" said the friend, lighting upon it with every appearance of admiring astonishment: "Isn't that a ——?" And a rich, splendid name settled like an unknown bird on the tree.

"Yes, I believe it is," said Father lightly. He knew nothing whatever about the names of fruit trees.

"Great Scott!" said the friend again. "They're wonderful apples. Nothing like 'em—and you're going to have a tip-top crop. Marvellous apples! You can't beat 'em!"

"No, they're very fine—very fine," said Father carelessly, but looking upon 30 the tree with new and lively interest.

"They're rare—they're very rare. Hardly ever see 'em in England nowadays," said the visitor and set a seal on Father's delight. For Father was a self-made

---

DIFFERENTIATED INSTRUCTION

FOR ENGLISH LEARNERS
Assessment Practice: Work Backward
Prepare students by having them read the questions *before* reading the passage. Have pairs find unfamiliar words in test directions and questions and follow these steps:

1. Write each word on an index card.
2. Look up the meaning in a dictionary and write it on the back of the card.
3. Use the cards to practice the words with partners and to teach them to others.

Test-Taking Strategies: Focus Your Reading
Tell students that reading test questions before reading the passage can help them focus their reading. As an example, ask students how many multiple-choice questions contain the word *apple* or *apples*. (five) Point out that the word *apples* does not appear in the passage until line 16, after which it appears often. Discuss how students can use this clue to know when to start reading closely.

man and the price he had to pay for everything was so huge and so painful that nothing rang so sweet to him as to hear his purchase praised. He was young and sensitive still. He still wondered whether in the deepest sense he got his money's worth. He still had hours when he walked up and down in the moonlight half deciding to "chuck this confounded rushing to the office every day—and clear out—clear out once and for all." And now to discover that he'd a valuable apple-tree thrown in with the orchard—an apple-tree that this
40 Johnny from England positively envied!

"Don't touch that tree! Do you hear me, children!" said he, bland and firm; and when the guest had gone, with quite another voice and manner:

"If I catch either of you touching those apples you shall not only go to bed—you shall each have a good sound whipping." Which merely added to its magnificence.

Every Sunday morning after church Father, with Bogey and me tailing after, walked through the flower garden, down the violet path, past the lace-bark tree, past the white rose and syringa bushes, and down the hill to the orchard. The apple-tree—like the Virgin Mary—seemed to have been miraculously
50 warned of its high honour, standing apart from its fellows, bending a little under its rich clusters, fluttering its polished leaves, important and exquisite before Father's awful eye. His heart swelled to the sight—we knew his heart swelled. He put his hands behind his back and screwed up his eyes in the way he had. There it stood—the accidental thing—the thing that no one had been aware of when the hard bargain was driven. It hadn't been counted in, hadn't in a way been paid for. If the house had been burned to the ground at that time it would have meant less to him than the destruction of his tree. And how we played up to him, Bogey and I,—Bogey with his scratched knees pressed together, his hands behind his back, too, and a round cap on his head with
60 "H.M.S. Thunderbolt" printed across it.

The apples turned from pale green to yellow; then they had deep pink stripes painted on them, and then the pink melted all over the yellow, reddened, and spread into a fine clear crimson.

At last the day came when Father took out of his waistcoat pocket a little pearl pen-knife. He reached up. Very slowly and very carefully he picked two apples growing on a bough.

"By Jove! They're warm," cried Father in amazement. "They're wonderful apples! Tip-top! Marvellous!" he echoed. He rolled them over in his hands.

GO ON

ITEM ANALYSIS

COMPREHENSION AND WRITTEN RESPONSE	ITEMS	UNIT PAGES
Theme	1, 3, 8	402–407, 409, 473
Symbol	4, 6, 7	402–407, 427
Make Inferences	2, 5, 6	427
Draw Conclusions	1, 4, 8	409

VOCABULARY	ITEMS	UNIT PAGES
Context Clues	1, 2, 3, 4, 5	457
Suffixes	6, 7, 8	421

GRAMMAR	ITEMS	UNIT PAGES
Independent and Subordinate Clauses	1, 2, 3, 4	445

FOR LESS–PROFICIENT READERS

Assessment Support Consider these options for completing the Assessment Practice:

- Have students "work backward" to review the test questions *before* reading the passage.

- Select random questions in the Assessment, and have students demonstrate how and where to look for answers.

- Ask students to locate unfamiliar vocabulary words in the Assessment. Elicit their meanings from the class.

- Have students record useful testing words and definitions in their journals for later reference.

- Read the selections or parts of them aloud to aid in student comprehension.

McDougal Littell
Assessment System

After checking student readiness with this Assessment Practice, you may administer the complete Unit 4 Test in order to more thoroughly evaluate student mastery of unit goals.

Comprehension

Model a thinking process for answering multiple-choice questions.

1. **D *is correct*.** *Lines 29–30 show that he is becoming interested in the tree's value. The next paragraph explains his motivation. A is incorrect because the father and friend had just discovered the tree. B is partly true, but it is not the father's reason for valuing the tree. C is completely untrue.*

2. **A *is correct*.** *B is completely untrue. C is incorrect, because the father only worries about this at the beginning. D is incorrect, since the father never thinks the tree is worth more than his house, even though he may value the tree more.*

3. **A *is correct*.** *The father's anticipation about the apples builds during the story; then the apples are a disappointment. B is only partly true, since it does not address the father's pride in the tree. C refers only to a detail. D is incorrect, since little in the story suggests caring for the tree.*

4. **C *is correct*.** *The narrator says the apples are floury and bitter. A and D are incorrect; the narrator never says the apples are small or that they smell like flowers. B is incorrect, because the apples turn red.*

5. **B *is correct*.** *A is incorrect; the narrator never states this. C and D are both untrue; the children lied cheerfully in order to mislead their father. They clearly care what he thinks.*

6. **A *is correct*.** *The father grows to value the tree even more than his house. B is incorrect, because the story is not about the children's obedience. C is incorrect, since the visitor was wrong. D is totally untrue.*

"Look at that!" he said. "Not a spot—not a blemish!" And he walked
70 through the orchard with Bogey and me stumbling after, to a tree-stump under the wattles. We sat, one on either side of Father. He laid one apple down, opened the pearl pen-knife and neatly and beautifully cut the other in half.

"By Jove! Look at that!" he exclaimed.

"Father!" we cried, dutiful but really enthusiastic, too. For the lovely red colour had bitten right through the white flesh of the apple; it was pink to the shiny black pips lying so justly in their scaly pods. It looked as though the apple had been dipped in wine.

"Never seen *that* before," said Father. "You won't find an apple like that in a
80 hurry!" He put it to his nose and pronounced an unfamiliar word. "Bouquet! What a bouquet!" And then he handed to Bogey one half, to me the other.

"Don't *bolt* it!" said he. It was agony to give even so much away. I knew it, while I took mine humbly and humbly Bogey took his.

Then he divided the second with the same neat beautiful little cut of the pearl knife.

I kept my eyes on Bogey. Together we took a bite. Our mouths were full of a floury stuff, a hard, faintly bitter skin—a horrible taste of something dry. . . .

"Well?" asked Father, very jovial. He had cut his two halves into quarters and was taking out the little pods. "Well?"
90 Bogey and I stared at each other, chewing desperately. In that second of chewing and swallowing a long silent conversation passed between us—and a strange meaning smile. We swallowed. We edged near Father, just touching him.

"Perfect!" we lied. "Perfect—Father! Simply lovely!"

But it was no use. Father spat his out and never went near the apple-tree again.

Comprehension

DIRECTIONS *Answer these questions about "The Apple-Tree."*

1. What makes the apple tree seem valuable to the father?
   A His children love the tree.
   B He has never seen a tree like it before.
   C He has always wanted an apple tree.
   D His friend tells him that it is rare.

2. As the apples on the tree ripen, the father
   A becomes more and more proud of owning the apple tree
   B begins to lose interest in the apple tree
   C worries that his children will somehow harm the apple tree
   D knows that the tree is worth more than his house

3. What is the main theme of the story?
   A If your expectations are too high, you may end up disappointed.
   B Beautiful apple trees often produce bitter fruit.
   C Telling the truth is always the best policy.
   D When you own something, you must constantly take care of it.

4. How are the ripe apples different from what the characters expect?
   A They are small instead of large.
   B The apples are pale pink instead of red.
   C They taste bitter instead of sweet.
   D The apples smell like flowers instead of fruit.

5. Why do the children lie to their father about how the apple tastes?
   A They are afraid of being punished.
   B They don't want him to be disappointed.
   C They want to trick him into liking the apple.
   D They don't care what he thinks.

6. What does the apple tree symbolize after the visitor praises it?
   A the father's power
   B the children's obedience
   C the visitor's wisdom
   D the fruit's sweetness

Written Response

SHORT RESPONSE
Write three or four sentences to answer the question.

7. Give one reason why the author calls the apple tree the Forbidden Tree. Support your idea about why the author uses this symbol with an example from the text or from your own knowledge.

EXTENDED RESPONSE
Write two or three paragraphs to answer the question.

8. Explain why the father believes his friend's statement that the apples are rare and will be marvelous. Support your answer with three details from the story.

GO ON

501

Written Response

Possible short response:

7. *In the story, the father tells the children to stay away from the tree. In addition, the tree is in a secluded part of the orchard and is valuable. From my knowledge about the Bible, I know that the fruit from the tree of knowledge in the Garden of Eden was forbidden.*

Possible extended response:

8. *The response should provide a sound reason to explain why the father believes his friend's statement. Reasons may include, for example, that the friend's admiration of the tree seems sincere to the father, that the father wants to impress his friend, or that the father is glad that there is something of value on his property. The details should support the stated reason. For example, for the reasons above, students may say that the friend seems to know a lot about fruit trees, including a rich name for the tree; that the friend, who had come from England where the tree is rare, envies the tree; or that the father feels that having a valuable tree on the property demonstrates that he got his money's worth when he purchased it.*

DIFFERENTIATED INSTRUCTION

FOR ENGLISH LEARNERS

Review Academic Vocabulary On the board, list the academic vocabulary shown in italics. Then give the examples in random order and have students match the examples with the vocabulary. Elicit additional examples from students.

- *context clues:* Unlike the other trees, the catalpa had flowers. One apple, the Granny Smith, is green instead of red.

- *symbol:* flag (patriotism); sunrise (beginning); flowing river (life)

- *theme:* Honesty is always best. Pride can be a terrible thing.

Vocabulary

1. **B is correct.** The context mentions two other fruits. We can eliminate A because it has nothing to do with the context. C and D are mentioned earlier in the sentence but are not related by any clear clues.

2. **A is correct.** Cherries, damsons, and plums are a series. We can eliminate B since transparent yellow describes plums. Vegetable garden (C) and under a cloud (D) are not related to the context clue "was planted with."

3. **B is correct.** The context clue is "with their streaming sickle-shaped leaves," which directly follows the word gums. All other answer choices can be eliminated.

4. **D is correct.** We can eliminate A, B, and C because the word blue describes the tree, and the words streaming and sickle describe the leaves, which suggests a plant.

5. **C is correct.** In the story, the word windfalls is followed by types of fruits. We can eliminate A, since the words broken branches do not appear near windfalls, and B because clumps of grass is not related to windfalls in the sentence. The last choice appears nowhere and so cannot be correct.

6. **C is correct.** It supports the father's feelings that the tree is special. We can eliminate A and B, since hugeness and light do not relate to the paragraph, and D because it has nothing to do with trees.

7. **B is correct.** B supports the idea that the tree has great value. A could possibly be true, but nothing in the text supports it. We can eliminate C and D because the narrator and Bogey are enthusiastic in line 75.

8. **B is correct.** Father's exclamations show that he thinks the apple should be savored. We can eliminate A since he has not yet tasted the apple and C since bitter does not relate to the excerpt. We can also eliminate D. Since no one has tasted the apple, Father cannot be triumphant.

Vocabulary

DIRECTIONS *Use context clues to answer the following questions.*

1. Which is the most likely meaning of *damson* from line 3?
   A a type of cloud
   B a kind of fruit
   C an orchard
   D a vegetable garden

2. Which nearby words give a clue to the meaning of *damson?*
   A *cherries* and *plums*
   B *transparent yellow*
   C *vegetable garden*
   D *under a cloud*

3. Which is the most likely meaning of *gums* from line 12?
   A strong colors
   B a certain type of tree
   C a structure in the mouth
   D chewy substances

4. Which nearby word gives the best clue to the meaning of *gums?*
   A *blue*
   B *streaming*
   C *sickle*
   D *leaves*

5. Use context clues to figure out what *windfalls* refers to in line 16.
   A broken branches
   B clumps of thick grass
   C fallen fruit
   D injured birds

DIRECTIONS *Use context clues and your knowledge of suffixes to answer the following questions.*

6. What is the most likely meaning of the word *magnificence* as it appears in the following quotation from lines 43–45?

   "If I catch either of you touching those apples you shall not only go to bed—you shall each have a good sound whipping." Which merely added to its <u>magnificence</u>.

   A hugeness
   B bright light
   C grand quality
   D lack of power

7. What is the meaning of *humbly* as it appears in the following quotation from lines 82–83?

   "Don't *bolt* it!" said he. It was agony to give even so much away. I knew it, while I took mine <u>humbly</u> and <u>humbly</u> Bogey took his.

   A full of joy
   B in a respectful manner
   C under pressure
   D out of a sense of kindness

8. Read the following two excerpts from the selection. Which word means nearly the same as the word *jovial* in line 88?

   "Never seen *that* before," said Father. "You won't find an apple like that in a hurry!" He put it to his nose and pronounced an unfamiliar word. "Bouquet! What a bouquet!" And then he handed to Bogey one half, to me the other.

   ———————

   "Well?" asked Father, very <u>jovial</u>. He had cut his two halves into quarters and was taking out the little pods. "Well?"

   A smug   C bitter
   B cheerful   D triumphant

502

DIFFERENTIATED INSTRUCTION

FOR ENGLISH LEARNERS

Assessment Vocabulary Review the following words and phrases used in the directions or items:

- *symbolize:* stand as a symbol for
- *support your idea:* provide details from the passage as reasons for your statement
- *suffix:* word part that appears at the end of a word to form a new word
- *rewrite:* write again in a different form

- *independent clause:* a group of words that could stand alone as a sentence because it contains both a subject and a verb
- *subordinate clause:* a group of words that could not stand alone as a sentence because the group lacks either a subject or a verb

Grammar & Style

DIRECTIONS *Read the passage and answer the questions that follow.*

> (1) Nadia walked down the street. (2) She heard a noise behind her. (3) She considered her options. (4) She decided to run. (5) But it was dark now. (6) She was in an unfamiliar part of town. (7) Suddenly, she felt hot breath on the back of her leg. (8) She poised herself to kick. (9) Then she realized it was just a dog. (10) Had she really been so afraid of a friendly little beagle? (11) Or had something else been behind her too?

1. Choose the correct way to rewrite sentences 1 and 2 as one sentence containing one independent clause and one subordinate clause. Choose D if no other answer choice is correct.

   A Nadia walked down the street, hearing a noise behind her.

   B Nadia walked down the street, she heard a noise behind her.

   C As Nadia walked down the street, she heard a noise behind her.

   D None of the above

2. Choose the correct way to rewrite sentences 3 and 4 as one sentence containing one independent clause. Choose D if no other answer choice is correct.

   A She considered her options and decided to run.

   B She considered her options, and then she decided to run.

   C She considered her options; she decided to run.

   D None of the above

3. Choose the correct way to rewrite sentences 5 and 6 as one sentence containing two independent clauses. Choose D if no other answer choice is correct.

   A Since it was dark now, this part of town was unfamiliar.

   B But it was dark now, and she was in an unfamiliar part of town.

   C Because it was dark now, she realized she was in an unfamiliar part of town.

   D None of the above

4. Choose the correct way to rewrite sentences 7–9 as one sentence containing one subordinate clause and two independent clauses. Choose D if no other answer choice is correct.

   A Suddenly, she felt hot breath on the back of her leg, and as she poised herself to kick, she realized it was just a dog.

   B Suddenly, she felt hot breath on the back of her leg, poised herself to kick, and realized it was just a dog.

   C Suddenly, she felt hot breath on the back of her leg, then she poised herself to kick, and then she realized it was just a dog.

   D None of the above

STOP

503

ANSWERS

Grammar & Style

1. **C is correct.** C contains a subordinate clause, "As Nadia walked down the street," and an independent clause, "she heard a noise behind her." A contains both kinds of clauses, but the subordinate clause is incorrectly stated and does not modify Nadia. B contains two independent clauses, so it is incorrect. D is incorrect because one of the answer choices is correct.

2. **A is correct.** A has one independent clause with a compound predicate. B and C both contain two independent clauses, so both are incorrect. D is incorrect because one of the answer choices is correct.

3. **B is correct.** B contains two independent clauses, since both parts of the sentence have a subject and a verb. Both A and C each contain one independent clause and one subordinate clause, so both are incorrect. D is incorrect, because one of the answer choices is correct.

4. **A is correct.** A is the only answer choice with one subordinate clause ("and as she poised herself to kick") and two independent clauses ("she felt hot breath on the back of her leg" and "she realized it was just a dog"). B is one independent clause with a compound predicate, and C contains three independent clauses. D is incorrect, because one of the answer choices is correct.

FOR LESS–PROFICIENT READERS

Assessment Support: Independent Clauses and Subordinate Clauses

- Review that an independent clause has a subject or subjects and a verb or verbs and can stand alone as a sentence. Show several examples from "The Apple-Tree," such as those in lines 65–66. Help students identify the subject and verb in each.
- Follow a similar procedure with subordinate clauses, using the sentence in lines 56–57 ("If the house . . ."). Emphasize the subordinating conjunction *if*.
- Remind students to look carefully at the instructions for each item. Have them ask themselves how many clauses of each type are asked for.
- Suggest that students count the number of independent and subordinate clauses in each answer choice. This will eliminate incorrect options.

INTRODUCE *GREAT READS*

In Unit 4, students have discussed a number of big questions. Invite students to tell which question they found most intriguing and why, and then focus attention on the three that appear on this page. Discuss the recommended books and their summaries, pointing out how each connects to the related question. Encourage students to choose one or more of these "great reads" to read independently.

ⓘ ClassZone.com

To find additional books that match students' interests and ability levels, visit the Literature Center at **ClassZone.com**.

Ideas for Independent Reading

Which of the themes in this unit has the most importance in your life? Discover how these themes affect others in the following books.

How do expectations affect performance?

Music of the Heart
by Roberta Gaspari

No one expected Gaspari's students to succeed at the violin. But she and her kids—more than one thousand over the years—proved that expectations and talent can lead to good music.

Gifted Hands
by Ben Carson, M.D. with Cecil Murphy

Carson's mother expected him to do something worthwhile with his life. He did not disappoint her. In 1987, the surgeon helped complete the first successful separation of Siamese twins joined at the head.

Lanterns: A Memoir of Mentors
by Marian Wright Edelman

The lawyer, civil rights activist, and founder of the Children's Defense Fund honors the famous and not-so-famous people in her life who kept her expectations high while she struggled to make a difference.

Why do we hurt the ones we love?

The Kite Runner
by Khaled Hosseini

Amir and Hassan grow up together in Afghanistan. Amir fails his friend Hassan before leaving for America. He returns years later to try to make up for his betrayal.

The Once and Future King
by T. H. White

In this retelling of the legend of King Arthur, Queen Guinevere loves both her husband Arthur and the knight Lancelot, Arthur's best friend. Though each one loves the other two, all three suffer terribly.

This Boy's Life
by Tobias Wolff

Divorce may be necessary for adults, but the children in the family often get hurt. The award-winning author remembers his struggle to grow up and find himself while frequently separated from his father.

What are you really good at?

One Writer's Beginnings
by Eudora Welty

In this memoir, Welty brings to life her family, her younger self, and the American South in the early 1900s. She also conveys her love for stories—those she found in books as well as those she heard on long, hot summer afternoons.

I'd Rather Teach Peace
by Colman McCarthy

As a *Washington Post* columnist, McCarthy has written for many years on nonviolence as a way of life. Here he talks about teaching peace to students, prisoners, and others.

The Other Side of the Mountain
by Evans G. Valens

Valens tells the inspiring true story of skier Jill Kinmont who found a way to reshape her life after a crippling accident.

Ideas Made Visible

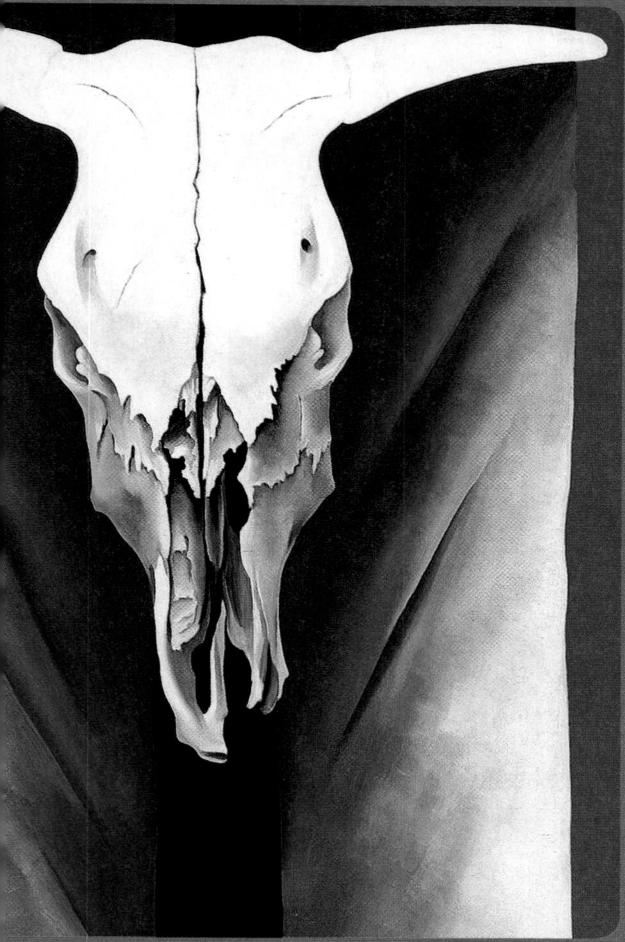

AUTHOR'S PURPOSE

- In Nonfiction
- In Media
- In Fiction

505

About the Art Georgia O'Keeffe (1887–1986) painted *Cow's Skull: Red, White, and Blue* in 1931. For more information, see page 529.

For help in planning this unit, see

 RESOURCE MANAGER UNIT 5 pp. 1–11

INTRODUCE THE UNIT

An idea is an abstract concept; it is personal and internal. Yet some people share their ideas with the world—and they often do so in ways that are clear and memorable. For example, painters, photographers, and architects make their ideas come alive through paint, film, and construction materials. Writers bring their ideas to life through words.

Invite students to describe how they express their ideas. Ask them to identify purposes that prompt them to bring their ideas to life. Then have students consider how the pictures on this page share ideas. Discuss these questions:

- What colors are in the painting? What might those colors mean?
- What is memorable about the architecture in the photograph?
- Does either image strike you as strongly positive or negative? Explain.
- Why do you think each artist whose work is represented on this page decided to share a visual idea in the way shown?

Tell students that as they read this unit, they will explore not only *how* writers make their ideas visible for readers but also *why* they do so. In each selection, therefore, students will consider the **author's purpose** for writing.

UNIT 5

Skills Trace

SKILLS STRAND	Critical Reading Workshop: Author's Purpose pp. 508–513	Island Morning pp. 514–523 Descriptive Essay *Level: Average*	Georgia O'Keeffe pp. 524–533 Biographical Essay *Level: Challenging*	Who Killed the Iceman?/Skeletal Sculptures pp. 534–545 Magazine Article/ Process Description *Level: Easy*	The Lost Boys pp. 546–555 Magazine Article *Level: Average*
Literary Analysis		Diction pp. 515, 516, 518, 519, 522 Review: Tone p. 520	Tone pp. 525, 528, 530, 531		
Reading and Informational Texts	Author's Purpose and Perspective pp. 508–510, 512–513 Recognize Patterns of Organization and Format pp. 510–513 Analyze the Literature pp. 509, 510, 511, 512–513 Compare Texts pp. 512–513	Analyze Patterns of Organization pp. 515, 519, 520, 522	Identify Implied Main Ideas pp. 525, 526, 531	Text Features pp. 535, 536, 537, 538, 543, 544 Take Notes pp. 535, 536, 537, 541, 544 Review: Monitor pp. 539, 540	Author's Purpose pp. 547, 548, 552, 554 Interpret Graphic Aids pp. 547, 548, 550, 553, 554 Review: Connect pp. 553, 554
Vocabulary	Academic Vocabulary pp. 508, 510		Word Acquisition pp. 525, T525, 532 Context Clues p. T525 Analogies p. 532 Latin and Greek Roots (*gen*) p. 532	Word Acquisition pp. 535, T535, 545 Context Clues p. T535 Suffixes (*-ology*) p. 545	Word Acquisition pp. 547, T547, 555 Context Clues p. T547 Latin Roots (*fract*) p. 555
Writing, Grammar, and Style		Sentence Flow pp. 518, 523 Coordinating Conjunctions pp. 518, 523	Descriptive Language pp. 528, 533 Concrete and Abstract Nouns pp. 528, 533		
Speaking, Listening, Viewing, and Media	Discuss pp. T508–T511	Discuss pp. 514, T516–T521, 522 Analyze Visuals pp. 516, T519, 521	Discuss pp. 524, T526–T530, 531 Analyze Visuals pp. 526, 529, 530	Discuss pp. 534, T536–T543, 544	Discuss pp. 546 T548–T553, 554 Analyze Visuals p. T548

505A **Assessment-Based Planning:** Skills in red are assessed on the Unit 5 Test. **T** = Teacher's Edition page

Media Study: News Reports pp. 556–559	The Open Window pp. 560–567	from The House on Mango Street pp. 568–575	Writing Workshop: Problem-Solution Essay pp. 576–583	
TV Newscast/Web News Report	Short Story Level: Challenging	Fiction Level: Average		**Skills Assessed on the Unit 5 Test:** **Literary Analysis** • Recognize and analyze author's perspective • Analyze how tone and diction reveal an author's purpose and perspective
	Tone and Author's Purpose pp. 561, 562, 565, 566 Review: Point of View pp. 564, 566	Author's Perspective pp. 569, 573, 574, 575 Review: Tone pp. 572, 575		**Reading and Informational Texts** • Identify and analyze author's purpose • Predict • Take notes • Analyze patterns of organization
	Predict pp. 561, 564, 566	Make Inferences About Character pp. 569, 570, 572, 575	Analyze a Problem-Solution Essay pp. 577–578, 582	• Use text features to locate and comprehend information **Vocabulary** • Use knowledge of Greek and Latin roots to understand words • Complete analogies
Academic Vocabulary (TV Newscast and Web News Report) p. 557				**Writing, Grammar, and Style** • Write a problem-solution essay • Use descriptive language • Use adverbs to create descriptive details
	Descriptive Details p. 567 Adverbs pp. 565, 567		Write a Problem-Solution Essay pp. 579–582 Transition Words pp. 577, 582 Punctuation in Compound Sentences p. 582	• Use coordinating conjunctions and sentence combining to improve sentence flow • Additional writing and grammar skills
Discuss pp. 556, 559 Interpret and Evaluate Information in TV and Web News Formats pp. 557–558 Create a News Segment p. 559	Discuss pp. 560, T562–T565, 566 Analyze Visuals p. 562	Discuss pp. 568, T570–T574, 575 Analyze Visuals pp. 570, T573	Discuss pp. 576–578, 582 Produce a Video Documentary p. 583	**Speaking, Listening, Viewing, and Media** • Analyze visual information

⊘ For additional lesson planning help, see **Easy Planner DVD.**

505B

OBJECTIVES
- establish prior knowledge about the reasons writers write
- discuss the author's **purpose** in written materials

Why do writers WRITE?

Read and discuss the question and the first paragraph. Point out that a writer's purpose sometimes is fairly obvious, as in these examples:

- an ad for a new car (to persuade)
- a story about a funny event at school (to entertain)
- a bicycle repair manual (to inform)

Note that sometimes a writer will have more than one purpose, but one purpose will be the strongest. Also explain that students sometimes may need to interpret symbolism or other literary devices before determining a writer's purpose.

ACTIVITY If students have kept reading and/or writing journals, encourage them to review recent entries as they answer the questions. Use students' responses to identify several broad **purposes** for writing: to entertain, to inform, to persuade, and to express personal thoughts and feelings.

CHECK UNDERSTANDING Have students name the **purposes** for writing that have been introduced on this page. Ask them to give an additional example of a form of writing meant to fulfill each purpose.

Unit Resources

Why do writers WRITE?

A letter to the editor. A research paper. An e-mail to a friend. Any of these writing products might come from your pen or computer and be shared with others or kept to yourself. The reasons that any individual writes are as varied as the personality and goals of the writer. But the writer always has a **purpose** for crafting words in a particular form and in a particular way.

ACTIVITY List five things you have read and five things you have written in the last month. Answer the following:

- Which did you read to get information? Which did you write to provide information?

- Which tried to persuade you? Which did you write to persuade someone else?

- Which did you write to express how you felt?

Think about your answers. For which purpose did you most often read? For which purpose did you most often write? Are you surprised?

506

 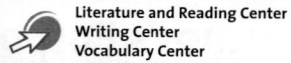
Preview Unit Goals

LITERARY ANALYSIS	• Identify and analyze tone and diction
	• Recognize and analyze an author's perspective
READING	• Use reading strategies, including predicting
	• Make inferences
	• Analyze patterns of organization, including chronological order and comparison and contrast
	• Use text features to locate and comprehend information
	• Identify and analyze an author's purpose
	• Interpret graphic aids
	• Identify an implied main idea
WRITING AND GRAMMAR	• Write a problem-solution essay
	• Use nouns, adverbs, and conjunctions correctly
SPEAKING, LISTENING, AND VIEWING	• Interpret and evaluate how events and information are presented in nonprint sources
	• Create a news segment
	• Produce a video documentary
VOCABULARY	• Use word roots to understand the meaning of words
	• Use Greek suffixes to understand specialized vocabulary
ACADEMIC VOCABULARY	• tone • diction
	• author's perspective • author's purpose
	• text features • patterns of organization

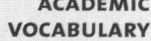

507

Preview Unit Goals

These goals outline the main skills addressed in this unit. Have students familiarize themselves with the list in preparation for the selections. Remind students of the use of color coding to distinguish the skill strands.

Draw students' attention to the Academic Vocabulary terms. Ask volunteers to define any familiar words. Have students record the terms in their journals, along with a preliminary definition for each. Throughout the unit, have students review each term and confirm the definitions by using the terms in writing and speaking.

ADDITIONAL UNIT GOALS

These skills will be taught in this unit but are not the major focus of the unit:

Literary Analysis
• Genre study: descriptive essay, biographical essay, short story, vignette, magazine article

Reading
• Take notes
• Identify characteristics of a magazine article

Writing and Grammar
• Support a point of view persuasively
• Add transition words to improve flow
• Use descriptive language and descriptive details in writing
• Use sentence combining to improve flow
• Punctuate compound sentences correctly

Speaking, Listening, and Viewing
• Analyze media presentations for bias
• Compare how different media cover the same event
• Identify characteristics of news formats

DIFFERENTIATED INSTRUCTION

FOR ENGLISH LEARNERS

Academic Vocabulary Use the copy master to help students learn the Academic Vocabulary listed on this page.

1. Read aloud each term. Have students find it on their copy master.

2. Discuss the meanings or examples shown, and complete the chart as a class.

3. Have students work in small groups to complete the remaining activities.

Additional Academic Vocabulary Use the copy master to help students learn academic words they will use in subsequent lessons and on the Assessment Practice. Follow the same procedure as for the Academic Vocabulary copy master.

 RESOURCE MANAGER—Copy Masters
Academic Vocabulary p. 9
Additional Academic Vocabulary p. 10

Focus and Motivate

OBJECTIVES

- identify and analyze author's purpose
- recognize and analyze author's perspective
- recognize and analyze patterns of organization
- use text features to locate and comprehend information

Teach

Part 1: Author's Purpose and Perspective

Author's Purpose Explain that students can identify an author's purpose by thinking about the author's main reason for writing. Suggest that students ask themselves, "What did the author most likely hope to accomplish?"

To identify and analyze author's purpose, readers may want to consider

- subject
- author's tone
- intended audience
- details and words
- effect on readers

Using this chart as a model, help students analyze various works, such as a newspaper article, an editorial, a short story, and an essay.

Title	Purpose
Subject	
Author's tone	
Intended audience	
Details, words	
Effect	

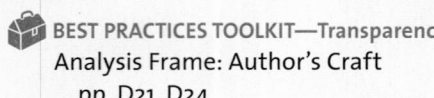 **BEST PRACTICES TOOLKIT—Transparency**
Analysis Frame: Author's Craft
pp. D21, D24

Author's Purpose

Before architects draft their blueprints, they need to understand the purpose of the proposed building. Are they designing a stadium to seat screaming spectators or a library for quiet study? This purpose drives every decision that architects make, from the layout of their buildings to the design. Like architects, writers carefully construct their stories and essays with a specific purpose in mind. Recognizing this purpose is essential to understanding everything you read.

Part 1: Author's Purpose and Perspective

An **author's purpose** is what the writer hopes to achieve by crafting a particular work. Although a writer may have more than one purpose, usually one purpose stands out. A writer's purpose could be any of the following:

- to inform or explain
- to persuade
- to express thoughts or feelings
- to entertain

You can uncover an author's purpose by looking at the choices the writer made. Every choice—from the subject and the tone to the particular words and details—is a clue that can reveal the purpose. Another clue is your reaction to what you read. For instance, if you are convinced by an argument to fight for a cause, then the author's primary purpose is probably to persuade.

AUTHOR'S PURPOSE	CLUES IN THE WRITING
TO INFORM OR EXPLAIN Examples: encyclopedia or magazine articles, documentaries, instruction manuals, Web sites	• facts and statistics • directions • steps in a process • diagrams or illustrated explanations
TO PERSUADE Examples: editorials, TV ads, political speeches	• a statement of opinion • supporting evidence • appeals to emotion • a call to action
TO ENTERTAIN Examples: short stories, novels, plays, humorous essays, movies	• suspenseful or exciting situations • humorous or fascinating details • intriguing characters
TO EXPRESS THOUGHTS OR FEELINGS Examples: personal essays, poems, diaries, journals	• thoughtful descriptions • insightful observations • the writer's personal feelings

---

DIFFERENTIATED INSTRUCTION

For general guidelines on differentiating instruction, see

 BEST PRACTICES TOOLKIT
Differentiated Instruction pp. 31–38

FOR LESS-PROFICIENT READERS

Note Taking For students who need help with note taking, hand out the note-taking copy master for Part 1 before reading the text. Have students read each paragraph silently. Then, as you discuss the main points of the text, have students record them on the copy master.

Visualize Have students use free-form mapping to associate the author's purposes on page 508 with examples and writing clues for these purposes.

 RESOURCE MANAGER—Copy Master
Note Taking p. 15

MODEL 1: TO INFORM OR EXPLAIN

Writing that informs or explains typically leaves you feeling more knowledgeable. As you read this article, look for clues that suggest its purpose.

from WEB MASTERS

Nonfiction article by **Joe Bower**

Spiderwebs are flexible yet strong, ultrasensitive, adaptable to different settings, and able to span great distances (compared with the size of their makers). They perform a variety of impressive functions, the most obvious of which is capturing prey.

5 Not all of the world's estimated 37,000 known spider species make webs. In fact, arachnologists categorize spiders based on this ability. Tarantulas and jumping spiders belong to the large group that doesn't make webs. Instead, these arachnids, which are sometimes referred to as wandering spiders, stalk or ambush their prey.

Close Read

1. Which words and phrases suggest that this is an informative article? One word has been boxed.

2. Identify one other clue that suggests the author's purpose is to inform or explain.

MODEL 2: TO EXPRESS THOUGHTS OR FEELINGS

This essay also focuses on spiders, but the writer does not include a single fact or statistic. How do the details, the language, and the writer's tone help you understand her feelings about spiders?

from Weaving THE WORLD

Personal essay by **Janisse Ray**

Every night the spiders weave the world back together. This morning I see webs whole again, shining freshly gossamer in the new sun, webs we tore down last night accidentally, setting up the tent on the platform. All day paddling, we have been watching for them—zippers and bananas and crabs, colorful and intriguing.

5 They are everywhere, stitching leaves to trees, and trees to shrubs, and shrubs to ground. . . .

The spiders have adapted to their fragility, their vulnerability; when we humans bungle into their webs, they scurry off, up a single thread into a sweet bay. They have no new technologies, no new economies. Across the

10 prairies they spin and spin, as they have done for thousands of years, holding this outrageously glorious world together.

Close Read

1. Examine the boxed details that the writer uses to describe spiders and their webs. How do these details differ from those in "Web Masters"?

2. Is the writer's attitude toward spiders admiring or matter-of-fact? Support your answer.

MODEL 1: TO INFORM OR EXPLAIN

Close Read

1. *Possible answer: Words and phrases that suggest that this is an informative article include "estimated 37,000 known spider species" (line 5), "in fact," "arachnologists" (line 6), and "which are sometimes referred to as wandering spiders" (line 8).*

2. *Possible answer: Other clues that suggest the author's purpose are his inclusion of a statistic, the "nonfiction article" byline, the matter-of-fact tone, and facts presented in a straightforward manner.*

MODEL 2: TO EXPRESS THOUGHTS OR FEELINGS

Close Read

1. *Possible answer: The boxed details are the writer's personal observations rather than verifiable facts and statistics. Words and phrases all have very positive—not neutral—connotations. Readers can tell that the writer is marveling at spiders and their place in the world.*

2. *Possible answer: The writer's tone is admiring, not matter-of-fact, as evidenced by words and phrases such as "spiders weave the world back together" (line 1), "colorful and intriguing" (line 4), and "holding this outrageously glorious world together" (line 11). The writer makes spiders seem both graceful in their movements and an important part of this world.*

FOR LESS–PROFICIENT READERS

Analysis Support: Author's Purpose Have students list as many facts and statistics as they can find in "Web Masters." **Possible answer:** *Spiderwebs are flexible, strong, ultrasensitive, adaptable, and "able to span great distances"; webs capture prey; there are 37,000 spider species; tarantulas and jumping spiders "stalk or ambush their prey" rather than make webs.*

Next, challenge students to identify facts and statistics in "Weaving the World." Elicit that Model 2 has few, if any, facts and no statistics. Ask what this difference suggests about the author's purpose. **Possible answer:** *The purpose is not to inform or explain.*

Teach

RECOGNIZING AUTHOR'S PERSPECTIVE

Different Perspectives To highlight the idea that perspectives may differ sharply even when purposes are the same, write this sentence on the board, or use another one that focuses on an issue over which students are divided:

> It is dangerous to talk on a cell phone while driving.

- Have the class form groups based on whether they agree or disagree with the statement.
- Have groups complete this chart by suggesting perspective-specific examples suitable for a persuasive essay on the subject. Then have them compare their charts.

Perspective Clues	Examples
Focus	
Word choice	
Tone	

 BEST PRACTICES TOOLKIT—Transparency
Two-Column Chart p. A25

Part 2: Organization and Format

Patterns of Organization After students read the chart, discuss with them that these patterns of organization can vary. For example, although chronological order usually proceeds forward in time, an author of a nonfiction article may begin by describing an event and then explaining what led up to it, while an author of fiction may use flashback. Similarly, an author using comparison-contrast may first present similarities and then describe differences. Or, the author may focus on differences first and then discuss similarities. Point out that authors choose the approach that best serves their purpose.

CHECK UNDERSTANDING

Have students describe two reasons for using a particular pattern of organization.

RECOGNIZING AUTHOR'S PERSPECTIVE

Even if they have similar purposes, no two writers will approach a topic in the same way. Their perspectives influence what they write and how they write it. An **author's perspective** is the lens through which a writer looks at a topic. This lens is colored by the writer's experiences, values, and feelings.

Consider the two excerpts on the previous page. Factual articles, such as "Web Masters," usually don't reveal a writer's viewpoint. However, essays, such as "Weaving the World," include clues that convey an author's perspective. Notice how the following clues reveal a writer who appreciates nature.

- **Focus of Essay** Instead of focusing on spiders' creepy qualities, the writer marvels at their ability to create webs from nothing.
- **Word Choice** Words and phrases such as "colorful and intriguing" and "vulnerability" reveal the writer's fascination with the wonders of nature.
- **Tone** A writer's **tone** is his or her attitude toward a subject. The words and details in "Weaving the World" reflect an admiring tone—not a fearful one.

Part 2: Organization and Format

To achieve their purpose, writers choose particular patterns of organization, such as **cause-effect** and **classification**. Recognizing these patterns can help you determine an author's purpose, locate information, and understand relationships between ideas. Here are two common patterns.

CHRONOLOGICAL	COMPARISON-CONTRAST
What It Does • Describes events in time order	**What It Does** • Highlights similarities and differences between two or more subjects
Why Writers Use It • To explain a sequence of events in an easy-to-follow way • To tell a suspenseful or exciting story	**Why Writers Use It** • To show the benefits of one subject over another • To compare an unfamiliar subject with a familiar one
How to Recognize It • Look for signal words such as *before, finally, first, next,* and *then.*	**How to Recognize It** • Look for signal words such as *also, and, but, in contrast, unlike,* and *while.*

In addition to these patterns, writers of nonfiction use **text features** to help you understand a topic. Imagine a scientific article without **subheadings, captions,** and **boldfaced type** to guide you. Who wouldn't be confused?

DIFFERENTIATED INSTRUCTION

FOR LESS–PROFICIENT READERS
Note Taking For those students who need help, hand out the note-taking copy master for Part 2. Read and discuss the text. Assist students in completing their note-taking copy master as needed.

 RESOURCE MANAGER—Copy Master
Note Taking p. 16

FOR ADVANCED LEARNERS/PRE–AP
Identify Pattern Combinations Have students identify works they have read in which the author combines two or more patterns of organization. Challenge students to explain how the pattern combinations help the authors accomplish their purpose.

MODEL: CLASSIFICATION ORGANIZATION

In this scientific article, the writer uses classification organization to group information by common characteristics. As you read, think about how this organization, with the help of the text features, helps you digest the information.

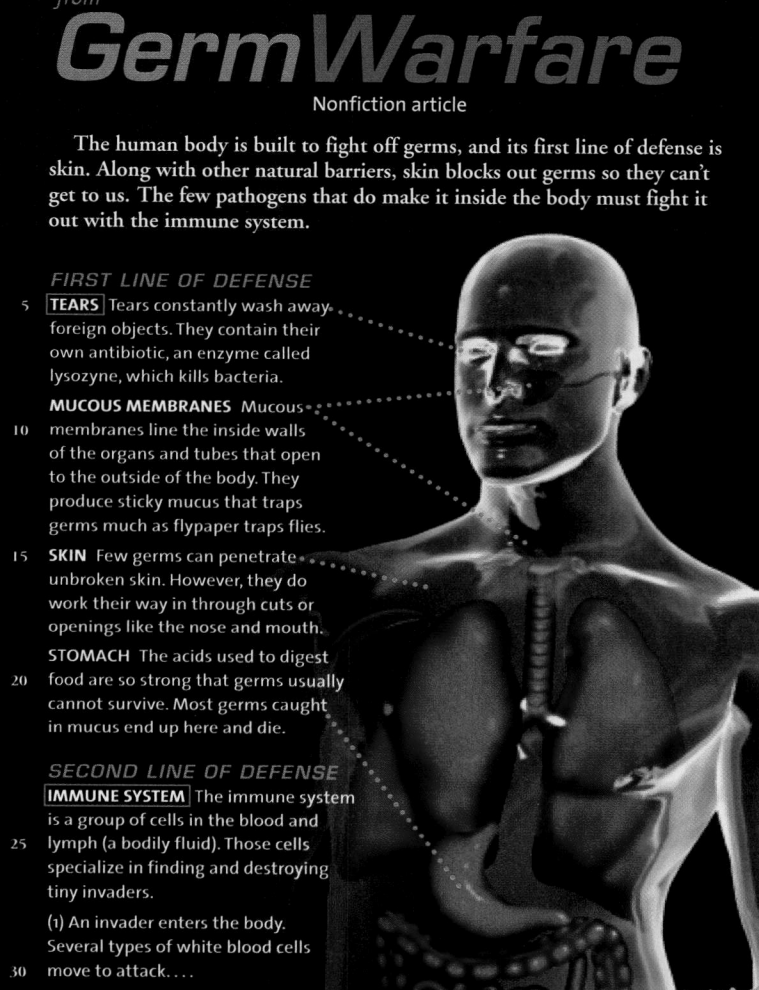

from

GermWarfare

Nonfiction article

The human body is built to fight off germs, and its first line of defense is skin. Along with other natural barriers, skin blocks out germs so they can't get to us. The few pathogens that do make it inside the body must fight it out with the immune system.

FIRST LINE OF DEFENSE

5 **TEARS** Tears constantly wash away foreign objects. They contain their own antibiotic, an enzyme called lysozyne, which kills bacteria.

MUCOUS MEMBRANES Mucous
10 membranes line the inside walls of the organs and tubes that open to the outside of the body. They produce sticky mucus that traps germs much as flypaper traps flies.

15 **SKIN** Few germs can penetrate unbroken skin. However, they do work their way in through cuts or openings like the nose and mouth.

STOMACH The acids used to digest
20 food are so strong that germs usually cannot survive. Most germs caught in mucus end up here and die.

SECOND LINE OF DEFENSE

IMMUNE SYSTEM The immune system is a group of cells in the blood and
25 lymph (a bodily fluid). Those cells specialize in finding and destroying tiny invaders.

(1) An invader enters the body. Several types of white blood cells
30 move to attack. . . .

Close Read

1. Into what two main categories is the information grouped? Explain how you can tell.

2. Notice the boldfaced words used throughout the article. Two have been boxed. What purpose do they serve?

3. What does the information in the annotated diagram add to your understanding of mucous membranes?

MODEL: CLASSIFICATION ORGANIZATION

Close Read

1. *Possible answer: Information is presented in two categories: the body's two lines of defense against intrusive germs. The heads "First Line of Defense" and "Second Line of Defense" are clues to the organization.*

2. *Possible answer: Boldfaced words identify each element of the body's first and second lines of defense. Readers can see at a glance which parts of the body help fight germs.*

3. *Possible answer: The annotated diagram shows readers exactly where mucous membranes are located—information many readers might not know. The annotation (lines 10–15) explains how the mucous membranes function to trap germs.*

DIFFERENTIATED INSTRUCTION

FOR LESS–PROFICIENT READERS

Comprehension: Classification Write these items on the board and have students explain what the items have in common that enables the writer to group them together: *tears, mucous membranes, skin, stomach*

Concept Support On the board, list the italicized terms. Then give the examples in random order for students to classify.

- *cause-effect:* The rainstorm flooded roads.
- *classification:* There are two kinds of medicine for the illness.
- *chronological order:* Jake arrived at the party after Emily.
- *comparison-contrast:* It is generally warmer in Florida than in Vermont.

Practice and Apply

Part 3: Compare Texts
Close Read

1. **Possible answer:** *Alvarez is sharing her personal thoughts and feelings. Through these details, she is probably trying to recreate for readers a common fear: having something go awry on an airplane. The details that Alvarez includes are probably intended to make readers smile or at least see the humor in the situation. Alvarez is describing an experience—facing an emergency on a plane and not having paid attention to the emergency procedures and drills—that many people can relate to.*

2. **Possible answer:** *Alvarez's tone might be described as honest and lightly humorous. Three details that convey the tone include "Oh Lord, I thought, this is it!" (line 3), "something that really worries me: when confident-looking businessmen look worried" (lines 13–14), and "I would have already died of terror" (line 21).*

3. **Possible answer:** *Alvarez's purpose is to express her thoughts and feelings. The details mentioned above are all observations about a personal experience.*

4. **Possible answer:** *Alvarez is writing from the perspective of someone who has been through this suspenseful, fearful situation and can still find something to smile about. She has a good-natured perspective on this experience.*

If students need help . . . Have students reread lines 19–21. Discuss how these lines reveal that the author has flown before ("I never paid attention") and how her lighthearted tone suggests that she can laugh about such experiences.

Part 3: Compare Texts

What happens when lightning strikes an airplane? Both of the following excerpts answer this question, but their similarities end there. As you read, use what you have just learned about clues—details, tone, and choice of words—to determine each author's purpose and perspective.

from Aha Moment
Essay by **Julia Alvarez**

I was in the tiny bathroom in the back of the plane when I felt the slamming jolt, then the horrible swerve that threw me against the door. Oh Lord, I thought, this is it! Somehow I managed to unbolt the door and scramble out. The flight attendants, already strapped in, waved wildly for me

5 to sit down. As I lunged ahead toward my seat, passengers looked up at me with the stricken expression of creatures who know they are about to die.

"I think we got hit by lightning," the girl in the seat next to mine said. She was from a small town in east Texas, and this was only her second time on an airplane. She had won a trip to England by competing in a high school

10 geography bee and was supposed to make a connecting flight when we landed in Newark.

In the next seat, at the window, sat a young businessman who had been confidently working. Now he looked worried—something that really worries me: when confident-looking businessmen look worried. The laptop was put

15 away. "Something's not right," he said.

The pilot's voice came over the speaker. I heard vaguely through my fear, "Engine number two . . . hit . . . emergency landing . . . New Orleans." When he was done, the voice of a flight attendant came on, reminding us of the emergency procedures she had reviewed before takeoff. Of course I never paid

20 attention to this drill, always figuring that if we ever got to the point where we needed to use life jackets, I would have already died of terror.

Now we began a roller-coaster ride through the thunderclouds. I was ready to faint, but when I saw the face of the girl next to me I pulled myself together. I reached for her hand and reassured her that we were going to make it. "What a

25 story you're going to tell when you get home!" I said. "After this, London's going to seem like small potatoes."

Close Read

1. Reread the boxed details. Is Alvarez reporting "just the facts" or is she sharing personal impressions? Explain the intended effect of these details.

2. Although Alvarez describes a frightening experience, her tone is not fearful. Identify the tone and three details that convey it.

3. Do you think Alvarez's primary purpose is to persuade, to entertain, to inform, or to express thoughts and feelings? Support your answer.

4. Consider the descriptions in lines 1–3 and 19–21, as well as Alvarez's tone. What can you infer about her perspective?

DIFFERENTIATED INSTRUCTION

FOR LESS–PROFICIENT READERS
Vocabulary Support Introduce these words from "Aha Moment." Have students read the context for each word and suggest a synonym to replace it:

- *jolt* (line 2), "bump"
- *swerve* (line 2), "sharp turn"
- *lunged* (line 5), "dove"
- *stricken* (line 6), "worried" or "scared"

FOR ENGLISH LEARNERS
Vocabulary: Idioms Help students use context clues to determine the meanings of these idioms in the essay: *pulled myself together* (line 23), "calmed myself down"; *make it* (line 24), "survive"; *like small potatoes* (line 26), "not very difficult."

Now read this article, and compare it to Alvarez's dramatic account.
Use the clues in the text to identify the author's purpose and perspective.

Aircraft Built to Shrug Off Lightning Strike

Newspaper article by **Tom McNamee**

The most common areas for lightning to strike a plane include the wing tips and the fuselage nose.

Lightning strikes airplanes now and again, but seldom with tragic results.

In a typical year, lightning
5   causes only a handful of aircraft accidents in the United States, and occasionally none at all. From 1983 through 1995, 29 accidents resulted in 37 deaths. But a 30th
10 accident proved the exception. On Aug. 2, 1985, lightning struck a Lockheed L-1011 as it came in for a landing at Dallas-Fort Worth International Airport, slamming
15 the jet to the ground and killing 137 passengers.

One witness on the ground, an aviation weather expert, recalled seeing "lightning from cloud to
20 cloud." Another witness said the plane exploded even before crashing into "just a big ball of fire."

A Plane's Built-in Protection

As a rule, however, the laws of nature favor aircraft in a collision
25 with lightning. Lightning's electrical charge usually spreads across the entire outer skin of the craft, robbing it of its concentrated power, before it is shed like rainwater.
30 The metallic skin of some aircraft is ideal for conducting and diluting an electrical charge. And planes with skins made of lighter-weight composite materials, such as

35 graphite, are commonly fitted with an underlying metal mesh to collect and route the charge. . . .

Aircraft Size and Condition

As a rule, larger planes are least threatened by lightning, said Donald
40 Kemp, retired chief of accident investigations for the Federal Aviation Administration. Larger aircraft have more surface area to absorb lightning's electrical charge,
45 and they are fitted with pencil-like "shedders" on the back of the wings to collect and "bleed off" electricity.

"If a plane is in proper condition, you shouldn't have a problem,"
50 Kemp said.

Close Read

1. How do the boxed details in this article differ from those in "Aha Moment"?

2. Identify two text features that the writer uses. What information do these features convey?

3. What is the author's purpose? Describe two clues that helped you determine that purpose.

4. Consider the writer's tone and the details in this article. Do they tell you anything about the writer's perspective? Explain your answer.

Close Read

1. *Possible answer:* The boxed details are facts and statistics rather than personal observations.

2. *Possible answer:* The title of the article conveys the main idea—generally what the article is about. The subheads tell the main idea of each section. Students might also identify the caption and the photo as text features.

3. *Possible answer:* The author's purpose is to inform and explain. Two clues are the statistics about aircraft accidents; the "newspaper article" byline; straightforward, objective language; and quotes from experts and witnesses.

4. *Possible answer:* Readers do not get a sense of the writer behind the words. The tone is objective, the details factual; the writer is simply reporting the facts in a neutral way without revealing anything about himself.

Assess and Reteach

Assess

Ask students to identify the purpose and perspective of previously read works of nonfiction and fiction. Have them identify organization patterns and text features in these works.

Reteach

For students who are unable to apply the workshop skills to previously read works, select from these reteaching options.

1. Review with students the note-taking copy masters for this lesson. Have students restate the information in the copy masters in their own words and provide examples.

2. Refer students to one or more recently read selections. Help students identify the author's purpose and perspective by asking questions such as these:

   • Why did the author write this selection?

   • For what audience is the selection written?

   • What is the subject of the selection?

   • What is the author's tone?

Next, ask questions to guide students' identification of organization patterns and text features.

FOR LESS–PROFICIENT READERS

Analysis Support: Author's Purpose and Perspective Have students create a chart to compare and contrast the models on pages 512 and 513 in terms of facts, details, focus, tone, and language. Then, using the information in the chart, help students draw conclusions about differences in the authors' purposes and perspectives.

FOR ENGLISH LEARNERS

Comprehension: Generalization Write these words and phrases on the board: *seldom* (line 2), *typical* (line 4), *As a rule* (lines 23 and 38), *usually* (line 26), and *most common* (photo caption). Have students find these words and phrases in the text and then use Think-Pair-Share to clarify what generalization the writer is making in each context.

 BEST PRACTICES TOOLKIT—Transparency
Think-Pair-Share p. A18

Focus and Motivate

OBJECTIVES

Literary Analysis
- explore the key idea of **home**
- analyze diction
- read a descriptive essay

Reading
- analyze patterns of organization (comparison and contrast, chronological)

Grammar and Writing
- use coordinating conjunctions to improve sentence flow
- use writing to analyze literature

SUMMARY

In her descriptive essay "Island Morning," Jamaica Kincaid recalls how she spent mornings in Antigua, her childhood island home. She goes on to describe her mornings on the island where she lives now, as an adult: Manhattan. Kincaid's detailed observations paint a vivid picture of the islands' different lifestyles.

What place do you call HOME?

Pose the question. As students read the **KEY IDEA,** elicit details that students associate with **home.** Extend the discussion by asking what elements—for example, family members and possessions—combine to create the feeling that a place is "home." Conclude by having students complete the **QUICKWRITE** and share their responses.

Island Morning
Descriptive Essay by Jamaica Kincaid

What place do you call HOME?

KEY IDEA The word *home* can mean many different things. When you think about your home, you might envision the building you live in or your own familiar neighborhood. You may picture the streets of your hometown or the landscape of your home country. *Home* can include the people you care about and your memories of growing up. It can even be a place where you no longer live that still feels more like home than where you live today.

QUICKWRITE What does the word *home* bring to mind? In a short paragraph, describe the first image—be it person, place, or thing—you picture when you think of *home*. If you'd like, attach a sketch to accompany your description.

514

Selection Resources

RESOURCE MANAGER UNIT 5

Plan and Teach pp. 17–24

Literary Analysis
Summary pp. 25, 26†*
Diction pp. 27, 28†*
Question Support p. 32*

Reading
Analyze Patterns of Organization
pp. 29, 30†*
Reading Check p. 31
Reading Fluency p. 34

Grammar and Writing
Improve Sentence Flow p. 33

Assessment
Selection Tests A, B/C pp. 35*, 37*
Test Generator CD

BEST PRACTICES TOOLKIT

Differentiated Instruction
pp. 31–38*

Scaffolding Instruction
pp. 43–46*

Graphic Organizers/Strategies
Word Squares • Three-Column Journal • Comparison Matrix • Classification Chart

Reading Support
Audio Anthology CD*

Technology
Literature and Vocabulary Centers at **ClassZone.com**
Write*Smart* CD

* Resources for Differentiation   † Also in Spanish

LITERARY ANALYSIS: DICTION

Diction includes both a writer's choice of words as well as syntax, or the way those words are arranged into sentences. Jamaica Kincaid arranges words in unique ways, often using repetition to create rhythmic sounds. Describing her neighbors' morning routine, she writes,

All of these different people doing all these different things did this one thing: they were all up and about by half past five in the morning.

As you read, look for other passages in which Kincaid creates unusual sentences or chooses words to establish rhythm as well as imagery.

Review: **Tone**

READING SKILL: ANALYZE PATTERNS OF ORGANIZATION

To show relationships between ideas, writers arrange their information in an order that emphasizes those relationships. In this essay, Kincaid uses both **comparison and contrast** and **chronological order.**

- When organizing according to comparison and contrast, Kincaid presents all of the details about one subject or place and then all of the details about another.
- When Kincaid uses chronological order, she presents events in the order in which they typically occur.

As you read, record **signal words** that help you identify both patterns of organization that Kincaid uses in this essay.

Signal Words	Pattern of Organization
"by *six o'clock*" (line 29)	chronological order
"I *now* live in . . ." (line 93)	comparison and contrast

Author Online

Leaving the Island
Jamaica Kincaid is the name Elaine Potter Richardson chose for herself when she began writing. Born on Antigua, a small Caribbean island that was then a British colony, Kincaid was educated in British schools. Although she was often at the top of her class, her mother removed her from school at age 17 against her wishes and sent her to America to support the family.

**Jamaica Kincaid
born 1949**

Musical Musings
When she arrived in America, Kincaid explains, "I didn't know there was such a world as the literary world. I didn't know anything, except maybe how to put one foot in front of the other." She broke ties with her family and took a number of different jobs—and was fired from each one. In 1976, Kincaid landed a job at the *New Yorker,* a literary magazine, where her unique and resilient writing voice emerged. Much of Kincaid's writing expresses her anger at colonialism and the British disregard for her identity as an African-Caribbean woman. Her prose is celebrated for its lyrical beauty. "My work," she says, "is a chord that develops in many different ways."

 MORE ABOUT THE AUTHOR
For more on Jamaica Kincaid, visit the **Literature Center** at **ClassZone.com.**

Background
History of Antigua Kincaid's birthplace, a small island in the eastern Caribbean, was a British colony for over 300 years. In 1981, Antigua united with a small neighboring island to become Antigua and Barbuda, an independent state. Most Antiguans have African heritage, as they are descendants of slaves brought to the island centuries ago to work in the tobacco and sugarcane fields.

ISLAND MORNING **515**

Teach

STANDARDS FOCUS

LITERARY ANALYSIS

● DICTION
For instructional support, read aloud this example:

> Home should be a place of safety, a shelter from life's storms. Home should be a refuge, a sanctuary, a fortress.

Ask students how the writer's diction sets a tone. ***Possible answer:*** *The writer chooses words carefully and uses rhythm and repetition to establish a comforting tone.*

CHECK UNDERSTANDING Have pairs of students use this example or the example on page 515 as the model for an original sentence. Discuss the results.

READING SKILL

■ ANALYZE PATTERNS OF ORGANIZATION
Review the explanation, making sure that students understand the difference in purpose between the two patterns. After discussing the examples of signal words, elicit other words and phrases that signal patterns of organization, such as these:

Comparison and contrast: *similarly, like, both, however, on the other hand*

Chronological order: *first, next, later, then, in the morning, after supper*

CHECK UNDERSTANDING Discuss the type and effectiveness of the pattern of organization in **About the Author.**

R RESOURCE MANAGER—Copy Master
Analyze Patterns of Organization
p. 29 (for student use while reading the selection)

DIFFERENTIATED INSTRUCTION

FOR LESS-PROFICIENT READERS
Reinforce the Concept Explain that comparison emphasizes *similarities* between people, places, or things, whereas contrast emphasizes *differences.* Point out that comparisons and contrasts sometimes are directly stated but at other times must be inferred from details.

FOR ADVANCED LEARNERS/PRE–AP
Extend the Concept Point out that both patterns of organization can have variations. For example, a writer who uses comparison and contrast may make point-by-point comparisons instead of exhausting one topic before describing the other. A writer using chronological order may include flashbacks. Have students name topics whose development might use these variations.

Practice and Apply

ANALYZE VISUALS

Possible answer: The bright colors, busy people, and whimsical animals create a happy mood— a feeling that the people enjoy their active lives. The cheerful mood is underscored by the lush trees and plants, which provide the fruits and vegetables that the people are gathering (and perhaps taking to market, as described in Kincaid's opening paragraph).

About the Art Rodrigue Mervilus was born in St. Marc, Haiti, in 1947. *Harvest Scene with Twelve People* is typical of the painter's depictions: busy, brightly colored scenes featuring rounded figures. The painting captures the flavor of many other West Indian islands, such as Antigua, Kincaid's home.

LITERARY ANALYSIS

A DICTION

Possible answer: By listing each fruit and vegetable separately, Kincaid emphasizes the abundance and diversity of items grown on the island. Listing the items in this way, repeating the word and *instead of using commas to separate the items, strengthens the stylistic rhythm of her language.*

Island MORNING
Jamaica Kincaid

> I grew up on an island in the West Indies which has an area of a hundred and eight square miles. On the island were many sugarcane fields and a sugar-making factory and a factory where both white and dark rum were made. There were cotton fields, but there were not as many cotton fields as there were sugarcane fields. There were arrowroot[1] fields and tobacco fields, too, but there were not as many arrowroot fields and tobacco fields as there were cotton fields. Some of the fifty-four thousand people who lived on the island grew bananas and mangoes and eddoes and dasheen and christophine[2] and sweet potatoes and white potatoes and plums and guavas and papaws and
> 10 limes and lemons and oranges and grapefruits, and every Saturday they would bring them to the market, which was on Market Street, and they would sell the things they had grown. This was the only way many of them could make **A** a living, and, though it sounds like farming, they weren't farmers in the way a Midwestern wheatgrower is a farmer, and they don't think of the plots of land on which they grew these things as The Farm. Instead, the plots of land were called The Ground. They might say, "Today, me a go up ground." The Ground was often many miles away from where they lived, and they got there not by taking a truck or some other kind of automotive transportation but by riding a donkey or by walking. A small number—a very small number—of the fifty-
> 20 four thousand people worked in banks or in offices. The rest of them—the ones who didn't grow things that were sold in the market on Saturday or work in the factories or in the fields, the banks or the offices—were carpenters or

---

1. **arrowroot:** a West Indian plant from which a starch is derived, for use in cooking and medicine.
2. **eddoes and dasheen and christophine:** eddoes and dasheen are plants with edible corms, or small bulblike growths. Christophine is a fruit-growing plant.

ANALYZE VISUALS
Examine the painting on page 517. What **mood** do the bright colors, busy people, and whimsical animals create? Explain your answer.

1 Targeted Passage

A DICTION
Reread lines 7–12 aloud. What is the effect of listing each fruit and vegetable separately instead of simply referring to the crops as a group?

Detail of *Harvest Scene with Twelve People*,
R. Mervilus. Oil on canvas.
Private collection. © SuperStock.

DIFFERENTIATED INSTRUCTION

FOR ALL STUDENTS

Interest Stations Post these assignments for students to work on independently:

- Debate: Where would you prefer to grow up, a Caribbean island or a city?
- Represent Kincaid's island home in various media.
- Write to Jamaica Kincaid.

To help students, see

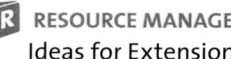 **RESOURCE MANAGER**
Ideas for Extension pp. 22–23

FOR LESS–PROFICIENT READERS

In combination with the *Audio Anthology CD,* use one or more Targeted Passages (pp. 516, 520, 521) to ensure that students focus on key events, concepts, and skills. Targeted Passages are also good for English learners.

1 Targeted Passage [Lines 1–12]

This passage introduces Kincaid's childhood home.

- Where did Jamaica Kincaid grow up?

BACKGROUND

Antigua Jamaica Kincaid's birthplace, in the eastern West Indies, was named by Christopher Columbus in honor of a church in Seville, Spain. The British colonized the island in 1632. Antigua and two smaller neighboring islands, Barbuda and Redonda, became the independent nation of Antigua and Barbuda in 1981.

Lines 7–12
DISCUSSION PROMPTS

Use these prompts to focus on Kincaid's list of home-grown produce:

Connect Test your memory: Which flowers, plants, or trees that grow in your neighborhood can you name right now? *Answers will vary.*

Apply Why is Kincaid's list more than just a test of her memory? *Possible answer: The list has a point—namely, that the islanders sold this abundance in the market.*

Evaluate How important are these lines to your understanding of Kincaid's childhood home? Explain. *Possible answer: The sentence presents the island as a place of abundance and Kincaid's childhood there as positive in at least one respect.*

Lines 1–31
REINFORCE *KEY IDEA:* HOME

Discuss Does Kincaid's description suggest that she has fond memories of **home?** Why or why not? *Possible answer: Students should offer support for either view.*

- How large and how heavily populated was that place?
- What major businesses were there?
- What kinds of crops did many islanders grow? How did they make use of the things that they grew?

FOR ENGLISH LEARNERS

Key Academic Vocabulary Use Word Squares to teach these words: *transportation* (line 18), *automatic* (line 28), *devotion* (line 72), *definition* (line 94), *vehicles* (line 102), *identically* (line 106).

 BEST PRACTICES TOOLKIT—Transparency
   Word Squares p. E10

Prereading For prereading instruction for English learners, see

 BEST PRACTICES TOOLKIT
   Scaffolding Reading Instruction pp. 43–46

FOR ADVANCED LEARNERS/PRE–AP

Pre-AP Exercises in the bottom channel provide additional challenge for students. Use these suggestions for small groups or individuals.

ADDITIONAL GUIDELINES

For more help with differentiation and tips for classroom management, see

 BEST PRACTICES TOOLKIT
   Differentiated Instruction pp. 31–38

B DICTION

Possible answer: *By repeating the phrase, the author emphasizes the routine, active lives of the people. The repetition also maintains the kind of rhythm that is characteristic of Kincaid's style.*

If students need help . . . Stress the purpose of the repetition by putting the details in these lines into chart form, as shown:

Got up . . .	On . . .	To go to . . .
early	weekdays	work or school
early	Saturdays	market
early	Sundays	church

 BEST PRACTICES TOOLKIT—Transparency
Three-Column Journal p. B10

Extend the Discussion How does Kincaid keep the idea of getting up early every day from sounding unpleasant?

C GRAMMAR AND STYLE

Coordinating Conjunctions Writers use coordinating conjunctions to connect elements of equal or nearly equal status and to combine ideas. For example, in lines 33–35, Kincaid uses *but* to combine the idea of the sun's rising with the idea that the air remains cool. Combining these ideas into one sentence creates a more flowing style than a series of short, simple sentences would do. Ask students to locate the appearances of *and* and *but* in these lines. Urge them to watch for other places in the text in which Kincaid uses coordinating conjunctions to combine ideas and make sentences flow.

---

masons or servants in the new hotels for tourists which were appearing suddenly all over the island, or servants in private homes, or seamstresses, or tailors, or shopkeepers, or fishermen, or dockworkers, or schoolchildren. All of these different people doing all these different things did this one thing: they were all up and about by half past five in the morning, and they did this without the help of an alarm clock or an automatic clock radio. Every morning—workday, Saturday, or Sunday—the whole island was alive by six o'clock. People got up
30 early on weekdays to go to work or to school; they got up early on Saturday to go to market; and they got up early on Sunday to go to church. **B**

It is true that the early morning is the most beautiful time of day on the island. The sun has just come up and is immediately big and bright, the way the sun always is on the island, but the air is still cool from the night; the sky is deep, cool blue (like the sea, it gets lighter as the day wears on, and then it gets darker, until by midnight it looks black); the red in the hibiscus and the flamboyant[3] flowers seems redder; the green of the trees and grass seems greener. If it is December, there is dew everywhere: dew on the painted red galvanized rooftops;[4] dew on my mother's upside-down washtubs; dew on the stones that
40 make up her stone heap (a round mound of big and little stones in the middle of our yard; my mother spreads out soapy white laundry on these stones, so that the hot sun will bleach them even whiter); dew on the vegetables in my mother's treasured (to her, horrible to me) vegetable garden. But it wasn't to admire any of these things that people got up so early. I had never, in all the time I lived there, heard anyone say, "What a beautiful morning." Once, just the way I had read it in a book, I stretched and said to my mother, "Oh, isn't it a really lovely morning?" She didn't reply to that at all, but she pulled my eyelids this way and that and then said that my sluggish liver was getting even more sluggish. I don't know why people got up so early, but I do know that they took great pride in
50 this. It wasn't unusual at all to hear one woman say to another, "Me up since way 'fore day mornin'," and for the other woman to say back to her, with a laugh, "Yes, my dear, you know de early bird ketch de early worm." **C**

In our house, we got up every day at half past five. This is what got us up: every morning, Mr. Jarvis—a dockworker who lived with his wife (she sold sweets she made herself to schoolchildren at the bus depot just before they boarded buses that would take them back to their homes in the country) and their eight children in a house at the very end of our street—would take his herd of goats to pasture. At exactly half past five, he and his goats reached our house. We heard the cries of the goats and the sound the stake at the end of the chain tied around their
60 necks made as it dragged along the street. Above the sound of what my mother called "the early morning racket," we could hear Mr. Jarvis whistling. Mostly, he whistled the refrain of an old but popular calypso[5] tune. The words in the refrain were "Come le' we go, Soukie, Come le' we go." If we heard only the crying of

---

3. **flamboyant:** another name for the royal poinciana (poin′sē-ăn′ə) tree, known for its huge red flowers.

4. **galvanized rooftops:** metal roofs coated with a layer of zinc to prevent rust.

5. **calypso** (kə-lĭp′sō): a type of West Indian music based on African rhythms, often with lyrics about local events or personalities.

B DICTION
Reread lines 28–31. What effect is created by the **repetition** of the phrase "got up early"?

C GRAMMAR AND STYLE
Reread lines 32–50. Kincaid creates long, fluid sentences by using the **coordinating conjunctions** *and* and *but*.

DIFFERENTIATED INSTRUCTION

FOR ENGLISH LEARNERS

Language: Conversational English Patterns Ask students to say these sentences from the essay in Standard English:

- *Today, me a go up ground* (line 16)
- *Me up since way 'fore day mornin'* (lines 50–51)
- *Yes, my dear, you know de early bird ketch de early worm* (line 52)
- *Come le' we go* (line 63)

Language: Punctuation and Print Clues Point out the appearance of a colon in lines 26, 38, and 121. Explain that writers often use this mark of punctuation to introduce something: a list, for example, or a definition, explanation, or conclusion. Discuss Kincaid's reason for using a colon in each of the sentences just noted.

Farm in Haiti, Roosevelt. Oil on canvas. Private collection. © SuperStock.

the goats and the sound of their chain, we knew it was Mr. Jarvis's son Nigel, a rude wharf-rat boy, who was taking the goats to pasture. **D**

We weren't the only ones who got up to the sound of Mr. Jarvis and his goats. Mr. Gordon, a man who grew lettuce and sold most of it to the new hotels and who lived right next to us, would get up soon after Mr. Jarvis passed. He would throw open all the windows and all the doors in his house, and he would turn on 70 his radio and tune it to a station in St. Croix,[6] a station which at that hour played American country-and-Western music. It may have been from this that my mother developed her devotion to the music of Hank Williams.[7] Mr. Gordon was very nice to my family, but that didn't prevent me from deciding that he resembled a monkey, and so I nicknamed him Monkey Lettuce. I called him this only behind his and my parents' back, of course. We never tuned our radio to the station in St. Croix. Instead, at exactly seven o'clock, my parents turned on our radio and tuned it to the station on our island. A man's voice would say, "It is seven o'clock." Then another voice, a completely different voice, would say, "This is BBC London."[8] Then we would listen to the news being broadcast. At 80 around that time, we sat down to eat breakfast. **E**

---

6. **St. Croix** (kroi): an island in the Caribbean Sea, one of the U.S. Virgin Islands.
7. **Hank Williams:** American songwriter, known for many country-and-Western hits, who died at the age of 29.
8. **BBC London:** the British Broadcasting Corporation, based in London, broadcasts in many areas that are part of the Commonwealth of Nations.

D DICTION
Reread lines 61–65. Compare the dialect in the song Kincaid quotes with Kincaid's own words, such as "a rude wharf-rat boy." Describe how they differ.

E PATTERNS OF ORGANIZATION
Identify the pattern of organization used in lines 75–80, and cite the specific words that signal this pattern. How does the organization help you to follow the events Kincaid describes?

ANALYZE VISUALS

Activity Ask students how the mood of the painting matches the mood of Kincaid's description. *Possible answer: Both works suggest a mood of serenity.*

About the Art *Farm in Haiti,* painted by Haitian artist Roosevelt, is an example of the spontaneous folk art for which many Caribbean artists are famous.

LITERARY ANALYSIS

D DICTION

Possible answer: The dialect in the song (line 63) uses repetition and contractions to create a rhythmic, conversational sound. The lyrics, however, are not descriptive. Kincaid's own words, such as "rude wharf-rat boy" (line 65), are less rhythmic and conversational than the song's lyrics, but they present a vivid descriptive image.

READING SKILL

E PATTERNS OF ORGANIZATION

Possible answers: The terms at exactly seven o'clock, then *(two appearances), and* at around that time *signal chronological order. This pattern of organization helps readers understand the time sequence of the events that Kincaid is describing.*

If students need help . . . Read through the passage with students, one sentence at a time. Model how to identify the first signal words (*at exactly seven o'clock*). Elicit the other signal words, prompting if necessary.

FOR ENGLISH LEARNERS
Vocabulary: Phrasal Verbs Have students use a dictionary to find and report on the meanings of these phrasal verbs from pages 518 and 519: *got up* (line 29), *come up* (line 33), *wears on* (line 35), *make up* (line 40), *throw open* (line 69), *turn on* (line 69).

Language: Pronoun Referents Explain the referents for *this* (line 71), *that* (line 73), *this* (line 74), and *this* (line 79).

FOR ADVANCED LEARNERS/PRE–AP
Analyze Details Have students reread and reflect upon the paragraph that begins with line 66. Ask them to write a statement explaining how the details in the paragraph add to the reader's understanding of the author. Invite students to compare their statements in small groups.

2 Targeted Passage

I now live in Manhattan. The only thing it has in common with the island where I grew up is a geographical definition. Certainly no one I know gets up at half past five, at six o'clock, at seven o'clock, at half past seven, at eight o'clock. I know one person who sleeps all day and stays up all night. I know another person who has to take a nap if he gets up before noon. And how easy it is, I have noticed, to put a great distance between you and a close friend if you should call that friend before ten in the morning. **F**

100 I wake up, still, without an alarm, at half past five. In the neighborhood in which I live, it is very quiet at that hour. It is not romantic at all to hear nothing in the city. At around six o'clock, I begin to hear the sound of moving vehicles. Trucks. I know they are trucks because the sound I hear is a rumbling sound that only trucks make. The sound sometimes comes from streets far away. If I get up and look out, I might not see anyone. If I see anyone, it is always two or three men together, dressed identically, in tight black leather pants, a black leather jacket, a black leather cap, and black leather boots. They will walk very quickly down my street as if they are in a great hurry. When I look out, I never notice the early light playing on the street or on the brownstone houses across
110 the street from me. In Manhattan, I notice only whether it is sunny or bright or cloudy and gray or raining or snowing. I never notice things like gradations of light,[10] but my friends tell me that they are there.

Between six and seven, I sit and read women's magazines. I read articles about Elizabeth Taylor's new, simple life, articles about Mary Tyler Moore, articles about Jane Pauley, articles about members of the Carter family, articles about Candice Bergen, articles about Doris Day, articles about Phyllis Diller, and excerpts from Lana Turner's autobiography.[11] I know many things about these people—things that they may have forgotten themselves and things that, should we ever meet, they might wish I would forget also. At seven o'clock, I **G**

---

9. **Ovaltine:** a nutritious chocolate drink.
10. **gradations of light:** shades of light; light that changes by very small degrees from lighter to darker.
11. **Elizabeth Taylor's ... Turner's autobiography:** The people named are actors, journalists, musicians, and other celebrities of the time, whose exploits would have made it into the pages of popular magazines.

F PATTERNS OF ORGANIZATION
Reread lines 93–99. Which pattern of organization does the author use to highlight the differences between Antigua and Manhattan? Identify the word or phrase that signals a shift in subject.

G TONE
How would you describe Kincaid's tone, or attitude, in lines 113–119? Explain your answer.

READING SKILL

F PATTERNS OF ORGANIZATION

Possible answer: The author uses comparison and contrast. The word that signals the shift is now *(line 93), but* in common *(line 93) also signals the pattern.*

LITERARY ANALYSIS: *Review*

G TONE

Possible answer: Kincaid's tone is disdainful. It reflects her realization that her daily reading habit is not a very worthwhile or productive use of time.

If students need help . . . Ask:

- Do the people that Kincaid is reading about have a direct bearing on her life? *Possible answer: The people may be famous, but they probably have no direct bearing on Kincaid's life.*
- Is what Kincaid is learning about these people important? How can you tell? *Possible answer: It is trivial. She says that these people probably wish that she would forget what she is learning about them (lines 117–119).*

Extend the Discussion Review lines 53–92. What might Kincaid be doing in Antigua during this same time of day?

DIFFERENTIATED INSTRUCTION

FOR LESS–PROFICIENT READERS
2 Targeted Passage [Lines 81–92]

This passage describes how Kincaid spends early mornings in her island home. It sets up a contrast with the description in the Targeted Passage on page 521.

- What kinds of activities fill Kincaid's early morning?
- Where does she go after completing her chores and eating breakfast?

- Why might you describe this as a pleasant scene?

FOR ENGLISH LEARNERS

Culture: Clarify Explain that the song that Kincaid mentions in lines 91–92 is a traditional British hymn. Its inclusion is a reminder that Britain ruled Antigua as a colony from 1632 to 1956.

Brownstones, Patti Mollica. © Patti Mollica/SuperStock.

120 watch the morning news for one whole hour. I watch the morning news for two reasons: it makes me feel as if I am living in Chicago, and on the morning news I see and hear the best reports on anything having to do with pigs. I don't know why the morning news makes me feel as if I am living in Chicago and not, say, Cleveland, but there it is. I love Chicago and would like to live there, but only for an hour. Some days, after watching the morning news, my head is filled with useless (to me) but interesting information about pigs. Some of the information, though, is good only for a day. Then, for half an hour, I watch Captain Kangaroo. I love Captain Kangaroo and have forgiven him for saying to Chastity Bono, when they were both guests on her parents' television show,[12] "Now, let me lay this on you, Chastity."[13] Surely a grown man, even if

130 he is a children's hero (perhaps because he is a children's hero), shouldn't talk like that.

Then it is half past eight and no longer early morning in Manhattan, either.

October 17, 1977

ANALYZE VISUALS
Compare this painting with the one on page 519. How well does each capture the **setting** Kincaid describes? Consider the colors and lines in both paintings, as well as each artist's depiction of light.

❸ Targeted Passage

---

12. **Captain Kangaroo . . . television show:** Captain Kangaroo, a.k.a. Bob Keeshan, was the host of a long-running television program for children. Chastity Bono is the daughter of Sonny Bono and Cher, pop singers who hosted a variety TV show in the 1970s.

13. **"Now, let me . . . Chastity":** Captain Kangaroo was using a slang expression of the time. Used mostly by young people, it meant, "Now, let me tell you something."

ANALYZE VISUALS

Possible answer: The painting on page 521 captures some of the feeling of the setting but only a few of Kincaid's details. For example, Kincaid talks about the early-morning quiet, broken by the sound of trucks, and about the few pedestrians she might see. The buildings in the painting (brownstones, as in Kincaid's description) seem to be bathed in early-morning light, but no streets, vehicles, or pedestrians are shown. Similarly, through its use of light and color, the painting on page 519 captures the farming life and the feeling of the island setting that Kincaid describes.

About the Art New York artist Patti Mollica is known for her urban landscapes. *Brownstones*, which dramatically highlights the buildings' shapes, angles, patterns, and colors, is typical of her work. Perhaps the buildings in this painting are similar to those that Kincaid mentions in lines 109–110.

SELECTION WRAP-UP

SUMMARIZE Ask students to reiterate Kincaid's concept of "home" and how she conveys it through her comparison of New York and Antigua.

⭐ **CRITIQUE** Have students decide whether Kincaid's descriptions provide a balanced account of both places.

READING FLUENCY

Distribute the copy master and have students work in pairs or groups to practice fluency.

🅡 **RESOURCE MANAGER—Copy Master**
Reading Fluency p. 34

FOR LESS-PROFICIENT READERS
❸ Targeted Passage [Lines 120–128]

This passage describes how Kincaid spends part of her early mornings in Manhattan. It contrasts with the description in the Targeted Passage on page 520.

• Why does Kincaid watch the morning news?

• How does she describe the information she watches about pigs? Why do you think she says this?

FOR ENGLISH LEARNERS

Language: Punctuation Point out Kincaid's use of parentheses in lines 54–56, 83–87, 126, and 131. Explain that these parentheses add interesting but not essential explanations and observations to her descriptions. Then work with students to write two or three original sentences that include information in parentheses.

Practice and Apply

After Reading

For additional support of post-reading questions, use these copy masters:

R RESOURCE MANAGER—Copy Masters

Reading Check p. 31 (to check understanding of the selection)

Diction p. 27 (for practice of literary analysis standards focus)

Question Support p. 32 (After Reading questions adapted for English learners and less-proficient readers)

For additional questions, see page 21.

ANSWERS

Comprehension

1. *Kincaid compares and contrasts her childhood home, the island of Antigua, with her current home, Manhattan.*

2. *Most people were up by 5:30 A.M. and busy by 6:00 A.M. (lines 26–29).*

3. *Life in Manhattan is nothing like life on Antigua. The times of getting up are different, as are the early-morning sights and sounds and people's priorities.*

Literary Analysis

Possible answers:

4. ■ **STANDARDS FOCUS** *Analyze Patterns of Organization Answers will vary but will probably focus on the early-morning activities in the two places. Opinions should be supported with specific evidence.*

5. *Kincaid grew up in an agricultural environment on a Caribbean island (lines 1–12). Manhattan life, with its big buildings and rumbling trucks (lines 100–112), must seem somewhat confining and grim. If she had grown up in a big city, she would be more accustomed to her surroundings.*

6. *Unlike her friends, Kincaid grew up in a place where the weather usually was bright and sunny (lines 33–34). Manhattan weather conditions are far more variable, so Kincaid focuses simply on whether the day is bright or gray (lines 110–111). The fact that she doesn't notice things like gradations of light suggests that she feels somewhat detached from her Manhattan home.*

Comprehension

1. **Recall** What does Kincaid compare and contrast in this essay?

2. **Recall** What time did most people in Kincaid's home country start their day?

3. **Clarify** Explain why the author feels that the only thing Manhattan and Antigua share is "a geographical definition" of being an island.

Literary Analysis

4. **Analyze Patterns of Organization** To **compare and contrast** Antigua and Manhattan, Kincaid includes many of the same kinds of details in her description of each place. Use the chart you created as you read to find examples of these points of comparison. In your opinion, which one highlights similarities and differences between the two islands most effectively? Support your opinion with evidence.

5. **Analyze Author's Perspective** An author's perspective is the way he or she looks at a topic. How might Kincaid's childhood experiences in Antigua have influenced her perspective on living in New York? If she had grown up in a big city, would her new home seem less foreign to her? Use evidence from the text to support your answer.

6. **Draw Conclusions** Reread lines 100–112. Why do the author's friends in Manhattan notice the gradations of light, while she herself does not? What might this tell you about her feelings toward Manhattan as her **home?** Explain your answer.

7. **Evaluate Diction** Kincaid frequently uses lists and repetition to achieve her unique style. In a chart like the one shown, record three examples of such usage. Then complete your chart by briefly explaining the effect created by each example.

Example of Kincaid's Diction	Effect Created
"Certainly no one I know gets up at <u>half past five</u>, at <u>six o'clock</u>, at <u>seven o'clock</u>, at <u>half past seven</u>, at <u>eight o'clock</u>" (lines 94–96)	Kincaid's use of repetition here helps emphasize how solitary her mornings in New York are. It gives the paragraph a reflective, lonely tone.

Literary Criticism

8. **Critical Interpretations** The literary critic Suzanne Freeman has said that Kincaid's "singsong style" produces "images that are as sweet and mysterious as the secrets that children whisper in your ear." In your opinion, does this comment apply to Kincaid's depiction of her island birthplace? Cite details and description from the selection to support your opinion.

---

7. ● **STANDARDS FOCUS** *Diction Examples of such usage include lines 7–10, which spotlight Antigua's agricultural variety and create a sense of satisfaction and delight; lines 20–25, which emphasize diversity through a range of occupations; and lines 113–117, which present the subjects of magazine articles to suggest why Kincaid finds them trivial.*

Literary Criticism

Possible answer:

8. *Answers will vary, but students should support their opinions by suggestions of a "singsong style" (such as the lists in lines 5–10 and 22–25).*

Reading-Writing Connection

Expand your knowledge of "Island Morning" by responding to these prompts.
Then use **Revision: Grammar and Style** to improve your writing.

WRITING PROMPTS	SELF-CHECK
A. Short Response: Support an Opinion Which place do you think Jamaica Kincaid calls **home?** In your opinion, does she seem more attached to her island birthplace or to her new city? Write a **one- or two-paragraph response,** citing evidence from the text to support your opinion.	*A strong response will . . .* • clearly state an opinion about which place Kincaid prefers • offer specific words and phrases from the selection to support your opinion
B. Extended Response: Compare and Contrast Choose one of the two mornings Kincaid describes and compare it with your own daily routine. Use the rich details presented in the selection to write a **three-to-five-paragraph comparison.**	*A successful comparison will . . .* • discuss at least three features of Kincaid's morning, citing details from the text • explain how Kincaid's routine is similar to or different from your own

REVISION: GRAMMAR AND STYLE

IMPROVE SENTENCE FLOW Review the **Grammar and Style** note on page 518. Jamaica Kincaid uses **coordinating conjunctions** to join independent clauses and connect ideas. She creates long sentences and achieves a conversational style.

Like Kincaid, use the coordinating conjunctions *and, but, for, nor, or, so,* and *yet* when you want to combine shorter sentences or connect ideas. In the following excerpt, notice how the author uses *and* to join two independent clauses and *but* to connect ideas:

> *The Ground was often many miles away from where they lived, and they got there not by taking a truck or some other kind of automotive transportation but by riding a donkey or by walking.* (lines 16–19)

Notice how the revisions in red help to improve the flow of this first draft. Revise your responses to the prompts by using similar techniques.

STUDENT MODEL

My house is home to a family of seven. There is only one bathroom. All five
of us kids race crazily down the hall every weekday morning. My older sister
almost always gets there first. The rest of us stand blinking and yawning in
the hallway. We drift slowly downstairs to the kitchen.

> **WRITING TOOLS**
> For prewriting, revision, and editing tools, visit the **Writing Center** at ClassZone.com.

DIFFERENTIATED INSTRUCTION

FOR LESS–PROFICIENT WRITERS

For Prompt A:

• Help students determine their opinions based on Kincaid's words and on the implied underlying feelings. For example, ask whether Kincaid sounds positive or negative in lines 93–112.

• Work with students to write a sentence that clearly states their opinions.

• Help students review possible supporting details from the text.

For Prompt B:

• Suggest that students limit their responses to three paragraphs.

• Present some details to which students might relate. For example, point out the early-morning activities on Antigua or the television viewing in Manhattan.

• Encourage peer reviews in which students can consider ways to make their comparisons clearer.

Reading-Writing Connection

WRITING PROMPTS

• For Prompt A, encourage students to apply what they have learned in the Critical Reading Workshop (pages 508–513) to this assignment. For example, ask students to consider Kincaid's purpose and perspective as she describes each place.

• For Prompt B, have students adapt the Comparison Matrix or the Classification Chart for use as they identify and group details. Remind students to choose a main idea for the comparison as a whole as well as a topic sentence for each paragraph.

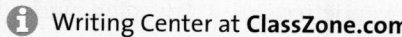

BEST PRACTICES TOOLKIT—Transparencies
Comparison Matrix p. A24
Classification Chart p. B17

For writing support, see

🔘 Write*Smart* CD

ℹ️ Writing Center at **ClassZone.com**

REVISION: GRAMMAR AND STYLE

• Elicit, or be prepared to share, sentences that illustrate the use of the coordinating conjunctions.

• After discussing the student model, write this paragraph on the board. Have students use coordinating conjunctions to improve the flow. (For more on coordinating conjunctions, see **Grammar Handbook,** page R46.)

> *My alarm goes off at 6:30, but I don't leap out of bed. There's no point. My sister is already in the bathroom, so I'll have to wait anyway.*

📋 RESOURCE MANAGER—Copy Master
Improve Sentence Flow p. 33

Assess and Reteach

Assess

📋 RESOURCE MANAGER—Copy Masters
Selection Test A pp. 35–36
Selection Test B/C pp. 37–38

🔘 Test Generator CD

Reteach

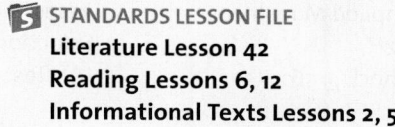

📄 STANDARDS LESSON FILE
Literature Lesson 42
Reading Lessons 6, 12
Informational Texts Lessons 2, 5

Focus and Motivate

OBJECTIVES

Literary Analysis
- explore the key idea of **inspiration**
- analyze tone
- read a biographical essay

Reading
- identify implied main ideas

Vocabulary
- build vocabulary for reading and writing
- use knowledge of the word root *gen* to help unlock meaning *(also an EL language objective)*

Grammar and Writing
- use concrete and abstract nouns to strengthen descriptive language
- use writing to analyze literature

SUMMARY

In "Georgia O'Keeffe," Joan Didion shows how this remarkable artist defied conventions of the early twentieth century. Spending much of her life in the relative isolation of the south-west United States, O'Keeffe used bold colors to paint subjects that many critics of the time considered unworthy. Today, however, her work is viewed as imaginative and inspiring.

What is the source of INSPIRATION?

Ask the question. After students read the **KEY IDEA**, elicit that an **inspiration** is anyone or anything (an object, an event, a thought) that sparks a creative idea. Introduce the **QUICKWRITE** and the varied applications of the term *artist*. Then have students complete the activity and share the results.

Selection Resources

Georgia O'Keeffe
Biographical Essay by Joan Didion

What is the source of INSPIRATION?

KEY IDEA What drives painters to create vibrant pictures? What compels movie directors to invent alien worlds or makes songwriters dream up meaningful lyrics? Artists find **inspiration** in their daily lives, in nature, or even in the work of other artists.

QUICKWRITE Think of the most powerful work by your favorite artist, be it a painter, a dancer, an actor, an author, or a musician. What do you think inspired the artist to create this work? Whether it's a song about the person who broke his heart or a huge mural of her neighborhood, try to imagine the inspiration behind the art. Describe your artist's source of inspiration in a short paragraph.

524

R RESOURCE MANAGER UNIT 5

Plan and Teach pp. 39–46

Literary Analysis
Summary pp. 47†*, 48‡*
Tone pp. 49, 50†*
Question Support p. 57*

Reading
Identify Implied Main Ideas
pp. 51, 52†*
Reading Check p. 56

Vocabulary
Study p. 53*
Practice p. 54
Strategy p. 55

Grammar and Writing
Use Descriptive Language p. 59

Assessment
Selection Tests A, B/C pp. 61*, 63*
⊘ Test Generator CD

BEST PRACTICES TOOLKIT

Differentiated Instruction
pp. 31–38*

Scaffolding Instruction
pp. 43–46*

Graphic Organizers/Strategies
Definition Mapping • Read Aloud/
Think Aloud

Reading Support
⊘ Audio Anthology CD*

Technology
ⓘ Literature and Vocabulary
Centers at **ClassZone.com**

⊘ Write*Smart* CD

LITERARY ANALYSIS: TONE

Tone is a writer's attitude toward his or her subject. Just as people often speak in a particular tone of voice, such as sarcastic or amused, writers create a tone with their choice of words. As you read "Georgia O'Keeffe," record details that help you identify Joan Didion's tone. Look for the following:

- unusual words Didion uses to describe O'Keeffe
- emphasized or repeated words and phrases
- details about O'Keeffe's life Didion chooses to include

Details from the Text	Tone Established
Didion describes O'Keeffe as "this angelic rattlesnake." (lines 63–64)	

READING SKILL: IDENTIFY IMPLIED MAIN IDEAS

The **main idea** is the most important idea in a paragraph or essay. Often, the main idea is not directly stated but **implied** by supporting details. As you read, use these strategies to identify and understand Didion's main ideas:

- Identify the specific topic of each paragraph or section.
- Examine all the details the author includes in that section.
- Ask what idea or message the details convey about the topic.
- State the idea or message in a sentence.

VOCABULARY IN CONTEXT

Didion's vibrant portrait of Georgia O'Keeffe is enhanced by her use of the words shown in bold. To see how many words you already know, restate each phrase, using a different word or words for each boldfaced term.

1. a **condescending** attitude toward teenagers
2. witness the **genesis** of an idea
3. scorned with a **derisive** laugh
4. bitter **rancor** between enemies
5. painted with bright, **immutable** colors

Author Online

A Sharp Eye
Joan Didion's keen observations of American society have earned her popularity and critical acclaim. Whether on the antiwar movement of the 1960s or American politics in the aftermath of September 11, Didion's insights have earned her a prominent place in American literature. They have also served a more personal purpose. "I write," she says, "entirely to find out what I'm thinking."

Joan Didion
born 1934

Speak for Yourself Didion's work, which includes essays, novels, and screenplays, spans four decades. The author is a firm believer in the power of language. She warns young people not to "settle for other people's words" but rather to voice their own opinions. "I am still committed," Didion declares, "to the idea that the ability to think for one's self depends on one's mastery of the language."

 MORE ABOUT THE AUTHOR
For more on Joan Didion, visit the **Literature Center at ClassZone.com.**

Background
Artistic Flair Georgia O'Keeffe (1887–1986) was a significant 20th-century American painter intrigued by the idea of "filling space in a beautiful way." Although she was born in Wisconsin, she is most closely associated with New Mexico, where she spent much of her life. In the Southwest, O'Keeffe painted what she saw: clouds, desert flowers, bones, and rocks. Some of O'Keeffe's most famous paintings are dramatic close-ups of flowers.

GEORGIA O'KEEFFE   **525**

Teach

STANDARDS FOCUS

LITERARY ANALYSIS

TONE

For instructional support, read aloud this example:

> The visitors to the museum stared as if hypnotized by the massive, colorful painting. They gasped at the daring beauty of the masterpiece.

Have students identify the words and phrases that set a tone of awe. ***Possible answer: "stared as if hypnotized," "massive," "gasped," "daring beauty," and "masterpiece"***

CHECK UNDERSTANDING Elicit details that might change the tone of the example.

 RESOURCE MANAGER—Copy Master
Tone p. 49 (for student use while reading the selection)

READING SKILL

IDENTIFY IMPLIED MAIN IDEAS

List these ideas on the board:

> Love can be an inspiration.
> Love is painful.
> Finding true love is an impossibility.

Ask students which idea would be implied in a paragraph about writing love songs or love poetry.
Possible answer: Love can be an inspiration.

CHECK UNDERSTANDING Ask students why these details probably would not support the other ideas well.

VOCABULARY SKILL

VOCABULARY IN CONTEXT

DIAGNOSE WORD KNOWLEDGE To determine preteaching needs, have all students complete Vocabulary in Context. ***Possible answers:***
1. *superior or belittling,* 2. *beginning,*
3. *mocking,* 4. *resentment or hostility,*
5. *permanent*

PRETEACH VOCABULARY Use the Vocabulary Study copy master to help students predict the meaning of each boldfaced word in the copy master.

1. Read the first sentence in Part A aloud, emphasizing *condescending.*
2. Point out the word "smug." Elicit possible meanings for *condescending,* such as "looking down upon."
3. Repeat the procedure for the other items in Part A.

RESOURCE MANAGER—Copy Master
Vocabulary Study p. 53

For general guidelines on differentiating vocabulary instruction and for alternative vocabulary activities for students not needing vocabulary preteaching, see

BEST PRACTICES TOOLKIT
Scaffolding Vocabulary Instruction pp. 43–46
Vocabulary Center at ClassZone.com

ANALYZE VISUALS

Possible answer: The many paintbrushes indicate that O'Keeffe is an avid painter. Her posture suggests that she thinks deeply and carefully. Her calm, piercing look implies that she is determined and unafraid.

About the Art The photography of Alfred Stieglitz (1864–1946) played a major role in the recognition of photography as an art form.

READING SKILL

Ⓐ IMPLIED MAIN IDEAS

Possible answer: *Didion's daughter realized that style is character and that the boldness of O'Keeffe's painting reflected O'Keeffe's bold character.*

If students need help . . . Point out that the main idea of a paragraph often is stated or suggested in the first sentence or two. As students reread the first two sentences of this paragraph, help them see the emphasis on Didion's daughter. Note key comments such as "the painting was the painter as the poem is the poet."

Lines 7–13
REINFORCE *KEY IDEA:* INSPIRATION

Discuss In what sense was the "Sky Above Clouds" canvas an **inspiration** to Didion's daughter? *Possible answer: It filled her with awe and made her feel that talking to O'Keeffe was very important—presumably, because she wanted to know the artist better, perhaps because the painting stirred her own creative impulses.*

Georgia O'Keeffe

JOAN DIDION

"Where I was born and where and how I have lived is unimportant," Georgia O'Keeffe told us in the book of paintings and words published in her ninetieth year on earth. She seemed to be advising us to forget the beautiful face in the Stieglitz photographs.[1] She appeared to be dismissing the rather **condescending** romance that had attached to her by then, the romance of extreme good looks and advanced age and deliberate isolation. "It is what I have done with where I have been that should be of interest." I recall an August afternoon in Chicago in 1973 when I took my daughter, then seven, to see what Georgia O'Keeffe had done with where she had been. One of the vast O'Keeffe "Sky Above Clouds"
10 canvases floated over the back stairs in the Chicago Art Institute that day, dominating what seemed to be several stories of empty light, and my daughter looked at it once, ran to the landing, and kept on looking. "Who drew it," she whispered after a while. I told her. "I need to talk to her," she said finally.

My daughter was making, that day in Chicago, an entirely unconscious, but quite basic assumption about people and the work they do. She was assuming that the glory she saw in the work reflected a glory in its maker, that the painting was the painter as the poem is the poet, that every choice one made alone—every word chosen or rejected, every brush stroke laid or not laid down—betrayed one's character. *Style is character.* It seemed to me that afternoon that I had rarely
20 seen so instinctive an application of this familiar principle, and I recall being pleased not only that my daughter responded to style as character but that it was Georgia O'Keeffe's particular style to which she responded: this was a hard woman who had imposed her 192 square feet of clouds on Chicago. Ⓐ

---

1. **Stieglitz** (stēg'lĭts) **photographs:** American photographer Alfred Stieglitz, O'Keeffe's husband, took and exhibited many photographs of O'Keeffe.

condescending
(kŏn'dĭ-sĕn'dĭng) *adj.*
assuming an air of superiority

❶ **Targeted Passage**

ANALYZE VISUALS
Examine this 1932 Stieglitz photograph of O'Keeffe. List three **traits** you would attribute to O'Keeffe based solely on this photograph.

Ⓐ **IMPLIED MAIN IDEAS**
Reread lines 14–23 and think about the details Didion includes about her daughter's reaction to O'Keeffe's work. What is the main idea of the paragraph?

DIFFERENTIATED INSTRUCTION

FOR ALL STUDENTS

Learning Center In your classroom or school library, create a Learning Center on the life and work of Georgia O'Keeffe. Provide books and online articles as well as photos and prints of her work.

To help students, see

R RESOURCE MANAGER
Ideas for Extension pp. 44–45

FOR LESS–PROFICIENT READERS

In combination with the *Audio Anthology CD,* use one or more Targeted Passages (pp. 526, 528, 530) to ensure that students focus on key events, concepts, and skills. Targeted Passages are also good for English learners.

❶ **Targeted Passage [Lines 1–7]**

This passage introduces the subject of Didion's essay, focusing on that subject's individualistic view of life.

BACKGROUND

Women at the Turn of the Century O'Keeffe was born into an era in which girls learned cooking, cleaning, and caring for children from their mothers. Women were rarely encouraged to obtain formal education beyond secondary school. At the time that O'Keeffe attended college, in fact, only about one out of every five university degrees went to women.

Cultural Connection Georgia O'Keeffe brought new vitality to what had been a traditionally "safe" art form for women in the United States: painting flowers. Likewise, during O'Keeffe's time, women artists in other countries found **inspiration** from traditional art forms of their cultures and transformed them into something boldly original. The Swiss artist Sophie Taeuber-Arp (1889–1943) was famous for her designs for marionettes, embroidery, even furniture. The lush, often fantastical paintings of Mexican artist Frida Kahlo (1910–1954) were often inspired by the folk art of her people, especially the colorful costumes, delicate lace, and vivid embroidery done by women. Invite students to share the artistic traditions of their own cultures, and explain how their creation and design are inspiring.

- What was Georgia O'Keeffe's profession?
- What three "romances" did she not seem to care about? Why?
- What did she think that people should find interesting about her? What does that statement tell you about her personality?

FOR ENGLISH LEARNERS

Key Academic Vocabulary Use Definition Mapping to teach these words: *isolation*

(line 6), *dominating* (line 11), *style* (line 19), *contemporaries* (line 32), *appreciation* (line 37), *exhibition* (line 39).

 BEST PRACTICES TOOLKIT—Transparency Definition Mapping p. E6

Prereading For prereading instruction for English learners, see

 BEST PRACTICES TOOLKIT Scaffolding Reading Instruction pp. 43–46

FOR ADVANCED LEARNERS/PRE–AP

Pre-AP Exercises in the bottom channel provide additional challenge for students. Use these suggestions for small groups or individuals.

ADDITIONAL GUIDELINES

For more help with differentiation and tips for classroom management, see

BEST PRACTICES TOOLKIT Differentiated Instruction pp. 31–38

"Hardness" has not been in our century a quality much admired in women, nor in the past twenty years has it even been in official favor for men. When hardness surfaces in the very old we tend to transform it into "crustiness" or eccentricity, some tonic pepperiness to be indulged at a distance. On the evidence of her work and what she has said about it, Georgia O'Keeffe is neither "crusty" nor eccentric. She is simply hard, a straight shooter, a woman clean of received wisdom and open to what she sees. This is a woman who could early on dismiss most of her contemporaries as "dreamy," and would later single out one she liked as "a very poor painter." (And then add, apparently by way of softening the judgment: "I guess he wasn't a painter at all. He had no courage and I believe that to create one's own world in any of the arts takes courage.") This is a woman who in 1939 could advise her admirers that they were missing her point, that their appreciation of her famous flowers was merely sentimental. "When I paint a red hill," she observed coolly in the catalogue for an exhibition that year, "you say it is too bad that I don't always paint flowers.
40 A flower touches almost everyone's heart. A red hill doesn't touch everyone's heart." This is a woman who could describe the **genesis** of one of her most well-known paintings—the "Cow's Skull: Red, White and Blue" owned by the Metropolitan—as an act of quite deliberate and **derisive** orneriness. "I thought of the city men I had been seeing in the East," she wrote. "They talked so often of writing the Great American Novel—the Great American Play—the Great American Poetry. . . . So as I was painting my cow's head on blue I thought to myself, 'I'll make it an American painting. They will not think it great with the red stripes down the sides—Red, White and Blue—but they will notice it.'"

50 The city men. The men. They. The words crop up again and again as this astonishingly aggressive woman tells us what was on her mind when she was making her astonishingly aggressive paintings. It was those city men who stood accused of sentimentalizing her flowers: "I made you take time to look at what I saw and when you took time to really notice my flower you hung all your associations with flowers on my flower and you write about my flower as if I think and see what you think and see—and I don't." *And I don't.* Imagine those words spoken, and the sound you hear is *don't tread on me.* "The men" believed it impossible to paint New York, so Georgia O'Keeffe painted New York. "The men" didn't think much
60 of her bright color, so she made it brighter. The men yearned toward Europe so she went to Texas, and then New Mexico. The men talked about Cézanne,[2] "long involved remarks about the 'plastic quality' of his form and color," and took one another's long involved remarks, in the view of this angelic rattlesnake in their midst, altogether too seriously. "I can paint one of those C

---

2. **Cézanne** (sā-zăn'): Paul Cézanne, late-19th-century French painter whose style and study of shapes influenced new art movements in the early 20th century.

B GRAMMAR AND STYLE

Concrete and Abstract Nouns Point out other abstract nouns in these lines, including *hardness, century, quality, favor, crustiness, eccentricity,* and *pepperiness.* Explain that descriptions of art often include abstract nouns, as well, and that many of those nouns express a positive or negative opinion. Discuss what the abstract nouns *finesse, beauty, essence, emotion, aggression, balance,* and *depth* might suggest about a work of art.

LITERARY ANALYSIS

C TONE

Possible answer: *Repeated words and phrases include* astonishingly aggressive, take time/took time, my flower, think and see, and I don't, so she, *and especially* the men. *Together, such expressions create a strong, defiant tone. They emphasize O'Keeffe's independent spirit and her determination not to be dictated to by the men in the arts of her day.*

If students need help . . . Use Think Aloud to model how students might identify key words and phrases and determine the tone that they suggest. For example, you might begin by recognizing the repeated use of *astonishingly aggressive* in lines 50–52 and inferring that the expression suggests a confrontational attitude.

🛠 BEST PRACTICES TOOLKIT—Transparency
Read Aloud/Think Aloud p. A34

B GRAMMAR AND STYLE
Reread lines 30–31. Didion uses both **concrete nouns,** such as *woman,* and **abstract nouns,** such as *wisdom,* to discuss O'Keeffe. Concrete nouns add substance to abstract ideas.

genesis (jĕn'ĭ-sĭs) *n.* the origin or coming into being (of something)

derisive (dĭ-rī'sĭv) *adj.* expressing contempt or ridicule

C TONE
Think about the words and phrases that Didion italicizes or repeats in lines 50–64. How would you describe her tone? Explain your answer.

DIFFERENTIATED INSTRUCTION

FOR LESS–PROFICIENT READERS

2 **Targeted Passage [Lines 24–38]**

In this passage, Didion identifies and begins to support her interpretation of O'Keeffe's essential trait: her hardness.

- What are two other words for *hardness*? How well does Didion think these other words describe O'Keeffe? Explain.

- How did O'Keeffe show hardness to most of her contemporaries? to her admirers?

FOR ENGLISH LEARNERS

Culture: Connect This essay mentions two of the most famous museums in the United States: the Chicago Art Institute (line 10; known officially as the Art Institute of Chicago) and the Metropolitan (line 43; known officially as The Metropolitan Museum of Art and located in New York City). Have students name any famous museums in their home country or in other cities in the United States.

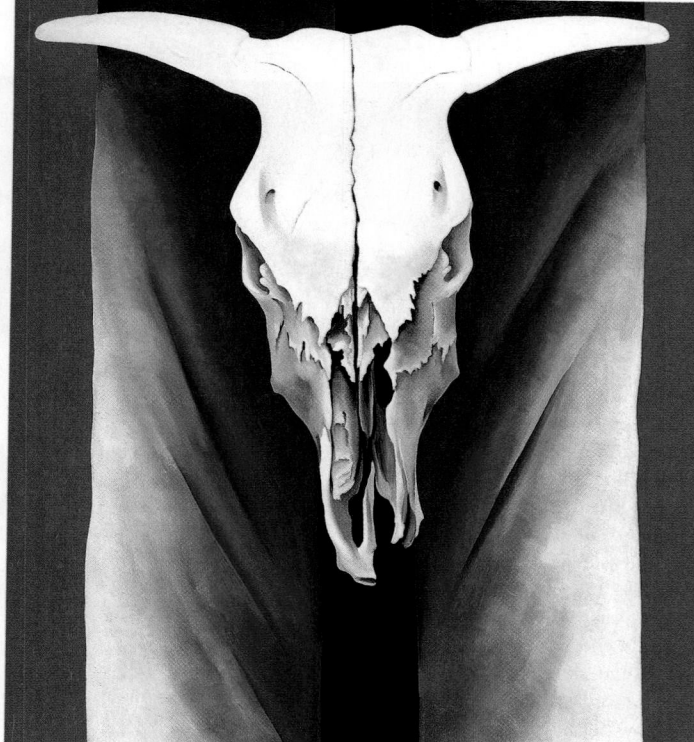

Cow's Skull: Red, White, and Blue (1931), Georgia O'Keeffe. Oil on canvas, 39⅞" × 35⅞". The Metropolitan Museum of Art, Alfred Stieglitz Collection, 1952. © 2007 Georgia O'Keeffe Museum/Artists Rights Society (ARS), New York. Photo © Georgia O'Keeffe/Metropolitan Museum of Art (52.203).

ANALYZE VISUALS
Reread lines 41–49. What message do you think O'Keeffe was sending to the "city men" when she painted this piece? Explain your answer, citing details from the text as well as the painting.

dismal-colored paintings like the men," the woman who regarded herself always as an outsider remembers thinking one day in 1922, and she did: a painting of a shed "all low-toned and dreary with the tree beside the door." She called the act of **rancor** "The Shanty" and hung it in her next show. "The men seemed to approve of it," she reported fifty-four years later, her contempt 70 undimmed. "They seemed to think that maybe I was beginning to paint. That was my only low-toned dismal-colored painting."

   Some women fight and others do not. Like so many successful guerrillas[3] in the war between the sexes, Georgia O'Keeffe seems to have been equipped early with an **immutable** sense of who she was and a fairly clear understanding that she would be required to prove it. On the surface her upbringing was conventional. She was a child on the Wisconsin prairie who played with china dolls and painted watercolors with cloudy skies because sunlight was too hard to paint and, with her brother and sisters, listened every night to her mother read stories of the Wild West, of Texas, of Kit Carson and Billy the Kid.[4] She

rancor (răng'kər) *n.* bitter and deep ill will

immutable (ĭ-myōō'tə-bəl) *adj.* unchanging

---

3. **guerrillas** (gə-rĭl'əz): members of irregular military units who work to undermine the enemy using tactics such as surprise raids.

4. **Kit Carson and Billy the Kid:** Carson was a scout in the American West; Billy the Kid was an outlaw.

ANALYZE VISUALS

Possible answer: O'Keeffe places the flower in the center and makes it so large that it dominates the painting. Her colors focus attention on the dramatically bright flower.

About the Art The jimson weed is a common desert plant in the American Southwest. Its flowers are large and beautiful, but all parts of the plant are toxic and can be fatal if eaten.

---

80 told adults that she wanted to be an artist and was embarrassed when they asked what kind of artist she wanted to be: she had no idea "what kind." She had no idea what artists did. She had never seen a picture that interested her, other than a pen-and-ink Maid of Athens[5] in one of her mother's books, some Mother Goose illustrations printed on cloth, a tablet cover that showed a little girl with pink roses, and the painting of Arabs on horseback that hung in her grandmother's parlor.

90 At thirteen, in a Dominican convent, she was mortified when the sister corrected her drawing. At Chatham Episcopal Institute in Virginia she painted lilacs and sneaked time alone to walk out to where she could see the line of the Blue Ridge Mountains on the horizon. At the Art Institute in Chicago she was shocked by the presence of live models and wanted to abandon anatomy lessons. At the Art Students League in New York one of her fellow students advised her that, since he

100 would be a great painter and she would end up teaching painting in a girls' school, any work of hers was less important than modeling for him. Another painted over her work to show her how the Impressionists[6] did trees. She had not before heard how the Impressionists did trees and she did not much care.

Jimson Weed (1932), Georgia O'Keeffe. The Georgia O'Keeffe Museum, Santa Fe, New Mexico. © 2007 Georgia O'Keeffe Museum/Artists Rights Society (ARS), New York. Photo © Art Resource, New York.

At twenty-four she left all those opinions behind and went for the first time to live in Texas, where there were no trees to paint and no one to tell her how not to paint them. In Texas there was only the horizon she craved. In Texas

110 she had her sister Claudia with her for a while, and in the late afternoons they would walk away from town and toward the horizon and watch the evening star come out. "That evening star fascinated me," she wrote. "It was in some way very exciting to me. My sister had a gun, and as we walked she would throw bottles in the air and shoot as many as she could before they hit the ground. I had nothing but to walk into nowhere and the wide sunset space with the star. Ten watercolors were made from that star." In a way one's interest is compelled as much by the sister Claudia with the gun as by the painter Georgia with the star, but only the painter left us this shining record. Ten watercolors were made from that star. ∾ **D**

ANALYZE VISUALS

O'Keeffe is celebrated for her ability to make even flowers look strong and imposing. Explain how she creates this air of strength, considering elements such as the flower's size, position, and color.

3 Targeted Passage
D TONE
Reread lines 107–119. What is the "shining record" Didion refers to? Describe the tone conveyed by the writer's **word choice**.

---

5. **Maid of Athens:** the subject of a love poem by 19th-century English writer George Gordon, Lord Byron.

6. **Impressionists:** members of an influential 19th-century French school of painting who focused on depicting quick visual impressions and conveying how light influenced the scenes they painted.

LITERARY ANALYSIS

D TONE

Possible answer: The "shining record" is O'Keeffe's series of paintings of the evening star. Didion's word choice expresses a tone of respect, appreciation, and admiration of the artist.

SELECTION WRAP–UP

SUMMARIZE Have students explain why Didion feels that O'Keeffe was an important artist.

⭐ **CRITIQUE** Ask students if they found reading this biography inspirational. Ask them to explain their responses.

DIFFERENTIATED INSTRUCTION

FOR LESS–PROFICIENT READERS
3 Targeted Passage [Lines 107–119]

This concluding passage ties O'Keeffe's independent spirit and love of beauty to the American Southwest.

- When O'Keeffe went to Texas, what did she leave behind? What things and attitudes did she want to find there?
- What did she do in the late afternoons?
- How can you tell that the evening star was important to her?

FOR ENGLISH LEARNERS

Culture: Clarify Tell students that *evening star* (lines 111–119) is another name for the planet Venus, which can be seen in the western sky in most parts of the United States. Ask them to name some well-known astronomical features in the sky over their home countries. For example, in South America, the brightest stars in the group that we call the Big Dipper are known as Las Tres Marías.

Comprehension

1. **Recall** What anecdote, or short personal story, does Didion tell at the beginning of this essay?

2. **Clarify** What did O'Keeffe's critics tend to think of her work?

Literary Analysis

3. **Paraphrase** O'Keeffe asserts, "Where I was born and where and how I have lived is unimportant. It is what I have done with where I have been that should be of interest." Paraphrase this quotation. Then explain what O'Keeffe meant.

4. **Understand Motives** What inspired O'Keeffe to act the way she did? For each action described in the chart, identify O'Keeffe's motive, or **inspiration.** Use a graphic organizer like the one shown to record your answers.

Motive ⟶	Action
	O'Keeffe paints "Cow's Skull: Red, White, and Blue" (line 42).
	O'Keeffe uses even brighter colors in her paintings (line 60).
	O'Keeffe moves to the Southwest (line 108).

5. **Identify Implied Main Idea** Reread lines 72–106. Examine the details in this paragraph. What is the implied main idea conveyed by these details? Use evidence from the text to support your answer.

6. **Analyze Characterization** Didion reveals her subject's traits using the same methods of characterization used by fiction writers. Identify at least two methods of characterization Didion uses in this selection. Then explain which of O'Keeffe's traits are revealed in each case, citing evidence from the text.

7. **Analyze Tone** Review the chart you filled in as you read. How does Didion's tone help convey the ideas she wants to express about O'Keeffe?

Literary Criticism

8. **Author's Style** Joan Didion has remarked that "writing is hostile in that you're trying to make somebody see something the way you see it, trying to impose your idea, your picture." In what ways might this essay be considered "hostile"? Did Didion achieve her goal of making you see Georgia O'Keeffe the same way she does? Explain your answer.

Just as fiction writers give background information that illuminates character traits, Didion gives details about O'Keeffe's childhood and education that shaped her independent artistic spirit (lines 72–106).

7. ● **STANDARDS FOCUS** *Tone* Didion's serious, informative tone shows the respect and admiration that she feels and wants readers to feel for O'Keeffe.

Literary Criticism
Possible answer:

8. The essay is "hostile" in that Didion tried to overcome O'Keeffe's early critics. Didion achieved her goal by showing the reader the reasons for O'Keeffe's orneriness and the great art that resulted from her defiance of convention.

Practice and Apply

After Reading

For additional support of post-reading questions, use these copy masters:

R RESOURCE MANAGER—Copy Masters
  Reading Check p. 56 (to check understanding of the selection)
  Identify Implied Main Ideas p. 51 (for practice of reading skill standards focus)
  Question Support p. 57 (After Reading questions adapted for English learners and less-proficient readers)

  For additional questions, see page 43.

ANSWERS

Comprehension

1. *She tells how her daughter was impressed by an O'Keeffe painting while visiting an art museum.*

2. *They thought that her colors were too bright and that she sentimentalized her flowers.*

Literary Analysis
Possible answers:

3. *"Don't look at where I have come from. Look at what I have accomplished." O'Keeffe meant that her achievements show her character and strength better than her background does.*

4. *Row 1: She wanted to paint an American painting, to make it noticeable, and to be ornery.*

  Row 2: She wanted to defy the men who did not like her use of bright colors.

  Row 3: She wanted to be in a place where no one would tell her what or how to paint.

5. ● **STANDARDS FOCUS** *Identify Implied Main Ideas In spite of obstacles, O'Keeffe was determined to be an artist. Those obstacles included her narrow exposure to art and literature and the discouraging comments that came from teachers and other art students.*

6. *Just as fiction writers use dialogue to reveal character traits, Didion uses O'Keeffe's words to show her independence and defiance of convention (lines 34–35, 54–57) and her love for nature (lines 112–116).*

ANSWERS

Vocabulary in Context

VOCABULARY PRACTICE

1. *condescending*
2. *derisive*
3. *immutable*
4. *rancor*
5. *genesis*

R RESOURCE MANAGER—Copy Master
Vocabulary Practice p. 54

VOCABULARY IN WRITING

Suggest that students begin by listing topics that interest them about O'Keeffe, including those that were discussed briefly or that were only implied in the essay.

VOCABULARY STRATEGY: THE WORD ROOT
gen (also an EL language objective)

- Point out that the root *gen* is pronounced differently in different words. Ask volunteers to demonstrate by pronouncing each word in the web.

- For each item in the activity, help students use their knowledge of the root in combination with context clues (such as *family tree* in item 1 and *brand names* in item 2) to determine word meaning.

Possible answers:

1. *genealogist*
2. *generic*
3. *gene*
4. *genocide*
5. *generate*

R RESOURCE MANAGER—Copy Master
Vocabulary Strategy p. 55

ⓘ Vocabulary Center at **ClassZone.com**
Additional Vocabulary Activities

Vocabulary in Context

VOCABULARY PRACTICE

Determine the relationship between the first pair of words in each analogy. Then write the vocabulary word that best completes the second pair.

1. *Tolerant* is to *easygoing* as *smug* is to _____.
2. *Contemptuous* is to *speech* as _____ is to *remark*.
3. *Filth* is to *squalor* as _____ is to *permanent*.
4. *Embrace* is to *affection* as *insult* is to _____.
5. *Birth* is to *death* as _____ is to *termination*.

WORD LIST
condescending
derisive
genesis
immutable
rancor

VOCABULARY IN WRITING

Imagine you had gotten the chance to interview Georgia O'Keeffe while she was still alive. Write three questions that you would have liked to ask the artist about her life and work. Use at least three vocabulary words in your questions.

> **EXAMPLE SENTENCE**
>
> *How did you respond to people who expressed **derisive** attitudes about your paintings?*

VOCABULARY STRATEGY: THE WORD ROOT *gen*

The vocabulary word *genesis* contains the Greek root *gen*, which means "birth, race, or origin." *Gen* is also a Latin root with a similar meaning. The root *gen* is found in a number of English words. To understand the meaning of words with *gen,* use context clues as well as your knowledge of the root.

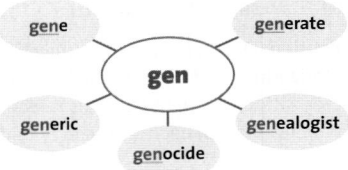

PRACTICE Choose the word from the word web that best completes each sentence. Use context clues to help you or, if necessary, consult a dictionary.

1. They hired a _____ to trace their family tree.
2. _____ products are usually less expensive than those with brand names.
3. The defective _____ that he inherited led to a serious blood disease.
4. _____ is the attempt to destroy a race of people.
5. They could not _____ enough interest in their project to get financial backing for it.

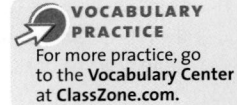
VOCABULARY PRACTICE
For more practice, go to the **Vocabulary Center** at **ClassZone.com**.

DIFFERENTIATED INSTRUCTION

FOR ENGLISH LEARNERS
Vocabulary: Roots Have students work with dictionaries in home language groups to create word webs like the one in the Vocabulary Strategy section, showing these additional English words with the root *gen: gender, generation, genetics, genome, pathogen, primogeniture, progeny,* and *regenerate.*

FOR ADVANCED LEARNERS/PRE–AP
Vocabulary Practice Challenge students to use the key academic vocabulary words listed in the **FOR ENGLISH LEARNERS** note on page T527 to write their own analogies. Have students trade their analogies with a partner to complete.

Reading-Writing Connection

Improve your understanding of "Georgia O'Keeffe" by responding to these prompts. Then use **Revision: Grammar and Style** to improve your writing.

WRITING PROMPTS	SELF-CHECK
A. Short Response: Evaluate Characterization What character trait does Didion highlight in her essay on Georgia O'Keeffe? How effective are the details the author includes to illustrate this trait? Write a **one- or two-paragraph response,** citing evidence from the text.	**A strong evaluation will . . .** • explain which character trait Didion emphasizes • establish criteria for judging the effectiveness of the details Didion uses
B. Extended Response: Describe Inspiration In your opinion, what was O'Keeffe's main source of **inspiration?** Write **three to five paragraphs** discussing the objects or ideas that compelled O'Keeffe to paint. Use details from the text as well as the paintings featured in this selection to support your analysis.	**A successful discussion will . . .** • consider different possible inspirations, such as the natural world and the artist's relationship with her critics • explain how O'Keeffe's inspiration drove her to create

REVISION: GRAMMAR AND STYLE

USE DESCRIPTIVE LANGUAGE Review the **Grammar and Style** note on page 528. A **concrete noun** names an object that can be seen, heard, smelled, touched, or tasted and is useful for conveying tangible information. An **abstract noun** names an idea or quality, making it useful for conveying feelings and traits. Didion uses both types of nouns to form a complete picture of Georgia O'Keeffe.

Concrete Nouns: *She was a child on the Wisconsin prairie who played with china dolls and painted watercolors....* (lines 76–77)

Abstract Nouns: *She appeared to be dismissing the rather condescending romance that had attached to her by then, the romance of extreme good looks and advanced age and deliberate isolation.* (lines 4–6)

The revisions in red incorporate a mix of concrete and abstract nouns to enhance the description. Use similar techniques to revise your responses to the prompts.

> **STUDENT MODEL**
>
> One source of O'Keeffe's inspiration was her conflict with her male critics.
>
> O'Keeffe ~~was very independent.~~ She refused to ~~listen to her critics.~~ Though
>
> critics praised her painting "The Shanty," O'Keeffe would not paint others ~~.~~
> *just to earn their praise.*
> like it.

WRITING TOOLS
For prewriting, revision, and editing tools, visit the **Writing Center** at ClassZone.com.

GEORGIA O'KEEFFE **533**

Reading-Writing Connection

WRITING PROMPTS

• For Prompt A, have students review the O'Keeffe quotations in lines 1–7 and 54–57, which point to her independence and defiance of convention.

• For Prompt B, encourage students to consider how negative criticism can be one source of inspiration. Suggest that they include examples of how O'Keeffe took action in response to criticism.

For writing support, see

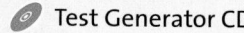 WriteSmart CD

 Writing Center at **ClassZone.com**

REVISION: GRAMMAR AND STYLE

• After students examine the student model, have them explain how the details in red improve the description.

• Write this bland passage on the board and ask students to improve it, using a mix of concrete and abstract nouns. (For more on nouns, see **Grammar Handbook,** page R52.)

Visiting the museum was ~~great~~ an inspirational experience. ~~I saw lots of beauty~~ The beautiful paintings and sculptures sent my imagination soaring. I enjoyed the nineteenth-century American ~~pieces~~ landscapes the most.

R RESOURCE MANAGER—Copy Master
   Use Descriptive Language p. 59

Assess and Reteach

Assess

R RESOURCE MANAGER—Copy Masters
   Selection Test A pp. 61–62
   Selection Test B/C pp. 63–64

Test Generator CD

Reteach

S STANDARDS LESSON FILE
   Literature Lesson 45: Tone
   Reading Lesson 4: Recognizing Main Idea and Details
   Vocabulary Lesson 6: Word Parts: Anglo-Saxon and Greek
   Writing Lesson 22: Descriptive Writing

FOR LESS–PROFICIENT WRITERS

For Prompt A:

• List several character traits that might be chosen as the topic for the essay.

• Have students choose one trait and look for three details that show this trait. Remind students to give the line numbers of supporting details that they cite.

For Prompt B:

Suggest this organization for responses:

Opening paragraph: State several sources of inspiration and identify one to explore.

Middle paragraph(s): Show how that source affected O'Keeffe's life and/or work.

Closing paragraph: Restate the source of inspiration and summarize its importance.

Focus and Motivate

OBJECTIVES

Elements of Nonfiction
- explore the key idea **investigate**
- use text features to locate and comprehend information
- read a magazine article and a process description

Reading
- take notes on a text

Vocabulary
- build vocabulary for reading and writing
- use the Greek suffix *-ology* to understand words *(also an EL language objective)*

Grammar and Writing
- use writing to analyze nonfiction

SUMMARIES

"Who Killed the Iceman?" This *National Geographic* article presents the mystery of a 5,000-year-old mummy found frozen in an Italian glacier. As archaeologists examine it, they discover a wound and speculate about its role in the death of the "Iceman."

"Skeletal Sculptures" Donna M. Jackson's article explains how forensic anthropologists reconstruct facial features on a skull cast to help detectives identify human remains.

How do scientists UNLOCK *the past?*

Lead into the *KEY IDEA* by asking the question. After students read the paragraph and complete the *DISCUSS* activity, have them write a definition of **investigate.**

Selection Resources

Who Killed the Iceman?
Magazine Article

Skeletal Sculptures
Process Description by Donna M. Jackson

How do scientists UNLOCK *the past?*

KEY IDEA Everyone knows bones and corpses can't talk. Or can they? As you may know from true-crime shows or sci-fi thrillers, human remains often have their own stories to tell. As police detectives unravel intricate cases and scientists **investigate** unexplained phenomena, these remains often tell stories that help piece the past together.

DISCUSS What types of criminal or scientific investigation do you know about? With a partner, choose one to discuss. List the methods investigators use to track down the truth. Then briefly explain the purpose of each method.

Criminal Investigation

Method	Purpose
1. Finger-printing	Identify suspect
2.	
3.	

534

● ELEMENTS OF NONFICTION: TEXT FEATURES

Text features are design elements that highlight the organization and key information of a text. They can help you preview what you'll read and recognize key ideas.

- **Subheadings** signal the beginning of a new topic or section. They often identify the focus of the text that follows them.
- **Graphic aids,** such as maps and photographs, present information visually. They are frequently accompanied by **captions,** which describe or clarify the information.
- **Numbered lists** often consist of steps in a process that should be followed in order.

As you read, use the text features mentioned to help you find and comprehend the important information in each article.

● READING STRATEGY: TAKE NOTES

When you **take notes,** your goal should be to record a text's main ideas and key information in a way that is easy to understand and remember. Since text features highlight main ideas and key information, including them in your notes can help.

As you read each section of "Who Killed the Iceman?" jot down its subheading. Then record the important details included in the section.

As you read "Skeletal Sculptures," note the key information in each step.

Review: **Monitor**

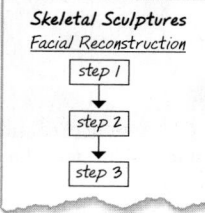

Who Killed the Iceman?
Background
- He was frozen for 5,000 years.
- Hikers found him in 1991 on the border between Austria and Italy.

Skeletal Sculptures
Facial Reconstruction
step 1
↓
step 2
↓
step 3

▲ VOCABULARY IN CONTEXT

Find a word that could be used in each newspaper headline.

WORD LIST	anthropology	compile	refute
	artifact	presumed	

1. Woman **Thought** Guilty of Murder
2. New Study to **Pull Together** Years of Research
3. Unusual **Object** Found in Archaeological Dig
4. **Science** Spotlight: Ancient Tribes
5. Scholar to **Deny Accuracy of** Theory

Background

Stumbling onto a Mummy

"Who Killed the Iceman?" chronicles some of the theories surrounding the death of a man who met his demise around 3000 B.C. The "Iceman," the oldest frozen mummy ever found, was discovered by German hikers vacationing in the Alps. When they spied a body embedded in the ice, the hikers assumed they had found the remains of a mountain climber who'd met a dismal fate. They had no idea they'd stumbled onto a 5,000-year-old relic. The Iceman now resides at the South Tyrol Museum of Archaeology in Bolzano, Italy.

Rescue workers and forensic experts examine the Iceman.

Crime-Fighting Scientists
"Skeletal Sculptures" describes how forensic anthropologists help police track down the truth. Anthropology is the scientific study of humans—our origins, behavior, environment, and physical features. Forensics is the use of science to solve crimes. Forensic anthropologists use their knowledge of human characteristics to assist in cracking tough cases involving human remains. The scientists identify the victim's age, sex, race, and physical characteristics. They also determine the likely cause of death, which makes them an integral part of many murder investigations.

 BUILDING BACKGROUND
To learn more about the Iceman and forensics, visit the **Literature Center** at **ClassZone.com.**

Teach

STANDARDS FOCUS

ELEMENTS OF NONFICTION

● TEXT FEATURES

For instructional support, have students scan the two selections to see that all of the features mentioned in the text are used. To reinforce the text, ask students to brainstorm for other types of writing that might include the text features listed. *Possible answers: history and science texts, encyclopedias, magazine articles, how-to guides, product information manuals*

CHECK UNDERSTANDING Have students suppose that such text features were missing from the genres that they listed. Discuss why the absence might make the writing more difficult to understand.

READING STRATEGY

● TAKE NOTES

Point out that by taking notes in the manner described, students are making use of text features (in these cases, subheadings and numbered lists/steps). Explain that a note does not have to be a complete sentence but that it should express an idea clearly. Urge students to include the page number with each note for later reference.

CHECK UNDERSTANDING Ask students to speculate about how they might use their notes at some time in the future.

R RESOURCE MANAGER—Copy Master
Take Notes p. 77 (for student use while reading the selection)

VOCABULARY SKILL

▲ VOCABULARY IN CONTEXT

DIAGNOSE WORD KNOWLEDGE To determine preteaching needs, have all students complete Vocabulary in Context. Point out that the boldfaced words in the headlines are synonyms for the vocabulary words. *Possible answers:* **1.** *presumed,* **2.** *compile,* **3.** *artifact,* **4.** *anthropology,* **5.** *refute*

PRETEACH VOCABULARY Use the Vocabulary Study copy master to help students predict meanings for each boldfaced word in the copy master.

1. Read aloud the first pair of sentences.
2. Point out "human cultures and their characteristics." Elicit meanings for *anthropology,* such as "the study of human cultures and characteristics."
3. Repeat the procedure for the other items.

R RESOURCE MANAGER—Copy Master
Vocabulary Study p. 79

For general guidelines on differentiating vocabulary instruction and for alternative vocabulary activities for students not needing vocabulary preteaching, see

BEST PRACTICES TOOLKIT
Scaffolding Vocabulary Instruction pp. 43–46
ℹ Vocabulary Center at **ClassZone.com**

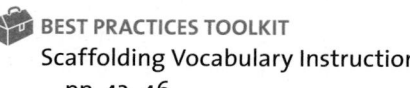

ELEMENTS OF NONFICTION

Ⓐ TEXT FEATURES

Possible answer: The mummy looks more lifelike than would be expected from a 5,000-year-old body. It is surprising that the body is a mummy, with skin, rather than just a skeleton.

If students need help . . . Explain that the photograph and its caption clarify the title of the article. Ask students to identify the Iceman and to explain their reasoning.

Extend the Discussion What features of the scene help explain why the mummy remained undiscovered for 5,000 years?

READING STRATEGY

Ⓑ TAKE NOTES

Possible answer: The most important information is that the Iceman is 5,000 years old, that he was found in 1991 in a mountain glacier on the border of Austria and Italy, and that scientists have determined that he died in battle or was murdered or sacrificed.

If students need help . . . Help them paraphrase the first sentence and the last sentence of the paragraph. Model turning the paraphrases into notes, deciding which details to include and which to omit.

FROM NATIONAL GEOGRAPHIC MAGAZINE

WHO KILLED THE ICEMAN?

Ⓐ TEXT FEATURES
Examine this **photograph** and its accompanying **caption.** Does the 5,000-year-old mummy look as you expected him to, or does his appearance surprise you? Explain your answer.

Ⓑ TAKE NOTES
What is the most important information provided in the section labeled "Background"? Be sure to record each section's essential details in your notes.
Targeted Passage ①

Among the first to reach the scene, these mountaineers used makeshift tools to help free the mummy.

Background

He spent some 5,000 years frozen in a mountain glacier on the Austro-Italian border before passing hikers discovered him, sprawled in the melting snow, in 1991. He now resides in a refrigerated room at a museum in Italy. Over the 11 years since his discovery the Iceman mummy has been examined from every possible angle. But not until this past summer did those studying his still frozen body notice a crucial piece of evidence that dramatically rewrites his story: "Ötzi," nicknamed for the Ötztal Alps where he was found, didn't freeze to death in a sudden snow storm while tending sheep as some had suggested. Instead he was killed, a victim of warfare, murder, or human sacrifice. Ⓑ

DIFFERENTIATED INSTRUCTION

FOR ALL STUDENTS

Expert Groups Allow students to become experts or members of expert groups by researching and choosing a way to share additional information about one of these topics.

- human civilization in Europe 5,000 years ago
- various methods of mummification
- other recent mummy investigations
- mummies in folklore and film

FOR LESS–PROFICIENT READERS

In combination with the *Audio Anthology CD,* use one or more Targeted Passages (pp. 536, 539, 540, 543) to ensure that students focus on key events, concepts, and skills. Targeted Passages are also good for English learners.

① Targeted Passage [Lines 5–9]

This passage sets up the mystery in this true story: the fact that the understanding of the Iceman's death has changed.

Clues Discovered

10 X-rays reveal an arrowhead buried deep in the Iceman's left shoulder—an injury that could not possibly have been self-inflicted. This discovery consequently led archaeologists to believe that the Iceman had been killed. The wound, visible as a small dark smudge beneath the mummy's leathery skin, had been overlooked in all previous examinations. Though no arrow shaft protrudes from the wound and no blood marks the arrow's entrance, it's now clear that the Iceman was shot in the back. But who did it? And why?

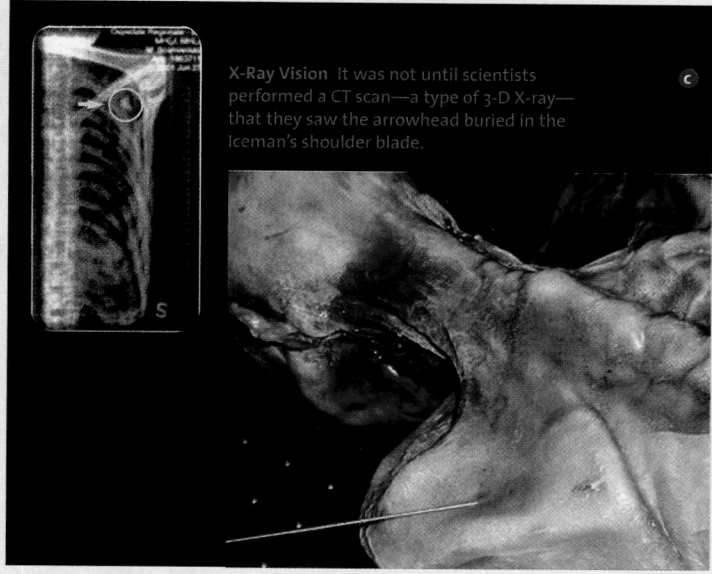

X-Ray Vision It was not until scientists performed a CT scan—a type of 3-D X-ray—that they saw the arrowhead buried in the Iceman's shoulder blade.

Differing Theories

"There's no way anyone can ever really know," says archaeologist Johan Reinhard, a National Geographic Society explorer-in-residence. "It might have been murder. Or it might have been ritual sacrifice."[1]

20 Reinhard knows mummies. Among the many he has discovered is the Inca "ice maiden," a victim of sacrifice, on the frozen slopes of Peru's Nevado Ampato[2] in 1995. His experience studying mountain cultures in the Andes, the Himalayas, and elsewhere has convinced him that the Iceman's death was not a random killing.

---

1. **ritual sacrifice:** a sacrifice that is part of a religious ceremony.
2. **Nevado Ampato** (nə-vä'dō äm-pä'tō): a volcano in the Central Andes.

WHO KILLED THE ICEMAN? **537**

"Look at where he died," Reinhard says. "It's a prominent pass, between two of the highest peaks in the Ötztal Alps. This is the kind of place where people from mountain cultures have traditionally made offerings to their mountain gods. We know that mountain worship was important in prehistoric Europe during the Bronze Age," he says. "And there is good
30 evidence that it may also have played a role earlier, in the Copper Age."[3]

Reinhard's interpretation seems to answer questions about **artifacts** found with the mummy that have long puzzled experts. For example, breaking objects was a ceremonial practice in Neolithic[4] Europe. This might explain the broken arrows lying near the mummy. The Iceman's copper ax—the oldest prehistoric ax in Europe with its bindings and handle intact—is also significant. Its copper had to have been mined, and mountains, as the source of valuable metals used to make tools, "were worshiped by miners throughout the world," says Reinhard. "This helps explain why the ax was left with the body after the killing." Murderers would likely have taken something so
40 useful with them. But people performing a ritual might have left it for the Iceman's use in the afterlife or as a tribute to the gods.

artifact (är′tə-făkt′) *n.* something created by humans, usually for a practical purpose

Ⓔ TEXT FEATURES
Examine the **map** that accompanies this article. What information does it convey? List two details you can learn from this graphic aid.

Where Ötzi Died

SWITZERLAND · AUSTRIA · Innsbruck · Ötztal Alps · Venice · ITALY

Ötzi was found at approximately 10,500 feet in the Ötztal Alps on the border between Austria and Italy. After closely examining Ötzi's clothing and possessions—including a sheath and dagger (shown at right)—archaeologists realized they had uncovered a 5,300-year-old find.

3. **Bronze Age . . . Copper Age:** The Bronze Age in Europe, when bronze tools began to be used, lasted roughly from 3500 B.C. to 1000 B.C. The Copper Age overlaps with the earliest part of the Bronze Age.
4. **Neolithic** (nē′ə-lĭth′ĭk): having to do with the prehistoric period when food growing began, but before metal tools were used—about 4000 B.C. in Europe.

ELEMENTS OF NONFICTION

Ⓔ TEXT FEATURES

Possible answer: The map indicates where the mummy was found. The caption gives the altitude of that location. The photograph shows what the Iceman's dagger looked like.

Lines 31–41
DISCUSSION PROMPTS

Use these prompts to help students grasp the importance of artifacts in learning more about the Iceman:

Connect How might artifacts that you carry provide information about your life? Give examples. *Possible answer: Textbooks might show students' grade level and approximate age. Certain jewelry might indicate their religion. Certain clothing might show that they live in a cold place or a warm place. Pencils and pens might indicate that they can write.*

Analyze What information do the artifacts that the Iceman carried reveal about his life? *Possible answer: The ax indicates that his people knew how to work with copper. The broken arrows and the ax may indicate that he (or his murderers) had a ceremonial religion.*

Synthesize What artifacts might help prove one theory about the Iceman's death over another? Explain. *Possible answer: If the Iceman had been found with more religious tokens, the "ritual sacrifice" theory would be more plausible. If he had carried arrows that were different from the broken ones, the "murder" theory would be more plausible.*

DIFFERENTIATED INSTRUCTION

FOR ENGLISH LEARNERS

Language: Verb Tenses Point out these verbs used in lines 36–41:

- *had to have been mined* (line 36)
- *were worshiped* (line 37)
- *would . . . have taken* (line 39)
- *might have left* (line 40)

Explain that some of these verb forms are common in language used to express theories and hypotheses.

FOR ADVANCED LEARNERS/PRE–AP

Hypothesize Ask students to reread this page, paying particular attention to details about where the Iceman was discovered. Have students use these details to propose an alternative hypothesis that explains the location of the find, the artifacts that accompanied the body, and the Iceman's wound. Students' hypotheses should draw upon textual evidence for support. Discuss hypotheses that volunteers offer to share.

Another clue: The Iceman's body was found in a naturally formed trench along the pass. Prior explanations had him taking shelter there from sudden bad weather. "But the trench is not deep and is at a high point of the pass. It
50 would have been a poor place to sit out a storm," explains Reinhard. Perhaps, instead, the Iceman was buried there by whoever killed him, which would account for the body's being so well preserved. **F**

Reinhard's ideas have not been met with enthusiasm by European experts. In contrast
60 with his beliefs, the mummy's caretaker, pathologist Eduard Egarter Vigl of South Tyrol Museum of Archaeology, believes that Ötzi may have been fleeing from an attacker, saying, "The Iceman was hit by an arrow from behind." Others maintain that arrows aren't efficient means of ritual killing and that no clear evidence of any other Copper Age sacrifice exists.

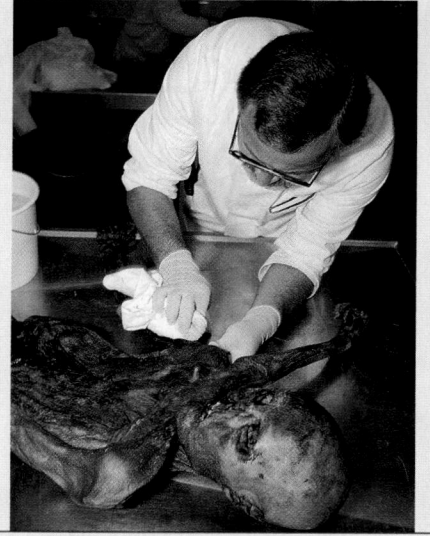
A scientist examines the skeletal remains of the Iceman.

So Who Killed the Iceman?

"They view the idea of human sacrifice as too sensational," says Reinhard. "But they can't **refute** what I've pointed out, and I believe my theory better explains the known facts.

"I know it's controversial," he admits. "But it's time to **compile** all the
70 evidence and reexamine it from a different perspective. Let's look at these artifacts not only relative to each other but also within social, sacred, and geographical contexts."

F MONITOR
One important part of monitoring your reading is **evaluating** the information that's provided. Do you find Reinhard's theory convincing? Why or why not?

 Targeted Passage

refute (rĭ-fyo͞ot′) v. to prove false by argument or evidence

compile (kəm-pīl′) v. to put together by gathering from many sources

Discuss How have researchers' investigations helped refute the idea that the Iceman died while taking shelter from bad weather?
Possible answer: *In studying the location where the mummy was found, researchers have learned that the pass was an exposed place, not one where the Iceman might have taken shelter from a storm.*

READING STRATEGY: *Review*

F MONITOR

Possible answer: *Reinhard's theory—that the Iceman was killed as a human sacrifice, rather than simply murdered—is convincing. He points out that the Iceman died in the kind of place where prehistoric people made human sacrifices. He argues that the Iceman's valuable copper ax, found near his body, would probably have been taken by murderers, while it might have been left by people performing a ritual killing. Finally, Reinhard argues that the trench where the Iceman's body was found suggests that he was buried there after his death and was not taking shelter from a storm.*

If students need help . . .

1. Guide students as they use Main Idea and Details to record the clues in lines 25–56.

2. Have students note Reinhard's professional qualifications.

3. Discuss the reputation of *National Geographic*, the publisher of the article.

BEST PRACTICES TOOLKIT—Transparency
Main Idea and Details p. B6

FOR LESS–PROFICIENT READERS
2 Targeted Passage [Lines 59–65]

This passage presents arguments against Reinhard's theory of ritual sacrifice as the cause of the Iceman's death.

- What are the professional qualifications of Eduard Egarter Vigl?

- What does Vigl believe the Iceman was doing when he was killed?

- How do others argue against ritual killing as the cause of his death?

FOR ENGLISH LEARNERS

Comprehension: Contrast Point out that this article expresses several opinions about what happened to the Iceman. Work with small groups of students to list the opinions and to find contrasts among them. As students work, point out transitions that signal contrast, such as *Though* (line 14), *Or* (line 19), *But* (lines 47, 67, and 69), *instead* (line 52), and *In contrast* (line 59).

G MONITOR

Possible answer: *Facial reconstruction is a "last resort" because it is a guess at the victim's appearance, meant to trigger the memory of someone who can identify the victim when no other clues point to the victim's identity.*

If students need help . . . Work through a diagram such as this to clarify the reasons for and results of facial reconstruction.

```
          ┌─────────────────┐
          │  A skeleton is  │
          │  unidentified.  │
          └─────────────────┘
           │               │
  ┌────────────────┐  ┌────────────────┐
  │ The police need │  │  Police want to │
  │  a new lead in a│  │ publish a likeness│
  │   crime case.   │  │  in the media.  │
  └────────────────┘  └────────────────┘
           │               │
          ┌─────────────────┐
          │    SKELETAL     │
          │   SCULPTURE     │
          └─────────────────┘
           │               │
  ┌────────────────┐  ┌────────────────┐
  │  The sculpture  │  │   Details can   │
  │  hints at the   │  │ provide clues to│
  │  identity of the│  │  investigators. │
  │     victim.     │  └────────────────┘
  └────────────────┘
           │
   ┌──────────────────┐
   │ Someone recognizes│
   │  the likeness and │
   │  has information  │
   │  about the victim.│
   └──────────────────┘
```

anthropology
(ăn'thrə-pŏl'ə-jē) *n.* the science or study of human beings, including their physical characteristics and cultures

G MONITOR

As you read, stop to **clarify:** why does Dr. Charney call facial reconstruction "a last resort at identification"?

Skeletal SCULPTURES

Dr. Michael Charney is an expert in forensic[1] **anthropology.** His expertise has enabled him to take a few pieces of a skeleton found in Missouri and compile a portrait of a five-foot, 120-pound Asian woman in her mid-twenties. Still, that isn't enough to identify her.

10 The dead woman's "face" needs to be brought back to life.

Reconstructing the likeness of a person in clay, using the skull as a guide, is a last resort at identification, Dr. Charney says. It gives police a new lead to follow, a visual clue that can be photographed and displayed in the media.

Facial reconstruction is not
20 an identifying tool, he warns. The goal is to trigger someone to recognize the model and to identify the person through scientific means.

"All that's needed is a general recognition that it looks like so-and-so," he says. **G**

Before re-creating a face, Dr. Charney and forensic sculptor
30 Nita Bitner search the skull for signs of disease, injury, and structural defects.

"We look for things that shouldn't be there," Bitner says. "Sometimes we find broken noses, cuts, or dentures." These

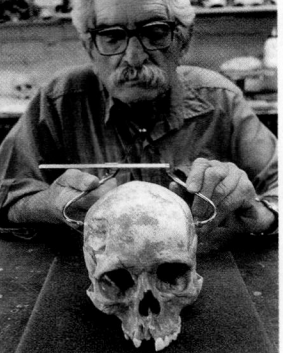

Dr. Michael Charney measures a skull with spreading calipers.

affect the face's appearance and aid in the identification process. If the nose bone is curved to one
40 side, for example, it's important to show it in the face because it's a distinguishing feature.

"We have to be careful, however, not to include anything that happened at the time of death," Bitner notes, "because it wouldn't be recognizable to others."

Age also influences how a face is built. Wrinkled skin, which
50 might help illustrate an older person, is often incorporated into a sculpture for accuracy.

After studying the Missouri woman's skull, Bitner makes a latex mold and pours a plaster cast. Now she's ready to sculpt the face.

1 Targeted Passage

1. **forensic:** having to do with applying scientific methods to crime investigation.

DIFFERENTIATED INSTRUCTION

FOR LESS–PROFICIENT READERS

1 Targeted Passage [Lines 43–56]

This passage identifies challenges in the work of Nita Bitner, the forensic sculptor.

- How does Bitner prepare to sculpt a face? Why do you think that she doesn't use the victim's actual skull?

- Why is it important for her to include wrinkles on some sculptures?

- What kinds of details would she want to avoid? Why?

FOR ADVANCED LEARNERS/PRE–AP

Synthesize Information Ask students to suppose that they are considering a career as a forensic sculptor. Have them supplement information from this article with original research to write an interview with a forensic sculptor. Questions and answers should focus on the training needed for and tasks involved in the job. Students may print out their interviews for classmates to read or perform them with a partner for the class.

1. Forensic sculptor Nita Bitner begins a facial restoration by cutting round rubber pegs into different lengths. The pegs, called landmarks, represent the thickness of the soft tissue (muscle, fat, and skin) at different points on the face. These tissue depths, which vary for men and women of varying ages, were first calculated from corpses by nineteenth-century scientists and later updated. **H**

2. She then glues the rubber pegs to the skull cast.

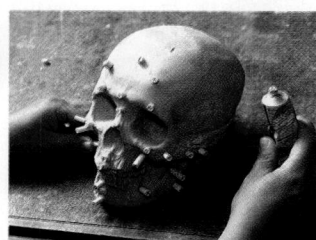

3. Bitner "connects the dots" with strips of modeling clay. When attaching the strips of clay, she begins at the forehead and works her way down to the cheekbones, nasal area, chin, and mouth.

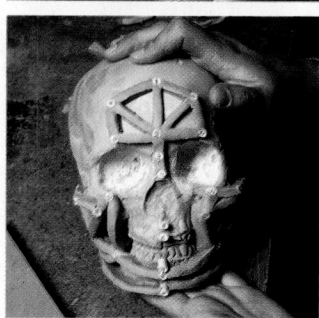

4. Once the dots are connected, Bitner fills in the spaces with clay and fleshes out the face. Now the prominent cheekbones of the Missouri woman become strikingly clear. Suddenly her broad face and delicate nose emerge.

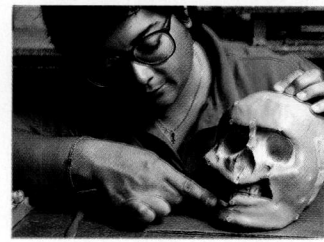

H TAKE NOTES
As you read the numbered items in this section, record the steps of the process in your notes. For each step, include only the **details** that are most important.

SKELETAL SCULPTURES **541**

READING STRATEGY

H TAKE NOTES

Possible answer: Step 1—Bitner cuts rubber pegs as landmarks. *Step 2*—She glues the pegs to the skull cast. *Step 3*—She uses clay strips to connect the pegs. *Step 4*—She fills in the gaps. *Step 5*—She smooths the clay. *Step 6*—She sets the eyes. *Step 7*—She sculpts eyelids. *Step 8*—She sculpts the sides of the nose. *Step 9*—She measures the width of the nose. *Step 10*—She molds the upper lip. *Step 11*—She adds a wig and scarf. *Step 12*—The finished sculpture is photographed.

Steps 1–4
REINFORCE *KEY IDEA:* INVESTIGATE

Discuss How does Bitner use forensic investigation to help her reconstruct a victim's face? *Possible answer: Bitner combines what she knows about the subject's race, gender, and approximate age with calculations of tissue depth, which differ for men and women of varying ages. Based upon this information, she uses rubber pegs and modeling clay to flesh out a likeness of the deceased person.*

FOR ENGLISH LEARNERS

Comprehension: Transitions Point out that the word *step* indicates a sequence of details. Then help students pick out these other words in the steps that help clarify the sequence: *begins* (Step 1); *then* (Step 2); *When* (Step 3); *Once, Now* (Step 4); *As* (Step 5); *Next* (Step 7); *then* (Step 8); *Now* (Step 10); *will, will then* (Step 11); *now* (Step 12).

Steps 1–12
DISCUSSION PROMPTS

Use these prompts to help students grasp the difficulty of facial reconstruction:

Connect Think about the distinguishing features of your face. How would an acquaintance describe you? *Students should identify characteristics of their appearance that are unique.*

Analyze What are some possible problems with facial reconstruction? *Possible answer: The sculptor might not know about such distinguishing features as scars, tattoos, or hairstyles. Furthermore, if the sculptor does not have enough information about the victim, the reconstruction might present the victim as looking too old or too young.*

Evaluate What qualities must sculptor Nita Bitner have in order to be good at her work? How can you tell? *Possible answer: Bitner must be meticulous about details, for she has to notice very small irregularities on each skull. She must be logical, for she is required to use clues to interpret facts. She must be artistic, for she needs to visualize tissues and shapes that are not present.*

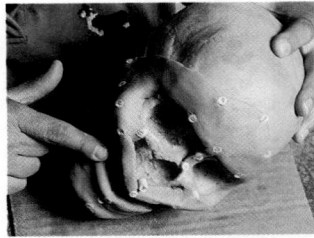

5. As Bitner smooths the clay with her thumb and fingers, the face develops like a photograph.

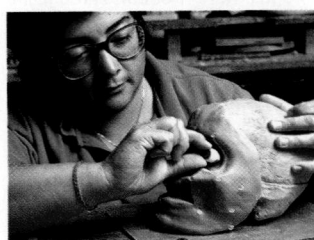

6. Bitner sets the plastic brown eyes in their sockets.

7. Next come the eyelids.

8. Bitner then sculpts the sides of the nose.

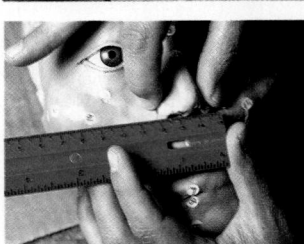

9. She measures the nose with a ruler to ensure it is the correct width.

DIFFERENTIATED INSTRUCTION

FOR LESS–PROFICIENT READERS

Use Visuals Discuss how the photographs clarify details or give additional details about the process of facial reconstruction. For example, the photographs show how the face is sculpted by hand rather than by machine, how the sculptor uses specialized tools to create details, and how precise measurements are important to completing the sculpture.

10. Now it's time to mold the upper lip.

11. The face is nearly complete. Because the Missouri woman is **presumed** to be Asian, Bitner will add a black wig. She will then add a scarf for a finishing touch.

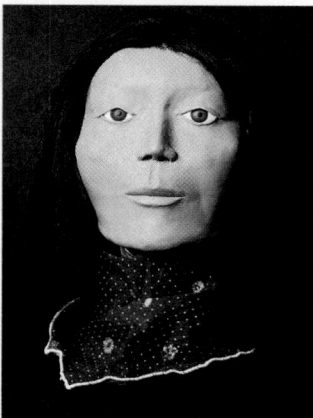

12. The model is now ready to be photographed and publicized in the media so that millions of amateur detectives can help solve the riddle of her identity. ❶

❷ Targeted Passage

presumed (prĭ-zōōmd′) *adj.* thought to be true **presume** *v.*

❶ TEXT FEATURES
Review the **photographs** illustrating the process. Which step do you think is the most critical for transforming a skull into a recognizable human face? Explain your answer.

ELEMENTS OF NONFICTION

❶ TEXT FEATURES

***Possible answers:** Step 4 is important because it is fundamental—the basic fleshing out of the face. Step 7, the creation of eyelids, would be especially important for an Asian face. The nose (Step 8) and the lips (Step 10) are also important because the unique characteristics of these features would be crucial to identifying a face.*

Extend the Discussion Even with a very skilled sculptor, the finished face might look different from the face of the victim. Do you think that facial reconstruction could hinder the investigation of a crime? Explain.

SELECTION WRAP–UP

SYNTHESIZE Ask students to make a statement about the contributions of forensic science in providing answers to the questions surrounding the deaths of mysterious victims.

⭐ **CRITIQUE** Have students explain whether they found each article interesting. Then ask them to rate the effectiveness of the two articles together.

FOR LESS–PROFICIENT READERS

❷ Targeted Passage [Step 12]

This passage explains how the sculpture will be used after it is completed.

- What will happen to the sculpture now?
- How will the media use the photograph of the sculpture?
- Who will be interested in viewing the sculpture? Which viewers are most likely to interest police, and why?

FOR ADVANCED LEARNERS/PRE–AP

Compare and Contrast [small-group option] Ask students whether a forensic sculptor is primarily an artist or a scientist and how the skills are different. Have students list the aspects of the job that require one or both sets of skills. Invite students to share their responses; then come to a class consensus.

Practice and Apply

After Reading

For additional support of post-reading questions, use these copy masters:

R RESOURCE MANAGER—Copy Masters

Reading Check p. 83 (to check understanding of the selections)

Text Features p. 75 (for practice of elements of nonfiction standards focus)

Question Support p. 85 (After Reading questions adapted for English learners and less-proficient readers)

For additional questions, see page 69.

ANSWERS

Comprehension

1. *The Iceman was found in the Ötztal Alps. "Ötzi" is short for "Ötztal."*

2. *Reinhard theorizes that the Iceman was killed as part of a ritual sacrifice.*

3. *Facial reconstruction is the re-creation of a face from a skull cast. Detectives use it to help identify skeletal remains.*

Critical Analysis

Possible answers:

4. ■ **STANDARDS FOCUS** *Take Notes*
Paragraphs should include key points from the 12 steps.

5. *Disagreement is helpful because it encourages deeper inquiry. Without disagreement, for instance, Reinhard might have accepted the original theory about the Iceman's death and might never have discovered the arrowhead in the mummy's back.*

6. ● **STANDARDS FOCUS** *Text Features*
The reader would have gotten an accurate idea about how and where the mummy was found and about the discovery of the arrowhead. The reader would have missed details about Reinhard's theory.

7. *X-ray imaging: shows the arrowhead lodged in the Iceman's back; **The analysis of where the body was found:** suggests that the Iceman was not seeking shelter from a storm; **Evaluating the artifacts:** helps date the Iceman and suggests that his death had a religious significance. Students should provide reasonable support for their choices of most effective method.*

After Reading

Comprehension

1. **Recall** Why is the Iceman nicknamed Ötzi?

2. **Summarize** What is Johan Reinhard's theory about how the Iceman died?

3. **Clarify** What is facial reconstruction, and for what is it used?

Critical Analysis

4. **Summarize Notes** Review the notes you took as you read "Skeletal Sculptures." Using your notes, write one or two paragraphs summarizing the process of facial reconstruction.

5. **Draw Conclusions** In your opinion, is disagreement between scientists helpful or harmful to further investigation? Use evidence from "Who Killed the Iceman?" to support your conclusion.

6. **Analyze Text Features** Think about the information communicated by the text features in "Who Killed the Iceman?" If you had simply scanned the title, subheads, and graphic aids, would you have had an accurate idea of what the article was about? What information would you have missed? Explain.

7. **Evaluate** Examine the methods of **investigation** listed in the chart shown. Complete the chart, noting the information each method provided to the scientists studying the Iceman. In your opinion, which method yielded the most crucial information? Cite details to support your answer.

Method of Investigation	Information Provided
X-rays of Ötzi's shoulder	
Analysis of where the body was found	
Evaluation of artifacts found with the Iceman's body	

Reading-Writing Connection

WRITING PROMPT	SELF-CHECK
Short Response: Compare and Contrast How do Reinhard's theories about the mummy's death differ from those of the other scientists mentioned in "Who Killed the Iceman?" Using your notes and examples from the text, write **one or two paragraphs** comparing and contrasting Reinhard's theories with the other scientists' beliefs.	*A successful comparison will . . .* <ul><li>clearly explain each of the differing theories</li><li>offer specific details from the text to support your comparison</li></ul>

Reading-Writing Connection

WRITING PROMPT

- Provide students with a Venn Diagram. Encourage them to reread the article, noting Reinhard's theories in one circle and other scientific theories in the other circle. Where the circles overlap, students should note any similarities between the two camps.

- Suggest that students organize their essays by explaining all the similarities first and the differences next.

 BEST PRACTICES TOOLKIT—Transparency
Venn Diagram p. A26

For ideas for writing, see

i Writing Center at **ClassZone.com**

Vocabulary in Context

VOCABULARY PRACTICE

Decide whether these statements are true or false.

WORD LIST
anthropology
artifact
compile
presumed
refute

1. A wildflower originally identified centuries ago is an ancient **artifact.**

2. If I **refute** an argument, I make a convincing case against it.

3. To write a good report, you should **compile** information from several sources.

4. A person interested in animal behavior might want to study **anthropology.**

5. Someone **presumed** to be at fault has already been proved wrong.

VOCABULARY IN WRITING

Imagine you were the first scientist to reach the scene when the Iceman was discovered. Write four sentences you might have used if you had had to file a report about the discovery. Use at least three vocabulary words in your sentences.

> **EXAMPLE SENTENCE**
>
> The Iceman's copper axe is an **artifact** that will help me determine just how old this mummy is.

VOCABULARY STRATEGY: SPECIALIZED FIELDS, OR "OLOGIES"

The words for many fields of study, such as *anthropology,* end with the Greek suffix *-ology,* meaning "study of." The word for the person doing the studying often ends in *-ologist,* as in *anthropologist.* Many of these words, such as *toxicology* (the study of poisons), are recognizable because they have a familiar root. Others, like *penology* (the study of prisons), have a Greek or Latin root you may have to learn.

PRACTICE Choose the word in parentheses that fits each sentence. Use context clues, your knowledge of roots, or, if necessary, a dictionary.

1. Because his grandfather had Alzheimer's disease, Jeremy decided to specialize in (gerontology, geology).

2. A (cosmetologist, criminologist) was brought in to examine the murder scene.

3. If you study (ornithology, psychology), you will become an expert on birds.

4. Please have your hearing checked by an (audiologist, ecologist).

5. Ed, an amateur (cytologist, herpetologist), viewed lizards, snakes, and turtles near the beach.

6. Learning a little about (meteorology, oncology) helped me anticipate thunderstorms.

VOCABULARY PRACTICE
For more practice, go to the **Vocabulary Center** at ClassZone.com.

WHO KILLED THE ICEMAN? / SKELETAL SCULPTURES **545**

ANSWERS

Vocabulary in Context
VOCABULARY PRACTICE

1. *false*	4. *false*
2. *true*	5. *false*
3. *true*	

R RESOURCE MANAGER—Copy Master
Vocabulary Practice p. 80

VOCABULARY IN WRITING

Point out that a scientist would make detailed observations and that students' sentences should do the same. For example, a scientist would observe details about the exact time and location of the discovery, the weather, and the condition of the body.

VOCABULARY STRATEGY: SPECIALIZED FIELDS OR "OLOGIES" (also an EL language objective)

After students have read the paragraph, help them use their knowledge of word parts and context clues to complete the **PRACTICE** activity. Urge students to use a dictionary to identify any unfamiliar fields of study.

Possible answers:

1. *gerontology*	4. *audiologist*
2 *criminologist*	5. *herpetologist*
3. *ornithology*	6. *meteorology*

R RESOURCE MANAGER—Copy Master
Vocabulary Strategy p. 81

ℹ Vocabulary Center at **ClassZone.com**
Additional Vocabulary Activities

Assess and Reteach

Assess

R RESOURCE MANAGER—Copy Masters
Selection Test A pp. 87–88
Selection Test B/C pp. 89–90

⊘ Test Generator CD

Reteach

S STANDARDS LESSON FILE
Informational Texts Lesson 1: Text Features
Vocabulary Lesson 10: Word Families and Derivatives

DIFFERENTIATED INSTRUCTION

FOR ENGLISH LEARNERS

Vocabulary: Cognates Create a Two-Column Chart on the board. Help students list more fields of study in the first column and titles of people who study them in English in the second column. In both columns, allow students to list the home-language equivalents of each field.

💼 BEST PRACTICES TOOLKIT—Transparency
Two-Column Chart p. A25

FOR ADVANCED LEARNERS/PRE–AP

Analyze Terminology Challenge students to locate similar-seeming words that end with *-ology,* along with a definition for each word, as in *ethnology* (the study of race)/*ethology* (the study of animal behavior) and *nephology* (the study of clouds)/*nephrology* (the study of kidneys). Have students exchange lists and try to match each word with its definition.

545

OBJECTIVES

Elements of Nonfiction
- explore the key idea of a **refugee**
- identify and analyze author's purpose
- identify characteristics of a magazine article
- read a magazine article

Reading
- interpret graphic aids

Vocabulary
- build vocabulary for reading and writing
- use knowledge of the Latin root *fract* to help unlock meaning *(also an EL language objective)*

Grammar and Writing
- use writing to analyze literature

SUMMARY

"The Lost Boys" describes the plight of orphaned African boys who fled Sudan during a hostile civil war. Sara Corbett's article presents the challenges faced by the roughly 10,000 survivors. It then focuses on the three Dut brothers, refugees who have been resettled in Fargo, North Dakota, and who are trying to adjust to their new life.

How far would you go to find FREEDOM?

Introduce the **KEY IDEA** by asking the question and having students read the paragraph. Make sure that students understand the term *refugee* before they begin the **DISCUSS** activity. As they read the article, urge students to connect their responses to the situation faced by the Sudanese boys.

Selection Resources

The Lost Boys

Magazine Article by Sara Corbett

How far would you go to find FREEDOM?

KEY IDEA It's impossible for most of us to imagine what it would be like to be a **refugee**—someone who faces terrible danger in his or her home country and flees in search of freedom and protection. What would you do if you were imprisoned for your religious or political beliefs or harassed about the color of your skin? What would it take to make you leave your home and seek refuge in a strange, new place?

DISCUSS With a partner, discuss what it might be like to be forced to leave your home, your friends, your family, and everything familiar to you. Describe the one thing you would take with you if you had to leave quickly, and explain what you think you would miss most.

546

R RESOURCE MANAGER UNIT 5

Plan and Teach pp. 91–98

Literary Analysis
Summary pp. 99†*, 100‡*
Author's Purpose pp. 101, 102†*
Question Support p. 111*

Reading
Interpret Graphic Aids
pp. 103, 104†*
Reading Check p. 109

Vocabulary
Study p. 105*
Practice p. 106
Strategy p. 107

Assessment
Selection Tests A, B/C pp. 113*, 115*
Test Generator CD

BEST PRACTICES TOOLKIT

Differentiated Instruction
pp. 31–38*

Scaffolding Instruction
pp. 43–46*

Graphic Organizers/Strategies
Word Questioning • Two-Column Chart

Technology
Literature and Vocabulary Centers at **ClassZone.com**
WriteSmart CD

Reading Support
Audio Anthology CD*

InterActive
READER & WRITER
- Integrated Test Practice
- Related Nonfiction Readings
McDougal Littell LITERATURE

---

* Resources for Differentiation   † Also in Spanish   ‡ In Haitian Creole and Vietnamese

● ELEMENTS OF NONFICTION: AUTHOR'S PURPOSE

An **author's purpose** is what he or she hopes to achieve by writing a particular work. An author might write for any of several purposes:

- to persuade
- to inform or explain
- to entertain
- to express thoughts and feelings

In fact, an author may have more than one purpose for writing a given piece. For example, an author could be attempting to persuade you to register to vote while also expressing feelings about democracy. Understanding the purpose of a text is essential to getting the most out of what you read. As you read "The Lost Boys," use a chart to identify the purpose of key passages in the text.

Passage	Purpose
"According to U.S. State Department estimates, some 17,000 boys were separated from their families...." (lines 27–29)	inform

■ READING SKILL: INTERPRET GRAPHIC AIDS

Magazine articles like "The Lost Boys" often include **graphic aids**—such as charts, maps, and photographs—that present key information.

- As you read, examine the **photographs** in this article. Consider the subjects' body language and facial expressions. What do they tell you about the subjects' feelings or experiences?
- As you study the **map** in this article, note details about Sudan. Where is this country? What features appear on the map? What else does the map communicate?

Review: **Connect**

▲ VOCABULARY IN CONTEXT

The words listed here are crucial to understanding the Lost Boys' journey to freedom. Place each word in the column where it belongs. Define each word you know.

WORD LIST	boon	fractious	posse
	exodus	marauding	subsist

Know Well	Think I Know	Don't Know

Background

A Devastating Division
The young refugees profiled in this article are from Sudan, the largest country in Africa. Sudan has been torn apart by Africa's longest-running civil war. Their country devastated by war and ravaged by religious conflicts, over 4 million Sudanese people have been driven from their homes, 2 million have died, and thousands more have been forced into slavery. Since 1955, Sudan's Islamic fundamentalist government has fought against groups of rebels from southern Sudan. The government is intent on imposing Islamic law on the people of Sudan, while the southern Sudanese groups demand religious freedom and economic power. Peace talks aimed at ending the war have produced glimmers of hope, and on May 26, 2004, a power-sharing agreement was signed by both sides. However, further crisis broke out in western Sudan shortly thereafter, plunging the country back into chaos and creating more orphans and refugees.

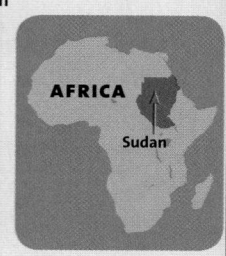

AFRICA

Sudan

 BUILDING BACKGROUND
To learn more about the Lost Boys of Sudan, visit the **Literature Center** at **ClassZone.com.**

THE LOST BOYS **547**

Teach

STANDARDS FOCUS

ELEMENTS OF NONFICTION

● AUTHOR'S PURPOSE

Reinforce the concept by asking students to explain the author's purpose or purposes for each of these kinds of writing: a newspaper editorial, a humorous short story, an encyclopedia article, a letter to the editor. *Possible answers: editorial— persuade and inform; story—entertain; article—inform; letter—express thoughts, inform, persuade*

CHECK UNDERSTANDING Ask students to identify the author's purpose or purposes in other selections that they have read as a class.

 RESOURCE MANAGER—Copy Master
Author's Purpose p. 101 (for student use while reading the selection)

READING SKILL

■ INTERPRET GRAPHIC AIDS

Have students preview "The Lost Boys" by answering the questions about the graphic aids used in the article. Call on volunteers to explain why they might choose a chart, map, or photograph to illustrate a piece of writing and help the writing achieve its purpose.

CHECK UNDERSTANDING Have students identify examples of graphic aids in one of their other textbooks and explain how each one facilitates understanding.

VOCABULARY SKILL

▲ VOCABULARY IN CONTEXT

DIAGNOSE WORD KNOWLEDGE To determine preteaching needs, have all students complete **Vocabulary in Context.** Check students' definitions against those on the selection pages: *boon* (p. 552), *exodus* (p. 550), *fractious* (p. 550), *marauding* (p. 550), *posse* (p. 550), *subsisting* (p. 551).

PRETEACH VOCABULARY Use the Vocabulary Study copy master to help students predict meanings for each boldfaced word in the copy master.

1. Read the first item aloud, emphasizing *boon*.
2. Point out the words *drink* and *thirsty*. Elicit possible meanings for *boon,* such as "an advantage that meets a need."
3. Repeat the procedure for the other items.

 RESOURCE MANAGER—Copy Master
Vocabulary Study p. 105

For general guidelines on differentiating vocabulary instruction and for alternative vocabulary activities for students not needing vocabulary preteaching, see

 BEST PRACTICES TOOLKIT
Scaffolding Vocabulary Instruction pp. 43–46
 Vocabulary Center at **ClassZone.com**

ANALYZE VISUALS

Activity After students have read the article, ask them to suggest other photographs that might have appeared here. **Possible answers:** *a photograph of the brothers in Africa, boarding the airplane, or walking through the airport in Minneapolis*

READING SKILL

Ⓐ GRAPHIC AIDS

Possible answer: *Their facial expressions and body language suggest that the brothers feel uneasy in their new surroundings.*

ELEMENTS OF NONFICTION

Ⓑ AUTHOR'S PURPOSE

Possible answer: *Beginning with an anecdote helps readers better perceive the subject matter in human terms—that is, to see Sudan's victims as real people.*

If students need help . . . Relate the question to a topic from students' social studies curriculum. For example, discuss how reading a timeline of events that led to the American Revolution is different from reading stories about the men and women who were part of the move to independence. Which kind of reading would students prefer, and why? *Answers will vary, but students should recognize that real-life stories encourage a personal connection.*

Extend the Discussion Does beginning the article with an anecdote help Sara Corbett, the writer, achieve her purpose? Explain.

The Lost Boys

SARA CORBETT

THESE YOUNG AFRICAN REFUGEES SURVIVED LIONS, CROCODILES, AND STARVATION. NOW THEY'RE STARTING LIFE OVER IN AMERICA.

One evening in late January, Peter Dut, 21, leads his two teenage brothers through the brightly lit corridors of the Minneapolis airport, trying to mask his confusion. Two days earlier, the brothers, refugees from Africa, had encountered their first light switch and their first set of stairs. An aid worker in Nairobi[1] had demonstrated the flush toilet to them—also the seat belt, the shoelace, the fork. And now they find themselves alone in Minneapolis, three bone-thin African boys confronted by a swirling river of white faces and rolling suitcases.

Finally, a traveling businessman recognizes their uncertainty. "Where are you flying to?" he asks kindly, and the eldest brother tells him in halting,
10 bookish English. A few days earlier, they left a small mud hut in a blistering-hot Kenyan refugee camp, where they had lived as orphans for nine years after walking for hundreds of miles across Sudan.[2] They are now headed to a new home in the U.S.A. "Where?" the man asks in disbelief when Peter Dut says the city's name. "Fargo? North Dakota? You gotta be kidding me. It's too cold there. You'll never survive it!"

And then he laughs. Peter Dut has no idea why. Ⓑ

In the meantime, the temperature in Fargo has dropped to 15 below. The boys tell me that, until now, all they have ever known about cold is what they felt grasping a bottle of frozen water. An aid worker handed it to them one day
20 during a "cultural orientation" session at the Kakuma[3] Refugee Camp, a place where the temperature hovers around 100 degrees.

Peter Dut and his two brothers belong to an unusual group of refugees referred to by aid organizations as the Lost Boys of Sudan, a group of roughly 10,000 boys who arrived in Kenya in 1992 seeking refuge from their country's

---

1. **Nairobi** (nī-rō′bē): the capital city of Kenya, a country in Africa.
2. **Sudan:** a country in eastern Africa northwest of Kenya.
3. **Kakuma** (kə-kōō′mä).

548 UNIT 5: AUTHOR'S PURPOSE

Ⓐ GRAPHIC AIDS
This **photograph** was taken shortly after the Dut brothers arrived in North Dakota. What do their facial expressions and body language suggest about their comfort level in their new surroundings?

❶ Targeted Passage

Ⓑ AUTHOR'S PURPOSE
The writer begins this article with an **anecdote** instead of immediately presenting statistics about Sudan. How does this choice affect your perception of the subject matter?

DIFFERENTIATED INSTRUCTION

FOR ALL STUDENTS

Anchor Activity Provide independent learning opportunities for students to do research on the Lost Boys and how their lives have changed since arriving in the United States. When they have completed their research, ask them to share their results with the class. For further details, see

Ⓡ RESOURCE MANAGER
Ideas for Extension pp. 96–97

FOR LESS–PROFICIENT READERS

In combination with the *Audio Anthology CD,* use one or more Targeted Passages (pp. 548, 550, 553) to ensure that students focus on key events, concepts, and skills. Targeted Passages are also good for English learners.

❶ Targeted Passage [Lines 1–16]

This passage introduces the Dut brothers. It addresses the challenges that they have faced in the past and are facing now.

 From where have the Dut brothers come? Where are they going?

 What changes in climate will the brothers experience?

 What else about life in the United States do you know will be new to them?

BACKGROUND

Sudan's People The great majority of the Sudanese people are Muslims. There is a Christian minority, but many Sudanese also practice a variety of traditional animist religions. These divisions occur to a large extent along geographic lines, with most of northern Sudan made up of Muslims and dominated by Islamic culture, while most of southern Sudan consists of Christians and followers of indigenous religions.

The Dinka Many of the Lost Boys were from the Dinka tribe. These native people of Sudan make up approximately 12 percent of the total population. The Dinka, who have lived in the region of the White Nile for some ten centuries, derive their living mainly from raising cattle, sheep, and goats. They are generally tall, have a thin build, and are known for their courage.

Lines 8–16
REINFORCE *KEY IDEA:* REFUGEE

Discuss How well does the businessman understand what it means to be a **refugee?** How can you tell? *Possible answer: He probably has little true understanding of the boys' life as refugees. Anything that he may have grasped about their circumstances from what Peter tells him seems to be lost in his amusement at their destination. It also is unlikely that the businessman has ever had to flee danger in his home country.*

FOR ENGLISH LEARNERS

Key Academic Vocabulary Use Word Questioning to teach these words: *survive* (line 15), *cultural* (line 20), *displaced* (line 68), *transition* (line 102), *coordinates* (line 102), *identity* (line 110).

BEST PRACTICES TOOLKIT—Transparency
Word Questioning p. E9

Prereading For prereading instruction for English learners, see

BEST PRACTICES TOOLKIT
Scaffolding Reading Instruction pp. 43–46

FOR ADVANCED LEARNERS/PRE–AP

Pre-AP Exercises in the bottom channel provide additional challenge for students. Use these suggestions for small groups or individuals.

ADDITIONAL GUIDELINES

For more help with differentiation and tips for classroom management, see

BEST PRACTICES TOOLKIT
Differentiated Instruction pp. 31–38

fractious civil war. The fighting pits a northern Islamic government against rebels in the south who practice Christianity and tribal religions.

The Lost Boys were named after Peter Pan's **posse** of orphans. According to U.S. State Department estimates, some 17,000 boys were separated from their families and fled southern Sudan in an **exodus** of biblical proportions after
30 fighting intensified in 1987. They arrived in throngs, homeless and parentless, having trekked about 1,000 miles from Sudan to Ethiopia, back to Sudan, and finally to Kenya. The majority of the boys belonged to the Dinka or Nuer tribes, and most were between the ages of 8 and 18. (Most of the boys don't know for sure how old they are; aid workers assigned them approximate ages after they arrived in 1992.)

② Targeted Passage

Along the way, the boys endured attacks from the northern army and **marauding** bandits, as well as lions who preyed on the slowest and weakest among them. Many died from starvation or thirst. Others drowned or were eaten by crocodiles as they tried to cross a swollen Ethiopian river. By the time
40 the Lost Boys reached the Kakuma Refugee Camp, their numbers had been cut nearly in half.

THE LOST BOYS' PERILOUS JOURNEY TO FREEDOM

SUDAN
AFRICA
Sudan
To U.S.
ETHIOPIA
CENTRAL AFRICAN REPUBLIC
250 km
250 miles
DEMOCRATIC REPUBLIC OF CONGO
UGANDA
Kakuma Refugee Camp
KENYA

C GRAPHIC AIDS
List two details included on the **map** that are not provided in the article. What do you think is the most important piece of information communicated by this map?

READING SKILL

C GRAPHIC AIDS

Possible answer: The map shows that Ethiopia is east of Sudan. It shows that Sudan also borders the Central African Republic, the Democratic Republic of Congo, Uganda, and Kenya. The most important information may be the locations of Sudan, Ethiopia, and Kenya because this information enables readers to better visualize the Lost Boys' trek.

Lines 27–41
DISCUSSION PROMPTS

Use these prompts to help students grasp the gravity of the refugees' circumstances:

Connect Have you or someone you know ever journeyed to a new place without a family member? What feelings and challenges were involved? *Challenges will vary; feelings may include excitement and/or fear.*

Analyze What challenges did the boys face on their journey, and what conclusion can you draw about the impact of such an experience on the survivors? *Possible answer: Challenges, such as lack of food and water, bandits, wild animals, risk of drowning, and witnessing so much death would make the experience traumatic.*

Evaluate These refugees were named "the Lost Boys" after the orphans in *Peter Pan*. Is this a fitting name? Why or why not? *Possible answers: Yes—because the refugees were orphans with nowhere to go. No—because their situation was too horrendous to be compared to a children's tale.*

DIFFERENTIATED INSTRUCTION

FOR LESS–PROFICIENT READERS

② Targeted Passage [Lines 27–35]

This passage introduces the Lost Boys and the extremity of their situation.

- Why have the Lost Boys left Sudan?
- What does the writer mean when she calls their journey "an exodus of biblical proportions"?
- What was the boys' condition when they arrived in Kenya?

FOR ENGLISH LEARNERS

Vocabulary: Suffixes Discuss the meaning of the suffixes in these words.

home*less* (line 30)   open*er* (line 60)

norma*l* (line 49)   govern*ment* (line 85)

Have small groups of students scan the article to locate other words with these suffixes. Then ask them to find three additional words for each of the prefixes from other sources. Compile a master list from the groups' findings.

In 1992, roughly 10,000 boys from Sudan poured into a refugee camp in Kenya.

Now, after nine years of **subsisting** on rationed corn mush and lentils and living largely ungoverned by adults, the Lost Boys of Sudan are coming to America. In 1999, the United Nations High Commissioner for Refugees, which handles refugee cases around the world, and the U.S. government agreed to send 3,600 of the boys to the U.S.—since going back to Sudan was out of the question. About 500 of the Lost Boys still under the age of 18 will be living in apartments or foster homes across the U.S. by the end of this year. The boys will start school at a grade level normal for their age, thanks to a
50 tough English-language program at their refugee camp. The remaining 3,100 Lost Boys will be resettled as adults. After five years, each boy will be eligible for citizenship, provided he has turned 21.

subsist (səb-sĭst′) v. to support oneself at a minimal level

NIGHTTIME IN AMERICA?
On the night that I stand waiting for Peter Dut and his brothers to land in Fargo, tendrils of snow are snaking across the tarmac. The three boys file through the gate without money or coats or luggage beyond their small backpacks. The younger brothers, Maduk, 17, and Riak, 15, appear petrified. As a social worker passes out coats, Peter Dut studies the black night through the airport window. "Excuse me," he says worriedly. "Can you tell me, please, is it now night or day?"
60 This is a stove burner. This is a can opener. This is a brush for your teeth. The new things come in a tumble. The brothers' home is a sparsely furnished, two-bedroom apartment in a complex on Fargo's south side. Rent is $445 a month. It has been stocked with donations from area churches and businesses: toothpaste, bread, beans, bananas.

Lines 42–52
REINFORCE *KEY IDEA:* REFUGEE
Discuss How might the Lost Boys' experience of being **refugees** in the United States differ from their experiences in the Kakuma Refugee Camp? *Possible answer: The settlement process may separate friends and even families. After "living largely ungoverned by adults" (line 43), those under the age of 18 will experience supervision in foster homes (line 48) and schools (line 49). Hopefully, their diet will be more plentiful than the rationed corn mush and lentils (line 42) they lived on before.*

ANALYZE VISUALS

Activity How does the photograph help you understand the experience of the Lost Boys as they arrived in the Kakuma Refugee Camp? *Possible answer: The photograph shows that the Lost Boys arrived by the thousands. Many are quite young and their arms are thin, suggesting that they have gone for months without proper nourishment. The looks on their faces and the position of their bodies suggest both fear and hope. Their arms are raised, as if in surrender, but they are moving forward, as if in anticipation of safety and the hope of a new life.*

FOR ENGLISH LEARNERS
Vocabulary: Word Associations Discuss these terms, made of words that often appear together: *aid worker* (line 4); *flush toilet* (line 5); *halting . . . English* (lines 9–10); *temperature hovers around _____ degrees* (line 21); *aid organizations* (line 23); *seeking refuge* (line 24); *eligible for citizenship* (lines 51–52); *sparsely furnished* (line 61); *terribly hungry* (line 71).

FOR ADVANCED LEARNERS/PRE–AP
Evaluate Point of View In line 53, Corbett shifts to a first-person point of view. Have students discuss why Corbett does so. Ask whether using a first-person point of view is necessary or desirable in this article, and why or why not.

D AUTHOR'S PURPOSE

Possible answer: *Corbett's main purpose is to inform or explain—specifically, to make clear to the reader just how drastically different the boys' new environment is from the life they have known. For example, the boys are used to "a lifetime of cooking . . . over a fire pit" and "have never opened a box" (lines 73–74).*

If students need help . . . Have students use a Two-Column Chart to analyze the possible purposes for these paragraphs:

Purpose	Evidence
to persuade	<u>None</u>
to entertain	<u>Little</u>: The "opening spree" is entertaining, but there is more to the paragraphs than that.
to inform or explain	<u>Much</u>: Corbett gives many factual details and explains how the Dut brothers did not understand what to do with packaged food.
to express thoughts and feelings	<u>Little</u>: Corbett's realization that she must be a teacher is a thought or feeling, but there is more to the paragraphs than that.

Extend the Discussion How does Sara Corbett hold her readers' attention while presenting this information?

📦 **BEST PRACTICES TOOLKIT—Transparency**
Two-Column Chart p. A25

A caseworker empties a garbage bag full of donated clothing, which looks to have come straight from the closet of an elderly man. I know how lucky the boys are: The State Department estimates that war, famine, and disease in southern Sudan have killed more than 2 million people and displaced another 4 million. Still I cringe to think of the boys showing up for school in these clothes.

70   The next day, when I return to the apartment at noon, the boys have been up since 5 and are terribly hungry. "What about your food?" I ask, gesturing to the bread and bananas and the box of cereal sitting on the counter.

Peter grins sheepishly. I suddenly realize that the boys, in a lifetime of cooking maize and beans over a fire pit, have never opened a box. I am placed in the role of teacher. And so begins an opening spree. We open potato chips. We open a can of beans. We untwist the tie on the bagged loaf of bread. Soon, the boys are seated and eating a hot meal. **D**

LIVING ON LEAVES AND BERRIES

The three brothers have come a long way since they fled their village in Sudan with their parents and three sisters—all of whom were later killed by Sudanese
80   army soldiers. The Lost Boys first survived a 6- to 10-week walk to Ethiopia, often subsisting on leaves and berries and the occasional **boon** of a warthog carcass. Some boys staved off dehydration by drinking their own urine. Many fell behind; some were devoured by lions or trampled by buffalo.

The Lost Boys lived for three years in Ethiopia, in UN-supported camps, before they were forced back into Sudan by a new Ethiopian government no longer sympathetic to their plight. Somehow, more than 10,000 of the boys miraculously trailed into Kenya's UN camps in the summer of 1992—as Sudanese government planes bombed the rear of their procession.

For the Lost Boys, then, a new life in America might easily seem to be the
90   answer to every dream. But the real world has been more complicated than that. Within weeks of arriving, Riak is placed in a local junior high; Maduk starts high school classes; and Peter begins adult-education classes.

REFUGEE BLUES

Five weeks later, Riak listens quietly through a lesson on Elizabethan history at school, all but ignored by white students around him.

Nearby at Fargo South High School, Maduk is frequently alone as well, copying passages from his geography textbook, trying not to look at the short skirts worn by many of the girls.

Peter Dut worries about money. The three brothers say they receive just $107 in food stamps each month and spend most of their $510 monthly cash
100   assistance on rent and utilities.

Resettlement workers say the brothers are just undergoing the normal transition. Scott Burtsfield, who coordinates resettlement efforts in Fargo through Lutheran Social Services, says: "The first three months are always the toughest. It really does get better."

552   UNIT 5: AUTHOR'S PURPOSE

D AUTHOR'S PURPOSE
What is Corbett's purpose in lines 70–77? Explain, citing specific details from the passage.

boon (bōōn) *n.* a benefit; blessing

DIFFERENTIATED INSTRUCTION

FOR ENGLISH LEARNERS

Language: Modifiers Point out compound adjectives with hyphens between two or more words: *6- to 10-week walk* (line 80); *adult-education classes* (line 92); *Nairobi-based relief consultant* (lines 107–108); *18-year-old Lost Boy* (lines 110–111). Ask students to find other hyphenated adjectives in the article. Explain that words ending in *-ly* are not hyphenated, as in *finely woven green tunic* (lines 116–117).

FOR ADVANCED LEARNERS/PRE-AP

Compare and Contrast Presentations Peter Dut is also one of the subjects of *Lost Boys of Sudan* (2003), an award-winning documentary by Megan Mylan and Jon Shenk. If a copy of the film is available from a local library, have a group of students watch it critically. Ask group members to show a clip in class and to compare and contrast Corbett's print article with the film.

Riak Dut, shown here in his school lunch line, eats alone most days.

The Lost Boys can only hope so; they have few other options. A return to southern Sudan could be fatal. "There is nothing left for the Lost Boys to go home to—it's a war zone," says Mary Anne Fitzgerald, a Nairobi-based relief consultant.

Some Sudanese elders have criticized sending boys to the U.S. They worry
110 their children will lose their African identity. One afternoon, an 18-year-old Lost Boy translated a part of a tape an elder had sent along with many boys: "He is saying: 'Don't drink. Don't smoke. Don't kill. Go to school every day, and remember, America is not your home.'" **F**

But if adjustment is hard, the boys also experience consoling moments.

One of these comes on a quiet Friday night last winter. As the boys make a dinner of rice and lentils, Peter changes into an African outfit, a finely woven green tunic, with a skullcap to match, bought with precious food rations at Kakuma.

Just then, the doorbell rings unexpectedly. And out of the cold tumble four
120 Sudanese boys—all of whom have resettled as refugees over the last several years. I watch one, an 18-year-old named Sunday, wrap his arms encouragingly around Peter Dut. "It's a hard life here," Sunday whispers to the older boy, "but it's a free life, too." ◦◦

E GRAPHIC AIDS
What can you **infer** about Riak's experiences at his junior high in North Dakota based on this photograph? Explain your answer.

F CONNECT
Think about what it's like to receive instructions from a parent or other adult. Do you think these taped messages will influence the boys? Explain.

③ Targeted Passage

THE LOST BOYS 553

READING SKILL

E GRAPHIC AIDS
Possible answer: It can be inferred that Riak is having trouble being accepted socially by the other students. As a result, he is isolated.

READING SKILL: Review

F CONNECT
Possible answer: The taped messages may have some influence, especially if the boys' culture encourages the respect of elders. However, the elders are far away. Peer pressure—and the desire for acceptance in a new environment—may be more influential.

SELECTION WRAP-UP

SUMMARIZE Ask students to sum up the many changes mentioned in this article that the Dut brothers faced.

⭐ **CRITIQUE** Have students evaluate the writer's presentation. Did Corbett provide enough information that readers truly could understand the Lost Boys' plight? What questions did she leave unanswered, and why?

FOR LESS–PROFICIENT READERS

③ Targeted Passage [Lines 114–123]

This concluding passage sets a positive tone as Peter Dut considers both his past and his future.

• On the Friday night described, how do Peter's clothing and dinner show that he values his African heritage?

• What does Peter have in common with the visitors who arrive?

• How might Sunday's words help Peter adjust to life in the United States?

FOR ENGLISH LEARNERS

Comprehension: Transitions Discuss the examples of contrast using the conjunction *but* in lines 90, 114, and 122–123. Then point out the idiomatic phrase *all but* in line 94. Explain that *all but* does not show contrast; instead, it is another way of saying *mostly* or *almost.*

Practice and Apply

After Reading

For additional support of post-reading questions, use these copy masters:

 RESOURCE MANAGER—Copy Masters
Reading Check p. 109 (to check understanding of the selection)
Interpret Graphic Aids pp. 103 (for practice of reading skill standards focus)
Question Support p. 111 (After Reading questions adapted for English learners and less-proficient readers)

For additional questions, see page 95.

ANSWERS

Comprehension

1. *The Lost Boys were seeking safety from a devastating civil war in their homeland.*

2. *The boys faced death from the northern army, bandits, and wild animals; from drowning; and from starvation or thirst.*

3. *He told Peter that life in America was difficult but "free." He meant that Peter now could make a life for himself without facing the daily dangers of civil war.*

Critical Analysis

Possible answers:

4. *Regardless of their view, students should support their responses with thoughtful reasons and details from the text.*

5. *Students should base their impressions on textual details and the photographs. Students may describe the brothers as uncertain in their new circumstances but determined to try their best.*

6. ■ **STANDARDS FOCUS** *Interpret Graphic Aids Students should recognize the usefulness of each graphic aid. For example, the map helps them visualize the boys' journey; the photographs emphasize the differences between the boys' lives as wandering refugees and their lives as students in the United States.*

7. ● **STANDARDS FOCUS** *Evaluate Author's Purpose Corbett's primary purpose is to inform and explain. She achieves this purpose by presenting facts and details that teach readers about the plight of the Lost Boys.*

After Reading

Comprehension

1. **Recall** Why did the Lost Boys leave Sudan?

2. **Summarize** What hardships did the boys endure as they fled from their homes in Sudan to the refugee camp in Kenya?

3. **Clarify** How did Peter Dut's friend comfort him at the end of the article?

Critical Analysis

4. **Connect** Think back to the discussion you had about what it might be like to be forced from your home. Did reading about these young **refugees** change your feelings at all? Explain why or why not, citing details from the selection.

5. **Analyze Characterization** How would you describe the Dut brothers? What details caused you to form this impression? Use a spider map like the one shown to record the details—such as the boys' words, or statements about them—that influenced your opinion. Then describe the brothers in one or two sentences.

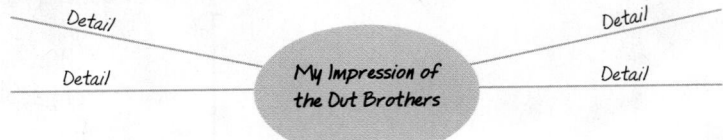

Detail   Detail

My Impression of the Dut Brothers

Detail   Detail

6. **Interpret Graphic Aids** Examine the **map** on page 550 and the **photographs** on pages 549, 551, and 553. Which was most effective at helping you understand the Lost Boys' experiences? Which had the strongest effect on you? Explain, describing the type of information conveyed by each graphic aid.

7. **Evaluate Author's Purpose** Review the chart you filled in as you read. What do you think is Corbett's primary purpose? Which purpose does she achieve most effectively? Explain your answers, citing evidence from the text.

Reading-Writing Connection

WRITING PROMPT	SELF-CHECK
Short Response: Analyze a Problem Of all the struggles these **refugees** faced in America, which do you think must have been the most difficult? Consider the alienation caused by culture shock, financial hardship, loneliness, and the new climate. Write **one or two paragraphs** explaining your view, citing evidence.	*A strong analysis will . . .* • demonstrate a thorough understanding of the boys' ordeal • incorporate relevant and convincing examples from the text to support your opinion

---

Reading-Writing Connection

WRITING PROMPT

• Review lines 1–7, 53–77, and 93–123, which emphasize the boys' alienation.

• Urge students to project themselves into the refugees' situation. Which challenges in their new life would students find most difficult? Why?

• Remind students to use textual evidence to support their views.

For ideas for writing, see

ℹ️ Writing Center at **ClassZone.com**

Vocabulary in Context

VOCABULARY PRACTICE

Choose the word that is not related in meaning to the other words.

1. migration, exodus, consolation, flight
2. boon, building, structure, edifice
3. conspiring, ravaging, plundering, marauding
4. amusement, posse, recreation, entertainment
5. subsist, survive, manage, reconsider
6. irritable, divisive, fractious, connected

WORD LIST

boon

exodus

fractious

marauding

posse

subsisting

VOCABULARY IN WRITING

Imagine you are a journalist writing about the conflict in Sudan. Write headlines that could appear above your story, using each vocabulary word at least once.

> **EXAMPLE HEADLINE**
> *Civil War Causes Exodus as Refugees Flee for Their Lives*

VOCABULARY STRATEGY: THE LATIN ROOT *fract*

The vocabulary word *fractious* contains the Latin root *fract*, which means "to break." This root may also appear as *frag* and *fring*. To understand the meaning of words with these root forms, use context clues and your knowledge of the root.

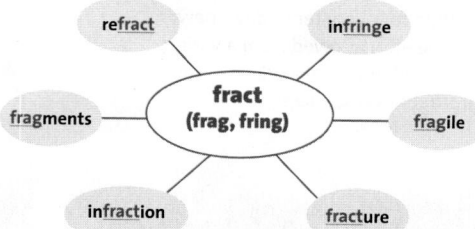

PRACTICE Choose the word from the word web that best completes each sentence. Use context clues to help you or, if necessary, check a dictionary.

1. Don't put _____ objects where children can reach them.
2. _____ of the shattered glass still lay on the floor.
3. The protesters feared that the police would _____ on their rights.
4. Because water will _____ light, a pencil in a glass of water will look broken.
5. Any serious _____ of the rules will be punished by a two-day suspension.
6. He suffered a hairline _____ of his collarbone.

VOCABULARY PRACTICE
For more practice, go to the **Vocabulary Center** at ClassZone.com.

DIFFERENTIATED INSTRUCTION

FOR ENGLISH LEARNERS

Vocabulary: Cognates Have students find all words in the Vocabulary Practice that have a similar form in their home language. You may want to point out that some words starting with *s* in English add an *e* at the beginning of the Spanish word (as in *structure/estructura*). As an alternative, have students think of words in their home languages with the root *fract* (*frag/fring*) and make word webs for each language.

FOR ADVANCED LEARNERS/PRE–AP

Vocabulary in Writing Ask students to use at least four vocabulary words in a paragraph to accompany one of their headlines. Have students compare their paragraphs to see how they used the words.

ANSWERS

Vocabulary in Context

VOCABULARY PRACTICE

1. *consolation*   4. *posse*
2. *boon*   5. *reconsider*
3. *conspiring*   6. *connected*

R RESOURCE MANAGER—Copy Master
Vocabulary Practice p. 106

VOCABULARY IN WRITING

Display several headlines from daily newspapers as a source of ideas. After pointing out the strong nouns and verbs, encourage students to choose precise, powerful nouns and verbs in their headlines.

VOCABULARY STRATEGY: THE LATIN ROOT *fract* (also an EL language objective)

- As you discuss the examples, point out that the root may appear anywhere in a word and that it can have prefixes and suffixes attached to it.
- As you review the **PRACTICE** items, call on volunteers to explain how they chose the correct word for each sentence.

Possible answers:

1. *fragile*   4. *refract*
2. *fragments*   5. *infraction*
3. *infringe*   6. *fracture*

R RESOURCE MANAGER—Copy Master
Vocabulary Strategy p. 107

ⓘ Vocabulary Center at **ClassZone.com**
Additional Vocabulary Activities

Assess and Reteach

Assess

R RESOURCE MANAGER—Copy Masters
Selection Tests A, B/C pp. 113–114, 115–116

⊘ Test Generator CD

Reteach

S STANDARDS LESSON FILE
Reading Lesson 3: Author's Purpose
Informational Texts Lesson 21: Reading Maps
Vocabulary Lesson 10: Word Families and Derivatives

Focus and Motivate

OBJECTIVES

Media Literacy

- explore the key concept of **news**
- view TV and Web news reports to understand how each medium's specific features deliver information and hold viewer attention
- create a script and plan for a video news segment to demonstrate understanding of news story features and structure

SUMMARY

These news reports recount the rescue of nine Pennsylvania coal miners to tell the following basic story. On Day 1 the men are trapped and nearly drown. On Day 2 rescuers drill an airshaft, providing oxygen and warmth to the miners. On Day 3, the rescuers start to drill a rescue tunnel, but their drill bit breaks. The trapped men begin writing farewell notes. That night the broken bit is replaced, and on Day 4 the drill breaks through. The men are soon brought one by one up to safety.

How do you get the NEWS?

To help students explore the **KEY IDEA,** ask them what **news** sources they use to get information about the world around them. For each news source mentioned, ask what techniques the source uses. Discuss how news on different media uses features such as photographs, diagrams, video, interviews, press conferences, and other elements.

BACKGROUND

How did teens learn about the trapped Pennsylvania miners? A 2003 study of more than 65,000 teens aged 13–18 showed the following: 48% ranked TV as their main news source; 9% cited the Internet; and 18% cited newspapers. Teens said newspapers were most accurate, fair, and informative, but TV news was most entertaining and easiest to use.

News Reports

TV Newscast Clip / Web News Report on ⊙ *MediaSmart* DVD

How do you get the NEWS?

KEY IDEA When you need to know the latest **news,** where do you turn? To the nearest TV or radio? To the Internet? To the nearest friend? Some people get their news through brief summaries, while others seek forms that are chock-full of details. The two news formats you'll explore, a segment of a TV newscast and an article from a news Web site, will shed light on the different ways the news media can cover the same event and the advantages and disadvantages of news formats.

Background

Digging for News The news event you'll investigate took place in Somerset, Pennsylvania, in 2002. Nine coal miners were trapped nearly 240 feet underground in a mineshaft that was filling up rapidly with icy water. Mining crews worked frantically to drill a rescue shaft and construct a basket of steel-wire mesh to transport each miner. During four very tense days, new developments about the rescue effort flowed from a variety of news sources, including TV- and radio-network newscasts, newspaper reports, and Internet news services.

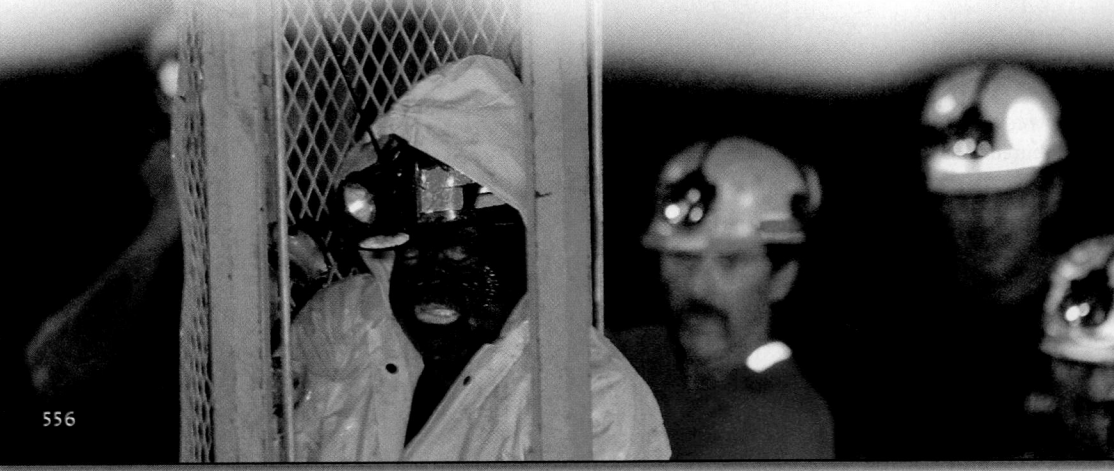

556

Media Study Resources

RESOURCE MANAGER UNIT 5

Plan and Teach pp. 117–120

Media Analysis
Summary pp. 121†*, 122‡*
Viewing Guide p. 123
Close Viewing p. 124
Viewing Activity p. 125
Produce Your Own Media p. 126

STANDARDS LESSON FILE

Media Lesson 11: Comparing News Formats
Media Lesson 20: Producing a Video

ℹ Media Center at **ClassZone.com**

MEDIA VIEWING
⊘ Media*Smart* DVD

---

* Resources for Differentiation   † Also in Spanish   ‡ In Haitian Creole and Vietnamese

Media Literacy: News Formats

News formats are packaged in a variety of ways, not only to deliver information but to get and keep an audience's attention. Shown below are features of two electronic news sources.

FEATURES OF A TV NEWSCAST

1 The **anchor** introduces the news story with a **lead-in.**

2 Then the scene cuts to **video footage,** which is shot and edited to illustrate the events of the news story. As the footage plays, the anchor or a **field reporter** describes the details.

3 The **voice-over** is the unseen reporter's voice that plays over the images. A voice-over makes a news story easy to follow.

4 **Sound bites,** brief statements from interviews with experts or witnesses, can provide details and stir emotions.

Advantages
- TV news stories can be aired as soon as the event is known.
- A typical news segment lasts 30 seconds to 2 minutes. This allows more news stories to be reported in a short period of time.
- Video and audio give a story immediacy and drama.

Disadvantages
- Because a news segment is short, it may not cover an event thoroughly enough.
- Sometimes stations "go live," or air a story, before all the facts are gathered.

FEATURES OF A WEB NEWS REPORT

1 **Menus** on the page help users to navigate the site.

2 The **lead,** the first sentence (or first few sentences), starts the report.

3 **Captions** explain the photographs or other visuals.

4 **Hyperlinks**—typically, highlighted words, phrases, or images—allow users to jump directly to updates or more information.

Quotations from those involved add human interest.

Advantages
- Breaking stories can be posted and updated at any time.
- Space is usually not a limitation. A Web news report can run for an indefinite length.
- **Streaming video** or **animations** bring the scene to life.

Disadvantages
- Web articles may not be accessible to everyone.
- Sometimes stories are posted so quickly that the facts may be inaccurate.

STRATEGIES FOR VIEWING

- In any news format, look for answers to the **5 W's** and the **H** questions: Who? What? Where? When? Why? and How?
- Be sure you can spot the **lead.** Try restating the lead in your own words to be sure it covers all the essential details.

Teach

Media Literacy

Discuss both TV newscasts and Web news reports. Ask students how TV newscasts generally progress. Who presents the news? Who and what do viewers see besides the newscasters? List terms on the board as students mention them, adding *anchor, video, reporter, voice-over,* and *sound bites* if necessary. Then ask students what elements they expect to find on a Web news report. How do they locate stories of interest? How can they find more details? Add terms to the board list, such as *menus* and *hyperlinks.* Then discuss the chart on page 557.

- **TV Newscast** To reinforce how different features of a TV newscast come together, ask students to improvise presenting a story about a football game. Have one student act as the anchor and provide a lead-in. Ask students what video footage they might see and what kind of commentary a field reporter might provide. Ask how voice-over might be used and what kinds of sound bites a reporter might try to get.

- **Web News Report** Ask students to imagine that they are getting information about the same football game, this time using an Internet news site. Ask how they would locate sports news and then specifically football news. Have students describe the screen on which the football story appears.

- **Advantages and Disadvantages** Have students describe the advantages and disadvantages of learning about the football story in each of these two formats.

⊘ Media*Smart* DVD

MEDIA STUDY: TEACHING OPTIONS

Teaching Option 1: The Basics (1-2 Days)

1. Begin the Media Study using the material provided on pages 556–557.
2. Show the Introduction on Media*Smart.* Then show the First Viewing. As they watch, have students use the Viewing Guide on page 558, along with the corresponding copy master on page 123 of the Resource Manager. Discuss their responses.
3. Return to the pupil book for the extension activities on page 559.

Teaching Option 2: In-Depth Study (2–3 Days)

1. Begin the Media Study using pages 556–557.
2. Show the Introduction and First Viewing from Media*Smart.* Continue on Media*Smart* with the Media Lessons, using the teacher notes available in the Resources section.
3. Show the Guided Analysis presentation. Have students record their observations on the Student Viewing Guide available in the Resources section from Media*Smart.*
4. Return to the pupil book, page 559.

Practice and Apply

VIEWING GUIDE

1. Before students view the TV news report and examine the Web news report, tell them that they will be asked to compare the way the two media deliver information and try to capture the audience's attention. Encourage them to watch and listen for these elements:

   - **leads** and how these draw audiences into the miners' dramatic story
   - **video footage** on TV that gives visual information about the rescue progress
   - **voice-overs** that help TV viewers follow the story and **captions** that explain Web images of the miners and the rescue
   - **sound bites** on TV and **quotations** on the Web that help viewers get to know the miners, their families, and their rescuers
   - **menus** and **hyperlinks** that help Web news readers locate information

2. Some students may not be able to link the labels for various TV news techniques with what they see in the news report. Help these students identify video footage, voice-over, and sound bite elements. Help them differentiate between an anchor and a field reporter.

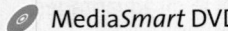 **RESOURCE MANAGER—Copy Masters**
   Viewing Guide p. 123
   Close Viewing p. 124
   Viewing Activity p. 125

Use this resource with the Viewing Guide:

📀 Media*Smart* DVD

ANSWERS

FIRST VIEWING: Comprehension

1. *A 240-foot shaft was drilled down to where the miners were trapped. They were raised through the shaft in a 21"-wide basket, one miner at a time.*

2. *Click on the link—the blue underlined words— "Randy Fogle."*

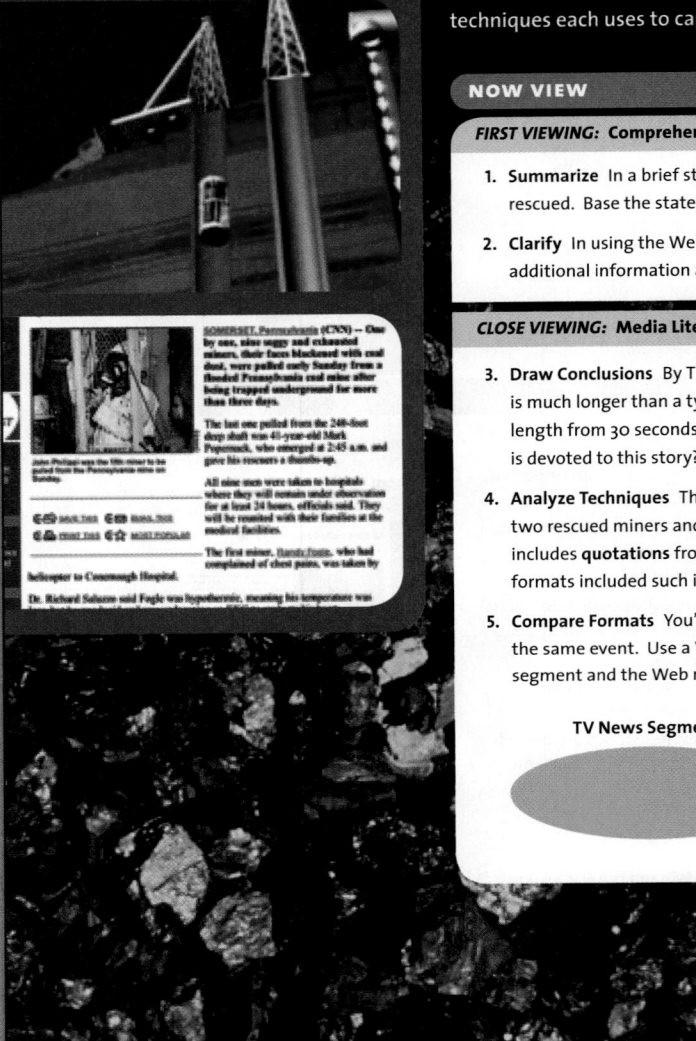

MediaSmart DVD
- **News Format 1:** "Nine Coal Miners Brought Up Safely"
- **Genre:** TV newscast
- **Running Time:** 4.5 minutes

- **News Format 2:** "All Nine Pulled Alive from Mine"
- **Genre:** Web news report

Viewing Guide for
News Reports

Both the NBC video clip and the CNN.com news report were originally presented the day after the rescue. The video clip, as an in-depth news feature, lasts longer than a typical news segment.

View the clip several times and take as much time as you need to look over the Web report. As you explore these two news formats, consider how each delivers the facts and take note of the specific techniques each uses to capture attention.

NOW VIEW

FIRST VIEWING: Comprehension

1. **Summarize** In a brief statement, describe how the coal miners were rescued. Base the statement on the TV newscast.

2. **Clarify** In using the Web news site, what would you need to do to find additional information about Randy Fogle?

CLOSE VIEWING: Media Literacy

3. **Draw Conclusions** By TV news standards, the newscast you've viewed is much longer than a typical news story. Basic news stories range in length from 30 seconds to 2 minutes. Why do you think so much time is devoted to this story?

4. **Analyze Techniques** The TV newscast includes **sound bites** from two rescued miners and from certain officials. The Web news report includes **quotations** from similar sources. Why do you think both news formats included such information?

5. **Compare Formats** You've examined how two news formats covered the same event. Use a Venn diagram to compare how the TV news segment and the Web news report are alike and different.

TV News Segment   Web News Report

Both

CLOSE VIEWING: Media Literacy
Possible answers:

3. *This story's unique and dramatic life-and-death qualities appealed to a national audience. The audience grew as the story played out over four days.*

4. *Quoting participants provides human interest and eyewitness details. Quoting others, such as experts, spokespeople, or the governor, gives different perspectives and details from other points of view.*

5. *TV news: extensive visuals and narrative convey the on-the-scene experience, provide a strong sense of the atmosphere, introduce people involved; perhaps more engaging because easier to watch* **Web news:** *dedicates more space to more thorough coverage of the event; allows for interactive links for more in-depth detail about the people and technology involved in the story* **Both:** *use credible sources; relay essential facts and details; provide visual images of the event*

Write or Discuss

Compare the News Formats Which news format—the TV news segment or the Web news report—is more effective at covering the rescue? Explain your opinion. Keep the following criteria in mind:

- the effectiveness of the lead in each format in delivering the important facts about the rescue
- the techniques used to capture and keep your interest
- the time or space limitations of each format

Produce Your Own Media

Create a News Segment Select an article from your school newspaper or from a community newspaper. Determine how you would create an update to the article in the form of a TV news segment. Then divide into teams to draft a script, conduct interviews, and plan to shoot the video footage of the segment.

HERE'S HOW Work in the assigned planning groups to address these questions:

- Who would be the anchor and the on-camera reporter?
- Whom would you interview for sound bites?
- What lead-in would your anchor provide?
- What voice-over would you need to include to structure the story?
- What video footage would you shoot?

MEDIA TOOLS
For help with creating a news segment, visit the **Media Center** at **ClassZone.com.**

STUDENT MODEL

WHAT VIEWERS SEE	WHAT VIEWERS HEAR	SHOT KEY
ON-CAMERA REPORTER BIANCA EXT—DAY 1. LS of reporter standing with a group of student protesters in a parking lot.	BIANCA: Since the start of the school year, a growing group of students at Optima High believe the school parking lot to be in need of a makeover. . . .	**LS** Long Shot **MS** Medium Shot **VWS** Very Wide Shot **EXT** Exterior
CUT TO: MS of BIANCA 2. Quickly zoom out to a VWS that reveals the potholes—some rather deep—dotting the lot.	BIANCA: . . . an extreme makeover.	

Tech Tip
You might use a design program to create a graphic for the report.

A LOT OF TROUBLE

559

Assess and Reteach

Write or Discuss

Compare the News Formats In their evaluations, students should address how well each medium conveyed the basic facts and identify techniques each medium used to capture audience interest. Students should also show an awareness of the general advantages and disadvantages of the two media. For example, students might point out how well the animations in the TV newscast conveyed information about drilling down to the miners but how time constraints limited the information given about the individual miners. They might note that the Web report enabled them to easily find additional information about Randy Fogle but that its minimal visuals reduced its impact. In addition, encourage students to include their own personal reactions to the TV newscast and the Web news report.

Produce Your Own Media

Rubric: Create a News Segment A strong plan for a TV news segment should have a script that clearly tells

- what viewers see and hear
- what the anchor's lead-in will be
- what the field reporter will say and do
- when sound bites will be used
- how and when voice-over will be used
- what video footage will be used
- the kinds of shots used when showing the anchor, the on-camera reporter, and the content of any video footage

R RESOURCE MANAGER—Copy Master
Produce Your Own Media p. 126

MEDIA STUDY WRAP–UP

Have students summarize what they have learned about TV newscasts and Web news reports. Encourage students to use terms such as *anchor, field reporter, lead-in, video footage, voice-over, sound bites, menu, lead, caption, hyperlink,* and *quotations* in the summary.

RETEACH

S STANDARDS LESSON FILE
Media Lesson 11: Comparing News Formats
Media Lesson 20: Producing a Video

Focus and Motivate

OBJECTIVES

Literary Analysis
- explore the key idea of a **guest**
- analyze tone and author's purpose
- read a short story

Reading
- make predictions about characters

Grammar and Writing
- use adverbs in writing descriptive details
- use writing to analyze literature

SUMMARY

On a mental health retreat to the country, Framton Nuttel visits an acquaintance of his sister whom he has never met. He is greeted by the woman's niece, Vera, who invents a story about her aunt in which the woman daily awaits the return of her long lost husband and brothers through the open window. When the husband and brothers arrive after a day of hunting, Nuttel believes he is seeing ghosts and flees.

How should you treat a GUEST?

Read the *KEY IDEA* question aloud. Then guide a discussion by asking students to describe a time when they were a **guest** in someone's home and were treated well. What did the host do to make them feel welcome and comfortable? Extend the discussion by having students complete the *DISCUSS* activity.

Selection Resources

The Open Window
Short Story by Saki

How should you treat a GUEST?

KEY IDEA You're sitting at home when the doorbell rings. Instead of the pizza-delivery guy you were expecting, it's an uninvited **guest**. If that guest happens to be your best friend, you now have someone fun to share your pizza with. If, however, that guest is someone you would rather not hang out with, what should you do?

DISCUSS In your opinion, do you have an obligation to treat a guest, invited or not, with hospitality? Discuss your opinion with a small group of classmates. Talk about the obligations you have as a host— especially to a guest you would rather not spend time with. Are there minimum standards you have to meet in order not to be rude? After you've discussed these questions, think about whether or not your opinion has changed and, if so, why.

560

RESOURCE MANAGER UNIT 5

Plan and Teach pp. 127–134

Literary Analysis
Summary pp. 135, 136†*
Tone and Author's Purpose
   pp. 137, 138†*
Question Support p. 142*

Reading
Predict pp. 139, 140†*
Reading Check p. 141
Reading Fluency p. 144

Grammar and Writing
Add Descriptive Details p. 143

Assessment
Selection Tests A, B/C pp. 145*, 147*
  Test Generator CD

BEST PRACTICES TOOLKIT

Differentiated Instruction
  pp. 31–38*

Scaffolding Instruction
  pp. 43–46*

Graphic Organizers/Strategies
Frayer Model • Character Analysis Chart

Reading Support
  Audio Anthology CD*

Technology
  Literature and Vocabulary Centers at **ClassZone.com**
  Write*Smart* CD

---

* Resources for Differentiation   † Also in Spanish

• LITERARY ANALYSIS: TONE AND AUTHOR'S PURPOSE

A writer's **tone,** or attitude toward a subject, can often reveal his or her **purpose.** Just as you might use one tone of voice to make a joke and another to criticize someone, writers use different tones to accomplish different purposes. A writer's tone may be playful or solemn, sarcastic or admiring. Figuring out the writer's tone can help you decide what his or her purpose might be. As you read Saki's famous short story "The Open Window," ask yourself

- Does the narrator's description of other characters reveal whether Saki is portraying them in a favorable or an unfavorable light?
- Does Saki use formal or informal language? What effect does this create?

Review: Point of View

■ READING STRATEGY: PREDICT

To make **predictions** about characters, try the following strategies:

- Think about each character's personality. How might someone with these traits respond to conflict or to new situations?
- Consider different characters' actions. What might happen as a result of these actions?
- Use your own experience. If you were ever in a situation similar to the one in the story, how did it turn out?

As you read "The Open Window," stop occasionally to predict what might happen next. Record text clues that help you make reasonable guesses, and check your predictions against what actually happens.

Text Clues	My Prediction	Actual Outcome
Mrs. Sappleton has had a "great tragedy." (line 26)	She will still be very sad, even though it happened years ago.	

Author Online

Also Known As …

"Saki" is the pen name of Hector Hugo Munro, a British author best known for his satirical short stories. Munro was born in Burma, a country in Asia then controlled by the British. When he was very young, his mother was killed in an accident. His father sent Munro and his siblings to England to be raised by their aunts, two old women who believed in old-fashioned discipline.

Saki
1870–1916

Saki's Saga
When he was 23, Munro returned to Burma to join the military police. Stricken with malaria a year later, he gave up his badge and his pet tiger cub and returned to England to try his hand at writing. As he embarked on his literary career, he picked up the name Saki from the *Rubáiyát,* a long poem by 12th-century Persian writer Omar Khayyám. Although he wrote nonfiction, political cartoons, novels, and plays, Saki is most famous for his short stories, which are praised for their whimsical humor and shrewd social criticism. When World War I began, the writer rushed to enlist. During a night march through France in 1916, he was shot and killed by a German sniper.

 MORE ABOUT THE AUTHOR
For more on Saki, visit the **Literature Center at ClassZone.com.**

Background

Ridiculing the Rich "The Open Window" depicts the world of the British upper class in the early 1900s. Saki, himself a member of the upper class, often ridiculed the customs of high society. For instance, he made fun of the fact that people were expected to present formal letters of introduction when visiting strangers and poked fun at the "nerve cure," a trip to the countryside to treat anxiety.

STANDARDS FOCUS

LITERARY ANALYSIS

● TONE AND AUTHOR'S PURPOSE

For instructional support, write some common author's purposes on the board, such as to inform, to persuade, and to entertain. Ask students what tones an author might use to achieve each purpose.

Possible answer: *to explain: deliberate and serious; to persuade: personal and positive; to entertain: informal and humorous.*

CHECK UNDERSTANDING Have students compare the tone and author's purpose they might find in a textbook, a newspaper editorial, and a children's book.

READING STRATEGY

■ PREDICT

To support instruction, read this passage aloud to students. Then ask students to predict what Ethan is up to in this passage:

Erica's two brothers had been arguing constantly lately. Her ten-year-old brother Ethan had threatened to do anything to get a room of his own. Now Erica wondered where he might be. Suddenly, a loud pounding came from the attic. Erica raced upstairs, flung open the door, and stared. There stood her brother, hammer in hand.

Possible answer: *Ethan is building his own room in the attic.*

CHECK UNDERSTANDING Have students define *prediction,* using a dictionary if necessary. Clarify any misunderstanding.

R RESOURCE MANAGER—Copy Master
Predict p. 139 (for student use while reading the selection)

DIFFERENTIATED INSTRUCTION

FOR LESS-PROFICIENT READERS

Concept Support After students read the discussion on tone and author's purpose, point out that they use and respond to tone every day. Read this statement aloud twice, using tone of voice first to express the imperative, and then excitement: "Class is beginning now." Ask students to identify the tone and the purpose it may imply. Have students provide other examples of how tone of speaking expresses a purpose or meaning.

FOR ENGLISH LEARNERS

Frayer Model To help students construct meaning and clarify understanding of the literary analysis and reading strategy concepts on this page, construct a Frayer Model on the board. Work with students to complete the organizer for each of the terms.

 BEST PRACTICES TOOLKIT—Transparency
Frayer Model p. A30

The Open Window

SAKI

"My aunt will be down presently, Mr. Nuttel," said a very self-possessed young lady of fifteen; "in the mean-time you must try and put up with me."

Framton Nuttel endeavored to say the correct something that should duly flatter the niece of the moment without unduly discounting the aunt that was to come. Privately he doubted more than ever whether these formal visits on a succession of total strangers would do much toward helping the nerve cure[1] which he was supposed to be undergoing. **Ⓐ**

"I know how it will be," his sister had said when he was preparing to migrate to this rural retreat; "you will bury yourself down there and not speak
10 to a living soul, and your nerves will be worse than ever from moping. I shall just give you letters of introduction to all the people I know there. Some of them, as far as I can remember, were quite nice."

Framton wondered whether Mrs. Sappleton, the lady to whom he was presenting one of the letters of introduction, came into the nice division.

"Do you know many of the people round here?" asked the niece, when she judged that they had had sufficient silent communion.

"Hardly a soul," said Framton. "My sister was staying here, at the rectory,[2] you know, some four years ago, and she gave me letters of introduction to some of the people here."

20 He made the last statement in a tone of distinct regret.

"Then you know practically nothing about my aunt?" pursued the self-possessed young lady.

"Only her name and address," admitted the caller. He was wondering whether Mrs. Sappleton was in the married or widowed state. An undefinable something about the room seemed to suggest masculine habitation.[3]

---

1. **nerve cure:** a treatment for nervousness or anxiety.
2. **the rectory** (rĕk′tə-rē): the parish priest's house.
3. **masculine habitation:** that men lived there.

Veil of Elegance, Peter Miller.
Private Collection. © The Bridgeman Art Library.

Ⓐ TONE AND AUTHOR'S PURPOSE

Paraphrase lines 3–7. So far, how would you describe Saki's tone, or his attitude toward this character? Explain your answer, citing evidence.

① Targeted Passage

ANALYZE VISUALS

The narrator describes the niece as "self-possessed," or confident and in control. In your opinion, does the young woman in this painting look self-possessed? Explain, citing the **details** that influenced your opinion.

LITERARY ANALYSIS

Ⓐ TONE AND AUTHOR'S PURPOSE

Possible answer: Framton Nuttel tries to think of something appropriate to say. In fact, he starts to wonder whether visiting total strangers will help him get over his nervous condition. Saki's tone shows that the character is thoughtful and kind. He shows this by including Nuttel's thoughts and his concern for the feelings of the niece.

If students need help . . . Ask students whether Nuttel is portrayed in a positive or negative manner in this passage. Have students consider the effect of the author's formal language on the character.

ANALYZE VISUALS

Possible answer: Yes, the subject looks self-possessed because she has a thoughtful expression on her face and sits in a relaxed, easy posture. She does not appear worried or tense.

About the Art The contemporary English artist Peter Miller uses light and color to create a thoughtful, serene mood in his work. In the painting, light streams from both the window and the lamp. The light is created with flickering colors that create a softness on the flowers, the outdoor scene, and the girl's clothing. In contrast, the artist draws chairs, furniture, and picture frames with sharp strokes and clean lines. The sharp lines and underlying structure of the furniture add strength to the overall softness of the painting.

DIFFERENTIATED INSTRUCTION

FOR ALL STUDENTS

Journal As they read, ask students to keep a journal noting questions, observations, and reflections about characters and situations. Ask students to refer to their notes when completing other activities that accompany the selection.

FOR LESS–PROFICIENT READERS

In combination with the *Audio Anthology CD*, use one or more Targeted Passages (pp. 562, 564, 565) to ensure that students focus on key story events, concepts, and skills. Targeted Passages are also good for English learners.

① Targeted Passage [Lines 15–22]

This passage shows what Nuttel knows about his host. It also introduces the character of the niece, giving her the information she needs to create a convincing tale.

"Her great tragedy happened just three years ago," said the child; "that would be since your sister's time."

"Her tragedy?" asked Framton; somehow in this restful country spot tragedies seemed out of place.

30 "You may wonder why we keep that window wide open on an October afternoon," said the niece, indicating a large French window[4] that opened on to a lawn.

"It is quite warm for the time of the year," said Framton; "but has that window got anything to do with the tragedy?" **B**

"Out through that window, three years ago to a day, her husband and her two young brothers went off for their day's shooting. They never came back. In crossing the moor to their favorite snipe-shooting ground they were all three engulfed by a treacherous piece of bog. It had been that dreadful wet summer, you know, and places that were safe in other years gave way suddenly without 40 warning. Their bodies were never recovered. That was the dreadful part of it." Here the child's voice lost its self-possessed note and became falteringly human. "Poor aunt always thinks that they will come back some day, they and the little brown spaniel that was lost with them, and walk in that window just as they used to do. That is why the window is kept open every evening till it is quite dusk. Poor dear aunt, she has often told me how they went out, her husband with his white waterproof coat over his arm, and Ronnie, her youngest brother, singing 'Bertie, why do you bound?' as he always did to tease her, because she said it got on her nerves. Do you know, sometimes on still, quiet evenings like this, I almost get a creepy feeling that they will all walk 50 in through that window—"

She broke off with a little shudder. It was a relief to Framton when the aunt bustled into the room with a whirl of apologies for being late in making her appearance.

"I hope Vera has been amusing you?" she said.

"She has been very interesting," said Framton. **C**

"I hope you don't mind the open window," said Mrs. Sappleton briskly; "my husband and brothers will be home directly from shooting, and they always come in this way. They've been out for snipe in the marshes today, so they'll make a fine mess over my poor carpets. So like you menfolk, 60 isn't it?"

She rattled on cheerfully about the shooting and the scarcity of birds, and the prospects for duck in the winter. To Framton it was all purely horrible. He made a desperate but only partially successful effort to turn the talk on to a less ghastly topic; he was conscious that his hostess was giving him only a fragment of her attention, and her eyes were constantly straying past him to the open window and the lawn beyond. It was certainly an unfortunate coincidence that he should have paid his visit on this tragic anniversary.

---

4. **French window:** a pair of windows that extend to the floor and open like doors.

564   UNIT 5: AUTHOR'S PURPOSE

B POINT OF VIEW
Is this story told from the **first-person** or the **third-person** point of view? Explain how you determined this, citing evidence.

C PREDICT
Will Nuttel say anything to Mrs. Sappleton about her "great tragedy"? Give reasons for your prediction.

2 Targeted Passage

Sidebar (left column)

LITERARY ANALYSIS: *Review*

B POINT OF VIEW

Possible answer: The story is told from the third-person point of view. The characters are referred to as "he," "she," "him," and "her." If the story were in the first person, the pronouns I, my, we, *and* mine *would be used.*

Lines 15–50
REINFORCE *KEY IDEA:* GUEST

Discuss How does Vera treat Nuttel when he is a **guest** in her home? *Possible answer: Vera is polite and friendly, showing genuine interest in him. However, her attitude seems excessive as she shares intimate details about her family with a man she has never met before.*

READING STRATEGY

C PREDICT

Possible answer: Nuttel will not say anything to Mrs. Sappleton about her tragedy. He is a sensitive and nervous character who would be careful not to upset Mrs. Sappleton.

If students need help . . . Ask students to summarize Mrs. Sappleton's tragedy. Then help them use the Character Analysis Chart to analyze Nuttel's personality and how he probably feels when he hears of the tragedy. Use this information as a text clue to make a prediction.

 BEST PRACTICES TOOLKIT—Transparency
Character Analysis Chart p. D5

DIFFERENTIATED INSTRUCTION

FOR LESS–PROFICIENT READERS

2 Targeted Passage [Lines 56–60]

This passage reveals how Mrs. Sappleton explains the "great tragedy" to her guest.

- Why is the window open?

- Where does Mrs. Sappleton believe her husband and brothers are?

- What has Nuttel been told about Mrs. Sappleton's husband and brothers?

FOR ENGLISH LEARNERS

Language: Modifiers Although both the British and Americans speak English, there are differences in how some words are used. For example, an American car has a hood and a trunk. A British car has a bonnet and a boot. For examples in this story, point out the uses of *quite* (lines 12, 33, and 45); *fine* (line 59); and *most* (line 95) and explain that these usages are more British than American. Have students think of other words that have several usages.

"The doctors agree in ordering me complete rest, an absence of mental excitement, and avoidance of anything in the nature of violent physical
70 exercise," announced Framton, who labored under the tolerably widespread delusion that total strangers and chance acquaintances are hungry for the least detail of one's ailments and infirmities, their cause and cure. "On the matter of diet they are not so much in agreement," he continued. **D**

"No?" said Mrs. Sappleton, in a voice which only replaced a yawn at the last moment. Then she suddenly brightened into alert attention—but not to what Framton was saying.

"Here they are at last!" she cried. "Just in time for tea, and don't they look as if they were muddy up to the eyes!"

Framton shivered slightly, and turned toward the niece with a look intended
80 to convey sympathetic comprehension. The child was staring out through the open window with dazed horror in her eyes. In a chill shock of nameless fear Framton swung round in his seat and looked in the same direction.

In the deepening twilight three figures were walking across the lawn toward the window; they all carried guns under their arms, and one of them was additionally burdened with a white coat hung over his shoulders. A tired brown spaniel kept close at their heels. Noiselessly they neared the house, and then a hoarse young voice chanted out of the dusk:

"I said, Bertie, why do you bound?"

Framton grabbed wildly at his stick and hat; the hall door, the gravel drive, and
90 the front gate were dimly noted stages in his headlong retreat. A cyclist coming along the road had to run into the hedge to avoid imminent collision. **E**

"Here we are, my dear," said the bearer of the white mackintosh, coming in through the window; "fairly muddy, but most of it's dry. Who was that who bolted out as we came up?"

"A most extraordinary man, a Mr. Nuttel," said Mrs. Sappleton; "could only talk about his illnesses, and dashed off without a word of goodbye or apology when you arrived. One would think he had seen a ghost."

"I expect it was the spaniel," said the niece calmly; "he told me he had a horror of dogs. He was once hunted into a cemetery somewhere on the banks
100 of the Ganges⁵ by a pack of pariah dogs⁶, and had to spend the night in a newly dug grave with the creatures snarling and grinning and foaming just above him. Enough to make anyone lose his nerve."

Romance⁷ at short notice was her specialty. ❧

---

5. **Ganges** (găn′jēz′): a large river in northern India.
6. **pariah** (pə-rī′ə) **dogs**: dogs that have escaped from their owners and become wild.
7. **romance**: highly imaginative fiction.

THE OPEN WINDOW **565**

D TONE AND AUTHOR'S PURPOSE
Is the language Saki uses to describe Nuttel's endless discussion of his health formal or informal? Explain the tone this language helps convey.

③ Targeted Passage

E GRAMMAR AND STYLE
Reread lines 89–91. Saki uses the **adverbs** *wildly* and *dimly* to emphasize Nuttel's desperate flight from the house.

THE OPEN WINDOW **565**

Practice and Apply

After Reading

For additional support of post-reading questions, use these copy masters:

R RESOURCE MANAGER—Copy Masters
  Reading Check p. 141 (to check under-
    standing of the selection)
  Tone and Author's Purpose p. 137 (for
    practice of literary analysis standards
    focus)
  Question Support p. 142 (After Reading
    questions adapted for English learners
    and less-proficient readers)

For additional questions, see page 131.

ANSWERS

Comprehension

1. *She keeps the window open because she be-lieves her husband and brothers will return from their hunting trip, one that took place three years before and during which they drowned.*

2. *Nuttel leaves abruptly because he believes he is seeing the ghosts of the husband and brothers. Vera explains his departure by inventing a story about his fear of dogs.*

3. *Vera is good at making up stories on the spur of the moment.*

Literary Analysis

Possible answers:

4. *First question: Vera wanted to know if he could have heard that she was good at inventing stories. Second question: She wanted to find out what information she would not be able to contradict in her invented story to make it plausible.*

5. ■ **STANDARDS FOCUS** *Predict Students should evaluate their predictions for accuracy and explain why any of their predictions were wrong.*

6. *We would not learn what happened after Nuttel left the room, nor would we learn of Vera's specialty for inventing stories at short notice.*

7. ● **STANDARDS FOCUS** *Tone and Author's Purpose Saki's purpose was to make fun of silly people like Nuttel. He might be try-ing to tell his readers that people like Mr. Nuttel are gullible, inexperienced, and dull*

After Reading

Comprehension

1. **Recall** Describe the "great tragedy" that Vera relates to Mr. Nuttel. According to Vera, why does her aunt keep the window open?

2. **Recall** Why does Nuttel leave so abruptly, and how does Vera explain his frantic departure?

3. **Paraphrase** Reread the story's final line. Then restate it in your own words.

Literary Analysis

4. **Draw Conclusions** A **surprise ending** is an unexpected twist at the end of a story. Reread lines 15–25 and think about Vera's behavior. Now that you know how "The Open Window" ends, what would you say was Vera's **motive** for asking Nuttel each question listed in the chart shown?

Vera's Question	Motive
"Do you know many of the people round here?" (line 15)	
"Then you know practically nothing about my aunt?" (line 21)	

5. **Evaluate Predictions** Review the chart you created as you read. How accurate were your predictions? If they were very accurate, describe the clues that allowed you to make such on-target guesses. If your predictions were off, explain how Saki caught you by surprise.

6. **Analyze Point of View** Saki uses a **third-person omniscient narrator** in "The Open Window." The narrator is an outside voice that gives you access to the thoughts and feelings of all the characters and relates events that may be happening simultaneously. How would the end of this story be different if it were told exclusively from Nuttel's point of view? Explain your answer.

7. **Analyze Tone and Author's Purpose** Think about Saki's use of formal language to describe silly situations, as well as his depiction of Mr. Nuttel. From Saki's tone, what can you infer about his purpose? Explain what he might be trying to tell his readers about people like Mr. Nuttel. Cite evidence from the text to support your analysis.

Literary Criticism

8. **Critical Interpretations** According to critic Rena Corb, the "successful ending" of this story depends on "the reader's belief, along with Nuttel's, that Vera is telling the truth." Whether you, like Nuttel, fell for Vera's story or you knew she was lying to her **guest** all along, explain why you agree or disagree with Corb's assertion. Support your opinion with evidence from the selection.

---

witted. In the passage in lines 89–91, Mr. Nuttel believes he is seeing the ghosts of the hunters. He is not clever enough to see through Vera's joke.

Literary Criticism

Possible answer:

8. *Corb is correct because if the reader thinks that Vera is not telling the truth, the end-ing is not surprising. Saki skillfully repeats the details of Vera's story—the clothing,*

the dog, and the hunting expedition three times: in Vera's story, when Mrs. Sappleton appears, and when the hunters appear. The repetition helps convince the reader that Vera's story is true.

Reading-Writing Connection

Extend your interaction with "The Open Window" by responding to these prompts. Then use **Revision: Grammar and Style** to improve your writing.

WRITING PROMPTS	SELF-CHECK
A. Short Response: Predict Nuttel's Reaction Imagine that Framton Nuttel learned the truth about the Sappleton "tragedy." How might he respond to the news? Write **one or two paragraphs** describing how Nuttel might feel and act upon learning that he had been tricked.	**A successful response will . . .** • describe in clear detail how Nuttel might act when he learns Vera has tricked him • convey what Nuttel might be thinking, based on the traits he exhibits in the story
B. Extended Response: Analyze Characters How would you describe the characters of Vera and her **guest,** Framton Nuttel? Is Vera deceitful or just imaginative? Is Nuttel stupidly gullible, or is he simply a trusting person? Write a **three-to-five-paragraph response,** citing evidence.	**A strong analysis will . . .** • discuss three features of each character's personality • use examples from the story to support your ideas

REVISION: GRAMMAR AND STYLE

ADD DESCRIPTIVE DETAILS Review the **Grammar and Style** note on page 565. Through his use of descriptive **adverbs,** Saki gives the reader a greater sense of the urgency with which Nuttel flees the scene.

Adverbs are used to modify verbs, adjectives, and other adverbs. Adverbs should accurately and descriptively convey where, when, how, or to what extent something is happening. In the following excerpts, notice how the adverbs Saki uses reveal important details about Vera's character:

> *"That was the dreadful part of it." Here the child's voice lost its self-possessed note and became falteringly human.* (lines 40–42)

> *"I expect it was the spaniel," said the niece calmly; "he told me he had a horror of dogs."* (lines 98–99)

Notice how the revisions in red make this first draft more descriptive. Revise your responses to the prompts by using similar techniques.

STUDENT MODEL

<u>cunningly</u>
Vera is ∧clever. She knows she will have a few minutes alone with Mr. Nuttel,
<u>spontaneously</u>   <u>clearly</u>
so she ∧decides to toy with him. She has ∧made up stories like this before, since
                                    <u>elaborately</u>
it takes her very little time to ∧describe the events to Mr. Nuttel.

WRITING TOOLS
For prewriting, revision, and editing tools, visit the **Writing Center** at ClassZone.com.

THE OPEN WINDOW **567**

DIFFERENTIATED INSTRUCTION

FOR LESS-PROFICIENT WRITERS

For Prompt A:

- Offer the following sentence frame as a paragraph starter: *When Nuttel learns that Vera has tricked him, he reacts by* _____. *The reason he reacts this way is* _____.

- Suggest that the first paragraph focus on Nuttel's reaction. The second paragraph should focus on quotations from the text that led to the prediction.

For Prompt B:

- Suggest that students organize their essays in this way:

  1. First paragraph: State a position about Vera and Nuttel.

  2. Second, third, and fourth paragraphs: Use one quotation per paragraph that supports the position statement.

  3. Fifth paragraph: Restate the position statement in a different way and summarize the text evidence.

Reading-Writing Connection

WRITING PROMPTS

- For Prompt A, encourage students to list words that describe Nuttel's character. As students write, they should use these character traits as a guide. Nuttel's reaction to being tricked should be consistent with the overriding character traits.

- For Prompt B, have students begin by locating several passages in the story that show how each character behaves. Direct them to use each passage as the basis of one paragraph of the essay.

For an extended writing activity, see
ℹ️ Carol Booth Olson's Reading-Writing Lesson Plans at **ClassZone.com**

REVISION: GRAMMAR AND STYLE
After students examine the model, ask them how the adverbs affect the writing. Then write these sentences on the board and have students revise them using adverbs.

Mrs. Sappleton wondered why Nuttel had come. (Mrs. Sappleton absently wondered . . .)

Mr. Nuttel wished he had not visited. (Mr. Nuttel mournfully wished . . .)

The hunters strode through the window. (The hunters strode happily . . .)

(For more on using adverbs, see **Grammar Handbook,** page R46.)

🅁 RESOURCE MANAGER—Copy Master
   Add Descriptive Details p. 143

Assess and Reteach

Assess

🅁 RESOURCE MANAGER—Copy Masters
   Selection Test A pp. 145–146
   Selection Test B/C pp. 147–148

💿 Test Generator CD

Reteach

🆂 STANDARDS LESSON FILE
   Literature Lesson 45: Tone
   Reading Lesson 3: Determining Author's Purpose
   Reading Lesson 1: Predicting

THE OPEN WINDOW **567**

Focus and Motivate

OBJECTIVES

Literary Analysis
- explore the key idea of **legacy**
- analyze author's perspective
- read a vignette

Reading
- make inferences

SUMMARY

In the first of three excerpts from *The House on Mango Street,* the narrator recalls how the house her family finally moved into did not live up to her expectations. In the second vignette, she reflects on the life of her great-grandmother, for whom she was named. In the final vignette, the narrator describes how and why she likes to make up stories.

What STORIES *will you tell your children?*

Introduce the ***KEY IDEA*** by pointing out that every family has its own particular **legacy.** Then introduce the question, and have students complete the ***PRESENT*** activity. Extend the discussion by asking why it is important for families to have and pass on legacies.

from The House on Mango Street

Fiction by Sandra Cisneros

What STORIES *will you tell your children?*

KEY IDEA Whether it's a tale about the sweet taste of victory or a description of a devastating loss, you have important stories to tell. These stories, if you choose to tell them, will someday be the next generation's **legacy**—stories, beliefs, and traditions passed on from one generation to the next.

PRESENT With a classmate, share a few stories you might want to tell your kids someday. Then pick your favorite—maybe it's the funniest, or the most outrageous, or the one that says the most about you. With a small group, take turns telling your chosen tales. Explain why these are the stories you would pass on to the next generation.

Selection Resources

RESOURCE MANAGER UNIT 5

Plan and Teach pp. 149–156

Literary Analysis
Summary pp. 157, 158†*
Author's Perspective pp. 159, 160†*
Question Support p. 164*

Reading
Make Inferences About Character pp. 161, 162†*
Reading Check p. 163
Reading Fluency p. 165

Assessment
Selection Tests A, B/C pp. 167*, 169*
Test Generator CD

BEST PRACTICES TOOLKIT

Differentiated Instruction pp. 31–38*

Scaffolding Instruction pp. 43–46*

Graphic Organizers/Strategies
Making Inferences • Word Questioning • Comparison Matrix

Technology
Literature and Vocabulary Centers at **ClassZone.com**
Write*Smart* CD

Reading Support
Audio Anthology CD*

InterActive
READER
& WRITER
• Integrated Test Practice
• Related Nonfiction Readings
McDougal Littell LITERATURE

* Resources for Differentiation † Also in Spanish

LITERARY ANALYSIS: AUTHOR'S PERSPECTIVE

Just as your own experiences influence the way you think about different issues, a writer's personal experiences affect the way he or she approaches a topic. When you analyze an **author's perspective,** you work to figure out how the writer looks at his or her subject. As you read this excerpt from *The House on Mango Street,* think about Sandra Cisneros's perspective on the narrator's circumstances.

- Pay attention to the writer's choice of details. In these vignettes, Cisneros describes a rundown house in vivid detail. What do her descriptions of its small windows, crumbling bricks, and tiny yard help emphasize?
- Consider direct statements of the narrator's thoughts or feelings. What kind of person is she?

As you read, consider what these details and statements reveal about Cisneros's ideas, as well as her feelings about what it's like to grow up in a place like the house on Mango Street.

Review: **Tone**

READING SKILL: MAKE INFERENCES ABOUT CHARACTER

Writers don't usually spell out every single thing their characters are thinking and feeling. They often leave it up to the reader to **make inferences** about what isn't directly stated. As you read the following vignettes, keep track of significant details that tell you something about the narrator's background, personality, and feelings. Then record what you can infer from these details.

Details from the Text	My Inferences
Esperanza's family has moved around a lot, and she doesn't sound very happy about that. (lines 1–3)	Esperanza probably wishes her family could just stay in one place and not move around so much.
When the family moves to Mango Street, they finally get their own house. But Esperanza says that "it's not the house we'd thought we'd get." (line 9)	

Author Online

Sandra Cisneros
born 1954

Defining Her Destiny
Sandra Cisneros grew up in a male-dominated household where her father and six brothers were the authority figures. She quietly rebelled against the traditional role she was expected to play as a Mexican-American female, writing in secret until she went away to college. The author now uses her work to give voice to the experiences of Mexican-American women. "I'm trying to write the stories that haven't been written," Cisneros explains. "I'm determined to fill a literary void."

Latina Power Much of Cisneros's writing deals with the shame of poverty and the guilt that comes with rejecting certain aspects of one's culture. Her poetry and prose have received critical acclaim. "I am a woman and I am a Latina," the author says proudly. "Those are the things that make my writing distinctive. Those are the things that give my writing power."

 MORE ABOUT THE AUTHOR
For more on Sandra Cisneros, visit the
Literature Center at ClassZone.com.

Background

No Place Like Home When Cisneros was young, her family moved frequently from Chicago to Mexico City and back again. She never remained in one place long enough to make close friends, and she longed for a "perfect" house like the ones she read about and saw on TV. When she was 11, Cisneros and her family finally moved into a shabby house in a poor Chicago neighborhood. The rundown house was not the dream home she had longed for. Esperanza Cordero, the narrator of *The House on Mango Street,* faces similar issues.

THE HOUSE ON MANGO STREET **569**

Teach

STANDARDS FOCUS

LITERARY ANALYSIS

● AUTHOR'S PERSPECTIVE

For instructional support, offer students an example and read this excerpt from the vignette:

> "I knew then I had to have a house. A real house. One I could point to. But this isn't it." (lines 44–45)

Ask students to explain how these sentences reflect the author's perspective.

Possible answer: She is disappointed and ashamed of this house and has aspirations to have a house of her own about which she can be proud.

CHECK UNDERSTANDING Ask students how the author's perspective might be different had she grown up in a family with more economic resources.

READING SKILL

■ MAKE INFERENCES ABOUT CHARACTER

Help students understand that making inferences involves making guesses about something that is not explicitly stated. Encourage students to confirm or revise their inferences about Esperanza as they read further and gather more information about her.

CHECK UNDERSTANDING Have students use the details from the second row of the chart to make an inference from Esperanza's statements about how she feels about the house.

R RESOURCE MANAGER—Copy Master
Make Inferences About Character
p. 161 (for student use while reading the selection)

DIFFERENTIATED INSTRUCTION

FOR LESS–PROFICIENT READERS

Vocabulary Support Elicit or provide the meanings of these words: *vignette*—"short descriptive literary sketch"; *inference*—"conclusion drawn from information in combination with personal knowledge and experience." Explain that *inference* comes from the verb *infer.*

Practice and Apply

ANALYZE VISUALS

Possible answer: On the one hand, the height-ened colors emphasize the run-down condition of the house. The sunlight shows the dilapi-dated door and crumbling brick. However, the house is also set off against the bright white snow on the front steps and the stark blue sky, suggesting that it is a shelter in a harsh world. On the other hand, part of the house is in shad-ow. This, together with the wavy lines of the painting, suggests that the house may not be in direct view, but may be a part of a memory.

READING SKILL

A MAKE INFERENCES ABOUT CHARACTER

Possible answer: The reader can infer that the family has limited financial resources, which compels them to live in a building that has broken pipes, and as a result, they had to use the washroom next door and carry water in empty milk jugs to use.

If students need help . . . Help students use the Making Inferences chart to find clues from details provided in the text and make inferences about the family.

Details from the Story	What I Know from Reading or Experience	My Inferences
"The water pipes broke . . . house was too old" (lines 10–11)	Broken water pipes can make life hard.	They prob-ably did not have enough money to live in a better place.

BEST PRACTICES TOOLKIT—Transparency
Making Inferences p. A13

The House on Mango Street

Sandra Cisneros

The House on Mango Street

We didn't always live on Mango Street. Before that we lived on Loomis on the third floor, and before that we lived on Keeler. Before Keeler it was Paulina, and before that I can't remember. But what I remember most is moving a lot. Each time it seemed there'd be one more of us. By the time we got to Mango Street we were six—Mama, Papa, Carlos, Kiki, my sister Nenny and me.

The house on Mango Street is ours, and we don't have to pay rent to anybody, or share the yard with the people downstairs, or be careful not to make too much noise, and there isn't a landlord banging on the ceiling with a broom. But even so, it's not the house we'd thought we'd get.

10 We had to leave the flat[1] on Loomis quick. The water pipes broke and the landlord wouldn't fix them because the house was too old. We had to leave fast. We were using the washroom next door and carrying water over in empty milk gallons. That's why Mama and Papa looked for a house, and that's why we moved into the house on Mango Street, far away, on the other side of town. **A**

They always told us that one day we would move into a house, a real house that would be ours for always so we wouldn't have to move each year. And our house would have running water and pipes that worked. And inside it would have real stairs, not hallway stairs, but stairs inside like the houses on TV. And

---

1. **flat:** an apartment on one floor of a building.

ANALYZE VISUALS
What effect is created by the heightened colors and blurred lines in this image? Explain your answer.

① Targeted Passage

A MAKE INFERENCES ABOUT CHARACTER
Reread lines 6–14. What can you infer about the family's economic circumstances? Explain your answer.

DIFFERENTIATED INSTRUCTION

FOR ALL STUDENTS

Enhancing Learning Styles Provide these projects for various learning preferences.

• **Verbal** Dramatize a conversation between Esperanza and her great-grandmother.

• **Visual** Design and furnish a house for Esperanza.

For further details on these projects, see

RESOURCE MANAGER
Ideas for Extension pp. 154–155

FOR LESS–PROFICIENT READERS

In combination with the *Audio Anthology CD,* use one or more Targeted Passages (pp. 570, 572, 573, 574) to ensure that students focus on key story events, concepts, and skills. Targeted Passages are also good for English learners.

① Targeted Passage [Lines 6–14]

This passage explains how the family came to live in the house on Mango Street and describes the flat they used to live in.

BACKGROUND

Disreputable Landlords Landlords like the one who refused to fix the broken water pipes in the flat on Loomis often buy rundown buildings for a small down payment and hold on to them just long enough to collect as much rent money as they can. Such "slumlords," as they are often called, invest little or no money in repairs and maintenance, knowing that eventually they will abandon the deteriorating building.

Lines 1–18
DISCUSSION PROMPTS

Use these prompts to help students understand the family's feelings about having a house of their own:

CONNECT Have you ever had to move or change schools or be in a situation where you had to make new friends? What challenges did you face? How did you feel? *Students' responses might include the difficulty in leaving someplace familiar, and perhaps having mixed emotions.*

ANALYZE How do you think the many moves and the difficult circumstances under which the family lived affected their family life? *Possible answer: It was probably very stressful and made life feel uncertain.*

EVALUATE The author could have begun the vignette with the second paragraph. How does the first paragraph enhance what the narrator says about owning a house in the second paragraph? *Possible answer: The description of the family's many moves helps the reader to more fully appreciate what owning a home meant to them after so much instability and so many changes.*

- Why did the family have to leave the flat on Loomis?

- Where did they move to?

- In what ways is the family's new home better than their old one?

FOR ENGLISH LEARNERS

Options for Reading Have students read the vignette "The House on Mango Street" carefully while they listen to it and two other vignettes on the *Audio Anthology CD*.

Prereading For prereading instruction for English learners, see

 BEST PRACTICES TOOLKIT
Scaffolding Reading Instruction pp. 43–46

FOR ADVANCED LEARNERS/PRE–AP

Pre-AP Exercises in the bottom channel provide additional challenge for students. Use these suggestions for small groups or individuals.

ADDITIONAL GUIDELINES

For more help with differentiation and tips for classroom management, see

BEST PRACTICES TOOLKIT
Differentiated Instruction pp. 31–38

THE HOUSE ON MANGO STREET **571**

B MAKE INFERENCES ABOUT CHARACTER

Possible answer: When the nun says "there," the narrator looks up and notices the paint peeling and wooden bars on the windows. Her reaction reveals that she feels ashamed and embarrassed to live there.

If students need help . . .

• Have students reread lines 34–36 and 40–41. Discuss the descriptive details, and ask what kind of mental image they create.

• Have students reread line 42. Ask them to paraphrase the narrator's reaction: "The way she said it made me feel like nothing."

Extend the Discussion Why do you think the author put the word *there* in italics (lines 39, 40, 42, and 43)?

C TONE

Possible answer: Striking words and phrases include "like the number nine" and "A muddy color" (line 48) and "songs like sobbing" (line 50). Cisneros's word choice conveys a sad, disconsolate tone, the feeling of longing for something that may never come.

Extend the Discussion The author makes several comparisons in lines 47–50. How do these comparisons express the narrator's feelings about her name?

---

we'd have a basement and at least three washrooms so when we took a bath we
20 wouldn't have to tell everybody. Our house would be white with trees around it, a great big yard and grass growing without a fence. This was the house Papa talked about when he held a lottery ticket and this was the house Mama dreamed up in the stories she told us before we went to bed.

> But the house on Mango Street is not the way they told it at all. It's small and red with tight steps in front and windows so small you'd think they were holding their breath. Bricks are crumbling in places, and the front door is so swollen you have to push hard to get in. There is no front yard, only four little elms the city planted by the curb. Out back is a small garage for the car we don't own yet and a small yard that looks smaller between the two buildings
> 30 on either side. There are stairs in our house, but they're ordinary hallway stairs, and the house has only one washroom. Everybody has to share a bedroom—Mama and Papa, Carlos and Kiki, me and Nenny.

2 Targeted Passage *continued*

Once when we were living on Loomis, a nun from my school passed by and saw me playing out front. The laundromat downstairs had been boarded up because it had been robbed two days before and the owner had painted on the wood YES WE'RE OPEN so as not to lose business.

Where do you live? she asked.

There, I said pointing up to the third floor.

You live *there*?

40 *There*. I had to look to where she pointed—the third floor, the paint peeling, wooden bars Papa had nailed on the windows so we wouldn't fall out. You live *there*? The way she said it made me feel like nothing. *There*. I lived *there*. I nodded. **B**

I knew then I had to have a house. A real house. One I could point to. But this isn't it. The house on Mango Street isn't it. For the time being, Mama says. Temporary, says Papa. But I know how those things go.

B MAKE INFERENCES ABOUT CHARACTER
Reread lines 33–43. Consider the narrator's reaction to the nun's remark. What do these lines reveal about the narrator's feelings?

My Name

In English my name means hope. In Spanish it means too many letters. It means sadness, it means waiting. It is like the number nine. A muddy color. It is the Mexican records my father plays on Sunday mornings when he is
50 shaving, songs like sobbing. **C**

It was my great-grandmother's name and now it is mine. She was a horse woman too, born like me in the Chinese year of the horse[2]—which is supposed to be bad luck if you're born female—but I think this is a Chinese lie because the Chinese, like the Mexicans, don't like their women strong.

My great-grandmother. I would've liked to have known her, a wild horse of a woman, so wild she wouldn't marry. Until my great-grandfather threw a sack over her head and carried her off. Just like that, as if she were a fancy chandelier. That's the way he did it.

C TONE
Reread lines 47–50. Identify striking words or phrases in this paragraph. What tone does Cisneros's **word choice** convey? Explain your answer.

---

2. **Chinese year of the horse:** In the traditional Chinese calendar, each succeeding year is named after 1 of 12 animals. People born in the year of the horse are thought to be energetic and quick-witted.

DIFFERENTIATED INSTRUCTION

FOR LESS–PROFICIENT READERS

2 Targeted Passage [Lines 24–32]

This passage contrasts the house on Mango Street with the narrator's expectations and shows how she feels about living there.

• What does the house look like?

• How is the house different from what the narrator had expected?

• How does the narrator feel about living in the house on Mango Street?

FOR ENGLISH LEARNERS

Key Academic Vocabulary Use Word Questioning to teach this word: *temporary* (line 46).

 BEST PRACTICES TOOLKIT—Transparency
Word Questioning p. E9

FOR ADVANCED LEARNERS/PRE–AP

Compare and Contrast Have students use a Comparison Matrix to compare Esperanza's expectations with the house her parents bought. Then have students write a brief essay that compares and contrasts an experience they have had in which the reality was different from their expectations. Encourage them to analyze what they learned from the experience.

 BEST PRACTICES TOOLKIT—Transparency
Comparison Matrix p. A24

And the story goes she never forgave him. She looked out the window her
60 whole life, the way so many women sit their sadness on an elbow. I wonder if
she made the best with what she got or was she sorry because she couldn't be
all the things she wanted to be. Esperanza. I have inherited her name, but I
don't want to inherit her place by the window. **D**

D AUTHOR'S PERSPECTIVE
Reread lines 51–63. What cultural expectations and values does Cisneros reveal in these paragraphs?

3 Targeted Passage

Lines 55–63
REINFORCE *KEY IDEA*: LEGACY
Discuss In what ways is the story of her great-grandmother a **legacy** to the narrator? **Possible answer:** *The narrator acknowledges her great-grandmother's defiance when she says that the older woman never forgave her husband for carrying her off to marry him. But, the narrator also expresses her determination not to "inherit her [great-grandmother's] place by the window" (line 63), meaning her sadness about how her life turned out.*

ANALYZE VISUALS

Activity Ask students whether they think the mood of the painting reflects Cisneros's tone. Why or why not? *Answers will vary, but students should support their responses with thoughtful reasons.*

About the Art Artist Lisa Reinke's *The Cashier* is typical of her brightly colored portraits. This bold, bright painting and the wavy lines emphasize the profile of a girl, whose serious and seemingly sad appearance may suggest the narrator of *The House on Mango Street*.

LITERARY ANALYSIS

D AUTHOR'S PERSPECTIVE

Possible answer: *Cisneros's narrative notes that "the Chinese, like the Mexicans, don't like their women strong" (line 54). The text also implies the dominant position of men when Cisneros describes how the "great-grandfather . . . carried her off . . . as if she were a fancy chandelier" (lines 56–58). The narrator then remarks that "so many women sit their sadness on an elbow" (line 60) and wonders if the great-grandmother was "sorry because she couldn't be all the things she wanted to be" (lines 61–62).*

FOR LESS–PROFICIENT READERS
3 Targeted Passage [Lines 59–63]
This passage tells the story of what happened to Esperanza's great-grandmother and shows Esperanza's feelings about it.

- What does the narrator wonder about her great-grandmother?
- What does the narrator inherit from her great-grandmother? What does she not want to inherit?

FOR ADVANCED LEARNERS/PRE–AP
Hypothesize Have students discuss to what extent the thoughts and observations on lines 59–63 are the fictional Esperanza's or Cisneros's own feelings. Ask students if they believe that the vignette of Esperanza's great-grandmother is a made-up tale or an account of events that actually happened in Cisneros's family.

At school they say my name funny as if the syllables were made out of tin and hurt the roof of your mouth. But in Spanish my name is made out of a softer something, like silver, not quite as thick as sister's name—Magdalena— which is uglier than mine. Magdalena who at least can come home and become Nenny. But I am always Esperanza.

I would like to baptize myself under a new name, a name more like the real 70 me, the one nobody sees. Esperanza as Lisandra or Maritza or Zeze the X. Yes. Something like Zeze the X will do.

Mango Says Goodbye Sometimes

I like to tell stories. I tell them inside my head. I tell them after the mailman says, Here's your mail. Here's your mail he said.

I make a story for my life, for each step my brown shoe takes. I say, "And so she trudged up the wooden stairs, her sad brown shoes taking her to the house she never liked."

I like to tell stories. I am going to tell you a story about a girl who didn't want to belong.

We didn't always live on Mango Street. Before that we lived on Loomis on 80 the third floor, and before that we lived on Keeler. Before Keeler it was Paulina, but what I remember most is Mango Street, sad red house, the house I belong but do not belong to.

I put it down on paper and then the ghost does not ache so much. I write it down and Mango says goodbye sometimes. She does not hold me with both arms. She sets me free. **E**

One day I will pack my bags of books and paper. One day I will say goodbye to Mango. I am too strong for her to keep me here forever. One day I will go away.

Friends and neighbors will say, What happened to that Esperanza? Where 90 did she go with all those books and paper? Why did she march so far away?

They will not know I have gone away to come back. For the ones I left behind. For the ones who cannot out. ❧

④ Targeted Passage

E AUTHOR'S PERSPECTIVE
Reread lines 83–85. What might the author be saying about the power of writing? Explain your answer.

E AUTHOR'S PERSPECTIVE

Possible answer: The author may be saying that writing for her is a way of expressing and releasing her feelings and a means to feel free of the difficult circumstances that constrain her.

Extend the Discussion Do you think that addressing the subject matter of *The House on Mango Street* in a *nonfiction* selection would have the same liberating power for the author? Why or why not?

SELECTION WRAP–UP

REFLECT Have students reflect on whether or not the Mango Street house is a **legacy** for the narrator. Have them support their responses with evidence from the text.

★ **CRITIQUE** The three vignettes are excerpts from a book-length work. Have students consider ways in which the vignettes are—and are not—related. Ask students to evaluate how well the three vignettes work together as a selection.

READING FLUENCY

Distribute the copy master and have students work in pairs or groups to practice fluency.

R RESOURCE MANAGER—Copy Master
Reading Fluency p. 165

DIFFERENTIATED INSTRUCTION

FOR LESS–PROFICIENT READERS

④ Targeted Passage [Lines 79–88]

This passage reveals Esperanza's feelings about the house on Mango Street, her reason for writing, and her intention to move away.

- Why does the narrator say that she does "not belong to" the house?

- What does she mean when she says, "I write it down and Mango says goodbye sometimes" (lines 83–84)?

- What does Esperanza hope to do in the future?

FOR ENGLISH LEARNERS

Comprehension: Comparisons Tell students that they will find many comparisons in the story. Point out "a wild horse of a woman" (lines 55–56), "as if . . . mouth" (lines 64–65), and "like silver" (line 66). Divide students into groups, assign each group a section of text, and have them identify other comparisons.

After Reading

Comprehension

1. **Recall** Describe Esperanza's house on Mango Street.

2. **Recall** What does Esperanza's name mean in English?

3. **Clarify** What does Esperanza mean when she refers to her home as "the house I belong but do not belong to"?

Literary Analysis

4. **Make Inferences About Character** Review the inferences you made about Esperanza as you read. Based on your inferences, what **conclusions** can you draw about this character? List the adjectives you would use to describe Esperanza, and then explain why you chose each. Cite evidence to support your conclusions.

5. **Understand Tone** How would you describe Cisneros's tone in these vignettes? Jot down words and phrases that stood out to you, and think about the tone they help create. Describe Cisneros's tone in a sentence or two.

6. **Interpret Text** Reread lines 51–63 and consider Esperanza's feelings about her **legacy.** She says she doesn't want to inherit her great-grandmother's "place by the window." What does she mean? What else doesn't she want to inherit? Explain your answer.

7. **Draw Conclusions** Consider Cisneros's statement on page 569 that she strives to "write the stories that haven't been written." On the basis of what you know about her, why do you think Cisneros chose to tell Esperanza's story? Explain your answer, citing evidence.

8. **Analyze Author's Perspective** Think about the details Cisneros includes in these vignettes, as well as Esperanza's feelings about her life. Then consider what you learned about Cisneros in the biography and background on page 569. What do you think is Cisneros's perspective on growing up poor? Use evidence from the selection as well as details from the biography to support your answer.

Literary Criticism

9. **Author's Style** Cisneros says that in writing *The House on Mango Street* she "was trying to write something that was a cross between fiction and poetry." In your opinion, are these vignettes more like verse or more like fiction? Consider the author's choice of words and details as well as what she communicates with each vignette. Defend your answer with evidence from the selection.

THE HOUSE ON MANGO STREET **575**

She writes so the "ghost does not ache so much" (lines 81–83).

6. *She doesn't want to be restricted in her activities by a dominating husband, as her great-grandmother was. She does not want to inherit a lifetime of regret, unable to pursue the things that she wants.*

7. *Esperanza's story is an example of giving "voice to the experiences of Mexican-American women" (page 569). In her portrayal of Esperanza, Cisneros suggests that Mexican-American females need not feel restricted to traditional roles; they need*

not "sit their sadness on an elbow" (line 60), as Esperanza's great-grandmother did.

8. ● **STANDARDS FOCUS** *Author's Perspective* Cisneros's childhood experience of moving into "a shabby house" in a poor Chicago neighborhood shaped her perspective on the pain of poverty and allowed her to vividly depict Esperanza's situation and feelings.

Literary Criticism

9. *Students may choose either answer, but they should support their opinions with evidence from the text.*

Practice and Apply

After Reading

For additional support of post-reading questions, use these copy masters:

R RESOURCE MANAGER—Copy Masters

Reading Check p. 163 (to check understanding of the selection)

Author's Perspective p. 159 (for practice of literary analysis standards focus)

Question Support p. 164 (After Reading questions adapted for English learners and less-proficient readers)

For additional questions, see page 153.

For additional exercises to challenge students, see:

ⓘ Power Thinking at **ClassZone.com**

ANSWERS

Comprehension

1. *It was a small, red house with tight steps, little windows, and crumbling bricks.*

2. *Esperanza means "hope" in English.*

3. *It is the house in which she lives with her family, but she does not feel a part of it.*

Literary Analysis

Possible answers:

4. ■ **STANDARDS FOCUS** *Make Inferences About Character* Esperanza's sensitivity, sense of legacy, and determination are shown by her feelings about the "sad red house," her connection to her great-grandmother, and her commitment to writing.

5. *Cisneros's tone is sad and wistful. For example, the narrator describes the house on Mango Street as "not the way they told it at all" (line 24). She says the house is "sad" and she does "not belong to it."*

Assess and Reteach

Assess

R RESOURCE MANAGER—Copy Masters
Selection Test A pp. 167–168
Selection Test B/C pp. 169–170

⊘ Test Generator CD

Reteach

S STANDARDS LESSON FILE
Literature Lesson 47: Author's Perspective
Reading Lesson 8: Making Inferences

THE HOUSE ON MANGO STREET **575**

Focus and Motivate

OBJECTIVES

- analyze a student model that reflects the key traits of problem-solution writing
- use the writing process to produce a problem-solution essay
- revise and edit, using a rubric for problem-solution writing
- plan and present a video documentary

WRITER'S ROAD MAP

WRITING PROMPTS 1 AND 2

Help students narrow their topics and choose problems appropriate to a short essay. Point out the need to narrow topics such as acid rain by focusing on certain effects or defining geographic areas.

ADDITIONAL PROMPTS

Use these prompts for practice with business writing and writing in the humanities.

WRITING PROMPT 3

Writing for the Real World Write a description of a problem with a product or service and tell ways to solve it. Try a complaint letter format.

Possible Subjects

- checkout lines that are too long
- tags that interfere with trying on clothing
- three-ring binders that break

WRITING PROMPT 4

Writing About Fine Art Artists must make two-dimensional subjects appear to have depth and must express mood in images. Find subjects in art books or use artwork that your teacher provides. Explain how the artist solved one of these problems.

Possible Subjects

- an impressionistic or abstract painting
- a cartoon or graphic novel

For additional writing prompts, see

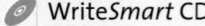 WriteSmart CD

 Writing Center at **ClassZone.com**

KEY TRAITS

Review the six **KEY TRAITS** with students, focusing primarily on ideas, organization, and word choice. Compare the list of traits with the rubric on page 582.

Writing Workshop

Problem-Solution Essay

What problems have you encountered in your life? How did you solve them? Writing about a problem can help you clarify possible solutions and persuade others to take action. To learn how to write about problems and solutions that matter to you, consult the **Writer's Road Map.**

WRITER'S ROAD MAP
Problem-Solution Essay

WRITING PROMPT 1

Writing for the Real World Problems exist at school, at home, in your community, and in the world at-large. Sometimes writing about a problem can help you find a solution. Choose a problem that deeply interests you, and write an essay in which you define the problem, examine its causes, and explore possible solutions.

Problems to Explore

- environmental issues, such as acid rain or noise pollution
- issues at school, such as video cameras in the hallways, locker searches, or metal detectors

WRITING PROMPT 2

Writing from Literature Sometimes, something you read makes you think about a problem in a new way. Choose a problem you found in a literary work that you want to explore. Write an essay in which you describe the problem and identify a possible solution.

Selections to Explore

- "Island Morning" (homesickness)
- "The Lost Boys" (adjusting to a new life)

 WRITING TOOLS
For prewriting, revision, and editing tools, visit the **Writing Center** at ClassZone.com.

KEY TRAITS

1. IDEAS

- States the problem in a clearly worded **thesis statement**
- Explores the **causes and effects** of the problem
- Addresses different **solutions**
- Chooses the **best solution** and supports it with relevant **details**

2. ORGANIZATION

- Shows the **significance** of the problem in the **introduction**
- Uses **transitions** to connect ideas
- Follows a consistent **organizational pattern**
- Concludes with a strongly stated **call to action**

3. VOICE

- **Tone** is suited to topic, audience, and purpose

4. WORD CHOICE

- Uses **precise words** to convey the problem and solution

5. SENTENCE FLUENCY

- Uses a variety of **sentence types**

6. CONVENTIONS

- Employs **correct grammar and usage**

Writing Workshop Resources

 RESOURCE MANAGER UNIT 5

Plan and Teach pp. 171–174
Prewriting–Editing pp. 175–179
Writing Rubric p. 180
Publishing with Technology p. 181
Writing Support p. 182

 **STANDARDS LESSON FILE**

Writing Lesson 26: Problem-Solution Essay

BEST PRACTICES TOOLKIT

Scaffolding Writing Instruction pp. 43–46*
Problem and Solution Charts • Cause-and-Effect Graphics • Writing Template: Problem and Solution • Reporter's Questions • Storyboard

TECHNOLOGY

 Easy Planner DVD
 Writing Center at **ClassZone.com**
WriteSmart CD

* Resources for Differentiation

Part 1: Analyze a Student Model

Karen Conboy
Belleplaine Academy

The Disappearing Arts

Walking down the halls at Belleplaine Academy isn't like it used to be. No new artwork decorates our school, and the paintings and sculptures from years past are becoming dusty. Instead of the sweet sounds of the swing choir or the sharps and flats of an orchestra tuning
5 up, there are only slamming doors and shuffling feet. Why? After the state legislature reduced funding for education, our local school board eliminated arts classes. Students must have a chance to learn about and practice fine arts, or we will miss out on a vital part of our education.

The two major causes of eliminating arts classes are money and
10 priorities. Our state has serious budget problems, and the first programs to get cut are so-called nonessential subjects, such as the arts and physical education. Many administrators and teachers believe that schools have to concentrate on traditional subjects, such as reading, history, math, and writing, so that students can get into college
15 and compete for jobs. As a result, the arts are a low priority; they're considered "extras."

However, the arts deserve to be a higher priority. Participating in the arts can help motivate and focus students. A Stanford University study showed that young people who participate in the arts are four times as
20 likely as nonparticipants to be recognized for academic achievement and more than four times as likely to perform community service. Learning to draw, paint, act, dance, sing, or play an instrument can build confidence. A chance to create or perform can encourage a reluctant student to keep attending school. Also, learning about the arts can give

KEY TRAITS IN ACTION

Vivid description in the introduction "hooks" the reader. **Thesis statement** explains the problem and its **significance.**

The writer explores the **causes and effects** of the problem.

Transitions connect ideas.

The writer provides relevant **statistics and reasons** to explain why her position is valid. **Tone** is appropriate to her audience—anyone who cares about education.

Teach

Part 1: Analyze a Student Model

Have students read the Student Model and **KEY TRAITS IN ACTION.** Then discuss the model with the class, pointing out specific examples of each trait and building on what students have already noted. You may also wish to incorporate these activities:

- **Thesis Statement** Write this weak thesis statement on the board:

  > When the local school board cut the art classes, it created a real problem.

  Ask a student to read this statement and lines 7–8 of the Student Model aloud. Ask what is missing from the thesis statement on the board and why this omission matters. **Possible answers:** *The thesis statement on the board identifies the problem but does not explain its significance or importance. Readers may have no idea why cutting art classes might cause a problem. Further, they may not care. The thesis statement in the Student Model gives details that help readers care.*

- **Transitions** Point out that the Student Model has more than one type of transition, including those showing cause-effect, time order, and comparison-contrast. Ask students to find some examples of each.

- **Relevant Details** Point out that the student author used statistics and reasons to explain her position. However, other kinds of details in a problem-solution essay might include **specific examples** that illustrate the problem or solution, **anecdotes** (brief stories that make a point or provide a specific example), and **expert testimony** (quotations or statements from experts in the field).

DIFFERENTIATED INSTRUCTION

For general guidelines on differentiating writing instruction, see

 BEST PRACTICES TOOLKIT
Scaffolding Writing Instruction pp. 43–46

FOR ENGLISH LEARNERS
Language: Skill Words Write these terms on the board and review them with students:

- *thesis statement:* one or two sentences stating the main idea of an essay. A problem-solution thesis identifies the problem and its importance.

- *significance:* importance

- *transitions:* words that show how ideas are related or joined. Transitions are sometimes called *signal words.* Identify examples on the

page and clarify the relationship each shows, such as cause-and-effect or comparison-contrast.

- *statistics:* facts that can be expressed by numbers, such as those in lines 19–21

- *precise words:* words that say exactly what the writer means; for example, *jogs* instead of *goes*

- *call to action:* a statement that urges readers to do something in response to the problem

- **Sentence Types** Point out other ways to vary sentence types, such as by connecting two sentences with a conjunction. As an example, review the GRAMMAR AND STYLE note on page 518 and the sentences to which it refers. Remind students that varying sentence types and structures creates more interesting writing.

  Ask students to find the following sentence types in the Student Model: a compound sentence, made up of two or more independent clauses joined by *and, but, so,* or *or*; a sentence with a compound subject; and a sentence with a compound predicate.

- **Relevant Details** Explain that relevant details are those that are directly related to the issue. Discuss what makes the writer's details relevant. *Possible answers: They support the solution, are possible, and are specific.*

- **Conclusion** Point out that a call to action is just one way to conclude a problem-solution essay. Other techniques include:

  Make a Prediction: The writer might predict a likely outcome if readers do or do not solve the problem or choose the correct solution.

  Ask a Question: The writer might ask a question that encourages readers to agree or disagree with the proposed solution.

For interactive student models, see

🖸 Write*Smart* CD

ℹ Writing Center at **ClassZone.com**

---

25 us new ideas about what careers to pursue after graduation.

How can we solve this problem? Some people want to pressure the state legislature to increase the amount of money it provides for education. They suggest letter-writing campaigns and even marching to the capitol. With more money, they argue, local school boards could 30 restore the programs and classes they've had to cut. The legislature has made it clear, however, that it can't provide money that it doesn't have.

We can't count on financial help from the state, so the best solution is to start thinking creatively and provide our own arts education. For example, students could start our own after-school and weekend arts 35 activities. We could plan visits to local art museums and galleries. We might also start student-run arts clubs, such as a photography club for students interested in learning how to shoot and print photos, or a theater club for those who want to see locally produced plays. Teachers can also get involved, sponsoring clubs and using online resources from 40 organizations such as Americans for the Arts to bring arts education into their classes. Furthermore, community members can be a valuable resource. Local artists, actors, and musicians might be persuaded to donate some time to teach young people about their particular crafts.

Budget cuts do not have to signal the end of arts education. We can 45 do for ourselves what the state is unable to do. With determination, passion, and creativity, we can fill the halls of Belleplaine with art and music once again.

> The writer **varies sentence types,** using an occasional question to add interest to her writing. She addresses **different solutions** to the problem.

> She offers what she considers **the best solution** and supports it with **relevant details.**

> A strong **conclusion** uses **precise words** (*determination, passion, creativity*) to **call** audience members **to action.**

2

DIFFERENTIATED INSTRUCTION

FOR ENGLISH LEARNERS

Comprehension: Transitions Review different types of transitional language. Help students locate transitions in the model and discuss the function that each serves. Then have students create sample sentences using these transitions:

- *Instead* (line 3) *contrasts* the sounds of the school with music education with the silence of the school without it

- *so* (lines 14, 32) highlights *cause-effect* links, telling why the school board made its choice and why students must act on their own

- *Also* (line 24) emphasizes a point by *adding detail*

- *For example* (lines 33–34) connects a detail to an idea by identifying it as an *example*

- *Furthermore* (line 41) connects *details* in a list to show that all relate to the same idea

To provide English learners with additional writing support, see

🅡 RESOURCE MANAGER—Copy Master Writing Support p. 182

Part 2: Apply the Writing Process

PREWRITING

What Should I Do?

What Does It Look Like?

1. Analyze the prompt.
Look closely at the prompt you chose on page 576. (Circle) the words that tell you what to do. Think about how you will choose a problem and how you will structure your essay.

▶ **WRITING PROMPT** Problems exist at school, at home, in your community, and in the world. Sometimes writing about a problem can help you find a solution. Choose a problem that deeply interests you, and write an essay in which you define the problem, examine its causes, and explore possible solutions.

It's clear from the prompt that my essay will be organized into three parts—the problem, its causes, and its solutions.

2. Consider possible problems.
Think of some general categories of problems to explore. List each category on a sheet of paper and under each write whatever specific problems come to mind. Put a star next to the problem you want to write about.

▶
Environment	Privacy	School
• the West Side landfill • summer ozone alerts	• no lockers at school • cameras in the mall's food court	✳ • no fine arts classes • security guards

3. Brainstorm possible solutions.
Now that you've selected a problem to write about, you need to consider possible solutions. Create a graphic organizer, such as a cluster diagram, to write down all the ways the problem might be solved.

TIP Don't edit as you brainstorm. Write down every possible solution you can think of.

▶
Protest at state capitol — Letters to representatives
More money from state — *No fine arts classes* — Get teachers involved
Bring in local artists — After-school activities

4. Collect supporting details.
Find details that support your solution. You might interview people, do research in newspapers or magazines, or check out relevant Internet sites.

▶
Ideas for Sources	Questions to Ask
• local newspaper • school librarian • the Internet	• What arts programs exist in our community? • What sources outside of school can help?

FOR ENGLISH LEARNERS
Writing: Analyzing Prompts Help students understand the three key verbs in the prompt that they may not understand in this context:

• *define:* decide and tell the nature of the problem and its important qualities

• *examine:* look carefully at the different parts

• *explore:* consider in some detail, such as by naming different possible results

FOR ADVANCED LEARNERS/PRE–AP
Choosing Problems [paired option] Urge students to select problems with multiple causes or multiple effects, such as rising ticket prices or violence in video games. Have students brainstorm in pairs, then use an organizer to list.

 BEST PRACTICES TOOLKIT—Transparency Cause-and-Effect Graphics p. B16

Practice and Apply

To support students during the writing process, use these copy masters:

R RESOURCE MANAGER—Copy Masters
Prewriting–Editing pp. 175–179
Writing Rubric p. 180
Writing Support p. 182 (for English learners)

Part 2: Apply the Writing Process

PREWRITING

1. Analyze the prompt. Stress that circling the parts of the task ensures that writers do not skip any elements. Urge students to complete this exercise, paying particular attention to verbs that identify tasks.

2. Consider possible problems. Students who have trouble thinking of categories or problems might think about topics that are often discussed on talk shows, on news shows, and with family members. Invite students with similar categories to exchange ideas.

3. Brainstorm possible solutions. Students may wish to work in pairs or small groups to brainstorm solutions orally before filling in graphic organizers. Make sure that they have noted the **TIP** in this step. Explain that editing limits the value of brainstorming, because although an idea may not be useful in itself, it may trigger another idea that is.

4. Collect supporting details. Briefly review with students the types of details they might use. Have them suggest possible sources for each.

• facts and statistics *(encyclopedias, almanacs, Internet)*

• reasons *(interviews, editorials)*

• expert testimony *(interviews, news stories)*

• examples *(newspapers, magazines, Internet)*

• anecdotes *(personal experience, interviews, newspapers)*

 **BEST PRACTICES TOOLKIT—Transparency** Problem and Solution Charts p. B20

For interactive graphic organizers, see

🖉 Write*Smart* CD

ℹ Writing Center at **ClassZone.com**

DRAFTING

1. Identify the problem and its significance. Tell students to consider their audience to determine how much detail they need to provide about the problem. Have them ask themselves these questions:

- How much does my audience know about the general topic or situation?
- What details about the specific problem should I provide?
- What details will help readers understand the significance of the problem?

2. Decide where to state your solution. Students who choose to state the solution immediately after the problem may want to use transitional phrases (*propose, reason for, problem, one answer, solution*) or sentences (*This problem has several causes. Solutions are few.*) to clarify that they are discussing solutions, not causes.

3. Explain causes and effects. Remind students to avoid the *false cause fallacy*, which means assuming that because one event followed another, the first event caused the second to happen. For example, computer use may rise, and math skills may fall, but rising computer use may not be the cause of the falloff in math skills.

4. Address different solutions. Explain that good problem-solution essays maintain a civil tone and avoid propaganda, which uses distorted, false, or misleading information. To be convincing, writers should acknowledge valid aspects of alternative solutions, then provide support to show why their solutions are better.

For a problem-solving writing template, see

📦 **BEST PRACTICES TOOLKIT—Transparency**
   Writing Template: Persuasive Writing:
   Problem and Solution pp. C16, C33

💿 Write*Smart* CD

ℹ️ Writing Center at **ClassZone.com**

What Should I Do?	What Does It Look Like?
1. Identify the problem and its significance. Early on in your essay, let your readers know what problem you are addressing. Also, give them some sense of why the problem is important to you.	Students must have a chance to learn about and practice fine arts, or we will miss out on a vital part of our education. — Problem / Significance
2. Decide where to state your solution. Some writers choose to state the solution right after they identify the problem. Other writers prefer to state the problem, discuss its causes, and then propose a solution.	(Paragraph 1) Local school board eliminated arts classes ... Problem (Paragraph 2) The two major causes ... Causes (Paragraph 4) How can we solve this problem? ... Solution
3. Explain causes and effects. Every problem has at least one cause. Likewise, an important problem has significant effects. Be sure to provide details, such as facts, statistics, examples, and quotations, to make causes and effects clear.	Causes: — Effects on Students: no money in budget → arts classes cut arts not a priority → money put toward more traditional subjects
4. Address different solutions. People see problems and solutions from different points of view. Discussing a variety of solutions lets your reader know that you've looked at the issue from all sides. **TIP** For more advice as you draft, consult the **key traits on page 576** and the **rubric and peer-reader questions on page 582.**	How can we solve this problem? Some people want to pressure the state legislature to increase the amount of money it provides for education. They suggest letter-writing campaigns and even marching to the capitol. With more money, they argue, local school boards could restore the programs and classes they've had to cut. The legislature has made it clear, however, that it can't provide money that it doesn't have.

DIFFERENTIATED INSTRUCTION

FOR LESS-PROFICIENT WRITERS
Deciding Where to State the Solution
To help students organize their essays, provide the following frame, explaining that it shows the organization of the student model. Have students follow this model to plan their own essays:

Beginning Paragraph
- Find an opening "hook."
- Identify the problem and why it matters.

Middle Paragraphs—Problem and Solutions
- Discuss causes and effects of the problem.
- Identify possible solutions.
- Suggest one solution as best.
- Provide details about this solution.

End Paragraphs
- Restate the problem and solution.
- State a call to action.

REVISING AND EDITING

What Should I Do?	What Does It Look Like?

1. Provide a "hook."
- Draw a box around the first two or three sentences of your essay. Do they capture your reader's attention?
- If not, add a vivid description, a bit of dialogue, or an interesting fact or statistic.

▶ *Walking down the halls at Belleplaine Academy isn't like it used to be. No new artwork decorates our school.* Instead of the sweet sounds of the swing choir, there are only slamming doors and shuffling feet. Why? After the state legislature reduced funding for education, our local school board eliminated arts classes.

2. Add supporting details.
- Underline supporting details in your essay.
- If you have few words or phrases underlined, add interesting facts, statistics, examples, or quotations to make your writing more informative.

▶ Many administrators and teachers believe that schools have to concentrate on traditional subjects so that students can get into college and compete for jobs.
, such as reading, history, math, and writing,

3. Address different solutions thoroughly.
- Number the parts of your essay where you discuss different solutions.
- Add additional solutions or details to further clarify your argument.

▶ For example, students could start our own ① after-school and weekend arts activities. We could plan visits to local art museums and galleries.
We might also start student-run arts clubs, such as ② a photography club or a theater club.

4. Strengthen the conclusion.
- Ask a peer reader to draw a wavy line under parts of your conclusion that seem weak or vague.
- How well does the conclusion sum up your ideas? Strengthen your conclusion so that it reinforces what has gone before.

See page 582: Ask a Peer Reader

▶ Budget cuts do not have to signal the end of arts education. We can do for ourselves what the state is unable to do. With determination, passion, and creativity, we can fill the halls of Belleplaine with art and music once again.

REVISING AND EDITING

1. Provide a "hook." Discuss additional ways to hook the attention of readers, such as
- a short anecdote that shows an effect of the problem
- an interesting question
- a new twist on a quotation or proverb

2. Add supporting details. In addition to cause-and-effect details, students might use comparison-contrast details to highlight either the problem or the solution. For example, they might compare a situation before and after a problem surfaced; they might compare and contrast possible solutions.

3. Address different solutions thoroughly. Students may be unsure how to add details to solutions. Suggest that they
- explain benefits and shortcomings of different solutions
- use descriptive language to illustrate the results of different solutions
- provide expert opinions on different solutions

4. Strengthen the conclusion. Point out that abstract nouns, which name ideas, can often help lend scale and importance to a conclusion, especially in the call for action.

For interactive revision tools, see

🔘 Write*Smart* CD

ℹ️ Writing Center at **ClassZone.com**

Review the **GRAMMAR AND STYLE** note on page 528 and the words to which it refers. Point out how the abstract ideas of *determination, passion,* and *creativity* in the Student Model elevate the call to action beyond the writer's literal meaning of "make our own art program." This invites readers to feel that participating in the solution is important.

FOR ENGLISH LEARNERS

Add Supporting Details Simplify the task of revising and editing by encouraging students to provide supporting details for only the problem, the best solution, and just one other solution. Then point out that one way to generate additional details is by using the Reporter's Questions. You may need to review the meaning of *how, who, what, where, when, why,* and *so what.* Have students answer these questions for the problem and the two solutions identified. From the answers, they can draw additional details to flesh out their ideas.

Students might work in pairs to generate details and to evaluate which to include.

 BEST PRACTICES TOOLKIT—Transparency Reporter's Questions p. C9

Preparing to Publish

Support for meeting the goals in the writing rubric is supplied throughout the Writing Workshop on pages 579–581.

For Rubric Bank, see

 WriteSmart CD

Writing Center at ClassZone.com

Assess and Reteach

S STANDARDS LESSON FILE
Writing Lesson 26: Problem-Solution Essay

Preparing to Publish **Problem-Solution Essay**

Apply the Rubric

A strong problem-solution essay . . .

☑ clearly identifies the problem

☑ helps the reader understand the issues involved

☑ analyzes the causes and effects of the problem

☑ includes relevant facts, statistics, examples, or quotations

☑ explores more than one possible solution

☑ persuasively supports the most suitable solution

☑ uses language and a tone that are appropriate to the audience

☑ uses a variety of sentence types

Ask a Peer Reader

• How would you describe the problem I wrote about?

• How could I explain the causes and effects more clearly?

• What could I add or subtract to improve my conclusion?

Add Transition Words

For Introducing Causes and Effects	
after	for this reason
as a result	if . . . then
because	since
before	so
consequently	therefore

Check Your Grammar

• Use a comma before the conjunction that joins the two main clauses of a compound sentence.

> Our state has serious budget problems, and the first programs to get cut are so-called nonessential subjects, such as the arts and physical education.

• Use a semicolon to join the parts of a compound sentence if no coordinating conjunction is used.

> As a result, the arts are a low priority ; they're considered "extras."

See page R63: Compound Sentences

Writing Online

PUBLISHING OPTIONS
For publishing options, visit the **Writing Center** at **ClassZone.com**.

ASSESSMENT PREPARATION
For writing and grammar assessment practice, go to the **Assessment Center** at **ClassZone.com**.

Producing a Video Documentary

A video documentary can dramatize the problem you explored and the solution you proposed. Follow these guidelines.

Planning the Documentary

1. **Create a script.** Use your essay as the basis for the **script** of your documentary. Your script will contain narration, stage directions, camera directions, and directions for inserting interviews.

2. **Create a storyboard.** Use sketches to illustrate, shot by shot, what viewers will see. Think about including various shots: **close-ups**, **medium shots**, and **establishing shots.**

Voice-over:
Students are missing out on an important part of a well-rounded education.

Voice-over:
Some people want to pressure the state legislature to increase education funding.

Voice-over:
But without financial help from the state, the best solution is to start thinking creatively.

Producing the Documentary

1. **Shoot the footage and record the voice-over.** Using your completed script and a digital camcorder, shoot the scenes that will make up your finished documentary. Get help from students and teachers who are willing to appear in your video. Record the voice-over—the narrative the viewers will hear.

2. **Wrap it up.** Using video-editing software, edit your documentary until you're satisfied with the sequence of scenes. Add a title screen, credits, and music if appropriate.

WRITING WORKSHOP   **583**

Assessment Practice

CHECK READINESS

Read aloud the paragraph under **ASSESS** and stress to students that this is not the full Unit Test, but a way for them to check their readiness for it. Then have students examine the skills listed under **REVIEW** and look back in the unit or in the **Student Resource Bank** for any skills they need to review.

READ THE SELECTIONS

Remind students to keep unit goals in mind as they read each passage, paying particular attention to these literary and reading skills:

- author's perspective
- author's purpose
- patterns of organization
- text features
- make inferences
- main ideas
- media: visual information

To help students focus on author's purpose, encourage them to ask questions such as

- What are some reasons that authors write stories? What purpose might the writers of selections have?
- What types of details helped you determine these purposes?

ANSWER THE QUESTIONS

Direct students to pages R93–R101 of the **Handbook** for Test-Taking Strategies. Tell students not to waste time looking for patterns in the answer choices of multiple-choice tests. Explain that editors vary the placement of correct answers to ensure that they are not predictable. Instead, students should carefully read all the choices and then eliminate any that are clearly wrong. They should then try to determine which of the remaining options is most accurate and complete. Remind students to refer back to the selection if necessary, because this can help them choose correct answers.

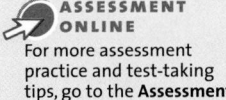

Assessment Practice

ASSESS
The practice test items on the next few pages match skills listed on the Unit Goals page (page 507) and addressed throughout this unit. Taking this practice test will help you assess your knowledge of these skills and determine your readiness for the Unit Test.

REVIEW
After you take the practice test, your teacher can help you identify any skills you need to review.

- Author's Perspective
- Author's Purpose
- Patterns of Organization
- Text Features
- Make Inferences
- Main Ideas
- Media: Visual Information
- Word Roots
- Technical/Specialized Vocabulary
- Concrete and Abstract Nouns
- Adverbs
- Coordinating Conjunctions

Reading Comprehension

DIRECTIONS *Read the following selections and then answer the questions.*

His Name Was Pete

William Faulkner

His name was Pete. He was just a dog, a fifteen-months-old pointer, still almost a puppy even though he had spent one hunting season learning to be the dog he would have been in another two or three if he had lived that long.

But he was just a dog. He expected little of the world into which he came without past and nothing of immortality either:—food (he didn't care what nor how little just so it was given with affection—a touch of a hand, a voice he knew even if he could not understand and answer the words it spoke); the earth to run on; air to breathe, sun and rain in their seasons and the covied quail which were his heritage long before he knew the earth and felt the sun,
10 whose scent he knew already from his staunch and faithful ancestry before he himself ever winded it. That was all he wanted. But that would have been enough to fill the eight or ten or twelve years of his natural life because twelve years are not very many and it doesn't take much to fill them.

Yet short as twelve years are, he should normally have outlived four of the kind of motorcars which killed him—cars capable of climbing hills too fast to avoid a grown pointer dog. But Pete didn't outlive the first of his four. He wasn't chasing it; he had learned not to do that before he was allowed on highways. He was standing on the road waiting for his little mistress on the horse to catch up, to squire her safely home. He shouldn't have been in the
20 road. He paid no road tax, held no driver's license, didn't vote. Perhaps his trouble was that the motorcar which lived in the same yard he lived in had a horn and brakes on it and he thought they all did. To say he didn't see the car because the car was between him and the late afternoon sun is a bad excuse because that brings the question of vision into it and certainly no one unable with the sun at his back to see a grown pointer dog on a curveless two-lane highway would think of permitting himself to drive a car at all, let alone one without either horn or brakes because next time Pete might be a human child and killing human children with motorcars is against the law.

No, the driver was in a hurry: that was the reason. Perhaps he had several
30 miles to go yet and was already late for supper. That was why he didn't have time to slow or stop or drive around Pete. And since he didn't have time to do that, naturally he didn't have time to stop afterward; besides Pete was only a dog flung broken and crying into a roadside ditch and anyway the car had passed him by then and the sun was at Pete's back now, so how could the driver be expected to hear his crying?

DIFFERENTIATED INSTRUCTION

FOR ENGLISH LEARNERS
Assessment Practice: Work Backward

Prepare students by having them read the questions *before* reading the passages. Have pairs find unfamiliar words in test directions and questions. Then follow these steps:

1. Write each word in a Knowledge Rating chart.

2. Have partners offer definitions of words they think they know. Fill in correct definitions.

3. Help students understand the meanings of the other words.

Culture: Clarify Identify the dog breeds mentioned: *pointer* (line 1 of "Pete"), *border collie* (line 1 of "Dog Proves..."), and *labradoodle* (Web page). Also explain the term *motorcar* (line 15 of "Pete"), an older word for an automobile.

 BEST PRACTICES TOOLKIT—Transparency Knowledge Rating p. E3

But Pete has forgiven him. In his year and a quarter of life he never had anything but kindness from human beings; he would gladly give the other six or eight or ten of it rather than make one late for supper.

Dog Proves As Smart As Average Toddler

Margaret Munro

A nine-year-old border collie with a 200-word "vocabulary" has provided scientific proof that dogs understand what their masters are saying, according to new research.

Knows Word Meanings

Rico knows the meaning of about 200 words and can infer and remember the meaning of new ones with the same ability as very young children, according to a report published in the journal *Science* yesterday.

Rico, who lives in Germany, can retrieve randomly chosen items from a collection of balls and toys. He understands requests to put toys in boxes and
10 bring them to certain people.

He can also fetch, by name, objects that he has never seen before.

A month after seeing them just once, he still remembered and fetched the new objects on demand, reported Julia Fischer and her colleagues with the Max Planck Institute for Evolutionary Anthropology.

Makes Inferences

The scientists say Rico's abilities provide evidence that dogs are capable of a type of learning and inference that has long been considered the domain of humans.

"There are some things that some people believe are uniquely human, such
20 as language acquisition," said Ms. Fischer. "Maybe it's not so special after all."

She said dogs appear to have innate and superior word-learning skills, which could help explain why they are such popular pets.

One of Canada's leading dog experts is impressed.

"It doesn't surprise me, but it's wonderful someone actually set out and spent all the time to plug that stuff into [Rico's] mind," said Dr. Stanley Coren, a psychologist at the University of British Columbia who has written extensively about the intelligence of dogs.

 GO ON

ITEM ANALYSIS

COMPREHENSION AND WRITTEN RESPONSES	ITEMS	UNIT PAGES
Author's Perspective	1, 3, 10	508–513, 569
Author's Purpose	4, 5, 11	508–513, 547, 561
Patterns of Organization	5, 6, 8	508–513, 515
Text Features	5, 8, 9	535
Make Inferences	1, 2, 3, 4, 5, 7	569
Main Ideas	2, 7, 11	525
Media: Visual Information	8, 9	547

VOCABULARY	ITEMS	UNIT PAGES
Word Roots	1, 2, 3, 4	532
Technical/Specialized Vocabulary	5, 6, 7, 8	545

WRITING AND GRAMMAR	ITEMS	UNIT PAGES
Concrete and Abstract Nouns	2, 5	533
Adverbs	3, 6	567
Coordinating Conjunctions	1, 4	523

FOR LESS–PROFICIENT READERS

Assessment Support Consider these options for completing the Assessment Practice:

- Have students "work backward" to review the test questions *before* reading the passages.
- Select random questions in the Assessment, and have students demonstrate how and where to look for the answers.
- Ask students to locate unfamiliar vocabulary words in the Assessment. Elicit their meanings from the class.
- Have students record useful testing words and definitions in their journals for later reference.
- Read the selections or parts of them aloud to aid in student comprehension.

McDougal Littell
Assessment System

After checking student readiness with this Assessment Practice, you may administer the complete Unit 5 Test in order to more thoroughly evaluate student mastery of unit goals.

ANSWERS

Comprehension

Model a thinking process for answering multiple-choice questions.

1. **C is correct.** *The author is clearly angry at the driver of the car. A is incorrect because the author never talks down to readers. B is incorrect, since the author is not yearning for the past in general. D is incorrect, since the author uses imagery (lines 8–11), personification (line 36), and other literary devices, rather than just stating facts.*

2. **D is correct,** *because it expresses the author's central idea. A, B, and C are details that support this idea.*

3. **B is correct.** *The author describes the driver as impatient and unfeeling. A is incorrect because the author is clearly not sympathetic with the driver. C is completely untrue. D is incorrect, because the author shows his sympathy for Pete by describing his cries.*

4. **C is correct.** *The author describes his feelings and is persuasive, in a sarcastic way. A is totally incorrect. The author makes no attempt to provide facts or entertain. B and D are also incorrect, because each is partially untrue. The author neither informs nor entertains.*

5. **A is correct.** *The subheadings provide information about things Rico can do. B, C, and D are not supported by any clues in the subheadings.*

6. **B is correct** *and is supported both by the title and by lines 5–6. A is completely incorrect. Although two scientists are mentioned, they are never contrasted, so C is incorrect. D is incorrect, because the two subjects are mentioned but not compared or contrasted.*

7. **C is correct.** *Faulkner describes Pete waiting for his mistress, and Munro describes a dog that fetches objects for a person. Pete has learned not to chase cars, so A is unsupported. B can be inferred only from Faulkner's essay. D is also unsupported, because the human is praised for patience and the dog is not ("Dog Proves As Smart as Average-Toddler," lines 22–23).*

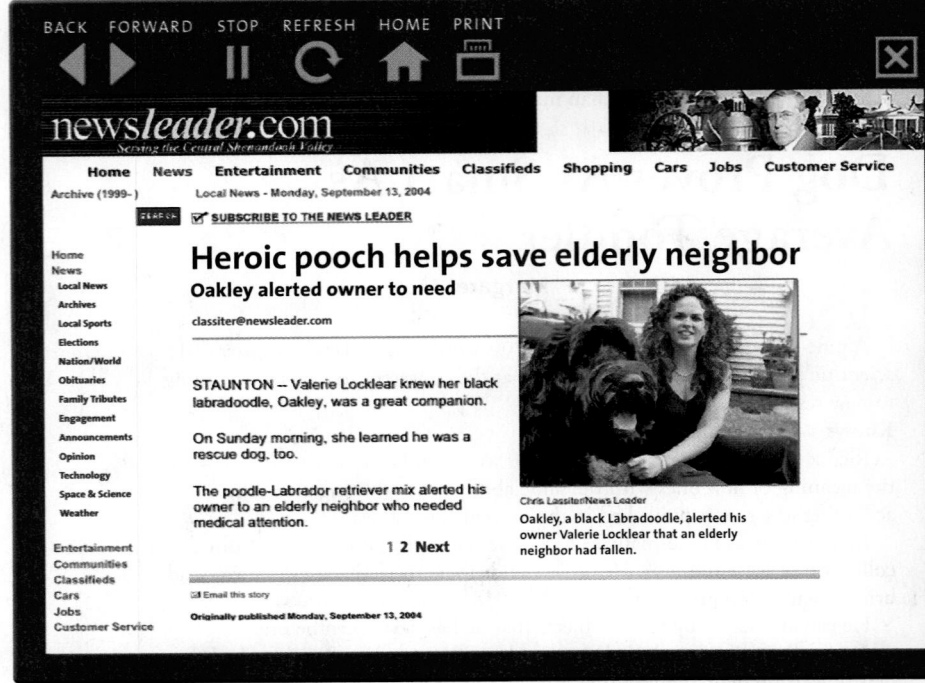

newsleader.com
Serving the Central Shenandoah Valley

Home | News | Entertainment | Communities | Classifieds | Shopping | Cars | Jobs | Customer Service

Archive (1999–)   Local News - Monday, September 13, 2004

☑ SUBSCRIBE TO THE NEWS LEADER

Home
News
   Local News
   Archives
   Local Sports
   Elections
   Nation/World
   Obituaries
   Family Tributes
   Engagement
   Announcements
   Opinion
   Technology
   Space & Science
   Weather
Entertainment
Communities
Classifieds
Cars
Jobs
Customer Service

Heroic pooch helps save elderly neighbor
Oakley alerted owner to need

classiter@newsleader.com

STAUNTON -- Valerie Locklear knew her black labradoodle, Oakley, was a great companion.

On Sunday morning, she learned he was a rescue dog, too.

The poodle-Labrador retriever mix alerted his owner to an elderly neighbor who needed medical attention.

1 2 Next

Chris Lassiter/News Leader
Oakley, a black Labradoodle, alerted his owner Valerie Locklear that an elderly neighbor had fallen.

✉ Email this story

Originally published Monday, September 13, 2004

Comprehension

DIRECTIONS *Answer these questions about the essay "His Name Was Pete."*

1. Which word best describes the author's tone throughout this essay?
   A superior
   B nostalgic
   C sarcastic
   D straightforward

2. What is the main idea of lines 14–28?
   A Pete didn't chase cars.
   B Pete shouldn't have been on the road.
   C Running over children is illegal.
   D There is no excuse for running over a dog.

3. In lines 34–35, the phrase "how could the driver" reveals the author's
   A sympathy with the driver
   B anger at the driver
   C feelings about cars
   D impatience with Pete

4. The author's two purposes in writing this essay were to
   A inform and entertain
   B inform and express feelings
   C persuade and express feelings
   D persuade and entertain

586

8. **C is correct.** *The title identifies the "heroic" one as a "pooch," the caption identifies the dog as a "black Labradoodle," and the photograph shows that the dog is large. A and B identify the victim, not the hero. D is incorrect because the dog's owner is a contributor to the rescue, not its main hero.*

9. **C is correct,** *because "Local News" is listed in the column on the left. A is incorrect, because the lead is on this page. B and D are also incorrect, because they are not shown as possibilities.*

DIRECTIONS *Answer these questions about the article "Dog Proves As Smart As Average Toddler."*

5. The subheadings "Knows Word Meanings" and "Makes Inferences" are clues that the author's primary purpose is to

   A inform or explain

   B persuade

   C entertain

   D express feelings

6. One way the author organizes the article is by comparing and contrasting

   A words and toys

   B dogs and children

   C scientists and research projects

   D pets and language acquisition

DIRECTIONS *Answer this question about both selections.*

7. Which one of the following statements would most likely be supported by both authors?

   A Most dogs are not as smart as Rico.

   B A dog should always be on a leash.

   C Dogs can interact with people.

   D Dogs are patient animals.

DIRECTIONS *Answer these questions about the news Web site.*

8. From the information in the photograph and the caption, you can identify that the hero of the story is

   A an elderly woman who fell down

   B someone who needed medical attention

   C a large black dog called a labradoodle

   D Valerie Locklear, a dog owner who lives in Staunton

9. Which of the following could you find by selecting a hyperlink from the menu on this Web site?

   A the lead to this story

   B a video clip of Oakley's rescue

   C more local news

   D more pictures of Oakley

Written Response

SHORT RESPONSE
Write three or four sentences to answer the question.

10. What was Faulkner's attitude toward the dog's death in "His Name Was Pete"? Support your answer with details from the essay.

EXTENDED RESPONSE
Write two or three paragraphs to answer the question.

11. Compare and contrast the main ideas of "His Name Was Pete" and "Dog Proves As Smart As Average Toddler." Name one way in which the selections are alike and one way in which they are different. Support your answer with two details from each of the selections.

GO ON ➡

587

Written Response

Possible short responses:

10. *The narrator is sad and angry that the car hit Pete.*

    He is sad because the dog was doing a good thing when he was hit. He was standing in the road waiting for the little girl on her horse to catch up with him so he could escort her home safely (lines 18–19). The driver was too busy to slow down for Pete or to stop when he hit him. Recalling Pete's kindness, the narrator implies that the dog gladly sacrificed his life so that the driver wouldn't be late for supper.

    You can feel the narrator's anger when he says, sarcastically, that Pete had no right to be in the road because he didn't pay taxes, hold a driver's license, or vote (line 20). He uses that same tone to suggest that one shouldn't be driving a car "without either horn or brakes" (line 27).

Possible extended response:

11. *The response should clearly state similarities and differences in the selections. Responses should contrast the purpose and tone of the selections by pointing out that "His Name Was Pete" is an emotional essay expressing sadness and anger with a sarcastic tone, while "Dog Proves As Smart . . ." is a factual report with an objective and balanced tone. Similarities might include that the main ideas of both selections focus on praiseworthy and intelligent dogs. Supporting details might include Pete's learning not to chase cars and Rico's understanding of 200 words.*

DIFFERENTIATED INSTRUCTION

FOR ENGLISH LEARNERS

Test-Taking Strategies: Understanding Instructions Read aloud the instructions for the Short Response, along with the sentences that make up the item. Discuss with students the tasks they must accomplish:

- Write 3–4 sentences.
- Answer the question. (Point out that there is not an actual question.)
- Support the answer with essay details.

Follow a similar procedure with the instructions for the Extended Response, making sure that students identify all the tasks:

- Compare the main ideas of the selections.
- Contrast the main ideas of the selections.
- Name one way they are alike and one way they are different.
- Use two details from each selection as support.

Vocabulary

1. **A is correct.** Since im- and in- mean "not," the word immortality is something like "not death." We can eliminate B and C, since they have nothing to do with life or death. The context in the story helps to eliminate D.

2. **C is correct.** The word birth directly relates to "born." The words humans in A, time in B, and memory in D reflect general concepts but do not relate to being born.

3. **D is correct.** A has nothing to do with knowing or knowledge. The words imagination and theory in B and C help to eliminate those choices, because both have to do with ideas, not knowledge.

4. **B is correct.** The context links "uniquely human" with "special." A and C can be eliminated, since they are unrelated to either of these ideas. Although lonely in D suggests "one," this does not fit in the context of the sentence.

5. **D is correct.** All the other answer choices deal with dogs' appearance or health. Only D mentions actions. Actions are behaviors, which are mentioned in the context.

6. **D is correct.** Because the context of the word specifically mentions intelligence, A can be eliminated. B and C can also be eliminated, because the psychologist was surprised that the dog learned so many words; therefore, he probably was not studying vocabulary or word-learning skills.

7. **C is correct.** A has nothing to do with the topic, so it can be eliminated. A report in a personal diary would not usually be published, so B can also be eliminated. D mentions transactions and not reports, so that cannot be correct either.

8. **C is correct.** A and B do not fit in the context, so they can be eliminated. A workshop (D) suggests a group of professionals that works together for a short time only. An institute (C), however, suggests the kind of established organization that would supply scientific research.

Vocabulary

DIRECTIONS *Use context clues and the word-root definitions to answer the following questions.*

1. The Latin word root *mort* means "death." What does *immortality* mean in line 5 of "His Name Was Pete"?
   A eternal life
   B great fame
   C good behavior
   D a promising future

2. The Latin word root *nat* means "born." What does *innate* mean in line 21 of "Dog Proves As Smart As Average Toddler"?
   A taught by humans
   B learned over time
   C present from birth
   D taken from memory

3. The Latin word root *scient* means "knowing." What does *scientific* mean in line 2 of "Dog Proves As Smart As Average Toddler"?
   A from animals
   B from imagination
   C based on theory
   D based on facts

4. The Latin word root *uni* means "one." What does *uniquely* mean in line 19 of "Dog Proves As Smart As Average Toddler"?
   A superficially
   B exclusively
   C partially
   D lonely

DIRECTIONS *Use context clues in the article "Dog Proves As Smart As Average Toddler" to help you answer the following questions about words in specialized fields.*

5. Anthropologists research the origins, behavior, and development of humans. If anthropologists studied dogs instead of people, they would most likely
   A groom dogs daily
   B dissect dogs who have died from an illness
   C increase the protein in dogs' diets
   D look at the actions and reactions of dogs

6. The word *psychologist* in line 26 refers to a person who studies
   A obedience in dogs
   B vocabulary words
   C word-learning skills
   D mental processes and behavior

7. In line 7 of the article, the term *journal* means
   A a ship's log
   B a personal diary
   C a magazine published periodically
   D an accounting ledger that lists transactions

8. The word *Institute* in line 14 most likely refers to
   A a pattern of behavior
   B an authoritative rule
   C an organization
   D a workshop

588

DIFFERENTIATED INSTRUCTION

FOR ENGLISH LEARNERS

Assessment Vocabulary Help students understand these words and phrases that are used in the directions or in the items:

- *tone:* attitude toward the subject
- *subheadings:* bold type that signals the start of a new topic or section
- *compare and contrast:* to show how two things are alike and different
- *hyperlink:* text that is clicked and then connects to another item, such as a piece of text or an image

- *context clues:* hints to a word's meaning found in the text around the word
- *concrete nouns:* nouns that name items that can be felt or identified with the senses
- *abstract nouns:* nouns that name ideas or concepts that cannot be sensed
- *adverb:* a word that tells more about a verb, an adjective, or another adverb
- *conjunction:* a word that links two or more words or phrases that have the same importance

Writing & Grammar

DIRECTIONS *Read the passage and answer the questions that follow.*

(1) For years, many people claimed that animals were not emotional. (2) Recently, scientists have documented what every pet owner already knows. (3) Animals can, indeed, feel emotions. (4) The author and former psychoanalyst Jeffrey Masson studies animal emotions in his book *When Elephants Weep.* (5) Masson describes an elephant that feels happy when drawing pictures. (6) He tells of a chimp that nursed its sick owner back to health. (7) Some scientists resist Masson's conclusions, but many believe that animals do feel emotions.

1. Choose the correct coordinating conjunction that can be used to combine sentences 1 and 2.

A and   C or

B but   D so

2. Identify the abstract noun in sentence 4.

A psychoanalyst

B Jeffrey Masson

C emotions

D book

3. Choose the correct way to rewrite sentence 5 by using an adverb.

A Masson describes an elephant that feels happy when playfully drawing pictures.

B Masson describes an elephant that feels happy when drawing fanciful pictures.

C Masson describes a talented elephant that feels happy when drawing pictures.

D Masson describes an elephant that draws happy pictures.

4. Choose the correct coordinating conjunction that can be used to combine sentences 5 and 6.

A or   C yet

B for   D and

5. Identify the two concrete nouns in sentence 7.

A conclusions, emotions

B scientists, animals

C emotions, scientists

D animals, conclusions

6. Choose the correct way to rewrite sentence 7 by using an adverb.

A Some stubborn scientists resist Masson's conclusions, but many believe that animals do feel emotions.

B Some scientists resist Masson's conclusions, and many believe that animals do feel emotions.

C Some scientists resist Masson's conclusions, but many believe that animals do feel something.

D Some scientists resist Masson's conclusions, but many strongly believe that animals do feel emotions.

STOP

589

ANSWERS

Writing & Grammar

1. **B is correct.** The first two sentences begin with For years and Recently, which are contrasted. A is incorrect because it adds something. C is incorrect because it offers an alternative. D suggests an effect, so it is also incorrect.

2. **C is correct.** C is the only abstract noun among the choices. The other options are all concrete nouns that can be sensed.

3. **A is correct.** The adverb playfully modifies the verb drawing. The other choices are adjectives, which modify nouns. Therefore, they are incorrect.

4. **D is correct.** Both sentences tell what Masson describes. The coordinating conjunction and combines similar ideas. A, B, and C can be eliminated.

5. **B is correct.** B is the only choice that supplies two concrete nouns. In A, both words are abstract. C and D each contain one abstract word—emotions and conclusions. Therefore, they are incorrect.

6. **D is correct.** D is the only answer choice that contains an adverb, strongly. A contains an additional adjective, stubborn. B changes the coordinating conjunction from but to and, and C substitutes a pronoun, something, for the noun emotions.

FOR ENGLISH LEARNERS

Assessment Support: Coordinating Conjunctions and Adverbs

- Remind students that a coordinating conjunction links words, phrases, and sentences. Show examples from "Dog Proves As Smart As Average Toddler" such as *and* (lines 4 and 8) and *but* (line 22). Have students identify the words or phrases that are linked by the conjunctions.

- List the conjunctions *and, but, or,* and *so* on the board. Have students take turns composing sentences orally using these conjunctions.

- Tell students that adverbs are words that tell more about verbs, adjectives, or even other adverbs. Adverbs often tell how, when, where, or to what extent. Write the words *very, quickly, there,* and *now* on the board. Use each in a sentence and ask students if the word tells *how, when, where,* or *to what extent.*

INTRODUCE *GREAT READS*

In Unit 5, students have discussed a number of big questions. Invite students to tell which question they found most intriguing and why, and then focus attention on the three that appear on this page. Discuss the recommended books and their summaries, pointing out how each connects to the related question. Encourage students to choose one or more of these "great reads" to read independently.

ClassZone.com
To find additional books that match students' interests and ability levels, visit the Literature Center at **ClassZone.com.**

UNIT 5
Great Reads

Ideas for Independent Reading
What ideas does each writer communicate in the following works?

What place do you call home?

Desert Solitaire
by Edward Abbey

Abbey's love song to the deserts of the southwestern United States has become a touchstone for writing about a place. This volume shows readers why the desert was Abbey's spiritual home.

Barrio Boy
by Ernesto Galarza

In this autobiography, Galarza describes his early years in western Mexico and his childhood in a barrio in Sacramento, California.

My Place
by Sally Morgan

Morgan was not told of her aboriginal heritage until she was 15. She wrote this highly personal memoir to show readers what Australia aboriginal people have endured as outsiders in their own land.

Why would people leave their homelands?

Picture Bride
By Yoshiko Uchida

In this novel, Hana Omiya journeys from Japan to the United States to escape a more restricted life in Japan. She finds that life in America has its own barriers to happiness and freedom.

Of Beetles and Angels: A Boy's Remarkable Journey from a Refugee Camp to Harvard
by Mawi Asgedom

Asgedom and his family fled civil war in Ethiopia in 1983. In 1999, he graduated from Harvard. His father's words, "Treat all people—even the most unsightly beetles—as though they were angels from heaven," have guided him.

How the García Girls Lo Their Accents
by Julia Alvarez

After the four García girls le the Dominican Republic, the eagerly embrace American culture, often to the dismay of their old-world parents.

What stories will you tell your children?

The Kitchen God's Wife
by Amy Tan

In this contemporary novel, a woman tries to communicate with her daughter by telling of her struggle for survival in the harsh world of China before and during World War II.

A Yellow Raft in Blue Water
by Michael Dorris

Three generations of Native American women share their lives and their secrets in three interwoven fictional narratives.

Fahrenheit 451
by Ray Bradbury

Four hundred fifty-one degrees Fahrenheit is the temperature at which book burn. Bradbury's classic novel considers an unname society in which ideas are s dangerous that people mu be "protected" from the stories of the past.

UNIT 6

Taking Sides

ARGUMENT AND PERSUASION

- In Nonfiction
- In Media
- Across Genres

591

About the Art Detail from *A Tempestuous Evening at the Maison de la Culture* by Albert Laforet (1937).

For help in planning this unit, see

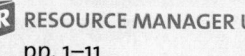 RESOURCE MANAGER UNIT 6
pp. 1–11

INTRODUCE THE UNIT

Civil rights hero Martin Luther King Jr. is considered one of the most powerful speakers of all time. His impassioned words persuaded hundreds of thousands of people to join in his peaceful demand for justice. Still, many people disagreed with King, and he had to argue his position often.

King's example suggests that people argue most strongly over issues that matter greatly to them. Invite students to apply that thought to the images on this page. Ask:

- What do you think is happening in each scene? If you were in that scene, what might you see and hear?
- Which scene shows "Taking Sides" in a calm, controlled way? in an angry way?
- Suppose that you were to create a scene of people arguing or being persuasive about something that matters greatly to them. Which of these images would it resemble more? Why?

Tell students that as they read this unit, they will learn some important techniques of **persuasive writing.** They will analyze how writers and speakers seek to influence. They also will practice being influential as they defend their own positions.

Skills Trace

SKILLS STRAND	Critical Reading Workshop: Argument and Persuasion pp. 594–599	I Have a Dream pp. 600–609 Speech Level: Challenging	Testimony Before the Senate pp. 610–619 Speech Level: Average	How Private Is Your Private Life?/The Privacy Debate: One Size Doesn't Fit All pp. 620–633 Magazine Article/ Newspaper Article Level: Average
Literary Analysis		Argument pp. 601, 602, 606, 608		
Reading and Informational Texts	Identify and Analyze the Elements of an Argument pp. 594–595, 599 Analyze Persuasive Techniques pp. 596–597, 599 Understand the Effects of Rhetorical Devices pp. 598,	Understand the Effects of Rhetorical Devices pp. 601, 604, 606, 608	Analyze Persuasive Techniques pp. 611, 612, 614, 617 Summarize Main Points pp. 611, 613, 614, 617	Distinguish Fact from Opinion pp. 621, 623, 624, 626, 628, 630, 631 Recognize and Analyze Bias pp. 621, 623, 627, 629, 631
Vocabulary	Academic Vocabulary pp. 594, 596, 598	Word Acquisition pp. 601, T601, 609 Context Clues p. T601 Specialized Vocabulary (Political Words) p. 609	Word Acquisition pp. 611, T611, 618 Context Clues p. T611 Dictionary Skills p. 618	Word Acquisition pp. 621, T621, 632 Context Clues p. T621 Specialized Vocabulary (Internet Words) p. 632
Writing, Grammar, and Style			Tone pp. 616, 619 Imperative Sentences pp. 616, 619	Rhetorical Devices pp. 630, 633 Parallelism pp. 630, 633
Speaking, Listening, Viewing, and Media	Discuss pp. 594–598	Discuss pp. 600, T602–T607, 608 Analyze Visuals pp. 602, 605, T607	Discuss p. 610 Analyze Visuals pp. 613, 615, T616	Discuss pp. 620, T622–T630, 631 Analyze Visuals pp. T622, T624, T625, T629, T630

Assessment-Based Planning: Skills in red are assessed on the Unit 6 Test. **T** = Teacher's Edition page

Media Study: Billy Thomas/ Life Is Calling pp. 634–637	Primal Screen/The Pedestrian pp. 638–649	Writing Workshop: Persuasive Speech pp. 650–657	
	Essay/Short Story *Level: Average*		**Skills Assessed on the Unit 6 Test:**
Public Service Announcements			**Literary Analysis** • Identify types of rhetorical devices and understand their effects
	Writer's Message Across Genres pp. 639, 640, 641, 642, 644, 645, 646, 647, 648		**Reading and Informational Texts** • Identify and analyze elements of an argument
	Set a Purpose for Reading pp. 639, 648 Compare Writers' Messages Across Genres p. 648	Analyze a Persuasive Speech pp. 651–652	• Analyze persuasive techniques • Distinguish fact from opinion • Summarize main ideas or points • Recognize bias • Compare writers' messages across genre
Academic Vocabulary (PSAs) pp. 634, 635			**Vocabulary** • Understand and use specialized vocabulary • Use a dictionary
	Write for Assessment p. 649	Write a Persuasive Speech pp. 650–657 Emotional Appeals pp. 650, 651, 655, 656 Modifiers p. 656	**Writing, Grammar, and Style** • Write a persuasive speech
Discuss pp. 634, 637 Analyze and Evaluate Persuasive Techniques in PSAs pp. 635–637 Create a PSA p. 637	Discuss pp. 638, T640–T647, 648 Analyze Visuals pp. 641, 642, T644, T646	Discuss pp. 650–652, 656 Present a Persuasive Speech p. 657	• Understand and use effective sentence types and structures, including imperative sentences, to set tone • Understand and use rhetorical devices, such as parallelism • Additional writing and grammar skills

For additional lesson planning help, see **Easy Planner DVD.**

OBJECTIVES
- establish prior knowledge about persuasive techniques
- consider the elements of an argument that have the greatest power to persuade

How can we INFLUENCE *others?*

Read and discuss the question and the paragraph. Help students connect to the explanation by asking them to think of times that they have seen advertising techniques like these used to influence an audience:

- citing a doctor's opinion of a product
- urging the audience to "join the crowd" by using a product
- citing facts and statistics
- appealing to the audience's fears

Ask students to explain how the poster and pins on this page attempt to influence an audience. ***Possible answer:*** *The poster and pins are meant to persuade people to vote. They influence their audience by suggesting that people can make their ideas heard and can solve problems by voting.*

ACTIVITY Urge students to make some notes or to freewrite about the occasion that they have in mind before they begin work on the chart. Afterward, use volunteers' responses to compile a list of persuasive "do's" and "don'ts."

CHECK UNDERSTANDING Elicit that the goal of persuasive writing is to influence the reader to take the writer's side.

How can we INFLUENCE *others?*

You convince your friend to see your side in an argument. You get your teacher to give you an extension on an assignment. You influence your classmates to vote for you in a school election. Each time you succeed in getting someone to side with you on an idea, a plan, or an action, you have practiced the art of **persuasion.** Similarly, whenever you purchase a product you saw advertised or go see a movie after viewing its trailer, the art of persuasion has influenced you.

ACTIVITY Recall a time when you were determined to get your way. Then fill in a chart like the one shown. Think about

- what worked to help you get your point across
- what information you supplied and how you organized it
- what techniques you used to convince your audience
- what you would have done differently if you were less successful than you had hoped

What Worked	What Didn't Work
• a logical argument	• whining

VOTE

Make them pay attention to us.
For more information or to volunteer: www.newvotersproject.org

NEW VOTERS PROJECT

Unit Resources

- **R** RESOURCE MANAGER UNIT 6
- BEST PRACTICES TOOLKIT
- **S** STANDARDS LESSON FILE
- Easy Planner DVD-ROM
- WriteSmart CD-ROM
- ClassZone.com
- Audio Anthology CD
- Multi-Language Academic Vocabulary Online
- eEdition DVD-ROM & Online
- McDougal Littell Assessment System
- Test Generator CD
- MediaSmart DVD-ROM

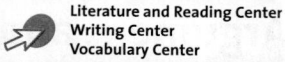

Online LITERATURE CLASSZONE.COM

Literature and Reading Center
Writing Center
Vocabulary Center

Preview Unit Goals

LITERARY ANALYSIS	• Compare and contrast the author's message across genres
READING	• Summarize • Distinguish fact from opinion • Recognize and analyze bias • Identify and analyze the elements of an argument—claim, support, reasons, evidence, and counterarguments • Analyze rhetorical devices—repetition, parallelism, and analogy • Analyze persuasive techniques, including emotional appeals
WRITING AND GRAMMAR	• Write a persuasive speech • Support a position and answer opposing views • Use persuasive language effectively • Understand and use appropriate sentence types • Understand and use parallelism
SPEAKING, LISTENING, AND VIEWING	• Present a persuasive speech • Create a persuasive print ad
VOCABULARY	• Understand and use specialized and technical vocabulary • Understand foreign words and phrases in English • Use a dictionary
ACADEMIC VOCABULARY	• argument • persuasive techniques • rhetorical devices • bias • fact and opinion • summarize

593

Preview Unit Goals

The goals on this page identify the main skills and strategies that students will meet in this unit's reading selections. Have students scan the list and consider what they already know about each goal. As you note the color-coding of each strand, urge students to watch for the colors to be repeated throughout the unit.

Point out the Academic Vocabulary at the bottom of the page. Call on volunteers to define familiar terms and to look up unfamiliar terms in a dictionary. Have students use their journals to record the terms and a definition for each. Throughout the unit, remind students to reinforce their understanding by using these terms in speaking and writing about the selections.

ADDITIONAL UNIT GOALS

These skills will be taught in this unit but are not the major focus of the unit:

Literary Analysis
- Evaluate allusion
- Genre study: science fiction, speech, public document, magazine article, newspaper article, nonfiction

Reading
- Set a purpose for reading

Writing and Grammar
- Write a compare-contrast essay
- Craft a strong thesis statement that explains a position
- Use appropriate sentence types to establish tone

Speaking, Listening, and Viewing
- View public service announcements
- Recognize persuasive media forms
- Identify a target audience

DIFFERENTIATED INSTRUCTION

FOR ENGLISH LEARNERS

Academic Vocabulary Use the copy master to help students learn the Academic Vocabulary listed on this page.

1. Read aloud each term. Have students find it on their copy master.
2. Discuss the meanings or examples shown, and complete the chart as a class.
3. Have students work in small groups to complete the remaining activities.

Additional Academic Vocabulary Use the copy master to help students learn terms they will use in subsequent lessons and on the Assessment Practice. Follow the same procedure as for the Academic Vocabulary copy master.

RESOURCE MANAGER—Copy Masters
Academic Vocabulary p. 9
Additional Academic Vocabulary p. 10

Focus and Motivate

OBJECTIVES

- identify and analyze elements of an argument
- analyze persuasive techniques
- understand rhetorical devices

Teach

Part 1: The Elements of an Argument

Claim and Support Explain that arguments are meant to influence readers or listeners—in other words, to cause them to think or act in a certain way. For example, campaigners offer arguments to support a candidate. An editorial may call for a change in an existing law. Stress that unless a claim is supported by solid facts or reasons, it remains nothing more than an opinion.

Ask students to cite examples of arguments meant to influence thought or action, such as advertisements, speeches, and letters to the editor. Have students use a chart to analyze the intent of two of these arguments.

Argument	Intent
This soap cleans better than any other soap.	To convince consumers to buy the soap

Reading an Argument To reinforce the notion that claims must be supported, draw a parallel with the legal system. Elicit that attorneys represent opposing positions, for which they provide evidence. This evidence is meant to influence a judge or jury.

 BEST PRACTICES TOOLKIT—Transparency
Analysis Frame: Persuasion pp. D21, D44

Argument and Persuasion

You encounter arguments and opinions everywhere. Friends share their views on controversial issues. Politicians explain why they deserve your vote. Ads claim that products can fix your problems. Which arguments have merit, and which are just cleverly persuasive? So many decisions you make depend on your ability to analyze arguments and recognize the techniques that are being used to persuade you.

Part 1: The Elements of an Argument

You've heard the word *argument* all your life. It suggests heated fights characterized by strong feelings and loud voices. In formal speaking and writing, however, an argument is not emotional. An **argument** expresses a position on an issue and supports the position with reasons and evidence. Sound arguments appeal strictly to reason, not emotions. They include these elements:

- the **claim**—the writer's or speaker's position on an issue
- the **support**—the reasons and evidence that support the claim

In addition to supporting the claim, strong arguments anticipate objections that opponents might raise and counter those objections with evidence.

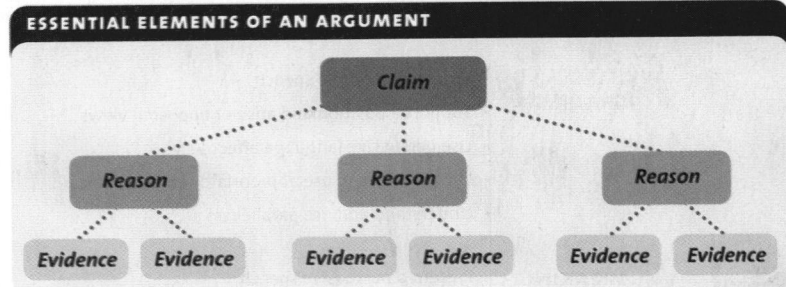

ESSENTIAL ELEMENTS OF AN ARGUMENT

STRATEGIES FOR READING AN ARGUMENT

- **Look for the claim.** Often, the claim is stated in the introduction or the conclusion of an argument. Make sure you look for clues in the title too. When the claim is not stated directly, ask yourself: What does the evidence tell me about the writer's or speaker's position?

- **Track the evidence.** Convincing arguments include a great deal of support. As a result, most arguments are not short. To keep track of the ideas, jot down the evidence that the writer or speaker uses to support his or her position. Look for facts, statistics, examples, anecdotes, and quotations from experts.

DIFFERENTIATED INSTRUCTION

For general guidelines on differentiating instruction, see

 BEST PRACTICES TOOLKIT
Differentiated Instruction pp. 31–38

FOR LESS–PROFICIENT READERS

Note Taking For students who need help with note taking, hand out the note-taking copy master for Part 1 before reading the text. Have students read each paragraph silently. Then, as you discuss the main points of the text, have students complete the copy master.

Distinguish Fact from Opinion Elicit or explain the difference between a fact (something that can be proved) and an opinion (someone's belief or judgment). Explain that only facts can support an argument. Write several statements on the board. Have students classify each statement as fact or opinion.

 RESOURCE MANAGER—Copy Master
Note Taking p. 15

MODEL: THE ELEMENTS OF AN ARGUMENT

In this testimony given before the Maryland Senate, the speaker makes a strong claim about the state's motorcycle helmet law. As you read, look for the elements that she uses to effectively prove her position.

from MOTORCYCLE HELMET BILL

Testimony before the Maryland Senate by **Janice Golec**

I respectfully urge you to oppose any legislation that weakens Maryland's current "all riders" motorcycle helmet law.

Motorcycle helmets help save lives and reduce critical head injuries, and laws requiring helmet use have a dramatic life-saving effect. This has been
5   proven in Maryland and every other state where all riders are required to wear helmets. In such states, death rates from head injuries are half what they are among cyclists in states with no helmet laws or laws which only apply to minors. Where helmet [laws] have been enacted, then repealed, death rates for motorcyclists rise in the absence of a helmet law.
10 This is hardly a fluke; the General Accounting Office, a non-partisan research agency of the U.S. Government, reviewed 46 studies of motorcycle helmets and helmet laws, and reported that every study comparing helmeted with non-helmeted crash victims found that helmeted riders had lower fatality rates, ranging from 28 percent to 73 percent lower. . . .
15 Helmet laws save taxpayers money, too. Studies in six states show that public funds pay up to 82 percent of the costs to treat orthopedic injuries sustained by motorcyclists. A Maryland study showed that acute care costs to non-helmeted riders averaged three times those of helmeted riders. . . .
A partial law is almost as bad as no law at all. Statistically speaking, there is
20 negligible difference in death and injury rates between states with no helmet law and states with partial laws. Because partial helmet laws are difficult for police to enforce, helmet-use rates for all riders remain low in states with restricted helmet laws.
Helmet law opponents love to talk about motorcyclists' right to decide whether
25 or not they will wear helmets, but some rights are not worth having. . . . To weaken Maryland's helmet law is to condemn 28—or more—Maryland motorcyclists to death. That's a right nobody should have.

Close Read

1. What is the speaker's claim, or position?

2. One reason that the speaker uses to prove her claim is boxed. Cite two pieces of evidence that support this reason.

3. Find another reason that the speaker uses to support her claim. What evidence supports this reason?

4. The speaker anticipates opponents' arguments in lines 19–27. How does she counter these viewpoints?

MODEL: THE ELEMENTS OF AN ARGUMENT

Close Read

1. *Possible answer:* Legislators should oppose laws that weaken Maryland's "all riders" motorcycle helmet law.

2. *Possible answer:* **Evidence 1:** In other states with all-rider laws, death rates from head injuries are half what they are in states with no helmet laws. **Evidence 2:** Helmeted riders have a lower fatality rate than non-helmeted crash victims, as reported in 46 studies of motorcycle helmets and helmet laws.

3. *Possible answer:* Another reason to oppose legislation that weakens the "all riders" law is that such laws save taxpayers money. Golec cites studies in six states that found that taxpayers end up paying for the majority of costs related to motorcyclists' orthopedic injuries.

   If students need help . . . Remind students that paragraphs often have topic sentences that state the main idea. Encourage them to find the topic sentence in the paragraph that begins on line 15 ("Helmet laws save taxpayers money, too"). Point out that the other sentences in the paragraph develop the topic sentence with supporting details.

4. *Possible answer:* Golec maintains that a partial law is almost as bad as no motorcycle helmet law. She says that partial laws are difficult for police to enforce, and therefore, many motorcyclists do not wear helmets. Golec also mentions the minimal difference between death and injury rates for motorcyclists in states with partial helmet laws and those with no laws. Finally, Golec anticipates that opponents will mention motorcyclists' right to decide whether to wear their helmets. She says that some rights are not worth having, especially when they put people's lives at risk.

FOR LESS-PROFICIENT READERS

Comprehension: Opposing Viewpoints
Explain that in lines 19–27, the speaker is anticipating two arguments that opponents might make. Help students use paragraph context to identify the opposing viewpoints. (*A partial helmet law would be adequate; motorcyclists have the right to decide whether they will wear helmets.*)

Concept Support

1. Draw a diagram similar to the one on page 594, but write each heading above the lozenge.

2. Help students list on the board key phrases from "Motorcycle Helmet Bill" that correspond to *claim, reason,* and *evidence.*

3. Have students write the phrases in the correct places in the diagram.

Teach

Part 2: The Craft of Persuasion

PERSUASIVE TECHNIQUES

Persuasion As students read the chart, have them reflect on each of the techniques and examples described. Elicit the purpose of each appeal—for example, to get someone's vote, to sell a product, to solicit money for charity, to encourage volunteers—and have students discuss whether the example is effective. To add to the discussion, some students may enjoy acting out each example in a way that exaggerates its appeal.

As you guide a discussion about the effectiveness of each example, ask students to describe an audience to which each might appeal. Extend the discussion by asking students to consider whether certain appeals work best with particular age groups. Ask, for example, which techniques might work best with teenagers, and why.

During your discussion, elicit from students additional examples for each of the techniques in the chart. Encourage students to draw from various sources, such as television and radio commercials, print advertisements, political speeches, essays, and editorials.

CHECK UNDERSTANDING

Have students brainstorm examples of persuasive techniques used in everyday interactions, as when peers urge one another to participate in an activity because "everyone's doing it."

Part 2: The Craft of Persuasion

Never underestimate the power of **persuasion**—that is, the art of swaying people's feelings, opinions, and actions. With compelling language, writers and speakers can enhance strong arguments or disguise the flaws in weak ones. To evaluate the real strength of an argument, you first need to recognize the persuasive techniques and rhetorical devices that are being used to sway you. Then you can objectively examine the evidence and determine your position.

PERSUASIVE TECHNIQUES

Consider where you have encountered the following persuasive techniques. What are their intended effects on readers, listeners, and viewers?

TECHNIQUES	EXAMPLES
Appeals by Association	
Bandwagon Appeal Taps into people's desire to belong	You have to come to the concert. Everyone's going to be there.
"Plain Folks" Appeal Implies that ordinary people are on "our side" or that a candidate is like an ordinary person	Senator Jacobs knows what it's like to struggle to make ends meet.
Testimonial Relies on endorsements from well-known people or satisfied customers	As an Olympic athlete, I need all the energy I can get. That's why I start my day with Grain Puffs.
Transfer Connects a product, a candidate, or a cause with a positive image or idea	Freedom is in your hands the minute you hit the road in a Mountainback XRV.
Emotional Appeals	
Appeals to Pity, Fear, or Vanity Uses words that evoke strong feelings, rather than facts and evidence, to persuade	**Appeal to Pity** For just one dollar a day, you can give a stray pet a second chance.
Appeal to Values	
Ethical Appeal Taps into people's values or moral standards	Volunteer today—because it's the right thing to do.
Word Choice	
Loaded Language Uses words with strongly positive or negative connotations to stir people's emotions	For the safety of our innocent children, we must protect our community from rampant crime.

596 UNIT 6: ARGUMENT AND PERSUASION

DIFFERENTIATED INSTRUCTION

FOR LESS–PROFICIENT READERS

Note Taking For students who need help, hand out the note-taking copy master for Part 2. Read and discuss the text. Assist students in completing their note-taking copy master as needed.

R RESOURCE MANAGER—Copy Master
Note Taking p. 16

FOR ENGLISH LEARNERS

Language: Skill Words On the board, list the italicized terms. Then give the examples in random order for students to classify.

- *Bandwagon Appeal:* Try Slick Gloss—it's what all the cool kids are wearing.
- *Testimonial:* I'm a fashion model, and I eat Fruit Flakes for breakfast every day.
- *Appeal to Fear:* The new Super-12 Lock will keep the bad guys out of your home!

MODEL 1: PERSUASION IN SPEECHES

In this speech, a government official pledges his commitment to promoting organ donation. What techniques does he use to win you over?

from The Gift of Life

Speech by **Tommy Thompson**

This month in Fresno, California, members of the Hispanic community gathered . . . to remember 19-year-old Maribel Cordova. Maribel had received an identification card this year and told her mother she wanted to become a donor.

Two weeks later, a damaged blood vessel in her head tragically cut her
5 life short.

Because of Maribel's selfless act, others lived. A 35-year-old man from Northern California received her lungs. A 66-year-old Southern California woman got her liver. . . .

These are the human experiences of hope out of loss, of life out of death,
10 that touch and motivate us, that drive us to do everything within our power to promote organ and tissue donation. Through education, outreach, science and the vitally important work of people like you, we will reach that future when organ donation is, quite simply, a fact of life.

Close Read

1. Find two examples of loaded language. One has been boxed.

2. Identify one other persuasive technique used in this speech. Cite details that helped you find it.

MODEL 2: PERSUASION IN THE MEDIA

Persuasive techniques are also at work in TV and magazine ads. How do the words and the visual in this print ad help convey a powerful message?

Make your home defensible against wildfires. Visit Firewise.org, where you can discover some simple things you can do to help protect your home and your loved ones. What have you got to lose, except everything.

Close Read

1. What persuasive technique is used in this ad? Cite specific details to support your answer.

2. Describe the intended effect of the ad on viewers.

MODEL 1: PERSUASION IN SPEECHES

Close Read

1. *Possible answer: Other examples of loaded language include "Maribel's selfless act" and "hope out of loss, of life out of death."*

2. *Possible answer: One other persuasive technique is ethical appeal, as evidenced by "through education, outreach, science and the vitally important work of people like you, we will reach that future . . . ."*

MODEL 2: PERSUASION IN THE MEDIA

Close Read

1. *Possible answer: Appeals to fear include "What have you got to lose, except everything" and the image of an ordinary home in flames.*

2. *Possible answer: The intended effect is to scare viewers into taking precautions with their homes. Also, the ad might prompt viewers to visit the Firewise Web site so they can find out other simple ways to protect their home from fires.*

DIFFERENTIATED INSTRUCTION

FOR LESS–PROFICIENT READERS

Analysis Support: Loaded Language Discuss with students how the title "The Gift of Life" is a metaphor that is an example of loaded language. Elicit or explain that both *gift* and *life* are words with positive connotations and that the phrase "gift of life" suggests the most valuable gift a person could give. Point out, too, that the speaker repeats the word *life* in lines 5, 9, and 13.

FOR ADVANCED LEARNERS/PRE–AP

Analyze Extended Meanings Explain that *donor, donate,* and *donation* all come from a Latin word meaning "gift." While these words typically refer to charitable gifts, they are also increasingly used in medical contexts, as in "blood donor" and "organ donation." Challenge students to identify other words that have such extended meanings. Discuss how new technologies expand our language.

RHETORICAL DEVICES

Repetition Elicit or provide other examples of the use of repetition for effect. For example, many students will be familiar with Martin Luther King Jr.'s "I Have a Dream" speech. Discuss how repetition not only emphasizes certain phrases and ideas but also creates a rhythm that makes key words more memorable.

Parallelism Have students read the Lyndon Baines Johnson quotation aloud to get a feeling for the rhythm created. Point out that repetition and parallelism are techniques often used together.

Analogy Elicit or explain the meaning of the Billy Joel analogy. Ask students whether the analogy expresses Joel's approval or disapproval of "American popular music today" and to explain why. Then ask why such an analogy is effective. *Possible answers: It expresses disapproval. It implies the music is not fresh. It creates a strong image in the listener's mind.*

Close Read

1. *Possible answer: The repeated question helps emphasize Truth's message about just how wrong "that man over there" is. Essentially, she is disproving the man's claim that women need to be helped because she does not need help.*

   If students need help ... Have students read Truth's words aloud, while listening for the repetition. Elicit that the phrase *And ain't I a woman?* underscores each point she makes.

2. *Possible answer: Parallelism occurs in the first two sentences: "helped into carriages"/ "helps me into carriages"; "lifted over ditches"/ "over mud-puddles"; "have the best place everywhere"/ "give me any best place." Also, many sentences begin with "I have" and "I could."*

RHETORICAL DEVICES

In addition to employing persuasive techniques, writers and speakers use **rhetorical devices** to emphasize their ideas. In these examples, notice how the wording makes the message memorable.

RHETORICAL DEVICE	EXAMPLE
REPETITION Uses the same word or words more than once for emphasis	Let there be justice for all. Let there be peace for all. Let there be work, bread, water and salt for all. —from "Glory and Hope" by Nelson Mandela
PARALLELISM Uses similar grammatical constructions to express ideas that are related or equal in importance. Often creates a rhythm.	We cannot, we must not, refuse to protect the right of every American to vote in every election. . . . And we ought not, and we cannot, and we must not wait another eight months before we get a bill. —from "We Shall Overcome" by Lyndon Baines Johnson
ANALOGY Makes a comparison between two subjects that are alike in some ways	Have you heard the canned, frozen and processed product being dished up to the world as American popular music today? —from a commencement address by Billy Joel

Sojourner Truth, a 19th-century leader in the antislavery and women's rights movements, made many powerful speeches. Here, Truth responds to men who had spoken against women's rights. How does her use of rhetorical devices enhance her message?

from And Ain't I a *Woman?*
Speech by **Sojourner Truth**

That man over there say that women needs to be helped into carriages, and lifted over ditches, and to have the best place everywhere. Nobody ever helps me into carriages, or over mud-puddles, or give me any best place! And ain't I a woman? Look at me! Look at my arm! I have ploughed, and planted, and gathered into barns, and no man could head me! And ain't I a woman? I could work as much and eat as much as a man—when I could get it—and bear the lash as well! And ain't I a woman? I have borne thirteen children, and seen 'em mos' all sold off to slavery, and when I cried out with my mother's grief, none but Jesus heard me! And ain't I a woman?

Close Read

1. Notice the boxed question that the speaker repeats. What is the effect of the repetition?

2. Find an example of parallelism. Identify the words, phrases, or sentences that are parallel.

598 UNIT 6: ARGUMENT AND PERSUASION

DIFFERENTIATED INSTRUCTION

FOR ADVANCED LEARNERS/PRE–AP

Use Rhetorical Devices Sojourner Truth used repetition and parallelism to make her speech more powerful. Challenge students to rewrite Truth's speech in more contemporary language while preserving her rhetorical devices. Have volunteers read their updated versions to the class. Discuss whether or not the students' versions are as powerful as the original.

598 UNIT 6: ARGUMENT AND PERSUASION

Part 3: Analyze the Text

In 1962, when President John F. Kennedy gave this stirring speech about space exploration, people were feeling threatened by the possibility of war with the Soviet Union. Using what you've just learned, analyze Kennedy's argument. What techniques does he use to persuade his audience?

from
The New Frontier
Speech by **John F. Kennedy**

No man can fully grasp how far and how fast we have come, but condense, if you will, the 50,000 years of man's recorded history in a time span of but a half century. Stated in these terms, we know very little about the first 40 years, except at the end of them advanced man had learned to use the skins
5 of animals to cover them. Then about 10 years ago, under this standard, man emerged from his caves to construct other kinds of shelter. Only five years ago man learned to write and use a cart with wheels. Christianity began less than two years ago. The printing press came this year, and then less than 2 months ago, during this whole 50-year span of human history, the steam engine
10 provided a new source of power.

Newton explored the meaning of gravity. Last month electric lights and telephones and automobiles and airplanes became available. Only last week did we develop penicillin and television and nuclear power, and now if America's new spacecraft succeeds in reaching Venus, we will have literally reached the
15 stars before midnight tonight.

This is a breathtaking pace, and such a pace cannot help but create new ills as it dispels old, new ignorance, new problems, new dangers. Surely the opening vistas of space promise high costs and hardships, as well as high reward. . . .

If this capsule history of our progress teaches us anything, it is that man, in
20 his quest for knowledge and progress, is determined and cannot be deterred. The exploration of space will go ahead, whether we join in it or not, and it is one of the great adventures of all time, and no nation which expects to be the leader of other nations can expect to stay behind in this race for space.

Those who came before us made certain that this country rode the first
25 waves of the industrial revolutions, the first waves of modern invention, and the first wave of nuclear power, and this generation does not intend to founder in the backwash of the coming age of space. We mean to be a part of it—we mean to lead it. For the eyes of the world now look into space, to the moon and to the planets beyond, and we have vowed that we shall not see it governed
30 by a hostile flag of conquest, but by a banner of freedom and peace. We have vowed that we shall not see space filled with weapons of mass destruction, but with instruments of knowledge and understanding.

Close Read

1. Summarize Kennedy's claim.

2. Does this speech mostly appeal to reason or to emotion? Explain your answer.

3. In lines 1–15, Kennedy uses a "capsule history" to describe a span of 50,000 years. Why might he begin with this analogy?

4. Identify one persuasive technique that Kennedy uses. Cite evidence to support your answer.

5. One example of parallelism has been boxed. What is its effect? Identify another example.

Practice and Apply

Part 3: Analyze the Text
Close Read

1. *Possible answer: Kennedy's claim is that the United States needs to emerge as a leader in the race for space.*

2. *Answers will vary, but students may say that Kennedy's speech appeals more to emotion than reason. Instead of facts and statistics, he opens with an analogy about progress, speaks about "high reward," stresses that the country cannot afford to stay behind, and says that space must be governed by a "banner of freedom and peace," not "a hostile flag of conquest."*

3. *Possible answer: Kennedy may want to emphasize the "breathtaking pace" of past progress and to show how far we've come in a short time.*

4. *Possible answers: He appeals to fear by saying that space could be "governed by a hostile flag of conquest" (lines 29–30). He also uses bandwagon appeal by implying that those who came before made sure that the U. S. "rode the first waves" (lines 24–25) of X, Y, and Z and that you should do the same.*

5. *Possible answers: The parallelism emphasizes that our predecessors were leaders in progress, which supports Kennedy's claim that the country should take a leadership role in exploring space. Other examples occur in lines 29–32.*

Assess and Reteach

Assess

Have students define and give examples of the persuasive techniques (page 596) and rhetorical devices (page 598) discussed.

Reteach

For students who are unable to apply the workshop skills to "The New Frontier," select from these reteaching options.

- Have students review the note-taking copy masters and restate the information in their own words. Help them identify examples.

- Have small groups summarize the persuasive techniques and rhetorical devices and identify examples of each.

FOR LESS–PROFICIENT READERS
Comprehension: Analogy After students read lines 1–15, discuss the idea of condensing "50,000 years . . . in a time span of but a half century" (lines 1–3). Display a timeline to help students visualize the concept, and guide students in locating on the timeline the events Kennedy mentions in his speech.

FOR ENGLISH LEARNERS
Comprehension: Contrast Call students' attention to the use of *but* in lines 30 and 31. Have students identify the items being contrasted (*hostile flag of conquest / banner of freedom and peace; weapons of mass destruction / instruments of knowledge and understanding*). Elicit or explain that the phrase *we shall not see* is used with *but* to form the parallel construction.

OBJECTIVES

Elements of Nonfiction
- explore the key idea of **vision**
- analyze an argument and its elements
- read a speech

Reading
- understand rhetorical devices

Vocabulary
- build vocabulary for reading and writing
- understand and use specialized vocabulary
  (also an EL language objective)

Grammar and Writing
- use writing to analyze literature

SUMMARY

In his historic "I Have a Dream" speech, delivered at the Lincoln Memorial in 1963, Dr. Martin Luther King Jr. presents a promise of freedom that has yet to be realized. He urges listeners to continue to press for freedom in the form of racial equality. He concludes by sharing his vision of an America in which racial differences do not matter and all people are "free at last."

Can a DREAM
change the world?

Ask the question. As students read the **KEY IDEA,** elicit that **vision** means seeing with the mind and heart what the world could become rather than seeing with the eyes what the world is now. After students have completed the **QUICKWRITE**, allow volunteers to share their responses.

I Have a Dream

Speech by Dr. Martin Luther King Jr.

Can a DREAM
change the world?

KEY IDEA Time and again someone has a dream, or **vision,** of how to make the world a better place. That vision finds expression in powerful words—words that stir others to find ways to improve our lives. In the speech you are about to read, Dr. Martin Luther King Jr. eloquently sets forth the vision he had for the future.

QUICKWRITE What is your vision for a better world? Does it involve better schools? safer communities? cleaner air? Write a paragraph describing your vision of how to change one aspect of the world.

600

RESOURCE MANAGER UNIT 6

Plan and Teach pp. 17–24

Elements of Nonfiction
Summary pp. 25†*, 26‡*
Argument pp. 27, 28†*
Question Support p. 35*

Reading
Understand Rhetorical Devices
   pp. 29, 30†*
Reading Check p. 34
Reading Fluency p. 37

Vocabulary
Study p. 31*
Practice p. 32
Strategy p. 33

Assessment
Selection Tests A, B/C pp. 39*, 41*
   Test Generator CD

BEST PRACTICES TOOLKIT

Differentiated Instruction
   pp. 31–38*

Scaffolding Instruction
   pp. 43–46*

Graphic Organizers/Strategies
Two-Column Chart • Definition Mapping • New Word Analysis • Argumentation • Mapping Main Ideas and Details

Technology
   Literature and Vocabulary Centers at **ClassZone.com**
   Write*Smart* CD

Reading Support
   Audio Anthology CD*

InterActive
READER & WRITER
• Integrated Test Practice
• Related Nonfiction Readings
McDougal Littell LITERATURE

---

* Resources for Differentiation   † Also in Spanish   ‡ Also in Haitian Creole and Vietnamese

● ELEMENTS OF NONFICTION: ARGUMENT

In an **argument**, a writer or speaker takes a position on an issue and provides support for the position by appealing strictly to reason. The position is referred to as the **claim**. The **support** for the claim may be reasons, evidence, or both. In "I Have a Dream," King makes the following claim about the status of African Americans in American society:

But one hundred years later [after the Emancipation Proclamation], *the Negro still is not free....*

As you read the speech, look for this claim and the reasons and evidence King provides to support it.

● READING SKILL: UNDERSTAND RHETORICAL DEVICES

Since arguments appeal only to reason, writers and speakers typically use more than just arguments to persuade. They also use rhetorical devices such as the following:

- **Repetition** is the repeated use of the same word or phrase. It is used primarily for emphasis.
- **Parallelism** is the repetition of similar grammatical structures, words, phrases, or sentences. It is used to show that ideas are related or equal in importance.
- An **analogy** is a point-by-point comparison of two subjects. It can help convey ideas that are hard to grasp.

As you read, write down examples of these devices and describe their effects, using a chart like the one shown.

Word, Phrase, or Sentence	Type of Device	Effect
"one hundred years later"	repetition	emphasizes how long African Americans have been denied their rights

▲ VOCABULARY IN CONTEXT

Martin Luther King Jr. chose the words shown in boldface to inspire his audience. Use the context to figure out the meaning of each word.

1. a **momentous** occasion
2. miss payments and **default** on a loan
3. felt **exalted** listening to great music
4. turned from protest to **militancy**
5. two evils **inextricably** joined
6. a **legitimate** excuse

Author Online

Crusader for Justice Preaching a philosophy of nonviolence, Dr. Martin Luther King Jr. became a catalyst for social change in the 1950s and 1960s. He galvanized people of all races to participate in boycotts, marches, and demonstrations against racial injustice. His moral leadership stirred the conscience of the nation and helped bring about the passage of the Civil Rights Act of 1964. In that same year he was awarded the Nobel Peace Prize. King continued his work for justice and equality until he was assassinated in 1968.

Dr. Martin Luther King Jr.
1929–1968

Inspirational Speaker An eloquent Baptist minister from Atlanta, King often used religious references in his speeches. On the night before his death, he told an audience in Memphis, Tennessee: "I've seen the Promised Land. I may not get there with you, but I want you to know tonight, that we as a people will get to the Promised Land."

 MORE ABOUT THE AUTHOR
For more on Dr. Martin Luther King Jr., visit the **Literature Center** at **ClassZone.com.**

Background

March on Washington In August 1963, thousands of Americans marched on Washington, D.C., to urge Congress to pass a civil rights bill. King delivered his "I Have a Dream" speech on the steps of the Lincoln Memorial before more than 200,000 people.

I HAVE A DREAM **601**

Teach

STANDARDS FOCUS

ELEMENTS OF NONFICTION

● ARGUMENT

For instructional support, ask students to imagine that their vision for changing the world involves feeding all who are hungry. Have them write a claim for this vision, using King's claim as a model. *Possible answer: Even though we have the technology to feed everyone, many people still go hungry.*

CHECK UNDERSTANDING Ask students to explain what roles a claim and its support have in an argument.

READING SKILL

● UNDERSTAND RHETORICAL DEVICES

Discuss the terms *repetition, parallelism,* and *analogy.* As students examine the chart, have them look ahead to see how *one hundred years later* is repeated in lines 8–13. For instructional support, have students locate and explain the purpose of a repeated term in the quotation in **Inspirational Speaker.** *Possible answer: King repeats Promised Land to emphasize the certainty of his vision.*

CHECK UNDERSTANDING Discuss why repetition, parallelism, and analogies can help make a speech effective.

 RESOURCE MANAGER—Copy Master
Understand Rhetorical Devices p. 29 (for student use while reading the selection)

VOCABULARY SKILL

▲ VOCABULARY IN CONTEXT

DIAGNOSE WORD KNOWLEDGE To determine preteaching needs, have all students complete Vocabulary in Context. *Possible answers:*
1. *great or important,* 2. *fail to fulfill a commitment,* 3. *lifted up,* 4. *hostility,* 5. *unable to be pulled apart,* 6. *reasonable or legal*

PRETEACH VOCABULARY Use the Vocabulary Study copy master to help students self-assess their knowledge of each boldfaced word in the copy master.

1. Read item 1 aloud, emphasizing *default.*

2. Point out the clues *promise to pay, promise,* and *does not give.* Elicit possible meanings for *default,* such as "fail to fulfill a commitment."

3. Repeat the procedure for items 2–6.

 RESOURCE MANAGER—Copy Master
Vocabulary Study p. 31

For general guidelines on differentiating vocabulary instruction and for alternative vocabulary activities for students not needing vocabulary preteaching, see

📋 BEST PRACTICES TOOLKIT
Scaffolding Vocabulary Instruction pp. 43–46
🛈 Vocabulary Center at **ClassZone.com**

ANALYZE VISUALS

Possible answer: King is calm, confident, and in control.

ELEMENTS OF NONFICTION

A ARGUMENT

King cites segregation (line 9), discrimination (line 10), and poverty (line 11) as evidence that African Americans do not enjoy complete freedom.

If students need help . . . Suggest that students use a Two-Column Chart to paraphrase King's claims, as in these examples.

I Read	My Paraphrase
"lives on a lonely island of poverty"	is isolated by being poor
"finds himself in exile"	set apart and sent away

🧰 **BEST PRACTICES TOOLKIT—Transparency**
Two-Column Chart p. A25

I HAVE A DREAM

DR. MARTIN LUTHER KING JR.

I am happy to join with you today in what will go down in history as the greatest demonstration for freedom in the history of our nation.

Five score[1] years ago, a great American, in whose symbolic shadow we stand today, signed the Emancipation Proclamation.[2] This **momentous** decree came as a great beacon light of hope to millions of Negro slaves who had been seared in the flames of withering injustice. It came as a joyous daybreak to end the long night of their captivity.

But one hundred years later, the Negro still is not free; one hundred years later, the life of the Negro is still sadly crippled by the manacles of segregation
10 and the chains of discrimination; one hundred years later, the Negro lives on a lonely island of poverty in the midst of a vast ocean of material prosperity; one hundred years later, the Negro is still languishing in the corners of American society and finds himself in exile in his own land. **A**

So we've come here today to dramatize a shameful condition. In a sense we've come to our nation's capital to cash a check. When the architects of our republic wrote the magnificent words of the Constitution and the Declaration of Independence, they were signing a promissory note[3] to which every American was to fall heir. This note was the promise that all men, yes, black men as well as white men, would be guaranteed the unalienable rights of life,
20 liberty, and the pursuit of happiness.

It is obvious today that America has **defaulted** on this promissory note insofar as her citizens of color are concerned. Instead of honoring this sacred obligation, America has given the Negro people a bad check, a check which has come back marked "insufficient funds." But we refuse to believe that the bank of justice is bankrupt. We refuse to believe that there are insufficient funds in

---

1. **five score:** 100; *score* means "twenty." (This phrasing recalls the beginning of Abraham Lincoln's Gettysburg Address: "Four score and seven years ago . . .")
2. **Emancipation Proclamation:** a document signed by President Lincoln in 1863, during the Civil War, declaring that all slaves in states still at war with the Union were free.
3. **promissory** (prŏm′ĭ-sôr′ē) **note:** a written promise to repay a loan.

ANALYZE VISUALS
What impression do you get of Martin Luther King Jr. from this photograph?

momentous
(mō-mĕn′təs) *adj.*
of great importance

1 Targeted Passage

A ARGUMENT
Reread lines 8–13. What evidence does King provide to **support** the **claim** that "the Negro still is not free"?

default (dĭ-fôlt′) *v.* to fail to keep a promise, especially a promise to repay a loan

August 28, 1963: Dr. Martin Luther King Jr. delivers his speech at the Lincoln Memorial during the March on Washington, D.C.

DIFFERENTIATED INSTRUCTION

FOR ALL STUDENTS
Learning Center Challenge students to create a "Dream On Display" museum exhibit. Include copies of historic photos, re-creations of signs the marchers carried, and buttons they wore. Use the Internet to find background information on the march, the civil rights movement, and the life of Dr. Martin Luther King Jr. For details, see

R RESOURCE MANAGER
Ideas for Extension pp. 22–23

FOR LESS–PROFICIENT READERS
In combination with the *Audio Anthology CD,* use one or more Targeted Passages (pp. 602, 605, 607) to ensure that students focus on key ideas, concepts, and skills. Targeted Passges are also good for English learners.

1 Targeted Passage [Lines 1–7]
This introductory passage establishes the historical context of King's speech.

BACKGROUND

"I Have a Dream" Ironically, the phrase that has come to define King's famous speech was not in the prepared version that he intended to deliver to the approximately 200,000 listeners who had gathered in front of the Lincoln Memorial on August 28, 1963 to protest racial injustice. As he stepped toward the podium after a long program of speeches and musical performances, King was informed that time would allow for him to speak extemporaneously if he wished. He delivered his prepared remarks and then, he reported later, a phrase came to him: "I have a dream." He had used it in speeches in Birmingham and Detroit in April and June of that year. But now, King repeated the phrase over and over, each time using it to introduce a vision of a more just nation, each time stirring the emotional response of his listeners. When he finished to thunderous applause, King had transformed his audience with the inspiration of his words and the power of his dream.

- What event took place 100 years before King gave this speech? Why was that event important to King's audience?

- What does King say about the historic importance of the event at which he is speaking? Do you think that he was right? Why or why not?

Options for Reading Read aloud the first two paragraphs of "I Have a Dream." Review the author and purpose of the speech. Then have learners listen to the *Audio Anthology CD* as they read along.

Key Academic Vocabulary Use Definition Mapping to practice these words: *demonstration* (line 2), *symbolic* (line 3), *discrimination* (line 10), *pursuit* (line 20), *insufficient* (line 24), *foundations* (line 43).

 BEST PRACTICES TOOLKIT—Transparency
Definition Mapping p. E6

Prereading For prereading instruction for English learners, see

 BEST PRACTICES TOOLKIT
Scaffolding Reading Instruction p. 43–46

FOR ADVANCED LEARNERS/PRE–AP

Pre-AP Exercises in the bottom channel provide additional challenges for students. Use these suggestions for small groups or individuals.

ADDITIONAL GUIDELINES
For more help with differentiation and tips for classroom management, see

BEST PRACTICES TOOLKIT
Differentiated Instruction p. 31–38

DISCUSSION PROMPTS

Use these prompts to help students focus on King's tone:

Connect If you had been in the audience, how might you have reacted to these words? Why? *Answers will vary, but students should consider responses to the resolute, even defiant, attitude in King's statements.*

Analyze In terms of content and emotion, what is the purpose of this paragraph? *Possible answer: The purpose is to bring King's introductory focus to a point of tension, some of which will be released in the next paragraph.*

Synthesize How does King use tone to appeal to his audience? *Possible answer: King's tone is both revolutionary and unifying. When he says that the struggle for equality will continue (lines 41–42) and will shake the country (line 43), his determined tone appeals to the need for radical change. He then appeals to a sense of unity, however, by looking optimistically to a "bright day of justice" (line 44) for all.*

READING SKILL

B RHETORICAL DEVICES

Possible answer: King uses repetition. By repeating now is the time *(lines 31, 32, 33, and 35), he stresses the urgency of the situation.*

If students need help . . . Read the lines aloud so that students can hear the repetition.

Extend the Discussion What else does King do in this paragraph to hold his listeners' attention and emphasize his message?

More than 200,000 marchers gather on the mall between the Washington Monument and the Lincoln Memorial. To the right, civil rights leaders march with King.

the great vaults of opportunity of this nation. And so we've come to cash this check, a check that will give us upon demand the riches of freedom and the security of justice.

We have also come to this hallowed spot to remind America of the fierce
30 urgency of now. This is no time to engage in the luxury of cooling off or to take the tranquilizing drug of gradualism.[4] Now is the time to make real the promises of democracy; now is the time to rise from the dark and desolate valley of segregation to the sunlit path of racial justice; now is the time to lift our nation from the quicksands of racial injustice to the solid rock of brotherhood; now is the time to make justice a reality for all of God's children. It would be fatal for the nation to overlook the urgency of the moment. This sweltering summer of the Negro's **legitimate** discontent will not pass until there is an invigorating autumn of freedom and equality. **B**

Nineteen sixty-three is not an end, but a beginning. And those who hope
40 that the Negro needed to blow off steam and will now be content will have a rude awakening if the nation returns to business as usual. There will be neither rest nor tranquility in America until the Negro is granted his citizenship rights. The whirlwinds of revolt will continue to shake the foundations of our nation until the bright day of justice emerges.

legitimate (lə-jĭt′ə-mĭt)
adj. justifiable; reasonable

B RHETORICAL DEVICES
Reread lines 29–38. What rhetorical device does King use, and what is the effect of using it?

---

4. **gradualism:** a policy of seeking to reach a goal slowly, in gradual stages.

604 UNIT 6: ARGUMENT AND PERSUASION

DIFFERENTIATED INSTRUCTION

FOR ENGLISH LEARNERS

Vocabulary: Idioms Use New Word Analysis to teach these idioms: *cooling off* (line 30), "calming down"; *blow off steam* (line 40), "release anger"; *rude awakening* (line 41), "shocking realization"; *business as usual* (line 41), "the normal routine"; *tied up with* (line 55), "connected to."

🧰 **BEST PRACTICES TOOLKIT—Transparency**
New Word Analysis p. E8

FOR ADVANCED LEARNERS/PRE–AP

Analyze Figurative Language King's speech is rich with figurative language, such as "the tranquilizing drug of gradualism," which he refers to in line 31. Ask students to choose one example of figurative language from King's speech and write a paragraph about how their choices helped them to understand King's message.

A young woman participates in the demonstration.

But there is something that I must say to my people, who stand on the worn threshold which leads into the palace of justice. In the process of gaining our rightful place we must not be guilty of wrongful deeds. Let us not seek to satisfy our thirst for freedom by drinking from the cup of bitterness and hatred. We must forever conduct our struggle on the high plain of dignity
50 and discipline. We must not allow our creative protests to degenerate into physical violence. Again and again we must rise to the majestic heights of meeting physical force with soul force. The marvelous new **militancy,** which has engulfed the Negro community, must not lead us to a distrust of all white people. For many of our white brothers, as evidenced by their presence here today, have come to realize that their destiny is tied up with our destiny. And they have come to realize that their freedom is **inextricably** bound to our freedom. We cannot walk alone. And as we walk, we must make the pledge that we shall always march ahead. We cannot turn back.

There are those who are asking the devotees of civil rights, "When will you
60 be satisfied?" We can never be satisfied as long as the Negro is the victim of the unspeakable horrors of police brutality; we can never be satisfied as long as our bodies, heavy with the fatigue of travel, cannot gain lodging in the motels of the highways and the hotels of the cities; we cannot be satisfied as long as the Negro's basic mobility is from a smaller ghetto to a larger one; we can never be satisfied as long as our children are stripped of their selfhood and robbed of

ANALYZE VISUALS
What do these photographs suggest about King's effectiveness as an orator and a leader? Explain.

② Targeted Passage

militancy (mĭl′ĭ-tənt-sē) *n.* the act of aggressively supporting a political or social cause

inextricably (ĭn-ĕk′strĭ-kə-blē) *adv.* in a way impossible to untangle

I HAVE A DREAM   **605**

ANALYZE VISUALS
Possible answers: The photograph of the huge crowd suggests that King was a powerful draw and a good speaker. The photograph of the marchers suggests that he understood how to work with others. The photograph of the young woman suggests that people looked to him as a leader and found hope in his words.

Activity Have students discuss why King and his fellow marchers wore suits. *Possible answer: King presented civil rights as a struggle for human dignity. Wearing suits was a way of symbolizing the dignity of that cause.*

Lines 45–58
DISCUSSION PROMPTS
Use these prompts to help students understand the audience for this speech:

Connect How do you react to King's words about violence? *Students might mention how violence could harm the cause of civil rights.*

Analyze What does King do in these lines to show that whites and blacks in his audience must work together? *Possible answer: King says that the freedom and destiny of whites are linked to that of blacks (lines 55–57).*

Synthesize How do these lines both send a message to King's followers and gain the support of a wider audience? *Possible answer: These lines show that hatred and bitterness are not the answer to the problem of racial inequality. They show the need for trust and cooperation.*

FOR LESS-PROFICIENT READERS
② Targeted Passage [Lines 45–58]
Several statements in this passage illustrate the dignity and highmindedness of the civil rights movement under King's leadership.

• What actions does King oppose?

• According to King, what thoughts should the Negro community have—and not have—toward white people?

• What does he mean when he uses the term *soul force* (line 52)?

FOR ADVANCED LEARNERS/PRE-AP
Analyze Style [paired-activity option]
Have students reread these two pages, considering how King's sentences vary in length, structure, and placement of key elements. As students comment, encourage them to note variations in sentence structures (simple, compound, complex, compound-complex) and sentence beginnings, in particular.

C ARGUMENT

***Possible answer:** police brutality, segregated hotels and motels, the existence of ghettos, "For Whites Only" signs, voting restrictions, and lack of concern for African Americans in the issues for which they are able to vote*

READING SKILL

D RHETORICAL DEVICES

***Possible answer:** "battered by the storms of persecution and staggered by the winds of police brutality" (lines 73–74); "sweltering with the heat of injustice, sweltering with the heat of oppression" (lines 88–89); and "by the color of their skin . . . by the content of their character" (lines 91–92)*

Lines 81–106
REINFORCE *KEY IDEA*: VISION

Discuss In these lines, King introduces his dream. Why is it appropriate to speak of his dream as a **vision**—that is, as something more than a dream? ***Possible answer:** King's dream is not just a fantasy; it is a vision because King has a plan that he believes can be carried out to make all of America a better place.*

---

their dignity by signs stating For Whites Only; we cannot be satisfied as long as the Negro in Mississippi cannot vote and a Negro in New York believes he has nothing for which to vote. No! No, we are not satisfied, and we will not be satisfied until "justice rolls down like waters and righteousness like a
70 mighty stream." **C**

I am not unmindful that some of you have come here out of great trials and tribulations. Some of you have come fresh from narrow jail cells. Some of you have come from areas where your quest for freedom left you battered by the storms of persecution and staggered by the winds of police brutality. You have been the veterans of creative suffering. Continue to work with the faith that unearned suffering is redemptive.[5] Go back to Mississippi. Go back to Alabama. Go back to South Carolina. Go back to Georgia. Go back to Louisiana. Go back to the slums and ghettos of our Northern cities, knowing that somehow this situation can and will be changed. Let us not wallow in the
80 valley of despair.

I say to you today, my friends, even though we face the difficulties of today and tomorrow, I still have a dream. It is a dream deeply rooted in the American dream. I have a dream that one day this nation will rise up and live out the true meaning of its creed, "We hold these truths to be self-evident; that all men are created equal." I have a dream that one day on the red hills of Georgia, sons of former slaves and the sons of former slave owners will be able to sit down together at the table of brotherhood. I have a dream that one day even the state of Mississippi, a state sweltering with the heat of injustice, sweltering with the heat of oppression, will be transformed into an oasis of freedom and
90 justice. I have a dream that my four little children will one day live in a nation where they will not be judged by the color of their skin, but by the content of their character. **D**

I have a dream today!

I have a dream that one day down in Alabama—with its vicious racists, with its Governor having his lips dripping with the words of interposition and nullification[6]—one day right there in Alabama, little black boys and black girls will be able to join hands with little white boys and white girls as sisters and brothers.

I have a dream today!

I have a dream that one day every valley shall be **exalted,** and every hill and
100 mountain shall be made low. The rough places will be plain and the crooked places will be made straight, "and the glory of the Lord shall be revealed, and all flesh shall see it together."

This is our hope. This is the faith that I go back to the South with. With this faith we will be able to hew out of the mountain of despair a stone of hope. With this faith we will be able to transform the jangling discords of our nation into a beautiful symphony of brotherhood. With this faith we will

---

5. **unearned suffering is redemptive:** undeserved suffering is a way of earning freedom or salvation.
6. **Governor . . . nullification:** Rejecting a federal order to desegregate the University of Alabama, Governor George Wallace claimed that the principle of nullification (a state's alleged right to refuse a federal law) allowed him to resist federal "interposition," or interference, in state affairs.

606 UNIT 6: ARGUMENT AND PERSUASION

C ARGUMENT
Identify the examples of racial injustice that King provides as **evidence** to convince his audience to share his views.

D RHETORICAL DEVICES
Reread lines 71–92. What examples of **parallelism** help make the expression of ideas concise and memorable?

exalted (ĭg-zôl'tĭd) *adj.* raised up **exalt** *v.*

DIFFERENTIATED INSTRUCTION

FOR LESS–PROFICIENT READERS
Comprehension Support [lines 81–92] To make sure that students understand this key paragraph, have them write the word *dream* six times on a sheet of paper, once for each appearance of *dream* as King describes it in the paragraph. In each case, ask students to note one thing that King says about his dream. Compare and discuss students' notes.

FOR ENGLISH LEARNERS
Language: Verb Tenses Explain that King favors certain verb tenses in various sections of this speech. Discuss with students how verb tenses make the speech more forceful in lines 71–75 (present perfect), lines 81–102 (present combined with future), lines 103–114 (future), and lines 122–138 (softened commands with *let*).

be able to work together, to pray together, to struggle together, to go to jail together, to stand up for
110 freedom together, knowing that we will be free one day. And this will be the day. This will be the day when all of God's children will be able to sing with new meaning, "My country 'tis of thee, sweet land of liberty, of thee I sing. Land where my fathers died, land of the pilgrims' pride, from every mountainside, let freedom ring."
120 And if America is to be a great nation, this must become true.

So let freedom ring from the prodigious hilltops of New Hampshire; let freedom ring from the mighty mountains of New York; let freedom ring from the heightening Alleghenies of Pennsylvania; let freedom ring from the snowcapped Rockies of
130 Colorado; let freedom ring from the curvaceous slopes of California. But not only that. Let freedom ring from Stone Mountain of Georgia; let freedom ring from Lookout Mountain of Tennessee; let freedom ring from every hill and molehill of Mississippi. "From every mountainside, let freedom ring."
And when this happens, and
140 when we allow freedom to ring,
when we let it ring from every village and every hamlet, from every state and every city, we will be able to speed up that day when all of God's children— black men and white men, Jews and Gentiles, Protestants and Catholics—will be able to join hands and sing in the words of the old Negro spiritual, "Free at last. Free at last. Thank God Almighty, we are free at last." ✐

❸ **Targeted Passage**

January 20, 2003: Marchers in St. Louis celebrate King's birthday, a national holiday.

Practice and Apply

After Reading

For additional support of post-reading questions, use these copy masters:

 RESOURCE MANAGER—Copy Masters

Reading Check p. 34 (to check understanding of the selection)

Argument p. 27 (for practice of elements of nonfiction standards focus)

Question Support p. 35 (After Reading questions adapted for English learners and less-proficient readers)

For additional questions, see page 21.

To challenge students further, see

🔘 **Bob Marzano's Power Thinking** Activities at **ClassZone.com**

ANSWERS

Comprehension

1. *King describes poverty (lines 8–13), police brutality (line 61), segregation (lines 61–66), ghettos (lines 63–64), and voting inequalities (lines 66–68).*

2. *King predicts that the struggle for civil rights will continue, disturbing the very foundations of the country (lines 39–44).*

3. *King's vision is of an America where all people live in brotherhood, justice, and freedom (lines 81–92 and 143–145).*

Critical Analysis

Possible answers:

4. ● **STANDARDS FOCUS** *Argument* **Example:** *"For Whites Only" signs (lines 65–66);* **Example:** *voting inequities (lines 66–68);* **Example:** *slums and ghettos (line 78)*

5. ■ **STANDARDS FOCUS** *Understand Rhetorical Devices* **Repetition:** *"No! No, we are not satisfied, and we will not be satisfied . . ." (lines 68–69). The repeated* no *and* not satisfied *emphasize King's frustration.* **Parallelism:** *"This is no time . . . . Now is the time . . ." (lines 30–35). The parallel structure sets up a contrast that stresses the urgency of the situation.*

6. *King means that America promised "unalienable rights" to all but has not honored that promise for African Americans. Instead, America has segregated African Americans and treated them unfairly.*

After Reading

Comprehension

1. **Recall** What examples of racial injustice does King describe?

2. **Clarify** What does King predict will happen if justice is denied African Americans?

3. **Summarize** What is King's dream, or **vision?**

Critical Analysis

4. **Analyze the Argument** On a graphic organizer like the one shown, list at least three examples of racial injustice that King uses as **support** for his **claim** that African Americans are not free.

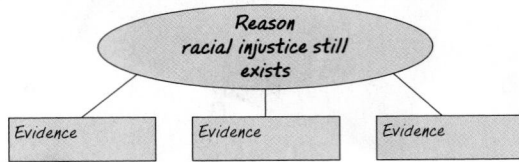

5. **Understand Rhetorical Devices** Review the chart you created as you read. Then identify an example of **repetition** or **parallelism** and explain the effect it creates.

6. **Understand an Analogy** Reread lines 14–28. In these paragraphs, King uses an analogy to compare a familiar object—a promissory note—to something abstract—the promise of equal rights. What does King mean when he says that America has given African Americans a "bad check"? Explain your answer.

7. **Evaluate an Allusion** Reread lines 81–85. An allusion is an indirect reference, within a work, to something that the audience or reader is expected to know. As King begins to explain his **vision**, he alludes to the Declaration of Independence, quoting its famous lines. How effective is this allusion? Support your evaluation.

Reading-Writing Connection

WRITING PROMPT	SELF-CHECK
Extended Response: Write an Analysis How would you account for the extraordinary acclaim King's speech has received, not only when it was first delivered but many years later? Write a **three-to-five-paragraph analysis** of the effectiveness of King's address. Consider both the strength of its logic and its emotional power.	*A strong analysis will . . .* • state the qualities that make the speech memorable • provide examples from the speech

---

7. *This allusion is effective because the Declaration of Independence is familiar to all Americans. Furthermore, King alludes to the document in lines 14–20, when he discusses how America has failed to keep its promise to African Americans; by quoting it again now, he is saying that the failure can be rectified.*

Reading-Writing Connection

WRITING PROMPT

Have students use an Argumentation frame to explore the logic of King's speech. Pairs

or small groups of students might work together to find and discuss examples of its emotional power. Students also may use Mapping Main Ideas and Details to plan their essays.

 BEST PRACTICES TOOLKIT—Transparencies

Argumentation p. B11

Mapping Main Ideas and Details p. C6

For an extended Reading-Writing Connection activity, see

ℹ️ Writing Center at **ClassZone.com**

Vocabulary in Context

VOCABULARY PRACTICE

Answer the questions to show your understanding of the vocabulary words.

1. Which would be more **momentous**—the birth of a baby or the first snow of the season in upstate New York?

2. If you **default** on a loan, do you sign up to borrow money or fail to make a payment?

3. If your teacher judges your doctor's note to be **legitimate,** would you be sent to the principal's office or allowed to miss gym?

4. Who would be more likely to support a course of **militancy**—a person starting a new job or a person unfairly denied an opportunity to work?

5. Which items are more likely to be **inextricably** linked—the products on a shelf at a grocery store, or the necklaces kept in a dresser drawer?

6. Would a high priestess or a herder be the more **exalted** member of a tribe?

WORD LIST
default
exalted
inextricably
legitimate
militancy
momentous

VOCABULARY IN WRITING

Assume that you had had the chance to interview King after he delivered his impassioned speech. Write several questions you might have asked him about his life and vision, using three or more vocabulary words. Here is an example.

> **EXAMPLE SENTENCE**
> *Can you describe a **momentous** event in your childhood?*

VOCABULARY STRATEGY: POLITICAL WORDS

Specialized vocabulary terms, such as *militancy,* often appear in political texts and articles. You will better understand world events if you know the exact meaning of such terms.

PRACTICE Use a dictionary to help you write the definition of each word listed. Then use each word in a sentence.

1. despot
2. geopolitics
3. imperialism
4. nationalism
5. theocracy

> **VOCABULARY PRACTICE**
> For more practice, go to the **Vocabulary Center** at **ClassZone.com.**

ANSWERS

Vocabulary in Context

VOCABULARY PRACTICE

1. *the birth of a baby*
2. *fail to make a payment*
3. *allowed to take gym*
4. *person denied work opportunity*
5. *necklaces kept in a dresser drawer*
6. *a high priestess*

R RESOURCE MANAGER—Copy Master
Vocabulary Practice p. 32

VOCABULARY IN WRITING

Call on volunteers to share their finished questions so that students can see the various ways in which the words have been used.

VOCABULARY STRATEGY: POLITICAL WORDS

Remind students to look at the part-of-speech labels.

Possible answers:

1. *tyrant*
2. *politics that reflect geographic factors*
3. *one nation taking over another*
4. *strong loyalty to and belief in one's nation*
5. *government of a state by divine guidance*

***Example of word used in sentence:** The despot shut down the press when it criticized him.*

R RESOURCE MANAGER—Copy Master
Vocabulary Strategy p. 33

ℹ Vocabulary Center at **ClassZone.com**
Additional Vocabulary Activities

Assess and Reteach

Assess

R RESOURCE MANAGER—Copy Masters
Selection Test A pp. 39–40
Selection Test B/C pp. 41–42

⊘ Test Generator CD

Reteach

S STANDARDS LESSON FILE
Informational Text Lesson 14: Elements of an Argument
Literature Lesson 36: Rhetorical Devices

DIFFERENTIATED INSTRUCTION

FOR ENGLISH LEARNERS

Vocabulary: Related Words Have students work with partners to find words that are related to some of these vocabulary words. For example, for *militancy,* students might note the related words *military, militant,* and *militia.* Interested pairs of students might work together to create a poster or other visual aid that catalogs their findings.

FOR ADVANCED LEARNERS/PRE–AP

Vocabulary in Writing Challenge students to write a coherent paragraph, with a clear main idea, that uses all the words. Allow students to share their paragraphs in small groups and discuss the ways in which they used the words.

Testimony Before the Senate

Speech by Michael J. Fox

OBJECTIVES

Elements of Nonfiction

- explore the key idea of a **pitch**
- analyze persuasive techniques
- read a speech/public document

Reading

- summarize the main points of a text

Vocabulary

- build vocabulary for reading and writing
- use a dictionary to determine the meaning of foreign words and phrases (*also an EL language objective*)

Grammar and Writing

- use appropriate sentence types to establish tone
- use writing to analyze literature

SUMMARY

In "Testimony Before the Senate," actor Michael J. Fox urges an increase in federal funding for Parkinson's disease research. Using facts and his personal experience as a victim of Parkinson's, Fox describes the devastating power of the disease and his expectation that a cure could be found soon—if the research were better funded.

How do you SELL AN IDEA?

Introduce the question. Have students read the *KEY IDEA* and comment on memorable commercials. After students complete the *DISCUSS* activity, compile a master list of persuasive techniques used to **pitch** products in commercials.

How do you SELL AN IDEA?

KEY IDEA Teenagers are a hot market—companies are always trying to convince them to buy something. You're familiar with commercials and ads that try to sell you a product. But are you aware that a great deal of energy and money is spent trying to sell you on people and ideas? People in almost every business work hard at crafting their **pitch.**

DISCUSS With a partner, brainstorm a list of times when you realized someone was trying to sell you an idea, an image, or a person's expertise. What techniques were used? Which ones worked?

Idea	Pitch Used
Say "no" to drugs.	Commercial about saving a friend who's drowning; features the slogan "Friends, the anti-drug."

610

Selection Resources

R RESOURCE MANAGER UNIT 6

Plan and Teach pp. 43–50

Elements of Nonfiction
Summary pp. 51†*, 52‡*
Persuasive Techniques pp. 53, 54†*
Question Support p. 61*

Reading
Summarize pp. 55, 56†*
Reading Check p. 60
Reading Fluency p. 63

Vocabulary
Study p. 57*
Practice p. 58
Strategy p. 59

Grammar and Writing
Set the Tone p. 62

Assessment
Selection Tests A, B/C pp. 65*, 67*
⊘ Test Generator CD

BEST PRACTICES TOOLKIT

Differentiated Instruction
pp. 31–38*

Scaffolding Instruction
pp. 43–46*

Graphic Organizers/Strategies
Word Questioning • Mapping
Main Idea and Details • Cluster
Diagram

Reading Support
⊘ Audio Anthology CD*

Technology
ⓘ Literature and Vocabulary Centers at **ClassZone.com**
⊘ Write*Smart* CD

* Resources for Differentiation   † Also in Spanish   ‡ Also in Haitian Creole and Vietnamese

● ELEMENTS OF NONFICTION: PERSUASIVE TECHNIQUES

Writers and speakers typically use more than just arguments to persuade. They use rhetorical devices and **persuasive techniques**—that is, messages and descriptions that appeal to people's emotions, values, and desires to belong to a particular group or be like a particular person.

In "Testimony Before the Senate," Michael J. Fox often uses the persuasive techniques that are classified as emotional appeals. **Emotional appeals** are descriptions designed to win support by appealing to people's feelings of compassion or, sometimes, fear. Here Fox appeals to our sense of pity:

There are doctors, teachers, policemen, nurses, and parents who are no longer able to work, to provide for their families, and live out their dreams.

As you read his testimony, look for other examples of emotional appeals.

● READING SKILL: SUMMARIZE

A **summary** is a brief retelling of the main ideas of a written or spoken text. When you summarize, use your own words to restate the main ideas. As you read Fox's speech, prepare to summarize it by jotting down main ideas and important details on a chart like the one shown.

Paragraph/Section 1
Main Idea:
Important Details:

↓

Paragraph/Section 2
Main Idea:
Important Details:

↓

▲ VOCABULARY IN CONTEXT

The following boldfaced words are key to understanding Michael J. Fox's persuasive plea. Restate each phrase, using a different word or words for the boldfaced term.

1. rejecting the **status quo**
2. a **meager** salary, which doesn't allow for luxuries
3. a **neurological** disorder causing tremors
4. **eradicate** poverty and other social problems

Author Online

Actor and Crusader A successful actor in both film and television—he received four Emmy Awards—Michael J. Fox was diagnosed with Parkinson's disease at the age of 30. In order to spend more time with his family and to promote Parkinson's research, he retired from acting in 2000. He went on to establish the Michael J. Fox Foundation for Parkinson's Research.

Michael J. Fox born 1961

 MORE ABOUT THE AUTHOR For more on Michael J. Fox, visit the **Literature Center** at **ClassZone.com.**

Background

Parkinson's Disease Parkinson's disease results from a loss of brain cells that produce dopamine, a chemical that transmits brain signals. The disease's many symptoms include tremors, slowness of movement, and problems with balance. Over time, walking and other ordinary activities become more and more difficult. The cause of Parkinson's is still unknown, and as yet no cure has been found. Unfortunately, the medications used to treat the disease often have serious side effects.

Teach

STANDARDS FOCUS

ELEMENTS OF NONFICTION

● PERSUASIVE TECHNIQUES

For instructional support, read aloud this example:

If you care about fire safety, vote to save Engine 12.

Have students explain how this emotional appeal is persuasive. *Possible answer: It appeals to people's concerns for their safety in the event of a fire.*

CHECK UNDERSTANDING Ask students to give an example of an emotional appeal about another topic.

READING SKILL

■ SUMMARIZE

Model this skill by summarizing *About the Author:*

After he was diagnosed with Parkinson's disease, Michael J. Fox gave up his successful acting career. He has become a powerful advocate for finding a cure for the disease.

Discuss which details from the text were included and which were omitted.

CHECK UNDERSTANDING Have students summarize the *Background* text.

 RESOURCE MANAGER—Copy Master Summarize p. 55 (for student use while reading the selection)

VOCABULARY SKILL

▲ VOCABULARY IN CONTEXT

DIAGNOSE WORD KNOWLEDGE To determine preteaching needs, have all students complete Vocabulary in Context. *Possible answers:*
1. *existing state of affairs,* 2. *small,*
3. *nerve (nervous system),* 4. *do away with*

PRETEACH VOCABULARY Use the Vocabulary Study copy master to help students predict the meaning of each boldfaced word in the copy master.

1. Read the first sentence in Part A aloud, emphasizing *status quo.*

2. Point out the phrase *resigned to accept.* Elicit possible meanings for *status quo.*

3. Repeat the procedure for the other items in Part A.

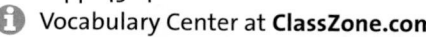 RESOURCE MANAGER—Copy Master Vocabulary Study p. 57

For general guidelines on differentiating vocabulary instruction and for alternative vocabulary activities for students not needing vocabulary preteaching, see

BEST PRACTICES TOOLKIT Scaffolding Vocabulary Instruction pp. 43–46
ⓘ Vocabulary Center at **ClassZone.com**

Practice and Apply

Lines 1–12
REINFORCE *KEY IDEA:* PITCH

Discuss How does Senator Specter indicate that the Subcommittee is open to listening to the **pitch** that Fox is about to make? ***Possible answer:*** *Specter mentions the acclaim that Fox has received (lines 1–5) and the fact that Fox has Parkinson's disease (lines 5–6), suggesting that Fox comes before the Subcommittee with some authority to address the issue. Specter also admits the need to cure the disease (lines 10–11). Finally, he thanks Fox for coming and says that the Subcommittee is looking forward to hearing Fox's testimony (lines 11–12).*

ELEMENTS OF NONFICTION

Ⓐ PERSUASIVE TECHNIQUES

Possible answer: *The persuasive technique is an appeal to vanity. Fox is trying to win over the senators, in part, by praising their leadership.*

If students need help . . . Have students review the chart that appears on page 596. Help them eliminate each persuasive technique that does not apply to these lines.

Extend the Discussion It is not uncommon for people who come before Congress to begin their testimony with words like these. Why is Fox's technique an effective opening for a speech to such an audience?

PARKINSON'S DISEASE RESEARCH AND TREATMENT

HEARING

BEFORE A
SUBCOMMITTEE OF THE
COMMITTEE ON APPROPRIATIONS
UNITED STATES SENATE
ONE HUNDRED SIXTH CONGRESS
FIRST SESSION

SPECIAL HEARING

Printed for the use of the Committee on Appropriations

Senator SPECTER. We have with us today Mr. Michael J. Fox, a successful actor for many years. First, as Alex P. Keaton, on the television series "Family Ties." You always work with a middle initial, do you not, Mr. Fox? Later in many movies, including "Back to the Future," and, most recently, on television again in the highly acclaimed "Spin City." Michael was diagnosed with Parkinson's in 1991, at the age of 30.

He has become very, very active in Parkinson's advocacy. One of the facts of life is that when someone like Michael J. Fox steps forward, it very heavily personalizes the problem, focuses a lot of public attention on it,
10 and has the public understanding of the need for doing whatever we can as a country to conquer this disease and many, many others. So we thank you for being here, Michael J. Fox, and look forward to your testimony.

Again, we will put the lights on, for 5 minutes, on testimony.

Mr. FOX. Mr. Chairman, Senator Harkin, and members of the Subcommittee—thank you for inviting me to testify today about the need for a greater federal investment in Parkinson's research. I would like to thank you, in particular, for your tremendous leadership in the fight to double funding for the National Institutes of Health.[1] Ⓐ

Ⓐ PERSUASIVE TECHNIQUES
What persuasive technique mentioned on page 596 in the Critical Reading Workshop is Fox using in lines 14–18?
Targeted Passage ①

---

1. **National Institutes of Health:** a government organization that conducts and supports research designed to improve the health of the nation.

UNIT 6: ARGUMENT AND PERSUASION

DIFFERENTIATED INSTRUCTION

FOR ALL STUDENTS

Expert Groups Allow students to become Experts or Expert Groups by researching and sharing additional information about one of these topics:

- Parkinson's disease
- the work of the Committee on Appropriations
- the Michael J. Fox Foundation for Parkinson's Research

FOR LESS–PROFICIENT READERS

In combination with the *Audio Anthology CD*, use one or more Targeted Passages (pp. 612, 615, 616) to ensure that students focus on key ideas, concepts, and skills. Targeted Passages are also good for English learners.

① **Targeted Passage [Lines 14–18]**

This passage presents Fox's first words and the goal for his speech.

- Who is Fox's audience?

UNIT 6: ARGUMENT AND PERSUASION

Michael J. Fox testifies before the U.S. Senate.

ANALYZE VISUALS
Think about your reaction to seeing a famous actor linked with a cause or product. Are you more willing to read this speech and consider its message because the author is a celebrity? Explain your answer.

Some, or perhaps most of you are familiar with me from 20 years of
20 work in film and television. What I wish to speak to you about today has little or nothing to do with celebrity—save for this brief reference.

When I first spoke publicly about my 8 years of experience as a person with Parkinson's, many were surprised, in part because of my age (although 30 percent of all Parkinson's patients are under 50, and 20 percent are under 40, and that number is growing). I had hidden my symptoms and struggles very well, through increasing amounts of medication, through surgery, and by employing the hundreds of little tricks and techniques a person with Parkinson's learns to mask his or her condition for as long as possible.

30 While the changes in my life were profound and progressive, I kept them to myself for a number of reasons: fear, denial for sure, but I also felt that it was important for me to just quietly "soldier on." **B**

When I did share my story, the response was overwhelming, humbling, and deeply inspiring. I heard from thousands of Americans affected by Parkinson's, writing and calling to offer encouragement and to tell me of their experience. They spoke of pain, frustration, fear and hope. Always hope.

B SUMMARIZE
Reread lines 22–32, and record the passage's important details in your chart. Then restate the main idea of the passage in your own words.

ANALYZE VISUALS

Possible answer: Yes; people generally would be more willing to consider a message coming from a celebrity whom they know and like than from a stranger.

BACKGROUND

Fox's Foundation The Michael J. Fox Foundation for Parkinson's Research looks for a cure through drug development, cell replacement therapy, and genetic discoveries. Since its founding, less than a year after Fox's 1999 testimony before the Senate, the organization has funded or directed more than $50 million in research.

READING SKILL

B SUMMARIZE

Possible answer: Important details may include the facts that many people were surprised when Fox spoke about his illness; that Fox was young when diagnosed; that he hid his symptoms well, like others who are able to hide their illness; and that he used a variety of methods to keep the secret for as long as possible. The main idea is that Fox, like many other Parkinson's victims, kept his illness a secret so successfully that many were surprised when they learned the truth.

If students need help . . . Explain that the main idea must be inferred by combining several details. Guide students as they record the details in their chart.

- What does Fox give as the reason for his testimony? What does that reason tell you about his purpose for speaking?

- To whom is he grateful? Why do you think that he opens his speech by expressing gratitude?

FOR ENGLISH LEARNERS

Key Academic Vocabulary Use Word Questioning to practice these words: *advocacy* (line 7), *federal* (line 16), *funding* (line 18),

techniques (line 27), *adequately* (line 47), *medical* (line 62).

 BEST PRACTICES TOOLKIT—Transparency
Word Questioning p. E9

Prereading For prereading instruction for English learners, see

 BEST PRACTICES TOOLKIT
Scaffolding Reading Instruction p. 43–46

FOR ADVANCED LEARNERS/PRE–AP

Pre-AP Exercises in the bottom channel provide additional challenges for students. Use these suggestions for small groups or individuals.

ADDITIONAL GUIDELINES

For more help with differentiation and tips for classroom management, see

 BEST PRACTICES TOOLKIT
Differentiated Instruction p. 31–38

C PERSUASIVE TECHNIQUES

Possible answer: *Fox is making a "plain folks" appeal, pointing out that Parkinson's disease affects a wide range of everyday Americans. Fox's list reminds senators that not all victims are celebrities.*

ANALYZE VISUALS

Activity In scenes such as this one, how does Fox come across to television viewers?
Possible answer: *Fox appears responsible, pleasant, socially conventional, and healthy.*

D SUMMARIZE

Possible answer: *Parkinson's disease can cause tremors and stiffness; the medicine can cause uncontrollable movement and slurred speech.*

If students need help . . . Have them reread lines 49–55 and then use Main Idea and Details notes to record the symptoms mentioned in the paragraph.

 BEST PRACTICES TOOLKIT—Transparency Mapping Main Idea and Details p. C6

What I understood very clearly is that the time for quietly "soldiering on" is through. The war against Parkinson's is a winnable war, and I am 40 resolved to play a role in that victory.

What celebrity has given me is the opportunity to raise the visibility of Parkinson's disease and focus more attention on the desperate need for more research dollars. While I am able, for the time being, to continue to do what I love best, others are not so fortunate. There are doctors, teachers, policemen, nurses, and parents who are no longer able to work, to provide for their families, and live out their dreams. **C**

C PERSUASIVE TECHNIQUES
In additon to appealing to the senators' pity, what does Fox appeal to by referring to the specific categories of "doctors, teachers, policemen, nurses, and parents"?

Fox starred in the sitcom *Spin City* from 1996 to 2000, when he retired from acting.

The one million Americans living with Parkinson's want to beat this disease. So do millions more Americans who have family members suffering from Parkinson's. But it won't happen until Congress adequately funds 50 Parkinson's research.

For many people with Parkinson's, managing their disease is a full-time job. It is a constant balancing act. Too little medicine causes tremors and stiffness. Too much medicine produces uncontrollable movement and slurring. And far too often, Parkinson's patients wait and wait for the medicines to "kick-in." New investigational therapies have helped some people like me control my symptoms, but in the end, we all face the same reality: the medicines stop working. **D**

For people living with Parkinson's, the **status quo** isn't good enough.

As I began to understand what research might promise for the future, 60 I became hopeful I would not face the terrible suffering so many with Parkinson's endure. But I was shocked and frustrated to learn that the

D SUMMARIZE
What challenges do people with Parkinson's face? Cite specific details.

status quo (stăt′əs kwō) *n.* the existing state of affairs

DIFFERENTIATED INSTRUCTION

FOR ENGLISH LEARNERS

Language: Pronoun Referents Ask students to identify the referents, either explicit or implicit, for the following pronouns: *you* (line 20); *many* (line 23); *his, her* (line 28); *They* (line 35); *others* (line 42); *their* (line 44); *it* (lines 47, 50, 97); *we* (lines 63, 64); *one* (line 84); *some* (line 87); *your* (line 92). If students cannot identify referents accurately, review the topic, using as models the sentences in which these pronouns appear.

amount of funding for Parkinson's research is so **meager.** Compared with the amount of federal funding going to other diseases, research funding for Parkinson's lags far behind.

In a country with a $15 billion investment in medical research we can and we must do better.

At present, Parkinson's is inadequately funded, no matter how one cares to spin it. Meager funding means a continued lack of effective treatments, slow progress in understanding the cause of the disease, and little chance
70 that a cure will come in time. I applaud the steps we are taking to fulfill the promise of the Udall Parkinson's Research Act, but we must be clear—we aren't there yet.

If, however, an adequate investment is made, there is much to be hopeful for. We have a tremendous opportunity to close the gap for Parkinson's. We are learning more and more about this disease. The scientific community
80 believes that with a significant investment in Parkinson's research, new discoveries and improved treatments strategies are close-at-hand. Many have called Parkinson's the most curable **neurological** disorder and the one expected to produce a breakthrough first. Scientists tell me that a cure is possible, some say even by the end
90 of the next decade—if the research dollars match the research opportunity.

Fox is greeted by Senators Paul Wellstone and Arlen Specter.

2 Targeted Passage

Mr. Chairman, you and the members of the Subcommittee have done so much to increase the investment in medical research in this country. I thank you for your vision. Most people don't know just how important this research is until they or someone in their family faces a serious illness. I know I didn't.

The Parkinson's community strongly supports your efforts to double medical research funding. At the same time, I implore you to do more for people with Parkinson's. Take up Parkinson's as if your life depended on it.
100 Increase funding for Parkinson's research by $75 million over current levels for the coming fiscal year.[2] Make this a down payment for a fully funded

meager (mē'gər) adj. lacking in quantity or quality

neurological (noor'ə-lŏj'ĭ-kəl) adj. having to do with the nervous system

---

2. **fiscal year:** a 12-month period—which may or may not coincide with the calendar year—during which a company or organization keeps accounting records.

Use these prompts to help students understand Fox's balanced tone:

Connect Think of a time when something on which you had set your hopes fell apart. How does that experience help you grasp what Fox says in lines 58–64? *Students should consider the disappointment and frustration implied in Fox's statement.*

Analyze What tone does Fox take as he describes the lack of federal funding for Parkinson's research? Cite evidence. *Possible answer: Fox's tone is firmly critical and yet respectful. He tells the Subcommittee that what has been done is not enough and that people are suffering as a result (lines 58–70). Still, his language is conservative, not fiery. Furthermore, he includes a word of gratitude for what the government has done (lines 70–72).*

Evaluate Did Fox take an appropriate tone in this passage? Explain. *Possible answer: Fox's tone was appropriate. If he were not critical, his plea would seem unimportant. At the same time, he needed to be respectful because of his audience's status and its power to grant his request.*

ANALYZE VISUALS

Activity How do the senators appear to respond to Fox in the photograph? *Possible answer: They appear interested in him and appreciative of his attention.*

FOR LESS–PROFICIENT READERS
2 Targeted Passage [Lines 73–91]

In this passage, Fox discusses the effect that increased funding could have on Parkinson's research.

- Why are scientists hopeful about finding a cure for Parkinson's disease?

- How soon might they find a cure?

- What do scientists need to make progress in finding a cure?

FOR ADVANCED LEARNERS/PRE–AP

Synthesize [small-group option] Review Fox's plea: "Take up Parkinson's as if your life depended on it" (line 97). Then ask students how they would "take up" the cause—for example, how they would raise money, conduct research, and support those suffering from the disease. Invite sharing of ideas for class discussion and evaluation.

Activity What can you infer about Parkinson's disease research from the photograph? ***Possible answer:*** *The research requires advanced technology.*

E GRAMMAR AND STYLE

Imperative Sentences Point out that Fox could have used declarative sentences (for example, *I would like you to increase funding . . .*). The imperative sentences, however, express respectful commands, making the plea direct and urgent. To check understanding, elicit that the second sentence in this group is imperative and that it seems more forceful than the other two:

> This research needs more funding.
> Increase funding for this research.
> Could you increase research funding?

SELECTION WRAP—UP

SUMMARIZE Have students identify the specific request that Fox makes of the Subcommittee.

⭐ **CRITIQUE** Have students evaluate the ending of the speech. Ask students how else Fox might have concluded his testimony.

READING FLUENCY

Distribute the copy master and have students work in pairs or groups to practice fluency.

R RESOURCE MANAGER—Copy Master
Reading Fluency p. 63

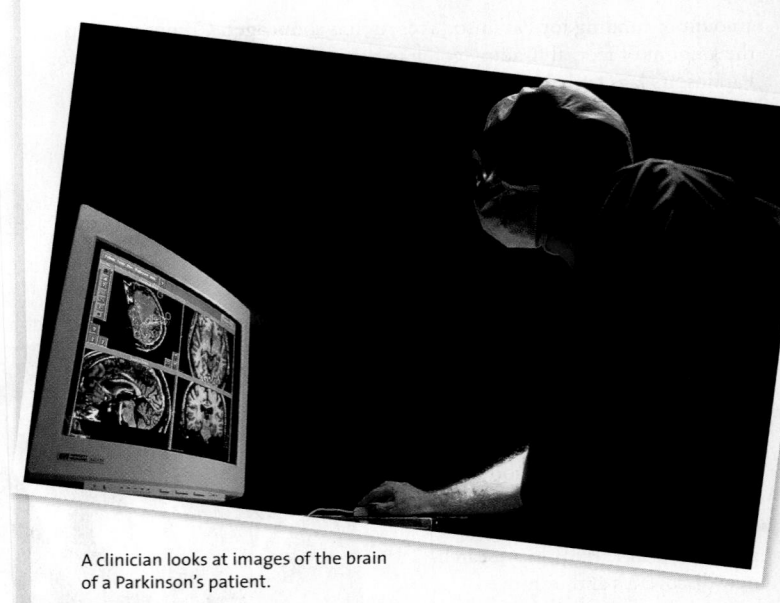

A clinician looks at images of the brain of a Parkinson's patient.

E GRAMMAR AND STYLE
Reread lines 97–103. Fox uses **imperative sentences** to urge Congress to increase research funding.

Targeted Passage

eradicate (ĭ-răd′ĭ-kāt′) *v.* to do away with completely

Parkinson's research agenda that will make Parkinson's nothing more than a footnote in medical textbooks. **E**

I would like to close on a personal note. Today you will hear from, or have already heard from, more than a few experts, in the fields of science, book-keeping and other areas. I am an expert in only one—what it is like to be a young man, husband, and father with Parkinson's disease. With the help of daily medication and selective exertion, I can still perform my job, in my case in a very public arena. I can still help out with the daily
110 tasks and rituals involved in home life. But I don't kid myself . . . that will change. Physical and mental exhaustion will become more and more of a factor, as will increased rigidity, tremor and dyskinesia.[3] I can expect in my 40s to face challenges most wouldn't expect until their 70s and 80s—if ever. But with your help, if we all do everything we can to **eradicate** this disease, in my 50s I'll be dancing at my children's weddings. And mine will be just one of millions of happy stories.

Thank you again for your time and attention.

Senator SPECTER. Thank you very much, Mr. Fox, for those very profound and moving words.

---

3. **dyskinesia** (dĭs′kə-nē′zhə): inability to control bodily movements.

DIFFERENTIATED INSTRUCTION

FOR LESS—PROFICIENT READERS
③ Targeted Passage [Lines 110–116]

This passage wraps up the speech and looks toward the future.

- At the end of the speech, what does Fox ask the senators to do?

- What will Fox be able to do if the disease is eradicated?

- Do you think the senators care if Fox dances at his children's weddings? Why is this ending effective?

Review Main Points Have students complete a Cluster Diagram to review the main points in Fox's testimony.

BEST PRACTICES TOOLKIT—Transparency
Cluster Diagram p. B18

Comprehension

1. **Recall** How did other people with Parkinson's disease respond to Fox when he made his condition known?

2. **Recall** What did Fox resolve to do after he shared his situation with the public?

3. **Clarify** Why is managing the disease a full-time job for people with Parkinson's?

Critical Analysis

4. **Summarize** Review the notes you took as you read. Then summarize what you learned about Parkinson's disease from reading Fox's testimony.

5. **Draw Conclusions** How does Fox's personal experience with Parkinson's help him make his **pitch** to his audience? Explain your answer.

6. **Analyze the Argument** Fox's **claim** is that Congress should increase federal spending for Parkinson's research. What reasons and evidence does he provide as **support** for his claim? Write them on a graphic organizer like the one shown.

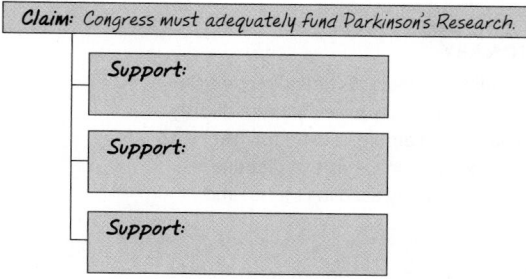

Claim: Congress must adequately fund Parkinson's Research.

Support:

Support:

Support:

7. **Analyze the Counterargument** What potential objection is Fox countering in lines 90–101?

8. **Evaluate Persuasive Techniques** Reread lines 102–114. Fox concludes his testimony by describing two contrasting visions of his future. What emotion does each vision create? What is the effect of concluding his speech with this **emotional appeal**?

9. **Synthesize** Does it strengthen or weaken a cause to have a celebrity associated with it? Would a plea from an ordinary person carry as much weight as one from a celebrity? Consider Michael J. Fox's association with Parkinson's research and think of other celebrities who support particular causes.

8. ● **STANDARDS FOCUS** *Persuasive Techniques* *The first vision, with Fox becoming more disabled, is sad and frightening. The second, with Fox dancing at his children's weddings, is happy and hopeful. The effect of this concluding emotional appeal is to make the senators feel the urgency of doing more to help find a cure.*

9. *Celebrity association strengthens a cause. A plea from an ordinary person would not carry as much weight as a plea from a celebrity because people immediately recognize the celebrity and may be influenced by his or her opinions.*

Practice and Apply

After Reading

For additional support of post-reading questions, use these copy masters:

R **RESOURCE MANAGER**—Copy Masters
   Reading Check p. 60 (to check understanding of the selection)
   Persuasive Techniques p. 53 (for practice of elements of nonfiction standards focus)
   Question Support p. 61 (After Reading questions adapted for English learners and less-proficient readers)

For additional questions, see page 47.

ANSWERS

Comprehension

1. *Other people with Parkinson's contacted Fox to encourage him and tell him of their experiences with the disease.*

2. *Fox resolved to dedicate himself to finding a cure for the disease.*

3. *Managing the disease is a full-time job because people with Parkinson's must monitor their condition all the time. They must constantly adjust their medications to control their symptoms.*

Critical Analysis

Possible answers:

4. ■ **STANDARDS FOCUS** *Summarize Parkinson's disease causes dyskinesia, or loss of bodily control. People with Parkinson's must manage their medications carefully and constantly. Eventually, medications become ineffective and sufferers can expect to display the severest symptoms of the disease.*

5. *Fox's personal experience makes him an expert on the difficulties of living with the disease. His pitch is more convincing because of his personal experience.*

6. *Support: Parkinson's research is inadequately funded. Support: Scientists believe that a rapid cure is possible if research is sufficiently funded. Support: The disease has devastated about a million American victims and their families.*

7. *Fox is countering the potential objection that the Subcommittee has already provided enough funding.*

ANSWERS

Vocabulary in Context

VOCABULARY PRACTICE

1. *neurological*   3. *meager*
2. *eradicate*   4. *status quo*

R RESOURCE MANAGER—Copy Master
Vocabulary Practice p. 58

VOCABULARY IN WRITING

Use these questions as prompts: What issues move you? What might you do to help?

VOCABULARY STRATEGY: USING A DICTIONARY *(also an EL language objective)*

Model how to locate etymology in a dictionary, using *status quo* as an example.

Possible answers:

1. ***Original Language:*** *French;* ***Original Meaning:*** *by the bill of fare;* ***Meaning in English:*** *with a separate price for each item on the menu*

2. ***Original Language:*** *Italian;* ***Original Meaning:*** *to the tooth;* ***Meaning in English:*** *cooked but still chewy*

3. ***Original Language:*** *Latin;* ***Original Meaning:*** *something for something;* ***Meaning in English:*** *one thing in return for another*

4. ***Original Language:*** *Spanish;* ***Original Meaning:*** *a pot;* ***Meaning in English:*** *a papier-mâché container filled with treats, and broken open*

5. ***Original Language:*** *French;* ***Original Meaning:*** *false step;* ***Meaning in English:*** *a social blunder*

6. ***Original Language:*** *Latin;* ***Original Meaning:*** *to this;* ***Meaning in English:*** *for this specific purpose*

7. ***Original Language:*** *Latin;* ***Original Meaning:*** *let the buyer beware;* ***Meaning in English:*** *one buys at one's own risk*

8. ***Original Language:*** *Italian;* ***Original Meaning:*** *in the cool;* ***Meaning in English:*** *outdoors*

R RESOURCE MANAGER—Copy Master
Vocabulary Strategy p. 59

ⓘ Vocabulary Center at **ClassZone.com**
Additional Vocabulary Activities

Vocabulary in Context

VOCABULARY PRACTICE

Write the word from the Word List that best completes each sentence.

1. _____ diseases can damage the brain.
2. The goal of medical research is to _____ these diseases.
3. A _____ increase in funding might slow progress toward finding a cure.
4. Clearly, it is important to progress instead of maintaining the _____.

WORD LIST
eradicate
meager
neurological
status quo

VOCABULARY IN WRITING

If you were given the chance, what important issue would you publicly support? Write a short paragraph identifying an issue and explaining its importance. Use at least two vocabulary words. You might start like this.

> **EXAMPLE SENTENCE**
>
> *We need to **eradicate** air pollution, especially in our big cities. . . .*

VOCABULARY STRATEGY: USING A DICTIONARY

A dictionary is an important tool for understanding terms that come directly from another language. The meaning of some foreign terms may have changed slightly since they were brought into English. *Status quo*, for example, is Latin for "the state in which" but means "the existing state of affairs" in English. A dictionary will have the definitions of many foreign terms commonly used in English, and some will include the term's etymology, or history.

PRACTICE Create a four-column chart with these headings: "Foreign Term," "Original Language," "Original Meaning," and "Meaning in English." Then, using a dictionary, fill in the chart for each term.

1. à la carte   5. faux pas
2. al dente   6. ad hoc
3. quid pro quo   7. caveat emptor
4. piñata   8. alfresco

➤ VOCABULARY PRACTICE
For more practice, go to the **Vocabulary Center** at **ClassZone.com**.

DIFFERENTIATED INSTRUCTION

FOR ENGLISH LEARNERS

Culture: Connect Invite students to think of words or expressions from their home languages or another language they know that they have heard used in English. Have them add these words to their Vocabulary Strategy Practice chart.

FOR ADVANCED LEARNERS/PRE–AP

Vocabulary in Writing Have students use each of the words from the Word List in a brief scripted dialogue. Ask students to exchange their dialogues with a partner for review and, if necessary, revision.

Reading-Writing Connection

Broaden your understanding of "Testimony Before the Senate" by responding to these prompts. Then use **Revision: Grammar and Style** to improve your writing.

WRITING PROMPTS	SELF-CHECK
A. Short Response: Prepare a Radio Message How would you persuade others to donate money for Parkinson's research? Using what you learned from "Testimony Before the Senate," write **a one- or two-paragraph message** for a radio broadcast that makes a **pitch** for raising money.	*A strong message will . . .* • clearly state the action you wish people to take • provide at least two reasons for taking the action
B. Extended Response: Write a Memo Imagine you are a senator who has just heard Fox's testimony. How would you respond? Write **a three-to-five-paragraph memo** to a fellow senator, describing your reaction and identifying the most convincing parts of Fox's testimony.	*A successful memo will . . .* • describe your reaction to the testimony • identify convincing parts of Fox's testimony

REVISION: GRAMMAR AND STYLE

SET THE TONE Review the **Grammar and Style** note on page 616. Fox uses **imperative sentences**—sentences that express a command or request—in his testimony. By using imperative sentences, rather than other sentence types, Fox creates a sense of directness and urgency. (The subject of imperative sentences is usually *you*, often understood rather than stated.)

Here is an example of one student's use of imperative sentences:

> *Take up the cause with me. Give full support to the Parkinson's community by increasing research funding.*

Now study the model. Notice how the revisions in red make the tone stronger and more urgent. Revise your responses to the prompts by employing similar techniques.

> **STUDENT MODEL**
> ~~You can~~ make a difference in the war against Parkinson's disease. ~~Your donation~~ will go to research for a cure. *Send in* Your

WRITING TOOLS
For prewriting, revision, and editing tools, visit the **Writing Center** at **ClassZone.com.**

FOR LESS–PROFICIENT WRITERS

For Prompt A:

• Suggest that students follow this structure: (1) define the disease; (2) explain how donations can help; (3) appeal for donations; and (4) explain how donations will be collected.

• Review Fox's call to action (lines 90–101), but remind students to make their message personal, not a mere parroting of Fox's message.

For Prompt B:

• Limit the length of the assignment to three paragraphs, with students identifying just two or three points in Fox's testimony.

• Have students work in pairs to identify convincing parts of Fox's testimony.

• Help students craft an introduction that has an appropriate tone and style.

Reading-Writing Connection

WRITING PROMPTS

• For Prompt A, urge students to use Fox's speech as a model, but remind them that the radio message must be concise. Nevertheless, they should use effective verbal strategies—vivid and descriptive language, imperative sentences, clear persuasive techniques—in preparing the message. After students have given their messages, have peers evaluate the informative and persuasive qualities of the oral presentations.

• For Prompt B, remind students that a memo is rather businesslike. The approach should be direct and formal.

For writing support, see

 Writing Center at **ClassZone.com**

REVISION: GRAMMAR AND STYLE

• Explain that imperative sentences should be used sparingly. To illustrate, discuss how the tone of Fox's testimony would have seemed angrier and been more unpleasant if most of his sentences had been imperative. (For more on tone, see **Reading Handbook**, page R21.)

• After discussing the student model, have students rewrite some declarative sentences from Fox's testimony as imperative sentences. Discuss the results. (For more on imperative sentences, see **Grammar Handbook**, page R59.)

R RESOURCE MANAGER—Copy Master
Set the Tone p. 62

Assess and Reteach

Assess

R RESOURCE MANAGER—Copy Masters
Selection Test A pp. 65–66
Selection Test B/C pp. 67–68

⊘ Test Generator CD

Reteach

S STANDARDS LESSON FILE
Research and Study Skill Lesson 13: Summarizing
Informational Texts Lesson 15: Persuasive Techniques
Writing Lesson 43: Tone and Voice
Vocabulary Lesson 24: Using Vocabulary Reference Sources

Focus and Motivate

OBJECTIVES

Elements of Nonfiction
- explore the key idea of **privacy**
- distinguish fact from opinion
- read a magazine article and a newspaper article

Reading
- recognize and analyze bias

Vocabulary
- build vocabulary for reading and writing
- understand and use specialized vocabulary (Internet words) *(also an EL language objective)*

Grammar and Writing
- use parallelism to express ideas that are related or of equal importance
- use writing to analyze literature

SUMMARIES

In "How Private Is Your Private Life?," Andrea Rock shows that the ways in which daily transactions are conducted make it practically impossible to keep personal information private.

In "The Privacy Debate: One Size Doesn't Fit All," Arthur M. Ahalt, a retired judge, explains the benefits of access to public records, noting that the privacy debate is not a simple matter.

Is PRIVACY *an illusion?*

Read the question and the **KEY IDEA.** Urge students to use their responses as a basis for their work on the **DEBATE** activity.

Selection Resources

How Private Is Your Private Life?
Magazine Article by Andrea Rock

The Privacy Debate: One Size Doesn't Fit All
Newspaper Editorial by Arthur M. Ahalt

Is PRIVACY *an illusion?*

KEY IDEA Your phone number appears in a hundred databases. Your favorite Web site keeps track of your every click. Do these advances in technology pose a threat to your **privacy?** Big Brother (along with 30 of his closest friends) may be watching you.

DEBATE With a small group, break into two teams and stage a debate over the question of personal privacy in today's society. Is your privacy at risk, or isn't it? Be prepared to back up your opinions with examples and other evidence.

PRIVATE PROPERTY KEEP OUT TRESPASSERS WILL BE PROSECUTED

620

RESOURCE MANAGER UNIT 6

Plan and Teach pp. 69–76

Elements of Nonfiction
Summary pp. 77†*, 78‡*
Fact and Opinion pp. 79, 80†*
Question Support p. 87*

Reading
Recognize Bias pp. 81, 82†*
Reading Check p. 86

Vocabulary
Study p. 83*
Practice p. 84
Strategy p. 85

Grammar and Writing
Use Rhetorical Devices p. 89

Assessment
Selection Tests A, B/C pp. 91*, 93*
Test Generator CD

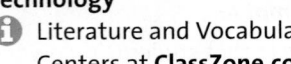 **BEST PRACTICES TOOLKIT**

Differentiated Instruction
pp. 31–38*

Scaffolding Instruction
pp. 43–46*

Graphic Organizers/Strategies
Definition Mapping • Two-Column Chart • Think-Pair-Share

Reading Support
Audio Anthology CD*

Technology
 Literature and Vocabulary Centers at **ClassZone.com**
WriteSmart CD

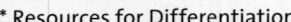

● ELEMENTS OF NONFICTION: FACT AND OPINION

Most persuasive writers use facts and opinions to support their claims. A **fact** is a statement that can be proved, or verified. An **opinion** is a statement that cannot be proved because it expresses a person's beliefs, feelings, or thoughts. It's important to distinguish facts from opinions because facts tend to be less disputable than opinions—unless the opinions come from experts. Can you distinguish the fact from opinion here?

The constant invasion of our privacy is an outrage.

According to a 1999 Wall Street Journal *poll, loss of privacy is the number-one concern of Americans.*

The first statement is an opinion. The second is a fact; it can be proved by consulting the 1999 *Wall Street Journal* poll.

As you read each of the following selections, identify the significant facts and opinions in a chart like the one shown.

Location	Example	Fact/Opinion
lines 2–3	A 1999 poll found that loss of privacy is the number-one concern of Americans.	Fact

▣ READING SKILL: RECOGNIZE BIAS

Bias is an unfair preference for or against a particular topic or issue. To detect bias, be on the lookout for the following:

- an argument in which the evidence is unbalanced, giving one side stronger or more adequate support than the other
- the presence of **loaded language**—words with intensely positive or negative connotations
- opinions stated as if they were facts
- the use of overgeneralizations, such as **stereotyping,** and other faulty reasoning (See **Reading Handbook,** page R24.)

▲ VOCABULARY IN CONTEXT

Which of the following words can be used to discuss
- the promotion of a cause?
- an unbiased discussion?
- something unsettling?
- a skilled talker?

WORD LIST		
advocacy	articulate	disconcerting
affiliate	awry	nonpartisan
anonymity	browser	pervasive
		surveillance

Background

Technology and Privacy Many Americans are becoming increasingly concerned that the miracles of technology have come at a high cost—namely, the loss of personal privacy. Internet companies, for example, can monitor Web sites to gather information about their visitors—information that can be sold to other companies for marketing purposes. In many large corporations, computer software can screen workers' e-mail messages. Some Americans want Congress to pass stronger privacy laws like those that have been established in other countries. In the United States, however, corporate opponents have lobbied successfully against such legislation.

"Meet the new head of security."

© Mike Baldwin/www.CartoonStock.com

BUILDING BACKGROUND
To learn more about technology and privacy, visit the **Literature Center** at **ClassZone.com.**

621

Teach

STANDARDS FOCUS

ELEMENTS OF NONFICTION

● FACT AND OPINION

After students read the *Background*, have them classify these related statements as either fact or opinion:

Internet companies can gather information about their visitors by monitoring Web sites. *(Fact)*

Technology is not worth the price we pay in privacy. *(Opinion)*

CHECK UNDERSTANDING Elicit that this statement is a fact: *Computer software can screen workers' e-mail.* Have students suggest an opinion related to that fact.

R RESOURCE MANAGER—Copy Master
Fact and Opinion p. 79 (for student use while reading the selections)

READING SKILL

▣ RECOGNIZE BIAS

For instructional support, write this chapter title on the board: *Government Snooping and You.* Elicit that *snooping* is loaded language. Discuss how the title might suggest a book whose author is biased.

CHECK UNDERSTANDING Ask students to suggest another chapter title that might appear in the same book.

R RESOURCE MANAGER—Copy Master
Recognize Bias p. 81 (for student use while reading the selections)

VOCABULARY SKILL

▲ VOCABULARY IN CONTEXT

DIAGNOSE WORD KNOWLEDGE To determine preteaching needs, have all students complete Vocabulary in Context. *Possible answers: cause: advocacy, nonpartisan, articulate; something unsettling: disconcerting, awry, surveillance; unbiased: nonpartisan, anonymity; skilled talker: articulate*

PRETEACH VOCABULARY Use the Vocabulary Study copy master to help students predict the meaning of each boldfaced word in the copy master.

1. Read item 1 aloud, emphasizing *advocacy*.
2. Point out the phrases *work to help* and *influencing the law.* Elicit possible meanings for *advocacy*, such as "helping people by exerting influence."
3. Repeat the procedure for items 2–10.

R RESOURCE MANAGER—Copy Master
Vocabulary Study p. 83

For general guidelines on differentiating vocabulary instruction and for alternative vocabulary activities for students not needing vocabulary preteaching, see

BEST PRACTICES TOOLKIT
Scaffolding Vocabulary Instruction pp. 43–46
ⓘ Vocabulary Center at **ClassZone.com**

BACKGROUND

A "Right" to Privacy? Students may be surprised to learn that the U.S. Constitution nowhere specifies privacy as a right. However, many Supreme Court cases have addressed a range of privacy issues. Court decisions and public discussion about the issues addressed have tended to give privacy Constitutional status. In particular, the Fourth Amendment (which protects Americans from "unreasonable searches and seizures") and the Fifth Amendment (which guards against self-incrimination and the taking of private property for public use) have been linked to privacy issues. Still, their application has not been interpreted consistently. As both Rock and Ahalt suggest, privacy remains difficult both to define and to protect.

ANALYZE VISUALS

Activity Have students explain what the boy in the picture is doing and what personal information he might be giving away. *Possible answer: The boy is using a telephone and a computer. He is holding a card—perhaps a library card, a membership card, or even a credit card. He may be giving away personal data, such as his address or date of birth. If the card is a credit card, he might be giving away private financial information. The boy also might be revealing such things as personal interests or preferences as a consumer.*

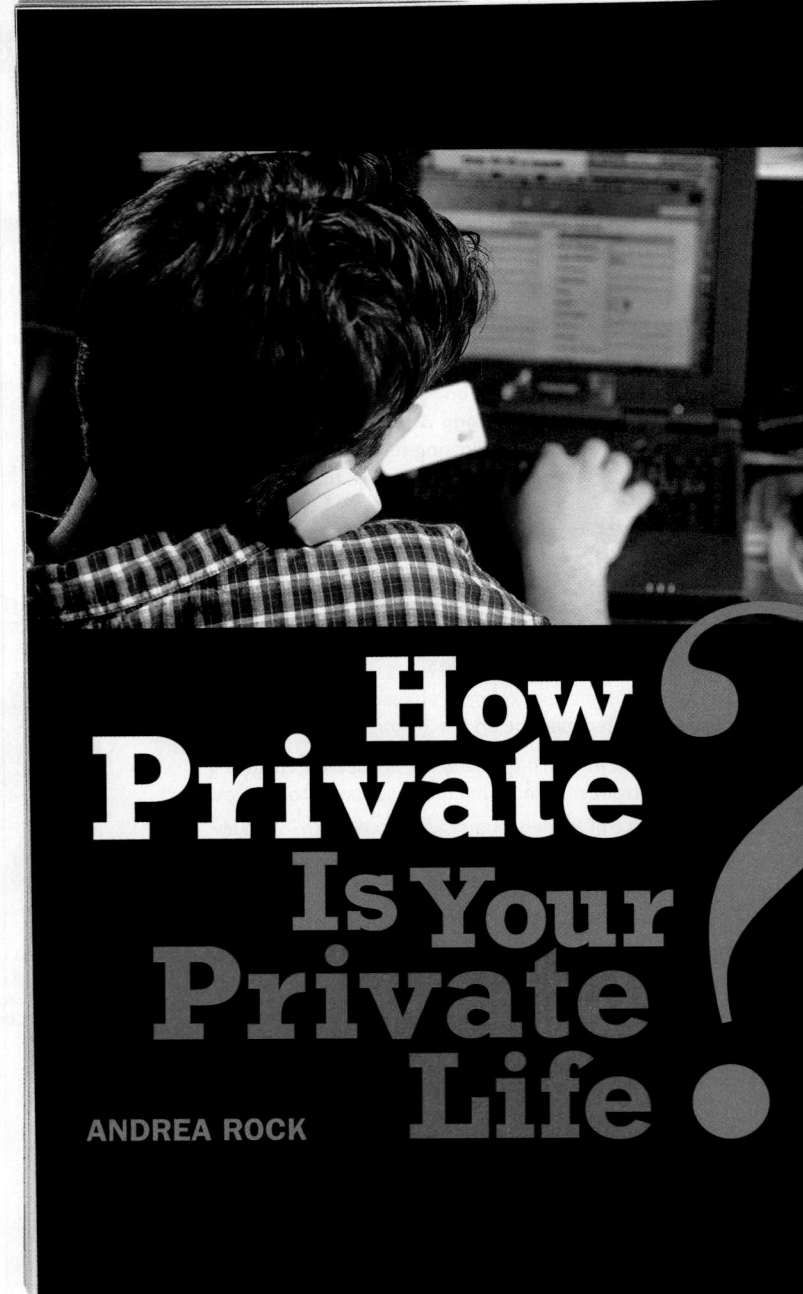

How Private
Is Your Private Life?

ANDREA ROCK

DIFFERENTIATED INSTRUCTION

FOR ALL STUDENTS
Journal As they read, ask students to keep a journal noting questions, observations, and reflections about issues raised by the selections. Ask students to refer to their notes when completing writing activities or participating in class discussion.

FOR LESS–PROFICIENT READERS
In combination with the *Audio Anthology CD,* use one or more Targeted Passages (pp. 623, 624, 627, 628, 630) to ensure that students focus on key ideas, concepts, and skills. Targeted Passages are also good for English learners.

When you go online, file an insurance claim or even eat out, you reveal personal information to strangers. Here's what you need to know about who's watching you—and how to protect yourself.

Rapid advances in technology have fostered an ever-growing assault on our private lives. A 1999 *Wall Street Journal* poll found that loss of privacy **A** ranked as Americans' number-one concern for the new century—ahead of depression, war and terrorism.

Regulators and lawmakers alike have proposed measures to safeguard privacy, but they face strong opposition from businesses whose aim is to collect as much information as possible about consumers' financial and medical histories, their shopping habits and other personal details. Companies profit by selling this information to advertisers and other
10 businesses, or simply by using it to tailor their own advertising.

To find out how **pervasive** the system really is, the editors of LHJ[1] asked me to see how often in a single day my activities resulted in a legal invasion of privacy. I was surprised by what I learned:

9:00 A.M.
After sending my two sons off to school, I go to the grocery store. At the register, I hand the cashier my supermarket discount card. Later, I discover that this card allows retailers to track exactly what I've purchased, how much I spend and how often I shop. These details can then be shared with product manufacturers so that coupons and other offers can be targeted to me. "People should be aware that when they use these cards, they are
20 literally selling their privacy," says Ari Schwartz, senior policy analyst at the Center for Democracy and Technology, an **advocacy** organization in Washington, D.C. Schwartz adds that his group has already seen cases where these records have been used in lawsuits. **B**

9:25 A.M.
After returning a video, I stop at the post office to mail an insurance claim form. Amazingly, the privacy of my video-rental records is protected by federal law, but not the data in my medical records. By signing the claim form, I authorize doctors to release sensitive information about myself to insurers and other third parties,[2] such as the Medical Information Bureau, which keeps records of health problems reported on some
30 insurance applications and informs insurers (on request) about pre-existing conditions.

---

1. **editors of LHJ:** The author was given this assignment by the editors of *Ladies' Home Journal.*
2. **release sensitive information . . . other third parties:** Congress attempted to address this problem by passing the Health Insurance Portability and Accountability Act, which makes the unauthorized release of medical information a crime.

HOW PRIVATE IS YOUR PRIVATE LIFE? **623**

A **RECOGNIZE BIAS**
Notice the phrase "ever-growing assault on our private lives." Does this **loaded language** portray technology as positive or negative? Explain.

1 Targeted Passage

pervasive (pər-vā'sĭv) *adj.* spreading widely through an area or group of people

advocacy (ăd'və-kə-sē) *adj.* involving public support for an idea or policy

B **FACT AND OPINION**
Reread lines 14–23. What facts are included here? Cite examples from the text.

---

1 Targeted Passage [Lines 1–13]

This introductory passage establishes the purpose of the article.

- What kinds of information about consumers do businesses want to collect? Why?
- How do many Americans feel about that practice? Why?
- What has Andrea Rock, the writer, been asked to find out? Who has asked her?

FOR ENGLISH LEARNERS

Key Academic Vocabulary Use Definition Mapping to teach these words: *technology* (line 1), *legal* (line 12), *policy* (line 20), *computer* (line 74), *security* (line 82).

 BEST PRACTICES TOOLKIT—Transparency Definition Mapping p. E6

Prereading For prereading instruction for English learners, see

 BEST PRACTICES TOOLKIT Scaffolding Reading Instruction p. 43–46

FOR ADVANCED LEARNERS/PRE–AP

Pre-AP Exercises in the bottom channel provide additional challenges for students. Use these suggestions for small groups or individuals.

ADDITIONAL GUIDELINES
For more help with differentiation and tips for classroom management, see

 BEST PRACTICES TOOLKIT Differentiated Instruction p. 31–38

Lines 26–34
REINFORCE *KEY IDEA:* PRIVACY

Discuss What good can come from sharing medical records? In your opinion, does that make the loss of **privacy** a good thing? Explain. ***Possible answer:*** *It is good that records are shared with insurers so that medical bills can be paid. It also is good that they are shared with other doctors and specialists so that the best care can be given. Opinions about the loss of privacy will vary but should be reasonably supported.*

ELEMENTS OF NONFICTION

C FACT AND OPINION

Possible answer: *The statement could be verified by reading the text of the law, either in a book or online.*

ANALYZE VISUALS

Activity Have students match the photograph to the text in lines 44–48. Then ask them to make an inference, based on the photograph. ***Possible answer:*** *The E-Z Pass makes it possible to create travel records for both individuals (the cars) and businesses (the trucks).*

Although my medical records can be shared with people I don't know, in about half the states in the U.S., I don't have the legal right to see them myself.

10:00 A.M.
I call the car dealer about the 1997 Subaru I just purchased. When I register a car or apply for a driver's license in New York, my name, address, date of birth and the model of my car may be sold to marketers, private investigators and others who access the state's database. Policies may vary by state, with some selling Social Security numbers, too.

40   The federal Driver's Privacy Protection Act of 1994 requires application forms to inform consumers that personal information may be disclosed to third parties and that they must be given an opportunity to prohibit such disclosures. **C**

Targeted Passage ②

C FACT AND OPINION
How could the statement in lines 41–43 be verified?

DIFFERENTIATED INSTRUCTION

FOR LESS–PROFICIENT READERS
② Targeted Passage [Lines 35–43]
This passage typifies the article's structure.
- What does the heading *10:00 A.M.* mean?
- What does the writer do at 10:00 A.M.?
- How does she relate that action to the release of personal information?
- What kind of factual information does Rock present next? Why?

FOR ENGLISH LEARNERS
Language: Print Cues Point out the conventions related to writing out numbers in *third parties* (line 42), *45th Street and Fifth Avenue* (line 49), and *twenty-second intervals* (line 50). Explain that numbers ten and below usually are written as words but that numbers above ten usually are written as numerals. Elicit that this practice has been followed in the first two examples but not in the third.

10:20 A.M.

On my way into New York City to meet a friend for lunch, I save time by paying the toll with my E-Z Pass, a radio tag that deducts the toll from my account. But using the pass means that a record of my travels is being kept. While it can help track criminals, the data could also be used to legally obtain personal information about law-abiding citizens.

11:30 A.M.

As I'm waiting to cross the corner of 45th Street and Fifth Avenue, I'm
50 being filmed by a hidden video camera. At twenty-second intervals, the device transmits the images onto an Internet site. The camera is operated by a private company simply for the use of promotional purposes and entertainment on its Web site, but **surveillance** cameras are increasingly being used by police and merchants to fight crime, as well.

surveillance (sər-vā′ləns) *adj.* having to do with close observation

"By the end of the decade, I imagine most public places will have surveillance cameras connected to a computer that spontaneously compares faces shown on a monitor with mug shots of people wanted by the police," says John Pike, a security analyst at the Federation of American Scientists, a private policy group in Washington D.C.

NOON

60 My friend Diane joins me at Daniel, a lovely French restaurant. In my research, I found out that tiny cameras strategically positioned in the

HOW PRIVATE IS YOUR PRIVATE LIFE? **625**

Lines 49–59
DISCUSSION PROMPTS

Use these prompts to help students link surveillance with technology:

Connect Where have you seen surveillance devices? *Students may mention places such as convenience stores and banks.*

Analyze How does the author contrast the use of the hidden camera on the corner of 45th Street and Fifth Avenue with surveillance cameras used by the police? *Possible answer: The camera that films the author transmits images to a private company for promotional and entertainment purposes; surveillance cameras fight crime.*

Evaluate How does the quotation from John Pike influence your views on the use of surveillance cameras? Explain. *Student answers may vary.*

ANALYZE VISUALS

Activity Have students note the relative size, placement, and clarity of the cars and cameras in this scene. Then have students use this information to analyze the photographer's purpose. *Possible answer: The cameras are in the foreground; they also are in focus and appear very large in relation to the cars. The photographer's purpose is to emphasize the watchfulness of the cameras.*

FOR ENGLISH LEARNERS

Language: Passive Voice Point out these examples of passive-voice verbs: *can be shared* (line 32); *may be sold* (line 37); *must be given* (line 42); *could . . . be used* (line 47); *[am] being filmed* (lines 49–50); *is operated* (line 51); and *are . . . being used* (lines 53–54). Explain that the passive voice is appropriate when the doer of the action is unknown or unimportant or when the writer is purposely withholding the doer's identity.

FOR ADVANCED LEARNERS/PRE–AP

Make Judgments [small-group option] Have students record the number of invasions of privacy that Rock experiences in the hours that her article covers. Then have students discuss whether her presentation is realistic. Students might compare and contrast her claims with their own experiences or the likely experiences of people they know.

FACT AND OPINION

Possible answer: fact: *Cameras allow chefs to watch diners (lines 61–62);* **opinion:** *"it's disconcerting to know that every bite I take is being filmed" (lines 63–64)*

If students need help . . . Model your thinking, using a Two-Column Chart.

Can Be Proved	Belief or Feeling
Diane = friend	restaurant is lovely
Daniel = French restaurant	food is delicious
chefs watch diners on cameras to time food delivery	being watched is disconcerting

🧰 **BEST PRACTICES TOOLKIT—Transparency**
Two-Column Chart p. A25

Lines 69–73
REINFORCE *KEY IDEA*: PRIVACY

Discuss Do you worry about your **privacy** when you use a cell phone? Why or why not?
Possible answers: *Yes; I didn't know that a radio receiver could pick up the signal. No; Almost no one is really interested in my phone conversations.*

---

disconcerting
(dĭs'kən-sûr'tĭng) *adj.*
causing one to feel confused or embarrassed
disconcert *v.*

⊙ FACT AND OPINION
Identify at least one fact and one opinion in lines 60–64.

---

ceiling allow the chefs to watch diners eating so that they can time their delivery of the courses. The food is delicious, but it's **disconcerting** to know that every bite I take is being filmed. ⊙

Diane tells me that a friend of hers just received a ticket by mail for running a red light six months earlier in Los Angeles. A police surveillance camera caught the license plate of the rental car, which the authorities used to track down his name and address.

1:30 P.M.

70 I use Diane's cell phone to leave a message for a friend, aware that my conversation could be intercepted by someone with a radio receiver. Says Pike: "If you are discussing something highly sensitive that you wouldn't want your prying neighbor or worst enemy to know, don't have that conversation on a cell or portable phone."

4:00 P.M.

After I check my e-mail on my home-office computer, my older son, Adam, visits a site that provides all the research he needs for his fifth-grade science project. I feel much more comfortable about his use of the Internet

DIFFERENTIATED INSTRUCTION

FOR ENGLISH LEARNERS
Vocabulary: Multiple-Meaning Words Using a dictionary for support, discuss the meaning in context for some or all of these multiple-meaning words: *records* (line 32), *right* (line 33), *parties* (line 42), *pass* (line 46), *track* (line 47), *twenty-second* (line 50), *simply* (line 52), *wanted* (line 57), *time* (line 62), *courses* (line 63), *caught* (line 67), *prying* (line 72), *cell* (line 73), *check* (line 74), and *check out* (line 94).

FOR ADVANCED LEARNERS/PRE–AP
Analyze an Allusion Review this statement from the *KEY IDEA* paragraph on page 620: "Big Brother . . . may be watching you." Explain that the term *Big Brother,* from George Orwell's novel *1984,* refers to a government that allows its citizens no privacy. Have students write and share a paragraph in which they discuss how the allusion applies to Rock's article.

now that a new federal law prohibits commercial Web sites from collecting personal information from children under thirteen without parental consent.

6:11 P.M.

80 I use online banking services to see if a recent deposit has been credited to my account. When I first signed up for this service, I was instructed to use my Social Security number as my customer access code. I avoid giving out that number when possible, but in this case, I had no choice. The bank protects my account information from hackers and other unauthorized third parties, but it does share that data with inside **affiliates,** such as brokerage partners.[3]

Consumer advocates say financial privacy has been further endangered by a federal law that made it easier for banks to merge with other financial firms, such as brokerages and insurance companies. Though the law
90 includes provisions to protect consumer privacy, critics say there are loopholes that could lead, for example, to a bank denying a loan to a customer because its health-insurance affiliate's data reveals that he or she is being treated for a life-threatening illness.

9:35 P.M.

When I visit *Amazon.com* to check out a book, a message on my computer screen says that the Web site is trying to place a "cookie," a tag that identifies me to an Internet company whenever I visit its site, on my hard drive. Normally, consumers don't receive this alert, but I've learned how to activate a feature on my computer's **browser** that will warn me every time a cookie is about to be placed, giving me the option of accepting it or not.
100 Adam and I have visited eleven Web sites today, accumulating forty-nine cookies in all.

Cookies can give you more than you bargained for. A Web site may share its data with an ad network, such as DoubleClick, which places banner ads on more than 1,800 Web sites. An online profile of you is created, which associates your computer with any sites you visit on that ad network, noting what you look at or buy. Your profile continues to expand and can be sold to anyone without your knowledge or consent. Visiting a gardening Web site just to learn about varieties of roses might trigger a deluge of seed catalogs in your mailbox later. **E**

10:45 P.M.

110 To wrap up, I return to my Excite home page to read my horoscope. "Your home is your castle," it says, "and you are the supreme ruler within its walls." After today, I'm not so sure.

---

3. **brokerage partners:** individuals or companies that buy and sell stocks or other assets for others.

affiliate (ə-fĭl′ē-ĭt) *n.* a person or an organization officially connected to a larger body

browser (brou′zər) *n.* a program used to navigate the Internet

❸ Targeted Passage

E RECOGNIZE BIAS
Reread lines 102–109. Loaded language can sometimes take the form of **hyperbole,** or exaggeration. Find an example of hyperbole in this paragraph. How might this influence a reader?

DISCUSSION PROMPTS
Use these prompts to help students understand the privacy issues related to sharing one's Social Security number:

Connect When have you been asked for your Social Security number? *Answers will vary.*

Apply Why do you think that Rock usually avoids giving out that number (lines 82–83)? *Possible answer: Rock regards that number as an important part of her identity. It also may be the best means of access to official— and private—data about her.*

Evaluate Based on the information that Rock presents, are her worries about giving out her Social Security number justified? Why or why not? *Possible answers: Yes; The information can be shared. No; She does not present enough facts about the abuse of the information.*

READING SKILL

E RECOGNIZE BIAS

Possible answer: Visiting a gardening Web site "might trigger a deluge of seed catalogs" (lines 107–109). Deluge (meaning "flood") is an example of hyperbole.

Extend the Discussion What other hyperbole might describe receiving a large number of unwanted items?

FOR LESS–PROFICIENT READERS

❸ Targeted Passage [Lines 94–109]

This passage explains how privacy is compromised on the Internet.

- What is a cookie? How does Rock gather cookies?

- Why does Rock have a browser alert about cookies?

- How can cookies be used to invade personal privacy?

FOR ENGLISH LEARNERS

Comprehension: Transitions Talk about how Rock incorporates examples into her article. Discuss her use of signal words or transitional words and phrases like *for example* (line 91) and *such as* (line 103), as well as her presentation of examples without such words (as in lines 107–109).

Title and Lines 1–10
DISCUSSION PROMPTS

Use these prompts to help students understand Ahalt's purpose in this article:

Connect What comes to your mind when you hear the phrase "privacy debate"? *Answers will vary.*

Analyze How does the Emerson quotation help clarify the title? How does Ahalt use the idea in that quotation? ***Possible answer:*** *The quotation suggests that people look at issues in different ways. Ahalt uses that idea to conclude that debates usually are more complex than people realize.*

Synthesize How does Ahalt probably view the idea of public use of private data? ***Possible answer:*** *Ahalt probably sees some reason to have access to private data.*

ELEMENTS OF NONFICTION

ⓕ FACT AND OPINION
Possible answer: *fact: "There are now 280 million Americans" (lines 32–33); opinion: "we're long past doing business at the corner store" (lines 33–35)*

The Privacy Debate
Arthur M. Ahalt

One Size Doesn't Fit All

anonymity
(ă'nə-nĭm'ĭ-tē) *n.* the condition of being unknown

ⓕ **FACT AND OPINION**
Identify a fact and an opinion in lines 27–36.

"One man's justice is another man's injustice," said Ralph Waldo Emerson, neatly summarizing the complexity of most debates.

Unfortunately, the current debate over privacy issues rarely illuminates both sides of this complex issue. Instead, we are told there should be no debate over the
10 need for privacy.

This article will explore the other side of the privacy debate and demonstrate the benefit of access and openness, particularly in the area of public records.

As a retired state circuit court judge with 17 years on the bench, I've observed firsthand the benefits to our judicial, government and
20 economic systems of open access to public records. Unfortunately, too many Americans seem willing to reduce such access in the name of privacy.

articulate (är-tĭk'yə-lĭt)
adj. able to speak clearly and coherently; well-spoken

Targeted Passage ④

Why is the siren call[1] of privacy so strong?

Maybe it stems from the impersonal nature of modern society, lack of community and
30 the rise of the global economy, all of which makes us wish for more **anonymity**. There now are 280 million Americans, and we're long past doing business at the corner store where everybody knew your name. ⓕ

Maybe technology is to blame, with credit cards and consumer information automated to move
40 consumers from the practical obscurity of paper records to huge computer databases.

Maybe it's some politicians, the media and any number of self-styled advocates and experts who traffic in scare headlines, breathless press releases and emotional soapbox speeches. It's no mystery—privacy concerns affect **articulate** middle
50 class citizens who buy papers and vote—creating a "squeaky" wheel that gets the grease.

---

1. **siren call:** alluring but possibly dangerous appeal (after the Sirens, mythological creatures whose irresistible songs lured sailors into danger).

DIFFERENTIATED INSTRUCTION

FOR LESS–PROFICIENT READERS
④ **Targeted Passage [Lines 25–52]**

This passage helps explain the public's worries about privacy. At the same time, it undermines the argument in favor of privacy.

• What three reasons does Arthur M. Ahalt, the writer, give to explain why people are so concerned about privacy?

• Does Ahalt believe that these are valid reasons? Do you agree?

FOR ENGLISH LEARNERS
Culture: Connect Discuss the meaning of these expressions from page 628:

• *siren call* (line 25)

• *corner store* (lines 34–35)

• *soapbox speeches* (lines 47–48)

• *a "squeaky" wheel that gets the grease* (lines 51–52)

Invite students to tell how they would describe a situation that each term suggests in their home languages or cultures.

Privacy is also a **nonpartisan** concern which neither political party owns, and represents an issue where conservatives and liberals often meet in unison. Media stories about privacy issues often are human-interest heart-tuggers that 60 sell and gather an audience. Think tanks, clearinghouses[2] and "experts" flock to issue press releases, hold seminars, appear on television and generally stoke the fires of paranoia[3] and emotionalism. **G**

In this atmosphere, confusion, fear and concern replace a balanced view of the privacy issue.

Politicians and the media quote 70 polls—"93 percent of people are concerned about privacy." Well, no doubt. (I would like to know about the 7 percent who are not

concerned about privacy, but that is another matter.) Those polls, however, don't appear to probe the trade-offs, such as "would you prefer a bank loan in three days or three months?" Most Americans 80 not only prefer to obtain immediate credit and debt, they demand it.

But instant credit and debt is more than a convenience; it's also the very basis of the underlying strength and power of our economic system, which moves at the speed of light as a direct result of the transparency of information available to economic decision 90 makers. Car, home and bank loans and the issuance of credit and debit cards can be made quickly because information about most of us is available. It's the source of our

nonpartisan
(nŏn-pär′tĭ-zən) *adj.* not supporting or controlled by any political group

G **RECOGNIZE BIAS**
Reread lines 53–65. Identify the **loaded language** in lines 53–58. What does the writer's language suggest about the people who raise concerns about invasions of privacy?

---

2. **think tanks, clearinghouses:** A think tank is a research institute organized to investigate social problems; a clearinghouse is an organization that collects and distributes information.

3. **stoke the fires of paranoia:** increase fear and suspicion.

FOR LESS-PROFICIENT READERS

Comprehension Support To clarify Ahalt's point in lines 82–90, present this statement:

transparency of information → quick financial decisions → a strong economic system

Help students express the statement in a sentence or two. *Possible answer: Because information is relatively easy to obtain, financial decision-makers can act quickly. Quick decisions keep the economy strong.*

FOR ADVANCED LEARNERS/PRE-AP

Compare and Contrast Tone [paired-activity option] Have students compare and contrast the tone of Ahalt's article with that of Rock's piece. Which writer seems more personal? more scornful? more sure of himself or herself? Have students identify several differences, as well as similarities. Remind students to support their points with textual evidence.

G **RECOGNIZE BIAS**

Possible answer: Loaded language in lines 43–48 includes "self-styled advocates and experts," "traffic in scare headlines, breathless press releases, and emotional soapbox speeches." This language suggests that the people who raise concerns about invasions of privacy are over-the-top sensationalists who appeal to an audience's fears instead of its reason.

Lines 69–81
REINFORCE *KEY IDEA*: PRIVACY

Discuss How is **privacy** at odds with our high-tech, commercial world? *Possible answer: Privacy may need to be traded for some benefits. For example, the ability to get credit fast depends on knowing quickly whether someone is a good credit risk.*

ANALYZE VISUALS

Activity Ask what the man is studying and how the photograph relates to the article.

Possible answer: The man is examining a fingerprint. Fingerprints are a means of identification that can be used to track a person's activities.

⊕ GRAMMAR AND STYLE

Have students locate the infinitive phrases in these lines, beginning with *to find ...* (line 109). Discuss how the parallelism creates a rhythm that helps readers distinguish—and remember—Ahalt's points.

ELEMENTS OF NONFICTION

❶ FACT AND OPINION

Possible answer: These lines state an opinion because they tell what Ahalt believes. His statement cannot be proved.

SELECTION WRAP–UP

SYNTHESIZE Ask students whether or how their feelings or knowledge about privacy issues changed as they read these articles.

⭐ **CRITIQUE** Have students compare their reactions to the two articles. For example, which did they find more informative? more interesting? more personally useful?

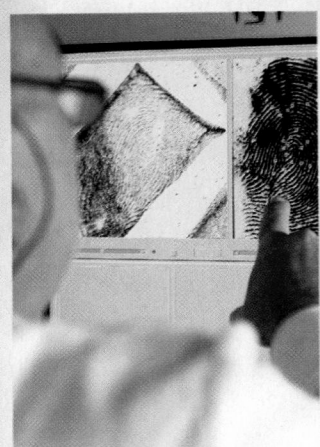

awry (ə-rī′) *adj.*
off course; wrong

retail sector's[7] strength. It's the reason we can buy and sell property in weeks; not months or years. Federal Trade Commission Chairman Tim Muris calls this system, which we 100 all take for granted, "the miracle of instant credit."

Economist Walter Kitchenman says that our consumer credit system is the "secret ingredient of the U.S. economy's resilience."

Aside from economic benefits, transparency also provides other specific benefits. It makes it possible to find absent spouses and 110 enforce child support payments; to screen day care workers and school bus drivers to keep our kids safe from substance abusers and child molesters; to check the background of bank tellers to avoid embezzlement; to connect heirs with fortunes; and to help prevent identity theft, and make it easier to fix if it occurs. ⊕

⊕ GRAMMAR AND STYLE
Reread lines 106–119. By using a series of infinitive phrases, the author establishes a **parallel structure** that emphasizes the benefits of open access to information.

❶ FACT AND OPINION
Is the author stating a fact or expressing an opinion in lines 133–137? How do you know?

120 There are real problems that affect real people in the privacy arena, but it's the classic case of bad news always selling, and good news remaining invisible.

Each day, billions of financial transactions occur in our economy. Do some go **awry?** Of course, but it is a small percentage. Unfortunately, no one wants 130 to read a headline "Today 299,999,033 Americans Did Not Suffer Privacy-Related Problems."

There is also a need to segment privacy from one huge ball of confusion into separate, more manageable and different issues, which require different approaches. ❶

Tracking Internet surfing and purchases is different from identity 140 theft, which is different from telemarketing calls, which is different from access to public records, which is also different from the use of Social Security numbers as a unique identifier.

Privacy supporters would have us believe that "one size fits all" when it comes to addressing matters of privacy.

150 I hold no portfolio on some of these issues, but as one who now is working directly in the area of public records accessibility, I am vitally concerned about access to these records and their contents.

Remember the old adage when you hear self-styled privacy experts expound on the need to keep information hidden: "for every 160 problem, there is a simple solution, which is usually wrong."

Targeted Passage ❺

7. **retail sector's:** of the branch of the nation's economy that deals with products people buy and use.

630 UNIT 6: ARGUMENT AND PERSUASION

DIFFERENTIATED INSTRUCTION

FOR LESS–PROFICIENT READERS

❺ **Targeted Passage [Lines 146–161]**

This concluding passage restates Ahalt's main idea.

- Where else in this article have you seen the expression *one size fits all?* Why does Ahalt repeat it here?

- What does Ahalt say about himself as an authority on the subject of privacy?

- What adage does Ahalt quote? Why?

FOR ENGLISH LEARNERS

Language: Punctuation Point out how the semicolon is used in place of the comma when items in a list are complex and already contain commas. Have students look at lines 108–119. Point out the *and* that introduces the final item in the series and the comma that the item contains. Compare this list to the one in lines 60–65, in which only commas are used.

Comprehension

1. **Recall** According to the author of "How Private Is Your Private Life?" what happens when a driver uses an E-Z Pass to pay a toll?

2. **Clarify** In the context of the Internet, what is a **cookie?**

3. **Summarize** According to the author of "The Privacy Debate: One Size Doesn't Fit All," how do we benefit from sacrificing some part of our **privacy?**

Critical Analysis

4. **Distinguish Fact from Opinion** Review the chart you filled in as you read. Does Andrea Rock rely more on fact or opinion in making her case? What about Arthur M. Ahalt? Cite evidence from the selections to support your answers.

5. **Analyze Argument** What question does Andrea Rock set out to explore? What conclusions does the bulk of her evidence support? How does she let readers know what she thinks by the end of her research day?

6. **Analyze Bias** Any piece of persuasive writing is likely to reflect the bias of its author. Which of the two articles do you think reflects a stronger bias? Support your answer with evidence from the texts.

7. **Identify Modes of Reasoning** The process of piecing together facts and other evidence to arrive at a logical conclusion or generalization is called **inductive reasoning.** Which of the two arguments you just read reaches its conclusion using inductive reasoning? Explain. (To learn more about inductive reasoning, see **Reading Handbook,** pages R22–R23.)

8. **Compare Texts** Which article do you find more convincing, and why?

9. **Make Judgments** How have these articles helped shape your thinking on the privacy issue? What does your reading experience suggest about the role that magazine articles and newspaper editorials can serve in civic life? Explain your answer.

6. ■ **STANDARDS FOCUS Recognize Bias**
Ahalt reflects a stronger bias. His writing is loaded with opinions but has few facts. For example, Ahalt says that only a few of the billions of daily financial transactions in the United States go awry (lines 125–128), but he does not give specifics. On the other hand, Rock doesn't only say that Web sites share data; she presents facts about DoubleClick (lines 102–107).

7. Rock's argument uses inductive reasoning. She gathers evidence throughout her day and then uses it to draw a conclusion at the end.

8. Ahalt is more convincing because he, as a judge, is an authority. Rock is more convincing because she gathers so many verifiable facts.

9. Rock's article shows how many ways our privacy can be invaded. Ahalt's article gives us good reasons to allow the invasion of privacy in some cases. Both articles serve a civic role in that they help readers think through the issue of privacy, which is related to citizenship.

Practice and Apply

After Reading
For additional support of post-reading questions, use these copy masters:

R RESOURCE MANAGER—Copy Masters
Reading Check p. 86 (to check understanding of the selections)
Fact and Opinion p. 79 (for practice of elements of nonfiction standards focus)
Question Support p. 87 (After Reading questions adapted for English learners and less-proficient readers)

For additional questions, see page 73.

ANSWERS

Comprehension
1. *The E-Z Pass establishes a travel record.*
2. *A cookie is a kind of ID tag that identifies users to those who create and maintain Web sites.*
3. *We benefit by being able to get credit quickly, a practice that keeps the economy strong. Other benefits are the ability to screen individuals for certain jobs (lines 111–116) and to help prevent identity theft (lines 117–118).*

Critical Analysis
Possible answers:

4. ● **STANDARDS FOCUS Fact and Opinion** *Rock relies heavily upon facts; Ahalt uses facts and opinions but emphasizes opinions.* **How Private . . . ?: fact:** *In about half of the states, citizens have no legal right to view their medical records (lines 33–34).* **opinion:** *"The [restaurant] food is delicious" (line 63).* **The Privacy Debate: fact:** *Access to records makes enforcing child support payments easier (lines 108–110).* **opinion:** *"[C]onfusion, fear and concern replace a balanced view of the privacy issue" (lines 66–68).*

5. *Rock wants to find out how often her privacy is legally invaded during a typical day. Her evidence supports the conclusion that the invasion is constant. She lets readers know of her concerns by stating that she is no longer sure that her home is her castle.*

ANSWERS

Vocabulary in Context

VOCABULARY PRACTICE

1. *assemble*	6. *enemy*
2. *fretfulness*	7. *broadcasting*
3. *inspiring*	8. *uneasy*
4. *browser*	9. *illogical*
5. *arrogant*	10. *advocacy*

> **R** RESOURCE MANAGER—Copy Master
> Vocabulary Practice p. 84

VOCABULARY IN WRITING

Suggest that students use *for example* as a transition to the anecdote. Students should recount the invasion of privacy with respect for the subject's privacy, especially if they plan to share the paragraph.

VOCABULARY STRATEGY: INTERNET WORDS

Explain that the Internet itself can provide definitions of Internet words. Suggest that students try *Internet glossary* as a search term. Note that definitions may vary from source to source.

Possible answers:

1. *a computer that stores information for client computers*
2. *a site that is a port of entry to the Web*
3. *a URL embedded in a document, meant to provide direct access to that URL*
4. *transmission of sounds and images via the Internet*
5. *a guide to accessing a site's content*
6. *wireless data communication; wireless networking (also called Wi-Fi)*

Other terms may include applet, blog, bookmark, domain name, FTP, netiquette, phishing, podcast, spyware, *and* worm.

> **R** RESOURCE MANAGER—Copy Master
> Vocabulary Strategy p. 85

> **i** Vocabulary Center at **ClassZone.com**
> Additional Vocabulary Activities

Vocabulary in Context

VOCABULARY PRACTICE

Choose the word that is not related in meaning to the other words.

1. awry, amiss, assemble, astray
2. namelessness, disguise, anonymity, fretfulness
3. distressing, embarrassing, disconcerting, inspiring
4. electrician, browser, plumber, carpenter
5. pervasive, widespread, arrogant, extensive
6. enemy, associate, affiliate, partner
7. broadcasting, spying, observing, surveillance
8. impartial, uneasy, nonpartisan, unbiased
9. articulate, illogical, eloquent, expressive
10. rejection, advocacy, rebuff, disdain

WORD LIST
advocacy
affiliate
anonymity
articulate
awry
browser
disconcerting
nonpartisan
pervasive
surveillance

VOCABULARY IN WRITING

In a paragraph, describe an invasion of privacy that someone you know has experienced. Use four or more vocabulary words. Here is a way to start.

> **EXAMPLE SENTENCE**
>
> **Anonymity** seems to be impossible in the world today.

VOCABULARY STRATEGY: INTERNET WORDS

You often hear Internet terms, but do you know what they actually mean? Some terms, like the vocabulary word *browser,* are common words used in specialized ways; other terms are unique to discussion of the Internet. To be Web literate, you need a working knowledge of basic Internet terms.

PRACTICE With a partner, write definitions for each term, and check them in a current dictionary or Web site glossary. Then list three other Internet terms you think your classmates should know, and define them.

1. server	4. Webcast
2. portal	5. site map
3. hyperlink	6. wireless fidelity

> **VOCABULARY PRACTICE**
> For more practice, go to the **Vocabulary Center** at **ClassZone.com.**

DIFFERENTIATED INSTRUCTION

FOR ENGLISH LEARNERS

Vocabulary Have students write the part of speech of each word on the Word List. Also ask students to identify any words in the list that have cognates in their home languages (such as the English *affiliate* and the Spanish *afiliado*).

FOR ADVANCED LEARNERS/PRE–AP

Vocabulary in Writing Have students consider the connotations of the words on the Word List. Then ask them to rank each word along a continuum for positive, neutral, or negative connotation. Invite students to compare and discuss their ideas.

Reading-Writing Connection

Explore the arguments presented in "How Private is Your Private Life?" and "The Privacy Debate: One Size Doesn't Fit All" by responding to these prompts. Then use **Revision: Grammar and Style** to improve your writing.

WRITING PROMPTS	SELF-CHECK
A. Short Response: Write a Critique Write a letter to one of the authors in which you explain how his or her piece could be made more convincing. In your critique, write **one or two paragraphs** describing your reaction to the article and your suggestions for improvement.	*A successful critique will . . .* • offer specific suggestions about what information to add or remove • contain well-supported advice about how to make the language more balanced or more powerful
B. Extended Response: Write an Argument Do you regard technology as a threat to your **privacy**? Why or why not? Write **three to five paragraphs** in which you argue your point.	*A strong argument will . . .* • clearly state a position • provide at least two supporting reasons

REVISION: GRAMMAR AND STYLE

USE RHETORICAL DEVICES Review the **Grammar and Style** note on page 630. **Parallelism**—the use of similar grammatical constructions to express ideas that are related or equal in importance—can add rhythm or emphasis to speech or writing. In the following example from "The Privacy Debate: One Size Doesn't Fit All," notice how the author uses a series of adjective clauses, all beginning with "which is," to emphasize how privacy needs differ:

> *Tracking Internet surfing and purchases is different from identity theft, which is different from telemarketing calls, which is different from access to public records, which is also different from the use of Social Security numbers as a unique identifier.* (lines 138–145)

Now study the model. Notice how the revisions in red add emphasis to the writer's ideas. Revise your response to Prompt B by using parallel structures.

STUDENT MODEL

The great privacy debate includes some pretty minor issues. *Why do we care if someone knows that we buy dog food?* ~~Some people don't consider their grocery purchases to be so~~ *Why do we* ~~private. Others don't~~ *someone knows that we drove down Fremont Highway on Tuesday?* care ~~if their comings and goings are tracked.~~

WRITING TOOLS

For prewriting, revision, and editing tools, visit the **Writing Center** at ClassZone.com.

FOR LESS–PROFICIENT WRITERS

For Prompt A:
Model this structure for the body of the letter:

> I enjoyed the article, but I feel that a few changes would make it even more convincing. For example, I think that _____ because _____. I also think that _____ because _____. Finally, I think that _____ because _____.

For Prompt B:
• Have pairs or small groups use a Two-Column Chart to generate points that could be made in an argument about how technology does or does not threaten their privacy.

• Have students write on their own, using notes from the chart as a starting place for their prewriting.

 **BEST PRACTICES TOOLKIT—Transparency** Two-Column Chart p. A25

Reading-Writing Connection

WRITING PROMPTS

• For Prompt A, have students who are writing to the same person approach the prewriting stage of the assignment as a Think-Pair-Share activity.

• For Prompt B, encourage students to create a working thesis statement that gives their position, along with a minimum of three supporting reasons, before they begin developing a draft.

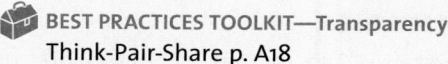 **BEST PRACTICES TOOLKIT—Transparency** Think-Pair-Share p. A18

For writing support, see

Writing Center at ClassZone.com

REVISION: GRAMMAR AND STYLE

After students analyze the two models, ask them to revise this passage for parallelism. Note that there may be more than one way to create parallelism in a given passage.

> *Some people say that most privacy issues are minor issues. Is knowledge of your bank statement a minor issue? Are unseen* ~~Unseen~~ *cameras* ~~are not unimportant~~ *a minor issue.? Is a* ~~A~~ *private conversation with a loved one* ~~is not~~ *a minor issue* ~~, either.~~ *?*

RESOURCE MANAGER—Copy Master Use Rhetorical Devices p. 88

Assess and Reteach

Assess

RESOURCE MANAGER—Copy Masters
Selection Test A pp. 91–92
Selection Test B/C pp. 93–94

Test Generator CD

Reteach

STANDARDS LESSON FILE
Reading Lesson 5: Distinguishing Fact from Opinion

Focus and Motivate

OBJECTIVES
Media Literacy
- explore the key idea of **promoting a cause**
- view two public service announcements (PSAs) to understand how they use persuasive techniques to define a target audience, deliver a message, and generate emotional appeals
- create a PSA to demonstrate understanding of persuasive visual techniques

SUMMARIES

The first PSA, "Billy Thomas," seeks support of Boys and Girls Clubs of America. Images of children having fun contrast with warning images such as police cars, and are interspersed with images of celebrity spokesman Denzel Washington expressing gratitude to his childhood Club and its leader, Billy Thomas. The second PSA, "Life Is Calling," asks people to join the Peace Corps. A voiceover asks questions about how far the viewer would go to help someone and for how long. Images take the viewer to very distant places with exotic peoples and landscapes.

How do you PROMOTE *a cause?*

To help students explore the **KEY IDEA,** ask them to share PSAs and their causes. Ask students what images, words, and music were used and what emotions were appealed to. You might focus on PSAs aimed at teens, such as about staying in school, drug use, underage drinking, or smoking.

BACKGROUND

PSAs began in the 1940s when the War Advertising Council was established to persuade Americans to support World War II. Messages such as "Keep 'em Rolling" and "Loose Lips Sink Ships" were designed to promote patriotism, security, and confidence. Today, non-profit organizations and government agencies use PSAs to promote awareness of issues such as literacy and human rights. The earliest PSAs appeared in donated media time and space, but today's PSAs run in both donated and purchased time.

Media Study

Billy Thomas
Life Is Calling

Public Service Announcements on **MediaSmart** DVD

How do you PROMOTE *a cause?*

KEY IDEA Have you ever wondered how you can get involved in your community? Perhaps you'd like to volunteer at a local soup kitchen, help restore a rundown building, or donate blood. The two public service announcements (PSAs) in this lesson **promote** worthy causes by inspiring viewers to get involved. See if they motivate you to take action.

Background

Making a Difference The PSAs you will view promote two well-known organizations. The first PSA, "Billy Thomas," is from the Boys and Girls Clubs of America, an organization that provides afterschool and weekend activities for boys and girls. The second PSA, "Life Is Calling," is part of a campaign for the Peace Corps, a government agency whose volunteers work in developing countries to help advance world peace.

WHAT'S GOING TO STOP YOUR KID FROM NOT WEARING A SEAT BELT?

BUCKLE UP.
A public service message from the Kansas Department of Transportation
Kansas Clicks

634

Media Study Resources

R RESOURCE MANAGER UNIT 6

Plan and Teach pp. 95–98

Media Analysis
Summary p. 99†*, 100‡*
Viewing Guide p. 101
Close Viewing p. 102
Viewing Activity p. 103
Produce Your Own Media p. 104

S STANDARDS LESSON FILE

Media Lessons 1, 3, 15

ℹ Media Center at **ClassZone.com**

MEDIA VIEWING
Ⓜ Media*Smart* DVD

---

* Resources for Differentiation   † Also in Spanish   ‡ In Haitian Creole and Vietnamese

Media Literacy: Persuasion in PSAs

Whether they're asking an audience to help end homelessness or to help save the environment, PSAs draw on many of the same techniques that are used in commercial advertising. Images, words, and music can attract an audience, but in order to raise awareness of important issues and get people to act, PSAs depend on **persuasive techniques.**

PERSUASIVE TECHNIQUES IN PUBLIC SERVICE ANNOUNCEMENTS

A **celebrity spokesperson** who possesses admirable qualities may appeal to a particular audience. ▶

◀ By giving a **testimonial,** or a personal recommendation, an individual directly associates himself or herself with the cause. For example,

Voice-over: Does it work? It did for me.

Images may represent ideas and values that appeal to a particular audience. Notice how this image conveys the idea of unity. ▶

◀ A **slogan** is a memorable phrase that helps an audience remember an organization's message. For example,

Life is calling. How far will you go?

STRATEGIES FOR ANALYZING PUBLIC SERVICE ANNOUNCEMENTS

- Make note of any words, images, and persuasive techniques that help you define the **target audience.** Ask yourself: Who might be interested in this cause?
- Pay attention to the delivery of the **message.** Ask yourself: Do the people, images, and words spoken help deliver a clear message? Is the information helpful to the viewer or listener?
- Be conscious of **emotional appeals**—messages that persuade an audience by creating strong feelings. Ask yourself: How do the words, images, symbols, and music create emotional appeal?
- Consider who the spokesperson is. Ask yourself: What qualities does this person possess? How might viewers identify with this person?
- Look for a logo to help you determine what group is behind the message. A **logo** is a unique symbol, name, or trademark that is associated with an organization. Ask yourself: When and where does the logo appear?

MEDIA STUDY   **635**

MEDIA STUDY: TEACHING OPTIONS

Teaching Option 1: The Basics (1–2 Days)
1. Begin the Media Study using the material provided on pages 634–635.
2. Show the Introduction on Media*Smart.* Then show the First Viewing. As they watch, have students use the Viewing Guide on page 636, along with the corresponding copy master on page 104 of the Resource Manager. Discuss their responses.
3. Return to the pupil book for the extension activities on page 637.

Teaching Option 2: In-Depth Study (2–3 Days)
1. Begin the Media Study using pages 634–635.
2. Show the Introduction and First Viewing from Media*Smart.* Then continue on Media*Smart* with the Media Lessons, using the teacher notes available in the Resources section.
3. Show the Guided Analysis presentation. Have students record their observations on the Student Viewing Guide available in the Resources section from Media*Smart.*
4. Return to the pupil book, page 637.

Teach

Media Literacy

Review with students the meaning of *persuasion* and ask them to recall especially persuasive PSAs. Ask what made these ads so persuasive. What kind of images and music were used? Was there a spokesperson and, if so, who was it? Was there a memorable slogan or symbol? Then discuss the techniques and strategies from page 635.

- **Celebrity Spokesperson and Testimonial** To reinforce the effect of celebrity spokespeople and testimonials, ask students to imagine an ad campaign to end world hunger. Ask them to contrast the impact of a celebrity such as Bono as spokesperson with that of an anonymous speaker.

- **Images** Recall the old adage "a picture is worth a thousand words." Help students recognize that PSAs, like all ads, need to be short. Strong images help PSAs convey ideas and values quickly and memorably.

- **Slogan** Review some highly successful slogans, such as "Only you can prevent forest fires" and "Friends don't let friends drive drunk." Stress that the slogans work because they are short, catchy, memorable, and make a clear point.

- **Target Audience** Discuss the difference between ads addressed to teens and ads addressed to their parents, both about a single issue such as drug use. Help students see that PSAs target particular audiences with different persuasive techniques.

- **Emotional Appeals** Point out that PSAs use emotional appeals to stress that support for the cause will bring personal satisfaction. Ask students to name values and desires that they think PSAs try to appeal to, such as self-respect and desires to be healthy, live in safety, and feel useful and helpful.

- **Logo** To be sure students recognize logos, have them identify the publisher's logo on this book. What does it mean?

◎ Media*Smart* DVD

Practice and Apply

VIEWING GUIDE

1. Before students view the two PSAs, tell them they will be asked to compare and contrast how the ads persuade people to support their causes. Encourage students to watch and listen for these elements and techniques:

   - a **celebrity spokesperson** and a **testimonial** that reflect a well-known actor's endorsement of the Boys and Girls Clubs

   - **images** that appeal to childhood memories or imagination of travel

   - **slogans** that deliver a message and encourage participation in life

   - how the interests and desires of the **target audiences** are addressed

   - how each **message** is delivered through words, images, and music, such as the continual line on maps and chalkboards that connects efforts of the Peace Corps

   - how **emotional appeals** that show young, impressionable children encourage viewers to act

   - **logos** that try to create unique symbols to associate with a cause

2. After students have viewed the PSAs, help them focus on different elements by showing the PSAs first with no sound, and then with only sound and no images.

R RESOURCE MANAGER—Copy Masters
   Viewing Guide p. 101
   Close Viewing p. 102
   Viewing Activity p. 103

Use this resource with the Viewing Guide:

Media*Smart* DVD

ANSWERS

FIRST VIEWING: Comprehension

Possible answers:

1. *He ran the Club that Denzel Washington belonged to as a child.*

2. *Peace Corps volunteer working in a field with local people*

MediaSmart DVD
- **PSA 1:** "Billy Thomas" from the Boys and Girls Clubs of America
- **PSA 2:** "Life Is Calling" from Peace Corps
- **Genre:** Public Service Announcements

636

Viewing Guide for
Public Service Announcements

In "Billy Thomas," Denzel Washington, a highly regarded actor who won an Academy Award in 2001, recalls a childhood experience. The second PSA, "Life Is Calling," poses a number of rhetorical questions designed to persuade viewers to volunteer and help those in need.
   The questions that follow will help you critically analyze these PSAs. Make sure to view each PSA several times.

NOW VIEW

FIRST VIEWING: Comprehension

1. **Clarify** Who exactly is Billy Thomas?

2. **Recall** Describe an image in "Life Is Calling" that creates a positive impression of the Peace Corps.

CLOSE VIEWING: Media Literacy

3. **Make Inferences** What impressions might viewers have of the Boys and Girls Clubs of America on the basis of Denzel Washington's testimonial? Use evidence from the PSA to support your views.

4. **Analyze Message** In "Life Is Calling," many of the images support the idea of going on a journey. Why might this idea appeal to the target audience?

5. **Compare and Contrast Audience** Describe the target audience for "Billy Thomas" and for "Life Is Calling." How are these audiences similar? How are they different? Think about the following characteristics: age, values, and background.

CLOSE VIEWING: Media Literacy

Possible answers:

3. *The Clubs are caring organizations—Images: children and Club volunteers together; They are possible refuges from danger—Images: Club children in safe surroundings but police car lights; Club children can learn and have fun—Images: children dancing and swimming*

4. *The Peace Corps' traditional audience is young people who might want to travel.*

5. *"Billy Thomas": primarily parents or adults who can contribute time or money*

   "Life Is Calling": primarily young adults

   Similarities: Both appeal to people with a desire to help others in need. **Differences:** *"Billy Thomas" uses a famous person's personal experience and calls for help close to home. "Life Is Calling" has a more global view and calls for help around the world.*

Write or Discuss

Evaluate Emotional Appeal The PSAs in this lesson use emotional appeal to persuade viewers. Choose one of the PSAs and make a list of the techniques that are used to create emotional appeal. In your opinion, which of these elements is most effective? As part of your evaluation, consider the following:

• the use of celebrity endorsement or voice-over to deliver the message
• the target audience and techniques used to appeal to this audience
• your reaction to the PSA and how you think the intended audience might react

Produce Your Own Media

Create a PSA The PSA shown in the professional model is from the National Crime Prevention Council. It is part of a campaign that encourages teens to get involved by taking an activity they enjoy and using it to help others in their community. Your job is to create a PSA like the one shown.

HERE'S HOW Think of a well-known organization or charity that supports an issue you care about. For example, if you're interested in helping cancer patients, you might want to create a PSA for the American Cancer Society.

• Consider the layout of your PSA, including the size and placement of visuals, text, and a slogan.
• Use catchy words and images that grab your audience's attention.

MEDIA TOOLS
For help with creating a PSA, visit the **Media Center** at **ClassZone.com.**

Tech Tip
Use your own photographs and photo-editing software to give your PSA a professional quality.

PROFESSIONAL MODEL

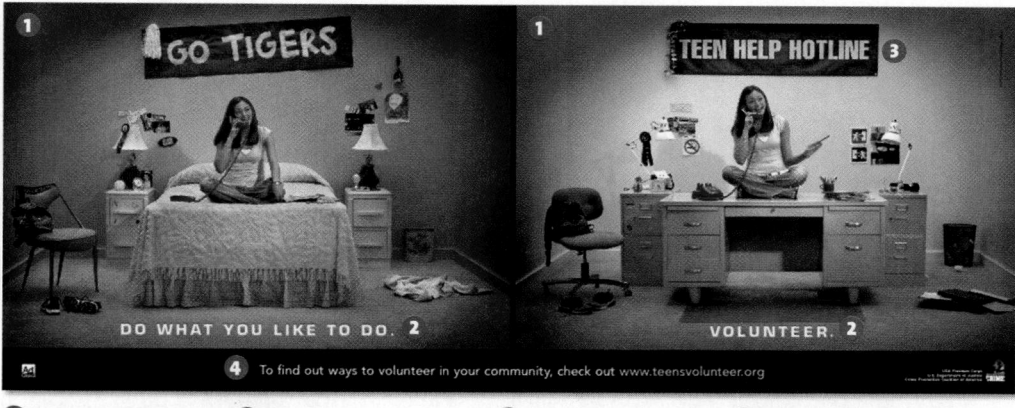

GO TIGERS
DO WHAT YOU LIKE TO DO. **2**

TEEN HELP HOTLINE **3**
VOLUNTEER. **2**

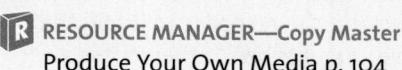 **4** To find out ways to volunteer in your community, check out www.teensvolunteer.org

1 "Before" and "after" images show how an activity can be used to help others.

2 A catchy slogan describes the message.

3 A sign identifies the volunteer activity.

4 The logo identifies the organization.

Assess and Reteach

Write or Discuss

Evaluate Emotional Appeal In their evaluations, students should address the persuasive techniques used to create emotional appeal, such as the relationship of a celebrity to the cause; images, music, and words that target the particular audience; and the specific emotions to which the ad appeals. They should compare how effective these techniques are in reaching viewers' emotions. For example, students might find Denzel Washington's personal relationship with the Boys Club and his memories highly effective. In "Life Is Calling," students may note that images of exotic faraway places successfully appeal to young people's urge for travel and adventure. Encourage students to include their own emotional reactions to the ad they choose.

Produce Your Own Media

Rubric: Create a PSA A strong PSA should have

• a clear message identifying the cause and encouraging action
• a catchy slogan that grabs viewers' attention and sticks in their memories
• eye-catching images that give information and/or call up an emotional response
• a clearly identifiable teen target audience
• a logo that clearly relates to the cause

R RESOURCE MANAGER—Copy Master
Produce Your Own Media p. 104

MEDIA STUDY WRAP–UP

Have students summarize what they have learned about the use of images, words, and music as persuasive techniques in PSAs. Encourage them to use terms such as *persuasion/persuasive, celebrity spokesperson, testimonial, image, slogan, target audience, message, emotional appeal,* and *logo* in their explanations.

RETEACH

S STANDARDS LESSON FILE
Media Lesson 1: Active Viewing Strategies
Media Lesson 3: Influence of Media on Society
Media Lesson 15: Analyzing Persuasive Techniques in Advertising

Focus and Motivate

OBJECTIVES

Literary Analysis
- explore the key idea of **television habit**
- analyze and compare writer's message across genres
- read an essay and a science fiction story

Reading
- set a purpose for reading

Grammar and Writing
- write a compare-contrast essay
- use writing to analyze literature

SUMMARIES

The author of "Primal Screen" argues that by choosing to spend many hours watching television, members of American families fail to interact well. As a result, American family life is declining.

As "The Pedestrian" opens, Leonard Mead sets out on his routine evening walk. He is alone on the street: In his world of A.D. 2053, everyone else is indoors, watching TV. When Mead explains his walk to the police car that stops him, he is arrested and taken to a psychiatric center.

Could we live without TELEVISION?

Read the question; then invite students to make some notes in response to it and the *KEY IDEA*. Have students revisit their notes after they have completed the *SURVEY* activity.

Selection Resources

Primal Screen
Essay by Ellen Goodman

The Pedestrian
Short Story by Ray Bradbury

Could we live without TELEVISION?

KEY IDEA Some of us spend a lot of our time watching television. According to research, the average American family is glued to the screen for more than seven hours a day. Is this **television habit** helping us or hurting us?

SURVEY How much time do you and your friends spend watching TV? Survey a small group of your classmates, tally their responses, and then discuss the results.

> **TV Viewing Habits**
> 1. How many hours do you watch TV each day?
> 2. How many hours do you watch TV each week?
> 3. How many TV sets does your family own?

638

RESOURCE MANAGER UNIT 6

Plan and Teach pp. 105–112

Literary Analysis
Summary pp. 113†*, 114‡*
Writer's Message Across Genres
pp. 115, 118†*
Question Support p. 121*

Reading
Reading Check p. 120
Reading Fluency p. 122

Assessment
Selection Tests A, B/C pp. 123*, 125*
 Test Generator CD

BEST PRACTICES TOOLKIT

Differentiated Instruction
pp. 31–38*

Scaffolding Instruction
pp. 43–46*

Graphic Organizers/Strategies
Main Idea and Details • Word Squares • Venn Diagram • Observation Chart • Peer Response Guide

Reading Support
 Audio Anthology CD*

Technology
ⓘ Literature Center at **ClassZone.com**
WriteSmart CD

---

* Resources for Differentiation   † Also in Spanish   ‡ Also in Haitian Creole and Vietnamese

LITERARY ANALYSIS: WRITER'S MESSAGE ACROSS GENRES

The essay and short story you are about to read are works of **social criticism,** or literature that addresses real-life issues— political, religious, economic, or social. However, while both selections comment on the same topic, the impact of television viewing, each has a different message, or main point, and conveys it through different methods. As you read, try to determine each **writer's message** by paying attention to the following:

In the Essay	In the Short Story
• direct statements	• setting and imagery
• facts, statistics, and other evidence, such as descriptions of people's behavior and interactions	• mood, sensory details, and word choice
	• characters
• explanations of causes and effects	• dialogue
• word choice	• plot—especially the nature of the conflict and its resolution
• tone	
• the writer's call to action at the end	• the lesson you take from the story

READING SKILL: SET A PURPOSE FOR READING

When you **set a purpose for reading,** you identify specific goals to accomplish as you read. For example, after reading these next two selections, you'll be asked to write an essay comparing each writer's message. To prepare for this essay, you'll want to read with the following goals in mind:

- to determine each writer's message
- to identify the similarities and differences in the two messages

Take a moment now to consider how you will accomplish these goals. Will you try to keep track of similarities and differences in the writers' messages as you read? Or do you need to determine each writer's message first and then review the selections to discover ways in which the messages differ?

Author Online

Ellen Goodman: Pioneering Newswoman

Ellen Goodman born 1941

After beginning her career as a research trainee at *Newsweek* in the early 1960s, Ellen Goodman broke into reporting and eventually became a columnist for the *Boston Globe.* Today her columns cover a wide range of topics— from politics to parenting—and appear in more than 450 newspapers across the country. Goodman rewards her readers with both good laughs and something to think about.

Ray Bradbury: Social Prognosticator

Ray Bradbury born 1920

Ray Bradbury is one of the best-known and most highly regarded writers of science fiction. His stories have been termed "warning fictions" because they often explore the dire consequences of society's dependence on technology. Though his stories are serious, Bradbury relishes writing them. "I write for fun," he has said. "I have fun with ideas."

 MORE ABOUT THE AUTHOR
For more on Ellen Goodman and Ray Bradbury, visit the **Literature Center** at **ClassZone.com.**

Teach

STANDARDS FOCUS

LITERARY ANALYSIS

● WRITER'S MESSAGE ACROSS GENRES

For instructional support, discuss the chart, using an essay and a short story that students have read to illustrate. For example, you might review the messages in Unit 4's "The Scarlet Ibis" (page 428) and "The Future in My Arms" (page 460). Discuss the methods that James Hurst and Edwidge Danticat used to convey those messages.

CHECK UNDERSTANDING Have students suggest topics for social criticism. Choose one topic and discuss how students might expect to see that topic covered in at least three genres.

RESOURCE MANAGER—Copy Master
Writer's Message Across Genres pp. 115–116 (for student use while reading the selections)

READING SKILL

■ SET A PURPOSE FOR READING

Ask students to identify what their purpose would be for reading these types of writing:

- a newspaper article *(to learn about current events)*
- a movie review *(to decide whether to see the movie)*
- an instruction manual *(to learn how to put something together or use something)*
- an e-mail or IM from a friend *(to keep in touch and get personal information)*

CHECK UNDERSTANDING Call on volunteers to name two pieces of writing that they have read so far today and to tell the purpose or goal for reading each one.

DIFFERENTIATED INSTRUCTION

FOR LESS–PROFICIENT READERS

Track Details Have students use a Main Idea and Details chart to record the details in each selection. When they have finished reading, ask them to summarize the details to write a statement about the writer's message.

 BEST PRACTICES TOOLKIT—Transparency
Main Idea and Details p. B6

FOR ADVANCED LEARNERS/PRE–AP

Evaluate a Reading Plan Have students write a plan for reading "Primal Screen" and "The Pedestrian," based on the **READING SKILL** discussion on this page. After they have read the selections and completed the assessment activities, ask them to review their plan and evaluate its effectiveness. Invite students to share what they have learned about setting a purpose for reading and establishing reading goals.

LITERARY ANALYSIS

Ⓐ WRITER'S MESSAGE

Possible answer: *By making this contrast, Goodman introduces the issue that real families, unlike the sitcom ones they are watching on TV, have trouble communicating and problem solving precisely because they are spending too much time watching TV.*

If students need help . . . Ask students to tell how the TV family is behaving. *(The TV family is communicating well and solving its problems.)* Then have students tell how the real family is behaving. *(Members of the real family are not solving problems or communicating at all except perhaps during commercials.)*

Lines 23–26
DISCUSSION PROMPTS

Use these prompts to help students grasp the main point of Goodman's argument:

Connect Does Goodman's description remind you of families you know? Explain. *Answers will vary.*

Analyze According to Goodman, which is worse: what families watch on TV or how long they watch TV? Why? *Possible answer: How long they watch is worse, according to Goodman. She believes that the more time family members watch TV, the less time they spend interacting with each other.*

Evaluate Do you think that Goodman's view is valid? Why or why not? *Possible answers: Yes, because the longer the TV is on, the less time there is for homework, conversation, hobbies, reading, or sleep. No, because people sometimes do other things even though a TV is on.*

Primal Screen

Ellen Goodman

Someday, I would like to see a television series about a family that sits around the set watching a series about a family that sits around the set.

It might not make the Nielsen top ten,[1] but it isn't such a strange idea. Especially when you think about what's going on right now.

Night after night, inside the tube, warm and wiggly families spend their prime time "communicating" like crazy and "solving problems" together like mad. Meanwhile, outside the tube, real families sit and wait for a commercial break just to talk to each other. Ⓐ

About the only subject that never comes up before our glazed eyes
10 is what the medium does to our family life. But, I suppose we already know that.

According to a recent Gallup Poll, television comes out as a major heavy in our family lives. On the scale of problems, TV didn't rate as bad as inflation, but it ran neck-and-neck with unemployment.

According to a recent Roper Poll, it even causes fights. When people were asked what husbands and wives argued about, money was the champion. But television was a strong contender. Considering how much more time we spend in front of the tube, that may not be such a shock.

To a certain extent, we blame the programs. In the Gallup Poll, for
20 example, people worried most about the overemphasis on sex and violence. But surely half of those fights between husbands and wives must be about the more fundamental issue of turning it off.

Deep down below our poll-taking consciousness, we know that the worst aspect of our addiction isn't what's on TV, but how long the TV is on. We can't help but be aware of what happens when we spend more time facing the screen than facing each other.

In that same Gallup Poll, a large number of us said that the way to improve family life is by sharing—sharing family needs, recreational activities and chores. But when you are watching, you aren't doing.
30 The only experience you are sharing is a vicarious one.

I am absolutely convinced that the average wife feels tuned out by the twelfth consecutive weekend sports event because she *is* being tuned out.

Ⓐ **WRITER'S MESSAGE**
Reread lines 5–8. What issue does the author introduce by contrasting sitcom families and real-life ones?

1. **Nielsen top ten:** the ten most-watched television shows, as determined by the Nielsen rating service.

DIFFERENTIATED INSTRUCTION

FOR ALL STUDDENTS

Anchor Activity Provide independent learning opportunities for students to prepare for and engage in a debate: To TV, or Not To TV? Assign students to opposing teams and assign roles as audience and judges as well. Allow time for presentation of arguments, rebuttals, and entire class discussion. For details, see

Ⓡ **RESOURCE MANAGER**
Ideas for Extension pp. 110–111

FOR LESS–PROFICIENT READERS

In combination with the *Audio Anthology CD*, use one or more Targeted Passages (pp. 641, 642, 645, 647) to ensure that students focus on key ideas, concepts, and skills. Targeted Passages are also good for English learners.

① Targeted Passage [Lines 49–58]

This passage presents Goodman's call to action.

The average kid develops that distant, slack-jawed, hypnotic, hooked stare because he or she *is* hooked.

In the same way, the people who spend night after night in front of the tube should worry about it. They've become an audience and not a family. Television simply presents us with one model of family life. Watching it makes us fit another model.

But the striking thing in all of this research about how we feel and
40 behave is the role of choice. On the one hand, we have real anxiety about what TV's doing to us. On the other hand, we allow it to happen. **B**

B WRITER'S MESSAGE
What is Goodman's message about excessive TV viewing?

ANALYZE VISUALS
What are your impressions of the family in this photograph?

We choose to turn it on and each other off. We choose peace and quiet when we let the kids watch TV instead of running around the living room. We choose to "relax" in the semi-comatose slump.

The average viewing time of the American child between six and sixteen years of age is twenty to twenty-four hours a week. A large percentage of parents place no restrictions on either the number of hours watched or the type of program viewed.

At the very least, we behave as if we were powerless to wrench each
50 other away.

I grant you that there are a lot of things that touch on our families that are totally out of our individual control. We can't regulate foreign affairs. We can't set the price for oil.

But a television set has a dial and a plug. And we have hands. It is absurd to let our feelings of impotence in the world start creeping into our private lives.

Just once, we ought to create a private show about a real-life family that kicked the habit.

1 Targeted Passage

Prereading for this story is found on page 638.

ANALYZE VISUALS

Possible answer: The dark, threatening sky; the lonely figure; and the plain, featureless homes create a somber mood.

About the Art Roger Brown (1941–1997), a prolific modern artist, lived and worked mainly in Chicago. His work includes painting, architecture, landscape design, theater sets, murals, and printmaking. Brown also created sculptures out of found, assembled, and painted objects.

LITERARY ANALYSIS

C WRITER'S MESSAGE

Possible answer: The imagery and figurative language compare the houses in which people are watching TV to death (the graveyard; the tomblike building) and to the supernatural (the flickering light; the gray phantoms). They suggest that Bradbury equates TV viewing with lifelessness.

If students need help . . . Use a web to clarify what Bradbury's details have in common.

- walking through a graveyard (line 12)
- gray phantoms on the walls (line 14)
- TV viewing removes you from the world of the living.
- faint glimmers of firefly light (line 13)
- whispers and murmurs from a tomblike building (lines 15–16)

THE PEDESTRIAN

Ray Bradbury

To enter out into that silence that was the city at eight o'clock of a misty evening in November, to put your feet upon that buckling concrete walk, to step over grassy seams and make your way, hands in pockets, through the silences, that was what Mr. Leonard Mead most dearly loved to do. He would stand upon the corner of an intersection and peer down long moonlit avenues of sidewalk in four directions, deciding which way to go, but it really made no difference; he was alone in this world of A.D. 2053, or as good as alone, and with a final decision made, a path selected, he would stride off, sending patterns of frosty air before him like the smoke of a cigar.

10   Sometimes he would walk for hours and miles and return only at midnight to his house. And on his way he would see the cottages and homes with their dark windows, and it was not unlike walking through a graveyard where only the faintest glimmers of firefly light appeared in flickers behind the windows. Sudden gray phantoms seemed to manifest upon inner room walls where a curtain was still undrawn against the night, or there were whisperings and murmurs where a window in a tomblike building was still open. **C**

Mr. Leonard Mead would pause, cock his head, listen, look, and march on, his feet making no noise on the lumpy walk. For long ago he had wisely changed to sneakers when strolling at night, because the dogs in intermittent
20 squads would parallel his journey with barkings if he wore hard heels, and lights might click on and faces appear and an entire street be startled by the passing of a lone figure, himself, in the early November evening.

ANALYZE VISUALS
What details in the painting help create a somber mood?

C WRITER'S MESSAGE
Reread lines 10–16. What do the **imagery** and the **figurative language** in this passage suggest about Bradbury's position on TV viewing?

(2) Targeted Passage

Detail of *Tourists Beware: New Buffalo Speed Trap* (1985), Roger Brown. Oil on canvas, 48″ × 48″. © The School of the Art Institute of Chicago and the Brown family.

DIFFERENTIATED INSTRUCTION

FOR LESS–PROFICIENT READERS
(2) Targeted Passage [Lines 17–22]

This passage emphasizes the difference between Leonard Mead, the main character, and the future world in which he lives.

- Why does Mr. Mead wear sneakers? For how long has he been doing so?
- Where are all the other people in this town?
- How would people react if they saw him taking his walk? Why?

FOR ADVANCED LEARNERS/PRE–AP
Analyze Imagery Point out that Bradbury uses many images of the natural world in this story. As students read, have them list examples in which the natural world is described or used in a comparison. Then ask students to write an analysis of these nature images that explains how Bradbury uses those references to make a point about the world of A.D. 2053.

BACKGROUND

Must-Have TV The technology that made today's TV possible was developed in the late 1920s. It was not until World War II ended, however, that the production of TV sets and the establishment of TV stations and programming began in earnest. By the end of 1950, the year in which Ray Bradbury wrote "The Pedestrian," there were 10.5 million TV sets in American homes—one set for every fourteen or fifteen Americans. It seemed that everyone wanted to be the first in the neighborhood to own a TV and to watch whatever limited programming was available. By 1950, too, the A. C. Nielsen Company was already surveying TV viewers' preferences—and some people were already warning about the influence of what by 1960 was called the "idiot box." It is little wonder that Bradbury found something ominous as he speculated about the future of this fledgling but captivating medium.

Lines 10–16
REINFORCE *KEY IDEA:* TELEVISION HABIT

Discuss "The Pedestrian" gives one writer's idea about how people would behave if a **television habit** took control of society. Is this scene of empty streets really possible, in your opinion? Explain. *Possible answer: Some students may argue that the scene does not seem possible. There always will be people who go out for entertainment or other reasons in the evenings.*

FOR LESS–PROFICIENT READERS

Make Connections Help pairs of students connect to the story's setting by completing a Venn Diagram that compares the world of "The Pedestrian" to the everyday world they know. Encourage students to think about the setting, character, and plot of the story as they create and then share their diagrams.

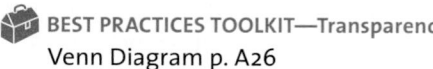 BEST PRACTICES TOOLKIT—Transparency
Venn Diagram p. A26

FOR ENGLISH LEARNERS

Comprehension: Transitions Explain that writers often tell about something by giving an example of what it is like. Point out a few of the many comparisons with forms of *like* in this story: "like" (line 9), "not unlike" (line 12), and the adjective "tomblike" (line 16). Ask small groups to search the rest of the story for comparisons and to share their findings.

Activity Point out that the painting on this page was created by the same artist, Roger Brown, who created the one on page 643. Ask students to tell how the paintings are similar and to name some adjectives that describe the artist's style. ***Possible answer:*** *Each painting features multiple houses that are identical to one another, and the multiple houses are the same in both paintings except for their color. In both paintings, the artist has used similar colors and tones, and the sky in each includes swirls and bright light shining behind dark shapes. The artist's style might be described using the adjectives* cartoon-like, stylized, fun, *or* funky.

Clouds Over Alabama or Midnight in Alabama (1994), Roger Brown. Oil on canvas, 48″ × 72″.
© The School of the Art Institute of Chicago and the Brown family.

On this particular evening he began his journey in a westerly direction, toward the hidden sea. There was a good crystal frost in the air; it cut the nose and made the lungs blaze like a Christmas tree inside; you could feel the cold light going on and off, all the branches filled with invisible snow. He listened to the faint push of his soft shoes through autumn leaves with satisfaction, and whistled a cold quiet whistle between his teeth, occasionally picking up a leaf as he passed, examining its skeletal pattern in the infrequent lamplights as he
30 went on, smelling its rusty smell.

"Hello, in there," he whispered to every house on every side as he moved. "What's up tonight on Channel 4, Channel 7, Channel 9? Where are the cowboys rushing, and do I see the United States Cavalry over the next hill to the rescue?"

The street was silent and long and empty, with only his shadow moving like the shadow of a hawk in midcountry. If he closed his eyes and stood very still, frozen, he could imagine himself upon the center of a plain, a wintry, windless Arizona desert with no house in a thousand miles, and only dry river beds, the streets, for company.

40 "What is it now?" he asked the houses, noticing his wrist watch. "Eight-thirty P.M.? Time for a dozen assorted murders? A quiz? A revue? A comedian falling off the stage?"

Was that a murmur of laughter from within a moon-white house? He hesitated, but went on when nothing more happened. He stumbled over a particularly uneven section of sidewalk. The cement was vanishing under flowers and grass. In ten years of walking by night or day, for thousands of miles, he had never met another person walking, not one in all that time. **D**

D WRITER'S MESSAGE
Consider the reason why Mead never encounters anyone on his nightly walks. How does this detail help you determine Bradbury's message?

D WRITER'S MESSAGE

Possible answer: *Mead never encounters anyone because everyone else spends evenings indoors, watching TV. This detail indicates Bradbury's view that television is powerful enough to control people's behavior and alienate them from the real world.*

If students need help . . . Review lines 31–34 and elicit that the people are watching TV. Then suggest possible interpretations of Bradbury's message—for example, "TV is entertaining," "TV is better than nature/real life," "TV provides everything that people need," and "Walking is useless." Allow students to reject each interpretation and to give reasons for their rejection before arriving at a more reasonable interpretation.

Extend the Discussion How would the people inside the houses probably react to Bradbury's message? Explain.

DIFFERENTIATED INSTRUCTION

FOR LESS-PROFICIENT READERS
Identify Sensory Details Have students use an Observation Chart to record details in lines 23–30 that involve human senses, such as sight (line 29), hearing (lines 26–28), touch (lines 24–26), and smell (line 30). Elicit that these details help establish the setting as a cold, pleasant autumn evening.

BEST PRACTICES TOOLKIT—Transparency
Observation Chart p. C7

FOR ENGLISH LEARNERS
Vocabulary: Multiple-Meaning Words
Review the fact that some English words have several meanings and that a reader must determine the correct meaning for a given context. Present these examples: *moved* (line 31), *plain* (line 37), *streams* (line 53), *block* (line 55), *force* (line 67), and *ill* (line 81). Ask students to define each word as used in context, using a dictionary to check.

He came to a cloverleaf intersection which stood silent where two main
highways crossed the town. During the day it was a thunderous surge of cars,
50 the gas stations open, a great insect rustling and a ceaseless jockeying for
position as the scarab-beetles,[1] a faint incense puttering from their exhausts,
skimmed homeward to the far directions. But now these highways, too, were
like streams in a dry season, all stone and bed and moon radiance.

He turned back on a side street, circling around toward his home. He
was within a block of his destination when the lone car turned a corner
quite suddenly and flashed a fierce white cone of light upon him. He stood
entranced, not unlike a night moth, stunned by the illumination, and then
drawn toward it.

A metallic voice called to him:

60 "Stand still. Stay where you are! Don't move!"

He halted.

"Put up your hands!"

"But—" he said.

"Your hands! Or we'll shoot!"

The police, of course, but what a rare, incredible thing; in a city of three
million, there was only one police car left, wasn't that correct? Ever since a year
ago, 2052, the election year, the force had been cut down from three cars to
one. Crime was ebbing; there was no need now for the police, save for this one
lone car wandering and wandering the empty streets.

70 "Your name?" said the police car in a metallic whisper. He couldn't see the
men in it for the bright light in his eyes.

"Leonard Mead," he said.

"Speak up!"

"Leonard Mead!"

"Business or profession?"

"I guess you'd call me a writer."

"No profession," said the police car, as if talking to itself. The light held him
fixed, like a museum specimen, needle thrust through chest.

"You might say that," said Mr. Mead. He hadn't written in years. Magazines
80 and books didn't sell any more. Everything went on in the tomblike houses at
night now, he thought, continuing his fancy. The tombs, ill-lit by television
light, where the people sat like the dead, the grey or multicolored lights
touching their faces, but never really touching *them.*

"No profession," said the phonograph voice, hissing. "What are you
doing out?"

"Walking," said Leonard Mead.

"Walking!"

"Just walking," he said simply, but his face felt cold.

"Walking, just walking, walking?"

90 "Yes, sir."

---

1. **scarab-beetles:** large beetles considered to be sacred in ancient Egypt.

③ Targeted Passage

Ⓔ WRITER'S MESSAGE
Why does the voice reply
"No profession" when
Mead says he is a writer?

Lines 70–90
DISCUSSION PROMPTS
Use these prompts to help students grasp
Mead's encounter with the police:

Connect Would you react as calmly as
Mead seems to be reacting to the police
car's challenge? *Students may feel that they
would be more defensive.*

Analyze Why does the police car treat Mead
with suspicion? *Possible answer: The car considers walking a suspicious activity because it
is abnormal in this society.*

Synthesize Why might taking a walk be
considered a threat to this society? *Possible
answer: A society that values conformity
would be threatened by any behavior outside
the norm because that behavior would encourage independent thinking.*

LITERARY ANALYSIS

Ⓔ WRITER'S MESSAGE

*Possible answer: Since people in this world
rarely buy magazines and books (lines
79–80), there seems to be no reason for
anyone to be a writer.*

If students need help . . . Have them
search for a clue in the next paragraph.
Discuss the thoughts that might have led
the police car to its conclusion.

Extend the Discussion Which other professions would be obsolete in Mead's world?
Which would be most important?

FOR LESS–PROFICIENT READERS

③ Targeted Passage [Lines 54–69]

This passage introduces the conflict that
takes the story to its climax.

- What confronts Mead just before he gets
home? Why is this challenger unusual?

- What does this challenger want Mead to
do? Why?

- What is this challenger's job? What might
your answer suggest about what will happen to Mead?

FOR ADVANCED LEARNERS/PRE–AP

Analyze Characterization [paired-activity
option] Ask students to reread Bradbury's
description in lines 81–83 of the people
inside the houses. Have them explain what
Bradbury means by comparing the people to
the dead and by saying that the television
lights do not touch them. Then ask students
to support an opinion about why Bradbury
might have chosen to characterize people in
this way.

Activity When students have finished reading "The Pedestrian," have them come back to this painting, also by Roger Brown (see **About the Art,** page 642). Ask them to explain how its details correspond with details in the text. *Possible answer: Only one person is on the street. In addition, the car seems to be in operation but apparently is unoccupied (unlike the houses).*

Detail of *Tourists Beware: New Buffalo Speed Trap* (1985), Roger Brown. Oil on canvas, 48″ × 48″. © The School of the Art Institute of Chicago and the Brown family.

"Walking where? For what?"

"Walking for air. Walking to see."

"Your address!"

"Eleven South Saint James Street."

"And there is air in your house, you have an air *conditioner,* Mr. Mead?"

"Yes."

"And you have a viewing screen in your house to see with?"

"No."

"No?" There was a crackling quiet that in itself was an accusation. **F**

100   "Are you married, Mr. Mead?"

"No."

"Not married," said the police voice behind the fiery beam. The moon was high and clear among the stars and the houses were gray and silent.

"Nobody wanted me," said Leonard Mead with a smile.

"Don't speak unless you're spoken to!"

Leonard Mead waited in the cold night.

646   UNIT 6: ARGUMENT AND PERSUASION

F WRITER'S MESSAGE
Notice the voice's reaction when Mead admits to not having a viewing screen. How important is TV viewing to the people of the future?

LITERARY ANALYSIS

F WRITER'S MESSAGE

Possible answer: The fact that the voice is suspicious and then accusingly quiet suggests that to the people of the future, TV viewing is so important that it is a requirement for acceptable behavior.

If students need help . . . Encourage students to cite at least one detail from the text that clarifies the importance of TV in this society.

Line 97
REINFORCE *KEY IDEA:* TELEVISION HABIT

Discuss Look at the word choice in the car's question. What does it suggest about this society's perception of the world? *Possible answer: Calling TV "a viewing screen . . . to see with" suggests that this society's perceptions are strictly controlled by television. The only "real" way of looking at the world is the way that TV presents it.*

DIFFERENTIATED INSTRUCTION

FOR ENGLISH LEARNERS

Vocabulary: Word Associations Point out how Bradbury joins adjectives to nouns in surprising combinations such as these: "rusty smell" (line 30), "a fierce white cone of light" (line 56), "a metallic whisper" (line 70), and "a crackling quiet" (line 99). Discuss the effect of each of these unusual descriptions.

"Just *walking*, Mr. Mead?"

"Yes."

"But you haven't explained for what purpose."

110 "I explained; for air, and to see, and just to walk."

"Have you done this often?"

"Every night for years."

The police car sat in the center of the street with its radio throat faintly humming.

"Well, Mr. Mead," it said.

"Is that all?" he asked politely.

"Yes," said the voice. "Here." There was a sigh, a pop. The back door of the police car sprang wide. "Get in."

"Wait a minute, I haven't done anything!"

120 "Get in."

"I protest!"

"Mr. Mead."

He walked like a man suddenly drunk. As he passed the front window of the car he looked in. As he had expected, there was no one in the front seat, no one in the car at all.

"Get in."

He put his hand to the door and peered into the back seat, which was a little cell, a little black jail with bars. It smelled of riveted steel. It smelled of harsh antiseptic; it smelled too clean and hard and metallic. There was nothing 130 soft there.

"Now if you had a wife to give you an alibi," said the iron voice. "But—"

"Where are you taking me?"

The car hesitated, or rather gave a faint whirring click, as if information, somewhere, was dripping card by punch-slotted card[2] under electric eyes. "To the Psychiatric Center for Research on Regressive Tendencies."[3] **G**

He got in. The door shut with a soft thud. The police car rolled through the night avenues, flashing its dim lights ahead.

They passed one house on one street a moment later, one house in an entire city of houses that were dark, but this one particular house had all of its 140 electric lights brightly lit, every window a loud yellow illumination, square and warm in the cool darkness.

"That's *my* house," said Leonard Mead.

No one answered him.

The car moved down the empty river-bed streets and off away, leaving the empty streets with the empty sidewalks, and no sound and no motion all the rest of the chill November night. ◡

G WRITER'S MESSAGE
What "crime" has Leonard Mead committed?

④ **Targeted Passage**

---

2. **punch-slotted card:** At the time this story was written, cards punched with coded holes were used to feed data into computers.

3. **Regressive Tendencies:** habits of acting in ways that belong to an earlier stage of human development, such as childhood.

THE PEDESTRIAN **647**

FOR LESS-PROFICIENT READERS

④ **Targeted Passage [Lines 138–146]**

This passage wraps up the story and reminds readers once again of the contrast between Mead and the rest of his society.

- What is different about Mead's house?
- What are the streets like after Mead is taken away?
- Who in Mead's world is aware of what has happened to him?

FOR ADVANCED LEARNERS/PRE-AP

Hypothesize Have students extend this story by writing another episode in Mead's life. Students may choose to write a scene in the police car, a scene in which Mead tries to explain himself to a psychiatrist, or a scene that may take place after his release from the psychiatric center. Invite students to share their sequels in small groups.

Practice and Apply

After Reading

For additional support of post-reading questions, use these copy masters:

R RESOURCE MANAGER—Copy Masters

Reading Check p. 120 (to check understanding of the selections)

Writer's Message Across Genres p. 117 (for practice of literary analysis standards focus)

Question Support p. 121 (After Reading questions adapted for English learners and less-proficient readers)

Additional selection questions are provided for teachers on page 109.

ANSWERS

Comprehension

1. *The city is busy by day. At night, however, everyone stays home watching TV, leaving the streets empty.*

2. *Mead seems suspicious because he is out walking at night, does not have a viewing screen, and is unmarried. These factors deviate from society's norm.*

3. *Goodman urges Americans to turn off the TV. By implication, she wants them to interact with their families more.*

Literary Analysis

Possible answers:

4. *To support her claim, Goodman says that half of married couples' fights about TV must be about whether to have the TV on at all rather than what to watch (lines 15–22). She also cites the statistic that American children watch 20–24 hours of TV each week and notes that parents allow that excessive viewing to happen (lines 42–48).*

5. *The title suggests that Goodman is using her essay to vent her deep (primal) frustration with the overuse of television (the screen).*

6. *The response that gets Mead into the most trouble is his revelation that he does not have a viewing screen. This fact makes Mead different from everyone else.*

7. ● STANDARDS FOCUS *Writer's Message Across Genres* Bradbury uses imagery *and figurative language to suggest that people of the future have given up thinking for themselves and accept whatever the*

Comprehension

1. **Recall** Describe the city where Leonard Mead walks in "The Pedestrian."

2. **Clarify** Why does Mead seem especially suspicious to the police car?

3. **Clarify** In "Primal Screen," what does Goodman urge Americans to do?

Literary Analysis

4. **Analyze Support** In "Primal Screen," Goodman claims that the **habit** of television watching is a more serious problem than the content of the programs. What evidence does she use to support this claim?

5. **Synthesize** The title of Goodman's essay, "Primal Screen," is a **pun,** or a play on words. It refers to primal scream therapy, a type of treatment in which patients scream to vent frustrations. Why do you think Goodman titled her column "Primal Screen"?

6. **Make Judgments** Of Leonard Mead's several responses to the police car, which do you think gets him into the most trouble? Why?

7. **Draw Conclusions About Writer's Message** Reread lines 79–83 in "The Pedestrian." Bradbury uses **imagery** and **figurative language** to describe the people of the future. In describing the future, what does he imply about the people of today?

Comparing Across Genres

Reflect on Your Purpose Now that you have read each selection, consider whether you have discovered enough similarities and differences in the writers' messages to compare and contrast them. If so, write your observations on a chart like the one shown. If not, reread the selections to gather more evidence and then fill in the chart.

Points of Comparison	In the Essay	In the Short Story
What is the writer's focus?	what television watching is doing to family life	what television is doing to American society in general
What problems are identified or portrayed?		
What solutions are recommended or suggested?		
What methods are used to convey the message?		

TV shows them. The implication is that people today may wind up like that if they fail to control their TV habit.

Comparing Across Genres

Possible answers:

● STANDARDS FOCUS *Set a Purpose for Reading* **In the Essay:** *Problem(s): the overuse of television and the perceived powerlessness to turn it off; Solution(s): turning off the set; Methods: persuasive language, statistics and other facts, and a strong call to action*

In the Short Story: Problem(s): the taking over of society by mind-numbing television programming; Solution(s): experiencing nature and thinking independently; Methods: setting, characters, dialogue, imagery, word choice

Writing for Assessment

1. READ THE PROMPT

In writing assessments, you will often be asked to compare and contrast two works that are similar in some way, such as the two examples of social criticism that you have just read. You are now going to practice writing an essay that involves this type of comparison.

> **PROMPT**
>
> Writers sometimes use literature to target faults or alarming trends in society. Consider Goodman's "Primal Screen" and Bradbury's "The Pedestrian." In a four- or five-paragraph essay, compare and contrast these works as examples of social criticism, identifying each writer's message and the techniques used to convey it. In your opinion, which work makes a stronger case? Support your analysis with details from the two works.

◀ **STRATEGIES IN ACTION**

*1. I need to summarize each **writer's message.***

*2. I have to identify the **methods** each writer uses to convey his or her message.*

*3. I need to determine the **similarities and differences** between the messages and methods.*

*4. I need to **evaluate** which message is more powerful or persuasive and **explain why.***

2. PLAN YOUR WRITING

- Review the chart you filled out for "Primal Screen" and "The Pedestrian" on page 648.
- Using your chart, find examples for the points you wish to develop in your essay. If necessary, review the selections again to look for more examples.
- Create an outline to organize your ideas.

3. DRAFT YOUR RESPONSE

Introduction Introduce the topic—literature as a tool of social criticism—and then explain that you will be comparing an essay and a short story, both on the subject of television viewing. Be sure to include the title and author of each work.

Body Use your outline to develop the key points of your essay. In one paragraph, for example, you might compare and contrast the solution each writer offers. Within each paragraph you write, give specific details to back up your points.

Conclusion Wrap up your essay with a restatement of your main idea and a brief summary of your main points.

Revision Check your use of signal words—such as *similarly, also, like, but,* and *while*—to make sure that your comparisons and contrasts are clear.

DIFFERENTIATED INSTRUCTION

FOR LESS–PROFICIENT WRITERS

Guide Revision Have students review their drafts with a partner, using the Peer Response Guide. Remind students to look for ways to improve and clarify the writing and to be constructive in their comments.

 BEST PRACTICES TOOLKIT—Transparency
Peer Response Guide p. C14

Writing For Assessment

1. *READ THE PROMPT*

- Have students read the prompt carefully, noting the verbs *compare, contrast, consider,* and *support.* Also discuss the importance of the nouns *message, techniques,* and *case.*

- Explain that **STRATEGIES IN ACTION** turns the prompt into a set of tasks. Urge students to use this approach whenever they respond to an essay question.

2. *PLAN YOUR WRITING*

- Direct students to use their chart details to develop their points.

- Urge students to have a main idea in mind as they plan. As they develop their plan, they can revise the main idea, but having one at the outset (for example, the third task under **STRATEGIES IN ACTION,** expressed as a main idea statement) can help them focus.

- Urge students to find at least one specific detail or example to illustrate each point.

- Suggest that students use complete sentences in their outlines.

3. *DRAFT YOUR RESPONSE*

- Remind students that although the styles of writing in these selections differ, the writers' messages are similar.

- Students may decide that one selection is stronger in some regards and the other is stronger in other regards. Suggest that in such a situation, students explain their opinions clearly and then summarize the position in the conclusion of the essay.

Assess and Reteach

Assess

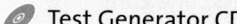 RESOURCE MANAGER—Copy Masters
Selection Test A pp. 123–124
Selection Test B/C pp. 125–126

Test Generator CD

Reteach

STANDARDS LESSON FILE
Writing Lesson 24: Comparison-Contrast Essay

Focus and Motivate

OBJECTIVES

- analyze a student model that reflects the key traits of a persuasive speech
- use the writing process to produce a persuasive speech
- revise and edit, using a rubric for persuasive speech writing
- plan and present a persuasive speech

WRITER'S ROAD MAP

WRITING PROMPTS 1 AND 2

Tell students that a good persuasive speech reflects the writer's genuine concern about the topic. Encourage students to choose a topic about which they care deeply.

ADDITIONAL PROMPTS

Use these prompts for practice with business writing and writing in the humanities.

WRITING PROMPT 3

Writing for the Real World Write a brief speech to introduce a business idea. Consider what you are "selling" and to whom.

Possible Situations
- proposal to potential investors in a new product
- presentation of an advertising campaign

WRITING PROMPT 4

Writing About Fine Art Write the text for a brief persuasive speech responding to the saying "A picture is worth a thousand words." Find supporting fine art works at an online museum, in a book, or in those provided by your teacher.

Possible Subjects
- a historic photograph with a strong message
- a painting by an American Realist

For additional writing prompts, see

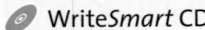 Write*Smart* CD

Writing Center at **ClassZone.com**

KEY TRAITS

Review the six *KEY TRAITS* with students, focusing mainly on ideas, organization, voice, and word choice. Compare the list of traits with the rubric on page 656.

Writing Workshop

Persuasive Speech

As you have seen in this unit, persuasive words can be powerful. They can change people's minds, convince people to take action, or even make a difference in the world. A good way to give your words this power is to write and deliver a heartfelt and well-reasoned speech about a topic that's important to you. To take the first steps to your personal podium, follow the **Writer's Road Map.**

WRITER'S ROAD MAP

Persuasive Speech

WRITING PROMPT 1

Writing from the Real World Sometimes an issue in your life or your community affects you so deeply that you must speak out to persuade others to see your point of view. Write a persuasive speech in which you attempt to convince your listeners to adopt your opinion or to take the action you propose.

Issues to Explore
- health issues, such as the link between obesity and fast food
- social problems, such as stereotyping
- problems in your community or school

WRITING PROMPT 2

Writing from Literature Choose an issue that was covered in a selection in this unit—an issue that matters to you. Write a persuasive speech in which you respond to the ideas expressed by the writer.

Selections to Explore
- "Primal Screen" (negative effects of television)
- "Testimony Before the Senate" (funding for medical research)

 WRITING TOOLS
For prewriting, revision, and editing tools, visit the **Writing Center** at **ClassZone.com**.

KEY TRAITS

1. IDEAS
- Clearly identifies the **issue**
- Presents a clear, logical, and forceful **claim,** or position, in a **thesis statement**
- Uses relevant and convincing details to **support** the position
- Anticipates and answers **opposing viewpoints** and counterclaims

2. ORGANIZATION
- Provides a memorable **introduction** to the issue
- Uses a consistent **organizational pattern**
- Concludes with a **summary** or a **call to action**

3. VOICE
- Uses a **tone** that is appropriate for the audience and purpose

4. WORD CHOICE
- Addresses the **audience** directly and uses **rhetorical devices** such as repetition and parallelism

5. SENTENCE FLUENCY
- Uses effective **sentence types and structures,** such as imperative sentences

6. CONVENTIONS
- Employs **correct grammar and usage**

Writing Workshop Resources

 RESOURCE MANAGER UNIT 6

Plan and Teach pp. 127–130
Prewriting–Editing pp. 131–135
Writing Rubric p. 136
Speaking and Listening p. 137
Writing Support p. 138*

 STANDARDS LESSON FILE

Writing Lessons 15–17, 30
Grammar Lesson 20

 BEST PRACTICES TOOLKIT

Scaffolding Writing Instruction pp. 43–46*
Main Idea and Details • Analysis Frame: Persuasion • Writing Template: Persuasive Writing: Editorial • Word Sorts

TECHNOLOGY
 Easy Planner DVD
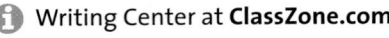 Writing Center at **ClassZone.com**
 Write*Smart* CD

* Resources for Differentiation

Part 1: Analyze a Student Model

Sara Jenkins
Danford High School

Bring Back Our Snacks

Superintendent Klein and other administrators, imagine how it would feel to arrive at your office and find the desk missing. You would probably be surprised and try to get it back. That's how I felt when I discovered that our school's three vending machines were removed
5 recently without warning. Let me explain why I believe the vending machines are important to students and should be brought back.

For **S**tarters—**S**—We need **S**nacks during **S**chool. High school students are growing rapidly and burn up enormous numbers of calories. Our half-hour lunch period is barely enough time to buy a hot lunch or
10 gulp down a sandwich, and we're hungry again before the next bell. We need quick energy to keep going and doing our best. As a result, we often go to the snack machines between classes. I did an informal survey of my homeroom and found that 67 percent of those students buy snacks or drinks from the vending machines at least once a day.

15 You might argue that the salty, fatty foods and sweet drinks available in the vending machines provide only empty calories—no real nutrition. It's hard to disagree with that point when reports of obesity in young people fill the media. There's a better solution, though: make nuts, dried fruit, or trail mix available instead of chips and candy; and fruit juice,
20 milk, or water instead of soft drinks. I'm not a junk-food junkie, and I don't think other students are either. When the munchies hit, we'd be happy to eat whatever came out of the machines.

Next—**N**—We **N**eed them **N**earby. In fact, snacks have to be available inside the school, since students aren't allowed to leave the
25 building during the day. You might say that students have to provide for

KEY TRAITS IN ACTION

Addresses the **audience** directly in an effective **introduction**. Presents the **claim** in a clear **thesis statement**.

Uses the letters of *snack* as a memorable **organizational pattern**.

Uses facts and a statistic as relevant and convincing **support**.

Anticipates and answers **opposing viewpoints** and counterclaims. Varied and sophisticated **sentence structures** help hold reader interest.

The writer introduces each of her points in a similar way. This parallelism is an effective **rhetorical device**.

WRITING WORKSHOP **651**

Part 1: Analyze a Student Model

Have students read the student model and ***KEY TRAITS IN ACTION***. Then discuss the model with the class, pointing out specific examples of each trait and building on what students have already noted. You may also wish to incorporate these activities:

- **Introduction** Explain that a good introduction captures the attention of the audience and generates interest in the subject. Students might consider using any of these ideas:
  - a startling fact, statement, or comparison
  - a lively anecdote
  - a mention of a timely or related event
  - a reason why the subject matters
  - a quotation or question
  - a first-person account

- **Rhetorical Devices** Point out that rhetorical devices are techniques for using language effectively and persuasively. Numerous such devices exist. Define these terms and have students find examples in the student model:

  analogy comparing similar items or situations to emphasize some point *(lines 1–2)*

  parallelism using the same grammatical form to state related ideas *(lines 18–20)*

  rhetorical question an unanswered question with an obvious answer *(lines 46–48)*

  alliteration the repetition of beginning consonant sounds *(lines 7, 23, 43)*

You may wish to review the **GRAMMAR AND STYLE** note on page 630 and to have students reread the series of infinitive phrases that the author uses to establish parallelism.

DIFFERENTIATED INSTRUCTION

For general guidelines on differentiating writing instruction, see

 BEST PRACTICES TOOLKIT
Scaffolding Writing Instruction
pp. 43–46

FOR ENGLISH LEARNERS

Language: Skill Words Write these terms on the board and review them with students:

- *thesis statement:* A sentence or two that states the essay's main idea. The thesis statement of a persuasive speech should be a clear statement of opinion on the topic.

- *opposing viewpoints:* what people might say if they disagreed with the writer's views; for example, that students are better off without snacks

- *rhetorical devices:* techniques to make persuasive arguments more effective; for examples, see **Rhetorical Devices** on this page.

- *organizational pattern:* the way a writer arranges the ideas and information; for example, the ideas in the model are organized by the letters in the word *snack*.

- *tone:* an expression of the writer's attitude toward a subject, such as *serious, humorous,* or *angry*

WRITING WORKSHOP **651**

- **Tone** Explain that *tone* is an expression of the writer's attitude toward a subject. The tone of a speech might be serious, angry, or even funny. If the tone is insulting, however, the ideas will be less effective. Tone is communicated in two ways: by word choice and by the type of details. To help students distinguish tone, write this sentence on the board:

  A small bunch of idiots trashed the machines, so it would be stupid to punish everyone.

  Ask a student to read these sentences and lines 38–39 of the student model. Ask students to compare the tone of the two, then discuss how tone can impact persuasiveness. **Possible answer:** *The lines on the board sound angry and insulting. The words* idiots *and* stupid *show a lack of respect both for the students and for the audience. Listeners will not want to hear the speaker's ideas if they feel insulted.*

- **Details** Details can include facts, examples, quotations, illustrations, and statistics. Students might include:
  - specific examples that illustrate a persuasive statement
  - descriptions of the setting if the speaker's position is not adopted
  - descriptions of how people will be affected if the speaker's position is not adopted
  - benefits of the speaker's position that will have a direct impact on the audience

- **Conclusion** Note that a summary or a call to action—a statement that urges readers to do something specific—are just two ways to end a persuasive speech. Other techniques include:

  Statement of Intent The writer might end by telling what he or she plans to do about the situation.

  A Brief, Memorable Phrase This could be a slogan, a proverb, or a brief quotation designed to stick in listeners' minds and remind them of a key point.

For interactive student models, see

- WriteSmart CD
- Writing Center at **ClassZone.com**

UNIT 6: ARGUMENT AND PERSUASION

---

their own nutritional needs. My response is that there's barely room in our lockers for our books, gym clothes, and jackets. Many of us have even started buying our lunches rather than eating the squashed remains of something brought from home.

30   **A**nd now—**A**—We can **A**ct like responsible **A**dults. I know that there have been some concerns about students using the vending-machine area as a hangout between classes. This loitering has led to congestion in the hallways and an increase in tardiness. If the machines were reinstalled, I'm sure students would agree to stop using the

35 snack center as a meeting place. We would remind each other of this condition and make a special effort to not be late to class.

    There also have been several instances of vandalism to the machines. Only a small number of students are responsible for these acts, and it's unfair for the rest of us to be punished on their account. One solution

40 to this problem would be to assign a hall monitor to the snack center. Since monitors are on duty throughout the building, one could easily be reassigned.

    Coming to—**C**—We **C**are and deserve to be **C**onsulted. The removal of the vending machines affects students directly, and we

45 should have been asked to take part in the decision-making process. How can we develop good judgment and learn to accept responsibility for our decisions if we aren't given the opportunity to practice those skills? People tend to live up to others' expectations of them, and if we aren't trusted, we may never become trustworthy. Bringing back the

50 vending machines would show your confidence in students and, at the same time, help us build self-confidence.

    And finally—**K**—We **K**now you respect us and will **K**eep our best interests in mind. All spelled out, that means: Bring back our **SNACK**s.

> Direct, serious **tone** shows awareness of and respect for the audience.

> Includes specific details and logic to **support** the statement.

> Effective **summary** makes a clear **call to action** and echoes the title. Imperative sentence at the end makes the message more forceful.

2

652   UNIT 6: ARGUMENT AND PERSUASION

DIFFERENTIATED INSTRUCTION

FOR ENGLISH LEARNERS

Comprehension: Transitions Help students identify different types of transitional words and phrases in the model. Point out the ones that link ideas within sentences, such as *and* (line 6), and within paragraphs, such as *As a result* (line 11). Then discuss transitions that link paragraphs to show their relationship. Identify some of these and help students think of other options for each:

- *For starters* (line 7) "First of all," "To begin," "One important reason is . . ."

- *You might argue* (line 15) "Some people believe," "Opponents claim"
- *Next* (line 23) "Second," "Also," "In addition," "Furthermore"
- *Coming to* (line 43) "Finally," "Most importantly"
- *And finally* (line 52) "In conclusion," "In short," "To summarize"

To provide English learners with additional writing support, see

R RESOURCE MANAGER—Copy Master
    Writing Support p. 138

Part 2: Apply the Writing Process

PREWRITING

What Should I Do?	What Does It Look Like?

1. Analyze the prompt.
Look back at the two prompts on page 650. Choose the one that appeals to you more. (Circle) words that tell you what kind of writing you will be doing. Underline details that help you focus your topic. Think about your **purpose** and **audience.** Who are you writing for, and why?

▶

WRITING PROMPT Sometimes an issue in your life or your community affects you so deeply that you must speak out to persuade others to see your point of view. Write a persuasive speech in which you attempt to convince your listeners to adopt your opinion or to take the action you propose.

I'm supposed to write a speech convincing listeners to agree with me about an issue that's important to me.

2. Zero in on your topic and purpose.
Make a list of situations that you feel strongly about. It's not enough to come up with a meaningful topic. You need to decide what change you want to advocate and what person or group you want to convince.

▶

Issues:
• *Drivers talking on cell phones*
• *Proposed skate-park*
• *Removal of school vending machines*

Goal: Return of vending machines
Audience: Superintendent and school administrators

3. Determine your supporting points.
List as many reasons for your position as you can. Ask yourself: What makes this issue worth debating? What are some possible solutions?

TIP Don't forget to consider opposing views. List arguments against your position and possible answers to those arguments.

▶

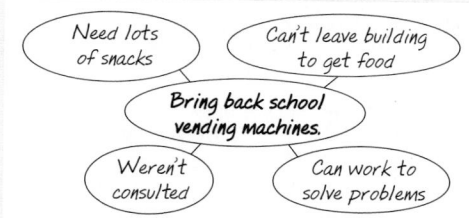

Need lots of snacks   *Can't leave building to get food*
Bring back school vending machines.
Weren't consulted   *Can work to solve problems*

4. Gather support for your position.
Look for facts, statistics, expert opinions, anecdotes, and logical arguments to lend weight to each supporting point. Think about how much audience members already know about the issue and what information they will need.

▶

Supporting point: Students need lots of snacks.
Details:
1. Students growing rapidly, burn calories
2. Lunch period only 30 minutes
3. Lots of students used machines. (How many students used them? Survey homeroom to find out)

FOR ENGLISH LEARNERS

Culture: Clarify Students from some cultures may hesitate to express personal opinions. Clarify that opinions are acceptable when they are expressed respectfully and can be supported by facts, statistics, or expert opinions. Review types of opinions that can and cannot be supported:

• Walls should be blue. (unsupportable)
• Students should wear uniforms. (supportable)
• Lunches should be free. (supportable)

FOR ADVANCED LEARNERS/PRE–AP

Supporting Opposing Views Invite students to write about a topic from the viewpoint opposing their personal feelings. Their goal is to create a powerful argument supporting the opposing view. Debate experience can be useful if students have been assigned views with which they disagree.

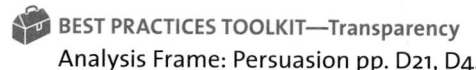 **BEST PRACTICES TOOLKIT—Transparency**
Analysis Frame: Persuasion pp. D21, D44

Practice and Apply

To support students during the writing process, use these copy masters.

R RESOURCE MANAGER—Copy Masters
Prewriting–Editing pp. 131–135
Writing Rubric p. 136
Writing Support p. 138 (for English learners)

Part 2: Apply the Writing Process

PREWRITING

1. Analyze the prompt. Ask questions that require students to identify the function of each marked section in the example, and point out that these are the questions to answer about any prompt:
  • What are you asked to write about?
  • What type of writing is expected?
  • What is the writing purpose?

2. Zero in on your topic and purpose. Encourage students to use three-column charts for this step. They should list all possible situations or issues in the first column. If they cannot fill both the second (goals) and third (audience) columns for a situation, they should reconsider the topic.

3. Determine your supporting points. Be sure that students read the **TIP** and identify at least one argument against their position.

4. Gather support for your position. Many persuasive arguments use the **deductive** method of organization. Writers begin with strong general statements about a position and then provide evidence to support the statements.

Encourage students to gather the most evidence for their most important points. A Main Idea and Details chart can help them see how much supporting evidence they have gathered.

BEST PRACTICES TOOLKIT—Transparency
Main Idea and Details p. B6

For interactive graphic organizers, see

🖉 Write*Smart* CD

ℹ Writing Center at **ClassZone.com**

DRAFTING

1. **Craft a strong, clear thesis statement.** Students should take the audience into account when they write their thesis statements. They may need to provide background context for an audience that is unfamiliar with the issue.

2. **Anticipate opposing views.** This activity would work well for pairs or small groups. Have students state their positions to one or more listeners. The students should provide no reasons at this point. The listeners should state reasons that oppose the students' positions. Writing students will then hear several opposing views.

3. **Make your points memorable.** A few strong supporting reasons will be more memorable than many weaker reasons. Tell students to imagine holding up the fingers on one hand as they list key reasons. If it takes more than one hand, students should focus on fewer reasons and try to strengthen them. One way to strengthen reasons is to use an expert's support, such as in a short, lively quotation.

   Discuss the **TIP** with students, asking them to suggest other ways a writer might make points in a memorable way.

   Ask students to review the **GRAMMAR AND STYLE** note on page 616 and to reread the imperative sentences that the author uses. Discuss how imperatives can emphasize ideas and make them memorable.

For a persuasive writing template, see

📁 **BEST PRACTICES TOOLKIT—Transparency**
   Writing Template: Persuasive Writing: Editorial pp. C16, C32

💿 WriteSmart CD

ℹ️ Writing Center at **ClassZone.com**

What Should I Do?

1. **Craft a strong, clear thesis statement.** Explain the issue, your position on it (in other words, your **claim**), and what you want your listeners to do about it. Be as clear and as forceful as you can. The working thesis statement will help guide your writing, but feel free to modify it as you go along.

What Does It Look Like?

▶ **Working thesis:** I was surprised that our school's three vending machines were removed recently without warning. Let me explain why I believe the vending machines are important to students and should be brought back.

2. **Anticipate objections by others.** Don't leave your listeners with unanswered questions. By anticipating and clearly answering opposing viewpoints, you have a much greater chance of persuading others to agree with you. Use a chart to think through opposing arguments and your answers.

▶

Who might object?	Possible objections	My arguments
School administrators	1. Snack foods lack nutrition.	1. Nuts, dried fruit, juice are fine.
	2. Students can bring snacks from home.	2. Lockers are too small.
	3. Students loiter near snack machines.	3. Students agree to avoid using that area as a meeting place.
	4. Machines have been vandalized.	4. Assign a hall monitor.

3. **Make your points memorable.** Because this is a speech, listeners hear your ideas only once. This writer began with an analogy (a point-by-point comparison of two things) directed at her target audience. Then she organized her essay in a way that makes each point easy to remember.

   TIP Words with repeated sounds at the beginning (alliteration) or at the end (rhyme) can help make your message memorable.

▶ **Analogy**

Superintendent Klein and other administrators, imagine how it would feel to arrive at your office and find the desk missing. You would probably be surprised and try to get it back. That's how I felt when I discovered that our school's three vending machines were removed recently without warning.

Parallelism

For Starters—S—We need Snacks during School.
Next—N—We Need them Nearby.

DIFFERENTIATED INSTRUCTION

FOR LESS–PROFICIENT WRITERS

Anticipating Opposing Views Students may not know how to organize both their reasons and those of people with opposing viewpoints. Distribute Writing Template: Persuasive Writing: to provide a starting point. Help students use the templates to create outlines for their essays.

FOR ENGLISH LEARNERS

Language: Parallelism To help students recognize parallel structure, provide them with several examples and non-examples. Discuss the parallel structure in each example:

Parallel: See<u>ing</u> is believ<u>ing</u>. (verb form)
Not: Seeing something will make you believe it.

Parallel: Waste <u>not</u>, want <u>not</u>. (verb + not)
Not: Do not waste, so you have what you want.

Parallel: <u>To live</u> is <u>to love</u>. (to + verb)
Not: All people alive love.

REVISING AND EDITING

What Should I Do?

1. Use emotional appeals wisely.
- Ask a peer reader which of your reasons are strongest and which are weakest.
- Underline words or phrases that are so emotionally charged or extreme that they may cause audience members to dismiss your entire message.
- Replace extreme statements with appeals supported by sound reasoning and evidence.

See page 656: Emotional Appeals

2. Shore up your support.
- Put [brackets] around statements of your ideas.
- Review each statement. Is it supported with explanations and details? If not, add facts, statistics, expert opinions, or reasons.

3. Make it clear, so they will hear.
- Read your speech aloud to identify sentences that are boring or bland.
- Use rhyme, repetition, parallelism, or other devices to help listeners remember your main points.

4. Sharpen your conclusion.
- Highlight your conclusion. Reread it, asking yourself: Does it summarize what has come before? Is it concise? Does it suggest a course of action?
- Edit your sentences so they summarize your points forcefully and call for action.

What Does It Look Like?

▶ ~~If you don't bring back the vending machines, we will continue to go hungry, day after day. How can you treat us so cruelly?~~ You might say that students have to provide for their own nutritional needs. My response is that there's barely room in our lockers for our books, gym clothes, and jackets. Many of us have even started buying our lunches rather than eating the squashed remains of something brought from home.

▶ [We need quick energy to keep going and doing our best. As a result, we often go to the snack machines between classes.]

I did an informal survey of my homeroom and found that 67 percent of those students buy snacks or drinks from the vending machines at least once a day.

▶ For Starters—S—We need Snacks during School. ~~The snacks have to be where we can buy them when we get hungry.~~
Next—N—We Need them Nearby.

▶ And finally—K—We Know you respect us and will Keep our best interests in mind. ~~Students (not administrators, staff, or teachers) use the vending machines, and you removed them when we weren't looking.~~
All spelled out, that means: Bring back our SNACKs.

WRITING WORKSHOP **655**

REVISING AND EDITING

1. Use emotional appeals wisely. Emotional appeals persuade by creating strong feelings rather than by using facts and evidence. Such appeals include:
- **appeal to fear** message that taps into people's fear of losing their safety or security (*At least we can control the safety of food in vending machines.*)
- **appeal to pity** message that taps into people's compassion (*Students in poor families may have no food at home.*)
- **appeal to vanity** message that taps into people's desire to feel good about themselves (*Vending machines allow you to treat your friends for less than a dollar.*)

2. Shore up your support. Tell students to consider two additional factors in choosing statements that need support:
- **Is the issue identified?** Would facts, anecdotes, quotations, or sensory details clarify the background or the current situation?
- **Is the writer's position stated?** What facts, quotations, illustrations, or explanations would more clearly state the position?

3. Make it clear, so they will hear. Each paragraph has at least one sentence that clearly states either the writer's position or a reason for it. Have students refer back to the student model to see how the author began many paragraphs with the main points.

4. Sharpen your conclusion. Students may wish to review their thesis statements to be sure that their conclusions recap and emphasize the main point they were trying to make.

For interactive revision tools, see

WriteSmart CD

Writing Center at **ClassZone.com**

FOR ENGLISH LEARNERS

Writing: Count and Noncount Nouns Some students may have trouble distinguishing between countable and noncountable nouns in listing supporting information. Thus, they may try to make noncountable nouns plural. (Students need *energies.* Such people need *helps.*)

Have students work with partners to identify each word as something that can be counted or something that cannot:

- information *(noncountable)*
- pride *(noncountable)*
- fame *(noncountable)*
- changes *(countable)*
- safety *(noncountable)*
- rules *(countable)*
- advice *(noncountable)*
- students *(countable)*

You might wish to have students start Word Sorts for count and noncount nouns.

 BEST PRACTICES TOOLKIT—Transparency
Word Sorts p. E5

Preparing to Publish

Support for meeting the goals in the writing rubric is supplied throughout the Writing Workshop on pages 653–655.

For Rubric Bank, see

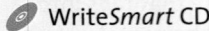 WriteSmart CD

ⓘ Writing Center at **ClassZone.com**

Assess and Reteach

ⓢ **STANDARDS LESSON FILE**

Writing Lesson 15: Writing a Thesis Statement
Writing Lesson 16: Writing Introductions
Writing Lesson 17: Writing Conclusions
Writing Lesson 30: Persuasive Writing
Grammar Lesson 20: Misplaced and Dangling Modifiers

Preparing to Publish **Persuasive Speech**

Apply the Rubric

A strong persuasive speech . . .

☑ has a strong introduction that identifies the issue and grabs listeners' attention

☑ explains the writer's claim in a clear, logical thesis statement

☑ addresses the audience directly in an appropriate tone

☑ supports ideas with convincing details, and answers opposing viewpoints

☑ uses persuasive techniques and rhetorical devices

☑ has a consistent organizational pattern

☑ concludes with a concise summary of ideas and a memorable call for action

☑ uses effective sentence types and structures

Ask a Peer Reader

• How would you restate my position on this issue?

• What details are needed to make my case stronger?

• Which of my persuasive techniques are best? Why?

Emotional Appeals

It's fine to try to create strong feelings when you deliver your speech. However, make sure your appeals don't make audience members feel manipulated.

• *Overemotional appeal to pity:* Do you want us to starve?

• *Effective appeal to pity:* Our half-hour lunch period is barely enough time to gulp down a sandwich, and we're hungry again before the next bell.

See page 596 for information on persuasive techniques.

Check Your Grammar

• Make sure that modifiers are placed near the words they modify. Misplaced modifiers confuse listeners and lessen the impact of your message.

I know that there have been some concerns (between classes) about students using the vending-machine area as a hangout. This loitering has led to congestion (and an increase in tardiness (in the hallways).

See page R59: Misplaced Modfiers

Writing Online

↱ **PUBLISHING OPTIONS**
For publishing options, visit the **Writing Center** at **ClassZone.com.**

ASSESSMENT PREPARATION
For writing and grammar assessment practice, go to the **Assessment Center** at **ClassZone.com.**

Presenting a Persuasive Speech

The hard part is over: you've already written a persuasive speech on an issue you feel strongly about. Now put your words into action by presenting them to an audience.

Planning the Speech

1. **Review your audience and purpose.** Remind yourself why you wrote your speech. Put yourself in the place of the audience members as you consider what information should be stressed and how.

2. **Support your argument with visuals.** Sara Jenkins used a poster like the one shown when she presented her speech. She also could have used a photograph of crowded lockers or a graph showing students' use of vending machines. Consider using posters, charts, graphs, or photographs to enhance your message. Mark your speech so you know when to refer to them.

3. **Take the time to rehearse.** Practice your speech alone and with friends and family. In the first case, stand in front of a mirror to see yourself as your audience will see you. In the second case, ask your audience for feedback.

S — We need Snacks during School.
N — We Need them Nearby.
A — We can Act like responsible Adults.
C — We deserve to be Consulted.
K — We Know you respect us.

Delivering the Speech

1. **Be deliberate in your delivery.** Speak slowly and pause after key ideas to allow the audience time to take in the information. Sara Jenkins paused after each of the main points shown in the poster.

2. **Connect with your audience.** When you address objections and counterclaims, make eye contact with audience members who may not agree with your ideas.

3. **Pay attention to audience reactions.** Make a mental note of techniques that do—or don't—go over well. Use what you learn this time to improve your next persuasive speech.

See page R79: Evaluate a Persuasive Speech

SPEAKING AND LISTENING

Ask students to read this page to get an overview of how to present a persuasive speech. Discuss the qualities of good visuals:

- large enough to be seen
- clear and simple
- support a point

If possible, have students listen to a well-known speech to hear the speed and the use of emphasis. Point out that speakers must give listeners time to process what they have heard.

Encourage students to mark their speeches to show points they wish to emphasize, places they will pause, and places they will refer to visuals.

Tell students to scan the audience for faces that look interested. These will encourage them, help them connect with the audience, and diminish stage fright.

Before students begin working, review this rubric with them so that they have clear goals:

Rubric A strong persuasive speech

- clearly states the writer's position on an issue
- supports that position with a variety of relevant, credible details
- presents details in an organized manner
- addresses opposing viewpoints respectfully
- includes visuals
- uses language and examples that are appropriate for the audience
- speaks clearly, using appropriate pace and volume

R RESOURCE MANAGER—Copy Master
Speaking and Listening p. 137

S STANDARDS LESSON FILE
Speaking and Listening Lesson 1: Preparing and Presenting a Speech
Speaking and Listening Lesson 8: Persuasive Speech

CHECK READINESS

Read aloud the paragraph under **ASSESS** and stress to students that this is not the full Unit Test, but a way for them to check their readiness for it. Then have students examine the skills listed under **REVIEW** and look back in the unit or in the **Student Resource Bank** for any they need to review.

READ THE SELECTIONS

Remind students to keep unit goals in mind as they read the passages, paying particular attention to these literary and reading skills:

- elements of argument
- persuasive techniques
- rhetorical devices
- fact and opinion
- summarize main idea

To help students focus on the elements and techniques of argument, encourage them to ask questions like these:

- What issue is the author writing about, and what stand does he take?
- What reasons does he give, and what evidence supports those reasons? What methods does he use to persuade readers to agree?

ANSWER THE QUESTIONS

Direct students to pages R93–R101 of the **Handbook** to review test-taking strategies.

- Tell students to always check their answers if they have time at the end of a test. First, they should make sure that they marked every answer and that they marked the intended answers. Then they should reread the answer choices for questions whose answers they were unsure of. If time allows, they should look back at the selection, because rereading may help them choose better answers than those they first chose.
- Remind students not to choose the first alternative that seems to fit when answering a multiple-choice question. Instead, they should read through all the choices, eliminate any that are clearly wrong, and then choose the *best* answer—the one that is most accurate and complete.

ASSESS
The practice test items on the next few pages match skills listed on the Unit Goals page (page 593) and addressed throughout this unit. Taking this practice test will help you assess your knowledge of these skills and determine your readiness for the Unit Test.

REVIEW
After you take the practice test, your teacher can help you identify any skills you need to review.

- Elements of Argument
- Persuasive Techniques
- Rhetorical Devices
- Fact and Opinion
- Summarize Main Idea
- Specialized and Technical Vocabulary
- Dictionary
- Imperative Sentences
- Parallelism

ASSESSMENT ONLINE
For more assessment practice and test-taking tips, go to the **Assessment Center** at ClassZone.com.

Reading Comprehension

DIRECTIONS *Read the following selection and then answer the questions.*

Appearances Are Destructive

Mark Mathabane

As public schools reopen for the new year, strategies to curb school violence will once again be hotly debated. Installing metal detectors and hiring security guards will help, but the experience of my two sisters makes a compelling case for greater use of dress codes as a way to protect students and promote learning.

Shortly after my sisters arrived here from South Africa I enrolled them at the local public school. I had great expectations for their educational experience. Compared with black schools under apartheid, American schools are Shangri-Las, with modern textbooks, school buses, computers, libraries, lunch programs and dedicated teachers.

10   But despite these benefits, which students in many parts of the world only dream about, my sisters' efforts at learning were almost derailed. They were constantly taunted for their homely outfits. A couple of times they came home in tears. In South Africa students were required to wear uniforms, so my sisters had never been preoccupied with clothes and jewelry.

They became so distraught that they insisted on transferring to different schools, despite my reassurances that there was nothing wrong with them because of what they wore.

I have visited enough public schools around the country to know that my sisters' experiences are not unique. In schools in many areas, brand names are
20   more familiar names to students than Zora Neale Hurston, Shakespeare and Faulkner. Many students seem to pay more attention to what's on their bodies than in their minds.

Teachers have shared their frustrations with me at being unable to teach those students willing to learn because classes are frequently disrupted by other students ogling themselves in mirrors, painting their fingernails, combing their hair, shining their gigantic shoes, or comparing designer labels on jackets, caps and jewelry.

The fiercest competition among students is often not over academic achievements, but over who dresses most expensively. And many students now
30   measure parental love by how willing their mothers and fathers are to pamper them with money for the latest fads in clothes, sneakers and jewelry.

Those parents without the money to waste on such meretricious extravagances are considered uncaring and cruel. They often watch in dismay and helplessness as their children become involved with gangs and peddle drugs to raise the money.

658   UNIT 6: ARGUMENT AND PERSUASION

DIFFERENTIATED INSTRUCTION

FOR ENGLISH LEARNERS
Assessment Practice: Work Backward Tell students to prepare by reading the questions before they read the passages. Have pairs find unfamiliar words in test directions and questions and follow these steps:

1. Write each word on an index card.
2. Find the meaning in a dictionary and write it on the back of the card.
3. Use the cards to practice words with partners and to teach them to others.

Culture: Clarify Write *dress codes* (line 4) on the board and explain that dress codes are sets of rules that govern how someone should dress. Provide examples, such as:

- Students must wear shirts.
- Students may not wear tank tops.
- Students must wear something on their feet.

Ask students to provide additional examples. Discuss reasons why schools might institute dress codes or decide not to have them.

When students are asked why they attach so much importance to clothing, they frequently reply that it's the cool thing to do, that it gives them status and earns them respect. And clothes are also used to send other messages, with girls thinking that the only things that make them attractive to boys are skimpy
40 dresses and gaudy looks, rather than intelligence and academic excellence.

The argument by civil libertarians that dress codes infringe on freedom of expression is misleading. We observe dress codes in nearly every aspect of our lives without any diminution of our freedoms—as demonstrated by flight attendants, bus drivers, postal employees, high school bands, military personnel, sports teams, Girl and Boy Scouts, employees of fast-food chains, restaurants and hotels.

In many countries where students outperform their American counterparts academically, school dress codes are observed as part of creating the proper learning environment. Their students tend to be neater, less disruptive in
50 class and more disciplined, mainly because their minds are focused more on learning and less on materialism.

It's time Americans realized that the benefits of safe and effective schools far outweigh any perceived curtailment of freedom of expression brought on by dress codes.

 GO ON

ITEM ANALYSIS

COMPREHENSION AND WRITTEN RESPONSE	ITEMS	UNIT PAGES
Elements of Argument	1, 2, 6, 11, 12, 16	594–599, 601
Persuasive Techniques	8, 10, 15	594–599, 611
Rhetorical Devices	4, 7, 9	601, 633
Fact and Opinion	3, 13, 14	621
Summarize Main Idea	1, 5, 9, 16	611

VOCABULARY	ITEMS	UNIT PAGES
Technical/Specialized Vocabulary	1, 2, 3	609, 632
Dictionary	4, 5, 6	618

WRITING AND GRAMMAR	ITEMS	UNIT PAGES
Imperative Sentences	2, 3	619
Parallelism	1, 4	601

FOR LESS–PROFICIENT WRITERS

Assessment Support Consider these options for completing the Assessment Practice:

- Have students "work backward" to review the test questions before reading the passage.
- Select random questions in the Assessment, and have students demonstrate how and where to look for the answers.

- Ask students to locate unfamiliar vocabulary words in the Assessment. Elicit their meanings from the class.
- Have students record useful testing words and definitions in their journals for later reference.
- Read the selection or parts of it aloud to aid in student comprehension.

McDougal Littell
Assessment System

After checking student readiness with this Assessment Practice, you may administer the complete Unit 6 Test in order to more thoroughly evaluate student mastery of unit goals.

Comprehension

Model a thinking process for answering multiple-choice questions.

1. **C is correct.** *It is the only answer choice supported by all of the paragraphs. A, B, and D are all details that support other ideas.*

2. **A is correct.** *The author tells what happened to his sisters. B and C are incorrect, because the author does not use statistics or deduction. D is incorrect, since no objections have been raised yet.*

3. **D is correct.** *This statement is an opinion that cannot be proved. A, B, and C are facts that can be proved or verified.*

4. **B is correct.** *The phrase "on their bodies" parallels the phrase "in their minds." A, C, and D are incorrect, because the lines do not have repetition, analogy, or rhetorical questions.*

5. **C is correct.** *It sums up what happened in the identified lines. A and D are incorrect, because they are only individual details. Although B is a reasonable inference, it is a detail, not a summary.*

6. **A is correct.** *The author uses teachers' statements to support his claim. B is incorrect because students' views are brought up later in the selection. C is incorrect because parents' views are inferred. D is incorrect because the author never mentions polls.*

7. **C is correct.** *The verb forms are repeated, which emphasizes what actions disrupt classes. A is not mentioned in the specified lines. Although these lines address one part of the relationship between students and teachers, the parallel verbs do not, so B is incorrect. D is incorrect because it reflects only one disruptive action, comparing designer labels.*

8. **A is correct.** *The word* fierce *suggests intensity and strength. B and C are relatively neutral words. Although* expensively *makes a judgment, the word is not emotionally charged, so D is incorrect.*

9. **D is correct.** *This answer is the only statement that sums up the statements in all the lines. A, B, and C do not relate to any statements, so they are incorrect.*

Comprehension

DIRECTIONS *Answer these questions about the selection.*

1. What is the author's main claim in this selection?
   A Teens demand too much money from their parents.
   B Schools need metal detectors and guards to curb school violence.
   C Dress codes will help protect students and promote learning.
   D American schools offer more advantages than South African schools.

2. In lines 10–19, the author supports his claim by
   A stating personal experience and observation
   B citing statistics about transfer students
   C using logical reasoning and deductions
   D countering the opposition's objections

3. Which of the following statements is an opinion?
   A "Shortly after my sisters arrived here from South Africa, I enrolled them at the local public school."
   B "A couple of times they came home in tears."
   C "I have visited enough public schools around the country. . . ."
   D "Many students seem to pay more attention to what's on their bodies than in their minds."

4. Which rhetorical device is used in the following sentence from lines 21–22?
   Many students seem to pay more attention to what's on their bodies than in their minds.
   A repetition
   B parallelism
   C analogy
   D rhetorical question

5. Which sentence summarizes lines 10–17?
   A The sisters often came home in tears from their new American school.
   B In South Africa, wearing uniforms improves the educational experience.
   C Being teased about their clothes ruined the sisters' experience.
   D There was nothing wrong with the sisters' clothing.

6. In lines 23–27, what new source of evidence does the author introduce to support his claim?
   A teachers
   B students
   C parents
   D polls

7. Parallelism is used in lines 23–27 to emphasize the
   A differences in the clothing students wear to school
   B relationship between the teachers and the students
   C disruption caused by the students' behavior
   D items with designer labels worn by the students

8. Which word in lines 28–29 gives strong emotional meaning to the author's opinion?
   A fiercest
   B academic
   C competition
   D expensively

10. **B is correct.** *The author shows that scary things, including involvement with gangs and drugs, can happen as a result of the emphasis on appearance. A is incorrect, because the author never appeals to readers' vanity. C and D are incorrect, because no group is described that readers would want to associate with.*

11. **C is correct.** *The author states this argument in the first sentence. A is incorrect, because it is not stated. B and D are both incorrect, because they are evidence used to support the author's position; neither is an opposing argument.*

12. **B is correct.** *This answer summarizes the author's response to the opposing argument. A, C, and D are incorrect because they represent unsupported opinions that the author never states.*

9. Which sentence summarizes the relationship between students and their parents, according to the author in lines 28–31?

A Students and their parents care more about clothes than about grades.

B Parents will do anything to help their children become popular.

C Parents reward their children when they do well in school.

D Students judge their parents by how much money the parents give them.

10. What persuasive technique does the author use in lines 32–35?

A emotional (vanity)

B emotional (fear)

C association (bandwagon)

D association ("plain folks")

11. What opposing argument does the author anticipate in lines 41–46?

A Our opinions affect how we view wearing uniforms.

B Our freedoms are not affected by dress codes.

C Dress codes reduce our freedom of expression.

D Many people observe dress codes for their jobs.

12. What evidence does the author present to counter the opposing argument in lines 41–46?

A Too many people are forced to follow dress codes for their jobs.

B People throughout our society follow dress codes without losing their freedom of expression.

C Civil libertarians have a fundamental misunderstanding of what freedom of expression means.

D Dress codes diminish our freedoms not just in school but also in sports and business.

13. Which of the following ideas from lines 47–51 is the author's opinion?

A In many countries, students perform better than Americans in school subjects.

B Schools in many countries of the world have dress codes.

C American students have academic counterparts in other countries.

D Students in other countries learn well because their minds are focused less on materialism.

Written Response

SHORT RESPONSE
Write three or four sentences to answer each question.

14. List three facts that the author uses in the essay to support his claim. List two opinions that the author uses to support his claim.

15. Give two examples of loaded language from the essay. Then replace each one with a neutral word or phrase.

EXTENDED RESPONSE
Write two or three paragraphs to answer the question.

16. Summarize the essay in your own words. Be sure to identify the claim, or main idea. Include reasons and evidence the author gives to support his claim.

GO ON →

661

13. **D is correct.** *It is the only opinion among the answer choices. A, B, and C are facts that can be proved.*

Written Response
Possible short responses:

14. *Facts: The author's sisters were taunted for their homely outfits (lines 11–12). Many people in the U.S. observe dress codes (lines 42–46). Students from many other countries wear uniforms and outperform American students academically (lines 47–49). Opinions: Because students seem to pay more attention to what they wear, they are not concerned with thinking or learning (lines 19–22). Students measure how much their parents love them by how much money the parents give them for clothing (lines 29–31). Students in other countries learn well because they are not thinking about clothes (lines 49–51).*

15. *Examples of loaded language include "meretricious extravagances" (lines 32–33), which could be replaced with expensive clothing; "skimpy" (line 39), which could be replaced with fashionable or summer; and "gaudy" (line 40), which could be replaced with colorful or stylish.*

Possible extended response:

16. *The response should include the main argument that school uniforms protect students and promote learning. It should list reasons that support this claim, such as the disruption caused by the emphasis on designer clothing, the fact that students with dress codes in other countries make better grades, and the fact that some students break the law to earn money for clothes. The response may end with the point that uniforms are required in many walks of life.*

DIFFERENTIATED INSTRUCTION

FOR ENGLISH LEARNERS
Review Academic Vocabulary List the italicized academic vocabulary on the board. Give examples in random order and have students match them with the terms. Elicit additional examples from students.

- *claim:* Schools should start later in the day.
- *summary:* Students often own a variety of footwear, including sneakers, sandals, and dress shoes.
- *fact:* July 4 is a holiday in the United States.

- *rhetorical device:* Why would students do this?
- *parallelism:* Students enjoy looking at clothes and trying on clothes.
- *specialized vocabulary:* Although the sneaker's shoelace is white, the aglet on the lace is red.
- *synonym:* The shoes are scarlet, or ruby, colored.
- *imperative sentence:* Wear a jacket.

Vocabulary

1. **C is correct.** *Since the term is followed by details that you might expect in a perfect school, Shangri-La must be a wonderful place. This eliminates A and B. D is not a good choice, because* suitable *is only average and not wonderful.*

2. **D is correct.** *The context mentions a concern with freedom of expression, which has to do with an individual's rights. Although A uses the term* express, *it has nothing to do with freedom. B and D have nothing to do with freedom of expression.*

3. **A is correct.** *The context specifically mentions dress codes, which limit what a person can wear. B and D are unrelated to clothing, and C involves being free* not *to buy clothes, so it is incorrect.*

4. **A is correct.** *The word* advantages *could be substituted for* benefits *in the sentence, and it would still make sense. None of the other choices makes sense in the context of the sentence.*

5. **B is correct.** Assistance *is the best answer, since the government has helped someone buy groceries in an emergency. A and C are incorrect, because groceries are a necessity, not a gain or profit. Although* advantage *can be a synonym for* benefits, *this meaning does not match the meaning of* benefits *as it is used in the example.*

6. **B is correct.** Everyone *is the subject of the sentence, and* benefits *is the verb.* Benefits *is used as a noun in A, C, and D. In A and D, it is the direct object of the main verb, and in C it is the subject of the sentence.*

Vocabulary

DIRECTIONS *Use context clues and your knowledge of specialized vocabularies to answer the following questions.*

> Compared with black schools under apartheid, American schools are <u>Shangri-Las</u>, with modern textbooks, school buses, computers, libraries, lunch programs and dedicated teachers.

1. What is the most likely meaning of *Shangri-Las* in lines 7–8 of the essay?
   - **A** flawed institutions
   - **B** average schools
   - **C** ideal places
   - **D** suitable locales

> The argument by <u>civil libertarians</u> that dress codes infringe on <u>freedom of expression</u> is misleading.

2. What does the term *civil libertarians* mean in line 41 of the essay?
   - **A** writers and artists who express themselves
   - **B** designers of casual and professional clothing
   - **C** enforcers of school safety requirements
   - **D** protectors of individuals' rights

3. There are many ways of defining the term *freedom of expression.* Choose the definition that best defines *freedom of expression* as it is used in lines 41–42.
   - **A** freedom to dress as one pleases
   - **B** freedom to speak or write anything
   - **C** freedom from spending money on outfits
   - **D** freedom from popularity contests

DIRECTIONS *Read this dictionary entry and answer the questions that follow.*

> **benefit** (bĕn´ə-fĭt) *noun* **1.** An advantage. **2.** A payment made or an entitlement available in accordance with a wage agreement, an insurance policy, or a public assistance program. **3.** A fund-raising public entertainment. **4.** *Archaic* A kindly deed. *verb* **1.** To be helpful or advantageous to. **2.** To derive benefit; profit. [From Latin *benefactum,* good deed.]
> **Synonyms:** *noun:* advantage, subsidy, assistance; *verb:* capitalize, profit, help, gain

4. Which definition best matches the meaning of the word *benefits* as it is used in line 10 of the essay?
   - **A** noun definition 1
   - **B** noun definition 2
   - **C** noun definition 3
   - **D** noun definition 4

5. Which word is a synonym for the word *benefits* in the following sentence?
   They bought groceries with the emergency government <u>benefits</u>.
   - **A** gains
   - **B** assistance
   - **C** profit
   - **D** advantage

6. In which sentence is the word *benefits* used as a verb?
   - **A** We are organizing three <u>benefits</u> to raise money for the zoo.
   - **B** Everyone <u>benefits</u> when students love learning and are focused on academic success.
   - **C** The <u>benefits</u> of good health should be taught to children at a young age.
   - **D** The company's profits boosted the <u>benefits</u> that all of the employees received.

DIFFERENTIATED INSTRUCTION

FOR ENGLISH LEARNERS

Assessment Vocabulary: Understanding Instructions Read aloud instructions that identify lines or that indicate specific information that students should include when taking a test. After each set of instructions, ask students how they might proceed. Help them develop useful strategies. For example, suppose you read aloud item 4 on page 660. Students might

- recall the definition of *rhetorical device*

- read the sentence
- read all the answer choices
- choose the best answer

Follow a similar procedure with the writing and vocabulary questions. For example, if you read aloud item 4 on this page, students might

- read the dictionary entry
- find *benefit* on line 10 of the essay
- read all the answer choices
- look at the dictionary entry again
- select the best answer

Grammar & Style

DIRECTIONS *Read this passage and answer the questions that follow.*

> (1) Why are people so afraid of stepping outside their social circles? (2) Every day in class, I notice how students congregate in separate groups. (3) Cheerleaders are in one corner. (4) There are art students who are in another corner. (5) Even though we might have different interests, that doesn't mean we can't try to find some common ground. (6) Breaking out of your mold can be good for you. (7) I recommend that you try speaking to someone you don't usually speak to. (8) Just go up to someone and start a conversation. (9) You might find that it's not so bad. (10) It's even possible that the two of you might like each other.

1. Choose how to rewrite sentence 4 so that its structure is parallel to that of sentence 3.
   - **A** Art students, who are in another group, also stand in a corner.
   - **B** Art students are in another corner.
   - **C** In another corner are art students.
   - **D** Art students, who are in another corner, are in a different group.

2. Choose how to rewrite sentence 6 as an imperative sentence.
   - **A** Sometimes it's good to break out of your mold.
   - **B** Why not break out of your mold?
   - **C** Molds are meant to be broken.
   - **D** Break out of your mold.

3. Choose how to rewrite sentence 7 as an imperative sentence.
   - **A** Speaking to someone you don't usually speak to is a good idea.
   - **B** What's wrong with speaking to someone you don't usually speak to?
   - **C** Try speaking to someone you don't usually speak to.
   - **D** Why don't you try speaking to someone you don't usually speak to?

4. Choose how to rewrite sentence 10 so that its structure is parallel to that of sentence 9.
   - **A** You might even find that the two of you like each other!
   - **B** That the two of you might like each other is a possibility.
   - **C** How could you not like each other?
   - **D** It would be impossible that the two of you wouldn't like each other.

STOP

ANSWERS
Grammar & Style

1. **B is correct.** *Sentence 3 contains just a subject followed by* are *followed by a prepositional phrase. Only B presents a sentence with the same form. A, C, and D have different grammatical patterns, so they are incorrect.*

2. **D is correct.** *Only D is an imperative sentence. A and C are both declarative sentences; they make statements. B asks a question.*

3. **C is correct.** *It is the only imperative sentence among the answer choices. A is a declarative sentence with the subject* Speaking to someone you don't usually speak to. *B and D are both questions, so they are incorrect.*

4. **A is correct.** *Sentence 9 begins with the words* You might find *followed by a noun clause. Only one answer choice follows that pattern. B begins with a noun clause; C is a question. Although D follows a similar pattern, the phrasing of the subject is different: the subject is* it *rather than* you.

FOR LESS-PROFICIENT READERS
Assessment Support: Parallel Structure
Remind students that writers use parallel structure, or similar grammatical forms, to express related ideas. Have them identify the parallel elements in these sentences:

- Cara likes *to sing, to dance,* and *to paint.*
- *Every morning, Van walks to school,* and *every afternoon he walks to work.*

Assessment Support: Imperative Sentences
Explain that an imperative sentence is a command or a request. Often, the subject of an imperative sentence is assumed to be *you.* Offer an example, such as *Sit next to me at lunch.* Then ask students to make up imperative sentences for these situations:

- if they want to be awakened at a certain time
- if they want a friend to call after school
- if they want a closer look at someone's ring

INTRODUCE *GREAT READS*

In Unit 6, students have discussed a number of big questions. Invite students to tell which question they found most intriguing and why, and then focus attention on the three that appear on this page. Discuss the recommended books and their summaries, pointing out how each connects to the related question. Encourage students to choose one or more of these "great reads" to read independently.

ⓘ ClassZone.com

To find additional books that match students' interests and ability levels, visit the Literature Center at **ClassZone.com**.

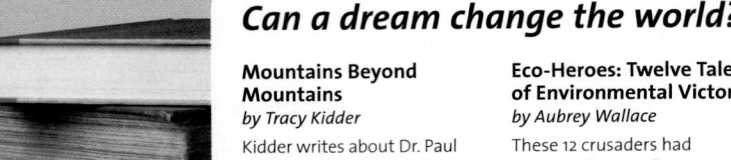

UNIT 6 Great Reads

Ideas for Independent Reading

How do you persuade others that your ideas have value? Read the following works to see how various individuals made their case.

Can a dream change the world?

Mountains Beyond Mountains
by Tracy Kidder

Kidder writes about Dr. Paul Farmer, whose dream of medical care as a human right—untied to financial status—has taken root in places such as Haiti, Russian and Peruvian prisons, and inner-city Boston.

Eco-Heroes: Twelve Tales of Environmental Victory
by Aubrey Wallace

These 12 crusaders had dreams of saving forests, cleaning up toxic waste, and preventing the slaughter of dolphins. All 12 have motivated others to dream and to work for change.

Eyes on the Prize: America's Civil Rights Years, 1954–1965
by Juan Williams

The dream to end Jim Crow segregation has deep roots. This book chronicles *Brown v. Board of Education*, the Montgomery bus boycott, sit-ins and freedom rides, and the courage of those engaged in the struggle.

How do you sell an idea?

Silent Spring
by Rachel Carson

In this groundbreaking book, Carson brought to the world's attention the fragility of our modern-day environment.

Still Me
by Christopher Reeve

Severely paralyzed in an accident, popular actor Reeve wrote and spoke eloquently about his condition. His activism led to increased research and breakthroughs in treating spinal cord injuries.

How the Other Half Lives
by Jacob Riis

Riis's writings and photographs of the poor in New York tenements of the late 19th century led to social reforms in the areas housing and fire prevention.

Is privacy an illusion?

The Right to Privacy
by Ellen Alderman and Caroline Kennedy

The authors present an overview of the ways in which our privacy has been invaded over the years, including the recent threats to privacy posed by cyberspace.

The Firm
by John Grisham

In this contemporary thriller, Mitch McDeere begins his legal career with a firm that seems to offer him everything—until he and his wife learn that their every move is under surveillance.

1984
by George Orwell

This novel portrays a chilling vision of a totalitarian society, a world in which the government can control individual thought and even reality itself.

664 UNIT 6: ARGUMENT AND PERSUASION

UNIT 7

Special Effects

THE LANGUAGE
OF POETRY

665

About the Art Christopher Myers created this image for his book *Wings* in 2000. For more information, see page 704.

For help with this unit, see

 RESOURCE MANAGER UNIT 7
pp. 1–11

INTRODUCE THE UNIT

When you hear the term *special effects,* you may think of *Star Wars, The Lord of the Rings,* or another blockbuster action movie. Moviemakers have their own bag of tricks to make ideas seem real or fantastic, but moviemaking is not the only genre to use special effects. Indeed, many people feel that poetry is the most effective of all genres for making unreal things seem real. Poets use imaginative language to evoke intense emotion, to help readers visualize improbable scenes, and to glorify even common objects. In poetry, language is the medium for creating special effects.

Invite students to consider how the term *special effects* applies to the images on this page. Ask:

- Which picture makes an impossible thing seem real?
- How is the boy in the artwork like the butterfly?
- What makes the photograph of the butterfly special?
- In what way is each image inspirational?

Explain to students that as they read the selections in this unit, they will see how the **language of poetry** creates special effects. They will learn to recognize and use these techniques—and, as a result, they will gain a greater appreciation for this special genre.

UNIT 7

Skills Trace

SKILLS STRAND	Literary Analysis Workshop: The Language of Poetry pp. 668–675	My Papa's Waltz/I Ask My Mother to Sing/ Grape Sherbet pp. 676–683 Poems *Level: Average*	Spring is like a perhaps hand/Elegy for the Giant Tortoises/Today pp. 684–691 Poems *Level: Average*	Linked selections 400-Meter Free Style/ Body Builders' Contest pp. 692–697 Concrete Poems *Level: Average*	The Night Poetry Rocked the House pp. 698–701 Magazine Article *Level: Average*
Literary Analysis	Form pp. 668–669, 674–675 Poetic Elements pp. 670–671, 674–675 Imagery and Figurative Language pp. 672–673, 674–675	Characteristics of Lyric Poetry pp. 677, 678, 681, 682 Imagery pp. 677, 680, 682	Characteristics of an Elegy pp. 685, 688, 691 Diction pp. 685, 686, 689, 691	Characteristics of Concrete Poetry pp. 693, 695, 697 Form pp. 693, 694, 696, 697	
Reading and Informational Texts	Analyze the Literature pp. 669, 671, 673, 674–675	Make Inferences pp. 677, 680, 681, 682	Paraphrase pp. 685, 688, 691 Read a Magazine Article p. 690	Connect pp. 693, 694, 697	Synthesize pp. 698, 699, 700, 701 Support an Opinion p. 701 Read a Magazine Article p. 699
Vocabulary	Academic Vocabulary pp. 668, 670–674				
Writing, Grammar, and Style		Descriptive Language p. 683 Participles and Participial Phrases p. 683			
Speaking, Listening, Viewing, and Media	Discuss pp. 668–673	Discuss pp. 676, T678–T681, 682 Analyze Visuals pp. 678, T680, T681	Discuss pp. 684, T686–T690, 691 Analyze Visuals pp. 686, T688, T689	Discuss pp. 692, T694–T696, 697 Analyze Visuals pp. T695, 696	Discuss pp. 698, T699–T700, 701

Assessment-Based Planning: Skills in red are assessed on the Unit 7 Test. **T** = Teacher's Edition page

For Poets/Ode to My Socks/egg horror poem pp. 702–713	O What Is That Sound pp. 714–719	The Seven Ages of Man/ The Road Not Taken pp. 720–725	Writing Workshop: Personal Response to a Poem pp. 726–733	Skills Assessed on the Unit 7 Test:
Poems *Level: Average*	Ballad *Level: Challenging*	Dramatic Monologue/Poem *Level: Challenging*		**Literary Analysis** • Analyze poetic structure and form • Analyze figurative language and imagery • Analyze sound devices • Analyze diction and its effects • Analyze tone
Characteristics of an Ode pp. 703, 709, 712 Figurative Language pp. 703, 704, 706, 707, 710, 712	Characteristics of a Ballad pp. 715, 718, 719 Sound Devices pp. 715, 716, 718, 719	Characteristics of a Dramatic Monologue pp. 721, 722, 725 Meter pp. 721, 723, 724, 725 Review: Rhyme Scheme pp. 722, 724		
Visualize pp. 703, 704, 708, 711, 712	Analyze Speakers pp. 715, 716, 719	Analyze Ideas in Poetry pp. 721, 724, 725	Analyze a Personal Response Essay pp. 727–728, 732	**Reading and Informational Texts** • Visualize • Make inferences • Paraphrase • Support an opinion • Analyze ideas in poetry
Conciseness p. 713 Infinitives and Infinitive Phrases p. 713			Write a Personal Response to a Poem pp. 726–732 Correction of Fragments p. 732 Active and Passive Voice p. 732	**Writing, Grammar, and Style** • Write a personal response to a poem • Use descriptive language, including participles and participial phrases • Write concisely, using infinitives and infinitive phrases • Additional writing and grammar skills
Discuss pp. 702, T704–T711, 712 Analyze Visuals p. 704	Discuss pp. 714, T716–T718, 719 Analyze Visuals p. 716	Discuss pp. 720, T722–T724, 725 Analyze Visuals pp. 723, T724	Discuss pp. T726–T728, 732 Create a Multimedia Presentation p. 733	

For additional lesson planning help, see **Easy Planner DVD.**

OBJECTIVES

- establish prior knowledge about poetry
- recall and discuss a favorite **poem**

What POEMS *do you remember?*

To introduce the page and illustrate the question, recite the opening lyrics of a few familiar songs, such as "This Land Is Your Land" and "You Are My Sunshine." Call on volunteers to answer each question. After students have read the paragraph, ask them why these songs—these poems set to music—are easy to remember. ***Possible answers:*** *The lines have a catchy rhythm or interesting rhymes; they bring a happy occasion to mind; they have been heard so often that they are hard to forget.*

ACTIVITY Point out that students need not choose a literary "classic"; rather, their choice should be a poem that is meaningful to them and that they can recite easily. As students share and discuss their examples, ask them to note the common qualities. Urge them to look for those qualities to reappear in the selections in this unit.

CHECK UNDERSTANDING Have students write a one- or two-sentence summary that explains why the **poem** they chose is a favorite.

What POEMS *do you remember?*

Snippets of a nursery rhyme, verses from a favorite bedtime story, lines from an old favorite song or commercial jingle—chances are that the words from these **poems** linger in your memory because you have heard them over and over again.

ACTIVITY Write down the words to one of your favorite poems. Choose from poems you have read, heard, or memorized. Answer the following questions:

- What is your poem about?
- Has it been set to music?
- Are there any words that rhyme or repeat?
- Do you picture anything when you read or hear the poem?
- What is your favorite part of the poem?

Discuss with your classmates the qualities your favorites have in common.

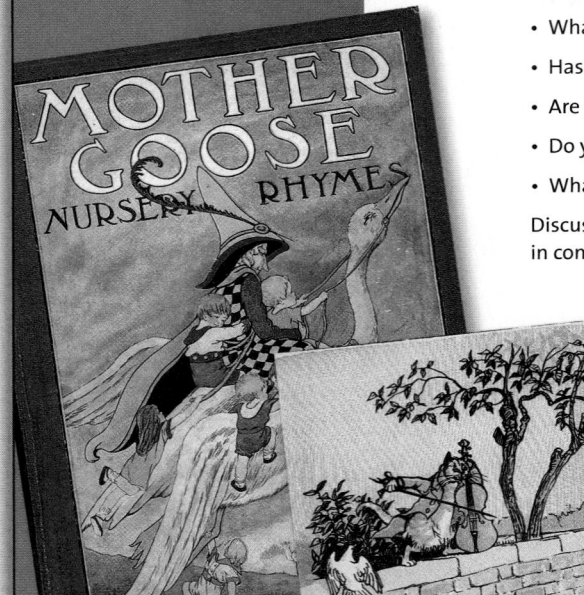

666

Unit Resources

 **RESOURCE MANAGER UNIT 7**

 **BEST PRACTICES TOOLKIT**

S **STANDARDS LESSON FILE**

- Easy Planner DVD-ROM
- Write*Smart* CD-ROM
- ClassZone.com
- Audio Anthology CD
- Multi-Language Academic Vocabulary Online

- eEdition DVD-ROM & Online
- McDougal Littell Assessment System
- Test Generator CD
- Media*Smart* DVD-ROM

 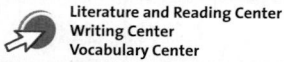

Preview Unit Goals

LITERARY ANALYSIS	• Recognize characteristics of a variety of forms of poetry, including lyric poetry, elegy, concrete poetry, ode, ballad, dramatic monologue, sonnet, free verse
	• Analyze form, including line and stanza
	• Analyze figurative language, including metaphor, simile, and personification; analyze imagery
	• Analyze sound devices, including repetition, alliteration, assonance, onomatopoeia, rhyme, rhythm, and meter
	• Analyze speaker
READING	• Use reading strategies, including visualizing and connecting
	• Make inferences
	• Synthesize ideas from multiple sources; paraphrase
WRITING AND GRAMMAR	• Write a personal response
	• Support key ideas with details and quotations
	• Use descriptive language effectively; write concisely
	• Use participles and participial phrases
	• Use infinitives and infinitive phrases
SPEAKING, LISTENING, AND VIEWING	• Create a multimedia presentation
ACADEMIC VOCABULARY	• line • imagery
	• stanza • visualize
	• figurative language • synthesize
	• sound devices • paraphrase
	• speaker

Preview Unit Goals

The goals on this page present an overview of this unit's skills and strategies. Encourage students to preview the skills as they prepare for the upcoming selections. Remind students that the colors for each skill strand create a code that students can track throughout the unit.

Draw students' attention to the Academic Vocabulary on the page. Students may find some of these words familiar, but they should try to record definitions that are relevant to the unit's discussion of poetry. Ask students to add these terms to their journals and to keep them in mind as they discuss and write about the poems that they read.

ADDITIONAL UNIT GOALS

These skills will be taught in this unit but are not the major focus of the unit:

Literary Analysis
• Analyze traditional vs. organic poetic forms
• Analyze hyperbole
• Analyze consonance and rhyme scheme
• Analyze diction and its effects
• Genre study: magazine article

Reading
• Read poetry strategically
• Analyze ideas in poetry
• Support an opinion
• Understand the function of a sidebar

Writing and Grammar
• Incorporate details (verbs)
• Use complete sentences
• Use active voice

DIFFERENTIATED INSTRUCTION

FOR ENGLISH LEARNERS

Academic Vocabulary Use the copy master to help students learn the Academic Vocabulary listed on this page.

1. Read aloud each term. Have students find it on their copy master.

2. Discuss the meanings or examples shown, and complete the chart as a class.

3. Have students work in small groups to complete the remaining activities.

Additional Academic Vocabulary Use the copy master to help students learn academic words they will use in subsequent lessons and on the Assessment Practice. Follow the same procedure as for the Academic Vocabulary copy master.

 RESOURCE MANAGER—Copy Masters
Academic Vocabulary p. 9
Additional Academic Vocabulary p. 10

Focus and Motivate

OBJECTIVES

- analyze traditional and organic form
- analyze meter and sound devices
- analyze imagery and figurative language

Teach

Part 1: Form

Traditional Poetry Read the Dickinson poem aloud, then explain that traditional poems are popular because of their regular, predictable rhythm and rhyme. Point out that other forms of traditional poetry also follow "rules," but these rules are more complex. Elicit or provide brief definitions and examples of these forms:

- *epic:* a long, narrative poem; examples: Homer's *Odyssey, The Song of Hiawatha*
- *ode:* a meditative or commemorative lyric poem; examples: poems of Keats and Shelley
- *ballad:* a narrative poem written to be sung or recited; example: Longfellow's *The Wreck of the Hesperus*
- *sonnet:* a 14-line poem having a set pattern of rhythm and rhyme; example: Shake-speare's sonnets
- *haiku:* a form of Japanese poetry having a set number of lines and syllables; example: poems of Basho Matsuo
- *limerick:* a light or humorous poem with a particular rhyme scheme; example: Ogden Nash's *Requiem*

Organic Poetry Explain that organic poetry is unpredictable; it doesn't follow the rules of traditional poetry. Elicit or provide brief definitions and examples of these forms:

- *free verse:* poetry that does not have regular meter
- *concrete poetry:* poetry that conveys meaning visually through the arrangement of letters and words

As students explore traditional and organic poetry, they may want to use a Classification Chart to record differences between the two forms.

 BEST PRACTICES TOOLKIT—Transparencies
Classification Chart p. B17

Analysis Frame: Poetic Form and Structure pp. D21, D40

The Language of Poetry

The poet Samuel Taylor Coleridge once described poetry as "the best words in their best order." Poets sear images into readers' minds, create unforgettable rhythms, and experiment with poetic forms. Whether they embrace the traditional rules of poetry, play with them, or break them altogether, poets use the techniques of their craft to inspire readers and communicate ideas. Experience these techniques in action by immersing yourself in the poetry of this unit.

Part 1: Form

Poetry is as much about form as it is about language and sound. *Form* refers to a poem's structure, or the way the words are arranged on the page. All poems are made up of series of **lines.** The length of the lines, where they break, and how they are punctuated all contribute to a poem's rhythm and meaning. In many poems, the lines are grouped into **stanzas,** which function like paragraphs in prose. Each stanza plays a part in conveying the overall message of a poem.

Poems come in a variety of forms, but they are usually talked about in terms of two categories—traditional and organic.

TRADITIONAL	ORGANIC
Characteristics  • follows fixed rules, such as a specified number of lines • has a regular pattern of rhythm and/or rhyme	**Characteristics** • does not follow established rules for form • does not have a regular pattern of rhythm and may not rhyme at all • may use unconventional spelling, punctuation, and grammar
▼	▼
Forms epic, ode, ballad, sonnet, haiku, limerick	**Forms** free verse, concrete poetry
▼	▼
Example Surgeons must be very careful When they take the knife! Underneath their fine incisions Stirs the Culprit—*Life!* —by Emily Dickinson	**Example** we're everyanything more than believe (with a spin leap alive we're alive) we're wonderful one times one —from "If Everything Happens That Can't Be Done" by E. E. Cummings

---

DIFFERENTIATED INSTRUCTION

For general guidelines on differentiating instruction, see

 BEST PRACTICES TOOLKIT
Differentiated Instruction pp. 31–38

FOR LESS–PROFICIENT READERS

Note Taking For students who need help with note taking, hand out the note-taking copy master before reading the page. Have students read each paragraph silently. Then,

as you discuss the main points of the text, have students complete the copy master.

 RESOURCE MANAGER—Copy Master
Note Taking p. 15

FOR ADVANCED LEARNERS/PRE–AP

Explore Forms Have students work independently to identify examples of the forms listed in the chart. Ask them to share their favorite examples with the class.

MODEL 1: TRADITIONAL FORM

For centuries, poets have written sonnets that explore everything from unrequited love to the mysteries of nature. There are several types of sonnets, but all of them have 14 lines and are written in a strict pattern of rhythm and rhyme. Read this poem, which is a **Petrarchan sonnet,** to determine the characteristics of this particular form.

Pretty Words
Poem by **Elinor Wylie**

Poets make pets of pretty, docile words:
I love smooth words, like gold-enamelled fish
Which circle slowly with a silken swish,
And tender ones, like downy-feathered birds:
5 Words shy and dappled, deep-eyed deer in herds,
Come to my hand, and playful if I wish,
Or purring softly at a silver dish,
Blue Persian kittens, fed on cream and curds.

I love bright words, words up and singing early;
10 Words that are luminous in the dark, and sing;
Warm lazy words, white cattle under trees;
I love words opalescent, cool, and pearly,
Like midsummer moths, and honied words like bees,
Gilded and sticky, with a little sting.

Close Read

1. How many lines make up the first stanza? How many are in the second stanza?

2. In the first stanza, each group of end-rhyming words is highlighted in the same color. Identify the end-rhyming words in the second stanza.

3. Compare the ideas expressed in the first stanza with those in the second one.

MODEL 2: ORGANIC FORM

Poems written in **free verse,** like the one shown, do not adhere to a regular pattern of rhythm and rhyme.

from **Beware: Do Not Read This Poem**
Poem by **Ishmael Reed**

the hunger of this poem is legendary
it has taken in many victims
back off from this poem
it has drawn in yr feet
5 back off from this poem
it has drawn in yr legs
back off from this poem

Close Read

1. Identify three characteristics that make this poem unconventional.

2. Even though the poet does not use punctuation, this poem has a natural rhythm. Read the poem aloud, using the rhythm you think is appropriate.

MODEL 1: TRADITIONAL FORM
Close Read

1. *There are eight lines in the first stanza, six in the second.*

2. *The end-rhyming words in the second stanza are "early" (line 9) and "pearly" (line 12); "trees" (line 11) and "bees" (line 13); "sing" (line 10) and "sting" (line 14).*

3. *Possible answer: In the first stanza, the poet expresses her love of "pretty, docile words"—words that are "smooth," "tender," "shy and dappled." In the second stanza, the poet expresses her love of "bright words"— words that "are luminous ... opalescent ... with a little sting." In both stanzas, she uses similes and metaphors to compare words to animals.*

MODEL 2: ORGANIC FORM
Close Read

1. *Possible answers: The poem has no punctuation or capitalization; the word your is abbreviated as "yr" (lines 4 and 6); the poem does not rhyme; the lines do not have a consistent pattern of syllables.*

2. *Possible answer: Make sure students' readings emphasize the staccato, pronounced rhythm that results from the end-stopped nature of the lines and the repetition of "back off from this poem."*

FOR LESS–PROFICIENT READERS

Language: Modifiers Call attention to the poet's use of adjectives in "Pretty Words" to describe words that she loves. Have students identify places where she uses pairs of adjectives (lines 1, 5, 11, 12, 14) and hyphenated adjectives (lines 2, 4, 5). Help students link each modifier to the noun it describes. Then discuss how the poet's careful choice of descriptive words helps to create images that convey her meaning.

FOR ADVANCED LEARNERS/PRE–AP

Synthesize: Free Verse Challenge students to write a free-verse poem about a person they admire. Encourage them to give their poems a natural rhythm rather than one based on a set pattern. Have volunteers read their poems to the class.

Teach

Part 2: Poetic Elements

SOUND DEVICES

After students read the chart, draw this chart on the board to help them reflect on the function of rhyme, rhythm, and sound devices in poems, prose, and popular music:

	Rhyme	Rhythm	Sound Devices
Poetry	✓	✓	✓
Prose			
Music			

- Place a check mark in each box as you review sound devices and their use in each literary form. Emphasize the characteristics that make poetry unique as you discuss similarities and differences. For example, poems are generally written in lines rather than in sentences, and poets tend to convey their ideas and feelings through strong images and comparatively few words.

- Help students understand that poetry, prose, and songs all use rhyme, rhythm, and sound devices, but to different degrees and for different purposes. For example, a poet might use alliteration and assonance to convey a particular feeling. A speechwriter might use repetition and rhythm to stress certain persuasive points. A songwriter might use alliteration to create a memorable phrase or lyric. Elicit or provide examples of the various techniques. (Edgar Allan Poe's "The Bells" is one excellent source. See page 671.)

CHECK UNDERSTANDING

Have students create their own examples of repetition, alliteration, assonance, and consonance.

Part 2: Poetic Elements

For a poet, deciding on a subject and form is just the beginning. Will the poem hum along at a steady beat or charge ahead with a bold rhythm? What images or sounds will convey a mood? Using sound devices and language, poets can convey meaning, make music, and tap into the senses.

SOUND DEVICES

Like music, language has rhythm. In poetry, the pattern of stressed and unstressed syllables in each line is what creates the **rhythm.** **Rhyme** also enhances the musical quality of a poem. It can occur at the ends of lines as **end rhyme** or within lines as **internal rhyme.**

A regular pattern of rhythm is called a **meter.** A regular pattern of rhyme is called a **rhyme scheme.** Meter is charted in a process called **scansion,** where stressed syllables are marked with a ´ and unstressed syllables with a ˘. A rhyme scheme is charted by assigning a letter of the alphabet to matching end rhymes. Notice how the meter and rhyme scheme are marked in these lines from "A Birthday" by Christina Rossetti:

My heart / is like / a sing / ing bird	a
Whose nest / is in / a wa/ tered shoot:	b
My heart / is like / an ap / ple-tree	c
Whose boughs / are bent/ with thick / set fruit;	b

Here are some other techniques that poets use to create sound effects.

SOUND DEVICE	EXAMPLE
REPETITION a sound, word, phrase, or line that is repeated for emphasis and unity ▶	back off from this poem it has drawn in yr feet back off from this poem —from "Beware: Do Not Read This Poem"
ALLITERATION repetition of consonant sounds at the beginnings of words ▶	Which circle slowly with a silken swish —from "Pretty Words"
ASSONANCE repetition of vowel sounds in words that don't end with the same consonant ▶	Words shy and dappled, deep-eyed deer in herds —from "Pretty Words"
CONSONANCE repetition of consonant sounds within and at the ends of words ▶	Whose nest is in a watered shoot —from "A Birthday"

DIFFERENTIATED INSTRUCTION

FOR LESS–PROFICIENT READERS

Note Taking For students who need help, hand out the note-taking copy master for Part 2. Read and discuss the text. Assist students in completing their note-taking copy master as needed.

R RESOURCE MANAGER—Copy Master
Note Taking p. 16

Analysis Support: Sound Devices To build understanding of sound devices, work with student pairs or small groups to create examples of repetition, alliteration, assonance, and consonance. If necessary, generate initial examples and have students identify them and add to them. For example, you might describe a "silent, slithery snake" and have students add alliteration, repetition, assonance, or consonance to the phrase. Ask volunteers to share the resulting examples.

MODEL 1: METER

To identify a poem's meter, you have to break each line into smaller units, called feet. A **foot** consists of one stressed syllable and one or two unstressed ones. Look at the type and the number of feet in each line. Then combine the terms listed on the side—for example, **trochaic trimeter** or **iambic pentameter**—to describe what you find. Scan this poem to determine its meter.

FIRE AND ICE

Poem by **Robert Frost**

Some say the world will end in fire,
Some say in ice.
From what I've tasted of desire
I hold with those who favor fire.
5   But if it had to perish twice,
I think I know enough of hate
To say that for destruction ice
Is also great
And would suffice.

METER

TYPES OF FEET
iamb (rĕSÍST)
trochee (ÁBsĕnt)
spondee (GÓAL LÍNE)

NUMBER OF FEET
trimeter (3)
tetrameter (4)
pentameter (5)

Close Read

1. What is the metrical pattern of the lines in the box?

2. What is the poem's rhyme scheme?

MODEL 2: OTHER SOUND DEVICES

Edgar Allan Poe wrote "The Bells" to experiment with the musical qualities of language. Read this excerpt aloud to get the full impact.

from The Bells

Poem by **Edgar Allan Poe**

Hear the sledges with the bells—
    Silver bells!
What a world of merriment their melody foretells!
    How they tinkle, tinkle, tinkle,
5   In the icy air of night!
    While the stars that oversprinkle
    All the Heavens, seem to twinkle
        With a crystalline delight;
    Keeping time, time, time,
10   In a sort of Runic rhyme, . . .

Close Read

1. Identify four examples of sound devices used in this poem.

2. What effects do these sound devices create? Explain how they add to Poe's description of the bells.

MODEL 1: METER
Close Read

1. *iambic tetrameter*

    If students need help . . . Have students read the boxed lines aloud, exaggerating the phrasing and stresses. Have them count the syllables, noting that there are eight syllables and that the first syllable in each foot is unstressed.

2. *abaabcbcb*

MODEL 2: OTHER SOUND DEVICES
Close Read

1. *Possible answer: Repetition: "tinkle, tinkle, tinkle" (line 4); alliteration: "What a world of merriment their melody" (line 3); assonance: "the icy air of night" (line 5); consonance: "crystalline delight" (line 8)*

2. *Possible answer: The devices suggest the sound of the bells, conveying their cheery, crisp, regular ringing. Use of the sound devices makes Poe's description come alive.*

DIFFERENTIATED INSTRUCTION

FOR ENGLISH LEARNERS
Language: Skill Words Point out the Greek combining forms *tri-*, in *trimeter*, meaning "three"; *tetra-*, in *tetrameter*, meaning "four"; and *penta-*, in *pentameter*, meaning "five." Also explain that *-meter* is a combining form too, meaning "measure." Have students define each complete word—*trimeter*, *tetrameter*, and *pentameter*—and put them in order from smallest to largest.

FOR ADVANCED LEARNERS/PRE–AP
Analyze Imagery Have students work in small groups to discuss Frost's imagery in "Fire and Ice," noting the senses to which the poet appeals. Then ask students to reflect on what feelings Frost associates with fire and what feelings he associates with ice. Also encourage students to discuss why it is often said that Frost's poems are deceptive in their apparent simplicity.

IMAGERY AND FIGURATIVE LANGUAGE

Word Pictures Explain that imagery and figurative language bring poetry to life by creating vivid pictures in the reader's mind. Have students practice understanding figurative language, using familiar figures of speech from everyday conversation. Ask them to identify the figure of speech in each of these expressions, explain its meaning, and describe the mood it conveys:

- March comes in like a lion, goes out like a lamb. (*simile; March begins with bad weather, but ends with good weather; wild, then gentle*)

- He's got a heart of stone. (*metaphor; He's unfeeling; emotionally cold*)

- The stack of bills was a mile high. (*hyperbole; There were too many bills; despair*)

- The morning sun smiled upon our arrival. (*personification; Our arrival went well; cheerful*)

Challenge students to provide additional examples of similes, metaphors, personification, and hyperbole or to identify examples in selections they have read.

You might also point out that sometimes metaphors are "extended." For example, a poet may write an entire poem in which a person's life is compared to a ship at sea, tossed about on the waves, sailing for points unknown, and so on.

IMAGERY AND FIGURATIVE LANGUAGE

Unlike prose, poetry is very concise: a limited number of words must carry a great deal of meaning. One of the ways poets expand their ability to make meaning is by using imagery and figurative language.

You've already learned how **imagery** in fiction evokes sensory experiences for readers by appealing to the five senses. Poets also use sensory details to illustrate and elaborate on their ideas and feelings. For example, look again at "Fire and Ice" on the preceding page. Robert Frost uses two powerful sensory details—fire and ice—to help you picture the end of the world. Not only can you probably visualize the world engulfed in flames or numbed by ice, but you can also probably imagine what each type of destruction would feel like. These details are enough to spark unsettling images in your mind.

Like imagery, **figurative language** opens up the mind to more than the literal meanings of words. In this example, notice how the figurative expression not only is more descriptive but also conveys a stronger emotion:

Literal: He was angry.

Figurative: He burned with anger.

FIGURATIVE LANGUAGE	EXAMPLE
SIMILE a comparison between two unlike things, containing the words *like*, *as*, or *as if* ▶	My heart is like a singing bird —from "A Birthday"
METAPHOR a comparison between two unlike things without the word *like* or *as* ▶	Poets make pets of pretty, docile words —from "Pretty Words"
PERSONIFICATION a description of an object, an animal, a place, or an idea in human terms ▶	it [this poem] has taken in many victims —from "Beware: Do Not Read This Poem"
HYPERBOLE an exaggeration for emphasis or humorous effect ▶	the hunger of this poem is legendary —from "Beware: Do Not Read This Poem"

DIFFERENTIATED INSTRUCTION

FOR LESS-PROFICIENT READERS
Concept Connect On the board, list the boldfaced terms. Then give the examples in random order for students to classify.

- *simile:* My uncle is as stubborn as a child.

- *metaphor:* Nicole is a machine at work, never needing to rest.

- *personification:* The black storm clouds rumbled their anger.

- *hyperbole:* Jim's arm is so strong he can throw a ball a mile.

Comprehension: Figurative Language To reinforce the difference between the four types of figurative language, write this sentence on the board:

My heart is like a stone.

Ask students to identify the figurative language (*simile*). Then help them change it into a metaphor. *(My heart is a stone.)* Work with students to change the base sentence to reflect personification and hyperbole.

MODEL 3: IMAGERY AND FIGURATIVE LANGUAGE

In this poem, the writer uses sensory details and figurative language to acquaint you with a vivid character. As you read, notice the contrasting images of Miss Rosie—what she was and what she has become. Also, pay attention to the poem's **speaker,** the voice that describes the character. How does the speaker's impression of Miss Rosie affect your perception of her?

miss rosie

Poem by **Lucille Clifton**

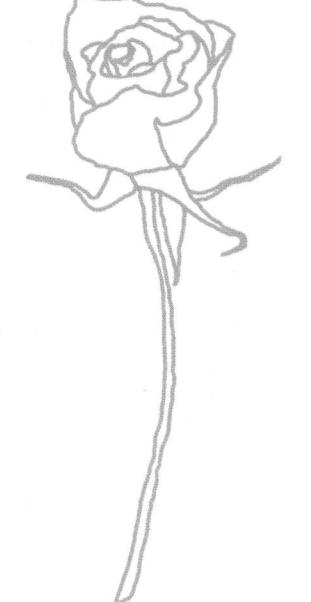

when i watch you
wrapped up like garbage
sitting, surrounded by the smell
of too old potato peels
5   or
when i watch you
in your old man's shoes
with the little toe cut out
sitting, waiting for your mind
10 like next week's grocery
i say
when i watch you
you wet brown bag of a woman
who used to be the best looking gal in georgia
15 used to be called the Georgia Rose
i stand up
through your destruction
i stand up

Close Read

1. Point out three unusual comparisons and identify them as similes or metaphors. What image of Miss Rosie does this figurative language convey?

2. Find the hyperbole and explain its effect.

3. Reread the boxed lines. What is the speaker's attitude toward Miss Rosie? Explain how it affects your impression of Miss Rosie.

MODEL 3: IMAGERY AND FIGURATIVE LANGUAGE

Close Read

1. *Possible answer: Comparisons:* "wrapped up like garbage" (line 2)—simile; "like next week's grocery" (line 10)—simile; "wet brown bag of a woman" (line 13)—metaphor. The language shows Miss Rosie as being alone, deteriorated, senile, pathetic.

2. "used to be the best looking gal in georgia" (line 14); effect: emphasizes just how far Miss Rosie has declined

   If students need help . . . Ask students what image of Miss Rosie "the best looking gal in georgia" suggests. Have them contrast this image with the one presented in lines 1–13.

3. *Possible answer: The speaker feels both saddened and distressed to witness Miss Rosie's "destruction," and also stands to honor Miss Rosie and what she was. Because we see Miss Rosie through the speaker's eyes, we tend to share the speaker's feelings.*

DIFFERENTIATED INSTRUCTION

FOR LESS–PROFICIENT READERS

Analysis Support: Speaker Read the poem aloud to the class. Then help students see how various sound devices contribute to the overall effect created by the speaker. For example, elicit or explain that the poem's stop-and-go rhythm and the speaker's repetition of the lines "when i watch you" and "i stand up" convey the speaker's feelings of distress.

Practice and Apply

Part 3: Analyze the Literature
Close Read

1. *The rhyme scheme is ababcdcdefefgg.*

2. *Possible answer: Two lines that reflect iambic pentameter are lines 2 and 11; lines that vary from the pattern include lines 1, 5, 9, and 14. Stressing words such as "Not" (lines 1, 5), "Love" (line 9), and "Look" (line 14) emphasizes the speaker's point that she's not like other girls who lock their loves away or harbor secrets behind a promise of fidelity.*

   If students need help... Have students read the poem aloud, listening for the metric pattern in each line. Remind students that iambic pentameter consists of five metric feet, each foot having one unstressed syllable followed by one stressed syllable.

3. *Possible answer: Lines 1–8 contain images of elaborate, bejeweled enclosures, locks, and secrecy; lines 9–12 contain images of openness, simplicity, kindness, and sharing.*

Part 3: Analyze the Literature

Now that you've learned about poetic forms and techniques, you're ready to see how everything works together in two distinctly different love poems.

The first poem is a Shakespearean sonnet, which has a rhyme scheme and organization different from those of the Petrarchan sonnet on page 669. A **Shakespearean sonnet** consists of three **quatrains**, or four-line units, and a final **couplet**, or pair of rhyming lines. Read the sonnet aloud first to understand what it is saying. Then read it again to analyze its poetic elements. What techniques are used to complement and extend the poem's meaning?

NOT IN A SILVER CASKET...

Poem by **Edna St. Vincent Millay**

Not in a silver casket cool with pearls
Or rich with red corundum[1] or with blue,
Locked, and the key withheld, as other girls
Have given their loves, I give my love to you;
5 Not in a lovers'-knot, not in a ring
Worked in such fashion, and the legend plain—
Semper fidelis,[2] where a secret spring
Kennels a drop of mischief for the brain:
Love in the open hand, no thing but that,
10 Ungemmed, unhidden, wishing not to hurt,
As one should bring you cowslips[3] in a hat
Swung from the hand, or apples in her skirt,
I bring you, calling out as children do:
"Look what I have!—And these are all for you."

---

1. **corundum:** an extremely hard mineral, red and blue forms of which are rubies and sapphires.
2. *Semper fidelis Latin:* always faithful.
3. **cowslips:** plants that have fragrant yellow flowers.

Close Read

1. Identify the rhyme scheme of the poem.

2. This poem is written in iambic pentameter. Find and scan two lines that reflect this meter. Then find two lines that vary from the pattern. What is the effect of the change in rhythm?

3. How do the images in lines 1–8 contrast with those in lines 9–12?

DIFFERENTIATED INSTRUCTION

FOR LESS–PROFICIENT READERS
Analysis Support: Form Draw a simple graphic organizer to help students visualize the Shakespearean sonnet's structure: three large boxes for each quatrain stacked above a smaller box for the couplet. Help students analyze the poem's meaning box by box. Write the meaning in the organizer.

- *first quatrain* (lines 1–4): other girls' love is elaborate love, but they keep it locked up.

- *second quatrain* (lines 5–8): the speaker gives her love plainly and forever, but with a hint of mystery

- *third quatrain* (lines 9–12): the speaker's love is open and simple like nature

- *couplet* (lines 13–14): the speaker feels that love should be expressed simply, freely, and openly

Now read this poem, which offers another perspective on love. As you read, notice how the sound devices, figurative language, and form help convey a heartfelt and sincere message.

I AM OFFERING THIS POEM

Poem by **Jimmy Santiago Baca**

I am offering this poem to you,
since I have nothing else to give.
Keep it like a warm coat
when winter comes to cover you,
5   or like a pair of thick socks
the cold cannot bite through,

      I love you,

I have nothing else to give you,
so it is a pot full of yellow corn
10   to warm your belly in winter,
it is a scarf for your head, to wear
over your hair, to tie up around your face,

      I love you,

Keep it, treasure this as you would
15   if you were lost, needing direction,
in the wilderness life becomes when mature;
and in the corner of your drawer,
tucked away like a cabin or hogan[1]
in dense trees, come knocking,
20   and I will answer, give you directions,
and let you warm yourself by this fire,
rest by this fire, and make you feel safe,

      I love you,

It's all I have to give,
25   and all anyone needs to live,
and to go on living inside,
when the world outside
no longer cares if you live or die;
remember,
30   I love you.

---

1. **hogan:** a one-room Navajo building that is used as a dwelling or for ceremonial purposes.

Close Read

1. Is this poem traditional or organic in form? Explain how you can tell.

2. Find four specific sound devices in the poem that give it unity and rhythm.

3. Identify the similes and metaphors in lines 1–12. A simile has been boxed. What qualities of the love poem do these comparisons help to emphasize?

4. Compare what these poems say about love. Cite similarities as well as differences.

FOR LESS–PROFICIENT READERS

Analysis Support: Meaning Help students explore the meaning of the last stanza. Explain what the poet means by the phrase "to go on living inside" (line 26). Note the contrast of "inside" with "outside" in line 27. Lead students to understand that the poet is speaking figuratively about feelings. Help students to paraphrase the stanza. *(Love is what I have to give. Love will help us feel okay even when the world ignores us.)*

FOR ENGLISH LEARNERS

Language: Pronoun Referents Make sure that students understand that the phrase "this poem" is the referent for the word *it* in lines 3, 9, 11, 14, and 24. Elicit or explain that the poem is also symbolic of the speaker's love, especially in the final stanza, when the speaker says that it's "all anyone needs." Thus, *it* refers to both the poem and the speaker's love.

Close Read

1. ***Possible answer:*** *The poem is organic in form. It has no regular pattern of rhythm or rhyme.*

2. ***Possible answer:*** *Repetition: "I love you" (lines 7, 13, 23, 30); alliteration: "when winter comes to cover you" (line 4); consonance: "like a pair of thick socks" (line 5); rhyme: "wear"/"hair" (lines 11–12), "give"/"live" (lines 24–25)*

3. ***Possible answer: Similes:*** *"like a warm coat" (line 3), "like a pair of thick socks" (line 5);* ***metaphors:*** *"[this poem] is a pot full of yellow corn" (line 9), "a scarf" (lines 11–12). The comparisons help to emphasize such qualities as warmth, comfort, nurturing, and protection.*

4. ***Possible answer:*** *Both poems suggest that love is something to be given freely and openly. Both also disparage ostentation in the expression of love and prefer simple and sincere declarations and offerings. Baca's poem suggests that love nurtures, protects, and directs in a harsh world and is "all anyone needs to live" (line 25); Millay's sonnet contrasts her simple, demonstrative love with the more calculated expression of "other girls" (line 3).*

Assess and Reteach

Assess

List on the board the boldfaced academic terms from pages 668–674. Have students explain the meaning of each term and, as appropriate, give examples from the poems.

Reteach

For students who are unable to apply the workshop skills to the poems, select from these reteaching options:

*   Provide specific examples of troublesome terms. Have students read these and follow your guidance in recognizing and analyzing the poetic forms and elements. Ask students to read poems aloud to hear sound devices.

*   Review with students the note-taking copy masters for this lesson. Have students restate the information in the copy masters in their own words. Help them identify examples.

Focus and Motivate

OBJECTIVES

Literary Analysis
- explore the key idea of **memories**
- recognize characteristics of lyric poetry
- analyze imagery
- read poems

Reading
- make inferences

Grammar and Writing
- use participles and participial phrases to enrich descriptive language
- use writing to analyze literature

SUMMARIES

"My Papa's Waltz" In this poem, the speaker shares a memory about his energetic romps with his father before bedtime.

"I Ask My Mother to Sing" The speaker of this poem describes how his mother and grandmother tearfully sing about a beautiful place in China that he has never seen.

"Grape Sherbet" In this poem, the speaker recalls a Memorial Day cookout when her father made grape sherbet. She reflects upon the importance of cherishing family memories and honoring the dead.

Who lives in your MEMORY?

Ask the question as a lead-in to discussing the *KEY IDEA*. Then have students jot down some notes about a vivid **memory** to use as they complete the *QUICKWRITE*.

Selection Resources

My Papa's Waltz
Poem by Theodore Roethke

I Ask My Mother to Sing
Poem by Li-Young Lee

Grape Sherbet
Poem by Rita Dove

Who lives in your MEMORY?

KEY IDEA What are some of your most vivid family **memories?** They might include a raucous pillow fight with your sister or a rained-out picnic with your cousins. These memories can take a special shape in your mind; some might linger as stories to tell, but others might remain simply a series of images. The following poems contain such images, boiled down to their essential qualities.

QUICKWRITE Choose a memory involving someone close to you and write a brief sketch of your recollection. Include sensory details as well as events that present a clear picture of your subject.

676

 RESOURCE MANAGER UNIT 7

Plan and Teach pp. 17–24

Literary Analysis
Imagery pp. 25, 26†*
Question Support p. 29*

Reading
Make Inferences pp. 27, 28†*
Reading Fluency p. 31

Grammar and Writing
Use Descriptive Language p. 30

Assessment
Selection Tests A, B/C pp. 33*, 35*
Test Generator CD

BEST PRACTICES TOOLKIT

Differentiated Instruction
pp. 31–38*

Graphic Organizers/Strategies
Draw It • Question Frames

Technology
Literature Center at **ClassZone.com**
Write*Smart* CD

Reading Support
Audio Anthology CD*

InterActive
READER & WRITER

• Integrated Test Practice
• Related Nonfiction Readings

McDougal Littell LITERATURE

---

* Resources for Differentiation   † Also in Spanish

● POETIC FORM: LYRIC POETRY

These three poems are all examples of **lyric poetry,** brief poems in which the speakers share personal thoughts and feelings on a subject. In ancient Greek, the word *lyric* referred to a type of poetry that expressed the feelings of a single singer, accompanied by a lyre, a small harplike instrument. Though no longer sung, lyric poems have a lot in common with songs, including

- a sense of rhythm and melody
- imaginative language
- the creation of a single, unified impression

Reading the following poems aloud will help you experience the imagery and the sounds of the language as the poets intended.

● LITERARY ANALYSIS: IMAGERY

One of the most important elements of any poem is its **imagery**—the words and phrases that appeal to one or more of the five senses. In addition to re-creating sensory experiences, however, imagery calls up particular ideas and emotions. In the following lines from "My Papa's Waltz," the imagery appeals to sight and hearing but also suggests certain feelings:

We romped until the pans
Slid from the kitchen shelf

These lines call up a sense of rowdy, out-of-control playtime. As you read, look for other images that evoke strong feelings.

● READING SKILL: MAKE INFERENCES

Lyric poems tend to be very condensed; in many cases, more is suggested than directly stated. It's particularly important, then, to make inferences about their meanings. When you encounter a puzzling line or stanza, think about the ideas and emotions suggested by the images. As you read each poem, write down the images and your inferences on a chart like the one shown.

"Grape Sherbet"		
Image	**My Associations**	**Inference**
"[Memorial Day] morning we galloped / through the grassed-over mounds / and named each stone / for a lost milk tooth."	• Memorial Day commemorates the dead. • Grassy mounds and stones are found in cemeteries	They are running through a cemetery.

Author Online

Theodore Roethke: Self-Taught Poet
Theodore Roethke learned to write verse by imitating other poets; he sought inspiration from his notebooks, where he had recorded his thoughts, feelings, and observations. He went on to earn a Pulitzer

Theodore Roethke
1908–1963

Prize and two National Book Awards. He once advised his readers to "listen" to his poems, "for they are written to be heard."

Li-Young Lee: Son of Chinese Exiles
After his parents fled China to escape political persecution, Li-Young Lee's family lived in several Asian countries before arriving in the United States in 1964. After college, Lee began to write poetry—about

Li-Young Lee
born 1957

love, family, and ordinary experiences.

Rita Dove: Poet Laureate
Rita Dove's first attempts as a writer came early: in third or fourth grade, she composed a science-fiction novel based on her classroom spelling lists. Her poetry collections have won many awards, including

Rita Dove
born 1952

a Pulitzer Prize in 1987. From 1993 to 1995, she served as U.S. poet laureate. Asked to name the most important quality for success, Dove replied, "I think that without imagination, we can go nowhere."

 MORE ABOUT THE AUTHOR
For more on these poets, visit the **Literature Center** at ClassZone.com.

677

Teach

STANDARDS FOCUS

LITERARY ANALYSIS

● IMAGERY

For instructional support, read aloud this poem:

Mama singing, children giggling,
Daddy chortling, stew bubbling;
Lightning flashing, rain dripping—
Darkness coming.

Have students identify details that appeal to the senses. ***Possible answer: Sight:*** *"Lightning flashing," "Darkness coming";* ***Sound:*** *"Mama singing," "children giggling," "stew bubbling," "Daddy chortling," "rain dripping";* ***Taste or smell:*** *"stew bubbling";* ***Touch:*** *"rain dripping"*

CHECK UNDERSTANDING Discuss the feelings that these images evoke.

READING SKILL

■ MAKE INFERENCES

Use the text under **Rita Dove: Poet Laureate** to model making inferences.

1. Dove had an imaginative childhood.
2. She says that she values imagination.
3. Her poems may offer an imaginative way of looking at life.

CHECK UNDERSTANDING Ask students to make an inference about Li-Young Lee or Theodore Roethke, based on the text under ***About the Authors.***

R RESOURCE MANAGER—Copy Master
Make Inferences p. 27 (for student use while reading the selections)

DIFFERENTIATED INSTRUCTION

FOR LESS-PROFICIENT READERS

Skill Words Review these terms that are often used in a discussion of poetry: *speaker, stanza, rhyme scheme, line length, impression, rhythm,* and *meter.* Call on volunteers to define any terms they know. Have students use a dictionary to locate the meanings of unfamiliar terms. Urge them to watch for some of these terms as they read and to use these terms as they discuss and write about the poems.

FOR ADVANCED LEARNERS/PRE-AP

Extend Poetic Form As you discuss what is meant by *lyric poetry,* challenge students to find examples of prose that could be described as lyrical because it reflects the qualities listed in the text. Descriptive short stories are a good starting place, but essays and "literary" nonfiction may yield rich examples too. Invite volunteers to read aloud a passage that they have found and to tell how it is marked by imagery, rhythm, and a unified impression.

677

Practice and Apply

ANALYZE VISUALS

Possible answer: The larger character is protective of the smaller character, as suggested by the fact that his very large hands encircle the child's hands. The scene may capture a memory from the painter's youth, as suggested by the photograph.

About the Art The poem scratched into the paint may be hard to read. It says

Ride by	Step by Step
from now	Life
and forever	Love
Back to Back	the journey

The words reflect the continuity of life that Haitian-American artist Francks Deceus (b. 1966) creates by juxtaposing the childhood photograph with the father and son—who seem to be dancing, like Roethke's speaker and his father.

My Papa's Waltz

THEODORE ROETHKE

The whiskey on your breath
Could make a small boy dizzy;
But I hung on like death:
Such waltzing was not easy.

5 We romped until the pans
Slid from the kitchen shelf;
My mother's countenance[1]
Could not unfrown itself.

The hand that held my wrist
10 Was battered on one knuckle;
At every step you missed
My right ear scraped a buckle.

You beat time on my head
With a palm caked hard by dirt,
15 Then waltzed me off to bed
Still clinging to your shirt.

ANALYZE VISUALS
What are your impressions of the characters depicted in the painting? Cite the details that create this impression.

A LYRIC POETRY
How does the **speaker** feel about his bedtime waltz with his father? Explain why you think as you do.

---

1. **countenance:** face or facial expression.

Detail of *Tender Moments* (2000), Francks Deceus. Mixed media. © Francks Deceus/The Bridgeman Art Library.

DIFFERENTIATED INSTRUCTION

For general guidelines on differentiating instruction, see

 BEST PRACTICES TOOLKIT
Differentiated Instruction pp. 31–38

FOR LESS–PROFICIENT READERS

Options for Reading Use the Draw It strategy to help students visualize the images in "My Papa's Waltz." Ask partners to read the poem aloud and share visual representations of what they read.

BEST PRACTICES TOOLKIT
Draw It p. A2

BACKGROUND

Roethke's Father Theodore Roethke was the son of Helen (Huebner) and Otto Roethke, a German immigrant who owned large commercial greenhouses in Saginaw, Michigan. Roethke's father was firm—sometimes fierce—with strangers, but affectionate and loyal to his family. Young Theodore viewed his father with a mixture of love and awe—characteristics that are reflected in "My Papa's Waltz."

REINFORCE *KEY IDEA:* MEMORIES

Discuss Why do you think the scene in "My Papa's Waltz" was so vivid among the poet's **memories?** *Possible answer: The scene was vivid and memorable because it was a happy time that the poet shared with his father. It was also emotionally charged, with a sometimes daring energy.*

ADDITIONAL TEACHING OPPORTUNITY

Appreciate Oral Poetry Point out that the impact of poetry changes somewhat when it is heard instead of read silently. To illustrate, read the poems in this lesson aloud, or choose students to read them aloud. Urge students to listen for enjoyment during a first reading. On a second reading, have them listen for and note examples of rhyme, vivid language and imagery, and characterization. Invite students to comment about how their perceptions changed when the poems were read aloud. (To learn more about appreciating oral poetry, see **Reading Handbook,** page R2.)

FOR ADVANCED LEARNERS/PRE–AP

Set a Poem to Music [small-group option] Remind students that lyric poetry was originally performed as song. Have interested students set to music a poem from this lesson or another poem of their choice. The music should mirror the emotions evoked by the poetry. Ask students to share their music by playing a recording or by performing it live for the class.

Prereading for this poem is found on page 676.

ANALYZE VISUALS

Activity Does this painting match the mood and imagery of the poem? Why or why not? *Possible answer: Yes, but in a suggestive rather than literal way. The painting reflects the poem's dreamy, nostalgic, and mournful mood. The painting's central image of a mother and child suggests the speaker's mother. The painting's fluid, translucent background suggests the poem's images of "spilling water" (line 11) and tears (line 13). The boat in the background evokes the poem's image of the speaker's father, who would "sway like a boat" if he were still alive to hear the singing (line 4).*

About the Art Hung Liu (b. 1948) emigrated from China to the United States in 1984. She mixes real and symbolic elements in paintings that explore personal subjects and her Chinese heritage.

LITERARY ANALYSIS

Ⓑ IMAGERY

Possible answer: The speaker can describe the images because they are described in the song. The feelings evoked are positive: awe at the sight of the structures and the lake and pleasure in the picnickers.

READING SKILL

Ⓒ MAKE INFERENCES

Possible answer: The women cry because the song evokes strong memories and a sense of longing for their homeland.

I Ask My Mother to Sing

LI-YOUNG LEE

Mother and Child by Grand Canal (2000), Hung Liu. Oil on canvas, 80″ × 80″. Courtesy Rena Bransten Gallery.

She begins, and my grandmother joins her.
Mother and daughter sing like young girls.
If my father were alive, he would play
his accordion and sway like a boat.

5 I've never been in Peking, or the Summer Palace,
nor stood on the great Stone Boat to watch
the rain begin on Kuen Ming Lake, the picnickers
running away in the grass. Ⓑ

But I love to hear it sung;
10 how the waterlilies fill with rain until
they overturn, spilling water into water,
then rock back, and fill with more.

Both women have begun to cry.
But neither stops her song. Ⓒ

Ⓑ **IMAGERY**
Reread lines 5–9. How is the **speaker** able to describe images of a place he's never seen? Describe the feelings evoked by the images.

Ⓒ **MAKE INFERENCES**
Why do the speaker's mother and grandmother start to cry during their song?

DIFFERENTIATED INSTRUCTION

FOR LESS–PROFICIENT READERS

Question the Poem Model the Question Frames strategy to help students better understand this poem. Pose such questions as these: "Are the women sad?" "Do they wish to go home?" and "Why don't they stop singing?" Have students read each stanza and pose their own questions about the events and emotions that the words evoke.

 BEST PRACTICES TOOLKIT—Transparency
Question Frames p. A33

FOR ENGLISH LEARNERS

Culture: Clarify Help students look in reference books and online sources to learn more about the references in lines 5–7: Peking, the Summer Palace, the great Stone Boat, and Kuen Ming Lake. In particular, help them locate images of some or all of these places. Discuss how knowing what the mother and grandmother are singing about affects their reading of the poem.

Grape Sherbet

RITA DOVE

The day? Memorial.
After the grill
Dad appears with his masterpiece—
swirled snow, gelled light.
5 We cheer. The recipe's
a secret and he fights
a smile, his cap turned up
so the bib resembles a duck.

That morning we galloped
10 through the grassed-over mounds
and named each stone
for a lost milk tooth. Each dollop
of sherbet, later,
is a miracle,
15 like salt on a melon that makes it sweeter.

Everyone agrees—it's wonderful!
It's just how we imagined lavender
would taste. The diabetic grandmother
stares from the porch,
20 a torch
of pure refusal. **D**

We thought no one was lying
there under our feet,
we thought it
25 was a joke. I've been trying
to remember the taste,
but it doesn't exist.
Now I see why
you bothered,
30 father. **E**

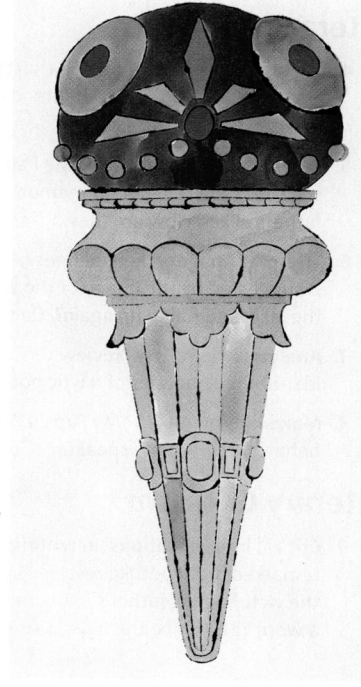

Ice Cream Dessert (1959), Andy Warhol © 2007 Andy Warhol Foundation for the Visual Arts/Artists Rights Society (ARS), New York. Photo © Corbis.

D MAKE INFERENCES
Reread lines 18–21. What does the image of the grandmother suggest about her actions?

E LYRIC POETRY
What feeling is the **speaker** expressing in this poem?

FOR ENGLISH LEARNERS

Vocabulary and Language Identify and define confusing words, concepts, and cultural details in "Grape Sherbet." Make sure students know what sherbet is. Discuss the meaning of Memorial Day and ask for parallels from students' home cultures. Also discuss the meaning of "fights a smile" (lines 6–7), "bib" (line 8), "grassed-over mounds" (line 10), "lost milk tooth" (line 12), and "salt on a melon" (line 15).

Prereading for this poem is found on page 676.

ANALYZE VISUALS

Activity In his depiction of an ice-cream cone, what other objects does the artist suggest?
Possible answer: The ice-cream cone looks like a fancy urn or building, and the ice cream scoop looks like a jewel.

About the Art Andy Warhol (1928–1987) was one of the pioneers of the pop art movement of the 1960s. *Ice Cream Dessert* is an early work that shows Warhol's fascination with the decorative qualities of popular objects.

READING SKILL

D MAKE INFERENCES

Possible answer: The image of the "torch of pure refusal" suggests that the grandmother acts with burning determination and perhaps some resentment at being left out.

POETIC FORM

E LYRIC POETRY

Possible answer: The speaker is expressing gratitude to her father for giving her happy memories and helping her see the importance of honoring the dead.

SELECTION WRAP–UP

SYNTHESIZE What message do all three poems convey about the importance of family and family memories?

★ CRITIQUE Which poem affects you most strongly? Explain your response.

READING FLUENCY

Distribute the copy master and have students work in pairs or groups to practice fluency.

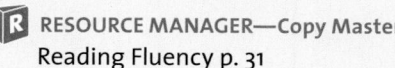 **RESOURCE MANAGER—Copy Master**
Reading Fluency p. 31

Practice and Apply

After Reading

For additional support of post-reading questions, use these copy masters:

R RESOURCE MANAGER—Copy Masters

    Imagery p. 25 (for practice of the literary analysis standards focus)

    Question Support p. 29 (After Reading questions adapted for English learners and less-proficient readers)

For additional questions, see page 21.

ANSWERS

Comprehension

1. *The speaker's mother frowns because she disapproves of the rowdy dancing.*

2. *The mother's song is about scenes from her homeland of China, especially a scene of rain filling the waterlilies at Kuen Ming Lake.*

3. *The main setting of "Grape Sherbet" is a backyard in which a cookout is taking place on a Memorial Day afternoon. In stanza 2, the setting is a cemetery.*

Literary Analysis

Possible answers:

4. ■ **STANDARDS FOCUS** *Make Inferences*
"My Papa's Waltz": The father's battered knuckle (line 10) and dirty palm (line 14) imply that the father works with his hands. "I Ask My Mother to Sing": The words "I've never been in Peking" (line 5) imply that the mother and grandmother are singing about China and longing for their homeland. "Grape Sherbet": The words "he fights a smile" (lines 6–7) suggest that the father was proud of his dessert.

5. *The experiences are alike in that both are happy memories of a lighthearted father. The experiences differ because in "Grape Sherbet," the speaker learns a life lesson from her father, but in "My Papa's Waltz," the speaker just has fun.*

6. ● **STANDARDS FOCUS** *Imagery* The *image of the waterlilies suggests that life is a cycle of happy and difficult events. The women's tears (line 13) reveal that their song of a happy memory also contains nostalgic sorrow.*

Comprehension

1. **Recall** In "My Papa's Waltz," why is the speaker's mother frowning?

2. **Clarify** In "I Ask My Mother to Sing," what is the mother's song about?

3. **Summarize** Describe the setting of "Grape Sherbet" as you visualize it.

Literary Analysis

4. **Make Inferences** Review the charts you made as you read. What key inferences helped you understand each poem? What clues did you use to make these inferences?

5. **Compare and Contrast** In "My Papa's Waltz" and "Grape Sherbet," the speakers recall childhood **memories.** How are their experiences with their fathers alike? How are they different?

6. **Interpret Imagery** Reread lines 9–12 in "I Ask My Mother to Sing." What idea is suggested by the image of the water lilies filling with water, spilling it into the lake, and filling up again? Consider the event described in the final stanza.

7. **Analyze Lyric Poetry** Review the definition of lyric poetry on page 677. Then identify the qualities of a lyric poem found in "I Ask My Mother to Sing."

8. **Make Judgments** In "My Papa's Waltz," how do you judge the father's behavior toward the **speaker?** Cite evidence to support your answer.

Literary Criticism

9. **Critical Interpretations** In writing about "My Papa's Waltz," one critic remarked that Roethke reveals "something of his own joy, and bafflement, as the victim of his father's exuberant energy." Do you consider *victim* too harsh a word to describe the boy's part in the evening waltz? Why or why not?

---

7. ● **STANDARDS FOCUS** *Lyric Poetry* The *lyric qualities are that the poem is brief, that the speaker shares personal thoughts, that it contains imaginative language (as in lines 5–12), and that it creates a unified impression of the women's song.*

8. *The father's behavior is loving and fun, even if he has whiskey on his breath and is a bit rough. The father "beats time" on the boy's head (line 13) in an affectionate way and puts his son to bed (line 15) in a tender way.*

Literary Criticism

Possible answer:

9. *The boy may be a victim in that he feels dizzy from the whiskey on his father's breath (lines 1–2) and has his ear scraped by his father's buckle (line 12). However, the scene seems to be a happy memory in which the boy participates willingly in the horseplay. Victim is too strong a word because it implies that the boy did not want to take part in the evening waltz and even that his father hurt him.*

Reading-Writing Connection

Increase your understanding of the family poems by responding to these prompts. Then use **Revision: Grammar and Style** to improve your writing.

WRITING PROMPTS	SELF-CHECK
A. Short Response: Write a Diary Entry The speaker in "My Papa's Waltz" notices his mother frowning during his waltz with his father. Write **one or two paragraphs** of a diary entry by the mother, recording her reaction to this dance.	**A meaningful entry will . . .** • provide images and details about the dance • describe the mother's thoughts and feelings
B. Extended Response: Analyze Relationships What message does each poem convey about the relationship between parents and children? Write **three to five paragraphs** discussing the ways this relationship is depicted in the three poems.	**A successful analysis will . . .** • clearly state the theme that each poet shares about parents and children • use quotations and details from the three poems as supporting evidence

REVISION: GRAMMAR AND STYLE

USE DESCRIPTIVE LANGUAGE One way to add interesting details to your writing is by using **participles** and **participial phrases.** A participle is a verb form that acts as an adjective. Present participles, as in "the *crying* baby," end in -*ing*, and past participles, as in "the freshly *washed* car," often end in -*ed*. A participial phrase consists of a participle and its modifiers and complements.

Here is an example of Rita Dove's use of participles in "Grape Sherbet":

> Dad appears with his masterpiece—
> *swirled* snow, *gelled* light. (lines 3–4)

Theodore Roethke uses a participial phrase in his poem "My Papa's Waltz":

> You beat time on my head
> With a palm *caked hard by dirt* (lines 13–14)

Notice how the revisions in red use participles to make this first draft more descriptive. Revise your responses to the prompts by using a similar technique.

STUDENT MODEL

Li-Young Lee describes a ~~sweet~~ *touching* scene between mother and son. The son shows an appreciation for his mother's past and the memory of his father*, deceased but not forgotten*.

> **WRITING TOOLS**
> For prewriting, revision, and editing tools, visit the **Writing Center** at ClassZone.com.

Reading-Writing Connection

WRITING PROMPTS

• For Prompt A, encourage students to take notes on each stanza, considering how the stanza's events may have appeared to the mother.

• For Prompt B, have students work in groups to state a theme for each poem. Have students freewrite individually about the parent/child relationship.

For writing support, see

ⓘ Writing Center at **ClassZone.com**

REVISION: GRAMMAR AND STYLE

1. As students examine the student model, point out that participles add variety to descriptions. They can also enhance the rhythm in writing, especially in poetry.

2. For practice, write the verbs *chill* and *amaze* on the board. Have students give the present participle and past participle of each. Then have them create a phrase using one of the new forms. ***Possible answer: chill:** chilling, chilled; the sweet, chilled dessert; **amaze:** amazing, amazed; an amazing accomplishment*

Ⓡ RESOURCE MANAGER—Copy Master
   Use Descriptive Language p. 30

Assess and Reteach

Assess

Ⓡ RESOURCE MANAGER—Copy Masters
   Selection Test A pp. 33–34
   Selection Test B/C pp. 35–36

Ⓢ Test Generator CD

Reteach

Ⓢ STANDARDS LESSON FILE
   Literature Lesson 18: Narrative vs. Lyric Poetry
   Literature Lesson 28: Imagery
   Reading Lesson 8: Making Inferences
   Writing Lesson 34: Elaborate with Sensory Details

DIFFERENTIATED INSTRUCTION

FOR LESS–PROFICIENT WRITERS

For Prompt A:

• Suggest that students focus on a single aspect of the poem that might concern the mother, such as seeing a mess in the kitchen or getting the boy put to bed.

• After students choose their subject, have them brainstorm emotions that a mother might have in relation to the scene.

• Remind students to write about those emotions in the first person.

For Prompt B:

Suggest that students approach each poem in a single paragraph. Paragraphs should cite the main theme and then show how this theme is demonstrated by giving examples from the poem.

Focus and Motivate

OBJECTIVES

Literary Analysis
- explore the key idea of **creativity**
- recognize characteristics of an elegy
- analyze diction and its effects
- read poems

Reading
- paraphrase lines of poetry

SUMMARIES

"Spring is like a perhaps hand" In this poem, the speaker likens the arrival of spring to a hand placing and rearranging things so that everything looks different.

"Elegy for the Giant Tortoises" In this elegy, the speaker laments the likely extinction of the giant tortoise. She has trouble visualizing them in the urban settings that surround her but is able to imagine them on the last day of their earthly existence.

"Today" In this poem, the speaker describes a spring day that is so perfect it fills him with a surging joy that makes him want to liberate everything around him.

Can you think
OUT OF THE BOX?

Read the question aloud. Then introduce the **KEY IDEA** by asking students, "What situations inspire your sense of **creativity?** Why?" Extend the discussion by having students complete the **PRESENT** activity.

Spring is like a perhaps hand
Poem by E. E. Cummings

Elegy for the Giant Tortoises
Poem by Margaret Atwood

Today
Poem by Billy Collins

Can you think
OUT OF THE BOX?

KEY IDEA Some of the best things in life are those unlike anything ever thought of before. Whether it's a brilliant invention (light bulb), a playful game (lizard boat), or an entertaining story (dog bites man), a new idea makes life more interesting and worthwhile. **Creativity** is a poet's bread and butter; a good poet always looks at things in a new way.

PRESENT With a small group, draw up a design for a new tool. Then share your invention with other groups and explain how it works.

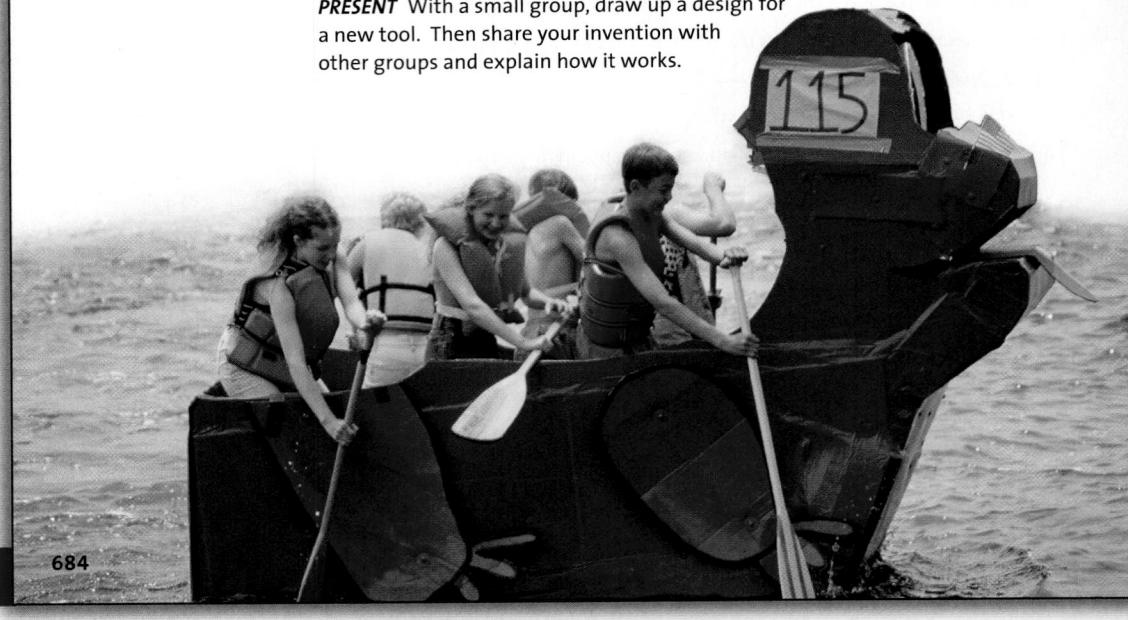

684

RESOURCE MANAGER UNIT 7

Plan and Teach pp. 37–44

Literary Analysis
Diction pp. 45, 46†*
Question Support p. 49*

Reading
Paraphrase pp. 47, 48†*

Assessment
Selection Tests A, B/C pp. 51*, 53*
Test Generator CD

BEST PRACTICES TOOLKIT

Differentiated Instruction
pp. 31–38*

Reading Support
Audio Anthology CD*

Technology
Literature Center at **ClassZone.com**
Write*Smart* CD

---

* Resources for Differentiation   † Also in Spanish

POETIC FORM: ELEGY

An **elegy** is a specific type of lyric poem. In an elegy, the speaker meditates about death, usually as a tribute to one who has recently died. Generally the tone is serious and the diction is formal. The second poem in this lesson is an elegy.

LITERARY ANALYSIS: DICTION

Poetry is known for its concise and exact use of language. When reading poetry, notice the **diction** (the choice of words) and the syntax (the order in which the words appear). For example, in "Today," Billy Collins describes his reaction to a spring day:

> . . . it made you want to throw
> open all the windows in the house

This particular use of words creates a sense of joy, freedom, and movement—more so than if he had simply said he felt like opening a window. Like any good poet, Collins has chosen his words carefully to create an intended effect. As you read these poems, notice the diction and the effects it creates.

READING STRATEGY: PARAPHRASE

Sometimes poems can be difficult to understand because of an unusual sentence structure. When you **paraphrase** a line or stanza in a poem, you rephrase the poet's words with your own words. Unlike a summary, a paraphrase is not necessarily shorter than the original text; it is simply a recasting of the same ideas. To paraphrase, you should

- find the main ideas and important details
- think of simpler or more familiar ways of saying what the writer has written
- rewrite sentences in standard, subject-verb order

As you read each of the poems that follow, create a chart in which you paraphrase difficult passages.

"Elegy for the Giant Tortoises"

Original Wording	Paraphrase
"on the road where I stand they will materialize, / plodding past me in a straggling line / awkward without water"	They [the tortoises] will appear on the road where I stand, walking slowly by in a scattered line, looking clumsy because they are not in the water.

Author Online

E. E. Cummings: Innovative and Popular Critics who praise Cummings rank him among the most innovative 20th-century poets. Believing in individuality and free expression, Cummings played with language, shaping it to fit his ideas. Though one of the most experimental of poets, he was enormously popular with the general public.

E. E. Cummings 1894–1962

Margaret Atwood: Canada's Treasure Margaret Atwood, a poet, novelist, essayist, and short story writer, has been called "a national heroine of the arts" in her native Canada. Her novels feature female characters searching for identity in a confusing and often threatening world. She is especially popular in Canada, where she has gained the status usually accorded only to movie stars and musicians.

Margaret Atwood born 1939

Billy Collins: "Most Popular Poet in America" Billy Collins's poetry appeals to a wide and ever-growing audience: high school students, fellow poets, literary critics, and general readers. According to one critic, "With his books selling briskly and his readings packing them in, Mr. Collins is the most popular poet in America."

Billy Collins born 1941

 MORE ABOUT THE AUTHOR For more on these poets, visit the **Literature Center at ClassZone.com.**

685

Teach

STANDARDS FOCUS

LITERARY ANALYSIS

● DICTION

For instructional support, write these lines on the board and read them aloud:

> In the museum of glass flowers
> nature's clock is stilled: forever
> flowers bud, arch, stretch, bloom
> this year, next year, a hundred years
> inside their cases: airless, dustless,
> colors unfading, leaves unwilted,
> upturned pollen faces
> forever unkissed by sun.

Ask students to identify the effect of the words *stilled, forever, never, airless, dustless, unfading, unwilted,* and *unkissed.* **Possible answers:** *The words convey a sense of timelessness, permanence, and perhaps staleness.*

CHECK UNDERSTANDING Ask students to identify the effect of the words *bud, arch, stretch,* and *bloom.*

READING STRATEGY

■ PARAPHRASE

Ask students to paraphrase the lines from the poem on the board. **Possible answer:** *At the natural history museum, flowers made of glass look as though they are growing and changing, but, in fact, they don't change at all.*

CHECK UNDERSTANDING Have students paraphrase another short poem.

📘 RESOURCE MANAGER—Copy Master
Paraphrase p. 47 (for student use while reading the selection)

DIFFERENTIATED INSTRUCTION

FOR LESS–PROFICIENT READERS

Skill Words Explain that the word *elegy* comes from the ancient Greek *elegos,* which means "song of mourning." Note that "mourning" is the process by which people come to terms with the death of someone they loved or admired. Explain that "Elegy for the Giant Tortoises" expresses sadness not about the death of a person but about the possible loss of a species of animals.

Practice and Apply

ANALYZE VISUALS

Possible answers: *Springlike elements in the painting include trees and leaves rendered in vibrant shades of pink, yellow, blue, orange, and brown; leaf and branch shapes; and textures that suggest clouds, sky, and water.*

About the Art California artist Laura Owens (b. 1970) is inspired by many sources, including film, computer, and television imagery. Her creative rendering of color is evident in this mixed-media painting, whose delicate and vivid hues suggest the spirit of springtime.

Spring is like a perhaps hand

E. E. Cummings

Spring is like a perhaps hand
(which comes carefully
out of Nowhere) arranging
a window, into which people look (while
5 people stare
arranging and changing placing
carefully there a strange
thing and a known thing here) and

changing everything carefully

10 spring is like a perhaps
Hand in a window
(carefully to
and fro moving New and
Old things, while
15 people stare carefully
moving a perhaps
fraction of flower here placing
an inch of air there) and

without breaking anything.

LITERARY ANALYSIS

A DICTION

Possible answer: *The words* fraction *and* inch *suggest small things or amounts; their use suggests that spring makes everything look new and different while making only small changes.*

If students need help . . . Explain that the word *inch* is used not in a literal sense but rather to connote a measure or increment small enough to be barely noticeable.

Untitled (2001), Laura Owens. Watercolor, color pencil, and photo on paper, 14" × 10". Courtesy Gavin Brown's enterprise, New York (LO 185d).

686 UNIT 7: THE LANGUAGE OF POETRY

DIFFERENTIATED INSTRUCTION

For general guidelines on differentiating instruction, see

📦 **BEST PRACTICES TOOLKIT**
Differentiated Instruction pp. 31–38

FOR LESS–PROFICIENT READERS

Options for Reading Read the poem aloud. Then have pairs of students reread the poem, with one student reading the parts that are outside the parentheses and the other student reading the parts that are inside the parentheses. Have students discuss how the two parts work together.

DISCUSSION PROMPTS

Use these prompts to help students understand the comparisons the speaker makes:

Connect Describe how something that you regularly observe in nature, such as a garden or a tree, changes from the last days of winter to the first days of spring. *Students might describe the brightening of colors and the way flowers and the leaves on trees suddenly appear.*

Analyze According to the speaker, in what ways is spring is like a hand? *Possible answer: Like a hand, spring arranges, changes, and places things. Both can rearrange things so that they appear entirely different. Moreover, a hand can move things quietly, gently, gradually, and delicately, much as spring gradually and delicately changes the world of nature.*

Synthesize Explain how Cummings arranges and rearranges his words to reinforce the idea of his comparison. *Possible answer: By arranging his words in unusual ways, Cummings makes his words spring to life, just as nature does in spring. The poet is "like a perhaps hand" that rearranges the conventional placement of words.*

REINFORCE *KEY IDEA:* CREATIVITY

Discuss How does Cummings's creative use of capitalization and punctuation help convey meaning? *Possible answer: By capitalizing "spring" and "hand" in one place and not another, Cummings changes the emphasis. He also adds emphasis to the words "nowhere," "new," and "old." By using no punctuation until the end of the last line, Cummings creates a breathless, nonstop rhythm that echoes the changes that the poem is describing.*

FOR LESS–PROFICIENT READERS
Comprehension Support

- Explain that Cummings often uses parts of speech in unconventional ways. For example, the adverb *perhaps* is used as an adjective to modify the noun *hand*. Discuss possible reasons for using *perhaps* as an adjective. Ask students to think of conventional adjectives that a poet might have used instead (*light, hesitant, unsure*).

- Point out Cummings's repetition of the adverb *carefully* (lines 2, 7, 9, and 15). Explain that in line 15, *carefully* is modifying *moving* in line 16, not *stare* in line 15. Ask students why Cummings might have chosen to break line 15 after *carefully* instead of *stare*. *Possible answer: He is being playful. By breaking the line after* carefully, *he keeps the reader off-balance, because at first we assume that "people are staring carefully."*

Prereading for this poem is found on page 684.

Elegy for the GIANT TORTOISES

MARGARET ATWOOD

Sea Turtle (about 1985), Andy Warhol. Synthetic polymer paint and silkscreen ink on canvas, 42" × 50". © Art Resource, New York/2007 Andy Warhol Foundation for the Visual Arts/Artists Rights Society (ARS), New York.

Let others pray for the passenger pigeon
the dodo, the whooping crane,[1] the eskimo:
everyone must specialize

I will confine myself to a meditation
5 upon the giant tortoises
withering finally on a remote island.

I concentrate in subway stations,
in parks, I can't quite see them,
they move to the peripheries of my eyes

10 but on the last day they will be there;
already the event
like a wave travelling shapes vision: **B**

on the road where I stand they will materialize,
plodding past me in a straggling line
15 awkward without water

their small heads pondering
from side to side, their useless armour
sadder than tanks and history,

in their closed gaze ocean and sunlight paralysed,
20 lumbering up the steps, under the archways
toward the square glass altars

where the brittle gods are kept,
the relics of what we have destroyed,
our holy and obsolete symbols. **C**

---

1. **the passenger pigeon / the dodo, the whooping crane:** extinct or extremely endangered birds.

688 UNIT 7: THE LANGUAGE OF POETRY

READING STRATEGY

B PARAPHRASE

Possible answer: I try but have trouble visualizing the tortoises in subway stations and parks, but on their last day of existence, that's where they'll be. I can already imagine the event.

POETIC FORM

C ELEGY

Possible answer: Religious language is appropriate in an elegy because, as a meditation about death, an elegy prompts religious thoughts (about the meaning of life and death) and often takes place in a religious setting.

B PARAPHRASE
Paraphrase lines 7–12. What does "the last day" refer to?

C ELEGY
Reread lines 20–24. Notice the religious language—*altars, gods, relics,* and *holy.* Why is such language appropriate in an elegy?

ANALYZE VISUALS

Activity Ask students what the image of the turtle in the print adds to their appreciation of the poem. *Possible answer: The image emphasizes how big and ponderous the related giant tortoise is, and how helpless, sad, and defenseless it would be in the face of extinction. The unusual color of the background suggests that the turtle in the print, like the one in the poem, is from the artist's imagination.*

About the Art Andy Warhol (1928–1987) is well known for his paintings of everyday objects. The starkly contrasting and unreal colors in this print help grab the viewer's attention and convey the strangeness of this creature.

688 UNIT 7: THE LANGUAGE OF POETRY

DIFFERENTIATED INSTRUCTION

FOR LESS–PROFICIENT READERS
Comprehension Support Remind students that there is no need to pause at the end of a line when reading poetry unless there is punctuation or a natural stopping point. Read the poem aloud a few lines at a time, and have students repeat the lines with the same intonation and rhythm.

FOR ADVANCED LEARNERS/PRE–AP
Irony Have students discuss what the speaker means when she says, "their useless armour / sadder than tanks and history" (lines 17–18). *Example: Armor is used for defense, but the tortoises are defenseless against their extinction, just as seemingly invincible armies (and their tanks) have been defeated.* Then have students identify the ultimate irony in the poem. *Example: After destroying the tortoises, we then honor and preserve them as relics in museum displays.*

TODAY

BILLY COLLINS

If ever there were a spring day so perfect,
so uplifted by a warm intermittent breeze

that it made you want to throw
open all the windows in the house

5 and unlatch the door to the canary's cage,
indeed, rip the little door from its jamb,

a day when the cool brick paths
and the garden bursting with peonies

seemed so etched in sunlight
10 that you felt like taking

a hammer to the glass paperweight
on the living room end table,

releasing the inhabitants
from their snow-covered cottage

15 so they could walk out,
holding hands and squinting

into this larger dome of blue and white, **D**
well, today is just that kind of day.

Flower (1964), Andy Warhol. Screenprint printed on white paper, 23″ × 23″.
© 2007 Andy Warhol Foundation for the Visual Arts/Artists Rights Society
(ARS), New York. © Art Resource, New York.

D DICTION
Reread lines 13–17. What
words does the speaker
use to characterize the
inhabitants of the glass
paperweight? What
sense or feeling is evoked
by this language?

ELEGY FOR . . . / TODAY **689**

DISCUSSION PROMPTS

Use these prompts to help students understand the connection between poetry and the role of the Poet Laureate:

Connect Have you ever felt "terrified" of poetry, as Rita Dove claims many people are? Why or why not? If so, do you feel this way now? Explain your answer. *Encourage students to refer to specific poems in their responses.*

Analyze Billy Collins encourages students to read poems aloud so they can "be simply enjoyed—not analyzed or interpreted." Do you think that it is possible to enjoy a poem fully without analyzing or interpreting it? Why or why not? *Some students might argue that a poem is best enjoyed as an immediate experience, without stopping to think about meanings. Other students might argue that poetry can be difficult to understand, and that it is hard to enjoy something you don't completely "get." Analyzing and interpreting a poem would therefore increase your enjoyment of it.*

Evaluate What can poets do to make poetry more popular? Are the kinds of things that Rita Dove and Billy Collins do effective? Give reasons for your answers. *Most students will say that visiting schools, giving readings, and hosting Web sites are all good ways to spread an appreciation and understanding of poetry. Students may also mention poetry slams and online magazines. Encourage students to be creative in thinking of other things poets might do to reach a wider audience.*

MAGAZINE ARTICLE Several poets in this unit have served as U.S. poet laureate. Read the following article to learn about this honorable and worthwhile position.

U.S. POET LAUREATES
Getting the Word Out

What should be the job of a national poet? Many readers suspect poets of being deliberately mysterious—of placing a hidden meaning behind a smokescreen of random line breaks and cryptic symbols. If that were true, then wouldn't a national poet keep these secrets under lock and key?

Not so. Every year since 1937, the U.S. Library of Congress has appointed a poet laureate to serve as the national poet. Apart from a few official duties, the poet is encouraged to continue to develop his or her own projects as well as promote the general appreciation of poetry. Some poet laureates have taken seriously their mission to dispel the poetry mystique.

Rita Dove, Poet Laureate from 1993–1995, visited schools and gave readings, presenting her complex poems in a down-to-earth manner.

"I really began to think about how poetry can reach every person. . . . If I can reduce the anxiety level of the audience out there and just read the poem as if it's an everyday thing . . . people would come up and say, 'I didn't realize poetry could be like that!' They [are] just terrified, that's all."

Billy Collins, Poet Laureate from 2001–2003, developed "Poetry 180," a website (www.loc.gov/poetry/180) featuring one poem for each day of the school year. He encourages students and teachers to read aloud a poem a day, with the strict rule that the poems are to be simply enjoyed—not analyzed or interpreted. Collins even helped establish a poetry channel for Delta Airlines.

"Well, there is always a temptation just to go to Washington and sit in this office and blow smoke rings for a year while I look out at the Capitol. But because of the excessive activism of my predecessors, it seems that an obligation falls my way to get out and light poetry bonfires and to spread the word of poetry."

Comprehension

1. **Recall** When does the speaker of "Elegy for the Giant Tortoises" expect to actually see these reptiles?

2. **Clarify** In "Today," what does "this larger dome" refer to?

3. **Clarify** What is the hand in "Spring is like a perhaps hand" doing?

Literary Analysis

4. **Paraphrase** Review your paraphrasing charts. Then read aloud one of your paraphrases and the original passage. Which version has the stronger impact?

5. **Examine Diction** What words and phrases in each poem strike you as vivid or unusual? What effect do they have on your understanding of the poem?

6. **Analyze an Elegy** Review the definition of an elegy on page 685. What characteristics of an elegy are found in "Elegy for the Giant Tortoises"? Why might Atwood have chosen this form for a poem about an endangered species?

7. **Draw Conclusions** In "Spring is like a perhaps hand," what qualities of spring does the **speaker** emphasize?

8. **Compare and Contrast** Tone is an expression of the writer's attitude toward his or her subject. For each poem, choose an adjective that best describes the tone, such as *bitter, sad, lighthearted,* or *playful.* Then list the words and phrases in each poem that help convey the tone. Which two poems are most different in tone? Explain your answer.

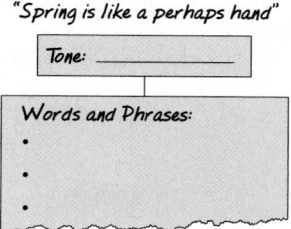

"Spring is like a perhaps hand"

Tone: _____

Words and Phrases:
-
-
-

Reading-Writing Connection

WRITING PROMPT	**SELF-CHECK**
Extended Response: Support an Opinion Which of the poems displays the most **creativity** in its treatment of its subject? Write **three to five paragraphs,** citing evidence to support your view.	*A strong evaluation will . . .* • provide criteria for evaluating creativity • evaluate each poem in terms of its creativity • present evidence such as diction, imagery, and figurative language

impending death of an entire species. Atwood's serious tone and formal diction are suitable for her somber subject.

7. *The speaker emphasizes the novelty, subtlety, and delicacy of spring.*

8. *"Spring": playful; "perhaps hand," "fraction of flower"; "Elegy": somber; "pray," "withering," "plodding," "useless armour," "sadder," "destroyed," "obsolete symbols"; "Today": joyful; "perfect," "bursting," "releasing the inhabitants." "Elegy . . ." and "Today" are the most different in tone.*

Reading-Writing Connection

WRITING PROMPT

To prepare for the assignment, have students list original or unusual uses of language from each poem. Have students use these examples to support their answers.

For ideas for writing, see

ⓘ Writing Center at **ClassZone.com**

After Reading

For additional support of post-reading questions, use these copy masters:

Ⓡ RESOURCE MANAGER—Copy Masters
Diction p. 45 (for practice of the literary analysis standards focus)
Question Support p. 49 (After Reading questions adapted for English learners and less-proficient readers)

Additional selection questions are provided for teachers on page 41.

ANSWERS

Comprehension

1. *She expects to see the tortoises on their last day of existence.*

2. *It refers to the sky above the real world.*

3. *The hand is arranging and placing the elements of spring.*

Literary Analysis

Possible answers:

4. ◼ **STANDARDS FOCUS** *Paraphrase Answers will vary.*

5. ● **STANDARDS FOCUS** *Diction In "Spring . . ." vivid and unusual phrases include "perhaps hand," "fraction of flower," and "inch of air." In "Elegy . . ." the phrases "sadder than tanks and history," "square glass altars," and "holy and obsolete symbols" are particularly vivid. In "Today" the image of "taking a hammer to the glass paperweight" is forceful and unusual.*

6. ● **STANDARDS FOCUS** *Elegy An elegy is about death, and "Elegy . . ." is about the*

Assess and Reteach

Assess

Ⓡ RESOURCE MANAGER—Copy Masters
Selection Test A pp. 51–52
Selection Test B/C pp. 53–54

◉ Test Generator CD

Reteach

Ⓢ STANDARDS LESSON FILE
Literature Lesson 16: Ode and Elegy
Study Skills Lesson 12: Paraphrasing

Focus and Motivate

OBJECTIVES

Literary Analysis
- explore the key idea of being a **competitor**
- recognize characteristics of concrete poetry
- analyze form
- read poems

Reading
- connect

SUMMARIES

"400-Meter Free Style" Maxine Kumin's concrete poem captures the simple, economical movements of a swimmer competing in a race, concentrating his efforts on achieving the fastest possible time.

"Bodybuilders' Contest" Wislawa Szymborska's humorous poem focuses on a muscular bodybuilder posing for, and winning, a competition.

What makes a great COMPETITOR?

Introduce the question, and have students read the **KEY IDEA.** Encourage students to explore the idea that a competitor's success usually involves some combination of talent, hard work, and luck. Have students complete the **DISCUSS** activity, giving reasons for the qualities they list. Then try to arrive at a class consensus regarding the most important qualities of a great **competitor.**

Selection Resources

400-Meter Free Style
Poem by Maxine Kumin

Bodybuilders' Contest
Poem by Wislawa Szymborska

What makes a great COMPETITOR?

KEY IDEA Does a great **competitor's** success mainly rely on natural talent? hard work? luck? The next two poems describe the experiences of two athletes pursuing athletic achievement.

DISCUSS With a partner, discuss your favorite kinds of competition. Then generate a list of qualities you think great competitors have in common. Present your list to other pairs to compare your ideas.

Qualities of a Great Competitor
1.
2.
3.
4.
5.

692

 **RESOURCE MANAGER UNIT 7**

Plan and Teach pp. 55–62

Literary Analysis
Form pp. 63, 64†*
Question Support p. 67*

Reading
Connect pp. 65, 66†*
Reading Fluency p. 68

Assessment
Selection Tests A, B/C pp. 69*, 71*
 Test Generator CD

BEST PRACTICES TOOLKIT

Differentiated Instruction
pp. 31–38*

Graphic Organizers/Strategies
Jigsaw Reading • Cluster Diagram
• Read-and-Say-Something

Reading Support
Audio Anthology CD*

Technology
Literature Center at **ClassZone.com**
WriteSmart CD

* Resources for Differentiation   † Also in Spanish

POETIC FORM: CONCRETE POETRY

Some poets go beyond the usual structural elements of line and stanza to write concrete poems. A **concrete poem** is one in which the poet uses visible shape to create a picture related to the poem's subject. For example, a concrete poem about stars might be written in the shape of a star. One of the poems you're about to read, "400-Meter Free Style," is a concrete poem.

LITERARY ANALYSIS: FORM

In poetry, **form** is the arrangement of words on a page. Poets use form deliberately to organize their thoughts, to help create rhythm, and to emphasize ideas and images. The two basic elements of form in poetry are **lines** and **stanzas.**

- **Lines:** The lines of a poem may be long or short. Poets manipulate line length to emphasize words and ideas and to establish rhythm.

- **Stanzas:** The lines of a poem may be grouped together in clusters known as stanzas. Poets use stanzas to organize important ideas and, in some cases, to develop rhyme schemes.

To understand how form can create a sense of rhythm in a poem, ask yourself the following questions:

- How long are the lines?
- Do the lines rhyme?
- Do the sentences always end at the end of a line?
- How many lines are in each stanza?

The two poems you are about to read have very different forms. "Bodybuilders' Contest" contains **couplets,** rhyming pairs of lines of equal length. "400-Meter Free Style," on the other hand, contains no rhyme but still has a strong rhythm. In each case, the form supports the poet's ideas.

As you read the poems in this lesson, notice the elements of form and how they affect the meaning.

READING STRATEGY: CONNECT

The poems you read will be more meaningful if you **connect** your own experiences to the ideas and feelings they express. For example, you might be on a swim team, or perhaps you have watched a swim meet like the one described in "400-Meter Free Style." Your own experience can help you understand the ideas expressed. As you read the following poems, make use of this strategy whenever appropriate.

Author Online

Maxine Kumin: Late Bloomer
Maxine Kumin didn't truly begin to write poetry until she was in her 30s. She did, however, have a few false starts before this. As a college freshman, she gave some of her poems to an instructor for comments. He returned the poems with a note that read, "Say it with flowers, but . . . don't try to write poems." Kumin didn't write poetry again for six years.

Maxine Kumin born 1925

Despite Bad Advice Kumin published her first poetry collection in 1961. Since then, she has published 14 volumes of poetry, as well as novels, essays, and children's books. She received a Pulitzer Prize in 1973 and was U.S. poet laureate from 1981 to 1982.

Wislawa Szymborska: Poland's Quiet Poet
Wislawa Szymborska was a renowned poet in her native Poland for many years before she became known in other countries. She was awarded the Nobel Prize in literature in 1996, which brought her international fame. Being thrust into the spotlight made the shy poet very uncomfortable. Today she lives quietly in Poland, where she continues to write and publish her poetry.

Wislawa Szymborska born 1923

 MORE ABOUT THE AUTHOR
For more on these poets, visit the **Literature Center** at ClassZone.com.

693

Teach

STANDARDS FOCUS

LITERARY ANALYSIS

CONCRETE POETRY

For instructional support, write these lines of poetry on the board, and then read them aloud:

The Runner
A few more yards, she told herself,
  her hunger for air was dire;
I'm nearly there, she urged herself,
  breathless
    gasping
      lungs on fire

Have students discuss how the lines of the poem help to create rhythm and emphasize the image of the runner. *Possible answer: The three short lines at the end seem to mimic the breathless pace of the runner, as if she doesn't have enough breath to speak one long line and is actually gasping the words. The way these short lines are stretched from left to right across the page also suggests the image of a runner in motion.*

CHECK UNDERSTANDING Ask students how the rhythm of this example would change if the poet had used one long line instead of three short ones.

READING STRATEGY

CONNECT

Ask students to reread the lines of poetry written on the board for the **LITERARY ANALYSIS** activity. What experiences help them connect to the action and sensations that the poet describes?

CHECK UNDERSTANDING Elicit examples of poems or songs that students have connected to because of their own experiences.

RESOURCE MANAGER—Copy Master
 Connect p. 65 (for student use while reading the selection)

400-Meter Free Style

Maxine Kumin

THE GUN full swing the swimmer catapults[1] and cracks
    s
    i
    x
5 feet away onto that perfect glass he catches at **(A)**
  a
  n
  d
throws behind him scoop after scoop cunningly moving
10   t
    h
    e
water back to move him forward. Thrift is his wonderful
  s
15 e
  c
ret; he has schooled out all extravagance. No muscle **(B)**
    r
    i
20   p
ples without compensation wrist cock to heel snap to
  h
  i
  s
25 mobile mouth that siphons[2] in the air that nurtures
    h
    i
    m
at half an inch above sea level so to speak.

---

1. **catapults** (kăt′ə-pŭlts′): springs.
2. **siphons** (sī′fənz): draws in, as if with a tube.

LITERARY ANALYSIS

(A) FORM

Possible answer: The poem's lines have endings in the same sense that each completed lap of the swimming pool has an "ending"—a brief pause that also marks the beginning of the next lap.

READING STRATEGY

(B) CONNECT

Students' responses should reflect the understanding that total concentration on a goal can maximize the likelihood of achieving that goal, while distractions can hamper performance.

Lines 13–29
REINFORCE *KEY IDEA*: COMPETITOR

Discuss How do these lines convey the amount of preparation this **competitor** has done for the race? *Possible answer: Through hard work, the competitor has "schooled out all extravagance" (line 17), meaning that there are no wasted movements. All of the swimmer's energy is applied toward the achievement of his goal.*

(A) FORM
Would you say that the **lines** in this poem have endings, or does the poem consist of one long line? Explain.

(B) CONNECT
The swimmer is completely focused on moving through the water as quickly and efficiently as possible. Think about a time when all your attention was focused on a single goal. Did it help you attain the goal?

DIFFERENTIATED INSTRUCTION

For general guidelines on differentiating instruction, see

 BEST PRACTICES TOOLKIT
Differentiated Instruction pp. 31–38

FOR LESS–PROFICIENT READERS

Options for Reading Have students listen to "400-Meter Free Style" on the *Audio Anthology CD* as they read along silently. Ask students why they think the poem is displayed on the page the way it is. Next, read the poem aloud a sentence at a time. Have students repeat what you have read, using the same intonation and rhythm.

```
30  T
    h
    e
    astonishing  whites  of  the  soles  of  his  feet  rise
                                                          a
35                                                        n
                                                          d
    salute  us  on  the  turns.  He  flips,  converts,  and  is  gone
    a
    l
40  l
    in  one.  We  watch  him  for  signs.  His  arms  are  steady  at
                                                               t
                                                               h
                                                               e
45  catch,  his  cadent³  feet  tick  in  the  stretch,  they  know
    t
    h
    e
    lesson  well.  Lungs  know,  too;  he  does  not  list  for
50                                                            a
                                                              i
                                                              r
    he  drives  along  on  little  sips  carefully  expended
    b
55  u
    t
    that  plum  red  heart  pumps  hard  cries  hurt  how  soon
                                                              i
                                                              t
60                                                            s
    near  one  more  and  makes  its  final  surge  Time:  4:25:9 ©
```

© CONCRETE POETRY
Describe the movement created by the arrangement of the poem's lines.

---

3. **cadent** (kād′nt): moving in a rhythmic pattern, or cadence.

BACKGROUND

Competitive Swimming While the sport of swimming has not achieved professional status, it has been established as an amateur sport since the 19th century (1837 in England) and became part of the modern Olympic Games in 1896. Today, USA Swimming, the national governing board in this country, claims 300,000 young members, and sponsors more than 7,000 meets each year.

Cultural Connection In the 19th century, while swimmers in England, the United States, Australia, and Canada were inventing swimming strokes of their own, observers reported more efficient maneuvers—especially certain overarm motions—by peoples of South America, the islands of the South Seas, and Hawaii. Finally, these observers persuaded colleagues to employ the techniques, and swimmers' times improved dramatically. Today, the study of stroke mechanics, body conditioning, and hydrodynamics helps swimmers to set new records all the time. Invite students to discuss swimming styles and other distinctive athletic traditions of their own cultures.

POETIC FORM

© CONCRETE POETRY

Possible answer: The poem's form parallels a swimming race. That is, the lines flip back and forth, just as swimmers swim back and forth completing laps.

ANALYZE VISUALS

Activity How does the swimmer's arm in this photograph connect to the visual form of the poem on the page? *Possible answer: The swimmer's arm makes a curved shape that matches the shape of the words that curve down at the ends and beginnings of lines.*

FOR LESS–PROFICIENT READERS

Vocabulary Support Have students explore the meanings of these words and phrases, using context clues and, as needed, the dictionary: "full swing" (line 1), "schooled out" (line 17), "heel snap" (line 21), "at the catch" (lines 41–45), "the stretch" (line 45), "list" (line 49), "drives" (line 53).

Comprehension Support Have students use the Jigsaw strategy to discuss and analyze the meaning of these images: "cracks . . . onto that perfect glass" (lines 1–5); "mobile mouth that siphons in the air . . . at half an inch above sea level" (lines 25–29); "astonishing whites of the soles of his feet rise and salute us" (lines 33–37); "flips, converts, and is gone all in one" (lines 37–41).

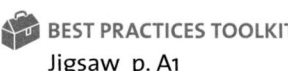 **BEST PRACTICES TOOLKIT**
Jigsaw p. A1

Prereading for this poem is found on page 692.

ANALYZE VISUALS

Possible answer: The painting suggests strength, power, and robust health.

About the Art Asian Pacific American artist Byron Spicer grew up in San Francisco in the 1960s and 1970s. The energy and diversity of the city influenced and inspired his imaginative artwork. Spicer paints numerous images at the same time and then assembles them in three-dimensional layers onto one panel. *Municipal Bonds* depicts a muscular physique suggestive of Szymborska's bodybuilder.

LITERARY ANALYSIS

D FORM

Possible answer: The poet divides her poem into three stanzas. The first stanza focuses on the bodybuilder's rippling muscles—the "ocean of his torso" (line 2). The second stanza describes his choreographed onstage movements for the contest. The third stanza reveals that he wins the competition.

If students need help... Help students use a Cluster Diagram to visualize the ideas presented in each of the three stanzas.

 BEST PRACTICES TOOLKIT—Transparency
Cluster Diagram p. B18

SELECTION WRAP—UP

SYNTHESIZE Ask students to consider how the athletes in these poems are represented as **competitors**, even though no opponent is ever described.

★ CRITIQUE Ask students which poem they think is more memorable, and why.

READING FLUENCY

Distribute the copy master and have students work in pairs or groups to practice fluency.

R RESOURCE MANAGER—Copy Master
Reading Fluency p. 68

BODYBUILDERS' CONTEST

Wislawa Szymborska

Municipal Bonds (2004), Byron Spicer. Mixed media, 45″ × 45″. © Byron Spicer.

From scalp to sole, all muscles in slow motion.
The ocean of his torso drips with lotion.
The king of all is he who preens[1] and wrestles
with sinews twisted into monstrous pretzels.

5   Onstage, he grapples with a grizzly bear
the deadlier for not really being there.
Three unseen panthers are in turn laid low,
each with one smoothly choreographed[2] blow.

He grunts while showing his poses and paces.
10 His back alone has twenty different faces.
The mammoth fist he raises as he wins
is tribute to the force of vitamins. **D**

Translated by Stanislaw Baranczak and Clare Cavanagh

---

1. **preens:** makes himself attractive and then shows off his appearance.
2. **choreographed** (kôr′ē-ə-grăft′): with the movements planned and arranged, as in a dance.

ANALYZE VISUALS
What qualities of a bodybuilder are reflected in the painting? Cite details.

D FORM
Notice the form of this poem. How has the poet used **stanzas** to organize her ideas?

DIFFERENTIATED INSTRUCTION

FOR LESS—PROFICIENT READERS

Support Comprehension Have students use the Read-and-Say-Something strategy to analyze the meaning and explain the humor in these lines: "From scalp to sole, all muscles in slow motion" (line 1); "sinews twisted into monstrous pretzels" (line 4); "a grizzly bear the deadlier for not really being there" (lines 5–6); "His back alone has twenty different faces" (line 10).

BEST PRACTICES TOOLKIT
Read-and-Say-Something p. D3

FOR ADVANCED LEARNERS/PRE—AP

Synthesize "Bodybuilders' Contest" was translated into English from Polish. Ask students what challenges the translators must have faced and why translating poetry is so much more difficult than translating prose. You may want to remind students that the English version consists of rhyming couplets. You may also want to point out that humor in one language does not always translate easily into another.

Comprehension

1. **Recall** In "Bodybuilders' Contest," what does the bodybuilder look like he is doing onstage?

2. **Recall** What is the very first thing that happens in "400-Meter Free Style"?

3. **Clarify** What "signs" has the speaker been watching for in "400-Meter Free Style"?

Literary Analysis

4. **Connect** What connections were you able to make to these two poems? Which athlete did you think was the better **competitor**? Explain.

5. **Analyze a Concrete Poem** In what ways does the shape of "400-Meter Free Style" reflect the poem's subject? Would the poem have as much impact if it were written in **stanzas** with clear line breaks? Explain.

6. **Interpret Imagery** Reread lines 30–41 in "400-Meter Free Style." How is the "salute" by the soles of the swimmer's feet in keeping with his other movements?

7. **Examine Sound Devices** In Kumin's poem, there are a number of sound devices, including **alliteration,** the repetition of consonant sounds at the beginning of words. Identify at least five examples of alliteration. What effect do they have when the poem is read aloud?

8. **Analyze Rhyme** "Bodybuilders' Contest" uses rhyming **couplets** to call attention to certain images in each stanza and to create humor. What humorous images are emphasized in the poem?

9. **Examine Form** The form of "Bodybuilders' Contest" is very controlled. In what ways does this form fit the subject of the poem?

Reading-Writing Connection

WRITING PROMPT	SELF-CHECK
Extended Response: Write a Concrete Poem Write your own **concrete poem** by first choosing a topic that suggests an object or an action, such as a bird or someone jumping. Then think of a simple **shape** that reflects that object or action. Draw an outline of the object, and write a poem to fit into the shape.	*A successful concrete poem will . . .* • focus on a single object or action • have a shape that closely connects to the subject • use precise, sensory words in a fresh and interesting way

7. *Examples of alliteration: "swing," "swimmer" (line 1); "catapults," "cracks" (line 1); "mobile mouth" (line 25); "sea," "so," "speak" (line 29); "lesson," "Lungs," "list" (line 49). The poem's alliteration unifies the flow of words.*

8. *The rhymes emphasize the images at the end of each couplet, such as the torso dripping with "lotion" (line 2), "sinews twisted into monstrous pretzels" (line 4), and "the force of vitamins" (line 12).*

9. ● **STANDARDS FOCUS** *Form The poem's controlled form matches the bodybuilder's controlled physique.*

Reading-Writing Connection

WRITING PROMPT

Tell students that they can also use the words and lines of their poems to form a shape. For example, a poem about baseball might be arranged to form a baseball diamond.

For ideas for writing, see

ⓘ Writing Center at **ClassZone.com**

After Reading

For additional support of post-reading questions, use these copy masters:

Ⓡ RESOURCE MANAGER—Copy Masters
Form p. 63 (for practice of the literary analysis standards focus)
Question Support p. 67 (After Reading questions adapted for English learners and less-proficient readers)

Additional selection questions are provided for teachers on page 59.

ANSWERS

Comprehension

1. *The bodybuilder looks like he is grappling with animals.*

2. *A gun fires, starting the race.*

3. *The speaker has been watching for signs that the swimmer is tiring or losing his concentration or rhythm.*

Literary Analysis
Possible answers:

4. ■ **STANDARDS FOCUS** *Connect Students should connect their own experiences to ideas in both poems and give reasons for their choices of the better competitor.*

5. ● **STANDARDS FOCUS** *Concrete Poetry The shape of the poem suggests a swimmer swimming laps. The poem would have less impact if it were written in stanzas because it would lose this visual connection.*

6. *The "salute" is part of the swimmer's flip turn, described in lines 37–41.*

Assess and Reteach

Assess

Ⓡ RESOURCE MANAGER—Copy Masters
Selection Test A pp. 69–70
Selection Test B/C pp. 71–72

Ⓢ Test Generator CD

Reteach

Ⓢ STANDARDS LESSON FILE
Literature Lesson 19: Structure of Poetry

Focus and Motivate

OBJECTIVES

Reading for Information

- synthesize information from multiple sources
- support an opinion
- read a magazine article
- understand the function of a sidebar

SUMMARY

In this article, a teenage girl recounts her experience as a participant in the finals of the National Youth Poetry Slam. She describes how, even though her team did not win, the competition provided an exciting and rewarding opportunity for self-expression.

What's the Connection?

Use the SQ3R graphic organizer to help students preview and read the article. Direct students to

- Scan the article for title, headings, and pictures. Also note the use of italics.
- Skim the article, and make predictions about what they think they will learn.
- Write questions based on their skim of the text. Example: What is a "poetry slam"?
- Answer the questions as they read.
- Summarize key points of the article.

 BEST PRACTICES TOOLKIT—Transparency SQ3R p. A23

Teach

Skill Focus: Synthesize

- Explain that a sidebar is meant to complement the main article—that is, extend the information in some way. Point out that "Not Your Father's Poetry" was written by someone other than the author of the main article, but that sometimes authors write one or more sidebars for their own articles.
- After students have read the article and the sidebar, discuss how the sidebar complements the main article.

 RESOURCE MANAGER—Copy Master Synthesize p. 81

The Night Poetry Rocked the House

Magazine Article

Use with "400-Meter Free Style" and "Bodybuilders' Contest," pages 694 and 696.

What's the Connection?

The last two poems brought to life two athletic competitions: a swim meet and a bodybuilders' contest. The article you are about to read will give you an idea of what it feels like to compete at a very different sort of event—a poetry slam.

Skill Focus: Synthesize

Magazine articles often include **sidebars**—news items or short features inserted near the main text. When you read a magazine article that has a sidebar, you need to **synthesize** the information from both the article and its sidebar. By putting together the facts, ideas, and details from each, you'll get a fuller understanding of the topic.

   How do you do that? What do you read first? Do you interrupt your reading of one piece to read the other? Here's how you can synthesize the ideas and details from "The Night Poetry Rocked the House" and the accompanying sidebar, "Not Your Father's Poetry."

- **Skim** both the main article and the sidebar to get a basic idea of what each is about and how each is organized.
- **Read** the main article from start to finish; then **summarize** its main ideas and details for yourself.
- **Note** any questions you have after reading the main article.
- **Read** the sidebar. As you read, ask yourself: What am I learning here that I did not learn from the main article?

After reading the sidebar, think about why the information in it was given separately from the main article. The answers you come up with may help you recognize the focus and strengths of the main article. For more help synthesizing the article and sidebar that follow, complete a chart like the one started here.

Source	Main Ideas & Information	Questions & New Information
1. "The Night Poetry Rocked the House"	Rachel Shapiro's last performance in the National Youth Poetry Slam in San Francisco is amazing.	What exactly is a poetry slam?

Selection Resources

 RESOURCE MANAGER UNIT 7

Plan and Teach pp. 73–78

Reading
Summary pp. 79†*, 80‡*
Synthesize pp. 81, 83†*
Reading Check p. 85*
Support an Opinion pp. 82, 84†
Question Support p. 87*

Assessment
Selection Tests A, B/C pp. 89*, 91*
⊙ Test Generator CD

Reading Support
⊙ Audio Anthology CD*

 BEST PRACTICES TOOLKIT
SQ3R • New Word Analysis
• Think-Pair-Share

---

* Resources for Differentiation   † Also in Spanish   ‡ In Haitian Creole and Vietnamese

The NIGHT POETRY ROCKED the HOUSE

Rachel Shapiro

We may not have won the national poetry slam—but that wasn't the point. **A**

We were brimming and overflowing with excitement. We had made it to the finals of the National Youth Poetry Slam in San Francisco, where more than 100 of the top teenage poets from across the country gathered to perform. It was 1 A.M., the last performance of the third and final round, and my team, representing
10 New York City, was about to go on, ending the entire weekend of inspiring words.

Onome, Casey, and I planned to perform a group piece that the three of us had written about women. *A girl thinks rich, thorough thoughts . . . Why doesn't she speak up in class?* We knew we would have points deducted because our piece was well over the
20 three-minute limit. But it didn't matter. We had something to say. We had a message to leave with San Francisco.

ELOQUENT WORDS

The three of us walked out on the stage gazing at the chandeliers and the 1,200 faces who cheered, who came to hear the voices of the young poets of the country. We performed on a stage blessed with the eloquent words of
30 skinny girls with proud, deep voices,

13-year-olds who roused the entire crowd, round women from Atlanta who sang amid their poetry; it was a stage ridden with confusion, rebirth, inspiration, talent, and pride.

Many words that night had shocked us with their brilliance. Now it was our turn. *Does she learn to dismiss her anger when/ he says he's sick of male-*
40 *bashing poems/ did she dump him when he bashed her?*

We had an open stage, a free forum to share the plight of the young girl who doesn't speak up in class—*who could never realize she was brilliant*—to speak of the silencing and submission of women—*Was she always this numb? Was she always this quiet?*—the abuse, the sellouts, and the lack of respect—
50 *Did her tears fall like raindrops/ outside a soundproof window?*

The words poured out with emotion and house-rocking force. We traded solos like a jazz trio; we jammed in counterpoint, in unison, in rhythm. *She was brilliant. Was she always this?* **B**

The second after we released the last word, the crowd was frozen, stunned. And then the room started to
60 shake with energy—in an instant my coach was onstage, people whom I had never met were hugging me, someone

A SYNTHESIZE
What do the title and the statement below it suggest the **main idea** of the article will be?

B SYNTHESIZE
Based on what you've read so far, how would you describe this poetry slam?

INFORMATIONAL ANALYSIS

A SYNTHESIZE

Possible answer: The title and the statement below it suggest that the article is about some kind of poetry competition—a competition that the writer did not win but from which she did gain some benefit.

If students need help . . . Elicit or explain the meaning of *rocked the house*: "caused great excitement in a theater or auditorium." Point out the word *won* in the statement, and elicit that this word implies a competition or contest.

INFORMATIONAL ANALYSIS

B SYNTHESIZE

Possible answer: The poetry slam is an exciting competition ("1,200 faces who cheered" [line 26]; "words poured out with emotion and house-rocking force" [line 53] and inspiring [line 11]). It is also entertaining to watch and listen to ("We traded solos like a jazz trio; we jammed in counterpoint, in unison, in rhythm" [lines 54–55]).

DIFFERENTIATED INSTRUCTION

FOR LESS–PROFICIENT READERS

Comprehension Support To make sure that students understand the writer's technique, ask what the italic type represents in lines 15–17, 38–41, and 44–51 (*excerpts from the performance of Rachel Shapiro's team*). Elicit or explain that each italicized quotation illustrates the immediately preceding text. Lead a class discussion of the italicized excerpts to help students understand their meanings.

FOR ENGLISH LEARNERS

Vocabulary: Idioms Use New Word Analysis to teach these idioms from the article: *had made it to* (line 2), "had reached"; *ridden with* (line 34), "full of"; *male-bashing* (lines 39–40), "verbally attacking males"; *dump him* (line 40), "get rid of him"; *sellouts* (line 49), "acts of betrayal or giving in."

🧰 **BEST PRACTICES TOOLKIT—Transparency**
New Word Analysis p. E8

700 UNIT 7: THE LANGUAGE OF POETRY

INFORMATIONAL ANALYSIS

C SYNTHESIZE

Possible answer: Poetry slams are different from more traditional poetry readings ("Not Your Father's Poetry"). They have become popular and widely accepted ("have come of age" [line 1]). They blend performance with competition (lines 9–13), which helps explain their popularity (lines 20–23).

INFORMATIONAL ANALYSIS

D SYNTHESIZE

Possible answer: The paragraph emphasizes the idea that winning "wasn't the point." What mattered was that the poetry slam gave participants an opportunity to express themselves and be heard.

C SYNTHESIZE
Skim the title and topic sentences of the sidebar. What do you think you will learn from it?

D SYNTHESIZE
What element of Shapiro's experience is emphasized in this paragraph?

Not Your Father's Poetry
By Bruce Weber/*The New York Times*

C Poetry slams have come of age. As poetry in general has surged in popularity in the United States, this offshoot has emerged as a way for passionate, mostly young people—representing a wide ethnic and racial range—to air their voices and for an evidently eager audience to hear and embrace them.

10 Slamming is a weird and lively amalgam of performance art, hip-hop concert, and—with its judges holding up numerical score cards—Olympic figure skating. It's a national grassroots movement, which began when a Chicago poet named Marc Smith held the first competitions in a bar in 1984.

The 11th annual National Poetry Slam was held in August, and the 3rd annual
20 National Youth Poetry Slam was held last spring.

Slam poetry has been boosted by, among other things, the popularity of rap music, the boom in stand-up comedy, and the proliferation of stage monologuists. At the same time, sales of poetry books have soared 30 percent in the last three years.

Watching others perform, says
30 Danny Solis, who has competed out of Albuquerque, New Mexico, "showed me that poetry could be something that lifts an audience to another place, like jazz, salsa or dance."

came up to us crying, saying, "Thank you. As a woman, I knew that had to be said, and you all said it so beautifully."

ARENAS OF SUPPORT

I knew then that it was real, and that it was necessary to find creative ways to express yourself, so that people,
70 especially adults, will take you seriously and realize that you have some monumental things to say as well. Poetry slams give poets arenas full of excitement and support that

encourage us, urge us to tell them what we have to say. **D**

We didn't win, but it couldn't have mattered less to me. When I think of the young men and women with
80 whom I shared the stage, and especially of my team, I think of an Adrienne Rich poem:

No one has imagined us. We want to live like trees,
Sycamores blazing through the sulfuric air,
dappled with scars still exuberantly budding.

DIFFERENTIATED INSTRUCTION

FOR LESS–PROFICIENT READERS

Vocabulary Support Have students use Think-Pair-Share strategy to explore the meanings of these words and phrases in the sidebar, using context clues and, as needed, the dictionary: *come of age* (line 1), *offshoot* (line 4), *embrace* (line 9), *amalgam* (line 11), *grassroots* (line 14), *proliferation* (line 25), *stage monologuists* (lines 25–26).

 BEST PRACTICES TOOLKIT—Transparency
Think-Pair-Share p. A18

FOR ADVANCED LEARNERS/PRE–AP

Evaluate Comparison Have students re-read lines 10–14. Then have them reflect on the accuracy of the writer's description of slamming. Direct students to work in small groups to do the research necessary to judge whether slamming can indeed be thought of as an "amalgam of performance art, hip-hop concert, and . . . Olympic figure skating" (lines 11–14). Have groups share their conclusions with the class.

Comprehension

1. **Recall** Why have these young poets gathered as described in "The Night Poetry Rocked the House"?

2. **Summarize** How was the National Youth Poetry Slam a rewarding experience for the author?

Critical Analysis

3. **Synthesize** Review the chart you filled in as you read the main article and the sidebar. What does the sidebar add to your understanding of Shapiro's poetry slam experience? Explain.

4. **Analyze Tone** Describe the tone of the main article and the tone of the sidebar. Why do you suppose their tones differ?

Read for Information: Support an Opinion

WRITING PROMPT

You have just read three very different portrayals of three very different forms of competition—a swim meet, a bodybuilders' contest, and a poetry slam. Which portrayal do you find the most compelling? What elements of that piece make it more interesting to you than the others?

To answer this prompt, follow these steps:

1. Decide which piece you find yourself caring the most about. Write a brief statement explaining why. This statement will be your **claim.**

2. Write down the elements of this piece that make it the most compelling of the three. These will be the **reasons** for your choice.

3. Find details in the selection that illustrate each of your reasons. These will be your **evidence.**

4. State your opinion and support it with your reasons and evidence. You may want to mention any strengths of the other selections, but also point out the reasons why—despite these strengths—they don't match up to your favorite.

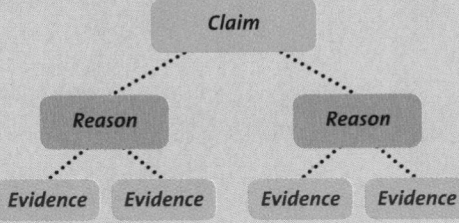

FOR LESS–PROFICIENT WRITERS

Read for Information To help students determine which piece they found most compelling and why, suggest that they jot down thoughts about each of the three as a brainstorming prewriting activity. Have students use three separate sheets of paper and then compare the results. The piece that generated the most specific and detailed notes is probably the one that made the strongest impression.

FOR ADVANCED LEARNERS/PRE–AP

Make Judgments Rachel Shapiro writes, "We didn't win, but it couldn't have mattered less to me" (lines 77–78). Have students discuss whether the swimmer in "400-Meter Free Style" or the bodybuilder in "Bodybuilders' Contest" would have felt the same way. Also have them explore whether Shapiro is being disingenuous in her statement.

Practice and Apply

For additional support of post-reading questions, use these copy masters:

R RESOURCE MANAGER—Copy Masters
Reading Check p. 85
Question Support p. 87
Support an Opinion p. 82

For additional questions, see page 76.

ANSWERS

Comprehension

1. *They are competing in the finals of a national poetry slam.*

2. *The author was inspired by the words of other poets and rewarded by the audience's positive response to her own performance.*

Critical Analysis

Possible answers:

3. ■ **STANDARDS FOCUS** *Synthesize The sidebar explains what poetry slams are, how they began, and why they've become so popular. These details flesh out Shapiro's account of her participation in a poetry slam.*

4. *The tone of the main article is enthusiastic and personal because it is a first-person account written by an actual participant. The tone of the sidebar is more subdued and objective because it is a newspaper article written by an observer.*

Read for Information: Support an Opinion

Writing Prompt *Students should support their opinions with evidence from the selections.*

Assess and Reteach

Assess

R RESOURCE MANAGER—Copy Masters
Selection Tests A, B/C pp. 89–90, 91–92

🖉 Test Generator CD

Reteach

S STANDARDS LESSON FILE
Informational Texts Lesson 1: Text Features
Reading Lesson 14: Synthesizing Information

Focus and Motivate

OBJECTIVES

Literary Analysis
- explore the key idea of **imagination**
- recognize characteristics of odes
- analyze figurative language (simile, metaphor, personification)
- read poems

Reading
- visualize poetic images and comparisons

Grammar and Writing
- use infinitives and infinitive phrases to incorporate details
- use writing to analyze literature

SUMMARIES

"For Poets" The speaker in this poem encourages poets to reach within themselves but also to "fly" with imagination.

"Ode to My Socks" In this ode, presented in English and Spanish, the speaker praises the virtues of a pair of hand-knit socks.

"egg horror poem" This poem describes the terror that refrigerated eggs feel as they wait to be made into meals for people.

What makes your IMAGINATION *soar?*

Ask the question and relate the **KEY IDEA** to the photograph. After students have completed the **QUICKWRITE**, call on volunteers to share responses, and ask how **imagination** influenced their descriptions.

Selection Resources

For Poets
Poem by Al Young

Ode to My Socks
Poem by Pablo Neruda

egg horror poem
Poem by Laurel Winter

What makes your IMAGINATION *soar?*

KEY IDEA It's easy to see why people might be inspired to creativity by something grand, like love or mountains, but **imagination** is not limited to the grand. A poet might see something as simple as a shoelace in a completely new way.

QUICKWRITE Write a short description of a familiar object as though you'd never seen it before. What does it make you think of? Use your imagination.

702

 **RESOURCE MANAGER UNIT 7**

Plan and Teach pp. 93–100

Literary Analysis
Figurative Language pp. 101, 102†*
Question Support p. 105*

Reading
Visualize pp. 103, 104†*

Grammar and Writing
Write Concisely p. 107

Assessment
Selection Tests A, B/C pp. 109*, 111*
Test Generator CD

 BEST PRACTICES TOOLKIT

Differentiated Instruction
pp. 31–38*

Graphic Organizers/Strategies
Read Aloud/Think Aloud • Venn Diagram • Cluster Diagram • Question Frames

Reading Support
Audio Anthology CD*

Technology
Literature Center at **ClassZone.com**
WriteSmart CD

---

* Resources for Differentiation   † Also in Spanish

POETIC FORM: ODE

A traditional **ode** is a poem that highly praises something— usually a person, an event, or an idea. Traditional odes are about serious subjects, and they have a formal tone. In this lesson, you'll read an ode by Pablo Neruda, who broke with tradition by writing odes about everyday objects—in this case a pair of cozy socks.

LITERARY ANALYSIS: FIGURATIVE LANGUAGE

Figurative language goes beyond the literal meaning of words, creating a comparison between two things not usually associated with one another. Such **figures of speech** allow the writer to characterize one of the two items in a particular, often unusual, way. Figurative language has three basic types, all found in Pablo Neruda's "Ode to My Socks."

- A **simile** compares two unlike things that have something in common, using the word *like* or *as*.

  two socks soft / as rabbits

- A **metaphor** directly compares two unlike things by saying that one thing actually *is* the other.

  my feet became / two woolen / fish

- **Personification** lends human qualities to an object, animal, or idea.

  my feet seemed / unacceptable to me, / two tired old / fire fighters

As you read, identify the figurative language used, and think of the qualities the comparision gives to the subject being described.

Poem	Passage	Figure of Speech	Meaning of Comparision
"For Poets"	"Breathe in trees"	metaphor	

READING STRATEGY: VISUALIZE

The process of forming a mental picture from a written description is called **visualizing**. Good readers visualize the images and comparisons in a poem to help them understand the poet's ideas. As you read the next three poems, pause frequently to visualize the images and comparisons you find.

Author Online

Al Young: A Man of Many Talents In his varied life, Al Young has written screenplays, essays, and novels, but poetry is his first love. "Poetry sweetens the tongue, deepens the heart, and expands the mind," he once said. "Even a writer of annual reports may draw richly from the conventions and techniques of poetry."

**Al Young
born 1939**

Pablo Neruda: Poetry and Politics Acclaimed both in his native Chile and internationally, Pablo Neruda's life was a mix of poetry and politics. After writing love poetry early in his career, Neruda turned to more political verse in the 1930s and 1940s.

**Pablo Neruda
1904–1973**

In the 1950s he began writing about everyday objects in a simple style that many people could understand and enjoy. Neruda was awarded the Nobel Prize in literature in 1971.

Laurel Winter: Sci-Fi/ Fantasy Poet "I grew up as an odd kid in the mountains of Montana," writes Laurel Winter. "I was klutzy and bookwormish and didn't always fit in." Today Winter is an award-winning writer.

**Laurel Winter
born 1959**

On writing science fiction and fantasy, she said, "To me as a writer, in fantasy everything is available. If you can think of it, you can write it."

 MORE ABOUT THE AUTHOR
For more on these poets, visit the **Literature Center at ClassZone.com.**

703

ANALYZE VISUALS

Possible answer: The boy in the image is flying, as the speaker recommends (line 17). The image shows sunlight, trees, and mountains, all of which are mentioned in the poem. Like the poem, the image depicts flying as an imaginative rather than literal activity.

About the Art Christopher Myers (b. 1975), is the son of author Walter Dean Myers.

LITERARY ANALYSIS

Ⓐ FIGURATIVE LANGUAGE

Possible answer: The speaker is really suggesting that poets extend themselves. In particular, they should become aware of the natural world that surrounds them.

If students need help . . . Discuss the figurative meaning of specific details. *Possible answer:* A "mole" (line 3) could mean a person who stays isolated in artistic work and hides from life experiences or other people. "Sunlight" (line 7) could stand for life with all its brightness and energy.

READING STRATEGY

Ⓑ VISUALIZE

Possible answer: These lines create mental pictures of creatures that move out of their comfort zone and extend themselves, as the speaker wants poets to do.

For Poets

AL YOUNG

Stay beautiful
but dont stay down underground too long
Dont turn into a mole
or a worm
5 or a root
or a stone

Come on out into the sunlight
Breathe in trees
Knock out mountains
10 Commune[1] with snakes
& be the very hero of birds Ⓐ

Dont forget to poke your head up
& blink
think
15 Walk all around
Swim upstream Ⓑ

Dont forget to fly

ANALYZE VISUALS
What elements of this image express the sentiments of this poem? Be specific.

Ⓐ FIGURATIVE LANGUAGE
In lines 7–11, the speaker is not offering literal advice. What is he really suggesting?

Ⓑ VISUALIZE
Reread lines 12–16. What mental pictures do these lines create?

---

1. **commune** (kə-myōōn'): communicate intimately.

From *Wings* (2000), Christopher Myers © 2000 Christopher Meyers. Reprinted by permission of Scholastic, Inc.

DIFFERENTIATED INSTRUCTION

For general guidelines on differentiating instruction, see

📦 **BEST PRACTICES TOOLKIT**
Differentiated Instruction pp. 31–38

FOR LESS–PROFICIENT READERS

Options for Reading Read "For Poets" aloud to help students appreciate its rhythm. Have students point out their favorite lines and explain why they feel that the lines are effective. Follow the same plan for "Ode to My Socks" and "egg horror poem," inviting students to be the readers.

DISCUSSION PROMPTS

Use these prompts to help students explore the speaker's advice to poets:

Connect What kinds of behaviors or attitudes might make a person become isolated or out of touch with the world? ***Possible answer:*** *working too hard, never trying new things, never exploring new places, never spending time with people from different backgrounds*

Analyze What does the speaker mean when he advises poets to "Stay beautiful" (line 1)? What advice is he offering when he cautions them against staying "underground too long" (line 2)? ***Possible answer:*** *The speaker means that poets should continue to nurture their pure, artistic sensibility—the trait that allows them to create poetry. However, they should not allow themselves to become too isolated or self-involved, because poets also need to experience life and other people if their poetry is to have any meaning.*

Evaluate Do you think that the speaker's two-part advice is valid for poets or other artists? How about everybody else? *Students should support their answers.*

FOR LESS–PROFICIENT READERS

Comprehension Support To make sure students understand that the speaker is urging a balanced view, discuss these questions:

- From the speaker's words, how can you tell that it's probably all right for poets to spend part of their time "underground"?
- According to the speaker, what do poets who spend all their time underground miss doing on land? in the air?

FOR ENGLISH LEARNERS

Language: Punctuation and Print Clues Note that in "For Poets," poet Al Young does not use any periods, apostrophes, or commas. He does use print cues, however, such as the ampersand (&) and capital letters. Suggest that Young may have kept the capital letters to mark his various thoughts but may have made the punctuation choices to emphasize a sense of urgency in sharing those thoughts with poets.

Prereading for this poem is found on page 702.

LITERARY ANALYSIS

C FIGURATIVE LANGUAGE

Possible answer: The similes are "soft as rabbits" (lines 6–7) and "slipped my feet into them as if into jewel cases" (lines 8–12). The first simile describes the socks' softness, as if the wool were as soft as the fur of rabbits. The second simile suggests the fine craftsmanship of the socks that were knit by Maru Mori and the value that the speaker places upon them as gifts.

If students need help . . . Have students search for the signal words *like* or *as*. Brainstorm for possible comparisons, then ask students to choose the comparisons that make the most sense to them.

Extend the Discussion Use a Venn Diagram to focus on one of the comparisons. For example, write *Socks* in one circle and *Jewel Cases* in the other. Have students fill in the diagram with details that show how the two objects are similar and different.

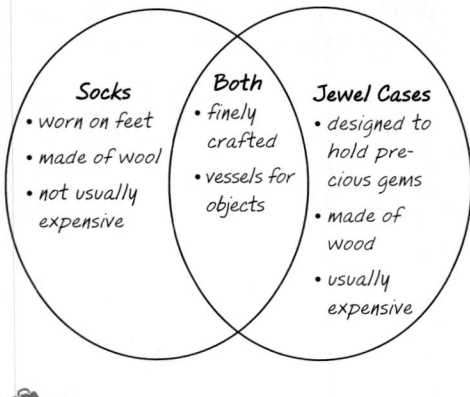

Socks
• worn on feet
• made of wool
• not usually expensive

Both
• finely crafted
• vessels for objects

Jewel Cases
• designed to hold precious gems
• made of wood
• usually expensive

🧰 **BEST PRACTICES TOOLKIT—Transparency**
Venn Diagram p. A26

ODE TO MY SOCKS

PABLO NERUDA

Maru Mori brought me
a pair
of socks
knitted with her own
5 shepherd's hands,
two socks soft
as rabbits.
I slipped
my feet into them
10 as if
into
jewel cases
woven
with threads of
15 dusk
and sheep's wool. **C**

Me trajo Maru Mori
un par
de calcetines
que tejió con sus manos
de pastora,
dos calcetines suaves
como liebres.
En ellos
metí los pies
como en
dos
estuches
tejidos
con hebras del
crepúsculo
y pellejo de ovejas.

C FIGURATIVE LANGUAGE
Identify the two **similes** in lines 1–16. What qualities of the socks is suggested by each simile?

706 UNIT 7: THE LANGUAGE OF POETRY

DIFFERENTIATED INSTRUCTION

FOR LESS–PROFICIENT READERS
Track Details As students read, have them complete a Cluster Diagram with comparisons and descriptive words that Neruda uses to describe the socks. Invite students to share their thoughts about the comparison or description that they consider the most imaginative, precise, unrealistic, and so on.

🧰 **BEST PRACTICES TOOLKIT—Transparency**
Cluster Diagram p. B18

FOR ENGLISH LEARNERS
Culture: Connect If any English learners speak Spanish as their first language, have them read aloud part or all of the Spanish version of this poem to the class. Have the rest of the class listen for the rhythm, alliteration, and assonance that is part of the original version of the poem.

Lines 17–40
REINFORCE *KEY IDEA*: IMAGINATION

Discuss Why do you think Neruda described his socks and feet with such **imagination**?
Possible answer: *Neruda may have wanted to show his appreciation to Maru Mori, who made the socks for him. He also may have wanted readers to understand that there is something wonderful about even the most ordinary objects.*

Audacious[1] socks,
my feet became
two woolen
20 fish,
two long sharks
of lapis[2] blue
shot
with a golden thread,
25 two mammoth blackbirds,
two cannons,
thus honored
were
my feet
30 by
these
celestial[3]
socks. **D**
They were
35 so beautiful
that for the first time
my feet seemed
unacceptable to me,
two tired old
40 fire fighters

Violentos calcentines,
mis pies fueron
dos pescados
de lana,
dos largos tiburones
de azul ultramarino
atravesados
por una trenza de oro,
dos gigantescos mirlos,
dos cañones:
mis pies
fueron honrados
de este modo
por
estos
celestiales
calcentines.
Eran
tan hermosos
que por primera vez
mis pies me parecieron
inaceptables
como dos decrépitos
bomberos, bomberos

D FIGURATIVE LANGUAGE
Reread lines 17–33. What unusual **metaphors** does the speaker use to emphasize the amazing nature of the socks?

---

1. **audacious** (ô-dā′shəs): bold or original.
2. **lapis:** the color of the stone lapis lazuli (lăp′ĭs lăz′ə-lē); bright blue.
3. **celestial** (sə-lĕs′chəl): heavenly.

LITERARY ANALYSIS

D FIGURATIVE LANGUAGE

Possible answer: *The speaker says that his socks have the power to transform his feet into fish, sharks, blackbirds, and cannons.*

If students need help . . . Remind students that a metaphor is a comparison in which one thing is said to be the same as another thing. (That is, one thing *is* the other, not one thing is *like* the other.) Have pairs of students look for such comparisons.

FOR ENGLISH LEARNERS
Vocabulary: Cognates A poem appearing in both English and Spanish offers a rich opportunity for comparing words with the same linguistic roots. These are a few of the words that you might explore in this poem:

- *cannons/cañones* (line 26)
- *honored/honrados* (lines 27 and 28)
- *unacceptable/inaceptables* (line 38)
- *temptation/tentación* (line 48)
- *doubly/doblemente* (line 83)

FOR ADVANCED LEARNERS/PRE–AP
Compare and Contrast Poets [small-group option] Tell students that Pablo Neruda's poetry is often compared to that of American poet Walt Whitman (1819–1892); in fact, Neruda said that Whitman was a source of great inspiration to him. Ask students to do some research on the connection, such as poetic style and choice of subject matter, and to share their findings with the class.

not worthy
of the woven
fire
of those luminous
45 socks.

Nonetheless,
I resisted
the strong temptation
to save them
50 the way schoolboys
bottle
fireflies,
the way scholars
hoard
55 sacred documents.
I resisted
the wild impulse
to place them
in a cage
60 of gold
and daily feed them
birdseed
and rosy melon flesh. **E**
Like explorers
65 who in the forest
surrender a rare
and tender deer
to the spit
and eat it
70 with remorse,
I stuck out
my feet
and pulled on
the
75 handsome
socks,
and
then my shoes.

indignos
de aquel fuego
bordado,
de aquellos luminosos
calcetines.

Sin embargo
resistí
la tentación aguda
de guardarlos
como los colegiales
preservan
las luciérnagas,
como los cruditos
coleccionan
documentos sagrados,
resistí
el impulso furioso
de ponerlos
en una jaula
de oro
y darles cada día
alpiste
y pulpa de melón rosado.
Como descubridores
que en la selva
entregan el rarísimo
venado verde
al asador
y se lo comen
con remordimiento,
estiré
los pies
y me enfundé
los
bellos
calcetines
y
luego los zapatos.

E VISUALIZE
Reread lines 46–63. As you visualize the images in these lines, think about what they have in common. What is the speaker saying about his socks?

READING STRATEGY

E VISUALIZE

Possible answer: All of the images describe delicate, exotic objects or creatures, protected or preserved in some way. The speaker is saying that even though his socks are special, he will resist the urge to enshrine them as sacred objects. Instead, he will wear them.

If students need help . . . Have them focus on one image at a time (lines 50–52, 53–55, and 56–63). Make sure they understand that each image shows someone saving something special.

DIFFERENTIATED INSTRUCTION

FOR LESS–PROFICIENT READERS

Clarify Comparisons Students may need help understanding the images in lines 46–70. Read each image aloud, and ask students to explain the comparison it makes. For lines 56–63, make sure students understand the unstated part of the metaphor: the speaker is comparing his socks to birds. Also point out that the image of the explorers (lines 64–70) is different from the other three images because it describes how the speaker feels about wearing, rather than saving, his special socks.

So this is
80 the moral of my ode:
twice beautiful
is beauty
and what is good doubly
good
85 when it is a case of two
woolen socks
in wintertime. **F**

Y es ésta
la moral de mi oda:
dos veces es belleza
la belleza
y lo que es bueno es doblemente
bueno
cuando se trata de dos calcentines
de lana
en el invierno.

F ODE
Traditional odes have a serious **tone,** or attitude toward the subject. What is the tone of this ode?

Translated by Margaret Sayers Peden

ODE TO MY SOCKS **709**

POETIC FORM

F ODE

Possible answer: *The tone is tongue in cheek. The poet is showing a dry humor through his intense study of a simple subject. His writing is not overtly humorous, but the topic is light, with little hidden meaning.*

If students need help . . . Suggest possible tones for students to accept or reject, such as angry, sad, mocking, happy, and funny.

FOR ADVANCED LEARNERS/PRE–AP

Oral Presentation Have students read several other odes by Pablo Neruda, such as "Ode to Salt," "Ode to Tomatoes," "Ode to Maize," and "Ode to a Large Tuna in the Market," collected in his *Odes to Common Things*. Ask students to select two or three of their favorite odes to share with the class in an oral presentation that includes a poetry reading and a brief analysis of the poems. Suggest that students focus their analyses on Neruda's tone and use of figurative language.

Prereading for this poem is found on page 702.

egg horror poem

LAUREL WINTER

small
white
afraid of heights
whispering
5 in the cold, dark carton
to the rest of the dozen. **G**
They are ten now.
Any meal is dangerous,
but they fear breakfast most.
10 They jostle in their compartments
trying for tiny, dark-veined cracks—
not enough to hurt much,
just anything to make them unattractive
to the big hands that reach in
15 from time to random time.
They tell horror stories
that their mothers,
the chickens,
clucked to them—
20 meringues,
omelettes,
egg salad sandwiches,
that destroyer of dozens,
the homemade angel food cake. **H**
25 The door opens.
Light filters into the carton,
"Let it be the milk,"
they pray.

LITERARY ANALYSIS

G FIGURATIVE LANGUAGE

Possible answer: An egg is being personified. The words "afraid" and "whispering" convey human qualities.

If students need help . . . Ask them which words in lines 3–4 go beyond what we normally associate with eggs.

LITERARY ANALYSIS

H FIGURATIVE LANGUAGE

Possible answer: All of these foods use eggs as a main ingredient. The eggs would be horrified because becoming part of such foods would mean that they would die.

G FIGURATIVE LANGUAGE
In lines 1–6, what object is being **personified?** Identify the words that convey human qualities.

H FIGURATIVE LANGUAGE
Reread lines 16–24. Why might meringues, omelettes, and the other foods mentioned in these lines seem horrifying to an egg?

DIFFERENTIATED INSTRUCTION

FOR LESS–PROFICIENT READERS

Clarify Meaning Winter uses some unusual but vivid verbs and verb forms in this poem, including *jostle* (line 10), *clucked* (line 19), *whirring* (line 41), and *huddle* (line 42). To check and refine understanding, invite volunteers to act out these verbs and verb forms as they imagine the action occurring in the poem.

FOR ENGLISH LEARNERS

Culture: Clarify Some students may be unfamiliar with meringues (line 20), omelettes (line 21), egg salad (line 22), or angel food cake (line 24). Describe each food, focusing on the importance of eggs as the main ingredient. You may wish to bring in a simple recipe for each food or provide samples of the food for students to taste. Students may also suggest how eggs are used in their home cultures.

But the carton opens,
30 a hand reaches in—
once,
twice.
Before they can even jiggle,
they are alone again,
35 in the cold,
in the dark,
new spaces hollow
where the two were.
Through the heavy door
40 they hear the sound of the mixer,
deadly blades whirring.

They huddle,
the eight,
in the cold,
45 in the dark,
and wait.

Lines 29–46
REINFORCE *KEY IDEA:* IMAGINATION

Discuss How does the poet use imagination to create suspense in these lines? *Possible answer: The poet uses imagination to personify the eggs as defenseless against impending danger. They are conscious of yet cannot protect themselves from the hand that reaches in to take them away (lines 29–33). They can only listen to "deadly blades" (line 41) and "huddle" (line 42) in the dark cold, and wait.*

READING STRATEGY

❶ VISUALIZE

Possible answer: First a person's hand reaches into the refrigerator, opens the egg carton, and removes two eggs. Then, inside the refrigerator, the remaining eight eggs miss the two that were taken and listen in horror to the sound of the whirring mixer that signals the gruesome death of those two eggs. Outside the refrigerator, a person is in the kitchen using an electric mixer to prepare food with those eggs.

SELECTION WRAP–UP

SYNTHESIZE Have students identify an audience to whom they would recommend each of these three poems. Ask them to explain each choice.

⭐ **CRITIQUE** Ask students to identify the element of each poem that they liked best, and to explain why.

FOR LESS–PROFICIENT READERS
Review Key Details Use the Question Frames strategy to help students review this poem. Pose questions such as, What do the eggs fear? Why do they want to have tiny cracks? How are the beginning and end of the poem the same? Have students pose and answer their own questions.

🧰 BEST PRACTICES TOOLKIT—Transparency
Question Frames p. A33

FOR ADVANCED LEARNERS/PRE–AP
Synthesize Would this poem translate to film? Have students explore the idea. Encourage students to be creative in their visual interpretations while maintaining the plot and tone of the poem. To convey their ideas for a short film, have students prepare a storyboard or have them write a paragraph explaining their plans. Invite students to share their interpretations with the class.

Practice and Apply

After Reading

For additional support of post-reading questions, use these copy masters:

R RESOURCE MANAGER—Copy Masters

Visualize p. 103 (for practice of the reading strategy standards focus)

Question Support p. 105 (After Reading questions adapted for English learners and less-proficient readers)

Additional selection questions are provided for teachers on page 97.

ANSWERS

Comprehension

1. *The danger is in turning into a mole, worm, root, or stone (lines 3–6).*

2. *The speaker compares his feet to fish, sharks, mammoth blackbirds, and cannons (lines 18–26) and to two old firefighters (lines 35–45).*

3. *The eggs' great fear is that they will be taken and cooked for people's food.*

Literary Analysis

Possible answers:

4. ■ **STANDARDS FOCUS** *Visualize*
   Students should support their answers with examples.

5. *The speaker means that poets should try to reach their highest potential. Flying may represent being imaginative and reaching artistic heights.*

6. *For the eggs, life is a scary waiting game (lines 3–5 and 46) in a cold, dark place (lines 35–36). They feel desperate and miserable, as shown in their prayer not to be taken (lines 27–28).*

7. *The onomatopoeic words are "whispering" (line 4), "jostle" (line 10), "cracks" (line 11), "clucked" (line 19), "jiggle" (line 33), and "whirring" (line 41).*

8. ● **STANDARDS FOCUS** *Ode "Ode to My Socks" is like a traditional ode because it offers praise. It is different from a traditional ode because its subject is an ordinary object, and its tone is light. Neruda's intent was for readers to become more appreciative of the world around them.*

Comprehension

1. **Recall** According to the speaker in "For Poets," what is the danger of staying underground too long?

2. **Recall** What two comparisons in "Ode to My Socks" involve the speaker's feet rather than his socks?

3. **Clarify** What is the eggs' great fear in "egg horror poem"?

Literary Analysis

4. **Visualize** Which poem creates the most vivid pictures in your mind? What specific images and comparisons in the poem create these pictures?

5. **Interpret Metaphor** What does the speaker in "For Poets" mean by telling poets, "Dont forget to fly"? What activity does flying represent?

6. **Interpret Personification** What is life like for the eggs described in "egg horror poem"? Describe your impressions and support your ideas with details from the poem.

7. **Identify Onomatopoeia** When words have sounds that echo their own meaning, as in *buzz* and *gargle*, it is known as onomatopoeia. Reread "egg horror poem" and identify the onomatopoetic words.

8. **Analyze an Ode** Reread the description of an ode on page 703. In what ways is "Ode to My Socks" like a traditional ode? In what ways is it different? What do you think Neruda's intent was in writing an ode to a pair of socks?

9. **Evaluate Figurative Language** Review the examples of figurative language you recorded in your chart. Which figures of speech do you find the most effective or compelling? Explain your preferences.

10. **Evaluate Ideas** Skim "Ode to My Socks" and "egg horror poem." Which poet shows more **imagination** in making an everyday object seem new or unusual? Support your opinion with details from the poems.

Literary Criticism

11. **Critical Interpretations** The critic Dean Rader wrote that "'Ode to My Socks' is a poem about poetry." He believes that Neruda's ode is commenting on "what poetry is and what it should be." If this is true, what is Neruda saying about poetry? Explain your ideas.

---

9. ● **STANDARDS FOCUS** *Figurative Language The comparisons in lines 46–63 of "Ode to My Socks" are compelling, as they compare the speaker's desire to save the socks to a schoolboy's desire to bottle fireflies, a scholar's desire to hoard documents, and a bird-lover's desire to cage and pamper a bird.*

10. *Accept either opinion, but make sure that students have supported their choices with evidence from the poems, including specific figures of speech and images.*

Literary Criticism

Possible answer:

11. *Neruda is saying that poetry has the power to bring attention to and beautify the smallest, most unimportant object.*

Reading-Writing Connection

Add to your understanding of the poems by responding to these prompts. Then use **Revision: Grammar and Style** to improve your writing.

WRITING PROMPTS	SELF-CHECK
A. **Short Response: Write a Poem** Using "egg horror poem" as a model, write a **five-to-ten-line poem** using an extended example of personification.	*An effective poem will . . .* • show the human qualities of a recognizable place, object, or animal • give insight into the subject that is not immediately obvious
B. **Extended Response: Give Advice** Think about the advice Al Young gives in "For Poets." What have you learned that you could pass along to someone younger or less experienced? You may even have your own advice for poets. Write **three to five paragraphs** explaining your advice.	*Good written advice will . . .* • respectfully explain what it takes to succeed • mention mistakes to avoid • give examples to support and clarify your points

REVISION: GRAMMAR AND STYLE

WRITE CONCISELY Because poetry typically consists of a compact, carefully chosen group of words, it benefits from the use of concise language. Other types of writing can also be improved when made concise. By incorporating **infinitives** and **infinitive phrases** into your writing, you can avoid unnecessary words. An infinitive is a verb form that begins with *to* and functions as a noun, an adjective, or an adverb. An infinitive phrase consists of an infinitive plus its modifiers and complements. Note the following examples:

> *Dont forget to fly* ("For Poets," line 17)

> *I resisted / the wild impulse / to place them / in a cage / of gold*
> ("Ode to My Socks," lines 56–60)

In the revisions in red, infinitives and infinitive phrases are used to combine sentences, making the writing more concise. Revise your responses to the prompts by making similar changes.

STUDENT MODEL

The kitchen at last settles down. ~~It wants~~ to nap.

The refrigerator hums softly in slumber.

It is happy ~~It wishes~~ to do nothing for a while.

WRITING TOOLS
For prewriting, revision, and editing tools, visit the **Writing Center** at ClassZone.com.

FOR POETS / ODE TO MY SOCKS / EGG HORROR POEM   **713**

Reading-Writing Connection

WRITING PROMPTS

• For Prompt A, provide class time for students to perform their finished poems. Remind them to use verbal techniques (such as pitch, rate, pause, and volume) and nonverbal techniques (such as posture and gestures) to enhance their presentations. Invite listeners to offer constructive feedback.

• For Prompt B, suggest that students review their drafts with a partner. Have partners point out areas that could be reworded to be clearer and to sharpen the approachable tone.

For writing support, see

🛈 Writing Center at **ClassZone.com**

REVISION: GRAMMAR AND STYLE

Have students analyze the examples and the student model. Then ask them to use infinitives or infinitive phrases to combine these pairs of sentences:

> *When I read poems, I feel inspired. ~~I want~~ to write poetry of my own.*

> *I have a few minutes. ~~I can~~ to write some poetry right now.*

R RESOURCE MANAGER—Copy Master
Write Concisely p. 107

Assess and Reteach

Assess

R RESOURCE MANAGER—Copy Masters
Selection Test A pp. 109–110
Selection Test B/C pp. 111–112

💿 Test Generator CD

Reteach

S STANDARDS LESSON FILE
Literature Lesson 16: Ode and Elegy
Literature Lessons 29, 30: Simile and Metaphor, Personification
Writing Lesson 41: Imagery and Figurative Language

713

Focus and Motivate

OBJECTIVES

Literary Analysis
- explore the key idea of **alarm**
- analyze sound devices
- recognize characteristics of a ballad
- read a ballad

Reading
- analyze speakers

SUMMARY

W. H. Auden's ballad "O What Is That Sound" is a dialogue between two speakers who may be a husband and wife or a pair of lovers. Watching the advance of "scarlet soldiers," the more apprehensive first speaker asks a series of questions, which the second speaker calmly answers. However, when it becomes clear that the soldiers are headed for their house, the second speaker takes flight, abandoning the other.

What triggers a sense of ALARM?

Lead into the *KEY IDEA* by asking the question. After students read the paragraph, ask what might cause a sense of **alarm** to gradually become more intense. Then have students complete the *QUICKWRITE,* and ask volunteers to share their paragraphs with the class.

O What Is That Sound
Poem by W. H. Auden

What triggers a sense of ALARM?

KEY IDEA Strange noises, flashing lights, the smell of something burning—any of these things would catch your attention. But would they set your heart pounding? At what point does something unusual become threatening? The following poem describes someone reacting to an approaching threat with a growing sense of **alarm.**

QUICKWRITE Imagine a situation that might cause you to panic. It could be something as dangerous as getting lost in the woods or as mild as forgetting to study for a quiz. Write a short paragraph describing your physical and mental reaction.

714

Selection Resources

 **RESOURCE MANAGER UNIT 7**

Plan and Teach pp. 113–120

Literary Analysis
Sound Devices pp. 121, 122†*
Question Support p. 125*

Reading
Analyze Speakers pp. 123, 124†*
Reading Fluency p. 126

Assessment
Selection Tests A, B/C pp. 127*, 129*
*Test Generator CD

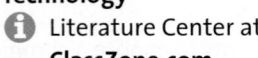 **BEST PRACTICES TOOLKIT**

Differentiated Instruction
pp. 31–38*

Reading Support
Audio Anthology CD

Technology
*Literature Center at
ClassZone.com
*Write*Smart* CD

---

* **Resources for Differentiation**   † Also in Spanish

POETIC FORM: BALLAD

W. H. Auden was a modern poet, but he used a traditional ballad form for "O What Is That Sound." A **ballad** is a narrative poem that is meant to be sung or recited. Typically, a traditional ballad focuses on a single tragic event and usually implies more than it tells explicitly. A ballad typically includes

- a setting, plot, and characters
- dialogue and repetition
- a regular and simple rhyme scheme (commonly *abab*, *abcb*, or *aabb*)

LITERARY ANALYSIS: SOUND DEVICES

Originally meant to be spoken or sung, poetry has a musical quality you won't always find in prose. This is no accident; poets use various **sound devices** to create rhythm and mood and to emphasize ideas in their poems. In "O What Is That Sound," W. H. Auden uses the following sound devices to help create suspense and meaning, as well as melody:

- **Rhyme:** similar sounds at the ends of lines (**end rhyme**) or within lines (**internal rhyme**)
- **Repetition:** words or phrases that are repeated (*drumming, drumming*)
- **Assonance:** repetition of vowel sounds within words that don't rhyme (*only soldiers*)

As you read this poem, look for examples of sound devices, and notice how they help create a feeling of anxiety.

READING SKILL: ANALYZE SPEAKERS

In this poem, everything you learn about the story and the characters' feelings comes from the dialogue between the two speakers. As you read, use the reactions of the speakers to imagine what is happening; also look for changes in either speaker's attitude. In a chart like the one shown, record what you infer about the speakers, including who they are and how they react to events—both early and then later on.

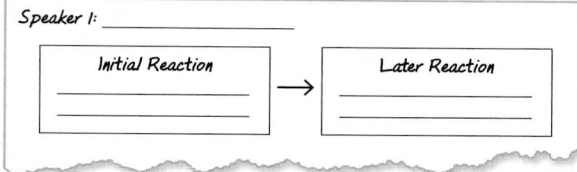

Speaker 1: _____

Initial Reaction		Later Reaction
_____	→	_____
_____		_____

Author Online

Admiration and Controversy
W. H. Auden is one of the giants of 20th-century poetry. Born in northern England, he first intended to study science but soon realized his talent for poetry. His early poems, among them "O What Is That Sound," attracted both admiration

W. H. Auden
1907–1973

and controversy. Perhaps Auden's most controversial act was moving to New York in 1939; he ultimately became a U.S. citizen. Some Englishmen never forgave him for leaving his country on the eve of World War II.

An Enduring Legacy In his poetry, Auden confronted the tumultuous ideas and events that rocked his age—Freudian psychology, Marxism, fascism, civil war, and world war. In winning the National Medal for Literature in 1967 he was praised for illuminating "our lives and times with grace, wit and vitality." After the terrorist attacks of September 11, 2001, Web sites and New York subway walls displayed two of his finest poems, "Musée des Beaux Arts" and "September 1, 1939."

 MORE ABOUT THE AUTHOR
For more on W. H. Auden, visit the **Literature Center** at ClassZone.com.

Background

Long Ago and Far Away? The references to drums, horses, and the red uniforms of soldiers in "O What Is That Sound" suggest a faraway time, perhaps around the time of the American Revolution. However, the poem was written in the 1930s, a decade that Auden called "the age of anxiety." Frightened by worldwide economic depression and the rise of fascism in Italy and Germany, ordinary citizens felt vulnerable to events beyond their control.

Teach

STANDARDS FOCUS

LITERARY ANALYSIS

● SOUND DEVICES

For instructional support, write this example on the board and read it aloud:

The Storm

Rumble . . . rumble, a crack and a flash—
    Take my hand, and for cover we'll dash.
Rumble . . . rumble, another bright flash—
    Run for shelter from the cold wind's lash.

Have students discuss how sound devices create rhythm and mood and emphasize ideas in this poem. ***Possible answer:*** *The repetition of "Rumble . . . rumble" and the end rhymes create rhythm; the repetition of the words* rumble *and* flash *emphasizes the approaching storm; the use of short, rhyming words underscores a mood of haste.*

CHECK UNDERSTANDING Elicit examples from poems and songs that create rhythm and mood through sound devices.

READING SKILL

▣ ANALYZE SPEAKERS

Explain that in prose, quotation marks generally show that a character is speaking. However, poets may choose not to use quotation marks. They may indicate who is speaking by other means—for example, by arrangement of lines or the use of italics. For example, in the lines of poetry used for the **LITERARY ANALYSIS** activity, the spoken lines (lines 2 and 4) are indented. Ask students what they can infer about the speaker's attitude in this example. ***Possible answer:*** *The speaker appears to be frightened by a storm.*

CHECK UNDERSTANDING Elicit examples of poems or songs that feature two or more speakers.

 RESOURCE MANAGER—Copy Master
Analyze Speakers p. 123 (for student use while reading the selection)

DIFFERENTIATED INSTRUCTION

FOR LESS–PROFICIENT READERS

Comprehension Support Write on the board these boldfaced terms used on page 715, and have students review their meaning: *rhyme, end rhyme, internal rhyme, repetition, assonance.* Elicit or provide examples of these sound devices from popular songs and familiar poems. Discuss how the devices help to create rhythm and mood and emphasize ideas in the songs and poems.

FOR ADVANCED LEARNERS/PRE–AP

Use Sound Devices Challenge students to write a poem of at least four lines using as many of the sound devices described on this page as possible. Have volunteers write their poems on the board and then read them to the class. Have the class identify the sound devices used.

Practice and Apply

ANALYZE VISUALS

Possible answer: The mood created by the painting is serious and purposeful. The slanted lines and angular shapes, suggesting rapid, unified motion toward a particular goal, contribute to this mood. The subject matter— armed soldiers quickly marching forward— also contributes to this mood, as does the artist's use of blue, red, and gray battlefield colors.

About the Art British artist Christopher Richard Wynne Nevinson (1889–1946) created some of the most striking paintings of World War I. His experiences as a volunteer ambulance driver during that war affected him deeply. His paintings tend to portray soldiers not as heroic fighters but as mechanized masses of men caught up in warfare. *Returning to the Trenches* suggests the relentless forward movement of troops heading into battle.

LITERARY ANALYSIS

Ⓐ SOUND DEVICES

Possible answer: Examples of assonance include "O" (line 9), "Only" (line 11), and "Or" (line 12); "usual" and "maneuvers" (line 11). The assonance contributes to the rhythm and flow of the poem. The repetition of long o sounds also creates a plaintive, mournful effect that reinforces the poem's meaning.

READING SKILL

Ⓑ ANALYZE SPEAKERS

Possible answer: The first speaker seems to feel apprehensive about the approaching soldiers, while the second speaker does not. The first speaker is sufficiently concerned to be asking one question after another, each of which the second speaker answers calmly and simply. In addition, the second speaker seems puzzled that the first speaker feels anxious enough to be kneeling (line 16).

O What Is That Sound

W. H. AUDEN

O what is that sound which so thrills the ear
    Down in the valley drumming, drumming?
Only the scarlet soldiers,[1] dear,
    The soldiers coming.

5   O what is that light I see flashing so clear
    Over the distance brightly, brightly?
Only the sun on their weapons, dear,
    As they step lightly.

O what are they doing with all that gear,
10   What are they doing this morning, this morning?
Only their usual maneuvers,[2] dear,
    Or perhaps a warning. Ⓐ

O why have they left the road down there,
    Why are they suddenly wheeling, wheeling?[3]
15 Perhaps a change in their orders, dear.
    Why are you kneeling? Ⓑ

ANALYZE VISUALS
What is the **mood** created by this painting? Identify the elements of subject matter, shape, and color that contribute to this mood.

Ⓐ SOUND DEVICES
Reread lines 9–12 aloud. Which of the lines in this stanza contains **assonance?** Identify the assonance, and explain its effect.

Ⓑ ANALYZE SPEAKERS
Do the two speakers seem to feel the same way about the approaching soldiers? Explain.

---

1. **scarlet soldiers:** a reference suggesting British soldiers, who wore bright red coats.
2. **maneuvers:** training exercises carried out by troops.
3. **wheeling:** turning around quickly so as to face in the opposite direction.

716   UNIT 7: THE LANGUAGE OF POETRY

Returning to the Trenches (1914), C. R. W. Nevinson. Oil on canvas, 51.2 cm × 76.8 cm. Gift of the Massey Collection of English Painting, 1946. © National Gallery of Canada, Ottawa/The Nevinson Estate/Bridgeman Art Library.

DIFFERENTIATED INSTRUCTION

For general guidelines on differentiating instruction, see

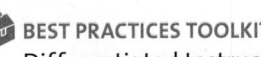 **BEST PRACTICES TOOLKIT**
Differentiated Instruction pp. 31–38

FOR LESS–PROFICIENT READERS

Options for Reading Divide students into two groups in preparation for a choral reading of the poem. Have one group take the role of the first speaker, reading the first two lines of each stanza. Have the second group take the role of the second speaker, reading the last two lines of each stanza.

Discuss How do the questions asked by the first speaker convey a growing sense of **alarm**?
Possible answer: *The questions suggest unexplained, possibly threatening behavior on the part of the soldiers. The questions in the fourth stanza, in particular, suggest alarm, because the soldiers have suddenly left the road, making the reader wonder where they are headed, and why.*

FOR LESS–PROFICIENT READERS

Concept Support Reinforce students' understanding of the ballad form by helping them complete a chart identifying narrative elements of the plot, setting, and characters in "O What Is That Sound."

Lines	Plot	Setting	Characters
1–4	soldiers coming		two speakers talking
5–8	they have weapons	daytime sun	
9–12		morning	

Detail of *Returning to the Trenches*. © National Gallery of Canada, Ottawa.

LITERARY ANALYSIS

❻ SOUND DEVICES

Answer: Lines 17 and 19—"care" and "dear"—create slant rhyme.

POETIC FORM

❼ BALLAD

Possible answer: "O What Is That Sound" is a traditional ballad—that is, it tells a story. The repetition, regular rhythm, and simple rhyme scheme are such that the poem lends itself to singing or recitation. The poem contains characters and dialogue, and, like many traditional ballads, it implies more than it explicitly states.

LITERARY ANALYSIS

❽ SOUND DEVICES

Possible answer: Rhyme: "door" (line 33) and "floor" (line 35); "turning" (line 34) and "burning" (line 36). **Repetition:** *"turning, turning" in line 34*

O haven't they stopped for the doctor's care,
    Haven't they reined their horses, their horses?
Why, they are none of them wounded, dear.
20   None of these forces. ❻

O is it the parson they want, with white hair,
    Is it the parson, is it, is it?
No, they are passing his gateway, dear,
    Without a visit.

25 O it must be the farmer who lives so near.
    It must be the farmer so cunning, so cunning?
They have passed the farmyard already, dear,
    And now they are running. ❼

O where are you going? Stay with me here!
30   Were the vows you swore deceiving, deceiving?
No, I promised to love you, dear,
    But I must be leaving.

O it's broken the lock and splintered the door,
    O it's the gate where they're turning, turning;
35 Their boots are heavy on the floor
    And their eyes are burning. ❽

❻ **SOUND DEVICES**
Slant rhyme refers to end rhymes that are not exact, as in "chair" and "cheer." Which two lines in this stanza create slant rhyme?

❼ **BALLAD**
What characteristics of a ballad do you find in this poem?

❽ **SOUND DEVICES**
Reread lines 33–36 aloud. What words in this stanza are emphasized by **rhyme** and **repetition**?

SELECTION WRAP–UP

REFLECT Ask students if they were surprised by the ending of the poem. Why or why not?

⭐ **CRITIQUE** Ask students whether they think the simplicity of the poem's language and structure adds to, or detracts from, the story the poem tells. Have students support their answers with details from the poem.

READING FLUENCY

Distribute the copy master and have students work in pairs or groups to practice fluency.

📋 RESOURCE MANAGER—Copy Master
Reading Fluency p. 126

DIFFERENTIATED INSTRUCTION

FOR ENGLISH LEARNERS
Vocabulary: Multiple-Meaning Words Have students look up these words in their dictionaries: *"gear"* (line 9); *"orders"* (line 15); *"forces"* (line 20); *"cunning"* (line 26); *"swore"* (line 30); *"burning"* (line 36). Then, for each word, have pairs of students write the meaning that best fits the context. Have volunteers read their definitions aloud. Discuss with the class whether the meaning chosen is correct.

FOR ADVANCED LEARNERS/PRE–AP
Interpret Throughout the poem, the second speaker has been an enigma, no less so in this last stanza. Ask students these questions: Is the second speaker a coward? Does the second speaker really love the first speaker as stated in line 31? If so, why does the second speaker place the first speaker in danger by not being more forthright about the troops? Ask students to write a short paragraph explaining their views on this mysterious figure.

Comprehension

1. **Recall** Whom do the speakers observe in the distance?

2. **Clarify** Which speaker seems calmer?

3. **Clarify** Reread the last stanza. What happens to the second speaker?

Literary Analysis

4. **Understand Poetry** What is happening in this poem? Briefly describe the actions that take place. Give possible reasons for these actions.

5. **Analyze Speakers** Review the chart you completed as you read. Who are the two speakers in the poem? What is their relationship? Describe what you inferred about the speakers' identities and their reactions to events. Be sure to support your **inferences** with details from the poem.

6. **Analyze Sound Devices** Reread the poem, looking for examples of **rhyme, repetition,** and **assonance.** Use a chart like the one shown to record two examples of each sound device. Which sound device is most effective in conveying a sense of anxiety and drama in the poem? Explain your thinking.

Sound Devices	Examples
Rhyme (internal or end)	
Repetition	
Assonance	

7. **Interpret Imagery** Reread lines 33–36 and note the words and phrases that describe the soldiers and their actions. On the basis of this imagery, what is your impression of the soldiers? Will they defend the speakers or attack them? Explain your answer.

8. **Evaluate a Ballad** In this ballad, one speaker asks a series of questions, and a second speaker gives answers. How does this pattern of **repetitive dialogue** affect the level of tension throughout the poem? What is the point of greatest tension? Cite evidence to support your answer.

Literary Criticism

9. **Historical Context** Auden wrote "O What Is That Sound" in the 1930s. During this decade, many European countries, including Germany and Italy, were being taken over by fascist dictators. These tyrannical leaders exercised complete control over every aspect of public and private life and used force, such as police or military terror, to crush opposition. In what ways does the poem reflect these political realities of the 1930s?

O WHAT IS THAT SOUND   **719**

Assonance: "stopped"/"doctor's," "must"/ "cunning." Most students will probably identify repetition as the most effective device for conveying anxiety and drama, because it emphasizes key words and phrases, as in lines 14, 22, 30, and 34.

7. The soldiers are on the attack, as evidenced by the fact that they broke the lock and splintered the door without ever calling out.

8. ● **STANDARDS FOCUS** *Ballad* The pattern heightens the tension, making readers feel as though they are sharing the experience with the speakers as it unfolds. The

tension reaches its greatest point in the eighth stanza, when the previously calm speaker realizes the danger is real and imminent, or perhaps in the final stanza, when the soldiers actually break in.

Literary Criticism

9. *Students should recognize that the brutal home invasion reflects the use of force in a totalitarian regime.*

Practice and Apply

After Reading

For additional support of post-reading questions, use these copy masters:

R RESOURCE MANAGER—Copy Masters
  Sound Devices p. 121
  Question Support p. 125

  Additional selection questions are provided for teachers on page 117.

ANSWERS

Comprehension

1. *The speakers see "scarlet soldiers"—probably British redcoats.*

2. *The second speaker seems calmer.*

3. *The second speaker abandons the first.*

Literary Analysis

Possible answers:

4. *Two people watch as soldiers approach. One person is apprehensive, while the other is calm. When it becomes clear that the soldiers pose a threat, the latter runs away. The soldiers then break down the door.*

5. ■ **STANDARDS FOCUS** *Analyze Speakers The two speakers are probably married or lovers, as shown by the second speaker's use of the word* dear. *While no clear threat is apparent, the second speaker remains calm. However, when the soldiers threaten their house (line 28), the second speaker abandons the first (lines 31–32), who expresses shock at this betrayal of "vows" (lines 29–30).*

6. ● **STANDARDS FOCUS** *Sound Devices Rhyme: "ear"/"dear," "drumming"/ "coming"; Repetition: "this morning, this morning," "wheeling, wheeling";*

Assess and Reteach

Assess

R RESOURCE MANAGER—Copy Masters
  Selection Test A pp. 127–128
  Selection Test B/C pp. 129–130

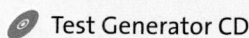 Test Generator CD

Reteach

S STANDARDS LESSON FILE
  Literature Lessons 14, 20–23

O WHAT IS THAT SOUND   **719**

Focus and Motivate

OBJECTIVES

Literary Analysis
- explore the key idea of a **journey**
- recognize characteristics of a dramatic monologue
- analyze rhythm (meter)
- read poems

Reading
- analyze ideas in poetry

SUMMARIES

"The Seven Ages of Man" In this dramatic monologue from Shakespeare's play *As You Like It,* a character named Jaques describes people as players on the world's stage who go through seven major periods, or "ages in their lives."

"The Road Not Taken" In this metaphorical poem, the speaker describes the choice he made when faced with two roads in a wood. By choosing to go down the less traveled road, he made a decision that affected the rest of his life.

Do you set your own COURSE?

Present the question. Then lead into the *KEY IDEA* by asking students for examples of a choice they or someone they know made that had a strong impact on their life **journeys.** Then have students complete the *ROLE-PLAY.*

Selection Resources

The Seven Ages of Man
Poem by William Shakespeare

The Road Not Taken
Poem by Robert Frost

Do you set your own COURSE?

KEY IDEA If life is a **journey,** then who's driving? Some people feel that they make their own choices about where to turn and how far to drive, while others feel they are simply following a course set by someone else. The poems that follow suggest two very different views of this question.

ROLE-PLAY Imagine you are applying for a job or preparing for a college interview. With a partner, take turns interviewing one another about your life goals. Where do you see yourself in 5 years? in 10 years? in 15 years? When answering these questions, explain what choices you may have to make in order to achieve these goals.

 RESOURCE MANAGER UNIT 7

Plan and Teach pp. 131–138

Literary Analysis
Meter pp. 139, 140†*
Question Support p. 143*

Reading
Analyze Ideas in Poetry
   pp. 141, 142†*
Reading Fluency p. 144

Assessment
Selection Tests A, B/C pp. 145*, 147*
Test Generator CD

BEST PRACTICES TOOLKIT

Differentiated Instruction
   pp. 31–38*

Graphic Organizers/Strategies
Cluster Diagram

Technology
Literature Center at **ClassZone.com**
WriteSmart CD

Reading Support
Audio Anthology CD*

InterActive
READER & WRITER
• Integrated Test Practice
• Related Nonfiction Readings
McDougal Littell LITERATURE

---

* Resources for Differentiation   † Also in Spanish

POETIC FORM: DRAMATIC MONOLOGUE

A **dramatic monologue** is a poem in which the speaker addresses a silent or absent listener, as if engaged in a private conversation. The speaker often reveals his or her own feelings, attitudes, motivations, and character traits in a moment of high intensity or deep emotion. "The Seven Ages of Man" is an example of a dramatic monologue; it is delivered by a character in Shakespeare's play *As You Like It*.

LITERARY ANALYSIS: METER

Rhythm is the pattern of stressed and unstressed syllables in a line of poetry. Rhythm that follows a regular pattern from line to line is called **meter**. The following lines from Shakespeare use a very even meter:

Thĕy hávĕ thĕir éxĭts ănd thĕir éntrăncĕs;

Ănd ónĕ mán ĭn hĭs tímĕ pláys mănỹ párts.

In the next example, from Frost, notice that the number of accents is the same in each line, but the rhythm varies slightly:

Ĭ shăll bĕ téllĭng thĭs wĭth ă sígh

Sómĕwhĕre ágĕs ănd ágĕs hénce

Why bother to use meter? For the same reasons that a songwriter bothers to use music: it sounds nice, it's easy to remember, and it allows for extra emphasis of words or phrases. Read the following poems aloud and tap your foot as you go. Then ask yourself these questions:

• Is the meter obvious or subtle? Is it close to normal speech?
• Where does the emphasis fall in each line?

Review: **Rhyme Scheme**

READING SKILL: ANALYZE IDEAS IN POETRY

You can better understand poems by looking for the **main idea** in each section. "The Seven Ages of Man" can be divided into seven sections—one for each "age." "The Road Not Taken" is already divided into four stanzas. As you read each poem, record the main idea of each "age" or stanza.

"The Seven Ages of Man"	
Age	*Main Idea*
1. infancy	
2. school-boy days	

Author Online

William Shakespeare: Timeless Greatness

William Shakespeare
1564–1616

Shakespeare is certainly the most famous writer in the world and arguably the greatest writer who ever lived. He wrote 37 plays, ranging from comedies to tragedies. He also published some of the most beautiful lyric poetry in the English language, including 154 sonnets, before he died at age 52. In his own time, theater audiences loved him and critics praised his incredible talent. But his contemporary Ben Jonson foresaw Shakespeare's indelible mark on the future: "He was not of an age, but for all time!"

Robert Frost: Beloved American Poet

Robert Frost
1874–1963

Declared America's poet laureate before the official creation of such a position, Robert Frost had become a beloved public figure by the time he died. The U.S. Senate passed a resolution honoring him, the state of Vermont named a mountain after him, and he was the first poet ever invited to recite his work at a presidential inauguration. Still, Frost is something of a puzzle. He was a modern poet who often used traditional rhyme and meter, a New England farmer whose folksy manner concealed an inner torment, and a man of ideas who valued both objectivity and a "tantalizing vagueness" in poetry.

 MORE ABOUT THE AUTHOR
For more on William Shakespeare and Robert Frost, visit the **Literature Center** at **ClassZone.com**.

721

Teach

STANDARDS FOCUS

LITERARY ANALYSIS

● METER

For instructional support, write these lines on the board and read them aloud. Have students tap their feet to mark each stressed syllable.

> The church bell peals so rich and strong,
> The city's noise just melts away;
> And here amid a crushing throng,
> My thoughts have drifted far astray.

Ask students how many stressed syllables are in each line. ***Answer: four stressed syllables***

CHECK UNDERSTANDING Provide students with examples of poems with regular meters, and have them identify where the emphasis falls in each line.

READING SKILL

■ ANALYZE IDEAS IN POETRY

For instructional support, have students identify the main idea of the stanza written on the board. ***Possible answer: The sound of church bells in a busy city sends the speaker's thoughts far from the surrounding noise and crowds.***

CHECK UNDERSTANDING Have students examine another stanza from a poem and state its main idea.

 RESOURCE MANAGER—Copy Master
Analyze Ideas in Poetry p. 141
(for student use while reading the selection)

DIFFERENTIATED INSTRUCTION

FOR LESS–PROFICIENT READERS

Dramatic Monologue Ask students to think of examples of songs in which a "speaker" expresses views as if engaged in a private conversation. Help students recognize the parallel between songs in which a speaker reveals his or her feelings and poems in which the speaker delivers a dramatic monologue.

Ⓐ DRAMATIC MONOLOGUE

Possible answer: *Jaques's descriptions of the infant as "Mewling and puking" (lines 5–6) and the schoolboy as "whining" and "creeping like snail unwillingly to school" (lines 7 and 8–9) show his negative attitude toward childhood.*

If students need help . . . Have them use a Cluster Diagram to focus on how the speaker describes what happens during each stage.

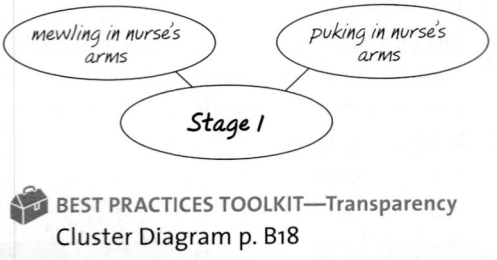

🧰 **BEST PRACTICES TOOLKIT—Transparency**
Cluster Diagram p. B18

Ⓑ RHYME SCHEME

Possible answer: *No. Lines 21 and 22 rhyme, but the other lines do not.*

Lines 1–5
DISCUSSION PROMPTS

Use these prompts to help students understand the metaphor that "All the world's a stage":

Connect In what situations are people like actors playing a part? *Students may mention jobs or family life.*

Analyze What "exits" and "entrances" do people make in life? *Possible answer: We exit at death and enter at birth; we also enter and exit various stages of life.*

Synthesize Jaques's view is that men and women are "merely players" (line 2). Is he a pessimist or a realist? Explain. *Some students may argue that Jaques is overly pessimistic because life involves more than just acting out a predetermined role. Others may argue that Jaques has a realistic view of our place in the world.*

THE SEVEN AGES OF MAN
William Shakespeare

JAQUES:
All the world's a stage,
And all the men and women merely players:
They have their exits and their entrances;
And one man in his time plays many parts,
5 His acts being seven ages. At first the infant,
Mewling[1] and puking in the nurse's arms.
And then the whining school-boy, with his satchel,
And shining morning face, creeping like snail
Unwillingly to school. And then the lover, Ⓐ
10 Sighing like furnace, with a woeful ballad[2]
Made to his mistress' eyebrow. Then a soldier,
Full of strange oaths, and bearded like the pard,[3]
Jealous in honor, sudden and quick in quarrel,
Seeking the bubble reputation[4]
15 Even in the cannon's mouth. And then the justice,
In fair round belly with good capon lin'd,[5]
With eyes severe, and beard of formal cut,
Full of wise saws and modern instances;[6]
And so he plays his part. The sixth age shifts
20 Into the lean and slipper'd pantaloon,[7]
With spectacles on nose and pouch on side,
His youthful hose well sav'd, a world too wide Ⓑ

Ⓐ **DRAMATIC MONOLOGUE**
Reread lines 5–9. Notice how Jaques describes the infant and the schoolboy. What do these descriptions reveal about his attitude toward childhood?

Ⓑ **RHYME SCHEME**
Does Shakespeare employ a rhyme scheme for this poem? Support your answer.

---

1. **mewling:** crying or whimpering.
2. **woeful ballad:** sad, sentimental song.
3. **pard:** leopard.
4. **bubble reputation:** reputation, which disintegrates as quickly as a bubble.
5. **with good capon** (kā'pŏn') **lin'd:** full of chicken.
6. **saws . . . instances:** old sayings and examples showing how they still apply.
7. **pantaloon** (păn'tə-lōōn'): a foolish old man.

DIFFERENTIATED INSTRUCTION

For general guidelines on differentiating instruction, see

🧰 **BEST PRACTICES TOOLKIT**
Differentiated Instruction pp. 31–38

FOR LESS–PROFICIENT READERS

Options for Reading Read the poems aloud to convey their mood and drama. You might also have students echo-read the poems in sections—by "ages" for the Shakespeare poem and by stanzas for the Frost poem.

The First and the Last Steps, Emilio Longoni. Private Collection. © Alinari/Art Resource, New York.

For his shrunk shank;[8] and his big manly voice,
Turning again toward childish treble,[9] pipes
25 And whistles in his sound. Last scene of all, **C**
That ends this strange eventful history,
Is second childishness and mere oblivion,[10]
Sans[11] teeth, sans eyes, sans taste, sans everything.

---

8. **youthful hose . . . shank:** The stockings of his youth are too large for his shrunken calves.

9. **treble:** a high-pitched voice.

10. **oblivion** (ə-blĭv′ē-ən): complete forgetfulness.

11. **sans** (säN) *French:* without.

ANALYZE VISUALS
After reading the poem, what connection can you see between the poem and this image?

C METER
Read aloud lines 20–25, tapping your foot at each stressed syllable. How many stressed syllables are in each line?

BACKGROUND
Jaques In Shakespeare's comedy *As You Like It,* the character Jaques has a melancholy view of life and judges others from the sidelines.

ANALYZE VISUALS
Possible answers: The painting, like the poem, focuses on stages of life, connecting childhood and old age.

About the Art Italian artist Emilio Longoni lived from 1859 to 1932.

LITERARY ANALYSIS

C METER
Answer: five

FOR LESS-PROFICIENT READERS
Vocabulary Support Point out that "second childishness" (line 27) is meant to connote helplessness and dependency. The connotations are different from those of the modern term *second childhood,* which suggests carefree playfulness.

FOR ADVANCED LEARNERS/PRE-AP
Analyzing Ancient Greek philosophers wrestled with the question as to whether fate determines character or character determines fate. Have students discuss which of these viewpoints the speaker in "The Seven Ages of Man" expresses. Which viewpoint do students support, and why?

Prereading for this poem is found on page 720.

ANALYZE VISUALS

Activity Ask students how the scenes in the poem and painting are similar. ***Possible answers:*** *In both scenes, a "road" goes through a wood, and one side of the road seems less grassy than the other. As in the poem, the wood in the painting could be described as "yellow," since it appears to be early spring when the new leaves look almost yellow.*

About the Art British artist William Samuel Jay lived from 1843 to 1933.

READING SKILL

D ANALYZE IDEAS

Possible answer: *The main idea is that people have to make choices (represented by the two roads).*

LITERARY ANALYSIS

E METER

Answer: *four pulses per line; words: "took," "other," "just," "fair" (line 6); "having," "perhaps," "better," "claim" (line 7); "because," "grassy," "wanted," "wear" (line 8); "as," "that," "passing," "there" (line 9); "worn," "really," "about," "same" (line 10)*

LITERARY ANALYSIS: *Review*

F RHYME SCHEME

Answer: *The rhyme scheme is abaab.*

SELECTION WRAP–UP

SYNTHESIZE Ask students how the speaker of each poem feels about people's choices in life.

⭐ **CRITIQUE** Have students choose the poem they feel is most relevant to their own life **journeys** and explain why.

READING FLUENCY

Distribute the copy master and have students work in pairs or groups to practice fluency.

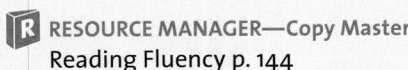 **RESOURCE MANAGER—Copy Master**
Reading Fluency p. 144

The Road Not Taken

In the Beechwoods, William Samuel Jay. Oil on canvas, 91.4 × 122 cm. Private collection. © Bourne Gallery, Reigate, Surrey/The Bridgeman Art Library.

ROBERT FROST

Two roads diverged[1] in a yellow wood,
And sorry I could not travel both
And be one traveler, long I stood
And looked down one as far as I could
5 To where it bent in the undergrowth; **D**

Then took the other, as just as fair,
And having perhaps the better claim,
Because it was grassy and wanted wear;
Though as for that the passing there
10 Had worn them really about the same, **E**

And both that morning equally lay
In leaves no step had trodden[2] black.
Oh, I kept the first for another day!
Yet knowing how way leads on to way,
15 I doubted if I should ever come back.

I shall be telling this with a sigh
Somewhere ages and ages hence:
Two roads diverged in a wood, and I—
I took the one less traveled by,
20 And that has made all the difference. **F**

---

1. **diverged:** branched out; went in different directions.
2. **trodden:** walked on or trampled.

D ANALYZE IDEAS
Reread lines 1–5. What main idea is the poet expressing here?

E METER
Read aloud lines 1-10, tapping your foot with each stressed syllable. How many pulses are in each line? Which words in the second stanza are emphasized by the pulses?

F RHYME SCHEME
What rhyme scheme does Frost use in this poem?

DIFFERENTIATED INSTRUCTION

FOR LESS–PROFICIENT READERS

Vocabulary Support Assign pairs of students to find a definition for each of the underlined words or phrases from the poem: "a yellow <u>wood</u>" (line 1), "<u>long</u> I stood" (line 3), "just as <u>fair</u>" (line 6), "<u>wanted wear</u>" (line 8), and "<u>ages and ages hence</u>" (line 17). Have students write their definitions on the board. Then ask other students to challenge these definitions until students arrive at a consensus.

Comprehension

1. **Recall** In "The Seven Ages of Man," which two stages follow infancy and childhood?

2. **Paraphrase** According to Jaques, what happens to people in the last stage of life?

3. **Recall** In "The Road Not Taken," where do Frost's roads diverge?

4. **Clarify** Which road does the speaker choose?

Literary Analysis

5. **Analyze Ideas** Look at the chart of main ideas that you filled out for each poem as you read. On the basis of these ideas taken together, what do you think is the **theme** of each poem?

6. **Interpret Extended Metaphor** An extended metaphor compares two unlike things at length and in a number of ways, sometimes throughout an entire work. In "The Seven Ages of Man," the speaker compares the world to a stage. What does this comparison imply about the speaker's view of life?

7. **Analyze Dramatic Monologue** "The Seven Ages of Man" comes from Shakespeare's play *As You Like It*. Other characters in this play refer to Jaques as "the melancholy Jaques." Do you agree that Jaques has a gloomy outlook on life? Support your answer with details from his **dramatic monologue.** What else can you **infer** about Jaques from his speech?

8. **Interpret Symbol** In "The Road Not Taken," both roads lead into the woods, so the speaker cannot see where they go. What do the woods symbolize?

9. **Compare Themes** How would Frost's speaker respond to Jaques' statement "All the world's a stage, / And all the men and women merely players"? Cite evidence to support your answer.

10. **Evaluate Meter** "The Seven Ages of Man" is written in **iambic pentameter,** which has five stressed syllables alternating with five unstressed syllables per line. It is said to be the closest meter to human speech in English. "The Road Not Taken" is written loosely in **iambic tetrameter,** which has only four stresses instead of five. Do you find one poem easier to read aloud than the other? Explain your answer.

Literary Criticism

11. **Author's Style** In many of Shakespeare's plays, there is a character who comments philosophically on the world of the characters and on the world at large. It is sometimes thought that this character is speaking for Shakespeare himself. Could Jaques's monologue be seen as giving voice to the playwright? Explain your answer, giving evidence from the text.

---

7. ● **STANDARDS FOCUS** *Dramatic Monologue His gloomy outlook is suggested by the ridicule he heaps upon man at each of his seven ages, from the puking infant to the debilitated old man; readers can infer that Jaques respects few people, if any.*

8. *The woods symbolize the unexplored and unmapped future—choices in life.*

9. *Frost's speaker would respond that people are able to shape the course of their own lives—that they are not simply playing an assigned role, predetermined by their age.*

10. ● **STANDARDS FOCUS** *Meter Students should support their answers by citing specific examples of the different meters.*

Literary Criticism

11. *Some students may cite Jaques's conviction and eloquence as evidence that he is giving voice to Shakespeare's own views.*

Practice and Apply

After Reading

For additional support of post-reading questions, use these copy masters:

R RESOURCE MANAGER—Copy Masters
Meter p. 139 (for practice of literary analysis standards focus)
Question Support p. 143 (After Reading questions adapted for English learners and less-proficient readers)

Additional selection questions are provided for teachers on page 135.

ANSWERS

Comprehension

1. *the lover and the soldier*

2. *People decline into a second childhood—forgetful and without teeth, sight, taste, or anything else.*

3. *in a forest*

4. *the road less traveled*

Literary Analysis

Possible answers:

5. ● **STANDARDS FOCUS** *Analyze Ideas **"The Seven Ages of Man"**: People's lives have seven predetermined stages. **"The Road Not Taken"**: People make choices in life without knowing what these choices will mean, but these choices often make all the difference in their lives.*

6. *The comparison implies that the speaker believes that people just play prescribed roles, with each role dictated by a given stage of life.*

Assess and Reteach

Assess

R RESOURCE MANAGER—Copy Masters
Selection Test A pp. 145–146
Selection Test B/C pp. 147–148

◎ Test Generator CD

Reteach

S STANDARDS LESSON FILE
Literature Lesson 22: Rhythm and Meter

Focus and Motivate

OBJECTIVES

- analyze a student model that reflects the key traits of a personal response
- use the writing process to produce a personal response
- revise and edit, using a rubric for writing a personal response
- create a multimedia presentation

WRITER'S ROAD MAP

WRITING PROMPTS 1 AND 2

Help students choose a prompt by listing poems from the unit or by brainstorming poems or songs that students remember reading or hearing. Point out that a poem or song may affect readers because of its theme, its language, or perhaps because it recalls a time in one's life.

ADDITIONAL PROMPTS

Use these prompts for practice with business writing and writing in the humanities:

WRITING PROMPT 3

Writing for the Real World Write a review of the Web site "Poetry 180, a poem a day for american high schools" for an online poetry journal. Choose two poems as examples to help explain your response to the poetry collection.

WRITING PROMPT 4

Writing About Fine Art Write several paragraphs for a fine arts magazine, giving your personal response to a painting, photograph, or other work of art. Find your subject at a museum's Web site or in a book.

Possible Subjects

- the photographs of Dorothea Lange, Irving Penn, or Walker Evans
- the artwork of Henri Matisse, Christo, or Roy Lichtenstein

For additional writing prompts, see

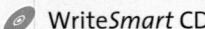 WriteSmart CD

 Writing Center at **ClassZone.com**

KEY TRAITS

Review the six **KEY TRAITS** with students, focusing primarily on ideas and organization. Compare the list of traits with the rubric on page 732.

Writing Workshop

Personal Response to a Poem

As you may have learned from the poems in this unit, it's hard to read a poem without reacting to it—positively or negatively. Just as you may want to share your reactions to a movie you've seen or a concert you've heard, you can share your reactions to a poem by writing a personal response. The **Writer's Road Map** can show you the way.

WRITER'S ROAD MAP

Personal Response to a Poem

WRITING PROMPT 1

Writing from Literature Choose a poem or group of poems that caused a strong emotional response in you. Write a personal response that helps you figure out the meaning of the poem or poems. If you wish, include information about how your own memories or experiences affected your reaction.

Poems to Explore
- "My Papa's Waltz"
- "Grape Sherbet"
- "The Road Not Taken"

WRITING PROMPT 2

Writing for the Real World Song lyrics are poems set to music. Write an essay for a music magazine in which you describe your response to a song or a type of music. Give readers specific examples of lyrics to show why the song or type of music matters to you.

Types of Music to Explore
- rap
- country and western

 WRITING TOOLS
For prewriting, revision, and editing tools, visit the **Writing Center** at **ClassZone.com**.

KEY TRAITS

1. **IDEAS**
   - Clearly presents an **overall response** to the poem or poems
   - Provides specific **details** and **quotations** to support the key ideas
   - **Elaborates** on the examples

2. **ORGANIZATION**
   - Begins by **identifying** the poem or group of poems
   - Includes an engaging **introduction** and a **conclusion** that summarizes the response

3. **VOICE**
   - **Tone** reflects the writer's personal reaction

4. **WORD CHOICE**
   - Uses **precise language** to convey the personal response

5. **SENTENCE FLUENCY**
   - Varies **sentence beginnings** to add interest and energy

6. **CONVENTIONS**
   - Employs **correct grammar and usage**

Writing Workshop Resources

 RESOURCE MANAGER UNIT 7

Plan and Teach pp. 149–152
Prewriting–Editing pp. 153–157
Writing Rubric p. 158
Publishing with Technology p. 159
Writing Support p. 160*

 STANDARDS LESSON FILE

Writing Lesson 15–17, 36

BEST PRACTICES TOOLKIT

Scaffolding Writing Instruction pp. 43–46*
Venn Diagram • T Chart • Analysis Frame:
Poetic Form and Structure • Writing Template:
Responding to Literature

TECHNOLOGY

 Easy Planner DVD

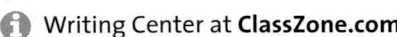 Writing Center at **ClassZone.com**

 WriteSmart CD

* Resources for Differentiation

Part 1: Analyze a Student Model

Leshon Reynolds
Wells High School

Two Views of Competition

When I play basketball, I play to win; but I also love to hear a cheering, shouting, stomping crowd of fans. The poems "400-Meter Free Style" by Maxine Kumin and "Bodybuilders' Contest" by Wislawa Szymborska are about athletes, and because I am an athlete, they caught
5 my attention. Both poems have to do with sports, and both are told from a spectator's point of view. However, because they portray athletes so differently, the poems made me think about the positive and negative aspects of competition.

Maxine Kumin's poem has a positive view of competition. "400-
10 Meter Free Style" is full of action: "full swing the swimmer catapults and cracks." The lines of the poem rush back and forth across the page like a swimmer in a race. The poem describes a talented swimmer. According to the speaker, "he has schooled out all extravagance," which means that he doesn't waste energy. His muscles, mouth, arms, feet, and lungs all know
15 exactly what to do as he surges forward. The speaker comments, "We watch him for signs." This could mean that the spectators are looking for indications that he is getting tired, or it could mean that the spectators admire him and look up to him. The poet seems to respect the swimmer for focusing all his energy and talent on one goal—to be as fast as
20 possible when competing. I respect the swimmer, too. He isn't interested in what the spectators think of him. All he cares about is the time on the clock. Similarly, in basketball, all that really matters is the final score.

In contrast, Wislawa Szymborska's poem has a negative view of

KEY TRAITS IN ACTION

Engaging **introduction identifies** the poems and states the writer's **overall response.**

Provides specific **details** and **quotations** from the poem so readers can understand the response.

Elaborates on the examples to explain his response. Thoughtful, sincere **tone** expresses the writer's personal reaction.

Part 1: Analyze a Student Model

Have students read the student model and **KEY TRAITS IN ACTION.** Then discuss the model with the class, pointing out specific examples of each trait and building on what students have already noted. You may also wish to incorporate these activities:

- **Overall Response** Write the following weak overall response on the board:

  Kumin's poem is about swimming, which is not my sport. However, I admired the poem. Szmborska's poem makes fun of body-building, although it is well written.

Have students read the response on the board and compare it to the student model. **Possible answer:** *The response on the board tells what the poems are about, but it does not give an overall impression about what the poems might mean. Also, the writer "admires" Kumin's poem but does not explain why. In the student model, the writer filters the poems through his own experience and gives a personal reaction. The last sentence tells how the poems caused the writer to think in a new way about the topic of competition.*

- **Tone** Remind students that tone refers to the attitude and feelings of the writer toward the subject. Have students look for phrases and sentences that illustrate the sincere, respectful tone of the model. **Possible answer: Paragraph 1:** *"and because I am an athlete, they caught my attention."* **Paragraph 2:** *The poem describes a talented swimmer; I respect the swimmer, too.*

DIFFERENTIATED INSTRUCTION

For general guidelines on differentiating writing instruction, see

 BEST PRACTICES TOOLKIT
Scaffolding Writing Instruction pp. 431–n46

FOR ENGLISH LEARNERS

Language: Skill Words Write these terms on the board and review them with students:

- *overall response:* the reader's thesis or main thoughts about what he or she has read

- *quotations:* the exact words used by a writer or a speaker—for example, "We watch him for signs."

- *elaborate:* to fully explain an idea by using examples and reasons. Share this example:

Like Maxine Kumin, I have always admired swimmers. Their training lets them race, full-speed ahead. When the speaker says, "We watch him for signs," I feel she is saying the spectators watch the swimmer, hoping not to see that he is getting tired or about to give up.

- **Sentence Beginnings** Remind students that varying sentence beginnings keeps writing from being repetitive, and therefore engages readers with the writer's ideas. To provide examples, ask students to find the following sentence beginnings in the first paragraph on this page:
  - a transitional word (*"However," line 25; "Maybe," line 34; "Instead," line 35*)
  - a transitional phrase (*"In the second stanza," line 28; "At first," line 33*)
  - a pronoun (*"He," line 27; "I," line 31*)
  - a compound subject (*"The bear and panthers," line 30*)
- **Conclusion** To illustrate how the model summarizes the writer's personal response to the poem, have students compare the first and last two sentences in the final paragraph to the opening paragraph. Point out how the writer weaves in his own athletic experiences with what he has learned from reading the poems. The writer also uses words and phrases that echo the main ideas he presented in the introduction.

For interactive student models, see

Write*Smart* CD

Writing Center at **ClassZone.com**

---

competition. "Bodybuilders' Contest" seems admiring at first. The
25 bodybuilder is "all muscles. . . . The king of all is he. . . ." However, the
speaker mocks the bodybuilder, saying that he "preens" and that his
sinews are "twisted into monstrous pretzels." He is someone to make
fun of, not someone to admire or fear. In the second stanza, the speaker
mentions that the bodybuilder's routine is "smoothly choreographed,"
30 but he doesn't actually do anything. The bear and panthers he fights
are imaginary. I believe the poet is saying that bodybuilding is vain
and pointless, no matter how much the bodybuilder practices or how
many prizes he wins. At first I agreed with this point of view, but I have
changed my mind. Posing *is* the bodybuilder's sport. Maybe battling the
35 imaginary animals is an expected part of the routine. Instead of a clock
or a final score, a group of judges decides who wins.

Reading these poems made me think about how I act on the
basketball court and how I view other players. Flashy moves and dunks
impress fans and teammates, much as the "poses and paces" do in
40 "Bodybuilders' Contest." But there's something to be said for efficiency,
for channeling every bit of energy into getting the job done, like the
swimmer in "400-Meter Free Style." Each poem gives a spectator's view
of a highly competitive athlete. Even though I love the cheers of the
crowd, I would rather be like the swimmer than the bodybuilder.

Uses **precise language** (*vain, pointless, battling*). Varied **sentence beginnings** create rhythm and flow.

Conclusion summarizes the response and explains what the writer learned.

2

DIFFERENTIATED INSTRUCTION

FOR ENGLISH LEARNERS

Comprehension: Transitions Check to make sure students recognize the transitions that begin sentences in the model. Point out that transitions can occur at the beginning of a sentence or in the middle.

1. Hold up a picture of a girl and a boy.
2. Provide a series of model sentences that include transitions. Write these transitions on the board.

The girl walks to school. **However,** the boy rides the bus. (*difference*)

The family includes May and Jason. **Last but not least,** there is Rick. (*importance*)

May enjoys sports. **For instance,** she plays basketball and soccer. (*examples*)

Both May and Jason are cheerful. (*similarity*)

Next, Jason practices guitar. (*time order*)

Another thing Jason likes is playing chess. (*connect ideas*)

3. Now hold up two new pictures and repeat the exercise. This time ask students to provide the sentences, using the words on the board to help them.

To provide English learners with additional writing support, see

R RESOURCE MANAGER—Copy Master
Writing Support p. 160

Part 2: Apply the Writing Process

PREWRITING

What Should I Do?	*What Does It Look Like?*

1. Note words or lines that puzzle or move you. Use a reading log to jot down lines and your understanding of them. (Circle) the quotations, questions, and comments that seem most important.

> **TIP** If the poem reminds you of an experience from your own life, think about including that information in your response.

Quotations	My Interpretations
"the swimmer catapults and cracks"	He's rushing back and forth like the lines in the poem.
"he has schooled out all extravagance"	He's a good swimmer because he doesn't waste energy.
"The (king) of all is he who preens and wrestles"	He's strong, but is the poet making fun of him?

2. Freewrite about the poem(s) and your reactions. Look at the quotations and interpretations you circled in step 1. What do they have in common? How are they different? Jot down your thoughts and feelings.

> 2 poems, both about athletes, I'm an athlete so that's why they interest me
> how are they different? is one poem positive & the other negative?

3. Draft a working thesis statement. Think about your interpretation of the poem(s). Draft a statement that explains your overall response.

> Working thesis statement:
> I'm an athlete, so the poems got my attention. Both are about athletes, but from the spectator's point of view. One shows a positive view of an athlete and the other is negative.

4. Look for more evidence. Reread the poems. Look for ideas, quotations, or devices (such as repetition) that support your thesis statement. For easy reference during drafting, use a chart or other graphic device to record these elements.

> Kumin poem: positive view
> 1. Powerful: "catapults and cracks"
> 2. Efficient: "schooled out all extravagance"
> 3. "We watch him for signs": we admire him, want to be like him?

FOR ENGLISH LEARNERS

Writing: Thesis Statement Have students use these sentence starters to help them state their thesis and develop their main points:

- My subject is _____.
- My thesis (overall response) is _____.
- The points I will explain are _____.
- For my first point, my evidence from the poem is _____.

FOR ADVANCED LEARNERS/PRE–AP

Contrast Form and Structure Have students contrast form and structure of the poems "Bodybuilders' Contest" and "400-Meter Free Style." Have them consider how these differences affect readers' responses to the poems. Urge students to develop the link between form, structure, and reader response in writing their own thesis statements.

 BEST PRACTICES TOOLKIT—Transparency Analysis Frame: Poetic Form and Structure pp. D21, D40

Practice and Apply

To support students during the writing process, use these copy masters:

 RESOURCE MANAGER—Copy Masters Prewriting–Editing pp. 153–157 Writing Rubric p. 158 Writing Support p. 159 (for English learners)

Part 2: Apply the Writing Process

PREWRITING

1. Note words or lines that puzzle or move you. Urge students to close their eyes and listen as a peer reads the poem aloud, then quickly jot down words or lines that make a strong impression. Then have them create a chart with circled words, as in the model. Point out that in the third quote in the chart, the word *preens* may give a clue that answers the writer's question.

2. Freewrite about the poem(s) and your reactions. Emphasize that students need not worry about sentence structure and grammar at this stage. They should focus on exploring ideas, using the examples they noted in Step 1 as a guide.

3. Draft a working thesis statement. Remind students that the thesis of a personal response should include the writer's reactions to the poems. Check students' statements to make sure they have written an overall response.

4. Look for more evidence. Ask students to review lines 23–28 of the model. Note how the interpretations and quotations support the writer's thesis that "Bodybuilders' Contest" has a negative view. Then have students note their evidence in a list or organizer. Suggest a Venn Diagram for students addressing two or more works.

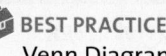 **BEST PRACTICES TOOLKIT—Transparencies** Venn Diagram p. A26 T Chart p. A25

For interactive graphic organizers, see

🖉 Write*Smart* CD

ⓘ Writing Center at **ClassZone.com**

DRAFTING

1. **Create a powerful introduction.** Remind students that an introduction should engage readers and introduce the subject. Students should avoid writing an attention-grabbing introduction that is not clearly related to the subject. Then display an introduction that begins with a quotation:

   "Full swing the swimmer catapults and cracks," writes Maxine Kumin in "400-Meter Free Style." In contrast to Kumin's positive view of an athlete, "Bodybuilders' Contest" . . .

2. **Organize your response.** Before students begin their drafts, explain that a poem's structure can suggest an organizational plan. If the poem builds toward a final important idea or strong image, presenting the ideas in the order in which they appear is a good choice. When a poem opens with its most important idea, it makes sense to organize a response from the most important ideas to the least important.

3. **Go beyond the evidence** Remind students to be specific and to elaborate on their comments and personal responses. Point out the sample response on page 730. The writer refers to a specific quotation, then elaborates by stating and explaining his reaction to the quotation.

For a personal response writing template, see

🧰 BEST PRACTICES TOOLKIT—Transparency
  Writing Template: Responding to Literature
    pp. C16, C38

💿 WriteSmart CD

ℹ️ Writing Center at ClassZone.com

DRAFTING

What Should I Do?	**What Does It Look Like?**
1. Create a powerful introduction. Grab readers' attention with an introduction that identifies the poem or poems you are responding to and outlines your response. **TIP** Consider opening with a quotation from the poem(s), a question to readers, or a vivid description from the poem(s) or your own life.	**A question** Have you ever won a game in front of a cheering crowd? If so, you may enjoy the two views of athletes presented in the poems "400-Meter Free Style" by Maxine Kumin and "Bodybuilders' Contest" by Wisława Szymborska. **A vivid description** When I play basketball, I play to win; but I also love to hear a cheering, shouting, stomping crowd of fans. . . .
2. Organize your response. Two ways of organizing your response are (1) to discuss the poem(s) using quotations and ideas in the order in which they appear in the poem, and (2) to discuss the most important quotation or idea first, then the second most important, and so on, ending with the least important quotation or idea in the poem(s). Because this writer included two poems in his response, he decided to discuss one poem at a time to avoid confusing his reader. Each idea or quotation is discussed in the order in which it appears in the poem.	*Introduction:* Poems present two views of competition. *Positive view: Kumin* 1. Powerful: "catapults and cracks" 2. Efficient: "schooled out all extravagance" 3. "We watch him for signs": We admire him, want to be like him? 4. My thoughts: I respect the swimmer. *Negative view: Szymborska* 1. Powerful: "all muscles" 2. Ridiculous: "preens," "monstrous" 3. Fights imaginary monsters 4. My thoughts: Poet is too harsh. *Conclusion:* Poems made me think about how I compete.
3. Go beyond the evidence. Don't just cite words and lines from the poem(s) that affected you. Explain how you reacted and why. **TIP** Stay focused on your response to the poem(s). Give readers only the information that supports your ideas.	The speaker mentioned that the bodybuilder's routine is "smoothly choreographed," but the animals he fights are imaginary. —*Quotation* I believe the poet is saying that bodybuilding is ridiculous. At first I agreed, but I have changed my mind. Posing *is* the bodybuilder's sport. Maybe battling the imaginary animals is part of the routine. —*Personal response*

DIFFERENTIATED INSTRUCTION

FOR LESS–PROFICIENT WRITERS

Choose an Organization To help students choose an organization, provide a frame for discussing the ideas in order of appearance, as in the student model. If students respond to one poem, they should ignore references to the second poem.

Beginning Paragraph—Introduction

• Name your subject or subjects.

• State your thesis. See page 729, number 3, for help with writing a thesis statement.

Middle Paragraphs—Personal Response
(Use ideas in order of appearance.)

• Present the first poem.

  —Present the first evidence in the text.
  —Give your interpretation.
  —Present the next evidence in the text.
  —Give your interpretation.

• Present the second poem.

  —Present the first evidence in the text.
  —Give your interpretation.
  —Present the next evidence in the text.
  —Give your interpretation.

End Paragraph—Conclusion

• Restate the subject or subjects.

• Write a conclusion that summarizes your response.

REVISING AND EDITING

What Should I Do?	What Does It Look Like?
1. Strengthen your support. • **Number** the reasons, examples, or explanations you provided. • If you don't have many numbers, **add supporting evidence** and elaboration.	▶ Maxine Kumin's poem has a positive view of competition. <u>It is full of action: "the swimmer catapults and cracks."</u> ① The swimmer is talented. "He has schooled out all extravagance," which means that he doesn't waste energy. ② His muscles, mouth, arms, feet, and lungs all know what to do as he surges forward. ③
2. Vary sentence beginnings. • Read aloud what you have written. Do many of your sentences have the same beginning? • **Highlight** sentences that begin the same way. • Rewrite the beginnings of some sentences to **create interest and fluency.**	▶ ~~He has to pose because it's part of his sport.~~ ~~He has to battle the imaginary animals.~~ Posing <u>is</u> the bodybuilder's sport. Maybe battling the imaginary animals is an expected part of the routine.

3. Eliminate vague vocabulary.
• Ask a peer reader to point out words and phrases in your response that lack detail.
• **[Bracket]** vocabulary that is weak and imprecise.
• **Replace** these words or phrases with strong, specific ones.
 	
See page 732: Ask a Peer Reader
	▶ I [like] the swimmer, too. He isn't interested in
	    ^respect
	        the spectators
	what [people] think of him.

4. Include appropriate transitions. • Look at the beginning and end of each paragraph. Have you included transitional words, phrases , or sentences that help the reader understand your message? • Draw a box around sentences that are not connected logically. • **Insert transitions** that show the relationship between ideas.	▶ Similarly, in basketball, all that really matters is the final score. ^In contrast, Wislawa Szymborska's poem has a negative view of competition.

REVISING AND EDITING

1. **Strengthen your support.** To highlight a good balance of examples and discussion, refer partners to the student model. Ask them to note the number of quotations used for support (*three or four*). Point out that the rest of the text contains discussion.

2. **Vary sentence beginnings.** Remind students that they can often vary sentence beginnings by simply inverting parts of a sentence or adding a transitional word or phrase. Refer students to the **Grammar and Style** note on page 214 to see how varying sentence beginnings can create more interesting writing.

3. **Eliminate vague vocabulary.** Encourage students to avoid weak or overused words and phrases such as *I think, I like, good,* and *interesting,* and instead use specific nouns, colorful adjectives, and precise, energetic verbs. Explain that the final peer reader questions on page 732 can help students find vagueness in their responses.

4. **Include appropriate transitions.** Point out that transitions between paragraphs show relationships between main ideas. Remind students that transitions may

   • connect ideas (*also, another*)
   • show importance (*more important, first, last but not least*)
   • show comparison/contrast (*both, like, however, unlike*)
   • give examples (*such as, like, for example*)
   • show cause and effect (*for that reason, so, therefore*).

For interactive revision tools, see

◉ Write*Smart* CD

ℹ️ Writing Center at **ClassZone.com**

FOR ENGLISH LEARNERS

Writing: Varying Sentence Beginnings

Provide sentence frames such as these to help students vary their sentence beginnings:

• He _____.
• Then, _____.
• However, the swimmer _____.
• The poem continues, "_____."
• Like _____, this poem _____.
• The swimmer also "_____."

Preparing to Publish

Support for meeting the goals in the writing rubric is supplied throughout the Writing Workshop on pages 729–731.

For Rubric Bank, see

 WriteSmart CD

Writing Center at **ClassZone.com**

Assess and Reteach

S STANDARDS LESSON FILE

Writing Lesson 15: Writing a Thesis Statement

Writing Lesson 16: Writing Introductions

Writing Lesson 17: Writing Conclusions

Writing Lesson 36: Elaborate with Incidents, Examples, and Quotations

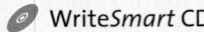
Preparing to Publish **Personal Response to a Poem**

Apply the Rubric

An effective personal response to a poem . . .

☑ begins by identifying the poem and stating an overall response

☑ provides information and specific details from the poem to support statements

☑ explains how and why lines from the poem elicited the personal response

☑ expresses ideas clearly in strong, precise language

☑ has a tone that reflects the writer's feelings

☑ creates fluency and interest with varied sentence beginnings

☑ concludes by effectively summarizing the response

Ask a Peer Reader

• How would you describe my reaction to the poem or poems?

• What evidence could I have included to make my statements more convincing?

• Which parts of my response could be more specific?

Check Your Grammar

• Use complete sentences. Correct any fragments—words or phrases that are punctuated as sentences but are missing a subject, a predicate, or both.

> He isn't interested in what the spectators think of him. *Just the time on the clock. In basketball too.*
>
> He isn't interested in what the spectators think of him. All he cares about is the time on the clock. Similarly, in basketball, all that really matters is the final score.

See page R64: Correcting Fragments

• Keep verbs in the active voice. Active verbs help make your response forceful and convincing.

> Teammates and fans *are impressed by* flashy moves and dunks.
>
> Flashy moves and dunks impress fans and teammates.

See page R57: Active and Passive Voice

Writing Online

 PUBLISHING OPTIONS
For publishing options, visit the **Writing Center** at **ClassZone.com.**

ASSESSMENT PREPARATION
For writing and grammar assessment practice, go to the **Assessment Center** at **ClassZone.com.**

Creating a Multimedia Presentation

Expand and strengthen your personal response to a poem by turning it into a multimedia presentation.

Planning the Presentation

1. **Know your technology.** Ask your teacher or your school's media specialist what authoring programs are available. An authoring program is a tool that lets you combine word processing with different types of media. Depending on the program, you might create a slide-show presentation or an interactive project with multiple links.

2. **Focus on your response.** Identify your main point about the poem(s). List quotations that illustrate that point.

3. **Gather media elements.** Find or create pictures, video clips, sound effects, words, and music that convey a mood or message similar to your response.

4. **Chart it out.** Make a flow chart that shows how your presentation will be organized. A slide-show presentation is usually linear, with one screen leading to another. An interactive presentation has branches like a tree, with each branch being a different choice that the user can make. See page 1231 for an example of this type of chart.

5. **Create a storyboard.** Sketch out, frame by frame, what your audience will see and hear. Specify the images, text, buttons, links, and sounds you will use. Think about whether you want to read lines from the poem as voice-overs or use them as onscreen text. See page 391 for an explanation of storyboarding.

Producing the Presentation

1. **Author the project.** Scan, download, or record the elements and use the authoring program to combine them.

2. **Test and revise.** Make sure that all information is correct and that all links work. Ask a few classmates to review your presentation before you give it.

3. **Present and reflect.** Present your project to an audience, or have small groups explore it on their own. Ask for feedback about small details and about the "big picture." What message did audience members take away from your presentation? Was that the message you wanted to send?

PUBLISHING WITH TECHNOLOGY

Ask students to read this page to get an overview of how to create a multimedia presentation. Students who choose this option should first familiarize themselves with the authoring software program they will use. Point out that a tutorial is usually included with a program.

Remind students to check copyright limits on written material, images, or sound files from the Internet. In some cases, students may use sound files in school projects without first obtaining copyright permission. Students should credit their sources in a Works Cited screen at the end of their presentation.

Before students begin working, review this rubric with them to help them focus on goals:

Rubric A strong multimedia presentation . . .

- contains accurate information from primary sources
- uses several media elements, attractively designed and combined in an effective order
- presents content in a logical order
- has a theme or main idea
- can be easily navigated and has links that work
- may be presented to an audience or explored by the audience without the creator's participation

R RESOURCE MANAGER—Copy Master
Publishing with Technology p. 159

S STANDARDS LESSON FILE

Media Lesson 20: Producing a Video
Media Lesson 22: Creating a Power Presentation

Assessment Practice

CHECK READINESS

Read aloud the paragraph under **ASSESS** and stress to students that this is not the full Unit Test but a way for them to check their readiness for it. Then, have students examine the skills listed under **REVIEW** and look back in the unit or in the **Student Resource Bank** for any skills they need to review.

READ THE SELECTIONS

Remind students to keep unit goals in mind as they read each poem, paying particular attention to these literary and reading skills:

- poetic structure and form
- sound devices
- figurative language
- imagery
- make inferences
- visualize

To help students focus on poetic elements, encourage them to ask questions like these:

- What tells you that these selections are poems? What poetic features do you notice even before you read the poems?
- How are these poems different from short stories or nonfiction articles? What is special about the way poets use language?

ANSWER THE QUESTIONS

Direct students to page R93–R101 of the **Handbook** to review test-taking strategies.

- Remind students not to choose the first alternative that seems to fit when answering a multiple-choice question. Instead, they should read through all the choices, eliminate any that are clearly wrong, and then choose the *best* answer—the one that is most accurate and complete.
- Remind students to use active reading strategies when they read test materials. For example, tell them to ask themselves questions as they read. Tell them to jot down these questions, answers, and other notes on scrap paper. After they have read the test questions, they should look back at the selection again, if necessary, because rereading may help them answer those questions.

Assessment Practice

ASSESS
The practice test items on the next few pages match skills listed on the Unit Goals page (page 667) and addressed throughout this unit. Taking this practice test will help you assess your knowledge of these skills and determine your readiness for the Unit Test.

REVIEW
After you take the practice test, your teacher can help you identify any skills you need to review.

- Poetic Structure/Form
- Sound Devices
- Figurative Language
- Imagery
- Make Inferences
- Visualize
- Participles and Participial Phrases
- Infinitives and Infinitive Phrases

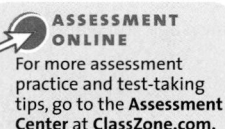

ASSESSMENT ONLINE
For more assessment practice and test-taking tips, go to the **Assessment Center** at ClassZone.com.

Reading Comprehension

DIRECTIONS *Read the following poems and then answer the questions.*

The Sower
Victor Hugo

Peaceful and cool, the twilight grey
Draws a dim curtain o'er the day,
While in my cottage-porch I lurk
And watch the last lone hour of work.

5 The fields around are bathed in dew,
And, with emotion filled, I view
An old man clothed in rags, who throws
The seed amid the channeled rows.

His shadowy form is looming now
10 High o'er the furrows of the plough;
Each motion of his arm betrays
A boundless faith in future days.

He stalks along the ample plain,
Comes, goes, and flings abroad the grain;
15 Unnoted, through the dreamy haze
With meditative soul I gaze.

At last, the vapours of the night
Dilate to heav'n the old man's height,
Till every gesture of his hand
20 Seems to my eyes sublimely grand!

Translated by George Murray

DIFFERENTIATED INSTRUCTION

FOR ENGLISH LEARNERS
Assessment Practice: Work Backward
Tell students to read questions before they read passages. Have pairs find unfamiliar words in test directions and questions and follow these steps:

1. Write each word on an index card.
2. Look up the meaning in a dictionary and write it on the back of the card.
3. Use the cards to practice the words with your partner and to teach them to others.

Culture: Connect Write *sower* on the board and explain that a sower is someone who sows, or spreads, seeds. Ask students what term they use in their home languages for people who plant seeds. Then lead a general discussion of work. Have students talk about the types of outdoor work they have seen in their home cultures, and have students compare this work to the kinds of outdoor work they see in their new communities.

To Be of Use

Marge Piercy

The people I love the best
jump into work head first
without dallying in the shallows
and swim off with sure strokes almost out of sight.
5 They seem to become natives of that element,
the black sleek heads of seals
bouncing like half-submerged balls.

I love people who harness themselves, an ox to a heavy cart,
who pull like water buffalo, with massive patience,
10 who strain in the mud and the muck to move things forward,
who do what has to be done, again and again.

I want to be with people who submerge
in the task, who go into the fields to harvest
and work in a row and pass the bags along,
15 who are not parlor generals and field deserters
but move in a common rhythm
when the food must come in or the fire be put out.

The work of the world is common as mud.
Botched, it smears the hands, crumbles to dust.
20 But the thing worth doing well done
has a shape that satisfies, clean and evident.
Greek amphoras for wine or oil,
Hopi vases that held corn, are put in museums
but you know they were made to be used.
25 The pitcher cries for water to carry
and a person for work that is real.

GO ON

ITEM ANALYSIS

COMPREHENSION AND WRITTEN RESPONSE	ITEMS	UNIT PAGES
Poetic Structure/Form	2, 3, 18	668–675, 693
Sound Devices	4, 6, 10, 11, 12	668–675, 715
Figurative Language	1, 8, 9, 14	668–675, 703
Imagery	5, 10, 11, 18	668–675, 677
Make Inferences	5, 12, 13, 16, 17	667
Visualize	7, 15, 17	703

WRITING AND GRAMMAR	ITEMS	UNIT PAGES
Participles and Participial Phrases	2, 3, 4, 7, 8	683
Infinitives and Infinitive Phrases	1, 5, 6, 9	713

FOR LESS−PROFICIENT READERS

Assessment Support Consider these options for completing the Assessment Practice:

- Have students "work backward" to review the test questions *before* reading the poems.
- Select random questions in the Assessment, and have students demonstrate how and where to look for the answers.
- Ask students to locate unfamiliar vocabulary words in the Assessment. Elicit the words' meanings from the class.
- For later reference, have students record useful testing words and definitions in their journals.
- Read the poems or parts of them aloud to aid in student comprehension.

McDougal Littell
Assessment System

After checking student readiness with this Assessment Practice, you may administer the complete Unit 7 Test in order to more thoroughly evaluate student mastery of unit goals.

Comprehension

Model a thinking process for answering multiple-choice questions.

1. **B is correct.** *It is the only metaphor among the answer choices. A and C describe the setting, so they are incorrect. D describes the sower's job, so it, too, is incorrect.*

2. **C is correct.** *A is completely untrue. B is untrue because each stanza contains only one complete sentence. D is untrue because each stanza is a complete sentence.*

3. **B is correct.** *All the other choices are untrue because the first two lines of each stanza end in the same sound (aa), not two different sounds (ab).*

4. **C is correct.** *The consonant sound d is repeated at the beginning of* draws *and* dim. *A is an example of consonance. B is an example of rhyme. D might be construed as words that create an image.*

5. **D is correct.** *The words "heav'n" and "sublimely" suggest nobility. A might be inferred from the entire poem but not from only the specified lines. B is completely untrue, while C cannot be inferred from anything in lines 17–20.*

6. **A is correct.** *The long o sound appears in both words of choice A. B and D are examples of consonance, while the words in C appear unrelated in sound.*

7. **A is correct.** *Every word in the answer choice describes an action that can be pictured. The other answer choices contain at least one word that cannot be pictured:* along, soul, through.

8. **B is correct.** *A is incorrect because the seals are not mentioned in line 3. The poem does not mention the work habits of seals, so C is incorrect. D is incorrect since the poem does not say the seals are having fun.*

9. **B is correct.** *It is the only answer choice that expresses a comparison using* like *or* as.

10. **A is correct.** *The repetition of "who" shows the emphasis on people rather than animals, so B is incorrect. C is incorrect because the speaker is making an analogy and not describing an actual task. D is also incorrect because the speaker emphasizes not strength but "massive patience," "muck," and the repetition of tasks, as shown by "again."*

Comprehension

DIRECTIONS *Answer these questions about "The Sower."*

1. The speaker uses a metaphor in lines 1–4 to compare the twilight to
   A a peaceful workplace
   B a dim curtain
   C a cottage-porch
   D a lonely job

2. Each stanza in "The Sower" is made up of
   A four lines that are incomplete sentences
   B four complete sentences that rhyme with each other
   C one complete sentence with rhyming parts
   D one part of a sentence that concludes in the last stanza

3. The rhyme scheme in every stanza of "The Sower" is
   A *abab*   C *abba*
   B *aabb*   D *abcd*

4. Which pair of words is an example of alliteration in the poem?
   A form, arm (lines 9, 11)
   B haze, gaze (lines 15, 16)
   C draws, dim (line 2)
   D furrows, plough (line 10)

5. From the image in lines 17–20, you can infer that the speaker
   A thinks that the old man is an amazing person
   B is frightened by the shadows that are on the field
   C hopes that he is not just dreaming about the farm
   D believes that the work of planting grain is noble

6. Which pair of words is an example of assonance in the poem?
   A old, clothed (line 7)
   B seed, amid (line 8)
   C stalks, ample (line 13)
   D seems, eyes (line 20)

7. Which group of words in lines 13–16 helps you visualize what the old man is doing in the field?
   A stalks, comes, goes, flings
   B along, ample, abroad, unnoted
   C plain, grain, dreamy, soul
   D he, through, haze, meditative

DIRECTIONS *Answer these questions about "To Be of Use."*

8. What is the most likely meaning of the metaphor in lines 1–7?
   A Seals and people like to swim long distances instead of wading in shallow water.
   B Some people immerse themselves in work in the way that seals immerse themselves in water.
   C Seals and people dive right into their work and have the same good work habits.
   D Some people have as much fun at work as seals do when they play around in the water.

9. Which of the following is an example of a simile in the poem?
   A "I love people who harness themselves"
   B "The work of the world is common as mud."
   C "I want to be with people who submerge / in the task"
   D "But the thing worth doing well done / has a shape that satisfies"

11. **B is correct.** *The m and u in "mud" and "muck" and the o in "who" and "move" draw attention to the obstacles that people struggle against. A is incorrect because "strain" does not necessarily suggest clumsiness. C and D are incorrect because "who" refers to humans, not animals.*

12. **C is correct.** *The sound at the beginning of "worth" and "well" shows their connection. A, B, and D are incorrect because no reward, difference, or beginning is mentioned or suggested.*

13. **A is correct.** *All of the poem's images relate to concrete, useful tasks. No answer but A relates to the totality of tasks. B, C, and D are incorrect because they describe only details of individual types of work.*

14. **D is correct.** *The pitcher's crying is a human activity. The corn, amphoras, and vase do nothing human, so A, B, and C are incorrect.*

10. In lines 8–11, the speaker uses the repetition of "who" and "again" to emphasize an image of

A people who diligently struggle to do their work

B sturdy animals that are trained to haul heavy loads

C the type of work that the speaker prefers to do

D people who are required to be physically strong to do their work

11. The assonance and alliteration used in line 10 help to create an image of

A people who are clumsy when they perform physical labor

B people who struggle against obstacles to accomplish their work

C animals that are forced to perform dangerous tasks

D animals that work alongside people on farms

12. The alliteration in "But the thing worth doing well done" (line 20) emphasizes the

A importance of rewarding people who do a good job

B different ways that people perform their jobs

C connection between working and doing a good job

D necessity of carrying out a job from the beginning to the end

13. The phrase "work that is real" in line 26 most likely refers to work that

A has a meaningful purpose

B is physically challenging

C includes making objects

D takes place outdoors

14. Which one of the following objects is personified in lines 22–26?

A corn   **C** vase

B amphoras   **D** pitcher

DIRECTIONS *Answer the following questions about both poems.*

15. Which type of work can you visualize from images in both poems?

A fishing   **C** farming

B logging   **D** building

16. The speakers of both poems would most likely agree with which one of the following statements?

A Outdoor occupations are dangerous.

B Workers' relationships are important.

C The best workers love their work.

D Work is something to be valued.

Written Response

SHORT RESPONSE
Write three or four sentences to answer the question.

17. List five words or phrases that help you visualize the time of day at which "The Sower" takes place. Why is visualizing that particular time of day important to this poem?

EXTENDED RESPONSE
Write two or three paragraphs to answer the question.

18. Compare the form of the poem "The Sower" with that of "To Be of Use." Explain how the line length, meter, and rhyme help convey the ideas and images of each poem.

737

---

15. C is correct. *"The Sower" describes planting; "To Be of Use" describes harvesting. Fishing might be suggested by water images and building by "mud," "muck," and "move" in Piercy's poem, but neither is directly mentioned there or in "The Sower," so A and D are incorrect. B is not mentioned in either poem.*

16. D is correct. *The comment that every gesture seems grand ("The Sower," lines 19–20) shows that the speaker values work. The remarks about loving hard workers shows the speaker of "To Be of Use" to value work. Nothing supports A or B. C is an inference that can be made from Piercy's poem but not from Hugo's, so it is incorrect.*

Written Response

Possible short responses:

17. *Words and phrases that help you visualize the time of day:* "twilight grey," "dim curtain," "last lone hour of work," "shadowy form," "dreamy haze," "vapours of the night"

Reasons for visualizing the time of day: Evening shadows make the worker appear larger than life. That is, the figure looks very big and important. His stature plays into the speaker's view of the farmer's work as noble. It is important to understand the perspective of the speaker on the porch. He watches the last of the day's work, the beginning of the evening, and rest.

Notes for extended response:

18. *Line lengths: "The Sower" has equal lines and stanzas (each stanza states one sentence), reinforcing the sower's steady progress. "To Be of Use" has variable line and stanza lengths, making up one or two sentences. The lengths underscore the variety of jobs.*

Meter: "The Sower" has the same meter line to line. The steadiness conveys grandeur, like regal music. The image of the farmer waving an arm underscores steadiness. "To Be of Use" has an uneven meter. The meter reflects different kinds of work.

Rhyme: "The Sower" uses a common, predictable rhyme scheme. It soothes as the words suggest a reliable worker. "To Be of Use" relies on alliteration and assonance; these devices also comfort us as we read about what the speaker values.

DIFFERENTIATED INSTRUCTION

FOR ENGLISH LEARNERS
Review Academic Vocabulary List the italicized academic vocabulary on the board. Give the examples in random order and have students match each example with the corresponding term. Elicit additional examples from students.

- *metaphor:* The pasture is a spotted carpet.
- *rhyme scheme:* aabba
- *alliteration:* Fat fruit flies flit about.

- *image:* A blue feather floats down onto white sand.
- *assonance:* seedy green weeds
- *simile:* Seeds scatter like frightened birds.
- *personification:* The wind shrieks angrily.
- *repetition:* Seeds sprout, leaves sprout, and plants sprout.
- *rhyme:* Boats float.
- *meter:* tickety-tock

Writing and Grammar

1. **C** *is correct.* To pursue *is an infinitive. Choice A offers a third-person present-tense verb, not an infinitive.* B *offers a participle.* D *is incorrect because the original sentence contains no infinitive.*

2. **A** *is correct.* Lacking meter or end rhymes *is a participial phrase.* B *contains a subordinate clause, while* C *contains an infinitive, so both are incorrect. The original contains no participial phrase, so* D *is incorrect.*

3. **C** *is correct. The word* arresting *is used as a participle.* A, B, *and the original sentence do not contain a participle, so all are incorrect.*

4. **B** *is correct. The word* admiring *is a participle.* A *adds an adjective, so it is incorrect.* C *substitutes a passive verb for an active verb, so it is incorrect.* D *is incorrect because the original sentence contains no participle.*

Writing and Grammar

DIRECTIONS *Read this passage and answer the questions that follow.*

(1) In her poem "For the Young Who Want To," Marge Piercy encourages young people who are in pursuit of their passion. (2) As is the case with many of Piercy's poems, the structure of this poem is organic. (3) Since it has no meter or end rhymes, it is difficult to memorize. (4) But its six stanzas are filled with strong statements that grab the reader's attention. (5) "Talent is what they say / you have after the novel / is published and favorably / reviewed," the poet states. (6) This assertion reflects Piercy's belief that artists receive praise from the public only after they have received the admiration of critics. (7) During the countless years that artists sacrifice so much time working on their art, their friends think it's just a hobby. (8) They keep asking artists when they are going to search for a real job. (9) As a result of this indirect form of criticism, artists sometimes seek to prove the legitimacy of their craft. (10) Piercy suggests that even though artists don't have licenses, they are still experts in their field. (11) She then points out that the real writer is the one who practices the craft of writing. (12) Finally, Piercy concludes that what drives an artist is loving the work, with or without recognition.

1. How would you change sentence 1 to include an infinitive?
   A Change "encourages" to "convinces."
   B Change "who are in pursuit of" to "pursuing."
   C Change "who are in pursuit of" to "to pursue."
   D No change is needed.

2. Choose the correct way to rewrite sentence 3 using a participial phrase.
   A Lacking meter or end rhymes, it is difficult to memorize.
   B Since it lacks both meter and end rhymes, it is difficult to memorize.
   C The lack of meter or end rhymes makes it difficult to memorize.
   D No change is needed.

3. How would you change sentence 4 to include a participle?
   A Change "grab" to "demand."
   B Change "strong" to "vivid."
   C Change "strong" to "arresting."
   D No change is needed.

4. How would you change sentence 6 to include a participle?
   A Change "of critics" to "of newspaper critics."
   B Change "the admiration of critics" to "compliments from admiring critics."
   C Change "receive praise from the public" to "are praised by the public."
   D No change is needed.

738

DIFFERENTIATED INSTRUCTION

FOR LESS–PROFICIENT READERS

Assessment Support: Participles Most participles end in -*ing* or -*ed*. They may appear alone or as part of a phrase. Have students identify the participle, if any, acting as an adjective in these sentences:

- Chen is a <u>published</u> poet. (*participle*)
- The <u>standing</u> student is Flo. (*participle*)
- Nora is reading a poetry book. (*none*)
- Otis sat, <u>waiting</u> quietly. (*participle*)
- The students had prepared well. (*none*)

Assessment Support: Infinitives Infinitives may appear alone or in phrases. Most contain the word *to*. Help students to distinguish infinitives and infinitive phrases from prepositional phrases in the following sentences:

- Mr. Gomez is able <u>to teach</u>. (*infinitive*)
- Julia walked <u>to the front</u> of the room. (*prepositional phrase*)
- <u>To illustrate meter</u>, Gil wrote two lines. (*infinitive phrase*)
- Pat likes <u>to write sonnets</u>. (*infinitive phrase*)

5. How would you change sentence 7 to include an infinitive?

   A Change "working" to "to work."

   B Change "sacrifice" to "are sacrificing."

   C Change "During the countless years" to "For the years."

   D No change is needed.

6. How would you change sentence 8 to include an infinitive?

   A Change "They keep asking artists" to "They wonder."

   B Change "going to search" to "searching."

   C Change "going to search" to "looking."

   D No change is needed.

7. Choose the correct way to rewrite sentence 9 using a participle.

   A As a result of this implied criticism, artists sometimes seek to prove the legitimacy of their craft.

   B As a result of this indirect form of criticism, artists sometimes seek to prove that their craft is legitimate.

   C As a result of this indirect form of criticism, artists sometimes are forced to prove the legitimacy of their craft.

   D No change is needed.

8. Choose the correct way to rewrite sentence 10 using a participial phrase.

   A Piercy suggests that although artists don't have licenses, they are still experts in their field.

   B Piercy suggests that even though artists don't have licenses, it doesn't mean they lack talent.

   C Piercy suggests that even though artists don't have licenses hanging on their walls, they are still experts in their field.

   D No change is needed.

9. Choose the correct way to rewrite sentence 12 using an infinitive phrase.

   A Finally, Piercy draws the conclusion that what drives an artist is loving the work, with or without recognition.

   B Finally, Piercy concludes that what drives an artist is the ability to love the work, with or without recognition.

   C Finally, Piercy concludes that what drives an artist is loving the work, whether or not the art is recognized.

   D No change is needed.

STOP

739

5. A *is correct.* To work *is an infinitive.* B *changes the present form of the verb to present progressive, which includes a participle, so it is incorrect.* C *replaces the prepositional phrase with another, so it is incorrect.* D *is incorrect because the original sentence has no infinitive.*

6. D *is correct.* *The original sentence already contains an infinitive,* to search. A *is incorrect because it replaces one verb with another, not an infinitive.* B *and* C *both remove an infinitive.*

7. A *is correct.* *The adjective* indirect *is changed to the participle* implied. *Neither* B *nor* C *contains a participle. The original sentence contains no participle, so* D *is incorrect.*

8. C *is correct.* Hanging on their walls *is a participial phrase that modifies* licenses. A, B, *and the original sentence do not contain a participial phrase, so all are incorrect.*

9. B *is correct.* To love the work *is an infinitive phrase that acts as an adjective modifying* ability. A, C, *and the original do not contain an infinitive phrase, so they are all incorrect.*

FOR ENGLISH LEARNERS

Test-Taking Strategies: Understanding Instructions

Read aloud the instructions for item 5, and model the steps students must take to answer such questions. Help them recognize that the first task is to see whether sentence 7 contains an infinitive. Students who do not understand the term *infinitive* should review it. Then do a think-aloud to show how to substitute the A, B, and C options and to select the correct choice.

Give students support as they go through the same steps for item 6. Ask what they should look for and where. Then work together to identify the changes in each answer choice. Finally, ask a student to do a think-aloud as he or she tries to determine the correct answer.

INTRODUCE *GREAT READS*

In Unit 7, students have discussed a number of big questions. Invite students to tell which question they found most intriguing and why, and then focus attention on the three that appear on this page. Discuss the recommended books and their summaries, pointing out how each connects to the related question. Encourage students to choose one or more of these "great reads" to read independently.

ℹ **ClassZone.com**

To find additional books that match students' interests and ability levels, visit the Literature Center at **ClassZone.com**.

Ideas for Independent Reading

Writers use poetic language in both the poetry and prose of the following selections.

What makes a strong competitor?

The Old Man and the Sea
by Ernest Hemingway

Hemingway's concise style depicts Santiago, a Cuban fisherman, as he battles a giant marlin. The competition does not end when Santiago lands the huge creature.

The Hot Zone
by Richard Preston

This suspenseful true account of dealing with an outbreak of Ebola virus serves as a warning to humankind. The struggle between viruses and humans is likely to intensify in the future.

The Big Year: A Tale of Man, Nature, and Fowl Obsession
by Mark Obmascik

A birding marathon in 1998 lasted for 365 days, during which bird watchers tried to set a new record for number of species seen worldwide. The author describes the marathon and three of the passionate competitors.

Where can your imagination take you?

About This Life
by Barry Lopez

The author's ability to see the natural world in fresh and startling ways makes him one of the nation's most valued naturalists and writers.

19 Varieties of Gazelle
by Naomi Shihab Nye

A Palestinian-American poet, Nye writes of animals, people, food, war and peace, and how life has changed in painful ways for Palestinians living in the occupied West Bank.

Spoon River Anthology
by Edgar Lee Masters

Under the sod of a Midwestern cemetery lie 244 souls. In this poetic classic, they speak to readers about their lives—full of disappointment and loss—and their inevitable deaths, some peaceful and some violent.

Do you set your own course?

We Die Alone: A WWII Epic of Escape and Endurance
by David Howarth

Norwegian commandos race for the Swedish border to escape from Nazi pursuers. This true account demonstrates the strength and endurance of the human spirit.

Great Expectations
by Charles Dickens

Set in 19th-century England, this novel depicts the rags-to-riches story of the orphan Pip. Pip dreams of becoming a gentleman, and a secret patron arranges for this to happen. When Pip moves to London to fulfill his "great expectations," he learns the true meaning of nobility and love.

In the Shadow of Man
by Jane Goodall

From her memoir we learn that when Goodall began chimpanzee research in 196 women didn't do primate studies. Her scientific discoveries paved the way for other women to do similar work.

UNIT 8

A Way with Words

AUTHOR'S STYLE AND VOICE

- • In Fiction
- • In Media
- • In Nonfiction
- • In Poetry
- • In Drama

741

About the Art Hyacinth Manning-Carner created *Tumbling Flowers* in 1954. For more information, see page 798.

For help in planning this unit, see

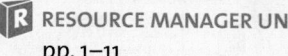 RESOURCE MANAGER UNIT 8
pp. 1–11

INTRODUCE THE UNIT

A person who speaks smoothly and easily is said to be "fluent." A person who chooses tactful, courteous words often is described as "well-spoken." A person who is said to have "a way with words" skillfully expresses ideas in clear, interesting ways. Ask students to think of someone they know or have read about who, in their opinion, has "a way with words." On the basis of those thoughts, invite students to share their ideas about what "a way with words" means.

Invite students to consider how the images on this page suggest various ways of using words. Use these discussion prompts:

- • How are the people in the photograph using words?
- • What details characterize the style of the artwork on the page?
- • How does the artwork convey an idea?
- • How does the style of communication in these images differ?

Tell students that as they read this unit, they will consider the various styles that writers use to express their ideas. They will look at different media and compare the **author's style and voice** in several literary selections.

SKILLS STRAND	Literary Analysis Workshop: Author's Style and Voice pp. 744–749	Where Have You Gone, Charming Billy? pp. 750–763 Short Story Level: Average	The Princess and the Tin Box pp. 764–769 Fable Level: Average	Media Study: from The Birds pp. 770–773 Film Clip	Going to Japan pp. 774–781 Essay Level: Average
Literary Analysis	Author's Style and Voice pp. 744–749	Realism pp. 751, 752, 754, 755, 761 Review: Point of View p. 756	Parody pp. 765, 766, 768, 769		Humor pp. 775, 776, 778, 779, 780
Reading and Informational Texts	Analyze the Literature pp. 745, 747–749	Analyze Sequence pp. 751, 755, 758, 759, 761 Read an Interview p. 760	Predict pp. 765, 768, 769		Summarize pp. 775, 779, 780
Vocabulary	Academic Vocabulary pp. 744, 746	Word Acquisition pp. 751, T751, 762 Context Clues p. T751 Prefixes (*in-*) p. 762		Academic Vocabulary pp. 771	Word Acquisition pp. 775, T775, 781 Context Clues p. T775 Connotation and Denotation (Word Choice) p. 781
Writing, Grammar, and Style		Supporting Details pp. 755, 763 Repetition for Effect pp. 755, 763			
Speaking, Listening, Viewing, and Media	Discuss pp. T744–T747	Discuss pp. 750, T752–T760, 761 Analyze Visuals pp. 752, 757, T759	Discuss pp. 764, T766–T768, 769 Analyze Visuals p. 766	Discuss pp. 770, 773 Style in Movies (Alfred Hitchcock's Cinematic Style) pp. 771–773 Analyze Visual Elements pp. 771–773 Create a Production Still p. 773	Discuss pp. 774, T776–T779, 780 Analyze Visuals p. 776

A Few Words pp. 782–789 Essay *Level: Challenging*	A narrow Fellow in the Grass/ "Hope" is the thing with feathers— pp. 790–795 Poems *Level: Challenging*	Luxury/Kidnap Poem pp. 796–801 Poems *Level: Average*	The Sneeze pp. 802–811 Drama *Level: Average*	Writing Workshop: Analysis of an Author's Style pp. 812–819	Skills Assessed on the Unit 8 Test:
Tone pp. 783, 784, 787	Dickinson's Style pp. 791, 792, 793, 795	Giovanni's Style pp. 797, 798, 800, 801	Farce pp. 803, T808, T810, 811		**Literary Analysis** • Identify elements of style, including word choice, sentence structure, and tone • Analyze style • Analyze the impact of style on meaning
Paraphrase pp. 783, 786, 787	Strategies for Reading Poetry pp. 791, 793 Read a Journal Article p. 794	Interpret Ideas in Poetry pp. 797, 798, 801	Visualize pp. 803, T804, T807, 811	Analyze a Literary Analysis pp. 813–814	**Reading and Informational Texts** • Visualize • Analyze sequence • Summarize
Word Acquisition pp. 783, T783, 788 Context Clues p. T783 Homonyms p. 788				Academic Vocabulary p. 818	**Vocabulary** • Use prefixes to help unlock word meaning • Understand and use homonyms
Variety in Sentence Types pp. 786, 789				Write an Analysis of an Author's Style pp. 812–819 Complete Sentences p. 818 Conciseness p. 818	**Writing, Grammar, and Style** • Write a literary analysis • Vary sentence types • Additional writing and grammar skills
Discuss pp. 782, T784–T786, 787 Analyze Visuals p. 786	Discuss pp. 790, T792–T794, 795	Discuss pp. 796, T798–T800, 801 Analyze Visuals pp. 798, T800	Discuss pp. 802, T804–T810, 811 Analyze Visuals pp. T805, T807	Deliver an Oral Interpretation p. 819	**Speaking, Listening, Viewing, and Media** • Analyze visual elements

⊙ For additional lesson planning help, see **Easy Planner DVD**.

OBJECTIVES
- establish prior knowledge about characteristics of **style**
- list similarities in the **style** of a particular artist

What is
STYLE?

Read and discuss the question and the paragraph. To illustrate differences in style, have students name a creative work that fits each of these stylistic descriptions:

- a movie that features extreme stunts and explosive action
- a song about personal thoughts, sung to subtle, possibly acoustic, accompaniment
- a clothing line known for its "retro" influences

Discuss how students chose their examples.

ACTIVITY As students meet in groups, urge them to choose an artist whom they all know and can discuss intelligently and to cite specific examples of that artist's work when they answer the questions. Have group representatives summarize the group's answers for a whole-class comparison.

CHECK UNDERSTANDING Have students define **style** in their own words and give an example of an artistic style.

What is
STYLE?

What draws you to a certain band's songs, a specific director's movies, or a particular writer's work? The answer to these questions can often be attributed to **style**. Style is what makes the work of writers and other creative people distinctive.

ACTIVITY With a small group, list artists—actors, songwriters, painters, authors, or directors—who have unique styles. Then pick one of these people and answer the following questions:

- What about the artist's work is distinctive? Are there characteristics that make his or her work immediately recognizable?
- What ties all of the artist's work together? For example, maybe your favorite songwriter uses the same imagery in all of his or her lyrics.
- What three words would you use to describe your artist's style?

Unit Resources

742

- **R** RESOURCE MANAGER UNIT 8
- **BEST PRACTICES TOOLKIT**
- **S** STANDARDS LESSON FILE

- Easy Planner DVD-ROM
- Write*Smart* CD-ROM
- ClassZone.com
- Audio Anthology CD
- Multi-Language Academic Vocabulary Online

- eEdition DVD-ROM & Online
- McDougal Littell Assessment System
- Test Generator CD
- Media*Smart* DVD-ROM

 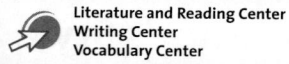
Preview Unit Goals

LITERARY ANALYSIS	• Identify and analyze elements of style, including word choice, tone, sentence structure, and figurative language
	• Analyze the impact of style on meaning
	• Analyze writers' styles
	• Analyze humor, parody, and farce
READING	• Use reading strategies, including visualizing and predicting
	• Summarize and paraphrase
	• Interpret ideas in poetry
WRITING AND GRAMMAR	• Write an analysis of an author's style
	• Support main points with examples from the text
	• Vary sentence types
SPEAKING, LISTENING, AND VIEWING	• Analyze Alfred Hitchcock's style in film
	• Analyze visual elements in film
	• Create a production still
	• Deliver a dramatic reading
VOCABULARY	• Use prefixes to help unlock meaning
	• Understand and use homonyms
ACADEMIC VOCABULARY	• elements of style • parody
	• realism • visual elements in film
	• irony • homonym
	• humor

743

Preview Unit Goals

This page expresses the main skills and strategies for Unit 8 as a set of goals. Have students preview the categories and goals, considering what experience they may already have with each goal. Be sure to point out the color-coding that identifies each strand throughout the unit.

Call on a volunteer to read the Academic Vocabulary terms aloud. Write definitions for the terms on the board, and have students record each term and its definition in their journals. As students read the selections in Unit 8, have them refer to their definitions as needed. Also encourage students to use these terms as they talk and write about the selections.

ADDITIONAL UNIT GOALS

These skills will be taught in this unit but are not the major focus of the unit:

Literary Analysis
• Analyze punctuation and grammar as elements of style
• Analyze sound devices, flashback, irony, extended metaphor, symbol, voice, and enjambment as elements of style
• Genre study: dramatic farce, short story, essay, poetry

Reading
• Use strategies for reading poetry
• Analyze sequence relationships

Writing and Grammar
• Use repetition effectively

Vocabulary
• Understand connotation and denotation of words

DIFFERENTIATED INSTRUCTION

FOR ENGLISH LEARNERS

Academic Vocabulary Use the copy master to help students learn the Academic Vocabulary listed on this page.

1. Read aloud each term. Have students find it on their copy master.

2. Discuss the meanings or examples shown, and complete the chart as a class.

3. Have students work in small groups to complete the remaining activities.

Additional Academic Vocabulary Use the copy master to help students learn academic words they will use in subsequent lessons and on the Assessment Practice. Follow the same procedure as for the Academic Vocabulary copy master.

> R RESOURCE MANAGER—Copy Masters
> Academic Vocabulary p. 9
> Additional Academic Vocabulary p. 10

Focus and Motivate

OBJECTIVES

- identify and analyze style
- analyze voice, including tone, word choice, and sentence structure

Teach

Part 1: What Is Style?

Common Styles Tell students that the four types of style are not rigid distinctions, but that thinking about them sharpens readers' awareness of the choices authors make—and the reasons for their choices—as they craft their own works.

Discuss the styles most likely to be found in these four examples, and elicit reasons an author or writer would choose those styles:

- a graduation speech *(The style would usually be formal overall because of the seriousness of the occasion. The speech might include informal elements, such as humorous anecdotes.)*
- a mystery about a 12-year-old detective, set in 2005 *(The style would probably be informal to mirror the speech and behavior of young people today, but the story would also include literary elements.)*
- an article on the health effects of traffic congestion *(The style would be journalistic because the author's main purpose is to convey information. The level of formality would vary depending on the publication.)*
- a novel set during the Civil War *(The style would be literary to create a rich portrayal of the historical setting and the dramatic, complex experiences of the characters.)*

List familiar books, articles, and documents with different styles in a chart. Have students check the main style or styles that apply to each, and discuss why the style suits the author's purpose.

Title	Formal	Informal

 BEST PRACTICES TOOLKIT—Transparency
Analysis Frame: Author's Craft pp. D21, D24

Author's Style and Voice

What makes classical music different from rap? How can you tell the difference between a spine-tingling Edgar Allan Poe story and a Stephen King thriller? The answer is style, or the unique elements that make everything—from music to writing—distinctive. Style is what helps you tell *Newsweek* from the *National Enquirer* or a Shakespearean sonnet from a poem by E. E. Cummings. Often, the style of what you read can affect you just as much as the substance.

Part 1: What Is Style?

In literature, **style** is the way a particular work is written—not what is said, but *how* it's said. A writer's style depends on many elements, including his or her choice of words, tone, and sentence structures. Does the writer use long sentences packed with flowery details or ones that are short and to the point? Is the tone laced with sarcasm, or is it sincere?

COMMON STYLE	EXAMPLE
FORMAL • uses sophisticated, abstract language • may use complex sentence structures • carefully observes rules of grammar	And was Mr. Rochester now ugly in my eyes? No, reader: gratitude and many associations, all pleasurable and genial, made his face the object I best liked to see. . . . —from *Jane Eyre* by Charlotte Brontë
Informal • sounds like everyday conversation • may use contractions and slang • may use simple sentences and fragments	Remember that boy you thought you could not live without? What was his name? Randy. You don't remember? —from *The Kitchen God's Wife* by Amy Tan
Journalistic • uses neutral words to report facts • often includes simple sentences • reader notices what's said, not who's talking	A lightning flash can happen in half a second. In that instant, the lightning flash superheats the surrounding air to a temperature five times hotter than that on the surface of the sun. —from *nationalgeographic.com*
Literary • may use imagery to convey a mood • often includes long, elaborate sentences • reader often gets to know the narrator— the voice that tells the story	The lightning quivered about the pinnacles of the ancient Hôtel de Ville, and shed flickering gleams over the open space in front. —from "The Adventure of the German Student" by Washington Irving

---

DIFFERENTIATED INSTRUCTION

For general guidelines on differentiating instruction, see

 BEST PRACTICES TOOLKIT
Differentiated Instruction pp. 31–38

FOR LESS–PROFICIENT READERS

Note Taking For students who need help with note taking, hand out the note-taking copy master before discussing this page. As volunteers read aloud each paragraph or chart section, discuss the main points, and have students record them on the copy master.

Relate Style to Other Media Help make the four styles concrete by asking students to relate them to other arts. Give examples to prompt students: TV sitcom or pop song— informal; opera or ballet—formal; literary or nature show or documentary—journalistic.

RESOURCE MANAGER—Copy Master
Note Taking p. 15

MODEL 1: STYLE

This excerpt comes from a famous novel about life on the Nebraska prairie. As you read, consider the common styles listed on the preceding page. Which style or styles do you think characterize the writing?

from
My Ántonia
Novel by **Willa Cather**

While the train flashed through never-ending miles of ripe wheat, by country towns and bright-flowered pastures and oak groves wilting in the sun, we sat in the observation car, where the woodwork was hot to the touch and red dust lay deep over everything. The dust and heat, the burning wind,
5 reminded us of many things. We were talking about what it is like to spend one's childhood in little towns like these, buried in wheat and corn, under stimulating extremes of climate: burning summers when the world lies green and billowy beneath a brilliant sky, when one is fairly stifled in vegetation, in the color and smell of strong weeds and heavy harvests; blustery winters with
10 little snow, when the whole country is stripped bare and gray as sheet-iron.

Close Read

1. Notice the sentence length and the use of imagery in the boxed text. On the basis of these details, how would you describe the style of this excerpt?

2. Identify another detail that helped you determine the style.

MODEL 2: STYLE

Here, another writer offers a different description of a prairie. As you read, consider how the writer's style compares with Willa Cather's in the excerpt from *My Ántonia*.

from
PRAIRYERTH
Nonfiction by **William Least Heat-Moon**

The Flint Hills are the last remaining grand expanse of tallgrass prairie in America. On a geologic map, their shape something like a stone spear point, they cover most of the two-hundred-mile longitude of Kansas from Nebraska to Oklahoma, a stony upland twenty to eighty miles wide. At their western
5 edge, the mixed-grass prairie begins and spreads a hundred or so miles to the shortgrass country of the high plains.

Close Read

1. Is this excerpt literary or journalistic? Support your answer.

2. Contrast Heat-Moon's style with Cather's. Identify at least two specific differences.

MODEL 1: STYLE
Close Read

1. *Possible answer: The style of this excerpt is literary. The entire passage is one long, graceful sentence filled with images that convey the power and beauty of summer's lushness (lines 6–9) and contrast it with the harsh barrenness of winter (lines 9–10).*

2. *Possible answer: Another clue to the literary style is the sentence "The dust and heat, the burning wind, reminded us of many things" (lines 4–5). This portrays the narrator as a person—someone who grew up in this setting and whose memories bring feelings of peace and nostalgia.*

MODEL 2: STYLE
Close Read

1. *Possible answer: This excerpt is journalistic, not literary. The writer focuses on specific facts, such as the shape, location, and width of the hills (lines 2–4) and how and where the vegetation changes (lines 4–6). Although he uses one simile, "like a stone spear point" (line 2), he mostly uses simple description, such as measurements—"twenty to eighty miles wide" (line 4)—and geographic terms, such as "tallgrass prairie" (line 1), "stony upland" (line 4), and "high plains" (line 6).*

2. *Possible answer: One specific difference between Heat-Moon's and Cather's styles is that Cather uses a great deal of imagery, whereas Heat-Moon uses very little. Another difference is in their sentence structures: Cather's sentences are much longer and more complex than Heat-Moon's. A third difference is that Cather's style gives the reader a sense of the narrator, whereas Heat-Moon's objective style draws little attention to the person behind the words.*

FOR LESS—PROFICIENT READERS
Comprehension: Figurative Language
Explain that authors create images with figurative language—words used for their associations beyond literal meaning. Discuss these phrases from Model 1 and explain what they help the reader to experience: *never-ending miles* (line 1), "seemingly endless plains"; *buried in wheat and corn* (line 6), "the fields were tall and endless"; *the world lies green and billowy* (lines 7–8), "the vegetation is lush"; *bare and gray as sheet-iron* (line 10), "cold, plain stillness."

FOR ADVANCED LEARNERS/PRE—AP
Analyze Styles Have students read the workshop independently and then work in small groups to identify examples of the four styles in their literature textbooks or other literature available in the classroom. Have them record short passages from their examples and point out the characteristics of the passage that fit the style.

Teach

Part 2: Style and Voice

Word Choice, Sentence Structure, and Tone

Point out to students that people speak in different styles and voices to friends, parents, teachers, strangers, and so on, and that writers also adjust their voice to suit their purpose and audiences. Challenge students to compose these sentences using an effective and appropriate voice:

- a teenage narrator of a humorous story describing a scary experience to a friend (*Example: It was—I mean, you can't believe how big that spider was! I was, like, let me out of here!*)

- a high-school student thanking a committee for an award or scholarship (*Example: Your generous gift allows me to fulfill my lifelong dream of attending college, and I will dedicate the next four years to making use of this opportunity.*)

- the anonymous narrator of a literary-style novel describing the weather (*Example: Lightning splintered the sky, thunder rumbled like barrels rolling down an alley, and the rain spilled down in sheets and raced along the gutters.*)

- a journalist writing about the background of a celebrity (*Example: She took her first ballet lesson at the age of three and performed in The Nutcracker Suite with the London Royal Ballet at the age of six.*)

Then discuss with students their choices of words, sentence structure, and tone in crafting the voice of each sentence. If necessary, have them review the chart on page 744 for terms that refer to different styles and their characteristics.

CHECK UNDERSTANDING

Have students describe their understanding of **voice**.

Part 2: Style and Voice

Almost every choice a writer makes contributes to the style of his or her work. These choices also help to create a **voice**, the personality that comes across on the page. The voice may be the writer's, or it may belong to a fictional character in a story.

Here, two writers express feelings about their craft. A close look at three key elements—word choice, sentence structure, and tone—in these passages can help you better understand each writer's unique style.

It is [the writer's] privilege to help man endure by lifting his heart, by reminding him of the courage and honor and hope and pride and compassion and pity and sacrifice which have been the glory of his past.
—William Faulkner, Nobel Prize acceptance speech, 1950

The very first thing I tell my new students on the first day of a workshop is that good writing is about telling the truth. We are a species that needs and wants to understand who we are. Sheep lice do not seem to share this longing, which is one reason they write so very little.
—Anne Lamott, *Bird by Bird*

WORD CHOICE

If you've ever struggled to find the perfect words to describe something, then you know how important **word choice** can be. A short boy can be *compact, shrimpy,* even *Lilliputian*—or just *short.* The **denotation** (literal meaning) is the same, but the **connotations** (emotional associations) are quite different.

In his speech, Faulkner uses formal, dramatic words and phrases—for example, "the glory of his past"—to emphasize the serious responsibility of writers. Lamott's writing, however, is more conversational. Her use of *I* and *we,* as well as phrases like "the very first thing," contributes to her personable style.

SENTENCE STRUCTURE

Sentences can be short and to the point (like Lamott's) or long and complex (like Faulkner's). In fact, the Faulkner excerpt is one long sentence that strings together *hope, courage,* and other weighty words with a series of *and*'s. This structure adds to the dramatic impact of the writing and helps to create its formal style.

TONE

Tone is a writer's attitude toward a subject, as expressed through choice of words and details. Faulkner's focus on the writer's "privilege" conveys a formal tone. Lamott, however, scampers playfully from truth to sheep lice. Such incongruous details help to create a humorous tone.

DIFFERENTIATED INSTRUCTION

FOR LESS–PROFICIENT READERS

Note Taking For students who need help, hand out the note-taking copy master for this page. As students read and discuss the main points, have them record them on the copy master.

 RESOURCE MANAGER—Copy Master
Note Taking p. 16

Concept Support Tell students that an attitude is a feeling toward something, such as angry, kind, or respectful. Then suggest a familiar subject, such as a neighbor's dog. Help students list positive and negative attitudes that a writer's tone could reflect toward the subject (*admiring, disapproving, caring, irritated*). Have students describe the subject, choosing words to craft a tone that reflects one of the attitudes listed.

MODEL 1: ELEMENTS OF STYLE

Sandra Cisneros has a unique and recognizable style of writing. As you read this excerpt, pay attention to her word choice and the structure of the sentences. To get the full effect of Cisneros's style, read the excerpt aloud. Does it sound like someone writing or like someone talking?

from Geraldo No Last Name

Vignette by **Sandra Cisneros**

She met him at a dance. Pretty too, and young. Said he worked in a restaurant, but she can't remember which one. Geraldo. That's all. Green pants and Saturday shirt. Geraldo. That's what he told her.

And how was she to know she'd be the last one to see him alive. An accident,
5   don't you know. Hit-and-run. Marin, she goes to all those dances. Uptown. Logan. Embassy. Palmer. Aragon. Fontana. The Manor. She likes to dance. She knows how to do cumbias and salsas and rancheras even. And he was just someone she danced with. Somebody she met that night. That's right.

That's the story. That's what she said again and again. Once to the hospital
10 people and twice to the police. No address. No name. Nothing in his pockets.

Close Read

1. Describe the structure of the sentences in the box. What effect do these sentences have on the style of the excerpt and the narrator's voice?

2. Find an example of word choice that would not belong in a story written in a formal style.

MODEL 2: ELEMENTS OF STYLE

Jane Austen is known for her "novels of manners," in which she recorded the details of 19th-century middle-class British life with irony and humor. How does her style of writing differ from Cisneros's?

from Pride and Prejudice

Novel by **Jane Austen**

Elizabeth Bennet had been obliged by the scarcity of gentlemen to sit down for two dances; and during part of that time, Mr. Darcy had been standing near enough for her to overhear a conversation between him and Mr. Bingley, who came from the dance for a few minutes to press his friend to join it.
5   "Come, Darcy," said he, "I must have you dance. I hate to see you standing about by yourself in this stupid manner. You had much better dance."

"I certainly shall not. You know how I detest it, unless I am particularly acquainted with my partner. At such an assembly as this, it would be insupportable. Your sisters are engaged, and there is not another woman in the
10 room whom it would not be a punishment to me to stand up with."

Close Read

1. What specific words and details in this excerpt help to convey a prim and proper tone?

2. Reread lines 1–4. What sentence structure does the writer use for the narrator's voice?

3. Rewrite the boxed text in a conversational style.

MODEL 1: ELEMENTS OF STYLE
Close Read

1. *Possible answer: The "sentences" in the box are mostly short fragments. The phrase "don't you know" (line 5) is an informal expression, and the double subject "Marin, she . . ." (line 5) is improper grammar. All of these elements give the passage an informal style and emphasize the voice of the narrator, which has the breathless, stream-of-consciousness sound of someone telling upsetting news to a friend.*

2. *Possible answer: Examples of word choice that would not belong in a story written in a formal style are "Saturday shirt" (line 3) and "hospital people" (lines 9–10). In a formal style, the narrator would have described what the shirt looked like and used the exact title of the person she spoke with at the hospital or a more formal term, such as "hospital staff."*

MODEL 2: ELEMENTS OF STYLE
Close Read

1. *Possible answer: Some of the words that convey a prim and proper tone are "obliged by the scarcity of gentlemen" (line 1), "particularly acquainted" (lines 7–8), "assembly" (line 8), and "insupportable" (line 9).*

2. *Possible answer: The passage begins with a long, complex sentence, which gives the narrator's voice a formal, literary quality.*

3. *Possible answer: Rewritten in a modern, informal, conversational style, the boxed text might read: "Absolutely not. I can't stand dancing with someone I don't know. Especially at this kind of party."*

DIFFERENTIATED INSTRUCTION

FOR LESS–PROFICIENT READERS

Comprehension: Plot If students have trouble following the fragmented style of the narrator in Model 1, have them work in pairs to list the events in order.

1. Marin went to a dance.

2. She danced with a boy named Geraldo.

3. Later that night, Geraldo was killed in a car accident.

4. Marin reported what she knew about him to the hospital staff and the police.

FOR ENGLISH LEARNERS

Vocabulary: Multiple-Meaning Words
Discuss the most common meanings of these words in Model 2: *obliged* (line 1), *press* (line 4), *engaged* (line 9).

1. Have students generate sentences using the different meanings of the words.

2. Ask students to identify the meaning intended in the model. (For *engaged*, accept either "occupied" or "pledged to marry" as a reasonable answer.)

Practice and Apply

Part 3: Analyze the Literature

Close Read

1. **Possible answer:** *In addition to the boxed phrases, three other examples of Wells's many vivid images are "big, grayish rounded bulk, the size, perhaps, of a bear, was rising slowly and painfully" (lines 1–2), "the lipless brim of which quivered . . . and dropped saliva" (lines 6–7), and "something fungoid in the oily brown skin" (lines 16–17).*

2. **Possible answer:** *The long string of repulsive images, linked in a single sentence, helps to emphasize the narrator's sense of fascination and horror.*

3. **Possible answer:** *Wells's style is literary. One literary element is his use of long, elaborate sentences, such as the one in lines 10–16. Another is his word choice. Wells describes the Martian in words chosen to convey the narrator's feelings, such as "strange horror" (lines 9–10), "Gorgon groups of tentacles" (line 12), "vital, intense, inhuman, crippled and monstrous" (line 16), and "unspeakably nasty" (line 18). Wells's style also contains formal elements. He uses sophisticated words such as "steadfastly" (line 4), "tentacular appendage" (line 8), "incessant" (line 12), and "tumultuous" (line 13), as well as proper grammar.*

Part 3: Analyze the Literature

Apply what you've just learned about style as you analyze these two excerpts. Though both writers take on the subject of outer space, they have distinctly different styles.

The first excerpt comes from a classic science fiction novel first published in 1898. As you read, pay attention to the elements—word choice, sentence structure, and tone—that reveal the writer's style.

> *from*
> # THE WAR OF THE WORLDS
> #### Novel by H. G. Wells
>
> A big, grayish rounded bulk, the size, perhaps, of a bear, was rising slowly and painfully out of the cylinder. As it bulged up and caught the light, it glistened like wet leather.
>
> Two large dark-colored eyes were regarding me steadfastly. The mass that
> 5 framed them, the head of the thing, was rounded, and had, one might say, a face. There was a mouth under the eyes, the lipless brim of which quivered and panted, and dropped saliva. The whole creature heaved and pulsated convulsively. A lank tentacular appendage gripped the edge of the cylinder, another swayed in the air.
>
> Those who have never seen a living Martian can scarcely imagine the strange
> 10 horror of its appearance. The peculiar V-shaped mouth with its pointed upper lip, the absence of brow ridges, the absence of a chin beneath the wedgelike lower lip, the incessant quivering of this mouth, the Gorgon groups of tentacles, the tumultuous breathing of the lungs in a strange atmosphere, the evident heaviness and painfulness of movement due to the greater gravitational energy
> 15 of the earth—above all, the extraordinary intensity of the immense eyes—were at once vital, intense, inhuman, crippled and monstrous. There was something fungoid in the oily brown skin, something in the clumsy deliberation of the tedious movements unspeakably nasty.

Close Read

1. One aspect of Wells's style is his use of vivid images to help you visualize the Martian. Three examples are boxed. Identify three additional examples.

2. Reread the sentence in lines 10–16. What do its structure and length help to emphasize?

3. Review the styles of writing on page 744. Which style or styles does Wells's writing display? Support your answer.

UNIT 8: AUTHOR'S STYLE AND VOICE

DIFFERENTIATED INSTRUCTION

FOR LESS–PROFICIENT READERS

Analysis Support: Sentence Structure and Word Choice Have students work in small groups to rewrite the sentence in lines 10–16 as a paragraph made up of short sentences in simple, neutral language. Paragraphs might begin "It had a V-shaped mouth with a pointed upper lip. Its lower lip was wedge-shaped, and it had no chin . . . ." Ask a group to read its paragraph aloud, then help students compare its effect with Wells's version.

Comprehension: Imagery Explain that a Gorgon is a character in Greek mythology who has snakes for hair. Anyone who looks into her eyes turns to stone. Then ask students to create a picture of the Martian. Urge them to capture the emotional content as well as the details of Wells's imagery.

In the next excerpt, the astronaut Sally Ride describes her feelings and impressions as she looked down on her home planet from space. How does her style compare with the one Wells used in *The War of the Worlds*?

from

Single Room, Earth View

Essay by **Sally Ride**

Everyone I've met has a glittering, if vague, mental image of space travel. And naturally enough, people want to hear about it from an astronaut: "How did it feel . . . ?" "What did it look like . . . ?" "Were you scared?" Sometimes, the questions come from reporters, their pens poised and their tape recorders
5 silently reeling in the words; sometimes, it's wide-eyed, ten-year-old girls who want answers. I find a way to answer all of them, but it's not easy.

Imagine trying to describe an airplane ride to someone who has never flown. An articulate traveler could describe the sights but would find it much harder to explain the difference in perspective provided by the new view from
10 a greater distance, along with the feelings, impressions, and insights that go with that new perspective. And the difference is enormous: Space flight moves the traveler another giant step farther away. Eight and one-half thunderous minutes after launch, an astronaut is orbiting high above the Earth, suddenly able to watch typhoons form, volcanos smolder, and meteors streak through
15 the atmosphere below.

While flying over the Hawaiian Islands, several astronauts have marveled that the islands look just like they do on a map. When people first hear that, they wonder what should be so surprising about Hawaii looking the way it does in the atlas. Yet, to the astronauts it is an absolutely startling sensation:
20 The islands really *do* look as if that part of the world has been carpeted with a big page torn out of Rand-McNally, and all we can do is try to convey the surreal quality of that scene.

In orbit, racing along at five miles per second, the space shuttle circles the Earth once every 90 minutes. I found that at this speed, unless I kept my nose
25 pressed to the window, it was almost impossible to keep track of where we were at any given moment—the world below simply changes too fast. If I turned my concentration away for too long, even just to change film in a camera, I could miss an entire land mass. It's embarrassing to float up to a window, glance outside, and then have to ask a crewmate, "What continent is this?"

Close Read

1. Reread the boxed sentence. What do you notice about its structure and Ride's choice of words? Explain whether these elements indicate a conversational style or a formal, academic one.

2. Consider the tone that Ride takes toward her subject. Is it enthusiastic or detached? Cite evidence to support your answer.

3. How would you characterize Ride's voice—the personality revealed through her writing? Explain.

4. Using examples from both excerpts, contrast Ride's and Wells's styles. Find three differences.

Close Read

1. ***Possible answer:*** *The boxed text contains a simple sentence followed by three very short questions. The words are also simple, and the sentence begins with "And." These elements create a conversational style.*

2. ***Possible answer:*** *Ride's tone is enthusiastic, as evidenced by words and phrases such as "marveled" (line 16), "absolutely startling sensation" (line 19), "surreal quality" (line 22), and "nose pressed to the window" (lines 24–25).*

3. ***Possible answer:*** *Ride's voice is candid, friendly, and enthusiastic. She is eager to answer questions (line 6), shows excitement in her descriptions (lines 12–15; 20–22), and has a sense of humor (lines 28–29).*

4. ***Possible answer:*** *Ride's style is informal and journalistic, while Wells's style is formal and literary. Specifically, Wells uses long, elaborate sentences, many sophisticated words, and a great deal of mood-evoking imagery. Ride uses simple sentences and familiar words, and she limits imagery in favor of more factual, neutral language.*

Assess and Reteach

Assess

Name two contrasting literature selections that the class has recently read. Ask students to describe the style and voice of each.

Reteach

For students who are unable to apply the workshop skills to recently read selections, use these reteaching options:

1. On the board, make a chart with columns headed *formal, informal, journalistic,* and *literary* and rows labeled *words, sentence structures, grammar, imagery,* and *sense of narrator.* Help students list the attributes of each style; for example, in the *words* row, write "sophisticated, abstract" under *formal* and "easy, familiar" under *informal.*

2. Ask students to review page 746 and its accompanying copy master. Have them meet in small groups to compose an answer to this question: What is voice, and what elements does a writer use to craft it? Have students share and refine their answers as a class.

FOR ENGLISH LEARNERS

Comprehension: Transitions Tell students that writers often make points by contrasting one thing or idea with another. Have students reread the sentence in line 6 of Ride's essay. Point out that in English the word *but* signals a contrast. In this sentence, Ride is contrasting her ability to answer questions with her struggle in doing it. Tell students that *yet* also signals a contrast.

Have students find other instances of *but* and *yet* in the selection and explain what is being contrasted. ***Possible answers:*** *contrast between ease of describing visual images and difficulty of describing thoughts and feelings associated with flight (line 8); contrast between what people would expect to experience and what astronauts actually experience (line 19)*

Focus and Motivate

OBJECTIVES

Literary Analysis
- explore the key idea of **fear**
- analyze realism
- read a short story

Reading
- analyze sequence

Vocabulary
- build vocabulary for reading and writing
- use the prefix *in-*

Grammar and Writing
- add supporting details, including repetition for emphasis
- use writing to analyze literature

SUMMARY

In "Where Have You Gone, Charming Billy?" Private First Class Paul Berlin, a soldier in Vietnam, heads with his unit toward the sea, where he hopes to find safety. During the journey, he reflects on the death a day earlier of Billy Boy Watkins, who became so terrified after stepping on a mine that he died of a heart attack.

Is FEAR *our worst enemy?*

Discuss the question with students. Ask them to name stories and movies with characters who experience **fear**. What frightens these characters? How do they behave while in the throes of **fear?** Extend the discussion by having students complete the **DISCUSS** activity.

Selection Resources

Where Have You Gone, Charming Billy?

Short Story by Tim O'Brien

Is FEAR *our worst enemy?*

KEY IDEA Your heart pounds. Your hands shake. Your stomach churns. Adrenaline floods your body. You are gripped by **fear,** and the way you react to it is as unique as your fingerprints. In "Where Have You Gone, Charming Billy?" a young soldier struggling through his first night in Vietnam tries desperately to combat his growing terror.

DISCUSS With a partner, discuss the different ways people respond to fear. Talk about negative reactions, like blind panic, as well as positive ones, such as increased concentration or sudden bursts of strength. Then decide whether you think fear elicits primarily positive reactions or mostly negative ones.

750

RESOURCE MANAGER UNIT 8

Plan and Teach pp. 17–24

Literary Analysis
Summary pp. 25†*, 26‡*
Realism pp. 27, 28†*
Question Support p. 35*

Reading
Analyze Sequence pp. 29, 30†*
Reading Check p. 34
Reading Fluency p. 37

Vocabulary
Study p. 31*
Practice p. 32
Strategy p. 33

Grammar and Writing
Add Supporting Details p. 36

Assessment
Selection Tests A, B/C pp. 39*, 41*
Test Generator CD

BEST PRACTICES TOOLKIT

Differentiated Instruction
pp. 31–38*

Scaffolding Instruction
pp. 43–46*

Graphic Organizers/Strategies
Word Squares • Sensory Notes • New Word Analysis • Two-Column Chart

Technology
Literature and Vocabulary Centers at **ClassZone.com**
Write*Smart* CD

Reading Support
Audio Anthology CD*

InterActive
READER & WRITER

• *Integrated Test Practice*
• *Related Nonfiction Readings*

McDougal Littell LITERATURE

---

* Resources for Differentiation   † Also in Spanish   ‡ Also in Haitian Creole and Vietnamese

LITERARY ANALYSIS: REALISM

You know that just as you and your friends have a style all your own, so do writers. A writer's style is the unique way he or she communicates ideas. This style is reflected in the dialogue, word choice, and sentence structure of every piece of writing. In this story, Tim O'Brien uses the style of **realism** to depict the horrors of combat as seen through the eyes of a young soldier. To make the story seem real to the reader, he uses

- dialogue that sounds natural, like actual speech
- vivid, realistic descriptions of what the soldier sees
- a mix of long and short sentences to communicate the soldier's thoughts and feelings

As you read, think about the way the characters talk to each other, and consider O'Brien's word choice and sentence structure. Note passages that seem particularly realistic to you.

Review: **Point of View**

READING SKILL: ANALYZE SEQUENCE

The **sequence** of a story is the order in which events occur. Sometimes a writer interrupts this order with a **flashback,** the account of an event that happened before the beginning of the story's action. A flashback provides more background information about the current situation and helps the reader understand the story's events. To identify a flashback, look for sudden changes in scene. As you read this story, keep track of its sequence of events by filling in a sequence chain like the one shown.

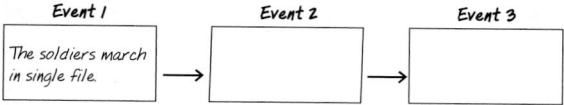

Event 1	Event 2	Event 3
The soldiers march in single file.		

▲ VOCABULARY IN CONTEXT

Restate each phrase, using a different word or words for the boldfaced term.

1. a secret mission depending on **stealth**
2. huge stalks of corn in the rich, **fecund** field
3. an argument too **diffuse** to understand
4. lying around in a state of **inertia**

Author Online

From Dull to Dangerous
"If you look in a dictionary under the word *boring*," Tim O'Brien says sarcastically, "you will find a little pen-and-ink illustration of Worthington, Minnesota, where I grew up." As a kid, O'Brien escaped from the quiet predictability of his

**Tim O'Brien
born 1946**

hometown by burying himself in books. Just after he graduated from a small Minnesota college, O'Brien's life got more exciting—but not in a way he ever would have chosen. He was drafted and sent to Vietnam.

Combat Zone O'Brien was strongly opposed to the Vietnam War and considered fleeing to Canada to avoid serving in the army. He knew, however, that failing to enlist would make him an outcast in his hometown. "That's a tough thing to do when you're that old," O'Brien says, "to decide to walk away from your whole history." He was shipped to Vietnam in 1969, and though some of his experiences there were gruesome, they inspired him to write. In 1973, O'Brien published his first book, an account of his time in Vietnam. The war has been the main subject of his writing ever since.

 MORE ABOUT THE AUTHOR
For more on Tim O'Brien, visit the **Literature Center at ClassZone.com.**

Background

Vietnam War This story takes place in the Southeast Asian country of Vietnam during a war in which over 58,000 Americans died. Rebels backed by Communist-ruled North Vietnam tried to take over South Vietnam in 1957. The U.S. entered the war as a South Vietnamese ally in 1964. Between 1965 and 1973, over 2 million Americans were sent to Vietnam. Few were prepared for the fear and anxiety that would overcome them.

751

Teach

STANDARDS FOCUS

LITERARY ANALYSIS

● REALISM

For instructional support, read aloud this example:

"I dunno. Folks aren't careful like they once was," said the man.

"Nope," said the second man. "Nobody's got the time—not a free minute."

Have students explain how natural dialogue and sentence structure create a sense of realism. ***Possible answer:*** *Short, interrupted sentences, slang, and inaccurate grammar make the conversation seem real.*

CHECK UNDERSTANDING Have students suggest how the first man might answer the second man in the example.

READING SKILL

■ ANALYZE SEQUENCE

To support instruction, write these sentences on the board:

Jake sat on a park bench, watching some kids playing baseball. A lanky boy raced to left field and made a diving catch. It reminded Jake of the last time he played ball with his brother.

Ask students to identify the shift in scene.

CHECK UNDERSTANDING Have students tell what the writer might describe next.

 RESOURCE MANAGER—Copy Master
Analyze Sequence p. 29 (for student use while reading the selection)

▲ VOCABULARY IN CONTEXT

DIAGNOSE WORD KNOWLEDGE To determine preteaching needs, have all students complete Vocabulary in Context. ***Possible answers:***
1. *secretive movement,* 2. *fertile,* 3. *unfocused,*
4. *inactivity*

PRETEACH VOCABULARY Use the Vocabulary Study copy master to help students predict meanings for each boldfaced word in the copy master.

1. Read item 1 aloud, emphasizing *stealth.*
2. Point out the context clues. Elicit possible meanings for *stealth,* such as "with great care not to be noticed."
3. Have students fill in the chart.
4. Repeat the procedure for items 2–4.

 RESOURCE MANAGER—Copy Master
Vocabulary Study p. 31

For general guidelines on differentiating vocabulary instruction and for alternative vocabulary activities for students not needing vocabulary preteaching, see

BEST PRACTICES TOOLKIT
Scaffolding Vocabulary Instruction pp. 43–46
Vocabulary Center at ClassZone.com

ANALYZE VISUALS

Possible answer: The painting is somewhat realistic. The soldier's posture is lifelike, and his clothing and ammunition look authentic. The setting is realistically depicted, though brushy and impressionistic in style. The dappled patches of greens, yellows, and browns suggest that the soldier is emerging from a dense forest into the sunlight—or perhaps into the glow of explosives. The mood of the painting is realistic in that it captures a soldier's exhaustion and despair. However, the painting is not realistic in the sense of portraying graphic violence or the gritty details of a soldier's life.

About the Art Colorado artist James E. Faulkner (b. 1945) has received awards for his wildlife paintings. His rich depiction of jungle foliage in this painting reflects his skill with natural backgrounds. Soldiers like Paul Berlin marched through similar terrain while on duty in Vietnam.

LITERARY ANALYSIS

Ⓐ REALISM

Possible answer: The mix of sentences mimics the way a real person might think about things. It provides a realistic depiction of a soldier trying to cope with the horrors he's confronting. It also helps to emphasize how desperately Paul longs to think about anything but war.

WHERE HAVE YOU GONE, *Charming Billy?*

TIM O'BRIEN

The platoon of twenty-six soldiers moved slowly in the dark, single file, not talking.

One by one, like sheep in a dream, they passed through the hedgerow, crossed quietly over a meadow and came down to the rice paddy.[1] There they stopped. Their leader knelt down, motioning with his hand, and one by one the other soldiers squatted in the shadows, vanishing in the primitive **stealth** of warfare. For a long time they did not move. Except for the sounds of their breathing, . . . the twenty-six men were very quiet: some of them excited by the adventure, some of them afraid, some of them exhausted from the long night
10 march, some of them looking forward to reaching the sea where they would be safe. At the rear of the column, Private First Class Paul Berlin lay quietly with his forehead resting on the black plastic stock of his rifle, his eyes closed. He was pretending he was not in the war, pretending he had not watched Billy Boy Watkins die of a heart attack that afternoon. He was pretending he was a boy again, camping with his father in the midnight summer along the Des Moines River. In the dark, with his eyes pinched shut, he pretended. He pretended that when he opened his eyes, his father would be there by the campfire and they would talk softly about whatever came to mind and then roll into their sleeping bags, and that later they'd wake up and it would be morning and there would
20 not be a war, and that Billy Boy Watkins had not died of a heart attack that afternoon. He pretended he was not a soldier. Ⓐ

---

1. **hedgerow . . . rice paddy:** A hedgerow is a thick hedge separating fields or farms; a rice paddy is a flooded field in which rice is grown.

752 UNIT 8: AUTHOR'S STYLE AND VOICE

ANALYZE VISUALS
Would you describe this painting as **realistic** or **abstract?** Cite details about the painting's subject, setting, and mood, as well as the artist's use of light and color.

stealth (stĕlth) *n.* cautious or secret action or movement

❶ Targeted Passage

Ⓐ REALISM
Reread lines 11–21, and consider O'Brien's use of both long and short sentences to convey Paul Berlin's thoughts. What effect does this stylistic choice create?

Infantry (1997), James E. Faulkner. Oil on canvas. Collection of Nature's Nest Gallery, Golden, Colorado. Photo courtesy of the artist.

DIFFERENTIATED INSTRUCTION

FOR ALL STUDENTS

Interest Stations Post these assignments for students to work on independently.

- **Create a Landscape: Realism** Illustrate a scene from the story.
- **Exploring Viewpoints: Speech** Write a speech Paul might give after a year in Vietnam.

For further details on these projects, see

R RESOURCE MANAGER
Ideas for Extension pp. 22–23

FOR LESS–PROFICIENT READERS

In combination with the *Audio Anthology CD,* use one or more Targeted Passages (pp. 752, 758, 759) to ensure that students focus on key story events, concepts, and skills. Targeted Passages are also good for English learners.

BACKGROUND

Vietnam's Geography Vietnam is generally mountainous with thick forests. South Vietnam, where this story takes place, is tropical with hot, wet summers. Winters tend to be dry and somewhat cooler. Flooding is common in some parts of the country. At the time of the Vietnam War, most Vietnamese were farmers, living in villages. The walls and roofs of their homes were made of palm leaves or straw. Rice has long been Vietnam's basic food; this crop grows in the kind of rice paddy that Paul Berlin wades through in the story.

---

① **Targeted Passage [Lines 1–21]**

This passage introduces the setting, the main character, and his internal conflict.

- Who is Paul Berlin?
- Where is he, and what is he doing?
- What is Paul Berlin pretending?
- Why is he pretending?

FOR ENGLISH LEARNERS

Reading: Background Students may need to know some basic facts about the Vietnam War. Before reviewing the **BACKGROUND** note, elicit prior knowledge from students.

Options for Reading Ask a question and have students scan designated text for the answer.

Prereading For prereading instruction for English learners, see

 BEST PRACTICES TOOLKIT
Scaffolding Reading Instruction pp. 43–46

FOR ADVANCED LEARNERS/PRE–AP

Pre-AP Exercises in the bottom channel provide additional challenge for students. Use these suggestions for small groups or individuals.

ADDITIONAL GUIDELINES

For more help with differentiation and tips for classroom management, see

 BEST PRACTICES TOOLKIT
Differentiated Instruction pp. 31–38

B REALISM

Possible answer: *Specific features that make the dialogue sound realistic include the use of short questions (line 30), short answers (line 31), interjections ("Hey!"), informal diction ("You got a lot to learn, buddy"), contractions, and shortened words ("sleepin'").*

Lines 36–44
DISCUSSION PROMPTS

Use these prompts to help students understand Paul's thoughts about what he will and will not tell his mother:

Connect Have you ever tried to describe a place to another person—how it looks, smells, and even sounds—but chosen not to describe how you were feeling in this place? Explain. *Answers will vary.*

Analyze Why would Paul plan to tell his mother about how things looked and smelled but not about how frightened he was? *Possible answer: He would want to share a part of his experience with her, but he would not want to upset her or to make her think less of him.*

Synthesize Why is Paul so focused on what he will and will not tell his mother? *Possible answer: It's a way of coping with this new experience, removing himself mentally to a safer place: at home with his mother.*

Lines 52–63
REINFORCE *KEY IDEA:* FEAR

Discuss What does Paul Berlin now know about **fear**? *Possible answer: He now knows that fear comes in different forms and degrees. He sees that fear can be as intense as the "bundled and tight" fear (line 59) that he felt when he watched Billy Boy Watkins die. But he also realizes that there are less intense, less specific fears—ghostly shapes, childhood nightmares, the boogieman (lines 56–57), as well as the fear of being afraid (line 63).*

In the morning, when they reached the sea, it would be better. The hot afternoon would be over, he would bathe in the sea and he would forget how frightened he had been on his first day at the war. The second day would not be so bad. He would learn.

There was a sound beside him, a movement and then a breathed: "Hey!" He opened his eyes, shivering as if emerging from a deep nightmare.

"Hey!" a shadow whispered. "We're *moving.* . . . Get up."

"Okay."

30 "You sleepin', or something?"

"No." He could not make out the soldier's face. With clumsy, concrete hands he clawed for his rifle, found it, found his helmet.

The soldier-shadow grunted. "You got a lot to learn, buddy. I'd shoot you if I thought you was sleepin'. Let's go." **B**

Private First Class Paul Berlin blinked.

Ahead of him, silhouetted against the sky, he saw the string of soldiers wading into the flat paddy, the black outline of their shoulders and packs and weapons. He was comfortable. He did not want to move. But he was afraid, for it was his first night at the war, so he hurried to catch up, stumbling once,
40 scraping his knee, groping as though blind; his boots sank into the thick paddy water and he smelled it all around him. He would tell his mother how it smelled: mud and algae and cattle manure and chlorophyll, decay, breeding mosquitoes and leeches as big as mice, the **fecund** warmth of the paddy waters rising up to his cut knee. But he would not tell how frightened he had been.

Once they reached the sea, things would be better. They would have their rear guarded by three thousand miles of ocean, and they would swim and dive into the breakers and hunt crayfish and smell the salt, and they would be safe.

He followed the shadow of the man in front of him. It was a clear night. Already the Southern Cross[2] was out. And other stars he could not yet name—
50 soon, he thought, he would learn their names. And puffy night clouds. There was not yet a moon. Wading through the paddy, his boots made sleepy, sloshing sounds, like a lullaby, and he tried not to think. Though he was afraid, he now knew that fear came in many degrees and types and peculiar categories, and he knew that his fear now was not so bad as it had been in the hot afternoon, when poor Billy Boy Watkins got killed by a heart attack. His fear now was **diffuse** and unformed: ghosts in the tree line, nighttime fears of a child, a boogieman in the closet that his father would open to show empty, saying "See? Nothing there, champ. Now you can sleep." In the afternoon it had been worse: the fear had been bundled and tight and he'd been on his hands and knees, crawling like an insect,
60 an ant escaping a giant's footsteps and thinking nothing, brain flopping like wet cement in a mixer, not thinking at all, watching while Billy Boy Watkins died.

Now as he stepped out of the paddy onto a narrow dirt path, now the fear was mostly the fear of being so terribly afraid again.

He tried not to think.

---

2. **Southern Cross:** a cross-shaped group of stars visible in the Southern Hemisphere.

754 UNIT 8: AUTHOR'S STYLE AND VOICE

B REALISM
Reread lines 26–34. What specific features of the characters' speech make this **dialogue** sound realistic? Explain, citing evidence to support your answer.

fecund (fē'kənd) *adj.* producing much growth; fertile

diffuse (dĭ-fyōōs') *adj.* unfocused

DIFFERENTIATED INSTRUCTION

FOR LESS–PROFICIENT READERS

Comprehension: Clarify Meaning Focus students' attention on the use of the conditional "would" in lines 22–25 and lines 41–44. Help students recognize that this usage refers to things that someone might hope will happen but which may not necessarily occur.

FOR ENGLISH LEARNERS

Key Academic Vocabulary Use Word Squares to teach these words: *categories* (line 53), *seek* (line 75), *adjust* (line 81), *enormous* (line 180), *stress* (line 180), *finally* (line 189).

 BEST PRACTICES TOOLKIT—Transparency Word Squares p. E10

There were tricks he'd learned to keep from thinking. Counting: He counted his steps, concentrating on the numbers, pretending that the steps were dollar bills and that each step through the night made him richer and richer, so that soon he would become a wealthy man, and he kept counting and considered the ways he might spend the money after the war and what he would do. He

70 would look his father in the eye and shrug and say, "It was pretty bad at first, but I learned a lot and I got used to it." Then he would tell his father the story of Billy Boy Watkins. But he would never let on how frightened he had been. "Not so bad," he would say instead, making his father feel proud. **C**

Songs, another trick to stop from thinking: *Where have you gone, Billy Boy, Billy Boy, Oh, where have you gone, charming Billy? I have gone to seek a wife, she's the joy of my life, but she's a young thing and cannot leave her mother,* and other songs that he sang in his thoughts as he walked toward the sea. And when he reached the sea he would dig a deep hole in the sand and he would sleep like the high clouds, and he would not be afraid any more.

80 The moon came out. Pale and shrunken to the size of a dime.

The helmet was heavy on his head. In the morning he would adjust the leather binding. He would clean his rifle, too. Even though he had been frightened to shoot it during the hot afternoon, he would carefully clean the breech and the muzzle and the ammunition so that next time he would be ready and not so afraid. In the morning, when they reached the sea, he would begin to make friends with some of the other soldiers. He would learn their names and laugh at their jokes. Then when the war was over he would have war buddies, and he would write to them once in a while and exchange memories. **D**

Walking, sleeping in his walking, he felt better. He watched the moon

90 come higher.

Once they skirted a sleeping village. The smells again—straw, cattle, mildew. The men were quiet. On the far side of the village, buried in the dark smells, a dog barked. The column stopped until the barking died away; then they marched fast away from the village, through a graveyard filled with conical-shaped burial mounds and tiny altars made of clay and stone. The graveyard had a perfumy smell. A nice place to spend the night, he thought. The mounds would make fine battlements, and the smell was nice and the place was quiet. But they went on, passing through a hedgerow and across another paddy and east toward the sea. **E**

He walked carefully. He remembered what he'd been taught: Stay off the

100 center of the path, for that was where the land mines and booby traps were planted, where stupid and lazy soldiers like to walk. Stay alert, he'd been taught. Better alert than inert. Ag-ile, mo-bile, hos-tile.[3] He wished he'd paid better attention to the training. He could not remember what they'd said about how to stop being afraid; they hadn't given any lessons in courage—not that he could remember—and they hadn't mentioned how Billy Boy Watkins would die of a heart attack, his face turning pale and the veins popping out.

---

3. **Better alert . . . hos-tile:** sayings and chants reminding soldiers to pay attention rather than be lifeless (inert), and to be light on their feet (agile), ready to move (mobile), and aggressive (hostile).

WHERE HAVE YOU GONE, CHARMING BILLY? **755**

C SEQUENCE
Summarize the story's events up to this point. Which events take place in Vietnam? Which are scenes the narrator imagines will happen in the future or remembers from his past?

D GRAMMAR AND STYLE
Reread lines 81–88. Notice O'Brien's repetition of "he would," which reflects Paul's way of coping with his current situation.

E REALISM
Reread lines 91–98. Identify the **sensory details**—details that appeal to the five senses—O'Brien includes. How do these details contribute to the vivid, realistic style of this story?

READING SKILL

C SEQUENCE

Possible answer: *Paul is marching at night with a platoon of soldiers in Vietnam. While the platoon stops by a rice paddy, Paul pretends he is still a boy, camping with his father. Another soldier chides Paul for daydreaming when he should be paying attention. As the platoon begins wading through the paddy, Paul recalls his terror over the death of a fellow soldier who died of a heart attack. He thinks of his father again and how he will tell him, when he's home again, that he wasn't afraid.*

D GRAMMAR AND STYLE

Analyze Repetition Repetition involves the repeated use of any language element. A writer may repeat sounds, words, phrases, clauses, sentences, or rhythmic patterns. Ask students to count the number of times O'Brien repeats "he would." What point do they think he is making? Then have students look for other examples of repetition.

LITERARY ANALYSIS

E REALISM

Possible answers: Smell: *straw, cattle, mildew, dark smells, perfumy graveyard, nice smell.* **Sound:** *dog barking, quiet place.* **Sight:** *conical-shaped burial mounds, tiny clay and stone altars, hedgerow, paddy. These sensory details make Paul's experience in Vietnam come alive for the reader.*

If students need help . . . Have them use the Sensory Notes chart.

 BEST PRACTICES TOOLKIT—Transparency Sensory Notes p. B9

FOR ENGLISH LEARNERS
Culture: Clarify You may wish to have students listen to a recording of the folk song "Billy Boy." Explain that it is actually a humorous song that has nothing to do with war.

FOR ADVANCED LEARNERS/PRE–AP
Repetition and Suspense Ask students to estimate and check how many times O'Brien has mentioned Billy Boy Watkins's death up to this point in the story. Discuss how this repetition builds suspense. What other effects does it have?

F POINT OF VIEW

Possible answer: The story is told from the third-person limited point of view, with the narrator describing Paul's thoughts and feelings. Without this detailed description, the reader would not develop such a strong attachment to Paul or understand his struggle to cope with his intense fear.

Lines 118–122
REINFORCE *KEY IDEA*: FEAR

Discuss Whom is Berlin trying to convince that he is not afraid? *Possible answer: He imagines how he will convince his father in the future, while trying to convince himself in the present.*

Lines 143–146
DISCUSSION PROMPTS

Use these prompts to help students understand why soldiers might avoid getting to know one another too well:

Connect In what kinds of situations might a person decide not to make an effort to get to know other people? *Students may suggest situations in which a person might get hurt by getting close to someone else.*

Analyze Why doesn't Paul care that he can't make out the man's face or know his name (lines 144–146)? *Possible answer: He does not want to get close to someone who may soon die.*

Evaluate Is Paul's strategy of not getting to know the other soldier a good one? Why or why not? *Possible answer: If the man dies, Paul will have insulated himself from feelings of shock, loss, and despair. On the other hand, Paul could benefit from connecting with another soldier and learning from his experience.*

Private First Class Paul Berlin walked carefully.

Stretching ahead of him like dark beads on an invisible chain, the string of shadow-soldiers whose names he did not yet know moved with the silence and
110 slow grace of smoke. Now and again moonlight was reflected off a machine gun or a wrist watch. But mostly the soldiers were quiet and hidden and faraway-seeming in a peaceful night, strangers on a long street, and he felt quite separate from them, as if trailing behind like the caboose on a night train, pulled along by **inertia,** sleepwalking, an afterthought to the war.

So he walked carefully, counting his steps. When he had counted to three thousand, four hundred and eighty-five, the column stopped.

One by one the soldiers knelt or squatted down.

The grass along the path was wet. Private First Class Paul Berlin lay back and turned his head so that he could lick at the dew with his eyes closed,
120 another trick to forget the war. He might have slept. "*I wasn't* afraid," he was screaming or dreaming, facing his father's stern eyes. "I wasn't afraid," he was saying. When he opened his eyes, a soldier was sitting beside him, quietly chewing a stick of Doublemint gum. **F**

"You sleepin' again?" the soldier whispered.

"No," said Private First Class Paul Berlin. . . .

The soldier grunted, chewing his gum. Then he twisted the cap off his canteen, took a swallow and handed it through the dark.

"Take some," he whispered.

"Thanks."
130 "You're the new guy?"

"Yes." He did not want to admit it, being new to the war.

The soldier grunted and handed him a stick of gum. "Chew it quiet—okay? Don't blow no bubbles or nothing."

"Thanks. I won't." He could not make out the man's face in the shadows.

They sat still and Private First Class Paul Berlin chewed the gum until all the sugars were gone; then the soldier said, "Bad day today, buddy."

Private First Class Paul Berlin nodded wisely, but he did not speak.

"Don't think it's always so bad," the soldier whispered. "I don't wanna scare you. You'll get used to it soon enough. . . . They been fighting wars a long
140 time, and you get used to it."

"Yeah."

"You will."

They were quiet awhile. And the night was quiet, no crickets or birds, and it was hard to imagine it was truly a war. He searched for the soldier's face but could not find it. It did not matter much. Even if he saw the fellow's face, he would not know the name; and even if he knew the name, it would not matter much.

"Haven't got the time?" the soldier whispered.

"No."

"Rats. . . . Don't matter, really. Goes faster if you don't know the time,
150 anyhow."

"Sure."

inertia (ĭ-nûr'shə) *n.* tendency to continue to do what one has been doing

F POINT OF VIEW
Identify the point of view from which this story is told. How might your impression of Paul be different if you didn't receive such detailed descriptions of his thoughts and feelings?

DIFFERENTIATED INSTRUCTION

FOR ENGLISH LEARNERS

Vocabulary: Idioms and Sayings Use New Word Analysis to teach these idioms from the story: *let on* (line 72), "reveal"; *tough as nails* (line 171), "strong, hard, tough"; *scared stiff* (lines 195, 229–230), "deeply afraid." Also point out the slang term *rats* (line 149), meaning "too bad." Encourage students to watch for additional slang expressions.

 BEST PRACTICES TOOLKIT—Transparency
New Word Analysis p. E8

FOR ADVANCED LEARNERS/PRE–AP

Figurative Language Have students reread and discuss O'Brien's description of the soldiers walking ahead of him (lines 108–110). Challenge students to imitate the author's style by using figurative language to describe a scene they have witnessed. Have them share their descriptions with the class.

"What's your name, buddy?"

"Paul."

"Nice to meet ya," he said, and in the dark beside the path they shook hands. "Mine's Toby. Everybody calls me Buffalo, though." The soldier's hand was strangely warm and soft. But it was a very big hand. "Sometimes they just call me Buff," he said.

And again they were quiet. They lay in the grass and waited. The moon was very high now and very bright, and they were waiting for cloud cover.

160 The soldier suddenly snorted.

"What is it?"

"Nothin'," he said, but then he snorted again. "A bloody *heart attack!*" the soldier said. "Can't get over it—old Billy Boy croaking from a lousy heart attack. . . . A heart attack—can you believe it?"

The idea of it made Private First Class Paul Berlin smile. He couldn't help it. "Ever hear of such a thing?"

"Not till now," said Private First Class Paul Berlin, still smiling.

"Me neither," said the soldier in the dark.

". . . Dying of a heart attack. Didn't know him, did you."

170 "No."

"Tough as nails."

Class of '67 (1987), Charlie Shobe. Oil on canvas. © Michael Tropea/National Vietnam Veterans Art Museum.

ANALYZE VISUALS
In this painting, the prone soldiers' boots take up the **foreground,** or front of the painting, while the standing soldiers are relegated to the **background.** What does this suggest about the message of the painting?

ANALYZE VISUALS

Possible answer: By highlighting the prone soldiers' boots in the foreground, the painting suggests that the dead are in the forefront of soldiers' minds. Who lived and who died was often just a matter of luck and chance, and soldiers, like those looking on in the background, lived in fear that they would be the next to die. The standard boots also evoke the anonymity of death.

About the Art American artist Charlie Shobe (b. 1940) served in the Marine Corps in Vietnam, from 1967 to 1968. Shobe's "paintings are of the horror show that was Vietnam . . . ." *Class of '67* refers to a specific incident in the hills between Khe Sanh and Laos in June 1968, when many American soldiers were killed. Shobe reflected that only a year earlier many of the dead had just been finishing high school.

FOR ENGLISH LEARNERS

Conversational English Patterns Discuss these usages with students and explain that such patterns are often heard in casual, spoken English: "What's your name, buddy?" (line 152); "Nice to meet ya" (line 154). Have students work with a partner to identify other conversational patterns in the selection.

FOR ADVANCED LEARNERS/PRE–AP

Analyze Point out that whenever he is referred to by name, Paul Berlin is almost always called "Private First Class Paul Berlin." Ask students to consider the effect of this device.

DISCUSSION PROMPTS

Use these prompts to help students understand Paul's giggling about Billy Boy's death:

Connect Have you ever giggled nervously in a situation where laughter was inappropriate? Explain. *Answers will vary.*

Analyze Why does Paul suddenly start giggling uncontrollably? *Possible answer: It strikes him as absurd that Billy Boy died of a "natural cause"—a heart attack—while in the midst of mortal danger. The telegram he imagines with its announcement that Billy was "scared to death in action" and "valiantly" died of fear seems laughably ironic. Paul is also giggling from nervousness.*

Synthesize What can you tell about Paul's own mental state from his sudden fit of giggling? *Possible answer: Paul is deeply shaken by Billy Boy's death and surprised by the intensity of his own fear.*

READING SKILL

G SEQUENCE

Possible answer: The story's chronological sequence is interrupted with a flashback to the events of the afternoon when Billy Boy stepped on a mine. The word "remembering" is a clue that Paul is going back to the past in his mind.

"Yeah."

"And what happens? A heart attack. Can you imagine it?"

"Yes," said Private First Class Paul Berlin. He wanted to laugh. "I can imagine it." And he imagined it clearly. He giggled—he couldn't help it. He imagined Billy's father opening the telegram: SORRY TO INFORM YOU THAT YOUR SON BILLY BOY WAS YESTERDAY SCARED TO DEATH IN ACTION IN THE REPUBLIC OF VIETNAM, VALIANTLY SUCCUMBING TO[4] A HEART ATTACK SUFFERED WHILE UNDER
180 ENORMOUS STRESS, AND IT IS WITH GREATEST SYMPATHY THAT . . . He giggled again. He rolled onto his belly and pressed his face into his arms. His body was shaking with giggles.

The big soldier hissed at him to shut up, but he could not stop giggling and remembering the hot afternoon, and poor Billy Boy, and how they'd been drinking Coca-Cola from bright-red aluminum cans, and how they'd started on the day's march, and how a little while later poor Billy Boy stepped on the mine, and how it made a tiny little sound—*poof*—and how Billy Boy stood there with his mouth wide-open, looking down at where his foot had been blown off, and how finally Billy Boy sat down very casually, not saying a word,
190 with his foot lying behind him, most of it still in the boot.

He giggled louder—he could not stop. He bit his arm, trying to stifle it, but remembering: "War's over, Billy," the men had said in consolation, but Billy Boy got scared and started crying and said he was about to die. "Nonsense," the medic said, Doc Peret, but Billy Boy kept bawling, tightening up, his face going pale and transparent and his veins popping out. Scared stiff. Even when Doc Peret stuck him with morphine,[5] Billy Boy kept crying. **G**

"Shut up!" the big soldier hissed, but Private First Class Paul Berlin could not stop. Giggling and remembering, he covered his mouth. His eyes stung, remembering how it was when Billy Boy died of fright.
200 "Shut up!"

But he could not stop giggling, the same way Billy Boy could not stop bawling that afternoon.

Afterward Doc Peret had explained: "You see, Billy Boy really died of a heart attack. He was scared he was gonna die—so scared, he had himself a heart attack—and that's what really killed him. I seen it before."

So they wrapped Billy in a plastic poncho, his eyes still wide-open and scared stiff, and they carried him over the meadow to a rice paddy, and then when the Medevac helicopter[6] arrived they carried him through the paddy and put him aboard, and the mortar rounds[7] were falling everywhere, and the
210 helicopter pulled up and Billy Boy came tumbling out, falling slowly and then faster, and the paddy water sprayed up as if Billy Boy had just executed a long

② Targeted Passage

G SEQUENCE
Reread lines 183–196. What happens to the story's sequence in these lines? Identify the clues that helped you form your answer.

---

4. **valiantly succumbing** (sə-kŭm′ĭng) **to:** bravely dying from.
5. **morphine** (môr′fēn′): a powerful drug used as a painkiller.
6. **Medevac** (mĕd′ĭ-văk′) **helicopter:** a helicopter used for transporting injured people to places where they can receive medical care. "Medevac" is a contraction of "medical evacuation."
7. **mortar rounds:** shells fired from small, portable cannons.

DIFFERENTIATED INSTRUCTION

FOR LESS–PROFICIENT READERS

② Targeted Passage [Lines 183–205]

This passage explains the mystery of Billy Boy's death.

- How did Billy Boy Watkins lose his foot?
- What was his reaction?
- Why did the men say, "War's over, Billy"?
- What really killed Billy Boy?

FOR ENGLISH LEARNERS

Vocabulary: Word Associations Help students understand the horror of Billy's reaction by focusing on the description of how his face looked: "mouth wide-open" (line 188); "face . . . pale and transparent" (lines 194–195); "veins popping out" (line 195).

and dangerous dive, as if trying to escape Graves Registration, where he would be tagged and sent home under a flag, dead of a heart attack.

"Shut up, . . . !" the soldier hissed, but Paul Berlin could not stop giggling, remembering: scared to death.

220   Later they waded in after him, probing for Billy Boy with their rifle butts, elegantly and delicately probing for Billy Boy in the stinking paddy, singing—some of them— *Where have you gone, Billy Boy, Billy Boy, Oh, where have you gone, charming Billy?* Then they found him. Green and covered with algae, his eyes still wide-open and scared

230 stiff, dead of a heart attack suffered while— **H**

"Shut up, . . . !" the soldier said loudly, shaking him.

But Private First Class Paul Berlin could not stop. The giggles were caught in his throat, drowning him in his own laughter: scared to death like Billy Boy.

Giggling, lying on his back, he saw the moon move, or the clouds moving across the moon. Wounded in action, dead of fright. A fine war story. He would tell it to his father, how Billy Boy had been scared to death, never letting on . . . He could not stop.

The soldier smothered him. He tried to fight back, but he was weak from the giggles.

240   The moon was under the clouds and the column was moving. The soldier helped him up. "You okay now, buddy?"

"Sure."

"What was so bloody funny?"

"Nothing."

"You can get killed, laughing that way."

"I know. I know that."

"You got to stay calm, buddy." The soldier handed him his rifle. "Half the battle, just staying calm. You'll get better at it," he said. "Come on, now."

He turned away and Private First Class Paul Berlin hurried after him. He

250 was still shivering.

He would do better once he reached the sea, he thought, still smiling a little. A funny war story that he would tell to his father, how Billy Boy Watkins was scared to death. A good joke. But even when he smelled salt and heard the sea, he could not stop being afraid. ❧

③ Targeted Passage

Chopper Lift-Out (1967), Ken McFadyen. Oil on canvas on hardboard, 30.6 cm × 48.2 cm.
© The Australian War Memorial Collection.

H SEQUENCE
What information has been communicated to the reader in this **flashback?** Explain, citing details from the text.

ANALYZE VISUALS

Activity Ask students how *Chopper Lift-Out* helps them understand the difficulty of airlifting Billy Boy's body. *Possible answer: The painting depicts the turbulence produced by the moving helicopter. It communicates the rapid and chaotic nature of helicopter landings and take-offs.*

About the Art Australian artist Ken McFadyen (1939–1997) was assigned to cover Australia's involvement in the Vietnam War for seven months, starting in mid-August 1967. He was expected to function as a combat soldier, if needed, and had to carry full combat equipment, along with his art materials.

READING SKILL

H SEQUENCE

Possible answer: The final flashback explains Billy Boy's death and describes its horrendous aftermath. This information further explains Paul's state of mind.

SELECTION WRAP—UP

REFLECT Ask students how the story leaves them feeling about war.

⭐ **CRITIQUE** Have students evaluate O'Brien's description of a soldier's mixed feelings and reactions to fear. Do his descriptions ring true? Why or why not?

READING FLUENCY

Distribute the copy masters and have students work in pairs or groups to practice fluency.

R RESOURCE MANAGER—Copy Master
Reading Fluency p. 37

FOR LESS—PROFICIENT READERS

③ Targeted Passage [Lines 240–254]

This passage concludes the story with a kind of "resolution" of Paul's inner conflict.

- What does Paul hope will happen when he reaches the sea?

- How does Paul imagine he will tell his father about the death of Billy Boy?

- How does Paul feel when he reaches the sea? Why?

- What is O'Brien saying about war?

FOR ADVANCED LEARNERS/PRE–AP

Compare and Contrast Have small groups discuss whether civilians cope with fear in the same way that soldiers do. What fears do ordinary people face? What coping mechanisms do they use? How are everyday reactions to fear the same and different from what soldiers experience?

DISCUSSION PROMPTS

Use these prompts to help students connect to O'Brien's attitudes as expressed in this interview:

Connect What kinds of memories make you feel nostalgia, or a longing for the past? *Students may mention childhood memories or past triumphs, such as winning a sports event.*

Analyze O'Brien notes that some veterans wish he had presented a more nostalgic view of the war. What does he mean? *Possible answer: A more romantic view would have focused on the fellowship among soldiers, fighting for the honor of one's country, and the gallantry of risking one's life. Instead, O'Brien focused on doing what one is forced to do and just surviving.*

Evaluate Do you agree with O'Brien's unromantic presentation of war? Give reasons for your answer. *Answers will vary, but students should thoughtfully refer to both the interview and the story to support their answers.*

INTERVIEW In this revealing interview, Tim O'Brien talks about two kinds of bravery and discusses the courage it took to make one frightening choice.

Tim O'Brien: *The Naked Soldier*

Douglas Novielli, Christopher Connal, and Jackson Ellis, Verbicide *Magazine*

Verbicide Do you think you would have pursued writing if you hadn't gone to Vietnam?

O'Brien Probably. It probably would've been something different. If I'd gone to Canada I'd be writing about that. Life provides you plenty of material, with girlfriends or whatever.

V Do you think you romanticize Vietnam at all?

O No. I think a lot of veterans think I haven't done that enough, but I refuse to do it.

V Is there a reason they think it should be romanticized?

O Yeah, they look back on it as more heroic, and with nostalgia, and they talk about the fellowship or fraternity among men, and there's some truth to that. But it's an artificial one; it's borne of necessity. Even if you don't like someone, you've got to trust them at night when they're on guard and you're sleeping. And you learn who to trust and who not to trust, and you bond that way. But I never found it very heroic, I just found it stone-man, gotta stay alive stuff. And that's all there was to it.

V Are soldiers heroes?

O In some ways. It's heroic just not to stop. Physically, there are always alternatives, I mean, just stop walking. What can they do? Court martial you, but they're not gonna kill you. It looks pretty attractive, especially in bad days when guys have been dropping like flies. . . .

You just keep humping. There's a weird heroism in that. Unglamorous kind of valor to just keep going, knowing you might die with every step, and just keep walking.

V Is the heroism there in your books to be interpreted if the reader wants it, or is it directly implied?

O I remember one part in *The Things They Carried* when I was talking about humping and just taking one step after the next, and at one point I called it a kind of courage, which it is, just to keep your legs moving. I'm kind of explicit about that kind of courage, but there are other kinds of courage just like there are kinds of truth. It took a lot of guts, for example, to go to Canada. Your whole hometown is going to think of you as a sissy or a coward, even though it's totally conscientious. So I admire the heroism and courage it took. I didn't have the guts to do it, to cross over the border.

V Do you still regret that?

O Yeah, you can't live your life over, but it would have been the right thing to do. I mean, think how hard it would be, even now it would be hard and I'm grown up. It was the thing that was worse than anything about the war, just going to it. Once you're in the war, it's pretty much what you'd expect. But, boy, making that decision, because you're in control of things. You can go in the army, or you can go to Canada. I never actually made that drive and went to the Rainy River.[1] That's invented. But it did happen in my head all summer long. I thought about driving to Canada.

---

1. **Rainy River:** a river on the U.S.– Canadian border. In O'Brien's short story "On the Rainy River," the main character drives to the river and considers whether he should cross the border into Canada and dodge the draft.

Comprehension

1. **Recall** According to Doc Peret, what causes the death of Billy Boy Watkins?

2. **Clarify** Why does Toby want to keep Paul quiet?

3. **Summarize** How does the story end?

Literary Analysis

4. **Draw Conclusions** Think back to the discussion you had about the different ways people respond to **fear.** Describe how Paul Berlin tries to combat his fear in this story. How successful is he? Cite evidence to support your conclusion.

5. **Identify Conflict** Is the main conflict in this story **internal** or **external?** Explain, citing details from the text to support your answer.

6. **Analyze Sequence** Review the chart you made as you read, and think about the **flashback** in lines 183–196, in which Paul recalls the death of Billy Boy Watkins in vivid detail. Why might O'Brien have used the flashback at this point in the story? What did it help you, the reader, understand?

7. **Analyze Realism** Find examples in the text that illustrate each element of **style** shown on the chart. Use your completed chart to explain how O'Brien's use of realism contributes to the reader's perceptions of Paul and his situation.

Element of Style	Examples from Text
Realistic dialogue	
Description featuring sensory details	
Passages made up of both long and short sentences	
Use of flashback	

8. **Synthesize** In "The Naked Soldier" on page 760, O'Brien talks about two different kinds of courage—the courage it took to serve in Vietnam and the courage it took to defy the draft and flee to Canada. In your opinion, which act was more courageous? Use evidence from both the story and the interview to support your opinion.

Literary Criticism

9. **Author's Style** In describing what he strives for when creating stories, O'Brien stated, "You aim for tension and suspense, a sense of drama, displaying in concrete terms the actions and reactions of human beings contesting problems of the heart." How successfully did O'Brien fulfill the above criteria in this story? Cite evidence from the selection to support your opinion.

"In the afternoon . . . not to think" (lines 58–64). Flashback: Students should cite Paul's flashback to Billy's death. All of these techniques make Paul seem like a real person and lend a sense of immediacy to his terrifying situation.

8. Answers will vary. Students should support their answers with references to the story and the interview.

Literary Criticism

9. Responses will vary. If students say that O'Brien accomplished this goal, they may cite tense, suspenseful scenes like the one in which Toby tries to make Paul stop giggling. They might discuss Paul's "problem of the heart," his terrible fear, and argue that O'Brien did a good job of depicting Paul's emotional response to that fear.

Practice and Apply

After Reading

For additional support of post-reading questions, use these copy masters:

R RESOURCE MANAGER—Copy Masters

Reading Check p. 34 (to check understanding of the selection)

Realism p. 27 (for practice of literary analysis standards focus)

Question Support p. 35 (After Reading questions adapted for English learners and less-proficient readers)

Additional selection questions are provided for teachers on page 21.

ANSWERS

Comprehension

1. *According to Doc Peret, Billy Boy died of a heart attack brought on by fear.*

2. *Paul's laughter might give away their position to the enemy.*

3. *Paul recovers from his hysterical laughing fit. Paul thinks his fear will lessen when they reach the sea, but it does not.*

Literary Analysis

Possible answers:

4. *Paul pretends he is not at war (lines 12–13), fantasizes about what will happen when it is over, and imagines it will be better when he reaches the sea (lines 45–47, 85–88). He is not successful; the last line of the story reveals that Paul "could not stop being afraid."*

5. *Internal—the main conflict is between Paul and his fear. Students should cite a few passages that deal with Paul's terror.*

6. ■ **STANDARDS FOCUS** *Analyze Sequence He uses the flashback toward the end to help the reader understand Paul's strange reaction—a fit of uncontrollable giggles—to Billy Boy's death. Paul's giggling helps him deal with that horrifying death and his own terror of dying.*

7. ● **STANDARDS FOCUS** *Realism Realistic dialogue: Students could cite any of Paul and Toby's conversations. Sensory details: "He would tell his mother how it smelled . . . (lines 41–44). Long and short sentences:*

ANSWERS

Vocabulary in Context

VOCABULARY PRACTICE

1. *stealth*
2. *fecund*
3. *diffuse*
4. *inertia*

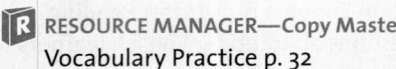 **RESOURCE MANAGER—Copy Master**
Vocabulary Practice p. 32

VOCABULARY IN WRITING

Remind students that all soldiers in the platoon went through experiences similar to Paul's. Suggest that students keep in mind the soldiers' feelings, along with what they know about Paul and Toby, as they write from the commanding officer's point of view.

VOCABULARY STRATEGY: WORDS THAT START WITH *in-*

For each item, have students look up in an unabridged dictionary the root word without the prefix. Some of these "roots" do not exist. In those cases, students should list the *in-* word in the first column.

Possible answers:

(words marked with asterisks have no positive form)

1. incorrigible: *not correctable*
2. inclement: *harsh*
3. insomnia*: *prolonged inability to sleep*
4. indolent*: *lazy*
5. insuperable: *unable to be overcome*
6. insipid*: *dull*
7. incognito*: *with one's true identity disguised*
8. incongruous: *seemingly unreasonable or unsuitable*

RESOURCE MANAGER—Copy Master
Vocabulary Strategy p. 33

ℹ️ Vocabulary Center at **ClassZone.com**
Additional Vocabulary Activities

Vocabulary in Context

VOCABULARY PRACTICE

WORD LIST
diffuse
fecund
inertia
stealth

Write the word from the Word List that best completes each sentence.

1. The soldiers moved with _____ across the countryside so that they would not be spotted by the enemy.
2. In spite of all the bombing it had suffered, the land they traveled through was still _____.
3. In their nervousness, it was hard to bring their _____ thoughts back into clear focus.
4. They relied on _____ and force of habit to keep them on the path.

VOCABULARY IN WRITING

Pretend that you are Paul Berlin's commanding officer, and write a paragraph describing the problems facing your platoon. Use at least two vocabulary words. You might start like this:

> **EXAMPLE SENTENCE**
> The **diffuse** attention of my soldiers is starting to worry me. . . .

VOCABULARY STRATEGY: WORDS THAT START WITH *in-*

The forms of certain words beginning with *in-* can sometimes cause confusion. When you see a word like *inertia*, for example, in which *in-* means "unable to" or "not," you might make the assumption that you can remove the prefix to form a word with an opposite, "positive" meaning. However, there is no such English word as *ertia*. To avoid writing incorrect antonyms for words with *in-*, always check a dictionary.

PRACTICE Create a two-column chart with these headings: "No Positive Form" and "Positive Form Not Often Used." Use a dictionary to place each word in the correct column. Then write a brief definition of each word.

1. incorrigible
2. inclement
3. insomnia
4. indolent
5. insuperable
6. insipid
7. incognito
8. incongruous

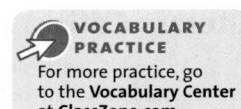 **VOCABULARY PRACTICE**
For more practice, go to the **Vocabulary Center** at **ClassZone.com**.

DIFFERENTIATED INSTRUCTION

FOR ENGLISH LEARNERS

Vocabulary: Home Language Equivalents for Word with *in-* Have students write home-language equivalents of the words in the two columns. Encourage them to write down additional words beginning with *in-*. Ask whether these words have English equivalents. If necessary, have them check them in a bilingual dictionary and report the results. List all the English words beginning with *in-* that the students generate.

FOR ADVANCED LEARNERS/PRE–AP

Vocabulary in Writing Ask students to use at least four of the *in-* words in a paragraph describing another soldier's experience in Paul Berlin's platoon.

Reading-Writing Connection

Demonstrate your knowledge of "Where Have You Gone, Charming Billy?" by responding to these prompts. Then use **Revision: Grammar and Style** to improve your writing.

WRITING PROMPTS	SELF-CHECK
A. Short Response: Write a Letter Think about Paul Berlin's deep desire to please his father and the **fear** he grapples with in this story. Using details from the text, pretend you are Paul and write a **one- or two-paragraph letter** home.	*A compelling letter will . . .* • describe Paul's experiences and how he's coping with being a soldier • sound as if it were written by Paul, on the basis of the traits he exhibits in the story
B. Extended Response: Analyze Realism O'Brien served in the Vietnam War for over a year, until an injury sustained in a grenade attack ended his enlistment. In your opinion, which details in this story could have been written only by someone who actually served in Vietnam? Which details seem to be products of the writer's artistic imagination? Citing evidence to support your opinion, write a **three-to-five-paragraph response.**	*A strong analysis will . . .* • consider the different details O'Brien includes in this story, such as sensory images and descriptions of the soldiers' feelings • cite relevant and convincing examples of both realistic and imaginative details

REVISION: GRAMMAR AND STYLE

ADD SUPPORTING DETAILS Review the **Grammar and Style** note on page 755. O'Brien depicts Paul as a frightened and inexperienced soldier by using details to provide a window into Paul's mental state. The **repetition** that marks Paul's thoughts reflects his continuing fear, anxiety, and denial. Here is an example from the story. Note that O'Brien repeats the verb *pretending:*

> *He was pretending he was not in the war, pretending he had not watched Billy Boy Watkins die of a heart attack that afternoon. He was pretending he was a boy again, camping with his father in the midnight summer along the Des Moines River.* (lines 12–16)

Notice how the revisions in red use repetition to reflect Paul's feelings of denial and anxiety. Revise your response to Prompt A by using similar techniques.

 WRITING TOOLS
For prewriting, revision, and editing tools, visit the **Writing Center** at ClassZone.com.

STUDENT MODEL

I'm exhausted and hungry, but I'm not afraid. Don't worry about me,
—*I don't worry about me*○
Dad⹁ I know I'll be home soon. *I'll be home sooner than you think*○

OR LESS PROFICIENT WRITERS

For Prompt A:

• Direct students to list three events Paul might describe to his father.

• Suggest that students describe these events in chronological order in the letter.

• Remind students that Paul does not want to reveal his fear to his father.

For Prompt B:

• Limit the assignment to two paragraphs.

• Encourage students to organize the first paragraph with descriptions of things the writer could know only from experience.

• Encourage students to organize the second paragraph with descriptions of things the writer could create from imagination.

• Have students work in small groups to brainstorm things that a writer would know from experience and things he could create from imagination.

Reading-Writing Connection

WRITING PROMPTS

• For Prompt A, suggest students reread some of Paul's thoughts involving his father (lines 14–21, 56–58, 69–73, 120–122, 235–237, 252–253). Encourage students to recreate Paul's ambivalence toward his fear and toward war.

• For Prompt B, encourage students to use a Two-Column Chart. In one column, students can note details of time, place, and reaction that might come from the imagination. In the second, they can insert details that could come only from experience.

 BEST PRACTICES TOOLKIT—Transparency
Two-Column Chart p. A25

For writing support, see

 Writing Center at **ClassZone.com**

REVISION: GRAMMAR AND STYLE

After students examine the lines from the story and the student model, write these lines on the board. Have students add repetition to accentuate feelings.

We walked for miles and miles—so many miles my soles wore thin. We passed through a rice paddy that smelled like mud and clay. I was looking forward to getting to the sea, really looking forward to it. Later we went through a village and then through another paddy. I was a little tired—to be honest, more than a little tired.

 RESOURCE MANAGER—Copy Master
Add Supporting Details p. 36

Assess and Reteach

Assess

 RESOURCE MANAGER—Copy Masters
Selection Test A pp. 39–40
Selection Test B/C pp. 41–42

Test Generator CD

Reteach

S STANDARDS LESSON FILE
Literature Lesson 46: Style and Syntax
Reading Lesson 6: Recognizing Sequence and Chronological Order
Vocabulary Lesson 1: Word Parts: Base Words, Prefixes, Suffixes, and Roots

Focus and Motivate

OBJECTIVES

Literary Analysis
- explore the key idea of **superficial**
- analyze parody
- read a short story

Reading
- make predictions about plot

SUMMARY

"Once upon a time," Thurber begins, a king had a beautiful daughter whom he spoiled with costly possessions. He offered her in marriage to the prince whose gift she liked best. Four rich princes bestowed lavish gifts, including a platinum jewel box. A fifth, handsome but poor, gave her a tin box. The princess chose the jewel box, since it was expensive and would hold many jewels.

Are DIAMONDS
really a girl's best friend?

Ask the question, and explain to students that "Diamonds Are a Girl's Best Friend" is the title of a song from the movie *Gentlemen Prefer Blondes*, starring Marilyn Monroe. Then read aloud the **KEY IDEA** and ask students if they agree that people who care about things like diamonds and clothes are **superficial.** Extend the discussion by having students complete the **PRESENT** activity.

Selection Resources

The Princess and the Tin Box
Fable by James Thurber

Are DIAMONDS
really a girl's best friend?

KEY IDEA For that matter, do clothes really make the man? We all know people who are **superficial** or shallow, concerned only with appearance rather than substance. In this takeoff on a fairy tale, James Thurber presents just such a person: a rich, spoiled princess.

PRESENT With a partner, create a "portrait" of a superficial person, using both words and images. Make your portrait as serious or as comically exaggerated as you like, but be sure to communicate how your subject thinks and acts. You can even outfit him or her in whatever clothes and accessories you think appropriate. After you've finished, pair up with another group and take turns presenting your portraits.

764

R RESOURCE MANAGER UNIT 8

Plan and Teach pp. 43–50

Literary Analysis
Summary pp. 51†*, 52‡*
Parody pp. 53, 54†*
Question Support p. 59*

Reading
Predict pp. 55, 56†*
Reading Check p. 57

Assessment
Selection Tests A, B/C pp. 61*, 63*
Test Generator CD

BEST PRACTICES TOOLKIT

Differentiated Instruction
pp. 31–38*

Scaffolding Instruction
pp. 43–46*

Graphic Organizers/Strategies
Two-Column Chart

Reading Support
Audio Anthology CD*

Technology
Literature Center at
ClassZone.com
Write*Smart* CD

---

* Resources for Differentiation   † Also in Spanish   ‡ In Haitian Creole and Vietnamese

LITERARY ANALYSIS: PARODY

Humorist James Thurber is known for his sly, skillful way of making fun of society. "The Princess and the Tin Box" begins in a very familiar way:

Once upon a time, in a far country, there lived a king whose daughter was the prettiest princess in the world.

With that opening sentence, readers immediately recognize that they have been whisked into a fairy tale. This particular tale, however, is a **parody**—a literary work that imitates another piece of literature in order to poke fun at it. To analyze this imitation fairy tale, be on the lookout for the following stylistic techniques:

- **Word Choice:** Notice how Thurber imitates the language used in fairy tales, as in the opening lines above.
- **Exaggeration:** Look for characters or situations exaggerated by the author for comic effect.
- **Irony:** Identify ironic plot twists, or moments when things happen very differently from the way you would expect.

As you read, look for evidence of these techniques. Think about the ways in which this parody resembles a typical fairy tale and the ways in which it does not.

READING STRATEGY: PREDICT

Fairy tales are usually pretty predictable. As you read this selection, jot down your impressions of the princess. Use these notes about the princess's character to make **predictions** about what will happen next in the story. After the last events have unfolded, ask yourself if this is the "happily ever after" you anticipated.

Author Online

Early Years One of the great humorists of American literature, James Thurber made a career out of poking fun at society. Despite a childhood eye injury that left him with lifelong vision problems, Thurber attended college and got early jobs as a clerk and then as a journalist.

**James Thurber
1894–1961**

In 1927, the *New Yorker*, a literary magazine, published one of his stories. He would write for the magazine for the rest of his life.

The *New Yorker* Years The *New Yorker* gave Thurber his fame, and he gave the magazine much of the sophisticated style it has today. Thurber often provided his own illustrations to accompany his writing. Although he did not consider himself an artist, his cartoons had a distinctive style and became as popular as his stories. Readers loved him for being so funny, but Thurber took humor seriously. "I write humor the way a surgeon operates," he said, "because it is a livelihood, because I have a great urge to do it, because many interesting challenges are set up, and because I have the hope it may do some good."

Last Years By the age of 57, Thurber's childhood eye injury had degenerated to almost total blindness. When his vision began to fail completely, Thurber started dictating stories to his secretary. His memory was so sharp that he could easily compose a 2,000-word story in his mind, remember it overnight, and dictate it to his secretary the next day. His friend and fellow-writer E. B. White described him this way: "During his happiest years, Thurber did not write the way a surgeon operates, he wrote the way a child skips rope, the way a mouse waltzes."

 MORE ABOUT THE AUTHOR
For more on James Thurber, visit the **Literature Center** at **ClassZone.com**.

Teach

STANDARDS FOCUS

LITERARY ANALYSIS

● PARODY

For instructional support, read aloud this example:

"Then I'll huff and I'll puff and I'll . . . you know," said the wheezing wolf. But the pig, whose house was built of reinforced concrete, merely yawned.

Have students identify the word choices that echo a well-known story. ***Possible answer:*** *"I'll huff and I'll puff and I'll," "wolf," "pig," "house"*

CHECK UNDERSTANDING Ask students to explain how exaggeration and irony contribute to the parody in the example.

READING STRATEGY

● PREDICT

To support instruction, read aloud this example:

In a story, a man in a dark hat and coat hides in an alley as an unsuspecting man walks up the sidewalk toward him.

Have students predict what will happen and cite reasons. ***Possible answer:*** *The first man may jump out and rob the second. Readers expect someone hiding in an alley, dressed in dark clothes, to be planning something sinister.*

CHECK UNDERSTANDING Elicit that predicting combines prior knowledge with text clues.

 RESOURCE MANAGER—Copy Master
Predict p. 55 (for student use while reading the selection)

DIFFERENTIATED INSTRUCTION

FOR LESS–PROFICIENT READERS

Concept Support Initiate a discussion of parody by having students cite fairy tales or folktales they know. Then explain that parodies combine language and ideas from the original work with exaggeration. Use this example:

Small Bunyan and his blue mouse, Blip, cleared the mighty weeds on the anthill.

Challenge students to parody a few lines from a familiar fairy tale or folktale.

FOR ENGLISH LEARNERS

Language: Skill Words Give these examples of exaggeration and irony:

- Her eyes got as big as dinner plates.
- After complaining about his meal, Julio cleaned his plate.

Discuss the effect of each, pointing out that eyes never get as big as plates, and after complaining about the meal, Julio's action is unexpected. Help students arrive at definitions of *exaggeration* and *irony*.

ANALYZE VISUALS

Possible answer: Thurber offers a stock image of romance and courtship: the prince kneels at the princess's feet, offering her a gift and his love. The viewer gets the feeling that Thurber is making fun of these romantic conventions.

About the Art James Thurber's childlike style cloaks a talent for conveying much information in a simple sketch. Robert Morsberger, Thurber's biographer, believes Thurber's illustrations for his fables represent the peak of his talent.

LITERARY ANALYSIS

Ⓐ PARODY

Possible answer: The princess throws pearls instead of rice at her brother's wedding; her slippers, bathroom, and bed are made of precious minerals and priceless gems. This exaggeration creates a comic effect.

If students need help . . . Read aloud the description of the princess's nursery (lines 5–8). Then ask students to describe a typical child's bedroom. Ask them why Thurber's description is comic.

THE *Princess* AND THE *Tin Box*

JAMES THURBER

Once upon a time, in a far country, there lived a king whose daughter was the prettiest princess in the world. Her eyes were like the cornflower, her hair was sweeter than the hyacinth, and her throat made the swan look dusty.

From the time she was a year old, the princess had been showered with presents. Her nursery looked like Cartier's window.[1] Her toys were all made of gold or platinum or diamonds or emeralds. She was not permitted to have wooden blocks or china dolls or rubber dogs or linen books, because such materials were considered cheap for the daughter of a king.

When she was seven, she was allowed to attend the wedding of her brother
10 and throw real pearls at the bride instead of rice. Only the nightingale, with his lyre of gold, was permitted to sing for the princess. The common blackbird, with his boxwood flute,[2] was kept out of the palace grounds. She walked in silver-and-samite slippers to a sapphire-and-topaz bathroom and slept in an ivory bed inlaid with rubies. Ⓐ

On the day the princess was eighteen, the king sent a royal ambassador to the courts of five neighboring kingdoms to announce that he would give his daughter's hand in marriage to the prince who brought her the gift she liked the most.

The first prince to arrive at the palace rode a swift white stallion and laid
20 at the feet of the princess an enormous apple made of solid gold which he had taken from a dragon who had guarded it for a thousand years. It was placed on a long ebony table set up to hold the gifts of the princess's suitors. The second prince, who came on a gray charger,[3] brought her a nightingale made

ANALYZE VISUALS
Thurber often sketched childlike line drawings like this one to accompany his stories. What basic ideas about love or courtship does he present in this sketch?

Ⓐ PARODY
Reread lines 1–14 and identify at least two examples of **exaggeration.** What is the effect of this stylistic technique? Explain your answer.

① Targeted Passage

---

1. **Cartier's** (kär-tyāz´) **window:** the show window of a well-known jewelry store.
2. **lyre** (līr) **of gold . . . boxwood flute:** The nightingale's voice is likened to a golden harp; the blackbird's voice is likened to a cheap wooden flute.
3. **charger:** warhorse.

The Princess and the Tin Box (1948), © James Thurber. © rer
1976 by Rosemary A. Thurber. Reprinted by arrangement
Rosemary A. Thurber and the Barbara Hogenson Ag

DIFFERENTIATED INSTRUCTION

FOR ALL STUDENTS

Enhancing Learning Styles Provide these projects for various learning preferences:

- **Verbal** Adapt the story for a dramatic reading.
- **Visual** Create a comic strip based on the story.

For further details on these projects, see

Ⓡ RESOURCE MANAGER
Ideas for Extension pp. 48–49

FOR LESS–PROFICIENT READERS

In combination with the *Audio Anthology CD,* use one or more Targeted Passages (pp. 766, 768) to ensure that students focus on key events, concepts, and skills. Targeted Passages are also good for English learners.

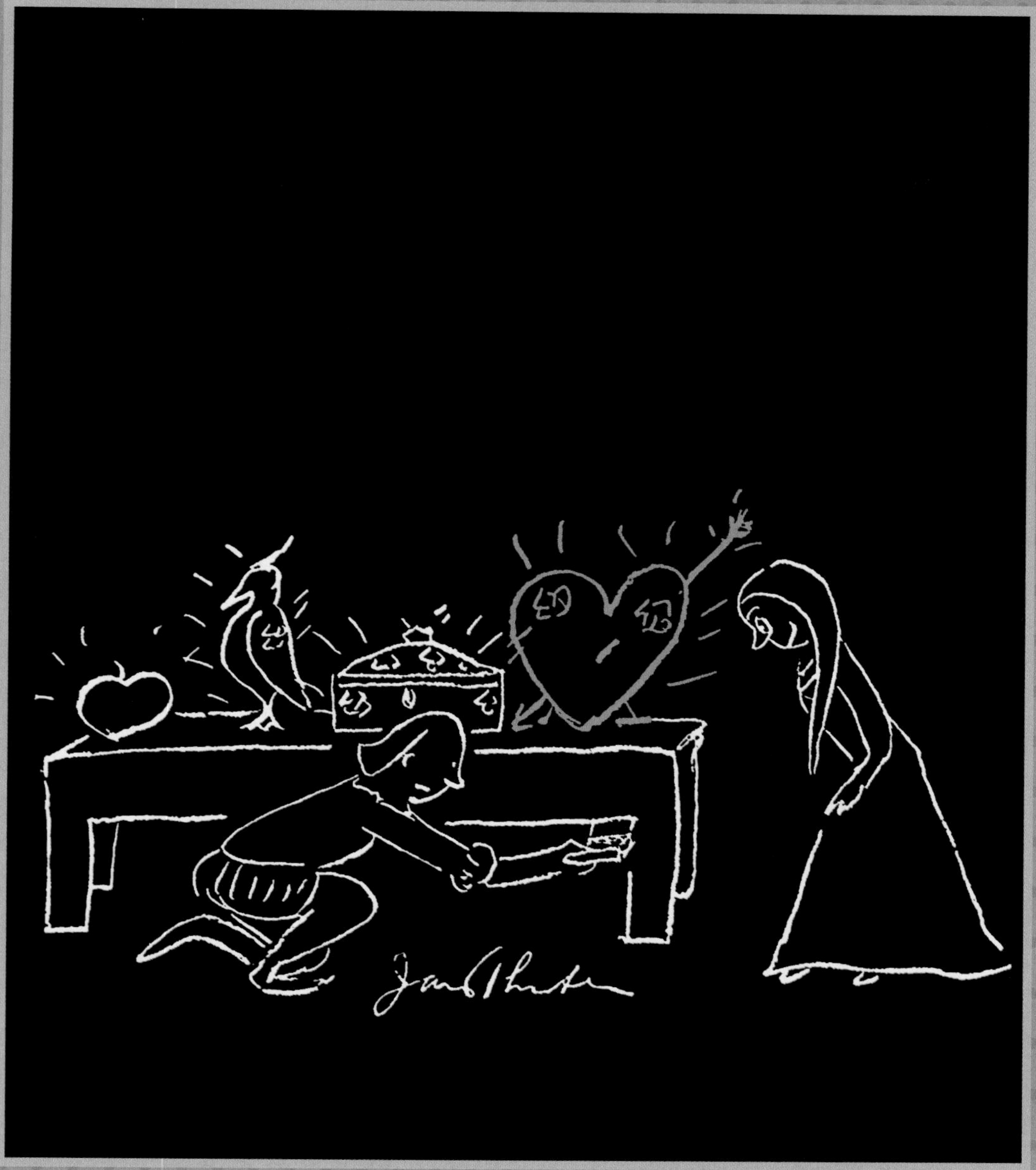

Fables and Fairy Tales "The Princess and the Tin Box" combines elements of fairy tales and fables. Fairy tales are a type of **folktale**—a traditional story that has been passed down from generation to generation by word of mouth. Fairy tales feature magical events and mainly one-dimensional human characters who are usually all good or all bad. While fables are also a type of folktale and also feature one-dimensional characters, these characters are usually animals rather than humans. A fable also offers a moral, or lesson about life, such as "It is dangerous to gossip" or "It is important to plan for the future."

REINFORCE *KEY IDEA:* SUPERFICIAL

Discuss Has the princess been raised to be **superficial?** Explain your answer, giving evidence from the story. *Possible answer: Yes, the princess has been raised to be superficial. She has been taught to prize wealth and appearances. Less exceptional things, such as the common blackbird (lines 11–12), are kept from her.*

---

① Targeted Passage [Lines 15–22]

This passage introduces the plot and further characterizes the king and the princess.

- What action does the king take that sets the plot in motion?

- What does the king's plan reveal about him and the princess?

- Based on the action of the first prince, what do you predict will happen next?

FOR ENGLISH LEARNERS

Reading: Background Ask students if they have read other stories about princes and princesses. Ask what type of person always marries the princess in these stories.

Options for Reading Have students read the tale aloud, taking turns with a partner.

Prereading For prereading instruction for English learners, see

 BEST PRACTICES TOOLKIT
Scaffolding Reading Instruction pp. 43–46

FOR ADVANCED LEARNERS/PRE–AP

Pre-AP Exercises in the bottom channel provide additional challenge for students. Use these suggestions for small groups or individuals.

ADDITIONAL GUIDELINES

For more help with differentiation and tips for classroom management, see

 BEST PRACTICES TOOLKIT
Differentiated Instruction pp. 31–38

LITERARY ANALYSIS

B PARODY

Possible answers: Plot: a marriage contest for the hand of the princess; the princes arrive on horseback, bearing gifts. Setting: "Once upon a time, in a far country (line 1). Characters: The poor prince is "the strongest and handsomest" (line 30).

READING STRATEGY

C PREDICT

Students may predict that, as in a typical fairy tale, virtue will win out and the princess will choose the poor but handsome prince.

If students need help . . . Explain that good readers check their predictions as they read. Then have students complete a Two-Column Chart like this one.

What I predicted	What happens
The princess will choose the poor prince's gift.	The princess chooses a rich prince.
The princess will discover the worth in ordinary things.	The princess is delighted with wealth and precious stones.

 BEST PRACTICES TOOLKIT—Transparency
Two-Column Chart p. A25

SELECTION WRAP-UP

REFLECT Remind students that a traditional fable teaches a moral lesson. Ask students why they think Thurber ends his fable with a moral that is the opposite of what we would expect.

★ **CRITIQUE** Ask students whether they find Thurber's moral satisfying, even if they do not find it morally uplifting. Why or why not?

---

of a thousand diamonds, and it was placed beside the golden apple. The third prince, riding on a black horse, carried a great jewel box made of platinum and sapphires, and it was placed next to the diamond nightingale. The fourth prince, astride a fiery yellow horse, gave the princess a gigantic heart made of rubies and pierced by an emerald arrow. It was placed next to the platinum-and-sapphire jewel box.

30 Now the fifth prince was the strongest and handsomest of all the five suitors, but he was the son of a poor king whose realm had been overrun by mice and locusts and wizards and mining engineers so that there was nothing much of value left in it. He came plodding up to the palace of the princess on a plow horse and he brought her a small tin box filled with mica and feldspar and hornblende[4] which he had picked up on the way. **B**

The other princes roared with disdainful laughter when they saw the tawdry[5] gift the fifth prince had brought to the princess. But she examined it with great interest and squealed with delight, for all her life she had been glutted with precious stones and priceless metals, but she had never seen tin
40 before or mica or feldspar or hornblende. The tin box was placed next to the ruby heart pierced with an emerald arrow. **C**

"Now," the king said to his daughter, "you must select the gift you like best and marry the prince that brought it."

The princess smiled and walked up to the table and picked up the present she liked the most. It was the platinum-and-sapphire jewel box, the gift of the third prince.

"The way I figure it," she said, "is this. It is a very large and expensive box, and when I am married, I will meet many admirers who will give me precious gems with which to fill it to the top. Therefore, it is the most valuable of all the
50 gifts my suitors have brought me and I like it the best."

The princess married the third prince that very day in the midst of great merriment and high revelry.[6] More than a hundred thousand pearls were thrown at her and she loved it.

Moral: All those who thought the princess was going to select the tin box filled with worthless stones instead of one of the other gifts will kindly stay after class and write one hundred times on the blackboard "I would rather have a hunk of aluminum silicate[7] than a diamond necklace." ~

---

4. **mica** (mī′kə) **and feldspar and hornblende** (hôrn′blĕnd′): three common minerals.
5. **tawdry** (tô′drē): flashy but cheap.
6. **revelry** (rĕv′əl-rē): noisy celebrating.
7. **aluminum silicate** (sĭl′ĭ-kāt′): a basically worthless chemical compound; refers to the mica, feldspar, and hornblende in the prince's box.

B PARODY
Think about the typical plot, setting, and characters of a fairy tale. Find three places where Thurber mimics these conventions in this story.

C PREDICT
Consider your impression of the princess and her reactions to her suitors' gifts. Do you think she will choose to marry the poor but handsome prince or one of the rich, snobby ones? Give reasons for your prediction.

② **Targeted Passage**

DIFFERENTIATED INSTRUCTION

FOR LESS-PROFICIENT READERS
② Targeted Passage [Lines 42–58]

This passage concludes the story with a twist that pokes fun at fables—and romantics.

- What does the king's statement (lines 42–43) lead you to expect will happen?
- How does the princess explain her choice (lines 47–50)? Is it a romantic choice? Why or why not?
- What punishment does the moral dole out for those who predicted the tin box?

FOR ENGLISH LEARNERS
Language: Verb Tenses Elicit from students that fairy tales are set in a magical past and so are always told in the past tense. Then form two teams and have them find irregular past tense verbs in the tale. Start by pointing out *saw* in line 36 as an example. Have each team compile a numbered list of the verbs, with line numbers. Discuss the list and announce which team identified the most verbs.

Comprehension

1. **Recall** What does the king do on his daughter's 18th birthday?

2. **Summarize** Describe the five gifts the suitors bring, which one the princess chooses to accept, and why.

3. **Paraphrase** Restate the moral of the story in your own words.

Literary Analysis

4. **Interpret Irony** Reread lines 54–58. How does the end of this story play against the reader's normal expectations of a fairy tale? Explain how the ending is ironic, citing evidence from the text.

5. **Analyze Parody** In a chart like the one shown, record examples of the **stylistic techniques** Thurber uses to parody a fairy tale. Use your completed chart to explain what human trait or quality Thurber is poking fun at in this story.

Stylistic Technique	Examples from the Text
Imitation of standard fairy tale language	
Exaggeration	
Irony	

6. **Evaluate Predictions** How accurately did you predict what would happen at the end of the story? Explain whether or not you think Thurber intended to take his readers by surprise, and why.

7. **Make Judgments** A **parody** is an imitation of a writer's style, a type of literature, or a specific work, and is usually designed to make fun of something. In your opinion, is humor an effective tool for social criticism? Can making a joke or commenting on something in a comic way ever help bring about change? Explain your answer.

Reading-Writing Connection

WRITING PROMPT

Short Response: Rewrite the Ending
What would have happened if the princess had made a different choice? How else could this story have ended? In **one or two paragraphs,** imagine an alternate ending to the story and create a new moral to go with it. Try to mimic Thurber's dry, comic style.

SELF-CHECK

An entertaining ending will . . .
- clearly convey what the princess's new choice is and explain why she chose as she did
- include a humorous moral written in a style similar to Thurber's

THE PRINCESS AND THE TIN BOX   769

Practice and Apply

After Reading
For additional support of post-reading questions, use these copy masters:

R RESOURCE MANAGER—Copy Masters
Reading Check p. 57 (to check understanding of the selection)
Parody p. 53 (for practice of literary analysis standards focus)
Question Support p. 59 (After Reading questions adapted for English learners and less-proficient readers)

Additional selection questions are provided for teachers on page 47.

ANSWERS

Comprehension

1. *The king announces that his daughter will wed the prince who gives her the gift she likes best.*

2. *The princes bring a golden apple, a diamond nightingale, a platinum-and-sapphire jewel box, a ruby heart, and a tin box filled with common minerals. The princess picks the jewel box because it is expensive and can hold many jewels.*

3. *Everyone who predicted the princess would choose the tin box should be punished for their naiveté.*

Literary Analysis
Possible answers:

4. *Readers expect love or virtue to triumph in fairy tales, but this ending ironically confounds our expectations by showing greed winning out.*

5. ● **STANDARDS FOCUS** *Parody Imitation of standard fairy tale language: "Once*

upon a time . . . " (lines 1–2). Exaggeration: "Her nursery looked like Cartier's window. Her toys were all made of gold or platinum or diamonds or emeralds" (lines 5–6). Irony: "The princess . . . picked up the present she liked the most. It was the . . . jewel box . . . " (lines 44–46). Thurber is making fun of superficiality and materialism.

6. ■ **STANDARDS FOCUS** *Predict* Predictions will vary. Thurber intended to surprise readers—that's why his parody is effective.

7. Some students may say that humor can be an effective tool for social change.

For example, some stand-up comics use pointed jokes about racism or sexism to spark conversations about these important topics. Others may say that only serious work can really drive social change.

Reading-Writing Connection

WRITING PROMPT
Encourage students to reread lines 42–58 to review the ending and Thurber's dry wit. Remind them to write an ironic ending.

Assess and Reteach

Assess
R RESOURCE MANAGER—Copy Masters
Selection Test A pp. 61–62
Selection Test B/C pp. 63–64
Test Generator CD

Reteach
S STANDARDS LESSON FILE
Literature Lesson 39: Parody and Satire
Reading Lesson 1: Predicting

THE PRINCESS AND THE TIN BOX   **769**

Focus and Motivate

OBJECTIVES

Media Literacy
- explore the key idea of **style**
- view a film clip to understand how Alfred Hitchcock used visual and editing techniques to create desired atmospheres and express particular themes
- create a production still to demonstrate understanding of Hitchcock's style

SUMMARY

This clip from *The Birds* opens from a bird's point of view high above a California town as fire spreads through the town's center. More and more birds cross the screen and begin to attack people rushing from a restaurant. The film's heroine, Melanie, seeks shelter in a phone booth, and from there, trapped and powerless, watches chaos and terror unfold around her. Two birds break the glass before a man finally pulls Melanie back to the safety of the restaurant.

What makes a director a master of STYLE?

To help students explore the **KEY IDEA**, ask them what they know about Hitchcock's films, such as *Rebecca, Rear Window, Spellbound, Vertigo,* or *North by Northwest.* Then broaden the discussion to more recent scary movies. Point out that Hitchcock invented many of the techniques that later directors used to create suspense.

BACKGROUND

Alfred Hitchcock is among the most widely known and influential directors in film history. From 1927 onward, he made cameo appearances in all of his movies, taking such roles as a man getting on a bus. Hitchcock's movie *Rebecca* received the Academy Award for Best Picture in 1940, though Hitchcock never received an Academy Award as Best Director. For his tombstone, Hitchcock suggested the words "This is what we do to bad little boys." His tombstone ultimately read "I'm in on a plot."

Media Study

from The Birds
Film Clip on **MediaSmart** DVD

What makes a director a master of STYLE?

KEY IDEA Long before there was a Steven Spielberg or a Peter Jackson, there was a world-class director known for creating spellbinding films. By viewing a clip from one of Alfred Hitchcock's most famous movies, you'll experience the **stylistic touches** that made this director a movie legend.

Background

Fear Factor Born in England in 1899, Alfred Hitchcock learned moviemaking from the ground up, beginning in the 1920s. In 1939, as a full-fledged director, he moved to the United States. Over the next three decades, the director crafted movies, and later produced two TV series, that earned him the titles of "master of suspense" and "master of the thriller." Hitchcock was known for engaging the minds and emotions of his audiences. The director once said, "They [fans of the thriller genre] want to put their toe in the cold waters of fear."

The Birds (1963)—considered Hitchcock's last great movie—portrays a California coastal town in which the bird population suddenly turns vicious. The movie is loosely based on the short story by suspense writer Daphne du Maurier.

770

Media Study Resources

R RESOURCE MANAGER UNIT 8

Plan and Teach pp. 65–68

Media Analysis
Summary pp. 69†*, 70‡*
Viewing Guide p. 71
Close Viewing p. 72
Viewing Activity p. 73
Produce Your Own Media p. 74

S STANDARDS LESSON FILE

Media Lesson 4: Analyzing Visuals in Film and TV
Media Lesson 6: Analyzing Editing in Film and TV

i Media Center at **ClassZone.com**

MEDIA VIEWING
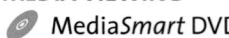 Media*Smart* DVD

* Resources for Differentiation   † Also in Spanish   ‡ In Haitian Creole and Vietnamese

Media Literacy: Style in Movies

A writer conveys his or her style primarily through carefully crafted words. A filmmaker achieves style through carefully selected images that can create specific meanings and trigger specific emotions. Director Alfred Hitchcock was often asked for insights into his craft. He once said, "Self-plagiarism is style." By this he meant that directors who consistently use and refine certain techniques from movie to movie can develop features recognizable as their own. To explore Hitchcock's style, it helps to have a sense of a director's basic techniques.

ELEMENTS OF STYLE	STRATEGIES FOR VIEWING	
Expressing Themes A director's stylistic techniques can be used to express particular themes or viewpoints that are characteristic of the director's work.	Become familiar with some common characteristics of Hitchcock's works. • Presentation of misfortune or evil as a fact of life • Ordinary, innocent people caught up in frightening circumstances • Threat of danger from unlikely settings, such as in a public place in full daylight • Fast-paced scenes in which tension builds • Probing exploration of a character's emotional or psychological state • Strong suspense mixed with humorous touches	*North by Northwest*  *The Birds* 
Creating Atmosphere A director can become known for trademark film techniques that he or she uses to convey meaning and to create an atmosphere.	Discover a few of Hitchcock's filming techniques. • Interpret **point of view** (POV) **shots,** which show what a character sees, and **reaction shots,** which show a character's response to whatever he or she faces. Hitchcock's POV shots allow viewers to slip into the role of a character and to identify with the character's predicament. • Watch for **camera placement.** For example, a camera placed at odd angles might portray a very confined setting or a confused state of mind. • Think about what the director is trying to achieve through the **pace** of the **editing.** Hitchcock was known for using **long takes** to promote reflection and **quick cuts** to increase tension.	*Rear Window* 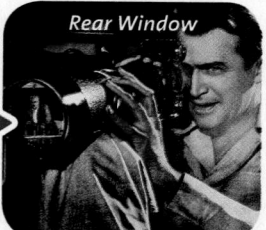 *Vertigo* 

MEDIA STUDY   **771**

MEDIA STUDY: TEACHING OPTIONS

Teaching Option 1: The Basics (1-2 Days)
1. Begin the Media Study using the material provided on pages 770–771.
2. Show the Introduction on Media*Smart*. Then show the First Viewing. As they watch, have students use the Viewing Guide on page 772, along with the corresponding copy master on page 71 of the Resource Manager. Discuss their responses.
3. Return to the pupil book for the extension activities on page 773.

Teaching Option 2: In-Depth Study (2–3 Days)
1. Begin the Media Study using pages 770–771.
2. Show the Introduction and First Viewing from Media*Smart*. Then continue on Media*Smart* with the Media Lessons, using the teacher notes available in the Resources section.
3. Show the Guided Analysis presentation. Have students record their observations on the Student Viewing Guide available in the Resources section from Media*Smart*.
4. Return to the pupil book, page 773.

Teach

Media Literacy

Ask students to define *style*. Students should recognize that *style* refers to the distinctive way in which someone does something. Ask students what might contribute to style in a movie. On the board, list answers students give, such as music, sound effects, and lighting. Make sure *camera shots, shot selection, pacing,* and *editing* are included in the list. Then discuss the chart on page 771.

- **Expressing Themes** To reinforce how themes can become part of a director's style, read aloud this synopsis of part of Hitchcock's *North by Northwest*. Ask students to identify which characteristic Hitchcock themes from the chart are found in the synopsis.

  Advertising executive Roger O. Thornhill stands up from lunch just as a "George Kaplan" is being paged. Three men seize him and take him to the mansion of enemy spy Philip Vandamm. Thornhill denies he is Kaplan and cannot answer Vandamm's questions. Next he is drugged and sent in a car down a treacherous mountain road, barely escaping death. Thornhill can't persuade the police or even his mother that his harrowing stories are true. The police cannot find Vandamm, and his mansion apparently belongs to United Nations ambassador Lester Townsend. Thornhill finds Townsend, who is soon knifed to death. Thornhill holds the knife!

- **Creating Atmospheres** Ask students to imagine they are directing this movie scene: A character is stood up by his girlfriend. The goal is to invite sympathy for the character and create an atmosphere of sorrow and disappointment. Ask students: How could point of view shots provide information? How could reaction shots generate sympathy for the character? How could camera angles help suggest disappointment and sadness? What pacing and editing suits such a scene?

@ Media*Smart* DVD

MEDIA STUDY   **771**

Practice and Apply

VIEWING GUIDE

1. Before students view the movie clip, tell them they will be asked to identify techniques Hitchcock uses to create an atmosphere of fear and helplessness. Ask them to watch for these elements:

   - **point of view shots** and **reaction shots** that show what Melanie sees and how she feels, especially inside the phone booth

   - **camera placement** that begins from above, then switches to Melanie's point of view, changing the mood and atmosphere of the clip

   - **shot selection, pacing, editing,** and **quick cuts** that generate increasing tension, such as the rapid sequence of different birds hitting the booth

2. Some students may not be able to link the techniques with what they see in the clip. Help these students connect the labels to specific examples in the clip.

R RESOURCE MANAGER—Copy Masters
Viewing Guide p. 71
Close Viewing p. 72
Viewing Activity p. 73

Use this resource with the Viewing Guide:

⊙ Media*Smart* DVD

ANSWERS

FIRST VIEWING: Comprehension

1. *The birds attack the phone booth more aggressively. Finally, a man brings Melanie to a restaurant for safety.*

2. *inside a phone booth*

CLOSE VIEWING: Media Literacy

Possible answers:

3. *She becomes progressively more panicked, wondering how she can escape from the attacking birds. She is also aghast at the scene outside the booth.*

4. *Hitchcock starts with an overhead shot of the entire scene and then uses medium and tight close-ups. He conveys increasing tension with quick edits.*

⊙ **MediaSmart** DVD
- **Film Clip:** from *The Birds*
- **Director:** Alfred Hitchcock
- **Genre:** Thriller
- **Running Time:** 2 minutes

772

Viewing Guide for
The Birds

Just before the start of the clip, main character Melanie Daniels is in a restaurant, overhearing anxious townspeople discussing the increasing threat of bird attacks. Then, through the windows, Melanie spots another attack in progress, which leads to a fiery explosion at a gasoline station.

   View the clip several times, and take as much time as you need to observe the events that take place. Keep the following questions in mind as you view.

NOW VIEW

FIRST VIEWING: Comprehension

1. **Summarize** What happens from the point at which the man crashes his car until the end of the clip?

2. **Recall** Where is Melanie in most of this scene?

CLOSE VIEWING: Media Literacy

3. **Make Inferences** Describe what you think are Melanie's thoughts and feelings as she witnesses the unfolding events.

4. **Analyze Techniques** What types of shots does Hitchcock use to convey the tense nature of Melanie's situation?

5. **Analyze Mood** In terms of mood and atmosphere, how is the very beginning of the clip different from the ending?

6. **Draw Conclusions** In folklore and other works of literature, the sighting of a bird often signals the coming of chaos. Why do you think a familiar device like the sighting of a bird would appeal to a director known for suspenseful thrillers?

7. **Evaluate Style** A **set piece** is a scene staged so skillfully that it serves as a textbook example of a filmmaking technique or style. The phone booth scene you've viewed is a famous set piece. Review the details about Hitchcock's work on page 771. Explain what examples of Hitchcock's style you think are effectively represented in this scene.

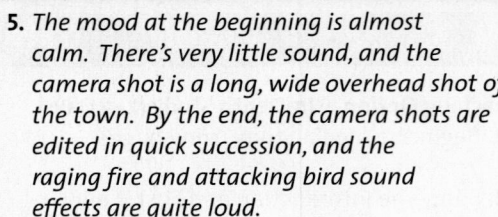

5. *The mood at the beginning is almost calm. There's very little sound, and the camera shot is a long, wide overhead shot of the town. By the end, the camera shots are edited in quick succession, and the raging fire and attacking bird sound effects are quite loud.*

6. *Birds are usually viewed as benevolent, so their use as an omen of chaos probably appealed to Hitchcock, who liked to present threats that come from unlikely places.*

7. *Ordinary people are caught up in frightening circumstances; danger threatens a normally peaceful setting; point of view shots, reaction shots, and close-ups build tension and take viewers inside characters' panic and fear; shot selection and pacing get faster as the action gets more intense.*

Write or Discuss

Analyzing Hitchcock's Style Here are more quotes from Alfred Hitchcock about his approach to moviemaking. Choose one that you think comes closest to the stylistic techniques used in the scene. Support your opinion with evidence.

- "Give them [the audience] pleasure—the same pleasure they have when they wake up from a nightmare."
- "If it's a good movie, the sound could go off and the audience would still have a perfectly clear idea of what was going on."
- "Always make the audience suffer as much as possible."

Produce Your Own Media

Create a Production Still Imagine you're part of a team promoting a new, Hitchcock-styled version of a fairy tale or folktale. Create a production still for the movie in the style of Hitchcock. A **production** or **promotional still** is a photograph taken during the making of a film. Sometimes a still shows an actual scene from the movie or an image that represents the highlights.

HERE'S HOW Here are a few suggestions for making the production still:

- Choose a familiar tale on which to base the production still.
- To add Hitchcock-flavored twists, think about how to take any familiar element of the tale to a thrilling extreme. Draw a sketch of a daytime setting that is ordinarily a safe public place. Then draw a sketch that includes elements of danger in the same setting.

MEDIA TOOLS

For help with creating a production still, visit the **Media Center** at **ClassZone.com**.

Tech Tip

Search the Internet for more images of Hitchcock's threatening settings.

PROFESSIONAL MODELS

These images are production stills from *North by Northwest.*

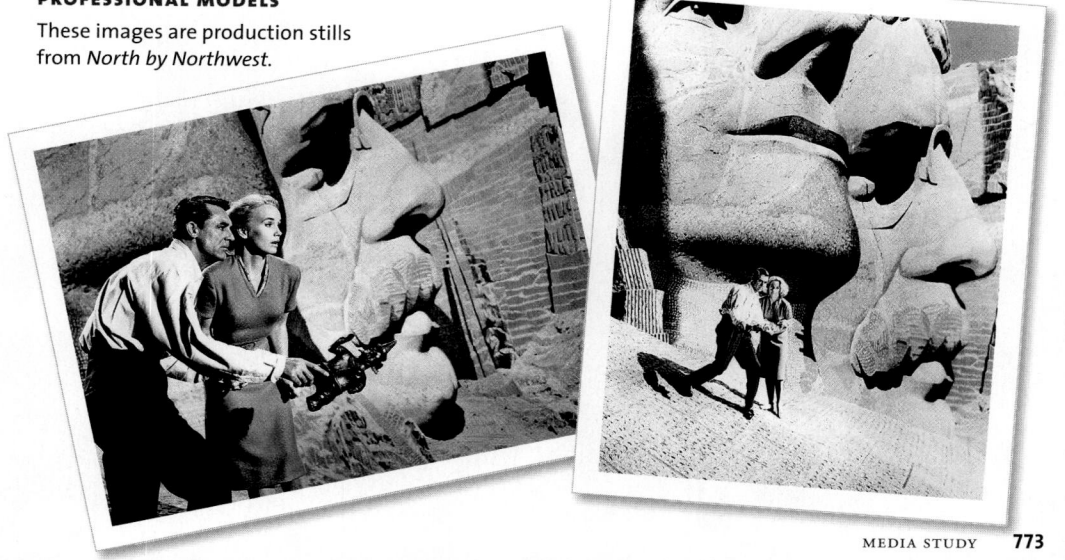

Assess and Reteach

Write or Discuss

Analyze Hitchcock's Style Students should cite specific elements from the clip to support their opinions. For example, for the second statement, students might point out that there is almost no sound in the clip. The quick cuts from inside the phone booth to horrific events outside would be enough to explain the situation and frighten the audience. For the last statement, students might point out how claustrophobic the phone booth is and the way in which point of view shots and reaction shots make the viewer suffer along with the main character. Encourage students to include their own personal reactions to the clip as support.

Produce Your Own Media

Rubric: Create a Production Still The production still should show a scene that

- represents a highlight from the story
- reflects a familiar tale but also includes a Hitchcock-type twist
- is dramatic
- encourages viewers to see the movie

R RESOURCE MANAGER—Copy Master
   Produce Your Own Media p. 74

MEDIA STUDY WRAP-UP

Have students summarize what they have learned about creating a style in movies. Encourage them to use terms such as *theme, atmosphere, point of view shots, reaction shots, camera placement, shot selection, pacing, editing,* and *quick cuts* in their explanations.

RETEACH

S STANDARDS LESSON FILE
   Media Lesson 4: Analyzing Visuals in Film and TV
   Media Lesson 6: Analyzing Editing in Film and TV

Focus and Motivate

OBJECTIVES

Literary Analysis
- explore the key idea of feeling **out of place**
- analyze humor
- read an essay

Reading
- summarize

Vocabulary
- build vocabulary for reading and writing
- understand connotation and denotation of words *(also an EL language objective)*

SUMMARY

"Going to Japan" is an amusing and thought-provoking essay in which Barbara Kingsolver describes a trip she took to Japan. She relates her experiences trying to fit into an unfamiliar culture and explains how she learned an important lesson about the value of forgiveness.

Have you ever felt
OUT OF PLACE?

Ask the question. After students have read the *KEY IDEA* paragraph, discuss situations in which a person might feel **out of place.** Have students complete the *QUICKWRITE.* Then encourage volunteers to share their paragraphs with the class.

Selection Resources

Going to Japan
Essay by Barbara Kingsolver

Have you ever felt
OUT OF PLACE?

KEY IDEA You know the feeling—that sinking sense of not quite fitting in. Pretty much everybody feels **out of place** at some point, whether it's at a party where you don't know anyone or on your first day at a new school in a new town. In "Going to Japan," Barbara Kingsolver describes a time when she felt totally out of her element. She relates the blunders she made as she tried to blend in.

QUICKWRITE In a paragraph, describe a situation in which you felt out of place. Include all the details you can remember—even the embarrassing ones! What about the situation made you feel self-conscious? Did you eventually relax and feel better, or were you uncomfortable the whole time?

R RESOURCE MANAGER UNIT 8

Plan and Teach pp. 75–82

Literary Analysis
Summary pp. 83†*, 84‡*
Humor pp. 85, 86†*
Question Support p. 94*

Reading
Summarize pp. 87, 88†*
Reading Check p. 93

Vocabulary
Study p. 89*
Practice p. 90
Strategy p. 91

Assessment
Selection Tests A, B/C pp. 95*, 97*
 Test Generator CD

BEST PRACTICES TOOLKIT

Differentiated Instruction
pp. 31–38*

Scaffolding Instruction
pp. 43–46*

Graphic Organizers/Strategies
Cluster Diagram • Word Squares
• Think-Pair-Share

Reading Support
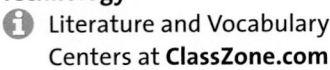 Audio Anthology CD*

Technology
🛈 Literature and Vocabulary Centers at **ClassZone.com**
WriteSmart CD

---

* Resources for Differentiation   † Also in Spanish   ‡ In Haitian Creole and Vietnamese

● LITERARY ANALYSIS: HUMOR

Have you ever used a joke to get your point across? Writers often use **humor** to convey a perspective on a topic. Humor is expressed through description and word choice that create surprise and amusement. The following techniques are common devices of humor:

- **Hyperbole:** exaggeration of the truth
- **Irony:** a contrast between what you expect to happen and what actually happens
- **Wordplay:** verbal wit, when a writer plays with words and word sounds

In this essay, Kingsolver presents an exaggerated account of how she felt out of place in Japan. "When I stepped on a streetcar," she writes, "a full head taller than all the other passengers, I became an awkward giant." As you read, consider how the writer felt Japanese people perceived her. Note passages that you find humorous.

● READING SKILL: SUMMARIZE

When you **summarize**, you use your own words to restate the main points and important details of what you've read. As you read, use a chart like the one shown to record the important details presented in each of the essay's three parts. In your own words, sum up the main point of each part.

Part	Details Included	Main Point
Part I: lines 1–15		
Part II: lines 16–59		
Part III: lines 60–91		

▲ VOCABULARY IN CONTEXT

The boldfaced words help Kingsolver turn her embarrassing experiences into funny anecdotes. Write sentences showing the meaning of each boldfaced word as you understand it.

1. showed defiance by speaking **brazenly**
2. felt **mortified** when her father sang in public
3. **cede** control to the new student council president
4. accepted his **abject** apology
5. a **baleful** and frightening threat

A Scientific Leaning Though Barbara Kingsolver began writing stories and essays as a child, she never dreamed she'd someday become a professional author. The writers she read, she explains, "were mostly old, dead men from England. It was inconceivable that I might grow up to be one of those myself." Kingsolver majored in biology in college, but also took one creative writing class—and found she loved it.

Barbara Kingsolver
born 1955

Writing for Change Kingsolver wrote her first novel holed up in a closet, typing while her husband slept. Her dedication paid off, and *The Bean Trees* was a critical and popular success. Kingsolver is now an award-winning author of essays, novels, and short stories. She believes that literature can be a force for social change. "I'm extremely interested in cultural difference," Kingsolver says, "in social and political history, and [in] the sparks that fly when people with different ways of looking at the world come together."

 MORE ABOUT THE AUTHOR
For more on Barbara Kingsolver, visit the **Literature Center** at **ClassZone.com**.

Background

Hiroshima On August 6, 1945, at a crucial moment in World War II, the U.S. dropped the first atomic bomb on the Japanese city of Hiroshima. The bomb destroyed the city and killed 80,000 people almost instantly; thousands more died later from radiation illness and other injuries. The city of Hiroshima has been rebuilt and is now at the center of a movement to abolish atomic weapons. Ground Zero, where the bomb fell, is now home to Peace Memorial Park.

Teach

STANDARDS FOCUS

LITERARY ANALYSIS

● HUMOR

To support instruction, read aloud this example:

> Eric was the kind of kid everyone referred to as a "brainiac." He was amazingly smart—*annoyingly* smart. I'm sure that as a toddler, he could fish the letters out of his alphabet soup and spell Latin phrases.

Have students explain how the writer uses humor to convey ideas. ***Possible answer:*** *The writer uses hyperbole to suggest how smart Eric is by exaggerating his ability.*

CHECK UNDERSTANDING Have students suggest examples of hyperbole, irony, and word play.

READING SKILL

■ SUMMARIZE

Use the paragraph under **A Scientific Leaning** to model summarizing: *Barbara Kingsolver never expected to become a professional author. In fact, she majored in biology in college.*

CHECK UNDERSTANDING Have students summarize **Writing for Change.**

🅡 RESOURCE MANAGER—Copy Master
Summarize p. 87 for student use while reading the selection

VOCABULARY SKILL

▲ VOCABULARY IN CONTEXT

DIAGNOSE WORD KNOWLEDGE To determine preteaching needs, have all students complete Vocabulary in Context. Students' sentences should reflect their understanding of the words as defined on the selection pages:
1. *brazenly* p. 778, 2. *mortified* p. 778, 3. *cede* p. 779, 4. *abject* p. 779, 5. *baleful* p. 779.

PRETEACH VOCABULARY Use the Vocabulary Study copy master to help students predict the meaning of each boldfaced word in the copy master.

1. Read item 1 aloud, emphasizing *brazenly*.
2. Point out the phrase "Although she meant to be polite." Elicit possible meanings for *brazenly*, such as "utterly."
3. Repeat the procedure for items 2–5.

🅡 RESOURCE MANAGER—Copy Master
Vocabulary Study p. 89

For general guidelines on differentiating vocabulary instruction and for alternative vocabulary activities for students not needing vocabulary preteaching, see

 BEST PRACTICES TOOLKIT
Scaffolding Vocabulary Instruction pp. 43–46
ⓘ Vocabulary Center at **ClassZone.com**

ANALYZE VISUALS

Possible answer: The top photograph shows a woman seated on a bench, while the background photographs are close-ups of shoes, with no person in sight. The woman in the top photograph is wearing Western-style clothing, while the shoes in the background photographs are traditional Japanese sandals. The top photo is set at an angle, and the woman's legs are slanting inward. The background photos are all aligned vertically, and the sandals themselves are vertical rather than slanting.

Ⓐ HUMOR

Possible answer: Kingsolver's breezy, informal tone suggests that this will be a humorous essay, as do the references to the "Aunt Zelda" game, with its silly lists of items (lines 1–2, 14–15).

If students need help . . .

- Have students draw a Cluster Diagram for each of the humor devices listed on page 775.

- In the circles around each word, have students list examples from the story as they read.

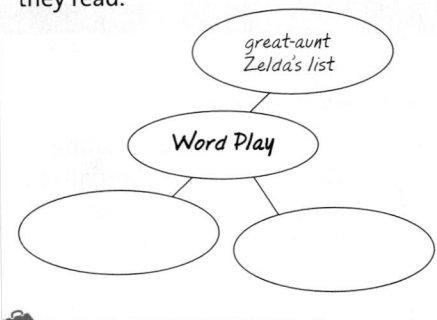

BEST PRACTICES TOOLKIT—Transparency
Cluster Diagram p. B18

Going to Japan

Barbara Kingsolver

My great-aunt Zelda went to Japan and took an abacus, a bathysphere, a conundrum, a diatribe, an eggplant. That was a game we used to play. All you had to do was remember everything in alphabetical order. Right up to Aunt Zelda.

Then I grew up and was actually invited to go to Japan, not with the fantastic Aunt Zelda but as myself. As such, I had no idea what to take. I knew what I planned to be doing: researching a story about the memorial at Hiroshima;[1] visiting friends; trying not to get lost in a place where I couldn't even read the street signs. Times being what they were—*any* times—I intended to do my
10 very best to respect the cultural differences, avoid sensitive topics I might not comprehend, and, in short, be anything but an Ugly American. When I travel, I like to try to blend in. I've generally found it helps to be prepared. So I asked around, and was warned to expect a surprisingly modern place.

My great-aunt Zelda went to Japan and took Appliances, Battery packs, Cellular technology. . . . That seemed to be the idea. Ⓐ

And so it came to pass that I arrived in Kyoto[2] an utter foreigner, unprepared. It's true that there are electric streetcars there, and space-age gas stations with uniformed attendants who rush to help you from all directions at once. There are also golden pagodas[3] on shimmering lakes, and Shinto shrines[4]

---

1. **the memorial at Hiroshima** (hĭ-rō′shə-mə): The Hiroshima Peace Memorial Park commemorates the deaths and destruction caused by the U.S. bombing of Hiroshima near the end of World War II.
2. **Kyoto** (kē-ō′tō): A Japanese city rich in history and culture, Kyoto was the nation's capital from 794 until 1868.
3. **pagodas** (pə-gō′dəz): sacred buildings of the Buddhist religion, typically towers with many levels.
4. **Shinto shrines**: shrines from the Shinto religion, one of the main religions of Japan.

776   UNIT 8: AUTHOR'S STYLE AND VOICE

ANALYZE VISUALS

Examine the collage on page 777. Name three elements that contribute to how out of place the photograph on top looks against the background images.

❶ Targeted Passage

Ⓐ HUMOR

What clues in lines 1–15 hint that this will be a humorous essay? Explain your answer, citing evidence.

FOR ALL STUDENTS

Expert Groups Allow students to become experts or members of expert groups by researching and sharing additional information about one of these topics. Suggest that they include pictures.

- the city of Kyoto, Japan
- Hiroshima, before, during, and after World War II
- Japanese customs and traditions

FOR LESS–PROFICIENT READERS

In combination with the *Audio Anthology CD*, use one or more Targeted Passages (pp. 776, 778, 779) to ensure that students focus on key events, concepts, and skills. Targeted Passages are also good for English learners.

❶ Targeted Passage [Lines 1–15]

This passage explains the reason for Kingsolver's trip, reveals her feelings about it, and introduces the "Aunt Zelda" game.

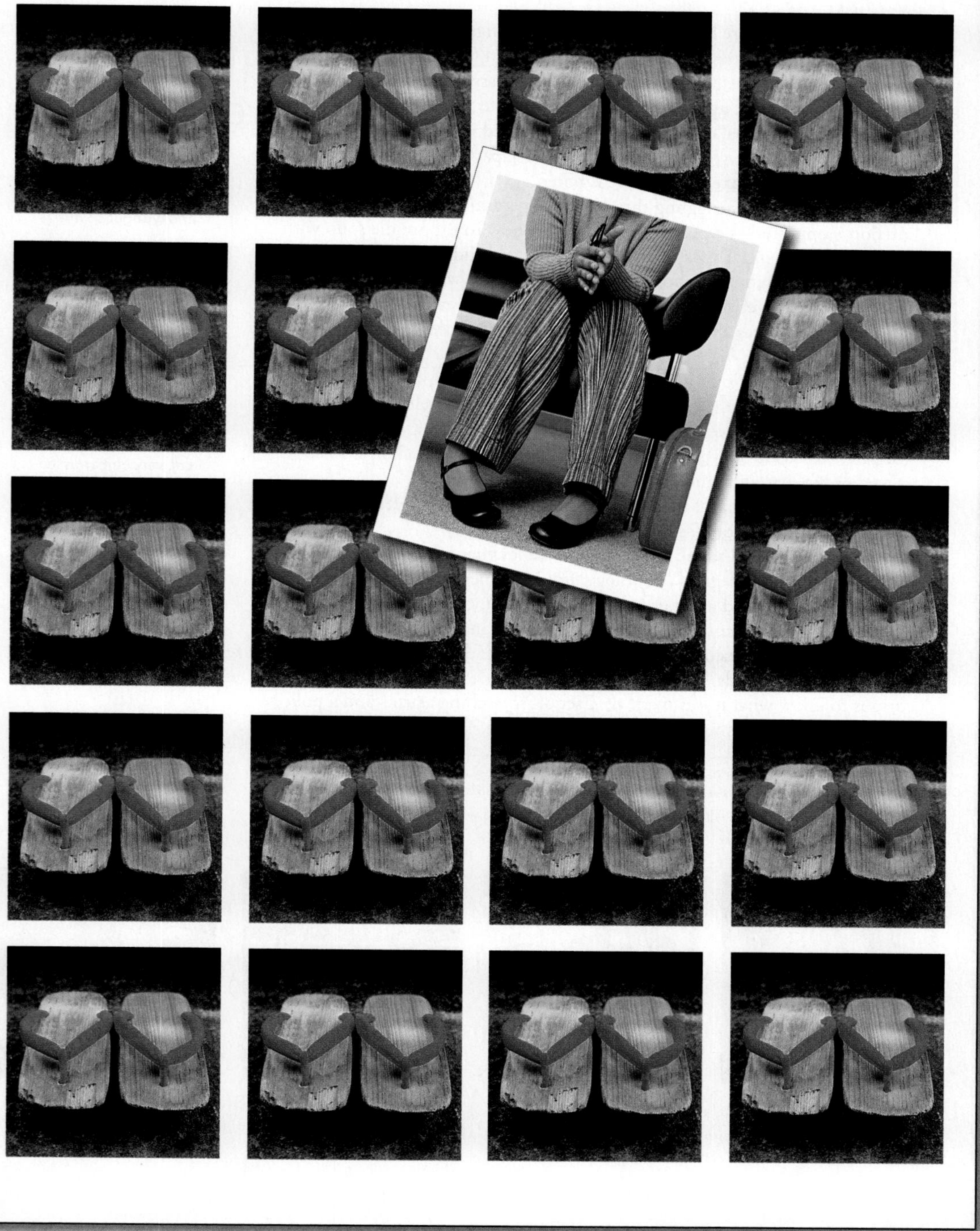

BACKGROUND

The Ugly American The term "Ugly American" (line 11) refers to an obnoxious, thoughtless American in a foreign country whose behavior offends the local people. The term comes from the 1958 bestseller *The Ugly American*, by Eugene Burdick and William Lederer. A collection of linked short stories set in Southeast Asia during the 1950s, the book was an attack on U.S. foreign policy and cultural arrogance in the period leading up to the Vietnam War. Ironically, the title character is a physically ugly American engineer who is in fact culturally sensitive—the very opposite of the type of American the book criticizes and the term has come to signify.

Lines 9–11
REINFORCE *KEY IDEA:* OUT OF PLACE

Discuss Kingsolver is determined to "respect the cultural differences" of Japan and not be an "Ugly American." How might being perceived as an Ugly American make an American visitor to a foreign country feel **out of place?** *Possible answer: An American visitor to a foreign country who was perceived as an Ugly American would not be welcomed by the local people and consequently might feel out of place—if that Ugly American were even aware of how he or she was perceived.*

- Why is the author going to Japan?
- What challenges does Kingsolver expect to face in Japan?
- How does the author feel about visiting a different culture?
- How are lines 1–2 and lines 14–15 similar? How are they different?

FOR ENGLISH LEARNERS

Key Academic Vocabulary Use Word Squares to teach these words: *topics* (line 10), *guidelines* (line 21), *infinite* (line 42), *approximately* (line 44), *presumption* (line 61).

 BEST PRACTICES TOOLKIT—Transparency Word Squares p. E10

Prereading For prereading instruction for English learners, see

 BEST PRACTICES TOOLKIT Scaffolding Reading Instruction pp. 43–46

FOR ADVANCED LEARNERS/PRE-AP

Pre-AP Exercises in the bottom channel provide additional challenge for students. Use these suggestions for small groups or individuals.

ADDITIONAL GUIDELINES

For more help with differentiation and tips for classroom management, see

 BEST PRACTICES TOOLKIT Differentiated Instruction pp. 31–38

DISCUSSION PROMPTS

Use these prompts to help students understand how Kingsolver feels in Japan:

Connect Think of a time when you were not sure what to do or say because you did not understand the "invisible guidelines" (line 21). How did you feel? *Students may mention experiences traveling or trying to fit in with a social group.*

Analyze How does Kingsolver's ignorance of Japanese customs lead to her embarrassment? *Possible answers: She crossed her arms, unintentionally signaling her boredom (lines 24–26); she ate soup "picturesquely wrong" (lines 28–29).*

Evaluate Do you think that Kingsolver could have avoided some of the embarrassment that she experienced? Explain your answer. *Possible answer: Yes—if she had prepared better for her trip, learning more about Japanese ways and expectations, she might have been able to avoid potentially embarrassing situations.*

LITERARY ANALYSIS

B HUMOR

Possible answer: Kingsolver changes the alphabetical list to fit with whatever anecdotes she is telling at that point in the essay. She chooses amusing items to include in the lists, such as "Altitude"—referring to her height—and "Bare-naked legs."

If students need help . . .

- Have students compare lines 39–40 with lines 14–15. Discuss how the lines are similar and how they differ.
- Have students read lines 21–24. Ask which item in line 39 refers to this anecdote.
- Have students read lines 34–38. Ask which item in line 39 refers to this anecdote.

---

20 in the forests. There are bamboo groves and nightingales. And finally there are more invisible guidelines for politeness than I could fathom. When I stepped on a streetcar, a full head taller than all the other passengers, I became an awkward giant. I took up too much space. I blended in like Igor would blend in with the corps de ballet in *Swan Lake.*[5] I bumped into people. I crossed my arms when I listened, which turns out to be, in Japanese body language, the sign for indicating **brazenly** that one is bored.

But I wasn't! I was struggling through my days and nights in the grip of boredom's opposite—i.e., panic. I didn't know how to eat noodle soup with chopsticks, and I did it most picturesquely *wrong.* I didn't know how to order, 30 so I politely deferred to my hosts and more than once was served a cuisine with heads, including eyeballs. I managed to wrestle these creatures to my lips with chopsticks, but it was already too late by the time I got the message that *one does not spit out anything.*

I undertook this trip in high summer, when it is surprisingly humid and warm in southern Japan. I never imagined that in such sweltering heat women would be expected to wear stockings, but every woman in Kyoto wore nylon stockings. Coeds in shorts *on the tennis court* wore nylon stockings. I had packed only skirts and sandals; people averted their eyes.

When I went to Japan I took my Altitude, my Bare-naked legs, my Callous 40 foreign ways. I was **mortified.** B

My hosts explained to me that the Japanese language does not accommodate insults, only infinite degrees of apology. I quickly memorized an urgent one, *"Sumimasen,"* and another for especially extreme cases, *"Moshi wake gozaimasen."*[6] This translates approximately to mean, "If you please, my transgression is so inexcusable that I wish I were dead."

I needed these words. When I touched the outside surface of a palace wall, curious to know what it was made of, I set off screeching alarms and a police car came scooting up the lawn's discreet gravel path. *"Moshi wake gozaimasen,*

② Targeted Passage

brazenly
(brā′zən-lē′) *adv.* boldly and without shame

mortified (môr′tə-fīd′) *adj.* very embarrassed; humiliated **mortify** *v.*

B HUMOR
Kingsolver repeats this alphabetical **word play** throughout the essay. How does this contribute to the humor of the piece? Explain your answer.

---

5. **Igor . . . corps de ballet** (kôr′də bǎ-lā′) **in** *Swan Lake:* Igor is the clumsy assistant in many Frankenstein movies. *Swan Lake* is a Russian ballet composed by Peter Ilich Tchaikovsky (chī-kôf′skē).

6. *Sumimasen* (soō-mē-mä-sěn′) . . . *Moshi wake gozaimasen* (mō-shē wä-kě gō-zī-mä-sěn).

DIFFERENTIATED INSTRUCTION

FOR LESS—PROFICIENT READERS

② Targeted Passage [Lines 21–33]

In this passage, Kingsolver describes some of the experiences that made her feel out of place during her visit.

- What experiences caused the author to feel out of place in Japan?
- Kingsolver's account is amusing, but do you think she found her experiences funny at the time? Explain.

FOR ENGLISH LEARNERS

Vocabulary: Phrasal Verbs Point out these phrasal verbs: *blend in* (line 23), *turns out* (line 25), *set off* (line 47), *fall short of* (line 73), *gave [myself] away* (line 77). Elicit or provide their meaning. Then have students find other examples in the essay and discuss their meaning.

Officer! Wish I were dead!" And in the public bath, try as I might, I couldn't
50 get the hang of showering with a hand-held nozzle while sitting fourteen inches
from a stranger. I sprayed my elderly neighbor with cold water. In the face.

"*Moshi wake gozaimasen,*" I declared, with feeling.

She merely stared, dismayed by the foreign menace. **G**

I visited a Japanese friend, and in her small, perfect house I spewed out
my misery. "Everything I do is wrong!" I wailed like a child. "I'm a blight
on your country."

"Oh, no," she said calmly. "To forgive, for us, is the highest satisfaction.
To forgive a foreigner, ah! Even better." She smiled. "You have probably made
many people happy here."

60 To stomp about the world ignoring cultural differences is arrogant, to
be sure, but perhaps there is another kind of arrogance in the presumption
that we may ever really build a faultless bridge from one shore to another,
or even know where the mist has **ceded** to landfall. When I finally arrived
at Ground Zero in Hiroshima, I stood speechless. What I found there was
a vast and exquisitely silent monument to forgiveness. I was moved beyond
words, even beyond tears, to think of all that can be lost or gained in the gulf
between any act of will and its consequences. In the course of every failure of
understanding, we have so much to learn.

I remembered my Japanese friend's insistence on forgiveness as the highest
70 satisfaction, and I understood it really for the first time: What a rich wisdom
it would be, and how much more bountiful a harvest, to gain pleasure not
from achieving personal perfection but from understanding the inevitability
of imperfection and pardoning those who also fall short of it. **D**

I have walked among men and made mistakes without number. When I
went to Japan I took my **Abject** goodwill, my **Baleful** excuses, my Cringing
remorse. I couldn't remember everything, could not even recite the proper
alphabet. So I gave myself away instead, evidently as a kind of public service.
I prepared to return home feeling empty-handed.

At the Osaka[7] Airport I sat in my plane on the runway, waiting to leave for
80 terra cognita,[8] as the aircraft's steel walls were buffeted by the sleet and winds
of a typhoon. We waited for an hour, then longer, with no official word from
the cockpit, and then suddenly our flight was canceled. Air traffic control in
Tokyo had been struck by lightning; no flights possible until the following day.

"We are so sorry," the pilot told us. "You will be taken to a hotel, fed, and
brought back here for your flight tomorrow."

As we passengers rose slowly and disembarked, we were met by an airline
official who had been posted in the exit port for the sole purpose of saying
to each and every one of us, "Terrible, terrible. *Sumimasen.*" Other travelers
nodded indifferently, but not me. I took the startled gentleman by the hands
90 and practically kissed him.

"You have no idea," I told him, "how thoroughly I forgive you." ❧

---

7. **Osaka** (ō-sä′kə).
8. **terra cognita** (tĕr′ə kŏg-nē′tə): Latin for "a familiar land or country."

GOING TO JAPAN   **779**

G HUMOR
Reread lines 49–53.
Do you think that
accidentally splashing
someone is grounds for
being labeled a "foreign
menace"? Identify the
humorous technique
Kingsolver uses here.

cede (sēd) *v.* to give up;
give way

3 Targeted Passage

D SUMMARIZE
What is Kingsolver's
main point in lines
69–73? Summarize the
feelings she expresses
about forgiveness in
this passage.

abject (ăb′-jĕkt′) *adj.*
exceedingly humble

baleful (bāl′fəl) *adj.*
evil; destructive

LITERARY ANALYSIS

G HUMOR

Possible answer: *No. Kingsolver is using hyperbole to make the anecdote amusing.*

Extend the Discussion What do you suppose the elderly woman was thinking before—and after—Kingsolver apologized?

READING SKILL

D SUMMARIZE

Possible answer: *People can derive far more satisfaction from accepting and forgiving human error than they can from striving to be perfect.*

If students need help . . .

• Discuss with students the meaning of the phrase "inevitability of imperfection" (lines 72–73).

• Point out that if imperfection is indeed inevitable, then striving for perfection can only lead to frustration. It would be much wiser to pardon "those who . . . fall short of it" (line 73).

SELECTION WRAP-UP

SUMMARIZE Ask students to summarize what they consider to be Kingsolver's purpose in writing "Going to Japan." If she has more than one purpose, which is the most important? Have students explain and support their answers.

⭐ **CRITIQUE** Ask students to explain what aspect of Kingsolver's essay they enjoyed the most and why.

FOR LESS-PROFICIENT READERS

3 Targeted Passage [Lines 63–73]

In this passage, Kingsolver describes her reaction to Ground Zero and summarizes what she learned as a result of visiting the site.

• What was the author's reaction to Ground Zero in Hiroshima?

• What did she come to understand about perfection and forgiveness as a result of her visit?

FOR ENGLISH LEARNERS

Vocabulary: Word Associations Use Think-Pair-Share to explore the meaning of these phrases: *And so it came to pass* (line 16), *try as I might* (line 49), *stood speechless* (line 64), *was moved beyond words* (lines 65–66), *'You have no idea'* (line 91). Elicit from students additional associations of the same type.

📦 **BEST PRACTICES TOOLKIT—Transparency** Think-Pair-Share p. A18

Practice and Apply

After Reading

For additional support of post-reading questions, use these copy masters:

R RESOURCE MANAGER—Copy Masters

Reading Check p. 93 (to check understanding of the selection)

Humor p. 85 (for practice of literary
analysis standards focus)

Question Support p. 94 (After Reading
questions adapted for English learners
and less-proficient readers)

Additional selection questions are
provided for teachers on page 79.

ANSWERS

Comprehension

1. *Kingsolver went to Japan to research a story about the memorial at Hiroshima and to visit friends.*

2. *Kingsolver was "a full head taller" than most Japanese people, "took up too much space," and "bumped into people" (lines 22–24); she "didn't know how to eat noodle soup with chopsticks" (lines 28–29); Japanese women wore stockings despite the heat, but Kingsolver did not (lines 35–38); Kingsolver "couldn't get the hang of showering with a hand-held nozzle" (lines 49–51).*

Literary Analysis

Possible answers:

3. *Kingsolver has just had a revelation about forgiveness (people gain far more from forgiving human error than from striving to be perfect), so when the official apologizes to her, she is touched and wants him to know "how thoroughly" she forgives him.*

4. *The essay's central irony is that Kingsolver is determined to blend in and "be anything but an Ugly American" (lines 11–12), yet she ends up making cultural blunders and feeling like a foreigner. For example, she is eager to please, but when she crosses her arms, she unintentionally signals boredom (lines 24–26). Ironically, Kingsolver makes people happy by doing things wrong, because in Japan "to forgive . . . is the highest satisfaction" (line 57). Another irony is that after begging others to forgive her, at the end of the essay, she is the one who is gratefully forgiving an airline official (lines 89–91).*

780 UNIT 8: AUTHOR'S STYLE AND VOICE

Comprehension

1. **Recall** Why did the author go to Japan?

2. **Recall** List three examples Kingsolver gives to illustrate her inability to blend in on her trip to Japan.

Literary Analysis

3. **Draw Conclusions** Why did Kingsolver react so strongly to the airline official's apology while her fellow travelers simply "nodded indifferently"? Explain, citing evidence from the selection to support your conclusion.

4. **Identify Irony** This essay is filled with examples of **situational irony,** the contrast between what a reader or character expects and what actually exists or happens. Identify three examples of situational irony and explain what is ironic about each.

5. **Summarize** Review the chart you filled in as you read. Taken together, what do the details you recorded reveal about Kingsolver's overall message? Summarize the author's **main point** in your own words.

6. **Analyze Tone** How would you describe Kingsolver's tone in this essay? Use a graphic like the one shown to record striking or unusual words and phrases from the essay. Then describe the tone Kingsolver's **word choice** helps create.

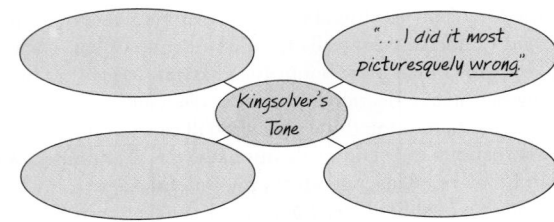

"...I did it most picturesquely wrong."

Kingsolver's Tone

7. **Evaluate Humor** Review the bulleted list of humorous techniques on page 775, and think about how Kingsolver uses humor to communicate her perspective. In your opinion, which technique best helps Kingsolver to convey her thoughts and feelings in a funny way? Give examples from the essay to support your answer.

Literary Criticism

8. **Different Perspectives** Kingsolver is a writer who has long been fascinated by cultural differences and who works to make others see these differences as unique and positive. Would someone less attuned to cultural differences have felt as **out of place** as Kingsolver did? Explain, citing evidence from "Going to Japan" to support your opinion.

780 UNIT 8: AUTHOR'S STYLE AND VOICE

---

5. ■ **STANDARDS FOCUS** *Summarize We all make mistakes, even when trying our best not to. We can derive far more benefit from accepting and forgiving inevitable human error than from striving to be perfect.*

6. *"I blended in like Igor . . ." (line 23); "I got the message that one does not spit out anything" (lines 32–33); "'I'm a blight on your country'" (lines 55–56). Such phrases create a humorous, self-mocking tone.*

7. ● **STANDARDS FOCUS** *Humor Students should support their opinions with examples from the text.*

Literary Criticism

8. *Some students might respond that Japanese culture is so different from American culture (as in its attitude toward apologizing) that even a person not particularly attuned to cultural differences would feel very out of place. Other students might say that Kingsolver was overly sensitive and that most people would have been less troubled than she by relatively minor cultural gaffes (such as eating noodle soup incorrectly).*

Vocabulary in Context

VOCABULARY PRACTICE

Decide whether these statements are true or false.

1. You might be **mortified** if you get the lowest test score in the class.
2. Hearing a **baleful** speech is likely to frighten or anger many people.
3. If you speak **brazenly,** your parents will probably compliment you on your politeness.
4. Mornings usually **cede** to afternoons.
5. **Abject** flattery has to do with praising someone's choice of clothing.

> **WORD LIST**
> abject
> baleful
> brazenly
> cede
> mortified

VOCABULARY IN WRITING

Write sentences describing the author's embarrassing mishaps in Japan. Use three or more vocabulary words.

> **EXAMPLE SENTENCE**
> Kingsolver was **mortified** by how clumsily she wielded her chopsticks.

VOCABULARY STRATEGY: APPROPRIATE WORD CHOICE

To communicate effectively, you should consider several factors when choosing your words. One is a word's **denotation**—its surface meaning or definition. The other is the word's **connotation,** or the overtone of meaning it carries beyond its surface definition. Saying that "Jake spoke *brazenly*," for example, has a stronger negative connotation than saying he spoke *boldly.* Another factor to consider is the formality of the situation. A word like *cede* is rather formal and might sound inappropriate in casual speech or writing.

PRACTICE Choose the word or phrase that is more appropriate in each situation.

1. In a negative review of a singer: Her voice was (shrill, high-pitched).
2. In a letter to a friend: We were (taken in by a con artist, duped by a charlatan).
3. In a formal report: Dr. White was (uptight, apprehensive) about the decision.
4. In a letter of recommendation: He has a (reserved, tight-lipped) but friendly manner.

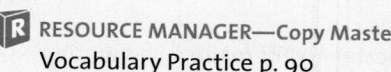 **VOCABULARY PRACTICE**
For more practice, go to the **Vocabulary Center** at ClassZone.com.

DIFFERENTIATED INSTRUCTION

FOR LESS–PROFICIENT READERS

Concept Support: Connotation To build understanding of the implied meanings of words, explore the differences between pairs of synonyms, such as *determined* and *stubborn, crowd* and *mob, meal* and *feast, skinny* and *slender.* Have students use the words in pairs of sentences and then compare their shades of meaning.

FOR ADVANCED LEARNERS/PRE–AP

Vocabulary in Writing Have students use at least four vocabulary words in a paragraph suggesting how *not* to feel out of place in new situations.

ANSWERS

Vocabulary in Context

VOCABULARY PRACTICE

1. *true*
2. *true*
3. *false*
4. *true*
5. *false*

R RESOURCE MANAGER—Copy Master
Vocabulary Practice p. 90

VOCABULARY IN WRITING

Suggest that students write sentences telling why each incident was embarrassing for the author.

VOCABULARY STRATEGY: APPROPRIATE WORD CHOICE *(also an EL language objective)*

Discuss with students how an author's word choice can affect tone.

Answers:

1. *shrill*
2. *taken in by a con artist*
3. *apprehensive*
4. *reserved*

R RESOURCE MANAGER—Copy Master
Vocabulary Strategy p. 91

i Vocabulary Center at **ClassZone.com**
Additional Vocabulary Activities

Assess and Reteach

Assess

R RESOURCE MANAGER—Copy Masters
Selection Test A pp. 95–96
Selection Test B/C pp. 97–98

CD Test Generator CD

Reteach

S STANDARDS LESSON FILE
Literature Lesson 38: Verbal and Dramatic Irony
Research and Study Skills Lesson 13: Summarizing
Vocabulary Lesson 17: Denotation and Connotation

Focus and Motivate

OBJECTIVES

Literary Analysis
- explore the key idea of being labeled **cute**
- analyze tone
- read an essay

Reading
- paraphrase

Vocabulary
- build vocabulary for reading and writing
- understand homonyms *(also an EL language objective)*

Grammar and Writing
- use varied sentence types
- use writing to analyze literature

SUMMARY

"A Few Words" is a strongly worded essay in which Mary Oliver declares that, despite what many people think, nothing in nature is "cute." Oliver asserts that humans should stop viewing themselves as powerful masters of nature and instead see themselves as one part of a greater natural whole.

Is "CUTE" a compliment?

To lead into the **KEY IDEA,** discuss the qualities associated with the word **cute.** Ask the question, and after students read the paragraph, discuss how people use *cute.* For example, is the word applied to adults or just children? Is it applied equally to both genders? Which animals are described as *cute?* Have students complete the **DEBATE** activity. Then discuss which team won, and why.

Selection Resources

A Few Words
Essay by Mary Oliver

Is "CUTE" a compliment?

KEY IDEA Before you answer, think about it: What does **cute** really mean? Can you be cute and still be taken seriously? still be strong? still be respected? In this essay, Mary Oliver has a few words to say about what happens when we label something *cute.*

DEBATE With a group of classmates, jot down what comes to mind when you think of something cute. Would you want to be described this way? Form two teams and square off to settle the question of whether or not *cute* is a compliment.

782

RESOURCE MANAGER UNIT 8

Plan and Teach pp. 99–106

Literary Analysis
Summary pp. 107†*, 108‡*
Tone pp. 109, 110†*
Question Support p. 117*

Reading
Paraphrase pp. 111, 112†*
Reading Check p. 116

Vocabulary
Study p. 113*
Practice p. 114
Strategy p. 115

Grammar and Writing
Vary Sentence Types p. 118

Assessment
Selection Tests A, B/C pp. 119*, 121*
  Test Generator CD

BEST PRACTICES TOOLKIT

Differentiated Instruction
  pp. 31–38*

Scaffolding Instruction
  pp. 43–46*

Graphic Organizers/Strategies
Two-Column Chart • Definition Mapping

Reading Support
  Audio Anthology CD*

Technology
  Literature and Vocabulary Centers at **ClassZone.com**
  Write*Smart* CD

---

* Resources for Differentiation   † Also in Spanish   ‡ In Haitian Creole and Vietnamese

LITERARY ANALYSIS: TONE

A writer's **tone**, or attitude toward a subject, can subtly sneak up on you as you read or boldly hit you over the head in the first paragraph. By noticing a writer's choice of words and details, you can detect and analyze his or her tone. Mary Oliver begins this essay by declaring, "Nothing in the forest is charming." Her blunt statement immediately challenges a common perception of the forest and establishes her tone. As you read "A Few Words," note striking words, details, and images that Oliver uses, and consider the tone they convey.

READING STRATEGY: PARAPHRASE

To understand difficult passages or sentences, it is sometimes helpful to **paraphrase**, or restate the writer's ideas in your own words. When you paraphrase, be sure to

- restate both the main idea and any important details
- use simpler words than those in the original text

As you read, paraphrase this essay's difficult passages in a chart like the one shown.

Passage	My Paraphrase
"Gardens are charming, and man-made grottos, and there is a tranquility about some scenes of husbandry and agriculture that is charming—orderly rows of vegetation, or lazy herds, or the stalks of harvest lashed and leaning together." (lines 1–4)	Man-made elements of nature, like gardens and grottos, are pleasant. Some farm scenes, like orderly rows of crops, tame animals, and harvested produce, look peaceful and calm.

▲ VOCABULARY IN CONTEXT

Mary Oliver uses these words to make her case about the perils of cuteness. To see how many you already know, choose the word that makes sense in each phrase.

WORD LIST	deftness	stalk
	diminutive	valorous

1. a _____ of wheat standing tall in the field
2. the _____ of a quarterback eluding tacklers
3. a _____ teddy bear among larger toys
4. _____ action in the face of danger

Author Online

A Natural Writer
Mary Oliver has been mesmerized by the natural world ever since she was a child growing up in Ohio. She has also always been enthralled by poetry. "I decided very early that I wanted to write," she says. "It was the most exciting thing, the most powerful thing, the most wonderful thing to do with my life." So she did it. Many years and countless awards later, Oliver still loves writing. "I feel writing is work, and I feel it's also play—bound together," she explains.

Mary Oliver
born 1935

Perfecting a Gift Oliver has been described as an "indefatigable guide to the natural world." An ardent observer of nature, she writes about the mysteries and wisdom that it reveals to us. For inspiration, she takes solitary walks in the fields and woods, which she calls part of her writing process. "Walks work for me," she explains. Critics and readers agree with her: Oliver is the winner of numerous awards, including the Pulitzer Prize and a National Book Award. Despite her success, Oliver confesses, "I never have felt yet that I've done it right. This is the marvelous thing about language. It can always be done better."

 MORE ABOUT THE AUTHOR
For more on Mary Oliver, visit the
Literature Center at **ClassZone.com.**

Teach

STANDARDS FOCUS

● TONE

For instructional support, read aloud this example:

> Many people think that squirrels are cute. I am *not* one of those people. I have a bird feeder in my yard, and no matter what I do to keep the bushy-tailed bandits away, they treat the feeder as their own private snack bar.

Have students describe the writer's tone. Ask what words and images help to create this tone. **Possible answer:** *The writer's tone is light but annoyed. "Bushy-tailed bandits" and "private snack bar" set the tone.*

CHECK UNDERSTANDING Ask students what words or phrases the writer might have used to convey a more serious tone.

READING STRATEGY

◼ PARAPHRASE

Use the first two sentences under **A Natural Writer** to model paraphrasing for students: *Mary Oliver has always been fascinated by nature and excited by poetry.*

CHECK UNDERSTANDING Have students paraphrase **Perfecting a Gift.**

 RESOURCE MANAGER—Copy Master
Paraphrase p. 111 (for student use while reading the selection)

VOCABULARY SKILL

▲ VOCABULARY IN CONTEXT

DIAGNOSE WORD KNOWLEDGE To determine preteaching needs, have all students complete Vocabulary in Context. *Answers:* **1.** *stalk,* **2.** *deftness,* **3.** *diminutive,* **4.** *valorous*

PRETEACH VOCABULARY Use the Vocabulary Study copy master to help students predict meanings for each boldfaced word in the copy master.

1. Read the first item in Part A aloud, emphasizing *deftness.*
2. Point out the phrase "quickly and accurately." Elicit possible meanings for *deftness,* such as "skill."
3. Repeat the procedure for the other items.

 RESOURCE MANAGER—Copy Master
Vocabulary Study p. 113

For general guidelines on differentiating vocabulary instruction and for alternative vocabulary activities for students not needing vocabulary preteaching, see

🧰 **BEST PRACTICES TOOLKIT**
Scaffolding Vocabulary Instruction pp. 43–46
ℹ Vocabulary Center at **ClassZone.com**

Practice and Apply

Lines 6–9
REINFORCE *KEY IDEA*: CUTE

Discuss Oliver describes a fox "carrying the soiled wing of a gull," as other foxes "grab onto it and pull." How does this image support her point that foxes "are not adorable, or charming, or **cute**"? *Possible answer: Oliver is making clear that foxes are wild animals that kill other animals to survive. There is nothing "cute" about such behavior.*

A Few Words
Mary Oliver

Nothing in the forest is charming. Gardens are charming, and man-made grottos,[1] and there is a tranquility about some scenes of husbandry[2] and agriculture that is charming—orderly rows of vegetation, or lazy herds, or the **stalks** of harvest lashed and leaning together.

And nothing in the forest is cute. The dog fox is not cute, nor the little foxes. I watch them as they run up and down the dune. One is carrying the soiled wing of a gull; the others grab onto it and pull. They fly in and out of the blond grasses, their small teeth snapping. They are not adorable, or charming, or cute.

10   The owl is not cute. The milk snake is not cute, nor the spider in its web, nor the striped bass. Neither is the skunk cute, and its name is not "Flower." Nor is there a rabbit in the forest whose name is "Thumper," who is cute.

Toys are cute. But animals are not toys. Neither are trees, rivers, oceans, swamps, the Alps, the mockingbird singing all night in the bowers of thorn, the snapping turtle, or the purple-fleshed mushroom. Ⓐ

Such words—"cute," "charming," "adorable"—miss the mark, for what is perceived of in this way is stripped of dignity, and authority. What is cute is entertainment, and replaceable. The words lead us and we follow: what is cute is **diminutive,** it is powerless, it is capturable, it is trainable, it is ours. It is all a

20 mistake. At our feet are the ferns—savage and resolute they rose, when the race of man was *nowhere* and altogether unlikely ever to be at all, in the terrifying shallows of the first unnamed and unnameable oceans. We find them pretty, delicate, and charming, and carry them home to our gardens.

Thus we manage to put ourselves in the masterly way—if nature is full of a hundred thousand things adorable and charming, diminutive and powerless, then who is in the position of power? We are! We are the parents, and the

---

1. **man-made grottos** (grŏt'ōz): artificial caves created for coolness and pleasure.
2. **husbandry** (hŭz'bən-drē): farming.

784   UNIT 8: AUTHOR'S STYLE AND VOICE

stalk (stôk) *n.* a stem or main axis of a plant

Ⓘ **Targeted Passage**

Ⓐ **TONE**
Reread lines 1–15. How would you describe Oliver's tone? Identify the words and images the author uses to create this tone.

diminutive
(dĭ-mĭn'yə-tĭv) *adj.*
very small

DIFFERENTIATED INSTRUCTION

FOR ALL STUDENTS

Anchor Activity Provide independent learning opportunities for students to research examples of wildlife. Invite students to share information as they respond to Oliver's essay. For further details on this project, see

Ⓡ **RESOURCE MANAGER**
Ideas for Extension pp. 104–105

FOR LESS–PROFICIENT READERS

In combination with the *Audio Anthology CD*, use one or more Targeted Passages (pp. 784, 786) to ensure that students focus on key events, concepts, and skills. Targeted Passages are also good for English learners.

BACKGROUND

Cute Ironically, like nature, *cute* is a word that has been tamed over centuries of its usage. *Cute* is a shortened version of *acute*, a word that dates back to the Middle Ages when it described a brief but severe disease. By the 1500s, *acute* meant penetrating or sharp-witted, and by the 1700s, someone who was cute was thought to be clever, even devious or sly. Our modern sense of cute as pleasing or attractive was first used as slang by American students in 1834.

Cultural Connection Unlike the callous observer that Oliver criticizes, many cultures do not consider nature as something that can be controlled or described as something distinct from ourselves. In traditional Japanese culture, there was no separate word for nature, because every living thing is inter-related. Native peoples in Australia speak of "feeling" the land. Many Native Americans believe that they possess the spirit of the land within them, and the land is a conscious, living being. Invite students to share traditional beliefs and values they may have learned about nature.

---

① Targeted Passage [Lines 1–20]

This passage introduces one of Oliver's main points: nothing in nature is "cute."

- What does Oliver consider to be "charming"?
- According to Oliver, what is and is not "cute"?
- According to Oliver, what is the problem with using the word *cute?*

FOR ENGLISH LEARNERS

Key Academic Vocabulary Use Definition Mapping to teach these words: *perceived* (line 17), *authority* (line 17), *notion* (line 27), *facilitates* (line 27), *benefit* (line 35), *physical* (line 39).

 BEST PRACTICES TOOLKIT—Transparency
Definition Mapping p. E6

Prereading For prereading instruction for English learners, see

 BEST PRACTICES TOOLKIT
Scaffolding Reading Instruction pp. 43–46

FOR ADVANCED LEARNERS/PRE–AP

Pre-AP Exercises in the bottom channel provide additional challenge for students. Use these suggestions for small groups or individuals.

ADDITIONAL GUIDELINES

For more help with differentiation and tips for classroom management, see

BEST PRACTICES TOOLKIT
Differentiated Instruction pp. 31–38

governors. The notion facilitates a view of the world as playground and laboratory, which is a meager view surely. And it is disingenuous, for it seems so harmless, so responsible. But it is neither. **B**

30   For it makes impossible the other view of nature, which is of a realm both sacred and intricate, as well as powerful, of which we are no more than a single part. Nature, the total of all of us, is the wheel that drives our world; those who ride it willingly might yet catch a glimpse of a dazzling, even a spiritual restfulness, while those who are unwilling simply to hang on, who insist that the world must be piloted by man for his own benefit, will be dragged around and around all the same, gathering dust but no joy. **C**

Humans or tigers, tigers or tiger lilies—note their differences and still how alike they are! Don't we all, a few summers, stand here, and face the sea and, with whatever physical and intellectual **deftness** we can muster, improve our
40   state—and then, silently, fall back into the grass, death's green cloud? What is cute or charming as it rises, as it swoons? Life is Niagara, or nothing. I would not be the overlord of a single blade of grass, that I might be its sister. I put my face close to the lily, where it stands just above the grass, and give it a good greeting from the stem of my heart. We live, I am sure of this, in the same country, in the same household, and our burning comes from the same lamp. We are all wild, **valorous,** amazing. We are, none of us, cute. ❧

GRAMMAR AND STYLE
Reread lines 24–29. Notice how Oliver uses a variety of **interrogative, exclamatory,** and **declarative sentences** to express her views on human arrogance.

PARAPHRASE
What is Oliver saying about human attitudes toward nature in lines 32–36? Paraphrase this sentence, breaking it down into several shorter sentences if necessary.

deftness (dĕft′nĭs) *n.* the quality of quickness and skillfulness

valorous (văl′ər-əs) *adj.* brave

ANALYZE VISUALS
Compare your reaction to these photographs with your reaction to the one on page 785. In your opinion, do these photos illustrate Oliver's message better than the one on the preceding page? Explain your answer.

B GRAMMAR AND STYLE

Make sure students understand the terms *interrogative, exclamatory,* and *declarative.* Then ask them to find the interrogative and exclamatory sentences in this paragraph. *(Interrogative: "Thus we manage . . . of power?" Exclamatory: "We are!")*

READING STRATEGY

C PARAPHRASE

Possible answer: Nature is more powerful than humans. Those who accept this and appreciate nature without trying to control it will experience its beauty and serenity. Those who try to control nature will fail and will miss out on nature's benefits.

If students need help . . . Have students read the whole sentence several times to get the gist. Then have them focus on each main part, rephrasing it as a separate sentence.

ANALYZE VISUALS

Students will probably feel that these photos do a better job of illustrating Oliver's message. Rather than showing a "cute" image of an animal, they depict the animal's fierce and predatory side.

SELECTION WRAP–UP

REFLECT Ask students whether Oliver's essay made them think about nature—and the word *cute*—in a new way. Encourage them to be specific in explaining their responses.

★ **CRITIQUE** Ask students whether they agree or disagree with Oliver's viewpoint, and to provide reasons to support their opinions.

DIFFERENTIATED INSTRUCTION

FOR LESS–PROFICIENT READERS

② **Targeted Passage [Lines 27–36]**

In this passage, Oliver states her view of nature: "sacred and intricate . . . powerful . . . the total of all of us."

- What two views of nature does Oliver describe?
- Which is her view? How do you know?
- According to Oliver, what is the place of humans in nature?

FOR ADVANCED LEARNERS/PRE–AP

Analyze Figurative Language Have students identify examples of figurative language in the last paragraph—for example, lines 40, 41, 44, and 45—and explain their meaning. Encourage students to explain the comparison in each figure of speech. Then ask them to consider whether Oliver's tilt toward poetic images in this paragraph adds to, or detracts from, her message.

Comprehension

1. **Recall** How does Oliver describe the foxes at the beginning of the essay?

2. **Recall** List three other animals or plants the author discusses.

3. **Clarify** In Oliver's view, if we see nature as made up of cute, powerless animals, then who is in a position of power?

Literary Analysis

4. **Draw Conclusions** Reread the essay's last line on page 786. Has "A Few Words" changed your opinion about what it means to label something *cute?* Do you think *cute* can ever be a compliment? Explain, citing lines from the essay you agree or disagree with.

5. **Analyze Tone** Describe Oliver's overall tone in this essay. As a reader, what can you tell about her attitude toward nature? Explain, citing evidence from the essay to support your analysis.

6. **Paraphrase** Review the paraphrasing chart you created as you read. Using your chart, summarize the main idea of this essay in your own words.

7. **Examine Author's Style** Oliver is most widely known for her poetry. In what way might this selection be described as poetic? In a chart like the one shown, record examples of the poetic elements Oliver uses in this essay. Use your completed chart to explain whether you think "A Few Words" is more like poetry or more like prose.

Poetic Element	Examples from the Text
Alliteration	• "At our feet are the ferns…" (line 20) • •
Metaphor	
Imagery	
Repetition	

Literary Criticism

8. **Critical Interpretations** Critics have praised Oliver's quest to, in the words of Holly Prado of the *L.A. Times Book Review,* "understand both the wonder and pain of nature." In your opinion, how well does Oliver explain both the beautiful and the not-so-beautiful aspects of the natural world? Support your answer with evidence from the selection.

of power" (line 26); "Niagara, or nothing" (line 41); "above the grass, and give it a good greeting" (lines 43–44). **Metaphor:** Oliver refers to the grass as "death's green cloud" (line 40) and nature as "the wheel that drives our world" (line 32); "Life is Niagara, or nothing" (line 41). **Imagery:** Oliver's images portray nature as both violent and beautiful: a fox "carrying the soiled wing of a gull" while other foxes "grab onto it and pull . . . , their small teeth snapping" (lines 6–8); "the purple-fleshed mushroom" (line 15). **Repetition:** "Nothing

in the forest is charming . . . . And nothing in the forest is cute" (lines 1, 5); "Humans or tigers, tigers or tiger lilies" (line 37). Students should cite evidence to support their view of Oliver's style.

Literary Criticism

8. Students may respond that Oliver does a good job of explaining both. She portrays the beautiful side of nature in her lyrical last paragraph, and she portrays its not-so-beautiful side in her description of the fox with a gull in its mouth (lines 6–8).

Practice and Apply

After Reading

For additional support of post-reading questions, use these copy masters:

R RESOURCE MANAGER—Copy Masters
Reading Check p. 116 (to check understanding of the selection)
Tone p. 109 (for practice of literary analysis standards focus)
Question Support p. 117 (After Reading questions adapted for English learners and less-proficient readers)

Additional selection questions are provided for teachers on page 103.

ANSWERS

Comprehension

1. *Oliver says that the "dog fox is not cute" and describes one fox with "the soiled wing of a gull" in its mouth as other foxes grab at it, "their small teeth snapping" (lines 5–8).*

2. **Possible answer:** *Oliver mentions the owl, the milk snake, and ferns.*

3. *We (humans) are.*

Literary Analysis

Possible answers:

4. *Students should explain their reasoning and cite relevant lines from the essay.*

5. ● **STANDARDS FOCUS** *Tone Oliver's overall tone can be described as direct, brisk, impassioned, and forceful, sometimes sounding almost angry, as in lines 10–13. When Oliver talks about nature, her tone turns admiring, even reverent: "a realm both sacred and intricate, as well as powerful, of which we are no more than a single part" (lines 30–32); "I would not be the overlord of a single blade of grass, that I might be its sister" (lines 41–42). Her tone reveals that she has great respect for nature, which she views as stunning and powerful, not something to be controlled, exploited, or undervalued.*

6. ■ **STANDARDS FOCUS** *Paraphrase Nothing in nature is cute or adorable. We should stop viewing nature as entertainment and stop trying to control it. Humans, animals, and plants are interconnected natural beings, wondrous entities that deserve respect.*

7. *Alliteration: "down the dune" (line 6); "At our feet are the ferns" (line 20); "position*

ANSWERS

Vocabulary in Context

VOCABULARY PRACTICE

1. *a*   3. *b*
2. *b*   4. *b*

 RESOURCE MANAGER—Copy Master
Vocabulary Practice p. 114

VOCABULARY IN WRITING

Help students focus their responses. Direct them to state Oliver's viewpoint clearly before they explain why they do or do not agree with it. Remind students to support their ideas with clear reasons and evidence from the essay.

VOCABULARY STRATEGY: HOMONYMS
(also an EL language objective)

Point out that homonyms are often, but not always, different parts of speech. To extend the activity, have students identify the parts of speech of each pair of homonyms. Then have them use each homonym in a sentence of their own.

Answers:

1. *row*   4. *hide*
2. *grave*   5. *mean*
3. *kind*   6. *mine*

 RESOURCE MANAGER—Copy Master
Vocabulary Strategy p. 115

ⓘ Vocabulary Center at **ClassZone.com**
Additional Vocabulary Activities

Vocabulary in Context

VOCABULARY PRACTICE

In which situation might you use each vocabulary word?

1. **diminutive:** (a) describing a miniature poodle, (b) listing the pros and cons of a school committee's proposal, (c) explaining how to draw trees
2. **stalk:** (a) explaining how to apply paint, (b) describing a field of corn, (c) listing the reasons you like bungee jumping
3. **valorous:** (a) telling about a peaceful day in the country, (b) describing how the hero of a movie saved the day, (c) detailing how to lay a brick sidewalk
4. **deftness:** (a) watching leaves fall in a windstorm, (b) describing how a runner broke away from the pack to win, (c) choosing a birthday card for your brother

WORD LIST
deftness
diminutive
stalk
valorous

VOCABULARY IN WRITING

Do you agree with Mary Oliver? Write a paragraph explaining why or why not. Use two or more vocabulary words. Here is a sample first sentence.

> **EXAMPLE SENTENCE**
>
> *Like Mary Oliver, I believe that thinking about animals as **diminutive**, helpless creatures is unjust. . . .*

VOCABULARY STRATEGY: HOMONYMS

Homonyms are words that have the same pronunciation and often the same spelling but different meanings. For example, the vocabulary word *stalk*, which means "a stem or main axis of a plant," looks and sounds just like the word *stalk*, meaning "to move threateningly or menacingly." Because they are pronounced and spelled the same way, homonyms can be confusing. The context of the sentence or passage can usually help you determine which of a set of homonyms is being used. However, sometimes it's difficult to figure out the meaning of a homonym from its context. In such cases, check a dictionary.

PRACTICE Identify the homonyms described by each pair of definitions. If you're stumped, figure out which word just one of the definitions describes. Then use a dictionary to find out if that word has any homonyms.

1. to move a boat forward with oars/a line of people or objects
2. place where a dead person is buried/very serious or solemn
3. a type of something/friendly and considerate
4. the skin of an animal/to conceal or keep secret
5. to intend to do something/unkind
6. belonging to me/an underground cavern from which gold is extracted

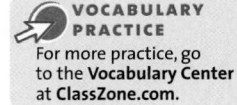

VOCABULARY PRACTICE
For more practice, go to the **Vocabulary Center** at **ClassZone.com.**

DIFFERENTIATED INSTRUCTION

FOR ENGLISH LEARNERS

Vocabulary: Homonyms Have same-language pairs or small groups list homonyms in their home languages. For languages where this is not possible, have students identify other English homonym pairs.

FOR ADVANCED LEARNERS/PRE–AP

Vocabulary in Writing Challenge students to use at least three vocabulary words in a paragraph written in Mary Oliver's style on the topic of nature's wonders.

Reading-Writing Connection

Increase your understanding of "A Few Words" by responding to these prompts.
Then use **Revision: Grammar and Style** to improve your writing.

WRITING PROMPTS	SELF-CHECK

A. Short Response: Analyze Tone
Did the tone of Oliver's essay make you more or less receptive to her ideas? Would you have agreed with her more if she'd tried to sweet-talk you into seeing things her way? In **one or two paragraphs**, describe how the author's tone affected your response to her message.

An effective analysis will . . .
- describe Oliver's tone in "A Few Words," using evidence from the selection to support your description
- reveal whether or not Oliver's tone affected how you feel about her views

B. Extended Response: Express an Opinion
Oliver makes the case that we do nature a disservice when we label it *cute*. Can this apply to calling a person *cute*, as well? Write a **three-to-five-paragraph response** explaining whether or not you think this label can be harmful to humans.

A strong response will . . .
- clearly state whether labeling a person *cute* can have negative repercussions
- use evidence from the text to support your opinion

REVISION: GRAMMAR AND STYLE

VARY SENTENCE TYPES Reread the **Grammar and Style** note on page 786. Oliver believes that some people have a very condescending view of nature. To express her outrage at this perception, she uses a variety of sentence types that allow her emotions to shine through. Here, Oliver enlists **imperative, interrogative,** and **declarative sentences** to get her point across:

> *Humans or tigers, tigers or tiger lilies—note their differences and still how alike they are! Don't we all, a few summers, stand here, and face the sea and, with whatever physical and intellectual deftness we can muster, improve our state— and then, silently, fall back into the grass, death's green cloud? What is cute or charming as it rises, as it swoons? Life is Niagara, or nothing.* (lines 37–41)

Notice how the revisions in red employ sentence types that more accurately reflect the emotions of the writer, making the statements more powerful. Revise your responses to the prompts by varying your sentence types.

STUDENT MODEL

I don't ~~think we should~~ refer to people as "cute." It belittles them
Why not
~~and it doesn't~~ take into account their achievements. ~~I think~~ we should give
people credit for something more worthwhile, like hard work.

WRITING TOOLS
For prewriting, revision, and editing tools, visit the **Writing Center** at **ClassZone.com.**

A FEW WORDS **789**

FOR LESS–PROFICIENT WRITERS

For Prompt A: Suggest that students imagine they are conversing with Mary Oliver. Help them reflect on these questions: Would Oliver's tone put them off? Would they think she was coming on too strong? Would a softer, friendlier tone be more likely to win agreement, or does her forceful style inspire them?

For Prompt B:
- Limit the length of the assignment to one or two paragraphs.
- Have students work in small groups to explore possible negative repercussions of being labeled *cute*.
- Encourage students to consider how different people might feel when they are called *cute*. Who would welcome the label? Who would not? Why?

Reading-Writing Connection

WRITING PROMPTS
- For Prompt A, encourage students to think about other ways in which Oliver might have expressed herself. Would a gentler approach have been more likely to win readers over?
- For Prompt B, encourage students to consider the significance of *who* is using the word *cute*. For example, one teen describing another as cute is very different from an employer calling an employee cute.

For writing support, see

🛈 Writing Center at **ClassZone.com**

REVISION: GRAMMAR AND STYLE
- After students examine the model, ask how the revisions strengthen the statements.
- Point out that Oliver sometimes poses a rhetorical question—a question with an obvious answer—and then answers it with an exclamatory sentence (lines 24–26).
- Write this passage on the board, and ask students to make it stronger by using a variety of sentence types.

> "~~I don't think it's appropriate for you to call me cute,~~ Don't call me cute!" said Ms. Davis. "~~Please notice that I never~~ Do I ever call you cute~~.~~? I am a grown woman~~, so~~. ~~I think I should be~~ Please treated me with more respect~~.~~!"

📑 RESOURCE MANAGER—Copy Master
Vary Sentence Types p. 118

Assess and Reteach

Assess

📑 RESOURCE MANAGER—Copy Masters
Selection Test A pp. 119–120
Selection Test B/C pp. 121–122

💿 Test Generator CD

Reteach

📄 STANDARDS LESSON FILE
Literature Lesson 45: Tone
Research and Study Skills Lesson 12: Paraphrasing
Vocabulary Lesson 20: Homonyms and Homographs
Writing Lesson 8: Creating Sentence Variety

OBJECTIVES

Literary Analysis
- explore the key idea of **insights**
- analyze Dickinson's style
- read poems

Reading
- read poetry for understanding

SUMMARIES

Dickinson uses descriptive and figurative language to depict the appearance and movements of a snake in "A narrow Fellow in the Grass." In a striking metaphor at the end of the poem, the speaker expresses fear at the sight of this "narrow Fellow." In "'Hope' is the thing with feathers—," Dickinson compares the abstract concept of hope with the concrete object of a bird through the use of extended metaphor. The speaker suggests that the bird's song, which "never stops," is the strongest reminder that hope is alive.

What is a poet's JOB?

Introduce the question, and have students read the **KEY IDEA.** Discuss with the class some examples of how poets can communicate **insights** about people, society, nature, or any other topic. In other words, what jobs do modern poets perform? Have students keep these examples in mind as they write want ads for the **PRESENT** activity.

A narrow Fellow in the Grass
"Hope" is the thing with feathers—
Poems by Emily Dickinson

What is a poet's JOB?

KEY IDEA Have you ever tried to describe something important, only to find yourself at a total loss for words? Some things are hard to explain, but certain people seem able to explain them anyway. Poets use their skill with language to communicate **insights,** or perceptive comments, about everything from emotions and adventure to animals and art.

PRESENT Write a want ad seeking a poet to communicate an insight you think is worth sharing. Include a description of what you want explained, the skills your poet should possess, and the kind of poetry you're looking for. Then pair up with a classmate and take turns presenting your ads.

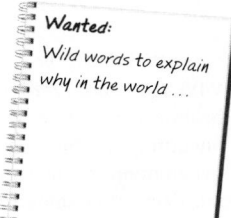

Wanted:
Wild words to explain
why in the world …

790

R RESOURCE MANAGER UNIT 8

Plan and Teach pp. 123–130

Literary Analysis
Dickinson's Style pp. 131, 132†*
Question Support p. 135*

Reading
Reading Poetry pp. 133, 134†*

Assessment
Selection Tests A, B/C pp. 137*, 139*
 Test Generator CD

 BEST PRACTICES TOOLKIT

Differentiated Instruction
pp. 31–38*

Reading Support
 Audio Anthology CD*

Technology
 Literature Center at
ClassZone.com
 Write*Smart* CD

---

* Resources for Differentiation   † Also in Spanish

LITERARY ANALYSIS: DICKINSON'S STYLE

Emily Dickinson's style is unmistakable. One of the originators of modern American poetry, she broke with tradition, creating a unique style all her own. Dickinson's poems are usually short—no more than 20 lines—but they often convey stunning insights in spite of their brevity. Distinct elements of Dickinson's style include

- dense stanzas that echo the **rhythms** of church hymns
- **slant rhymes,** or words that do not rhyme exactly
- unconventional capitalization that adds emphasis to certain words or phrases
- frequent use of dashes to highlight important words and break up the singsong rhythm of her poems
- original **figurative language,** including similes, metaphors, and personification

As you read, notice the poet's use of these elements, and consider the insights she communicates by using them.

READING STRATEGY: READING POETRY

The following suggestions can help you increase both your understanding and your enjoyment of Dickinson's poetry:

- Read the poems aloud to appreciate Dickinson's unique rhythm and imagery.
- Pay close attention to words that are capitalized for emphasis.
- Analyze the poet's use of figurative language.
- Pause when you encounter dashes, just as you would for a comma or a period in a more conventional poem.

Author Online

Emily Dickinson
1830–1886

Close to Home Except for a year she spent away at school, Emily Dickinson lived her entire life in the small community of Amherst, Massachusetts, with her family. She was very close to her older brother and younger sister. Though she adored her stern and principled father, she had a complicated relationship with her mother. By her 40s, Dickinson began to dress only in white and refused to leave her family's house. Except for the many letters she wrote and received, she withdrew from the world, living in isolation until her death.

A Private Poet After Dickinson's death, her sister Lavinia carried out the poet's wishes, burning all of her letters from family and friends. However, Lavinia rescued a little box filled with poems. Since her late teens or early 20s, Emily Dickinson had been writing poetry. She'd jot down her thoughts during the day—on scraps of paper, old recipes, and the backs of envelopes—and write all night by candlelight. Though she wrote 1,775 poems, Dickinson published only 7, anonymously, during her lifetime. The private poet left the world pondering her untold secrets.

A Rich Life The first volume of Emily Dickinson's poetry was published in 1890, four years after her death. Today, she is known as one of the most popular and influential U.S. poets. Even though Dickinson lived in isolation, her poems, according to 20th-century poet Allen Tate, reveal a life that was "one of the richest and deepest ever lived on this continent."

 MORE ABOUT THE AUTHOR
For more on Emily Dickinson, visit the **Literature Center** at ClassZone.com.

791

Teach

STANDARDS FOCUS

DICKINSON'S STYLE

To illustrate Dickinson's style, write these lines from "A narrow Fellow in the Grass" on the board:

The Grass divides as with a Comb—
A spotted shaft is seen—

Ask students to identify elements of Dickinson's style found in these lines. *Possible answer: the lines' regular, hymn-like rhythm; unconventional capitalization ("Grass," "Comb"); the use of dashes at the end of each line; figurative language (the grass is likened to a head of hair being divided by a comb)*

CHECK UNDERSTANDING What stylistic element common to Dickinson's poetry is not present in these lines?

READING POETRY

Return to the lines written on the board. Model for students how to read poetry. For example, read the lines aloud, emphasizing their rhythm and pausing at the dash. Then ask students what the figurative language in those lines suggests about the speaker's relationship with nature. *Possible answer: The use of personification suggests that nature is something that the speaker is familiar with, even close to.*

CHECK UNDERSTANDING Invite several volunteers to practice reading the lines aloud.

DIFFERENTIATED INSTRUCTION

FOR LESS—PROFICIENT READERS
Concept Support Help students understand the stylistic elements covered in the **LITERARY ANALYSIS** discussion.

- Point out that the hymnlike rhythm that Dickinson often uses consists of an alternating pattern of weak and strong beats. She frequently uses a four-beat line followed by a three-beat line.

- Explain that some slant rhymes include similar vowel sounds but different consonant sounds (*moon/goose*). Others include similar consonant sounds but different vowel sounds (*blade/blood*).

- Remind students that figurative language is language that uses one or more figures of speech to make an imaginative comparison between two things that are unlike yet have something in common.

A narrow
Fellow in the Grass

EMILY DICKINSON

A narrow Fellow in the Grass
Occasionally rides—
You may have met Him—did you not
His notice sudden is—

5 The Grass divides as with a Comb—
A spotted shaft is seen—
And then it closes at your feet
And opens further on— Ⓐ

He likes a Boggy Acre
10 A Floor too cool for Corn—
Yet when a Boy, and Barefoot—
I more than once at Noon
Have passed, I thought, a Whip lash
Unbraiding in the Sun
15 When stopping to secure it
It wrinkled, and was gone— Ⓑ

Several of Nature's People
I know, and they know me—
I feel for them a transport
20 Of cordiality—[1]

But never met this Fellow
Attended, or alone
Without a tighter breathing
And Zero at the Bone—

Ⓐ **DICKINSON'S STYLE**
What is the "narrow Fellow" Dickinson describes? Explain why you think the poet chose to capitalize certain words in the first two stanzas.

Ⓑ **DICKINSON'S STYLE**
Identify one example of **slant rhyme** in this stanza. What other distinctive features of Dickinson's style can you see in this poem? Support your answer with evidence.

---

1. **a transport of cordiality:** a very strong feeling of warmth and friendliness.

Lines 5–24
REINFORCE *KEY IDEA*: INSIGHTS

Discuss What **insights** has the speaker gained from her experience with snakes? *Possible answer: The speaker realizes that despite being familiar with "Several of Nature's People" (line 17), snakes inspire fear, possibly originating from the childhood experience described in lines 10–16.*

DIFFERENTIATED INSTRUCTION

For general guidelines on differentiating instruction, see

 BEST PRACTICES TOOLKIT
Differentiated Instruction pp. 31–38

FOR LESS–PROFICIENT READERS

Options for Reading Read aloud "A narrow Fellow in the Grass" and discuss with students the sound of the poem. Point out that certain aspects of Dickinson's style, particularly the rhythm, rhyme, and pauses, create this sound. Encourage students to explore the sound of Dickinson's style by working in small groups to perform a choral reading of the poem.

"Hope" is the thing with feathers—

EMILY DICKINSON

"Hope" is the thing with feathers—
That perches in the soul—
And sings the tune without the words—
And never stops—at all— **C**

5 And sweetest—in the Gale—is heard—
And sore[1] must be the storm—
That could abash[2] the little Bird
That kept so many warm—

I've heard it in the chillest land—
10 And on the strangest Sea—
Yet, never, in Extremity,[3]
It asked a crumb—of Me. **D**

C **DICKINSON'S STYLE**
What **metaphor** does
Dickinson present in the
first stanza? Explain
your answer.

D **READING POETRY**
Reread lines 11–12 aloud.
What is the effect of
Dickinson's unusual
punctuation and
capitalization in
these lines?

1. **sore:** severe
2. **abash:** cause to be upset or embarrassed.
3. **Extremity:** greatest need or danger.

Prereading for this poem is found on
page 790.

Lines 1–10
REINFORCE *KEY IDEA:* INSIGHTS
Discuss What **insight** does Dickinson communicate? *Possible answer: Dickinson communicates the insight that hope can be found everywhere.*

LITERARY ANALYSIS

C DICKINSON'S STYLE
Possible answer: The metaphor is "'Hope' is the thing with feathers" (line 1). The metaphor compares hope with a bird and is extended throughout the stanza with such words as "perches" (line 2) and "sings the tune" (line 3).

READING STRATEGY

D READING POETRY
Possible answer: The effect of Dickinson's unusual punctuation and capitalization is to establish breaks or pauses and to emphasize certain words or ideas. For example, capitalizing "Extremity" draws attention to the word, and placing a dash before "of Me" adds emphasis to the idea by breaking the rhythm of the final line.

SELECTION WRAP–UP

SYNTHESIZE Ask students to identify similarities between the two poems. *Possible answer: Both poems use figurative language, slant rhymes, a regular rhythm, unconventional capitalization, and dashes.*

⭐ **CRITIQUE** Have students discuss which element of Dickinson's style they found most interesting or effective, and why.

FOR LESS–PROFICIENT READERS
Syntax Explain that poets often rearrange the usual order of words to achieve a certain effect. For example, in "A narrow Fellow in the Grass," line 4 reverses the usual word order: "His notice sudden is" instead of "His notice is sudden." This inversion places "is" at the end of the line, creating a slant rhyme with "rides" in line 2. Suggest that students rearrange such lines for comprehension but then reread the poem as it is written to appreciate the effects of the inverted syntax.

FOR ADVANCED LEARNERS/PRE–AP
Evaluate Dickinson's Style [small-group option] Ask students to evaluate the unique stylistic elements that Dickinson employs in both poems. Students should first identify these stylistic elements and discuss their effects on reading and on comprehension. Then, have students critique the style, explaining their opinions of what does and does not enhance their reading experience and why.

DISCUSSION PROMPTS

Use these prompts to help students make connections between Emily Dickinson's life and her poetry:

Connect Recall a time in your life when you felt that someone had the wrong idea about you. How did the experience make you feel? *Students might say that they felt frustrated or embarrassed.*

Analyze What details did the writer include to provide a wider perspective on Dickinson's personality? *Possible answer: Details include her extensive correspondence, her popularity at parties, her visitors (including her mentor Higginson), her large library, and her busy work routine.*

Synthesize What kind of person do you think Emily Dickinson was? Based on the insights expressed in the two poems as well as the article you have just read, how would you answer the question presented in the article's final paragraph? Explain your interpretation. *Possible answer: Based on these two poems, Dickinson seems more of a fulfilled, although solitary, soul than a shy, troubled woman. This interpretation is supported by the playfulness of the first poem and the positive message of hope presented in the second poem.*

Reading for Information

JOURNAL ARTICLE Intrigued by the mysterious Ms. Dickinson? Read on to learn why some scholars think the poet was anything but solitary.

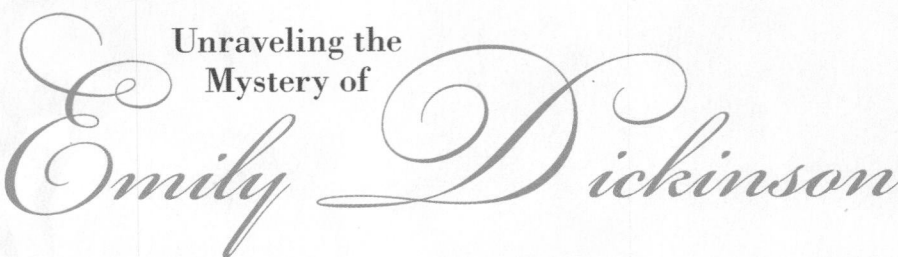

Unraveling the Mystery of

Emily Dickinson

> "I'm Nobody! Who are you?
> Are you—Nobody—too?"

These lines come from one of Emily Dickinson's famous poems. Imagine that a friend sent those words to you. Would you think your friend was feeling witty? contemplative? sad? Like the faceless e-mail and text messages sent between friends today, Dickinson's letters and poetry could be interpreted numerous ways by her friends. Scholars still debate Dickinson's mysterious words and life.

Many theories exist about her reasons for withdrawing from the world and her seclusion at the family home for the last 20 years of her life. Some say that it was an opportunity to concentrate her energies on her writing. Others believe it was a case of agoraphobia (fear of crowds). No one can prove which, if any, is correct, but the best available evidence is found in her correspondence. Some people even believe her letters indicate her life was far from antisocial. They suggest that it was her editors, who hoped to persuade the public that Dickinson was an upstanding single lady in accordance with her time, who perpetuated the notion of Dickinson as a recluse.

The sheer volume of her writing indicates she often wrote a few letters or poems each day, keeping in frequent touch with family and friends. Scholars also note the Dickinson house was an active gathering place, so Dickinson did not have to leave to socialize. Her best friend, Susan, lived next door for 30 years. Famous writers of Dickinson's time came to visit, as did some of her mentors. In addition, the household library contained nearly 1,000 books, and the grounds offered gardens and woods—some of her favorite spots to spend time when she wasn't helping with the household, working on her writing, or caring for her brother's children.

Although popularly characterized as a shy adult, as a child Dickinson was known for her sense of humor. An account of her meeting with literary critic Thomas Wentworth Higginson in 1870 shows her to be a talkative woman—Higginson found her draining. Of course, it could be that she was simply so excited to finally meet the famous mentor she had corresponded with for eight years. One friend commented that Dickinson was so surrounded by friends at a party that she couldn't even talk to her.

Despite their long correspondence—over 20 years—Higginson didn't know what to make of the mysterious poet. "She was much too enigmatical a being for me to solve in an hour's interview," he wrote in an article for the *Atlantic* after her death.

Was Emily Dickinson a shy, troubled woman; a fulfilled, solitary soul; or someone in between? Study her writing closely, and perhaps you will discover a clue.

Comprehension

1. **Recall** What are two places where the "narrow Fellow" can be found?

2. **Recall** List three ways Dickinson compares hope to a bird.

Literary Analysis

3. **Interpret Theme in Poetry** In one or two sentences, state the theme of each poem. Then explain which poem you think offers a more interesting or perceptive **insight.**

4. **Analyze Mood** Reread lines 17–24 of "A narrow Fellow in the Grass." How does the mood of the fourth stanza differ from that of the fifth? Explain which words or phrases contribute to the change in mood.

5. **Identify Symbol** A symbol is something that stands for more than itself. In "'Hope' is the thing with feathers—" what do "the Gale," "the chillest land," and "the strangest Sea" represent? Cite evidence to support your answer.

6. **Analyze Extended Metaphor** An extended metaphor compares two things at some length and in several ways. In "'Hope' is the thing with feathers—" Dickinson compares hope to a bird. How does she develop this metaphor throughout the poem? Use a graphic like the one shown to help organize your evidence.

```
( Hope is a bird. )
┌──────────────┐
│ stanza 1:    │
├──────────────┤
│ stanza 2:    │
├──────────────┤
│ stanza 3:    │
└──────────────┘
```

7. **Examine Emily Dickinson's Style** Review the bulleted list of Dickinson's stylistic hallmarks on page 791. Pick two elements of the poet's style and find examples of them in "A narrow Fellow in the Grass" and "'Hope' is the thing with feathers—." Then explain the effect created by each example.

Literary Criticism

8. **Author's Style** Dickinson's first volume of poetry, and each collection after that until 1955, consisted of "corrected" versions of her poems. In other words, editors "fixed" Dickinson's punctuation and capitalization. Acting as a 19th-century editor, rewrite one of Dickinson's poems using standard punctuation and capitalization. Read your finished product. Is there something missing? Do you prefer the poem Dickinson's way? Explain your answer.

6. **Stanza 1:** Hope is called "the thing with feathers" that "perches," or rests, in the soul. **Stanza 2:** The speaker likens the sound of birdsong during a storm to the hope that one feels during a difficult time in life. **Stanza 3:** The speaker explains that wherever she goes, the singing of birds is still present.

7. ● **STANDARDS FOCUS** *Dickinson's Style* The poet uses unusual capitalization that emphasizes key words ("Fellow," "Zero," "Me"); dashes that break up the rhythm; slant rhymes that create an off-kilter sound unity ("soul"/"all"); and figurative language that presents imaginative comparisons ("Zero at the Bone").

Literary Criticism

8. ■ **STANDARDS FOCUS** *Reading Poetry* Students might say that the "edited" version lacks the unique appeal of Dickinson's work. They may prefer the emphasis that unconventional capitalization adds to certain words or feel that the poem has more sound appeal when its rhythm is broken up by Dickinson's dashes.

Practice and Apply

After Reading

For additional support of post-reading questions, use these copy masters:

R RESOURCE MANAGER—Copy Masters
Dickinson's Style p. 131 (for practice of the literary analysis standards focus)
Question Support p. 135 (After Reading questions adapted for English learners and less-proficient readers)

Additional selection questions are provided for teachers on page 127.

ANSWERS

Comprehension

1. *The "narrow Fellow" can be found in a "Boggy Acre" or "A Floor too cool for Corn."*

2. *Like a bird, hope has "feathers," it "perches," and it "sings" sweetly.*

Literary Analysis

Possible answers:

3. *"A narrow Fellow . . .": Nature can be both familiar and fascinating, but it may scare us. "'Hope' . . . ": Like a bird that sings through the harshest weather, hope is always there and asks nothing of us in return. Students should support their choices for the more insightful poem.*

4. *The mood of the fourth stanza is light, but in the fifth stanza, the mood turns anxious as the speaker describes her fear. The phrases "tighter breathing" and "Zero at the Bone" contribute to that change.*

5. *They represent difficult times in one's life. The song is "sweetest" when heard in a "Gale" (line 5), suggesting that hope is most appreciated during difficult times.*

Assess and Reteach

Assess

R RESOURCE MANAGER—Copy Masters
Selection Test A pp. 137–138
Selection Test B/C pp. 139–140

🖫 Test Generator CD

Reteach

S STANDARDS LESSON FILE
Literature Lesson 46: Style and Syntax
Reading Lesson 2: Monitoring

Focus and Motivate

OBJECTIVES

Literary Analysis
- explore the key idea of **love poems**
- analyze Giovanni's style
- read poetry

Reading
- interpret ideas in poetry

SUMMARIES

In "Luxury," Giovanni considers the luxury of material wealth and technological advances and concludes that the ultimate luxury is the love of another person. Giovanni expresses her desire to capture her beloved in poetry, as she playfully manages to do just that in "Kidnap Poem."

What would win your HEART?

Introduce the question, and have students read the *KEY IDEA.* Then discuss whether **love poems** are preferable to the other suggestions for the purpose of winning students' hearts. Extend the discussion by having students complete the *QUICKWRITE* activity. Discuss how students' responses could be written as love poems.

Luxury
Kidnap Poem
Poems by Nikki Giovanni

What would win your HEART?

KEY IDEA What would it take to win you over? Candy and flowers? A pretty face? A sense of humor? What about **love poems**—could they ever help someone win your heart? The following poems are so passionate that if you answered no, you might change your mind after reading them.

QUICKWRITE What is the one thing someone could do to make you totally fall for him or her? In a paragraph, describe the act or gesture—be it grand and thrilling or small and ordinary—that would win your heart.

796

Selection Resources

 **RESOURCE MANAGER UNIT 8**

Plan and Teach pp. 141–148

Literary Analysis
Giovanni's Style pp. 149, 150†*
Question Support p. 153*

Reading
Interpret Ideas in Poetry
   pp. 151, 152†*
Reading Fluency p. 154

Assessment
Selection Tests A, B/C pp. 155*, 157*
 Test Generator CD

 BEST PRACTICES TOOLKIT

Differentiated Instruction
   pp. 31–38*

Graphic Organizers/Strategies
Venn Diagram • Cluster Diagram

Reading Support
Audio Anthology CD*

Technology
Literature Center at
   ClassZone.com
Write*Smart* CD

* Resources for Differentiation   † Also in Spanish

LITERARY ANALYSIS: GIOVANNI'S STYLE

Nikki Giovanni is a poet who goes by her own rules. "I want my writing to sound like I talk," she says. To that end, Giovanni employs a conversational style that breaks with convention. Most of her work consists of lyric poetry written in **free verse,** which lacks a regular rhyme and meter and often sounds like natural speech. Giovanni's unique style also includes

- a deliberate lack of punctuation and capitalization
- stanzas and lines of varying length
- simple language and clear metaphors
- the use of sound devices such as **alliteration** and **repetition** to create a distinct rhythm

As you read, look for evidence of these techniques, and think about how Giovanni's style helps her communicate her message.

READING SKILL: INTERPRET IDEAS IN POETRY

The key to understanding and interpreting poetry is often digesting little chunks at a time. Working through a poem slowly can help you extract its meaning and its message. As you read "Luxury" and "Kidnap Poem," write down interesting stanzas and unusual phrases. Then record what you think each means.

Phrase or Stanza	Meaning
i suppose living in a materialistic society luxury to some would be having more than what you need ("Luxury," lines 1–5)	People in money-centered societies think excess equals luxury.

Author Online

Family Ties Yolande Cornelia Giovanni Jr. was nicknamed Nikki by her older sister. Giovanni's close-knit family moved from Tennessee to Ohio just after she was born, but they often returned to visit her dynamic, outspoken grandmother, who was a huge influence on the poet. Giovanni says her grandmother, a great storyteller, was also "the only person I know for sure whose love I did not have to earn."

Nikki Giovanni born 1943

Young and Driven Giovanni always suspected she'd be famous one day. Her drive led her to Fisk University, but her independent spirit got her kicked out after just one semester. Giovanni eventually returned to Fisk, where she became active in the civil rights movement. A year after graduating with honors, Giovanni published *Black Feeling, Black Talk*, her first book of poetry. The book was inspired both by the death of her grandmother and by the poet's increasing outrage at the way African Americans were treated in the U.S. Giovanni was determined to change society through her poetry. Writing, according to Giovanni, is the easy part. "Then," she says, "comes the hard part: you have to find someone to read it."

The Journey Much of Giovanni's early work consisted of militant calls to action and angry demands for racial equality. While she hasn't lost her political edge, Giovanni's later poetry also explores more personal territory, delving into family, love, and loneliness. Giovanni battled cancer in the 1990s, but after successful surgery, she resumed her work. Writing poetry, Giovanni says, "is a journey without end."

MORE ABOUT THE AUTHOR
For more on Nikki Giovanni, visit the **Literature Center** at ClassZone.com.

DIFFERENTIATED INSTRUCTION

FOR LESS–PROFICIENT READERS

Review with students that a metaphor is a figure of speech that compares two dissimilar things without using *like* or *as*. Write these examples on the board:

- the curtain of night
- a blanket of love
- kidnap your heart

Discuss the meaning of each metaphor. Make sure students understand the two things that are being compared.

Teach

STANDARDS FOCUS

LITERARY ANALYSIS

● GIOVANNI'S STYLE

To illustrate Giovanni's style, write these lines from "Luxury" on the board:

> i have thought if only
> i could become rich and famous
>   i would
> live luxuriously in new york

Ask students to identify elements of Giovanni's style found in the lines on the board. ***Possible answer:*** *a lack of capitalization and punctuation; lines of varying length; simple language; alliteration and repetition ("live luxuriously," the repetition of "i" throughout the stanza)*

CHECK UNDERSTANDING Ask students how elements of Giovanni's style help create the sound of natural speech.

READING SKILL

■ INTERPRET IDEAS IN POETRY

Point out that, particularly in free verse, poets pay close attention to where they break their lines, since they do not have to follow a meter or rhyme scheme. Line breaks create chunks of meaning by setting off key words or phrases. Ask students how the varying line lengths in the poem on the board help convey meaning. ***Possible answer:*** *The varying line lengths and the use of enjambment convey a sense of incompleteness, as if the speaker can only experience fulfillment in something yet to occur in her life*

CHECK UNDERSTANDING Ask students how the poem would be different if Giovanni divided her lines into complete sentences.

RESOURCE MANAGER—Copy Master Interpret Ideas in Poetry p. 151 (for student use while reading the selections)

Practice and Apply

ANALYZE VISUALS

Possible answer: Yes, the painting is luxurious. The figures look as if they are resting in each other's arms. They seem to glow, like a couple in love. The golden arch that surrounds them; the flowers that cascade around them; and the rich, jewel-toned colors and patterns of their clothing all create a sense of luxury.

About the Art In *Tumbling Flowers* and *Sleeping Couple I* (page 800), Hyacinth Manning-Carter uses lush, sunny colors and ethnic patterns that reflect her culture.

LITERARY ANALYSIS

A GIOVANNI'S STYLE

Possible answer: Elements of Giovanni's style include the lack of punctuation and capitalization; lines and stanzas of varying lengths (lines 1–14); informal language ("nth degree," line 9); and repetition ("living" in lines 1 and 6, "having" in lines 4 and 12).

If students need help . . . Have them reread page 797 and see which stylistic elements they can find in the first two stanzas.

READING SKILL

B INTERPRET IDEAS IN POETRY

Possible answer: The idea is similar to that in previous stanzas: what is luxury? But the idea of luxury to the poet now is not about material things, but rather, love.

If students need help . . . Have them use a Venn Diagram to compare the idea of luxury in the first part of the poem with the idea of luxury in the last stanza.

- having more than what you need
- having someone there to push buttons for you

luxury

you held me one evening

🧰 BEST PRACTICES TOOLKIT—Transparency
Venn Diagram p. A26

Luxury
Nikki Giovanni

i suppose living
in a materialistic society
luxury
to some would be having
5 more than what you need

living in an electronic age seeing
the whole world by
    pushing a button
the *nth* degree[1] might
10   perhaps be
adequately represented
    by having
someone there to push
the buttons for you ⒜

15 i have thought if only
i could become rich and famous
    i would
live luxuriously in new york
    knowing
20 famous people eating
in expensive restaurants calling
long distance anytime i want

but you held me
one evening and now i know
25 the ultimate luxury
of your love ⒝

---

1. **the *nth* degree:** the ultimate degree of something; as much or as far as possible.

ANALYZE VISUALS
Does this painting seem **luxurious** to you? Consider its colors, shapes, and textures, as well as the figures it depicts. Explain your opinion, citing details.

⒜ GIOVANNI'S STYLE
What elements of Giovanni's distinctive style are apparent so far in this poem? Explain your answer, referring to specific lines for evidence.

⒝ INTERPRET IDEAS IN POETRY
Reread lines 23–26. How does the idea expressed in this stanza compare with the ideas in previous stanzas of the poem?

Tumbling Flowers (1954), Hyacinth Manning-Carner.
© Hyacinth Manning-Carner/SuperStock.

DIFFERENTIATED INSTRUCTION

For general guidelines on differentiating instruction, see

🧰 **BEST PRACTICES TOOLKIT**
Differentiated Instruction pp. 31–38

FOR LESS–PROFICIENT READERS
Options for Reading Read the poem aloud for enjoyment and to capture its style. Tell students to listen for the poem's simple, conversational language.

FOR ADVANCED LEARNERS/PRE–AP
Writing Poetry Encourage students to write a poem using Giovanni's conversational, free verse style, on any emotion they are comfortable exploring. After students have written their poems, discuss the ways in which free verse affected how they were able to express their ideas. How would their poems have been different in content or tone if they had used a more structured style? Ask volunteers to read their poems to the class.

DISCUSSION PROMPTS

Use these prompts to explore the contrast that the speaker sets up between conventional ideas of luxury and her own interpretation:

Connect What is your definition of *luxury*? Give some examples of specific things that you consider luxuries. *Students may define* luxury *as something expensive and perhaps unnecessary. They may mention the latest technological equipment, expensive cars or SUVs, trendy clothing, and fancy jewelry.*

Analyze Why might having someone else "push the buttons for you" (lines 13–14) be considered the "*nth* degree" (line 9) of luxury? *Possible answer: Technology has become so advanced that we expect our machines to do everything for us as we simply sit back and watch. Some people may be so lazy that they don't even want to have to push a button to turn on the machine or make it work. Having someone else push the buttons would be the ultimate luxury for those people because it would free them from all effort.*

Evaluate Do you think that the speaker has a valid insight about our technology-driven society, or is she off the mark? Explain. *Students who feel that she is off the mark may cite the popularity of interactive video games as evidence that people still want to "push the buttons." Other students may feel that she is using exaggeration to make a valid point.*

REINFORCE *KEY IDEA:* LOVE POEMS

Discuss How can love be considered the "ultimate luxury"? Do you agree with the idea expressed in this **love poem**? Why or why not? *Possible answer: Love is more valuable than any material possession, so it is the "ultimate luxury" in the sense that it is the most valuable thing in the world. Students who disagree with this idea may say that love is not a luxury because it is a necessity—something people can't live without.*

FOR ENGLISH LEARNERS

Language: Punctuation and Print Cues The lack of punctuation and capitalization in this poem may confuse English learners. Read through each stanza with students, pointing out missing punctuation and capital letters. After reviewing the poem, have students paraphrase each stanza, using conventional punctuation and capitalization.

FOR ADVANCED LEARNERS/PRE–AP

Analyze a Quotation Tell students that Nikki Giovanni has called love "the only true adventure." Have students write a brief essay analyzing Giovanni's view of love and explain whether they agree or disagree with her statement. Have students share their essays with a partner.

ANALYZE VISUALS

Activity In what ways does this painting reflect the imagery and theme of the poem? *Possible answer: The speaker says that she wants to wrap her beloved in colors (line 16), and in the painting, the two figures are wrapped in a colorful blanket. Their physical closeness suggests a loving relationship that matches the theme of love in the poem.*

LITERARY ANALYSIS

G GIOVANNI'S STYLE

Possible answer: The short phrases help create a driving rhythm, which adds to the intensity of the feelings the speaker expresses.

If students need help . . . Have them read the poem aloud with a partner, listening for its rhythm, and then discuss how the poem's rhythm supports the speaker's feelings about her subject.

SELECTION WRAP–UP

SYNTHESIZE Ask students to compare and contrast the message about love in the two poems.

⭐ **CRITIQUE** Have students evaluate each poem by rating it from 1 (did not like) to 5 (liked a lot). Then ask them to support their evaluations.

READING FLUENCY

Distribute the copy master and have students work in pairs or groups to practice fluency.

R RESOURCE MANAGER—Copy Master
Reading Fluency p. 154

Kidnap POEM

NIKKI GIOVANNI

Sleeping Couple I (2000), Hyacinth Manning-Carner.
© Hyacinth Manning-Carner/SuperStock.

ever been kidnapped
by a poet
if i were a poet
i'd kidnap you
5 put you in my phrases and meter
you to jones beach
or maybe coney island[1]
or maybe just to my house
lyric you in lilacs
10 dash you in the rain
blend into the beach
to complement my see[2] G
play the lyre[3] for you
ode you with my love song
15 anything to win you
wrap you in the red Black green
show you off to mama
yeah if i were a poet i'd kid
nap you

G GIOVANNI'S STYLE
Read lines 9–12 aloud. Describe the **rhythm** created by Giovanni's use of short phrases like "lyric you in lilacs" and "dash you in the rain." How does the rhythm help communicate her ideas in this poem?

---

1. **jones beach . . . coney island:** beach and amusement areas on the outskirts of New York City.

2. **complement my see:** complete or perfect my kingdom.

3. **lyre** (līr): stringed instrument like a small, U-shaped harp.

DIFFERENTIATED INSTRUCTION

FOR LESS–PROFICIENT READERS

Comprehension Support Reread the poem with students and help them complete a Cluster Diagram showing the ways the speaker plans to express her love.

BEST PRACTICES TOOLKIT—Transparency
Cluster Diagram p. B18

ode you with my love song
meter you to jones beach
dash you in the rain
To win your love
lyric you in lilacs
blend into the beach
play the lyre for you

Comprehension

1. **Recall** What is the "ultimate luxury" described toward the end of the first poem?

2. **Recall** List three things the speaker of "Kidnap Poem" says she would do if she were a poet.

Literary Analysis

3. **Interpret Ideas in Poetry** Review the chart you filled in as you read. Using the interpretations you recorded, summarize the main message, or **theme,** of each poem.

4. **Analyze Voice** Voice refers to a writer's unique use of language that allows you to "hear" a personality in his or her writing. How would you characterize the voice of the speaker in "Luxury"? Consider the point of view from which the poem is told and the language it uses, as well as the poem's rhythm and message.

5. **Analyze Diction** Reread lines 5–14 of "Kidnap Poem." Consider Giovanni's unconventional use of words like *meter, lyric,* and *ode.* How does Giovanni's unusual word usage help her communicate her message about the power of poetry? Support your answer with evidence from the poem.

6. **Examine Giovanni's Style** Think about the poet's description of her own writing on page 797, and review the bulleted list of Giovanni's trademarks. Which stylistic elements help create Giovanni's loose, conversational style in "Kidnap Poem"? Explain your answer, citing evidence.

7. **Compare and Contrast** In terms of **style,** how are "Luxury" and "Kidnap Poem" similar? In what ways do they differ? Think about the form and rhythm of each poem, as well as the language Giovanni uses in each. Cite specific examples from both poems to support your comparison.

Literary Criticism

8. **Critical Interpretations** Rapper, singer, and actress Queen Latifah discovered Giovanni's poetry at age 14. "Nikki's poems struck me," Latifah explains. "I could feel her. I liked how some of the things she wrote were so clever and cool. I liked how she threw a little bit of rhythm around. All her poetry seemed to be real and to have love in it." After reading "Luxury" and "Kidnap Poem," do you agree or disagree with this description? Explain, citing evidence from both poems.

Practice and Apply

After Reading
For additional support of post-reading questions, use these copy masters:

RESOURCE MANAGER—Copy Masters
Giovanni's Style p. 149 (for practice of literary analysis standards focus)
Question Support p. 153 (After Reading questions adapted for English learners and less-proficient readers)

Additional selection questions are provided for teachers on page 145.

ANSWERS

Comprehension
1. *love*
2. *Possible answer:* "kidnap you," "lyric you in lilacs," "dash you in the rain"

Literary Analysis
Possible answers:

3. ■ STANDARDS FOCUS *Interpret Ideas in Poetry* "Luxury": Love, not material wealth, is what makes our lives rich. "Kidnap Poem": Love can make us want to do extraordinary things for the one we love; poetry, like love, has the power to sweep us off our feet.

4. *Her voice is intense, wise, and street-smart.*

5. *By using nouns as verbs (meter, lyric, and ode), Giovanni makes poetry seem powerful and surprising. By using them in the context of wooing someone, she also makes these academic poetic terms—and thus poetry itself—seem passionate and enticing.*

6. ● STANDARDS FOCUS *Giovanni's Style* Students should cite examples of simple language and irregular line lengths that create a loose, fluid, conversational style.

7. *Both poems lack capitalization and punctuation and contain simple language and lines of varying length. However, "Luxury" has four stanzas, while "Kidnap Poem" is one long stanza. "Kidnap Poem" also uses more unusual diction (nouns as verbs) than "Luxury." Students should find examples of each style similarity and difference.*

Literary Criticism
8. *Answers will vary. Students may cite the driving rhythm of "Kidnap Poem" to support Queen Latifah's assertion that Giovanni "thr[ows] a little bit of rhythm around." They may say that Giovanni's simple, everyday language makes her poems sound "real," and they may point out that both poems are about love. Students may also note Giovanni's clever, unconventional use of language in "Kidnap Poem."*

Assess and Reteach

Assess
RESOURCE MANAGER—Copy Masters
Selection Test A pp. 155–156
Selection Test B/C pp. 157–158
Test Generator CD

Reteach
STANDARDS LESSON FILE
Literature Lesson 46: Style and Syntax
Reading Lesson 2: Monitoring
Reading Lesson 8: Making Inferences

Focus and Motivate

OBJECTIVES

Literary Analysis
- explore the key idea of how people make us **laugh**
- recognize characteristics of farce
- read a play

Reading
- visualize

SUMMARY

In "The Sneeze," Cherdyakov, a clerk in the Ministry of Public Parks, is seated at a play behind the head of the Ministry, General Brassilhov. Because the clerk wants to impress his boss, he is mortified when he sneezes on him. Cherdyakov apologizes profusely, but he cannot forget the incident. Twice he visits the General to apologize, only irritating him. When Cherdyakov sneezes on his boss again, the General hurls abuse at him. A devastated Cherdyakov returns home and dies.

Who makes you LAUGH?

Introduce the question, and have students read the *KEY IDEA*. Then discuss the various ways—sight gags, word plays, silly voices—in which people make us **laugh**. Continue the exploration by having students complete the *QUICKWRITE* activity and compare their lists.

The Sneeze
Drama by Neil Simon

Based on a story by Anton Chekhov

Who makes you LAUGH?

KEY IDEA Whether it's your best friend or a professional comedian, who makes you laugh—*really* **laugh?** What does this person do that you find so funny? If you get a kick out of ridiculous characters bumbling into trouble because of their out-of-control bodily functions, you'll love "The Sneeze."

QUICKWRITE Think about the last time you succumbed to helpless laughter—the kind that makes you gasp for breath and clutch your stomach. What set you off? Create your own top-ten list describing the things and the people you find funniest.

802

Selection Resources

 RESOURCE MANAGER UNIT 8

Plan and Teach pp. 159–166

Literary Analysis
Summary pp. 167†*, 168‡*
Farce pp. 169, 170†*
Question Support p. 174*

Reading
Visualize pp. 171, 172†*
Reading Check p. 173

Assessment
Selection Tests A, B/C pp. 175*, 177*
Test Generator CD

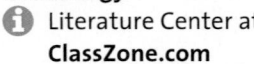 **BEST PRACTICES TOOLKIT**

Differentiated Instruction
pp. 31–38*

Scaffolding Instruction
pp. 43–46*

Graphic Organizers/Strategies
Two-Column Chart • Word
Questioning • Jigsaw • T Chart

Reading Support
Audio Anthology CD*

Technology
Literature Center at
ClassZone.com

WriteSmart CD

---

* Resources for Differentiation   † Also in Spanish   ‡ In Haitian Creole and Vietnamese

● LITERARY ANALYSIS: FARCE

A **farce** is a humorous play that prompts laughter by presenting ridiculous situations, comic dialogue, and physical humor—in this case, an enormous sneeze. Often, the purpose of a farce is simply to keep the audience laughing. However, sometimes the writer of a farce has the goal of poking fun at someone or something in particular. To spot a farce, look for

- absurd plots driven by humorous conflicts
- exaggerated behavior and language
- characters who often exhibit just one comic trait or quality
- clever wordplay, including puns and double meanings
- physical comedy

As you read "The Sneeze," think about how it exhibits these features. Note situations or characters that you find especially funny.

● READING STRATEGY: VISUALIZE

When you **visualize,** you use details, description, and dialogue to create mental pictures of what you read. Visualizing the hilarity of this play can help you interpret and enjoy it. Try the following:

- Read the stage directions to get a mental picture of the setting and actions taking place.
- Pay attention to the narrator's description of the other characters. Do you get an image of how they might look and behave?
- To help you picture the characters, try mentally casting your favorite comedic actor in the lead role.
- Use your own imagination and sense of humor.

As you read, keep track of the details that help you visualize different aspects of the play.

Details from the Text	My Visualization
"He is in his mid-thirties, mild-mannered and unassuming." (lines 4–5)	I picture a timid-looking, boring man with a pale, slightly anxious face.

Author Online

Popular Playwright
Neil Simon, one of America's most popular dramatists, was born on the 4th of July in New York City. He began writing comedy sketches for radio during the 1940s, then migrated to television and finally to the theater. Most of Simon's plays are set in his hometown of New York City and deal with the domestic problems of middle-class Americans.

Neil Simon
born 1927

Russian Master
One of his country's greatest authors, Anton Chekhov was born to a poor family in Russia. He enrolled in medical school as a young man, but his family needed his financial support, so he began writing comical sketches and selling them to magazines. Writing, not medicine, became his career. Chekhov wrote short stories and one-act farces before turning to the full-length plays that made him a legend.

Anton Chekhov
1860–1904

Background

A Team . . . Sort of Neil Simon's *The Good Doctor* is a series of dramatic sketches based on Chekhov's stories. The sketches are tied together through the character of the Writer, who reveals his ideas for stories to the audience. "The Sneeze" is one of those sketches. Simon has jokingly referred to Chekhov as "my non-consenting collaborator."

 MORE ABOUT THE AUTHOR
For more on the authors, visit the
Literature Center at ClassZone.com.

THE SNEEZE **803**

Teach

STANDARDS FOCUS

LITERARY ANALYSIS

● FARCE

For instructional support, read aloud this example:

> Carlton stepped up to the next rung on the ladder, carefully holding the paint can so as not to spill a drop.
>
> "Why can't we hire a professional?" his wife called from inside the house.
>
> "Stop worrying. I know what I'm do—." Just then, he had slipped down three rungs and dumped blue paint all over himself.

Have students identify the element or elements of farce in this example. *Possible answer: The main farcical element is physical comedy—the husband falling off the ladder and spilling paint all over himself. The husband also seems to be a comic character who exhibits overconfidence despite his own incompetence.*

CHECK UNDERSTANDING Elicit other examples of farcical humor from stories, movies, and television shows.

READING STRATEGY

■ VISUALIZE

To support instruction, read aloud this sentence:

> Melinda was about 20, with curly hair and inquiring eyes.

Then ask students either to draw a sketch or to write a description of Melinda. Compare and discuss students' visualizations of Melinda.

CHECK UNDERSTANDING Ask students to explain what clues help them visualize characters in works of fiction.

RESOURCE MANAGER—Copy Master
Visualize p. 171 (for student use while reading the selection)

DIFFERENTIATED INSTRUCTION

FOR LESS–PROFICIENT READERS

Concept Support After students have read the instruction about visualizing, stress that the strategy relies on information gathered by all the senses, not just the sense of sight. For example, the description of Cherdyakov as "mild-mannered and unassuming" (line 5) could suggest that he speaks softly, a trait perceived by the sense of hearing. Urge students to use all their senses in visualizing.

Concept Support Clarify the meaning of these terms related to farce:

- *exaggerated:* overdone or overstated, beyond what is believable
- *puns:* plays on words based on different meanings of the same word or two different words that sound alike
- *physical humor* or *physical comedy:* humor that depends on physical actions, such as when a character slips on a banana peel or is hit in the face with a pie

Practice and Apply

Lines 1–32

READING STRATEGY

● VISUALIZE

Unlike many plays, "The Sneeze" has no introductory description of characters or setting. How does Simon help readers visualize the characters, setting, and actions? ***Possible answer:*** *Simon's Writer acts as a narrator. In lines 1–3, 12–18, and 20–23, the Writer introduces Cherdyakov and the General and describes the setting—"the very best section of the theater for the opening night performance" (lines 16–17). In addition, Simon uses stage directions to describe Cherdyakov, the setting, and the actions of the characters, as in lines 3–12, 18–20, 24–26, and 31–32.*

If students need help . . . Work with them to find examples in the text to complete a Two-Column Chart like this one.

Play Element	Visual Clues
Characters	"He is in his mid-thirties" (line 4)
Setting	"very best section of the theater" (lines 16–17)
Actions	"peruses her program" (line 9)

📋 **BEST PRACTICES TOOLKIT—Transparency**
Two-Column Chart p. A25

THE SNEEZE

NEIL SIMON

FROM *THE GOOD DOCTOR*

BASED ON A STORY BY ANTON CHEKHOV

Writer. If Ivan Ilyitch Cherdyakov,[1] a civil servant, a clerk in the Ministry of Public Parks, had any passion in life at all, it was the theater. (*Enter* Ivan Cherdyakov *and his* Wife. *He is in his mid-thirties, mild-mannered and unassuming. He and his* Wife *are dressed in their best, but are certainly no match for the grandeur around them. They are clearly out of their element here. They move into their seats. As his* Wife *peruses her program,* Cherdyakov *is
10 beaming with happiness as he looks around and in back at the theater and its esteemed audience. He is a happy man tonight.*) He certainly had hopes and ambitions for higher office and had dedicated his life to hard work, zeal and patience. Still, he would not deny himself his one great pleasure. So he purchased two tickets in the very best section of the theater for the opening night performance of Rostov's *The Bearded Countess.*[2] (*A splendidly uniformed* General *and his* Wife *enter, looking for
20 their seats.*) As fortune would have it, into the theater that night came His Respected Superior, General Mikhail Brassilhov,[3] the Minister of Public Parks himself.

(*The* General *and his* Wife *take their seats in the first row, the* General *directly in front of* Cherdyakov.)

Cherdyakov (*leans over to the* General). Good evening, General.

General (*turns, looks at* Cherdyakov *coldly*).
30 Hmm? . . . What? Oh, yes. Yes. Good evening.

(*The* General *turns front again, looks at his program.*)

Cherdyakov. Permit me, sir. I am Cherdyakov . . . Ivan Ilyitch. This is a great honor for me, sir.

General (*turns; coldly*). Yes.

Cherdyakov. Like yourself, dear General, I too serve the Ministry of Public Parks . . . That is to say, I serve *you*, who is indeed *himself* the Minister of Public Parks. I am the Assistant Chief Clerk in
40 the Department of Trees and Bushes.

General. Ahh, yes. Keep up the good work . . . Lovely trees and bushes this year. Very nice.

① Targeted Passage

---

1. **Ivan Ilyitch Cherdyakov** (ē-vän′ ĭl-yēch′ chĕrd′yə-kəv).
2. **Rostov's *The Bearded Countess:*** a made-up author and play.
3. **Mikhail Brassilhov** (mē′kä-ēl′ bräs′ĭl-əv).

804 UNIT 8: AUTHOR'S STYLE AND VOICE

DIFFERENTIATED INSTRUCTION

FOR ALL STUDENTS

Anchor Activity Provide independent learning opportunities for students to learn about point of view. Ask students to write three journal entries form the point of view of either Cherdyakov or the General. Invite students to share their entries with the class. For further details, see

📘 **RESOURCE MANAGER**
Ideas for Extension pp. 164–165

FOR LESS–PROFICIENT READERS

In combination with the *Audio Anthology CD*, use one or more Targeted Passages (pp. 804, 807, 810) to ensure that students focus on key events, concepts, and skills. Targeted Passages are also good for English learners.

① Targeted Passage [Lines 1–23]

This passage introduces the play's setting and describes the characters.

BACKGROUND

Aaaaahchoo! Sneezing is the involuntary, explosive expulsion of air from the nose and mouth, usually caused by nasal irritation. Scientists estimate that the force of an average sneeze is roughly 100 miles per hour, comparable to the force of hurricane winds. Like Cherdyakov in the play "The Sneeze," many have believed for centuries that a sneeze was an omen of things to come, both good and bad. In 400 B.C., a soldier's sneeze at the end of General Xenophon's speech convinced Athenians that the gods were happy, and they followed the general into battle. The custom of uttering a blessing after a sneeze spans many religions and dates back centuries, arising in part from the belief that a sneeze was strong enough to expel the soul from the body.

ANALYZE VISUALS

Activity After students have read page 804, ask them to look at the photograph, think about the play's title, and predict what will happen. Suggest that they consider whose sneeze the title refers to and what the consequences of the sneeze might be. *Students may predict that Cherdyakov sneezes and sprays the General.*

- What is the setting?
- What characters are introduced?
- Why is Cherdyakov "a happy man tonight"?
- Why are Cherdyakov and his wife "out of their element"?

FOR ENGLISH LEARNERS

Key Academic Vocabulary Use Word Questioning to teach these words: *element* (line 8), *assistant* (line 39), *proportion* (line 128), *motivation* (line 231), *committed* (line 236).

 BEST PRACTICES TOOLKIT—Transparency Word Questioning p. E9

Prereading For prereading instruction for English learners, see

 BEST PRACTICES TOOLKIT Scaffolding Reading Instruction pp. 43–46

FOR ADVANCED LEARNERS/PRE–AP

Pre-AP Exercises in the bottom channel provide additional challenge for students. Use these suggestions for small groups or individuals.

ADDITIONAL GUIDELINES

For more help with differentiation and tips for classroom management, see

 BEST PRACTICES TOOLKIT Differentiated Instruction pp. 31–38

Lines 80–110
REINFORCE *KEY IDEA:* LAUGH

Discuss What aspects of Simon's description of the sneeze are likely to make people **laugh?**
Possible answer: Simon uses exaggeration and figurative language to describe the event, saying it came "like a bolt from a gray thundering sky" (lines 81–82) and calling it "monstrous" (line 86). He emphasizes the General's "completely bald head" (line 88) and creates a humorous image with "Your complete head is splattered" (lines 108–109). Simon then adds to the humor by having Cherdyakov agree with the General that his sneeze is disgusting.

Lines 84–116
DISCUSSION PROMPTS

Use these prompts to help students understand the interaction between Cherdyakov and the General:

Connect Have you ever accidentally sneezed or spilled something on someone? How did you feel? *Responses should show a grasp of such embarrassing situations.*

Analyze Why does Cherdyakov make so much of the sneeze? *Possible answer: Cherdyakov had hoped to establish a more personal relationship with his boss, making a favorable impression on him, and now he is mortified by what he has done.*

Evaluate Do you think that Cherdyakov's apologies and actions after the sneeze make matters better or worse? Explain your answer. *Possible answer: The clerk's actions make matters worse. The General repeatedly tries to put the incident behind him and is getting irritated by Cherdyakov's focus on it.*

(*The* General *turns back.* Cherdyakov *sits back, happy, grinning like a cat. The* General's Wife *whispers to him and he shrugs back. Suddenly the unseen curtain rises on the play and they all applaud.* Cherdyakov *leans forward again.*)

Cherdyakov. My wife would like very much to say hello, General. This is she. My wife, Madame
50 Cherdyakov.

Wife (*smiles*). How do you do?

General. My pleasure.

Wife. *My* pleasure, General.

General. How do you do?

(*He turns front, flustered.* Cherdyakov *beams at his* Wife; *then*)

Cherdyakov (*to the* General's Wife). Madame Brassilhov—my wife, Madame Cherdyakov.

Wife. How do you do, Madame Brassilhov?

60 **Madame Brassilhov** (*coldly*). How do you do?

Wife. I just had the pleasure of meeting your husband.

Cherdyakov (*to* Madame Brassilhov). And I am my wife's husband. How do you do, Madame Brassilhov?

(*The* Writer *"shushes" them.*)

General (*to the* Writer). Sorry. Terribly sorry.

(*The* General *tries to control his anger as they all go back to watching the play.*)

70 **Cherdyakov.** I hope you enjoy the play, sir.

General. I will if I can watch it.

(*He is getting hot under the collar. They all go back to watching the performance.*)

Writer. Feeling quite pleased with himself for having made the most of this golden opportunity, Ivan Ilyitch Cherdyakov sat back to enjoy *The Bearded Countess.* He was no longer a stranger to the Minister of Public Parks. They had become, if one wanted to be generous about the matter,

80 familiar with each other . . . And then, quite suddenly, without any warning, like a bolt from a gray thundering sky, Ivan Ilyitch Cherdyakov reared his head back, and—

Cherdyakov. AHHHHHHHH—CHOOOOOOOO!!! (Cherdyakov *unleashes a monstrous sneeze, his head snapping forward. The main blow of the sneeze discharges on the back of the* General's *completely bald head. The* General *winces and his hand immediately goes to his now-*
90 *dampened head.*) Ohhh, my goodness, I'm *sorry,* your Excellency! I'm so terribly sorry!

(*The* General *takes out his handkerchief and wipes his head.*)

General. Never mind. It's all right.

Cherdyakov. *All right?* . . . It certainly is *not* all right! It's unpardonable. It was monstrous of me—

General. You make too much of the matter. Let it rest.

100 (*He puts away his handkerchief.*)

Cherdyakov (*quickly takes out his own handkerchief*). How can I let it rest? It was inexcusable. Permit me to wipe your neck, General. It's the least I can do.

(*He starts to wipe the* General's *head. The* General *pushes his hand away.*)

General. Leave it be! It's all right, I say.

Cherdyakov. But I splattered you, sir. Your complete head is splattered. It was an accident,
110 I assure you—but it's *disgusting!*

Writer. Shhhh!

General. I'm sorry. My apologies.

Cherdyakov. The thing is, your Excellency, it came completely without warning. It was out of my nose before I could stifle it.

Madame Brassilhov. Shhh!

DIFFERENTIATED INSTRUCTION

FOR ENGLISH LEARNERS

Vocabulary: Idioms Use a Jigsaw strategy by dividing students into home groups of five and assigning one of these idioms to a student in each group: *golden opportunity* (line 75), "excellent chance"; *make too much of* (line 98), "give too much importance to"; *Let it rest* (line 99), "forget about it"; *Leave it be* (line 107), "leave it alone."

Then have students reassemble into expert groups, and have each expert group determine its idiom's meaning. Have experts return to their home groups, whose students should then work together to create definitions and example sentences for the five idioms. Have groups share and compare their definitions and sentences.

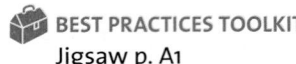 **BEST PRACTICES TOOLKIT**
Jigsaw p. A1

Cherdyakov. Shhh, yes, certainly. I'm sorry . . . (*He sits back, nervously. He blows his nose with his handkerchief. Then* Cherdyakov *leans forward.*) It's not a cold, if that's what you were worrying about, sir. Probably a particle of dust in the nostril—

General. Shhh! ❷ **Targeted Passage**

(*They watch the play in silence, and* Cherdyakov *sits back, unhappy with himself.*)

Writer. But try as he might, Cherdyakov could not put the incident out of his mind. The sneeze, no more than an innocent anatomical accident,[4] grew out of all proportion in his mind, until it resembled the angry roar of a cannon aimed squarely at the enemy camp. He played the incident back in his mind, slowing the procedure down so he could view again in horror the infamous deed.

(Cherdyakov, *in slow motion, repeats the sneeze again, but slowed down so that it appears to us as one frame at a time. It also seems to be three times as great in intensity as the original sneeze. The* General, *also in slow motion, reacts as though he has just taken a fifty-pound hammer blow at the base of his skull.*) *They all go with the slow motion of the "sneeze" until it is completed, when the unseen curtain falls and they applaud. They all rise and begin to file out of the theater, chattering about the lovely evening they have just spent.*)

General. Charming . . . Charming.

Madame Brassilhov. Yes, charming.

General. Charming . . . Simply charming. Wasn't it charming, my dear?

Madame Brassilhov. I found it utterly charming.

(Cherdyakov *stands behind them tapping the* General.)

Writer. I was completely charmed by it.

---

4. **innocent anatomical accident:** A biological act over which Cherdyakov had no control.

Cherdyakov (*still tapping away at the* General). Excuse me, Excellency—

General. Who's tapping? Somebody's tapping me. Who's that tapping?

Cherdyakov. I'm tapping, sir. I'm the tapper . . . Cherdyakov.

Madame Brassilhov (*quickly pulls the* General *back*). Stand back, dear, it's the sneezer.

Cherdyakov. No, no, it's all right. I'm all sneezed out . . . I was just concerned about your going out into the night air with a damp head.

General. Oh, that. It was a trifle. A mere faux pas. Forget it, young man. Amusing play, don't you think? Did you find it amusing?

Cherdyakov. Amusing? Oh, my goodness, yes. Ha, ha. So true. Ha, ha. I haven't laughed as much in years. Ha, ha, ha . . .

General. Which part interested you the most?

Cherdyakov. The sneeze. When I sneezed on you. It was unforgivable, sir.

General. Forget it, young man. Come, my dear. It looks like rain. I don't want to get my head wet again.

Madame Brassilhov. You shouldn't let people sneeze on you, dear. You're not to be sneezed at.

(*They are gone.*)

Cherdyakov. I'm ruined! Ruined! He'll have me fired from Trees and Bushes. They'll send me down to Branches and Twigs.

Wife. Come, Ivan.

Cherdyakov. What?

Wife. You mustn't let it concern you. It was just a harmless little sneeze. The General's probably forgotten it already.

Cherdyakov. Do you really think so?

Wife. No! I'm scared, Ivan.

THE SNEEZE **807**

Lines 125–144

READING STRATEGY

■ **VISUALIZE**

How does Simon help readers visualize and therefore understand Cherdyakov's perception of events? *Possible answer: Simon first has the Writer explain Cherdyakov's feelings in lines 125–133, emphasizing how in Cherdyakov's mind, the incident has grown "out of all proportion" and resembles "the angry roar of a cannon" (lines 128–129). Then in his stage directions (lines 134–144), Simon describes the images running through Cherdyakov's mind.*

Extend the Discussion What exaggerated comparisons does Simon make in lines 134–144 to enhance the description of the sneeze as Cherdyakov sees it?

ANALYZE VISUALS

Activity Ask students how the photographs displayed on pages 806–810 relate in general to the play and in particular to lines 134–142. *Possible answer: Cherdyakov's sneeze is the central incident in the play. The photographs show a well-dressed man sneezing, an image suggestive of Cherdyakov. In lines 134–142, the stage directions describe how Cherdyakov replays the sneeze in his mind in slow motion, "one frame at a time." The photographs displayed are a frame-by-frame sequence of a sneeze and are repeated on each successive page of the play as they are in Cherdyakov's mind.*

About the Art The images at the top of pages 806–810 are taken from *The Edison Kinetoscopic Record of a Sneeze.* The film is less than a minute long and was shot in 1894 at Thomas Edison's early motion picture studio in New Jersey. It starred Fred Ott, an Edison employee known for his comic sneezes. *The Sneeze*, as it is popularly known, is the earliest surviving motion picture to be copyrighted and is sometimes cited as the first example of a close-up shot in movies.

FOR LESS–PROFICIENT READERS

❷ **Targeted Passage [Lines 123–140]**

This passage shows Cherdyakov distorting the reality as he obsesses over the sneeze.

• Why doesn't Cherdyakov just sit back and enjoy the play?

• How is Cherdyakov's memory of the sneeze different from the actual sneeze?

• What examples of farcical exaggeration appear in this passage?

FOR ADVANCED LEARNERS/PRE–AP

Analyze Figurative Language In lines 126–130 and 137–140, Simon uses figurative language to make amusing comparisons. Discuss what Simon conveys with these comparisons. Have students create original figures of speech that would convey similar ideas. Invite students to share their comparisons with the class.

● FARCE

Explain how the dialogue on this page combines word play and exaggeration to create humor. *Possible answer: Word play: The Writer says that Cherdyakov's career had "been blown away" (line 193), a pun referring to the sneeze. Later Cherdyakov reminds the General that they met under "'explosive' circumstances" (lines 222–223), another pun on the sneeze. Cherdyakov refers to the General as "your kindship" (line 238), an unintentional play on the words* kindness *and* worship. *Exaggeration: Cherdyakov exaggerates when he tells his wife that people of their own class "love sneezing on each other" (lines 196–197). Cherdyakov's apology is nonstop exaggeration. For example, he insists that "there was no political or antisocial motivation" behind his sneeze (lines 230–231) and that it was merely "a nonpartisan, nonviolent act of God" (lines 231–232). Referring to his nose, he proclaims, "I curse the day the protuberance formed itself on my face" (lines 232–233). Cherdyakov continues to overdo his apology when he sputters, "I worship the chair you sit on and the uniform you wear that sits on the chair that I worship" (lines 257–259).*

Lines 229–238
REINFORCE *KEY IDEA:* LAUGH

Discuss Why is Cherdyakov's response to the General likely to make people **laugh**? *Possible answer: Cherdyakov's response is highly exaggerated. He refers to the sneeze as "a nonpartisan, nonviolent act of God" and calls his nose "hateful." Then he grabs it and tells the General to exile his nose, "but absolve the innocent body behind it."*

Writer. And so they walked home in despair.

190 **Cherdyakov.** Perhaps I should send him a nice gift. Maybe some Turkish towels.

Writer. Cherdyakov's once-promising career had literally been blown away.

Cherdyakov (*as they arrive home*). Why did this happen to me? Why did I go to the theater at all? Why didn't I sit in the balcony with people of our own class? They love sneezing on each other.

Wife. Come to bed, Ivan.

Cherdyakov. Perhaps if I were to call on the
200 General and explain matters again, but in such a charming, honest and self-effacing manner, he would have no choice but to forgive me . . .

Wife. Maybe it's best not to remind him, Ivan.

Cherdyakov. No, no. If I ever expect to become a gentleman, I must behave like one.

Writer. And so the morning came. It so happened this was the day the General listened to petitions, and since there were fifty or sixty petitions ahead of Cherdyakov, he waited from morning till late,
210 late afternoon . . .

(Cherdyakov *moves into the office set.*)

General. Next! . . . NEXT!

Cherdyakov. I'm not next, your Excellency . . . I'm last.

General. Very well, then . . . Last!

Cherdyakov. That's me, sir.

General. Well, what is your petition?

Cherdyakov. I have no petition, sir. I'm not a petitioner.

220 **General.** Then you waste my time.

Cherdyakov. Do you not recognize me, sir? We met last night under rather "explosive" circumstances . . . I am the splatterer.

---
5. **Gesundheit** (gə-zŏŏnt'hīt'): German for "good health," this term is often used after someone sneezes.

General. The what?

Cherdyakov. The sneezer. The one who sneezed. The sneezing splatterer.

General. Indeed? And what is it you want now? A *Gesundheit?*[5]

Cherdyakov. No, Excellency . . . Your forgiveness.
230 I just wanted to point out there was no political or antisocial motivation behind my sneeze. It was a nonpartisan, nonviolent act of God. I curse the day the protuberance formed itself on my face. It's a hateful nose, sir, and I am not responsible for its indiscretions . . . (*grabbing his own nose*) Punish that which committed the crime, but absolve the innocent body behind it. Exile my nose, but forgive me, your kindship. Forgive me.

General. My dear young man, I'm not angry with
240 your nose. I'm too busy to have time for your nasal problems. I suggest you go home and take a hot bath—or a cold one—take *something,* but don't bother me with this silly business again . . . Gibber, gibber gibber, that's all I've heard all day. (*going offstage*) Gibber, gibber, gibber, gibber . . . (Cherdyakov *stands alone in the office sobbing.*)

Cherdyakov. Thank you, sir. God bless you and your wife and your household. May your days be sweet and may your nights be better than your days.

250 **Writer.** The feeling of relief that came over Cherdyakov was enormous . . .

Cherdyakov. May the birds sing in the morning at your window and may the coffee in your cup be strong and hot . . .

Writer. The weight of the burden that was lifted was inestimable . . .

Cherdyakov. I worship the chair you sit on and the uniform you wear that sits on the chair that I worship . . .

260 **Writer.** He walked home, singing and whistling like a lark. Life was surely a marvel, a joy, a heavenly paradise . . .

DIFFERENTIATED INSTRUCTION

FOR ENGLISH LEARNERS

Vocabulary: Suffixes Direct students' attention to the words *tapper* (line 157), *sneezer* (line 225), and *splatterer* (line 226). Elicit the definition of each word ("someone who taps," "someone who sneezes," and "someone who splatters"). Call attention to the suffix *-er,* and explain that it means "one who does an action." Then divide students into small groups, and have groups list other "doer" words ending in *-er, -or* (such as *actor*), or *-ar* (such as *liar*). Challenge groups to create a T Chart listing the action verbs on the left and the nouns naming those who do these actions on the right. The group that can list the most correct entries within a set time limit wins.

 BEST PRACTICES TOOLKIT—Transparency T Chart p. A25

Cherdyakov. Oh, God, I am happy!

Writer. And yet—

Cherdyakov. And yet—

Writer. When he arrived home, he began to think . . .

Cherdyakov. Have I been the butt of a cruel and thoughtless joke?

270 **Writer.** Had the Minister toyed with him?

Cherdyakov. If he had no intention of punishing me, why did he torment me so unmercifully?

Writer. If the sneeze meant so little to the Minister, why did he deliberately cause Cherdyakov to writhe in his bed?

Cherdyakov. . . . to twist in agony the entire night?

Writer. Cherdyakov was furious!

Cherdyakov. I AM FURIOUS!

280 **Writer.** He foamed and fumed and paced the night through, and in the morning he called out to his wife, "SONYA!"

Cherdyakov. SONYA! (*She rushes in.*) I have been humiliated.

Wife. *You,* Ivan? Who would humiliate *you?* You're such a kind and generous person.

Cherdyakov. Who? I'll tell you who! General Brassilhov, the Minister of Public Parks.

Wife. What did he do?

290 **Cherdyakov.** The swine! I was humiliated in such subtle fashion, it was almost indiscernible. The man's cunning is equal only to his cruelty. He practically forced me to come to his office to grovel and beg on my knees. I was reduced to a gibbering idiot.

Wife. You were that reduced?

---

6. **humiliated by *I* . . . humiliate *he*:** Cherdyakov uses an incorrect pronoun, and the Writer mimics him.

Cherdyakov. I must go back and tell him what I think of him. The lower classes must speak up . . . (*He is at the door.*) The world must be made

300 safe so that men of all nations and creeds, regardless of color or religion, will be free to sneeze on their superiors! It is *he* who will be humiliated by *I!*

Writer. And so, the next morning, Cherdyakov came to humiliate *he.*[6]

(*Lights up on the* General *at his desk.*)

General. Last! (Cherdyakov *goes to the* General's *desk. He stands there glaring down at the* General *with a faint trace of a smile on his lips. The* General *looks up.*) Well?

310 **Cherdyakov** (*smiles*). Well? Well, you say? . . . Do you not recognize me, your Excellency? Look at my face . . . Yes. You're quite correct. It is I once again.

General (*looks at him, puzzled*). It is you once again who?

Cherdyakov (*confidentially*). Cherdyakov, Excellency. I have returned, having taken neither a hot bath nor a cold one.

General. Who let this filthy man in? What is it?

320 **Cherdyakov** (*on top of the situation now*). What is it? . . . What is it, you ask? You sit there behind your desk and ask, What is it? You sit there in your lofty position as General and Minister of Public Parks, a member in high standing among the upper class and ask me, a lowly civil servant, What is it? You sit there with full knowledge that there is no equality in this life, that there are those of us who serve and those that are served, those of us that obey and those that are obeyed, those of us who bow and those that

330 are bowed to, that in this life certain events take place that cause some of us to be humiliated and those that are the cause of that humiliation . . . and still you ask, "WHAT IS IT?"!

General (*angrily*). *What is it?* Don't stand there gibbering like an idiot! What is it you want?

Lines 263–315
DISCUSSION PROMPTS

Use these prompts to help students understand why Cherdyakov goes to see the General again:

Connect Have you ever reacted one way to something a person said or did but then reacted altogether differently later on? Why did your reaction change? Which proved more accurate: your initial feelings or your subsequent reaction? *Responses should reflect an understanding of such situations.*

Analyze Cherdyakov's mood turns from "happy" (line 263) to "furious" (line 278) in no time at all. Explain why. *Possible answer: As Cherdyakov reflects on recent events, he decides that the General has humiliated and "toyed with" (line 270) him. Cherdyakov attributes his self-inflicted mental anguish to the General's behavior rather than to his own obsessiveness.*

Evaluate Do you think there is any truth to Cherdyakov's conclusion that the General meant to humiliate him in "subtle fashion"? Support your answer. *Possible answer: Nothing in the play suggests that the General meant to humiliate Cherdyakov. The General did not even remember Cherdyakov when he came to his office on the morning after the sneeze. He tells Cherdyakov that he is not angry—much as he had at the theater the night before—and that Cherdyakov should not bother him again. Even when Cherdyakov returns the second time, the General still does not understand who he is or why he has come.*

FOR ENGLISH LEARNERS

Vocabulary: Word Associations Review the meanings of these phrases from the play: "The thing is . . ." (line 113), "try as he might" (line 125), "simply charming" (line 147), and "singing and whistling like a lark" (lines 260–261). Then have pairs of students create and perform brief dialogues using the phrases.

Lines 336–352
REINFORCE *KEY IDEA:* LAUGH

Discuss How does the final exchange between Cherdyakov and the General show how people make us **laugh?** *Possible answer: Instead of telling off the General, as the reader anticipates, Cherdyakov apologizes yet again. The General's abusive tirade (lines 340–344) is also humorous. The comical climax occurs when Cherdyakov sneezes again—right in the General's face (line 345). Then the General starts calling him comically inventive, insect-derived names, such as "son-in-law of a bed bug" (line 350).*

Lines 345–366

LITERARY ANALYSIS

● **FARCE**

How does the ending of the play illustrate the qualities of farce? *Possible answer: The ending reflects exaggeration to the point of absurdity.*

Extend the Discussion How else might Simon have ended the play?

SELECTION WRAP–UP

REFLECT Ask students which character they found more sympathetic: Cherdyakov or the General. Students should give reasons to support their responses.

 **CRITIQUE** Ask students if they enjoyed the farcical elements of "The Sneeze," and to explain why or why not. Urge students to give specific reasons for their opinions.

Cherdyakov. *I'll tell you what I want!* . . . I wanted to apologize again for sneezing on you . . . I wasn't sure I made it clear. It was an accident, an accident, I assure you . . .

340 **General** (*stands and screams out*). Out! Out, you idiot! Fool! Imbecile! Get out of my sight! I never want to see you again. If you ever cross my line of vision I'll have you exiled forever . . . WHAT'S YOUR NAME?

Cherdyakov. Ch—Cherdyakov!

(*It comes out as a sneeze in the* General's *face.*)

General (*wiping himself*). You germ spreader! You maggot! You insect! You are lower than an insect. You are the second cousin to a cockroach! The
350 son-in-law of a bed bug! You are the nephew of a ringworm! You are nothing, nothing, do you hear me? . . . *NOTHING!*

(Cherdyakov *backs away, and returns home.*)

Writer. At that moment, something broke loose inside of Cherdyakov . . . Something so deep and vital, so organic, that the damage that was done seemed irreparable . . . Something drained from him that can only be described as the very life force itself . . . (Cherdyakov *takes off his coat. He*
360 *sits on the sofa, head in hands.*) The matter was over, for once, for all, forever. What happened next was quite simple . . . (Cherdyakov *lies back on the sofa.*) Ivan Ilyitch Cherdyakov arrived at home . . . removed his coat . . . lay down on the sofa—and died! (Cherdyakov's *head drops and his hand falls to the floor.*)

Blackout

❸ **Targeted Passage**

---

810   UNIT 8: AUTHOR'S STYLE AND VOICE

DIFFERENTIATED INSTRUCTION

FOR LESS–PROFICIENT READERS
❸ **Targeted Passage [Lines 345–366]**

This passage concludes the play, as Cherdyakov's second sneeze causes the General to explode, which in turn leads to Cherdyakov's absurd death.

- Why does the General lose his temper and yell at Cherdyakov?

- How does Cherdyakov react to the General's outburst?

FOR ADVANCED LEARNERS/PRE–AP
Updating the Play Simon's 1973 play is based on a Chekhov story set in 19th-century Russia. Ask students to write a paragraph or two suggesting how Simon might have set "The Sneeze" in contemporary America. If students are familiar with Simon's plays, encourage them to consider how Simon might have adapted "The Sneeze" to reflect his own cultural background and literary themes.

Comprehension

1. **Recall** Where does the opening scene of the play take place?

2. **Summarize** How does the General react when Cherdyakov sneezes?

3. **Recall** Why does Cherdyakov go to see the General in his office the next morning?

4. **Clarify** How does the play end?

Literary Analysis

5. **Visualize** Review the chart you filled in as you read. Which scene or situation in the play were you able to picture most vividly? Write a short paragraph describing the details. If you'd like, create a sketch to accompany your paragraph.

6. **Draw Conclusions** What is the role of the Writer in "The Sneeze"? Explain the function he performs, citing evidence to support your answer.

7. **Analyze Farce** Which element of farce made you **laugh** the most? Using a chart like the one shown, record examples of ridiculous situations, exaggerated behavior or language, and physical comedy that appear in "The Sneeze." What in particular does Neil Simon seem to be mocking?

Ridiculous Situations	Exaggerated Behavior/Language	Physical Comedy
•	•	•
•	•	•

8. **Identify Dramatic Irony** Dramatic irony occurs when the audience (or the reader) knows more information about a character or a situation than the characters themselves know. Find an example of dramatic irony in the play, and explain what makes it ironic.

Literary Criticism

9. **Author's Style** Neil Simon has said, "My idea of the ultimate achievement in a comedy is to make a whole audience fall onto the floor, writhing and laughing so hard that some of them pass out." Did he accomplish this goal with "The Sneeze"? Cite evidence from the play to support your opinion.

THE SNEEZE **811**

Practice and Apply

After Reading

For additional support of post-reading questions, use these copy masters:

R RESOURCE MANAGER—Copy Masters
Reading Check p. 173 (to check understanding of the selection)
Farce p. 169 (for practice of literary analysis standards focus)
Question Support p. 174 (After Reading questions adapted for English learners and less-proficient readers)

Additional selection questions are provided for teachers on page 163.

ANSWERS

Comprehension

1. *The opening scene occurs at the theater.*

2. *He is understanding but gets irritated as Cherdyakov keeps frantically apologizing.*

3. *Cherdyakov visits the General to apologize for the sneeze so that he won't fire him.*

4. *Cherdyakov sneezes on the General again, the General screams insults at him, and Cherdyakov goes home and dies.*

Literary Analysis
Possible answers:

5. ■ **STANDARDS FOCUS** *Visualize Students should cite details from the play.*

6. *The Writer serves as the narrator, giving background (lines 74–83), making humorous comments (lines 192–193), and occasionally joining in the dialogue (line 111).*

Assess and Reteach

Assess

R RESOURCE MANAGER—Copy Masters
Selection Test A pp. 175–176
Selection Test B/C pp. 177–178
Test Generator CD

Reteach

S STANDARDS LESSON FILE
Literature Lesson 38: Verbal and Dramatic Irony
Literature Lesson 25: Elements of Drama

7. ● **STANDARDS FOCUS** *Farce Ridiculous Situations: Cherdyakov's excessive apologies (lines 90–121, 221–238); his slow-motion reenactment of the sneeze (lines 125–144); his rapid transition from "happy" to "furious" (lines 263–279); his abrupt death (lines 363–366). Exaggerated Behavior/Language: Cherdyakov and his wife's overly polite introduction at the theater (lines 33–71); the description of the first sneeze (lines 80–90); Cherdyakov's excessive apologies; the General's abusive tirade (lines 340–352). Physical Comedy: the first sneeze; Cherdyakov's slow-motion re-* *enactment of the sneeze; the second sneeze (line 345). Simon mocks the human tendencies to blow events out of proportion and to misinterpret other people.*

8. *Cherdyakov thinks the General has intentionally humiliated him, but the audience realizes the General doesn't even remember Cherdyakov, who is humiliating himself.*

Literary Criticism

9. *Students may cite any of the farcical elements listed for answer 7.*

Focus and Motivate

OBJECTIVES

- analyze a student model that reflects the key traits of analysis of an author's style
- use the writing process to produce an analysis of an author's style
- revise and edit, using a rubric for writing an analysis of an author's style
- deliver an oral presentation

WRITER'S ROAD MAP

WRITING PROMPTS 1 AND 2

Help students choose a prompt by reviewing literature from the unit or by brainstorming people whose songs, works of art, or films would make good subjects for an analysis of style. Make sure students understand that they are to analyze the style of the individual's work, not the style of the person.

ADDITIONAL PROMPTS

Use these prompts for practice with business writing and writing in the humanities:

WRITING PROMPT 3

Writing from Media Write an analysis of the style in a work of journalism. Keep in mind the medium's purpose and audience.

Possible Subjects

- a prime time news anchor
- a regular newspaper editorial column
- a radio talk show

WRITING PROMPT 4

Writing About Food Write an analysis of the style of a good meal you enjoyed recently. Keep in mind that the meal need not be elaborate or expensive, but it should be distinctive in taste and preparation.

Possible Subjects

- a meal enjoyed in a restaurant
- a home-cooked meal

For additional writing prompts, see

- WriteSmart CD
- Writing Center at **ClassZone.com**

KEY TRAITS

Review the six *KEY TRAITS* with students, focusing primarily on **ideas** and **word choice**. Compare the list of traits with the rubric on page 818.

Writing Workshop
Analysis of an Author's Style

Every writer—and human being—has a unique way of experiencing life and sharing his or her experience. As you've learned in this unit, exploring the elements that make up this uniqueness can help you understand and appreciate literary works. Use the **Writer's Road Map** to get started writing an analysis of an author's style.

WRITER'S ROAD MAP
Analysis of an Author's Style

WRITING PROMPT 1

Writing from Literature Choose a piece of literature and write an analysis of the author's style. If you can, read several pieces by the same author. Your analysis should help readers understand important elements of that author's style, such as word choice, sentence structure, tone, figurative language, and imagery.

Authors to Explore

- Tim O'Brien, "Where Have You Gone, Charming Billy?"
- Barbara Kingsolver, "Going to Japan"
- Emily Dickinson, "A narrow Fellow in the Grass"

WRITING PROMPT 2

Writing for the Real World Style isn't limited to writing. Choose a creative person you know about and write an analysis of his or her distinctive style. Explain how that style communicates the individual's personality, values, or message.

People to Consider

- artists
- musicians
- actors or film directors

 WRITING TOOLS
For prewriting, revision, and editing tools, visit the **Writing Center** at ClassZone.com.

KEY TRAITS

1. IDEAS

- Presents a **thesis statement** that identifies the main points of the analysis
- Uses relevant **details** to support the main points
- **Elaborates** on the details to explain the style

2. ORGANIZATION

- Identifies the author and literary work (or the person being analyzed) in an engaging **introduction**
- Provides enough **information** about the literary work (or the person) for readers to follow the analysis
- **Concludes** with a summary of the ideas and offers insights into the author's (or person's) style

3. VOICE

- Speaks directly to the reader in an active, engaging **voice**

4. WORD CHOICE

- Uses precise **terms** to describe and analyze the style

5. SENTENCE FLUENCY

- Uses a variety of **sentence structures**

6. CONVENTIONS

- Employs **correct grammar and usage**

Writing Workshop Resources

 **RESOURCE MANAGER UNIT 8**

Plan and Teach pp. 179–182
Prewriting–Editing pp. 183–187
Writing Rubric p. 188
Speaking and Listening p. 189
Writing Support p. 190*

 **STANDARDS LESSON FILE**

Writing Lesson 27: Analysis Essay
Grammar Lesson 2: Avoiding Run-Ons

 BEST PRACTICES TOOLKIT

Scaffolding Writing Instruction pp. 43–46*
T Chart • Classification Chart • Writing Template: Literary Analysis

TECHNOLOGY

- Easy Planner DVD
- Writing Center at **ClassZone.com**
- WriteSmart CD

* Resources for Differentiation

Part 1: Analyze a Student Model

Leslie Wu
Reagan High School

Nikki Giovanni's Notable Style

Have you ever been kidnapped by a poet? Nikki Giovanni asks this surprising question in "Kidnap Poem." In that poem and in "Luxury," Giovanni uses an informal, personal, playful style of writing to explore the importance of love.

5   Giovanni's informal tone creates a sense of closeness and familiarity. Both poems are free verse rather than a more structured style, with line breaks in the middle of a thought or even in the middle of a word ("i'd kid / nap you"). There is no punctuation in either poem except for contractions, which make the writing sound more like spoken language.

10 Simple, direct language adds to the conversational tone. Words and phrases such as "rich and famous" and "maybe coney island / or maybe just to my house" are straightforward and fairly easy to understand. The poems' loosely structured, casual style makes sense because in each poem the speaker is addressing a loved one. "Kidnap Poem" is a love poem, or

15 maybe even a love song. The main message of "Luxury" is that love is more important than power, wealth, and fame.

    Another important aspect of this poet's style has to do with point of view. Giovanni uses the first-person point of view in both poems. The speaker addresses the loved one as "you" rather than using a name or

20 giving any details about the person. This technique makes both poems sound like a close, personal conversation. "Luxury" and "Kidnap Poem" make the reader feel as if he or she is eavesdropping on two people who know each other very well. These are extremely personal poems about love and relationships.

KEY TRAITS IN ACTION

Introduction includes an intriguing question and identifies the author and literary works. **Thesis statement** presents the elements of the author's style.

Supports a main point about the author's style with relevant **details** from the poems, and **elaborates** on the details to explain the effect on readers.

Writer uses precise **terms** in her analysis.

Teach

Part 1: Analyze a Student Model

Have students read the student model and **KEY TRAITS IN ACTION.** Then discuss the model with the class, pointing out specific examples of each trait and building on what students have already noted. You may also wish to incorporate these activities:

- **Thesis Statement** Write this incomplete thesis statement on the board:

  > Nikki Giovanni's poems have a unique style. She uses a casual style to explore the theme of love.

  Ask a student to read this statement and lines 3–4 of the student model. Then ask students to compare the two. ***Possible answer:*** *The thesis statement on the board begins with a generalization and gives little specific information about the author's style and theme. The thesis statement in the model uses a literary term* (informal) *to describe the author's style and briefly identifies the author's theme.*

- **Terms** Have students refer to the Terms for Writing About Literary Style on page 818. Review the meaning of terms highlighted on page 813. Clarify that in the *first-person point of view,* the speaker uses the word *I.* The speaker is the voice in a poem. Ask students to find other literary terms used on page 813.

  - *informal* (line 3)
  - *tone* (line 5)
  - *line breaks* (lines 6–7)
  - *the speaker* (line 14)

DIFFERENTIATED INSTRUCTION

For general guidelines on differentiating writing instruction, see

BEST PRACTICES TOOLKIT
Scaffolding Writing Instruction
pp. 43–46

FOR ENGLISH LEARNERS

Language: Skill Words Write these terms on the board and review them with students:

- *literary terms:* words that describe a literary genre or style, such as *informal,* and *tone*
- *voice:* a writer's unique style of expression, which reveals his or her personality, beliefs, and attitudes
- *thesis statement:* one or two sentences stating the main idea of an essay. In an analysis

of an author's style, the thesis statement names the most important elements of the author's style and tells how they help convey the author's message, or theme. Share this example:

> The poet uses an informal style to explain her message that love is more important than anything else.

- **Sentence Structures** Remind students of these strategies for varying sentence structure:
  - Use both simple and complex sentences.
  - Include both short and long sentences.
  - Begin sentences in different ways.

Point out that sentences can begin with a quotation, with descriptive words, and with transitions. Have partners find these sentence beginnings in lines 25–39:

   Transitions

   Lines 25–26: *A third; For example*

   Lines 34–35: *In "materialistic society"*

   Line 37: *Although*

   Descriptive Words

   Line 32: *Playful, thought-provoking*

- **Information** Throughout the student model, the writer gives examples and quotations from the two poems to show readers what the poems are like. This information supports the writer's analysis of the poem's style. Have students look in the first paragraph on page 814 to find four quotations from "Kidnap Poem" and two quotations and an example from "Luxury."

For interactive student models, see

Write*Smart* CD

Writing Center at **ClassZone.com**

---

25   A third stylistic similarity the poems share is playful imagery. For example, in "Kidnap Poem," Giovanni uses poetry terms in unusual ways: "put you in my phrases and meter / you to jones beach," "lyric you in lilacs / dash you in the rain," "ode you with my love song." Giovanni *is* a poet, so the speaker's repeated comment "if i were a poet"

30   shows a teasing and flirtatious attitude. The speaker seems to be saying that she will use all the techniques that poets have perfected throughout the centuries to write a love song. Playful, thought-provoking images in "Luxury" have to do with modern life: "living in an electronic age seeing / the whole world by / pushing a button." In "materialistic

35   society," the speaker suggests, true luxury might be having pushbutton gadgets to do everything—and also having someone to push the buttons for you. Although the middle two stanzas are playful, "Luxury" ends with a more serious message. The speaker concludes that even though luxuries are appealing, love means far more.

40   An author's style helps to bring out the meaning of the work. By analyzing the different elements of Nikki Giovanni's style, a reader can better understand why she constructed her poems in this way and what meaning she is conveying to her audience. In "Kidnap Poem" and "Luxury," Nikki Giovanni uses tone, point of view, and imagery to

45   deliver her message that love is "the ultimate luxury."

2

The variety of **sentence structures** creates interest and flow. Writer provides enough **information** about the poems for reader to understand the analysis.

Writer's **voice** is straightforward and confident as she analyzes imagery and meaning.

Concludes with an insightful summary of the author's style.

DIFFERENTIATED INSTRUCTION

FOR ENGLISH LEARNERS

Comprehension: Transitions Help students recognize transitions by pointing out the transitions and transitional phrases in the model. To help familiarize students with the uses of transitions, use this activity:

1. Write these sentences on the board and underline the transitional words and phrases:

   Both poems have a playful tone. *(comparison that shows similarity)*

For example, "Fly" is about a bee. *(introduces an example)*

When the speaker says, "I buzz it," it means "I understand." *(introduces an example)*

The second poem also uses imagery. *(shows order)*

Although the poem is humorous, it has a serious message. *(contrast that shows difference)*

2. Now ask students to provide sentences using the underlined transition words on the board to help them.

To provide English learners with additional writing support, see

R RESOURCE MANAGER—Copy Master Writing Support p. 190

Part 2: Apply the Writing Process

Practice and Apply

PREWRITING

What Should I Do?	What Does It Look Like?

1. Choose and examine a subject for analysis.
If you are responding to Prompt 1, keep an ongoing reader's log, listing elements of the work that catch your attention, along with your questions or comments. Indicate in your log how your understanding of the work developed or changed with each reading.

If you are responding to Prompt 2, freewrite about a person whose style interests you. What makes that person's style interesting or significant?

▶

Details about Nikki Giovanni's Poems	Comments
• no punctuation	• makes poems hard to read but got used to it
• "if i were a poet"	• but Giovanni *is* a poet— is she making a joke?
• "ode you with my love song"	• uses poetry terms in unusual ways
• "the ultimate luxury / of your love"	• Oh, "Luxury" is about love.

2. Focus on the aspects of style you want to analyze.
For Prompt 1, review the elements of literary style and their definitions in the Literary Analysis Workshop on pages 744–747. Think about other elements of literary style you have learned about this year. Use a graphic organizer to list style elements and examples from the literary work.

For Prompt 2, make some notes about how specific aspects of the person's style reflect his or her personality or values. For example, how do a singer's lyrics reflect his or her beliefs?

See page 818: Terms for Writing About Literary Style

▶

Style Element	"Kidnap Poem"	"Luxury"
Tone	• informal, simple words, loose structure	• mostly simple words, loose structure has four stanzas
Point of view	• first person, talking directly to a loved one	• first person, talking directly to a loved one
Imagery	• fun, teasing, "lyric you in lilacs"	• about modern technology, but message is that love is more important

3. Develop a working thesis statement.
Your thesis should identify the main points that you plan to analyze. Continue refining or modifying this statement as you draft.

▶

Working thesis statement:
Nikki Giovanni's "Kidnap Poem" and "Luxury" are both about love. Each poem uses a relaxed, fun style to get the author's message across.

WRITING WORKSHOP **815**

To support students during the writing process, use these copy masters:

R RESOURCE MANAGER—Copy Masters
Prewriting–Editing pp. 183–187
Writing Rubric p. 188
Writing Support p. 190 (for English learners)

Part 2: Apply the Writing Process

PREWRITING

1. Reread the literary work several times.
Suggest that students leave space between items they note in their logs after their first reading. They can then add comments in roughly the same order after their second reading. Students who choose visual or audio works should be sure to repeat their viewing or listening.

2. Focus on the aspects of style you want to analyze. Suggest that students scan Units 1–7 for Literary Analysis elements that might apply to their analyses. If students analyze an author's style in two works, have them note when literary elements appear in only one work.

 BEST PRACTICES TOOLKIT—Transparencies
T Chart p. A25
Classification Chart p. B17

For interactive graphic organizers, see

🔘 Write*Smart* CD

ℹ️ Writing Center at **ClassZone.com**

3. Develop a working thesis statement.
Ask students to compare the working thesis statement on page 815 to the thesis statement in lines 3–4 on page 813 to see how a working thesis is refined. Check that students' thesis statements are viable before they begin writing.

FOR ENGLISH LEARNERS
Writing: Thesis Statement Have students use these sentence starters to help them develop their thesis statements and support:

• My subject is _____, by _____.

• The two elements of the author's style I will discuss are _____ and _____.

• The author's style fits the author's message about _____.

FOR ADVANCED LEARNERS/PRE–AP
Synthesize: Aspects of Style Have students read forward in this book to learn about additional style elements. Then challenge them to analyze these style elements in literary work. Invite students to use their essays to teach these style elements to the class.

DRAFTING

1. Organize your ideas. Explain that the student model uses point-by-point organization to discuss the author's style from least important to most important. Explain that this is a good choice because the tone and imagery in each poem is the same. Clarify that the purpose of students' writing is to analyze the author's style, not to directly compare two works in a comparison-contrast essay.

2. Back up each statement with examples from the literary work. Point out lines 29–30 as an excellent example of making an interesting point and backing it up with an example from the poem. Then suggest that students look on page 814 to find quotations the writer includes from "Luxury" that support her point about playful imagery. Display models of correct ways to include quotations.

- In "Shiny Man," the robot "whistles" and "frolics." *(quoted words from a poem)*

- Chapin sings, "Make me a moon / And please make it soon." *(two consecutive lines of a song lyric)*

3. End with a strong conclusion. Point out that this conclusion includes a summary of the elements the writer discussed and a quote that highlights the point about theme made in the thesis statement.

For a literary analysis writing template, see

🧰 BEST PRACTICES TOOLKIT—Transparency
Writing Template: Literary Analysis
pp. C16, C30
💿 Write*Smart* CD
ℹ️ Writing Center at **ClassZone.com**

DRAFTING

What Should I Do?	*What Does It Look Like?*

1. Organize your ideas.
Think about how you can present your ideas to make your analysis clear to readers. You could discuss style elements in the order of their importance. If you are comparing two or more works by one writer, you could proceed one work at a time.

▶

ORDER OF IMPORTANCE (LEAST TO MOST)

1. *Tone in both poems*
   - *loosely structured*
   - *mostly simple language*
   - *affects meaning: Both are about love.*
2. *Point of view in both*
   - *first person*
   - *affects meaning: extremely personal*
3. *Imagery in both*
   - *playful, creative*
   - *affects meaning: Love is important.*

COMPARING TWO OR MORE WORKS

1. *"Kidnap Poem"*
   - *tone: informal, flirtatious*
   - *point of view: first person*
   - *imagery: playful*
   - *message: The speaker will use poets' techniques to write a love song.*
2. *"Luxury"*
   - *tone: informal*
   - *point of view: first person*
   - *imagery: playful, about a pushbutton society*
   - *message: Love is the ultimate luxury.*

2. Back up each statement with examples.
Every point you make about the author's style should be supported with examples and details. Be sure to explain exactly how and why each detail supports your analysis.

▶

A third stylistic similarity the poems share is playful imagery. — Identifies element of style

For example, in "Kidnap Poem," Giovanni uses poetry terms in unusual ways: "meter / you to jones beach," "lyric you in lilacs." — Gives example of imagery

The speaker seems to be saying that she will use all the techniques that poets have perfected throughout the centuries to write a love song. — Explains how style affects meaning

3. End with a strong conclusion.
Summarize your analysis and offer an overall insight about style and meaning.

TIP Before revising, consult the key traits on page 812 and the rubric and peer-reader questions on page 818.

▶

By analyzing the different elements of Nikki Giovanni's style, a reader can better understand the meaning she is conveying. In "Kidnap Poem" and "Luxury," Nikki Giovanni uses tone, point of view, and imagery to deliver her message that love is "the ultimate luxury."

DIFFERENTIATED INSTRUCTION

FOR LESS–PROFICIENT WRITERS

Organize Your Ideas Have students follow this frame to plan their analyses. Explain that it uses order of importance organization, as in the student model.

Beginning Paragraph—Introduction
- Name the titles of the work(s) and author.
- State your thesis. See page 815, number 3, for help with writing a thesis statement.

Middle Paragraphs
- Name the second most important style element.
  —Present examples from the work(s).
  —Discuss the examples.
- Name the *most* important style element.
  —Present examples from the work(s).
  —Discuss the examples.

End Paragraph
- Restate the subject(s) and author.
- Write a conclusion that summarizes your analysis.
- Include an overall insight about the author's style.

REVISING AND EDITING

What Should I Do?

1. Make your introduction engaging.
- [Bracket] the first few sentences of your introduction.
- Review the bracketed text. If you are just stating the obvious, insert some details to make your analysis more interesting.

TIP Consider beginning with a powerful quotation or a question to readers.

2. Add appropriate transitions.
- Highlight the transitional words and phrases that signal a new topic.
- If you have few or no highlights, add transitions that clarify how ideas are connected.

3. Include enough information about the literary work.
- Ask a peer reader to underline confusing passages that need more explanation.
- Add details to help readers understand your points.

See page 818: Ask a Peer Reader

4. Vary the structures of your sentences.
- Draw a box around consecutive sentences that all begin the same way.
- Rewrite some of these sentences to make your writing more rhythmic and interesting.

What Does It Look Like?

> ["Luxury" and "Kidnap Poem" are the poems I read. They're both about love and have a similar style.] Have you ever been kidnapped by a poet? Nikki Giovanni asks this surprising question in "Kidnap Poem."

> Another important aspect of this poet's style has to do with point of view. Giovanni uses the first-person point of view in both poems.
> A third stylistic similarity the poems share is playful imagery. For example, In "Kidnap Poem," Giovanni uses poetry terms in unusual ways.

> "Luxury" ends with a more serious message. The speaker concludes that even though luxuries are appealing, love means far more.

> The speaker describes a "materialistic society." The speaker suggests that true luxury might be having pushbutton gadgets to do everything. Also, having someone to push the buttons for you would be even better. In "materialistic society," the speaker suggests, true luxury might be having pushbutton gadgets to do everything—and also having someone to push the buttons for you.

REVISING AND EDITING

1. Make your introduction engaging. Refer students to the model for an introduction that begins with a question. Then remind students of these other strategies for writing a lively introduction:
- Begin by making a startling statement.
- Tell an anecdote that will engage readers.

2. Add appropriate transitions. Have students check that they have used the best transitions to link ideas. If students find that their analyses are overloaded with transitions, suggest that they explore a more logical organization of ideas.

3. Include enough information about the literary work. Remind students that a good analysis clearly explains the thoughts or reasoning the writer uses to reach conclusions. Students who choose *WRITING PROMPT 2* should address and explain such elements of style as
- art: form, subject matter, color, line
- music: lyrics, theme, vocal style, phrasing
- acting/film directing: subject matter, visual style

4. Vary the structures of your sentences. Have students look for consecutive sentences that begin with nouns, the same nouns, or the same transitions.

For interactive revision tools, see
- WriteSmart CD
- Writing Center at **ClassZone.com**

FOR ENGLISH LEARNERS
Writing: Vary Sentence Structure Provide sentence frames such as these to help students vary their sentence beginnings:
- The poem is _____.
- "_____" suggests that _____.
- In the second story, _____.
- The style is _____.
- Both songs _____.
- For example, _____.

Preparing to Publish

Support for meeting the goals in the writing rubric is supplied throughout the Writing Workshop on pages 815–817.

For Rubric Bank, see

 WriteSmart CD

ℹ️ Writing Center at ClassZone.com

Assess and Reteach

Ⓢ STANDARDS LESSON FILE

Writing Lesson 8: Creating Sentence Variety

Writing Lesson 15: Writing a Thesis Statement

Writing Lesson 27: Analysis Essay

Writing Lesson 36: Elaborate with Incidents, Examples, and Quotations

Grammar Lesson 2: Avoiding Run Ons

Apply the Rubric

A strong analysis of style . . .

☑ identifies the author and literary work (or the person being analyzed) in the introduction

☑ clarifies the main points of the analysis in a strong thesis statement

☑ supports ideas with relevant details and information

☑ uses precise terms to define and analyze style

☑ has a confident, engaging voice

☑ varies sentence structures for rhythm

☑ concludes by summarizing the analysis and offering insight into the individual's style

Ask a Peer Reader

- What are the main points of my analysis?
- Which statements need to be supported with more information?

Terms for Writing About Literary Style

Term	Definition
Diction	choice of words
Imagery	sensory and figurative language
Point of view	angle from which the story is told
Sentence structure	type and length of sentences
Tone	writer's attitude toward the subject

Check Your Grammar

- Run-on sentences make your analysis confusing.

  > Giovanni's informal tone creates a _Both_ sense of closeness and familiarity, both poems are free verse.

- Eliminate unnecessary words. If your analysis is too short, add more quotations and examples.

  > What I am trying to say is that the main message of the poem "Luxury" is that love is more important than other things such as power, wealth, and fame.

See page R64–R65: Writing Complete Sentences

Writing Online

PUBLISHING OPTIONS
For publishing options, visit the **Writing Center** at **ClassZone.com.**

ASSESSMENT PREPARATION
For writing and grammar assessment practice, go to the **Assessment Center** at **ClassZone.com.**

Delivering an Oral Interpretation

Delivering a reading of a literary work can make an author's style come alive for your audience.

Planning the Oral Interpretation

1. **Choose passages that clearly illustrate the style.** Find material that includes several style elements and that your audience can understand without explanation or background information.
2. **Mark up the selection.** Highlight words to stress, and indicate places where you would like to change your pacing and emphasis. Add punctuation marks if you need to.

> play the lyre for you,
> ode you with my love song,
> anything to win you! ← smile   Yellow = Use emphasis.
> wrap you in the red Black green   Blue = Pick up the pace.
> show you off to mama ← pause
> yeah if i were a poet i'd kid
> nap you

3. **Read into a tape recorder.** Practice your delivery by speaking into a tape recorder.
4. **Rehearse in front of a mirror.** See and hear yourself as your audience will. Go over any difficult words, and practice your pacing, tone, emphasis, and gestures until they come naturally.

Delivering the Oral Interpretation

1. **Maintain eye contact with your listeners.** If you are using notes, hold them in front of you so that you can glance at them while keeping your head and body directed at your audience.
2. **Reveal the author's style by using your voice, facial expressions, and gestures.** Depending on the content of your reading, you might smile, frown, or point during part of your presentation.

   See page R80: Evaluate an Oral Interpretation

SPEAKING AND LISTENING

Ask students to read this page to get an overview of how to prepare for and deliver an oral interpretation. Students who choose this option may first want to listen to an audiotape of a writer reading his or her own work to familiarize themselves with effective reading techniques.

Before students begin working, review this rubric with them so that they have clear goals:

Rubric A strong oral interpretation

- reflects thorough familiarity with the content and tone of the literary work
- is well-rehearsed and delivered clearly with good pronunciation
- engages the audience by maintaining eye contact
- uses effective emphasis, pacing, gestures, and facial expressions that reveal the author's style

R RESOURCE MANAGER—Copy Master
Speaking and Listening p. 189

S STANDARDS LESSON FILE
Speaking and Listening Lesson 9: Oral Interpretation

Assessment Practice

CHECK READINESS

Read aloud the paragraph under **ASSESS** and stress to students that this is not the full Unit Test, but a way for them to check their readiness for it. Then have students examine the skills listed under **REVIEW** and look back in the unit or in the **Student Resource Bank** for any skills they need to review.

READ THE SELECTIONS

Remind students to keep unit goals in mind as they read each passage, paying particular attention to these literary and reading skills:

- style
- word choice
- sentences
- tone
- media: visual elements

To help students focus on elements of style while reading, encourage them to ask themselves questions such as

- What elements make one writer's work different from another's? What are some of the elements that clearly define a writer's style?
- What qualities make a writer's work lively and interesting?

ANSWER THE QUESTIONS

Direct students to pages R93–R101 of the **Handbook** to review test-taking strategies.

- Urge students to use active reading strategies when they read test materials. For example, before they read a passage, suggest that they skim the questions that follow it. Knowing the questions that must be answered will help students focus their reading.
- When students are ready to answer the multiple-choice questions, remind them not to choose the first alternative that seems to fit. Instead, they should read through all the choices, eliminate any that are clearly wrong, and then choose the *best* answer—the one that is the most accurate.

Assessment Practice

ASSESS
The practice test items on the next few pages match skills listed on the Unit Goals page (page 743) and addressed throughout this unit. Taking this practice test will help you assess your knowledge of these skills and determine your readiness for the Unit Test.

REVIEW
After you take the practice test, your teacher can help you identify any skills you need to review.

- Style
  - Word Choice
  - Sentence Structure
  - Tone
- Media: Visual Elements
- Homonyms
- Prefixes
- Sentence Types

> **ASSESSMENT ONLINE**
> For more assessment practice and test-taking tips, go to the **Assessment Center** at ClassZone.com.

Reading Comprehension

DIRECTIONS *Read the following selections and then answer the questions.*

The two characters in this excerpt from The Sea Wolf *have escaped from the cruel captain of the* Ghost, *a seal-hunting schooner. They are adrift in a small sailing boat hundreds of miles off the coast of Japan.*

from The Sea Wolf
Jack London

Maud's condition was pitiable. She sat crouched in the bottom of the boat, her lips blue, her face gray and plainly showing the pain she suffered. But ever her eyes looked bravely at me, and ever her lips uttered brave words.

The worst of the storm must have blown that night, though little I noticed it. I had succumbed and slept where I sat in the stern-sheets. The morning of the fourth day found the wind diminished to a gentle whisper, the sea dying down and the sun shining upon us. Oh, the blessed sun! How we bathed our poor bodies in its delicious warmth, reviving like bugs and crawling things after a storm. We smiled again, said amusing things, and waxed optimistic
10 over our situation. Yet it was, if anything, worse than ever. We were farther from Japan than the night we left the *Ghost*. Nor could I more than roughly guess our latitude and longitude. At a calculation of a two-mile drift per hour, during the seventy and odd hours of the storm, we had been driven at least one hundred and fifty miles to the northeast. But was such calculated drift correct? For all I knew, it might have been four miles per hour instead of two. In which case we were another hundred and fifty miles to the bad.

Where we were I did not know, though there was quite a likelihood that we were in the vicinity of the *Ghost*. There were seals about us, and I was prepared to sight a sealing schooner at any time. We did sight one, in the afternoon,
20 when the northwest breeze had sprung up freshly once more. But the strange schooner lost itself on the sky-line and we alone occupied the circle of the sea.

Came days of fog, when even Maud's spirit drooped and there were no merry words upon her lips; days of calm, when we floated on the lonely immensity of sea, oppressed by its greatness and yet marveling at the miracle of tiny life, for we still lived and struggled to live; days of sleet and wind and snow-squalls, when nothing could keep us warm; or days of drizzling rain, when we filled our water-breakers from the drip of the wet sail.

DIFFERENTIATED INSTRUCTION

FOR ENGLISH LEARNERS
Assessment Practice: Work Backward

Prepare students by having them read the questions *before* reading the passages. Have pairs find and define unfamiliar words in test directions and questions, following these steps:

1. Write each word on an index card and divide the cards among pairs of students. Tell students that they are going to define these words.

2. Instruct students to work individually to make an initial determination of each word's meaning. Then have students confer with their partners and check their work by using a dictionary.

3. Have students then share the words and definitions with the entire class, who can confirm the definitions or suggest others.

from Pilgrim at Tinker Creek

Annie Dillard

It was just this time last year that we had the flood. It was Hurricane Agnes, really, but by the time it got here, the weather bureau had demoted it to a tropical storm. I see by a clipping I saved that the date was June twenty-first, the solstice, midsummer's night, the longest daylight of the year; but I didn't notice it at the time. Everything was so exciting, and so very dark.

All it did was rain. It rained, and the creek started to rise. The creek, naturally, rises every time it rains; this didn't seem any different. But it kept raining, and, that morning of the twenty-first, the creek kept rising.

That morning I'm standing at my kitchen window. Tinker Creek is out of
10 its four-foot banks, way out, and it's still coming. The high creek doesn't look like our creek. Our creek splashes transparently over a jumble of rocks; the high creek obliterates everything in flat opacity. It looks like somebody else's creek that has usurped or eaten our creek and is roving frantically to escape, big and ugly, like a blacksnake caught in a kitchen drawer. The color is foul, a rusty cream. Water that has picked up clay soils looks worse than other muddy waters, because the particles of clay are so fine; they spread out and cloud the water so that you can't see light through even an inch of it in a drinking glass.

Everything looks different. Where my eye is used to depth, I see the flat water, near, too near. I see trees I never noticed before, the black verticals of
20 their rain-soaked trunks standing out of the pale water like pilings for a rotted dock. The stillness of grassy banks and stony ledges is gone; I see rushing, a wild sweep and hurry in one direction, as swift and compelling as a waterfall. The Atkins kids are out in their tiny rain gear, staring at the monster creek. It's risen up to their gates; the neighbors are gathering; I go out.

I hear a roar, a high windy sound more like air than like water, like the run-together whaps of a helicopter's propeller after the engine is off, a high million rushings. The air smells damp and acrid, like fuel oil, or insecticide. It's raining.

GO ON

ITEM ANALYSIS

COMPREHENSION AND WRITTEN RESPONSE	ITEMS	UNIT PAGES
Style		
Word Choice	4, 5, 7, 8, 11, 12	744–749, 781
Sentences	1, 5, 7, 8, 11, 12	744–749, 789
Tone	2, 3, 4, 6, 7, 11, 12	744–749, 783
Media: Visual Elements	9, 10	803

VOCABULARY	ITEMS	UNIT PAGES
Homonyms	1, 2, 3	788
Prefixes	4, 5, 6	762

WRITING AND GRAMMAR	ITEMS	UNIT PAGES
Sentence Types	1, 2, 3, 4	789

FOR LESS–PROFICIENT READERS

Assessment Support Consider these options for completing the Assessment Practice:

- Have students "work backward" to review the test questions *before* reading the passages.

- Select random questions in the Assessment and have students demonstrate *how* and *where* to look for the answers.

- Ask students to locate unfamiliar vocabulary words in the Assessment. Elicit the words' meanings from the class.

- Have students record useful testing words and definitions in their journals for later reference.

- Read the selections or parts of them aloud to aid in student comprehension.

Comprehension

Model a thinking process for answering multiple-choice questions.

1. **C is correct.** The first sentence is only four words long, but the next has more than 20 words; thus, the mix of long and short sentences is evident right away, contradicting A and B. D is incorrect because there are only a few short sentences in the first two paragraphs and no short sentences in the final two paragraphs.

2. **A is correct.** The narrator delights in the "blessed sun" and says that he and Maud "waxed optimistic." D is incorrect because although the mood becomes gloomier later in the selection, it is not glooamy at this point. B and C are not supported by any details or word choices in the selection.

3. **B is correct.** The sentence immediately before this one is hopeful; the sentences that follow identify the narrator's concerns. A is incorrect because it expresses optimism rather than doubt. Although C and D relate to doubt, both appear after the shift in tone already has occurred.

4. **A is correct.** These words have a formal, serious tone, as does the entire sentence. Although *marveling might be considered sentimental* in a different context, here it is used in the context of a philosophical question, so B is incorrect. Similarly, *struggled might be considered playful* in a different context, but here it is used in the context of a fight for survival, so C is incorrect. D is incorrect because nothing in the words suggests confidence.

5. **B is correct.** In these lines, the reader sees the flood through Dillard's eyes. A is incorrect because a scientist would not make the comparisons made here; rather, he or she would focus on objective facts and figures. No description of an actual kitchen is given, so C is incorrect. Dillard compares the creek to a snake but does not describe a literal snake, so D also is incorrect.

6. **C is correct.** Dillard explains exactly why the water looks so bad. Her tone is matter-of-fact, not melodramatic or humorous, so A and B are incorrect. The descriptive context suggests that Dillard is being factual rather than sarcastic, so D also can be eliminated.

7. **A is correct.** The first-person point of view

Comprehension

DIRECTIONS *Answer these questions about the excerpt from* The Sea Wolf.

1. The author's style in *The Sea Wolf* can be characterized by his use of
   A all long sentences
   B all short sentences
   C a mix of long and short sentences
   D mostly very short sentences

2. Which word best describes the tone of lines 5–9?
   A hopeful   C frenzied
   B suspicious   D gloomy

3. In which of the following sentences from lines 9–12 does the tone shift to reveal the narrator's doubts?
   A "We smiled again, said amusing things, and waxed optimistic over our situation."
   B "Yet it was, if anything, worse than ever."
   C "We were farther from Japan than the night we left the *Ghost*."
   D "Nor could I more than roughly guess our latitude and longitude."

4. Notice the verbs *drooped, oppressed, marveling,* and *struggled* in lines 22–27. What tone do these words convey?
   A serious   C playful
   B sentimental   D confident

822

makes the tone conversational, as if Dillard were talking directly to the reader. Also, she describes shapes, colors, and sounds in detail. There are few explanations and no sense of despair—only wonder—so B is incorrect. C also can be eliminated, because Dillard uses ordinary words and puts them together without sarcasm. Such words as exciting *(line 5)*, obliterates *(line 12)*, usurped *(line 13)*, foul *(line 14)*, wild *(line 22)*, and acrid *(line 27)* have strong connotations, so D also is incorrect.

8. **B is correct.** Both writers use vivid language to describe the setting and events. Although Dillard uses a flashback, London does not, so A is incorrect. Since neither selection contains dialogue, C can be eliminated. D also is incorrect, because no contractions appear in London's passage.

9. **D is correct.** Clearly, the man is racing toward his car; viewers can assume the reason, based on the tornado in the image. No evidence supports A, B, or C: The man is not running away from the tornado; no hurt friend is visible; the viewer cannot tell whether the tornado is coming or going, but based on the man's speed, it may be coming toward him.

DIRECTIONS *Answer these questions about the excerpt from* Pilgrim at Tinker Creek.

5. The author's sentences and word choices in lines 12–14 help you

   A look at the flood objectively, like a scientist

   B experience the flood with the author

   C imagine what the author's kitchen looks like

   D see a snake that crawled out of the creek

6. Which word best describes the tone of the sentence in lines 15–17?

   A melodramatic   **C** informative

   B humorous   **D** sarcastic

7. The author's style can best be characterized by her use of

   A descriptive language and a conversational tone

   B long explanations and words that convey despair

   C flowery language and a sarcastic tone

   D neutral words and simple sentences

DIRECTIONS *Answer this question about both selections.*

8. Which of the following elements of style is found in both selections?

   A flashbacks   **C** realistic dialogue

   B vivid language **D** contractions

DIRECTIONS *Answer these questions about the photograph.*

9. Notice the visual elements in this photograph. What story does the photo tell?

   A A man thinks he can run down a tornado.

   B After his friend is hurt, a man runs for help.

   C A newly formed tornado is moving away from the man.

   D A man is running toward his car to get out of the tornado's path.

10. What is the effect of the blurred figure in the photograph?

   A It helps highlight the landscape surrounding the tornado.

   B It focuses the viewer's attention on the power of nature.

   C It conveys a sense of motion, urgency, and fear.

   D It puts less emphasis on the car, the fence, and the person.

Written Response

SHORT RESPONSE
Write three or four sentences to answer the following question.

11. Both authors chose to repeat words or phrases in their selections. Identify one word or phrase from each selection that is repeated. Why are these words repeated?

EXTENDED RESPONSE
Write two or three paragraphs to answer the following question.

12. Compare how each author uses these elements of style: word choice, sentences, tone. How are the authors' styles different or alike? Use examples from the selections to support your answer.

GO ON ➡

---

10. C is correct. *The blurring suggests speed and movement, which imply that the man is scared. The man is blurred, but the rest of the picture is not, so the landscape is not emphasized any more than the tornado or the car. Therefore, A can be eliminated. The blurring also does nothing to show the power of nature, so B is incorrect. D cannot be true, because the blurring has no effect on the car and fence.*

Written Response

Possible short response:

11. *An author uses repetition to emphasize an idea or image and to make the language more lyrical. London, for example, repeats* days of *in lines 22–27 to show how long the journey is and to demonstrate how the characters experience time in terms of weather and the conditions of the sea. Dillard repeats* rain *and* rise *in lines 6–8 to emphasize the connection between the continuous rain and the rising water level in the creek. She also repeats* creek *numerous times, which keeps the reader's attention focused on it.*

Possible extended response:

12. *Jack London and Annie Dillard have written pieces that have many similarities. Both authors use vivid, expressive language, including London's description of people enjoying the sun's "delicious warmth, reviving like bugs" (line 8) and Dillard's description of foul water as being "rusty cream" (line 15). In addition, both authors vary the lengths of their sentences. Most of London's short sentences are statements of fact or short, impressionistic observations, such as his opening: "Maud's condition was pitiable." His longer sentences include descriptions and explanations. Dillard also writes long, descriptive sentences, such as when she compares the creek to a blacksnake (lines 12–14).*

The two authors create very different tones, however. London's passage has a journalistic, almost formal tone. Using formal language, such as succumbed *and* diminished, *the narrator talks about latitude, longitude, and hourly drift. Dillard's passage has a more dramatic, folksy tone; it is marked by an easy conversational style, as when she writes, "I see by a clipping I saved" (line 3).*

DIFFERENTIATED INSTRUCTION

FOR ENGLISH LEARNERS

Review Academic Vocabulary On the board, list these academic vocabulary terms. Then give the examples in random order and have students match the examples with the terms on the board. Elicit additional examples from students.

- *elements of style:* In an essay, an author frequently asks thought-provoking questions or presents examples as lists.

- *humor:* In a story, an author's word choices reveal a tone that is meant to make the reader laugh.

- *visual elements:* The lighting in an image draws the viewer's attention to an unexpected detail.

- *homonym:* Last night's <u>live</u> broadcast was a panel discussion on how to <u>live</u> with a debilitating disease.

Vocabulary

1. **A is correct.** Both sentences use *banks* in the context of waterways. B can be eliminated because *banks* is used as a verb. Neither C nor D has any relationship to waterways, so both are incorrect.

2. **C is correct.** Dillard talks about particles being *fine*. In A, *fine* is a noun, so it can be eliminated. B and D have no connection to anything related to particles, so they also are incorrect. The boat mentioned in D might suggest water, but *fine* in that sentence describes the people, not the water.

3. **D is correct.** In A and C, *light* is an adjective; in B, *light* is a verb. Since the correct answer needs to have *light* as a noun, A, B, and C can be eliminated. Also, the passage refers to *light* as something that one can see, and only D uses *light* in this sense.

4. **A is correct.** Since the prefix *re-* means "again" and *viv* means "to live," *revive* must mean something like "living again," which would eliminate B and D. Of the other two possibilities, only A makes sense in context.

5. **D is correct.** Since the prefix *im-* means "not" or "unable" and *mens* means "to measure," *immensity* must have a meaning like "a quality that is not measurable." Neither B nor C has anything to do with size or measurement. A also is incorrect, because the passage says that the sea was calm.

6. **A is correct.** The root *liter*, meaning "letter," might suggest writing, but the prefix *ob-* rules out that answer, so B can be eliminated. C may appear possible because it suggests negativity, but *opposes* does not fit the context of the sentence. D does not reflect the meaning of either the prefix or the root and so is incorrect.

Vocabulary

DIRECTIONS *Use context clues and your knowledge of homonyms to answer the following questions.*

> That morning I'm standing at my kitchen window. Tinker Creek is out of its four-foot <u>banks</u>, way out, and it's still coming.

1. Which sentence uses *banks* as it is used in line 10 of *Pilgrim at Tinker Creek*?
   A A number of colorful houseboats are moored along the banks of the channel.
   B Luis banks the plane toward the south to give us a clear view of the canyon.
   C Sonia heads the finance ethics division for all of our North American banks.
   D The two banks of elevators are on the north and west sides of the building.

> Water that has picked up clay soils looks worse than other muddy waters, because the particles of clay are so <u>fine</u>; they spread out and cloud the water so that you can't see <u>light</u> through even an inch of it in a drinking glass.

2. Which sentence uses *fine* as it is used in line 16 of *Pilgrim at Tinker Creek*?
   A Solana paid her library fine yesterday.
   B It was such a fine day that we decided to walk to town.
   C The recipe called for fresh cinnamon, ground as fine as powder.
   D "We are fine!" they yelled from the boat.

3. Which sentence uses *light* as it is used in line 17 of *Pilgrim at Tinker Creek*?
   A The menu called for a light supper.
   B I heard him yell, "Light the fire!"
   C She gave him a light tap on the shoulder.
   D We searched by the light of the moon.

DIRECTIONS *Use context clues and your knowledge of prefixes to answer the following questions.*

> How we bathed our poor bodies in its delicious warmth, <u>reviving</u> like bugs and crawling things after a storm.

4. The prefix *re-* means "again," and the root *viv* means "to live." What does the word *reviving* mean in line 8 of *The Sea Wolf*?
   A coming back to life
   B no longer living
   C having lived before
   D unable to live

> Came days of fog, when even Maud's spirit drooped and there were no merry words upon her lips; days of calm, when we floated on the lonely <u>immensity</u> of sea, oppressed by its greatness and yet marveling at the miracle of tiny life . . .

5. The prefix *im-* means "not" or "unable," and the Latin root *mens* means "to measure." What does the word *immensity* mean in line 24 from *The Sea Wolf*?
   A waves too rough to navigate
   B awesome character
   C hollowed-out shape
   D area too vast to determine

> Our creek splashes transparently over a jumble of rocks; the high creek <u>obliterates</u> everything in flat opacity.

6. The prefix *ob-* means "against," and the Latin root *liter* means "letter." What does *obliterates* mean in line 12 of *Pilgrim at Tinker Creek*?
   A erases   C opposes
   B writes   D drowns

DIFFERENTIATED INSTRUCTION

FOR ENGLISH LEARNERS
Assessment Support: Sentence Types

- Write the words *declarative, interrogative, exclamatory,* and *imperative* on the board. Remind students that these words describe different types of sentences.

- Review with students that many sentences can make statements; that is, they *declare* that something is so. Call on volunteers to identify some declarative sentences in the excerpt on page 821.

- Discuss the fact that some sentences *interrogate,* or ask questions; others *exclaim,* or show strong emotion; and still others issue *commands.* As you review each type of sentence, point out that punctuation sometimes offers a clue. Draw a period, a question mark, and an exclamation point on the board. As each sentence type is discussed, have students suggest examples and identify the punctuation with which each example would end.

Writing & Grammar

DIRECTIONS *Read this passage and answer the questions that follow.*

(1) I wasn't prepared for the massive destruction of Hurricane Ivan. (2) What began as a tropical depression eventually caused billions of dollars in damage and the deaths of 130 people. (3) The hurricane swept across the Caribbean, slamming into St. Vincent, Barbados, and Jamaica! (4) Another hard-hit place was my country, Grenada. (5) By the time it reached the capital, St. George's, Ivan was traveling at 140 miles per hour. (6) Virtually every major building in St. George's suffered structural damage. (7) I saw trees ripped from the ground and people displaced from their homes. (8) People wonder how they can avoid this kind of destruction. (9) The best thing to do is never find yourself in the path of a hurricane.

1. How might the writer revise sentence 2 to make it interrogative?

   A What began as a tropical depression eventually caused billions of dollars in damage and the deaths of 130 people!

   B Imagine that what began as a tropical depression eventually caused billions of dollars in damage and the deaths of 130 people.

   C How could I foresee that what began as a tropical depression would eventually cause billions of dollars in damage and the deaths of 130 people?

   D No change is needed.

2. How might the writer revise sentence 5 to make it exclamatory?

   A Was Ivan traveling at 140 miles per hour when it reached the capital, St. George's?

   B Traveling at 140 miles per hour, Ivan reached the capital, St. George's.

   C By the time it reached the capital, St. George's, Ivan was traveling at 140 miles per hour!

   D No change is needed.

3. How might the writer revise sentence 6 to make it declarative?

   A Did you know that virtually every major building in St. George's suffered structural damage?

   B Virtually every major building in St. George's suffered structural damage!

   C Take note that every major building in St. George's suffered structural damage.

   D No change is needed.

4. How might the writer revise sentence 9 to make it imperative?

   A Never find yourself in the path of a hurricane.

   B I recommend that you never find yourself in the path of a hurricane!

   C Have you ever found yourself in the path of a hurricane?

   D No change is needed.

STOP

825

Writing & Grammar

1. **C is correct.** C is an interrogative sentence; it turns the statement in sentence 2 into a question. A is incorrect because it is an exclamatory sentence. B can be eliminated because it is an imperative sentence. D also can be eliminated, because sentence 2 is declarative, not interrogative.

2. **C is correct.** C changes the declarative sentence 5 into an exclamatory sentence. A is incorrect because it is an interrogative sentence, indicated by the inverted word order and the question mark at the end. B is rewritten but is still declarative, and therefore incorrect; it merely states that Ivan reached the capital. Since sentence 5 is not exclamatory, D can be eliminated.

3. **D is correct.** Since sentence 6 already is declarative, no change is needed, and D is correct. A would make the sentence interrogative, B would make it exclamatory, and C would make it imperative; thus, all are incorrect.

4. **A is correct.** A is the only sentence that gives a command; furthermore, its subject is not stated but is understood to be *you*. B is incorrect because it is exclamatory, and C is incorrect because it is interrogative. D is incorrect because sentence 9 is declarative, not imperative.

FOR ENGLISH LEARNERS

Test-Taking Strategies: Understanding Instructions Read aloud the instructions for the first item; then model a strategy for answering such questions. In this case, students first should recall or review the meaning of *interrogative*. They should then locate and read sentence 2 in the passage and identify it as declarative (making a statement) rather than interrogative (asking a question). Invite students to explain how they would decide which alternatives to eliminate. Support students as they follow the model for item 2.

INTRODUCE *GREAT READS*

In Unit 8, students have discussed a number of big questions. Invite students to tell which question they found most intriguing and why, and then focus attention on the three that appear on this page. Discuss the recommended books and their summaries, pointing out how each connects to the related question. Encourage students to choose one or more of these "great reads" to read independently.

ℹ ClassZone.com

To find additional books that match students' interests and ability levels, visit the Literature Center at **ClassZone.com**.

UNIT 8 Great Reads

Ideas for Independent Reading

Highly individualistic writing styles are apparent in the following works.

Is fear our worst enemy?

One Day in the Life of Ivan Denisovich
by Alexandr Solzhenitsyn

The author's indictment of the Soviet gulags, in which he was once a prisoner, shows that hunger, cold, and humiliation are just as powerful as fear.

Things Fall Apart
by Chinua Achebe

Okonkwo, the main character in Achebe's novel of the effects of colonialism on Nigeria, fears the dissolution of his world and his own powerlessness to resist it.

Ethan Frome
by Edith Wharton

Ethan Frome is locked into a sterile marriage that keeps him from finding love with Mattie. This famous novel suggests that isolation and loneliness are the enemies of human fulfillment.

Have you ever felt out of place?

All Creatures Great and Small
by James Herriot

In the well-known veterinarian's first collection, he lands a position in the Yorkshire Dales. He can't understand the dialect, the farmers think he's crazy, and he makes a mess of the first dates with his eventual wife. But his patients love him.

Brave New World
by Aldous Huxley

In this classic novel's vision of the future, Bernard Marx feels out of place in the World State, in which everything—feelings, childbirth, human experience—is artificial. Can he escape?

Red Scarf Girl: A Memoir of the Cultural Revolution
by Ji-li Jiang

The author's world was turned upside down during China's Cultural Revolution. At first she accepted the spying, humiliation, and fear. Then, as dangerous as it was, she determined that she would think for herself.

Who makes you laugh?

I'm a Stranger Here Myself
by Bill Bryson

After living in Britain for 20 years, Bryson returned to the United States with a fresh eye for the absurdities of U.S. life.

Funny Letters from Famous People
by Charles Osgood

Popular broadcaster Charles Osgood offers us the witty remarks of notable people from Abraham Lincoln to Andy Rooney.

The Wit and Wisdom of Mark Twain
edited by Alex Ayres

This anthology compiles the most humorous excerpts of Twain's fiction, speeches, and letters.

Putting It in Context

UNIT

HISTORY, CULTURE, AND THE AUTHOR

- In Nonfiction
- In Fiction
- In Poetry

827

About the Art Louise Freshman Brown created the collage *Jazz Player III* in 1991. For more information, see page 905.

For help in planning this unit, see

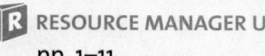 RESOURCE MANAGER UNIT 9
pp. 1–11

INTRODUCE THE UNIT

People sometimes ask, "What is the context?" The answer often depends on what you are talking about. For example, the context of a conversation often refers to the circumstances that brought the people together to talk. The context of a story includes the time and place in which it is set, and the characters' background. The context of a painting includes the artist's biography and his or her motivation for creating the art. The context of a political argument includes the issues of the day and the personal views of the people involved. In each case, a reader, viewer, or listener can understand ideas more clearly by putting them in context.

Invite students to consider how the painting and the photograph on this page relate to the matter of context. To elicit ideas, ask:

- How are the painting and the photograph similar?

- What can you tell about the setting of each image? How might the differences affect your thoughts about the musicians in the images?

- What other questions might you ask to put each image in context?

Tell students that in this unit, they will read works of nonfiction, fiction, and poetry. They will consider the context of each selection's **history, culture,** and **author.**

UNIT 9

Skills Trace

SKILLS STRAND	Literary Analysis Workshop: History, Culture, and the Author pp. 830–835	from Angela's Ashes pp. 836–851 Memoir *Level: Average*	Revisiting Sacred Ground pp. 852–861 Essay *Level: Challenging*	Blues Ain't No Mockin Bird pp. 862–873 Short Story *Level: Challenging*	*Linked selections* American History pp. 874–887 Short Story *Level: Average*
Literary Analysis	Context Within the Literature pp. 830–831, 834–835 Historical and Cultural Influences, The Writer's Background pp. 832–835	Memoir pp. 837, 838, 840, 842, 843, 844, 845, 849	Cultural Symbol pp. 853, 856, 857, 859, 860	Voice and Dialect pp. 863, 864, 868, 870, 872	Influence of Author's Background pp. 875, 876, 881, 885, 886 Review: Character p. 879
Reading and Informational Texts	Analyze the Literature pp. 831, 833–835	Use Allusions to Make Inferences pp. 837, 843, 847, 849 Read a Magazine Article p. 848 Review: Draw Conclusions pp. 840, 849	Monitor pp. 853, 854, 858, 860	Draw Conclusions pp. 863, 866, 869, 871, 872	Connect pp. 875, 878, 882, 884, 886
Vocabulary	Academic Vocabulary p. 832	Vocabulary Acquisition pp. 837, T837, 850 Context Clues p. T837 Latin Roots (*fid*) p. 850	Vocabulary Acquisition pp. 853, T853, 861 Context Clues p. T853 Greek Roots (*cosmo*) p. 861		Vocabulary Acquisition pp. 875, T875, 887 Context Clues p. T875 Idioms p. 887
Writing, Grammar, and Style		Conciseness p. 851 Gerunds pp. 843, 851		Word Choice pp. 869, 873 Vivid Verbs pp. 869, 873	
Speaking, Listening, Viewing, and Media	Discuss pp. 830–833	Discuss pp. 836, 838–848, 849 Analyze Visuals pp. 838, T842, T845	Discuss pp. 852, 854–859, 860 Analyze Visuals pp. 854, T857	Discuss pp. 862, 864–871, 872 Analyze Visuals pp. 864, 867, T869	Discuss pp. 874, 876–885, 886 Analyze Visuals pp. 876, 880, T883, T885

Assessment-Based Planning: Skills in red are assessed on the Unit 9 Test. **T** = Teacher's Edition page

Four Days in November pp. 888–893 Newspaper Article/Diary Entry/Magazine Article/ Political Cartoon *Level: Average*	The Tropics in New York/ Theme for English B pp. 894–901 Poems *Level: Average*	Haiku/Haiku/Honku pp. 902–907 Haiku *Level: Average*	Writing Workshop: Persuasive Essay pp. 908–915
	Harlem Renaissance Literature pp. 895, 898, 900, 901	Characteristics of Haiku pp. 903, 907 Historical and Cultural Context pp. 903, 904, 905, 906, 907	
Synthesize pp. 888, 889, 890, 891, 892, 893 Summarize Information from Multiple Sources p. 893	Strategies for Reading Poetry pp. 895, 896, 899, 901 Read a Magazine Article p. 900	Interpret Imagery pp. 903, 904, 907	Analyze a Persuasive Essay pp. 909–910, 914
			Write a Persuasive Essay pp. 908–915 Errors in Reasoning p. 914 Interrogative Pronouns p. 914
Discuss pp. 888, 889–892, 893	Discuss pp. 894, 896–900, 901 Analyze Visuals pp. T897, T899	Discuss pp. 902, 904–906, 907 Analyze Visuals pp. T904, T905, T906	Discuss pp. 908–910 Debate an Issue p. 915

**Skills Assessed on
the Unit 9 Test:**

Literary Analysis
- Analyze the
  influence of
  an author's
  background
- Analyze the
  influence of
  historical and
  cultural context
- Identify and
  analyze voice and
  dialect

**Reading and
Informational Texts**
- Draw conclusions
- Synthesize
- Summarize
  information from
  multiple sources

Vocabulary
- Use knowledge of
  Greek and Latin
  roots to unlock
  word meaning
- Use context clues
  to determine the
  meaning of idioms

**Writing, Grammar,
and Style**
- Write a persuasive
  essay
- Use sound logic
  and persuasive
  language
- Use gerunds and
  gerund phrases to
  write concisely
- Choose effective
  words, such as
  vivid verbs
- Additional writing
  and grammar skills

For additional lesson
planning help, see **Easy
Planner DVD.**

OBJECTIVES

- establish prior knowledge about how personal experiences shape personality
- consider how history has shaped an influential person

What SHAPES *who you are?*

Introduce the page by reading the question aloud. As students read the opening paragraph, encourage them to take a few notes in which they apply the factors to themselves. If you are comfortable doing so, share an example from your own life or the life of someone you know.

ACTIVITY Suggest several possibilities to get students started, such as the historical figures Pocahontas and Dr. Martin Luther King Jr. and the film character Indiana Jones. Using one of these examples, model the ***ACTIVITY*** by writing on the board the answers to the questions. After students answer the questions for their own choice following your example, invite volunteers to share their insights with the class.

CHECK UNDERSTANDING Have students summarize the reasons that context helps readers understand the experiences of an individual.

What SHAPES *who you are?*

What helped make you the individual you are today? Your family, friends, and personal experiences probably played key roles. But broader factors—like the neighborhood you grew up in and the decade you were born into—have also influenced who you are.

ACTIVITY Think of someone who has made a strong impression on you—either a historical figure, a fictional character, or someone you know. Consider how the following factors may have shaped that person:

- **When he or she grew up.** How would his or her daily life have been different from our lives today?

- **Where he or she is from.** Was the person from a bustling city or a tiny town? a peaceful island or a war-torn nation?

- **What happened during his or her lifetime.** Maybe the person grew up during the Great Depression, fled Europe during the Holocaust, or turned 18 in the midst of the Vietnam War.

Sandra Cisneros

The House on Mango Street

"Sandra Cisneros is one of the most brilliant of today's young writers. Her work is sensitive, alert, nuanceful... rich with music and picture."—Gwendolyn Brooks

828

Unit Resources

- **R** RESOURCE MANAGER UNIT 9
- BEST PRACTICES TOOLKIT
- **S** STANDARDS LESSON FILE

- Easy Planner DVD-ROM
- Write*Smart* CD-ROM
- ClassZone.com
- Audio Anthology CD
- Multi-Language Academic Vocabulary Online

- eEdition DVD-ROM & Online
- McDougal Littell Assessment System
- Test Generator CD
- Media*Smart* DVD-ROM

 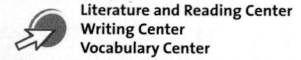
Preview Unit Goals

LITERARY ANALYSIS	• Analyze influence of author's background
	• Analyze influence of historical and cultural context
	• Recognize how cultures and time periods are represented in literature
	• Identify and interpret cultural symbols
	• Identify and analyze allusions, voice, and dialect
READING	• Make inferences and draw conclusions
	• Synthesize
WRITING AND GRAMMAR	• Write a persuasive essay
	• Use gerunds and gerund phrases to write concisely
	• Use vivid verbs
SPEAKING, LISTENING, AND VIEWING	• Debate an issue
VOCABULARY	• Use knowledge of word roots to help unlock word meanings
	• Use context clues to determine meanings of idioms
ACADEMIC VOCABULARY	• author's background • dialect
	• historical and cultural context • summarize and synthesize
	• cultural symbol • gerund and gerund phrase
	• allusion • word root
	• voice • idiom

829

Preview Unit Goals

Explain that the goals listed on this page reflect the main skills focus of Unit 9. To prepare for the unit, have students familiarize themselves with the list and set some goals for themselves. Draw their attention to the color that designates each skill set here and throughout the unit.

Point out the Academic Vocabulary. Invite students to write the list in their journal, along with a definition for each term. Urge students to return to and refine the definitions as they read, discuss, and write about the selections in Unit 9.

ADDITIONAL UNIT GOALS

These skills will be taught in this unit but are not the major focus of the unit:

Literary Analysis
• Read and identify the characteristics of memoirs, essays, short stories, and poetry
• Analyze literature in relation to a literary movement
• Genre study: newspaper article, diary entry, magazine article, political cartoon, essay

Reading
• Use reading strategies including monitoring, connecting, and reading poetry aloud
• Identify main ideas
• Interpret imagery
• Summarize information from multiple sources

Writing and Grammar
• Choose effective words

DIFFERENTIATED INSTRUCTION

FOR ENGLISH LEARNERS

Academic Vocabulary Use the copy master to help students learn the Academic Vocabulary.

1. Read aloud each term. Have students find it on their copy master.

2. Discuss the meanings or examples shown, and complete the chart as a class.

3. Have students work in small groups to complete the remaining activities.

Additional Academic Vocabulary Use the copy master to help students learn academic words they will use in subsequent lessons and on the Assessment Practice. Follow the same procedure as for the Academic Vocabulary copy master.

 RESOURCE MANAGER—Copy Masters
Academic Vocabulary p. 9
Additional Academic Vocabulary p. 10

Focus and Motivate

OBJECTIVES

- recognize culture and time period in literature
- analyze the influence of historical and cultural context
- analyze the influence of author's background

Teach

Part 1: Context Within the Literature

Context Explain that context provides a way for authors to create worlds that differ from readers' worlds. Use this activity to clarify:

- Write on the board a familiar title from students' lists. Then ask students to identify differences between the story context and their own lives in each of these areas: physical environment, clothing, work, education, pastimes, values/dreams, challenges/dangers. Record students' ideas on the board.

- Discuss how the differences in context add to students' reading experiences and their understanding of the literature. Create an Understanding Context word web like this one:

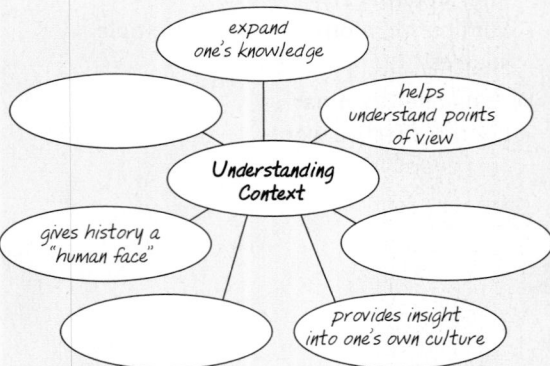

History, Culture, and the Author

You are a product of your time. In other words, who you are depends on the year you were born, the places you've lived, and the people—both family and friends—who surround you. Similarly, writers are influenced by the experiences and events they themselves live through. By examining clues within the literature you read, you can learn about a culture or time period, or about how both may have affected the writer. Armed with more knowledge, such as information about the events that inspired a story, you can often see literature in a new light.

Part 1: Context Within the Literature

Think about stories that have introduced you to other times and places, such as Harper Lee's *To Kill a Mockingbird,* set in the South in the 1930s. Unless you had researched small Southern towns in the early 20th century, you probably would have little understanding of that time and place. Yet by analyzing details in the novel, you can learn about the world the writer created.

In nonfiction, writers often provide these details directly. Fiction writers, however, use details of setting and plot and vivid language to acquaint you with the times and places they describe. Notice how Bret Harte brings the Old West to life in his short story "The Outcasts of Poker Flat."

"THE OUTCASTS OF POKER FLAT"

> From this single sentence, you begin to get a sense of a small Western town in the 1850s and can start to question the values of the time. (Is gambling a common pastime?)

As Mr. John Oakhurst, gambler, stepped into the main street of Poker Flat on the morning of the twenty-third of November, 1850, he was conscious of a change in its moral atmosphere. . . .

> The dialect lets you hear how people in Poker Flat sounded.

"It's agin justice," said Jim Wheeler, "to let this yer young man from Roaring Camp—an entire stranger—carry away our money."

> Imagery helps you imagine what the Old West was like at this time.

The road . . . lay over a steep mountain range. It was distant a day's severe travel. In that advanced season, the party soon passed out of the moist, temperate regions of the foot-hills into the dry, cold, bracing air of the Sierras.

DIFFERENTIATED INSTRUCTION

For general guidelines on differentiating instruction, see

BEST PRACTICES TOOLKIT
Differentiated Instruction pp. 31–38

FOR LESS–PROFICIENT READERS

Note Taking For students who need help with note taking, hand out the note-taking copy master before discussing this page. As volunteers read aloud each section, discuss the main points, and have students record them on the copy master.

Analysis Support: Context Point out what these details about period and culture in "The Outcasts of Poker Flat" reveal:

- the town names Poker Flat and Roaring Camp (*importance of gambling; rugged life*)
- Jim Wheeler's dialect and statement (*little education; unsophisticated sense of justice*)

RESOURCE MANAGER—Copy Master
Note Taking p. 15

MODEL 1: READING NONFICTION

As you read this excerpt, notice the writer's descriptions of people and places, as well as details about historical events and cultural traditions.

from THE NAMES *of* Women

Biographical essay by **Louise Erdrich**

Ikwe is the word for woman in the language of the Anishinabe, my mother's people, whose descendants, mixed with and married to French trappers and farmers, are the Michifs of the Turtle Mountain reservation in North Dakota. Every Anishinabe *Ikwe,* every mixed-blood descendant like me, who can trace

5 her way back a generation or two, is the daughter of a mystery. The history of the woodland Anishinabe—decimated by disease, fighting Plains Indian tribes to the west and squeezed by European settlers to the east—is much like most other Native American stories, a confusion of loss, a tale of absences, of a culture that was blown apart and changed so radically in such a short time that

10 only the names survive.

Close Read

1. Review the boxed text. What does it tell you about what life was like for the Anishinabe people?

2. What does the writer's choice of words (such as *decimated* and *loss*) reveal about her feelings toward her subject?

MODEL 2: READING FICTION

As you read this excerpt, ask yourself: What do the details tell me about the time and place? What can I infer about the characters' values?

from

The Son from AMERICA

Short story by **Isaac Bashevis Singer**

The village of Lentshin was tiny—a sandy marketplace where the peasants of the area met once a week. It was surrounded by little huts with thatched roofs or shingles green with moss. The chimneys looked like pots. Between the huts there were fields, where the owners planted vegetables or pastured their goats.

5 In the smallest of these huts lived old Berl, a man in his eighties, and his wife, who was called Berlcha (wife of Berl). Old Berl was one of the Jews who had been driven from their villages in Russia and had settled in Poland. In Lentshin, they mocked the mistakes he made while praying aloud. He spoke with a sharp "r." He was short, broad-shouldered, and had a small white beard,

10 and summer and winter he wore a sheepskin hat, a padded cotton jacket, and stout boots. He walked slowly, shuffling his feet. He had a half acre of field, a cow, a goat, and chickens.

The couple had a son, Samuel, who had gone to America forty years ago.

Close Read

1. How would you describe the village of Lentshin?

2. What does the description of old Berl tell you about the people of Lentshin and their culture?

3. The boxed text is a clue to the historical period. Many Jews left Russia following persecution in the 1880s. Find another clue that helps identify the time.

MODEL 1: READING NONFICTION
Close Read

1. *Possible answer: Life was extremely difficult for the Anishinabe. They suffered from disease, hostile neighboring tribes, and encroaching European settlers (lines 6–7). Their culture was "blown apart" (line 9) so that now "only the names survive" (line 10).*

2. *Possible answer: The author's use of the word* decimated *(line 6), which has connotations of merciless brutality, suggests anger. The word* squeezed *(line 7) also indicates anger. Her use of* loss *(line 8) suggests deep sadness and regret. It also reveals why the surviving names are important to her.*

MODEL 2: READING FICTION
Close Read

1. *Possible answer: The village of Lentshin is a tiny rural community inhabited by poor peasants who live very simply (lines 1–4).*

2. *Possible answers: The description of old Berl reveals that religious traditions were very important to the culture of Lentshin. When Berl did not follow the traditions correctly, the people made fun of him (line 8). The mention of Berl's accent (lines 8–9) suggests that the small community of Lentshin viewed newcomers as outsiders.*

3. *Possible answer: Line 13 provides a clue that identifies the time period: "The couple had a son . . . who had gone to America forty years ago." As many Jews left Russia in the 1880s, the story is probably set in the 1920s.*

FOR ENGLISH LEARNERS

Comprehension: Transitions Tell students that Singer uses spatial words to help readers picture the layout of the village. Point out the word *surrounded* in line 2. Give its meaning, and ask a volunteer to sketch on the board a map of the location of the huts relative to the marketplace. Then have students find the signal words in lines 3–5 that help to locate the fields (*Between,* line 3), gardens and pastures (*where,* line 4), and Berl himself (*In,* line 5). Ask a volunteer to revise the map, adding the fields and gardens between the huts and marking the smallest hut as Berl's. Have students describe what the map shows, using the words *surrounded, between, where,* and *in.* Finally, have students repeat the process with Model 1.

Teach

Part 2: Context Outside the Literature

Historical and Cultural Influences After students read the section, copy these charts on the board, omitting the examples shown in lightface:

Historical Influences	
Political U.S. internment of Japanese citizens	**Social** the women's movement
Economic the Great Depression	**Environmental** the effects of pollution

Cultural Influences	
Ethnicity struggles to fit in while maintaining identity	**Values/Beliefs** the writer's religion
Technology world-altering inventions, such as the railroad or computers	**Arts/Entertainment** popular culture such as rock 'n' roll and baseball

Make these concepts concrete. Help students generate examples of factors that have influenced the writers of familiar literature. Note their examples in the squares, or use the examples provided to prompt ideas. Ask students to identify examples that reflect **The Writer's Background** and discuss how these specific factors might influence a particular writer.

CHECK UNDERSTANDING

Have students suggest historical and cultural influences that might affect their own writing.

Part 2: Context Outside the Literature

Consider a story about a soldier who grapples with the horrors of World War II. By looking within the text, you can probably learn some details about the war. But what happens when you discover that the writer himself was a soldier in that war? With a little background, you can often uncover new levels of meaning.

HISTORICAL AND CULTURAL INFLUENCES

Writers respond to the world around them: events, such as the first landing of humans on the moon; places, such as the battlefield at Gettysburg; and social conditions, such as racial discrimination. For this reason, it can be helpful to think about a work's **historical** and **cultural contexts**—that is, the social and cultural conditions that may have influenced the work. For instance, consider Dr. Martin Luther King's "I have a dream" speech, which he delivered to a crowd of around 250,000 at the March on Washington on August 28, 1963. King's message of peace and hope becomes more impressive when you discover that he spoke just months after the assassination of another civil rights leader.

CONTEXT	LITERATURE
Two months before the March on Washington, the civil rights leader Medgar Evers was assassinated. Concerned about violence, President John F. Kennedy considered canceling the march.	"We must forever conduct our struggle on the high plain of dignity. . . ."

As you read any text, ask

- What significant events were taking place at the time this text was written?
- What were the predominant values in the society of the time?

THE WRITER'S BACKGROUND

Personal factors can also affect a writer's work. A writer who grew up poor in the rural South will have been influenced by his or her experiences, as will a writer who spent years working on a nature preserve in Africa. Gender, ethnicity, national identity, family—all these factors help shape a writer's view of the world.

CONSIDERING A WRITER'S BACKGROUND

First analyze the clues within the text. Ask
- What values are conveyed? (Look for direct commentary as well as characters' actions.)
- What is the tone? (Notice characters and ideas that are respected or criticized.)

Then consider how a writer's background may be mirrored in his or her work. Ask
- What do I know about the writer's personal history?
- How does this information shed light on my reading?

832   UNIT 9: HISTORY, CULTURE, AND THE AUTHOR

DIFFERENTIATED INSTRUCTION

FOR LESS–PROFICIENT READERS
Note Taking For students who need help, hand out the note taking copy master for this page. As students read and discuss the main points, have them record these on the copy master. Provide assistance as needed.

📖 RESOURCE MANAGER—Copy Master
Note Taking p. 16

Comprehension: Syntax To help students understand the syntax of "The Butterfly," have them work in pairs and take turns reading it aloud two or three times. Note that the first four lines do not contain complete sentences. Remind students that commas, line breaks, and stanza breaks signal pauses.

832   UNIT 9

MODEL 1: INTERPRETING POETRY

As you read this poem, look at details such as imagery and setting to help you interpret its meaning.

The Butterfly

Poem by **Pavel Friedmann**

The last, the very last,
So richly, brightly, dazzlingly yellow.
  Perhaps if the sun's tears would sing
  against a white stone . . .

5   Such, such a yellow
Is carried lightly 'way up high.
It went away I'm sure because it wished to
  kiss the world goodbye.

For seven weeks I've lived in here,
10   Penned up inside this ghetto
But I have found my people here.
The dandelions call to me
And the white chestnut candles in the court.
Only I never saw another butterfly.

15   That butterfly was the last one.
Butterflies don't live in here,
  In the ghetto.

Close Read

1. Look at the boxed text. How does it help you understand the speaker's description of the butterfly in lines 1–8?
2. What might the butterfly symbolize in the poem?

MODEL 2: UNDERSTANDING THE CONTEXT

Now read this background information about the era in which "The Butterfly" was written.

BACKGROUND Beginning in 1941 when the Holocaust was sweeping across Europe, Adolf Hitler rounded up Jews from Czechoslovakia and many other countries and moved them to the small Czech town of Terezin—the "ghetto" Pavel Friedmann describes in his poem. Originally home to about 7,000
5   people, Terezin eventually held more than 550,000 Jews at one time. Under such conditions, thousands died from starvation and disease. Thousands more were shipped to the Auschwitz death camp. Friedmann was 21 years old when he arrived in the town of Terezin. He died two years later at Auschwitz.

Close Read

1. How does this information change your interpretation of the poem?
2. What is the theme of the poem? Support your answer with information from the background as well as details from the poem.

MODEL 1: INTERPRETING POETRY
Close Read

1. *Possible answer: The boxed text clarifies that the speaker's confinement in the ghetto magnifies his appreciation for the butterfly's beauty and freedom. It also helps the reader understand the sadness in the images "the sun's tears" (line 3) and "it wished to kiss the world goodbye" (lines 7–8).*

2. *Possible answer: The butterfly might symbolize lost freedom, hope, the spirit, or the continuity of life.*

MODEL 2: UNDERSTANDING THE CONTEXT
Close Read

1. *Possible answer: The background gives readers a more explicit understanding of the specific ghetto from which Friedmann writes. This understanding adds meaning to the repeated word "last" (lines 1 and 15), which suggests that the speaker anticipates his own death.*

2. *Possible answer: The poem's theme is the fragility of freedom, as symbolized by the butterfly. There is life and beauty in the ghetto—people, dandelions, white chestnut candles (lines 11–13), but not freedom; freedom flutters lightly away (lines 6–8). The butterfly is the last one because "Butterflies don't live in here, / In the ghetto" (lines 16–17). This theme reflects the historical context of the poem: for the Jews at Terezin, freedom had ended suddenly and permanently.*

DIFFERENTIATED INSTRUCTION

FOR LESS–PROFICIENT READERS

Comprehension: Interpreting Symbols Before students read Model 1, remind them that a symbol is an object that stands for an idea. Explain that a symbol works well when its qualities call to mind the idea. As they read, have students list qualities of the butterfly.

Qualities	Behavior
beautiful	leaves the ghetto
light	never returns
can fly	

Comprehension: Interpreting Theme Before students answer question 2 for Model 2, remind them that a theme in a work of literature is a message or idea about life or human nature that the work as a whole imparts. Ask students to name some common themes in literature, movies, or TV shows. *(the triumph of good over evil, the tragedy of war, the power of love, the wonder or power of nature)*

Practice and Apply

Part 3: Analyze the Literature

Close Read

1. **Possible answer:** *Lines 29–32 in the Background on page 835 clarify the imagery in the boxed lines by describing the memorial in more literal terms.*

2. **Possible answer:** *According to the Background, the names on the wall were placed in the order in which the soldiers died as a way of "highlighting the individual sacrifices that made up the war" (lines 32–36). The effect of this arrangement on the speaker of the poem is to make him imagine the endless series of individual, agonizing deaths, a vision so disturbing that he starts to leave: "They are in the order of dying, / An alphabet of—somewhere— screaming. / I start to walk out" (lines 24–26).*

Part 3: Analyze the Literature

From the title of this poem, you know it is about the "Vietnam Wall." Think about what you may already know about the wall and read through the poem a first time. Then read the background information on the next page. How does the background information change or enhance your understanding of the poem? Read the poem again before answering the **Close Read** questions.

THE VIETNAM WALL

Poem by **Alberto Ríos**

I
Have seen it
And I like it: The magic,
The way like cutting onions
5 It brings water out of nowhere.
Invisible from one side, a scar
Into the skin of the ground
From the other, a black winding
Appendix line.
10   A dig.
        An archaeologist can explain.
The walk is slow at first
Easy, a little black marble wall
Of a dollhouse,
15 A smoothness, a shine
The boys in the street want to give.
One name. And then more
Names, long lines, lines of names until
They are the shape of the U.N. building
20 Taller than I am: I have walked
Into a grave.
And everything I expect has been taken away, like that, quick:
        The names are not alphabetized.
        They are in the order of dying,
25   An alphabet of—somewhere—screaming.
I start to walk out. I almost leave
But stop to look up names of friends,
My own name. There is somebody
Severiano Ríos.
30 Little kids do not make the same noise
Here, junior high school boys don't run
Or hold each other in headlocks.

No rules, something just persists
Like pinching on St. Patrick's Day
35 Every year for no green.
        No one knows why.
Flowers are forced
Into the cracks
Between sections.
40 Men have cried
At this wall.
I have
Seen them.

DIFFERENTIATED INSTRUCTION

FOR LESS–PROFICIENT READERS

Comprehension: Imagery Imagery contributes to historical and cultural context. Help students understand these images from the poem:

- "like cutting onions / It brings water out of nowhere" (lines 4–5) (*It makes one suddenly weep.*)

- "a black winding / Appendix line" (lines 8–9) (*refers to a scar left by an appendectomy*)

- "a shine / The boys in the street want to give" (lines 15–16) (*refers to boys who earn money by shining shoes*)

- "Like pinching on St. Patrick's Day / Every year for no green" (lines 34–35) (*refers to a schoolchildren's tradition of pinching anyone who does not wear green on St. Patrick's Day*)

BACKGROUND

Vietnam: THE WAR AND THE WALL

The Vietnam War was one of the most controversial and divisive wars in U.S. history. During the major years of combat, 1964–1972, more
5   than 58,000 Americans were killed or missing in action. The United States spent about $200 billion to support the South Vietnamese government against soldiers from
10 both North and South Vietnam fighting to unite the country under Communist rule. Two years after the withdrawal of U.S. troops, North Vietnamese forces overran the south
15 and united the country. Many in the United States questioned the worth of our involvement in the war.

In 1979, a group was organized to create the Vietnam Veterans
20 Memorial to honor the U.S. soldiers who died in the war. Some hoped that the construction of a memorial would help to heal the wounds at home caused by the war.

25 A young Yale University student named Maya Ying Lin won a nationwide competition to design the memorial. Lin's abstract design consisted of two walls of polished
30 black granite plunging on a slant into the ground to meet at a 125° angle. The names of the soldiers were carved into the granite in the order that they died, highlighting
35 the individual sacrifices that made up the war. A walkway running the length of each 246-foot wall allows visitors not only to read the names but to touch them and leave
40 messages and other mementos.

When U.S. involvement in the Vietnam War ended in 1973, the poet Alberto Ríos was 21 years old— the same age as the young Severiano
45 Ríos whose name the speaker notices on the wall. Corporal Ríos died from small-arms fire on April 2, 1970, in Tay Ninh, South Vietnam.

Close Read

1. Reread the boxed lines of the poem. What information in the background helped you to understand the imagery in these lines?

2. According to the background, why were soldiers' names placed in their particular order on the wall? Explain the effect their arrangement has on the speaker of the poem.

3. Why might the speaker of the poem be moved by the sight of the name Severiano Ríos on the wall?

4. According to the background, what was the purpose of the Vietnam Veterans Memorial? After reading Ríos's poem, do you think the wall accomplishes that purpose? Support your answer.

Close Read

3. **Possible answer:** The speaker of the poem might be moved by the name Severiano Ríos on the wall (lines 28–29) because Ríos is his own last name. According to the Background, the poet was 21 years old when the war ended (lines 41–43). Perhaps seeing his name intensifies his awareness that he himself could have fought and died in the war.

4. **Possible answer:** According to the Background, the purpose of the memorial was "to honor the U.S. soldiers who died in the war" and to help "heal the wounds at home" caused by divided feelings over the war (lines 20–24). Ríos's poem seems to suggest that the wall has accomplished this purpose. Rather than mentioning the political controversy generated by the war, he focuses on the dignity of the long columns of names (line 18), the respect the wall inspires among visitors (lines 30–36), and the sanctuary it provides for personal memorializing (lines 37–39) and emotional catharsis (lines 40–43).

Assess and Reteach

Assess

Ask students to describe the historical context of the poem and explain how that context was important to fully understanding the poem.

Reteach

For students who are unable to apply the workshop skills to the poem and background selection, use these reteaching activities:

1. Have students review their note-taking copy masters for pages 830 and 832. Ask them to define the terms *historical context* and *cultural context* and to explain why these are important to readers.

2. Return briefly to the two excerpts on page 831 and the poems on pages 833 and 834. Ask students what knowledge of history and of the writer's background deepened their own understanding of each work.

FOR LESS–PROFICIENT READERS

Comprehension: Paragraph Structure Remind students that paragraphs in informative writing usually contain one main idea and supporting details. Have students reread the first paragraph in the Background and state the main idea. *(The Vietnam War was controversial.)* Ask how the writer supports this idea. *(The writer gives reasons—the enormous cost in lives and money and the war's eventual failure.)*

FOR ADVANCED LEARNERS/PRE–AP

Research Context Have students read the workshop independently. Ask them to choose a work of literature they have read and to do research into the historical context or the author's background. Have them explain what insights they gained about the literature from this new information.

Focus and Motivate

OBJECTIVES

Literary Analysis
- explore the key idea of **friendships**
- analyze characteristics of a memoir
- read a memoir and a magazine article

Reading
- make inferences from allusions

Vocabulary
- build vocabulary for reading and writing
- use knowledge of the Latin word root *fid* to help unlock meaning (*also an EL language objective*)

Grammar and Writing
- use gerunds and gerund phrases to write concisely
- use writing to analyze literature

SUMMARY

Frank McCourt recalls a hospital stay when he was ten. He is isolated in his hospital room to recover from typhoid. Despite the disapproval of nurses and nuns, Frank becomes friends with a girl in the next room and with the janitor, Seamus. The girl thrills Frank by reciting most of "The Highwayman," and after her death, Seamus learns and recites the poem's last lines for him.

How does FRIENDSHIP *begin?*

Lead into the *KEY IDEA* by asking the question. Have students read the paragraph and complete the *QUICKWRITE.* Then have them compare how their various **friendships** began.

Selection Resources

---

from **Angela's Ashes**
Memoir by Frank McCourt

How does FRIENDSHIP *begin?*

KEY IDEA Old friends, new friends, close friends, best friends—what makes two people connect? Whether it's a simple act of kindness or the discovery of a shared interest, something special happens to turn a mere acquaintance into a friend. In his memoir *Angela's Ashes*, writer Frank McCourt describes two **friendships** that develop under unusual circumstances.

QUICKWRITE Have you ever formed an unlikely friendship? Perhaps it was with someone much older or much younger than you—or simply with someone very different from you. Write a paragraph about the circumstances under which your friendship formed.

RESOURCE MANAGER UNIT 9

Plan and Teach pp. 17–24

Literary Analysis
Summary pp. 25†*, 26‡*
Memoir pp. 27, 28†*
Question Support p. 35*

Reading
Use Allusions to Make Inferences pp. 29, 30†*
Reading Check p. 34
Reading Fluency p. 37

Vocabulary
Study p. 31*
Practice p. 32
Strategy p. 33

Grammar and Writing
Write Concisely p. 36

Assessment
Selection Tests A, B/C pp. 39*, 41*
Test Generator CD

BEST PRACTICES TOOLKIT

Differentiated Instruction pp. 31–38*

Scaffolding Instruction pp. 43–46*

Graphic Organizers/Strategies
Spider Map • Word Squares
• T Chart • Two-Column Chart

Reading Support
Audio Anthology CD*

Technology
Literature and Vocabulary Centers at **ClassZone.com**
Write*Smart* CD

---

* Resources for Differentiation   † Also in Spanish   ‡ In Haitian Creole and Vietnamese

● LITERARY ANALYSIS: MEMOIR

Frank McCourt was born in New York, but he grew up in Limerick, Ireland, as he describes in his memoir *Angela's Ashes*. A **memoir** is a form of autobiographical writing in which a writer shares his or her personal experiences and observations of significant events and people. Often informal or even intimate in tone, memoirs usually give readers insights into the influence of history on people's lives.

In this selection, McCourt recalls being hospitalized with typhoid, a highly infectious, life-threatening illness. As you read, think about the impact of this event on his life. In addition, note what you learn about Irish history and culture, especially the influence of the Roman Catholic Church.

■ READING SKILL: USE ALLUSIONS TO MAKE INFERENCES

One way Frank McCourt adds meaning to his writing is through allusions. An **allusion** is a reference to a well-known person, place, event, or literary work. It depends on shared knowledge of both the writer and the reader. For example, a writer might refer to a character as having the patience of Job—a biblical figure who endured great suffering without losing his faith in God. Writers use allusions

- to help characterize people or situations
- to evoke ideas or feelings in the reader's mind
- to clarify or highlight important ideas, including the theme

As you read, look for allusions. What can you infer from them? Develop a chart like the one shown.

Allusion	Significance	Inference
"Oh, yes, he knows Roddy McCorley. He'll sing it for me...." (line 134)	Refers to a folk song about Roddy McCorley, a famous Irish labor leader of the late 1700s	Seamus loves music and is very patriotic.

Review: **Draw Conclusions**

▲ VOCABULARY IN CONTEXT

Use context clues to figure out the meanings of the words in bold.

1. The **relapse** of his illness put him back in the hospital.
2. Her persuasive speech **induced** me to support her cause.
3. **Torrents** of rain caused the roads to flood.
4. The officer's **perfidy** led him to be charged with treason.

Author On|ine

Frank McCourt born 1930

A Spellbinding Storyteller Frank McCourt worked as a messenger, a barkeeper, a laborer, and an actor, but it was as a high school writing teacher that he gained his reputation as a consummate storyteller. Columnist Dennis Dugan noted that McCourt "has a way of finding incredible humor in the worst situations"—a trait that has helped him throughout his life. McCourt's advice to students to "write what you know" eventually led him to tell his own story.

Late-Blooming Writer Frank McCourt was 60 years old when he completed his first book, the Pulitzer Prize–winning *Angela's Ashes*. He waited so long to write this memoir of childhood because he needed time to come to terms with his early, poverty-stricken years with an alcoholic father. "I had attitudes and these attitudes had to be softened. I had to get rid of them, I had to become, as it says in the Bible, as a child. The child started to speak in this book. And that was the only way to do it, without judging." The success of *Angela's Ashes* led him to continue his memoir in *'Tis*.

MORE ABOUT THE AUTHOR
For more on Frank McCourt, visit the **Literature Center at ClassZone.com.**

Background

Catholic Ireland in the Mid-1900s When Frank McCourt was growing up in Ireland, the Roman Catholic Church held a firm grip on Irish society. Recognized by Ireland's constitution as the "guardian of the faith," the church operated the schools and hospitals; it had such pervasive influence on society that Irish law did not permit divorce, and censorship of books and films was common.

Teach

STANDARDS FOCUS

LITERARY ANALYSIS

● MEMOIR

To guide students, ask them to reread **Literary Analysis: Memoir** and *About the Author* with these questions in mind: What kind of attitude do you expect McCourt to show in his memoir? Why would his experiences make for a rich memoir? How might time affect memory? ***Possible answer:*** *McCourt might be reflective. His childhood probably had many challenges. Time can give a writer perspective.*

CHECK UNDERSTANDING Ask students to name single incidents that they might include in memoirs of their lives so far. Ask why they would include them.

READING SKILL

■ USE ALLUSIONS TO MAKE INFERENCES

For instructional support, write this sentence on the board. Help students find and explain the allusion.

> Joe must have had Mercury's wings the day he won the race.

Possible answer: *Mercury was a Roman god who had wings on his feet. The allusion suggests that Joe ran exceptionally fast.*

R **RESOURCE MANAGER—Copy Master**
Use Allusions to Make Inferences p. 29 (for student use while reading the selection)

VOCABULARY SKILL

▲ VOCABULARY IN CONTEXT

DIAGNOSE WORD KNOWLEDGE To determine preteaching needs, have all students complete Vocabulary in Context. ***Possible answers:***
1. *setback, return to a previous condition;*
2. *encouraged, tempted;* 3. *flood, violent flow;*
4. *disloyalty, betrayal*

PRETEACH VOCABULARY Use the Vocabulary Study copy master to help students determine word meaning using context clues.

1. Read item 1 aloud, emphasizing *induced*.
2. Point out the phrase "led her to talk." Elicit possible meanings for *induced*, such as "caused."
3. Have students fill in the chart.
4. Repeat the procedure for items 2–4.

R **RESOURCE MANAGER—Copy Master**
Vocabulary Study p. 31

For general guidelines on differentiating vocabulary instruction and for alternative vocabulary activities for students not needing vocabulary preteaching, see

BEST PRACTICES TOOLKIT
Scaffolding Vocabulary Instruction pp. 43–46

 Vocabulary Center at **ClassZone.com**

ANALYZE VISUALS

Possible answer: The photograph suggests that the memoir's time period is the first half of the 20th century and that its subject is childhood events. Support includes the photograph being black and white, creased with age, and showing only boys dressed in old-fashioned clothes.

LITERARY ANALYSIS

Ⓐ MEMOIR

Possible answer: *Readers can infer that economic conditions were harsh. The narrator and Mam go to the hospital in the doctor's car, indicating they have no car. Mam cries, "am I to lose the whole family?" (lines 3–4), suggesting the family has lost other members because it cannot afford good medical care. The narrator remarks on "cool white sheets" (line 6), indicating they are very different from what he has at home.*

If students need help . . . Reread the lines with students as they list clues in a Spider Map.

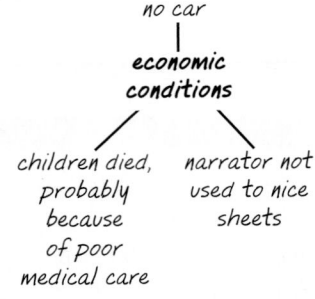

no car

economic conditions

children died, probably because of poor medical care

narrator not used to nice sheets

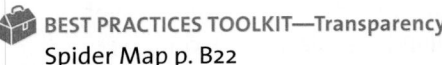

BEST PRACTICES TOOLKIT—Transparency
Spider Map p. B22

Extend the Discussion What other information about economic conditions does the class photograph give you?

Angela's Ashes

FRANK McCOURT

Mam comes with Dr. Troy. He feels my forehead, rolls up my eyelids, turns me over to see my back, picks me up and runs to his motor car. Mam runs after him and he tells her I have typhoid fever. Mam cries, . . . am I to lose the whole family? Will it ever end? She gets into the car, holds me in her lap and moans all the way to the Fever Hospital at the City Home.[1]

The bed has cool white sheets. The nurses have clean white uniforms and the nun, Sister Rita, is all in white. Dr. Humphrey and Dr. Campbell have white coats and things hanging from their necks which they stick against my chest and all over. I sleep and sleep but I'm awake when they bring in jars of
10 bright red stuff that hang from tall poles above my bed and they stick tubes into my ankles and the back of my right hand. Sister Rita says, You're getting blood, Francis. Soldier's blood from the Sarsfield Barracks.

Mam is sitting by the bed and the nurse is saying, You know, missus, this is very unusual. No one is ever allowed into the Fever Hospital for fear they'd catch something but they made an exception for you with his crisis coming. If he gets over this he'll surely recover. Ⓐ

I fall asleep. Mam is gone when I wake but there's movement in the room and it's the priest, Father Gorey, from the Confraternity[2] saying Mass at a table in the corner. I drift off again and now they're waking me and pulling down the
20 bedclothes. Father Gorey is touching me with oil and praying in Latin. I know it's Extreme Unction[3] and that means I'm going to die and I don't care. They wake me again to receive Communion. I don't want it, I'm afraid I might get sick. I keep the wafer on my tongue and fall asleep and when I wake up again it's gone.

It's dark and Dr. Campbell is sitting by my bed. He's holding my wrist and looking at his watch. He has red hair and glasses and he always smiles when he talks to me. He sits now and hums and looks out the window. His eyes close and he snores a little. . . .

---

1. **Mam cries, . . . City Home:** The Fever Hospital was a special section of the Limerick City Home Hospital where patients who had fever-related illnesses like typhoid were treated. The McCourt family had already lost a baby daughter and twin boys to childhood disease.
2. **Confraternity** (kŏn'frə-tûr'nĭ-tē): a religious society or association.
3. **Extreme Unction** (ŭngk'shən): a Roman Catholic sacrament given to a person thought to be near death.

838 UNIT 9: HISTORY, CULTURE, AND THE AUTHOR

ANALYZE VISUALS
What does this class photograph tell you about the time period and subject of this memoir?

Ⓐ MEMOIR
Reread lines 1–16. What **inferences** can you make about economic conditions in Ireland at this time?

① Targeted Passage

Frank McCourt (right front) in the playground of Leamy's school in Limerick, Ireland, about 1938.

Reprinted with permission of Scribner, a division of Simon and Schuster, from *Angela's Ashes: A Memoir* by Frank McCourt. © 1996 by Frank McCourt.

DIFFERENTIATED INSTRUCTION

FOR ALL STUDENTS
Expert Groups Allow students to become experts or members of expert groups by researching and choosing a way to share information about one of these topics:

- typhus and diphtheria
- social conditions in Ireland in the 1940s
- Irish patriotic songs and poems
- the Irish potato famine

FOR LESS–PROFICIENT READERS
In combination with the *Audio Anthology CD*, use one or more Targeted Passages (pp. 838, 843, 844, 846, 847) to ensure that students focus on key story events, concepts, and skills. Targeted Passages are also good for English learners.

① Targeted Passage [Lines 17–23]

This passage provides the first suggestion of the important role Catholicism plays in Frank's life.

BACKGROUND

Anglo-Irish Relations In the 1500s, the king of England became king of Ireland. He and later rulers tried to force Protestantism on the largely Catholic population. They gave Irish lands to English and Protestant settlers. The conflicts became religious as Protestants gained property and political rights that Catholics lost. During the potato famine in the 1840s, England did little to help the starving Irish. In 1921, rising up against British rule, Ireland was divided into two parts. Ulster, in the north, remained part of Britain. The rest became the Irish Free State, which gained self-government in the British Empire and full independence by 1949.

- Why does Father Gorey visit Frank?
- How does Frank react to receiving Extreme Unction?
- How does Frank react when Father Gorey makes him receive Communion?
- What can you tell from this passage about the role of Catholicism in Frank's life?

FOR ENGLISH LEARNERS

Key Academic Vocabulary Use Word Squares to teach these words: *recover* (line 16), *internal* (line 112), *job* (line 118), *circumstances* (line 155), *collapsed* (line 256), *concentrate* (line 290).

 BEST PRACTICES TOOLKIT—Transparency
Word Squares p. E10

Prereading For prereading instruction for English learners, see

BEST PRACTICES TOOLKIT
Scaffolding Reading Instruction pp. 43–46

FOR ADVANCED LEARNERS/PRE–AP

Pre-AP Exercises in the bottom channel provide additional challenge for students. Use these suggestions for small groups or individuals.

ADDITIONAL GUIDELINES

For more help with differentiation and tips for classroom management, see

 BEST PRACTICES TOOLKIT
Differentiated Instruction pp. 31–38

B MEMOIR

Possible answer: The Catholic Church had a great influence over Irish children and their education. Sister Rita, who is a nun, emphasizes that Frank's recovery has largely resulted from the prayers of "Hundreds of boys saying the rosary" for him (lines 31–34). These boys attend a Catholic-run school.

If students need help . . . Have them reread lines 31–34. Discuss the reasons Sister Rita gives for Frank's recovery.

READING SKILL: *Review*

C DRAW CONCLUSIONS

Possible answer: Frank's relationship with his father seems distant. When Frank's father kisses him, Frank is thrilled because it is the first time this has happened (lines 54–55). The affection is apparently unusual in their relationship, though it reveals that Frank's father loves him.

---

ister Rita's white habit is bright in the sun that comes in the window. She's holding my wrist, looking at her watch, smiling.
30 Oh, she says, we're awake, are we? Well, Francis, I think we've come through the worst. Our prayers are answered and all the prayers of those hundreds of little boys at the Confraternity. Can you imagine that? Hundreds of boys saying the rosary[4] for you and offering up their communion. **B**

My ankles and the back of my hand are throbbing from the tubes bringing in the blood and I don't care about boys praying for me. I can hear the swish of Sister Rita's habit and the click of her rosary beads when she leaves the room. I fall asleep and when I wake it's dark and Dad is sitting by the bed with his hand on mine.

40 Son, are you awake?

I try to talk but I'm dry, nothing will come out and I point to my mouth. He holds a glass of water to my lips and it's sweet and cool. He presses my hand and says I'm a great old soldier and why wouldn't I? Don't I have the soldier's blood in me?

The tubes are not in me anymore and the glass jars are gone.

Sister Rita comes in and tells Dad he has to go. I don't want him to go because he looks sad. When he looks sad it's the worst thing in the world and I start crying. Now what's this? says Sister Rita. Crying with all that soldier blood in you? There's a big surprise for you tomorrow, Francis. You'll never
50 guess. Well, I'll tell you, we're bringing you a nice biscuit[5] with your tea in the morning. Isn't that a treat? And your father will be back in a day or two, won't you, Mr. McCourt?

Dad nods and puts his hand on mine again. He looks at me, steps away, stops, comes back, kisses me on the forehead for the first time in my life and I'm so happy I feel like floating out of the bed. **C**

The other two beds in my room are empty. The nurse says I'm the only typhoid patient and I'm a miracle for getting over the crisis.

The room next to me is empty till one morning a girl's voice says, Yoo hoo, who's there?
60 I'm not sure if she's talking to me or someone in the room beyond.

Yoo hoo, boy with the typhoid, are you awake?

I am.

Are you better?

I am.

Well, why are you here?

I don't know. I'm still in the bed. They stick needles in me and give me medicine.

What do you look like?

I wonder, What kind of a question is that? I don't know what to tell her.

---

4. **rosary** (rō′zə-rē): a series of prayers repeated by Roman Catholics as a form of devotion to the Virgin Mary—usually counted off on a string of beads as they are said.

5. **biscuit:** cookie.

B MEMOIR
Reread lines 28–34. What do you learn about the Catholic Church's influence over Irish children and their education at this time?

C DRAW CONCLUSIONS
How would you describe Frank's relationship with his father? Cite details to support your answer.

DIFFERENTIATED INSTRUCTION

FOR ENGLISH LEARNERS

Culture: Clarify McCourt introduces many elements of Irish Catholicism in the mid-1900s. Ask students to work in small groups to list elements under the categories *Key People* and *Rituals/Objects* on a T Chart. After comparing charts, ask students to add to them as they read the rest of the selection.

BEST PRACTICES TOOLKIT—Transparency
T Chart p. A25

FOR ADVANCED LEARNERS/PRE–AP

Analyze Attitudes Ask students what Dad means when he says that Frank has "soldier's blood" in him (lines 43–44). As students read, have them note references to and by Frank about being a soldier. After they have finished reading the selection, ask them to write a brief paragraph about what it might have meant to Frank to have the soldier's blood in him.

70   Yoo hoo, are you there, typhoid boy?

    I am.

    What's your name?

    Frank.

    That's a good name. My name is Patricia Madigan. How old are you?

    Ten.

    Oh. She sounds disappointed.

    But I'll be eleven in August, next month.

    Well, that's better than ten. I'll be fourteen in September. Do you want to know why I'm in the Fever Hospital?

80   I do.

    I have diphtheria[6] and something else.

    What's something else?

    They don't know. They think I have a disease from foreign parts because my father used to be in Africa. I nearly died. Are you going to tell me what you look like?

    I have black hair.

    You and millions.

    I have brown eyes with bits of green that's called hazel.

    You and thousands.

90   I have stitches on the back of my right hand and my two feet where they put in the soldier's blood.

    Oh, . . . did they?

    They did.

    You won't be able to stop marching and saluting.

    There's a swish of habit and click of beads and then Sister Rita's voice. Now, now, what's this? There's to be no talking between two rooms especially when it's a boy and a girl. Do you hear me, Patricia?

    I do, Sister.

    Do you hear me, Francis?

100   I do, Sister.

    You could be giving thanks for your two remarkable recoveries. You could be saying the rosary. You could be reading *The Little Messenger of the Sacred Heart*[7] that's beside your beds. Don't let me come back and find you talking. She comes into my room and wags her finger at me. Especially you, Francis, after thousands of boys prayed for you at the Confraternity. Give thanks, Francis, give thanks. She leaves and there's silence for awhile. Then Patricia whispers, Give thanks, Francis, give thanks, and say your rosary, Francis, and I laugh so hard a nurse runs in to see if I'm all right. She's a very stern nurse from the County Kerry[8] and she frightens me. What's this, Francis? Laughing? What is
110 there to laugh about? Are you and that Madigan girl talking? I'll report you to

---

6. **diphtheria** (dǐf-thǐr′ē-ə): a highly infectious disease caused by the bacterium *Corynebacterium diphtheriae*. It is spread by infected secretions from the nose and throat and can create toxins that destroy the heart and nervous system.

7. ***The Little . . . Heart:*** a Roman Catholic magazine.

8. **County Kerry:** a largely rural county to the west of Limerick.

ANGELA'S ASHES   **841**

Lines 58–94
REINFORCE *KEY IDEA:* FRIENDSHIPS

Discuss What is unusual about how the friendship between Frank and Patricia starts? *Possible answer: The two are in separate hospital rooms and can't see each other (lines 58–59) and are a boy and girl of different ages. Their friendship may develop out of their similarities—both are sick and alone in a hospital.*

Lines 70–97
DISCUSSION PROMPTS

Use these prompts to help students understand the importance of the first conversation between Frank and Patricia:

Connect How would you feel if you were alone in a hospital? *Students will probably respond that they would be lonely or frightened.*

Analyze Based on their conversation, how do you think Frank feels talking to Patricia? *Possible answer: Talking to Patricia probably comforts Frank and lifts his spirits.*

Evaluate Sister Rita doesn't want Patricia and Frank to talk to each other. What do her restrictions reveal about her character? *Possible answer: Sister Rita's restrictions show her to be conscientious but somewhat unfeeling. While quiet activities can foster healing, the infirmary setting seems scary, and companionship can be soothing and healthy.*

FOR ENGLISH LEARNERS

Language: Contractions Have individual students identify contractions in the last paragraph on this page—*that's* and *Don't* (line 103), *there's* (line 106), *I'm* and *She's* (line 108), *What's* (line 109), and *I'll* (line 110)—and read the sentences containing the contractions, substituting the long forms. Then have students hunt for additional contractions in the selection, call out the line numbers, and repeat the process.

FOR ADVANCED LEARNERS/PRE-AP

Dialogue: Dramatic Reading McCourt offers no description as to how the disclosure in lines 70–93 is delivered. Challenge students to break into pairs and deliver dramatic readings of these lines to the class. Remind them to imagine how each character is feeling at that moment and to deliver the lines in such a way that makes the characters seem realistic.

A Limerick hospital in the early part of the 20th century

ANALYZE VISUALS

Activity Ask students how this photograph helps them visualize Frank's experience in the hospital. *Possible answer: The photograph shows a very plain and somewhat run-down hospital in Limerick in the early 1900s. This is probably much like the hospital that Frank stays in when he is ill.*

Sister Rita. There's to be no laughing for you could be doing serious damage to your internal apparatus.[9]

She plods out and Patricia whispers again in a heavy Kerry accent, No laughing, Francis, you could be doin' serious damage to your internal apparatus. Say your rosary, Francis, and pray for your internal apparatus.

Mam visits me on Thursdays, I'd like to see my father, too, but I'm out of danger, crisis time is over, and I'm allowed only one visitor. Besides, she says, he's back at work at Rank's Flour Mills and please God this job will last a while with the war on and the English desperate for flour. She brings me a chocolate
120 bar and that proves Dad is working. She could never afford it on the dole.[10] He sends me notes. He tells me my brothers are all praying for me, that I should be a good boy, obey the doctors, the nuns, the nurses, and don't forget to say my prayers. He's sure St. Jude pulled me through the crisis because he's the patron saint of desperate cases and I was indeed a desperate case. ⓓ

Patricia says she has two books by her bed. One is a poetry book and that's the one she loves. The other is a short history of England and do I want it? She gives it to Seamus,[11] the man who mops the floors every day, and he brings it to me. He says, I'm not supposed to be bringing anything from a diphtheria room to a typhoid room with all the germs flying around and hiding between
130 the pages and if you ever catch diphtheria on top of the typhoid they'll know and I'll lose my good job and be out on the street singing patriotic songs with a tin cup in my hand, which I could easily do because there isn't a song ever written about Ireland's sufferings I don't know. . . .

Oh, yes, he knows Roddy McCorley.[12] He'll sing it for me right enough but he's barely into the first verse when the Kerry nurse rushes in. What's this,

---

9. **internal apparatus:** the internal organs of the body.

10. **on the dole:** living on government unemployment payments.

11. **Seamus** (shā'məs).

12. **Roddy McCorley:** a song about Roddy McCorley, a local leader during an Irish uprising. McCorley was hanged by the English in 1798.

ⓓ **MEMOIR**
Reread lines 116–124. What details describe Frank's family and the role of religion in their lives?

LITERARY ANALYSIS

ⓓ **MEMOIR**

Possible answer: Mam praying to God that Dad will hold on to his job, and Dad's message that people are praying for him, that he should obey the nuns and say his prayers, and that St. Jude has pulled him through show that the family is religious (lines 117–124).

Lines 125–133
REINFORCE *KEY IDEA*: FRIENDSHIPS

Discuss How does the friendship with Patricia develop? How does the friendship with Seamus begin? Do these **friendships** follow ordinary patterns? Explain. *Possible answer: The friendship with Patricia develops through sharing books (lines 125–126). Friendship often develops when people share interests. The friendship with Seamus begins because he helps the children communicate with each other (lines 126–128). Helping someone is often the basis for the beginning of a friendship.*

DIFFERENTIATED INSTRUCTION

FOR ENGLISH LEARNERS

Language: Conversational English Patterns Point out that Irish speech patterns can differ from American English patterns. Show students these examples and help them paraphrase the sentences containing them into American English: "There's to be no" (line 111); "right enough" (line 134); "Isn't it a great pity" (line 148); "to be had" (line 150); "'twould" (line 228); "'twas" (line 235); "'Tis" (line 237).

FOR ADVANCED LEARNERS/PRE–AP

Analyze Social Context Ask students to locate and share the words to the song "Roddy McCorley." Have students work in groups to summarize the song's story. Then have students discuss what this song and its popularity show about the Ireland of the 1940s. Have groups share their conclusions with one another and with the class.

Seamus? Singing? Of all the people in this hospital you should know the rules against singing. I have a good mind to report you to Sister Rita.

Ah, . . . don't do that, nurse.

Very well, Seamus. I'll let it go this one time. You know the singing could
140 lead to a **relapse** in these patients.

When she leaves he whispers he'll teach me a few songs because singing is good for passing the time when you're by yourself in a typhoid room. He 🄴 says Patricia is a lovely girl the way she often gives him sweets from the parcel her mother sends every fortnight.[13] He stops mopping the floor and calls to Patricia in the next room, I was telling Frankie you're a lovely girl, Patricia, and she says, You're a lovely man, Seamus. He smiles because he's an old man of forty and he never had children but the ones he can talk to here in the Fever Hospital. He says, Here's the book, Frankie. Isn't it a great pity you have to be reading all about England after all they did to us, that there isn't a history of
150 Ireland to be had in this hospital. 🄵

The book tells me all about King Alfred and William the Conqueror and all the kings and queens down to Edward, who had to wait forever for his mother, Victoria, to die before he could be king. The book has the first bit of Shakespeare I ever read.

*I do believe, **induced** by potent circumstances*
That thou art mine enemy.

The history writer says this is what Catherine, who is a wife of Henry the Eighth, says to Cardinal Wolsey, who is trying to have her head cut off. I don't know what it means and I don't care because it's Shakespeare and it's like
160 having jewels in my mouth when I say the words. If I had a whole book of Shakespeare they could keep me in the hospital for a year. 🄶

> Patricia says she doesn't know what induced means or potent circumstances and she doesn't care about Shakespeare, she has her poetry book and she reads to me from beyond the wall a poem about an owl and a pussycat that went to sea in a green boat with honey and money[14] and it makes no sense and when I say that Patricia gets huffy and says that's the last poem she'll ever read to me. She says I'm always reciting the lines from Shakespeare and they make no sense either. Seamus stops mopping again and tells us we shouldn't be fighting over poetry because we'll have enough to fight about when we grow up and
> 170 get married. Patricia says she's sorry and I'm sorry too so she reads me part of another poem which I have to remember so I can say it back to her early in the morning or late at night when there are no nuns or nurses about,

② **Targeted Passage**

*The wind was a **torrent** of darkness among the gusty trees,*
The moon was a ghostly galleon tossed upon cloudy seas,
The road was a ribbon of moonlight over the purple moor,

---

13. **fortnight:** two weeks.

14. **a poem . . . money:** "The Owl and the Pussycat," a humorous poem by the 19th-century British poet and artist Edward Lear.

---

relapse (rē'lăps) *n.* a worsening of an illness after a partial recovery

🄴 **GRAMMAR AND STYLE**
Reread lines 139–142. Notice McCourt's use of the **gerund** *singing.* A gerund is a verb form that ends in *–ing* and is used as a noun.

🄵 **ALLUSIONS**
Here Seamus refers to the troubled relationship between England and Ireland. What does this reveal about him? about Irish culture?

induced (ĭn-dōōst') *adj.* led on; persuaded **induce** *v.*

🄶 **MEMOIR**
What does this first encounter with Shakespeare reveal about Frank?

torrent (tôr'ənt) *n.* a heavy, uncontrolled outpouring

🄴 **GRAMMAR AND STYLE**
Recognize Gerunds Without exception, all gerunds end in *-ing.* However, all present participles also end in *-ing.* Gerunds can be subjects, objects, or subject complements, while present participles act as modifiers or complete progressive verbs. Note that using gerunds in writing helps bring variety to it. Have students locate other gerunds in the selection.

READING SKILL

🄵 **ALLUSIONS**
Possible answer: Seamus knows history well and loves his country (lines 148–150). This suggests that ordinary Irish people are politically active and passionately patriotic.

LITERARY ANALYSIS

🄶 **MEMOIR**
Possible answer: Frank's first encounter with Shakespeare reveals his love of language and poetry. Shakespeare's words are like "jewels in [his] mouth" (line 160).

FOR LESS–PROFICIENT READERS
② Targeted Passage [Lines 162–172]

This passage gives more information about Patricia and describes what the relationship between the two children is like.

- How do Frank and Patricia make up after an argument? Is it hard? Explain.
- What interests do the children share?
- Based on their interactions, why do you think the children like each other?

FOR ENGLISH LEARNERS
Culture: Clarify Read full versions of both "The Owl and the Pussycat" and "The Highwayman" to students, or have English speakers do so. As an alternative, you might bring sound recordings or picture books with the poems to class for students. Have students discuss and summarize the stories in both poems.

And the highwayman came riding
Riding riding
The highwayman came riding, up to the old inn-door.
He'd a French cocked-hat on his forehead,
180   *a bunch of lace at his chin,*
A coat of the claret velvet, and breeches of brown doe-skin,
They fitted with never a wrinkle, his boots were up to the thigh.
And he rode with a jeweled twinkle,
His pistol butts a-twinkle,
His rapier hilt a-twinkle, under the jeweled sky.[15]

Every day I can't wait for the doctors and nurses to leave me alone so I can learn a new verse from Patricia and find out what's happening to the highwayman and the landlord's red-lipped daughter. I love the poem because it's exciting and almost as good as my two lines of Shakespeare. The redcoats
190 are after the highwayman because they know he told her, I'll come to thee by moonlight. . . . **H**

I'd love to do that myself, come by moonlight for Patricia in the next room. . . . She's ready to read the last few verses when in comes the nurse from Kerry shouting at her, shouting at me, I told ye there was to be no talking between rooms. Diphtheria is never allowed to talk to typhoid and visa versa. I warned ye. And she calls out, Seamus, take this one. Take the by.[16] Sister Rita said one more word out of him and upstairs with him. We gave ye a warning to stop the blathering but ye wouldn't. Take the by, Seamus, take him.

Ah, now, nurse, sure isn't he harmless. 'Tis only a bit o' poetry.
200   Take that by, Seamus, take him at once. **I**

He bends over me and whispers, Ah, . . . I'm sorry, Frankie. Here's your English history book. He slips the book under my shirt and lifts me from the bed. He whispers that I'm a feather. I try to see Patricia when we pass through her room but all I can make out is a blur of dark head on a pillow.

Sister Rita stops us in the hall to tell me I'm a great disappointment to her, that she expected me to be a good boy after what God had done for me, after all the prayers said by hundreds of boys at the Confraternity, after all the care from the nuns and nurses of the Fever Hospital, after the way they let my mother and father in to see me, a thing rarely allowed, and this is how I
210 repaid them lying in the bed reciting silly poetry back and forth with Patricia Madigan knowing very well there was a ban on all talk between typhoid and diphtheria. She says I'll have plenty of time to reflect on my sins in the big ward upstairs and I should beg forgiveness for my disobedience reciting a pagan English poem about a thief on a horse and a maiden with red lips who commits a terrible sin when I could have been praying or reading the life of a saint. She made it her business to read that poem so she did and I'd be well advised to tell the priest in confession.

---

15. **The wind . . . jeweled sky:** the opening lines of "The Highwayman," a romantic, action-packed narrative poem by the 20th-century British writer Alfred Noyes.

16. **by:** boy (spelled to indicate the nurse's dialectal pronunciation).

844   UNIT 9: HISTORY, CULTURE, AND THE AUTHOR

LITERARY ANALYSIS

H MEMOIR

Possible answer: As in "The Highwayman," the children seem to be starting a romance but are separated by outside forces. Frank wants to visit Patricia like the highwayman wants to visit Bess (line 192).

LITERARY ANALYSIS

I MEMOIR

Possible answer: The nurse's dialect makes her a little hard to understand but also makes her sound old-fashioned and rather harsh. It helps readers hear her voice (lines 194–198).

REINFORCE KEY IDEA: FRIENDSHIPS

How do Seamus and Sister Rita differ in their understanding of the **friendship** between Frank and Patricia? What does this difference show about who they are as people? *Possible answer: Seamus, who appreciates poetry, understands the romance between the two. Sister Rita sees the friendship as a problem, a constant infraction of the rules. Seamus is a kind-hearted romantic. Sister Rita, while dedicated, values rules and discipline.*

H MEMOIR
In what ways is Frank and Patricia's situation like that of the characters in "The Highwayman"?

③ Targeted Passage

I MEMOIR
Reread lines 193–200. McCourt uses **dialect** to provide a realistic portrayal of the nurse. How does this influence your reaction to her?

DIFFERENTIATED INSTRUCTION

FOR LESS–PROFICIENT READERS

③ Targeted Passage [Lines 192–200]

This passage describes how Frank and Patricia are separated.

• Why does the nurse make Frank move?

• How does Seamus react when he's asked to move Frank?

• What kind of attitude does the nurse show toward the children?

FOR ADVANCED LEARNERS/PRE–AP

Analyze Character Ask students to analyze what Sister Rita finds objectionable in "The Highwayman." Have student pairs read "The Highwayman," then discuss these questions: What makes "The Highwayman" a "pagan English poem"? What about the poem makes Sister Rita think Frank must confess he has read it?

A children's ward typical of British and Irish hospitals in the 1940s

ANALYZE VISUALS

Activity Ask students what the photograph suggests about how children in England and Ireland were viewed by adults in the 1940s.
Possible answer: The placement of an older child in a crib suggests that children were treated as babies long after leaving infancy. The lack of curtains or screens suggests that adults felt children did not need privacy.

The Kerry nurse follows us upstairs gasping and holding on to the banister. She tells me I better not get the notion she'll be running up to this part of the
220 world every time I have a little pain or a twinge.

There are twenty beds in the ward, all white, all empty. The nurse tells Seamus put me at the far end of the ward against the wall to make sure I don't talk to anyone who might be passing the door, which is very unlikely since there isn't another soul on this whole floor. She tells Seamus this was the fever ward during the Great Famine[17] long ago and only God knows how many died here brought in too late for anything but a wash before they were buried and there are stories of cries and moans in the far reaches of the night. She says 'twould break your heart to think of what the English did to us, that if they didn't put the blight[18] on the potato they didn't do much to take it off.
230 No pity. No feeling at all for the people that died in this very ward, children suffering and dying here while the English feasted on roast beef and guzzled the best of wine in their big houses, little children with their mouths all green from trying to eat the grass in the fields beyond, God bless us and save us and guard us from future famines. **J**

Seamus says 'twas a terrible thing indeed and he wouldn't want to be walking these halls in the dark with all the little green mouths gaping at him. The nurse takes my temperature, 'Tis up a bit, have a good sleep for yourself now that you're away from the chatter with Patricia Madigan below who will never know a gray hair.[19]
240 She shakes her head at Seamus and he gives her a sad shake back.

J MEMOIR
Reread lines 221–234. What insights do you get about the sufferings the Irish endured during the famine and its lasting effect on their culture?

---

17. **Great Famine** (făm′ĭn): a devastating food shortage in Ireland in the late 1840s, caused by a failure of the potato crop. Over a million Irish people died of starvation during the famine, and about 1.5 million emigrated, mainly to the United States.

18. **blight**: a plant disease—in this case, the one that destroyed the Irish potato crop.

19. **never know a gray hair**: won't live to be old.

ANGELA'S ASHES   **845**

LITERARY ANALYSIS

J MEMOIR

Possible answer: The nurse's remarks indicate there was great suffering during the Great Famine. The memory of that suffering and England's lack of help continued to haunt Ireland in the 1940s.

If students need help . . .

• Direct them to footnotes 17 and 18 for additional background about the Great Famine.

• Reread lines 221–234 with students, highlighting details that refer to the Great Famine. Discuss what images these create of the Irish experience at that time and how such an experience would make people feel.

Extend the Discussion What is ironic about the nurse's criticism of the attitude of the English toward Irish children?

FOR ADVANCED LEARNERS/PRE–AP

Secret Note Imagine that Frank could have slipped a note to Patricia. Perhaps Seamus might have delivered it. How might Frank have described his surroundings? his feelings for Patricia? Have students write a note that Frank might have written. Have them read their notes aloud to the class.

Lines 237–246
DISCUSSION PROMPTS

Use these prompts to help students understand Frank's feelings toward the nurses and nuns and his reactions to the idea that Patricia might die:

Recall What does the nurse tell Seamus about Patricia? How does Frank respond to this news? *Possible answer: The nurse tells Seamus that Patricia is dying. Frank is upset by this but hides it from the adults.*

Analyze Why does Frank feel he can't "cry over this girl"? *Possible answer: The adults think Frank won't realize that Patricia is dying. Also, they believe they have ended an inappropriate friendship by moving Frank. Frank worries that crying over Patricia will reveal that he still cares about her and that he will be scolded for this (lines 241–246).*

Synthesize How do these lines help you to understand what Patricia really means to Frank? *Possible answer: Patricia brought romance and beauty into Frank's lonely and isolated world.*

Nurses and nuns never think you know what they're talking about. If you're ten going on eleven you're supposed to be simple like my uncle Pat Sheehan who was dropped on his head. You can't ask questions. You can't show you understand what the nurse said about Patricia Madigan, that she's going to die, and you can't show you want to cry over this girl who taught you a lovely poem which the nun says is bad.

The nurse tells Seamus she has to go and he's to sweep the lint from under my bed and mop up a bit around the ward. Seamus tells me . . . that you can't catch a disease from a poem. . . . He never heard the likes of it, a little
250 fella shifted upstairs for saying a poem and he has a good mind to go to the *Limerick Leader*[20] and tell them print the whole thing except he has this job and he'd lose it if ever Sister Rita found out. Anyway, Frankie, you'll be outa here one of these fine days and you can read all the poetry you want though I don't know about Patricia below, I don't know about Patricia. . . .

He knows about Patricia in two days because she got out of the bed to go to the lavatory when she was supposed to use a bedpan and collapsed and died in the lavatory. Seamus is mopping the floor and there are tears on his cheeks and he's saying, 'Tis a dirty rotten thing to die in a lavatory when you're lovely in yourself. She told me she was sorry she had you reciting that poem and getting
260 you shifted from the room, Frankie. She said 'twas all her fault.

It wasn't, Seamus.

I know and didn't I tell her that.

(4) Targeted Passage

Patricia is gone and I'll never know what happened to the highwayman and Bess, the landlord's daughter. I ask Seamus but he doesn't know any poetry at all especially English poetry. He knew an Irish poem once but it was about fairies and had no sign of a highwayman in it. Still he'll ask the men in his local pub where there's always someone reciting something and he'll bring it back to me. Won't I be busy meanwhile reading my short history of England
270 and finding out all about their **perfidy.** That's what Seamus says, perfidy, and I don't know what it means and he doesn't know what it means but if it's something the English do it must be terrible.

perfidy (pûr'fĭ-dē) *n.* treachery; betrayal of trust

He comes three times a week to mop the floor and the nurse is there every morning to take my temperature and pulse. The doctor listens to my chest with the thing hanging from his neck. They all say, And how's our little soldier today? A girl with a blue dress brings meals three times a day and never talks to me. Seamus says she's not right in the head so don't say a word to her.

The July days are long and I fear the dark. There are only two ceiling lights in the ward and they're switched off when the tea tray is taken away
280 and the nurse gives me pills. The nurse tells me go to sleep but I can't because I see people in the nineteen beds in the ward all dying and green around their mouths where they tried to eat grass and moaning for soup

---

20. *Limerick Leader:* a newspaper published in Limerick.

DIFFERENTIATED INSTRUCTION

FOR LESS–PROFICIENT READERS
(4) Targeted Passage [Lines 255–261]

This passage describes Patricia's death and Seamus's reaction to it.

- How does Patricia die?
- How does Seamus react to her death?
- What does Patricia tell Seamus before she dies?

FOR ENGLISH LEARNERS
Culture: Clarify Make sure that students recognize the anti-English feelings of the Irish. Direct students to reread lines 269–272 as one example of these feelings. Then have them look for other examples of anti-English feelings or direct them to read and comment on the feelings expressed in lines 148–150, 227–234, and 320–322.

Protestant soup[21] any soup and I cover my face with the pillow hoping they won't come and stand around the bed clawing at me and howling for bits of the chocolate bar my mother brought last week. **K**

No, she didn't bring it. She had to send it in because I can't have any more visitors. Sister Rita tells me a visit to the Fever Hospital is a privilege and after my bad behavior with Patricia Madigan and that poem I can't have the privilege anymore. She says I'll be going home in a few weeks and my job is
290 to concentrate on getting better and learn to walk again after being in bed for six weeks and I can get out of bed tomorrow after breakfast. I don't know why she says I have to learn how to walk when I've been walking since I was a baby but when the nurse stands me by the side of the bed I fall to the floor and the nurse laughs, See, you're a baby again.

I practice walking from bed to bed back and forth back and forth. I don't want to be a baby. I don't want to be in this empty ward with no Patricia and no highwayman and no red-lipped landlord's daughter. I don't want the ghosts of children with green mouths pointing bony fingers at me and clamoring for bits of my chocolate bar.

300 Seamus says a man in his pub knew all the verses of the highwayman poem and it has a very sad end. Would I like him to say it because he never learned how to read and he had to carry the poem in his head? He stands in the middle of the ward leaning on his mop and recites,

Tlot-tlot, in the frosty silence! Tlot-tlot in the echoing night!
Nearer he came and nearer! Her face was like a light!
Her eyes grew wide for a moment, she drew one last deep breath,
Then her finger moved in the moonlight,
Her musket shattered the moonlight,
Shattered her breast in the moonlight and warned him—with her death.

310 He hears the shot and escapes but when he learns at dawn how Bess died he goes into a rage and returns for revenge only to be shot down by the redcoats.

Blood-red were his spurs in the golden noon; wine-red was his velvet coat,
When they shot him down on the highway,
Down like a dog on the highway,
And he lay in his blood on the highway, with a bunch of lace at his throat.

Seamus wipes his sleeve across his face and sniffles. He says, There was no call at all to shift you up here away from Patricia when you didn't even know what happened to the highwayman and Bess. 'Tis a very sad story and when I said it to my wife she wouldn't stop crying the whole night till we went to bed.
320 She said there was no call for them redcoats to shoot that highwayman, they are responsible for half the troubles of the world and they never had any pity on the Irish, either. Now if you want to know any more poems, Frankie, tell me and I'll get them from the pub and bring 'em back in my head. ☙

---

21. **Protestant soup:** soup provided by the English to the starving Irish during the famine, often in return for renouncing Catholicism and joining the Protestant faith.

ANGELA'S ASHES **847**

K **ALLUSIONS**
Reread lines 280–285 and identify the allusions McCourt makes to tragic events that occurred during the Great Famine. Why do you think McCourt includes these references?

⑤ Targeted Passage

READING SKILL

K **ALLUSIONS**

Possible answer: The broad allusion to "people in the nineteen beds . . ." (line 281) and the specific allusion to "Protestant soup" (line 283) both refer to hunger and illness during the Great Famine. The allusions show that these events haunt young Frank.

SELECTION WRAP–UP

REFLECT Have students think about how a childhood experience like this one might affect a person's attitudes in later years. How might one feel about the treatment of hospital patients? about the impact of poetry? about the value of friendships?

★ CRITIQUE Have students share which episodes within the selection they found the most memorable and explain why.

READING FLUENCY

Distribute the copy masters and have students work in pairs or groups to practice fluency.

R RESOURCE MANAGER—Copy Master
Reading Fluency p. 37

FOR LESS–PROFICIENT READERS

⑤ Targeted Passage [Lines 300–323]

This passage concludes the selection with the end of the poem "The Highwayman" and Seamus's reactions to it.

• What happens to Bess and the highwayman at the end of the poem?

• How does Seamus feel about Patricia not being able to read the end of the poem to Frank?

• What sad events are summed up in the final paragraph?

FOR ADVANCED LEARNERS/PRE–AP

Compare and Contrast Context Have students think about the two friendships Frank develops in the hospital. How are they similar? different? What does he take and give to each one? Have students break into small groups to discuss these questions and then share their conclusions with the class.

ANGELA'S ASHES **847**

MAGAZINE ARTICLE As a high school teacher, Frank McCourt encouraged his students to write from their experiences. Years later, he recalled the honesty and bravery of their writing and found the inspiration to write his own memoir.

DISCUSSION PROMPTS

Use these prompts to help students understand why McCourt wrote *Angela's Ashes:*

Connect Do you ever feel frustrated when you try to write? Are you sometimes afraid that you just won't get it right? Describe your feelings about writing. *Answers will vary. Encourage students to cite specific situations in their responses.*

Analyze What were the most important ideas about writing that McCourt passed on to his students? What were the most important ideas McCourt gained from his students? *Possible answer: Students learned that everyone has a story to tell, to write about things they know, to find their own voices, and to dig deep. They gained inspiration and courage. McCourt recognized that his students were doing what he should be doing and was inspired by their courage. He learned to follow his own advice.*

Evaluate McCourt learned from his students just as they learned from him. In your view, who gained more, McCourt or his students? *Possible answer: McCourt may have gained more from his students than they did from him because he gained perspective from reading their work, recognized the many good stories he had to tell as he shared them with his classes, and gained courage by seeing his students challenge themselves.*

THE EDUCATION of
Frank McCourt
By Barbara Sande Dimmitt

The bell rang in the faculty lounge at Stuyvesant High School in Manhattan. When McCourt began teaching at the prestigious public high school in 1972, he joked that he'd finally made it to paradise. . . .

The bits and pieces that bubbled into his consciousness enlivened the stories he told in class. "Everyone has a story to tell," he said. "Write about what you know with conviction, from the heart. Dig deep," he urged. "Find your own voice and dance your own dance!"

On Fridays the students read their compositions aloud. To draw them out, McCourt would read excerpts from his duffel bag full of notebooks. "You had such an interesting childhood, Mr. McCourt," they said. "Why don't you write a book?" They threw his own words back at him: "It sounds like there's more to that story; dig deeper . . ."

McCourt was past 50 and painfully aware of the passage of time. But despite his growing frustration at his [own memoir begun six years earlier], he never tired of his students' work.

Over the years some talented writers passed through McCourt's popular classes. Laurie Gwen Shapiro was one of them. He decided she was coasting along on her technical skills. "You're capable of much more," McCourt told her. "Try writing something that's meaningful to you for a change."

Near the end of the semester, McCourt laid an essay—graded 100—on Laurie's desk. "If Laurie is willing to read her essay," he announced to the class, "I think we'll all benefit."

Laurie began to read a portrait of love clouded by anger and shame. She told of her father, partially paralyzed, and of resenting his inability to play with her or help her ride a bicycle. The paper shook in her trembling hands, and McCourt understood all too well what it cost her to continue. She also admitted she was embarrassed by her father's limp. The words, McCourt knew, were torn straight from her soul.

When Laurie finished, with tears streaming down her face, the students broke into applause. McCourt looked around the room, his own vision blurred.

These young people have been giving you lessons in courage, he thought. When will you dare as mightily as they?

It was October 1994. Frank McCourt, now retired, sat down and read his book's new opening, which he had written a few days before and still found satisfying. But many blank pages lay before him. *What if I never get it right?* he wondered grimly.

He stared at the logs glowing in the fireplace and could almost hear students' voices from years past, some angry, some defeated, others confused and seeking guidance. "It's no good, Mr. McCourt. I don't have what it takes."

Then Frank McCourt, author, heard the steadying tones of Frank McCourt, teacher:

Of course you do. Dig deeper. Find your own voice and dance your own dance.

He scribbled a few lines. "I'm in a playground on Classon Avenue in Brooklyn with my brother Malachy. He's two, I'm three. We're on the seesaw." In the innocent voice of an unprotected child who could neither comprehend nor control the world around him, Frank McCourt told his tale of poverty and abandonment.

Comprehension

1. **Recall** Why is Frank in the hospital?

2. **Recall** What rules does Frank break?

3. **Clarify** What happens to Patricia Madigan?

4. **Clarify** According to "The Education of Frank McCourt," who or what finally prompted McCourt to complete *Angela's Ashes*?

Literary Analysis

5. **Understand Memoir** Frank develops two **friendships** in the hospital. What is the basis for each friendship? Give reasons to support your response.

6. **Draw Conclusions About Character** What kind of a man is Seamus? Support your answer with examples of his actions and his words.

7. **Analyze Character Motives** What motivates Sister Rita to forbid Frank to talk to Patricia? Considering Patricia's fate, were Sister Rita's actions justified? Cite details to support your response.

8. **Use Allusions to Make Inferences** Review the allusions and inferences you recorded in your chart as you read. What would your reading experience have been like if McCourt had not included these allusions?

9. **Identify Author's Perspective** On the basis of the numerous **allusions** to Catholic clergy, rituals, practices, and beliefs in this selection, what do you think is McCourt's view of the Catholic Church and its influence on Irish culture and society in the 1940s? Explain your answer.

10. **Evaluate Voice** A writer's unique style of expression is called voice. In *Angela's Ashes*, McCourt writes in the "innocent voice of an unprotected child." How effective is this voice in relating not only events from McCourt's childhood but also his adult feelings about these events?

Literary Criticism

11. **Critical Interpretations** One critic has said that while reading *Angela's Ashes* "you never know whether to weep or roar—and find yourself doing both at once." Did you think any of the incidents described in this selection were at the same time sad and humorous? Cite examples to support your answer.

ANGELA'S ASHES **849**

Practice and Apply

After Reading
For additional support of post-reading questions, use these copy masters:

RESOURCE MANAGER—Copy Masters
Reading Check p. 34 (to check understanding of the selection)
Memoir p. 27 (for practice of literary analysis standards focus)
Question Support p. 35 (After Reading questions adapted for English learners and less-proficient readers)
For additional questions, see page 21.

ANSWERS

Comprehension
1. *Frank is in the hospital with typhoid.*
2. *Frank breaks the rules about talking between rooms and talking with a girl.*
3. *Patricia dies.*
4. *McCourt's students' courage prompted him to complete the book. He decided to follow the same advice he gave students.*

Literary Analysis
Possible answers:
5. ● STANDARDS FOCUS *Memoir The friendship with Patricia is based on a shared experience of being sick in a hospital (lines 58–85) and shared feelings about poetry (lines 125–126). The friendship with Seamus is based on a love of poetry and song (lines 132–135), Seamus's love for children, and his role as intermediary between the children (lines 201–202).*
6. *Seamus is kindhearted and loves children. Examples: He brings books to Frank, feels sad over Patricia's death (lines 255–260), and memorizes the end of "The Highwayman" to recite for Frank (lines 300–303).*
7. *Sister Rita is motivated by the idea that talking, laughing, and singing are bad for the health (lines 111–112) and by the desire to exert authority. Sister Rita's actions may have contributed to Patricia's death, as she would have stayed in bed if talking to Frank.*
8. ■ STANDARDS FOCUS *Use Allusions to Make Inferences Students should note that allusions help establish the significance of the Church and the impact of English oppression on Irish culture.*

9. *McCourt implies is that people are both nourished and confined by the Church, especially by the authoritative nuns.*
10. *The use of the "innocent voice" is very effective, but also deceptive. We are reading a child's voice, but one crafted by an adult with the experience of a lifetime. For example, McCourt shapes his image of discovering poetry with adult perspectives (lines 158–161).*

Literary Criticism
Possible answer:
11. *Serious and humorous moments include Frank and Patricia's matter-of-fact discussion of their illnesses during which Patricia calls Frank "typhoid boy" (line 70); the nurse's scolding about talking, including the idea that it can do "damage to your internal apparatus" (lines 111–112); and Seamus's comments about getting fired and singing patriotic songs on the street (lines 131–133).*

ANGELA'S ASHES **849**

ANSWERS

Vocabulary in Context

VOCABULARY PRACTICE

1. *a*   3. *b*

2. *b*   4. *a*

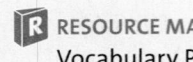 RESOURCE MANAGER—Copy Master
Vocabulary Practice p. 32

VOCABULARY IN WRITING

Have students brainstorm words describing
what Patricia was like. Words might include
friendly, funny, quirky, outgoing, and *fun-
loving.* Then have students create their
paragraphs.

**VOCABULARY STRATEGY: THE LATIN WORD
ROOT** *fid (also an EL language objective)*

- Encourage students to look for other word
parts they know, such as the prefix *in-,*
meaning "not," in *infidel.*

- Suggest that students use dictionaries for
any word meanings they cannot figure out.

Possible answers:

1. *fidelity*   4. *fiduciary*

2. *confidant*   5. *infidel*

3. *affidavit*

RESOURCE MANAGER—Copy Master
Vocabulary Strategy p. 33

ℹ Vocabulary Center at **ClassZone.com**
Additional Vocabulary Activities

Vocabulary in Context

VOCABULARY PRACTICE

Write the letter of the phrase that best clarifies the meaning of the
boldfaced word.

1. Experiencing a **relapse** of the flu usually means that (a) one will be sick for a
little longer, (b) it is time for a flu shot, (c) it is time to go back to school or work.

2. A **torrent** of water could most likely be produced by (a) a leaky hose,
(b) a large rain cloud, (c) a spray bottle.

3. Experiencing an act of **perfidy** might make you (a) get interested in mountain
climbing, (b) feel angry and betrayed, (c) decide to read historical fiction.

4. If you have **induced** a friend to join you on a boring errand, you are probably
good at (a) persuading others, (b) staying on schedule, (c) working alone.

WORD LIST
induced
perfidy
relapse
torrent

VOCABULARY IN WRITING

Imagine what Seamus might say to Patricia's parents about her time in the
hospital. What anecdotes or words of comfort might he share? Write a
paragraph that expresses his sentiments, using at least two vocabulary words.
Here is an example.

> **EXAMPLE SENTENCE**
>
> Well, Missus, your Patricia was a lovely girl. I cried a **torrent**
> of tears over her passing.

VOCABULARY STRATEGY: THE LATIN ROOT *fid*

The word *perfidy* contains the Latin root *fid,* which means "faith;
trust; belief." This root is found in a number of English words. To
understand the meaning of words with *fid,* use context clues as
well as your knowledge of the root.

fiduciary   perfidy
affidavit   **fid**   fidelity
confidant   infidel

PRACTICE Write the word from the word web that best completes
each sentence. Use context clues to help you or, if necessary, consult
a dictionary.

1. The _____ of the sound from those speakers is amazing; the music
sounds like a live concert.

2. Everyone needs a trusted _____, someone to rely on.

3. A (An) _____ is usually sworn to in front of a public official.

4. In a (an) _____ agreement, one party holds money or property in
trust for another.

5. You shouldn't call Leo a (an) _____ just because he doesn't believe
in your religion.

**VOCABULARY
PRACTICE**
For more practice, go
to the **Vocabulary Center**
at **ClassZone.com**.

DIFFERENTIATED INSTRUCTION

FOR ENGLISH LEARNERS

Vocabulary: Cognates Point out that the
Spanish cognates *fidelidad* and *perfidia* are
similar to the English words *fidelity* and
perfidy. Invite students who speak Latin-
based languages to look for and explain
additional words in the selection that are
similar to those in their languages. Have
students teach the non-English versions of
these words to the class.

FOR ADVANCED LEARNERS/PRE–AP

Vocabulary in Writing Ask students to use
the words containing the root *fid* in a short
paragraph. Challenge them to find and
include additional words based on this root.

Reading-Writing Connection

Increase your understanding of the people portrayed in *Angela's Ashes* by responding to these prompts. Then use **Revision: Grammar and Style** to improve your writing.

WRITING PROMPTS	SELF-CHECK

A. Short Response: Write an Argument
Sister Rita is in charge of patient care, while Seamus takes care of the building. Who is the more caring person? Write **one or two paragraphs** in which you explain why Sister Rita or Seamus is the more compassionate person.

▸ *A successful argument will...*
• identify the person who is more compassionate
• provide examples of his or her behavior to support the choice

B. Extended Response: Write a Dialogue
Imagine the conversation in which Sister Rita tells Mam that she can no longer visit her son because he was reciting a poem with a girl. Write **one page of dialogue** that includes Mam's reaction.

▸ *A strong dialogue will...*
• portray a likely exchange between the two people
• reflect the speech characteristics of the two people

REVISION: GRAMMAR AND STYLE

WRITE CONCISELY Review the **Grammar and Style** note on page 843. A gerund is a verb form that ends in *-ing* and acts as a noun. A **gerund phrase** consists of a gerund plus its modifiers and complements. Because gerunds can be used to replace entire groups of words, they often help to make writing more concise.

Here are two examples of McCourt's use of gerund phrases:

> *I practice walking from bed to bed back and forth back and forth.*
> (line 295)

> *He stops mopping the floor and calls to Patricia....* (lines 144–145)

Notice how the revisions in red insert gerunds and a gerund phrase to make the writing more concise. Revise your responses to the prompts by employing similar techniques.

STUDENT MODEL
reciting poetry is good for
Seamus thinks that ~~Patricia and Frank should be able to recite~~

~~poetry to each other~~ while Sister Rita believes that patients
refrain from talking or laughing.
~~shouldn't talk with each other or laugh with each other.~~

WRITING TOOLS
For prewriting, revision, and editing tools, visit the **Writing Center** at ClassZone.com.

FOR LESS-PROFICIENT WRITERS

For Prompt A:

Suggest students organize their argument this way:

1. Begin by stating which person is more compassionate.
2. Describe three ways in which this person is compassionate.
3. Describe three ways in which the second person is not compassionate.

For Prompt B:

1. Limit the assignment to one paragraph.
2. Have students work in pairs to complete their dialogues.
3. Have students act out the parts of Sister Rita and Mam before they begin writing.
4. List some of the exchanges on the board so that pairs can refer to them as they write.

Reading-Writing Connection

WRITING PROMPTS

• For Prompt A, suggest students reread some of the passages involving Sister Rita (lines 28–34, 95–106, 205–217, 286–291) and Seamus (lines 126–150, 196–204, 247–272, 300–323). Encourage students to think about how the two act toward the patients. Students might use a Two-Column Chart to list Sister Rita's and Seamus's actions and ideas.

• For Prompt B, urge students to reread what Sister Rita and Mam say to understand their points of view and speaking patterns. (Sister Rita: lines 30–34, 95–106, 205–217, 286–291; Mam: lines 3–4, 116–124)

🧰 BEST PRACTICES TOOLKIT—Transparency
  Two-Column Chart p. A25

REVISION: GRAMMAR AND STYLE

• After students review page 843, elicit and list examples of gerunds.

• Write these lines on the board. Have students rewrite them using gerunds.

Sister Rita believes that ~~the most important thing is to talk to the children about being good Catholics~~. talking to the children about being good Catholics is the most important thing. Seamus believes ~~that the children should be allowed to enjoy each other~~. in allowing the children to enjoy each other.

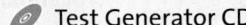

Ⓡ RESOURCE MANAGER—Copy Master
  Write Concisely p. 36

Assess and Reteach

Assess

Ⓡ RESOURCE MANAGER—Copy Masters
  Selection Test A pp. 39–40
  Selection Test B/C pp. 41–42

💿 Test Generator CD

Reteach

Ⓢ STANDARDS LESSON FILE
  Literature Lesson 35: Allusion
  Literature Lesson 47: Author's Perspective
  Reading Lesson 8: Making Inferences

Focus and Motivate

OBJECTIVES

Literary Analysis
- explore the key idea of something **sacred**
- identify and interpret cultural symbols
- read an essay

Reading
- monitor comprehension

Vocabulary
- build vocabulary for reading and writing
- use the Greek word root *cosmo* to help unlock meaning *(also an EL language objective)*

SUMMARY

Accompanied by his friend Chuck, author N. Scott Momaday follows the migration route of his Kiowa ancestors from Montana to Oklahoma. They head to the Medicine Wheel, a sacred site in the Bighorn Mountains. On a forest road they meet Jurg, who is also seeking the ring of stones. Later, Momaday and Chuck journey to Devil's Tower, a monolith also sacred to the Kiowa.

What makes something SACRED?

Introduce the question and have students read the *KEY IDEA*. Ask them to identify **sacred** objects or places they have visited or know about. Extend the discussion by having students complete the *QUICKWRITE*.

Revisiting Sacred Ground
Essay by N. Scott Momaday

What makes something SACRED?

KEY IDEA The word *sacred* means "holy" or "associated with divine power." Different religions and cultures hold different objects and places sacred. In "Revisiting Sacred Ground," Native American author N. Scott Momaday describes a journey to a sacred place that has spiritual significance for his people, the Kiowa.

QUICKWRITE Imagine that you have been invited into a sacred place. What do you need to know? How should you behave? List your ideas on how to act in this special location.

> **Being in a Sacred Place**
> 1. Be silent, or speak softly, to allow people to think or to absorb the feeling of the place.
> 2.
> 3.

852

Selection Resources

R RESOURCE MANAGER UNIT 9

Plan and Teach pp. 43–50

Literary Analysis
Summary pp. 51†*, 52‡*
Cultural Symbol pp. 53, 54†*
Question Support p. 61*

Reading
Monitor pp. 55, 56†*
Reading Check p. 60

Vocabulary
Study p. 57*
Practice p. 58
Strategy p. 59

Assessment
Selection Tests A, B/C pp. 63*, 65*
Test Generator CD

BEST PRACTICES TOOLKIT

Differentiated Instruction
pp. 31–38*

Scaffolding Instruction
pp. 43–46*

Graphic Organizers/Strategies
New Word Analysis • Three-Column Journal • Think-Pair-Share • Open Mind

Reading Support
Audio Anthology CD*

Technology
Literature and Vocabulary Centers at **ClassZone.com**
Write*Smart* CD

* Resources for Differentiation   † Also in Spanish   ‡ In Haitian Creole and Vietnamese

● LITERARY ANALYSIS: CULTURAL SYMBOL

You already know that a symbol is an object, a place, or a person that has meaning beyond itself. A **cultural symbol** is one that has shared meaning for an entire culture. In "Revisiting Sacred Ground," N. Scott Momaday incorporates many cultural symbols that are important to the Kiowa and other Plains tribes. These cultural symbols include

- places, such as the Black Hills and the Bighorn Mountains
- animals, such as the deer and the coyote
- concepts, such as the four directions
- objects, such as prayer bundles

As you read, note the significance of these cultural symbols. What do these symbols tell you about Momaday's heritage and the way he feels about it?

● READING STRATEGY: MONITOR

When you read, you can increase your comprehension by pausing occasionally to check, or **monitor,** how well you understand the text. As you read "Revisiting Sacred Ground," use the following strategies to monitor your comprehension:

- Reread difficult passages.
- Write down questions you may have about the content.

Make a chart like the one shown to record your questions, and answer them, when possible, from information found in the text.

Questions	Answers
Why is the Medicine Wheel significant to the author?	

▲ VOCABULARY IN CONTEXT

Restate each phrase, using a different word or words for the boldfaced term.

1. ill will and **alienation** within the family
2. suggest **cosmetic** changes to the plan
3. **sauntering** lazily through the park
4. a fender-bender causing **negligible** damage
5. visited an ancient **petrified** forest
6. the **inherent** sweetness of honey
7. a **monolith** standing alone in the desert
8. **engender** goodwill by his kindness

Author Online

Poet with a Native Voice
N. Scott Momaday was born in Oklahoma and raised on Southwestern Indian reservations. His mother was a teacher and writer of children's stories, and his father was an art teacher. Even though Momaday won a Pulitzer Prize for his novel *House Made*

N. Scott Momaday born 1934

of Dawn, he thinks of himself primarily as a poet—and as a Native American.

Harmony with Nature Momaday's Kiowa heritage inspires both his poetry and his prose, which often portray the Native American view that people need to live in harmony with nature. "I believe that the Indian has a [unique] understanding of the physical world and of the earth as a spiritual entity," says Momaday. "The whole world view of the Indian is predicated upon the principle of harmony in the universe."

 MORE ABOUT THE AUTHOR For more on N. Scott Momaday, visit the **Literature Center** at **ClassZone.com.**

Background

The Nomadic Kiowa As of the 1600s, the Kiowa were living as nomadic hunters in what is now western Montana. Around 1700, they moved to the Black Hills of present-day eastern Wyoming and southwestern South Dakota and then migrated to the southern Great Plains. When the U.S. government moved Native Americans onto reservations by the late 1800s, the Kiowa settled in reservations in Oklahoma. However, many sites in their former homelands, where traditions originated or important tribal events occurred, still have spiritual significance to the Kiowa.

Teach

STANDARDS FOCUS

LITERARY ANALYSIS

● CULTURAL SYMBOL

To support instruction, read aloud this example:

> The Washington Monument's white stone cut into the blue sky. As the old man gazed at the peak of the obelisk, a tingle traveled along the skin of his arms.

Explain that all cultures have important symbols. Ask students to note the meaning of the cultural symbol above. ***Possible answer:*** *The Washington Monument symbolizes our first president, and thus, our nation's origin.*

CHECK UNDERSTANDING Elicit other widely known symbols of the nation.

READING STRATEGY

■ MONITOR

Help students see how monitoring can help readers better comprehend a text. Read aloud the ***About the Author*** text. Guide students in asking questions. ***Possible answers:*** *Why is it helpful for us to know that Momaday's culture is important to him? What does Momaday mean by "harmony in the universe"?*

CHECK UNDERSTANDING Have students read the ***Background*** and write questions to monitor their understanding.

 RESOURCE MANAGER—Copy Master Monitor p. 55 (for student use while reading the selection)

VOCABULARY SKILL

▲ VOCABULARY IN CONTEXT

DIAGNOSE WORD KNOWLEDGE To determine preteaching needs, have all students complete Vocabulary in Context. ***Possible answers:***
1. *isolation;* 2. *decorative rather than functional;* 3. *walking in a slow, relaxed manner;* 4. *not important enough to merit attention;* 5. *turned into stone;* 6. *built-in;* 7. *something made from a single large stone;* 8. *to bring into existence*

PRETEACH VOCABULARY Use the Vocabulary Study copy master to help students predict meanings for each boldfaced word:

1. Read the first sentence in Part A aloud, emphasizing *alienation.*
2. Point out the phrases "lived easily in its environment" and "no alienation from its wild surroundings." Then elicit possible meanings for *alienation.*
3. Repeat the approach for the other items.

RESOURCE MANAGER—Copy Master Vocabulary Study p. 57

For general guidelines on differentiating vocabulary instruction and for alternative vocabulary activities for students not needing vocabulary preteaching, see

BEST PRACTICES TOOLKIT Scaffolding Vocabulary Instruction pp. 43–46

ⓘ Vocabulary Center at **ClassZone.com**

ANALYZE VISUALS

Possible answer: The landscape of the photograph is wide, majestic, mountainous, rocky, and somewhat arid, connecting the earth and sky. Student responses will vary about what it symbolizes to them, but could include the beauty of nature, the majesty of creation, the distance from human society, or the purity and cleanliness of wilderness.

Ⓐ MONITOR

Student answers will vary but should be phrased as questions. Sample questions include: What does Momaday's Kiowa ancestry mean to him? How does he know about his ancestors' journey? Why does he feel a need to see what his ancestors saw on their journey?

Extend the Discussion Why may people want to visit places where their ancestors lived?

Revisiting SACRED GROUND

N. Scott Momaday

There is great good in returning to a landscape that had extraordinary meaning in one's life. It happens that we return to such places in our minds irresistibly. There are certain villages and towns, mountains and plains that, having seen them, walked in them, lived in them, even for a day, we keep forever in the mind's eye. They become indispensable to our well-being; they define us, and we say, I am who I am because I have been there, or there. There is good, too, in actual, physical return.

Some years ago I made a pilgrimage into the heart of North America. I began the journey proper in western Montana. From there I traveled across the
10 high plains of Wyoming into the Black Hills, then southward to the southern plains, to a cemetery at Rainy Mountain, in Oklahoma. It was a journey made by my Kiowa[1] ancestors long before. In the course of their migration they became the people of the Great Plains, and theirs was the last culture to evolve in North America. They had been for untold generations a mountain tribe of hunters. Their ancient nomadism, which had determined their way of life even before they set foot on this continent, perhaps thirty thousand years ago, was raised to its highest level of expression when they entered upon the Great Plains and acquired horses. Their migration brought them to a golden age. At the beginning of their journey they were a people of hard circumstances,
20 often hungry and cold, fighting always for sheer survival. At its end, and for a hundred years, they were the lords of the land, a daring race of centaurs[2] and buffalo hunters whose love of freedom and space was profound.

Recently I returned to the old migration route of the Kiowas. I had in me a need to behold again some of the principle landmarks of that long, prehistoric quest, to descend again from the mountain to the plain. Ⓐ

With my close friend Chuck I drove north to the Montana-Wyoming border. I wanted to intersect the Kiowa migration route at the Bighorn Medicine Wheel, high in the Bighorn Mountains. We gradually ascended

ANALYZE VISUALS
How would you describe the landscape of the Bighorn Mountains in this photo? What might it **symbolize** to you?

❶ Targeted Passage

Ⓐ MONITOR
After reading lines 8–25, **question** yourself about what the writer's journey may represent to him.

---

1. **Kiowa** (kī'ə-wō').
2. **centaurs** (sĕn'tôrz'): in Greek mythology, creatures that were half man and half horse.

854 UNIT 9: HISTORY, CULTURE, AND THE AUTHOR

FOR ALL STUDENTS
Expert Groups Allow students to become experts or members of expert groups by researching and choosing a way to share information about one of these topics:

- the Bighorn Medicine Wheel
- Native American religious rituals
- medicine bundles

FOR LESS–PROFICIENT READERS
In combination with the *Audio Anthology CD*, use one or more Targeted Passages (pp. 854, 856, 859) to ensure that students focus on key events, concepts, and skills. Targeted Passages are also good for English learners.

❶ Targeted Passage [Lines 1–7]

In this passage, the writer explains that the places people love contribute to who they are and what is important to them.

BACKGROUND

The Kiowa and Horses The Kiowa's affinity for horses is perhaps the greatest among the Plains Native Americans. Possibly over an intra-tribe dispute, a faction of the Kiowa moved south from Montana with the Kiowa Apache and began living with the Crow nation. The Crow taught the Kiowa to ride horses and to hunt buffalo. The Kiowa readily adopted the practices that they learned from the Crow. For years, they held more horses than any other Plains nation.

- In what ways can people return to special places, according to Momaday?
- Why might people keep certain places "forever in the mind's eye"?
- What does Momaday think about people's identities in relation to places?

FOR ENGLISH LEARNERS

Key Academic Vocabulary Use New Word Analysis to teach these words: *migration* (line 12), *evolve* (line 13), *design* (line 64), *equation* (line 66), *conformation* (line 130).

 BEST PRACTICES TOOLKIT —Transparency New Word Analysis p. E8

Prereading For prereading instruction for English learners, see

 BEST PRACTICES TOOLKIT Scaffolding Reading Instruction pp. 43–46

FOR ADVANCED LEARNERS/PRE–AP

Pre-AP Exercises in the bottom channel provide additional challenge for students. Use these suggestions for small groups or individuals.

ADDITIONAL GUIDELINES

For more help with differentiation and tips for classroom management, see

 BEST PRACTICES TOOLKIT Differentiated Instruction pp. 31–38

B CULTURAL SYMBOL

Possible answer: The deer could be an indication that they are doing the right thing, that they are on the right track, or that nature (the divine) approves of their quest.

If students need help . . . What words in lines 38–43 have positive connotations?

Lines 44–69
DISCUSSION PROMPTS

Use these prompts to help students understand the author's experiences on his journey:

Connect Imagine the sudden calm and silence after the bitter wind. How might you feel if this happened to you in a special place? *Students' answers should reflect an understanding of the author's sensitivity to the setting.*

Analyze How does Momaday's language change when he begins to describe weather changes at the Medicine Wheel? *Possible answer: Once at the Medicine Wheel, Momaday's factual description of the meeting with Jurg and the wheel itself becomes more atmospheric with phrases such as "a profound silence" (line 69).*

Evaluate Momaday uses heightened language to describe certain events and conditions in this passage. Is this language effective in helping you visualize the experience? Cite examples. *Students' answers will vary but should include specific examples from the passage.*

---

to eight thousand feet on a well-maintained but winding highway. Then we
30 climbed sharply, bearing upon timberline. It was early October, and although
the plain below had been comfortable, even warm at midday, the mountain
air was cold, and much of the ground was covered with snow. We turned off
the pavement, on a dirt road that led three miles to the Medicine Wheel. The
road was forbidding; it was narrow and winding, and the grades were steep
and slippery; here and there the shoulders fell away into deep ravines. But at
the same time something wonderful happened: we crossed the line between
civilization and wilderness. Suddenly the earth persisted in its original being.
Directly in front of us a huge white-tailed buck crossed our path, ambling
without haste into a thicket of pines. As we drove over his tracks we saw four
40 does above on the opposite bank, looking down at us, their great black eyes
bright and benign, curious. There seemed no wariness, nothing of fear or
alienation. Their presence was a good omen, we thought; somehow in their
attitude they bade us welcome to their sphere of wilderness. **B**

There was a fork in the road, and we took the wrong branch. At a steep,
hairpin curve we got out of the car and climbed to the top of a peak. An icy
wind whipped at us; we were among the bald summits of the Bighorns. Great
flumes of sunlit snow erupted on the ridges and dissolved in spangles on
the sky. Across a deep saddle we caught sight of the Medicine Wheel. It was
perhaps two miles away.
50   When we returned to the car we saw another vehicle approaching. It was
a very old Volkswagen bus, in much need of repair, **cosmetic** repair at least.
Out stepped a thin, bearded young man in thick glasses. He wore a wool cap,
a down parka, and well-worn hiking boots. "I am looking for the Medicine
Wheel," he said, having nodded to us. He spoke softly, with a pronounced
accent. His name was Jurg, and he was from Switzerland; he had been traveling
for some months in Canada and the United States. Chuck and I shook his
hand and told him to follow us, and we drove down into the saddle. From
there we climbed on foot to the Medicine Wheel.

The Medicine Wheel is a ring of stones, some fifty feet in diameter. Stone
60 spokes radiate from the center to the circumference. Cairns[3] are placed at
certain points on the circumference, one in the center, and one just outside
the ring to the southwest. We do not know as a matter of fact who made the
wheel or to what purpose. It had been proposed that it is an astronomical
observatory, a solar calendar, and the ground design of a Kiowa Sun Dance
lodge.[4] What we know without doubt is that it is a sacred expression, an
equation of man's relation to the cosmos.

There was a great calm upon that place. The hard, snow-bearing wind that
had burned our eyes and skin only minutes before had died away altogether.
The sun was warm and bright, and there was a profound silence. On the wire

---

alienation (āl'yə-nā'shən) *n.* a feeling of separation or isolation

B CULTURAL SYMBOL
Native Americans believe animals are representatives of higher powers who impart wisdom to humans. What might the appearance of the deer represent to the author in this setting?

cosmetic (kŏz-mĕt'ĭk) *adj.* decorative rather than functional

2 Targeted Passage

---

3. **cairns** (kârnz): mounds of rough stones built as memorials or landmarks.
4. **Kiowa Sun Dance lodge:** For the annual Sun Dance ceremony, the most important Kiowa religious rite through much of the 19th century, Kiowa members built a sweat lodge for their purification and self-renewal.

DIFFERENTIATED INSTRUCTION

FOR LESS–PROFICIENT READERS

2 Targeted Passage [Lines 44–58]

In this passage, Momaday relates events that precede his arrival at the Medicine Wheel.

- How does Momaday describe the summits of the Bighorns?
- How does he make the setting sound beautiful?
- Who do the two men meet on the trail?
- How do they help the stranger?

FOR ENGLISH LEARNERS

Language: Modifiers Have students record modifiers about nature in a Three-Column Journal like this one:

Animals	Weather	Land
white-tailed buck (line 38)	icy wind (lines 45–46)	bald summits (line 46)
four does (lines 39–40)	snow-bearing wind (line 67)	black planes of forest (line 76)

 BEST PRACTICES TOOLKIT—Transparency
Three-Column Journal p. B10

Reaching 80 feet across, the Medicine Wheel sits atop a ridge of Medicine Mountain in north-central Wyoming.

ANALYZE VISUALS

Activity Have students study the photograph and then draw parallels to other similar sacred places from other cultures throughout history. *Students may draw parallels to places such as Stonehenge or Easter Island.*

70 fence which had been erected to enclose and protect the wheel were fixed offerings, small prayer bundles. Chuck and Jurg and I walked about slowly, standing for long moments here and there, looking into the wheel or out across the great distances. We did not say much; there was little to be said. But we were deeply moved by the spirit of that place. The silence was such that it must be observed. To the north we could see down to timberline, to the snowfields and draws that marked the black planes of forest among the peaks of the Bighorns. To the south and west the mountains fell abruptly to the plains. We could see thousands of feet down and a hundred miles across the dim expanse.

80   When we were about to leave, I took from my pocket an eagle-bone whistle that my father had given me, and I blew it in the four directions. The sound was very high and shrill, and it did not break the essential silence. As we were walking down we saw far below, crossing our path, a coyote **sauntering** across the snow into a wall of trees. It was just there, a wild being to catch sight of, and then it was gone. The wilderness, which had admitted us with benediction let us go. **C**

saunter (sôn′tər)
v. to walk in a slow, relaxed manner

C CULTURAL SYMBOL
Many ceremonies of the Plains Indians begin with a call to the four directions, which represent different powers or ways of perceiving. Why does the narrator call to the four directions?

REVISITING SACRED GROUND   **857**

LITERARY ANALYSIS

C CULTURAL SYMBOL

Possible answer: *By blowing the whistle in the four directions, he is marking this moment as a sacred one and asking to be endowed with the four powers or ways of perceiving.*

FOR ENGLISH LEARNERS
Vocabulary: Phrasal Verbs Point out these passive-voice phrasal verbs: "had been pro-posed" (line 63) and "had been erected" (line 70). Explain that passive voice removes the action-doer. Using Think-Pair-Share, have students write five passive-voice sentences, exchange them, and read each other's sentences aloud.

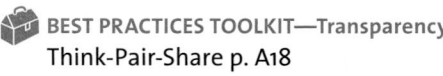 **BEST PRACTICES TOOLKIT—Transparency**
Think-Pair-Share p. A18

FOR ADVANCED LEARNERS/PRE–AP
Analyze Tone Have students analyze the tone of lines 67–86, using these questions:
• How does Momaday's diction affect tone?
• How does the tone of this passage support the author's message?
• How does the tone affect the mood?

D MONITOR

Discuss how Momaday conveys the vast-ness of the land relative to the negligible human-made objects.

If students need help . . . Use an Open Mind graphic organizer to model how students might think through the question.

says human-made things are "negligible"

"overwhelmed" makes fences and houses seem puny

landscape like ocean—really big

revelation of infinity— I can't think that big

🧰 BEST PRACTICES TOOLKIT—Transparency
Open Mind p. D9

Lines 100–125
DISCUSSION PROMPTS

Use these prompts to help students appreciate how Momaday feels about the Black Hills:

Connect Think of a place that impresses you in some way. How would you describe it? *Accept descriptions that point out the remarkable attributes of a place.*

Analyze How does Momaday make the Black Hills seem special? Cite details. *Possible answer: He cites impressive facts, such as the Black Hills' 2-billion-year age; he uses vivid language, like "an island . . . in the vast sea of grasses" (lines 103–104); and he tells of their sacredness to tribes.*

Evaluate How does the author's ancestry influence the purpose of each paragraph? Does he achieve his purpose? *Possible answer: Because of his ancestry, Momaday feels a special kinship with the land that cannot be duplicated by those newer to the region. In lines 100–108, he tries to give the hills an epic stature. In lines 109–115, he aims to show the triviality of the explorers' visits to the hills. In lines 116–125, he tries to show how Native Americans revered the hills.*

858 UNIT 9

When we came within a stone's throw of the highway, Chuck and I said goodbye to Jurg, but not before he had got out his camp stove and boiled water for tea. There in the dusk we enjoyed a small ceremonial feast of tea
90 and crackers. The three of us had become friends. Only later did I begin to understand the extraordinary character of that friendship. It was the friendship of those who come together in recognition of the sacred. If we never meet again, I thought, we shall not forget this day.

On the plains the fences and roads and windmills and houses seemed almost **negligible,** all but overwhelmed by the earth and sky. It is a landscape of great clarity; its vastness is that of the ocean. It is the near revelation of infinity. Antelope were everywhere in the grassy folds, grazing side by side with horses and cattle. Hawks sailed above, and crows scattered before us. The place names were American—Tensleep, Buffalo, Dull Knife, Crazy Woman, Spotted Horse. **D**
100 The Black Hills are an isolated group of mountains in South Dakota and Wyoming. They lie very close to both the geographic center of the United States, if you include Alaska and Hawaii, and the geographic center of the North American continent. They form an island, an elliptical area of nearly six thousand square miles, in the vast sea of grasses that is the northern Great Plains. The Black Hills are a calendar of geologic time[5] that is truly remarkable. Their foundation rocks are much older than the sedimentary layers[6] of which the Americas are primarily formed. An analysis of this foundation, made in 1964, indicates an age of between two and three billion years.

A documented record of exploration in this region is found in the Lewis
110 and Clark journals, 1804–1806. The first white party known definitely to have entered the Black Hills proper was led by Jedidiah Smith in 1823. The diary of this expedition, kept by one James Clyman, is notable. Clyman reports a confrontation between Jedidiah Smith and a grizzly bear, in which Smith lost one of his ears. There is also reported the discovery of a **petrified** ("putrified," as Clyman has it) forest in which petrified birds sing petrified songs.

The Lakotas, or Teton Sioux, called these mountains *Paha Sapa,* "hills that are black." Other tribes, beside the Kiowas and the Sioux, thought of the Black Hills as sacred ground, a place that is crucial in their past. The Arapahos[7] lived here. So did the Cheyennes. Bear Butte, near Sturgis, South Dakota, on
120 the northeast edge of the Black Hills, is the Cheyennes' sacred mountain. It remains, like the Medicine Wheel, a place of the greatest spiritual intensity. So great was thought to be the power **inherent** in the Black Hills that the Indians did not camp there. It was a place of rendezvous, a hunting ground, but above all an inviolate, sacred ground. It was a place of thunder and lightning, a dwelling place of the gods.

On the edge of the Black Hills nearest the Bighorn Mountain is Devil's Tower, the first of our national monuments. The Lakotas called it *Mateo*

---

negligible (nĕg'lĭ-jə-bəl) *adj.* not large or important enough to merit attention

D MONITOR
Reread lines 94–99 and note how the writer describes man-made objects in relation to nature.

petrified (pĕt'rə-fīd') *adj.* turned into stone
petrify v.

inherent (ĭn-hîr'ənt) *adj.* forming part of the essential nature of something; built-in

---

5. **geologic time:** the period of time defined by the formation and development of the earth.
6. **sedimentary layers:** layers of earth and stone deposited by wind, water, and ice.
7. **Arapahos** (ə-răp'ə-hōz').

DIFFERENTIATED INSTRUCTION

FOR ENGLISH LEARNERS

Vocabulary: Idioms Offer practice with idioms such as "as a matter of fact" (line 62), "stone's throw" (line 87), "more or less" (line 138), and "on our minds" (line 156). Choose three other idioms, and write each, with its line number, on the back of an index card. Divide the cards among small groups. Have each group write two sentences using their idioms on the front of each of their cards. Have groups exchange cards and write

sentences until all groups have practiced each idiom.

Tepee, "Grizzly Bear Lodge." The Kiowas called it *Tsoai,* "Rock Tree." Devil's Tower is a great **monolith** that rises high above the timber of the Black Hills.
130 In conformation it closely resembles the stump of a tree. It is a cluster of rock columns of phonolite porphyry[8] 1,000 feet across at the base and 275 feet across at the top. It rises 865 feet above the high ground upon which it stands and 1,280 feet above the Belle Fourch River, which runs in the valley below.

It has to be seen to be believed. "There are things in nature that **engender** an awful quiet in the heart of man; Devil's Tower is one of them." I wrote these words almost twenty years ago. They remain true to my experience. Each time I behold this *Tsoai* anew I am more than ever in awe of it.

Two hundred years ago, more or less, the Kiowas came upon this place. They were moved to tell a story about it:

140   *Eight children were there at play, seven sisters and their brother. Suddenly the boy was struck dumb; he trembled and began to run upon his hands and feet. His fingers became claws, and his body was covered with fur. Directly there was a bear where the boy had been. The sisters were terrified; they ran, and the bear after them. They came to the stump of a great tree, and the tree spoke to them. It bade them climb upon it, and as they did so it began to rise into the air. The bear came to kill them, but they were just beyond its reach. It reared against the tree and scored the bark all around with its claws. The seven sisters were borne into the sky, and they became the stars of the Big Dipper.* **E**

This story, which I have known from the time I could first understand
150 language, exemplifies the sacred for me. The storyteller, that anonymous man who told the story for the first time, succeeded in raising the human condition to the level of universal significance. Not only did he account for the existence of the rock tree, but in the process he related his people to the stars.

When Chuck and I had journeyed over this ground together, when we were about to go our separate ways, I reminded him of our friend Jurg, knowing well enough that I needn't have; Jurg was on our minds. I can't account for it. He had touched us deeply with his trust, not unlike that of the wild animals we had seen, and with his generosity of spirit, his concern to see beneath the surface of things, his attitude of free, clear, direct, disinterested kindness.
160   "Did he tell us what he does?" I asked. "Does he have a profession?"
"I don't think he said." Chuck replied. "I think he's a pilgrim."
"Yes."
"Yes." ❧

---

8. **phonolite porphyry** (fō′nə-līt′ pôr′fə-rē): a type of hard volcanic rock with fairly large crystals, set in a fine-grained groundmass.

---

monolith (mŏn′ə-lĭth′) *n.* something, such as a monument, made from a single large stone

engender (ĕn-jĕn′dər) *v.* to bring into existence

E CULTURAL SYMBOL
How does the story of the origin of *Tsoai* reflect the Kiowa belief in people's kinship with nature?

❸ Targeted Passage

Lines 140–153
REINFORCE KEY IDEA: SACRED

Discuss What ideas in the Kiowa story does Momaday see as **sacred,** and what do they share with stories in other cultures? *Possible answer: Momaday sees explaining the wondrous and linking people to the heavens as sacred. Trying to understand how things came into existence is a theme that appears in the stories of many cultures and religions.*

LITERARY ANALYSIS

E CULTURAL SYMBOL

Possible answer: The story reflects the Kiowa belief in kinship with nature in that the people are transformed into natural entities.

SELECTION WRAP–UP

SUMMARIZE Read aloud the final lines of the selection (lines 154–163). Ask how these lines summarize Momaday's own experience.

⭐ **CRITIQUE** Have students evaluate Momaday's explanation of why and how he views places as sacred. Do you agree or disagree with his view of what is sacred?

FOR LESS–PROFICIENT READERS
❸ Targeted Passage [Lines 154–163]

In this passage, the writer expresses how he and Chuck feel about Jurg.

- How does Momaday know that Chuck is thinking about Jurg?
- What did Momaday and Chuck admire about Jurg?
- What may have caused the men to become so close so quickly?
- What do the men mean by "pilgrim"?

FOR ADVANCED LEARNERS/PRE–AP
Analyze Symbolic Meaning Have students read lines 126–153 closely and analyze the symbolic significance of Devil's Tower to the author's thematic message, or thesis. Why does Momaday choose to retell this story within his essay? Within the story itself, what might the tower represent? What might the boy and girls represent? In retelling the tale, how does Momaday "[relate] his people to the stars" (line 153)?

Practice and Apply

After Reading

For additional support of post-reading questions, use these copy masters:

> **R** RESOURCE MANAGER—Copy Masters
> Reading Check p. 60 (to check understanding of the selection)
> Cultural Symbol p. 53 (for practice of literary analysis standards focus)
> Question Support p. 61 (After Reading questions adapted for English learners and less-proficient readers)
>
> For additional questions, see page 47.

ANSWERS

Comprehension

1. *He describes his own pilgrimage to the Bighorn Medicine Wheel.*

2. *He wants to make the same journey his Kiowa ancestors made.*

3. *They meet a fellow pilgrim named Jurg.*

4. *They all seek a sacred place and experience.*

Literary Analysis

Possible answers:

5. ■ **STANDARDS FOCUS** *Monitor Students should make mention of reading closely to find answers to their questions.*

6. ● **STANDARDS FOCUS** *Cultural Symbol journey: respect for Kiowa traditions ("They become indispensable to our well-being" [line 5]); deer: nature's welcome ("bade us welcome" [line 43]); Medicine Wheel: "man's relation to cosmos" (line 66); coyote: spirit (wilderness letting the men go [lines 83–86]); Devil's Tower: the Kiowa's relation to the stars (Tsoai story [lines 140–148]).*

7. *Momaday sees the deer as nature's welcome and the coyote as its farewell blessing.*

8. *On his journey, Momaday honors ancestors, practices the Kiowa's relation to nature by noting the omens of the white-tailed deer and the coyote, pays respect to a sacred place, and recalls the story of the* Tsoai.

9. *Momaday's perspective on the relationship between people and nature is defined by the Kiowa tradition. (Many passages support this.)*

Comprehension

1. **Recall** What journey does Momaday describe?

2. **Recall** Why does he want to make this journey?

3. **Recall** Whom do Momaday and Chuck meet at the Medicine Wheel?

4. **Clarify** Why is the friendship between the three men significant to Momaday?

Literary Analysis

5. **Monitor** Review the questions and answers you listed as you read. How many questions were you able to answer from further reading in the text? For questions without answers, how would you go about finding the answers?

6. **Interpret Cultural Symbols** Momaday mentions a number of places, animals, and objects that are considered **sacred** to the Kiowa. Explain what these symbols represent to Momaday's heritage. Cite evidence from the text.

7. **Draw Conclusions** Momaday describes seeing deer upon entering the site of the Medicine Wheel and a coyote upon leaving. Why is the appearance of the animals meaningful to Momaday at those particular points in his journey?

8. **Analyze Cultural Context** In many Native American traditions, quests helped people define their relationship with the world around them. How does Momaday's journey fit within this tradition?

9. **Analyze Author's Perspective** An author's perspective is the unique combination of ideas, values, and beliefs that influences the way he or she looks at a topic. After reading this essay, how would you define Momaday's perspective on the relationship between people and the natural world? Cite evidence from the text to support your answers.

10. **Evaluate Word Choice** At the end of the selection, Chuck says he thinks Jurg is a "pilgrim." What does he mean by this? Why is this description appropriate?

Literary Criticism

11. **Different Perspectives** Momaday describes the land and its creatures as being responsive to him. For example, he says the "wilderness, which had admitted us with benediction let us go" and the deer "bade us welcome." How does this viewpoint differ from the typical Anglo-American perspective?

---

10. *Chuck means Jurg is traveling in search of the sacred. The description is apt, since Jurg did not talk of the material world and had an unspoken bond with his fellow pilgrims.*

Literary Criticism

Possible answer:

11. *The typical Anglo-American does not view animals as having this sort of intentional, intelligent, or thinking relationship with humans.*

Vocabulary in Context

VOCABULARY PRACTICE

Determine whether these statements are true or false.

1. If I'm experiencing **alienation** from a friend, it's likely I'm not getting along with him.
2. A woman who **saunters** down the street is probably in a hurry.
3. A large car is a good example of a **monolith.**
4. An **inherent** quality of granite is its hardness.
5. If a committee submits a **cosmetic** reform proposal, it is suggesting major changes.
6. One small critical comment on a long essay would be considered **negligible.**
7. If I **engender** something, I build it with brick and mortar.
8. You would not expect a **petrified** bird to fly.

WORD LIST
alienation
cosmetic
engender
inherent
monolith
negligible
petrified
saunter

VOCABULARY IN WRITING

Write a paragraph about the feelings Momaday experienced during his journey. Use three or more vocabulary words. You might start this way.

> **EXAMPLE SENTENCE**
> The _inherent_ nobility of the Medicine Wheel made a great impression on Momaday. . . .

VOCABULARY STRATEGY: THE GREEK WORD ROOT *cosmo*

The vocabulary word *cosmetic* stems from the Greek word root *cosm*, from the Greek word *kosmos*, meaning "order." This root is found in a number of English words. To understand the meaning of words with *cosm*, use context clues as well as your knowledge of the root.

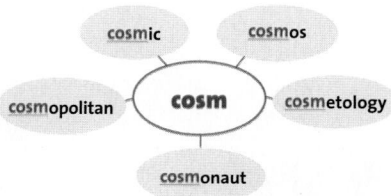

PRACTICE Write the word from the word web that best completes each sentence. Use word structure and context clues to help you. If necessary, consult a dictionary.

1. Astronomers make an academic study of the _____.
2. After leaving the space station, the _____ had to spend several weeks being reconditioned for life on Earth.
3. My cousin wants to study _____ and become a hairstylist.
4. New York is a very _____ city; people come there from all over the world.
5. _____ dust covered the ground near the fallen meteorite.

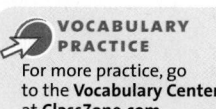

> **VOCABULARY PRACTICE**
> For more practice, go to the **Vocabulary Center** at **ClassZone.com.**

DIFFERENTIATED INSTRUCTION

FOR ENGLISH LEARNERS

Writing: Definitions Organize students in pairs to work again with the Vocabulary Practice activity. Ask each pair to write new sentences for the *false* items in the activity. Then have two pairs work together. One pair reads the target word and the sentence they have created. A student from the other pair then gives the definition of the target word.

FOR ADVANCED LEARNERS/PRE-AP

Vocabulary in Writing Challenge students to use at least four vocabulary words in a brief essay about a landscape that has personal meaning for them.

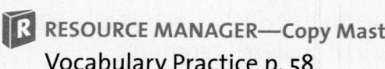

ANSWERS

Vocabulary in Context

VOCABULARY PRACTICE

1. *true*	**5.** *false*
2. *false*	**6.** *true*
3. *true*	**7.** *false*
4. *true*	**8.** *true*

R RESOURCE MANAGER—Copy Master
Vocabulary Practice p. 58

VOCABULARY IN WRITING

Suggest that students consider the subject of cultural traditions and focus on Momaday's reasons for making his journey.

VOCABULARY STRATEGY: THE GREEK WORD ROOT *cosmo* (also an EL language objective)

• Have students use context to find each word's part of speech.

Possible answers:

1. *cosmos*   4. *cosmopolitan*
2. *cosmonaut*   5. *Cosmic*
3. *cosmetology*

R RESOURCE MANAGER—Copy Master
Vocabulary Strategy p. 59

i Vocabulary Center at **ClassZone.com**
Additional Vocabulary Activities

Assess and Reteach

Assess

R RESOURCE MANAGER—Copy Masters
Selection Test A pp. 63–64
Selection Test B/C pp. 65–66

⊘ Test Generator CD

Reteach

S STANDARDS LESSON FILE
Literature Lesson 31: Symbol and Symbolism
Literature Lesson 47: Author's Perspective
Reading Lesson 2: Monitoring
Vocabulary Lesson 6: Word Parts: Anglo-Saxon and Greek

Focus and Motivate

OBJECTIVES

Literary Analysis
- explore the key idea of **self-respect**
- analyze voice and dialect
- read a short story

Reading
- draw conclusions

Grammar and Writing
- use vivid verbs as effective words in writing
- use writing to analyze literature

SUMMARY

Granny is not happy when a reporter and cameraman come filming her property without asking. Granddaddy Cain arrives with a dead hawk. After dispatching the hawk's furious mate, Granddaddy Cain calmly takes the camera, exposes the film, and then politely asks the men to step out of Granny's garden.

How important is SELF-RESPECT?

Introduce the question. Have students read the **KEY IDEA** and demonstrate understanding by giving examples of actions that show **self-respect**. Begin the **DISCUSS** activity as a group by drawing a word web on the board. Have students complete the web independently.

Selection Resources

Before Reading

Blues Ain't No Mockin Bird

Short Story by Toni Cade Bambara

How important is SELF-RESPECT?

KEY IDEA When you treat someone with respect, you treat him or her with regard and esteem. When you have **self-respect,** you treat yourself with regard and esteem, and you can often gain others' respect in return. In "Blues Ain't No Mockin Bird," Toni Cade Bambara explores how an African-American family respond with self-respect when their privacy is invaded.

DISCUSS Think of a situation you have seen or read about in which someone showed self-respect in the face of ridicule or embarrassment. What did that person do? With a small group of classmates, discuss the situation and the way the person behaved. Then generate a word web detailing actions or behaviors that show self-respect. What is gained by displaying these behaviors?

Acts of Self-Respect

speaking up for yourself

remaining calm

The **3** Pillars of Self-Esteem — Suraiya Nathani

BELIEVE IN YO... A Guide to Self Re...

The Power of YOU by Erik Koelle

THE SELF-ESTEEM HANDBOOK — The Power of Self-Esteem — J.D. H...

I'm Terrific Learning Self-Respect — Kurt Devloeminck

862

RESOURCE MANAGER UNIT 9

Plan and Teach pp. 67–74

Literary Analysis
Summary pp. 75†*, 76‡*
Voice and Dialect pp. 77, 78†*
Question Support p. 82*

Reading
Draw Conclusions pp. 79, 80†*
Reading Check p. 81*

Grammar and Writing
Choose Effective Words p. 83

Assessment
Selection Tests A, B/C pp. 85*, 87*
Test Generator CD

BEST PRACTICES TOOLKIT

Differentiated Instruction
pp. 31–38*

Scaffolding Instruction
pp. 43–46*

Graphic Organizers/Strategies
Definition Mapping • Cluster Diagram • Word Squares • Whip Around • T Chart

Technology
Literature Center at **ClassZone.com**
WriteSmart CD

Reading Support
Audio Anthology CD*

InterActive READER & WRITER
• Integrated Test Practice
• Related Nonfiction Readings
McDougal Littell LITERATURE

---

* Resources for Differentiation   † Also in Spanish   ‡ In Haitian Creole and Vietnamese

LITERARY ANALYSIS: VOICE AND DIALECT

When you pick up the telephone, you probably recognize the voice of your best friend immediately; no one else sounds exactly like him or her. Similarly, writers have a distinct voice in their writing. **Voice** is a writer's unique style of expression.

In "Blues Ain't No Mockin Bird," the narrator seems to be talking personally to the reader. Bambara creates the narrator's voice through the use of **dialect**—a form of language as it is spoken in a particular geographic area or by a particular social or ethnic group. In writing, dialect can be reflected in specific pronunciations, vocabulary, idioms or expressions, and grammatical constructions.

For example, in "Blues Ain't No Mockin Bird," Bambara captures the cadence, or rhythm, of rural Southern black speech in the 1960s.

> . . . and Granny was onto the steps, the screen door bammin soft and scratchy against her palms.

As you read the story, notice how the author uses dialect to create the narrator's distinctive voice.

READING SKILL: DRAW CONCLUSIONS

Many of Bambara's stories feature strong African-American female characters and reflect social issues of concern to African Americans. This story was published in 1971—a time when issues of racial equality and civil rights influenced many writers.

As you read "Blues Ain't No Mockin Bird," record details that give you clues about social issues. Then use those details to help you draw conclusions about the writer's beliefs regarding the issues she presents. Ask yourself the following questions:

- Who are the characters? Do they represent stereotypes, real people, or the writer's ideals?
- What do the characters say to each other? What types of issues are at the heart of their dialogue?
- What is the conflict? Does the conflict reflect a social issue unique to the time when the writer lived?

Author Online

Wide-Ranging Career Toni Cade Bambara's lifework spanned many arenas. As a social activist, she became a respected leader in the civil rights and feminist movements of the 1960s and 1970s. She was a social worker, teacher, theater director, and filmmaker as

Toni Cade Bambara 1939–1995

well as a writer of short stories, novels, and scripts. Her writing reflects the wide range of her experiences as well as her deep commitment to the welfare of African Americans. In 1981, she won the American Book Award for her novel *The Salt Eaters*.

Supportive Parenting Born Miltona Mirkin Cade in 1939, Toni Cade Bambara adopted the African name Bambara in 1970. She was raised by her mother in New York City, and after attending Queens College there, she studied in Europe and lived in the Harlem and Brooklyn sections of New York. Bambara credited her mother as her main inspiration in life.

 MORE ABOUT THE AUTHOR For more on Toni Cade Bambara, visit the **Literature Center** at ClassZone.com.

Background

Racism in the South The civil rights movement of the 1950s and 1960s sought to end decades of racial discrimination against African Americans in the South. This discrimination took many forms, including segregation in education, housing, and public places. Although laws and court rulings from the 1940s through the 1960s made such discrimination illegal, African Americans still faced prejudice, restrictions, and physical and verbal intimidation.

Teach

STANDARDS FOCUS

LITERARY ANALYSIS

● VOICE AND DIALECT

For instructional support, read aloud this example:

> Runnin fer the porch ain't goin to stop them bees. They lookin fer your hide and won't take no for an answer.

Have students identify the evidence of dialect and the details that convey the writer's voice. *Possible answer: Dialect is conveyed by* Runnin, fer, ain't, goin, them, They, lookin, *and* hide. *Together, these words convey the author's voice.*

CHECK UNDERSTANDING Ask students to identify their own local dialect.

READING SKILL

■ DRAW CONCLUSIONS

Have students read the first sentence under **Supportive Parenting.** What conclusions can they draw about the author's values? *Possible answer: The author feels connected to her African heritage.*

CHECK UNDERSTANDING Ask students to name clues in the sentences that helped them draw their conclusions.

 RESOURCE MANAGER—Copy Master Draw Conclusions p. 79 (for student use while reading the selection)

DIFFERENTIATED INSTRUCTION

FOR LESS–PROFICIENT READERS

Concept Support: Dialect Explain that the best way to understand dialect is to read it aloud slowly. Readers should also look at context to try to identify unusual word forms and define unfamiliar words. Model this process with the italicized text from page 863. Help students paraphrase the text. *(Possible answer: Granny stomped up the steps, pushing the scratchy screen door and letting it bang behind her.)*

FOR ENGLISH LEARNERS

Concept Support: Draw Conclusions Be sure students know the importance of the racial conflicts that the author coped with in the 1960s and 1970s. Read *Background* with them and answer questions they may have about racial conflicts in America during this time period.

ANALYZE VISUALS

Possible answer: The setting is a red-hot afternoon, probably in a Southern cotton field. The man's stooped posture and his loose hold on the hoe suggests that he is tired and perhaps discouraged. Yet his calm, intent expression as he pauses in his labor to study the cotton flower also conveys a feeling of self-respect and centeredness.

About the Art The second of ten children, Benny Andrews (b. 1930) grew up in rural Georgia in a family of sharecroppers. After serving in the Korean War and receiving a B.F.A. at the Art Institute of Chicago, Andrews moved to New York City where he became recognized as both an influential artist and educator. The imagery in Andrews's work is often drawn from memories of his family and childhood in Georgia.

LITERARY ANALYSIS

Ⓐ VOICE AND DIALECT

Possible answer: Student responses should include some of these examples: g dropped off *-ing endings ("stompin" "swingin," "waitin," "tap-dancin"); "making the cakes drunk," referring to soaking cakes in rum;* ain't; *"Me and Cathy" rather than "Cathy and I"; "station wagon'd been roamin" for "station wagon had been roaming"; and "lassoed to his shoulder."*

If students need help . . . Have them read each sentence slowly, looking for words that depart from standard English. Help them paraphrase the meaning of each sentence.

BLUES AIN'T NO MOCKIN BIRD

Toni Cade Bambara

The puddle had frozen over, and me and Cathy went stompin in it. The twins from next door, Tyrone and Terry, were swingin so high out of sight we forgot we were waitin our turn on the tire. Cathy jumped up and came down hard on her heels and started tap-dancin. And the frozen patch splintered every which way underneath kinda spooky. "Looks like a plastic spider web," she said. "A sort of weird spider, I guess, with many mental problems." But really it looked like the crystal paperweight Granny kept in the parlor. She was on the back porch, Granny was, making the cakes drunk. The old ladle dripping rum into the Christmas tins, like it used to drip maple syrup into the pails when we
10 lived in the Judson's woods, like it poured cider into the vats when we were on the Cooper place, like it used to scoop buttermilk and soft cheese when we lived at the dairy.

"Go tell that man we ain't a bunch of trees."

"Ma'am?"

"I said to tell that man to get away from here with that camera." Me and Cathy look over toward the meadow where the men with the station wagon'd been roamin around all mornin. The tall man with a huge camera lassoed to his shoulder was buzzin our way. Ⓐ

"They're makin movie pictures," yelled Tyrone, stiffenin his legs and twistin
20 so the tire'd come down slow so they could see.

"They're makin movie pictures," sang out Terry.

"That boy don't never have anything original to say," say Cathy grown-up.

By the time the man with the camera had cut across our neighbor's yard, the twins were out of the trees swingin low and Granny was onto the steps, the screen door bammin soft and scratchy against her palms. "We thought we'd get a shot or two of the house and everything and then—"

ANALYZE VISUALS
Consider the **setting** depicted in this painting, as well as the subject's posture and expression. What feelings do these elements convey? Explain.

❶ Targeted Passage

Ⓐ VOICE AND DIALECT
Reread lines 1–18. Identify the distinctive vocabulary and grammar that characterize the narrator's dialect.

Detail of *Cotton Choppers* (1965), Benny Andrews. Oil on canvas, 25″ × 35″. © ACA Galleries, New York.

864 UNIT 9: HISTORY, CULTURE, AND THE AUTHOR

DIFFERENTIATED INSTRUCTION

FOR ALL STUDENTS
Enhancing Learning Styles Provide these projects for various learning preferences:

- **Visual** Create a frieze that illustrates a scene from the story.
- **Musical** Compose a ballad that retells events from the story.

For further details on these projects, see

R RESOURCE MANAGER
Ideas for Extension pp. 72–73

FOR LESS–PROFICIENT READERS
In combination with the *Audio Anthology CD*, use one or more Targeted Passages (pp. 864, 869, 871) to ensure that students focus on key ideas, concepts, and skills. Targeted Passages are also good for English learners.

❶ Targeted Passage [Lines 1–12]

This passage introduces the characters, the time period, and the season of the year.

- Who are Cathy, Tyrone, and Terry? How do they feel about one another?

BACKGROUND

The Food Stamp Program Granny is offended by the reporter's suggestion that her home could be part of the promotion of the Food Stamp Program, but many benefited from its services. The first Food Stamp Program began in the 1930s under the policies of President Roosevelt's New Deal as a way of helping the very poor. The program ended in 1943, but was reopened during the 1960s and 1970s.

Cultural Connection Many nations have no organized food relief program for their citizens. Organizations such as the International Federation of Red Cross and Red Crescent Societies work around the world to bring food relief to victims of drought, earthquakes, and other disasters that emphasize poverty. Since the 1970s, the Red Cross has brought food relief to countries all over the world. Ask students to share any knowledge they might have about food relief services overseas.

- What time of year does the story take place? How can you tell?

- Where has the family lived before living in their current house? What can you tell about the family from the places they have lived?

FOR ENGLISH LEARNERS

Key Academic Vocabulary Use Definition Mapping to teach these words: *mental* (line 6), *plus* (line 103), *invisible* (line 131).

 BEST PRACTICES TOOLKIT—Transparency
Definition Mapping p. E6

Prereading For prereading instruction for English learners, see

BEST PRACTICES TOOLKIT
Scaffolding Reading Instruction pp. 43–46

FOR ADVANCED LEARNERS/PRE–AP

Pre-AP Exercises in the bottom channel provide additional challenge for students. Use these suggestions for small groups or individuals.

ADDITIONAL GUIDELINES

For more help with differentiation and tips for classroom management, see

 BEST PRACTICES TOOLKIT
Differentiated Instruction pp. 31–38

B DRAW CONCLUSIONS

Possible answer: The men want to show poor people growing their own vegetables as a way to show that food stamps are not really necessary. Evidence: He says he is from the county, that his film is for the food stamp campaign. He notes that Granny grows her own vegetables, and says "If more folks did that, see, there'd be no need—" (lines 56–57). The implied end to his statement is "to give them food stamps to help them buy food."

If students need help . . . Ask students how they think the smiling man intended to end his sentence.

Lines 27–57
REINFORCE *KEY IDEA:* SELF–RESPECT

Discuss How does Granny show her feeling of **self-respect** to the smiling man? How does the man react? *Possible answer: The smiling man calls Granny "aunty," rather than "ma'am" or another respectful term. Granny shows her self-respect when she tells him she is not related to him. Then, when he asks for a statement, she does not reply. The smiling man does not understand her reactions and continues to disrespect Granny.*

"Good mornin," Granny cut him off. And smiled that smile.

"Good mornin," he said, head all down the way Bingo does when you yell at him about the bones on the kitchen floor. "Nice place you got here, aunty. 30 We thought we'd take a—"

"Did you?" said Granny with her eyebrows. Cathy pulled up her socks and giggled.

"Nice things here," said the man, buzzin his camera over the yard. The pecan barrels, the sled, me and Cathy, the flowers, the printed stones along the driveway, the trees, the twins, the toolshed.

"I don't know about the thing, the it, and the stuff," said Granny, still talkin with her eyebrows. "Just people here is what I tend to consider."

Camera man stopped buzzin. Cathy giggled into her collar.

"Mornin, ladies," a new man said. He had come up behind us when we 40 weren't lookin. "And gents," discoverin the twins givin him a nasty look. "We're filmin for the county," he said with a smile. "Mind if we shoot a bit around here?"

"I do indeed," said Granny with no smile. Smilin man was smiling up a storm. So was Cathy. But he didn't seem to have another word to say, so he and the camera man backed on out the yard, but you could hear the camera buzzin still. "Suppose you just shut that machine off," said Granny real low through her teeth, and took a step down off the porch and then another.

"Now, aunty,"[1] Camera said, pointin the thing straight at her.

"Your mama and I are not related."

50 Smilin man got his notebook out and a chewed-up pencil. "Listen," he said movin back into our yard, "we'd like to have a statement from you . . . for the film. We're filmin for the county, see. Part of the food stamp campaign. You know about the food stamps?"

Granny said nuthin.

"Maybe there's somethin you want to say for the film. I see you grow your own vegetables," he smiled real nice. "If more folks did that, see, there'd be no need—" **B**

Granny wasn't sayin nuthin. So they backed on out, buzzin at our clothesline and the twins' bicycles, then back on down to the meadow. The 60 twins were danglin in the tire, lookin at Granny. Me and Cathy were waitin, too, cause Granny always got somethin to say. She teaches steady with no let-up. "I was on this bridge one time," she started off. "Was a crowd cause this man was goin to jump, you understand. And a minister was there and the police and some other folks. His woman was there, too."

"What was they doin?" asked Tyrone.

"Tryin to talk him out of it was what they was doin. The minister talkin about how it was a mortal sin,[2] suicide. His woman takin bites out of her own hand and not even knowin it, so nervous and cryin and talkin fast."

---

1. **aunty:** a derogatory term of address once commonly used for black women in the South.
2. **mortal sin:** in many religions, an extremely serious offense against the laws of God.

866 UNIT 9: HISTORY, CULTURE, AND THE AUTHOR

B DRAW CONCLUSIONS
What is the men's purpose for making the film? What evidence in the text helped you draw that conclusion?

DIFFERENTIATED INSTRUCTION

FOR ENGLISH LEARNERS

Language: Multiple-Meaning Words Have pairs use a Cluster Diagram to map the various definitions of each of the following words. Help students use dictionaries and your suggestions to fill in the outer circles with definition ideas: *head* (line 28), *grow* (line 55), *stalks* (line 124), *ducks* (line 142), *figure* (line 157), *hand* (line 174), *face* (line 180), *chest* (line 192), *throws* (line 201).

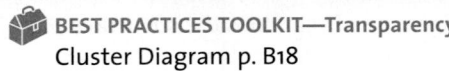 BEST PRACTICES TOOLKIT—Transparency
Cluster Diagram p. B18

Brothers (1934), Malvin Gray Johnson. Smithsonian American Art Museum, Washington, D.C. Photo © Smithsonian American Art Museum, Washington, D.C./Art Resource, New York.

ANALYZE VISUALS
Look at the way the artist mixes colors in this painting—for example, on the boys' sleeves and overalls, as well as on the fence. What effect does this create? How well, in your opinion, does this technique fit the subject matter of the painting? Explain.

"So what happened?" asked Tyrone.

70 "So here comes . . . this person . . . with a camera, takin pictures of the man and the minister and the woman. Takin pictures of the man in his misery about to jump, cause life so bad and people been messin with him so bad. This person takin up the whole roll of film practically. But savin a few, of course."

"Of course," said Cathy, hatin the person. Me standin there wonderin how Cathy knew it was "of course" when I didn't know and it was *my* grandmother.

After a while Tyrone said, "Did he jump?"

"Yeh, did he jump?" say Terry all eager.

ANALYZE VISUALS

Possible answer: The mix of colors makes the clothing and fence look dirty and worn rather than clean or freshly painted. Since the farm boys look like they work close to the earth, the technique fits the subject matter.

About the Art Malvin Gray Johnson (1896–1934) painted *Brothers* in 1934. It was painted from sights Johnson saw on a journey through rural Virginia. Johnson's trip was funded by the Public Works of Art project and helped him show one rural African-American community. The oil painting shows two young boys sharing a cane bench, though the younger boy has only half a seat.

FOR LESS–PROFICIENT READERS

Comprehension Support Have students read lines 62–75, in which Granny tells a story about how a cameraman invaded the privacy of a suicidal man. Lead students in a group to figure out what Granny is teaching by the story. Have them decide what the ending of that story might be.

FOR ADVANCED LEARNERS/PRE–AP

Analyze Tone Ask students to identify the tone of this story. Then have them break up into groups and have them discuss how that tone contributed to their appreciation of the setting, characters, and subject matter of the story.

And Granny just stared at the twins till their faces swallow up the eager and they don't even care any more about the man jumpin. Then she goes back onto the porch and lets the screen door go for itself. I'm lookin to Cathy to finish the story cause she knows Granny's whole story before me even. Like she knew about how come we move so much and Cathy ain't nothin but a third cousin we picked up on the way last Thanksgivin visitin. But she knew it was on account of people drivin Granny crazy till she'd get up in the night and start packin. Mumblin and packin and wakin everybody up sayin, "Let's get on away from here before I kill me somebody." Like people wouldn't pay her for things like they said they would. Or Mr. Judson bringin us boxes of old clothes and raggedy magazines. Or Mrs. Cooper comin in our kitchen and touchin everything and sayin how clean it all was. Granny goin crazy, and Granddaddy Cain pullin her off people sayin, "Now, now, Cora." But next day loadin up the truck, with rocks all in his jaw, madder than Granny in the first place. **ⓒ**

"I read a story once," said Cathy soundin like Granny teacher. "About this lady Goldilocks who barged into a house that wasn't even hers. And not invited, you understand. Messed over the people's groceries and broke up the people's furniture. Had the nerve to sleep in the folks' bed."

"Then what happened?" asked Tyrone. "What they do, the folks, when they come in to all this mess?"

"Did they make her pay for it?" asked Terry, makin a fist. "I'd've made her pay me."

I didn't even ask. I could see Cathy actress was very likely to just walk away and leave us in mystery about this story which I heard was about some bears.

"Did they throw her out?" asked Tyrone, like his father sounds when he's bein extra nasty-plus to the washin-machine man.

"Woulda," said Terry. "I woulda gone upside her head with my fist and—"

"You woulda done whatcha always do—go cry to Mama, you big baby," said Tyrone. So naturally Terry starts hittin on Tyrone, and next thing you know they tumblin out the tire and rollin on the ground. But Granny didn'y say a thing or send the twins home or step out on the steps to tell us about how we can't afford to be fightin amongst ourselves. She didn't say nuthin. So I get into the tire to take my turn. And I could see her leanin up against the pantry table, starin at the cakes she was puttin up for the Christmas sale, mumblin real low and grumpy and holdin her forehead like it wanted to fall off and mess up the rum cakes.

Behind me I hear before I can see Granddaddy Cain comin through the woods in his field boots. Then I twist around to see the shiny black oilskin cuttin through what little left there was of yellows, reds, and oranges. His great white head not quite round cause of this bloody thing high on his shoulder, like he was wearin a cap on sideways. He takes the shortcut through the pecan grove, and the sound of twigs snapping overhead and underfoot travels clear and cold all the way up to us. And here comes Smilin and Camera up behind

---

LITERARY ANALYSIS

ⓒ VOICE AND DIALECT

Possible answer: "With rocks all in his jaw" *suggests that Granddaddy Cain is clenching his jaw in anger.*

If students need help . . . Ask these questions to help them clarify the idiom:

- What might rocks in one's jaw look like?
- What is happening in Granddaddy Cain's face to make it look like it has rocks in it?
- What emotion does Granddaddy Cain feel when he has "rocks all in his jaw?"

Lines 78–91
DISCUSSION PROMPTS

Use these prompts to help students understand some of the events in Granny's life:

Connect Have you ever been offended by someone even though you knew that person was trying to be nice? *Accept all reasonable responses.*

Analyze What do people do for Granny that makes her mad? Explain. *Students should recognize that a gift of old clothes and raggedy magazines and Mrs. Cooper's compliments about cleanliness made Granny mad. They make her feel pitied.*

Evaluate What might Granny do instead of moving out of her house when she gets mad? *Possible answer: Granny feels such anger that she fears she will kill someone if she does not move. Instead of moving, she could control her anger and swallow the disrespect she feels. She could resolve to show the well-intentioned landlords that she does not deserve their disrespect.*

ⓒ VOICE AND DIALECT
An **idiom** is a common phrase whose meaning is different from the meaning of its individual words. On the basis of the context, identify the meaning of the idiom "with rocks all in his jaw."

DIFFERENTIATED INSTRUCTION

FOR LESS–PROFICIENT READERS

Comprehension Support: Characterization Point out that the author calls Cathy "Cathy grown-up" (line 22), "soundin like Granny teacher" (line 92), "Cathy actress" (line 100), and "Cathy dreamer" (line 206). Ask students to discuss why the author uses this treatment to characterize Cathy. Explain that these all refer to the same person. Discuss what it tells readers about Cathy.

FOR ENGLISH LEARNERS

Vocabulary: Idioms Have small groups use Word Squares to learn these idioms: *smiling up a storm* (lines 43–44), *talk him out of it* (line 66), *messin with him* (line 72), *in the first place* (line 91), *Had the nerve to* (line 95), *throw her out* (line 102), *can't afford to* (line 109), *go for him* (line 121), *every which way* (line 140).

 BEST PRACTICES TOOLKIT—Transparency Word Squares p. E10

him like they was goin to do somethin. Folks like to go for him sometimes. Cathy say it's because he's so tall and quiet and like a king. And people just can't stand it. But Smilin and Camera don't hit him in the head or nuthin. **D** They just buzz on him as he stalks by with the chicken hawk slung over his shoulder, squawkin, drippin red down the back of the oilskin. He passes the porch and stops a second for Granny to see he's caught the hawk at last, but she's just starin and mumblin, and not at the hawk. So he nails the bird to the toolshed door, the hammerin crackin through the eardrums. And the bird flappin himself to death and droolin down the door to paint the gravel in the

130 driveway red, then brown, then black. And the two men movin up on tiptoe like they was invisible or we were blind, one. **E**

"Get them persons out of my flower bed, Mister Cain," say Granny moanin real low like at a funeral.

"How come your grandmother calls her husband 'Mister Cain' all the time?" Tyrone whispers loud and noisy and from the city and don't know no better. Like his mama, Miss Myrtle, tell us never mind the formality as if we had no better breeding than to call her Myrtle, plain. And then this awful thing—a giant hawk—come wailin up over the meadow, flyin low and tilted and screamin, zigzaggin through the pecan grove, breakin branches and hollerin,

140 snappin past the clothesline, flyin every which way, flyin into things reckless with crazy.

Woodshed (1944), Andrew Wyeth. Collection of the Brandywine River Museum. Bequest of C. Porter Schutt, 1995. © Andrew Wyeth.

 Targeted Passage

D DRAW CONCLUSIONS
The narrator says that people like to "go for" her grandfather because he is "tall and quiet and like a king" and the "people just can't stand it." What "people" does she mean, and why do they resent the man's regal appearance?

E GRAMMAR AND STYLE
Reread lines 124–125. Notice how Bambara chooses imaginative, **vivid verbs,** such as "buzz" and "stalks," to enhance the image of Granddaddy carrying the chicken hawk.

E GRAMMAR AND STYLE
Vivid Verbs Point out that some of the vivid verbs are effective because they sound like what they mean, such as *buzz* (line 124), *mumblin* (line 127), and *wailin* (line 138). Ask students how this style improves the writing. To extend the activity, have students list vivid verbs used throughout the story.

ANALYZE VISUALS
Activity Ask students what part of the story the painting depicts and how it helps them understand the story. *Possible answer: The painting shows how Granddaddy Cain hammered the hawk on the tool shed. This helps readers picture how this is done.*

About the Art *Woodshed* by Andrew Wyeth (born 1917) was painted in 1944, near the end of World War II. It shows a sense of anxiety and death that people of this time period often experienced.

Lines 134–137
REINFORCE *KEY IDEA:* SELF–RESPECT

Discuss How does Granny show respect to Granddaddy Cain? How can you tell that Tyrone's family does not share the same values about **self-respect**? *Possible answer: Granny calls Granddaddy Cain "Mister Cain." Tyrone's mother allows the narrator to call her "Myrtle" instead of "Miss Myrtle."*

FOR LESS–PROFICIENT READERS

 Targeted Passage [Lines 121–133]

This passage introduces the character of Granddaddy Cain.

- What does Granddaddy Cain look like? How is he different from other people?

- What does Granddaddy Cain bring with him from the field? What does he do with it?

- What does Granny ask Granddaddy Cain to do?

FOR ENGLISH LEARNERS

Language: English Conversational Patterns
Point out that these phrases are not standard English. With a Whip Around strategy, read each phrase in context and have a student change it to standard English: *we ain't a bunch of trees* (line 13), *Granny gonna bust through that screen* (lines 157–158), *all around these parts* (line 182).

 **BEST PRACTICES TOOLKIT**
Whip Around p. B1

🕞 VOICE AND DIALECT

Possible answer: *The run-on sentence makes the writing sound like casual spoken language rather than written language.*

Lines 164–180
REINFORCE *KEY IDEA*:
SELF–RESPECT

Discuss How does Granddaddy Cain show **self-respect** in dealing with the reporter and the cameraman? **Possible answer:** *Granddaddy Cain shows self-respect by demanding respect from the two men. He looks straight at them and confidently holds his large hand out for the camera, knowing that he deserves their compliance.*

"He's come to claim his mate," say Cathy fast, and ducks down. We all fall quick and flat on the gravel driveway, stones scrapin my face. I squinch my eyes open again at the hawk on the door, tryin to fly up out of her death like it was just a sack flown into by mistake. Her body holdin her there on that nail, though. The mate beatin the air overhead and clutchin for hair, for heads, for landin space.

150 The camera man duckin and bendin and runnin and fallin, jigglin the camera and scared. And Smilin jumpin up and down swipin at the huge bird, tryin to bring the hawk down with just his raggedy ole cap. Granddaddy Cain straight up and silent, watchin the circles of the hawk, then aimin the hammer off his wrist. The giant bird fallin, silent and slow. Then here comes Camera and Smilin all big and bad now that the awful screechin thing is on its back and broken, here they come. And Granddaddy Cain looks up at them like it was the first time noticin, but not payin them too much mind[3] cause he's listenin, we all listening, to that low groanin music comin from the porch. And we figure any minute, somethin in my back tells me any minute now, Granny gonna bust through that screen with somethin in her hand and murder on her mind. So Granddaddy say above the buzzin, but quiet, "Good day,

160 gentlemen." Just like that. Like he'd invited them in to play cards and they'd stayed too long and all the sandwiches were gone and Reverend Webb was droppin by and it was time to go. 🕞

They didn't know what to do. But like Cathy say, folks can't stand Grandaddy tall and silent and like a king. They can't neither. The smile the men smilin is pullin the mouth back and showin the teeth. Lookin like the wolf man, both of them. Then Granddaddy holds his hand out—this huge hand I used to sit in when I was a baby and he'd carry me through the house to my mother like I was a gift on a tray. Like he used to on the trains. They called the other men just waiters. But they spoke of Granddaddy separate and said,

170 The Waiter. And said he had engines in his feet and motors in his hands and couldn't no train throw him off and couldn't nobody turn him around. They were big enough for motors, his hands were. He held that one hand out all still and it gettin to be not at all a hand but a person in itself.

"He wants you to hand him the camera," Smilin whispers to Camera, tiltin his head to talk secret like they was in the jungle or somethin and come upon a native that don't speak the language. The men start untyin the straps, and they put the camera into that great hand speckled with the hawk's blood all black and crackly now. And the hand don't even drop with the weight, just the fingers move, curl up around the machine. But Granddaddy lookin straight at

180 the men. They lookin at each other and everywhere but at Granddaddy's face.

"We filmin for the county, see," say Smilin. "We puttin together a movie for the food stamp program . . . filmin all around these parts. Uhh, filmin for the county."

🕞 VOICE AND DIALECT
Reread lines 160–162. Notice the grammatical construction of this sentence. What effect does the use of a long chain of clauses have on the voice of the narrator?

---

3. **not payin them too much mind:** barely noticing them; ignoring them.

DIFFERENTIATED INSTRUCTION

FOR ENGLISH LEARNERS
Language: Verb Tenses Point out that characters, like many native English speakers, often use present tense in place of past tense verbs when speaking. Pose these examples: *Then here comes Camera and Smilin all big and bad* (lines 152–153); *But like Cathy say* (line 163). Assign story pages to student pairs. Ask them to find all possible examples, read them aloud as written, and then rewrite them with the correct form in the past.

FOR ADVANCED LEARNERS/PRE–AP
Analyze Alternative Perspectives Have students consider the events of the story from the point of view of the reporter. Then, have them write the narration that the reporter would have written to accompany his documentary's scene at the Cains' house. Ask volunteers to share their narration.

"Can I have my camera back?" say the tall man with no machine on his shoulder, but still keepin it high like the camera was still there or needed to be. "Please, sir." **G**

Then Granddaddy's other hand flies up like a sudden and gentle bird, slaps down fast on top of the camera and lifts off half like it was a calabash[4] cut for sharing.

"Hey," Camera jumps forward. He gathers up the parts into his chest and everything unrollin and fallin all over. "Whata tryin to do? You'll ruin the film." He looks down into his chest of metal reels and things like he's protectin a kitten from the cold.

"You standin in the misses' flower bed," say Granddaddy. "This is our own place."

The two men look at him, then at each other, then back at the mess in the camera man's chest, and they just back off. One sayin over and over all the way down to the meadow, "Watch it, Bruno. Keep ya fingers off the film." Then Granddaddy picks up the hammer and jams it into the oilskin pocket, scrapes his boots, and goes into the house. And you can hear the squish of his boots headin through the house. And you can see the funny shadow he throws from the parlor window onto the ground by the string-bean patch. The hammer draggin the pocket of the oilskin out so Granddaddy looked even wider. Granny was hummin now—high, not low and grumbly. And she was doin the cakes again, you could smell the molasses from the rum.

"There's this story I'm goin to write one day," say Cathy dreamer. "About the proper use of the hammer."

"Can I be in it?" Tyrone say with his hand up like it was a matter of first come, first served.

"Perhaps," say Cathy, climbin onto the tire to pump us up. "If you there and ready."

G DRAW CONCLUSIONS
Why does the camera man add "Please, sir" to his request for the camera?

3 Targeted Passage

4. **calabash** (kăl′ə-băsh′): a fruit whose dried shell is used to make things like bottles, bowls, and rattles.

READING SKILL

G DRAW CONCLUSIONS

Possible answer: *The cameraman is trying to show respect to Granddaddy Cain in the hopes of appeasing his anger.*

SELECTION WRAP-UP

REFLECT Have students think about how the cameraman responds to Granddaddy Cain. Why did the cameraman give his camera to Granddaddy Cain? What did he think Granddaddy Cain would do with it?

★ CRITIQUE Have students decide if Granny and Granddaddy Cain handled the situation with the reporter and cameraman well. Ask them to suggest alternative approaches.

FOR LESS–PROFICIENT READERS

3 Targeted Passage [Lines 187–205]

This passage includes the climax of the story in which Granddaddy Cain breaks the camera.

- What does Granddaddy Cain do to the movie camera?
- How does the cameraman react?
- How does Granny feel after the camera is broken?

FOR ENGLISH LEARNERS

Language: Transitions Point out that Bambara uses similes frequently. Review that a simile is a comparison linked by *like,* as in this example: *Granddaddy's other hand flies up like a sudden and gentle bird* (line 187). Assign selection pages to groups of students and have them list similes in a T Chart with headings *Compares* ________ and *To* ________.

BEST PRACTICES TOOLKIT—Transparency
T Chart p. A25

BLUES AIN'T NO MOCKIN BIRD 871

Practice and Apply

After Reading

For additional support of post-reading questions, use these copy masters:

R RESOURCE MANAGER—Copy Masters

Reading Check p. 81 (to check understanding of the selection)

Voice and Dialect p. 77 (for practice of literary analysis standards focus)

Question Support p. 82 (After Reading questions adapted for English learners and less-proficient readers)

For additional questions, see page 71.

ANSWERS

Comprehension

1. *Smilin man and Camera man are from the county and making a film for the food stamp campaign. They are probably white, whereas the Cains are African American.*

2. *They film Granny's yard even though she tells them not to, they call her "aunty," and they are patronizing and disrespectful.*

3. *He takes it from them, pulls it into two pieces, and exposes the film.*

Literary Analysis

Possible answers:

4. *If he hadn't come home, the men probably would have continued to film.*

5. *The anecdote and the Goldilocks story are inspired by the county men: the first is about people taking pictures to satisfy their own needs before those of the subject; the second is about nosy strangers who meddle.*

6. *Cathy is going to write about using a hammer to punish disrespectful people for meddling or to keep them away.*

7. ● STANDARDS FOCUS *Voice and Dialect Student charts will vary. Their analyses should note that the narrator's voice is informal, conversational, and energetic; reflects an African-American dialect; and contains idioms and figurative images that create vivid mental pictures.*

8. ■ STANDARDS FOCUS *Draw Conclusions Bambara is concerned about racism and class discrimination. Her respectful (even admiring) use of dialect and the depiction of strong African-American characters sug-*

Comprehension

1. **Recall** Who are Smilin man and Camera man?

2. **Recall** What do they do that offends Granny?

3. **Recall** What does Granddaddy Cain do to their camera?

Literary Analysis

4. **Predict** What might have happened if Granddaddy Cain had not come home when he did?

5. **Interpret Text** Reread lines 62–95. How do the anecdotes about the suicide attempt and Goldilocks relate to the events in the story?

6. **Make Inferences** What does Cathy mean at the end when she says she is going to write a story about "the proper use of the hammer"?

7. **Analyze Voice and Dialect** Create a chart with examples of the distinctive vocabulary, pronunciation, grammar, and idioms that characterize the narrator's dialect. How would you describe the narrator's voice?

Distinctive Characteristics of Narrator's Dialect			
Vocabulary	Pronunciation	Grammar	Idioms
bammin	stompin	me and Cathy went	smiling up a storm
	kinda		

8. **Draw Conclusions About Values and Beliefs** Review the conclusions you drew about social issues presented in the story. What conclusions can you draw about Bambara's values and beliefs concerning those social issues? Cite evidence from the story to support your conclusions.

9. **Evaluate Characters** How do Granny and Granddaddy Cain demonstrate their **self-respect?** Cite evidence from the text to support your response.

Literary Criticism

10. **Critical Interpretations** One critic stated that Bambara "presents black culture as embattled but unbowed" in her stories. How does that comment apply to "Blues Ain't No Mockin Bird"? Support your interpretation with evidence from the text.

---

gest that she values the rural African-American culture.

9. *Granny speaks her mind and is not intimidated by the visitors' patronizing; she has no use for people who refuse to pay for services or otherwise disrespect the family (lines 85–91). Granddaddy carries himself "tall and quiet and like a king" (line 122). He deals with the unwelcome visitors with quiet but fierce strength, demanding their camera, pulling it in two, explaining briefly*

but clearly what they are doing wrong, and showing them that they are unwelcome.

Literary Criticism

10. *The black characters in this story are embattled because they have experience dealing with people who disrespect them, including the visitors in the story, those who refuse to pay for services, and people who offer charity in a patronizing manner. However, they continue to face such people with quiet strength and self-assurance.*

Reading-Writing Connection

Demonstrate your understanding of the characters portrayed in "Blues Ain't No Mockin Bird" by responding to these prompts. Then use **Revision: Grammar and Style** to improve your writing.

WRITING PROMPTS

SELF-CHECK

A. Short Response: Analyze Action
Why do you think Granddaddy smashes the man's camera? Do you think his action is justifiable, or do you think he is overreacting? Write **one or two paragraphs** in which you argue your point.

A successful analysis will . . .
- clearly state your opinion of Granddaddy's behavior
- discuss the concept of **self-respect**
- use examples from the story to support your opinion

B. Extended Response: Describe Granny
How would you describe Granny's attitude and behavior? Identify two of her character traits in **a three-to-five-paragraph response.** Be sure to include examples from the story to support your characterization.

A strong characterization will . . .
- include descriptive language that accurately conveys Granny's personality
- use at least two examples from the story to illustrate each of the traits

REVISION: GRAMMAR AND STYLE

CHOOSE EFFECTIVE WORDS Review the **Grammar and Style** note on page 869. Bambara brings life to her story by peppering it with a series of **vivid verbs.** Follow Bambara's example by choosing words that add liveliness and depth to your writing; avoid words that are too bland or generic. Both you and your reader will find the end result far more satisfying. Here is another example of how Bambara effectively uses vivid verbs in her descriptions:

> *Then Granddaddy's other hand flies up like a sudden and gentle bird, slaps down fast on top of the camera and lifts off half like it was a calabash cut for sharing.* (lines 187–189)

Notice how the revisions in red enhance the description in this first draft. Revise your responses to the prompts by similarly incorporating vivid verbs.

STUDENT MODEL

Granny seems like a grumpy person. She ~~talks under her breath~~ *mumbles* all the time and refuses to smile. She doesn't hide her dislike for the two men who come to film them and ~~tells~~ *commands* Granddaddy to get them out of her flower bed.

WRITING TOOLS
For prewriting, revision, and editing tools, visit the **Writing Center** at ClassZone.com.

DIFFERENTIATED INSTRUCTION

FOR LESS–PROFICIENT WRITERS

For Prompt A:

Offer these sentence starters to help students begin their thesis statements:

- Granddaddy was overreacting when he broke the man's camera because . . .
- Granddaddy was justified in breaking the man's camera because . . .

For Prompt B:

- Limit the length of the essay to three paragraphs, with students identifying just one of Granny's characteristics.
- Have students work in small groups to determine Granny's strongest characteristics and evidence to support each one.
- Help students craft a closing paragraph that summarizes the information covered in the essay.

Reading-Writing Connection

WRITING PROMPTS

- For Prompt A, urge students to write a thesis statement that unifies the paragraphs. Remind them that each sentence should support the thesis statement with examples or reasons. After students finish, have them discuss their positions in small groups.

- For Prompt B, have students write one paragraph to focus on each trait they choose. Explain that the introduction and the conclusion should summarize the qualities mentioned in the paragraphs and should synthesize Granny's character.

For writing support, see

Writing Center at **ClassZone.com**

REVISION: GRAMMAR AND STYLE

- Explain that vivid verbs can energize writing and allow readers to visualize the scene clearly. To illustrate, have a volunteer tell how he or she pictured the scene in the story where the hawk attacked the farm. Point out that the scene is easy to visualize because the author effectively uses vivid verbs.

- After discussing the student model, write these sentences on the board. Have students replace common verbs with vivid verbs.

The men ~~stepped~~ bumbled onto the flower bed, ~~breaking~~ smashing petals and ~~bumping into~~ crushing stalks. Their heels ~~dug into~~ gouged the soil leaving deep holes among the flowers.

R RESOURCE MANAGER—Copy Master
Choose Effective Words p. 83

Assess and Reteach

Assess

R RESOURCE MANAGER—Copy Masters
Selection Test A pp. 85–86
Selection Test B/C pp. 87–88

Test Generator CD

Reteach

S STANDARDS LESSON FILE
Literature Lesson 43: Dialogue and Dialect
Literature Lesson 47: Author's Perspective
Reading Lesson 9: Drawing Conclusions
Writing Lesson 40: Word Choice

Focus and Motivate

OBJECTIVES

Literary Analysis
- explore the key idea of **connection**
- analyze influence of author's background
- read a short story

Reading
- connect

Vocabulary
- build vocabulary for reading and writing
- use context clues to determine the meaning of idioms *(also an EL language objective)*

SUMMARY

Fourteen-year-old Elena and her family live in a tenement in Paterson, New Jersey, home to many Puerto Rican immigrants like them. Elena is infatuated with Eugene, a boy from Georgia who lives in a neighboring house. On the day that President Kennedy is assassinated, Elena goes to Eugene's house to study. His mother coldly turns her away, rejecting her perhaps because of her race and her socioeconomic class. Later that evening Elena tries to feel grief for the President, but cries really for herself.

When do WORLD EVENTS hit home?

Introduce the question, and have students read the *KEY IDEA.* Discuss the kinds of world events that cause people to feel a personal **connection,** and why. Continue the exploration by having students complete the *QUICKWRITE.*

Selection Resources

American History
Short Story by Judith Ortiz Cofer

When do WORLD EVENTS hit home?

KEY IDEA Once in a while, large numbers of people feel such a **connection** to a news event that they stop everything. The selection you are about to read takes place on November 22, 1963, when the assassination of President John F. Kennedy stunned and distressed an entire nation.

QUICKWRITE List world events that have captured your attention. Then choose one that really "hit home" and write about where you were, what you were doing, and what your reactions were when you first learned about the event.

> World Events That Caught Our Attention
> 1. Terrorist attacks of September 11, 2001
> 2. Russian school hostage crisis in September 2004
> 3.

874

RESOURCE MANAGER UNIT 9

Plan and Teach pp. 89–96

Literary Analysis
Summary pp. 97†*, 98‡*
Influence of Author's Background
  pp. 99, 100†*
Question Support p. 108*

Reading
Connect pp. 101, 102†*
Reading Check p. 107

Vocabulary
Study p. 103*
Practice p. 104
Strategy p. 105

Assessment
Selection Tests A, B/C pp. 109*, 111*
Test Generator CD

BEST PRACTICES TOOLKIT

Differentiated Instruction
  pp. 31–38*

Scaffolding Instruction
  pp. 43–46*

Graphic Organizers/Strategies
Definition Mapping • New Word Analysis • Y Chart • Cluster Diagram

Reading Support
Audio Anthology CD*

Technology
Literature and Vocabulary Centers at **ClassZone.com**
Write*Smart* CD

---

* Resources for Differentiation   † Also in Spanish   ‡ In Haitian Creole and Vietnamese

● LITERARY ANALYSIS: INFLUENCE OF AUTHOR'S BACKGROUND

An **author's background**—that is, the writer's life experiences and cultural heritage—shapes his or her perspective on the world and inevitably influences what he or she writes, whether it is fiction or nonfiction. For example, Judith Ortiz Cofer was born in Puerto Rico but moved at a young age to Paterson, New Jersey. She sets many of her stories in Paterson, featuring Puerto Rican–born Americans.

Before you read "American History," learn more about Cofer from the biography on this page. Then, as you read the story, look for the following:

• references to places you know Cofer has lived or visited
• characters whose beliefs, values, or heritage echo Cofer's
• events and circumstances that are similar to Cofer's own

Review: **Character**

● READING STRATEGY: CONNECT

Good readers **connect** what they know about a person, place, or situation to what they are reading in order to understand it better. As you read "American History," connect your own life experiences to what you find in the story—the characters' circumstances, actions, and feelings. Record your connections on a chart such as the one begun here.

Detail from Story	Connection	Better Understanding
tenement	I read about tenements in social studies— large, rundown apartment buildings with poor tenants.	El Building must be big and rundown.

▲ VOCABULARY IN CONTEXT

Try to guess the meaning of each boldfaced word from its context.

1. soft music and **muted** conversation
2. **hierarchy** of command
3. **maneuvering** the car
4. **infatuated** and in love
5. **vigilant** protection
6. **enthralled** by the movie
7. **distraught** at losing her job
8. **resigned** to failing
9. a **dilapidated** shack
10. seeking **solace** in prayer

Author Online

**Judith Ortiz Cofer
born 1952**

A Child of Two Cultures It's no wonder that Judith Ortiz Cofer writes about what it's like to be a Puerto Rican girl growing up in a mainland U.S. city. "I write about the things I have known," she says. Cofer was born in Puerto Rico but moved at a young age to Paterson, New Jersey, where she lived in a large apartment building known by its residents as *El Building*. Whenever her father, a navy man, was on active duty, however, her mother would take the family back to Puerto Rico to live with their grandmother. Her father pushed her to adopt American ways, while her mother counseled her to hold on to Puerto Rican customs.

The Power of Words Cofer first became aware of the power of storytelling during visits with her grandmother, who Cofer says "could silence an entire room when she said 'Tengo un cuento' ('I have a story to tell')." Cofer especially loves writing poetry, because in a poem "every word weighs a ton."

Background

A Great Loss "American History" takes place on the day of President John F. Kennedy's assassination. The president's death deeply saddened the Puerto Rican–American community because, as Cofer points out, "President Kennedy was a saint to these people." Not only was he a charming young father and husband, but his goals were their dreams. He pledged to fight racial discrimination in the United States, raise the standard of living, and wipe out communism in Latin American countries.

 MORE ABOUT THE AUTHOR AND BACKGROUND
For more on Judith Ortiz Cofer and John F. Kennedy, visit the **Literature Center** at **ClassZone.com**.

AMERICAN HISTORY **875**

Teach

STANDARDS FOCUS

LITERARY ANALYSIS

● INFLUENCE OF AUTHOR'S BACKGROUND

To guide students, read aloud this example:

Carl frowned at his image in the mirror. If only he had the money to buy decent clothes. Maybe then the kids would accept him, instead of mocking his appearance.

Ask students how the writer's background may have influenced his portrayal of Carl. *Possible answer: The writer may have once been too poor to buy nice clothing.*

CHECK UNDERSTANDING Elicit other examples of childhood experiences that can affect an author's portrayal of a character.

READING STRATEGY

◼ CONNECT

Use the text in **The Power of Words** to model the concept of connecting. Say:

I think about someone who can silence an entire room with a story. With this person in mind, I can better understand how Cofer might be influenced by observing her grandmother.

CHECK UNDERSTANDING Ask students how finding similarities between characters and actual people can help them understand the characters.

[R] **RESOURCE MANAGER**—Copy Master
Connect p. 101 (for student use while reading the selection)

VOCABULARY SKILL

▲ VOCABULARY IN CONTEXT

DIAGNOSE WORD KNOWLEDGE To determine preteaching needs, have all students complete Vocabulary in Context. Check students' definitions against those on the selection pages. *Possible answers:* 1. *quiet,* 2. *chain,* 3. *handling,* 4. *attracted,* 5. *watchful,* 6. *charmed,* 7. *upset,* 8. *prepared,* 9. *broken down,* 10. *comfort*

PRETEACH VOCABULARY Use the Vocabulary Study copy master to help students predict the meaning of each boldfaced word.

1. Read item 1 aloud, emphasizing *dilapidated.*
2. Point out the phrase *clean and well cared for,* the word *old,* and the signal word *unlike.* Elicit possible meanings for *dilapidated,* such as "rundown."
3. Have students record their predictions.
4. Repeat the procedure for items 2–10.

[R] **RESOURCE MANAGER**—Copy Master
Vocabulary Study p. 103

For general guidelines on differentiating vocabulary instruction and for alternative vocabulary activities for students not needing vocabulary preteaching, see

 BEST PRACTICES TOOLKIT
Scaffolding Vocabulary Instruction pp. 43–46
[i] Vocabulary Center at **ClassZone.com**

ANALYZE VISUALS

Possible answer: The images depict the last moments of President John F. Kennedy's life before his assassination in Dallas, Texas on November 22, 1963. Setting the images on a filmstrip background gives viewers a sense of immediacy, as if they are seeing a moment-by-moment replay of history.

LITERARY ANALYSIS

❶ AUTHOR'S BACKGROUND

*Possible answer: Based on **About the Author** (page 875), the "Puerto Rican tenement known as El Building" (lines 2–3) in Paterson, New Jersey, appears to come directly from the author's background. In addition, Cofer herself had been one of the "new immigrants just up from the island" (lines 6–7). Finally, Cofer (born 1952) was 11 years old when Kennedy was assassinated (1963), so she probably recalls the details in lines 8–15 from her own childhood experiences.*

American History

JUDITH ORTIZ COFER

I once read in a "Ripley's Believe It or Not" column that Paterson, New Jersey, is the place where the Straight and Narrow (streets) intersect. The Puerto Rican tenement known as *El Building* was one block up from Straight. It was, in fact, the corner of Straight and Market; not "at" the corner, but *the* corner. At almost any hour of the day, El Building was like a monstrous jukebox, blasting out *salsas*[1] from open windows as the residents, mostly new immigrants just up from the island,[2] tried to drown out whatever they were currently enduring with loud music. But the day President Kennedy was shot there was a profound silence in El Building; even the abusive tongues of viragoes,[3] the
10 cursing of the unemployed, and the screeching of small children had been somehow **muted.** President Kennedy was a saint to these people. In fact, soon his photograph would be hung alongside the Sacred Heart and over the spiritist altars[4] that many women kept in their apartments. He would become part of the **hierarchy** of martyrs they prayed to for favors that only one who had died for a cause would understand. ❶

On the day that President Kennedy was shot, my ninth grade class had been out in the fenced playground of Public School Number 13. We had been given "free" exercise time and had been ordered by our P.E. teacher, Mr. DePalma, to "keep moving." That meant that the girls should jump rope and the boys
20 toss basketballs through a hoop at the far end of the yard. He in the meantime would "keep an eye" on us from just inside the building.

---

1. *salsas* (säl'säs): Latin-American dance tunes.
2. **the island:** Puerto Rico.
3. **abusive tongues of viragoes** (və-rä'gōz): hurtful comments of noisy, scolding women.
4. **alongside the Sacred Heart . . . spiritist altars:** The Sacred Heart, an image showing the physical heart of Jesus Christ, symbolizes Christ's love to some Roman Catholics. Spiritist altars are places of worship set up to observe spiritism, a set of religious beliefs based on the idea that spirits of the dead communicate with the living.

876 UNIT 9: HISTORY, CULTURE, AND THE AUTHOR

Background, top, center © Corbis;
bottom © Bettmann/Corbis

ANALYZE VISUALS
Consider the images on page 877. Why might the artist have chosen to place the photographs on a filmstrip background? Describe the effect created by this technique.

❶ Targeted Passage

muted (myoo'tĭd) *adj.* softened or muffled

hierarchy (hī'ə-rär'kē) *n.* a body of persons having authority

❶ AUTHOR'S BACKGROUND
Reread lines 1–15. What story elements appear to come from the author's background? Explain.

DIFFERENTIATED INSTRUCTION

FOR ALL STUDENTS
Expert Groups Allow students to become experts or members of expert groups by researching and choosing a way to share information about one of these topics:

- President John F. Kennedy's assassination
- reactions to President Kennedy's death

FOR LESS–PROFICIENT READERS
In combination with the *Audio Anthology CD,* use one or more Targeted Passages (pp. 876, 879, 881, 885) to ensure that students focus on key events, concepts, and skills. Targeted Passages are also good for English learners.

❶ Targeted Passage [Lines 1–15]
This passage introduces the setting of the story and links the plot with Kennedy's assassination.

A Tragic Loss John Fitzgerald Kennedy (1917–1963) was the youngest person ever to be elected President. He was shot to death by an assassin (Lee Harvey Oswald), on November 22, 1963, after less than three years in office. Many Americans who were alive at the time can still recall where they were and what they were doing when they learned of the president's assassination.

Lines 8–15
REINFORCE *KEY IDEA:* CONNECTION

Discuss What do the details that Cofer provides in these lines suggest about the **connection** people felt with Kennedy? Explain. *Possible answer: People felt a very strong connection with Kennedy. His death shocked the community into silence, and people displayed his photograph with religious reverence.*

- What is El Building? Where is it located?
- Who are the main occupants of El Building?
- When does the story take place?
- How did Kennedy's assassination affect the people of El Building?

FOR ENGLISH LEARNERS

Reading: Background Display a map and show students the location of Puerto Rico and its proximity to New Jersey. Explain that many Puerto Ricans migrated to New York and New Jersey during the 1940s and 1950s in pursuit of job opportunities.

Prereading For prereading instruction for English learners, see

 BEST PRACTICES TOOLKIT
Scaffolding Reading Instruction pp. 43–46

FOR ADVANCED LEARNERS/PRE–AP

Pre-AP Exercises in the bottom channel provide additional challenge for students. Use these suggestions for small groups or individuals.

ADDITIONAL GUIDELINES

For more help with differentiation and tips for classroom management, see

 BEST PRACTICES TOOLKIT
Differentiated Instruction pp. 31–38

It was a cold gray day in Paterson. The kind that warns of early snow. I was miserable, since I had forgotten my gloves, and my knuckles were turning red and raw from the jump rope. I was also taking a lot of abuse from the black girls for not turning the rope hard and fast enough for them.

"Hey, Skinny Bones, pump it, girl. Ain't you got no energy today?" Gail, the biggest of the black girls had the other end of the rope, yelled, "Didn't you eat your rice and beans and pork chops for breakfast today?"

The other girls picked up the "pork chop" and made it into a refrain: "pork
30 chop, pork chop, did you eat your pork chop?" They entered the double ropes in pairs and exited without tripping or missing a beat. I felt a burning on my cheeks and then my glasses fogged up so that I could not manage to coordinate the jump rope with Gail. The chill was doing to me what it always did; entering my bones, making me cry, humiliating me. I hated the city, especially in winter. I hated Public School Number 13. I hated my skinny flat-chested body, and I envied the black girls who could jump rope so fast that their legs became a blur. They always seemed to be warm while I froze. **B**

There was only one source of beauty and light for me that school year. The only thing I had anticipated at the start of the semester. That was seeing
40 Eugene. In August, Eugene and his family had moved into the only house on the block that had a yard and trees. I could see his place from my window in El Building. In fact, if I sat on the fire escape I was literally suspended above Eugene's backyard. It was my favorite spot to read my library books in the summer. Until that August the house had been occupied by an old Jewish couple. Over the years I had become part of their family, without their knowing it, of course. I had a view of their kitchen and their backyard, and though I could not hear what they said, I knew when they were arguing, when one of them was sick, and many other things. I knew all this by watching them at mealtimes. I could see their kitchen table, the sink, and the stove. During
50 good times, he sat at the table and read his newspapers while she fixed the meals. If they argued, he would leave and the old woman would sit and stare at nothing for a long time. When one of them was sick, the other would come and get things from the kitchen and carry them out on a tray. The old man had died in June. The last week of school I had not seen him at the table at all. Then one day I saw that there was a crowd in the kitchen. The old woman had finally emerged from the house on the arm of a stocky, middle-aged woman, whom I had seen there a few times before, maybe her daughter. Then a man had carried out suitcases. The house had stood empty for weeks. I had had to resist the temptation to climb down into the yard and water the flowers the old
60 lady had taken such good care of.

By the time Eugene's family moved in, the yard was a tangled mass of weeds. The father had spent several days mowing, and when he finished, from where I sat, I didn't see the red, yellow, and purple clusters that meant flowers to me. I didn't see this family sit down at the kitchen table together. It was just the mother, a red-headed tall woman who wore a white uniform—a nurse's,

B CONNECT
Think about a time when you continued to do something even though you were miserable doing it. Why might the narrator continue to turn the jump rope?

READING STRATEGY

B CONNECT

Possible answer: The narrator probably continued to turn the jump rope because she was already being taunted by the other girls and did not want to draw any more attention to herself.

If students need help . . . Have them use the chart introduced on page 875.

Detail from Story	Connection	Better Understanding
Elena gets teased		

Lines 22–40
DISCUSSION PROMPTS

Use these prompts to help students understand the narrator and how her situation makes her feel:

Connect Think about a time when you found it hard to fit into a social situation. How did the experience affect you? *Answers should demonstrate an understanding of the frustrations involved in trying to fit into certain social situations.*

Analyze How does the narrator feel about her life in Paterson? Explain. *Possible answer: For the most part, she is very unhappy there. She "hated the city, especially in winter," and she hates her school (lines 34–35). She appears to be having a difficult time fitting in with the other girls. Her "one source of beauty and light" (line 38) is seeing Eugene, a boy she likes.*

Evaluate Do you think the narrator is a "typical" teenager? Give reasons for your answer. *Possible answer: The narrator does seem like a typical teenager in several ways. Like so many other teens, she is very concerned about how she appears to her peers. She also appears to have a crush on a boy. However, she may be atypical in that she doesn't seem to have any close friends.*

DIFFERENTIATED INSTRUCTION

FOR ENGLISH LEARNERS

Culture: Connect Ask students whether children jump rope or do a similar activity in their home culture. If so, ask what kinds of rhymes the children say or sing. Have students explore such rhymes with other speakers of the same home language.

Key Academic Vocabulary Use Definition Mapping to teach these words: *source* (line 38), *suspended* (line 42), *couple* (line 45), *apparent* (line 207), *logic* (line 207), *restraint* (line 246).

 BEST PRACTICES TOOLKIT—Transparency Definition Mapping p. E6

I guessed it was; the father was gone before I got up in the morning and was never there at dinner time. I only saw him on weekends when they sometimes sat on lawn chairs under the oak tree, each hidden behind a section of the newspaper; and there was Eugene. He was tall and blond, and he wore glasses.

70 I liked him right away because he sat at the kitchen table and read books for hours. That summer, before we had even spoken one word to each other, I kept him company on my fire escape.

Once school started I looked for him in all my classes, but P.S. 13 was a huge, overpopulated place and it took me days and many discreet questions to discover that Eugene was in honors classes for all his subjects; classes that were not open to me because English was not my first language, though I was a straight A student. After much **maneuvering**, I managed "to run into him" in the hallway where his locker was—on the other side of the building from mine—and in study hall at the library where he first seemed to notice me, but

80 did not speak; and finally, on the way home after school one day when I decided to approach him directly, though my stomach was doing somersaults. **C**

I was ready for rejection, snobbery, the worst. But when I came up to him, practically panting in my nervousness, and blurted out: "You're Eugene. Right?" he smiled, pushed his glasses up on his nose, and nodded. I saw then that he was blushing deeply. Eugene liked me, but he was shy. I did most of the talking that day. He nodded and smiled a lot. In the weeks that followed, we walked home together. He would linger at the corner of El Building for a few minutes then walk down to his two-story house. It was not until Eugene moved into that house that I noticed that El Building blocked most of the sun, and that the only

90 spot that got a little sunlight during the day was the tiny square of earth the old woman had planted with flowers.

I did not tell Eugene that I could see inside his kitchen from my bedroom. I felt dishonest, but I liked my secret sharing of his evenings, especially now that I knew what he was reading since we chose our books together at the school library.

One day my mother came into my room as I was sitting on the windowsill staring out. In her abrupt way she said: "Elena, you are acting 'moony.'" *Enamorada*[5] was what she really said, that is—like a girl stupidly **infatuated**. Since I had turned fourteen . . . , my mother had been more **vigilant** than

100 ever. She acted as if I was going to go crazy or explode or something if she didn't watch me and nag me all the time about being a *señorita*[6] now. She kept talking about virtue, morality, and other subjects that did not interest me in the least. My mother was unhappy in Paterson, but my father had a good job at the bluejeans factory in Passaic[7] and soon, he kept assuring us, we would be moving to our own house there. Every Sunday we drove out to the suburbs of Paterson, Clifton, and Passaic, out to where people mowed grass on Sundays

---

5. *enamorada* (ĕ-nä'mô-rä'dä) *Spanish:* in love.
6. *señorita* (sĕ'nyô-rē'tä) *Spanish:* young lady.
7. *Passaic* (pə-sā'ĭk).

maneuvering
(mə-nōō'vər-ĭng) *n.* an action skillfully designed to achieve a goal
maneuver *v.*

C CHARACTER
In what ways are the narrator and Eugene similar? In what ways do they differ? Explain.

 Targeted Passage

infatuated
(ĭn-făch'ōō-ā'tĭd) *adj.* possessed by an unreasoning love or attraction

vigilant (vĭj'ə-lənt) *adj.* on the alert; watchful

C CHARACTER

Possible answer: Elena and Eugene are both good students (lines 75–77) and both enjoy reading books (lines 43, 70–71). However, Eugene's first language is English, while Elena's is Spanish (line 76). Students might also note that Eugene's family seems to have more money than Elena's, since "Eugene and his family had moved into the only house on the block that had a yard and trees" (lines 40–41), while Elena lives in El Building, a tenement.

If students need help . . . Use a Y Chart to help students identify similarities and differences between Elena and Eugene.

Elena speaks Spanish as her first language and lives in a tenement.

Eugene speaks English and lives in a house with a yard.

Both are good students who enjoy reading books.

BEST PRACTICES TOOLKIT—Transparency Y Chart p. A27

FOR LESS–PROFICIENT READERS

2 Targeted Passage [Lines 77–101]

In this passage, Elena initiates a relationship with Eugene.

- How did Elena think Eugene might react when she approached him?
- Did Eugene react as Elena had expected? Explain your answer.
- Do you agree with Elena's mother that her daughter is "*enamorada*"? Why or why not?

FOR ENGLISH LEARNERS

Vocabulary: Idioms Use New Word Analysis to teach these idioms from the story: *run into* (line 77), "meet"; *my stomach was doing somersaults* (line 81), "I was feeling very nervous"; *moony* (line 97), "dreamy"; *Most of all* (line 123), "especially"; *get close to* (line 233), "develop a relationship with."

 BEST PRACTICES TOOLKIT—Transparency New Word Analysis p. E8

ANALYZE VISUALS

Possible answer: The girl's white dress and the white pages of her book cause the girl and her book to stand out against the colorful background. Like the protagonist in the story, this girl, too, likes to read. In addition, the girl in the painting has an air of loneliness or isolation about her—a feeling that the protagonist of the story shares.

About the Art Armenian artist Simon Samsonian is known for his cubist-impressionist work. The balance and harmony of *Little Girl Reading* are typical of his oil paintings. The girl in this sharply focused portrait brings to mind the narrator of "American History," who likes to sit out on her fire escape in the summer and read library books (lines 42–44).

Little Girl Reading #3 (1973), Simon Samsonian. Oil on canvas, 42″ × 32″. Private collection, New York.

DIFFERENTIATED INSTRUCTION

FOR ENGLISH LEARNERS

Culture: Connect After students have read lines 128–135 on page 881, ask what similarities there may be between Eugene's family and Elena's. Elicit or explain that both families have come from another place and are trying to adjust to new surroundings. Discuss the idea that although many immigrants are happy to be living in a new country and feel that their lives have improved, they may still miss their homeland intensely and have difficulty adjusting to their new home.

in the summer, and where children made snowmen in the winter from pure white snow, not like the gray slush of Paterson which seemed to fall from the sky in that hue. I had learned to listen to my parents' dreams, which were
110 spoken in Spanish, as fairy tales, like the stories about life in the island paradise of Puerto Rico before I was born. I had been to the island once as a little girl, to grandmother's funeral, and all I remembered was wailing women in black, my mother becoming hysterical and being given a pill that made her sleep two days, and me feeling lost in a crowd of strangers all claiming to be my aunts, uncles, and cousins. I had actually been glad to return to the city. We had not been back there since then, though my parents talked constantly about buying a house on the beach someday, retiring on the island—that was a common topic among the residents of El Building. As for me, I was going to go to college and become a teacher. **D**

120 　　But after meeting Eugene I began to think of the present more than of the future. What I wanted now was to enter that house I had watched for so many years. I wanted to see the other rooms where the old people had lived, and where the boy spent his time. Most of all, I wanted to sit at the kitchen table with Eugene like two adults, like the old man and his wife had done, maybe drink some coffee and talk about books. I had started reading *Gone with the Wind*.[8] I was **enthralled** by it, with the daring and the passion of the beautiful girl living in a mansion, and with her devoted parents and the slaves who did everything for them. I didn't believe such a world had ever really existed, and I wanted to ask Eugene some questions since he and his parents, he had told me,
130 had come up from Georgia, the same place where the novel was set. His father worked for a company that had transferred him to Paterson. His mother was very unhappy, Eugene said, in his beautiful voice that rose and fell over words in a strange, lilting way. The kids at school called him "the hick" and made fun of the way he talked. I knew I was his only friend so far, and I liked that, though I felt sad for him sometimes. "Skinny Bones" and the "Hick" was what they called us at school when we were seen together.

　　The day Mr. DePalma came out into the cold and asked us to line up in front of him was the day that President Kennedy was shot. Mr. DePalma, a short, muscular man with slicked-down black hair, was the science teacher, P.E.
140 coach, and disciplinarian at P.S. 13. He was the teacher to whose homeroom you got assigned if you were a troublemaker, and the man called out to break up playground fights, and to escort violently angry teen-agers to the office. And Mr. DePalma was the man who called your parents in for "a conference."

　　That day, he stood in front of two rows of mostly black and Puerto Rican kids, brittle from their efforts to "keep moving" on a November day that was turning bitter cold. Mr. DePalma, to our complete shock, was crying. Not just silent adult tears, but really sobbing. There were a few titters from the back of the line where I stood shivering.

8. ***Gone with the Wind:*** a 1936 novel, written by Margaret Mitchell and set in the South during and immediately after the Civil War.

D AUTHOR'S BACKGROUND
Reread lines 103–119. Think back to what you learned about Cofer in the biography on page 875. What experiences and circumstances from Cofer's life are echoed in Elena's life? Explain.

enthralled (ĕn-thrôld′) *adj.* charmed greatly
enthrall *v.*

3 Targeted Passage

D AUTHOR'S BACKGROUND

Possible answer: Like Cofer, Elena is "a Puerto Rican girl growing up in a mainland U.S. city," having *"moved at a young age to Paterson, New Jersey, where she lived in a large apartment building known . . . as El Building"* (**A Child of Two Cultures,** *p. 875). Cofer's mother continued to feel a strong pull to Puerto Rico and Puerto Rican customs, while her father "pushed her to adopt American ways." This is perhaps echoed in the story by Elena's father's repeated assurances that the family would be moving into their own house in the suburbs (lines 104–105).*

If students need help . . .

- Have them reread **A Child of Two Cultures** (page 875).
- Direct students to list key ideas and details from page 875 that describe Cofer but could also apply to Elena's life.
- Students may also benefit from completing and comparing Cluster Diagrams for Cofer and Elena to help them see similarities.

Extend the Discussion What differences can you find between Cofer's life and family and Elena's?

 BEST PRACTICES TOOLKIT—Transparency Cluster Diagram p. B18

FOR LESS–PROFICIENT READERS
3 Targeted Passage [Lines 125–136]

This passage provides background information about Eugene and his family.

- Where are Eugene and his family from?
- Why did they move to Paterson?
- Why does it sound to Elena that Eugene speaks "in a strange, lilting way"?
- Why do you think the kids call Eugene the "Hick"?

FOR ADVANCED LEARNERS/PRE–AP
Analyze Theme One of the underlying themes of "American History" is the idea of people having hopes and dreams. Have students write a brief essay analyzing this theme in the story. Encourage them to consider the hopes and dreams of Elena and her mother and father as well as those of all of the American people in relation to President Kennedy. Then have them read their essays aloud in class.

E CONNECT

Possible answer: *The students are probably reacting this way because they feel uncomfortable seeing a teacher cry and they don't know how else to react.*

Lines 175–197
DISCUSSION PROMPTS

Use these prompts to help students understand Elena's feelings:

Connect Think about a time when you had conflicting feelings. How does your experience help you understand the way that Elena feels? *Answers should demonstrate an understanding of how conflicting feelings can pull a person in different directions.*

Analyze How does Cofer use descriptive details about Eugene's house to capture the sense of conflict in this scene? *Possible answer: El Building overshadows Eugene's house, casting it in darkness. This foreshadows the resentment or prejudice that Eugene's family may feel toward El Building's occupants.*

Synthesize Why do you think Elena is surprised by her mother's reaction? *Possible answer: Elena is caught up in her own teenage world, unaware of the gravity of the events unfolding around her.*

"Listen," Mr. DePalma raised his arms over his head as if he were about 150 to conduct an orchestra. His voice broke, and he covered his face with his hands. His barrel chest was heaving. Someone giggled behind me.

"Listen," he repeated, "something awful has happened." A strange gurgling came from his throat, and he turned around and spat on the cement behind him.

"Gross," someone said, and there was a lot of laughter. **E**

"The President is dead, you idiots. I should have known that wouldn't mean anything to a bunch of losers like you kids. Go home." He was shrieking now. No one moved for a minute or two, but then a big girl let out a "Yeah!" and ran to get her books piled up with the others against the brick wall of the 160 school building. The others followed in a mad scramble to get to their things before somebody caught on. It was still an hour to the dismissal bell.

A little scared, I headed for El Building. There was an eerie feeling on the streets. I looked into Mario's drugstore, a favorite hangout for the high school crowd, but there were only a couple of old Jewish men at the soda-bar talking with the short order cook in tones that sounded almost angry, but they were keeping their voices low. Even the traffic on one of the busiest intersections in Paterson—Straight Street and Park Avenue—seemed to be moving slower. There were no horns blasting that day. At El Building, the usual little group of unemployed men were not hanging out on the front stoop making it difficult 170 for women to enter the front door. No music spilled out from open doors in the hallway. When I walked into our apartment, I found my mother sitting in front of the grainy picture of the television set.

She looked up at me with a tear-streaked face and just said: "*Dios mio,*"[9] turning back to the set as if it were pulling at her eyes. I went into my room.

Though I wanted to feel the right thing about President Kennedy's death, I could not fight the feeling of elation that stirred in my chest. Today was the day I was to visit Eugene in his house. He had asked me to come over after school to study for an American history test with him. We had also planned to walk to the public library together. I looked down into his yard. The oak tree 180 was bare of leaves and the ground looked gray with ice. The light through the large kitchen window of his house told me that El Building blocked the sun to such an extent that they had to turn lights on in the middle of the day. I felt ashamed about it. But the white kitchen table with the lamp hanging just above it looked cozy and inviting. I would soon sit there, across from Eugene, and I would tell him about my perch just above his house. Maybe I should.

In the next thirty minutes I changed clothes, put on a little pink lipstick, and got my books together. Then I went in to tell my mother that I was going to a friend's house to study. I did not expect her reaction.

"You are going out *today?*" The way she said "today" sounded as if a storm 190 warning had been issued. It was said in utter disbelief. Before I could answer, she came toward me and held my elbows as I clutched my books.

---

9. *Dios mio* (dyōs mē'ō) *Spanish:* my God.

E CONNECT
Reread lines 144–155 and think about how different people receive bad news. Why do you think the students are reacting this way to Mr. DePalma?

DIFFERENTIATED INSTRUCTION

FOR LESS–PROFICIENT READERS
Vocabulary Support Point out the following terms in the story and explain their meanings: *eerie* (line 162), "strange or mysterious"; *short order cook* (line 165), "a cook who prepares food quickly"; *elation* (line 176), "joy, delight."

FOR ENGLISH LEARNERS
Vocabulary: Compound Words Point out some of the compound words in the story, such as *homeroom* (line 140), *troublemaker* (line 141), *playground* (line 142), *drugstore* (line 163), *hangout* (line 163), *soda-bar* (line 164), and *streetlight* (line 252). Ask students to find others. Then have students in home-language groups list examples of similar words in their language and share their meanings with the class.

Rag in Window (1959), Alice Neel. 33″ × 24″. Gift of the Estate of Arthur M. Bullowa 1993.
Courtesy of the Philadelphia Museum of Art.

ANALYZE VISUALS

Activity Ask students in what ways the painting reminds them of the setting of "American History." ***Possible answer:*** *The bleak view brings to mind the tenement in the story, and the snow in the painting suggests the "cold gray day" (line 22) that Elena describes.*

About the Art Although American artist Alice Neel (1900–1984) is best known for her portraits, she also painted street scenes and still lifes. Her realistic style is evident in *Rag in Window,* which shows the cheerless view from her apartment in Spanish Harlem, a view that perhaps suggests what life was like for many of the residents of El Building in the story.

"*Hija,*[10] the President has been killed. We must show respect. He was a great man. Come to church with me tonight."

She tried to embrace me, but my books were in the way. My first impulse was to comfort her, she seemed so **distraught,** but I had to meet Eugene in fifteen minutes.

distraught (dĭ-strôt′) *adj.* deeply upset

"I have a test to study for, Mama. I will be home by eight."

---

10. **hija** (ē′hä) *Spanish:* daughter.

Culture: Clarify Ask Spanish-speaking students to pronounce and explain the meaning of Spanish words in the story, such as *Enamorada* (line 98), *Hija* (line 192), *Niña* (line 198), *Verde-Esperanza* (line 213), and *luto* (line 246).

Discuss What does Elena's mother mean when she says, "You are forgetting who you are, *Niña*" (line 198). Why do you think her tone is "resigned"? ***Possible answer:*** *Elena's mother is aware of the discrimination that her daughter will face. However, she knows that Elena is young and must learn of it herself.*

"You are forgetting who you are, *Niña*.[11] I have seen you staring down at that boy's house. You are heading for humiliation and pain." My mother said this in Spanish and in a **resigned** tone that surprised me, as if she had no intention of stopping me from "heading for humiliation and pain." I started for the door. She sat in front of the TV holding a white handkerchief to her face.

I walked out to the street and around the chainlink fence that separated El Building from Eugene's house. The yard was neatly edged around the little walk that led to the door. It always amazed me how Paterson, the inner core of the city, had no apparent logic to its architecture. Small, neat, single residences like this one could be found right next to huge, **dilapidated** apartment buildings like El Building. My guess was that the little houses had been there first, then the immigrants had come in droves, and the monstrosities had been raised for them—the Italians, the Irish, the Jews, and now us, the Puerto Ricans and the blacks. The door was painted a deep green: *verde,* the color of hope, I had heard my mother say it: *Verde-Esperanza.* I knocked softly. A few suspenseful moments later the door opened just a crack. The red, swollen face of a woman appeared. She had a halo of red hair floating over a delicate ivory face—the face of a doll—with freckles on the nose. Her smudged eye make-up made her look unreal to me, like a mannequin seen through a warped store window.

"What do you want?" Her voice was tiny and sweet-sounding, like a little girl's, but her tone was not friendly.

"I'm Eugene's friend. He asked me over. To study." I thrust out my books, a silly gesture that embarrassed me almost immediately.

"You live there?" She pointed up to El Building, which looked particularly ugly, like a gray prison with its many dirty windows and rusty fire escapes. The woman had stepped halfway out and I could see that she wore a white nurse's uniform with St. Joseph's Hospital on the name tag.

"Yes. I do."

She looked intently at me for a couple of heartbeats, then said as if to herself, "I don't know how you people do it." Then directly to me: "Listen. Honey. Eugene doesn't want to study with you. He is a smart boy. Doesn't need help. You understand me. I am truly sorry if he told you you could come over. He cannot study with you. It's nothing personal. You understand? We won't be in this place much longer, no need for him to get close to people—it'll just make it harder for him later. Run back home now."

I couldn't move. I just stood there in shock at hearing these things said to me in such a honey-drenched voice. I had never heard an accent like hers, except for Eugene's softer version. It was as if she were singing me a little song.

"What's wrong? Didn't you hear what I said?" She seemed very angry, and I finally snapped out of my trance. I turned away from the green door, and heard her close it gently. **F**

11. ***Niña*** (nē'nyä) *Spanish*: little girl.

resigned (rĭ-zīnd') *adj.* marked by acceptance of a condition or action as unavoidable

dilapidated (dĭ-lăp'ĭ-dā'tĭd) *adj.* broken down and shabby

F CONNECT
Reread lines 228–240. Think about how you and people you know react to confrontation. Why does Elena become so entranced with Eugene's mother's voice?

Detail of *Loneliness* (1970), Alice Neel. Oil on canvas, 80" x 38". Gift of Arthur M. Bullowa, in honor of the 50th Anniversary of the National Gallery of Art. Photo by Lyle Peterzell. Image © 2005 Board of Trustees, National Gallery of Art, Washington, D.C.

Activity Ask students how the mood of the painting matches the mood of the story at the end. ***Possible answer:*** *Elena is miserable because of her encounter with Eugene's mother. The sadness and loneliness that she feels match the emptiness of the scene depicted in the painting.*

About the Art *Loneliness* is another still life by American artist Alice Neel (see page 883).

Our apartment was empty when I got home. My mother was in someone else's kitchen, seeking the <u>solace</u> she needed. Father would come in from his late shift at midnight. I would hear them talking softly in the kitchen for hours that night. They would not discuss their dreams for the future, or life in Puerto Rico, as they often did; that night they would talk sadly about the young widow and her two children, as if they were family. For the next few days, we would observe *luto* in our apartment; that is, we would practice restraint and silence—no loud music or laughter. Some of the women of El Building would wear black for weeks. **G**

solace (sŏl'ĭs) *n.* comfort from sorrow or misfortune

250   That night, I lay in my bed trying to feel the right thing for our dead President. But the tears that came up from a deep source inside me were strictly for me. When my mother came to the door, I pretended to be sleeping. Sometime during the night, I saw from my bed the streetlight come on. It had a pink halo around it. I went to my window and pressed my face to the cool glass. Looking up at the light I could see the white snow falling like a lace veil over its face. I did not look down to see it turning gray as it touched the ground below. ❧

G AUTHOR'S BACKGROUND
What **inferences** can you make about Puerto Rico culture from the description of mourning in lines 241–249?

④ Targeted Passage

LITERARY ANALYSIS

G AUTHOR'S BACKGROUND

Possible answer: *Readers can infer that the Puerto Rican culture treats a person's death with great seriousness and respect. They avoid music, laughter, and merriment for a period of time, and some wear black to symbolize mourning.*

SELECTION WRAP–UP

REFLECT   What do you think Elena has learned from her encounter with Eugene's mother?

⭐ **CRITIQUE**   Have students evaluate the ending of the story. Discuss whether the plot was or was not resolved in an effective way.

FOR LESS–PROFICIENT READERS

④ Targeted Passage [Lines 250–257]

This passage concludes the story with Elena in tears, not because of Kennedy's death but as a result of her encounter with Eugene's mother.

- What does Elena mean when she says that she was "trying to feel the right thing for our dead President"?

- Explain what Elena means when she says that her tears "were strictly for [herself]."

FOR ADVANCED LEARNERS/PRE–AP

Analyze Symbolism   Compare lines 105–109 with lines 254–256. Have students discuss the symbolic significance of snow in the story. Ask why Cofer includes in line 255 the specific detail that Elena "did not look down."

Practice and Apply

After Reading

For additional support of post-reading questions, use these copy masters:

R RESOURCE MANAGER—Copy Masters

Reading Check p. 107 (to check understanding of the selection)

Influence of Author's Background p. 99 (for practice of literary analysis standards focus)

Question Support p. 108 (After Reading questions adapted for English learners and less-proficient readers)

For additional questions, see page 93.

ANSWERS

Comprehension

1. *Elena is attracted to Eugene because he likes to read books, as she does. When Elena approaches him, Eugene smiles and blushes; he likes her, but he is shy.*

2. *President Kennedy is assassinated.*

3. *Elena's greatest concern on this day is her study date with Eugene at his house.*

Literary Analysis

Possible answers:

4. *Eugene's mother looks down on Elena as an immigrant who lives in a dilapidated tenement. She points with disdain at El Building, then says "I don't know how you people do it" (line 229). Aside from the fact that Elena is in a lower socioeconomic class, Eugene's mother may be rejecting her because she is Puerto Rican.*

5.

WHO	Is Separated HOW	From WHOM
Elena	• She can't turn rope fast enough. • They call her names. • They jump rope better.	the black girls
	• English is not her first language.	honors classes
	• In honors classes. • He lives in a house; she lives in a tenement. • His mother rejects her.	Eugene

---

After Reading

Comprehension

1. **Recall** What attracts Elena to Eugene? How does he respond to her?

2. **Recall** What world event happens on November 22, 1963?

3. **Summarize** What is Elena's greatest personal concern on this day?

Literary Analysis

4. **Draw Conclusions** What do you think is the real reason that Eugene's mother turns Elena away? Explain why you think as you do.

5. **Understand a Character's Social Context** Elena faces a variety of social barriers. What are these barriers and how are they demonstrated or enforced? Record your answers in a chart like the one shown.

WHO	Is Separated HOW	from WHOM
Elena	• • •	the black girls

6. **Analyze the Influence of the Author's Background** Reread Cofer's biography and Background on page 875. Identify three descriptive passages in the story that refer to events or circumstances that actually occurred in Cofer's life.

7. **Connect Literature to Life Experiences** Refer to the chart you created as you read. Did the connections you made while reading improve your understanding of Elena and her situation? Explain.

8. **Make Judgments** Elena is far more preoccupied with her private loss than with the loss affecting the entire nation. Do you think this is reasonable? Explain why or why not.

Literary Criticism

9. **Historical Context** When President Kennedy died, many Americans felt that their chance to realize the dreams and hopes he had championed, such as racial equality, died with him. Why might Cofer have chosen to set Elena's story on the day of the president's assassination?

---

6. ● **STANDARDS FOCUS** *Influence of Author's Background* Descriptive passages might include lines 1–15, 162–171, 206–212.

7. ■ **STANDARDS FOCUS** *Connect* Students' answers should reflect their understanding of how making personal connections aids understanding of characters and situations.

8. *Students may feel Elena's response is reasonable, because most fourteen-year-olds tend to be self-centered and not involved with current events. Others may feel that Elena's response is not reasonable, because even a fourteen-year-old should react*

more strongly to an event of such obvious magnitude.

Literary Criticism

9. *Possible answer: Cofer might have chosen to set the story on the day of the assassination to draw a parallel between America's loss of hopes and dreams and Elena's loss. This parallel is reinforced by Kennedy's association with racial equality and Eugene's mother's likely rejection of Elena at least in part because of her race.*

Vocabulary in Context

VOCABULARY PRACTICE

Write the letter of the word that is most different in meaning from the others.

1. (a) spellbound, (b) enthralled, (c) considerate, (d) thrilled
2. (a) cowardly, (b) watchful, (c) observant, (d) vigilant
3. (a) muted, (b) noisy, (c) deafening, (d) boisterous
4. (a) consolation, (b) solace, (c) depression, (d) sympathy
5. (a) rejecting, (b) jockeying, (c) maneuvering, (d) strategizing
6. (a) hierarchy, (b) order, (c) religion, (d) classification
7. (a) perplexed, (b) infatuated, (c) surprised, (d) confounded
8. (a) fired, (b) accepting, (c) resigned, (d) submissive
9. (a) enlivened, (b) entertained, (c) amused, (d) distraught
10. (a) dilapidated, (b) antique, (c) decaying, (d) neglected

WORD LIST

dilapidated
distraught
enthralled
hierarchy
infatuated
maneuvering
muted
resigned
solace
vigilant

VOCABULARY IN WRITING

Two different responses to Kennedy's death are described in this story. Using three or more vocabulary words, write a paragraph describing these responses.

> **EXAMPLE SENTENCE**
>
> *Many in Elena's community were **distraught** at the president's death. . . .*

VOCABULARY STRATEGY: IDIOMS

An idiom is a phrase whose overall meaning is different from the grammatical or logical meaning of its individual parts. For example, the narrator of this story says, "That summer, . . . I kept him company on my fire escape." "Kept him company" is an idiomatic expression.

If you run into an unfamiliar idiom, you can often use context clues to figure out its meaning. Otherwise, consult a dictionary. Many dictionaries list idioms at the end of the entry for the main word in the idiom. So *kept him company* would be explained under *keep*, as part of a list like this:

> —*idioms:* **for keeps** To hold indefinitely: *He gave me the book for keeps.* **keep an eye on** To watch over attentively. **keep (someone) company** To accompany or stay with.

PRACTICE Identify the idiom in each sentence and write a definition of it. Use context clues or a dictionary.

1. Your advice flies in the face of good sense.
2. Her shoe fell off, so she finished her dance routine on a wing and a prayer.
3. No one will follow those rules unless you put some teeth into them.
4. Winning this contract will really put him on the map in our community.

> **VOCABULARY PRACTICE**
> For more practice, go to the **Vocabulary Center** at ClassZone.com.

ANSWERS

Vocabulary in Context

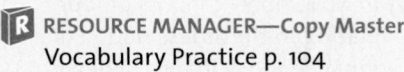

VOCABULARY PRACTICE

1. *c*	6. *c*
2. *a*	7. *b*
3. *a*	8. *a*
4. *c*	9. *d*
5. *a*	10. *b*

R RESOURCE MANAGER—Copy Master
Vocabulary Practice p. 104

VOCABULARY IN WRITING

Encourage students to plan their paragraph before beginning to write. Suggest that they focus on one response at a time, rather than trying to describe both at once. Review with students words and phrases used to signal contrast, such as *but, however,* and *on the other hand.*

VOCABULARY STRATEGY: IDIOMS *(also an EL language objective)*

Elicit additional examples of familiar idioms. Have students define them and use them in sentences.

Possible answers:

1. *flies in the face of,* "goes against"
2. *on a wing and a prayer,* "as best she could"
3. *put some teeth into,* "enforce"
4. *put him on the map,* "make him known"

R RESOURCE MANAGER—Copy Master
Vocabulary Strategy p. 105

i Vocabulary Center at **ClassZone.com**
Additional Vocabulary Activities

Assess and Reteach

Assess

R RESOURCE MANAGER—Copy Masters
Selection Test A pp. 109–110
Selection Test B/C pp. 111–112

Test Generator CD

Reteach

S STANDARDS LESSON FILE
Literature Lesson 47: Author's Perspective
Vocabulary Lesson 22: Idioms

DIFFERENTIATED INSTRUCTION

FOR LESS–PROFICIENT READERS

Vocabulary Practice To build students' comprehension, elicit or explain the meaning of each correct word choice (that is, the word most different in meaning from the others), and then have students use the word in a sentence. Expand the activity by exploring how synonyms in the practice set have similar, but not identical, meanings.

FOR ADVANCED LEARNERS/PRE–AP

Vocabulary in Writing Challenge students to use at least four vocabulary words in a paragraph written about Elena from Eugene's point of view.

Focus and Motivate

OBJECTIVES

Reading for Information

- synthesize
- summarize information from multiple texts
- identify main ideas
- read a newspaper article, diary entry, magazine article, and political cartoon

SUMMARY

"Four Days in November" consists of four selections relating to the assassination of President John F. Kennedy in 1963: a news article reporting the event; a diary entry recounting the event from Lady Bird Johnson's point of view; a magazine article written on the 40th anniversary of Kennedy's death; and a political cartoon reacting to the assassination.

What's the Connection?

Use a KWL chart to prepare students for the four selections. In the first column, have students note what they know (K) about John F. Kennedy and his assassination. In the second column, have them write questions about what they want to know (W). After reading, have students use the third column to record what they have learned (L).

 BEST PRACTICES TOOLKIT—Transparency KWL p. A21

Teach

Skill Focus: Synthesize

As you discuss the benefits that can come from reading different texts on the same topic, explain that readers need to know the genre of each information source and consider its content accordingly. For example, a newspaper article will provide an objective account of events, whereas a diary entry will include the writer's personal perceptions and opinions.

 RESOURCE MANAGER—Copy Master Synthesize p. 121

Reading for Information

Four Days in November

- Newspaper Article, page 889
- Diary Entry, page 890
- Magazine Article, page 891
- Political Cartoon, page 892

Use with "American History," page 876.

What's the Connection?

"American History" takes place on the day that President John F. Kennedy was killed. The nonfiction selections you are about to read will add to your sense of how that tragic event affected those close to the president and the nation at large.

Skill Focus: Synthesize

When you read different texts on the same topic, you **synthesize** information—that is, you put together the facts, ideas, and details you get from each of them. As a result, you gain a fuller understanding of the topic than you would get if you relied on only one text.

Here's how to synthesize the information from the pieces about President Kennedy's assassination:

- Summarize the main ideas in each selection.
- Jot down any questions that occur to you as you read a selection; look for answers to those questions in other selections.
- Ask yourself why certain information might appear in one selection but not another.
- Reread the selections to answer your questions and fill in gaps in your understanding.

For more help synthesizing, complete a chart like the one started here as you read the selections that follow. Begin by writing down any questions "American History" raised for you.

Source	Main Ideas	Questions & New Information
"American History"	Everybody is sad that the president is dead, but Elena winds up feeling bad for her own personal reasons.	Did students really get dismissed early from school? Did teachers cry?
"President Dead"	The president was killed by a sniper on the afternoon of November 22, 1963. Governor Connally was also shot.	Did Gov. Connally live? Did the president get to say anything to his wife before he died?

Selection Resources

 RESOURCE MANAGER UNIT 9

Plan and Teach pp. 113–117

Reading
Summary pp. 119†*, 120‡*
Synthesize pp. 121, 123†*
Reading Check p. 125
Summarize Information from Multiple Sources pp. 122, 124†*
Question Support p. 126*

Assessment
Selection Tests A, B/C pp. 127*, 129*
 Test Generator CD

Reading Support
 Audio Anthology CD*

BEST PRACTICES TOOLKIT
KWL • Reciprocal Teaching • Think-Pair-Share

---

* Resources for Differentiation   † Also in Spanish   ‡ In Haitian Creole and Vietnamese

THE DALLAS TIMES HERALD FINAL EDITION

CONTINUOUSLY PUBLISHED FOR 87 YEARS   THE TIMES 1876   THE HERALD 1886   CONSOLIDATED 1898

87th year—No. 292   ★★ DALLAS, TEXAS, FRIDAY EVENING, NOVEMBER 22, 1963   3 PARTS   PRICE FIVE CENTS

PRESIDENT DEAD

Connally Also Hit by Sniper

President Kennedy greets supporters upon his arrival in Forth Worth.

BY GEORGE CARTER

President Kennedy died of assassin's bullets in Dallas Friday afternoon.

The President and Gov. John Connally were ambushed as they drove in the President's open convertible in a downtown motorcade.

Two priests announced shortly before 1:30 that the President was dead.

Bullets apparently came from a high-powered rifle in a building at Houston and Elm.

A man was arrested and taken to the sheriff's office.

The President immediately clutched his chest and slumped into the arms of his wife. Gov. Connally, apparently shot in the chest, fell to the floor under his wife's feet.

Secret service agents immediately dispatched the motorcade at high speed to Parkland Hospital.

Gov. Connally was reported in critical condition.

Witnesses standing on a balcony at the courthouse gave this account of what they saw:

The motorcade had just turned into Houston Street from Main Street when a shot rang out. Pigeons flew up from the street. Then, two more shots rang out and Mr. Kennedy fell to the floor of the car.

READING FOR INFORMATION   **889**

A SYNTHESIZE
The following news article appeared in the day's final edition of the *Dallas Times Herald*. As you read, think about the information it supplies that you didn't already know.

B SYNTHESIZE
News articles often begin by answering the questions *who, what, where, when,* and *how.* Which of those questions are answered at the start of this article? Record any unanswered questions on your chart.

INFORMATIONAL ANALYSIS

A SYNTHESIZE

Ask students about how much time passed between Kennedy's death and publication of this article. Also discuss what key fact the article does not contain and possible reasons why. **Possible answer:** *Only a few hours had passed since Kennedy's death. The article does not give the name of the suspected assassin, perhaps because authorities had not yet positively identified him.*

If students need help . . .

- Direct their attention to the parts of the masthead that identify the date and edition.
- Remind students that they already know from "American History" that November 22, 1963, was the day on which Kennedy died. Elicit or explain that *final edition* means that this is the last edition published that same day.

INFORMATIONAL ANALYSIS

B SYNTHESIZE

Possible answer: *The questions answered are* who (President Kennedy, Governor Connally; lines 3–4); *what* (shot by assassin, with Kennedy killed; lines 1–6); *where* (Dallas; line 2); *when* (Friday afternoon; line 2); *and* how (high-powered rifle; line 10). *The unanswered question is* why, *but it is possible that there are additional answers to the other questions.*

DIFFERENTIATED INSTRUCTION

FOR LESS–PROFICIENT READERS

Options for Reading Use Reciprocal Teaching with small groups of students, especially for the diary entry and magazine article. In each group, the leader reads a paragraph or two aloud, asks questions about events in the text, and asks another group member to summarize. Before moving on, the leader also asks if clarification is needed and works to clarify.

BEST PRACTICES TOOLKIT—Transparency
Reciprocal Teaching p. A35

FOR ADVANCED LEARNERS/PRE–AP

Compare and Contrast Reports [paired-activity option] News of Kennedy's death sped around the world through radio, TV, and newspapers. Seven presidents before him also died in office. Have students find out who they were and how they died. Then ask students to choose one of those presidents and locate information about how (and how quickly) news of his death spread. Have students share the

information, comparing it to what they know about the reporting of Kennedy's death.

A White House Diary

by Lady Bird Johnson C

DALLAS **Friday, November 22, 1963**

It all began so beautifully. After a drizzle in the morning, the sun came out bright and clear. We were driving into Dallas. In the lead car were President and Mrs. Kennedy, John and Nellie Connally, a Secret Service car full of men, and then our car with Lyndon and me and Senator Ralph Yarborough.

The streets were lined with people—
10 lots and lots of people—the children all smiling, placards, confetti, people waving from windows. . . .

Then, almost at the edge of town, on our way to the Trade Mart for the Presidential luncheon, we were rounding a curve, going down a hill, and suddenly there was a sharp, loud report. It sounded like a shot. The sound seemed to me to come from a
20 building on the right above my shoulder. A moment passed, and then two more shots rang out in rapid succession. There had been such a gala air about the day that I thought the noise must come from firecrackers—part of the celebration. Then the Secret Service men were suddenly down in the lead car. Over the car radio system, I heard "Let's get out of here!" and our
30 Secret Service man, Rufus Youngblood, vaulted over the front seat on top of Lyndon, threw him to the floor, and said, "Get down."

Senator Yarborough and I ducked our heads. The car accelerated terrifically—faster and faster. Then, suddenly, the brakes were put on so hard that I wondered if we were going to make it as we wheeled left and went
40 around the corner. We pulled up to a building. I looked up and saw a sign, "HOSPITAL." Only then did I believe that this might be what it was. Senator Yarborough kept saying in an excited voice, "Have they shot the President? Have they shot the President?" I said something like, "No, it can't be."

As we ground to a halt—we were still the third car—Secret Service men
50 began to pull, lead, guide, and hustle us out. I cast one look over my shoulder and saw in the President's car a bundle of pink, just like a drift of blossoms, lying on the back seat. It was Mrs. Kennedy lying over the President's body. D

The Secret Service men rushed us to the right, then to the left, and then onward into a quiet room in the
60 hospital—a very small room. It was lined with white sheets, I believe. . . .

[The Secret Service] began to lead me up one corridor and down another. Suddenly I found myself face to face with Jackie in a small hallway. . . . I don't think I ever saw anyone so much alone in my life. I went up to her, put my arms around her, and said . . . something like "God, help us all.". . .
70 I turned and went back to the small white room where Lyndon was. Mac Kilduff, the President's press man on this trip, and Kenny O'Donnell were coming and going. I think it was from Kenny's face that I first knew the truth and from Kenny's voice that I first heard the words "The President is dead." Mr. Kilduff entered and said to Lyndon, "Mr. President."

Special Report

BY KENNETH T. WALSH

NOVEMBER 24, 2003

In the days immediately after 9/11, Americans in large numbers showed up at the John F. Kennedy Library and Museum in Boston, apparently looking for strength and hope at a time of national peril and sorrow. They were drawn in particular to a film recounting the Cuban missile crisis, when Kennedy guided the nation
10 through a confrontation with the Soviet Union that could easily have led to nuclear war. Many visitors seemed comforted by the idea that prudent leadership and common sense could make all the difference, even in the worst of times. **F**

The fact that Kennedy still has such a hold on America's imagination comes as no surprise to historians and other
20 observers of popular culture. This connection will become even more apparent in the coming weeks as the nation marks the 40th anniversary of his assassination, on Nov. 22, 1963.

Yet the reasons for his mystique are less clear. The fact that he was assassinated in the prime of life goes only so far in explaining it. President William McKinley, another popular
30 leader, was murdered in 1901, but his death generated no vast outpouring of emotion and no enduring sense of a lost legacy. In contrast, millions of Americans still recall where they were when they heard that Kennedy had

been shot. (I was attending history class at St. Rose High School in Belmar, N.J., when the principal came on the public-address system and,
40 choking back tears, told us what had happened. Everyone marched to our nearby church, and we spent the next few hours praying for the president's survival and, a bit later, his soul.) **G**

We all seem to have vivid memories of his funeral, carried on live television, with those unforgettable images of his grieving widow and his young son saluting smartly when his father's
50 cortege passed by.

"Kennedy is frozen in our memory at age 46," says historian Robert Dallek, author of *An Unfinished Life: John F. Kennedy 1917–1963.* "People don't realize that this past May 29 he would have been 86 years of age."

Some deft PR by the White House helped to create his charismatic aura in the first place. He and his advisers
60 quickly grasped the power of the new medium of television, and the handsome, eloquent young leader quickly mastered it and went on to convey an image of optimism and charm that still surrounds him today. His performances at live press conferences are remembered as tours de force. His speeches are used as brilliant examples of political
70 communication. And if his legislative

E SYNTHESIZE
On the 40th anniversary of Kennedy's assassination, *U.S. News & World Report* featured this special report. As you read, consider what this perspective adds to your understanding of Kennedy and his tragic death.

F SYNTHESIZE
Summarize the main ideas and details in lines 1–16.

G SYNTHESIZE
Reread the first sentence of the third paragraph. What does this **topic sentence** suggest about Walsh's focus for the rest of the article? Turn that sentence into a question and read on to find an answer.

INFORMATIONAL ANALYSIS

E SYNTHESIZE

After students have read the article, ask how the passage of time enables Walsh to offer new insights into Kennedy's time in office and into his legacy. *Possible answer: Walsh can see Kennedy from a historical perspective. He recognizes, for example, that "Kennedy governed prior to the age of cynicism" that followed his presidency (lines 111–116).*

INFORMATIONAL ANALYSIS

F SYNTHESIZE

Possible answer: After September 11, 2001, Americans came to the John F. Kennedy Library and Museum, hoping for inspiration. They saw Kennedy's leadership during the Cuban missile crisis as a sign of strength during national trauma.

INFORMATIONAL ANALYSIS

G SYNTHESIZE

Possible answer: The sentence suggests that Walsh will focus on exploring the reasons for the Kennedy "mystique." The sentence might be posed as this question: Why did a mystique develop around John F. Kennedy?

FOR LESS–PROFICIENT READERS

Vocabulary Support Have students use a Think-Pair-Share activity to explore the meaning of these words and phrases using context clues and, as needed, a dictionary: *confrontation* (line 10), *prudent* (line 13), *mystique* (line 25), *prime of life* (line 27), *legacy* (line 33), *cortege* (line 50), *deft* (line 57), *charismatic aura* (line 58), *eloquent* (line 62), *tours de force* (lines 67–68).

🧰 **BEST PRACTICES TOOLKIT—Transparency**
Think-Pair-Share p. A18

FOR ADVANCED LEARNERS/PRE–AP

Analyze a Symbol [small-group option]
In the first paragraph of this article, Walsh presents the Cuban missile crisis as a symbol of national stress and presidential leadership. Have students research the Cuban missile crisis, which occurred when the United States learned in 1962 that the Soviet Union planned to install ballistic missiles in Cuba. Ask students to report on the crisis and its resolution and to offer insights on the symbolic importance of the event.

record fell short, his ideas about ending the Cold War and achieving racial equality at home, at least under the law, eventually took root and became reality.

Further, his glamorous wife, Jacqueline, reinforced the exciting image of Camelot, especially in contrast to his solid but dull
80 predecessor, Dwight Eisenhower. Ike had been the oldest man to serve as president up until that time; Kennedy was the youngest ever elected to the office. The White House never let anyone forget it.

"One of the things President Kennedy did was instill in the American people the idea they could make a difference," says Deborah Leff,
90 director of the Kennedy Library and Museum. ". . . It was a time when you saw America striving to be its best."

For his part, Kennedy said in one of his famous speeches, at American University on June 10, 1963: "No problem of human destiny is beyond human beings. Man's reason and spirit have often solved the seemingly unsolvable—and we believe they can
100 do it again."

The tragic Kennedy mythology was reinforced when his brother Robert was assassinated in 1968 and, later, when his son, John F. Kennedy Jr., died in a plane crash in 1999. All of this perpetuated the idea that the Kennedys, despite all their advantages, were not immune from life's calamities. This deepened their connection to the
110 rest of us.

Yet Kennedy governed prior to the age of cynicism brought on by the Vietnam War, the Watergate scandal,

H **SYNTHESIZE**
What is the cartoonist suggesting about the connection between Presidents Lincoln and Kennedy? If you can't answer the question, record it in your chart and consider reading further to find an answer.

and the wrenching social changes of the past four decades (including, of course, his own assassination). Perhaps not even Kennedy could have emerged from this era unscathed had he lived and remained in public life.

120 "The sudden end to Kennedy's life and presidency has left us with tantalizing 'might have beens,'" Dallek writes. "Yet even setting these aside and acknowledging some missed opportunities and false steps, it must be acknowledged that the Kennedy thousand days spoke to the country's better angels, inspired visions of a less divisive nation and world, and
130 demonstrated that America was still the last best hope of mankind." It is a legacy any president would be proud of.

H

This famous cartoon by Bill Mauldin appeared in the *Chicago Sun-Times* the day after Kennedy was assassinated.

DIFFERENTIATED INSTRUCTION

FOR LESS–PROFICIENT READERS

Vocabulary Support Have students work in small groups to define these words and phrases and then use them in sentences: *predecessor* (line 80), *instill* (line 87), *perpetuated* (line 106), *calamities* (line 108), *cynicism* (line 112), *unscathed* (line 118), *tantalizing* (line 122), *"might have beens"* (line 122), *false steps* (line 125), *better angels* (line 128).

FOR ENGLISH LEARNERS

Vocabulary: Idioms Have students work in pairs to write a sentence for each of these idioms: *make all the difference* (line 15), "bring about a good result"; *has . . . a hold on* (lines 17–18), "is able to retain influence over"; *goes only so far* (lines 27–28), "does not completely"; *took root* (line 74), "became accepted"; *For his part* (line 93), "as far as he was concerned."

Comprehension

1. **Recall** What facts do you learn from "President Dead" that you did not learn from the short story "American History"?

2. **Recall** What was Mrs. Johnson's reaction to these events?

3. **Summarize** According to Kenneth Walsh, why did so many Americans show up at the John F. Kennedy Library and Museum in Boston in the days immediately after September 11, 2001?

Critical Analysis

4. **Synthesize** What does the political cartoon add to your understanding of how Kennedy's loss affected the nation? Explain.

5. **Evaluate** Which of the selections you just read do you think is the best source of information about the assassination of President Kennedy? Explain.

Read for Information: Summarize Information from Multiple Sources

WRITING PROMPT

On the basis of the information in the selections you just read, describe the emotional impact of John F. Kennedy's assassination on the people of the United States.

To answer this prompt, you will first need to synthesize information on this topic. Then you will need to summarize that information. Following these steps can help:

1. Review your chart to identify any main ideas that have to do with people's emotional reactions to the assassination.

2. Reread the selections with the prompt in mind. Record any direct statements or facts that add to your understanding of the topic.

3. Study the information you have compiled, looking for similarities in people's reactions as well as the range of those reactions.

4. Summarize the emotional impact of this event on the nation.

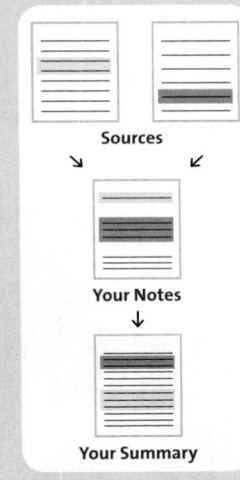

Sources

↓   ↙

Your Notes

↓

Your Summary

Practice and Apply

For additional support of post-reading questions, use these copy masters:

RESOURCE MANAGER—Copy Masters
Reading Check p. 125
Question Support p. 126
Summarize Information from Multiple Sources p. 122

For additional questions, see page 116.

ANSWERS

Comprehension

1. *The reader learns where and how the assassination occurred and that Governor Connally also was shot.*

2. *Mrs. Johnson was shocked, confused, and deeply saddened.*

3. *Americans were seeking comfort by recalling Kennedy's optimism and his leadership during the Cuban missile crisis.*

Critical Analysis
Possible answers:

4. ■ **STANDARDS FOCUS** *Synthesize The cartoon suggests that the assassination was not only a historic event but also a symbolic one—an event that united Americans but that did so through tragedy.*

5. *Students should recognize that the sources provide different kinds of information.*

Read for Information

Writing Prompt *Possible answer: The Kennedy assassination was a huge emotional blow to the people of the United States. Kennedy had symbolized energy and optimism; the fact that he was taken so suddenly left Americans longing for leadership and inspiration.*

Assess and Reteach

Assess

RESOURCE MANAGER—Copy Masters
Selection Tests A, B/C pp. 127, 129

Test Generator CD

Reteach

STANDARDS LESSON FILE
Reading Lesson 14: Synthesizing Information

Study Skills Lesson 13: Summarizing

FOR LESS—PROFICIENT WRITERS
Read for Information

- Encourage students to start by summarizing the emotional impact in a clearly written topic sentence. Explain that they can revise their sentences as they develop their responses, but writing the topic sentence first will help them focus on relevant information as they review the selections.

- Remind students to support their topic sentences with evidence from the selections.

FOR ADVANCED LEARNERS/PRE–AP
Read for Information Have students integrate information from at least one additional outside source in their written responses to the writing prompt. As volunteers share their work with the class, have them describe the additional source and explain how it added to their understanding.

Focus and Motivate

OBJECTIVES

Literary Analysis
- explore the key idea of **heritage**
- analyze Harlem Renaissance literature

Reading
- read poetry for understanding
- read a magazine article

SUMMARIES

The speaker of **"The Tropics in New York"** describes a display of fruits and other tropical goods in a New York store window. These sights inspire vivid memories of another place and make the speaker long for home.

In **"Theme for English B,"** the speaker explores a writing assignment given by a college professor. By pondering self-identity and the idea of truth, the speaker reveals intimate details of what his life is like as an African American in the early 1900s.

How does HERITAGE *shape identity?*

Introduce the question, and have students read the *KEY IDEA.* Then, discuss with students some of the things that comprise one's **heritage,** such as one's ethnicity, family traditions, religious practices, and belief systems. Encourage them to consider these aspects of their own heritages as they complete the *QUICKWRITE.*

Selection Resources

The Tropics in New York
Poem by Claude McKay

Theme for English B
Poem by Langston Hughes

How does HERITAGE *shape identity?*

KEY IDEA Your identity is certainly shaped by your personal experiences, but your **heritage** also has something to do with it. No matter who you are, your family and the culture in which you grew up shaped the person you are today, as well as the person you will be in the future. In the poems "The Tropics in New York" and "Theme for English B," two African-American writers explore and celebrate the importance of their heritage.

QUICKWRITE What is your heritage, and how important has it been in shaping your identity? Jot down your thoughts, and then write a paragraph describing how your heritage has influenced who you are.

894

 **RESOURCE MANAGER UNIT 9**

Plan and Teach pp. 131–138

Literary Analysis
Harlem Renaissance Literature
   pp. 139, 140†*
Question Support p. 143*

Reading
Reading Poetry pp. 141, 142†*
Reading Fluency p. 144

Assessment
Selection Tests A, B/C pp. 145*, 147*
 Test Generator CD

 **BEST PRACTICES TOOLKIT**

Differentiated Instruction
   pp. 31–38*

Graphic Organizers/Strategies
Read Aloud • Analysis Frame:
Poetic Form and Structure

Reading Support
  Audio Anthology CD*

Technology
  Literature Center at
   ClassZone.com
  Write*Smart* CD

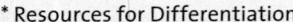 * Resources for Differentiation   † In Spanish

LITERARY ANALYSIS: HARLEM RENAISSANCE LITERATURE

In the early 1920s, a literary movement known as the **Harlem Renaissance** took root in the New York City neighborhood known as Harlem. African-American writers, artists, and musicians created works that expressed their own heritage, style, and voice rather than mimicking the style and voice of white culture.

Claude McKay and Langston Hughes were key writers in this movement. Both poets were concerned with the social issues facing African Americans. McKay, who grew up on the tropical island of Jamaica, wrote poetry that reflected the lush landscape and the rhythms of life on the island. Langston Hughes experimented with bringing the rhythms of blues and jazz music into his poetry. As you read these poems, note the following:

- images that are unique to the cultural background of the writer
- ideas or cultural experiences that are expressed through the speaker
- words or cultural ideas that are unique to the time period

READING STRATEGY: READING POETRY

Rhythm and melody play an important role in most poetry, including the poetry of the Harlem Renaissance. In fact, you can find in these poems sounds and rhythms that continue to occur in contemporary African-American poetic forms. After reading each poem silently, read the poems aloud. Notice the rhythms created by the words as well as the sounds of the words in combination. Jot down examples of **sound devices,** such as alliteration, assonance, repetition, and rhyme.

"The Tropics in New York"	
Example	Type of Sound Device
"dewy dawns"	alliteration

Author Online

Claude McKay: From Rural Jamaican to World Traveler The 11th child of peasant farmers, Claude McKay was born and raised in Jamaica. By the time he came to the United States in 1912 to attend college, he had published two volumes of verse in Jamaican dialect. He moved to New York in 1914, and by the early 1920s he had emerged as one of the first inspirational voices of the Harlem Renaissance movement. McKay lived and traveled widely as a poet, novelist, and journalist.

Claude McKay
1889–1948

Langston Hughes: Spokesman for the Common People Born in Joplin, Missouri, Langston Hughes moved often during his youth and grew up in various Midwestern cities. Like Claude McKay, Hughes became a world traveler, but he lived in New York's Harlem neighborhood at several points in his life. He was deeply influenced by the sights and sounds of Harlem and played a key role in the Harlem Renaissance. Hughes's poetry focuses on the experiences of ordinary black people in America and reflects his love of blues and jazz music.

Langston Hughes
1902–1967

 MORE ABOUT THE AUTHOR For more on Claude McKay and Langston Hughes, visit the **Literature Center** at **ClassZone.com.**

895

Teach

STANDARDS FOCUS

LITERARY ANALYSIS

● HARLEM RENAISSANCE LITERATURE

After students read the page, ask them what the common elements are in Claude McKay's and Langston Hughes's lives. Ask how these elements relate to Harlem Renaissance literature. *Possible answer: Both men are African American. Both men lived in Harlem, New York, at some time in their lives. Harlem is where the largely African-American Harlem Renaissance movement began.*

CHECK UNDERSTANDING What ideas about culture do you expect to read in the poems of McKay and Hughes?

READING STRATEGY

■ READING POETRY

For instructional support, write these lines on the board:

> Before we leave, we'll feast with ease.
> Feasting on fat fishes,
> Splayed on Grandma's special dishes.

Read the lines aloud, emphasizing rhythm, rhyme, and other sound devices. Then, ask students to identify the sound devices in the lines. *Possible answer: Alliteration— Feasting/fat/fishes; Assonance—we/leave/ feast/ease; Rhyme—fishes/dishes*

CHECK UNDERSTANDING Invite several volunteers to read the lines aloud.

R RESOURCE MANAGER—Copy Master Reading Poetry p. 141 (for student use while reading the selections)

DIFFERENTIATED INSTRUCTION

FOR LESS-PROFICIENT READERS

Concept Support Review the meanings of the skill words discussed under **Reading Poetry.** Explain that *alliteration* refers to repeated use of a similar consonant sound. *Assonance* refers to repeated use of a similar vowel sound. Confirm that students can recognize rhyme when they hear it.

BACKGROUND

Claude McKay immigrated to the United States from Jamaica, an island nation in the West Indies section of the Caribbean Sea. The island population features a majority of people descended from enslaved Africans brought by European traders. In addition, people of Spanish, French, and English descent live on Jamaica. Once colonized by Great Britain, Jamaica gained independence in 1962. This colonial heritage leaves most Jamaicans speaking English. Many also speak Creole—a blend of French, Spanish, and West African languages. The culture blends these several influences.

READING STRATEGY

READING POETRY

Possible answer: The word and *is repeated in a way that emphasizes the rhythm of the poem.*

If students need help . . . Read the first stanza aloud for students, using your voice to emphasize the word *and*. Repeat, having students read aloud with you.

REINFORCE *KEY IDEA:* HERITAGE

Discuss What aspects of the speaker's **heritage** does he reveal in the poem? How do you know that these things reflect his heritage? *Possible answer: The speaker reveals physical characteristics of his homeland in the poem. He uses the word* memories *to illustrate that the poem's images are not something that he is currently experiencing. He continues to explain that these memories make him "hungry for the old, familiar ways" (line 11), a phrase that further suggests one's heritage.*

The Tropics in New York
CLAUDE McKAY

Bananas ripe and green, and ginger-root,
    Cocoa in pods and alligator pears,
And tangerines and mangoes and grape fruit,
    Fit for the highest prize at parish fairs,

5 Set in the window, bringing memories
    Of fruit-trees laden by low-singing rills,
And dewy dawns, and mystical blue skies
    In benediction over nun-like hills.

My eyes grow dim, and I could no more gaze;
10   A wave of longing through my body swept,
And, hungry for the old, familiar ways,
    I turned aside and bowed my head and wept.

A READING POETRY
Reread lines 1–4 aloud. What word is repeated in a way that emphasizes the rhythm?

896   UNIT 9: HISTORY, CULTURE, AND THE AUTHOR

DIFFERENTIATED INSTRUCTION

For general guidelines on differentiating instruction, see

📦 BEST PRACTICES TOOLKIT
   Differentiated Instruction pp. 31–38

FOR LESS–PROFICIENT READERS

Options for Reading Read aloud "The Tropics in New York," vocally emphasizing the poem's rhythm and melody. Then, draw students' attention to the end rhymes in the first stanza. Point out that such repetitive rhymes help to establish a strong rhythm in a poem. Using the Read Aloud strategy, guide students in performing an echo reading of the poem by reading aloud a few lines at a time and having students repeat the lines with the same intonation and rhythm.

📦 BEST PRACTICES TOOLKIT—Transparency
   Read Aloud p. A34

897

Activity Ask students to identify elements of the art that reflect their ideas about "the tropics." *Possible answer: The bold colors in the painting reflect the vivid colors associated with places like the Caribbean Islands, where jewel-toned waters meet sandy, white beaches peppered with lush, green trees. The bright colors also lend the idea of ripeness to the illustrated fruits.*

About the Art *Tropical Fruit* was created by Barbara Maslen and features fruits often found in the tropics: citrus, kiwi, and papaya.

DISCUSSION PROMPTS

Use these prompts to help students connect their experiences to those described in the poem:

Connect What ideas, images, sights, or smells do you associate with your hometown? What might you see or experience in another place that would remind you of the place you live now? *Students' answers will vary.*

Analyze What kind of memories might the fruit be calling up for the speaker? *Possible answer: The fruit most likely reminds the speaker of his homeland and "old, familiar ways" (line 11).*

Evaluate In the beginning of the poem, the speaker is looking at fruit in a store window. At the end, he is weeping. Is it plausible that such a reaction would occur in real life, or has it been dramatized for literary purposes? *Possible answer: A person's reaction to an object that brings back strong memories could be very intense. It is entirely possible that the sight of a banana could bring a person to tears if it recalled a happier time.*

FOR LESS–PROFICIENT READERS

Vocabulary Support Explain the following terms from the poem:

- *parish fairs* (line 4), fairs or festivals, held by a religious community to help raise money for its church.
- *laden* (line 6), loaded with a heavy burden
- *rills* (line 6), small streams or creeks
- *mystical* (line 7), spiritual; magical
- *benediction* line 8, an act of blessing

Language Support Have students work in pairs to identify nouns and their modifiers in the poem. They can complete a chart like this one:

Nouns	Modifiers
bananas	ripe, green

Tell students that not all nouns will have a modifier and that some may have more than one. Point out that vivid nouns and modifiers help poets create strong images.

897

Lines 1–20, 25–28
REINFORCE *KEY IDEA:* HERITAGE

Discuss What aspects of the speaker's heritage does he reveal in the poem? How does the speaker feel about his heritage? *Possible answer: The speaker shares that he is an African American and that he was born in North Carolina. He also reveals that living in Harlem (specifically) and New York (in general) has been influential for him. At some points in the poem, the speaker seems to have a matter-of-fact attitude about his heritage; at other points, he seems to express pride in it.*

LITERARY ANALYSIS

Ⓑ HARLEM RENAISSANCE

Possible answer: In lines 6–15, we learn that the speaker is 22 years old, African American, and was born in Winston-Salem, North Carolina. We also learn that the speaker went to school in Winston-Salem, then in Durham, North Carolina, and then at Columbia University in New York City. The speaker is the only African-American student in the class. The speaker lives at the Harlem Branch YMCA.

Theme for
English B
Langston Hughes

The instructor said,

   Go home and write
   a page tonight.
   And let that page come out of you—
5   Then, it will be true.

I wonder if it's that simple?
I am twenty-two, colored, born in Winston-Salem.
I went to school there, then Durham,[1] then here
to this college on the hill above Harlem.[2]
10 I am the only colored student in my class.
The steps from the hill lead down into Harlem,
through a park, then I cross St. Nicholas,
Eighth Avenue, Seventh, and I come to the Y,
the Harlem Branch Y, where I take the elevator
15 up to my room, sit down, and write this page: Ⓑ

It's not easy to know what is true for you or me
at twenty-two, my age. But I guess I'm what
I feel and see and hear. Harlem, I hear you:
hear you, hear me—we two—you, me talk on this page.
20 (I hear New York, too.) Me—who?

Ⓑ HARLEM RENAISSANCE
Reread lines 6–15. What do you learn about the speaker in these lines?

---

1. **Winston-Salem . . . Durham:** cities in North Carolina.
2. **this college on the hill above Harlem:** Columbia University in New York City.

DIFFERENTIATED INSTRUCTION

FOR LESS–PROFICIENT READERS
Options for Reading Read aloud "Theme for English B" and then point out that the poem sounds more like normal speech than some other poems students may have read. (You might wish to compare the rhythm to that of "The Tropics in New York.") Start an echo reading of the poem by reading aloud a few lines and having students repeat the lines with the same intonation and rhythm.

FOR ADVANCED LEARNERS/PRE–AP
Analyze Poetic Structure Ask students to analyze the structure of "Theme for English B," using the Poetic Form and Structure analysis frame. They should focus on the arrangement and length of words and lines, and how these elements affect readers. Ask students to consider why Hughes chose to change form and structure during the poem.

🧰 **BEST PRACTICES TOOLKIT—Transparency**
Analysis Frame: Poetic Form and
Structure pp. D21, D40

Young Man Studying (Portrait of Langston Hughes) (1932), Hilda Wilkinson Brown. Oil on canvas.
Photo by Gregory R. Staley © Lilian T. Burwell/Howard University.

ANALYZE VISUALS

Activity Ask students how the portrait reflects the speaker's description of himself.
Possible answer: The portrait shows a young African-American man studying.

About the Art *Young Man Studying* is subtitled "(Portrait of Langston Hughes)." Painted in oil on canvas in 1932 by Hilda Wilkinson Brown, the painting shows Hughes in a thoughtful, contemplative moment, perhaps writing poetry.

Well, I like to eat, sleep, drink, and be in love.
I like to work, read, learn, and understand life.
I like a pipe for a Christmas present,
or records—Bessie, bop, or Bach.[3]
25 I guess being colored doesn't make me not like
the same things other folks like who are other races.
So will my page be colored that I write?
Being me, it will not be white. **C**
But it will be
30 a part of you, instructor.
You are white—
yet a part of me, as I am a part of you.
That's American.
Sometimes perhaps you don't want to be a part of me.
35 Nor do I often want to be a part of you.
But we are, that's true!
As I learn from you,
I guess you learn from me—
although you're older—and white—
40 and somewhat more free.

This is my page for English B.

C READING POETRY
Reread lines 16–28.
What sound devices
do you recognize
in these lines?

---

3. **Bessie, bop, or Bach:** Bessie Smith was a leading jazz and blues singer of the 1920s and early 1930s. Bop is a style of jazz that became popular in the 1940s. Johann Sebastian Bach was an 18th-century German composer.

THEME FOR ENGLISH B   **899**

READING STRATEGY

C READING POETRY

Possible answer: The sound devices in these lines include assonance (eat, sleep, be, read); alliteration (hear, Harlem, hear; Bessie, bop, Bach); and rhyme (true, you, two, too, who).

If students need help . . . Have student pairs read aloud lines 16–28 to each other several times. Suggest that students listen for one sound device during each reading.

SELECTION WRAP-UP

SYNTHESIZE Have students think about the personal information these poets share in their works. Then, ask students to name other writers or artists that infuse their works with personal information.

★ **CRITIQUE** Have students discuss which poet they feel they know better after reading these poems: McKay or Hughes.

READING FLUENCY

Distribute the copy master and have students work in pairs or groups to practice fluency.

R RESOURCE MANAGER—Copy Master
Reading Fluency p. 144

FOR LESS–PROFICIENT READERS

Language Support Ask students to study the punctuation marks in "Theme for English B." Point out that "Theme for English B" is meant to sound as if the speaker were talking to his instructor in a natural, easy way. Explain that the periods and commas tell readers when to pause or stop completely. These marks can help to make the reading of a poem both easy and expressive.

Have students work in pairs to practice reading the poem aloud. Remind students to use the punctuation marks, not the line breaks, as a guide. Have the listening partner take notes on the reading and then offer advice for improvement. Once both students have practiced, have them read aloud the poem to you and offer them further advice and guidance.

DISCUSSION PROMPTS

Use these prompts to help students make connections between the Harlem Renaissance and the poems by McKay and Hughes:

Connect Recall a time in your life when you felt part of a community, or simply that you "belonged." In your opinion, what makes people feel this way? *Students might say that people feel like they "belong" when they are surrounded by people with similar interests, experiences, and beliefs.*

Analyze Why might McKay and Hughes have felt that they "belonged" in Harlem at the time of the Harlem Renaissance? *Possible answer: In Harlem at that time, McKay and Hughes found themselves surrounded by other African Americans who celebrated their ethnicity and culture.*

Evaluate How might McKay's and Hughes's work be different if the Harlem Renaissance had not taken place? *Answers will vary but should include an awareness of the far-reaching cultural influences of the Harlem Renaissance and the important role of a supportive community in the creative process.*

Reading for Information

MAGAZINE ARTICLE This article sheds further light on the Harlem Renaissance and its groundbreaking influence.

THE HARLEM RENAISSANCE:

A Cultural Explosion

From the "stompin'" jazz performances at the Savoy Ballroom to the lavish, racially-integrated literary events at the Dark Tower, 1920s Harlem in New York City hosted a vibrant cultural scene known as the Harlem Renaissance.

Scholars disagree about the exact dates of the Harlem Renaissance but generally place this cultural revolution between 1919 and the mid-1930s. The Harlem Renaissance represented a movement that was occurring throughout the country, as African Americans explored artistic, political, and social acts to raise race consciousness. Black people experiencing poverty and racial tension, particularly in the rural South, flocked to Harlem in the hopes of creating a more unified, self-determined community.

Harlem's population quickly exploded, despite high rents there. The "city within a city" drew residents from as far as Africa and the West Indies, as its influence spread throughout the world. The result was a strong community of African-American businesses, churches, schools, and civic and entertainment centers. Although Harlemites had problems and differences, residents drew together to enjoy "strolling" (a pastime that involved dressing up to walk the neighborhood and meet neighbors), parades (which could occur a few times in one day and involve the whole crowd), and rent parties (hosted by tenants hoping to earn enough money from a cover charge to pay the month's rent).

During the Harlem Renaissance, African Americans from all walks of life, as well as other audiences, developed greater appreciation for both the folk and more sophisticated aspects of black culture. Musical forms such as jazz and the blues swelled in popularity. Plays by African Americans appeared on Broadway, black artists gained prominence, and black writers published more books than during any previous era.

Some of the Harlem Renaissance's most prominent figures, such as poet Langston Hughes, drew inspiration from "the low-down folks," a term he used to describe the masses. Hughes, who experimented with dialect and music in his writing, believed African Americans needed to be proud of their individuality and blackness. Others, such as the scholar W. E. B. DuBois, felt that African-American art should serve the political purpose of portraying its people in the best possible light, in order to show equality with whites and to defy stereotypes. Despite these differences, writers of the movement found enough in common to support one another.

The Harlem Renaissance suffered when the stock market crashed in 1929 and wealthy white patrons from New York City's uptown neighborhoods no longer frequented Harlem's clubs. Other factors, such as race riots, the repeal of Prohibition, and growing dissent affected the movement as well. Today the Harlem Renaissance remains a powerful influence among artists such as Nobel Prize winner Toni Morrison, Pulitzer Prize winner Alice Walker, Poet Laureate Rita Dove, and many others.

900 UNIT 9: HISTORY, CULTURE, AND THE AUTHOR

Comprehension

1. **Recall** In "The Tropics in New York," what do the fruits in the window remind the speaker of?

2. **Recall** What causes him to weep?

3. **Recall** In "Theme for English B," what instructions are given to the speaker?

4. **Summarize** What aspect of his identity does he discuss?

Literary Analysis

5. **Examine Title** Consider the title of "The Tropics in New York." How does it affect your understanding of the poem?

6. **Draw Conclusions** In "Theme for English B," the speaker says that he and the instructor are part of each other. What does he mean? Explain.

7. **Analyze Theme** In your own words, explain the theme of the poem "Theme for English B." What is the message the poet wants to convey? Support your answer with evidence from the text.

8. **Identify Tone** A poet's choice of words and details conveys a certain tone, or attitude toward the subject. Identify the tone of each poem by completing a chart like the one shown.

"The Tropics in New York"	
Tone of Poem	Words/Details That Convey Tone
sad, nostalgic	

9. **Understand Sound in Poetry**
Review the sound devices you recorded as you read the two poems. How does noticing these sound devices affect the way you perceive these poems?

10. **Interpret Harlem Renaissance Literature** Writers of the Harlem Renaissance explored and celebrated their African-American **heritage.** What does the article "The Harlem Renaissance: A Cultural Exlplosion" add to your understanding of these two poems? Be specific.

Literary Criticism

11. **Biographical Context** Claude McKay grew up in a Jamaican town populated mainly by blacks. When he went to work in the city of Kingston, with a greater proportion of whites, he was shocked by the racism he encountered. He later went to the United States with great optimism about the opportunity he might find "even for a Negro," but he was quickly disillusioned about the conditions for black Americans: "It was the first time I had ever come face to face with such manifest, implacable hate of my race." What does this knowledge about his life add to your perception of the homesickness described in "The Tropics in New York"? Explain.

8. **"The Tropics in New York": Words/Details:** "dewy dawns"; "mystical blue skies"; "eyes grow dim"; "wave of longing"; "hungry for the old, familiar ways"; "bowed my head and wept." **"Theme for English B": Tone:** calm, serious; **Words/Details:** speaker's life details, likes and interests

9. ■ **STANDARDS FOCUS** *Reading Poetry* In "The Tropics in New York," the sound devices recall a spiritual song or prayer. The rhyme scheme builds to the final line and emphasizes its power. "Theme for English B" sounds more like a conversation, except

in lines 18–20, where the rhythm of repetition is briefly musical.

10. ● **STANDARDS FOCUS** *Harlem Renaissance Literature* The article places the poems in a cultural time frame beyond the poets' personal experiences.

Literary Criticism

11. Students might say that McKay's disappointment at finding racism in America sharpens the poignancy of the homesickness expressed in the poem.

Practice and Apply

After Reading

For additional support of post-reading questions, use these copy masters:

R RESOURCE MANAGER—Copy Masters
Harlem Renaissance Literature p. 139 (for practice of literary analysis standards focus)
Question Support p. 143 (After Reading questions adapted for English learners and less-proficient readers)

For additional questions, see page 135 .

ANSWERS

Comprehension

1. *The fruits remind the speaker of home: of fruit trees, dawns, blue skies, and hills.*

2. *The speaker weeps because he longs for "the old, familiar ways" and misses home.*

3. *The speaker is told to write a page from his heart, a page that is "true."*

4. *The speaker discusses several aspects of his identity, but especially his racial identity.*

Literary Analysis
Possible answers:

5. *The title notes the poem's New York setting, far from the speaker's home in the tropics. It explains the speaker's longing.*

6. *The speaker likely means that both are American, so share aspects of culture.*

7. *The message is that the instructor and student—a white American and a black American—are connected. Students should cite lines 31–40 as evidence.*

Assess and Reteach

Assess

R RESOURCE MANAGER—Copy Masters
Selection Test A pp. 145–146
Selection Test B/C pp. 147–148

💿 Test Generator CD

Reteach

S STANDARDS LESSON FILE
Literature Lesson 47: Author's Perspective

Focus and Motivate

OBJECTIVES

Literary Analysis
- explore the key idea of being **concise**
- analyze historical and cultural context
- read haiku

Reading
- interpret imagery

SUMMARIES

"Haiku" by Matsuo Bashō In these three haiku, Bashō connects images from nature to the human experience.

"Haiku" by Richard Wright Wright uses the haiku form to explore the sensory experiences of urban living.

"Honku" by Aaron Naparstek Naparstek uses a modified haiku form to comment on the effects of technology.

How many WORDS *do you need?*

Ask the question. Once students have read the **KEY IDEA,** have a volunteer define the word **concise.** Ask students to give examples of other times writers must be concise—for example, a photo caption or news headline. Have students practice their ability to be concise by completing the **QUICKWRITE.**

Selection Resources

R RESOURCE MANAGER UNIT 9

Plan and Teach pp. 149–156

Literary Analysis
Historical and Cultural Context
   pp. 157, 158†*
Question Support p. 161*

Reading
Interpret Imagery pp. 159, 160†*

Assessment
Selection Tests A, B/C pp. 163*, 165*
⊘ Test Generator CD

🧰 BEST PRACTICES TOOLKIT

Differentiated Instruction
   pp. 31–38*

Graphic Organizers/Strategies
Read Aloud/Think Aloud
• Comparison Matrix

Reading Support
⊘ Audio Anthology CD*

Technology
ℹ️ Literature Center at
   ClassZone.com
⊘ Write*Smart* CD

* Resources for Differentiation   † Also in Spanish

Haiku
Poems by Matsuo Bashō

Haiku
Poems by Richard Wright

Honku
Poems by Aaron Naparstek

How many WORDS *do you need?*

KEY IDEA Sometimes a few words can leave a big impression. Even three short lines can contain a thoughtful observation about life. Poets of haiku are masters of being **concise** in this way. In this lesson, you'll read the works of three poets from very different places and time periods who use the tiny three-line haiku to create unforgettable images and express powerful ideas.

QUICKWRITE Can you create a vivid or unusual image from only three or four words? Choose a few of the words pictured here, and arrange them to create a striking image or idea.

| CORN | SEPTEMBER | YELLOW | STANDS |
| FLOWER | STALKS | AMONG | RED |

Milk
Bread
Eggs

POETIC FORM: HAIKU

Haiku originated in Japan hundreds of years ago. Over time, many poets in many cultures have used and adapted the form. But the haiku still presents a challenge with its strict rules about form and content. It requires

- three unrhymed lines of five, seven, and five syllables
- two common images, usually from nature, that are juxtaposed to suggest a greater meaning
- an allusion to a season, as in the phrase "Heat waves shimmering," which suggests summer

As you read, note how each poet uses and experiments with each of these characteristics.

LITERARY ANALYSIS: HISTORICAL AND CULTURAL CONTEXT

The poets Matsuo Bashō and Richard Wright lived in vastly different times and places, and Aaron Naparstek's world is vastly different from theirs. The varied social conditions that inspired these poets to write their poems is the **historical** or **cultural context** of their work.

Before you read each group of poems, read about the author to learn historical and cultural details that will help you interpret the poetry. Then read the poems, focusing on their imagery, symbolism, word choice, and themes. Notice how these elements reflect the life, times, and culture of the poet.

READING SKILL: INTERPRET IMAGERY

Imagery consists of words and phrases that appeal to a reader's sense of sight, hearing, touch, smell, or taste. In haiku, the imagery has added weight because the form is so brief; each word and phrase is critical to the meaning. As you read, follow these steps to find deeper meaning in each poem.

1. Record the images in the poem.
2. Identify the mood, idea, or feeling the images evoke.
3. Explain the meaning of the images.

Record details in a chart as shown.

First Haiku by Bashō: "Harvest Moon"		
Imagery	Mood, Idea, or Feeling	Meaning
the moon walking around the pond all night	mood—quiet or serene; idea—moon stays all night	Nature is abundant and constant.

Author Online

Matsuo Bashō: Japanese Haiku Master
A samurai before he was a poet, Matsuo Bashō elevated haiku from a popular social pastime into a literary art form. Bashō brought the gentle spirit of Zen Buddhism to both his writing and his life. He spent his later life writing poetry as he journeyed through Japan.

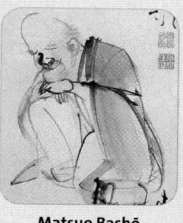

**Matsuo Bashō
1644–1694**

Richard Wright: African-American Novelist
Considered one of the most important black authors of the 1900s, Richard Wright is best known for his novel *Native Son* and his autobiography *Black Boy*. He also wrote short stories, essays, and poetry about life in Northern ghettos and racial oppression of blacks.

**Richard Wright
1908–1960**

Aaron Naparstek: Activism Meets Poetry
Fed up with the noise created by motorists in his Brooklyn neighborhood, Aaron Naparstek began writing "honku"— haiku about honking cars—and taping them to lampposts. Others began posting their own honkus, and a movement was born. In 2003 Naparstek published *Honku: The Zen Antidote to Road Rage*.

**Aaron Naparstek
born 1970**

 MORE ABOUT THE AUTHOR
For more on these poets, visit the **Literature Center** at **ClassZone.com**.

DIFFERENTIATED INSTRUCTION

FOR LESS–PROFICIENT READERS

Review the terms discussed in the haiku instruction. Confirm that students can identify syllables and recognize rhyme. Explain that *juxtaposed* means "to place two things together to highlight a similarity or contrast." Remind students that an allusion is a reference to knowledge the writer thinks readers will have. For example, a poem may allude to a specific mountain and assume that readers know its legends or history.

Teach

STANDARDS FOCUS

LITERARY ANALYSIS

● HISTORICAL AND CULTURAL CONTEXT

For instructional support, write these lines on the board:

> And in this deep chill,
> the warmth of the Midwest soul
> welcomes me back home.

Ask students to hypothesize about the life context of the poem's speaker. *Possible answer: The speaker probably lived in the Midwest and then moved away for a while. He or she finds comfort in the region and is happy to be back home.*

CHECK UNDERSTANDING Ask students to identify details in the poem that support this hypothesis about context.

READING SKILL

■ INTERPRET IMAGERY

Focus students' attention once more on the haiku written on the board. Ask them to identify the imagery in the poem and to explain which sense it mostly appeals to. *Possible answer: The image of a cold winter day is presented. This imagery appeals to the sense of touch or feeling. It may also appeal secondarily to the sense of sight.*

CHECK UNDERSTANDING Discuss with students the deeper meaning implied by the juxtaposition of the words *chill* and *warmth*.

R RESOURCE MANAGER—Copy Master
Interpret Imagery p. 159 (for student use while reading the selections)

Practice and Apply

ANALYZE VISUALS

Activity Ask students how the artwork and Bashō's haiku are similar. ***Possible answer:*** *The artwork reflects images present in the haiku. The moon is shown peeking through the clouds. The plants are brown and look dead. The brown and yellow tones convey a feeling of autumn.*

About the Art Point out to students that this six-fold screen—painted with ink, color, and gold leaf—is one of a pair. It was created during the same time period in which Bashō lived. The painter is unknown.

Millet Fields with the Sun and the Moon (Early Edo period, 1600s), Anonymous. Pair of six-fold screens, painted, 150.5 cm. × 348.8 cm. Restricted gift of the Rice Foundation, 1989. Reproduction, The Art Institute of Chicago.

H A I K U

Matsuo Bashō

Harvest moon—
walking around the pond
all night long.

Heat waves shimmering
one or two inches
above the dead grass.

You could turn this way,
I'm also lonely
this autumn evening.

LITERARY ANALYSIS

Ⓐ HISTORICAL AND CULTURAL CONTEXT

How does Bashō use nature to express his own feelings at any given moment? ***Possible answer:*** *Bashō presents images from nature that might reflect or provoke the feelings that he is trying to express. For example, an autumnal full moon reflecting off the surface of a pond might inspire a feeling of loneliness or restlessness.*

READING SKILL

◼ INTERPRET IMAGERY

Have students use a reflection chart to record imagery from Bashō's second haiku and express their thoughts about each image.

Imagery	Thoughts About It

Possible answer: Imagery: *dry, shimmering heat; dead grass.* *Students' thoughts will vary.*

 HISTORICAL AND CULTURAL CONTEXT
Author: Matsuo Bashō
Time: mid- to late 1600s
Place: Japan
Development of haiku: Bashō established the tradition of focusing the content of haiku on nature. The haiku on this page do not reflect the five-seven-five syllable pattern because they are translations from Japanese.

904 UNIT 9: HISTORY, CULTURE, AND THE AUTHOR

DIFFERENTIATED INSTRUCTION

For general guidelines on differentiating instruction, see

BEST PRACTICES TOOLKIT
Differentiated Instruction pp. 31–38

FOR LESS–PROFICIENT READERS

Options for Reading: Partner Reading Begin by reading the poems aloud to convey their moods to students. Then have students work in pairs to read the Bashō and Wright haiku in alternating lines. Next, have students work in groups of three to read each complete haiku aloud. Have groups discuss how the poems should be read and what each means. If students wish, they may also listen to the selections on the *Audio Anthology CD* as a reading guide.

BEST PRACTICES TOOLKIT—Transparency
Read Aloud/Think Aloud p. A34

Jazz Player III (1991), Louise Freshman Brown. Collage. © SuperStock

Haiku

RICHARD WRIGHT

From a tenement,
The blue jazz of a trumpet
Weaving autumn mists. **ⓑ**

Twisting violently,
A lost kite seeks its freedom
From telegraph wires.

Standing in the crowd
In a cold drizzling rain,—
How lonely it is.

ⓑ HISTORICAL AND CULTURAL CONTEXT
Author: Richard Wright
Time: mid-1900s
Place: United States
Evolution of haiku: Wright uses the traditional form but adapts the content to reflect on urban life rather than nature.

Prereading for these poems is found on page 902.

ANALYZE VISUALS

Activity Which Wright haiku connects most immediately to the artwork? Explain.
Possible answer: The painting, depicting a trumpet player, connects most immediately to the first haiku. The background suggests that the jazz player might well be playing "from a tenement." Even the painting's dominant blue colors evoke one of the haiku's images: "The blue jazz of a trumpet."

About the Art A painter and mixed-medium artist, Louise Freshman Brown has work featured in numerous U.S. and European museums and galleries. Currently, she is a professor of art at the University of North Florida, Jacksonville.

LITERARY ANALYSIS

ⓑ HISTORICAL AND CULTURAL CONTEXT

How does Wright use the urban environment to describe a sense of loneliness?
Possible answer: In the second haiku, Wright presents the image of a lone kite struggling against telegraph wires, an image that suggests modern technology in an urban environment. In the third haiku, the speaker seems to get lost "in the crowd."

Third haiku
REINFORCE *KEY IDEA:* CONCISE

Discuss What is the main idea conveyed in the third haiku? How does the **concise** haiku form help the speaker to reinforce this idea?
Possible answer: The speaker appears to feel alone and insignificant in a crowd. Because the haiku is concise, the feeling is highlighted instead of buried amidst a lot of text.

FOR ADVANCED LEARNERS/PRE–AP

Compare and Contrast Theme Ask students to work independently to identify and analyze the theme (or themes) conveyed by each of the three haiku by each of the three poets. Then, ask students to use a Comparison Matrix to evaluate which poet used imagery most effectively to convey those themes to readers. Have students summarize their conclusions in a one- to two-page literary analysis. Then, have students share their ideas with one another and discuss the similarities and differences in their analyses.

 BEST PRACTICES TOOLKIT—Transparency
Comparison Matrix p. A24

Prereading for these poems is found on page 902.

ANALYZE VISUALS

Activity How do the two images relate to Naparstek's haiku? *Possible answer: The traffic and crowds of people both reflect images in the three haiku. They illustrate the crowded and noisy images Naparstek conveys.*

LITERARY ANALYSIS

ⓒ HISTORICAL AND CULTURAL CONTEXT

What are the poet's concerns about modern life and technology, and how do his modifications of form help express these concerns? *Possible answer: Whereas traditional haiku connect nature to an observation on the human condition, Naparstek adds another layer to the form by connecting modern technology to nature, which in turn offers a comment on human experience. By eliminating much of the form's capitalization and punctuation, Naparstek seems to reflect the hurried lifestyles that many 21st-century people lead.*

SELECTION WRAP–UP

SYNTHESIZE Ask students what all of these poems have in common aside from the similarities in structural form.

⭐ **CRITIQUE** Ask students which poet's haiku they respond to more readily. Why?

HONKU — Aaron Naparstek

clinton street autos
honk, guzzle and burn away
our crisp, clean spring days ⓒ

Morning commuters
follow measured lines, honking—
how like geese we are

When the light turns green
like a leaf on a spring wind
the horn blows quickly

ⓒ HISTORICAL AND CULTURAL CONTEXT
Author: Aaron Naparstek
Time: early 2000s
Place: New York City
Evolution of haiku: Naparstek modifies the form by eliminating end punctuation and, sometimes, capitalization and adapts its contents to reflect concerns about modern life and technology.

DIFFERENTIATED INSTRUCTION

FOR LESS–PROFICIENT READERS
Options for Reading Read aloud the three "honku" by Aaron Naparstek, and discuss with students how the lack of punctuation affects the reading. Suggest that each haiku is like a poetic sentence that conveys a single thought. Then, have students practice reading the poems independently, and ask volunteers to read them aloud.

Vocabulary Support Discuss with students the different meanings these words can convey depending on their part of speech:

- *street*—noun; slang adjective
- *clean*—verb; adjective
- *spring*—noun; verb; adjective
- *like*—verb; conjunction

Ask students to define each word on their own, or help them use a dictionary to understand the differences in meaning.

Comprehension

1. **Recall** What subject is common to all three of the "honku" by Aaron Naparstek?

2. **Recall** What kind of music is mentioned in the first haiku by Richard Wright?

3. **Clarify** What season is suggested in the first poem by Matsuo Bashō?

Literary Analysis

4. **Interpret Imagery** Review the chart in which you analyzed the imagery in the haiku. How do the three poets differ in the kinds of imagery they use and the moods they create?

5. **Compare and Contrast Word Choice** Notice the use of verbs in all three sets of poems. Which two sets are the most similar? different? How do the verbs affect the messages of the poems? Explain your answer.

6. **Evaluate Figurative Language** In **personification,** an animal, object, or idea is given human attributes. Identify three examples of personification in these poems, and explain how each strengthens or weakens the writer's message.

7. **Recognize Cultural and Historical Context** For each poet, write a brief summary of how his cultural and historical background may have influenced the images and themes in the haiku.

8. **Analyze Poetic Form** In **haiku,** the image presented is often symbolic of a greater truth or meaning. In the second haiku by Richard Wright, what does the kite trapped in the wires symbolize? Explain your answer, citing evidence from the text.

9. **Interpret Ambiguity** When a situation can be interpreted in more than one way, it has the quality of ambiguity. In the first haiku by Bashō, note the ambiguity in the first two lines. Who is walking around the pond—the moon, the speaker, or both? Explain your answer.

10. **Evaluate** Matsuo Bashō wrote his haiku in the 1600s. Do the poems seem dated, or are they timeless? Explain your answer.

Literary Criticism

11. **Critical Interpretations** Author Aaron Naparstek says that "haiku poems are sort of the perfect little sound bytes. They fit our culture." Using what you know about the haiku and about American culture, explain what Naparstek might mean by that statement. How do the characteristics of the haiku seem well suited to contemporary American culture?

night, which adds to the sense of loneliness. Wright's kite seeking freedom suggests human desire to escape technology. The "behavior" of Naparstek's cars reinforces modernization's negative aspects.

7. ● **STANDARDS FOCUS Historical and Cultural Context** Bashō's poems reflect a quiet stillness that might be inspired by his practice of Zen Buddhism. Wright's poems reflect life in an urban setting—the setting in which he lived. Naparstek wrote his poems in response to the frustrations of urban living.

8. The kite symbolizes the desire to escape from the modern world.

9. Students should support answers with words from the poem.

10. Students' answers will vary.

Literary Criticism
Possible answer:

11. Naparstek is referring to our modern attention span: we only have patience to digest short messages. Like sound bytes, the "honku" are simple and to the point.

Practice and Apply

After Reading
For additional support of post-reading questions, use these copy masters:

R RESOURCE MANAGER—Copy Masters
Historical and Cultural Context p. 157 (for practice of literary analysis standards focus)
Question Support p. 161 (After Reading questions adapted for English learners and less-proficient readers)

For additional questions, see page 153.

ANSWERS

Comprehension

1. *The three "honku" are all about cars honking in city traffic.*

2. *Wright mentions jazz in the first haiku.*

3. *Autumn is suggested in Bashō's first poem.*

Literary Analysis
Possible answers:

4. ■ **STANDARDS FOCUS Interpret Imagery** *Bashō uses natural imagery to create a quiet, wistful, solitary mood. Wright uses urban and natural imagery to also create a wistful, solitary mood. Naparstek uses noisy urban imagery of cars and natural imagery to create a wistful mood with an element of whimsy.*

5. *The verbs in Bashō's and Wright's poems are more similar. They end in -ing and describe movement in nature. Both sets of verbs reflect the poems' messages of loneliness or solitude. Naparstek's poems use harsh verbs that convey a distaste for aspects of urban life.*

6. *Bashō describes the moon "walking" all*

Assess and Reteach

Assess

R RESOURCE MANAGER—Copy Masters
Selection Test A pp. 163–164
Selection Test B/C pp. 165–166

⊘ Test Generator CD

Reteach

S STANDARDS LESSON FILE
Literature Lesson 13: Haiku
Literature Lesson 28: Imagery

Focus and Motivate

OBJECTIVES

- analyze a student model that reflects the key traits of a persuasive essay
- use the writing process to produce a persuasive essay
- revise and edit, using a rubric for writing a persuasive essay
- debate an issue

WRITER'S ROAD MAP

WRITING PROMPTS 1 AND 2

Help students choose a prompt by brainstorming current issues of interest *and* controversy related to their school or community, or to young people in society as a whole. If students know of literature related to these issues, urge them to share and discuss it. Point out that there must be two opposing views of the issue that they choose.

ADDITIONAL PROMPTS

Use these prompts for practice with business writing and writing in the humanities:

WRITING PROMPT 3

Writing for the Real World Write a persuasive essay directed to a business leader in response to an issue discussed in a newspaper or television editorial.

Possible Subjects
- global warming
- the energy crisis
- online privacy

WRITING PROMPT 4

Writing About Fine Art Choose a type of artwork or music that you think is valuable and deserves recognition. Write an essay that persuades your audience to agree with you.

Possible Subjects
- graffiti art
- a style of music, such as sampling
- quilting

For additional writing prompts, see

- WriteSmart CD
- Writing Center at ClassZone.com

KEY TRAITS

Review the six **KEY TRAITS** with students, focusing primarily on ideas and organization. Compare the list of traits with the rubric on page 914.

Writing Workshop

Persuasive Essay

"We must clean up toxic waste now!" "Vote for me!" "My client is innocent!" When an issue affects you deeply, you want to convince others to agree with you. Expressing your thoughts on a topic that is significant to you, as writers in this unit have done, can change your life and your community. To learn how to persuade others effectively, take a look at the **Writer's Road Map.**

WRITER'S ROAD MAP
Persuasive Essay

WRITING PROMPT 1

Writing for the Real World Choose an issue you feel strongly about. Write a persuasive essay in which you explain the issue and attempt to convince readers to support your position.

Issues to Explore
- new restrictions on teenage drivers
- discrimination in various forms
- censorship of student newspapers

WRITING PROMPT 2

Writing from Literature Sometimes reading a work of literature can give you a whole new perspective on an issue. Using something you have read as a springboard, write a persuasive essay about an issue that is meaningful to you.

Issues to Explore
- medical treatment of children (*Angela's Ashes*)
- racial discrimination ("Blues Ain't No Mockin Bird" and "American History")
- preserving the sacred places of different cultures ("Revisiting Sacred Ground")

 WRITING TOOLS For prewriting, revision, and editing tools, visit the **Writing Center at ClassZone.com.**

KEY TRAITS

1. IDEAS
- Presents a **thesis statement** that makes a **claim,** or takes a position, on a clearly identified issue
- Uses **relevant and convincing reasons and evidence** to support the position
- Anticipates and addresses **opposing arguments** and objections

2. ORGANIZATION
- Describes the issue in a **strong introduction**
- Uses **transitions** to create a **consistent organizational pattern**
- Concludes by **summarizing** the position or issuing a **call to action**

3. VOICE
- Reflects the **writer's commitment** to his or her opinion
- Addresses the **audience** directly

4. WORD CHOICE
- Uses **persuasive language** effectively

5. SENTENCE FLUENCY
- Varies **sentence beginnings**

6. CONVENTIONS
- Employs **correct grammar and usage**

Writing Workshop Resources

 RESOURCE MANAGER UNIT 9

Plan and Teach pp. 167–170
Prewriting–Editing pp. 171–175
Writing Rubric p. 176
Speaking and Listening p. 177
Writing Support p. 178*

 **STANDARDS LESSON FILE**

Writing Lesson 30
Informational Texts Lesson 12
Speaking and Listening Lesson 10

 BEST PRACTICES TOOLKIT

Scaffolding Writing Instruction pp. 43–46*
Two-Column Chart • Analysis Frame: Persuasion • Writing Template: Persuasive Essay

TECHNOLOGY
- Easy Planner DVD
- Writing Center at **ClassZone.com**
- WriteSmart CD

* Resources for Differentiation

Part 1: Analyze a Student Model

Daniel Carpenter
Concord West High School

Curfews: Fairness and the Facts

Two weeks ago, the Concord City supervisors proposed a new law that discriminates against young people who have done nothing wrong. The new law would establish a curfew for anyone under age 18. The weekday curfew would be 10:00 P.M. to 5:00 A.M., and the weekend
5 curfew would last from 11:00 P.M. until 5:00 A.M. Anyone violating curfew would be fined $50. The proposed law has two serious flaws: it is based on feelings instead of facts, and it violates the rights of Concord's young people and their parents.

According to Supervisor Ellen Baxter, the main reason for the law is
10 to prevent juvenile crime. This includes crimes committed by juveniles and crimes committed against juveniles. If minors are off the streets at night, she says, Concord's crime rate would drop.

Her argument sounds good, but unfortunately, the facts do not support it. A study by two university professors, William Ruefle and
15 Kenneth Mike Reynolds, showed there is almost no evidence that curfews lowered crime rates. In fact, the FBI reported recently that most juvenile crimes take place between 3:00 P.M. and 6:00 P.M.—not at night.

Supervisor Frank Angelo says that there are no reasons for youth to be outside late at night. They should be home studying, he says, and
20 spending time with their families. Supervisor Angelo was quoted in the *Concord Clarion* saying, "Anything kids want to do at 11:30 at night can just as easily be done at 8:30."

Supervisor Angelo's argument also ignores the facts. Teenagers have many good reasons to be out at night. Some have part-time jobs that

KEY TRAITS IN ACTION

Strong **introduction** is tailored to the interest of **audience** members (Daniel Carpenter's classmates and teacher).

Thesis statement makes a clear, detailed **claim**.

Throughout the essay, the writer clearly explains **opposing arguments** and rebuts them with relevant **facts, statistics, and expert opinions**.

Organization is easy to follow—opposing argument followed by answer to that argument.

Teach

Part 1: Analyze a Student Model

Have students read the student model and **KEY TRAITS IN ACTION**. Then discuss the model with the class, pointing out specific examples of each trait and building on what students have already noted. You may also wish to incorporate these activities:

- **Introduction** Note that lines 1–8 introduce the essay's issue and state the writer's position. They give details and state a thesis with two supporting arguments.

- **Facts, Statistics, and Expert Opinions** Write this ineffective counterargument on the board:

  > Her argument sounds good, but she is wrong. Curfews don't prevent crime. We don't need curfews because they don't stop crime. They keep people glued to clocks.

  Ask a student to read this statement and lines 14–17 of the model, then compare the two. **Possible answer:** *The statement on the board includes several reasoning errors. The second sentence is an overgeneralization that can't be proven. The third sentence proves nothing and repeats earlier text. The model uses an expert opinion and facts to support the view that curfews don't work.*

- **Organization** To show clear organization in the model, have students list arguments in each paragraph, and identify them as opposing arguments or counterarguments.

DIFFERENTIATED INSTRUCTION

For general guidelines on differentiating writing instruction, see

 BEST PRACTICES TOOLKIT
Scaffolding Writing Instruction pp. 43–46

FOR ENGLISH LEARNERS

Language: Skill Words Write these terms on the board and review them with students:

- *position:* an opinion for or against an issue
- *expert opinions:* opinions or facts given by people who know a lot about a subject
- *facts and statistics:* information that can be proven, and numerical information such as what time most juvenile crime takes place

- *opposing arguments:* the evidence given by others who have the opposite view from that of the writer
- *counterarguments:* the evidence the writer gives to disprove the opposing arguments
- *call to action:* the writer's request to readers to do, think, or say something in response to the essay
- *ethical belief:* a view based on ideas about right and wrong

- **Transitions** Share transitions useful for persuasive writing, including *for these reasons* (to state a position); *according to, first, also, for instance* (to present evidence); and *however, even though, but* (to present contrasting views).

  Then ask students to locate the following transitions in the student model and tell how they link ideas in the paragraphs.

  according to (line 9)
  also (line 23)
  finally (line 29)
  however (line 33)

- **Persuasive Language** Point out that persuasive writing may appeal to the audience by making arguments based on reason, ethics, or emotion, or on a combination of all three. Explain that when writers appeal only to emotions, their argument will lack good evidence and therefore not be effective.

- **Call to Action** Ask students to identify the call to action in the model. Remind them that good persuasive writing leaves readers with a suggestion about an action they can take to help solve a problem.

For interactive student models, see
  WriteSmart CD
  Writing Center at **ClassZone.com**

25 don't end until 9:00 or 10:00. Some participate in activities sponsored by youth groups or church groups. Some may be responding to family emergencies. Why should teens have to risk being arrested and fined just for living their lives?

Finally, Mayor Erika Snow said that she supported the proposed law
30 because it was "just good government." Providing a safe place to live is the city government's most important task, she said.

It is true, as Mayor Snow says, that the city has a responsibility to keep its citizens safe. However, that doesn't mean the city can violate parental or constitutional rights. The city government has no business
35 telling parents when their children must be home. That's a decision for parents to make. Also, the U.S. Constitution says that citizens' private lives should be free from unnecessary government interference. It makes no sense to punish teenagers for problems they haven't caused.

Juvenile crime is a problem in many places, including Concord, but
40 curfews are not the solution. The proper response to juvenile crime is to arrest the criminals, not to put law-abiding young people under house arrest. I encourage those of you who believe the curfew law is unfair and distorts the facts to write to your city supervisors and make your opinions known.

Transitions connect ideas. **Varied sentence beginnings** help keep the essay interesting.

The writer uses **persuasive language** to make an effective appeal based on ethical belief. The essay is forceful but not bullying.

Conclusion **summarizes** the writer's position, suggests a more effective response to the problem, and issues a **call to action** that addresses the **audience** directly.

2

DIFFERENTIATED INSTRUCTION

FOR ENGLISH LEARNERS

Comprehension: Transitions Help students recognize transitions by pointing out the transitions and transitional phrases in the model. To help familiarize students with the uses of transitions, use this activity:

1. Hold up pictures of a girl, labeled *For,* and a woman, labeled *Against.*

2. Display the appropriate picture as you read each sentence containing a transition.

I believe that teens are good drivers. (*for*)

However, the city council wants to put limits on teen drivers. (*against*)

Even though teens pass a driver's test, they have many accidents. (*against*)

According to the council, teens have too little experience. (*against*)

For these reasons, the council says teens should drive with an adult for one year. (*against*)

First, teens have the legal right to drive. (*for*)

Teens have accidents, **but** so do adults. (*for*)

Although they are new drivers, most teens have good eyesight and quick reflexes. (*for*)

Finally, teens often drive to work or school, and adults aren't always available. (*for*)

3. Now repeat the exercise, this time asking students to provide the sentences.

To provide English learners with additional writing support, see

  RESOURCE MANAGER—Copy Master
  Writing Support p. 178

Part 2: Apply the Writing Process

PREWRITING

What Should I Do?

1. Analyze the prompt.
Study the prompt you chose on page 908. (Circle) the part of the prompt that tells you what you will be writing. Then underline words and phrases in the prompt that help you focus your thoughts.

2. Think about what really matters to you.
List some questions that explore your current state of mind. Think of issues in your school, neighborhood, community, state, or region. Place a star next to any issue that might make a suitable topic for your persuasive essay.

> **TIP** Remember, to be effective, your argument must have two sides to it.

3. Develop a working thesis statement.
Spend some time crafting a thesis that includes a **claim**—a forceful statement of your position. Your thesis should reflect the tone and point of view of the rest of the essay. The writer of the student model wanted to concentrate on two main points, so he built his thesis around them.

4. Gather support material.
You're going to need strong reasons and solid evidence to support your position. If you need facts and statistics, you might try using an Internet search engine.

What Does It Look Like?

▶ **WRITING PROMPT** Choose an issue you feel strongly about. (Write a persuasive essay) in which you explain the issue and attempt to convince readers to support your position.

> *The key here is to find an issue I really care about so that my passion for my position comes through loud and clear.*

▶ *1. What's bothering me at school?*
geometry class, Richie Franklin, ✳ backpack searches, rising cafeteria prices
2. What's been happening in the community lately?
vandalism, ✳ proposed curfew law, new community center

▶ *The proposed curfew law is a terrible idea.*
1. The people proposing the law are basing it on their feelings about young people and crime, not the facts.
2. The law would violate our rights and our parents' rights.

▶ *Possible Sources*
- *Article in Concord Clarion*
- *Ask school librarian for research tips.*
- *Internet search keywords: "curfew," "teen curfew," "juvenile crime," "Constitutional rights of juveniles"*

FOR ENGLISH LEARNERS

Writing: Thesis Statement Have students use these sentence starters to help them develop their thesis statements and support:

- My topic is _____.
- My position is that _____.
- My first main point is _____.
- My second main point is _____.

FOR ADVANCED LEARNERS/PRE–AP

Synthesize Support Material Have students use Analysis Frame: Persuasion to explore their topics in depth. Urge them to research creatively, such as by conducting interviews, citing published editorials, or utilizing many different types of sources. Have students cite sources with parenthetical notes and a list of works cited.

 BEST PRACTICES TOOLKIT—Transparency
Analysis Frame: Persuasion pp. D21, D44

Practice and Apply

To support students during the writing process, use these copy masters:

R **RESOURCE MANAGER—Copy Masters**
Prewriting–Editing pp. 171–175
Writing Rubric p. 176
Writing Support p. 178 (for English learners)

Part 2: Apply the Writing Process

PREWRITING

1. Analyze the prompt. Make sure students understand their chosen prompt. Stress the importance of commitment to the topic, explaining that this helps writers more effectively meet the prompt requirements.

2. Think about what really matters to you. Have students work in groups to brainstorm ideas for common prompts, making sure they have noted the **TIP**. Remind students to narrow their topic to a specific issue. For example:

- "backpack searches" instead of "school rules"
- "discrimination against athletes" instead of "discrimination at school"

3. Develop a working thesis statement. Have students identify two or more thesis-supporting arguments. Urge them to think of opposing arguments as they list points of support. Make sure students have workable plans before they begin writing.

4. Gather support material. Suggest that students list supporting information in a Two-Column Chart. Have them list their evidence under *Support* or *Oppose*. Remind students that they need to present both sides fairly to avoid being biased.

BEST PRACTICES TOOLKIT—Transparency
Two-Column Chart p. A25

For interactive graphic organizers, see

📀 Write*Smart* CD

ℹ️ Writing Center at **ClassZone.com**

DRAFTING

1. **Plan your organization.** Point out that the model uses Pattern 2 and that the counterarguments are outlined in the thesis statement. Explain that one challenge of using Pattern 1 is that readers are initially persuaded by the opposing arguments. The writer must then overcome their views with especially strong counterarguments.

2. **Use persuasive language.** To illustrate good examples of strong persuasive language, have partners find examples in lines 40–45 of the student model. *(not the solution, proper response, arrest the criminals, unfair and distorts the facts)*

3. **Support key ideas.** Suggest that students note the **TIP** and review the material *before* they begin drafting. Remind students that statements such as "everybody thinks" and "people should" are not reasons, but generalizations. Stress also the need to accurately cite facts, statistics, and expert opinions.

For a persuasive essay writing template, see

📁 BEST PRACTICES TOOLKIT—Transparency
Writing Template: Persuasive Essay
pp. C16, C31

🖉 WriteSmart CD

ℹ️ Writing Center at **ClassZone.com**

DRAFTING

What Should I Do?	What Does It Look Like?

1. Plan your organization.
Two common ways to organize the body of a persuasive essay are shown here. In both cases, the writer places his strongest argument last.

- **Pattern 1** Present all opposing arguments, then refute them with counterarguments.
- **Pattern 2** Raise one opposing argument and immediately counter it, then raise another opposing argument and counter it.

▶

PATTERN 1

Introduction and Thesis
Opposing Arguments:
- Deters juvenile crime
- No need for teens to be out
- Government must keep citizens safe.

Counterarguments:
- Facts show curfews don't deter juvenile crime.
- Many good reasons for teens to be out
- Curfews violate citizens' rights.

Conclusion

PATTERN 2

Introduction and Thesis
Opposing Argument 1:
Deters juvenile crime
Counterargument 1: Facts say otherwise.
Opposing Argument 2: No need for teens to be out
Counterargument 2:
Many good reasons
Opposing Argument 3:
Government must keep citizens safe.
Counterargument 3:
Curfews violate citizens' rights.
Conclusion

2. Use persuasive language.
Don't be hesitant or vague. Use language that shows your commitment to and strong feelings about your argument.

See page 596: Persuasive Techniques

▶

The city government has no business telling parents when their children must be home. That's a decision for parents to make.

3. Support key ideas.
If you want your audience to be truly persuaded, you must offer convincing support for what you say. Back up your arguments with strong reasons and convincing facts, statistics, and expert opinions.

TIP Before revising, consult the **key traits on page 908** and the **rubric and peer-reader questions on page 914.**

▶

Her argument sounds good, but unfortunately, the facts do not support it. ⎤ Key idea

A study by two university professors, William Ruefle and Kenneth Mike Reynolds, showed there is almost no evidence that curfews lowered crime rates. ⎦ Supporting evidence (expert opinion)

DIFFERENTIATED INSTRUCTION

FOR LESS–PROFICIENT WRITERS

Plan an Organization Have students follow this frame to plan their essays. Recall that it uses Pattern 2, as does the student model.

Beginning Paragraph
- Introduce the topic.
- State your thesis. See page 911, number 3, for help with writing a thesis statement.

Middle Paragraphs—Key Arguments
(number of paragraphs will vary)

- Paragraph 1
  —Present Opposing Argument 1.
  —Explain the opposing argument.

- Paragraph 2
  —Present Counterargument 1.
  —Present reason, fact, or expert opinion.
  —Present second reason, fact, or expert opinion.

- Paragraph 3
  —Present Opposing Argument 2.
  —Explain the opposing argument.

- Paragraph 4
  —Present Counterargument 2.
  —Present reason, fact, or expert opinion.
  —Present second reason, fact, or expert opinion.

End Paragraph
- Summarize your position.
- Include a call to action addressed to the audience.

REVISING AND EDITING

What Should I Do?

1. Be alert for errors in reasoning.
- Put [brackets] around statements that are not based on sound reasoning. Watch out for statements that are too broad to prove. These often include words and phrases such as *everyone, every time, no one,* and *none.*

See page 914: Errors in Reasoning

2. Fully develop supporting material.
- <u>Underline</u> the key idea in each paragraph.
- Reread the material supporting each key idea. Add reasons, facts, or statistics if needed. This writer supported his idea with three specific reasons.

3. Use precise vocabulary.
- Read your essay aloud. (Circle) words and phrases that seem vague or overused.
- Replace circled words and phrases with language that is precise and reflects your strong feelings about the subject.

4. Write a strong conclusion.
- Have a peer reader draw a <u>wavy line</u> under parts of your conclusion that are weak or that need details.
- Revise the conclusion to make sure it includes a call to action. Most conclusions also include a concise restatement of the position.

See page 914: Ask a Peer Reader

What Does It Look Like?

Juvenile crime is a problem in many areas, including Concord, but curfews are not the solution. [Everyone knows that curfews are a bad idea] The proper response to juvenile crime is to arrest the criminals, not to put law-abiding young people under house arrest.

Teenagers have many good reasons to be out at night. Why should teens have to risk being arrested and fined just for living their lives?

Some have part-time jobs that don't end until 9:00 or 10:00. Some participate in activities sponsored by youth groups or church groups. Some may be responding to family emergencies.

The proper response to juvenile crime is to (look) arrest the criminals, (for the bad ones) not to put (the rest of us) law-abiding young people under house arrest.

including Concord, but curfews are not the solution. Juvenile crime is a problem in many places. The proper response to juvenile crime is to arrest the criminals, not to put law-abiding young people under house arrest. I encourage those of you who believe the curfew law is unfair and distorts the facts to write to your city supervisors and make your opinions known.

REVISING AND EDITING

1. Be alert for errors in reasoning. Refer students to page 914, Errors in Reasoning, and discuss the list before students revise. Then, have students replace bracketed text with sound reasons, facts, statistics, or expert opinions.

2. Fully develop supporting material. Caution students that supporting material must be relevant to the topic and not just restate the writer's position. Students who cannot identify two solid pieces of support for an idea should revise the paragraph's topic sentence until they can support it.

3. Use precise vocabulary. Point out the revision to "the rest of us." Explain that the student avoided a generalization and made his argument more convincing by being specific. Remind students that the language in a persuasive essay
- is formal in tone
- uses words and phrases that show conviction
- uses specific words and elaboration
- avoids overgeneralizations

4. Write a strong conclusion. Stress that after reading a writer's arguments and support, the audience should be convinced that the issue is important enough to merit action. Explain that the call to action directs readers to concrete efforts, harnessing the energy a writer has created.

For interactive revision tools, see

WriteSmart CD

Writing Center at **ClassZone.com**

FOR ENGLISH LEARNERS

Writing: Conclusion Provide sentence frames such as these to help students develop their conclusions:
- My topic is _____.
- To restate my position, I _____.
- The issue could be solved by _____.
- I hope my audience will _____.

Preparing to Publish

Support for meeting the goals in the writing rubric is supplied throughout the Writing Workshop on pages 911–913.

For Rubric Bank, see

 WriteSmart CD

Writing Center at **ClassZone.com**

Assess and Reteach

S STANDARDS LESSON FILE
Writing Lesson 30: Persuasive Writing
Informational Texts Lesson 12: Inductive vs. Deductive Reasoning

---

Preparing to Publish **Persuasive Essay**

Apply the Rubric

A strong persuasive essay . . .

☑ has an attention-getting introduction

☑ states the issue and the writer's opinion in a thesis statement

☑ is sensibly organized

☑ supports opinions with reasons and evidence

☑ raises and refutes opposing arguments and objections

☑ addresses the audience directly

☑ uses persuasive language that shows the writer's commitment

☑ concludes with a summary or a call to action

Ask a Peer Reader

- Did my argument convince you? Why or why not?

- Which point is strongest? Did I use it in the right place?

- Does my essay seem biased? If so, could you explain how and why?

- How can I improve my conclusion?

Errors in Reasoning

Circular Reasoning trying to prove a statement by repeating it using different words ("Curfew laws are unnecessary because we don't need them.")

Overgeneralization a statement that is too broad or general to prove ("Nobody supports curfews.")

Either/Or Fallacy claiming there is one possible outcome to an action when there may be several ("Either this law passes or there will be no safety.")

False Cause assuming that one event led to another just because the second event followed the first ("Merrillville passed a curfew law, and there hasn't been a burglary there in months.")

See page R24: Identifying Faulty Reasoning

Check Your Grammar

- Use *who* as the subject of a sentence.

> *Who is responsible for making laws?*

Who is the subject of the verb *is*.

- Use *whom* as an object in a sentence.

> *For whom is this law intended?*

Whom is the object of the preposition *for*.

See page R54: Interrogative Pronouns

Writing Online

 PUBLISHING OPTIONS
For publishing options, visit the **Writing Center** at **ClassZone.com.**

ASSESSMENT PREPARATION
For writing and grammar assessment practice, go to the **Assessment Center** at **ClassZone.com.**

Debating an Issue

Further explore your feelings about your topic by debating the issue.

Planning the Debate

1. **Set up teams.** A traditional debate requires two two-person teams and a moderator. Debate participants are usually assigned to a team without regard for how each member feels about the issue.

2. **Write a clear resolution.** A resolution is a statement of the issue to be debated. Example: *The city of Concord should establish a curfew for residents under age 18.*

3. **Decide who will take the affirmative and negative positions.** The affirmative team argues in favor of the resolution. This team needs to present two to four reasons backed by strong supporting evidence. The negative team argues that the resolution should be rejected. This team must present two to four reasons backed by strong evidence to show that a problem does not exist or that a solution is already in place.

4. **Appoint a moderator.** The moderator states the resolution, introduces the debate participants, and sets and enforces time limits for speakers.

5. **Plan your position and rebuttal speeches carefully.** Do research to identify the main differences between your position and that of the opposing team. Use your research to develop specific reasons and to identify evidence to support your position. A position speech explains your argument, and a rebuttal speech rebuilds that argument after the opposing team has attacked it. When planning your rebuttal speech, think of ways that the opposition may attack your argument and decide on the best ways to respond.

Presenting the Debate

1. **Maintain eye contact.** Don't look at just one audience member— let your gaze shift from one person to another.

2. **Vary your pace and your facial expressions.** Expressions showing surprise, sadness, or disbelief can make your presentation more effective.

   See page R79: Evaluate a Team in a Debate

SPEAKING AND LISTENING

Ask students to read this page to get an overview of how to prepare for and participate in a debate. You may want to suggest that students first listen to a recording of a debate. Students can find debates online using the key words "debate" and "audio" in a search engine.

Before students begin working, review this rubric with them so that they understand their goals:

Rubric Participants in a debate should

- stay focused on the resolution
- demonstrate a clear understanding of the topic
- participate with respect for the moderator and other team members
- present position and rebuttal statements that are clear, strong, and accurate
- support two to four different points with facts, statistics, relevant examples, and expert opinions
- use appropriate facial gestures and maintain eye contact with the audience
- speak clearly and at an appropriate pace

R RESOURCE MANAGER—Copy Master
Speaking and Listening p. 177

S STANDARDS LESSON FILE
Speaking and Listening Lesson 10:
Debate

Assessment Practice

CHECK READINESS

Read aloud the paragraph under **ASSESS** and stress to students that this is not the full Unit Test, but a way for them to check their readiness for it. Then have students examine the skills listed under **REVIEW** and look back in the unit or in the **Student Resource Bank** for any skills they need to review.

READ THE SELECTIONS

Remind students to keep unit goals in mind as they read the passage and the supplementary selections, paying particular attention to these literary and reading skills:

- author's background
- historical and cultural context
- draw conclusions
- synthesize
- multiple sources

To help students focus on various background materials, discuss these questions:

- Why might knowing something about the time and place in which a story is set help you understand the story better?
- What kinds of details from an author's life might you expect to see reflected in a story?

ANSWER THE QUESTIONS

Direct students to pages R93–R101 of the **Handbook** to review test-taking strategies.

- Remind students to identify unfamiliar words by scanning a passage before they read in depth and then using context clues and a dictionary to check meanings. Also remind students to decode words by recognizing prefixes, suffixes, and roots.

- When students are ready to answer the multiple-choice questions, remind them not to choose the first alternative that seems to fit. Instead, they should read through all the choices, eliminate any that are clearly wrong, and then choose the *best* answer—the one that is the most accurate.

ASSESS
The practice test items on the next few pages match skills listed on the Unit Goals page (page 829) and addressed throughout this unit. Taking this practice test will help you assess your knowledge of these skills and determine your readiness for the Unit Test.

REVIEW
After you take the practice test, your teacher can help you identify any skills you need to review.

- Author's Background
- Historical and Cultural Context
- Draw Conclusions
- Synthesize
- Multiple Sources
- Idioms
- Greek and Latin Roots
- Gerunds and Gerund Phrases
- Vivid Verbs

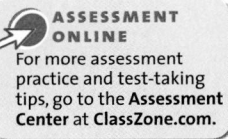

ASSESSMENT ONLINE
For more assessment practice and test-taking tips, go to the **Assessment Center** at ClassZone.com.

Reading Comprehension

DIRECTIONS *Read the excerpt from the novel* All Quiet on the Western Front *and the two supplementary background selections. The Historical Background material will help you understand what was happening in Europe when the story takes place. The Author's Background material will help you understand what life experiences might have influenced the author to write this novel. Use this supplementary material to help you answer the questions.*

In All Quiet on the Western Front, *Erich Maria Remarque brings to life the horrors of combat and the tragic effects of World War I on his generation. The following excerpt from the novel recounts a conversation among young soldiers stationed along the front.*

from All Quiet on the Western Front
Erich Maria Remarque

Albert cleans his nails with a knife. We are surprised at this delicacy. But it is merely pensiveness. He puts the knife away and continues: "That's just it. Kat and Detering and Haie will go back to their jobs because they had them already. Himmelstoss too. But we never had any. How will we ever get used to one after this, here?"—he makes a gesture toward the front.

"What we'll want is a private income, and then we'll be able to live by ourselves in a wood," I say, but at once feel ashamed of this absurd idea.

"But what will really happen when we go back?" wonders Müller, and even he is troubled.

10 Kropp gives a shrug, "I don't know. Let's get back first, then we'll find out." We are all utterly at a loss. "What could we do?" I ask.

"I don't want to do anything," replies Kropp wearily. "You'll be dead one day, so what does it matter? I don't think we'll ever go back."

"When I think about it, Albert," I say after a while rolling over on my back, "when I hear the word 'peace-time,' it goes to my head: and if it really came, I think I would do some unimaginable thing—something, you know, that it's worth having lain here in the muck for. But I can't even imagine anything. All I do know is that this business about professions and studies and salaries and so on—it makes me sick, it is and always was disgusting. I don't see anything 20 at all, Albert."

All at once everything seems to me confused and hopeless.

Kropp feels it too. "It will go pretty hard with us all. But nobody at home seems to worry much about it. Two years of shells and bombs—a man won't peel that off as easy as a sock."

DIFFERENTIATED INSTRUCTION

FOR ENGLISH LEARNERS
Assessment Practice: Work Backward

Prepare students by having them read the questions *before* reading the passage. Have pairs find unfamiliar words in test directions and questions.

1. Write each word on an index card.
2. Look up the meaning in a dictionary and write it on the back of the card.
3. Use the cards to practice the words with your partner and to teach them to others.

Test-Taking Strategies: Frame the Story

Suggest that as students read the excerpt from *All Quiet on the Western Front,* they take rough notes on setting, plot, conflict, character, and theme. Framing the story in this way will help students focus their reading, comprehend what they read, and answer questions about it. Students should note the main idea and author's purpose in each supplementary selection, as well.

We agree that it's the same for everyone; not only for us here, but everywhere, for everyone who is of our age; to some more, and to others less. It is the common fate of our generation.

Albert expresses it: "The war has ruined us for everything."

He is right. We are not youth any longer. We don't want to take the world
30 by storm. We are fleeing. We fly from ourselves. From our life. We were eighteen and had begun to love life and the world; and we had to shoot it to pieces. The first bomb, the first explosion, burst in our hearts. We are cut off from activity, from striving, from progress. We believe in such things no longer, we believe in the war.

Historical Background

World War I erupted in Europe in 1914. It was fueled by the nationalism and militarism that were rampant on the European continent. Millions of young soldiers entered a war that would not be fought as earlier wars had been. New technologies—machine guns and advanced artillery—forced troops from both sides into an elaborate system of trenches. On the western front, these trenches stretched for hundreds of miles through France and Belgium and were the bloody battlefields where the Central Powers and the Allies fought each other. Craters and barbed-wire marked the barren no man's land between the lines of trenches. Troops lived in and fought from these muddy, rat-infested trenches for months at a time. They suffered from the ravages of the seasons as well as from diseases such as trench fever, a debilitating illness spread by lice. Surprise charges from the trenches to engage the enemy in hand-to-hand battle were met by bursts of machine-gun fire and clouds of poison gas. By the end of the war, about 8.5 million soldiers had lost their lives; millions more were missing.

Those soldiers who survived the war became a generation that felt it had been robbed of its youth. The discontented German soldiers found it difficult to settle back into mainstream civilian life, especially given the economic troubles that beset Germany after its defeat. Many returning soldiers on both sides were disillusioned by the war and by their elders, who had not prepared them for its grim realities.

Author's Background

Erich Maria Remarque was born in Germany in 1898. His family was poor, but Remarque was a bright student with a keen interest in music, literature, and art. He decided to pursue a teaching career, but his college studies were interrupted in 1916, when he was drafted into the German army for service in World War I.

GO ON ➡

ITEM ANALYSIS

COMPREHENSION AND WRITTEN RESPONSE	ITEMS	UNIT PAGES
Author's Background	2, 7, 8	832–835, 875
Historical and Cultural Context	1, 3, 6, 7, 8	832–835, 853, 903
Draw Conclusions	1, 4, 5, 6, 7	863
Synthesize	3, 6, 7, 8	888
Multiple Sources	1, 2, 3, 6, 7, 8	893

VOCABULARY	ITEMS	UNIT PAGES
Idioms	1, 2, 3	887
Greek and Latin Roots	4, 5, 6	850, 861

WRITING AND GRAMMAR	ITEMS	UNIT PAGES
Gerunds and Gerund Phrases	1, 2, 6	851
Vivid Verbs	3, 4, 5	873

FOR LESS-PROFICIENT READERS

Assessment Support Consider these options for completing the Assessment Practice:

- Have students "work backward" to review the test questions *before* reading the passage and the supplementary selections.

- Select random questions in the Assessment and have students demonstrate *how* and *where* to look for the answers.

- Ask students to locate unfamiliar vocabulary words in the Assessment. Elicit the words' meanings from the class.

- Have students record useful testing words and definitions in their journals for later reference.

- Read aloud the passage and the supplementary selections, or parts of them, to aid in student comprehension.

McDougal Littell
Assessment System

After checking student readiness with this Assessment Practice, you may administer the complete Unit 9 Test in order to more thoroughly evaluate student mastery of unit goals.

Comprehension

Model a thinking process for answering multiple-choice questions.

1. **B is correct.** Muck (line 17) is a mixture of mud, vegetation, and filth; it would have characterized the trenches where the soldiers lay. A, C, and D neither state nor imply anything about trench warfare. A is incorrect because it shows Müller's thoughts about the future. C is incorrect because it shows the narrator's desire to escape thoughts of the war. D is incorrect because it shows how the war, as a whole, affected the narrator and his friends.

2. **D is correct.** In **Author's Background,** readers learn that Remarque had trouble finding a career after the war. Being born into a poor family probably would have influenced him to want the financial security of a job, so A is incorrect. B can be eliminated because the narrator probably would not have decided to train to become a teacher if the idea of a profession, studies, and salaries made him sick. C is incorrect because **Author's Background** does not make a connection between Remarque's injury and a lack of interest in a career.

3. **C is correct.** Kropp says in lines 23–24 that after fighting in a war, soldiers do not adjust to postwar life easily. A is a true statement, but it is not the correct answer, because nationalism and militarism were feelings that led to the war itself, not to how soldiers felt after leaving the war. B and D are also true statements but are not correct answers because they state facts about the war but ignore any reference to soldiers' feelings before, during, or after the war.

4. **A is correct.** In this statement, Albert summarizes the conversation about how the soldiers' lives have changed for the worse, and A best captures that sentiment. B is incorrect because the war has not yet ended when Albert makes the statement. C is incorrect because not being interested in anything but the war is not the same as being ruined by the war. D is incorrect because it contradicts Albert's statement.

5. **B is correct.** Context is the key to interpreting this statement. Just before the statement, the narrator says that because the soldiers have been cut off from activity, striving, and progress, they no longer believe in these things (lines 32–33). The only thing left to believe in, as B suggests, is the war itself. A, C, and D are not correct because the soldiers never discuss whom they support, what the issues are, or how they feel about the part that they have played in the war.

The 18-year-old Remarque was assigned to a trench unit near the western front, the region in northern France where the bloody fighting was deadlocked. He saw many of his friends killed or wounded in battle, and he himself was severely injured. After the war, Remarque had trouble finding a career. He took on odd jobs, including substitute teaching, writing advertising copy, and working as associate editor of a sports magazine. He faltered when he took his first steps as a novelist in 1920, but he surprised everyone with the publication of *All Quiet on the Western Front* in 1929. In this book, Remarque brought to life the horrors of combat and the tragic effects the war had on his generation. The novel made a deep impression on readers around the world.

Comprehension

DIRECTIONS *Use the Historical Background and Author's Background information to help you answer these questions about the excerpt from* All Quiet on the Western Front.

1. Which of the following quotations from the excerpt indicates that the soldiers were engaged in trench warfare?

   A "'But what will really happen when we go back?' wonders Müller, and even he is troubled." (lines 8–9)

   B . . . "I think I would do some unimaginable thing—something, you know, that it's worth having lain here in the muck for." (lines 16–17)

   C "We don't want to take the world by storm. We are fleeing. We fly from ourselves. From our life." (lines 29–30)

   D "We were eighteen and had begun to love life and the world; and we had to shoot it to pieces." (lines 30–32)

2. Which fact from the author's life probably had the greatest influence on what he wrote in lines 17–20?

   "But I can't even imagine anything. All I do know is that this business about professions and studies and salaries and so on—it makes me sick, it is and always was disgusting. I don't see anything at all, Albert."

   A his birth into a poor family at the turn of the century

   B his decision to go to college to become a teacher

   C the artillery injury he got during the war

   D the difficult time he had finding a career after the war

3. Which of the following facts from the Historical Background material best reflects what Kropp means in lines 23–24?

   "Two years of shells and bombs—a man won't peel that off as easy as a sock."

   A World War I was fueled by nationalism and militarism.

   B New types of weapons were used in World War I.

   C Returning soldiers had trouble adjusting to civilian life.

   D Millions of soldiers were killed or wounded in combat.

4. Which conclusion might you draw about the soldiers who fought in World War I from Albert's statement in line 28?

"The war has ruined us for everything."

A They lost their enthusiasm for life.

B They could not find work after the war.

C They were not interested in anything but the war.

D They enjoyed their wartime experiences.

5. In line 34, what does the narrator most likely mean by "we believe in the war"?

A The soldiers support Germany and the Central Powers in the war.

B The soldiers can't see beyond their immediate experience in the war.

C The soldiers really don't believe in the issues being fought over in the war.

D The soldiers are proud of their part in the war.

6. Which consequence of the war is the author most likely referring to in lines 29–33?

A that the war robbed his generation of their youth

B that some nations suffered severely from the effects of the war

C that new technology changed warfare

D that the war had serious economic effects on the modern world

Written Response

SHORT RESPONSE
Write three or four sentences to answer this question.

7. Reread lines 6–7. What does the narrator most likely mean when he says, "What we'll want is a private income, and then we'll be able to live by ourselves in a wood"? Cite one fact from the Historical Background material and one fact from the Author Background material to support your interpretation of this statement.

EXTENDED RESPONSE
Write two or three paragraphs to answer this question.

8. Describe three characters' views that reflect the author's life and times. Give specific examples from *All Quiet on the Western Front* and use the Historical Background and Author's Background evidence to support your answer.

 GO ON

919

DIFFERENTIATED INSTRUCTION

FOR ENGLISH LEARNERS

Assessment Vocabulary To help students understand the Comprehension questions, teach or review these key vocabulary words:

- Item 1: *excerpt*, "part of a story; passage"
- Item 1: *were engaged*, "participated"
- Item 3: *reflects*, "makes clear; reveals"
- Item 4: *conclusion*, "a judgment or decision reached by reasoning"
- Item 6: *consequence*, "result; effect"

- Item 7: *cite*, "quote or otherwise present as evidence"
- Item 7: *interpretation*, "explanation of the meaning of something"

---

6. A *is correct.* *In lines 25–27, Remarque prefaces the narrator's commentary by having him say that the soldiers' situation is true of "everyone who is of our age .... It is the common fate of our generation." Then, in line 29, he makes a specific reference to the loss of youth. B, C, and D are all factual statements; however, they are not correct answers, because throughout the excerpt, Remarque focuses upon the soldiers whose personal lives have been ruined, not upon the war's international impact or its technological or economic aspects.*

Written Response

Possible short response:

7. *The narrator expresses a desire to withdraw from the world. He wants a private income because he cannot imagine holding a job (lines 17–19), and he wants to flee from his life (line 30). He has lost his enthusiasm for the future. The Historical Background essay notes that German soldiers, like this fictional narrator, found it difficult to adjust to civilian life after World War I. The Author's Background notes that Remarque, like other veterans, had trouble settling into a career after he served; in a sense, he fulfills the narrator's words.*

Possible extended response:

8. *Kropp is pessimistic (lines 12–13, 22–23), Albert is fatalistic and despairing (lines 4–5, 28), and the narrator is philosophical (lines 29–34). The Historical Background suggests that their feelings are similar to those of many other young German soldiers, who felt they had been lured into the war without being prepared for its grim realities. The Author's Background shows that Remarque was part of that generation that the soldiers in the passage exemplify—young adults whose war experience profoundly changed their lives and made the postwar years very difficult.*

Vocabulary

1. **C is correct.** In this passage, the soldiers are filled with questions and confusion as they consider what the future holds for them; perplexed *refers to a confused state of mind.* B is incorrect because although the soldiers' comments can be interpreted as a hint at deprivation, the fact and nature of that deprivation do not become clear until later in the conversation. There is no evidence for A or D.

2. **A is correct.** The idea of peace-time, the opposite of war, would please the war-weary narrator. B, C, and D can be eliminated because they all make the concept of peace negative instead of positive.

3. **D is correct.** The narrator uses this idiom as part of his acknowledgment that the soldiers' lives have been ruined by the war and that they no longer have high expectations. A is incorrect because the soldiers already have experienced violence, and they want to escape it. B can be eliminated because the narrator implies that the soldiers do want something more than war in their lives (lines 29–34). Although the soldiers seem to be angry about their situation, C is incorrect because living in anger is an internal experience whereas "taking the world by storm" is an external experience.

4. **B is correct.** Bomb *is closest to* bombos *in sound and meaning; it is an explosive weapon.* A and C are incorrect because although explosion and burst *may involve sound, neither word contains the same set of letters.* D is incorrect because absurd *has nothing to do with sound.*

5. **A is correct.** Generation, *meaning "a group of people born around the same time,"* is closest in spelling to genos *and has a related meaning.* B, C, and D can be eliminated because the meanings of disgusting, gesture, *and* imagine *have nothing to do with "birth."*

6. **A is correct.** Pensiveness, *which means "deep and serious thought,"* is the closest match to pensare. B, C, and D are incorrect because they do not share similarities with the root pensare, *either in meaning or spelling.*

Vocabulary

DIRECTIONS *Use context clues and your knowledge of idioms to answer the following questions.*

1. In line 11, the soldiers are described as being "utterly at a loss." Which of the following words best defines that idiom?

   A vanished

   B deprived

   C perplexed

   D injured

2. In line 15, the narrator says that the word *peace-time* "goes to my head." Which of the following phrases best defines that idiom?

   A makes me overjoyed

   B confuses me

   C angers me

   D causes me pain

3. In lines 29–30, the narrator says, "We don't want to take the world by storm." The idiom "take the world by storm" means

   A cause trouble violently

   B look for happiness

   C live in anger

   D achieve success quickly

DIRECTIONS *Use the Greek and Latin word definitions to answer the following questions.*

4. The Greek word *bombos* means "a deep and hollow sound." Which of the following words from the excerpt most likely comes from the Greek word *bombos?*

   A explosion

   B bomb

   C burst

   D absurd

5. The Greek word *genos* means "birth." Which of the following words from the excerpt most likely comes from the Greek word *genos?*

   A generation

   B disgusting

   C gesture

   D imagine

6. The Latin word *pensare* means "to consider." Which of the following words from the excerpt most likely comes from the Latin word *pensare?*

   A pensiveness

   B private

   C peace-time

   D professions

DIFFERENTIATED INSTRUCTION

FOR ENGLISH LEARNERS

Review Academic Vocabulary On the board, list the academic vocabulary from the unit. Then give the examples in random order and have students classify them. Elicit additional examples from students.

- *author's background:* At the age of 18, during World War I, Erich Maria Remarque was drafted into the German army.

- *historical and cultural context:* German soldiers who returned from the war had a difficult time adjusting to civilian life.

- *idiom:* "His heart is in the right place" means that he has good intentions.

- *word root:* The Latin *port,* meaning "to carry," is found in the words *transportation* and *portfolio.*

- *gerund and gerund phrase:* For me, <u>studying</u> means <u>reviewing class notes</u> and <u>asking myself questions about the material.</u>

Writing & Grammar

DIRECTIONS *Read the passage and answer the questions that follow.*

> (1) Wars are fought and won not just on the battlefield but on the home front as well. (2) In addition to requiring military forces, wars need to be financed and need supplies. (3) So it was with the entry of the United States into World War I. (4) The government decided that to sell Liberty Bonds was a good way to raise money. (5) Throughout cities and towns, colorful posters <u>asked</u> citizens to contribute to the war effort. (6) Many people <u>took</u> the opportunity to become involved. (7) Young men enlisted, and women knit socks for soldiers. (8) Children <u>collected</u> tin and paper. (9) In addition, many families took steps to cut out expensive purchases and to plant "victory gardens."

1. Choose the correct way to rewrite sentence 2 by adding a gerund.

   A In addition to requiring military forces, wars need financing and supplies.

   B Wars require military forces and need to be financed and supplied.

   C In addition to requiring military forces, wars have to be financed and need supplies.

   D In addition to requiring military forces, wars need to be financed and need to be supplied.

2. Choose the correct way to rewrite sentence 4 by using a gerund phrase.

   A The government decided that to sell Liberty Bonds was a good solution to raise money.

   B The government decided that selling Liberty Bonds was a good way to raise money.

   C The government was deciding to sell Liberty Bonds as a good way to raise money.

   D The government was going out to sell Liberty Bonds as a good way to raise money.

3. Choose a more vivid verb to replace the underlined word in sentence 5.

   A told   **C** requested

   B urged   **D** invited

4. Choose a more vivid verb to replace the underlined word in sentence 6.

   A accepted   **C** seized

   B sought   **D** liked

5. Choose a more vivid verb to replace the underlined word in sentence 8.

   A obtained   **C** carried

   B gathered   **D** scavenged

6. Choose the correct way to rewrite sentence 9 by using two gerund phrases.

   A In addition, many families cut out purchases that were expensive and planted victory gardens.

   B To cut out purchases that were expensive and to plant victory gardens were additional steps taken by many families.

   C In addition, many families participated by cutting out expensive purchases and planting victory gardens.

   D In addition, many families were taking steps to cut out purchases that were expensive and to plant victory gardens.

STOP

921

ANSWERS

Writing & Grammar

1. A is correct. Financing *makes the sentence parallel with two nouns,* financing *and* supplies, *as the direct object of the verb* need. B *does not contain a gerund. In C and D, the introductory phrase has the same gerund as the original sentence, but the rest of the sentence uses various combinations of verbs, not gerunds.*

2. B is correct. *The gerund* selling *is the subject of the adjective clause* that selling Liberty Bonds was a good way to raise money. A *contains no gerund.* C *and* D *use* -ing *forms as verbs, not nouns.*

3. B is correct. Urge *is the strongest word because it means "to insist vigorously," usually with the strong intention of accomplishing a goal.* A *is incorrect because* told *is a command.* C *is incorrect because* requested *implies the use of a courteous manner in expressing a need.* D *is incorrect because* invited *suggests that someone else is given permission to fulfill a need or desire.*

4. C is correct. Seized *is the most vivid choice because it means "took hold of suddenly, with force."* A *is incorrect because* accepted *means "received something that is offered."* B *is incorrect because* sought *is too tentative for the meaning of the sentence.* D *is out of place because* liked *is not a synonym for* took.

5. D is correct. Scavenged, *"searched through for usable materials," indicates some challenge in the task.* A *is incorrect because* obtained *means "gained possession of."* B *is incorrect because* gathered, *meaning "picked," sounds as if the material were readily available.* C *is incorrect because* carried *means "took from one place to another."*

6. C is correct. *The two gerund phrases* cutting out expensive purchases *and* planting victory gardens *are objects of the preposition* by. *Neither* A *nor* B *contains gerund phrases.* D *has an* -ing *form of the verb* take, *but it is used as part of a verb phrase (*were taking*).*

FOR LESS-PROFICIENT READERS
Assessment Support: Gerunds

- Review with students that a gerund is a verb form ending in *-ing* that is used as a noun. Like a noun, a gerund can function as a subject, a direct object, an indirect object, a predicate nominative, or the object of a preposition. Ask students to locate and identify the function of the gerund in line 33 of the excerpt from *All Quiet on the Western Front.* **Possible answer:** *striving; object of a preposition*

- Have students locate and identify the function of the gerunds in these sentences:

   The soldiers thought about fleeing the war and themselves. **Possible answer:** *fleeing; object of a preposition*

   Surviving was their only goal. **Possible answer:** *surviving; subject*

   Albert enjoyed cleaning his fingernails with a knife. **Possible answer:** *cleaning; direct object*

INTRODUCE *GREAT READS*

In Unit 9, students have discussed a number of big questions. Invite students to tell which question they found most intriguing and why, and then focus attention on the three that appear on this page. Discuss the recommended books and their summaries, pointing out how each connects to the related question. Encourage students to choose one or more of these "great reads" to read independently.

ⓘ ClassZone.com

To find additional books that match students' interests and ability levels, visit the Literature Center at **ClassZone.com**.

Ideas for Independent Reading

Which of the questions in Unit 9 intrigued you the most? Continue exploring them with these additional works.

How does friendship begin?

Watership Down
by Richard Adams

Adams's unusual novel describes how rabbits Fiver, Hazel, and Bigwig form a friendship in the face of danger. They must flee human encroachment and warlike rabbits to find a new and safe homeland.

A Separate Peace
by John Knowles

A New England boarding school is the setting for the developing friendship between studious Gene and athletic Phineas. This is a novel of personal growth and the loss of innocence.

The Beekeeper's Apprentice
by Laurie R. King

Mary, a 15-year-old orphan, stumbles across Sherlock Holmes as he is watching bees. They become friends and she helps the famous detective solve mysteries.

When do world events hit home?

Refuge: An Unnatural History of Family and Place
by Terry Tempest Williams

Williams chronicles the seasons around the Great Salt Lake near her Utah home. She also sees a connection between the high number of family members with cancer—herself included—and their proximity to 1950s atom bomb testing.

Small Wonder
by Barbara Kingsolver

In the wake of the events of September 11, 2001, the author writes about reasons to have hope. She considers children, conservation projects, gardening, and a new definition of the word *patriotism*.

A World of Hurt: Between Innocence and Arrogance in Vietnam
by Mary Reynolds Powell

The author, an army nurse i
Vietnam, recalls the steps t
led her to becoming an anti
war activist. She describes
several friends who were w
her in Vietnam and who ha
taken the same journey.

How does heritage shape identity?

Dust Tracks on a Road: An Autobiography
by Zora Neale Hurston

Hurston, a writer born in poverty in the American South, wrote during the Harlem Renaissance. She helped preserve African-American heritage as a novelist, a folklorist, and an anthropologist.

The Names: A Memoir
by N. Scott Momaday

Momaday, a Kiowa Indian, comes from a family of storytellers. His memoir extols the value of words and the voice of the speaker. He writes in many voices to tell of his childhood and youth.

Lest Innocent Blood be Shed
by Philip Hallie

The people of Le Chambon,
France, were descended
from Huguenots. They
had suffered persecution
themselves and during Wo
War II chose to protect the
Jews in their midst. They
saved over 4,500 people fr
the Nazi concentration cam

UNIT 10

Shakespearean Drama

THE TRAGEDY OF ROMEO AND JULIET

- In Drama
- In Media
- In Poetry

923

For help in planning this unit, see

RESOURCE MANAGER UNIT 10
pp. 1–11

INTRODUCE THE UNIT

What an immense literary range William Shakespeare had! His works include broad comedy, gripping tragedy, academic history, ardent love poetry, and poignant social criticism. Invite students to name some of Shakespeare's plays; as they do, note that most of his plays are instantly known by title and have been performed around the world countless times. Indeed, Shakespearean references have become part of our cultural vocabulary.

Explain that both the photograph and the painting portray a young couple in love. The photograph on the right shows Romeo and Juliet, perhaps Shakespeare's most famous—and most tragic—young couple. Use these questions to get students thinking about the drama that the images suggest:

- How would you describe the facial expressions visible in each couple?
- What other details in both images suggest the drama of love?
- Can you guess the famous Shakespearean scene that the image on the right depicts?

Tell students that in this unit, they will read the **Shakespearean drama** *The Tragedy of Romeo and Juliet*. They will also read an ancient poem that helped inspire the drama and a critical review of a filmed version of the play.

About the Art French artist Adolphe-William Bouguereau (1825–1905) created *The Proposal* in 1872. During some showings, the painting has been called *Faust and Marguerite*, the lovers from Goethe's famous poem *Faust*. However, Bouguereau did not identify the lovers, and the association with Faust is speculative.

923

SKILLS STRAND	Shakespeare's World pp. 926–929 Article Level: Average	Literary Analysis Workshop: Shakespearean Drama pp. 930–937	The Tragedy of Romeo and Juliet, Act One pp. 938–967 Drama Level: Challenging	The Tragedy of Romeo and Juliet, Act Two pp. 968–991 Drama Level: Challenging	The Tragedy of Romeo and Juliet, Act Three pp. 992–1017 Drama Level: Challenging	The Tragedy of Romeo and Juliet, Act Four pp. 1018–1033 Drama Level: Challenging
Literary Analysis		Characteristics of Shakespearean Drama and Tragedy pp. 930–937 The Language of Shakespeare, Including Blank Verse, Allusions, and Word Play pp. 932–933	Shakespearean Drama—Aside pp. 939, 944, 967; Blank Verse pp. 951, 963, 967; Pun p. 958; Tragedy p. 957 Character pp. 946, 955, 967, 973, 975, 980, 990, 991, 994, 996, 1016, 1017, 1018, 1026, 1036, 1041	Shakespearean Drama—Allusion p. 987; Aside p. 991; Soliloquy pp. 971, 991; Tragedy p. 990 Character pp. 973, 975, 980, 991	Shakespearean Drama—Allusion pp. 999, 1017; Dramatic Irony p. 1000; Tragedy pp. 994, 996, 998, 1001, 1007, 1008 Character pp. 994, 996, 1016, 1017	Shakespearean Drama—Character pp. 1018, 1026; Comic Relief pp. 1023, 1033; Dramatic Irony pp. 1023, 1033; Pun p. 1031; Tragedy p. 1024
Reading and Informational Texts	Read to Interpret Literature in Relationship to Its Period pp. 926–929 Strategies for Understanding an Informational Article pp. 926–929 Understand the Influence of Author Background p. 929	Strategies for Reading Shakespearean Drama and Tragedy pp. 934–935 Paraphrase pp. 934–937 Analyze the Literature pp. 933, 935, 936–937	Strategies for Reading Shakespearean Drama pp. 939, 967	Strategies for Reading Shakespearean Drama p. 991 Summarize p. T968	Strategies for Reading Shakespearean Drama p. 1017 Predict p. T992 Review p. T1018	Strategies for Reading Shakespearean Drama p. 1033 Review p. T1018
Vocabulary		Academic Vocabulary pp. 930, 932				
Writing, Grammar, and Style				Parallelism p. 970		
Speaking, Listening, Viewing, and Media	Discuss pp. 926–929 Analyze Visuals pp. T927, T928	Discuss pp. T930–T931	Discuss pp. 938, T940–T966 Casting p. 949 Costumes p. 959 Analyze Visuals pp. T941, T954, T962, T965	Discuss pp. T968–T990, 991 Set Design p. 985 Analyze Visuals pp. T968, T974, T979	Discuss pp. T992–1016 Blocking p. 1009 Analyze Visuals pp. T992, T998	Discuss pp. 1018–1032, 1033 Promotion p. 1025 Analyze Visuals pp. T1019, T1029

The Tragedy of Romeo and Juliet, Act Five pp. 1034–1051	Linked selections		Pyramus and Thisbe pp. 1062–1069	Writing Workshop: Comparison-Contrast Essay pp. 1070–1077
	Media Study: from Romeo and Juliet pp. 1052–1055	Great Movies: Romeo and Juliet pp. 1056–1061		
Drama Level: Challenging	Film Clip	Critical Review Level: Average	Myth Level: Average	
Shakespearean Drama—Tragedy pp. 1034, 1040, 1048, 1050; Soliloquy pp. 1038, 1050; Character pp. 1036, 1041			Myth pp. 1063, 1064, 1067, 1068, 1069 Review: Narrative Poem p. 1067	
Strategies for Reading Shakespearean Drama p. 1050 Clarify p. 1034		Analyze a Critical Review pp. 1055, 1056–1057, 1059, 1060, 1061 Compare and Contrast p. 1061	Sequence pp. 1063, 1066, 1067, 1069	Analyze a Comparison-Contrast Essay pp. 1071–1072, 1076
	Academic Vocabulary (Film) p. 1053			Academic Vocabulary (Film) p. 1076
Create Rhythm p. 1051 Parallelism p. 1051				Write a Comparison-Contrast Essay pp. 1070–1077 Quotation Marks p. 1076
Discuss pp. T1034–T1049, 1050 Lighting p. 1039 Analyze Visuals pp. T1035, T1049	Discuss pp. 1052, 1055 Evaluate Mise en Scène pp. 1053–1055 Create a Visual Treatment p. 1055		Discuss pp. 1062, T1064–T1068, 1069 Analyze Visuals p. 1064	Stage a Scene p. 1077

Skills Assessed on the Unit 10 Test:

Literary Analysis
- Identify characteristics of Shakespearean tragedy and drama
- Identify characteristics of myth
- Identify character foils
- Identify and analyze a tragic hero
- Identify and analyze Shakespearean language, including word play, blank verse, and allusions

Reading and Informational Texts
- Paraphrase a passage
- Keep track of events, cause-and-effect relationships as lead to outcome, and relationships and roles
- Understand a sequence of events

Writing, Grammar, and Style
- Write a comparison-contrast essay
- Use parallelism to create rhythm or cadence
- Use a consistent organizational pattern
- Support ideas with relevant details
- Additional writing and grammar skills

For additional lesson planning help, see **Easy Planner DVD.**

OBJECTIVES

- establish prior knowledge about **love stories**
- list memorable **love stories**

What is the ultimate LOVE STORY?

Introduce the page by reading aloud the question and the opening paragraph. Point out that couples and their love stories appear throughout the world's poetry, folklore, song lyrics, history, and even cartoons, as in these examples:

Cinderella and Prince Charming

Orpheus and Eurydice

Beauty and the Beast

John and Abigail Adams

Sarah and Abraham

Using these examples, explain that some couples fall in love at first sight. Some have a long, loving friendship; others have a turbulent love that is complicated by a variety of differences. Invite student comments and additional examples.

ACTIVITY Before partners make their choices about the ultimate **love story,** have them consider their criteria. For example, does the ultimate love story have the happiest ending? the greatest compatibility between the lovers? the greatest ability to overcome hardship? the greatest potential for marriage? Invite students to share and compare their choices.

CHECK UNDERSTANDING As you review the question at the top of the page, elicit that the **love stories** that students chose need not be famous, only memorable.

Unit Resources

What is the ultimate LOVE STORY?

From cynics to sentimentalists, almost everyone can appreciate a good **love story.** These stories are everywhere, from great literary masterpieces to last week's made-for-TV movie. One of the most famous love stories ever written is William Shakespeare's *Romeo and Juliet,* the tale of two reckless teenagers who fall in love at first sight. It is a story that has captivated readers and audiences for over 400 years.

ACTIVITY With a partner, think of a few love stories you remember reading or watching. Whether it's an old-fashioned fairy tale or a modern romantic comedy, a tear-jerker novel or a film featuring the couple you love to hate, which story do you remember most vividly? Working together, make a list of titles and then settle on the tale *you* consider the ultimate love story.

R RESOURCE MANAGER UNIT 10

BEST PRACTICES TOOLKIT

S STANDARDS LESSON FILE

- Easy Planner DVD-ROM
- Write*Smart* CD-ROM
- ClassZone.com
- Audio Anthology CD
- Multi-Language Academic Vocabulary Online

- eEdition DVD-ROM & Online
- McDougal Littell Assessment System
- Test Generator CD
- Media*Smart* DVD-ROM

 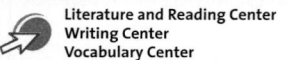
Preview Unit Goals

<table>
<tr><td>LITERARY ANALYSIS</td><td>• Identify the characteristics of Shakespearean drama and tragedy
• Identify and analyze Shakespearean language, including word play and blank verse
• Identify and analyze character foils and the tragic hero
• Identify and analyze soliloquies, asides, and allusions
• Analyze influence of historical and cultural context
• Interpret literature in relation to its literary period</td></tr>
<tr><td>READING</td><td>• Use strategies for reading Shakespearean drama, including keeping track of events and character relationships
• Paraphrase passages as an aid to comprehension
• Identify and analyze a critical review
• Compare and contrast a critical review with your own response</td></tr>
<tr><td>WRITING AND GRAMMAR</td><td>• Compare a film with a play
• Understand and use parallel structure</td></tr>
<tr><td>SPEAKING, LISTENING, AND VIEWING</td><td>• Identify, analyze, and evaluate mise en scène
• Create a visual treatment
• Stage a scene</td></tr>
<tr><td>ACADEMIC VOCABULARY</td><td>• tragedy   • soliloquy and aside
• tragic hero   • allusion
• character foil   • paraphrase
• word play and blank verse   • critical review</td></tr>
</table>

925

Preview Unit Goals

Point out to students that these goals reflect the main skills and strategies taught in Unit 10. Have students read through the list and consider what they already may know about each goal. Review the color-coding of the skill strands, reminding students that this coding will reappear throughout the unit.

Invite students to read the Academic Vocabulary terms silently. Ask them to record the words in their journals, with a definition for each word. Throughout the unit, encourage students to return to their lists to refine or clarify their original definitions.

ADDITIONAL UNIT GOALS

These skills will be taught in this unit but are not the major focus of the unit:

Literary Analysis
• Identify the characteristics of a myth
• Identify the characteristics of narrative poetry
• Identify and analyze comic relief and dramatic irony
• Identify protagonist and antagonist
• Identify iambic pentameter
• Analyze tragedy
• Analyze influence of author background
• Genre study: drama, myth, blank verse, narrative poetry

Reading
• Study a cast of characters, a synopsis/summary, stage directions, and marginal notes
• Make notes
• Keep track of cause-effect relationships as they lead to an outcome
• Note character traits
• Note punctuation and phrasing

Writing and Grammar
• Create rhythm in writing

Speaking, Listening, and Viewing
• View a feature film
• Compare and contrast a film with a play

DIFFERENTIATED INSTRUCTION

FOR ENGLISH LEARNERS

Academic Vocabulary Use the copy master to help students learn the Academic Vocabulary listed on this page.

1. Read aloud each term. Have students find it on their copy master.
2. Discuss the meanings or examples shown, and complete the chart as a class.
3. Have students work in small groups to complete the remaining activities.

Additional Academic Vocabulary Use the copy master to help students learn academic words they will use in subsequent lessons and on the Assessment Practice. Follow the same procedure as for the Academic Vocabulary copy master.

 RESOURCE MANAGER—Copy Masters
Academic Vocabulary p. 9
Additional Academic Vocabulary p. 10

Shakespeare's World

OBJECTIVES

Reading for Information

- understand the influence of author background
- analyze the influence of historical and cultural context
- read genre: read a nonfiction article to interpret literature in relation to its period
- use reading strategies, such as previewing
- make generalizations
- make inferences
- compare and contrast
- identify main ideas
- summarize
- analyze graphic aids and a cartoon

READING STRATEGY

■ PREVIEW

Have students preview the article by examining it quickly. Suggest that they look at the illustrations and read the heads and subheads. Discuss their initial impressions of the article. After students have read the article, have them compare and contrast their first impressions with what they learned from reading it in detail.

READING SKILL

■ MAKE GENERALIZATIONS

Have students make a general assessment of the era in which Shakespeare wrote.
Possible answer: The era in which Shakespeare wrote was a period of relative political stability under Queen Elizabeth I and intense intellectual and cultural activity.

England in Shakespeare's Day

Renaissance Man
William Shakespeare is widely considered to be the greatest writer in the English language and the greatest playwright of all time. His plays have been produced more often and in more countries than those of any other author.

**William Shakespeare
1564–1616**

Shakespeare lived in England during the flowering of intellectual activity known as the Renaissance. The European Renaissance was marked by a renewed interest in science, commerce, philosophy, and the arts. Basic to Renaissance thinking was a new emphasis on the individual and on freedom of choice. The Renaissance movement began in 14th-century Italy and gradually moved north and west toward England, where it reached its peak during the reign of Queen Elizabeth I. Shakespeare started his literary career during Elizabeth's reign, a period that lasted from 1558 to 1603 and is often called the Elizabethan Age.

All Hail the Queen Elizabeth was the last member of England's royal house of Tudor. Her grandfather, King Henry VII, brought stability and prosperity to his kingdom, and it was during his reign that Renaissance ideas began taking hold in England. However, political and religious problems surfaced during the reign of Elizabeth's father, Henry VIII, and continued into the early years of Elizabeth's own reign. Luckily, Elizabeth proved to be a strong monarch, able to guide England along a more moderate and prosperous course. It was a course that most Elizabethans, including Shakespeare, seem to have appreciated.

Like her grandfather and father before her, Elizabeth I was a strong supporter of English culture. As a result, artists of all types—including playwrights, poets, painters, sculptors, musicians, and architects—were held in high esteem. Taking the cue from their monarch, members of England's upper class often became patrons, or financial sponsors, of the arts. In the early 1590s, Shakespeare began acting in and writing plays for a theater company sponsored by two men who had both held the office of lord chamberlain, a high-ranking position in Elizabeth's court. The company was called the Lord Chamberlain's Men, and Elizabeth herself attended some of its productions.

**Queen Elizabeth I
1533–1603**

Theater in Shakespeare's Day

A Writer for All Time Though acting companies toured throughout England, London was the center of the Elizabethan stage. In 1576, well before Shakespeare became affiliated with the Lord Chamberlain's Men, the company built England's first theater in the suburbs of London; by the end of the 1590s, London boasted more theaters than any other European capital. One reason the London theaters did so well was that they attracted an audience of rich and poor alike. In fact, the Elizabethan theater was one of the few forms of entertainment available to working-class people of the day, and one of the few places where the working class and the educated upper class could mix. Shakespeare appealed to English audience members of all classes by including a great deal of variety in his plays: poetic speeches, exciting action, fast-paced humor, vivid character portrayals, and wise observations about human nature. Thus, while he was respected by the rich and powerful people of his day, he also became very popular with the common people.

Around the Globe In 1599, Shakespeare and the other shareholders of the Lord Chamberlain's Men became joint owners of the company's new home, the Globe Theatre. The Globe was a three-story wooden structure with an open-air courtyard in the center. Actors performed on a raised platform stage. The theater could hold 3,000 spectators, many of whom stood in the part of the courtyard near the stage, known as the pit. These customers paid the lowest admission charge, usually just a penny. Richer theatergoers paid more and sat in the inner balconies, which surrounded most of the courtyard. Audiences became emotionally involved in performances, openly showing their pleasure or their disappointment. They cheered, booed, hissed, and even threw rotten vegetables. They applauded agile sword fighting and dramatic sound effects, such as blares of trumpets, drum rolls, and claps of thunder.

THE GLOBE

This illustration shows what scholars believe the Globe Theatre looked like.

1. raised platform stage
2. pit
3. courtyard
4. inner balconies

927

◼ COMPARE AND CONTRAST

After students have read the section **Theater in Shakespeare's Day** (pp. 927–928), ask them how theater in Shakespeare's time differed from theater today. ***Possible answer:*** *In Shakespeare's time, many of the spectators stood near the stage instead of sitting in orderly rows. The staging was rather simple, with little scenery and no artificial lighting. Furthermore, women's roles were played by young men. Just the same, audience members identified so strongly with what was happening on the stage that they cheered, booed, hissed, and sometimes even threw things at the actors.*

◼ IDENTIFY MAIN IDEAS

Ask students to identify the main idea of the section **Impact on Language.** ***Possible answer:*** *Shakespeare greatly enriched the English language by including in his plays both the language of his day and words and expressions that he coined himself.*

ANALYZE VISUALS

Activity Which elements of the cartoon evoke a Shakespearean play? Which element does not? Explain. ***Possible answer:*** *The castle-like setting and the Elizabethan costumes evoke a Shakespearean play. The caption does not, because it uses contemporary slang rather than Shakespearean language.*

Elizabethan theater relied heavily on the audience's imagination. Most theaters had no curtains, no artificial lighting, and very little scenery. Instead, props, sound effects, and sometimes lines of dialogue let the audience know when and where a scene took place. However, while the staging was simple, it was hardly dull. Swords, shields, brightly colored banners, and elegant costumes often added to the spectacle. The costumes also helped audiences imagine that women were playing the female roles, which in fact were played by young male actors. In Shakespeare's day, no women belonged to English acting companies—it was considered improper for women to appear on stage. The boys who played female roles underwent rigorous training in acting, singing, and dancing. Before one could play a role such as Juliet in a first-rate company, he had to learn to move gracefully and speak convincingly.

HIS WORDS LIVE ON
Shakespeare continues to influence modern culture, as the following images demonstrate.

Actors from a popular 1993 film based on Shakespeare's *Much Ado About Nothing*

Impact on Language

Word Master Shakespeare was a master of dramatic language and a great experimenter with spoken English. He was clever and imaginative, playing with words and their meanings and creating striking images that, once heard or read, are rarely forgotten.

Shakespeare contributed more words, phrases, and expressions to the English language than any other writer. Some of these words were his own invention, including *assassination, bump,* and *lonely.* Other expressions might have been part of the everyday speech of Elizabethan England, but Shakespeare was the first to use them in writing, and their inclusion in his plays gave them a permanent place in the language.

Many of these phrases and expressions have become so common that people use them without realizing that they are quoting Shakespeare. In fact, the expressions have become "household words"— a term first used in Shakespeare's historical play *Henry V.* Other expressions that have become part of the language include "dead as a doornail" (*Henry VI, Part 2*), "laughingstock" (*The Merry Wives of Windsor*), and "for goodness' sake" (*Henry VIII*). Shakespeare's fine ear for the English language prompted the British writer George Orwell to call him a "word musician."

"He's, like, 'To be or not to be,' and I'm, like, 'Get a life.'"

A cartoon from the *New Yorker* magazine does a takeoff on *Hamlet.*

More About the Man

The Bard of Avon Although Shakespeare is probably the most famous writer who ever lived, it is largely through his plays and poetry that we know him. The known facts about his personal life are surprisingly few. We know that he came from Stratford-on-Avon, a small town on the river Avon about 90 miles northwest of London. His father was a glove maker who later became the town's mayor; his mother was a distant relative of a wealthy family who lived just outside town. Church records indicate that Shakespeare was baptized on April 26, 1564, which suggests that he was born a few days earlier. He probably went to the local grammar school, although school records no longer exist. There he would have studied Latin and read works by ancient Roman writers, such as Virgil and Seneca.

Making His Way At 18, Shakespeare married Anne Hathaway, a local farmer's daughter. The couple had a daughter named Susanna in 1583 and boy and girl twins named Hamnet and Judith two years later. There are no records of what Shakespeare did in the next seven years, which some scholars call the "lost years" of his life. During that time he apparently left his family back in Stratford, where they could live comfortably, and made his way to London, center of the theater world. He probably joined a theater company and traveled with it as an actor. When next we hear of Shakespeare, it is as a successful playwright and sometime actor in London. His earliest plays include *Richard III* and *The Comedy of Errors;* he also was writing lyric and narrative poetry. In 1593 he published his long poem *Venus and Adonis,* apparently written during the 1592–1593 season, when London's theaters were shut because of an outbreak of the plague.

Fame and Fortune By 1596, the year *Romeo and Juliet* was probably first performed, ten of Shakespeare's plays had already been produced in London, and he was a shareholder in the Lord Chamberlain's Men. Shakespeare's plays helped make the theater company the most successful of its day. In 1599, he became part owner of London's popular new Globe Theatre. In 1603, when James I succeeded Elizabeth I on the throne of England, the new king himself became the patron of Shakespeare's theater company, which became known as the King's Men. Shakespeare's business interests and revenues from plays brought him a good deal of money, enough to purchase a beautiful home for his family in Stratford. He also may have purchased a coat of arms for his father, an important symbol that allowed his father to move officially into the ranks of gentlemen.

The End In 1609, Shakespeare took advantage of his fame by publishing his sonnets, a series of poems about love and friendship that most scholars feel he wrote in the 1590s. Shakespeare also began spending more time in Stratford, retiring there permanently in 1613. He wrote no plays after that year; his last complete plays are believed to be *Cymbeline, The Tempest, The Winter's Tale,* and *Henry VIII.* While there are no documentary records of the date of his death, the monument that marks his grave indicates that he died on April 23, 1616.

 MORE ABOUT THE AUTHOR
For more on William Shakespeare, visit the **Literature Center** at **ClassZone.com.**

OTHER PLAYS BY WILLIAM SHAKESPEARE

- *Hamlet*
- *Julius Caesar*
- *King Lear*
- *Macbeth*
- *A Midsummer Night's Dream*
- *Much Ado About Nothing*
- *Othello*
- *Richard II*
- *Twelfth Night*

BACKGROUND

Biographical Clues Although the amount of factual information about Shakespeare is small compared to that of some other great literary figures, it is surprisingly large for a person of his modest social standing in life. Many scholars have looked for personal details about Shakespeare's life in the words of his sonnets. From those poems, some scholars assert that Shakespeare suffered from insomnia, and that he loved music. Perhaps the reason that his character is so elusive is that Shakespeare was a master of portraying the diverse aspects of human nature, not just the aspects that he saw in himself.

Focus and Motivate

OBJECTIVES

- identify characteristics of Shakespearean drama and tragedy, including characters and soliloquy
- identify and analyze Shakespearean language, including blank verse, allusion, and word play

Teach

Part 1: Characteristics of Shakespearean Tragedy

Characters Remind students that drama develops plot and characters through dialogue and action. Students learn about characters by what they say and do. A protagonist and antagonist create the conflict that drives the plot. Note that Shakespeare's plays often have many minor characters as well as major ones. Often, a foil is a minor character.

Tell students that one way to keep track of characters is by listing them and their qualities in two-column charts. Students might underline names of main characters and make more detailed notes about them.

Character	Traits and Qualities

 BEST PRACTICES TOOLKIT—Transparency
Two-Column Chart p. A25

Dramatic Conventions Use this activity to help students understand the dramatic conventions that are described:

- Suggest scenarios for a soliloquy and an aside and ask volunteers to improvise dialogue for them. For example, tell students that a character is feeling hopeful about the future. What might the character say?
- Ask students to give examples of dramatic irony or comic relief from television shows or films.
- Discuss what each convention adds to the drama.

 BEST PRACTICES TOOLKIT—Transparency
Core Analysis Frame: Drama pp. D21, D42

Shakespearean Drama

"If we wish to know the force of human genius," the writer William Hazlitt once proclaimed, "we should read Shakespeare." Though he wrote them over 400 years ago, Shakespeare's 37 plays are arguably as popular today as they were in Elizabethan times; they still draw avid fans to packed theaters. Shakespeare's comedies and histories remain crowd-pleasing classics, but his tragedies are perhaps his most powerful plays. One of Shakespeare's most famous tragedies is *The Tragedy of Romeo and Juliet,* the story of two lovestruck teenagers from feuding families.

Part 1: Characteristics of Shakespearean Tragedy

A **tragedy** is a drama that ends in catastrophe—most often death—for the main characters. Shakespearean tragedies, however, offer more than just despair; they also include comic moments that counter the overall seriousness of the plot. Familiarize yourself with the characters and dramatic conventions of Shakespearean tragedy before you begin reading *Romeo and Juliet.*

CHARACTERS

Tragic Hero
- is the **protagonist,** or central character—the one with whom audiences identify
- usually fails or dies because of a character flaw or a cruel twist of fate
- often has a high rank or status; shows strength while facing his or her destiny

Antagonist
- is the force working against the protagonist
- can be another character, a group of characters, or something nonhuman, such as nature or society

Foil
- is a character whose personality and attitude contrast sharply with those of another character
- highlights both characters' traits—for example, a timid character can make a talkative one seem even chattier

DRAMATIC CONVENTIONS

Soliloquy
- is a speech given by a character alone on stage
- lets the audience know what the character is thinking or feeling

Aside
- is a character's remark, either to the audience or to another character, that others on stage do not hear
- reveals the character's private thoughts

Dramatic Irony
- is when the audience knows more than the characters—for example, the audience is aware of Romeo and Juliet's tragic demise long before the characters themselves face it
- helps build suspense

Comic Relief
- is a humorous scene or speech intended to lighten the mood
- serves to heighten the seriousness of the main action by contrast

---

DIFFERENTIATED INSTRUCTION

For general guidelines on differentiating instruction, see

 BEST PRACTICES TOOLKIT
Differentiated Instruction pp. 31–38

FOR LESS–PROFICIENT READERS

Note Taking For students who need help with note taking, hand out the note-taking copy master before discussing this page. Explain that students will be learning about many new terms in this lesson. As you

discuss each definition on this spread, have students record notes on the copy master. When you teach pages 932–933, reintroduce the copy master and have students complete its remaining items.

 RESOURCE MANAGER—Copy Master
Note Taking p. 15

MODEL 1: CHARACTER IN TRAGEDY

In this excerpt, Romeo—the young protagonist of the play and a member of the Montague family—complains to his cousin, Benvolio, about a problem that is plaguing him. What do you learn about Romeo's personality?

from Act One, SCENE 1

Lines 153–161

Benvolio. Good morrow, cousin.

Romeo.   Is the day so young?

Benvolio. But new struck nine.

Romeo.   Ay me! sad hours seem long.

155 Was that my father that went hence so fast?

Benvolio. It was. What sadness lengthens Romeo's hours?

Romeo. Not having that which having makes them short.

Benvolio. In love?

Romeo. Out—

160 **Benvolio.** Of love?

Romeo. Out of her favor where I am in love.

Close Read

1. What is Romeo experiencing that most readers could relate to?

2. What possible weakness or flaw does Romeo's attitude hint at?

MODEL 2: SOLILOQUY

Through this soliloquy, readers gain access to the thoughts and feelings of Juliet, a Capulet and therefore a hated enemy of any Montague.

from Act Three, SCENE 2

Lines 20–31

20 **Juliet.** . . . Come, gentle night; come, loving, black-browed night;
Give me my Romeo; and, when he shall die,
Take him and cut him out in little stars,
And he will make the face of heaven so fine
That all the world will be in love with night
25 And pay no worship to the garish sun.
O, I have bought the mansion of a love,
But not possessed it; and though I am sold,
Not yet enjoyed. So tedious is this day
As is the night before some festival
30 To an impatient child that hath new robes
And may not wear them. . . .

Close Read

1. What does the imagery in lines 20–25 reveal about Juliet's feelings for Romeo?

2. Reread the boxed text. What is Juliet's mood as she waits for Romeo? Point out specific words and details that reveal her state of mind.

MODEL 1: CHARACTER IN TRAGEDY
Close Read

1. *Possible answer:* Romeo is feeling sad that the girl he loves does not love him. He refers to sadness in line 154 and gives the reason in line 161, when he says, "Out of her favor where I am in love."

2. *Answers will vary, but students may suggest that Romeo is impatient or that he overdramatizes the ups and downs of his love life.*

MODEL 2: SOLILOQUY
Close Read

1. *Possible answer:* The imagery shows Juliet's high regard for Romeo. She envisions that even after death he would make night so wonderful that "all the world" would love him as much as she does.

2. *Possible answer:* Juliet is in an impatient mood. Her use of the word "tedious" to describe the day and her simile comparing herself to "an impatient child" reveal her own state of mind as she waits for night to bring Romeo to her.

FOR ENGLISH LEARNERS

Language: Skill Words On the board, list and define the academic vocabulary terms shown in italics. Then give the examples in random order and have students match them to the vocabulary.

- *imagery:* the sky was black velvet
- *character:* Romeo, Juliet, Benvolio
- *dialogue:* Oh, I cannot wait much longer!
- *stage directions:* Midnight in the church-yard. A bell chimes softly.

FOR ADVANCED LEARNERS/PRE–AP

Evaluate Characters Have students discuss which character is more sympathetic, Romeo or Juliet. Have students consider both of the characters' attitudes and words. Tell students to give reasons for their responses and to support their evaluations with evidence from the models.

Part 2: The Language of Shakespeare

Blank Verse To help students understand the concept of stressed and unstressed syllables in iambic pentameter, read the two italicized lines aloud again. Tap a pencil or ruler at every stressed syllable. Have students count aloud the taps in each line.

Allusion and Word Play To illustrate the concept of an allusion, point out that the character of Romeo has now become an allusion. People often refer to a man in love as a Romeo. Write *allusion* and *illusion* on the board, noting the difference in the spelling and meaning; an illusion is a false perception.

Write this pun on the board:

> Time flies like an arrow. Fruit flies like
> a banana.

Ask which words have more than one meaning (*flies, like*). Then discuss how the knowledge of the two meanings creates the humorous surprise.

CHECK UNDERSTANDING

Have students sum up what they have learned about the characteristics of Shakespearean drama and the language of Shakespeare.

Part 2: The Language of Shakespeare

Shakespeare's plays deal with experiences and emotions that are easy to relate to, but his language can be challenging for modern readers to decipher. However, once you get past the play's unfamiliar language, learn the rhythm of its poetry, and discover how to decode Shakespeare's allusions and puns, you will come to appreciate the romance, drama, and humor that await you.

BLANK VERSE

Shakespeare wrote his plays primarily in **blank verse,** the form of poetry that most resembles natural speech. Blank verse is made up of unrhymed lines of **iambic pentameter,** a type of meter that has five unstressed syllables (˘), each followed by a stressed syllable (ʹ). Read the following lines aloud, making sure to emphasize each stressed syllable:

> *Yet tell me not, for I have heard it all.*
>
> *Here's much to do with hate but more with love.*

While this pattern is the general rule, it is often broken. Variations in the rhythm prevent the play from sounding monotonous. Breaks in the pattern also help to emphasize important ideas or dramatic moments. As you read, pay close attention to places where characters speak in rhyming poetry instead of unrhymed prose.

ALLUSION AND WORD PLAY

An **allusion** is a reference, within a work, to something that the audience is expected to know. Shakespeare's audience was familiar with Greek and Roman mythology as well as the Bible, so he sprinkled references to these works throughout his plays. In this romantic tragedy, Shakespeare included allusions to Venus, the Roman goddess of love.

Shakespeare was also a master of clever **puns,** or jokes that result from multiple word meanings or rhyming sounds. In Act One, a depressed Romeo puns on two meanings of the word *light* when he offers to carry a torch: "Being but heavy, I will bear the light."

ELIZABETHAN WORDS TO KNOW

Chances are you don't need an Elizabethan glossary to figure out that *dost* means "does." Other words and expressions, however, can prove more of a challenge. Here is a list of words that you should expect to encounter often as you read:

'a: he.

an, and: if.

anon: soon; right away.

aught: anything.

coz: short for *cousin;* used to refer to relatives or close friends.

ere: before.

e'er: ever.

god-den: good evening.

God gi' go-den: God give you a good evening.

hence: from here.

hie: hurry.

hither: here.

marry: a short form of "by the Virgin Mary" and so a mild exclamation.

morrow: morning.

naught: nothing.

o'er: over.

prithee: pray thee, or please.

sirrah: a term used to address a servant.

soft: be still; quiet; wait a minute.

thither: there.

whence: where.

wherefore: why.

wot: know.

yond, yonder: over there.

DIFFERENTIATED INSTRUCTION

FOR ENGLISH LEARNERS

Language: Punctuation Direct students' attention to the apostrophe in the second line of the italicized example and in the list of **Elizabethan Words to Know.** Point out that an apostrophe can signal ownership or missing letters, such as the missing *i* in *Here's.* Have students find examples of each use on these pages (*e'er, o'er, Cupid's*).

Culture: Clarify Draw attention to line 6 in Model 1 on page 933. Point out that the language is English that contains word forms no longer used, such as *thou* and *art*. Urge student pairs to use context to define these words. Have pairs find other examples of outdated English. Help the class create a master list and decode the meanings of the examples.

MODEL 1: BLANK VERSE

The fact that Shakespeare wrote in verse should not intimidate you. Since iambic pentameter is fairly close to English speech patterns, it can be spoken naturally, without much awkwardness. Read the following excerpt aloud to get a feel for its rhythm.

---

from Act Two, SCENE 2

Lines 2–6

But soft! What light through yonder window breaks?
It is the East, and ⟨Juliet is the sun!⟩
Arise, fair sun, and kill the envious moon,
5 Who is already sick and pale with grief
That thou her maid art far more fair than she.

Close Read

1. Reread the excerpt, tapping your foot at each stressed syllable. How many stressed syllables are in each line?

2. Point out a place where the pattern breaks. One example has been ⟨boxed.⟩ What ideas are emphasized by these variations in rhythm?

MODEL 2: ALLUSION AND WORD PLAY

For a tragedy, *Romeo and Juliet* contains quite a bit of humor. In the first two acts, much of the comedy comes courtesy of Mercutio, who clowns around, trying to make his friend Romeo laugh. Look for several puns and an allusion in this comic conversation.

---

from Act One, SCENE 4

Lines 13–22

Mercutio. Nay, gentle Romeo, we must have you dance.
Romeo. Not I, believe me. You have dancing shoes
15 With nimble ⟨soles;⟩ I have a ⟨soul⟩ of lead
So stakes me to the ground I cannot move.
Mercutio. You are a lover. Borrow Cupid's wings
And soar with them above a common bound.
Romeo. I am too sore enpierced with his shaft
20 To soar with his light feathers, and so bound
I cannot bound a pitch above dull woe.
Under love's heavy burden do I sink.

Close Read

1. Identify the allusion in this excerpt, and describe the mental image it conjures up for you. Why do you think Shakespeare included this reference?

2. One example of a pun has been ⟨boxed.⟩ Find one other example and explain the play on words.

MODEL 1: BLANK VERSE
Close Read

1. *Possible answer: There are five stressed syllables in each line.*

2. *Possible answer: The pattern also breaks at the word "envious" in line 4. These breaks add variety to the rhythm. They also help to emphasize Juliet's beauty, which is equated with sun and daylight and which makes even the moon envious.*

MODEL 2: ALLUSION AND WORD PLAY
Close Read

1. *Possible answer: Mercutio alludes to Cupid, the winged Roman god of love, when he suggests that Romeo soar on the wings of love. Students may say the allusion conjures up a mental image of a flying Cupid, piercing hearts with his arrows and making people fall in love. Shakespeare probably included this reference because the play is a tragedy about love.*

2. *Possible answer: Romeo makes the pun that he is too sore to soar. Students should also recognize that* bound *is used in different ways, although they may not know the three meanings: a common* bound, *which means "leaping upright"; so* bound, *meaning "to be tied down"; and* bound *a pitch, which means "leap the height a falcon reaches when it soars."*

If students need help . . . Explain that they do not need to catch every break in rhythm, every allusion, or every pun to understand a scene. Encourage students to take turns paraphrasing the dialogue in Model 2. Point out that most people enjoy allusions and word play only after they have grasped the meaning of a particular scene or excerpt.

FOR ENGLISH LEARNERS

Culture: Allusions Students from other cultures will likely struggle with allusions. Identify the allusion to Cupid in line 17 of Model 2, explaining that Cupid was the god of love in ancient Roman myths. Discuss why he might be mentioned in a play about love.

Language: Conversational English Patterns

Point out that Shakespeare often changes the usual order of words in sentences. Using Model 1, line 1 as an example, note that today, people would say, "What light breaks through that window?" Have students find another example of a verb placed at the end of a sentence (Model 2, line 22).

Teach

Part 3: Reading Shakespearean Drama

Reading Drama As you discuss such features as the cast of characters and stage directions, display actual elements from additional plays that students have read or will read. Point out that stage directions may contain important information about how a character appears or speaks, as well as details about the setting. Remind students that most dramas—not only Shakespearean plays—contain these elements.

Reading Shakespearean Tragedy Point out to students that Shakespearean tragedies have five acts and that the plot stages are divided among the acts. The exposition and rising action, for example, usually occur in Act One. Suggest that students use a Plot Diagram to track the plot throughout the play.

 BEST PRACTICES TOOLKIT—Transparency
Plot Diagram p. D10

Reading Shakespeare's Language Point out that students will not read plays the same way they read novels. For example, suggest that they pause to look at the marginal notes on each page *before* reading the page. This way, they will have some idea of the meanings of certain terms or speeches before reading them in context. Students should use a similar pre-reading strategy with paraphrasing, reading a group of lines completely before attempting to paraphrase its parts in order to get help from context.

Part 3: Reading Shakespearean Drama

As you read *Romeo and Juliet,* you will encounter tools and strategies on every page. The following tips will show you how to make the most of them:

READING DRAMA

- Study the opening **cast of characters** to see who's in the play.
- Read the **stage directions** to find out where a scene takes place as well as who's on stage and what they're doing. Stage directions in *Romeo and Juliet* are minimal, so you'll sometimes have to infer what's happening from the dialogue.
- Visualize the setting and the action by noting key details in the stage directions and the **synopsis** at the beginning of every scene.

READING SHAKESPEAREAN TRAGEDY

- Keep track of the characters' relationships, such as whether they are friends, relatives, or enemies. Also think about what role a character has—tragic hero, antagonist, foil, or comic relief. This will help you interpret his or her speech and actions.
- Note important character traits revealed through **dialogue, soliloquies,** and **asides** as well as the action. Consider whether the characters exhibit any flaws or weaknesses.
- Look for cause-and-effect relationships between events, especially those events that lead to the tragic outcome. Track them in a graphic like the one shown.

Cause	Effect
As part of a plan to cheer up Romeo, Benvolio and other Montagues bring him to a party that the Capulets are throwing.	At the party, Romeo sees Juliet for the first time and falls madly in love.

READING SHAKESPEARE'S LANGUAGE

- Use the **marginal notes** to help you figure out unfamiliar words and unusual sentence structures. In a chart like this one, record difficult lines and then rephrase them to read like modern speech.
- **Paraphrase** passages to help clarify their meaning. Remember, when you paraphrase something, you restate the main ideas using your own words.
- Just as when you read poetry, don't automatically stop reading when you come to the end of a line. Look carefully at each line's punctuation and consider the meaning of the complete sentence or phrase.

Text	What It Really Says	What It Means
"O Romeo, Romeo! wherefore art thou Romeo?" Juliet, Act Two, Scene 2, line 33	"Why are you Romeo?"	Why do you have to be a Montague, an enemy of my family?

934   UNIT 10: SHAKESPEAREAN DRAMA

DIFFERENTIATED INSTRUCTION

FOR LESS–PROFICIENT READERS
Note Taking For students who need help with note taking, hand out the second note-taking copy master before discussing this page. Clarify that this copy master addresses strategies for reading Shakespearean plays. Explain that it lists steps that readers should take. As they read this page, they should pay attention to how the steps can help them.

R RESOURCE MANAGER—Copy Master
Note Taking p. 16

FOR ADVANCED LEARNERS/PRE–AP
Analyze Drama Have students choose a soliloquy or other monologue from this or another Shakespearean tragedy and read it carefully to clarify its meaning. Challenge students to develop a reading that makes the meaning clear to an audience. Allow practice time, then invite students to perform dramatic readings for the class.

MODEL: READING SHAKESPEAREAN DRAMA

This fight scene takes place in a public square in Verona, the city in which the play is set. Sampson and Gregory, servants of the Capulets, have gotten into a heated argument with Abram and Balthasar, servants of the Montagues. Use the strategies you learned on the preceding page and what you already know about tragedy to analyze this episode.

from Act One, SCENE 1

Lines 51–67

[*Enter* Benvolio, *nephew of Montague and first cousin of Romeo.*]

Gregory [*aside to* Sampson]. Say "better." Here comes one of my master's kinsmen.

Sampson. Yes, better, sir.

Abram. You lie.

55 **Sampson.** Draw, if you be men. Gregory, remember thy swashing blow.
[*They fight.*]

Benvolio. Part, fools! [*beats down their swords*]
Put up your swords. You know not what you do.
[*Enter* Tybalt, *hot-headed nephew of Lady Capulet and first cousin of Juliet.*]

Tybalt. What, art thou drawn among these heartless hinds?

60 Turn thee, Benvolio! look upon thy death.

Benvolio. I do but keep the peace. Put up thy sword,
Or manage it to part these men with me.

Tybalt. What, drawn, and talk of peace? I hate the word
As I hate hell, all Montagues, and thee.

65 Have at thee, coward!
[*They fight.*]
[*Enter several of both houses, who join the fray; then enter* Citizens *and* Peace Officers, *with clubs.*]

Officer. Clubs, bills, and partisans! Strike! beat them down!

Citizens. Down with the Capulets! Down with the Montagues!

51–52 Gregory notices that Tybalt, a Capulet, is arriving.

59–65 Tybalt does not understand that Benvolio is trying to stop the fight. He challenges Benvolio.

59 heartless hinds: cowardly servants.

63 drawn: with your sword out.

65 Have at thee: Defend yourself.

66 bills, and partisans: spears.

Close Read

1. First, read through this excerpt. Then describe the setting, characters, and action you visualized as you read. Cite details from the dialogue and stage directions that helped you form a mental image.

2. What is Benvolio trying to do when Tybalt enters? Support your answer.

3. Using the marginal notes as necessary, paraphrase Tybalt's speech in the boxed lines. Why does Tybalt hate Benvolio so much?

4. How would you characterize Tybalt on the basis of this excerpt? In what way is he different from Benvolio? Cite details from the text to support your answer.

LITERARY ANALYSIS WORKSHOP **935**

MODEL: READING SHAKESPEAREAN DRAMA
Close Read

1. *Answers will vary, but students should describe a public square in a city. These details are in the synopsis on page 934 and the text on page 935. A small conflict between servants escalates into a heated fight between Benvolio and Tybalt, who is described as "hot-headed" in the stage directions following line 58. His challenge to Benvolio backs up this description. Then additional people enter, according to the stage directions following line 65.*

2. *Possible answer: Benvolio is trying to stop a fight between the Montagues' and Capulets' servants. He tells the servants to "part" and he beats down their swords, telling them to put them away. He probably draws his own sword from its scabbard to accomplish this, because Tybalt mentions the drawn sword.*

3. *Possible answer: A paraphrased version might read, "What, you wave a sword and talk of peace? I hate peace, just as I hate hell, all Montagues, and you. Get ready to fight, coward!" Tybalt hates all Montagues, so when he sees Benvolio with his drawn sword, he assumes the worst.*

4. *Possible answer: Tybalt is described as "hot-headed," and his actions and speech support this. He quickly picks a fight with Benvolio and does not listen when Benvolio asks him to put away his sword or use it to help him maintain peace. Benvolio seems like a reasonable person who wants to maintain peace.*

If students need help . . . Break the page down into these separate parts: the servants enter and fight, Benvolio tries to stop them, Tybalt enters and goads Benvolio into a fight, others join in and criticize both families.

DIFFERENTIATED INSTRUCTION

FOR ENGLISH LEARNERS

Culture: Clarify List *thou, thee, thy, thine,* and *thyself* on the board. Explain that these are older forms of the pronoun *you* and were usually used between people who were friends or relatives. Write a second list next to the first: *you* (subject), *you* (object), *your, yours, yourself.* Have students create oral sentences using a form of *you* and then restating the sentence using the appropriate form of *thou.*

FOR ENGLISH LEARNERS

Language: Punctuation Remind students that punctuation helps show how something is said. As an example, read Benvolio's outburst in line 57. Remind students that exclamation marks show strong feeling. Follow a similar procedure with question marks.

Practice and Apply

Part 4: Analyze the Literature
Close Read

1. *Answers will vary depending on the chosen passage. Examples include:* **Capulet, lines 13–24:** *"Welcome, gentlemen. Ladies who are able will dance with you. Ah ha, ladies! Which of you refuse to dance? We'll just assume that anyone who shies away from dancing has corns. Can I come near you now? Welcome, gentlemen! Long gone are the days since I wore a mask and courted the ladies. But you are welcome to dance . . . . Come on, ladies, hit the dance floor!"* **Romeo, lines 42–51:** *"She is so beautiful that the torches can learn to shine from her. She is like a rich, sparkling jewel. She is too beautiful for Earth! She stands out from others like a white dove traveling with crows. Since the dance is done, I'll watch where she goes. By touching her hand, my own will be blessed. I didn't know what love was until this moment. Before tonight, I never saw true beauty!"* **Tybalt, lines 52–57:** *"I can tell by Romeo's voice that he's a Montague. Get my sword, boy! How dare he come here, hiding behind a mask, to mock our party! It won't be a sin if I kill him, because I have to defend the honor of my people."*

2. **Possible answer:** *Capulet seems like a jovial and outgoing man. He goes out of his way to make his guests feel welcome, and he tries hard to get the party going. You see these qualities when he teases the ladies, calls for the musicians to play, and jokes about his past exploits. At the same time, he seems a bit bossy, barking orders to the servants.*

Part 4: Analyze the Literature

Apply the skills you've learned in this workshop as you analyze a longer excerpt from the beginning of the tragedy. This scene takes place at a costume party hosted by the Capulets. Disguised by their masks, Romeo and other Montagues have crashed the party. The important moment that follows—when Romeo notices Juliet from across the room and falls in love at first sight—sets the course of tragic events in motion.

from # Act One, SCENE 5

Lines 14–62

[Maskers *appear with* Capulet, Lady Capulet, Juliet, *all the* Guests, *and* Servants.]

Capulet. Welcome, gentlemen! Ladies that have their toes
15 Unplagued with corns will have a bout with you.
Ah ha, my mistresses! which of you all
Will now deny to dance? She that makes dainty,
She I'll swear hath corns. Am I come near ye now?
Welcome, gentlemen! I have seen the day
20 That I have worn a visor and could tell
A whispering tale in a fair lady's ear,
Such as would please. 'Tis gone, 'tis gone, 'tis gone!
You are welcome, gentlemen! Come, musicians, play.
A hall, a hall! give room! and foot it, girls.
[*Music plays and they dance.*]
25 More light, you knaves! and turn the tables up,
And quench the fire, the room is grown too hot.
Ah, sirrah, this unlooked-for sport comes well.
Nay, sit, nay, sit, good cousin Capulet,
For you and I are past our dancing days.
30 How long is't now since last yourself and I
Were in a mask?
Second Capulet. By'r Lady, thirty years.
Capulet. What, man? 'Tis not so much, 'tis not so much!

14–27 Capulet welcomes his guests and invites them all to dance. At the same time, like a good host, he is trying to get the party going. He alternates talking with his guests and telling the servants what to do.

17–18 She that . . . corns: Any woman too shy to dance will be assumed to have corns, ugly and painful growths on the toes.

20 visor: mask.

28–38 Capulet and his relative watch the dancing as they talk of days gone by.

Close Read

1. Choose a passage with several unfamiliar or Elizabethan words. Paraphrase the passage, using the marginal notes and the word list on page 932 as necessary.

2. Consider Capulet's behavior toward his guests and his treatment of his servants. How would you describe Capulet? Support your answer with details from the text.

936 UNIT 10: SHAKESPEAREAN DRAMA

DIFFERENTIATED INSTRUCTION

FOR LESS–PROFICIENT READERS
Analysis Support: Marginal Notes Point out that marginal notes often provide a very brief summary of a scene or speech. Have students read all the marginal notes on page 936 before reading the dialogue. Discuss what students learned from the notes. After they read the dialogue, have them match up lines from the play with details mentioned in the notes.

Analysis Support: Comic Relief Remind students that even tragedies have comic relief, or humorous moments. Ask students to identify the comic relief in Capulet's speech (the reference to corns) and contrast it with the fury that Tybalt expresses later in the scene. Have students compare such banter with jokes that appear in action or adventure films.

936 UNIT 10: SHAKESPEAREAN DRAMA

'Tis since the nuptial of Lucentio,
Come Pentecost as quickly as it will,
35 Some five-and-twenty years, and then we masked.
Second Capulet. 'Tis more, 'tis more! His son is elder, sir;
His son is thirty.
Capulet.   Will you tell me that?
His son was but a ward two years ago.
Romeo [*to a* Servingman]. What lady's that, which doth enrich the hand
40 Of yonder knight?
Servant. I know not, sir.

Romeo. O, she doth teach the torches to burn bright!
It seems she hangs upon the cheek of night
Like a rich jewel in an Ethiop's ear—
45 Beauty too rich for use, for earth too dear!
So shows a snowy dove trooping with crows
As yonder lady o'er her fellows shows.
The measure done, I'll watch her place of stand
And, touching hers, make blessed my rude hand.
50 Did my heart love till now? Forswear it, sight!
For I ne'er saw true beauty till this night.

Tybalt. This, by his voice, should be a Montague.
Fetch me my rapier, boy. What, dares the slave
Come hither, covered with an antic face,
55 To fleer and scorn at our solemnity?
Now, by the stock and honor of my kin,
To strike him dead I hold it not a sin.
Capulet. Why, how now, kinsman? Wherefore storm you so?
Tybalt. Uncle, this is a Montague, our foe;
60 A villain, that is hither come in spite,
To scorn at our solemnity this night.
Capulet. Young Romeo is it?
Tybalt.   'Tis he, that villain Romeo.

---

33 nuptial: marriage.

39–40 Romeo has spotted Juliet across the dance floor and is immediately entranced by her beauty.

44–45 Ethiop's ear: the ear of an Ethiopian (African); **for earth too dear:** too precious for this world.

52–57 Tybalt recognizes Romeo's voice and tells his servant to get his sword (**rapier**). He thinks Romeo has come to make fun of (**fleer**) their party.

Close Read

3. Reread the boxed text. How is the pattern of Romeo's smitten speech different from the pattern of earlier lines in this scene?

4. Reread lines 52–57. What does Tybalt want to do to Romeo? Explain what has made Tybalt so enraged.

5. Tybalt is just one of many antagonists working against Romeo and Juliet. Cite details that reveal Tybalt's searing hatred of Romeo.

6. Given what you know about the characters' personalities, what do you think might happen next between Romeo and Tybalt? Support your prediction with evidence.

Close Read

3. *Possible answer: Unlike earlier lines, Romeo's speech is written in rhymed couplets, or pairs, of iambic pentameter. This change emphasizes the shift from typical party banter to Romeo's realization that he has fallen in love at first sight.*

4. *Possible answer: Tybalt wants to kill Romeo. He is furious, because he thinks that Romeo has come disguised by a mask to mock Capulet's party.*

5. *Possible answer: Details that reveal Tybalt's hatred include his asking for his sword, his assumption that Romeo has come only to make fun of them, his assertion that killing Romeo would be no sin, and Capulet's line "Wherefore storm you so?" (lines 58–59)*

6. *Predictions will vary, but students will probably predict some type of conflict between Romeo and Tybalt because Tybalt is so hot-headed and angry and because he has mentioned killing Romeo.*

Assess and Reteach

Assess

Ask students to briefly summarize what they have read of the play and to tell how they learned the information: through stage directions, dialogue, or marginal notes.

Reteach

For students who are unable to apply the workshop skills to the excerpts from *Romeo and Juliet*, review with them the note-taking copy masters for this lesson:

- Ask students to look at the text and identify examples of a protagonist, antagonist, soliloquy, stage direction, marginal note, and synopsis.

- Discuss what steps students might follow when starting to read a Shakespearean tragedy.

FOR ENGLISH LEARNERS

Vocabulary: Multiple-Meaning Words Write these words from the play on the board:

- Act 1, Scene 1: "drawn" (line 63). Explain that *drawn* is a form of *draw*.

- Act 1, Scene 5: "swear" (line 18), "play" (line 23), "storm" (line 58)

Have student pairs find these words in dictionaries and choose the best meaning for the context in the play. Ask volunteers to read the meaning they chose. Invite the class to consider and decide if that meaning is correct.

Focus and Motivate

OBJECTIVES

Literary Analysis
- explore the key idea of **love** and **hate**
- identify characteristics of Shakespearean drama and tragedy
- identify and analyze blank verse, iambic pentameter, word play, protagonists, antagonists, tragic heroes, character foils, soliloquies, asides, allusions, dramatic irony, and comic relief

Reading
- read a Shakespearean drama
- understand sequence of events

Grammar and Writing
- use parallel structure to create cadence
- use writing to analyze literature

SUMMARY

The Tragedy of Romeo and Juliet tells of two teenagers who fall in love despite the feud between their families. They are married in secret by a friar who hopes that the union will end the feud. His goal is met, but through bitter irony: Believing that Juliet has died, Romeo kills himself; finding Romeo dead, Juliet kills herself. The families reconcile in grief.

Is LOVE *stronger than* HATE?

Introduce the question and ask students for initial responses to the scenario of **love** and **hate** in the paragraph. As groups prepare for the *DEBATE* activity, encourage them to support their arguments with examples.

Selection Resources

The Tragedy of Romeo and Juliet
Drama by William Shakespeare

Is LOVE *stronger than* HATE?

KEY IDEA It sounds like a story ripped from the tabloids. Two teenagers fall in **love** at a party. Then they learn that their parents **hate** each other. The teenagers' love is forbidden, so not surprisingly, they cling to each other even more tightly. Murder and suffering ensue, and by the end, a whole town is in mourning. What love can—and cannot—overcome is at the heart of *Romeo and Juliet*, considered by many to be the greatest love story of all time.

DEBATE People say that love conquers all. Is this statement true, or is it just a cliché? How powerful *is* love? Discuss this topic in a small group. Talk about instances in which love has brought people together as well as times when hate has driven them apart. Then form two teams and debate the age-old question, Is love stronger than hate?

 **RESOURCE MANAGER UNIT 10**

Plan and Teach pp. 17–20, 37–40, 53–56, 69–72, 85–88

Literary Analysis
Summary pp. 23†*, 24‡*, 41†*, 42‡*, 57†*, 58‡*, 73†*, 74‡*, 89†*, 90‡*
Shakespearean Drama pp. 25, 26†*, 43, 44†*, 59, 60†*, 75, 76†*, 91, 92†*
Question Support pp. 31*, 48*, 64*, 80*, 96*

Reading Keeping Track of the Characters p. 21
Reading Shakespearean Drama pp. 27, 28†*, 45, 46†*, 61, 62†*, 77, 78†*, 93, 94†*
Reading Check pp. 29, 47, 63, 79, 95
Reading Fluency p. 32

Grammar and Writing Create Rhythm p. 97

Assessment
Selection Tests A, B/C pp. 33*, 35*, 49*, 51*, 65*, 67*, 81*, 83*, 99*, 101*
 Test Generator CD

 **BEST PRACTICES TOOLKIT**

Differentiated Instruction pp. 31–38*

Graphic Organizers/Strategies
Cluster Diagram • Character Analysis Chart • Venn Diagram • Making Inferences • Sequence Chain • Open Mind • Plot Diagram • Problem and Solution Charts • Classification Chart • Two-Column Chart • Main Idea and Details • Reporter's Questions

Reading Support
 Audio Anthology CD*

Technology
🛈 Literature Center at **ClassZone.com**
 Write*Smart* CD

* Resources for Differentiation   † Also in Spanish   ‡ In Haitian Creole and Vietnamese

LITERARY ANALYSIS: SHAKESPEAREAN DRAMA

You can probably guess that a **tragedy** isn't going to end with the words "and they all lived happily ever after." Shakespearean tragedies are dramas that end in disaster—most often death—for the main characters. The conflicts in a tragedy are usually set in motion by the main characters' actions, but fate can also play a part in the catastrophic course of events. As you read *Romeo and Juliet*, pay attention to specific characteristics of Shakespearean drama.

- Notice what **soliloquies** and **asides** reveal about the characters. Reading these is like being around when someone is "thinking out loud"—you may learn valuable information about characters' private thoughts.

- Watch for and analyze **allusions**. Once you decode them, they add an extra layer of meaning to certain passages.

- Consider Shakespeare's use of **comic relief** to ease the tension of certain scenes. Think of the comic episodes as brief breaks that allow you to absorb earlier events in the plot and get ready for new developments.

- Pay attention to the rhythm of each line. Shakespeare wrote his plays in **blank verse,** a poetic form that resembles the rhythm of natural speech.

READING STRATEGY: READING SHAKESPEAREAN DRAMA

Though his plays can sweep you away, Shakespeare's English is sometimes hard for modern readers to understand. These strategies can help:

- Read the synopsis, or summary, of each scene to get an idea of what happens in that part of the play.

- Use the marginal notes to figure out the meanings of unfamiliar words, unusual grammatical structures, and allusions.

- Keep track of events to make the plot easier to follow. All the events in *Romeo and Juliet* take place in six days. As you read, use a chart to record plot developments and interactions between characters.

Sunday	Monday	Tuesday	Wednesday	Thursday	Friday
street brawl					

Overview

Act One We meet the Montagues and the Capulets, two long-feuding families in the Italian city of Verona. At the beginning of the play, Romeo, a Montague, is in love with Rosaline. Juliet, a Capulet, is asked by her parents to consider marrying Paris. Romeo and Juliet meet at a masked ball and fall in love, each later realizing that the other is from the enemy family.

Act Two Forced to meet in secret, Romeo and Juliet declare their love to each other and decide to get married. Romeo visits Friar Laurence, a priest, and asks him to perform the wedding. Aided by Juliet's nurse, Romeo and Juliet meet and marry in secret.

Act Three During a street fight, Juliet's cousin Tybalt kills Romeo's friend Mercutio. Romeo loses his temper and kills Tybalt; he then flees, realizing with horror what he has done. Romeo is banished from Verona under pain of death. Juliet grieves the double loss of her cousin and her husband. With the help of Friar Laurence and the nurse, Romeo and Juliet make plans to flee to Mantua, another city. Her parents, not knowing she is already married to Romeo, order her to marry Paris.

Act Four A distraught Juliet visits Friar Laurence for help and threatens to kill herself. He gives her a potion that will not kill her but put her into a deathlike sleep for two days, with the plan that Romeo will rescue her from the family tomb when she awakens. Friar Laurence sends a letter to Romeo in Mantua, describing this plan. Juliet takes the potion. Her family finds her and prepares her burial, believing her dead.

Act Five Romeo does not get Friar Laurence's letter before he hears of Juliet's death and believes it is real. Grief stricken, he returns to Verona. He finds Juliet in her deathlike sleep, takes real poison, and dies. Juliet awakens and, finding Romeo dead, kills herself with his dagger. When the families realize what has happened, Lord Capulet and Lord Montague agree to end their feud.

ROMEO AND JULIET **939**

Teach

STANDARDS FOCUS

LITERARY ANALYSIS

● SHAKESPEAREAN DRAMA

Define characteristics as needed. Then read aloud this excerpt from *Romeo and Juliet*, Act Two, Scene 2. Explain that Romeo is speaking to himself when he sees Juliet appear on her balcony.

> But soft! What light through yonder window breaks?
> It is the East, and Juliet is the sun!

Ask students which characteristics of Shakespearean drama the lines illustrate. *Possible answer: The lines are a soliloquy spoken in blank verse.*

CHECK UNDERSTANDING Ask students to name other characteristics of Shakespearean drama.

READING STRATEGY

■ READING SHAKESPEAREAN DRAMA

Explain that the Prologue (p. 941) serves as a synopsis of the play as a whole; then point out the synopsis of Act One, Scene 1 (page 942). Use the Prologue to model the use of marginal notes. Elicit that much of what is said in the Prologue probably would be recorded in the last day or days in the chart.

CHECK UNDERSTANDING Have students explain the three strategies in their own words. Invite volunteers to share how they have used these strategies in the past.

R RESOURCE MANAGER—Copy Master
  Reading Shakespearean Drama p. 27
  (for student use while reading the selection)

DIFFERENTIATED INSTRUCTION

FOR LESS-PROFICIENT READERS

Preview Point out that *Romeo and Juliet* is such a famous play that most productions assume that audience members already know some of its key plot events, especially the ending. Have students work with partners to read the *Overview* and check each other's understanding of the summaries before they begin reading the play itself.

FOR ENGLISH LEARNERS

Concept Support Remind students of some terms that are used in the reading of dramatic works, including *cast, prologue, chorus, act, scene, stage, stage directions,* and *curtain*. Help students define each term. Point out that stage directions for this play appear in brackets and italics (except for names of characters).

Practice and Apply

READING STRATEGY

◼ MONITOR

Suggest that students place a bookmark at this page, which lists the play's cast of characters. Doing so will help them refer to the list easily if they become uncertain about who a character is or to which side of the feud he or she belongs. In addition, urge students to make use of the Tracking the Characters copy master as they read.

 RESOURCE MANAGER—Copy Master
Keeping Track of the Characters p. 21

GO BEHIND THE CURTAIN

As students read and discuss the sidebar, explain that *stagecraft* refers to theatrical devices and techniques. Then have students turn to page 949, the first appearance of the **Behind the Curtain** feature, and tell what the photographs show. *Possible answer: The photographs show different actors who have been cast as Romeo and Juliet.* Point out that casting is just one of the many elements of stagecraft.

BACKGROUND

The story of Romeo and Juliet had been told by several writers by the time William Shakespeare produced his play between 1594 and 1596. *The Tragicall Historye of Romeus and Juliet,* for example, was written by a now nearly forgotten English poet named Arthur Brooke and was published in 1562. Shakespeare used virtually all of Brooke's major characters and kept the setting of Verona in the 1300s, but added his own unique artistry to the characters and the story.

THE TRAGEDY OF
Romeo & Juliet

WILLIAM SHAKESPEARE

GO BEHIND THE CURTAIN

One Play, Many Productions
The images at the top of page 941 capture five different interpretations of *Romeo and Juliet.* Though the productions were staged at different times in different countries, each director had the same goal: to thrill audiences with Shakespeare's timeless tale of two reckless, lovesick teenagers. As you read the play, you will discover many more images from a variety of productions. You'll also encounter **Behind the Curtain** feature pages that will help you explore the stagecraft used to create moving theatrical productions of this famous play.

TIME
The 14th century

CAST

THE MONTAGUES
Lord Montague (mŏn'tə-gyōō')
Lady Montague
Romeo, son of Montague
Benvolio (bĕn-vō'lē-ō), nephew of Montague and friend of Romeo
Balthasar (bäl'thə-sär'), servant to Romeo
Abram, servant to Montague

THE CAPULETS
Lord Capulet (kăp'yōō-lĕt')
Lady Capulet
Juliet, daughter of Capulet
Tybalt (tĭb'əlt), nephew of Lady Capulet
Nurse to Juliet
Peter, servant to Juliet's nurse
Sampson, servant to Capulet
Gregory, servant to Capulet
An Old Man of the Capulet family

PLACE
Verona (və-rō'nə) and Mantua (măn'chōō-ə) in northern Italy

OTHERS
Prince Escalus (ĕs'kə-ləs), ruler of Verona
Mercutio (mĕr-kyōō'shē-ō), kinsman of the prince and friend of Romeo
Friar Laurence, a Franciscan priest
Friar John, another Franciscan priest
Count Paris, a young nobleman, kinsman of the prince
Apothecary (ə-pŏth'ĭ-kĕr'ē)
Page to Paris
Chief Watchman
Three Musicians
An Officer
Chorus
Citizens of Verona, **Gentlemen** and **Gentlewomen** of both houses, **Maskers, Torchbearers, Pages, Guards, Watchmen, Servants,** and **Attendants**

DIFFERENTIATED INSTRUCTION

FOR LESS–PROFICIENT READERS

Read Aloud Have students take turns reading aloud the cast list to gain an oral familiarity with the names. Remind students that *Montague* and *Capulet* are family names and that each family dislikes the other intensely. Emphasize that keeping track of family alliances will be important to understanding Shakespeare's plot.

FOR ENGLISH LEARNERS

Vocabulary: Outdated Forms Have students begin a language journal for their reading of *Romeo and Juliet.* Point out that some words and expressions in this play are not used in modern English. Still, they are important to understanding the play, and their modern equivalents are worth knowing. Model a journal entry using *Apothecary* from the cast list. Have students look up the definition and add it to their journals.

Prologue

The Chorus is one actor who serves as a narrator. He enters from the back of the stage to introduce and explain the theme of the play. His job is to "hook" the audience's interest by telling them just enough to quiet them down and make them eager for more. In this prologue, or preview, the narrator explains that the play will be about a feud between two families (the Capulets and the Montagues). In addition, the narrator says that the feud will end in tragedy. As you read the prologue, determine what the tragedy will be.

[*Enter* Chorus.]

Chorus. Two households, both alike in dignity,
In fair Verona, where we lay our scene,
From ancient grudge break to new mutiny,
Where civil blood makes civil hands unclean.
5 From forth the fatal loins of these two foes,
A pair of star-crossed lovers take their life,
Whose misadventured piteous overthrows
Doth with their death bury their parents' strife.
The fearful passage of their death-marked love,
10 And the continuance of their parents' rage,
Which, but their children's end, naught could remove,
Is now the two hours' traffic of our stage,
The which if you with patient ears attend,
What here shall miss, our toil shall strive to mend.

[*Exit.*]

3–4 ancient . . . unclean: A new outbreak of fighting (**mutiny**) between families has caused the citizens of Verona to have one another's blood on their hands.

6 star-crossed: doomed. The position of the stars when the lovers were born was not favorable. In Shakespeare's day, people took astrology very seriously.

7 misadventured: unlucky.

11 but: except for; **naught:** nothing.

12 the two hours' . . . stage: what will be shown on the stage in the next two hours.

14 what . . . mend: The play will fill in the details not mentioned in the prologue.

Get Into the Act

SUMMARY

Act One opens with a street brawl between the feuding Capulets and Montagues. Then Romeo enters, pining with unrequited love for Rosaline. In the meantime, Capulet and his wife are considering a marriage between their daughter Juliet and Count Paris. The Capulets give a party that evening, and Romeo attends, uninvited. There he meets and instantly falls in love with Juliet, as does she with him. Only later does each learn that the other comes from the rival family.

ANALYZE VISUALS

Activity What can you predict about the play's events from these photographs? *Possible answer: You can predict love between Romeo and Juliet, violence, poisoning, and death.*

READING STRATEGY

 SUMMARIZE

After allowing time for review of the marginal notes, ask students to summarize what the Chorus explains. ***Possible answer:*** *The Chorus explains that the play will show how a family feud causes the death of two lovers and how the feud ends in their deaths.*

Resources for Act One

R RESOURCE MANAGER UNIT 10

Plan and Teach pp. 17–20

Literary Analysis
Summary pp. 23†*, 24‡*
Shakespearean Drama pp. 25, 26†*
Question Support p. 31*

Reading
Keeping Track of Characters p. 21
Reading Shakespearean Drama
   pp. 27, 28†*
Reading Check p. 29
Reading Fluency p. 32

Assessment
Selection Tests A, B/C pp. 33*, 35*
Test Generator CD

BEST PRACTICES TOOLKIT

Differentiated Instruction
   pp. 31–38*

Graphic Organizers/Strategies
Cluster Diagram • Character
Analysis Chart • Venn Diagram

Reading Support
Audio Anthology CD*

Technology
Literature Center at
ClassZone.com
Write*Smart* CD

* Resources for Differentiation   † Also in Spanish   ‡ In Haitian Creole and Vietnamese

Practice and Apply

ANALYZE VISUALS

Activity How does the photograph capture the relationship between Romeo and Juliet?

Possible answer: *The characters are looking up, as if they aspire to a happy dream. Their bodies, however, face in opposite directions, symbolizing the feud between their families. Their faces seem to meet and blend, perhaps illustrating the commitment of love that the two share.*

Act One

SCENE 1 *A public square in Verona.*

As the scene opens, two young Capulet servants swagger across the stage, joking and bragging. When they happen to meet servants from the rival house of Montague, a quarrel begins that grows into an ugly street fight. Finally the ruler of Verona, Prince Escalus, appears. He is angry about the violence in his city and warns that the next offenders will receive the death penalty. The crowd fades away, and the stage is set for the entrance of Romeo, heir of the Montague family. Romeo, infatuated and miserable, can talk of nothing but his love for Rosaline and her cruelty in refusing to love him back.

[*Enter* Sampson *and* Gregory, *servants of the house of Capulet, armed with swords and bucklers (shields).*]

Sampson. Gregory, on my word, we'll not carry coals.

Gregory. No, for then we should be colliers.

Sampson. I mean, an we be in choler, we'll draw.

Gregory. Ay, while you live, draw your neck out of collar.

5 **Sampson.** I strike quickly, being moved.

Gregory. But thou art not quickly moved to strike.

Sampson. A dog of that house of Montague moves me.

Gregory. To move is to stir, and to be valiant is to stand. Therefore, if thou art moved, thou runnest away.

10 **Sampson.** A dog of that house shall move me to stand. I will take the wall of any man or maid of Montague's.

Gregory. That shows thee a weak slave, for the weakest goes to the wall.

Sampson. 'Tis true; and therefore women, being the weaker 15 vessels, are ever thrust to the wall. Therefore push I will Montague's men from the wall and thrust his maids to the wall.

Gregory. The quarrel is between our masters and us their men.

Sampson. 'Tis all one. I will show myself a tyrant. When I have fought with the men, I will be cruel with the maids: I will cut 20 off their heads.

Gregory. The heads of the maids?

Sampson. Ay, the heads of the maids, or their maidenheads. Take it in what sense thou wilt.

Gregory. They must take it in sense that feel it.

1–2 we'll not carry coals: we won't stand to be insulted. **Colliers,** those involved in the dirty work of hauling coal, were often the butt of jokes.

3–4 in choler: angry; **collar:** a hangman's noose.

① **Targeted Passage**

11 take the wall: walk nearest to the wall. People of higher rank had the privilege of walking closer to the wall, to avoid any water or garbage in the street. *What claim is Sampson making about himself and anyone from the rival house of Montague?*

14–24 Sampson's tough talk includes boasts about his ability to overpower women.

Romeo and Juliet in the Anželika Cholina Dance Theatre's 2003 production

---

DIFFERENTIATED INSTRUCTION

FOR LESS–PROFICIENT READERS

Preview Read through the italicized scene synopsis to give students an overview of Scene 1. Help them create a sequence chain to organize the plot events.

> Capulet and Montague servants fight.
>
> ↓
>
> Prince Escalus breaks up the fight.
>
> ↓
>
> Romeo enters, upset about being jilted.

FOR ENGLISH LEARNERS

Vocabulary Support The feud between the Montagues and Capulets is central to the play. Make sure that students understand that a feud is a long-standing disagreement. Then teach these interrelated words in the scene synopsis:

- *rival,* "opposing," "enemy"
- *quarrel,* "fight or argument"
- *offenders,* "people who commit a crime"
- *death penalty,* "execution as punishment"

Task Support Call attention to the question in the marginal note for line 11. Briefly discuss the explanation for the expression "take the wall." *Possible answer: Sampson is claiming that no Montague can force him to the nasty side of the walk, for he is superior to anyone from the Montague clan.*

BACKGROUND

***Romeo and Juliet* in Its Time** Although *Romeo and Juliet* is set in Verona in the 1300s, it is important to remember that Shakespeare wasn't primarily interested in accurately portraying life in Italy in the Middle Ages. He was more interested in presenting a play that his English audience of the 1590s could relate to. He was aware that his audience could understand the characters and events of his play—feuding families, arranged marriages, secretive friars, shady apothecaries, duels, and fate—only through their own knowledge and experience. Like feud-torn Verona, England at that time was a place of strife, suspicion, and revenge. After the defeat of the Spanish Armada in 1588, a Spanish reprisal seemed imminent. Many suspected that Roman Catholic sympathizers were plotting to overthrow the Protestant Queen Elizabeth. Moreover, plague and repeated crop failure had led to economic depression, widespread unemployment, vagrancy, crime, and social conditions similar to those Shakespeare describes toward the end of the play. As students read, have them pay attention to the details Shakespeare weaves into his play to make its tragic tale of "star-crossed" love realistic and relevant.

For general guidelines on differentiating instruction, see

BEST PRACTICES TOOLKIT
   Differentiated Instruction pp. 31–38

FOR LESS–PROFICIENT READERS

In combination with the *Audio Anthology CD*, use one or more Targeted Passages (pp. 942, 951, 963, 966) to ensure that students focus on key story events, concepts, and skills. Targeted Passages are also good for English learners.

① Targeted Passage [Lines 7–16]

This passage sets up the family feud by showing how even the Capulet servants express ill will toward the Montagues.

- Who owns the dog that moves Sampson to stand?

- Which members of the Montague clan will Sampson oppose? What would he like to do to them?

- Does Gregory agree with Sampson? How can you tell?

944   UNIT 10: SHAKESPEAREAN DRAMA

25 **Sampson.** Me they shall feel while I am able to stand;
and 'tis known I am a pretty piece of flesh.

Gregory. 'Tis well thou art not fish; if thou hadst, thou hadst
been poor-John. Draw thy tool! Here comes two of the house
of Montagues.

[*Enter* Abram *and* Balthasar, *servants to the Montagues.*]

30 **Sampson.** My naked weapon is out. Quarrel! I will back thee.

Gregory. How? turn thy back and run?

Sampson. Fear me not.

Gregory. No, marry. I fear thee!

Sampson. Let us take the law of our sides; let them begin.

35 **Gregory.** I will frown as I pass by, and let them take it as they list.

Sampson. Nay, as they dare. I will bite my thumb at them;
which is disgrace to them, if they bear it.

Abram. Do you bite your thumb at us, sir?

Sampson. I do bite my thumb, sir.

40 **Abram.** Do you bite your thumb at us, sir?

Sampson [*aside to* Gregory]. Is the law of our side if I say ay?

Gregory [*aside to* Sampson]. No.

Sampson. No, sir, I do not bite my thumb at you, sir; but I bite
my thumb, sir.

45 **Gregory.** Do you quarrel, sir?

Abram. Quarrel, sir? No, sir.

Sampson. But if you do, sir, I am for you. I serve as good a man
as you.

Abram. No better.

50 **Sampson.** Well, sir.

[*Enter* Benvolio, *nephew of Montague and first cousin of Romeo.*]

Gregory [*aside to* Sampson]. Say "better." Here comes one of my
master's kinsmen.

Sampson. Yes, better, sir.

Abram. You lie.

55 **Sampson.** Draw, if you be men. Gregory, remember thy
swashing blow. **Ⓐ**

[*They fight.*]

Benvolio. Part, fools! [*beats down their swords*]
Put up your swords. You know not what you do.

28 poor-John: a salted fish, considered fit only for poor people to eat.

33 marry: a short form of "by the Virgin Mary" and so a mild exclamation.

34–44 Gregory and Sampson decide to pick a fight by insulting the Montague servants with a rude gesture (**bite my thumb**).

51–52 Gregory notices that Tybalt, a Capulet, is arriving. *Why do you think Gregory and Sampson behave more aggressively as soon as they realize that Tybalt is approaching?*

Ⓐ ASIDE
Contrast what the servants say openly in lines 35–56 with what they say in **asides,** or whispers to each other. What does this contrast reveal about Sampson and Gregory?

944   UNIT 10: SHAKESPEAREAN DRAMA

Ⓐ ASIDE

Possible answer: When Sampson and Gregory speak openly, their words are bold and rash. In contrast, the words that they speak in asides are cautious and rather timid. The contrast reveals that these characters are not as brave as they claim to be.

If students need help . . . Have three volunteers (taking the roles of Sampson, Gregory, and Abram) read aloud the dialogue in lines 35–56, with lowered voices for the asides. Discuss how the volume and tone suggest the Capulet servants' public and private emotions.

Lines 55–58
REINFORCE *KEY IDEA:* LOVE AND HATE

Discuss How does Benvolio show that he may not be as obsessed with **hate** as are the other characters in this scene? *Possible answer: Instead of drawing his sword and fighting alongside Abram and Balthasar against Sampson and Gregory, Benvolio urges them to stop, and he physically beats down their swords.*

DIFFERENTIATED INSTRUCTION

FOR ENGLISH LEARNERS
Vocabulary: Outdated Forms Remind students that Shakespearean English contains terms that are not used today. Provide these terms and their definitions. Then have students reread the lines noted and substitute the definitions for the words.

- *'tis* (line 26), "it is"
- *thee* (line 30), "you"
- *Put up* (line 58), "put away"
- *art thou* (line 59), "are you"

Task Support Have students read the question in the marginal note for lines 51–64. Elicit that "one of my master's kinsmen" (lines 51–52) refers to Tybalt, not Benvolio (who has just entered the scene). *Possible answer: Gregory and Sampson are outnumbered—three Montagues to two Capulets. Tybalt's arrival gives the Capulets a better chance at winning the fight that they have provoked.*

[*Enter* Tybalt, *hot-headed nephew of Lady Capulet and first cousin of Juliet.*]

Tybalt. What, art thou drawn among these heartless hinds?
60 Turn thee, Benvolio! look upon thy death.

Benvolio. I do but keep the peace. Put up thy sword,
Or manage it to part these men with me.

Tybalt. What, drawn, and talk of peace? I hate the word
As I hate hell, all Montagues, and thee.
65 Have at thee, coward!

[*They fight.*]

[*Enter several of both houses, who join the fray; then enter* Citizens *and* Peace Officers, *with clubs.*]

Officer. Clubs, bills, and partisans! Strike! beat them down!

Citizens. Down with the Capulets! Down with the Montagues!

[*Enter old* Capulet *and* Lady Capulet.]

Capulet. What noise is this? Give me my long sword, ho!

Lady Capulet. A crutch, a crutch! Why call you for a sword?

70 **Capulet.** My sword, I say! Old Montague is come
And flourishes his blade in spite of me.

[*Enter old* Montague *and* Lady Montague.]

Montague. Thou villain Capulet!—Hold me not, let me go.

Lady Montague. Thou shalt not stir one foot to seek a foe.

[*Enter* Prince Escalus, *with attendants. At first no one hears him.*]

Prince. Rebellious subjects, enemies to peace,
75 Profaners of this neighbor-stained steel—
Will they not hear? What, ho! you men, you beasts,
That quench the fire of your pernicious rage
With purple fountains issuing from your veins!
On pain of torture, from those bloody hands
80 Throw your mistempered weapons to the ground
And hear the sentence of your moved prince.
Three civil brawls, bred of an airy word
By thee, old Capulet, and Montague,
Have thrice disturbed the quiet of our streets
85 And made Verona's ancient citizens
Cast by their grave beseeming ornaments
To wield old partisans, in hands as old,
Cankered with peace, to part your cankered hate.
If ever you disturb our streets again,
90 Your lives shall pay the forfeit of the peace.

59–65 Tybalt does not understand that Benvolio is trying to stop the fight. He challenges Benvolio.

59 heartless hinds: cowardly servants.

63 drawn: with your sword out.

65 Have at thee: Defend yourself.

66 bills, and partisans: spears.

69 A crutch . . . sword: You need a crutch more than a sword.

74–81 The prince is furious about the street fighting caused by the feud. He orders the men to drop their weapons and pay attention.

77 pernicious: destructive.

82–90 Three . . . peace: The prince holds Capulet and Montague responsible for three recent street fights, each probably started by an offhand remark or insult (**airy word**). He warns that they will be put to death if any more fights occur.

ROMEO AND JULIET: ACT ONE, SCENE 1   **945**

FOR LESS–PROFICIENT READERS
Paraphrasing Shakespeare Have students re-read the marginal note for lines 74–81. Model a paraphrase of lines 76–78: *Can't they hear me? Hey! Listen, you animals, whose fiery anger will not be satisfied until you have shed blood!* Then invite volunteers to paraphrase lines 79–81. *Possible answer: Unless you want to be tortured, drop your weapons and listen to my decision.*

FOR ENGLISH LEARNERS
Vocabulary Support Define and discuss these phrases from the prince's speech:
- *neighbor-stained steel* (line 75), "sword with a fellow-citizen's blood on it"
- *purple fountains* (line 78), "spurts of blood"
- *wield old partisans* (line 87), "handle old weapons with a broad blade and long shaft"
- *cankered hate* (line 88), "feud" (literally, "diseased hate")

Lines 66–73
REINFORCE *KEY IDEA:* LOVE AND HATE

Discuss In what sense does **love** win over **hate** in this scene between the heads of the Montague and the Capulet families? ***Possible answer:*** *Love wins over hate in the sense that the love that Lady Capulet and Lady Montague have for their husbands is able to stop the hatred between the two men from erupting into more violence.*

Lines 74–90
DISCUSSION PROMPTS
Use these prompts to help students explore the role of Prince Escalus:

Connect What kinds of officials in American society today would serve the same functions as Prince Escalus? ***Possible answer:*** *The same functions would be served by a mayor (Prince Escalus is the head of the city's government), a police chief (he also has the power to enforce the law and to take offenders into custody), and a judge (he has the power to declare offenders guilty and even sentence them to death).*

Analyze Why is Prince Escalus upset about what has just happened? Cite evidence from his speech. ***Possible answer:*** *Prince Escalus is upset for several reasons: It is just the most recent episode in a series of violent fights (line 82–84); the violence has upset the citizens of Verona, especially the older ones (lines 84–88); and both parties have demonstrated that they will not be bound by his laws (lines 74–76).*

Synthesize How might Prince Escalus's threat in line 90 hint at a price that neither party could understand at this moment? ***Possible answer:*** *By threatening that Montague and Capulet will pay with their lives, the Prince is foreshadowing not their death but the death of their children. The two enemies will instead pay with their grief.*

For this time all the rest depart away.
You, Capulet, shall go along with me;
And, Montague, come you this afternoon,
To know our farther pleasure in this case,
95 To old Freetown, our common judgment place.
Once more, on pain of death, all men depart.

[*Exeunt all but* Montague, Lady Montague, *and* Benvolio.]

Montague. Who set this ancient quarrel new abroach?
Speak, nephew, were you by when it began?

Benvolio. Here were the servants of your adversary
100 And yours, close fighting ere I did approach.
I drew to part them. In the instant came
The fiery Tybalt, with his sword prepared;
Which, as he breathed defiance to my ears,
He swung about his head and cut the winds,
105 Who, nothing hurt withal, hissed him in scorn. **B**
While we were interchanging thrusts and blows,
Came more and more, and fought on part and part,
Till the Prince came, who parted either part.

Lady Montague. O, where is Romeo? Saw you him today?
110 Right glad I am he was not at this fray.

Benvolio. Madam, an hour before the worshiped sun
Peered forth the golden window of the East,
A troubled mind drave me to walk abroad,
Where, underneath the grove of sycamore
115 That westward rooteth from the city's side,
So early walking did I see your son.
Towards him I made, but he was ware of me
And stole into the covert of the wood.
I—measuring his affections by my own,
120 Which then most sought where most might not be found,
Being one too many by my weary self—
Pursued my humor, not pursuing his,
And gladly shunned who gladly fled from me.

Montague. Many a morning hath he there been seen,
125 With tears augmenting the fresh morning's dew,
Adding to clouds more clouds with his deep sighs;
But all so soon as the all-cheering sun
Should in the farthest East begin to draw
The shady curtains from Aurora's bed,
130 Away from light steals home my heavy son
And private in his chamber pens himself,
Shuts up his windows, locks fair daylight out,

B CHARACTER

Possible answers: *According to Benvolio, Tybalt is "fiery" (line 102), or easily angered. Benvolio says that Tybalt entered with sword at the ready and that he quickly began to fight. If Tybalt runs into Benvolio or another Montague again, he probably will try to fight again, despite the decree of Prince Escalus.*

If students need help . . . Write these terms from Benvolio's speech on the board: "fiery" (line 102), "sword prepared" (line 102), "breathed defiance" (line 103), "cut the winds" (line 104), "hurt" (line 105), and "hissed" (line 105). Discuss the negative impression that these words make.

---

exeunt: the plural form of *exit*, indicating that more than one person is leaving the stage.

97 Who . . . abroach: Who reopened this old argument?

99 adversary: enemy.

100 ere: before.

B CHARACTER
According to Benvolio, what kind of person is Tybalt? **Predict** how Tybalt might act if he runs into Benvolio—or any other Montague—again.

107 on part and part: some on one side, some on the other.

110 fray: fight.

113 drave: drove.

115 rooteth: grows.

117–123 made: moved; **covert:** covering. Romeo saw Benvolio coming and hid in the woods. Since Benvolio himself was seeking solitude, he decided to respect Romeo's privacy and did not go after him. *What does this action tell you about Benvolio?*

124–135 Romeo has been seen wandering through the woods at night, crying. At dawn he returns home and locks himself in his darkened room. Montague feels that this behavior is a bad sign and that his son needs guidance.

129 Aurora's bed: Aurora was the goddess of the dawn.

DIFFERENTIATED INSTRUCTION

FOR LESS–PROFICIENT READERS
Inverted Word Order Explain that Shakespeare often inverted the word order of sentences, stating the verb before the subject. (This was not the pattern of everyday Elizabethan speech.) Encourage students to "translate" such sentences by restating them with the subject first. Model these examples:

• *come you this afternoon* (line 93), "you come this afternoon"

• *Here were the servants of your adversary* (line 99), "the servants of your adversary were here"

Then ask pairs of students to restate these lines for the class:

• "Saw you him today?" (line 109) **Possible answer:** *You saw him today?*

• "And private in his chamber pens himself" (line 131) **Possible answer:** *and pens himself in his private chamber*

FOR ENGLISH LEARNERS
Task Support Point out the question in the marginal note for lines 117–123. Ask students to imagine themselves in Benvolio's place, saying these words, and then to speculate about the feelings behind the words. **Possible answer:** *The action suggests that Benvolio is considerate. He also seems to have a mild temperament and may prefer to avoid confrontations.*

And makes himself an artificial night.
Black and portentous must this humor prove
135 Unless good counsel may the cause remove.

Benvolio. My noble uncle, do you know the cause?

Montague. I neither know it nor can learn of him.

Benvolio. Have you importuned him by any means?

Montague. Both by myself and many other friends;
140 But he, his own affections' counselor,
Is to himself—I will not say how true—
But to himself so secret and so close,
So far from sounding and discovery,
As is the bud bit with an envious worm
145 Ere he can spread his sweet leaves to the air
Or dedicate his beauty to the sun.
Could we but learn from whence his sorrows grow,
We would as willingly give cure as know.

[*Enter* Romeo *lost in thought.*]

Benvolio. See, where he comes. So please you step aside,
150 I'll know his grievance, or be much denied.

Montague. I would thou wert so happy by thy stay
To hear true shrift. Come, madam, let's away.

[*Exeunt* Montague *and* Lady.]

Benvolio. Good morrow, cousin.

Romeo.   Is the day so young?

Benvolio. But new struck nine.

Romeo.   Ay me! sad hours seem long.
155 Was that my father that went hence so fast?

Benvolio. It was. What sadness lengthens Romeo's hours?

Romeo. Not having that which having makes them short.

Benvolio. In love?

Romeo. Out—

160 **Benvolio.** Of love?

Romeo. Out of her favor where I am in love.

Benvolio. Alas that love, so gentle in his view,
Should be so tyrannous and rough in proof!

Romeo. Alas that love, whose view is muffled still,
165 Should without eyes see pathways to his will!
Where shall we dine?—O me! What fray was here?—
Yet tell me not, for I have heard it all.

134 **portentous:** indicating evil to come; threatening.

138 **importuned:** asked in an urgent way.

140 **his own affections' counselor:** Romeo keeps to himself.

143–148 **so far from ... know:** Finding out what Romeo is thinking is almost impossible. Montague compares his son to a young bud destroyed by the bite of a worm before it has a chance to open its leaves. Montague wants to find out what is bothering Romeo so he can help him.

152 **shrift:** confession.

153 **cousin:** any relative or close friend. The informal version is *coz.*

157–163 *Why has Romeo been so depressed?*

162–164 **love:** references to Cupid, the god of love, typically pictured as a blind boy with wings and a bow and arrow. Anyone hit by one of his arrows falls in love instantly. Cupid looks sweet and gentle, but in reality he can be a harsh master.

Lines 124–148
DISCUSSION PROMPTS

Use these prompts to help students understand the relationship between the characters of Montague and Romeo:

Connect How would you feel if someone close to you was acting the way that Romeo is described as acting in lines 124–135? *Students should note Romeo's depression and should recognize Montague's desire to understand and ease his son's pain.*

Analyze How has Montague tried to help his son? Why do you think that he has not been successful? **Possible answer:** *Montague has tried to find out why Romeo is so sad, but Romeo will not speak to him about it. The reason may be that Montague considers Romeo somewhat immature—as when he comments, "I will not say how true" (line 141) and when he compares Romeo to a young bud (line 144).*

Evaluate Does Montague have a good reason to worry about his son? Explain. **Possible answer:** *Montague has a good reason to worry, since Romeo is withdrawn, seems sad, and is keeping silent; however, Montague doesn't have enough information to judge the nature or severity of the problem. He is feeling the natural impulse to expect the worst.*

FOR LESS-PROFICIENT READERS
Paraphrasing Shakespeare Model this paraphrase of lines 143–146: *Romeo won't let us hear or find out about what's bothering him. The situation is just like a budding flower that has been bitten by a worm before it can blossom in the air and sunshine.* Then call on volunteers to paraphrase lines 147–148. **Possible answer:** *If we could find out what's making him [Romeo] so sad, we'd be happy to help him.*

FOR ENGLISH LEARNERS
Task Support Point out the marginal question for lines 157–163. Before students answer, have them note the numerous times that the word *love* appears in the lines in question. **Possible answer:** *Romeo is depressed because he is in love with someone who does not love him in return.*

REINFORCE *KEY IDEA:* LOVE AND HATE

Discuss What is Romeo's opinion of **love?** Cite evidence. *Possible answer: Romeo's opinion is that love is a violent, contradictory thing. For example, he refers to love as "Misshapen chaos of well-seeming forms" (line 172) and as "A madness most discreet" (line 186). Romeo does not feel that love is necessarily good, for he calls it both "A choking gall, and a preserving sweet" (line 187). His negative view is perhaps best summed up in his statement that "Love is a smoke raised with the fume of sighs" (line 183).*

Here's much to do with hate, but more with love.
Why then, O brawling love! O loving hate!
170 O anything, of nothing first create!
O heavy lightness! serious vanity!
Misshapen chaos of well-seeming forms!
Feather of lead, bright smoke, cold fire, sick health!
Still-waking sleep, that is not what it is!
175 This love feel I, that feel no love in this.
Dost thou not laugh?

Benvolio.   No, coz, I rather weep.

Romeo. Good heart, at what?

Benvolio.   At thy good heart's oppression.

Romeo. Why, such is love's transgression.
Griefs of mine own lie heavy in my breast,
180 Which thou wilt propagate, to have it prest
With more of thine. This love that thou hast shown
Doth add more grief to too much of mine own.
Love is a smoke raised with the fume of sighs;
Being purged, a fire sparkling in lovers' eyes;
185 Being vexed, a sea nourished with lovers' tears.
What is it else? A madness most discreet,
A choking gall, and a preserving sweet.
Farewell, my coz.

Benvolio.   Soft! I will go along.
An if you leave me so, you do me wrong.

190 **Romeo.** Tut! I have lost myself; I am not here:
This is not Romeo, he's some other where.

Benvolio. Tell me in sadness, who is that you love?

Romeo. What, shall I groan and tell thee?

Benvolio.   Groan? Why, no;
But sadly tell me who.

195 **Romeo.** Bid a sick man in sadness make his will.
Ah, word ill urged to one that is so ill!
In sadness, cousin, I do love a woman.

Benvolio. I aimed so near when I supposed you loved.

Romeo. A right good markman! And she's fair I love.

200 **Benvolio.** A right fair mark, fair coz, is soonest hit.

Romeo. Well, in that hit you miss. She'll not be hit
With Cupid's arrow. She hath Dian's wit,
And, in strong proof of chastity well armed,
From Love's weak childish bow she lives unharmed.

168–176 Romeo, confused and upset, tries to describe his feelings about love. He uses phrases like "loving hate" and other contradictory expressions.

176–182 Benvolio expresses his sympathy for Romeo. Romeo replies that this is one more problem caused by love. He now feels worse than before because he must carry the weight of Benvolio's sympathy along with his own grief.

184 purged: cleansed (of the smoke).
185 vexed: troubled.

187 gall: something causing bitterness or hate.

188 Soft: Wait a minute.

192 sadness: seriousness.

201–204 She'll . . . unharmed: The girl isn't interested in falling in love. She is like Diana, the goddess of chastity, who fended off Cupid's arrows.

DIFFERENTIATED INSTRUCTION

FOR ENGLISH LEARNERS

Vocabulary Support Have students reread the marginal note for lines 168–176. Emphasize that speaking in opposites shows Romeo's confusion over the fact that love, which should make him happy, has made him miserable. Model the restatement of *heavy lightness* (line 171) as "what should feel light feels heavy." Then guide students to restate these other opposites.

- *serious vanity* (line 171), "What should be unimportant is serious"
- *Feather of lead* (line 173), "A lightweight feather feels as heavy as lead"
- *bright smoke* (line 173), "Dark smoke is actually bright"
- *cold fire* (line 173), "Fire, which should be hot, is now cold"

Behind the Curtain

Casting

Even plays as timeless as Shakespearean dramas need powerful performances to bring them to life. Examine these photographs, and think about the choices the directors made when **casting,** or selecting, the pairs of actors for the roles of Juliet and Romeo. If you were in charge of casting a production of *Romeo and Juliet,* which pair would you choose, and why?

The Royal Shakespeare Company's 1992 production

A 2004 coproduction of the Chicago Shakespeare Theater and Second City

e Cottesloe Theatre's 2000 production

BEHIND THE CURTAIN

Casting Point out to students that the choice of an actor to play a role is often partly determined by the actor's age, race, and physical features, such as height and overall build. Casting is a particular challenge in *Romeo and Juliet,* as the characters are described as young teenagers. Casting directors must decide whether or not they wish to give the lead roles to youthful actors, or if older actors might present certain dramatic possibilities. For example, the Romeo in the Chicago Shakespeare Theater and Second City coproduction has strong facial features and a shaved head; this couple seems older than the couples in the other photographs. By making distinctive casting choices, a director imposes a personal interpretation upon Shakespeare's text. *Accept any answer that is reasonably supported by details from the photographs. For example, casting an interracial couple in the roles might symbolize and emphasize the differences between the feuding families, and casting the smiling, somewhat animated couple might emphasize the youthful enthusiasm of Romeo and Juliet and the play's touches of humor.*

FOR ADVANCED LEARNERS/PRE–AP

Make Judgments Have students do an Internet search to locate photographs from various professional, community, and college productions of *Romeo and Juliet.* As they did for the photographs on this page, ask students to think about the choices that the directors of their researched productions made when casting the play. Have students meet in small groups to share their opinions about the casting choices.

REINFORCE *KEY IDEA:* LOVE AND HATE

Discuss We already know that Romeo will kill himself over his **love** for Juliet. In what sense does Romeo's state of mind in this scene foreshadow his death? *Possible answer: We can see from this scene that Romeo is driven by his emotions. These qualities foreshadow his suicide. He is depressed over Rosaline's refusal to accept him. He later will kill himself rather than face life without Juliet.*

BACKGROUND

Families Wealthy Renaissance families relied upon clearly defined roles as well as carefully arranged alliances for stability and power. Families were usually ruled by strong fathers who arranged marriages for their children, sometimes with the fathers of other wealthy families, or else, in the case of his daughters, with an adult male who possessed wealth or political power. A father was also expected to provide a dowry, a gift of money or valuables to the groom. Wives were expected to produce children, preferably male ones, in order to secure an heir to the family's fortunes. They were also expected to support their husbands in their choice of potential spouses for the children. Children were expected to obey their parents without question.

---

205 She will not stay the siege of loving terms,
   Nor bide the encounter of assailing eyes,
   Nor ope her lap to saint-seducing gold.
   O, she is rich in beauty; only poor
   That, when she dies, with beauty dies her store.

210 **Benvolio.** Then she hath sworn that she will still live chaste?

   Romeo. She hath, and in that sparing makes huge waste;
   For beauty, starved with her severity,
   Cuts beauty off from all posterity.
   She is too fair, too wise, wisely too fair,
215 To merit bliss by making me despair.
   She hath forsworn to love, and in that vow
   Do I live dead that live to tell it now.

   Benvolio. Be ruled by me: forget to think of her.

   Romeo. O, teach me how I should forget to think!

220 **Benvolio.** By giving liberty unto thine eyes:
   Examine other beauties.

   Romeo.   'Tis the way
   To call hers (exquisite) in question more.
   These happy masks that kiss fair ladies' brows,
   Being black, puts us in mind they hide the fair.
225 He that is strucken blind cannot forget
   The precious treasure of his eyesight lost.
   Show me a mistress that is passing fair,
   What doth her beauty serve but as a note
   Where I may read who passed that passing fair?
230 Farewell. Thou canst not teach me to forget.

   Benvolio. I'll pay that doctrine, or else die in debt.

   [*Exeunt.*]

205–207 She will not . . . saint-seducing gold: She is not swayed by Romeo's declaration of love, his adoring looks, or his wealth.

212–213 For beauty . . . posterity: By denying herself love and marriage, she wastes her beauty, which will not be passed on to future generations.

215–216 to merit . . . despair: The girl will reach heaven (**bliss**) by being so virtuous, which causes Romeo to feel hopelessness or despair; **forsworn to:** sworn not to.

220–221 *What is Benvolio's advice?*

221–222 'Tis . . . more: That would only make me appreciate my own love's beauty more.

223 Masks were worn by Elizabethan women to protect their complexions from the sun.

227–229 Show me . . . that passing fair: A woman who is exceedingly (**passing**) beautiful will only remind me of my love, who is even prettier.

231 I'll pay . . . debt: I'll convince you you're wrong, or die trying.

SCENE 2   *A street near the Capulet house.*

This scene opens with Count Paris, a young nobleman, asking Capulet for permission to marry his daughter, Juliet. Capulet says that Juliet is too young but gives Paris permission to court her and try to win her heart. He also invites Paris to a party he is giving that night.

   Romeo finds out about the party and discovers that Rosaline, the girl who rejected him, will be present. Benvolio urges Romeo to go to the party to see how Rosaline compares with the other women.

[*Enter* Capulet *with* Paris, *a kinsman of the Prince, and* Servant.]

Capulet. But Montague is bound as well as I,
In penalty alike; and 'tis not hard, I think,
For men so old as we to keep the peace.

1 bound: obligated.

DIFFERENTIATED INSTRUCTION

FOR LESS–PROFICIENT READERS

Preview Model creating a cartoon to record key details in the synopsis for Scene 2.

Count Paris:
May I marry Juliet?

Capulet:
No. She's too young. You may court her, though. Come to our party tonight.

Invite students to create a cartoon to synthesize the rest of the synopsis.

FOR ENGLISH LEARNERS

Task Support As students consider the marginal question for lines 220–221, clarify that Benvolio is responding to Romeo's request in line 219. Help students paraphrase Benvolio's reply. *Possible answer: You can forget Rosaline if you let your eyes look beyond her. Consider the other beautiful girls around here.*

Paris. Of honorable reckoning are you both,
5 And pity 'tis you lived at odds so long.
But now, my lord, what say you to my suit?

Capulet. But saying o'er what I have said before:
My child is yet a stranger in the world,
She hath not seen the change of fourteen years;
10 Let two more summers wither in their pride
Ere we may think her ripe to be a bride.

Paris. Younger than she are happy mothers made.

Capulet. And too soon marred are those so early made.
The earth hath swallowed all my hopes but she;
15 She is the hopeful lady of my earth.
But woo her, gentle Paris, get her heart;
My will to her consent is but a part.
An she agree, within her scope of choice
Lies my consent and fair according voice. **C**

20 This night I hold an old accustomed feast,
Whereto I have invited many a guest,
Such as I love, and you among the store,
One more, most welcome, makes my number more.
At my poor house look to behold this night
25 Earth-treading stars that make dark heaven light.
Such comfort as do lusty young men feel
When well-appareled April on the heel
Of limping Winter treads, even such delight
Among fresh female buds shall you this night
30 Inherit at my house. Hear all, all see,
And like her most whose merit most shall be;
Which, on more view of many, mine, being one,
May stand in number, though in reck'ning none.
Come, go with me. [*to* Servant, *giving him a paper*]
                    Go, sirrah, trudge about
35 Through fair Verona; find those persons out
Whose names are written there, and to them say,
My house and welcome on their pleasure stay.

[*Exeunt* Capulet *and* Paris.]

Servant. Find them out whose names are written here! It is
written that the shoemaker should meddle with his yard and the
40 tailor with his last, the fisher with his pencil and the painter
with his nets; but I am sent to find those persons whose names
are here writ, and can never find what names the writing person
hath here writ. I must to the learned. In good time!

---

4 **reckoning:** reputation.

6 **what say . . . suit:** Paris is asking for Capulet's response to his proposal to marry Juliet.

10 **let two more summers . . . pride:** let two more years pass.

2 Targeted Passage

14 **The earth . . . she:** All my children are dead except Juliet.

16 **woo her:** try to win her heart.

18–19 **An . . . voice:** I will give my approval to the one she chooses.

20 **old accustomed feast:** a traditional or annual party.

C BLANK VERSE
Reread lines 16–19 aloud, tapping your foot at each stressed syllable. How many stressed syllables are in each line?

29–33 **among . . . none:** Tonight at the party you will witness the loveliest young girls in Verona, including Juliet. When you see all of them together, your opinion of Juliet may change.

34 **sirrah:** a term used to address a servant.

38–43 The servant cannot seek out the people on the list because he cannot read. In his remarks he confuses the craftsmen and their tools, tapping a typical source of humor for Elizabethan comic characters.

43 **In good time:** What luck (a reference to the arrival of Romeo and Benvolio, who will be able to help the servant read the list).

ROMEO AND JULIET: ACT ONE, SCENE 2 **951**

Lines 4–19
DISCUSSION PROMPTS

Use these prompts to help students understand the character of Capulet and his arrangement with Count Paris:

Recall What is Capulet's answer to Paris? *Possible answer: Capulet answers that Juliet is too young to marry (lines 9–11). He urges Paris to wait another two years (line 10). He also says that Juliet's consent must be part of the decision (lines 17–18).*

Analyze What does his response show about Capulet's character? *Possible answer: Capulet is a loving father who greatly cares about his daughter's happiness. He is protective of his daughter, in part because she is his only surviving child (line 14). He is also respectful of his daughter's feelings and opinions, as shown by his statement that she must have choice in the matter (lines 17–18).*

Synthesize Based on what you know about the era in which the play takes place, are some of Capulet's attitudes toward his daughter surprising? Explain why or why not. *Possible answer: His attitudes seem surprisingly modern. Arranged marriages were common at the time, yet Capulet wants his daughter to have some choice in the matter (lines 17–18). In addition, girls were married at a very young age, but he does not want to rush Juliet into marriage.*

LITERARY ANALYSIS

C BLANK VERSE

Possible answer: There are five stressed syllables in each line.

If students need help . . . Write the lines on the board. Work with students to put a strike mark above each stressed syllable.

FOR LESS–PROFICIENT READERS

2 Targeted Passage [Lines 6–19]

This passage offers insight into the kind of life that Juliet is expected to have.

• How long does Capulet want Juliet to wait before getting married?

• Does he think that Juliet will someday become a wife and mother? Explain.

• What must Paris do before Capulet gives his consent to marry Juliet?

REINFORCE *KEY IDEA:* LOVE AND HATE

Discuss To what does Benvolio compare **love** in these lines? How do his words apply to Romeo's thoughts about Rosaline? *Possible answer: Benvolio compares love to an infection and a poison. He says that a love that is going badly can be driven out by introducing a new love. The application is clear: Rosaline is the source of Romeo's pain, but finding another person to love will make that pain go away.*

[*Enter* Benvolio *and* Romeo.]

Benvolio. Tut, man, one fire burns out another's burning;
45 One pain is lessened by another's anguish;
Turn giddy, and be holp by backward turning;
One desperate grief cures with another's languish.
Take thou some new infection to thy eye,
And the rank poison of the old will die.

50 **Romeo.** Your plantain leaf is excellent for that.

Benvolio. For what, I pray thee?

Romeo.   For your broken shin.

Benvolio. Why, Romeo, art thou mad?

Romeo. Not mad, but bound more than a madman is;
Shut up in prison, kept without my food,
55 Whipped and tormented and—God-den, good fellow.

Servant. God gi' go-den. I pray, sir, can you read?

Romeo. Ay, mine own fortune in my misery.

Servant. Perhaps you have learned it without book. But
I pray, can you read anything you see?

60 **Romeo.** Ay, if I know the letters and the language.

Servant. Ye say honestly. Rest you merry!

[*Romeo's joking goes over the clown's head. He concludes that*
Romeo *cannot read and prepares to seek someone who can.*]

Romeo. Stay, fellow; I can read. [*He reads.*]
"Signior Martino and his wife and daughters;
County Anselmo and his beauteous sisters;
65 The lady widow of Vitruvio;
Signior Placentio and his lovely nieces;
Mercutio and his brother Valentine;
Mine uncle Capulet, his wife, and daughters;
My fair niece Rosaline and Livia;
70 Signior Valentio and his cousin Tybalt;
Lucio and the lively Helena."
[*gives back the paper*]
A fair assembly. Whither should they come?

Servant. Up.

Romeo. Whither?

75 **Servant.** To supper, to our house.

Romeo. Whose house?

Servant. My master's.

Romeo. Indeed I should have asked you that before.

44–49 Tut, man . . . die: Romeo and Benvolio are still discussing Romeo's love problems. Benvolio says Romeo should find a new love—that a "new infection" will cure the old one.

55 god-den: good evening. Romeo interrupts his lament to talk to the servant.

56 God gi' go-den: God give you a good evening.

69 Rosaline: This is the woman that Romeo is in love with. Mercutio, a friend of both Romeo and the Capulets, is also invited to the party.

72 whither: where.

DIFFERENTIATED INSTRUCTION

FOR ENGLISH LEARNERS

Vocabulary: Outdated Forms Discuss these examples of Shakespearean terms that have passed from use: *thy* (line 48), "your"; *pray* (line 51), "ask," "beg"; *Ay* (line 57), "yes"; *Ye* (line 61), "you"; *Stay* (line 62), "wait"; *Whither* (line 74), "where."

FOR ADVANCED LEARNERS/PRE–AP

Analyze Character and Plot The reference passes by almost too quickly to register, but lines 68–69 reveal that Romeo's beloved Rosaline is a Capulet—a member of the rival clan. Have students comment about how this information (1) sheds light on Romeo's character (and possibly Rosaline's feelings toward him) and (2) helps set up Romeo's reaction to the news (revealed at the end of Act One) that Juliet is a Capulet.

Servant. Now I'll tell you without asking. My master is the great
80 rich Capulet; and if you be not of the house of Montagues, I
pray come and crush a cup of wine. Rest you merry!

[*Exit.*]

Benvolio. At this same ancient feast of Capulet's
Sups the fair Rosaline whom thou so lovest,
With all the admired beauties of Verona.
85 Go thither, and with unattainted eye
Compare her face with some that I shall show,
And I will make thee think thy swan a crow.

Romeo. When the devout religion of mine eye
Maintains such falsehood, then turn tears to fires;
90 And these, who, often drowned, could never die,
Transparent heretics, be burnt for liars!
One fairer than my love? The all-seeing sun
Ne'er saw her match since first the world begun.

Benvolio. Tut! you saw her fair, none else being by,
95 Herself poised with herself in either eye;
But in that crystal scales let there be weighed
Your lady's love against some other maid
That I will show you shining at this feast,
And she shall scant show well that now shows best.

100 **Romeo.** I'll go along, no such sight to be shown,
But to rejoice in splendor of mine own.

[*Exeunt.*]

81 crush a cup of wine: slang for "drink some wine."

85 unattainted: unbiased; unprejudiced.

88–91 When . . . liars: If the love I have for Rosaline, which is like a religion, changes because of such a lie (that others may be more beautiful), let my tears be turned to fire and my eyes be burned.

94–99 Tut . . . best: You've seen Rosaline alone; now compare her with some other women. *How does Benvolio think Rosaline will measure up against the other girls?*

100–101 Romeo agrees to go to the party, but only to see Rosaline.

SCENE 3   *Capulet's house.*

In this scene, you will meet Juliet, her mother, and her nurse. The nurse, a merry and slightly crude servant, has been in charge of Juliet since her birth. Once she starts talking, she can't stop. Just before the party, Juliet's mother asks if Juliet has thought about getting married. Lady Capulet is matchmaking, trying to convince her daughter that Paris would make a good husband. Juliet responds just as you might if your parents set up a blind date for you—without much enthusiasm.

[*Enter* Lady Capulet *and* Nurse.]

Lady Capulet. Nurse, where's my daughter? Call her forth to me.

Nurse. Now, by my maidenhead at twelve year old,
I bade her come. What, lamb! what, ladybird!
God forbid! Where's this girl? What, Juliet!

[*Enter* Juliet.]

5 **Juliet.** How now? Who calls?

3–4 what: a call like "Hey, where are you?"

ROMEO AND JULIET: ACT ONE, SCENE 3   **953**

ANALYZE VISUALS

Activity What can you infer from the photograph about the relationship between Juliet and her nurse? *Possible answer: Juliet shows her love for the nurse through her hug. The nurse shows her affection for Juliet in her dreamy smile; she shows her protective feelings for Juliet in her act of placing her hands over Juliet's.*

Nurse. Your mother.

Juliet. Madam, I am here. What is your will?

Lady Capulet. This is the matter—Nurse, give leave awhile,
We must talk in secret. Nurse, come back again;
10 I have remembered me, thou's hear our counsel.
Thou knowest my daughter's of a pretty age.

Nurse. Faith, I can tell her age unto an hour.

Lady Capulet. She's not fourteen.

Nurse.   I'll lay fourteen of my teeth—
And yet, to my teen be it spoken, I have but four—
15 She's not fourteen. How long is it now
To Lammastide?

Lady Capulet.   A fortnight and odd days.

8–11 **give leave . . . counsel:** Lady Capulet seems flustered or nervous, not sure whether she wants the nurse to stay or leave; **of a pretty age:** of an attractive age, ready for marriage.

14 **teen:** sorrow.

16 **Lammastide:** August 1, a religious feast day. It is two weeks (**a fortnight**) away.

Juliet and her nurse in the 1994 production of the Shakespeare Theatre in Washington, D.C.

954   UNIT 10: SHAKESPEAREAN DRAMA

DIFFERENTIATED INSTRUCTION

FOR ENGLISH LEARNERS

Vocabulary: Outdated Forms Encourage students to add these outdated terms to their language journals. (See the **For English Learners** activity on page 940.) Then have them reread the lines noted and substitute the definitions for the words.

- *give leave* (line 8), "leave [us] alone"
- *thou's* (line 10), "you should"
- *Thou knowest* (line 11), "you know"
- *Faith* (line 12), "believe me"

- *Yea* (line 42), "indeed"
- *quoth* (line 42), "said"
- *wit* (line 43), "sense"
- *Wilt thou not* (line 44), "won't you"
- *I warrant, an I should live* (line 47), "I swear [promise], if I should live"
- *hold thy peace* (line 50), "stop," "be quiet"
- *when thou comest to age* (line 57), "when you're grown up"

Nurse. Even or odd, of all days in the year,
Come Lammas Eve at night shall she be fourteen.
Susan and she (God rest all Christian souls!)
20 Were of an age. Well, Susan is with God;
She was too good for me. But, as I said,
On Lammas Eve at night shall she be fourteen;
That shall she, marry; I remember it well.
'Tis since the earthquake now eleven years;
25 And she was weaned (I never shall forget it),
Of all the days of the year, upon that day.
For I had then laid wormwood to my dug,
Sitting in the sun under the dovehouse wall.
My lord and you were then at Mantua—
30 Nay, I do bear a brain—But, as I said,
When it did taste the wormwood on the nipple
Of my dug and felt it bitter, pretty fool,
To see it tetchy and fall out with the dug!
Shake, quoth the dovehouse! 'Twas no need, I trow,
35 To bid me trudge.
And since that time it is eleven years,
For then she could stand alone; nay, by the rood,
She could have run and waddled all about;
For even the day before, she broke her brow;
40 And then my husband (God be with his soul!
'A was a merry man) took up the child.
"Yea," quoth he, "dost thou fall upon thy face?
Thou wilt fall backward when thou has more wit,
Wilt thou not, Jule?" And, by my holidam,
45 The pretty wretch left crying, and said "Ay."
To see now how a jest shall come about!
I warrant, an I should live a thousand years,
I never should forget it. "Wilt thou not, Jule?" quoth he,
And, pretty fool, it stinted, and said "Ay." **D**
50 **Lady Capulet.** Enough of this. I pray thee hold thy peace.
   Nurse. Yes, madam. Yet I cannot choose but laugh
To think it should leave crying and say "Ay."
And yet, I warrant, it had upon its brow
A bump as big as a young cock'rel's stone;
55 A perilous knock; and it cried bitterly.
"Yea," quoth my husband, "fallst upon thy face?
Thou wilt fall backward when thou comest to age,
Wilt thou not, Jule?" It stinted, and said "Ay."

17–49 The nurse begins to babble about various memories of Juliet's childhood. She talks of her own dead daughter, Susan, who was the same age as Juliet. Susan probably died in infancy, leaving the nurse available to become a wet nurse to (that is, breastfeed) Juliet. She remembers an earthquake that happened on the day she stopped breast-feeding Juliet (**she was weaned**).

27 laid wormwood to my dug: applied wormwood, a plant with a bitter taste, to her breast in order to discourage the child from breastfeeding.

33 tetchy: touchy; cranky.
34–35 Shake . . . trudge: When the dove house shook, I knew enough to leave.

37 by the rood: by the cross of Christ (a mild oath).

39 broke her brow: cut her forehead.

42–49 "Yea" . . . "Ay": To quiet Juliet after her fall, the nurse's husband made a crude joke, asking the baby whether she'd fall the other way (on her back) when she was older. Although at three Juliet didn't understand the question, she stopped crying (**stinted**) and innocently answered "Yes." The nurse finds the story so funny that she can't stop retelling it.

D CHARACTER
So far, how would you describe the nurse? List three **traits** this character exhibits.

55 perilous: hazardous; dangerous.

ROMEO AND JULIET: ACT ONE, SCENE 3   955

LITERARY ANALYSIS

D CHARACTER
Possible answer: The nurse is religious, as suggested by her references to God in lines 19, 20, and 40. She also acts very familiarly toward Lady Capulet, even though she is the woman's servant. Most notably, she has a crude sense of humor, revealed in her great enjoyment of the suggestive story that she tells in lines 37–46 and mentions again in lines 47–49 and lines 51–58. Her earthiness makes her a foil to the formal, refined Lady Capulet and to the less mature but mannerly Juliet.

If students need help . . . Use a Character Analysis Chart to help students note what they know about the nurse. Discuss how she is similar to and different from other characters that students have met thus far in Act One.

 BEST PRACTICES TOOLKIT—Transparency Character Analysis Chart p. D5

FOR LESS–PROFICIENT READERS
Inverted Word Order Point out the repetition of "shall she" in the nurse's speech (lines 18, 22, and 23). Explain that in each case, the words seem like a question to the modern ear, but that, in fact, they are statements. Have a volunteer read the lines aloud, changing *shall she* to *she shall*.

FOR ENGLISH LEARNERS
Concept Support Explain that at the time that this play takes place, most European upper-class marriages were arranged by families for social and economic reasons. Because life spans were shorter than they are today, people married younger, and parents often made marriage plans for their children long before the wedding occurred. Romantic love was not seen as a requirement for a sound marriage.

BACKGROUND
Dating the Play Some scholars believe that the nurse's mention of an earthquake in lines 24 and 34–36 is a clue as to when Shakespeare wrote *Romeo and Juliet*. On April 6, 1580, an earthquake frightened Londoners badly. The nurse's references to the 11 years that have passed since that event—an event that the audience would have remembered—suggest a date of 1591 for *Romeo and Juliet*.

DISCUSSION PROMPTS

Use these prompts to help students analyze Lady Capulet's speech about Paris:

Connect Has a parent or family member ever tried to persuade you to do something that you did not want to do? How might that experience help you understand Lady Capulet's speech to Juliet? *Most students will recall such a persuasive speech. The experience might help them understand that Lady Capulet is trying to get her own way without starting an argument with Juliet.*

Analyze What features of Paris does Lady Capulet emphasize? *Possible answer: Lady Capulet emphasizes Paris's good looks and, to a lesser extent, his wealth.* What do you suppose is Lady Capulet's real motivation at this moment? *Possible answer: Although Lady Capulet probably wants Juliet to be happy, she also wants Juliet to marry someone who is socially acceptable and who can provide for her (lines 94–95).*

Evaluate Do you think that Lady Capulet provides a strong and effective argument in favor of Paris? Why or why not? *Students may suggest that his handsomeness would be persuasive to a young teenager. They may say that this approach is likely to be more successful than an outright demand from Lady Capulet would be.*

Lines 82–87
REINFORCE *KEY IDEA:* LOVE AND HATE

Discuss Lady Capulet describes Paris's looks to persuade Juliet to take an interest in him. What do her words have in common with what Romeo has said about **love** in Scenes 1 and 2? *Possible answer: Both characters' words have indicated a belief that love springs from physical attractiveness.*

Juliet. And stint thou too, I pray thee, nurse, say I.

60 **Nurse.** Peace, I have done. God mark thee to his grace!
Thou wast the prettiest babe that e'er I nursed.
An I might live to see thee married once,
I have my wish.

Lady Capulet. Marry, that "marry" is the very theme
65 I came to talk of. Tell me, daughter Juliet,
How stands your disposition to be married?

Juliet. It is an honor that I dream not of.

Nurse. An honor? Were not I thine only nurse,
I would say thou hadst sucked wisdom from thy teat.

70 **Lady Capulet.** Well, think of marriage now. Younger than you,
Here in Verona, ladies of esteem,
Are made already mothers. By my count,
I was your mother much upon these years
That you are now a maid. Thus then in brief:
75 The valiant Paris seeks you for his love.

Nurse. A man, young lady! lady, such a man
As all the world—why he's a man of wax.

Lady Capulet. Verona's summer hath not such a flower.

Nurse. Nay, he's a flower, in faith—a very flower.

80 **Lady Capulet.** What say you? Can you love the gentleman?
This night you shall behold him at our feast.
Read o'er the volume of young Paris' face,
And find delight writ there with beauty's pen;
Examine every several lineament,
85 And see how one another lends content;
And what obscured in this fair volume lies
Find written in the margent of his eyes.
This precious book of love, this unbound lover,
To beautify him only lacks a cover.
90 The fish lives in the sea, and 'tis much pride
For fair without the fair within to hide.
That book in many's eyes doth share the glory,
That in gold clasps locks in the golden story;
So shall you share all that he doth possess,
95 By having him making yourself no less.

Nurse. No less? Nay, bigger! Women grow by men.

Lady Capulet. Speak briefly, can you like of Paris' love?

Juliet. I'll look to like, if looking liking move;
But no more deep will I endart mine eye

64 Marry ... "marry": two different usages of the same word—the first meaning "by the Virgin Mary" and the second meaning "to wed."

73–74 I was ... maid: I was your mother at about your age, yet you are still unmarried.

77 a man of wax: a man so perfect he could be a wax statue, of the type sculptors once used as models for their works.

82–89 Read ... cover: Lady Capulet uses an extended metaphor that compares Paris to a book that Juliet should read.

84 every several lineament: each separate feature (of Paris' face).

87 margent ... eyes: She compares Paris' eyes to the margin of a page, where notes are written to explain the content.

88–91 This ... hide: This beautiful book (Paris) needs only a cover (wife) to become even better. He may be hiding even more wonderful qualities inside.

96 The nurse can't resist commenting that women get bigger (pregnant) when they marry.

98 I'll look ... move: I'll look at him with the intention of liking him, if simply looking can make me like him.

99 endart: look deeply, as if penetrating with a dart.

DIFFERENTIATED INSTRUCTION

FOR LESS–PROFICIENT READERS

Compare and Contrast Ask students to reread Capulet's conversation with Paris on page 951. Use a Venn Diagram to help students compare how Capulet and his wife are alike and how they differ on the subject of Juliet's marriage.

 BEST PRACTICES TOOLKIT—Transparency
Venn Diagram p. A26

Capulet
Does not want Juliet to marry too early
Believes that young mothers are marred

Both
Wish for Juliet's happiness
Look for Juliet's consent to marry

Lady Capulet
Encourages Juliet to become a bride and mother
Is interested in Paris's money

100 Than your consent gives strength to make it fly. **E**

[*Enter a* Servingman.]

Servingman. Madam, the guests are come, supper served up, you called, my young lady asked for, the nurse cursed in the pantry, and everything in extremity. I must hence to wait. I beseech you follow straight.

105 **Lady Capulet.** We follow thee. [*Exit* Servingman.] Juliet, the County stays.

Nurse. Go, girl, seek happy nights to happy days.

[*Exeunt.*]

SCENE 4 *A street near the Capulet house.*

It is the evening of the Capulet masque, or costume ball. Imagine the guests proceeding through the darkened streets with torches to light the way.

Romeo and his friends Mercutio and Benvolio join the procession. Their masks will prevent Romeo's and Benvolio's being recognized as Montagues. Mercutio and Benvolio are in a playful, partying mood, but Romeo is still depressed by his unanswered love for Rosaline. Romeo has also had a dream that warned him of the harmful consequences of this party. He senses trouble.

[*Enter* Romeo, Mercutio, Benvolio, *with five or six other* Maskers; Torchbearers.]

Romeo. What, shall this speech be spoke for our excuse?
Or shall we on without apology?

Benvolio. The date is out of such prolixity.
We'll have no Cupid hoodwinked with a scarf,
5 Bearing a Tartar's painted bow of lath,
Scaring the ladies like a crowkeeper;
Nor no without-book prologue, faintly spoke
After the prompter, for our entrance;
But let them measure us by what they will,
10 We'll measure them a measure, and be gone.

Romeo. Give me a torch. I am not for this ambling;
Being but heavy, I will bear the light.

Mercutio. Nay, gentle Romeo, we must have you dance.

Romeo. Not I, believe me. You have dancing shoes
15 With nimble soles; I have a soul of lead
So stakes me to the ground I cannot move.

Mercutio. You are a lover. Borrow Cupid's wings
And soar with them above a common bound.

Romeo. I am too sore enpierced with his shaft
20 To soar with his light feathers, and so bound

ROMEO AND JULIET: ACT ONE, SCENE 4 **957**

E TRAGEDY

How might Lady Capulet's desire for Juliet to marry Paris lead to **conflict** later in the play? Explain your answer.

103–104 extremity: great confusion; **straight:** immediately.

105 the County stays: Count Paris is waiting for you.

1–10 What, shall this . . . be gone: Romeo asks whether they should send a messenger announcing their arrival at the party. Benvolio replies that this custom is out of date. He says that they'll dance one dance with the partygoers (**measure them a measure**) and then leave.

12 heavy: sad. Romeo makes a joke based on the meanings of *heavy* and *light*.

14–32 Romeo continues to talk about his sadness, while Mercutio jokingly makes fun of him to try to cheer him up.

ⓕ PUN

Possible answer: *In line 12, Romeo makes a pun by using the word* heavy *to mean both "sad" and "of great weight" and the word* light *to mean "luminous" and "of little weight." In line 15, Romeo's pun comes from pairing the words* soul *and* soles *when explaining his unhappiness. In lines 19–20, Romeo puns on the words* sore *("in pain") and* soar *("fly"). The effect of the puns is to lighten the mood. Although Romeo is sad, his puns show that he can nevertheless joke with his friends.*

If students need help . . . Read lines 11–22 aloud, emphasizing the words in the puns. Point out that the first pun is based on two different multiple-meaning words: *heavy* and *light.* Then explain that both the second and third puns are based on homophones, or words that sound alike but are spelled differently and have different meanings: *soles* and *soul* and *sore* and *soar.*

I cannot bound a pitch above dull woe.
Under love's heavy burden do I sink. ⓕ

Mercutio. And, to sink in it, should you burden love—
Too great oppression for a tender thing.

25 **Romeo.** Is love a tender thing? It is too rough,
Too rude, too boist'rous, and it pricks like thorn.

Mercutio. If love be rough with you, be rough with love.
Prick love for pricking, and you beat love down.
Give me a case to put my visage in.

30 A visor for a visor! What care I
What curious eye doth quote deformities?
Here are the beetle brows shall blush for me.

Benvolio. Come, knock and enter, and no sooner in
But every man betake him to his legs.

35 **Romeo.** A torch for me! Let wantons light of heart
Tickle the senseless rushes with their heels;
For I am proverbed with a grandsire phrase,
I'll be a candle-holder and look on;
The game was ne'er so fair, and I am done.

40 **Mercutio.** Tut, dun's the mouse, the constable's own word!
If thou art Dun, we'll draw thee from the mire
Of, save your reverence, love, wherein thou stickst
Up to the ears. Come, we burn daylight, ho!

Romeo. Nay, that's not so.

Mercutio.   I mean, sir, in delay
45 We waste our lights in vain, like lamps by day.
Take our good meaning, for our judgment sits
Five times in that ere once in our five wits.

Romeo. And we mean well in going to this masque;
But 'tis no wit to go.

Mercutio.   Why, may one ask?

50 **Romeo.** I dreamt a dream tonight.

Mercutio.   And so did I.

Romeo. Well, what was yours?

Mercutio.   That dreamers often lie.

Romeo. In bed asleep, while they do dream things true.

Mercutio. O, then I see Queen Mab hath been with you.
She is the fairies' midwife, and she comes
55 In shape no bigger than an agate stone
On the forefinger of an alderman,
Drawn with a team of little atomies

ⓕ PUN
Identify two puns in lines 11–22. What effect do they have on the **mood** of this scene?

29–32 Give . . . for me: Give me a mask for an ugly face. I don't care if people notice my appearance. Here, look at my bushy eyebrows.

34 betake . . . legs: dance.

35–38 Let . . . look on: Let playful people tickle the grass (**rushes**) on the floor with their dancing. I'll follow the old saying (**grandsire phrase**) and just be a spectator.

40–43 Tut . . . daylight: Mercutio jokes, using various meanings of the word *dun*, which sounds like Romeo's last word, *done.* He concludes by saying they should not waste time (**burn daylight**).

53–95 This famous speech is yet one more attempt by Mercutio to cheer up Romeo. He talks of Mab, queen of the fairies, a folktale character well-known to Shakespeare's audience. His language includes vivid descriptions, puns, and satires of people; and ultimately he gets caught up in his own wild imaginings. It is not necessary to understand everything Mercutio says to recognize the beauty of this born storyteller's tale.

55 agate stone: jewel for a ring.

57 atomies: tiny creatures.

DIFFERENTIATED INSTRUCTION

FOR LESS–PROFICIENT READERS

Paraphrasing Shakespeare Draw students' attention to the marginal note that summarizes lines 53–95. Help students paraphrase lines 53–58 to read something like this: *I see that Queen Mab has visited you. She is the helper of fairies and is smaller than the stone on a ring. She rides a tiny carriage pulled by tiny creatures, bringing sweet dreams to sleeping people.*

FOR ENGLISH LEARNERS

Vocabulary Support Mercutio's speech in lines 53–95 includes many unusual descriptions of Queen Mab's appearance. Work with students to restate the descriptions, as in these examples:

- Mab's size: only as big as the stone in an alderman's ring (lines 55–56)
- her wagon's spokes: long spider legs (line 59)
- the cover of her coach: grasshopper wings (line 60)

- the harness: webs of tiny spiders (line 61)
- her collars: moonbeams (line 62)
- her whip: crickets' bones (line 63)
- her driver: a small gray gnat (bug), not even half as big as a little worm (lines 64–65)
- her chariot: a hazelnut shell (line 67)

Behind the Curtain

Costume Design

Classic dramas such as *Romeo and Juliet* can be staged in many different ways. **Costumes** are one means of making a production distinctive. Think about the interpretations of the play pictured here. (Note: The middle shot is of Romeo and Juliet in the midst of the famous balcony scene, coming up in Act Two—and the ladder serves as the balcony!) How are the different costume choices in these photographs appropriate for the different productions?

Romeo and Juliet in the Globe Theatre's 2004 production

Romeo and Juliet in the Globe Theatre's 2000 production

Romeo and Juliet in the Royal Ballet's 2003 production

ROMEO AND JULIET: ACT ONE, SCENE 4   **959**

BEHIND THE CURTAIN

Costume Design Point out that costumes can reflect such time periods as, for example, the Renaissance, the Roaring Twenties, or the Old West. Costumes can reflect geographical settings such as, a Chinese village, a Caribbean island, or an American high school. Costumes may suggest the attitudes of the characters or a director's unique interpretation of a play. Elicit that the costumes in the Globe Theatre's 2004 production are from the Renaissance era and that the Royal Ballet production uses traditional ballet costuming. Note that the costuming in the Globe Theatre's 2000 production shows a more modern interpretation, with all-white costumes and unusual makeup and headgear. *Possible answer: In each case, the costumes are appropriate for the production. For the Royal Ballet, the costumes reflect and allow for flowing ballet movements. The costuming in the Globe Theatre's 2000 production reflects an alternative interpretation of Shakespeare's text. The costumes in the Globe Theatre's 2004 production aim for a more historical interpretation of the play.*

FOR ADVANCED LEARNERS/PRE–AP

Reinterpret the Play Remind students that costumes play a very visible role in a production's interpretation of a play. Then ask students to reinterpret *Romeo and Juliet* by designing costumes that reflect a specific era or geographical setting. After allowing time for research, have students draw their costuming ideas or write a detailed description. Invite students to share their costuming ideas with the class.

ROMEO AND JULIET: ACT ONE, SCENE 4   **959**

Athwart men's noses as they lie asleep;
Her wagon spokes made of long spinners' legs,

59 **spinners' legs:** spiders' legs.

60 The cover, of the wings of grasshoppers;
Her traces, of the smallest spider's web;
Her collars, of the moonshine's wat'ry beams;
Her whip, of cricket's bone; the lash, of film;
Her wagoner, a small grey-coated gnat,

61 **traces:** harness.

65 Not half so big as a round little worm
Pricked from the lazy finger of a maid;
Her chariot is an empty hazelnut,
Made by the joiner squirrel or old grub,
Time out o' mind the fairies' coachmakers.

68 **joiner:** carpenter.

70 And in this state she gallops night by night
Through lovers' brains, and then they dream of love;
O'er courtiers' knees, that dream on curtsies straight;
O'er lawyers' fingers, who straight dream on fees;
O'er ladies' lips, who straight on kisses dream,
75 Which oft the angry Mab with blisters plagues,
Because their breaths with sweetmeats tainted are.
Sometime she gallops o'er a courtier's nose,
And then dreams he of smelling out a suit,
And sometime comes she with a tithe-pig's tail

77–78 **Sometimes she ... suit:** Sometimes Mab makes a member of the king's court dream of receiving special favors.

80 Tickling a parson's nose as 'a lies asleep,
Then dreams he of another benefice.
Sometime she driveth o'er a soldier's neck,
And then dreams he of cutting foreign throats,
Of breaches, ambuscadoes, Spanish blades,

81 **benefice:** a well-paying position for a clergyman.

84 **ambuscadoes:** ambushes; **Spanish blades:** high-quality Spanish swords.

85 Of healths five fathom deep; and then anon
Drums in his ear, at which he starts and wakes,
And being thus frighted, swears a prayer or two
And sleeps again. This is that very Mab
That plaits the manes of horses in the night

89 **plaits:** braids.

90 And bakes the elflocks in foul sluttish hairs,
Which once untangled much misfortune bodes.
This is the hag, when maids lie on their backs,
That presses them and learns them first to bear,
Making them women of good carriage.
95 This is she—

Romeo.   Peace, peace, Mercutio, peace!
Thou talkst of nothing.

Mercutio.   True, I talk of dreams;
Which are the children of an idle brain,
Begot of nothing but vain fantasy;
Which is as thin of substance as the air,
100 And more inconstant than the wind, who woos

96–103 **True ... South:** Mercutio is trying to keep Romeo from taking his dreams too seriously.

DISCUSSION PROMPTS

Use these prompts to help students analyze Mercutio's famous speech:

Recall What is Mercutio's explanation for where dreams come from? ***Possible answer:*** *Mercutio's explanation is that dreams come from Queen Mab, the queen of the fairies, who visits people while they are sleeping, riding her wagon made from "an empty hazelnut" (line 67). The content of a person's dreams is determined by which part of the body she gallops over or through, or perhaps which body part she tickles.*

Analyze What do Mercutio's comments about Queen Mab reveal about his character? ***Possible answer:*** *Mercutio's comments reveal that he is very imaginative, that he is playful, and perhaps that he loves to hear himself talk (for Romeo finally has to tell him to stop talking).*

Evaluate In your opinion, does this passage help the play? Why or why not? ***Possible answers:*** *Yes. It reveals the dreamy, imaginative character of Mercutio and lightens Romeo's dark mood. No. It slows down the play's action.*

DIFFERENTIATED INSTRUCTION

FOR ENGLISH LEARNERS

Concept Support Point out that according to Mercutio, Queen Mab brings dreams to many types of people. Model several of the pairings in lines 70–88, as shown.

- Through lovers' brains: they dream of love (line 71).
- Over lawyers' fingers: they dream of fees, the money they charge (line 73).
- Over ladies' lips: they dream of kisses (line 74).
- Tickling a parson's (minister's) nose: he dreams of receiving more money in exchange for his work (lines 79–81).

Have students similarly identify the dream of a soldier and two dreams of a courtier. ***Possible answer:*** *A soldier dreams of killing foreigners and of adventures at sea (lines 82–88). One courtier dreams of being able to make a proper curtsy (line 72); another, of receiving a royal favor (lines 77–78).*

Even now the frozen bosom of the North
And, being angered, puffs away from thence,
Turning his face to the dew-dropping South.

Benvolio. This wind you talk of blows us from ourselves.
105 Supper is done, and we shall come too late.

Romeo. I fear, too early; for my mind misgives
Some consequence, yet hanging in the stars,
Shall bitterly begin his fearful date
With this night's revels and expire the term
110 Of a despised life, closed in my breast,
By some vile forfeit of untimely death.
But he that hath the steerage of my course
Direct my sail! On, lusty gentlemen!

Benvolio. Strike, drum.

[*Exeunt.*]

106–111 Romeo, still depressed, fears that some terrible event caused by the stars will begin at the party. Remember the phrase "star-crossed lovers" from the prologue on page 941.

SCENE 5 *A hall in Capulet's house; the scene of the party.*

This is the scene of the party at which Romeo and Juliet finally meet. Romeo and his friends, disguised in their masks, arrive as uninvited guests. As he watches the dancers, Romeo suddenly sees Juliet and falls in love at first sight. At the same time, Tybalt recognizes Romeo's voice and knows he is a Montague. Tybalt alerts Capulet and threatens to kill Romeo. Capulet, however, insists that Tybalt behave himself and act like a gentleman. Promising revenge, Tybalt leaves. Romeo and Juliet meet and kiss in the middle of the dance floor. Only after they part do they learn each other's identity.

[*Servingmen come forth with napkins.*]

First Servingman. Where's Potpan, that he helps not to take away? He shift a trencher! he scrape a trencher!

Second Servingman. When good manners shall lie all in one or two men's hands, and they unwashed too, 'tis a foul thing.

5 **First Servingman.** Away with the joint-stools, remove the court-cupboard, look to the plate. Good thou, save me a piece of marchpane and, as thou lovest me, let the porter let in Susan Grindstone and Nell. Anthony, and Potpan!

Second Servingman. Ay, boy, ready.

10 **First Servingman.** You are looked for and called for, asked for and sought for, in the great chamber.

Third Servingman. We cannot be here and there too. Cheerly, boys! Be brisk awhile, and the longer liver take all.

[*Exeunt.*]

1–13 These opening lines are a comic conversation among three servants as they work.

2 trencher: wooden plate.

6–7 plate: silverware and silver plates; **marchpane:** marzipan, a sweet made from almond paste.

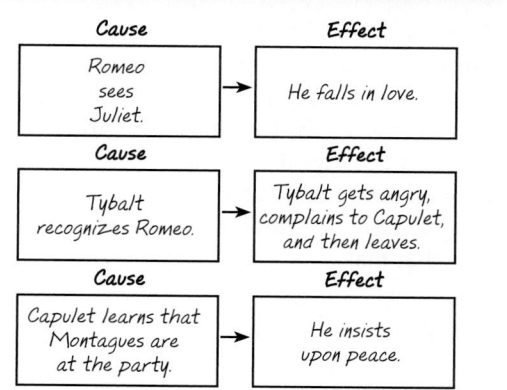

ANALYZE VISUALS

Activity Look closely at the costumes. What do they indicate to you about this production of *Romeo and Juliet*? **Possible answer:** *The costumes indicate that the masked ball was not done as a full masquerade, but with simple masks. The production was done in somewhat stylized period dress, adapted to the needs of ballet dancers.*

[Maskers *appear with* Capulet, Lady Capulet, Juliet, *all the* Guests, *and* Servants.]

Capulet. Welcome, gentlemen! Ladies that have their toes
15 Unplagued with corns will have a bout with you.
Ah ha, my mistresses! which of you all
Will now deny to dance? She that makes dainty,
She I'll swear hath corns. Am I come near ye now?
Welcome, gentlemen! I have seen the day
20 That I have worn a visor and could tell
A whispering tale in a fair lady's ear,
Such as would please. 'Tis gone, 'tis gone, 'tis gone!
You are welcome, gentlemen! Come, musicians, play.
A hall, a hall! give room! and foot it, girls.

[*Music plays and they dance.*]

25 More light, you knaves! and turn the tables up,
And quench the fire, the room is grown too hot.
Ah, sirrah, this unlooked-for sport comes well.
Nay, sit, nay, sit, good cousin Capulet,
For you and I are past our dancing days.
30 How long is't now since last yourself and I
Were in a mask?

Second Capulet. By'r Lady, thirty years.

Capulet. What, man? 'Tis not so much, 'tis not so much!

14–27 Capulet welcomes his guests and invites them all to dance. At the same time, like a good host, he is trying to get the party going. He alternates talking with his guests and telling the servants what to do.

17–18 She that . . . corns: Any woman too shy to dance will be assumed to have corns, ugly and painful growths on the toes.

20 visor: mask.

28–38 Capulet and his relative watch the dancing as they talk of days gone by.

Guests dance at the Capulets' ball in the Royal Ballet's 1996 production.

DIFFERENTIATED INSTRUCTION

FOR ENGLISH LEARNERS

Vocabulary: Outdated Forms Urge students to continue adding outdated terms to their language journals. (See the **For English Learners** activity on page 940.) Have students check their understanding by creating original sentences that use the terms in a way that makes sense.

- *hath* (line 18), "has"
- *knaves* (line 25), "fools"
- *sirrah* (line 27), "sir," "sire"
- *is't* (line 30), "is it"
- *By'r Lady* (line 32), "By Our Lady" (a reference to the Virgin Mary)
- *ward* (line 38), "young person who is still under a guardian's care"
- *Forswear* (line 50), "Deny"
- *hither* (line 54), "here"
- *kin* (line 56), "relatives"
- *hold* (line 57), "consider"

'Tis since the nuptial of Lucentio,
Come Pentecost as quickly as it will,
35 Some five-and-twenty years, and then we masked.

Second Capulet. 'Tis more, 'tis more! His son is elder, sir;
His son is thirty.

Capulet.   Will you tell me that?
His son was but a ward two years ago.

Romeo [*to a* Servingman]. What lady's that, which doth enrich
     the hand
40 Of yonder knight?

Servant. I know not, sir.

> **Romeo.** O, she doth teach the torches to burn bright!
> It seems she hangs upon the cheek of night
> Like a rich jewel in an Ethiop's ear—
> 45 Beauty too rich for use, for earth too dear!
> So shows a snowy dove trooping with crows
> As yonder lady o'er her fellows shows.
> The measure done, I'll watch her place of stand
> And, touching hers, make blessed my rude hand.
> 50 Did my heart love till now? Forswear it, sight!
> For I ne'er saw true beauty till this night. **G**

Tybalt. This, by his voice, should be a Montague.
Fetch me my rapier, boy. What, dares the slave
Come hither, covered with an antic face,
55 To fleer and scorn at our solemnity?
Now, by the stock and honor of my kin,
To strike him dead I hold it not a sin.

Capulet. Why, how now, kinsman? Wherefore storm you so?

Tybalt. Uncle, this is a Montague, our foe;
60 A villain, that is hither come in spite
To scorn at our solemnity this night.

Capulet. Young Romeo is it?

Tybalt.   'Tis he, that villain Romeo.

Capulet. Content thee, gentle coz, let him alone.
'A bears him like a portly gentleman,
65 And, to say truth, Verona brags of him
To be a virtuous and well-governed youth.
I would not for the wealth of all this town
Here in my house do him disparagement.
Therefore be patient, take no note of him.
70 It is my will; the which if thou respect,

33 **nuptial:** marriage.

39–40 Romeo has spotted Juliet across the dance floor and is immediately entranced by her beauty.

③ Targeted Passage

44–45 **Ethiop's ear:** the ear of an Ethiopian (African); **for earth too dear:** too precious for this world.

G BLANK VERSE
Romeo's awestruck speech is in rhymed couplets, not blank verse. Why do you think Shakespeare chose to use rhymed verse here? Explain your answer.

52–57 Tybalt recognizes Romeo's voice and tells his servant to get his sword (**rapier**). He thinks Romeo has come to make fun of (**fleer**) their party. *What does Tybalt want to do to Romeo?*

64 **portly:** dignified.

68 **do him disparagement:** speak critically or insultingly to him.

LITERARY ANALYSIS

G BLANK VERSE

Possible answer: *Shakespeare chose to use rhymed verse because he wanted to draw attention to this moment in the play. The change in poetic style underscores two facts: (1) Romeo's depression suddenly has been replaced with adoration; and (2) This moment is a turning point in Romeo's life. Furthermore, the rhymed verse seems more romantic because it is sweet and easy to listen to.*

If students need help . . . Have students point out the word that ends each line in lines 42–51. Call on volunteers to say each rhyming pair ("bright"/"night," "ear"/ "dear," and so on) aloud. Invite another volunteer to read the entire passage aloud.

Lines 59–68
REINFORCE *KEY IDEA:* LOVE AND HATE

Discuss Why does Capulet refuse to let Tybalt act upon his **hate** for Romeo? *Possible answer: Capulet says that Romeo is behaving himself (line 64) and that he does not want to cause a scene at his own party by confronting Romeo (lines 67–68).*

FOR LESS–PROFICIENT READERS

③ Targeted Passage [Lines 42–51]

In this passage, Romeo first sees Juliet and declares his sudden love, even though he has not yet met her.

- To what objects does Romeo compare Juliet? How are these objects similar?

- What does Romeo imagine will happen when he touches Juliet's hand?

- How does Romeo feel about Rosaline now? How can you tell?

FOR ENGLISH LEARNERS

Task Support Call attention to the question in the marginal note for lines 52–57. Point out the definition of *rapier;* then have students reread what Tybalt says immediately after sending his servant to get the rapier. ***Possible answer:*** *Tybalt wants to use his sword to kill Romeo.*

Show a fair presence and put off these frowns,
An ill-beseeming semblance for a feast.

Tybalt. It fits when such a villain is a guest.
I'll not endure him.

Capulet.   He shall be endured.
75 What, goodman boy? I say he shall. Go to!
Am I the master here, or you? Go to!
You'll not endure him? God shall mend my soul!
You'll make a mutiny among my guests!
You will set cock-a-hoop! You'll be the man.

80 **Tybalt.** Why, uncle, 'tis a shame.

Capulet.   Go to, go to!
You are a saucy boy. Is't so, indeed?
This trick may chance to scathe you. I know what.
You must contrary me! Marry, 'tis time.—
Well said, my hearts!—You are a princox—go!
85 Be quiet, or—More light, more light!—For shame!
I'll make you quiet; what!—Cheerly, my hearts!

Tybalt. Patience perforce with willful choler meeting
Makes my flesh tremble in their different greeting.
I will withdraw; but this intrusion shall,
90 Now seeming sweet, convert to bitter gall.

[*Exit.*]

Romeo. If I profane with my unworthiest hand
This holy shrine, the gentle fine is this:
My lips, two blushing pilgrims, ready stand
To smooth that rough touch with a tender kiss.

95 **Juliet.** Good pilgrim, you do wrong your hand too much,
Which mannerly devotion shows in this;
For saints have hands that pilgrims' hands do touch,
And palm to palm is holy palmers' kiss.

Romeo. Have not saints lips, and holy palmers too?

100 **Juliet.** Ay, pilgrim, lips that they must use in prayer.

Romeo. O, then, dear saint, let lips do what hands do!
They pray; grant thou, lest faith turn to despair.

Juliet. Saints do not move, though grant for prayers' sake.

Romeo. Then move not while my prayer's effect I take.
105 Thus from my lips, by thine my sin is purged.

[*kisses her*]

Juliet. Then have my lips the sin that they have took.

72 semblance: outward appearance.

75 goodman boy: a term used to address an inferior; **Go to:** Stop, that's enough!

79 set cock-a-hoop: cause everything to be upset.

82–83 scathe: harm; **I know ... contrary me:** I know what I'm doing! Don't you dare challenge my authority.

84–86 Capulet intersperses his angry speech to Tybalt with comments to his guests and servants.

87–90 Patience ... gall: Tybalt says he will restrain himself, but his suppressed anger (**choler**) makes his body shake. *What do you think he will do about his anger?*

91–108 Romeo and Juliet are in the middle of the dance floor, with eyes only for each other. They touch the palms of their hands together. Their conversation revolves around Romeo's comparison of his lips to pilgrims who have traveled to a holy shrine. Juliet goes along with the comparison.

105 purged: washed away.

Lines 91–107
DISCUSSION PROMPTS

Use these prompts to help students analyze the first encounter between Romeo and Juliet:

Connect Recall your first meeting with someone who later became close to you. How were your words different from the words spoken in Romeo and Juliet's first meeting? *Students should identify the usual awkwardness of first meetings and should contrast that way of talking with the gentle poetry of Romeo and Juliet's first meeting.*

Analyze What are the religious references in the dialogue? What is meant by them? *Possible answer: Romeo calls Juliet a holy shrine (line 92) and a saint (line 101). He says that his lips are pilgrims (line 93). Juliet calls Romeo a pilgrim (line 95). Romeo says that his sin is purged by Juliet's kiss (line 105). The references show that even though these teenagers have just met, they already idolize each other.*

Synthesize What do you think each lover has learned about the other in this brief scene? *Possible answer: Each lover has learned that the other has a similar sense of humor and religious intensity. They both sense a mutual physical attraction and emotional intensity as well.*

DIFFERENTIATED INSTRUCTION

FOR LESS–PROFICIENT READERS
Paraphrasing Shakespeare Have students re-read the marginal note for lines 84–86. Then model a paraphrase of Capulet's mix of angry and friendly words, as shown:

- *Well said, friends!—You are a conceited fighter—Dance! (line 84)*

- *Keep quiet or I will . . . —Let's turn up the lights!—Shame on you! (line 85)*

- *I'll force you to be quiet!—Enjoy the party, my darlings! (line 86)*

FOR ENGLISH LEARNERS
Task Support Have students read the marginal note and question for lines 87–90. Remind students that when they met Tybalt in Scene 1, they saw him refuse to let Benvolio talk him out of a fight. *Possible answer: He will suppress his anger for the moment and will leave the party, but he will not let the anger go. It will boil over at another place and time.*

Romeo and Juliet in the Shakespeare & Company's 2004 Spring Tour Production

Romeo. Sin from my lips? O trespass sweetly urged!
Give me my sin again.

[*kisses her*]

Juliet.   You kiss by the book.

Nurse. Madam, your mother craves a word with you.

110 **Romeo.** What is her mother?

Nurse.   Marry, bachelor,
Her mother is the lady of the house.
And a good lady, and a wise and virtuous.
I nursed her daughter that you talked withal.
I tell you, he that can lay hold of her
115 Shall have the chinks.

Romeo.   Is she a Capulet?
O dear account! my life is my foe's debt.

108 **kiss by the book:** Juliet could mean "You kiss like an expert, someone who has studied and practiced." Or she could be teasing Romeo, meaning "You kiss coldly, as though you had learned how by reading a book."

109 At the nurse's message, Juliet walks to her mother.

115 **shall have the chinks:** shall become rich.

116 **my life ... debt:** my life belongs to my enemy.

ANALYZE VISUALS

Activity Do the actors in this photograph match your vision of Romeo and Juliet? Explain why or why not. *Students should provide reasonable support for their opinions.* What physical features would you look for if you were casting the play? *Students should name physical qualities that would influence their decision, such as youth and innocence.*

FOR ADVANCED LEARNERS/PRE–AP

Analyze a Motif Review Romeo's comment about hands in lines 48–49. Have students write a paragraph in which they relate that comment to his first words to Juliet in line 91 and to what both Romeo and Juliet say about hands in their brief conversation (including their pun about "holy palmers" in lines 98–99). Have students share their analyses of this motif in small groups.

Lines 136–139
REINFORCE *KEY IDEA:*
LOVE AND HATE

Discuss What great irony has Juliet just begun to grasp about **love** and **hate**?

Possible answer: Juliet has just begun to grasp the great irony that it is possible—and, indeed, her fate—to love someone whom you have been taught to hate.

ACT ONE WRAP-UP

PREDICT Have students make predictions about what may happen if Capulet and Montague learn that Romeo and Juliet have fallen in love. *Possible answer: They will forbid the lovers to meet. They may well be angry that the two do not understand the impossibility of their love.*

⭐ **CRITIQUE** Ask students to recall the events in *Romeo and Juliet* so far. Ask them what events they consider the most memorable or the most important. Then ask them to explain their choices.

READING FLUENCY

Distribute the copy master and have students work in pairs or groups to practice fluency.

📕 RESOURCE MANAGER—Copy Master
Reading Fluency p. 32

Benvolio. Away, be gone, the sport is at the best.

Romeo. Ay, so I fear; the more is my unrest.

Capulet. Nay, gentlemen, prepare not to be gone;
120 We have a trifling foolish banquet towards.

[*They whisper in his ear.*]

Is it e'en so? Why then, I thank you all.
I thank you, honest gentlemen. Good night.
More torches here! [*Exeunt* Maskers.] Come on then, let's to bed.
Ah, sirrah, by my fay, it waxes late;
125 I'll to my rest.

[*Exeunt all but* Juliet *and* Nurse.]

Juliet. Come hither, nurse. What is yond gentleman?

Nurse. The son and heir of old Tiberio.

Juliet. What's he that now is going out of door?

Nurse. Marry, that, I think, be young Petruchio.

130 **Juliet.** What's he that follows there, that would not dance?

Nurse. I know not.

Juliet. Go ask his name.—If he be married,
My grave is like to be my wedding bed.

Nurse. His name is Romeo, and a Montague,
135 The only son of your great enemy.

Juliet. My only love, sprung from my only hate!
Too early seen unknown, and known too late!
Prodigious birth of love it is to me
That I must love a loathed enemy.

140 **Nurse.** What's this? what's this?

Juliet.   A rhyme I learnt even now
Of one I danced withal.

[*One calls within, "Juliet."*]

Nurse.   Anon, anon!
Come, let's away; the strangers all are gone.

[*Exeunt.*]

120 **towards:** coming up.

126–130 Juliet asks the nurse to identify various guests as they leave. *What does she really want to know?*

137–138 **Too early...too late:** I fell in love with him before I learned who he is; **prodigious:** abnormal; unlucky. *How does Juliet feel about the fact that she's fallen in love with the son of her father's enemy?*

④ **Targeted Passage**

DIFFERENTIATED INSTRUCTION

FOR LESS-PROFICIENT READERS

④ **Targeted Passage [Lines 134–144]**

In this passage, Juliet's thrill over her first meeting with Romeo is challenged by the realization that Romeo is a Montague.

- What is wrong with Juliet's new love? How do you think that her feelings about him have changed?
- How can you tell that Juliet is worried about the future?

- Why does she hide from her nurse the truth about what has happened?

FOR ENGLISH LEARNERS

Task Support As you call attention to the question in the marginal note for lines 126–130, elicit that Juliet may be trying to distract her nurse by first expressing interest in two other party guests. *Possible answer: Juliet really wants to know the identity of the young man with whom she has just exchanged words of love (Romeo).*

Task Support Have students read the question in the marginal note for lines 137–138. Read aloud the explanation for the lines, especially the meaning of *prodigious*. *Possible answer: Juliet feels unhappy that she did not learn Romeo's identity until after she had fallen in love with him. She seems confused about what to do next.*

Comprehension

1. **Recall** What warning does Prince Escalus give the Capulets and the Montagues?

2. **Recall** What agreement do Paris and Lord Capulet reach?

3. **Recall** Why does Romeo go to the Capulets' party?

4. **Clarify** What is the chief obstacle to Romeo and Juliet's love?

Literary Analysis

5. **Reading Shakespearean Drama** Review the chart you created. Which events in Act One seem most important in setting up **conflicts** in the plot?

6. **Identify Character Foils** A foil is a character who highlights, through sharp contrast, the qualities of another character. Identify two characters in Act One who are foils for each other. What do you learn about the characters by seeing them in contrast to one another?

7. **Analyze Foreshadowing** Examine the examples of foreshadowing listed in the chart. To clarify your understanding of the examples, try paraphrasing them. Then explain what event each ominous passage foreshadows.

Foreshadowing	Paraphrase	What It Hints At
I fear, too early; for my mind misgives Some consequence, yet hanging in the stars, Shall bitterly begin his fearful date With this night's revels and expire the term Of a despised life, closed in my breast, By some vile forfeit of untimely death. - Romeo (Act One, Scene 4, lines 106–111)		
My grave is like to be my wedding bed. - Juliet (Act One, Scene 5, line 133)		

8. **Evaluate Blank Verse** Find and copy a group of four lines of blank verse in Act One, marking the unstressed (˘) and the stressed (´) syllables in each line. Then explain whether the lines show the typical **iambic pentameter** pattern or contain rhythmic variations. In your opinion, does the passage accurately capture the sound of spoken English? Explain.

Literary Criticism

9. **Critical Interpretations** Works with tremendous critical acclaim can sometimes fail to live up to our expectations. Who hasn't been disappointed after hype? According to critic Robert Graves, the "remarkable thing about Shakespeare is that he is really very good—in spite of all the people who say he is very good." Is *Romeo and Juliet* living up to your expectations? Explain.

eagerness to fight. Lady Capulet's dignity and short, direct statements contrast with the nurse's light, crude chatter. Mercutio's high spirits and playfulness contrast with Romeo's lovesick melancholy.

7. *Paraphrases will vary. The first passage hints at Romeo's death, the ultimate result of his seeing and meeting Juliet at that night's party. The second passage hints at Juliet's death, which comes soon after her marriage.*

8. ● **STANDARDS FOCUS** *Evaluate Blank Verse* Students should use scansion marks

to mark the stressed and unstressed syllables and should note variations in the meter. Students may feel that iambic pentameter sounds stylized yet is still more like spoken English than other meters.

Literary Criticism

9. *Students should offer a clear opinion about why the play is or is not living up to their expectations. They may suggest it is too soon to tell, since at the end of Act One, Romeo and Juliet have just met.*

Practice and Apply

After Reading

For additional support of post-reading questions, use these copy masters:

R **RESOURCE MANAGER**—Copy Masters

Reading Check p. 29 (to check understanding of the selection)

Shakespearean Drama p. 25 (for practice of literary analysis standards focus)

Question Support p. 31 (After Reading questions adapted for English learners and less-proficient readers)

For additional questions, see page 19.

ANSWERS

Comprehension

1. *The prince warns that if there is another violent outburst, the head of each family will be executed as punishment.*

2. *They agree that Paris may woo Juliet but will wait two years before marrying her.*

3. *Romeo goes in hopes of seeing Rosaline.*

4. *The chief obstacle is their families' feud.*

Literary Analysis

Possible answers:

5. ■ **STANDARDS FOCUS** *Reading Shakespearean Drama The opening brawl between the Capulets and Montagues is the key event in setting up conflicts, because it reveals the hatred that threatens Romeo and Juliet's love. Talk of a match between Juliet and Paris and the first meeting of Romeo and Juliet are other conflict-producing events.*

6. *Tybalt and Benvolio, Lady Capulet and the nurse, and Mercutio and Romeo are foils. Benvolio's peaceful nature highlights Tybalt's*

Assess and Reteach

Assess

R **RESOURCE MANAGER**—Copy Masters

Selection Test A pp. 33–34
Selection Test B/C pp. 35–36

Test Generator CD

Reteach

S **STANDARDS LESSON FILE**

Literature Lessons 25, 26, 35, 38

Practice and Apply

Get Into the Act

SUMMARY

A Prologue summarizes Act One; then Act Two begins. After the party, Romeo comes to Capulet's garden. He sees Juliet at her balcony, and the two declare their love. Juliet promises to marry Romeo if he can arrange the ceremony. Romeo enlists the help of Friar Laurence, who sees in the marriage a way to end the Montague-Capulet feud. Later, Romeo reveals his plan to Juliet's nurse. The lovers meet and marry at Friar Laurence's cell.

ANALYZE VISUALS

Activity What can you infer from this photograph about the characters and setting of *Romeo and Juliet*? *Possible answer: The reader can identify the Elizabethan setting from the style of the costumes and the richness of the set. The actors' poses suggest their love for one another.*

READING STRATEGY

■ SUMMARY

Have several students share in reading the Prologue aloud. Then ask students to summarize the main action of Act Two. *Possible answer: Romeo has found a new love in Juliet. There are challenges to their love, but their passion drives them to find a way to be together.*

Resources for Act Two

 RESOURCE MANAGER UNIT 10

Plan and Teach pp. 37–40

Literary Analysis
Summary pp. 41†*, 42‡*
Shakespearean Drama pp. 43, 44†*
Question Support p. 48*

Reading
Reading Shakespearean Drama
pp. 45, 46†*
Reading Check p. 47

Assessment
Selection Tests A, B/C pp. 49*, 51*
 Test Generator CD

BEST PRACTICES TOOLKIT

Differentiated Instruction
pp. 31–38*

Graphic Organizers/Strategies
Making Inferences • Character
Analysis Chart • Sequence Chain •
Open Mind

Reading Support
 Audio Anthology CD*

Technology
ⓘ Literature Center at
ClassZone.com
 Write*Smart* CD

---

* Resources for Differentiation   † Also in Spanish   ‡ In Haitian Creole and Vietnamese

---

Prologue

In a sonnet the Chorus summarizes what has happened so far in the play. He reviews how Romeo and Juliet have fallen in love and suggests both the problems and the delights they now face. He also includes hints about what will result from the events of Act One.

[*Enter* Chorus.]

Chorus. Now old desire doth in his deathbed lie,
And young affection gapes to be his heir.
That fair for which love groaned for and would die,
With tender Juliet matched, is now not fair.
5 Now Romeo is beloved, and loves again,
Alike bewitched by the charm of looks;
But to his foe supposed he must complain,
And she steal love's sweet bait from fearful hooks.
Being held a foe, he may not have access
10 To breathe such vows as lovers use to swear,
And she as much in love, her means much less
To meet her new beloved anywhere;
But passion lends them power, time means, to meet,
Temp'ring extremities with extreme sweet.

[*Exit.*]

> **1–4 Now . . . fair:** Romeo's love for Rosaline (**old desire**) is now dead. His new love (**young affection**) replaces the old. Compared to Juliet, Rosaline no longer seems so beautiful.

> **6** *What attracted Romeo and Juliet to each other?*

> **7 but . . . complain:** Juliet, a Capulet, is Romeo's supposed enemy, yet she is the one to whom he must plead (**complain**) his love.

> **14 temp'ring . . . sweet:** moderating great difficulties with extreme delights.

Act Two

SCENE 1   *A lane by the wall of Capulet's orchard.*

Later in the evening of the party, Romeo returns alone to the Capulet home, hoping for another glimpse of Juliet. He climbs the wall and hides outside, in the orchard. Meanwhile, Benvolio and Mercutio come looking for him, but he remains hidden behind the wall. Mercutio makes fun of Romeo and his lovesick condition. Keep in mind that Mercutio and Benvolio think Romeo is still in love with Rosaline, since they know nothing about his meeting with Juliet.

[*Enter* Romeo *alone.*]

Romeo. Can I go forward when my heart is here?
Turn back, dull earth, and find thy center out.

[*climbs the wall and leaps down within it*]

[*Enter* Benvolio *with* Mercutio.]

Benvolio. Romeo! my cousin Romeo! Romeo!

> **1–2 Can . . . out:** How can I leave when Juliet is still here? My body (**dull earth**) has to find its heart (**center**).

Balcony scene from the Globe Theatre's 2004 production

Use these prompts to help students understand why Romeo disappears without telling his friends:

Connect Have you ever felt like avoiding your friends? How does that feeling help you understand Romeo as this scene opens? *Students should identify with Romeo's desire for privacy.*

Analyze Consider Romeo's plans as Act Two opens. Why do you think Romeo does not want to talk to Mercutio and Benvolio at this time? *Possible answer: He probably doesn't want to face their questions, their teasing, and perhaps their attempts to keep him from seeing Juliet again.*

Evaluate In your opinion, is hiding from his friends a wise thing for Romeo to do? Defend your answer. *Possible answers: Yes. Romeo's friends probably would keep him away from Juliet. No. Romeo is acting upon a moment's passion, and his friends probably could help him look at the situation more realistically.*

DIFFERENTIATED INSTRUCTION

For general guidelines on differentiating instruction, see

BEST PRACTICES TOOLKIT
Differentiated Instruction pp. 31–38

FOR LESS–PROFICIENT READERS

In combination with the *Audio Anthology CD*, use one or more Targeted Passages (pp. 971, 975, 986, 990) to ensure that students focus on key story events, concepts, and skills. Targeted Passages are also good for English learners.

Preview Have students use a chart like this to organize the Scene 1 synopsis:

	Want(s) . . .	Will . . .
Romeo	to see Juliet again	hide in Capulet's orchard
Benvolio & Mercutio	to find Romeo	look for him near Capulet's home

FOR ENGLISH LEARNERS

Task Support Point out the marginal question for line 6 of the Prologue. Make sure students understand that in the first part of the sonnet, the Chorus is referring to Romeo's previous love: Rosaline. *Possible answer: Romeo and Juliet were attracted by each other's physical appearance ("the charm of looks").*

Mercutio.   He is wise,
And, on my life, hath stol'n him home to bed.

5 **Benvolio.** He ran this way, and leapt this orchard wall.
Call, good Mercutio.

Mercutio.   Nay, I'll conjure too.
Romeo! humors! madman! passion! lover!
Appear thou in the likeness of a sigh;
Speak but one rhyme, and I am satisfied!
10 Cry but "Ay me!" pronounce but "love" and "dove";
Speak to my gossip Venus one fair word, ◆
One nickname for her purblind son and heir,
Young Adam Cupid, he that shot so trim
When King Cophetua loved the beggar maid!
15 He heareth not, he stirreth not, he moveth not;
The ape is dead, and I must conjure him.
I conjure thee by Rosaline's bright eyes,
By her high forehead and her scarlet lip,
By her fine foot, straight leg, and quivering thigh,
20 And the demesnes that there adjacent lie,
That in thy likeness thou appear to us!

Benvolio. An if he hear thee, thou wilt anger him.

Mercutio. This cannot anger him. 'Twould anger him
To raise a spirit in his mistress' circle
25 Of some strange nature, letting it there stand
Till she had laid it and conjured it down.
That were some spite; my invocation
Is fair and honest and in his mistress' name
I conjure only but to raise up him.

30 **Benvolio.** Come, he hath hid himself among these trees
To be consorted with the humorous night.
Blind is his love, and best befits the dark.

Mercutio. If love be blind, love cannot hit the mark.
Now will he sit under a medlar tree
35 And wish his mistress were that kind of fruit
As maids call medlars when they laugh alone.
Oh, Romeo, that she were, O, that she were
An open et cetera, thou a pop'rin pear!
Romeo, good night. I'll to my truckle bed;
40 This field-bed is too cold for me to sleep.
Come, shall we go?

Benvolio.   Go then, for 'tis in vain
To seek him here that means not to be found.

[*Exeunt.*]

A GRAMMAR AND STYLE

Parallelism Explain that writers use parallelism not only to create rhythm, but also to connect related ideas or details. Elicit that "Speak," "Cry," "pronounce," and "Speak" are the imperative-mood verbs in lines 9–11 and that each refers to a form of verbal communication. Then have students identify two other examples of parallelism in this speech by Mercutio and discuss the way in which each uses the rhythm it creates. *Possible answer:*
Two other examples of parallelism are line 15 and lines 17–19. The rhythm of the first example emphasizes the verbs ("heareth," "stirreth," "moveth"). The rhythm of the second example emphasizes Rosaline's physical features ("bright eyes," "high forehead," "scarlet lip," "fine foot," "straight leg," "quivering thigh").

---

6 conjure: use magic to call him.

8–21 Appear . . . us: Mercutio jokes about Romeo's lovesickness. He tries to make Romeo appear by suggestively naming parts of Rosaline's body.

◆ **GRAMMAR AND STYLE**
In lines 8–11, Shakespeare creates rhythm through **parallelism,** or the use of similar grammatical structures to express related ideas. Notice how each of these lines begins with a verb in the imperative mood.

20 demesnes: areas; **adjacent:** next to.

23–29 'Twould . . . raise up him: It would anger him if I called a stranger to join his beloved (**mistress**), but I'm only calling Romeo to join her.

31 to be . . . night: to keep company with the night, which is as gloomy as Romeo is.

34 medlar: a fruit that looks like a small brown apple.

39 truckle bed: trundle bed, a small bed that fits in beneath a bigger one.

DIFFERENTIATED INSTRUCTION

FOR LESS–PROFICIENT READERS

Paraphrasing Shakespeare Draw students' attention to Mercutio's "Romeo, good night" in line 39 and to his declared intention of going to bed. Help students paraphrase Benvolio's closing comment in lines 42–43 to read something like this: *Yes, let's go home. It's no use to keep looking for Romeo if he intends to hide from us.*

Preview Read through the italicized scene synopsis with students to provide an overview of Scene 2. Check their understanding of the events mentioned by listing these events in random order and having students put them into the correct order (the order shown here).

Romeo hides in Capulet's garden.

↓

Juliet comes to her balcony and speaks her thoughts about Romeo's being a Montague.

↓

Romeo reveals his presence and declares his love for Juliet.

↓

Juliet declares that she loves him too.

↓

Romeo leaves to arrange their wedding.

SCENE 2 *Capulet's orchard.*

The following is one of the most famous scenes in all literature. The speeches contain some of the most beautiful poetry Shakespeare ever wrote.

Juliet appears on the balcony outside her room. She cannot see Romeo, who stands in the garden just below. At the beginning of the scene, both characters are speaking private thoughts to themselves. Romeo, however, can hear Juliet as she expresses her love for him despite his family name. Eventually, he speaks directly to her, and they declare their love for each other. Just before dawn Romeo leaves to make plans for their wedding.

[*Enter* Romeo.]

Romeo. He jests at scars that never felt a wound.

[*Enter* Juliet *above at a window.*]

But soft! What light through yonder window breaks?
It is the East, and Juliet is the sun!
Arise, fair sun, and kill the envious moon,
5 Who is already sick and pale with grief
That thou her maid art far more fair than she.
Be not her maid, since she is envious;
Her vestal livery is but sick and green,
And none but fools do wear it; cast it off.
10 It is my lady; O, it is my love!
O that she knew she were!
She speaks, yet she says nothing. What of that?
Her eye discourses; I will answer it.
I am too bold; 'tis not to me she speaks.
15 Two of the fairest stars in all the heaven,
Having some business, do entreat her eyes
To twinkle in their spheres till they return.
What if her eyes were there, they in her head?
The brightness of her cheek would shame those stars
20 As daylight doth a lamp; her eyes in heaven
Would through the airy region stream so bright
That birds would sing and think it were not night.
See how she leans her cheek upon her hand!
O that I were a glove upon that hand,
25 That I might touch that cheek! **B**

Juliet.   Ay me!

Romeo.   She speaks.
O, speak again, bright angel! for thou art
As glorious to this night, being o'er my head,
As is a winged messenger of heaven

---

1 He jests ... wound: Romeo has overheard Mercutio and comments that Mercutio makes fun of love because he has never been wounded by it.

2–9 But soft ... cast it off: Romeo sees Juliet at the window. For a moment he is speechless (**soft:** be still), but then he describes her beauty in glowing images.

① Targeted Passage

13–14 Her eye ... speaks: Romeo shifts back and forth between wanting to speak to Juliet and being afraid.

15–22 Two of ... not night: Romeo compares Juliet's eyes to stars in the sky.

B SOLILOQUY
To whom is Romeo speaking in lines 2–25? Explain what this soliloquy tells you about Romeo's thoughts.

25 Juliet begins to speak, not knowing that Romeo is nearby.

26–32 thou art ... of the air: He compares Juliet to an angel (**winged messenger of heaven**) who stands on (**bestrides**) the clouds.

ROMEO AND JULIET: ACT TWO, SCENE 2 **971**

Lines 1–25

REINFORCE *KEY IDEA:* LOVE AND HATE

Discuss Near the end of Scene 1 (lines 30–34), Benvolio and Mercutio both spoke about Romeo's "blind" love. How does Romeo's description of Juliet at the beginning of Scene 2 suggest that Benvolio and Mercutio might be right? *Possible answer: Romeo's description is dominated by exaggeration. For example, he says that the moon is jealous of Juliet's beauty (lines 4–6), that Juliet speaks with the stars (lines 14–17), and that her eyes could light up the sky (lines 20–22). Romeo's love is "blind" in the sense that Romeo is not seeing Juliet realistically.*

LITERARY ANALYSIS

B SOLILOQUY

Possible answer: Romeo is speaking to himself, giving voice to his thoughts. The soliloquy reveals that Romeo is enraptured by Juliet's beauty, that he idealizes her, that he is uncertain about how to communicate with her, and that he wants to touch her.

If students need help ... Have a student look up and share the definition of *soliloquy.* Elicit that Romeo has not yet made his presence known to Juliet, the only other person in this scene. Then guide students through a Making Inferences chart to relate Romeo's comments to his likely thoughts.

 BEST PRACTICES TOOLKIT—Transparency Making Inferences p. A13

FOR LESS–PROFICIENT READERS

① Targeted Passage [Lines 2–25]

The figurative language in this classic soliloquy emphasizes the poetic nature of Romeo's love.

- Who is the "fair sun" (line 4)? Why, according to Romeo, does this sun make the moon envious?

- With whom does Romeo imagine that Juliet is speaking? about what topic?

- As he finishes his speech, why does Romeo wish that he were a glove on Juliet's hand?

FOR ADVANCED LEARNERS/PRE–AP

Compare and Contrast Criticism [paired-activity option] It is not surprising that one of the most famous scenes in literature has had much literary criticism written about it. Challenge students to locate two critics' writings about this scene. After they have read the criticisms, have students compare and contrast the authors' views and arguments, either in an essay or as part of a larger oral presentation.

DISCUSSION PROMPTS

Use these prompts to explore Juliet's philosophical musing about names and Romeo's response to it:

Connect How strongly do you identify with your family name? Why might you give it up? *Some students may say that their family name is very important and that they would never give it up, even in marriage. Others might be willing to give it up if doing so would achieve something important.*

Analyze How does Juliet feel about Romeo's name? about names in general? *Possible answer: Juliet feels that Romeo's name is hateful, since the Montagues are enemies of the Capulets, but that Romeo himself is not an enemy (lines 38–39). She feels that names are artificial labels that do not indicate the true nature of the things to which they are applied (lines 40–47). Does Romeo agree with her? How can you tell? Possible answer: Romeo agrees, for he offers to give up his name (lines 49–51).*

Synthesize Since some Capulets can identify Romeo by sight (Act One, Scene 5), it is doubtful that a name change would improve Romeo's situation. Why, then, do you think that Shakespeare included this speech? *Possible answer: Shakespeare included this speech to show that the young lovers are above their families' feud and want to try to separate themselves from it.*

Unto the white-upturned wond'ring eyes
30 Of mortals that fall back to gaze on him
When he bestrides the lazy-pacing clouds
And sails upon the bosom of the air.

Juliet. O Romeo, Romeo! wherefore art thou Romeo?
Deny thy father and refuse thy name!
35 Or, if thou wilt not, be but sworn my love,
And I'll no longer be a Capulet.

Romeo [*aside*]. Shall I hear more, or shall I speak at this?

Juliet. 'Tis but thy name that is my enemy.
Thou art thyself, though not a Montague.
40 What's Montague? It is nor hand, nor foot,
Nor arm, nor face, nor any other part
Belonging to a man. O, be some other name!
What's in a name? That which we call a rose
By any other name would smell as sweet.
45 So Romeo would, were he not Romeo called,
Retain that dear perfection which he owes
Without that title. Romeo, doff thy name;
And for that name, which is no part of thee,
Take all myself.

Romeo.   I take thee at thy word.
50 Call me but love, and I'll be new baptized;
Henceforth I never will be Romeo.

Juliet. What man art thou that, thus bescreened in night,
So stumblest on my counsel?

Romeo.   By a name
I know not how to tell thee who I am.
55 My name, dear saint, is hateful to myself,
Because it is an enemy to thee.
Had I it written, I would tear the word.

Juliet. My ears have yet not drunk a hundred words
Of that tongue's utterance, yet I know the sound.
60 Art thou not Romeo, and a Montague?

Romeo. Neither, fair saint, if either thee dislike.

Juliet. How camest thou hither, tell me, and wherefore?
The orchard walls are high and hard to climb,
And the place death, considering who thou art,
65 If any of my kinsmen find thee here.

33 wherefore: why. Juliet asks why Romeo is who he is—someone from her enemy's family. *What does Juliet ask Romeo to do? What does she promise to do?*

43–47 Juliet tries to convince herself that a name is just a meaningless word that has nothing to do with the person. She asks Romeo to get rid of (**doff**) his name.

52–53 Juliet is startled that someone hiding (**bescreened**) nearby hears her private thoughts (**counsel**).

63–65 *What warning does Juliet give Romeo?*

DIFFERENTIATED INSTRUCTION

FOR ENGLISH LEARNERS

Task Support Direct students to the question in the marginal note for line 33. Have a volunteer read lines 34–36 aloud. *Possible answer: Juliet asks Romeo to separate from his family and give up the Montague name. If he will not, she says, she will swear her love to him and turn against her family.*

Task Support As you have students read the marginal question for lines 63–65, ask them to consider the identity of the "kinsmen" to whom Juliet refers in line 65. *Possible answer: Juliet warns that her Capulet relatives will kill Romeo, the Montague, if they find him in Capulet's garden.*

Romeo. With love's light wings did I o'erperch these walls;
For stony limits cannot hold love out,
And what love can do, that dares love attempt.
Therefore thy kinsmen are no let to me.

70 **Juliet.** If they do see thee, they will murder thee.

Romeo. Alack, there lies more peril in thine eye
Than twenty of their swords! Look thou but sweet,
And I am proof against their enmity.

Juliet. I would not for the world they saw thee here.

75 **Romeo.** I have night's cloak to hide me from their sight;
And but thou love me, let them find me here.
My life were better ended by their hate
Than death prorogued, wanting of thy love. **⦿**

Juliet. By whose direction foundst thou out this place?

80 **Romeo.** By love, that first did prompt me to enquire.
He lent me counsel, and I lent him eyes.
I am no pilot, yet, wert thou as far
As that vast shore washed with the farthest sea,
I would adventure for such merchandise.

85 **Juliet.** Thou knowest the mask of night is on my face;
Else would a maiden blush bepaint my cheek
For that which thou hast heard me speak tonight.
Fain would I dwell on form—fain, fain deny
What I have spoke; but farewell compliment!

90 Dost thou love me? I know thou wilt say "Ay";
And I will take thy word. Yet, if thou swearst,
Thou mayst prove false. At lovers' perjuries,
They say Jove laughs. O gentle Romeo,
If thou dost love, pronounce it faithfully.

95 Or if thou thinkst I am too quickly won,
I'll frown, and be perverse, and say thee nay,
So thou wilt woo; but else, not for the world.
In truth, fair Montague, I am too fond,
And therefore thou mayst think my 'havior light;

100 But trust me, gentleman, I'll prove more true
Than those that have more cunning to be strange.
I should have been more strange, I must confess,
But that thou overheardst, ere I was ware,
My true love's passion. Therefore pardon me,

105 And not impute this yielding to light love,
Which the dark night hath so discovered.

66–69 With . . . me: Love helped me climb (**o'erperch**) the walls. Neither walls nor your relatives are a hindrance (**let**) to me.

72–73 Look . . . enmity: Smile on me, and I will be defended against my enemies' hatred (**enmity**).

78 than death . . . love: than my death postponed (**prorogued**) if you don't love me.

⦿ CHARACTER
Reread lines 75–78, and explain what Romeo means. Do you think he is seriously thinking of death here, or is he just exaggerating because he's head over heels in love? Explain.

85–89 Thou . . . compliment: Had I known you were listening, I would have gladly (**fain**) behaved more properly, but now it's too late for good manners (**farewell compliment**). *Why is Juliet embarrassed that Romeo overheard her?*

92–93 At . . . laughs: Jove, the king of the gods, laughs at lovers who lie to each other.

95–101 Or if . . . strange: You might think I've fallen in love too easily and that I'm too outspoken. But I'll be truer to you than those who play games to hide their real feelings (**be strange**).

LITERARY ANALYSIS

⦿ CHARACTER

Possible answer: *Romeo means that he would rather die quickly at the hands of the Capulets than to continue living with the knowledge that Juliet does not love him. Although Romeo is probably exaggerating, he made similarly rash statements when he was pining for Rosaline. It is clear that Romeo is led by his passions.*

If students need help . . . Have students compare this speech to Romeo's previous speech (lines 71–73) before asking the Literary Analysis question. Then call on volunteers to paraphrase each line of the speech in lines 75–78.

FOR LESS–PROFICIENT READERS
Inverted Word Order Explain that inverted word order can mean moving sentence elements other than verbs out of their traditional positions. Have students restate line 66 and the sentence that begins in the middle of line 92, placing the prepositional phrases in a traditional position. ***Possible answer:*** *I o'erperched these walls with love's light wings; They say Jove laughs at lovers' perjuries.*

FOR ENGLISH LEARNERS
Task Support Have students read the marginal note and question for lines 85–89. Point out lines 86–87, in which Juliet speaks of blushing with embarrassment. ***Possible answer:*** *Juliet is embarrassed that Romeo overheard her because she did not mean to let him know her personal thoughts. She feels that she has given away too much information about her feelings for Romeo.*

FOR ADVANCED LEARNERS/PRE–AP
Analyze Meter Remind students that iambic pentameter (a ten-syllable line with alternating unstressed and stressed syllables) is meant to imitate the sound of spoken English. Then ask students to analyze the meter of the romantic lines of the balcony scene. Have students consider and then share their thoughts about how Shakespeare keeps the lovers' speeches from sounding "sing-songy" and, therefore, insincere.

Activity What features of the photograph make this famous scene recognizable?

Possible answer: A man has climbed a balcony to speak with a young woman. The two seem to be fascinated with each other. These features combine to identify the balcony scene of Romeo and Juliet.

If students need help... Ask leading questions, such as "Who is in the photograph?" "How are they dressed?" and "What emotions do their faces reveal?"

Romeo. Lady, by yonder blessed moon I swear,
That tips with silver all these fruit-tree tops—

Juliet. O, swear not by the moon, the inconstant moon,
110 That monthly changes in her circled orb,
Lest that thy love prove likewise variable.

Romeo. What shall I swear by?

Juliet.   Do not swear at all;
Or if thou wilt, swear by thy gracious self,
Which is the god of my idolatry,
115 And I'll believe thee.

109–111 *Why doesn't Juliet want Romeo to swear by the moon?*

Balcony scene from the Seattle Repertory Theatre's 2003 production

974   UNIT 10: SHAKESPEAREAN DRAMA

DIFFERENTIATED INSTRUCTION

FOR LESS–PROFICIENT READERS

Inverted Word Order In lines 108 and 147, Shakespeare adds interest and emphasis to sentences by placing the phrase that names a direct object in an unusual position. Call on volunteers to "translate" these lines. *Possible answer: That tips all these fruit-tree tops with silver; And I'll lay all my fortunes at thy foot.*

FOR ENGLISH LEARNERS

Task Support Read aloud the marginal question for lines 109–111. Discuss the meanings of "inconstant", "changes", and "variable", then elicit that the moon's appearance changes as it passes through its monthly phases. *Possible answer: Juliet doesn't want Romeo to swear by the moon because the moon constantly changes. If his love is similar to the moon, it will be variable and therefore untrustworthy.*

Romeo.   If my heart's dear love—

Juliet. Well, do not swear. Although I joy in thee,
I have no joy of this contract tonight.
It is too rash, too unadvised, too sudden;
Too like the lightning, which doth cease to be
120 Ere one can say "It lightens." Sweet, good night!
This bud of love, by summer's ripening breath,
May prove a beauteous flow'r when next we meet.
Good night, good night! As sweet repose and rest
Come to thy heart as that within my breast! **D**

125 **Romeo.** O, wilt thou leave me so unsatisfied?

Juliet. What satisfaction canst thou have tonight?

Romeo. The exchange of thy love's faithful vow for mine.

Juliet. I gave thee mine before thou didst request it;
And yet I would it were to give again.

130 **Romeo.** Wouldst thou withdraw it? For what purpose, love?

Juliet. But to be frank and give it thee again.
And yet I wish but for the thing I have.
My bounty is as boundless as the sea,
My love as deep; the more I give to thee,
135 The more I have, for both are infinite.
I hear some noise within. Dear love, adieu!

[Nurse *calls within.*]

Anon, good nurse! Sweet Montague, be true.
Stay but a little, I will come again.
[*Exit.*]

Romeo. O blessed, blessed night! I am afeard,
140 Being in night, all this is but a dream,
Too flattering-sweet to be substantial.

[*Re-enter* Juliet, *above.*]

Juliet. Three words, dear Romeo, and good night indeed.
If that thy bent of love be honorable,
Thy purpose marriage, send me word tomorrow,
145 By one that I'll procure to come to thee,
Where and what time thou wilt perform the rite;
And all my fortunes at thy foot I'll lay
And follow thee my lord throughout the world.

Nurse [*within*]. Madam!

150 **Juliet.** I come, anon.—But if thou meanst not well,
I do beseech thee—

117 **I have ... contract:** I am concerned about this declaration of love (**contract**).

D CHARACTER
Reread lines 116–124, and describe Juliet's attitude at this point. How does she feel about Romeo? Why does she seem uneasy about their relationship?

137–138 **anon:** right away. Juliet calls to her nurse but asks Romeo to wait, as she will come back soon.

143–146 **If that ... rite:** I'll send a messenger to you tomorrow. If your intention is to marry me, tell the messenger where and when the ceremony will be.

2 Targeted Passage

150–151 **But if ... thee:** Juliet is still worried that Romeo is not serious.

LITERARY ANALYSIS

D CHARACTER

Possible answer: Juliet loves Romeo and is joyful (line 116) to know that he loves her. However, she seems uneasy about their relationship because everything is happening so quickly (lines 117–118). She is afraid that a love that begins so suddenly will disappear too soon (lines 119–120).

If students need help . . . Have a volunteer read lines 116–124 aloud. Ask other students to paraphrase the speech. In addition, relate this question to the marginal question for lines 109–111 on page 974.

FOR LESS–PROFICIENT READERS

2 Targeted Passage [Lines 142–148]

This passage advances the plot by revealing a plan for the lovers' next meeting.

- What kind of message may Romeo send to Juliet the next day? How will Juliet receive that message?

- What specific information will Romeo send to Juliet?

- What is Juliet willing to do when she receives that message? Why?

FOR ENGLISH LEARNERS

Vocabulary Support Explain to students that some of Shakespeare's words are similar to modern English but are changed to fit the meter of the lines. Illustrate with these examples from Scene 2: "'havior" (line 99), "flow'r" (line 122), "falc'ner's" (line 158), and "Rememb'ring" (line 174).

Lines 165–170
REINFORCE *KEY IDEA:* LOVE AND HATE

Discuss By nine o'clock the next morning, wedding plans for these young lovers may be in place. Do you think that a marriage between Romeo and Juliet is possible, given the fact that their families **hate** each other?

Possible answer: *The lovers plan to wed in secret, which is the only possible way for the marriage to happen. When the news becomes public, the families' hate may lead both sides to become very angry.*

Nurse [*within*]. Madam!

Juliet. By-and-by I come.—
To cease thy suit and leave me to my grief.
Tomorrow will I send.

Romeo. So thrive my soul—

Juliet. A thousand times good night! [*Exit.*]

155 **Romeo.** A thousand times the worse, to want thy light!
Love goes toward love as schoolboys from their books;
But love from love, towards school with heavy looks.
[*Enter* Juliet *again, above.*]

Juliet. Hist! Romeo, hist! O for a falc'ner's voice
To lure this tassel-gentle back again!
160 Bondage is hoarse and may not speak aloud;
Else would I tear the cave where Echo lies,
And make her airy tongue more hoarse than mine
With repetition of my Romeo's name.
Romeo!

165 **Romeo.** It is my soul that calls upon my name.
How silver-sweet sound lovers' tongues by night,
Like softest music to attending ears!

Juliet. Romeo!

Romeo. My sweet?

Juliet. What o'clock tomorrow
Shall I send to thee?

Romeo. By the hour of nine.

170 **Juliet.** I will not fail. 'Tis twenty years till then.
I have forgot why I did call thee back.

Romeo. Let me stand here till thou remember it.

Juliet. I shall forget, to have thee still stand there,
Rememb'ring how I love thy company.

175 **Romeo.** And I'll still stay, to have thee still forget,
Forgetting any other home but this.

Juliet. 'Tis almost morning. I would have thee gone—
And yet no farther than a wanton's bird,
That lets it hop a little from her hand,
180 Like a poor prisoner in his twisted gyves,
And with a silk thread plucks it back again,
So loving-jealous of his liberty.

Romeo. I would I were thy bird.

156–157 Love . . . looks: The simile means that lovers meet as eagerly as schoolboys leave their books; lovers separate with the sadness of boys going to school.

158–163 Hist . . . name: Listen, Romeo, I wish I could speak your name as loudly as a falconer calls his falcon (**tassel-gentle**), but because of my parents I must whisper. **Echo** was a nymph in Greek mythology whose unreturned love for Narcissus caused her to waste away till only her voice was left.

177–182 I would . . . liberty: I know you must go, but I want you close to me like a pet bird that a thoughtless child (**wanton**) keeps on a string.

DIFFERENTIATED INSTRUCTION

FOR ENGLISH LEARNERS
Concept Support Romeo and Juliet plan to run away to marry without parental knowledge or consent. Discuss Romeo and Juliet's rationale for this action. Then invite students to share their thoughts about how various cultures might view the wisdom of this decision.

FOR ADVANCED LEARNERS/PRE–AP
Analyze a Speech Ask students to reread Juliet's final words in Scene 2. Then have students write a brief analysis of her speech, focusing on (1) Juliet's repeated fear of killing Romeo with love (line 184, but see also lines 63–65) and (2) the meaning and importance of the oxymoron "sweet sorrow" (line 185). Invite students to compare their analyses to see if their interpretations agree.

Juliet. Sweet, so would I.
Yet I should kill thee with much cherishing.
185 Good night, good night! Parting is such sweet sorrow,
That I shall say good night till it be morrow.

[*Exit.*]

Romeo. Sleep dwell upon thine eyes, peace in thy breast!
Would I were sleep and peace, so sweet to rest!
Hence will I to my ghostly father's cell,
190 His help to crave and my dear hap to tell.

[*Exit.*]

189–190 ghostly father: spiritual adviser or priest; **dear hap:** good fortune.

SCENE 3   *Friar Laurence's cell in the monastery.*

Romeo goes from Capulet's garden to the monastery where Friar Laurence lives. The friar knows Romeo well and often gives him advice. As the scene begins, Friar Laurence is gathering herbs in the early morning. He talks of good and bad uses for herbs. Keep this in mind, since Friar Laurence's skill at mixing herbs becomes important later in the play. Romeo tells the friar that he loves Juliet and wants to marry her. The friar is amazed that Romeo has forgotten about Rosaline so easily and suggests that Romeo might be acting in haste. Eventually, however, he agrees to marry Romeo and Juliet, hoping that the marriage will end the feud between their families.

[*Enter Friar Laurence alone, with a basket.*]

Friar Laurence. The grey-eyed morn smiles on the frowning night,
Chequ'ring the Eastern clouds with streaks of light;
And flecked darkness like a drunkard reels
5 From forth day's path and Titan's fiery wheels.
Now, ere the sun advance his burning eye
The day to cheer and night's dank dew to dry,
I must upfill this osier cage of ours
With baleful weeds and precious-juiced flowers.
10 The earth that's nature's mother is her tomb,
What is her burying grave, that is her womb;
And from her womb children of divers kind
We sucking on her natural bosom find;
Many for many virtues excellent,
15 None but for some, and yet all different.
O, mickle is the powerful grace that lies
In plants, herbs, stones, and their true qualities;
For naught so vile that on the earth doth live
But to the earth some special good doth give;

1–30 Friar Laurence begins his speech by describing how night changes into day. He then speaks of the herbs he is collecting. The friar is particularly fascinated with the idea that in herbs as well as man both good and evil can exist.

4 Titan is the god whose chariot pulls the sun into the sky each morning.

7 osier cage: willow basket.

9–12 The earth . . . find: The same earth that acts as a tomb is also the womb, or birthplace, of various useful plants that people can harvest.

15–18 mickle: great. The friar says that nothing from the earth is so evil that it doesn't do some good.

ROMEO AND JULIET: ACT TWO, SCENE 3   **977**

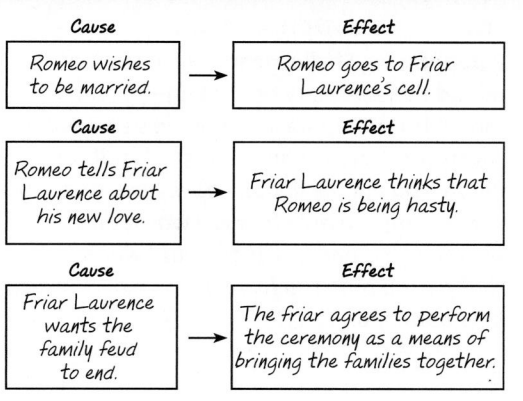

Use these prompts to discuss Romeo's visit with Friar Laurence:

Connect Think of a confidant—someone you can go to when you need to talk. How is Friar Laurence like that person? *Students may feel that both are caring, wise people.*

Analyze Why is Friar Laurence a particularly good character to counsel Romeo? *Possible answer: Friar Laurence is perceptive. He notices immediately that Romeo is "distempered" (line 33), or upset. He also demands that Romeo be "plain" (line 55), or honest, with him. It seems clear that the friar's manner has won Romeo's respect, affection, and trust.*

Synthesize By acting as a counselor and performing the marriage of these young lovers, what risk does Friar Laurence take? *Possible answer: Friar Laurence risks angering both powerful families. As a result, there may be greater violence instead of peace in Verona—and some of that violence might be directed at him.*

Nor aught so good but, strained from that fair use,
20 Revolts from true birth, stumbling on abuse.
Virtue itself turns vice, being misapplied,
And vice sometime's by action dignified.
Within the infant rind of this small flower
Poison hath residence, and medicine power;
25 For this, being smelt, with that part cheers each part;
Being tasted, slays all senses with the heart.
Two such opposed kings encamp them still
In man as well as herbs—grace and rude will;
And where the worser is predominant,
30 Full soon the canker death eats up that plant.

[*Enter* Romeo.]

Romeo. Good morrow, father.

Friar Laurence.   Benedicite!
What early tongue so sweet saluteth me?
Young son, it argues a distempered head
So soon to bid good morrow to thy bed.
35 Care keeps his watch in every old man's eye,
And where care lodges sleep will never lie;
But where unbruised youth with unstuffed brain
Doth couch his limbs, there golden sleep doth reign.
Therefore thy earliness doth me assure
40 Thou art uproused with some distemp'rature;
Or if not so, then here I hit it right—
Our Romeo hath not been in bed tonight.

Romeo. That last is true, the sweeter rest was mine.

Friar Laurence. God pardon sin! Wast thou with Rosaline?

45 **Romeo.** With Rosaline, my ghostly father? No.
I have forgot that name, and that name's woe.

Friar Laurence. That's my good son! But where hast thou been then?

Romeo. I'll tell thee ere thou ask it me again.
I have been feasting with mine enemy,
50 Where on a sudden one hath wounded me
That's by me wounded. Both our remedies
Within thy help and holy physic lies.
I bear no hatred, blessed man, for, lo,
My intercession likewise steads my foe.

55 **Friar Laurence.** Be plain, good son, and homely in thy drift.
Riddling confession finds but riddling shrift.

23–26 Within . . . heart: He holds a flower that can be used either as a poison or as a medicine. If the flower is smelled, its fragrance can improve health in each part of the body; if it is eaten, it causes death.

28 grace and rude will: good and evil. Both exist in people as well as in plants.

31 Benedicite (bĕ′nĕ-dī′sĭ-tē′): God bless you.

33–42 it argues . . . tonight: Only a disturbed (**distempered**) mind could make you get up so early. Old people may have trouble sleeping, but it is not normal for someone as young as you. Or were you up all night?

44 God . . . Rosaline: The friar is shocked that Romeo has not been to bed yet. *Where does he think Romeo has been?*

49–56 Romeo tries to explain the situation, asking for help both for himself and his "foe" (Juliet). The friar does not understand Romeo's convoluted language and asks him to speak clearly so that he can help.

DIFFERENTIATED INSTRUCTION

FOR LESS–PROFICIENT READERS
Paraphrasing Shakespeare Have students reread the summary of lines 49–56. Then model this paraphrase of Romeo's somewhat confusing words in lines 48–52: *I'll tell you before you ask me again: I have been to a party at my enemy's home. I was suddenly wounded by someone there, but I wounded that person too. You have the cure that will help both of us.*

FOR ENGLISH LEARNERS
Task Support Have students read the marginal note and question for line 44. Point out Romeo's comment about "sweeter rest" (line 43), and explain that Friar Laurence probably hears many people confess their sins. *Possible answer: Friar Laurence thinks that Romeo has spent the night in a romantic encounter with Rosaline.*

Romeo. Then plainly know my heart's dear love is set
On the fair daughter of rich Capulet;
As mine on hers, so hers is set on mine,
60 And all combined, save what thou must combine
By holy marriage. When, and where, and how
We met, we wooed, and made exchange of vow,
I'll tell thee as we pass; but this I pray,
That thou consent to marry us today.

65 **Friar Laurence.** Holy Saint Francis! What a change is here!
Is Rosaline, that thou didst love so dear,
So soon forsaken? Young men's love then lies
Not truly in their hearts, but in their eyes.

66–68 What is Friar Laurence saying in these lines?

Friar Laurence counsels Romeo in the University of Victoria's 1998 production.

Activity What assumptions can you make about Friar Laurence from details in this photograph? Explain your assumptions.
Possible answer: *The reader can assume that Friar Laurence is interested in plants, for he is holding a plant and has a drawing of a plant on his easel. From his robe and his cross necklace, the reader can assume that he belongs to a Christian religious order. His pose suggests that he is an instructor or counselor to Romeo.*

FOR LESS–PROFICIENT READERS

Explore Characters Have pairs or small groups of students read Friar Laurence's lines carefully. Then have them work together to fill out a Character Analysis Chart about him. Students can add notes and explore this character further as he reappears in later scenes.

 BEST PRACTICES TOOLKIT—Transparency
Character Analysis Chart p. D5

FOR ENGLISH LEARNERS

Task Support Draw attention to the marginal question for lines 66–68. Ask a volunteer to read the lines aloud for the class. ***Possible answer:*** *Friar Laurence is saying that he is surprised that Romeo has so quickly forgotten about his former love. From this event he concludes that love is a function of a young man's attraction, not of his heart.*

❷ CHARACTER

Possible answer: Friar Laurence agrees to help Romeo because he is motivated to help end the feud between the Capulet and Montague families.

If students need help . . . Discuss these questions:

- What does Friar Laurence mean when he says that Rosaline "knew well / Thy love did read by rote, that could not spell" (lines 87–88)? *Possible answer: He means that Rosaline understood that Romeo's love was immature or not the real thing.*

- What do you think is the friar's tone of voice when he calls Romeo "young waverer" (line 89)? *Possible answer: His tone probably is kindly, especially as the words are part of an invitation.*

- According to Friar Laurence, why might Romeo's marriage to Juliet be a happy thing? *Possible answer: The marriage might turn the "rancor" (bitterness) between the families into love.*

Jesu Maria! What a deal of brine
70 Hath washed thy sallow cheeks for Rosaline!
How much salt water thrown away in waste,
To season love, that of it doth not taste!
The sun not yet thy sighs from heaven clears,
Thy old groans ring yet in mine ancient ears.
75 Lo, here upon thy cheek the stain doth sit
Of an old tear that is not washed off yet.
If e'er thou wast thyself, and these woes thine,
Thou and these woes were all for Rosaline.
And art thou changed? Pronounce this sentence then:
80 Women may fall when there's no strength in men.
    Romeo. Thou chidst me oft for loving Rosaline.
    Friar Laurence. For doting, not for loving, pupil mine.
    Romeo. And badest me bury love.
    Friar Laurence.   Not in a grave
To lay one in, another ought to have.
85 **Romeo.** I pray thee chide not. She whom I love now
Doth grace for grace and love for love allow.
The other did not so.
    Friar Laurence.   O, she knew well
Thy love did read by rote, that could not spell.
But come, young waverer, come go with me.
90 In one respect I'll thy assistant be;
For this alliance may so happy prove
To turn your households' rancor to pure love. **❷**
    Romeo. O, let us hence! I stand on sudden haste.
    Friar Laurence. Wisely, and slow. They stumble that run fast.
    [*Exeunt.*]

69 brine: salt water—that is, the tears that Romeo has been shedding for Rosaline.

80 Women . . . men: If men are so weak, women may be forgiven for sinning.

81–82 chidst: scolded. The friar replies that he scolded Romeo for being lovesick, not for loving.

85–88 She whom . . . spell: Romeo says that the woman he loves feels the same way about him. That wasn't true of Rosaline. The friar replies that Rosaline knew that he didn't know what real love is.

91–92 For this . . . prove: this marriage may work out so well; **rancor:** bitter hate.

❷ CHARACTER
Why does Friar Laurence agree to help Romeo marry Juliet, despite his worry that Romeo falls in love too easily? Explain the friar's **motives.**

SCENE 4 *A street.*

Several hours after his meeting with Friar Laurence, Romeo meets Benvolio and Mercutio in the street. He is excited and happy; his mood is key to the comic nature of this scene, which includes much talk of swordplay and many suggestive jokes. Mercutio makes fun of Tybalt and teases Romeo. The nurse comes to carry a message from Romeo to Juliet. Romeo tells her that Juliet should meet him at Friar Laurence's cell for their secret marriage ceremony.

[*Enter* Benvolio *and* Mercutio.]
    Mercutio. Where the devil should this Romeo be?
Came he not home tonight?

DIFFERENTIATED INSTRUCTION

FOR LESS–PROFICIENT READERS

Preview Ask a volunteer to read aloud the italicized scene synopsis. Help students organize the events of Scene 4 into a Sequence Chain.

 BEST PRACTICES TOOLKIT—Transparency
Sequence Chain p. B21

Romeo meets friends to talk and joke.

↓

Juliet's nurse arrives to speak to Romeo.

↓

Romeo tells the nurse of his plan to marry Juliet secretly at Friar Laurence's cell.

Benvolio. Not to his father's. I spoke with his man.

Mercutio. Why, that same pale hard-hearted wench, that Rosaline,
5 Torments him so that he will sure run mad.

Benvolio. Tybalt, the kinsman to old Capulet,
Hath sent a letter to his father's house.

Mercutio. A challenge, on my life.

Benvolio. Romeo will answer it.

10 **Mercutio.** Any man that can write may answer a letter.

Benvolio. Nay, he will answer the letter's master, how he dares,
being dared.

Mercutio. Alas, poor Romeo, he is already dead! stabbed with a
white wench's black eye; shot through the ear with a love song;
15 the very pin of his heart cleft with the blind bow-boy's butt-shaft;
and is he a man to encounter Tybalt?

Benvolio. Why, what is Tybalt?

Mercutio. More than Prince of Cats, I can tell you. O, he's the
courageous captain of compliments. He fights as you sing
20 pricksong—keeps time, distance, and proportion; rests me his
minim rest, one, two, and the third in your bosom! the very
butcher of a silk button, a duelist, a duelist! a gentleman of the
very first house, of the first and second cause. Ah, the immortal
passado! the *punto reverso!* the *hay!*

25 **Benvolio.** The what?

Mercutio. The pox of such antic, lisping, affecting fantasticoes—
these new tuners of accent! "By Jesu, a very good blade! a very
tall man! a very good whore!" Why, is not this a lamentable thing,
grandsire, that we should be thus afflicted with these strange flies,
30 these fashion-mongers, these perdona-mi's, who stand so much
on the new form that they cannot sit at ease on the old bench?
O, their bones, their bones!

[*Enter* Romeo, *no longer moody.*]

Benvolio. Here comes Romeo! here comes Romeo!

Mercutio. Without his roe, like a dried herring. O, flesh, flesh,
35 how art thou fishified! Now is he for the numbers that Petrarch
flowed in. Laura, to his lady, was but a kitchen wench (marry,
she had a better love to berhyme her), Dido a dowdy, Cleopatra
a gypsy, Helen and Hero hildings and harlots, Thisbe a grey eye

---

3 **man:** servant.

6–12 **Tybalt . . . dared:** Tybalt, still angry about Romeo's crashing the Capulet party, has sent a letter challenging Romeo to a duel. Benvolio says that Romeo will do more than answer the letter; he will accept Tybalt's challenge and fight him.

15 **blind bow-boy's butt-shaft:** Cupid's dull practice arrow. Mercutio suggests that Romeo fell in love with very little work on Cupid's part.

18–24 **More than . . . hay:** Mercutio mocks Tybalt's name. **Prince of Cats** refers to a cat in a fable, named Tybalt, who was known for his slyness. Then Mercutio makes fun of Tybalt's fancy new style of dueling, comparing it to precision singing (**pricksong**). *Passado, punto reverso,* and *hay* were terms used in the new dueling style.

26–32 **The pox . . . their bones:** Mercutio continues to make fun of people who embrace new styles and new manners of speaking.

34–39 **without his roe:** only part of himself (Mercutio makes fun of Romeo's name and his lovesickness); **numbers:** verses. Mercutio mentions Petrarch, who wrote sonnets to his love, Laura. According to Mercutio, Romeo's feelings for Rosaline are so intense that great loves in literature—Laura, Dido, and others—could never measure up.

Lines 18–32
DISCUSSION PROMPTS

Use these discussion prompts to help students understand Mercutio's perception of Tybalt:

Recall Why did Tybalt send a letter challenging Romeo to a duel? *Because Romeo showed up uninvited at the Capulets' party, an intrusion that was considered disrespectful.*

Analyze According to Mercutio, why is Tybalt particularly dangerous? *Possible answer: Tybalt is a master duelist and knows the calculated moves needed to destroy an opponent. "A gentleman of the very first house" (lines 22–23), Tybalt is also a "butcher of a silk button" (line 22), a skilled swordsman, and a dangerous man.*

Evaluate Does Mercutio's assessment of Tybalt seem like an objective assessment? *Possible answer: Mercutio is objective enough to be wary of Tybalt's skill as a duelist, but he also harbors a personal resentment of Tybalt and his fancy dueling style.*

FOR ENGLISH LEARNERS

Concept Support To help students understand that another fight is brewing, organize students into pairs. Ask one student in the pair to look for the lines at the beginning of Scene 4 that refer to the challenge (lines 6–12). Ask the other student to look for the lines that involve swordplay (lines 13–24). Have students work together to rephrase or otherwise work out the meaning of the lines.

FOR ADVANCED LEARNERS/PRE-AP

Analyze Allusions [small-group option] Have students reread Mercutio's speech in lines 34–39 and the marginal note about it. Then ask them to do more research about the allusions that Mercutio makes in these lines— to Laura, Dido, Cleopatra, Helen, Hero, and Thisbe. Invite students to give a brief oral report on their findings and to share a few comments about the point that Mercutio is making by using these allusions.

REINFORCE *KEY IDEA:* LOVE AND HATE

Discuss After Scenes 2 and 3, which focus on words of romance and plans for a marriage, Scene 4 opens with witty talk and comedy. In what sense, however, is there still a focus upon **love?** How does the dialogue reveal this focus? ***Possible answer:*** *There is still a focus on love, but for the moment it is the love between friends rather than romantic love. The dialogue between Romeo and Mercutio is full of jokes and funny threats (line 61). These characters could not jest with each other so personably if they were not friends who love each other.*

---

or so, but not to the purpose. Signior Romeo, *bon jour!* There's
40 a French salutation to your French slop. You gave us the
counterfeit fairly last night.

   Romeo. Good morrow to you both. What counterfeit did I give you?

   Mercutio. The slip, sir, the slip. Can you not conceive?

45 **Romeo.** Pardon, good Mercutio. My business was great, and in such a case as mine a man may strain courtesy.

   Mercutio. That's as much as to say, such a case as yours constrains a man to bow in the hams.

   Romeo. Meaning, to curtsy.

50 **Mercutio.** Thou hast most kindly hit it.

   Romeo. A most courteous exposition.

   Mercutio. Nay, I am the very pink of courtesy.

   Romeo. Pink for flower.

   Mercutio. Right.

55 **Romeo.** Why, then is my pump well-flowered.

   Mercutio. Well said! Follow me this jest now till thou hast worn out thy pump, that, when the single sole of it is worn, the jest may remain, after the wearing, solely singular.

   Romeo. Oh, single-soled jest, solely singular for the singleness!

60 **Mercutio.** Come between us, good Benvolio! My wits faint.

   Romeo. Switch and spurs, switch and spurs! or I'll cry a match.

   Mercutio. Nay, if our wits run the wild-goose chase, I am done; for thou hast more of the wild goose in one of thy wits than, I am sure, I have in my whole five. Was I with you there for the
65 goose?

   Romeo. Thou wast never with me for anything when thou wast not there for the goose.

   Mercutio. I will bite thee by the ear for that jest.

   Romeo. Nay, good goose, bite not!

70 **Mercutio.** Thy wit is a very bitter sweeting; it is a most sharp sauce.

   Romeo. And is it not, then, well served in to a sweet goose?

   Mercutio. O, here's a wit of cheveril, that stretches from an inch narrow to an ell broad!

39–44 *bon jour:* "Good day" in French; **There's . . . last night:** Here's a greeting to match your fancy French trousers (**slop**). You did a good job of getting away from us last night. (A piece of counterfeit money was called a **slip**.)

44–81 In these lines, Romeo and Mercutio have a battle of wits. They keep trying to top each other with funnier comments and cleverer puns.

55 *pump:* shoe; *well-flowered:* Shoes were "pinked," or punched out in flowerlike designs.

61 *Switch . . . match:* Keep going, or I'll claim victory.

64–65 *Was . . . goose:* Have I proved that you are a foolish person?

73 *cheveril:* kidskin, which is flexible. Mercutio means that a little wit stretches a long way.

DIFFERENTIATED INSTRUCTION

FOR ENGLISH LEARNERS

Vocabulary Support Point out the complicated word play in this scene. In lines 46–52, the friends enjoy some word play using the related words *courtesy* (lines 46 and 52), *curtsy* (line 49), and *courteous* (line 51). In lines 57–59, the friends repeat the words *single* and *sole* in five different variations. Help students find other examples of word play in this scene.

FOR ADVANCED LEARNERS/PRE–AP

Evaluate a Scene Remind students that according to the summary on page 939, Mercutio will soon die at the hand of Tybalt. Have pairs of students discuss Act Two, Scene 4, focusing on Mercutio, and then write a joint evaluation of its importance to the plot of the play. After students have read Act Three, ask the same pairs of students to reread and refine their evaluations.

75 **Romeo.** I stretch it out for that word "broad," which, added to the goose, proves thee far and wide a broad goose.

Mercutio. Why, is not this better now than groaning for love? Now art thou sociable, now art thou Romeo; now art thou what thou art, by art as well as by nature. For this driveling love is like
80 a great natural that runs lolling up and down to hide his bauble in a hole.

Benvolio. Stop there, stop there!

Mercutio. Thou desirest me to stop in my tale against the hair.

Benvolio. Thou wouldst else have made thy tale large.

85 **Mercutio.** O, thou art deceived! I would have made it short; for I was come to the whole depth of my tale, and meant indeed to occupy the argument no longer.

[*Enter* Nurse *and* Peter, *her servant. He is carrying a large fan.*]

Romeo. Here's goodly gear!

Mercutio. A sail, a sail!

90 **Benvolio.** Two, two! a shirt and a smock.

Nurse. Peter!

Peter. Anon.

Nurse. My fan, Peter.

Mercutio. Good Peter, to hide her face; for her fan's the fairer of
95 the two.

Nurse. God ye good morrow, gentlemen.

Mercutio. God ye good-den, fair gentlewoman.

Nurse. Is it good-den?

Mercutio. 'Tis no less, I tell ye, for the bawdy hand of the dial is
100 now upon the prick of noon.

Nurse. Out upon you! What a man are you!

Romeo. One, gentlewoman, that God hath made himself to mar.

Nurse. By my troth, it is well said. "For himself to mar," quoth'a? Gentlemen, can any of you tell me where I may find the young
105 Romeo?

Romeo. I can tell you; but young Romeo will be older when you have found him than he was when you sought him. I am the youngest of that name, for fault of a worse.

80–81 **great natural:** an idiot, like a jester or clown who carries a fool's stick (**bauble**).

88–89 **goodly gear:** something fine to joke about; **a sail:** Mercutio likens the nurse in all her petticoats to a huge ship coming toward them.

93 Fans were usually carried only by fine ladies. The nurse is trying to pretend that she is more than a servant.

Lines 77–81
REINFORCE *KEY IDEA:* LOVE AND HATE

Discuss In these lines, Mercutio expresses his relief that Romeo seems to be himself again. What is Mercutio's opinion about people who brood over **love?** Why do you think that he feels this way? *Possible answer: Mercutio's opinion is best shown in his reference to "driveling love" (line 79), which indicates that he found Romeo's moodiness over love ridiculous and irritating. (Students may also remember that Mercutio has already ridiculed Romeo's pining for Rosaline.) Mercutio may feel this way because he has never been in love and, therefore, has not experienced the passions that Romeo feels.*

FOR ADVANCED LEARNERS/PRE–AP

Mercutio and Friar Laurence Even though they possess very different personalities, Mercutio and Friar Laurence share a closeness to Romeo. After students have finished reading Scene 4, challenge them to reread Scene 3, as well as Mercutio's speech in lines 53–95 in Scene 4 of Act One. Then ask them to write two to three paragraphs comparing and contrasting the approaches that Friar Laurence and Mercutio take in responding to Romeo's moods and offer an assessment as to why each is important in Romeo's life.

DISCUSSION PROMPTS

Use these prompts to explore the way in which the young men treat Juliet's nurse:

Connect When have you seen someone treated with disrespect? How does that memory help you understand this scene? *Students may recall a time when they saw one person make fun of another. Students should recognize the verbal abuse that Mercutio, in particular, directs at the nurse.*

Analyze What can you tell about Mercutio and Benvolio, who ridicule the nurse? Who treats her worse? Why do you think they are so unkind? *Possible answer: Mercutio and Benvolio's behavior shows that they are playful and bawdy. It also reveals them to be class conscious, for they ridicule the low standing of the nurse. Mercutio says more and so is the worse of the two. They are probably being unkind as a way of showing off in front of each other.*

Synthesize Romeo is not nearly as unkind as are his friends. In fact, once his friends leave, he is respectful to the nurse and even offers her an apology of sorts (lines 129–130). How do you explain his behavior? *Possible answer: Romeo's behavior is better because he knows why the nurse has come, whereas his friends do not. He probably does not want the nurse to take a bad report back to Juliet; besides, when Mercutio isn't around to egg him on, Romeo seems to display a pleasant personality.*

Nurse. You say well.

110 **Mercutio.** Yea, is the worst well? Very well took, i' faith! wisely, wisely.

Nurse. If you be he, sir, I desire some confidence with you.

Benvolio. She will endite him to some supper.

Mercutio. A bawd, a bawd, a bawd! So ho!

115 **Romeo.** What hast thou found?

Mercutio. No hare, sir; unless a hare, sir, in a lenten pie, that is something stale and hoar ere it be spent.

[*sings*]

> "An old hare hoar,
> And an old hare hoar,
120   Is very good meat in Lent.
> But a hare that is hoar,
> Is too much for a score
> When it hoars ere it be spent."

Romeo, will you come to your father's? We'll to dinner thither.

125 **Romeo.** I will follow you.

Mercutio. Farewell, ancient lady. Farewell, [*sings*] lady, lady, lady.

[*Exeunt* Mercutio *and* Benvolio.]

Nurse. Marry, farewell! I pray you, sir, what saucy merchant was this that was so full of his ropery?

Romeo. A gentleman, nurse, that loves to hear himself talk and 130 will speak more in a minute than he will stand to in a month.

Nurse. An 'a speak anything against me, I'll take him down, an 'a were lustier than he is, and twenty such Jacks; and if I cannot, I'll find those that shall. Scurvy knave! I am none of his flirt-gills; I am none of his skainsmates. [*turning to* Peter] And thou must 135 stand by too, and suffer every knave to use me at his pleasure?

Peter. I saw no man use you at his pleasure. If I had, my weapon should quickly have been out, I warrant you. I dare draw as soon as another man, if I see occasion in a good quarrel, and the law on my side.

112–113 confidence: The nurse means *conference;* she uses big words without understanding their meaning; **endite:** Benvolio makes fun of the nurse by using this word rather than *invite.*

114–124 Mercutio calls the nurse a **bawd,** or woman who runs a house of prostitution. His song uses the insulting puns **hare,** a rabbit or prostitute, and **hoar,** old.

128 ropery: roguery, or jokes.

133–134 The nurse is angry that Mercutio treated her like one of his loose women (**flirt-gills**) or his gangsterlike friends (**skainsmates**).

DIFFERENTIATED INSTRUCTION

FOR LESS–PROFICIENT READERS

Paraphrasing Shakespeare Have students reread the marginal note for lines 133–134. Model a paraphrase of lines 131–133: *And if he insults me, I'll fight and defeat him, for I am stronger [lustier] than he and twenty of his friends, put together, are; and if I can't defeat him, I'll find someone who will.* Then call on volunteers to paraphrase the nurse's words to Peter (lines 134–135) and Peter's reply (lines 136–139).

Possible answer:

Nurse. And is it right for you to stand around and do nothing, letting every rascal treat me as he wishes?

Peter. I didn't see anyone treat you as he wished. If I had seen that, I guarantee that I would have drawn my weapon [to defend you]. I am as willing to fight as anyone, if the right argument presents itself, and I am acting within the law.

The Orlando-UCF Shakespeare Festival's 1992 production

The Royal Shakespeare Company's 1992 production

The University of South Carolina's 1999 production

Set Design

Often, set designers recreate the world of *Romeo and Juliet* in strikingly unique ways. Designers of the productions pictured here created radically different **sets** for the balcony scene. List three adjectives you would use to describe each set. What factors might make a designer choose to create one of these particular set styles?

985

BEHIND THE CURTAIN

Set Design Explain that sets are the platforms, walls, and building structures that help create the world within a play. Point out that it is not unusual for set designers to avoid a completely realistic "look." To illustrate this point, draw students' attention to the photographs of the Royal Shakespeare Company's 1992 production and the University of South Carolina's 1999 production. In both cases, the sets require the audience to use its imagination to fill in details. The Orlando-UCF Shakespeare Festival's 1992 production, however, has a much more realistic set, including a real balcony. ***Possible answer:*** *The Orlando-UCF Shakespeare Festival's set is realistic, romantic, and rich; the Royal Shakespeare Company's set is modern, abstract, and geometric; the University of South Carolina's set is stark, bare, otherworldly. In determining a set style, a set designer might consider the actual setting of the work, any interpretation that the director wants to give it, and the production's budget.*

FOR ADVANCED LEARNERS/PRE–AP

Create a Set Design Have groups of students choose a scene they have read and design a creative but appropriate set. Have students use graph paper for an overhead view, as well as drawings that show how the set will look from the front. Encourage students to add details such as colors, fabrics, and foliage that would be part of the set. Display the set designs and compare designs created for the same scene.

REINFORCE *KEY IDEA:*
LOVE AND HATE

Discuss How is Nurse's **love** for Juliet shown in her response to Romeo? ***Possible answer:*** *She is protective and honest about her feelings. The nurse reminds Romeo that Juliet is young, and should he "deal double" (line 146) with her, it would show him up as "weak" and of poor character. Nurse is of a lower social class than Romeo, so she cannot legitimately threaten him. Still, she is brutally honest in telling him that leading Juliet into a "fool's paradise" (line 144)—that is, a false promise—would be a "very gross kind of behavior" (lines 144–145).*

140 **Nurse.** Now, afore God, I am so vexed that every part about me quivers. Scurvy knave! Pray you, sir, a word; and as I told you, my young lady bade me enquire you out. What she bid me say, I will keep to myself; but first let me tell ye, if ye should lead her into a fool's paradise, as they say, it were a very gross kind of
145 behavior, as they say; for the gentlewoman is young; and therefore, if you should deal double with her, truly it were an ill thing to be offered to any gentlewoman, and very weak dealing.

Romeo. Nurse, commend me to thy lady and mistress. I protest unto thee—

150 **Nurse.** Good heart, and i' faith I will tell her as much. Lord, Lord! she will be a joyful woman.

Romeo. What wilt thou tell her, nurse? Thou dost not mark me.

Nurse. I will tell her, sir, that you do protest, which, as I take it, is a gentlemanlike offer.

155 **Romeo.** Bid her devise
Some means to come to shrift this afternoon;
And there she shall at Friar Laurence' cell
Be shrived and married. Here is for thy pains.

Nurse. No, truly, sir; not a penny.

160 **Romeo.** Go to! I say you shall.

Nurse. This afternoon, sir? Well, she shall be there.

Romeo. And stay, good nurse, behind the abbey wall.
Within this hour my man shall be with thee
And bring thee cords made like a tackled stair,
165 Which to the high topgallant of my joy
Must be my convoy in the secret night.
Farewell. Be trusty, and I'll quit thy pains.
Farewell. Commend me to thy mistress.

Nurse. Now God in heaven bless thee! Hark you, sir.

170 **Romeo.** What sayst thou, my dear nurse?

Nurse. Is your man secret? Did you ne'er hear say,
Two may keep counsel, putting one away?

Romeo. I warrant thee my man's as true as steel.

Nurse. Well, sir, my mistress is the sweetest lady. Lord, Lord!
175 when 'twas a little prating thing—O, there is a nobleman in town, one Paris, that would fain lay knife aboard; but she, good soul, had as lief see a toad, a very toad, as see him. I anger her

142–147 The nurse warns Romeo that he'd better mean what he said about marrying Juliet. She holds back her news while she tries to decide if Romeo's love is genuine.

148 commend me: give my respectful greetings.

155–159 Romeo tells the nurse to have Juliet come to Friar Laurence's cell this afternoon, using the excuse that she is going to confess her sins (**shrift**). There she will receive forgiveness for her sins (**be shrived**) and be married.

3 Targeted Passage

164–165 tackled stair: rope ladder; **topgallant:** highest point.

167–172 quit thy pains: reward you. The nurse then asks Romeo if his servant can be trusted, then quotes the saying that two can keep a secret but not three.

174–177 The nurse begins to babble about Paris' proposal but says that Juliet would rather look at a toad than at Paris.

DIFFERENTIATED INSTRUCTION

FOR LESS–PROFICIENT READERS

3 Targeted Passage [Lines 155–168]

This passage lays out the specifics of Romeo's plan for marrying Juliet.

- To whom is Romeo speaking? Why does he tell his plan to this person?

- When and where does Romeo want Juliet to meet him?

- What will he send to the nurse first? Why do you think it will be needed?

Infer Action Explain that Shakespeare uses relatively few stage directions and that readers sometimes must infer action from his dialogue. In lines 158–160, for example, the dialogue implies that Romeo is putting a coin into the nurse's hand to thank her for her help, that she may shake her head and try to give it back, and that Romeo may then use a gesture to underscore his insistence upon her keeping the gift.

sometimes, and tell her that Paris is the proper man; but I'll
warrant you, when I say so, she looks as pale as any clout in the
180 versal world. Doth not rosemary and Romeo begin both with a
letter?

Romeo. Ay, nurse, what of that? Both with an R.

Nurse. Ah, mocker! that's the dog's name. R is for the—No; I
know it begins with some other letter; and she hath the prettiest
185 sententious of it, of you and rosemary, that it would do you good
to hear it.

Romeo. Commend me to thy lady.

Nurse. Ay, a thousand times. [*Exit* Romeo.] Peter!

Peter. Anon.

190 **Nurse.** Peter, take my fan, and go before, and apace.

[*Exeunt.*]

179–186 **clout:** old cloth; **the versal world:**
the entire world; **Doth not . . . hear it:**
The nurse tries to recall a clever saying
that Juliet made up about Romeo and
rosemary, the herb for remembrance, but
cannot remember it. She is sure that the
two words couldn't begin with *R* because
this letter sounds like a snarling dog;
sententious: The nurse means *sentences*.

190 **apace:** quickly.

SCENE 5   *Capulet's orchard.*

*Juliet is a nervous wreck, having waited for more than three hours for the nurse to
return. When the nurse does arrive, she simply won't come to the point. Juliet gets
more and more upset, until the nurse finally reveals the wedding arrangements.*

[*Enter* Juliet.]

Juliet. The clock struck nine when I did send the nurse;
In half an hour she promised to return.
Perchance she cannot meet him. That's not so.
O, she is lame! Love's heralds should be thoughts,
5 Which ten times faster glide than the sun's beams
Driving back shadows over lowering hills.
Therefore do nimble-pinioned doves draw Love,
And therefore hath the wind-swift Cupid wings. **F**
Now is the sun upon the highmost hill
10 Of this day's journey, and from nine till twelve
Is three long hours; yet she is not come.
Had she affections and warm youthful blood,
She would be as swift in motion as a ball;
My words would bandy her to my sweet love,
15 And his to me.
But old folks, many feign as they were dead—
Unwieldy, slow, heavy, and pale as lead.
[*Enter* Nurse *and* Peter.] O God, she comes! O honey nurse,
what news?

4–6 **Love's . . . hills:** Love's messengers
should be thoughts, which travel ten
times faster than sunbeams.

7 **nimble-pinioned . . . Love:** Swift-winged
doves pull the chariot of Venus, goddess
of love.

F **ALLUSION**
What do Juliet's allusions to Venus
and to Cupid emphasize about her
state of mind as she waits for the
nurse to return?

14 **bandy:** toss.

16 **feign as:** act as if.

LITERARY ANALYSIS

F **ALLUSION**

Possible answer: *Juliet's allusions to the
goddess of love (Love, or Venus) and to the
god of love (Cupid, Venus's son) emphasize
her obsession with Romeo, her idealized
view of love, and her nervousness as she
waits for news about the wedding
arrangements.*

If students need help . . . Make sure that
students understand who Venus (Love)
and Cupid are, according to classical
mythology. Discuss what might cause a
person to talk about the "gods of love."

FOR LESS–PROFICIENT READERS

Preview As you read through the Scene 5
synopsis, use an Open Mind diagram to help
students identify Juliet's emotions.

 BEST PRACTICES TOOLKIT—Transparency
Open Mind p. D9

nervous waiting for nurse

excited/anxious about
wedding arrangements

happy to see nurse

frustrated with nurse's
stalling

impatient to hear news

DISCUSSION PROMPTS

Use these prompts to provide insight into the relationship between Juliet and her nurse:

Connect How do people often feel about asking someone to do them a big favor? How do you think Juliet feels toward her nurse? *Students should understand that asking a big favor leads to feelings of gratitude. Juliet feels grateful to her nurse for meeting with Romeo, but she also becomes frustrated with the nurse for withholding Romeo's news.*

Analyze What reason might the nurse have for teasing Juliet by not telling her the news right away? *Possible answer: The nurse might be teasing Juliet because she enjoys the power that withholding the news gives her. By not revealing the information, she forces Juliet to beg her for it.*

Evaluate Who do you think is the wiser counselor—Friar Laurence or the nurse? Explain. *Possible answer: Both characters are confidants of the lovers, and both are in favor of the marriage. Friar Laurence may be the wiser counselor, however: he is educated, he is not an employee of one of the families involved, and he is able to see beyond the wedding itself to a greater good that might come from the marriage.*

Hast thou met with him? Send thy man away.

20 **Nurse.** Peter, stay at the gate.

[*Exit* Peter.]

Juliet. Now, good sweet nurse—O Lord, why lookst thou sad?
Though news be sad, yet tell them merrily;
If good, thou shamest the music of sweet news
By playing it to me with so sour a face.

25 **Nurse.** I am aweary, give me leave awhile.
Fie, how my bones ache! What a jaunce have I had!

Juliet. I would thou hadst my bones, and I thy news.
Nay, come, I pray thee speak. Good, good nurse, speak.

Nurse. Jesu, what haste! Can you not stay awhile?
30 Do you not see that I am out of breath?

Juliet. How art thou out of breath when thou hast breath
To say to me that thou art out of breath?
The excuse that thou dost make in this delay
Is longer than the tale thou dost excuse.
35 Is thy news good or bad? Answer to that.
Say either, and I'll stay the circumstance.
Let me be satisfied, is't good or bad?

Nurse. Well, you have made a simple choice; you know not how
to choose a man. Romeo? No, not he. Though his face be better
40 than any man's, yet his leg excels all men's; and for a hand and a
foot, and a body, though they be not to be talked on, yet they are
past compare. He is not the flower of courtesy, but, I'll warrant
him, as gentle as a lamb. Go thy ways, wench; serve God. What,
have you dined at home?

45 **Juliet.** No, no. But all this did I know before.
What say he of our marriage? What of that?

Nurse. Lord, how my head aches! What a head have I!
It beats as it would fall in twenty pieces.
My back o' t'other side—ah, my back, my back!
50 Beshrew your heart for sending me about
To catch my death with jauncing up and down!

Juliet. I' faith, I am sorry that thou art not well.
Sweet, sweet, sweet nurse, tell me, what says my love?

21–22 The nurse teases Juliet by putting on a sad face as if the news were bad.

25–26 give me . . . I had: Leave me alone for a while. I ache all over because of the running back and forth I've been doing.

36 I'll . . . circumstance: I'll wait for the details.

38 simple: foolish.

50–51 Beshrew . . . down: Curse you for making me endanger my health by running around. *Considering the nurse's feelings for Juliet, do you think this is really an angry curse? Explain.*

DIFFERENTIATED INSTRUCTION

FOR ENGLISH LEARNERS

Task Support Have students read the marginal note and question for lines 50–51. Urge students to think of the tone of the characters' conversation thus far. *Possible answer: No, this curse is not sincerely angry. The nurse is thrilled to bring Juliet the message, but at the moment, she is having a bit of fun by making Juliet wait.*

Vocabulary Support Shakespeare often uses elliptical language. Work with students to add the "missing" words to these lines. *See boldfacing in each possible answer.*

- *Line 23,* **Possible answer:** *If* **the news be good,** . . .

- *Line 27,* **Possible answer:** . . . *and I* **had** *thy news.*

- *Lines 54–55,* **Possible answer:** *Your love says, like an honest gentleman, and a courteous*

gentleman, and a kind **gentleman,** *and a handsome* **gentleman,** *and, I warrant, a virtuous* **gentleman—**

- *Line 71,* **Possible answer:** . . . *I must* **hie [go]** *another way.*

Nurse. Your love says, like an honest gentleman, and a courteous,
55 and a kind, and a handsome, and, I warrant, a virtuous—Where
is your mother?

Juliet. Where is my mother? Why, she is within.
Where should she be? How oddly thou repliest!
"Your love says, like an honest gentleman,
60 'Where is your mother?'"

Nurse.   O God's Lady dear!
Are you so hot? Marry come up, I trow.
Is this the poultice for my aching bones?
Hence forward do your messages yourself.

Juliet. Here's such a coil! Come, what says Romeo?

65 **Nurse.** Have you got leave to go to shrift today?

Juliet. I have.

Nurse. Then hie you hence to Friar Laurence' cell;
There stays a husband to make you a wife.
Now comes the wanton blood up in your cheeks:
70 They'll be in scarlet straight at any news.
Hie you to church; I must another way,
To fetch a ladder, by the which your love
Must climb a bird's nest soon when it is dark.
I am the drudge, and toil in your delight;
75 But you shall bear the burden soon at night.
Go; I'll to dinner; hie you to the cell.

Juliet. Hie to high fortune! Honest nurse, farewell.

[*Exeunt.*]

61–62 **Marry ... bones:** Control yourself! Is this the treatment I get for my pain?

64 **coil:** fuss.

67–68 **Then hie ... a wife:** Then go quickly to Friar Laurence's cell, where Romeo is waiting to marry you.

71–73 The nurse will get the ladder that Romeo will use to climb to Juliet's room after they are married.

SCENE 6   *Friar Laurence's cell.*

Friar Laurence cautions Romeo to be more sensible in his love for Juliet. When she arrives, the two confess their love to each other and prepare to be married by Friar Laurence.

[*Enter* Friar Laurence *and* Romeo.]

Friar Laurence. So smile the heavens upon this holy act
That after-hours with sorrow chide us not!

Romeo. Amen, amen! But come what sorrow can,
It cannot countervail the exchange of joy
5 That one short minute gives me in her sight.
Do thou but close our hands with holy words,
Then love-devouring death do what he dare—
It is enough I may but call her mine.

1–2 **So smile ... us not:** May heaven so bless this act that we won't regret it in the future (**after-hours**).

4 **countervail:** outweigh.

ROMEO AND JULIET: ACT TWO, SCENE 6   **989**

G TRAGEDY

Possible answer: Romeo will not take the friar's advice. Shakespearean tragedies end in death for the main characters, so if moderation is the key to a long love (line 14), Romeo will not be moderate.

ACT TWO WRAP-UP

REFLECT Have students consider the relationship between Romeo and Juliet. Ask them to reflect upon whether their marriage has a solid foundation.

⭐ **CRITIQUE** Ask students what aspects of the play they have found to be the most realistic and why. Then ask them what aspects of the play they have found the most difficult to believe or imagine. Have them provide examples to explain their responses.

Friar Laurence. These violent delights have violent ends
10 And in their triumph die, like fire and powder,
Which, as they kiss, consume. The sweetest honey
Is loathsome in his own deliciousness
And in the taste confounds the appetite.
Therefore love moderately: long love doth so;
15 Too swift arrives as tardy as too slow. **G**

[*Enter* Juliet.]

Here comes the lady. O, so light a foot
Will ne'er wear out the everlasting flint.
A lover may bestride the gossamer
That idles in the wanton summer air,
20 And yet not fall; so light is vanity.

Juliet. Good even to my ghostly confessor.

Friar Laurence. Romeo shall thank thee, daughter, for us both.

Juliet. As much to him, else is his thanks too much.

Romeo. Ah, Juliet, if the measure of thy joy
25 Be heaped like mine, and that thy skill be more
To blazon it, then sweeten with thy breath
This neighbor air, and let rich music's tongue
Unfold the imagined happiness that both
Receive in either by this dear encounter.

30 **Juliet.** Conceit, more rich in matter than in words,
Brags of his substance, not of ornament.
They are but beggars that can count their worth;
But my true love is grown to such excess
I cannot sum up sum of half my wealth.

35 **Friar Laurence.** Come, come with me, and we will make short work;
For, by your leaves, you shall not stay alone
Till Holy Church incorporate two in one.

[*Exeunt.*]

9–15 These...slow: The friar compares Romeo's passion to gunpowder and the fire that ignites it—both are destroyed—then to honey, whose sweetness can destroy the appetite. He reminds Romeo to practice moderation in love.

G TRAGEDY
Consider what you know about Shakespearean tragedy. Do you think Romeo will take the advice Friar Laurence gives him in lines 9–15? Explain.

18–20 A lover...vanity: A lover can walk across a spider's web (**gossamer**) without falling.

23 as much to him: I give the same greeting to Romeo that he offers to me.

24–29 if the measure...encounter: If you are as happy as I am and have more skill to proclaim it, then sweeten the air by singing of our happiness to the world.

30–31 Conceit...ornament: True understanding (**conceit**) needs no words.

④ Targeted Passage

37 till Holy Church...one: till you are joined in marriage in a religious ceremony.

DIFFERENTIATED INSTRUCTION

FOR LESS-PROFICIENT READERS
④ Targeted Passage [Lines 24–37]

This passage presents the moment before the wedding (which takes place offstage).

• How does Romeo want Juliet to express her joy?

• What does Juliet say she cannot "sum up"? Why?

• According to Friar Laurence, what power will join Romeo and Juliet? Why is this an important statement?

Comprehension

1. **Recall** Who challenges Romeo to a duel, and why?

2. **Recall** What important message from Romeo does the nurse bring to Juliet?

3. **Clarify** Why does Friar Laurence agree to marry Romeo and Juliet despite his reservations? Explain what he hopes this marriage will accomplish.

Literary Analysis

4. **Reading Shakespearean Drama** Examine the events you recorded in your chart as you read Act Two. Which events seem most crucial in escalating the **conflicts** in the plot? Explain your answer.

5. **Make Inferences About Character Motives** Why do Romeo and Juliet rush to get married after declaring their love? Support your inference with evidence from the text. Then explain whether you think the young lovers get married too soon, and why or why not.

6. **Analyze Soliloquy and Aside** Identify at least one soliloquy and one aside in Act Two and record them in a chart like the one shown. Complete the chart by explaining what each example reveals about the character speaking.

Scene and Lines	Character Who Speaks	Soliloquy or Aside?	What Is Revealed?
Scene 2, lines 1–25	Romeo		

7. **Analyze Character Development** Compare Romeo's behavior before he meets Juliet with his behavior after they declare their love for each other. What do you learn about Romeo from the change in his behavior?

Literary Criticism

8. **Author's Style** Shakespeare is often praised for his masterly use of **figurative language**, or language that communicates ideas beyond the ordinary, literal meaning of the words. Find two examples of particularly striking figurative language in Act Two and discuss what makes each example effective.

ROMEO AND JULIET: ACT TWO **991**

6. ● **STANDARDS FOCUS** *Analyze Soliloquy and Aside* *Scene 2, lines 1–25 is a soliloquy in which Romeo reveals his love for Juliet. Scene 2, line 37 is an aside in which Romeo wonders whether he should speak to Juliet or hear more of her private thoughts.*

7. *Before Romeo meets Juliet, he is moody, pessimistic, and passive. After declaring his love, he is joyful and positive, and he takes action. This change in behavior suggests that Romeo is easily moved by his emotions and is quick to change his mind.*

Literary Criticism
Possible answer:

8. *In Scene 2, line 121, Juliet compares her love for Romeo to a flower bud. It is an effective comparison because their love is new and full of hope, just as a bud is new growth that holds out hope of a beautiful flower. In Scene 5, line 43, the nurse says that Romeo is gentle as a lamb. It is an effective comparison because it means more than it intends: like a sacrificial lamb, Romeo ultimately will lose his life.*

Practice and Apply

After Reading
For additional support of post-reading questions, use these copy masters:

R RESOURCE MANAGER—Copy Masters
Reading Check p. 47 (to check understanding of the selection)
Shakespearean Drama p. 43 (for practice of literary analysis standards focus)
Question Support p. 48 (After Reading questions adapted for English learners and less-proficient readers)

For additional questions, see page 39.

ANSWERS

Comprehension

1. *Tybalt challenges Romeo to a duel because he is angry that Romeo came to Capulet's party.*

2. *Juliet will meet Romeo at Friar Laurence's cell, where they will marry.*

3. *Friar Laurence hopes that the marriage will mend the feud between the families.*

Literary Analysis
Possible answers:

4. ■ **STANDARDS FOCUS** *Reading Shakespearean Drama* *Romeo and Juliet secretly marry, making the situation more tense. Tybalt challenges Romeo; their conflict escalates into a possible fight.*

5. *Students might say that the lovers rush to marry because they are swept away by love, that their families' feud prevents them from courting in the usual manner, or that they fear being discovered by their parents. Students may offer varying responses to the second part of the question.*

Assess and Reteach

Assess

R RESOURCE MANAGER—Copy Masters
Selection Test A pp. 49–50
Selection Test B/C pp. 51–52

Test Generator CD

Reteach

S STANDARDS LESSON FILE
Literature Lessons 25, 26, 35, 38

Practice and Apply

Get Into the Act

SUMMARY

As Act Three begins, Capulets and Montagues clash again. Tybalt kills Mercutio; enraged, Romeo kills Tybalt. Prince Escalus banishes Romeo, but Friar Laurence promises that he will try to make things right and bring Romeo home again. Meanwhile, the Capulets grieve for Tybalt, and Capulet promises Count Paris that Juliet will marry him in three days. When Juliet refuses, he threatens to disown her.

ANALYZE VISUALS

Activity What elements of this production's stagecraft reveal that the audience is intended to realize that this duel is meant to be a grim moment in the play? *Possible answer: The literal darkness of both the set and the costumes suggests that this is a dark moment, figuratively speaking, in the plot of Shakespeare's narrative.*

READING STRATEGY

■ PREDICT

Review the fact that Act Two ended with a scene of love and happiness. Ask students to make a prediction about the type of scene to which Shakespeare will take us next. *Possible answer: Shakespeare will introduce a contrasting scene—something that reminds us of the family feud and the challenges that the newlyweds face.*

Resources for Act Three

Act Three

SCENE 1 *A public place.*

Act Two ends with the joyful Romeo and Juliet secretly married. Their happiness, however, is about to end abruptly. In this scene, Mercutio, Benvolio, and Romeo meet Tybalt on the street. Tybalt insults Romeo, but Romeo, who has just returned from his wedding, remains calm. Mercutio, on the other hand, is furious with Tybalt, and they begin to fight. As Romeo tries to separate them, Tybalt stabs Mercutio, who later dies. Romeo then challenges Tybalt, kills him, and flees. The prince arrives and demands an explanation. He announces that Romeo will be killed if he does not leave Verona immediately.

[*Enter* Mercutio, Benvolio, Page, *and* Servants.]

Benvolio. I pray thee, good Mercutio, let's retire.
The day is hot, the Capulets abroad,
And if we meet, we shall not scape a brawl,
For now, these hot days, is the mad blood stirring.

5 **Mercutio.** Thou art like one of those fellows that, when he enters the confines of a tavern, claps me his sword upon the table and says "God send me no need of thee!" and by the operation of the second cup draws him on the drawer, when indeed there is no need.

10 **Benvolio.** Am I like such a fellow?

Mercutio. Come, come, thou art as hot a Jack in thy mood as any in Italy; and as soon moved to be moody, and as soon moody to be moved.

Benvolio. And what to?

15 **Mercutio.** Nay an there were two such, we should have none shortly, for one would kill the other. Thou! why, thou wilt quarrel with a man that hath a hair more or a hair less in his beard than thou hast. Thou wilt quarrel with a man for cracking nuts, having no other reason but because thou hast hazel eyes.
20 What eye but such an eye would spy out such a quarrel? Thy head is as full of quarrels as an egg is full of meat; and yet thy head hath been beaten as addle as an egg for quarreling. Thou hast quarreled with a man for coughing in the street, because he hath wakened thy dog that hath lain asleep in the sun. Didst
25 thou not fall out with a tailor for wearing his new doublet before Easter? with another for tying his new shoes with old riband? And yet thou wilt tutor me from quarreling!

3–4 we shall . . . stirring: We shall not avoid a fight, since the heat makes people ill-tempered.

7–8 by the . . . drawer: feeling the effects of a second drink, is ready to fight (**draw on**) the waiter who's pouring the drinks (**drawer**).

12–13 as soon moved . . . to be moved: as likely to get angry and start a fight.

15–27 Mercutio teases his friend by insisting that Benvolio is quick to pick a fight, though everyone knows that Benvolio is gentle and peace loving.

25 doublet: jacket.
26 riband: ribbon or laces.

Mercutio and Tybalt duel in the 2004 coproduction of the Chicago Shakespeare Theater and Second City.

Ⓡ RESOURCE MANAGER UNIT 10

Plan and Teach pp. 53–56
Literary Analysis
Summary pp. 57†*, 58‡*
Shakespearean Drama pp. 59, 60†*
Question Support p. 64*
Reading
Reading Shakespearean Drama
   pp. 61, 62†*
Reading Check p. 63

Assessment
Selection Tests A, B/C pp. 65*, 67*
⊙ Test Generator CD

🧰 BEST PRACTICES TOOLKIT

Differentiated Instruction
   pp. 31–38*

Graphic Organizers/Strategies
Sequence Chain • Plot Diagram •
Problem and Solution Charts •
Classification Chart • Cluster
Diagram

Reading Support
⊘ Audio Anthology CD*

Technology
ⓘ Literature Center at
   ClassZone.com
⊘ Write*Smart* CD

---

* Resources for Differentiation   † Also in Spanish   ‡ In Haitian Creole and Vietnamese

Lines 1–4
REINFORCE *KEY IDEA:* LOVE AND HATE

Discuss Based on these opening lines, what will be the focus of Scene 1: **love** or **hate?** Explain your answer. *Possible answer: Hate will probably be the focus of Scene 1. Benvolio speaks of a possible brawl with the Capulets (lines 2–3) and comments upon the "mad blood stirring" on this day (line 4).*

BACKGROUND

Shakespeare and Duels The weapon used most often for duels in Shakespeare's time was the rapier, as shown in the photograph. A rapier was terribly dangerous. Its pointed tip frequently meant a fatal outcome in duels. Nevertheless, Elizabethans respected duels as a way to defend one's honor, to prove one's innocence, to counter an injury or insult, or to defend some other personal claim. Elizabethans believed that justice could be determined by the outcome of a duel and that rejecting a challenge to a duel was shameful. In Scene 1, Tybalt's challenge addresses the wrong that he felt took place when the Montagues came, uninvited, to the Capulet party. By rejecting the challenge, Romeo shames his family and friends—a fact that helps to explain why Mercutio rises to Tybalt's challenge.

DIFFERENTIATED INSTRUCTION

For general guidelines on differentiating instruction, see

🧰 **BEST PRACTICES TOOLKIT**
Differentiated Instruction pp. 31–38

FOR LESS–PROFICIENT READERS
In combination with the *Audio Anthology CD*, use one or more Targeted Passages (pp. 995, 1002, 1006, 1015) to ensure that students focus on key story events, concepts, and skills.

Preview Draw students' attention to the italicized scene synopsis. Have them use a Sequence Chain to familiarize themselves with the events of Scene 1.

Mercutio, Benvolio, and Romeo meet Tybalt.
↓
| Tybalt insults Romeo. |
↓
| Mercutio gets angry and fights Tybalt. |
↓

Tybalt kills Mercutio.
↓
| Romeo challenges Tybalt and kills him. |
↓
| Prince Escalus punishes Romeo with banishment from Verona. |

🧰 **BEST PRACTICES TOOLKIT—Transparency**
Sequence Chain pp. B21

Ⓐ TRAGEDY

Possible answers: Tybalt is largely responsible: He makes the initial challenge, and he calls Romeo a villain (line 56). Mercutio is largely responsible: He goads Tybalt (lines 35–50); and after Romeo tries to avoid a fight, Mercutio draws his sword first (line 70).

Ⓑ CHARACTER

Possible answer: Romeo's motive for not wanting to fight Tybalt is that he has married Juliet, Tybalt's cousin. He does not want conflict with the Capulets, to whom he is now related. Juliet, the nurse, and Friar Laurence are the only other characters who know this reason.

If students need help . . . Review the cast of characters (page 940). Elicit that both Juliet and Tybalt are Capulets and that they are cousins. Remind students, too, that Romeo married Juliet at the end of Act Two.

Benvolio. An I were so apt to quarrel as thou art, any man should buy the fee simple of my life for an hour and a quarter.

30 **Mercutio.** The fee simple? O simple!

[*Enter* Tybalt *and others.*]

Benvolio. By my head, here come the Capulets. Ⓐ

Mercutio. By my heel, I care not.

Tybalt. Follow me close, for I will speak to them. Gentlemen, good den. A word with one of you.

35 **Mercutio.** And but one word with one of us? Couple it with something; make it a word and a blow.

Tybalt. You shall find me apt enough to that, sir, an you will give me occasion.

Mercutio. Could you not take some occasion without giving?

40 **Tybalt.** Mercutio, thou consortest with Romeo.

Mercutio. Consort? What, dost thou make us minstrels? An thou make minstrels of us, look to hear nothing but discords. Here's my fiddlestick; here's that shall make you dance. Zounds, consort!

45 **Benvolio.** We talk here in the public haunt of men.
Either withdraw unto some private place
And reason coldly of your grievances,
Or else depart. Here all eyes gaze on us.

Mercutio. Men's eyes were made to look, and let them gaze.
50 I will not budge for no man's pleasure, I.

[*Enter* Romeo.]

Tybalt. Well, peace be with you, sir. Here comes my man.

Mercutio. But I'll be hanged, sir, if he wear your livery.
Marry, go before to field, he'll be your follower!
Your worship in that sense may call him man.

55 **Tybalt.** Romeo, the love I bear thee can afford
No better term than this: thou art a villain.

Romeo. Tybalt, the reason that I have to love thee
Doth much excuse the appertaining rage
To such a greeting. Villain am I none.
60 Therefore farewell. I see thou knowst me not. Ⓑ

Tybalt. Boy, this shall not excuse the injuries
That thou hast done me; therefore turn and draw.

Romeo. I do protest I never injured thee,
But love thee better than thou canst devise

28–29 An I . . . quarter: If I picked fights as quickly as you do, anybody could own me for the smallest amount of money.

Ⓐ TRAGEDY
As you read lines 31–79, think about the play's mounting **conflict.** Ask yourself: Who is responsible for starting this sword fight? Cite evidence to support your viewpoint.

40–44 consortest: keep company with. Tybalt means "You are friends with Romeo." Mercutio pretends to misunderstand him, assuming that Tybalt is insulting him by calling Romeo and him a **consort,** a group of traveling musicians. He then refers to his sword as his **fiddlestick,** the bow for a fiddle.

45–48 *What does Benvolio want Tybalt and Mercutio to do?*

51–54 When Romeo enters, Mercutio again pretends to misunderstand Tybalt. By **my man,** Tybalt means "the man I'm looking for." Mercutio takes it to mean "my servant." (**Livery** is a servant's uniform.) He assures Tybalt that the only place Romeo would follow him is to the dueling field.

57–59 I forgive your anger because I have reason to love you.

Ⓑ CHARACTER
What **motive** does Romeo have for not wanting to fight Tybalt? Who else knows about this motive?

61 boy: an insulting term of address.

DIFFERENTIATED INSTRUCTION

FOR LESS–PROFICIENT READERS
Inverted Word Order Explain that in some lines, Shakespeare places the negative word at the end of the sentence. To illustrate, have students read lines 32 and 59–60 and locate the words "not" and "none". Call on volunteers to restate the lines, moving the negative to a more traditional place. *Possible answer: By my heel, I don't care (line 32); I am no villain. / Therefore farewell. I see you do not know me (lines 59–60).*

FOR ENGLISH LEARNERS
Task Support Point out the marginal question for lines 45–48. Remind students that Benvolio showed himself to be a peacemaker in the play's opening scene. *Possible answer: Benvolio wants Tybalt and Mercutio either to go and settle their quarrel privately, without violence, or to go their separate ways.*

65 Till thou shalt know the reason of my love;
And so, good Capulet, which name I tender
As dearly as mine own, be satisfied.

Mercutio. O calm, dishonorable, vile submission!
Alla stoccata carries it away.

[*draws*]

70 Tybalt, you ratcatcher, will you walk?

Tybalt. What wouldst thou have with me?

Mercutio. Good King of Cats, nothing but one of your nine lives.
That I mean to make bold withal, and, as you shall use me
hereafter, dry-beat the rest of the eight. Will you pluck your
75 sword out of his pilcher by the ears? Make haste, lest mine be
about your ears ere it be out.

Tybalt. I am for you.

[*draws*]

Romeo. Gentle Mercutio, put thy rapier up.

Mercutio. Come, sir, your *passado!*

[*They fight.*]

80 **Romeo.** Draw, Benvolio; beat down their weapons.
Gentlemen, for shame! forbear this outrage!
Tybalt, Mercutio, the Prince expressly hath
Forbid this bandying in Verona streets.
Hold, Tybalt! Good Mercutio!

[Tybalt, *under Romeo's arm, thrusts* Mercutio *in, and flies with his* Men.]

Mercutio.   I am hurt.
85 A plague o' both your houses! I am sped.
Is he gone and hath nothing?

Benvolio.   What, art thou hurt?

Mercutio. Ay, ay, a scratch, a scratch. Marry, 'tis enough.
Where is my page? Go, villain, fetch a surgeon.

[*Exit* Page.]

Romeo. Courage, man. The hurt cannot be much.

90 **Mercutio.** No, 'tis not so deep as a well, nor so wide as a church
door; but 'tis enough, 'twill serve. Ask for me tomorrow, and you
shall find me a grave man. I am peppered, I warrant, for this
world. A plague o' both your houses! Zounds, a dog, a rat, a
mouse, a cat, to scratch a man to death! A braggart, a rogue, a

---

66 **tender:** cherish.

68–70 Mercutio assumes that Romeo is afraid to fight. *Alla stoccata* is a move used in sword fighting; Mercutio is suggesting that Tybalt has won the battle of words with Romeo. Mercutio then dares Tybalt to step aside and fight (**walk**).

72–74 **nothing but . . . eight:** I intend to take one of your nine lives (as a cat supposedly has) and give a beating to the other eight.

1 **Targeted Passage**

79 *passado:* a sword-fighting maneuver.

80–84 Romeo wants Benvolio to help him stop the fight. They are able to hold back Mercutio.

83 **bandying:** fighting.

85 **A plague . . . sped:** I curse both the Montagues and the Capulets. I am destroyed.

90–96 Even as he lies dying, Mercutio continues to joke and make nasty remarks about Tybalt. He makes a pun on the word *grave.*

Lines 70–87
DISCUSSION PROMPTS

Use these prompts to discuss the duel between Tybalt and Mercutio:

Recall Why do Tybalt and Mercutio fight? *Possible answer: Tybalt insults Romeo, who refuses to fight. Mercutio becomes angry and draws his rapier.*

Analyze Do you think that Tybalt intended to fight and kill Mercutio? Why or why not? *Possible answers: No. Mercutio challenged Tybalt and drew his weapon, forcing Tybalt to defend himself. Yes. Tybalt has expressed hatred toward Romeo and would probably enjoy hurting Romeo in any way possible— including killing one of Romeo's friends.*

Evaluate Was the fight between Mercutio and Tybalt fair? What factors made it fair or unfair? *Possible answers: The fight was fair because the opponents were armed and fought one on one. It was unfair because Mercutio was not a member of either family and because Mercutio was held back by Romeo and Benvolio, unintentionally giving Tybalt the chance to deliver a fatal wound.*

FOR LESS–PROFICIENT READERS

Paraphrasing Shakespeare Have students reread the summary of lines 80–84. Then model this paraphrase of Romeo's attempt to stop the fight: *Use your sword, Benvolio; use it to beat down their swords. Shame on you! Stop this fight! Tybalt, Mercutio, remember that the prince has forbidden our fighting in Verona's streets. Stop, Tybalt! Stop, Mercutio!* Invite students to suggest other wordings.

1 **Targeted Passage [Lines 77–87]**

This passage, which presents the fight between Tybalt and Mercutio, is a turning point in the play.

- What is Romeo's role in the fight? What does he say and do?

- What happens to Mercutio? Why do you think he cries, "A plague o' both your houses!" (line 85)?

- What does Tybalt do? Why?

Possible answer: *Mercutio repeats the curse "A plague o' both your houses" (lines 85, 93, and 99). The curse foreshadows disaster for both the Capulet and Montague families.*

If students need help . . . Make sure that they understand the correct meaning of *curse* in this context—namely, "a wish for terrible things to happen to someone." In addition, define *plague* and *houses* as the words are used in this context.

Possible answer: *A desire to avenge Mercutio drives Romeo to challenge Tybalt.*

If students need help . . . Read lines 115–122 aloud. Discuss these questions:

- Who is "alive in triumph" (line 115)? **Answer:** *Tybalt*

- Why does Romeo refer to his action as "fire-eyed fury" (line 117)? **Possible answer:** *Romeo is overwhelmed with anger at Mercutio's death.*

- According to lines 119–122, why hasn't Mercutio's soul departed yet? **Possible answer:** *Mercutio's soul is waiting for the soul of Tybalt or Romeo—whoever is killed in the fight—to accompany him.*

---

95 villain, that fights by the book of arithmetic! Why the devil came
you between us? I was hurt under your arm.

Romeo. I thought all for the best.

Mercutio. Help me into some house, Benvolio,
Or I shall faint. A plague o' both your houses! **C**
100 They have made worms' meat of me. I have it,
And soundly too. Your houses!

[*Exit, supported by* Benvolio.]

Romeo. This gentleman, the Prince's near ally,
My very friend, hath got this mortal hurt
In my behalf—my reputation stained
105 With Tybalt's slander—Tybalt, that an hour
Hath been my kinsman, O sweet Juliet,
Thy beauty hath made me effeminate
And in my temper softened valor's steel!

[*Reenter* Benvolio.]

Benvolio. O Romeo, Romeo, brave Mercutio's dead!
110 That gallant spirit hath aspired the clouds,
Which too untimely here did scorn the earth.

Romeo. This day's black fate on mo days doth depend;
This but begins the woe others must end.

[*Reenter* Tybalt.]

Benvolio. Here comes the furious Tybalt back again.

115 **Romeo.** Alive in triumph, and Mercutio slain?
Away to heaven respective lenity,
And fire-eyed fury be my conduct now!
Now, Tybalt, take the "villain" back again
That late thou gavest me, for Mercutio's soul
120 Is but a little way above our heads,
Staying for thine to keep him company.
Either thou or I, or both, must go with him. **D**

Tybalt. Thou, wretched boy, that didst consort him here,
Shalt with him hence.

Romeo.   This shall determine that.

[*They fight*. Tybalt *falls*.]

125 **Benvolio.** Romeo, away, be gone!
The citizens are up, and Tybalt slain.
Stand not amazed. The Prince will doom thee death
If thou art taken. Hence, be gone, away!

C TRAGEDY
What curse does Mercutio repeat three times in this scene? Explain what this ominous curse might **foreshadow.**

102–108 This gentleman . . . valor's steel: My friend has died protecting my reputation against a man who has been my relative for only an hour. My love for Juliet has made me less manly and brave.

110 aspired: soared to.

112–113 This day's . . . must end: This awful day will be followed by more of the same.

116 respective lenity: considerate mildness.

D CHARACTER
What drives Romeo to challenge Tybalt to fight?

124 The sword fight probably goes on for several minutes, till Romeo runs his sword through Tybalt.

DIFFERENTIATED INSTRUCTION

FOR LESS–PROFICIENT READERS
Paraphrasing Shakespeare Have students reread the summary of lines 102–108. Then help students paraphrase lines 102–105, the moment when Romeo realizes what has happened to Mercutio. **Possible answer:** *Mercutio, a gentleman, is a close friend of the Prince and is my friend. He has been fatally hurt because of me, after I was insulted by Tybalt.*

FOR ADVANCED LEARNERS/PRE–AP
Analyze Character Point out that Mercutio dies without knowing of Romeo's marriage to Juliet. Ask students to consider these questions: Would Mercutio's attitude or actions have been different if he had known? Might he have avoided the duel that killed him? Then have students write a paragraph or two in response, citing details to support their position. Invite students to compare their analyses in small groups.

Romeo. O, I am fortune's fool!

Benvolio.   Why dost thou stay?

[*Exit* Romeo.]

[*Enter* Citizens.]

130 **Citizen.** Which way ran he that killed Mercutio?
Tybalt, that murderer, which way ran he?

Benvolio. There lies that Tybalt.

Citizen.   Up, sir, go with me.
I charge thee in the Prince's name obey.

[*Enter* Prince *with his* Attendants, Montague, Capulet, *their* Wives,
and others.]

Prince. Where are the vile beginners of this fray?

135 **Benvolio.** O noble Prince, I can discover all
The unlucky manage of this fatal brawl.
There lies the man, slain by young Romeo,
That slew thy kinsman, brave Mercutio.

Lady Capulet. Tybalt, my cousin! O my brother's child!
140 O Prince! O cousin! O husband! O, the blood is spilled
Of my dear kinsman! Prince, as thou art true,
For blood of ours shed blood of Montague.
O cousin, cousin!

Prince. Benvolio, who began this bloody fray?

145 **Benvolio.** Tybalt, here slain, whom Romeo's hand did slay.
Romeo, that spoke him fair, bid him bethink
How nice the quarrel was, and urged withal
Your high displeasure. All this—uttered
With gentle breath, calm look, knees humbly bowed—
150 Could not take truce with the unruly spleen
Of Tybalt deaf to peace, but that he tilts
With piercing steel at bold Mercutio's breast;
Who, all as hot, turns deadly point to point,
And, with a martial scorn, with one hand beats
155 Cold death aside and with the other sends
It back to Tybalt, whose dexterity
Retorts it. Romeo he cries aloud,
"Hold, friends! friends, part!" and swifter than his tongue,
His agile arm beats down their fatal points,
160 And 'twixt them rushes; underneath whose arm
An envious thrust from Tybalt hit the life

129 I am fortune's fool: Fate has made a fool of me.

135–136 Benvolio says he can tell (**discover**) what happened.

141–142 as thou . . . Montague: If your word is good, you will sentence Romeo to death for killing a Capulet.

146–147 Romeo, that . . . was: Romeo talked calmly (**fair**) and told Tybalt to think how trivial (**nice**) the argument was.

150–151 could . . . peace: could not quiet the anger of Tybalt, who would not listen to pleas for peace.

156–157 whose dexterity retorts it: whose skill returns it.

159–160 his agile . . . rushes: He rushed between them and pushed down their swords.

Lines 145–168
REINFORCE *KEY IDEA:* LOVE AND HATE

Discuss According to Benvolio's story, in what sense did **hate** prove stronger than **love** in the encounter with Tybalt? *Possible answer: Romeo and Benvolio, as peacemakers, tried to stop Tybalt. However, Tybalt's hate and Mercutio's goading enflamed the conflict between the families and caused the death of Mercutio. Only then was Romeo's love for peace overcome by hate for Tybalt.*

BACKGROUND

The "Unruly Spleen" Why does Benvolio blame Tybalt's spleen for his refusal to listen to an appeal for peace (lines 150–151)? Elizabethans considered the spleen an important part of the body. Drawing upon ideas from classical medicine, they believed that the spleen contained and controlled "black bile," a fluid (called a humor) that caused bad temper and violent outbursts. If the spleen was not working properly—if it was "unruly," as Benvolio says—black bile could control a person's behavior. Although these beliefs would not have excused Tybalt's actions, they would have helped to explain them.

FOR LESS–PROFICIENT READERS

Explore Motivation Students will grasp this scene better if you help them connect each character's emotions with the events that inspired them. For example, Lady Capulet is very sad about Tybalt's death and is angry with Romeo. Benvolio is very sad about Mercutio's death, but he tries to be honest in his account of the events. Prince Escalus is very angry about the violence in the city and the violation of his decree.

ⓔ TRAGEDY

Possible answer: Lady Capulet thinks that Benvolio is lying because she cannot imagine that one Montague would endanger another by telling the truth. Her accusation (lines 169–170) can be paraphrased in this way: "Benvolio is related to the Montagues. His love for his family makes him tell lies about what happened." Lady Capulet begs the Prince to execute Romeo for killing Tybalt (line 174).

ANALYZE VISUALS

Activity What do the opulent scarlet costumes worn by Lady Capulet and Tybalt indicate about the Capulet family? Why do you think the director of the production made this costuming choice? *Possible answer: The costumes indicate the Capulet family's high social status and wealth. The director probably wanted costumes that immediately let the audience know that the Capulets were important, influential people in Verona.*

Of stout Mercutio, and then Tybalt fled,
But by-and-by comes back to Romeo,
Who had but newly entertained revenge,
165 And to't they go like lightning; for, ere I
Could draw to part them, was stout Tybalt slain;
And, as he fell, did Romeo turn and fly.
This is the truth, or let Benvolio die.

Lady Capulet. He is a kinsman to the Montague;
170 Affection makes him false, he speaks not true.
Some twenty of them fought in this black strife,
And all those twenty could but kill one life.
I beg for justice, which thou, Prince, must give.
Romeo slew Tybalt; Romeo must not live. **ⓔ**

175 **Prince.** Romeo slew him; he slew Mercutio.
Who now the price of his dear blood doth owe?

Montague. Not Romeo, Prince; he was Mercutio's friend;
His fault concludes but what the law should end,
The life of Tybalt.

164 entertained: thought of.

ⓔ TRAGEDY
Why does Lady Capulet think Benvolio is lying? **Paraphrase** the accusation she makes, and explain what she begs the prince to do.

178–179 Romeo is guilty only of avenging Mercutio's death, which the law would have done anyway.

Lady Capulet mourns Tybalt in the Royal Shakespeare Company's 2004 production.

998 UNIT 10: SHAKESPEAREAN DRAMA

DIFFERENTIATED INSTRUCTION

FOR LESS–PROFICIENT READERS
Inverted Word Order Point out lines 166, 167, and 176, in which Shakespeare alters the placement of the verb in the sentence. Have students read the lines aloud, changing the order to suit a modern ear. *Possible answer: stout Tybalt was slain; Romeo did turn and fly; Who now owes the price of his dear blood?*

FOR ENGLISH LEARNERS
Concept Support Help students compare the families' attempts to sway Prince Escalus. Discuss how Lady Capulet appeals to his sense of honor (lines 142–143) and stretches the truth (lines 171–172) as she cries for the death of Romeo, whereas Montague tries to justify Romeo's actions by arguing that he merely carried out the sentence that the prince himself would have decreed against Tybalt (lines 178–179).

Prince.   And for that offense
180 Immediately we do exile him hence.
I have an interest in your hate's proceeding,
My blood for your rude brawls doth lie a-bleeding;
But I'll amerce you with so strong a fine
That you shall all repent the loss of mine.
185 I will be deaf to pleading and excuses;
Nor tears nor prayers shall purchase out abuses.
Therefore use none. Let Romeo hence in haste,
Else, when he is found, that hour is his last.
Bear hence this body, and attend our will.
190 Mercy but murders, pardoning those that kill.
[*Exeunt.*]

179–190 The prince banishes Romeo from Verona. He angrily points out that one of his own relatives is dead because of the feud and declares that Romeo will be put to death unless he flees immediately.

SCENE 2 *Capulet's orchard.*

The scene begins with Juliet impatiently waiting for night to come so that Romeo can climb to her bedroom on the rope ladder. Suddenly the nurse enters with the terrible news of Tybalt's death and Romeo's banishment. Juliet mourns for the loss of her cousin and her husband and threatens to kill herself. To calm her, the nurse promises to find Romeo and bring him to Juliet before he leaves Verona.

[*Enter* Juliet *alone.*]

Juliet. Gallop apace, you fiery-footed steeds,
Toward Phoebus' lodging! Such a wagoner
As Phaëton would whip you to the West,
And bring in cloudy night immediately.
5 Spread thy close curtain, love-performing night,
That runaways' eyes may wink, and Romeo
Leap to these arms, untalked of and unseen. **ⓕ**
Lovers can see to do their amorous rites
By their own beauties; or, if love be blind,
10 It best agrees with night. Come, civil night,
Thou sober-suited matron, all in black,
And learn me how to lose a winning match,
Played for a pair of stainless maidenhoods.
Hood my unmanned blood bating in my cheeks
15 With thy black mantle; till strange love, grown bold,
Think true love acted simple modesty.
Come, night; come, Romeo, come; thou day in night;
For thou wilt lie upon the wings of night
Whiter than new snow on a raven's back.
20 Come, gentle night; come, loving, black-browed night;
Give me my Romeo; and, when he shall die,
Take him and cut him out in little stars,

2–3 Phoebus: Apollo, the god of the sun; **Phaëton:** a mortal who lost control of the sun's chariot when he drove it too fast.

ⓕ ALLUSION
Paraphrase lines 1–7. Why does Juliet allude to Phoebus and Phaëton in this **soliloquy?**

14–16 Hood . . . modesty: Juliet asks that the darkness hide her blushing cheeks on her wedding night.

Lines 179–184
REINFORCE *KEY IDEA:* LOVE AND HATE

Discuss How do **love** and **hate** play a role in the prince's decision to banish Romeo?
Possible answer: The prince's love of his cousin Mercutio demands he take action against those involved, hence his interest in allowing "hate's proceeding" (line 181). Still, the prince hates violence, and so does not call for Romeo's execution, as others have urged him to do.

LITERARY ANALYSIS

ⓕ ALLUSION

Possible answer: Paraphrase of lines 1–7: "Ride quickly, you fast horses, to the house of Phoebus. If only Phaëton were driving, you would be faster, and night would come sooner. Bring darkness for love, so that Romeo can come to me without having anyone see him." By alluding to Phoebus and Phaëton, Juliet is implying that divine powers should be on the lovers' side.

If students need help . . . Help them paraphrase the passage, one line at a time. Review the marginal note, which points out that both Phoebus and Phaëton are godlike. Then ask the Literary Analysis question.

FOR LESS–PROFICIENT READERS

Preview Call on a volunteer to read aloud the italicized scene synopsis for the class. Help students complete a Plot Diagram to track the events in Scene 2.

 BEST PRACTICES TOOLKIT—Transparency
Plot Diagram p. D10

Climax: Juliet threatens suicide.

Rising Action: The nurse brings news about Tybalt and Romeo.

Falling Action: The nurse calms Juliet.

Background: Juliet waits for night.

Resolution: The nurse promises to bring Romeo to Juliet before he leaves Verona.

And he will make the face of heaven so fine
That all the world will be in love with night
25 And pay no worship to the garish sun.
O, I have bought the mansion of a love,
But not possessed it; and though I am sold,
Not yet enjoyed. So tedious is this day
As is the night before some festival
30 To an impatient child that hath new robes
And may not wear them. Oh, here comes my nurse,

[*Enter* Nurse, *wringing her hands, with the ladder of cords in her lap.*]

And she brings news; and every tongue that speaks
But Romeo's name speaks heavenly eloquence.
Now, nurse, what news? What hast thou there? the cords
35 That Romeo bid thee fetch?

Nurse.   Ay, ay, the cords.

Juliet. Ay me! what news? Why dost thou wring thy hands?

Nurse. Ah, well-a-day! he's dead, he's dead, he's dead!
We are undone, lady, we are undone!
Alack the day! he's gone, he's killed, he's dead!

40 **Juliet.** Can heaven be so envious? **G**

Nurse.   Romeo can,
Though heaven cannot. O Romeo, Romeo!
Who ever would have thought it? Romeo!

Juliet. What devil art thou that dost torment me thus?
This torture should be roared in dismal hell.
45 Hath Romeo slain himself? Say thou but "I,"
And that bare vowel "I" shall poison more
Than the death-darting eye of a cockatrice.
I am not I, if there be such an "I,"
Or those eyes shut, that make thee answer "I."
50 If he be slain, say "I," or if not, "no."
Brief sounds determine of my weal or woe.

Nurse. I saw the wound, I saw it with mine eyes,
(God save the mark!) here on his manly breast.
A piteous corse, a bloody piteous corse;
55 Pale, pale as ashes, all bedaubed in blood,
All in gore blood. I swounded at the sight.

Juliet. O, break, my heart! poor bankrout, break at once!
To prison, eyes; ne'er look on liberty!
Vile earth, to earth resign; end motion here,
60 And thou and Romeo press one heavy bier!

26–27 **I have . . . possessed it:** Juliet protests that she has gone through the wedding ceremony (**bought the mansion**) but is still waiting to enjoy the rewards of marriage.

34 **the cords:** the rope ladder.

37–42 **well-a-day:** an expression used when someone has bad news. The nurse wails and moans without clearly explaining what has happened, leading Juliet to assume that Romeo is dead.

G DRAMATIC IRONY
How is Juliet's belief that her new husband is dead an example of dramatic irony?

45–50 Juliet's "I" means "aye," or "yes." A **cockatrice** is a mythological beast whose glance kills its victims.

51 **my weal or woe:** my happiness or sorrow.

53–56 **God . . . mark:** an expression meant to scare off evil powers, similar to "Knock on wood"; **corse:** corpse; **swounded:** fainted.

57–60 Juliet say her heart is broken and bankrupt (**bankrout**). She wants to be buried with Romeo, sharing his burial platform (**bier**).

LITERARY ANALYSIS

G DRAMATIC IRONY

Possible answer: Juliet's belief that her new husband is dead is an example of dramatic irony because although he is not yet dead, he will be by the end of the play. It is also ironic because in this scene, Juliet mistakenly thinks that Romeo is dead. Later, it will be Romeo who mistakenly thinks that Juliet is dead.

If students need help . . . Define the term *dramatic irony.* Refer students to the Prologue that opens the play and to what it says about the play's outcome. Discuss what students know about death in this story that Juliet herself does not yet know.

DIFFERENTIATED INSTRUCTION

FOR ENGLISH LEARNERS

Vocabulary Support Direct students' attention to lines 45–50, in which Shakespeare uses homophones: the pronoun *I*, the word *eye*, and the implied word *aye*. Point out that this is not humorous word play; rather, Shakespeare mixes the words to indicate Juliet's confusion. Go through lines 45–50 especially slowly, paraphrasing to clear up any misunderstandings.

Nurse. O Tybalt, Tybalt, the best friend I had!
O courteous Tybalt! honest gentleman!
That ever I should live to see thee dead!

Juliet. What storm is this that blows so contrary?
65 Is Romeo slaughtered, and is Tybalt dead?
My dear-loved cousin, and my dearer lord?
Then, dreadful trumpet, sound the general doom!
For who is living, if those two are gone?

Nurse. Tybalt is gone, and Romeo banished;
70 Romeo that killed him, he is banished.

Juliet. O God! Did Romeo's hand shed Tybalt's blood?

Nurse. It did! it did! alas the day, it did!

Juliet. O serpent heart, hid with a flow'ring face!
Did ever dragon keep so fair a cave?
75 Beautiful tyrant! fiend angelical!
Dove-feathered raven! wolvish-ravening lamb!
Despised substance of divinest show!
Just opposite to what thou justly seemst,
A damned saint, an honorable villain!
80 O nature, what hadst thou to do in hell
When thou didst bower the spirit of a fiend
In mortal paradise of such sweet flesh?
Was ever book containing such vile matter
So fairly bound? O, that deceit should dwell
85 In such a gorgeous palace!

Nurse.   There's no trust,
No faith, no honesty in men; all perjured,
All forsworn, all naught, all dissemblers.
Ah, where's my man? Give me some aqua vitae.
These griefs, these woes, these sorrows make me old.
90 Shame come to Romeo!

Juliet.   Blistered be thy tongue
For such a wish! He was not born to shame.
Upon his brow shame is ashamed to sit;
For 'tis a throne where honor may be crowned
Sole monarch of the universal earth.
95 O, what a beast was I to chide at him! **H**

Nurse. Will you speak well of him that killed your cousin?

Juliet. Shall I speak ill of him that is my husband?
Ah, poor my lord, what tongue shall smooth thy name
When I, thy three-hours' wife, have mangled it?
100 But wherefore, villain, didst thou kill my cousin?
That villain cousin would have killed my husband.

73–85 Juliet's contradictory phrases here show how she feels conflicting feelings about the events the nurse has described. *What is Juliet's first reaction to the news that Romeo has killed Tybalt?*

81 bower . . . fiend: give a home to the spirit of a demon.

87 all . . . dissemblers: All are liars and pretenders.

88 aqua vitae: brandy.

H TRAGEDY
Compare Juliet's initial reaction to the news of Tybalt's death with her response to the nurse in lines 90–95. What **internal conflict** is Juliet wrestling with in this scene?

Lines 73–85
REINFORCE *KEY IDEA:* LOVE AND HATE

Discuss What does this speech by Juliet suggest about the nature of her **love** for Romeo, or about the nature of love in general?
Possible answer: *Juliet's hateful words suggest that her love for Romeo is immature and, perhaps, that she can fall out of love as easily as she fell into it. In more general terms, the speech suggests that although love is a strong emotion, grief can overpower love in times of crisis.*

LITERARY ANALYSIS

H TRAGEDY

Possible answer: *Juliet's initial reaction to the news of Tybalt's death is to denounce Romeo. When she hears the nurse's condemnation, however, she reverses her position, defending Romeo and condemning her cousin. Juliet is wrestling with an internal conflict about whether her loyalty should lie with her husband or with her family.*

FOR ENGLISH LEARNERS

Vocabulary Support Juliet's speech in lines 73–85 is filled with oxymorons. Using "fiend angelical" (line 75) and "honorable villain" (line 79) as examples, explain that an oxymoron is a phrase in which words have opposing meanings and yet make sense when put together. Help students locate other oxymorons in this passage. Elicit that the oxymorons show that Juliet feels both love and hate for Romeo at this moment.

Task Support Have students read the marginal note and question for lines 73–85. Explain that Juliet has just realized (in line 71) that Romeo has killed Tybalt. ***Possible answer:*** *Juliet's first reaction to the news is to be angry with Romeo and to assume that he is really an evil person who is merely pretending to be good.*

Back, foolish tears, back to your native spring!
Your tributary drops belong to woe,
Which you, mistaking, offer up to joy.
105 My husband lives, that Tybalt would have slain;
And Tybalt's dead, that would have slain my husband.
All this is comfort; wherefore weep I then?
Some word there was, worser than Tybalt's death,
That murdered me. I would forget it fain;
110 But O, it presses to my memory
Like damned guilty deeds to sinners' minds!
"Tybalt is dead, and Romeo—banished."
That "banished," that one word "banished,"
Hath slain ten thousand Tybalts. Tybalt's death
115 Was woe enough, if it had ended there;
Or, if sour woe delights in fellowship
And needly will be ranked with other griefs,
Why followed not, when she said "Tybalt's dead,"
Thy father, or thy mother, nay, or both,
120 Which modern lamentation might have moved?
But with a rearward following Tybalt's death,
"Romeo is banished"—to speak that word
Is father, mother, Tybalt, Romeo, Juliet,
All slain, all dead. "Romeo is banished"—
125 There is no end, no limit, measure, bound,
In that word's death; no words can that woe sound.
Where is my father and my mother, nurse?

Nurse. Weeping and wailing over Tybalt's corse.
Will you go to them? I will bring you thither.

130 **Juliet.** Wash they his wounds with tears? Mine shall be spent,
When theirs are dry, for Romeo's banishment.
Take up those cords. Poor ropes, you are beguiled,
Both you and I, for Romeo is exiled.
He made you for a highway to my bed;
135 But I, a maid, die maiden-widowed.
Come, cords; come, nurse. I'll to my wedding bed;
And death, not Romeo, take my maidenhead!

Nurse. Hie to your chamber. I'll find Romeo
To comfort you. I wot well where he is.
140 Hark ye, your Romeo will be here at night.
I'll to him; he is hid at Laurence' cell.

Juliet. O, find him! give this ring to my true knight
And bid him come to take his last farewell.

[*Exeunt.*]

102–106 Juliet is uncertain whether her tears should be of joy or of sorrow.

114–127 Juliet says that if the news of Tybalt's death had been followed by the news of her parents' deaths, she would have felt normal (**modern**), or expected, grief. To follow the story of Tybalt's death with the terrible news of Romeo's banishment creates a sorrow so deep it cannot be expressed in words.

132 beguiled: cheated.

135–137 I...maidenhead: I will die a widow without ever really having been a wife. Death, not Romeo, will be my husband.

139 wot: know.

② **Targeted Passage**

Lines 100–114
DISCUSSION PROMPTS

Use these prompts to help students understand Juliet's conflicted grief:

Connect Think of some unexpected news that made you or someone you know very sad. How does that experience help you understand Juliet's reaction to the news of Tybalt's death and Romeo's banishment? *Students should express some empathy for Juliet's shock and grief.*

Analyze Why is Juliet happy? Why is she sad? *Possible answer: Juliet is happy that Romeo is not dead. She is sad about the violence, sad about Tybalt's death, and especially sad about the fact that Romeo has been banished from Verona.*

Synthesize By this point in the scene, what decision has Juliet made about her loyalty? How does her decision threaten her relationship with her nurse? *Possible answer: By this point, Juliet has decided to be loyal to her husband, even though they have been married for only a few hours. To this point, the nurse has mourned Tybalt and condemned Romeo; if she does not support Romeo, she will be at odds with Juliet and will lose Juliet's trust.*

DIFFERENTIATED INSTRUCTION

FOR LESS–PROFICIENT READERS
② **Targeted Passage [Lines 138–143]**

In this passage, Juliet and the nurse make a plan to bring the lovers together.

- Where is Romeo hiding?
- What is the nurse going to do and say after she leaves Juliet?
- Why does Juliet call the coming night Romeo's "last farewell" (line 143)?

FOR ENGLISH LEARNERS
Vocabulary: Outdated Forms Urge students to continue adding outdated terms to their language journal. (See the **For English Learners** activity on p. 940.) Provide these terms and their definitions. Then have students reread the lines noted and substitute the definitions for the words.

- *would have slain* (lines 105 and 106), "wanted to kill"

- *fain* (line 109), "happily"
- *needly will be* (line 117), "must be"
- *corse* (line 128), "corpse"
- *thither* (line 129), "there"
- *hark ye* (line 140), "listen" (a command)

SCENE 3 *Friar Laurence's cell.*

Friar Laurence tells Romeo of his banishment, and Romeo collapses in grief. When he learns from the nurse that Juliet, too, is in despair, he threatens to stab himself. The friar reacts by suggesting a plan. Romeo is to spend a few hours with Juliet and then escape to Mantua. While he is away, the friar will announce the wedding and try to get a pardon from the prince.

[*Enter* Friar Laurence.]

Friar Laurence. Romeo, come forth; come forth, thou fearful man.
Affliction is enamored of thy parts,
And thou art wedded to calamity.

[*Enter* Romeo.]

Romeo. Father, what news? What is the Prince's doom?
5 What sorrow craves acquaintance at my hand
That I yet know not?

Friar Laurence.   Too familiar
Is my dear son with such sour company.
I bring thee tidings of the Prince's doom.

Romeo. What less than doomsday is the Prince's doom?

10 **Friar Laurence.** A gentler judgment vanished from his lips—
Not body's death, but body's banishment.

Romeo. Ha, banishment? Be merciful, say "death";
For exile hath more terror in his look,
Much more than death. Do not say "banishment."

15 **Friar Laurence.** Hence from Verona art thou banished.
Be patient, for the world is broad and wide.

Romeo. There is no world without Verona walls,
But purgatory, torture, hell itself.
Hence banished is banish'd from the world,
20 And world's exile is death. Then "banishment,"
Is death misterm'd. Calling death "banishment,"
Thou cuttst my head off with a golden axe
And smilest upon the stroke that murders me.

Friar Laurence. O deadly sin! O rude unthankfulness!
25 Thy fault our law calls death; but the kind Prince,
Taking thy part, hath rushed aside the law,
And turned that black word death to banishment.
This is dear mercy, and thou seest it not.

Romeo. 'Tis torture, and not mercy. Heaven is here,
30 Where Juliet lives; and every cat and dog
And little mouse, every unworthy thing,
Live here in heaven and may look on her;
But Romeo may not. More validity,

2 affliction...parts: Trouble loves you.

4 doom: sentence.

9 doomsday: death.

10 vanished: came.

17–23 There is...murders me: Being exiled outside Verona's walls is as bad as being dead. And yet you smile at my misfortune.

24–28 The angry friar reminds Romeo that by law he should have gotten the death penalty. The prince has shown Romeo mercy.

ROMEO AND JULIET: ACT THREE, SCENE 3   **1003**

Lines 29–33
REINFORCE *KEY IDEA:* LOVE AND HATE

Discuss At the end of Scene 1, Prince Escalus chose to banish Romeo rather than execute him for killing Tybalt. In what sense does Romeo's **love** make him ungrateful for the prince's mercy? *Possible answer: Romeo has such great love for Juliet that any separation from her feels like a death sentence. He is ungrateful because the prince's decision, even if it was merciful, will separate him from Juliet.*

FOR LESS–PROFICIENT READERS

Preview After students have read the Scene 3 synopsis, have them use Problem and Solution Charts to record its key events.

 BEST PRACTICES TOOLKIT—Transparency
Problem and Solution Charts p. B20

| Romeo has been banished from Verona. |

| Friar Laurence will announce the wedding and try to get a pardon for Romeo after Romeo leaves Verona. |

More honorable state, more courtship lives
35 In carrion flies than Romeo. They may seize
On the white wonder of dear Juliet's hand
And steal immortal blessing from her lips,
Who, even in pure and vestal modesty,
Still blush, as thinking their own kisses sin;
40 But Romeo may not—he is banished.
This may flies do, when I from this must fly;
They are free men, but I am banished.
And sayst thou yet that exile is not death?
Hadst thou no poison mixed, no sharp-ground knife,
45 No sudden mean of death, though ne'er so mean,
But "banished" to kill me—"banished"?
O friar, the damnèd use that word in hell;
Howling attends it! How hast thou the heart,
Being a divine, a ghostly confessor,
50 A sin-absolver, and my friend professed,
To mangle me with that word "banished"?

Friar Laurence. Thou fond mad man, hear me a little speak.

Romeo. O, thou wilt speak again of banishment.

Friar Laurence. I'll give thee armor to keep off that word;
55 Adversity's sweet milk, philosophy,
To comfort thee, though thou art banished.

Romeo. Yet "banished"? Hang up philosophy!
Unless philosophy can make a Juliet,
Displant a town, reverse a prince's doom,
60 It helps not, it prevails not. Talk no more.

Friar Laurence. O, then I see that madmen have no ears.

Romeo. How should they, when that wise men have no eyes?

Friar Laurence. Let me dispute with thee of thy estate.

Romeo. Thou canst not speak of that thou dost not feel.
65 Wert thou as young as I, Juliet thy love,
An hour but married, Tybalt murdered,
Doting like me, and like me banishèd,
Then mightst thou speak, then mightst thou tear thy hair,
And fall upon the ground, as I do now,
70 Taking the measure of an unmade grave.

[Nurse *knocks within.*]

Friar Laurence. Arise; one knocks. Good Romeo, hide thyself.

Romeo. Not I; unless the breath of heartsick groans
Mist-like infold me from the search of eyes.

[*knock*]

33–35 More validity ... than Romeo: Even flies that live off the dead (**carrion**) will be able to get closer to Juliet than Romeo will.

44–46 Hadst ... to kill me: Couldn't you have killed me with poison or a knife instead of with that awful word *banished*? *Why does Romeo think banishment is a worse punishment than death?*

52 fond: foolish.

54–56 The friar offers philosophical comfort and counseling (**adversity's sweet milk**) as a way to overcome hardship.

63 dispute: discuss; **estate:** situation.

72–73 Romeo will hide only if his sighs create a mist and shield him from sight.

1004 UNIT 10: SHAKESPEAREAN DRAMA

Lines 53–70
DISCUSSION PROMPTS

Use these prompts to help students understand Friar Laurence's attempts to console Romeo:

Connect Have you or anyone you know ever tried to calm someone who was particularly upset? How does that experience help you understand the role of Friar Laurence in this scene? *Students may describe the difficulty in getting a person to move beyond his or her emotions and be rational.*

Analyze How does the friar attempt to help Romeo deal with his grief about being banished? Is he successful? *Possible answer: Friar Laurence attempts to console Romeo with philosophy, possibly to encourage Romeo to think rationally about his situation.*

Evaluate Do Romeo and Friar Laurence seem as close in this scene as they have been? Explain. *Possible answer: Students may note that the closeness is strained, as the friar's attempts to console Romeo are well meaning but intellectual, and Romeo alludes to this when he says that the friar shouldn't comment on feelings he doesn't understand (line 64).*

DIFFERENTIATED INSTRUCTION

FOR ENGLISH LEARNERS

Task Support As students consider the blue marginal question for lines 44–46, remind them that *banishment* means forcing a person to leave a place, never to return. *Possible answer: Romeo thinks that banishment is worse than death because he must live with the knowledge that Juliet is alive but that he cannot be with her. He believes that if he were dead, he would not have the pain of longing for Juliet.*

1004 UNIT 10: SHAKESPEAREAN DRAMA

Friar Laurence. Hark, how they knock! Who's there? Romeo, arise;
75 Thou wilt be taken.—Stay awhile!—Stand up;

[*knock*]

Run to my study.—By-and-by!—God's will,
What simpleness is this.—I come, I come!

[*knock*]

Who knocks so hard? Whence come you? What's your will?

Nurse [*within*]. Let me come in, and you shall know my errand.
80 I come from Lady Juliet.

Friar Laurence.   Welcome then.

[*Enter Nurse.*]

Nurse. O holy friar, O, tell me, holy friar,
Where is my lady's lord, where's Romeo?

Friar Laurence. There on the ground, with his own tears made
    drunk.

Nurse. O, he is even in my mistress' case,
85 Just in her case! O woeful sympathy!
Piteous predicament! Even so lies she,
Blubb'ring and weeping, weeping and blubbering.
Stand up, stand up! Stand, an you be a man.
For Juliet's sake, for her sake, rise and stand!
90 Why should you fall into so deep an O?

Romeo [*rises*]. Nurse—

Nurse. Ah sir! ah sir! Well, death's the end of all.

Romeo. Spakest thou of Juliet? How is it with her?
Doth not she think me an old murderer,
95 Now I have stained the childhood of our joy
With blood removed but little from her own?
Where is she? and how doth she? and what says
My concealed lady to our canceled love?

Nurse. O, she says nothing, sir, but weeps and weeps;
100 And now falls on her bed, and then starts up,
And Tybalt calls; and then on Romeo cries,
And then down falls again.

Romeo.   As if that name,
Shot from the deadly level of a gun,
Did murder her; as that name's cursed hand
105 Murdered her kinsman. O tell me, friar, tell me,
In what vile part of this anatomy
Doth my name lodge? Tell me, that I may sack
The hateful mansion.

[*draws his dagger*]

84–85 he is even...her case: He is acting the same way that Juliet is.

90 into so deep an O: into such deep grief.

96 blood...from her own: the blood of a close relative of hers.

98 concealed lady: secret bride.

102 that name: the name Romeo.

106–108 in what vile part...mansion: Romeo asks where in his body (**anatomy**) his name can be found so that he can cut the name out. *What is Romeo about to do?*

FOR ENGLISH LEARNERS
Task Support Point out the question in the marginal note for lines 106–108. Have students reread that note, reread lines 106–108, and then read the stage direction that follows line 108 *(draws his dagger)*. **Possible answer:** *Romeo is about to stab himself with his dagger.*

FOR ADVANCED LEARNERS/PRE–AP
Evaluate Meter [paired-activity option] Remind students that in previous scenes, the nurse's speeches have been written in prose. In lines 84–90, however, she speaks in blank verse. Have students evaluate her lines and share their ideas about (1) why Shakespeare might have changed her speech pattern and (2) whether Shakespeare is being inconsistent in portraying her character.

BACKGROUND
Guns Romeo's statement that the mention of his name to Juliet was like a "Shot from the deadly level of a gun" (line 103) alludes to technological advances in firearms made around the time of the play's production. The "hand gonne," used in the 15th century, resembled a small cannon and was difficult and dangerous to use. By the 1570s, however, smaller muskets such as the snaphaunce used a trigger to strike a flint against a metal surface, igniting a spark, lighting the gunpowder, and firing the projectile, thereby assuring a deadlier aim. While firearms are never used in *Romeo and Juliet,* they are referred to as a figurative way of describing the explosive nature of passions and emotions (see line 132).

REINFORCE *KEY IDEA:* LOVE AND HATE

Discuss According to Friar Laurence, why should Romeo's marriage—his commitment to a lifelong **love**—prevent him from killing himself? *Possible answer: By taking marriage vows, Romeo has promised to cherish his love for Juliet. Friar Laurence argues that Romeo should not kill that love through suicide. If he kills himself, the friar says, he will also destroy the thing for which he cares the most.*

Friar Laurence.   Hold thy desperate hand.
    Art thou a man? Thy form cries out thou art;
110 Thy tears are womanish, thy wild acts denote
    The unreasonable fury of a beast.
    Unseemly woman in a seeming man!
    Or ill-beseeming beast in seeming both!
    Thou hast amazed me. By my holy order,
115 I thought thy disposition better tempered.
    Hast thou slain Tybalt? Wilt thou slay thyself?
    And slay thy lady too that lives in thee,
    By doing damned hate upon thyself?
    Why railst thou on thy birth, the heaven, and earth?
120 Since birth and heaven and earth, all three do meet
    In thee at once; which thou at once wouldst lose.
    Fie, fie, thou shamest thy shape, thy love, thy wit,
    Which, like a usurer, aboundst in all,
    And usest none in that true use indeed
125 Which should bedeck thy shape, thy love, thy wit.
    Thy noble shape is but a form of wax,
    Digressing from the valor of a man;
    Thy dear love sworn but hollow perjury,
    Killing that love which thou hast vowed to cherish;
130 Thy wit, that ornament to shape and love,
    Misshapen in the conduct of them both,
    Like powder in a skilless soldier's flask,
    Is set afire by thine own ignorance,
    And thou dismembered with thine own defense.
135 What, rouse thee, man! Thy Juliet is alive,
    For whose dear sake thou wast but lately dead.
    There art thou happy. Tybalt would kill thee,
    But thou slewest Tybalt. There art thou happy.
    The law, that threatened death, becomes thy friend
140 And turns it to exile. There art thou happy.
    A pack of blessings light upon thy back;
    Happiness courts thee in her best array;
    But, like a misbehaved and sullen wench,
    Thou poutst upon thy fortune and thy love.
145 Take heed, take heed, for such die miserable.
    Go get thee to thy love, as was decreed,
    Ascend her chamber, hence and comfort her.
    But look thou stay not till the watch be set,
    For then thou canst not pass to Mantua,
150 Where thou shalt live till we can find a time
    To blaze your marriage, reconcile your friends,
    Beg pardon of the Prince, and call thee back
    With twenty hundred thousand times more joy

108–125 Hold thy . . . bedeck thy shape, thy love, thy wit: You're not acting like a man. Would you send your soul to hell by committing suicide (**doing damned hate upon thyself**)? Why do you curse your birth, heaven, and earth? You are refusing to make good use of your advantages, just as a miser refuses to spend his money.

126–134 The friar explains how by acting as he is, Romeo is misusing his shape (his outer form or body), his love, and his wit (his mind or intellect).

135–140 The friar tells Romeo to count his blessings instead of feeling sorry for himself. He lists the things Romeo has to be thankful for. *What three blessings does the friar mention?*

③ Targeted Passage

148–149 look . . . Mantua: Leave before the guards take their places at the city gates; otherwise you will not be able to escape to Mantua.

151 blaze . . . friends: announce your marriage and get the families (**friends**) to stop feuding.

DIFFERENTIATED INSTRUCTION

FOR LESS–PROFICIENT READERS

③ Targeted Passage [Lines 146–152]

This passage presents Friar Laurence's solution to Romeo's problem.

- According to Friar Laurence's plan, where will Romeo go after seeing Juliet? When will he leave?
- What will Friar Laurence do while Romeo is in Mantua?
- Whose help will the friar seek? Why?

FOR ENGLISH LEARNERS

Task Support Have students read the marginal note and question for lines 135–140. Then point out the repeated "There art thou happy" in lines 135–140. *Possible answer: The three blessings are that Juliet is alive, that Romeo was not killed by Tybalt, and that the prince is only exiling him instead of executing him for killing Tybalt.*

Than thou wentst forth in lamentation.
155 Go before, nurse. Commend me to thy lady,
And bid her hasten all the house to bed,
Which heavy sorrow makes them apt unto.
Romeo is coming.

Nurse. O Lord, I could have stayed here all the night
160 To hear good counsel. O, what learning is!
My lord, I'll tell my lady you will come.

Romeo. Do so, and bid my sweet prepare to chide.

[Nurse *offers to go and turns again.*]

Nurse. Here is a ring she bid me give you, sir.
Hie you, make haste, for it grows very late.

[*Exit.*]

165 **Romeo.** How well my comfort is revived by this!

Friar Laurence. Go hence; good night; and here stands all your
state:
Either be gone before the watch be set,
Or by the break of day disguised from hence.
Sojourn in Mantua. I'll find out your man,
170 And he shall signify from time to time
Every good hap to you that chances here.
Give me thy hand. 'Tis late. Farewell; good night.

Romeo. But that a joy past joy calls out on me,
It were a grief so brief to part with thee.
175 Farewell. ❶

[*Exeunt.*]

SCENE 4 *Capulet's house.*
In this scene, Paris visits the Capulets, who are mourning the death of Tybalt.
He says he realizes that this is no time to talk of marriage. Capulet, however,
disagrees; he decides that Juliet should marry Paris on Thursday, three days
away. He tells Lady Capulet to inform Juliet immediately.

[*Enter* Capulet, Lady Capulet, *and* Paris.]

Capulet. Things have fall'n out, sir, so unluckily
That we have had no time to move our daughter.
Look you, she loved her kinsman Tybalt dearly,
And so did I. Well, we were born to die.
5 'Tis very late; she'll not come down tonight.

162 bid . . . chide: Tell Juliet to get ready to scold me for the way I've behaved.

166–171 and here . . . here: This is what your fate depends on: either leave before the night watchmen go on duty, or get out at dawn in a disguise. Stay awhile in Mantua. I'll find your servant and send messages to you about what good things are happening here.

❶ **TRAGEDY**
Despite Romeo and Juliet's anguish, their problem at this point seems solvable. **Summarize** the plan that has been made to resolve their dilemma.

1–2 Things have . . . our daughter: Such terrible things have happened that we haven't had time to persuade (**move**) Juliet to think about your marriage proposal.

ROMEO AND JULIET: ACT THREE, SCENE 4 **1007**

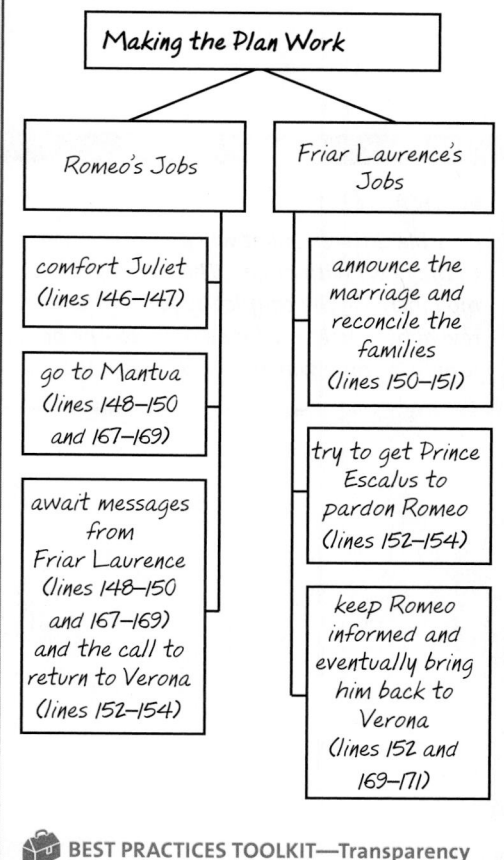

Lines 12–14
REINFORCE *KEY IDEA:* LOVE AND HATE

Discuss How does Capulet understand the role of **love** when he offers Juliet in marriage to Count Paris? *Possible answer: Capulet assumes that Juliet's love is something he is free to offer to whomever he wishes. What seems more important is obedience. Capulet has every confidence that Juliet will "be ruled" (line 13) by him and agree to the marriage.*

❶ TRAGEDY

Possible answer: Juliet will probably react to the news with anger. This turn of events may increase the conflict by forcing Juliet to reveal her secret marriage or to escape her family in some way to avoid marrying Paris.

I promise you, but for your company,
I would have been abed an hour ago.

   Paris. These times of woe afford no time to woo.
Madam, good night. Commend me to your daughter.

10 **Lady Capulet.** I will, and know her mind early tomorrow;
Tonight she's mewed up to her heaviness.

   [Paris *offers to go and* Capulet *calls him again.*]

   Capulet. Sir Paris, I will make a desperate tender
Of my child's love. I think she will be ruled
In all respects by me; nay more, I doubt it not.

15 Wife, go you to her ere you go to bed;
Acquaint her here of my son Paris' love
And bid her (mark you me?) on Wednesday next—
But, soft! what day is this?

   Paris.   Monday, my lord.

   Capulet. Monday! ha, ha! Well, Wednesday is too soon.

20 A Thursday let it be—a Thursday, tell her,
She shall be married to this noble earl.
Will you be ready? Do you like this haste?
We'll keep no great ado—a friend or two;
For hark you, Tybalt being slain so late,

25 It may be thought we held him carelessly,
Being our kinsman, if we revel much.
Therefore we'll have some half a dozen friends,
And there an end. But what say you to Thursday?

   Paris. My lord, I would that Thursday were tomorrow.

30 **Capulet.** Well, get you gone. A Thursday be it then. ❶
Go you to Juliet ere you go to bed;
Prepare her, wife, against this wedding day.
Farewell, my lord.—Light to my chamber, ho!
Afore me, it is so very very late

35 That we may call it early by-and-by.
Good night.

   [*Exeunt.*]

8 Sad times are not good times for talking of marriage.

11 Tonight she is locked up with her sorrow. *What do Juliet's parents think is causing this sorrow?*

12 desperate tender: bold offer.

16 Capulet is so sure that Juliet will accept Paris that he calls Paris "son" already.

23 no great ado: no big festivity.

❶ **TRAGEDY**
Predict how Juliet will react to the news that her parents have promised her to Paris. How might this turn of events add to the play's mounting **conflict**?

34–35 it is . . . by-and-by: It's so late at night that soon we'll be calling it early in the morning.

DIFFERENTIATED INSTRUCTION

FOR ENGLISH LEARNERS

Task Support Draw students' attention to the question in the marginal note about line 11. Ask students to review Juliet's emotional speeches in Scene 2. *Possible answer: Juliet's parents think that Juliet's sorrow is due to Tybalt's death.*

FOR ENGLISH LEARNERS

Vocabulary: Outdated Forms Discuss these examples of Shakespearean terms that have passed from use:

- *abed* (line 7), "in bed"
- *ere* (line 15), "before" (at an earlier time)
- *mark you* (line 17), "pay attention [to]"
- *we held him carelessly* (line 25), "we cared little about him"
- *get you gone* (line 30), "leave"
- *afore* (line 34), "before" (in front of)

Behind the Curtain

The Clarence Brown Theatre's 2003 production

The Seattle Repertory Theatre's 2003 production

The Bolshoi Ballet's 2004 production

Stage Combat

A character's movements can convey as much as his or her words. In fight scenes, **blocking** is used to decide exactly how the actors will move. From a stylistic point of view, how are the movements captured in these photographs different? Which fight looks most realistic, and why?

BEHIND THE CURTAIN

Possible answer: From a stylistic point of view, the movements in the Seattle Repertory Theatre's production appear fierce. In contrast, the movements in the Clarence Brown Theatre's production are more disciplined. The movements in the Bolshoi Ballet's production seem carefully choreographed and elegant. The most realistic fight is in the photograph from the Seattle Repertory Theatre because the movements are the most aggressive and the actors' faces portray the most emotion.

Stage Combat The object of stage combat is to portray physical fighting among characters. It can be difficult to stage fights effectively, because the audience realizes that the actors will not really be hurt and therefore will not be easily convinced by the fight. For this reason, some productions, such as that of the Bolshoi Ballet, stage the combat without fierce aggression, allowing the audience to imagine the ferocity of the fight. In the other two images, the scene has been blocked to create excitement and tension, yet with few characters on the stage, to ensure the actors' safety.

FOR ADVANCED LEARNERS/PRE–AP

Research Stage Combat [small-group option]
Have students research and prepare an oral presentation about creating realistic stage combat. Topics might include information on props such as trick daggers or swords made of blunted plastic, theatrical punches and tumbles, choreographing movement, and schools that teach classes in stage combat.

Lines 17–25
REINFORCE *KEY IDEA:*
LOVE AND HATE

Discuss Think about the proverb *Love is blind.* How does Romeo's **love** blind him and put him in danger? *Possible answer: Romeo is "blinded" by love in the sense that he is willing to be captured and killed if staying means pleasing Juliet.*

SCENE 5   *Capulet's orchard.*

Romeo and Juliet have spent the night together, but before daylight, Romeo leaves for Mantua. As soon as he leaves, Lady Capulet comes in to tell Juliet of her father's decision—that she will marry Count Paris on Thursday. Juliet is very upset and refuses to go along with the plan. Juliet's father goes into a rage at her disobedience and tells her that she will marry Paris or he will disown her.

The nurse advises Juliet to wed Paris, since her marriage to Romeo is over and Paris is a better man anyway. Juliet, now angry with the nurse, decides to go to Friar Laurence for help.

[*Enter* Romeo *and* Juliet *above, at the window.*]

Juliet. Wilt thou be gone? It is not yet near day.
It was the nightingale, and not the lark,
That pierced the fearful hollow of thine ear.
Nightly she sings on yond pomegranate tree.
5 Believe me, love, it was the nightingale.

Romeo. It was the lark, the herald of the morn;
No nightingale. Look, love, what envious streaks
Do lace the severing clouds in yonder East.
Night's candles are burnt out, and jocund day
10 Stands tiptoe on the misty mountain tops.
I must be gone and live, or stay and die.

Juliet. Yond light is not daylight; I know it, I.
It is some meteor that the sun exhales
To be to thee this night a torchbearer
15 And light thee on thy way to Mantua.
Therefore stay yet; thou needst not to be gone.

Romeo. Let me be ta'en, let me be put to death.
I am content, so thou wilt have it so.
I'll say yon grey is not the morning's eye,
20 'Tis but the pale reflex of Cynthia's brow;
Nor that is not the lark whose notes do beat
The vaulty heaven so high above our heads.
I have more care to stay than will to go.
Come, death, and welcome! Juliet wills it so.
25 How is't, my soul? Let's talk; it is not day.

Juliet. It is, it is! Hie hence, be gone, away!
It is the lark that sings so out of tune,
Straining harsh discords and unpleasing sharps.
Some say the lark makes sweet division;
30 This doth not so, for she divideth us.
Some say the lark and loathed toad changed eyes;
O, now I would they had changed voices too,

2 It was...lark: The nightingale sings at night; the lark sings in the morning. *What is Juliet trying to get Romeo to believe?*

9 night's candles: stars.

12–25 Juliet continues to pretend it is night to keep Romeo from leaving. Romeo gives in and says he'll stay if Juliet wishes it, even if staying means death.

20 reflex of Cynthia's brow: reflection of the moon. Cynthia is another name for Diana, the Roman goddess of the moon. She was often pictured with a crescent moon on her forehead.

26 Romeo's mention of death frightens Juliet, and she urges him to leave quickly.

29 division: melody.

31–34 I wish the lark had the voice of the hated (**loathed**) toad, since its voice is frightening us apart and acting as a morning song for hunters (**hunt's-up**).

1010   UNIT 10: SHAKESPEAREAN DRAMA

DIFFERENTIATED INSTRUCTION

FOR LESS–PROFICIENT READERS

Preview Have students read the italicized scene synopsis aloud. Then have them fill in a Cluster Diagram in which they note the opinion that each character takes as it relates to Juliet's future.

 BEST PRACTICES TOOLKIT—Transparency
Cluster Diagram p. B18

Nurse: Juliet should give up on Romeo and marry Paris.

Lady Capulet: Juliet must marry Paris.

Juliet's Future

Capulet: Juliet must marry Paris or be disowned.

Juliet: I refuse to marry Paris. I'll ask Friar Laurence for help.

FOR ENGLISH LEARNERS

Task Support As students read the marginal note and question about line 2, remind them that Romeo and Juliet have just spent their wedding night together. *Possible answer: Juliet is trying to get Romeo to believe that it is still night and, therefore, that he does not have to leave her yet.*

Since arm from arm that voice doth us affray,
Hunting thee hence with hunt's-up to the day!
35 O, now be gone! More light and light it grows.

Romeo. More light and light—more dark and dark our woes!

[*Enter* Nurse, *hastily.*]

Nurse. Madam!

Juliet. Nurse?

Nurse. Your lady mother is coming to your chamber.
40 The day is broke; be wary, look about.

[*Exit.*]

Juliet. Then, window, let day in, and let life out.

Romeo. Farewell, farewell! One kiss, and I'll descend.

[*He starts down the ladder.*]

Juliet. Art thou gone so, my lord, my love, my friend?
I must hear from thee every day in the hour,
45 For in a minute there are many days.
O, by this count I shall be much in years
Ere I again behold my Romeo!

Romeo. Farewell!
I will omit no opportunity
50 That may convey my greetings, love, to thee.

Juliet. O, thinkst thou we shall ever meet again?

Romeo. I doubt it not; and all these woes shall serve
For sweet discourses in our time to come.

Juliet. O God, I have an ill-divining soul!
55 Methinks I see thee, now thou art below,
As one dead in the bottom of a tomb.
Either my eyesight fails, or thou lookst pale.

Romeo. And trust me, love, in my eye so do you.
Dry sorrow drinks our blood. Adieu! adieu!

[*Exit.*]

60 **Juliet.** O Fortune, Fortune! all men call thee fickle.
If thou art fickle, what dost thou with him
That is renowned for faith? Be fickle, Fortune,
For then I hope thou wilt not keep him long
But send him back.

Lady Capulet [*within*]. Ho, daughter! are you up?

65 **Juliet.** Who is't that calls? It is my lady mother.
Is she not down so late, or up so early?
What unaccustomed cause procures her hither?

46 **much in years:** very old.

54–56 **I have ... tomb:** Juliet sees an evil vision of the future. *What is her vision?*

59 **Dry ... blood:** People believed that sorrow drained the blood from the heart, causing a sad person to look pale.

60–62 **fickle:** changeable in loyalty or affection. Juliet asks fickle Fortune why it has anything to do with Romeo, who is the opposite of fickle.

67 **What ... hither:** What unusual reason brings her here?

BACKGROUND

Fickle Fortune When Juliet speaks of "Fortune" (lines 60–62), she is not referring to wealth. Instead, she is appealing to a personified cosmic force that greatly influenced Elizabethan thinking. Although Elizabethans believed that God had ordered the universe, they also believed that God used Fortune to raise and lower (as if on a wheel) the circumstances of individuals. In this speech, Juliet recognizes the role of Fortune in bringing her and Romeo into difficulty. She then prays that Fortune will soon raise their circumstances and grant them a happy outcome.

FOR ENGLISH LEARNERS

Task Support Point out the question in the marginal note for lines 54–56. Call on a volunteer to read lines 54–56 aloud, then have students focus on line 56. *Possible answer: Juliet's vision is of Romeo as a corpse in a tomb.*

REINFORCE *KEY IDEA:* LOVE AND HATE

Discuss How can Juliet's words to her mother be words of **hate** and words of **love** at the same time? Cite evidence. *Possible answer: Juliet's words, carefully chosen, sound to her mother like words of hatred toward Romeo. We, the audience, know more about the situation than Lady Capulet does, however. We realize that Juliet is voicing the desires of her heart—namely, that she wishes that she could touch Romeo (lines 85–86), that she could see him (line 94), that she could go to him (lines 99–100), and that she could give him her love (line 101–102).*

[*Enter* Lady Capulet.]

Lady Capulet. Why, how now, Juliet?

Juliet.   Madam, I am not well.

Lady Capulet. Evermore weeping for your cousin's death?
70 What, wilt thou wash him from his grave with tears?
An if thou couldst, thou couldst not make him live.
Therefore have done. Some grief shows much of love;
But much of grief shows still some want of wit.

Juliet. Yet let me weep for such a feeling loss.

75 **Lady Capulet.** So shall you feel the loss, but not the friend
Which you weep for.

Juliet.   Feeling so the loss,
I cannot choose but ever weep the friend.

Lady Capulet. Well, girl, thou weepst not so much for his death
As that the villain lives which slaughtered him.

80 **Juliet.** What villain, madam?

Lady Capulet.   That same villain Romeo.

Juliet [*aside*]. Villain and he be many miles asunder.—
God pardon him! I do, with all my heart;
And yet no man like he doth grieve my heart.

Lady Capulet. That is because the traitor murderer lives.

85 **Juliet.** Ay, madam, from the reach of these my hands.
Would none but I might venge my cousin's death!

Lady Capulet. We will have vengeance for it, fear thou not.
Then weep no more. I'll send to one in Mantua,
Where that same banished runagate doth live,
90 Shall give him such an unaccustomed dram
That he shall soon keep Tybalt company;
And then I hope thou wilt be satisfied.

Juliet. Indeed I never shall be satisfied
With Romeo till I behold him—dead—
95 Is my poor heart so for a kinsman vexed.
Madam, if you could find out but a man
To bear a poison, I would temper it;
That Romeo should, upon receipt thereof,
Soon sleep in quiet. O, how my heart abhors
100 To hear him named and cannot come to him,
To wreak the love I bore my cousin Tybalt
Upon his body that hath slaughtered him!

Lady Capulet. Find thou the means, and I'll find such a man.
But now I'll tell thee joyful tidings, girl.

69–70 *What does Lady Capulet think Juliet is crying about?*

72–73 have . . . wit: Stop crying (**have done**). A little grief is evidence of love, while too much grief shows a lack of good sense (**want of wit**).

81–102 In these lines Juliet's words have double meanings. To avoid lying to her mother, she chooses her words carefully. They can mean what her mother wants to hear—or what Juliet really has on her mind.

89 runagate: runaway.

90 unaccustomed dram: poison.

93–102 Dead could refer either to Romeo or to Juliet's heart. Juliet says that if her mother could find someone to carry a poison to Romeo, she would mix (**temper**) it herself.

DIFFERENTIATED INSTRUCTION

FOR LESS–PROFICIENT READERS

Paraphrasing Shakespeare Have students paraphrase Juliet's aside in lines 81–83, which reveals her real emotions. *Possible answer: Romeo is far from being a villain. May God forgive him, as I do with all my heart. Still, no man makes me more unhappy (by being away from me).* Then ask students to paraphrase Lady Capulet's words in lines 88–91. Elicit that she plans to send an assassin to Mantua to poison Romeo.

FOR ENGLISH LEARNERS

Task Support As students read the marginal question about lines 69–70, point out that this is the first time that Lady Capulet has spoken to Juliet since Juliet learned of Tybalt's death, from the nurse, in Scene 2. *Possible answer: Lady Capulet thinks that Juliet is crying about the death of Tybalt, her cousin.*

105 **Juliet.** And joy comes well in such a needy time.
What are they, I beseech your ladyship?

Lady Capulet. Well, well, thou hast a careful father, child;
One who, to put thee from thy heaviness,
Hath sorted out a sudden day of joy
110 That thou expects not nor I looked not for.

Juliet. Madam, in happy time! What day is that?

Lady Capulet. Marry, my child, early next Thursday morn
The gallant, young, and noble gentleman,
The County Paris, at Saint Peter's Church,
115 Shall happily make thee there a joyful bride.

Juliet. Now by Saint Peter's Church, and Peter too,
He shall not make me there a joyful bride!
I wonder at this haste, that I must wed
Ere he that should be husband comes to woo.
120 I pray you tell my lord and father, madam,
I will not marry yet; and when I do, I swear
It shall be Romeo, whom you know I hate,
Rather than Paris. These are news indeed!

Lady Capulet. Here comes your father. Tell him so yourself,
125 And see how he will take it at your hands.

[*Enter* Capulet *and* Nurse.]

Capulet. When the sun sets the air doth drizzle dew,
But for the sunset of my brother's son
It rains downright.
How now? a conduit, girl? What, still in tears?
130 Evermore show'ring? In one little body
Thou counterfeitst a bark, a sea, a wind:
For still thy eyes, which I may call the sea,
Do ebb and flow with tears; the bark thy body is,
Sailing in this salt flood; the winds, thy sighs,
135 Who, raging with thy tears and they with them,
Without a sudden calm will overset
Thy tempest-tossed body. How now, wife?
Have you delivered to her our decree?

Lady Capulet. Ay, sir; but she will none, she gives you thanks.
140 I would the fool were married to her grave!

Capulet. Soft! take me with you, take me with you, wife.
How? Will she none? Doth she not give us thanks?
Is she not proud? Doth she not count her blest,
Unworthy as she is, that we have wrought
145 So worthy a gentleman to be her bridegroom?

121–123 Juliet mentions Romeo to show her mother how strongly opposed she is to marrying Paris, yet what she really means is that she loves Romeo.

127 the sunset . . . son: the death of Tybalt.

129–137 conduit: fountain. Capulet compares Juliet to a boat (**bark**), an ocean, and the wind because of her excessive crying.

141 take me with you: let me understand you.

REINFORCE KEY IDEA: LOVE AND HATE

Discuss What has Juliet done to cause her father's anger? Is Capulet's **hate** well founded? *Possible answer:* Juliet has caused her father's anger by rejecting his choice for her husband. His disappointment or confusion might be well founded, for choosing a husband for her is part of his traditional role as her father. His hatred, however, goes too far, and it is a dramatic change from his loving, doting demeanor seen earlier in the play. Capulet's anger seems to be founded on the realization that Juliet refuses to be ruled by him. Capulet does not realize that Juliet's response does not express a rejection of his authority as much as it expresses fear of her own unhappiness and betrayal of her secret marriage.

Juliet. Not proud you have, but thankful that you have.
Proud can I never be of what I hate,
But thankful even for hate that is meant love.

   Capulet. How, how, how, how, choplogic? What is this?
150 "Proud"—and "I thank you"—and "I thank you not"—
And yet "not proud"? Mistress minion you,
Thank me no thankings, nor proud me no prouds,
But fettle your fine joints 'gainst Thursday next
To go with Paris to Saint Peter's Church,
155 Or I will drag thee on a hurdle thither.
Out, you green-sickness carrion! out, you baggage!
You tallow-face!

   Lady Capulet. Fie, fie; what, are you mad?

   Juliet. Good father, I beseech you on my knees,

[She kneels down.]

Hear me with patience but to speak a word.

160   **Capulet.** Hang thee, young baggage! disobedient wretch!
I tell thee what—get thee to church a Thursday
Or never after look me in the face.
Speak not, reply not, do not answer me!
My fingers itch. Wife, we scarce thought us blest
165 That God had lent us but this only child;
But now I see this one is one too much,
And that we have a curse in having her.
Out on her, hilding!

   Nurse.   God in heaven bless her!
You are to blame, my lord, to rate her so.

170   **Capulet.** And why, my Lady Wisdom? Hold your tongue,
Good Prudence. Smatter with your gossips, go!

   Nurse. I speak no treason.

   Capulet.   O, God-i-god-en!

   Nurse. May not one speak?

   Capulet.   Peace, you mumbling fool!
Utter your gravity o'er a gossip's bowl,
175 For here we need it not.

   Lady Capulet.   You are too hot.

   Capulet. God's bread! it makes me mad. Day, night, late, early,
At home, abroad, alone, in company,
Waking or sleeping, still my care hath been
To have her matched; and having now provided
180 A gentleman of princely parentage,

146–148 Not proud . . . meant love: I'm not pleased, but I am grateful for your intentions.

149–157 In his rage, Capulet calls Juliet a person who argues unnecessarily over fine points (**choplogic**) and says she is a spoiled child (**minion**). He tells her to prepare herself (**fettle your fine joints**) for the wedding or he'll haul her there in a cart for criminals (**hurdle**). He calls her an anemic piece of dead flesh (**green-sickness carrion**) and a coward (**tallow-face**).

164 My fingers itch: I feel like hitting you.

168 hilding: a good-for-nothing person.

171 smatter: chatter.

174 Utter . . . bowl: Save your words of wisdom for a gathering of gossips.

179 matched: married.

DIFFERENTIATED INSTRUCTION

FOR LESS–PROFICIENT READERS

Explore Character Students may be surprised to hear Lady Capulet's cruel statement, "I have done with thee" (line 204). Guide students through her earlier statements (lines 124–125, 139–140, 157, and 175). Discuss how she goes from frustration with Juliet's stubbornness to attempts to calm her husband to a realization that she cannot support both Juliet and her husband, and finally, a decision to stand by her husband.

FOR ENGLISH LEARNERS

Concept Support Have students reread the nurse's words and Capulet's reaction to them. Point out that although the nurse has been part of the Capulet household since Juliet was a baby, if not longer, she is still a household servant. Capulet does not hesitate to insult her when she rises to Juliet's defense and speaks to him as an equal.

Of fair demesnes, youthful, and nobly trained,
Stuffed, as they say, with honorable parts,
Proportioned as one's thought would wish a man—
And then to have a wretched puling fool,
185 A whining mammet, in her fortunes tender,
To answer "I'll not wed, I cannot love;
I am too young, I pray you pardon me"!
But, an you will not wed, I'll pardon you.
Graze where you will, you shall not house with me.
190 Look to't, think on't; I do not use to jest.
Thursday is near; lay hand on heart, advise:
An you be mine, I'll give you to my friend;
An you be not, hang, beg, starve, die in the streets,
For, by my soul, I'll ne'er acknowledge thee,
195 Nor what is mine shall never do thee good.
Trust to't. Bethink you. I'll not be forsworn.
[*Exit.*]

Juliet. Is there no pity sitting in the clouds
That sees into the bottom of my grief?
O sweet my mother, cast me not away!
200 Delay this marriage for a month, a week;
Or if you do not, make the bridal bed
In that dim monument where Tybalt lies.

Lady Capulet. Talk not to me, for I'll not speak a word.
Do as thou wilt, for I have done with thee.
[*Exit.*]

205 **Juliet.** O God!—O nurse, how shall this be prevented?
My husband is on earth, my faith in heaven.
How shall that faith return again to earth
Unless that husband send it me from heaven
By leaving earth? Comfort me, counsel me.
210 Alack, alack, that heaven should practice stratagems
Upon so soft a subject as myself!
What sayst thou? Hast thou not a word of joy?
Some comfort, nurse.

Nurse.   Faith, here it is.
Romeo is banish'd; and all the world to nothing
215 That he dares ne'er come back to challenge you;
Or if he do, it needs must be by stealth.
Then, since the case so stands as now it doth,
I think it best you married with the County.
O, he's a lovely gentleman!
220 Romeo's a dishclout to him. An eagle, madam,

184 **puling:** crying.
185 **mammet:** doll.

189–195 Capulet swears that he'll kick Juliet out and cut her off financially if she refuses to marry.

196 **I'll not be forsworn:** I will not break my promise to Paris.

207–211 Juliet is worried about the sin of being married to two men. She asks how heaven can play such tricks (**practice stratagems**) on her.

213–222 The nurse gives Juliet advice. She says that since Romeo is banished, he's no good to her; Juliet should marry Paris. Romeo is a dishcloth (**dishclout**) compared to Paris.

④ **Targeted Passage**

Lines 176–196
DISCUSSION PROMPTS
Use these prompts to discuss Capulet's harsh words to his daughter:

Recall What good qualities about Paris does Capulet name? *Possible answer: Paris is of a good family (line 180), owns good land ("fair demesnes," line 181), and is handsome, young, and well educated (lines 181–183).*

Analyze How do you think Juliet feels when her father demands that she marry Paris? *Students may suggest that Juliet feels desperate and powerless against her father's demand.*

Synthesize Paris is a kinsman of Prince Escalus. What effect might that relationship have upon Capulet's anger toward Juliet? *Possible answer: By marrying Juliet to Paris, Capulet may feel that he will gain favor with the prince, especially when it comes to the feud with the Montagues. If this is indeed his plan, he is probably furious that Juliet is thwarting it by refusing to marry Paris.*

BACKGROUND

Bigamy Juliet's nurse counsels her to marry Count Paris, even though she is legally married to Romeo. Elizabethan England frowned upon divorce. Many people in unhappy marriages, especially those who were, like the nurse, among the poorer classes, abandoned their spouses and married again. Notice that the nurse urges Juliet to consider Romeo ("your first") dead (line 225). Fraudulent claims of death were common when justifying remarriage.

FOR LESS–PROFICIENT READERS
④ **Targeted Passage [Lines 213–219]**

In this passage, the nurse begins her attempt to change Juliet's mind.

- According to the nurse, what is the status of Juliet's marriage with Romeo?

- What specific action does the nurse suggest that Juliet take?

- What is the nurse's opinion of Paris?

Inverted Word Order Remind students that Shakespeare sometimes inverts word order to maintain poetic meter. Point out line 199, in which Juliet pleads with her mother. As written, the line is an example of iambic pentameter. Have students reorder the words so that the line sounds more natural. *Possible answer: O my sweet mother, [do] not cast me away!* Point out that the new line does not follow the poetic meter.

Hath not so green, so quick, so fair an eye
As Paris. Beshrew my very heart,
I think you are happy in this second match,
For it excels your first; or if it did not,
225 Your first is dead—or 'twere as good he were
As living here and you no use of him.

Juliet. Speakst thou this from thy heart?

Nurse. And from my soul too; else beshrew them both.

Juliet. Amen!

230 **Nurse.** What?

Juliet. Well, thou hast comforted me marvelous much.
Go in; and tell my lady I am gone,
Having displeased my father, to Laurence' cell,
To make confession and to be absolved.

235 **Nurse.** Marry, I will; and this is wisely done.

[*Exit.*]

Juliet. Ancient damnation! O most wicked fiend!
Is it more sin to wish me thus forsworn,
Or to dispraise my lord with that same tongue
Which she hath praised him with above compare
240 So many thousand times? Go, counselor!
Thou and my bosom henceforth shall be twain. **Ⓚ**
I'll to the friar to know his remedy.
If all else fail, myself have power to die.

[*Exit.*]

222 beshrew: curse.

223–225 This new marriage will be better than the first, which is as good as over.

229 Amen: I agree—that is, curse your heart and soul.

236–238 ancient damnation: old devil; **dispraise:** criticize.

241 Thou . . . twain: I'll no longer tell you my secrets.

Ⓚ CHARACTER
How has Juliet's relationship with the nurse changed? Citing details from their **interactions,** explain the main reason for the change.

LITERARY ANALYSIS

Ⓚ CHARACTER

Possible answer: Juliet now views the nurse as an adversary instead of a close confidant. The change occurred after lines 214–226, when the nurse supported Juliet's parents' demand that she marry Paris and gave Juliet a detailed argument about the superiority of Paris over Romeo.

ACT THREE WRAP–UP

SYNTHESIZE Ask students to think of reasons that all of the characters in contact with Juliet have turned on her, including her mother, father, and nurse. Encourage students to cite details that explain the motivation of the characters.

★ **CRITIQUE** Ask students to re-examine their feelings about the characters of Romeo and Juliet. Have their feelings changed, either positively or negatively, toward either one? If so, have students explain why.

DIFFERENTIATED INSTRUCTION

FOR ADVANCED LEARNERS/PRE–AP

Synthesize a Solution Have students reread the nurse's solution to Juliet's problem. Then ask them to consider how they might have advised Juliet if they had been in the nurse's place. Have students write the speech that they would have given to Juliet, with a clear solution and reasonable supporting arguments; then invite students to compare their speeches in small groups.

Comprehension

1. **Recall** How is Romeo accidentally responsible for Mercutio's death?

2. **Recall** Why does Prince Escalus banish Romeo from Verona?

3. **Recall** What promise does Lord Capulet make to Paris?

4. **Clarify** Why does Lord Capulet become so enraged with Juliet?

Literary Analysis

5. **Reading Shakespearean Drama** Review your list detailing the events in Act Three. What event in this act causes the most problems for Romeo and Juliet? Cite evidence to support your answer.

6. **Analyze Character Motivation** What is Romeo's motivation for killing Tybalt? What are the consequences of this action? Citing evidence, explain whether you think Romeo's behavior is justified revenge or a disastrous mistake.

7. **Interpret Allusions** Find two allusions in Act Three, and record them in a chart like the one shown. Complete the chart by describing what each allusion is a reference to and explaining what each means.

Scene and Lines	Allusion	Meaning
Scene 1, lines 70–72	**Mercutio.** . . . Tybalt, you ratcatcher, will you walk? **Tybalt.** What wouldst thou have with me? **Mercutio.** Good King of Cats, nothing but one of your nine lives.	In Act Two, Scene 4, there was an allusion to a cat named Tybalt in a common story of the time. Mercutio alludes to this story again here to taunt Tybalt and make him want to fight.

8. **Evaluate Characters** Compare and contrast the behaviors of the nurse and Friar Laurence in Act Three. On the basis of their actions and interactions with other characters, which of the two would you trust more if you were Romeo or Juliet? Explain, citing evidence from the play.

Literary Criticism

9. **Philosophical Context** In the first three acts of *Romeo and Juliet,* both the Chorus and the characters make frequent references to the role of fate in life. How does this notion of fate differ from contemporary views? Do people still think this way today? Explain your answer.

ROMEO AND JULIET: ACT THREE **1017**

7. *Scene and Lines: Scene 5, line 20; **Allusion:** Romeo—'Tis but the pale reflex of Cynthia's brow; **Meaning:** "Cynthia" is the Roman goddess of the moon. The distancing effect of the allusion anticipates the lovers' separation. **Scene and Lines:** Scene 5, lines 60–64; **Allusion:** Juliet—O Fortune, Fortune! . . . send him back; **Meaning:** Fortune was believed to be fickle. Playing on this word, which means "liable to change affections," and on the image of Fortune as a woman who has taken her love, Juliet expresses hope that Fortune will soon tire of Romeo and return him to her.*

8. *Friar Laurence does not waver in his views, but the nurse is easily manipulated. Students may choose Friar Laurence as the more trustworthy confidant because he seems to have more integrity.*

Literary Criticism

9. *Students may suggest that most people today have a different view: they believe that they can shape their "fate" through hard work, honesty, and proper behavior.*

Practice and Apply

After Reading

For additional support of post-reading questions, use these copy masters:

R RESOURCE MANAGER—Copy Masters

Reading Check p. 63 (to check understanding of the selection)

Shakespearean Drama p. 59 (for practice of literary analysis standards focus)

Question Support p. 64 (After Reading questions adapted for English learners and less-proficient readers)

For additional questions, see page 55.

ANSWERS

Comprehension

1. *When Romeo comes between Mercutio and Tybalt, trying to stop the fight, Tybalt is able to fatally wound Mercutio.*

2. *as punishment for killing Tybalt*

3. *that Juliet will marry Paris on Thursday*

4. *Juliet refuses to marry Paris.*

Literary Analysis

Possible answers:

5. ■ **STANDARDS FOCUS** *Reading Shakespearean Drama Romeo's slaying of Tybalt is the most problematic event, for it sends Romeo into exile.*

6. *Romeo's motivation is his desire to avenge Mercutio's death. The consequences are Romeo's banishment and separation from Juliet. Romeo's behavior is a disastrous mistake: had he not sought revenge, the law would have put Tybalt to death, and Romeo would not have been banished.*

Assess and Reteach

Assess

R RESOURCE MANAGER—Copy Masters

Selection Test A pp. 65–66

Selection Test B/C pp. 67–68

📀 Test Generator CD

Reteach

S STANDARDS LESSON FILE

Literature Lessons 25, 26, 35, 38

ROMEO AND JULIET: ACT THREE **1017**

Practice and Apply

Get Into the Act

SUMMARY

Act Four opens with Juliet's plea for Friar Laurence's help. He offers her a drug that will make her appear dead for 42 hours, after which Romeo will take her to Mantua. Juliet returns home and apologizes to her father; delighted, he advances the wedding date. Juliet drinks the drug that night and is discovered the next morning, apparently dead. Despite some comic relief, Act Four ends with lamentation.

Resources for Act Four

Act Four

SCENE 1 *Friar Laurence's cell.*

When Juliet arrives at Friar Laurence's cell, she is upset to find Paris there making arrangements for their wedding. When Paris leaves, the panicked Juliet tells the friar that if he has no solution to her problem, she will kill herself. The friar explains his plan. Juliet will drink a potion he has made from his herbs, which will put her in a deathlike coma. When she wakes up two days later in the family tomb, Romeo will be waiting for her, and they will escape to Mantua together.

[*Enter* Friar Laurence *and* Paris.]

Friar Laurence. On Thursday, sir? The time is very short.

Paris. My father Capulet will have it so,
And I am nothing slow to slack his haste.

Friar Laurence. You say you do not know the lady's mind.

5 Uneven is the course; I like it not.

Paris. Immoderately she weeps for Tybalt's death,
And therefore have I little talked of love;
For Venus smiles not in a house of tears.
Now, sir, her father counts it dangerous

10 That she do give her sorrow so much sway,
And in his wisdom hastes our marriage
To stop the inundation of her tears,
Which, too much minded by herself alone,
May be put from her by society.

15 Now do you know the reason of this haste.

Friar Laurence [*aside*]. I would I knew not why it should be
    slowed.—
Look, sir, here comes the lady toward my cell.

[*Enter* Juliet.]

Paris. Happily met, my lady and my wife!

Juliet. That may be, sir, when I may be a wife.

20 **Paris.** That may be must be, love, on Thursday next.

Juliet. What must be shall be.

Friar Laurence.   That's a certain text.

Paris. Come you to make confession to this father?

Juliet. To answer that, I should confess to you.

2–3 My . . . haste: Capulet is eager to have the wedding on Thursday and so am I.

4–5 You . . . course: You don't know how Juliet feels about this. It's a very uncertain (**uneven**) plan.

A CHARACTER
What is the friar's real **motive** for wanting to slow down the wedding preparations?

13–14 which . . . society: which, thought about too much by her in privacy, may be put from her mind if she is forced to be with others. *According to Paris, why does Capulet want Juliet to marry so quickly?*

19–28 Juliet once again chooses her words carefully to avoid lying and to avoid telling her secret.

Friar Laurence mixes a potion in the Royal Shakespeare Company's 1995 production.

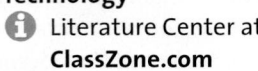

BACKGROUND

Sleeping Potions While the sleeping potion that the friar proposes is never described specifically, Elizabethan audiences might well have surmised that it involved a medicinal plant known as mandragora, or mandrake. As Juliet remarks in lines 47–48 of Scene 3, it was popularly believed that the mandrake screamed when uprooted, and anyone who heard the sound perished or went insane. Popular belief held that mandrake could only be uprooted when pulled by a black dog attached to it by a cord. Once freed from the earth, mandrake was often mixed with opium or hemlock and served as a popular and powerful anesthetic. The friar, being an herbalist, would have had access to all of these ingredients.

ANALYZE VISUALS

Activity What details in the photograph reveal the seriousness of Friar Laurence's business? *Possible answer: The friar's expression shows that he is concentrating. The lighting is dramatic, suggesting an ominous event.*

DIFFERENTIATED INSTRUCTION

For general guidelines on differentiating instruction, see

 BEST PRACTICES TOOLKIT
Differentiated Instruction pp. 31–38

FOR LESS–PROFICIENT READERS
In combination with the *Audio Anthology CD*, use one or more Targeted Passages (pp. 1020, 1023, 1026, 1031) to ensure that students focus on key story events, concepts, and skills.

Preview Have students use a Two-Column Chart to organize the Scene 1 synopsis.

Character	Action
Paris	plans wedding with Juliet
Juliet	threatens suicide and begs the friar for help
Friar	explains plan for reuniting Juliet with Romeo

BEST PRACTICES TOOLKIT—Transparency
Two-Column Chart p. A25

FOR ENGLISH LEARNERS

Task Support Point out the question in the marginal note for lines 13–14. Ask students to remember how Juliet was acting just before Lady Capulet announced the wedding plans in Act Three, Scene 5. *Possible answer: Paris believes that Capulet wants Juliet to marry so that she will be distracted from her grief over Tybalt.*

REINFORCE *KEY IDEA:* LOVE AND HATE

Discuss How does Paris's expression of **love** compare to Romeo's expression of love when he first met Juliet? ***Possible answer:*** *Like Romeo, Paris praises Juliet's beauty (lines 29 and 32). However, unlike Romeo, Paris's expression of love is much less emotional. He does not use poetry or show his complete idolatry of Juliet as Romeo did. Paris also discusses his ownership and control of Juliet, which Romeo did not do.*

Paris. Do not deny to him that you love me.

25 **Juliet.** I will confess to you that I love him.

Paris. So will ye, I am sure, that you love me.

Juliet. If I do so, it will be of more price,
Being spoke behind your back, than to your face.

Paris. Poor soul, thy face is much abused with tears.

30 **Juliet.** The tears have got small victory by that,
For it was bad enough before their spite.

Paris. Thou wrongst it more than tears with that report.

Juliet. That is no slander, sir, which is a truth;
And what I spake, I spake it to my face.

35 **Paris.** Thy face is mine, and thou hast slandered it.

Juliet. It may be so, for it is not mine own.
Are you at leisure, holy father, now,
Or shall I come to you at evening mass?

Friar Laurence. My leisure serves me, pensive daughter, now.
40 My lord, we must entreat the time alone.

Paris. God shield I should disturb devotion!
Juliet, on Thursday early will I rouse ye.
Till then, adieu, and keep this holy kiss.
[Exit.]

Juliet. O, shut the door! and when thou hast done so,
45 Come weep with me—past hope, past cure, past help!

Friar Laurence. Ah, Juliet, I already know thy grief;
It strains me past the compass of my wits.
I hear thou must, and nothing may prorogue it,
On Thursday next be married to this County.

50 **Juliet.** Tell me not, friar, that thou hearst of this,
Unless thou tell me how I may prevent it.
If in thy wisdom thou canst give no help,
Do thou but call my resolution wise
And with this knife I'll help it presently.
55 God joined my heart and Romeo's, thou our hands;
And ere this hand, by thee to Romeo's sealed,
Shall be the label to another deed,
Or my true heart with treacherous revolt
Turn to another, this shall slay them both.

60 Therefore, out of thy long-experienced time,

25 *Whom does "him" refer to in this line?*

30–31 The tears . . . spite: The tears haven't ruined my face; it wasn't all that beautiful before they did their damage.

35 Paris says he owns Juliet's face (since she will soon marry him). Insulting her face, he says, insults him, its owner.

47–48 compass: limit; **prorogue:** postpone.

① Targeted Passage

52–53 If in . . . wise: If you can't find a way to help me, at least agree that my plan is wise.

56–67 And ere this hand . . . of remedy: Before I sign another wedding agreement (**deed**), I will use this knife to kill myself. If you, with your years of experience (**long-experienced time**), can't help me, I'll end my sufferings (**extremes**) and solve the problem myself.

DIFFERENTIATED INSTRUCTION

FOR LESS–PROFICIENT READERS

① Targeted Passage [Lines 50–59]

This passage reveals Juliet's fragile state of mind as she asks for Friar Laurence's help.

- Why is Juliet so upset?

- What help does Juliet want from Friar Laurence?

- What is Juliet prepared to do if Friar Laurence does not help her? How does she want him to feel about her decision?

FOR ENGLISH LEARNERS

Task Support Direct students to the marginal question about line 25. Help students understand the scene by having two students read lines 22–28 aloud. Remind students that Juliet is choosing her words carefully so that she can speak the truth without giving away her secret. ***Possible answer:*** *Juliet uses "him" to refer to Romeo, but Paris thinks that "him" refers to Friar Laurence.*

Give me some present counsel; or, behold,
'Twixt my extremes and me this bloody knife
Shall play the umpire, arbitrating that
Which the commission of thy years and art
65 Could to no issue of true honor bring.
Be not so long to speak. I long to die
If what thou speakst speak not of remedy.

Friar Laurence. Hold, daughter, I do spy a kind of hope,
Which craves as desperate an execution
70 As that is desperate which we would prevent.
If, rather than to marry County Paris,
Thou hast the strength of will to slay thyself,
Then is it likely thou wilt undertake
A thing like death to chide away this shame,
75 That copest with death himself to scape from it;
And, if thou darest, I'll give thee remedy.

Juliet. O, bid me leap, rather than marry Paris,
From off the battlements of yonder tower,
Or walk in thievish ways, or bid me lurk
80 Where serpents are; chain me with roaring bears,
Or shut me nightly in a charnel house,
O'ercovered quite with dead men's rattling bones,
With reeky shanks and yellow chapless skulls;
Or bid me go into a new-made grave
85 And hide me with a dead man in his shroud—
Things that, to hear them told, have made me tremble—
And I will do it without fear or doubt,
To live an unstained wife to my sweet love.

Friar Laurence. Hold, then. Go home, be merry, give consent
90 To marry Paris. Wednesday is tomorrow.
Tomorrow night look that thou lie alone:
Let not the nurse lie with thee in thy chamber.
Take thou this vial, being then in bed,
And this distilled liquor drink thou off;
95 When presently through all thy veins shall run
A cold and drowsy humor; for no pulse
Shall keep his native progress, but surcease;
No warmth, no breath, shall testify thou livest;
The roses in thy lips and cheeks shall fade
100 To paly ashes, thy eyes' windows fall

71–76 If, rather than . . . remedy: If you are desperate enough to kill yourself, then you'll be daring enough to try the deathlike solution that I propose.

77–88 Juliet gives a lengthy list of things she would do rather than marry Paris. **charnel house:** a storehouse for bones from old graves; **reeky shanks:** stinking bones; **chapless:** without jaws. The description in lines 84–88 comes closer to Juliet's future than she knows.

89–120 The friar explains his plan.

93 vial: small bottle.

96–106 humor: liquid; **no pulse . . . pleasant sleep:** Your pulse will stop (**surcease**), and you will turn cold, pale, and stiff, as if you were dead; this condition will last for 42 hours.

Lines 77–88
DISCUSSION PROMPTS
Use these prompts to explore the depths of Juliet's desperation:

Connect Think of a time when you had to do something that you did not want to do. How does that memory help you understand how Juliet feels about marrying Paris? *Students may identify with Juliet's gloom and rising panic, especially as she lists terrible preferences to the marriage.*

Analyze How would the actions in Juliet's list get her out of the marriage with Paris? *Possible answer: Leaping from the tower's battlements (lines 77–78) would kill her; she might also die by going near serpents or bears (lines 79–80). Becoming a thief (line 79) would either cause Paris to reject her or would require her to live in hiding. Going into a charnel house or a new grave (lines 81–85) would make her seem insane, probably causing Paris to reject her.*

Evaluate Why is Juliet so dramatically upset? Does she really dislike Paris so intensely, or does she simply want to avoid the shame of betraying her husband? *Possible answer: In lines 87–88, Juliet says that she would do these things so that she could "live an unstained wife." From this line, it appears that she does not hate Paris; rather, she does not want to betray Romeo. The play indicates Juliet's feelings about what Paris represents, but it offers little to suggest her feelings about Paris as an individual.*

FOR LESS–PROFICIENT READERS
Comprehension Support [lines 90–91] To make sure that students understand this part of the friar's plan, discuss why he doesn't suggest that Juliet take the sleeping potion that same night. Elicit that he needs time to get a message to Romeo and get Romeo back to Verona before the effects wear off. Refer to this point about timing again when Capulet moves the wedding to Wednesday (Scene 2, line 24).

Inverted Word Order Remind students that sometimes Shakespeare's word order needs to be revised before it sounds correct to the modern ear. Have students revise the word order in lines 92–94. *Possible answer: [Do] not let the nurse lie with thee in thy chamber. / [Thou] Take this vial, being then in bed, / And drink off this distilled liquor.*

Scene 2, Lines 17–22
DISCUSSION PROMPTS

Use these prompts to discuss Juliet's apology to her father:

Recall What reason does Juliet give for offering an apology to her father? ***Possible answer:*** *She says that she has learned from Friar Laurence that she should repent of her disobedience to him.*

Analyze What is the real reason for Juliet's apology? ***Possible answer:*** *The real reason is to fool her father so that she may be left in peace to follow through with Friar Laurence's plan.*

Evaluate By making an apology, Juliet regains her father's favor. Why do you think Capulet is so quickly convinced? ***Possible answer:*** *Capulet is convinced because he hears what he longs to hear—namely, the words "Henceforward I am ever ruled by you" (line 22).*

Like death when he shuts up the day of life;
Each part, deprived of supple government,
Shall, stiff and stark and cold, appear like death;
And in this borrowed likeness of shrunk death
105 Thou shalt continue two-and-forty hours,
And then awake as from a pleasant sleep.
Now, when the bridegroom in the morning comes
To rouse thee from thy bed, there art thou dead.
Then, as the manner of our country is,
110 In thy best robes uncovered on the bier
Thou shalt be borne to that same ancient vault
Where all the kindred of the Capulets lie.
In the meantime, against thou shalt awake,
Shall Romeo by my letters know our drift;
115 And hither shall he come; and he and I
Will watch thy waking, and that very night
Shall Romeo bear thee hence to Mantua.
And this shall free thee from this present shame,
If no inconstant toy nor womanish fear
120 Abate thy valor in the acting it.

Juliet. Give me, give me! O, tell me not of fear!

Friar Laurence. Hold! Get you gone, be strong and prosperous
In this resolve. I'll send a friar with speed
To Mantua, with my letters to thy lord.

125 **Juliet.** Love give me strength! and strength shall help afford.
Farewell, dear father.

[*Exeunt.*]

107–112 *According to the friar's plan, what will happen when Paris comes to wake Juliet?*

111–112 same ancient vault . . . lie: same ancient tomb where all members of the Capulet family are buried.

114 drift: plan.

119–120 inconstant toy: foolish whim; **abate thy valor:** weaken your courage.

SCENE 2 *Capulet's house.*

Capulet is making plans for the wedding on Thursday. Juliet arrives and apologizes to him, saying that she will marry Paris. Capulet is so relieved that he reschedules the wedding for the next day, Wednesday.

[*Enter* Capulet, Lady Capulet, Nurse, *and* Servingmen.]

Capulet. So many guests invite as here are writ.

[*Exit a* Servingman.]

Sirrah, go hire me twenty cunning cooks.

Servingman. You shall have none ill, sir; for I'll try if they can lick their fingers.

1–8 Capulet is having a cheerful conversation with his servants about the wedding preparations. One servant assures him that he will test (**try**) the cooks he hires by making them taste their own food (**lick their fingers**).

1022 UNIT 10: SHAKESPEAREAN DRAMA

DIFFERENTIATED INSTRUCTION

FOR LESS–PROFICIENT READERS

Preview Call on a volunteer to read aloud the italicized scene synopsis. Help students create a Sequence Chain like this to organize the events in Scene 2:

 BEST PRACTICES TOOLKIT—Transparency
Sequence Chain p. B21

```
Capulet is planning the wedding.
           |
           v
Juliet arrives and apologizes.
           |
           v
Juliet agrees to marry Paris.
           |
           v
Capulet reschedules the wedding for
Wednesday—the next day.
```

FOR ENGLISH LEARNERS

Task Support As you direct students to the marginal question for lines 107–112, make sure that they understand the words "bridegroom", "bier", "borne", and "vault". ***Possible answer:*** *When Paris arrives in the morning, he will find Juliet seemingly dead. Then her body will be carried to the Capulet family vault.*

1022 UNIT 10: SHAKESPEAREAN DRAMA

5 **Capulet.** How canst thou try them so?

Servingman. Marry, sir, 'tis an ill cook that cannot lick his own
fingers. Therefore he that cannot lick his fingers goes not with
me.

Capulet. Go, begone.

[*Exit* Servingman.]

10 We shall be much unfurnished for this time.
What, is my daughter gone to Friar Laurence?

Nurse. Ay, forsooth.

Capulet. Well, he may chance to do some good on her.
A peevish self-willed harlotry it is.

[*Enter* Juliet.]

15 **Nurse.** See where she comes from shrift with merry look.

Capulet. How now, my headstrong? Where have you been gadding?

Juliet. Where I have learnt me to repent the sin
Of disobedient opposition
To you and your behests, and am enjoined
20 By holy Laurence to fall prostrate here
To beg your pardon. Pardon, I beseech you!
Henceforward I am ever ruled by you.

Capulet. Send for the County. Go tell him of this.
I'll have this knot knit up tomorrow morning.
25 **Juliet.** I met the youthful lord at Laurence' cell
And gave him what becomed love I might,
Not stepping o'er the bounds of modesty.

Capulet. Why, I am glad on't. This is well. Stand up.
This is as't should be. Let me see the County.
30 Ay, marry, go, I say, and fetch him hither.
Now, afore God, this reverend holy friar,
All our whole city is much bound to him. **C**

Juliet. Nurse, will you go with me into my closet
To help me sort such needful ornaments
35 As you think fit to furnish me tomorrow?

Lady Capulet. No, not till Thursday. There is time enough.

Capulet. Go, nurse, go with her. We'll to church tomorrow.

[*Exeunt* Juliet *and* Nurse.]

B COMIC RELIEF
Think about the purpose that
comic relief serves. Why might
Shakespeare have chosen to begin
this scene with a light, humorous
conversation?

10 unfurnished: unprepared.

14 A silly, stubborn girl she is.

19 behests: orders; **enjoined:**
commanded.

24 I'll have this wedding scheduled for
tomorrow morning.

2 Targeted Passage

C DRAMATIC IRONY
What is ironic about Capulet's praise
of Friar Laurence?

36–39 Lady Capulet urges her husband
to wait until Thursday as originally
planned. She needs time to get food
(**provision**) ready for the wedding party.

LITERARY ANALYSIS

B COMIC RELIEF

Possible answer: *Shakespeare might have
chosen to begin the scene with humor to
break away from the heavy, dark ending to
Scene 1. Light conversation is also appropriate for planning a party, the focus of
the scene.*

LITERARY ANALYSIS

C DRAMATIC IRONY

Possible answer: *Capulet's praise of Friar
Laurence is ironic because the friar has
taken many secret actions for which
Capulet would condemn him, if only he
knew of them. The friar has married Juliet
to Romeo, is scheming to overturn Romeo's
sentence of banishment, and is conspiring
with Juliet to trick Capulet into believing
that she is dead.*

If students need help . . . Have them use
Main Idea and Details notes to record the
actions that Friar Laurence has taken up
to this point in the play. After they have
reviewed the details, help them craft a
main idea statement that expresses
what Capulet would think if he knew of
these actions.

BEST PRACTICES TOOLKIT—Transparency
Main Idea and Details p. B6

FOR LESS–PROFICIENT READERS

2 Targeted Passage [Lines 23–37]

By presenting Capulet's response to Juliet's
apology, this passage introduces a further
complication to the story.

- How does Capulet react to the apology?
Which words show his feelings?

- When will the wedding take place? Was this
the original plan? How does Juliet's mother
feel about Capulet's decision?

- Who will help Juliet prepare for the wedding? Does Capulet approve?

FOR ENGLISH LEARNERS

Vocabulary: Outdated Forms Urge students
to continue adding outdated terms to their
language journals. (See the **For English Learners** activity on page 940.) Provide these terms
and their definitions. Then have students
reread the lines noted and substitute the
definitions for the words.

- *writ* (line 1), "written"

- Sirrah (line 2), "hey, you" (a call to someone
inferior)

- *try* (lines 3 and 5), "test"

- *Ay, forsooth* (line 12), "Yes, it's true"

- *gadding* (line 16), "wandering"

- *learnt* (line 17), "learned"

- *prostrate* (line 20), "face down" (showing
humility and reverence)

- *Henceforward* (line 22), "from now on"

- *becomed* (line 26), "appropriate"

- *needful* (line 34), "necessary"

ⓓ TRAGEDY

Possible answer: *Moving the wedding up by one day threatens to undermine Friar Laurence's plan. Juliet will not be able to wait until Wednesday night to take the sleeping potion. Furthermore, it will be very difficult, perhaps impossible, for Friar Laurence to get word to Romeo about Juliet's feigned death and his plan to have Romeo come and take her to Mantua.*

If students need help . . . Explain that Mantua is almost 40 miles from Verona. Discuss how long students think it would take for a message to travel that distance in Shakespeare's time.

Lady Capulet. We shall be short in our provision.
'Tis now near night.

Capulet.   Tush, I will stir about,
40 And all things shall be well, I warrant thee, wife.
Go thou to Juliet, help to deck up her.
I'll not to bed tonight; let me alone.
I'll play the housewife for this once. What, ho!
They are all forth; well, I will walk myself
45 To County Paris, to prepare him up
Against tomorrow. My heart is wondrous light,
Since this same wayward girl is so reclaimed. ⓓ

[*Exeunt.*]

39–46 Capulet is so set on Wednesday that he promises to make the arrangements himself.

ⓓ **TRAGEDY**
Think about how the **plot** of this tragedy is unfolding. What does moving the wedding up by one day do to Friar Laurence's plan?

SCENE 3 *Juliet's bedroom.*

Juliet sends her mother and the nurse away and prepares to take the drug the friar has given her. She is confused and frightened but finally puts the vial to her lips and drinks.

[*Enter* Juliet *and* Nurse.]

Juliet. Ay, those attires are best; but, gentle nurse,
I pray thee leave me to myself tonight;
For I have need of many orisons
To move the heavens to smile upon my state,
5 Which, well thou knowest, is cross and full of sin.

[*Enter* Lady Capulet.]

Lady Capulet. What, are you busy, ho? Need you my help?

Juliet. No madam; we have culled such necessaries
As are behooveful for our state tomorrow.
So please you, let me now be left alone,
10 And let the nurse this night sit up with you;
For I am sure you have your hands full all
In this so sudden business.

Lady Capulet.   Good night.
Get thee to bed and rest, for thou hast need.

[*Exeunt* Lady Capulet *and* Nurse.]

Juliet. Farewell! God knows when we shall meet again.
15 I have a faint cold fear thrills through my veins
That almost freezes up the heat of life.
I'll call them back again to comfort me.
Nurse!—What should she do here?
My dismal scene I needs must act alone.

3 orisons: prayers.

7–8 we have . . . tomorrow: We have picked out (**culled**) everything appropriate for the wedding tomorrow.

17–19 In her fear, Juliet starts to call the nurse back but realizes that she must be alone to drink the poison.

DIFFERENTIATED INSTRUCTION

FOR LESS-PROFICIENT READERS

Paraphrasing Shakespeare Draw students' attention to the marginal note for lines 39–46, which explains how Capulet takes over the preparations for the wedding. Help students paraphrase his comments in lines 39–41 to read something like this: *Nonsense! I will get busy, and everything will be fine. I guarantee it, wife. You go to Juliet and help her choose her finest clothes [for the wedding].*

Preview As you read through the Scene 3 synopsis, use an Open Mind diagram to help students identify Juliet's actions and emotions.

🧰 BEST PRACTICES TOOLKIT—Transparency
Open Mind p. D9

Juliet's actions
sends mother and nurse away
prepares to take Friar Laurence's drug
drinks the potion

Juliet's emotions
confusion
fear
determination

The Seattle Repertory Theatre, 2003

LOVE CONQUERS EVERYTHING.
EXCEPT STAB WOUNDS AND POISONING.

WILLIAM SHAKESPEARE
OMEO & JULIET

The Arkansas Repertory Theatre, 2004

The National Theater of Poland, 1996

Promotion

Imagine that you knew nothing about the story of the star-crossed lovers. What clues about the play do each of these **promotional** posters provide? Which poster would most make you want to see the play? Explain your answers.

1025

BEHIND THE CURTAIN

Promotion Discuss the fact that effective promotional materials must give enough information about a play to entice an audience to attend the performance but not so much information that they give away the whole story. Ask how the promotional pieces shown here contain messages that are clear only to people who are familiar with the play. *Possible answer: The Arkansas Repertory Theatre's poster uses the rose motif, an important image in Juliet's famous soliloquy (Act Two, Scene 2) about the importance of names: "A rose by any other name . . . ." The Seattle Repertory Theatre's poster offers a witty caption, compelling lettering, and images of weapons, suggesting the violence in the tale. The National Theater of Poland's poster contains a mysterious image of the lovers unfolding from a flower. It reveals little information about the plot of the play. Answers will vary, but students should identify the features that make their chosen poster appealing.*

FOR ADVANCED LEARNERS/PRE–AP

Contrast and Evaluate [small-group option] Ask students to research print and Internet sources to find more than one poster that advertises the same play or movie. Have them contrast these promotional materials, determine the message of each one, and decide which one is the most effective. To extend the activity, challenge students to create a poster that they think does an even better job of promoting the play or movie.

Come, vial.
   What if this mixture do not work at all?
   Shall I be married then tomorrow morning?
   No, no! This shall forbid it. Lie thou there.

   [*lays down a dagger*]

   What if it be a poison which the friar
25 Subtly hath ministered to have me dead,
   Lest in this marriage he should be dishonored
   Because he married me before to Romeo?
   I fear it is; and yet methinks it should not,
   For he hath still been tried a holy man. **E**
30 How if, when I am laid into the tomb,
   I wake before the time that Romeo
   Come to redeem me? There's a fearful point!
   Shall I not then be stifled in the vault,
   To whose foul mouth no healthsome air breathes in,
35 And there die strangled ere my Romeo comes?
   Or, if I live, is it not very like
   The horrible conceit of death and night,
   Together with the terror of the place—
   As in a vault, an ancient receptacle
40 Where for this many hundred years the bones
   Of all my buried ancestors are packed;
   Where bloody Tybalt, yet but green in earth,
   Lies fest'ring in his shroud; where, as they say,
   At some hours in the night spirits resort—
45 Alack, alack, is it not like that I,
   So early waking—what with loathsome smells,
   And shrieks like mandrakes torn out of the earth,
   That living mortals, hearing them, run mad—
   O, if I wake, shall I not be distraught,
50 Environed with all these hideous fears,
   And madly play with my forefathers' joints,
   And pluck the mangled Tybalt from his shroud,
   And, in this rage, with some great kinsman's bone
   As with a club dash out my desp'rate brains?
55 O, look! methinks I see my cousin's ghost
   Seeking out Romeo, that did spit his body
   Upon a rapier's point. Stay, Tybalt, stay!
   Romeo, I come! this do I drink to thee.

   [*She drinks and falls upon her bed within the curtains.*]

23 This shall forbid it: A dagger will be her alternative means of keeping from marrying Paris.

24–57 Juliet lists her various doubts and fears about what she is about to do.

E **CHARACTER**
In her anxious state, what does Juliet suspect about Friar Laurence's **motives** for giving her the potion? Do you think she really believes this to be true? Explain.

36–43 Juliet fears the vision (**conceit**) she might have on waking in the family tomb and seeing the rotting body of Tybalt.

45–54 She fears that the smells together with the sounds of ghosts screaming might make her lose her mind and commit bizarre acts. Mandrake root was thought to look like the human form and to scream when pulled from the ground.

③ **Targeted Passage**
57 stay: stop.

LITERARY ANALYSIS

E CHARACTER

Possible answer: Juliet suspects that Friar Laurence, motivated by fear of being dishonored for his role in the plot, has given her a potion that really will kill her. She probably does not really believe this: In lines 28–29, she reminds herself that the friar is a holy man and can be trusted.

Lines 30–58
DISCUSSION PROMPTS

Use these prompts to discuss Juliet's internal conflict before she takes the sleeping potion:

Recall What is Juliet afraid of as she prepares to drink the potion? *Possible answer: She is afraid that she will wake up before Romeo arrives. If she does, she fears that she will suffocate or that she will go crazy at the sight of the corpses and kill herself with the bone of a nearby corpse.*

Analyze What emotions does Juliet display when she overcomes her fear and drinks the potion? *Possible answer: She shows courage, bravery, love for Romeo, and devotion to her marriage.*

Evaluate Are the fears that Juliet expresses in lines 45–54 justified? Explain. *Some students may feel that waking up in a family cemetery would stir up the imagination and fears of most people. Others might find that lines such as 49–52 express fears that go beyond what is reasonable.*

DIFFERENTIATED INSTRUCTION

FOR LESS–PROFICIENT READERS

③ Targeted Passage [Lines 55–58]

In this passage, Juliet musters her courage and drinks Friar Laurence's potion.

- Who is the ghost that Juliet imagines she sees? What is it doing, and why?

- What does Juliet mean when she says, "I come!" (line 58)?

- What fateful action does Juliet take as Scene 3 concludes?

SCENE 4   *Capulet's house.*

It is now the next morning, nearly time for the wedding. The household is happy and excited as everyone makes final preparations.

[*Enter* Lady Capulet *and* Nurse.]

Lady Capulet. Hold, take these keys and fetch more spices, nurse.

Nurse. They call for dates and quinces in the pastry.

[*Enter* Capulet.]

Capulet. Come, stir, stir, stir! The second cock hath crowed,
The curfew bell hath rung, 'tis three o'clock.
5 Look to the baked meats, good Angelica;
Spare not for cost.

Nurse.   Go, you cot-quean, go,
Get you to bed! Faith, you'll be sick tomorrow
For this night's watching.

Capulet. No, not a whit. What, I have watched ere now
10 All night for lesser cause, and ne'er been sick.

Lady Capulet. Ay, you have been a mouse-hunt in your time;
But I will watch you from such watching now.

[*Exeunt* Lady Capulet *and* Nurse.]

Capulet. A jealous hood, a jealous hood!

[*Enter three or four* Servants, *with spits and logs and baskets.*]
                          Now, fellow,
What is there?

15 **First Servant.** Things for the cook, sir; but I know not what.

Capulet. Make haste, make haste. [*Exit* Servant.] Sirrah, fetch
   drier logs.
Call Peter; he will show thee where they are.

Second Servant. I have a head, sir, that will find out logs
And never trouble Peter for the matter.

20 **Capulet.** Mass, and well said, merry whoreson, ha!
Thou shalt be loggerhead. [*Exit* Servant.] Good faith, 'tis day.
The County will be here with music straight,
For so he said he would. [*music within*] I hear him near.
Nurse! Wife! What, ho! What, nurse, I say!

2 pastry: the room where baking is done.

5 good Angelica: In his happy mood, Capulet even calls the nurse by her name.

6 cot-quean: The nurse playfully refers to Capulet as a "cottage quean," or housewife. This is a joke about his doing women's work (arranging the party).

11–13 Lord and Lady Capulet joke about his being a woman chaser (**mouse-hunt**) as a young man. He makes fun of her jealousy (**jealous hood**).

20–23 The joking between Capulet and his servants includes the mild oath **Mass**, short for "by the Mass," and **loggerhead**, a word for a stupid person as well as a pun, since the servant is searching for drier logs. **straight:** right away.

BACKGROUND

Elizabethan Wedding Feasts The Capulets have reason to hurry as they prepare overnight for the wedding. Elizabethan wedding feasts typically had three or more large courses, each of which offered at least two meat dishes (including animals that are rarely eaten today—such as peacock, swan, hedgehog, and songbirds—and which sometimes were prepared for show rather than for eating). Several pastry offerings, a sweet, and wine were also served. The food preparation alone could take several days. During such a feast, a wealthy family employed many servants with specific tasks. For example, a bread trencher provided fresh bread to guests to replace bread that had gone stale during the meal.

FOR LESS–PROFICIENT READERS
Preview After students read the italicized scene synopsis, have them fill in a Reporter's Questions chart to record its key events.

 BEST PRACTICES TOOLKIT—Transparency
Reporter's Questions p. C9

Who is in this scene?	the Capulet household
What are they doing?	preparing for the wedding
Where does the scene take place?	at Capulet's house
When does the scene take place?	the next morning
Why are they hurrying?	almost time for the ceremony
How do they feel?	happy and excited

[*Reenter* Nurse.]

25 Go waken Juliet; go and trim her up.
I'll go and chat with Paris. Hie, make haste,
Make haste! The bridegroom he is come already:
Make haste, I say.

[*Exeunt.*]

SCENE 5 *Juliet's bedroom.*

*The joyous preparations suddenly change into plans for a funeral when the nurse
discovers Juliet on her bed, apparently dead. Lord and Lady Capulet, Paris, and the
nurse are overcome with grief. Friar Laurence tries to comfort them and instructs
them to bring Juliet's body to the Capulet family tomb. The scene abruptly switches
to humor, in a foolish conversation between the servant Peter and the musicians
hired to play at the wedding.*

[*Enter* Nurse.]

Nurse. Mistress! what, mistress! Juliet! Fast, I warrant her, she.
Why, lamb! why, lady! Fie, you slugabed!
Why, love, I say! madam! sweetheart! Why, bride!
What, not a word? You take your pennyworths now,
5 Sleep for a week; for the next night, I warrant,
The County Paris hath set up his rest
That you shall rest but little. God forgive me,
Marry and amen, how sound is she asleep!
I needs must wake her. Madam, madam, madam!
10 Aye, let the County take you in your bed,
He'll fright you up, i' faith. Will it not be?

[*opens the curtains*]

What, dressed and in your clothes and down again?
I must needs wake you. Lady! lady! lady!
Alas, alas! Help, help! my lady's dead!
15 O well-a-day that ever I was born!
Some aqua vitae, ho! My lord! my lady!

[*Enter* Lady Capulet.]

Lady Capulet. What noise is here?

Nurse.   O lamentable day!

Lady Capulet. What is the matter?

Nurse.   Look, look! O heavy day!

Lady Capulet. O me, O me! My child, my only life!
20 Revive, look up, or I will die with thee!
Help! help! Call help.

1–11 The nurse chatters as she bustles around the room. She calls Juliet a **slugabed,** or sleepyhead, who is trying to get her **pennyworths,** or small portions, of rest now, since after the wedding Paris won't let her get much sleep. When Juliet doesn't answer, the nurse opens the curtains that enclose the bed.

17 lamentable: filled with grief.

[*Enter* Capulet.]

Capulet. For shame, bring Juliet forth; her lord is come.

Nurse. She's dead, deceased; she's dead! Alack the day!

Lady Capulet. Alack the day, she's dead, she's dead, she's dead!

25 **Capulet.** Ha! let me see her. Out alas! she's cold,
Her blood is settled, and her joints are stiff;
Life and these lips have long been separated.
Death lies on her like an untimely frost
Upon the sweetest flower of all the field.

30 **Nurse.** O lamentable day!

Lady Capulet.   O woeful time!

Capulet. Death, that hath ta'en her hence to make me wail,
Ties up my tongue and will not let me speak.

[*Enter* Friar Laurence *and* Paris, *with* Musicians.]

Friar Laurence. Come, is the bride ready to go to church?

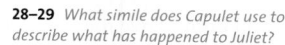

28–29 *What simile does Capulet use to describe what has happened to Juliet?*

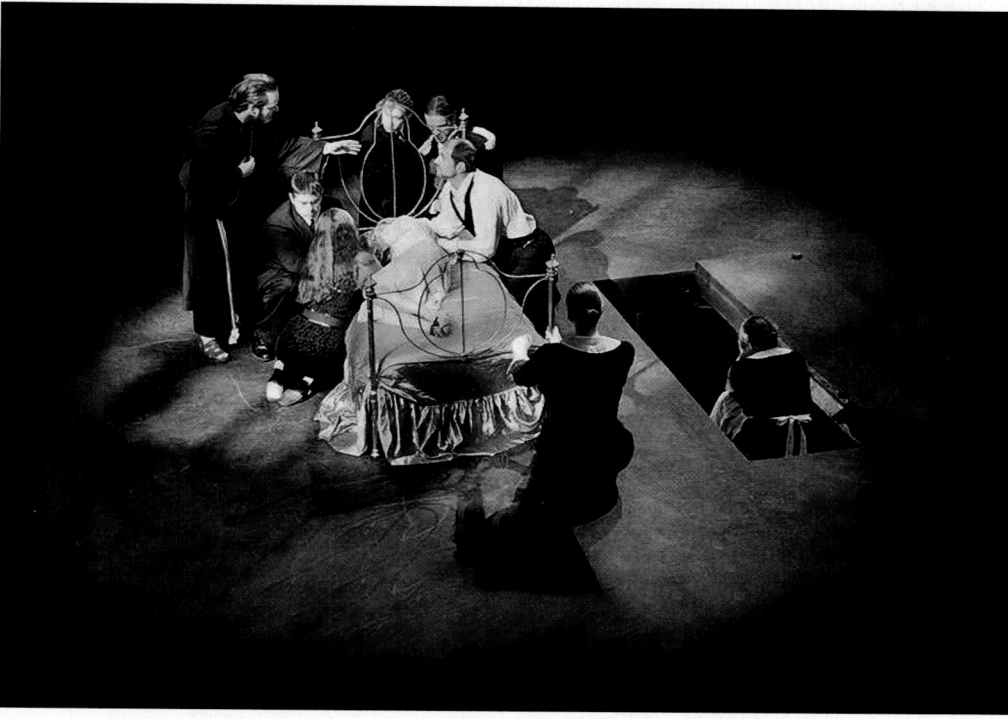

Friar Laurence and the Capulets mourn for Juliet in the University of Victoria's 1998 production.

ANALYZE VISUALS

Activity What details about the costumes and the poses of the actors in the photograph convey a solemn mood? *Possible answer: The actors are dressed in dark clothing (except for Juliet, whose light clothing provides a contrast) and have grim looks on their faces. Almost everyone is huddled around the bed in which Juliet lies; the exception is the nurse, who sits apart, her head in her hands. All of these details help convey the solemnity and grief caused by Juliet's apparent death.*

FOR ENGLISH LEARNERS

Task Support Point out the marginal question for lines 28–29. Remind students that a simile is a comparison that uses the words *like* or *as;* then have students reread lines 28–29 to find one of those words and the descriptions that it connects. ***Possible answer:*** *Capulet compares Juliet's death to an unexpected frost that kills the sweetest flower in a field.*

DISCUSSION PROMPTS

Use these prompts to explore Friar Laurence's words to the Capulets:

Connect Have you ever heard someone offering words of comfort about a person's death? Do you find Friar Laurence's words comforting? Why or why not? *Students should cite specific phrases from the text to support their answers.*

Analyze According to Friar Laurence, what is the highest form of human advancement? *Possible answer: The highest form of human advancement is to live in heaven (lines 73–74).*

Synthesize How might Friar Laurence's advice to the family be different if he did not know that Juliet was alive? *Possible answers: Friar Laurence might not encourage the family to take Juliet's body to the tomb quickly. He might express greater regret and loss. He might sympathize more with the grief-stricken family.*

Capulet. Ready to go, but never to return.
35 O son, the night before thy wedding day
Hath death lain with thy wife. See, there she lies,
Flower as she was, deflowered by him.
Death is my son-in-law, Death is my heir;
My daughter he hath wedded. I will die
40 And leave him all. Life, living, all is Death's.

   Paris. Have I thought long to see this morning's face,
And doth it give me such a sight as this?

   Lady Capulet. Accursed, unhappy, wretched, hateful day!
Most miserable hour that e'er time saw
45 In lasting labor of his pilgrimage!
But one, poor one, one poor and loving child,
But one thing to rejoice and solace in,
And cruel Death hath catched it from my sight!

   Nurse. O woe! O woeful, woeful, woeful day!
50 Most lamentable day, most woeful day
That ever, ever I did yet behold!
O day! O day! O day! O hateful day!
Never was seen so black a day as this.
O woeful day! O woeful day!

55 **Paris.** Beguiled, divorced, wronged, spited, slain!
Most detestable Death, by thee beguiled,
By cruel, cruel thee quite overthrown!
O love! O life! not life, but love in death!

   Capulet. Despised, distressed, hated, martyred, killed!
60 Uncomfortable time, why camest thou now
To murder, murder our solemnity?
O child! O child! my soul, and not my child!
Dead art thou, dead! alack, my child is dead,
And with my child my joys are buried!

65 **Friar Laurence.** Peace, ho, for shame! Confusion's cure lives not
In these confusions. Heaven and yourself
Had part in this fair maid! now heaven hath all,
And all the better is it for the maid.
Your part in her you could not keep from death,
70 But heaven keeps his part in eternal life.
The most you sought was her promotion,
For 'twas your heaven she should be advanced;
And weep ye now, seeing she is advanced
Above the clouds, as high as heaven itself?
75 O, in this love, you love your child so ill

40 Life . . . Death's: My life, my possessions, and everything else of mine belongs to Death.

44–48 Most miserable . . . my sight: This is the most miserable hour that time ever saw on its long journey. I had only one child to make me happy, and Death has taken (**catched**) her from me.

55 beguiled: tricked.

60–61 why . . . solemnity: Why did Death have to come to murder our celebration?

65–78 The friar comforts the family. He says that the cure for disaster (**confusion**) cannot be found in cries of grief. Juliet's family and heaven once shared her; now heaven has all of her. All the family ever wanted was the best for her; now she's in heaven—what could be better than that? It is best to die young, when the soul is still pure, without sin.

DIFFERENTIATED INSTRUCTION

FOR ENGLISH LEARNERS
Concept Support Have students review the mourning in this scene by writing a one-sentence summary of each character's speech. Begin with these examples:

- Capulet says that his daughter is now the bride of Death (lines 34–40).
- Paris complains that he has waited for this wedding morning and now sees this terrible sight (lines 41–42).

FOR ADVANCED LEARNERS/PRE–AP
Inverted Word Order Shakespeare inverts word order for effect, for emphasis, and to better fit with his poetic meter. Discuss his reason for doing so in lines 56, 60, 63, 65, and 73. *Possible answer: The inversions in lines 56 and 65 conform to meter. The inversion in line 60 creates a dramatic effect. The inversion in line 63 creates emphasis (on dead). The inversion in line 73 creates emphasis (on weep and now).*

That you run mad, seeing that she is well.
She's not well married that lives married long,
But she's best married that dies married young.
Dry up your tears and stick your rosemary
80 On this fair corse, and, as the custom is,
In all her best array bear her to church;
For though fond nature bids us all lament,
Yet nature's tears are reason's merriment.

Capulet. All things that we ordained festival
85 Turn from their office to black funeral—
Our instruments to melancholy bells,
Our wedding cheer to a sad burial feast;
Our solemn hymns to sullen dirges change;
Our bridal flowers serve for a buried corse;
90 And all things change them to the contrary.

Friar Laurence. Sir, go you in; and, madam, go with him;
And go, Sir Paris. Every one prepare
To follow this fair corse unto her grave.
The heavens do lower upon you for some ill;
95 Move them no more by crossing their high will.

[*Exeunt* Capulet, Lady Capulet, Paris, *and* Friar.]

First Musician. Faith, we may put up our pipes, and be gone.

Nurse. Honest good fellows, ah, put up, put up,
For well you know this is a pitiful case.

[*Exit.*]

Second Musician. Aye, by my troth, the case may be amended. **F**

[*Enter* Peter.]

100 **Peter.** Musicians, oh, musicians, "Heart's ease, heart's ease." Oh,
an you will have me live, play "Heart's ease."

First Musician. Why "Heart's ease"?

Peter. Oh, musicians, because my heart itself plays "My heart is
full of woe." Oh, play me some merry dump, to comfort me.

105 **First Musician.** Not a dump we, 'tis no time to play now.

Peter. You will not, then?

First Musician. No.

Peter. I will then give it you soundly.

79–80 **stick...corse:** Put rosemary, an herb, on her corpse.

82–83 **though...merriment:** Though it's natural to cry, common sense tells us we should rejoice for the dead.

84 **ordained festival:** intended for the wedding.

88 **sullen dirges:** sad, mournful tunes.

④ Targeted Passage

94–95 **The heavens...will:** The fates (**heavens**) frown on you for some wrong you have done. Don't tempt them by refusing to accept their will (Juliet's death).

F PUN
Reread lines 96–99. The musician is talking about the case for his instrument. What "case" is the nurse referring to?

100–138 After the tragedy of Juliet's "death," Shakespeare injects a light and witty conversation between Peter and the musicians. Peter asks them to play "Heart's Ease," a popular song of the time, or a **dump,** a slow dance melody. They refuse to play, and insults and puns are traded. Peter says that instead of money he'll give them a jeering speech (**gleek**), and he insults them by calling them minstrels. In return they call him a servant. Then both make puns on notes of the musical scale, re and fa.

LITERARY ANALYSIS

F PUN

Possible answer: The "case" is the situation of Juliet's apparent death.

If students need help... Give students this example of a pun: "How these bugs are flying around my ears! If only I weren't so bugged." Explain that here the word play doesn't reveal itself until the second appearance of the word *bug*. The same is true in lines 96–99: There is no humor in the nurse's use of the word *case*, but when the second musician uses the same word in a different way the pun becomes apparent.

FOR LESS-PROFICIENT READERS
Paraphrasing Shakespeare Draw students' attention to the words of consolation from Friar Laurence in lines 65–78. Elicit that an effective paraphrase of his words in lines 77–78 might read something like this: *A woman who dies after having been married for a short time is better off than a woman who lives as a wife for a long time.*

④ Targeted Passage [Lines 84–95]

In this passage, Capulet and Friar Laurence conclude this scene's grieving mood.

• What does Friar Laurence say should be done with Juliet?

• What things for Juliet's wedding will now be used for her funeral?

• How does Friar Laurence suggest that Juliet's "death" may be her family's fault? Do you think that he means it?

SUMMARIZE Have students consider the Capulets' horrifying discovery. Ask them how Friar Laurence's plan is—and is not—going as anticipated.

⭐ **CRITIQUE** Ask students whether the risks that Juliet has taken are justified in her desperate attempt to avoid marriage with Paris. Could Juliet have gotten out of the situation any other way? Encourage students to cite details from Act Three, Act Four, or both to support their opinions.

First Musician. What will you give us?

110 **Peter.** No money, on my faith, but the gleek. I will give you the minstrel.

First Musician. Then will I give you the serving creature.

Peter. Then will I lay the serving creature's dagger on your pate. I will carry no crotchets. I'll re you, I'll fa you, do you note me?

113 **pate:** top of the head.

115 **First Musician.** An you re us and fa us, you note us.

Second Musician. Pray you put up your dagger, and put out your wit.

Peter. Then have at you with my wit! I will drybeat you with an iron wit, and put up my iron dagger. Answer me like men:

120   "When griping grief the heart doth wound
          And doleful dumps the mind oppress,
          Then music with her silver sound—"

Why "silver sound"? Why "music with her silver sound"?—What say you, Simon Catling?

125 **First Musician.** Marry, sir, because silver hath a sweet sound.

Peter. Pretty! What say you, Hugh Rebeck?

Second Musician. I say "silver sound" because musicians sound for silver.

Peter. Pretty too! What say you, James Soundpost?

130 **Third Musician.** Faith, I know not what to say.

Peter. Oh, I cry you mercy, you are the singer. I will say for you. It is "music with her silver sound" because musicians have no gold for sounding.

          "Then music with her silver sound
135   With speedy help doth lend redress."

[*Exit.*]

First Musician. What a pestilent knave is this same!

136 **pestilent:** bothersome; irritating.

Second Musician. Hang him, Jack! Come, we'll in here. Tarry for the mourners, and stay dinner.

[*Exeunt.*]

DIFFERENTIATED INSTRUCTION

FOR ENGLISH LEARNERS
Vocabulary Support Help students decipher the word play in the comic ending to Act Four by defining these terms:

- *gleek* (line 110), "insult"
- *pate* (line 113), "top of the head"
- *crochets* (line 114), "stubborn ideas"
- *doleful* (line 121), "sad"
- *redress* (line 135), "correction"
- *Tarry* (line 137), "wait"

Comprehension

1. **Recall** What reason does Paris give for Lord Capulet's decision to move up the wedding?

2. **Recall** At first, what does Juliet believe is the only solution to her problem?

3. **Summarize** What plan does Friar Laurence devise for Juliet, and what reservations does Juliet have about this plan?

Literary Analysis

4. **Reading Shakespearean Drama** Review the events you recorded as you read Act Four, and think about how the characters' interactions drive the plot forward. If the nurse had accompanied Juliet to Friar Laurence's cell, do you think Juliet would have made a different decision? Explain.

5. **Make Judgments** Do you feel sympathy for the Capulets, the nurse, and Paris when they express grief over Juliet's death? Why or why not?

6. **Identify Dramatic Irony** Dramatic irony exists when the reader or viewer knows something that one or more of the characters do not. Find three examples of dramatic irony in Act Four and record them in a chart like the one shown. Then explain how these ironic moments contribute to the building tension in the play.

Scene and Lines	Dramatic Irony
Scene 1, lines 24–28	Paris asks Juliet to confess to Friar Laurence that she loves him, and Juliet carefully avoids denying it. We know that Juliet loves Romeo, not Paris.

7. **Recognize Protagonist and Antagonist** If Romeo and Juliet are the protagonists of this play, who or what is the antagonist? Keep in mind that an antagonist can be a character, a group of characters, a set of circumstances, or even society as a whole. Use details from the play to support your answer.

8. **Evaluate Comic Relief** The humorous exchange between Peter and the musicians at the end of Act Four is an example of comic relief. It lightens the mood after the grief-filled speeches that follow the discovery of Juliet's body. If you were producing a stage or film version of *Romeo and Juliet,* would you cut this passage, or do you think it serves an important purpose? Explain.

Literary Criticism

9. **Different Perspectives** How might older and younger audiences differ in their assessment of Romeo's and Juliet's actions? Explain your opinion, citing specific actions and interactions in the play.

ROMEO AND JULIET: ACT FOUR **1033**

6. *Examples should follow this pattern: **Scene and Line:** Scene 1, line 6; **Dramatic Irony:** Paris thinks that Juliet grieves for Tybalt. We know that she cries for Romeo. Other examples include Scene 2, lines 17–22, and Scene 3, lines 1–13. The irony builds tension because readers sense that the unfolding tragedy is unavoidable.*

7. *Students might say that the lovers' parents, the family feud, or Fortune itself is the antagonist. Be sure they support their answers.*

8. *Students should offer a reasonable defense for their views—either that the scene needs this moment of comic relief or that the humor is too distracting.*

Literary Criticism

9. *Students may feel that a younger audience may identify with the strong passion of the lovers, whereas an older audience may feel frustrated that the lovers cannot find a more moderate course of action.*

Practice and Apply

After Reading

For additional support of post-reading questions, use these copy masters:

R RESOURCE MANAGER—Copy Masters
Reading Check p. 79 (to check understanding of the selection)
Shakespearean Drama p. 75 (for practice of literary analysis standards focus)
Question Support p. 80 (After Reading questions adapted for English learners and less-proficient readers)

For additional questions, see page 71.

For additional exercises to challenge students, see

ⓘ Power Thinking at **ClassZone.com**

ANSWERS

Comprehension

1. *Paris says that Capulet acts out of concern over Juliet's grief for Tybalt.*

2. *suicide*

3. *Friar Laurence gives Juliet a sleeping potion that will make her appear dead; when she awakens, Romeo will take her to Mantua. Juliet fears that Romeo will not arrive in time.*

Literary Analysis
Possible answers:

4. ■ **STANDARDS FOCUS** *Reading Shakespearean Drama Juliet might not have shared her feelings; Friar Laurence might not have suggested such a drastic plan.*

5. *Accept all reasonable responses. Some students may suggest that they have more sympathy for the nurse and for Paris than for Juliet's parents.*

Assess and Reteach

Assess

R RESOURCE MANAGER—Copy Masters
Selection Test A pp. 81–82
Selection Test B/C pp. 83–84

💿 Test Generator CD

Reteach

S STANDARDS LESSON FILE
Literature Lessons 25, 26, 35, 38

Practice and Apply

Get Into the Act

SUMMARY

As Act Five opens, Romeo learns that Juliet has died, and he returns to Verona. Meanwhile, Friar Laurence learns that his message to Romeo was not delivered. Determined to join Juliet, Romeo kills Paris at the tomb, drinks poison, and dies beside Juliet. Friar Laurence arrives just as Juliet awakens but flees when he hears people coming. After he leaves, Juliet kills herself with Romeo's dagger. Finally, the prince determines what has happened, and Capulet and Montague make peace.

LITERARY ANALYSIS

A TRAGEDY

Possible answer: Lines 1–11 may be paraphrased like this: "If dreams can be trusted, I will learn happy news. Today I feel cheerful. I dreamed that Juliet found me dead (how strange!) and kissed me awake, and I found myself an emperor. How sweet is love!" The part of the dream in which Juliet kisses Romeo's corpse foreshadows the tragedy.

Resources for Act Five

Act Five

SCENE 1 *A street in Mantua.*

Balthasar, Romeo's servant, comes from Verona to tell him that Juliet is dead and lies in the Capulets' tomb. Since Romeo has not yet received any word from the friar, he believes Balthasar. He immediately decides to return to Verona in order to die next to Juliet. He sends Balthasar away and sets out to find a pharmacist who will sell him poison.

[*Enter* Romeo.]

Romeo. If I may trust the flattering truth of sleep,
My dreams presage some joyful news at hand.
My bosom's lord sits lightly in his throne,
And all this day an unaccustomed spirit
5 Lifts me above the ground with cheerful thoughts.
I dreamt my lady came and found me dead
(Strange dream that gives a dead man leave to think!)
And breathed such life with kisses in my lips
That I revived and was an emperor.
10 Ah me! how sweet is love itself possessed,
When but love's shadows are so rich in joy! **A**

[*Enter Romeo's servant*, Balthasar, *booted*.]

News from Verona! How now, Balthasar?
Dost thou not bring me letters from the friar?
How doth my lady? Is my father well?
15 How fares my Juliet? That I ask again,
For nothing can be ill if she be well.

Balthasar. Then she is well, and nothing can be ill.
Her body sleeps in Capels' monument,
And her immortal part with angels lives.
20 I saw her laid low in her kindred's vault
And presently took post to tell it you.
O, pardon me for bringing these ill news,
Since you did leave it for my office, sir.

Romeo. Is it e'en so? Then I defy you, stars!
25 Thou knowst my lodging. Get me ink and paper
And hire posthorses. I will hence tonight.

Balthasar. I do beseech you, sir, have patience.
Your looks are pale and wild and do import
Some misadventure.

1–5 If I may . . . cheerful thoughts: If I can trust my dreams, something joyful is about to happen. My heart (**bosom's lord**) is happy and I am content.

A TRAGEDY
Paraphrase lines 1–11. What part of Romeo's seemingly happy dream **foreshadows** the tragic events to come?

1 Targeted Passage
17–19 Balthasar replies that Juliet is well, since although her body lies in the Capulets' (**Capels'**) burial vault, her soul (**her immortal part**) is with the angels.

21 presently took post: immediately rode (to Mantua).

23 you did . . . office: you gave me the duty of reporting important news to you.

24 I . . . stars: Romeo angrily challenges fate, which has caused him so much grief.

28–29 import some misadventure: suggest that something bad will happen.

Romeo and Juliet in the 1994 production of the Shakespeare Theatre in Washington, D.C.

RESOURCE MANAGER UNIT 10

Plan and Teach pp. 85–88

Literary Analysis
Summary pp. 89†*, 90‡*
Shakespearean Drama pp. 91, 92†*
Question Support p. 96*

Reading
Reading Shakespearean Drama
   pp. 93, 94†*
Reading Check p. 95

Grammar and Writing
Create Rhythm p. 97

Assessment
Selection Tests A, B/C pp. 99*, 101*
Test Generator CD

BEST PRACTICES TOOLKIT

Differentiated Instruction
   pp. 31–38*

Graphic Organizers/Strategies
Problem and Solution Charts
• Sequence Chain • Classification
Chart

Reading Support
Audio Anthology CD*

Technology
Literature Center at
ClassZone.com
Write*Smart* CD

---

* Resources for Differentiation   † Also in Spanish   ‡ In Haitian Creole and Vietnamese

Activity How does the photograph capture both the harshness and the tenderness of Romeo's and Juliet's deaths? ***Possible answer:*** *The harshness of death is seen in Juliet's awkward pose, with head lolling back and arms splayed. This harshness is tempered by the tenderness of Romeo's embrace and the scattered roses.*

DIFFERENTIATED INSTRUCTION

For general guidelines on differentiating instruction, see

📦 BEST PRACTICES TOOLKIT
Differentiated Instruction pp. 31–38

FOR LESS–PROFICIENT READERS

In combination with the *Audio Anthology CD,* use one or more Targeted Passages (pp. 1034, 1042, 1049) to ensure that students focus on key story events, concepts, and skills.

Preview Have students use a chart like this to organize the Scene 1 synopsis:

ROMEO . . .
Hears the report of Juliet's death
Does not hear Friar Laurence's message
Believes Balthasar's report
Decides to go to Verona and kill himself
Looks for a pharmacist to sell him poison

① Targeted Passage [Lines 17–23]

This passage uses Balthasar's news to set the tragic conclusion of the play in motion.

- What information has Balthasar brought? How does he know it?

- Why does Balthasar bring the news to Romeo? Why does he ask forgiveness for doing so?

B CHARACTER

Possible answer: Romeo means that he will go to where Juliet is buried and kill himself beside her. As is consistent with his character, Romeo plunges into action without thinking of options (such as consulting Friar Laurence) or the consequences of returning to Verona.

If students need help . . . Discuss whether Romeo was impulsive or thoughtful when he followed Juliet to her balcony, married Juliet, and sought revenge for Mercutio's death. Connect those impulsive events to the impulsiveness that Romeo now shows.

BACKGROUND

Apothecaries In Shakespeare's time, apothecaries were the lowest level of medical practitioners, below physicians and surgeons. Apothecaries were sometimes known as a physician's cook, because they prepared and dispensed the drugs prescribed by a physician. Others, however, dispensed fraudulent prescriptions to those who could barely afford them. The apothecary in *Romeo and Juliet* is clearly one beset by poverty but not necessarily dishonesty. His shop is shabby but contains legitimate ingredients used in prescriptions. Romeo notices "old cakes of roses" (line 47), which would have been used to treat ailments of the head.

Romeo.   Tush, thou art deceived.
30 Leave me and do the thing I bid thee do.
Hast thou no letters to me from the friar?
Balthasar. No, my good lord.
Romeo.   No matter. Get thee gone
And hire those horses. I'll be with thee straight.
[*Exit* Balthasar.]
Well, Juliet, I will lie with thee tonight. **B**
35 Let's see for means. O mischief, thou art swift
To enter in the thoughts of desperate men!
I do remember an apothecary,
And hereabouts he dwells, which late I noted
In tattered weeds, with overwhelming brows,
40 Culling of simples. Meager were his looks,
Sharp misery had worn him to the bones;
And in his needy shop a tortoise hung,
An alligator stuffed, and other skins
Of ill-shaped fishes; and about his shelves
45 A beggarly account of empty boxes,
Green earthen pots, bladders, and musty seeds,
Remnants of packthread, and old cakes of roses
Were thinly scattered, to make up a show.
Noting this penury, to myself I said,
50 "An if a man did need a poison now
Whose sale is present death in Mantua,
Here lives a caitiff wretch would sell it him."
O, this same thought did but forerun my need,
And this same needy man must sell it me.
55 As I remember, this should be the house.
Being holiday, the beggar's shop is shut.
What, ho! apothecary!
[*Enter* Apothecary.]
Apothecary.   Who calls so loud?
Romeo. Come hither, man. I see that thou art poor.
Hold, there is forty ducats. Let me have
60 A dram of poison, such soon-speeding gear
As will disperse itself through all the veins
That the life-weary taker may fall dead,
And that the trunk may be discharged of breath
As violently as hasty powder fired
65 Doth hurry from the fatal cannon's womb.
Apothecary. Such mortal drugs I have; but Mantua's law
Is death to any he that utters them.

B CHARACTER
What does Romeo mean in line 34? Explain whether he thoughtfully considers his options or plunges immediately into action.

35–40 Let's . . . means: Let me find a way (to join Juliet in death); **apothecary:** pharmacist; **tattered weeds:** ragged clothes; **culling of simples:** selecting herbs.

47 cakes of roses: rose petals pressed together to create a perfume.

49 penury: poverty.

50–52 "An if a man . . . sell it him": Though it is a crime to sell poison in Mantua, the apothecary is such a miserable (**caitiff**) wretch that he would probably do it for the money.

59 ducats: gold coins.

60–65 Romeo wants fast-acting (**soon-speeding**) poison that will work as quickly as gunpowder exploding in a cannon.

67 any . . . them: any person who dispenses or sells them.

DIFFERENTIATED INSTRUCTION

FOR ENGLISH LEARNERS

Concept Support As students read Romeo's description of the apothecary (lines 37–54), help them locate and discuss these expressions that indicate his poverty:

- *tattered weeds* (line 39), "ragged clothes"

- *Meager were his looks* (line 40), "he looked puny and thin"

- *worn him to the bones* (line 41), "made him thin through hardship"

- *needy* (line 42), "poorly stocked and ugly"

- *beggarly account* (line 45), "kind of inventory that a penniless person would have"

- *penury* (line 49), "poverty"

- *this same needy man* (line 54), "this man who needs money"

Romeo. Art thou so bare and full of wretchedness
And fearest to die? Famine is in thy cheeks,
70 Need and oppression starveth in thine eyes,
Contempt and beggary hangs upon thy back:
The world is not thy friend, nor the world's law;
The world affords no law to make thee rich;
Then be not poor, but break it and take this.
75 **Apothecary.** My poverty but not my will consents.

Romeo. I pay thy poverty and not thy will.

Apothecary. Put this in any liquid thing you will
And drink it off, and if you had the strength
Of twenty men, it would dispatch you straight.

80 **Romeo.** There is thy gold—worse poison to men's souls,
Doing more murder in this loathsome world,
Than these poor compounds that thou mayst not sell.
I sell thee poison; thou hast sold me none.
Farewell. Buy food and get thyself in flesh.
85 Come, cordial and not poison, go with me
To Juliet's grave; for there must I use thee.

[*Exeunt.*]

72–74 Romeo urges the apothecary to improve his situation by breaking the law and selling him the poison.

75 I'm doing this for the money, not because I think it's right.

79 **dispatch you straight:** kill you instantly.

85 Romeo refers to the poison as a **cordial,** a drink believed to be good for the heart. *Why does he refer to it in this way?*

SCENE 2 *Friar Laurence's cell in Verona.*

Friar Laurence's messenger arrives, saying that he was unable to deliver the letter to Romeo. Friar Laurence, his plans ruined, rushes to the Capulet vault before Juliet awakes. He intends to hide her in his room until Romeo can come to take her away.

[*Enter* Friar John.]

Friar John. Holy Franciscan friar, brother, ho!

[*Enter* Friar Laurence.]

Friar Laurence. This same should be the voice of Friar John.
Welcome from Mantua. What says Romeo?
Or, if his mind be writ, give me his letter.

5 **Friar John.** Going to find a barefoot brother out,
One of our order to associate me,
Here in this city visiting the sick,
And finding him, the searchers of the town,
Suspecting that we both were in a house
10 Where the infectious pestilence did reign,
Sealed up the doors, and would not let us forth,
So that my speed to Mantua there was stayed.

5–12 Friar John explains why he did not go to Mantua. He had asked another friar (**barefoot brother**), who had been caring for the sick, to go with him. The health officials of the town, believing that the friars had come into contact with a deadly plague (**infectious pestilence**), locked them up to keep them from infecting others.

Lines 59–75
DISCUSSION PROMPTS

Use these prompts to discuss Romeo's interaction with the apothecary:

Connect Have you ever been faced with a difficult choice? How does that experience help you understand the choice that the apothecary must make? *Students should identify the choice the apothecary must make regarding his poverty and his life.*

Analyze Which of these two characters has a greater fear of death? *Possible answer: The apothecary has a greater fear of death: he considers the death penalty for selling poison (lines 66–67). Romeo does not fear death. He is determined to buy the poison.*

Evaluate What does the apothecary's hesitancy to give Romeo the poison reveal about his character? *Possible answer: The apothecary is worried about what will happen if the authorities find out that he has sold an illegal substance. His hesitancy reveals that he cares about his own well-being and not Romeo's.*

BACKGROUND

"Infectious Pestilence" The streets of medieval and Renaissance cities were basically open sewers as well as communal garbage dumps and were largely responsible for breeding the rats whose infected fleas spread the plague or "Black Death." While no one really understood the nature of the plague's contagion, one of the few successful efforts to control it was to board up houses containing infected residents and quarantine the inhabitants.

FOR LESS-PROFICIENT READERS
Preview Have students read the Scene 2 synopsis and then use Problem and Solution Charts to record its key events.

BEST PRACTICES TOOLKIT—Transparency
Problem and Solution Charts p. B20

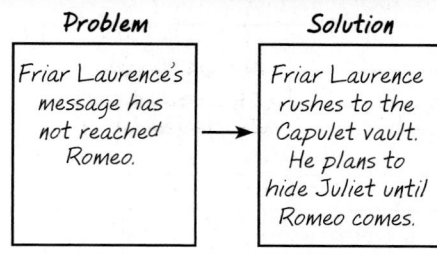

Problem

Friar Laurence's message has not reached Romeo.

Solution

Friar Laurence rushes to the Capulet vault. He plans to hide Juliet until Romeo comes.

FOR ENGLISH LEARNERS
Task Support Draw students' attention to the question in the marginal note for line 85. Explain that in his current state of mind, Romeo thinks that he can do no better than to die with Juliet. *Possible answer: Romeo refers to the poison as a cordial because it will end the pain in his heart from the loss of Juliet. The poison will be good because it will take him out of a world in which she no longer exists.*

Friar Laurence. Who bare my letter, then, to Romeo?

Friar John. I could not send it—here it is again—

15 Nor get a messenger to bring it thee,
So fearful were they of infection.

Friar Laurence. Unhappy fortune! By my brotherhood,
The letter was not nice, but full of charge,
Of dear import, and the neglecting it

20 May do much danger. Friar John, go hence,
Get me an iron crow and bring it straight
Unto my cell.

Friar John.   Brother, I'll go and bring it thee.

[*Exit.*]

Friar Laurence. Now must I to the monument alone.
Within this three hours will fair Juliet wake.

25 She will beshrew me much that Romeo
Hath had no notice of these accidents;
But I will write again to Mantua,
And keep her at my cell till Romeo come—
Poor living corse, closed in a dead man's tomb! **C**

[*Exit.*]

13 **bare:** carried (bore).

18–20 The letter wasn't trivial (**nice**) but contained a message of great importance (**dear import**). The fact that it wasn't sent (**neglecting it**) may cause great harm.

21 **iron crow:** crowbar.

25–26 **She ... accidents:** She will be furious with me when she learns that Romeo doesn't know what has happened.

C SOLILOQUY
Explain what you learn about the friar's new plan in this soliloquy. Why is it essential that the friar reach Juliet before Romeo does?

SCENE 3   *The cemetery that contains the Capulets' tomb.*

In the dark of night Paris comes to the cemetery to put flowers on Juliet's grave. At the same time Romeo arrives, and Paris hides. Paris assumes that Romeo is going to harm the bodies. He challenges Romeo, they fight, and Romeo kills Paris. When Romeo recognizes the dead Paris, he lays his body inside the tomb as Paris requested. Romeo declares his love for Juliet, drinks the poison, and dies. Shortly after, Friar Laurence arrives and discovers both bodies. When Juliet wakes up, the friar urges her to leave with him before the guard comes. Juliet refuses, and when the friar leaves, she kills herself with Romeo's dagger. The guards and the prince arrive, followed by the Capulets and Lord Montague, whose wife has just died of grief because of Romeo's exile. Friar Laurence explains what has happened. Capulet and Montague finally end their feud and promise to erect statues honoring Romeo and Juliet.

[*Enter* Paris *and his* Page *with flowers and a torch.*]

Paris. Give me thy torch, boy. Hence, and stand aloof.
Yet put it out, for I would not be seen.
Under yond yew tree lay thee all along,
Holding thine ear close to the hollow ground.

1 **aloof:** some distance away.

LITERARY ANALYSIS

C SOLILOQUY

Possible answer: *We learn that the friar will greet Juliet when she awakens and will hide her in his cell until Romeo arrives. It is essential that the friar reach Juliet first because Romeo believes that she is really dead. If Romeo reaches her first, he may harm himself.*

DIFFERENTIATED INSTRUCTION

FOR LESS–PROFICIENT READERS
Preview Have students read the scene synopsis carefully. Track the many events of Scene 3 using a Sequence Chain.

Paris brings flowers to Juliet's grave.

↓

Romeo arrives at the cemetery.

↓

Romeo fights with and kills Paris.

↓

Romeo grieves over Juliet's body and then kills himself.

↓

Friar Laurence arrives at the tomb.

↓

Juliet awakens but refuses to leave.

↓

When Friar Laurence leaves, Juliet stabs herself with Romeo's dagger.

↓

The families and Prince Escalus arrive, and Friar Laurence reveals the truth.

↓

The Capulets and Montagues end their feud.

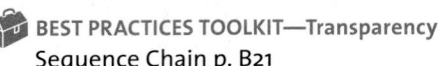 **BEST PRACTICES TOOLKIT—Transparency**
Sequence Chain p. B21

Behind the Curtain

Lighting

Directors use a variety of techniques to make a play's **lighting** effective. For example, spotlights can illuminate one character while leaving others in semi-darkness, and effects such as candles or prominent shadows can help create specific moods. What is distinctive about the lighting in each of these shots? Explain the effect each technique produces.

The Royal Shakespeare Company's 2004 production

The Royal Opera House's 2000 Covent Garden production

The Shakespeare Israeli Company's 1994 production

1039

REINFORCE *KEY IDEA:* LOVE AND HATE

Discuss How does Paris indicate that he indeed has **love** for Juliet? *Possible answer: Paris indicates his love by bringing flowers to the tomb and promising to continue to do so (even though he is not obligated to do so).*

5 So shall no foot upon the churchyard tread
   (Being loose, unfirm, with digging up of graves)
   But thou shalt hear it. Whistle then to me,
   As signal that thou hearst something approach.
   Give me those flowers. Do as I bid thee, go.
10 **Page** [*aside*]. I am almost afraid to stand alone
   Here in the churchyard; yet I will adventure.

   [*withdraws*]

   Paris. Sweet flower, with flowers thy bridal bed I strew

   [*He strews the tomb with flowers.*]

   (O woe! thy canopy is dust and stones)
   Which with sweet water nightly I will dew;
15 Or, wanting that, with tears distilled by moans.
   The obsequies that I for thee will keep
   Nightly shall be to strew thy grave and weep.

   [*The Page whistles.*]

   The boy gives warning something doth approach.
   What cursed foot wanders this way tonight
20 To cross my obsequies and true love's rite?
   What, with a torch? Muffle me, night, awhile.

   [*withdraws*]

   [*Enter Romeo and Balthasar with a torch, a mattock, and a crow of iron.*]

   Romeo. Give me that mattock and the wrenching iron.
   Hold, take this letter. Early in the morning
   See thou deliver it to my lord and father.
25 Give me the light. Upon thy life I charge thee,
   Whate'er thou hearest or seest, stand all aloof
   And do not interrupt me in my course.
   Why I descend into this bed of death
   Is partly to behold my lady's face,
30 But chiefly to take thence from her dead finger
   A precious ring—a ring that I must use
   In dear employment. Therefore hence, be gone.
   But if thou, jealous, dost return to pry
   In what I farther shall intend to do,
35 By heaven, I will tear thee joint by joint
   And strew this hungry churchyard with thy limbs.
   The time and my intents are savage-wild,
   More fierce and more inexorable far
   Than empty tigers or the roaring sea. **D**

12–17 Paris promises to decorate Juliet's grave with flowers, as he does now, and sprinkle it with either perfume (**sweet water**) or his tears. He will perform these honoring rites (**obsequies**) every night.

20 cross: interfere with.
21 muffle: hide.

mattock . . . iron: an ax and a crowbar.

32 in dear employment: for an important purpose.

33 jealous: curious.

37–39 Romeo's intention is more unstoppable (**inexorable**) than hungry (**empty**) tigers or the waves of an ocean.

D **TRAGEDY**
Reread lines 25–39 and think about how tragedies usually end for the main characters. Paraphrase the two reasons Romeo gives for going into the tomb. What third reason does he hint at?

LITERARY ANALYSIS

D TRAGEDY

Possible answer: Tragedies usually end with the death of the main characters. Romeo gives Balthasar two reasons for going into the tomb: he wants to see Juliet's face (line 29) and he wants to take a ring from her finger (lines 30–32). In lines 34 and 37, he hints at a third reason, which he stated in Scene 1: to kill himself with poison and die beside Juliet's dead body.

DIFFERENTIATED INSTRUCTION

FOR LESS–PROFICIENT READERS
Paraphrasing Shakespeare Have students paraphrase lines 12–15, in which Paris reveals his feelings for Juliet. *Possible answer: You are my sweet flower, and I will place flowers where you lie. (How sad it is that your bed is made of dust and stones!) Each night I will bring water to the flowers, or I will water the flowers with my tears.*

FOR ADVANCED LEARNERS/PRE–AP
Hypothesize In Scene 1, Balthasar left Romeo in Mantua after he delivered his news but before Romeo bought the poison. Ask students to imagine that Balthasar knows about the poison, after all. Have them meet in small groups to discuss what Balthasar might say and do—and whether it would make a difference in the story's outcome. Have groups compare responses and come to a consensus.

40 **Balthasar.** I will be gone, sir, and not trouble you.

Romeo. So shalt thou show me friendship. Take thou that.
Live, and be prosperous; and farewell, good fellow.

Balthasar [*aside*]. For all this same, I'll hide me hereabout.
His looks I fear, and his intents I doubt.
[*withdraws*]

45 **Romeo.** Thou detestable maw, thou womb of death,
Gorged with the dearest morsel of the earth,
Thus I enforce thy rotten jaws to open,
And in despite I'll cram thee with more food.
[*Romeo opens the tomb.*]

Paris. This is that banish'd haughty Montague
50 That murdered my love's cousin—with which grief
It is supposed the fair creature died—
And here is come to do some villainous shame
To the dead bodies. I will apprehend him.
Stop thy unhallowed toil, vile Montague!
55 Can vengeance be pursued further than death?
Condemned villain, I do apprehend thee.
Obey, and go with me; for thou must die.

Romeo. I must indeed; and therefore came I hither.
Good gentle youth, tempt not a desp'rate man.
60 Fly hence and leave me. Think upon these gone;
Let them affright thee. I beseech thee, youth,
Put not another sin upon my head
By urging me to fury. O, be gone!
By heaven, I love thee better than myself.
65 For I come hither armed against myself.
Stay not, be gone. Live, and hereafter say
A madman's mercy bid thee run away.

Paris. I do defy thy conjuration
And apprehend thee for a felon here.

70 **Romeo.** Wilt thou provoke me? Then have at thee, boy! **E**
[*They fight.*]

43 *Who else besides Balthasar is hiding in the cemetery at this point?*

45–49 Romeo addresses the tomb as though it were devouring people. He calls it a hateful stomach (**detestable maw**) that is filled (**gorged**) with Juliet, the **dearest morsel of the earth.** He uses his crowbar to open its **rotten jaws** and moves to enter the tomb.

49–53 Recognizing Romeo, Paris speaks these first few lines to himself. He is angry with Romeo, believing that Romeo's killing Tybalt caused Juliet to die of grief.

58–67 Romeo rejects Paris' challenge. He tells Paris to think of those already killed and to leave before Romeo is forced to kill him too. Romeo swears that he has come to harm himself, not Paris.

68 I reject your appeal.

E **CHARACTER**
Consider what you know about Romeo's **traits** and **flaws.** Is Romeo at fault for fighting Paris? Why or why not?

FOR ENGLISH LEARNERS

Task Support After students read the marginal question for line 43, elicit what Paris says to his page before Romeo and Balthasar arrive on the scene. *Possible answer: Besides Balthasar, Paris and his page are hiding in the cemetery.*

Concept Support Make sure students understand that in lines 49–57, Paris identifies with the Capulets. He refers to Romeo with a family insult (line 49), believes the Capulets' story about why Juliet died (lines 50–51), assumes that Romeo has come to desecrate the tomb (lines 52–53), and assumes the responsibility of defending the family's honor by taking Romeo into custody (lines 56–57).

LITERARY ANALYSIS

E **CHARACTER**

Possible answer: *Romeo's chief traits are his impulsiveness and his great passion. His main flaw is that he acts without thinking about consequences or alternatives. Romeo is true to his character when he fights Paris because he is acting upon his passion and his impulsiveness. Students might say that Romeo is not at fault because Paris provokes him, or that he is at fault because he does not explain his intentions clearly to Paris after being challenged.*

If students need help . . . Offer these suggestions of traits and flaws and allow students to accept or reject each one: *stubborn, calm, understanding, kind, hate-filled, defensive, belligerent, trustworthy, passionate, impulsive, idealistic, selfish, loyal.* Discuss how any suggestions that students accept might point to Romeo's

Lines 88–120
DISCUSSION PROMPTS

Use these prompts to discuss Romeo's state of mind at this moment in the play:

Connect Have you ever been surprised by decisions that you or someone you know made under great stress? What conditions at this point in the story might weaken Romeo's judgment? *Students may suggest that the late hour, worry, and grief probably cause Romeo great stress and compromise his judgment.*

Analyze What features of Juliet's face, mentioned by Romeo, should lead Romeo to doubt his intent to commit suicide? *Possible answer: Romeo notices that Juliet's cheeks and lips are red and that she does not look dead at all (lines 94–96).*

Synthesize What does Romeo hope to accomplish by killing himself? *Possible answer: Romeo says that by killing himself he will repay Tybalt for murdering him and will be able to protect Juliet from becoming Death's lover (lines 97–107).*

Page. O Lord, they fight! I will go call the watch.
[*Exit.*]

Paris. O, I am slain! [*falls*] If thou be merciful,
Open the tomb, lay me with Juliet.
[*dies*]

Romeo. In faith, I will. Let me peruse this face.
75 Mercutio's kinsman, noble County Paris!
What said my man when my betossed soul
Did not attend him as we rode? I think
He told me Paris should have married Juliet.
Said he not so? or did I dream it so?
80 Or am I mad, hearing him talk of Juliet,
To think it was so? O, give me thy hand,
One writ with me in sour misfortune's book!
I'll bury thee in a triumphant grave.
A grave? O, no, a lantern, slaughtered youth,
85 For here lies Juliet, and her beauty makes
This vault a feasting presence full of light.
Death, lie thou there, by a dead man interred.

[*lays* Paris *in the tomb*]
How oft when men are at the point of death
Have they been merry! which their keepers call
90 A lightning before death. O, how may I
Call this a lightning? O my love! my wife!
Death, that hath sucked the honey of thy breath,
Hath had no power yet upon thy beauty.
Thou art not conquered. Beauty's ensign yet
95 Is crimson in thy lips and in thy cheeks,
And death's pale flag is not advanced there.
Tybalt, liest thou there in thy bloody sheet?
O, what more favor can I do to thee
Than with that hand that cut thy youth in twain
100 To sunder his that was thine enemy?
Forgive me, cousin! Ah, dear Juliet,
Why art thou yet so fair? Shall I believe
That unsubstantial Death is amorous,
And that the lean abhorred monster keeps
105 Thee here in dark to be his paramour?
For fear of that I still will stay with thee
And never from this palace of dim night

74–78 Romeo discovers that the man he has just killed is Paris, who he vaguely remembers being told was supposed to marry Juliet.

 Targeted Passage

82 Romeo notes that, like himself, Paris has been a victim of bad luck

84–87 Romeo will bury Paris with Juliet, whose beauty fills the tomb with light. Paris' corpse (**Death**) is being buried (**interred**) by a dead man in that Romeo expects to be dead soon.

94 **ensign:** sign.

98–100 **O, what . . . enemy:** I can best repay you (Tybalt) by killing your enemy (myself) with the same hand that cut your youth in two (**twain**).

102–105 Romeo can't get over how beautiful Juliet still looks. He asks whether Death is loving (**amorous**) and whether it has taken Juliet as its lover (**paramour**).

DIFFERENTIATED INSTRUCTION

FOR LESS–PROFICIENT READERS
Targeted Passage [Lines 71–87]

In this passage, Romeo removes one more obstacle between himself and Juliet: Paris.

- Who wins the fight between Paris and Romeo?

- When does Romeo figure out who Paris is? How did he find out that Paris was going to marry Juliet?

- What does Romeo do and say after killing Paris?

FOR ADVANCED LEARNERS/PRE–AP
Analyze Staging Explain that the original staging of this scene is unclear. A trap door in the stage may have opened into the (unseen) tomb beneath; in that case, Romeo would have given his final speech before disappearing below stage, and Juliet then would have risen through the trap door. There are many other possibilities. Have students write and share a paragraph or two describing how they would stage this scene.

Depart again. Here, here will I remain
With worms that are thy chambermaids. O, here
110 Will I set up my everlasting rest
And shake the yoke of inauspicious stars
From this world-wearied flesh. Eyes, look your last!
Arms, take your last embrace! and, lips, O you
The doors of breath, seal with a righteous kiss
115 A dateless bargain to engrossing death!
Come, bitter conduct; come, unsavory guide!
Thou desperate pilot, now at once run on
The dashing rocks thy seasick weary bark!
Here's to my love! [drinks] O true apothecary!
120 Thy drugs are quick. Thus with a kiss I die.
[falls]

[Enter Friar Laurence, with lantern, crow, and spade.]

Friar Laurence. Saint Francis be my speed! how oft tonight
Have my old feet stumbled at graves! Who's there?

Balthasar. Here's one, a friend, and one that knows you well.

Friar Laurence. Bliss be upon you! Tell me, good my friend,
125 What torch is yond that vainly lends his light
To grubs and eyeless skulls? As I discern,
It burneth in the Capels' monument.

Balthasar. It doth so, holy sir; and there's my master,
One that you love.

Friar Laurence. Who is it?

Balthasar. Romeo.

130 **Friar Laurence.** How long hath he been there?

Balthasar. Full half an hour.

Friar Laurence. Go with me to the vault.

Balthasar. I dare not, sir.
My master knows not but I am gone hence,
And fearfully did menace me with death
If I did stay to look on his intents.

135 **Friar Laurence.** Stay then; I'll go alone. Fear comes upon me.
O, much I fear some ill unthrifty thing.

111–112 **shake . . . flesh:** rid myself of the burden of an unhappy fate (**inauspicious stars**). *On what does Romeo blame his imminent death?*

115 **dateless:** eternal; never-ending. Romeo means that what he is about to do can never be undone.

117–118 Romeo compares himself to the pilot of a ship (**bark**) who is going to crash on the rocks because he is so weary and sick.

132–134 **My master . . . intents:** My master told me to go away and threatened me with death if I watched what he did.

136 **unthrifty:** unlucky.

ROMEO AND JULIET: ACT FIVE, SCENE 3   **1043**

Lines 110–120
REINFORCE *KEY IDEA:* LOVE AND HATE

Discuss Does Romeo really prove his **love** for Juliet by drinking the poison? What action might he have taken to show his love more effectively? ***Possible answer:*** *Perhaps Romeo's refusal to live without Juliet is the greatest proof of his love. On the other hand, killing himself is an act of despair. If Romeo were less impulsive—if he could look beyond this moment of grief—he might have decided that he could honor Juliet and show his love for her more effectively by working to end the feud between their families.*

FOR ENGLISH LEARNERS

Task Support Have students read the marginal note and question for lines 111–112. Remind students that the play's Prologue refers to Romeo and Juliet as "star-crossed lovers" and that various characters have spoken of the role of Fortune in events. ***Possible answer:*** *Romeo blames his death on an unkind cosmic force, which he calls "the yoke of inauspicious stars" (line 111).*

Balthasar. As I did sleep under this yew tree here,
I dreamt my master and another fought,
And that my master slew him.

Friar Laurence.   Romeo!

[*stoops and looks on the blood and weapons*]

140 Alack, alack, what blood is this which stains
The stony entrance of this sepulcher?
What mean these masterless and gory swords
To lie discolored by this place of peace?

[*enters the tomb*]

Romeo! O, pale! Who else? What, Paris too?
145 And steeped in blood? Ah, what an unkind hour
Is guilty of this lamentable chance!
The lady stirs.

[Juliet *rises.*]

Juliet. O comfortable friar! where is my lord?
I do remember well where I should be,
150 And there I am. Where is my Romeo?

Friar Laurence. I hear some noise. Lady, come from that nest

140–143 Alack . . . place of peace? Why are these bloody swords lying here at the tomb (**sepulcher**), a place that should be peaceful? (The swords are also **masterless,** or without their owners.)

148 comfortable: comforting.

Romeo and Juliet in the 2004
production of the Globe Theatre

DIFFERENTIATED INSTRUCTION

FOR LESS–PROFICIENT READERS

Summarize Plot Help students develop this list of characters whose deaths are a part of Scene 3:

- **Lady Montague:** dead of grief over Romeo's banishment

- **Paris:** killed in a duel with Romeo

- **Romeo:** poisoned by his own hand in grief for Juliet

- **Juliet:** self-inflicted stab wound after realizing that Romeo is dead

Of death, contagion, and unnatural sleep.
A greater power than we can contradict
Hath thwarted our intents. Come, come away.
155 Thy husband in thy bosom there lies dead;
And Paris too. Come, I'll dispose of thee
Among a sisterhood of holy nuns.
Stay not to question, for the watch is coming.
Come, go, good Juliet. I dare no longer stay.

160 **Juliet.** Go, get thee hence, for I will not away.
[*Exit* Friar Laurence.]
What's here? A cup, closed in my true love's hand?
Poison, I see, hath been his timeless end.
O churl! drunk all, and left no friendly drop
To help me after? I will kiss thy lips.
165 Haply some poison yet doth hang on them
To make me die with a restorative.
[*kisses him*]
Thy lips are warm!

Chief Watchman [*within*]. Lead, boy. Which way?

Juliet. Yea, noise? Then I'll be brief. O happy dagger!
[*snatches Romeo's dagger*]
170 This is thy sheath; there rust, and let me die.
[*She stabs herself and falls.*]
[*Enter* Watchmen *with the* Page *of Paris.*]

Page. This is the place. There, where the torch doth burn.

Chief Watchman. The ground is bloody. Search about the
churchyard.
Go, some of you; whoe'er you find attach.
[*Exeunt some of the* Watch.]
Pitiful sight! here lies the County slain;
175 And Juliet bleeding, warm, and newly dead,
Who here hath lain this two days buried.
Go, tell the Prince; run to the Capulets;
Raise up the Montagues; some others search.
[*Exeunt others of the* Watch.]
We see the ground whereon these woes do lie,
180 But the true ground of all these piteous woes
We cannot without circumstance descry.
[*Reenter some of the* Watch, *with* Balthasar.]

153–154 A greater . . . intents: A greater force than we can fight (**contradict**) has ruined our plans (**thwarted our intents**).

156–157 I'll dispose . . . nuns: I'll find a place for you in a convent of nuns.

158–159 *Why is the friar so anxious to leave?*

162 timeless: happening before its proper time.

163 churl: miser.

165 haply: perhaps.

173 attach: arrest.

178 raise up: awaken.

179–181 We see . . . descry: We see the earth (**ground**) these bodies lie on. But the real cause (**true ground**) of these deaths is yet for us to discover (**descry**).

Lines 151–160
DISCUSSION PROMPTS

Use these prompts to explore the role of Friar Laurence in this scene:

Recall What does Friar Laurence propose to do with Juliet? Why? *Possible answer: He wants to send her to a convent of nuns where she can be protected. He fears the approach of the guard who will hand her over to her father, and her father's severe reaction.*

Analyze Why does Friar Laurence flee the scene so hastily? *Possible answer: Friar Laurence has broken the law by helping Romeo return from exile. It seems possible that he might be held partially responsible for the death of Paris, if not others. He is also responsible for the secret marriage and the pretended death of Juliet, and so severe punishment almost certainly awaits him.*

Evaluate Do Friar Laurence's actions in this scene negate his earlier role as counselor and confidant to Juliet? Explain. *Some students may answer no, as the friar tries to protect Juliet in his offer to place her in a convent. By fleeing, he saved himself and could continue to work on her behalf. Other students may answer yes. If he really cared about Juliet, the friar would have stayed to console her over the death of Romeo and continue to beg for her safety, even after the guards apprehended her.*

FOR ENGLISH LEARNERS

Task Support After students read the marginal question about lines 158–159, have them review line 71, in which the page runs from the fight between Romeo and Paris to call the watch. *Possible answer: Friar Laurence is afraid that the watch will find him in the vault. He probably doesn't want to have to explain the bodies or be implicated in their deaths.*

FOR ADVANCED LEARNERS/PRE–AP

Analyze Character Critics have remarked that Friar Laurence serves as a kind of surrogate parent to both Romeo and Juliet. After students have finished reading the play, challenge them to write two to three paragraphs expressing their views on the role of Friar Laurence and the degree to which he was or wasn't a positive presence in the lives of Romeo and Juliet.

REINFORCE *KEY IDEA:* LOVE AND HATE

Discuss Prince Escalus refers to "this foul murder" (line 198), and the chief watchman says that Romeo has been "slaughtered" (line 199). Both the prince and the watchman seem to interpret the scene as one of **hate.** In what ironic sense is it actually a scene of **love**? ***Possible answer:*** *Romeo has killed Paris, reluctantly, in order to be with his beloved Juliet. He then has killed himself rather than live without Juliet's love, and Juliet has killed herself rather than live without Romeo's love.*

Second Watchman. Here's Romeo's man. We found him in the churchyard.

Chief Watchman. Hold him in safety till the Prince come hither.

[*Reenter* Friar Laurence *and another* Watchman.]

Third Watchman. Here is a friar that trembles, sighs, and weeps.
185 We took this mattock and this spade from him
As he was coming from this churchyard side.

Chief Watchman. A great suspicion! Stay the friar too.

[*Enter the* Prince *and* Attendants.]

Prince. What misadventure is so early up,
That calls our person from our morning rest?

[*Enter* Capulet, Lady Capulet, *and others*.]

190 **Capulet.** What should it be, that they so shriek abroad?

Lady Capulet. The people in the street cry "Romeo,"
Some "Juliet," and some "Paris"; and all run,
With open outcry, toward our monument.

Prince. What fear is this which startles in our ears?

195 **Chief Watchman.** Sovereign, here lies the County Paris slain;
And Romeo dead, and Juliet, dead before,
Warm and new killed.

Prince. Search, seek, and know how this foul murder comes.

Chief Watchman. Here is a friar, and slaughtered Romeo's man,
200 With instruments upon them fit to open
These dead men's tombs.

Capulet. O heavens! O wife, look how our daughter bleeds!
This dagger hath mista'en, for, lo, his house
Is empty on the back of Montague,
205 And it missheathed in my daughter's bosom!

Lady Capulet. O me! this sight of death is as a bell
That warns my old age to a sepulcher.

[*Enter* Montague *and others*.]

Prince. Come, Montague; for thou art early up
To see thy son and heir now early down.

210 **Montague.** Alas, my liege, my wife is dead tonight!
Grief of my son's exile hath stopped her breath.
What further woe conspires against mine age?

Prince. Look, and thou shalt see.

Montague. O thou untaught! what manners is in this,
215 To press before thy father to a grave?

182–187 The guards arrest Balthasar and Friar Laurence as suspicious characters.

194 startles: causes alarm.

203–205 This dagger...in my daughter's bosom: This dagger has missed its target. It should rest in the sheath (**house**) that Romeo wears. Instead it is in Juliet's chest.

210 liege: lord.

214–215 what manners...grave: What kind of behavior is this, for a son to die before his father?

DIFFERENTIATED INSTRUCTION

FOR ADVANCED LEARNERS/PRE–AP
Evaluate Resolution (Part 1) Have students skim these last pages and determine that of the play's main characters, only the nurse and Benvolio appear to be absent from the resolution. What distinguishes these two is that each is the best friend of one of the lovers. Ask students either to defend Shakespeare's omission of these characters or to explain how the two could have been incorporated into the conclusion.

Prince. Seal up the mouth of outrage for a while,
Till we can clear these ambiguities
And know their spring, their head, their true descent;
And then will I be general of your woes
220 And lead you even to death. Meantime forbear,
And let mischance be slave to patience.
Bring forth the parties of suspicion.

Friar Laurence. I am the greatest, able to do least,
Yet most suspected, as the time and place
225 Doth make against me, of this direful murder;
And here I stand, both to impeach and purge
Myself condemned and myself excused.

Prince. Then say at once what thou dost know in this.

Friar Laurence. I will be brief, for my short date of breath
230 Is not so long as is a tedious tale.
Romeo, there dead, was husband to that Juliet;
And she, there dead, that Romeo's faithful wife.
I married them; and their stol'n marriage day
Was Tybalt's doomsday, whose untimely death
235 Banish'd the new-made bridegroom from this city;
For whom, and not for Tybalt, Juliet pined.
You, to remove that siege of grief from her,
Betrothed and would have married her perforce
To County Paris. Then comes she to me
240 And with wild looks bid me devise some mean
To rid her from this second marriage,
Or in my cell there would she kill herself.
Then gave I her (so tutored by my art)
A sleeping potion; which so took effect
245 As I intended, for it wrought on her
The form of death. Meantime I writ to Romeo
That he should hither come as this dire night
To help to take her from her borrowed grave,
Being the time the potion's force should cease.
250 But he which bore my letter, Friar John,
Was stayed by accident, and yesternight
Returned my letter back. Then all alone
At the prefixed hour of her waking
Came I to take her from her kindred's vault;
255 Meaning to keep her closely at my cell
Till I conveniently could send to Romeo.
But when I came, some minute ere the time
Of her waking, here untimely lay
The noble Paris and true Romeo dead.
260 She wakes; and I entreated her come forth

216–221 Seal . . . patience: Stop your emotional outbursts until we can find out the source (**spring**) of these confusing events (**ambiguities**). Wait (**forbear**) and be patient, and let's find out what happened.

223–227 Friar Laurence confesses that he is most responsible for these events. He will both accuse (**impeach**) himself and clear (**purge**) himself of guilt.

236 It was Romeo's banishment, not Tybalt's death, that made Juliet so sad.

248 borrowed: temporary.

254 kindred's: family's.

Lines 223–269
DISCUSSION PROMPTS
Use these prompts to explore Friar Laurence's defense before Prince Escalus:

Summarize Summarize Friar Laurence's explanation of the deaths of Romeo, Juliet, and Paris. *Possible answer: Friar Laurence retells the tale of Romeo's marriage to Juliet, his banishment, Juliet's plea for help, and their fateful deaths.*

Analyze Why is it appropriate that Friar Laurence be the one to explain the events that led to the three deaths? *Possible answer: Friar Laurence is an appropriate source because he has been involved in many of the steps of the lovers' relationship and has taken great risks to get them together. The fact that he is neither a Capulet nor a Montague means that he can relate the events objectively.*

Evaluate Does Friar Laurence think he has done anything wrong? Should he think so? *Possible answer: Friar Laurence thinks that he has done wrong but that his actions are excusable (lines 226–227). Since the lovers followed his plans, Friar Laurence is probably more culpable than he allows in this speech.*

FOR ENGLISH LEARNERS
Vocabulary: Outdated Forms Have students add these words to their language journals. (See the **For English Learners** activity on page 940.) After they record each term and its definition, have them reread the lines and substitute the definitions for the words.

- *Banish'd* (line 235), "Banished"
- *perforce* (line 238), "by necessity"
- *wrought* (line 245), "worked" (made happen)
- *writ* (line 246), "wrote"
- *stayed* (line 251), "detained"
- *yesternight* (line 251), "last night"
- *prefixed* (line 253), "prearranged"
- *conveniently* (line 256), "in a proper way"

And bear this work of heaven with patience;
But then a noise did scare me from the tomb,
And she, too desperate, would not go with me,
But, as it seems, did violence on herself.
265 All this I know, and to the marriage
Her nurse is privy; and if aught in this
Miscarried by my fault, let my old life
Be sacrificed, some hour before his time,
Unto the rigor of severest law.

270 **Prince.** We still have known thee for a holy man.
Where's Romeo's man? What can he say in this?

Balthasar. I brought my master news of Juliet's death;
And then in post he came from Mantua
To this same place, to this same monument.
275 This letter he early bid me give his father,
And threatened me with death, going in the vault,
If I departed not and left him there.

Prince. Give me the letter. I will look on it.
Where is the County's page that raised the watch?
280 Sirrah, what made your master in this place?

Page. He came with flowers to strew his lady's grave;
And bid me stand aloof, and so I did.
Anon comes one with light to ope the tomb;
And by-and-by my master drew on him;
285 And then I ran away to call the watch.

Prince. This letter doth make good the friar's words,
Their course of love, the tidings of her death;
And here he writes that he did buy a poison
Of a poor 'pothecary, and therewithal
290 Came to this vault to die and lie with Juliet.
Where be these enemies? Capulet, Montague,
See what a scourge is laid upon your hate,
That heaven finds means to kill your joys with love!
And I, for winking at your discords too,
295 Have lost a brace of kinsmen. All are punished. ⑥

Capulet. O brother Montague, give me thy hand.
This is my daughter's jointure, for no more
Can I demand.

265–269 **and to . . . law:** Her nurse can bear witness to this secret marriage. If I am responsible for any of this, let the law punish me with death.

270 *How does the Prince respond to the friar's acceptance of blame?*

273 **in post:** at full speed.

279–280 The Prince asks for Paris' servant, who notified the guards (**raised the watch**). Then he asks the servant why Paris was at the cemetery.

283–285 **Anon . . . call the watch:** Soon (**anon**) someone with a light came and opened the tomb. Paris drew his sword, and I ran to call the guards.

292–295 **See what . . . punished:** Look at the punishment your hatred has brought on you. Heaven has killed your children (**joys**) with love. For shutting my eyes to your arguments (**discords**), I have lost two relatives. We have all been punished.

⑥ **TRAGEDY**
Reread lines 291–295. On what does the prince blame all the deaths? What **theme,** or message, might this passage suggest?

297–298 **jointure:** dowry, the payment a bride's father traditionally made to the groom. Capulet means that no one could demand more of a bride's father than he has already paid.

LITERARY ANALYSIS

⑥ TRAGEDY

Possible answer: *The prince blames the deaths on the enmity between the Capulets and Montagues. The theme may be that hatred hurts the person who hates as well as the person who is hated, or that hatred will be punished by the destruction of joy.*

If students need help . . . Discuss these questions:

- What "joys" does the prince refer to in line 293?
- What does the prince mean when he says that these "joys" have been killed with love?
- What scourge, or punishment, does the prince describe?
- Why and how has the prince also been punished in these events?

DIFFERENTIATED INSTRUCTION

FOR ENGLISH LEARNERS

Task Support Have students read the marginal question for line 270 and then reread line 270 itself. Explain that a person in a religious order was thought to answer to the laws of heaven even more than to human laws. ***Possible answer:*** *The prince dismisses the friar's acceptance of blame. Since the friar is a holy man, the prince implies, his character is above reproach.*

Concept Support Have students carefully read these last two pages of the play and the marginal notes. Then have them work in pairs to write a speech-by-speech summary of the ending. Use these sentences to start:

- The prince forgives the friar.
- Balthasar says that he has a letter from Romeo to his father.
- The prince takes the letter and asks why Paris was at the cemetery.

Montague.   But I can give thee more;
For I will raise her statue in pure gold,
300 That whiles Verona by that name is known,
There shall no figure at such rate be set
As that of true and faithful Juliet.

Capulet. As rich shall Romeo's by his lady's lie—
Poor sacrifices of our enmity!

305 **Prince.** A glooming peace this morning with it brings.
The sun for sorrow will not show his head.
Go hence, to have more talk of these sad things;
Some shall be pardoned, and some punished;
For never was a story of more woe
310 Than this of Juliet and her Romeo.
[*Exeunt.*]

③ Targeted Passage

301 at such rate be set: be valued so highly.

303–304 Capulet promises to do for Romeo what Montague will do for Juliet. Their children have become sacrifices to their hatred (**enmity**).

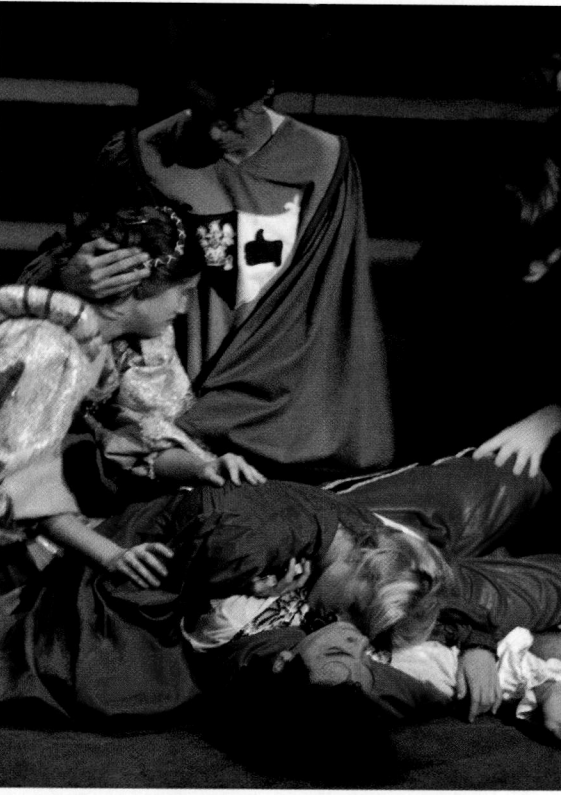

The Capulets and Lord Montague mourn their children's deaths in an Austin, Texas, high school production.

ANALYZE VISUALS

Activity What elements of stagecraft contribute to the mood and energy of the closing scene in this production? *Possible answer: The costumes show that the play has a traditional Elizabethan setting. The vivid colors and opulent fabrics convey the high social standing of the characters. The bodies of Romeo and Juliet are spotlighted, making them the focus of the scene.*

ACT FIVE WRAP-UP

SYNTHESIZE Ask students to comment on how love and hate play a role in the events of Act Five. Ask them which of the two they believed in the end to be stronger and why.

⭐ **CRITIQUE** Have students discuss the reasons that Romeo and Juliet have become symbols of great love. Encourage students to share why they think this drama has retained its power over the centuries.

FOR LESS-PROFICIENT READERS

③ Targeted Passage [Lines 298–310]

In this concluding passage, the families settle their feud and make plans to honor Romeo and Juliet.

- What will Montague do to honor Juliet? What will Capulet do to honor Romeo?

- How will their actions settle the feud?

- How will Prince Escalus follow up on what has happened?

FOR ADVANCED LEARNERS/PRE-AP

Evaluate Resolution (Part 2) Is this feud really over? Point out that both Capulet and Montague speak out of sudden grief and in the presence of the condemning Prince Escalus. In some productions of the play, the actors' body language suggests that the reconciliation is reluctant or even temporary. Ask students to write a paragraph about why it matters that the reconciliation be genuine and lasting; then have them compare responses in small groups.

Practice and Apply

After Reading

For additional support of post-reading questions, use these copy masters:

R RESOURCE MANAGER—Copy Masters

Reading Check p. 95 (to check understanding of the selection)

Shakespearean Drama p. 91 (for practice of literary analysis standards focus)

Question Support p. 96 (After Reading questions adapted for English learners and less-proficient readers)

For additional questions, see page 87.

For additional exercises to challenge students, see

ℹ Power Thinking at **ClassZone.com**

ANSWERS

Comprehension

1. *plague quarantines in Verona*

2. *Paris thinks that Romeo is an enemy of the Capulets and has come to desecrate the tomb.*

3. *Paris challenges and is killed by Romeo, who places Paris's body in the tomb. Romeo poisons himself in the tomb, thinking that Juliet is dead. Juliet stabs herself in the tomb when she realizes that Romeo is dead.*

Literary Analysis

Possible answers:

4. ■ **STANDARDS FOCUS** *Reading Shakespearean Drama The death of Romeo, Juliet, and Paris and the families' reconciliation make up the resolution of the play. There is satisfaction in the fact that the feuding seems to end and the families finally seem to realize how wrong they have been. On the other hand, their reconciliation has only begun, and it may not be strong enough to make up for the death and loss in the play.*

5. *Students may suggest that they would find Friar Laurence worthy of punishment, even though Prince Escalus pardoned him. Students may also identify a punishment for Capulet and Montague, noting that their feud resulted in many deaths.*

6. *Answers will vary. In Scene 1, lines 1–11, Romeo describes his happy dream. The soliloquy shows his deep love for Juliet; it also increases the sense of irony, for the*

Comprehension

1. **Recall** What prevents Friar John from delivering the letter to Romeo?

2. **Recall** Why does Paris attack Romeo at the Capulets' tomb?

3. **Summarize** How do the bodies of Paris, Romeo, and Juliet all end up in the Capulets' tomb? Explain how each character loses his or her life.

Literary Analysis

4. **Reading Shakespearean Drama** In Shakespearean drama, the **resolution,** or final plot stage, occurs in the last act. Look back at the chart you completed as you read. Describe the events that make up the resolution of this tragedy. Do you think this sequence of events brings the play to a satisfying conclusion? Explain your answer.

5. **Make Judgments** In the play's final speech, Prince Escalus declares, "Some shall be pardoned, and some punished." If you were the ruler of Verona, whom would you pardon, and whom would you punish? Explain.

6. **Identify Soliloquy** Identify a soliloquy in Act Five. Citing specific lines of the play, explain what you learn about the character who is speaking.

7. **Analyze Tragedy** In a tragedy, the hero or heroine usually has a character flaw that leads to his or her downfall. Is this true of Romeo and Juliet? Cite evidence from the tragedy to support your explanation.

8. **Examine Universal Theme** Many of the themes in *Romeo and Juliet* are universal—they are as relevant today as they were in the 1590s. Examine the values and experiences shown, and think about how each is presented in *Romeo and Juliet.* Complete the chart by stating how each topic is conveyed as a theme in the play. Which theme do you find most relevant today?

Value or Experience	Statement of Theme
Fate	There are forces in life over which people have no control.
Family ties	
Friendship	
Love	

Literary Criticism

9. **Critical Interpretations** *Romeo and Juliet,* according to the critic F. M. Dickey, is "a drama of love and hate." Of these two feelings, the critic maintains, "love overshadows the other dramatically, since it is the passion of the protagonists and since Shakespeare has lavished his most moving poetry upon the love scenes." Do you agree that **love** overshadows **hate** in this play? Support your conclusion with evidence from the text.

---

audience knows that some of his comments have meanings that are yet to be revealed.

7. *Some students may feel that rashness is their chief flaw. Others may mention the couple's overly romantic attitudes or their disobedience of social expectations.*

8. *Family ties: are strong, but romantic love is stronger. Friendship: Hate can ruin everything, even the best of friendships. Love: doesn't care who your family is; anyone, even sworn enemies, can fall in love. Relevance will depend upon students' interpretations of the themes.*

Literary Criticism

Possible answer:

9. *Some students may agree that love overshadows hate, for the reasons listed. These students may cite as evidence any of the scenes in which the lovers speak to each other. Other students may argue that since the lovers were destroyed by family hatred, hate is stronger than love.*

Reading-Writing Connection

Increase your understanding of *The Tragedy of Romeo and Juliet* by responding to these prompts. Then use **Revision: Grammar and Style** to improve your writing.

WRITING PROMPTS | SELF-CHECK

A. Short Response: Write Blank Verse
What if Romeo had taken slower-acting poison? Imagine that Juliet wakes before the poison kills Romeo, so that he is able to utter his last words of love to her. Write **six to eight lines of blank verse** in which Romeo says goodbye to Juliet before dying.

A successful verse will . . .
- be written in iambic pentameter (for help with this, turn back to page 932)
- mimic the lyric language of Shakespeare and sound like something Romeo would say

B. Extended Response: Analyze Tragedy
How does Shakespeare portray both **love** and **hate** as causes of violence in *Romeo and Juliet*? Write a **three-to-five-paragraph response** describing how the writer presents each emotion as a cause of catastrophe.

A strong analysis will . . .
- explore how each emotion contributes to the bloody resolution of the play
- include detailed evidence from the play as support

REVISION: GRAMMAR AND STYLE

CREATE RHYTHM Review the **Grammar and Style** note on page 970. **Parallelism** is the repetition of grammatical structures—phrases or clauses, for example. Shakespeare's use of parallelism creates cadence, or a balanced, rhythmic flow. Here are two examples from the play. The first contains a series of four past-tense verbs, each followed by the word *for*. In the second, Shakespeare uses the three parallel adjectives *stiff*, *stark* and *cold*. Think about how these passages might sound without the parallelism.

> ***First Servingman.*** *You are looked for and called for, asked for and sought for,* in the great chamber. (Act One, Scene 5, lines 10–11)

> ***Friar Laurence.*** . . . *Each part, deprived of supple government,*
> *Shall,* *stiff and stark and cold,* *appear like death;* (Act Four, Scene 1, lines 102–103)

Now consider how the revision in red makes use of parallelism to improve the rhythm of this first draft. Revise your responses to the prompts by using parallelism whenever possible.

STUDENT MODEL

All of the deaths in the play—the murders of Mercutio, Tybalt, and
of Romeo and Juliet
Paris and the suicides—result largely from someone's acting out of love.

WRITING TOOLS
For prewriting, revision, and editing tools, visit the **Writing Center** at ClassZone.com.

ROMEO AND JULIET **1051**

DIFFERENTIATED INSTRUCTION

FOR LESS–PROFICIENT WRITERS

For Prompt A:
1. Suggest that students write a first draft, in prose, and then manipulate their language by substituting words and phrases that fit the meter.
2. Remind students that they need not be concerned about creating rhymes.
3. Remind students that they can shorten words or invert word order, as Shakespeare often did, to fit the meter.

For Prompt B:
1. Limit the length of the assignment to three paragraphs, with students identifying just two or three of the most important violent episodes.
2. Help students craft an introduction that has an appropriate tone and style.
3. Urge pairs of students to discuss how they plan to support their ideas and then meet again to review their responses.

Reading-Writing Connection

WRITING PROMPTS

- For Prompt A, students might begin by making lists of key words and figurative phrases (for example, *you are like . . .* or *our love is like . . .*) that could be used in their stanzas.

- For Prompt B, encourage students to use a Classification Chart. Under the headings *ove* and *ate*, students can categorize the acts of violence that result from each powerful emotion.

BEST PRACTICES TOOLKIT—Transparency
Classification Chart p. B17

For an extended writing activity, see
Carol Booth Olson's Reading-Writing Lesson Plans at **ClassZone.com**

REVISION: GRAMMAR AND STYLE

1. Elicit that the parallel elements in the first example are phrases of a verb + *for*; in the second example, the parallel elements are one-word adjectives. More important, since the elements in each example are phrased in the same way, they create an ear-pleasing cadence.

2. Have students identify the cadence in the student model. *Possible answer:* The ca dence comes f rom the murders of names and the s uicides of names.

3. For practice, have students rewrite this sentence, using parallelism to improve its cadence:

   > Romeo intended to enter the cemetery, where he would find Juliet; then he would drink the poison. *Possible answer: Romeo intended to enter the cemetery, find Juliet, and drink the poison.*

RESOURCE MANAGER—Copy Master
Create Rhythm p. 97

Assess and Reteach

Assess

RESOURCE MANAGER—Copy Masters
Selection Tests A, B/C pp. 99–100, 101–102
Test Generator CD

Reteach

STANDARDS LESSON FILE
Literature Lessons 25, 26, 35, 38

ROMEO AND JULIET **1051**

Focus and Motivate

OBJECTIVES

Media Literacy

- explore the key idea of **Hollywood**
- view a clip from the movie *Romeo and Juliet* to recognize how directors use elements of mise en scène, such as lighting, setting, props, costumes, and action, to create their visions
- create a visual treatment for *The Tragedy of Romeo and Juliet*

SUMMARY

This clip from *Romeo and Juliet* shows the famous balcony scene in Shakespeare's tragedy. Romeo is beneath Juliet's window when she appears on the balcony. Juliet, unaware of Romeo, despairs that the two are separated because of their names. Romeo responds, surprising her, and the two confess their love. Juliet says she will send someone the next day at nine to see if Romeo intends to marry her. They restate their love, and Romeo leaves to find Father Laurence to help him.

Why does HOLLYWOOD *love Shakespeare?*

To help students explore the **KEY IDEA**, ask them what elements **Hollywood** producers look for in scripts. List ideas on the board, such as action, intrigue, high drama, love, and hate. Ask students which of these elements appear in Shakespeare's plays, and invite students to describe examples.

BACKGROUND

More than 250 films based on Shakespeare and his plays have been produced. Between 1907 and 2000, 61 film adaptations and 21 TV adaptations were made of *Hamlet* alone. Other versions of *Romeo and Juliet* include those by George Cukor (1935), Renato Castellani (1954), Armando Acosta (1990), and Baz Luhrmann (1996). More than 13 notable films based on Shakespeare's work were made in the 1990s. Some films are faithful to their source, while others feature radical departures. Zeffirelli's 1967 version of *The Taming of the Shrew,* for example, followed the original play closely, while the 1999 film *10 Things I Hate About You* reset the story in a contemporary high school.

Why does HOLLYWOOD *love Shakespeare?*

KEY IDEA Shakespeare's *Tragedy of Romeo and Juliet* has all the ingredients for a successful **Hollywood** adaptation: timeless, universal themes; vibrant characters; an exotic setting; and a string of misunderstandings that ultimately lead to tragedy. Now that you have read the play version of *Romeo and Juliet*, notice the choices the film director makes in bringing this play to the screen.

Background

Love at First Sight Some would argue that the true mark of a great movie is its ability to leave a long-lasting impression on its audience. When viewers and critics were first introduced to Franco Zeffirelli's *Romeo and Juliet* in 1968, the reaction was unanimous praise. Everything about the film—from the romantic setting to the playful yet sometimes somber music—captivated audiences. In addition, Zeffirelli did what no other director had done before. He cast as his leads two young, unknown actors who were 16 and 17 years old when filming began. By taking a risk on these young actors, Zeffirelli created an interpretation filled with innocence, liveliness, and passion.

1052

Media Study Resources

R **RESOURCE MANAGER UNIT 10**

Plan and Teach pp. 103–106

Media Analysis
Summary pp. 107†*, 108‡*
Viewing Guide p. 109
Close Viewing p. 110
Viewing Activity p. 111
Produce Your Own Media p. 112

S **STANDARDS LESSON FILE**
Media Lessons 1, 4, 5

ℹ Media Center at **ClassZone.com**

MEDIA VIEWING
 Media*Smart* DVD

---

* Resources for Differentiation   † Also in Spanish   ‡ In Haitian Creole and Vietnamese

Media Literacy: Shakespearean Drama in Movies

Long before a director can call out, "Lights, camera, action!" he or she must have a vision for the film. Together with a filmmaking crew, a director plans every detail of a movie, including the lighting, setting, props, costumes, and action. The arrangement and use of these filmmaking elements is known as **mise en scène** (mēz′ än sĕn′). Notice how the following elements of mise en scène in the film clip shape our understanding of Shakespearean drama.

ELEMENTS OF MISE EN SCÈNE

1 **Lighting** can be used to create a mood or a dramatic effect. It can also make a scene look realistic and can draw viewers' attention to an important object or person.

2 The **setting** and **props** build certain expectations in viewers' minds and establish a location. For example, an exotic setting can help create an atmosphere of romance or love.

3 A character's **facial expressions, body language,** and **actions** convey what he or she is thinking or feeling.

4 A director deliberately positions characters within a **frame** to indicate the nature of the characters' relationship. For example, characters who don't trust each other may be placed at opposite ends of the frame.

5 In a Shakespearean movie, **costumes** may provide clues about characters' social status and may also indicate a specific time period. A director can also experiment with costumes to reflect a character's personality.

MEDIA STUDY: TEACHING OPTIONS

Teaching Option 1: The Basics (1–2 Days)
1. Begin the Media Study using the material provided on pages 1052–1053.
2. Show the Introduction on Media*Smart*. Then show the First Viewing. As they watch, have students use the Viewing Guide on page 1054, along with the corresponding copy master on page 109 of the Resource Manager. Discuss their responses.
3. Return to the pupil book for the extension activities on page 1055.

Teaching Option 2: In-Depth Study (2–3 Days)
1. Begin the Media Study using pages 1052–1053).
2. Show the Introduction and First Viewing from Media*Smart*. Then continue on Media*Smart* with the Media Lessons, using the teacher notes available in the Resources section.
3. Show the Guided Analysis presentation. Have students record their observations on the Student Viewing Guide available in the Resources section from Media*Smart*.
4. Return to the pupil book, page 1055.

Media Literacy

Review with students the definition of *mise en scène*. Students should recognize that directors seek a certain look to their films and hope to convey particular ideas or emotions. Ask students what specific elements directors use to create their unique visions. On the board, list students' answers, which may include such elements as lighting and sets. Make sure setting, props, facial expressions, body language, actions, frame, and costumes are included in the list. Then discuss the chart on page 1053.

- **Lighting** To reinforce the impact of lighting, ask students to imagine an empty room first brightly lit and then dark and shadowy. What different moods do the two kinds of lighting convey? Suppose a boy enters the room. What difference would it make if the director directed light on the boy or left the boy in shadow?

- **Setting and Props** Have students imagine a beach on a clear summer day and then a school cafeteria. What differences in the kind of story they will expect do they immediately recognize?

- **Facial Expressions, Body Language, and Actions** Have volunteers describe likely reactions to the sudden appearance of a gorilla and identify actions people might take in response. Discuss how facial expressions, body language, and actions convey such a situation.

- **Frame** Have volunteers draw these movie scenes: (1) teacher and student, (2) close friends, (3) captains of rival football teams. Have other students imagine the scene being portrayed and provide a brief description of the pivotal moment that the frame captures.

- **Costumes** Have students think about costumes they have seen in movies. Ask them to describe costumes they would expect in movies about: (1) an international high school in 2080, (2) a factory outside of London in 1890, (3) a sailing expedition in 2006. Discuss how the costumes reflect the time period and setting.

Media*Smart* DVD

Practice and Apply

VIEWING GUIDE

1. Before students view the movie clip, tell them they will be asked to identify techniques that create the director's vision. Have them watch for these elements:

   - **camera shots** that establish the scene and develop Romeo's and Juliet's emotions and reactions
   - **lighting and sound** that establish the romantic mood between the lovers
   - **music** that stirs the viewers' emotions about the young lovers

2. Some students may struggle to isolate the director's techniques. Help these students focus on the camera shots and lighting by playing the clip without sound. Then help them isolate the use of sound and music by listening to the soundtrack only.

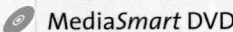 RESOURCE MANAGER—Copy Masters

Viewing Guide p. 109
Close Viewing p. 110
Viewing Activity p. 111

Use this resource with the Viewing Guide:

Media*Smart* DVD

ANSWERS

FIRST VIEWING: Comprehension

Possible answers:

1. *The setting is the back of Juliet's house, a stone villa with a wide balcony above an orchard. The action takes place on the balcony or in the orchard.*

2. *The director begins with a long wide shot of the orchard. In a second long wide shot, we see Romeo in the orchard. We then see a medium-angle shot of Romeo's view. Next we see close-ups of Romeo, interspersed with panning shots of Juliet's house. This follows Romeo's view as he moves through the orchard. Romeo is finally able to see Juliet on the balcony.*

CLOSE VIEWING: Media Literacy

Possible answers:

3. *The moonlight effect through the orchard trees creates an intimate, romantic mood.*

4. *The setting in the clip is lush and heavily forested. The balcony is longer and wider and allows for greater movement than the one in the text.*

MediaSmart DVD
- **Film Clip:** *Romeo and Juliet*
- **Director:** Franco Zeffirelli
- **Rating:** PG
- **Genre:** Drama
- **Running Time:** 11 minutes

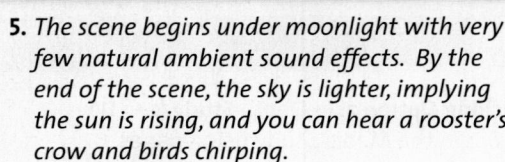

Viewing Guide for
Romeo and Juliet

The scene you're about to view is perhaps the most well-known one in all of Shakespeare's plays—the balcony scene.

Because of the length of the clip, you may wish to view the scene once for the story. During any additional viewings, concentrate on such elements as mise en scène, camera shots, and sound. Keep the following questions in mind as you view.

NOW VIEW

FIRST VIEWING: Comprehension

1. **Summarize** Describe the setting of the clip in your own words.

2. **Clarify** What types of **shots** does the director use in the beginning of the clip to establish the scene?

CLOSE VIEWING: Media Literacy

3. **Interpret Mood** What kind of mood do you think the **lighting** creates?

4. **Analyze Setting** How does the setting compare with what you envisioned?

5. **Analyze Director's Techniques** How does the director show that time has passed from the beginning to the end of this scene? Consider how the director uses **lighting** and **sounds** to show the passing of time.

6. **Evaluate Music** Zeffirelli uses music throughout the movie to stir viewers' emotions. When is music used, and how effectively is it used, in this scene?

5. *The scene begins under moonlight with very few natural ambient sound effects. By the end of the scene, the sky is lighter, implying the sun is rising, and you can hear a rooster's crow and birds chirping.*

6. *Quiet music plays as a backdrop as first Romeo and then Juliet speak alone. The music fades out when the two see and begin talking to each other. Low, gentle music begins again with Romeo's vow of love, then swells with Juliet's declaration and the lovers' embrace. Then frivolous, lighthearted music* plays as the nurse calls Juliet away and Romeo happily swings from a branch. The music becomes flowing with the lovers' next embrace, and the scene ends with a mournful swelling at the lovers' parting. Zeffirelli effectively uses music to make viewers alternately feel passion, joy, and sadness.*

Write or Discuss

Evaluate Mise en Scène In your opinion, is Zeffirelli's film version of the balcony scene appealing and believable? Why or why not? Cite specific examples from the clip to support your view. Think about

- the actors' physical appearance, actions, and movements
- the details of the setting, costumes, and props
- the camera shots of the scene

Produce Your Own Media

Create a Visual Treatment Imagine you're filming a modern adaptation of *The Tragedy of Romeo and Juliet.* Before you begin filming, you'll want to create a **visual treatment,** a series of images that visually represent key scenes from the play. With a small group, determine who will be the costume designer, the set designer, and the cast of characters. Then choose six key scenes from the play that you want to photograph.

HERE'S HOW Use the professional model and the following tips to help you visualize the elements of **mise en scène:**

- **Characters:** What is the relationship between the characters, and how will you position them within the frame?
- **Setting:** What elements of the setting will convey a specific time or place?
- **Costumes:** What clues do the costumes reveal about the characters?
- **Lighting:** How does the lighting create a mood?

MEDIA TOOLS

For help with creating a visual treatment, visit the **Media Center** at **ClassZone.com.**

Tech Tip

If you have access to photo-editing software, use it to edit your pictures after the photo shoot.

PROFESSIONAL MODEL

Assess and Reteach

Write or Discuss

Evaluate Mise en Scène In their opinion statements, students should cite specific examples from the clip that support their views. For example, if students find the scene appealing and believable, they might point out that the actors are close to the ages of Romeo and Juliet in the play and that both actors are very attractive. They might point to the wealthy appearance of the villa and its orchard and to the period costumes as elements that make the scene believable. They might point to the panning shot in the opening to reveal Juliet as something making the scene appealing and to the natural facial expressions in close-ups as characters speak, react, and embrace.

Produce Your Own Media

Rubric: Create a Visual Treatment A strong visual treatment should include images that

- convey a clear description of each key scene
- position characters within frames in ways that show their relationships
- use elements of setting to establish time and place
- use costumes to give information about characters
- use lighting to establish mood

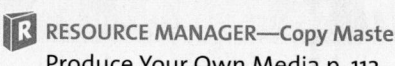

RESOURCE MANAGER—Copy Master
Produce Your Own Media p. 112

MEDIA STUDY WRAP–UP

Have students summarize what they have learned about using elements of mise en scène to create a vision on film. Encourage them to use terms such as *lighting, setting, props, facial expressions, body language, actions, framing,* and *costumes* in their explanations.

RETEACH

STANDARDS LESSON FILE

Media Lesson 1: Active Viewing Strategies
Media Lesson 4: Analyzing Visuals in Film and TV
Media Lesson 5: Analyzing Sound in Film and TV

Focus and Motivate

OBJECTIVES

Reading for Information

- analyze a critical review
- compare and contrast
- read a film review

SUMMARY

In this critical review, Roger Ebert argues that Franco Zeffirelli's 1968 *Romeo and Juliet* will long endure as a great movie. He compares it to other film versions of the play and discusses the success of its stagecraft.

What's the Connection?

Use an Anticipation Guide to prepare students for the selection. Have students respond to these statements before and after reading:

- Only experienced actors can convey the language of Shakespeare effectively.
- A good reason to cast unknown actors is so that you can pay them less money.
- Zeffirelli needed more experience before directing *Romeo and Juliet*.

 BEST PRACTICES TOOLKIT—Transparency Anticipation Guide p. A14

Teach

Skill Focus: Analyze a Critical Review

Elicit that like other kinds of persuasive writing, the purpose of a critical review is to encourage the reader to agree with the writer. In this case, Roger Ebert will use several techniques to persuade readers to agree with his evaluation of a famous film treatment of *Romeo and Juliet*.

 RESOURCE MANAGER—Copy Master Analyze a Critical Review p. 121

Reading for Information

Great Movies: *Romeo and Juliet*

Critical Review by Roger Ebert

Use with *Romeo and Juliet*, page 940.

What's the Connection?

You've just discovered why filmmakers love Shakespeare: plays like *Romeo and Juliet* present directors with terrific material to work with. You've also explored the choices one director, Franco Zeffirelli, made to transform Shakespeare's classic drama into a big-screen blockbuster. How do critics think Zeffirelli's movie measures up? Read to find out one movie reviewer's opinion.

Skill Focus: Analyze a Critical Review

A **critical review** is an essay in which the writer gives his or her opinions about a movie, a play, a book, a TV show, or another work. A critical review typically includes these elements:

- the name of the work and its creator
- a description of the work
- a clearly stated opinion of the work
- reasons that support the opinion
- examples or details that illustrate the reasons

A critical review may include other elements as well, like background information on the work's creator or descriptions of how audiences reacted when the work was released. The heart of a review, however, is the writer's opinion and the reasons and examples he or she uses to back it up.

As you read this critical review, use a chart like the one shown to record Roger Ebert's opinion and the main reasons he gives to support it. Keep track of the examples and details from the movie that Ebert uses to illustrate each reason.

Ebert's Opinion:	
Reason	**Examples or Details**
Reason 1:	
Reason 2:	

Selection Resources

 RESOURCE MANAGER UNIT 10

Plan and Teach pp. 113–117

Reading
Summary pp. 119†*, 120‡*
Analyze a Critical Review pp. 121, 123†*
Reading Check p. 125
Compare and Contrast pp. 122, 124†*
Question Support p. 126*

Assessment
Selection Tests A, B/C pp. 127*, 129*

 Test Generator CD

 BEST PRACTICES TOOLKIT
Anticipation Guide • Main Idea and Details

---

* **Resources for Differentiation**   † **Also in Spanish**   ‡ **In Haitian Creole and Vietnamese**

GREAT MOVIES

Romeo and Juliet

BY ROGER EBERT

"Romeo and Juliet" is always said to be the first romantic tragedy ever written, but it isn't really a tragedy at all. It's a tragic misunderstanding, scarcely fitting the ancient requirement of tragedy that the mighty fall through their own flaws. Romeo and Juliet have no flaws, and aren't old enough to be blamed if they did. They die because of the pigheaded 10 quarrel of their families, the Montagues and the Capulets. By writing the play, Shakespeare began the shaping of modern drama, in which the fates of ordinary people are as crucial as those of the great. The great tragedies of his time, including his own, involved kings, emperors, generals. Here, near the dawn of his career, perhaps remembering a sweet early romance before his forced marriage 20 to Anne Hathaway, he writes about teenagers in love.

"Romeo and Juliet" has been filmed many times in many ways; Norma Shearer and Leslie Howard starred in the beloved 1936 Hollywood version, and modern transformations include Robert Wise's "West Side Story" (1961), which applies the plot to Manhattan gang warfare; Abel Ferrara's 30 "China Girl" (1987), about a forbidden romance between a girl of Chinatown and a boy of Little Italy; and Baz Luhrmann's "William Shakespeare's Romeo & Juliet" (1996), with California punk gangs on Verona Beach. But the favorite film version is likely to re-

Zeffirelli cast two young, unknown actors instead of more experienced stars in his 1968 film.

main, for many years, Franco Zeffirelli's 1968 production. **A**

His crucial decision, in a film where 40 almost everything went well, was to cast actors who were about the right age to play the characters (as Howard and Shearer were obviously not). As the play opens, Juliet "hath not seen the change of 14 years," and Romeo is little older. This is first love for Juliet, and Romeo's crush on the unseen Rosalind is forgotten the moment he sees **B**

A CRITICAL REVIEW
In lines 1–38, Ebert introduces the play and provides information about other film versions of it. What opinion about Zeffirelli's film does Ebert state in lines 35–38?

B CRITICAL REVIEW
What was Zeffirelli's "crucial decision"? Paraphrase the first reason Ebert gives to support his opinion of the movie.

DIFFERENTIATED INSTRUCTION

FOR LESS–PROFICIENT READERS

Build Comprehension To check their understanding—and to complete the chart on page 1056—have students first read the selection independently. Next, ask them to meet in pairs to share their understanding of Ebert's ideas and arguments. Finally, have partners work together to list Ebert's reasons and to explain how he supports each one.

FOR ENGLISH LEARNERS

Culture: Connect In lines 22–35, Ebert gives examples of how Shakespeare's story has been translated into various cultural settings. Invite students to draw upon their own cultural background and suggest how they might adapt *Romeo and Juliet* to an audience with strong ties to that background.

INFORMATIONAL ANALYSIS

A CRITICAL REVIEW

Possible answer: Ebert feels that Zeffirelli's film version of Romeo and Juliet *will remain the favorite for many years.*

INFORMATIONAL ANALYSIS

B CRITICAL REVIEW

Possible answer: Zeffirelli's "crucial decision" was to cast actors of about the same age as the characters of Romeo and Juliet in the play (lines 39–43). A paraphrase might read like this: "Zeffirelli planned well, but the best part of his plan was to cast actors who were about the same age as Romeo and Juliet themselves were (instead of actors who were well known but older)."

If students need help . . . Point out the term "crucial decision," which appears in quotation marks in the question. Explain that the use of quotation marks means that the question includes some of Ebert's own words. If students scan the paragraph for the term "crucial decision," they should find the answer to the question rather quickly.

DISCUSSION PROMPTS

Use these prompts to discuss the altering of an original script when creating the film version of a play:

Connect Have you ever watched a movie that seemed to drag on and on? What are some reasons that a director might choose to make a movie or play shorter? *Accept any reasonable answers. Students should recognize the drawbacks not only of tedious scenes but also of unnecessary scenes.*

Analyze Do you agree with Ebert's argument that Shakespeare "might have understood" cutting the verbal description of Juliet's funeral (lines 69–77)? Why or why not? *Possible answer: There is no evidence that reveals Shakespeare's opinion about cutting his plays, but as Ebert says, Shakespeare "took such wholesale liberties with his own sources" (lines 76–77). Also, film is a visual medium. It seems reasonable to cut the verbal description of a scene that might be more powerful if shown rather than merely described.*

Evaluate How much can a director change about a play before it is no longer an interpretation and, instead, becomes a different story? Can scenes be rearranged? Can characters be combined or omitted? Can the storyline remain the same without the original dialogue? *Possible answers: Yes. Shakespeare's plays are so timeless that nearly any interpretation of them can reflect the spirit of the play. No. If the original script is not followed, the performance is no longer what Shakespeare intended.*

Olivia Hussey as Juliet proclaims her love in the balcony scene.

Juliet at the masked ball: "I ne'er saw
50 true beauty until this night." After a well-publicized international search, Zeffirelli cast Olivia Hussey, a 16-year-old from Argentina, and Leonard Whiting, a British 17-year-old.

They didn't merely look their parts, they embodied them in the freshness of

> ## Hussey and Whiting were so good because they didn't know any better.

their personalities, and although neither was a trained actor, they were fully equal to Shakespeare's dialogue for
60 them; Anthony Holden's new book *William Shakespeare: The Man Behind the Genius* contrasts "the beautiful simplicity with which the lovers speak at their moments of uncomplicated happiness," with "the ornate rhetorical

flourishes which fuel so much else in the play"—flourishes that Zeffirelli severely pruned, trimming about half the play. He was roundly criticized for his
70 edits, but much that needs describing on the stage can simply be shown on-screen, as when Benvolio is shown witnessing Juliet's funeral and thus does not need to evoke it in a description to the exiled Romeo. Shakespeare, who took such wholesale liberties with his own sources, might have understood.

What is left is what people love the play for—the purity of the young lovers'
80 passion, the earthiness of Juliet's nurse, the well-intentioned plans of Friar Laurence, the hot-blooded feud between the young men of the families, the cruel irony of the double deaths. And there is time, too, for many of the great speeches, including Mercutio's poetic evocation of Mab, the queen of dreams.

Hussey and Whiting were so good because they didn't know any better.
90 Another year or two of experience, perhaps, and they would have been too intimidated to play the roles. It was my good fortune to visit the film

DIFFERENTIATED INSTRUCTION

FOR LESS–PROFICIENT READERS
Explore Parallelism Have students reread the paragraph that begins at line 78. Then discuss how Ebert uses parallelism to make his list of characteristics of *Romeo and Juliet* both clear and pleasant to read. Provide these first two items in the list:

- *the purity of the young lovers' passion*
- *the earthiness of Juliet's nurse*

As students list the other items, discuss the cadence and consistency of the parallelism.

FOR ENGLISH LEARNERS
Multiple-Meaning Words Remind students that when an English word has several meanings, students should use context clues to determine the correct meaning. Point out the use of "pruned" (line 68), "roundly" (line 69), and "wholesale" (line 76). Ask students to give the most common definition for each word. Then have them define the word as it is used in the sentence in which it appears. In both cases, allow students to refer to a dictionary if necessary.

set, in a small hill town an hour or so outside Rome, on the night when the balcony scene was filmed. I remember Hussey and Whiting upstairs in the old hillside villa, waiting for their call, unaffected, uncomplicated. And when
100 the balcony scene was shot, I remember the heedless energy that Hussey threw into it, take after take, hurling herself almost off the balcony for hungry kisses. (Whiting, balanced in a tree, needed to watch his footing.) **C**

Between shots, in the overgrown garden, Zeffirelli strolled with the composer Nino Rota, who had written the music for most of Fellini's films
110 and now simply hummed the film's central theme, as the director nodded. Pasqualino De Santis, who was to win an Oscar for his cinematography, directed his crew quietly, urgently, trying to be ready for the freshness of the actors instead of making them wait for technical quibbles. At dawn, drinking strong coffee as cars pulled around to take his actors back to Rome, Zeffirelli
120 said what was obvious: That the whole movie depended on the balcony and the crypt scenes, and he felt now that his casting decision had proven itself, and that the film would succeed.

It did, beyond any precedent for a film based on Shakespeare, even though Shakespeare is the most filmed writer in history. The movie opened in the tumultuous year of 1968, a
130 time of political upheaval around the world, and somehow the story of the star-crossed lovers caught the mood of rebellious young people who had wearied of their elders' wars. "This of all works of literature eternizes the ardor of young love and youth's aggressive spirit," wrote Anthony Burgess. **D**

Zeffirelli, born in Florence in 1923, came early to the English language
140 through prewar experiences hinted at in the loosely autobiographical "Tea with Mussolini" (1999). His crucial early artistic influence was Laurence Olivier's "Henry V" (1945), which inspired him to go into the theater; he has had parallel careers directing plays, films and operas. Before the great

Leonard Whiting as Romeo gazes adoringly at his Juliet.

C CRITICAL REVIEW
Reread lines 88–105. Why does Ebert think Hussey and Whiting were so successful at bringing the star-crossed lovers to life?

D CRITICAL REVIEW
Why does Ebert think audiences—particularly young people—were so taken with the movie when it premiered in 1968?

DIFFERENTIATED INSTRUCTION

FOR ADVANCED LEARNERS/PRE–AP

Make Judgments Zeffirelli believes that the success of his movie depends on the balcony and crypt scenes (lines 120–122). Is this statement true of *Romeo and Juliet* as a play? Have two teams of students choose opposing sides of the question; prepare appropriate arguments, with evidence from the play as support; and debate the issue.

C CRITICAL REVIEW

Possible answer: *Hussey and Whiting were successful because their youthfulness and their lack of experience gave them great energy for playing their parts and kept them from being intimidated by the very famous roles.*

If students need help . . .

1. Have them use a Main Idea and Details chart to record Ebert's impressions of the two actors. Then work with students to try out various main idea statements until they find one that they consider satisfying.

2. To check their answers, have students compare them with what Ebert says in lines 55–60 about Hussey and Whiting's freshness and inexperience.

BEST PRACTICES TOOLKIT—Transparency Main Idea and Details p. B6

D CRITICAL REVIEW

Possible answer: *Ebert thinks that the movie attracted young people because it opened at a time when they were interested in seeing a story about young people who rebel against the values of their parents.*

If students need help . . . Explain that during the 1960s and 1970s, the United States was embroiled in a controversial war in Vietnam, which was heatedly protested by thousands of young people.

E CRITICAL REVIEW

Possible answer: Ebert praises the costuming. He argues that the costumes are essential because they allow bright color to enter the film, adding life to scenes that otherwise would be filled with dark, neutral colors and earth tones (lines 172–175).

If students need help . . . Urge them not to focus too much on the names of the characters and actors mentioned in these lines. Explain that Ebert includes these details to support the main idea, then use the description of Juliet's costumes (lines 180–183) to model the thinking involved in realizing that Ebert names the characters so that he can classify their costumes.

E CRITICAL REVIEW
Reread lines 168–186. What aspect of the film does Ebert praise in this paragraph? Explain why he found this element essential to the movie's success.

---

success of "Romeo and Juliet," he first visited Shakespeare for the shaky but high-spirited "Taming of the Shrew" (1967), with Burton and Taylor. Later he directed Placido Domingo in "Otello" (1986), Verdi's opera, and directed Mel Gibson in "Hamlet" (1990).

Something fundamental has changed in films about and for young people.

"Romeo and Juliet" remains the magical high point of his career. To see it again is to luxuriate. It is intriguing that Zeffirelli in 1968 focused on love, while Baz Luhrmann's popular version of 1996 focused on violence; something fundamental has changed in films about and for young people, and recent audiences seem shy of sex and love but eager for conflict and action. I wonder if a modern Friday night audience would snicker at the heart-baring sincerity of the lovers. . . .

The costumes by Danilo Donati won another Oscar for the film (it was also nominated for best picture and director), and they are crucial to its success; they are the avenue for color and richness to enter the frame, which is otherwise filled with gray and ochre stones and the colors of nature. The nurse (Pat Heywood) seems enveloped in a dry goods' sale of heavy fabrics, and Mercutio (John McEnery) comes flying a handkerchief that he uses as a banner, disguise and shroud. Hussey's dresses, with low bodices and simple patterns, set off her creamy skin and long hair; Whiting is able to inhabit his breeches, blouse and codpiece with the conviction that it is everyday clothing, not a costume. **E**

The costumes and everything else in the film—the photography, the music, above all Shakespeare's language—is so voluptuous, so sensuous. The stagecraft of the twinned death scenes is of course all contrivance; the friar's potion works with timing that is precisely wrong, and yet we forgive the manipulation because Shakespeare has been able to provide us with what is theoretically impossible, the experience of two young lovers each grieving the other's death. When the play was first staged in London, Holden writes, Shakespeare had the satisfaction "of seeing the groundlings moved to emotions far beyond anything before known in the theater." Why? Because of craft and art, yes, but also because Romeo and Juliet were not distant and august figures, not Caesars, Othellos or Macbeths, but a couple of kids in love, as everyone in the theater had known, and everyone in the theater had been.

Whiting and Hussey in Donati's sumptuous costumes

DIFFERENTIATED INSTRUCTION

FOR ENGLISH LEARNERS

Culture: Clarify Some terms in Ebert's description of the characters' Elizabethan costumes may need clarification. Define these words that relate to clothing of that era:

- *shroud* (line 180), "something that conceals, protects, or screens"
- *bodices* (line 181), "fitted parts of dresses that extend from the waist to the shoulder"
- *breeches* (line 184), "trousers extending to the knee"
- *blouse* (line 184), "a loose-fitting garment resembling a long shirt"

Comprehension

1. **Recall** What is Ebert's opinion of Franco Zeffirelli's film adaptation of *Romeo and Juliet*?

2. **Paraphrase** Reread lines 198–209. According to Ebert, why have audiences been so moved by the story of *Romeo and Juliet* ever since it was first staged?

Critical Analysis

3. **Analyze a Critical Review** Look at the chart you filled in as you read. What are the main reasons that Ebert gives to support his opinion of the film? Describe at least two examples or details that Ebert uses to illustrate each reason.

4. **Identify Author's Purpose** What do you think was Ebert's primary purpose in writing this critical review of a film that came out more than 35 years ago? Support your conclusion with evidence from the review.

5. **Evaluate an Opinion** Do you agree with Ebert that "Romeo and Juliet have no flaws" and that they die only "because of the pigheaded quarrel of their families"? Explain your answer.

Read for Information: Compare and Contrast

WRITING PROMPT

What did you think about the casting of Olivia Hussey and Leonard Whiting in Zeffirelli's film version of *Romeo and Juliet*, and how would you rate their performances in the balcony scene? How are your opinions similar to and different from Ebert's?

To answer this prompt, you will have to **compare and contrast,** or explain similarities and differences. To explore the similarities and differences between your views and those expressed by Ebert, follow these steps:

1. Consider your reactions to the movie's two main characters and their acting in the balcony scene. Sum up your opinion, and give at least two reasons for it. Identify details from the scene that support your opinion.

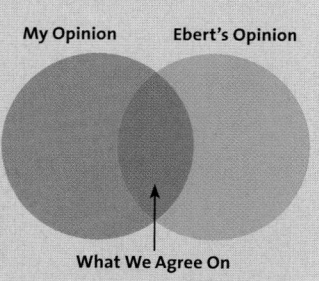

My Opinion   Ebert's Opinion

What We Agree On

2. Review each of Ebert's main points and the evidence he gives to back them up. Which do you agree with? Which do you disagree with?

For additional support of post-reading questions, use these copy masters:

R RESOURCE MANAGER—Copy Masters
Reading Check p. 125
Question Support p. 126
Compare and Contrast p. 122

For additional questions, see page 116.

ANSWERS

Comprehension

1. *Ebert thinks that Zeffirelli's film will remain a favorite for many years.*

2. *Audiences identify with Romeo and Juliet.*

Critical Analysis

Possible answers:

3. ▪ **STANDARDS FOCUS** *Critical Review* See Skill Focus: Analyze a Critical Review *on page 1056.*

4. *Ebert wanted to convince readers that the film belongs in the category of Great Movies. He names other versions and argues that Zeffirelli's is better.*

5. *Yes. Romeo and Juliet's love would not have been fatal but for the feud. No. Romeo is impulsive, Juliet is stubborn, and both base their love on physical attraction.*

Read for Information: Compare and Contrast

Writing Prompt *Possible answer: Hussey and Whiting are energetic and natural. However, they are so young that it is hard for a modern audience to accept their feelings as real. Ebert feels that the actors' youth was an asset.*

Assess

 RESOURCE MANAGER—Copy Masters
Selection Tests A, B/C pp. 127–128, 129–130

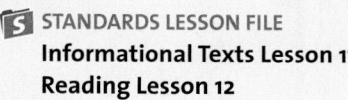 Test Generator CD

Reteach

S STANDARDS LESSON FILE
Informational Texts Lesson 17
Reading Lesson 12

FOR LESS–PROFICIENT WRITERS

Read for Information Have students answer these questions to compare their reactions to the balcony scene with Ebert's reaction:

- Did the actors seem at ease with Shakespeare's dialogue?

- How would you describe each actor's energy in this scene?

- Can you identify with the actors as teenagers in love?

FOR ADVANCED LEARNERS/PRE–AP

Read for Information Have students extend their essay to discuss their opinion not just of the acting but also of the costuming and other elements of stagecraft in the balcony scene. Ask students to compare their opinions of these elements with what Ebert says about them, as well.

Focus and Motivate

OBJECTIVES

Literary Analysis
- explore the key idea of **classic stories**
- identify the characteristics of a myth
- read a myth
- read a narrative poem

Reading
- understand sequence of events

Grammar and Writing
- use writing to analyze literature

SUMMARY

This myth, told in a narrative poem, is set in ancient Babylon. There, the love between Pyramus and Thisbe is forbidden by their parents. Still, the lovers make a plan to meet by speaking through a crack in a shared wall. Thisbe arrives first and drops her shawl as she runs from a lioness, who tears it apart. Pyramus arrives and finds the bloody, shredded shawl. Believing Thisbe to be dead, he stabs himself. Thisbe returns, grieves his death, and then stabs herself.

What makes a CLASSIC STORY?

Lead into the *KEY IDEA* by asking the question. Have students suggest various definitions of *classic* before they complete the *DISCUSS* activity. Ask groups to share their lists of characteristics of **classic stories.**

Selection Resources

Pyramus and Thisbe
Myth Retold by Ovid

What makes a CLASSIC STORY?

KEY IDEA Two teenagers fall madly in love, but their parents forbid them to see each other. Defying their families, they plan to run away together, but a series of misunderstandings leads to their disastrous demise. Sound familiar? Some stories are so universally appealing that they appear over and over, in everything from ancient myths to Shakespearean drama to modern soap operas. "Pyramus and Thisbe" is one of these **classic stories.**

DISCUSS What are some other examples of classic stories? In a small group, talk about situations that are replayed in fairy tales and bedtime stories, in movies and books, and on TV shows and Broadway stages. What do these stories share? Thrilling plots? Insurmountable conflicts? Happy endings? With your group, come up with a list detailing five characteristics of a classic story.

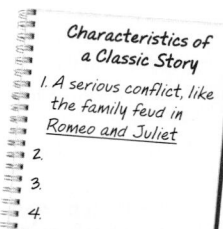

Characteristics of a Classic Story
1. A serious conflict, like the family feud in Romeo and Juliet
2.
3.
4.

1062

R RESOURCE MANAGER UNIT 10

Plan and Teach pp. 131–138

Literary Analysis
Summary pp. 139†*, 140‡*
Myth pp. 141, 142†*
Question Support p. 146*

Reading
Sequence pp. 143, 144†*
Reading Check p. 145

Assessment
Selection Tests A, B/C pp. 147*, 149*
 Test Generator CD

BEST PRACTICES TOOLKIT

Differentiated Instruction
pp. 31–38*

Graphic Organizers/Strategies
Character Traits and Textual Evidence • Plot Diagram • Venn Diagram

Reading Support
Audio Anthology CD*

Technology
Literature Center at **ClassZone.com**
 Write*Smart* CD

---

* Resources for Differentiation   † Also in Spanish   ‡ In Haitian Creole and Vietnamese

LITERARY ANALYSIS: MYTH

Why does the sun rise in the east every morning? What makes thunderstorms strike so violently? Why do the seasons change? Different cultures throughout time have attempted to answer similar questions about the world. Frequently, these questions became the bases of myths. A **myth** is a traditional story usually created to explain why the world is the way it is or why things in nature happen as they do. Myths are also a form of entertainment that people have enjoyed since ancient times. The stories myths tell are filled with colorful characters, suspenseful plots, and daring adventures. Most myths share these basic characteristics:

- They explain how things connected with nature or humans came to be.
- They tell about supernatural beings or events.
- They present lessons or morals.

"Pyramis and Thisbe" is a classic myth, here retold in the form of a narrative poem. As you read this myth, notice what it attempts to explain. Also, consider the lesson the myth teaches about the value of love.

Review: **Narrative Poem**

READING SKILL: SEQUENCE

Timing is everything—especially when it comes to myths. The tragic action in "Pyramus and Thisbe" all takes place in two days. As you read this myth, look for signal words, such as *later, then,* and *after,* that make the sequence of events clear. Record the myth's main events in a sequence chain like this one.

| Pyramus and Thisbe fall in love. | → | | → | |

Author Online

Ovid
43 B.C.–A.D. 17

A Bright Start Ovid is considered to be one of the greatest poets of antiquity. But if Ovid's father had had his way, his son would have followed a very different career path. Ovid's father was determined to see his son become a public official in the Roman Empire. He sent Ovid to Rome to study rhetoric and law under the best teachers. Instead of studying, Ovid followed his natural inclinations and focused on writing poetry. Luckily, he achieved success with his first work, the *Amores*, a series of short, witty poems about a love affair. The poet quickly became popular in fashionable Roman society.

A Lasting Legacy "Pyramus and Thisbe" is taken from the *Metamorphoses*, Ovid's masterpiece. A long narrative poem, the *Metamorphoses* retells many of the most important myths from ancient Greece and Rome. Ovid breathed new life into the old stories, shaping them in imaginative ways and strengthening their structure. Ovid's retellings have inspired writers for centuries—including Shakespeare.

A Grim End Before Ovid was able to publish the *Metamorphoses*, disaster struck. In A.D. 8, the emperor Augustus banished him from Rome and sent him to live in exile in Tomis, a desolate fishing village on the edge of the Roman Empire. The exact reason for this cruel punishment is unknown, but in many of the poems Ovid wrote while in exile, he begs for permission to return to Rome. His pleas fell on deaf ears. Ovid died in exile in A.D. 17.

 MORE ABOUT THE AUTHOR
For more on Ovid, visit the **Literature Center** at ClassZone.com.

Teach

STANDARDS FOCUS

LITERARY ANALYSIS

● MYTH

For instructional support, have students identify mythical elements in this summary of a classic myth:

> Arachne was so proud of her weaving that she challenged the goddess Athena to a weaving contest. When Arachne wove a design that showed the gods' follies, the angry Athena punished her by turning her into the first spider.

Possible answer: *The mythical elements include how spiders came to be, a super-natural creature (Athena), and a lesson about vanity.*

CHECK UNDERSTANDING Have students explain in their own words how a myth differs from other kinds of stories.

READING SKILL

■ SEQUENCE

Have students create a sequence chart from the details about Ovid in **A Bright Start.** *Possible main events: Ovid's father sent him to Rome to study. Ovid wrote poetry instead. Ovid achieved success with Amores. Ovid became fashionable.*

CHECK UNDERSTANDING Have students create a sequence chart from details in **A Grim End.**

R RESOURCE MANAGER—Copy Master
Sequence p. 143 (for student use while reading the selection)

DIFFERENTIATED INSTRUCTION

FOR LESS–PROFICIENT READERS

Concept Support Point out to students that many characters from ancient Greek and Roman myths are already familiar, partly because many names in astronomy come from mythical characters. List these names on the board and ask students to tell what they know about any of them.

Amazon	Cyclops	Pegasus
Atlas	Hercules	Phoenix
Cupid	Jupiter	Venus

Research a Connection Shakespeare was not the only Renaissance writer to borrow from Ovid's *Metamorphoses*, nor was "Pyramus and Thisbe" the only story that he borrowed. Ask a group of students to do some research on Shakespeare's use of Ovid. Have them prepare and present to the class a visual aid that shows the connection and that explains why the *Metamorphoses* was such a popular resource.

Practice and Apply

ANALYZE VISUALS

Possible answer: The artist conveys a sense of separation by using a dark background and a light foreground and by presenting Thisbe alone. The lovers' longing to be together is suggested in Thisbe's intense, concerned expression as she presses against the crack.

About the Art John William Waterhouse (1849–1917), who was born in Rome but spent most of his life in England, painted *Thisbe* (1909). Waterhouse's art reveals his interest in classic literature. He had a particular interest in *femme fatales*, women who led their men into tragedy. He featured such women in several paintings, including *Echo and Narcissus*, *Circe Offering the Cup to Ulysses*, and *Cleopatra*.

LITERARY ANALYSIS

Ⓐ MYTH

Possible answer: The lovers' parents are keeping them apart and have forbidden their marriage (line 11). Pyramus and Thisbe overcome these barriers by communicating through a crack in a shared wall (lines 17–22). Based on the text so far, the story may teach a lesson about the enduring power of love.

If students need help . . . Have them work in pairs to paraphrase the six sentences in the story so far. Offer assistance with defining difficult words and sorting through complicated phrasing.

Pyramus and Thisbe
Ovid

The house of Pyramus[1] and that of Thisbe[2]
stood side by side within the mighty city
ringed by the tall brick walls Semíramis
had built[3]—so we are told. If you searched all
5 the East, you'd find no girl with greater charm
than Thisbe; and no boy in Babylon
was handsomer than Pyramus. They owed
their first encounters to their living close
beside each other—but with time, love grows.
10 Theirs did—indeed they wanted to be wed,
but marriage was forbidden by their parents:
yet there's one thing that parents can't prevent:
the flame of love that burned in both of them.
They had no confidant—and so used signs:
15 with these each lover read the other's mind:
when covered, fire acquires still more force.

The wall their houses shared had one thin crack,
which formed when they were built and then was left;
in all these years, no one had seen that cleft;
20 but lovers will discover every thing:
you were the first to find it, and you made
that cleft a passageway which speech could take. Ⓐ
For there the least of whispers was kept safe:
it crossed that cleft with words of tenderness.
25 And Pyramus and Thisbe often stood,
he on this side and she on that; and when
each heard the other sigh, the lovers said:
"O jealous wall, why do you block our path?
Oh wouldn't it be better if you let
30 our bodies join each other fully or,
if that is asking for too much, just stretched
your fissure wide enough to let us kiss!

---

1. **Pyramus** (pĭr′ə-məs).
2. **Thisbe** (thĭz′bē).
3. **the mighty city . . . had built:** the walled city of Babylon (băb′ə-lən), the ruins of which are south of Baghdad, Iraq. In Greek mythology, it was founded by Semíramis (sə-mĭr′ə-məs), a powerful Assyrian queen.

ANALYZE VISUALS
Explain how this painting conveys a sense of Pyramus and Thisbe's separation and their longing to be together. Consider the painter's use of light and color, as well as Thisbe's expression and Pyramus' absence.

Ⓐ MYTH
What is keeping Pyramus and Thisbe apart, and what do they do to overcome these barriers? From what you've read so far, decide what lesson about love this myth might teach.

Thisbe, John William Waterhouse. Whitford and Hughes, London. © The Bridgeman Art Library.

DIFFERENTIATED INSTRUCTION

For general guidelines on differentiating instruction, see

 BEST PRACTICES TOOLKIT
Differentiated Instruction pp. 31–38

FOR LESS–PROFICIENT READERS

Options for Reading Read the first stanza of the poem aloud to give students an idea of the rhythm of its language. Have volunteers take turns reading several more lines of the poem. Lead students to see that this translation of "Pyramus and Thisbe" (like *Romeo and Juliet*) is presented in blank verse (unrhymed iambic pentameter) to suggest a storyteller's natural speech.

BACKGROUND

Ovid and Shakespeare The myth of Pyramus and Thisbe helped inspire Shakespeare's *Romeo and Juliet.* However, Shakespeare also wrote a spoof of Ovid's tale for *A Midsummer Night's Dream,* with comic characters playing Pyramus, Thisbe, the lion, the moon, and the wall through which the lovers speak. Evidence suggests that *A Midsummer Night's Dream* was first performed just one season after *Romeo and Juliet,* so Shakespeare may have written the comic scene while he was working on or just after he finished *Romeo and Juliet.*

REINFORCE *KEY IDEA:* CLASSIC STORIES

Discuss "Pyramus and Thisbe" is set in ancient Babylon. What does this fact suggest about the universal appeal of **classic stories?** *Possible answer: This fact suggests that the universal appeal of a classic story is based on elements other than the story's setting.*

FOR ENGLISH LEARNERS

Language: Pronoun Referents Students may find this myth less challenging if they can identify pronoun referents. Draw students' attention to each of these pronouns and ask students to name its referent:

- *that* (line 1), "house"
- *Theirs* (line 10), "Pyramus and Thisbe's love"
- *that* (line 26), "side"
- *each* (line 27), "lover"

FOR ADVANCED LEARNERS/PRE–AP

Evaluate Tone Direct students to the comments that the speaker makes about love in lines 12–13 and 16. Elicit that these comments inject a somewhat "teachy" tone into the storytelling. As students read on, ask them to decide how strong this tone is in the myth as a whole. When they have finished reading, invite students to share their thoughts about how this tone adds to or detracts from the telling of the story.

And we are not ungrateful: we admit
our words reach loving ears." And having talked
35 in vain, the lovers still remained apart.
Just so, one night, they wished each other well,
and each delivered kisses to the wall—
although those kisses could not reach their goal.
But on the morning after, when firstlight
40 had banished night's bright star-fires from the sky
and sun had left the brine-soaked[4] meadows dry,
again they took their places at the cleft.
Then, in low whispers—after their laments—
those two devised this plan: they'd circumvent
45 their guardians' watchful eyes[5] and, cloaked by night,
in silence, slip out from their homes and reach
a site outside the city. Lest each lose
the other as they wandered separately
across the open fields, they were to meet
50 at Ninus' tomb[6] and hide beneath a tree
in darkness; for beside that tomb there stood
a tall mulberry[7] close to a cool spring,
a tree well weighted down with snow-white berries. **B**
Delighted with their plan—impatiently—
55 they waited for the close of day. At last
the sun plunged down into the waves, and night
emerged from those same waves.

                        Now Thisbe takes
great care, that none detect her as she makes
her way out from the house amid the dark;
60 her face is veiled; she finds the tomb; she sits
beneath the tree they'd chosen for their tryst.
Love made her bold. But now a lioness
just done with killing oxen—blood dripped down
her jaws, her mouth was frothing—comes to slake
65 her thirst at a cool spring close to the tree.
By moonlight, Thisbe sees the savage beast;
with trembling feet, the girl is quick to seek
a shadowed cave; but even as she flees,
her shawl slips from her shoulders. Thirst appeased,
70 the lioness is heading for the woods
when she, by chance, spies the abandoned shawl

---

4. **brine-soaked:** dew-covered.

5. **they'd circumvent . . . eyes:** They would sneak past their parents.

6. **Ninus'** (nī′nəs) **tomb:** According to Greek legend, King Ninus was Semiramis' husband. When he died, she marked his burial place with a tall monument outside the walls of Babylon.

7. **mulberry:** a type of tree that produces small, sweet berries, which are usually deep red or purple in color.

1066 UNIT 10: SHAKESPEAREAN DRAMA

Lines 43–57
DISCUSSION PROMPTS

Use these prompts to explore the lovers'
thinking as they devise their plan:

Connect How might you feel if you were
forbidden to see someone who was close to
you? In what way do Pyramus and Thisbe
show such feelings? *Students should recognize the lovers' desire to be together and their
rebellious thoughts and decision.*

Analyze Why do the lovers decide to meet
at Ninus's tomb? How does this location
foreshadow later story events? *Possible
answer: The lovers plan to meet at Ninus's
tomb because it is outside the city and
because they can hide under a tree there.
The location foreshadows the fact that both
lovers will die there.*

Evaluate Do you think that Pyramus and
Thisbe would be as interested in one
another if their love were not forbidden?
Explain. *Possible answer: Pyramus and
Thisbe probably would be interested in each
other, but the fact that their love is forbidden
may add to the attraction. The lovers seem
to enjoy the planning of the secret meeting
and are impatient to carry out the plan
(line 54).*

B SEQUENCE
Explain the steps in the
lovers' plan. Where and
when do they decide
to meet?

DIFFERENTIATED INSTRUCTION

FOR LESS–PROFICIENT READERS

Explore Narrative Poetry Help students get a
better grasp of the nature of narrative poetry
by discussing ways in which "Pyramus and
Thisbe" is both like a poem and like a prose
story. Help them list characteristics of poetry
(such as stanza form and poetic meter)
and of prose fiction (such as conflict and a
sequence of plot events) that they recognize
as they read.

FOR ENGLISH LEARNERS

Language: Verb Tenses Most stories are told
with past-tense verbs; in "Pyramus and Thisbe,"
however, the tense switches between past
and present. Have students follow along as
you point out these changes in lines 58, 73,
107, and 128. Explain that the use of the
present tense, although unusual, heightens
the dramatic energy in the parts of the story
in which it appears.

upon the ground and, with her bloodstained jaws,
tears it to tatters.

        Pyramus had left
a little later than his Thisbe had,
75 and he could see what surely were the tracks
of a wild beast left clearly on deep dust.
His face grew ashen. And when he had found
the bloodstained shawl, he cried: "Now this same night
will see two lovers lose their lives: she was
80 the one more worthy of long life: it's I
who bear the guilt for this. O my poor girl,
it's I who led you to your death; I said
you were to reach this fearful place by night;
I let you be the first who would arrive.
85 O all you lions with your lairs beneath
this cliff, come now, and with your fierce jaws feast
upon my wretched guts! But cowards talk **C**
as I do—longing for their death but not
prepared to act." At this he gathered up
90 the bloody tatters of his Thisbe's shawl
and set them underneath the shady tree
where he and she had planned to meet. He wept
and cried out as he held that dear shawl fast:
"Now drink from my blood, too!" And then he drew
95 his dagger from his belt and thrust it hard
into his guts. And as he died, he wrenched
the dagger from his gushing wound. He fell,
supine, along the ground. The blood leaped high;
it spouted like a broken leaden pipe
100 that, through a slender hole where it is worn,
sends out a long and hissing stream as jets
of water cleave the air. And that tree's fruits,
snow-white before, are bloodstained now; the roots
are also drenched with Pyramus' dark blood,
105 and from those roots the hanging berries draw
a darker, purple color. **D**

        Now the girl
again seeks out the tree: though trembling still,
she would not fail his tryst;[8] with eyes and soul
she looks for Pyramus; she wants to tell
110 her lover how she had escaped such perils. **E**
She finds the place—the tree's familiar shape;
but seeing all the berries' color changed,

---

8. **fail his tryst:** neglect to meet him.

C SEQUENCE
Reread lines 73–87. What does Pyramus think has happened to Thisbe? Explain why Pyramus blames himself for this disaster.

D MYTH
Reread lines 96–106. Which events in this section seem supernatural?

E NARRATIVE POEM
Like fiction, narrative poetry often includes statements about the main characters. Describe the key traits of Pyramus and Thisbe, using specific words and phrases from the poem.

READING SKILL

C SEQUENCE

Possible answer: Pyramus thinks that the lioness has killed Thisbe. He blames himself because he had helped devise the plan that brought her to this place and because it was he that Thisbe had come to this place to meet.

LITERARY ANALYSIS

D MYTH

Possible answer: The leaping of blood from Pyramus's wound (line 98) and the color change of the mulberries (lines 102–106) seem supernatural.

If students need help . . . Define difficult words in the passage, such as "wrenched" (line 96), "supine" (line 98), and "cleave" (line 102).

LITERARY ANALYSIS: *Review*

E NARRATIVE POEM

Possible answer: Pyramus is tender with Thisbe when he speaks through the crack (line 24); he is grief-stricken when he finds her shawl (lines 92–93). Thisbe's love makes her bold (line 62), but she trembles when she sees the lioness (line 67); and although she is still trembling from that encounter, she is brave enough to return to the meeting place (lines 106–108).

If students need help . . . Use a Character Traits and Textual Evidence diagram to help students explore these characters' traits.

 BEST PRACTICES TOOLKIT—Transparency
Character Traits and Textual Evidence p. D6

FOR LESS–PROFICIENT READERS

Comprehension Support To clarify the rising action in lines 66–77, write these statements on the board:

Thisbe runs away → the lioness rips her shawl apart → Pyramus finds the shawl

Help students express the statements in a sentence or two. *Possible answer: After Thisbe runs away, the lioness rips her shawl apart. Then Pyramus finds the shawl.*

FOR ENGLISH LEARNERS

Comprehension: Transitions Remind students that certain signal terms can help them track story events. Point out words and phrases that establish a setting (such as "one night" in line 36 and "At last" in line 55), that show that one event follows another (such as "But now" in line 62 and "And then" in line 94), and that indicate that some events are happening at the same time (such as "even as" in line 68 and "as" in line 96).

Discuss How can "Pyramus and Thisbe" be considered one of the world's **classic stories**?
Possible answer: The story is classic because it has a universal appeal. Readers from a wide range of cultures and eras can sympathize with the lovers' desire to be together and can feel sorry that things go so terribly wrong for them.

LITERARY ANALYSIS

F MYTH

Possible answer: The mulberry tree, stained with the lovers' blood, will continue to produce purple instead of white berries to signify the lovers' sad end and to help people remember their deaths (lines 144–146).

SELECTION WRAP–UP

REFLECT Ask students how this myth made them feel about the concept of fate and the power of love.

⭐ **CRITIQUE** Ask students to find a purpose in this myth beyond explaining why the mulberry tree has purple berries. Have them state in their own words what they think is the moral of "Pyramus and Thisbe."

---

she is not sure. And as she hesitates,
she sights the writhing body on the ground—
115 the bloody limbs—and, paler than boxwood,[9]
retreats; she trembles—even as the sea
when light wind stirs its surface. She is quick
to recognize her lover; with loud blows
she beats her arms—though they do not deserve
120 such punishment. She tears her hair, enfolds
her love's dear form; she fills his wounds with tears
that mingle with his blood; and while she plants
her kisses on his cold face, she laments:
"What struck you, Pyramus? Why have I lost
125 my love? It is your Thisbe—I—who call
your name! Respond! Lift up your fallen head!"
He heard her name; and lifting up his eyes
weighed down by death, he saw her face—and then
he closed his eyes again.

　　　　　　　　　She recognized
130 her own shawl and his dagger's ivory sheath.
She cried: "Dear boy, you died by your own hand:
your love has killed you. But I, too, command
the force to face at least this task: I can
claim love, and it will give me strength enough
135 to strike myself. I'll follow you in death;
and men will say that I—unfortunate—
was both the cause and comrade of your fate.
Nothing but death could sever you from me;
but now death has no power to prevent
140 my joining you. I call upon his parents
and mine; I plead for him and me—do not
deny to us—united by true love,
who share this fatal moment—one same tomb.
And may you, mulberry, whose boughs now shade
145 one wretched body and will soon shade two,
forever bear these darkly colored fruits
as signs of our sad end, that men remember
the death we met together." With these words, **F**
she placed the dagger's point beneath her breast,
150 then leaned against the blade still warm with her
dear lover's blood. The gods and parents heard
her prayer, and they were stirred. Her wish was granted.

Translated by Allen Mandelbaum

---

9. **boxwood:** a white or light yellow type of wood.

F MYTH
Why does the mulberry tree produce deep red berries?

DIFFERENTIATED INSTRUCTION

FOR LESS–PROFICIENT READERS
Review the Plot Have students review the plot of this narrative poem by completing a Plot Diagram.

 BEST PRACTICES TOOLKIT—Transparency Plot Diagram p. D10

Background: Pyramus and Thisbe, forbidden lovers, make secret plans to meet.
Rising Action: Thisbe hides from a lioness and drops her shawl, which the lioness shreds.
Climax: Pyramus finds the shawl, thinks that Thisbe is dead, and kills himself.
Falling Action: Thisbe finds the dying Pyramus and kills herself.
Resolution: Mulberry bushes have purple berries in memory of the lovers' deaths.

Comprehension

1. **Recall** Describe how Pyramus and Thisbe communicate with each other at the beginning of the myth. Why can't they just talk face to face?

2. **Summarize** What secret plan do Pyramus and Thisbe make?

3. **Clarify** What happens to ruin the lovers' plan?

Literary Analysis

4. **Make Judgments** As she decides to take her own life, Thisbe says, "I can / claim love, and it will give me strength enough / to strike myself." Both Pyramus and Thisbe seem to think that taking their own life is a strong or brave thing to do. If you had been with them that night, how could you have talked them into making a different decision? Explain.

5. **Analyze Sequence** Review the sequence chain you created as you read. How might the myth's ending have been different if Pyramus had left for the rendezvous at the same time Thisbe did? Cite evidence to support your answer.

6. **Analyze Myth** Use a chart like the following to explain how each characteristic of myth appears in "Pyramus and Thisbe."

Characteristic of Myth	In "Pyramus and Thisbe"
Explains how something connected to humans or nature came to be	
Tells about supernatural beings or events	
Presents a lesson or moral	

7. **Evaluate Theme** "Pyramus and Thisbe" is an ancient myth, passed down orally and in writing for generations before Ovid recorded it some 2,000 years ago. Explain whether you think the theme, or message, of this **classic story** is still relevant to contemporary audiences.

Reading-Writing Connection

WRITING PROMPT

Extended Response: Compare and Contrast
Many great writers have looked to myths for inspiration. "Pyramus and Thisbe" was retold by Ovid long before Shakespeare wrote *Romeo and Juliet*, and Ovid was one of Shakespeare's favorite authors. Compare and contrast *Romeo and Juliet* with "Pyramus and Thisbe" in terms of plot, conflict, characters, and theme.

SELF-CHECK

A strong comparison will . . .
- clearly present the selections' similarities and differences
- cite evidence from both myth and play
- state whether the selections are more alike or more different

---

Practice and Apply

After Reading

For additional support of post-reading questions, use these copy masters:

R RESOURCE MANAGER—Copy Masters
Reading Check p. 145 (to check understanding of the selection)
Myth p. 141 (for practice of literary analysis standards focus)
Question Support p. 146 (After Reading questions adapted for English learners and less-proficient readers)

For additional questions, see page 135.

ANSWERS

Comprehension

1. *Pyramus and Thisbe communicate by whispering through a crack in a shared wall. They cannot talk face to face because their parents have forbidden their love.*

2. *Pyramus and Thisbe make a plan to meet at night outside of the city.*

3. *A lioness scares Thisbe away from the meeting place, and Pyramus assumes that she is dead when he finds her shawl, which the lioness has shredded.*

Literary Analysis

Possible answers:

4. *Pyramus might have been persuaded to look for Thisbe's remains, which would have allowed time for her to return. Thisbe might have responded to a plea to honor her love by creating an impressive burial site for Pyramus instead of taking her life.*

5. ■ **STANDARDS FOCUS** *Sequence If the lovers had left at the same time, they might*

Assess and Reteach

Assess

R RESOURCE MANAGER—Copy Masters
Selection Test A pp. 147–148
Selection Test B/C pp. 149–150

⊙ Test Generator CD

Reteach

S STANDARDS LESSON FILE
Literature Lesson 18: Narrative vs. Lyric Poetry
Reading Lesson 6: Recognizing Sequence and Chronological Order

---

have met happily and married. On the other hand, both of them might have been killed by the lioness.

6. ● **STANDARDS FOCUS** *Myth* **Something connected to humans or nature:** *why mulberries are purple in color;* **Supernatural being or event:** *The mulberries darkened after Pyramus's blood spilled on them;* **Lesson or moral:** *Passion can be so strong that it destroys those who feel it.*

7. *The myth remains a classic story because people today can relate to the great power of love and because they still feel great sadness when young love is destroyed by tragedy.*

Reading-Writing Connection

WRITING PROMPT
Encourage students to use a Venn Diagram as they compare the selections and gather evidence. Offer two methods of organization: (1) discussing one selection and then going on to discuss the second or (2) comparing both works, point by point, at the same time.

⊡ BEST PRACTICES TOOLKIT—Transparency
Venn Diagram p. A26

Focus and Motivate

OBJECTIVES

- analyze a student model that reflects the key traits of comparison-contrast writing
- use the writing process to produce a comparison-contrast essay
- revise and edit, using a rubric for comparison-contrast writing
- plan and present a scene from a play

WRITER'S ROAD MAP

WRITING PROMPTS 1 AND 2

Help students choose a prompt by reviewing the specified scenes for key events and mood. Provide alternative film adaptation titles. For example, students might enjoy a more modern version of *Romeo and Juliet*. List these options as well:

- *Roots*
- *Pride and Prejudice*
- *Jurassic Park*
- *Harry Potter*

ADDITIONAL PROMPTS

Use these prompts for practice with real-world writing and writing in the humanities:

WRITING PROMPT 3

Writing from the Real World Write a short review comparing two high-tech products for possible purchase.

Possible Subjects
- two personal music devices
- two video games
- two Web browsers

WRITING PROMPT 4

Writing About Fine Art Write the text for a Web page about an artist or musician that compares two works by a single artist.

Possible Subjects
- paintings created by an artist at very different stages in his or her career
- a live concert and recorded work by a musician

For additional writing prompts, see

 Write*Smart* CD

 Writing Center at **ClassZone.com**

KEY TRAITS

Review the six **KEY TRAITS** with students, focusing mainly on ideas and organization. Compare the list of traits with the rubric on page 1076.

Writing Workshop

Comparing a Play and a Film

Plays, novels, and short stories often provide inspiration for filmmakers. However, a film script is not the same as a literary source. In this workshop, you will compare and contrast part of a film with the literary work that inspired it. The **Writer's Road Map** will start you on your way.

WRITER'S ROAD MAP

Comparing a Play and a Film

WRITING PROMPT 1

Writing from Literature Write an essay in which you compare and contrast one scene from the Italian filmmaker Franco Zeffirelli's adaptation of *Romeo and Juliet* with the same scene in Shakespeare's play. Your comparison might discuss plot, setting, mood, characters, dialogue, lighting, costumes, or camera angles.

Scenes to Compare
- opening scene in the public square
- Romeo and Juliet's meeting
- balcony scene

WRITING PROMPT 2

Writing for the Real World Choose a book you have read and enjoyed. Compare and contrast it with a film it inspired. Your comparison might discuss plot, setting, mood, characters, dialogue, lighting, costumes, or camera angles.

Subjects to Consider
- *To Kill a Mockingbird*
- *The Lord of the Rings*
- *A Separate Peace*

 WRITING TOOLS
For prewriting, revision, and editing tools, visit the **Writing Center** at **ClassZone.com**.

KEY TRAITS

1. IDEAS
- Engaging **introduction** names the works being compared and clearly states the **focus** of the comparison
- Supports ideas with relevant **details** from the two works
- Presents a **thesis statement** that identifies important similarities and differences
- Provides **background information** for the reader where it is needed

2. ORGANIZATION
- Follows a consistent **organizational pattern**
- Uses **transitions** to connect ideas
- Ends with a summary and a broader **conclusion** about ideas or techniques in the two works

3. VOICE
- Uses a **tone** that is appropriate for the audience and purpose

4. WORD CHOICE
- Uses precise **literary and media terms** to discuss the written work and the film

5. SENTENCE FLUENCY
- Varies **sentence beginnings** for pacing and interest

6. CONVENTIONS
- Employs **correct grammar and usage**

Writing Workshop Resources

 RESOURCE MANAGER UNIT 10

Plan and Teach pp. 151–154
Prewriting–Editing pp. 155–159
Writing Rubric p. 160
Speaking and Listening p. 161
Writing Support p. 162*

 STANDARDS LESSON FILE

Writing Lesson 24: Comparison-Contrast Essay

 BEST PRACTICES TOOLKIT

Scaffolding Writing Instruction pp. 43–46*
Analysis Frame • Writing Templates • List-Group-Label

TECHNOLOGY
 Easy Planner DVD
 Writing Center at **ClassZone.com**
 Write*Smart* CD

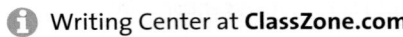

* Resources for Differentiation

Part 1: Analyze a Student Model

Lucas LaPaglia
Lakeview Academy of the Arts

A Night in Fair Verona

William Shakespeare's play *Romeo and Juliet* is a timeless and tragic tale of old grudges and young love. I recently read the play for my literature class, and then I watched a film version, directed in 1968 by the Italian filmmaker Franco Zeffirelli. I compared Act One, Scene 5, in
5 the play and the film and found differences in setting, plot, and dialogue that affect the meaning and the impact of the work. I learned that, while a filmmaker has to sacrifice some details to keep the running time reasonable, he or she can use scenery, music, and acting to create a vivid, fresh interpretation of what is on the page.

10 The setting is similar in the play and the film—a party at Capulet's house. However, what you have to imagine as you read the play is vividly presented onscreen. Colorfully costumed guests dance to traditional music in the film version. Blazing torches in the great hall are like Romeo's description of Juliet: "O, she doth teach the torches to
15 burn bright!" They symbolize the passion that will flare up this night.

Zeffirelli's camera also helps set the scene. The camera moves in rhythm to the music, swaying to the right and left while the dancers circle, drawing viewers into the scene as if they, too, are dancing in Capulet's house. During the dancing, the film cuts (jumps back and forth) from
20 Juliet's face to Romeo's, emphasizing their attraction to each other.

As for the plot, Zeffirelli remains mostly faithful to Shakespeare's design for Scene 5. However, there is one important exception. The filmmaker adds a song as a backdrop for the meeting and first kisses between Juliet and Romeo. A young man sings these words to the guests:
25   What is a youth? Impetuous fire.
          What is a maid? Ice and desire.

KEY TRAITS IN ACTION

Interesting **introduction** clearly states the **focus** of the essay. **Thesis statement** identifies what aspects of the play and the film are being compared.

Uses **point-by-point organization.** This paragraph covers the first point, comparison of setting. Varied **sentence beginnings** add interest.

Relevant **details** support the comparison.

Transitional words and phrases connect ideas. Formal **tone** is appropriate for audience (teacher and perhaps classmates).

Teach

Part 1: Analyze a Student Model

Have students read the **Student Model** and *KEY TRAITS IN ACTION.* Then discuss the model with the class, pointing out specific examples of each trait and building on what students have already noted. You may also wish to incorporate these activities:

- **Introduction** Explain that a good introduction identifies the works for comparison and elements for discussion, and then tells why this matters. Have students analyze the introduction in lines 1–9. Have them identify the lines in which the works are named (lines 1, 3–4), the element identified (line 5), and why this matters (lines 6–9).

- **Organization and Details** Point out that the student model clearly shows the organization at the beginning. In the thesis statement, the writer mentions "setting, plot, and dialogue," and he begins the body by discussing setting. Ask students what topic will probably be discussed next (*plot*), and have them skim the next few paragraphs to verify this.

- **Details** Discuss different details the writer has included for support.
  - **examples:** specific scenes from the film that prove the statement that the settings are similar
  - **sensory details:** details that describe sights, sounds, and movements of both people and the camera
  - **direct quotations:** words, phrases, or sentences from the play

---

DIFFERENTIATED INSTRUCTION

For general guidelines on differentiating writing instruction, see

 BEST PRACTICES TOOLKIT
Scaffolding Writing Instruction pp. 43–46

FOR ENGLISH LEARNERS

Language: Skill Words Write these terms on the board and review them with students:

- *point-by-point organization:* In this essay, the writer organizes by main idea and details. A main idea is stated and then details that support it are provided.

- *transitions:* words and phrases that show how ideas are related

- *literary and media terms:* words and phrases that identify elements of literature—such as *setting, plot,* and *characters*—or of film—such as *slow motion* and *close-up*

- *tone:* the writer's attitude toward his subject. A tone can be humorous, formal, or excited, for instance.

- **Background Information** Tell students to consider their audience's knowledge level in choosing the amount of background information that is needed. Students who have read the play need less background information than readers who have never heard of the play. Discuss background information students would include for an audience unfamiliar with Shakespeare or the play. ***Possible answers:*** *Students might mention the characters' ages, the play's time period, or the fact that it is a tragedy.*

- **Precise Terms** Help students brainstorm a vocabulary of precise filmmaking terms, such as these:
  - what you see (***Possible answers:*** *scenes, settings, actors, action*)
  - descriptions of what the camera does (***Possible answers:*** *fade in, cut, low camera angle, close-up, establishing shot, pan, dissolve*)
  - sound and music (***Possible answers:*** *soundtrack, dialogue, audio, voice over*)

  Record the terms on the board so students can refer to them during drafting and revising.

  Remind students to use precise terms to discuss the literary elements as well. Review the **GRAMMAR AND STYLE** note on page 970 as an example. Clarify that students should define *parallelism* if discussing Shakespeare's language.

For interactive student models, see

Write*Smart* CD

Writing Center at **ClassZone.com**

The youth, of course, is Romeo, and Juliet is the maid. The song reflects the feelings of Romeo and Juliet, and as it is sung, Zeffirelli's film cuts back and forth from the singer to the young lovers kissing and
30 proclaiming their desire for each other.

Perhaps the biggest difference between the play and the movie involves dialogue. Zeffirelli leaves out some of Shakespeare's text because a filmmaker is able to show what a playwright has to explain in dialogue or stage directions. For example, at the beginning of the scene,
35 Capulet encourages his guests to dance. Zeffirelli deletes this dialogue and simply shows people dancing. Another example involves Tybalt's outrage at Romeo's presence at the party. Instead of Shakespeare's many heated exchanges between Capulet and Tybalt, Zeffirelli demonstrates Tybalt's anger by showing his face in close-up shots, scowling with
40 rage. There is no need for dialogue; the actor's expression demonstrates Tybalt's hatred of Romeo. During the rest of the scene, the film cuts back again and again to Tybalt scowling directly into the camera—and, of course, directly at the viewer—reinforcing his ill feelings.

The rest of the movie follows the pattern evident in Scene 5. After
45 watching the movie, I understood that Shakespeare intended his play to be performed, not just read. Zeffirelli uses the tools of filmmaking to bring the setting, plot, and dialogue of *Romeo and Juliet* to life on the screen.

> Provides helpful **background information** about the play.

> Employs **precise terms** from the language of filmmaking.

> **Conclusion** not only summarizes the comparison but also includes a broader judgment about techniques in the two works.

2

1072 UNIT 10: SHAKESPEAREAN DRAMA

DIFFERENTIATED INSTRUCTION

FOR ENGLISH LEARNERS

Comprehension: Transitions Display a pen, a pencil, a cup, and a glass. Ask which items are alike and which are different. List these transitions on the board: *both, too, similar, also.* Explain that they can be used to show how things are alike. Have students use the transition words to tell how certain items are alike. Follow a similar procedure with transitions that emphasize contrast: *although, but, difference, however.* Then have students find

transitional words or phrases in the student model. Have them tell whether each shows a likeness or difference. ***Possible answers:*** *"similar," likeness* (line 10); *"However," difference* (line 22); *"difference," difference* (line 31); *"Instead of," difference* (line 37)

To provide English learners with additional writing support, see

 **RESOURCE MANAGER**—**Copy Master**
   Writing Support p. 162

1072 UNIT 10: SHAKESPEAREAN DRAMA

Part 2: Apply the Writing Process

PREWRITING

What Should I Do?	What Does It Look Like?

1. Choose a scene from the film.
Watch the film actively, taking notes as you do so. List those scenes that especially interest you or that seem the most different from those in the literary work. Draw a star next to the scene you decide to write about.

See page 1076: Techniques of Filmmaking

> ✳ *1. Act One, Scene 5: Romeo meets Juliet.*
> * *replaces some of Shakespeare's dialogue with lively action*
> * *includes a song*
> *2. Act Two, Scene 2: the balcony scene*
> * *mostly faithful to the play; some deletions*
> * *scene lit with soft blue light*
> *3. Act Five, Scene 3: Romeo and Juliet die.*
> * *duel with Paris cut*
> * *Friar's remarks moved to church steps*

2. Note differences between the film and the text.
Once you have chosen a scene to write about, reread that scene in the literary work. How are the setting, plot, and dialogue similar and different in the text and the movie? What techniques has the filmmaker used—lighting, music, and camera movements, for example—to bring the text to life on the screen?

> **TIP** If you're watching the movie on DVD, turn on the English subtitles or the closed captioning. Then you can compare what the actors in the movie say with what the author wrote.

> *Similarities/differences:*
> * *Setting is pretty much the same.*
> * *A special dance is added; a song is added when Romeo and Juliet meet.*
> * *Some dialogue is deleted; new dialogue is added at the beginning of the scene.*
>
> *Film techniques:*
> * *The hall is brightly lit by torches.*
> * *The camera seems to dance with the dancers.*
> * *Music plays throughout the scene.*
> * *The film cuts back and forth to different characters.*

3. Write a thesis statement.
Now that you've analyzed the similarities and differences between the text and the movie, write a thesis statement that tells your reader the focus of your comparison. You can refine your thesis as you draft and revise your essay.

> *I compared Act One, Scene 5, in the play and the film and found differences in setting, plot, and dialogue. These differences affect the meaning and the impact of the work.*

FOR ENGLISH LEARNERS

Writing: Thesis Statement Have students use sentence starters to help them develop a thesis statement.

* I will write about (act, scene) _____.
* My essay will focus on _____ and _____.
* The effect of the likenesses/differences is _____.
* The point I want to make is _____.

FOR ADVANCED LEARNERS/PRE–AP

Have students use the Core Analysis Frame: Drama to provide ideas for more challenging thesis statements.

 BEST PRACTICES TOOLKIT—Transparency
  Core Analysis Frame: Drama pp. D21, D42

Practice and Apply

To support students during the writing process, use these copy masters:

R RESOURCE MANAGER—Copy Masters
  Prewriting–Editing pp. 155–159
  Writing Rubric p. 160
  Writing Support p. 162 (for English learners)

Part 2: Apply the Writing Process

PREWRITING

1. Choose a scene from the film. Students may begin with the text if they wish, but in either case they should select a scene that affects them strongly. Point out that they can find the act and scene number later by looking at the text.

2. Note differences between the film and the text. Encourage pairs of students to experiment with different graphic organizers to help them generate ideas.

 BEST PRACTICES TOOLKIT—Transparencies
  Sensory Notes p. B9
  Y Chart p. A27
  Comparison Matrix p. A24
  Classification Chart p. B17

Discuss the **TIP** with students, pointing out that students can also use DVD features such as freeze frames and slow motion to analyze the film.

3. Write a thesis statement. Have volunteers deconstruct the model thesis statement to identify its parts.

* the act and scene
* the literary elements
* the reason why these matter

Suggest that students begin writing their own thesis statements by listing these three parts. They can then turn the list into a sentence. Remind students that they may revise their thesis statements after they finish drafting if they notice additional elements that they wish to cover.

For interactive graphic organizers, see

 Write*Smart* CD

 Writing Center at **ClassZone.com**

DRAFTING

1. Organize your ideas. Review the advantages of each type of organization. Note that subject-by-subject organization allows writers to focus on one subject or work at a time, which may be an advantage if the film and play are very different. Point-by-point organization stresses individual elements in each work, but requires writers to clearly indicate which work is being discussed.

2. Include effective transitions. Review alternative methods to show transitions.

- repeat a key word or phrase
- use phrasing that links the last line of a paragraph with the first line of the next
- use parallel sentence structure

3. Select evidence to support your comparison. Point out that the student model uses words and phrases that show how the evidence is connected to the writer's main ideas. Then ask students to find three ways of citing evidence. *Possible answers: within quotation marks (lines 14–15); in a block quote (lines 25–26; summarized or described (lines 35–43).*

Discuss how to punctuate each type and when it would be appropriate.

For comparison-contrast writing templates, see

BEST PRACTICES TOOLKIT—Transparencies
Writing Template: Compare-Contrast
   pp. C16, C23, C24

WriteSmart CD

Writing Center at **ClassZone.com**

DRAFTING

What Should I Do?	What Does It Look Like?

1. Organize your ideas.
You can organize your comparison in many ways. Two common methods of organization are shown here.

- **Subject-by-Subject Organization**
  Discusses characteristics of the first subject before moving on to the next subject

- **Point-by-Point Organization**
  Compares or contrasts both subjects, one point at a time

SUBJECT BY SUBJECT

Subject A: Play
1. *Setting:* Capulet's house
2. *Plot:* Romeo meets Juliet.
3. *Dialogue:* original text

Subject B: Film
1. *Setting:* same as play, with lighting, music, costumes
2. *Plot:* same, but includes singer and song not in play
3. *Dialogue:* some deletions from play

POINT BY POINT

Point 1: Setting
   Play: Capulet's house
   Film: same as play, with lighting, music, costumes
Point 2: Plot
   Play: Romeo meets Juliet.
   Film: same, but includes singer and song not in play
Point 3: Dialogue
   Play: original text
   Film: some deletions

2. Include effective transitions.
Transitional words and phrases, such as *like, unlike, just as, while, in contrast, on the other hand,* and *however,* can signal comparisons and show the reader how ideas are connected.

> However, there is one important exception.
> Perhaps the biggest difference between the play and the movie involves dialogue.

3. Select evidence to support your comparison.
Whenever you tell your reader that something is similar to or different from something else, you have to provide supporting evidence, such as a quotation or an example.

TIP Before you begin revising, study the key traits on page 1070 and the **rubric and peer-reader questions on page 1076.**

> Perhaps the biggest difference between the play and the movie involves dialogue. — *Comparison*
>
> Instead of Shakespeare's many heated exchanges between Capulet and Tybalt, Zeffirelli demonstrates Tybalt's anger by showing his face in close-up shots, scowling with rage. There is no need for dialogue; the actor's expression demonstrates Tybalt's hatred of Romeo. — *Supporting example*

DIFFERENTIATED INSTRUCTION

FOR LESS–PROFICIENT WRITERS

Organize Your Ideas To help students with point-by-point organization, provide this frame and explain that it mirrors the student model's organization. Have students follow the model to plan their essays.

Beginning Paragraph

- Name the two subjects and the focus.
- State your thesis. Refer to your notes or graphic organizer for item 2 on page 1073.

Middle Paragraphs—Points to Compare (number will vary)

- Make the first point.
  —Provide evidence from the text.
  —Connect the evidence and main idea.

- Make the next point.
  —Provide evidence from the text.
  —Connect the evidence and main idea.

End Paragraph

- Restate the subjects and summarize the comparison.
- Make a judgment or observation about the meaning or importance of the differences and similarities.

REVISING AND EDITING

What Should I Do?	What Does It Look Like?

1. Check the flow of your ideas.
- Draw [boxes] around the transitional words and phrases you have used to signal comparisons and connect ideas.
- If your essay lacks boxes, add transitions to make your ideas flow more smoothly.

▶ *They symbolize the passion that will flare up this night.*
Zeffirelli's camera ^also^ *helps set the scene.*

2. Keep your tone polite and formal.
- As you revise, keep in mind that your essay is a formal comparison. Read your essay aloud, highlighting slang expressions and language that is too casual or conversational.
- Replace highlighted words and phrases with language appropriate for your audience and purpose.

▶ *~~Still, there's one pretty big change.~~*
However, there is one important exception.

A young ~~guy~~ ^man^ *sings these words to the guests:*

3. Evaluate your evidence.
- Number each piece of supporting evidence you have used in your essay.
- If you don't have many numbers, add information to make your points clearer.

▶ *Zeffirelli's camera also helps set the scene.*
1. The camera moves in rhythm to the music.
2. During the dancing, the film cuts from Juliet's face to Romeo's, emphasizing their attraction to each other.

4. Define technical terms as necessary.
- Underline technical terms you have used to compare the literary work and the film.
- Have you defined terms that your audience might not know? Add definitions wherever needed to make your writing clear.

▶ *During the dancing, the film <u>cuts</u>* ^(jumps back and forth)^ *from Juliet's face to Romeo's, emphasizing their attraction to each other.*

REVISING AND EDITING

1. **Check the flow of your ideas.** Point out that students should look not only for transitions that signal comparison or contrast, but also for ones that signal examples—*thus, to illustrate, for instance*—or additional information—*in addition, moreover, furthermore, besides.*

2. **Keep your tone polite and formal.** Explain that **tone** is communicated both by word choice and by the type of details. To help students distinguish tone, write these sentences on the board:

   The camera jumps all over the place.

   The quick camera movements are distracting.

   Ask a student to read the sentences and compare their tones. Discuss slang terms students have identified and ways to state these ideas in formal English.

3. **Evaluate your evidence.** Point out that each main idea should be supported by at least one piece of evidence. If students cannot find evidence for a point, they should consider eliminating it.

4. **Define technical terms as necessary.** Encourage students to review the terms they brainstormed when the student model was analyzed.

For interactive revision tools, see

✐ Write*Smart* CD

ⓘ Writing Center at **ClassZone.com**

FOR ENGLISH LEARNERS

Recognizing Tone English learners may have trouble distinguishing formal language from casual or slang language. Lead a List-Group-Label activity. Have students identify and list descriptive words and phrases from their essays. Then have them work with partners or small groups to classify terms as either *formal* or *informal.*

🛠 **BEST PRACTICES TOOLKIT—Transparency**
   List-Group-Label p. A15

Preparing to Publish

Support for meeting the goals in the writing rubric is supplied throughout the Writing Workshop on pages 1073–1075.

For Rubric Bank, see

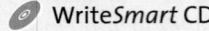 WriteSmart CD

 Writing Center at ClassZone.com

Assess and Reteach

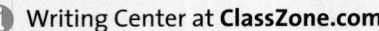 STANDARDS LESSON FILE
Writing Lesson 24: Comparison-Contrast Essay

Apply the Rubric

A strong essay comparing a play and a film . . .

☑ has a clear thesis statement that identifies the focus of the comparison

☑ includes relevant evidence and background information to support the writer's thesis

☑ follows a clear, logical organizational pattern

☑ connects ideas with transitions

☑ varies sentence beginnings

☑ maintains an appropriate tone

☑ uses literary and media terms correctly

☑ summarizes the writer's thesis and feelings in a satisfying conclusion

Ask a Peer Reader

- What makes my introduction either engaging or weak?

- Can you explain the focus of my comparison in your own words?

- Which evidence in my essay do you find most compelling?

Techniques of Filmmaking

Lighting: Soft lighting can make a scene more romantic; long shadows can make a scene mysterious or frightening.

Sound: Music and sound effects can establish mood. For example, lively music and laughing guests add to a party scene.

Camera Shots and Angles: Filmmakers use different camera shots (close-ups, pans, and long shots) and camera angles (from above, from below, or from the side).

Check Your Grammar

- When quoting a single line of verse, use quotation marks.

> Romeo describes Juliet this way: " O, she doth teach the torches to burn bright! "

- When quoting two or more lines of verse, indent the lines and don't use quotation marks.

> A young man sings these words to the guests:
>   What is a youth? Impetuous fire.
>   What is a maid? Ice and desire.

Writing Online

 PUBLISHING OPTIONS
For publishing options, visit the **Writing Center** at **ClassZone.com.**

ASSESSMENT PREPARATION
For writing and grammar assessment practice, go to the **Assessment Center** at **ClassZone.com.**

Staging a Scene

When you and your classmates stage a scene, you learn firsthand the craft that goes into a play or a film. These guidelines will help you.

Planning to Stage the Scene

1. **Choose your cast.** Hold a "casting call," with your classmates as the aspiring actors.
2. **Decide what scenery and props you will need.** You don't need lots of scenery and props to stage your scene. A coat of arms on the wall and a table and chairs, for example, are all that's needed to suggest a room in a wealthy household.

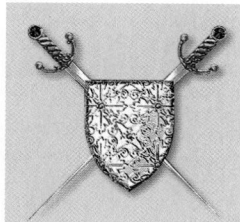

3. **Prepare the script.** Create an annotated version of the script for your scene. The annotations should include stage directions, such as where the actors should stand and how they should speak. Make copies of the script for all the actors.
4. **Rehearse the scene.** Bring the actors together as often as needed to run through the scene. Each rehearsal is an opportunity to fine-tune the action and improve the quality of the acting. Rehearse until the scene achieves your vision of what it should look and sound like.

   TIP Shakespeare's dialogue can be difficult to understand and deliver. Ask your teacher or your school's drama teacher for help with pronunciation and rhythm.

Presenting the Scene

1. **Use a narrator.** A narrator can introduce the scene and provide background information.
2. **Speak clearly.** The actors should enunciate each word and speak loudly enough to be heard in the back of the room.
3. **Show emotion.** Emotions—happiness, sorrow, amazement, anger—are the core of an actor's performance. Laughter or tears can help actors connect with an audience.

   See page R80: Evaluate an Oral Interpretation

SPEAKING AND LISTENING

Ask students to read this page to get an overview of how to stage a Shakespearean scene. Discuss which students will perform on stage and which will work on directing, scenery, and props. The director and actors should work together to create the annotated script. Make sure that the script includes the narrator's dialogue as well as that of the other actors. Before students rehearse, you may wish to discuss the **TIP** and whether students would benefit from help.

Allow time for students to prepare the scenery and props and hold several rehearsals. Before students begin work, review this rubric with them so that they have clear goals:

Rubric A strong staged scene

- shows evidence of planning and rehearsal
- includes any necessary props and scenery
- provides background information, either through a narrator or some other means
- contains dialogue and narration that is delivered using appropriate volume and speed
- features actors who use voice and movement to communicate characters and their emotions

R RESOURCE MANAGER—**Copy Master**
Speaking and Listening p. 161

Assessment Practice

CHECK READINESS

Read aloud the paragraph under **ASSESS** and stress to students that this is not the full Unit Test, but a way for them to check their readiness for it. Then have students examine the skills listed under **REVIEW** and look back in the unit or in the **Student Resource Bank** for any skills they need to review.

READ THE SELECTION

Remind students to keep unit goals in mind as they read the passage, paying particular attention to these literary and reading skills:

- characteristics of tragedy
- conflict
- character motivation
- character foil
- tragic hero
- Shakespearean language
- blank verse
- word play
- paraphrase

To help students focus on characteristics of tragedy while reading, encourage them to ask questions such as

- Why does Romeo react so strongly to being banished? Is he right to be so upset?
- What is the conflict between Romeo and the friar?

ANSWER THE QUESTIONS

Direct students to pages R93–R101 of the **Handbook** to review test-taking strategies.

- Remind students not to choose the first alternative that seems to fit when answering a multiple-choice question. Instead, they should read through all the choices, eliminate any that are clearly wrong, and then choose the *best* answer—the one that is most accurate and complete.
- Tell students that if they have extra time, they should reread each question, looking for key words that give clues about the answer.

Assessment Practice

ASSESS

The practice test items on the next few pages match skills listed on the Unit Goals page (page 925) and addressed throughout this unit. Taking this practice test will help you assess your knowledge of these skills and determine your readiness for the Unit Test.

REVIEW

After you take the practice test, your teacher can help you identify any skills you need to review.

- Characteristics of Tragedy
  - Conflict
  - Character Motivation
  - Character Foil
  - Tragic Hero
- Shakespearean Language
  - Blank Verse
  - Word Play
- Paraphrase
- Parallelism

ASSESSMENT ONLINE

For more assessment practice and test-taking tips, go to the **Assessment Center** at **ClassZone.com**.

Reading Comprehension

DIRECTIONS *Read the following selection and then answer the questions.*

from The Tragedy of Romeo and Juliet

William Shakespeare

Friar Laurence's cell.
In Act Three, Scene 3, Friar Laurence tells Romeo of his banishment for the murder of Tybalt, and Romeo collapses in grief. Then he learns from the nurse that Juliet, too, is in despair.

[*Enter* Friar Laurence.]

Friar Laurence. Romeo, come forth; come forth, thou fearful man.
Affliction is enamored of thy parts,
And thou art wedded to calamity.

[*Enter* Romeo.]

Romeo. Father, what news? What is the Prince's doom?
5 What sorrow craves acquaintance at my hand
That I yet know not?

Friar Laurence.   Too familiar
Is my dear son with such sour company.
I bring thee tidings of the Prince's doom.

Romeo. What less than doomsday is the Prince's doom?

10 **Friar Laurence.** A gentler judgment vanished from his lips—
Not body's death, but body's banishment.

Romeo. Ha, banishment? Be merciful, say "death";
For exile hath more terror in his look,
Much more than death. Do not say "banishment."

15 **Friar Laurence.** Hence from Verona art thou banished.
Be patient, for the world is broad and wide.

Romeo. There is no world without Verona walls,
But purgatory, torture, hell itself.
Hence banished is banish'd from the world,
20 And world's exile is death. Then "banishment,"
Is death misterm'd. Calling death "banishment,"
Thou cuttst my head off with a golden axe
And smilest upon the stroke that murders me.

DIFFERENTIATED INSTRUCTION

FOR ENGLISH LEARNERS
Assessment Practice: Work Backward

Prepare students by having them read the questions *before* reading the passages. Have pairs find unfamiliar words in test directions and questions and follow these steps:

1. Write each word on an index card.
2. Look up the meaning in a dictionary and write it on the back of the card.
3. Use the cards to practice the words with a partner or to teach them to others.

Friar Laurence. O deadly sin! O rude unthankfulness!
25 Thy fault our law calls death; but the kind Prince,
Taking thy part, hath rushed aside the law,
And turned that black word death to banishment.
This is dear mercy, and thou seest it not.

Romeo. 'Tis torture, and not mercy. Heaven is here,
30 Where Juliet lives; and every cat and dog
And little mouse, every unworthy thing,
Live here in heaven and may look on her;
But Romeo may not. More validity,
More honorable state, more courtship lives
35 In carrion flies than Romeo. They may seize
On the white wonder of dear Juliet's hand
And steal immortal blessing from her lips,
Who, even in pure and vestal modesty,
Still blush, as thinking their own kisses sin;
40 But Romeo may not—he is banished.
This may flies do, when I from this must fly;
They are free men, but I am banished.
And sayst thou yet that exile is not death?
Hadst thou no poison mixed, no sharp-ground knife,
45 No sudden mean of death, though ne'er so mean,
But "banished" to kill me—"banished"?
O friar, the damned use that word in hell;
Howling attends it! How hast thou the heart,
Being a divine, a ghostly confessor,
50 A sin-absolver, and my friend professed,
To mangle me with that word "banished"?

Friar Laurence. Thou fond mad man, hear me a little speak.

Romeo. O, thou wilt speak again of banishment.

Friar Laurence. I'll give thee armor to keep off that word;
55 Adversity's sweet milk, philosophy,
To comfort thee, though thou art banished.

Romeo. Yet "banished"? Hang up philosophy!
Unless philosophy can make a Juliet,
Displant a town, reverse a prince's doom,
60 It helps not, it prevails not. Talk no more.

Friar Laurence. O, then I see that madmen have no ears.

ITEM ANALYSIS

COMPREHENSION AND WRITTEN RESPONSE	ITEMS	UNIT PAGES
Characteristics of Tragedy		
Conflict	3, 4, 10	930–937
Character Motivation	13	930–937
Character Foil	9	930–937
Tragic Hero	8, 12	930–937
Shakespearean Language		
Blank Verse	5	932–933, 939
Word Play	1, 6	932–933
Paraphrase	2, 7, 11	934

WRITING AND GRAMMAR	ITEMS	UNIT PAGES
Parallelism	1, 2, 3	1051

FOR LESS–PROFICIENT READERS

Assessment Support Consider these options for completing the Assessment Practice:

- Have students "work backward" to review the test questions *before* reading the passages.

- Select random questions in the Assessment and have students demonstrate *how* and *where* to look for the answers.

- Ask students to locate unfamiliar vocabulary words in the Assessment questions.

- Have students record useful testing words and definitions in their journals for later reference.

- Read the selections or parts of them aloud to aid in student comprehension.

McDougal Littell
Assessment System

After checking student readiness with this Assessment Practice, you may administer the complete Unit 10 Test in order to more thoroughly evaluate student mastery of unit goals.

Romeo. How should they, when that wise men have no eyes?

Friar Laurence. Let me dispute with thee of thy estate.

Romeo. Thou canst not speak of that thou dost not feel.
65 Wert thou as young as I, Juliet thy love,
An hour but married, Tybalt murdered,
Doting like me, and like me banished,
Then mightst thou speak, then mightst thou tear thy hair,
And fall upon the ground, as I do now,
70 Taking the measure of an unmade grave.

[Nurse *knocks within.*]

Friar Laurence. Arise; one knocks. Good Romeo, hide thyself.

Romeo. Not I; unless the breath of heartsick groans
Mist-like infold me from the search of eyes.

[*knock*]

Friar Laurence. Hark, how they knock! Who's there? Romeo, arise;
75 Thou wilt be taken.—Stay awhile!—Stand up;

[*knock*]

Run to my study.—By-and-by!—God's will,
What simpleness is this.—I come, I come!

[*knock*]

Who knocks so hard? Whence come you? What's your will?

Nurse [*within*]. Let me come in, and you shall know my errand.
80 I come from Lady Juliet.

Friar Laurence.   Welcome then.

[*Enter* Nurse.]

Nurse. O holy friar, O, tell me, holy friar,
Where is my lady's lord, where's Romeo?

Friar Laurence. There on the ground, with his own tears made
    drunk.

Nurse. O, he is even in my mistress' case,
85 Just in her case! O woeful sympathy!
Piteous predicament! Even so lies she,
Blubb'ring and weeping, weeping and blubbering.
Stand up, stand up! Stand, an you be a man.
For Juliet's sake, for her sake, rise and stand!
90 Why should you fall into so deep an O?[1]

---

1. **into so deep an O:** into such deep grief.

DIFFERENTIATED INSTRUCTION

DIFFERENTIATED INSTRUCTION

FOR ENGLISH LEARNERS

Assessment Vocabulary To help students understand questions on pages 1081–1082, teach or review these key vocabulary words:

- Item 1: *excerpt*, "part of a story; passage"
- Item 5: *phrase*, "a group of words that lacks a subject and verb"
- Item 6: *contrasting*, "showing differences"
- Item 11: *paraphrase*, "state main ideas and supporting details in you own words"

Romeo [*rises*]. Nurse—

Nurse. Ah sir! ah sir! Well, death's the end of all.

Romeo. Spakest thou of Juliet? How is it with her?
Doth not she think me an old murderer,
95 Now I have stained the childhood of our joy
With blood removed but little from her own?
Where is she? and how doth she? and what says
My concealed lady to our canceled love?

Nurse. O, she says nothing, sir, but weeps and weeps;
100 And now falls on her bed, and then starts up,
And Tybalt calls; and then on Romeo cries,
And then down falls again.

Comprehension

DIRECTIONS *Answer these questions about the excerpt from* Romeo and Juliet.

1. Which line from the excerpt contains a play on words?

  A "What less than doomsday is the Prince's doom?" (line 9)

  B "There is no world without Verona walls. . . ." (line 17)

  C "This is dear mercy, and thou seest it not." (line 28)

  D "O, she says nothing, sir, but weeps and weeps; . . ." (line 99)

2. When Friar Laurence says "Thy fault our law calls death" (line 25), he means that

  A the law says the punishment for Romeo's crime is death

  B according to the law, death is a fault, not a crime

  C Romeo's death would be Friar Laurence's fault

  D it is Romeo's fault that he has been sentenced to death

3. The conflict in lines 17–28 presents two views of

  A jealousy

  B banishment

  C murder

  D the law

4. Which statement best describes why Friar Laurence disagrees with Romeo in lines 24–28?

  A He hopes to keep Romeo from acting rashly or causing more harm.

  B He blames Romeo for all that has gone wrong and wants to punish him.

  C He thinks Romeo is ignorant of the law and needs to learn the facts.

  D He thinks that Juliet deserves a better husband than Romeo.

GO ON

1081

ANSWERS

Comprehension
Model a thinking process for answering multiple-choice questions.

1. **A is correct.** Romeo's play on words involves the prince's doom, or final decision, and Romeo's doomsday, or death. In B, Romeo states that there is no world outside of Verona for him. Banishment is death. In C, the friar reprimands Romeo for not seeing the difference between the mercy of banishment and death. In D, the nurse simply reports Juliet's actions. None of these three answers demonstrate a play on words.

2. **A is correct.** The friar explains that Romeo's crime demands the death penalty. B is not what the friar says. C is not something the friar is claiming; he knows full well that Romeo killed Tybalt. D is inaccurate because Romeo has been banished rather than sentenced to death.

3. **B is correct.** Romeo sees banishment as more frightening than death, while Friar Laurence believes that Romeo should feel lucky he was saved from death. A and C are not correct because the two men are not discussing jealousy or murder. D is not the conflict because Romeo has clearly broken the law. It is his punishment that causes the conflict.

4. **A is correct.** The friar's role here is that of mediator. He points out that the Prince has been kind to Romeo by choosing banishment rather than death. B is not correct, because the friar assigns no blame. He thinks Romeo should be thrilled that he has escaped death. C is not correct because other than mentioning what the law calls for, the friar spends most of his time explaining the more positive aspects of banishment. D is not correct because Juliet is not mentioned.

FOR ENGLISH LEARNERS
Review Academic Vocabulary On the board, list the academic vocabulary shown in italics. Then provide examples in random order for students to classify.

- *play on words* (item 1): "If love be rough with you, be rough with love; / Prick love for pricking and you beat love down."
- *conflict* (item 3): the Montagues versus the Capulets
- *blank verse* (item 5): "But soft! What light through yonder window breaks?"
- *pun* (item 6): the argument in the opening scene of the play between the servants Sampson and Gregory (collier/choler)
- *foil* (item 9): Benvolio (calm and sensible) and Romeo (moody, emotional)
- *character flaw* (item 12): Romeo's idealism and defiance of fate

5. B is correct. *The word* mouse *and the first syllable of the word* every *are two stressed syllables that follow each other, varying from the usual rhythm of iambic pentameter.*

6. D is correct. *Romeo plays on the words* fly *(an insect), and* fly, *meaning "to go through the air." He implies that flies are better off than he is, since they may land on Juliet's hand, but he, in banishment, cannot have this pleasure. A is incorrect since it is too general. B and C are only partly correct.*

7. A is correct. *Unable or unwilling to listen, Romeo is acting like a "madman," or insane person. B is incorrect because while madness causes Romeo's "deafness," deafness is not a sign of madness. C is incorrect because* madman *refers to an insane person, not to an angry one; also, the friar is talking to Romeo, not to a nameless "someone." D is not correct, since the friar says nothing about Romeo's anger.*

8. C is correct. *Romeo is absorbed in his own problem and emotions. He shows no generosity or dignity so A and B are not correct. D is incorrect since Romeo is heated with emotion in this scene and not at all cold.*

9. B is correct. *The friar is trying to reason with an irrational Romeo. A is not correct because Laurence is not cynical—he is trying to highlight positive aspects of banishment. Romeo is the opposite of hopeful. C and D are incorrect, since Romeo and Laurence do not display these traits in the scene.*

10. C is correct. *Romeo is concerned with what Juliet will think of him and how his act of murder has caused her pain. A, B, and D are incorrect, since Romeo does not speak of these things at all.*

Written Response

Possible short responses:

11. *Friar Laurence tells Romeo that the work of great thinkers can help him cope with his forced exile. Like a coat of armor, philosophy will shield him. Like a sweet drink, it can remove exile's bitterness.*

---

5. In lines 29–36, which phrase breaks the pattern of blank verse?

  A "But Romeo may not."

  B "And little mouse, every unworthy thing . . ."

  C "Where Juliet lives; . . ."

  D "On the white wonder of dear Juliet's hand . . ."

6. What is Shakespeare contrasting in the pun in lines 41–42?

  "This may flies do, when I from this must fly;
They are free men, but I am banished."

  A insects and humans

  B flies and free men

  C Juliet and Romeo

  D flies and Romeo

7. What does Friar Laurence mean by "madmen have no ears" (line 61)?

  A An irrational person won't listen to advice.

  B Deafness in a person is a sign of madness.

  C Friar Laurence is angry at someone who doesn't listen.

  D Romeo's anger is a sign of madness.

8. Which trait does Romeo exhibit most strongly in this excerpt?

  A generosity

  B dignity

  C self-absorption

  D coldness

9. Which statement best describes Friar Laurence's role as a foil to Romeo in this excerpt?

  A Laurence is cynical; Romeo is hopeful.

  B Laurence is reasonable; Romeo is emotional.

  C Laurence is fearful; Romeo acts bravely.

  D Laurence is comic; Romeo is tragic.

10. In lines 94–96, Romeo laments killing Tybalt. This murder intensifies Romeo's conflict between

  A remaining loyal to Friar Laurence and upholding family responsibilities

  B being in love with Juliet and feeling guilty for leaving Rosaline

  C defending his personal honor and being worthy of Juliet

  D performing religious duties and keeping his obligations to the Prince

Written Response

short response *Write three or four sentences to answer each question.*

11. Paraphrase lines 54–56 and identify which character is speaking.

  "I'll give thee armor to keep off that word;
Adversity's sweet milk, philosophy,
To comfort thee, though thou art banished."

12. What character flaw of Romeo's does the nurse call attention to in lines 84–90? Support your answer with details from the excerpt.

EXTENDED RESPONSE *Write two to three paragraphs to answer this question.*

13. Why does Romeo disagree with Friar Laurence's advice in line 16: "Be patient, for the world is broad and wide"? Discuss Romeo's motivation for rejecting this advice and support your answer with details from the excerpt.

---

12. *The nurse scolds Romeo for being too emotional. She implies that his response is weak by telling him, "Stand, an you be a man" (line 88). She compares his display of grief to Juliet's and seems to be frustrated or annoyed with the behavior. She refers to their "Blubb'ring and weeping, weeping and blubbering" (line 87) as if they are children.*

Possible extended response:

13. *Friar Laurence suggests that Romeo's situation is not that bad; Romeo's life has been spared, and he can go anywhere to let time heal his grief. Romeo, however, can't imagine life away from Verona and Juliet (lines 29–30). As a result, he equates banishment with death (lines 43–46).*

UNIT 10: SHAKESPEAREAN DRAMA

Writing & Grammar

DIRECTIONS *Read the passage and answer the questions that follow.*

> (1) The musical *West Side Story* is based on Shakespeare's play *Romeo and Juliet*. (2) Unlike the play, however, both *West Side Story*'s Broadway production and its Hollywood adaptation set the 14th-century tale of Italian lovers in 20th-century New York. (3) *Romeo and Juliet* features two wealthy and prominent families, while the depiction of working-class people is the focus of *West Side Story*. (4) In the musical, Romeo becomes "Tony," and filling the shoes of Juliet is "Maria." (5) Many aspects of *Romeo and Juliet* are updated in *West Side Story*. (6) An opulent house becomes a crowded tenement. (7) A duel becomes a street fight. (8) Maria uses a fire escape instead of a balcony. (9) In this way, *West Side Story* represents a modern urban tragedy.

1. Choose the best way to rewrite sentence 3 so that its elements are parallel.

   A *Romeo and Juliet* features wealthier and more prominent families, while working-class people are the focus of *West Side Story*.

   B *Romeo and Juliet* features two families that are wealthy and prominent, while working-class people are focused on in *West Side Story*.

   C *Romeo and Juliet* features two wealthy and prominent families, while *West Side Story* focuses on working-class people.

   D *Romeo and Juliet* features two wealthy and prominent families; working-class people are the focus of *West Side Story*.

2. Choose the best way to rewrite sentence 4 so that its elements are parallel.

   A In the musical, Romeo becomes "Tony," while "Maria" is busy filling the shoes of Juliet.

   B In the musical, Romeo becomes "Tony," and Juliet becomes "Maria."

   C In the musical, Romeo becomes "Tony," with "Maria" trying to fill the shoes of Juliet.

   D In the musical, Romeo becomes "Tony," and "Maria" and Juliet are each other.

3. Choose the best way to rewrite sentence 8 so that its structure is parallel to that of sentences 6 and 7.

   A A fire escape was a balcony in the play.

   B A fire escape is a modern-day balcony in *West Side Story*.

   C A balcony becomes a fire escape.

   D Balconies and fire escapes are the same thing.

STOP

1083

ANSWERS

Writing & Grammar

1. **C is correct.** *The sentence has parallel subjects:* Romeo and Juliet, West Side Story; *parallel verbs:* features, focuses; *and parallel objects:* families, people. A *is not correct because the first part of the sentence is active, while the second part is passive. It also includes the incomplete comparison* wealthier and more prominent. B *is not correct because* Romeo and Juliet *is the subject of the first part of the sentence, and* West Side Story *is the object of the second part. The same is true for* D, *which substitutes a semicolon for a comma and conjunction (while).*

2. **B is correct.** *The order of both parts of the sentence is subject/verb/object. Two independent clauses are joined with a coordinating conjunction.* A *is not correct because the clause "while 'Maria' is busy filling the shoes of Juliet" is in subject/verb/modifier order. In* C, *the two independent clauses become one independent and one dependent. In* D, *the second part of the sentence makes no sense.*

3. **C is correct.** *Sentences 6 and 7 set the pattern of subject/becomes/predicate noun. C is the only sentence that repeats that pattern. A, B, and D all use different linking verbs (was, is, and are) to connect the subject and predicate noun.*

DIFFERENTIATED INSTRUCTION

FOR ENGLISH LEARNERS

Assessment Support: Parallelism

Define parallelism as a similarity of grammatical form in two or more elements of a compound sentence. Post this sentence:

> <u>Wherever</u> *ideas are connected* with coordinating or correlative conjunctions, <u>wherever</u> *elements are compared*, and <u>wherever</u> *items are arranged* in a list, the elements should match each other in structure.

Use the underlined and italicized text to clarify parallelism. Then give students sentences like this one:

> Romeo matures as a result of his love for Juliet and he was involved in the feud.

Ask a volunteer to revise for parallelism. ***Possible answer:*** *Romeo matures as a result of his love for Juliet and his involvement in the feud.*

INTRODUCE *GREAT READS*

In Unit 10, students have discussed a number of big questions. Invite students to tell which question they found most intriguing and why, and then focus attention on the two that appear on this page. Discuss the recommended books and their summaries, pointing out how each connects to the related question. Encourage students to choose one or more of these "great reads" to read independently.

ⓘ ClassZone.com

To find additional books that match students' interests and ability levels, visit the Literature Center at **ClassZone.com**.

UNIT 10
Great Reads

Ideas for Independent Reading

Find out who inspired Shakespeare and who Shakespeare inspired, and read more of his classic plays.

West Side Story
by Leonard Bernstein, Irving Schulman, and Stephen Sondheim

Sondheim, Schulman, and Bernstein move the story of *Romeo and Juliet* to 1950s New York City, where gang warfare dominates the West Side. Tony and Maria meet at a school dance and instantly fall in love. At first their happiness erases all else from their minds, but the harsh realities of their lives cannot be kept at bay. In some parts of the play, the authors are faithful to Shakespeare's plot; in others, they take greater liberty. In either case, the power of true love remains a resonant theme.

Othello
by William Shakespeare

The mastermind in this Shakespearean tragedy is not Fate but a jilted assistant in the army. Othello, a military general, is choosing a new lieutenant; he passes over Iago in favor of another man in his battalion. Iago vows revenge on both of them. He tells Othello that the new lieutenant is romantically involved with Othello's beloved wife, Desdemona. Though both protest to the contrary, Othello's jealously blinds him to reason and reality, with devastating consequences.

Metamorphoses
by Ovid

Metamorphoses is a collection of stories in which love causes physical transformation. One tale of thwarted love, "Pyramus and Thisbe," was an inspiration for *Romeo and Juliet*. The characters in the myths are sometimes brought closer together by their transformations, but sometimes they are pushed apart or separated forever. Ovid's tone, like Shakespeare's, changes suddenly from humorous to tragic and back again, allowing him to constantly surprise and entertain his readers.

The Wings of the Dove
by Henry Jame

Kate Croy is desperately in love with Merton Densher. Kate's family claims that Merton is too poor and will keep Kate from rising in the world, but the two have promised each other that they will somehow marry. When a wealthy, gravely ill young woman befriends Kate and falls in love with Merton, Kate plans to use the woman's feelings and friendship to meet her own needs. In *Romeo and Juliet,* overt tragedy and political strife change the lives of lovers. In *The Wings of the Dove,* subtle and intimate personal interactions cause love itself to change.

A Midsummer Night's Dream
by William Shakespeare

In this play, Shakespeare ta a comic and magical appro to forbidden love. Four young people have run aw from the Athenian court to escape an impending force marriage. Far from their homes, they fall asleep in forest on a summer evenir There they are visited by Puck, a devilish spirit who will use magic to change their passions and their liv While their passions are as forceful as those of Rome and Juliet, the results are b funnier and more hopeful.

A Natural History of Lo
by Diane Ackerman

In this book, Ackerman studies and explores the ways in which love has bee portrayed through the age *A Natural History of Love* discusses the lessons that can be taken from tales of love throughout history, be from historical romances a from such fictional roman as Romeo and Juliet's, and examines how love has been treated throughout history. Both a poet and a journalist, Ackerman uses poetic language in writing this detailed and thoroug history of a subject that ha significance for every read

UNIT 11

Epic Poetry

THE ODYSSEY

1085

For help in planning this unit, see

 RESOURCE MANAGER UNIT 11
pp. 1–11

INTRODUCE THE UNIT

What do we mean when we describe a story or an event as "epic"? Broadly speaking, epics reveal powerful qualities, such as heroism, majesty, and bravery. They tell stories of great horror, great tragedy, great triumph, or any combination of the three. More specifically, narrative poems such as Homer's *Iliad* and *Odyssey,* Milton's *Paradise Lost,* and Dante's *Divine Comedy* are considered epics because they share a dignified style and a subject that is important to a large group of readers. Epic characteristics can appear in modern-day events, too. For example, the exploration of space has been called an epic journey because of its heroic nature and the way that it represents the aspirations of humanity as a whole.

Invite students to consider how the pictures on this page illustrate the meaning of the word *epic.* Ask:

- What is happening in each picture?
- The people shown are travelers. What qualities might they share?
- What danger or potential for tragedy can you see in each scene? What courage or potential for triumph can you see?

Tell students that as they read the *Odyssey* in this unit, they will consider the importance of the story to the ancient Greeks. They also will explore its epic qualities and think about why it has become perhaps the most famous of all epic tales.

About the Art Alessandro Allori (1535–1607) painted this fresco of Odysseus' journey around 1580. For more information, see pages 1136–1137.

UNIT 11

Skills Trace

SKILLS STRAND	Homer's World pp. 1088–1093 — Informational Article	Literary Analysis Workshop: The Epic pp. 1094–1101	The Wanderings of Odysseus from the Odyssey pp. 1102–1139 — Epic Poem Level: Challenging
Literary Analysis	Influence of Author's Background p. 1090 Influence of Historical and Cultural Context pp. 1088–1090	Characteristics of the Epic pp. 1094–1095 The Language of Homer (Epic Simile, Epithet, Allusions) pp. 1096–1097	Epic Hero pp. 1103, 1104, 1108, 1110, 1116, 1118, 1120, 1121, 1123, 1129, 1133, 1134, 1135, 1138 Epic Simile pp. 1106, 1119, 1124, 1138 Epithet pp. 1109, 1113, 1116, 1122, 1138 Allusion pp. 1115, 1119, 1126, 1138
Reading and Informational Texts	Read to Interpret Literature in Relation to Its Period pp. 1088–1093 Set a Purpose for Reading pp. T1088, T1093 Monitor p. T1091 Make Inferences pp. T1088, T1090, T1092, T1093 Identify Main Ideas pp. T1089, T1090, T1092 Analyze Graphic Aid (Map) p. 1091	Strategies for Reading an Epic pp. 1098–1099 Analyze the Literature pp. 1100–1101	Strategies for Reading an Epic Poem pp. 1103, 1105, 1107, 1111, 1125, T1127, T1131 Predict pp. 1105 Visualize Imagery p. 1107
Vocabulary		Academic Vocabulary pp. 1094, 1096, 1098	Word Acquisition pp. 1103, T1103, 1139 Context Clues p. T1103 Prefixes (fore-) p. 1139
Writing, Grammar, and Style			
Speaking, Listening, Viewing, and Media	Discuss pp. T1088–T1093 Analyze Visuals pp. T1089, T1091, T1093	Discuss pp. T1094–T1099	Discuss pp. 1102, T1104–T1137, 1138 Analyze Visuals pp. 1104, 1106, 1110, T1116, T1120, T1124, 1127, 1130, 1136

Assessment-Based Planning: Skills in red are assessed on the Unit 11 Test. **T** = Teacher's Edition page

The Homecoming
from the **Odyssey**
pp. 1140–1169

Epic Poem
Level: Challenging

Characteristics of an Epic pp. 1141, 1144, 1146, 1147, 1149, 1153, 1154, 1155, 1156, 1158, 1159, 1160, 1162, 1165, 1167

Archetype pp. 1150, 1153, 1164, 1167

Epic Simile p. 1165

Conflict p. T1163

Summarize pp. 1141, 1167

Visualize Imagery p. T1151

Read a Poem p. 1166

Word Acquisition pp. 1141, T1141, 1168

Latin Roots (*solus*) p. 1168

Descriptive Details (Figurative Language) pp. 1156, 1169

Discuss pp. 1139, 1140, T1142–T1166, 1167

Analyze Visuals pp. 1142, T1145, 1146, 1148, 1150, 1154, 1156, 1160, 1162

Writing Workshop: Subject Analysis
pp. 1170–1177

Analyze a Subject Analysis pp. 1171–1172

Write a Subject Analysis pp. 1170–1177

Parallel Structure p. 1176

Indefinite Pronouns p. 1176

Discuss pp. T1170–T1172, 1176

Prepare and Present an Oral Report p. 1177

Skills Assessed on the Unit 11 Test:

Literary Analysis
- Identify and analyze epic hero
- Identify and analyze epic settings
- Identify and analyze epic themes
- Identify and analyze archetypes
- Identify and analyze epic similes, epithets, and allusions
- Identify and analyze epic plots

Reading and Informational Texts
- Summarize plot

Vocabulary
- Use prefixes to help determine word meaning
- Use word roots to help determine word meaning

Writing, Grammar, and Style
- Write a subject analysis
- Use figurative language to add descriptive details
- Additional writing and grammar skills

For additional lesson planning help, see **Easy Planner DVD.**

OBJECTIVES

- establish prior knowledge about the importance of a **journey**
- discuss literature and media presentations that depict a **journey**

Is it the JOURNEY
or the DESTINATION?

To introduce the page, read the question and then restate it as "Which is more important: the goal itself, or the things that you learn as you work toward the goal?" As students read the opening paragraph, discuss examples of high-school moments that students have come to appreciate or that they think they will appreciate even more in the future. Then relate the paragraph to the photograph by discussing what the climber might have learned during his **journey** to the top of the mountain.

ACTIVITY Model the activity, using a familiar story that involves a **journey**. (The *Lord of the Rings* trilogy is a good choice: the destination is Mount Doom and the goal, the destruction of the One Ring; but the journey teaches lessons about teamwork, courage, selflessness, perseverance, and more.) After students have completed the activity, call on volunteers to share their responses.

CHECK UNDERSTANDING Confirm that students understand the metaphor of a **journey** in this context. Have them explain why the journey can be even more important than the destination.

Unit Resources

Is it the JOURNEY
or the DESTINATION?

If attending high school is a journey, then the ultimate destination is graduation. As you strive to cross that finish line, you'll face new experiences, build friendships, and even run into some frustrating roadblocks. As you consider this journey, what do you think is more important—reaching your goal and clutching that diploma in your hand, or taking time to appreciate the many moments (both good and bad) that will lead up to graduation day?

ACTIVITY With a classmate, think of books, movies, or TV shows that depict a journey of some sort—whether it's a quest to find a long-lost family member, a struggle to make it safely back home, or a mission to fulfill an important dream. Which seems more important to the story, the destination the character strives to reach or the journey itself?

1086

R RESOURCE MANAGER UNIT 11	⊘ Easy Planner DVD-ROM	⊘ eEdition DVD-ROM & Online
□ BEST PRACTICES TOOLKIT	⊘ Write*Smart* CD-ROM	ⓘ McDougal Littell Assessment System
S STANDARDS LESSON FILE	ⓘ ClassZone.com	⊘ Test Generator CD
	⊘ Audio Anthology CD	⊘ Media*Smart* DVD-ROM
	ⓘ Multi-Language Academic Vocabulary Online	

Preview Unit Goals

LITERARY ANALYSIS	• Identify and evaluate characteristics of an epic • Identify and analyze epic hero and archetypes • Identify and analyze epic similes, epithets, and allusions • Identify and analyze plot, setting, and theme in an epic
READING	• Use strategies for reading an epic • Summarize plot
WRITING AND GRAMMAR	• Write a subject analysis • Use figurative language to add descriptive detail • Use parallel construction • Use correct subject-verb agreement
SPEAKING, LISTENING, AND VIEWING	• Deliver an oral report
VOCABULARY	• Use prefixes and word roots to help determine the meanings of unfamiliar words
ACADEMIC VOCABULARY	• epic • epithet • epic hero • allusion • archetypes • subject analysis • epic simile

Preview Unit Goals

The main skills and strategies taught in Unit 11 are presented on this page. Have a volunteer read the goals aloud while students read along silently and consider what they already know about each skill and term. Remind students about the color-coding of the skills strands, as well.

Model the strategy of copying the Academic Vocabulary and writing a preliminary definition for each term. Suggest that students use their journals for this purpose. Encourage them to use the terms in discussions and in writing. Also urge students to revisit each term throughout the unit and to refine its meaning.

DIFFERENTIATED INSTRUCTION

FOR ENGLISH LEARNERS

Academic Vocabulary Use the copy master to help students learn the Academic Vocabulary.

1. Read aloud each term. Have students find it on their copy master.

2. Discuss the meaning or example shown, and complete the chart as a class.

3. Have students work in small groups to complete the remaining activities.

Additional Academic Vocabulary Use the copy master to help students learn academic words they will use in subsequent lessons and on the Assessment Practice. Follow the same procedure as for the Academic Vocabulary copy master.

 RESOURCE MANAGER—Copy Masters
Academic Vocabulary p. 9
Additional Academic Vocabulary p. 10

Homer's World

OBJECTIVES

READING FOR INFORMATION

- understand the influence of author background
- analyze the influence of historical and cultural context
- read genre: read nonfiction article to interpret literature in relationship to its period
- set a purpose for reading
- monitor reading
- make inferences
- identify main ideas
- analyze fine art and a map

READING STRATEGY

■ SET A PURPOSE FOR READING

Point out to students that their reason for reading "Homer's World" is to enable them to read the *Odyssey* with increased understanding and enjoyment. Ask students to look over the article quickly, and suggest how it might prepare them for reading the *Odyssey*. List their ideas on the board. After reading, encourage them to add to this list.

BACKGROUND

Ancient Troy Troy, also known as Ilium, was an ancient seaport on the Aegean Sea in present-day Turkey. In the 1870s and 1880s, Heinrich Schliemann, a wealthy German businessman, excavated the site of ancient Troy. His findings suggest that the story of the Trojan War may be based on fact.

READING SKILL

■ MAKE INFERENCES

Ask students what they can infer about Odysseus' character from information in the section **The Trojan War.** *Possible answer: Odysseus was a clever, intelligent leader, skilled at outwitting his enemies.*

HOMER'S WORLD

The acropolis of Athens, Greece, was the high point of the city and a place to worship the goddess Athena, the city's patroness.

Examining the Homeric Epics

Composed in Greece around 750–725 B.C., the *Iliad* and the *Odyssey* are perhaps the greatest masterpieces of the epic form, narrative poetry about a hero's adventures. Both stories were first told orally, perhaps even sung, and it may not have been until several generations later that they were set down in writing. The poems are traditionally credited to a blind poet named Homer. Although there have been many translations of the poems into English, Robert Fitzgerald's verse renderings are considered among the best at capturing the poems' high drama and intense emotions. Three important elements of the plot of each epic are the Trojan War, the heroism of Odysseus, and the interference of the gods.

The Trojan War This legendary war seems to have occurred sometime around 1200 B.C. The earliest literary accounts of it, found in the *Iliad* and the *Odyssey,* are elaborated in later classical literature.

According to legend, the Trojan War began after Paris, a Trojan prince, kidnapped the beautiful Helen from her husband, Menelaus (měn´ə-lā´əs), the king of Sparta. Menelaus recruited kings and soldiers from all over Greece to help him avenge his honor and recover his wife. The Greeks held Troy under siege for ten years.

The *Iliad* takes place during the tenth year of this war. It tells the story of the Greek warrior Achilles and his quarrel with Menelaus' brother Agamemnon, ending with the death and funeral of Paris' brother Hector.

After Hector's death, the Greeks brought the war to an end thanks to the cleverness of Odysseus, ruler of the island of Ithaca. To break the ten-year stalemate, Odysseus thought of a scheme to make the Trojans think that the Greeks had finally given up. He ordered a giant wooden horse to be built and left at the gates of Troy. The Trojans, waking to find it there—without a Greek in sight—assumed that the enemy had fled and left them a peace offering. They took the horse inside the city, only to discover, too late, that it was filled with Greek soldiers and that Troy was doomed.

Giovanni Domenico Tiepolo's *The Procession of the Trojan Horse into Troy,* painted in 1773

The Heroic Story of Odysseus The *Odyssey* deals with Odysseus' adventures as he makes his way home from Troy and with events that take place on Ithaca just before and after his return. The first excerpts that you will read depict some of the wanderings of Odysseus after his departure from Troy with a fleet of 12 ships carrying about 720 men. This time his opponents are not military ones. Instead, he encounters various monsters who try to devour him and enchanting women who try to keep him from his wife, Penelope. The final excerpts describe Odysseus' homecoming and his reunion with Penelope and his son, Telemachus. In addition to great strength and courage, what sets Odysseus apart from others is a special quality that has been called his craft or guile: the ingenious tricks he uses to get himself out of difficult situations.

The Intervention of the Gods and Goddesses
Adding another dimension to the human struggles recounted in Homer's epics are the conflicts among the gods and goddesses on Mount Olympus (ə-lĭm′pəs). In Homer's time, most Greeks believed that their gods not only took an active interest in human affairs but also behaved in recognizably human ways, often engaging in their own trivial quarrels and petty jealousies. For example, Athena, the goddess of war and practical wisdom, supported the Greek cause in the Trojan War and championed Odysseus, while Aphrodite (ăf′rə-dī′tē), the goddess of love, sided with Paris and his fellow Trojans. The story of Odysseus' return from Troy contains some notable instances of divine interference. Odysseus has Athena on his side, but he has displeased the gods who were on the side of Troy. Furthermore, as you will see, he angers another god during one of his first adventures and still another later on. As a result, he is forced to suffer many hardships before he manages to return home.

To Homer's audience, the *Odyssey,* with its interfering gods and goddesses and its strange lands and creatures, must have seemed as full of mystery and danger as science fiction and fantasy adventures seem to people today. Just as we can imagine aliens in the next galaxy or creatures created in a laboratory, the ancient Greeks could imagine monsters living just beyond the boundaries of their known world. It was not necessary for them to believe that creatures such as one-eyed giants did exist, but only that they might.

This detail of a late 18th-century frieze depicts several Greek gods and goddesses.

Eros	**Aphrodite**	**Apollo**	**Athena**	**Muses**
God of love (also known as Cupid)	Goddess of love and mother of Eros	God of music, poetry, and prophecy	Goddess of war, wisdom, and cleverness	Daughters of Zeus (three shown here), often viewed as sources of divine inspiration

HOMER'S WORLD **1089**

■ MAIN IDEA

Remind students that writers sometimes state the main idea of a paragraph or longer piece of writing in a topic sentence. Ask students which sentence in **The Heroic Story of Odysseus** states its main idea. *Possible answer: The first sentence states the main idea.* Which sentence states the main idea of **The Intervention of the Gods and Goddesses**? *Possible answer: The first sentence states the main idea.* Have students reread each section with its main idea in mind.

BACKGROUND

Greek Mythology Our knowledge of Greek mythology begins with Homer's epics, the oldest written record of ancient Greece. Greek mythology does not comprise a religious document, like the Bible or Quran, for example. Some Greek myths explain a natural feature or occurrence, such as the existence of a constellation or the eruption of a volcano. Others are pure entertainment.

ANALYZE VISUALS

The image is an oil painting on plaster. It represents a procession of mythological figures. Ask students how the figures on this wall painting differ from Homer's depiction of the Greek gods and goddesses. *Possible answer: The frieze is an idealized vision of the mythological figures, showing their beauty and grace. By contrast, Homer depicted the pettiness and flaws of the gods, who could be mean-spirited, jealous, and vain.*

BACKGROUND

The World of the *Odyssey* Although Homer probably composed the *Odyssey* in the 8th century B.C., scholars believe that the epic recreates Greece's Bronze Age, an era that had ended some 500 years earlier. During that era, warrior chieftains, much like Odysseus, lived in elaborate palaces and conducted colonizing expeditions to expand trade and territory.

Homer: The Epic Poet

Shadowy Figure Although the ancient Greeks credited a man named Homer with composing the *Iliad* and the *Odyssey,* scholars have long debated whether Homer really existed. There are many theories about who Homer may have been and when and where he may have lived. According to ancient accounts, he lived sometime between 900 and 700 B.C., possibly on the island of Chios in the eastern Aegean Sea, and he was blind. Most modern scholars agree that the Homeric poems are the work of one or two exceptionally talented bards—singers who made up their verses as they sang.

Oral History Homer's epics are all that remains of a series of poems that told the whole story of the Trojan War. In later centuries, the *Iliad* and the *Odyssey* were memorized by professional reciters, who performed them at religious festivals throughout Greece. They were also the first works read by Greek schoolchildren. By 300 B.C. many slightly different versions of the poems existed, and scholars began to work at restoring them to their original form.

Models for the Ages Homer's epics became models for many later writers, including the Roman poet Virgil, who wrote his own epic in Latin. Poets throughout English literature, from Chaucer in the Middle Ages to Shakespeare in the Renaissance to Keats in the Romantic era, have found inspiration in Homer's epics. Moreover, by helping to shape classical Greek culture, the epics contributed to the development of many later Western ideas and values.

A Living Tradition Artists of all kinds continue to be inspired by Homer's work. In 1922, the Irish writer James Joyce published his groundbreaking novel *Ulysses* ("Ulysses" is a Latin form of Odysseus' name), in which he turned a day in the life of an ordinary man into an Odyssean journey. In 2000, the Coen brothers' film *O Brother, Where Art Thou?* told the story of a Depression-era Ulysses, an escaped convict returning home to prevent his wife from marrying another man. The 2004 movie *Troy* is a more straightfoward adaptation of Homer's *Iliad.*

 MORE ABOUT THE AUTHOR
For more on Homer, visit the **Literature Center** at ClassZone.com.

A scene from the 2004 movie *Troy*; a bust of Homer

People and Places of the *Odyssey*

You will find it helpful to become familiar with important people and places in the *Odyssey* before you begin reading. The map identifies real places mentioned in the poem, such as Troy, Sparta, and Ithaca. It also shows where later readers have thought that some of the imaginary lands visited by Odysseus could have been located, after applying Mediterranean geography to Homer's descriptions. Following is a list of important characters. All Greek names used in Robert Fitzgerald's translation have been changed from their original spelling to a more familiar, Latinized spelling.

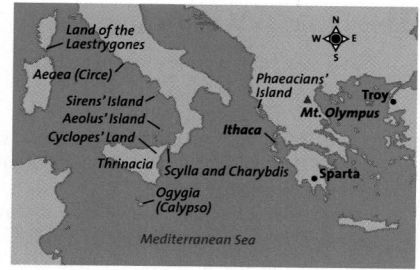

IMPORTANT CHARACTERS IN THE *ODYSSEY* *(in order of mention)*

BOOK 1
Helios (hē′lē-ŏs′)—the sun god, who raises his cattle on the island of Thrinacia (thrĭ-nā′shə)

Zeus (zōōs)—the ruler of the Greek gods and goddesses; father of Athena and Apollo

Telemachus (tə-lĕm′ə-kəs)—Odysseus' son

Penelope (pə-nĕl′ə-pē)—Odysseus' wife

BOOK 5
Hermes (hûr′mēz)—the god of invention, commerce, and cunning; messenger of the gods

Calypso (kə-lĭp′sō)—a sea goddess who lives on the island of Ogygia (ō-gĭj′yə)

Laertes (lā-ûr′tēz)—Odysseus' father

BOOK 9
Alcinous (ăl-sĭn′ō-əs)—the king of the Phaeacians (fē-ā′shənz)

Circe (sûr′sē)—a goddess and enchantress who lives on the island of Aeaea (ē-ē′ə)

Cicones (sĭ-kō′nēz)—allies of the Trojans, who live at Ismarus (ĭs-măr′əs)

Lotus Eaters—inhabitants of a land Odysseus visits

Cyclopes (sī-klō′pēz)—a race of one-eyed giants; an individual member of the race is a Cyclops (sī′klŏps)

Apollo (ə-pŏl′ō)—the god of music, poetry, prophecy, and medicine

Poseidon (pō-sīd′n)—the god of the seas, earthquakes, and horses; father of the Cyclops who battles Odysseus

BOOK 10
Aeolus (ē′ə-ləs)—the guardian of the winds

Laestrygones (lĕs′trĭ-gō′nēz)—cannibal inhabitants of a distant land

Eurylochus (yŏŏ-rĭl′ə-kəs)—a trusted officer of Odysseus'

Persephone (pər-sĕf′ə-nē)—the wife of Hades, ruler of the underworld

Tiresias (tī-rē′sē-əs) of Thebes (thēbz)—a blind prophet whose spirit Odysseus visits in the underworld

BOOK 11
Elpenor (ĕl-pē′nôr)—one of Odysseus' crew, killed in an accident

BOOK 12
Sirens (sī′rənz)—creatures, part woman and part bird, whose songs lure sailors to their death

Scylla (sĭl′ə)—a six-headed sea monster who devours sailors

Charybdis (kə-rĭb′dĭs)—a dangerous whirlpool personified as a female sea monster

BOOK 16
Athena (ə-thē′nə)—the goddess of war, wisdom, and cleverness; goddess of crafts

Eumaeus (yōō-mē′əs)—a servant in Odysseus' household

BOOK 17
Argos (är′gŏs)—Odysseus' dog

BOOKS 21—23
Antinous (ăn-tĭn′ō-əs)—a suitor of Penelope's

Eurymachus (yŏŏ-rĭm′ə-kəs)—a suitor of Penelope's

Philoetius (fĭ-lē′shəs)—a servant in Odysseus' household

Amphinomus (ăm-fĭn′ə-məs)—a suitor of Penelope's

Eurynome (yŏŏ-rĭn′ə-mē)—a female servant in Odysseus' household

Eurycleia (yŏŏr′ĭ-klē′ə)—an old female servant, still loyal to Odysseus

ANALYZE VISUALS

Ask students what information the map shows that is not in the text under **People and Places of the *Odyssey*?** *Possible answer: The map shows that the seas around Greece are dotted with islands and that Greece is close to Troy. The map also helps the reader to understand why the sea profoundly influenced life in Greece.*

READING STATEGY

■ **MONITOR READING**

Suggest that students bookmark **Important Characters in the *Odyssey*** to use as a reference as they read.

ALTERED SPELLINGS

The following is a list of altered spellings of characters' names taken from Fitzgerald's *Odyssey* and used in this selection:

Original	Altered
Antiklos	Anticlus
Deïphobos	Deiphobus
Andraimon	Andraemon
Thoas	<no change>
Olympos	Olympus
Meneláos	Menelaus
Agamémnon	Agamemnon
Akhaians	Achaeans
Ithaka	Ithaca
Thrinákia	Thrinacia
Mount Neion	<no change>
Doulíkhion	Dulichium
Samê	Same
Zakynthos	Zacynthus
Aiaia	Aeaea
Malea	<no change>
Kythera	Cythera

(List continues on page 1092.)

Why did the two artists use seascapes in their depictions of the *Odyssey*? **Possible answer:** *A seascape offers an opportunity to explore color and light; moreover, the sea is central to the plot and setting of the epic.*

ALTERED SPELLINGS LIST *(cont.)*:

Original	Altered
Euanthês	Euanthes
Maron	<no change>
Ísmaros	Ismarus
Kronos	Cronus
Erebos	Erebus
Amphitritê	Amphitrite
Phaêthousa	Phaethusa
Lampetía	Lampetia
Neaira	Neaera
Perimêdês	Perimedes
Politês	Polites
Pylos	<no change>
Hêlios	Helios
Telémakhos	Telemachus
Penélopê	Penelope
Hermês	Hermes
Kalypso	Calypso
Laërtês	Laertes
Alkínoös	Alcinous
Kirkê	Circe
Kikonês	Cicones
Lotos Eaters	Lotus Eaters

(List continues on page 1105.)

What is the main idea of the section **The *Odyssey* in Art**? **Possible answer:** *The* Odyssey *has inspired artists from the seventh century B.C. through modern times.*

The *Odyssey* in Art

Artists have been representing images from the *Odyssey* since the seventh century B.C., when Greek artists painted Odyssean images and scenes as decoration on ceramic urns and vases. Since then, artists have continued to tell Odysseus' story in painting, sculpture, and other media.

Throughout the unit, you will see how numerous artists have interpreted this epic in a range of styles and forms. As you look at the art illustrating each episode, ask yourself what the artists were trying to show about each part of the story and what their own attitudes toward characters and events may have been.

Looking at Art You've seen how understanding a writer's craft can help you appreciate the beauty and meaning of a literary text. In the same way, knowing about artists' techniques can help you understand and appreciate their work. The following list of terms and related questions may help you identify and think about the choices each artist made. Consider how these choices have contributed to the meaning and beauty of each piece.

Term	Questions
composition	What shape or space is emphasized?
material	Has the artist used paint, clay, pencil, ink, or some other material?
function	Is the piece useful, decorative, or both?
color	Does the piece have a broad palette (range of colors) or a limited one?
line	Are the lines clean, simple, rough, ornate, or jagged?
shape	Does the piece have large, bold shapes or smaller, more complex ones? Are they geometric or organic (free-form)?
texture	In painting, are the brush strokes distinct or smooth looking? In sculpture or ceramics, is the surface polished or rough?
scale	Does the piece show large things or small ones?
representation	Are the images realistic, stylized, or abstract?

Landscapes When you look at a Homeric landscape, ask questions like the ones that follow. See if the answers help you understand each artist's purpose.

- Which of the following two landscapes is more **realistic?** How so?
- What **material** has each artist used? Which do you prefer, and why?
- Look at the **composition** of each piece. What part of the scene is emphasized in the painting? What is emphasized in the collage?
- Describe the **mood** and **tone** of each piece. Which is more lush, and which is more spare? Consider the techniques that created these differences.

200s: *Ulysses and the Sirens*, Roman. Mosaic, 130 cm x 344 cm. Musée du Bardo, Tunis, Tunisia. © Bridgeman Art Library.

About 1650: *Ulysses Returns Chryseis to Her Father,* Claude Lorrain. Oil painting.

Portraiture As you look at a portrait, ask yourself what the image suggests about the character or characters being depicted. Try to identify the techniques that helped the artist create that impression.

- What does the **position** of the characters tell you about the scene rendered in terra cotta?
- Consider the difference in **dimension** between the two pieces; one is flat, while the other is in **relief.** How does that difference affect the feel of each piece?
- The pastel drawing is a highly **abstract** figure, as opposed to a realistic one. What do you think of it? Why might an artist choose such an abstract style?

Narrative Art Most of the artwork in this selection tells a story in one way or another. Consider how the artist's choices affect your sense of the events portrayed in each work.

- One of the following pieces is a decorative scene painted on a useful object, and the other is a book illustration. How does each piece's **function** affect its **style?**
- Compare the **backgrounds** on which the two scenes are painted. How does each background affect the way you view and understand the scene?
- Which scene makes more sense to you? Explain.

About 460–450 B.C.: Terra cotta plaque showing the return of Odysseus

1931–1932: *Ulysses,* Georges Braque. Pastel drawing.

About 450–440 B.C.: Clay urn showing Odysseus slaying Penelope's suitors

About 1915: Illustration from *Tales of the Gods and Heroes* by Sir G. W. Cox, Innes Fripp. Hermes, messenger of Zeus, urges the nymph Calypso to release Odysseus.

ANALYZE VISUALS

Ask students to choose which artistic rendering best illustrates the characters from the *Odyssey. Students' answers will vary but should cite specific elements from the piece.*

READING SKILL

■ **MAKE INFERENCES**

What can you learn about ancient Greece by studying the plaque and urn from that period? ***Possible answer:*** *The plaque and urn reveal information about the clothing, hairstyles, and tools of the ancient Greeks. They also demonstrate the high level of skill in different art forms.*

READING STRATEGY

■ **SET A PURPOSE FOR READING**

Ask students how "Homer's World" helped them accomplish their purpose of getting ready to read the *Odyssey. **Possible answer:** Students may say that "Homer's World" provided historical and geographical background, that it gave them an overview of the characters, that it provided images that will help them visualize events and characters, and that it stimulated their interest in reading the story.*

Focus and Motivate

OBJECTIVES

- identify epic characteristics, such as epic hero, plot, setting, archetypes, and themes
- identify and analyze epic language, such as epic similes, epithets, and allusions
- understand techniques for reading epics, such as visualizing, noting sound devices, and identifying character traits

Teach

Part 1: Characteristics of the Epic

Epic Hero and Plot Explain that an epic is more than a good adventure story; an epic has an outcome that affects an entire nation or even the world. Its scale is vast, covering many countries or worlds. The hero may have super-human abilities but still has human flaws. Such flaws make the hero more appealing than a perfect character, because the audience can identify with him.

- Brainstorm a list of stories from literature or film that might fit this description.
- Draw a web on the board and test each example against the qualities of an epic:

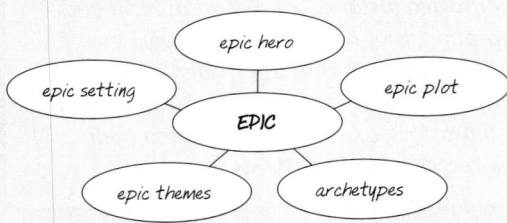

Epic Archetypes and Themes Ask students why they enjoy films, television shows, and stories about heroes who overcome great odds. Point out that people enjoyed such stories long before films, televisions, or even novels existed.

- Identify additional archetypes, such as the warrior princess or the traitorous friend.
- Discuss how archetypes, which are quickly recognizable, yield stories with wide appeal.
- Point out that themes of universal concern also generate stories with wide appeal.

Literary Analysis Workshop

The Epic

Extraordinary heroes and hideous monsters. Brutal battles and dangerous voyages. Spectacular triumphs and crushing defeats. The epic tradition, still very much alive in today's movies and novels, began thousands of years ago with the orally told epic poem. In ancient Greece, listeners crowded around poet-storytellers to hear about the daring exploits of a hero named Odysseus. With its storm-tossed seas, powerful evildoers, and narrow escapes, it's no wonder that Homer's *Odyssey* remains one of most famous epics in Western literature. It captivates us because it is a compelling narrative and a window into a time and place quite different from our own.

Part 1: Characteristics of the Epic

In literature, an **epic** is a long narrative poem. It recounts the adventures of an **epic hero,** a larger-than-life figure who undertakes great journeys and performs deeds requiring remarkable strength and cunning. As *you* journey through many episodes from the *Odyssey*, expect to encounter the following elements.

THE EPIC AT A GLANCE

EPIC HERO
- Possesses superhuman strength, craftiness, and confidence
- Is helped and harmed by interfering gods
- Embodies ideals and values that a culture considers admirable
- Emerges victorious from perilous situations

EPIC PLOT
Involves a long journey, full of complications, such as
- strange creatures
- large-scale events
- divine intervention
- treacherous weather

EPIC SETTING
- Includes fantastic or exotic lands
- Involves more than one nation

ARCHETYPES
All epics include archetypes—characters, situations, and images that are recognizable in many times and cultures:
- sea monster
- buried treasure
- epic hero
- wicked temptress
- suitors' contest
- loyal servant

EPIC THEMES
Reflect such universal concerns as
- courage
- a homecoming
- loyalty
- the fate of a nation
- beauty
- life and death

DIFFERENTIATED INSTRUCTION

For general guidelines on differentiating instruction, see

 BEST PRACTICES TOOLKIT
Differentiated Instruction pp. 31–38

FOR LESS–PROFICIENT READERS

Note Taking For students who need help with note taking, hand out the note-taking copy master before discussing the instructions in Part 1. Then have students read the first paragraph. Review the meaning of

narrative and explain that an epic poem is a very specific kind of narrative poem; it has a number of distinguishing elements. As you discuss the elements identified in the chart, have students record notes on their copy masters.

 RESOURCE MANAGER—Copy Master
Note Taking p. 15

MODEL: CHARACTERISTICS OF THE EPIC

Here, the Greek (Achaean) king Menelaus is speaking to his wife, Helen. He recalls the moment when he and Odysseus hid with their fellow soldiers inside a giant wooden horse, waiting to attack the Trojans. Formerly a Trojan herself, Helen stood outside the horse and called to the soldiers inside, mimicking the voices of their wives. As you read, notice the characteristics of an epic that are revealed.

from BOOK 4: *The Red-Haired King and His Lady*

"In my life I have met, in many countries,
foresight and wit in many first rate men,
but never have I seen one like Odysseus
for steadiness and a stout heart. Here, for instance,
5 is what he did—had the cold nerve to do—
inside the hollow horse, where we were waiting,
picked men all of us, for the Trojan slaughter,
when all of a sudden, you came by—I dare say
drawn by some superhuman
10 power that planned an exploit for the Trojans;
and Deiphobus, that handsome man, came with you.
Three times you walked around it, patting it everywhere,
and called by name the flower of our fighters,
making your voice sound like their wives, calling.
15 Diomedes and I crouched in the center
along with Odysseus; we could hear you plainly;
and listening, we two were swept
by waves of longing—to reply, or go.
Odysseus fought us down, despite our craving,
20 and all the Achaeans kept their lips shut tight,
all but Anticlus. Desire moved his throat
to hail you, but Odysseus' great hands clamped
over his jaws, and held. So he saved us all,
till Pallas Athena led you away at last."

Close Read

1. King Menelaus mentions several heroic traits that Odysseus exhibited while carrying out his plan to defeat the Trojans. One trait has been boxed. Identify two more.

2. What archetype does Helen represent? Explain your answer.

3. Reread lines 8–10 and 23–24. Explain how the gods interfered in the episode that Menelaus is describing.

MODEL: CHARACTERISTICS OF THE EPIC

Close Read

1. *Possible answers: Other heroic traits mentioned by Menelaus in his description of Odysseus include "foresight and wit" (line 2), "steadiness and a stout heart" (line 4), and the strength to fight down everyone, including Anticlus (lines 19–24).*

   If students need help . . . Explain that a hero's traits are shown in many different ways: through actions, words, and other people's descriptions. Ask what specific qualities Menelaus mentions in lines 2 and 4. Point out too that in line 23 Menelaus credits Odysseus with saving them all.

2. *Possible answer: Helen represents the beautiful temptress whom no man—except Odysseus—can resist. This is evident when she walks around the horse, mimics their wives' voices, and creates "waves of longing" (lines 12–18).*

3. *Possible answer: The gods interfered at two points. First, some god or goddess on the side of the Trojans seemed to have influence over Helen's behavior, as evidenced by the words "drawn by some superhuman power that planned an exploit for the Trojans" (lines 9–10). Then later, the goddess Athena led Helen away at last from the men who were hiding (lines 23–24).*

FOR LESS–PROFICIENT READERS

Comprehension: Point of View and Pronouns
Make sure students understand the pronoun referents in the model. Reread the first line of the instructional text to clarify who is speaking in the model. Then ask a volunteer to read the first line of the model aloud. Ask who is referenced with the pronoun *I*. Repeat with other pronouns in the model: *he* (line 5), *we* (line 6), *you* (line 8), *it* (line 12), *his* (line 21), and *he* (line 23).

FOR ADVANCED LEARNERS/PRE–AP

Evaluate Genre Explain that historically, epics were presented orally. Have students work in small groups to identify features that make this passage especially suitable for oral presentation, such as the way descriptions lend themselves to visualization and the rhythm and sounds of the words. Afterward, have students take turns identifying and giving examples of features that enhance oral presentations.

Teach

Part 2: The Language of Homer

Translations Tell students that all the model passages are from the 1961 Robert Fitzgerald translation.

Poetic Elements Explain that *epithet* has another meaning: it can mean "an abusive or nasty phrase." In addition, because students may confuse *allusion* with *illusion*, write both words on the board and clarify the difference.

Point out that authors use similes, epithets, and allusions as different means for expressing ideas indirectly. For example, a writer might compare a robe to a butterfly's wings or to the skin of a poisonous snake. Discuss how each comparison would affect listeners.

Ask students to make up epithets that they would like used to describe themselves, such as "Kim, builder of friendships" or "Duane, singer of songs." Encourage them to be playful but accurate. Ask how epithets might help others form opinions about each student.

To illustrate what an allusion might add, ask students what allusion they would use to refer to the *Odyssey*. Would they call it the *Star Wars* of its day, for example, or something else? Ask how the choice of allusion might affect someone's views of the *Odyssey*.

Part 2: The Language of Homer

Because the language of Homer was ancient Greek, what you will read is an English translation. The *Odyssey* has been translated many times, and each translator has interpreted it differently. Read these two versions of the opening of Book 2. The first is written in verse and has a more formal tone—closer to the original—while the second is written in prose and is less formal.

TRANSLATION 1

When primal Dawn spread on the eastern sky
her fingers of pink light, Odysseus' true son
stood up, drew on his tunic and his mantle,
slung on a sword-belt and a new-edged sword,
tied his smooth feet into good rawhide sandals,
and left his room, a god's brilliance upon him.

—translated by Robert Fitzgerald (1961)

TRANSLATION 2

Dawn came, showing her rosy fingers through the early mists, and Telemachus leapt out of bed. He dressed himself, slung a sharp sword over his shoulder, strapt a stout pair of boots on his lissom feet, and came forth from his chamber like a young god.

—translated by W. H. D. Rouse (1937)

The Greeks who first experienced the *Odyssey* did not read a written version; they heard it as a live performance. Singing or reciting, a poet kept the audience enthralled with **epic similes, epithets,** and **allusions.**

- A **simile** is a comparison between two unlike things, using the word *like* or *as*. Homer often develops a simile at great length, so that it goes on for several lines. This is known as an **epic simile.** In this passage from Book 20, an angry Odysseus is compared to a sausage being roasted over a fire.

> His rage
> held hard in leash, submitted to his mind,
> while he himself rocked, rolling from side to side,
> as a cook turns a sausage, big with blood
> and fat, at a scorching blaze, without a pause,
> to broil it quick: so he rolled left and right, . . .

- An **epithet** is a brief descriptive phrase used to characterize a particular person or thing. When a poet needed to fill out a line, he'd add an epithet with the right meter and number of syllables. Odysseus is known by various epithets, including "son of Laertes" and "raider of cities."

- An **allusion** is a reference to a famous person, place, or event. To help his audience picture what he described, a poet might have made an allusion to something they already knew. For instance, when Odysseus' son first sees the palace of Menelaus, he says, "This is the way the court of Zeus must be." Every Greek would have understood this allusion to the ruler of the gods.

DIFFERENTIATED INSTRUCTION

FOR LESS–PROFICIENT READERS
Note Taking For students who need help with note taking, hand out the note-taking copy master before beginning the instruction on this page. Point out that the copy master is to be used for Parts 2 and 3 of this workshop. As you discuss the terms and ideas in both parts, have students record notes on their copy masters.

R RESOURCE MANAGER—Copy Master
Note Taking p. 16

FOR ENGLISH LEARNERS
Culture: Allusions Students from other cultures may have particular difficulty recognizing certain allusions. As they read, have students jot down the names of people, places, or events with which they are unfamiliar. Afterward, they can meet in small groups to compare their notes and to learn more about the names they recorded.

MODEL 1: EPIC SIMILE

In this excerpt, Odysseus is watching the performance of a bard (a poet like Homer himself). Suddenly he finds himself listening to the story of the fall of Troy and of his own part in it. Notice the epic simile that is developed over this entire passage.

---

from BOOK 8: *The Songs of the Harper*

And Odysseus
let the bright molten tears run down his cheeks,
weeping [like] the way a wife mourns for her lord
on the lost field where he has gone down fighting
5   the day of wrath that came upon his children.
   At sight of the man panting and dying there,
   she slips down to enfold him, crying out;
   then feels the spears, prodding her back and shoulders,
   and goes bound into slavery and grief.
10   Piteous weeping wears away her cheeks:
   but no more piteous than Odysseus' tears,
   cloaked as they were, now, from the company.

Close Read

1. What two things are being compared in this epic simile?

2. In the boxed lines, the wife cries first for her dying husband, then for herself. Consider what this might suggest about Odysseus' feelings. What might the epic hero be crying about?

MODEL 2: EPITHET

Here, the goddess Athena speaks to her father, Zeus, on behalf of Odysseus. Reminding Zeus of sacrifices made to him during the Trojan War, she begs him to let Odysseus return home. Athena has told Zeus that Odysseus is so homesick that he "longs to die."

---

from BOOK 1: *A Goddess Intervenes*

"Are you not moved by this, Lord of Olympus?
Had you no pleasure from Odysseus' offerings
beside the Argive ships, on Troy's wide seaboard?
O Zeus, what do you hold against him now?"

5   To this the summoner of cloud replied:

"My child, what strange remarks you let escape you.
Could I forget that kingly man, Odysseus?
There is no mortal half so wise; no mortal
gave so much to the lords of open sky."

Close Read

1. One epithet of Zeus is boxed. Find another.

2. What epithet does Zeus use to refer to Odysseus?

MODEL 1: EPIC SIMILE
Close Read

1. *Possible answer: A weeping Odysseus is being compared to a wife who first weeps for her husband, who has died on the battlefield.*

2. *Possible answer: The comparison emphasizes Odysseus' deep love for whomever he cries for. He is probably crying for his comrades who died in the Trojan War and perhaps for his family.*

MODEL 2: EPITHET
Close Read

1. *Possible answer: Another epithet used to describe Zeus is "the summoner of cloud" (line 5).*

2. *Possible answer: Zeus refers to Odysseus as "that kingly man" (line 7).*

FOR ENGLISH LEARNERS

Language: Punctuation Draw attention to *Odysseus'* in line 11 of Model 1. Note that the apostrophe shows possession. Usually a singular noun takes an apostrophe plus *s* to show possession. However, multi-syllabic Greek names that end in *s* are exceptions to this rule. Have students find additional examples of an apostrophe alone signaling ownership (*Odysseus'*, Model 2, line 2; *Telemachus'*, Model, page 1099, before line 10).

Practice and Apply

Part 3: Reading the Epic

Use a Cluster Diagram to show students how an epic can be read in different ways. Draw a circle on the board and write *Odyssey* in the center. Add a section for narrative as you discuss how an epic can be read as narrative. Then add sections as you discuss other ways an epic can be read.

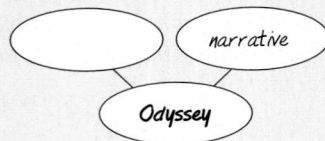

 BEST PRACTICES TOOLKIT—Transparency
Cluster Diagram p. B18

Reading the Epic as Narrative Point out to students that an epic is a bit like a soap opera: a cast of characters appears in numerous episodes that address narrow plot issues yet each are part of a larger story. Ask students for examples of television shows that have one basic premise—such as a character trying to solve one basic problem—which inspires the plots of the separate episodes.

Reading the Epic as Poetry Remind students that in figurative language, words are not always used in their literal sense but may instead be used to symbolize ideas and to evoke emotions in listeners. Ask why imagery would be so useful in a poem that was spoken aloud to a group of people.

Reading the Epic as a Reflection of its Time Ask students to identify modern heroes, fictional or real-life. Then ask what these heroes show about our society's values. Encourage students to choose heroes that reflect a variety of values, such as respect for intelligence, strength, leadership, and money.

CHECK UNDERSTANDING

Have students summarize the characteristics of the epic and describe what poetic elements are found in the *Odyssey*.

Part 3: Reading the Epic

Reading the *Odyssey* is a complex experience. On one level, the poem is an action-packed narrative that makes readers eagerly anticipate the hero's homecoming. On another level, it's a work of art to be appreciated and analyzed. Use the following strategies to help you make the most of your journey through the epic.

READING THE EPIC AS NARRATIVE

- Note the changing narrators. Who is telling the story at any given point? Consider how the different narrators deepen your understanding of characters and events.
- **Visualize** the action and the settings by using details in the text.
- Track the events and conflicts and try to **predict** the outcomes.
- Use a chart like the one shown to keep track of the characters, including gods and goddesses and Odysseus' friends and foes. What does each do to either help or harm him?

STRATEGIES IN ACTION

Characters Who Help Odysseus	Characters Who Harm Odysseus
Athena (goddess) • pleads with Zeus to help Odysseus escape Calypso's island	Poseidon (god) • stirs up nasty weather to create problems for Odysseus

READING THE EPIC AS POETRY

- Try reading the lines aloud, as the epic was originally performed.
- Read the lines for their sense, just as you would read prose. Follow the punctuation, and remember that the end of a line does not always mean the end of a thought.
- Listen for sound devices such as **alliteration, assonance, consonance,** and **rhyme** and notice how they reinforce meaning. (Although the sound devices in English aren't the same as those in the original Greek, they do reflect the translator's attempt to capture the spirit and technique of Homer's verse.)
- Consider how the **imagery** and **figurative language**—especially the **epic similes**—help you understand characters and events.

from BOOK 4: *The Red-Haired King and His Lady*

but never have I seen one like Odysseus for steadiness and a stout heart. . . .

Alliteration: The repeated "s" sound emphasizes the strength of the epic hero.

READING THE EPIC AS A REFLECTION OF ITS TIME

- Pay attention to the **character traits** of Odysseus, the epic hero, by looking closely at how he behaves and how he is described. What do these traits tell you about the values of the time?
- Think about what you've learned of Greek history. What events may have influenced Homer?
- Remember that in Homer's time most Greeks believed that the gods took an active interest in human affairs and themselves behaved much like humans. How are these religious beliefs apparent in the epic?

Odysseus' Traits	Evidence
strong, skilled, and swift	frequently referred to as "master mariner and soldier"
quick-witted; thinks on his feet	described as "strategist" when he responds to a difficult question posed by Calypso (Book 5)

DIFFERENTIATED INSTRUCTION

FOR ENGLISH LEARNERS

Language: Skill Words On the board, list the academic vocabulary shown in italics. Then give the examples in random order and have students match them to the vocabulary.

- *alliteration:* sailing the seven seas
- *assonance:* eight were taken away
- *consonance:* the tick of a clock
- *rhyme:* better letter
- *imagery:* the sea exploded onto the rocky shore
- *figurative language:* jewels sparkled like stars in a velvety night sky
- *character trait:* bravery, intelligence, thoughtfulness, loyalty

MODEL: READING THE EPIC

Odysseus has been gone from his homeland for years, and all except his family believe him dead. Young men make themselves at home in Odysseus' castle while vying to marry his "widow," Penelope. Odysseus' son, Telemachus, calls an assembly to discuss the situation. The following excerpt is an exchange between Telemachus and one of Penelope's suitors.

from BOOK 2: *A Hero's Son Awakens*

Telemachus addresses the crowd, complaining of the suitors' behavior.

"No; these men spend their days around our house
killing our beeves and sheep and fatted goats,
carousing, soaking up our good dark wine,
not caring what they do. They squander everything.
5 We have no strong Odysseus to defend us,
and as to putting up a fight ourselves—
we'd only show our incompetence in arms.
Expel them, yes, if I only had the power;
the whole thing's out of hand, insufferable."

A suitor responds to Telemachus' heated accusation.

10 "You want to shame us, and humiliate us,
but you should know the suitors are not to blame—
it is your own dear, incomparably cunning mother.
For three years now—and it will soon be four—
she has been breaking the hearts of the Achaeans,
15 holding out hope to all, and sending promises
to each man privately—but thinking otherwise.

Here is an instance of her trickery:
she had her great loom standing in the hall
and the fine warp of some vast fabric on it;
20 we were attending her, and she said to us:
'Young men, my suitors, now my lord is dead,
let me finish my weaving before I marry,
or else my thread will have been spun in vain.
It is a shroud I weave for Lord Laertes,
25 when cold death comes to lay him on his bier.
The country wives would hold me in dishonor
if he, with all his fortune, lay unshrouded.'
We have men's hearts; she touched them; we agreed.
So every day she wove on the great loom—
30 but every night by torchlight she unwove it;
and so for three years she deceived the Achaeans."

Close Read

1. Try to visualize the suitors at Odysseus' home by using details in lines 1–9. Describe the image that the lines conjured up in your mind.

2. Note the two speakers. What does Telemachus accuse the suitors of doing? How does one suitor defend his and the other suitors' actions?

3. Identify two examples of sound devices in the boxed text.

4. What do the accusations made in this excerpt tell you about Greek values?

5. How would you describe Penelope? Cite details that help you to understand the traits Greeks prized in a woman.

LITERARY ANALYSIS WORKSHOP **1099**

MODEL: READING THE EPIC
Close Read

1. **Possible answer:** *Although answers will vary, students should describe the suitors as lazy and wasteful. According to Telemachus, they lie around the house all day, eating, drinking, and "not caring what they do."*

2. **Possible answer:** *Telemachus accuses the suitors of being wasteful and taking advantage of the situation. The suitor defends his and others' actions by pointing out that the length of their stay is Penelope's fault. The suitor claims that she is leading them on, saying that she will marry again once she has finished weaving a shroud for Laertes. However, every night she unweaves what she wove during the day.*

3. **Possible answer:** *Two examples of sound devices include the assonance (repetition of the long o sound) and alliteration (repetition of the h sound) in holding and hope, and the consonance (repetition of the s sound) in "sending promises."*

4. **Possible answer:** *The accusations suggest that Greeks condemned laziness or living off of others. The suitor's description of Penelope's actions suggests that deception was not viewed favorably but that loyalty to a spouse was an admired value.*

5. **Possible answer:** *Penelope is an honorable, loyal wife. She refuses to let her husband's father lie "unshrouded," and she does not want other women to hold her in dishonor. However, Penelope is also shrewd and clever. She does not want to anger her suitors, so she stalls for time by destroying her weaving, which means that the shroud is never completed.*

If students need help . . . Briefly summarize each section before students read it.

DIFFERENTIATED INSTRUCTION

FOR LESS–PROFICIENT READERS
Comprehension: Characters Draw attention to the title of the model. Clarify that Telemachus is the son of Odysseus. Then draw attention to the italic notes in the model, asking volunteers to read them aloud. Before students read independently, have them describe the situation and identify who is speaking which lines.

FOR ENGLISH LEARNERS
Vocabulary: Multiple-Meaning Words
Identify these multiple-meaning words: *addresses* (first italic line), *arms* (line 7), and *touched* (line 28). In groups of three, have students look up the meanings of the words. Then have them create a sentence for at least two meanings of each word. One sentence should use the meaning that is used in the model.

Practice and Apply

Part 4: Analyze the Literature

Close Read

1. **Possible answer:** *Through his actions, Odysseus shows extreme cunning and a lack of trust. He creates an elaborate ruse simply to test someone's loyalty. The ruse also shows that Odysseus is creative.*

2. **Possible answer:** *The imagery in the boxed lines serves to emphasize how frigid and wintry the weather is. The use of "black" and "white," coupled with the use of the words "wintry," "sleet," "frost," and "ice," all create a feeling of cold desolation.*

3. **Possible answer:** *The "soldier," who is actually Odysseus pretending, uses the epithets "Son of Laertes and the gods of old" (line 28) and "master mariner and soldier" (line 29) to address Odysseus.*

   If students need help . . . Remind them that Odysseus is pretending to be an anonymous soldier, so he has invented an entirely new person. As a result, there are actually two Odysseuses in this model—the new person and the Odysseus who is described by that person.

Part 4: Analyze the Literature

Here, Odysseus returns to his homeland at last, disguised as an old beggar. The first person he approaches is Eumaeus, his head swineherd. Welcoming the unknown beggar in the name of his missing lord, Eumaeus gives him a hot meal, a drink, and a place to sleep. To test the faithful swineherd and to try to keep warm in the frigid cold, the disguised Odysseus devises a story. Through the story, he hopes to encourage Eumaeus to give him—a supposed stranger—the cloak off his back. As you read this excerpt, use what you've learned to make sense of the episode.

from BOOK 14: *Hospitality in the Forest*

                                                "Listen," he said,
"Eumaeus, and you others, here's a wishful
tale that I shall tell. The wine's behind it,
vaporing wine, that makes a serious man
5 break down and sing, kick up his heels and clown,
or tell some story that were best untold.
But now I'm launched, I can't stop now.
                                           Would god I felt

the hot blood in me that I had at Troy!
Laying an ambush near the walls one time,
10 Odysseus and Menelaus were commanders
and I ranked third. I went at their request.
We worked in toward the bluffs and battlements
and, circling the town, got into canebrakes,
thick and high, a marsh where we took cover,
15 hunched under arms.
                     The northwind dropped, and night
came black and wintry. A fine sleet descending
whitened the cane like hoarfrost, and clear ice
grew dense upon our shields. The other men,
all wrapt in blanket cloaks as well as tunics,
20 rested well, in shields up to their shoulders,
but I had left my cloak with friends in camp,
foolhardy as I was. No chance of freezing hard,
I thought, so I wore kilts and a shield only.
But in the small hours of the third watch, when stars
25 that rise at evening go down to their setting,
I nudged Odysseus, who lay close beside me;
he was alert then, listening, and I said:

'Son of Laertes and the gods of old,
Odysseus, master mariner and soldier,
30 I cannot hold on long among the living.

Close Read

1. Think about why Odysseus is telling Eumaeus this elaborate story. Through his plan of action, what traits does he display? Explain.

2. Reread the boxed text and visualize the imagery used to describe the setting. What does the imagery serve to emphasize?

3. What epithets does the soldier use to address Odysseus in the story?

DIFFERENTIATED INSTRUCTION

FOR LESS–PROFICIENT READERS

Analysis Support: Details Help students recognize the various speakers in this model. Point out that in the first eight lines, Odysseus sets his trap and explains why he is telling this story. Then, in lines 9–11, he identifies himself as third in command. It is this character who tells the rest of the story. Later, in line 51, the speaker switches to Eumaeus. Have students identify the lines that he says.

Afterward, discuss with students whether they think such a charade would actually work. Encourage them to give reasons for their responses.

The cold is making a corpse of me. Some god
inveigled me to come without a cloak.
No help for it now; too late.'

                                        Next thing I knew

   he had a scheme all ready in his mind—
35 and what a man he was for schemes and battles!
   Speaking under his breath to me, he murmured:

   'Quiet; none of the rest should hear you.'

                                             Then,

   propping his head on his forearm, he said:

   'Listen, lads, I had an ominous dream,
40 the point being how far forward from our ships
   and lines we've come. Someone should volunteer
   to tell the corps commander, Agamemnon;
   he may reinforce us from the base.'

                                    At this,

   Thoas jumped up, the young son of Andraemon,
45 put down his crimson cloak and headed off,
   running shoreward.

                       Wrapped in that man's cloak
   how gratefully I lay in the bitter dark
   until the dawn came stitched in gold! I wish
   I had that sap and fiber in me now!"

50 Then—O my swineherd!—you replied, Eumaeus:

   "That was a fine story, and well told,
   not a word out of place, not a pointless word.
   No, you'll not sleep cold for lack of cover,
   or any other comfort one should give
55 to a needy guest. However, in the morning,
   you must go flapping in the same old clothes.
   Shirts and cloaks are few here; every man
   has one change only. When our prince arrives,
   the son of Odysseus, he will make you gifts—
60 cloak, tunic, everything—and grant you passage
   wherever you care to go."

                              On this he rose

   and placed the bed of balsam near the fire,
   strewing sheepskins on top, and skins of goats.
   Odysseus lay down. His host threw over him
65 a heavy blanket cloak, his own reserve
   against the winter wind when it came wild.

Close Read

4. What quality does Odysseus attribute to himself in telling this tale? Cite specific details to support your answer.

5. Reread lines 31–33 and 39–46. What do you learn about how the ancient Greeks perceived their gods and ominous dreams?

6. Think about where else you have encountered a character like Eumaeus. What archetype does he represent? Explain.

Close Read

4. **Possible answer:** *In lines 33–35, the "soldier" describes Odysseus as clever and quick-thinking in difficult situations. He says that Odysseus "had a scheme all ready in his mind."*

5. **Possible answer:** *Lines 31–33 suggest that Greeks felt the gods were responsible for some human actions. The soldier says that some god tricked him into coming without his cloak. In lines 39–46, Odysseus describes an "ominous dream" about the course they are on. He urges a volunteer to warn Agamemnon. That Thoas volunteered so eagerly suggests that he believed that such dreams were real warnings that should be heeded.*

6. **Possible answer:** *Eumaeus represents the archetype of the faithful servant or sidekick. Students may recall television shows, films, or novels in which they have encountered such an archetype.*

Assess and Reteach

Assess

Have students identify epic elements in Book 14 of the *Odyssey*.

Reteach

For students who are unable to apply the workshop skills to the excerpts from the *Odyssey*, select from these reteaching options:

1. Display one blank note-taking copy master for this lesson.
   - Ask students which parts were hard to complete. Focus instruction on only those parts.
   - Have students work in teams to take turns identifying details for sections on the copy masters. Tell one group to suggest details. Then have another group either confirm the choice or offer an alternative.
   - Follow a similar procedure with the second copy master.

2. Review with students the main elements of an epic poem, including the language used by Homer. Help students identify these elements in the models.

FOR ADVANCED LEARNERS/PRE–AP

Evaluate On the basis of the models they have read, have students discuss whether the *Odyssey* would make a good adventure film. Have them first develop criteria for a good adventure film and then rate the *Odyssey* based on those criteria. Remind students that films sometimes make changes in language, setting, and plot details, while trying to maintain the overall sense of the original.

Focus and Motivate

OBJECTIVES

Literary Analysis
- explore the key idea of a **hero**
- read and analyze an epic poem
- identify, analyze, and evaluate characteristics of an epic hero

Reading
- use strategies for reading an epic poem
- summarize

Vocabulary
- build vocabulary for reading and writing
- use words with the prefix *fore-* (also an EL language objective)

Grammar and Writing
- use figurative language

SUMMARY

Books 1–12 After the Greek victory over Troy, Odysseus sails for home with his warriors. They wander for many years. All are killed except Odysseus, who is held captive by the goddess Calypso. Then he sails to the island of King Alcinous, to whom he tells of his adventures with the Lotus Eaters, the Cyclops, Circe, and the underworld. Finally, he tells about the Sirens and Scylla and Charybdis.

What is a HERO?

Ask the question and have students provide and discuss possible answers. Then read the *KEY IDEA* paragraph aloud. Ask students to suggest situations in which someone may prove to be a **hero**. Do those situations require strength, courage, or other qualities? Continue the exchange by having students complete the *DISCUSS* activity.

Selection Resources

The Wanderings of Odysseus
from the Odyssey
Epic Poem by Homer
Translated by Robert Fitzgerald

What is a HERO?

KEY IDEA When you hear the word *hero,* who comes to mind? Do you think of someone with unusual physical strength? great courage? a rare talent? In Homer's *Odyssey,* you'll meet one of the classic heroes of Western literature—Odysseus, a man with many heroic traits as well as human faults.

DISCUSS Work with a small group to make a list of people who are generally considered heroes. Discuss the heroic qualities of each. Which qualities seem essential to every hero?

1102

R RESOURCE MANAGER UNIT 11

Plan and Teach pp. 17–24

Literary Analysis
Summary pp. 25, 26†*, 27‡*, 28‡*
Epic Hero pp. 29, 30†*
Question Support p. 37*

Reading
Reading an Epic Poem pp. 31, 32†*
Reading Check p. 36
Reading Fluency p. 38

Vocabulary
Study p. 33*
Practice p. 34
Strategy p. 35

Assessment
Selection Tests A, B/C pp. 39*, 41*
⊘ Test Generator CD

📦 BEST PRACTICES TOOLKIT

Differentiated Instruction
pp. 31–38*

Scaffolding Instruction
pp. 43–46*

Graphic Organizers/Strategies
Character Traits and Textual
Evidence • Sequence Chain
• T Chart • Comparison Matrix
• Story Map

Reading Support
⊘ Audio Anthology CD*

Technology
ⓘ Literature and Vocabulary Centers at **ClassZone.com**
⊘ Write*Smart* CD

---

* Resources for Differentiation   **† Also in Spanish**   **‡ In Haitian Creole and Vietnamese**

LITERARY ANALYSIS: EPIC HERO

The **epic hero** is a larger-than-life character, traditionally a man, who pursues long and dangerous adventures. Alternately aided and blocked by the gods, he carries the fate of his people on his shoulders. The epic hero is an **archetypal** character—one found in works across time and cultures. Odysseus, one of the most famous heroes in Western culture, has shaped our ideas about the traits that a hero should have.

- extraordinary strength and courage
- cleverness and deceit, also known as guile
- extreme confidence and a tendency to dismiss warnings

Every epic hero embodies the values of his culture. As you read the *Odyssey*, consider how Odysseus faces various conflicts. What does this tell you about his character? What do his character traits tell you about what the ancient Greeks found admirable?

READING STRATEGY: READING AN EPIC POEM

The strategies for reading an epic are very similar to those for reading any narrative poem.

- Keep track of the events.
- Visualize the **imagery.**
- Notice how the **figurative language,** including **epic similes,** can make the story more vivid and interesting.
- Read difficult passages more than once. Use the side notes for help in comprehension.
- Read the poem aloud, as it was originally conveyed.

As you read, keep a list of major events and consider whether they lead Odysseus any closer to home.

VOCABULARY IN CONTEXT

Place each of the following words in the appropriate column.

WORD LIST			
	abominably	assuage	meditation
	adversary	beguiling	ponderous
	appalled	foreboding	profusion
	ardor	harried	travail

Know Well	Think I Know	Don't Know

Overview

Book 1: A Goddess Intervenes The poet introduces Odysseus, a successful warrior who, after conquering the city of Troy, has wandered the seas for many years. Now he wants only to return safely to his home and family.

Book 5: Calypso, the Sweet Nymph Odysseus has been held captive for many years by the goddess Calypso on her island. Zeus sends the god Hermes to order her to release Odysseus; she offers her advice and helps him build a raft on which he can sail to Scheria, his next destination.

Book 9: New Coasts and Poseidon's Son Odysseus has met King Alcinous and begins telling him of his adventures since leaving Troy. He relates the tale of the Lotus Eaters and his encounter with the brutal Cyclops, a son of the sea-god Poseidon. Odysseus continues his tales in Books 10–12.

Book 10: Circe, the Grace of the Witch Eventually, Odysseus and his men arrive at the island home of Circe, a goddess and enchantress. She detains the men for a year, allowing them to go home only if they will visit the land of the dead and hear a prophecy from the ghost of Tiresias.

Book 11: The Land of the Dead Odysseus and his crew travel to the underworld, where Tiresias warns Odysseus against stealing the cattle of Helios, god of the sun. According to the prophecy, if Odysseus raids the cattle, he will lose his ship and crew and return home only after many years alone at sea.

Book 12: The Sirens; Scylla and Charybdis Odysseus and his men return to Circe's island, where she advises him on how to get past the bewitching Sirens and the horrible sea monsters Scylla and Charybdis. He successfully evades the Sirens but does not escape the monsters without losing some of his men.

Teach

STANDARDS FOCUS

LITERARY ANALYSIS

EPIC HERO

Direct students to the *Overview.* Have a volunteer read the summary of Book 1. Ask students what traits Odysseus shows by his resolve to return home. ***Possible answer:*** *toughness, steadfastness, determination.*

CHECK UNDERSTANDING Continue this process with the other book summaries in the overview.

READING STRATEGY

READING AN EPIC POEM

Have students make a timeline of each book to track events and monitor their comprehension. For practice, have them create a timeline of the major events from Books 1–12 as summarized in the *Overview.*

CHECK UNDERSTANDING Ask students to use the overview to identify "obstacles" and "helpers" of Odysseus.

 RESOURCE MANAGER—Copy Master
Reading an Epic Poem p. 31 (for student use while reading the selection)

VOCABULARY SKILL

VOCABULARY IN CONTEXT

DIAGNOSE WORD KNOWLEDGE To determine preteaching needs, have all students complete Vocabulary in Context. Refer to the definitions on the selection pages: *abominably* (p. 1132), *adversary* (p. 1121), *appalled* (p. 1116), *assuage* (p. 1126), *beguiling* (p. 1124), *foreboding* (p. 1125), *harried* (p. 1104), *meditation* (p. 1120), *ponderous* (p. 1116), *profusion* (p. 1117), *travail* (p. 1135).

PRETEACH VOCABULARY Use the Vocabulary Study copy master to help students predict the meanings for each boldfaced word in the copy master.

1. Read the first two sentences aloud, emphasizing the word *travail.*
2. Point out the phrase "hard labor." Elicit possible meanings for *travail.*
3. Have students record their predictions.
4. Repeat the procedure for the rest of the passage.

 RESOURCE MANAGER—Copy Master
Vocabulary Study p. 33

For general guidelines on differentiating vocabulary instruction and for alternative vocabulary activities for students not needing vocabulary preteaching, see

 BEST PRACTICES TOOLKIT
Scaffolding Vocabulary Instruction pp. 43–46
Vocabulary Center at **ClassZone.com**

Practice and Apply

BOOK 1:
A Goddess Intervenes

Sing in me, Muse, and through me tell the story
of that man skilled in all ways of contending,
the wanderer, **harried** for years on end,
after he plundered the stronghold
5 on the proud height of Troy.
                      He saw the townlands
and learned the minds of many distant men,
and weathered many bitter nights and days
in his deep heart at sea, while he fought only
to save his life, to bring his shipmates home.
10 But not by will nor valor could he save them,
for their own recklessness destroyed them all—
children and fools, they killed and feasted on
the cattle of Lord Helios, the Sun,
and he who moves all day through heaven
15 took from their eyes the dawn of their return. **Ⓐ**

Of these adventures, Muse, daughter of Zeus,
tell us in our time, lift the great song again. . . .

*The story of Odysseus begins with the goddess Athena's appealing to Zeus
to help Odysseus, who has been wandering for ten years on the seas, to find
his way home to his family on Ithaca. While Odysseus has been gone, his son,
Telemachus, has grown to manhood and his wife, Penelope, has been besieged
by suitors wishing to marry her and gain Odysseus' wealth. The suitors have
taken up residence in her home and are constantly feasting on the family's cattle,
sheep, and goats. They dishonor Odysseus and his family. Taking Athena's
advice, Telemachus travels to Pylos for word of his father. Meanwhile, on
Ithaca, the evil suitors plot to kill Telemachus when he returns.*

1 Muse: a daughter of Zeus, credited with divine inspiration.

harried (hăr'ēd) *adj.* tormented; harassed **harry** *v.*

11–13 their own recklessness . . . the Sun: a reference to an event occurring later in the poem—an event that causes the death of Odysseus' entire crew.

Ⓐ EPIC HERO
This invocation (lines 1–15) introduces us to Odysseus, "that man skilled in all ways of contending." What **traits** is he shown to have?

ANALYZE VISUALS
This 1930s print, *The Ship of Odysseus*, is part of an *Odyssey* series by Francois-Louis Schmied. What qualities of this ship has Schmied emphasized with his use of color and shape? Explain.

The Ship of Odysseus, Francois-Louis Schmied. From *Homer the Odyssey*, published Paris (1930–1933). Color lithograph. The Stapleton Collection. © Bridgeman Art Library. © 2007 Artists Rights Society (ARS), New York/ADAGP, Paris.

1104   UNIT 11: THE ODYSSEY

DIFFERENTIATED INSTRUCTION

FOR LESS–PROFICIENT READERS
Preview Read aloud the Book 1 synopsis at the bottom of the page. To give students a clear idea of the plot, help them list the events in a Sequence Chain.

 BEST PRACTICES TOOLKIT—Transparency
Sequence Chain p. B21

FOR ENGLISH LEARNERS
Task Support Review with students all side-column notes, especially those that paraphrase the text.

Get Into the Book
SUMMARY

Book 1 introduces Odysseus, gives a brief overview of his epic struggle to return home, and tells the reader what has been happening at home during Odysseus' long absence.

ALTERED SPELLINGS LIST *(cont.)*:

Original	Altered
Kyklopês	Cyclopes
Kyklops	Cyclops
Polyphêmos	Polyphemus
Apollo	<no change>
Poseidon	<no change>
Aiolos	Aeolus
Laistrygonês	Laestrygones
Eurylokhos	Eurylochus
Perséphonê	Persephone
Teirêsias	Tiresias
Elpênor	Elpenor
Seirênês	Sirens
Skylla	Scylla
Kharybdis	Charybdis
Athena	<no change>
Eumaios	Eumaeus
Argos	<no change>
Philoítios	Philoetius
Antínoös	Antinous
Eurymakhos	Eurymachus

(List concludes on page 1106.)

READING STRATEGY

⬛ PREDICT

Remind students that making and revising predictions can help them concentrate on details and follow the sequence of events. Ask them to predict what will happen to Odysseus' shipmates. *Possible answer: They will be killed or die of other causes because of their recklessness in feasting on the cattle of Helios.*

FOR LESS–PROFICIENT READERS

Minor Characters Remind students to refer back to the list **Important Characters in the Odyssey** on page 1091 during reading. Ask them where the ancient Greeks believed Helios (line 13) pastured his cattle. (*the island of Thrinacia*)

ALTERED SPELLINGS LIST (cont.):

Original	Altered
Amphínomos	Amphinomus
Eurynomê	Eurynome
Eurykleia	Eurycleia
Télemos	Telemus
Eurymos	Eurymus
Antikleía	Anticlea
Autólykos	Autolycus
Parnassos	Parnassus
Kroníon	Cronion
Hephaistos	Hephaestus
Aktoris	Actoris

LITERARY ANALYSIS

ⓑ EPIC SIMILE

Possible answer: The simile compares the flight of a seagull, fishing in the waves, to Hermes' trip to Calypso. The comparison conveys Hermes' dexterity, speed, and supreme confidence as messenger of the gods.

If students need help . . . Point out that a gull is a sea bird. Ask students to visualize a seagull flying between waves and dipping into the water to catch a fish.

ANALYZE VISUALS

Possible answer: The painter has characterized Calypso as a vibrant free spirit, at ease in nature. The wispy white fabric of her dress suggests a connection with the clouds—boundless, beautiful, and uncontained, like Calypso herself.

About the Art Lawyer-turned-artist George Hitchcock (1850–1913) left the United States to study art in Paris. In the early 1880s, he settled in Egmond, the Netherlands. His paintings of Dutch life and scenery won him acclaim. Later, he employed a decorative, impressionist style in his paintings, as he did in this 1906 portrait of Calypso in a meadow.

BOOK 5:
Calypso, the Sweet Nymph

For seven of the ten years Odysseus has spent wandering the Mediterranean Sea, he has been held captive by the goddess Calypso on her island. As Book 5 begins, Zeus sends the god Hermes to tell Calypso to release Odysseus. However, she is only to help him build a raft. He must sail for 20 days before landing on the island of Scheria, where he will be helped in his effort to return home.

No words were lost on Hermes the Wayfinder,
who bent to tie his beautiful sandals on,
ambrosial, golden, that carry him over water
or over endless land in a swish of the wind,
5 and took the wand with which he charms asleep—
or when he wills, awake—the eyes of men.
So wand in hand he paced into the air,
shot from Pieria down, down to sea level,
and veered to skim the swell. A gull patrolling
10 between the wave crests of the desolate sea
will dip to catch a fish, and douse his wings;
no higher above the whitecaps Hermes flew ⓑ
until the distant island lay ahead,
then rising shoreward from the violet ocean
15 he stepped up to the cave. Divine Calypso,
the mistress of the isle, was now at home.
Upon her hearthstone a great fire blazing
scented the farthest shores with cedar smoke
and smoke of thyme, and singing high and low
20 in her sweet voice, before her loom a-weaving,
she passed her golden shuttle to and fro.
A deep wood grew outside, with summer leaves
of alder and black poplar, pungent cypress.
Ornate birds here rested their stretched wings—
25 horned owls, falcons, cormorants—long-tongued
beachcombing birds, and followers of the sea.
Around the smoothwalled cave a crooking vine
held purple clusters under ply of green;
and four springs, bubbling up near one another
30 shallow and clear, took channels here and there
through beds of violets and tender parsley.

1-6 Hermes (hûr'mēz): the messenger of the gods, also known for his cleverness and trickery.

8 Pieria (pī-îr'ē-ə): an area next to Mount Olympus, home of the gods.

ⓑ EPIC SIMILE
Identify the epic simile in lines 9–12. What does this comparison tell you about Hermes?

① Targeted Passage

ANALYZE VISUALS
How has the painter characterized Calypso in this 1906 portrait? Consider any relationship between her white dress and the white clouds.

28 purple clusters: grapes.

Calypso (about 1906), George Hitchcock. Oil on canvas, 111 cm × 89 cm. © Indianapolis Museum of Art, Indianapolis, Indiana/Bridgeman Art Library.

DIFFERENTIATED INSTRUCTION

For general guidelines on differentiating instruction, see

 BEST PRACTICES TOOLKIT
Differentiated Instruction pp. 31–38

FOR LESS–PROFICIENT READERS
In combination with the *Audio Anthology CD*, use one or more Targeted Passages (pp. 1106, 1113, 1118, 1123, 1130, and 1136) to ensure that students focus on key events, concepts, and skills. Targeted Passages are also good for English learners.

① Targeted Passage [Lines 15–31]

This passage describes the home of Calypso, who has held Odysseus captive for the past seven years.

- In what kind of dwelling does Calypso live?
- What relationship does she appear to have with nature?
- What do you know about Calypso from this first description?

Even a god who found this place
would gaze, and feel his heart beat with delight:
so Hermes did; but when he had gazed his fill
35 he entered the wide cave. Now face to face
the magical Calypso recognized him,
as all immortal gods know one another
on sight—though seeming strangers, far from home.
But he saw nothing of the great Odysseus,
40 who sat apart, as a thousand times before,
and racked his own heart groaning, with eyes wet
scanning the bare horizon of the sea. . . .

Calypso invites Hermes to her table for food and drink, asking why he has come.
Hermes explains that he has brought with an order from Zeus that Calypso must
not detain Odysseus any longer but send him on his way home. She reluctantly
obeys, agreeing to offer Odysseus her advice about how to get home.

The strong god glittering left her as he spoke,
and now her ladyship, having given heed
45 to Zeus's mandate, went to find Odysseus
in his stone seat to seaward—tear on tear
brimming in his eyes. The sweet days of his life time
were running out in anguish over his exile,
for long ago the nymph had ceased to please.
50 Though he fought shy of her and her desire,
he lay with her each night, for she compelled him.
But when day came he sat on the rocky shore
and broke his own heart groaning, with eyes wet
scanning the bare horizon of the sea. **C**
55 Now she stood near him in her beauty, saying:

"O forlorn man, be still.
Here you need grieve no more; you need not feel
your life consumed here; I have pondered it,
and I shall help you go. . . ."

60 Swiftly she turned and led him to her cave,
and they went in, the mortal and immortal.
He took the chair left empty now by Hermes,
where the divine Calypso placed before him
victuals and drink of men; then she sat down
65 facing Odysseus, while her serving maids
brought nectar and ambrosia to her side.
Then each one's hands went out on each one's feast
until they had their pleasure; and she said:

C EPIC HERO
Reread lines 43–54. Which
of Odysseus' qualities is
emphasized here?

LITERARY ANALYSIS

C EPIC HERO

Possible answer: *These lines emphasize*
Odysseus' loyalty and determination.
Although he is the captive of the beautiful
Calypso, he still longs for home and looks
to the horizon.

If students need help . . . Ask them who
would have the advantage in a contest: a
goddess with magical powers or a human?
What would it take for the human to win?

DIFFERENTIATED INSTRUCTION

FOR LESS–PROFICIENT READERS

Text Digests Read line by line through the
italicized text digests (after line 42 and after
line 86) to make sure students understand
how the intervening plot connects with the
events they are reading.

"Son of Laertes, versatile Odysseus,
70 after these years with me, you still desire
your old home? Even so, I wish you well.
If you could see it all, before you go—
all the adversity you face at sea—
you would stay here, and guard this house, and be
75 immortal—though you wanted her forever,
that bride for whom you pine each day.
Can I be less desirable than she is?
Less interesting? Less beautiful? Can mortals
compare with goddesses in grace and form?"

80 To this the strategist Odysseus answered:

"My lady goddess, here is no cause for anger.
My quiet Penelope—how well I know—
would seem a shade before your majesty,
death and old age being unknown to you,
85 while she must die. Yet, it is true, each day
I long for home, long for the sight of home. . . ." **D**

*With Calypso's help, Odysseus builds a raft and sets out to sea. For 17 days he sails
until he is in sight of Scheria. For 3 more days he is pummeled by storms and finally
swims for the island. He makes it safely ashore and crawls to rest under some bushes.*

A man in a distant field, no hearthfires near,
will hide a fresh brand in his bed of embers
to keep a spark alive for the next day;
90 so in the leaves Odysseus hid himself,
while over him Athena showered sleep
that his distress should end, and soon, soon.
In quiet sleep she sealed his cherished eyes.

D EPITHET
Reread Odysseus' answer to Calypso
in lines 81–86. Why do you think
he is referred to in line 80 as "the
strategist Odysseus"? Explain.

LITERARY ANALYSIS

D EPITHET

Remind students that an epithet is a
descriptive term or phrase used like a title
to characterize a person. ***Possible answer:***
*He is referred to as "the strategist Odysseus"
because of his shrewd, diplomatic way of
handling people and situations. In lines
81–86, Odysseus cleverly flatters Calypso,
allaying her jealousy and anger, while he
remains loyal to Penelope. The epithet
also supports Calypso's reference to him as
"versatile Odysseus" (line 69).*

Lines 69–79
DISCUSSION PROMPTS

Use these prompts to help students understand Calypso's final attempt to convince
Odysseus to stay with her:

Connect Are you influenced by flattery
when someone is trying to persuade you to
do something? *Students may acknowledge
the power of flattery.*

Analyze In addition to flattery, what strategies does Calypso use to try to convince
Odysseus to stay with her? ***Possible answer:***
*She tries to frighten him about the dangers
he will face, to bribe him with immortality,
and to instill guilt in him about insulting her.*

Synthesize What do these lines reveal
about Odysseus and Calypso? ***Possible answer:*** *They reveal how hard Calypso worked
to win Odysseus' heart and how Odysseus
needed great willpower to resist her. The
lines show that the two were well-matched
competitors: willful, clever, and tough.*

FOR ENGLISH LEARNERS

Vocabulary Support Point out to students
examples of words and phrases that are now
used infrequently and that evoke a time long
past. Encourage them to use context to determine their meaning. Examples include:

• *had gazed his fill* (line 34), "had looked long
enough"

• *her ladyship* (line 44), "a woman of high
rank"

• *having given heed* (line 44), "having paid
attention to"

• *victuals* (line 64), "food"

• *nectar and ambrosia* (line 66), "the drink
and food of the gods"

• *pine* (line 76), "long"

• *hearthfires* (line 87), "fires in fireplaces"

BOOK 9:
New Coasts and Poseidon's Son

In Books 6–8, Odysseus is welcomed by King Alcinous, who gives a banquet in his honor. That night the king begs Odysseus to tell who he is and what has happened to him. In Books 9–12, Odysseus relates to the king his adventures.

"I AM LAERTES' SON"

"What shall I
say first? What shall I keep until the end?
The gods have tried me in a thousand ways.
But first my name: let that be known to you,
5 and if I pull away from pitiless death,
friendship will bind us, though my land lies far.

I am Laertes' son, Odysseus.

Men hold me
formidable for guile in peace and war:
this fame has gone abroad to the sky's rim.
10 My home is on the peaked sea-mark of Ithaca
under Mount Neion's wind-blown robe of leaves,
in sight of other islands—Dulichium,
Same, wooded Zacynthus—Ithaca
being most lofty in that coastal sea,
15 and northwest, while the rest lie east and south.
A rocky isle, but good for a boy's training;
I shall not see on earth a place more dear,
though I have been detained long by Calypso,
loveliest among goddesses, who held me
20 in her smooth caves, to be her heart's delight,
as Circe of Aeaea, the enchantress,
desired me, and detained me in her hall.
But in my heart I never gave consent.
Where shall a man find sweetness to surpass
25 his own home and his parents? In far lands
he shall not, though he find a house of gold. ⓔ

ANALYZE VISUALS
This sculpture of Odysseus was produced in Rome sometime between A.D. 4 and 26. How would you describe the expression on his face?

7–8 hold me formidable for guile: consider me impressive for my cunning and craftiness.

11–13 Mount Neion's (nē'ŏnz'); **Dulichium** (dōō-lĭk'ē-əm); **Same** (sä'mē); **Zacynthus** (zə-sĭn'thəs).

18–26 Odysseus refers to two beautiful goddesses, Calypso and Circe, who have delayed him on their islands. (Details about Circe appear in Book 10.) At the same time, he seems nostalgic for his family and homeland, from which he has been separated for 18 years—10 of them spent fighting in Troy.

ⓔ EPIC HERO
Reread lines 24–26. What does Odysseus value most highly?

Detail of *Ulysses* from the *Polyphemos* group (second century B.C.), Hagesandros, Polydoros, and Athenodoros. Sperlonga, Italy. © Araldo de Luca/Corbis.

DIFFERENTIATED INSTRUCTION

FOR LESS–PROFICIENT READERS
Preview Read line by line through the italicized synopsis of Books 6–12 at the top of page 1110 to give students a clear idea of the plot of this part of the *Odyssey*. Help them organize the events in a simple Sequence Chain.

🧰 **BEST PRACTICES TOOLKIT—Transparency**
Sequence Chain p. B21

King Alcinous welcomes Odysseus.

↓

The king begs Odysseus to share his adventures.

↓

Odysseus tells his story.

Get Into the Book
SUMMARY
Book 9 begins with Odysseus telling of his raid on the Cicones and his loss of 72 men. Then he explains how he avoided disaster in the Land of the Lotus Eaters. Finally, he describes their exploration of the land of the Cyclopes—giant, one-eyed monsters—where they are trapped in a cave by the Cyclops Polyphemus, who eats two men at every meal. Odysseus blinds the monster and works out a clever escape from the cave. Sailing away, Odysseus calls back and taunts Polyphemus, who prays to his father, the sea god Poseidon, to take revenge on Odysseus.

READING STRATEGY

■ READING AN EPIC POEM
Remind students that the *Odyssey* is meant to be read orally, as it was in ancient Greece. In Books 9–12, Odysseus relates his adventures. Ask students to imagine how Odysseus would speak. Have them characterize his voice and presentation. ***Possible answer: Odysseus' voice would be strong and deep, and he would speak with great confidence and self-control. A leader, he would enjoy being the center of attention and know how to keep his audience's interest. His presentation would be dramatic and poignant.***

CULTURAL CONNECTION
Outside of Greece, oral poetry has existed in many cultures. Between the 9th and 13th centuries, Icelandic poets developed a form of oral poetry called Skaldic, which praised leaders, memorialized the dead, and retold history and lineage. In Africa, the priests of the Yoruba tribe must memorize poems exactly to pass down the wisdom and history the poems contain. Invite students to share examples of festivals or contests where poets must recite their work from memory.

FOR ADVANCED LEARNERS/PRE–AP
Narrative The book opens as Odysseus begins to tell his tale to King Alcinous. Write a narrative describing Odysseus' arrival at the king's court. Describe Odysseus from Alcinous' point of view. How might the king have told of Odysseus' arrival, his appearance, and what prompted him to tell his story?

DISCUSSION PROMPTS

Use these prompts to help students understand the challenge presented by the Lotus Eaters to Odysseus and his men:

Connect Think of a situation that turned out to be different from what it seemed at first. How does this help you understand the reaction of Odysseus' men to the Lotus Eaters? *Responses should demonstrate an understanding that appearances can be deceptive and connect to Odysseus' experience with the Lotus Eaters.*

Analyze Odysseus devotes only about 25 lines to the Lotus Eaters. Why do you think he didn't extend his description of this adventure? *Possible answer: The Lotus Eaters were not aggressive, evil, or a powerful foe, and Odysseus was not called upon to use his guile or demonstrate his prowess in battle or as a leader of his men. It was just one more adventure among many and so he told the story quickly and efficiently.*

Evaluate Do you think Odysseus handled the situation with the Lotus Eaters effectively? Was he too lenient or too harsh? *Possible answer: Odysseus neutralized the situation quickly. He did not overreact, and nobody was hurt. He showed strong leadership.*

What of my sailing, then, from Troy?

What of those years
of rough adventure, weathered under Zeus? . . ."

Odysseus explains that soon after leaving Troy, he and his crew land near Ismarus, the city of the Cicones. The Cicones are allies of the Trojans and therefore enemies of Odysseus. Odysseus and his crew raid the Cicones, robbing and killing them, until the Ciconian army kills 72 of Odysseus' men and drives the rest out to sea. Delayed by a storm for two days, Odysseus and his remaining companions then continued their journey.

THE LOTUS EATERS

"I might have made it safely home, that time,
30 but as I came round Malea the current
took me out to sea, and from the north
a fresh gale drove me on, past Cythera.
Nine days I drifted on the teeming sea
before dangerous high winds. Upon the tenth
35 we came to the coastline of the Lotus Eaters,
who live upon that flower. We landed there
to take on water. All ships' companies
mustered alongside for the mid-day meal.
Then I sent out two picked men and a runner
40 to learn what race of men that land sustained.
They fell in, soon enough, with Lotus Eaters,
who showed no will to do us harm, only
offering the sweet Lotus to our friends—
but those who ate this honeyed plant, the Lotus,
45 never cared to report, nor to return:
they longed to stay forever, browsing on
that native bloom, forgetful of their homeland.
I drove them, all three wailing, to the ships,
tied them down under their rowing benches,
50 and called the rest: 'All hands aboard;
come, clear the beach and no one taste
the Lotus, or you lose your hope of home.'
Filing in to their places by the rowlocks
my oarsmen dipped their long oars in the surf,
55 and we moved out again on our sea faring.

THE CYCLOPS

In the next land we found were Cyclopes,
giants, louts, without a law to bless them.
In ignorance leaving the fruitage of the earth in mystery
to the immortal gods, they neither plow

30 Malea (mă-lē'ä).

32 Cythera (sǐ-thîr'ə).

38 mustered: assembled; gathered.

44–52 those who ate . . . hope of home.
How do the Lotus Eaters pose a threat to Odysseus and his men?

56 Cyclopes (sī-klō'pēz): refers to the creatures in plural; *Cyclops* is singular.

DIFFERENTIATED INSTRUCTION

FOR ENGLISH LEARNERS

Text Digest Read aloud the two italicized text digests to ensure that students understand the intervening plot. After reading the first digest (after line 28), ask them what they can infer about Odysseus as a warrior. *Possible answer: He is aggressive, harsh, and without pity.*

Task Support Direct students' attention to the side note for lines 44–52. *Possible answer: The lotuses that they eat cause the sailors to forget their intentions.*

60 nor sow by hand, nor till the ground, though grain—
   wild wheat and barley—grows untended, and
   wine-grapes, in clusters, ripen in heaven's rain.
   Cyclopes have no muster and no meeting,
   no consultation or old tribal ways,
65 but each one dwells in his own mountain cave
   dealing out rough justice to wife and child,
   indifferent to what the others do. . . ."

58–67 *Why doesn't Odysseus respect the Cyclopes?*

Across the bay from the land of the Cyclopes was a lush, deserted island. Odysseus and his crew landed on the island in a dense fog and spent days feasting on wine and wild goats and observing the mainland, where the Cyclopes lived. On the third day, Odysseus and his company of men set out to learn if the Cyclopes were friends or foes.

"When the young Dawn with finger tips of rose **F**
   came in the east, I called my men together
70 and made a speech to them:

                          'Old shipmates, friends,
   the rest of you stand by; I'll make the crossing
   in my own ship, with my own company,
   and find out what the mainland natives are—
   for they may be wild savages, and lawless,
75 or hospitable and god fearing men.'

   At this I went aboard, and gave the word
   to cast off by the stern. My oarsmen followed,
   filing in to their benches by the rowlocks,
   and all in line dipped oars in the gray sea.

F EPITHET
Notice the descriptive phrase used to characterize the dawn in line 68. What does this description tell you about the dawn?

77 stern: the rear end of a ship.

80 As we rowed on, and nearer to the mainland,
   at one end of the bay, we saw a cavern
   yawning above the water, screened with laurel,
   and many rams and goats about the place
   inside a sheepfold—made from slabs of stone
85 earthfast between tall trunks of pine and rugged
   towering oak trees.
                          A prodigious man
   slept in this cave alone, and took his flocks
   to graze afield—remote from all companions,
   knowing none but savage ways, a brute
90 so huge, he seemed no man at all of those
   who eat good wheaten bread; but he seemed rather
   a shaggy mountain reared in solitude.
   We beached there, and I told the crew

82 screened with laurel: partially hidden by laurel trees.

② **Targeted Passage**

91–92 *What does Odysseus' metaphor imply about the Cyclops?*

LITERARY ANALYSIS

F EPITHET

Possible answer: The description tells us that it was the start of dawn ("young Dawn"); the dawn was colorful, with reddish rays brightening the horizon.

BACKGROUND

Sailing The ancient Greeks used two kinds of ship: the galley and the sailboat, or cargo boat. The galley, which was propelled by tiers of rowers, was used primarily in battles. As shown in the image on page 1105, galleys were painted black with pitch and had no raised decks. They were propelled by a sail attached to a large mast at the center of the ship or by rowers who sat on benches (line 78) and rowed with oars fastened with leather oarlocks. Sailboats, like the one Odysseus builds on page 1109, depended solely on the wind and so were used less often.

FOR LESS–PROFICIENT READERS

② Targeted Passage [Lines 80–92]

This passage introduces the setting of Odysseus' next adventure and foreshadows his great conflict with the Cyclops.

- What did Odysseus see as they approached land?

- What words does Odysseus use to describe the Cyclops?

FOR ENGLISH LEARNERS

Text Digest After reading the text digest (after line 67), ask them why Odysseus waited three days before he set out to learn about the Cyclops. *Possible answer: He bided his time to plan his moves and perhaps to rest his men.*

Task Support Direct students' attention to the side note for lines 58–67. *Possible answer: The Cyclopes are lawless creatures with no sense of community and no drive to cultivate the land.*

Task Support Direct students' attention to the side note for lines 91–92. *Possible answer: The Cyclops is as large as a mountain.*

Lines 96–115
REINFORCE *KEY IDEA:* HERO

Discuss Odysseus has been referred to as "the Strategist." How does he reveal that trait in this passage? *Possible answer: He plans for potential conflict with the Cyclops: he leaves guards with his ship, and he brings along Maron's irresistible drink as a possible weapon to use against the giants.* What other qualities does Odysseus reveal in this passage? *Possible answer: He shows that he can be kind and gracious to a friend like Maron (lines 99–100).*

BACKGROUND

Food and Drink The soil in many parts of ancient Greece was poor for growing most crops. However, the Greek farmers could grow wheat, barley, grapes, and olive trees. Olives and olive oil were a major part of the Greek diet. Grapes were used to make wine, which could be served at any meal. In addition, the ancient Greeks kept goats for milk and cheese, and kept chickens for meat and eggs. Many kinds of seafood were also eaten on a regular basis. Food and drink were also used as gifts, tribute to conquerors, and offerings to deities. Notice how a rare wine is given as tribute to Odysseus (lines 96–111) for sparing a family during his conquest of Ismarus, and Odysseus in turn uses the wine in his attempts to win over the Cyclops. Later, Odysseus and his men burn an offering (line 133) that was most likely food.

---

     to stand by and keep watch over the ship;
95 as for myself I took my twelve best fighters
     and went ahead. I had a goatskin full
     of that sweet liquor that Euanthes' son,
     Maron, had given me. He kept Apollo's
     holy grove at Ismarus; for kindness
100 we showed him there, and showed his wife and child,
     he gave me seven shining golden talents
     perfectly formed, a solid silver winebowl,
     and then this liquor—twelve two-handled jars
     of brandy, pure and fiery. Not a slave
105 in Maron's household knew this drink; only
     he, his wife and the storeroom mistress knew;
     and they would put one cupful—ruby-colored,
     honey-smooth—in twenty more of water,
     but still the sweet scent hovered like a fume
110 over the winebowl. No man turned away
     when cups of this came round.
                   A wineskin full

     I brought along, and victuals in a bag,
     for in my bones I knew some towering brute
     would be upon us soon—all outward power,
115 a wild man, ignorant of civility.

     We climbed, then, briskly to the cave. But Cyclops
     had gone afield, to pasture his fat sheep,
     so we looked round at everything inside:
     a drying rack that sagged with cheeses, pens
120 crowded with lambs and kids, each in its class:
     firstlings apart from middlings, and the 'dewdrops,'
     or newborn lambkins, penned apart from both.
     And vessels full of whey were brimming there—
     bowls of earthenware and pails for milking.
125 My men came pressing round me, pleading:
                     'Why not

     take these cheeses, get them stowed, come back,
     throw open all the pens, and make a run for it?
     We'll drive the kids and lambs aboard. We say
     put out again on good salt water!'

                       Ah,
130 how sound that was! Yet I refused. I wished
     to see the caveman, what he had to offer—
     no pretty sight, it turned out, for my friends.

97–98 Euanthes (yōō-ăn′thēz); **Maron** (măr′ŏn′).

101 talents: bars of gold or silver of a specified weight, used as money in ancient Greece.

112 victuals (vĭt′lz): food.

121–122 The Cyclops has separated his lambs into three age groups.

123 whey: the watery part of milk, which separates from the curds, or solid part, during the making of cheese.

129 good salt water: the open sea.

130–132 *Why does Odysseus refuse his men's "sound" request?*

DIFFERENTIATED INSTRUCTION

FOR ENGLISH LEARNERS

Task Support Direct students' attention to the side note for lines 130–132. Explain that one trait of an epic hero is a tendency to dismiss warnings. *Possible answer: Odysseus' curiosity about "the caveman" caused him to refuse his men's "sound" request. Also, Odysseus may have been intrigued by the challenge of confronting this prodigious brute in a battle of brains against brawn.*

We lit a fire, burnt an offering,
and took some cheese to eat; then sat in silence
135 around the embers, waiting. When he came
he had a load of dry boughs on his shoulder
to stoke his fire at suppertime. He dumped it
with a great crash into that hollow cave,
and we all scattered fast to the far wall.
140 Then over the broad cavern floor he ushered
the ewes he meant to milk. He left his rams
and he-goats in the yard outside, and swung
high overhead a slab of solid rock
to close the cave. Two dozen four-wheeled wagons,
145 with heaving wagon teams, could not have stirred
the tonnage of that rock from where he wedged it
over the doorsill. Next he took his seat
and milked his bleating ewes. A practiced job
he made of it, giving each ewe her suckling;
150 thickened his milk, then, into curds and whey,
sieved out the curds to drip in withy baskets,
and poured the whey to stand in bowls
cooling until he drank it for his supper.
When all these chores were done, he poked the fire,
155 heaping on brushwood. In the glare he saw us.

'Strangers,' he said, 'who are you? And where from?
What brings you here by sea ways—a fair traffic?
Or are you wandering rogues, who cast your lives
like dice, and ravage other folk by sea?'

160 We felt a pressure on our hearts, in dread
of that deep rumble and that mighty man.
But all the same I spoke up in reply:

'We are from Troy, Achaeans, blown off course
by shifting gales on the Great South Sea;
165 homeward bound, but taking routes and ways
uncommon; so the will of Zeus would have it.
We served under Agamemnon, son of Atreus—
the whole world knows what city
he laid waste, what armies he destroyed. **G**
170 It was our luck to come here; here we stand,
beholden for your help, or any gifts
you give—as custom is to honor strangers.
We would entreat you, great Sir, have a care
for the gods' courtesy; Zeus will avenge
175 the unoffending guest.'

133 burnt an offering: burned a portion of the food as an offering to secure the gods' goodwill. (Such offerings were frequently performed by Greek sailors during difficult journeys.)

151 withy baskets: baskets made from twigs.

157 fair traffic: honest trading.

G ALLUSION
Reread lines 163–169. Agamemnon was the Greek king who led the war against the Trojans. Consider what Odysseus says about Agamemnon; what point is he making about himself by claiming this association?

172–175 It was a sacred Greek custom to honor strangers with food and gifts. Odysseus is warning the Cyclops that Zeus will punish anyone who mistreats a guest.

THE WANDERINGS OF ODYSSEUS: BOOK 9 **1115**

Activity Ask students whether they think the painting depicts the pitiless cannibal of Homer's *Odyssey*. ***Possible answer:*** *The painting shows a subdued Cyclops in a whimsical presentation; it is much different from the brutish savage of Homer's tale.*

About the Art Odilon Redon (1840–1916) was one of the foremost symbolist painters of his period. This painting is a detail of *The Cyclops*. The full illustration shows Polyphemus looking down on the sleeping Galatea. In Greek myth, the Cyclops falls hopelessly in love with this charming sea nymph, who mocks him.

LITERARY ANALYSIS

Ⓗ EPIC HERO

Possible answer: *Odysseus now knows with certainty that the Cyclops has no qualms about mistreating his guests or their property; he lies to protect the ship.*

LITERARY ANALYSIS

Ⓘ EPITHET

Possible answer: *The epithet of "young Dawn with fingertips of rose" is repeated in lines 211–212.*

He answered this
from his brute chest, unmoved:

'You are a ninny,
or else you come from the other end of nowhere,
telling me, mind the gods! We Cyclops
care not a whistle for your thundering Zeus
180 or all the gods in bliss; we have more force by far.
I would not let you go for fear of Zeus—
you or your friends—unless I had a whim to.
Tell me, where was it, now, you left your ship—
around the point, or down the shore, I wonder?'

185 He thought he'd find out, but I saw through this,
and answered with a ready lie:

'My ship?

Poseidon Lord, who sets the earth a-tremble,
broke it up on the rocks at your land's end.
A wind from seaward served him, drove us there.
190 We are survivors, these good men and I.' Ⓗ

Neither reply nor pity came from him,
but in one stride he clutched at my companions
and caught two in his hands like squirming puppies
to beat their brains out, spattering the floor.
195 Then he dismembered them and made his meal,
gaping and crunching like a mountain lion—
everything: innards, flesh, and marrow bones.
We cried aloud, lifting our hands to Zeus,
powerless, looking on at this, **appalled**;
200 but Cyclops went on filling up his belly
with manflesh and great gulps of whey,
then lay down like a mast among his sheep.
My heart beat high now at the chance of action,
and drawing the sharp sword from my hip I went
205 along his flank to stab him where the midriff
holds the liver. I had touched the spot
when sudden fear stayed me: if I killed him
we perished there as well, for we could never
move his **ponderous** doorway slab aside.
210 So we were left to groan and wait for morning.

When the young Dawn with fingertips of rose
lit up the world, the Cyclops built a fire Ⓘ
and milked his handsome ewes, all in due order,

1116 UNIT 11: THE ODYSSEY

Detail of *The Cyclops* (about 1914) Odilon Redon. Oil on canvas. Kroller-Muller Museum, Otterlo, Netherlands. © Peter Will/SuperStock.

178–182 *What is the Cyclopes' attitude toward the gods?*

Ⓗ **EPIC HERO**
Reread lines 185–190. Why does Odysseus lie to the Cyclops about his ship?

appalled (ə-pôld') *adj.* filled with dismay; horrified **appall** *v.*

ponderous (pŏn'dər-əs) *adj.* heavy in a clumsy way; bulky

207–210 *Why doesn't Odysseus kill the Cyclops right now?*

Ⓘ **EPITHET**
What **epithet** is repeated in lines 211–212? Look for more repetitions like this one.

DIFFERENTIATED INSTRUCTION

FOR ENGLISH LEARNERS

Task Support Direct students to the question in the side note for lines 178–182. ***Possible answer:*** *The Cyclopes' attitude toward the gods is disrespectful. The Cyclops has no regard for, or fear of, the Olympians.* Point out that the Cyclops' arrogance foreshadows trouble: the gods will likely punish such disrespect.

Task Support Direct students to the question for lines 207–210. ***Possible answer:*** *Odysseus doesn't kill the Cyclops because only Ployphemus is strong enough to move the slab that blocks the mouth of the cave.*

FOR ADVANCED LEARNERS/PRE–AP

Analyze Repetition Remind students that poets often use repetition. Ask them to discuss the effect of the repetition of the dawn epithet. Then have students create an original epithet for the passage of time.

putting the sucklings to the mothers. Then,
215 his chores being all dispatched, he caught
another brace of men to make his breakfast,
and whisked away his great door slab
to let his sheep go through—but he, behind,
reset the stone as one would cap a quiver.
220 There was a din of whistling as the Cyclops
rounded his flock to higher ground, then stillness.
And now I pondered how to hurt him worst,
if but Athena granted what I prayed for.
Here are the means I thought would serve my turn:

225 a club, or staff, lay there along the fold—
an olive tree, felled green and left to season
for Cyclops' hand. And it was like a mast
a lugger of twenty oars, broad in the beam—
a deep-sea-going craft—might carry:
230 so long, so big around, it seemed. Now I
chopped out a six foot section of this pole
and set it down before my men, who scraped it;
and when they had it smooth, I hewed again
to make a stake with pointed end. I held this
235 in the fire's heart and turned it, toughening it,
then hid it, well back in the cavern, under
one of the dung piles in **profusion** there.
Now came the time to toss for it: who ventured
along with me? whose hand could bear to thrust
240 and grind that spike in Cyclops' eye, when mild
sleep had mastered him? As luck would have it,
the men I would have chosen won the toss—
four strong men, and I made five as captain.

At evening came the shepherd with his flock,
245 his woolly flock. The rams as well, this time,
entered the cave: by some sheep-herding whim—
or a god's bidding—none were left outside.
He hefted his great boulder into place
and sat him down to milk the bleating ewes
250 in proper order, put the lambs to suck,
and swiftly ran through all his evening chores.
Then he caught two more men and feasted on them.
My moment was at hand, and I went forward
holding an ivy bowl of my dark drink,
255 looking up, saying:

216 brace: pair.

218–219 The Cyclops reseals the cave with the massive rock as easily as an ordinary human places the cap on a container of arrows.

226 left to season: left to dry out and harden.

228 lugger: a small, wide sailing ship.

profusion (prə-fyōō′zhən) *n.* abundance

238–243 *What does Odysseus plan to do to the Cyclops?*

Lines 225–247
DISCUSSION PROMPTS

Use these prompts to help students understand how a combination of careful planning and good luck is pushing the momentum toward Odysseus' advantage:

Recall What three things happened that showed luck was on Odysseus' side? *Possible answer: First: Odysseus found the olive tree in the cave. Second: The four men Odysseus would have chosen to help him all won the toss. Third: The Cyclops brought all the rams into the cave, not just the youngest.*

Analyze How does Odysseus take advantage of his good luck? What do his reactions reflect about his character? *Possible answer: Odysseus quickly formulates a plan based on the tools he has available, namely, the olive tree and the rams. His actions reflect his intelligence.*

Evaluate Which do you think will be most important to the outcome of Odysseus' conflict with the Cyclops: careful planning or good luck? *Possible answer: Both good luck and good planning will contribute to the outcome.*

FOR ENGLISH LEARNERS

Task Support Call attention to the question in the side note for lines 238–243. Make sure students understand that Odysseus has made a six-foot-long stake with a pointed end (lines 230–234) from the olive tree that the Cyclops left in the cave. *Possible answer: Odysseus plans to push the stake into the Cyclops' single eye after he falls asleep.*

'Cyclops, try some wine.
Here's liquor to wash down your scraps of men.
Taste it, and see the kind of drink we carried
under our planks. I meant it for an offering
if you would help us home. But you are mad,
260 unbearable, a bloody monster! After this,
will any other traveller come to see you?'

He seized and drained the bowl, and it went down
so fiery and smooth he called for more:

'Give me another, thank you kindly. Tell me,
265 how are you called? I'll make a gift will please you.
Even Cyclopes know the wine-grapes grow
out of grassland and loam in heaven's rain,
but here's a bit of nectar and ambrosia!'

Three bowls I brought him, and he poured them down.
270 I saw the fuddle and flush come over him,
then I sang out in cordial tones:

                                        'Cyclops,
you ask my honorable name? Remember
the gift you promised me, and I shall tell you.
My name is Nohbdy: mother, father, and friends,
275 everyone calls me Nohbdy.'

                                        And he said:
'Nohbdy's my meat, then, after I eat his friends.
Others come first. There's a noble gift, now.' **J**

Even as he spoke, he reeled and tumbled backward,
his great head lolling to one side: and sleep
280 took him like any creature. Drunk, hiccupping,
he dribbled streams of liquor and bits of men.

Now, by the gods, I drove my big hand spike
deep in the embers, charring it again,
and cheered my men along with battle talk
285 to keep their courage up: no quitting now.
The pike of olive, green though it had been,
reddened and glowed as if about to catch.
I drew it from the coals and my four fellows
gave me a hand, lugging it near the Cyclops
290 as more than natural force nerved them; straight
forward they sprinted, lifted it, and rammed it

UNIT 11: THE ODYSSEY

255–261 *Why does Odysseus offer the Cyclops the liquor he brought from the ship?*

268 nectar (nĕk'tər) **and ambrosia** (ăm-brō'zhə): the drink and food of the gods.

270 fuddle and flush: the state of confusion and redness of the face caused by drinking alcohol.

③ **Targeted Passage**

J EPIC HERO
Say the name *Nohbdy* out loud and listen to what it sounds like. What might Odysseus be planning? Consider what this tells you about his **character**.

286 the pike: the pointed stake.

J EPIC HERO

Possible answer: *The name* Nohbdy *sounds like "nobody." Odysseus is concealing his identity, which tells us that he is planning ahead, possibly setting some trap for the Cyclops. Odysseus didn't mention the name* Nohbdy *until after the Cyclops' wits had been dulled by three drinks. These moves show that Odysseus is both clever and careful in his planning.*

DIFFERENTIATED INSTRUCTION

FOR LESS–PROFICIENT READERS
③ Targeted Passage [Lines 264–281]

This passage illustrates how Odysseus' plan depends on the Cyclops' carelessness.

- How many bowls of wine did the Cyclops drink?
- Why didn't Odysseus tell Cyclops his name as soon as he asked?
- Why did the Cyclops believe that Odysseus' name was Nohbdy?

- Why did the Cyclops trust Odysseus, drink his wine, and ask for more?

FOR ENGLISH LEARNERS

Task Support Point out the question in the side note for lines 255–261. **Possible answer:** *He offers the wine, knowing that Cyclops won't be able to resist and counting on its sleep-inducing effect.*

deep in his crater eye, and I leaned on it
turning it as a shipwright turns a drill
in planking, having men below to swing
295 the two-handled strap that spins it in the groove.
So with our brand we bored that great eye socket
while blood ran out around the red hot bar.
Eyelid and lash were seared; the pierced ball
hissed broiling, and the roots popped.

                                         In a smithy
300 one sees a white-hot axehead or an adze
plunged and wrung in a cold tub, screeching steam—
the way they make soft iron hale and hard—:
just so that eyeball hissed around the spike. **K**
The Cyclops bellowed and the rock roared round him,
305 and we fell back in fear. Clawing his face
he tugged the bloody spike out of his eye,
threw it away, and his wild hands went groping;
then he set up a howl for Cyclopes
who lived in caves on windy peaks nearby.
310 Some heard him; and they came by divers ways
to clump around outside and call:

                                   'What ails you,
Polyphemus? Why do you cry so sore
in the starry night? You will not let us sleep.
Sure no man's driving off your flock? No man
315 has tricked you, ruined you?'

                              Out of the cave
the mammoth Polyphemus roared in answer:

'Nohbdy, Nohbdy's tricked me, Nohbdy's ruined me!'

To this rough shout they made a sage reply:

'Ah well, if nobody has played you foul
320 there in your lonely bed, we are no use in pain
given by great Zeus. Let it be your father,
Poseidon Lord, to whom you pray.' **L**

                            So saying
they trailed away. And I was filled with laughter
to see how like a charm the name deceived them.
325 Now Cyclops, wheezing as the pain came on him,
fumbled to wrench away the great doorstone

---

299 smithy: blacksmith's shop.

300 adze (ădz): an axlike tool with a curved blade.

K EPIC SIMILE
Find the epic similes in lines 292–297 and lines 299–303. What two things are being compared in each case? What are the effects of this **figurative language?**

310 divers: various.

312 Polyphemus (pŏl′ə-fē′məs): the name of the Cyclops.

318 sage: wise.

319–322 Odysseus' lie about his name has paid off. *What do the other Cyclopes assume to be the source of Polyphemus' pain?*

L ALLUSION
What do you learn about Polyphemus from the allusion in lines 321–322?

LITERARY ANALYSIS

K EPIC SIMILE

Possible answer: In lines 292–297, Odysseus compares pushing and turning the spike in the Cyclops' eye socket to a ship carpenter turning a drill in a plank on a ship's deck. In lines 299–303, he compares the hissing of the Cyclops' eye to the steam given off by a white-hot axehead that is dipped in a cold tub of water.

Lines 292–299
REINFORCE *KEY IDEA:* HERO

Discuss What leadership qualities does Odysseus, the **hero,** display in this passage? Remind students that Greek warriors won honor through noble deeds, and that honor, they believed, was the greatest good.
Possible answer: Odysseus joins his men in the maneuver, leaning on the spike himself, rather than removing himself from harm's way. In displaying such bravery and confidence, he acts as an inspiring role model for his men.

LITERARY ANALYSIS

L ALLUSION

Possible answer: The reader learns that the Cyclops is the son of Poseidon. Point out that during the Trojan War, the Greeks had incurred the anger of Poseidon; the god of the sea was responsible for Odysseus' long journey and suffering.

FOR ENGLISH LEARNERS

Task Support Draw students' attention to the question in the side note for lines 319–322. Reread Cyclops' response ("Nohbdy, Nohbdy's tricked me, Nohbdy's ruined me!").
Possible answer: The other Cyclopes assume that no one is hurting Polyphemus. They think it must be some injury or sickness imposed by Zeus.

FOR ADVANCED LEARNERS/PRE–AP

Compare and Contrast Point out that Polyphemus and Odysseus are not entirely dissimilar. Have students work in pairs and create a Comparison Matrix that shows the similarities and differences between the two. Tell them to consider personal as well as physical features. Have pairs discuss their findings and share their results with the class.

 BEST PRACTICES TOOLKIT—Transparency
Comparison Matrix p. A24

and squatted in the breach with arms thrown wide
for any silly beast or man who bolted—
hoping somehow I might be such a fool.
330 But I kept thinking how to win the game:
death sat there huge; how could we slip away?
I drew on all my wits, and ran through tactics,
reasoning as a man will for dear life,
until a trick came—and it pleased me well.
335 The Cyclops' rams were handsome, fat, with heavy
fleeces, a dark violet.

Three abreast

I tied them silently together, twining
cords of willow from the ogre's bed;
then slung a man under each middle one
340 to ride there safely, shielded left and right.
So three sheep could convey each man. I took
the woolliest ram, the choicest of the flock,
and hung myself under his kinky belly,
pulled up tight, with fingers twisted deep
345 in sheepskin ringlets for an iron grip.
So, breathing hard, we waited until morning.

When Dawn spread out her finger tips of rose
the rams began to stir, moving for pasture,
and peals of bleating echoed round the pens
350 where dams with udders full called for a milking.
Blinded, and sick with pain from his head wound,
the master stroked each ram, then let it pass,
but my men riding on the pectoral fleece
the giant's blind hands blundering never found.
355 Last of them all my ram, the leader, came,
weighted by wool and me with my **meditations.**
The Cyclops patted him, and then he said:

'Sweet cousin ram, why lag behind the rest
in the night cave? You never linger so,
360 but graze before them all, and go afar
to crop sweet grass, and take your stately way
leading along the streams, until at evening
you run to be the first one in the fold.
Why, now, so far behind? Can you be grieving
365 over your Master's eye? That carrion rogue
and his accurst companions burnt it out
when he had conquered all my wits with wine.
Nohbdy will not get out alive, I swear.

1120 UNIT 11: THE ODYSSEY

This 1910 color print depicts Odysseus taunting
Polyphemus as he and his men make their escape.

Detail of *Odysseus and Polyphem* (1910), after L. du Bois-
Reymond. Color print. From *Sagen des klasseschen Altertums* by
Karl Becker, Berlin. © akg-images.

LITERARY ANALYSIS

EPIC HERO

Remind students that Odysseus was the
mastermind behind the Trojan horse, which
broke the stalemate and won the war for
Greece. Ask them how this situation, and
the plan that he devises, is similar. **Possible
answer:** *Odysseus and his men are at a kind
of stalemate with the Cyclops. They have
neutralized but not defeated him. Odysseus
again thinks of a trick, this time to deceive
the Cyclops. Once again, his clever planning
will fool a formidable foe.*

ANALYZE VISUALS

Activity Compare this depiction of the Cyclops
with the one on page 1116. How do they differ?
Which do you think better illustrates Polyphemus? **Possible answer:** *The expression of the
Cyclops in the painting on page 1116 and the
soft colors make the creature seem harmless.
The Cyclops on page 1120, however, is depicted
as strong and threatening, using bold colors
to highlight his strong physique. Students'
opinions on which painting is more effective
will vary.*

DIFFERENTIATED INSTRUCTION

FOR ENGLISH LEARNERS
Vocabulary: Outdated Forms Call attention to
these words and phrases (on pages 1120–1121)
that are now rarely used and that suggest a
bygone time. Work with students to use context clues to determine their meaning:

- *so* (line 359), "this way"
- *afar* (line 360), "far away"
- *carrion rogue* (line 365), "rotten, dishonest
person"

- *accurst* (line 366), "damned"
- *I should have rest* (lines 372–373), "I would
be free"

Oh, had you brain and voice to tell
370 where he may be now, dodging all my fury!
Bashed by this hand and bashed on this rock wall
his brains would strew the floor, and I should have
rest from the outrage Nohbdy worked upon me.'

He sent us into the open, then. Close by,
375 I dropped and rolled clear of the ram's belly,
going this way and that to untie the men.
With many glances back, we rounded up
his fat, stiff-legged sheep to take aboard,
and drove them down to where the good ship lay. **N**
380 We saw, as we came near, our fellows' faces
shining; then we saw them turn to grief
tallying those who had not fled from death.
I hushed them, jerking head and eyebrows up,
and in a low voice told them: 'Load this herd;
385 move fast, and put the ship's head toward the breakers.'
They all pitched in at loading, then embarked
and struck their oars into the sea. Far out,
as far off shore as shouted words would carry,
I sent a few back to the **adversary:**

390 'O Cyclops! Would you feast on my companions?
Puny, am I, in a Caveman's hands?
How do you like the beating that we gave you,
you damned cannibal? Eater of guests
under your roof! Zeus and the gods have paid you!'

395 The blind thing in his doubled fury broke
a hilltop in his hands and heaved it after us.
Ahead of our black prow it struck and sank
whelmed in a spuming geyser, a giant wave
that washed the ship stern foremost back to shore.
400 I got the longest boathook out and stood
fending us off, with furious nods to all
to put their backs into a racing stroke—
row, row, or perish. So the long oars bent
kicking the foam sternward, making head
405 until we drew away, and twice as far.
Now when I cupped my hands I heard the crew
in low voices protesting:

                          'Godsake, Captain!

Why bait the beast again? Let him alone!'

N EPIC HERO
What **character traits** has Odysseus
demonstrated in his dealings with
Polyphemus?

385 **put . . . the breakers:** turn the ship
around so that it is heading toward the
open sea.

adversary (ăd′vər-sĕr′ē)
n. an opponent; enemy

390–394 Odysseus assumes that
the gods are on his side.

395–403 The hilltop thrown by
Polyphemus lands in front of the ship,
causing a huge wave that carries the
ship back to the shore. Odysseus uses
a long pole to push the boat away from
the land.

406 **cupped my hands:** put his hands
on either side of his mouth in order to
magnify his voice.

LITERARY ANALYSIS

N EPIC HERO

Possible answer: *Odysseus has demonstrated leadership, bravery, and cunning in his dealings with Polyphemus. His actions also reveal his curiosity and his tendency to be rash and even foolhardy.*

FOR LESS–PROFICIENT READERS

Paraphrasing Homer Have students reread the summaries of lines 390–394 and lines 395–403. Then model how to paraphrase lines 390–394: *You were going to eat up all my friends and take me in your hands. So, how do you like having us beat you? The gods have punished you for mistreating your guests.*

Invite volunteers to paraphrase lines 395–403: *The blind Cyclops tore off the top of a hill and threw it at us. It landed in front of our ship and sent up a geyser; a wave washed us back to shore. I pushed us away with a pole and ordered my men to row for their lives.*

'That tidal wave he made on the first throw
410 all but beached us.'

'All but stove us in!'

'Give him our bearing with your trumpeting,
he'll get the range and lob a boulder.'

'Aye

He'll smash our timbers and our heads together!'

I would not heed them in my glorying spirit,
415 but let my anger flare and yelled:

'Cyclops,

if ever mortal man inquire
how you were put to shame and blinded, tell him
Odysseus, raider of cities, took your eye:
Laertes' son, whose home's on Ithaca!' ◉

420 At this he gave a mighty sob and rumbled:

'Now comes the weird upon me, spoken of old.
A wizard, grand and wondrous, lived here—Telemus,
a son of Eurymus; great length of days
he had in wizardry among the Cyclopes,
425 and these things he foretold for time to come:
my great eye lost, and at Odysseus' hands.
Always I had in mind some giant, armed
in giant force, would come against me here.
But this, but you—small, pitiful and twiggy—
430 you put me down with wine, you blinded me.
Come back, Odysseus, and I'll treat you well,
praying the god of earthquake to befriend you—
his son I am, for he by his avowal
fathered me, and, if he will, he may
435 heal me of this black wound—he and no other
of all the happy gods or mortal men.'

Few words I shouted in reply to him:
'If I could take your life I would and take
your time away, and hurl you down to hell!
440 The god of earthquake could not heal you there!'

At this he stretched his hands out in his darkness
toward the sky of stars, and prayed Poseidon:

Side Notes

◉ **EPITHET**
Notice that Odysseus uses the warlike **epithet** "raider of cities" in his second boast to the Cyclops. What **trait** does he display in revealing so much about himself?

421 Now comes . . . of old: Now I recall the destiny predicted long ago.

421–430 Now comes . . . you blinded me: Polyphemus tells of a prophecy made long ago by Telemus, a prophet who predicted that Polyphemus would lose his eye at the hands of Odysseus. *How have the actual events turned out differently from what Polyphemus expected?*

432 the god of earthquake: Poseidon.
433 avowal: honest admission.

Left Margin

LITERARY ANALYSIS

◉ EPITHET

Possible answer: In revealing this information, Odysseus displays his pride. It is a rash, foolhardy action: the Cyclops may use this information to cause Odysseus trouble with his father, Poseidon, who is already angry with the Greek.

Lines 437–440
REINFORCE *KEY IDEA:* HERO

Discuss Odysseus was a great **hero.** Are his faults of heroic proportions? Or are they failings that you would expect most people to share? *Possible answer: Odysseus' faults are not shared by most ordinary people. His fatal flaw is his excessive pride, as well as his tendency to act at times without thinking of consequences. Both traits bring him bad luck. Thus, Odysseus is responsible for much of the misfortune he suffers.*

DIFFERENTIATED INSTRUCTION

FOR LESS–PROFICIENT READERS
Paraphrasing Homer Have students reread the summary of lines 421–430. Then paraphrase lines 421–426: *Now Telemus' prophecy has come true. He said that one day I would lose my eye at the hands of Odysseus.* Then ask a volunteer to paraphrase lines 427–430: *I always thought it would be a great giant, not a weakling who used wine to weaken me and then blinded me.*

FOR ENGLISH LEARNERS
Task Support Direct students' attention to the side note for lines 421–430. Help them answer the question. *Possible answer: Polyphemus expected Odysseus to be a "giant, armed in giant force" and not a frail human.*

'O hear me, lord, blue girdler of the islands,
if I am thine indeed, and thou art father:
445 grant that Odysseus, raider of cities, never
see his home: Laertes' son, I mean,
who kept his hall on Ithaca. Should destiny
intend that he shall see his roof again
among his family in his father land,
450 far be that day, and dark the years between.
Let him lose all companions, and return
under strange sail to bitter days at home.' ℗

℗ EPIC HERO
Reread lines 437–452. Paraphrase Polyphemus' curse. How has Odysseus brought this curse upon himself?

In these words he prayed, and the god heard him.
Now he laid hands upon a bigger stone
455 and wheeled around, titanic for the cast,
to let it fly in the black-prowed vessel's track.
But it fell short, just aft the steering oar,
and whelming seas rose giant above the stone
to bear us onward toward the island.

There

455 titanic for the cast: drawing on all his enormous strength in preparing to throw.

457 aft: behind.

459 the island: the deserted island where most of Odysseus' men had stayed behind.

460 as we ran in we saw the squadron waiting,
the trim ships drawn up side by side, and all
our troubled friends who waited, looking seaward.
We beached her, grinding keel in the soft sand,
and waded in, ourselves, on the sandy beach.
465 Then we unloaded all the Cyclops' flock
to make division, share and share alike,
only my fighters voted that my ram,
the prize of all, should go to me. I slew him
by the sea side and burnt his long thighbones
470 to Zeus beyond the stormcloud, Cronus' son,
who rules the world. But Zeus disdained my offering;
destruction for my ships he had in store
and death for those who sailed them, my companions.

④ **Targeted Passage**

470 Cronus' son: Zeus' father, Cronus, was a Titan, one of an earlier race of gods.

Now all day long until the sun went down
475 we made our feast on mutton and sweet wine,
till after sunset in the gathering dark
we went to sleep above the wash of ripples.

When the young Dawn with finger tips of rose
touched the world, I roused the men, gave orders
480 to man the ships, cast off the mooring lines;
and filing in to sit beside the rowlocks
oarsmen in line dipped oars in the gray sea.
So we moved out, sad in the vast offing,
having our precious lives, but not our friends."

483 offing: the part of the deep sea visible from the shore.

LITERARY ANALYSIS

℗ **EPIC HERO**

Possible answer: *Paraphrase: May Odysseus the son of Laertes and conqueror of cities never again see Ithaca, his home. And if the fates decree that he does return home, may that day be far from now, may the time between be troubled with the loss of his companions. May his homecoming be by strange passage, and upon his arrival, may he find chaos. Odysseus has brought this curse on himself by provoking Polyphemus with his boasting—not once but three times, despite the warnings of his men (lines 390–394 and lines 415–419)—his anger, and his taunts (lines 437–440). Odysseus' pride will cost him dearly.*

FOR LESS–PROFICIENT READERS

④ Targeted Passage [Lines 453–473]

This passage shows the resolution of Odysseus' great conflict with Polyphemus.

• What did the Cyclops do after cursing Odysseus?

• What happened to Odysseus' ship?

• What did Odysseus and his crew do after they landed?

FOR ADVANCED LEARNERS/PRE–AP

Foreshadowing Have students list all the prophecies mentioned in Book 9. Then have them talk about these questions: What effect does the knowledge that Odysseus' men are doomed have on the story? Why do you think Homer may have given this information rather than keeping his audience in the dark?

ANALYZE VISUALS

Activity Ask students what qualities of Circe are captured in this painting. *Possible answer: The painting reveals her beauty and charm. There is mischief in her eyes, suggesting that danger lurks beneath the lovely surface.*

About the Art German painter Franz von Struck (1863–1928) used myth and imagination in his Art Nouveau works. A painter, sculptor, and designer, von Struck influenced a generation of important painters, including Albers, Kandinsky, and Klee.

LITERARY ANALYSIS

◎ EPIC SIMILE

Possible answer: The simile compares the drugged wolves and mountain lions, shaking their tails and looking up at Odysseus' men, to tame dogs that wag their tails and fawn on their masters when fed at the table. The point of the comparison is to show the power of Circe's magic, which can turn vicious predators into pets. This description inspires awe and fear of Circe and her great hall.

BOOK 10:
Circe, the Grace of the Witch

Detail of *Tilla Durieux as Circe* (about 1912–1913), Franz von Struck. Oil on paper, 53.5 cm × 46.5 cm. Private collection. Photo © akg-images.

Odysseus and his men next land on the island of Aeolus, the wind king, and stay with him a month. To extend his hospitality, Aeolus gives Odysseus two parting gifts: a fair west wind that will blow the fleet of ships toward Ithaca, and a great bag holding all the unfavorable, stormy winds. Within sight of home, and while Odysseus is sleeping, the men open the bag, thinking it contains gold and silver. The bad winds thus escape and blow the ships back to Aeolus' island. The king refuses to help them again, believing now that their voyage has been cursed by the gods.

The discouraged mariners next stop briefly in the land of the Laestrygones, fierce cannibals who bombard the fleet of ships with boulders. Only Odysseus, his ship, and its crew of 45 survive the shower of boulders. The lone ship then sails to Aeaea, home of the goddess Circe, who is considered by many to be a witch. There, Odysseus divides his men into two groups. Eurylochus leads one platoon to explore the island, while Odysseus stays behind on the ship with the remaining crew.

"In the wild wood they found an open glade,
around a smooth stone house—the hall of Circe—
and wolves and mountain lions lay there, mild
in her soft spell, fed on her drug of evil.
5   None would attack—oh, it was strange, I tell you—
but switching their long tails they faced our men
like hounds, who look up when their master comes
with tidbits for them—as he will—from table.
Humbly those wolves and lions with mighty paws
10 fawned on our men—who met their yellow eyes
and feared them. ◎   In the entrance way they stayed
to listen there: inside her quiet house
they heard the goddess Circe.
                              Low she sang

in her **beguiling** voice, while on her loom
15 she wove ambrosial fabric sheer and bright,

10 fawned on: showed affection for.

◎ EPIC SIMILE
In lines 6–11, notice the simile involving Circe's wolves and mountain lions. What is the point of this comparison? How does it affect your impression of Circe's hall?

beguiling (bĭ-gī'lĭng) *adj.* charming; pleasing **beguile** *v.*

15 ambrosial: fit for the gods.

DIFFERENTIATED INSTRUCTION

FOR LESS–PROFICIENT READERS

Preview Read aloud the italicized synopsis that begins Book 10, and help students create a Story Map of the characters and events. They can complete the organizer as they read.

Characters: Odysseus, Aeolus, the Laestrygones, Circe, Eurylochus

Events:

1. Odysseus and crew stay with Aeolus.
2. Aeolus gives Odysseus two parting gifts.
3. The men open a bag with bad winds.
4. The winds blow them back to Aeolus.
5. The Laestrygones destroy all the ships but one.
6. The ship sails to Circe's home, Aeaea.
7. Eurylochus explores the island with some men.

 **BEST PRACTICES TOOLKIT—Transparency** Story Map p. D14

by that craft known to the goddesses of heaven.
No one would speak, until Polites—most
faithful and likable of my officers, said:

17 **Polites** (pə-lī'tēz).

'Dear friends, no need for stealth: here's a young weaver
20 singing a pretty song to set the air
a-tingle on these lawns and paven courts.
Goddess she is, or lady. Shall we greet her?'

So reassured, they all cried out together,
and she came swiftly to the shining doors
25 to call them in. All but Eurylochus—
who feared a snare—the innocents went after her.
On thrones she seated them, and lounging chairs,
while she prepared a meal of cheese and barley
and amber honey mixed with Pramnian wine,
30 adding her own vile pinch, to make them lose
desire or thought of our dear father land.
Scarce had they drunk when she flew after them
with her long stick and shut them in a pigsty—
bodies, voices, heads, and bristles, all
35 swinish now, though minds were still unchanged.
So, squealing, in they went. And Circe tossed them
acorns, mast, and cornel berries—fodder
for hogs who rut and slumber on the earth.

23–26 If you were among this group, whom would you follow—Polites or Eurylochus? Why?

27–36 What happens to the men after they drink Circe's magic potion?

Down to the ship Eurylochus came running
40 to cry alarm, foul magic doomed his men!
But working with dry lips to speak a word
he could not, being so shaken; blinding tears
welled in his eyes; **foreboding** filled his heart.
When we were frantic questioning him, at last
45 we heard the tale: our friends were gone. . . ."

foreboding (fôr-bō'dǐng) *n.* a sense of approaching evil

Eurylochus tells Odysseus what has happened and begs him to sail away from Circe's island. Against this advice, however, Odysseus rushes to save his men from the enchantress. On the way, he meets the god Hermes, who gives him a magical plant called moly to protect him from Circe's power. Still, Hermes warns Odysseus that he must make the goddess swear she will play no "witches' tricks." Armed with the moly and Hermes' warning, Odysseus arrives at Circe's palace.

Circe gives Odysseus a magic drink, but it does not affect him and he threatens to kill her with his sword. Circe turns the pigs back into men but puts them all into a trance. They stay for one year, until Odysseus finally begs her to let them go home. She replies that they must first visit the land of the dead and hear a prophecy from the ghost of Tiresias.

Get Into the Book
SUMMARY

Book 10 recants how Odysseus and his crew visit the wind king, Aeolus. He sends them off with a fair wind and a bag of violent winds. One night, close to home, the men open the bag. The winds blow the ship back to Aeolus, who refuses to help them again. Next, the Laestrygones destroy all their ships but one. Odysseus sails his last ship to Aeaea, home of Circe. He sends Eurylochus to explore the island with a platoon. Circe offers them food and drink, which they accept, despite Eurylochus' warning. Her brew turns them into pigs. Eurylochus tells Odysseus, who hurries to save his men. A magical plant from Hermes protects him from Circe. She releases his crew but exacts a price: they must visit the ghost of Tiresias in the land of the dead to hear a prophecy.

READING STRATEGY

■ READING AN EPIC POEM
Remind students that an important strategy for reading any narrative poem is keeping track of events. Ask students to complete the Story Map they started with the preview and use it to summarize Book 10.

FOR ENGLISH LEARNERS

Task Support Point out the question in the side note for lines 23–26. *Some students may acknowledge Circe's magic; others may suggest that they would have learned from their experience with the Lotus Eaters not to trust strangers.*

Task Support Draw students' attention to the side-note question for lines 27–36. **Possible answer:** *They turn into swine; then*

Circe forces them into a pigsty and feeds them food fit for hogs.

Text Digests Read line by line through the italicized text digest at the end of page 1125 to make sure students understand the plot of the rest of Book 10.

Possible answer: The shades are literally featureless shadows. By contrast, Odysseus is dressed in full regalia; his clothing and weapons are presented in detail. His body, face, and limbs are well-defined and solid.

About the Art Giovanni Stradano (1523–1605) painted *Ulysses Descending into the Underworld* in a Mannerist style. Mannerism developed during the late Renaissance. Using the masters of the Renaissance, such as Michelangelo and Raphael, for inspiration, Mannerist artists created idealized and highly refined work.

LITERARY ANALYSIS

Ⓡ ALLUSION

Possible answer: The reference to the myth of Hades and Persephone reminds us that Hades is determined, ruthless, and self-centered. It helps to create the impression of the underworld as a gloomy, dark, and frightening place. It also reinforces the sense of foreboding.

BACKGROUND

Death and the Underworld The land of the dead was ruled by the god Hades, who was also the god of earth's fertility. His kingdom was also called Hades, and it was divided into two regions. The first region, called Erebus, was where a person's spirit (or psyche) passed at death. The second region was called Tartarus. It was separated from the land of the living by the river Styx. An old boatman named Charon transported the dead across the river to Hades. The land of the dead was also guarded by a three-headed, dragon-tailed dog named Cerberus.

BOOK 11:
The Land of the Dead

Odysseus and his crew set out for the land of the dead. They arrive and find the place to which Circe has directed them.

"Then I addressed the blurred and breathless dead,
vowing to slaughter my best heifer for them
before she calved, at home in Ithaca,
and burn the choice bits on the altar fire;
5 as for Tiresias, I swore to sacrifice
a black lamb, handsomest of all our flock.
Thus to **assuage** the nations of the dead
I pledged these rites, then slashed the lamb and ewe,
letting their black blood stream into the wellpit.
10 Now the souls gathered, stirring out of Erebus,
brides and young men, and men grown old in pain,
and tender girls whose hearts were new to grief;
many were there, too, torn by brazen lanceheads,
battle-slain, bearing still their bloody gear.
15 From every side they came and sought the pit
with rustling cries; and I grew sick with fear.
But presently I gave command to my officers
to flay those sheep the bronze cut down, and make
burnt offerings of flesh to the gods below—
20 to sovereign Death, to pale Persephone. Ⓡ
Meanwhile I crouched with my drawn sword to keep
the surging phantoms from the bloody pit
till I should know the presence of Tiresias.

One shade came first—Elpenor, of our company,
25 who lay unburied still on the wide earth
as we had left him—dead in Circe's hall,
untouched, unmourned, when other cares compelled us.
Now when I saw him there I wept for pity
and called out to him:

assuage (ə-swāj′) *v.* to calm or pacify

10 Erebus (ĕr′ə-bəs): a region of the land of the dead, also known as the underworld or Hades. Hades is also the name of the god of the underworld.

18 flay: to strip off the outer skin of.

Ⓡ ALLUSION
In lines 17–20, Odysseus makes a sacrifice to "sovereign Death," or Hades, and "pale Persephone" (pər-sĕf′ə-nē), his bride, who was kidnapped and forced to live with him for six months of every year. Her mother, goddess of the harvest, grieves during that time, causing winter to fall. What does this background information tell you about Hades? Consider how this information affects your impression of the underworld.

DIFFERENTIATED INSTRUCTION

FOR LESS–PROFICIENT READERS
Preview Read aloud the italicized synopsis of Book 11 at the top of page 1126 to give students a clear idea of the plot from the end of Book 10 to Odysseus' descent to the underworld. Ask students to recall what task Circe had set for Odysseus to perform in the land of the dead. *(to hear a prophecy from the ghost of Tiresias)*

Ulysses Descending into the Underworld (16th century), Giovanni Stradano. Fresco. Palazzo Vecchio, Florence. Photo © Scala/Art Resource, New York.

'How is this, Elpenor,
30 how could you journey to the western gloom
swifter afoot than I in the black lugger?'

He sighed, and answered:

'Son of great Laertes,
Odysseus, master mariner and soldier,
bad luck shadowed me, and no kindly power;
35 ignoble death I drank with so much wine.
I slept on Circe's roof, then could not see
the long steep backward ladder, coming down,
and fell that height. My neck bone, buckled under,
snapped, and my spirit found this well of dark.
40 Now hear the grace I pray for, in the name
of those back in the world, not here—your wife
and father, he who gave you bread in childhood,
and your own child, your only son, Telemachus,
long ago left at home.

ANALYZE VISUALS
This 16th-century painting illustrates the descent of Ulysses (Odysseus) into the underworld. How has the artist distinguished between Ulysses and the dead, also known as shades?

Get Into the Book
SUMMARY
Book 11 describes how Odysseus and his crew travel to the underworld to meet with the blind sage Tiresias, as Circe has demanded. Odysseus meets Elpenor, a shipmate who had died in an accident, and promises to give him a proper burial. Then Tiresias tells him that his crew will return to Ithaca only if they avoid stealing from Helios' herd. Odysseus speaks with many other spirits, including his mother, who had died of a broken heart.

READING STRATEGY

■ READING AN EPIC POEM
Point out to students that visualizing the imagery will help them understand and remember the opening of Book 11. Ask them what words or images appeal to the senses in lines 10–16. What mood do these words and images create? ***Possible answer: The main image is of a crowd of many souls, coming "from every side": brides, young men, old men, tender girls "new to grief," wounded warriors with "their bloody gear." The sound of the shadows' "rustling cries" and Odysseus' admission that he "grew sick with fear" also draw on the senses. The accumulation of words and ghastly images helps to create a mood of fear and foreboding.***

FOR ADVANCED LEARNERS/PRE–AP

Analyze Ask students to reflect on the similarities and differences between Persephone's forced abduction and Odysseus' reluctant descent into the underworld. Encourage students to investigate details of the Hades-Persephone-Demeter myth to include in their analysis.

DISCUSSION PROMPTS

Use these prompts to help students understand the mix of emotions Odysseus would have felt as he waited in the underworld for Tiresias:

Connect Have you or anyone you know during a moment of crisis or tension bumped into an old friend or a family member? *Responses should demonstrate an understanding that the bad timing and bad location might cause discomfort, worry, and even pain.*

Analyze What does the reader learn about Odysseus from his encounters with Elpenor and Anticlea? *Possible answer: The reader learns that Odysseus commanded the respect of his crew and in turn felt responsibility for them. We learn from his response to Elpenor that he is a dutiful and gracious leader and from his grief over his mother that he is a devoted son.*

Evaluate How well do you think Odysseus handled his meetings with Elpenor and Anticlea? *Possible answer: Odysseus handled these trying situations with patience, respect, and grace. It must have been a shock to see his lost crewmate and to learn of his mother's death. Nevertheless, he maintained control, operating calmly in the midst of personal loss and the horrors of the underworld.*

When you make sail

45 and put these lodgings of dim Death behind,
you will moor ship, I know, upon Aeaea Island;
there, O my lord, remember me, I pray,
do not abandon me unwept, unburied,
to tempt the gods' wrath, while you sail for home;
50 but fire my corpse, and all the gear I had,
and build a cairn for me above the breakers—
an unknown sailor's mark for men to come.
Heap up the mound there, and implant upon it
the oar I pulled in life with my companions.'

55 He ceased, and I replied:

'Unhappy spirit,

I promise you the barrow and the burial.'

So we conversed, and grimly, at a distance,
with my long sword between, guarding the blood,
while the faint image of the lad spoke on.
60 Now came the soul of Anticlea, dead,
my mother, daughter of Autolycus,
dead now, though living still when I took ship
for holy Troy. Seeing this ghost I grieved,
but held her off, through pang on pang of tears,
65 till I should know the presence of Tiresias.
Soon from the dark that prince of Thebes came forward
bearing a golden staff; and he addressed me:

'Son of Laertes and the gods of old,
Odysseus, master of land ways and sea ways,
70 why leave the blazing sun, O man of woe,
to see the cold dead and the joyless region?
Stand clear, put up your sword;
let me but taste of blood, I shall speak true.'

At this I stepped aside, and in the scabbard
75 let my long sword ring home to the pommel silver,
as he bent down to the sombre blood. Then spoke
the prince of those with gift of speech:

'Great captain,

a fair wind and the honey lights of home
are all you seek. But anguish lies ahead;
80 the god who thunders on the land prepares it,
not to be shaken from your track, implacable,

50–51 fire my corpse . . . cairn: Elpenor wants Odysseus to hold a funeral for him.

58 with my long sword . . . blood: the ghosts are attracted to the blood of the sacrifice; Odysseus must hold them at bay with his sword.

66 prince of Thebes: Tiresias, the blind seer, comes from the city of Thebes (thēbz).

DIFFERENTIATED INSTRUCTION

FOR ENGLISH LEARNERS

Paraphrase Make sure that students understand Tiresias' prophecy. Have small groups paraphrase sections of the prophecy: lines 77–90, lines 91–104, and lines 105–116. Invite them to create cartoon frames to illustrate each part of the prophecy. Circulate to check comprehension and to make sure each group has identified the key elements. Students can draw the international "No" symbol (x) between frames to indicate what Tiresias

tells Odysseus that he and his men should not do and the word *or* between frames to show what will happen if they do.

in rancor for the son whose eye you blinded.
One narrow strait may take you through his blows:
denial of yourself, restraint of shipmates.
85 When you make landfall on Thrinacia first
and quit the violet sea, dark on the land
you'll find the grazing herds of Helios
by whom all things are seen, all speech is known.
Avoid those kine, hold fast to your intent,
90 and hard seafaring brings you all to Ithaca.
But if you raid the beeves, I see destruction
for ship and crew. Though you survive alone,
bereft of all companions, lost for years,
under strange sail shall you come home, to find
95 your own house filled with trouble: insolent men
eating your livestock as they court your lady.
Aye, you shall make those men atone in blood!
But after you have dealt out death—in open
combat or by stealth—to all the suitors,
100 go overland on foot, and take an oar,
until one day you come where men have lived
with meat unsalted, never known the sea,
nor seen seagoing ships, with crimson bows
and oars that fledge light hulls for dipping flight.
105 The spot will soon be plain to you, and I
can tell you how: some passerby will say,
"What winnowing fan is that upon your shoulder?"
Halt, and implant your smooth oar in the turf
and make fair sacrifice to Lord Poseidon:
110 a ram, a bull, a great buck boar; turn back,
and carry out pure hekatombs at home
to all wide heaven's lords, the undying gods,
to each in order. Then a seaborne death
soft as this hand of mist will come upon you
115 when you are wearied out with rich old age,
your country folk in blessed peace around you.
And all this shall be just as I foretell.' . . ." **S**

*Odysseus speaks to the shade of his mother. She tells him that Penelope and
Telemachus are still grieving for him and that his father, Laertes, has moved
to the country, where he, too, mourns his son. Odysseus' mother explains that
she died from a broken heart. Odysseus also speaks with the spirits of many
great ladies and men who died, as well as those who were being punished
for their earthly sins. Filled with horror, Odysseus and his crew set sail.*

89–91 kine; beeves: two words for cattle.

**101–102 where men have lived with meat
unsalted:** refers to an inland location
where men do not eat salted (preserved)
meat as sailors do aboard a ship.

S EPIC HERO
An epic hero's fate is often a matter
of great importance to the gods
and to the hero's homeland. In lines
77–117, Odysseus' fate is the subject
of a prophecy by Tiresias, a blind
seer who now dwells among the
dead. A prophecy such as this can
serve as **foreshadowing** in an epic
or other story. Do you think that
Odysseus' fate will unfold exactly as
Tiresias foretells it? Explain why you
think as you do.

**Lines 89–91
ADDITIONAL TEACHING
OPPORTUNITY: ETYMOLOGY**
Remind students that etymology is the study
of the origins and historical development of
words. Explain that there are many word
variations that have become obsolete. For
example, *kine* is a Middle English plural of
cow, and *beeves* is the plural of *beef*.

LITERARY ANALYSIS

S EPIC HERO
Point out that in mythology, Tiresias was
the blind prophet and holy man of the
Greek city of Thebes. He made several
famous predictions and warnings in addition to his words to Odysseus. Tiresias
predicted, for example, that Hercules
would become a great hero. ***Possible
answer:*** *In the* Odyssey, *the predictions
of wise men carry great weight. Tiresias'
predictions are likely to come to pass.*

FOR LESS–PROFICIENT READERS

Text Digests Read aloud the italicized text
digest at the bottom of page 1129. Ask students to summarize what Odysseus learned
about his family during his visit to the underworld. ***Possible answer:*** *Odysseus learned
that this wife, his son, and his father were still
alive but that his mother had died of a broken
heart. He learned that his home is under assault by rude suitors. He also learned that he
will ultimately see his family again and prevail
over those who wish him harm.*

Possible answer: *The depiction of the Sirens as huge birds of prey with women's faces conveys incongruent qualities: beauty and horror, delicacy and strength, allure and repulsiveness. It provides a strong visual image for understanding the power and intensity of their song. Bound to the mast, even the strong-willed Odysseus seems to bend to their will.*

About the Art British artist John William Waterhouse (1849–1917) was the son of a painter. He had a lifelong interest in classical, historical, and literary subjects, including the *Odyssey*. Like other Pre-Raphaelite artists, Waterhouse was fascinated by tragic or powerful *femmes fatales*—"dangerous women"— as evidenced by the painting *Ulysses and the Sirens*.

Lines 4–12
REINFORCE *KEY IDEA*: HERO

Discuss Odysseus learns from Circe about the terrible danger that the Sirens present to any sailor who hears their song. Ask students what they have learned about Odysseus that suggests he will listen to the Sirens' song.
Possible answer: *Odysseus' great curiosity often leads him to accept unnecessary challenges. Just as he chose to meet the Cyclops, so he will choose to hear the Sirens' song.*

BOOK 12:
The Sirens; Scylla and Charybdis

Odysseus and his men return to Circe's island. While the men sleep, Circe takes Odysseus aside to hear about the underworld and to offer advice.

"Then said the Lady Circe:

'So: all those trials are over.

                    Listen with care

to this, now, and a god will arm your mind.
Square in your ship's path are Sirens, crying
5 beauty to bewitch men coasting by;
woe to the innocent who hears that sound!
He will not see his lady nor his children
in joy, crowding about him, home from sea;
the Sirens will sing his mind away
10 on their sweet meadow lolling. There are bones
of dead men rotting in a pile beside them
and flayed skins shrivel around the spot.
                      Steer wide;

keep well to seaward; plug your oarsmen's ears
with beeswax kneaded soft; none of the rest
15 should hear that song.

                    But if you wish to listen,
let the men tie you in the lugger, hand
and foot, back to the mast, lashed to the mast,
so you may hear those harpies' thrilling voices;
shout as you will, begging to be untied,
20 your crew must only twist more line around you
and keep their stroke up, till the singers fade.
What then? One of two courses you may take,
and you yourself must weigh them. I shall not
plan the whole action for you now, but only
25 tell you of both.

This detail from a 19th-century painting shows Odysseus tied to the mast of his ship to protect him from the Sirens' tempting song. Notice that his men have all covered their ears. How does the artist's depiction of the Sirens affect your understanding of the story? Explain.

2–3 In Circe, Odysseus has found a valuable ally. In the next hundred lines, she describes in detail each danger that he and his men will meet on their way home.

5️⃣ **Targeted Passage**

14 kneaded (nĕ'dĭd): squeezed and pressed.

18 those harpies' thrilling voices: the delightful voices of those horrible female creatures.

Detail of *Ulysses and the Sirens* (1891), John William Waterhouse. Oil on canvas, 100 cm × 201.7 cm. National Gallery of Victoria, Melbourne, Australia. Photo © Bridgeman Art Library.

DIFFERENTIATED INSTRUCTION

FOR LESS–PROFICIENT READERS
Review Read the italicized introduction to Book 12 at the top of page 1130. Ask students to recall how Circe had treated Odysseus and his men during their previous stay on her island.
Possible answer: *Circe had turned a platoon of Odysseus' men into swine and attempted to do the same to Odysseus. After that, she held them in a trance for a year. Then she forced Odysseus to go to the underworld to hear Tiresias' prophecy.*

FOR ADVANCED LEARNERS/PRE–AP
Debate Present this topic for discussion: Did the Greeks believe in free will or in predestination? Ask students to base their conclusions on evidence from the *Odyssey*.

Book 12 narrates how Circe advises Odysseus on what he must do to survive the Sirens and Scylla and Charybdis. Odysseus orders his men to put beeswax in their ears, so they can avoid the Sirens' tantalizing song. He listens, tied to the mast. Then Odysseus navigates past Scylla to avoid Charybdis, sacrificing six men. Finally, they come to Thrinacia, where Odysseus' starving men steal Helios' cattle, despite Circe's warning. As a result, all but Odysseus are lost at sea. He drifts to Calypso's island.

READING STRATEGY

■ READING AN EPIC POEM

Remind students to read all side notes to improve their comprehension. Have them use the side notes to answer these questions: In what way is Circe a valuable ally? *(She warns Odysseus of the dangers he and his men will meet on the way.)* How can Odysseus soften the beeswax? *(by kneading it)* What is another name for the Sirens? *(harpies)*

⑤ Targeted Passage [Lines 4–21]

This passage explains the danger of the Sirens and how Odysseus can avoid that danger and listen to their song.

- What happens to sailors who hear the Sirens?

- How can Odysseus protect his men from this danger?

- How can he listen to their song and survive?

Lines 26–70
DISCUSSION PROMPTS

Use these prompts to help students understand the choices that Odysseus must make in order to pass Scylla and Charybdis without disaster:

Connect What is it like to be faced with a "no-win proposition"—where you lose something important no matter what decision you make? *Responses should reflect an understanding that a no-win proposition is unpleasant, stressful, and difficult: nobody likes being faced with a decision that will lead inevitably to loss.*

Analyze Are all the "courses" Circe suggests equal? *Possible answer: No one can pass the Prowling Rocks or Charybdis. Though Scylla will eat some of Odysseus' men, their ship can pass by her.*

Evaluate What course should Odysseus choose? Give your reasons. *Possible answer: Odysseus should pass by Scylla. In a sense, he has no other choice; passing by her is the only way he can continue homeward.*

                                        Ahead are beetling rocks
and dark blue glancing Amphitrite, surging,
roars around them. Prowling Rocks, or Drifters,
the gods in bliss have named them—named them well.
Not even birds can pass them by. . . .

30   A second course
lies between headlands. One is a sharp mountain
piercing the sky, with stormcloud round the peak
dissolving never, not in the brightest summer,
to show heaven's azure there, nor in the fall.
35 No mortal man could scale it, nor so much
as land there, not with twenty hands and feet,
so sheer the cliffs are—as of polished stone.
Midway that height, a cavern full of mist
opens toward Erebus and evening. Skirting
40 this in the lugger, great Odysseus,
your master bowman, shooting from the deck,
would come short of the cavemouth with his shaft;
but that is the den of Scylla, where she yaps
abominably, a newborn whelp's cry,
45 though she is huge and monstrous. God or man,
no one could look on her in joy. Her legs—
and there are twelve—are like great tentacles,
unjointed, and upon her serpent necks
are borne six heads like nightmares of ferocity,
50 with triple serried rows of fangs and deep
gullets of black death. Half her length, she sways
her heads in air, outside her horrid cleft,
hunting the sea around that promontory
for dolphins, dogfish, or what bigger game
55 thundering Amphitrite feeds in thousands.
And no ship's company can claim
to have passed her without loss and grief; she takes,
from every ship, one man for every gullet.

The opposite point seems more a tongue of land
60 you'd touch with a good bowshot, at the narrows.
A great wild fig, a shaggy mass of leaves,
grows on it, and Charybdis lurks below
to swallow down the dark sea tide. Three times
from dawn to dusk she spews it up
65 and sucks it down again three times, a whirling
maelstrom; if you come upon her then
the god who makes earth tremble could not save you.

25 beetling: jutting or overhanging.

26 glancing Amphitrite (ăm'fĭ-trī'tē): sparkling seawater. (Amphitrite is the goddess of the sea and the wife of Poseidon. Here, Circe uses the name to refer to the sea itself.)

31 headlands: points of land jutting out into the sea; promontories.

34 heaven's azure (ăzh'ər): the blue sky.

abominably (ə-bŏm'ə-nə-blē) *adv.* in a hateful way; horribly

43–55 Circe presents a very unpleasant image of Scylla. *To get a better idea of what Odysseus and his crew will be up against, try using this detailed description to either visualize or draw a picture of Scylla.*

66 maelstrom (māl'strəm): a large, violent whirlpool.

DIFFERENTIATED INSTRUCTION

FOR ENGLISH LEARNERS

Task Support To prepare students for completing the task for lines 43–55, help them break down and categorize the description of Scylla: *Sound:* horrible yaps, like those of a newborn animal (lines 43–44); *size:* huge and monstrous (line 45); *appearance:* 12 huge, unjointed legs, like tentacles (lines 46–48), six necks that look like a serpent's (lines 48–49), sharp fangs in triple rows (line 50), deep black throats (lines 50–51); *food:* dolphins, dogfish, or bigger game (lines 54–55).

No, hug the cliff of Scylla, take your ship
through on a racing stroke. Better to mourn
70 six men than lose them all, and the ship, too.'

So her advice ran; but I faced her, saying:

'Only instruct me, goddess, if you will,
how, if possible, can I pass Charybdis,
or fight off Scylla when she raids my crew?'

75 Swiftly that loveliest goddess answered me:

'Must you have battle in your heart forever?
The bloody toil of combat? Old contender,
will you not yield to the immortal gods?
That nightmare cannot die, being eternal
80 evil itself—horror, and pain, and chaos;
there is no fighting her, no power can fight her,
all that avails is flight.

                      Lose headway there
along that rockface while you break out arms,
and she'll swoop over you, I fear, once more,
85 taking one man again for every gullet. ❶
No, no, put all your backs into it, row on;
invoke Blind Force, that bore this scourge of men,
to keep her from a second strike against you.

Then you will coast Thrinacia, the island
90 where Helios' cattle graze, fine herds, and flocks
of goodly sheep. The herds and flocks are seven,
with fifty beasts in each.

                       No lambs are dropped,
or calves, and these fat cattle never die.
Immortal, too, their cowherds are—their shepherds—
95 Phaethusa and Lampetia, sweetly braided
nymphs that divine Neaera bore
to the overlord of high noon, Helios.
These nymphs their gentle mother bred and placed
upon Thrinacia, the distant land,
100 in care of flocks and cattle for their father.

Now give those kine a wide berth, keep your thoughts
intent upon your course for home,
and hard seafaring brings you all to Ithaca.
But if you raid the beeves, I see destruction
105 for ship and crew.

---

82 all . . . flight: all you can do is flee.

❶ EPIC HERO
Summarize the exchange between Odysseus and Circe in lines 68–85. What is Circe's advice to Odysseus? Do you think he will follow her advice? Explain.

87 invoke . . . men: pray to the goddess Blind Force, who gave birth to Scylla.

89 coast: sail along the coast of.

95–96 Phaethusa (fā'ə-thōō'sə); **Lampetia** (lăm-pē'shə); **Neaera** (nē-ē'rə).

101–105 Circe warns Odysseus not to steal Helios' fine cattle because Helios will take revenge.

LITERARY ANALYSIS

❶ EPIC HERO

Possible answer: Circe advises Odysseus to pass by Scylla and accept the loss of six men. She points out that trying to fight the monster will only cost him more men. Odysseus will pass Scylla, but he will not heed her warning about avoiding a fight. In the past, he has turned his back on such sound warnings.

FOR LESS–PROFICIENT READERS
Paraphrasing Homer Have students reread the summary of lines 101–105 in the side column. Then model how to paraphrase lines 101–102: *Stay away from those cattle, and think only about your journey.* Invite volunteers to paraphrase lines 103–105: *And then you will all get back to Ithaca. But if you steal the beef, your ship and crew will be destroyed.*

FOR ENGLISH LEARNERS
Task Support Help students to paraphrase lines 76–88 in preparation for answering the literary analysis question: *Stop thinking about fighting, because you cannot kill that nightmarish monster. Instead, flee by rowing quickly so she cannot strike again.*

LITERARY ANALYSIS

Ⓤ EPIC HERO

Remind students that both Circe and Tiresias offered Odysseus the same warning about Helios: His men and ship will be destroyed if they steal his cattle, and only Odysseus will return to Ithaca.

Possible answer: *Odysseus has some limited power to steer his fate. He can heed the advice himself and can try to influence his men, but he cannot control their actions.*

Rough years then lie between
you and your homecoming, alone and old,
the one survivor, all companions lost.' . . ." Ⓤ

At dawn, Odysseus and his men continue their journey. Odysseus decides to tell the men only of Circe's warnings about the Sirens, whom they will soon encounter. He is fairly sure that they can survive this peril if he keeps their spirits up. Suddenly, the wind stops.

"The crew were on their feet
briskly, to furl the sail, and stow it; then,
110 each in place, they poised the smooth oar blades
and sent the white foam scudding by. I carved
a massive cake of beeswax into bits
and rolled them in my hands until they softened—
no long task, for a burning heat came down
115 from Helios, lord of high noon. Going forward
I carried wax along the line, and laid it
thick on their ears. They tied me up, then, plumb
amidships, back to the mast, lashed to the mast,
and took themselves again to rowing. Soon,
120 as we came smartly within hailing distance,
the two Sirens, noting our fast ship
off their point, made ready, and they sang. . . .

The lovely voices in **ardor** appealing over the water
made me crave to listen, and I tried to say
125 'Untie me!' to the crew, jerking my brows;
but they bent steady to the oars. Then Perimedes
got to his feet, he and Eurylochus,
and passed more line about, to hold me still.
So all rowed on, until the Sirens
130 dropped under the sea rim, and their singing
dwindled away.
My faithful company
rested on their oars now, peeling off
the wax that I had laid thick on their ears;
then set me free.
But scarcely had that island
135 faded in blue air than I saw smoke
and white water, with sound of waves in tumult—
a sound the men heard, and it terrified them.
Oars flew from their hands; the blades went knocking
wild alongside till the ship lost way,
140 with no oarblades to drive her through the water.

Ⓤ EPIC HERO
Reread lines 104–107, and reconsider your thoughts about Tiresias' prophecy. Do you think Odysseus has the power to steer his fate? Explain.

117–118 plumb amidships: exactly in the center of the ship.

ardor (är′dər) *n.* passion

126 Perimedes (pĕr′ĭ-mē′dēz).

134–139 The men panic when they hear the thundering surf.

DIFFERENTIATED INSTRUCTION

FOR LESS–PROFICIENT READERS

Text Digest Have a volunteer read aloud the italicized text at the top of page 1134. Ask students why Odysseus told his men only of Circe's warnings about the Sirens. ***Possible answer:*** *He wanted them to concentrate on getting past the Sirens, not to worry about anything else.*

Well, I walked up and down from bow to stern,
trying to put heart into them, standing over
every oarsman, saying gently,

                                     'Friends,
have we never been in danger before this?
145 More fearsome, is it now, than when the Cyclops
penned us in his cave? What power he had!
Did I not keep my nerve, and use my wits
to find a way out for us?

                              Now I say
by hook or crook this peril too shall be
150 something that we remember.

                          Heads up, lads!
We must obey the orders as I give them.
Get the oarshafts in your hands, and lay back
hard on your benches; hit these breaking seas.
Zeus help us pull away before we founder.
155 You at the tiller, listen, and take in
all that I say—the rudders are your duty;
keep her out of the combers and the smoke;
steer for that headland; watch the drift, or we
fetch up in the smother, and you drown us.'

160 That was all, and it brought them round to action.
But as I sent them on toward Scylla, I
told them nothing, as they could do nothing.
They would have dropped their oars again, in panic,
to roll for cover under the decking. Circe's
165 bidding against arms had slipped my mind,
so I tied on my cuirass and took up
two heavy spears, then made my way along
to the foredeck—thinking to see her first from there,
the monster of the gray rock, harboring
170 torment for my friends. I strained my eyes
upon that cliffside veiled in cloud, but nowhere
could I catch sight of her.

                          And all this time,
in **travail**, sobbing, gaining on the current,
we rowed into the strait—Scylla to port
175 and on our starboard beam Charybdis, dire
gorge of the salt sea tide. By heaven! when she
vomited, all the sea was like a cauldron
seething over intense fire, when the mixture
suddenly heaves and rises. **Ⓥ**

154 founder: sink.

157 combers: breaking waves.

158–159 watch . . . smother: keep the
ship on course, or it will be crushed in
the rough water.

travail (trə-vāl') n. painful effort

176 gorge: throat; gullet.

Ⓥ EPIC HERO
Consider Odysseus' behavior in lines
108–179. Do you think he is a good
leader? Explain your opinion.

Lines 141–164
DISCUSSION PROMPTS
Use these prompts to help students understand how Odysseus leads his crew out of
danger:

Connect Have you ever been in a situation
where it was important to do everything
exactly as you were told? How does that
help you understand the importance of
the crew's obeying Odysseus? *Students'
responses should reflect an understanding of
the importance of following orders in order
to get through a task.*

Analyze On the basis of their actions, do
you think the crew trusts Odysseus? *Possible
answers: Yes, the crew falls into action as
soon as Odysseus explains their orders. No,
Odysseus must withhold the truth from them
in order to keep them from hiding in fear.*

Evaluate Does Odysseus lead effectively by
withholding the truth? *Possible answers:
Yes, he tells his men only what they must
know in order to save the ship and most of
the crew. No, Odysseus should have told
them of their fate and trusted their actions.*

LITERARY ANALYSIS

Ⓥ EPIC HERO

*Possible answer: Odysseus is an excellent
leader. When the men falter in turbulent
waters, Odysseus keeps his head and cajoles
them into going back to their duties. He
uses Circe's information judiciously. He tells
them what they need to know but holds
back unhelpful, disturbing information.
Thus, he acts as a good role model, displaying wisdom, composure, patience, and
bravery.*

FOR ADVANCED LEARNERS/PRE–AP
Characterization Only a few of Odysseus'
shipmates are identified by name. In Book 12,
Odysseus mentions Perimedes and Eurylochus (lines 126–127). Ask students to recall
what we know about these men. Discuss
why the narrative rarely focuses on Odysseus'
shipmates. Ask students to rewrite one adventure from Book 12 from the point of view
of Eurylochus.

REINFORCE *KEY IDEA:* HERO

As Odysseus' ship nears Scylla, he forgets Circe's warning and takes up spears and ties on his cuirass (lines 166–167). Ask students why Odysseus does not attempt to stop the monster when they finally pass Scylla.
Possible answer: *Odysseus must have realized that Circe was right: any effort to fight Scylla would have cost him more men.*

ANALYZE VISUALS

Possible answer: *This painting is not as "realistic" as Waterhouse's* Ulysses and the Sirens. *Waterhouse portrayed two sides of these female monsters—both their beauty and their horror. By contrast, the painting of Scylla is concerned only with the monster's horror. Also, Waterhouse's painting is rich in detail, whereas Allori's fresco lacks the specific details of the clothing, the ship, and the expressions of the subjects.*

About the Art Alessandro Allori (1535–1607) painted this fresco in about 1580, near the end of the Renaissance. It is in the style known as Mannerism. Remind students that Mannerist artists tended to create works that were idealized and refined. Their paintings were often made for rich patrons.

The shot spume
180 soared to the landside heights, and fell like rain.

But when she swallowed the sea water down
we saw the funnel of the maelstrom, heard
the rock bellowing all around, and dark
sand raged on the bottom far below.
185 My men all blanched against the gloom, our eyes
were fixed upon that yawning mouth in fear
of being devoured.
                    Then Scylla made her strike,
whisking six of my best men from the ship.
I happened to glance aft at ship and oarsmen
190 and caught sight of their arms and legs, dangling
high overhead. Voices came down to me
in anguish, calling my name for the last time.

A man surfcasting on a point of rock
for bass or mackerel, whipping his long rod
195 to drop the sinker and the bait far out,
will hook a fish and rip it from the surface
to dangle wriggling through the air:
                                    so these
were borne aloft in spasms toward the cliff.

She ate them as they shrieked there, in her den,
200 in the dire grapple, reaching still for me—
and deathly pity ran me through
at that sight—far the worst I ever suffered,
questing the passes of the strange sea.
                                    We rowed on.
The Rocks were now behind; Charybdis, too,
205 and Scylla dropped astern. . . ."

Odysseus tries to persuade his men to bypass Thrinacia, the island of the sun god, Helios, but they insist on landing. Driven by hunger, they ignore Odysseus' warning not to feast on Helios' cattle. This disobedience angers the sun god, who threatens to stop shining if payment is not made for the loss of his cattle. To appease Helios, Zeus sends down a thunderbolt to sink Odysseus' ship. Odysseus alone survives. He eventually drifts to Ogygia, the home of Calypso, who keeps him on her island for seven years. With this episode, Odysseus ends the telling of his tale to King Alcinous.

179 **shot spume:** flying foam.

185 **blanched:** became pale.

189 **aft:** toward the rear of the ship.

⑥ **Targeted Passage**

198 **borne aloft in spasms:** lifted high while struggling violently.

200 **grapple:** grasp.

ANALYZE VISUALS
Apart from depicting a different narrative moment, how does this 16th-century painting differ from the one on page 1131? Be specific in describing the differences in style and mood.

DIFFERENTIATED INSTRUCTION

FOR LESS–PROFICIENT READERS

⑥ **Targeted Passage [Lines 193–198]**

In this passage, a simile illustrates the powerlessness of the men caught in Scylla's grasp.

- To what does Homer compare the men hanging in the air?

- How does the image express their hopelessness?

- Fishing is an ordinary activity. How does this add to the horror of the simile?

Text Digests Read aloud the italicized text digest at the bottom of page 1136. Ask students to explain what happened to Odysseus after leaving Scylla and Charybdis behind.
Possible answer: *Odysseus' starving men feasted on Helios' cattle. As punishment, Zeus sank their ship. Only Odysseus lived, drifting to Calypso's island.*

Scylla and Charybdis from the *Ulysses Cycle* (1580), Alessandro Allori. Fresco. Banca Toscana (Palazzo Salviati), Florence. Photo © Erich Lessing/Art Resource, New York.

SELECTION WRAP-UP

PREDICT Ask students to predict what will happen to Odysseus after he leaves Alcinous. Have them explain their reasoning.

⭐ **CRITIQUE** Ask students if they think Odysseus is a believable character. Have them give specific examples to support their opinions.

READING FLUENCY

Distribute the copy masters and have students work in pairs or in groups to practice fluency.

🅡 **RESOURCE MANAGER—Copy Master**
  Reading Fluency p. 38

Practice and Apply

After Reading

For additional support of post-reading questions, use these copy masters:

RESOURCE MANAGER—Copy Masters
Reading Check p. 36 (to check understanding of the selection)
Epic Hero p. 29 (for practice of literary analysis standards focus)
Question Support p. 37 (After Reading questions adapted for English learners and less-proficient readers)

For additional questions, see page 21.

For additional exercises to challenge students, see

ⓘ Power Thinking at **ClassZone.com**

ANSWERS

Comprehension

1. *Odysseus longs for his home and family.*

2. *Odysseus and his men blind Polyphemus and escape by hiding under his sheep.*

3. *They turn into pigs.*

4. *Tiresias predicts that Odysseus will lose his crew and ship.*

5. *Odysseus survives the Sirens by blocking his men's ears with beeswax; he avoids Charybdis and sacrifices six men to pass Scylla.*

Literary Analysis
Possible answers:

6. ● **STANDARDS FOCUS** *Epic Hero*
Strengths: guile, determination, bravery, leadership, self-sacrifice; weaknesses: pride, stubbornness, unwillingness to listen to advice. Odysseus' traits seem fitting for an epic hero: his weaknesses represent his strengths taken too far.

7. *"that man skilled in all ways of contending" (Book 1, line 2), aggressive, brave; "the wanderer" (Book 1, line 3), curiosity; "son of Laertes, versatile Odysseus" (Book 5, line 69), multitalented, family pride; "the strategist" (Book 5, line 80), clever; "raider of cities" (Book 9, line 418), ruthless, warlike; "master mariner and soldier" (Book 11, line 33), multitalented; "master of land ways and sea ways" (Book 11, line 69), multitalented.*

8. *Odysseus' pride and anger cause him to taunt Polyphemus. He cares because Polyphemus killed his men and insulted him.*

Comprehension

1. **Recall** Why does Odysseus want to leave Calypso and her island?

2. **Recall** How does Odysseus escape from Polyphemus?

3. **Recall** What happens to Eurylochus' men after they drink Circe's wine?

4. **Recall** What does Tiresias predict will happen if Odysseus raids the herds of Helios?

5. **Summarize** How does Odysseus survive the dangers posed by the Sirens, Scylla, and Charybdis?

Literary Analysis

6. **Analyze Epic Hero** Create a two-column chart to analyze Odysseus' strengths and weaknesses. To what extent do the traits in each column seem fitting for an epic hero? Explain.

Strengths	Weaknesses
shows loyalty in his desire to reach home	pride

7. **Analyze Epithets** Identify at least five epithets used to describe Odysseus in Part 1. For each epithet, explain what it tells you about his **character.**

8. **Understand Character Motivation** After Odysseus escapes from Polyphemus, he makes sure that Polyphemus knows who outwitted him. Why does he care? What are the consequences of Odysseus' behavior?

9. **Interpret Epic Simile** Reread the epic simile on page 1136, lines 193–198, which describes the men being caught by Scylla. Explain what two items are being compared. What does the comparison help to emphasize?

10. **Interpret Allusions** In the opening lines of Book 1, the poet calls upon Muse, a daughter of Zeus often credited with inspiration. Why would he open the epic in this way? What does this allusion tell you about him as a poet?

11. **Examine Theme** One theme of the adventures described in Part 1 is that a hero must rely on clever deceit, or guile, to survive. Explain how this theme is conveyed. Can you identify any other themes in Part 1?

Literary Criticism

12. **Critical Interpretations** In discussing Homer's use of epic similes, the critic Eva Brann contends that "similes do much the same work in Homeric epic as do the gods, who also beautify and magnify human existence." Think about how the gods interact with humans in the *Odyssey*. Do you agree that they "beautify and magnify" human existence? Then consider the epic similes you have encountered so far; how might they be seen to do the same? Explain whether or not you think Brann is making a worthwhile comparison.

The consequences: the continued wrath of Poseidon.

9. *The two items being compared are the hooking of a fish by a fisherman and the capturing of Odysseus' trapped men by Scylla. The comparison emphasizes the size and strength of Scylla, the powerlessness of the men, and the men's hopelessness.*

10. *Calling upon Muse emphasizes the seriousness of the task. The allusion also tells us that Homer is respectful of the gods.*

11. *Odysseus uses guile in his encounters with the Cyclops, Circe, and the Sirens. Other* themes: *be careful of whom you trust; treat guests honorably; do not enrage the gods.*

Literary Criticism
Possible answer:

12. *The comparison is apt: the concern and involvement of the gods adds significance to the trials and actions of Odysseus. So, too, the similes uplift the deeds and trials of the mortals and make them resonate.*

Vocabulary in Context

VOCABULARY PRACTICE

Decide whether the words in each pair are synonyms or antonyms.

1. harried/calmed
2. appalled/dismayed
3. profusion/shortage
4. ardor/indifference
5. assuage/soothe
6. adversary/friend

7. ponderous/awkward
8. travail/relaxation
9. beguiling/entrancing
10. foreboding/prediction
11. abominably/atrociously
12. meditation/contemplation

WORD LIST
abominably
adversary
appalled
ardor
assuage
beguiling
foreboding
harried
meditation
ponderous
profusion
travail

VOCABULARY IN WRITING

Write a paragraph describing one of the tricks Odysseus uses to escape from danger. Use four or more vocabulary words. Here is a sample beginning.

> **EXAMPLE SENTENCE**
>
> *Odysseus had been warned about the Sirens' **beguiling** him.*

VOCABULARY STRATEGY: WORDS WITH THE PREFIX *fore-*

The prefix *fore-*, which means "earlier," "in front of," or "beforehand," is used in forming numerous English words. In *foreboding*, it is combined with the verb *bode*, "to give signs of something." *Fore-* is also combined with many common words, as in *forehead* and *foretell*. Recognizing this prefix when it appears in words can help you determine their meanings.

PRACTICE Choose a word from the box to complete each sentence. Refer to a dictionary if you need help.

1. Our _____ came to this land looking for freedom.
2. Diandra tried to _____ Jack before he walked right into the trap.
3. In the _____ of the painting was a large house; behind the house was a barn.
4. Casual comments early in a story often _____ coming events.
5. The tennis star's strong _____ made her a formidable opponent.
6. To _____ a quick vote on the issue, the committee voted to study it further.
7. In what way was the horse and buggy the _____ of the automobile?

WORDS WITH *fore-*
forefathers
foreground
forehand
forerunner
foreshadow
forestall
forewarn

VOCABULARY PRACTICE
For more practice, go to the **Vocabulary Center** at **ClassZone.com**.

DIFFERENTIATED INSTRUCTION

FOR ENGLISH LEARNERS

Vocabulary Have partners write sentences with six words from the word list. Then call out each word and ask volunteers to read their sentences.

FOR ADVANCED LEARNERS/PRE–AP

Vocabulary Practice Challenge Have students write a description of one of Odysseus' adversaries, using as many of the words from the word list as possible.

ANSWERS

Vocabulary in Context

VOCABULARY PRACTICE

1. *antonyms*
2. *synonyms*
3. *antonyms*
4. *antonyms*
5. *synonyms*
6. *antonyms*

7. *synonyms*
8. *antonyms*
9. *synonyms*
10. *synonyms*
11. *synonyms*
12. *synonyms*

R RESOURCE MANAGER—Copy Master
Vocabulary Practice p. 34

VOCABULARY IN WRITING

Ask volunteers to recall the tricks that Odysseus played on Polyphemus, Circe, and the Sirens. Suggest that they pick words that relate to one of these tricks. As they write, they should use those words.

VOCABULARY STRATEGY: WORDS WITH THE PREFIX *fore-* (also an EL language objective)

Review the words in the box. Urge students to use what they know about each root word to come up with a definition for each word.

Possible answers:

1. *forefathers*
2. *forewarn*
3. *foreground*
4. *foreshadow*

5. *forehand*
6. *forestall*
7. *forerunner*

R RESOURCE MANAGER—Copy Master
Vocabulary Strategy p. 35

i Vocabulary Center at **ClassZone.com**
Additional Vocabulary Activities

Assess and Reteach

Assess

R RESOURCE MANAGER—Copy Masters
Selection Test A pp. 39–40
Selection Test B/C pp. 41–42
Test Generator CD

Reteach

S STANDARDS LESSON FILE
Literature Lessons 17, 28, 29, 32, 35
Vocabulary Lesson 2

Focus and Motivate

OBJECTIVES

Literary Analysis
- explore the key idea of a **homecoming**
- read and analyze an epic poem
- identify, analyze, and evaluate characteristics and features of an epic poem

Reading
- use strategies for reading an epic poem
- summarizing

Vocabulary
- build vocabulary for reading and writing
- use words with the Latin root *solus (also an EL language objective)*

Grammar and Writing
- use figurative language
- use writing to analyze literature

SUMMARY

Books 16–23 When Odysseus returns home, Athena disguises him as a beggar to help him surprise Penelope's suitors. Tired from her long ordeal, Penelope proposes to marry the winner of an archery contest. Odysseus, still in disguise, wins the contest and kills the evil suitors. He must pass one last test: to prove his identity to Penelope.

How does it feel to come HOME *again?*

Read the question. To lead into the *KEY IDEA,* have students look at the picture on page 1140. What details convey the intensity of the moment? What emotions do the people project? How can you tell this is a **homecoming?** Then have students complete the *QUICKWRITE.*

Selection Resources

The Homecoming
from the **Odyssey**

Epic Poem by Homer

Translated by Robert Fitzgerald

How does it feel to come HOME *again?*

KEY IDEA If you spend enough time at any airport or bus station, you're bound to witness an emotional scene. A long-awaited **homecoming** can touch us more deeply than almost anything. Imagine a traveler who's been away for years, whose family thought he might never return. What kind of scene might you expect at his homecoming?

QUICKWRITE Recall a time when you or someone you know returned home after some time away. Write a brief description of the scene, and explain the emotions that went along with it.

1140

 **RESOURCE MANAGER UNIT 11**

Plan and Teach pp. 43–50

Literary Analysis
Summary pp. 51, 52†*, 53‡*, 54‡*
Characteristics of an Epic
   pp. 55, 56†*
Question Support p. 63*

Reading
Summarizing pp. 57, 58†*
Reading Check p. 62

Vocabulary
Study p. 59*
Practice p. 60
Strategy p. 61

Grammar and Writing
Add Descriptive Details p. 64

Assessment
Selection Tests A, B/C pp. 65*, 67*
 Test Generator CD

 BEST PRACTICES TOOLKIT

Differentiated Instruction
   pp. 31–38*

Scaffolding Instruction
   pp. 43–46*

Graphic Organizers/Strategies
Sequence Chain • Character Traits and Textual Evidence

Reading Support
 Audio Anthology CD*

Technology
 Literature and Vocabulary Centers at **ClassZone.com**
 Write*Smart* CD

---

* Resources for Differentiation   † Also in Spanish   ‡ In Haitian Creole and Vietnamese

LITERARY ANALYSIS: CHARACTERISTICS OF AN EPIC

In the simplest terms, an epic is a long adventure story. An epic **plot** spans many years and involves a long journey. Often, the fate of an entire nation is at stake. An epic **setting** spans great distances and foreign lands. Epic **themes** reflect timeless concerns, such as courage, honor, life, and death.

Epics also contain **archetypes,** or patterns found in works across different cultures and time periods. As explained in Part 1, the epic hero is an archetype. So is the notion of a heroic journey. Other archetypes are also found in the *Odyssey*.

- intervention by gods
- descent into the underworld
- floods and storms
- heroic battles against monsters

As you read the second part of the *Odyssey*, look for these and other archetypes. Consider where else you might have encountered them in literature, art, or film.

READING STRATEGY: SUMMARIZING

Writing a **plot summary**—a brief retelling of a story—is a good way to make sure you're following the events of a narrative. An epic consists of many episodes, each with its own set of characters, conflicts, and resolution. As you read, record information that will help you summarize each episode.

Episode: *Father and Son*	
Characters: *Odysseus, Eumaeus*	**Setting:** *Odysseus' homeland of Ithaca*
Conflict:	**Resolution:**

▲ VOCABULARY IN CONTEXT

Replace the words in bold with synonyms from the word list.

WORD LIST	adversity	desolation	revulsion
	aloof	implacable	tremulous
	commandeer	restitution	
	contemptible	revelry	

1. It's **disgusting** to be **shaky** in the face of **hardship.**
2. He felt an **unforgiving hatred** for his captors.
3. Don't act **distant;** forget **sorrow** and join the **celebration!**
4. He could **seize** enemy ships as **repayment** for wrongs.

Overview

Book 16: Father and Son Sent safely on his way by King Alcinous, Odysseus reaches Ithaca. The goddess Athena disguises him as an old man so that he may surprise the evil suitors who are courting his wife, Penelope. Odysseus greets Eumaeus, his faithful swineherd, and Telemachus, his own son, returned home after many years abroad.

Book 17: The Beggar and the Manor Disguised as a beggar, Odysseus returns to his home.

Book 21: The Test of the Bow Not recognizing the beggar as her husband, and weary from grief and waiting, Penelope proposes an archery contest to the suitors, with marriage to her as the prize. Still disguised as an old man, Odysseus beats them all in the contest.

Book 22: Death in the Great Hall With Telemachus and Eumaeus at his side, Odysseus sheds his disguise and does battle with the suitors, showing them no mercy.

Book 23: The Trunk of the Olive Tree Hardened by years of waiting, Penelope is not convinced that this man is really her husband. She tests him, playing a trick that only Odysseus would recognize. Odysseus passes the test, and husband and wife are reunited.

Penelope weaving at her loom.

THE HOMECOMING **1141**

Teach

STANDARDS FOCUS

LITERARY ANALYSIS

● CHARACTERISTICS OF AN EPIC

Ask students to identify specific examples of archetypes from Part 1. ***Possible answer: Part 1 is a heroic journey. Interventions: Athena and Zeus on Odysseus' behalf; Poseidon against. Descent into the underworld: to see Tiresias. Storms: bad winds escape from Aeolus' bag; Zeus sends storms after the men eat Helios' cattle. Monsters: Cyclops, Sirens, Scylla***

CHECK UNDERSTANDING Have students list examples of archetypes from literature, art, or film.

READING STRATEGY

■ SUMMARIZING

Have students review lines 130–190 in Book 9 "The Wanderings of Odysseus" and fill out a chart like the one shown on the student page.

CHECK UNDERSTANDING Have students summarize the *Overview* on this page in three or four sentences.

R RESOURCE MANAGER—Copy Master
Summarizing p. 57 (for student use while reading the selection)

VOCABULARY SKILL

▲ VOCABULARY IN CONTEXT

DIAGNOSE WORD KNOWLEDGE To determine preteaching needs, have all students complete Vocabulary in Context. Check students' definitions against those on the selection pages. ***Possible answers: 1.*** *contemptible, tremulous, adversity;* ***2.*** *implacable, revulsion;* ***3.*** *aloof, desolation, revelry;* ***4.*** *commandeer, restitution*

PRETEACH VOCABULARY Use the Vocabulary Study copy master to help students predict meanings for each boldfaced word in the copy master.

1. Read item 1 aloud, emphasizing *adversity.*
2. Point out that "survive" and "so much hardship" give clues to the word's meaning.
3. Have students try to figure out what the word means.
4. Repeat the procedure for items 2–10.

R RESOURCE MANAGER—Copy Master
Vocabulary Study p. 59

For general guidelines on differentiating vocabulary instruction and for alternative vocabulary activities for students not needing vocabulary preteaching, see

 BEST PRACTICES TOOLKIT
Scaffolding Vocabulary Instruction pp. 43–46

ⓘ Vocabulary Center at **ClassZone.com**

REINFORCE *KEY IDEA:* HOMECOMING

Discuss Point out that Odysseus has been gone from his home for 20 years. What changes does Odysseus find on his **homecoming?** *Possible answer: All of the people from his former life have grown older. His son is now a tall man. Furthermore, Ithaca has changed to the extent that Odysseus does not even recognize his island (text digest).*

ANALYZE VISUALS

Possible answer: The bold colors and out-stretched arms of Athena capture the urgency of Athena's proclamation as she warns Telemachus of the suitors' murderous plot.

About the Art One of the most significant artists of the 20th century, Marc Chagall (1887–1985) worked in painting, sculpture, ceramics, and stained glass. Born in Russia to a deeply religious Jewish family, Chagall later became a citizen of France. Chagall's distinctive use of color and form blends expressionism, surrealism, and cubism. In addition to his series of lithographs from the *Odyssey,* he created many prints illustrating biblical works and other literary classics.

PART TWO: THE HOMECOMING

BOOK 16:
Father and Son

In Books 13–15, King Alcinous and his friends send Odysseus on his way home. Odysseus sleeps while the rowers bring him to Ithaca. When he awakens, he fails to recognize his homeland until Athena appears and tells him that he is indeed home. She disguises him as an old man, so that he can surprise the suitors, and then urges him to visit his faithful swineherd, Eumaeus. The swineherd welcomes the disguised Odysseus and tells him about what has been happening in Odysseus' home. Athena goes to Telemachus and tells him to return home. She warns him of the suitors' plot to kill him and advises him to stay with the swineherd for a night. Telemachus does as she bids.

But there were two men in the mountain hut—
Odysseus and the swineherd. At first light
blowing their fire up, they cooked their breakfast
and sent their lads out, driving herds to root
5 in the tall timber.
               When Telemachus came,
the wolvish troop of watchdogs only fawned on him
as he advanced. Odysseus heard them go
and heard the light crunch of a man's footfall—
at which he turned quickly to say:
                                 "Eumaeus,
10 here is one of your crew come back, or maybe
another friend: the dogs are out there snuffling
belly down; not one has even growled.
I can hear footsteps—"
                              But before he finished
his tall son stood at the door.

ANALYZE VISUALS
Review the information given in the summary at the top of this page. What do you think Marc Chagall wanted to capture in this painting?

Athene and Telemach, from *Odyssey II* (1975), Marc Chagall. Lithograph on Arches paper. 16.9″ × 13″. Photograph by George R. Staley. © 2007 Artists Rights Society (ARS), New York.

DIFFERENTIATED INSTRUCTION

FOR LESS–PROFICIENT READERS
Preview Read through the italicized synopsis of Books 13–15 at the top of the page to give students a clear idea of the intervening plot. Help them organize the plot events in a Sequence Chain.

BEST PRACTICES TOOLKIT—Transparency
Sequence Chain p. B21

Alcinous gets Odysseus home.

↓

Athena disguises Odysseus as an old man.

↓

Athena warns Telemachus of danger.

Get Into the Book

SUMMARY

Book 16 begins when Odysseus comes to the mountain hut of his swineherd, Eumaeus. Telemachus arrives and they share a meal. After the swineherd leaves to tell Penelope that her son is safe, Odysseus reveals his identity to Telemachus. A tearful reunion ensues.

BACKGROUND

Home and Family A palace like the one belonging to Odysseus was known as a *megaron* and stood in the center of town. The chief held court in a large chamber with a circular hearth, and retainers slept in a vestibule outside. Husbands and wives often lived in separate chambers within the home and engaged in separate activities. For example, a husband might arrange a party for his male friends from which wives and daughters were excluded. Children stayed in the women's chambers with their mothers. At an appropriate age, boys moved out of the women's chambers. They attended school while girls stayed home to learn how to cook, to weave, and to care for children.

FOR LESS–PROFICIENT READERS

Minor Characters Refer students to the character list on page 1091 and have them preview the characters whom they will be meeting in Books 16–23. Ask students whether they think Athena is an apt ally for Odysseus. Why or why not? *Possible answer: Athena, the goddess of war, wisdom, and cleverness, personifies the qualities that we associate with Odysseus: aggressiveness, astuteness, and cunning.*

FOR ADVANCED LEARNERS/PRE–AP

Irony Odysseus returns to Ithaca after 20 years. Have students discuss how the passage of time presents many opportunities for irony.

15 rose in surprise, letting a bowl and jug
   tumble from his fingers. Going forward,
   he kissed the young man's head, his shining eyes
   and both hands, while his own tears brimmed and fell.
   Think of a man whose dear and only son,
20 born to him in exile, reared with labor,
   has lived ten years abroad and now returns:
   how would that man embrace his son! Just so
   the herdsman clapped his arms around Telemachus **Ⓐ**
   and covered him with kisses—for he knew
25 the lad had got away from death. He said:

   "Light of my days, Telemachus,
   you made it back! When you took ship for Pylos
   I never thought to see you here again.
   Come in, dear child, and let me feast my eyes;
30 here you are, home from distant places! **Ⓑ**
   How rarely anyway, you visit us,
   your own men, and your own woods and pastures!
   Always in the town, a man would think
   you loved the suitors' company, those dogs!"

35 Telemachus with his clear candor said:

   "I am with you, Uncle. See now, I have come
   because I wanted to see you first, to hear from you
   if Mother stayed at home—or is she married
   off to someone and Odysseus' bed
40 left empty for some gloomy spider's weaving?"

   Gently the forester replied to this:

   "At home indeed your mother is, poor lady,
   still in the women's hall. Her nights and days
   are wearied out with grieving."

                                    Stepping back
45 he took the bronze-shod lance, and the young prince
   entered the cabin over the worn door stone.
   Odysseus moved aside, yielding his couch,
   but from across the room Telemachus checked him:

   "Friend, sit down; we'll find another chair
50 in our own hut. Here is the man to make one!"

Ⓐ EPIC
Reread lines 19–23. What **theme** is being developed in this **epic simile**?

27 when you took ship for Pylos: Ten years earlier, Telemachus went to Pylos (pī'läs') in search of knowledge about Odysseus' whereabouts.

Ⓑ EPIC
Reread lines 26–30. How do these lines indicate an epic **setting**?

① Targeted Passage

LITERARY ANALYSIS

Ⓐ EPIC

Possible answer: The simile compares Eumaeus' reunion with Telemachus to a father meeting with his only son after ten years' absence. The simile explains Eumaeus' relationship with Telemachus: he had been like a father to the boy. It develops the theme that family relationships are deep and enduring. It also prepares us for Odysseus' reunion with his son.

LITERARY ANALYSIS

Ⓑ EPIC

Possible answer: These lines indicate a journey to strange and distant lands—an epic setting. They suggest that Telemachus has been engaged in his own epic voyage during his father's absence and that he shares the heroic traits of his father.

Extend the Discussion What do these lines suggest about Telemachus' character?

DIFFERENTIATED INSTRUCTION

FOR LESS–PROFICIENT READERS

In combination with the *Audio Anthology CD*, use one or more Targeted Passages (pp. 1144, 1150, 1158, 1162, 1165) to ensure that students focus on key story events, concepts, and skills. Targeted Passages are also good for English learners.

① Targeted Passage [Lines 26–50]

This passage introduces Telemachus and develops the character of Eumaeus.

- What words does the narrator use to describe Telemachus?

- How does Telemachus treat Eumaeus? How does he treat Odysseus? What does this tell us about him?

- Why might Odysseus and Penelope have chosen a swineherd to help raise their son?

The swineherd, when the quiet man sank down,
built a new pile of evergreens and fleeces—
a couch for the dear son of great Odysseus—
then gave them trenchers of good meat, left over
55 from the roast pork of yesterday, and heaped up
willow baskets full of bread, and mixed
an ivy bowl of honey-hearted wine.
Then he in turn sat down, facing Odysseus,
their hands went out upon the meat and drink
60 as they fell to, ridding themselves of hunger. . . .

*Telemachus sends the swineherd to let his mother know he has returned safely.
Athena appears and urges Odysseus to let Telemachus know who he really is.*

                                    Saying no more,
she tipped her golden wand upon the man,
making his cloak pure white and the knit tunic
fresh around him. Lithe and young she made him,
65 ruddy with sun, his jawline clean, the beard
no longer grew upon his chin. And she
withdrew when she had done.

Detail of *Goddess Athena Disguises Ulysses as Beggar* (18th century), Giuseppe
Bottani. Civiche Racc d'Arte, Pavia, Italy. Photo © Dagli Orti /The Art Archive.

DISCUSSION PROMPTS
Use these prompts to help students understand the function of the dinner scene:

Connect Have you ever shared a meal during which you knew something the others had yet to find out? How does this help you understand Odysseus' situation? *Responses should reflect an understanding of how it feels to keep a secret from others.*

Analyze What is ironic about this scene? What effect does the irony have? ***Possible answer:*** *Odysseus is eating with his son for the first time in 20 years. Telemachus treats Eumaeus like a father, while his real father is a stranger. Only Odysseus knows the truth. The irony increases the suspense.*

Synthesize How does this meal compare with other important meals in the* Odyssey*? ***Possible answer:*** *Earlier meals—with the Lotus Eaters, with Circe, with the Cyclops— were often violent or suspenseful, while this one is quiet. Like the other meals, this one marks a point where Odysseus must make decisions and take action. If he hopes to regain his home and family, it must be the right decision.*

ANALYZE VISUALS

About the Art Italian Baroque master Giuseppe Bottani (1717–1784) is known for delicate brushwork and bright colors. He produced many religious and secular works. Ask students to compare this picture of Athena with the other 18th-century depiction on page 1089. ***Possible answer:*** *Both works show Athena in classical attire. Bottani's work is looser and more vibrant than the posed figures on the frieze. It also depicts a specific scene from the* Odyssey *in an elaborate and beautiful setting.*

FOR ENGLISH LEARNERS

Concept Support To make sure students understand the extended scene with Eumaeus, Odysseus, and Telemachus (lines 1–60), list the events: 1. Odysseus goes to Eumaeus' mountain home; 2. Athena sends Telemachus to Eumaeus' home; 3. Odysseus thinks Telemachus' footsteps are those of one of Eumaeus' men; 4. Eumaeus greets Telemachus like a long-lost son; 5. Telemachus asks about his mother; 6. Eumaeus says she is waiting for Odysseus; 7. Telemachus enters, Odysseus moves, and Telemachus stops him; 8. Eumaeus makes a couch for Telemachus; 9. They all sit down to a meal.

ANALYZE VISUALS

About the Art The mosaic of Odysseus and Telemachus is from first-century A.D. Rome. Romans used mosaics to decorate their walls and floors. Roman artists often copied the subject matter and techniques of painting in their mosaics. *Possible answer: The tiles are clustered in similar ways for the two men, highlighting similarities in facial features, coloring, and size. The images are flat and not realistic, but the placement and appearance of the figures make them look like father and son.*

Then Lord Odysseus ●
reappeared—and his son was thunderstruck.
Fear in his eyes, he looked down and away
70 as though it were a god, and whispered:

                    "Stranger,

you are no longer what you were just now!
Your cloak is new; even your skin! You are
one of the gods who rule the sweep of heaven!
Be kind to us, we'll make you fair oblation
75 and gifts of hammered gold. Have mercy on us!"

The noble and enduring man replied:

"No god. Why take me for a god? No, no.
I am that father whom your boyhood lacked
and suffered pain for lack of. I am he."

80 Held back too long, the tears ran down his cheeks
as he embraced his son.

● EPIC
What supernatural event is described in lines 61–67?

74 oblation: sacrifice

ANALYZE VISUALS
This detail of an ancient Roman mosaic shows Odysseus (Ulysses) and Telemachus. How does the technique of clustering colored tiles together affect the kind of image that can be created? Be specific.

Ulysses and His Son Telemachus (A.D. first century). Mosaic.
Kunsthistorisches Museum, Vienna. © Erich Lessing/Art Resource, New York.

DIFFERENTIATED INSTRUCTION

FOR ADVANCED LEARNERS/PRE–AP
Analyze Ask students how Odysseus shows himself to be "noble and enduring" (line 76) in his first conversation with Telemachus. How is your understanding of his character deepened by this interaction?

FOR LESS–PROFICIENT READERS
Concept Support Help students recall these terms related to the elements of plot: *conflict,* "a struggle between opposing forces, either internal or external"; *resolution,* "the final outcome of events and conflicts and tying up of loose ends."

Only Telemachus,
uncomprehending, wild
with incredulity, cried out:

"You cannot
be my father Odysseus! Meddling spirits
85 conceived this trick to twist the knife in me!
No man of woman born could work these wonders
by his own craft, unless a god came into it
with ease to turn him young or old at will.
I swear you were in rags and old,
90 and here you stand like one of the immortals!" **D**

Odysseus brought his ranging mind to bear
and said:

"This is not princely, to be swept
away by wonder at your father's presence.
No other Odysseus will ever come,
95 for he and I are one, the same; his bitter
fortune and his wanderings are mine.
Twenty years gone, and I am back again
on my own island. . . ."

Then, throwing
100 his arms around this marvel of a father
Telemachus began to weep. Salt tears
rose from the wells of longing in both men,
and cries burst from both as keen and fluttering
as those of the great taloned hawk,
105 whose nestlings farmers take before they fly.
So helplessly they cried, pouring out tears,
and might have gone on weeping so till sundown. . . . **E**

*Telemachus lets Odysseus know that they face more than 100 suitors. Odysseus
tells Telemachus to return home. He will follow—still disguised as an old man—
and Telemachus must pretend not to know him. He must also lock away
Odysseus' weapons and armor.*

D EPIC
Reread lines 61–90. What central
conflict is beginning to find
resolution in this scene? What
elements indicate the importance of
this moment?

91 brought his ranging mind to bear:
took control of his wandering thoughts.

E EPIC
Reread lines 99–107. What striking
character trait is emphasized in both
Odysseus and Telemachus? Why is
this unusual?

D EPIC

*Possible answer: The scene between
Odysseus and Telemachus begins to resolve
Odysseus' long struggle to be reunited with
his family and to return to his own home.
The supernatural elements elevate the
moment, infusing it with a mysterious,
fateful quality.*

E EPIC

*Possible answer: The emotional depth of
both characters is striking. Their feelings
of longing and loss are emphasized in this
passage. Such an open display of emotion
is unusual for a hero and his son. Until
now, Odysseus has kept these feelings
at bay.*

If students need help . . . Have them fill
out a Character Traits and Textual Evidence
chart for either character.

Character Trait: Emotional	
Quote (line 101): "Telemachus began to weep."	Explanation: He is very happy to see his father.
Quote (line 102): "wells of longing"	Explanation: The men have wanted to see each other for a very long time.

BEST PRACTICES TOOLKIT—Transparency
Character Traits and Textual Evidence
p. D6

FOR LESS–PROFICIENT READERS

Text Digest Read aloud the text digest
that follows line 107 to make sure students
understand how Odysseus brings Telemachus
into his plan. Ask them why Odysseus told
Telemachus to pretend not to know him and
to lock away the weapons. *Possible answer:
Odysseus doesn't want the suitors to find out
about his arrival so that he can keep the advantage of surprise. If the weapons and armor
are locked away, the suitors won't have access
to them.*

FOR ENGLISH LEARNERS

Concept Support To help students understand Odysseus' and Telemachus' behavior
when they are reunited, ask students to focus
on the extended simile in lines 103–107. Ask
them what their sobs are compared to here.
*Possible answer: Their sobs are compared to
the cries of a helpless hawk whose nestlings
are taken by farmers before the young hawks
can fly.*

ANALYZE VISUALS

Possible answer: Both pieces use a polished coppery color on velvety black for a rich, elegant effect. Both pieces show the flow of the clothing. Both depict a scene from Odysseus' homecoming. The modern image is neoclassical, employing the style of ancient Greece for more modern purposes: Odysseus is meditative and emotional. The black background heightens the sadness of the moment, and the copper color visually links the two figures and reinforces their emotional tie. The late-19th-century artist illustrated a quiet, nostalgic scene, whereas the urn painter depicted a violent one.

Lines 18–27
REINFORCE *KEY IDEA:* HOMECOMING

Discuss How did Odysseus feel about seeing his old dog? Why didn't he let Eumaeus know? *Possible answer: Odysseus felt sad and nostalgic seeing this once vibrant puppy, now so old and badly treated. He couldn't tell Eumaeus because he feared that the swineherd might give away his secret, intentionally or inadvertently.*

BOOK 17:
The Beggar at the Manor

Telemachus returns home, and Odysseus and the swineherd soon follow. Odysseus is still diguised as a beggar.

While he spoke

an old hound, lying near, pricked up his ears
and lifted up his muzzle. This was Argos,
trained as a puppy by Odysseus,
5 but never taken on a hunt before
his master sailed for Troy. The young men, afterward,
hunted wild goats with him, and hare, and deer,
but he had grown old in his master's absence.
Treated as rubbish now, he lay at last
10 upon a mass of dung before the gates—
manure of mules and cows, piled there until
fieldhands could spread it on the king's estate.
Abandoned there, and half destroyed with flies,
old Argos lay.

But when he knew he heard

15 Odysseus' voice nearby, he did his best
to wag his tail, nose down, with flattened ears,
having no strength to move nearer his master.
And the man looked away,
wiping a salt tear from his cheek; but he
20 hid this from Eumaeus. Then he said:

"I marvel that they leave this hound to lie
here on the dung pile;
he would have been a fine dog, from the look of him,
though I can't say as to his power and speed
25 when he was young. You find the same good build
in house dogs, table dogs landowners keep
all for style."

And you replied, Eumaeus:

"A hunter owned him—but the man is dead
in some far place. If this old hound could show

ANALYZE VISUALS
This illustration of Odysseus and his dog comes from the late 19th or early 20th century. Compare it with the scene depicted on the clay urn shown on page 1093. What elements do the two pieces have in common?

DIFFERENTIATED INSTRUCTION

FOR LESS–PROFICIENT READERS
Preview Read aloud the italicized synopsis at the top of the page to give students a clear idea of the intervening plot. To check their comprehension, ask them where Telemachus, Odysseus, and Eumaeus are at the start of Book 17. *Possible answer: back at Odysseus' home in Ithaca*

Ulysses and His Dog (about 1900). © Bettman/Corbis.

30   the form he had when Lord Odysseus left him,
  going to Troy, you'd see him swift and strong.
  He never shrank from any savage thing
  he'd brought to bay in the deep woods; on the scent
  no other dog kept up with him. Now misery
35   has him in leash. His owner died abroad,
  and here the women slaves will take no care of him.
  You know how servants are: without a master
  they have no will to labor, or excel.
  For Zeus who views the wide world takes away
40   half the manhood of a man, that day
  he goes into captivity and slavery." **F**

  Eumaeus crossed the court and went straight forward
  into the mégaron among the suitors;
  but death and darkness in that instant closed
45   the eyes of Argos, who had seen his master,
  Odysseus, after twenty years. . . .

Odysseus enters his home as a beggar, and the suitors mock and abuse him.
Penelope asks to speak with the beggar, but Odysseus puts her off until nightfall.

F EPIC
Reread lines 28–41. Eumaeus still
does not know that he is speaking to
Odysseus in disguise. This is known
as **dramatic irony**—when the reader
knows more than a character knows.
What event does this speech cause
you to anticipate?

43 mégaron: the main hall of a palace
or house

THE HOMECOMING: BOOK 17   **1149**

Get Into the Book
SUMMARY

In Book 17 Odysseus, still disguised as a
beggar, arrives with Telemachus at his
home. Eumaeus follows. Seeing his dog,
Argos, now old and mistreated, saddens
Odysseus. When he enters his home, the
suitors ridicule him.

LITERARY ANALYSIS

F EPIC

*Possible answer: The reader knows that
Odysseus is not only alive but also walking
and talking to Eumaeus, who believes him
to be dead. The fact that neither Eumaeus
nor Telemachus had seen through Odysseus' disguise sets up the possibility that
it will also fool Penelope and her suitors.
Eumaeus' speech causes us to anticipate
this meeting.*

FOR LESS-PROFICIENT READERS

Text Digest Read aloud the italicized text
digest at the end of page 1149 to make sure
students understand what happens right
after Odysseus enters his home. Ask them
what we learn about the suitors from the
way they treat Odysseus. *Possible answer:
The suitors are crude bullies. They assume
that Odysseus is helpless because he appears
to be a poor beggar, and they have no
sympathy for him.*

FOR ADVANCED LEARNERS/PRE-AP

Point of View In the scene where Odysseus
sees his old dog, the narrator switches point
of view several times (lines 1–41). Have students discuss how the changing point of view
increases the poignancy of the scene.

Possible answer: *The painting emphasizes Penelope's purity, her sturdiness, her sadness, and her grief. The text, too, emphasizes her strength, as she lifts the heavy bow in its bowcase (lines 14–15), as well as her sadness, as she sinks down and sobs (line 18).*

About the Art Swiss-born artist Angelica Kauffman (1741–1807) studied in Italy and settled in Britain. One of the few 18th-century women to achieve distinction as an artist, she was part of Sir Joshua Reynolds's circle. Even so, she suffered discrimination: Kauffman was not allowed to take life classes or attend meetings of the Royal Academy, although she was a founding member.

LITERARY ANALYSIS

Ⓖ ARCHETYPE

Possible answer: *The image of a bull bellowing in a field is an archetypal male image. The bull suggests strength, anger, power. Its bellowing indicates both a warning and a challenge. The bull represents Odysseus and reminds us that he is preparing to defend his home and family.*

BOOK 21:
The Test of the Bow

In Books 18–20, Odysseus observes the suitors and finds that two in particular, Antinous and Eurymachus, are rude and demanding. Penelope asks Odysseus the beggar for news of her husband. He says he has heard that Odysseus is on his way home. Penelope, however, has given up hope for Odysseus' return. She proposes an archery contest to the suitors, with marriage to her as the prize. She enters the storeroom and takes down the heavy bow that Odysseus left behind.

Now the queen reached the storeroom door and halted.
Here was an oaken sill, cut long ago
and sanded clean and bedded true. Foursquare
the doorjambs and the shining doors were set
5   by the careful builder. Penelope untied the strap
around the curving handle, pushed her hook
into the slit, aimed at the bolts inside
and shot them back. Then came a rasping sound
as those bright doors the key had sprung gave way—
10 a bellow like a bull's vaunt in a meadow— Ⓖ
followed by her light footfall entering
over the plank floor. Herb-scented robes
lay there in chests, but the lady's milkwhite arms
went up to lift the bow down from a peg
15 in its own polished bowcase.
                                    Now Penelope

sank down, holding the weapon on her knees,
and drew her husband's great bow out, and sobbed
and bit her lip and let the salt tears flow.
Then back she went to face the crowded hall,
20 tremendous bow in hand, and on her shoulder hung
the quiver spiked with coughing death. Behind her
maids bore a basket full of axeheads, bronze
and iron implements for the master's game.
Thus in her beauty she approached the suitors,
25 and near a pillar of the solid roof

1150   UNIT 11: THE ODYSSEY

ANALYZE VISUALS
This is a detail from an 18th-century portrait of Penelope. What qualities are emphasized in this portrait, and how do they compare with qualities emphasized in the text on this page? Explain.

② **Targeted Passage**

Ⓖ **ARCHETYPE**
Reread lines 8–10. What archetypal image do you recognize in these lines? Explain how this image helps to build **suspense**.

15–18 Notice that Penelope still grieves for Odysseus, even after 20 years.

21 quiver (kwĭv´ər): a case in which arrows are carried. *What is meant by "the quiver spiked with coughing death"?*

22–23 axeheads . . . game: metal heads of axes (without handles) that Odysseus employs in a display of archery skill.

Detail of *Penelope Weeping Over the Bow of Ulysses* (about 1779), Angelica Kauffmann. Wolverhampton Art Gallery, Wolverhampton, United Kingdom (OP 531).

DIFFERENTIATED INSTRUCTION

FOR LESS–PROFICIENT READERS
② Targeted Passage [Lines 5–25]

This passage introduces Penelope and illustrates her conflict:

- What words are used to describe Penelope?
- How can you tell that she is physically strong?
- Why is she carrying the bow?
- How can you tell that she still loves

Odysseus?

FOR ENGLISH LEARNERS

Task Support Direct students' attention to the question in the side note for line 21.
Possible answer: *A quiver holds arrows; these weapons have the potential for killing, especially in Odysseus' hands. They foreshadow his revenge. "Coughing death" suggests that an arrow may pierce someone's lungs.*

Get Into the Book
SUMMARY

Book 21 tells how Penelope sobs when she takes out Odysseus' bow for a contest to win her hand in marriage. While the suitors try to string the bow, Odysseus enlists the help of Eumaeus and Philoetius. Despite the suitors' protests, which are followed by their jeers, Odysseus gets the bow. He strings it and carries out Penelope's task. Then, with his son by his side, Odysseus faces his enemies.

■ VISUALIZE IMAGERY

Have students pay attention to the words and images used to describe Odysseus' storeroom as you reread lines 1–15. Challenge them to recall specific visual details of the doorway and storeroom. What other senses does the scene appeal to? Explain. ***Possible answer:*** *It appeals to the senses of hearing and smell: sound of bolts, rasping sound of the doors, Penelope's light footfall; the smell of herb-scented robes.*

FOR ADVANCED LEARNERS/PRE–AP

Women Characters Have students compare and contrast the different types of women in the *Odyssey:* Penelope, the archetype of loyalty and patience, and the *femme fatales*—Circe, Calypso, and the Sirens.

DISCUSSION PROMPTS

Use these prompts to help students understand Penelope's long ordeal and her decision to hold the contest:

Recall What has Penelope decided to do? *She has decided to take Odysseus' heavy bow and see which of the suitors is able to string it and accurately make a difficult shot.*

Analyze What is Penelope's attitude toward the suitors? Why is she having this contest? *Possible answer: She seems to feel some resentment for the way they took over her home. She has reached a point of desperation, needing to resolve the situation.*

Evaluate Do you think Penelope's contest is a good way to resolve her ordeal? *Possible answer: She seems to have little choice but to take some action, having no one to protect her and knowing that her son is at risk. She may hope that none of the suitors can manage her husband's bow.*

Lines 41–56
REINFORCE *KEY IDEA:* HOMECOMING

Discuss How might Odysseus assess his chances at the end of his encounter with Eumaeus and Philoetius? *Possible answer: Odysseus knows that he is greatly outnumbered. However, he has the support of trusty servants and of his son. He also knows that the suitors are struggling with his bow. Moreover, he holds the advantage of surprise, everyone believing him dead. The element of surprise has worked well for him in the past.*

---

she paused, her shining veil across her cheeks,
her maids on either hand and still,
then spoke to the banqueters:

> "My lords, hear me:
suitors indeed, you **commandeered** this house
30 to feast and drink in, day and night, my husband
being long gone, long out of mind. You found
no justification for yourselves—none
except your lust to marry me. Stand up, then:
we now declare a contest for that prize.
35 Here is my lord Odysseus' hunting bow.
Bend and string it if you can. Who sends an arrow
through iron axe-helve sockets, twelve in line?
I join my life with his, and leave this place, my home,
my rich and beautiful bridal house, forever
40 to be remembered, though I dream it only."...

Despite heating and greasing the bow, the lesser suitors prove unable to string it. The most able suitors, Antinous and Eurymachus, hold off. While the suitors are busy with the bow, Odysseus—still disguised as an old beggar—goes to enlist the aid of two of his trusted servants, Eumaeus, the swineherd, and Philoetius, the cowherd.

Two men had meanwhile left the hall:
swineherd and cowherd, in companionship,
one downcast as the other. But Odysseus
followed them outdoors, outside the court,
45 and coming up said gently:

> "You, herdsman,
and you, too, swineherd, I could say a thing to you,
or should I keep it dark?
> No, no; speak,
my heart tells me. Would you be men enough
to stand by Odysseus if he came back?
50 Suppose he dropped out of a clear sky, as I did?
Suppose some god should bring him?
Would you bear arms for him, or for the suitors?"

The cowherd said:

> "Ah, let the master come!
Father Zeus, grant our old wish! Some courier
55 guide him back! Then judge what stuff is in me
and how I manage arms!"

commandeer (kŏm'ən-dîr') *v.* to take control of by force

35–37 Note that the contest has two parts: first the suitor must bend the heavy bow and string it—a task that requires immense strength and skill—and then he must shoot an arrow straight through the holes in 12 axe heads set up in a row.

DIFFERENTIATED INSTRUCTION

FOR LESS-PROFICIENT READERS

Text Digest Read the italicized text digest after line 40 to make sure students understand the intervening plot. Then ask them why Odysseus chooses this moment to test the allegiance of Eumaeus and Philoetius. *Possible answer: The suitors are occupied with the bow and not paying attention to the beggar or his cohorts.*

Likewise Eumaeus
fell to praying all heaven for his return,
so that Odysseus, sure at least of these,
told them:

"I am at home, for I am he.
60 I bore **adversities,** but in the twentieth year
I am ashore in my own land. I find
the two of you, alone among my people,
longed for my coming. Prayers I never heard
except your own that I might come again.
65 So now what is in store for you I'll tell you:
If Zeus brings down the suitors by my hand
I promise marriages to both, and cattle,
and houses built near mine. And you shall be
brothers-in-arms of my Telemachus. ⓗ
70 Here, let me show you something else, a sign
that I am he, that you can trust me, look:
this old scar from the tusk wound that I got
boar hunting on Parnassus. . . ."

Shifting his rags
75 he bared the long gash. Both men looked, and knew,
and threw their arms around the old soldier, weeping,
kissing his head and shoulders. He as well
took each man's head and hands to kiss, then said—
to cut it short, else they might weep till dark—

80 "Break off, no more of this.
Anyone at the door could see and tell them.
Drift back in, but separately at intervals
after me.

Now listen to your orders:
when the time comes, those gentlemen, to a man,
85 will be dead against giving me bow or quiver.
Defy them. Eumaeus, bring the bow
and put it in my hands there at the door.
Tell the women to lock their own door tight.
Tell them if someone hears the shock of arms
90 or groans of men, in hall or court, not one
must show her face, but keep still at her weaving.
Philoetius, run to the outer gate and lock it.
Throw the cross bar and lash it.". . . ⓘ

---

adversity (ăd-vûr'sĭ-tē) *n.* hardship; misfortune

ⓗ **ARCHETYPE**
Identify the **trait** that Odysseus values so highly in these two servants. Where else in film or literature have you encountered these archetypal characters?

73 Parnassus (pär-năs'əs): a mountain in central Greece.

ⓘ **EPIC**
Identify the **plot stage** in lines 84–93. What do you think is about to happen?

THE HOMECOMING: BOOK 21 **1153**

ANALYZE VISUALS

Possible answer: *Odysseus, aiming at the iron axes, takes center stage. The suitors, by comparison, seem small, even childlike, crowded together in the shadows. They all face the courtyard, riveted on the ax heads through which Odysseus must shoot his arrow. The sky and courtyard are luminous and colorful, suggesting a favorable outcome.*

About the Art Newell Convers Wyeth (1882–1945) was a prolific American illustrator and painter. His works were paired with dozens of famous classics, including many works of Robert Louis Stevenson. In 1929, he illustrated the *Odyssey*. Wyeth has been heralded as one of the greatest painters of American outdoor life and among the top illustrators of his day.

Possible answer: *The primary conflict in lines 94–104 is between Odysseus, who hopes to reclaim his home and family, and the rude suitors who want to displace him and kill his son.*

Odysseus the beggar asks the suitors if he might try the bow. Worried that the old man may show them up, they refuse, but Penelope urges them to let Odysseus try. At Telemachus' request, Penelope leaves the men to settle the question of the bow among themselves. Two trusted servants lock the doors of the room, and Telemachus orders the bow be given to Odysseus.

ANALYZE VISUALS
How does 20th-century-artist N. C. Wyeth show suspense in this detail from the painting *The Trial of the Bow*? Be specific.

Detail of *The Trial of the Bow* (1929), N. C. Wyeth. Illustration from *The Odyssey of Homer*, translated by George Herbert Palmer. © 1929 by Houghton Mifflin Company.

                      And Odysseus took his time,
95 turning the bow, tapping it, every inch,
for borings that termites might have made
while the master of the weapon was abroad.
The suitors were now watching him, and some
jested among themselves:

                         "A bow lover!"

100 "Dealer in old bows!"

                          "Maybe he has one like it
at home!"

                  "Or has an itch to make one for himself."

"See how he handles it, the sly old buzzard!"

And one disdainful suitor added this:

"May his fortune grow an inch for every inch he bends it!" Ⓙ

Ⓙ EPIC
What is is the primary **conflict** in lines 94–104?

DIFFERENTIATED INSTRUCTION

FOR LESS–PROFICIENT READERS
Text Digest Read the italicized text digest at the top of page 1154 to make sure students understand the intervening plot. Ask them why the servants locked the doors of the room. *Possible answer: to make sure that the suitors cannot escape when Odysseus exacts his revenge*

FOR ADVANCED LEARNERS/PRE–AP
Present a Poem Have students read a poem based on the *Odyssey* and then present it to the class, analyzing the poem's connection to characters, scenes, or themes in Homer's epic. Suggest that students present one of these poems: "Ulysses," by Alfred, Lord Tennyson; "Ithaka," by C. P. Cavafy; "An Ancient Gesture," by Edna St. Vincent Millay; "Odysseus to Telemachus," by Joseph Brodsky; "Circe's Power," by Louise Glück; or "Odysseus," by W.S. Merwin.

105 But the man skilled in all ways of contending,
    satisfied by the great bow's look and heft,
    like a musician, like a harper, when
    with quiet hand upon his instrument
    he draws between his thumb and forefinger
110 a sweet new string upon a peg: so effortlessly
    Odysseus in one motion strung the bow.
    Then slid his right hand down the cord and plucked it,
    so the taut gut vibrating hummed and sang
    a swallow's note.
                              In the hushed hall it smote the suitors
115 and all their faces changed. Then Zeus thundered
    overhead, one loud crack for a sign.
    And Odysseus laughed within him that the son
    of crooked-minded Cronus had flung that omen down.
    He picked one ready arrow from his table
120 where it lay bare: the rest were waiting still
    in the quiver for the young men's turn to come.
    He nocked it, let it rest across the handgrip,
    and drew the string and grooved butt of the arrow,
    aiming from where he sat upon the stool.
                                        Now flashed
125 arrow from twanging bow clean as a whistle
    through every socket ring, and grazed not one,
    to thud with heavy brazen head beyond.
                                        Then quietly
    Odysseus said:

                              "Telemachus, the stranger
    you welcomed in your hall has not disgraced you.
130 I did not miss, neither did I take all day
    stringing the bow. My hand and eye are sound,
    not so **contemptible** as the young men say.
    The hour has come to cook their lordships' mutton—
    supper by daylight. Other amusements later,
135 with song and harping that adorn a feast."

    He dropped his eyes and nodded, and the prince
    Telemachus, true son of King Odysseus,
    belted his sword on, clapped hand to his spear,
    and with a clink and glitter of keen bronze
140 stood by his chair, in the forefront near his father. **K**

---

106 heft: weight.

107–111 In this epic simile, Odysseus' stringing of the bow is compared to the stringing of a harp. *What qualities of Odysseus does this comparison emphasize?*

114 smote: struck; affected sharply.

115–116 The thunder, a sign from Zeus, indicates that the gods are on Odysseus' side.

118 Cronus (krō′nəs): Zeus' father.

122 nocked it: placed the arrow's feathered end against the bowstring.

127 brazen: made of brass.

contemptible (kən-tĕmp′tə-bəl) *adj.* deserving of scorn; despicable

K EPIC
Book 21 ends with the image of father and son standing side by side facing more than 100 enemies. How can this be considered an epic moment?

Lines 94–97 and 115–132
REINFORCE *KEY IDEA*: HOMECOMING

Discuss What details does the narrator use to suggest that Odysseus is relishing this part of his **homecoming**? *Possible answer: He takes his time inspecting the bow; he laughs at the crack of thunder; after completing both tasks with the bow, he speaks quietly to his son.*

LITERARY ANALYSIS

K EPIC

Possible answer: This is an epic moment because Odysseus is making a heroic stand against an enemy that greatly outnumbers him in order to defend home, hearth, and honor against those who have scorned and abused him and his family. He must bring to bear all of his heroic traits—bravery, strength, determination, and cunning—in order to vanquish the enemy.

FOR ENGLISH LEARNERS

Task Support Direct students' attention to the question in the side note for lines 107–111.
Possible answer: Odysseus shows himself to be a true "master of the weapon" (line 97). Self-assured, strong, and athletic, with a virtuoso's touch, he makes the task look easy, though many suitors had failed.

Possible answer: *Odysseus, in the foreground, appears godlike and heroic, overshadowing the other men. The background is an impression-istic cauldron of hot colors—fiery reds, "white-hot" whites, and yellows—that suggest the hellish perdition to which the godlike Odysseus is sending the evil suitors.*

About the Art *The Slaughter of the Suitors,* like *The Trial of the Bow* (page 1154), is one of N. C. Wyeth's 1929 illustrations for the *Odyssey.*

🄛 GRAMMAR AND STYLE

Possible answer: *The metaphor compares the falling arrows to pouring rain. This detail illustrates that Odysseus is an able warrior who knows well how to prepare for battle. He is indeed "the wiliest fighter of the islands" (line 1).*

Analyze Description Emphasize that the *Odyssey* is rich in metaphors and other figurative language that helps readers visualize events as they are described.

LITERARY ANALYSIS

🄜 EPIC

After students finish reading lines 7–15, ask them whether Odysseus seems to have the support of Apollo. **Possible answer:** *Odysseus does indeed seem to have Apollo's support, given that he made the shot for which he invoked Apollo's name (line 6).*

BOOK 22:
Death in the Great Hall

Now shrugging off his rags the wiliest fighter of the islands
leapt and stood on the broad door sill, his own bow in his hand.
He poured out at his feet a rain of arrows from the quiver 🄛
and spoke to the crowd:

　　　　　　"So much for that. Your clean-cut game is over.
5　Now watch me hit a target that no man has hit before,
　if I can make this shot. Help me, Apollo." 🄜

　He drew to his fist the cruel head of an arrow for Antinous
　just as the young man leaned to lift his beautiful drinking cup,
　embossed, two-handled, golden: the cup was in his fingers:
10　the wine was even at his lips: and did he dream of death?
　How could he? In that **revelry** amid his throng of friends
　who would imagine a single foe—though a strong foe indeed—
　could dare to bring death's pain on him and darkness on his
　　　eyes?
　Odysseus' arrow hit him under the chin
15　and punched up to the feathers through his throat.

　Backward and down he went, letting the winecup fall
　from his shocked hand. Like pipes his nostrils jetted
　crimson runnels, a river of mortal red,
　and one last kick upset his table
20　knocking the bread and meat to soak in dusty blood.

　Now as they craned to see their champion where he lay
　the suitors jostled in uproar down the hall,
　everyone on his feet. Wildly they turned and scanned
　the walls in the long room for arms; but not a shield,
25　not a good ashen spear was there for a man to take and throw.
　All they could do was yell in outrage at Odysseus:

ANALYZE VISUALS
What stylistic elements of Wyeth's *The Slaughter of the Suitors* emphasize the conflict? Explain.

🄛 GRAMMAR AND STYLE
Identify the **metaphor** in line 3. What does this detail add to the description of Odysseus as a warrior?

🄜 EPIC
Note that Odysseus calls upon the help of the god Apollo, who was, among other things, the supporter and protector of archers. The bow was his sacred weapon.

revelry (rĕv′əl-rē) *n.* noisy merrymaking; festivity

18 runnels: streams.

7–20 *Why does Odysseus kill Antinous first? Why does he do it in such a sudden, terrible way?*

23–25 Earlier, in preparation for this confrontation, Odysseus and Telemachus removed all the weapons and shields that were hanging on the walls.

The Slaughter of the Suitors (1929), N. C. Wyeth. Illustration from *The Odyssey of Homer,* translated by George Herbert Palmer. © 1929 by Houghton Mifflin Company.

DIFFERENTIATED INSTRUCTION

FOR ENGLISH LEARNERS

Task Support Draw students' attention to the question in the side note for lines 7–20. **Possible answer:** *Odysseus has just watched Antinous' merrymaking with a "throng of friends" (line 11) and sees that he is about to drink from Odysseus' beautiful golden cup (line 8); Antinous' behavior insults Odysseus. His sudden, horrifying death reflects Odysseus' anger at the way the suitors have dishonored him and his family.*

Get Into the Book

SUMMARY

Book 22 begins when Odysseus kills Antinous as Antinous carouses with the other suitors. Eurymachus tries to placate and bargain with Odysseus, to no avail. Odysseus, backed by Telemachus, Eumaeus, and Philoetius, slaughters the suitors, with some help from Athena.

BACKGROUND

Arms and Armor The battle equipment gathered up by Telemachus in lines 110 and following is typical of the lightweight, effective armaments used during the Greek Bronze Age. Warriors went into battle protected by helmets that were fronted by nasal guards and cheek pieces, and topped by horsetails. Greaves covered the legs, and body armor or corselets covered the upper body. All were made of thin sheets of bronze that could bend to fit. Warriors also wore bucklers, or leather shields, strapped to their arm and carried bronze-tipped ash-wood spears that could be thrown from a distance. Broadswords needed to be held with both hands, but nobles carried shorter, single-handed swords for easier use. Bows like the one Odysseus used were made of wood covered with strips of goat-horn.

FOR ADVANCED LEARNERS/PRE–AP
Epithets Have students identify the epithets used to characterize Odysseus during the homecoming part of the *Odyssey*. How do they compare with those used during his wanderings? To what extent do these epithets help to foreshadow important scenes?

"Foul! to shoot at a man! That was your last shot!"

"Your own throat will be slit for this!"

"Our finest lad is down!
You killed the best on Ithaca."

"Buzzards will tear your eyes out!"

③ Targeted Passage

30 For they imagined as they wished—that it was a wild shot,
    an unintended killing—fools, not to comprehend
    they were already in the grip of death.
    But glaring under his brows Odysseus answered:

    "You yellow dogs, you thought I'd never make it
35 home from the land of Troy. You took my house to plunder,
    twisted my maids to serve your beds. You dared
    bid for my wife while I was still alive.
    Contempt was all you had for the gods who rule wide heaven,
    contempt for what men say of you hereafter.
40 Your last hour has come. You die in blood." **N**

    As they all took this in, sickly green fear
    pulled at their entrails, and their eyes flickered
    looking for some hatch or hideaway from death.
    Eurymachus alone could speak. He said:

45 "If you are Odysseus of Ithaca come back,
    all that you say these men have done is true.
    Rash actions, many here, more in the countryside.
    But here he lies, the man who caused them all.
    Antinous was the ringleader; he whipped us on
50 to do these things. He cared less for a marriage
    than for the power Cronion has denied him
    as king of Ithaca. For that
    he tried to trap your son and would have killed him.
    He is dead now and has his portion. Spare
55 your own people. As for ourselves, we'll make
    restitution of wine and meat consumed,
    and add, each one, a tithe of twenty oxen
    with gifts of bronze and gold to warm your heart.
    Meanwhile we cannot blame you for your anger." **O**

60 Odysseus glowered under his black brows
    and said:

N EPIC
Paraphrase Odysseus' speech in lines 34–40. What reasons does he give for killing the suitors?

42 entrails: internal organs.

47 rash: foolish; thoughtless.

51 Cronion (krō′nē-ŏn′): Zeus, the son of Cronus.

restitution (rĕs′tĭ-tōō′shən) *n.* a making good for loss or damage; repayment

57 tithe: payment.

O EPIC
What is Eurymachus' **motivation** in lines 45–59? What is his strategy for achieving his goal?

N EPIC

Possible answer: Odysseus says that the suitors are cowards who stole his goods and tried to take his wife, because they believed he was dead. He tells them they are going to die, because they showed no regard for what was right and thereby dishonored him and themselves.

O EPIC

Possible answer: Eurymachus' motivation is the wish to save himself and his friends. He tries to mollify Odysseus by saying that his reasons for being angry are correct, but that only Antinous, as ringleader, was to blame, and Antinous is dead. He reminds Odysseus that despite their errors, he and the other suitors are of Ithaca, Odysseus' own people. He also promises that the suitors will pay him for everything they consumed and an additional 20 oxen each, as well as bronze and gold.

DIFFERENTIATED INSTRUCTION

FOR LESS–PROFICIENT READERS
③ **Targeted Passage [Lines 27–33]**

This passage illustrates how Odysseus' plan counts on the element of surprise.

- Why did the suitors think Odysseus' killing of Antinous was "a wild shot"?
- Why does the narrator call them "fools"?

Paraphrasing Homer To help students paraphrase Odysseus' speech in lines 34–40, model how to paraphrase lines 34–37: *You cowards believed I was dead, so you stole from my home and tried to marry my wife.* Invite volunteers to paraphrase lines 38–40: *You didn't care that what you did was wrong; now you are going to die.*

"Not for the whole treasure of your fathers,
all you enjoy, lands, flocks, or any gold
put up by others, would I hold my hand.
There will be killing till the score is paid.
65 You forced yourselves upon this house. Fight your way out,
or run for it, if you think you'll escape death.
I doubt one man of you skins by."

They felt their knees fail, and their hearts—but heard
Eurymachus for the last time rallying them.

70 "Friends," he said, "the man is **implacable.**
Now that he's got his hands on bow and quiver
he'll shoot from the big door stone there
until he kills us to the last man.

                                Fight, I say,
let's remember the joy of it. Swords out!
75 Hold up your tables to deflect his arrows.
After me, everyone: rush him where he stands.
If we can budge him from the door, if we can pass
into the town, we'll call out men to chase him.
This fellow with his bow will shoot no more."

80 He drew his own sword as he spoke, a broadsword of fine
    bronze,
honed like a razor on either edge. Then crying hoarse and loud
he hurled himself at Odysseus. But the kingly man let fly
an arrow at that instant, and the quivering feathered butt
sprang to the nipple of his breast as the barb stuck in his liver.
85 The bright broadsword clanged down. He lurched and fell
    aside,
pitching across his table. His cup, his bread and meat,
were spilt and scattered far and wide, and his head slammed
    on the ground.
Revulsion, anguish in his heart, with both feet kicking out,
he downed his chair, while the shrouding wave of mist closed
    on his eyes.

90 Amphinomus now came running at Odysseus,
broadsword naked in his hand. He thought to make
the great soldier give way at the door.
But with a spear throw from behind Telemachus hit him
between the shoulders, and the lancehead drove
95 clear through his chest. He left his feet and fell
forward, thudding, forehead against the ground. ●

THE HOMECOMING: BOOK 22   **1159**

61–67 *Why do you think Odysseus rejects Eurymachus' explanation and offer of restitution?*

67 skins by: sneaks away.

implacable (ĭm-plăk'ə-bəl) *adj.* impossible to soothe; unforgiving

revulsion (rĭ-vŭl'shən) *n.* a sudden feeling of disgust or loathing

88–89 Eurymachus' death is physically painful, but he also has "revulsion, anguish in his heart." *What do you think causes this emotional pain?*

90 Amphinomus (ăm-fĭn'ə-məs): one of the suitors.

93–100 Telemachus proves to be a valuable help to his father.

℗ EPIC
How has the battle with the suitors taken on epic proportions?

Lines 70–84
DISCUSSION PROMPTS
Use these prompts to help students understand that Eurymachus has heroic qualities that make him a formidable enemy:

Connect Have you ever met a person that you disliked yet couldn't help admiring in some way? How does this enhance your understanding of Eurymachus? *Responses should reflect an understanding that people may have admirable qualities or achievements and yet be flawed in their behavior, attitude, or personality.*

Analyze What heroic qualities does Eurymachus possess? *Possible answer: He is strong and brave, thinks on his feet, and enjoys a good fight, which are heroic qualities.*

Evaluate Do you think that Eurymachus is a good leader? Explain your opinion. *Possible answer: Yes, he is a good leader. He keeps his head, effectively cajoles the other men to act, and is a model of bravery and confidence. No, he was an intruder in the house of Odysseus and set his men up for retribution and revenge.*

LITERARY ANALYSIS

℗ EPIC

Possible answer: Eurymachus has rallied the suitors—nearly 100 of them. Odysseus, his son, and the two servants face terrifying odds. Odysseus' heroic traits—bravery, cunning, and strength—must now come into play. The gods have already shown signs that they are on Odysseus' side, in Zeus' thunderbolt (Book 21, lines 115–118) and Apollo's apparent response to his plea for help (Book 22, lines 5–6). The interest of the gods heightens the epic proportions of the battle.

FOR ENGLISH LEARNERS

Task Support Direct students' attention to the question in the side note for lines 61–67. *Possible answer: Odysseus probably doesn't believe that Antinous caused all the trouble. He may also consider all the men responsible for going along, regardless of Antinous' role. His anger is too deep to accept restitution for the dishonor they caused him.* Also point out the question in the side note for lines 88–89. *Possible answer: Eurymachus feels anguish,* realizing that he had brought this disaster on himself by disregarding what was right and dishonoring Odysseus and his family.

Possible answer: *The mood is somber, sad, dark, and oppressive. The black lines and colors heighten this mood. The black lines suggest death and set into relief the blood red and fading yellow. These colors signify the ebbing of blood and of life from the victims.*

About the Art One of England's greatest sculptors, Henry Spencer Moore (1898–1986) drew *Death of the Suitors: The Odyssey.* Moore's most famous sculptures are massive reclining figures that swoop and swirl like the hills and valleys of a landscape. Moore periodically turned to drawing. The piece on page 1161 was among a number of works completed during World War II, when the Germans were blitzing London.

LITERARY ANALYSIS

◎ EPIC

Possible answer: *Telemachus shows that he is the son of Odysseus in character and action as well as in blood. He is brave, able, and quick of foot and mind.*

Telemachus swerved around him, leaving the long dark spear
planted in Amphinomus. If he paused to yank it out
someone might jump him from behind or cut him down with
    a sword
100 at the moment he bent over. So he ran—ran from the tables
to his father's side and halted, panting, saying:

"Father let me bring you a shield and spear,
a pair of spears, a helmet.
I can arm on the run myself; I'll give
105 outfits to Eumaeus and this cowherd.
Better to have equipment."

                                 Said Odysseus:

"Run then, while I hold them off with arrows
as long as the arrows last. When all are gone
if I'm alone they can dislodge me."

                                 Quick
110 upon his father's word Telemachus
ran to the room where spears and armor lay.
He caught up four light shields, four pairs of spears,
four helms of war high-plumed with flowing manes,
and ran back, loaded down, to his father's side.
115 He was the first to pull a helmet on
and slide his bare arm in a buckler strap.
The servants armed themselves, and all three took their stand
beside the master of battle. ◎
                        While he had arrows
he aimed and shot, and every shot brought down
120 one of his huddling enemies.
But when all barbs had flown from the bowman's fist,
he leaned his bow in the bright entry way
beside the door, and armed: a four-ply shield
hard on his shoulder, and a crested helm,
125 horsetailed, nodding stormy upon his head,
then took his tough and bronze-shod spears. . . .

The suitors make various unsuccessful attempts to expel Odysseus from his post at the door. Athena urges Odysseus on to battle, yet holds back her fullest aid, waiting for Odysseus and Telemachus to prove themselves. Six of the suitors attempt an attack on Odysseus, but Athena deflects their arrows. Odysseus and his men seize this opportunity to launch their own attack, and the suitors begin to fall. At last Athena's presence becomes known to all, as the shape of her shield becomes visible

113 helms: helmets.

◎ EPIC
How does Telemachus conduct himself in this **conflict** with the suitors?

DIFFERENTIATED INSTRUCTION

FOR ENGLISH LEARNERS
Vocabulary Support Point out phrasal verbs on page 1160: *yank (it) out* (line 98), "pull (the arrow) out"; *jump (him) from behind* (line 99), "come from behind to attack (him)"; *cut (him) down* (line 99), "kill (him)"; *hold (them) off* (line 107), "keep (them) at bay"; *brought down* (line 119), "shot down; struck down."

above the hall. The suitors, recognizing the intervention of the gods on Odysseus'
behalf, are frantic to escape but to no avail. Odysseus and his men are compared to
falcons who show no mercy to the flocks of birds they pursue and capture. Soon the
room is reeking with blood. Thus the battle with the suitors comes to an end, and
Odysseus prepares himself to meet Penelope.

Death of the Suitors: The Odyssey (1944), Henry Spencer Moore. Black chalk, wash, and ink on paper, 13.3 cm ×
28.8 cm. Cecil Higgins Art Gallery, Bedford, Bedfordshire, United Kingdom. Photo © Bridgeman Art Library.
© The Henry Moore Foundation. This image may not be reproduced or altered without prior consent from the
Henry Moore Foundation.

Discuss How is the role of Athena crucial to
Odysseus' **homecoming?** *Possible answer:*
Athena has been performing supernatural feats
to disguise and protect Odysseus. She finally
challenges Odysseus to prove himself and act
on his own behalf, thus realizing his own physi-
cal and emotional strength. She then rewards
him by displaying her shield and frightening
the suitors.

FOR LESS–PROFICIENT READERS

Text Digest Read aloud the italicized text
digest that follows line 126 to make sure
students understand the intervening plot.
Then ask them why Athena might have aided
Odysseus when the six suitors tried to attack
him. *Possible answer: At six to one, the fight*
had become unfair, so Athena decided to even
the odds for Odysseus.

BOOK 23:
The Trunk of the Olive Tree

Greathearted Odysseus, home at last,
was being bathed now by Eurynome
and rubbed with golden oil, and clothed again
in a fresh tunic and a cloak. Athena
5 lent him beauty, head to foot. She made him
taller, and massive, too, with crisping hair
in curls like petals of wild hyacinth
but all red-golden. Think of gold infused
on silver by a craftsman, whose fine art
10 Hephaestus taught him, or Athena: one
whose work moves to delight: just so she lavished
beauty over Odysseus' head and shoulders.
He sat then in the same chair by the pillar,
facing his silent wife, and said:

                                    "Strange woman,

15 the immortals of Olympus made you hard,
harder than any. Who else in the world
would keep **aloof** as you do from her husband
if he returned to her from years of trouble,
cast on his own land in the twentieth year?

20 Nurse, make up a bed for me to sleep on.
Her heart is iron in her breast."

                                    Penelope

spoke to Odysseus now. She said:

                                    "Strange man,

if man you are . . . This is no pride on my part
nor scorn for you—not even wonder, merely.
25 I know so well how you—how he—appeared
boarding the ship for Troy. But all the same . . . ®

2 Eurynome (yŏŏ-rĭn′ə-mē): a female servant.

④ **Targeted Passage**

10 Hephaestus (hĭ-fĕs′təs): the god of metalworking.

11 lavished: showered.

15 immortals of Olympus: the gods, who live on Mount Olympus.

aloof (ə-lōōf′) *adj.* distant; remote; standoffish

® **EPIC**
Reread lines 22–26. What do you think is the **motivation** for Penelope's skepticism about this man who claims to be the husband she hasn't seen in 20 years? Consider her experiences in his absence.

Detail of plaque with the return of Odysseus (about 460–450 B.C.). Classical Greek. Melian. Terracotta, height 7 ³/₈". Fletcher Fund, 1930. © The Metropolitan Museum of Art (30.11.9).

DIFFERENTIATED INSTRUCTION

FOR LESS–PROFICIENT READERS
④ **Targeted Passage [Lines 1–16]**

This passage sets up the scene for Odysseus' meeting with Penelope.

• What did Athena do to get Odysseus ready to meet his wife?

• Why did the goddess go to such lengths to make Odysseus handsome?

• Why does Odysseus need the help of a goddess now?

• Do you think Odysseus' beauty will melt Penelope's heart? Give your reasons.

Confirm Understanding Help students to answer the Literary Analysis question as fully as possible. On the board, list their ideas about Penelope's motivation. Then direct their attention to pages 1164–1165, lines 58–67. Ask them to discuss how their explanations compare with Penelope's.

Get Into the Book

SUMMARY

In Book 23 Odysseus bathes and, with Athena's help, dresses to meet Penelope. Instead of embracing him, however, Penelope holds back, testing him one last time. Odysseus proves his identity with information to which no one else was privy: nobody could have moved their bed, because one post was built from the trunk of an olive tree, still rooted in the ground.

● CONFLICT

Encourage students to discuss the new conflict that Odysseus faces at the beginning of Book 23. How is this conflict different from his other struggles in the homecoming section of the *Odyssey*? How is it ironic? ***Possible answer:*** *This conflict involves proving his identify to his wife. The conflict is not a physical struggle but an emotional one between Odysseus and Penelope. It is ironic that he must prove himself to his wife after struggling all these years to get back to her. Penelope is a formidable adversary, possessing many of the heroic traits of her husband—determination, persistence, loyalty, bravery, and guile. Odysseus' happiness depends upon the outcome of this final conflict, a "battle of the sexes." His preparations in the opening of this book show how seriously he takes the encounter.*

Discuss How are Penelope's actions similar to those of Athena at Odysseus' homecoming? How are they different? ***Possible answer:** Penelope's actions are similar in that like Athena, Penelope tests Odysseus by making him prove himself. They are different in that Penelope acts out of the insecurity of a mortal, being not at all sure of the identity of the man in front of her. Athena acts out of the power and privilege of a goddess.*

LITERARY ANALYSIS

Ⓢ ARCHETYPE

***Possible answer:** Penelope wanted to check Odysseus' reaction when she told her servant to move his bed and make it up; this would be impossible, because Odysseus had made one bedpost from an olive tree still rooted in the ground. Only he would have known this. Penelope's actions show caution and guile, traits expected of archetypal heroic characters.*

Make up his bed for him, Eurycleia.
Place it outside the bedchamber my lord
built with his own hands. Pile the big bed
30 with fleeces, rugs, and sheets of purest linen."

With this she tried him to the breaking point,
and he turned on her in a flash raging:

"Woman, by heaven you've stung me now!
Who dared to move my bed?
35 No builder had the skill for that—unless
a god came down to turn the trick. No mortal
in his best days could budge it with a crowbar.
There is our pact and pledge, our secret sign,
built into that bed—my handiwork
40 and no one else's!
                                        An old trunk of olive
grew like a pillar on the building plot,
and I laid out our bedroom round that tree,
lined up the stone walls, built the walls and roof,
gave it a doorway and smooth-fitting doors.
45 Then I lopped off the silvery leaves and branches,
hewed and shaped that stump from the roots up
into a bedpost, drilled it, let it serve
as model for the rest. I planed them all,
inlaid them all with silver, gold and ivory,
50 and stretched a bed between—a pliant web
of oxhide thongs dyed crimson.
                                        There's our sign!
I know no more. Could someone else's hand
have sawn that trunk and dragged the frame away?"

Their secret! as she heard it told, her knees
55 grew **tremulous** and weak, her heart failed her.
With eyes brimming tears she ran to him,
throwing her arms around his neck, and kissed him, Ⓢ
murmuring:

                        "Do not rage at me, Odysseus!
No one ever matched your caution! Think
60 what difficulty the gods gave: they denied us
life together in our prime and flowering years,
kept us from crossing into age together.
Forgive me, don't be angry. I could not
welcome you with love on sight! I armed myself

27–30 The bed, built from the trunk of an olive tree still rooted in the ground, is actually unmovable.

50–51 a pliant web . . . crimson: a network of ox-hide straps, dyed red, stretched between the sides of the bed to form a springy base for the bedding.

tremulous (trĕm′yə-ləs) *adj.* marked by trembling or shaking

Ⓢ ARCHETYPE
How has Penelope tricked Odysseus into proving his identity? What do her actions suggest about archetypal characters?

DIFFERENTIATED INSTRUCTION

FOR ADVANCED LEARNERS/PRE–AP
Debate Have students discuss whether Penelope is a fitting match for Odysseus. Elaborate on characteristics such as caution, bravery, cleverness, and patience, finding examples in the selection for both characters.

65   long ago against the frauds of men,
     impostors who might come—and all those many
     whose underhanded ways bring evil on!
     Helen of Argos, daughter of Zeus and Leda,
     would she have joined the stranger, lain with him,
70   if she had known her destiny? known the Achaeans
     in arms would bring her back to her own country?
     Surely a goddess moved her to adultery,
     her blood unchilled by war and evil coming,
     the years, the **desolation;** ours, too.

75   But here and now, what sign could be so clear
     as this of our own bed?
     No other man has ever laid eyes on it—
     only my own slave, Actoris, that my father
     sent with me as a gift—she kept our door.
80   You make my stiff heart know that I am yours." **T**

     Now from his breast into his eyes the ache
     of longing mounted, and he wept at last,
     his dear wife, clear and faithful, in his arms,
     longed for
            as the sunwarmed earth is longed for by a swimmer
85   spent in rough water where his ship went down
     under Poseidon's blows, gale winds and tons of sea.
     Few men can keep alive through a big surf
     to crawl, clotted with brine, on kindly beaches
     in joy, in joy, knowing the abyss behind:
90   and so she too rejoiced, her gaze upon her husband,
     her white arms round him pressed as though forever. . . . **U**

Odysseus and Penelope tell each other about all that happened to them while Odysseus was away. Then Odysseus visits his father, Laertes, to give him the good news of his safe return. Meanwhile, the townspeople, angry about the deaths of the young suitors, gather to fight Odysseus. In the end, Athena steps in and makes peace among them all.

68 Argos (är'gŏs); **Leda** (lē'də).

desolation (dĕs'ə-lā'shən) *n.* lonely grief; misery

78 Actoris (ăk-tôr'ĭs).

T EPIC
Reread lines 58–80. What **traits** of Penelope's does this speech reveal?

5 Targeted Passage

U EPIC SIMILE
What is Penelope compared to in these final lines?

T EPIC

Possible answer: This speech reveals Penelope's thoughtfulness, her self-awareness, her loyalty, her strength, and her underlying tenderness.

U EPIC SIMILE

Possible answer: Penelope is compared to a safe shore, where a tired, shipwrecked swimmer comes to rest after a monumental struggle for survival in tumultuous seas.

SELECTION WRAP-UP

REFLECT Ask students how the ending would have been different if Penelope had not been so cautious. Would it have been as effective? Why or why not?

★ CRITIQUE Have students rate the *Odyssey* as an adventure story, with 1 being the least adventurous and 5 being the most exciting.

FOR LESS-PROFICIENT READERS
5 Targeted Passage [Lines 75–91]

This passage concludes the epic with Odysseus' and Penelope's reunion.

- What does Penelope mean by her "stiff heart"?
- How is Penelope different from Helen of Argos?
- What worries do Odysseus and Penelope still have to face?

Text Digest Read the italicized text digest that follows line 91 to make sure students understand how loose threads of the *Odyssey* are wrapped up.

DISCUSSION PROMPTS

Use these prompts to help students see how both the *Odyssey* and Dorothy Parker's "Penelope" reflect on Penelope's bravery:

Connect Do you appreciate bravery that does not require facing physical danger? Tell why or why not. *Many students may say that they don't often notice bravery that does not involve facing danger, because it may not be obvious or vivid enough to draw their attention.*

Analyze Is the last line of the poem ironic? Give your reasons. ***Possible answer:*** *Yes, the last line is ironic. Odysseus is indeed known for his bravery. The irony is that Penelope's fame derives mostly from her devotion and loyalty; yet she was brave in the way she faced the suitors, watched out for her son's safety, and endured her ordeal for 20 years.*

Evaluate The power of the poem derives from its understatement. Do you think the understatement is effective in revealing the suffering that Penelope endured during her husband's long absence? ***Possible answer:*** *The understatement is effective in revealing Penelope's suffering. By compressing Odysseus' trials and adventures into five lines that minimize his ordeal, the poem suggests that Penelope, too, suffered emotional trials and tribulations that her five lines do not hint at.*

Dorothy Parker, an American writer of the early 20th century, wrote many poems offering a woman's perspective on life. In "Penelope," Parker imagines what Odysseus' wife might have thought about his journeys.

PENELOPE

DOROTHY PARKER

In the pathway of the sun,
   In the footsteps of a breeze,
Where the world and sky are one,
   He shall ride the silver seas,
5   He shall cut the glittering wave.
I shall sit at home, and rock;
Rise, to heed a neighbor's knock;
Brew my tea, and snip my thread;
Bleach the linen for my bed.
10   They will call him brave.

Comprehension

1. **Recall** Why is Telemachus fearful when his father first reveals his identity?

2. **Recall** How does Odysseus react when Argos recognizes him?

3. **Recall** Who helps Odysseus fight the suitors?

4. **Clarify** Why does Penelope test Odysseus?

Literary Analysis

5. **Summarize the Plot** Review the chart you created as you read these episodes about Odysseus' homecoming. Use the chart to write a plot summary of Part 2; feel free to use the overview on page 1141 as a starter.

6. **Analyze Character** Why do you think Penelope devises the contest with the bow? What does this contest reveal about her character?

7. **Examine Archetypes** Think about other contests you have encountered in literature or film. Would you say that the contest of the bow is archetypal? Explain why or why not.

8. **Analyze Universal Theme** The *Odyssey* has themes reflecting timeless and universal concerns, such as courage and honor, good and evil, life and death, and the importance of home. Choose one of these topics. What message about this topic does Homer convey? Give evidence from the text to support your answer.

9. **Evaluate Epic Characteristics** One thing that all epics have in common is tremendous **scale**. Everything about an epic is big: an extended and complicated plot, a long journey over great distances, powerful gods and horrible monsters, and major universal themes. Identify one aspect each of epic **plot, setting, character,** and **theme** in the *Odyssey*. Which do you consider most impressive? Give reasons for your choice.

10. **Compare and Contrast Texts** In Dorothy Parker's poem "Penelope," is the attitude toward Odysseus similar to or different from Penelope's attitude in the *Odyssey* excerpts you have just read? Cite evidence to support your answer.

Literary Criticism

11. **Social Context** Assume that Odysseus represents the ancient Greeks' ideal of a man and that Penelope represents their ideal of a woman. In what ways are the characters similar to and different from the ideal man and woman of today?

life or death. **Most impressive:** *theme, made memorable by powerful characters, setting, and plot*

10. *In the* Odyssey, *Penelope loves Odysseus without the obvious bitterness or irony that is central to Parker's poem. In Book 21, Penelope weeps when she pulls Odysseus' bow from its case (lines 5–18), and she describes her home as her "bridal house" (line 39). In Book 23, when she realizes it is indeed Odysseus before her, she weeps and kisses him (lines 54–67).*

Literary Criticism
Possible answer:

11. **Similar:** *The ideal man and the ideal woman, then and now, are strong, brave, intelligent, and admired.* **Different:** *The Greeks' ideal woman spent her time in domestic pursuits. The ideal man went out into the world. Today, the ideal man and the ideal woman share a balance of domestic and worldly pursuits.*

Practice and Apply

After Reading
For additional support of post-reading questions, use these copy masters:

R RESOURCE MANAGER—Copy Masters
Reading Check p. 62 (to check understanding of the selection)
Characteristics of an Epic p. 55 (for practice of literary analysis standards focus)
Question Support p. 63 (After Reading questions adapted for English learners and less-proficient readers)

For additional questions, see page 47.

For additional exercises to challenge students, see

ⓘ Power Thinking at **ClassZone.com**

ANSWERS

Comprehension

1. *He fears that the transformed Odysseus is a god who might harm him.*

2. *Odysseus wipes a tear from his cheek but hides his emotions from Eumaeus.*

3. *Telemachus, Eumaeus, and Philoetius fight beside him; Athena intervenes.*

4. *She tests Odysseus to check his identity.*

Literary Analysis
Possible answers:

5. ■ **STANDARDS FOCUS** *Summarizing Athena disguises Odysseus as a beggar. Penelope has promised to marry the winner of an archery contest. At Eumaeus' home, Odysseus reveals his identity to Telemachus. Then he goes home, wins the contest, and kills the suitors. Penelope tests Odysseus to prove his identity.*

6. *She devises the test to get rid of the suitors, believing that none will pass the test. She is crafty and not easily deceived.*

7. ● **STANDARDS FOCUS** *Characteristics of an Epic The contest is archetypal, pitting a worthy underdog (Odysseus) against bullies who underestimate him.*

8. *Homer conveys the message that good will win out over evil. (See answer to* **7.***)*

9. ● **STANDARDS FOCUS** *Plot: Odysseus travels 20 years to return home.* **Setting:** *the known world and beyond* **Character:** *Odysseus—heroic in strength, bravery, cunning* **Theme:** *People have little control over*

ANSWERS

Vocabulary in Context

VOCABULARY PRACTICE

1. *false*	6. *false*
2. *false*	7. *false*
3. *true*	8. *true*
4. *true*	9. *true*
5. *false*	10. *false*

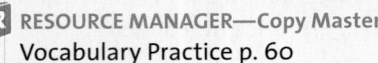 **RESOURCE MANAGER—Copy Master**
Vocabulary Practice p. 60

VOCABULARY IN WRITING

Ask volunteers to recall palace events at which the servants were present. Suggest that they choose one or two vocabulary words that the servants might associate with each event. When students write their paragraph, they should use those words.

VOCABULARY STRATEGY: THE LATIN WORD ROOT *solus* (also an EL language objective)

Review the words in the word web. Have students use what they know about each word to come up with a working definition. Possibilities include *soliloquy*, "a monologue; speaking to oneself"; *desolation*, "loneliness; misery"; *sole*, "only; one and only"; *solitude*, "space to oneself; time alone"; *solitaire*, "a card game played by oneself"; *solo*, "alone; on one's own."

Answers:

1. *solo*	4. *sole*
2. *solitaire*	5. *soliloquy*
3. *solitude*	

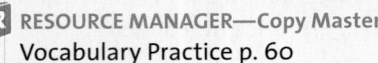 RESOURCE MANAGER—Copy Master
Vocabulary Strategy p. 61

ⓘ Vocabulary Center at **ClassZone.com**
Additional Vocabulary Activities

Vocabulary in Context

VOCABULARY PRACTICE

Decide whether each item is true or false.

1. A person making **restitution** is trying to get revenge.
2. If I **commandeer** your boat, I have asked your permission before taking it.
3. A person who acts **aloof** often is unwilling to make friends.
4. One might feel **desolation** at the death of a close relative.
5. If I feel **revulsion** for you, I enjoy spending time with you.
6. **Adversity** is a serious skin condition.
7. A **tremulous** person tends to have very steady hands.
8. If my anger is **implacable,** I am not going to get over it soon.
9. New Year's Eve is a common night for **revelry.**
10. Being kind to a pet is **contemptible** behavior.

WORD LIST
adversity
aloof
commandeer
contemptible
desolation
implacable
restitution
revelry
revulsion
tremulous

VOCABULARY IN WRITING

Using four or more vocabulary words, write a paragraph to describe how Odysseus' old servants feel about events going on in the palace. You might start like this.

> **EXAMPLE SENTENCE**
> The servants felt a strong <u>revulsion</u> toward the suitors in the palace.

VOCABULARY STRATEGY: THE LATIN WORD ROOT *solus*

The vocabulary word *desolation* contains a form of the Latin root *solus*, which means "alone." This root is found in numerous other English words. To understand the meaning of words formed from *solus*, use context clues as well as your knowledge of the root.

PRACTICE Insert the word from the word web that best completes each sentence. Use context clues to help you or, if necessary, consult a dictionary.

1. After months of training with an instructor, he was ready for his first _____ flight.
2. Jeannette often plays a game of _____ on her computer.
3. Rupert lived on a desert island because he wanted _____.
4. The _____ requirement for joining the club is that you are 13 or older.
5. An actor delivering a _____ generally stands on the stage alone.

Word web: *soliloquy*, *desolation*, *sole*, *solitude*, *solitaire*, *solo* connected to **solus**

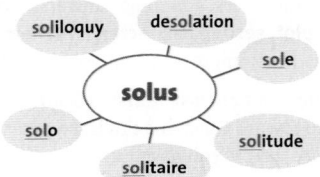 **VOCABULARY PRACTICE**
For more practice, go to the **Vocabulary Center** at **ClassZone.com**.

DIFFERENTIATED INSTRUCTION

FOR ENGLISH LEARNERS
Vocabulary: Latin Word Root *solus* After students complete the vocabulary practice with the Latin root *solus*, have them work in home-language groups. Ask them to create word webs with the same root word in those languages, including as many words as possible. Encourage them to then write the English equivalent for each word. Invite volunteers to present their webs to the class.

FOR ADVANCED LEARNERS/PRE–AP
Vocabulary Practice Challenge Have students write a note that Penelope might have written to a relative, describing the situation in her home before Odysseus' return. Tell them to use as many of the words from the word list as possible.

Reading-Writing Connection

Engage with the main characters in the *Odyssey* by responding to these prompts. Then use **Revision: Grammar and Style** to improve your writing.

WRITING PROMPTS	SELF-CHECK
A. Short Response: Write a Monologue What do you think Penelope's hopes for the future might be after Odysseus' **homecoming?** Write a **stanza** (at least ten lines) in the style of the *Odyssey* in which Penelope expresses her dreams for her future years with Odysseus.	***An effective stanza will . . .*** • mimic the style of Homer's writing • express Penelope's likely hopes for the future
B. Extended Response: Evaluate a Character Is Odysseus someone who would be admired by young people today? Write a **three-to-five-paragraph response** in which you describe Odysseus' behavior and attitudes and explain why people would or would not look up to him today.	***A successful response will . . .*** • clearly introduce an opinion • describe aspects of Odysseus' attitudes and actions • give reasons why young people today would or would not admire him

REVISION: GRAMMAR AND STYLE

ADD DESCRIPTIVE DETAILS Review the **Grammar and Style** note on page 1156. Similes and metaphors are types of **figurative language**—they communicate ideas beyond their literal meaning. A **simile** is a comparison that uses the **prepositions** *like* or *as*. A **metaphor** directly compares two things by saying or suggesting that one thing *is* another. Using figurative language can make your readers see things in a new way. Here are two examples.

> "Like pipes his nostrils jetted
> crimson runnels, a river of mortal red. . . ." (simile, Book 22, lines 17–18)

> "'Her heart is iron in her breast.'" (metaphor, Book 23, line 21)

Notice how the revisions in red use figurative language to add interesting descriptive details to this first draft. Revise your response to prompt A by incorporating different types of figurative language.

STUDENT MODEL

We have missed one another for many years.

Like two pieces of the same puzzle,
We have been separated
∧
and then joined again.

WRITING TOOLS
For prewriting, revision, and editing tools, visit the **Writing Center** at ClassZone.com.

FOR LESS–PROFICIENT WRITERS

For Prompt A:

• Help students list some dreams Penelope might have about her and Odysseus, their home, their son, their grandchildren.

• Help students write one line of a stanza.

• Suggest that students begin with one of the models, changing it slightly.

• Limit the length of the stanza to five lines.

For Prompt B:

• Help students to brainstorm a list of actions taken by Odysseus. Discuss how they feel about the way Odysseus behaved in one of these actions.

• Ask students to think about Odysseus' attitude in one of these actions. Discuss how they feel about his attitude.

• Limit the length of the assignment to no more than two paragraphs.

Reading-Writing Connection

WRITING PROMPTS

• For Prompt A, encourage students to reread Penelope's speech to Odysseus in Book 23, lines 58–80, to help them get a feel for the style of Homer's writing and the rhythms of Penelope's speech.

• For Prompt B, have students use a three-column chart to list Odysseus' attitudes, actions, and their opinions/responses to each one.

For an extended writing activity, see Carol Booth Olson's Reading-Writing Lesson Plans at **ClassZone.com**

REVISION: GRAMMAR AND STYLE

• After students review the student model, ask them to identify the type of figurative language used there. (*a simile*) Ask them to revise the same model by turning the simile into a metaphor. (*We are two puzzle pieces, long separated, now joined.*)

• Write this model on the board. Have students complete it by comparing the future to a hearth fire; encourage them to use the comparison as a simile and then as a metaphor.

I dream of a future together that is as bright and warm as the fire in our hearth.

Our future is a hearth fire that fills me with warmth and happiness.

R RESOURCE MANAGER—Copy Master
Add Descriptive Details p. 64

Assess and Reteach

Assess

R RESOURCE MANAGER—Copy Masters
Selection Test A pp. 65–66
Selection Test B/C pp. 67–68

S Test Generator CD

Reteach

S STANDARDS LESSON FILE
Literature Lessons 2, 12, 17, 29, 32
Research and Study Skills Lesson 13
Vocabulary Lessons 7, 8

Focus and Motivate

OBJECTIVES

- analyze a student model that reflects the key traits of subject analysis writing
- use the writing process to produce a subject analysis essay
- revise and edit, using a rubric for subject analysis writing
- plan and present an oral report

WRITER'S ROAD MAP

WRITING PROMPTS 1 AND 2

Review with students some of the literary elements that they discussed while reading the *Odyssey*: archetypes, epic heroes, epithets, allusions, and other characteristics. Point out that any of these could be analyzed in depth. Link this approach to Prompt 2 by asking students to identify possible subelements of the listed topics.

ADDITIONAL PROMPTS

Use these prompts for practice with business writing and writing in the humanities:

WRITING PROMPT 3

Writing for the Real World Write the text of a critical business letter to a company producing a form of news media. Analyze the form and convey a conclusion about it.

Possible Subjects
- television newscast
- newspaper front page
- online news source

WRITING PROMPT 4

Writing About Fine Art Write a review about artwork that conveys a message about society. Use subject analysis to ask and answer a question about that message.

Possible Subjects
- an important news photograph
- an illustration on a poster, book, or CD
- a political or editorial cartoon

For additional writing prompts, see

- WriteSmart CD
- Writing Center at **ClassZone.com**

KEY TRAITS

Review the six *KEY TRAITS* with students, focusing mainly on ideas and organization. Compare the list of traits with the rubric on page 1176.

Writing Workshop

Subject Analysis

Have you ever taken something apart and put it back together? When you write a subject analysis, you break a subject into different elements and draw a conclusion about what you found. Writing a subject analysis can deepen your understanding of a complex literary work such as the *Odyssey*. To get started, consult the **Writer's Road Map**.

WRITER'S ROAD MAP

Subject Analysis

WRITING PROMPT 1

Writing from Literature Choose a topic related to the *Odyssey* that you would like to understand better. Write a subject analysis in which you examine the parts of your topic in detail.

Subjects to Consider
- women in the *Odyssey*
- monsters in the *Odyssey*
- Odysseus' strengths and failings as a leader

WRITING PROMPT 2

Writing for the Real World Taking something apart and examining its separate parts is a good way to understand almost anything, from an electronic device to a political concept. Write an analysis of a subject you consider important. Be sure your analysis identifies and explores the significant parts of your subject.

Subjects to Consider
- scientific concepts, such as carbon dating
- medical issues, such as a flu epidemic
- social issues, such as voter turnout

WRITING TOOLS
For prewriting, revision, and editing tools, visit the **Writing Center** at **ClassZone.com**.

KEY TRAITS

1. **IDEAS**
   - Presents a **thesis statement** that identifies the main points of the analysis
   - Uses **evidence** to support and explain the main points

2. **ORGANIZATION**
   - Identifies the subject of the analysis in an engaging **introduction**
   - Uses **transitions** to connect ideas
   - Follows a consistent **organizational pattern**
   - Concludes by **summarizing** and showing the **significance** of the analysis

3. **VOICE**
   - **Tone** adds interest and is appropriate for the purpose and audience

4. **WORD CHOICE**
   - Uses words that are **specific** and **accurate**

5. **SENTENCE FLUENCY**
   - Varies **sentence structure and length**

6. **CONVENTIONS**
   - Employs **correct grammar and usage**

1170 UNIT 11: THE ODYSSEY

Writing Workshop Resources

 RESOURCE MANAGER UNIT 11

Plan and Teach pp. 69–72
Prewriting–Editing pp. 73–77
Writing Rubric p. 78
Speaking and Listening p. 79
Writing Support p. 80*

 **STANDARDS LESSON FILE**

Writing Lessons 9, 36
Grammar Lesson 5
Speaking and Listening Lessons 1, 12

 BEST PRACTICES TOOLKIT

Scaffolding Writing Instruction pp. 43–46*
Venn Diagram • Reporter's Questions
• Spider Map • Analysis Frame: Theme
• Writing Template: Subject Analysis

TECHNOLOGY
- Easy Planner DVD
-  Writing Center at **ClassZone.com**
- WriteSmart CD

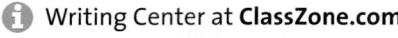 * Resources for Differentiation

Part 1: Analyze a Student Model

Ted Jorgenssen
Park West High School

Are You a Hero?

Everyone has heroes. We read about them in books and see them on the news or in the movies. We might even live next door to one. What qualities do these people share? Some display great strength and courage. Some put others' lives ahead of their own. Some show honesty and
5 humility in difficult situations. I believe that only someone with all of these traits is truly a hero. This definition may seem obvious, but it can lead to surprising conclusions. Often, people considered to be heroes are not, while others who don't see themselves as special are truly heroic. Someday, you may even find out that you are someone's hero.

10 One individual who has always been considered a hero is Odysseus, the main character of Homer's *Odyssey*. When we examine him on the basis of the characteristics listed above, however, he falls short. Odysseus does have great strength and courage. He resists the Sirens, blinds and escapes from the Cyclops, survives Scylla and Charybdis, and returns
15 home after 20 years.

However, Odysseus survives by putting his own life above the lives of others. Because of his love of battle, he ignores advice from his men and the gods. Not one of the 720 men he left Ithaca with returns alive. In failing to fulfill the vow "to bring his shipmates home," which he makes
20 at the start of his journey, he fails to fulfill the second criterion of a hero.

Odysseus also shows little honesty or humility. He enjoys hiding and disguising himself—in the wooden horse during the Trojan War, under the Cyclops's sheep, and as a beggar on his return to Ithaca—and is proud of his deception. In his arrogance, he forgets that he survives

KEY TRAITS IN ACTION

Engaging **introduction** captures reader interest. **Thesis statement** presents the main points of analysis (the three qualities that make a person a hero).

Provides specific **evidence** to support the opinion that Odysseus is strong and brave.

Tone is straightforward and sincere. Varied **sentence structure and length** provide rhythm and interest.

WRITING WORKSHOP **1171**

Teach

Part 1: Analyze a Student Model

Have students read the student model and *KEY TRAITS IN ACTION.* Then discuss the model with the class, pointing out specific examples of each trait and building on what students have already noted. You may also wish to incorporate these activities:

- **Evidence** Point out that writers can choose among many different types of evidence:
  - **sensory details,** which tell how things look, sound, smell, taste, and feel
  - **examples,** specific instances from the text that prove a statement
  - **anecdotes,** brief stories that reveal character or make some point
  - **facts,** statements that can be proved true
  - **quotations,** words and phrases copied directly from the text

  Ask which type of evidence is given in the highlighted text (*examples*) and in the other paragraphs on this page (*examples, quotations*).

- **Tone** Explain that tone is an expression of the writer's attitude toward a subject. It may be serious, angry, or humorous, for example. Tone is conveyed by the writer's choice of words. To help students distinguish tone, write the following sentence on the board:

  > All the shipmates of Odysseus wind up dead, despite his promise to bring them all home. He's a total flop as a hero.

  Have students read the sentences and compare them to lines 18–20 of the student model. *Possible answer: The lines on the board sound irritable and childish. The words "wind up dead" and "flop" show lack of respect for the literature and the essay's audience.*

WRITING WORKSHOP **1171**

- **Transitions** Tell students that transitions are words and phrases that help readers understand how ideas are related. Draw attention to the highlighted phrases in lines 29 and 31. Point out that both show a contrast of ideas. Have students suggest other words that might show comparison or contrast. *Possible answers: both, like, similarly, on the other hand* Point out that transitions can also show time order. Have students identify a time order transitional phrase in the student model. *Possible answer: Two years ago (line 33)*

- **Specific, Accurate Words** Help students discriminate between general or vague words and specific, accurate ones. Ask students to compare the highlighted words in lines 36–37 with the phrase "undergoing lots of procedures." *Possible answers: The highlighted words help readers understand exactly what Jerry had to suffer through— not only three operations but also hundreds of hours of physical therapy.*

  Review the GRAMMAR AND STYLE note on page 1156, pointing out that a metaphor can also help readers understand a situation, person, or place.

- **Explaining the Significance** Point out that one mistake many students make is to summarize some element of a work and then fail to point out its significance. Read these sentences aloud and ask which is a summary and which shows the significance of some literary element.

  - All 720 men perished during the time that the *Odyssey* covers. (*summary*)
  - The deception and arrogance shown by Odysseus are less than heroic. (*significance*)

For interactive student models, see

- WriteSmart CD
- Writing Center at **ClassZone.com**

---

25 many adventures because of help from the god Hermes and the goddesses Athena and Circe. Odysseus is reunited with his wife, but his return is achieved through selfishness and dishonesty. In the final analysis, he is no hero.

In contrast to Odysseus, my brother Jerry has never commanded
30 a fleet of ships or wandered hundreds of miles from home. Jerry is a teenager unknown outside of my community. However, he is heroic in a way that Odysseus never could be.

Two years ago, Jerry was riding his bike when a car hit him. One minute he was a regular 14-year-old, and the next he was in the
35 hospital, facing pain and fears that most of us can't even imagine. He has shown a hero's strength and courage in undergoing three operations and hundreds of hours of painful physical therapy.

Although Jerry has many problems to worry about, he turns his attention to others. He talks with other accident victims on the phone
40 and sends them e-mails and instant messages. He gives advice about how to deal with frustrating physical therapy sessions. He suggests what to say to friends who don't know how to act around somebody recovering from a major injury. Jerry thinks it is ridiculous that I consider him to be a hero. "I went through something that most people
45 don't experience," he said. "It makes sense to try to help somebody else who's going through the same thing."

That's what makes a hero—bravery, unselfishness, honesty, and humility. Whether our heroes are famous or unknown, or from literature or real life, they have qualities that we admire and try to
50 achieve. Whose hero are you?

2

Writer uses a compare-contrast strategy as he continues to analyze the characteristics of a hero. **Transitions** make the organization clear.

Specific, accurate words give the reader a precise understanding of the situation.

Concludes by **summarizing** and explaining the **significance** of the analysis. Question refers back to the title of the essay.

DIFFERENTIATED INSTRUCTION

FOR ENGLISH LEARNERS

Comprehension: Transitions Help students identify different types of signal words and phrases in the model. Point out that some transitions, such as *and,* can link ideas within sentences. Have students identify some of these and suggest alternatives.
Possible answers: "while" (line 8), alternatives: but, on the other hand; *"because" (line 17), alternatives:* since, as a result of

Follow a similar procedure with transitions that show how paragraphs are related.
Possible answers: "also" (line 21), alternatives: in addition, more importantly, furthermore; *"in contrast to" (line 29), alternative:* unlike; *"although" (line 38), alternatives:* even though, despite this, still

To provide English learners with additional writing support, see

R RESOURCE MANAGER—Copy Master
Writing Support p. 80

Part 2: Apply the Writing Process

PREWRITING

What Should I Do?	**What Does It Look Like?**

1. Brainstorm ideas for your analysis.
Use a graphic organizer to identify aspects of the *Odyssey* that intrigue you. Highlight the topics that you'd like to analyze further.

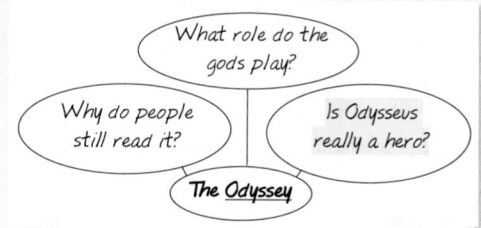

What role do the gods play?

Why do people still read it?

Is Odysseus really a hero?

The Odyssey

2. Focus on a topic and freewrite about it.
After choosing the subject you want to analyze, freewrite about it to examine the elements it is made up of.

Odysseus has a lot of exciting adventures, but he isn't a very nice person. He doesn't really take care of his men, and he is always using trickery to get his way. All he really seems to care about is himself. So what are the things that make someone a hero?

3. Explore your topic.
Think about how your topic breaks down into parts. Creating a list or chart can help.

TIP You might list the distinguishing characteristics of your topic, as this writer has done. Other approaches include comparing and contrasting your topic with a related subject, breaking your topic into a series of steps or stages, or writing an extended definition of your topic.

Qualities of a Hero
- *brave, honest, strong*
- *should not boast or be proud*
- *should care about others*

Heroes in Literature and in Real Life
- *Is Odysseus a hero?*
- *Is my brother Jerry a hero?*

4. Create a working thesis statement.
Review the information you have gathered, and condense your ideas into a statement that explains the main idea of your analysis. Your working thesis is a forecast of what points your essay will cover.

Working thesis statement:

Everybody has heroes. Some have strength and courage. Some put others' lives ahead of their own. Some show honesty and humility in difficult situations. I believe that only someone with all of these traits is a hero.

FOR ENGLISH LEARNERS
Writing: Thesis Statement Have students use these sentence starters to help them explore subject elements and choose a focus:
- I was surprised that _____.
- The significant _____ (parts) all suggest that _____.
- This _____ (aspect) points out that _____.
- Compared to other _____ (literary works, inventions, etc.), _____.

FOR ADVANCED LEARNERS/PRE–AP
Suggest that students try looking at the subject from a specific point of view, such as a feminist, historical, or minority perspective. Suggest that students use Analysis Frame: Theme to provide ideas.

BEST PRACTICES TOOLKIT—Transparency
Analysis Frame: Theme pp. D21, D32

Practice and Apply

To support students during the writing process, use these copy masters:

R RESOURCE MANAGER—Copy Masters
Prewriting–Editing pp. 73–77
Writing Rubric p. 78
Writing Support p. 80 (for English learners)

Part 2: Apply the Writing Process

PREWRITING

1. Brainstorm ideas for your analysis. Two other useful techniques would be clustering or listing. Suggest that students create a cluster that shows all the literary elements they can identify, such as *epic hero*, *setting*, and so on. Then have them note personal responses to each element.

2. Focus on a topic and freewrite about it. Remind students that during freewriting they are to keep their pencils moving and not stop to edit their thoughts. When the time is up, have them go over what they wrote and circle or underline words and phrases that suggest ideas.

3. Explore your topic. Encourage students to use one or more graphic organizers to generate ideas and subtopics. Reference the **TIP** for possible methods of organization, but urge students to look beyond these ideas.

BEST PRACTICES TOOLKIT—Transparencies
Venn Diagram p. A26
Reporter's Questions p. C9
Spider Map p. B22

For interactive graphic organizers, see
Write*Smart* CD
Writing Center at ClassZone.com

4. Create a working thesis statement. Have students analyze the thesis statement in lines 2–6, identifying the main idea and the points that the writer will cover. *Possible answers: the qualities that heroes share: strength, courage, honesty, and humility* Point out that this thesis statement provides a brief preview of what will follow.

DRAFTING

1. **Grab your reader's attention.** Discuss several ways students might begin their essays: with a personal anecdote, an unusual or startling detail, an analogy, or a quotation. Then draw attention to the **TIP**, pointing out that many people write the title last.

2. **Outline.** Students might begin their outlines by listing the topics and main points they will cover, then arrange the order.

3. **Elaborate.** Discuss other ways to elaborate, such as with facts, sensory details, personal feelings, definitions, anecdotes, and quotations. Have students identify some ways the student author elaborated. *Possible answer: fact (line 18), personal response (lines 31–32), anecdote (lines 33–37), quotation (lines 44–46)*

   For practice elaborating, have students work in teams to suggest different ways they might elaborate on one of these statements:

   - The world of the *Odyssey* existed only in the imagination of its author.
   - People have not really changed in thousands of years.

4. **Go beyond a summary.** Point out that a good conclusion connects readers to the essay's subject by answering the questions "So what? Why should I care?" Suggest that students consider ending with a question, as in the model; a prediction; a useful comparison; or a thoughtful quotation.

For a subject analysis writing template, see

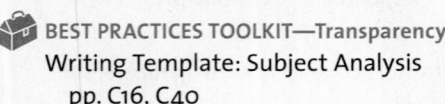

BEST PRACTICES TOOLKIT—Transparency
   Writing Template: Subject Analysis
      pp. C16, C40

Write*Smart* CD

Writing Center at ClassZone.com

What Should I Do?	What Does It Look Like?
1. Grab your reader's attention. Draw your reader into your analysis from the first sentence. Make a statement or ask a question that provokes curiosity, surprise, or agreement. **TIP** A catchy title can intrigue a reader.	**Are You a Hero?** *Everyone has heroes. We read about them in books and see them on the news or in the movies. We might even live next door to one. What qualities do these people share?*
2. Outline. An informal outline can help you organize your analysis. Ask yourself: Which parts of my subject do I want to discuss? How do those parts work together?	**Analysis of a hero** *1. List characteristics. 2. Odysseus is not a hero. • strong and brave • not concerned about others • not honest or humble 3. Jerry is a hero. • brave • helps others • modest 4. Conclusion: Good qualities are more important than fame.*
3. Elaborate. Don't just state the facts. Show readers how each idea relates to the topic as a whole by giving examples, comparing and contrasting, and evaluating each part of the analysis.	*Odysseus survives by putting his own life above the lives of others.* ┤Key point *He ignores advice from his men and the gods. Not one of the 720 men he left Ithaca with returns alive. In failing to fulfill the vow "to bring his shipmates home," which he makes at the start of his journey, he fails to fulfill the second criterion of a hero.* ┤2 examples + quotation
4. Go beyond a summary. Your conclusion should show readers why they should care about and remember what you have written. **TIP** Before revising, consult the key traits on page 1132 and the rubric and peer-reader questions on page 1138.	*That's what makes a hero—bravery, unselfishness, honesty, and humility.* ┤Summary *Whether our heroes are famous or unknown, they have qualities that we admire and try to achieve. Whose hero are you?* ┤Significance + question for reader

---

DIFFERENTIATED INSTRUCTION

FOR LESS–PROFICIENT WRITERS

Outline To help students organize their ideas, guide them in creating outlines. Have them answer the following questions and use their answers to generate informal outlines:

- What is your thesis statement, or the main point of your essay?
- What points do you want to analyze?
- What do you want to say about the first point?

- What evidence supports this idea?
- What do you want to say about the next point?
- What evidence supports this?
- What conclusion do you draw from these points?

REVISING AND EDITING

What Should I Do?

1. Eliminate irrelevant information.
- Ask a peer reader to <u>underline</u> statements that seem to be unnecessary or off the topic.
- Replace these sentences with examples, quotations, or other appropriate details.

See page 1176: Ask a Peer Reader

2. Connect ideas with transitions.
- Highlight transitional words and phrases, such as *first*, *after*, *however*, and *in contrast to*.
- If your essay has few highlights, add transitional words or phrases to show how ideas are related.

3. Be specific.
- Circle boring, general words and phrases, such as *a lot*, *some*, *very*, *really*, and *things*.
- Choose specific, accurate words that get your point across.

4. Fine-tune your tone.
- Read your essay aloud. [Bracket] words or phrases that are too slangy or that make you seem uncertain of your opinions.
- Substitute formal vocabulary that is appropriate for a subject analysis.

What Does It Look Like?

> One individual who has always been considered a hero is Odysseus, ~~He is also called Ulysses, and the American president Ulysses S. Grant was named after him.~~
> the main character of Homer's <u>Odyssey</u>.

> When we examine Odysseus on the basis of the characteristics listed above, however, he falls short.

> Although
> ^Jerry has many problems to worry about, He turns his attention to others.

> Odysseus is (very) strong and (really) brave. He has to deal with the Sirens, the Cyclops, and Scylla and Charybdis. It takes him a (long time) to get back home.
> Odysseus does have great strength and courage. He resists the Sirens, blinds and escapes from the Cyclops, survives Scylla and Charybdis, and returns home after 20 years.

> Jerry thinks I am [kind of a goof] for calling him a hero. [I guess] he went through something that is [sort of weird.]
> Jerry thinks it is ridiculous that I consider him to be a hero. "I went through something that most people don't experience," he said.

REVISING AND EDITING

1. Eliminate irrelevant information. Discuss ways that peer readers can be helpful:
- tell what you think the main idea is
- identify interesting or helpful points
- ask questions about confusing parts
- provide specific, focused feedback

2. Connect ideas with transitions. Discuss different ways students can connect ideas, such as by repeating key words or linking sentences with pronouns such as *these* or *this*. Ask students to generate a list of transitions that they might use.

3. Be specific. Help students discriminate between boring, general words and specific, accurate words. List these words on the board and ask students to suggest more precise alternatives:
- good (**Possible answers:** *honorable, loyal, virtuous*)
- character (**Possible answers:** *soldier, hero, monster, sidekick*)
- nice (**Possible answers:** *kind, helpful, generous*)
- went (**Possible answers:** *sailed, raced, wandered*)

4. Fine-tune your tone. Remind students that an analysis is a formal piece of writing that should be written with appropriately formal language. Suggest that they use the type of language suited to speaking with a respected adult. Such language would
- contain no slang and few contractions
- avoid catch phrases and trite, overused expressions
- use complex sentence structure and an academic vocabulary

For interactive revision tools, see

🖉 Write*Smart* CD

ℹ️ Writing Center at **ClassZone.com**

FOR ENGLISH LEARNERS

Transitions Provide sentence frames such as these to help students use transitions in their writing:
- While some _____, others _____.
- Through this _____ (identify subject), readers discover _____.
- However, _____.
- The best example of this is _____.
- In contrast to _____, _____.
- In addition to this, _____.
- As these details show, _____.

Preparing to Publish

Support for meeting the goals in the writing rubric is supplied throughout the Writing Workshop on pages 1170–1175.

For Rubric Bank, see

 WriteSmart CD

ℹ️ Writing Center at **ClassZone.com**

Assess and Reteach

S **STANDARDS LESSON FILE**

Writing Lesson 9: Revising for Parallelism

Writing Lesson 36: Elaborate with Incidents, Examples, and Quotations

Grammar Lesson 5: Verb Agreement with Indefinite Pronouns

Preparing to Publish Subject Analysis

Apply the Rubric

A strong subject analysis . . .

☑ presents the main points of the subject being analyzed in a clear thesis statement

☑ develops ideas logically, connecting them with appropriate transitions

☑ includes evidence to support ideas

☑ has a tone that is tailored to the audience and purpose

☑ maintains interest by using strong, specific vocabulary

☑ varies sentence structures and lengths

☑ goes beyond a mere summary of ideas to show the significance of the subject

Ask a Peer Reader

• What are my main points?

• Which part of my analysis has the strongest support? Which lacks convincing evidence?

• Does my analysis include unnecessary information?

Check Your Grammar

• Use parallel structure. Sentence parts that have the same function should have the same form.

> He resists the Sirens, blinds and escapes from the Cyclops, survives Scylla and Charybdis, and returns home after 20 years.

> Jerry talks with other accident victims. He gives advice about how to deal with physical therapy. He suggests what to say to friends who don't know how to act around somebody recovering from a major injury.

See page R64: Parallel Structure

• Make sure that indefinite-pronoun subjects have the correct verbs. Remember that the indefinite pronouns *all, any, more, most, none,* and *some* can take either singular or plural verbs depending on the noun they refer to.

> Everyone has heroes. What qualities do these people share? Some display great strength and courage. Most are not well known. All are worthy of respect.

See page R54: Indefinite Pronouns

Writing Online

 PUBLISHING OPTIONS
For publishing options, visit the **Writing Center** at **ClassZone.com.**

ASSESSMENT PREPARATION
For writing and grammar assessment practice, go to the **Assessment Center** at **ClassZone.com.**

Delivering an Oral Report

To make your subject analysis even more interesting and to reach a broader audience than you can in writing, present it as an oral report.

Planning the Oral Report

1. **Decide what information to cover.** Find out who your audience will be and how long you will be expected to talk. Tailor your presentation to those guidelines. If your teacher expects you to answer questions afterwards, think of what the most likely questions will be and how you will answer them.

2. **Collect or create visuals to illustrate your points.** Consider creating a flip chart, poster, or slide presentation.

3. **Rehearse your report.** Run through your report several times in front of family or friends. Consider having someone time you. Be sure you can incorporate the visuals easily and naturally into your presentation.

Qualities of a Hero	Odysseus
Strong and brave	Yes
Puts others first	No
Honest and humble	No

Delivering the Oral Report

1. **Speak directly to your audience.** Don't talk to your shoes or to the ceiling. If possible, have a friend in the audience signal you if you begin rushing through what you have to say.

2. **Avoid "um" and "uh."** It's okay to pause for a moment and take a breath instead of filling every second of your presentation with speech.

3. **Use facial expressions for emphasis.** For example, if your topic is funny or entertaining, don't be afraid to smile.

4. **Ask for feedback.** Find out what a few audience members thought of your report. You may learn about weaknesses that you can correct the next time you speak before a group.

5. **Evaluate your performance.** Turn to page R78 to read about what qualities make an oral report effective.

SPEAKING AND LISTENING

Ask students to read this page to get an overview of how to present an oral report. Ask students what types of speakers they enjoy hearing. Responses may include speakers who:

- quickly come to the point
- avoid speaking in a monotone
- speak with enough volume to be heard and slowly enough to be understood
- demonstrate enthusiasm for the subject as well as knowledge of it

Then discuss the qualities of good visuals. Help students recognize that these should be simple, as well as large enough to be clearly visible. Allow time for students to practice their speeches. Encourage them to rehearse in front of a mirror before practicing in front of friends or family. Suggest that they use note cards rather than prepared scripts, because note cards promote natural-sounding speech.

Before students begin working, review this rubric with them so that they understand their goals:

Rubric A strong oral report

- shows evidence of planning, research, and rehearsal
- contains supporting evidence for each key idea
- includes visuals that illustrate specific points
- is delivered clearly, with appropriate emphasis, pacing, and volume
- is addressed to the audience, as shown by eye contact and facial expressions
- provides an opportunity for questions

R RESOURCE MANAGER—Copy Master
Speaking and Listening p. 79

S STANDARDS LESSON FILE
Speaking and Listening Lesson 1:
Preparing and Presenting a Speech

Speaking and Listening Lesson 12:
Active Listening

Assessment Practice

CHECK READINESS

Read aloud the paragraph under **ASSESS** and stress to students that this is not the full Unit Test but a way for them to check their readiness for it. Then have students examine the skills listed under **REVIEW** and look back in the unit or in the **Student Resource Bank** for any skills they need to review.

READ THE SELECTIONS

Remind students to keep unit goals in mind as they read the passage, paying particular attention to these literary and reading skills:

- characteristics of an epic
  setting
  conflict
  theme
- epic hero
- summarize

To help students focus on the epic hero, urge them to consider these questions:

- Which details in this selection show Odysseus' words and actions?
- What character traits do those details reveal?

ANSWER THE QUESTIONS

Direct students to pages R93–R101 of the **Handbook** to review test-taking strategies.

- As students prepare to answer the multiple-choice questions, remind them not to choose the first alternative that seems to fit. Instead, they should read through all the choices, eliminate any that are clearly wrong, and then choose the *best* answer—the one that is the most accurate.
- Remind students to take a little time to plan their written responses before writing them. Students can use simple prewriting strategies such as listing ideas or making a concept web. When they have finished writing, they should take time to proofread their work, as well.

ASSESS
The practice test items on the next few pages match skills listed on the Unit Goals page (page 1087) and addressed throughout this unit. Taking this practice test will help you assess your knowledge of these skills and determine your readiness for the Unit Test.

REVIEW
After you take the practice test, your teacher can help you identify any skills you need to review.

- Characteristics of an Epic
  - Setting
  - Conflict
  - Theme
- Epic Hero
- Summarize
- Prefixes
- Latin Roots
- Figurative Language

ASSESSMENT ONLINE
For more assessment practice and test-taking tips, go to the **Assessment Center** at ClassZone.com.

Reading Comprehension

DIRECTIONS *Read the following excerpt from Book 9 of the* Odyssey *and then answer the questions.*

from The Odyssey
Homer

Blinded, and sick with pain from his head wound,
the master stroked each ram, then let it pass,
but my men riding on the pectoral fleece
the giant's blind hands blundering never found.
5 Last of them all my ram, the leader, came,
weighted by wool and me with my meditations.
The Cyclops patted him, and then he said:

'Sweet cousin ram, why lag behind the rest
in the night cave? You never linger so,
10 but graze before them all, and go afar
to crop sweet grass, and take your stately way
leading along the streams, until at evening
you run to be the first one in the fold.
Why, now, so far behind? Can you be grieving
15 over your Master's eye? That carrion rogue
and his accurst companions burnt it out
when he had conquered all my wits with wine.
Nohbdy will not get out alive, I swear.
Oh, had you brain and voice to tell
20 where he may be now, dodging all my fury!
Bashed by this hand and bashed on this rock wall
his brains would strew the floor, and I should have
rest from the outrage Nohbdy worked upon me.'

He sent us into the open, then. Close by,
25 I dropped and rolled clear of the ram's belly,
going this way and that to untie the men.
With many glances back, we rounded up
his fat, stiff-legged sheep to take aboard,
and drove them down to where the good ship lay.
30 We saw, as we came near, our fellows' faces
shining; then we saw them turn to grief
tallying those who had not fled from death.

DIFFERENTIATED INSTRUCTION

FOR ENGLISH LEARNERS
Assessment Practice: Work Backward

Prepare students by having them read the questions *before* reading the passage. Have pairs find unfamiliar words in test directions and questions and follow these steps:

1. Write each word on an index card.
2. Look up the meaning in a dictionary and write it on the back of the card.

3. Use the cards to practice the words with your partner and to teach them to others.

I hushed them, jerking head and eyebrows up,
and in a low voice told them: 'Load this herd;
35 move fast, and put the ship's head toward the breakers.'
They all pitched in at loading, then embarked
and struck their oars into the sea. Far out,
as far off shore as shouted words would carry,
I sent a few back to the adversary:

40 'O Cyclops! Would you feast on my companions?
Puny, am I, in a Caveman's hands?
How do you like the beating that we gave you,
you damned cannibal? Eater of guests
under your roof! Zeus and the gods have paid you!'

45 The blind thing in his doubled fury broke
a hilltop in his hands and heaved it after us.
Ahead of our black prow it struck and sank
whelmed in a spuming geyser, a giant wave
that washed the ship stern foremost back to shore.
50 I got the longest boathook out and stood
fending us off, with furious nods to all
to put their backs into a racing stroke—
row, row, or perish. So the long oars bent
kicking the foam sternward, making head
55 until we drew away, and twice as far.
Now when I cupped my hands I heard the crew
in low voices protesting:

                    'Godsake, Captain!
Why bait the beast again? Let him alone!'

'That tidal wave he made on the first throw
60 all but beached us.'

                    'All but stove us in!'

'Give him our bearing with your trumpeting,
he'll get the range and lob a boulder.'

                    'Aye

He'll smash our timbers and our heads together!'
I would not heed them in my glorying spirit,
65 but let my anger flare and yelled:

ITEM ANALYSIS

COMPREHENSION AND WRITTEN RESPONSE	ITEMS	UNIT PAGES
Characteristics of an Epic	1, 5, 7, 8, 9	1094–1101, 1103, 1141
Setting	1, 9	1094–1101
Conflict	5, 8	1094–1101
Theme	7	1094–1101
Epic Hero	3, 6, 7	1094–1101, 1103, 1141
Summarize	2, 4, 8	1141

VOCABULARY	ITEMS	UNIT PAGES
Prefixes	1, 2, 3, 4	1139
Latin Roots	5, 6, 7, 8	1168

WRITING AND GRAMMAR	ITEMS	UNIT PAGES
Figurative Language	1, 2, 3, 4	1169

FOR LESS–PROFICIENT READERS

Assessment Support Consider these options for completing the Assessment Practice:

- Have students "work backward" to review the test questions *before* reading the passage.

- Select random questions in the Assessment and have students demonstrate *how* and *where* to look for the answers.

- Ask students to locate unfamiliar vocabulary words in the Assessment. Elicit the words' meanings from the class.

- Have students record useful testing words and definitions in their journals for later reference.

- Read the selection or parts of it aloud to aid in student comprehension.

McDougal Littell
Assessment System

After checking student readiness with this Assessment Practice, you may administer the complete Unit 11 Test in order to more thoroughly evaluate student mastery of unit goals.

Comprehension

Model a thinking process for answering multiple-choice questions.

1. **A is correct.** It is not the cave itself but its resident that matters, for one of the characteristics that qualifies the *Odyssey* as an epic poem is its inclusion of monsters and other supernatural beings. The settings described in B, C, and D might appear in some epics but are not specific to epics.

2. **C is correct.** The prisoners' escape plan— clinging to the underside of the rams—is described at the start of the passage. A can be eliminated because it is the Cyclops who calls upon Poseidon (lines 91–102). B is incorrect because the escape is made in the daytime (lines 8–12). D is incorrect because the prisoners are never said to roll boulders.

3. **D is correct.** In this passage, Odysseus shows cunning in overseeing the theft of the Cyclops' sheep. A is incorrect because Odysseus does not rely much on physical strength, nor is he seeking adventure. B is incorrect because stealing the sheep is an act of dishonesty. C can be eliminated because Odysseus here does not call upon the gods for help.

4. **C is correct.** Odysseus' actions are described in lines 50–52. A is incorrect because Odysseus blinds the Cyclops in an earlier scene. B is incorrect because the Cyclops, not Odysseus, tries to flood the ship (lines 45–49). D is incorrect because Odysseus taunts the Cyclops from the sea in the lines that follow the passage cited.

5. **B is correct.** The men's begging words are presented in lines 57–63. A and C can be disqualified because the men do not disagree with Odysseus about where to hide from the Cyclops or whether or not to kill it. D is untrue.

6. **A is correct.** In line 64, Odysseus says that his "glorying spirit" led him to declare his name. B is incorrect because while revealing his name is unwise, it is bold. C is incorrect because Odysseus is honest in revealing his true name. D can be eliminated because Odysseus avenges nothing by revealing his name.

'Cyclops,

if ever mortal man inquire
how you were put to shame and blinded, tell him
Odysseus, raider of cities, took your eye:
Laertes' son, whose home's on Ithaca!'

70 At this he gave a mighty sob and rumbled:

'Now comes the weird upon me, spoken of old.
A wizard, grand and wondrous, lived here—Telemus,
a son of Eurymus; great length of days
he had in wizardry among the Cyclopes,
75 and these things he foretold for time to come:
my great eye lost, and at Odysseus' hands.
Always I had in mind some giant, armed
in giant force, would come against me here.
But this, but you—small, pitiful and twiggy—
80 you put me down with wine, you blinded me.
Come back, Odysseus, and I'll treat you well,
praying the god of earthquake to befriend you—
his son I am, for he by his avowal
fathered me, and, if he will, he may
85 heal me of this black wound—he and no other
of all the happy gods or mortal men.'

Few words I shouted in reply to him:
'If I could take your life I would and take
your time away, and hurl you down to hell!
90 The god of earthquake could not heal you there!'

At this he stretched his hands out in his darkness
toward the sky of stars, and prayed Poseidon:

'O hear me, lord, blue girdler of the islands,
if I am thine indeed, and thou art father:
95 grant that Odysseus, raider of cities, never
see his home: Laertes' son, I mean,
who kept his hall on Ithaca. Should destiny
intend that he shall see his roof again
among his family in his father land,
100 far be that day, and dark the years between.

Let him lose all companions, and return
under strange sail to bitter days at home.'

DIFFERENTIATED INSTRUCTION

FOR ENGLISH LEARNERS

Assessment Vocabulary To help students understand the Comprehension questions, teach or review these key vocabulary words:

- Item 3: *quality,* "character trait" (See Item 6.)
- Item 5: *develops,* "happens; arises"
- Item 7: *revealed,* "made clear"

To help students understand the Written Response questions, teach or review these key vocabulary words:

- Items 8, 9: *support,* "give reasons for"
- Items 8, 9: *details,* "specific words, events, or images"
- Item 9: *role,* "function (of a character)"

Comprehension

DIRECTIONS *Answer these questions about the excerpt from the* Odyssey.

1. The cave mentioned in line 9 is an epic setting because it is
   A home to a fantastic, archetypal creature
   B a beautiful, hidden location
   C a rugged, barren land formation
   D an imaginary but believable place

2. Which statement summarizes the escape plan for Odysseus and his men?
   A They beg Poseidon to make the Cyclops free them.
   B They blind the Cyclops and then sneak away during the night.
   C They hide in the rams' wool and let the rams carry them past the Cyclops.
   D They roll boulders down a hill to distract the Cyclops, and then run.

3. Which quality of an epic hero does Odysseus display in lines 24–35?
   A strength in pursuit of adventure
   B honesty in the face of conflict
   C dependence on the gods
   D cunning in the face of danger

4. Which statement summarizes Odysseus' heroic actions in lines 45–55?
   A He blinds the Cyclops with a boathook.
   B He throws a boulder that causes a wave to flood the ship.
   C He single-handedly pushes the ship out to sea while urging his men to row.
   D He taunts the Cyclops from the shore while the ship is sinking.

5. What conflict develops between Odysseus and his men in lines 56–69?
   A They disagree about where to hide from the Cyclops.
   B The men beg Odysseus to stop taunting the Cyclops, but he continues.
   C They disagree about whether or not to kill the Cyclops.
   D The men want to steal the Cyclops' sheep without telling Odysseus.

6. Which character trait causes Odysseus to reveal his name to the Cyclops?
   A pride   **C** dishonesty
   B cowardice   **D** vengefulness

7. Which theme of the *Odyssey* is revealed in the Cyclops' speech in lines 75–80?
   A the rescue of a nation from invaders
   B a hero's loyalty to his friends
   C the victorious homecoming of a hero
   D a hero's triumph over a powerful opponent

Written Response

SHORT RESPONSE *Write three or four sentences to answer this question.*

8. Briefly summarize the conflict between Odysseus and the Cyclops. Support your answer with details from the excerpt.

EXTENDED RESPONSE *Write two or three paragraphs to answer this question.*

9. Explain the importance of the sea and the role of Poseidon in this excerpt. Support your answer with details from the excerpt.

 **GO ON**

1181

7. **D is correct.** *The fact that the Cyclops expected to be defeated by a giant emphasizes Odysseus' greatness. A is incorrect because the Cyclops has not invaded Odysseus' nation; indeed, Odysseus is a trespasser on the Cyclops' island. B is incorrect because although Odysseus is a loyal friend, these lines do not mention that trait. C is incorrect because the scene concerns Odysseus' escape, not his homecoming.*

Written Response

Possible short response:

8. *This conflict pits human brains against monstrous brawn. The Cyclops traps Odysseus and his men in a cave, but Odysseus enables his men to escape by hiding them among the Cyclops' rams (lines 1–4). When Odysseus taunts the monster (lines 40–45), the Cyclops hurls a hilltop at the ship (lines 45–46). Finally, the Cyclops prays that Poseidon will end the conflict in a way that he himself cannot (lines 91–102).*

Possible extended response:

9. *The sea is a key element in this excerpt because it is both a means of escape for Odysseus and his men and a danger to them. The Cyclops tries to use the sea against the escaping prisoners, first by causing a huge wave to wash over the ship (lines 45–49) and then by praying to Poseidon, god of the sea, to cause them harm (lines 91–102).*

Poseidon is a key player in this scene because he is the god of the sea and the Cyclops' father. As such, Poseidon may desire to fulfill the prayer of his son, whom Odysseus has harmed, and, especially since Odysseus travels by sea, Poseidon has the means to fulfill the Cyclops' wish that Odysseus be kept from his home (lines 95–96) or that he return home only after many years, at the cost of his companions' lives, and "under strange sail" (lines 97–102).

FOR ENGLISH LEARNERS

Review Academic Vocabulary On the board, list the academic vocabulary shown in italics. Then give the examples in random order and have students classify them. Elicit other examples from students.

- *setting:* This story takes place in the years following the Trojan War.
- *epic:* Odysseus has a series of amazing adventures as he journeys toward home.
- *conflict:* He must overcome many enemies during his travels.
- *epic hero:* Since he is braver and more clever than average people, Odysseus triumphs.
- *theme:* His deep desire to return to his family illustrates the power of love.

Vocabulary

1. B is correct. Untying reverses the action of tying; in line 26, untie refers to freeing the men from their ropes. A describes the prefix re-, not un-. C is incorrect, because untie refers to an action, not to an object. D is incorrect because untie does not involve going against something.

2. D is correct. The context of line 36—loading a ship and rowing away—verifies the meaning. A is incorrect because the men are leaving, not staying. B is incorrect because they are rowing away from land rather than toward it. C suggests that embarked relates to the sound of barking, but that meaning makes no sense in this context.

3. D is correct. In line 82, the Cyclops falsely tells Odysseus that he will get Poseidon to help—become friendly to—Odysseus. A can be eliminated; it suggests the opposite meaning. B is incorrect because be- does not imply begging. C shares a partial meaning with D but is incorrect because the meaning of be- implies finding a friend, not just looking for one.

4. A is correct. The context discusses Odysseus' turning again toward home. B is incorrect because the context does not imply any meaning of regarding. C implies that return means "different turn," and D implies that return means "more turn"; both meanings make less sense in the context of Odysseus' return home than "turn again" does.

5. A is correct. The context describes a huge wave overwhelming the ship, and such a wave would be foaming with bubbles. B, C, and D name possible descriptions of a wave but have nothing to do with the meaning of spuma.

6. B is correct. The context contrasts mortal humans with gods, and the chief difference is that humans die but gods do not. A has a related meaning but is a weaker choice, since all people are subject to death whether their lives are long or short. C comes from the same root as mortal but does not make sense in context. D reflects the meaning of the root but is not implied by the context.

Vocabulary

DIRECTIONS *Use context clues and your knowledge of prefixes to answer the following questions.*

1. The prefix *un-* in the word *untie* in line 26 most likely means

   A performs an action over again

   B reverses a specified action

   C removes a specific thing

   D goes against something

2. The prefix *em-* means "to put onto." What does the word *embarked* mean in line 36?

   A stayed on shore

   B rowed toward land

   C made a loud noise

   D got onto a ship

3. The prefix *be-* means "to make." The word *befriend* in line 82 means to

   A form a rivalry

   B beg for companionship

   C look for friendship

   D become friends with

4. The prefix *re-* in the word *return* in line 101 most likely means

   A again

   B regarding

   C different

   D more

DIRECTIONS *Use context clues and your knowledge of Latin words and roots to answer the following questions.*

5. The Latin word *spuma* means "foam." What is the most likely meaning of *spuming* as it is used in line 48?

   A bubbling

   B rising

   C shooting

   D raging

6. *Mortal* comes from the Latin root *mer,* which means "to die." What is the most likely meaning of *mortal* as it is used in line 86?

   A short-lived

   B subject to death

   C morbid

   D deadly

7. The Latin root *civ* means "citizen." Which of the following words most likely comes from that root?

   A carrion (line 15)

   B companions (line 16)

   C crew (line 56)

   D cities (line 95)

8. The Latin word *destinare* means "to determine." What is the most likely meaning of *destiny* as it is used in line 97?

   A shame

   B fate

   C privilege

   D misfortune

1182

7. D is correct. Dwellers in cities often are called "citizens." Additionally, cities sounds more like civ than does carrion, companions, or crew. A has nothing specifically in common with citizens. B is incorrect because citizenship and companionship are not closely related concepts. C is incorrect because citizenship has to do with cities and nations, not with boats.

8. B is correct. Fate determines whether Odysseus "shall see his roof again" (line 98). A and C can be disqualified because neither shame nor privilege will determine whether Odysseus returns home safely. D is incorrect because misfortune suggests "bad luck," a weaker concept than determination.

Writing & Grammar

DIRECTIONS *Read the passage and answer the questions that follow.*

> (1) Ithaca, an island west of the Greek mainland, was the home of Odysseus. (2) Today, the island's rugged terrain and other physical features still mirror those described in the *Odyssey.* (3) Ancient ruins lie south of the narrow isthmus that gives Ithaca its distinctive shape. (4) On a hilltop in Pilikáta, you may view the three seas and mountains that Odysseus saw from his palace. (5) The Fountain of Arethusa, mentioned in the *Odyssey,* is a spring located beneath a towering sea cliff. (6) You may visit this spring by hiking along steep mountain paths. (7) Visiting these sites allows a person to trace the ancient travels of Odysseus.

1. Which rewrite of sentence 3 includes a simile?

A Ancient ruins lie south of the isthmus that gives Ithaca an hourglass shape.

B Ancient ruins lie south of the narrow isthmus that separates Ithaca in two.

C Ancient ruins lie south of the narrow isthmus that divides Ithaca like the neck of an hourglass.

D Ancient ruins lie south of the narrow isthmus that separates Ithaca into north and south.

2. Which rewrite of sentence 4 includes a metaphor?

A A Pilikáta hilltop view offers a scenic landscape of the three seas and mountains that Odysseus saw from his palace.

B On a hilltop in Pilikáta the view is a landscape painting of the three seas and mountains that Odysseus saw from his palace.

C In Pilikáta, the hilltop view is like the view of the three seas and mountains that Odysseus saw from his palace.

D On a hilltop in Pilikáta the view features the three raging seas and towering mountains that Odysseus saw from his palace.

3. Which rewrite of sentence 5 includes a simile?

A The Fountain of Arethusa, mentioned in the *Odyssey,* is a spring located beneath a towering sea cliff that stands like a watchful guardian.

B The Fountain of Arethusa, mentioned in the *Odyssey,* is a spring located beneath a towering sea cliff of jagged rocks.

C The Fountain of Arethusa, a spring that flows beneath a towering sea cliff, is mentioned in the *Odyssey.*

D The Fountain of Arethusa, mentioned in the *Odyssey,* is a cool, fresh spring located beneath a towering sea cliff.

4. Which rewrite of sentence 7 includes a metaphor?

A Visiting these sites is like tracking the travels of Odysseus in ancient times.

B To visit these sites is to walk through the pages of the *Odyssey* itself.

C Visiting these sites makes one remember the travels of Odysseus.

D To visit these sites is to recall Odysseus' travels in ancient times.

STOP

ANSWERS
Writing & Grammar

1. C *is correct.* Like the neck of an hourglass *is a simile for the shape of the isthmus.* A *is incorrect because* hourglass shape *is a metaphor, not a simile.* B *and* D *contain no figurative comparisons.*

2. B *is correct.* The phrase the view is a landscape painting *is a comparison that does not use signal words—a metaphor.* A *and* D *are literal descriptions that do not use figurative comparisons.* C *is phrased as a simile; furthermore, it offers a literal rather than a figurative comparison.*

3. A *is correct.* The comparison between a cliff and a guardian is figurative; the use of like *makes it a simile.* B, C, *and* D *are literal, not figurative, comparisons and do not use signal words.*

4. B *is correct.* The phrase to walk through the pages *is figurative, for a person cannot literally walk through a book; the absence of signal words identifies the figurative language as a metaphor.* A *uses the word* like, *which is a clue that the comparison is not a metaphor, and the comparison between visiting the sites and tracking Odysseus' travels is more literal than figurative.* C *and* D *use literal language.*

INTRODUCE *GREAT READS*

In Unit 11, students have discussed two big questions. Invite students to tell which question they found more intriguing and why, and then focus attention on this page. Discuss the recommended books and their summaries, pointing out how each connects to the related question. Encourage students to choose one or more of these "great reads" to read independently.

ⓘ ClassZone.com

To find additional books that match students' interests and ability levels, visit the Literature Center at **ClassZone.com**.

UNIT **11**
Great Reads

Ideas for Independent Reading

Read more epic tales, and see how Homer's masterpiece has inspired contemporary writers.

The Iliad
by Homer

In the *Iliad*, Homer writes of the events that preceded the *Odyssey*—the actual battles and conflicts during the Trojan War. Menelaus and his brother, Agamemnon, struggle for power; Agamemnon fights with his greatest warrior, Achilles; Achilles shows loyalty to his closest friend, Patroclos; Odysseus commands his powerful army. The *Iliad* shows what the men in the *Odyssey* have left behind them, depicting the greater and smaller aspects of ancient war.

The Aeneid
by Virgil

Odysseus had tremendous difficulty returning home. What was the experience of the Trojans, who no longer had a home? Defeated in the Trojan War, Aeneas and his companions set sail at the instruction of the gods on Mount Olympus. The goddess Venus, Aeneas' mother, has told them they must found a new city. That city will eventually become the center of a new and majestic power—the Roman Empire. However, they are waylaid by storms, the wrath and vengefulness of the goddess Juno, and Aeneas' affection for Dido, the queen of Carthage in northern Africa.

The Epic of Gilgamesh
translated by Stephen Mi

The Epic of Gilgamesh is t oldest known piece of wr in the world. Experts bel it preceded **the *Odyssey*** b at least a thousand years was found written on bro clay tablets in the ruined of Nineveh. Gilgamesh, great but selfish king of U (modern-day Iraq), has hi transformed by his frienc with Enkidu. Together, th two bring peace to his ci battle monsters similar t those encountered in Homer's work, and go on quest for immortality.

Omeros
by Derek Walcott

Walcott, a Caribbean-American poet and playwright, resets **the *Odyssey*** in contemporary St. Lucia. This book-length poem follows contemporary characters—fishermen, a household servant, a seer—who share traits and names with those in Homer's work, as they travel through the Caribbean Islands, Europe, and the United States. Throughout the book, the poet himself addresses Omeros (Greek for "Homer") as a source of inspiration. Like Odysseus' traveling companions, all the characters are, in one way or another, searching for a home.

Cold Mountain
by Charles Frazier

This novel has been called "an American *Odyssey*." Inman, a Confederate soldier in the Civil War, has been severely wounded and leaves the army, walking home to Ada, whom he loved before going to war. The journey is difficult, and Inman is consistently waylaid by others in the South who have been affected by the war. Like Odysseus, Inman must use all the cunning and determination he has to make it home. Like Penelope, Ada must figure out how to live without the love she had relied upon, knowing he might never return to her.

The Hero with a Thousand Faces
by Joseph Campbell

What makes a hero? Do heroes embody the same ideals, even in different s contexts? Joseph Campbe examines heroes, looking at sources that range fro Greek mythology to fairy tales and Eastern philoso and claims that the hero timeless. No matter how story changes, Campbell the hero is a constant fig his attributes are similar and equally significant through time.

1184 UNIT 11: THE ODYSSEY

UNIT 12

The Power of Research

RESEARCH WORKSHOPS

- Research Strategies
- Writing Research Papers

1185

For help in planning this unit, see

R RESOURCE MANAGER UNIT 12
pp. 1–7

INTRODUCE THE UNIT

This unit is divided into two parts. The **Research Strategies Workshop,** pages 1188–1209, introduces students to strategies they can use to do both academic and everyday research. Students learn about selecting and using various electronic and print resources. As they learn, they also apply the information in hands-on activities designed to help them gain proficiency in using these various research tools and strategies.

The **Writing Workshop,** pages 1210–1233, provides a framework for students to apply the strategies they have learned to an academic writing assignment: a research paper. After analyzing a student model, students are guided through a step-by-step process in writing their own research papers.

Research Strategies Workshop
pp. 1188–1209

SKILLS STRAND	
Research and Study Skills	Plan and Focus Research pp. 1189–1190
	Develop Research Questions p. 1190
	Use the Internet to Select Relevant Sites pp. 1191–1193, 1208
	Navigate Relevant Internet Sites p. 1193
	Use Library or Media Center Resources pp. 1194–1200, 1208
	Distinguish Between Primary and Secondary Sources p. 1196
	Use Parts of a Book to Locate Information p. 1200
	Choose and Evaluate Information and Sources by Applying Evaluation Criteria pp. 1201–1205, 1209
	Use Evaluation Criteria to Evaluate a Web Site pp. 1202–1203
	Use Evaluation Criteria to Evaluate Nonfiction Books and Periodicals pp. 1204–1205, 1209
	Collect Data for a Report pp. 1206–1208
Vocabulary	Academic Vocabulary pp. 1191, 1992, 1193, 1194, 1195, 1196, 1197, 1199
Speaking, Listening, Viewing, and Media	Discuss pp. 1188, T1189–T1209

Assessment-Based Planning: Skills in red are assessed on the Unit 12   Test. **T** = Teacher's Edition page

SKILLS STRAND

**Writing Workshop:
Research Paper**
pp. 1210–1233

**Reading and
Informational Texts**

Analyze a Research Paper pp. 1211–1216

**Writing,
Grammar,
and Style**

Write a Research Paper pp. 1210–1233

Narrow a Research Topic p. 1217

Locate and Evaluate Relevant Sources p. 1218

Make Source Cards p. 1219

Take Notes p. 1220

Summarize and Paraphrase Information pp. 1212, 1220

Quote Directly and Avoid Plagiarism pp. 1213, 1214, 1221, 1227

Write a Thesis Statement pp. 1222, 1226

Organize and Outline Information p. 1222

Use Transitions to Connect Ideas pp. 1215, 1226

Support Ideas with Reasons pp. 1213, 1223, 1226

Document Sources pp. 1224, 1227

Prepare a Works Cited List pp. 1225, 1227–1229

Format a Research Paper p. 1230

**Speaking, Listening,
Viewing, and Media**

Discuss pp. 1210–1216, 1230

Create a Web Site pp. 1231–1233

**Skills Assessed on
the Unit 12 Test:**

**Reading and
Informational Texts**
• Analyze and
  evaluate a research
  paper

**Research and Study
Skills**
• Use the Internet
  to select and
  navigate relevant
  sites
• Use library
  and reference
  sources to locate
  information
• Distinguish
  between primary
  and secondary
  sources
• Evaluate Web sites
  and other sources
  of information
• Collect data for
  a report

**Writing, Grammar,
and Style**
• Narrow a research
  topic
• Take notes and
  document sources
• Organize
  information for
  a report
• Summarize
  and paraphrase
  information to
  avoid plagiarism
• Prepare a works
  cited list
• Use transitions to
  connect ideas
• Support ideas
  with reasons
• Additional writing
  skills

✐ For additional lesson
planning help, see **Easy
Planner DVD.**

OBJECTIVES

- establish prior knowledge about **research** strategies
- list personal research tasks and explain how each was completed

Why do RESEARCH?

Read the question. Then read and discuss the introductory paragraph, emphasizing the ways in which **research** is part of daily life. Elicit or explain that even such minor questions as "What time does the movie start?" and "How long should this food cook in the microwave?" require research of some sort. Invite students to suggest additional examples of everyday research questions.

ACTIVITY Encourage students to recall different places they have gone—the mall, the supermarket, sports events, and so on—and explore links between these places and doing **research.** For example, discuss what kind of research students might do when shopping for clothing. Have students make some notes about how they go about getting answers to their questions.

CHECK UNDERSTANDING Ask students how doing research is important for success not only in school but also in their daily lives.

Why do RESEARCH?

When you look up movie reviews, gather information for a report, or explore careers in computer animation, you are doing **research** to answer questions you have. No matter what your questions are, there are resources available to help you find the answers. You just need to know how to access those resources.

ACTIVITY Make a list of the research challenges or problems you have had over the past week. Next to each question, write the answer and how you found it. Think about topics in the following areas:

- school assignments
- local and national news
- consumer products and services
- movies and television programs

Unit Resources

- **R** RESOURCE MANAGER UNIT 12
- **B** BEST PRACTICES TOOLKIT
- **S** STANDARDS LESSON FILE

- Easy Planner DVD-ROM
- Write*Smart* CD-ROM
- ClassZone.com
- Audio Anthology CD
- Multi-Language Academic Vocabulary Online

- eEdition DVD-ROM & Online
- McDougal Littell Assessment System

Preview Unit Goals

DEVELOPING RESEARCH SKILLS	• Plan research • Use library and media center resources • Distinguish between primary and secondary sources • Use parts of a book to locate information • Evaluate information and sources, including nonfiction books, newspaper articles, and Web sites • Collect your own data
WRITING	• Write a research paper • Narrow your research topic • Locate and evaluate sources • Take notes • Make source cards • Summarize and paraphrase • Quote directly and avoid plagiarism • Document sources • Prepare a Works Cited list • Format your paper
SPEAKING, LISTENING, AND VIEWING	• Create a Web site
VOCABULARY	• research paper • plagiarism • research topic • documentation • sources • Works Cited list • source cards • Web site

Preview Unit Goals

An overview of the main skills and strategies discussed in Unit 12 appears on this page. Remind students that previewing will help them get more from their reading. As students skim the list to preview the skills that this unit will cover, urge them to apply two or three of the skills to the **Activity** on the preceding page. Note that in this unit, too, color-coding marks the skills strands.

Model for students the strategy of copying the Academic Vocabulary and writing a preliminary definition for each term. Suggest that students use their journals for this purpose. Encourage students to use the terms in discussions and in writing. Also urge students to review the terms throughout the unit, revising their preliminary definitions as needed.

ADDITIONAL UNIT GOALS

These skills will be taught in this unit but are not the major focus of the unit:

Developing Research Skills

• Use the Internet, including searching the Web and selecting and exploring relevant sites

• Evaluate information and sources, using criteria such as currency, accuracy, credibility of author, bias, coverage, and relevance

---

DIFFERENTIATED INSTRUCTION

FOR ENGLISH LEARNERS

Academic Vocabulary for the Internet Use the first page of the copy master to help students learn the Academic Vocabulary listed on page 1191.

1. Read aloud each term. Have students find it on their copy master.

2. Discuss the meanings or examples shown, and complete the chart as a class.

3. Have students work in small groups to complete the remaining activities.

Academic Vocabulary for the Library Use the second page of the copy master to help students learn the Academic Vocabulary listed on page 1194. Follow the same procedure as for the first copy master.

R RESOURCE MANAGER—Copy Masters
Academic Vocabulary pp. 6–7

Focus and Motivate

Tell students that this unit presents strategies that will help them with all kinds of research, not just research for school assignments. Explain that the unit is divided into two parts:

- the **Research Strategies Workshop,** in which students will learn to select and use print and electronic resources, as well as find activities that will strengthen their ability to use reference sources and tools

- the **Writing Workshop,** in which students will apply the strategies to write a research paper

OBJECTIVES

- explore the key idea of **research**
- explore strategies for planning and carrying out research
- identify and explore print, nonprint, and electronic resources
- distinguish between primary and secondary sources
- evaluate information and sources by applying evaluation criteria

How can I FIND *what I need?*

Introduce the question and have students read the *KEY IDEA.* Elicit or explain that an effective, efficient researcher can find *useful* information in a reasonable amount of time. Extend the discussion by having students complete the *QUICKWRITE* and inviting volunteers to share a few of their subjects.

How can I FIND *what I need?*

KEY IDEA Finding the information you need can be a challenge. For example, typing a single word or phrase into an Internet search engine could yield tens of thousands of pages to look at. You need to find a way to do **research** efficiently and effectively.

QUICKWRITE Knowing how to do research can help you in many situations. For example, the student handbook pages shown here illustrate a situation requiring research. The skills you will learn in this unit will help you do almost any kind of research. Right now, make a list of subjects that intrigue you. Then choose one or two of them to investigate as you learn research skills.

> **Graduation Requirement**
> **COMMUNITY SERVICE**
>
> All students must complete at least ten hours of community service work by the end of each school year. Service must be completed for
>
> a nonprofit organization within 15 miles of the school. Students must submit a written description of what service they plan to perform, what agency or organization will benefit, and why performing this service would help the community.
>
> 28 STUDENT HANDBOOK
>
> STUDENT HANDBOOK 29

1188

Research Workshop Resources

RESOURCE MANAGER UNIT 12

Plan and Teach pp. 9–11, 14
Develop Research Questions p. 15
Search Relevant Web Sites p. 16
Navigate Relevant Web Sites p. 17
Use Library and Media Center
   Sources p. 18
Determine Primary and
   Secondary Sources p. 19
Identify Bias p. 20
Use Parts of a Book to Locate
   Information p. 21

Evaluate Web Sites p. 22
Evaluate Nonfiction Books p. 23
Evaluate Periodicals p. 24

STANDARDS LESSON FILE
Reading Lessons 5, 17
Research and Study Skills
   Lessons 1–8
Vocabulary Lesson 24
Media Lessons 17–18
Speaking and Listening Lesson 11

BEST PRACTICES TOOLKIT

Differentiated Instruction
   pp. 31–38*

Graphic Organizers/Strategies
Reciprocal Teaching • Reporter's Questions • Mapping Main Ideas and Details • Question and Answer Note Taking • Interactive Notes • Reflection Chart • Jigsaw • Y Chart • T Chart • New Word Analysis • Comparison Matrix • Cluster Diagram

Technology
- Easy Planner DVD
- Write*Smart* CD

* Resources for Differentiation

Planning Your Research

How Do I Begin? You have a general idea of what you want to accomplish, but you're not sure where to begin. What are the first steps to take?

Getting Started

Just as when preparing for a trip or studying for a test, you will have a better research experience if you make a plan and carry out each step as completely as you can.

CLARIFY YOUR GOAL

What do you want your research to achieve? Your first step is to list your general and specific goals.

> **GENERAL GOAL:** *find volunteer work with a nonprofit organization*
>
> **SPECIFIC NEEDS:**
>
> **Time:** *Saturday afternoons are best.*
>
> **Preferences:** *working with animals, working outdoors*
>
> **Limitations:** *Where can 15-year-olds volunteer? Check age requirements. Also, I'll have to walk or bike.*
>
> **SPECIFIC GOAL:** *I want to do volunteer work on weekends, either with animals or in the outdoors, for a nonprofit organization that is near my home.*

GET AN OVERVIEW

Now that you have a goal, the next step is to get a broad overview of your subject.

- **Talk to people.** To explore volunteering, for example, you might talk to students who have already volunteered or to a school counselor.

- **Try the Internet.** Choose **keywords**—specific words and phrases from your goal statement that are related to your subject. For example, you might use the word *volunteer* and the name of your city or town. Plug them into search engines and explore related Web sites.

- **Visit your school's media center or the local public library.** Share your goal with the research librarian.

- **Think creatively.** Does the phone book list places you might call for information? Is there a local business that you might visit?

As you explore your subject, you may decide to change the focus of your research. For instance, Web sites of local volunteer organizations may list opportunities to work with special-needs children, an option you may not have considered.

> **RESEARCH TOOLS**
> For research tools and strategies, visit the **Research Center** at ClassZone.com.

RESEARCH STRATEGIES WORKSHOP **1189**

Planning Your Research
Getting Started

CLARIFY YOUR GOAL

- Point out that the examples in this unit relate to the community service scenario introduced on page 1188.

- Illustrate the difference between general goals and specific goals by presenting several general goals and having the class (or small groups) refine them into specific goals. Examples of general goals might include *tutor students* and *improve the neighborhood;* related specific goals might include *tutor elementary students in math* and *start a litter patrol in my neighborhood.*

GET AN OVERVIEW

- Discuss the kinds of information students might expect to collect from people, from the Internet, and from the media center or public library.

- Point out that each source of information has advantages and disadvantages. For example, talking to someone might provide first-hand information, but the facts might be mixed with statements of opinion. Students will learn more about evaluating sources on pages 1201–1205.

- Have students preview the content of the Research Strategies Workshop by skimming the heads and graphics on pages 1190–1209.

DIFFERENTIATED INSTRUCTION

FOR ALL STUDENTS

Enhance Learning Styles This unit can be adapted to suit various learning styles.

- **Tactile** Maximize students' opportunities to "learn by doing" at the computer.

- **Interpersonal** Have small groups apply a Reciprocal Teaching strategy.

- **Visual** Have students use graphic organizers to record ideas and information.

 **BEST PRACTICES TOOLKIT—Transparency**
Reciprocal Teaching p. A35

FOR LESS-PROFICIENT READERS

Concept Support The skills in this workshop are presented in the context of community service. To be sure that students understand some key concepts, write these terms on the board, then elicit or provide the meaning and several examples of each:

- *volunteer work:* work performed by choice rather than for pay; examples: stuffing envelopes for a political candidate, assisting the activities director at a nursing home, reshelving books at the library

- *community service:* volunteer work performed to benefit a local area and its people; examples: tutoring disadvantaged children, planting flowers to beautify the neighborhood, collecting canned goods for the town's food bank

- *nonprofit organization:* an organization that operates to perform a service rather than make a financial profit; examples: ASPCA, American Red Cross, United Way

RESEARCH STRATEGIES WORKSHOP **1189**

Focusing Your Research

DEVELOP RESEARCH QUESTIONS

- Model the use of Reporter's Questions to brainstorm this starter list of questions:

  Who would have the best information?

  What are the requirements?

  Where would I be working?

  Why is this service needed?

  When would I be working?

  How can I apply for the position?

 BEST PRACTICES TOOLKIT—Transparency
Reporter's Questions p. C9

- Have students refine the list, making the questions as specific as possible.
- Help students look for key terms in the new questions. Compare these terms, which signal specific facts that they will want to find, to keywords in an Internet search.

CHOOSE A NOTE-TAKING METHOD

Discuss the note-taking methods in the text.

Note Cards Preview the note cards on page 1220.

Category Chart Explain that this chart also helps students to retrieve facts quickly.

Pro-Con Chart Compare this chart to the thought process that students go through when they make decisions.

Additional Note-Taking Methods Point out some other note-taking methods. For example, students also might take notes using a Mapping Main Ideas and Details or Question and Answer Note Taking.

 BEST PRACTICES TOOLKIT—Transparencies
Mapping Main Ideas and Details p. C6
Question and Answer Note Taking p. B7

 STANDARDS LESSON FILE
Research and Study Skills Lesson 1:
Research Questions and Topic

Research and Study Skills Lesson 8:
Source Cards and Note Cards

 RESOURCE MANAGER—Copy Master
Develop Research Questions p. 15

Focusing Your Research

Now that you have a better sense of what you want to find out, you can direct your research in more specific ways.

DEVELOP RESEARCH QUESTIONS

Develop a set of specific questions to help you narrow the focus of your research. You may think of more key terms as you draft your questions.

> - Which nonprofit organizations in the Sacramento area help stray animals or do animal rescue?
> - Which of these organizations are looking for volunteers?
> - What requirements do volunteers have to meet? Are there age limitations or time requirements?

CHOOSE A NOTE-TAKING METHOD

To avoid drowning in a sea of facts, figures, and details, record the information you find in a way that matches your purpose. Here are some examples:

- If you are doing research for a formal report, you should probably use **note cards.** See page 1220 to learn more about this method.
- Use a **category chart** to help you compare details.

Name and Address of Animal Shelter	Age Requirements	Hours per Week Required	Other Details
CARE Shelter for Animals, 3832 Bradley Rd.	16+	No minimum	Web site: careshelters.org
Happy Tails, 1560 Broadway	14+	10 hr/week	Saturdays OK

- Consider a **pro-con chart** if you want to examine two options.

Volunteering at CARE Shelter for Animals	
Advantages:	**Disadvantages:**
• can get there on my bike	• must be at least 16 years old, so I'd have to wait until my birthday in January
• no minimum number of hours	• dogs and cats only; no exotic animals
Volunteering at Happy Tails	
Advantages:	**Disadvantages:**
• has dogs, cats, and exotic animals	• have to take two buses to get there
• lets 14-year-olds volunteer	• must volunteer at least one weekday after school and every Saturday

---

DIFFERENTIATED INSTRUCTION

FOR ADVANCED LEARNERS/PRE–AP
Demonstrate Note-Taking Methods Assign each of several groups of students a specific note-taking method not already discussed, such as Interactive Notes or a Reflection Chart. Have each group prepare and present a class demonstration that explains the method and why it might be used and gives clear examples of how the method might be used with specific topics.

 BEST PRACTICES TOOLKIT—Transparencies
Interactive Notes p. B4
Reflection Chart p. B8

Using the Internet

How Can I Find the Best Online Resources? The Internet is a great place to find a vast amount of information quickly. How can you target your search so that you don't get lost?

Understanding the Web

You probably know that the World Wide Web is accessible through the Internet, a vast system of linked computers. The Web includes literally hundreds of millions of Web sites and billions of Web pages.

Each type of Web site has its own purpose. One clue to the purpose is the URL, or "address," of a Web page. Each Web address includes an abbreviation that tells you what type of site the page is in.

WEB ABBREVIATIONS AND MEANINGS

.COM   commercial organization—product information and sales; some personal sites; some combinations of products and information, such as World Book Online

.EDU   education—information about schools, courses, campus life, and research projects; may also include students' personal sites

.GOV   U.S. government—official sites of the White House, the CIA, and many other government agencies

.MIL   U.S. military—official sites of the armed forces, the Department of Defense, and related agencies

.NET   network—product information and sales

.ORG   organization—charities, libraries, and other nonprofit organizations; also political parties

SEARCH THE WEB

Keyword Search Start with a **search engine,** a Web site that allows you to look for information by using a phrase or term related to your subject. This kind of search is called a **keyword search.** Here are some search tips:

- Be as specific as possible. Instead of *volunteering,* try *volunteer programs in Sacramento.* Look at your research questions for ideas.

- Some search engines allow you to replace letters at the end of a word with an asterisk. For example, a search for the keyword *volunt** will find sites that contain *volunteer, voluntary,* and *volunteerism.*

- Enclose an exact phrase in quotation marks. For example, a search for *"volunteer with animals"* will find sites that include those three words in that order.

TIP Search engines often have "Advanced Search" or "Search Tips" links that you can click for more information.

ACADEMIC VOCABULARY FOR THE INTERNET
- World Wide Web
- Web site
- URL (uniform resource locator, also called Web address)
- search engine
- keyword search
- menu
- hyperlink or link
- icon

Using the Internet
Understanding the Web

ACADEMIC VOCABULARY FOR THE INTERNET

Write the terms on the board. Elicit preliminary definitions, but urge students to refine those definitions as they meet the terms on pages 1191–1193.

WEB ABBREVIATIONS AND MEANINGS

- Have students read the abbreviations and meanings. Note that this is a partial listing.

- Have small groups of students work at classroom computers to find an example of each type of site. (Groups might begin with www.cnn.com, www.health.harvard.edu, and www.irs.gov.) Ask groups to share a piece of information found at each site.

SEARCH THE WEB

Keyword Searches Brainstorm a list of familiar search engines, such as Google, Yahoo!, and ASK Jeeves. After pointing out the , have students use each search engine to try the searches described in the text. Compare their findings. Then challenge students to conduct searches using key terms from the specific research questions that they developed for page 1190. Again, ask students to use various search engines and compare results.

 STANDARDS LESSON FILE

Media Lesson 17: Understanding the Basics of Web Sites

Research and Study Skills Lesson 4: Using a Web Site for Research

---

FOR LESS-PROFICIENT READERS

Comprehension Support Use a Jigsaw strategy by dividing the class into "home groups" of five students each and assigning one or two Web abbreviations to a student in each group. Then have students reassemble into "expert groups," each group working at classroom computers to find examples of their Web type(s). Have "experts" return to their home groups and share their favorite examples.

BEST PRACTICES TOOLKIT
Jigsaw p. A1

FOR ENGLISH LEARNERS

Oral Language Explain to students that in spoken English, the suffixes of the Web site addresses presented on this page are pronounced "dot com," "dot e-d-u," "dot guv," "dot mil," "dot net," and "dot org."

Getting a Home Page Students can make their favorite search engine their home page—the page that opens when they access the Internet. To make Dogpile® their home page, for example, they can go to www.dogpile.com and click on "Tools and Tips." Then have them follow the instructions provided.

To check understanding, ask

- Once you have input your preferences for your home page, what must you do to save them? *Possible answer: click OK*

- After you have saved your changes, how can you go directly to your new home page? *Possible answer: by clicking the Home button on the browser toolbar*

Boolean Searches To conduct Boolean searches, have students use the key terms they developed for the research questions on page 1190. Point out the **TIP** about metasearch engines.

SELECT RELEVANT SITES

Review the meaning of *URL*.

Close Read

Possible answers:

1. *The words used were* volunteer, Sacramento, *and* animals. *The combination effectively specifies the type of volunteer activities* (animals) *and the location* (Sacramento).

2. *The total number of sites found was 59. This is too large a number to open and read every item, but it is a manageable number to review for relevance and usefulness.*

3. *The first three sites are relevant. The fourth one is not (because of location).*

RESOURCE MANAGER—Copy Master Search Relevant Web Sites p. 16

Boolean Search A Boolean search allows you to specify the relationships among keywords and phrases.

- **AND search:** The AND tells the search engine to find all documents that contain every word (*volunteer* AND *animals*). Some search engines use a plus sign instead (*+volunteer +animals*).

- **OR search:** The OR broadens the search to include all documents that contain either word (*cats* OR *dogs*).

- **NOT search:** A NOT excludes unwanted terms from the search (*pets* NOT *breeders*). Some search engines use a minus sign (*+pets –breeders*).

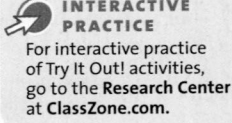
TIP Use a metasearch engine to scan multiple search engines simultaneously. See page 1208 for more information.

SELECT RELEVANT SITES

Your search may result in a list that puts what the search engine considers the most relevant sites at the top of the page. Most search engines base relevance on how often your search terms appear on a particular page and on whether any or all of your search terms appear in the page's URL. However, just because a site is at the top of a list doesn't mean it's the most relevant site for you. Read the full entries in the list, looking for words that are related to your needs.

TR IT OUT! *Look at Search Engine Results*

A search for volunteer opportunities in one community resulted in a number of possibilities. Which ones would you choose to explore?

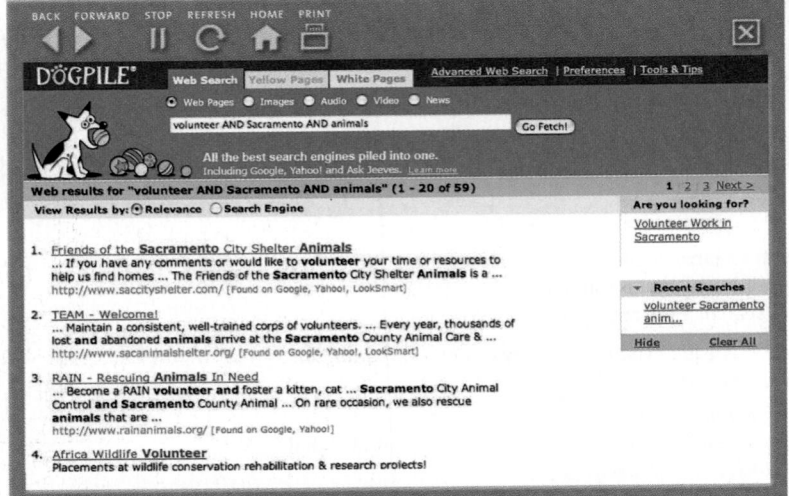

INTERACTIVE PRACTICE For interactive practice of Try It Out! activities, go to the **Research Center** at **ClassZone.com.**

Close Read

1. Which three words were used in this Boolean search? What makes them an effective combination?

2. What was the total number of sites found? Is this a manageable number of sites to open and read? Why or why not?

3. Of the four sites shown, which are relevant to volunteer work with animals in Sacramento? Which one of the sites is not relevant?

DIFFERENTIATED INSTRUCTION

FOR LESS-PROFICIENT READERS

Concept Support Assess and reinforce students' understanding of keyword searches and Boolean searches by having them work in small groups to create a chart summarizing what they have learned and making clear the differences between the two kinds of searches. Encourage students to include specific examples of searches. Have groups exchange and compare their finished charts.

Task Support Reinforce the application of Boolean search techniques by working with students to conduct searches of increasing specificity. For example, search first for *volunteers* AND *animals,* then for *volunteers* AND *cats* OR *dogs,* and then for *volunteers* AND *cats* OR *dogs* NOT *puppies.* Have students record the number of "hits" for each search and observe how the total decreases as the search becomes more specific.

EXPLORE WEB SITES

Once you have chosen a site to look at, you have to know how to read it and how to use the special features it contains. Most Web pages have features that aren't used in books.

- **Hyperlinks** are usually underlined or highlighted words. Clicking on a link leads you to related information on another page on the site or on a different site.
- **Icons** are pictures that can be clicked on to take you to another page.
- Most Web pages include at least one **menu**, or list of choices. These are often on one side of the page, at the top, or at the bottom.

TIP To evaluate the usefulness and accuracy of the information on a Web site, use the evaluation guidelines on page 1202.

TR IT OUT! *Read a Web Site*

Let's say you choose to visit the second site that the search engine listed. Take a close look at the site's home page and see what information you can find.

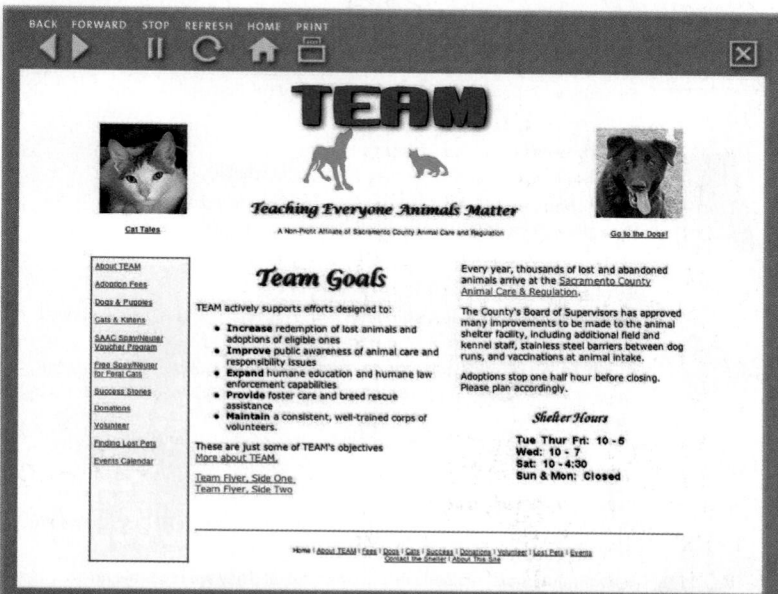

Close Read

1. Is this site a useful one for someone looking for volunteer work with animals in Sacramento? Give reasons for your answer.
2. Where would you click to learn more about this organization's objectives and goals?
3. This site has menus on the left side of the page and at the bottom. Which link would you click to find out about volunteer opportunities?
4. Where would you click to find out who created this site and when it was last updated? Why is that information important?

EXPLORE WEB SITES

If classroom computers are available, have students go to the actual Web site displayed on page 1193: www.sacanimalshelter.org. Mention the **TIP** and encourage students to evaluate these features as you discuss them:

Hyperlinks Explain that hyperlinks provide fast connections to information that visitors to a site often want to find. For example, clicking on "Success Stories" (in the left-hand sidebar) takes you to a page with photographs of people and the animals that they have adopted. Have students identify hyperlinks on the Dogpile.com site shown on page 1192.

Icons Explain that icons serve the same purpose as hyperlinks. For example, clicking on the small photograph of the dog takes you to a page with information about adoptable dogs and puppies.

Menus Point out the menus along the left-hand side and across the bottom of this site. Explain that each menu item is a hyperlink.

Close Read

Possible answers:

1. *The site is a good match, because one of TEAM's goals is to "Maintain a consistent, well-trained corps of volunteers."*
2. *To learn more about the organization, you would click on the link "About TEAM."*
3. *You would click on the link "Volunteer" (at the bottom) to learn about such opportunities.*
4. *You would click on "About This Site" at the bottom to find this information. The information is important because it helps the user judge whether the information is current and reliable.*

S STANDARDS LESSON FILE
Media Lesson 17: Understanding the Basics of Web Sites

R RESOURCE MANAGER—Copy Master
Navigate Relevant Web Sites p. 17

FOR LESS—PROFICIENT READERS

Comprehension Support Direct groups to input a Web address, such as www.un.org/english, www.nytimes.com, or www.archives.gov. Then have students create an oversize mock-up of the home page on poster paper. Ask them to label features of the page, using the terms and information presented on page 1193. Create a classroom display of the groups' finished posters and invite student discussion.

FOR ADVANCED LEARNERS/PRE—AP

Create a Home Page Have students design the home page of a personal Web site. Encourage them to be creative, including graphics as well as text. The page should contain at least one menu, several hyperlinks and icons, a description of the site, the identity of the creator, and any other features that the student wants to include. Call on volunteers to present and explain their home page to the class.

Using the Library or Media Center

ACADEMIC VOCABULARY FOR THE LIBRARY

Read the terms aloud; then invite volunteers to share situations in which they have found these resources helpful when using school or community libraries. Elicit preliminary definitions that can be refined as students read and discuss the page.

Understanding Today's Library

LIBRARY AND MEDIA CENTER RESOURCES

Display or demonstrate the use of each library resource on this page. Explain that students will learn more about each type of information on the next several pages.

Books Explain that nonfiction books focus on factual explanations and real-life stories. Nonfiction books are usually more reliable resources than fiction books, due to the imaginative nature of fiction.

Periodicals Have students name newsmagazines and subject-area magazines that they might use for a research project. Invite students who have used microfilm or microfiche in past projects to comment on those resources.

Reference Discuss the different kinds of information presented in the references listed. Point out the organization of information in each resource.

Electronic Resources Ask students to suggest research topics for which some of these resources might be appropriate.

Other Resources Urge students to consult with a librarian about the use and usefulness of some of these resources for the topic they have chosen. For example, students might use audio resources to research a famous speech.

> **R RESOURCE MANAGER—Copy Master**
> Use Library and Media Center Sources p. 18

ACADEMIC VOCABULARY FOR THE LIBRARY
- reference sources
- abstract
- catalog
- database
- table of contents
- bibliography
- index

Using the Library or Media Center

What Information Can I Find at the Library? Let's say you find information on animal shelters and begin to volunteer at one. You meet veterinarians and veterinary technicians, and you begin to wonder about a career in veterinary medicine. Now you have a new topic—one that requires in-depth research.

Understanding Today's Library

Libraries and media centers today are information supersources. They offer access to print, audio-visual, electronic, and human resources. Here is a quick look at the many types of information libraries have to offer.

LIBRARY AND MEDIA CENTER RESOURCES

BOOKS

Nonfiction books are organized by subject. See "Library Sleuth" on page 1208 to learn about the two systems for classifying nonfiction books.

Fiction books are organized alphabetically by the authors' last names.

NEWSPAPERS AND PERIODICALS

Periodicals include magazines, newsletters, and scholarly journals.

Microforms are periodicals, newspapers, and reports stored on film (microfilm) or cards (microfiche) and viewable on special machines.

REFERENCE SOURCES

Reference books include dictionaries, encyclopedias, atlases, and almanacs. These usually cannot be checked out of the library.

Search tools include databases, directories, indexes, and the library's online catalog. One search tool that can save you time is an index of abstracts. An **abstract** is a short summary of a journal article. By looking at abstracts, you can determine which articles are most closely related to your topic.

ELECTRONIC RESOURCES

DVDs and videos of documentaries and other films and television shows are available at most libraries for free or for a small fee.

E-books are books available in electronic form. They are readable on a personal computer or on various hand-held electronic devices.

Audio resources include books, music, and speeches on CDs or in MP3 files.

CD-ROMs of encyclopedias, maps, and other resources are available at many libraries.

OTHER RESOURCES

Your library may have a careers section, a college search section, maps, music scores, genealogy resources, and many other items. Most libraries have special sections for both young adults and children.

DIFFERENTIATED INSTRUCTION

FOR LESS—PROFICIENT READERS

Understanding Today's Library Arrange one or more visits to the school library or media center. Before students visit, help them create a list of questions to be answered. Then ask a librarian or center director to conduct a tour and explain resources available for student use. Answer questions not covered during the tour. Invite each student to share something that he or she learned about research resources during this activity.

FOR ADVANCED LEARNERS/PRE—AP

Present Academic Vocabulary Assign groups of students two or three terms from the Academic Vocabulary list. Instruct each group to use the information in the text, their own knowledge, and additional resources to teach the term to the class. Encourage groups to illustrate the meaning of each term through examples, illustrations, or additional facts.

Finding What You Need

All the different departments and resources in your local library can seem overwhelming. Where should you start? Ask a librarian, or consult the library's online resources.

THE RESEARCH LIBRARIAN

Librarians are experts in finding information. These experts can help you

- define what you need to know
- locate print, electronic, and audio-visual sources of information
- use the library's resources and operate equipment
- use interlibrary catalogs to expand your research to other libraries

THE LIBRARY'S CATALOG

The catalog is your road map to the library's vast resources. There are four ways to search for a source:

- author • title • subject • keyword

In addition to a source's author, title, and publication date, the catalog entry may include a brief summary of its content and the subject categories it addresses. The entry will also indicate where it is shelved and whether it is available.

TRY IT OUT! *Search a Library Catalog*

This example of a catalog entry shows information about a specific book.

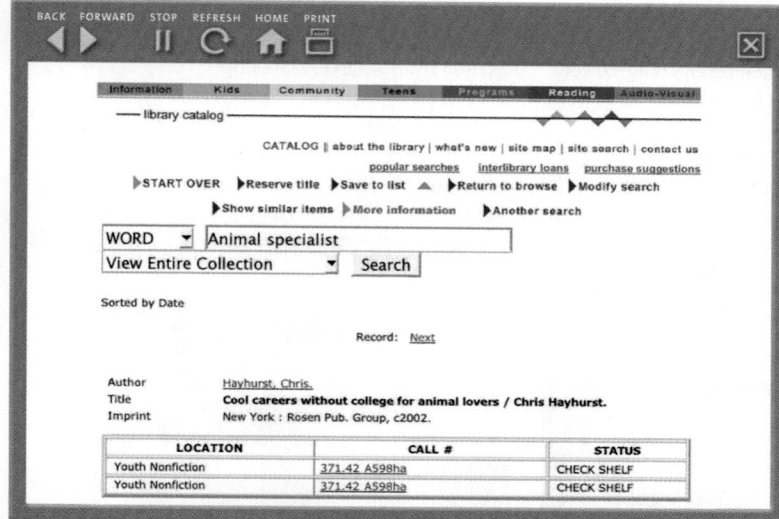

Close Read

1. What search term did this student use? List some other search terms that might produce similar results.

2. Is the book *Cool Careers* available at this library? How can you tell?

3. When was this book published? How do you know?

FOR ENGLISH LEARNERS

Vocabulary Support Write these terms on the board. Ask groups of students to define each term, using context clues, prior knowledge, and a dictionary. Have groups share and compare their definitions.

- *online:* connected to or available through a computer system
- *catalog:* listing of books and other resources
- *interlibrary:* between or shared by libraries

FOR ADVANCED LEARNERS/PRE–AP

Map Out the Library Have students visit the school or public library to explore and take note of its layout and facilities. Then have students work individually or in pairs to create a detailed map of the library and the various resources that it offers. Encourage students to make the map as clear and precise as possible. Work with students to create a format for sharing the completed maps.

Finding What You Need

THE RESEARCH LIBRARIAN

Brainstorm questions to ask a research librarian—for example, "Where can I find a news article published 50 years ago?" or "What should I do if my library does not have the book I need?"

THE LIBRARY'S CATALOG

Make these points as you discuss the different kinds of online searches:

Author Searching by an author's last name will produce a list of works by that author. Use an author's full name, because some authors have the same last name, such as Charlotte Brontë and Emily Brontë. Different search engines will use different formats for entering an author's name. Some may require the last name first (Twain, Mark), while others require the first name first (Mark Twain).

Title Searching by title will produce a list of books and other materials with that title. Use the full title, because many works have similar titles. Point out that titles are listed alphabetically, but not by the articles *a* and *the* that appear at the beginning of some titles.

Subject Searching by subject may produce a long list of entries. The more specific the subject, the more relevant the list will be.

Keyword Searching for a combination of two or three keywords will produce results in much the same way that Internet searches do. For example, searching on "Austen Prejudice" will produce not only Jane Austen's novel *Pride and Prejudice,* but also books about the novel, audiobooks, films of the novel, and so on.

Close Read

Possible answers:

1. *The student used the search term "animal specialist." Other search terms might be "veterinarian" or "veterinary technician."*

2. *The book is available; the status line says "CHECK SHELF." If the book were not available, the status line would say, "CHECKED OUT" and might give the date it is due.*

3. *The book was published in 2002, as indicated in the "Imprint" line.*

📄 STANDARDS LESSON FILE
Research and Study Skills Lesson 2: Using Library Catalogs

Choosing Sources

PRIMARY AND SECONDARY SOURCES

Point out that the terms *primary source* and *secondary source* usually apply only to non-fiction sources.

Primary Sources Primary sources can provide vivid details and personal accounts of an event. For example, reading the words of an earthquake victim enables a researcher to see the event through the victim's eyes and understand better the impact of the event.

Secondary Sources Secondary sources can help a researcher put an event in context. For example, a soldier in a war (primary source) can only tell about his or her experiences. However, a history book (secondary source) can address the war on a larger scale and place it in a historical context.

Comparing Sources Point out that evaluating and comparing sources can help students judge a source's accuracy and bias. Distinguishing the type of resource and the source of information can help students find reliable information. For example, an encyclopedia entry on World War I might be more objective and reliable than an interview with an American protester of the war.

To check understanding, direct students to identify both a primary source and a secondary source that relate to the same subject. Use a Y Chart to note students' comments and comparisons about the information that the two sources would be likely to provide.

 BEST PRACTICES TOOLKIT—Transparency
Y Chart p. A27

 STANDARDS LESSON FILE
Research and Study Skills Lesson 5:
Using Primary and Secondary Sources

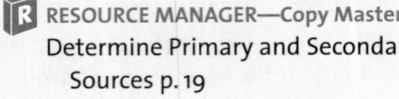 RESOURCE MANAGER—Copy Master
Determine Primary and Secondary
Sources p. 19

Choosing Sources

You have arrived at the library and looked at the online catalog. You're amazed at the amount of information available on your subject. How can you find which sources best fit your needs?

PRIMARY AND SECONDARY SOURCES

One of the first steps in choosing a source is to determine whether it is a primary or a secondary source. This chart explains the differences.

PRIMARY SOURCES	SECONDARY SOURCES
Definition: materials written or created by people who were present at events, either as participants or as observers	**Definition:** records of events that were written or created after the events occurred by people who were not directly involved in the events
▼	▼
Advantages: firsthand information; can help the researcher understand the attitudes and beliefs of a particular time period; may contain very specific information	**Advantages:** sometimes include excerpts from many primary sources; often have a broad perspective and many viewpoints; good for getting an overview of a topic
▼	▼
Disadvantages: limited perspective; may need interpretation; may be biased	**Disadvantages:** only as reliable as the sources used; may be biased
▼	▼
Often used when researching: current events, biographical information	**Often used when researching:** complex or technical subjects, ancient history
▼	▼
Examples: letters, diaries, speeches, travelogues, photographs, autobiographies, interviews, e-mails, public documents such as census data, first-person newspaper and magazine articles	**Examples:** encyclopedias, textbooks, biographies, some newspaper and magazine articles, documentaries and other films

DIFFERENTIATED INSTRUCTION

FOR LESS–PROFICIENT READERS

Concept Support Distribute a primary source and a secondary source—for example, an eyewitness account of an event and a news article describing the same event—to small groups of students. Have each group use a T Chart to compare the two and make observations about the differences.

 BEST PRACTICES TOOLKIT—Transparency
T Chart p. A25

FOR ENGLISH LEARNERS

Vocabulary: Cognates Note the similarity between the English words *primary, secondary,* and *reference* and the Spanish words *primario, secundario,* and *referencia.* Then have pairs of students apply New Word Analysis to help them define these terms: *primary source, secondary source,* and *reference work.* Encourage students to use context clues.

 BEST PRACTICES TOOLKIT—Transparency
New Word Analysis p. E8

REFERENCE SOURCES

A good first step in finding primary and secondary sources is to examine the library's reference collection. Reference works can give you a good overview of a topic and help you identify people, dates, and publications associated with your topic. They can also help you focus your topic and develop research questions. Many types of reference works are available on CD-ROMs and online. Ask a research librarian for help.

REFERENCE SOURCES	EXAMPLES
ENCYCLOPEDIAS **General:** Detailed articles on many topics **Specialized:** Articles on topics in a specific field, such as medicine, art, or careers	*Encyclopaedia Britannica* *The World Book Encyclopedia* *Encyclopedia of Careers and Vocational Guidance*
DICTIONARIES **General:** Word meanings, origins, spellings, pronunciations, and usage **Specialized:** Terms used in a specific field, such as medicine or music	*The American Heritage Student Dictionary* *Delmar's Veterinary Technician Dictionary*
ALMANACS AND YEARBOOKS Facts and statistics	*The World Almanac and Book of Facts*
THESAURI Synonyms and antonyms	*Webster's New World Thesaurus* *Roget's II: The New Thesaurus*
BIOGRAPHICAL REFERENCES Detailed information on the lives and careers of noteworthy people	*Native American Women*
ATLASES Maps and geographic information	*Rand McNally Classroom Atlas*
DIRECTORIES Names, addresses, and phone numbers of people and organizations	Telephone books; lists of business organizations, agencies, and publications
INDEXES Alphabetical lists of information, usually subjects, authors, and titles	*Readers' Guide to Periodical Literature* *New York Times Index*

RESEARCH STRATEGIES WORKSHOP **1197**

REFERENCE SOURCES

Elicit or provide examples of research tasks for which each reference source might be helpful. Use examples such as these to fill in a T Chart that associates each reference source with appropriate tasks:

Encyclopedias: find biographical information about a famous person; gather background information for a research paper

Dictionaries: check spelling and pronunciation of a technical term

Almanacs and Yearbooks: gather economic data about foreign nations; find statistics for past U.S. national elections

Thesauri: identify synonyms to add variety to a piece of writing

Biographical References: learn more about a historical person; read about a favorite author

Atlases: locate an unfamiliar country; determine distance between cities

Directories: find contact information for a local business; identify agencies or publications serving a particular need

Indexes: identify magazine or journal articles about a particular subject; find a book review

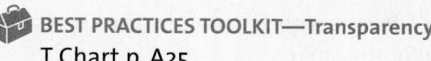 BEST PRACTICES TOOLKIT—Transparency
T Chart p. A25

S STANDARDS LESSON FILE
Research and Study Skills Lesson 3: Using Reference and Search Tools

Vocabulary Lesson 24: Using Vocabulary Reference Sources

FOR LESS–PROFICIENT READERS

Comprehension Support Ask pairs or small groups to review the chart on this page. Then have each pair or group create an outline that places each type of reference source in at least one of these categories:

- Facts About People
- Facts About Places
- Facts About Events
- Facts About Words

Have students present and discuss the results.

FOR ADVANCED LEARNERS/PRE–AP

Demonstrate Reference Sources Have students work in pairs. Assign each pair one or two reference sources; then instruct pairs to prepare and present a class demonstration of each reference source. Presentations should describe the key features of each source and demonstrate how to use the source effectively.

DATABASES

Have students read the description of databases. Then elicit or provide examples of research activities for which databases would be helpful. For example, students might use a database for tasks such as these:

- To find education-related articles, using a Department of Education database (www.eric.ed.gov)
- To gather health-related information, using a National Institutes of Health database (www.nlm.nih.gov/medlineplus)
- To find articles about genetic research, using a database of scientific information (www.scirus.com/srsapp)

Close Read

Possible answers:

1. *The first or third match might be most useful. The first is the most recent; the third is older but may be more relevant. Similarly, the second match or the last match may be least useful. The second may be too narrowly focused; the last may be too out of date.*

If students need help . . . Have them ask

- How relevant is each source to the keywords used for the search?
- How recent is each source?
- How broad or limited in scope is each source likely to be?

2. *The information is organized by date, in descending order. This organization makes spotting the most current source easy, but it also may cause a researcher to overlook an older but more useful source.*

3. *You would click on "Limit search."*

DATABASES

What Are They? A database is a collection of information arranged so that it is easy to search. You may be familiar with some free online databases, such as the Internet Movie Database. Other databases require a subscription, but your local library may have access to them. For instance, InfoTrac is a database of articles from newspapers, magazines, and journals. America's Newspapers contains articles from about 270 American newspapers. The Veterinary Medical Database is a collection of case histories of individual animals that have been given veterinary care.

Why Are They Useful? One advantage to using databases rather than search engines is that database searches are more targeted. Unlike search engines, databases have no advertisements. Also, most databases are collections of specific types of material—only newspaper articles, only scientific papers, and so on.

When Do I Use Them? Use databases when you have narrowed your topic considerably and have a good idea of what information you are seeking. Ask a librarian which databases are available to you.

TRY IT OUT! *Examine a Database*

A search of InfoTrac brought up the following information about veterinary technicians.

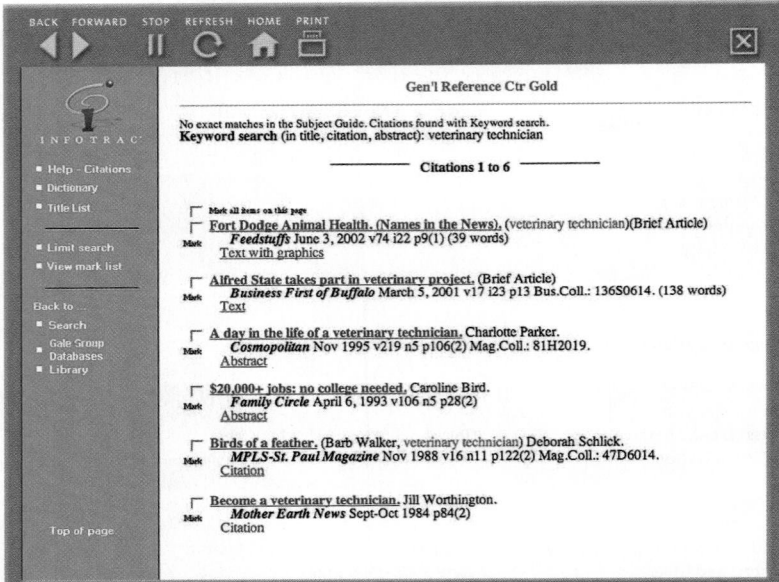

Close Read

1. InfoTrac found six matches for the keywords. Which of these matches might be most useful? least useful? Why?

2. Is the information organized alphabetically or by date? What are the advantages or disadvantages of this organization?

3. Which menu item on the left would you click on to make your search more specific?

DIFFERENTIATED INSTRUCTION

FOR LESS–PROFICIENT READERS

Explore Databases If classroom computers are available, guide students as they go to an online database, such as the Internet Movie Database (www.imdb.com), for first-hand experience. Call students' attention to the on-screen menus, hyperlinks, and icons; have students review the functions of each. Invite students to perform and comment on some sample searches.

FOR ADVANCED LEARNERS/PRE–AP

Analyze Databases [paired-activity option] Have students investigate several databases and report their findings and observations to the class. Students should consider each database's range of information, ease of use, and special features.

NEWSPAPERS AND PERIODICALS

Newspapers are publications that contain news and advertising and that are published daily, weekly, or very frequently. Publications that are issued at regular intervals of more than one day are **periodicals.** Magazines and journals are examples of periodicals.

TYPES OF SOURCES	EXAMPLES
MAGAZINES General: For most readers Specialized: Articles on specific topics	*Time, Newsweek, Parade* *Horse Illustrated* *Popular Mechanics*
NEWSPAPERS General: For most readers in a particular geographic area Specialized: For readers interested in a particular topic, such as finance	*Fort Worth Star-Telegram* *Los Angeles Times* *Wall Street Journal*
JOURNALS Journals present specialized information and are designed for experts. Journals are usually more formal than magazines and have fewer advertisements.	*American Journal of Veterinary Research* *Journal of Interactive Media in Education*

Here are tips to help you find an article on your topic:

- Ask the research librarian about specialized magazines or journals that may contain articles on your topic.

- Use databases of articles, such as InfoTrac, to help you find information on your topic in newspapers and magazines. If the database doesn't provide the full articles, you can ask at the periodicals desk for the specific issues you want to see.

DOCUMENTARIES AND OTHER FILMS

Your list of possible sources may include some titles on DVD or videotape. How can you quickly assess whether these sources are worth watching?

- Is the source **fiction** or **nonfiction?** To identify a nonfiction film, read the library's online catalog description. Look for the word *documentary* or *interview*. A fictional film probably would not have enough factual information to serve as a reliable source.

- Does the film contain the kind of **information** you need? Check the online catalog description and the front and back covers of the DVD or videocassette. Does the film include **primary sources,** such as interviews or speeches?

NEWSPAPERS AND PERIODICALS

If possible, bring in an assortment of newspapers and periodicals for students to examine or have students list newspapers and magazines with which they are familiar. Divide the class into small groups, asking each group to answer these questions about each periodical as specifically as possible:

- What is the purpose of the periodical?
- How frequently is the periodical published?
- Who are the intended readers?
- What does the advertising in the periodical suggest about the periodical's readers?
- Does the periodical present facts, opinions, or a mix of both?
- What are the periodical's most notable features? For example, are there striking photographs? interesting first-person articles? well-researched statistical tables?

Follow up with a class discussion that encourages students to compare their findings and suggest specific research tasks for which various periodicals would be useful.

DOCUMENTARIES AND OTHER FILMS

- Explain that a documentary is a factual film that dramatically presents or analyzes key events, people's lives, or social conditions, for example. Point out that documentaries often are good sources of information but that they may reflect the bias of the filmmaker.

- Note that some films are "based on" facts but may contain fictionalized elements, as well. Such films are not reliable sources.

- Elicit or provide examples of documentaries and other films. Discuss why each documentary would or would not be a useful reference.

FOR ADVANCED LEARNERS/PRE–AP

Compare and Contrast Films [small-group option] Have students compare fiction and nonfiction films about particular subjects. For example, students might compare *Jaws* with a documentary about sharks or compare a war movie with a documentary about the same war. Have students summarize their findings in an oral report to the class, making clear why one film would make a more reliable source than the other.

Encourage students to use a graphic organizer, such as a Comparison Matrix, in their presentations. Comparisons should include references to factual content and should point out instances of distortion and bias.

 BEST PRACTICES TOOLKIT—Transparency
Comparison Matrix p. A24

NONFICTION BOOKS

In addition to using the illustrations on this page, have individual students or pairs of students refer to a nonfiction book as you lead a discussion of the book parts described. Direct students to find the corresponding parts in their books as you discuss these questions:

- What can you learn from examining the book's title, chapter titles, and headings?
- What is the copyright date? Point out that some books have revision dates.
- What information can you get from the table of contents and the index?
- How can a bibliography or list of recommended readings help?
- How can a glossary help? What types of books are likely to have glossaries?

Close Read

Possible answers:

1. *The subtitle makes clear that the book focuses on certain types of careers that involve working with animals.*

2. *This book was published in 2006. Because it is recent, it is likely to be a useful source.*

3. *The book probably includes interviews, as suggested by the inclusion of "Meet a _____" features in the table of contents.*

4. *The book includes such information. The index lists "jobs in" under the heading "Animal shelters." Since there is only a single page reference, however, the book probably contains only a little information.*

R **RESOURCE MANAGER—Copy Master**
Use Parts of a Book to Locate Information
p. 21

NONFICTION BOOKS

Your library search may result in a list of book titles and call numbers. How can you quickly determine which books have the information you're seeking?

- Read each book's **title** (and **subtitle,** if there is one) and skim chapter titles and headings to get an idea of the general subject matter.
- Check the **copyright page** for the date of publication. If you need up-to-the-minute information, don't depend on a book that is several years old.
- Examine the **table of contents** at the front of the book and the **index** at the back for terms related to your subject. Is there sufficient information on your subject or very little?
- Many books also have **bibliographies** or lists of **recommended readings.** These can give you ideas for other sources to consult.
- If the book contains difficult technical terms, look for a **glossary** at the back. This section lists specialized terms and their definitions.

TRY IT OUT! *Examine the Parts of a Book*

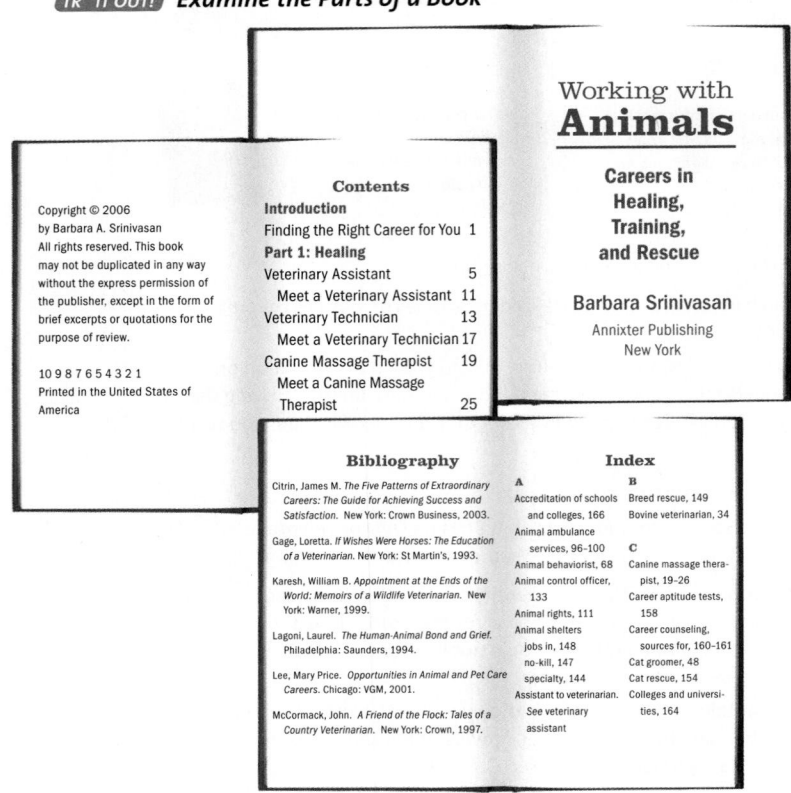

1200 UNIT 12: THE POWER OF RESEARCH

Close Read

1. How does the subtitle of this book help you understand its content?

2. When was this book published? Is it recent enough to be a useful source?

3. Does this book include interviews with people employed in certain jobs? How do you know?

4. Does this book include information on jobs in animal shelters? How do you know?

FOR LESS–PROFICIENT READERS

Comprehension Support To check students' grasp of the book parts, supplement the Close Read with these questions:

1. Who wrote the book? *Answer: Barbara A. Srinivasan*

2. What kind of warning appears on the copyright page? *Answer: a warning about how the book may and may not be duplicated*

3. How long is the chapter about the work of a veterinary technician? *Answer: six pages (pages 13–18)*

4. Which book in the bibliography would probably be least helpful when it comes to up-to-date information? Explain. *Possible answer: The book by Loretta Gage might have the least up-to-date information; its copyright is 13 years earlier than that of Srinivasan's book.*

FOR ADVANCED LEARNERS/PRE–AP

Evaluate Book Parts Divide students into small groups; then have each group locate three nonfiction books about the same subject. Ask students to compare the books and reach a consensus about the most useful source for a research paper. Invite each group to share its evaluation, supporting the evaluation with specific reasons.

Evaluating Information

How Can I Tell If the Information I Find Can Be Trusted? Now that you have found a number of useful sources, how can you figure out which ones are credible and reliable?

Applying General Evaluation Guidelines

No matter what kind of source you have chosen—in print or online—or where you have found it, you need to look at it critically before deciding whether you can trust the information it contains.

EVALUATING SOURCES

Is the information up-to-date?	Look for a copyright date or a "last updated" reference. Recent information is critical in some fields, such as science, medicine, and sports. Older publications can be helpful for historical topics.
Is the information accurate?	Can the facts be verified by more than one source? Most print and online encyclopedias, dictionaries, directories, and almanacs are considered reliable because they are updated regularly and go through a rigorous review process.
What are the author's credentials?	Does the author have a position or job title that qualifies him or her as an expert on the topic? Has he or she written other materials on this topic?
What kinds of materials does the publisher produce?	University presses usually publish information that is carefully researched. Magazines that publish trendy articles and gossip are not as reliable as newsmagazines or science magazines.
Could the source be biased?	Why does the source exist? Does the author mention his or her goals in a foreword, preface, or introduction? Is the author's purpose to inform, to persuade, to entertain, or some combination of these? Does the author use loaded language, such as "Millions of people are joining the fight against this unforgivable injustice"?
How much information does the source cover?	Does the source give an overview or detailed information? Does the material support other information you have read or add new information? Start by looking at the table of contents, menu, or index.
Is the source relevant?	Does the source cover aspects of the topic that interest you? Is it written at a level you can understand?

FOR LESS–PROFICIENT READERS

Vocabulary Support Elicit or provide the meanings of these terms:

- *credentials:* knowledge, skill, or experience that qualifies a person as an expert

- *loaded language:* language with positive or negative connotations, designed to stir people's feelings

FOR ADVANCED LEARNERS/PRE–AP

Analyze Fact, Opinion, and Bias [paired-activity option] Instruct students to read a magazine article or newspaper editorial and analyze its mix of factual information and opinion. Have students use a T Chart to list facts and opinions and to comment on signs of subtle bias in the piece. Work with students to create a format for sharing their findings.

BEST PRACTICES TOOLKIT
T Chart p. A25

Evaluating Information
Applying General Evaluation Guidelines

EVALUATING SOURCES

Discuss the chart, providing clarification and additional instruction as needed. Consider including these comments and activities:

Up-to-date Information Ask students why a five-year-old publication would be an acceptable source of information about Abraham Lincoln but not about a current president. *Possible answer: Lincoln lived so long ago that the facts about him are well established, but a current president's story is not yet complete. Elicit additional examples of topics that would or would not require current information.*

Accuracy Stress the importance of distinguishing fact from opinion when evaluating accuracy. Also urge students to find a second, confirming source for any questionable material. Note that accuracy and reliability are particular concerns when doing Internet research because anyone can post a Web site. (Guidelines for evaluating Web sites appear on page 1202.)

Bias Explain that bias may be obvious or subtle. For instance, the writer of an article about popular music may express a distaste for rap music (1) by saying so directly, (2) by discussing several kinds of music in detail but giving just a few lines to rap music at the end of the article, or (3) by using words with negative connotations to describe rap music or its performers.

S STANDARDS LESSON FILE
Reading Lesson 5: Distinguishing Fact from Opinion

Reading Lesson 17: Author's Credibility

R RESOURCE MANAGER—Copy Master
Identify Bias p. 20

Evaluating Specific Sources

EVALUATE WEB SITES

Discuss the information about evaluating Web sites, providing clarification as needed. If possible, have students visit various *.com*, *.net*, and *.org* Web sites and examine actual examples.

Commercial Web Sites Explain that commercial Web sites can be informative at some times but misleading at others. For example, some commercial sites mix facts with product claims or sales pitches, or they make unsubstantiated or exaggerated statements; other sites, such as those of some organizations, may present facts primarily as part of persuasive arguments to influence your thinking. Call students' attention to the **TIP** about knowing who created a site. Also encourage students to question any content that seems questionable and to check it against a second, trustworthy source.

Personal Web Sites As you discuss the **TIP** regarding personal Web sites, point out that obtaining information from a personal Web site is like getting information from an individual—that is, the person may or may not be a reliable source. (See pages 1206–1207.) Urge students not to accept as fact any statement made by an unknown source unless they can verify the information elsewhere.

S STANDARDS LESSON FILE
Research and Study Skills Lesson 7:
Evaluating Electronic Sources
Media Lesson 18: Evaluating Web Sites

R RESOURCE MANAGER—Copy Master
Evaluate Web Sites p. 22

Evaluating Specific Sources

The evaluation guidelines on the previous page apply to every source you use. The questions and tips on these pages will help you evaluate specific types of sources.

EVALUATE WEB SITES

Web sites are often a mix of helpful information and attempts to promote points of view or to sell products or services.

Commercial Web Sites As you learned on page 1191, sites with URLs containing *.com* or *.net* are sometimes for-profit sites. When you look at a commercial site, ask yourself these questions:

- **Who is the author?** Look for a menu link called "About This Site" or "Contact Us."
- **Why was the site created?** If the site was designed to sell you something, the site creators may have omitted any negative information about the product.

TIP Knowing who created a site can help you figure out why the site exists and whether it is appropriate to use in your research.

Organization (.org) Web Sites These sites may represent particular points of view. Although many are nonprofit organizations, such as the Red Cross, political parties also have *.org* in their domain names. Ask yourself these questions:

- **Who created the site, and when was it last updated?** Look for a link titled "About Us" or "Mission Statement." If there is no way to identify the creator of the site, then you should be cautious about the content.
- **Are statements of fact supported by examples and evidence?** Look for links to supporting evidence from respected institutions or publications.

Personal Web Sites Because anyone can post anything on the World Wide Web, there are millions of personal Web sites. Some have misleading URLs. For example, students and faculty members can set up personal Web sites on a university's server, and their Web addresses will contain the university's URL. However, these sites might not be reviewed, evaluated, or in any way sanctioned by the institution.

TIP Not all personal Web sites are unreliable, but be cautious.

- **How can I tell if a site is personal when its address contains the name of an institution?** Look for a forward slash and tilde (/~) and a name or initials following *.edu* in the URL.
- **What does the lack of an official institution logo tell me?** Don't expect the information to have been reviewed or approved by the institution.
- **What does it mean if links in the site don't work or are mostly links to other items by the same author?** The author may be careless, or he or she may lack outside support.

DIFFERENTIATED INSTRUCTION

FOR ENGLISH LEARNERS
Task Support Have students compare two Web sites on the same topic, one in English and one in their home language. Suggest that they study aspects such as differences in structure and the way information is presented. Help them with any Internet-related terms that they may not be familiar with.

FOR ADVANCED LEARNERS/PRE–AP
Evaluate a Web Site Have pairs of students use the criteria in the text to create a Web site evaluation checklist. Ask students to identify a Web site related to a topic that interests them. Then have them use their checklist to evaluate the Web site, refining the checklist as they do so. Invite students to combine their individual checklists into a master checklist that they can share with the class.

TRY IT OUT! *Examine Web Sites*

Examine this Web site. What does it offer a visitor?

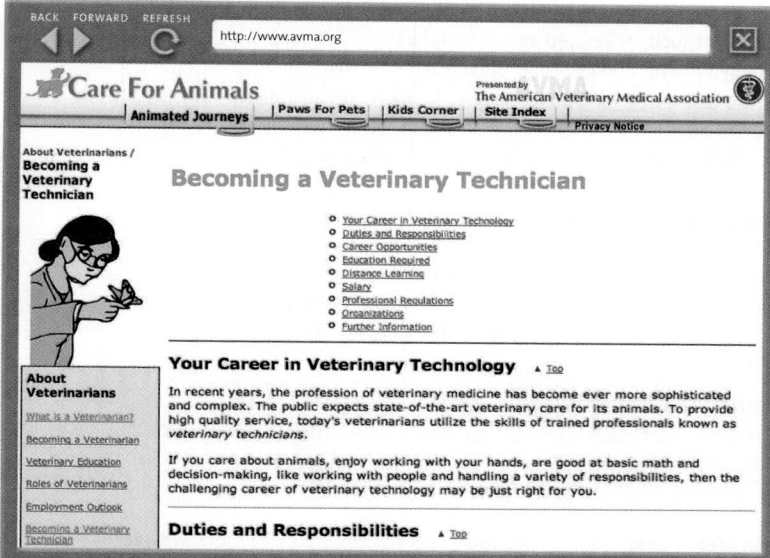

Close Read

1. Who created this site?
2. What is the purpose of the site?
3. Who is the intended audience?
4. What clues tell you that it is a nonprofit site?

TIP To get to a site's home page from a page with a long URL, simply delete everything after the domain name (such as *www.avma.org*) and press Enter. The home page will come up.

Here is an example of a personal Web site. What does it offer?

Close Read

1. How reliable are the statistics about homeless animals? Give reasons for your answer.
2. Does Dunstan Community College support the efforts of the site's creator? How can you tell?

As you present the **TIP**, refer students to the URL abbreviations on page 1191.

Close Read

Possible answers:

1. *The American Veterinary Medical Association (AVMA) created the site.*
2. *The main purpose of this screen of the Web site is to provide information about a career in veterinary technology.*
3. *The intended audience of this screen of the Web site is anyone wanting career information about veterinary technology.*
4. *The URL is .org, which generally is associated with nonprofit sites. Furthermore, no products or services are being advertised on this screen.*

If students need help . . . ask

- What is the URL? What Web sites usually have such a URL? *Possible answer: The URL is www.avma.org. Nonprofit organizations usually have such a URL.*
- What is one way to recognize a for-profit site? *Possible answer: the presence of advertising*

Close Read

Possible answers:

1. *The statistics are not very reliable or useful. The first point is vague and general, with no factual support. The second point refers to a study, but the conductors of the study are not identified. Moreover, a 1990 study on this topic would be out of date today.*
2. *The site displays no official logo of Dunston Community College, so there is no reason to believe that it has been reviewed or approved by the college.*

FOR ADVANCED LEARNERS/PRE–AP

Create a Site Guide Have students work in small groups to develop a guide to interesting Web sites that pertain to the subjects that they are studying this year. The guide should explain the features of each site, describe the kind of information that it offers, and evaluate the site's usefulness and reliability. Groups can add the guides to the classroom library as a permanent reference.

For a challenge, invite groups to create a Web site that presents the information and includes a link to each site listed.

EVALUATE NONFICTION BOOKS

As you lead a class discussion of this page, ask students about the various sources that they use to write their papers and reports. For example, what kinds of nonfiction books would they be likely to use for learning about a person's life? *Possible answer: a biography, autobiography, encyclopedia, or biographical reference book*

Copyright Ask students why a book that has been updated many times over a period of years is likely to be reliable. *Possible answer: The author has had multiple opportunities to correct errors and update information.*

Author's Qualifications Remind students to consider an author's knowledge, skill, and experience. Ask students how these factors can help shape the content and tone of a book. *Possible answer: An author who is strong in one or more of these qualities is likely to provide deeper insight into a subject than is a writer who has done only book research.*

Close Read

Possible answers:

1. *The book is about career options in the veterinary field.*

2. *The author has been a veterinarian for eight years and has been a veterinary assistant.*

3. *The book was published recently; the back cover proclaims that it is the 7th Edition, "Revised and updated for 2008."*

4. *Examine the table of contents, the index, and perhaps the preface.*

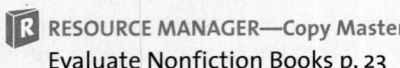 RESOURCE MANAGER—Copy Master
Evaluate Nonfiction Books p. 23

EVALUATE NONFICTION BOOKS

Nonfiction books are one of the best sources of in-depth information.

- **When was the book last copyrighted or updated?** Check the **copyright notice,** which is usually on the back of the title page. Also look on the copyright page or on the cover for a statement such as "revised and updated edition." A book that has gone through many updates and printings is likely to be reliable.

- **What sources did the writer use?** Look for a **bibliography.** Some books include an **appendix**—a collection of additional material on the subject. Notes within the book, such as **footnotes, endnotes,** or **cross-references,** can also give you clues about sources.

- **What are the author's qualifications?** Look for an author's biography on the book jacket or at the beginning or end of the book. The author may have written a **preface,** a short introductory essay that explores the purpose of the book, the intended audience, and the research on which the book is based. If the source is a biography, find out if the author is related to the person he or she has written about.

TRY IT OUT! *Examine a Nonfiction Book*

Use what you have learned about nonfiction books and about the parts of a book (page 1200) to help you evaluate whether this book is a relevant source for someone interested in a career involving work with animals.

Alexander Rutkowski has been a veterinarian for eight years. Many young people have told him that they would like to work with animals but don't know what qualifications they need or how to find jobs in the field. This book explains what educational and employment opportunities exist. It also describes Dr. Rutkowski's own experiences as a pet owner, veterinary assistant, veterinary student, and vet.

Close Read

1. What is this book about?

2. What qualifies the author to write a book on this topic?

3. Was this book published recently? How do you know?

4. What other parts of the book should you examine to determine if it is a worthwhile source? (Hint: See page 1200.)

DIFFERENTIATED INSTRUCTION

FOR LESS–PROFICIENT READERS

Comprehension Support To check students' understanding about an author's use of sources, distribute several nonfiction books to pairs of students. Ask students to identify examples of bibliographies, appendices, footnotes, and endnotes. Then have students write four statements, each one summarizing the type of information that one of these features contains. Have pairs of students exchange and compare their summary statements.

FOR ADVANCED LEARNERS/PRE–AP

Evaluating Usefulness [paired-activity option] Ask students to brainstorm questions that they can ask themselves to decide whether or not a particular book will be useful. Offer these examples: *When was the book written? Does the book have an index so that I can locate information quickly? Is the book clearly written? Does the book have helpful illustrations?* Have students choose their best questions to create a "Ten Questions" chart.

EVALUATE NEWSPAPERS AND PERIODICALS

Newspapers and periodicals can be good sources of up-to-the-minute, easy-to-read information. Different publications are available in a print edition, online, or on microfilm or microfiche. Evaluating an article can be tricky, because you need to assess the publication, the author of the specific article, and the content. Here are some basic questions to ask:

TIP Even the most reliable publications may contain errors. Whenever possible, check facts in more than one source.

- **Is the source well-known and respected?** Most large-circulation newspapers and national magazines are reliable sources. Beware of sensationalist publications such as the *National Enquirer,* however.

- **When was it published?** Old is not necessarily bad. Out-of-date newspaper and magazine articles can provide rich information on historical events.

- **Who is the author?** You can usually assume that articles by staff writers or contributing editors are as reliable as the source they're published in.

- **Was the article reprinted from another source?** If so, make sure the original source—for example, *Scientific American* or a news service such as the Associated Press (AP)—is reliable.

- **Can the facts in the article be verified?** Consult other sources, either on paper, online, or in person.

TRY IT OUT! *Examine a Newspaper Article*

Use what you have learned about evaluating sources as you examine this article.

---

from The Dallas Morning News

Animal ER

For injured pets, 'round-the-clock clinics provide a haven and hope

BY ALINE MCKENZIE, STAFF WRITER

It's an ordinary night. One of life-and-death situations, tears and relief, small miracles. Meals eaten on the fly, calm during lulls.

Animals don't time their ills and injuries to convenient office hours.

So when regular veterinarians are off duty, the after-hours emergency animal clinics take over. From kennel cough to surgery, every night brings a different mix.

"It's just something I've always wanted to do, just as a kid," says Dr. Michelle

Hazlewood, 32. "I've always loved animals."

"Neither of us could go back into a regular day practice," says Dr. Kathleen Bowe, 38. The variety and the excitement beat the ordinary well-animal care of a day job, she says.

The two are the vets on duty this night at the Emergency Animal Clinic of Collin County in Plano, one of a
See ANIMALS, page B2

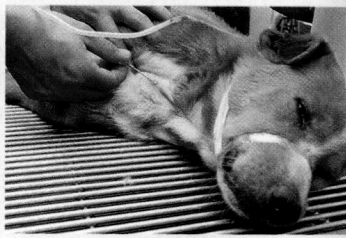
Buster the dog donates blood.

Close Read

1. What kind of veterinary clinic is the focus of this article?

2. Knowing that Dallas is a large city in Texas and that the *Dallas Morning News* is its major newspaper, would you expect this to be a reliable source of information?

3. How could a reader verify the facts in an article like this?

1205

FOR ADVANCED LEARNERS/PRE–AP

Demonstrate Evaluation Techniques Have small groups of students prepare and present a demonstration of the evaluation guidelines on this page. Students might choose one of these approaches:

- Use the text information to evaluate two articles, including one that lacks credibility.

- Create a "how-to" video that explains how to implement the evaluation guidelines.

- Develop an oral presentation that uses graphic organizers and other visual aids to reteach the ideas on this page.

Instruct students to include information about how to go about consulting another source to verify the facts in an article. Have students use text information, their own knowledge and experience, and additional resources to create a clear how-to presentation.

EVALUATE NEWSPAPERS AND PERIODICALS

Distribute assorted periodicals for students to examine and compare. Divide the class into small groups to discuss these questions:

- Which periodicals are well-known and respected? Which would *not* be reliable?

- When was each periodical published? Does the publication date limit its usefulness? Why or why not?

- Are the authors of the articles reliable sources of information? Why or why not?

- Did any of the articles originally appear elsewhere? If so, why did the periodical reprint it?

- How could you verify the facts in the articles? Call students' attention to the **TIP** about checking facts in more than one source.

Follow up with a class discussion in which students compare their observations. Elicit or provide examples of research tasks for which various publications might be used.

Close Read

Possible answers:

1. *The article focuses on an after-hours emergency animal clinic.*

2. *The article probably is reliable. Stories in large-circulation major newspapers generally are viewed as reliable.*

3. *A reader could call the clinic or do an Internet search about the clinic featured in the article.*

4. *The e-mail address would allow readers to ask questions or verify facts.*

S STANDARDS LESSON FILE
Research and Study Skills Lesson 6: Evaluating Print Sources

R RESOURCE MANAGER—Copy Master
Evaluate Periodicals p. 24

Collecting Your Own Data
Using People as Primary Sources

FIELD RESEARCH AND OBSERVATION

Ask students what skills they need to carry out field research and observation. ***Possible answer:*** *listening skills, note-taking skills, attention to detail, interpersonal skills*

Have students read through the sample field notes. Then discuss these questions:

- What kinds of information did the observer record? ***Possible answer:*** *number of people working at the shelter, number of animals there and what kinds, who's in charge*

- What conclusion can you draw from the field notes? ***Possible answer:*** *The CARE Shelter is a busy place, with many people taking care of 50–70 dogs and cats—and with a need for volunteers.*

INTERVIEWS

Elicit examples of various kinds of research projects, such as finding a part-time job or writing a research paper about a foreign country. For each project, ask students to identify people whom they might interview. Draw a simple Cluster Diagram of possible interview subjects for each project.

 BEST PRACTICES TOOLKIT—Transparency
Cluster Diagram p. B18

 STANDARDS LESSON FILE
Speaking and Listening Lesson 11:
Interview

Collecting Your Own Data

What If I Need to Gather Information Firsthand? Sometimes the answers to your questions cannot be found on a Web site or in a library. How can you collect original data?

Using People as Primary Sources

For some topics, your own observations and data will be your best source of information. The following techniques can turn you into your own search engine.

FIELD RESEARCH AND OBSERVATION

Any focused, purposeful observations you make can be considered field research. For instance, you might visit an animal shelter or a veterinarian's office to learn about careers in veterinary medicine, or you might listen to a **lecture** at school about veterinary careers. If you wish to make a visit, be sure to call ahead to ask permission and to make an appointment. For some research projects, you may want to set up a **field study** in which you make observations and collect specific types of data.

> *Notes on Visit to CARE Shelter for Animals, 10/21/2006*
>
> - *staff : 4 full-time employees plus 8 to 12 part-time volunteers*
> - *provides medical care for 20 to 30 dogs plus 30 to 40 cats; no rabbits, rodents, wild animals, or exotic animals*
> - *Dogs are in individual cages, but most cats are 3 or 4 to a cage.*
> - *"no-kill" shelter, which means that animals stay until they are adopted*
> - *Jackie Kirchner coordinates all the volunteers. The shelter needs people to clean cages and to feed and exercise the animals.*
> - *Ms. Kirchner says that Kyle Faris, their veterinary technician, would probably agree to an interview.*

INTERVIEWS

Try talking with people who have experience in what you are researching. For example, you could interview a veterinary assistant, a veterinary technician, and a veterinarian about their jobs. You might interview someone in person, over the telephone, or by e-mail. First, ask if the person is willing to talk with you, and then set a date and time for the interview. Prepare a list of clear, open-ended questions that must be answered with specific information, not just yes or no. Take thorough notes during the interview. Here are some sample interview questions.

DIFFERENTIATED INSTRUCTION

FOR LESS–PROFICIENT READERS

Concept Support Invite a reporter from the school newspaper or a community newspaper to come to class and speak to students about interview techniques, note taking, and listening skills. Have students get ready for the visit by preparing a list of questions to ask the reporter. Follow up with a discussion in which students share what they have learned from the talk.

FOR ADVANCED LEARNERS/PRE–AP

Do a Field Study Ask students to choose a community activity or exhibit that they would like to research. For example, students might investigate a community gardening project or the public library's new art exhibit. Ask students to visit the activity or exhibit to make observations and collect information. Have them use their field research to write a report. Then work with students to create a format for sharing the reports in class.

Questions for Kyle Faris

1. How long have you been a veterinary technician?
2. What is the best part of the job? Why?
3. What is the worst part of the job? Why?
4. What kind of education and work experience would I need to become a veterinary technician?

See page R81–R82: Interview

If you are able to identify an expert, you may wish to send a politely worded, specific question by e-mail or letter. You can gain an inside track to a group of experts by joining a relevant Internet discussion group, also called a list server. For instance, VETMED is a discussion group about veterinary medicine.

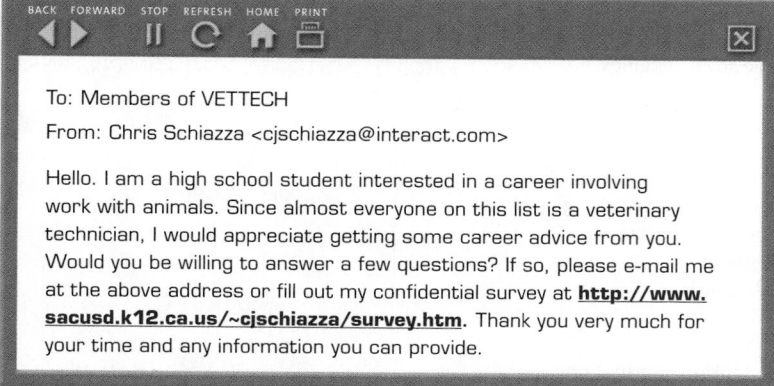

To: Members of VETTECH

From: Chris Schiazza <cjschiazza@interact.com>

Hello. I am a high school student interested in a career involving work with animals. Since almost everyone on this list is a veterinary technician, I would appreciate getting some career advice from you. Would you be willing to answer a few questions? If so, please e-mail me at the above address or fill out my confidential survey at **http://www.sacusd.k12.ca.us/~cjschiazza/survey.htm**. Thank you very much for your time and any information you can provide.

SURVEYS AND QUESTIONNAIRES

You can collect survey and questionnaire information by telephone, by mail, by e-mail, through a Web site, or in person. Keep the names of participants confidential to protect their privacy.

TIP Stay safe—give only an e-mail address for people to use in responding to your survey. Do not give your home address or telephone number.

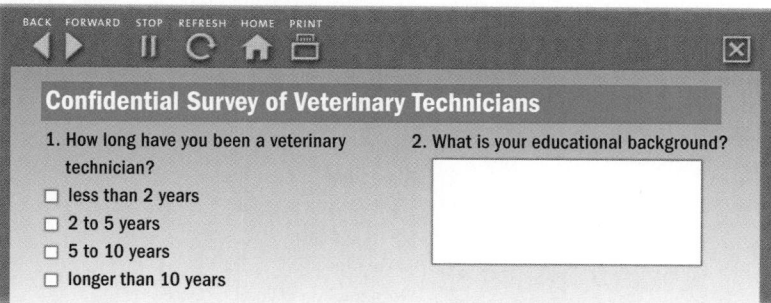

DIFFERENTIATED INSTRUCTION

FOR LESS–PROFICIENT READERS

Develop Interview Skills Brainstorm with students for questions that an interviewer might ask a teenager about his or her interests or plans for the future. Instruct students to list the questions on paper or on index cards. Then have pairs of students interview each other, drawing their questions from the brainstormed list. Afterward, discuss with students what they have learned about the interview process from conducting these interviews.

Share these interviewing tips with students:

- Do research ahead of time about the person whom you are interviewing and the topics that you plan to discuss. Ask students why such preparation is important. ***Possible answer:*** *Knowledge about the person and the topic leads to better questions and shows that the interviewer is serious.*

- Write each question on an index card, allowing space to record the response. Alternatively, ask permission in advance to audiotape or videotape the interview. Be flexible about the order in which you ask questions, however, and be ready to ask follow-up questions as you listen to what the person says. Ask students why such flexibility is important. ***Possible answer:*** *Interesting information and insights might result if the person is allowed to volunteer additional ideas.*

- If you are not taping the interview, save some time at the end of the interview to summarize and confirm important points. Also, consider asking the person to suggest sources of additional information.

- If you conduct an interview by e-mail or letter, use formal language, proper grammar, and correct capitalization and punctuation.

- Always remember to thank people whom you interview. Sending a polite thank-you note after the interview is appropriate, too.

SURVEYS AND QUESTIONNAIRES

Explain to students that surveys should contain specific questions and should not be overly long or complicated. Brief, straightforward surveys are most likely to get a response. Call students' attention to the **TIP** regarding survey safety.

Research Tips and Strategies

Web Watch

Discuss the search tool options, using one or more of these activities. Make sure that students understand the differences between search engines, metasearch engines, and directories.

- Have pairs of students use and compare some of the sources listed. For example, ask students to conduct an identical keyword search using Google, Dogpile, and About.com. Have them compare results, noting similarities and differences.

- As a class, have students share and compare their observations about various tools and sites that they have used. Ask students which tools and sites they found most helpful, and why.

- Invite students to explore the Internet Public Library (www.ipl.org). Discuss the sources of information available at the site and the types of research projects for which this site would prove most useful.

Library Sleuth

Share with the class examples of nonfiction books as they are classified under the Dewey decimal system and under the Library of Congress system. Make sure that students know which system is used (1) in the school library and (2) in the community public library system.

 STANDARDS LESSON FILE
Research and Study Skills Lesson 3:
Using Reference and Search Tools

Research Tips and Strategies

Web Watch

Knowing what search tools to use is crucial to finding information on the World Wide Web.

Search Engines

Search engines differ in speed, size of database, method of searching, and other variables. Never use only one search engine.

- Altavista • Excite • Teoma • Google

Metasearch Engines

A metasearch tool can save you time by sending a search to multiple search engines simultaneously.

- Vivismo • Dogpile • Metacrawler

Directories

Directories are useful when you are researching a general topic, because they arrange Internet resources into subject categories.

- Galaxy • About.com • Yahoo!

Virtual Libraries

At a virtual library, you can look up information in encyclopedias, directories, and indexes. You can even e-mail a question to a librarian.

- Internet Public Library
- Librarians' Index to the Internet

Other Web Resources

Library catalogs: Library of Congress
Encyclopedias: Encyclopaedia Britannica Online
Newspaper archives: New York Times Index
News associations: Associated Press
Specialized databases: Medline

Library Sleuth

Two basic systems are used to classify nonfiction books. Most high school and public libraries use the Dewey decimal system; university and research libraries generally use the Library of Congress system.

DEWEY DECIMAL SYSTEM

000–099	General works
100–199	Philosophy and psychology
200–299	Religion
300–399	Social sciences
400–499	Language
500–599	Natural sciences and mathematics
600–699	Technology (applied sciences)
700–799	Arts and recreation
800–899	Literature and rhetoric
900–999	Geography and history

LIBRARY OF CONGRESS SYSTEM

A	General works
B	Philosophy, psychology, religion
C	History
D	General and Old World history
E–F	American history
G	Geography, anthropology, recreation
H	Social sciences
J	Political science
K	Law
L	Education
M	Music
N	Fine arts
P	Language and literature
Q	Science
R	Medicine
S	Agriculture
T	Technology
U	Military science
V	Naval science
Z	Bibliography and library science

DIFFERENTIATED INSTRUCTION

FOR LESS–PROFICIENT READERS

Concept Support Invite an experienced librarian to speak to students about the Dewey decimal system and the Library of Congress system. Also ask the librarian to discuss with students how the advent of the Internet has changed the librarian's job and expanded the research capabilities of library users.

FOR ADVANCED LEARNERS/PRE–AP

Create a Search Tools Bulletin Board Have students work together to create a bulletin-board display of search tools for finding information on the World Wide Web and tips for using them. Information should be based on the content on this page as well as preceding content in the Research Strategies Workshop. Students should include specific examples to illustrate the key points in the display.

Checklist for Evaluating Sources

☑ The information is relevant to the topic you are researching.

☑ The information is up-to-date. (This point is especially important when researching time-sensitive fields such as science, medicine, and sports.)

☑ The information is from an author who is qualified to write about this topic.

☑ The information is from a trusted source that is updated or reviewed regularly.

☑ The author's or institution's purpose for writing is clear.

☑ The information is written at the right level for your needs. For example, a children's book is probably too simplistic, while a scientific paper may be too complex.

☑ The information has the level of detail you need—neither too general nor too specific.

☑ The facts can be verified in more than one source.

Sharing Your Research

At last you have established your research goal, located sources of information, evaluated the materials, and taken notes on what you learned. Now you have a chance to share the results with the people in your world—and even beyond. Here are some options:

• Use presentation software to create a power presentation for your classmates, friends, or family.

• Publish your research findings on your own Web site.

• Develop a newsletter or brochure summarizing your information.

• Explain what you learned in an oral presentation to your classmates or to people in your community.

• Write up your research in a formal research paper. **See the following pages.** ▶

See pages 1231–1233: Creating a Web Site

Checklist for Evaluating Sources

Review with students the checklist items, which summarize what students have learned. Have students explain the importance of each item on the list, giving examples as appropriate.

Sharing Your Research

Discuss the options for sharing research. Create a master list by adding to that list other possible options that students suggest—for example:

• Create a manual or introductory guide to your topic. If you speak more than one language, consider making it a bilingual publication.

• Prepare a presentation that makes your research accessible to children.

• Find a classmate who chose a related topic. Collaborate on an oral presentation that links your research.

• Use your research to support a cause that matters to you. Write an editorial or persuasive speech that includes that research.

Have students consider the pros and cons of each option on the master list. For example, which one(s) would communicate information to the greatest number of people? Which one(s) would allow for the most creativity? Then ask students to pick and rank their top three options and to explain their choices.

 STANDARDS LESSON FILE

Research and Study Skills Lesson 6: Evaluating Print Sources

Research and Study Skills Lesson 7: Evaluating Electronic Sources

FOR LESS–PROFICIENT READERS

Comprehension Support Assess and reinforce students' understanding of the Research Strategies Workshop by having them work in small groups to create a graphic/visual summary of what they have learned about planning and carrying out research. Have groups share their graphic displays with the class.

Focus and Motivate

OBJECTIVES

- analyze a student model that reflects the key traits of research papers
- use the writing process to produce a research paper
- revise and edit, using a rubric for research papers
- create a Web site

WRITER'S ROAD MAP

WRITING PROMPTS 1 AND 2

To help students choose a prompt that will result in an effective research paper, direct them to the sample questions. Explain that the more excited they are about their writing topic, the better their research paper is likely to be; in other words, their enthusiasm for their topic will be evident in both their research and their writing.

ADDITIONAL PROMPTS

Use these prompts for practice with investigative writing and writing in the humanities:

WRITING PROMPT 3

Writing About the Working World Write a research paper that investigates career and job opportunities in a particular field of endeavor, such as transportation, graphic design, or medicine. Include information about training, duties and responsibilities, hours, salary, and related work aspects.

WRITING PROMPT 4

Writing About Fine Art In an online museum or a book, find an artist whose work interests you. Write a research paper in which you describe the artist's life and work and analyze two of the artist's most famous creations.

For additional writing prompts, see

- WriteSmart CD
- Writing Center at **ClassZone.com**

KEY TRAITS

Review the six *KEY TRAITS* with students, focusing on ideas and organization. Compare the list of traits with the rubric on page 1230.

Writing Workshop

Research Paper

Now that you have thoroughly explored a variety of research strategies, you are ready for your next challenge: the formal research paper. Perhaps you will have the opportunity to learn more about people, places, or events in history, science, or art. You can even choose a great literary work and explore one aspect of it in depth. To start your investigation, refer to the **Writer's Road Map.**

WRITER'S ROAD MAP
Research Paper

WRITING PROMPT 1

Writing from Literature Formulate a question about the *Odyssey* or another literary work that you would like to explore in detail. Write a research paper that includes data from at least five sources and has Works Cited list.

Questions Related to the *Odyssey*
- What is the role of women in the *Odyssey*?
- What kinds of weapons, armor, and ships did the ancient Greeks have?
- How did the discovery of the ruins of Troy change our understanding of the *Odyssey*?

WRITING PROMPT 2

Writing for the Real World Write a research paper that investigates an idea or a question that interests you. Your paper should present your own ideas and interpretations as well as factual information. Include data from at least five sources and provide a Works Cited list.

Questions to Investigate
- How has the Internet changed the music industry?
- Are genetically modified foods safe to eat?

 RESEARCH TOOLS
For research help and citation guidelines, go to the **Research Center** at **ClassZone.com.**

KEY TRAITS

1. IDEAS
- Presents a **thesis statement** that identifies the governing idea of the entire paper
- Supports the thesis with **evidence,** including **quotations** and **paraphrases**
- Synthesizes information from **multiple sources**
- Includes the **writer's own ideas and interpretations**

2. ORGANIZATION
- Has a focused **introduction**
- Has a logical **organizational pattern** and **transition words**
- Includes a satisfying and thoughtful **conclusion**

3. VOICE
- Maintains a **tone** that is appropriate for the topic, audience, and purpose

4. WORD CHOICE
- Uses **precise language** to convey ideas clearly

5. SENTENCE FLUENCY
- Varies **sentence lengths and structures**

6. CONVENTIONS
- Employs **correct grammar and usage**
- **Credits sources**
- Uses **correct formats and style**

Writing Workshop Resources

 RESOURCE MANAGER UNIT 12

Plan and Teach pp. 9, 12–14
Prewriting–Editing pp. 25–35
Publishing with Technology p. 36
Writing Support p. 37*

 **STANDARDS LESSON FILE**

Writing Lessons 2, 14–18, 21, 35–37
Research and Study Skills Lessons 9–10, 12–13, 16
Media Lesson 21

 BEST PRACTICES TOOLKIT

Scaffolding Writing Instruction pp. 43–46*
Reporter's Questions • Cluster Diagram • Microtheme • Writing Template: Informative Essay • Analysis Frame • Classification Chart

TECHNOLOGY
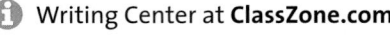
- Easy Planner DVD
- Writing Center at **ClassZone.com**
- WriteSmart CD

* Resources for Differentiation

Part 1: Analyze a Student Model

Bergstrom 1

Ilona Bergstrom
Mr. Grant
English 9
10 May 2008

The Mystery of the <u>Odyssey</u>

Everybody loves a great adventure story, especially one that has everything—monsters, gods, bloody battles, raging storms, and, finally, a happy ending. The <u>Odyssey</u> by Homer is that kind of adventure story. For modern readers, though, it is also an intriguing mystery.
5 Did the places Homer described really exist? We may never know for certain which places in the <u>Odyssey</u> are real and which are fiction, but investigating the events and geography of Odysseus' wanderings can lead to a better understanding of this great literary work.

As readers begin the <u>Odyssey</u>, we are swept into a journey that is so
10 exciting that we suffer along with Odysseus (or Ulysses, as he is known in Latin) and rejoice when he finally returns home. Only after closing the book do we step back to consider our earlier questions.

The <u>Odyssey</u> is full of fantastic creatures, gods, and events—such as Odysseus' battle with the Cyclops—that seem too amazing to be true.
15 The third-century-B.C. astronomer Eratosthenes, for example, thought that Homer's story was totally imaginary (Knox 25; "Homeric Legend"). Many people throughout history have tried to identify a real setting for the tale, though. The Greek poet Hesiod, who lived in the eighth century B.C., probably not long after the <u>Odyssey</u> was written, thought
20 that Odysseus' wanderings took him around Italy and Sicily. Other

KEY TRAITS IN ACTION

Presents the subject of the report in a clear **thesis statement.**

Teach

Part 1: Analyze a Student Model

Point out that the formatting of the student model research paper—margins, line spacing, and so on—has been modified to fit the textbook page. For formatting guidelines, students should consult the *MLA Handbook for Writers of Research Papers* or the "Format Your Paper" feature on page 1230.

Have students read the student model and **KEY TRAITS IN ACTION.** Then discuss the model with the class, noting specific examples of each trait and building on what students have already noted. You may also want to incorporate these activities:

- **Thesis Statement** Point out that the thesis statement often appears in the first paragraph but that it usually is not the opening sentence. Ask students why the thesis statement appears so early. *Possible answer: The thesis statement identifies the governing idea of the research paper, so presenting it at the beginning makes the focus of the paper immediately clear.*

Lead students to see that this thesis statement consists of two parts: a clause that provides a context (lines 5–6), followed by a clause that specifies the reason for writing the paper (lines 7–8). It is the second clause that dictates the kind of information that the writer will provide.

Finally, discuss the characteristics of an effective thesis statement. Elicit or explain that this thesis statement is clear, specific, and interesting enough to encourage the reader to keep reading.

DIFFERENTIATED INSTRUCTION

For general guidelines on differentiating writing instruction, see

 BEST PRACTICES TOOLKIT
Scaffolding Writing Instruction
pp. 43–46

FOR ENGLISH LEARNERS

Language: Skill Words Write these terms on the board and review them with students:

- *thesis:* the governing idea, or main focus, that the writer will attempt to prove—for example, the thesis of this paper is that information about the events and geography in the *Odyssey* can make the work easier to understand

- *thesis statement:* the sentence that states the thesis—for example, lines 5–8 of the student model

- **Organizational Pattern** Elicit that the subheadings are helpful because they serve as guideposts for the reader, indicating what content will follow.

  Point out that subheadings should be specific enough to convey, or at least suggest, major ideas. To reinforce the concept, ask students why the subheadings "So Many Theories" and "A Puzzling Situation" would not have been as effective as the ones that appear on page 1212. ***Possible answer:*** *The suggested subheadings are too general. The first would leave readers wondering, "Many theories about <u>what</u>?" The second is even more vague and gives no clear indication of the text that follows.*

- **Paraphrasing** Point out that paraphrasing information from research sources is an alternative to quoting directly and that it is an often-used method of supporting main ideas in nonfiction writing.

  Have students identify the credited sources of the paraphrased details in lines 32–41. Explain that the Works Cited list on page 1216 gives complete information about these sources. ***Possible answer:*** *The details in lines 34–36 come from works by Severin and by Struck; the details in lines 38–40, from a work by Knox; the details in lines 40–41, from another work by Severin.*

Bergstrom 2

historians throughout the ages have thought he traveled to other places in the Mediterranean Sea or even the Atlantic Ocean ("Homeric Legend").

25 The debate has continued into modern times. About the only thing people seem to agree on is that Troy existed where Homer said it was and that the Trojan War took place sometime between 1300 and 1200 B.C. (Knox 5; Nardo 20; Wilford D1). The reason they agree is that archaeologists have found proof. Heinrich Schliemann first excavated the ruins of Troy in the 1870s, and other layers of the site have been identified since then (Nardo 16). It is what happened after

30 Odysseus left Troy—and where it happened—that remains a mystery.

Many Theories About <u>Odyssey</u> Locations

To try to solve this mystery, people have to assume that the events reported in the <u>Odyssey</u> actually did happen. Unfortunately, though, Homer's descriptions of places are often vague and confusing. Unlike the

35 events of the Trojan War, which took place on land, Odysseus' sea voyage left no traces (Severin 17; Struck). Therefore, all of the ideas historians have come up with about where the events occurred are just guesses.

Interestingly, these guesses have been literally all over the map, ranging from the North to the South Pole and from Norway to South

40 Africa (Knox 25). One sea captain claims that he identified every location described in the <u>Odyssey</u> along the coast of the Adriatic Sea (Severin 22).

Focus on the Mediterranean

Other historians have looked for the location of the <u>Odyssey</u> closer to Homer's own Mediterranean home. According to the literary expert

> Synthesizes information from **multiple sources.** Uses correct parenthetical documentation **formats.**

> Subheadings clarify major ideas and provide structure for a logical **organizational pattern.**

> Supports main ideas with specific details **paraphrased** from and correctly **credited** to the sources.

Bergstrom 3

45 George Steiner, the story seems to take place in the waters surrounding
Greece, Italy, and Egypt, though he admits, "The geography of the tale
is a riddle" (9). For example, in Book Four of the <u>Odyssey</u>, Menelaus
describes the island of Pharos as "as far out as the distance a hollow ship
can make in a whole day's sailing" (Homer 74). However, Pharos is

50 now connected to the mainland of Egypt. Even the Greek geographer
and historian Strabo, who lived from 63 B.C. to A.D. 23, was puzzled by
Homer's geography (Severin 18).

The explorer Tim Severin compared many theories of Odysseus'
route with nautical maps and concluded that "Ulysses' vessel jumps

55 up and down the length of the Mediterranean like the knight on a
chessboard. It skips over inconvenient land masses, skids around capes,
travels at speeds that would do credit to a modern cruise liner . . ." (22).
Between lines 134 and 135 in Book Ten (Homer 155), for example,
Odysseus somehow manages to get from one side of the island of Ithaca

60 to the other without stopping off there, "as though he had sailed right
by his homeland" (Severin 240). One explanation is that the <u>Odyssey</u>
actually describes two separate voyages and that the adventures after line
135 of Book Ten were based on the stories of another Greek hero, Jason,
and his Argonauts ("Homeric Legend").

65 **Retracing Odysseus' Route**

Even so, none of the theories Severin examined were formulated by
sailors, and he thought that the best way to discover the route taken by
Odysseus was to try to retrace it. Using a replica of a Bronze Age ship

> Includes a lively **quotation** from the source to support a main idea and add interest.

- **Quotations** Explain that the student writer included this quotation because it is nicely worded and contains a vivid, memorable simile. Ask students to identify the simile. ***Answer:*** *Severin, the author, compares the movements of Ulysses' ship to the movements of a "knight on a chessboard."* Note that the knight is the only chess piece capable of moving over other pieces. Then ask students what main idea the quotation supports. ***Possible answer:*** *The quotation supports the idea that Odysseus' voyage could not have happened exactly as Homer suggests it did.*

Remind students that direct quotations are an alternative to paraphrasing. To illustrate the difference, have students paraphrase the quotation in lines 54–57, restating the same meaning in their own words. ***Possible answer:*** *Ulysses' ship could not have moved around the Mediterranean Sea in exactly the way Homer described. Land masses would have blocked Ulysses' route, and the ship could not have traveled at such a fast speed.*

DIFFERENTIATED INSTRUCTION

FOR ENGLISH LEARNERS

Language: Skill Words Write these terms from pages 1212–1213 on the board and review them to ensure students' understanding:

- *organizational pattern:* the way in which the content of a research paper is organized—for example, chronological order, order of importance, comparison and contrast, problem and solution, or cause and effect

- *paraphrase:* to restate an author's words, using different words to give the same meaning—as the writer does in lines 38–41 of the model. Explain that *paraphrase* can be a verb or a noun.

- *credit (sources):* to acknowledge the use of an author's words or ideas—as the writer does with parenthetical documentation in lines 40 and 41 of the student model.

- *quotation:* an author's words, repeated exactly from a book or other source, enclosed in quotation marks—as done in lines 54–57 of the student model.

- **Tone** Remind students that tone refers to a writer's attitude toward his or her subject. Point out that the student writer's tone is appropriate for a research paper.

  Have students think about the writer's tone as they reread lines 66–73. Ask them to describe the tone in their own words and to explain how that tone is created. ***Possible answer:*** *The writer's choice of words and details conveys a serious, thoughtful feeling. The writer is trying to explain clearly what Severin did.*

- **Writer's Original Interpretation** Discuss how the student writer has woven a personal interpretation into the paper. Ask students what original ideas the writer has added and what facts serve as the basis for those ideas. ***Possible answer:*** *The writer explains that Severin found a channel near Cape Scylla that long ago might have caused whirlpools. She suggests that Homer may have based the whirlpool Charybdis on this channel, exaggerating its power in order to make the story more exciting. The writer further suggests that Homer may have wanted his "larger-than-life hero" to contend with a "larger-than-life" problem.*

Bergstrom 4

he had built, Severin set sail from Troy. He took the most direct route
70 to the present-day island of Ithaca, assuming that's what Odysseus
would have done in his haste to return home after the long Trojan War
(Burgess; Severin 22-23). He used both physical landmarks and local
folk tales to help him trace the places and events in Homer's story.

> Straightforward **tone** conveys ideas objectively and understandably.

   Severin did manage to locate many places and things mentioned in
75 the <u>Odyssey</u>, such as Scylla and Charybdis, described in Book Twelve:

> On one side was Scylla, and on the other side was shining
> Charybdis, who made her terrible ebb and flow of the sea's
> water. When she vomited it up, like a cauldron over a strong
> fire, the whole sea would boil up in turbulence (Homer 191).

> Correctly indents and documents a long **quotation.**

80   Cape Scylla still exists, and Severin found the cave of the monster
that ate six of Odysseus' men. According to Homer, Charybdis was
just across a narrow channel. Today, however, the channel is too wide
to create the violent whirlpools described in the <u>Odyssey</u>. Severin did
locate a narrow channel a little south of Cape Scylla that may have
85 caused whirlpools in ancient times, though (199). It's possible that
Homer used this place as the basis for Charybdis, exaggerating its power
to make the story more exciting. After all, a larger-than-life hero needs
larger-than-life problems to struggle with.

> Provides the **writer's original interpretation** and summary of ideas.

   The land of the Lotus-Eaters also turned out to be where other
90 people had thought it was—past the island of Cythera in Tunisia
(Burgess). Severin used Homer's mention of "wild goats beyond
number" in Book Nine (Homer 140) to locate Odysseus' next stop, the
island of the Cyclopes, on present-day Crete. The savage people

---

DIFFERENTIATED INSTRUCTION

FOR ENGLISH LEARNERS

Language: Skill Words Write these terms from pages 1214 and 1215 on the board and review them to ensure students' understanding:

- *tone:* the expression of a writer's attitude toward the subject—for example, serious, objective, angry, conversational, or humorous

- *original interpretation:* the writer's own ideas and inferences, based on what he or she has learned through research

- *transitions:* words and phrases that connect ideas and guide the reader from one

thought to the next—for example, *On the other hand* (line 95) and *In the end* (line 100)

- *sentence structure:* the complexity of a sentence—that is, whether it is simple, compound, complex, or compound-complex

- *conclusion:* the ending of a research paper, in which the writer usually provides a summary of important ideas—for example, lines 106–119 in the student model (Point out that a conclusion does not necessarily contain a quotation.)

Bergstrom 5

described by Homer were nothing like the civilized Cyclops of
95 folklore, however (Severin 86). On the other hand, Severin failed to
find anything like Calypso's island, Ogygia. For this reason, he agreed
with other scholars that Homer may have created it and Odysseus'
imprisonment there to help explain why the hero had been wandering
for so long (Severin 243).

100   In the end, Severin was unable to trace Odysseus' journey exactly
and found many parts of Homer's tale puzzling. He concluded that "the
geographies of folklore and navigation overlapped" (245). Although he
didn't set out to prove whether the <u>Odyssey</u> was real or imagined, his
findings suggest that it was a mixture of both.

105 **An Unsolved Mystery**
        What conclusions can modern readers draw from these confusing
and conflicting ideas about the <u>Odyssey</u>? Robert Fagles, a well-known
translator and scholar of Homer, gives probably the best summary of the
possibilities—and of the <u>Odyssey</u>'s lasting influence and interest:
110   I think it's altogether likely that, however "mythological"
            the Greek experience may seem, it nevertheless stems from
            experience. Was that experience actual or imagined, or a
            combination of the two? I don't think we'll ever know. . . .
            Homer's period in history was in fact a time of exploration
115   and new settlements, and these events survive in the
            [Odyssey], strikingly dramatized by Homer's incorporation of
            the fabulous, the Cyclops, the witches, and the other monsters
            and seductresses. All of it is stranger than fiction, as we'd say,
            and even more compelling than fact.

> **Transitions** show how ideas are related.

> Varied **sentence lengths and structures** integrate information from several sources while creating interest and flow.

> **Conclusion** provides a thoughtful summary.

- **Transitions** Explain that transitional words and phrases, such as *however* and *On the other hand* (line 95), may appear at the beginning, in the middle, or at the end of a sentence and can serve a variety of purposes. For example, they can add information (*in addition, also*), give an example (*for instance*), show sequence (*first, next*), offer a comparison (*similarly*), or introduce a conclusion (*therefore*). Ask students to identify other transitions on this page of the student model. *Possible answers:* For this reason (*line 96*), In the end (*line 100*)

- **Conclusion** Point out that the student writer chose to end this research paper with a direct quotation. Explain that because the source is online (refer students to the Works Cited list on page 1216), no page reference is given. Ask students whether they think that the writer should have paraphrased instead of quoting directly, and why or why not. *Accept all reasonable responses.*

    Explain that the conclusion to a research paper usually summarizes or reinforces the paper's most important ideas. In addition, a strong conclusion encourages readers to think about what they have read. Point out that in these respects the conclusion to a research paper is similar to the conclusion that students would write for an essay.

For interactive student models, see
🖎 Write*Smart* CD
ℹ️ Writing Center at **ClassZone.com**

FOR ENGLISH LEARNERS

Comprehension: Transitions List on the board transitional words and phrases that are often used in research papers, such as *for example, for instance, such as, another, for this reason, as a result, however,* and *although.*

1. Call students' attention to contextual examples in lines 13–14, 18, 36, 47, 49, 58, and 66 of the student model.

2. Work with students to use transitional words and phrases from the list in original sentences such as these:

- The author of the *Odyssey* is referred to as Homer; _____, the work's true authorship is debatable. ***Possible answer:*** *however*

- There are many traditions about Homer. _____, it is said that he was born in Smyrna and that he was blind. ***Possible answer:*** *For instance*

To provide English learners with additional writing support, see

📕 **RESOURCE MANAGER—Copy Master**
Writing Support p. 37

Explain to students that the term *Works Cited* refers to a list of all the works that a writer quotes from, or directly refers to, in a research paper. Point out that the list includes both print and nonprint sources. Have students identify the nonprint sources in this Works Cited list. ***Possible answer:*** *three online sources and a CD-ROM*

Also explain that *Works Cited* is a term based on MLA style guidelines for documentation; that *MLA* stands for Modern Language Association; and that MLA style is widely used by schools as well as by many magazines, journals, and newsletters. Tell students that they will learn about MLA documentation guidelines in Part 2 of this Writing Workshop.

Ask students how the Works Cited list is organized. ***Possible answer:*** *The list is alphabetized by the authors' last name or, when a work has no identified author, by title.* Have students identify the one source not listed by an author's last name. ***Possible answer:*** *"Homeric Legend"* Point out that a Works Cited list is similar, but not identical, to a bibliography: a bibliography would include *all* of the sources that a writer used, including sources used just to verify facts or gather background information.

Review with students how the works that are listed are referred to parenthetically in the research paper. Point out that a parenthetical citation usually includes the name of the author and the page number on which the information or quotation appears. Have students look back at several parenthetical citations and find their corresponding entries in the Works Cited list.

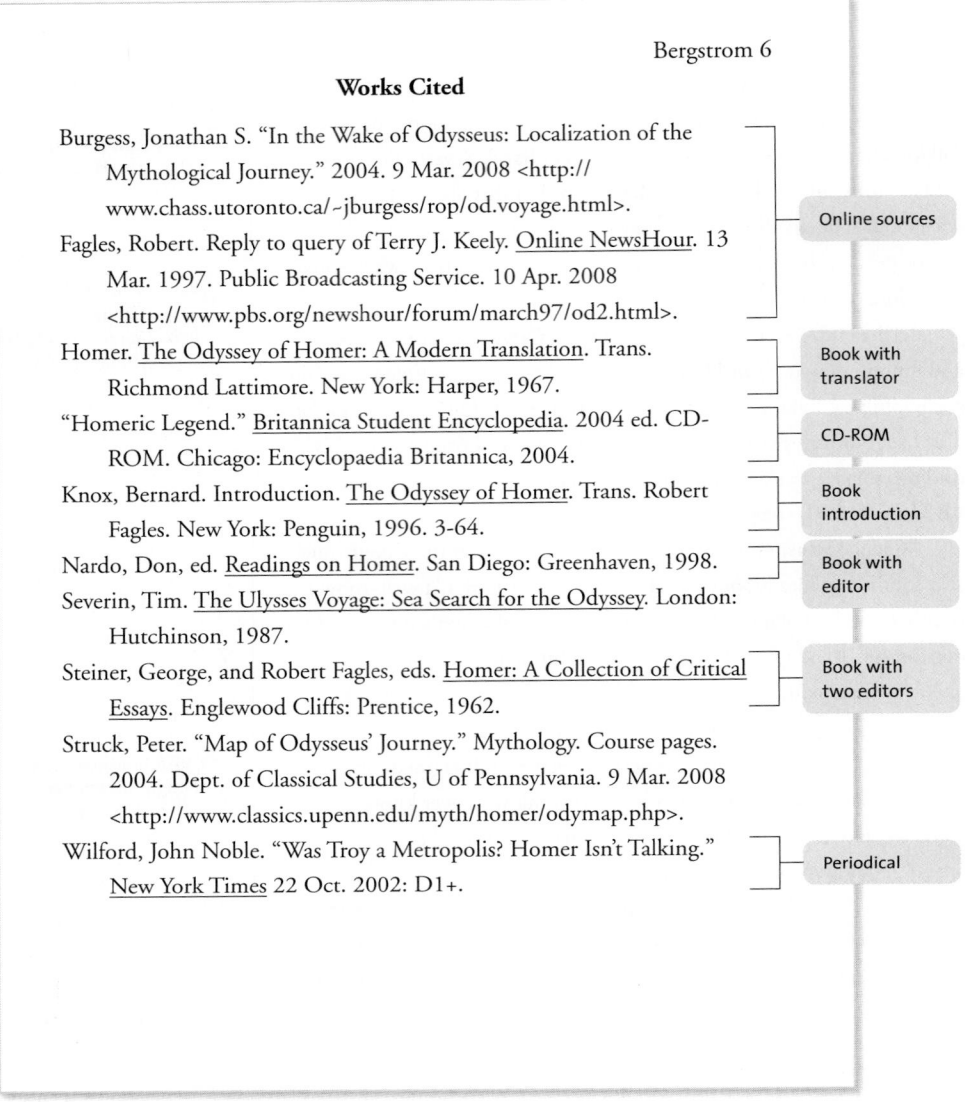

Works Cited

Burgess, Jonathan S. "In the Wake of Odysseus: Localization of the Mythological Journey." 2004. 9 Mar. 2008 <http://www.chass.utoronto.ca/~jburgess/rop/od.voyage.html>.

Fagles, Robert. Reply to query of Terry J. Keely. Online NewsHour. 13 Mar. 1997. Public Broadcasting Service. 10 Apr. 2008 <http://www.pbs.org/newshour/forum/march97/od2.html>.

Homer. The Odyssey of Homer: A Modern Translation. Trans. Richmond Lattimore. New York: Harper, 1967.

"Homeric Legend." Britannica Student Encyclopedia. 2004 ed. CD-ROM. Chicago: Encyclopaedia Britannica, 2004.

Knox, Bernard. Introduction. The Odyssey of Homer. Trans. Robert Fagles. New York: Penguin, 1996. 3-64.

Nardo, Don, ed. Readings on Homer. San Diego: Greenhaven, 1998.

Severin, Tim. The Ulysses Voyage: Sea Search for the Odyssey. London: Hutchinson, 1987.

Steiner, George, and Robert Fagles, eds. Homer: A Collection of Critical Essays. Englewood Cliffs: Prentice, 1962.

Struck, Peter. "Map of Odysseus' Journey." Mythology. Course pages. 2004. Dept. of Classical Studies, U of Pennsylvania. 9 Mar. 2008 <http://www.classics.upenn.edu/myth/homer/odymap.php>.

Wilford, John Noble. "Was Troy a Metropolis? Homer Isn't Talking." New York Times 22 Oct. 2002: D1+.

Online sources

Book with translator

CD-ROM

Book introduction

Book with editor

Book with two editors

Periodical

DIFFERENTIATED INSTRUCTION

FOR LESS–PROFICIENT READERS

Comprehension Support To check students' grasp of the items on the Works Cited list, ask

1. In which city was Tim Severin's book published? ***Answer:*** *London*

2. What kind of CD-ROM does the student writer cite? ***Answer:*** *the CD-ROM of the Britannica Student Encyclopedia*

3. What kind of work did John Noble Wilford write, and when and where was it published? ***Answer:*** *He wrote a newspaper article, published in 2002 in the* New York Times.

4. Which Homeric scholar appears on the list three times? ***Answer:*** *Robert Fagles* For which source did he serve as a translator? as an editor? ***Answer:*** The Odyssey of Homer *and* Homer: A Collection of Critical Essays, *respectively*

FOR ENGLISH LEARNERS

Language: Skill Words Write these terms from this page on the board and review them to ensure students' understanding:

- *online source:* an informational resource published on the Internet—for example, the Web site of a company or organization or the online edition of an encyclopedia

- *periodical:* a publication that is issued on a regular basis (such as daily or monthly)—for example, a magazine or newspaper

Part 2: Apply the Writing Process

PREWRITING

What Should I Do?

1. Analyze the prompt. Reread the prompts on page 1210 and pick the one that interests you. (Circle) the words that tell you what to do. <u>Underline</u> the important details about the assignment.

2. Brainstorm possible topics and narrow your focus. Use a graphic organizer to explore topics that you'd like to research and write about. Focus on one that can be covered in detail in a short research paper.

> **TIP** Check the catalogs in your school and local libraries, and databases such as InfoTrac, to see how much information is available on your topic. If there's too little, broaden your focus; if there's too much, you may need to limit it.

3. Develop research questions. Make a list of questions that you want to answer in your report. Keep these questions in mind as you do your research.

What Does It Look Like?

▶ **WRITING PROMPT** <u>Formulate a question</u> about the *Odyssey* or another literary work that you would like to <u>explore in detail</u>. Write a (research paper) that includes <u>data from at least five sources</u> and has a Works Cited list.

> I'm supposed to do research and write a paper about some aspect of the <u>Odyssey</u> or another piece of literature. I have to use in-depth information from at least five sources in the body of the paper and list the sources at the end.

▶

```
        humans        goddesses
            the role of
              women          fact or fiction?
                  The Odyssey
        Odysseus            monsters
      Too broad        Scylla    Cyclops
                              Too narrow
```

▶ **Research Questions**

1. How much of the <u>Odyssey</u> is real, and how much is made up?

2. If any of the events are real, where did they take place?

3. If events were made up, what were they based on?

4. Has anyone ever tried to duplicate Odysseus' journey?

FOR LESS—PROFICIENT WRITERS

Brainstorm Possible Topics After students have read the page, help them visualize topics for themselves by using a Cluster Diagram. Work with students to follow these steps, which show how the graphic on page 1217 was developed:

1. Write a possible topic inside a circle.

2. Make a list of ideas related to this topic.

3. Group these ideas into related clusters. Choose a key term that identifies each.

4. Write the key terms in smaller circles around the topic circle. Draw lines connecting each circle to the topic circle.

5. Write words relating to the key terms around the smaller circles. Circle these words, too, and draw lines connecting them to the key term circles.

6. If students find that their topic is not working, have them repeat the process with a different possible topic.

📦 **BEST PRACTICES TOOLKIT—Transparency**
Cluster Diagram p. B18

Practice and Apply

To support students during the writing process, use these copy masters:

📘 **RESOURCE MANAGER—Copy Masters**
Prewriting–Editing pp. 25–35
Publishing with Technology p. 36
Writing Support p. 37 (for English learners)

Part 2: Apply the Writing Process

PREWRITING

1. Analyze the prompt. After students have copied their writing prompt and marked its key elements, have them restate the prompt in their own words, as shown in the sample Analysis.

2. Brainstorm possible topics and narrow your focus. Encourage students to include as many topics as they can without being concerned yet about which topic will work best. Then direct them to evaluate each possibility, eliminating choices that are unacceptable, unworkable, or simply less desirable. In this way, students gradually will zero in on a viable topic that interests them. Also invite students to try the **TIP** and report on the results to the class.

3. Develop research questions. Use the Reporter's Questions organizer to help students get started. Remind students that they need not come up with a question for every question word—and that some question words may generate more than one question. Also point out that some questions may be useful even if they do not fit neatly into the Reporter's Questions format, such as the text example *Has anyone ever tried to duplicate Odysseus' journey?*

📦 **BEST PRACTICES TOOLKIT—Transparency**
Reporter's Questions p. C9

📘 **RESOURCE MANAGER—Copy Masters**
Narrowing a Research Topic p. 25
Prewriting p. 26

For interactive graphic organizers, see
💿 Write*Smart* CD

ℹ️ Writing Center at **ClassZone.com**

RESEARCHING

1. **Look for possible sources.** Review with students the wide range of research sources that are available to them, as discussed on pages 1191–1200. Point out that the initial goal is to look for sources that are not just interesting, but also informative and relevant for their topic. Ask students why it is a wise idea to identify a variety of sources. *Possible answers: A variety of sources will provide different kinds of information and reflect different authors' viewpoints; consulting different sources enables the writer to compare and verify data.*

2. **Evaluate each source.** Divide the class into four groups. Have each group prepare and present a brief summary of one part of these guidelines for evaluating sources presented on pages 1201–1205. That is, assign one group to cover each of these:
   • general evaluation guidelines (p. 1201)
   • evaluation of Web sites (pp. 1202–1203)
   • evaluation of nonfiction books (p. 1204)
   • evaluation of periodicals (p. 1205)
   Encourage students to include visual aids, such as reference charts, in their presentations.

As you discuss the "Reasons for Rejecting Sources," ask students to read the **TIP** and then explain why each of the four sources was rejected. *Possible answer: (1) cannot depend on the site's accuracy; (2) unknown author qualifications, so cannot trust information; (3) information may be out of date; (4) should use primary, not secondary, source for the* Odyssey.

📖 RESOURCE MANAGER—Copy Master
Sources p. 27

RESEARCHING

What Should I Do?	*What Does It Look Like?*

1. Look for possible sources.
Begin gathering information about your topic by searching the World Wide Web and your school and local libraries. Try to select only those reference materials that are most likely to contain the information you need. For example, you might consult an atlas to trace Odysseus' journey, and refer to an encyclopedia to learn about Homeric legends. Keep a list indicating the name of each source and the place where you found it, adding comments that will help you use the sources later.

After locating and making comments on the sources, go on to the next step—evaluating each source for usefulness and reliability.

See pages 1189–1200 for more information about selecting appropriate reference works and research tools.

Sources	Comments
World Wide Web (bookmarked)	
"Geography in the Odyssey." Wikipedia[1]	lots of info
"Map of Odysseus' Journey"	go to "Background" link
"About the Odyssey." Gradesaver [2]	compares several sources
"In the Wake of Odysseus: Localization of the Mythological Journey"	
"Synesthesia and Homer's World"	far-out theory
"Homer's Odyssey Resources on the Web." Robot Wisdom [3]	guide to other sources
School Library	
"Homeric Legend." Britannica Student Encyclopedia CD-ROM	study "Analysis" section
The Odyssey of Homer: A Modern Translation. Trans. Richmond Lattimore (883 HOM)	easy reading
Public Library	
The Odyssey of Homer. Trans. Robert Fagles (88301 Homer)	great introduction by B. Knox
Tales from the Odyssey. Mary Pope Osborne [4]	retelling of Odyssey
"Was Troy a Metropolis? Homer Isn't Talking." New York Times	scientific evidence

2. Evaluate each source.
Carefully examine and evaluate each source you have identified. Ask yourself if the information it contains is reliable, specifically addresses your topic, and is the right level for your audience. Eliminate unsuitable sources, noting why you rejected each one.

TIP In considering a source, ask yourself questions such as these: Is this a primary or a secondary source? What are the author's qualifications? What biases might he or she have? How up-to-date is the information? Who is the intended audience? For more information on evaluating sources, see the Research Strategies Workshop, pages 1201–1205.

Reasons for Rejecting Sources

[1] Disclaimer says "Wikipedia makes no guarantee of validity."

[2] No credentials given for author of the article; statements may be unreliable.

[3] Site not updated since 2002; also, information really confusing.

[4] Too elementary; should use primary source.

DIFFERENTIATED INSTRUCTION

FOR LESS-PROFICIENT WRITERS

Evaluate Sources Help students apply the **TIP** on this page. For each source (or category of sources) in the sample list, model and then have students consider these questions:

• Does this source contain reliable information? What about the author's background helps me make this decision?

• Who is the intended audience for this information? Is the information presented at a level that is appropriate for my audience?

• Is the source biased? How can I tell?

• Does the information relate directly to my specific topic?

• Is the information up-to-date? How do I know?

• Is this a primary source or a secondary source?

• If I were to keep this source, how might I use it in the paper?

RESEARCHING

What Should I Do?

3. Make source cards.
Once you have sorted through your initial list of sources, record important information about each of the "keepers" on an index card. Include the following information, numbering each card in the top right-hand corner:

World Wide Web source
- author (if given)
- title of Web page or article
- publication information for any print version
- date created or posted
- name of any institution or organization responsible for the site
- date accessed
- URL

Book
- author or editor
- title
- location and publisher
- year of publication
- library call number

Encyclopedia article
- author (if given)
- title of article
- name and year of encyclopedia
- location and publisher (if CD-ROM)

Periodical article
- author
- title of article
- name and date of periodical
- page numbers of article

What Does It Look Like?

World Wide Web source

> ③
> Burgess, Jonathan S. "In the Wake of Odysseus: Localization of the Mythological Journey." 2004. 9 Mar. 2008 <http://www.chass.utoronto.ca/~jburgess/rop/odvoyage.html>.

Book

> ⑥
> Severin, Tim. The Ulysses Voyage: Sea Search for the Odyssey. London: Hutchinson, 1987. 883.01 S49

Encyclopedia article

> ①
> "Homeric Legend." Britannica Student Encyclopedia. 2004 ed. CD-ROM. Chicago: Encyclopaedia Britannica, 2004.

Periodical article

> ④
> Wilford, John Noble. "Was Troy a Metropolis? Homer Isn't Talking." New York Times 22 Oct. 2002: D1+.

3. Make source cards. Explain that a source card is a record of the bibliographic data about a particular source. Note that students will need this information (1) if they need to double-check their facts while writing or revising and (2) when they prepare their Works Cited list.

Call students' attention to the sample source cards in the text. Point out the numbers in the top right-hand corner. Explain that numbering source cards makes it easy to use them in conjunction with note cards; that is, when taking research notes, students should write the number of each source card on the corresponding note card. Then they can quickly determine what information came from which source.

For each type of source listed, call on volunteers to identify where the pieces of information listed in the text appear on the sample source card. For additional practice, have pairs of students refer to the models as they work together to create their own source cards for a Web source, a nonfiction book, an encyclopedia article, and a periodical article.

FOR ENGLISH LEARNERS

Language: Skill Words Students have come across these terms earlier in the unit, but you should review the terms here to ensure students' understanding:

- *Web page:* a page or screen displayed at an Internet site on the World Wide Web
- *URL ("uniform resource locator"):* the address of a document or Web site on the Internet
- *call number:* a combination of letters, numbers, or both assigned to a library book to indicate its location in the library
- *CD-ROM:* an optical disk containing recorded data
- *periodical:* a publication that is issued on a regular basis

4. Take notes. Be sure that students understand the difference between note cards and source cards and that they grasp how the two work together. Ask students to identify the source of the information on the note cards on this page and to explain how they were able to do so. ***Possible answer:*** *The number 1 in the top right-hand corner of the note cards indicates that the information comes from source 1. The source card with the same number on page 1219 identifies the source as "Homeric Legend," an encyclopedia article.*

Remind students that if they need to re-check their information later, they can do so by referring to the source cards. To pinpoint the location of the facts and examples that they use, students should include on each note card the page (the page number of a printed work or the section title of a nonprint work) on which the information appears.

Explain that when students record ideas, details, and examples on note cards, they do not always have to write complete sentences, even when summarizing. Short phrases often are sufficient, as in these examples:

- *Smith born 1947—London, England*
- *Age 6—came to the U.S.*

As you discuss the **TIP**, emphasize that such comments are meant to help students organize information or write the paper. Discuss how comments that connect or compare information from various sources can prove especially helpful.

R RESOURCE MANAGER—Copy Masters
   Paraphrase and Summary 1 p. 28
   Paraphrase and Summary 2 p. 29

RESEARCHING

What Should I Do?

4. Take notes.
Read through your sources, looking for information that addresses your research questions and for new facts and expert opinions. Record each piece of information on a separate index card so that you can try different ways of organizing your ideas as you draft your report. On each card, include

- the main idea
- the number of the source (from its source card)
- a page number, section name, or other way of locating the information

TIP You also might want to add comments to your note cards about information that is puzzling or that supports or contradicts what you already know.

Restatements
Unless you are quoting material from the source directly, be sure to restate it in your own words. There are two ways to do this: in a paraphrase or in a summary.

Paraphrase—captures all the ideas of the original and is about the same length

Summary—presents the main idea of the original; may include key facts and statistics but is shorter because it omits unnecessary details

What Does It Look Like?

Original source

> The vividly fictional characteristics of the story have not prevented critics, past and present, from seeking to place it in a specific geographic context. Hesiod, who wrote later than Homer, believed that Odysseus and his ships sailed around in the general area of Italy and Sicily, to the west of . . .
>
> "Homeric Legend." *Britannica Student Encyclopedia* CD-ROM

Paraphrase

> *Early ideas—Italy and Sicily*   ①
>
> *Although the Odyssey includes many fantastic creatures and events, people throughout history have tried to identify a real setting for the tale. Hesiod, a writer who came after Homer, thought that Odysseus' journey took him around Italy and Sicily. (Section: "Analysis of the Odyssey")*
> *NOTE: Who was Hesiod? Look him up.*

Summary

> *Early ideas—Italy and Sicily*   ①
>
> *The early writer Hesiod believed that the Odyssey took place near Italy and Sicily. (Section: "Analysis of the Odyssey")*
> *NOTE: Modern explorer Tim Severin agrees.*

DIFFERENTIATED INSTRUCTION

FOR LESS−PROFICIENT WRITERS

Take Notes Choose a paragraph from a non-fiction book. Divide the class into two groups. Have one group paraphrase the paragraph and the other group summarize it. After groups share the results, discuss the differences between directly quoting, paraphrasing, and summarizing. Repeat, using another paragraph, but switch the tasks. After results have been shared, extend the discussion by asking students when they would choose to quote, paraphrase, or summarize text.

FOR ADVANCED LEARNERS/PRE−AP

Create a Note-Taking Guide Invite groups of students to draw upon this text, possibly other research-skills resources, and their own experience to write a clear, engaging "how-to" guide for novice note-takers. The guide should include tips about recognizing helpful information, as well as instructions and examples about paraphrasing and summarizing. Invite groups to present their guide and then add it to the classroom library as a permanent reference.

RESEARCHING

What Should I Do?

5. Quote well-stated ideas directly.
Sometimes, information in a source is expressed so powerfully that you want to use the author's own words. In recording direct quotations on your note cards, be sure to copy the material exactly as it appears in the original and to enclose it in quotation marks.

TIP If you want to leave out phrases or sentences within a quotation, insert three ellipsis points (...) in place of the omitted material. If you need to add a word or phrase to clarify an idea, enclose it in brackets ([ ]).

6. Avoid plagiarism.
Plagiarism, or the unauthorized use of others' words or ideas, is not honest. To avoid plagiarism, you must document the sources of any ideas that aren't common knowledge. You must do this whether you are paraphrasing, summarizing, or directly quoting the material.

TIP Remember that quoting word for word several sentences or more without documenting the source is not the only type of plagiarism. When you use special phrases someone else wrote, you must credit the source. For example, if your source includes the phrases "Alexandrian geographer," "ports of call," and "wild-goose chase," and you use any of these phrases without citing the source, you are plagiarizing.

What Does It Look Like?

> **Odyssey's odd geography** ⑥
>
> Explorer Tim Severin compared many theories of Odysseus' route with nautical maps and concluded that "Ulysses' vessel jumps up and down the length of the Mediterranean like the knight on a chessboard. It skips over inconvenient land masses, skids around capes, [and] travels at speeds that would do credit to a modern cruise liner ..." (22).

Original source

> Odysseus' wanderings in the west have inspired many attempts to plot his course and identify his ports of call. This wild-goose chase had begun already in the ancient world, as we know from ... the great Alexandrian geographer Eratosthenes, who said that you would be able to chart the course of Odysseus' wanderings when you found the cobbler who sewed the bag in which Aeolus confined the winds.
>
> Knox, Bernard. Introduction. *The Odyssey of Homer*. Trans. Robert Fagles

Plagiarized

> The great Alexandrian geographer Eratosthenes said that trying to identify Odysseus' ports of call would be a wild-goose chase.

Correctly documented

> The third-century-B.C. astronomer Eratosthenes, for example, thought that Homer's story was totally imaginary (Knox 25).

5. Quote well-stated ideas directly. Review the difference between a direct quotation and a paraphrase. Remind students that when a direct quotation appears in a paper, it is enclosed in quotation marks *unless* it is a long quotation; in that case, it gets extra indentation, as in lines 76–79 and 110–119 of the student model.

Call students' attention to the **TIP**. Point out the use of ellipses in lines 57 and 113 and the use of brackets in line 116 of the student model. Ask students why *Odyssey* appears in brackets. ***Possible answer:*** *For clarity, the writer inserted the title in place of another word, perhaps* book *or* poem.

6. Avoid plagiarism. Stress that plagiarism is unacceptable because it is the theft of someone else's words or ideas. Define *common knowledge* as "facts that can be found rather easily in numerous sources and that are likely to be known by many people." Point out that plagiarism can occur as a part of the note-taking process or when incorporating research into the paper itself.

After discussing the **TIP**, remind students that to avoid plagiarism, they must document these types of information:

- facts that are not common knowledge
- authors' ideas that interpret or draw conclusions from the facts

R RESOURCE MANAGER—Copy Masters
Avoid Plagiarism 1 p. 30
Avoid Plagiarism 2 p. 31

FOR ADVANCED LEARNERS/PRE–AP

Quote Ideas Directly Ask small groups of students to prepare an instructional presentation of punctuation guidelines for quotations. Students should cover rules for the placement of quotation marks in conjunction with periods, commas, semicolons, question marks, and exclamation points. Presentations also should cover the punctuation of lengthy quotations and the use of ellipses and brackets. Direct students to include charts that display simple, specific examples. You also may wish to have students choose their examples from nonfiction selections in this textbook that students have read in the past few months. During the presentation, help listeners practice their note-taking skills as they record key points.

7. Craft a working thesis statement. Review with students that an effective thesis statement is clear and specific, is interesting, encourages the reader to read on, and links to the writing prompt.

After students have read the sample working thesis statement, ask them why the writer crossed out the three questions. *Possible answer: As the attached note indicates, the writer has "so much info about places" that the logical question to focus on is "Did the places Homer described really exist?" In addition, trying to deal with all four questions probably would have resulted in too much material to cover in one paper.*

Help students compare the working thesis statement on this page with the final thesis statement on page 1211. Discuss how the student writer improved the wording and made the thesis statement more specific.

8. Organize and outline your material. As you discuss the sample outline, explain that outlining is a flexible process. For example, students might have had a rough outline in mind when they began their research.

Call students' attention to the **TIP**. Encourage students to use the outline approach that works best for them. Emphasize, however, that whatever the approach, students should (1) identify main ideas and (2) have sufficient information to support those ideas.

R RESOURCE MANAGER—Copy Master
Write a Thesis Statement p. 32

What Should I Do?	*What Does It Look Like?*

7. Craft a working thesis statement.
Review the material you've gathered from your sources. Write a working thesis statement that describes the main idea you want to explore in your research paper. You may have to rework your statement several times to define a topic that is neither too broad nor too narrow. You'll probably also continue to refine it as you draft your report.

TIP Your paper should not include information that is unrelated to your thesis. If you discover an interesting new angle as you research, then you need to revise your thesis to match it.

▶ **Working Thesis Statement**

People have come up with many different answers to questions such as these: ~~Who was Homer? Why did he write the Odyssey? Were the characters he described real?~~ Did the places Homer described really exist? We may never know for sure how much of the *Odyssey* is real and how much is made up, but doing some investigating can help us understand the book better.

I have so much info about places. I should focus on that.

8. Organize and outline your material.
Read through your note cards and collect them into groups that address similar main ideas. Then arrange the main ideas in an order that shows the relationships between those ideas and develops them logically. Try several arrangements to find the one that works best. These main ideas will become the Roman numerals of your outline. Then separate each group of cards into subgroups to create the sublevels of your outline. As you draft, use the entries in your outline to create the topic sentences and supporting details of your report.

TIP You can also outline your material by using a graphic organizer or grouping the ideas into questions and answers.

▶ **The Mystery of the *Odyssey***

I. Great adventure story
    A. Based on real places?
    B. Investigate to understand *Odyssey* better
II. Early theories
    A. Imaginary
    B. Real
        1. Italy and Sicily
        2. Other Mediterranean sites; the Atlantic
        3. Schliemann proved Troy real
III. Modern ideas
    A. All over the map
    B. Mediterranean (Severin)
        1. Re-created Odysseus' voyage
        2. Identified some sites, not others
IV. Conclusion
    A. Homer's era a time of exploration
    B. Unsolved mystery

DIFFERENTIATED INSTRUCTION

FOR LESS–PROFICIENT WRITERS

Organize and Outline Your Material Have students use the Microtheme organizer to help them plan their research papers. For the Introduction, suggest that students think of two or three different approaches to writing their thesis statements. Remind students that the points that they make in the Main Body must support their theses.

BEST PRACTICES TOOLKIT—Transparency
Microtheme p. C13

FOR ADVANCED LEARNERS/PRE–AP

Demonstrate an Outline at Work [paired-activity option] Have students illustrate the value of an outline by applying the outline on this page to the student model on pages 1211–1215. Ask students to copy the outline and then, next to each point, note the line numbers of the student model that the point covers. Invite students to exchange and compare annotated outlines.

DRAFTING

What Should I Do?	*What Does It Look Like?*

1. Draft your introduction.
You've already created a working thesis statement, so that's a good place to begin your report. Don't worry about writing the perfect opening at this stage. The important thing is to clearly state what you want to accomplish in the paper and to get your ideas flowing.

> The <u>Odyssey</u> by Homer is a real adventure story. For modern readers, though, it is also an intriguing mystery. Did the places Homer described really exist?

2. Incorporate facts, ideas, and quotations from your notes.
Using your outline as a guide, incorporate the material on your note cards into a draft of your report. As you add information to your draft, include the source and page number of that information. For instructions on how to do this, see "Document your sources" on the next page.

TIP Don't just plop a quotation into the middle of your paper. Use these techniques instead:

- Introduce the quotation.
  As Severin says, . . .
- Insert phrases or words into a sentence.
  The story is "a cunning weave" . . .

Note card

> Mediterranean ⑤
> The story of Odysseus' voyage home is "a cunning weave." It is hard to get into because it is full of complications and irony. The story seems to be set in the waters around Greece, Italy, and Egypt. "The geography of the tale is a riddle" (9).

Draft

> Other historians have looked for the location of the <u>Odyssey</u> closer to Homer's own Mediterranean home. According to the literary expert George Steiner, the story seems to take place in the waters surrounding Greece, Italy, and Egypt, though he admits, "The geography of the tale is a riddle" (9).

3. Share your own ideas and interpretations.
Writing a report involves more than just stringing together the information you found. It also involves analyzing the ideas of others and making your own interpretations. You should, however, use the facts, examples, and other evidence you found to support your ideas.

> Severin did locate a narrow channel south of Cape Scylla that may have caused whirlpools in ancient times (199). It's possible that Homer used this place as the basis for Charybdis, exaggerating its power to make the story more exciting. After all, a larger-than-life hero needs larger-than-life problems to struggle with.

DRAFTING

1. **Draft your introduction.** Help students compare the drafted introduction on this page with the final version on page 1211. Discuss how the student writer made the final version more developed and more engaging. Point out the writer's use of details to interest the reader: "monsters, gods, bloody battles, raging storms, and, finally, a happy ending" (lines 2–3).

2. **Incorporate facts, ideas, and quotations from your notes.** Have students compare the sample note card and draft, then discuss the **TIP**. Summarize this point by explaining that if students do adequate research and create a good working outline, the actual writing should go smoothly. This is a point worth stressing because students often think—mistakenly—that they can save time by jumping ahead to writing.

3. **Share your own ideas and interpretations.** Encourage students to think carefully about the research information that they have gathered. What personal observations can they make? What connections can they find? What conclusions can they draw? Stress that what makes one research paper different from another is not just the information presented, but also the personal insight that the writer brings to the paper.

For a writing template that can be adapted to a research paper, see

BEST PRACTICES TOOLKIT—Transparency
Writing Template: Informative Essay
pp. C16, C29

Write*Smart* CD

Writing Center at ClassZone.com

RESOURCE MANAGER—Copy Master
Use Quotations Effectively p. 33

4. **Document your sources.** After students have examined the text, examples, and **TIP**, refer them to the student model on pages 1211–1215. Help students classify each use of parenthetical documentation as an example of one or more of these situations:

- author's name and page number (lines 16, 29, 36, 40, 41, 49, 52, 58, 61, 79, 92, 95, 99)
- author's name but no page number (lines 36, 72, 91)
- author already mentioned in sentence (lines 47, 57, 85, 102)
- author unknown (lines 16, 22, 64)
- more than one source supporting an idea (lines 16, 26, 36, 72)

5. **Extend and interpret.** Remind students to use their note cards to write comments to themselves. For example, if students draw a conclusion or make a connection as they are carrying on their research, they should jot it down for possible use at this point.

ADDITIONAL TEACHING OPPORTUNITY

Using the HELP Function: Encourage students to use the HELP function of their word processing software to learn how to carry out tasks that can help them write, revise, and edit their work. For example, students can consult HELP to get directions for finding and replacing, cutting and pasting, and formatting text.

Divide the class into small groups and assign each group a particular word processing function. Have groups consult HELP to learn how to perform the function. Then have them demonstrate to the class what they have learned, explaining why the function is useful.

DRAFTING

What Should I Do?

4. **Document your sources.**
   Indicate the source of each specific idea in parentheses at the end of the sentence. This parenthetical documentation will help readers find the original information. In general, include the **author's last name** and the **page number** (Severin 22). Here are some special cases:

   - **Author already mentioned in the sentence**— use only the page number (22).
   - **Author unknown**—use a shortened title of the work ("Homeric Legend").
   - **Multiple authors**—use last names for up to three authors (Steiner and Fagles 12). For more than three authors, use the first author's last name and *et al.* (Greene et al. 45).
   - **More than one work by an author**—include the name of the work (Jones, <u>Readings</u> 39).
   - **More than one source supporting an idea**— include citations for all sources, separated by semicolons (Knox 5; Nardo 20; Wilford D1).

   TIP Highlight each parenthetical citation in color to help you compile your Works Cited list later.

5. **Extend and interpret.**
   As you draft your report, weave together ideas from your various sources. Compare and contrast them and add your own interpretations, observations, and conclusions.

What Does It Look Like?

> According to the literary expert George Steiner, the story seems to take place in the waters surrounding Greece, Italy, and Egypt, though he admits, "The geography of the tale is a riddle" (9).
> — Author mentioned in sentence

> For example, in Book Four of the <u>Odyssey</u>, Menelaus describes the island of Pharos as "as far out as the distance a hollow ship can make in a whole day's sailing" (Homer 74).
> — Basic documentation —author and page number

> One explanation is that the <u>Odyssey</u> actually describes two separate voyages and that the adventures after line 135 of Book Ten were based on the stories of another Greek hero, Jason, and his Argonauts ("Homeric Legend").
> — No page number in source

> About the only thing people seem to agree on is that Troy existed where Homer said it was and that the Trojan War took place sometime between 1300 and 1200 B.C. (Knox 5; Nardo 20; Wilford D1). The reason they agree is that archaeologists have found proof.
> — Synthesizes information from multiple sources

DIFFERENTIATED INSTRUCTION

FOR ENGLISH LEARNERS

Vocabulary: Latin Abbreviations Explain that italicized Latin abbreviations often appear in research papers and other documents. Have students work in groups with dictionaries to define each of these abbreviations: *et al.* (*et alii*—"and others"), *e.g.* (*exempli gratia*—"for example"), *i.e.* (*id est*—"that is"), A.D. (*Anno Domini*—"in the year of the Lord"). When groups have finished, have them compare their definitions.

FOR ADVANCED LEARNERS/PRE–AP

Follow Software Instructions Point out that research papers often display statistical information in graphic form. Have students follow the instructions in a software program to help them convert statistics into graphs or pie charts as appropriate and report on the experience.

DRAFTING

What Should I Do?

6. Create a thoughtful conclusion.
An effective conclusion should go beyond restating the facts presented in your report. It should leave readers with something solid and interesting to think about, such as the overall importance of your topic, questions about it that remain unanswered, or suggestions for additional research.

TIP A powerful quotation, an exciting anecdote, or a provocative question can help make your conclusion memorable.

7. Prepare a Works Cited list.
After you have finished a draft of your research paper, go through it and collect the source cards for all the parenthetical documentation you included. (If you highlighted these references during drafting, they will be easy to find.) Alphabetize the cards by the author's last names (by work titles where the author's names are unknown), and copy the information on the cards onto a list. For instructions on preparing and formatting a Works Cited list, see "MLA Citation Guidelines" on pages 1228–1229.

What Does It Look Like?

▶ What conclusions can modern readers draw from these confusing and conflicting ideas about the <u>Odyssey</u>? Robert Fagles, a well-known translator and scholar of Homer, gives probably the best summary of the possibilities—and of the <u>Odyssey</u>'s lasting influence and interest:

> I think it's altogether likely that, however "mythological" the Greek experience may seem, it nevertheless stems from experience. Was that experience actual or imagined, or a combination of the two? I don't think we'll ever know. . . . All of it is stranger than fiction, as we'd say, and even more compelling than fact.

▶ **Works Cited**

Burgess, Jonathan S. "In the Wake of Odysseus: Localization of the Mythological Journey." 2004. 9 Mar. 2008 <http://www.chass.utoronto.ca/~jburgess/rop/od.voyage.html>.

Fagles, Robert. Reply to query of Terry J. Keely. <u>Online NewsHour</u>. 13 Mar. 1997. Public Broadcasting Service. 10 Apr. 2008 <http://www.pbs.org/newshour/forum/march97/od2.html>.

Homer. <u>The Odyssey of Homer: A Modern Translation</u>. Trans. Richmond Lattimore. New York: Harper, 1967.

"Homeric Legend." <u>Britannica Student Encyclopedia</u>. 2004 ed. CD-ROM. Chicago: Encyclopaedia Britannica, 2004.

6. Create a thoughtful conclusion. Discuss the twofold purpose of a conclusion for this kind of writing as well as the suggestions in the **TIP**. Then ask students whether they think that the quotation from Robert Fagles was a good choice for concluding the student model, and why. *Accept all reasonable responses, but encourage students to support their answers with clear reasons.* Invite students to suggest other ways in which the student writer might have concluded the paper.

7. Prepare a Works Cited list. After students have examined the text and examples, have them review the complete Works Cited list on page 1216. Remind students that *MLA* stands for *Modern Language Association* and that MLA style is widely used by schools and various publications. Also note the variety of sources cited, pointing out that consulting a variety of sources often helps make both the research and the final paper more interesting.

FOR ENGLISH LEARNERS

Prepare a Works Cited List Give students practice in alphabetizing entries for a Works Cited list, reminding them to use work titles when no author is named. For example, present these partial entries (taken from pages 1228–1229) in mixed order and have students arrange them alphabetically, as shown:

- <u>Greek Literature: An Overview.</u>

- Heubeck, Alfred, Stephanie West, and J. B. Hainsworth. <u>A Commentary on Homer's Odyssey.</u>

- "Homer." <u>The World Book Encyclopedia.</u>

- Severin, Tim. "The Quest for Ulysses."

- Steiner, George, and Robert Fagles, eds. <u>Homer: A Collection of Critical Essays.</u>

- Struck, Peter. "Map of Odysseus' Journey."

REVISING AND EDITING

1. **Make your introduction a "grabber."** Point out that a "grabber" introduction is common to many kinds of writing. Then challenge students to rewrite the opening of the student model as a question. *Possible answer: Do you enjoy adventure tales about monsters, fierce battles, and raging storms? Do you like stories with happy endings? Most readers will answer YES—and that answer helps explain why Homer's* Odyssey *remains popular today.*

2. **Hone your thesis statement.** Point out that the original thesis statement, expressed as a question, is too broad and does not have a specific enough governing idea. Discuss the **TIP**, emphasizing that a thesis statement must signal a task that is significant but still provable within the length of a research paper. The thesis statement that has been added in red achieves that purpose, and the question now serves to introduce it.

3. **Show how ideas are connected.** Direct students' attention to the edited example (which became lines 34–37 in the student model) and ask how the changes improve the student's draft. *Possible answer: Adding the "Unlike" phrase makes it clear that the writer is making a comparison. Adding "Therefore" shows that the second sentence draws a conclusion from the first.*

4. **Support your ideas with details.** Note that statistics, facts, details, reasons, quotations, paraphrases, and anecdotes are among the kinds of evidence that writers can use.

REVISING AND EDITING

What Should I Do?	**What Does It Look Like?**
1. Make your introduction a "grabber." • Highlight the first sentence of your introduction. • Ask yourself if this beginning would "hook" your reader. • Consider starting with a question, a powerful quotation, or a lively image.	▶ *Everybody loves a great adventure story, especially one that has everything—monsters, gods, bloody battles, raging storms, and, finally, a happy ending.* ~~The Odyssey by Homer is a real adventure story.~~ *For modern readers, though, it is also an intriguing mystery.* *that kind of*
2. Hone your thesis statement. • Underline your thesis statement. • Make sure you have explained clearly and completely what you will investigate or discuss. **TIP** Your thesis is the governing idea of your paper. In other words, it sets boundaries on what your paper will cover.	▶ *Did the places Homer described really exist? We may never know for certain which places in the Odyssey are real and which are fiction, but investigating the events and geography of Odysseus' wanderings can lead to a better understanding of this great literary work.*
3. Show how ideas are connected. • Ask a peer reader to draw a ⬚box⬚ around sentences or paragraphs whose logical connection is unclear. • Add transitions or more information to show how the ideas are related. **See page 1230:** Ask a Peer Reader	▶ *Unlike the events of the Trojan War, which* *The Trojan War took place on land, Odysseus' sea voyage left no traces (Severin 17; Struck).* *Therefore,* *All of the ideas historians have come up with about where the events occurred are just guesses.*
4. Support your ideas with details. • Reread your paper. Ask yourself: Did I provide reasons and evidence to support my ideas? • Add reasons and evidence in places where support is missing.	▶ *Many people throughout history have tried to identify a real setting for the tale. The Greek poet Hesiod, who lived in the eighth century BC, probably not long after the Odyssey was written, thought that Odysseus' wanderings took him around Italy and Sicily.*

DIFFERENTIATED INSTRUCTION

FOR LESS–PROFICIENT WRITERS

Revising and Editing (1–4) Help students turn the points on this page into a checklist like this one, which students can use for self- and peer assessment:

• Will my introduction "grab" my readers' attention and make them want to continue reading?

• Does my thesis statement clearly and completely explain what my paper is about?

• Do my ideas seem logically organized and connected?

• Do I use transitional words and phrases where needed?

• Do I support my ideas with details, reasons, and evidence, including quotations and paraphrases?

REVISING AND EDITING

What Should I Do?	*What Does It Look Like?*

5. Document others' ideas correctly.
- (Circle) ideas or quotations from your sources that are not documented.
- Follow guidelines for parenthetical documentation.

▶ In the end, Severin was unable to trace Odysseus' journey exactly and found many parts of Homer's tale puzzling. He concluded that ⌈"the geographies of folklore and navigation overlapped"⌉ (245). Although he didn't set out to prove whether the Odyssey was real or imagined, his findings suggest that it was a mixture of both.

6. Eliminate unnecessary words.
- Ask a peer reader to draw a wavy line under words or phrases that do not add new information to a sentence or that can be stated more simply.
- Delete unnecessary information and simplify complicated statements.

See page 1230: Ask a Peer Reader

▶ As readers begin reading the ~~epic poem known as the~~ Odyssey, we are swept into a journey that is so ~~very~~ exciting that we ~~feel suffering~~ along with Odysseus.
suffer

7. Adjust your tone.
- [Bracket] passages that have an inappropriate tone for a research paper because they are too casual or slangy.
- Substitute words or phrases that are objective and serious, yet lively.

▶ used this place as the basis for Charybdis, exaggerating its power
It's possible that Homer ^[could've figured out the whole idea of Charybdis from this spot]. [So weird!] [Then he just made a mountain out of a molehill] to make the story more exciting.

8. Check the parenthetical documentation.
- Look through the paper for all the places you used parenthetical documentation.
- Check that you have punctuated the references correctly.

See page 1224: Document your sources.

▶ Incorrect: (Knox, 25, "Homeric Legend.").
Correct: (Knox 25; "Homeric Legend").

Incorrect: (Knox, 5, Nardo, 20; Wilford, D1).
Correct: (Knox 5; Nardo 20; Wilford D1).

5. Document others' ideas correctly. Remind students to document not only direct quotations but also paraphrases and summaries of others' ideas. Parenthetical documentation enables readers to find complete information about the source in the Works Cited list.

6. Eliminate unnecessary words. Suggest to students that after writing their papers, they allow some time to pass before attempting to revise and edit them. Returning to the papers with a fresh eye will make it easier to spot places that need editing.

7. Adjust your tone. Remind students that a serious, thoughtful, objective tone is appropriate for a research paper. As you urge students to use this tone consistently throughout the paper, discuss some of the ways in which students can keep their language lively without changing tone—for example, concrete nouns, vivid verbs and adjectives, active instead of passive verbs, and a mix of sentence structures.

8. Check the parenthetical documentation. Discuss the correct use of periods, commas, semicolons, and quotation marks in the examples. Note, too, that pages 1228–1229 present the MLA citation guidelines.

For interactive revision tools, see

Write*Smart* CD

Writing Center at **ClassZone.com**

FOR LESS–PROFICIENT WRITERS

Revising and Editing (5–8) Extend the checklist started on page 1226 by helping students turn the points on this page into questions like these:

- Do I correctly document ideas and words from my sources?
- Do I avoid unnecessary words?
- Does all of my information relate to my main ideas?

- Are my sentences clear without being too complicated?
- Is my tone appropriate for a research paper?
- Are all of my documentation references correctly formatted and punctuated?
- Do I include some of my own ideas and interpretations?
- Does my paper end with a thoughtful conclusion?

FOR ADVANCED LEARNERS/PRE–AP

Compare and Contrast Analyses [small-group option] Students may have used an Analysis Frame in conjunction with nonfiction selections in this textbook. Have them apply it and then the guidelines on pages 1226–1227 to the student model (pages 1211–1216). Then ask students to share their insights with the class.

 BEST PRACTICES TOOLKIT—Transparency
Analysis Frame: Informational Nonfiction
pp. D21, D46

REVIEW MLA GUIDELINES
BOOKS

Point out these details to students:

- When a book by two or three authors or editors is cited, only the first person is listed with the last name first; the others are listed with the first name first.

- When listing an author and a translator or editor, give the author's name before the book's title and the other name or names after the title.

PARTS OF BOOKS

Point out that short works, such as poems and short stories, are designated by quotation marks, not underlining or italics.

MLA Citation Guidelines

Here are some basic forms for citing sources. Use these forms on your source, or bibliography, cards and in the Works Cited list that appears at the end of your paper.

BOOKS

One author
Severin, Tim. <u>The Ulysses Voyage: Sea Search for the Odyssey</u>. London: Hutchinson, 1987.

Two authors or editors
Steiner, George, and Robert Fagles, eds. <u>Homer: A Collection of Critical Essays</u>.
    Englewood Cliffs: Prentice, 1962.

Three authors
Heubeck, Alfred, Stephanie West, and J. B. Hainsworth. <u>A Commentary on Homer's Odyssey</u>.
    New York: Oxford UP, 1988.

Four or more authors
The abbreviation et al. *means "and others."* Use et al. *instead of listing all the authors.*
Melick, Peter, et al. <u>The Odyssey Explained</u>. New York: Garden UP, 1997.

No author given
<u>Greek Literature: An Overview</u>. New York: Sunrise, 1993.

An author and a translator
Homer. <u>The Odyssey of Homer: A Modern Translation</u>. Trans. Richmond Lattimore.
    New York: Harper, 1967.

An author, a translator, and an editor
La Fontaine, Jean de. <u>Selected Fables</u>. Trans. Christopher Wood. Ed. Maya Slater.
    New York: Oxford UP, 1995.

PARTS OF BOOKS

An introduction, a preface, a foreword, or an afterword written by someone other than the author(s) of a work
Knox, Bernard. Introduction. <u>The Odyssey of Homer</u>. Trans. Robert Fagles.
    New York: Penguin, 1996. 3-64.

A poem, a short story, an essay, or a chapter in a collection of works by one author
Sappho. "He Is More Than a Hero." <u>The Works of Sappho</u>. Trans. Edward Osmond.
    New York: Garden UP, 1990. 53.

A poem, a short story, an essay, or a chapter in an anthology of works by several authors
Solonos, Costa. "Journeys." Trans. Carl Foreman. <u>Greek Voices</u>. Ed. Katharine Greene and
    Gerald Spencer. London: Greenwood, 1985. 83-85.

DIFFERENTIATED INSTRUCTION

FOR ENGLISH LEARNERS

Vocabulary Support Write these terms on the board. Elicit or provide the meaning of each:

- *preface:* the introduction to a book or other work, usually written by the author to explain his or her purpose for writing

- *foreword:* the introduction to a book or other work, often written by someone other than the author

- *afterword:* a section that sometimes follows the main body of a book or other work, often containing comments written by someone other than the author

- *anthology:* a collection of literary pieces or passages within a single book

A novel or a play in a collection
Sophocles. <u>Antigone</u>. <u>The Three Theban Plays</u>. Trans. Robert Fagles. New York:
    Penguin, 1984.

MAGAZINES, NEWSPAPERS, AND ENCYCLOPEDIAS

An article in a newspaper
Wilford, John Noble. "Was Troy a Metropolis? Homer Isn't Talking." <u>New York Times</u>
    22 Oct. 2002: D1+.

An article in a magazine
Severin, Tim. "The Quest for Ulysses." <u>National Geographic</u> Aug. 1986: 194-225.

An article in an encyclopedia
"Homer." <u>The World Book Encyclopedia</u>. 2000 ed.

MISCELLANEOUS NONPRINT SOURCES

An interview
Baldwin, Richard. Personal interview. 9 June 2004.

A video recording
<u>The Odyssey of Troy</u>. Videocassette. A&E Home Video, 1994.

ELECTRONIC PUBLICATIONS

A CD-ROM
"Homeric Legend." <u>Britannica Student Encyclopedia</u>. 2004 ed. CD-ROM. Chicago:
    Encyclopaedia Britannica, 2004.

A document from an Internet site
Entries for online sources should contain as much of the information shown as available.

Author or compiler   Title or description of document
Fagles, Robert. Reply to query of Terry J. Keely.

     Title of site and date of document   Site sponsor   Date of access
Online NewsHour. 13 Mar. 1997. Public Broadcasting Service. 10 Apr. 2008

          Complete URL enclosed in angle brackets. Break only after a slash.
<http://www.pbs.org/newshour/forum/march97/od2.html>.

Struck, Peter. "Map of Odysseus' Journey." Mythology. Course pages. 2004. Dept. of
    Classical Studies, U of Pennsylvania. 9 Mar. 2008 <http://www.classics.upenn.edu/
    myth/homer/odymap.php>.

MAGAZINES, NEWSPAPERS, AND ENCYCLOPEDIA

Note these details:

- The names of newspapers and magazines are underlined (or italicized), but titles of articles appear within quotation marks.

- When citing a periodical article, include the page numbers on which the article appears.

MISCELLANEOUS NONPRINT SOURCES

Invite students to suggest other miscellaneous nonprint sources. ***Possible answers:*** *a radio talk show, a movie, a speech*

ELECTRONIC PUBLICATIONS

- Have students explain how the listing for the *Britannica Student Encyclopedia* CD-ROM differs from the listing for the *World Book Encyclopedia* article. ***Possible answer:*** *The* Britannica *listing identifies the source as a CD-ROM and includes the location and publisher.*

- Suggest that students take the time to study the examples of how to document online sources, as such documentation can be confusing. Stress the importance of providing a complete, accurate URL.

- Have students work in pairs to practice documenting several online sources.

FOR ENGLISH LEARNERS
Vocabulary Support Write these terms on the board. Elicit or provide the meaning of each:

- *compiler:* a person who gathers materials, such as documents or statistics, from one or more sources

- *site sponsor:* the person or organization responsible for a Web site

- *angle brackets:* marks (< >) used to enclose words or characters in certain situations—in this case, when citing a Web site

Preparing to Publish

Support for meeting the goals in the writing rubric is supplied throughout the Writing Workshop on pages 1217–1229.

For Rubric Bank, see

 WriteSmart CD

ℹ️ Writing Center at **ClassZone.com**

🅡 RESOURCE MANAGER—Copy Masters
Ask a Peer Reader p. 34
Proofreading and Editing p. 35

Assess and Reteach

🆂 STANDARDS LESSON FILE

Writing Lesson 2: Limiting or Expanding a Topic
Writing Lesson 14: Coherence in Paragraphs
Writing Lesson 15: Writing a Thesis Statement
Writing Lesson 16: Writing Introductions
Writing Lesson 17: Writing Conclusions
Writing Lesson 18: Unity in Compositions
Writing Lesson 21: Integrating Quotations
Writing Lesson 35: Elaborate with Facts and Statistics
Writing Lesson 36: Elaborate with Incidents, Examples, and Quotations
Writing Lesson 37: Elaborate with Visuals
Research and Study Skills Lesson 9: Avoiding Plagiarism
Research and Study Skills Lesson 10: Documentation
Research and Study Skills Lesson 12: Paraphrasing
Research and Study Skills Lesson 13: Summarizing
Research and Study Skills Lesson 16: Outlining a Paper

Preparing to Publish **Research Paper**

Apply the Rubric

A strong research paper . . .

☑ has a lively introduction
☑ presents the controlling idea of the paper in a clear thesis statement
☑ supports the thesis with quotations, paraphrases, and other evidence from multiple sources
☑ uses quotations effectively
☑ credits sources correctly
☑ develops ideas in a logical organizational pattern
☑ includes the writer's own interpretations of the material
☑ has a tone appropriate for the topic, audience, and purpose
☑ uses precise language and varied sentence lengths and structures
☑ has a thoughtful conclusion

Ask a Peer Reader

- Which part of my paper did you find most interesting? Why?
- Which ideas need clarification?
- Which aspects of my subject would you like to know more about?

Format Your Paper

Follow these guidelines in preparing the final draft of your research paper:

- Leave one-inch margins at top, bottom, and sides of each page (except for page numbers).

- On separate lines, type your name, your teacher's name, the class, and the date at the top left of the first page.

- On each page, type your last name and the page number one-half inch from the top, aligned at the right-hand corner.

- Double-space all text, including quotations and the Works Cited list.

- Indent paragraphs one-half inch (or five spaces) from the left margin.

- Indent set-off quotations one inch (or ten spaces) from the left margin.

- Begin your Works Cited list on a separate page, and indent the second and subsequent lines of entries one-half inch (or five spaces). End each entry with a period.

See the *MLA Handbook for Writers of Research Papers* for additional formatting guidelines.

Writing On|ine

 PUBLISHING OPTIONS
For publishing options, visit the **Writing Center** at **ClassZone.com**.

ASSESSMENT PREPARATION
For writing and grammar assessment practice, go to the **Assessment Center** at **ClassZone.com**.

Creating a Web Site

You can use the World Wide Web to share your research with the world. The Web also lets you supplement your research paper with pictures, audio, and video.

Planning the Web Site

1. **Decide on a topic for your Web site.** Choose a subject that interests you and that lends itself to various kinds of media elements. For example, a Web site about monsters in the *Odyssey* could have many different media types: images of the monsters, sound effects, and maps showing the monsters' locations.
2. **Who is your audience?** Other students? People who are unfamiliar with your topic? Will your site inform, persuade, or entertain?
3. **Research your subject.** Find media elements to illuminate your topic. You may find maps, photographs, music, animation—even video clips. Use library resources and at least two Internet search engines.

Organizing the Web Site

1. **Create a flow chart.** A flow chart will help you figure out how to group information, where to make links, how everything will fit together, and how many pages you will need. Here is an example for a site about monsters in the *Odyssey*.

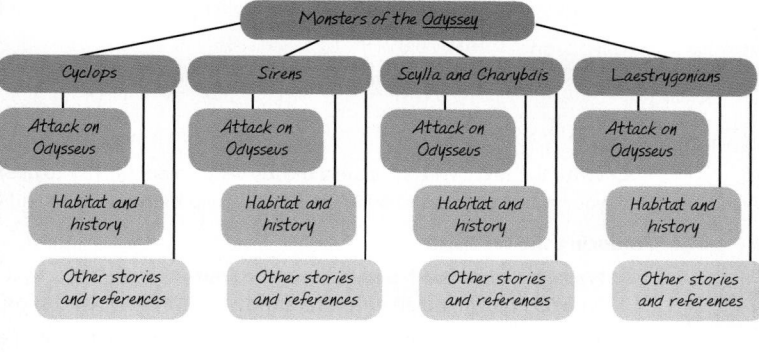

continued

PUBLISHING WITH TECHNOLOGY

Ask students to read pages 1231–1233 to get an overview of how to plan, organize, and produce a Web site. Students who choose this option should familiarize themselves with the features of personal Web sites and the technology used to create them.

Before students begin working, review this rubric to help them understand their goals:

Rubric An effective Web site

- has a definite audience and purpose
- blends a variety of media types
- is well researched and logically organized
- avoids unnecessary distractions
- is primarily visual, with easy-to-read text

Have students use the rubric to evaluate each other's Web sites.

Planning the Web Site

- Since a Web site is largely a visual medium, students should choose a subject with visual possibilities.
- Point out that a site may serve more than one purpose—for example, to inform *and* to entertain—but students should try to decide on one *main* purpose.
- Encourage students to do research to identify a variety of media elements.

Organizing the Web Site

- Encourage students to use a Classification Chart, or other graphic organizer to help them plan their Web site. Suggest that students experiment with different arrangements to see what works best.

BEST PRACTICES TOOLKIT—Transparency Classification Chart p. B17

RESOURCE MANAGER—Copy Master Publishing with Technology p. 36

STANDARDS LESSON FILE **Media Lesson 21:** Creating a Web Site

- Compare storyboarding a Web site to story-boarding a movie or creating a comic strip. Point out that even though a Web site is not really "narrative" in nature, it nonetheless has a sequence that a storyboard can capture.

- Emphasize that the visual and audio elements of the Web site should work together, not compete with each other. Also caution students to avoid overload. Packing in too many elements can cause user confusion or make a site annoyingly busy.

Producing the Web Site

- Direct students' attention to the warning about using elements from certain sources. Explain that it is not always clear what material is copyrighted, who the copyright holder is, or under what conditions material may be used. When in doubt, students should check with a teacher or school computer specialist before adding materials to their project file.

2. **Storyboard the pages.** Draw rough sketches of how you want your pages to look. Each storyboard frame should indicate the placement of text, images, buttons, and links.

> **TIP** Avoid distractions like flashing text or constant background music. All elements should be relevant to your purpose.

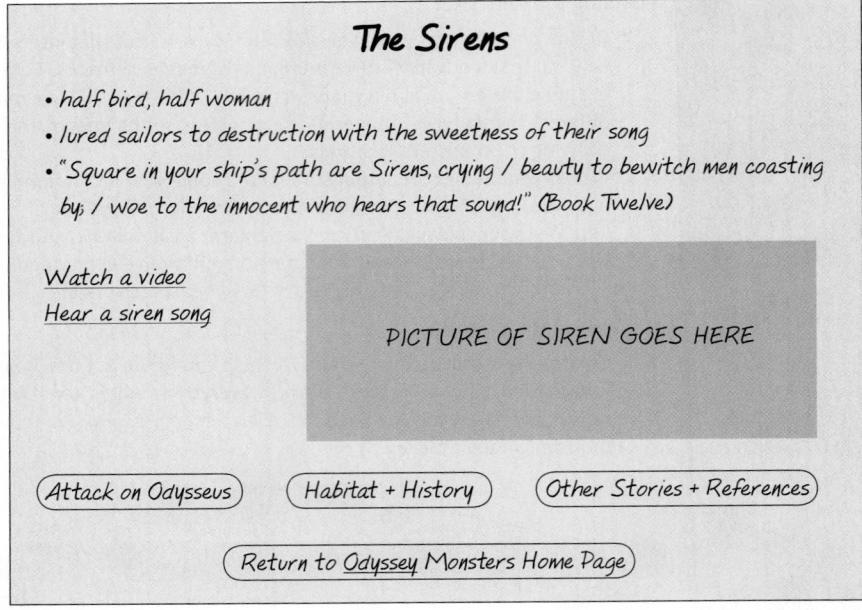

The Sirens

- *half bird, half woman*
- *lured sailors to destruction with the sweetness of their song*
- *"Square in your ship's path are Sirens, crying / beauty to bewitch men coasting by; / woe to the innocent who hears that sound!" (Book Twelve)*

Watch a video
Hear a siren song

PICTURE OF SIREN GOES HERE

(Attack on Odysseus) (Habitat + History) (Other Stories + References)

(Return to *Odyssey* Monsters Home Page)

3. **Write the text.** Web sites are a mostly visual medium. Try to use visuals to convey your ideas. Charts and bulleted lists can help keep text brief and to the point.

Producing the Web Site

1. **Prepare your research materials for the Web.** Ask your school's computer specialist for help in scanning graphics and saving CD-ROM elements to your project file.

   Note: Be careful when using elements from sources like the Internet, books, and magazines. These sources often contain copyrighted material that must be cited on a Works Cited page. (See page 1225.) Some materials require permission from the creators, and many media elements on the Internet have terms-and-conditions statements. These statements may specify that students can use the media elements in school projects.

2. **Choose an authoring program.** An authoring program allows you to combine media elements into a Web document. Your school may have an authoring program, or you can download a program from the Internet. (Check with your school's computer specialist first.) Import your media elements into the program. Choose colors, fonts, buttons, and layout. Keep these guidelines in mind:

- Text should be easy to read. Use a font size of 12 points or larger, and choose contrasting colors for the text and the background.
- Buttons with the same function should have the same design.

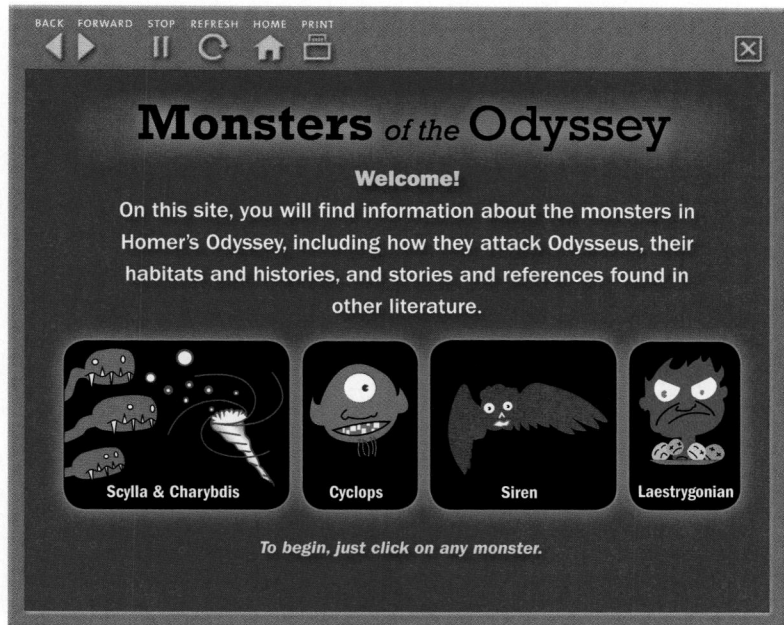

3. **Test and revise your site.** Proofread every screen and check for faulty links. Ask yourself and classmates the following questions: Where is the navigation confusing? Which visual or audio elements are helpful? Which are distracting? Use the feedback to revise and improve your site.

4. **Upload your site.** Make your site available for viewing either on your school's internal server or on the World Wide Web. Ask your school's computer specialist for permission.

- Encourage students to try out different fonts and color combinations to see which ones are most effective.
- Direct students' attention to the sample Web page: "Monsters of the Odyssey." Have students evaluate the page for clarity and design. Ask what they might do differently if they were presenting the same material.
- Compare testing and revising a preliminary site to revising and editing the draft of a piece of writing. Point out that, like a piece of writing, the screens need to present clear, error-free, and easy-to-follow text. With screens, however, students also need to evaluate the effectiveness of visuals and the accuracy and effectiveness of links.

Student Resource Bank

Reading Handbook — R2
1 Reading Literary Texts — R2
2 Reading Informational Texts: Text Features — R3
3 Reading Informational Texts: Patterns of Organization — R8
4 Reading Informational Texts: Forms — R14
5 Reading Persuasive Texts — R21
6 Adjusting Reading Rate to Purpose — R27

Writing Handbook — R28
1 The Writing Process — R28
2 Building Blocks of Good Writing — R30
3 Descriptive Writing — R34
4 Narrative Writing — R36
5 Expository Writing — R37
6 Persuasive Writing — R40
7 Workplace and Technical Writing — R42

Grammar Handbook — R46
Quick Reference: Parts of Speech — R46
Quick Reference: The Sentence and Its Parts — R48
Quick Reference: Punctuation — R49
Quick Reference: Capitalization — R51
1 Nouns — R52
2 Pronouns — R52
3 Verbs — R55
4 Modifiers — R57
5 The Sentence and Its Parts — R59
6 Phrases — R60
7 Verbals and Verbal Phrases — R60
8 Clauses — R62
9 The Structure of Sentences — R63
10 Writing Complete Sentences — R64
11 Subject-Verb Agreement — R65

Vocabulary and Spelling Handbook — R68
1 Using Context Clues — R68
2 Analyzing Word Structure — R69
3 Understanding Word Origins — R70
4 Synonyms and Antonyms — R70
5 Denotation and Connotation — R71
6 Analogies — R71
7 Homonyms and Homophones — R71
8 Words with Multiple Meanings — R72
9 Specialized Vocabulary — R72
10 Using Reference Sources — R72
11 Spelling Rules — R72
12 Commonly Confused Words — R75

Speaking and Listening Handbook — R76
1 Speech — R76
2 Different Types of Oral Presentations — R78
3 Other Types of Communication — R81
4 Active Listening — R82

Media Handbook — R84
1 Five Core Concepts in Media Literacy — R84
2 Media Basics — R85
3 Film and TV — R86
4 News — R88
5 Advertising — R90
6 Elements of Design — R91
7 Evaluating Media Messages — R92

Test-Taking Handbook — R93
1 General Test-Taking Strategies — R93
2 Critical Reading — R94
3 Writing — R99
4 Essay — R101

Glossary of Literary Terms — R102

Glossary of Reading & Informational Terms — R115

Glossary of Vocabulary in English & Spanish — R121

Pronunciation Key — R130

Index of Fine Art — R131

Index of Skills — R133

Index of Titles and Authors — R150

Acknowledgments — R152

Art Credits — R158

Reading any text—short story, poem, magazine article, newspaper, Web page— requires the use of special strategies. For example, you might plot events in a short story on a diagram, while you may need to use text features to spot main ideas in a magazine article. You also need to identify patterns of organization in the text. Using such strategies can help you read different texts with ease and also help you understand what you're reading.

❶ Reading Literary Texts

Literary texts include short stories, novels, poems, and dramas. Literary texts can also be biographies, autobiographies, and essays. To appreciate and analyze literary texts, you will need to understand the characteristics of each type of text.

1.1 READING A SHORT STORY
Strategies for Reading

- Read the title. As you read the story, you may notice that the title has a special meaning.

- Keep track of events as they happen. Plot the events on a diagram like this one.

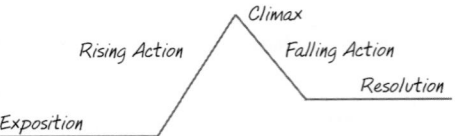

- From the details the writer provides, **visualize** the characters. **Predict** what they might do next.

- Look for specific adjectives that help you visualize the **setting**—the time and place in which events occur.

1.2 READING A POEM
Strategies for Reading

- Notice the **form** of the poem, or the number of its lines and their arrangement on the page.

- Read the poem aloud a few times. Listen for **rhymes** and **rhythms.**

- **Visualize** the images and comparisons.

- **Connect** with the poem by asking yourself what message the poet is trying to send.

- Create a word web or another **graphic organizer** to record your reactions and questions.

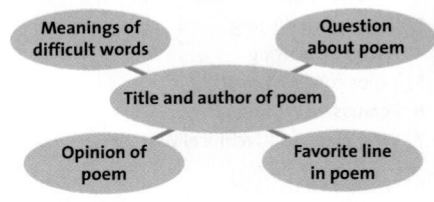

1.3 READING A PLAY
Strategies for Reading

- Read the stage directions to help you **visualize** the setting and characters.

- **Question** what the title means and why the playwright chose it.

- Identify the main conflict (struggle or problem) in the play. To **clarify** the conflict, make a chart that shows what the conflict is and how it is resolved.

- **Evaluate** the characters. What do they want? How do they change during the play? You may want to make a chart that lists each character's name, appearance, and traits.

1.4 READING LITERARY NONFICTION
Strategies for Reading

- If you are reading a biography, an autobiography, or another type of biographical writing, such as a diary or memoir, use a family tree or word web to keep track of the people mentioned.

- When reading an essay, **evaluate** the writer's ideas and reasoning. Does the writer present a thesis statement? identify the main points? support opinions with facts?

2 Reading Informational Texts: Text Features

An **informational text** is writing that provides factual information. Informational materials, such as chapters in textbooks and articles in magazines, encyclopedias, and newspapers, usually contain elements that help the reader recognize their purposes, organizations, and key ideas. These elements are known as **text features.**

2.1 UNDERSTANDING TEXT FEATURES

Text features are design elements of a text that indicate its organizational structure or otherwise make its key ideas and information understandable. Text features include titles, headings, subheadings, boldface type, bulleted and numbered lists, and graphic aids, such as charts, graphs, illustrations, and photographs. Notice how the text features help you find key information on the textbook page shown.

A The **title** identifies the topic.

B A **subheading** indicates the start of a new topic or section and identifies the focus of that section.

C **Boldface type** is used to make key terms obvious.

D A **bulleted list** shows items of equal importance.

E **Graphic aids,** such as graphs, illustrations, photographs, charts, diagrams, maps, and timelines, often clarify ideas in the text.

F A **caption,** or the text that accompanies a graphic aid, gives information about the graphic aid that isn't necessarily obvious from the image itself.

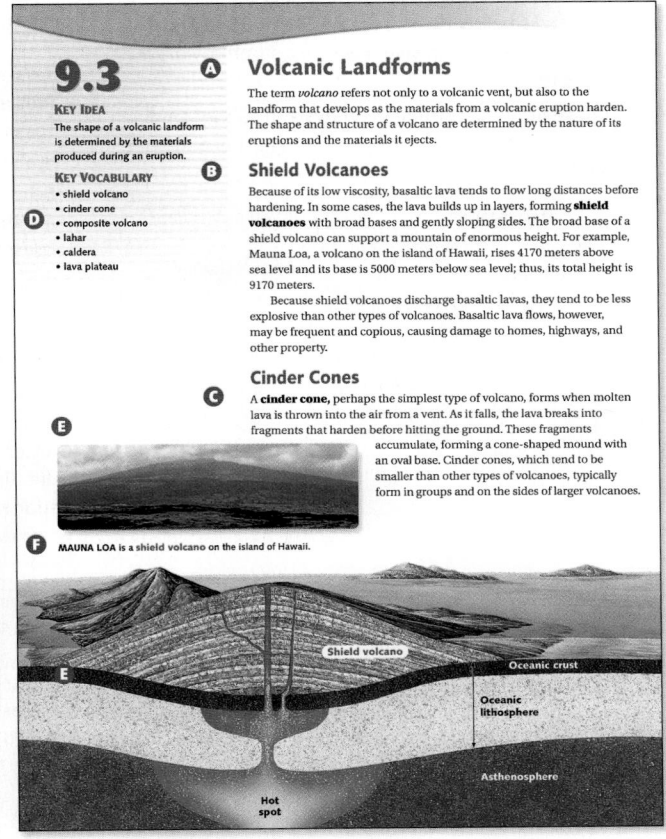

9.3

A **Volcanic Landforms**

The term *volcano* refers not only to a volcanic vent, but also to the landform that develops as the materials from a volcanic eruption harden. The shape and structure of a volcano are determined by the nature of its eruptions and the materials it ejects.

KEY IDEA
The shape of a volcanic landform is determined by the materials produced during an eruption.

KEY VOCABULARY **B**
• shield volcano
D • cinder cone
• composite volcano
• lahar
• caldera
• lava plateau

Shield Volcanoes

Because of its low viscosity, basaltic lava tends to flow long distances before hardening. In some cases, the lava builds up in layers, forming **shield volcanoes** with broad bases and gently sloping sides. The broad base of a shield volcano can support a mountain of enormous height. For example, Mauna Loa, a volcano on the island of Hawaii, rises 4170 meters above sea level and its base is 5000 meters below sea level; thus, its total height is 9170 meters.

Because shield volcanoes discharge basaltic lavas, they tend to be less explosive than other types of volcanoes. Basaltic lava flows, however, may be frequent and copious, causing damage to homes, highways, and other property.

Cinder Cones

C A **cinder cone,** perhaps the simplest type of volcano, forms when molten lava is thrown into the air from a vent. As it falls, the lava breaks into fragments that harden before hitting the ground. These fragments accumulate, forming a cone-shaped mound with an oval base. Cinder cones, which tend to be smaller than other types of volcanoes, typically form in groups and on the sides of larger volcanoes.

E

F **MAUNA LOA is a shield volcano on the island of Hawaii.**

Shield volcano

Oceanic crust

Oceanic lithosphere

Asthenosphere

Hot spot

PRACTICE AND APPLY

1. What are the subheadings on the textbook page shown?

2. What are the key terms on the page? How do you know?

3. What does the illustration tell you about shield volcanoes? Can you find this information elsewhere on the page?

PRACTICE AND APPLY

ANSWERS

1. *Shield Volcanoes, Cinder Cones*

2. *The key terms,* shield volcanoes *and* cinder cone, *are in boldface type.*

3. ***Possible answer:*** *The illustration shows how shield volcanoes form. This information can also be found in the section subtitled "Shield Volcanoes."*

2.2 USING TEXT FEATURES

You can use text features to locate information, to help you understand it, and to categorize it. Just use the following strategies when you encounter informational text.

Strategies for Reading

- Scan the title, headings, and subheadings to get an idea of the main concepts and the way the text is organized.

- Before you begin reading the text more thoroughly, read any questions that appear at the end of a lesson or chapter. Doing this will help you set a purpose for your reading.

- Turn subheadings into questions. Then use the text below the subheadings to answer the questions. Your answers will be a summary of the text.

- Take notes by turning headings and subheadings into main ideas. You might use a chart like the following.

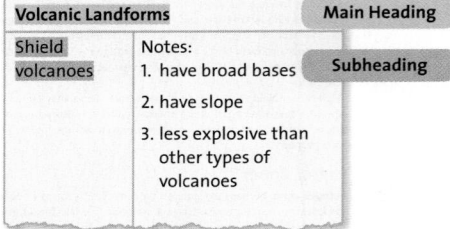

2.3 TURNING TEXT HEADINGS INTO OUTLINE ENTRIES

You can also use text features to take notes in outline form. The following outline shows how one student used text headings from the sample page on page R3. Study the outline and use the strategies that follow to create an outline based on text features.

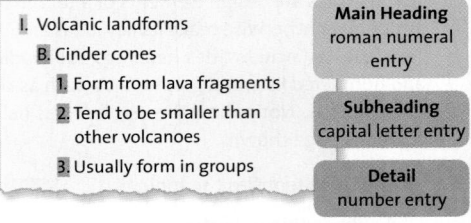

Strategies for Using Text Headings

- Preview the headings and subheadings in the text to get an idea of what different kinds there are and what their positions might be in an outline.

- Be consistent. Note that subheadings that are the same size and color should be used consistently in Roman-numeral or capital-letter entries in the outline. If you decide that a chapter heading should appear with a Roman numeral, then that's the level at which all other chapter headings should appear.

- Write the headings and subheadings that you will use as your Roman-numeral and capital-letter entries first. As you read, fill in numbered details from the text under the headings and subheadings in your outline.

PRACTICE AND APPLY

Reread *The Lost Boys,* pages 548–553. Use text features in the selection to take notes in outline form.

Preview the subheadings in the text to get an idea of the different kinds. Write the headings and subheadings you are using as your Roman-numeral and capital-letter entries first. Then fill in the details.

PRACTICE AND APPLY

ANSWERS

Students' outlines will vary. They should follow the format on page R4 and include a main idea for each roman numeral entry, a subheading for each capital letter entry, and one or more details for each numbered entry. The following is an example of a partial outline:

I. A new life

  A. Fargo, North Dakota

  B. Lost Boys of Sudan

    1. Civil war

    2. Exodus from Sudan

    3. Kakuma Refugee Camp

  C. Agreement between United Nations and United States

    1. Lost Boys sent to America

    2. Foster care and school

    3. Citizenship

II. Nighttime in America

  A. Meeting the social worker

  B. New home

    1. Fargo's south side

    2. Donations

    3. Food

III. Living on Leaves and Berries

  A. Family is killed

  B. Ethiopia

2.4 GRAPHIC AIDS

Information is communicated not only with words but also with graphic aids. **Graphic aids** are visual representations of verbal statements. They can be charts, webs, diagrams, graphs, photographs, or other visual representations of information. Graphic aids usually make complex information easier to understand. For that reason, graphic aids are often used to organize, simplify, and summarize information for easy reference.

Graphs

Graphs are used to illustrate statistical information. A **graph** is a drawing that shows the relative values of numerical quantities. Different kinds of graphs are used to show different numerical relationships.

Strategies for Reading

Ⓐ Read the title.

Ⓑ Find out what is being represented or measured.

Ⓒ In a circle graph, compare the sizes of the parts.

Ⓓ In a line graph, study the slant of the line. The steeper the line, the faster the rate of change.

Ⓔ In a bar graph, compare the lengths of the bars.

A **circle graph,** or **pie graph,** shows the relationships of parts to a whole. The entire circle equals 100 percent. The parts of the circle represent percentages of the whole.

MODEL: CIRCLE GRAPH

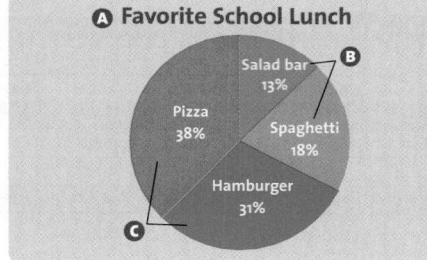

Line graphs show changes in numerical quantities over time and are effective in presenting trends such as attendance at a drama fair from 2003 to 2007. A line graph is made on a grid. Here, the vertical axis indicates quantity, and the horizontal axis shows years. Points on the graph indicate data. The line that connects the points highlights a trend or pattern.

MODEL: LINE GRAPH

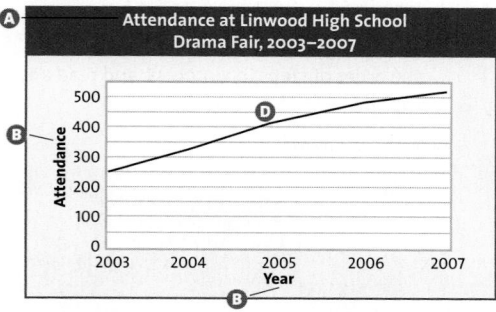

In a **bar graph,** vertical or horizontal bars are used to show or compare categories of information, such as the gestation periods of certain mammals. The lengths of the bars indicate the quantities.

MODEL: BAR GRAPH

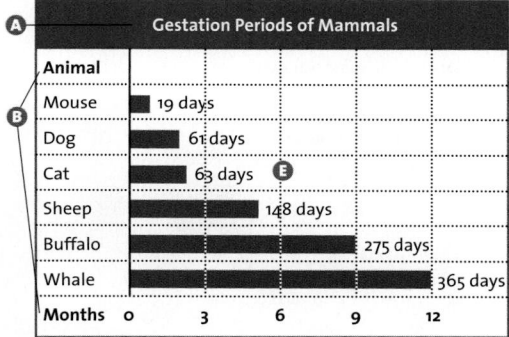

WATCH OUT! Evaluate carefully the information presented in graphs. For example, circle graphs show major factors and differences well but tend to minimize smaller factors and differences.

Diagrams

A **diagram** is a drawing that shows how something works or how its parts relate to one another.

A **picture diagram** is a picture or drawing of the subject being discussed.

Strategies for Reading

Ⓐ Read the title.

Ⓑ Read each label and look at the part it identifies.

Ⓒ Follow any arrows or numbers that show the order of steps in a process, and read any captions.

MODEL: PICTURE DIAGRAM

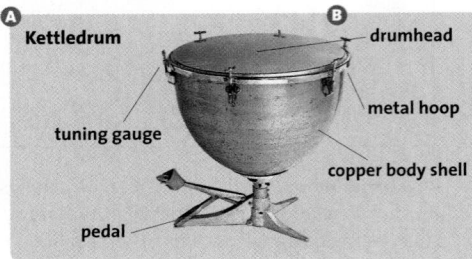

Ⓐ **Kettledrum**
Ⓑ drumhead
metal hoop
tuning gauge
copper body shell
pedal

In a **schematic diagram,** lines, symbols, and words are used to help readers visualize processes or objects they wouldn't normally be able to see.

MODEL: SCHEMATIC DIAGRAM

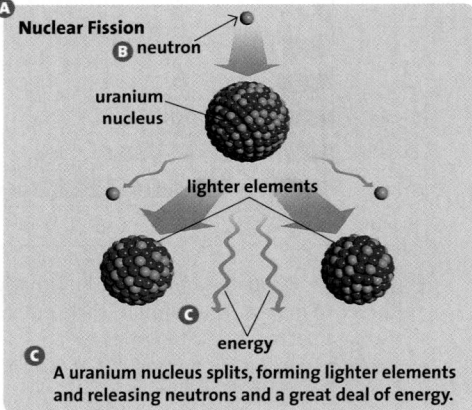

Ⓐ **Nuclear Fission**
Ⓑ neutron
uranium nucleus
lighter elements
Ⓒ energy
Ⓒ A uranium nucleus splits, forming lighter elements and releasing neutrons and a great deal of energy.

Charts and Tables

A **chart** presents information, shows a process, or makes comparisons, usually in rows or columns. A **table** is a specific type of chart that presents a collection of facts in rows and columns and shows how the facts relate to one another.

Strategies for Reading

Ⓐ Read the title to learn what information the chart or table covers.

Ⓑ Study column headings and row labels to determine the categories of information presented.

Ⓒ Look down columns and across rows to find specific information.

MODEL: CHART

Ⓐ Sounds in Poetry	
Ⓑ **Technique**	**Example**
Onomatopoeia	the slow **clip clop** of the ox Ⓒ
Alliteration	**r**ough **r**eaches of **r**anch and sky
Assonance	the c**o**stly t**o**ssing of l**o**st dreams
Consonance	his meager nuggets of begrudging praise
Rhyme	A truth that's told with bad **intent** Beats all the lies you can **invent**.

MODEL: TABLE

Ⓐ Bus Route 333: Grand Avenue				Weekday Mornings— EASTBOUND	
Ⓑ Lawrence Station	Chestnut St. Mall	Grand & Lincoln	Memorial Hospital	Grand & Delaware	Three Rivers Station
Ⓒ 4:57 A.M.	5:03 A.M.	5:06 A.M.	5:10 A.M.	5:16 A.M.	5:19 A.M.
5:38	5:44	5:48	5:53	5:59	6:02
5:55	6:02	6:06	6:11	6:18	6:22
6:15	6:22	6:26	6:31	6:38	6:42
6:35	6:42	6:46	6:51	6:58	7:02
7:00	7:08	7:13	7:19	7:28	7:33
7:15	7:23	7:28	7:34	7:43	7:48

Maps

A **map** visually represents a geographic region, such as a state or country. It provides information about areas through lines, colors, shapes, and symbols. There are different kinds of maps.

- **Political maps** show political features, such as national borders.
- **Physical maps** show the landforms in areas.
- **Road or travel maps** show roads and highways.
- **Thematic maps** show information on a specific topic, such as climate, weather, or natural resources.

Strategies for Reading

Ⓐ Read the title to find out what kind of map it is.

Ⓑ Read the labels to get an overall sense of what the map shows.

Ⓒ Look at the **key** or **legend** to find out what the symbols and colors on the map stand for.

MODEL: WEATHER MAP

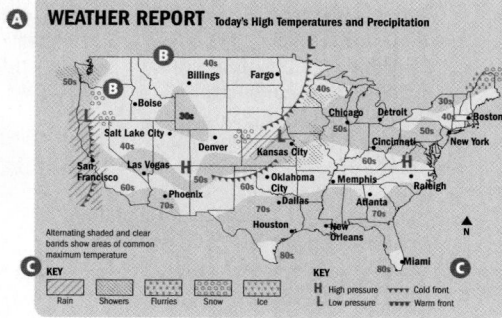

MODEL: POLITICAL MAP

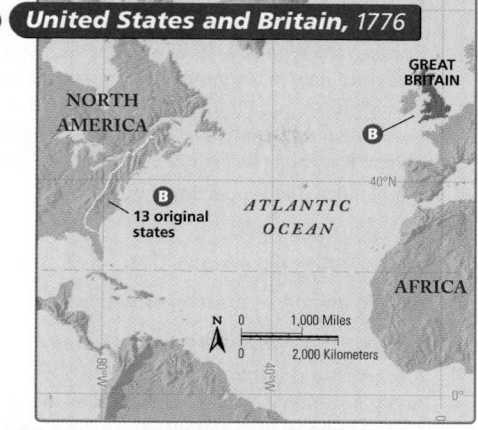

PRACTICE AND APPLY

Use the graphic aids shown on pages R5–R7 to answer the following questions:

1. What was the approximate attendance at the Linwood High School Drama Fair in 2005?
2. Is there more than one tuning gauge on a kettledrum?
3. What is the least favorite lunch according to the circle graph?
4. Write a definition of *alliteration*, using the information in the chart.
5. Use the bus schedule to figure how long your trip would be if you boarded the bus at Lawrence Station at 7:15 A.M. and got off the bus at Memorial Hospital.
6. According to the weather map, which states have temperatures in the 80s?
7. Using the scale on the political map, find the approximate number of miles from the 13 original states across the Atlantic Ocean to Great Britain.

PRACTICE AND APPLY

ANSWERS

1. *Approximately 400*
2. *Yes*
3. *Salad bar*
4. *Possible answer: Alliteration is the repetition of the same sound or letter at the beginning of words.*
5. *19 minutes*
6. *Texas and Florida*
7. *Approximately 3,000 miles*

3 Reading Informational Texts: Patterns of Organization

Reading any type of writing is easier once you recognize how it is organized. Writers usually arrange ideas and information in ways that best help readers see how they are related. There are several common patterns of organization:

- main idea and supporting details
- chronological order
- cause-effect organization
- compare-and-contrast organization

3.1 MAIN IDEA AND SUPPORTING DETAILS

Main idea and supporting details is a basic pattern of organization in which a central idea about a topic is supported by details. The **main idea** is the most important idea about a topic that a particular text or paragraph conveys. **Supporting details** are words, phrases, or sentences that tell more about the main idea. The main idea may be directly stated at the beginning and then followed by supporting details or may be merely implied by the supporting details. It may also be stated after it has been implied by supporting details.

Strategies for Reading

- To find a stated main idea in a paragraph, identify the paragraph's topic. The topic is what the paragraph is about and can usually be summed up in one or two words. The word, or synonyms of it, will usually appear throughout the paragraph. Headings and subheadings are also clues to the topics of paragraphs.

- Ask: What is the topic sentence? The topic sentence states the most important idea, message, or information the paragraph conveys about this topic.

- To find an implied main idea, ask yourself: Whom or what did I just read about? What do the details suggest about the topic?

- Formulate a sentence stating this idea and add it to the paragraph. Does your sentence convey the main idea?

Notice how the main idea is expressed in each of the following models.

MODEL: MAIN IDEA STATED IN THE BEGINNING

Some of the most impressive of all human achievements took place during the prehistoric period called the Stone Age. [**Main idea**] These accomplishments included the invention of tools and pottery, as well as the development of farming. Stone chopping tools date from the early Stone Age—2.5 million to 8000 B.C. Polished tools, pottery, and agriculture were developed during the late Stone Age—8000 to 3000 B.C. [**Supporting details**]

MODEL: MAIN IDEA IMPLIED BY SUPPORTING DETAILS

Imagine that the 102-story Empire State Building represents the history of the earth. Each story is the equivalent of about 40 million years. The earth was formed at the ground floor. Not until floor 30 or so did the first single-celled organism appear. The first dinosaurs arose at the base of the radio antenna. Mammals appeared on earth about three-quarters of the way up the antenna. The ancestors of modern humans did not appear until the tip of the antenna—about 40,000 years ago. [**Supporting details**]

[**Implied main idea: Humans have existed for only a small percentage of the history of the planet.**]

MODEL: MAIN IDEA STATED AFTER IT HAS BEEN IMPLIED BY SUPPORTING DETAILS

Scientists believe that Cro-Magnons planned their hunts carefully. Cro-Magnons studied animals' habits. They also developed advanced language skills, which improved their ability to cooperate and plan. [**Supporting details**] These survival skills helped the Cro-Magnon population to grow and thrive. [**Main idea**]

Read each paragraph, and then do the following:

1. Identify the main idea in the paragraph, using one of the strategies discussed on the previous page.

2. Identify whether the main idea is stated or implied in the paragraph.

> It was deeply unnerving. It took us over two hours to cover six-tenths of a mile of trail. By the time we reached solid ground at a place called Bearpen Gap, the snow was four or five inches deep and accumulating fast. The whole world was white, filled with dime-sized snowflakes that fell at a slant before being caught by the wind and hurled in a variety of directions. We couldn't see more than fifteen or twenty feet ahead, often not even that.
> —Bill Bryson, *A Walk in the Woods*

> For many people with Parkinson's managing their disease is a full-time job. It is a constant balancing act. Too little medicine causes tremors and stiffness. Too much medicine produces uncontrollable movement and slurring. And far too often, Parkinson's patients wait and wait for the medicines to "kick-in."
> —Michael J. Fox, testimony before the Senate

3.2 CHRONOLOGICAL ORDER

Chronological order is the arrangement of events in their order of occurrence. This type of organization is used in fictional narratives, historical writing, biographies, and autobiographies. To indicate the order of events, writers use words such as *before, after, next,* and *later* and words and phrases that identify specific times of day, days of the week, and dates, such as *the next morning, Tuesday,* and *on July 4, 1776.*

Strategies for Reading

- Look in the text for headings and subheadings that may indicate a chronological pattern of organization.
- Look for words and phrases that identify times, such as *in a year, three hours earlier, in 202 B.C.,* and *the next day.*
- Look for words that signal order, such as *first, afterward, then, during,* and *finally,* to see how events or steps are related.
- Note that a paragraph or passage in which ideas and information are arranged chronologically will have several words or phrases that indicate time order, not just one.
- Ask yourself: Are the events in the paragraph or passage presented in time order?

Notice the words and phrases that signal time order in the first two paragraphs of the following model.

MODEL

Dynasties of China from 202 B.C. to A.D. 1279

The Han dynasty ruled China from 202 B.C. to A.D. 220. (A dynasty is a series of rulers from a single family.) For more than 350 years after the Han dynasty collapsed, no emperor was able to unite northern and southern China. Then, in 589, Emperor Sui Wendi created a strong central government and laid the foundation for a golden age of China under the Tang and Song dynasties. Literature, poetry, architecture, sculpture, painting, and dance all flourished during this period.

The Tang dynasty ruled China for almost 300 years, from 618 to 907. The first important Tang emperor, Tang Taizong, held the throne from 626 until 649. During his reign, China regained its northern and western lands. After 660 or so, the real power in China was Empress Wu Zhao, although a series of weak emperors actually sat on the throne. Under her leadership, Chinese armies overran

Events

Time words and phrases

Order words and phrases

PRACTICE AND APPLY
ANSWERS

1. *Possible answers: Paragraph 1: The blizzard obscured the trail and made hiking in the woods dangerous. Paragraph 2: For many people with Parkinson's, managing their disease is a full-time job.*

2. *In the first paragraph, the main idea is implied. In the second paragraph, the main idea is stated.*

Korea before 668. By 690, Wu Zhao had become emperor in her own right, the only woman to hold that title.

By the mid-700s, the Tang emperors had begun losing control over their huge empire. Arab armies defeated the Chinese on their far western frontier in 751. For the next 150 years, China suffered attacks on its borders and internal rebellions. Then, in 907, Chinese rebels burned the capital city of Ch'ang-an and murdered the child emperor, ending the Tang dynasty.

Much of China was reunited in 960 under the first Song emperor, Song Taizu. However, in the early 1100s, the Song lost all of northern China to the Jurchen people. The Song established a new capital in the coastal city of Hangzhou, where they continued to rule from 1127 to 1279. During this century and a half, southern China became a prosperous trading center.

The 600 years of Song and Tang rule were years of great growth. Copper coins and paper money came into regular circulation. High-quality schools were established to train government workers. Standard editions of great works of literature were published. Although both dynasties included periods of turmoil, their cultural and economic accomplishments are still impressive today.

PRACTICE AND APPLY

Refer to the last three paragraphs of the preceding model to do the following:

1. List at least eight words in the paragraphs that indicate time or order.

2. Plot the events in the paragraphs on a timeline, using the dates mentioned. Some events may overlap.

3. A writer may use more than one pattern of organization in a text. In the last paragraph of the model, what pattern of organization does the writer use? How does this pattern contribute to your understanding of the passage?

PRACTICE AND APPLY

ANSWERS

1. *Possible answers:* "By the mid-700s"; "in 751"; "For the next 150 years"; "Then, in 907"; "in 960"; "in the early 1100s"; "from 1127 to 1279"; "During this century and a half"; "The 600 years of Song and Tang rule"

2. To help students create a timeline, show them one or two examples. Students should include the following events in their timelines: *751: Arab armies defeat China on the western frontier; 907: Chinese rebels burn the capital city of Ch'ang-an and murder the child emperor; 960: China reunited under the first Song emperor, Song Taizu; 960–1279: Song Dynasty; Early 1100s: Song loses all of northern China to the Jurchen people; 1127: New capital established at Hangzhou*

3. *Possible answer:* The writer organizes the paragraph using a main idea and supporting details. This pattern conveys the cultural and economic significance of the Song and Tang dynasties.

3.3 CAUSE-EFFECT ORGANIZATION

Cause-effect organization is a pattern of organization that establishes causal relationships between events, ideas, and trends. Cause-effect relationships may be directly stated or merely implied by the order in which the information is presented. Writers often use the cause-effect pattern in historical and scientific writing. Cause-effect relationships may take several forms.

One cause with one effect

One cause with multiple effects

Multiple causes with a single effect

A chain of causes and effects

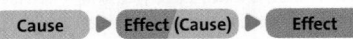

Strategies for Reading

- Look for headings and subheadings that indicate a cause-effect pattern of organization, such as "Effects of Population Density."

- To find the effect or effects, read to answer the question, What happened?

- To find the cause or causes, read to answer the question, Why did it happen?

- Look for words and phrases that help you identify specific relationships between events, such as *because, since, had the effect of, led to, as a result, resulted in, for that reason, due to, therefore, if . . . then,* and *consequently.*

- Evaluate each cause-effect relationship. Do not assume that because one event happened before another, the first event caused the second event.

- Use graphic organizers like the diagrams shown to record cause-effect relationships as you read.

Notice the words that signal causes and effects in the following model.

MODEL

The Lasting Effects of the Krakatau Eruption

In 1883, the massive explosion of a volcano called Krakatau resulted in tens of thousands of deaths as well as long-term changes in climate conditions.

> Causes
>
> Signal words
>
> Effects

Krakatau, also called Krakatoa, takes up much of a small island called Rakata. Part of the country of Indonesia, Rakata lies between the islands of Java and Sumatra in the Indian Ocean. Until 1883, Krakatau was a huge volcano, with a height of about 6,000 feet above sea level.

At 10:00 A.M. on August 27, 1883, a huge eruption destroyed most of Krakatau. As a result of the explosion, volcanic ash spewed into the air as high as 50 miles above the volcano.

The effects of the explosion were deadly. The blast caused nearly five cubic miles of rock fragments to be released into the air. In the region of the blast, the sun was not visible for the next two and a half days. Burning ash and rocks killed thousands. Tsunamis, underwater earthquakes, struck Java and Sumatra causing waves up to 120 feet. Because of the ash, rocks, and waves, about 36,000 people lost their lives.

The destruction at Krakatau had effects around the world. People in Australia, more than 2,000 miles away, heard the boom. Weather forecasters all over the planet detected sudden increases in atmospheric pressure. A series of tsunamis resulting from the blast reached as far as Hawaii and South America. Some scientists believe that dust from Krakatau may have been the reason the world experienced unseasonably cool weather for months after the eruption.

PRACTICE AND APPLY

Refer to the preceding model to do the following.

1. Use the pattern of one cause with multiple effects illustrated on page R10 to make a graphic organizer showing the main cause described in the text and at least three effects of that cause.

2. List at least four words and phrases that the writer uses to signal causes and effects in the last two paragraphs.

3.4 COMPARE-AND-CONTRAST ORGANIZATION

Compare-and-contrast organization is a pattern of organization that serves as a framework for examining similarities and differences in two or more subjects. A writer may use this pattern of organization to analyze two or more subjects, such as characters or movies, in terms of their important points or characteristics. These points or characteristics are called points of comparison. The compare-and-contrast pattern of organization may be developed in either of two ways:

Point-by-point organization—The writer discusses one point of comparison for both subjects, then goes on to the next point.

Subject-by-subject organization—The writer covers all points of comparison for one subject and then all points of comparison for the next subject.

Strategies for Reading

- Look in the text for headings, subheadings, and sentences that may suggest a compare-and-contrast pattern of organization, such as "Plants Share Many Characteristics." These will help you identify where similarities and differences are addressed.

- To find similarities, look for words and phrases such as *like, similarly, both, also,* and *in the same way.*

- To find differences, look for words and phrases such as *unlike, but, on the other hand, in contrast,* and *however.*

PRACTICE AND APPLY

ANSWERS

1. *Possible answers (on graphic organizer):* Cause: In 1883, Krakatau, a volcano on an island in Indonesia, erupted in a massive explosion. Effects: volcanic ash spewed as high as 50 miles into the air; blast released nearly five cubic miles of rock fragments into the air; sun was not visible for two and a half days; tsunamis struck Sumatra, Java, Hawaii, and South America; about 36,000 people lost their lives; atmospheric pressure over the entire planet suddenly increased

2. *Possible answers:* effects; caused; Because of; had effects; resulting from; may have been the reason

• Use a graphic organizer, such as a Venn diagram or a compare-and-contrast chart, to record points of comparison and similarities and differences.

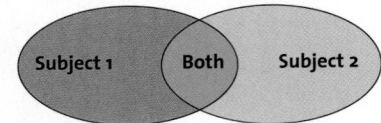

	Subject 1	Subject 2
Point 1		
Point 2		
Point 3		

Read the following models. As you read, use the signal words and phrases to identify the similarities and differences between the subjects and how the details are organized in each text.

MODEL 1

Pyramids in Egypt and the Americas

The pyramid is perhaps the most well-known accomplishment of ancient peoples. When most people think of these amazing structures, they think of Egypt. However, Egypt was not the only place where pyramids were built. Pyramids were also constructed in the Americas, mainly in Central America and South America. — **Subjects**

Most pyramid construction in Egypt took place between 2686 and 2345 B.C. In contrast, most Central American and South American pyramids were built much later. — **Contrast words and phrases**
So far, only one pyramid of the Americas has been found to be similar in age to the Egyptian pyramids. A pyramid in Caral, Peru, has been dated to 2627 B.C. — **Comparison words and phrases**

The Pyramid of the Sun at Teotihuacán, Mexico, and the Great Pyramid at Giza, Egypt, measure nearly the same at their base. Egyptian pyramids are taller, however. The Great Pyramid originally reached a height of 481 feet, while the tallest pyramid in the Americas is 216 feet high. Even the pyramid at Caral is only one-eighth the height of the Great Pyramid.

Pyramids in Egypt and the Americas have major structural differences as well. Pyramids in the Americas have receding steps that resemble the layers of a cake. Egyptian pyramids, on the other hand, have smooth sides that connect in a point at the top.

Egyptian pyramids were always part of larger groups of buildings, including temples and houses. Similarly, American pyramids were built in the middle of cities. However, pyramids in the Americas typically served as temples and were the sites of human and animal sacrifices. In contrast, all Egyptian pyramids were built to be royal burial chambers.

Modern scientists are amazed at the size and durability of these structures. Many pyramids took as long as 20 years to build, requiring millions of stone blocks and thousands of laborers. Pyramids in Egypt and in the Americas were both outstanding accomplishments of the civilizations that created them.

MODEL 2

The Governments of Rome and the United States

After fighting the Revolutionary War, Americans were faced with the task of creating a new government. The vision of the new nation as a republic—a government in which citizens rule through their elected representatives—was based on the republic of ancient Rome. The republican governments of Rome and the United States have both similarities and differences.

Subjects

Comparison words and phrases

Contrast words and phrases

The guiding principles of the government of Rome were recorded in the Twelve Tables, a list of legal rules. Only adult male landowners could be citizens, and only they could vote. The government was divided into three branches—executive, legislative, and judicial. The executive branch was made up of two consuls, or leaders, chosen by the legislative assembly to serve one-year terms. The legislative branch was divided into three houses: a 300-member Senate chosen from the aristocracy, a Centuriate Assembly of citizen-soldiers, and a Tribal Assembly of general citizens. All assembly members served life terms. The judicial branch consisted of eight judges chosen by the Centuriate Assembly for one-year terms.

Like the republic of Rome, the government of the United States is based on a code of laws, the U.S. Constitution, which gives its citizens the right to select their leaders. However, U.S. citizens now include all native-born and naturalized persons, not just adult male landowners as in Rome. The U.S. government also consists of an executive, a legislative, and a judicial branch. In contrast to the Roman consuls, the U.S. executive is one person—a president elected by citizens for a four-year term. The legislative branch includes only two houses rather than Rome's three—

a Senate, whose 100 members are elected by the people for six-year terms, and a House of Representatives whose members are elected for two-year terms. These legislators all serve shorter terms than their Roman counterparts. However, the federal judges in the U.S. judicial branch are appointed by the president to life terms, in contrast to the Roman judges' single-year appointments.

PRACTICE AND APPLY

Refer to the preceding models to answer the following questions:

1. Which model is organized by subject? Which model is organized by points of comparison?

2. Identify at least two words or phrases in each model that signal a compare-and-contrast pattern of organization. Do not choose words or phrases that have already been highlighted.

3. List at least three points that the writer of each model compares and contrasts.

4. Use a Venn diagram or a compare-and-contrast chart to identify at least two points of comparison and their similarities and differences in model 2.

PRACTICE AND APPLY

ANSWERS

1. *Model 2 is organized by subject. Model 1 is organized by points of comparison.*

2. ***Possible answers: Model 1:*** *only, nearly the same, while, differences, as well, on the other hand, and Similarly.* ***Model 2:*** *both, Only, All, rather than, and than*

3. ***Possible answers:*** *Model 1: construction of the pyramids in Egypt and South America; height and measurement of the pyramids; structural differences of the pyramids; cultural purpose and function of the pyramids. Model 2: guiding principles of Roman and U.S. governments; citizenship; branches of government*

4. Students should create a Venn diagram or a compare-and-contrast chart like the ones shown on page R12. ***Possible answers: Roman Government:*** *only adult male landowners could be citizens and could vote; executive branch consisted of two consuls; consuls were chosen by the legislative assembly; consuls served for one year; legislative branch was divided into three houses; all assembly members served life terms; judges were chosen by the Centuriate Assembly; judges served for one year.* ***U.S. Government:*** *all native-born and naturalized citizens can vote; president is elected by citizens and serves a four-year term; legislative branch includes two houses; senators serve a six-year term; representatives serve a two-year term; federal judges are appointed by the president and serve a life term.* ***Similarities:*** *only citizens elect their officials; government was divided into three branches: executive, legislative, and judicial; government is based on a code of law.*

4 Reading Informational Texts: Forms

Magazines, newspapers, Web pages, and consumer, public, and workplace documents are all examples of informational materials. To understand and analyze informational texts, pay attention to text features and patterns of organization.

4.1 READING A MAGAZINE ARTICLE

Because people often skim magazines, magazine publishers use devices to attract attention to articles.

Strategies for Reading

A Notice whether **graphic aids** or **quotations** attract your attention. Sometimes a publisher pulls a quotation out of the text and displays it to get your attention. Such quotations are called **pull quotes.**

B Once you decide that you're interested in the article, read the title and other headings to find out more about its topic and organization.

C Notice whether the article has a **byline,** a line naming the author.

D Sometimes an article will be accompanied by a **sidebar,** a short article that presents additional information. This sidebar also has a **title.** Is your understanding of the main article enhanced by the information in the sidebar?

PRACTICE AND APPLY

ANSWERS

1. *Possible answers: the angry faces at the top of the page; the image of the football players*

2. *The subtitle states, "Parents become violent and abusive during kids' games"*

3. *The pull quote is taken from the last paragraph in the article.*

B Is "youth sports rage" on the rise?

Parents become violent and abusive during kids' games

C by Belinda Liu

The news stories are frightening. In Virginia, the mother of a soccer player assaults a 14-year-old referee and is fined. In Pennsylvania, a "midget league" football game results in a brawl involving about 100 players and spectators. Accounts of "youth sports rage" are reported in Britain, Canada, Australia, and New Zealand.

Are spectators at youth sports becoming more violent? Some observers believe they are.

"There have always been problem parents in kids' sports," explains soccer coach Larry Fiore. "But the vast majority of parents, coaches, and athletes act appropriately."

However, some factors are making the problem worse, believes sports psychologist Theresa Mathelier. "Sports are getting more expensive for parents in terms of equipment, traveling, and coaching," she explains. "The tendency now is to start kids in organized sports earlier and to get them to specialize in one sport."

As a result, Mathelier says, "a few parents get unrealistic ideas about college scholarships and professional careers in sports. They start to live through their kids, and if something goes wrong, they blow up."

A *"Parents should be role models."*

Fiore and Mathelier both say that it is rarely the athletes who cause the problems. Serena Terell, a 15-year-old soccer player, agrees. "It's so embarrassing when the parents yell and curse," Serena explains, adding that her parents always behave themselves. "Their kids just want them to stop. After all, it's only a game, and parents should be role models."

D STOPPING SPORTS RAGE: STEPS YOU CAN TAKE

Here are steps that some groups have taken to prevent youth sports rage.

- The National Youth Sports Safety Foundation has created a Sport Parent Code of Conduct. Penalties range from a verbal warning to a season suspension for parents.
- Some soccer leagues designate one day as "Silent Sunday." Spectators are not allowed to cheer or even talk until the game is over.
- Some coaches choose one parent to be in charge of crowd control. This parent patrols the bleachers or sidelines, making sure that fans of his or her team behave.

PRACTICE AND APPLY

1. Which graphic aids in the article attracted your attention?

2. What heading other than the title tells you what the article is about?

3. From what part of the article is the pull quote taken?

4.2 READING A TEXTBOOK

Each textbook that you use has its own system of organization based on the content in the book. Often an introductory unit will explain the book's organization and special features. If your textbook has such a unit, read it first.

Strategies for Reading

Ⓐ Before you begin reading the lesson or chapter, read any **questions** that appear at the end of it. Then use the questions to set your purpose for reading.

Ⓑ **Read slowly and carefully** to better understand and remember the ideas presented in the text. When you come to an unfamiliar word, first try to figure out its meaning from **context clues.** If necessary, find the meaning of the word in a **glossary** in the textbook or in a dictionary.

For more information, see the **Vocabulary and Spelling Handbook,** *pages R68 and R72.*

Ⓒ Use the book's graphic aids, such as illustrations, diagrams, and captions, to clarify your understanding of the text.

Ⓓ Take notes as you read. Use text features such as **subheadings** and boldfaced terms to help you organize your notes. Use graphic organizers, such as cause-effect charts, to help you clarify relationships among ideas.

PRACTICE AND APPLY

1. How would you find the definition of *pyroclastic*?

2. Where on the page can you find out the names of different composite volcanoes?

3. Use the text to answer the second question in the Section Review.

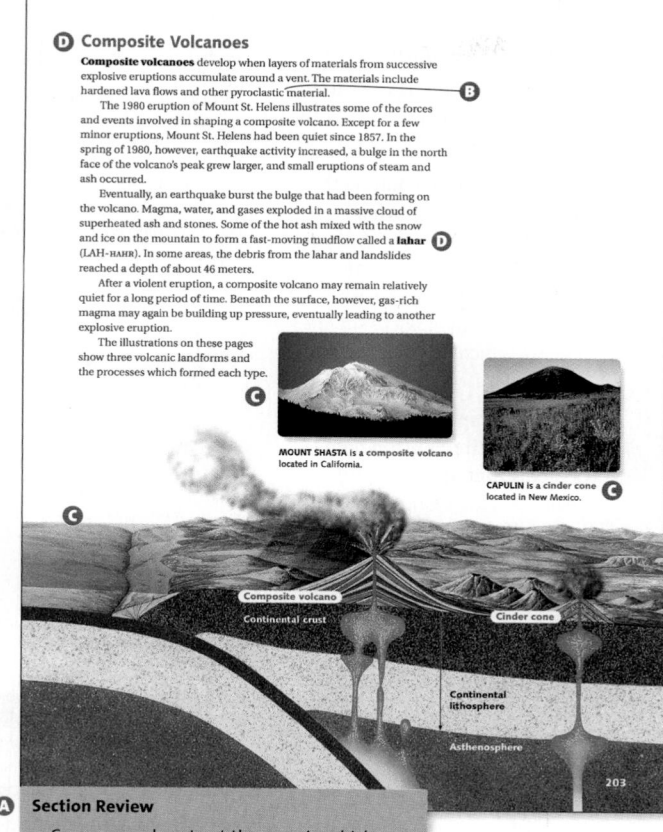

Ⓓ Composite Volcanoes

Composite volcanoes develop when layers of materials from successive explosive eruptions accumulate around a vent. The materials include hardened lava flows and other pyroclastic material. **Ⓑ**

The 1980 eruption of Mount St. Helens illustrates some of the forces and events involved in shaping a composite volcano. Except for a few minor eruptions, Mount St. Helens had been quiet since 1857. In the spring of 1980, however, earthquake activity increased, a bulge in the north face of the volcano's peak grew larger, and small eruptions of steam and ash occurred.

Eventually, an earthquake burst the bulge that had been forming on the volcano. Magma, water, and gases exploded in a massive cloud of superheated ash and stones. Some of the hot ash mixed with the snow and ice on the mountain to form a fast-moving mudflow called a **lahar** **Ⓓ** (LAH-hahr). In some areas, the debris from the lahar and landslides reached a depth of about 46 meters.

After a violent eruption, a composite volcano may remain relatively quiet for a long period of time. Beneath the surface, however, gas-rich magma may again be building up pressure, eventually leading to another explosive eruption.

The illustrations on these pages show three volcanic landforms and the processes which formed each type.

MOUNT SHASTA is a composite volcano located in California.

CAPULIN is a cinder cone **Ⓒ** located in New Mexico.

Composite volcano
Continental crust
Cinder cone
Continental lithosphere
Asthenosphere

203

Ⓐ Section Review

- Compare and contrast the ways in which shield volcanoes and cinder cones are formed.

- **Critical Thinking** Describe the formation of a composite volcano.

- **Writing** The eruption of Mount Rainier, a composite volcano, could pose a serious threat to local residents. Write a description of the potential hazards that people living near Mount Rainier might face.

PRACTICE AND APPLY

ANSWERS

1. *Possible answers: using context clues; looking up the word in a glossary of the textbook; looking for the word in a dictionary*

2. *Possible answers: in the main text of the section titled "Composite Volcanoes"; in the captions on the graphic aids; in the Section Review*

3. *Possible answer: Gas-rich magma builds up pressure, eventually causing an explosive eruption. Material from that eruption, such as hardened lava flows and other pyroclastic material, accumulates around the vent at the top of the volcano to form layers.*

4.3 READING A CONSUMER DOCUMENT

Consumer documents are printed materials that accompany products and services. They usually provide information about the use, care, operation, or assembly of the products they accompany. Some common consumer documents are contracts, warranties, manuals, instructions, and schedules. Two examples of consumer documents follow.

Strategies for Reading

Ⓐ Read the **subheadings** to learn what process each section of the instructions explains.

Ⓑ Look for **numbers** or **letters** that indicate the order in which the steps should be followed. If you do not find letters or numbers, look for signal words such as *first, next, then,* and *finally* to see the order in which the steps should be followed.

Ⓒ Words that appear in **all capital letters** are often button names or labels that appear on the device you are being shown how to use. If there is an illustration or diagram, try to match the capitalized words in the instructions to words or symbols in the graphic aid.

Ⓓ Look for **verbs that describe actions** you should take, such as *press, select, set,* and *turn.*

Ⓔ Pay attention to **warnings** or **notes** that describe potential problems.

INSTRUCTIONS FOR OPERATING A TELEVISION REMOTE CONTROL

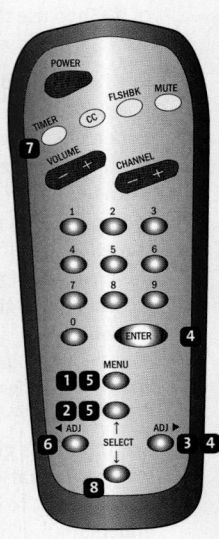

Ⓐ **SETTING THE SLEEP TIMER**

Ⓑ 1. Press the MENU key. The Setup menu will appear on your television.

Ⓒ 2. Select the Timer Setup on your screen by using the UP/DOWN arrows on your remote control.

3. Now press the RIGHT or LEFT arrow. A menu of the Timer Setup will appear on the screen.

4. Sleep Timer: Use the RIGHT/LEFT arrows to program the length of time until the TV shuts down. You can select any time from ten minutes to four hours. Press ENTER to return to TV viewing.

Ⓐ **SETTING THE ON/OFF TIMER**

5. Follow steps 1–3 above to get to the Timer Setup menu. Using the UP/DOWN arrows on the remote control, select On Time on your screen.

Ⓒ 6. Press the RIGHT or LEFT arrow to adjust the time your television will turn on automatically.

Ⓓ 7. Press the TIMER button to choose either A.M. or P.M.

8. Repeat steps 5–7 to set Off Time. Use the UP/DOWN arrows to select the On/Off Timer, and activate the timer by pressing a RIGHT/LEFT arrow.

Ⓔ **WARNING:** The On/Off Timer will not work until the clock on your television has been set.

PRACTICE AND APPLY

Reread the page from the manual for a television remote control and then answer the following questions:

1. What do these instructions explain how to do?

2. According to the instructions, what happens when the Enter button is pressed?

3. What button allows the user to select A.M. or P.M.?

PRACTICE AND APPLY

ANSWERS

1. *The instructions show how to set the sleep timer and how to set the on/off timer using a television remote control.*

2. *When the ENTER button is pressed, the remote allows you to exit the menu and return to TV viewing.*

3. *the TIMER button*

The instructions on this page are from a manual for operating a graphing calculator.

Strategies for Reading

(A) Read the **heading** to learn the kind of operation this section of the manual explains.

(B) Look at any **introductory text** to get an overview of what the numbered steps will cover.

(C) Look for **numbers** that indicate the order in which the steps should be followed.

(D) Look for **verbs that describe actions** you should take, such as *press, position,* and *select.*

(E) Examine **graphic aids** that illustrate steps. If you have trouble completing the process, the graphic aids can help you pinpoint what you are doing wrong.

INSTRUCTIONS FOR OPERATING A GRAPHING CALCULATOR

(A) Zooming on the Graph

(B) You can magnify the viewing WINDOW around a specific location by using the ZOOM instructions, thus making it easier to help identify maximums, minimums, roots, and intersections of functions.

1. Press ZOOM to display the ZOOM menu.

   This menu is typical of TI-82 menus. To select an item, you may either press the number to the left of the item, or you may press ▼ until the item number is highlighted and then press ENTER.

   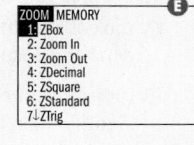

(C) 2. To zoom in, press 2. The graph is displayed again. The cursor has changed to indicate that you are using a ZOOM instruction.

   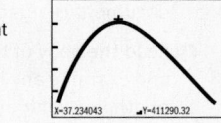

(D) 3. Use ◄, ▲, ►, and ▼ to position the cursor near the maximum value of the function and press ENTER.

   The new viewing WINDOW is displayed. It has been adjusted in both the X and Y directions by factors of 4, the values for ZOOM factors.

   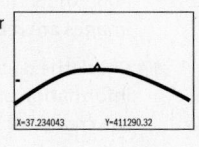

4. Press WINDOW to display the new WINDOW settings.

   WINDOW FORMAT
   Xmin=24.734042...
   Xmax=49.734042...
   Xsc1=10
   Ymin=348790.32...
   Ymax=473790.32...
   Ysc1=100000

PRACTICE AND APPLY

Reread the page from the manual and then answer the following questions:

1. What does this page explain how to do?

2. According to the instructions, how do you select a menu item?

3. What key should you press to zoom in?

4. What key should you press to display new window settings?

Refer to the documents on pages R16–R17 to answer the following questions.

5. Compare the document on page R16 with the document on this page. In terms of text features and organization, are they more alike or more different? Support your answer.

6. Do you think the directions for the remote control would be clearer if the steps below "Setting the On/Off Timer" were also numbered 1–4? Why or why not?

PRACTICE AND APPLY

ANSWERS

1. *The instructions explain how to use a graphing calculator to zoom in on a graph.*

2. *Press the number of the item; press the down arrow to highlight the item, then press ENTER.*

3. *Press the "2" key.*

4. *Press the WINDOW key.*

5. ***Possible answers:*** *The documents are more different than they are alike. While both documents provide numbers to show the steps involved, the graphing calculator document appears more organized and easier to follow. For example, in the graphing calculator document, each step is accompanied by a visual representation that helps the reader see what is actually happening. The graphing calculator document also uses less text than the television remote document to explain each step. Finally, whereas the visuals on the calculator document are well-organized and help the reader understand each step, the image of the remote control is not very useful.*

6. ***Possible answer:*** *Yes, if the steps were numbered 1–4, readers would recognize the two sets of directions as two separate functions.*

4.4 READING A PUBLIC DOCUMENT

Public documents are documents that are written for the public to provide information that is of public interest or concern. These documents are often free. They can be federal, state, or local government documents. They can be speeches or historical documents. They may even be laws, posted warnings, signs, or rules and regulations. The following is one type of public document.

Strategies for Reading

Ⓐ Look at the **title** to determine what the document is about.

Ⓑ Look for **subheadings** to identify main ideas and topics and to determine how the document is organized.

Ⓒ Read the body of the document and examine any **illustrations** or other **graphic aids.** Think about how the text and the images are related.

Ⓓ Check the document to find information on how to contact the creator or source of the document.

Ⓐ Rules of the Road for Cyclists
Follow these rules when you are bicycling in our area.

Ⓑ Be Visible

Don't Ride Against Traffic: Motorists may not see you on the wrong side of the road.

Use Hand Signals: These let drivers know what you plan to do. Be polite—and be safer, too!

Protect Yourself: Local laws require you to wear a helmet while cycling. If you are riding at night, your bike must have a headlight and a rear reflector.

Ⓑ Ride Defensively

Watch for Vehicles: Cars and trucks may pull out suddenly.

Obey Traffic Signs and Signals: They apply to you as well as to drivers. For example, don't go straight in a lane marked "Right Turn Only." **Ⓒ**

Don't Weave Between Parked Cars: Drivers may not see you as you move back into traffic.

Thank you for being a courteous cyclist!

Ⓓ Buena Vista County Parks Department (602) 555-6367 www.buenavistacounty.az.gov/parksdept

Para los hispanohablantes, llame por favor a (602) 555-6388.

PRACTICE AND APPLY

Refer to the document shown to answer the following questions.

1. Into what two subtopics is the information organized? What are the main ideas covered within each subtopic?

2. What appears to be the purpose of this document?

3. Many people may find the rules of the road for cyclists easier to follow than the directions for operating a TV remote control on page R16 or those for operating a graphing calculator on page R17. How do the text features used in "Rules of the Road for Cyclists" make it effective in communicating its message? In your answer, be sure to address each of the following features:
   - graphic aids
   - subheadings
   - use of color
   - arrangement of words and visuals on the page

For more information, see **Reading Informational Texts: Text Features,** *pages R3–R7.*

PRACTICE AND APPLY

ANSWERS

1. *The two subtopics are "Be Visible" and "Ride Defensively." The main ideas covered in the first subtopic include riding against traffic, using hand signals, and protecting oneself. In the second subtopic, the main ideas include watching for vehicles, obeying traffic signs and signals, and weaving between cars.*

2. *The purpose of the document is to explain the rules of riding bicycles on the road.*

3. ***Possible answers:*** *The illustrations are simple but help illustrate the point of each rule. The subheadings divide the rules into two categories. The use of color makes it easier to skim the subheadings and main ideas. The arrangement of words and visuals makes it easier to visualize and understand each rule.*

4.5 READING A WORKPLACE DOCUMENT

Workplace documents are materials that are produced or used within a workplace, usually to aid in the functioning of a business. These may be documents generated by a business to monitor itself, such as minutes of a meeting or a sales report. These documents may also explain company policies, organizational structures, and operating procedures. Workplace documents include memos, business letters, job applications, and résumés.

Strategies for Reading

A Read a workplace document slowly and carefully, as it may contain **details** that should not be overlooked.

B Notice how to contact the creator of the document. You will need this information to clear up anything that you don't understand.

C **Take notes** to help you remember times, dates, deadlines, and actions required. In particular, note whether you are expected to respond to the document, whether there is a deadline for your response, and to whom you should address your reply.

PRACTICE AND APPLY

Refer to both workplace documents to answer the following questions:

1. Why might the letter from Fred Fenton be classified as a workplace document?

2. According to the details in Fenton's letter, what actions should the yearbook staff take?

3. How does the author of the memo use text features, such as graphics and headings, to get his message across clearly and quickly?

4. What actions is the recipient of the memo expected to take?

LETTER

B **Famous Fred's Bike Store**
7451 East Trenton Boulevard
Cupertino, CA 95014
voice (408) 555-BIKE
fax (408) 555-3658
info@famousfreds.net

January 14, 2008 **A**

Yearbook Staff
James Madison High School
300 Elmwood Avenue
Cupertino, CA 95014

Dear Yearbook Staff:

C I would like to buy an advertisement in your upcoming yearbook. Would you call me at the above number to discuss the layout and cost of the ad. I also need to know whether you require camera-ready copy **A** and art, plus the total measurement, in inches or picas, of a full-page ad. I look forward to hearing from you. **C**

Yours truly,

Fred Fenton
Fred Fenton

MEMO

To: Rayna Jordan
B **From:** Mr. Jeff Kniffen, Yearbook Adviser
Re: Customer Letter
Date: January 21, 2008

C Rayna, please call Mr. Fenton with the prices for the ads for the yearbook. The chart below shows the price breakdown.

Size of ad	Price
1/4 page (3 1/2" W x 5" H)	$75.00
1/2 page (7 1/2" W x 5" H)	$125.00
1 full page (7 1/2" W x 10" H)	$200.00

Also, let him know that we do need camera-ready copy and art. Don't forget to tell him what the deadlines are for submitting the **A** ad and paying for it.

Thanks.

READING HANDBOOK **R19**

PRACTICE AND APPLY

ANSWERS

1. **Possible answer:** The letter can be classified as a workplace document because it is written in the form of a business letter, including a business address, date, greeting, body, and closing.

2. The letter asks the yearbook staff to call Mr. Fenton with the price of a full-page ad, the requirements for the copy and art, and the measurements of a full-page ad.

3. **Possible answer:** The author uses a graphic aid to organize important information and to make it stand out from the rest of the text. The headings help the reader scan for information that pertains to the price and measurement of each ad.

4. **Possible answer:** The recipient is expected to call Mr. Fenton with the price of each ad, inform him about camera-ready copy and art, and mention the deadline and payment schedule for submitting ads.

4.6 READING ELECTRONIC TEXT

Electronic text is any text that is in a form that a computer can store and display on a screen. Electronic text can be part of Web pages, CD-ROMs, search engines, and documents that you create with your computer software. Like books, Web pages often provide aids for finding information. However, each Web page is designed differently, and information is not in the same location on each page. It is important to know the functions of different parts of a Web page so that you can easily find the information you want.

Strategies for Reading

Ⓐ Look at the **title** of a page to determine what topics it covers.

Ⓑ For an online source, such as a Web page or search engine, note the **Web address,** known as a **URL** (Universal Resource Locator). You may want to make a note of it if you need to return to that page.

Ⓒ Look for a **menu bar** along the top, bottom, or side of a Web page. Clicking on an item in a menu bar will take you to another part of the Web site.

Ⓓ Notice any hyperlinks to related pages. **Hyperlinks** are often underlined or highlighted in a contrasting color. You can click on a hyperlink to get to another page—one that may or may not have been created by the same person or organization.

Ⓔ For information that you want to keep for future reference, save documents on your computer or print them. For online sources, you can pull down the **Favorites** or **Bookmarks** menu and bookmark pages so that you can easily return to them or print the information you need. Printing the pages will allow you to highlight key ideas on a hard copy.

PRACTICE AND APPLY

1. What is the URL of the Web page shown?
2. How do you know that the Web site has information for different audiences?
3. What would you do to view an article about astronauts?

PRACTICE AND APPLY

ANSWERS

1. *http://www.nasa.gov/home/index.html*
2. *The menu bar on the top left side of the Web page provides information for different audiences.*
3. *Click the hyperlink "View Article" under "World Book @ NASA Feature Topic."*

5 Reading Persuasive Texts

5.1 ANALYZING AN ARGUMENT

An **argument** expresses a position on an issue or problem and supports it with reasons and evidence. Being able to analyze and evaluate arguments will help you distinguish between claims you should accept and those you should not. A sound argument should appeal strictly to reason. However, arguments are often used in texts that also contain other types of persuasive devices. An argument includes the following elements:

- A **claim** is the writer's position on an issue or problem.

- **Support** is any material that serves to prove a claim. In an argument, support usually consists of reasons and evidence.

- **Reasons** are declarations made to justify an action, decision, or belief—for example, "My reason for thinking we will be late is that we can't make it to the appointment in five minutes."

- **Evidence** is the specific references, quotations, facts, examples, and opinions that support a claim. Evidence may also consist of statistics, reports of personal experience, or the views of experts.

- A **counterargument** is an argument made to oppose another argument. A good argument anticipates opposing claims and provides counterarguments to disprove or answer them.

Claim	I believe my curfew should be extended from 11 P.M. to midnight on Saturday night.
Reason	I don't have enough time to spend with my friends on weekdays because of homework and my job.
Evidence	On weekends I spend four hours doing homework and four hours at my job.
Counterargument	I know that it's difficult for you to sleep when I'm out late, but you need to trust that I'll be home by midnight and give me a chance to prove it.

Read the following editorial and use a chart like the one shown to identify the claim, reason, evidence, and counterargument.

On the second Monday in October, Americans celebrate Columbus Day. We honor the Italian explorer who has been credited with discovering the Americas in 1492. Some people, however, think that we need to look more closely at what Christopher Columbus actually did and at his place in our history. I am one of those people.

First of all, although we honor Columbus as the first European to set foot in the Americas, he may not have been the first. Archaeologists have found Norse ruins in Greenland and what is now Newfoundland, dating from around A.D. 1000. This evidence seems to prove that Vikings actually reached the North American continent nearly 500 years before Columbus ever left the shores of Spain.

Second, although Columbus did reach the Americas, he did not discover them. Millions of people were already living here when he arrived.

Defenders of Columbus argue that, in a way, he did discover the Americas. Even if he wasn't the first person, or even the first European, to set foot on the land, his voyages made the rest of the world aware of the Americas. In the years following Columbus' voyages, Europeans came to establish colonies and to explore the land.

I argue that this spread of culture brought great harm as well as great good to the Americas. The Europeans who came to the Americas brought deadly diseases with them. The native people had no immunity to such diseases as mumps, measles, smallpox, and typhus. As a result, hundreds of thousands of them died.

In conclusion, I don't suggest that people should boycott their local Columbus Day parades. I do think, though, that we should create a more balanced picture of the man we're honoring.

PRACTICE AND APPLY

ANSWERS

Students should create a chart like the one on page R21. The chart should include details similar to the ones below.

Claim: *We need to look more closely at what Christopher Columbus actually did and his place in our history.*

Reason: *We honor Columbus as the first European to set foot in the Americas when he may not have been the first.*

Evidence: *Archaeologists found Norse ruins in Greenland and in what is now Newfoundland, dating from A.D. 1000. This evidence seems to prove that Vikings reached North America almost 500 years before Columbus.*

Evidence: *Although Columbus did reach the Americas, he did not discover them. Millions of people were already living here when he arrived.*

Counterargument: *Even though he may not have been the first European to set foot on American soil, Columbus' voyages made the rest of the world aware of the Americas.*

PRACTICE AND APPLY

ANSWERS

Appeals by Association: *snob appeal; appeal to loyalty; testimonial*

Emotional Appeals: *appeal to vanity, appeal to patriotism*

Word Choice: *glittering generality*

5.2 RECOGNIZING PERSUASIVE TECHNIQUES

Persuasive texts typically rely on more than just the logical appeal of an argument to be convincing. They also rely on **persuasive techniques**—devices that can sway you to adopt a position or take an action. Persuasive techniques are used in advertising, political speeches, films, and fundraisers. The chart shown here explains several ways a writer may attempt to sway you to adopt his or her position. Learn to recognize these techniques, and you will be less likely to be influenced by them.

Persuasive Technique	Example
Appeals by Association	
Bandwagon appeal Uses the argument that a person should believe or do something because "everyone else" does	More and more people are making the switch to Discountline long-distance service.
Testimonial Relies on endorsements from well-known people or satisfied customers	Pierre DuPont, world-class rock climber, would be left hanging without DuraTwine rope.
Snob appeal Taps into people's desire to be special or part of an elite group	Treat yourself to Tropical Paradise because after all, you deserve the best under the sun.
Transfer Connnects a product, candidate, or cause with a positive emotion or idea	Freedom . . . you can feel it the instant you put your hands on the wheel of a Farnsworth 4 × 4 SL.
Appeal to loyalty Relies on people's affiliation with a particular group	This car is made in America by Americans.
Emotional Appeals	
Appeals to pity, fear, or vanity Use strong feelings, rather than facts, to persuade	Without more police, we'll be at the mercy of thieves.
Word Choice	
Glittering generality Makes a generalization that includes a word or phrase with positive connotations to promote a product or idea.	A vote for Evan Smith is a vote for democracy.

Identify the persuasive techniques used in the model.

Indiana and Issun Boshi— Building Another Great Team

Indiana is basketball country. Names like Bobby Knight, Larry Bird, and Isiah Thomas have added greatness to the game for over a quarter century.

That's why Issun Boshi, Japan's leading automobile company, chose Indiana as its U.S. teammate. The new plant will produce 150,000 new vehicles a year, built by 25,000 hard-working Hoosiers just like you. In addition, many of those workers will be driving the cars they make at a special discount—that's only fair; that's the American way. It's how we play the game.

Just ask Indiana sportscaster Wally Elliot, who says, "Issun Boshi and Hoosier pride— now that's what I call an expansion team."

5.3 ANALYZING LOGIC AND REASONING

When you evaluate an argument, you need to look closely at the writer's logic and reasoning. To do this, it is helpful to identify the type of reasoning the writer is using.

The Inductive Mode of Reasoning

When a writer leads from specific evidence to a general principle or generalization, that writer is using **inductive reasoning.** Here is an example of inductive reasoning.

SPECIFIC FACTS

Fact 1 The American Society of Composers, Authors, and Publishers (ASCAP) was formed on Friday, February 13, 1914, to collect royalties on copyrighted music.

Fact 2 The licensing of the first female flight instructor took place on Friday, October 13, 1939.

Fact 3 On Friday, February 13, 1948, Orville Wright announced that he was giving the famous flying machine *Kitty Hawk* to the Smithsonian Institution.

GENERALIZATION

Good things can happen on Friday the 13th.

Strategies for Determining the Soundness of Inductive Arguments

Ask yourself the following questions to evaluate an inductive argument:

- **Is the evidence valid and sufficient support for the conclusion?** Inaccurate facts lead to inaccurate conclusions.

- **Does the conclusion follow logically from the evidence?** From the facts listed in the previous example, the conclusion that good things happen only on Friday the 13th would be too broad a generalization.

- **Is the evidence drawn from a large enough sample?** Even though there are only three facts listed above, the sample is large enough to support the claim. If you wanted to support the conclusion that only good things happen on Friday the 13th, the sample is not large enough.

The Deductive Mode of Reasoning

When a writer arrives at a conclusion by applying a general principle to a specific situation, the writer is using **deductive reasoning.** Here's an example.

Journalism that stretches the truth is deceptive.	General principle or premise

▼

Hollywood Snoop Magazine stretches the truth.	Specific situation

▼

Hollywood Snoop Magazine practices deceptive journalism.	Specific conclusion

Strategies for Determining the Soundness of Deductive Arguments

Ask yourself the following questions to evaluate a deductive argument:

- **Is the general principle actually stated, or is it implied?** Note that writers often use deductive reasoning in an argument without stating the general principle. They just assume that readers will recognize and agree with the principle. So you may want to identify the general principle for yourself.

- **Is the general principle sound?** Don't just assume the general principle is sound. Ask yourself whether it is really true.

- **Is the conclusion valid?** To be valid, a conclusion in a deductive argument must follow logically from the general principle and the specific situation.

The following chart shows two conclusions drawn from the same general principle.

All team members wore school colors on Friday.	
Accurate Deduction	**Inaccurate Deduction**
Mara is on the volleyball team; therefore Mara wore school colors on Friday.	Jaime wore school colors on Friday; therefore Jaime is on a school team.

Jaime could have worn school colors in support of a team without being a member.

PRACTICE AND APPLY

Identify the mode of reasoning used in the following paragraph.

> . . . America has digitized, and there's no going back. Worldwide there are almost 200 million people on the Internet. In the United States alone, 80 million. . . . A third of wired Americans now do at least some of their shopping on the Net, and some are already consulting doctors on the Net, listening to radio on the Net, making investments on the Net, getting mortgages on the Net. . . . Each of these activities is impressive, but the aggregate effect is a different kind of life.
> —*Newsweek,* September 20, 1999

PRACTICE AND APPLY

ANSWER

Deductive reasoning

Identifying Faulty Reasoning

Sometimes an argument at first appears to make sense but isn't valid because it is based on a fallacy. A **fallacy** is an error in logic. Learn to recognize these common fallacies.

TYPE OF FALLACY	DEFINITION	EXAMPLE
Circular reasoning	Supporting a statement by simply repeating it in different words	Teenagers should avoid fad diets, because it is important for **adolescents to stay away from popular weight-loss plans.**
Either/or fallacy	A statement that suggests that there are only two choices available in a situation that really offers more than two options	**Either** students should be allowed to leave school to have lunch at nearby fast-food restaurants, **or** they should be allowed to choose the cafeteria menu.
Oversimplification	An explanation of a complex situation or problem as if it were much simpler than it is	Making the team depends on **whether the coach likes you.**
Overgeneralization	A generalization that is too broad. You can often recognize overgeneralizations by the use of words such as *all, everyone, every time, anything, no one,* and *none.*	**No one** cares that there is not enough parking downtown.
Stereotyping	A dangerous type of overgeneralization. Stereotypes are broad statements about people on the basis of their gender, ethnicity, race, or political, social, professional, or religious group.	The only thing **the members of that political party** care about is big business.
Attacking the person or name-calling	An attempt to discredit an idea by attacking the person or group associated with it. Candidates often engage in name-calling during political campaigns.	**My opponent is not smart enough** to be mayor.
Evading the issue	Refuting an objection with arguments and evidence that do not address its central point	Yes, I broke my campaign promise not to raise taxes, **but higher taxes have led to increases in police patrols, paved highways, and smaller class size in schools.**
Non sequitur	A statement that uses irrelevant "proof" to support a claim. A non sequitur is sometimes used to win an argument by diverting the reader's attention to proof that can't be challenged.	I know I'll pass math. **Mr. Gray is my math teacher and my football coach.**
False cause	The mistake of assuming that because one event occurred after another event in time, the first event caused the second one to occur	The mayor declared a get-tough crime policy, and sure enough, **crime rates dropped.**
False analogy	A comparison that doesn't hold up because of a critical difference between the two subjects	She walks to the store and back every day, **so surely she can walk in the 10K race.**
Hasty generalization	A conclusion drawn from too little evidence or from evidence that is biased	That corner must be dangerous. **There were two car accidents there last week.**

Look for examples of logical fallacies in the following argument. Identify each one and explain why you identified it as such.

> Watching television causes a child's grades to drop. What other conclusion can be drawn? Money-hungry media moguls produce horrible programming just to sell advertising time. These programs interfere with children's thinking. If you say television isn't bad for children, you would probably say the earth is flat. Parents who care should at least limit their children's viewing. The most responsible parents should turn off the TV—permanently. They can either unplug the TV or expect their children to become uneducated slugs.

5.4 EVALUATING PERSUASIVE TEXTS

Learning how to evaluate persuasive texts and identify bias will help you become more selective when doing research and also help you improve your own reasoning and arguing skills. **Bias** is an inclination for or against a particular opinion or viewpoint. A writer may reveal a strongly positive or negative opinion on an issue by presenting only one way of looking at it or by heavily weighting the evidence on one side of the argument. Additionally, the presence of either of the following is often a sign that a writer is biased:

Loaded language consists of words with strongly positive or negative connotations that are intended to influence a reader's attitude.

EXAMPLE: *The safety of our children depends on our driving the savage criminals out of this horrible neighborhood.* (*Savage* and *horrible* have very negative connotations.)

Propaganda is any form of communication that is so distorted that it conveys false or misleading information. Some politicians create and distribute propaganda. Many logical fallacies, such as name-calling, the either/or fallacy, and false causes are often used in propaganda. The

following example shows an oversimplification. The writer uses one fact to support a particular point of view but does not reveal another fact that does not support that viewpoint.

EXAMPLE: *Since the new park opened, vandalism in the area has increased by 10 percent. Clearly, the park has had a negative impact on the area.* (The writer does not include the fact that the vandalism was caused by people who were not drawn into the area by the park.)

*For more information, see **Identifying Faulty Reasoning**, page R24.*

Strategies for Evaluating Evidence

It is important to have a set of standards by which you can evaluate persuasive texts. Use the questions below to help you critically assess facts and opinions that are presented as evidence.

- **Are the facts presented verifiable?** Facts can be proved by eyewitness accounts, authoritative sources such as encyclopedias and almanacs, experts, or research.
- **Are the opinions presented well informed?** Any opinions offered should be supported by facts, be based on research or eyewitness accounts, or be the opinions of experts on the topic.
- **Is the evidence thorough?** Thorough evidence leaves no reasonable questions unanswered. If a choice is offered, background for making the choice should be provided. If taking a side is called for, all sides of the issue should be presented.
- **Is the evidence biased?** Be alert to evidence that contains loaded language and other signs of bias.
- **Is the evidence authoritative?** The people, groups, or organizations that provided the evidence should have credentials that support their authority.
- **Is it important that the evidence be current?** Where timeliness is crucial, as in the areas of medicine and technology, the evidence should reflect the latest developments in the areas.

PRACTICE AND APPLY
ANSWERS
Possible answers:

1. *Oversimplification:* "Watching television causes a child's grades to drop." *Explanation:* The explanation for the problem, a drop in children's grades, is oversimplified. Not all children's grades drop.

2. *Attacking the Person or Name-Calling:* "Money-hungry media moguls produce horrible programming." *Explanation:* The writer is attempting to discredit media moguls by attacking them and using harsh language.

3. *False Analogy:* "If you say television isn't bad for children, you would probably say the earth is flat." *Explanation:* The writer compares two subjects that have nothing in common.

4. *Either/Or Fallacy and Stereotyping:* "They can either unplug the TV or expect their children to become uneducated slugs." *Explanation:* The either/or fallacy suggests that there is only one alternative to watching television (unplugging the TV). The term *uneducated slug is a stereotype of children who watch television.*

PRACTICE AND APPLY

ANSWERS

Possible answers:

Facts: A study by economists William Landes and Lewis Solomon found little evidence to show that compulsory attendance laws increase attendance rates.

Opinions: Kids who are forced to be in school because of attendance laws are to blame for the reduced quality of instruction in school. Poor attenders are almost always failing. The ability to expel students contributes to a positive climate in schools.

Elements of bias: "Why are students who show up late for tests, fill in answers randomly, and then snooze for the rest of the period allowed to jeopardize school test scores and reduce the quality of instruction for motivated kids?" "Why not tell poor attenders . . . 'You're done. You don't belong here.'"

PRACTICE AND APPLY

ANSWERS

Students' responses will vary, but they should evaluate the strength of the claim, the evidence supporting the claim, and the counterarguments.

Possible answers: Overall, the editorial does not illustrate a very strong argument. The claim—that animal testing is unnecessary and cruel and that it must be stopped—reveals a heavily biased opinion. The writer uses words and phrases with a negative connotation and emotional or biased tone (for example, "unnecessary, cruel," and "must be stopped"). In addition, many of the statements presented as facts are inappropriate and not supported by sound evidence. Finally, the author does not adequately refute counterarguments with logical arguments or evidence. Instead, the writer engages in name-calling and faulty reasoning.

Read the argument below. Identify the facts, opinion, and elements of bias.

Why are students who show up late for tests, fill in answers randomly, and then snooze for the rest of the period allowed to jeopardize school test scores and reduce the quality of instruction for motivated kids? The answer is simple—compulsory attendance laws. These laws say that kids must be in school. But a study by economists William Landes and Lewis Solomon found little evidence that such laws increase attendance rates at all. Why not tell poor attenders, who are almost always failing too, "You're done. You don't belong here." Private schools do it, and the ability to expel students contributes to a positive climate.

Strategies for Determining a Strong Argument

Make sure that all or most of the following statements are true:

- The argument presents a claim or thesis.
- The claim is connected to its support by a general principle that most readers would readily agree with. Valid general principle: *It is the job of a school to provide a well-rounded physical education program.* Invalid general principle: *It is the job of a school to produce healthy, physically fit people.*
- The reasons make sense.
- The reasons are presented in a logical and effective order.
- The claim and all reasons are adequately supported by sound evidence.
- The evidence is adequate, accurate, and appropriate.
- The logic is sound. There are no instances of faulty reasoning.
- The argument adequately anticipates and addresses reader concerns and counterclaims with counterarguments.

Use the preceding criteria to evaluate the strength of the following editorial.

According to veterinarian and animal-rights advocate Dr. Michael W. Fox, more than 100 million animals are used each year in laboratory tests. These animals are used to study such things as the causes and effects of illnesses and to test drugs. This unnecessary and cruel animal testing must be stopped.

The most important reason to stop this testing is that it's wrong to make living creatures suffer. Even though they can't talk or use tools as people do, animals have feelings. Zoologist Ann Speirs says that animals may suffer even more than people do, because they can't understand what's happening to them.

People who favor animal research argue that the medical advances gained justify animal experimentation. They also say that the suffering experienced by the animals is minor. People like that are dumber than any guinea pig or rat.

Another important reason to stop this testing is that everybody knows it isn't reliable. Many drugs that help animals are harmful to people. One example is the drug thalidomide. After it was tested in animals in the 1950s and early 1960s, it was given to pregnant women. More than 10,000 of these women gave birth to handicapped babies. The process works the other way, too. Many drugs that help people kill animals. Two common examples are penicillin and aspirin.

Animal testing also affects the environment. The Animal Protection Service says that a quarter of a million chimpanzees, monkeys, and baboons are taken from their natural homes and used in laboratory experiments every year. Those animals will never be able to reproduce, and whole species may become extinct.

A final reason for not using animals in experiments is that there are other research methods available. Two examples are using bits of animal tissue and cells and using computer models.

In conclusion, animal testing has to stop because it just can't go on.

6 Adjusting Reading Rate to Purpose

You may need to change the way you read certain texts in order to understand what you read. To properly adjust the way you read, you need to be aware of what you want to get out of what you are reading. Once you know your purpose for reading, you can adjust the speed at which you read in response to your purpose and the difficulty of the material.

Determine Your Purpose for Reading

You read different types of materials for different purposes. You may read a novel for enjoyment. You may read a textbook unit to learn a new concept or to master the content for a test. When you read for enjoyment, you naturally read at a pace that is comfortable for you. When you read for information, you need to read material more slowly and thoroughly. When you are being tested on material, you may think you have to read fast, especially if the test is being timed. However, you can actually increase your understanding of the material if you slow down.

Determine Your Reading Rate

The rate at which you read most comfortably is called your **independent reading level.** It is the rate that you use to read materials that you enjoy. To learn to adjust your reading rate to read materials for other purposes, you need to be aware of your independent reading level. You can figure out your reading level by following these steps:

1. Select a passage from a book or story you enjoy.
2. Have a friend or classmate time you as you begin reading the passage silently.
3. Read at the rate that is most comfortable for you.
4. Stop when your friend or classmate tells you one minute has passed.
5. Determine the number of words you read in that minute and write down the number.
6. Repeat the process at least two more times, using different passages.
7. Add the numbers and divide the sum by the number of times your friend timed you.

Reading Techniques for Informational Material

Use the following techniques to adapt your reading for informational texts, to prepare for tests, and to better understand what you read:

- **Skimming** is reading quickly to get the general idea of a text. To skim, read only the title, headings, graphic aids, highlighted words, and first sentence of each paragraph. In addition, read any introduction, conclusion, or summary. Skimming can be especially useful when taking a test. Before reading a passage, you can skim questions that follow it in order to find out what is expected and better focus on the important ideas in the text.

  When researching a topic, skimming can help you determine whether a source has information that is pertinent to your topic.

- **Scanning** is reading quickly to find a specific piece of information, such as a fact or a definition. When you scan, your eyes sweep across a page, looking for key words that may lead you to the information you want. Use scanning to review for tests and to find answers to questions.

- **Changing pace** is speeding up or slowing down the rate at which you read parts of a particular text. When you come across familiar concepts, you might be able to speed up without misunderstanding them. When you encounter unfamiliar concepts or material presented in an unpredictable way, however, you may need to slow down to process and absorb the information better.

WATCH OUT! Reading too slowly can affect your ability to comprehend what you read. Make sure you aren't just reading one word at a time. Practice reading phrases.

PRACTICE AND APPLY

Find an article in a magazine or textbook. Skim the article. Then answer the following questions:

1. What did you notice about the organization of the article from skimming it?
2. What is the main idea of the article?

PRACTICE AND APPLY

ANSWERS

Accept answers that provide an accurate description of the article and its main ideas.

Writing is a process, a journey of discovery in which you can explore your thoughts, experiment with ideas, and search for connections. Through writing, you can explore and record your thoughts, feelings, and ideas for yourself alone or you can communicate them to an audience.

> **WRITING TOOLS**
> Go to the **Writing Center** at **ClassZone.com** for interactive models, publishing ideas, and other support.

1 The Writing Process

The writing process consists of the following stages: prewriting, drafting, revising and editing, proofreading, and publishing. These are not stages that you must complete in a set order. Rather, you may return to an earlier stage at any time to improve your writing.

1.1 PREWRITING

In the prewriting stage, you explore what you want to write about, what your purpose for writing is, whom you are writing for, and what form you will use to express your ideas. Ask yourself the following questions to get started.

Topic	• Is my topic assigned, or can I choose it?
	• What would I be interested in writing about?
Purpose	• Am I writing to entertain, to inform, or to persuade—or some combination of these?
	• What effect do I want to have on my readers?
Audience	• Who is the audience?
	• What might the audience members already know about my topic?
	• What about the topic might interest them?
Format	• What format will work best? Essay? Poem? Speech? Short story? Article? Research paper?

Find Ideas for Writing

- Browse through magazines, newspapers, and Web sites.
- Start a file of articles you want to save for future reference.
- With a group, brainstorm as many ideas as you can. Compile your ideas into a list.
- Interview someone who is an expert on a particular topic.

- Write down anything that comes into your head.
- Use a cluster map to explore subordinate ideas that relate to a general topic.

Organize Ideas

Once you've chosen a topic, you will need to compile and organize your ideas. If you are writing a description, you may need to gather sensory details. Or you may need to record information from different sources for an essay or a research paper. To record notes from sources you read or view, use any or all of these methods:

- **Summarize:** Briefly retell the main ideas of a piece of writing in your own words.
- **Paraphrase:** Restate all or almost all of the information in your own words.
- **Quote:** Record the author's exact words.

Depending on what form your writing takes, you may also need to arrange your ideas in a certain pattern.

*For more information, see the **Writing Handbook**, pages R34–R41.*

1.2 DRAFTING

In the drafting stage, you put your ideas on paper and allow them to develop and change as you write. You don't need to worry about correct grammar and spelling at this stage. There are two ways that you can draft:

Discovery drafting is a good approach when you are not quite sure what you think about your subject. You just start writing and let your feelings and ideas lead you in developing the topic.

Planned drafting may work better if you know that your ideas have to be arranged in a certain way, as in a research paper. Try making a writing plan or an informal outline before you begin drafting.

1.3 REVISING AND EDITING

The revising and editing stage allows you to polish your draft and make changes in its content, organization, and style. Use the questions that follow to assess problems and determine what changes would improve your work:

- Does my writing have a **main idea** or central focus? Is my thesis clear?

- Have I used **precise** nouns, verbs, and modifiers?

- Have I incorporated **adequate detail** and **evidence?** Where might I include a telling detail, a revealing statistic, or a vivid example?

- Is my writing **unified?** Do all ideas and supporting details pertain to my main idea or advance my thesis?

- Is my writing clear and **coherent?** Is the flow of sentences and paragraphs smooth and logical?

- Have I used a consistent **point of view?**

- Do I need to add **transitional words, phrases,** or sentences to clarify relationships among ideas?

- Have I used a **variety of sentence types?** Are they well constructed? What sentences might I combine to improve the rhythm of my writing?

- Have I used a **tone** appropriate for my audience and purpose?

1.4 PROOFREADING

When you are satisfied with your revision, proofread your paper for mistakes in grammar, usage, and mechanics. You may want to do this several times, looking for a different type of mistake each time. Use the following questions to help you correct errors:

- Have I corrected any errors in **subject-verb agreement** and **pronoun-antecedent agreement?**

- Have I double-checked for errors in **confusing word pairs,** such as *it's/its, than/then,* and *too/to?*

- Have I corrected any **run-on sentences** and **sentence fragments?**

- Have I followed rules for **correct capitalization?**

- Have I used **punctuation marks** correctly?

- Have I checked the **spellings of all unfamiliar words** in the dictionary?

TIP If possible, don't begin proofreading just after you've finished writing. Put your work away for at least a few hours. When you return to it, it will be easier for you to identify and correct mistakes.

*For more information, see the **Grammar Handbook** and the **Vocabulary and Spelling Handbook**, pages R46–R75.*

Use the proofreading symbols in the chart to mark changes on your draft.

Proofreading Symbols	
∧ Add letters or words.	/ Make a capital letter lowercase.
⊙ Add a period.	¶ Begin a new paragraph.
≡ Capitalize a letter.	⌐ Delete letters or words.
⌒ Close up space.	∿ Switch the positions of letters or words.
∧ Add a comma.	

1.5 PUBLISHING AND REFLECTING

Always consider sharing your finished writing with a wider audience. Reflecting on your writing is another good way to finish a project.

Publishing Ideas
- Post your writing on a Weblog.

- Create a multimedia presentation and share it with classmates.

- Publish your writing in a school newspaper, local newspaper, or literary magazine.

- Present your work orally in a report, speech, reading, or dramatic performance.

Reflecting on Your Writing
Think about your writing process and whether you would like to add what you have written to your writing portfolio. You might attach a note in which you answer questions like these:

- Which parts of the process did I find easiest? Which parts were more difficult?

- What was the biggest problem I faced during the writing process? How did I solve the problem?

- What changes have occurred in my writing style?

- Have I noticed any features in the writing of

published authors or my peers that I can apply to my own work?

1.6 PEER RESPONSE

Peer response consists of the suggestions and comments you make about the writing of your peers and also the comments and suggestions they make about your writing. You can ask a peer reader for help at any time in the writing process.

Using Peer Response as a Writer

- Indicate whether you are more interested in feedback about your ideas or about your presentation of them.

- Ask questions that will help you get specific information about your writing. Open-ended questions that require more than yes-or-no answers are more likely to give you information you can use as you revise.

- Encourage your readers to be honest.

Being a Peer Reader

- Respect the writer's feelings.

- Offer positive reactions first.

- Make sure you understand what kind of feedback the writer is looking for, and then respond accordingly.

For more information on the writing process, see the ***Introductory Unit,*** *pages 16–19.*

2 Building Blocks of Good Writing

Whatever your purpose in writing, you need to capture your reader's interest and organize your thoughts clearly.

2.1 INTRODUCTIONS

An introduction should present a thesis statement and capture your reader's attention.

Kinds of Introductions

There are a number of ways to write an introduction. The one you choose depends on who the audience is and on your purpose for writing.

Make a Surprising Statement Beginning with a startling statement or an interesting fact can arouse your reader's curiosity about a subject, as in the following model.

> **MODEL**
>
> W. H. Auden is one of the major poets of the 20th century. Until he was 14 years old, however, Auden's greatest interests were machinery and mining. He intended to become a mining engineer.

Provide a Description A vivid description sets a mood and brings a scene to life for your reader.

Here, details about heating the air for a hot-air balloon set the tone for a narrative about a balloon ride.

> **MODEL**
>
> Whoosh! The red and yellow flame shot up into the great nylon cone. The warm air filled the balloon so that the cooler air below held the apparatus aloft. A soft breeze helped to push the balloon and basket along. The four passengers hardly noticed the noise or the heat as they stared in awe at the hilly farmland and meandering streams below.

Pose a Question Beginning with a question can make your reader want to read on to find out the answer. The following introduction asks a question about the breadth of a popular author's imagination.

> **MODEL**
>
> Between 1915 and 1973, Agatha Christie wrote 184 works of crime fiction. How was it possible for her to create so many clever plots that depend on intricate puzzles, clues, and solutions?

Relate an Anecdote Beginning with an anecdote, or brief story, can hook your reader and help you make a point in a dramatic way. The following anecdote introduces a firsthand account of a rescue from a burning apartment building.

MODEL

A red light began blinking. A siren started up slowly but built to a screeching pitch. Twenty-five sleepy faces appeared a few at a time in the hallway. As I recall, each of us looked to left and right almost in unison, as if watching an imaginary tennis match that would give some clue to the source of this midnight disturbance.

Address the Reader Speaking directly to your reader establishes a friendly, informal tone and involves the reader in your topic.

MODEL

Find out how to maintain your cardiovascular system while enjoying yourself. Come to a free demonstration of Fit for Life at the community center, Friday night at 7:00 P.M.

Begin with a Thesis Statement A thesis statement expressing a main idea may be woven into both the beginning and the end of a piece of nonfiction writing. The following thesis statement introduces a literary analysis.

MODEL

In "The Great Taos Bank Robbery," Tony Hillerman presents eccentric characters in loving detail. It is clear that he has affection for the hapless criminals as well as for the fascinated, easygoing townspeople.

TIP To write the best introduction for your paper, you may want to try more than one of the methods and then decide which is the most effective for your purpose and audience.

2.2 PARAGRAPHS

A paragraph is made up of sentences that work together to develop an idea or accomplish a purpose. Whether or not it contains a topic sentence stating the main idea, a good paragraph must have unity and coherence.

Unity

A paragraph has unity when all the sentences support and develop one stated or implied idea. Use the following techniques to create unity in your paragraphs:

Write a Topic Sentence A topic sentence states the main idea of the paragraph; all other sentences in the paragraph provide supporting details. A topic sentence is often the first sentence in a paragraph. However, it may also appear later in a paragraph or at the end, to summarize or reinforce the main idea, as shown in the model that follows.

MODEL

Tomás lifted the skimmer baskets and emptied the collection of bugs and leaves. Then he filled the small vials with water and carefully measured four different solutions to test the pH, chlorine, total alkalinity, and acid demand. Next, he got out the equipment for vacuuming. Tomás had not realized that taking care of a swimming pool would require so much time and effort.

Relate All Sentences to an Implied Main Idea A paragraph can be unified without a topic sentence as long as every sentence supports an implied, or unstated, main idea. In the model, all the sentences work together to create a unified impression of baking an apple pie.

MODEL

The chef carefully poured in the mixture of freshly sliced apples, sugar, flour, salt, cinnamon, and nutmeg. Then she floured her hands again before adding strips of pastry in crisscrosses over the top. She dotted some butter all around the top and sprinkled on a little more sugar and cinnamon. Finally she placed the masterpiece in the oven.

Coherence

A paragraph is coherent when all its sentences are related to one another and each flows logically to the next. The following techniques will help you achieve coherence in paragraphs:

- Present your ideas in the most logical order.
- Use pronouns, synonyms, and repeated words to connect ideas.
- Use transitional devices to show relationships among ideas.

In the model shown here, the writer used some of these techniques to create a unified paragraph.

> **MODEL**
>
> Just the name "alligator snapping turtle" brings to mind a ferocious, frightening creature. The alligator snapping turtle can grow to more than 200 pounds. In fact, whereas common snapping turtles rarely weigh 30 pounds, alligator snappers have been recorded with weights up to 300 pounds.

2.3 TRANSITIONS

Transitions are words and phrases that show connections between details. Clear transitions help show how your ideas relate to one another.

Kinds of Transitions

The types of transitions you choose depend on the ideas you want to convey.

Time or Sequence Some transitions help to clarify the sequence of events over time. When you are telling a story or describing a process, you can connect ideas with such transitional words as *first, second, always, then, next, later, soon, before, finally, after, earlier, afterward,* and *tomorrow.*

> **MODEL**
>
> The orchestra members were seated. At first, the sounds conflicted with one another as the players tuned and tested their instruments. Then, the concertmaster stood and played one note on her violin. Next, all the instruments tuned to that tone, so that one great sound on the same pitch filled the auditorium.

Spatial Relationships Transitional words and phrases such as *in front, behind, next to, along, nearest, lowest, above, below, underneath, on the left,* and *in the middle* can help your reader visualize a scene.

> **MODEL**
>
> Gardeners have kept the tall-grass maze in perfect order. They have mowed the paths that weave in and out within the 15-foot diameter of the maze. On the left, a clearly marked entrance invites walkers to try the maze. At the center, a small clump of clover signals to the careful observer that the path winds toward the exit on the right.

Degree of Importance Transitional words such as *mainly, strongest, weakest, first, second, most important, least important, worst,* and *best* may be used to rank ideas or to show degrees of importance.

> **MODEL**
>
> Nathan has several qualifications that make him a good candidate for class representative; his greatest strength is his tolerance of more than one point of view.

Compare and Contrast Words and phrases such as *similarly, likewise, also, like, as, neither ... nor,* and *either ... or* show similarity between details. *However, by contrast, yet, but, unlike, instead, whereas,* and *while* show difference. Note the use of both types of transitions in the model.

> **MODEL**
>
> Like dogs, cats are wonderful pets. Dogs give unconditional affection and have a great desire to please. You will find out, however, that there is no substitute for the comfort of a cat's purr.

TIP Both *but* and *however* can be used to join two independent clauses. When *but* is used as a coordinating conjunction, it is preceded by a comma. When *however* is used as a conjunctive adverb, it is preceded by a semicolon and followed by a comma.

Cause and Effect When you are writing about a cause-effect relationship, use transitional words and phrases such as *since, because, thus, therefore, so, due to, for this reason,* and *as a result* to help clarify that relationship and make your writing coherent.

MODEL

Because a tree fell across the electric wires Monday night, we lost our electricity for four hours.

2.4 CONCLUSIONS

A conclusion should leave readers with a strong final impression.

Kinds of Conclusions

Good conclusions sum up ideas in a variety of ways. Here are some techniques you might try.

Restate Your Thesis A good way to conclude an essay is by restating your thesis, or main idea, in different words. The following conclusion restates the thesis introduced on page R31.

MODEL

The kind humor with which Hillerman portrays the would-be bank robbers as well as the curious townspeople in "The Great Taos Bank Robbery" shows his affection for all his characters.

Ask a Question Try asking a question that sums up what you have said and gives your reader something new to think about. This question concludes a request to consider a visit to a place of educational entertainment.

MODEL

If you enjoy science experiments and you like puzzles, shouldn't you plan to visit the Magic House soon?

Make a Recommendation When you are persuading your audience to take a position on an issue, you can conclude by recommending a specific course of action.

MODEL

Today's youth are at risk of damaging their hearing by listening to very loud music. Consider turning down the bass and turning down the volume on your headphones.

Make a Prediction Readers are concerned about matters that may affect them and therefore are moved by a conclusion that predicts the future.

MODEL

If this state continues to permit landowners to drain wetlands, we will see a tremendous decline in the numbers and variety of wildlife.

Summarize Your Information Summarizing reinforces your main idea, leaving a strong, lasting impression. The model concludes with a statement that summarizes a literary analysis of the works of Agatha Christie.

MODEL

Although there are a few examples of unrealistic situations in Agatha Christie's novels, for the most part each story is well crafted, providing an excellent plot and entertaining reading.

2.5 ELABORATION

Elaboration is the process of developing an idea by providing specific supporting details that are relevant and appropriate to the purpose and form of your writing.

Facts and Statistics A fact is a statement that can be verified, and a statistic is a fact expressed as a number. Make sure the facts and statistics you supply are from reliable, up-to-date sources.

MODEL

Female cicadas cut little slits in the bark of twigs and lay their eggs inside the slits. The eggs hatch after 6 to 10 weeks. When the eggs hatch, the nymphs drop from the trees.

Sensory Details Details that show how something looks, sounds, tastes, smells, or feels can enliven a description, making readers feel they are actually experiencing what you are describing.

MODEL

About 4:00 in the afternoon, the racket would begin in earnest. The cicadas must have dozed all day, but they seemed to awake in the heat of the afternoon to begin their persistent mating screeches. In lush suburban areas with large trees, the din was almost deafening.

Incidents From our earliest years, we are interested in hearing "stories." One way to illustrate a point powerfully is to relate an incident or tell a story, as shown in the example.

MODEL

The pavement was slippery from the rain, but I was going to miss the bus if I didn't run. As I rushed toward the bus stop, I tripped and fell on the sidewalk close to the curb. Now I had dirt on my skirt. As I got up from the pavement, the bus roared past me, splashing muddy water on my skirt and shoes.

Examples An example can help make an abstract idea concrete or can serve to clarify a complex point for your reader.

MODEL

Many fiction writers use real locations for their settings. For example, Tony Hillerman uses cities and towns in New Mexico and Arizona for his mystery novels.

Quotations Choose quotations that clearly support your points, and be sure that you copy each quotation word for word. Remember always to credit the source.

MODEL

The sky looks blue because air is not completely transparent. In *The Cosmological Milkshake,* Robert Ehrlich explains that "a fraction of sunlight is scattered by the molecules of the atmosphere, with blue light scattered the most." Even without smog and other forms of pollution, the sky would still look blue.

3 Descriptive Writing

Descriptive writing allows you to paint word pictures about anything, from events of global importance to the most personal feelings. It is an essential part of almost every piece of writing.

> **RUBRIC: Standards for Writing**
>
> **Successful descriptive writing should**
> - have a clear focus and sense of purpose
> - use sensory details and precise words to create a vivid image, establish a mood, or express emotion
> - present details in a logical order

3.1 KEY TECHNIQUES

Consider Your Goals What do you want to accomplish with your description? Do you want to show why something is important to you? Do you want to make a person or scene more memorable? Do you want to explain an event?

Identify Your Audience Who will read your description? How familiar are they with your subject? What background information will they need? Which details will they find most interesting?

Think Figuratively What figures of speech might help make your description vivid and interesting? What simile or metaphor comes to mind? What imaginative comparisons can you make? What living thing does an inanimate object remind you of?

Gather Sensory Details Which sights, smells, tastes, sounds, and textures make your subject come alive? Which details stick in your mind when you observe or recall your subject? Which senses does it most strongly affect?

You might want to use a chart like the one shown here to collect sensory details about your subject.

Sights	Sounds	Textures	Smells	Tastes

Create a Mood What feelings do you want to evoke in your readers? Do you want to soothe them with comforting images? Do you want to build tension with ominous details? Do you want to evoke sadness or joy?

3.2 OPTIONS FOR ORGANIZATION

Option 1: Spatial Order Choose one of these options to show the spatial order of elements in a scene you are describing.

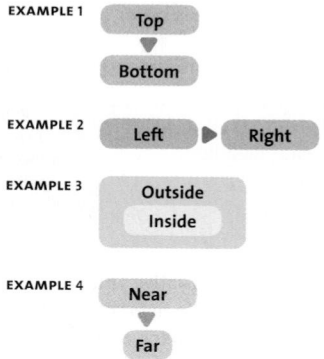

MODEL

The tour group squeezed through the door and into the long, narrow entryway. The leader began describing what they would see when it was their turn to enter the great center room. Some in the group tried to steal a glimpse of the enormous spectacle just ahead of them. At the end of the hall, a light illuminated a magnificent marble sculpture.

*For more information, see **Transitions**, page R32.*

Option 2: Order of Impression Order of impression is the order in which you notice details.

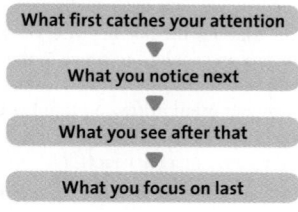

MODEL

When I first looked at the painting, I saw a brightly illuminated, sophisticated face looking toward me and well-manicured hands turning the pages of a book. The longer I looked at the painting, the more I saw. I noticed that a letter seems to have just been opened, read, and set down. Before long my eyes fastened on bits of paper or maybe flower petals that might have come with the letter. At this point, I studied the expression on the young man's face. He seems very serious, maybe sad or worried. Suddenly, I really wanted to know more about this subject. I stared at the painting a long time.

TIP Use transitions that help readers understand the order of the impressions you are describing. Some useful transitions are *after, next, during, first, before, finally,* and *then.*

Option 3: Order of Importance You can use order of importance as the organizing structure for a description.

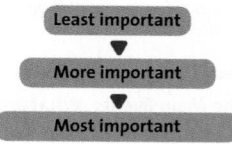

MODEL

Annaliese tried to dredge up from her memory everything about the accident. She remembered unimportant details, like the song that was playing on her radio before the truck loomed up ahead. She remembered her panic as she steered into the guardrail. Gradually she recalled more important information—her conservative speed, the fact that the truck was coming toward her on the wrong side of the road, the driver's long beard. Finally, when she closed her eyes and really concentrated, she could remember the license-plate number at eye level as the truck zoomed by.

*For more information, see **Transitions**, page R32.*

4 Narrative Writing

Narrative writing tells a story. If you write a story from your imagination, it is a fictional narrative. A true story about actual events is a nonfictional narrative. Narrative writing can be found in short stories, novels, news articles, personal narratives, and biographies.

> **RUBRIC: Standards for Writing**
>
> **A successful narrative should**
> - hook the reader's attention with a strong introduction
> - include descriptive details and dialogue to develop the characters, setting, and plot
> - have a clear beginning, middle, and end
> - have a logical organization, with clues and transitions that help the reader understand the order of events
> - maintain a consistent tone and point of view
> - use language that is appropriate to the audience
> - demonstrate the significance of events or ideas

*For more information, see **Writing Workshop: Personal Narrative**, pages 168–175, and **Writing Workshop: Short Story**, pages 384–391.*

4.1 KEY TECHNIQUES

Identify the Main Events What are the most important events in your narrative? Is each event needed to tell the story?

Describe the Setting When do the events occur? Where do they take place? How can you use setting to create mood and to set the stage for the characters and their actions?

Depict Characters Vividly What do your characters look like? What do they think and say? How do they act? What details can show what they are like?

TIP Dialogue is an effective way of developing characters in a narrative. As you write dialogue, choose words that express your characters' personalities and that show how the characters feel about one another and about the events in the plot.

4.2 OPTIONS FOR ORGANIZATION

Option 1: Chronological Order One way to organize a piece of narrative writing is to arrange the events in chronological order, as shown in the following example.

EXAMPLE

Kid Turner is missing from the ranch. Fearing that he is hurt, Jake and Edna Mae set out to search for him.

As a thunderstorm approaches, they find his horse and backtrack up a dry wash.

They find Turner just as the storm breaks. He has a broken leg, and he can't drag himself out of the dry wash.

They carry him out of the riverbed and find shelter under a rock ledge. As they watch, a flash flood surges over the riverbed where Turner had been lying.

Introduction
Characters and setting

▼

Event 1

▼

Event 2

▼

End
Perhaps showing the significance of the events

Option 2: Flashback In narrative writing, it is also possible to introduce events that happened sometime before the beginning of the story. You can use a flashback to show how past events led up to the present situation or to provide background about a character or event. Use clue words such as *last summer, as a young girl, the previous school year,* and *his earliest memories* to let your reader know that you are interrupting the main action to describe earlier events.

Notice how the flashback interrupts the action in the model.

MODEL

At the trials for the first big meet of the school year, Shayna was anxious to prove to the coach that she could be a leader on the track team. During warm-ups, her mind drifted back to her disastrous showing in the final meet last year, when she had dropped a baton in a relay race.

Option 3: Focus on Conflict When a fictional narrative focuses on a central conflict, the story's plot may be organized as shown in the following example.

EXAMPLE

Before a championship basketball game, two players arrive at the school gym an hour before the rest of the team. The players are identical twins, but their personalities couldn't be more different. Mark is outgoing and impulsive, while Matt is thoughtful and shy.

> **Describe main characters and setting.**

As they prepare for the game, Matt notices a man enter the locker room and give Mark a wad of cash. In the first quarter of the game, Matt notices that his brother is missing shots on purpose. He realizes that Mark has taken cash to lose the game.

> **Present conflict.**

- Matt has a chance at a basketball scholarship if they win the championship.
- Mark needs money to buy a car.
- Matt and Mark have always supported each other's goals.

> **Relate events that make conflict complex and cause characters to change.**

During halftime, Matt reminds Mark of a family story in which their grandfather chose honor and integrity over easy money. When the game resumes, Mark plays to win.

> **Present resolution or outcome of conflict.**

5 Expository Writing

Expository writing informs and explains. You can use it to evaluate the effects of a new law, to compare two movies, to analyze a piece of literature, or to examine the problem of greenhouse gases in the atmosphere. There are many types of expository writing. Think about your topic and select the type that presents the information most clearly.

5.1 COMPARISON AND CONTRAST

Compare-and-contrast writing examines the similarities and differences between two or more subjects. You might, for example, compare and contrast two short stories, the main characters in a novel, or two movies.

> **RUBRIC: Standards for Writing**
> **Successful compare-and-contrast writing should**
> - hook the reader's attention with a strong introduction
> - clearly identify the subjects that are being compared and contrasted
> - include specific, relevant details
> - follow a clear plan of organization
> - use language and details appropriate to the audience
> - use transitional words and phrases to clarify similarities and differences

Options for Organization

Compare-and-contrast writing can be organized in different ways. The examples that follow demonstrate point-by-point organization and subject-by-subject organization.

Option 1: Point-by-Point Organization

EXAMPLE

I. Both women want something that they cannot afford. **[Point 1]**
   Subject A Mathilde in "The Necklace": new dress and fancy jewelry to go to a ball
   Subject B Della in "The Gift of the Magi": special Christmas present for her husband

II. Both make sacrifices that turn out to be ironic. **[Point 2]**
   Subject A Mathilde: works for years to replace a necklace that turns out to be a cheap imitation
   Subject B Della: sells her hair to buy a chain for a watch that her husband has sold

Option 2: Subject-by-Subject Organization

EXAMPLE

I. Mathilde in "The Necklace" — **Subject A**

   Point 1/Wish: new dress and fancy jewelry to go to a ball

   Point 2/Ironic Sacrifice: works for years to replace a necklace that turns out to be a cheap imitation

II. Della in "The Gift of the Magi" — **Subject B**

   Point 1/Wish: special Christmas present for her husband

   Point 2/Ironic Sacrifice: sells her hair to buy a chain for a watch that her husband has sold

*For more information, see **Writing Workshop: Comparison-Contrast Essay**, pages 284–291.*

5.2 CAUSE AND EFFECT

Cause-effect writing explains why something happened, why certain conditions exist, or what resulted from an action or a condition. You might use cause-effect writing to explain a character's actions, the progress of a disease, or the outcome of a war.

> **RUBRIC: Standards for Writing**
>
> **Successful cause-effect writing should**
>
> - hook the reader's attention with a strong introduction
> - clearly state the cause-and-effect relationship
> - show clear connections between causes and effects
> - present causes and effects in a logical order and use transitions effectively
> - use facts, examples, and other details to illustrate each cause and effect
> - use language and details appropriate to the audience

Options for Organization

Your organization will depend on your topic and your purpose for writing.

Option 1: Effect-to-Cause Organization If you want to explain the causes of an event, such as the closing of a factory, you might first state the effect and then examine its causes.

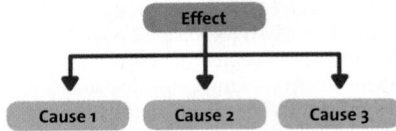

Option 2: Cause-to-Effect Organization If your focus is on explaining the effects of an event, such as the passage of a law, you might first state the cause and then explain the effects.

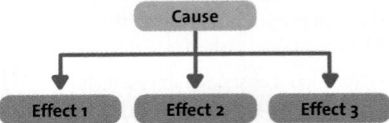

Option 3: Cause-Effect Chain Organization Sometimes you'll want to describe a chain of cause-effect relationships to explore a topic, such as the disappearance of tropical rain forests or the development of home computers.

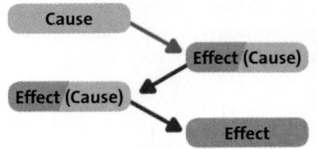

TIP Don't assume that a cause-effect relationship exists just because one event follows another. Look for evidence that the later event could not have happened if the first event had not caused it.

5.3 PROBLEM-SOLUTION

Problem-solution writing clearly states a problem, analyzes the problem, and proposes a solution to the problem. It can be used to identify and solve a conflict between characters, investigate global warming, or tell why the home team keeps losing.

> **RUBRIC: Standards for Writing**
>
> **Successful problem-solution writing should**
>
> - hook the reader's attention with a strong introduction
> - identify the problem and help the reader understand the issues involved
> - analyze the causes and effects of the problem
> - include quotations, facts, and statistics
> - explore possible solutions to the problem and recommend the best one(s)
> - use language, details, and a tone appropriate to the audience

Options for Organization

Your organization will depend on the goal of your problem-solution piece, your intended audience, and the specific problem you have chosen to address. The organizational methods that follow are effective for different kinds of problem-solution writing.

Option 1: Simple Problem-Solution

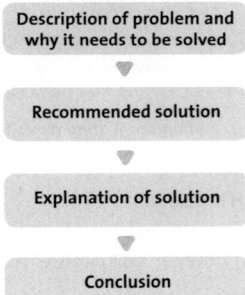

Option 2: Deciding Between Solutions

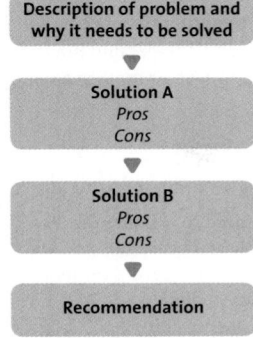

5.4 ANALYSIS

In writing an analysis, you explain how something works, how it is defined, or what its parts are.

> **RUBRIC: Standards for Writing**
>
> **A successful analysis should**
>
> - hook the reader's attention with a strong introduction
> - clearly define the subject and its parts
> - use a specific organizing structure to provide a logical flow of information
> - show connections among facts and ideas through transitional words and phrases
> - use language and details appropriate for the audience

Options for Organization

Organize your details in a logical order appropriate to the kind of analysis you're writing. Use one of the following options:

Option 1: Process Analysis A process analysis is usually organized chronologically, with steps or stages in the order they occur. You might use a process analysis to explain how to bake a pie, prepare for a test, or replace a windowpane.

EXAMPLE

Repairing a window is easy.   **Introduce process.**

You will need to measure the frame and purchase a new pane. You will also need to buy glazing compound and glazier's points.   **Give background.**

Step 1: Remove broken glass and clean frame.   **Explain steps.**

Step 2: Put glazing compound in frame; set new glass.

Step 3: Push in glazier's points to secure glass.

Step 4: Apply glazing compound to space where glass meets frame.

Option 2: Definition Analysis You can organize the details of a definition analysis in order of importance or impression. Use a definition analysis to explain a quality (such as proficiency), the distinguishing features of a sonnet, or the features of a lever.

EXAMPLE

A lever is a simple machine that allows a person to move heavy loads with less effort.   **Introduce term and definition.**

Feature 1: Force

Feature 2: Fulcrum (pivot point)   **Explain features.**

Feature 3: Load

Option 3: Parts Analysis The following parts analysis explains the parts of the intestinal tract.

EXAMPLE

The intestinal tract breaks food into particles the body can use.   **Introduce subject.**

Part 1: Mouth, esophagus, stomach

Part 2: Small intestine   **Explain parts.**

Part 3: Large intestine, appendix, rectum

*For more information, see **Writing Workshop: Analysis of an Author's Style,** pages 812–819.*

6 Persuasive Writing

Persuasive writing allows you to use the power of language to inform and influence others. It includes speeches, persuasive essays, newspaper editorials, advertisements, and critical reviews.

RUBRIC: Standards for Writing

Successful persuasive writing should

- hook the reader's attention with a strong introduction
- state the issue and the writer's position
- give opinions and support them with facts or reasons
- have a reasonable and respectful tone
- answer opposing views
- use sound logic and effective language
- conclude by summing up reasons or calling for action

*For more information, see **Writing Workshop: Persuasive Speech,** pages 650–657.*

6.1 KEY TECHNIQUES

Clarify Your Position What do you believe about the issue? How can you express your opinion most clearly?

Know Your Audience Who will read your writing? What do they already know and believe about the issue? What objections to your position might they have? What additional information might they need? What tone and approach would be most effective?

Support Your Opinion Why do you feel the way you do about the issue? What facts, statistics, examples, quotations, anecdotes, or expert opinions support your view? What reasons will convince your readers? What evidence can answer their objections?

Ways to Support Your Argument	
Statistics	facts that are stated in numbers
Examples	specific instances that explain points
Observations	events or situations you yourself have seen
Anecdotes	brief stories that illustrate points
Quotations	direct statements from authorities

*For more information, see **Identifying Faulty Reasoning**, page R24.*

Begin and End with a Bang How can you hook your readers and make a lasting impression? What memorable quotation, anecdote, or statistic will catch their attention at the beginning or stick in their minds at the end? What strong summary or call to action can you conclude with?

MODEL

Beginning

If you want to spend an evening with your neighbors, seeing a live performance or shopping for homemade crafts, will you come to the community center? Probably not. It's too hot!

End

Many people put hours and weeks into providing our town with entertainment. Often only a few people attend these events at the community center because the building is too hot on summer evenings. One "cool" solution would be to purchase an air-conditioning system.

6.2 OPTIONS FOR ORGANIZATION

In a two-sided persuasive essay, you want to show the weaknesses of other opinions as you explain the strengths of your own.

Option 1: Reasons for Your Opinion

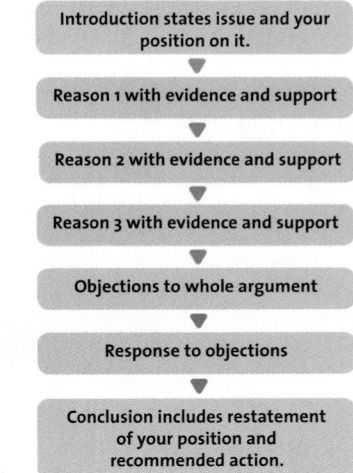

Option 2: Point-by-Point Basis

Business writing is writing done in a workplace to support the work of a company or business. Several types of formats, such as memos, letters, e-mails, applications, and bylaws, have been developed to make communication easier.

> **RUBRIC: Standards for Writing**
>
> **Successful business writing should**
> - be courteous
> - use language that is geared to its audience
> - state the purpose clearly in the opening sentences or paragraph
> - have a formal tone and not contain slang, contractions, or sentence fragments
> - use precise words
> - present only essential information
> - present details in a logical order
> - conclude with a summary of important points

7.1 KEY TECHNIQUES

Think About Your Purpose Why are you doing this writing? Do you want to promote yourself to a college admissions committee or a job interviewer? Do you want to order or complain about a product? Do you want to set up a meeting or respond to someone's ideas? Are you writing bylaws for an organization?

Identify Your Audience Who will read your writing? What background information will they need? What tone or language is appropriate?

Use a Pattern of Organization That Is Appropriate to the Content If you have to compare and contrast two products in a memo, you can use the same compare-and-contrast organization that you would use in an essay.

Support Your Points What specific details might clarify your ideas? What reasons do you have for your statements?

Finish Strongly How can you best sum up your statements? What is your main point? What action do you want the recipients to take?

Revise and Proofread Your Writing Just as you are graded on the quality of an essay you write for a class, you will be judged on the quality of your writing in the workplace.

7.2 MATCHING THE FORMAT TO THE OCCASION

E-mail messages, memos, and letters have similar purposes but are used in different situations. The chart shows how each format can be used.

Format	Occasion
Memo	Use to send correspondence **inside** the workplace only.
E-mail message	Use to send correspondence **inside or outside** the company.
Letter	Use to send correspondence **outside** the company.

TIP Remember that e-mail messages in the workplace require formal language and standard spelling, capitalization, and punctuation.

PRACTICE AND APPLY

Refer to the documents on page R43 to complete the following:

1. Draft a response to the letter. Then revise your letter as necessary according to the rubric at the beginning of this section. Make sure you have included the necessary information and have written in an appropriate tone. Proofread your letter for grammatical errors and spelling mistakes. Follow the format of the model and use appropriate spacing between elements.

2. Write a memo in response to the memo. Tell the recipient what actions you have taken. Follow the format of the model.

PRACTICE AND APPLY

ANSWERS

1. *Students' letters should include a heading, inside address, salutation, body, and closing. Students should thank Mr. D'Amato for submitting the letter and application. They should also schedule an interview with the applicant.*

2. *Students should model the memo on page R43. In their replies, students should indicate that they have sent out a brochure to Kerry Takata and have contacted the Pennsylvania alumni group regarding Tom Martinez.*

7.3 FORMATS

Business letters usually have a formal tone and a specific format as shown below. The keys to writing a business letter are to get to the point as quickly as possible and to present your information clearly.

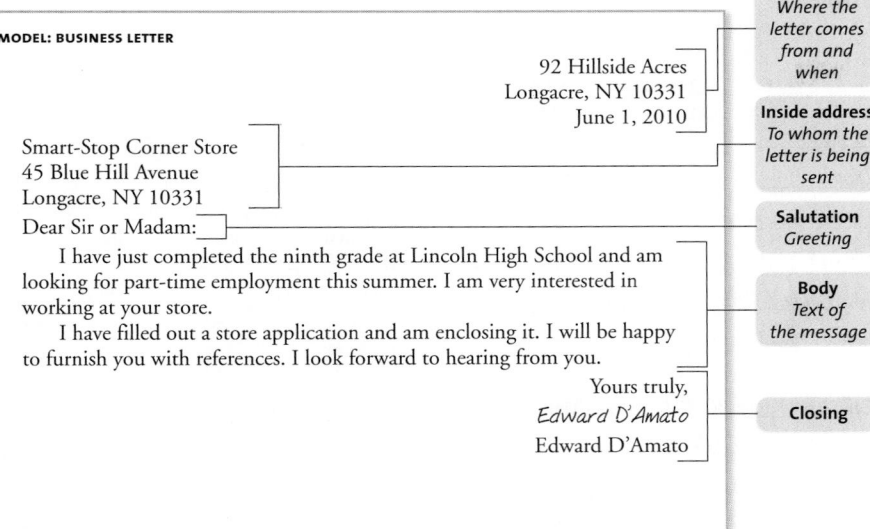

MODEL: BUSINESS LETTER

92 Hillside Acres
Longacre, NY 10331
June 1, 2010

Smart-Stop Corner Store
45 Blue Hill Avenue
Longacre, NY 10331

Dear Sir or Madam:

    I have just completed the ninth grade at Lincoln High School and am looking for part-time employment this summer. I am very interested in working at your store.

    I have filled out a store application and am enclosing it. I will be happy to furnish you with references. I look forward to hearing from you.

Yours truly,
Edward D'Amato
Edward D'Amato

Heading
Where the letter comes from and when

Inside address
To whom the letter is being sent

Salutation
Greeting

Body
Text of the message

Closing

Memos are often used in workplaces as a way of conveying information in a direct and concise manner. They can be used to announce or summarize meetings and to request actions or specific information.

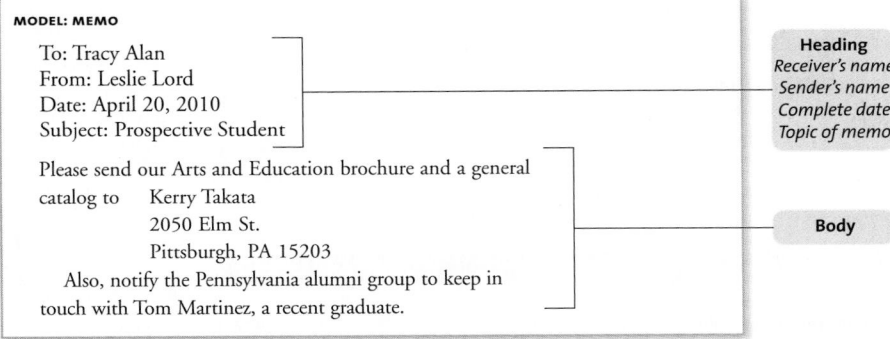

MODEL: MEMO

To: Tracy Alan
From: Leslie Lord
Date: April 20, 2010
Subject: Prospective Student

Please send our Arts and Education brochure and a general catalog to   Kerry Takata
            2050 Elm St.
            Pittsburgh, PA 15203
Also, notify the Pennsylvania alumni group to keep in touch with Tom Martinez, a recent graduate.

Heading
Receiver's name
Sender's name
Complete date
Topic of memo

Body

TIP Don't forget to write the topic of your memo in the subject line. This will help the receiver determine the importance of your memo.

When you apply for a job, you may be asked to fill out an application form. Application forms vary, but most of them ask for similar kinds of information. (If you are mailing your application, you may want to include a brief letter.)

MODEL: JOB APPLICATION

EASY-STOP CORNER STORE
EMPLOYMENT APPLICATION

Date _June 1, 2008_

Name _Daniel_ _Allen_ _Geraci_
　　　FIRST　　　　　　　　MIDDLE　　　　　　LAST

Address _53 Sunset Path_ _Austin,_ _Texas_ _75207_
　　　　　STREET　　　　　　CITY　　　　　STATE　　ZIP

Phone _214-443-9447_ Social Security Number _535-89-7779_

Date of Birth _July 7, 1993_ Place of Birth _Dallas, Texas_

Have you been employed here before? ____ Yes _x_ No

AVAILABILITY
Date You Can Start _June 30, 2010_ Full Time ____ Part Time _x_ Summer _x_

Total Hours Available per Week _20_

If hired, and you are under 16, can you furnish proof of age and/or a work permit?

_x_ Yes ____ No

EDUCATION
Highest Grade Completed (circle one)

Middle 6 7 8　　High ⑨ 10 11 12　　College 13 14 15 16

College _N/A_ From _N/A_ To _N/A_

High School _James Bowie_ From _2007_ To _2008_

Middle School _Fulmore Middle School_ From _2004_ To _2007_

REFERENCES

1 _____

PRACTICE AND APPLY

Refer to the documents on pages R44 and R45 to complete the following:

1. Visit a business and request an employment application for a job you would like to have. Make sure you understand what each question is asking before you begin to write. Fill out the application as neatly and completely as possible.

2. Write a set of bylaws for an organization that you already belong to or one that you would like to form. Follow the format of the document on page R45.

PRACTICE AND APPLY

ANSWERS

1. *Have students fill out the application. Encourage them to verify that the information is correct before turning in their applications.*

2. *Students' bylaws should include a mission statement, a description of activities, membership requirements, election laws, rules for meetings, and other pertinent information.*

Sometimes you may have to write technical documents, such as a list of procedures for conducting a meeting, a manual on rules of behavior, or the minutes of a meeting. These documents contain written descriptions of rules, regulations, and meetings and enable organizations and businesses to run smoothly.

These bylaws for a drama club include a description of the organization and detailed information about how the club operates. The writer began each section with a heading, so that readers could easily find information. The writer was also very specific, so that readers would not misunderstand the rules.

MODEL: BYLAWS DOCUMENT

Central High School Drama Club Bylaws

We, the current members of the Central High School Drama Club, create the following laws for our organization. Our members include actors, scenery designers, makeup artists, costume designers, lighting and sound specialists, stagehands, and stage managers.

MISSION STATEMENT: To provide an organization through which members of the dramatic arts program at Central High School heighten awareness of theater in the school and provide entertainment for the community

ACTIVITIES
- Biweekly meetings to talk about concerns and programming
- Publicity for upcoming school productions
- Performances, including two major drama productions

MEMBERSHIP REQUIREMENTS

To qualify for membership in the Drama Club, a candidate must
- be enrolled as a student at Central High School
- complete ten hours of participation in a school or community production

To remain a member of the Drama Club, an individual must
- actively contribute to the goals of the club
- complete a minimum of five hours of production participation each year

OFFICER ELECTION LAWS

Each year the members will vote for a president, a vice-president, a treasurer, and a secretary.
1. Each individual running for office must be nominated by another Drama Club member.
2. To be elected, a nominee must receive a majority of the votes.

RULES OF ORDER FOR MEETINGS
1. All meetings will be conducted according to *Robert's Rules of Order*.
2. A quorum of five members must be present for discussion of business items and voting.
3. The president will call the meeting to order.
4. The secretary will record, distribute, and manage meeting minutes.

Writing that has a lot of mistakes can confuse or even annoy a reader. A business letter with a punctuation error might lead to a miscommunication and delay a reply. Or a sentence fragment might lower your grade on an essay. Paying attention to grammar, punctuation, and capitalization rules can make your writing clearer and easier to read.

Quick Reference: Parts of Speech

PART OF SPEECH	FUNCTION	EXAMPLES
Noun	names a person, a place, a thing, an idea, a quality, or an action	
Common	serves as a general name, or a name common to an entire group	poet, novel, love, journey
Proper	names a specific, one-of-a-kind person, place, or thing	Lewis, Jackson, Pleasant Street, Stanley Cup
Singular	refers to a single person, place, thing, or idea	child, park, flower, truth
Plural	refers to more than one person, place, thing, or idea	children, parks, flowers, truths
Concrete	names something that can be perceived by the senses	roof, flash, Dublin, battle
Abstract	names something that cannot be perceived by the senses	intelligence, fear, joy, loneliness
Compound	expresses a single idea through a combination of two or more words	haircut, father-in-law, Christmas Eve
Collective	refers to a group of people or things	army, flock, class, species
Possessive	shows who or what owns something	Strafford's, Bess's, children's, witnesses'
Pronoun	takes the place of a noun or another pronoun	
Personal	refers to the person making a statement, the person(s) being addressed, or the person(s) or thing(s) the statement is about	I, me, my, mine, we, us, our, ours, you, your, yours, she, he, it, her, him, hers, his, its, they, them, their, theirs
Reflexive	follows a verb or preposition and refers to a preceding noun or pronoun	myself, yourself, herself, himself, itself, ourselves, yourselves, themselves
Intensive	emphasizes a noun or another pronoun	(same as reflexives)
Demonstrative	points to one or more specific persons or things	this, that, these, those
Interrogative	signals a question	who, whom, whose, which, what
Indefinite	refers to one or more persons or things not specifically mentioned	both, all, most, many, anyone, everybody, several, none, some
Relative	introduces an adjective clause by relating it to a word in the clause	who, whom, whose, which, that

PART OF SPEECH	FUNCTION	EXAMPLES
Verb	expresses an action, a condition, or a state of being	
Action	tells what the subject does or did, physically or mentally	run, reaches, listened, consider, decides, dreamed
Linking	connects the subject to something that identifies or describes it	am, is, are, was, were, sound, taste, appear, feel, become, remain, seem
Auxiliary	precedes the main verb in a verb phrase	be, have, do, can, could, will, would, may, might
Transitive	directs the action toward someone or something; always has an object	The storm **sank** the ship.
Intransitive	does not direct the action toward someone or something; does not have an object	The ship **sank.**
Adjective	modifies a noun or pronoun	**strong** women, **two** epics, **enough** time
Adverb	modifies a verb, an adjective, or another adverb	walked **out, really** funny, **far** away
Preposition	relates one word to another word	at, by, for, from, in, of, on, to, with
Conjunction	joins words or word groups	
Coordinating	joins words or word groups used the same way	and, but, or, for, so, yet, nor
Correlative	used as a pair to join words or word groups used the same way	both . . . and, either . . . or, neither . . . nor
Subordinating	introduces a clause that cannot stand by itself as a complete sentence	although, after, as, before, because, when, if, unless
Interjection	expresses emotion	wow, ouch, hurrah

Quick Reference: The Sentence and Its Parts

The diagrams that follow will give you a brief review of the essentials of a sentence and some of its parts.

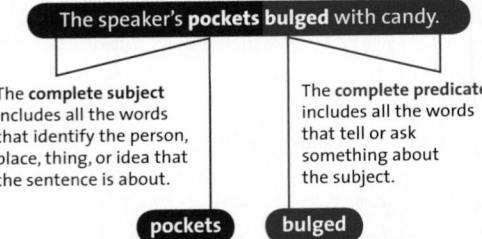

The speaker's **pockets bulged** with candy.

The **complete subject** includes all the words that identify the person, place, thing, or idea that the sentence is about.

The **complete predicate** includes all the words that tell or ask something about the subject.

pockets

bulged

The **simple subject** tells exactly whom or what the sentence is about. It may be one word or a group of words, but it does not include modifiers.

The **simple predicate**, or **verb**, tells what the subject does or is. It may be one word or several, but it does not include modifiers.

Every word in a sentence is part of a complete subject or a complete predicate.

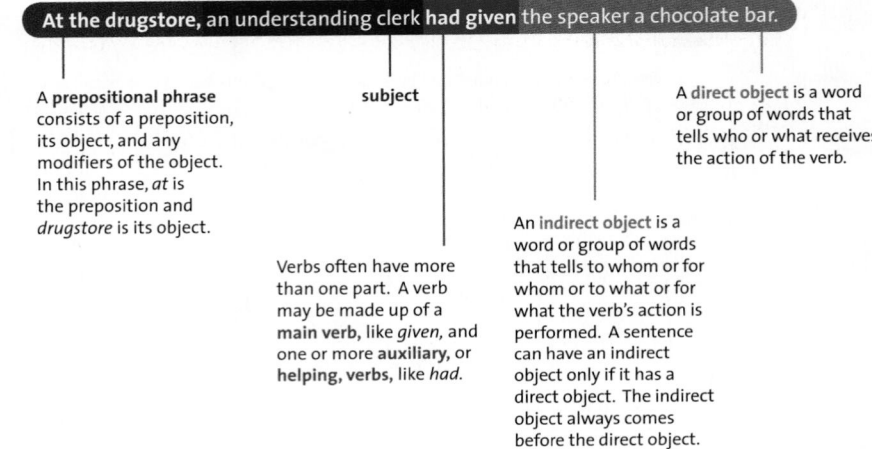

At the drugstore, an understanding clerk **had given** the speaker a chocolate bar.

A **prepositional phrase** consists of a preposition, its object, and any modifiers of the object. In this phrase, *at* is the preposition and *drugstore* is its object.

subject

A **direct object** is a word or group of words that tells who or what receives the action of the verb.

An **indirect object** is a word or group of words that tells to whom or for whom or to what or for what the verb's action is performed. A sentence can have an indirect object only if it has a direct object. The indirect object always comes before the direct object.

Verbs often have more than one part. A verb may be made up of a **main verb**, like *given*, and one or more **auxiliary**, or **helping**, **verbs**, like *had*.

Quick Reference: Punctuation

MARK	FUNCTION	EXAMPLES
End Marks period, question mark, exclamation point	ends a sentence	We can start now. When would you like to leave? What a fantastic hit!
period	follows an initial or abbreviation **Exception:** postal abbreviations of states	Mrs. Dorothy Parker, McDougal Littell Inc., C. P. Cavafy, P.M., A.D., lb., oz., Blvd., Dr. NE (Nebraska), NV (Nevada)
period	follows a number or letter in an outline	I. Volcanoes A. Central-vent 1. Shield
Comma	separates part of a compound sentence	I had never disliked poetry, but now I really love it.
	separates items in a series	She is brave, loyal, and kind.
	separates adjectives of equal rank that modify the same noun	The slow, easy route is best.
	sets off a term of address	Maria, how can I help you? You must do something, soldier.
	sets off a parenthetical expression	Hard workers, as you know, don't quit. I'm not a quitter, believe me.
	sets off an introductory word, phrase, or dependent clause	Yes, I forgot my key. At the beginning of the day, I feel fresh. While she was out, I was here. Having finished my chores, I went out.
	sets off a nonessential phrase or clause	Ed Pawn, the captain of the chess team, won. Ed Pawn, who is the captain, won. The two leading runners, sprinting toward the finish line, finished in a tie.
	sets off parts of dates and addresses	Mail it by May 14, 2010, to the Hauptman Company, 321 Market Street, Memphis, Tennessee.
	follows the salutation and closing of a letter	Dear Jim, Sincerely yours,
	separates words to avoid confusion	By noon, time had run out. What the minister does, does matter. While cooking, Jim burned his hand.
Semicolon	separates items that contain commas in a series	We spent the first week of summer vacation in Chicago, Illinois; the second week in St. Louis, Missouri; and the third week in Albany, New York.
	separates parts of a compound sentence that are not joined by a coordinating conjunction	The last shall be first; the first shall be last. I read the Bible; however, I have not memorized it.
	separates parts of a compound sentence when the parts contain commas	After I ran out of money, I called my parents; but only my sister was home, unfortunately.

MARK	FUNCTION	EXAMPLES
Colon	introduces a list	Those we wrote were the following: Dana, John, and Will.
	introduces a long quotation	Abraham Lincoln wrote: "Four score and seven years ago, our fathers brought forth on this continent a new nation. . . ."
	follows the salutation of a business letter	To Whom It May Concern: Dear Leonard Atole:
	separates certain numbers	1:28 P.M., Genesis 2:5
Dash	indicates an abrupt break in thought	I was thinking of my mother—who is arriving tomorrow—just as you walked in.
Parentheses	enclose less important material	It was so unlike him (John is always on time) that I began to worry. The last World Series game (did you see it?) was fun.
Hyphen	joins parts of a compound adjective before a noun	The not-so-rich taxpayer won't stand for this!
	joins part of a compound with *all-*, *ex-*, *self-*, or *-elect*	The ex-firefighter helped rescue him. Our president-elect is self-conscious.
	joins part of a compound number (to ninety-nine)	Today, I turned twenty-one.
	joins part of a fraction	My cup is one-third full.
	joins a prefix to a word beginning with a capital letter	Which Pre-Raphaelite painter do you like best? It snowed in mid-October.
	indicates that a word is divided at the end of a line	How could you have any reasonable expect-ations of getting a new computer?
Apostrophe	used with *s* to form the possessive of a noun or an indefinite pronoun	my friend's book, my friends' books, anyone's guess, somebody else's problem
	replaces one or more omitted letters in a contraction or numbers in a date	don't (omitted *o*), he'd (omitted *woul*), the class of '99 (omitted *19*)
	used with *s* to form the plural of a letter	I had two A's on my report card.
Quotation Marks	set off a speaker's exact words	Sara said, "I'm finally ready." "I'm ready," Sara said, "finally." Did Sara say, "I'm ready"? Sara said, "I'm ready!"
	set off the title of a story, article, short poem, essay, song, or chapter	I liked McLean's "Marine Corps Issue" and Roethke's "My Papa's Waltz." I like Joplin's "Me and Bobby McGee."
Ellipses	replace material omitted from a quotation	"When in the course of human events . . . and to assume among the powers of the earth. . . ."
Italics	indicate the title of a book, play, magazine, long poem, opera, film, or TV series, or the name of a ship	*The House on Mango Street, Hamlet, Newsweek, the Odyssey, Madama Butterfly, Gone with the Wind, Seinfeld,* USS *Constitution*

Quick Reference: Capitalization

CATEGORY	EXAMPLES
People and Titles	
Names and initials of people	Amy Tan, W. H. Auden
Titles used before names	Professor Holmes, Senator Long
Deities and members of religious groups	Jesus, Allah, Buddha, Zeus, Baptists, Roman Catholics
Names of ethnic and national groups	Hispanics, Jews, African Americans
Geographical Names	
Cities, states, countries, continents	Philadelphia, Kansas, Japan, Europe
Regions, bodies of water, mountains	the South, Lake Baikal, Mount Everest
Geographic features, parks	Great Basin, Yellowstone National Park
Streets and roads, planets	318 East Sutton Drive, Charles Court, Jupiter, Pluto
Organizations, Events, Etc.	
Companies, organizations, teams	Ford Motor Company, Boy Scouts of America, St. Louis Cardinals
Buildings, bridges, monuments	Empire State Building, Eads Bridge, Washington Monument
Documents, awards	Declaration of Independence, Stanley Cup
Special named events	Mardi Gras, World Series
Government bodies, historical periods and events	U.S. Senate, House of Representatives, Middle Ages, Vietnam War
Days and months, holidays	Thursday, March, Thanksgiving, Labor Day
Specific cars, boats, trains, planes	Porsche, *Mississippi Queen*, *Stourbridge Lion*, Concorde
Proper Adjectives	
Adjectives formed from proper nouns	French cooking, Freudian psychology, Edwardian age, Midwestern university
First Words and the Pronoun *I*	
First word in a sentence or quotation	This is it. He said, "Let's go."
First word of sentence in parentheses that is not within another sentence	The spelling rules are covered in another section. (Consult that section for more information.)
First words in the salutation and closing of a letter	Dear Madam, Very truly yours,
First word in each line of most poetry Personal pronoun *I*	Then am I A happy fly If I live Or if I die.
First word, last word, and all important words in a title	*A Tale of Two Cities*, "The World Is Too Much with Us"

For more help with pronouns, see

G GRAMMAR FOR WRITING
pp. 9–13, 178–207

For more help with nouns, see

G GRAMMAR FOR WRITING
pp. 6–8

1 Nouns

A **noun** is a word used to name a person, a place, a thing, an idea, a quality, or an action. Nouns can be classified in several ways.

*For more information on different types of nouns, see **Quick Reference: Parts of Speech**, page R46.*

1.1 COMMON NOUNS

Common nouns are general names, common to entire groups.

1.2 PROPER NOUNS

Proper nouns name specific, one-of-a-kind people, places, and things.

Common	Proper
guitarist, museum, lake, month	B. B. King, Rock and Roll Hall of Fame, Lake Pontchartrain, February

*For more information, see **Quick Reference: Capitalization**, page R51.*

1.3 SINGULAR AND PLURAL NOUNS

A noun may take a singular or a plural form, depending on whether it names a single person,

Singular	Plural
stage, city, foot	stages, cities, feet

place, thing, or idea or more than one. Make sure you use appropriate spellings when forming plurals.

*For more information, see **Forming Plural Nouns**, page R74.*

1.4 POSSESSIVE NOUNS

A **possessive noun** shows who or what owns something.

*For more information, see **Forming Possessives**, page R74.*

2 Pronouns

A **pronoun** is a word that is used in place of a noun or another pronoun. The word or word group to which the pronoun refers is called its **antecedent.**

2.1 PERSONAL PRONOUNS

Personal pronouns change their form to express person, number, gender, and case. The forms of these pronouns are shown in the following chart.

	Nominative	Objective	Possessive
Singular			
First person	I	me	my, mine
Second person	you	you	your, yours
Third person	she, he, it	her, him, it	her, hers, his, its
Plural			
First person	we	us	our, ours
Second person	you	you	your, yours
Third person	they	them	their, theirs

2.2 AGREEMENT WITH ANTECEDENT

Pronouns should agree with their antecedents in number, gender, and person.

If an antecedent is singular, use a singular pronoun.
> EXAMPLE: *I lost my new **cell phone**. I may have left it on the bus.*

If an antecedent is plural, use a plural pronoun.
> EXAMPLES: *Take the **snacks** out of the grocery bag and put them in the pantry.*
> ***Delores and Arnetta** rode their bikes to the park.*

The gender of a pronoun must be the same as the gender of its antecedent.
> EXAMPLE: *The **man** thought he left his hat in the room. He ran back to it to look for the hat.*

The person of the pronoun must be the same as the person of its antecedent. As the chart in Section 2.1 shows, a pronoun can be in first-, second-, or third-person form.
> EXAMPLE: *You folks will have to go to the stadium to buy your tickets for the concert.*

GRAMMAR PRACTICE

Rewrite each sentence so that the underlined pronoun agrees with its antecedent.

1. The story "A Sound of Thunder" tells about a man who travels back in time and <u>its</u> adventures.
2. The man behind the desk warns Eckels, "If you disobey instructions, there will be a stiff penalty upon <u>our</u> return."
3. Eckels panics at the size of the dinosaur and <u>his</u> enormous teeth.
4. Travis looks at Eckels's shoes and notices dirt on <u>it</u>.
5. Travis feels <u>they</u> has to kill Eckels, so he shoots him.

2.3 PRONOUN CASE

Personal pronouns change form to show how they function in sentences. Different functions are shown by different **cases.** The three cases are **nominative, objective,** and **possessive.** For examples of these pronouns, see the chart in Section 2.1.

A **nominative pronoun** is used as a subject or a predicate nominative in a sentence.

An **objective pronoun** is used as a direct object, an indirect object, or the object of a preposition.

SUBJECT   OBJECT
He will lead them to us.
OBJECT OF PREPOSITION

A **possessive pronoun** shows ownership. The pronouns *mine, yours, hers, his, its, ours,* and *theirs* can be used in place of nouns.
EXAMPLE: *This horse is mine.*

The pronouns *my, your, her, his, its, our,* and *their* are used before nouns.
EXAMPLE: *This is my horse.*

WATCH OUT! Many spelling errors can be avoided if you watch out for *its* and *their.* Don't confuse the possessive pronoun *its* with the contraction *it's,* meaning "it is" or "it has." The homonyms *they're* (a contraction of *they are*) and *there* ("in that place" or an expletive) are often mistakenly used for *their.*

TIP To decide which pronoun to use in a comparison, such as "He tells better tales than (I *or* me)," fill in the missing word(s): *He tells better tales than I tell.*

GRAMMAR PRACTICE

Replace the underlined words in each sentence with an appropriate pronoun and identify the pronoun as nominative, objective, or possessive.

1. In "The Necklace," <u>Mme. Loisel</u> was not happy about her life.
2. Mme. Loisel married a clerk but wished <u>the couple</u> could be wealthy.
3. She hated <u>the apartment's</u> dirty walls.
4. One evening <u>Mme. Loisel's</u> husband said, "I have something for you."
5. Mme. Loisel's reaction to the party invitation was puzzling to <u>M. Loisel</u>.

2.4 REFLEXIVE AND INTENSIVE PRONOUNS

These pronouns are formed by adding *-self* or *-selves* to certain personal pronouns. Their forms are the same, and they differ only in how they are used.

A **reflexive pronoun** follows a verb or preposition and reflects back on an earlier noun or pronoun.
EXAMPLES: *He likes himself too much.*
She is now herself again.

Intensive pronouns intensify or emphasize the nouns or pronouns to which they refer.
EXAMPLES: *They themselves will educate their children.*
You did it yourself.

WATCH OUT! Avoid using *hisself* or *theirselves.* Standard English does not include these forms.
NONSTANDARD: *The sniper kept hisself hidden behind a chimney.*
STANDARD: *The sniper kept himself hidden behind a chimney.*

GRAMMAR PRACTICE
ANSWERS
1. *The story "A Sound of Thunder" tells about a man who travels back in time and <u>his</u> adventures.*
2. *The man behind the desk warns Eckels, "If you disobey instructions, there will be a stiff penalty upon <u>your</u> return."*
3. *Eckels panics at the size of the dinosaur and <u>its</u> enormous teeth.*
4. *Travis looks at Eckels's shoes and notices dirt on <u>them</u>.*
5. *Travis feels <u>he</u> has to kill Eckels, so he shoots him.*

GRAMMAR PRACTICE
ANSWERS
1. *she; nominative*
2. *they; nominative*
3. *its; possessive*
4. *her; possessive*
5. *him; objective*

2.5 DEMONSTRATIVE PRONOUNS

Demonstrative pronouns point out things and persons near and far.

	Singular	Plural
Near	this	these
Far	that	those

2.6 INDEFINITE PRONOUNS

Indefinite pronouns do not refer to specific persons or things and usually have no antecedents. The chart shows some commonly used indefinite pronouns.

Singular	Plural	Singular or Plural	
another	both	all	most
anybody	few	any	none
no one	many	more	some
neither	several		

TIP Indefinite pronouns that end in *one, body,* or *thing* are always singular.

INCORRECT: *Did everybody play their part well?*
CORRECT: *Did everybody play his or her part well?*

If the indefinite pronoun might denote either a male or a female, *his or her* may be used to refer to it, or the sentence may be recast.

EXAMPLES: *Did everybody play his or her part well?*
Did all the students play their parts well?

2.7 INTERROGATIVE PRONOUNS

An **interrogative pronoun** tells a reader or listener that a question is coming. The interrogative pronouns are *who, whom, whose, which,* and *what.*

EXAMPLES: *Who is going to rehearse with you?*
From whom did you receive the script?

TIP *Who* is used as a subject; *whom,* as an object. To find out which pronoun you need to use in a question, change the question to a statement.

QUESTION: *(Who/Whom) did you meet there?*
STATEMENT: *You met (?) there.*

Since the verb has a subject (*you*), the needed word must be the object form, *whom.*

EXAMPLE: *Whom did you meet there?*

WATCH OUT! A special problem arises when you use an interrupter, such as *do you think,* within a question.

EXAMPLE: *(Who/Whom) do you think will win?*

If you eliminate the interrupter, it is clear that the word you need is *who.*

2.8 RELATIVE PRONOUNS

Relative pronouns relate, or connect, adjective clauses to the words they modify in sentences. The noun or pronoun that a relative clause modifies is the antecedent of the relative pronoun. Here are the relative pronouns and their uses.

	Subject	Object	Possessive
Person	who	whom	whose
Thing	which	which	whose
Thing/Person	that	that	whose

Often short sentences with related ideas can be combined by using a relative pronoun to create a more effective sentence.

SHORT SENTENCE: *Poe wrote "The Raven."*
RELATED SENTENCE: *"The Raven" is one of the most famous poems in American literature.*
COMBINED SENTENCE: *Poe wrote "The Raven," which is one of the most famous poems in American literature.*

GRAMMAR PRACTICE

Write the correct form of each incorrect pronoun.

1. Whom has read "The Gift of the Magi"?

2. Jim needs money for a present for Della, so he takes his watch to the pawnshop hisself.

3. Would anybody else sell their watch to buy a Christmas present?

4. He chooses a beautiful pair of them jeweled combs for Della's hair.

5. Della sells her long hair to buy a watch chain for himself.

GRAMMAR PRACTICE

ANSWERS

1. *Who has read "The Gift of the Magi"?*

2. *Jim needs money for a present for Della, so he takes his watch to the pawnshop himself.*

3. *Would anybody else sell his or her watch to buy a Christmas present?*

4. *He chooses a beautiful pair of those jeweled combs for Della's hair.*

5. *Della sells her long hair to buy a watch chain for him.*

2.9 PRONOUN REFERENCE PROBLEMS

The referent of a pronoun should always be clear. Avoid problems by rewriting sentences.

An **indefinite reference** occurs when the pronoun *it, you,* or *they* does not clearly refer to a specific antecedent.

> UNCLEAR: *In the new production of* Romeo and Juliet, *you have more experienced actors.*
>
> CLEAR: *The new production of* Romeo and Juliet *has more experienced actors.*

A **general reference** occurs when the pronoun *it, this, that, which,* or *such* is used to refer to a general idea rather than a specific antecedent.

> UNCLEAR: *Jenna takes acting lessons. This has improved her chances of getting a part in the school play.*
>
> CLEAR: *Jenna takes acting lessons. The lessons have improved her chances of getting a part in the school play.*

Ambiguous means "having more than one possible meaning." An **ambiguous reference** occurs when a pronoun could refer to two or more antecedents.

> UNCLEAR: *Odysseus escaped from Cyclops, and he blinded him.*
>
> CLEAR: *Odysseus escaped from Cyclops, and he blinded Cyclops.*

GRAMMAR PRACTICE

Rewrite the following sentences to correct indefinite, ambiguous, and general pronoun references.

1. In Miss Lottie's yard you don't have any grass.
2. Miss Lottie plants marigolds. This makes her barren yard look strange.
3. Lizabeth and her brother throw stones at the marigolds, which ends Miss Lottie's planting.
4. Miss Lottie stares at Lizabeth as if she is strange.

3 Verbs

A **verb** is a word that expresses an action, a condition, or a state of being.

For more information, see **Quick Reference: Parts of Speech,** page R47.

3.1 ACTION VERBS

Action verbs express mental or physical activity.

> EXAMPLE: *Mr. Cho slept with the window open.*

3.2 LINKING VERBS

Linking verbs join subjects with words or phrases that rename or describe them.

> EXAMPLE: *When he awoke the next morning, his bed was wet from the rain.*

3.3 PRINCIPAL PARTS

Action and linking verbs typically have four principal parts, which are used to form verb tenses. The principal parts are the **present,** the **present participle,** the **past,** and the **past participle.**

Action verbs and some linking verbs also fall into two categories: regular and irregular. A **regular verb** is a verb that forms its past and past participle by adding *-ed* or *-d* to the present form.

Present	Present Participle	Past	Past Participle
risk	(is) risking	risked	(has) risked
solve	(is) solving	solved	(has) solved
drop	(is) dropping	dropped	(has) dropped
carry	(is) carrying	carried	(has) carried

An **irregular verb** is a verb that forms its past and past participle in some other way than by adding *-ed* or *-d* to the present form.

Present	Present Participle	Past	Past Participle
begin	(is) beginning	began	(has) begun
break	(is) breaking	broke	(has) broken
go	(is) going	went	(has) gone

3.4 VERB TENSE

The **tense** of a verb indicates the time of the action or state of being. An action or state of being can occur in the present, the past, or the future. There are six tenses, each expressing a different range of time.

GRAMMAR PRACTICE

ANSWERS

1. *Miss Lottie's yard doesn't have any grass.*
2. *Possible answer: Miss Lottie plants marigolds. The marigolds make her barren yard look strange.*
3. *Possible answer: Lizabeth and her brother throw stones at Miss Lottie's marigolds. Miss Lottie stops planting marigolds.*
4. *Miss Lottie stares at Lizabeth as if Lizabeth is strange.*

For more help with verbs, see

 GRAMMAR FOR WRITING
pp. 14–16, 128–155

The **present tense** expresses an action or state that is happening at the present time, occurs regularly, or is constant or generally true. Use the present part.

> NOW: *That snow looks deep.*
> REGULAR: *It snows every day.*
> GENERAL: *Snow falls.*

The **past tense** expresses an action that began and ended in the past. Use the past part.

> EXAMPLE: *The storyteller finished his tale.*

The **future tense** expresses an action or state that will occur. Use *shall* or *will* with the present part.

> EXAMPLE: *They will attend the next festival.*

The **present perfect tense** expresses an action or state that (1) was completed at an indefinite time in the past or (2) began in the past and continues into the present. Use *have* or *has* with the past participle.

> EXAMPLE: *Poetry has inspired many readers.*

The **past perfect tense** expresses an action in the past that came before another action in the past. Use *had* with the past participle.

> EXAMPLE: *He had built a fire before the dog ran away.*

The **future perfect tense** expresses an action in the future that will be completed before another action in the future. Use *shall have* or *will have* with the past participle.

> EXAMPLE: *They will have read the novel before they see the movie version of the tale.*

An auxiliary verb is not used with a past-tense irregular verb, but it is always used with a past-participle irregular verb.

> INCORRECT: *I have saw her before.* (*Saw* is the past tense form and shouldn't be used with *have*.)
> CORRECT: *I have seen her somewhere before.*
> INCORRECT: *I seen her before.* (*Seen* is the past participle form of an irregular verb and shouldn't be used without an auxiliary verb.)

3.5 PROGRESSIVE FORMS

The progressive forms of the six tenses show ongoing actions. Use forms of *be* with the present participles of verbs.

PRESENT PROGRESSIVE: *She is rehearsing her lines.*
PAST PROGRESSIVE: *She was rehearsing her lines.*
FUTURE PROGRESSIVE: *She will be rehearsing her lines.*
PRESENT PERFECT PROGRESSIVE: *She has been rehearsing her lines.*
PAST PERFECT PROGRESSIVE: *She had been rehearsing her lines.*
FUTURE PERFECT PROGRESSIVE: *She will have been rehearsing her lines.*

WATCH OUT! Do not shift from tense to tense needlessly. Watch out for these special cases.

- In most compound sentences and in sentences with compound predicates, keep the tenses the same.

> INCORRECT: *His boots freeze, and he shook with cold.*
> CORRECT: *His boots freeze, and he shakes with cold.*

- If one past action happens before another, do shift tenses.

> INCORRECT: *They wished they started earlier.*
> CORRECT: *They wished they had started earlier.*

GRAMMAR PRACTICE

Rewrite each sentence, using a form of the verb in parentheses. Identify each form that you use.

1. Many people (benefit) from the civil rights movement.
2. Martin Luther King Jr. (remain) a towering figure in the history of nonviolent protest.
3. King (become) the leader of the Montgomery bus boycott.
4. When he (speak) to the crowds in Washington, D.C., more than 200,000 people heard his words.
5. Our class (read) his speech "I Have a Dream."

Rewrite each sentence to correct an error in tense.

6. It is a chilly morning as Rosa Parks went to work.
7. She leaves her job early and was preparing to go out of town.
8. She boarded the bus and is taking a seat in the "colored" section.
9. After several more stops, there are no more seats in the front of the bus.
10. Rosa Parks refused to give up her seat and is arrested.

GRAMMAR PRACTICE

ANSWERS

1. *Many people benefited from the civil rights movement. (past tense)*
2. *Martin Luther King Jr. remains a towering figure in the history of nonviolent protest. (present tense)*
3. *King became the leader of the Montgomery bus boycott. (past tense)*
4. *When he spoke to the crowds in Washington, D.C., more than 200,000 people heard his words. (past tense)*
5. *Our class read his speech "I Have a Dream." (past tense)* **Alternate answer:** *Our class is reading his speech "I Have a Dream." (present progressive)*
6. *It was a chilly morning as Rosa Parks went to work.*
7. *She left her job early and prepared to go out of town.*
8. *She boarded the bus and took a seat in the "colored" section.*
9. *After several more stops, there were no more seats at the front of the bus.*
10. *Rosa Parks refused to give up her seat and was arrested.*

3.6 ACTIVE AND PASSIVE VOICE

The voice of a verb tells whether its subject performs or receives the action expressed by the verb. When the subject performs the action, the verb is in the **active voice.** When the subject is the receiver of the action, the verb is in the **passive voice.**

Compare these two sentences:

ACTIVE: *Richard Wilbur wrote "The Writer."*

PASSIVE: *"The Writer" was written by Richard Wilbur.*

To form the passive voice, use a form of *be* with the past participle of the verb.

WATCH OUT! Use the passive voice sparingly. It can make writing awkward and less direct.

AWKWARD: *"The Writer" is a poem that was written by Richard Wilbur.*

BETTER: *Richard Wilbur wrote the poem "The Writer."*

There are occasions when you will choose to use the passive voice because

- you want to emphasize the receiver: *The king was shot.*

- the doer is unknown: *My books were stolen.*

- the doer is unimportant: *French is spoken here.*

4 Modifiers

Modifiers are words or groups of words that change or limit the meanings of other words. Adjectives and adverbs are common modifiers.

4.1 ADJECTIVES

Adjectives modify nouns and pronouns by telling which one, what kind, how many, or how much.

WHICH ONE: *this, that, these, those*
EXAMPLE: *That bird is a scarlet ibis.*

WHAT KIND: *small, sick, courageous, black*
EXAMPLE: *The sick bird sways on the branch.*

HOW MANY: *some, few, ten, none, both, each*
EXAMPLE: *Both brothers stared at the bird.*

HOW MUCH: *more, less, enough, fast*
EXAMPLE: *The bird did not have enough strength to remain perched.*

4.2 PREDICATE ADJECTIVES

Most adjectives come before the nouns they modify, as in the examples above. A **predicate adjective,** however, follows a linking verb and describes the subject.

EXAMPLE: *My friends are very intelligent.*

Be especially careful to use adjectives (not adverbs) after such linking verbs as *look, feel, grow, taste,* and *smell.*

EXAMPLE: *The bread smells wonderful.*

4.3 ADVERBS

Adverbs modify verbs, adjectives, and other adverbs by telling where, when, how, or to what extent.

WHERE: *The children played outside.*
WHEN: *The author spoke yesterday.*
HOW: *We walked slowly behind the leader.*
TO WHAT EXTENT: *He worked very hard.*

Adverbs may occur in many places in sentences, both before and after the words they modify.

EXAMPLES: *Suddenly the wind shifted.*

The wind suddenly shifted.

The wind shifted suddenly.

4.4 ADJECTIVE OR ADVERB?

Many adverbs are formed by adding *-ly* to adjectives.

EXAMPLES: *sweet, sweetly; gentle, gently*

However, *-ly* added to a noun will usually yield an adjective.

EXAMPLES: *friend, friendly; woman, womanly*

4.5 COMPARISON OF MODIFIERS

Modifiers can be used to compare two or more things. The form of a modifier shows the degree of comparison. Both adjectives and adverbs have **comparative** and **superlative** forms.

The **comparative form** is used to compare two things, groups, or actions.

EXAMPLES: *His father's hands were stronger than his own.*

His father was more courageous than the other man.

For more help with modifiers, see

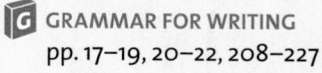 **GRAMMAR FOR WRITING** pp. 17–19, 20–22, 208–227

The **superlative form** is used to compare more than two things, groups, or actions.

> EXAMPLES: *His father's hands were the strongest in the family.*
>
> *His father was the most courageous of them all.*

4.6 REGULAR COMPARISONS

Most one-syllable and some two-syllable adjectives and adverbs have comparatives and superlatives formed by adding *-er* and *-est*. All three-syllable and most two-syllable modifiers have comparatives and superlatives formed with *more* or *most*.

Modifier	Comparative	Superlative
small	smaller	smallest
thin	thinner	thinnest
sleepy	sleepier	sleepiest
useless	more useless	most useless
precisely	more precisely	most precisely

WATCH OUT! Note that spelling changes must sometimes be made to form the comparatives and superlatives of modifiers.

> EXAMPLES: *friendly, friendlier* (Change *y* to *i* and add the ending.)
>
> *sad, sadder* (Double the final consonant and add the ending.)

4.7 IRREGULAR COMPARISONS

Some commonly used modifiers have irregular comparative and superlative forms. They are listed in the following chart. You may wish to memorize them.

Modifier	Comparative	Superlative
good	better	best
bad	worse	worst
far	farther *or* further	farthest *or* furthest
little	less *or* lesser	least
many	more	most
well	better	best
much	more	most

4.8 PROBLEMS WITH MODIFIERS

Study the tips that follow to avoid common mistakes:

Farther* and *Further Use *farther* for distances; use *further* for everything else.

Double Comparisons Make a comparison by using *-er/-est* or by using *more/most*. Using *-er* with *more* or using *-est* with *most* is incorrect.

> INCORRECT: *I like her more better than she likes me.*
>
> CORRECT: *I like her better than she likes me.*

Illogical Comparisons An illogical or confusing comparison results when two unrelated things are compared or when something is compared with itself. The word *other* or the word *else* should be used when comparing an individual member to the rest of a group.

> ILLOGICAL: *The narrator was more curious about the war than any student in his class.* (implies that the narrator isn't a student in the class)
>
> LOGICAL: *The narrator was more curious about the war than any other student in his class.* (identifies that the narrator is a student)

Bad* vs. *Badly *Bad*, always an adjective, is used before a noun or after a linking verb. *Badly*, always an adverb, never modifies a noun. Be sure to use the right form after a linking verb.

> INCORRECT: *Ed felt badly after his team lost.*
>
> CORRECT: *Ed felt bad after his team lost.*

Good* vs. *Well *Good* is always an adjective. It is used before a noun or after a linking verb. *Well* is often an adverb meaning "expertly" or "properly." *Well* can also be used as an adjective after a linking verb when it means "in good health."

> INCORRECT: *Helen writes very good.*
>
> CORRECT: *Helen writes very well.*
>
> CORRECT: *Yesterday I felt bad; today I feel well.*

Double Negatives If you add a negative word to a sentence that is already negative, the result will be an error known as a double negative. When using *not* or *-n't* with a verb, use *any-* words, such as

anybody or *anything*, rather than *no-* words, such as *nobody* or *nothing*, later in the sentence.

INCORRECT: *We haven't seen nobody.*

CORRECT: *We haven't seen anybody.*

Using *hardly*, *barely*, or *scarcely* after a negative word is also incorrect.

INCORRECT: *They couldn't barely see two feet ahead.*

CORRECT: *They could barely see two feet ahead.*

Misplaced Modifiers Sometimes a modifier is placed so far away from the word it modifies that the intended meaning of the sentence is unclear. Prepositional phrases and participial phrases are often misplaced. Place modifiers as close as possible to the words they modify.

MISPLACED: *We found the child in the park who was missing.* (The child was missing, not the park.)

CLEARER: *We found the child who was missing in the park.*

Dangling Modifiers Sometimes a modifier doesn't appear to modify any word in a sentence. Most dangling modifiers are participial phrases or infinitive phrases.

DANGLING: *Looking out the window, his brother was seen driving by.*

CLEARER: *Looking out the window, Josh saw his brother driving by.*

GRAMMAR PRACTICE

Choose the correct word or words from each pair in parentheses.

1. *The House on Mango Street* gives (better, more better) insight into Mexican-American culture than any other book I've read.

2. Sandra Cisneros's family moved so often that she hardly had (any, no) friends.

3. She felt (bad, badly) that she didn't live in a perfect house like the ones she saw on TV.

4. At one time Cisneros didn't think (nothing, anything) was positive about belonging to a different culture.

GRAMMAR PRACTICE

Rewrite each sentence that contains a misplaced or dangling modifier. Write "correct" if the sentence is written correctly.

1. The house on Loomis Street belongs to Esperanza's family with the broken water pipes.

2. Esperanza has to carry water from the house in empty milk jugs.

3. A nun asks Esperanza where she lived.

4. Feeling bad about the nun's reaction, the house is no longer good enough for Esperanza.

5 The Sentence and Its Parts

A **sentence** is a group of words used to express a complete thought. A complete sentence has a subject and a predicate.

For more information, see **Quick Reference: The Sentence and Its Parts**, *page R48.*

5.1 KINDS OF SENTENCES

There are four basic types of sentences.

Type	Definition	Example
Declarative	states a fact, a wish, an intent, or a feeling	Joan Bauer understands youths.
Interrogative	asks a question	Did you read "Pancakes"?
Imperative	gives a command or direction	Read the story.
Exclamatory	expresses strong feeling or excitement	The story is funny!

5.2 COMPOUND SUBJECTS AND PREDICATES

A compound subject consists of two or more subjects that share the same verb. They are typically joined by the coordinating conjunction *and* or *or*.

EXAMPLE: *A short story or novel will keep you engaged.*

A compound predicate consists of two or more predicates that share the same subject. They too are typically joined by a coordinating conjunction, usually *and*, *but*, or *or*.

GRAMMAR PRACTICE

ANSWERS

1. *better*

2. *any*

3. *bad*

4. *anything*

GRAMMAR PRACTICE

ANSWERS

1. *The house with the broken water pipes on Loomis Street belongs to Esperanza's family.*

2. *correct*

3. *A nun asks Esperanza where she lives.*

4. *Feeling bad about the nun's reaction, Esperanza no longer thinks the house is good enough.*

For more help with the sentence and its parts, see

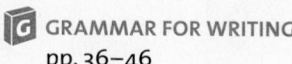 **GRAMMAR FOR WRITING**
   pp. 36–46

For more help with phrases, see

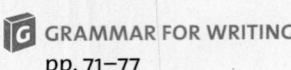

GRAMMAR FOR WRITING
pp. 64–70

For more help with verbals and verbal
phrases, see

GRAMMAR FOR WRITING
pp. 71–77

EXAMPLE: *The class finished all the poetry but did
not read the short stories.*

5.3 COMPLEMENTS

A **complement** is a word or group of words that
completes the meaning of the sentence. Some
sentences contain only a subject and a verb.
Most sentences, however, require additional
words placed after the verb to complete the
meaning of the sentence. There are three kinds of
complements: direct objects, indirect objects, and
subject complements.

Direct objects are words or word groups that
receive the action of action verbs. A direct object
answers the question *what* or *whom*.

EXAMPLES: *The students asked many questions.*
(Asked what?)
The teacher quickly answered the students.
(Answered whom?)

Indirect objects tell to whom or what or for whom
or what the actions of verbs are performed.
Indirect objects come before direct objects. In
the examples that follow, the indirect objects are
highlighted.

EXAMPLES: *My sister usually gave her friends good
advice.* (Gave to whom?)
Her brother sent the store a heavy package.
(Sent to what?)

Subject complements come after linking verbs
and identify or describe the subjects. A subject
complement that names or identifies a subject
is called a **predicate nominative.** Predicate
nominatives include **predicate nouns** and
predicate pronouns.

EXAMPLES: *My friends are very hard workers.*
The best writer in the class is she.

A subject complement that describes a subject is
called a **predicate adjective.**

EXAMPLE: *The pianist appeared very energetic.*

6 Phrases

A **phrase** is a group of related words that does not
contain a subject and a predicate but functions in
a sentence as a single part of speech.

6.1 PREPOSITIONAL PHRASES

A **prepositional phrase** is a phrase that consists
of a preposition, its object, and any modifiers of
the object. Prepositional phrases that modify
nouns or pronouns are called **adjective phrases.**
Prepositional phrases that modify verbs, adjectives,
or adverbs are **adverb phrases.**

ADJECTIVE PHRASE: *The central character of the story
is a villain.*

ADVERB PHRASE: *He reveals his nature in the first scene.*

6.2 APPPOSITIVES AND APPOSITIVE PHRASES

An **appositive** is a noun or pronoun that identifies
or renames another noun or pronoun. An
appositive phrase includes an appositive and
modifiers of it.

An appositive can be either **essential** or
nonessential. An **essential appositive** provides
information that is needed to identify what is
referred to by the preceding noun or pronoun.

EXAMPLE: *The book is about the author Richard
Wright.*

A **nonessential appositive** adds extra information
about a noun or pronoun whose meaning is
already clear. Nonessential appositives and
appositive phrases are set off with commas.

EXAMPLE: *The book, an autobiography, tells how he
began writing.*

7 Verbals and Verbal Phrases

A **verbal** is a verb form that is used as a noun,
an adjective, or an adverb. A **verbal phrase**
consists of a verbal along with its modifiers and
complements. There are three kinds of verbals:
infinitives, participles, and **gerunds.**

7.1 INFINITIVES AND INFINITIVE PHRASES

An **infinitive** is a verb form that usually begins with *to* and functions as a noun, an adjective, or an adverb. An **infinitive phrase** consists of an infinitive plus its modifiers and complements. The examples that follow show several uses of infinitive phrases.

NOUN: *To know her is my only desire.* (subject)
I'm planning to walk with you. (direct object)
Her goal was to promote women's rights. (predicate nominative)

ADJECTIVE: *We saw his need to be loved.* (adjective modifying *need*)

ADVERB: *She wrote to voice her opinions.* (adverb modifying *wrote*)

Because *to*, the sign of the infinitive, precedes infinitives, it is usually easy to recognize them. However, sometimes *to* may be omitted.

EXAMPLE: *Let no one dare [to] enter this shrine.*

7.2 PARTICIPLES AND PARTICIPIAL PHRASES

A **participle** is a verb form that functions as an adjective. Like adjectives, participles modify nouns and pronouns. Most participles are present-participle forms, ending in *-ing,* or past-participle forms ending in *-ed* or *-en.* In the examples below, the participles are highlighted.

MODIFYING A NOUN: *The dying man had a smile on his face.*

MODIFYING A PRONOUN: *Frustrated, everyone abandoned the cause.*

Participial phrases are participles with all their modifiers and complements.

MODIFYING A NOUN: *The dogs searching for survivors are well trained.*

MODIFYING A PRONOUN: *Having approved your proposal, we are ready to act.*

7.3 DANGLING AND MISPLACED PARTICIPLES

A participle or participial phrase should be placed as close as possible to the word that it modifies. Otherwise the meaning of the sentence may not be clear.

MISPLACED: *The boys were looking for squirrels searching the trees.*

CLEARER: *The boys searching the trees were looking for squirrels.*

A participle or participial phrase that does not clearly modify anything in a sentence is called a **dangling participle.** A dangling participle causes confusion because it appears to modify a word that it cannot sensibly modify. Correct a dangling participle by providing a word for the participle to modify.

DANGLING: *Running like the wind, my hat fell off.* (The hat wasn't running.)

CLEARER: *Running like the wind, I lost my hat.*

7.4 GERUNDS AND GERUND PHRASES

A **gerund** is a verb form ending in *-ing* that functions as a noun. Gerunds may perform any function nouns perform.

SUBJECT: *Running is my favorite pastime.*

DIRECT OBJECT: *I truly love running.*

INDIRECT OBJECT: *You should give running a try.*

SUBJECT COMPLEMENT: *My deepest passion is running.*

OBJECT OF PREPOSITION: *Her love of running keeps her strong.*

Gerund phrases are gerunds with all their modifiers and complements.

SUBJECT: *Wishing on a star never got me far.*

OBJECT OF PREPOSITION: *I will finish before leaving the office.*

APPOSITIVE: *Her avocation, flying airplanes, finally led to full-time employment.*

GRAMMAR PRACTICE

ANSWERS

1. *"Daughter of Invention," a short story, was written by Julia Alvarez.*

2. *The narrator loves writing to record her experiences.*

3. *She will appear at an assembly to give a speech.*

4. *Working feverishly for hours, she finally finishes her speech.*

5. *Feeling proud, she reads her speech to her parents.*

For more help with clauses, see

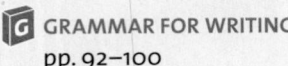
GRAMMAR FOR WRITING
pp. 92–100

---

8 Clauses

A **clause** is a group of words that contains a subject and a predicate. There are two kinds of clauses: independent clauses and subordinate clauses.

8.1 INDEPENDENT AND SUBORDINATE CLAUSES

An **independent clause** can stand alone as a sentence, as the word *independent* suggests.

> **INDEPENDENT CLAUSE:** *Taos is famous for its Great Bank Robbery.*

A sentence may contain more than one independent clause.

> **EXAMPLE:** *Many people remember the robbery, and they will tell you all about it.*

In the preceding example, the coordinating conjunction *and* joins two independent clauses.

For more information, see Coordinating Conjunction, page R47.

A **subordinate clause** cannot stand alone as a sentence. It is subordinate to, or dependent on, an independent clause.

> **EXAMPLE:** *Although the two men needed cash, they didn't get it from the bank.*

The highlighted clause cannot stand by itself.

8.2 ADJECTIVE CLAUSES

An **adjective clause** is a subordinate clause used as an adjective. It usually follows the noun or pronoun it modifies.

> **EXAMPLE:** *Tony Hillerman is someone whom millions know as a mystery writer.*

Adjective clauses are typically introduced by the relative pronoun *who, whom, whose, which,* or *that.*

For more information, see Relative Pronouns, page R54.

> **EXAMPLES:** *A person who needs money should get a job.*
>
> *The robbers, whose names were Gomez and Smith, had guns.*

An adjective clause can be either essential or nonessential. An **essential adjective clause** provides information that is necessary to identify the preceding noun or pronoun.

> **EXAMPLE:** *One robber wore a disguise that was meant to fool Taos's residents.*

A **nonessential adjective clause** adds additional information about a noun or pronoun whose meaning is already clear. Nonessential clauses are set off with commas.

> **EXAMPLE:** *The suspects, who drove away in a pickup truck, sideswiped a car driven by a minister.*

> **TIP** The relative pronouns *whom, which,* and *that* may sometimes be omitted when they are objects in adjective clauses.
>
> **EXAMPLE:** *Hillerman is a writer [whom] millions enjoy.*

8.3 ADVERB CLAUSES

An **adverb clause** is a subordinate clause that is used to modify a verb, an adjective, or an adverb. It is introduced by a subordinating conjunction.

For examples of subordinating conjunctions, see Noun Clauses, page R63.

Adverb clauses typically occur at the beginning or end of sentences.

> **MODIFYING A VERB:** *When we need you, we will call.*
>
> **MODIFYING AN ADVERB:** *I'll stay here where there is shelter from the rain.*
>
> **MODIFYING AN ADJECTIVE:** *Roman felt as good as he had ever felt.*

8.4 NOUN CLAUSES

A **noun clause** is a subordinate clause that is used as a noun. A noun clause may be used as a subject, a direct object, an indirect object, a predicate nominative, or the object of a preposition. Noun clauses are introduced either by pronouns, such as *that, what, who, whoever, which,* and *whose,* or by subordinating conjunctions, such as *how, when, where, why,* and *whether.*

*For more information, see **Quick Reference: Parts of Speech,** page R47.*

TIP Because the same words may introduce adjective and noun clauses, you need to consider how a clause functions within its sentence. To determine if a clause is a noun clause, try substituting *something* or *someone* for the clause. If you can do it, it is probably a noun clause.

EXAMPLES: *I know whose woods these are.* ("I know *something.*" The clause is a noun clause, direct object of the verb *know.*)

Give a copy to whoever wants one. ("Give a copy to *someone.*" The clause is a noun clause, object of the preposition *to.*)

GRAMMAR PRACTICE

Add descriptive details to each sentence by writing the type of clause indicated in parentheses.

1. My aunt has an interesting hobby. (adjective clause)
2. She works on her craft at night. (adverb clause)
3. She writes. (noun clause)
4. She has written several books. (adjective clause)
5. I asked her to write a story about me. (adverb clause)

9 The Structure of Sentences

When classified by their structure, there are four kinds of sentences: simple, compound, complex, and compound-complex.

9.1 SIMPLE SENTENCES

A **simple sentence** is a sentence that has one independent clause and no subordinate clauses.

The fact that such a sentence is called simple does not mean that it is uncomplicated. Various parts of simple sentences may be compound, and simple sentences may contain grammatical structures such as appositive and verbal phrases.

EXAMPLES: *Ray Bradbury, a science fiction writer, has written short stories and novels.* (appositive and compound direct object)

The narrator, recalling the years of his childhood, tells his story. (participial phrase)

9.2 COMPOUND SENTENCES

A **compound sentence** consists of two or more independent clauses. The clauses in compound sentences are joined with commas and coordinating conjunctions (*and, but, or, nor, yet, for, so*) or with semicolons. Like simple sentences, compound sentences do not contain any subordinate clauses.

EXAMPLES: *I enjoyed Bradbury's story "The Utterly Perfect Murder," and I want to read more of his stories.*

The narrator has lived a normal, complete life; however, he decides to kill his childhood playmate.

WATCH OUT! Do not confuse compound sentences with simple sentences that have compound parts.

EXAMPLE: *A subcommittee drafted a document and immediately presented it to the entire group.* (Here *and* joins parts of a compound predicate, not a compound sentence.)

9.3 COMPLEX SENTENCES

A **complex sentence** consists of one independent clause and one or more subordinate clauses. Each subordinate clause can be used as a noun or as a modifier. If it is used as a modifier, a subordinate clause usually modifies a word in the independent clause, and the independent clause can stand alone. However, when a subordinate clause is a noun clause, it is a part of the independent clause; the two cannot be separated.

GRAMMAR PRACTICE

ANSWERS

Possible answers:

1. *My aunt, who lives in Baltimore, has an interesting hobby.*
2. *She works on her craft at night when she can't sleep.*
3. *She writes whenever she gets an idea.*
4. *She has written several books that have become bestsellers.*
5. *When I visited my aunt last summer, I asked her to write a story about me.*

For more help with the structure of sentences, see

 GRAMMAR FOR WRITING
pp. 101–109

MODIFIER: *One should not complain unless one has a better solution.*

NOUN CLAUSE: *We sketched pictures of whomever we wished.* (The noun clause is the object of the preposition *of* and cannot be separated from the rest of the sentence.)

9.4 COMPOUND-COMPLEX SENTENCES

A **compound-complex sentence** contains two or more independent clauses and one or more subordinate clauses. Compound-complex sentences are, simply, both compound and complex. If you start with a compound sentence, all you need to do to form a compound-complex sentence is add a subordinate clause.

COMPOUND: *All the students knew the answer, yet they were too shy to volunteer.*

COMPOUND-COMPLEX: *All the students knew the answer that their teacher expected, yet they were too shy to volunteer.*

9.5 PARALLEL STRUCTURE

When you write sentences, make sure that coordinate parts are equivalent, or **parallel,** in structure.

NOT PARALLEL: *Erin loved basketball and to play hockey.* (*Basketball* is a noun; *to play hockey* is a phrase.)

PARALLEL: *Erin loved basketball and hockey.* (*Basketball* and *hockey* are both nouns.)

NOT PARALLEL: *He wanted to rent an apartment, a new car, and traveling around the country.* (*To rent* is an infinitive, *car* is a noun, and *traveling* is a gerund.)

PARALLEL: *He wanted to rent an apartment, to drive a new car, and to travel around the country.* (*To rent, to drive,* and *to travel* are all infinitives.)

⑩ Writing Complete Sentences

Remember, a sentence is a group of words that expresses a complete thought. In writing that you wish to share with a reader, try to avoid both sentence fragments and run-on sentences.

10.1 CORRECTING FRAGMENTS

A **sentence fragment** is a group of words that is only part of a sentence. It does not express a complete thought and may be confusing to a reader or listener. A sentence fragment may be lacking a subject, a predicate, or both.

FRAGMENT: *Waited for the boat to arrive.* (no subject)

CORRECTED: *We waited for the boat to arrive.*

FRAGMENT: *People of various races, ages, and creeds.* (no predicate)

CORRECTED: *People of various races, ages, and creeds gathered together.*

FRAGMENT: *Near the old cottage.* (neither subject nor predicate)

CORRECTED: *The burial ground is near the old cottage.*

In your writing, fragments may be a result of haste or incorrect punctuation. Sometimes fixing a fragment will be a matter of attaching it to a preceding or following sentence.

FRAGMENT: *We saw the two girls. Waiting for the bus to arrive.*

CORRECTED: *We saw the two girls waiting for the bus to arrive.*

10.2 CORRECTING RUN-ON SENTENCES

A **run-on sentence** is made up of two or more sentences written as though they were one. Some run-ons have no punctuation within them. Others may have only commas where conjunctions or stronger punctuation marks are necessary. Use your judgment in correcting run-on sentences, as you have choices. You can make a run-on two sentences if the thoughts are not closely connected. If the thoughts are closely related, you can keep the run-on as one sentence by adding a semicolon or a conjunction.

RUN-ON: *We found a place for the picnic by a small pond it was three miles from the village.*

MAKE TWO SENTENCES: *We found a place for the picnic by a small pond. It was three miles from the village.*

For more help with writing complete sentences, see

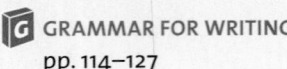 GRAMMAR FOR WRITING
pp. 114–127

RUN-ON: *We found a place for the picnic by a small pond it was perfect.*

USE A SEMICOLON: *We found a place for the picnic by a small pond; it was perfect.*

ADD A CONJUNCTION: *We found a place for the picnic by a small pond, and it was perfect.*

WATCH OUT! When you form compound sentences, make sure you use appropriate punctuation: a comma before a coordinating conjunction, a semicolon when there is no coordinating conjunction. A very common mistake is to use a comma alone instead of a comma and a conjunction. This error is called a **comma splice.**

INCORRECT: *He finished the apprenticeship, he left the village.*

CORRECT: *He finished the apprenticeship, and he left the village.*

11 Subject-Verb Agreement

The subject and verb in a clause must agree in number. Agreement means that if the subject is singular, the verb is also singular, and if the subject is plural, the verb is also plural.

11.1 BASIC AGREEMENT

Fortunately, agreement between subjects and verbs in English is simple. Most verbs show the difference between singular and plural only in the third person of the present tense. In the present tense, the third-person singular form ends in *-s.*

Present-Tense Verb Forms	
Singular	**Plural**
I sleep	we sleep
you sleep	you sleep
she, he, it sleeps	they sleep

11.2 AGREEMENT WITH *BE*

The verb *be* presents special problems in agreement, because this verb does not follow the usual verb patterns.

Forms of *Be*			
Present Tense		**Past Tense**	
Singular	**Plural**	**Singular**	**Plural**
I am	we are	I was	we were
you are	you are	you were	you were
she, he, it is	they are	she, he, it was	they were

11.3 WORDS BETWEEN SUBJECT AND VERB

A verb agrees only with its subject. When words come between a subject and a verb, ignore them when considering proper agreement. Identify the subject, and make sure the verb agrees with it.

EXAMPLES: *A story in the newspapers tells about the 1890s.*

Dad as well as Mom reads the paper daily.

11.4 AGREEMENT WITH COMPOUND SUBJECTS

Use plural verbs with most compound subjects joined by the word *and.*

EXAMPLE: *My father and his friends read the paper daily.*

To confirm that you need a plural verb, you could substitute the plural pronoun *they* for *my father and his friends.*

If a compound subject is thought of as a unit, use a singular verb. Test this by substituting the singular pronoun *it.*

EXAMPLE: *Peanut butter and jelly [it] is my brother's favorite sandwich.*

Use a singular verb with a compound subject that is preceded by *each, every,* or *many a.*

EXAMPLE: *Each novel and short story seems grounded in personal experience.*

When the parts of a compound subject are joined by *or, nor,* or the correlative conjunctions *either . . . or* or *neither . . . nor,* make the verb agree with the noun or pronoun nearest the verb.

EXAMPLES: *Cookies or ice cream is my favorite dessert.*

Either Cheryl or her friends are being invited.

Neither ice storms nor snow is predicted today.

For more help with subject-verb agreement, see

 GRAMMAR FOR WRITING
pp. 156–177

11.5 PERSONAL PRONOUNS AS SUBJECTS

When using a personal pronoun as a subject, make sure to match it with the correct form of the verb *be*. (See the chart in Section 11.2.) Note especially that the pronoun *you* takes the forms *are* and *were*, regardless of whether it is singular or plural.

WATCH OUT! *You is* and *you was* are nonstandard forms and should be avoided in writing and speaking. *We was* and *they was* are also forms to be avoided.

INCORRECT: *You was a good student.*

CORRECT: *You were a good student.*

INCORRECT: *They was starting a new school.*

CORRECT: *They were starting a new school.*

11.6 INDEFINITE PRONOUNS AS SUBJECTS

Some indefinite pronouns are always singular; some are always plural.

Singular Indefinite Pronouns			
another	either	neither	one
anybody	everybody	nobody	somebody
anyone	everyone	no one	someone
anything	everything	nothing	something
each	much		

EXAMPLES: *Each of the writers was given an award.*
Somebody in the room upstairs is sleeping.

Plural Indefinite Pronouns			
both	few	many	several

EXAMPLES: *Many of the books in our library are not in circulation.*
Few have been returned recently.

Still other indefinite pronouns may be either singular or plural.

Singular or Plural Indefinite Pronouns		
all	more	none
any	most	some

The number of the indefinite pronoun *any* or *none* often depends on the intended meaning.

EXAMPLES: *Any of these topics has potential for a good article.* (any one topic)
Any of these topics have potential for good articles. (all of the many topics)

The indefinite pronouns *all, some, more, most,* and *none* are singular when they refer to quantities or parts of things. They are plural when they refer to numbers of individual things. Context will usually give a clue.

EXAMPLES: *All of the flour is gone.* (referring to a quantity)
All of the flowers are gone. (referring to individual items)

11.7 INVERTED SENTENCES

Problems in agreement often occur in inverted sentences beginning with *here* or *there*; in questions beginning with *how, when, why, where,* or *what*; and in inverted sentences beginning with phrases. Identify the subject—wherever it is—before deciding on the verb.

EXAMPLES: *There clearly are far too many cooks in this kitchen.*
What is the correct ingredient for this stew?
Far from the embroiled cooks stands the master chef.

GRAMMAR PRACTICE

Locate the subject of each verb in parentheses in the sentences below. Then choose the correct verb form.

1. Many Greeks sail home from Troy, but few (struggles, struggle) as hard as Odysseus to get there.

2. Neither Odysseus nor his men (know, knows) what dangers lie ahead.

3. There (is, are) more dangers awaiting him than there (is, are) gods to save him.

4. Everybody who has read about Odysseus' trials (knows, know) what he endured.

5. There (is, are) few friends who can help him during his ten-year odyssey.

6. The herds of the Cyclops Polyphemus (gives, give) Odysseus an idea for escape.

7. Does anyone (escapes, escape) the spell of Circe?

8. Standing before the hogs that are his friends (is, are) Odysseus.

9. Some of the winds (blows, blow) favorably, but many (blows, blow) ill.

10. Penelope, Telemachus, and the suitors (awaits, await) Odysseus upon his return.

11.8 SENTENCES WITH PREDICATE NOMINATIVES

When a predicate nominative serves as a complement in a sentence, use a verb that agrees with the subject, not the complement.

EXAMPLES: *The speeches of Martin Luther King Jr. are a landmark in American civil rights history.* (*Speeches* is the subject—not *landmark*—and it takes the plural verb *are*.)

One landmark in American civil rights history is the speeches of Martin Luther King Jr. (The subject is *landmark*—not *speeches*—and it takes the singular verb *is*.)

11.9 *DON'T* AND *DOESN'T* AS AUXILIARY VERBS

The auxiliary verb *doesn't* is used with singular subjects and with the personal pronouns *she, he,* and *it*. The auxiliary verb *don't* is used with plural subjects and with the personal pronouns *I, we, you,* and *they*.

SINGULAR: *She doesn't know Martin Luther King's famous "I Have a Dream" speech.*

Doesn't the young woman read very much?

PLURAL: *We don't have the speech memorized.*

Don't speakers usually memorize their speeches?

11.10 COLLECTIVE NOUNS AS SUBJECTS

Collective nouns are singular nouns that name groups of persons or things. *Team,* for example, is the collective name of a group of individuals. A collective noun takes a singular verb when the group acts as a single unit. It takes a plural verb when the members of the group act separately.

EXAMPLES: *Our team usually wins.* (The team as a whole wins.)

Our team vote differently on most issues. (The individual members vote.)

11.11 RELATIVE PRONOUNS AS SUBJECTS

When the relative pronoun *who, which,* or *that* is used as a subject in an adjective clause, the verb in the clause must agree in number with the antecedent of the pronoun.

SINGULAR: *I didn't read the **poem** about fireworks that was assigned.*

The antecedent of the relative pronoun *that* is the singular *poem*; therefore, *that* is singular and must take the singular verb *was*.

PLURAL: ***William Blake and Amy Lowell,** who are very different from each other, are both outstanding poets.*

The antecedent of the relative pronoun *who* is the plural compound subject *William Blake and Amy Lowell*. Therefore *who* is plural, and it takes the plural verb *are*.

GRAMMAR PRACTICE

ANSWERS

1. *struggle*
2. *know*
3. *are; are*
4. *knows*
5. *are*
6. *give*
7. *escape*
8. *is*
9. *blow; blow*
10. *await*

The key to becoming an independent reader is to develop a toolkit of vocabulary strategies. By learning and practicing the strategies, you'll know what to do when you encounter unfamiliar words while reading. You'll also know how to refine the words you use for different situations—personal, school, and work.

Being a good speller is important when communicating your ideas in writing. Learning basic spelling rules and checking your spelling in a dictionary will help you spell words that you may not use frequently.

VOCABULARY PRACTICE
For more practice, go to the **Vocabulary Center** at ClassZone.com.

1 Using Context Clues

The context of a word is made up of the punctuation marks, words, sentences, and paragraphs that surround the word. A word's context can give you important clues about its meaning.

1.1 GENERAL CONTEXT

Sometimes you need to infer the meaning of an unfamiliar word by reading all the information in a passage.

> After twelve hours without food, I was so *ravenous* that I ate four slices of pizza, two bowls of cereal, and an ice-cream sundae.

You can figure out from the context that *ravenous* means "extremely hungry."

1.2 SPECIFIC CONTEXT CLUES

Sometimes writers help you understand the meanings of words by providing specific clues such as those shown in the chart.

1.3 IDIOMS, SLANG, AND FIGURATIVE LANGUAGE

An **idiom** is an expression whose overall meaning is different from the meaning of the individual words. **Slang** is informal language in which made-up words and ordinary words are used to mean something different from their meanings in formal English. **Figurative language** is language that communicates meaning beyond the literal meaning of the words. Use context clues to figure out the meanings of idioms, slang, and figurative language.

> The mosquitoes *drove us crazy* on our hike through the woods. (idiom; means "bothered")

> That's a really *cool* backpack that you're wearing. (slang; means "excellent" or "first-rate")

> I was angry. *Heat rose under my skin* until I felt as if *searing flames were threatening to engulf my whole body.* (figurative language; hot skin and flames symbolize anger)

Specific Context Clues		
Type of Clue	**Key Words/ Phrases**	**Example**
Definition or restatement of the meaning of the word	or, which is, that is, in other words, also known as, also called	His first conjecture, **or guess,** was correct.
Example following an unfamiliar word	such as, like, as if, for example, especially, including	She loved macabre stories, **such as those by Edgar Allan Poe and Stephen King.**
Comparison with a more familiar word or concept	as, like, also, similar to, in the same way, likewise	Despite his physical suffering, his mind was as **lucid** as any **rational** person's.
Contrast with a familiar word or experience	unlike, but, however, although, on the other hand, on the contrary	Unlike her **clumsy** partner, she was an agile dancer.
Cause-and-effect relationship in which one term is familiar	because, since, when, consequently, as a result, therefore	**Because** this perfume has such a sharp scent, **I will buy** the one with a subtle fragrance.

For more information, see **Vocabulary Strategy: Using Context Clues,** pages 371 and 457.

1.3 IDIOMS, SLANG, AND FIGURATIVE LANGUAGE

Use this opportunity to have students identify and use figurative meanings of words. For each word in the list below, have students first identify the literal meaning and then use the same word in a figurative sense:

dirt

fire

water

snake

gold

2 Analyzing Word Structure

Many words can be broken into smaller parts. These word parts include base words, roots, prefixes, and suffixes.

2.1 BASE WORDS

A **base word** is a word part that by itself is also a word. Other words or word parts can be added to base words to form new words.

2.2 ROOTS

A **root** is a word part that contains the core meaning of the word. Many English words contain roots that come from older languages such as Greek, Latin, Old English (Anglo-Saxon), and Norse. Knowing the meaning of the word's root can help you determine the word's meaning.

Root	Meaning	Examples
bi (Greek)	life	biography
gramm (Greek)	letter, something written	grammar
grad (Latin)	step, degree	graduate
man (Latin)	hand	manual
hēadfod (Old English)	head, top	headfirst

*For more information, see **Vocabulary Strategy: Word Roots**, pages 49, 204, 340, 532, and 555.*

2.3 PREFIXES

A **prefix** is a word part attached to the beginning of a word. Most prefixes come from Greek, Latin, or Old English.

Prefix	Meaning	Examples
pre-	before	**pre**school
ex-	out, from	**ex**tend
re-	again, back	**re**turn

*For more information, see **Vocabulary Strategy: Prefixes**, page 92.*

2.4 SUFFIXES

A **suffix** is a word part that appears at the end of a root or base word to form a new word. Some suffixes do not change word meaning. These suffixes are

- added to nouns to change the number of persons or objects
- added to verbs to change the tense
- added to modifiers to change the degree of comparison

Suffix	Meaning	Examples
-s, -es	to change the number of a noun	snack + s = snacks
-d, -ed, -ing	to change verb tense	walk + ed = walked
-er, -est	to change the degree of comparison in modifiers	wild + er = wilder fast + est = fastest

Other suffixes can be added to a root or base to change the word's meaning. These suffixes can also determine a word's part of speech.

Suffix	Meaning	Examples
-age	action or process	pilgrimage
-able	ability	enjoyable
-ize	to make	criticize

*For more information, see **Vocabulary Strategy: Suffixes**, page 421.*

Strategies for Understanding Unfamiliar Words

- Look for any prefixes or suffixes. Remove them to isolate the base word or the root.
- See if you recognize any elements—prefix, suffix, root, or base—of the word. You may be able to guess its meaning by analyzing one or two elements.
- Consider the way the word is used in the sentence. Use the context and the word parts to make a logical guess about the word's meaning.
- Consult a dictionary to see whether you are correct.

3.1 ETYMOLOGIES

Have students research the etymology of these words:

audience

butterfly

chronic

despot

inquire

pretty

imperial

cosmology

speak

qualm

3.3 WORDS FROM CLASSICAL MYTHOLOGY

Have students look up the etymology of each word and locate the myth associated with it. Use the information from the myth to explain the origin and meaning of each word.

3 Understanding Word Origins

3.1 ETYMOLOGIES

Etymologies show the origin and historical development of a word. When you study a word's history and origin, you can find out when, where, and how the word came to be.

> **dra•ma** (drä′mə) *n.* **1.** A work that is meant to be performed by actors. **2.** Theatrical works of a certain type or period in history. [Late Latin *drāma, drāmat-,* from Greek *drān,* to do or perform.]
>
> **for•mi•car•y** (fôr′mĭ-kĕr′ē) *n., pl.* **-ies** A nest of ants; an anthill. [Medieval Latin *formīcārium,* from Latin *formīca,* ant.]
>
> **lock²** (lŏk) *n.* **1a.** A length or curl of hair; a tress. **b.** The hair of the head. Often used in the plural. **2.** A small wisp or tuft, as of wool or cotton. [Middle English, from Old English *locc.*]

For more information, see Vocabulary Strategy: Etymologies, page 282.

3.2 WORD FAMILIES

Words that have the same root make up a word family and have related meanings. The chart shows a common Greek and a common Latin root. Notice how the meanings of the example words are related to the meanings of their roots.

Latin Root	*vid, vis:* "see"
English	**vision** eyesight
	video visual portion of a televised broadcast
	visible possible to see
Greek Root	*phonē:* "sound"
English	**homophone** word that sounds like another word
	phonetics the study of speech sounds
	telephone a device that converts voice into a form that can be transmitted as sound waves

For more information, see Vocabulary Strategy: Word Family, pages 131 and 354.

3.3 WORDS FROM CLASSICAL MYTHOLOGY

The English language includes many words from classical mythology. You can use your knowledge of Greek, Roman, and Norse myths to understand the origins and meanings of these words. For example, *herculean task* refers to the strongman Hercules. Thus *herculean task* probably means "a job that is large or difficult." The chart shows a few common words from mythology.

Greek	Roman	Norse
Achilles' heel	academy	Thursday
pandemonium	volcano	berserk
muse	cupid	rune
Midas touch	floral	valkyrie

3.4 FOREIGN WORDS

The English language has grown to include words from diverse languages such as French, Dutch, Spanish, Italian, Portuguese, and Chinese. Many of these words stayed the way they were in their original languages.

French	Dutch	Spanish	Italian
ballet	boss	canyon	diva
beret	caboose	rodeo	carnival
mirage	dock	salsa	spaghetti

4 Synonyms and Antonyms

4.1 SYNONYMS

A **synonym** is a word with a meaning similar to that of another word. You can find synonyms in a thesaurus or a dictionary. In a dictionary, synonyms are often given as part of the definition of the word. The following word pairs are synonyms:

happy/joyful   sad/unhappy

angry/mad   beautiful/lovely

4.2 ANTONYMS

An **antonym** is a word with a meaning opposite that of another word. The following word pairs are antonyms:

best/worst   well/ill

light/dark   happy/sad

5 Denotation and Connotation

5.1 DENOTATION

A word's dictionary meaning is called its **denotation.** For example, the denotation of the word *rascal* is "an unethical, dishonest person."

5.2 CONNOTATION

The images or feelings you connect to a word add a finer shade of meaning, called **connotation.** The connation of a word goes beyond its basic dictionary definition. Writers use connotations of words to communicate positive or negative feelings.

Positive	Neutral	Negative
gaze	look	glare
slender	thin	scrawny
playful	active	rowdy

Make sure you understand the denotation and connotation of a word when you read it or use it in your writing.

*For more information, see **Vocabulary Strategy: Denotation and Connotation,** pages 76, 324, and 444.*

6 Analogies

An **analogy** is a comparison between two things that are similar in some way but are otherwise dissimilar. Analogies are sometimes used in writing when unfamiliar subjects or ideas are explained in terms of familiar ones. Analogies often appear on tests as well, usually in a format like this:

bird : fly ::   A) boat : water
              B) bear : cave
              C) fish : scales
              D) fish : swim
              E) sparrow : wings

Follow these steps to determine the correct answer:

- Read the first half of the analogy as "*bird* is to *fly* as...."
- Read the answer choices as *"boat* is to *water,"* *"bear* is to *cave,"* and so on.
- Ask yourself how the words *bird* and *fly* are related. (A bird can fly.)
- Ask yourself which of the choices shows the same relationship. (A boat can't water and a bear can't cave, but a fish can swim. Therefore, the answer is D.)

7 Homonyms and Homophones

7.1 HOMONYMS

Homonyms are words that have the same spelling and sound but have different meanings.

The girl had to stoop to find her ball under the stoop.

Stoop can mean "a small porch," but an identically spelled word means "to bend down." Because the words have different meanings, each word has its own dictionary entry.

The lawyer argued the case of the missing jewelry case.

Case can mean "evidence in support of a claim." However, another identically spelled word means "container." Each word has a different meaning and its own dictionary entry.

Sometimes only one of the meanings of a homonym may be familiar to you. Use context clues to help you figure out the meaning of an unfamiliar word.

7.2 HOMOPHONES

Homophones are words that sound alike but have different meanings and spellings. The following homophones are frequently misused:

it's/its   they're/their/there

to/too/two   stationary/stationery

Many misused homophones are pronouns and contractions. Whenever you are unsure whether to write *your* or *you're* and *who's* or *whose*, ask yourself if you mean *you are* or *who is/has*. If you do, write the contraction. For other homophones, such as *fair* and *fare*, use the meaning of the word to help you decide which one to use.

8 Words with Multiple Meanings

Some words have acquired additional meanings over time that are based on the original meaning.

> *Thinking of the horror movie made my skin creep.*
> *I saw my little brother creep around the corner.*

These two uses of *creep* have different meanings, but both of them have the same origin. You will find all the meanings of *creep* listed in one entry in the dictionary.

*For more information, see **Vocabulary Strategy: Multiple-Meaning Words**, page 248.*

9 Specialized Vocabulary

Specialized vocabulary is special terms suited to a particular field of study or work. For example, science, mathematics, and history all have their own technical or specialized vocabularies. To figure out specialized terms, you can use context clues and reference sources, such as dictionaries on specific subjects, atlases, or manuals.

*For more information, see **Vocabulary Strategy: Specialized Vocabulary**, pages 263 and 545.*

10 Using Reference Sources

10.1 DICTIONARIES

A **general dictionary** will tell you not only a word's definitions but also its pronunciation, parts of speech, and history and origin. A **specialized dictionary** focuses on terms related to a particular field of study or work. Use a dictionary to check the spelling of any word you are unsure of in your English class and for other subjects as well.

*For more information, see **Vocabulary Strategy: Using a Dictionary**, page 618.*

10.2 THESAURI

A **thesaurus** (plural, thesauri) is a dictionary of synonyms. A thesaurus can be especially helpful when you find yourself using the same modifiers over and over again.

10.3 SYNONYM FINDERS

A **synonym finder** is often included in word-processing software. It enables you to highlight a word and be shown a display of its synonyms.

10.4 GLOSSARIES

A **glossary** is a list of specialized terms and their definitions. It is often found in the back of a book and sometimes includes pronunciations. Many textbooks contain glossaries. In fact, this textbook has three glossaries: the **Glossary of Literary Terms,** the **Glossary of Reading and Informational Terms,** and the **Glossary of Vocabulary in English & Spanish.** Use these glossaries to help you understand how terms are used in this textbook.

11 Spelling Rules

11.1 WORDS ENDING IN A SILENT *E*

Before adding a suffix beginning with a vowel or *y* to a word ending in a silent *e,* drop the *e* (with some exceptions).

> amaze + -ing = amazing
> love + -able = lovable
> create + -ed = created
> nerve + -ous = nervous

Exceptions: *change + -able = changeable; courage + -ous = courageous*

When adding a suffix beginning with a consonant to a word ending in a silent *e,* keep the *e* (with some exceptions).

> late + -ly = lately
> spite + -ful = spiteful
> noise + -less = noiseless
> state + -ment = statement

Exceptions: *truly, argument, ninth, wholly, awful, and others.*

When a suffix beginning with *a* or *o* is added to a word with a final silent *e,* the final *e* is usually retained if it is preceded by a soft *c* or a soft *g.*

> **bridge + -able = bridgeable**
> **peace + -able = peaceable**
> **outrage + -ous = outrageous**
> **advantage + -ous = advantageous**

When a suffix beginning with a vowel is added to words ending in *ee* or *oe,* the final silent *e* is retained.

> **agree + -ing = agreeing**　**free + -ing = freeing**
> **hoe + -ing = hoeing**　**see + -ing = seeing**

11.2 WORDS ENDING IN *Y*

Before adding most suffixes to a word that ends in *y* preceded by a consonant, change the *y* to *i.*

> **easy + -est = easiest**
> **crazy + -est = craziest**
> **silly + -ness = silliness**
> **marry + -age = marriage**

Exceptions: *dryness, shyness,* and *slyness.*

However, when you add *-ing,* the *y* does not change.

> **empty + -ed = emptied**　but
> **empty + -ing = emptying**

When adding a suffix to a word that ends in *y* preceded by a vowel, the *y* usually does not change.

> **play + -er = player**
> **employ + -ed = employed**
> **coy + -ness = coyness**
> **pay + -able = payable**

11.3 WORDS ENDING IN A CONSONANT

In one-syllable words that end in one consonant preceded by one short vowel, double the final consonant before adding a suffix beginning with a vowel, such as *-ed* or *-ing.* These are sometimes called 1+1+1 words.

> **dip + -ed = dipped**　　**set + -ing = setting**
> **slim + -est = slimmest**　**fit + -er = fitter**

The rule does not apply to words of one syllable that end in a consonant preceded by two vowels.

> **feel + -ing = feeling**　　**peel + -ed = peeled**
> **reap + -ed = reaped**　　**loot + -ed = looted**

In words of more than one syllable, double the final consonant when (**1**) the word ends with one consonant preceded by one vowel and (**2**) the word is accented on the last syllable.

> **be•gin´　per•mit´　　re•fer´**

In the following examples, note that in the new words formed with suffixes, the accent remains on the same syllable:

> **be•gin´ + -ing　=　be•gin´ning　=　beginning**
> **per•mit´ + -ed　=　per•mit´ted　=　permitted**

Exceptions: In some words with more than one syllable, though the accent remains on the same syllable when a suffix is added, the final consonant is nevertheless not doubled, as in the following examples:

> **tra´vel + er　=　tra´vel•er　=　traveler**
> **mar´ket + er　=　mar´ket•er　=　marketer**

In the following examples, the accent does not remain on the same syllable; thus, the final consonant is not doubled:

> **re•fer´ + -ence　=　ref´er•ence　=　reference**
> **con•fer´ + -ence　=　con´fer•ence　=　conference**

11.4 PREFIXES AND SUFFIXES

When adding a prefix to a word, do not change the spelling of the base word. When a prefix creates a double letter, keep both letters.

> **dis- + approve　=　disapprove**
> **re- + build　=　rebuild**
> **ir- + regular　=　irregular**
> **mis- + spell　=　misspell**
> **anti- + trust　=　antitrust**
> **il- + logical　=　illogical**

When adding *-ly* to a word ending in *l,* keep both *l*'s. When adding *-ness* to a word ending in *n,* keep both *n*'s.

> **careful + -ly　=　carefully**
> **sudden + -ness　=　suddenness**
> **final + -ly　=　finally**
> **thin + -ness = thinness**

11.5 FORMING PLURAL NOUNS

To form the plural of most nouns, just add -s.

prizes   dreams   circles   stations

For most singular nouns ending in **o**, add -s.

solos   halos   studios   photos   pianos

For a few nouns ending in **o**, add -es.

heroes   tomatoes   potatoes   echoes

When the singular noun ends in **s, sh, ch, x,** or **z,** add -es.

**waitresses   brushes   ditches
axes   buzzes**

When a singular noun ends in **y** with a consonant before it, change the **y** to **i** and add -es.

**army—armies   candy—candies
baby—babies   diary—diaries
ferry—ferries   conspiracy—conspiracies**

When a vowel (**a, e, i, o, u**) comes before the **y,** just add -s.

**boy—boys   way—ways
array—arrays   alloy—alloys
weekday—weekdays   jockey—jockeys**

For most nouns ending in **f** or **fe,** change the **f** to **v** and add -es or -s.

**life—lives   calf—calves   knife—knives
thief—thieves shelf—shelves loaf—loaves**

For some nouns ending in **f,** add -s to make the plural.

roofs   chiefs   reefs   beliefs

Some nouns have the same form for both singular and plural.

deer   sheep   moose   salmon   trout

For some nouns, the plural is formed in a special way.

**man—men   goose—geese
ox—oxen   woman—women
mouse—mice   child—children**

For a compound noun written as one word, form the plural by changing the last word in the compound to its plural form.

stepchild—stepchildren   firefly—fireflies

If a compound noun is written as a hyphenated word or as two separate words, change the most important word to the plural form.

**brother-in-law—brothers-in-law
life jacket—life jackets**

11.6 FORMING POSSESSIVES

If a noun is singular, add **'s.**

mother—my mother's car   Ross—Ross's desk

Exception: The **s** after the apostrophe is dropped after *Jesus', Moses',* and certain names in classical mythology *(Zeus')*. These possessive forms can thus be pronounced easily.

If a noun is plural and ends with **s,** just add an apostrophe.

**parents—my parents' car
the Santinis—the Santinis' house**

If a noun is plural but does not end in **s,** add **'s.**

**people—the people's choice
women—the women's coats**

11.7 SPECIAL SPELLING PROBLEMS

Only one English word ends in **-sede:** *supersede*. Three words end in **-ceed:** *exceed, proceed,* and *succeed*. All other verbs ending in the sound "seed" are spelled with **-cede.**

concede   precede   recede   secede

In words with **ie** or **ei,** when the sound is long **e** (as in *she*), the word is spelled **ie** except after **c** (with some exceptions).

i before *e*	thief	relieve	field
	piece	grieve	pier
except after *c*	conceit	perceive	ceiling
	receive	receipt	
Exceptions:	either	neither	weird
	leisure	seize	

Commonly Confused Words

WORDS	DEFINITIONS	EXAMPLES
accept/except	The verb *accept* means "to receive or believe"; *except* is usually a preposition meaning "excluding."	**Except** for some of the more extraordinary events, I can **accept** that the *Odyssey* recounts a real journey.
advice/advise	*Advise* is a verb; *advice* is a noun naming that which an *adviser* gives.	I **advise** you to take that job. Whom should I ask for **advice?**
affect/effect	As a verb, *affect* means "to influence." *Effect* as a verb means "to cause." If you want a noun, you will almost always want *effect*.	Did Circe's wine **affect** Odysseus' mind? It did **effect** a change in Odysseus' men. In fact, it had an **effect** on everyone else who drank it.
all ready/already	*All ready* is an adjective meaning "fully ready." *Already* is an adverb meaning "before or by this time."	He was **all ready** to go at noon. I have **already** seen that movie.
allusion/illusion	An *allusion* is an indirect reference to something. An *illusion* is a false picture or idea.	There are many **allusions** to the works of Homer in English literature. The world's apparent flatness is an **illusion**.
among/between	*Between* is used when you are speaking of only two things. *Among* is used for three or more.	**Between** *Hamlet* and *King Lear,* I prefer the latter. Emily Dickinson is **among** my favorite poets.
bring/take	*Bring* is used to denote motion toward a speaker or place. *Take* is used to denote motion away from such a person or place.	**Bring** the books over here, and I will **take** them to the library.
fewer/less	*Fewer* refers to the number of separate, countable units. *Less* refers to bulk quantity.	We have **less** literature and **fewer** selections in this year's curriculum.
leave/let	*Leave* means "to allow something to remain behind." *Let* means "to permit."	The librarian will **leave** some books on display but will not **let** us borrow any.
lie/lay	To *lie* is "to rest or recline." It does not take an object. *Lay* always takes an object.	Rover loves to **lie** in the sun. We always **lay** some bones next to him.
loose/lose	*Loose* (lo͞os) means "free, not restrained"; *lose* (lo͞oz) means "to misplace or fail to find."	Who turned the horses **loose?** I hope we won't **lose** any of them.
precede/proceed	*Precede* means "to go or come before." Use *proceed* for other meanings.	Emily Dickinson's poetry **precedes** that of Alice Walker. You may **proceed** to the next section of the test.
than/then	Use *than* in making comparisons; use *then* on all other occasions.	Who can say whether Amy Lowell is a better poet **than** Denise Levertov? I will read Lowell first, and **then** I will read Levertov.
their/there/they're	*Their* means "belonging to them." *There* means "in that place." *They're* is the contraction for "they are."	**There** is a movie playing at 9 P.M. **They're** going to see it with me. Sakara and Erin drove away in **their** car after the movie.
two/too/to	*Two* is the number. *Too* is an adverb meaning "also" or "very." Use *to* before a verb or as a preposition.	Meg had **to** go to town, **too.** We had **too** much reading **to** do. **Two** chapters is **too** many.

Effective oral communication occurs when the audience understands a message the way the speaker intends it. Good speakers and listeners do more than just talk and hear. They use specific techniques to present their ideas effectively, and they are attentive and critical listeners.

1 Speech

In school, in business, and in community life, a speech is one of the most effective means of communicating.

1.1 AUDIENCE, PURPOSE, AND OCCASION

When developing and delivering a speech, your goal is to deliver a focused, coherent presentation that conveys your ideas clearly and relates to the background of your audience. By understanding your audience, you can tailor your speech to them appropriately and effectively.

- **Know Your Audience** What kind of group are you presenting to? Fellow classmates? A group of teachers? What are their interests and backgrounds? Understanding their different points of view can help you organize the information so that they understand and are interested in it.

- **Understand Your Purpose** Keep in mind your purpose for speaking. Are you trying to persuade the audience to do something? Perhaps you simply want to entertain them by sharing a story or experience. Your reason for giving the speech will guide you in organizing your thoughts and deciding on how to deliver it.

- **Know the Occasion** Are you speaking at a special event? Is it formal? Will others be giving speeches besides you? Knowing what the occasion is will help you tailor the language and the length for the event.

1.2 PREPARING YOUR SPEECH

There are several approaches to preparing a speech. Your teacher may tell you which one to use.

Manuscript	Prepare a complete script of the speech in advance and use it to deliver the speech. Use for formal occasions, such as graduation speeches and political addresses, and to present technical or complicated information.
Memory	Prepare a written text in advance and then memorize it in order to deliver the speech word for word. Use for short speeches, as when introducing another speaker or accepting an award.
Extemporaneous	Prepare the speech and deliver it using an outline or notes. Use for informal situations, for persuasive messages, and to make a more personal connection with the audience.

1.3 DRAFTING YOUR SPEECH

If you are writing your speech beforehand, rather than working from notes, use the following guidelines to help you:

- **Create a Unified Speech** Do this first by organizing your speech into paragraphs, each of which develops a single main idea. Then make sure that just as all the sentences in a paragraph support the main idea of the paragraph, all the paragraphs in your speech support the main idea of the speech.

- **Use Appropriate Language** The subject of your speech—and the way you choose to present it—should match your audience, your purpose, and the occasion. You can use informal language, such as slang, to share a story with your classmates. For a persuasive speech in front of a school assembly, use formal, standard American English. If you are giving an informative

presentation, be sure to explain any terms that the audience may not be familiar with.

- **Provide Evidence** Include relevant facts, statistics, and incidents; quote experts to support your ideas and opinions. Elaborate—provide specific details, perhaps with visual or media displays—to clarify what you are saying.

- **Emphasize Important Points** To help your audience follow the main ideas and concepts of your speech, be sure to draw attention to important points. You can use rhyme, repetition, and other rhetorical devices.

- **Use Precise Language** Use precise language to convey your ideas, and vary the structure and length of your sentences. You can keep the audience's attention with a word that elicits strong emotion. You can use a question or interjection to make a personal connection with the audience.

- **Start Strong, Finish Strong** As you begin your speech, consider using a "hook"—an interesting question or statement meant to capture your audience's attention. At the end of the speech, restate your main ideas simply and clearly. Perhaps conclude with a powerful example or anecdote to reinforce your message.

- **Revise Your Speech** After you write your speech, revise, edit, and proofread it as you would a written report. Use a variety of sentence structures to achieve a natural rhythm. Check for correct subject-verb agreement and consistent verb tense. Correct run-on sentences and sentence fragments. Use parallel structure to emphasize ideas. Make sure you use complete sentences and correct punctuation and capitalization, even if no one else will see it. Your written speech should be clear and error-free. If you notice an error in your notes during the speech, you may not remember what you actually wanted to say.

1.4 DELIVERING YOUR SPEECH

Confidence is the key to a successful presentation. Use these techniques to help you prepare and present your speech:

Prepare

- **Review Your Information** Reread your notes and review any background research. You'll feel more confident during your speech.

- **Organize Your Notes** Some people prefer to include only key points. Others prefer the entire script. Write each main point, or each paragraph, of your speech on a separate numbered index card. Be sure to include your most important evidence and examples.

- **Plan Your Visual Aids** If you are planning on using visual aids, such as slides, posters, charts, graphs, video clips, overhead transparencies, or computer projections, now is the time to design them and decide how to work them into your speech.

Practice

- **Rehearse** Rehearse your speech several times, possibly in front of a practice audience. Maintain good posture by standing with your shoulders back and your head up. If you are using visual aids, practice handling them. Adapt your rate of speaking, pitch, and tone of voice to your audience and setting. Glance at your notes to refresh your memory, but avoid reading them word for word. Your style of performance should express the purpose of your speech. Use the following chart to help you.

Purpose	Pace	Pitch	Tone
To persuade	fast but clear	even	urgent
To inform	using plenty of pauses	even	authoritative
To entertain	usually building to a "punch"	varied to create characters or drama	funny or dramatic

- **Use Audience Feedback** If you had a practice audience, ask them specific questions about your delivery: Did I use enough eye contact? Was my voice at the right volume? Did I stand straight, or did I slouch? Use the audience's comments to evaluate the effectiveness of your delivery and to set goals for future rehearsals.

- **Evaluate Your Performance** When you have finished each rehearsal, evaluate your performance. Did you pause to let an important point sink in or use gestures for emphasis? Make a list of the aspects of your presentation that you will try to improve for your next rehearsal.

Present

- **Begin Your Speech** Try to look relaxed and smile.

- **Make Eye Contact** Try to make eye contact with as many audience members as possible. This will establish personal contact and help you determine if the audience understands your speech.

- **Remember to Pause** A slight pause after important points will provide emphasis and give your audience time to think about what you're saying.

- **Speak Clearly** Speak loud enough to be heard clearly, but not so loud that your voice is overwhelming. Use a conversational tone.

- **Maintain Good Posture** Stand up straight and avoid nervous movements that may distract the audience's attention from what you are saying.

- **Use Expressive Body Language** Use facial expressions to show your feelings toward your topic. Lean forward when you make an important point; move your hands and arms for emphasis. Use your body language to show your own style and reflect your personality.

- **Watch the Audience for Responses** If they start fidgeting or yawning, speak a little louder or get to your conclusion a little sooner. Use what you learn to evaluate the effectiveness of your speech and to decide what areas need improvement for future presentations.

Respond to Questions

Depending on the content of your speech, your audience may have questions. Follow these steps to make sure that you answer questions in an appropriate manner:

- Think about what your audience may ask and prepare answers before your speech.

- Tell your audience at the beginning of your speech that you will take questions at the end. This helps avoid audience interruptions that may make your speech hard to follow.

- Call on audience members in the order in which they raise their hands.

- Repeat each question before you answer it to ensure that everyone has heard it. This step also gives you time to prepare your answer.

2 Different Types of Oral Presentations

2.1 INFORMATIVE SPEECH

When you deliver an informative speech, you give the audience new information, provide a better understanding of information, or enable the audience to use the information in a new way. An informative speech is presented in an objective way.

*For more information, see **Speaking and Listening: Delivering an Oral Report,** page 1177.*

Use the following questions to evaluate the presentation of a peer or a public figure, or your own presentation.

> **Evaluate an Informative Speech**
> - Did the speaker have a specific, clearly focused topic?
> - Did the speaker take the audience's previous knowledge into consideration?
> - Did the speaker cite sources for the information?
> - Did the speaker communicate the information objectively?
> - Did the speaker explain technical terms?
> - Did the speaker use visual aids effectively?
> - Did the speaker anticipate and address any audience concerns or misunderstandings?

2.2 PERSUASIVE SPEECH

When you deliver a persuasive speech, you offer a thesis or clear statement on a subject, you provide relevant evidence to support your position, and you attempt to convince the audience to accept your point of view.

*For more information, see **Speaking and Listening: Presenting a Persuasive Speech,** page 657.*

Use the following questions to evaluate the presentation of a peer or a public figure, or your own presentation.

Evaluate a Persuasive Speech

- Did the speaker present a clear thesis or argument?
- Did the speaker anticipate and address audience concerns, biases, and counterarguments?
- Did the speaker use sound logic and reasoning in developing the argument?
- Did the speaker support the argument with valid evidence, examples, facts, expert opinions, and quotations?
- Did the speaker use rhetorical devices, such as emotional appeals, to support assertions?
- Did the speaker hold the audience's interest with an effective voice, facial expressions, and gestures?
- Is your reaction to the speech similar to other audience members'?

2.3 DEBATE AN ISSUE

A debate is a balanced argument covering both sides of an issue. In a debate, two teams compete to win the support of the audience. In a formal debate, two teams, each with two members, present their arguments on a given proposition or policy statement. One team argues for the proposition or statement and the other argues against it. Each debater must consider the proposition closely and must research both sides of it. To argue persuasively either for or against a proposition, a debater must be familiar with both sides of the issue.

*For more information, see **Speaking and Listening: Debating an Issue,** page 915.*

Use the following guidelines to evaluate a debate.

Evaluate a Team in a Debate

- Did the team prove that a significant problem does or does not exist? How thorough was the analysis?
- How did the team convince you that the proposition is or is not the best solution to the problem?
- How effectively did the team present reasons and evidence supporting the case?
- How effectively did the team rebut arguments made by the opposing team?
- Did the speakers maintain eye contact and speak at an appropriate rate and volume?
- Did the speakers observe proper debate etiquette?

PRACTICE AND APPLY

View a political debate for a local, state, or national election. Use the preceding criteria to evaluate it.

2.4 NARRATIVE SPEECH

When you deliver a narrative speech, you tell a story or present a subject using a story-type format. A good narrative keeps an audience informed and entertained. It also allows you to deliver a message in a creative way.

*For more information, see **Speaking and Listening: Presenting an Informal Speech,** page 175.*

Use the following questions to evaluate a speaker or your own presentation.

Evaluate a Narrative Speech

- Did the speaker choose a context that makes sense and contributes to a believable narrative?
- Did the speaker locate scenes and incidents in specific places?
- Does the plot flow well?
- Did the speaker use words that convey the appropriate mood and tone?
- Did the speaker use sensory details that allow the audience to experience the sights, sounds, and smells of a scene and the specific actions, gestures, and thoughts of the characters?
- Did the speaker use a range of narrative devices to keep the audience interested?
- Is your reaction to the presentation similar to other audience members'?

2.5 DESCRIPTIVE SPEECH

Description is part of most presentations. In a descriptive speech, you describe a subject that you are personally involved with. A good description will enable your listeners to tell how you feel toward your subject through the images you provide.

Use the following questions to evaluate a speaker or your own presentation.

Evaluate a Descriptive Speech

- Did the speaker make clear his or her point of view toward the subject being described?
- Did the speaker use sensory details, figurative language, and factual details?
- Did the speaker use tone and pitch to emphasize important details?
- Did the speaker use facial expressions to emphasize his or her feelings toward the subject?
- Did the speaker change vantage points to help the audience see the subject from another position?
- Did the speaker change perspectives to show how someone else might feel toward the subject or place?

2.6 ORAL INTERPRETATION

When you perform an oral reading, you use appropriate vocal intonations, facial expressions, and gestures to bring a literature selection to life.

For more information, see **Speaking and Listening: Delivering an Oral Interpretation,** *page 819.*

Use the following questions to evaluate an artistic performance by a peer or a public presenter, a media presentation, or your own performance.

Evaluate an Oral Interpretation

- Did the speaker speak clearly, enunciating each word carefully?
- Did the speaker maintain eye contact with the audience?
- Did the speaker control his or her volume, projecting without shouting?
- Did the speaker vary the rate of speech appropriately to express emotion, mood, and action?
- Did the speaker use a different voice for the character(s)?
- Did the speaker stress important words or phrases?
- Did the speaker use voice, tone, and gestures to enhance meaning?
- Did the speaker's presentation allow you to identify and appreciate elements of the text such as character development, rhyme, imagery, and language?

PRACTICE AND APPLY

Listen to an oral reading by a classmate or view a dramatic performance in a theater or on television. Use the preceding criteria to evaluate it.

2.7 ORAL RESPONSE TO LITERATURE

An oral response to literature is a personal, analytic interpretation of a writer's story, novel, poem, or drama. It demonstrates to an audience a solid and comprehensive understanding of what that piece means to you.

For more information, see **Speaking and Listening: Participating in a Panel Discussion,** *page 497.*

Use the following questions to evaluate a speaker or your own presentation.

Evaluate an Oral Response to Literature

- Did the speaker choose an interesting piece that he or she understands and feels strongly about?
- Did the speaker make a judgment that shows an understanding of significant ideas from the text?
- Did the speaker direct the audience to specific parts of the piece that support his or her idea?
- Did the speaker identify and analyze the use of artistic elements such as imagery, figurative language, and character development?
- Did the speaker demonstrate an appreciation of the author's style?
- Did the speaker discuss any ambiguous or difficult passages and the impact of those passages on the audience?

PRACTICE AND APPLY

Listen as a classmate delivers an oral response to a selection you have read. Use the preceding criteria to evaluate the presentation.

❸ Other Types of Communication

3.1 CONVERSATION

Conversations are informal, but they are important means of communicating. When two or more people exchange messages, it is equally important that each person contribute and actively listen.

3.2 GROUP DISCUSSION

Successful groups assign a role to each member. These roles distribute responsibility among the members and help keep discussions focused.

Leader or Chairperson
- Introduces topic
- Explains goal or purpose
- Participates in discussion and keeps it on track
- Helps resolve conflicts
- Helps group reach goal

Recorder
- Takes notes on discussion
- Reports on suggestions and decisions

- Organizes and writes up notes
- Participates in discussion

Participants
- Contribute relevant facts or ideas to discussion
- Respond constructively to one another's ideas
- Reach agreement or vote on final decision

Guidelines for Discussion
- Be informed about the topic.
- Participate in the discussion.
- Ask questions and respond appropriately to questions.
- Don't talk while someone else is talking.
- Support statements and opinions with facts and examples.
- Listen attentively; be courteous and respectful of others' viewpoints.
- Work toward the goal; avoid getting sidetracked by unrelated topics.

*For more information, see **Speaking and Listening: Participating in a Panel Discussion**, page 497.*

3.3 INTERVIEW

An **interview** is a formal type of conversation with a definite purpose and goal. To conduct a successful interview, use the following guidelines:

Prepare for the Interview
- Select your interviewee carefully. Identify who has the kind of knowledge and experience you are looking for.
- Set a time, a date, and a place. Ask permission to tape-record the interview.
- Learn all you can about the person you will interview or the topic you want information on.
- Prepare a list of questions. Create questions that encourage detailed responses instead of yes-or-no answers. Arrange your questions in order from most important to least important.
- Arrive on time with everything you need.

Conduct the Interview

- Ask your questions clearly and listen to the responses carefully. Give the person whom you are interviewing plenty of time to answer.
- Be flexible; follow up on any responses you find interesting.
- Avoid arguments; be tactful and polite.
- Even if you tape an interview, take notes on important points.
- Thank the person for the interview, and ask if you can call with any follow-up questions.

Follow Up on the Interview

- Summarize your notes or make a written copy of the tape recording as soon as possible.
- If any points are unclear or if information is missing, call and ask more questions while the person is still available.
- Select the most appropriate quotations to support your ideas.
- If possible, have the person you interviewed review your work to make sure you haven't misrepresented what he or she said.
- Send a thank-you note to the person in appreciation of his or her time and effort.

Evaluate an Interview

You can determine how effective your interview was by asking yourself these questions:

- Did you get the type of information you were looking for?
- Were your most important questions answered to your satisfaction?
- Were you able to keep the interviewee focused on the subject?

---

4 Active Listening

Active listening is the process of receiving, interpreting, evaluating, and responding to a message. Whether you listen to a class discussion or a formal speech, use the following strategies to get as much as you can from the message.

Listening with a Purpose		
Situation	**Reason for Listening**	**How to Listen**
A friend tells a joke.	enjoyment	Maintain eye contact; react to the joke.
You and a friend are trying to go to a concert.	to make plans	Identify goals and problems; listen closely to each other's ideas.

Before Listening

- Learn what the topic is beforehand. You may need to read background information about the topic or learn technical terms in order to interpret the speaker's message.
- Think about what you know or want to know about the topic.
- Have a pen and paper or a laptop computer to take notes.
- Establish a purpose for listening.

While Listening

- Focus your attention on the speaker. Your facial expressions and body language should demonstrate your interest in hearing the topic. Ignore barriers such as room temperature and noise.
- Listen for the speaker's purpose (usually stated at the beginning), which alerts you to main ideas.
- To help you interpret the speaker's message, listen for words or phrases that signal important points, such as *to begin with, in addition, most important, finally,* and *in conclusion.*
- Listen carefully for explanations of technical terms. Use these terms to help you understand the speaker's message.
- Listen for ideas that are repeated for emphasis.
- Take notes. Write down only the most important points.
- If possible, use an outline or list format to organize main ideas and supporting points.
- Note comparisons and contrasts, causes and effects, or problems and solutions.

- As you take notes, use phrases, abbreviations, and symbols to keep up with the speaker.

- To aid your comprehension, note how the speaker uses word choice, voice pitch, posture, and gestures to convey meaning.

After Listening

- Ask relevant questions to clarify anything that was unclear or confusing.

- Review your notes right away to make sure you understand what was said.

- Summarize and paraphrase the speaker's ideas.

- You may also wish to compare your interpretation of the speech with the interpretations of others who listened to it.

4.1 CRITICAL LISTENING

Critical listening involves interpreting and analyzing a spoken message to judge its accuracy and reliability. You can use the following strategies as you listen to messages from advertisers, politicians, lecturers, and others:

- **Determine the Speaker's Purpose** Think about the background, viewpoint, and possible motives of the speaker. Separate facts from opinions. Listen carefully to details and evidence that a speaker uses to support the message.

- **Listen for the Main Idea** Figure out the speaker's main message before allowing yourself to be distracted by seemingly convincing facts and details.

- **Recognize the Use of Persuasive Techniques** Pay attention to a speaker's choice of words. Speakers may slant information to persuade you to buy a product or accept an idea. Persuasive devices such as inaccurate generalizations, either/or reasoning, and bandwagon or snob appeal may represent faulty reasoning and provide misleading information.

*For more information, see **Persuasive Techniques,** pages 596 and R22.*

- **Observe Nonverbal Messages** A speaker's gestures, facial expressions, and tone of voice should reinforce the message. If they don't, you should doubt the speaker's sincerity and his or her message's reliability.

- **Give Appropriate Feedback** An effective speaker looks for verbal and nonverbal cues from you, the listener, to gauge how the message is being received. For example, if you understand or agree with the message, you might nod your head. If possible, during or after a presentation, ask questions to clarify understanding.

4.2 VERBAL FEEDBACK

At times you will be asked to give direct feedback to a speaker. You may be asked to evaluate the way the speaker delivers the presentation as well as the content of the presentation.

Evaluate Delivery

- Did the speaker articulate words clearly and distinctly?
- Did the speaker pronounce words correctly?
- Did the speaker vary his or her rate?
- Did the speaker's voice sound natural and not strained?
- Was the speaker's voice loud enough?

Evaluate Content

Here's how to give constructive suggestions for improvement:

Be Specific Don't make statements like "Your charts need work." Offer concrete suggestions, such as "Please make the type bigger so we can read the poster from the back of the room."

Discuss Only the Most Important Points Don't overload the speaker with too much feedback about too many details. Focus on important points, such as:

- Is the topic too advanced for the audience?
- Are the supporting details well organized?
- Is the conclusion weak?

Give Balanced Feedback Tell the speaker not only what didn't work but also what did work: "Consider dropping the last two slides, since you covered those points earlier. The first two slides got my attention."

MEDIA TOOLS

For more information, visit the **Media Center** at **ClassZone.com**.

Every day you are exposed to hundreds of images and messages from television, radio, movies, newspapers, and the Internet. What is the effect of all this media? What do you need to know to be a smart media consumer? Being media literate means that you have the ability to think critically about media messages. It means that you are able to analyze and evaluate media messages and how they influence you and your world. To become media literate, you'll need the tools to study media messages.

1 Five Core Concepts in Media Literacy

from The Center for Media Literacy

The five concepts of media literacy provide you with the basic questions you can consider when examining media messages.

All media messages are "constructed." All media messages are made by someone. In fact, they are carefully thought out and researched and have attitudes and values built into them. Much of the information that you use to make sense of the world comes from the media. Therefore, it is important to know how a medium is put together so you can better understand the message it conveys.

Media messages are constructed using a creative language with its own rules. Each means of communication—whether it is film, television, newspapers, magazines, radio, or the Internet—has its own language and design. Therefore, the contents of a message must use the language and design of the medium that conveys the message. Thus, the medium actually shapes the message. For example, a horror film may use music to heighten suspense, or a newspaper may use a big headline to signal the significance of a story. Understanding the language of each medium can increase your enjoyment of it as well as alert you to obvious and subtle influences.

Different people experience the same media messages differently. Personal factors such as age, education, and experience will affect the way a person responds to a media message. How many times has your interpretation of a film or book differed from that of a friend? Everyone interprets media messages through his or her own lens.

Media have embedded values and points of view. Media messages carry underlying values, which are purposely built into them by the creators of the message. For example, a commercial's main purpose may be to persuade you to buy something, but it also conveys the value of a particular lifestyle. Understanding both the core message and the embedded point of view will help you decide whether to accept or reject the message.

Most media messages are constructed to gain profit and/or power. The creators of media messages often provide a commodity, such as information or entertainment, in order to make money. The bigger the audience, the higher the cost of advertising. Consequently, media outlets want to build large audiences in order to bring in more revenue from advertising. For example, a television network will create programming to appeal to the largest audience possible, in the hope that the viewer ratings will attract more advertising dollars.

2 Media Basics

2.1 MESSAGE

When a film or TV show is created, it becomes a media product. Each media product is created to send a **message,** or an expression of belief or opinion, that serves a specific purpose. In order to understand the message, you will need to deconstruct it.

Deconstruction is the process of analyzing a media presentation. To analyze a media presentation you will need to look at its content, its purpose, the audience it's aimed at, and the techniques and elements that are used to create certain effects.

2.2 AUDIENCE

A **target audience** is a specific group of people that a product or presentation is aimed at. The members of a target audience usually share certain characteristics, such as age, gender, ethnic background, values, or lifestyle. For example, a target audience may be males, ages 15 to 20, who live in urban areas and engage in sports.

Demographics are the characteristics of a population, including age, gender, profession, income, education, ethnicity, and geographical location. Media decision makers use demographics to shape their content to suit the needs and tastes of a target audience.

Nielsen ratings are the system used to track TV audiences and their viewing preferences. Nielsen Media Research, the company that provides this system, monitors TV viewing in a random sample of 5,000 U.S. households selected to represent the population as a whole.

2.3 PURPOSE

The **purpose,** or intent, of a media presentation is the reason it was made. Most media have more than one purpose. However, every media message has a **core purpose.** To discover that purpose, think about why its creator paid for and produced the message. For example, an ad might entertain you with humor, but its core purpose is to persuade you to buy something.

2.4 TYPES AND GENRES OF MEDIA

The term *media* refers to television, newspapers, magazines, radio, movies, and the Internet. Each is a **medium,** or means, for carrying information, entertainment, and advertisements to a large audience.

Each type of media has different characteristics, strengths, and weaknesses. Understanding how different types of media work and the role they play will help you become more informed about the choices you make in response to the media.

For more information, see **Types of Media,** *page 12.*

2.5 PRODUCERS AND CREATORS

People who control the media are known as **gatekeepers.** Gatekeepers decide what information to share with the public and the ways it will be presented. The following diagram gives some examples.

Who Controls the Media?

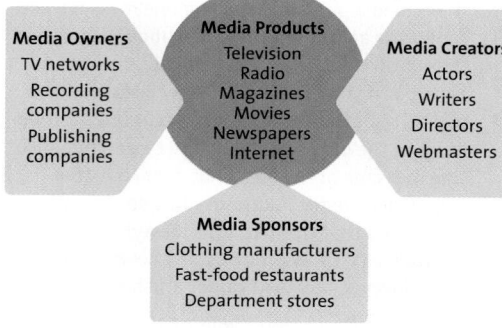

Media Owners
TV networks
Recording companies
Publishing companies

Media Products
Television
Radio
Magazines
Movies
Newspapers
Internet

Media Creators
Actors
Writers
Directors
Webmasters

Media Sponsors
Clothing manufacturers
Fast-food restaurants
Department stores

Some forms of media are independently owned, while others are part of a corporate family. Some corporate families might own several different kinds of media. For example, a company may own three radio stations, five newspapers, a publishing company, and a small television station. Often a corporate "parent" decides the content for all of its holdings.

2.6 LAWS GOVERNING MEDIA

Four main laws and policies affect the content, delivery, and use of mass media.

The First Amendment to the Constitution forbids Congress to limit speech or the press.

Copyright law protects the rights of authors and other media creators against the unauthorized publishing, reproduction, and selling of their works.

Laws prohibit **censorship,** any attempt to suppress or control people's access to media messages.

Laws prohibit **libel,** the publication of false statements that damage a person's reputation.

2.7 INFLUENCE OF MEDIA

By sheer volume alone, media influences our very existence, values, opinions, and beliefs. Our environment is saturated with media messages from television, billboards, radio, newspapers, magazines, video games, and so on. Each of these media products is selling one message and conveying another—a message about values—in the subtext. For example, a car ad is meant to sell a car, but if you look closer, you will see that it is using a set of values, such as a luxurious lifestyle, to make the car attractive to the target audience. One message of the ad is that if you buy the car, you'll have the luxurious lifestyle. The other message is that the luxurious lifestyle is good and desirable. TV shows, movies, and news programs also convey subtexts of values and beliefs.

Media can also shape your opinions about the world. For example, news about crime shapes our understanding about how much and what type of crime is prevalent in the world around us. TV news items, talk show interviews, and commercials may shape our perception of a political candidate, a celebrity, an ethnic group, a country, or a regional area. As a consequence, our knowledge of someone or someplace may be completely based on the information we receive from the television.

3 Film and TV

Films and television programs come in a variety of types. Films include comedies, dramas, documentaries, and animated features. Televison programs cover an even wider array, including dramas, sitcoms, talk shows, reality shows, newscasts, and so on. Producers of films and producers of television programs rely on many of the same elements to convey their messages. Among these elements are scripts, visual and sound elements, special effects, and editing.

3.1 SCRIPT AND WRITTEN ELEMENTS

The writer and editor craft a story for television or film using a script and storyboard. A **script** is the text or words of a film or television show. A **storyboard** is a device often used to plan the shooting of a film and to help the director envision and convey what the finished product will look like. It consists of a sequence of sketches showing what will appear in the film's shots, often with explanatory notes and dialogue written beside or underneath them, as shown in the example.

*For more information, see **Media Study: Produce Your Own Media,** page 109.*

Shot type: LS (long shot)
Action: Black Rider races dangerously fast.
Audio: Horse screeches. Silence.

Shot type: MS (medium shot)
Action: Camera zooms in to show image of Black Rider. Audio: Music plays to indicate danger.

3.2 VISUAL ELEMENTS

Visual elements in film and television include camera shots, angles, and movements, as well as film components such as mise en scène, set design, props, and visual special effects.

A **camera shot** is a single, continuous view taken by a camera. **Camera angle** is the angle at which the camera is positioned during the recording of a shot or image. Each angle is carefully planned to create an effect. The chart shows what different shots are used for.

Camera Shot/Angle	Effect
Establishing shot introduces viewers to the location of a scene, usually by presenting a wide view of an area	establishes the setting of a film
Close-up shot shows a detailed view of a person or object	helps to create emotion and make viewers feel as if they know the character
Medium shot shows a view wider than a close-up but narrower than an establishing or long shot	shows part of an object or a character from the knees or waist up
Long shot is a wide view of a scene, showing the full figure(s) of a person or group and their surroundings	allows the viewer to see the "big picture" and shows the relationship between characters and the environment
Reaction shot shows someone reacting to something that occurred in a previous shot	allows the viewer to see how the subject feels in order to create empathy in the viewer
Low-angle shot looks up at an object or person	makes a character, object, or scene appear more important or threatening
High-angle shot looks down on an object or person	makes a character, object, or scene seem vulnerable or insignificant
Point-of-view (POV) shot shows a part of the story through a character's eyes	helps viewers identify with that character

Camera movement can create energy, reveal information, or establish a mood. The following chart shows some of the ways filmmakers move the camera to create an effect.

Camera Movement	Effect
Pan–a shot in which the camera scans a location from right to left or left to right	reveals information by showing a sweeping view of an area
Tracking shot–a shot in which the camera moves with the subject	establishes tension or creates a sense of drama
Zoom–the movement of the camera as it closes in or moves farther away from the subject	captures action or draws the viewer's attention to detail

Mise en scène is a French term that refers to the arrangement of actors, props, and action on a film set. It is used to describe everything that can be seen in a frame, including the setting, lighting, visual composition, costumes, and action.

Framing is capturing people and objects within the "frame" of a screen or image. Framing is what the camera sees.

Composition is the arrangement of objects, characters, shapes, and colors within a frame and the relationship of the objects to one another.

3.3 SOUND ELEMENTS

Sound elements in film and television include music, voice-over, and sound effects.

Music may be used to set the mood and atmosphere in a scene. Music can have a powerful effect on the way viewers feel about a story. For example, fast-paced music helps viewers feel excited during an action scene.

Voice-over is the voice of the unseen commentator or narrator of a film, TV program, or commercial.

Sound effects are the sounds added to films, TV programs, and commercials during the editing process. Sound effects, such as laugh tracks or the sounds of punches in a fight scene, can create humor, emphasize a point, or contribute to the mood.

3.4 SPECIAL EFFECTS

Special effects include computer-generated animation, manipulated video images, and fast- or slow-motion sequences in films, TV programs, and commercials.

Animation on film involves the frame-by-frame photography of a series of drawings or objects. When these frames are projected—at a rate of 24 per second—the illusion of movement is achieved.

A **split screen** is a special-effects shot in which two or more separate images are shown in the same frame. One example is when two people, actually a distance apart, are shown talking to each other.

3.5 EDITING

Editing is the process of selecting and arranging shots in a sequence. The editor decides which scenes or shots to use, as well as the length of each shot, the number of shots, and their sequence. Editing establishes pace, mood, and a coherent story.

Cut is the transition from one shot to another. To create excitement, editors often use quick cuts, which are a series of short shots strung together.

Dissolve is a transitional device in which one scene fades into another.

Fade-in is a transitional device in which a white or black shot fades in to reveal the beginning of a new scene.

Fade-out is a transitional device in which a shot fades to darkness to end a scene.

Jump cut is an abrupt and jarring change from one shot to another. A jump cut shows a break in time or continuity.

Pace is the length of time each shot stays on the screen and the rhythm that is created by the transitions between shots. Short, quick cuts create a fast pace in a story. Long cuts slow down a story.

4 News

The **news** is information on events, people, and places in your community, your region, the nation, and the world. The news can be categorized by type, as shown in the chart.

Type	Description	Examples
Hard news	fact-based accounts of current events	local newspapers, newscasts, online wire services
Soft news	human-interest stories and other accounts that are less current or urgent than hard news	magazines and tabloid TV shows such as *Sports Illustrated, Access Hollywood*
News features	stories that elaborate on news reports	documentaries such as history reports on PBS
Commentary and opinion	essays and perspectives by experts, professionals, and media personalities	editorial pages, personal Web pages

4.1 CHOOSING THE NEWS

Newsworthiness is the significance of an event or action that makes it worthy of media reporting. Journalists and their editors usually weigh the following criteria in determining which stories should make the news:

Timeliness is the quality of being very current. Timely events usually take priority over previously reported events. For example, a car accident with fatalities will be timely on the day it occurs. Because of its timeliness it may be on the front page of a newspaper or may be the lead story on a newscast.

Widespread impact refers to the importance of an event and the number of people it could affect. The more widespread the impact of an event, the more likely it is to be newsworthy.

Proximity gauges the nearness of an event to a particular city, region, or country. People tend to be more interested in stories that take place locally and affect them directly.

Human interest is a quality of stories that cause readers or listeners to feel emotions such as happiness, anger, or sadness. People are interested in reading stories about other people.

Uniqueness refers to uncommon events or circumstances that are likely to be interesting to an audience.

Compelling video and **photographs** grab people's attention and stay in their minds.

4.2 REPORTING THE NEWS

While developing a news story, a journalist makes a variety of decisions about how to construct the story, such as what information to include and how to organize it. The following elements are commonly used in news stories:

5 *W*'s and *H* are the six questions reporters answer when writing news stories—*who, what, when, where, why,* and *how.* It is a journalist's job to answer these questions in any type of news report. These questions also serve as a structure for writing and editing a story.

Inverted pyramid is the means of organizing information according to importance. In the inverted-pyramid diagram below, the most important information (the answers to the 5 *W*'s and *H*) appears at the top of the pyramid. The less important details appear at the bottom. Not all stories are reported using the inverted-pyramid form. The form remains popular, however, because it enables a reader to get the essential information without reading the entire story. Notice the following example.

Marcus Albright, star guard for the Streaking Impalas, scored the winning basket in an 87–86 come-from-behind victory over the Rovers.

The Impalas had trailed by as many as 15 points with just over four minutes left in the game.

Albright dominated the last three minutes with four three-pointers.

Angle or slant is the point of view from which a story is written. Even an objective report must have an angle.

Consider these two headlines that describe the same house fire.

Family Heirlooms Destroyed in Fire

Firefighters Slow to Respond to Fire

The first headline focuses on facts about the family's loss and has a human-interest angle. The second headline focuses on an opinion about the firefighters' response time and has a negative slant.

Standards for News Reporting

The ideal of journalism is to present news in a way that is objective, accurate, and thorough. The best news stories contain the following elements:

- **Objectivity** The story takes a balanced point of view on the issues; it is not biased, nor does it reflect a specific attitude or opinion.

- **Accuracy** The story presents factual information that can be verified.

- **Thoroughness** The story presents all sides of an issue; it includes background information, telling *who, what, when, where, why,* and *how.*

Balanced Versus Biased Reporting

Objectivity in news reporting can be measured by how balanced or biased the story is.

Balanced reporting means that all sides of an issue are represented equally and fairly.

A balanced news story

- represents people and subjects in a neutral light

- treats all sides of an issue equally

- does not include inappropriate questions, such as "Will you seek counseling after this terrible tragedy?"

- does not show stereotypes or prejudice toward people of a particular race, gender, age, religion, or other group

• does not leave out important background information that is needed to establish a context or perspective

Biased reporting is reporting in which one side is favored over another or in which the subject is unfairly represented. Biased reporting may show an overly negative view of a subject, or it may encourage racial, gender, or other stereotypes and prejudices. Sometimes biased reporting is apparent in the journalist's choice of sources.

Sources are the people interviewed for the news report and also any written materials and documents the journalist used for background information. From each source, the journalist gets a different point of view. To decide whether news reporting is balanced or biased, you will need to pay attention to the sources. For a news story on a new medicinal drug, for instance, if the journalist's only source is a representative from the company that made the drug, the report may be biased. But if the journalist also includes the perspective of someone neutral, such as a scientist who is objectively studying the effects of drugs, the report may be more balanced. The following chart shows which sources are credible.

Sources for News Stories	
Credible Sources	**Weak Sources**
• experts in a field • people directly affected by the reported event (eyewitnesses) • published reports that are specifically mentioned or shown	• unnamed or anonymous sources • people who are not involved in the reported event (for example, people who heard about a story from a friend) • research, data, or reports that are not specifically named or are referred to only in vague terms (for example, "Research shows that …")

5 Advertising

Advertising is a sponsor's paid use of various media to promote products, services, or ideas. Some common forms of advertising are shown in the chart.

Type of Ad	Characteristic
Billboard	large outdoor advertising sign
Print ad	typically appears in magazines and newspapers; uses eye-catching graphics and persuasive copy
Flyer	print ad that is circulated by hand or mail
Infomercial	an extended ad on TV that usually includes detailed product information, demonstrations, and testimonials
Public service announcement	a message aired on radio or TV to promote ideas that are considered to be in the public interest
Political ad	broadcast on radio or TV to promote political candidates
Trailer	a short film promoting an upcoming movie, TV show, or video game

Marketing is the process of transferring products and services from producer to consumer. It involves determining the packaging and pricing of a product, how it will be promoted and advertised, and where it will be sold. One way companies market their product is by becoming media sponsors.

Sponsors pay for their products to be advertised. These companies hire advertising agencies to create and produce specific campaigns for their products. They then buy television or radio airtime or magazine, newspaper, or billboard space to feature ads where the target audience is sure to see them. Because selling time and space to advertisers generates much of the income the media need to function, the media need advertisers just as much as advertisers need the media.

Product placement is the intentional and identifiable featuring of brand-name products in movies, television shows, video games, and other media. The intention is to have viewers feel positive about a product because they see a favorite character using it. Another purpose may be to promote product recognition.

5.1 PERSUASIVE TECHNIQUES

Persuasive techniques are the methods used to convince an audience to buy a product or adopt an idea. Advertisers use a combination of visuals, sound, special effects, and words to persuade their target audience. Recognizing the following techniques can help you evaluate persuasive media messages and identify misleading information:

Emotional appeals use strong feelings rather than factual evidence to persuade consumers. An example of any emotional appeal is, "Is your home safe? ProAlarm systems will make sure it is."

Bandwagon appeals use the argument that a person should believe or do something because "everyone else" does. These appeals take advantage of people's desire to be socially accepted by other people. Purchasing a popular product seems less risky to those concerned about making a mistake. An example of a bandwagon appeal is "More and more people are making the switch to Discountline long-distance service."

Slogans are memorable phrases used in advertising campaigns. Slogans substitute catchy phrases for factual information.

Logical appeals rely on logic and facts, appealing to a consumer's reason and his or her respect for authority. Two examples of logical appeals are expert opinions and product comparison.

Celebrity ads use one of the following two categories of spokesperson:

- **Celebrity authorities** are experts in a particular field. Advertisers hope that audiences will transfer the respect or admiration they have for the person to the product. For example, a famous chef may endorse a particular brand of cookware. The manufacturers of the cookware want you to think that it is a good product because a cooking expert wouldn't endorse pots and pans that didn't work.

- **Celebrity spokespeople** are famous people who endorse a product. Advertisers hope that audiences will associate the product with the celebrity.

Product comparison is comparing a product and its competition. Often mentioned by name, the competing product is portrayed as inferior. The intended effect is for people to question the quality of the competing product and to believe the featured product is superior.

6 Elements of Design

The design of a media message is just as important as the words are in conveying the message. Like words, visuals are used to persuade, inform, and entertain.

Graphics and images, such as charts, diagrams, maps, timelines, photographs, illustrations, and symbols, present information that can be quickly and easily understood. The following basic elements are used to give meaning to visuals:

Color can be used to highlight important elements such as headlines and subheads. It can also create mood, because many colors have strong emotional or psychological impacts on the reader or viewer. For example, warm colors more readily draw the eye and are often associated with happiness and comfort. Cool colors are often associated with feelings of peace and contentment or sometimes with sadness.

Lines—strokes or marks—can be thick or thin, long or short, and smooth or jagged. They can focus attention and create a feeling of depth. They can frame an object. They can also direct a viewer's eye or create a sense of motion.

Texture is the surface quality or appearance of an object. For example, an object's texture can be glossy, rough, wet, or shiny. Texture can be used to create contrast. It can also be used to make an object look "real." For example, a pattern on

wrapping paper can create a feeling of depth even though the texture is only visual and cannot be felt.

Shape is the external outline of an object. Shapes can be used to symbolize living things or geometric objects. They can emphasize visual elements and add interest. Shapes can symbolize ideas.

Notice how this movie poster uses design elements:

- **Lines** The reader's eyes are led downward to the cityscape and film's title by the vertical line or ray of light.
- **Shape** The spacecraft's shape immediately suggests a flying saucer. It may also symbolize a friendly or unfriendly visitor.
- **Color** Deep blues and purples lend an air of mystery and also make the central ray of light stand out.

7 Evaluating Media Messages

Being able to respond critically to media images and messages will help you evaluate the reliability of the content and make informed decisions. Here are six questions to ask about any media message:

Who made—and who sponsored—this message, and for what purpose? The source of the message is a clue to its purpose. If the source of the message is a private company, that company may be trying to sell you a product. If the source is a government agency, that agency may be trying to promote a program or philosophy. To discover the purpose, think about why its creator paid for and produced the message.

Who is the target audience and how is the message specifically tailored to it? Think about the age group, ethnic group, gender, and/or profession the message is targeting. Decide how it relates to you.

What are the different techniques used to inform, persuade, entertain, and attract attention? Analyze the elements, such as humor, music, special effects, and graphics, that have been used to create the message. Think about how visual and sound effects, such as symbols, color, photographs, words, and music, support the purpose behind the message.

What messages are communicated (and/or implied) about certain people, places, events, behaviors, lifestyles, and so forth? The media try to influence who we are, what we believe in, how we view things, and what values we hold. Look or listen closely to determine whether certain types of behavior are being depicted and if judgments or values are communicated through those behaviors. What are the biases in the message?

How current, accurate, and credible is the information in this message? Think about the reputation of the source. Note the broadcast or publication date of the message and whether the message might change quickly. If a report or account is not supported by facts, authoritative sources, or eyewitness accounts, you should question the credibility of the message.

What is left out of this message that might be important to know? Think about what the message is asking you to believe. Also think about what questions come to mind as you watch, read, or listen to the message.

Strategies and Practice for the SAT, ACT, and Other Standardized Tests

The test items in this section are modeled after test formats that are used on the SAT. The strategies presented here will help you prepare for that test and others. This section offers general test-taking strategies and tips for answering multiple-choice items, as well as short-response and extended-response questions in critical reading and writing. It also includes guidelines and samples for impromptu writing and essay writing. For each test, read the tips in the margin. Then apply the tips to the practice items. You can also apply the tips to Assessment Practice Tests in this book.

❶ General Test-Taking Strategies

- Arrive on time and be prepared. Be sure to bring either sharpened pencils with erasers or pens—whichever you are told to bring.

- If you have any questions, ask them before the test begins. Make sure you understand the test procedures, the timing, and the rules.

- Read the test directions carefully. Look at the passages and questions to get an overview of what is expected.

- Tackle the questions one at a time rather than thinking about the whole test.

- Refer back to the reading selections as needed. For example, if a question asks about an author's attitude, you might have to reread a passage for clues.

- If you are not sure of your answer, make a logical guess. You can often arrive at the correct answer by reasoning and eliminating wrong answers.

- As you fill in answers on your answer sheet, make sure you match the number of each test item to the numbered space on the answer sheet.

- Don't look for patterns in the positions of correct choices.

- Only change an answer if you are sure your original choice is incorrect. If you do change an answer, erase your original choice neatly and thoroughly.

- Look for main ideas as you read passages. They are often stated at the beginning or the end of a paragraph. Sometimes the main idea is implied.

- Check your answers and reread your essay.

2 Critical Reading

Most tests contain a critical reading section that measures your ability to read, understand, and interpret passages. The passages may be either fiction or nonfiction, and they can be 100 words or 500 to 800 words. They are drawn from literature, humanities, social studies, and natural sciences.

Directions: Read the following passage. Base your answers to questions 1 and 2 on what is stated or implied in the passage.

PASSAGE

By global or historical standards, much of what Americans consider poverty is luxury. A rural Russian is not considered poor if he cannot afford a car and his home has no central heating; a rural American is. Most impoverished people in the world would be dazzled by the apartments, telephones, television sets, running water, clothing, and other amenities that surround the poor in America. But that does not mean that the poor are not poor, or that those on the edge of poverty are not truly on the edge of a cliff.

—David Shipler, *The Working Poor*

1 stem

1. The (main) idea of this paragraph is that **2**

3 choices

(A) the definition of poverty can differ from one country to another

(B) no one in America is really poor

(C) many people in Russia are very poor

(D) being poor is like falling off a cliff

(E) running water and central heating are basic amenities

2. What does the author mean when he says that those on the edge of poverty are standing on the edge of a cliff? **5**

(A) Poor people sometimes feel suicidal.

(B) For poor people, life can be risky and uncertain.

(C) Being poor is like looking down into a black hole. **4**

(D) Many poor people are homeless.

(E) It is hard to pull yourself up out of poverty.

Tips: Multiple Choice

A multiple-choice question consists of a stem and a set of choices. On some tests, there are four choices. On the SAT, there are five choices. The stem is usually in the form of a question or an incomplete sentence. One of the choices correctly answers the question or completes the sentence.

1 Read the stem carefully and try to answer the question without looking at the choices.

2 Pay attention to key words in the stem. They may direct you to the correct answer. Question 1 is looking for the "main idea." Choices (D) and (E) focus on minor details.

3 Read all the choices before deciding on the correct answer.

4 After reading all of the choices, eliminate any that you know are incorrect. In question 2, you can safely eliminate choice (C), because the passage says nothing about a black hole.

5 Some questions ask you to interpret a figure of speech. Poor people are not actually "on the edge of a cliff," but that image reinforces the author's point of view that a life of poverty is filled with risk and uncertainty.

Answers: 1. (A), **2.** (B)

Directions: Base your answers to questions 1 through 3 on the two passages below.

PASSAGE 1

Contemporary students now sample the once-exotic sounds of African pennywhistle, Tuvian throat singing, or Scandinavian mandolin as casually as they choose between tacos, pizza, and sushi. . . . Madonna's *Ray of Light*, for example, borrowed from bhangra, an Indian-inflected dance music. . . . Some fear that globalization will destroy cultural diversity, resulting in a world ruled by American exports. Yet the world-music scene suggests an alternative, where global popular culture enters our marketplace with help from American youth.

—Henry Jenkins, "Culture Goes Global"

PASSAGE 2

As the unrivaled global superpower, America exports its culture on an unprecedented scale. From music to media, film to fast food, language to literature and sport, the American idea is spreading inexorably, not unlike the influence of empires that preceded it. The difference is that today's technology flings culture to every corner of the globe with blinding speed. Sometimes, U.S. ideals get transmitted—such as individual rights, freedom of speech, and respect for women—and local cultures are enriched. At other times, materialism or worse becomes the message and local traditions get crushed.

—"In 2,000 Years, Will the World Remember Disney or Plato?"
The Christian Science Monitor

---

1. Which statement best describes the attitudes of the authors of Passages 1 and 2 toward the spread of U.S. culture to other countries?
   (A) Only the author of Passage 1 sees this trend as positive.
   (B) Only the author of Passage 2 sees this trend as positive.
   (C) Neither author sees this trend as positive.
   (D) Both authors see this trend as positive.
   (E) Both authors see positive and negative aspects of this trend.

2. The author of Passage 1 claims that
   (A) globalization will destroy cultural diversity
   (B) students and musicians are influenced by music from other cultures
   (C) non-Westerners prefer American culture to their own
   (D) American ideals are spreading around the world
   (E) pop musicians fear globalization

3. The author of Passage 2 believes that
   (A) freedom of speech will have a negative effect on local traditions
   (B) international music is a problem for American culture
   (C) local traditions can be crushed by American culture
   (D) other cultures have no interest in American culture
   (E) American influence abroad has been uniformly negative

Tips: Two Passages

Questions are sometimes based on a pair of related passages. Sometimes the passages have completely different views. At other times, the passages describe different aspects of the same subject.

❶ Before reading the passages, skim the questions to see what information you will need.

❷ Look for topic sentences in each passage. Ask yourself whether the passage supports or refutes its topic sentence. Passage 1 refutes its topic sentence, while Passage 2 supports its topic sentence.

❸ Focus on key words, especially ones that are used in both passages (though possibly in different forms). You can figure out that *globe* is the root word of *global* and *globalization*. If *globe* refers to the earth, then *global* means "worldwide," and *globalization* means "the process of making worldwide."

❹ Look for clues about an author's attitude toward a subject in the author's choice of words and examples. In Passage 2, the author's use of the word *flings* suggests that he has some negative feelings about the spread of American culture.

Answers: 1. (E), **2.** (B), **3.** (C)

Directions: Read the following passage. Base your answers to questions 1 through 3 on what is stated or implied in the passage. Then base your answer to question 4 on your knowledge of types of writing.

In the following passage, the narrator recalls her childhood growing up in Puerto Rico.

PASSAGE

❶—I had not meant to start a contest of wills between my parents when I mentioned my dreams of playing the piano to Papi. My hands seemed to yearn for action, moving constantly as I talked, seeking textures when I sat reading a book, digging fearlessly into holes on walls, dipping into containers, drawers, boxes with lids that didn't quite close. Since I loved music, learning to play piano seemed like a good choice, even though I'd never actually seen a piano, let alone had any idea of what it took to play one.

❷ When I mentioned it to Papi, he was excited. The idea of a concert career for me appealed to his vision of himself as a poet and of me as more than a spunky tomboy. He took it upon himself to find me a teacher and **❷**—came up with the principal at my new school, an elderly gentleman with thinning hair and a thick mustache that seemed pasted on his delicate features. We wouldn't have to pay anything, Papi said, because "he's willing to give you lessons in exchange for some carpentry on his porch."

On Sunday afternoon I set off with Papi for my first piano lesson. I had never seen a teacher outside of school, and as we neared Don Luis's house, I was scared and dug my thumbnail into the other nails to scrape out any dirt that might have escaped the scratchy bristles of Mami's vegetable brush.

"Buenas!" he greeted us. I held on to Papi's hand as to a lifeline, not **❸** trusting my knocking knees to hold me up. But Don Luis's warm smile soon melted my fear into awe at finding myself in his house, away from the unpleasant implications of a student face-to-face with the school principal.

His house was detached from those around it, surrounded by flowers **❹** that bloomed in splendid colors and overwhelming fragrances. The inside was small but as ornate as the yard, with lace curtains, glass-topped tables, invitingly curvy furniture, and, dominating the back wall, an enormous reddish-brown piano, lustrous and dust free, majestic against a fabric-covered wall. I looked at Papi, who winked at me and smiled. We shared the joy of being in this room, in the home of an artist, a person whose life was gracious and carefree, whose furnishings and decorations were as impractical as ours were utilitarian.

—Esmeralda Santiago, *When I Was Puerto Rican*

Tips: Reading Text

❶ Identify the narrator's point of view. In the first-person point of view, the narrator is a character in the story and describes people and events as he or she experiences them, using the pronouns *I* and *me*. In the third-person point of view, the narrator is outside of the story and uses pronouns such as *he, she,* and *they.*

❷ Notice the characters who are presented in a passage. The characters in this passage are the narrator, Papi, and the principal. Look for details about personality such as appearance, feelings, actions, and things that a character owns.

❸ Find words that contribute to the mood or atmosphere of a passage. When the narrator says she held onto Papi's hand "as to a lifeline," she conveys her fear.

❹ Look at details that describe the setting of a narrative passage. The details in this passage take the reader inside the piano teacher's home.

Answers: **1.** (C), **2.** (E), **3.** (A), **4.** (B)

1. What was Papi's vision of his daughter?
   (A) He envisioned her as a poet.
   (B) He saw her as nothing more than a tomboy.
   (C) He believed she could have a musical career.
   (D) He wanted her to become a teacher.
   (E) He thought she was spoiled.

2. How would you describe the narrator's feelings before her first piano lesson?
   (A) She felt that the piano lessons were a mistake.
   (B) She felt humble because her family didn't own a piano.
   (C) She was embarassed because she had never seen a piano.
   (D) She felt proud because her father was able to arrange free lessons.
   (E) She was scared because the piano teacher was the principal of her school.

3. The narrator wanted to play piano
   (A) to find an outlet for her nervous energy
   (B) to impress her father
   (C) to test her will against her parents' will
   (D) to develop discipline by practicing an instrument
   (E) to prove she was not a tomboy

4. The last paragraph of the passage is an example of what kind of writing?
   (A) persuasive
   (B) descriptive
   (C) expository
   (D) dramatic
   (E) analytic

The critical reading section may also feature sentence-completion questions that test your knowledge of vocabulary. They may also measure your ability to figure out how different parts of a sentence logically fit together.

Directions: Choose the word or set of words that, when inserted, best fits the meaning of each of the following sentences.

1. The personal computer, which was a _____ tool just 30 years ago, has had a _____ impact on our lives since then. **❶**
   - (A) forgotten . . profound
   - (B) fledgling . . huge
   - (C) whimsical . . significant **❷**
   - (D) negligible . . munificent
   - (E) practical . . healthy

2. Today there is _____ evidence that the earth orbits the sun, (but) before the telescope was invented, facts to back that claim were _____. **❸**
   - (A) mammoth . . tenuous
   - (B) ample . . unstinting
   - (C) dynamic . . credible
   - (D) circumstantial . . incalculable
   - (E) copious . . scant

3. The island of Alcatraz was once the _____ of an _____ federal prison.
   - (A) topography . . idyllic
   - (B) portal . . impromptu
   - (C) locale . . eclectic
   - (D) site . . infamous **❹**
   - (E) milieu . . illicit

4. The woman left food every day for a colony of _____ cats that lived behind her barn, but they shied away from her nonetheless.
   - (A) feral **❺**
   - (B) affectionate
   - (C) fierce
   - (D) indoor
   - (E) docile

Tips: Sentence Completion

❶ When you are completing sentences with two words missing, look at both blanks and think about what kinds of words will fill them.

❷ If one of the words in an answer choice is wrong, you can eliminate that whole set of words from consideration. In sentence 1, *significant* makes sense, but *whimsical* does not.

❸ Look for key words or phrases that link the ideas in a sentence. The word *but* signals that the two parts of the sentence express contrasting ideas.

❹ A prefix can change the meaning of a word. Someone becomes famous for doing something positive but infamous for doing something negative. An artist might be famous; a criminal would be infamous.

❺ If you don't know the exact meaning of a word, you can look for clues in the sentence. For sentence 4, you can ask yourself: What kind of cat lives outdoors and shies away from people? *Feral* means "untamed" and is the best answer to that question.

Answers: 1. (B), **2.** (E), **3.** (D), **4.** (A)

3 Writing

To measure your ability to express ideas clearly and correctly, tests ask you to identify errors in grammar and usage and to improve sentences and paragraphs.

Directions: Select the one underlined part that must be changed to make the following sentence correct. There is no more than one error in the sentence. If the sentence is correct as written, select answer choice E.

1. Since the first dinosaur bones <u>collected</u> in 19th-century England,
❷   (A)

dinosaur remains—<u>ranging from bone fragments to nearly complete skeletons</u>— ❶
❸   ❹ (B)

have been <u>unearthed</u> on every continent <u>except</u> Antarctica. No error
(C)   (D)   (E)

Directions: Determine whether the underlined section of the following sentence needs improvement. If it does, select the best change presented in the choices below the sentence. Note that Choice A repeats the original phrase.

2. The author of a definitive work on Abraham Lincoln, Carl Sandburg is renowned as a biographer <u>as well as for his poetry</u>. ❻
   - (A) as well as for his poetry ❺
   - (B) as well as a poet
   - (C) as well as for being a poet
   - (D) and for being a poet
   - (E) and also for poetry

Directions: Read the passage below and select the best answer to the question that follows the passage.

(1) Scott Joplin was an African-American pianist and composer. (2) He is regarded as the father of ragtime, a form of popular music. (3) Joplin wanted to establish his name with more serious music. (4) His opera titled *Treemonisha* received the Pulitzer Prize for music in 1976, 59 years after the composer's death. (5) It is considered the first truly American opera.

3. What is the best way to combine sentences 2 and 3?
   - (A) He is regarded as the father of ragtime, a form of popular music, so Joplin wanted to establish his name with more serious music.
   - (B) He is regarded as the father of ragtime, a form of popular music; Joplin wanted to establish his name with more serious music.
   - (C) He is regarded as the father of ragtime, a form of popular music, but Joplin wanted to establish his name with more serious music. ❼
   - (D) Rather than being regarded as the father of ragtime, a form of popular music, Joplin wanted to establish his name with more serious music.
   - (E) He is regarded as the father of ragtime, a form of popular music, and Joplin wanted to establish his name with more serious music.

Tips: Grammar and Style

❶ Read the entire sentence or passage to grasp its overall meaning. Pay particular attention to any underlined portions.

❷ Parenthetical thoughts can be inserted between dashes to interrupt the main flow of a sentence.

❸ Use prefixes to help you understand unfamiliar words. In test item 1, *un-*, for example, means "a reverse action." To unearth is to dig up.

❹ Don't confuse words that look or sound alike. *Except* means "other than"; *accept* means "to receive willingly."

❺ In choosing a revision, read through all of the choices before you and decide which one is best. Choose this answer (A) only if the sentence is correct as it appears originally.

❻ Parallelism is an important part of sentence structure. In test item 2, *biographer* and *poet* are both nouns and both descriptions of Sandburg.

❼ Know the meanings of conjunctions.

Answers: 1. (A), **2.** (B), **3.** (C)

Some tests may measure your understanding of a passage by asking you to write a response.

> **Directions:** Read the passage. Then answer the questions that follow.

> When I was a boy my grandfather died, and he was a sculptor. He was also a very kind man who had a lot of love to give the world, and he helped clean up the slum in our town; and he made toys for us and he did a million things in his lifetime; he was always busy with his hands. . . .
>
> Everyone must leave something behind when he dies, my grandfather said. A child or a book or a painting or a house or a wall built or a pair of shoes made. Or a garden planted. Something your hand touched some way so your soul has somewhere to go when you die, and when people look at that tree or that flower you planted, you're there. It doesn't matter what you do, he said, so long as you change something from the way it was before you touched it into something that's like you after you take your hands away. The difference between the man who just cuts lawns and a real gardener is in the touching, he said. The lawn-cutter might just as well not have been there at all; the gardener will be there a lifetime.
>
> —Ray Bradbury, *Fahrenheit 451*

SHORT RESPONSE

What things does the grandfather say we can create that will live after we die? Write a sentence that names two of those things.

> **SAMPLE SHORT RESPONSE**
>
> The grandfather says we can live on in a book we write or a house we build. **❶**

EXTENDED RESPONSE

What does the grandfather mean when he says, "Everyone must leave something behind when he dies"? Write one or two paragraphs to answer this question.

> **SAMPLE EXTENDED RESPONSE**
>
> The grandfather in this passage believes that people should create things that they will be remembered for. The things we create, whether they are **❸** works of art or the children we raise, express our individuality. Just as we leave fingerprints when we touch something, we leave a part of ourselves in the things we create. A person who creates something of worth or **❷** beauty will be remembered for generations to come. For that reason, the grandfather is urging his grandchild to make a difference with his life.

Tips: Responding to Writing Prompts

❶ Short-response prompts are often fact based rather than interpretive. Get right to the point in your answer, and stick to the facts.

❷ Make sure that you write about the assigned topic. Support your answer with details from the passage, such as a quotation, a paraphrase, or an example.

❸ When you are writing an extended response, build your paragraphs around clear topic sentences that will pull your ideas together.

❹ If you are asked to interpret a passage, don't just copy the author's words. Try to express the ideas in your own words. Express your ideas clearly, so that the reader understands your viewpoint.

❺ Proofread your response for errors in capitalization, punctuation, spelling, or grammar.

4 Essay

To determine how well you can develop and support your thoughts, many tests ask you to write an essay in response to an assignment, or prompt. The essay will represent a first draft and will be scored based on the following:

- **Focus** Establish a point of view in the opening paragraph.
- **Organization** Maintain a logical progression of ideas.
- **Support for ideas** Use details and examples to develop an argument.
- **Style/word choice** Use words accurately and vary sentences.
- **Grammar** Use standard English and proofread for errors.

Think carefully about the issue presented in these quotations and the assignment that follows.

> No slogan of democracy; no battle cry of freedom is more stirring than the American parent's simple statement which all of you have heard so many times: 'I want my child to go to college.' —Lyndon Baines Johnson
>
> Everybody can be great. Because anybody can serve. You don't have to have a college degree to serve. —Dr. Martin Luther King Jr.

Assignment: What is your view on the idea that a college education is needed to be successful in our society? Plan and write an essay in which you develop your point of view on this issue. Support your position with examples from your reading, your experience, or current events.

SAMPLE ESSAY

Some people believe that everyone needs a college degree. Education is important, but I don't think a four-year university education is needed to be ❶ successful in our society.

Electricians, plumbers, and carpenters go through specialized training in their fields. They don't need to be college graduates to do their work. Blue-collar workers are the backbone of our society. Where would we be if no one took vocational training? Who would repair our cars and unclog our sinks? The college-educated professional won't do it. Unskilled work is important, too. Dishwashers and taxi drivers may not have even a high school education, but many people rely on the services they provide. ❸

On the other hand, a practical education combined with some college ❷ courses in business administration might mean the difference between being an electrician and owning a successful electrical contracting business. Bill Gates is a good example. He started building computers from kits when he was in high school. He went to Harvard for a while, but he dropped out so that he could pursue his own idea of creating an operating system for personal ❸ computers. He invented DOS (disk operating system) and founded Microsoft.

In conclusion, people should have a chance to receive the highest level of education that their potential and effort allow. It's great to have some college experience, because it exposes you to new people and new ideas, but it is not ❹ necessary for everyone to receive a four-year university education.

Tips: Writing an Essay

The SAT test allows only 25 minutes for you to write an essay. So before you begin writing, take a few minutes to gather your thoughts. Write down the main points you want to make. Allow time to reread your essay before you hand it in. Make sure your handwriting is legible.

❶ When you're writing a persuasive essay, state your point of view in the introduction.

❷ Take the opposing point of view into consideration and respond to it.

❸ Use examples in the body of your essay to clarify your points and strengthen your arguments.

❹ Make sure your essay has a conclusion, even if it's just a single sentence. A conclusion pulls your ideas together and lets the reader know you've finished.

❺ Allow enough time to reread what you have written. If you have to make a correction, do so neatly and legibly.

Glossary of Literary Terms

Act An act is a major division within a play, similar to a chapter in a book. Each act may be further divided into smaller sections, called scenes. Plays can have as many as five acts, as in Shakespeare's *Romeo and Juliet*. Neil Simon's *The Sneeze* is a one-act play.

Allegory An allegory is a work with two levels of meaning—a literal one and a symbolic one. In such a work, most of the characters, objects, settings, and events represent abstract qualities. Personification is often used in traditional allegories. As in a fable or a parable, the purpose of an allegory may be to convey truths about life, to teach religious or moral lessons, or to criticize social institutions.

Alliteration Alliteration is the repetition of consonant sounds at the beginning of words. Note the repetition of the *d* sound in these lines.

> Deep into that darkness peering, long I stood there
>   wondering, fearing,
> Doubting, dreaming dreams no mortal ever dared to
>   dream before
> —Edgar Allan Poe, "The Raven"

See pages 139, 670, 797.
See also **Consonance.**

Allusion An allusion is an indirect reference to a famous person, place, event, or literary work. The title of Maya Angelou's autobiography *I Know Why the Caged Bird Sings* is an allusion to the poem "Sympathy" by Paul Laurence Dunbar.
See pages 238, 608, 837, 933, 1096.

Analogy An analogy is a point-by-point comparison between two things that are alike in some respect. Often, writers use analogies in nonfiction to explain unfamiliar subjects or ideas in terms of familiar ones.
See also **Extended Metaphor; Metaphor; Simile.**

Antagonist An antagonist is a principal character or force in opposition to a **protagonist,** or main character. The antagonist is usually another character but sometimes can be a force of nature, a set of circumstances, some aspect of society, or a force within the protagonist. In "The Most Dangerous Game," General Zaroff is the antagonist.
See pages 370, 930.

Archetype An archetype is a pattern in literature that is found in a variety of works from different cultures throughout the ages. An archetype can be a plot, a character, an image, or a setting. For example, the association of death and rebirth with winter and spring is an archetype common to many cultures.

Aside In drama, an aside is a short speech directed to the audience, or another character, that is not heard by the other characters on stage. In Act Four, Scene 1, of *Romeo and Juliet*, Paris is urging that his marriage to Juliet take place soon. Friar Laurence expresses his uneasiness in an aside.

> Friar Laurence [*aside*]. I would I knew not why it
>   should be slowed.—
> Look, sir, here comes the lady toward my cell.
> —William Shakespeare, *Romeo and Juliet*

See pages 939, 1018.
See also **Soliloquy.**

Assonance Assonance is the repetition of vowel sounds within nonrhyming words. An example of assonance is the repetition of the *u* sound in the following line.

> Only their usual maneuvers, dear
> —W. H. Auden, "O What Is That Sound"

Author's Perspective An author's perspective is a unique combination of ideas, values, feelings, and beliefs that influences the way the writer looks at a topic. **Tone,** or attitude, often reveals an author's perspective. Julia Alvarez in "Daughter of Invention" writes from a perspective that reflects her feelings about being an immigrant in America.
See pages 361, 459, 508, 569.
See also **Author's Purpose; Tone.**

Author's Purpose A writer usually writes for one or more of these purposes: to express thoughts or feelings, to inform or explain, to persuade, to entertain. For example, Pat Mora's purposes for writing "A Voice" are to express her feelings and to explain.
See also **Author's Perspective.**

Autobiography An autobiography is a writer's account of his or her own life. In almost every case, it is told from the first-person point of view. Generally, an autobiography focuses on the most significant events and people in the writer's life over a period of time. Richard Wright's *Black Boy* is an autobiography. Shorter autobiographical narratives include **journals, diaries,** and **letters.** An **autobiographical**

essay, another type of short autobiographical work, focuses on a single person or event in the writer's life.

See pages 9, 111, 236.

See also **Memoir.**

Ballad A ballad is a type of narrative poem that tells a story and was originally meant to be sung or recited. Because it tells a story, a ballad has a setting, a plot, and characters. **Traditional ballads** are written in four-line stanzas with regular rhythm and rhyme. **Folk ballads** were composed orally and handed down by word of mouth. These ballads usually tell about ordinary people who have unusual adventures or perform daring deeds. A **literary ballad** is a poem written by a poet in imitation of the form and content of a folk ballad. "O What Is That Sound" is an example of a literary ballad.

Biography A biography is the true account of a person's life, written by another person. As such, a biography is usually told from a third-person point of view. The writer of a biography usually researches his or her subject in order to present accurate information. The best biographers strive for honesty and balance in their accounts of their subjects' lives.

Blank Verse Blank verse is unrhymed poetry written in **iambic pentameter.** That is, each line of blank verse has five pairs of syllables. In most pairs, an unstressed syllable is followed by a stressed syllable. The most versatile of poetic forms, blank verse imitates the natural rhythms of English speech. Much of Shakespeare's drama is in blank verse.

> Bŭt sŏft! Whăt líght thrŏugh yóndĕr wíndŏw bréaks?
> Ĭt ĭs thĕ Éast, ănd Júlĭĕt ĭs thĕ sún!
> —William Shakespeare, *Romeo and Juliet*

See also **Iambic Pentameter.**

Cast of Characters In the script of a play, a cast of characters is a list of all the characters in the play, usually in order of appearance. It may include a brief description of each character.

Character Characters are the individuals who participate in the action of a literary work. Like real people, characters display certain qualities, or **character traits;** they develop and change over time; and they usually have **motivations,** or reasons, for their behaviors.

> **Main characters:** Main characters are the most important characters in literary works. Generally, the plot of a short story focuses on one main character, but a novel may have several main characters.

Minor characters: The less prominent characters in a literary work are known as minor characters. Minor characters support the plot. The story is not centered on them, but they help carry out the action of the story and help the reader learn more about the main character.

Dynamic character: A dynamic character is one who undergoes important changes as a plot unfolds. The changes occur because of his or her actions and experiences in the story. The change is usually internal and may be good or bad. Main characters are usually, though not always, dynamic.

Static character: A static character is one who remains the same throughout a story. The character may experience events and have interactions with other characters, but he or she is not changed because of them.

Round character: A round character is one who is complex and highly developed, having a variety of traits and different sides to his or her personality. Some of the traits may create conflict in the character. Round characters tend to display strengths, weaknesses, and a full range of emotions. The writer provides enough detail for the reader to understand their feelings and emotions.

Flat character: A flat character is one who is not highly developed. A flat character is a one-sided character: he or she usually has one outstanding trait, characteristic, or role. Flat characters exist mainly to advance the plot, and they display only the traits needed for their limited roles. Minor characters are usually flat characters.

See pages 79, 186, 207, 233.

See also **Characterization.**

Characterization The way a writer creates and develops characters' personalities is known as characterization. There are four basic methods of characterization:

- The writer may make direct comments about a character's personality or nature through the voice of the narrator.
- The writer may describe the character's physical appearance.
- The writer may present the character's own thoughts, speech, and actions.
- The writer may present pertinent thoughts, speech, and actions of other characters.

See pages 188, 237, 275.

See also **Character.**

Chorus In early Greek tragedy, the chorus commented on the actions of the characters in a drama. In some Elizabethan plays, such as Shakespeare's *Romeo and Juliet,* the role of the chorus is taken by a single actor who serves

as a narrator and speaks the lines in the **prologue** (and sometimes in an **epilogue**). The chorus serves to foreshadow or summarize events.

Climax In a plot, the climax is the point of maximum interest or tension. Usually the climax is a turning point in the story, which occurs after the reader has understood the **conflict** and become emotionally involved with the characters. The climax sometimes, but not always, points to the **resolution** of the conflict. In "American History" by Judith Ortiz Cofer, the climax occurs when Elena encounters Eugene's mother at the door of Eugene's house.
See pages 420, 876.
See also **Plot.**

Comedy A comedy is a dramatic work that is light and often humorous in tone, usually ending happily with a peaceful resolution of the main conflict. A comedy differs from a farce by having a more believable plot, more realistic characters, and less boisterous behavior.

Comic Relief Comic relief consists of humorous scenes, incidents, or speeches that are included in a serious drama to provide a reduction in emotional intensity. Because comic relief breaks the tension, it allows an audience to prepare emotionally for events to come. Shakespeare often uses this device in his tragedies.
Example: In many of Shakespeare's plays, a scene involving a fool, or bawdy interplay among common folks or between a servant and his or her master, provides comic relief. Comic relief in *Romeo and Juliet* is provided by the nurse in Act Two, Scene 5, when she returns to Juliet after learning the wedding plans from Romeo. Although Juliet is anxious to hear of the plans, which the audience already knows, the nurse deliberately withholds the information until the end of the scene.

Complication A complication is an additional factor or problem introduced into the rising action of a story to make the conflict more difficult. Often, a plot complication makes it seem as though the main character is getting farther away from the thing he or she wants.

Conflict A conflict is a struggle between opposing forces. Almost every story has a main conflict—a conflict that is the story's focus. An **external conflict** involves a character pitted against an outside force, such as nature, a physical obstacle, or another character. An **internal conflict** is one that occurs within a character.
Examples: In "The Most Dangerous Game" by Richard Connell, Rainsford is in conflict with General Zaroff. In Doris Lessing's "Through the Tunnel," Jerry is torn between the

safety of familiar beach surroundings and the challenge of swimming through the tunnel.
See pages 24, 53, 54, 328, 761.
See also **Plot.**

Connotation A connotation is an attitude or a feeling associated with a word, in contrast to the word's **denotation,** which is its literal, or dictionary, meaning. The connotations of a word may be positive or negative. For example, *enthusiastic* has positive associations, while *rowdy* has negative ones. Connotations of words can have an important influence on style and meaning and are particularly important in poetry.

Consonance Consonance is the repetition of consonant sounds within and at the end of words, as in "lonely afternoon." Consonance is unlike rhyme in that the vowel sounds preceding or following the repeated consonant sounds differ. Consonance is often used together with **alliteration, assonance,** and **rhyme** to create a musical quality, to emphasize certain words, or to unify a poem.
See also **Alliteration.**

Couplet A couplet is a rhymed pair of lines. A couplet may be written in any rhythmic pattern.

> From what I've tasted of desire
> I hold with those who favor fire.
> —Robert Frost, "Fire and Ice"

See also **Stanza.**

Critical Essay *See* **Essay.**

Denotation *See* **Connotation.**

Dénouement *See* **Falling Action.**

Dialect A dialect is a form of language that is spoken in a particular geographic area or by a particular social or ethnic group. A group's dialect is reflected in its pronunciations, vocabulary, expressions, and grammatical structures. Writers use dialects to capture the flavors of locales and to bring characters to life, re-creating the way they actually speak. In "Two Kinds" by Amy Tan, the narrator's mother uses grammatical constructions that are not common in English and therefore speaks a kind of dialect.

> "Who ask you be genius?" she shouted. "Only ask you be your best. For your sake. You think I want you be genius?"
> —Amy Tan, "Two Kinds"

Dialogue Dialogue is written conversation between two or more characters. Writers use dialogue to bring characters to life and to give readers insights into the characters' qualities, traits, and reactions to other characters. Realistic, well-paced dialogue also advances the plot of a narrative. In fiction, dialogue is usually set off with quotation marks. In drama, stories are told primarily through dialogue. Playwrights use stage directions to indicate how they intend the dialogue to be interpreted by actors.

Diary A diary is a daily record of a writer's thoughts, experiences, and feelings. As such, it is a type of autobiographical writing. The terms *diary* and *journal* are often used synonymously.

Diction A writer's or speaker's choice of words and way of arranging the words in sentences is called diction. Diction can be broadly characterized as formal or informal. It can also be described as technical or common, abstract or concrete, and literal or figurative. A writer for *Scientific American* would use a more formal, more technical, and possibly more abstract diction than would a writer for the science section of a local newspaper.

See pages 515, 605.

See also **Style.**

Drama Drama is literature in which plots and characters are developed through dialogue and action; in other words, it is literature in play form. Drama is meant to be performed. Stage plays, radio plays, movies, and television programs are types of drama. Most plays are divided into acts, with each act having an emotional peak, or climax. Certain modern plays, such as *The Sneeze*, have only one act. Most plays contain stage directions, which describe settings, lighting, sound effects, the movements and emotions of actors, and the ways in which dialogue should be spoken.

Dramatic Irony *See* **Irony.**

Dramatic Monologue A dramatic monologue is a lyric poem in which a speaker addresses a silent or absent listener in a moment of high intensity or deep emotion, as if engaged in private conversation. The speaker proceeds without interruption or argument, and the effect on the reader is that of hearing just one side of a conversation. This technique allows the poet to focus on the feelings, personality, and motivations of the speaker. The poem known as "The Seven Ages of Man," spoken by Jaques, a character in Shakespeare's play *As You Like It,* is a dramatic monologue.

See page 721.

See also **Lyric Poetry; Soliloquy.**

Dynamic Character *See* **Character.**

Elegy An elegy is an extended meditative poem in which the speaker reflects on death—often in tribute to a person who has died recently—or on an equally serious subject. Most elegies are written in formal, dignified language and are serious in tone.

Epic An epic is a long narrative poem on a serious subject, presented in an elevated or formal style. It traces the adventures of a great hero whose actions reflect the ideals and values of a nation or race. Epics address universal concerns, such as good and evil, life and death, and sin and redemption. The *Odyssey* is an epic.

Epic Hero An epic hero is a larger-than-life figure who embodies the ideals of a nation or race. Epic heroes take part in dangerous adventures and accomplish great deeds. Many undertake long, difficult journeys and display great courage and superhuman strength.

See page 1094.

Epic Simile An epic simile (also called a Homeric simile) is a long, elaborate comparison that often continues for a number of lines.

> Just as a farmer's hunger grows, behind
> the bolted plow and share, all day afield,
> drawn by his team of winedark oxen: sundown
> is benison for him, sending him homeward
> stiff in the knees from weariness, to dine;
> just so the light on the sea rim gladdened
> Odysseus.
>
> —Homer, *Odyssey*

See page 1096.

See also **Simile.**

Epilogue An epilogue is a short addition at the end of a literary work, often dealing with the future of the characters. The concluding speech by Prince Escalus in *Romeo and Juliet* serves as an epilogue.

Epithet An epithet is a brief phrase that points out traits associated with a particular person or thing. In the *Odyssey*, Odysseus is often called "the master strategist."

See page 1096.

Essay An essay is a short work of nonfiction that deals with a single subject. Some essays are **formal**—that is, tightly structured and written in an impersonal style. Others are **informal,** with a looser structure and a more personal

style. Generally, an **expository essay** presents or explains information and ideas. A **personal essay** is typically an informal essay in which the writer expresses his or her thoughts and feelings about a subject, focusing on the meaning of events and issues in his or her own life. In a **reflective essay**, the author makes a connection between a personal observation or experience and a universal idea, such as love, courage, or freedom. A **critical essay** evaluates a situation, a course of action, or a work of art. In a **persuasive essay**, the author attempts to convince readers to adopt a certain viewpoint or to take a particular stand.

See pages 8, 458, 514, 524, 774, 783.

Exposition Exposition is the first stage of a plot in a typical story. The exposition provides important background information and introduces the setting and the important characters. The conflict the characters face may also be introduced in the exposition, or it may be introduced later, in the rising action.

See page 24.
See also **Plot**.

Expository Essay *See* **Essay**.

Extended Metaphor An extended metaphor is a figure of speech that compares two essentially unlike things at some length and in several ways. It does not contain the word *like* or *as*. For example, in "The Seven Ages of Man" by William Shakespeare, an extended metaphor compares the world to a stage.

> All the world's a stage,
> And all the men and women merely players
> —William Shakespeare, *As You Like It*

See also **Metaphor**.

External Conflict *See* **Conflict**.

Fable A fable is a brief tale told to illustrate a moral or teach a lesson. Often the moral of a fable appears in a distinct and memorable statement near the tale's beginning or end. "The Princess and the Tin Box" by James Thurber is a humorous fable.

See also **Moral**.

Falling Action In a plot, the falling action follows the climax and shows the results of the important action that happened at the climax. Tension eases as the falling action begins; however, the final outcome of the story is not yet fully worked out at this stage. Events in the falling action lead to the **resolution**, or **dénouement**, of the plot. In "American History" by Judith Ortiz Cofer, the falling action begins when the narrator turns away from the door of Eugene's house.

See page 24.
See also **Climax; Plot**.

Fantasy Fantasy is a type of fiction that is highly imaginative and portrays events, settings, or characters that are unrealistic. The setting might be a nonexistent world, the plot might involve magic or the supernatural, and the characters might employ superhuman powers.

Farce Farce is a type of exaggerated comedy that features an absurd plot, ridiculous situations, and humorous dialogue. The main purpose of a farce is to keep an audience laughing. The characters are usually stereotypes, or simplified examples of individual traits or qualities. Comic devices typically used in farces include mistaken identity, deception, physical comedy, wordplay—such as puns and double meanings—and exaggeration.

Fiction Fiction is prose writing that consists of imaginary elements. Although fiction can be inspired by actual events and real people, it usually springs from writers' imaginations. The basic elements of fiction are plot, character, setting, and theme. The novel and short story are forms of fiction.

See also **Character; Novel; Plot; Setting; Short Story; Theme**.

Figurative Language Figurative language is language that communicates meanings beyond the literal meanings of words. In figurative language, words are often used to symbolize ideas and concepts they would not otherwise be associated with. Writers use figurative language to create effects, to emphasize ideas, and to evoke emotions. Simile, metaphor, extended metaphor, hyperbole, and personification are examples of figurative language.

See pages 703, 791, 991.
See also **Hyperbole; Metaphor; Onomatopoeia; Personification; Simile**.

First-Person Point of View *See* **Point of View**.

Flashback A flashback is an account of a conversation, an episode, or an event that happened before the beginning of a story. Often, a flashback interrupts the chronological flow of a story to give the reader information needed for the understanding of a character's present situation.

Example: In "Where Have You Gone, Charming Billy?" Tim O'Brien uses flashbacks to help capture the thought process

of the main character as he copes with the realities of his wartime experience.

Foil A foil is a character who provides a striking contrast to another character. By using a foil, a writer can call attention to certain traits possessed by a main character or simply enhance a character by contrast. In Shakespeare's *Romeo and Juliet*, Mercutio serves as a foil to Romeo.

Foreshadowing Foreshadowing is a writer's use of hints or clues to suggest events that will occur later in a story. The hints and clues might be included in a character's dialogue or behavior, or they might be included in details of description. Foreshadowing creates suspense and makes readers eager to find out what will happen. For example, in Stephen King's teleplay *Sorry, Right Number,* the opening camera close-up and the first line of dialogue seem to hint that the telephone and Bill's health will be important in the play.

Form *Form* refers to the principles of arrangement in a poem—the ways in which lines are organized. Form in poetry includes the following elements: the length of lines, the placement of lines, and the grouping of lines into stanzas. *See also* **Stanza.**

Free Verse Free verse is poetry that does not contain regular patterns of rhythm or rhyme. The lines in free verse often flow more naturally than do rhymed, metrical lines and thus achieve a rhythm more like that of everyday speech. Although free verse lacks conventional meter, it may contain various rhythmic and sound effects, such as repetitions of syllables or words. Free verse can be used for a variety of subjects. Billy Collins's poem "Today" is an example of free verse.
See pages 669, 797.
See also **Meter; Rhyme.**

Genre The term *genre* refers to a category in which a work of literature is classified. The major genres in literature are fiction, nonfiction, poetry, and drama.

Haiku Haiku is a form of Japanese poetry in which 17 syllables are arranged in three lines of 5, 7, and 5 syllables. The rules of haiku are strict. In addition to the syllabic count, the poet must create a clear picture that will evoke a strong emotional response in the reader. Nature is a particularly important source of inspiration for Japanese haiku poets, and details from nature are often the subjects of their poems.

> Harvest moon—
> walking around the pond
> all night long.
>
> —Bashō

Hero A hero is a main character or protagonist in a story. In older literary works, heroes tend to be better than ordinary humans. They are typically courageous, strong, honorable, and intelligent. They are protectors of society who hold back the forces of evil and fight to make the world a better place. In modern literature, a hero may simply be the most important character in a story. Such a hero is often an ordinary person with ordinary problems.

Historical Fiction A short story or novel can be classified as historical fiction when the settings and details of the plot include real places and real events of historical importance. Historical figures may appear as major or minor characters, as Napoleon does in Leo Tolstoy's classic novel *War and Peace.* In historical fiction, the setting generally influences the plot in important ways.

Horror Fiction Horror fiction contains strange, mysterious, violent, and often supernatural events that create suspense and terror in the reader. Edgar Allan Poe and Stephen King are famous authors of horror fiction.

Humor In literature, there are three basic types of humor, all of which may involve exaggeration or irony. **Humor of situation** arises out of the plot of a work. It usually involves exaggerated events or situational irony, which arises when something happens that is different from what was expected. **Humor of character** is often based on exaggerated personalities or on characters' failure to recognize their own flaws, a form of dramatic irony. **Humor of language** may include sarcasm, exaggeration, puns, or verbal irony, in which what is said is not what is meant.
See page 775.
See also **Irony.**

Hyperbole Hyperbole is a figure of speech in which the truth is exaggerated for emphasis or humorous effect.

Iambic Pentameter Iambic pentameter is a metrical pattern of five feet, or units, each of which is made up of two syllables, the first unstressed and the second stressed. Iambic pentameter is the most common meter used in English poetry; it is the meter used in blank verse and in the sonnet. The following lines are examples of iambic pentameter.

> My lips, two blushing pilgrims, ready stand
>   —William Shakespeare, *Romeo and Juliet*

See pages 725, 932.
See also **Blank Verse; Sonnet.**

Idiom An idiom is a common figure of speech whose meaning is different from the literal meaning of its words. For example, the phrase "raining cats and dogs" does not literally mean that cats and dogs are falling from the sky; the expression means "raining heavily."

Imagery Imagery consists of descriptive words and phrases that re-create sensory experiences for the reader. Imagery usually appeals to one or more of the five senses—sight, hearing, smell, taste, and touch—to help the reader imagine exactly what is being described. The imagery in the poem "Incident in a Rose Garden" by Donald Justice helps the reader to see Death, who wears a black coat, black gloves, and a black hat. Truman Capote uses vivid imagery appealing to multiple senses in order to re-create the childhood of the narrator in "A Christmas Memory."
See pages 145, 273, 304, 309, 379, 677.

Internal Conflict *See* **Conflict.**

Interview An interview is a conversation conducted by a writer or reporter, in which facts or statements are elicited from another person, recorded, and then broadcast or published. "Tim O'Brien: The Naked Soldier" is an example of an interview.
See page 760.

Irony Irony is a special kind of contrast between appearance and reality—usually one in which reality is the opposite of what it seems. One type of irony is **situational irony,** a contrast between what a reader or character expects and what actually exists or happens. The unexpected twist in the outcome of "The Gift of the Magi" by O. Henry is an example of situational irony. Another type of irony is **dramatic irony,** where the reader or viewer knows something that a character does not know. **Verbal irony** exists when someone knowingly exaggerates or says one thing and means another.
See pages 95, 780, 811.

Journal *See* **Diary.**

Limited Point of View *See* **Point of View.**

Line The line is the core unit of a poem. In poetry, line length is an essential element of the poem's meaning and rhythm. **Line breaks,** where a line of poetry ends, may coincide with grammatical units. However, a line break may also occur in the middle of a grammatical or syntactical unit, creating a meaningful pause or emphasis. Poets use a variety of line breaks to play with sense, grammar, and syntax and thereby create a wide range of effects.

Literary Criticism Literary criticism is a form of writing in which works of literature are compared, analyzed, interpreted, or evaluated. Two common forms of literary criticism are book reviews and critical essays.

Literary Nonfiction Literary nonfiction is nonfiction that is recognized as being of artistic value or that is about literature. Autobiographies, biographies, essays, and eloquent speeches typically fall into this category.

Lyric Poetry A lyric poem is a short poem in which a single speaker expresses personal thoughts and feelings. Most poems other than dramatic and narrative poems are lyric poems. In ancient Greece, lyric poetry was meant to be sung. Modern lyrics are usually not intended for singing, but they are characterized by strong melodic rhythms. Lyric poetry has a variety of forms and covers many subjects, from love and death to everyday experiences. Langston Hughes's "Theme for English B" and Pat Mora's "A Voice" are examples of lyric poems.

Memoir A memoir is a form of autobiographical writing in which a writer shares his or her personal experiences and observations of significant events or people. Often informal or even intimate in tone, memoirs usually give readers insight into the impact of historical events on people's lives. *Angela's Ashes* by Frank McCourt is a memoir.
See pages 165, 837.
See also **Autobiography.**

Metaphor A metaphor is a figure of speech that makes a comparison between two things that are basically unlike but have something in common. Unlike similes, metaphors do not contain the word *like* or *as.* In "Ode to My Socks," Pablo Neruda uses metaphors to compare his socks to multiple objects, including "two long sharks of lapis blue."
See also **Extended Metaphor; Figurative Language; Simile.**

Meter Meter is a regular pattern of stressed and unstressed syllables in a poem. The meter of a poem emphasizes the musical quality of the language. Each unit of meter, known as a **foot,** consists of one stressed syllable and one or two unstressed syllables. In representations of meter, a stressed syllable is indicated by the symbol ´; an unstressed syllable, by the symbol ˘. The four basic types of metrical feet are the **iamb,** an unstressed syllable followed by a stressed syllable (˘´); the **trochee,** a stressed syllable

followed by an unstressed syllable (⌣⌣); the **anapest,** two unstressed syllables followed by a stressed syllable (⌣⌣⌣); and the **dactyl,** a stressed syllable followed by two unstressed syllables (⌣⌣⌣).

See pages 671, 721.

See also **Rhythm.**

Mise en Scène *Mise en scène* is a term from the French that refers to the various physical aspects of a dramatic presentation, such as lighting, costumes, scenery, makeup, and props.

Mood In a literary work, mood is the feeling or atmosphere that a writer creates for the reader. Descriptive words, imagery, and figurative language contribute to the mood of a work, as do the sound and rhythm of the language used. In "The Cask of Amontillado," Edgar Allan Poe creates a mood of dread and horror.

See pages 304, 343, 361.

See also **Tone.**

Moral A moral is a lesson taught in a literary work, such as a fable. For example, the moral "Do not count your chickens before they are hatched" teaches that one should not count on one's fortunes or blessings until they appear. In James Thurber's "The Princess and the Tin Box," the moral, like the fable itself, is satirical.

See also **Fable.**

Motivation *See* **Character.**

Myth A myth is a traditional story, usually concerning some superhuman being or unlikely event, that was once widely believed to be true. Frequently, myths were attempts to explain natural phenomena, such as solar and lunar eclipses or the cycle of the seasons. For some peoples, myths were both a kind of science and a religion. In addition, myths served as literature and entertainment, just as they do for modern-day audiences.

Greek mythology forms much of the background in Homer's *Odyssey.* For example, the myth of the judgment of Paris describes events that led to the Trojan War. The goddesses Athena, Hera, and Aphrodite asked a mortal—Paris—to decide which of them was the most beautiful. Paris chose Aphrodite and was rewarded by her with Helen, wife of the Greek king Menelaus.

Narrative Nonfiction Narrative nonfiction is writing that reads much like fiction, except that the characters, setting, and plot are real rather than imaginary. Its purpose is usually to entertain or to express opinions or feelings. Narrative nonfiction includes, but is not limited to, autobiographies, biographies, memoirs, diaries, and journals. *Seabiscuit* by Laura Hillenbrand is an example of narrative nonfiction.

See page 122.

Narrative Poetry Narrative poetry tells a story or recounts events. Like a short story or a novel, a narrative poem has the following elements: plot, characters, setting, and theme. "The Raven" by Edgar Allan Poe is a narrative poem.

Narrator The narrator of a story is the character or voice that relates the story's events to the reader.

See also **Persona; Point of View.**

Nonfiction Nonfiction is writing that tells about real people, places, and events. Unlike fiction, nonfiction is mainly written to convey factual information, although writers of nonfiction shape information in accordance with their own purposes and attitudes. Nonfiction can be a good source of information, but readers frequently have to examine it carefully in order to detect biases, notice gaps in the information provided, and identify errors in logic. Nonfiction includes a diverse range of writing—newspaper articles, letters, essays, biographies, movie reviews, speeches, true-life adventure stories, advertising, and more.

Novel A novel is an extended work of fiction. Like a short story, a novel is essentially the product of a writer's imagination. Because a novel is considerably longer than a short story, a novelist can develop a wider range of characters and a more complex plot.

Example: In John Knowles's novel *A Separate Peace,* Gene's character develops as he struggles with guilt that resulted from the "accident" that crippled Phineas.

Novella A novella is a work of fiction that is longer than a short story but shorter than a novel. A novella differs from a novel in that it concentrates on a limited cast of characters, a relatively short time span, and a single chain of events. The novella is an attempt to combine the compression of the short story with the development of the novel.

Ode An ode is a complex lyric poem that develops a serious and dignified theme. Odes appeal to both the imagination and the intellect, and many commemorate events or praise people or elements of nature.

Omniscient Point of View *See* **Point of View.**

Onomatopoeia Onomatopoeia is the use of words whose sounds echo their meanings, such as *buzz, whisper, gargle,* and *murmur.* Onomatopoeia as a literary technique goes

beyond the use of simple echoic words, however. Skilled writers, especially poets, choose words whose sounds intensify images and suggest meanings.

Oxymoron An oxymoron is a special kind of concise paradox that brings together two contradictory terms. In *Romeo and Juliet,* each of the phrases "brawling love," "loving hate," "bright smoke," and "feather of lead" is an oxymoron.

Paradox A paradox is a seemingly contradictory or absurd statement that may nonetheless suggest an important truth.

Parallelism Parallelism is the use of similar grammatical constructions to express ideas that are related or equal in importance.

> Go back to Mississippi. Go back to Alabama. Go back to South Carolina. Go back to Georgia. Go back to Louisiana. Go back to the slums and ghettos of our Northern cities. . . .
> —Martin Luther King Jr., "I Have a Dream"

Parallel Plot A parallel plot is a particular type of plot in which two stories of equal importance are told simultaneously. The story moves back and forth between the two plots.

Parody A parody is an imitation of another work, a type of literature, or a writer's style, usually for the purpose of poking fun. It may serve as an element of a larger work or be a complete work in itself. The purpose of parody may be to ridicule through broad humor, deploying such techniques as exaggeration or the use of inappropriate subject matter. Such techniques may even provide insights into the original work. "The Princess and the Tin Box" by James Thurber is a parody of the typical moralistic fairy tale.

Persona A persona is a voice that a writer assumes in a particular work. A persona is like a mask worn by the writer, separating his or her identity from that of the speaker or the narrator. It is the persona's voice—not the writer's voice— that narrates a story or speaks in a poem.
See also **Narrator; Speaker.**

Personal Essay *See* **Essay.**

Personification Personification is a figure of speech in which human qualities are given to an object, animal, or idea. In "Incident in a Rose Garden" by Donald Justice, death is personified as someone who wears black and grins. In the following line by Shakespeare, morning is personified.

> The grey-eyed morn smiles on the frowning night
> —William Shakespeare, *Romeo and Juliet*

See pages 672, 703.
See also **Figurative Language.**

Persuasive Essay *See* **Essay.**

Play *See* **Drama.**

Plot The sequence of events in a story is called the plot. A plot focuses on a central **conflict** or problem faced by the main character. The actions that the characters take to resolve the conflict build toward a climax. In general, it is not long after this point that the conflict is resolved and the story ends. A plot typically develops in five stages: exposition, rising action, climax, falling action, and resolution.
See pages 24, 79.
See also **Climax; Exposition; Falling Action; Rising Action.**

Poetry Poetry is a type of literature in which words are carefully chosen and arranged to create certain effects. Poets use a variety of sound devices, imagery, and figurative language to express emotions and ideas.
See also **Alliteration; Assonance; Ballad; Free Verse; Imagery; Meter; Rhyme; Rhythm; Stanza.**

Point of View *Point of view* refers to the method of narration used in a short story, novel, narrative poem, or work of nonfiction. In a work told from a **first-person** point of view, the narrator is a character in the story, as in "The Cask of Amontillado" by Edgar Allan Poe. In a work told from a **third-person** point of view, the narrative voice is outside the action, not one of the characters. If a story is told from a **third-person omniscient,** or all-knowing, point of view, as in "The Gift of the Magi" by O. Henry, the narrator sees into the minds of all the characters. If events are related from a **third-person limited** point of view, as in Doris Lessing's "Through the Tunnel," the narrator tells what only one character thinks, feels, and observes.
See pages 186, 193.
See also **Narrator.**

Prologue A prologue is an introductory scene in a drama. Some Elizabethan plays include prologues that comment on the theme or moral point that will be revealed in the play. The prologue is a feature of all Greek drama.

Prop   The word *prop*, originally an abbreviation of the word *property*, refers to any physical object that is used in a drama. In the teleplay *Sorry, Right Number*, a telephone is an important prop.

Prose   Generally, *prose* refers to all forms of written or spoken expression that are not in verse. The term, therefore, may be used to describe very different forms of writing—short stories as well as essays, for example.

Protagonist   A protagonist is the main character in a work of literature—the character who is involved in the central conflict of the story. Usually, the protagonist changes after the central conflict reaches a climax. He or she may be a hero and is usually the one with whom the audience tends to identify. In Judith Ortiz Cofer's "American History," Elena is the protagonist as well as the narrator.

Pun   A pun is a joke that comes from a play on words. It can make use of a word's multiple meanings or of a word's sound. In *Romeo and Juliet*, when Mercutio is fatally wounded, he says, "Ask for me tomorrow, and you shall find me a grave man," with a pun on the word *grave*, meaning both "solemn" and "a tomb."

Quatrain   A quatrain is a four-line stanza, or group of lines, in poetry. The most common stanza in English poetry, the quatrain can have a variety of meters and rhyme schemes.

Realistic Fiction   Realistic fiction is fiction that is a truthful imitation of ordinary life. "Through the Tunnel" by Doris Lessing and "A Christmas Memory" by Truman Capote are examples of realistic fiction.

Recurring Theme   *See* **Theme.**

Reflective Essay   *See* **Essay.**

Refrain   A refrain is one or more lines repeated in each stanza of a poem.
See also **Stanza.**

Repetition   Repetition is a technique in which a sound, word, phrase, or line is repeated for emphasis or unity. Repetition often helps to reinforce meaning and create an appealing rhythm. The term includes specific devices associated with both prose and poetry, such as alliteration and parallelism.
See pages 670, 715.
See also **Alliteration; Parallelism; Sound Devices.**

Resolution   *See* **Falling Action.**

Rhetorical Devices   Rhetorical devices are techniques writers use to enhance their arguments and communicate more effectively. Rhetorical devices include **analogy, parallelism, rhetorical questions,** and **repetition.**
See also **Analogy; Repetition; Rhetorical Questions,** *Glossary of Reading and Informational Terms, page R119.*

Rhyme   Rhyme is the occurrence of similar or identical sounds at the end of two or more words, such as *suite, heat,* and *complete*. Rhyme that occurs within a single line of poetry is **internal rhyme.** Rhyme that occurs at the ends of lines of poetry is called **end rhyme.** End rhyme that is not exact but approximate is called **slant rhyme,** or **off rhyme.** Notice the following example of slant rhyme involving the words *care* and *dear.*

> O haven't they stopped for the doctor's <u>care</u>,
>   Haven't they reined their horses, their horses?
> Why, they are none of them wounded, <u>dear</u>.
>   None of these forces.
>   —W. H. Auden, "O What Is That Sound"

See pages 670, 716, 791.

Rhyme Scheme   A rhyme scheme is a pattern of end rhymes in a poem. A rhyme scheme is noted by assigning a letter of the alphabet, beginning with *a*, to each line. Lines that rhyme are given the same letter. Notice the rhyme scheme of the first stanza of this famous poem.

> Two roads diverged in a yellow wood,   *a*
> And sorry I could not travel both   *b*
> And be one traveler, long I stood   *a*
> And looked down one as far as I could   *a*
> To where it bent in the undergrowth   *b*
>   —Robert Frost, "The Road Not Taken"

See page 670.

Rhythm   Rhythm is a pattern of stressed and unstressed syllables in a line of poetry. Poets use rhythm to bring out the musical quality of language, to emphasize ideas, to create moods, to unify works, and to heighten emotional responses. Devices such as alliteration, rhyme, assonance, consonance, and parallelism often contribute to creating rhythm.
See pages 670, 791.
See also **Meter.**

Rising Action Rising action is the stage in a plot in which the conflict develops and story events build toward a climax. During this stage, complications arise that make the conflict more intense. Tension grows as the characters struggle to resolve the conflict.

See page 24.

See also **Plot.**

Satire Satire is a literary technique in which ideas, customs, behaviors, or institutions are ridiculed for the purpose of improving society. Satire may be gently witty, mildly abrasive, or bitterly critical, and it often involves the use of irony and exaggeration to force readers to see something in a critical light.

Scansion Scansion is the notation of stressed and unstressed syllables in poetry. A stressed syllable is indicated by the symbol ´; an unstressed syllable, by the symbol ˘. Using scansion can help you determine the rhythm and meter of a poem.

See page 670.

See also **Meter.**

Scene In drama, the action is often divided into acts and scenes. Each scene presents an episode of the play's plot and typically occurs at a single place and time.

See also **Act.**

Scenery Scenery is a painted backdrop or other structures used to create the setting for a play.

Science Fiction Science fiction is fiction in which a writer explores unexpected possibilities of the past or the future, using known scientific data and theories as well as his or her creative imagination. Most science fiction writers create believable worlds, although some create fantasy worlds that have familiar elements. Ray Bradbury, the author of "A Sound of Thunder," is a famous writer of science fiction.

See also **Fantasy.**

Screenplay A screenplay is a play written for film.

Script The text of a play, film, or broadcast is called a script.

Sensory Details Sensory details are words and phrases that appeal to the reader's senses of sight, hearing, touch, smell, and taste. For example, the sensory detail "a fine film of rain" appeals to the senses of sight and touch. Sensory details stimulate the reader to create images in his or her mind.

See also **Imagery.**

Setting Setting is the time and place of the action of a story. Some stories, such as "The Open Window" by Saki,

have only minimal descriptions of setting. In other works, such as Eugenia Collier's "Marigolds" and Edgar Allan Poe's "The Cask of Amontillado," settings are described in detail and become major contributors to the stories' overall effect.

See pages 302, 309, 361.

See also **Fiction.**

Short Story A short story is a work of fiction that centers on a single idea and can be read in one sitting. Generally, a short story has one main conflict that involves the characters, keeps the story moving, and stimulates readers' interest.

See also **Fiction.**

Simile A simile is a figure of speech that makes a comparison between two unlike things, using the word *like* or *as*.

> I am offering this poem to you,
> since I have nothing else to give.
> Keep it <u>like a warm coat</u>
> When winter comes to cover you
> —Jimmy Santiago Baca, "I Am Offering This Poem"

See pages 672, 703.

See also **Epic Simile; Figurative Language; Metaphor.**

Situational Irony See **Irony.**

Soliloquy In drama, a soliloquy is a speech in which a character speaks his or her thoughts aloud. Generally, the character is on the stage alone, not speaking to other characters and perhaps not even consciously addressing an audience. At the beginning of Act Two, Scene 3, of *Romeo and Juliet*, Friar Laurence has a long soliloquy. Shakespeare makes use of soliloquies in many of his plays.

See also **Aside; Dramatic Monologue.**

Sonnet A sonnet is a lyric poem of 14 lines, commonly written in **iambic pentameter.** Sonnets are often classified as Petrarchan or Shakespearean. The Shakespearean, or Elizabethan, sonnet consists of three quatrains, or four-line units, and a final couplet. The typical rhyme scheme is *abab cdcd efef gg.*

See also **Iambic Pentameter; Rhyme Scheme.**

Sound Devices Sound devices, or uses of words for their auditory effect, can convey meaning and mood or unify a work. Some common sound devices are **alliteration, assonance, consonance, meter, onomatopoeia, repetition, rhyme,** and **rhythm.** The following lines contain alliteration, repetition, assonance, consonance, rhyme, and rhythm, all of which combine to help convey both meaning and mood.

> O what is that sound which so thrills the ear
> Down in the valley drumming, drumming:
> Only the scarlet soldiers, dear,
> The soldiers coming.
> —W. H. Auden, "O What Is That Sound"

See pages 139, 715.

See also **Alliteration; Assonance; Consonance; Meter; Onomatopoeia; Repetition; Rhyme; Rhythm.**

Speaker In poetry the speaker is the voice that "talks" to the reader, similar to the narrator in fiction. The speaker is not necessarily the poet. For example, in Pat Mora's "A Voice," the experiences related may or may not have happened to the poet.

See pages 269, 673, 715.

See also **Persona.**

Speech A speech is a talk or public address. The purpose of a speech may be to entertain, to explain, to persuade, to inspire, or any combination of these aims. "I Have a Dream" by Martin Luther King Jr. was written and delivered in order to inspire an audience.

See pages 600, 610.

Stage Directions A play typically includes instructions called stage directions, which are usually printed in italic type. They serve as a guide to directors, set and lighting designers, performers, and readers. When stage directions appear within passages of dialogue, parentheses are usually used to set them off from the words spoken by characters.

> Jeff *gets up, walks to the window, and looks out into the dark. He's really upset.* Dennis *and* Connie, *in the grand tradition of older brothers and sisters, are delighted to see it.*
> —Stephen King, *Sorry, Right Number*

See pages 7, 150, 934.

Stanza A stanza is a group of two or more lines that form a unit in a poem. A stanza is comparable to a paragraph in prose. Each stanza may have the same number of lines, or the number of lines may vary. "The Road Not Taken" by Robert Frost is divided into four stanzas.

See also **Couplet; Form; Poetry; Quatrain.**

Static Character *See* **Character.**

Stereotype In literature, a simplified or stock character who conforms to a fixed pattern or is defined by a single trait is known as a stereotype. Such a character does not usually demonstrate the complexity of a real person. Familiar stereotypes in popular literature include the absent-minded professor and the busybody.

Stream of Consciousness Stream of consciousness is a literary technique developed by modern writers, in which thoughts, feelings, moods, perceptions, and memories are presented as they randomly flow through a character's mind.

Structure Structure is the way in which the parts of a work of literature are put together. In poetry, structure involves the arrangement of words and lines to produce a desired effect. A common structural unit in poetry is the stanza, of which there are numerous types. In prose, structure is the arrangement of larger units or parts of a work. Paragraphs, for example, are basic units in prose, as are chapters in novels and acts in plays. The structure of a poem, short story, novel, play, or nonfictional work usually emphasizes certain important aspects of content.

See also **Act; Stanza.**

Style Style is the particular way in which a work of literature is written—not *what* is said but *how* it is said. It is the writer's unique way of communicating ideas. Many elements contribute to style, including word choice, sentence structure and length, tone, figurative language, and point of view. A literary style may be described in a variety of ways, such as formal, informal, journalistic, conversational, wordy, ornate, poetic, or dynamic.

Surprise Ending A surprise ending is an unexpected plot twist at the end of a story. The surprise may be a sudden turn in the action or a piece of information that gives a different perspective to the entire story. O. Henry is famous for using this device, as exemplified in his story "The Gift of the Magi."

See pages 96, 146.

Suspense Suspense is the excitement or tension that readers feel as they wait to find out how a story ends or a conflict is resolved. Writers create suspense by raising questions in readers' minds about what might happen next. The use of **foreshadowing** is one way in which writers create suspense.

See page 107.

See also **Foreshadowing.**

Symbol A symbol is a person, a place, an object, or an activity that stands for something beyond itself. For example, a flag is a colored piece of cloth that stands for a country. A white dove is a bird that represents peace.

Example: In "Through the Tunnel" by Doris Lessing, the rocky bay represents challenge, danger, and adulthood; the beach represents safety and Jerry's childhood.

See pages 323, 327, 402, 427, 853.

Tall Tale A tall tale is a humorously exaggerated story about impossible events, often involving the supernatural abilities of the main character. Stories about folk heroes such as Pecos Bill and Paul Bunyan are typical tall tales.

Teleplay A teleplay is a play written for television. In a teleplay, scenes can change quickly and dramatically. The camera can focus the viewer's attention on specific actions. The camera directions in teleplays are much like the stage directions in stage plays.

See page 149.

Theme A theme is an underlying message about life or human nature that a writer wants the reader to understand. It is a perception about life or human nature that the writer shares with the reader. In most cases, themes are not stated directly but must be inferred. A theme may imply how a person should live but should not be confused with a **moral.** The theme of "The Scarlet Ibis" by James Hurst might be expressed as "Pride, love, and cruelty are often intermingled in human relationships."

  Recurring themes are themes found in a variety of works. For example, authors from varying backgrounds might convey similar themes having to do with the importance of family values. **Universal themes** are themes that are found throughout the literature of all time periods. For example, the *Odyssey* and *The Lord of the Rings* both contain a universal theme relating to the hero's search for truth, goodness, and honor.

See pages 107, 402, 467.

See also **Moral.**

Third-Person Point of View *See* **Point of View.**

Tone Tone is the attitude a writer takes takes toward a subject. Unlike mood, which is intended to shape the reader's emotional response, tone reflects the feelings of the writer. A writer communicates tone through choice of words and details. Tone may often be described by a single word, such as *serious, humorous, formal, informal, somber, sarcastic, playful, ironic, bitter,* or *objective.* For example, the tone of "Grape Sherbet" by Rita Dove might be described as tender and loving, whereas the tone of Mary Oliver's essay "A Few Words" might be described as persistent and somewhat angry.

See pages 525, 561, 746, 783.

See also **Author's Perspective; Mood.**

Tragedy A tragedy is a dramatic work that presents the downfall of a dignified character (**tragic hero**) or characters who are involved in historically or socially significant events. The events in a tragic plot are set in motion by a decision that is often an error in judgment (**tragic flaw**) on the part of the hero. Succeeding events are linked in a cause-and-effect relationship and lead inevitably to a disastrous conclusion, usually death. Shakespeare's *Romeo and Juliet* is a tragedy.

Tragic Flaw *See* **Tragedy.**

Tragic Hero *See* **Tragedy.**

Traits *See* **Character.**

Turning Point *See* **Climax.**

Understatement Understatement is a technique of creating emphasis by saying less than is actually or literally true. It is the opposite of **hyperbole,** or exaggeration. One of the primary devices of irony, understatement can be used to develop a humorous effect, to create satire, or to achieve a restrained tone.

See also **Hyperbole; Irony.**

Universal Theme *See* **Theme.**

Verbal Irony *See* **Irony.**

Voice Voice is a writer's unique use of language that allows a reader to "hear" a human personality in the writer's work. Elements of style that contribute to a writer's voice include sentence structure, **diction,** and **tone.** Voice can reveal much about the author's personality, beliefs, and attitudes.

See pages 801, 863.

Word Choice *See* **Diction.**

Glossary of Reading & Informational Terms

Almanac *See* **Reference Works.**

Analogy *See Glossary of Literary Terms, page R102.*

Argument An argument is speech or writing that expresses a position on an issue or problem and supports it with reasons and evidence. An argument often takes into account other points of view, anticipating and answering objections that opponents of the position might raise.
See also **Claim; Counterargument; Evidence.**

Assumption An assumption is an opinion or belief that is taken for granted. It can be about a specific situation, a person, or the world in general. Assumptions are often unstated.

Author's Message An author's message is the main idea or theme of a particular work.
See also **Main Idea; Theme,** *Glossary of Literary Terms, page R114.*

Author's Perspective *See Glossary of Literary Terms, page R102.*

Author's Position An author's position is his or her opinion on an issue or topic.
See also **Claim.**

Author's Purpose *See Glossary of Literary Terms, page R102.*

Autobiography *See Glossary of Literary Terms, page R102.*

Bias Bias is an inclination toward a particular judgment on a topic or issue. A writer often reveals a strongly positive or strongly negative opinion by presenting only one way of looking at an issue or by heavily weighting the evidence. Words with intensely positive or negative connotations are often a signal of a writer's bias.

Bibliography A bibliography is a list of books and other materials related to the topic of a text. Bibliographies can be good sources of works for further study on a subject.
See also **Works Consulted.**

Biography *See Glossary of Literary Terms, page R103.*

Business Correspondence Business correspondence includes all written business communications, such as business letters, e-mails, and memos. In general, business correspondence is brief, to the point, clear, courteous, and professional.

Cause and Effect A **cause** is an event or action that directly results in another event or action. An **effect** is the direct or logical outcome of an event or action. Basic **cause-and-effect relationships** include a single cause with a single effect, one cause with multiple effects, multiple causes with a single effect, and a chain of causes and effects. The concept of cause and effect also provides a way of organizing a piece of writing. It helps a writer show the relationships between events or ideas.
See also **False Cause,** *Reading Handbook, page R24.*

Chronological Order Chronological order is the arrangement of events in their order of occurrence. This type of organization is used in both fictional narratives and in historical writing, biography, and autobiography.

Claim In an argument, a claim is the writer's position on an issue or problem. Although an argument focuses on supporting one claim, a writer may make more than one claim in a work.

Clarify Clarifying is a reading strategy that helps a reader to understand or make clear what he or she is reading. Readers usually clarify by rereading, reading aloud, or discussing.

Classification Classification is a pattern of organization in which objects, ideas, or information is presented in groups, or classes, based on common characteristics.

Cliché A cliché is an overused expression. "Better late than never" and "hard as nails" are common examples. Good writers generally avoid clichés unless they are using them in dialogue to indicate something about characters' personalities.

Compare and Contrast To compare and contrast is to identify similarities and differences in two or more subjects. Compare-and-contrast organization can be used to structure a piece of writing, serving as a framework for examining the similarities and differences in two or more subjects.

Conclusion A conclusion is a statement of belief based on evidence, experience, and reasoning. A **valid conclusion** is a conclusion that logically follows from the facts or statements upon which it is based. A **deductive conclusion** is one that follows from a particular generalization or premise. An **inductive conclusion** is a broad conclusion or generalization that is reached by arguing from specific facts and examples.

Connect Connecting is a reader's process of relating the content of a text to his or her own knowledge and experience.

Consumer Documents Consumer documents are printed materials that accompany products and services. They are intended for the buyers or users of the products or services and usually provide information about use, care, operation, or assembly. Some common consumer documents are applications, contracts, warranties, manuals, instructions, package inserts, labels, brochures, and schedules.

Context Clues When you encounter an unfamiliar word, you can often use context clues as aids for understanding. Context clues are the words and phrases surrounding the word that provide hints about the word's meaning.

Counterargument A counterargument is an argument made to oppose another argument. A good argument anticipates opposing viewpoints and provides counterarguments to refute (disprove) or answer them.

Credibility *Credibility* refers to the believability or trustworthiness of a source and the information it contains.

Critical Review A critical review is an evaluation or critique by a reviewer or critic. Different types of reviews include film reviews, book reviews, music reviews, and art-show reviews.

Database A database is a collection of information that can be quickly and easily accessed and searched and from which information can be easily retrieved. It is frequently presented in an electronic format.

Debate A debate is basically an argument—but a very structured one that requires a good deal of preparation. In academic settings, *debate* usually refers to a formal argumentation contest in which two opposing teams defend and attack a proposition.
See also **Argument.**

Deductive Reasoning Deductive reasoning is a way of thinking that begins with a generalization, presents a specific situation, and then advances with facts and evidence to a logical conclusion. The following passage has a deductive argument imbedded in it: "All students in the drama class must attend the play on Thursday. Since Ava is in the class, she had better show up." This deductive argument can be broken down as follows: generalization— all students in the drama class must attend the play on Thursday; specific situation—Ava is a student in the drama class; conclusion—Ava must attend the play.
See also **Analyzing Logic and Reasoning,** *Reading Handbook, pages R22–R23.*

Dictionary *See* **Reference Works.**

Draw Conclusions To draw a conclusion is to make a judgment or arrive at a belief based on evidence, experience, and reasoning.

Editorial An editorial is an opinion piece that usually appears on the editorial page of a newspaper or as part of a news broadcast. The editorial section of a newspaper presents opinions rather than objective news reports.
See also **Op-Ed Piece.**

Either/Or Fallacy An either/or fallacy is a statement that suggests that there are only two possible ways to view a situation or only two options to choose from. In other words, it is a statement that falsely frames a dilemma, giving the impression that no options exist but the two presented—for example, "Either we stop the construction of a new airport, or the surrounding suburbs will become ghost towns."
See also **Identifying Faulty Reasoning,** *Reading Handbook, page R24.*

Emotional Appeals Emotional appeals are messages that evoke strong feelings—such as fear, pity, or vanity—in order to persuade instead of using facts and evidence to make a point. An **appeal to fear** is a message that taps into people's fear of losing their safety or security. An **appeal to pity** is a message that taps into people's sympathy and compassion for others to build support for an idea, a cause, or a proposed action. An **appeal to vanity** is a message that attempts to persuade by tapping into people's desire to feel good about themselves.
See also **Recognizing Persuasive Techniques,** *Reading Handbook, page R22.*

Encyclopedia *See* **Reference Works.**

Essay *See Glossary of Literary Terms, page R105.*

Evaluate To evaluate is to examine something carefully and judge its value or worth. Evaluating is an important skill for gaining insight into what you read. A reader can evaluate the actions of a particular character, for example, or can form an opinion about the value of an entire work.

Evidence Evidence is the specific pieces of information that support a claim. Evidence can take the form of facts, quotations, examples, statistics, or personal experiences, among others.

Expository Essay *See* **Essay,** *Glossary of Literary Terms, page R105.*

Fact versus Opinion A **fact** is a statement that can be

proved or verified. An **opinion,** on the other hand, is a statement that cannot be proved because it expresses a person's beliefs, feelings, or thoughts.

See also **Inference; Generalization.**

Fallacy A fallacy is an error in reasoning. Typically, a fallacy is based on an incorrect inference or a misuse of evidence. Some common logical fallacies are **circular reasoning, either/or fallacy, oversimplification, overgeneralization,** and **stereotyping.**

See also **Either/Or Fallacy, Logical Appeal, Overgeneralization; Identifying Faulty Reasoning,** *Reading Handbook, page R24.*

Faulty Reasoning *See* **Fallacy.**

Feature Article A feature article is a main article in a newspaper or a cover story in a magazine. A feature article is focused more on entertaining than informing. Features are lighter or more general than hard news and tend to be about human interest or lifestyles.

Functional Documents *See* **Consumer Documents; Workplace Documents.**

Generalization A generalization is a broad statement about a class or category of people, ideas, or things, based on a study of only some of its members.

See also **Overgeneralization.**

Government Publications Government publications are documents produced by government organizations. Pamphlets, brochures, and reports are just some of the many forms these publications may take. Government publications can be good resources for a wide variety of topics.

Graphic Aid A graphic aid is a visual tool that is printed, handwritten, or drawn. Charts, diagrams, graphs, photographs, and maps can all be graphic aids.

See also **Graphic Aids,** *Reading Handbook, pages R5–R7.*

Graphic Organizer A graphic organizer is a "word picture"—that is, a visual illustration of a verbal statement—that helps a reader understand a text. Charts, tables, webs, and diagrams can all be graphic organizers. Graphic organizers and graphic aids can look the same. For example, a table in a science article will not be constructed differently from a table that is a graphic organizer. However, graphic organizers and graphic aids do differ in how they are used. Graphic aids are the visual representations that people encounter when they read informational texts. Graphic organizers are visuals that people construct to help them understand texts or organize information.

Historical Documents Historical documents are writings that have played a significant role in human events or are themselves records of such events. The Declaration of Independence, for example, is a historical document.

How-To Book A how-to book is a book that is written to explain how to do something—usually an activity, a sport, or a household project.

Implied Main Idea *See* **Main Idea.**

Index The index of a book is an alphabetized list of important topics and details covered in the book and the page numbers on which they can be found. An index can be used to quickly find specific information about a topic.

Inductive Reasoning Inductive reasoning is the process of logically reasoning from specific observations, examples, and facts to arrive at a general conclusion or principle.

See also **Analyzing Logic and Reasoning,** *Reading Handbook, pages R22–R23.*

Inference An inference is a logical assumption that is based on observed facts and one's own knowledge and experience.

Informational Nonfiction Informational nonfiction is writing that provides factual information. It often explains ideas or teaches processes. Examples include news reports, science textbooks, software instructions, and lab reports.

Internet The Internet is a global, interconnected system of computer networks that allows for communication through e-mail, listservers, and the World Wide Web. The Internet connects computers and computer users throughout the world.

Journal A journal is a periodical publication issued by a legal, medical, or other professional organization. Alternatively, the term may be used to refer to a diary or daily record.

Loaded Language Loaded language consists of words with strongly positive or negative connotations intended to influence a reader's or listener's attitude.

Logical Appeal A logical appeal relies on logic and facts, appealing to people's reasoning or intellect rather than to their values or emotions. Flawed logical appeals—that is, errors in reasoning—are considered logical fallacies.

See also **Fallacy.**

Logical Argument A logical argument is an argument in which the logical relationship between the support and the claim is sound.

Main Idea A main idea is the central or most important idea about a topic that a writer or speaker conveys. It can be the central idea of an entire work or of just a paragraph. Often, the main idea of a paragraph is expressed in a topic sentence. However, a main idea may just be implied, or suggested, by details. A main idea and supporting details can serve as a basic pattern of organization in a piece of writing, with the central idea about a topic being supported by details.

Make Inferences *See* **Inference.**

Monitor Monitoring is the strategy of checking your comprehension as you are reading and modifying the strategies you are using to suit your needs. Monitoring may include some or all of the following strategies: **questioning, clarifying, visualizing, predicting, connecting,** and **rereading.**

Narrative Nonfiction *See Glossary of Literary Terms, page R109.*

News Article A news article is a piece of writing that reports on a recent event. In newspapers, news articles are usually written concisely and report the latest news, presenting the most important facts first and then more detailed information. In magazines, news articles are usually more elaborate than those in newspapers because they are written to provide both information and analysis. Also, news articles in magazines do not necessarily present the most important facts first.

Nonfiction *See Glossary of Literary Terms, page R109.*

Op-Ed Piece An op-ed piece is an opinion piece that usually appears opposite ("op") the editorial page of a newspaper. Unlike editorials, op-ed pieces are written and submitted by named writers.

Organization *See* **Pattern of Organization.**

Overgeneralization An overgeneralization is a generalization that is too broad. You can often recognize overgeneralizations by the appearance of words and phrases such as *all, everyone, every time, any, anything, no one,* and *none.* Consider, for example, this statement: "None of the sanitation workers in our city really care about keeping the environment clean." In all probability, there are many exceptions; the writer can't possibly know the feelings of every sanitation worker in the city.

See also **Identifying Faulty Reasoning,** *Reading Handbook, page R24.*

Overview An overview is a short summary of a story, a speech, or an essay. It orients the reader by providing a preview of the text to come.

Paraphrase Paraphrasing is the restating of information in one's own words.

See also **Summarize.**

Pattern of Organization A pattern of organization is a particular arrangement of ideas and information. Such a pattern may be used to organize an entire composition or a single paragraph within a longer work. The following are the most common patterns of organization: **cause-and-effect, chronological order, compare-and-contrast, classification, deductive, inductive, order of importance, problem-solution, sequential,** and **spatial.**

See also **Cause and Effect; Chronological Order; Classification; Compare and Contrast; Problem-Solution Order; Sequential Order; Reading Informational Texts: Patterns of Organization,** *Reading Handbook, pages R8–R13.*

Periodical A periodical is a publication that is issued at regular intervals of more than one day. For example, a periodical may be a weekly, monthly, or quarterly journal or magazine. Newspapers and other daily publications generally are not classified as periodicals.

Personal Essay *See* **Essay,** *Glossary of Literary Terms, page R105.*

Persuasion Persuasion is the art of swaying others' feelings, beliefs, or actions. Persuasion normally appeals to both the intellect and the emotions of readers. **Persuasive techniques** are the methods used to influence others to adopt certain opinions or beliefs or to act in certain ways. Types of persuasive techniques include emotional appeals, logical appeals, and loaded language. When used properly, persuasive techniques can add depth to writing that's meant to persuade. Persuasive techniques can, however, be misused to cloud factual information, disguise poor reasoning, or unfairly exploit people's emotions in order to shape their opinions.

See also **Emotional Appeals; Loaded Language; Logical Appeal; Recognizing Persuasive Techniques,** *Reading Handbook, page R22.*

Predict Predicting is a reading strategy that involves using text clues to make a reasonable guess about what will happen next in a story.

Primary Source *See* **Sources.**

Prior Knowledge Prior knowledge is the knowledge a reader already possesses about a topic. This information might come from personal experiences, expert accounts, books, films, or other sources.

Problem-Solution Order Problem-solution order is a pattern of organization in which a problem is stated and analyzed and then one or more solutions are proposed and examined. Writers use words and phrases such as *propose, conclude, reason for, problem, answer,* and *solution* to connect ideas and details when writing about problems and solutions.

Propaganda Propaganda is a form of communication that may use distorted, false, or misleading information. It usually refers to manipulative political discourse.

Public Documents Public documents are documents that were written for the public to provide information that is of public interest or concern. They include government documents, speeches, signs, and rules and regulations. *See also* **Government Publications.**

Reference Works General reference works are sources that contain facts and background information on a wide range of subjects. More specific reference works contain in-depth information on a single subject. Most reference works are good sources of reliable information because they have been reviewed by experts. The following are some common reference works: **encyclopedias, dictionaries, thesauri, almanacs, atlases, chronologies, biographical dictionaries,** and **directories.**

Review *See* **Critical Review.**

Rhetorical Devices *See Glossary of Literary Terms, page R111.*

Rhetorical Questions Rhetorical questions are those that do not require a reply. Writers use them to suggest that their arguments make the answer obvious or self-evident.

Scanning Scanning is the process of searching through writing for a particular fact or piece of information. When you scan, your eyes sweep across a page, looking for key words that may lead you to the information you want.

Secondary Source *See* **Sources.**

Sequential Order A pattern of organization that shows the order in which events or actions occur is called sequential order. Writers typically use this pattern of organization to explain steps or stages in a process.

Setting a Purpose The process of establishing specific reasons for reading a text is called setting a purpose.

Sidebar A sidebar is additional information set in a box alongside or within a news or feature article. Popular magazines often make use of sidebar information.

Signal Words Signal words are words and phrases that indicate what is to come in a text. Readers can use signal words to discover a text's pattern of organization and to analyze the relationships among the ideas in the text.

Sources A source is anything that supplies information. **Primary sources** are materials written by people who were present at events, either as participants or as observers. Letters, diaries, autobiographies, speeches, and photographs are primary sources. **Secondary sources** are records of events that were created sometime after the events occurred; the writers were not directly involved or were not present when the events took place. Encyclopedias, textbooks, biographies, most newspaper and magazine articles, and books and articles that interpret or review research are secondary sources.

Spatial Order Spatial order is a pattern of organization that highlights the physical positions or relationships of details or objects. This pattern of organization is typically found in descriptive writing. Writers use words and phrases such as *on the left, to the right, here, over there, above, below, beyond, nearby,* and *in the distance* to indicate the arrangement of details.

Speech *See Glossary of Literary Terms, page R113.*

Stereotyping Stereotyping is a type of overgeneralization. Stereotypes are broad statements made about people on the basis of their gender, ethnicity, race, or political, social, professional, or religious group.

Summarize To summarize is to briefly retell, or encapsulate, the main ideas of a piece of writing in one's own words. *See also* **Paraphrase.**

Support Support is any material that serves to prove a claim. In an argument, support typically consists of reasons and evidence. In persuasive texts and speeches, however, support may include appeals to the needs and values of the audience.

Supporting Detail *See* **Main Idea.**

Synthesize To synthesize information is to take individual pieces of information and combine them with other pieces

of information and with prior knowledge or experience to gain a better understanding of a subject or to create a new product or idea.

Text Features Text features are design elements that indicate the organizational structure of a text and help make the key ideas and supporting information understandable. Text features include headings, boldface type, italic type, bulleted or numbered lists, sidebars, and graphic aids such as charts, tables, timelines, illustrations, and photographs.

Thesaurus *See* **Reference Works.**

Thesis Statement In an argument, a thesis statement is an expression of the claim that the writer or speaker is trying to support. In an essay, a thesis statement is an expression, in one or two sentences, of the main idea or purpose of the piece of writing.

Topic Sentence The topic sentence of a paragraph states the paragraph's main idea. All other sentences in the paragraph provide supporting details.

Visualize Visualizing is the process of forming a mental picture based on written or spoken information.

Web Site A Web site is a collection of "pages" on the World Wide Web that is usually devoted to one specific subject. Pages are linked together and are accessed by clicking hyperlinks or menus, which send the user from page to page within the site. Web sites are created by companies, organizations, educational institutions, branches of the government, the military, and individuals.

Workplace Documents Workplace documents are materials that are produced or used within a work setting, usually to aid in the functioning of the workplace. They include job applications, office memos, training manuals, job descriptions, and sales reports.

Works Cited A list of works cited lists names of all the works a writer has referred to in his or her text. This list often includes not only books and articles but also nonprint sources.

Works Consulted A list of works consulted names all the works a writer consulted in order to create his or her text. It is not limited just to those works cited in the text.
See also **Bibliography.**

Glossary of Vocabulary in English & Spanish

abject (ăb-jĕkt′) *adj.* exceedingly humble
   abyecto *adj.* sumamente pobre

abominably (ə-bŏm′ə-nə-blē) *adv.* in a hateful way; horribly
   abominablemente *adv.* de manera odiosa u horrible

abscond (ăb-skŏnd′) *v.* to go away suddenly and secretly
   fugarse *v.* huir de repente

abysmal (ə-bĭz′məl) *adj.* very bad
   pésimo *adj.* desastroso; atroz

acclimatization (ə-klī′mə-tĭ-zā′shən) *n.* the act of getting accustomed to a new climate or environment
   aclimatación *s.* acción de acostumbrarse a un nuevo clima o ambiente

adulation (ăj′ə-lā′shən) *n.* excessive praise or flattery
   adulación *s.* halago exagerado

adversary (ăd′vər-sĕr′ē) *n.* an opponent; enemy
   adversario *s.* opositor; enemigo

adversity (ăd-vûr′sĭ-tē) *n.* hardship; misfortune
   adversidad *s.* infortunio; desgracia

advocacy (ăd′və-kə-sē) *adj.* involving public support for an idea or policy
   defensa *s.* apoyo público a una idea o medida

affiliate (ə-fĭl′ē-ĭt) *n.* a person or an organization officially connected to a larger body
   afiliado *s.* persona u organización conectada oficialmente con una entidad

aghast (ə-găst′) *adj.* filled with shock or horror
   horrorizado *adj.* muy atemorizado

agile (ăj′əl) *adj.* able to move quickly and easily
   ágil *adj.* capaz de moverse con rapidez y facilidad

alienation (āl′yə-nā′shən) *n.* a feeling of separation or isolation
   alienación *s.* sensación de separación o aislamiento

aloof (ə-lōōf′) *adj.* distant; remote; standoffish
   distante *adj.* remoto; indiferente

amenity (ə-mĕn′ĭ-tē) *n.* something that adds to one's comfort or convenience
   comodidad *s.* cosa que aumenta el confort

analytic (ăn′ə-lĭt′ĭk) *adj.* using logical reasoning or analysis
   analítico *adj.* que usa razonamiento o análisis lógico

annihilate (ə-nī′ə-lāt′) *v.* to destroy completely
   aniquilar *v.* destruir por completo

anonymity (ăn′ə-nĭm′ĭ-tē) *n.* the condition of being unknown
   anonimato *s.* condición de no ser conocido

anthem (ăn′thəm) *n.* an uplifting song or hymn
   himno *s.* composición musical solemne

anthropology (ăn′thrə-pŏl′ə-jē) *n.* the science or study of human beings, including their physical characteristics and cultures
   antropología *s.* ciencia que estudia las características físicas y las culturas de los seres humanos

aperture (ăp′ər-chər) *n.* an opening, such as a hole or a gap
   abertura *s.* agujero o grieta

aplomb (ə-plŏm′) *n.* poise; self-assurance
   aplomo *s.* serenidad; circunspección

appalled (ə-pôld′) *adj.* filled with dismay; horrified **appall** *v.*
   asombrado *adj.* pasmado; asustado **asombrar** *v.*

archaic (är-kā′ĭk) *adj.* very old or unfashionable
   arcaico *adj.* muy antiguo o pasado de moda

ardor (är′dər) *n.* passion
   ardor *s.* pasión

arduous (är′jōō-əs) *adj.* requiring much effort; difficult
   arduo *adj.* que requiere mucho esfuerzo; difícil

articulate (är-tĭk′yə-lĭt) *adj.* able to speak clearly and coherently; well-spoken
   elocuente *adj.* que se expresa con claridad y convicción

artifact (är′tə-făkt′) *n.* something created by humans, usually for a practical purpose
   artefacto *s.* objeto creado por los seres humanos, usualmente con propósitos prácticos

askew (ə-skyōō′) *adj.* crooked; to one side
   torcido *adj.* chueco; que se inclina hacia un lado

assertion (ə-sûr′shən) *n.* a statement
   aseveración *s.* declaración; afirmación

assuage (ə-swāj′) *v.* to calm or pacify
   calmar *v.* tranquilizar o mitigar

awry (ə-rī′) *adj.* off course; wrong
   sesgado *adj.* desviado; torcido

baleful (bāl′fəl) *adj.* evil; destructive
 torvo *adj.* funesto; siniestro

banal (bə-năl′) *adj.* commonplace; trite
 banal *adj.* común; trillado

beguiling (bǐ-gī′lǐng) *adj.* charming; pleasing **beguile** *v.*
 encantador *adj.* seductor; atrayente **encantar** *v.*

benign (bǐ-nīn′) *adj.* good; kindly
 benigno *adj.* bondadoso; amable

boon (bo͞on) *n.* a benefit; blessing
 beneficio *s.* gran ayuda; bendición

bravado (brə-vä′dō) *n.* a false show of courage or defiance
 bravata *s.* alarde; demostración falsa de valor o valentía

brazenly (brā′zən-lē) *adv.* boldly and without shame
 descaradamente *adv.* con descaro y frescura

browser (brou′zər) *n.* a program used to navigate the Internet
 browser *s.* programa para desplazarse en la Internet

buffeted (bŭf′ǐ-tǐd) *adj.* knocked about or struck **buffet** *v.*
 golpeado *adj.* empujado o azotado **golpear** *v.*

cadence (kād′ns) *n.* a balanced, rhythmic flow
 cadencia *s.* repetición regular de sonidos o movimientos

cascade (kă-skād′) *v.* to fall or flow like a waterfall
 precipitarse *v.* caer o deslizarse como una cascada

cavort (kə-vôrt′) *v.* to leap or romp about
 retozar *v.* saltar; divertirse

cede (sēd) *v.* to give up; give way
 ceder *v.* conceder; rendirse

chronicle (krŏn′ǐ-kəl) *n.* a record of events
 crónica *s.* registro de sucesos

clamor (klăm′ər) *n.* a noisy outburst; outcry
 clamor *s.* conjunto de gritos o ruidos fuertes

clarity (klăr′ǐ-tē) *n.* clearness
 claridad *s.* transparencia

commandeer (kŏm′ən-dîr′) *v.* to take control of by force
 confiscar *v.* tomar por la fuerza

compile (kəm-pīl′) *v.* to put together by gathering from many sources
 compilar *v.* reunir de muchas fuentes

condescending (kŏn′dǐ-sĕn′dǐng) *adj.* assuming an air of superiority
 condescendiente *adj.* que asume un aire de superioridad

condiment (kŏn′də-mənt) *n.* a sauce, relish, or spice used to season food
 condimento *s.* salsa o especia para sazonar la comida

condone (kən-dōn′) *v.* to forgive or overlook
 condonar *v.* perdonar, olvidar o ignorar

contemptible (kən-tĕmp′tə-bəl) *adj.* deserving of scorn; despicable
 despreciable *adj.* que merece desdén o desprecio; vil

contrition (kən-trǐsh′ən) *n.* a feeling of regret for doing wrong
 contrición *s.* arrepentimiento por haber actuado mal

correlate (kôr′ə-lāt′) *v.* to figure out or create a relationship between two items or events
 correlacionar *v.* establecer una relación entre dos puntos o sucesos

cosmetic (kŏz-mĕt′ǐk) *adj.* decorative rather than functional
 cosmético *adj.* decorativo más que funcional

coveted (kŭv′ǐ-tǐd) *adj.* greedily desired or wished for **covet** *v.*
 codiciado *adj.* que se desea con envidia **codiciar** *v.*

crass (krăs) *adj.* crude; unrefined
 craso *adj.* burdo; grosero

crevasse (krǐ-văs′) *n.* a deep crack or split in a glacier
 grieta *s.* hendidura profunda, especialmente en un glaciar

cultivated (kŭl′tə-vā′tǐd) *adj.* refined or cultured in manner
 cultivado *adj.* refinado o de modales cultos

daunted (dôn′tǐd) *adj.* discouraged **daunt** *v.*
 amilanado *adj.* intimidado **amilanar** *v.*

debut (dā-byo͞o′) *n.* first public performance or showing
 debut *s.* estreno; primera presentación

default (dǐ-fôlt′) *v.* to fail to keep a promise, especially a promise to repay a loan
 incumplir *v.* no cumplir una promesa, especialmente no pagar un préstamo

deftness (dĕft′nǐs) *n.* the quality of quickness and skillfullness
 destreza *s.* agilidad y habilidad

degenerate (dĭ-jĕn'ər-ĭt) *n.* a corrupt or vicious person
  degenerado *s.* persona corrupta o viciosa

degradation (dĕg'rə-dā'shən) *n.* condition of being brought to a lower level; humiliation
  degradación *s.* pérdida de status y dignidad; humillación

demeanor (dĭ-mē'nər) *n.* a way of behaving; manner
  comportamiento *s.* conducta externa

derisive (dĭ-rī'sĭv) *adj.* expressing contempt or ridicule
  desdeñoso *adj.* que expresa burla o ridículo

desolation (dĕs'ə-lā'shən) *n.* lonely grief; misery
  desolación *s.* dolor en soledad; desgracia

dialect (dī'ə-lĕkt') *n.* a variety of a standard language unique to a certain region or social group
  dialecto *s.* variedad de una lengua que se habla en una región o que habla un grupo social

diffuse (dĭ-fyōōs') *adj.* unfocused
  difuso *adj.* vago e impreciso

dilapidated (dĭ-lăp'ĭ-dā'tĭd) *adj.* broken down and shabby
  dilapilado *adj.* en ruinas

diminutive (dĭ-mĭn'yə-tĭv) *adj.* very small
  diminuto *adj.* muy pequeño

disarming (dĭs-är'mĭng) *adj.* removing or overcoming suspicion; inspiring confidence
  apaciguador *adj.* tranquilizador; que elimina sospechas; que crea confianza

disclaimer (dĭs-klā'mər) *n.* a denial of responsibility or knowledge
  descargo *s.* repudiación de responsabilidad o conocimiento

disconcerting (dĭs'kən-sûr'tĭng) *adj.* causing one to feel confused or embarrassed **disconcert** *v.*
  desconcertante *adj.* que causa confusión, malestar o desconcierto **desconcertar** *v.*

disconsolate (dĭs-kŏn'sə-lĭt) *adj.* extremely depressed or dejected
  desconsolado *adj.* extremadamente triste

discordant (dĭ-skôr'dnt) *adj.* having a disagreeable or clashing sound
  discordante *adj.* disonante; de sonidos desagradables; sin armonía

dispirited (dĭ-spĭr'ĭ-tĭd) *adj.* dejected
  desanimado *s.* abatido

distraught (dĭ-strôt') *adj.* deeply upset
  perturbado *adj.* profundamente molesto

doggedness (dô'gĭd-nĭs) *n.* persistence; stubbornness
  obstinación *s.* persistencia; tenacidad

droll (drōl) *adj.* amusingly odd or comical
  divertido *adj.* gracioso y curioso

encore (ŏn'kōr') *n.* a repeated or additional performance
  bis *s.* repetición

engender (ĕn-jĕn'dər) *v.* to bring into existence
  engendrar *v.* causar; originar

enthralled (ĕn-thrôld') *adj.* charmed greatly **enthrall** *v.*
  cautivado *adj.* encantado **cautivar** *v.*

eradicate (ĭ-răd'ĭ-kāt') *v.* to do away with completely
  erradicar *v.* acabar por completo

evanesce (ĕv'ə-nĕs') *v.* to disappear; vanish
  desvanecerse *v.* desaparecer; disiparse

exalted (ĭg-zôl'tĭd) *adj.* raised up **exalt** *v.*
  exaltado *adj.* elevado **exaltar** *v.*

exhilarate (ĭg-zĭl'ə-rāt') *v.* to make merry or lively
  regocijar *v.* alegrar; levantar el ánimo

exhortation (ĕg'zôr-tā'shən) *n.* a communication strongly urging that something be done
  exhortación *s.* palabras que inducen a una acción

exodus (ĕk'sə-dəs) *n.* a mass departure
  éxodo *s.* partida en masa

exotic (ĭg-zŏt'ĭk) *adj.* excitingly strange
  exótico *adj.* extraño; curioso

expansive (ĭk-spăn'sĭv) *adj.* outgoing; showing feelings openly and freely
  expansivo *adj.* comunicativo; que muestra sus sentimientos

expendable (ĭk-spĕn'də-bəl) *adj.* not worth keeping; not essential
  prescindible *adj.* que no es esencial

exuberance (ĭg-zōō'bər-əns) *n.* condition of unrestrained joy
  exuberancia *s.* euforia; exaltación

falter (fôl'tər) *v.* to hesitate from lack of courage or confidence
  vacilar *v.* titubear por falta de valor o de confianza

fecund (fē'kənd) *adj.* producing much growth; fertile
  fecundo *adj.* fértil; abundante

fiasco (fē-ăs'kō) *n.* a complete failure
  fiasco *s.* fracaso total

flay (flā) *v.* to whip or lash
  desollar *v.* despellejar a latigazos

foreboding (fôr-bō'dĭng) *n.* a sense of approaching evil
  presentimiento *s.* sentimiento de que algo malo sucederá

fractious (frăk'shəs) *adj.* hard to manage or hold together; unruly
  quisquilloso *adj.* cascarrabias; rebelde

frenetically (frə-nĕt'ĭk-lē) *adv.* in a frenzied or frantic way
  frenéticamente *adv.* de modo frenético o desenfrenado

futile (fyo͞ot'l) *adj.* having no useful result
  fútil *adj.* inútil; sin resultados útiles

gamut (găm'ət) *n.* an entire range or series
  gama *s.* serie; variedades

genesis (jĕn'ĭ-sĭs) *n.* the origin or coming into being (of something)
  génesis *s.* origen o principio de una cosa

goad (gōd) *v.* to drive or urge
  provocar *v.* urgir; instar

harried (hăr'ēd) *adj.* tormented; harassed **harry** *v.*
  agobiado *adj.* atribulado; acosado **agobiar** *v.*

heresy (hĕr'ĭ-sē) *n.* an action or opinion contrary to what is generally thought of as right
  herejía *s.* acto u opinión contrario a lo que se considera correcto

hierarchy (hī'ə-rär'kē) *n.* a body of persons having authority
  jerarquía *s.* grupo de personas de autoridad

homely (hōm'lē) *adj.* characteristic of home life; simple; everyday
  casero *adj.* característico de la vida hogareña; sencillo

hypothesis (hī-pŏth'ĭ-sĭs) *n.* an assumption made in order to test its possible consequences
  hipótesis *s.* suposición que se pone a prueba

illiteracy (ĭ-lĭt'ər-ə-sē) *n.* a lack of ability to read and write
  analfabetismo *s.* desconocimiento de la lectura y escritura

imminent (ĭm'ə-nənt) *adj.* about to occur
  inminente *adj.* que está por ocurrir

immolation (ĭm'ə-lā'shən) *n.* death or destruction
  inmolación *s.* muerte o destrucción

immutable (ĭ-myo͞o'tə-bəl) *adj.* unchanging
  inmutable *adj.* que no cambia

imperative (ĭm-pĕr'ə-tĭv) *adj.* absolutely necessary
  imperativo *adj.* absolutamente necesario

implacable (ĭm-plăk'ə-bəl) *adj.* impossible to soothe; unforgiving
  implacable *adj.* desalmado; despiadado; que no perdona

impotent (ĭm'pə-tənt) *adj.* powerless; lacking strength or vigor
  impotente *adj.* sin poder o capacidad; carente de fuerza o vigor

impunity (ĭm-pyo͞o'nĭ-tē) *n.* freedom from penalty or harm
  impunidad *s.* falta de castigo, penalidad o daño

inaudibly (ĭn-ô'də-blē) *adv.* in a way that is impossible to hear
  inaudiblemente *adv.* de modo que no se oye

inaugurate (ĭn-ô'gyə-rāt') *v.* to make a formal beginning of
  inaugurar *v.* dar principio o estrenar

incessantly (ĭn-sĕs'ənt-lē) *adv.* without interruption; continuously
  incesantemente *adv.* continuamente; sin parar

incredulous (ĭn-krĕj'ə-ləs) *adj.* doubtful; disbelieving
  incrédulo *adj.* no creyente

increment (ĭn'krə-mənt) *n.* a small, slight growth or increase
  incremento *s.* pequeño aumento o crecimiento

induced (ĭn-do͞ost') *adj.* led on; persuaded **induce** *v.*
  inducido *adj.* persuadido; convencido **inducir** *v.*

inept (ĭn-ĕpt') *adj.* generally incompetent
  inepto *adj.* incompetente

inertia (ĭ-nûr'shə) *n.* tendency to continue to do what one has been doing
  inercia *s.* tendencia a continuar haciendo lo que se ha estado haciendo

inevitability (ĭn-ĕv′ĭ-tə-bĭl′ĭ-tē) *n.* something that is certain to happen
  inevitabilidad *s.* lo que no se puede evitar

inexplicably (ĭn-ĕk′splĭ-kə-blē) *adv.* in a way that is difficult or impossible to explain
  inexplicablemente *adv.* de modo difícil o imposible de explicar

inextricably (ĭn-ĕk′strĭ-kə-blē) *adv.* in a way impossible to untangle
  inextricablemente *adv.* de manera imposible de descifrar o desenredar

infallibility (ĭn-făl′ə-bĭl′ĭ-tē) *n.* an inability to make errors
  infalibilidad *s.* incapacidad para cometer errores

infatuated (ĭn-făch′ōō-ā′tĭd) *adj.* possessed by an unreasoning love or attraction
  encaprichado *adj.* locamente enamorado o atraído irracionalmente hacia una persona

infinitesimally (ĭn′fĭn-ĭ-tĕs′ə-mə-lē) *adv.* in amounts so small as to be barely measurable
  infinitesimalmente *adv.* en cantidades tan pequeñas que casi no se puede medir

infuse (ĭn-fyōōz′) *v.* to fill, as if by pouring
  infundir *v.* llenar

inherent (ĭn-hîr′ənt) *adj.* forming part of the essential nature of something; built-in
  inherente *adj.* que por naturaleza es parte esencial de algo

inhospitable (ĭn-hŏs′pĭ-tə-bəl) *adj.* not welcoming; hostile
  inhóspito *adj.* hostil; que rechaza

inquisitive (ĭn-kwĭz′ĭ-tĭv) *adj.* curious; inquiring
  inquisitivo *adj.* curioso; preguntón

instigate (ĭn′stĭ-gāt′) *v.* to stir up; provoke
  instigar *v.* provocar; incitar

insubordinate (ĭn′sə-bôr′dn-ĭt) *adj.* disobedient to a superior
  insubordinado *adj.* desobediente a un superior

insurmountable (ĭn′sər-moun′tə-bəl) *adj.* impossible to overcome
  insuperable *adj.* insalvable; infranqueable

intuitive (ĭn-tōō′ĭ-tĭv) *adj.* based on what seems to be true without conscious reasoning; instinctive
  intuitivo *adj.* que se conoce sin razonamiento consciente; instintivo

lament (lə-mĕnt′) *v.* to express grief or deep regret
  lamentar *v.* expresar dolor o profundo arrepentimiento

lavish (lăv′ĭsh) *adj.* extravagant; more than is needed
  espléndido *adj.* extravagante; despilfarrador

leer (lîr) *v.* to give a sly, evil glance
  mirar de reojo *v.* lanzar una mirada lasciva o maliciosa

legitimate (lə-jĭt′ə-mĭt) *adj.* justifiable; reasonable
  legítimo *adj.* justificable; razonable

malfunctioning (măl-fŭngk′shə-nĭng) *adj.* not working or operating properly **malfunction** *v.*
  dañado *adj.* que no funciona bien **dañar** *v.*

maneuvering (mə-nōō′vər-ĭng) *n.* an action skillfully designed to achieve a goal **maneuver** *v.*
  maniobras *s.* acciones diseñadas para alcanzar una meta **maniobrar** *v.*

marauding (mə-rô′dĭng) *adj.* roaming about in search of plunder **maraud** *v.*
  saqueador *adj.* que merodea en busca de botín **saquear** *v.*

meager (mē′gər) *adj.* lacking in quantity or quality
  escaso *adj.* poco, insuficiente en cantidad y número

meditation (mĕd′ĭ-tā′shən) *n.* the act of being in serious, reflective thought
  meditación *s.* reflexión atenta y profunda

mesmerizing (mĕz′mə-rīz′ĭng) *adj.* holding one's attention in an almost hypnotic manner **mesmerize** *v.*
  fascinante *adj.* que capta la atención de forma casi hipnótica **fascinar** *v.*

militancy (mĭl′ĭ-tənt-sē) *n.* the act of aggressively supporting a political or social cause
  militancia *s.* apoyo enérgico a una causa política o social

misnomer (mĭs-nō′mər) *n.* an inaccurate or incorrect name
  incorrección *s.* nombre erróneo o incorrecto

momentous (mō-mĕn′təs) *adj.* of great importance
  trascendental *adj.* de gran importancia

monolith (mŏn′ə-lĭth′) *n.* something, such as a monument, made from a single large stone
    monolito *s.* monumento u objeto tallado de un solo bloque de piedra

mortified (môr′tə-fīd′) *adj.* very embarrassed; humiliated **mortify** *v.*
    mortificado *adj.* avergonzado; apenado **mortificar** *v.*

muted (myōō′tĭd) *adj.* softened or muffled
    apagado *adj.* débil o suave

negligible (nĕg′lĭ-jə-bəl) *adj.* not large or important enough to merit attention
    insignificante *adj.* que no merece atención; desdeñable

neurological (nŏŏr′ə-lŏj′ĭ-kəl) *adj.* having to do with the nervous system
    neurológico *adj.* relacionado con el sistema nervioso

noncommittal (nŏn′kə-mĭt′l) *adj.* not committing oneself; not revealing what one thinks
    indefinido *adj.* evasivo; que no revela su opinión o propósito

nonpartisan (nŏn-pär′tĭ-zən) *adj.* not supporting or controlled by any political group
    independiente *adj.* no afiliado a un grupo político

nostalgia (nŏ-stăl′jə) *n.* bittersweet longing for things from the past
    nostalgia *s.* recuerdo triste del pasado

optimal (ŏp′tə-məl) *adj.* most favorable; best
    óptimo *adj.* sumamente favorable; lo mejor

ostensibly (ŏ-stĕn′sə-blē) *adv.* seemingly; to all outward appearances
    aparentemente *adv.* en apariencia

paradox (păr′ə-dŏks′) *n.* a statement or an event that sounds impossible but seems to be true
    paradoja *s.* afirmación o suceso que suena imposible pero parece verdadero

paramount (păr′ə-mount′) *adj.* of highest importance
    primordial *adj.* de suma importancia

paraphernalia (păr′ə-fər-nāl′yə) *n.* the articles needed for a particular event or activity
    parafernalia *s.* conjunto de artículos necesarios para una actividad

pauper (pô′pər) *n.* a poor person, especially one who depends on public charity
    pobre *s.* indigente; persona que depende de la caridad pública

perfidy (pûr′fĭ-dē) *n.* treachery; betrayal of trust
    perfidia *s.* traición; abuso de confianza

persistence (pər-sĭs′təns) *n.* the act of refusing to stop or be changed
    persistencia *s.* constancia; perseverancia

pervasive (pər-vā′sĭv) *adj.* spreading widely through an area or group of people
    penetrante *adj.* que todo lo invade; dominante

perverse (pər-vûrs′) *adj.* stubbornly contrary; wrong; harmful
    perverso *adj.* malvado; vil

petrified (pĕt′rə-fīd′) *adj.* turned into stone **petrify** *v.*
    petrificado *adj.* convertido en piedra **petrificar** *v.*

plagiarized (plā′jə-rīzd′) *adj.* copied from someone else's writings **plagiarize** *v.*
    plagiado *adj.* copiado de los escritos de otro **plagiar** *v.*

poignantly (poin′yənt-lē) *adv.* in a profoundly moving manner
    emocionadamente *adv.* de manera muy conmovedora

ponderous (pŏn′dər-əs) *adj.* heavy in a clumsy way; bulky
    pesado *adj.* lento y torpe; sin gracia

posse (pŏs′ē) *n.* a band
    banda *s.* grupo; cuadrilla

potent (pōt′nt) *adj.* powerful
    potente *adj.* poderoso

precariously (prĭ-kâr′ē-əs-lē) *adv.* insecurely; in a dangerous or unstable way
    precariamente *adv.* peligrosamente; de manera incierta o insegura

preclude (prĭ-klōōd′) *v.* to make impossible, especially by taking action in advance
    imposibilitar *v.* impedir mediante un acto realizado con anticipación; prevenir

presumed (prĭ-zōōmd′) *adj.* thought to be true **presume** *v.*
    supuesto *adj.* presunto; que se cree que es verdad **suponer** *v.*

privation (prī-vā′shən) *n.* the lack of a basic necessity or a comfort of life
   privación *s.* carencia de lo básico o de comodidades

prodigy (prŏd′ə-jē) *n.* a person who is exceptionally talented or intelligent
   prodigio *s.* persona con inteligencia o talento especiales

profusion (prə-fyōō′zhən) *n.* abundance
   profusión *s.* abundancia

promontory (prŏm′ən-tôr′ē) *n.* a high ridge of land or rock jutting out into a body of water
   promontorio *s.* altura de tierra que avanza dentro del mar

prosaic (prō-zā′ĭk) *adj.* dull; commonplace
   prosaico *adj.* vulgar; corriente

prospects (prŏs′pĕkts′) *n.* chances or possibilities, especially for financial success
   perspectivas *s.* oportunidades o posibilidades, especialmente de éxito o ganancia

protégé (prō′tə-zhā′) *n.* a person who is guided or supported by an older or more influential person
   protegido *s.* persona guiada o financiada por una persona mayor o de más influencia

prudence (prōōd′ns) *n.* the use of good judgment and common sense
   prudencia *s.* juicio y sentido común

quarry (kwôr′ē) *n.* the object of a hunt; prey
   presa *s.* objeto de la cacería

rabid (răb′ĭd) *adj.* uncontrollable; fanatical
   rabioso *adj.* furibundo; fanático

rancor (răng′kər) *n.* bitter and deep ill will
   rencor *s.* sentimiento persistente de animosidad o de resentimiento

ransack (răn′săk′) *v.* to search or examine vigorously
   registrar *v.* buscar por todas partes

ravage (răv′ĭj) *n.* serious damage
   estrago *s.* daño grave

reconnoiter (rē′kə-noi′tər) *v.* to make a preliminary inspection
   reconocer *v.* hacer una inspección preliminar del terreno o de una situación

refute (rĭ-fyōōt′) *v.* to prove false by argument or evidence
   refutar *v.* demostrar una falsedad con argumento o evidencia

reiterate (rē-ĭt′ə-rāt′) *v.* to repeat
   reiterar *v.* repetir

relapse (rē′lăps) *n.* a worsening of an illness after a partial recovery
   recaída *s.* empeoramiento de una enfermedad después de una recuperación parcial

repose (rĭ-pōz′) *v.* to lie dead or at rest
   reposar *v.* yacer muerto o en descanso

reproach (rĭ-prōch′) *n.* blame; criticism
   reproche *s.* reprimenda; crítica

resigned (rĭ-zīnd′) *adj.* marked by acceptance of a condition or action as unavoidable
   resignado *adj.* que acepta algo como inevitable

resilient (rĭ-zĭl′yənt) *adj.* strong but flexible; able to withstand stress without injury
   elástico *adj.* fuerte pero flexible; que tolera presión

restitution (rĕs′tĭ-tōō′shən) *n.* a making good for loss or damage; repayment
   restitución *s.* reposición que se da por algo perdido o dañado

retaliate (rĭ-tăl′ē-āt′) *v.* to pay back an injury in kind
   tomar represalias *v.* contraatacar; responder con agresión

retribution (rĕt′rə-byōō′shən) *n.* something given in repayment, usually as a punishment
   castigo *s.* represalia; merecido

retrieve (rĭ-trēv′) *v.* to find and return safely
   recuperar *v.* rescatar; salvar

revelry (rĕv′əl-rē) *n.* noisy merrymaking; festivity
   juerga *s.* jolgorio; festejo alegre y ruidoso

reverie (rĕv′ə-rē) *n.* a state of daydreaming
   ensueño *s.* sueño despierto; ensoñación

revulsion (rĭ-vŭl′shən) *n.* a sudden feeling of disgust or loathing
   repugnancia *s.* sentimiento repentino de asco o desprecio

sacrilegious (săk′rə-lĭj′əs) *adj.* disrespectful toward a sacred person, place, or thing
   sacrílego *adj.* irrespetuoso hacia una persona, lugar o cosa sagrada

saunter (sôn′tər) *v.* to walk in a slow, relaxed manner
   pasear *v.* caminar de una forma lenta y relajada

scenario (sĭ-nâr′ē-ō′) *n.* a description of a possible course of action or events
   panorama *s.* descripción de un curso posible de acción

scruple (skrōō′pəl) *n.* a feeling of uneasiness that keeps a person from doing something
   escrúpulo *s.* malestar provocado por la conciencia o por los principios personales

serene (sə-rēn′) *adj.* calm; peaceful
   sereno *adj.* calmo; con paz

sever (sěv′ər) *v.* to cut off
   arrancar *v.* partir; cortar por completo

singularity (sĭng′gyə-lăr′ĭ-tē) *n.* something peculiar or unique
   singularidad *s.* rareza; peculiaridad

solace (sŏl′ĭs) *n.* comfort from sorrow or misfortune
   solaz *s.* consuelo frente al dolor o el infortunio

solicitously (sə-lĭs′ĭ-təs-lē) *adv.* in a manner expressing care or concern
   solícitamente *adv.* con preocupación e interés

spartan (spär′tn) *adj.* simple, plain, and frugal
   espartano *adj.* sencillo y frugal

squalor (skwŏl′ər) *n.* a filthy, shabby, and wretched condition, as from poverty
   escualidez *s.* condición sucia y miserable

squander (skwŏn′dər) *v.* to spend or use wastefully
   despilfarrar *v.* desperdiciar; gastar o usar algo descuidadamente

stagnating (stăg′nā′tĭng) *adj.* becoming foul or rotten from lack of movement **stagnate** *v.*
   estancado *adj.* putrefacto por falta de movimiento **estancar** *v.*

stalk (stôk) *n.* a stem or main axis of a plant
   tallo *s.* tronco o eje central de una planta

stark (stärk) *adj.* complete or utter; extreme
   marcado *adj.* absoluto; extremo

status quo (stăt′əs kwō) *n.* the existing state of affairs
   statu quo *s.* estado actual

stealth (stĕlth) *n.* cautious or secret action or movement
   secreto *s.* conducta callada u oculta

steel (stēl) *v.* to make hard or strong
   templar *v.* endurecer; fortalecer

stoicism (stō′ĭ-sĭz′əm) *n.* indifference to pleasure or pain; a lack of visible emotion
   estoicismo *s.* indiferencia ante el dolor o placer

subliminal (sŭb-lĭm′ə-nəl) *adj.* below the level of consciousness
   subliminal *adj.* por debajo de la conciencia

subside (səb-sīd′) *v.* to decrease in amount or intensity; settle down
   calmarse *v.* tranquilizarse; disminuir

subsist (səb-sĭst′) *v.* to support oneself at a minimal level
   subsistir *v.* vivir con lo mínimo

suffuse (sə-fyōōz′) *v.* to gradually spread through or over
   envolver *v.* extenderse gradualmente

superannuated (sōō′pər-ăn′yōō-ā′tĭd) *adj.* obsolete with age
   caduco *adj.* que se ha vuelto obsoleto con el tiempo

supplication (sŭp′lĭ-kā′shən) *n.* a humble request or prayer
   súplica *s.* ruego; solicitud o petición humilde; rezo

surrogate (sûr′ə-gĭt) *adj.* serving as a substitute
   suplente *adj.* que sustituye

surveillance (sər-vā′ləns) *adj.* having to do with close observation
   vigilante *adj.* que hace una observación detallada

sustenance (sŭs′tə-nəns) *n.* food or provisions that sustain life
   sustento *s.* alimentos para vivir

tangible (tăn′jə-bəl) *adj.* capable of being touched or felt; having actual form and substance
   tangible *adj.* que puede tocarse o sentirse; que tiene forma o sustancia real

taut (tôt) *adj.* pulled or drawn tight
   tenso *adj.* tirante

termination (tûr′mə-nā′shən) *n.* an end, limit, or edge
   terminación *s.* fin de algo; límite u orilla

torrent (tôr′ənt) *n.* a heavy, uncontrolled outpouring
   torrente *s.* aguacero fuerte

transcend (trăn-sĕnd′) *v.* to pass beyond the limits of
   transcender *v.* ir más allá de los límites

travail (trə-vāl′) *n.* painful effort
   congoja *s.* esfuerzo doloroso

tremulous (trĕm′yə-ləs) *adj.* marked by trembling or shaking
   trémulo *adj.* tembloroso

trepidation (trĕp′ĭ-dā′shən) *n.* nervous fear
   trepidación *s.* incertidumbre; nerviosismo

uncanny (ŭn-kăn′ē) *adj.* so remarkable as to seem supernatural
   extraordinario *adj.* tan asombroso que parece sobrenatural

undulate (ŭn′jə-lāt′) *v.* to move in waves or in a smooth, wavelike motion
   ondular *v.* moverse en olas

unequivocal (ŭn′ĭ-kwĭv′ə-kəl) *adj.* allowing no doubt or misunderstanding
   inequívoco *adj.* que no admite duda o malentendido

unnerving (ŭn-nûr′vĭng) *adj.* causing loss of courage
unnerve *v.*
   desconcertante *adj.* que pone nervioso **desconcertar** *v.*

valorous (văl′ər-əs) *adj.* brave
   valeroso *adj.* valiente

veneer (və-nîr′) *v.* to cover with a thin layer of material
   enchapar *v.* cubrir con una fina capa de un material fino

vestibule (vĕs′tə-byōōl′) *n.* a small entryway within a building
   vestíbulo *s.* pequeña entrada en un edificio

vexation (vĕk-sā′shən) *n.* irritation; annoyance
   molestia *s.* irritación o ira

vigilant (vĭj′ə-lənt) *adj.* on the alert; watchful
   alerta *adj.* atento para evitar un peligro

wry (rī) *adj.* dryly humorous, often with a bit of irony
   irónico *adj.* de un humor seco; sardónico

zealous (zĕl′əs) *adj.* intensely enthusiastic
   fervoroso *adj.* intensamente dedicado y entusiasta

Pronunciation Key

Symbol	Examples	Symbol	Examples	Symbol	Examples
ă	**a**t, g**a**s	m	**m**an, see**m**	v	**v**an, sa**ve**
ā	**a**pe, d**ay**	n	**n**ight, mitte**n**	w	**w**eb, tw**i**ce
ä	f**a**ther, b**a**rn	ng	si**ng**, ha**ng**er	y	**y**ard, law**y**er
âr	f**air**, d**are**	ŏ	**o**dd, n**o**t	z	**z**oo, rea**s**on
b	**b**ell, ta**b**le	ō	**o**pen, r**oa**d, gr**ow**	zh	trea**s**ure, gara**ge**
ch	**ch**in, lun**ch**	ô	**a**wful, b**ou**ght, h**o**rse	ə	**a**wake, ev**e**n, penc**i**l,
d	**d**ig, bore**d**	oi	c**oi**n, b**oy**		pil**o**t, foc**u**s
ĕ	**e**gg, t**e**n	ŏŏ	l**oo**k, f**u**ll	ər	p**er**form, lett**er**
ē	**e**vil, s**ee**, m**ea**l	ōō	r**oo**t, gl**ue**, thr**ou**gh		
f	**f**all, lau**gh**, **ph**rase	ou	**ou**t, c**ow**	**Sounds in Foreign Words**	
g	**g**old, bi**g**	p	**p**ig, ca**p**	KH	*German* i**ch**, au**ch**;
h	**h**it, in**h**ale	r	**r**ose, sta**r**		*Scottish* lo**ch**
hw	**wh**ite, every**wh**ere	s	**s**it, fa**c**e	N	*French* e**n**tre, bo**n**, fi**n**
ĭ	**i**nch, f**i**t	sh	**sh**e, ma**sh**	œ	*French* f**eu**, c**œu**r;
ī	**i**dle, m**y**, tr**i**ed	t	**t**ap, hopp**ed**		*German* sch**ö**n
îr	d**ear**, h**ere**	th	**th**ing, wi**th**	ü	*French* **u**tile, r**ue**;
j	**j**ar, **g**em, ba**dge**	*th*	**th**en, o**th**er		*German* gr**ü**n
k	**k**eep, **c**at, lu**ck**	ŭ	**u**p, n**u**t		
l	**l**oad, ratt**le**	ûr	f**ur**, **ear**n, b**ir**d, w**o**rm		

Stress Marks

′ This mark indicates that the preceding syllable receives the primary stress. For example, in the word *language,* the first syllable is stressed: lăng′gwĭj.

‚ This mark is used only in words in which more than one syllable is stressed. It indicates that the preceding syllable is stressed, but somewhat more weakly than the syllable receiving the primary stress. In the word *literature,* for example, the first syllable receives the primary stress, and the last syllable receives a weaker stress: lĭt′ər-ə-chŏŏr′.

Adapted from *The American Heritage Dictionary of the English Language,* fourth edition. Copyright © 2000 by Houghton Mifflin Company. Used with the permission of Houghton Mifflin Company.

INDEX OF FINE ART

ix *top*, xxvi, 899   *Young Man Studying* (1932), Hilda Wilkinson Brown.

xii *right*, 271   *Girls from Guadalupita, New Mexico*, Miguel Martinez.

xiv *right*, 329   *La Jolla Cove* (1922), Alson Clark.

xviii *left*, 521   *Brownstones*, Patti Mollica.

xviii *right*, 519   *Farm in Haiti*, Roosevelt.

xx *left*, 591   *A Tempestuous Evening at the Maison de la Culture* (1937), Albert Lafloret.

xxii *left*, 689   *Flower* (1964), Andy Warhol.

xxiv *right*, 753   *Infantry* (1997), James E. Faulkner.

xxiv *left*, 799   *Tumbling Flowers* (1954), Hyacinth Manning-Carner.

xxx *right*, 1131   Detail from *Ulysses and the Sirens* (1891), John William Waterhouse.

2 *right*, 1094 *top*, 1111   Head and bust fragment of Odysseus (4–26).

3 *right*, 679   *Tender Moments* (2000), Francks Deceus.

21, 141   *Raven* (1994), Jim Dine.

38   *Orinoco Jungle Life* (1894), A. Goering.

46   *Blue Morpho Butterfly* (1864–1865), Martin Heade.

71   *Tree Circle* (1992), Peter Schroth.

81   *Reader with Green Hat* (1909), Henri Charles Manguin.

85   *La Mere de l'artiste* (1889), Paul Gauguin.

87   *Pedro Mañach* (1901), Pablo Picasso.

89   *The Third of May, 1808* (1814), Francisco de Goya y Lucientes.

97   *The Kiss* (1891), Edouard Vuillard.

98   *Woman Combing Her Hair*, Edgar Degas.

113   *Alley* (1942), Jacob Lawrence.

114   *Woman Worker* (1951), Charles White.

144   *Red Passion* (1986), Jim Dine.

145   *The Back of a Man with a Rose*, René Magritte.

183 *left*, 209   *Louise Augusta, Queen of Prussia* (1801), Marie Louise Elisabeth Vigée-LeBrun.

211   *A Paris Street, Rain* (1877), Gustave Caillebotte.

213   *The Ball*, Victor Gilbert.

216   *The Laundress* (1869), Edgar Degas.

225, 232 *left*   *Inspiration* (1994), Daniel Nevins.

228, 232 *right*   *Healing* (1996), Daniel Nevins.

239   *Woman with Umbrella*, Bill Farnsworth.

241   *Ancilla with an Orange* (1956), Dod Procter.

244   *Lemonade* (2002), Michele Hausman.

272   *Navajo Power Plant* (1990), Shonto Begay.

299, 349   Burial niches with fresco of Christ Pantocrator.

311   *Anna Kuerner* (1971), Andrew Wyeth.

312   *Wild Dog Mushroom* (1974), Bob Timberlake.

315   Detail of *Winter Sun* (1971), Bob Timberlake.

316   *Mrs. Dorset's Kitchen* (1973), Bob Timberlake.

318   Detail of *Another World* (1974), Bob Timberlake.

321   *Christmas Orange* (1975), Bob Timberlake.

333   *Reflections* (1970), Ken Danby.

336–337 *top*   *Ice Blue* (1981), Susan Shatter.

399 *left*, 461   *Mama's Cradle*, April Harrison.

411   *Full Spittoon* (1974), Bob Timberlake.

415   *Field of Hope*, Charly Palmer.

418   *New Dreams* (2002), Ernest Crichlow.

429   *Richard at Age Five* (1944), Alice Neel.

431   *Cypress Swamp, Texas* (1940), Florence McClung.

436   *Autumn Embers (Frosted Scarlet Sage)* (1944), Charles Burchfield.

463   *Circle of Joy*, Keith Mallett.

468   *Plum Blossoms by Moonlight*, Ma Yuan.

505 *left*, 529   *Cow's Skull: Red, White, and Blue* (1931), Georgia O'Keeffe.

517   Detail of *Harvest Scene with Twelve People*, R. Mervilus.

530   *Jimson Weed* (1932), Georgia O'Keeffe.

563   *Veil of Elegance*, Peter Miller.

573   *The Cashier* (2003), Lisa Reinke.

643, 646   Detail of *Tourists Beware: New Buffalo Speed Trap* (1985), Roger Brown.

644   *Clouds Over Alabama or Midnight in Alabama* (1994), Roger Brown.

666 *right*   *The Cow Jumped Over the Moon* (1885), Randolph Caldecott.

680   *Mother and Child by Grand Canal* (2000), Hung Liu.

681   *Ice Cream Dessert* (1959), Andy Warhol.

687   Untitled (2001), Laura Owens.

688   *Sea Turtle* (1985), Andy Warhol.

696, 698   *Municipal Bonds* (2004), Byron Spicer.

717, 718   *Returning to the Trenches* (1914–1915), C. R. W. Nevinson.

723   *The First and the Last Steps*, Emilio Longoni.

724   *In the Beechwoods*, William Samuel Jay.

742–743   *The Persistence of Memory* (1931), Salvador Dali.

757   *Class of '67* (1987), Charlie Shobe.

759   *Chopper Lift-Out* (1967), Ken McFadyen.

767   *The Princess and the Tin Box* (1948), James Thurber.

800   *Sleeping Couple I* (2000), Hyacinth Manning-Carner.

827 *left*, 905   *Jazz Player III* (1991), Freshman Brown.

865   *Cotton Choppers* (1965), Benny Andrews.

867   *Brothers* (1934), Malvin Gray Johnson.

869   *Woodshed* (1944), Andrew Wyeth.

880   *Little Girl Reading #3* (1973), Simon Samsonian.

883   *Rag in the Window* (1959), Alice Neel.

885   Detail of *Loneliness* (1970), Alice Neel.

903 *top*   *Portrait of Bashō*, Kameda Bosai.

904   *Millet Fields with the Sun and the Moon* (1600s), Chinese.

923 *left*   *The Proposal* (1872), Adolphe-William Bouguereau.

924 *center left*   *Francesca da Rimini* (1837), William Dyce.

924 *bottom left*   *A Bridal Couple* (about 1490), Southern Germany.
1063   *Ovid* (1500–1503), Duomo, Orvieto, Italy.
1065   *Thisbe,* John William Waterhouse.
1085 *left,* 1137   *Scylla and Charybdis,* from the *Ulysses Cycle*
                        (1580), Alessandro Allori.
1088 *bottom*   *Procession of Trojan Horse into Troy,* G.D. Tiepolo.
1089   Detail of a frieze representing a procession of
                        mythological divinites, muses, graces, etc.
                        French.
1090 *right*   *Homer* (about 150 B.C.).
1092 *top,* 1143   *Ulyssess and the Sirens* (200s), Roman.
1092 *bottom,* 1094   *Ulysses Returns Chryseis to Her Father,*
third   Claude Lorrain.
1093 *top left,* 1163 Plaque with the return of Odysseus (about
                        460–450 B.C.). Classical Greek.
1093 *bottom left*   *Ulysses* (1931–1932), Georges Braque.
1093 *top right*   *Odysseus Slaying the Suitors* (400s B.C.),
                        Penelope Painter.
1093 *bottom right*   Illustration by Innes Fripp in *Tales of the Gods
                        and Heroes* by Sir G.W. Cox.
1094 *second*   *Odysseus and Polyphemus* (1896), Arnold Bocklin.
1094 *fourth,* 1124   Detail of *Tilla Durieux as Circe* (about 1912–
                        1913), Franz von Struck.

1094 *fifth,* 1105   *The Ship of Odysseus,* Francois-Louis Schmeid.
1107   *Calypso* (about 1906), George Hitchcock.
1116   *The Cyclops* (about 1914), Odilon Redon.
1120   *Odysseus and Polyphem* (1910), L. du Bois-
                        Reymond.
1127   *Ulysses Descending into the Underworld* (1500s),
                        Giovanni Stradano.
1141   *Penelope Embroidering* (1903), Mrs. H. de Rudder.
1143   *Athene and Telemach,* from *Odyssey II* (1975),
                        Marc Chagall.
1145   Detail of *Goddess Athena Disguises Ulysses as
                        Beggar,* Giuseppe Bottani.
1146   *Ulysses and His Son Telemachus* (A.D. first century).
1151   Detail of *Penelope Weeping over the Bow of Ulysses*
                        (about 1779), Angelica Kauffmann.
1154   Detail of *The Trail of the Bow* (1929), N. C. Wyeth.
1157   *The Slaughter of the Suitors* (1929), N. C. Wyeth.
1161   *Death of the Suitors: The Odyssey* (1944),
                        Henry Spencer Moore.

Index of Skills

A

Abbreviations
  periods in, R49
  postal, R49
  Web, 1191
Academic vocabulary, 23, 185, 301, 401, 507, 593, 667, 743, 829, 925, 1087, 1187. *See also* Specialized vocabulary.
Act (in a play), 7, R102
Active listening, R82–R83
Active voice. *See* Voice.
Adjective clauses, 243, 249, R62
Adjective phrases, R60
Adjectives, 93, 490, 491, 495, R47, R57
  versus adverbs, R57
  avoiding too many, 205
  choosing, 495
  commas and, R49
  precise, 170, 196, 205, 284, 286
  predicate, R57, R60
  proper, R51
  sensory, 390
Adverb clauses, R62
Adverb phrases, R60
Adverbs, 93, 490, 491, 495, 565, 567, R47, R57
  versus adjectives, R57
  choosing, 495
  relative, 249
Advertising, 4, 10, 634–637, R90–R91
  audience and cost of, R84
  billboard, R90
  celebrities in, 635–636, R91
  flyer, R90
  infomercial, R90
  marketing, R90
  persuasive techniques in, 596, 635, R22, R91
  political ad, R90
  print ad, R90
  product comparison, R91
  product placement, R91
  promotional posters, 1025
  public service announcement, 634–637, R90
  sponsors, R90
  trailer, R90
  types of, R90–R91
Aesthetics and literary criticism. *See* Literary criticism.
Affixes. *See* Prefixes; Suffixes.

Agreement
  pronoun-antecedent, R52
  subject-verb agreement, R65–R67
Allegory, R102
Alliteration, 139, 142, 654, 670, 697, 797, 895, 1098, R102. *See also* Sound devices.
Allusions, 95, 103, 608, 932, 933, 939, 987, 999, 1017, 1096, 1115, 1119, 1126, 1138, R102
  author's perspective and, 849
  to make inferences, 837, 843, 847, 849
Almanacs, 1197. *See also* References.
Ambiguity, interpreting, 907
Analogy, 598, 601, 608, 654, R71, R102. *See also* Rhetorical devices.
  false, R24
Analysis, writing, 490–497, 608, 726–733, 812–819, 1051, 1170–1177, R37–R40
  definition, R40
  process, R40
Anapest, R109
Anecdotes, 447, 452, 454, 548, R30–R31
Angle, in news reporting, R89
Anglo-Saxon affix, 1139
Animation, 557, R88
Antagonist, 370, 930, 1033, R102
Antecedent-pronoun agreement, R52
Antonyms, 118, 176, 292, 392, 498, 584, 658, 734, 820, 916, 1078, 1178, R71
Apostrophes, R50
Appeals
  by association, 596, R22
  to authority, R91
  bandwagon, 596, R22, R91
  emotional, 596, 611, 617, 635, 637, 655, 656, R22, R91, R116
  ethical, 596
  to fear, 596, R22, R116
  logical, R91, R117
  to loyalty, R22
  to pity, 596, R22, R116
  "plain folks," 596
  to values, 596, R116
  to vanity, R22
Appearance in oral presentations, R77–R78
Applications, job, R44
Appositives, R60
Approaches to literature. *See* Literary criticism.
Archetypes, 1094, 1103, 1141, 1150, 1153, 1164, 1167, R102

Arguments, 601, 602, 606, R115. *See also* Appeals; Persuasive writing.
  analysis of, 608, 617, 631, R21, R26
  claim, 594, 601, 608, 909, 911, R115
  counterarguments, 617, 650, 651, 654, 661, R21, R116
  counterclaims, 650, 651
  deductive, R23, R116
  elements of, 594, 595
  by emotion, 596, 611, 617, 635, 637, 655, R22, R91, R116
  ethical, 596
  evidence, 594, R21
  faulty, R24
  general principle, R23
  inductive, 631, R22–R23, R117
  logical, R118
  opposing, 908, 909
  reasons, 594, 595, 599, 601, 617, 633, 653, 655, R21, R41
  strategies for determining strong, R26
  strategies for reading, 594, R21
  support, 594, 601, 608, 911, 912, R21, R119
  writing, 633, 851
Art. *See* Visuals.
Articles (part of speech), 220
Articles (written). *See* Feature articles; Journal articles; Magazine articles; News articles; Newspapers, articles in.
Articulation. *See* Speaking strategies.
Artistic effects. *See* Media presentations.
Aside, 930, 934, 939, 944, 991, R102
Assessment Practice
  reading comprehension, 176–179, 292–297, 392–397, 498–503, 584–589, 658–663, 734–739, 820–825, 916–921, 1078–1083, 1178–1183
  vocabulary, 180, 296, 396, 502, 588, 662, 824, 920, 1182
  writing and grammar, 181, 283, 295, 297, 395, 397, 489, 501, 587, 589, 649, 661, 737–739, 823, 825, 919, 921, 1082, 1083, 1181, 1183, R101
Assonance, 670, 715, 716, 719, 895, 1098, R102
Assumptions, R115
Atlases, 1197. *See also* References.
Attitudes, comparing, 205, 231
Audience, 285, 650, 651, 1033
  media, 636, R85
  speaking and listening, 657, 1177, R76, R78, R83

target, 635, R85
writing, 16, 635, 908, 909, R34, R41,
R42
Authority. *See* Arguments; Sources.
Author's background, 832, 875, 876, 881,
885, 886
Author's intent. *See* Author's purpose.
Author's message, 377, 639–648, R115
Author's perspective, 361, 362, 366, 370,
459, 460, 462, 464, 510, 522, 569,
573, 574, 575, 849, 860, R102
Author's point of view. *See* Author's
perspective.
Author's position, R21, R40–R41, R115.
See also Author's perspective; Author's
purpose; Claims.
Author's purpose, 121, 122, 126, 130, 377,
506, 508, 509, 547, 548, 552, 554,
561, 562, 565, 566, 1061, R85, R102
Author's style. *See* Style.
Author's viewpoint. *See* Author's perspective.
Autobiographical essay, R102–R103
Autobiography, 4, 8, 9, 111, 114, 115,
R102–R103. *See also* Memoirs.
characterization in, 237, 238, 242, 245,
247
dialogue in, 111, 114, 117
interpreting, 117
narrative techniques in, 117

B

Ballad, 715, 718, 719, R103
Bandwagon appeal, 596, R22, R91
Bar graphs, R5
Base words, R69
Bias, 621, R115
analysis, 631
in evidence, R25
recognizing, 621, 623, 627, 629, 1201,
R25
in reporting, R90
Bibliography, 1200, 1204, R115. *See also*
Works cited.
MLA citation guidelines, 1228–1229
Biographical context, 247, 273, 323, 901
Biographical essay, 1197
Biographical references, 1197. *See also*
References.
Biography, 4, 8, R103
suspense in, 121, 124, 127, 129, 130
Blank verse, 932, 933, 939, 951, 963, 967,
1051, R103
Boldface type, as text feature, 510, R3
Boolean searches, 1192
Brainstorming, 19, 52, 287, 387, 389, 446,
579, 610, 1173, 1217
Bulleted list, as text feature, R3

Business and technical writing, R42–R43
audience, R42
correspondence, R115
formats for, R43–R45
key techniques, R42
rubric for, R42
Bylaws, R45
Bylines, R14

C

Calculator, graphing, R17
Call to action, 652, 908, 910
Camera shots in film and video, 107, 1076
camera movement, R87
close-up, 109, 357, 358, 391, R87
establishing, 391, R87
extreme long, 109
high-angle, 107, 108, 109, R87
long, 109, 771, R87
low-angle, 107, 108, 109, R87
medium, 109, 391, R87
pan, R87
point-of-view, 107, 108, 109, 771, R87
reaction, 771, R87
tracking shot, R87
zoom, R87
Capitalization
in outlines, 422
quick reference chart, R51
in quotations, 496
Captions
as text features, 510, 535, 536, R3
in Web news report, 557
Career-related writing. *See* Business and
technical writing.
Case, pronoun
nominative, R53
objective, R53
possessive, R53
Casting, 949
Cast of characters, 934, R103
Cause-and-effect organization, 111, 262,
576, 577, R10–R11, R38, R115. *See
also* Patterns of organization.
setting and, 364
in Shakespearean tragedy, 934
in writing, 582, R38
Cause-and-effect relationships, reading, 111,
112, 116, 262
CD-ROMs, of reference works, 1194
Censorship, R86
Chain of events, 342, R38. *See also* Cause-
and-effect organization.
Characterization, 235, 238, 242, 243, 245,
533, 873, R103
across genres, 275, 278, 279, 280, 281
in autobiography, 237, 247

in biography, 275, 278, 279, 281
methods of, 188, 189, 235, 237, 247,
275, 278, 279, 281, 339, 427, 533,
683, 1016, 1053
in poetry, 275, 280, 281
Characters, 384, 879, 946, 955, 973, 975,
980, 996, 1016, 1041, 1055, R103. *See
also* Character types; Characterization.
actions of, 188, 189, 341, 445
analysis of, 203, 220, 233, 235, 325, 339,
341, 443, 445, 567, 683, 849, 991,
1017, 1033, 1167
archetypes, 1103, 1150, 1153, 1164,
1167, R102
cast of, 934, R103
comparing and contrasting, 75, 91, 130,
218, 233
creating memorable, 184, 387
creating realistic, 167, 387
describing, 873
details in creating, 323
development, 991
dialogue in revealing, 388
drawing conclusions about, 323, 480,
485, 840, 849
evaluating, 93, 872, 1017, 1169, R116
facial expressions, body language, and
actions of, 1053
humor of, R107
making inferences about, 270, 353, 427,
428, 430, 432, 433, 434, 437, 441,
569, 570, 572, 575, 680, 991, 1016
motivation of, 190, 207, 212, 215, 217,
218, 247, 531, 849, 980, 991, 994,
1017, 1018, 1026, 1138, 1158, 1162
in narrative poetry, 145, 1067
in narrative writing, R36
physical appearance of, 188, 189
plot and, 79, 82, 86, 89, 91
point of view and, 186–187, 223, 226,
226, 229, 233, R110
reactions of other, 188
relationships between, 339, 427, 683,
1016
settings in influencing, 302, 303
social context of, 886, 1167
study, 251, 252, 254, 256, 258, 262
theme and, 404, 474
thoughts of, 188, 189
in tragedy, 931, 1036, 1040
traits. *See* Character traits.
for video presentation, 391
words of, 188, 189
Character study, 251, 252, 254, 256, 258,
262
Character traits, 75, 188–189, 196, 200,
224, 226, 233, 237, 242, 249, 252,

258, 955, 1041, 1098, 1121, 1147, 1153, R103
evaluating, 203, 370
Character types
antagonist, 370, 930, 1033, R102
archetypal, 1094, 1103, 1150, 1153, 1164, 1167, R102
dynamic, 203, R103
epic hero, 1094, 1103, 1104, 1108, 1110, 1116, 1118, 1120, 1121, 1123, 1129, 1133, 1134, 1135, 1138, R105
flat, 233, R103
foils, 930, 967, R107
main, 233, 930, R103, R107
minor, 233, R103
protagonist, 370, 930, 1033, R111
round, 233, R103
static, 203, R103
tragic hero, 930, 934, R114
Charts. *See* Graphic aids; Graphic organizers.
Choice of words. *See* Diction; Word choice.
Chorus, R103–R104
Chronological order, 26, 172, 510, 515, R9–R10, R36, R115. *See also* Patterns of organization.
signal words for, 515, 519, 520, R9
Circle graph. *See* Graphic aids; Graphic organizers.
Circular reasoning, 914, R24, R117. *See also* Fallacy; Reasoning.
Citation of sources. *See* MLA citation guidelines; Works cited.
Claims, 594, 601, 602, 608, 651, 701, 908, 909, 911, R21, R115
in reading argument, looking for, 594
Clarifying, as reading strategy, 86, 223, 230, 540, R115. *See also* Monitoring.
Clarity, 655, R122
Classification, 511, R115
Classificatory writing. *See* Expository writing.
Clauses, R62–R63
adjective, 243, 249, R62
adverb, R62
essential, R62
as fragments. *See* Sentence fragments.
independent (main), 434, 445, R62
nonessential, R62
noun, R63
punctuation of, R49
subordinate (dependent), 434, 445, R62
Cliché, R115
Climax, 24, R104. *See also* Plot.
analysis of, 420
conflict at, 25
suspense in, 111
Cluster diagram, 17
Coherence in compositions and paragraphs, R31–R32

Colons, 496, R50
Combining sentences. *See* Conjunctions, coordinating.
Comedy, 4, R104. *See also* Tragedy.
Comic relief, 930, 939, 1023, 1033, R104. *See also* Humor.
Commas
in addresses, R49
adjectives and, R49
appositives and, R60
to avoid confusion, R49
with clauses, R49, R62
in compound sentences, 582, R49, R60
in dates, R49
in dialogue, 174
in direct address, R49
in letters, R49
with parenthetical expressions, R49
with phrases, 290, 496, R49
quick reference chart, R49
with quotation marks, 174, 290, 496
in series, R49
Comma splices, R65
Commercials. *See* Advertising.
Commonly confused words, R58, R71–R72, R75
Comparative form of modifiers, R57
Compare and contrast, reading and thinking, 267, 383, 489, 523, 1069, R11–R13, R115
across genres, 274–283, 472–489, 638–649
analyzing, 75, 130, 383, 471, 682, 691, 907, 1167
of attitudes, 205, 231
of audience, 636, 1033
of characters, 75, 91, 130, 218
of cultures, 456
of film and written versions, 359, 1070–1077
of literary works, 233, 247, 383, 443
in poetry, 682, 691, 801
of speakers, 273
of texts, 353, 1167
of word choice, 907
Comparison-and-contrast organization, R11–R13, R115. *See also* Analogy; Arguments.
point-by-point, 1071, 1074, R11
signal words for, 290, 515, R32
subject-by-subject, 1074, R11
of texts, 512
Comparison-contrast essay, 284–291
Comparisons, illogical, R58
Complements, R60
subject, R60
Complications of plot, 62, 70, R104
Comprehension. *See* Assessment; Reading skills and strategies.

Computer software. *See* Software.
Conciseness in writing, 341, 713, 851
Conclusions, 170, 490, 492, 578, 726, 728, 812, 814, 816, 908, 910, 913, 1070, 1072, 1170, 1172, 1210, 1215, 1225, R115
deductive, R23, R115, R116
drawing, 48, 75, 91, 103, 193, 194, 198, 203, 233, 261, 262, 281, 284, 286, 323, 332, 334, 409, 412, 413, 416, 417, 419, 420, 480, 485, 522, 544, 558, 566, 575, 648, 691, 761, 772, 780, 787, 811, 840, 849, 860, 863, 866, 869, 871, 872, 886, 901, R116
inductive, R22–R23, R115, R117
kinds of, R33
in own writing, 384, 386, 388, 494, 581, 655, 816, 913, 1225, R33
in speeches, R77
valid, R115
Concrete poetry, 693, 695, 697
Conflict, 24, 761, R104
analyzing, 53, 54, 57, 62, 68, 70, 72, 75, 339, 487, 761
in building suspense, 57, 70
central, 384, 386
characterization and, 243
at climax, 25
in epic poems, 1147, 1154, 1160
in exposition, 25
external, 24, 456, 761, R104
identifying, 176, 262, 292, 339, 392, 498, 584, 658, 734, 820, 916, 1078, 1178
internal, 24, 140, 456, 481, 761, 1001, R104
in narrative poetry, 144, 145
in narrative writing, R37
in plot, 24, 53, 54, 57, 62, 68, 70, 72, 75, 79, 111, 149, 957, 967
resolution of, 130, 386, 1050
setting and, 303
theme and, 404, 478, 481, 487, 489
in tragedy, 957, 991, 994, 996, 1001, 1008, 1016
Conjunctions
coordinating, 518, 523, 582, R47, R49, R59
correlative, R47
subordinating, R47, R63
Connecting, 11, 12, 14, 223, 231, 257, 379, 382, 383, 553, 554, 693, 694, 697, 875, 878, 882, 884, 886, 1166, R115
Connotation, 76, 324, 444, 746, 781, R71, R104. *See also* Denotation.
Consonance, 670, 1098, R104
Consumer documents, 8, R16, R17, R116. *See also* Technical writing; Workplace documents.

Content-area vocabulary. *See* Academic vocabulary; Specialized vocabulary.
Context clues, 371, 457, R15, R68, R116. *See also* Vocabulary, in context.
　biographical, 247, 901
　cause-and-effect, R68
　comparison, R68
　contrast, R68
　cultural, 903, 904, 905, 906, 907
　definition or restatement, R68
　examples as, R68
　general context, R68
　historical, 130, 471, 719, 830–835, 886, 903, 904, 905, 906, 907
　social, 420, 464, 886, 1167
　specific, R68
　word roots and, 204
Contractions, 40, 50
Contracts, R116
Conventions, grammar, 18, 168, 284, 384, 490, 576, 650
Conversational tone, in informal speech, 175
Copyright law, R86
Copyright page, 1200, 1204
Correspondence, business, R42–R43, R115
Costumes, 357, 959, 1053, 1055
　analyzing, in media literacy, 358
　design of, 959
Counterarguments, 650, 651, 654, 661, R21, R116
　analysis of, 617
Couplet, 674, 693, 697, 963, R104, R112, R113
Credibility, R90, R116. *See also* Sources.
Crisis. *See* Climax.
Critical analysis
　allusions in, 95, 103, 608, 837, 843, 847, 849, 932, 933, 939, 987, 999, 1017
　analogies in, 598, 601, 608, 654, R71, R102
　argument in, 608, 617
　of author's message, 377
　author's purpose in, 377, 554, 1061
　bias in, 631
　characterization in, 554
　compare and contrast of cultures in, 456
　conflict analysis in, 456
　counterargument in, 617
　critical review in, 1061
　distinguishing fact from opinion, 631, R116–R117
　drawing conclusions, 544, 617, 840, 849, 860
　evaluation, 48, 544, 893
　graphic aids in, 554
　implied main ideas in, 456
　making inferences in, 425
　making judgments in, 425, 456, 631

modes of reasoning in, 631
mood in, 137
opinions in, 1061
of outline, 425
primary sources in, 377
rhetorical devices in, 608
sequence in, 456
summarizing in, 544, 617
synthesizing in, 617, 701, 888, 889, 890, 891, 892, 893
texts, 544, 631
tone in, 137, 701, 1175
Critical essays, R106
Critical interpretation, 48, 75, 91, 103, 117, 147, 218, 233, 339, 353, 370, 522, 566, 682, 712, 787, 849, 872, 907, 967, 1050, 1138
Critical listening, R83
Critical reading. *See* Reading skills and strategies; Test-taking strategies.
Critical reviews, 1056, 1057, 1059, 1060, 1061, R116
Critical thinking. *See* Reading skills and strategies; Critical analysis.
Criticism. *See* Literary criticism.
Critique, writing, 633
Cultural contexts, 832, 860, 903, 904, 905, 906, 907
Cultural symbols, 853, 856, 857, 859, 860
Currency of sources. *See* Sources.

D

Dactyl, R109
Dashes, R50
Data, collecting own, 1206–1207
Databases, 1198, R116. *See also* References.
Debates, 620, 915, 782, 938, R79, R116
　appointing moderator, 915
　evaluating, R79
　planning, 915
　presenting, 915
　resolution in, 915
Deconstruction, of media presentation, R85
Deductive arguments, R23, R116
Deductive conclusion, R115, R116
Deductive reasoning, R23, R116
Definition analysis, R40
Degree of importance, R32, R35
Delivery. *See* Speaking strategies.
Demographics, R85
Denotation, 76, 324, 746, 781, R71, R104. *See also* Connotation.
Dénouement. *See* Resolution.
Derivations of words, R69. *See also* Word parts, analyzing.
Descriptive language, 249, 533, 683. *See also* Details.

Descriptive speech, R80
Descriptive writing, 105, 205, R34–R35. *See also* Writing skills and strategies.
　key techniques in, R34–R35
　options for organization, R35
　rubric for, R34
Details, 169, 170, 171, 241, 436
　analysis of, 327, 328, 330, 332, 335, 339
　descriptive, 77, 249, 327, 384, 385, 390, 567, 1169
　relevant, 169
　sensory, 170, 171, 304, 672, 755, R33, R34, R112
　supporting, 205, 288, 289, 422, 494, 562, 652, 653, 655, 656, 763, 1070, 1226, R8
　vivid, 169, 172
Dewey decimal system, 1208
Diagrams, 795, R6. *See also* Graphic aids; Graphic organizers.
　interpreting, 251, 255, 260, 262
　picture diagrams, R6
　schematic diagrams, R6
　of story events, R2
　strategies for reading, R6
　Venn, 75, 233, 287, R12
Dialect, 457, 830, 844, 863, 864, 868, 870, 872, R104. *See also* Standard English.
Dialogue, 934, R105. *See also* Monologue.
　in autobiographies, 111, 114, 117, 119
　in characterization, 388, R36
　contractions in, 40, 50
　creating, 167, 341
　in drama, 7, 149, 166, 167, 803, 934, 1058, 1077, R105
　in film, 107
　making believable, 50, 389
　punctuation in, 174
　realistic, 50, 111, 754
　repetitive, 719
　revising and editing, 50, 389
　sentence fragments in, 50
　Shakespearean, 934, 1058, 1077
　writing, 50, 167–169, 341, 851
Diary, 77, 683, 890, R105
Diction, 515, 516, 518, 519, 522, 685, 686, 689, 691, 801, R105. *See also* Word choice.
Dictionary, 340, 618, 1197, R72. *See also* References.
　idioms in, 887
Directions
　in consumer document, R16–R17
　stage, 934, R113
Direct objects, R48, R60
Directories, 1197, 1208. *See also* References.
Director's techniques, 1053, 1054
Discovery drafting, R28

Discussion, 11, 446, R81
  class, 326, 378
  group, 342, R81
  guidelines, R81
  listening skills and, R81, R82–R83
  panel, 497
  partner, 534, 546, 610, 692, 750
  role of leader, R81
  role of participants, R81
  role of recorder, R81
  small-group, 110, 192, 236, 274, 426,
    472, 560, 862, 1062, 1102
Documentaries, 1199. *See also* Media; Media
    presentations; Sources.
Documenting sources. *See* Works cited.
Documents
  consumer, R16, R17, R116
  public, R18, R119
  workplace, R19, R42–R45, R120
Double negatives, R58–R59
Drafting techniques, 17, 172, 288, 388, 489,
    494, 580, 654, 729, 730, 815, 816,
    912, 1074, 1174, 1223–1225, R28
Drama, 4, 7, R105
  act, 7, R102, R105, R112
  aside, 930, 934, 939, 944, 991, R102
  characteristics of, 7, 149, 803, 930–937,
    R105
  comedies, 4, R104
  comic relief, 930, 939, 1023, 1033, R104
  dialogue, 7, 149, 166, 167, 803, 934,
    1058, 1077, R105
  dramatic irony, 95, 353, 357, 358, 811,
    930, 1000, 1023, 1033, 1149, R108
  farce, 4, 803, 811, R106
  interpretation of, 166, 811, 939, 967,
    991, 1017, 1033, 1050, 1051
  plot in, 149, 166
  scene, 7, R102, R105, R112
  Shakespearean, 923–1083
  soliloquy, 930, 931, 934, 939, 971, 991,
    999, 1038, 1050, R112
  stage directions, 7, 150, 803, 934, R113
  strategies for reading, R2, 934–935, 939,
    967, 991, 1017, 1033, 1050
  themes in, 1048, 1050
  tragedy, 4, 930–931, 939, 957, 990, 994,
    996, 998, 1001, 1007, 1008, 1024,
    1034, 1040, 1048, 1050, 1051, R114
  types of, 4
Dramatic irony, 95, 353, 357, 358, 811, 930,
    1000, 1023, 1033, 1149, R108
Dramatic monologue, 721, 722, 725, R105.
    See also Soliloquy.
Drawing conclusions. *See* Conclusions,
    drawing.
Dynamic character, 203, R103

E

Editing, of films and video, 107, 108, 391,
    583, R88
  cut, 107, 108, 771, R88
  dissolve, R88
  fade-in, R88
  fade-out, R88
  jump cut, R88
  pace, 107, 108, 771, R88
  split screen, R88
Editing, of writing. *See* Revising and editing.
Editorials, 508, 628–631, R40, R88, R116
  newspaper, 628–630
Effect, 111, R115. *See also* Cause-and-effect
    organization.
Effect-to-cause organization, R38
Either/or fallacy, 914, R24, R117
Elaboration, 727, 1174, R33–R34
  examples in, R34
  facts and statistics in, R33
  incidents in, R34
  quotations in, R34
  responding to questions and
  sensory details in, R33–R34
Electronic card catalog, 1195
Electronic mail (e-mail), R42
Electronic media. *See also* Multimedia
    presentations; References; Research.
  card catalog, 1195
  Internet, 632, 1189, 1191–1193, R117
Electronic sources. *See* References.
Electronic text, R20
  strategies for reading, R20
Elegy, 685, 688, 691, R105
Ellipses, 496, R50
E-mail, R42
Emotional appeals, 596, 611, 617, 637, 655,
    656, R22, R91, R116
Encyclopedia, 1197. *See also* References.
End rhyme, 670, 715, R111
Enunciation, 1077, R78
Epic hero, 1094, 1103, 1104, 1108, 1110,
    1116, 1118, 1120, 1121, 1123, 1129,
    1133, 1134, 1135, 1138, R105
Epic poetry, 1094–1095, R105
  archetypes in, 1094, 1141, 1150, 1153,
    1164, 1167
  characteristics of, 1094–1095, 1141,
    1144, 1146, 1147, 1149, 1153, 1154,
    1155, 1156, 1158, 1159, 1160, 1162,
    1165, 1167
  characters in, 1167
  conflict in, 1147, 1154, 1160
  epic heroes in, 1094, 1103, 1104, 1108,
    1110, 1116, 1118, 1120, 1121, 1123,
    1129, 1133, 1134, 1135, 1138, R105
  plot in, 1094, 1141, 1153, 1167

  reading, 1098–1099, 1103, 1141
  settings in, 1094, 1141, 1144, 1167
  themes in, 1094, 1138, 1141, 1144, 1167
Epic similes, 1096, 1097, 1103, 1106, 1119,
    1124, 1138, 1144, R105
Epilogue, R104, R105
Epithets, 1096, 1097, 1109, 1113, 1116,
    1122, 1138, R105
Eponyms, 488
Essay questions in assessment. *See*
    Assessment; Writing for assessment.
Essays, literary, 177, 360–371, 446–457,
    458–464, 514–522, 524–532, 584,
    600–609, 638–641, 658, 774–781,
    782–788, 821, 852–861, 1056–1061
  autobiographical, R102–R103
  biographical, 1197
  critical, R106
  expository, R106
  formal, 8, R105
  informal, 8, R105–R106
  personal, 8, R106
  persuasive, 8, 908–914, R106
  reflective, R106
  writer's message in, 639
Essays, writing, R37–R40
  analysis, 490–497, 726–733, 812–819,
    1170–1177
  comparison-contrast, 284–291, 1068–
    1075, R37–R38
  personal response, 726–763
  persuasive, 650–657, 908–915, R40–R41
  problem-solution, 576–583, R39
Ethical appeal, 596
Etymologies, 282, 488, R70. *See also* Word
    origins.
Evaluation, 218, 539, R79, R116
  of arguments, 608, 617, 631, R21, R26
  of information, 262, 372, 544, 637, 657,
    893, 1193, 1201–1205, 1209, 1218,
    R25–R26, R92
  of literature, 48, 77, 117, 130, 166, 203,
    218, 247, 273, 323, 339, 353, 370,
    377, 383, 420, 455, 471, 522, 554,
    566, 608, 617, 712, 719, 725, 772,
    780, 849, 860, 872, 907, 967, 1017,
    1033, 1061, 1069, 1167
  of writing, 174, 290, 390, 496, 582, 732,
    818, 914, 1076, 1176, 1230
Everyday texts. *See* Consumer documents;
    Job applications; Public documents;
    Workplace documents.
Evidence, 490, 491, 594, 596, 601, 602, 608,
    617, 701, 908, 909, 1210, R21, R116
  bias in, 621, R25, R115
  citing, 377
  collecting, 287, 493, 729, 1188–1209

evaluating, 621, 631, 1075, R23, R25
  expert opinions, 909
  providing, in speeches, R77
  tracking, in reading argument, 594
Exaggeration, 765, 766, 769
Exclamation points, 174, R49
Expert opinion, 621, 909, R25, R41
Explanatory writing, 508, 509, 547. *See also*
    Expository writing.
Exposition, of plot, 24, 25, 36, R106. *See*
    also Plot.
Expository texts. *See* Nonfiction.
Expository writing, student, R37–R40
    analysis, 490–497, 726–733, 812–819,
      1170–1177, R39–R40
    cause and effect, R32, R38
    comparison and contrast in, 283,
      284–291, 489, 649, 1068–1075, R32,
      R37–R38
    options for organization, R37–R40
    problem-solution, 576–583, R39
    research papers, 1210–1233
    rubric for, 174, 290, 496, 582, 732, 818,
      914, 1076, 1176, 1230, R37
Expressive writing. *See* Narrative writing.
Extemporaneous speeches, R76. *See also* Oral
    presentations.
Extended metaphor, 725, 795, R106
External conflict, 24, 456, 761, R104
Eye contact, 819, 915, R78

F

Fable, R106
Facial expression in speeches, 819, 915
Facts, 621, 909, R116–R117. *See also*
    Supporting statements.
    in elaboration, R33
    versus opinion, 623, 624, 626, 628, 630,
      631, R25, R116–R117
    recognizing, 621
    verifying, R25
Fallacy, 914, R24, R117
Falling action, 24, 31, 130, R106. *See also*
    Plot.
False analogy, R24
False cause, 914, R24
Fantasy, R106
Farce, 4, 803, 811, R106
Faulty reasoning, R24
Fear, appeal to, 596, R22, R116
Feature articles, 4, 8, 264–267, 422–425,
    889, R117
Feedback. *See* Peer response.
Fiction, strategies for reading, 11–15, 831.
    See also Reading skills and strategies.
Fiction, types of, 4, 5
    fable, R106

fantasy, R106
historical, 831, R107
horror, R107
novellas, 4, 5, R109
novels, 4, 5, R109
realistic, R111
science, 5, 33, 639, 642–647, R112
short stories, 4, 5, 13–14, R112
tall tales, R114
Field research, 1206
Figurative language, 642, 648, 672, 673,
    703, 704, 706, 707, 710, 712, 791,
    991, 1098, 1103, 1119, 1169, R68,
    R106
  in descriptive writing, R34
  epic similes, 1096, 1097, 1098, 1103,
    1106, 1119, 1124, 1138, 1144, R105
  epithets, 1096, 1097, 1109, 1113, 1116,
    1122, 1138, R105
  extended metaphor, 725, 795, R106
  hyperbole, 627, 672, 775, R107, R114
  metaphor, 672, 703, 707, 712, 793,
    1156, 1169, R108
  paradox, 281, R110
  personification, 117, 672, 703, 710, 712,
    907, R110
  similes, 672, 703, 706, 1096, 1169, R112
Figure of speech. *See* Figurative language.
Film reviews, 1056–1061
Films, 1199, R86–R88. *See also* Camera shots
    in film and video; Media elements and
    techniques.
  comparing with plays, 1070–1077
  differences between text and, 359, 1073
  documentaries, 1199
  editing of, 107, 108, 391, 583, R88
  feature, 4, 10
  irony in, 357
  mood in, 357, 772, 1054
  script and written elements, R86, R112
  setting in, 357, 1054
  sound in, 107, 1054, 1076, R87
  storyboard, 109, 391, 583, R86
  style in, 771, 773
  suspense in, 106, 107, 109
  visual elements in, R87
First Amendment, R86
First-person narrator. *See* Narrators.
First-person point of view. *See* Point of view.
Firsthand and expressive writing. *See*
    Narrative writing.
Flashbacks, 26, 27, 751, 759, 761, R36,
    R106–R107
Flat characters, 233, R103
Flow chart, 733, 1231
Fluency in writing, 168, 284, 384, 490, 523,
    576, 650, 908
Foils (character), 930, 967, R107

Folk ballads, R103
Folktales. *See* Oral tradition.
Foreground, 757
Foreign words in English, 618, R70
Foreshadowing, 26, 33, 34, 36, 37, 48, 121,
    166, 443, 967, 996, 1034, 1129, R107
  in creating suspense, 26, 33, 37, 75, 121,
    166, R107, R113
Form in poetry, 6, 668, 693, 694, 696, 697,
    R107
Formal language, 348, 355
Formatting
  research paper, 1230
  workplace documents, R42–R44
  works cited, 1228–1229
Forms of writing. *See* Writing skills and
    strategies.
Fragments. *See* Sentence fragments.
Framing (on screen), 668, 1053, R87
Freewriting, 17, 19, 729, 1173. *See also*
    Quickwriting.
Free verse, 668, 669, 797, R107
Functional documents, 8. *See also* Consumer
    documents; Workplace documents.
Functional reading, R3–R20

G

Generalizations, R117
  hasty, R24
  making, 267
  overgeneralization, 621, 914, R24, R117,
    R118
General pronoun reference, R55
Genre, 4, R107. *See also* Drama; Fiction;
    Informational texts; Nonfiction; Poetic
    forms.
  characterization across, 275, 278, 279,
    280, 281
  comparing across, 274–283, 472–489,
    638–649
  theme across, 473
  writer's message across, 639
Gerunds and gerund phrases, 843, 851, R61
Gestures, R79
Glittering generality, R22
Glossary, 1200, R15, R72
Government publications, R117
Grammar. *See also specific grammar concepts;*
    Grammar handbook, R46–R65.
  checking, 18, 174, 290, 390, 496, 582,
    656, 732, 818, 914, 1076, 1176
  style and, 40, 50, 69, 77, 82, 93, 105, 115,
    119, 167, 196, 205, 214, 220, 232, 235,
    243, 249, 316, 325, 331, 341, 348, 355,
    434, 445, 462, 465, 503, 518, 523, 528,
    533, 565, 567, 616, 619, 630, 633, 663,

683, 713, 755, 763, 786, 789, 843, 851, 869, 873, 970, 1051, 1156, 1169
Graphic aids, 535, R3, R5–R7, R117
captions, 510, 535, 536, 557, R3
charts, R6
in consumer documents, R17
diagrams, 251, 255, 260, 262, 287, R6
graphs, R5
interpreting, 251, 255, 260, 262, 547
maps, 538, 547, 550, 554, R7
photographs, 547, 548, 553, 554
pie graphs, R5
in public documents, R18
tables, R6
Graphic organizers, 11, 19, R117
balance scale, 326
cause-and-effect, 934
charts, 12, 15, 32, 33, 48, 53, 79, 91, 103, 111, 117, 130, 132, 139, 147, 171, 193, 207, 237, 251, 262, 264, 273, 275, 281, 287, 309, 327, 339, 343, 361, 370, 372, 379, 387, 409, 420, 427, 443, 447, 464, 471, 473, 487, 489, 493, 522, 525, 531, 544, 547, 561, 566, 569, 579, 592, 601, 611, 648, 654, 677, 685, 698, 703, 715, 719, 761, 775, 783, 787, 797, 803, 811, 815, 837, 853, 872, 875, 886, 888, 895, 903, 939, 967, 991, 1017, 1033, 1050, 1056, 1069, 1098, 1103, 1138, 1190, 1231, R6
cluster diagrams, 11, 17, 579
conclusion organizer, 409
diagrams, 233, 579, 780, 795
lists, 493
sequence chain, 342, 751, 1063
spider maps, 554
story maps or story graphs, 172, 387
timelines, 171
Venn diagrams, 75, 233, 287, 558, R12
webs, 52, 104, 204, 219, 236, 340, 387, 458, 466, 532, 555, 653, 780, 862, 1173, 1217
Graphing calculator, R17
Greek culture, words from, 234
Greek word parts, 104, 532, 545, 861, R69. *See also* Word roots.
Group discussion, R81
leadership, R81
participant roles, R81
skills, R81

H
Haiku, 4, 903–907, R107
Harlem Renaissance literature, 895, 898, 900, 901

Hasty generalization, R24
Hero, R107. *See also* Epic hero; Tragic hero
Hierarchical organization. *See* Order of importance.
Historical context of literature, 130, 471, 719, 830–835, 863, 886, 903–907, 926–929, 1088–1093
Historical documents, R117
Historical fiction, 831, R107
Historical perspective, 383
Homer
language of, 1096–1097
world of, 1088–1093
Homeric similes. *See* Epic similes.
Homonyms, 788, R71
Homophones, R71–R72
Horror fiction, R107
How-to books, R117
Humor, 775, 776, 778, 780, R107
Hyperbole, 627, 672, 775, R107, R114
Hyperlinks, 1193, R20
in Web news report, 557
Hyphens, R50

I
Iamb, 671, R108
Iambic pentameter, 671, 725, 932, 967, R103, R107, R112
Iambic tetrameter, 725
Icons, 1193
Ideas, 18, 384. *See also* Main ideas.
analysis of, 420, 425, 721, 724, 725
expressing, in writing, 16
finding, for writing, R28
flow of, 289, 1075
organizing, R28
in poetry, 797, 798, 801
supporting with details, 205, 288, 726, 1226, R8
Idioms, 868, 887, R68, R108
vocabulary development and, 887
Illogical comparisons, R58
Imagery, 6, 304, 642, 648, 672, 677, 830, 1103, R108
analysis of, 309, 313, 314, 323
in creating mood, 304, 379, 380, 428, R35
creating sensory, 304, 305, R34
evaluating, 323
interpreting, 273, 682, 697, 903, 907
in poetry, 672, 673, 677, 680, 682, 697, 1098
Independent clauses, 434, 445, R62
Independent reading level, R27
Indexes, 1197, R117. *See also* References.
as part of a book, 1200

Indirect objects, R48, R60
Inductive conclusion, R115
Inductive reasoning, 631, R22–R23, R117
Inferences, making, 12, 14, 34, 37, 41, 47, 48, 79, 80, 84, 87, 88, 90, 91, 108, 207, 208, 210, 218, 229, 231, 240, 260, 281, 312, 314, 317, 319, 322, 347, 369, 425, 443, 464, 471, 636, 677, 680, 681, 682, 719, 772, 837, 838, 872, R117
about author's purpose, 121, 122, 126, 130, 377, 508, 509, 547, 552, 554, 561, 562, 565, 566, 1061, R102
about characters, 353, 427, 428, 430, 432, 433, 434, 437, 441, 569, 570, 572, 575, 991
about speakers, 144, 270
allusions in, 837, 843, 847, 849
in memoirs, 837, 838, 849
Infinitives and infinitive phrases, 713, R61
Inflection. *See* Speaking strategies.
Informal language, 167, 389, 495, 565, 744, 1075, 1175, 1227, R68, R76
Information. *See also* Electronic media; References; Sources.
evaluating, 893, 1201–1205
gathering, in research, 1190–1195, 1206–1207, 1220
from multiple sources, 893
reading for, R27. (*See also* Reading for information.)
summarizing, 893, 1220, R33
Informational texts, 8, R3, R8. *See also* Consumer documents; Nonfiction; Public documents; Reading for information; Workplace documents.
Informative article. *See* News articles; Reading for information.
Informative writing, 508, 509, 547. *See also* Expository writing.
Instructional manuals, R16–R17, R45
Interjections, R47
Internal conflict, 24, 140, 456, 481, 761, 1001, R104
Internal rhyme, 143, 670, 715, R111
Internet, 586, 632, 651, 1189, 1191–1193, R117. *See also* Electronic media; References.
Interviews, 760, 1206–1207, R81–R82, R108
conducting, R82
evaluating, R82
following up on, R82
preparing for, R81
Intransitive verbs, R47
Introductions, 168, 169, 284, 285, 289, 384, 490, 491, 576, 577, 651, 726, 727,

812, 813, 817, 908, 909, 1070, 1071, 1170, 1171, 1210, 1226, R30–R31
  kinds of, 172, R30–R31
Irony, 95, 98, 102, 103, 147, 218, 347, 765, 769, 775, 780, R108
  dramatic, 95, 353, 357, 358, 811, 930, 1000, 1023, 1033, 1149, R108
  situational, 95, 103, 218, 780, R108
  verbal, 95, R108
Issues
  debating, 915
  evading, as logical fallacy, R24
Italics, R50. *See also* Formatting.

J

Job applications, R44, R116, R120
Journal articles, 794
Journaling, 11, 19
Journals, 1199, R117. *See also* References.
Judgments, making, 75, 91, 103, 130, 166, 323, 339, 353, 370, 425, 456, 487, 631, 648, 682, 769, 886, 1033, 1050, 1069

K

Keywords, 1189
Keyword search, 1191
Key traits of effective writing, 18, 168, 284, 384, 490, 576, 650, 726, 812

L

Language. *See also* Diction; Literary elements; Word choice.
  descriptive, 533, 683
  figurative, 642, 648, 672, 673, 703, 704, 706, 707, 710, 712, 791, 907, 991, 1098, 1103, 1119, 1169, R34, R68, R106
  formal, 348, 355
  humor of, R107
  informal, 167, 389, 495, 565, 744, 1075, 1175, 1227, R68, R76
  loaded, 596, 621, 623, 629, R25, R117
  persuasive, 908, 910, 912
  precise, 168, 170, 196, 205, 726, 728, R77
  sensory, 384, 385
  Shakespearean, 928, 932–933, 934
  using appropriate for speech, R76–R77
  using appropriate for writing, 355
Latin word parts. *See* Word parts.
  affixes, 91
  word roots, 49, 131, 176, 204, 219, 292, 340, 392, 498, 555, 584, 658, 734, 820, 850, 916, 1168, 1078, 1178, R69

Layout. *See* Formatting.
Lead
  in TV newscast, 557
  in Web news report, 557
Legend. *See* Oral tradition.
Letters
  business, R42–R43, R115
  published, 372
  writing, 465, 763, R43
Libel, R86
Library
  catalog in, 1195
  classification systems for books in, 1208
  research in, 1194–1200
Library of Congress classification system, 1208
Lighting, 357, 1039, 1053, 1054, 1055, 1076
Line graphs, R5
Lines, in poetry, 6, 668, 693, 694, R108
Listening skills. *See also* Speaking.
  active, R82–R83
  critical, R83
  note taking and, R82–R83
  rubric for evaluating oral presentations, R83
Literary analysis, 23, 24–31, 33, 48, 53, 75, 79, 91, 95, 103, 111, 117, 121, 130, 139, 147, 149, 166, 185-191, 193, 203, 207, 218, 223, 233, 237, 247, 262, 269, 273, 275, 281, 301, 302–306, 309, 323, 327, 339, 343, 353, 361, 370, 379, 383, 401, 402–407, 409, 420, 427, 443, 459, 464, 467, 471, 473, 487, 490, 496, 507, 515, 522, 525, 531, 561, 566, 569, 575, 593, 639, 648, 667, 668–675, 677, 682, 685, 691, 693, 697, 703, 712, 715, 719, 721, 725, 743, 744–749, 751, 761, 765, 769, 775, 780, 783, 787, 791, 795, 797, 801, 803, 811, 829, 830–835, 837, 849, 853, 860, 863, 872, 875, 886, 895, 901, 903, 907, 925, 930–937, 939, 967, 991, 1017, 1033, 1050, 1063, 1069, 1087, 1094–1101, 1103, 1138, 1141, 1167
Literary criticism, R108
  author's style, 166, 203, 443, 531, 575, 725, 747, 761, 787, 791, 792, 793, 795, 797, 798, 800, 801, 811, 991
  biographical context, 247, 273, 323, 901
  critical interpretation, 48, 75, 91, 103, 117, 147, 218, 233, 339, 353, 370, 522, 566, 682, 712, 787, 801, 849, 872, 907, 967, 1050, 1138
  cultural context, 832, 860, 903, 904, 905, 906, 907

different perspectives in, 262, 780, 860, 1033
historical context, 130, 471, 719, 830–835, 863, 886, 903–907, 926–929, 1088–1093
historical perspective, 383
philosophical context, 1017
social context, 420, 464, 886, 1167
Literary elements and devices. *See also* Characters; Conflict; Plot; Point of view; Settings; Theme.
  allegories, R102
  allusions, 95, 103, 849, 932, 933, 987, 999, 1017, 1096, 1115, 1119, 1126, 1138, R102
  ambiguity, 907
  archetypes, 1103, 1141, 1150, 1153, 1164, 1167, R102
  assonance, 715, 716, 719
  blank verse, 932, 933, 939, 963, 967, R103
  character foils, 930, 967, R107
  characterization, 237, 238, 242, 245, 247, 275, 278, 279, 280, 281, 531, 533, R103
  characters, 75, 79, 82, 86, 89, 91, 188–198, 200, 203, 207, 212, 215, 217, 218, 220, 224, 226, 233, 235, 237, 242, 249, 252, 258, 323, 370, 531, 849, 872, 955, 973, 975, 980, 994, 996, 1016,1017, 1018, 1026, 1036, 1041, 1098, 1121, 1138, 1147, 1153, 1158, 1162, 1167, R103
  comic relief, 930, 939, 1023, 1033, R104
  conflict, 24, 25, 53, 54, 57, 62, 68, 70, 72, 75, 79, 111, 262, 339, 487, 761, 957, 967, 991, 1008, 1147, 1154, 1160, R104
  cultural symbols, 853, 856, 857, 859, 860
  dialect, 457, 830, 863, 864, 868, 870, 872, R104
  dialogue, 168, 169, 934, R105
  diction, 515, 516, 518, 519, 522, 685, 686, 689, 691, 801
  dramatic irony, 95, 353, 357, 358, 811, 930, 1000, 1023, 1033, 1149, R108
  dramatic monologues, 725, R105
  epic characteristics, 1141, 1144, 1146, 1147, 1149, 1153, 1154, 1155, 1156, 1158, 1159, 1160, 1162, 1165, 1167, R105
  epic hero, 1094, 1103, 1104, 1108, 1110, 1116, 1118, 1120, 1121, 1123, 1129, 1133, 1134, 1135, 1138, R105
  epic similes, 1096, 1097, 1098, 1103, 1106, 1119, 1124, 1138, 1144, R105
  epithets, 1096, 1097, 1109, 1113, 1116, 1122, 1138, R105

extended metaphors, 725, 795, R106

figurative language, 672, 673, 703, 704, 706, 707, 710, 712, 791, 907, 991, 1098, 1103, 1119, 1169, R106. *See also* Figurative language.

flashbacks, 26, 27, 751, 759, 761, R36, R106–R107

foreshadowing, 26, 33, 34, 36, 37, 48, 75, 121, 166, 443, 967, 996, 1034, 1129, R107

form, 693, 694, 696, 697, R107

humor, 775, 776, 778, 780, R107

hyperbole, 627, 672, 775, R107, R114

imagery, 309, 310, 313, 314, 323, 379, 380, 672, 673, 677, 680, 682, 697, 719, 830, 903, 907, 1098, R108

irony, 95, 98, 102, 103, 147, 218, 347, 769, 775, 780, 811, R108

metaphors, 703, 707, 712, 793, 1156, 1169

meter, 721, 723, 724, 725, R108–R109

mood, 137, 343, 346, 348, 351, 353, 358, 361, 362, 364, 368, 370, 379, 380, 383, 428, 443, 795, 958, R109

parodies, 765, 766, 768, 769, R110

personification, 117, 703, 710, 712, 907

plot, 24, 31, 53, 79, 82, 86, 89, 91, 130, 149, 166, 1024, 1050, 1153, 1167, R110

point of view, 193, 203, 214, 218, 223, 226, 227, 229, 233, 269, 384, 385, 566, 756, R110

repetition, 139, 144, 715, 718, 719

rhyme, 139, 143, 697, 715, 718, 719, 722, 724, R111

rhyme scheme, 670, 722, 724, R111

rhythm, 139, 146, 670, 721, 791, 797, 800, 1051, R111

satire, R112

setting, 309, 310, 314, 319, 321, 323, 327, 330, 335, 339, 361, 362, 364, 368, 370, 409, 410, 414, 415, 417, 418, 420, 1053, 1054, 1055, R112

similes, 703, 706, 1096, 1169

situational irony, 95, 103, 218, 780, R107, R108

slant rhyme, 791, 792

soliloquy, 930, 931, 934, 939, 971, 991, 999, 1038, 1050, R112

sound devices, 147, 697, 715, 716, 718, 719, 797, 901

speakers, 139, 142, 147, 269, 270, 271, 272, 273, 383, 673, 678, 719, R113

stanzas, 693, 696

suspense, 33, 37, 106, 107, 109, 111, 121, 124, 127, 129, 130, 339, 370, 1150, R113

symbols, 91, 323, 327, 330, 335, 339, 420, 427, 430, 439, 440, 443, 725, 795, R114

themes, 48, 105, 409, 432, 443, 473, 725, 795, 901, 1048, 1069, 1138

themes, universal, 467, 469, 470, 471, 1050, 1167, R114

tone, 137, 520, 525, 528, 530, 531, 561, 562, 565, 566, 780, 783, 784, 787, 789, 901, R114

tragedy, 930–931, 936–937, 957, 994, 996, 998, 1001, 1007, 1008, 1024, 1034, 1040, 1048, 1050, 1051, R114

verbal irony, 95, R107, R108

voice, 801, 849, 863, 864, 868, 870, 872, R114

word choice, 860

word play, 775, 778

Literary nonfiction, 8, 110–118, 120–131, 165, 176–177, 236–279, 360–371, 446–457, 458–464, 514–522, 524–532, 584, 600–609, 638–641, 658, 774–781, 782–788, 821, 836–847, 852–861, 890, 1056–1061, R108. *See also* Narrative nonfiction.

   strategies for reading, R2

Literary techniques. *See* Literary elements and devices.

Loaded language, 596, 621, 623, 629, R25, R117

Logic. *See* Arguments; Reasoning.

Logical appeals, R91, R117

Logical argument, R118

Logical fallacy. *See* Fallacy.

Lyric poetry, 4, 677, 678, 681, 682, R108

M

Magazine articles, 51, 133, 221, 252–261, 536–539, 548–553, 622–627, 690, 698, 699–700, 848, 891, 900

   strategies for reading, 132, 698, R14

Magazines, 1199. *See also* References.

Main characters, R103. *See also* Characters.

Main ideas, 525, 537, 780, R8, R118

   identifying, 264, 265, 266, 267, 464, R8

   implied, 447, 451, 452, 454, 455, 456, 525, 526, 531, R31

   in outline, 1222

   in poetry, 685, 721, 724, 725

   summarizing, 544, 611, 775, 779, 780, R33

   and supporting details, 205, 288, 276, 1226, R8

Making inferences. *See* Inferences, making.

Manuals, R45

Manuscripts

   citing sources, 1229, 1230

   formatting of, 1230

Maps, 538, 547, 550, 554, R7

Margins, 1230

Media, 4, R85–R92. *See also* Films; Media elements and techniques; Media genres and types; Viewing skills and strategies.

   audience of, R85

   core concepts in media literacy, 10, R84

   demographics, R85

   editing of, 107, R88

   gatekeepers in, R85

   influence of, R86

   laws governing, R86

   message in, R84, R85, R92

   Nielsen ratings, R85

   persuasion in, 597, R84, R86, R91–R92

   producers and creators of, R85

   purpose of, 106–109, 356–359, 556–559, 634–637, 770–773, 1052–1055, R85

Media center, 1194–1200

Media elements and techniques, 733, R85–R92

   animation, 557, R88

   camera angles, 107–109, 771, 1076, R87

   camera shots, 107–109, 149, 359, 391, 559, 771, 1054, 1055, 1076, R87

   color, R91, R92

   composition, 357, R87

   costumes, 357, 358, 959, 1053, 1055

   design, R91–R92

   dialogue, 357

   editing, 391, 771, R88

   framing, 668, 1053, R87

   lighting, 357, 1039, 1053, 1054, 1055, 1076

   lines, R91, R92

   mise en scène, 1053, 1055, R87, R109

   music, 107, 357, 358, 1054, R87

   props, 357, 1053, R111

   script, 391, 583, 1077, R86, R112

   set design, 357, 358, 985

   shape, R92

   sound, 107, 108, 1054, 1076, R87

   sound bites, 557

   sound effects, 107, 357, 391, R87

   special effects, R88

   storyboard, 109, 391, 583, 733, 1232, R86

   texture, R91–R92

   voice-over narration, 391, 557, 583, R87

Media genres and types, 4, 10, R85

   advertising, 4, 10, R90–R91

   documentaries, 583

   feature films, 4, 10

   magazines, 10, 1199,

   news media, 10, 1199, 1205

   online information. *See* Internet.

radio messages, 619
TV newscast, 556–559, R86, R88
TV shows, 10
Web news report, 557
Web sites, 4, 10, 1202–1203, 1231–1233, R120
Media Handbook, R84-R92
Media literacy, 10, 108, 357, 635, 771, 772, 1053, R84
Media messages, R84, R85
evaluating, R92
viewing strategies for, 557, 558
Media presentations and products. *See also* Multimedia presentations.
creating, 1055
planning, 1055
producing, 359, 559, 1055
production design board, 359
production still, 773
promotional posters, 1025
promotional still, 773
storyboard, 109, 391, 583, 733, 1232, R86
video documentary, 583
video presentation, 391
Web site, 1231–1233, R120
Media study, 106–109, 356–359, 556–559, 597, 634–637, 770–773, 1052–1055
Memoirs, 165, 166, 447, 837, 838, 840, 842, 843, 844, 845, 849, R108. *See also* Autobiography.
Memorandums, R42–R43
formatting, R43
writing, 619
Menus, Web site, 557, 1193, R20
Metaphor, 672, 703, 707, 712, 1156, 1169, R108
extended, 725, 795, R106
Metasearch engines, 1192, 1208
Meter, 670, 671, 721, 723, 724, 725, R108–R109
anapest, R108
dactyl, R108
foot, 671, R108
iamb, 671, R108
iambic pentameter, 671, 725, 932, 967, R103, R107, R112
iambic tetrameter, 725
pentameter, 671
spondee, 671
tetrameter, 671
trimeter, 671
trochee, 671, R108–R109
Microfiche, 1194
Microform, 1194
Minor characters, R103
Mise en scène, R87, R109
elements of, 1053, 1055
evaluating, 1055

MLA citation guidelines, 1228–1229
Modifiers, 82, 93, 176, 292, 392, 498, 584, 658, 734, 820, 916, 1078, 1178, R57. *See also* Adjectives; Adverbs; Commonly confused words.
clauses. *See* Clauses.
comparative and superlative forms of, R57–R58
comparison of, R57–R58
dangling, R59
essential adjective clauses, R62
irregular comparison of, R58
nonessential adjective clauses, R62
phrases. *See* Phrases.
placement of, 656, R59
precise, 170, 176, 205
problems with, R58–R59
regular comparison of, R58
Monitoring, 12, 13, 223, 224, 227, 230, 231, 233, 234, 459, 460, 462, 539, 540, 853, 854, 858, 860, R118
Monologue
creating, 355
dramatic, 721, 722, 725, R105
writing, 1169
Mood, 140, 304, 384, 428, 443, 716, 795, 958, 1054, 1160, R109
analysis of, 137, 343, 346, 348, 351, 353, 358, 772
in descriptive writing, R35
evaluating, 383
imagery in creating, 304, 379, 380, R35
setting and, 304, 305, 358, 361, 362, 364, 368, 370
visuals in conveying, 194
Moral, R109
Motivation
of characters, 190, 207, 212, 215, 217, 218, 531, 849, 980, 994, 1017, 1018, 1026, 1138, 1158, 1162
interpreting, 119
making judgments about, 339
understanding, 247
Motives, 119, 247, 531
Movies. *See* Films.
Multimedia presentations. *See also* Media presentations and products; Oral presentations.
planning, 733
power presentation 291
producing, 733
Multiple-choice questions, R94
Multiple-meaning words, 248, R72
Multiple-step instructions. *See* Instructions.
Music, 107, 357, 358, 1054, R87
Mythology, words from classical, 234, R70
Myths, 1063, 1064, 1067, 1068, 1069, R109
characteristics of, 1069

N
Name-calling, as logical fallacy, R24
Narrative and expressive writing, R36–R37
advice, 713
alternative ending, 119, 769
analysis, 249, 445, 465, 554, 608, 683, 763, 789, 873, 1051
anecdotes, 447, 452, 454, R30–R31
blank verse, 932, 933, 939, 963, 967, 1051
character analysis, 93, 220, 325, 341, 445, 567, 1169
characterization, 235, 237, 238, 242, 245, 247, 533
conflict organization for, R37
critiques, 633
description, 105, 205, 873
dialogue, 50, 341, 851
diary, 77, 683, 890, R105
evaluating statements, 77
inspiration, 533
interpreting endings, 355
interpreting quotations, 235
key techniques in, 117, R36
letters, 465, 763
monologues, 355, 1169
motives, 119
options for organization, R36–R37
personal, 168–175
response, 567
rubric for, R36
scene, 93, 325
short stories, 384–391, R112
theme, 105
Narrative elements. *See* Character; Conflict; Plot; Point of view; Setting; Theme.
Narrative essay. *See* Essays.
Narrative nonfiction, 360–371, R36–R37, R109. *See also* Literary nonfiction.
Narrative poetry, 4, 139, 140, 142, 144, 145, 146, 147, 713, 1067, R109
characters in, 145
conflict in, 145
interpretation of, 147
speakers in, 139, 142, 147
surprise endings in, 146
Narrative speeches, 175, R79. *See also* Oral presentations.
Narrators, 103, 186, 353, R109
drawing conclusions about, 103
first-person, 186, 193, 203, 388
point of view of, 186, 193, 197, 201, 203, 214, 223, 226, 227, 229, 233, R110
in staging a scene, 1077
third-person, 186, 388
third-person omniscient, 203
Negatives, double, R58–R59

News, 10, R88–R90. *See also* Media genres and types.
  angle, R89
  balance in reporting, R89
  bias in reporting, R90
  choosing the news, R88
  commentary and opinion, R88
  editorial, 628–630, R116
  five W's and H, 557, R89
  human interest, R88
  inverted pyramid, R89
  newscast, 556–559, R86, R88
  newsworthiness, R88
  op-ed, R118
  proximity, R88
  reporting, 556–559, R88–R90
  slant, R89
  sources for, R90
  standards for reporting, R89
  timeliness, R88
  Web news reports, 557
  widespread impact, R88
News articles, 4, 8, 9, R118
News formats, 557, 558, 559
Newspapers, 1199
  articles in, 4, 8, 264–267, 422–425, 889, R117
  editorials in, 628–630, R116
  evaluating, 1205
News reports, 556–559, R88–R90
  viewing guide for, 558
Newsworthiness, R88
Nielsen ratings, R85
Nominative pronoun case, R53
Nonfiction, 4, 1194, 1200, R109
  argument in, 547, R115
  characterization in, 237, 247
  text features in, 535, 544, R3–R4
Nonfiction, strategies for reading, 831, R2
Nonfiction, types of
  autobiographies, 4, 8, 9, 111, 114, 115, 117, 237, 247, R102–R103
  biographies, 4, 8, 121, 276, R103
  critical reviews, 1056, 1057, 1059, 1060, 1061, R116
  diary, 77, 683, 890, R105
  editorials, 628–630, R40, R88, R116
  encyclopedia article, 1197
  essays, 4, 8. *See also* Essays.
  feature articles, 4, 8, R117
  functional documents, 8
  government publications, 595, 612, R117
  historical writing, 900
  interview, 760, 1206–1207, R81–R82, R108
  letter, 372
  literary, R108. *See also* Literary nonfiction.
  magazine articles, 51, 133, 221, 252–261,

536–539, 548–553, 622–627, 690, 698, 848, 891, 900, 1199
  memoirs, 165, 447, 837, 838, 840, 842, 843, 844, 845, 849, R108
  narrative, R36–R37, R109
  news articles, 4, 8, 9, 889, 1199, 1205, R118
  political cartoons, 892
  process description, 540–543
  speeches, 4, 8, 600, 610, R113
  travel narrative, 360
  workplace documents, 8, R19, R42–R45, R120
Non sequitur, R24
Note cards, 1190, 1219–1221, 1223
Notes. *See also* Graphic aids; Graphic organizers.
  in adapting informal speech, 175
  marginal, 934
  in reading consumer documents, R16
  in reading workplace documents, R19
  summarizing, 544
Note taking, 11, 535, 536, 537, 541, 1190, 1220, R4
  as study skill for writing, 1190, R28
Noun clauses, R63
Nouns, R46, R52
  abstract, 528, 533, R46
  collective, R46, R67
  common, R46, R52
  compound, R46
  concrete, 528, 533, R46
  direct address
  plural, R46, R52, R74
  possessive, R46, R52, R74
  precise, 170
  predicate, R60
  proper, R46, R52
  singular, R46, R52
Novellas, 4, 5, R109
Novels, 4, 5, R109

O

Objections, anticipating, 650, 651, 654, 661, R21, R116
Objective pronoun case, R53
Objectivity
  in news reporting, R89
  of sources. (*See* Sources, evaluating.)
Objects
  direct, R48, R60
  indirect, R48, R60
  of prepositions, R60
  use of *whom* as, in sentence, 914
Observations, 1206
Ode, 703, 709, 712, R109
Off rhyme, 718, 791, 792, R111

Online catalog, 1195
Online information. *See* Internet.
Onomatopoeia, 712, R109–R110
Op-ed pieces, R118
Opinion statement. *See* Persuasion.
Opinions, 621, R117
  evaluating, 1061
  expert, 621, 909, R25, R41
  expressing, 789
  versus facts, 623, 624, 626, 628, 630, 631, R25, R116–R117
  supporting, 523, 691, 701
Opposing argument, 909
Opposing viewpoint, 650, 651
Oral histories, 1090
Oral interpretation, 819, R80
Oral presentations. *See also* Speaking strategies.
  audience feedback, 1177, R78, R83
  debate, 620, 782, 938, R79, R116
  delivery of, R77–R78
  descriptive speech, R80
  evaluating, 1177, R78–R81, R83
  extemporaneous, R76
  informative speech, R78
  multimedia presentation, 733
  narrative speech, 175, R79
  oral interpretation, 819, R80
  oral reports, 1177
  oral response to literature, R80–R81
  panel discussions, 497
  persuasive speech, 597, 650–657, R79, R83
  preparing for, 1177, R76–R77
  props in, R111
  responding to questions, R78
  visual aids in, 657, 1177, R77
Oral tradition
  fables, R106
  folk ballad, R103
  myths, 1063, 1064, 1067, 1068, 1069, R109
  tall tales, R114
Order of importance, 816, R35
Order of impression, R35
Organizational patterns. *See* Patterns of organization.
Organizing. *See* Graphic organizers; Patterns of organization.
Origin of words, 234, 282, 488, R70. *See also* Word roots.
Outlines, 422, 423, 424, 425, 1174, 1222
  drafting from, 17, 1223
  for taking notes, R4
Overgeneralization, 621, 914, R24, R117, R118
Oversimplification, R24, R117
Overview, R118
Oxymoron, R110

P

Pace, 107, 108, 771, 915, R27, R88
Pacing. *See* Speaking strategies.
Pagination, 1230
Panel discussions, 497
Paradox, 281, R110
Paragraphs, R31–R32
   coherence of, R31–R32
   organizing, R31
   topic sentence in, R31, R120
   transitions in, R32–R33
   unity of, R31
Parallelism, 630, 654, 970, 1051, 1176, R64, R110
   as a rhetorical device, 598, 601, 606, 608, 633
Parallel plot, R110
Paraphrasing, 343, 344, 351, 419, 531, 562, 685, 688, 691, 783, 786, 787, 934, 967, 998, 1034, 1210, 1212, 1220, R118. *See also* Plagiarism.
Parentheses, R50
Parenthetical documentation, 1224, 1227
Parodies, 765, 766, 768, 769, R110
Participles and participial phrases, 683, R61
   dangling, R61
   misplaced, R61
   past, R55
   present, R55
Parts analysis, R40
Parts of a book, 1200
Parts of speech. *See also specific part of speech.*
   reference chart of, R46–R47
Passive voice. *See* Voice.
Past participle verb forms, 683, R55
Patterns of organization, 18, 284, 285, 490, 491, 494, 650, 651, 908, 909, 912, 1070, 1071, R8–R13, R118
   analysis of, 515, 519, 520, 522
   cause-effect, 262, 576, 577, R10–R11, R38, R115
   chronological, 26, 172, 510, 515, R9–R10, R36, R115
   classification, 511, R115
   comparison-contrast, 510, 515, 522, 523, 816, R11–R13, R37–R38, R115
   deductive, R23, R116
   effect-to-cause, R38
   hierarchical, 816, R35
   inductive, 631, R22–R23, R117
   main idea and supporting details, R8–R9
   order of importance, 816, R35
   order of impression, R35
   point-by-point, 288, 489, 1071, 1074, R11, R37, R41
   problem-solution, R39, R119
   reasons for opinion, R41

   sequential, R119
   spatial order, R35, R119
   subject-by-subject, 288, 1074, R11, R38
Peer response, 17, 19, 174, 290, 390, 496, 582, 656, 732, 818, 914, 1076, 1176, 1230, R30
Performing arts. *See* Drama.
Periodicals, 1194, 1199, 1205, R118. *See also* Magazines; Newspapers.
Periods, R49
   in abbreviations, R49
   with quotation marks, 290, 496
Persona, R110. *See also* Speakers.
Personal essay, 8, R106
Personal narratives, 168–175. *See also* Narrative writing.
Personification, 117, 672, 703, 710, 712, 907, R110
Perspective. *See also* Point of view.
   analysis of, 237, 240, 245, 247
   author's, 361, 362, 366, 370, 459, 460, 462, 464, 510, 522, 569, 573, 574, 575, 849, 860, R102
   in literary criticism, 262
Persuasion, 592, R118. *See also* Persuasive techniques.
   craft of, 596
   in the media, 597
   in public service announcements, 635
   text analysis of, 599, R25–R26
Persuasive arguments, R21. *See also* Arguments.
Persuasive essay, 8, 908–915, R106
Persuasive language, 908, 910, 912
Persuasive speeches, 597, 650–657, R79, R83
Persuasive techniques, 611, 612, 614, 617, R22, R91, R118. *See also* Persuasion.
   appeals by association, 596, R22
   appeals to loyalty, R22
   appeals to pity, fear, or vanity, 596, 611, R22, R116
   bandwagon appeals, 596, R22, R91
   celebrity ads, 635–636, R91
   emotional appeals, 596, 611, 617, 635, 637, 655, R22, R91, R116
   ethical appeals, 596
   evaluating, 617, R25–R26
   glittering generality, R22
   loaded language, 596, 621, 623, 629, R25, R117
   logical appeals, R91, R117
   "plain folks" appeal, 596
   product comparison, R91
   recognizing, R22
   slogans, 635, R91
   snob appeal, R22
   testimonial, 596, R22
   transfer, 596, R22
   word choice in, 596, R22

Persuasive writing, 508, 547, R40–R41. *See also* Arguments.
   arguments, 631, 851
   essay, 8, 908–915, R106. (*See also* Expository writing.)
   key techniques, R40–R41
   opinion statement, 789
   options for organizing, R41
   rubric for, R40
Philosophical assumptions, R115
Philosophical context, 1017
Photographs, 536, 537, 543, 547, 548, 553, 554, R3, R5, R117, R119, R120
Phrases, R60–R62
   adjective, R60
   adverb, R60
   appositive, R60
   gerund, 851, R61
   infinitive, 713, R61
   participial, 683, R61
   prepositional, 69, 77, 390, R48, R60
   verbal, R60–R61
Plagiarism, 1221. *See also* Parenthetical documentation; Works cited.
Planned drafting, R28
Plays. *See also* Drama.
   comparing films with, 1070–1077
   strategies for reading, 934–935, 939, 967, 991, 1017, 1033, 1050, R2
Plot, 24, 36, 176, 292, 384, 386, 392, 498, 584, 658, 734, 820, 916, 1024, 1078, 1178, R110
   character interactions and, 79, 82, 86, 89, 91
   climax of, 24, 25, 111, 420, R104
   as clue to theme, 404
   complications in, 62, 70, R104
   conflict in, 24, 53, 54, 57, 62, 68, 70, 72, 79, 111, 140, 149, 957, 967, 991, 1008, R104
   development of, 24
   in drama, 149, 166
   in epic poem, 1094, 1141, 1153, 1167
   exposition of, 36, R106
   falling action in, 24, 31, 130, R106
   in narrative poetry, R109
   parallel, R110
   resolution in, 24, 130, 386, 1050
   rising action in, 24, 53, R112
   summarizing, 1141, 1167
Plot chart, 939
Plot diagram, 166, 939
Plot summary, 1141, 1167
Poetic devices and elements, 6, R110. *See also* Poetic forms.
   alliteration, 139, 142, 670, 697, 797, 1098
   assonance, 670, 715, 716, 719, 1098
   consonance, 670, 1098

diction, 685, 686, 689, 691, 801
end rhyme, 670, 715, R111
figurative language, 672, 673, 703, 704, 706, 710, 712, 791, 907, 1098, 1103, 1119, 1169
form, 6, 668, 693, R107
ideas, 721, 797, 798, 801
imagery, 6, 672, 673, 677, 680, 682, 1098
inferences, 144, 677, 680, 681
internal rhyme, 143, 670, 715, R111
interpreting, 833
lines, 6, 668, 693, 694, R108
main ideas, 721
meter, 670, 671, 721, 723, 724, 725, R108–R109
personification, 117, 672, 703, 710, 712, 907, R110
repetition, 139, 144, 670, 715, 718, 719, R111
rhyme, 6, 139, 143, 670, 715, 718, 719, 1098, R111
rhythm, 6, 139, 146, 670, 721, 797, 800, R111
sound devices, 147, 670–671, 697, 797, R112–R113
speaker, 139, 142, 147, 467, 471, 673, 678, 691
stanzas, 6, 668, 693, 696, 697, 1169, R113
theme, 795, 901
tone, 709, 901
Poetic forms, 4, 668, 693, 694, 696, 697, R107
ballads, 715, 718, 719
blank verse, 932, 933, 939, 951, 963, 967, 1051, R103
concrete, 693, 695, 697
couplet, 674, 693, 697, R104
dramatic monologue, 721, 722, 725, R105
elegy, 685, 688, 691, R105
epic, 1088–1183, R105
free verse, 669, 797, R107
haiku, 4, 903, 904, 905, 906, 907, R107
lyric, 4, 677, 678, 681, 682, R108
narrative, 4, 139, 140, 142, 144, 146, 147, 1067, R109
ode, 703, 709, 712, R109
organic, 668, 669
Petrarchan sonnets, 669
sonnets, 4, R112
Shakespearean sonnets, 674
traditional, 668, 669
Poetry. *See also* Poetic devices and elements; Poetic forms.
personal response to, 726–732
strategies for reading, 269, 270, 273, 467, 468, 470, 791, 793, 895, 896, 899, R2
types of, 4
writing, 713

Point-by-point organization, 288, 489, 1071, 1074, R11, R37, R41
Point of view, 186, 193, 197, 201, 203, 214, 218, 223, 226, 227, 228, 229, 233, 269, 384, 756, R110
first-person, 186, 187, 193, 203, 233, 388, 564, R110
third-person, 186, 187, 385, 388, 564, R110
third-person limited, 223, R110
third-person omniscient, 203, 566, R110
Political cartoons, 892
Positions. *See* Author's position; Claims; Thesis statements.
Possessive case, R53
Possessive forms, R74
Posture, R78
Power presentations, 291. *See also* Oral presentations.
Predicate adjectives, R57, R60
Predicate nominatives, R60, R67
Predicates
complete, R48
compound, 331, 341, R59
simple, R48
Predicting, 12, 44, 56, 58, 63, 66, 70, 72, 95, 99, 100, 101, 103, 117, 124, 176, 199, 202, 217, 223, 265, 292, 392, 459, 460, 498, 561, 564, 566, 567, 584, 658, 734, 765, 768, 769, 820, 872, 916, 946, 1078, 1098, 1178, R33, R118
Preface, 1204
Prefixes, 92, 1139, R69, R73. *See also* Word parts.
Prejudice. *See* Bias.
Prepositional phrases, 69, 77, 390, R48, R60
Prepositions, 1169, R47, R48
Present participle verb forms, 683, R55
Presentations. *See* Oral presentations.
Previewing, 12
Prewriting, 17, 19, 171, 287, 387, 493, 579, 653, 729, 815, 911, 1073, 1173, 1217, R28. *See also* Graphic organizers; Writing process.
Primary sources, 372, 373, 374, 375, 376, 1196, 1199, R119
analysis of, 377
versus secondary sources, 1196, R119
using people as, 1206–1207
Prior knowledge, 12, R119
Problem-solution essay, 576–583
Problem-solution order, R39, R119
Procedures. *See* Business and technical writing.
Process analysis, R40
Process description, reading, 540–543

Producing, for submission and/or publication, 174, 290–291, 390–391, 496–497, 582–583, 656–657, 732–733, 818–819, 914–915, 1076, 1176, 1231–1233
Prologue, 941, R104, R110
Promotional posters, 1025
Prompts, responding to. *See* Reading-writing connection; Writing for assessment.
Pronoun-antecedent agreement, R52
Pronouns, R46, R52–R55
capitalization of *I*, R51
case of, R53
demonstrative, R46, R54
first-person, R52
forms, R52–R54
indefinite, 1176, R46, R54, R66
intensive, R46, R53
interrogative, R46, R54
nominative, R53
objective, R53
personal, R46, R52, R66
possessive, R53
predicate, R60
reference problems, R55
reflexive, R46, R53
relative, 249, R46, R54, R63, R67
second-person, R52
as subject of sentence, R66
third-person, R52
using too many, 220
verb agreement with, R66
Proofreading, R29. *See also* Revising and editing.
test responses, R93
Propaganda, R25, R119
Props, 357, 358, 1053, R111
Prose, R111
Protagonist, 370, 930, 1033, R111
Public documents, R18, R119. *See also* Editorials; Government publications; Nonfiction, types of; Speech.
strategies for reading, R18
Public service announcements, 634–637, R90
creating, 637
persuasion in, 635
strategies for analyzing, 635
viewing guide for, 636
Pull quotes, R14
Punctuation, R49–R50
apostrophes, R50
colons, 496, R50
commas, R49
dashes, R50
in dialogue, 174
ellipses, 496, R50
end marks, R49
exclamation points, R49

hyphens, R50
italics, R50
parentheses, R50
periods, R49
question marks, R49
quick reference chart, R49–R50
quotation marks, 174, 496, R50
semicolons, R49
Puns, 932, 958, 1031, R111
Purpose, 16, 506, R85, R119. *See also*
    Author's purpose.

Q

Qualities of a character. *See* Character traits.
Quatrain, 674, R111
Questioning, 223, 227, 459. *See also*
    Monitoring.
Question marks, R49
    in dialogue, 174
Questionnaires, 1207
Questions, 1190, 1217. *See also* Interviews;
    Research; Sentences.
    rhetorical, 462, 465, R119
Quickwriting, 32, 148, 206, 250, 268, 308,
    360, 408, 458, 466, 514, 524, 600,
    676, 702, 714, 774, 796, 802, 836,
    852, 874, 894, 902, 1140, 1188. *See
    also* Freewriting.
Quotation marks, 174, 290, R50
    commas with, 174, 290, 496
    periods with, 290, 496
    to set off speaker's exact words, R50
    for single line of verse, 1076
    with titles, R50
Quotations, 727, 1210, 1213, 1221. *See also*
    Plagiarism; Works cited.
    capitalization in, 496, R51
    colon to introduce, 496, R50
    in elaboration, R34
    ellipses in, 496, 1221, R50
    integrating, 1223
    interpreting, 235
    punctuating, 496

R

Radio message, preparing, 619
Radio transcript, 135–136
Reading comprehension, assessment practice,
    176–181, 292–297, 392–397, 498–503,
    584–589, 658–663, 734–739, 820–825,
    916–921, 1078–1083, 1178–1183
Reading for information. *See also*
    Informational texts; Reading skills and
    strategies.
    analysis of ideas, 425
    citing evidence, 377

compare and contrast, 267, 1061
critical reviews, 1056, 1057, 1059, 1060,
    1061, R116
diary entries, 890
drawing conclusions, 137
feature articles, 120, R117
identifying main ideas, 264, 265, 266,
    267, R8
interviews, 760, R108
journal articles, 794
letter, 372–377
magazine articles, 51, 133, 221, 252–261,
    536–539, 548–553, 690, 698, 848,
    891, 900, R14
making generalizations, 267
memoirs, 165, 837, 838, 840, 842, 843,
    844, 845, 849, R108
news articles, 8, 9, R118
newspaper articles, 264–267, 422–425,
    889
outline, 422
political cartoons, 892
primary sources, 372, 373, 374, 375, 376,
    377, R119
process description, 540–543
radio transcript, 135–136
summarizing information from multiple
    sources, 893
supporting an opinion, 701
synthesizing, 132, 133, 134, 135, 136,
    137, 698, 888, 889, 890, 891, 892,
    893, R119–R120
timeline, 134
Reading log, 729, 815
Reading rate, R27
Reading skills and strategies, 12, 15
    author's perspective, 361, 362, 366, 370,
        459, 460, 461, 462, 510, R102
    bias in, 621, R115
    cause and effect in, 111, 262
    clarifying, 86, 223, 230, 540, R115
    compare and contrast, 75, 91, 130,
        205, 218, 231, 233, 247, 267, 273,
        274–283, 353, 359, 383, 456, 471,
        472–489, 523, 638–649, 636, 682,
        691, 801, 907, 1033, 1070–1077,
        1069, 1167, R11–R13, R115
    connecting, 11, 12, 14, 223, 231, 257,
        379, 382, 383, 553, 554, 693, 694,
        875, 878, 882, 884, 886, 1166, R115
    critical, R94–R98
    details in, 327, 328, 330, 332, 335, 339
    drawing conclusions, 193, 194, 198, 203,
        261, 332, 334, 409, 412, 413, 416,
        417, 419, 420, 480, 485, 840, 849,
        863, 866, 869, 871, 872
    evaluating, 539, R116

graphic aids in, 15, 251, 255, 260, 547,
    R5, R117
implied main ideas, 525, 526, 531
main idea, 205, 264, 265, 266, 267, 276,
    288, 447, 451, 452, 454, 455, 456,
    464, 525, 526, 531, 537, 544, 611,
    685, 721, 724, 725, 775, 779, 780,
    1222, 1226, R8, R31, R33, R118
making inferences, 12, 14, 34, 37, 41, 47,
    48, 207, 208, 210, 218, 240, 260, 270,
    281, 312, 314, 317, 319, 322, 347,
    353, 369, 427, 428, 430, 432, 433,
    434, 437, 441, 569, 570, 572, 575,
    677, 680, 681
monitoring, 12, 13, 223, 224, 227, 230,
    231, 233, 459, 460, 462, 539, 540,
    853, 854, 858, 860, R118
note taking, 535, 536, 537, 541, 1220
organization patterns in, 515, 519, 520
pace, R27
paraphrasing, 343, 344, 351, 419, 562,
    685, 688, 783, 786, 787, 934, 967,
    998, 1034, 1220, R118
perspective in, 237, 240, 245, 247
predicting, 12, 44, 56, 58, 63, 66, 70, 72,
    95, 99, 100, 101, 103, 117, 124, 199,
    202, 217, 223, 265, 459, 460, 561,
    564, 566, 567, 765, 768, 946, 1098,
    R118
previewing, 12
rate, R27
reading poetry, 139, 269, 270, 273, 467,
    468, 470, 791, 793, 895, 896, 899,
    1103
reading Shakespearean drama, 939, 967,
    991, 1017, 1033, 1050
reading teleplays, 149, 166
rereading, 459, 462
rhetorical devices in, 601
scanning, R27, R119
sequence in, 33, 40, 42, 48, 447, 450, 452,
    456, 751, 1063, 1066, 1067, 1069
setting purpose for reading, 12, 275, 473,
    639, R119
skimming, 698, 700, R27
summarizing, 611, 613, 614, 775, 779,
    893, 1141, 1220, R119
synthesizing, 132, 133, 134, 135, 136,
    137, 698, 888, 889, 890, 891, 892,
    893, R119–R120
using prior knowledge, 15
visualizing, 12, 13, 53, 56, 57, 58, 63, 74,
    75, 223, 224, 703, 704, 708, 711, 712,
    803, 811, 1098, R120
Reading-writing connection, 50, 77, 93, 105,
    119, 167, 205, 220, 235, 249, 325, 341,
    355, 445, 465, 523, 533, 567, 619, 633,
    683, 713, 763, 789, 851, 873, 1051

Realism, 751, 752, 754, 755, 761, 763
Realistic fiction, R111
Reasoning
    analyzing, in persuasive texts, R22–R24
    circular, 914, R24, R117
    deductive, R23, R116
    errors in, 913, 914
    identifying faulty, R24
    inductive, 631, R22–R23, R117
    modes of, in critical analysis, 631
Reasons, for claim, 601, 602, 608, 651, 701
Recommendations, in conclusions, R33
Reference list. *See* Works cited.
Reference problems, of pronouns
    ambiguous, R55
    general, R55
    indefinite, R55
References, 1197, R72, R119. *See also*
        Sources.
    abstracts, 1194
    almanacs, 1197
    atlases, 1197
    audio, 1194
    biographical, 1197
    books, 1194, 1199
    CD-ROMs, 1194
    databases, 1198, R116
    dictionaries, 618, 1197, R72
    directories, 1197, 1208
    documentaries, 1199
    electronic card catalog, 1195
    electronic resources, 1194
    encyclopedias, 1197
    glossaries, 1200, R15, R72
    indexes, 1197, R117
    Internet, 632, 1189, 1191–1193, R117
    Internet discussion groups, 1207
    library, 1194
    listservers, R117
    microform, 1194
    periodicals, 1194, 1199, 1205
    synonym finders, R72
    thesauri, 1197, R72
    World Wide Web. *See* Internet.
    yearbooks, 1197
Refining. *See* Revising and editing.
Reflective essay, R106
Refrain, R111
Reliability of sources. *See* Sources, evaluating.
Repetition
    to add emphasis, 232, 235, 755, 763
    as rhetorical device, 139, 144, 598, 601,
        608, R111
    as sound device, 670, 715, 718, 719, 797,
        895, 896
Reports. *See* Research; Research papers.

Research, 1186–1209, 1218–1222
    collecting data, 1206–1207
    determining purpose of, 1189
    electronic media, 1194
    evaluating information, 893, 1201–1205,
        R116
    focusing, 1190
    gathering information for, 1190–1195,
        1206–1207
    Internet, 632, 1189, 1191–1193, R117
    in library or media center, 1194–1200
    note-taking method in, 1190
    personal interview, 760, 1206–1207,
        R81–R82, R108
    planning, 1189
    presenting, 1210–1230
    questions for, 1190
    sharing, 1209
    survey, 638, 1207
    tips and strategies, 1208–1209
    topics in, 1217
Research librarian, 1195
Research papers, 1210–1233
    citing sources, 1229–1230. *See also* Works
        cited.
    formatting of, 1230
    rubric for, 1230
    writing process, 1217–1227
Research questions, 1190, 1217
Resolution, in debate, 915
Resolution, plot, 130, 386, 1050, R106
Resources. *See* References; Sources.
Reviews
    critical, 1056–1061, R116
    film, 1056–1061
    writing, 167
Revising and editing, 17, 19, 50, 93, 105,
        119, 167, 173, 205, 220, 235, 289,
        325, 341, 355, 389, 445, 465, 495,
        523, 533, 567, 581, 619, 633, 655,
        683, 713, 731, 763, 789, 817, 851,
        873, 913, 914, 1051, 1075, 1083,
        1169, 1175, 1226–1227, R29, R77
Rhetorical devices, 604, 606, 633, 650, 651,
        R111
    alliteration, 139
    allusion, 95, 103, 608, 837, 843, 847,
        849, 932, 933, 939, 1017, 1096, 1115,
        1119, 1126, 1138, R102
    analogy, 598, 601, 608, 654, R71, R102
    parallelism, 598, 601, 606, 608, 633,
        R110
    puns, 932, 958, 1031, R111
    repetition, 139, 144, 598, 601, 608,
        R111
    rhetorical questions, 462, 465, R119
Rhetorical questions, 462, 465, R119

Rhyme, R111
    analyzing, 697
    end, 670, R111
    internal, 143, 670, 715, R111
    off, R111
    in poetry, 6, 139, 670, 697, 715, 718,
        719, 895, 1098
    slant, 718, 791, 792, R111
Rhyme scheme, 670, 722, 724, R111. *See
    also* Poetic forms; Sound devices.
Rhythm, 6, 139, 146, 670, 721, 791, 797,
        800, 1051, R111. *See also* Meter; Poetic
        forms.
Rising action, 24, 53, R112
Role-playing, 78, 720
Root words. *See* Word roots.
Round characters, 233, R103
Rubric, 17
    analysis of author's style, 818
    analysis writing, R39
    business writing, R42
    cause-effect writing, R38
    compare-and-contrast essay, 290, R37
    descriptive writing, R34
    literary analysis, 496
    narrative writing, R36
    personal narratives, 174
    personal response to poem, 732
    persuasive essay, 914
    persuasive speech, 656
    persuasive writing, R40
    play-film comparison, 1076
    problem-solution essay, 582
    for research paper, 1230
    short stories, 390
    subject analysis, 1176

S

Satire, R112
Scanning, R27, R119
Scansion, 670, R112. *See also* Meter.
Scene (in a play), 7, 1077, R112
Scenery, 1077, R112
Schematic diagram, R6
Science fiction, 5, 33, 639, 642–647, R112
Screenplays, R112
Screenwriter
Scripts, R112
    annotating, 1077
    for film and TV, R86
    rough, 391
    for video documentary, 583
    for video presentation, 391
Search engine, 1191, 1192, 1208
Secondary sources, 1196, R119

Self-check, 18, 50, 77, 93, 105, 119, 167, 205, 220, 235, 249, 325, 341, 355, 445, 465, 523, 533, 544, 554, 567, 608, 619, 633, 683, 691, 697, 713, 763, 769, 789, 851, 873, 1051, 1069, 1169

Semicolons, 582, R49

Sensory details, 170, 171, 173, 304, 672, 755, R33–R34, R112
  in descriptive writing, R33–R34
  elaborating with, R33–R34

Sensory language, 384, 385, 390

Sentence completion, R98

Sentence fluency, 18, 168, 284, 384, 490, 523, 576, 650, 726, 812, 908, 910

Sentence fragments, 40, 50, 732, R64

Sentences, R59–R60
  complements in, R60
  complete, 732, R64–R65
  complex, R63–R64
  compound, 582, R49, R63
  compound-complex, R64
  declarative, 786, 789, R59
  exclamatory, 786, R59
  imperative, 616, 619, 789, R59
  interrogative, 465, 786, 789, R59
  inverted, R66
  parallel structure, 1176, R64
  parts of (diagram), R48
  placement of modifiers, R61
  predicate, complete, R48
  predicate, compound, 331, 341, R59
  predicate, simple, R48
  run-on, 818, R64–R65
  simple, R63
  structure of, 169, 490, 492, 650, 651, 746, R63–R64
  subject, complete, R48
  subject, compound, R59
  subject, simple, R48
  topic, 137, R31, R120
  variety in, 18, 168, 169, 214, 220, 284, 285, 445, 490, 492, 495, 578, 726, 728, 731, 789, 812, 814, 817, 908, 910, 1070, 1170, 1171, 1210, 1215

Sequence, 176, 292, 392, 498, 584, 658, 734, 755, 758, 759, 761, 820, 916, 1063, 1066, 1067, 1069, 1078, 1178 R32
  analyzing, 33, 40, 42, 48, 751
  of events, 384, 386, 447, 450, 452, 456
  flashbacks, 26, 27, 751, 759, 761, R36, R106–R107
  foreshadowing, 26, 33, 34, 36, 37, 48, 75, 121, 166, 443, 967, 1034, 1129, R107, R113

Sequence chain, 342, 751, 1063

Sequence transitions, R32

Sequential order, R119

Set design, 357, 985. *See also* Media; Props.

Set piece, 772

Setting, 300, 302, 1053, 1054, 1055, R112. *See also* Time frame.
  analyzing, 323, 327, 339, 358, 361, 409
  character and, 302, 303
  in creating conflicts, 302, 303
  describing, in narrative writing, R36
  details of, 309, 310, 314, 319, 321, 323
  in epic poetry, 1094, 1141, 1144, 1167
  imagery in creating, 304, 305, 830
  influence of, 323, 420
  mood and, creating, 304, 305, 358, 361, 362, 364, 368, 370
  in movies, 357
  in short story, 302–307, 308, 326
  as symbol, 302, 327, 330, 335, 339
  theme and, 404, 409, 410, 414, 415, 417, 418, 420
  for video presentation, 391
  visualizing, 213, 223, 224, 1098, R120

Setting a purpose for reading, 275, 473, 639, R119

Shakespearean drama, 930–939, 968, 992, 1018, 1034, 1050
  literary analysis of, 939, 1051
  in movies, 1053
  reading, 934–935, 939, 967, 991, 1017, 1033, 1050

Shakespearean language, 932–933, 934

Shakespearean sonnet, 674, R112

Shakespearean tragedy, 930–931, 934, 939, 957, 994, 996, 998, 1001, 1007, 1008, 1024, 1033, 1034, 1040, 1048, 1050, 1051

Shakespeare's world, 926–929

Short stories, 28, 32, 52, 78, 94, 192, 206, 222, 292, 308, 326, 342, 405, 408, 426, 472, 498, 560, 642, 750, 862, 874
  reading, 4, 5, 13–14, R112
  strategies for reading, R2
  writing, 384–391,

Sidebars, 698, R14, R119

Signal words, R9, R119
  for cause and effect, 582, R32
  for chronological order, 515, R9
  for comparison and contrast, 290, 515
  for sequence of events, 447, 1063, R32

Similes, 672, 703, 706, 1096, 1169, R112
  epic, 1096, 1097, 1103, 1106, 1119, 1124, 1138, 1144, R105

Situational irony, 95, 103, 218, 780, R108

Skimming, 698, 700, R27

Slang, 167, 389, 495, 744, 1075, 1175, 1227, R68, R76

Slant, in news reporting, R89

Slant rhyme, 718, 791, 792, R111

Slogans, R91
  for public service announcements, 635

Snob appeal, R22

Social context, 420, 464, 886, 1167

Social criticism, 639

Software
  authoring (for Web sites), 1233
  photo-editing, 637, 1055
  presentation, 1209
  video-editing, 391, 583

Soliloquy, 930, 931, 934, 939, 971, 991, 999, 1038, 1050, R112

Solutions, 576–583, 578, R119

Sonnets, 4, R112
  Petrarchan, 669
  Shakespearean, 674, R112

Sound devices, 139, 147, 670–671, 715, 716, 718, 719, 895, 899, 901, R112–R113
  alliteration, 139, 142, 670, 697, 797, 895, 1098
  assonance, 670, 715, 716, 719, 895, 1098, R102
  consonance, 670, 1098, R104
  onomatopoeia, 712, R109–R110
  repetition, 139, 144, 670, 715, 718, 719, 895, 896, R111
  rhyme, 139, 143, 715, 718, 719, 895, 1098, R111
  rhyme scheme, 670, 715, 724, R111
  slant rhyme, 718, 791, 792, R111

Sound elements. *See* Media elements and techniques.

Source cards, 1219–1220
  MLA citation guidelines, 1228–1229

Sources, documenting, 1219, 1224. *See also* Parenthetical documentation; Works cited.

Sources, evaluating, 893, 1201–1205, 1218, R116, R119
  accuracy, 1201
  authority or authorship, 1201
  bias, 1201, R25
  checklist for, 1209
  coverage, 1201
  credibility, 1201, R90, R116
  currency, 1201
  for news stories, R90
  relevance, 1201

Sources, types of, R119, R120. *See also* References.
  databases, 1198, R116
  electronic, 1194
  field studies, 1206
  film, 1199
  government publications, R117
  Internet, 632, 1189, 1191–1193, R117
  interviews, 760, 1206–1207, R81–R82, R108

journals, 1199, R117
magazines, 1199
microforms, 1194
newspapers, 1199, 1205
observations, 1206
periodicals, 1194, 1199, 1205, R118
primary, 372, 373, 374, 375, 376, 377,
   1196, 1199, R119
questionnaires, 1207
reference books, 1194, 1197
secondary, 1196, R119
survey, 1207
Spatial order, R32, R35, R119
Speakers, 139, 142, 144, 147, 269–273, 383,
   467, 471, 673, 678, 691, 715, 716,
   719, R113
Speaking. *See also* Oral presentations;
   Speaking strategies.
  to entertain, R77
  to inform, R77
  listening and, 175, 497, 583, 657, 819,
    915, 1077, 1177, R82–R83
  to persuade, 657, R77, R79
Speaking strategies, R76–R78
  body language, R78
  emphasis, R77
  enunciation, 1077
  eye contact, 819, 915, R78
  facial expressions, 175, 819, 915, 1177
  gestures, 175, R78
  interpretation of text, 819, R80
  nonverbal, R78
  pace, 915, R77
  pitch, R77
  posture, R78
  time limit, 175
  tone, 175, R77
Special effects. *See* Media elements and
   techniques.
Specialized dictionaries, 1197, R72
Specialized vocabulary, 263, 545, R72. *See*
   also Academic vocabulary.
Speech, 4, 8, R76–R78, R113. *See*
   also Nonfiction, types of; Oral
   presentations; Speaking strategies.
Spelling
  commonly confused words, R75
  errors in, of pronouns, R53
  homonyms and, 788
  plural nouns, R74
  possessives, R74
  prefixes, R73
  rules for, R72–R74
  special problems, R74
  suffixes, R72–R73
  using resources for, R72
  words ending in a silent *e*, R72–R73

words ending in consonant, R73
words ending in *y*, R73
Spondee, 671
Stage combat, 1009
Stage design. *See* Props.
Stage directions, 7, 150, 803, 934, R113
Staging a scene, 1077
  blocking, 1009
Standard English. *See also* Dialect.
  capitalization, 496, R51
  conventions, 18
  grammar, R46–R67
  punctuation, 496, R49–R50
  sentence structure, R48, R63–R64
  spelling, R72–R74
Standards for writing. *See* Rubric.
Stanza, 6, 143, 668, 693, 696, 697, 1169,
   R113
Statement of purpose, 171
Static characters, 203, R103
Statistics, 577, 909
  in elaboration, R33
Stereotyping, 621, R24, R113, R119
Storyboards, 109, R86
  for multimedia presentation, 733
  for video presentation, 391, 583
  for Web site, 1232
Story maps or story graphs, 172, 387
Stream of consciousness, R113
Stress. *See* Speaking strategies.
Structure, R113. *See also* Patterns of
   organization.
Study skills
  note taking, 1190, R4, R28
  outlining, R4
  previewing, 12
  scanning, R27, R119
  skimming, 698, 700, R27
  summarizing, 376, 611, 613, 614, 617,
    698, 775, 779, 780, 1141, 1220, R119
Style, 742, 744, 745, 746, 761, R113
  analysis of author's, 166, 203, 725, 748,
    749, 797, 811, 812–819, 991
  grammar and, 40, 50, 69, 77, 82, 93,
    105, 115, 119, 167, 196, 205, 214,
    220, 232, 235, 243, 249, 316, 325,
    331, 341, 348, 355, 434, 445, 462,
    465, 503, 518, 523, 528, 533, 565,
    567, 616, 619, 630, 633, 663, 683,
    713, 755, 763, 786, 789, 843, 851,
    869, 873, 970, 1051, 1156, 1169
  in film, 771, 772, 773
Subheadings, 510, 535, 544, R3, R15
Subject analysis essay, 1170–1176
Subject-by-subject organization, 288, 1074,
   R11, R38
Subject complements, R60

Subjects
  complete, R48
  compound, R59
  indefinite pronouns as, 1176, R66
  personal pronouns as, R66
  of sentence, use of *who* as, 914
  simple, R48
Subject-verb agreement, R65–R67
  agreement with *be*, R65
  agreement with compound subjects, R65
  basic agreement, R65
  collective nouns as subject, R67
  don't and *doesn't* as auxiliary verbs, R67
  indefinite pronouns as subjects, 1176,
    R66
  inverted sentences, R66
  personal pronouns as subjects, R66
  relative pronouns as subjects, R67
  sentences with predicate nominatives,
    R67
  with words between subject and verb,
    R65
Subordinate character. *See* Minor characters.
Subordinate clauses, 434, 445, R62
Subtitles, 1200
Suffixes, 421, R69, R73
Summarizing, 376, 544, 611, 613, 614, 617,
   698, 775, 779, 780, 893, 908, 910,
   1007, 1141, 1167, 1170, 1172, 1220,
   R33, R119
Superlative form of modifiers, R57–R58
Support, 594, 601, 602, 608, 650, 651, 652,
   912, R21, R41, R119
  analysis of, 648
  gathering, for position, 653
  strengthening, 731
Supporting details, 205, 494, 726, 763, R8
  incorporating, 288
  in outlines, 422, 1222
Supporting statements, writing
  examples, 816, 1074, R34
  facts and statistics, 912, R33
Surprise ending, 103, R113
  in narrative poetry, 146
Surveys, 638, 1207
Suspense, R113
  analysis of, 339
  in biography, 121, 124, 127, 129, 130
  building, 1150
  climax and, 111
  conflict and, 57, 70
  foreshadowing and, 26, 33, 37, 75, 121,
    166, R107, R113
  interpreting, 370
  in movies, 106, 107, 109
Symbols, 91, 402, 403, 795, R114
  analysis of, 443
  as clue to theme, 404

cultural, 853, 856, 857, 859, 860
interpreting, 323, 443, 725
in literary analysis, 420, 427, 430, 439, 440
setting as, 302, 327, 330, 335, 339
Synonym finders, R72
Synonyms, 118, 176, 292, 392, 498, 584, 658, 734, 820, 916, 1078, 1178, R70
Syntax, 515, 685. *See also* Diction.
Synthesizing, 91, 103, 132, 133, 134, 135, 136, 137, 617, 648, 698, 699, 700, 701, 761, 888, 889, 890, 891, 892, 893, R119–R120

T

Table of contents, 1200
Tables, R6. *See also* Graphic aids; Graphic organizers.
Taking notes. *See* Note taking.
Tall tales, R114
Technical vocabulary. *See* Specialized vocabulary.
Technical writing, R45
  audience, R42
  bylaws, R45
  e-mail, R42
  instruction manual, R45
  letter, R43
  memo, R43
Technology
  Internet, 632, 1189, 1191–1193, R117
  publishing with, 291, 391, 733, 1231–1233
  video, 391
Teleplays, 148
  reading, 166, R114
Television, 10, 556–559, R86–R88. *See also* Media genres and types.
Tense. *See* Verb tense.
Test formats
  essay, R101
  extended response, R100
  multiple choice, R94
  short response, R100
Test-taking strategies, R93–R101. *See also* Assessment practice.
  critical reading, R94–R98
  essay, R101
  general, R93
  sentence completion, R98
  writing, R99–R101
Testimonial, 596, 635, R22
Textbooks, strategies for reading, R15
Text features, 510, 535, 536, 537, 538, 543, 544, R3–R4, R120
  boldface type, 510, R3
  bulleted list, R3

captions, 510, 535, 536, R3
comparing, R17
graphic aids, 251, 255, 260, 262, 535, R3, R117
headings, R3–R4
maps, 538, 547, 550, 554, R7
overviews, R118
pull quotes, R14
sidebars, 698, R119
strategies for using, R4
subheadings, 510, 535, 544, R3
subtitles, 1200
titles, 901, 1200, R3
visuals, R91–R92
Themes, 400, 402, 403, 404, 432, 476, 477, 480, 486, 487, 1048, 1069, R114. *See also* Author's message.
  across genres, 281, 473–487,
  analysis of, 48, 409, 443, 901
  characters as a clue to, 404, 474
  comparison of, 402, 467, 469, 470, 471, 725, 1050, 1167, R114
  conflict as clue to, 404, 478, 481
  in epic poetry, 1094, 1138, 1141, 1144, 1167
  in film, 771
  identifying, 404
  important statements as clue to, 404
  plot as clue to, 404
  in poetry, 467, 795
  recurring, R114
  setting as clue to, 404, 409, 410, 414, 415, 417, 418, 420
  symbols as clue to, 404
  title as clue to, 404, 483
  understanding, 105
  universal, 402, 467, 469, 470, 471, 1050, 1167, R114
Thesauri, 1197, R72. *See also* References.
Thesis statements, 284, 287, 490, 491, 576, 577, 650, 651, 812, 813, 908, 909, 1070, 1071, 1073, 1170, 1171, 1210, 1211, 1226, R31, R120
  drafting, 654
  in introduction, 285, R31
  restating in conclusion, R33
  working, 493, 729, 815, 911, 1173, 1222
Third-person narrators, 186, 388
Third-person point of view, 186, 187, 564, R110
  limited, 223, R110
  omniscient, 203, 218, 566, R110
Time frame, 302–303, 323, 830–835, 837–849
Timelines, 171. *See also* Chronological order.
Time order, 172. *See also* Chronological order.
Time periods. *See* Historical context of literature.

Time transition, R32
Titles, 1200, R3
  brainstorming, 389
  capitalization of, R51
  clarification of, 117
  as clue to theme, 404, 483
  examining, 901
  italics to set off, R50
  quotation marks to set off, R50
  for sidebars, R14
Tone, 137, 168, 169, 173, 285, 289, 490, 492, 495, 520, 525, 528, 530, 531, 561, 562, 565, 566, 576, 577, 650, 652, 701, 709, 726, 727, 746, 780, 783, 784, 787, 789, 901, 1070, 1075, 1170, 1171, 1175, 1210, 1214, 1227, R114
  analysis of, 137
  in author's perspective, 510
  in business letters, R42
  conversational, 175
  in delivering informal speech, 175
  monitoring, 289
  in poetry, 709, 901
  in speech, 175, R77
  word choice and, 530, 572, 780, 1175
Topic sentence, 137, R31, R120
Tragedy, 4, 930–931, 939, 957, 983, 990, 994, 996, 998, 1001, 1007, 1008, 1024, 1034, 1040, 1048, 1050, 1051, R114
  characters in, 930, 931, 991, 1036
Tragic flaw, 1050, R114
Tragic hero, 930, R114
Traits. *See* Character traits; Key traits of effective writing.
Transfer, 596, R22
Transitions, 286, 288, 577, 731, 817, 908, 910, 1070, 1071, 1074, 1170, 1172, 1175, 1210, 1215, 1226, R29, R32–R33
  cause and effect, 582, R32–R33
  commas to set off introductory, 290, R49
  compare and contrast, 290, R32
  degree of importance, R32
  spatial relationships, R32
  time or sequence, R32
Transitive verbs, R47
Trochee, 671, R108–R109
Turning point. *See* Climax.

U

Understatement, R114
Universal themes, 402, 467, 469, 470, 471, 1050, 1167, R114
URLs, 1191, R20
Usage. *See* Grammar Handbook.

V

Valid conclusion, R115
Validity of sources. *See* Sources, evaluating.
Vantage points. *See* Oral presentations.
Venn diagrams, 75, 233, 287, R12
Verb agreement. *See* Subject-verb agreement.
Verbal irony, 95, R108
Verbals and verbal phrases, R60–R62
    gerunds, 843, R61
    infinitives, 713, R61
    participles, 683, R55, R61
Verbs, R47, R48, R55–R57
    action, R47, R55
    auxiliary (helping), R47, R48, R56
    with compound subjects, R65
    intransitive, R47
    irregular, R55
    linking, R47, R55
    main, R48
    mood of
    objects of
    plural, R65
    precise, 102, 105, 170, 176, 292, 392, 498,
      584, 658, 734, 820, 916, 1078, 1178
    principal parts of, R55
    in reading consumer documents, R16, R17
    regular, R55
    sensory, 390
    singular, R65
    strong, in series, 115, 119, 176, 292, 392,
      498, 584, 658, 734, 820, 916, 1078,
      1178
    transitive, R47
    vivid, 869, 873
Verb tense, R55–R56
    choosing effective, 325
    errors in, R56
    future, R56
    future perfect, R56
    past, R56
    past perfect, R56
    present, 316, 325, R56
    present perfect, R56
    progressive forms, R56
    shifting, R56
Verifying information, 1205
Verse. *See* Poetic forms.
Video. *See* Media; Technology.
Video-editing software, 391, 583
Video presentations, 391
Viewing skills and strategies
    analyzing techniques, 558
    compare and contrast audience, 636
    comparing formats, 359, 558
    core concepts in media literacy, R84
    deconstructing media, R85
    drawing conclusions, 558
    5 W's and the H questions, 557

    making inferences, 636
    message analysis, 636, R92
    spotting lead, 557
Viewpoint. *See* Author's perspective; Bias.
Virtual libraries, 1208
Visual aids. *See also* Graphic aids.
    in oral presentations, 657, 117, R77
    in persuasive speech, 657
Visual effects, 391
Visual elements
    of film, 107–109, 356–359, 770–773,
      1052–1055, R87
    of TV, 556–559, R87
Visualizing, 12, 13, 53, 56, 57, 58, 63, 74,
    75, 149, 223, 224, 410, 703, 704, 708,
    711, 712, 803, 811, 1098, R120
Visuals, analysis of, 34, 43, 54, 65, 80, 89,
    96, 112, 122, 127, 128, 140, 194, 198,
    208, 213, 216, 224, 228, 238, 241,
    252, 259, 271, 276, 310, 316, 328,
    332, 344, 349, 362, 380, 410, 415,
    428, 436, 448, 460, 474, 516, 521,
    526, 529, 530, 562, 570, 602, 605,
    613, 641, 642, 678, 686, 696, 704,
    716, 723, 752, 757, 766, 776, 786,
    798, 838, 854, 864, 867, 876, 880,
    1064, 1092–1093, 1104, 1106, 1110,
    1127, 1130, 1136, 1142, 1146, 1148,
    1150, 1154, 1156, 1160, 1162
Vocabulary. *See also* Vocabulary skills and
    strategies.
    assessment practice, 180, 296, 396, 502,
      588, 662, 824, 920, 1182
    building your, 15
    in context, 33, 49, 53, 76, 79, 92, 95,
      104, 111, 118, 121, 131, 193, 204,
      207, 219, 223, 234, 237, 248, 251,
      263, 275, 282, 309, 324, 327, 340,
      343, 354, 361, 371, 409, 421, 427,
      444, 447, 457, 473, 488, 525, 532,
      535, 545, 546, 555, 601, 609, 611,
      618, 621, 632, 751, 762, 775, 781,
      783, 788, 837, 850, 853, 861, 875,
      887, 1103, 1139, 1141, 1168
    in writing, 49, 76, 92, 104, 118, 131,
      204, 219, 234, 248, 263, 282, 324,
      340, 354, 371, 421, 444, 457, 488,
      532, 545, 555, 609, 618, 632, 731,
      762, 781, 788, 850, 861, 887, 913,
      1139, 1168
Vocabulary skills and strategies, 15, R68–
    R75. *See also* Vocabulary.
    analogies, 598, 601, 608, 654, R71, R102
    antonyms, 118, R71
    base words, R69
    commonly confused words, R75
    connotation, 76, 324, 444, 781, R71,
      R104

    context clues, 371, 457, R68, R116
    denotation, 76, 324, 781, R71, R104
    dictionary, 618, R72
    foreign words in English, R70
    glossaries, 1200, R15, R72
    homonyms, 788, R71
    homophones, R71
    idioms, 887, R68, R108
    Internet words, 632
    multiple-meaning words, 248, R72
    political words, 609
    prefixes, 92, 762, 1139, R69
    root words. *See* word roots, *below.*
    specialized vocabulary, 263, 545, R72
    suffixes, 421, R69
    synonyms, 118, R70, R72
    word choice, 781
    word families, 131, 354, R70
    word origins, 234, 282, 488, R70
    word parts. *See* Word parts.
    word roots, 49, 104, 131, 204, 219, 340,
      354, 532, 555, 850, 861, 1168, R69
    words from Greek culture, 234
Voice. *See also* Oral presentations; Speaking
    strategies; Style.
    active, 384, 385, 389, 732, R57
    in literature, 746, 801, 812, 814, 849,
      863, 864, 868, 870, 872, 908, R114
    passive, R57
    in writing, 18, 168, 284
Volume. *See* Speaking strategies.

W

Webs (graphics), 52, 104, 204, 219, 236,
    340, 387, 458, 466, 532, 555, 653,
    780, 862, 1217
Web address, 1191, R20
Web sites, 4, 10, R120. *See also* Internet;
    References.
    evaluating, 1202–1203
    organizing, 1231–1232
    planning, 1231
    producing, 1232–1233
    reading, 1193
    writing text for, 1232
Word choice, 18, 576, 746, 765, 781, 812,
    860, 869–873, 1070. *See also* Diction.
    in author's perspective, 510
    compare and contrast of, 907
    in information sources
    making effective, 105
    in persuasive techniques, 596, R22, R91
    precise words, 102, 105, 168, 170, 196,
      205, 284, 286, 578, 726, 728, 812,
      813, 912, 1070, 1170, 1172, 1210
    tone and, 18, 530, 572, 746, 780, 1075,
      1175, R114

Word derivations. *See* Word families; Word parts; Word roots.

Word families, 131, 354, R70. *See also* Word roots.

Word order, 515, 685. *See also* Diction.

Word origins, 234, 282, 488, R70. *See also* Word roots.

Word parts, analyzing
  base words, R69
  prefixes, 92, 1139, R69
  roots, 49, 104, 131, 204, 219, 340, 354, 532, 555, 861, 1168, R69
  suffixes, R69

Word play, 775, 778, 932, 933

Word-processing software. *See* Software.

Word roots, R69
  Anglo-Saxon (Old English), R69
  Greek, 104, 532, 861, R69
  Latin, 49, 131, 204, 219, 340, 354, 555, 850, 1168, R69

Word structure. *See* Word roots.

Workplace and technical writing, R42–R45. *See also* Business writing.
  formats for, R43–R45
  key techniques in, R42
  matching the organization to the content, R42
  rubric for, R42

Workplace documents, 8, R19, R120. *See also* Business writing; Workplace and technical writing.
  strategies for reading, R19

Works cited, 1216, 1224, 1225, R120. *See also* Parenthetical documentation.
  direct quotations, 1213, 1214, 1221, 1223
  formatting, 1228–1229
  MLA citation guidelines, 1228–1229
  preparing list, 1224, 1225

Works consulted, R120

World Wide Web. *See* Internet.

Writer's message, 639, 640, 641, 642, 644, 645, 646, 647, 648. *See also* Author's message.

Writing
  across texts, 50, 220
  audience, 16, 284, 635, R34, R41, R42

format of, 16

goals in, R34

from literature, 168, 284, 384, 490, 576, 650, 726, 812, 908, 1070, 1170, 1210

peer response. *See* Peer response.

prompts, 19, 137, 171, 267, 489, 1217, R100

purpose of, 16

style, R113

Writing about literature, 168, 284, 384, 490, 576, 650, 726, 812, 908, 1070, 1170, 1210

Writing for assessment, 181, 283, 295, 297, 395, 397, 489, 501, 587, 589, 649, 737–739, 823, 825, 919, 921, 1082, 1083, 1181, 1183, R100, R101

Writing modes. *See* Descriptive writing; Expository writing; Narrative writing; Persuasive writing; Writing about literature.

Writing process, 17, R28–R29
  drafting, 17, 172, 288, 388, 489, 494, 580, 654, 729, 730, 816, 912, 1074, 1174, 1223–1225, R28
  evaluating, 17, 174, 290, 390, 496, 582, 656, 732, 818, 914, 1076, 1176, 1230, R34–R42
  peer response in, 17, 19, 174, 290, 390, 496, 582, 656, 732, 818, 914, 1076, 1176, 1230, R30
  prewriting, 17, 19, 52, 94, 148, 171, 206, 222, 287, 387, 493, 579, 653, 729, 815, 911, 1073, 1173, 1217, R28
  proofreading, R29
  publishing, 17, 174, 290–291, 390–391, 496–497, 582–583, 656–657, 732–733, 818–819, 914–915, 1076, 1176, 1231–1233, R29
  reflecting, R29–R30
  revising and editing, 17, 50, 93, 105, 119, 167, 173, 235, 289, 325, 341, 355, 389, 445, 495, 523, 533, 581, 619, 655, 731, 817, 851, 913, 1051, 1075, 1169, 1175, 1226–1227, R29

Writing skills and strategies. *See also* Reading-writing connection.
  analogies, 598, 601, 608, 654, R71, R102
  anecdotes, R30–R31
  cause and effect, 582, R32, R38, R115
  characters, creating, 167, 184, 323
  coherence, R31–R32
  compare and contrast, 284–291, 523, 544, 1061, 1069, R32, R115
  conciseness, 341, 713, 851
  description, 105, 205, R30, R34
  details, 168, 169, 384, 385, 390, 494, 726, 727, 812, 813, R33
  dialogue, 50, 167, 168, 169, 174, 341, 388, 851, R36
  elaboration, 727, 812, 813, 1174, R33–R34
  examples, 284, 286, 289, R34
  humor, R107
  organization. *See* Patterns of organization.
  parallelism, 598, 601, 606, 608, 630, 633, 654, 970, 1051, 1176, R64, R110
  precise language, 102, 105, 168, 170, 205, 284, 286, 578, 726, 728, 912
  quotations, 726, 727, 1210, 1213, 1221
  rhetorical devices, 604, 606, 633, 650, 651, R111
  rhetorical questions, 462, 465, R119
  sentence variety, 18, 168, 169, 214, 220, 284, 285, 445, 490, 492, 495, 578, 726, 728, 731, 789, 812, 814, 817, 908, 910, 1070, 1170, 1171, 1210, 1215
  style, R113
  tone, 18, 168, 173, 289, 490, 492, 495, 726, 727, 746, 1075, 1170, 1171, 1175, 1210, 1214, 1227
  transitions, 288, 731, 908, 910, 1070, 1071, 1074, 1175, 1210, 1215, 1227, R32
  unity, R31
  word choice, 18, 105, 510, 530, 572, 576, 746, 765, 780, 781, 812, 860, 907, 1070, 1075, 1170, 1172, 1175, 1210, R22

INDEX OF TITLES & AUTHORS

Page numbers that appear in italics refer to biographical information.

A

Ahalt, Arthur M., 628
All Nine Pulled Alive from Mine, 556
All Quiet on the Western Front, 916
Alvarez, Julia, 78, *79*
American History, 874
Angela's Ashes, 836
Angelou, Maya, 236, *237,* 246
Appearances Are Destructive, 658
Apple-Tree, The, 498
Atwood, Margaret, *685,* 688
Auden, W.H., 714, *715*

B

Bambara, Toni Cade, 862, *863*
Bashō, Matsuo, 902, *903*
Bauer, Joan, 192, *193*
Berry, Wendell, *379,* 382
Billy Thomas, 634
Birds, The, 770
Blind to Failure, 250
Blues Ain't No Mockin Bird, 862
Bodybuilders' Contest, 696
Bradbury, Ray, 32, *33, 639,* 642
Brinkley, Douglas, 274, *275*
Brooks, Gwendolyn, 293
Bryson, Bill, 360, *361*

C

Caged Bird, 246
Capote, Truman, 308, *309*
Cask of Amontillado, The, 342
Cask of Amontillado, The, 356
Ch'ien, T'ao, 466, *467*
Chekhov, Anton, 802, *803*
Christmas Memory, A, 308
Cisneros, Sandra, 568, *569*
Cofer, Judith Ortiz, 874, *875*
Collier, Eugenia, 408, *409*
Collins, Billy, *685,* 689
Connell, Richard, 52, *53*
Corbett, Sara, 546
Cummings, E.E., 684, *685*

D

Danticat, Edwidge, 458, *459*
Daughter of Invention, 78
Dickinson, Emily, 790, *791,* 793
Didion, Joan, 524, *525*
Different Level of Competition, A, 264
Dillard, Annie, 821
Dog Proves As Smart As Average Toddler, 585
Dove, Rita, *275,* 280, *677,* 681

E

Ebert, Roger, 1056
Education of Frank McCourt, The, 848
egg horror poem, 710
Elegy for the Giant Tortoises, 688

F

Faulkner, William 584
Few Words, A, 782
Fish Cheeks, 176
For Poets, 702
Four Good Legs Between Us, 133
400-Meter Free Style, 692
Fox, Michael J., 610, *611*
From Here to There: The Physics of Time Travel, 51
Frost, Robert, *721,* 724
Future in My Arms, The, 458

G

Georgia O'Keeffe, 524
Gift of the Magi, The, 94
Giovanni, Nikki, 796, *797,* 800
Going to Japan, 774
Goodman, Ellen, 638, *639*
Grape Sherbet, 681
Great Movies: Romeo and Juliet, 1056
Greenfield, Karl Taro, 250, *251*

H

Haiku (Bashō), 902
Haiku (Wright), 905
Hamadi, 222

Harlem Renaissance, The: A Cultural Explosion, 900
Henry, O., 94, *95*
Hillenbrand, Laura, 120, *121*
His Name Was Pete, 584
Hobbit, The, 392
Homer, *1090,* 1102, 1178
Honku, 906
"Hope" is the thing with feathers, 793
House on Mango Street, The, 568
How Private Is Your Private Life? 620
Hughes, Langston, *895,* 898
Hugo, Victor, 734
Hurst, James, 426, *427*

I

I Ask My Mother to Sing, 680
I Have a Dream, 600
I Know Why the Caged Bird Sings, 236
Incident in a Rose Garden, 145
Island Morning, 515

J

Jackson, Donna M., 540
Justice, Donald, *139,* 145

K

Kidnap Poem, 800
Kincaid, Jamaica, 514, *515*
King, Dr. Martin Luther Jr., 600, *601*
King, Stephen, 148, *149,* 165
Kingsolver, Barbara, 774, *775*
Kumin, Maxine, 692, *693*

L

Lee, Li-Young, *677,* 680
Lessing, Doris, 326, *327*
Levertov, Denise, 378, *379*
Life Is Calling, 634
Lincoln Weeping, 892
London, Jack, 820
Lord of the Rings, The, 106
Lost Boys, The, 546
Luxury, 796

M

Madgett, Naomi Long, 442
Mansfield, Katherine, 498
Marigolds, 408
Mark, Diane Mei Lin, *473*, 486
Math and After Math, 446
Mathabane, Mark, 658
Maud Martha, 293
Maupassant, Guy de, 206, *207*
McCourt, Frank, 836, *837*
McKay, Claude, 894 , *895*
Momaday, N. Scott, 852, *853*
Mora, Pat, 268, *269*
Most Dangerous Game, The, 52
Munro, Margaret, 585
My Father's Song, 272
My Heart Leaps Up, 469
My Papa's Waltz, 676

N

Namioka, Lensey, 446, *447*
Naparstek, Aaron, *903*, 906
Narrow Fellow in the Grass, A, 790
Necklace, The, 206
Neruda, Pablo, *703*, 706
Night Poetry Rocked the House, The, 698
Nine Coal Miners Brought Up Safely, 556
Nye, Naomi Shihab, 222, *223*

O

O What Is That Sound, 714
O'Brien, Tim, 750, *751*
Ode to My Socks, 706
Odyssey, The, 1102
Oliver, Mary, *467*, 470, 782, *783*
On Writing, 165
Open Window, The, 560
Ortiz, Simon J., *269*, 272
Ovid, 1062, *1063*

P

Pancakes, 192
Parker, Dorothy, 1166
Peace of Wild Things, The, 382
Pedestrian, The, 642
Penelope, 1166
Piedra, 177

Piercy, Marge, 735
Pilgrim at Tinker Creek, 821
Poe, Edgar Allan, 138, *139*, 342, *343*
Poem on Returning to Dwell in the Country, 466
Powder, 292
President Dead: Connally Also Hit by Sniper, 888
Primal Screen, 638
Princess and the Tin Box, The, 764
Privacy Debate, The: One Size Doesn't Fit All, 628
Pyramus and Thisbe, 1062

R

Races on the Radio: Santa Anita Handicap, 135
Raven, The, 138
Remarque, Erich Maria, 916
Revisiting Sacred Ground, 852
Rice and Rose Bowl Blues, 486
Rights to the Streets of Memphis, The, 110
Road Not Taken, The, 724
Rock, Andrea, 620
Roethke, Theodore, 676, *677*
Romeo and Juliet (film), 1052
Romeo and Juliet, The Tragedy of, 938, 1078
Rosa, 280
Rosa Parks, 274

S

Saki, 560, *561*
Scarlet Ibis, The, 426
Sea Wolf, The, 820
Seabiscuit (timeline), 134
Seabiscuit: An American Legend, 120
Seven Ages of Man, The, 720
Sharks, The, 378
Shakespeare, William, 720, *721, 926*, 938, 1078
Simon, Neil, 802, *803*
Skeletal Sculptures, 540
Sneeze, The, 802
Sorry, Right Number, 148
Soto, Gary, 177
Sound of Thunder, A, 32
Sower, The, 734

Sowing Change, 422
Special Report, 891
Spending Spree, 221
Spring is like a perhaps hand, 684
Stegner, Wallace, 372
Story Behind "The Cask of Amontillado," The, 352
Sun, The, 470
Szymborska, Wislawa, *693*, 696

T

Tan, Amy, 176, 472, *473*
Testimony Before the Senate, 610
Theme for English B, 898
Through the Tunnel, 326
Thurber, James, 764, *765*
Tim O'Brien: The Naked Soldier, 760
To Be of Use, 735
Today, 689
Tolkien, J.R.R., 392
Tropics in New York, The, 894
Two Kinds, 472

U

Unraveling the Mystery of Emily Dickinson, 794
U.S. Poet Laureates: Getting the Word Out, 690

V

Voice, A, 268

W

Walk in the Woods, A, 360
Where Have You Gone, Charming Billy? 750
White House Diary, A, 890
Who Killed the Iceman? 534
Wilderness Letter, 372
Winter, Laurel, *703*, 710
Wolff, Tobias, 292
Woman with Flower, 442
Wordsworth, William, *467*, 469
Wright, Richard, 110, *111, 903*, 905

Y

Young, Al, 702, *703*

ACKNOWLEDGMENTS

UNIT 1

Pollinger Limited: Excerpt from *The Splendid Outcast: Beryl Markham's African Stories* compiled and introduced by Mary S. Lovell. Copyright © 1987 by the Beryl Markham Estate. Reproduced by permission of Pollinger Limited and the proprietor.

Eugenia Collier: "Sweet Potato Pie," by Eugenia Collier from *Black World,* August 1972, pp. 54–62. Copyright © 1969 by Eugenia Collier. Reprinted by permission of the author.

Scholastic Inc.: "Checkouts" from *A Couple of Kooks and Other Stories* by Cynthia Rylant. Published by Orchard Books/Scholastic Inc. Copyright © 1990 by Cynthia Rylant. All rights reserved. Used by permission.

Don Congdon Associates, Inc.: Excerpt from "A Sound of Thunder" from *R is for Rocket* by Ray Bradbury. Copyright © 1952 by Crowell Collier Publishing, renewed 1980 by Ray Bradbury. Reprinted by permission of Don Congdon Associates, Inc.

Newsweek, Inc.: "From Here to There: The Physics of Time Travel," by Brad Stone, from *Newsweek,* March 16, 1998. Copyright © 1998 by Newsweek. Reprinted by permission of Newsweek, Inc.

Brandt & Hochman Literary Agents, Inc.: "The Most Dangerous Game" by Richard Connell. Copyright © 1924 by Richard Connell. Copyright renewed 1952 by Louise Fox Connell. Reprinted by permission of Brandt & Hochman Literary Agents, Inc.

Susan Bergholz Literary Services: "Daughter of Invention," from *How the Garcia Girls Lost Their Accents* by Julia Alvarez. Copyright © 1991 by Julia Alvarez. Published by Plume, an imprint of The Penguin Group (USA) and originally in hardcover by Algonquin Books of Chapel Hill. Reprinted by permission of Susan Bergholz Literary Services, New York. All rights reserved.

HarperCollins: Excerpt from *Black Boy* by Richard Wright. Copyright 1937, 1942, 1945 by Richard Wright; renewed 1973 by Ellen Wright. Reprinted by permission of HarperCollins Publishers Inc.

Random House, Inc.: Excerpt from *Seabiscuit: An American Legend* by Laura Hillenbrand. Copyright © 2001 by Laura Hillenbrand. Used by permission of Random House, Inc.

Laura Hillenbrand: "Four Good Legs Between Us," from *American Heritage,* July/August 1998, by Laura Hillenbrand. Copyright © 1998 by Laura Hillenbrand. Reprinted by permission of the author.

WGBH/Boston: Excerpt from "Timeline: Seabiscuit" from the American Experience Web site located at http://www.pbs.org/wgbh/amex/seabiscuit/timeline/timeline2.html. Copyright © 2003 by WGBH/Boston. Reprinted by permission of WGBH Educational Foundation.

NBC News Archives: Excerpt from the radio broadcast "Santa Anita Handicap," by Clem McCarthy and Buddy Twist. Copyright © 1937 by NBC News Archives. Reprinted by permission of NBC News Archives.

Alfred A. Knopf: "Incident in a Rose Garden" from *Collected Poems* by Donald Justice. Copyright © 2004 by Donald Justice. Reprinted by permission of Alfred A. Knopf, a division of Random House, Inc.

Stephen King: "Sorry, Right Number" by Stephen King. Copyright © 1993 by Stephen King. Reprinted with permission.

Simon & Schuster: Excerpt from *On Writing: A Memoir of the Craft* by Stephen King. Copyright © 2000 by Stephen King. Reprinted with the permission of Scribner, an imprint of Simon & Schuster Adult Publishing Group.

Sandra Dijkstra Literary Agency: "Fish Cheeks" by Amy Tan first appeared in *Seventeen* magazine. Copyright © 1987 by Amy Tan. Reprinted and digitalized with permission of the author and the Sandra Dijkstra Literary Agency.

Persea Books: Excerpt from "Piedra," from *The Effects of Knut Hamsun on a Fresno Boy: Recollections and Short Essays* by Gary Soto. Copyright © 1983, 1988, 2000 by Gary Soto. Reprinted by permission of Persea Books, Inc. (New York).

UNIT 2

Random House: Excerpt from *The Chocolate War* by Robert Cormier. Copyright © 1974 by Robert Cormier. Used by permission of Random House Children's Books, a division of Random House, Inc.

HarperCollins Publishers: Excerpt from "Life Without Go-Go Boots," by Barbara Kingsolver from *High Tide in Tucson: Essays from Now or Never.* Copyright © 1995 by Barbara Kingsolver. Reprinted by permission of HarperCollins Publishers Inc.

Excerpt from *To Kill a Mockingbird* by Harper Lee. Copyright © 1960 by Harper Lee. Forward copyright © 1993 by Harper Lee. Reprinted by permission of HarperCollins Publishers.

Bancroft Library: Excerpt from *Picture Bride* by Yoshiko Uchida. Copyright © 1987 by Yoshiko Uchida. Reprinted by permission of the Bancroft Library, University of California, Berkeley.

Sll/Sterling Lord Literistic, Inc.: "Pancakes," by Joan Bauer from *Trapped! Cages of Mind and Body* by Lois Duncan. Copyright © 1998 by Joan Bauer. Reprinted by permission of Sll/Sterling Lord Literistic, Inc.

Harcourt: "The Necklace" by Guy de Maupassant from *Adventures in Reading,* Laureate Edition, Grade 9. Copyright © 1963 by Harcourt, Inc., and renewed 1991. Reprinted by permission of the publisher. This material may not be reproduced in any form or by any means without prior written permission of the publisher.

Naomi Shihab Nye: "Hamadi" by Naomi Shihab Nye. Copyright © 1993 by Naomi Shihab Nye. First published in *America Street,* edited by Anne Mazer. Reprinted by permission of the author.

Random House, Inc.: Excerpt from "Sister Flowers," from *I Know Why the Caged Bird Sings* by Maya Angelou. Copyright © 1969 and renewed © 1997 by Maya Angelou. Used by permission of Random House, Inc.

"Caged Bird," from *Shaker, Why Don't You Sing?* by Maya Angelou. Copyright © 1983 by Maya Angelou. Used by permission of Random House, Inc.

Time: "Blind to Failure" by Karl Taro Greenfeld from *Time,* June 18, 2001. Copyright © 1991 by Time, Inc. Reprinted by permission.

Anne Stein: "A Different Level of Competition" by Anne Stein from *Chicago Tribune,* February 24, 2002. Copyright © 2002 by Anne Stein. Reprinted by permission of the author.

Arte Público Press: "A Voice," from *Communion* by Pat Mora. Copyright © 1991 by Pat Mora. Reprinted with permission of Arte Público Press, University of Houston.

Simon J. Ortiz: "My Father's Song," by Simon J. Ortiz from *Going for the Rain* originally published by Harper & Row Publishers, Inc. Copyright © 1976 by Simon J. Ortiz.

Penguin Group (USA) Inc.: Excerpt from "The Bus Boycott" from *Rosa Parks* by Douglas Brinkley. Copyright © 2000 by Douglas Brinkley. Used by permission of Viking Penguin, a division of Penguin Group (USA) Inc.

Rita Dove: "Rosa" by Rita Dove was first published in the *Georgia Review,* Winter 1998, and subsequently in *On the Bus with Rosa Parks,* published by W.W. Norton. Copyright © 1999 by Rita Dove. Reprinted by permission of the author.

Random House, Inc.: "Powder," from *The Night in Question* by Tobias Wolff. Copyright © 1996 by Tobias Wolff. Used by permission of Alfred A. Knopf, a division of Random House, Inc.

Brooks Permissions: "Description of Maud Martha," from *Blacks* by Gwendolyn Brooks. Copyright © 1945, 1949, 1953, 1960, 1963, 1969, 1970, 1971, 1975, 1981, 1987 by Gwendolyn Brooks Blakely. Reprinted by consent of Brooks Permissions.

UNIT 3

Harcourt, Inc.: Excerpt from *Nineteen Eighty-Four* by George Orwell. Copyright © 1949 by Harcourt, Inc., and renewed 1977 by Sonia Brownell Orwell. Reprinted by permission of the publisher. This material may not be reproduced in any form or by any means without the prior written permission of the publisher.

Arkham House Publishers: Excerpt from "The Music of Erich Zann" by H. P. Lovecraft, from *Masterpieces of Terror and the Supernatural,* selected by Marvin Kaye. Copyright © 1925. Used by permission of Arkham House Publishers, Inc., and Arkham's agent, JABberwocky Literary Agency.

Sabine R. Ulibarrí: Excerpt from "My Wonder Horse/Mi caballo mago." From *Tierra Amarilla: Stories of New Mexico* by Sabine R. Ullibarí, translated from the Spanish by Thelma Campbell Nason. Reprinted by permission of the author.

Random House, Inc.: "A Christmas Memory" by Truman Capote. Copyright © 1956 by Truman Capote. Used by permission of Random House, Inc.

HarperCollins Publishers and Jonathan Clowes: "Through the Tunnel," from *The Habit of Loving* by Doris Lessing. Copyright © 1954, 1955 by Doris Lessing, originally appeared in the *New Yorker.* Reprinted by permission of HarperCollins Publishers Inc. and the kind permission of Jonathan Clowes Ltd., London, on behalf of Doris Lessing.

The Estate of Edward Rowe Snow: Excerpt from "The Roving Skeleton of Boston Bay" by Edward Rowe Snow, from *Yankee* magazine. Reprinted by permission of Dorothy Snow Bicknell on behalf of the Estate of Edward Rowe Snow.

Broadway Books and Doubleday Canada: Excerpt from *A Walk in the Woods* by Bill Bryson. Copyright © 1997 by Bill Bryson. Used by the permission of Broadway Books, a division of Random House, Inc., and Doubleday Canada, a division of Random House of Canada Limited.

Doubleday: "Wilderness Letter" from *The Sound of Mountain Water* by Wallace Stegner. Copyright © 1969 by Wallace Stegner. Used by permission of Doubleday, a division of Random House, Inc.

New Directions: "The Sharks," from *Collected Earlier Poems 1940–1960* by Denise Levertov. Copyright © 1957, 1958, 1959, 1960, 1961, 1979 by Denise Levertov. Reprinted by permission of New Directions Publishing Corp.

Farrar, Straus and Giroux: "The Peace of Wild Things," from *Collected Poems: 1957–1982* by Wendell Berry. Copyright © 1985 by Wendell Berry. Reprinted by permission of North Point Press, a division of Farrar, Straus and Giroux, LLC.

Houghton Mifflin: Excerpt from *The Hobbit* by J.R.R. Tolkien. Copyright © 1937 by George Allen & Unwin Ltd. Copyright © 1966 by J.R.R. Tolkien. Copyright © renewed 1994 by Christopher R. Tolkien, John F.R. Tolkien, and Priscilla M.A.R. Tolkien. Copyright © restored 1996 by the Estate of J.R.R. Tolkien, assigned 1997 to the J.R.R. Tolkien Copyright Trust. Reprinted by permission of Houghton Mifflin Company. All rights reserved.

UNIT 4

PFD: "The Sniper," from *Spring Sowing* by Liam O'Flaherty. Copyright © 1924 by the Estate of Liam O'Flaherty. Reproduced by permission of PFD (www.pfd.co.uk) on behalf of the Estate of Liam O'Flaherty.

Eugenia Collier: "Marigolds," from *Breeder and Other Stories* by Eugenia Collier. Copyright © 1994 by Eugenia Collier. First published by Black Classic Press, Baltimore. Reprinted by permission of the author.

Donna Freedman: "Sowing Change" from *Chicago Tribune,* August 31, 2003, by Donna Freedman. Copyright © 2003 by Donna Freedman. Reprinted by permission of the author.

James Hurst: "The Scarlet Ibis" by James Hurst. Copyright © 1960 by the *Atlantic Monthly* and renewed 1988 by James Hurst. Reprinted by permission of James Hurst.

Naomi Long Madgett: "Woman With Flower," from *Star By Star* by Naomi Long Madgett. Copyright © 1965, 1970 by Naomi Long Madgett. Published originally by Lotus Press, Inc. Reprinted by permission of the author.

Ruth Cohen, Inc.: "Math and After Math" by Lensey Namioka from *Going Where I'm Coming From,* edited by Anne Mazer. Reprinted by permission of Lensey Namioka. All rights are reserved by the author.

Aragi Inc. and Edwidge Danticat: "The Future in My Arms" by Edwidge Danticat, first published in *Ebony* magazine. Reprinted by permission of Edwidge Danticat and Aragi Inc.

Thames & Hudson Ltd.: "Poem on Returning to Dwell in the Country," from *T'ao the Hermit: Sixty Poems by Tao Chien* by Tao Ch'ien, translated by William Acker. Copyright © 1952 by William Acker. Reprinted by kind permission of Thames & Hudson Ltd., London.

Beacon Press: "The Sun," from *New and Selected Poems* by Mary Oliver. Copyright © 1992 by Mary Oliver. Reprinted by permission of Beacon Press, Boston.

Penguin Group (USA) Inc.: "Two Kinds," from *The Joy Luck Club* by Amy Tan. Copyright © 1989 by Amy Tan. Used by permission of G. P. Putnam and Sons, a division of Penguin Group (USA) Inc.

Diane Mei Lin Mark: "Rice and Rose Bowl Blues" by Diane Mei Lin Mark. Copyright © by Diane Mei Lin Mark. Reprinted by permission of the author.

Random House, Inc.: "The Apple-Tree," from *The Scrapbook of Katherine Mansfield* by Katherine Mansfield. Copyright © 1939 by Alfred A. Knopf, a division of Random House, Inc., and renewed 1967 by Mrs. Mary Middleton Murry. Used by permission of Alfred A. Knopf, a division of Random House, Inc.

UNIT 5

Joe Bower: Excerpt from "Web Masters" by Joe Bower, *Audubon,* January-February 2002. Copyright © by Joe Bower 2002. Reprinted by permission of the author, who lives in Michigan and writes on environmental issues.

Janisse Ray: Excerpt from "Weaving the World" by Janisse Ray, *Audubon,* January-February 2002. Copyright © 2002 by Janisse Ray. Reprinted by permission of the author.

Kids Discover: "Germ Warfare" by *Kids Discover,* October 2003, Volume 13, Issue 10. Copyright © 2003, 2005 by Kids Discover. Reprinted by permission of Kids Discover. All rights reserved.

Susan Bergholz Literary Services: Excerpt from "Aha Moment" by Julia Alvarez, first published in *O, The Oprah Magazine* 1, no. 5 (November 2000). Copyright © 2000 by Julia Alvarez. Reprinted by permission of Susan Bergholz Literary Services, New York. All rights reserved.

Chicago Sun-Times: Excerpt from "Aircraft Built to Shrug Off Lightning Strike" by Tom McNamee, *Chicago Sun-Times,* May 9, 1996. Copyright © 1996 by Chicago Sun-Times, Inc. Reprinted by permission.

Farrar, Straus and Giroux: Excerpt from "Notes and Comments," from *Talk Stories* by Jamaica Kincaid. Copyright © 2001 by Jamaica Kincaid. Used by permission of Farrar, Straus and Giroux, LLC.

"Georgia O'Keeffe," from *The White Album* by Joan Didion. Copyright 1979 by Joan Didion. Used by permission of Farrar, Straus and Giroux, LLC.

National Geographic Society: "Who Killed the Iceman?" *National Geographic,* February 2002. Copyright © 2002 by National Geographic Society. Reprinted by permission of the National Geographic Society.

Little, Brown and Company: Excerpt from "Skeletal Sculptures" from *The Bone Detectives* by Donna Jackson. Copyright © 1996 by Donna Jackson (text) and Charlie Fellenbaum (photographs). By permission of Little, Brown and Company.

Scholastic Inc.: "The Lost Boys," by Sara Corbett, *New York Times Upfront* magazine. Copyright © 2001 by Scholastic Inc. and The New York Times Company. Reprinted by permission of Scholastic Inc.

Susan Bergholz Literary Services: "The House on Mango Street," "My Name," and "Mango Says Goodbye Sometimes," from *The House on Mango Street* by Sandra Cisneros. Copyright © 1984 by Sandra Cisneros, published by Vintage Books, a division of Random House, Inc., and in hardcover by Alfred A. Knopf in 1994. Used by permission of Susan Bergholz Literary Services, New York. All rights reserved.

Cable News Network: "All Nine Pulled Alive from Mine" by Jeff Flock and Jeff Goodell on CNN.com, July 28, 2002. Copyright © 2002 by CNN. Reprinted by permission of Cable News Network.

Random House, Inc.: "His Name Was Pete," from *Essays, Speeches, Letters* by William Faulkner, edited by James B. Meriwether. Copyright © 1965 by Random House, Inc. Used by permission of Random House, Inc.

Newsleader.com: "Heroic Pooch Helps Save Elderly Neighbor" by Chris Lassiter on newsleader.com, September 13, 2004. Reprinted by permission of Newsleader.com.

UNIT 6

Writers House LLC: "I Have a Dream" speech by Martin Luther King Jr. Copyright © 1963 by Martin Luther King Jr., copyright renewed 1991 by Coretta Scott King. Reprinted by arrangement with the Estate of Martin Luther King Jr., c/o Writers House as agent for the proprietor, New York, NY.

Ladies Home Journal: "How Private Is Your Private Life?" by Andrea Rock, *Ladies Home Journal,* October 2000. Copyright © 2000 by Andrea Rock. Reprinted with the permission of Ladies' Home Journal, Meredith Corporation.

The Washington Post Writers Group: "Primal Screen" by Ellen Goodman, the *Washington Post,* 1980. Copyright © 1980 by The Washington Post Writers Group. Reprinted with permission.

Don Congdon Associates, Inc.: "The Pedestrian" by Ray Bradbury. First published in *The Reporter,* August 7, 1951. Copyright © 1951 by The Fortnightly Publishing Company, renewed 1979 by Ray Bradbury. Reprinted by permission of Don Congdon Associates, Inc.

Mark Mathabane: "Appearances Are Destructive," by Mark Mathabane from the *New York Times,* August 26, 1993. Copyright © 1993 by Mark Mathabane. Reprinted by permission of the author.

UNIT 7

Lowenstein-Yost Associates, Inc.: "Beware: Do Not Read This Poem," by Ishmael Reed from *New and Collected Poems.* Copyright © 1989 by Antheneum. Permission granted by Lowenstein-Yost Associates, Inc.

Henry Holt and Company: "Fire and Ice," by Robert Frost from *The Poetry of Robert Frost,* edited by Edward Connery Lathem. Copyright © 1923, 1969 from Henry Holt and Company, copyright 1951 by Robert Frost. Reprinted by permission of Henry Holt and Company, LLC.

BOA Editions, Ltd.: "miss rosie," by Lucille Clifton from *Good Woman: Poems and a Memoir 1969–1980.* Copyright © 1987 by Lucille Clifton. Reprinted with the permission of BOA Editions, Ltd.

Elizabeth Barnett: "Sonnet XI," by Edna St. Vincent Millay from *Fatal Interview.* Copyright © 1931, 1958 by Edna St. Vincent Millay and Norman Millay Ellis. Used by permission of Elizabeth Barnett, Literary Executor. All rights reserved.

New Directions: "I Am Offering This Poem," by Jimmy Santiago Baca from *Immigrants In Our Own Land.* Copyright © 1982 by Jimmy Santiago Baca. Reprinted by permission of New Directions Publishing Corp.

Random House, Inc.: "My Papa's Waltz," by Theodore Roethke from *Complete Poems of Theodore Roethke.* Copyright © 1942 by Hearst Magazines, Inc. Used by permission of Doubleday, a division of Random House, Inc.

BOA Editions, Ltd.: "I Ask My Mother to Sing," from *Rose, poems by Li-Young Lee* by Li-Young Lee. Copyright © 1986 by Li-Young Lee. Reprinted by permission of BOA Editions, Ltd.

Rita Dove: "Grape Sherbet," by Rita Dove from *Museum* published by Carnegie-Mellon University Press. Copyright © 1983 by Rita Dove. Reprinted by permission of the author.

Liveright: "Spring is like a perhaps hand," by E. E. Cummings from *Complete Poems: 1904–1962.* Copyright © 1923, 1925, 1951, 1953, 1991 by the Trustees for the E. E. Cummings Trust. Copyright © 1976 by George James Firmage. Used by permission of Liveright Publishing Corporation.

Houghton Mifflin: "Elegy for the Giant Tortoises," by Margaret Atwood from *Selected Poems 1965–1975.* Copyright © 1976 by Margaret Atwood. Reprinted by permission of Houghton Mifflin Company. All rights reserved.

Random House, Inc.: "Today," by Billy Collins from *Nine Horses.* Copyright © 2002 by Billy Collins. Used by permission of Random House, Inc.

W. W. Norton: "400-Meter Freestyle," by Maxine Kumin from *Selected Poems 1960–1990.* Copyright © 1959 and renewed 1987 by Maxine Kumin. Used by permission of W. W. Norton & Company, Inc.

Harcourt, Inc.: "Bodybuilders' Contest," by Wislawa Szymborska, English translation by Stanislaw Baranczak and Clare Cavanaugh from *View with a Grain of Sand.* Copyright © 1993 by Wislawa Szymborska, English translation copyright 1995 by Harcourt, Inc. Reprinted by permission of the publisher. This material may not be reproduced in any form or by any means without the prior written permission of the publisher.

Scholastic: "The Night Poetry Rocked the House" by Rachel Shapiro from the *New York Times Upfront* magazine, September 4, 2000. Copyright © 2000 by Scholastic Inc. and The New York Times Company. Reprinted by permission of Scholastic Inc.

Al Young: "For Poets" by Al Young. Copyright © 1968, 1992 by Al Young. Reprinted by permission of the author.

University of California Press: "Ode to My Socks," by Pablo Neruda from *Selected Odes of Pablo Neruda,* translated by Margaret Sayers Peden. Copyright © 1990 by Regents of the University of California and Fundación Pablo Neruda. Reprinted by permission of the University of California Press.

Agencia Literaria Carmen Balcells: "Oda a los calcetines," by Pablo Neruda from *Nuevas odas elementales.* Copyright © 1956 by Fundación Pablo Neruda. Reprinted by permission of Agencia Literaria Carmen Balcells, S.A. on behalf of Fundación Pablo Neruda.

Laurel Winter: "egg horror poem," by Laurel Winter from *Nebula Awards: Showcase 2001,* edited by Robert Silverberg. Copyright © 2001 by Laurel Winter. Reprinted by permission of the author.

Random House, Inc.: "O What Is That Sound," by W. H. Auden from *Collected Poems* by W. H. Auden. Copyright © 1937 and renewed 1965 by W. H. Auden. Used by permission of Random House, Inc.

"To be of Use," by Marge Piercy from *Circles on the Water.* Copyright © 1982 by Marge Piercy. Used by permission of Alfred A. Knopf, a division of Random House, Inc.

UNIT 8

Random House, Inc.: Excerpt from *Bird by Bird* by Anne Lamott. Copyright © 1994 by Anne Lamott. Reprinted by permission of Random House, Inc.

Susan Bergholz: Excerpt from "Geraldo No Last Name" from *The House on Mango Stree*t by Sandra Cisneros. Copyright 1984 by Sandra Cisneros. Published by Vintage Books, a division of Random House, Inc., and in hardcover by Alfred A. Knopf in 1994. Reprinted by permission of Susan Bergholz Literary Services, New York. All rights reserved.

International Creative Management: Excerpt from "Single Room, Earth View" by Sally Ride from *Air & Space,* April/May 1986. Copyright © 1986 by Sally Ride. Reprinted by permission of International Creative Management, Inc.

Tim O'Brien: "Where Have You Gone, Charming Billy?" by Tim O'Brien, from *Redbook,* May 1975. Copyright © 1975 by Tim O'Brien. Reprinted by permission of the author.

Scissor Press: Interview with Tim O'Brien by Douglas Novielli, Chris Connal, and Jackson Ellis. From *Verbicide,* Issue 8. Copyright © 2003 by Scissor Press. Reprinted by permission of Scissor Press.

Barbara Hogenson Agency: "The Princess and the Tin Box," from *The Beast In Me and Other Animals* by James Thurber. Copyright © 1948 by James Thurber. Copyright renewed 1976 by Helen Thurber and Rosemary A. Thurber. Reprinted by arrangement with Rosemary A. Thurber and The Barbara Hogenson Agency. All rights reserved.

HarperCollins Publishers: "Going to Japan," from *Small Wonder: Essays* by Barbara Kingsolver. Copyright © 2002 by Barbara Kingsolver. Reprinted by permission of HarperCollins Publishers Inc.

Harcourt: "A Few Words," from *Blue Pastures* by MaryOliver. Copyright © 1995, 1992, 1991 by Mary Oliver. Reprinted by permission of Harcourt, Inc. This material may not be reproduced in any form or by any means without the prior written permission of the publisher.

Harvard University Press: "A Narrow Fellow in the Grass" and "'Hope' Is the Thing with Feathers" by Emily Dickinson from *The Poems of Emily Dickinson,* edited by Thomas H. Johnson, Cambridge, Mass.: The Belknap Press of Harvard University Press. Copyright © 1951, 1955, 1979 by the President and Fellows of Harvard College. Reprinted by permission of the publishers and the Trustees of Amherst College.

HarperCollins Publishers: "Luxury" and "Kidnap Poem" by Nikki Giovanni from *The Selected Poems of Nikki Giovanni.* Compilation copyright © 1996 by Nikki Giovanni. Reprinted by permission of HarperCollins Publishers, Inc.

Gary N. DaSilva: "The Sneeze" from *The Good Doctor,* by Neil Simon. Copyright © 1974 by Neil Simon, copyright renewed 2004 by Neil Simon. Professionals and amateurs are hereby warned that *The Good Doctor* is fully protected under the Berne Convention and the Universal Copyright Convention and is subject to royalty. All rights, including without limitation professional, amateur, motion picture, television, radio, recitation, lecturing, public reading and foreign translation rights, computer media rights and the right of reproduction, and electronic storage or retrieval, in whole or in part and in any form, are strictly reserved and none of these rights can be exercised or used without written permission from the copyright owner. Inquiries for stock and amateur performances should be addressed to Samuel French, Inc., 45 West 25th Street, New York, NY 10010. All other inquiries should be addressed to Gary N. DaSilva, 111 N. Sepulveda Blvd., Manhattan Beach, CA, 90266-6850.

UNIT 9

The Wylie Agency: Excerpt from "The Names of Women" by Louise Erdrich, originally published in *The Granta Book of the Family.* Copyright © 1995 by Louise Erdrich. Reprinted with permission of The Wylie Agency Inc.

Farrar, Straus and Giroux: Excerpt from "The Son from America," from *A Crown of Feathers and Other Stories* by Isaac Bashevis Singer. Copyright © 1973 by Isaac Bashevis Singer. Reprinted by permission of Farrar, Straus and Giroux, LLC.

Jewish Museum in Prague: Excerpt from "The Butterfly," by Pavel Friedmann from *… I Never Saw Another Butterfly: Children's Drawings and Poems from Terezin Concentration Camp 1942–1944.* Copyright © 1962 by the State Jewish Museum in Prague. Reprinted by permission of the Jewish Museum in Prague.

Alberto Ríos: "The Vietnam Wall," by Alberto Ríos from *The Lime Orchard Woman.* Copyright © 1988 by Alberto Ríos. Reprinted by permission of the author.

Simon & Schuster: Excerpt from *Angela's Ashes* by Frank McCourt. Copyright © 1996 by Frank McCourt. Reprinted with the permission of Scribner, an imprint of Simon & Schuster Adult Publishing Group.

Reader's Digest: Excerpt from "The Education of Frank McCourt," by Barbara Sande Dimmitt published in *Reader's Digest,* November 1977. Copyright © 1997 by The Reader's Digest Association, Inc. Reprinted with the permission of Reader's Digest.

N. Scott Momaday: "Revisiting Sacred Ground," by N. Scott Momaday from *The Man Made of Words.* Copyright © 1997 by N. Scott Momaday. Reprinted by permission of the author.

Random House, Inc.: "Blues Ain't No Mocking Bird," by Toni Cade Bambara from *Gorilla, My Love.* Copyright © 1971 by Toni Cade Bambara. Used by permission of Random House, Inc.

University of Georgia Press: "American History," from *The Latin Deli: Prose & Poetry* by Judith Oritz Cofer. Copyright © 1992 by Judith Ortiz Cofer. Reprinted by permission of the University of Georgia Press.

Dallas Morning News: Excerpt from "President Dead" by George Carter, from the *Dallas Times Herald,* November 22, 1963. Copyright © 1963 by The Dallas Times Herald. Reprinted by permission of the Dallas Morning News.

Lady Bird Johnson: Excerpt from *A White House Diary* by Lady Bird Johnson. Copyright © 1970 by Claudia T. Johnson. Reprinted by permission of Mrs. Lyndon B. Johnson.

U.S. News & World Report: "Dark Day" by Kenneth T. Walsh from *U.S. News & World Report,* November 24, 2003. Copyright © 2003 by U.S. News & World Report. Reprinted by permission of U.S. News & World Report.

Random House, Inc.: "Theme for English B," by Langston Hughes from *The Collected Poems of Langston Hughes.* Copyright © 1994 by The Estate of Langston Hughes. Used by permission of Alfred A. Knopf, a division of Random House, Inc.

HarperCollins Publishers: "Harvest moon—," "Heat waves shimmering," and "You could turn this way," by Matsuo Bashō from *The Essential Haiku: Versions of Bashō, Buson & Issa,* edited and with an introduction by Robert Hass. Introduction and selection copyright © 1994 by Robert Hass. Used by permission of HarperCollins Publishers, Inc.

Arcade Publishing: "From a tenement," "Twisting violently," and "Standing in the crowd," by Richard Wright from *Haiku: This Other World.* Copyright © 1998 by Ellen Wright, published by Arcade Publishing, New York, New York. Reprinted by permission of Richard Wright.

Aaron Naparstek: "clinton street autos," by Aaron Naparstek from www.honku.org. Copyright © 2003 by Aaron Naparstek. Reprinted by permission of the author.

Random House, Inc.: "Morning commuters," and "When the light turns green" from *HONKU* by Aaron Naparstek. Copyright © 2003 by Aaron Naparstek. Reprinted by permission of Villard Books, a division of Random House, Inc.

Pryor Cashman Sherman & Flynn LLP: Excerpt from *All Quiet on the Western Front* by Erich Maria Remarque. Copyright © 1929, 1930 by Little, Brown and Company, copyright renewed 1957, 1958 by Erich Maria Remarque. *Im Westen Nichts Neus* by Erich Maria Remarque. Copyright © 1928 by Ullstein A.G., copyright renewed 1957, 1958 by Erich Maria Remarque. Reprinted by permission of Pryor Cashman Sherman & Flynn LLP on behalf of the Estate of Erich Maria Remarque.

UNIT 10

Universal Press Syndicate: Excerpt from "Romeo and Juliet" by Roger Ebert, from the *Chicago Sun-Times,* September 17, 2000. Copyright © 2000 by The Ebert Company. Reprinted with permission. All rights reserved.

Harcourt, Inc.: Excerpt from *The Metamorphoses of Ovid: A New Verse Translation* by Allen Mandelbaum. English translation copyright © 1993 by Allen Mandelbaum. Reprinted by permission of Harcourt, Inc. This material may not be reproduced in any form or by any means without the prior written permission of the publisher.

UNIT 11

Farrar, Straus and Giroux: Excerpts from *The Odyssey* by Homer, translated by Robert Fitzgerald. Translation copyright © 1961, 1963 renewed 1989 by Benedict R. C. Fitzgerald on behalf of the Fitzgerald children. This edition © 1998 by Farrar, Straus & Giroux, LLC. Reprinted by permission of Farrar, Straus and Giroux, LLC.

Penguin Group (USA) Inc.: "Penelope," by Dorothy Parker from *The Portable Dorothy Parker,* edited by Brendan Gill. Copyright © 1928, renewed 1956 by Dorothy Parker. Used by permission of Viking Penguin Group (USA) Inc.

UNIT 12

Dallas Morning News: Excerpt from "Animal ER" by Aline McKenzie from the *Dallas Morning News,* January 19, 2005. Copyright © 2005 by The Dallas Morning News. Reprinted with the permission of The Dallas Morning News.

STUDENT RESOURCE BANK

Broadway Books and Doubleday Canada: Excerpt from *A Walk in the Woods* by Bill Bryson. Copyright © 1997 by Bill Bryson. Used by the permission of Broadway Books, a division of Random House, Inc. and Doubleday Canada, a division of Random House of Canada Limited.

Newsweek: Excerpt from "e-Life: How the Internet is Changing America" from *Newsweek,* September 20, 1999. Copyright © 1999 by Newsweek, Inc. All rights reserved. Reprinted by permission.

Center for Media Literacy: The "Five Core Concepts in Media Literacy" may be found in the *CML MediaLit Kit ™/Part I—Literacy for the 21st Century: An Overview and Orientation to Media Literacy Education.* Copyright © Center for Media Literacy. Reprinted by permission of Center for Media Literacy, whose Web site is located at www.medialit.org.

Project Look Sharp: "Six Questions to Ask About Any Media Message," from Project Look Sharp, Ithaca College. Copyright © Project Look Sharp. Reprinted by permission of Project Look Sharp, www.ithaca.edu/looksharp/resources.php.

Copyright Clearance Center: Excerpt from "Culture Goes Global," by Henry Jenkins from *Technology Review,* July/August 2001. Copyright © 1991 by Technology Review. Reprinted by permission of the Copyright Clearance Center.

Christian Science Monitor: Excerpt from "In 2000 Years, Will the World Remember Disney or Plato," from the *Christian Science Monitor,* January 15, 2004. Reprinted by permission of the author.

Don Congdon Associates, Inc.: Excerpt from *Fahrenheit 451* by Ray Bradbury. Copyright © 1953 by Ray Bradbury, copyright renewed 1981 by Ray Bradbury. Reprinted by permission of Don Congdon Associates, Inc.

CONSULTANTS

Title page © Brand X Pictures; Photo © Duane McCubrey; Photo © Mark Schmidt; Photo © Bruce Forrester; Photo © McDougal Littell; Photo © Howard Gollub; Photo © Tamra Stallings; Photo © Mark Schmidt; Photo © Robert J. Marzano; Photo © McDougal Littell; Photo © Dawson & Associates Photography; Photo © Gitchell's Studio; © Michael Romeo; Photo © Monica Ani; Photo © William McBride; Photo © Bill Caldwell; Photo © Gabriel Pauluzzi; Photo © Steven Scheffler.

TABLE OF CONTENTS

Contents in Brief verso *top* © Stone/Getty Images; *bottom* © Mary Rhodes/Animals Animals; **recto** *top, Young Man Studying* (Portrait of Langston Hughes) (1932), Hilda Wilkinson Brown. Oil on canvas. Photo by Gregory R. Staley. © Lilian T. Burwell/Howard University; *bottom* © The University of South Carolina Department of Theatre and Dance, Directed by Dennis Krausnick, Scenery by Kim Jennings, Lighting by Jim Hunter, Costumes by Kenneth Wolfe; **Unit 1 verso** *left* © Firefly Productions/Corbis; *right,* © Don Carstens/Brand X/Corbis; **recto** © PunchStock; **Unit 2 verso** *left* © Bettmann/Corbis; *right, Girls from Guadalupita, New Mexico,* Miguel Martinez. Oil pastel on paper, 30″ × 40″. Contemporary Southwest Galleries, Sante Fe, New Mexico; **recto** © PunchStock; **Unit 3 verso** *left* © Stone/Getty Images; *right, La Jolla Cove* (1922), Alson Clark. Private collection. Courtesy of the Laguna Art Museum; **recto** © PunchStock; **Unit 4 verso** *left* © Tom Salyer; *right* © Mary Rhodes/Animals Animals; **recto** © PunchStock; **Unit 5 verso** *left, Brownstones,* Patti Mollica. © Patti Mollica/SuperStock; *right, Farm in Haiti,* Roosevelt. Oil on canvas. Private collection. © SuperStock; **recto** © PunchStock; **Unit 6 verso** *left, A Tempestuous Evening at the Maison de la Culture* (1937), Albert Lafloret. Oil on canvas, 54 cm × 81 cm. Private collection. Photo © Bridgeman Art Library; *right* © Robert W. Kelley/Time Life Pictures/Getty Images; **recto** © PunchStock; **Unit 7 verso** *left, Flower* (1964), Andy Warhol. Screenprint printed on white paper, 23″ × 23″. © Art Resource, New York © 2007 Andy Warhol Foundation for the Visual Arts/Artists Rights Society (ARS), New York; *right* From *Wings* by Christopher Myers. © 2000 by Christopher Myers. Reprinted by permission of Scholastic, Inc.; **recto** © PunchStock; **Unit 8 verso** *left, Tumbling Flowers* (1954), Hyacinth Manning-Carner. © Hyacinth Manning-Carner/SuperStock; *right, Infantry* (1997), James E. Faulkner. Oil on canvas. Collection of Nature's Nest Gallery, Golden, Colorado. Courtesy of the artist; **recto** © PunchStock; **Unit 9 verso** *left* © Images.com/Corbis; *right, Young Man Studying* (Portrait of Langston Hughes) (1932), Hilda Wilkinson Brown. Oil on canvas. Photo by Gregory R. Staley. © Lilian T. Burwell/Howard University; **recto** © PunchStock; **Unit 10 verso** *left* © ArenaPal/Topham/The Image Works; *right* © The University of South Carolina Department of Theatre and Dance, Directed by Dennis Krausnick, Scenery by Kim Jennings, Lighting by Jim Hunter, Costumes by Kenneth Wolfe; **recto** © PunchStock; **Unit 11 verso** *left* © Araldo de Luca/Corbis; *right* Detail from *Ulysses and the Sirens* (1891), John William Waterhouse. Oil on canvas, 100 cm × 201.7 cm. National Gallery of Victoria, Melbourne, Australia. Photo © Bridgeman Art Library; **recto** © PunchStock.

INTRODUCTORY UNIT

1 *left,* From *Wings* by Christopher Myers. © 2000 by Christopher Myers. Reprinted by permission of Scholastic, Inc.; *top right* © MGM/The Kobal Collection; *lower right, Healing* (1996), Daniel Nevins. Oil on wood, 7.4″ × 9.0″. © Daniel Nevins/SuperStock; **2** *left* © ArenaPal/Topham/The Image Works; *right* © Araldo de Luca/Corbis; **3** *left, The Lord of the Rings: The Fellowship of the Ring* © 2001 New Line Productions, Inc. ™ The Saul Zaentz Company, d/b/a Tolkien Enterprises under license to New Line Productions, Inc. All rights reserved. Photo by Pierre Vinet. Photo appears courtesy of New Line Productions, Inc.; *right, Tender Moments* (2000), Francks Deceus. Mixed media. 101.6 cm × 101.6 cm. Haitian. Private Collection. Photo © The Bridgeman Art Library; **8** *top, upper center* © Bettmann/Corbis; *lower center* © Peter Turnley/Corbis; *bottom* Commuter Rail Division of the Regional Transportation Authority, d/b/a/ Metra; **10** *top to bottom* © Universal/The Kobal Collection; News footage of *All 9 Coal Miners Brought to Safety* courtesy of NBC News Archives; © NBC/courtesy Everett Collection, courtesy Kansas Department of Transportation, Bureau of Traffic Safety; © Tony Freeman/PhotoEdit; © Richard Thornton/Shutterstock; **11** © Jaume Gual/Age Fotostock America, Inc.; **15** *top* © Brian Hagiwara/Getty Images (Royalty-Free); *bottom* © Thinkstock/Getty Images; **16** *left* © Corbis; *center* © PhotoDisc; *right, collage left* © Time & Life Pictures/Getty Images; *center* Public Domain; *right* © Norbert Rosing/National Geographic Image Collection; **17** © Brian Mcweeney/Getty Images; **18** © Alain Choisnet/Getty Images; **19** *left* © Brian Mcweeney/Getty Images; *center* © Dex Image/Getty Images; *right* © Flying Colours, Ltd./Getty Images.

UNIT 1

21 *left, Raven* (1994), Jim Dine. Charcoal on wall, 128″ × 98 ¹/₂″. Kunstverein Ludwigsburg, Germany, destroyed. © 2007 Jim Dine/Artists Rights Society (ARS), New York; *right* © Firefly Productions/Corbis; **22–23** © Warner Brothers/The Kobal Collection; **22** *bottom left* From *The Perfect Storm* by Sebastian Junger. © 1997 by Sebastian Junger. Used by permission of W.W. Norton & Company, Inc.; **24** © Stockbyte/Royalty-Free; **32** © Reuters/Corbis; **33** © Bassouls Sophie/Corbis Sygma; **35** © Mary Evans Picture Library; **38** *Orinoco Jungle Life* (1894), A. Goering. Lithograph. © Mary Evans Picture Library; **42–43** Illustration by Steve Kirk/Wildlife Art Ltd. from *A Guide to Dinosaurs* © Weldon Owen Pty Ltd; **51** NASA; **52** AP/Wide World Photos; **53** © Schlesinger Library, Radcliffe College; **55** © Terry Deroy Gruber/Getty Images; **60** © Earl and Nazima Kowall/Corbis; **65** Detail of *Downtime,* Dale Kennington © Dale Kennington/SuperStock; **67** © Bertrand Demée/Getty Images/Amana America Inc.; © Lee Cates/Getty Images; **68** Man © Keith Goldstein/Getty Images/Amana America Inc.; forest © Photodisc/Getty Images; **73** © Wieteke Teppema/Getty Images; **78** © Jeff Greenberg/PhotoEdit; **79** AP/Wide World Photos; **94** © Michael Newman/PhotoEdit; **95** © Bettmann/Corbis; **97** *The Kiss* (1891),

Edouard Vuillard. Oil on paper mounted on board, 23 cm × 16.5 cm. Philadelphia Museum of Art, The Louis E. Stern Collection, 1963. © Philadelphia Museum of Art/Art Resource, New York. © 2007 Artists Rights Society (ARS), New York/ADAGP, Paris (1963-181-76); **101** © Royalty-Free/Corbis; **106** *The Lord of the Rings: The Fellowship of the Ring* © 2001 New Line Productions, Inc. ™ The Saul Zaentz Company, d/b/a Tolkien Enterprises under license to New Line Productions, Inc. All rights reserved. Photo by Pierre Vinet. Photo appears courtesy of New Line Productions, Inc.; **107** *The Lord of the Rings: The Fellowship of the Ring* © 2001 New Line Productions, Inc. ™ The Saul Zaentz Company, d/b/a Tolkien Enterprises under license to New Line Productions, Inc. All rights reserved. Photo appears courtesy of New Line Productions, Inc.; **108** *background* © Stone/Getty Images; *top, bottom, The Lord of the Rings: The Fellowship of the Ring* © 2001 New Line Productions, Inc. ™ The Saul Zaentz Company, d/b/a Tolkien Enterprises under license to New Line Productions, Inc. All rights reserved. Photo appears courtesy of New Line Productions, Inc.; **110** © Eric Gaillard/Reuters News Picture Archive; **111** © Corbis; **120** AP/Wide World Photos; **121** © Lauren Chelec; **123** © Bettmann/Corbis; **124** © Keeneland-Cook Association, Inc.; **126–127, 128, 132** © Bettmann/Corbis; **133** © Morgan Collection/Getty Images; **134** *top* © Hulton Archive/Getty Images; *bottom* © Bettmann/Corbis; **135** *left* © Bettmann/Corbis; *right* © Hulton Archive/Getty Images; **138** © Corbis; **139** *bottom* Photo by Nathaniel Justice; *top* © Bettmann/Corbis; **144** *Red Passion* (1996), Jim Dine. Cardboard relief intaglio. Image size 33 1/8" × 59". Paper size 39 1/2" × 63 7/8". Published by Pace Editions, Inc. Edition of 12 © 2007 Jim Dine/Artists Rights Society (ARS), New York; **145** *The Back of a Man with a Rose*, René Magritte. Private Collection Bloch, Santa Monica, CA. Photo © Superstock, Inc. © 2007 C. Herscovici, Brussels/Artists Rights Society (ARS), New York; **148** © Aaron Horowitz/Corbis; **149** © Seth Joel/Corbis; **151** © Joel Sartore/Getty Images; **153** © William Whitehurst/Corbis; **154** © Photodisc; **157** © Andrea Pistolesi/Getty Images; **161** © Royalty-Free/Corbis; **162** © Lorna Clark/Getty Images; **165** AP/Wide World Photos; **168, 174** © Craig Aurness/Corbis; **175** © Mary Kate Denny/PhotoEdit; **182** © Siede Preis/Photodisc/Getty Images.

UNIT 2

183 *left, Louise Augusta, Queen of Prussia* (1801), Marie Louise Elisabeth Vigée-LeBrun. Pastel, 51 cm × 41 cm. Stiftung Preussische Schlösser und Gärten Berlin-Brandenburg. Photo by J. P. Anders; *right* © BananaStock/Punchstock; **184** *left* Public Domain; *right* © Paul C. Chauncey/Corbis; **184–185** © Pawel Libera/Corbis; **193** Photo by Jim Lundquist; **195** © Peter M. Fisher/Corbis; **198** © Iconica Limited; **201** © Ian Kahn/Iconica; **206** © Mauro Panci/Corbis; **207** © Chris Hellier/Corbis; **221** © Dave Nagel/Stone/Getty Images; **222** © Photodisc Green/Getty Images; **223** Photo by Madison Nye; **236** © Gabe Palmer/Corbis; **237** © Mitchell Gerber/Corbis; **246** © Photodisc/Getty Images; **250** © Peter Turnley/Corbis; **251** © Amy Etra/Time Life Pictures/Getty Images; **253** © Didrik Johnck/Corbis; **255** © Chris Curry/Hedgehoghouse.com; **259, 264** © Didrik Johnck/Corbis; **265** © Adam Pretty/Getty Images; **268** © Jeff Greenberg/Age Fotostock America, Inc.; **269** *top* Courtesy Pat Mora/Photo by Cheron Bayman; *bottom* Photo by David Burkhalter. Reprinted by permission of the University of Arizona Press; **272** *Navajo Power Plant* (1990). © Shonto Begay/Avery Collection of American Indian Painting; **274** white gloves © Photodisc/Getty Images; Empress Michiko © Andy Rain-Pool/Getty

Images; man © Getty Images; frames © Image Farm, Inc.; working glove © Rubberball Productions/Getty Images; **275** *top* AP/Wide World Photos; *bottom* © Fred Viebahn/Rita Dove; **277** © Bettmann/Corbis; **280** From *Americans Who Tell The Truth*, Robert Shetterly. Used by permission of Dutton Children's Books, a division of Penguin Young Readers Group, a member of Penguin Group, Inc. All rights reserved. © Robert Shetterly; **284, 290** Joseph Sohm; ChromoSohm Inc./Corbis; **291** *left* © Jan von Holleben/Getty Images; *right* © SuperStock, Inc./SuperStock; **298** © Siede Preis/Photodisc/Getty Images.

UNIT 3

299 *left* Burial niches with fresco of Christ Pantocrator. Catacomb of San Callisto, Rome, Italy. Photo © Erich Lessing/Art Resource, New York; *right* © Keith Kapple/SuperStock; **300–301** © Sekai Bunka/Premium/Panoramic Images; **304** © The Kobal Collection; **309** © Slim Aarons/Getty Images; **311** © Getty Images/Royalty Free; **326** © Stanley Chou/Getty Images; **327** © Bettmann/Corbis; **329** *La Jolla Cove* (1922), Alson Clark. Private collection. Courtesy of the Laguna Art Museum; **342** © Photographer's Choice/Getty Images; **343** © Bettmann/Corbis; **345** © Stone/Getty Images; **349** Burial niches with fresco of Christ Pantocrator. Catacomb of San Callisto, Rome, Italy. Photo © Erich Lessing/Art Resource, New York; **350** © Punchstock; **352** © PhotoDisc/Getty Images; **356** © Nik Wheeler/Corbis; **357** *top, center, bottom* Footage from *Edgar Allan Poe: The Soul of Terror, The Cask of Amontillado*. Courtesy of Film Odyssey, Inc.; **358** *background* © Image Source/PictureQuest; *top left, bottom left* Footage from *Edgar Allan Poe: The Soul of Terror, The Cask of Amontillado*. Courtesy of Film Odyssey, Inc.; **359** *top left* © Photodisc; *top center* © Image Farm, Inc.; *top right* © PhotoDisc; *bottom left* © Brand X Pictures/Fotosearch Stock Photography; *bottom center, bottom right* © Photodisc, Inc.; **360** © Paul Katz/Index Stock Imagery/PictureQuest/Jupiterimages Corporation; **361** © Rick Friedman/Corbis; **363** © Patrik Giardino/Corbis; **364–365** © Ric Ergenbright/Ric Ergenbright Photography; **369** © Creatas/PictureQuest; **373** © Margaretta K. Mitchell; **378** © SuperStock; **379** *top* © Christopher Felver/Corbis; *bottom* Courtesy The Land Institute, Prairie Writers Circle; **381** © Kiefner/Premium Stock/PictureQuest/Jupiterimages Corporation; **382** © John Warden/Index Stock Imagery/PictureQuest/Jupiterimages Corporation; **384, 390** © Daryl Benson/Masterfile; **391** © Yang Liu/Corbis; **398** © Siede Preis/Photodisc/Getty Images.

UNIT 4

399 *left, Mama's Cradle,* April Harrison. Mixed media collage on canvas board, 14" × 18". © April Harrison; **400–401** © Richard Cummins/Corbis; **400** © Royalty-Free/Corbis; **402** © Kevin Anthony Horgan/Getty Images; **408** © Digital Vision Ltd./SuperStock; **409** © Olan Mills; **422** Full Spittoon (1974), Bob Timberlake. Watercolor. Private Collection. © Bob Timberlake; **423** Chicago Tribune photo by Warren Skalski; **426** FOXTROT © 1997 Bill Amend. Reprinted with permission of UNIVERSAL PRESS SYNDICATE. All rights reserved; **427** Courtesy of James Hurst; **435** © Vincent McIndoe/Images.com/Corbis; **438** © Mary Rhodes/Animals Animals; **442** © Sam Abell/National Geographic Image Collection; **446** © Spencer Grant/PhotoEdit; **447** © Richard McNamee; **449** © Keren Su/Corbis; **450** © Images.com/Corbis; **453** © Dean Conger/Corbis; **458** © Richard T. Nowitz/Corbis; **459** © Getty Images; **466** © Craig C. Sheumaker/PanStock/

PictureQuest/Jupiterimages Corporation; **467** *top* © ChinaStock; *center* The Granger Collection, New York; *bottom* Photo by Barbara Savage Cheresh; **468** *Viewing Plum Blossoms by Moonlight,* Ma Yuan. Southern Sung. John M. Crawford, Jr. Collection. Photo © Wan-go H. C. Weng/ Metropolitan Museum of Art, New York/Art Resource, New York; **469** © Bill Binzen/Corbis; **470** © Tom Salyer; **472** © Pete Saloutos/ Corbis; **473** *top* © Lawrence Lucier/Getty Images; *bottom* © Photo by Paul H. Mark; **475** *top* © Corbis; *left* © Getty Images; *right* © Rykoff Collection/Corbis; **478** *center* © Ed Sullivan Show/Photofest; *bottom* © Trinette Reed/Corbis; **481** © Richard Cummins/SuperStock; **484** © Catherine Karnow/Corbis; **486** Anthony-Masterson/Foodpix/Getty Images/Jupiterimages Corporation; **490, 496** © Richard Sisk/ Jupiterimages; **497** © Design Pics, Inc./Alamy Images; **504** © Siede Preis/Photodisc/Getty Images.

UNIT 5

505 *left, Cow's Skull: Red, White, and Blue* (1931), Georgia O'Keeffe. Oil on canvas, 39⅞″ × 35⅞″. The Metropolitan Museum of Art, Alfred Stieglitz Collection, 1952. Photo © Georgia O'Keeffe/ Metropolitan Museum of Art (52.203) © 2007 Georgia O'Keeffe Museum/Artists Rights Society (ARS), New York/Art Resource, New York; *right* © Joseph Sohm; Visions of America/Corbis; **506-507** *collage far left* © Creatas Images/Jupiterimages Corporation; *center left* © Karl Weatherly/Getty Images; *center* © Time & Life Pictures/Getty Images; *center right* Public Domain; *far right* © Norbert Rosing/National Geographic Image Collection; **511** © Matthew Frey/Wood Ronsaville Harlin; **513** © Erik Simonsen/Getty Images; **514** © Bryan and Cherry Alexander; **515** © Taro Yamasaki/Time Life Pictures/Getty Images; **524** © Abigail Pope/LuckyPix; **525** © Neville Elder/Corbis; **527** Phillips Collection/AP/Wide World Photos; **529** *Cow's Skull: Red, White, and Blue* (1931), Georgia O'Keeffe. Oil on canvas, 39⅞″ × 35⅞″. The Metropolitan Museum of Art, Alfred Stieglitz Collection, 1952. Photo © Georgia O'Keeffe/Metropolitan Museum of Art (52.203) © 2007 Georgia O'Keeffe Museum/Artists Rights Society (ARS), New York/Art Resource, New York; **530** *Jimson Weed* (1932), Georgia O'Keeffe. The Georgia O'Keeffe Museum, Santa Fe, New Mexico. © Art Resource, New York © 2007 Georgia O'Keeffe Museum/Artists Rights Society (ARS), New York; **534** © Reuters/Corbis; **535** © Corbis Sygma; **536** *top* © National Geographic Society. Reprinted by permission of the National Geographic Society; *bottom* © Hanny Paul/Gamma Press USA, Inc.; **537** *left* © Regional Hospital of Bolzano/South Tyrol Museum of Archaeology www.iceman.it; *right* © South Tyrol Museum of Archaeology; **538** *top* © GeoNova LLC; *bottom* © South Tyrol Museum of Archaeology; **539** © Hinterleitner Gerhard/Gamma Press USA, Inc.; **540–543** Photos from *The Bone Detective.* © Charles Fellenbaum, Boulder, Colorado; **546** AP/Wide World Photos; **549** © Jeff Riedel/Creative Photographers, Inc.; **551** © Hudson Derek/ Corbis Sygma; **553** © Jeff Riedel/Creative Photographers, Inc.; **556** AP/ Wide World Photos; **557** *top* News footage of *All 9 Coal Miners Brought to Safety* courtesy of NBC News Archives; *center* © by CNN. Reprinted by permission of Cable News Network; *bottom* © Getty Images; **558** *top left* News footage of *All 9 Coal Miners Brought to Safety* courtesy of NBC News Archives; *bottom left* Getty Images; *background* © Larry Lee Photography/Corbis; **559** © IT International Ltd./Jupiterimages Corporation; **560** © Andrew McKim/Masterfile; **561** The Granger Collection, New York; **568** © Mike Powell/Getty Images; **569** © Gene Blevins/Corbis; **576, 582** © Daryl Benson/Masterfile; **583** © Lon
C. Diehl/PhotoEdit; **586** © Daily News Leader. All rights reserved. Reproduced with the permission of Gannett Co., Inc. by NewsBank, Inc.; **590** © Siede Preis/Photodisc/Getty Images.

UNIT 6

591 *left, A Tempestuous Evening at the Maison de la Culture* (1937), Albert Lafloret. Oil on canvas, 54 cm × 81 cm. Private collection. Photo © The Bridgeman Art Library; *right* © Bettmann/Corbis; **592–593** © Spencer Platt/Getty Images; **592** *left* © New Voters Project; **597** © Ad Council; **600** © Alex Wong/Getty Images; **601** © Time Life Pictures/Getty Images; **603** © Bettmann/Corbis; **604–605** © Robert W. Kelley/Time Life Pictures/Getty Images; **604** *top left* © Paul Schutzer/Time Life Pictures/Getty Images; **605** *top right* © MPI/Getty Images; **607** AP/Wide World Photos; **610** © Tatsuyuki Tayama/ Fujifotos/The Image Works; **611** © Thierry Orban/Corbis Sygma; **613** © Ron Sachs/CNP/Corbis; **614** © Corbis Sygma; **615** © Ron Sachs/ CNP/Corbis; **616** © Eurelios/Phototake; **620** © Jeffrey Sylvester/Getty Images; **621** © Mike Baldwin/www.CartoonStock.com; **622** © Peter Ciresa/Index Stock Imagery; **624** AP/Wide World Photos; **625** © Reuters/Corbis; **626** © Ed Quinn/Corbis; **629** © The Image Bank/ Getty Images; **630** © Mauro Fermariello/Photo Researchers, Inc.; **634** Courtesy of Kansas Department of Transportation, Bureau of Traffic Safety; *background* © Tony Freeman/PhotoEdit; **635** *top, Billy Thomas* Public Service Announcement courtesy of Boys and Girls Clubs of America; *bottom, How Far Would You Go?* Public Service Announcement courtesy of Peace Corps of America; **636** *top left, Billy Thomas* Public Service Announcement courtesy of Boys and Girls Clubs of America; *bottom left, How Far Would You Go?* Public Service Announcement courtesy of Peace Corps of America; *background* © Layne Kennedy/ Corbis; **637** © Ad Council; **638** © Nicholas Rigg/Getty Images; **639** *top* © Washington Post Writers Group; *bottom* © Bassouls Sophie/ Corbis Sygma; **641** © Chip Simons/Getty Images; **650–656** © J. David Andrews/Masterfile; **657** © Pedro Coll/Age Fotostock America, Inc.; **664** © Siede Preis/Photodisc/Getty Images.

UNIT 7

665 *left* From *Wings* by Christopher Myers. © 2000 by Christopher Myers. Reprinted by permission of Scholastic, Inc.; *right* © Pete Turner/ Getty Images; **666** *right, The Cow Jumped Over the Moon* (1885), Randolph Caldecott. From *R. Caldecott's Second Collection of Pictures and Songs*/Mary Evans Picture Library; *left* The Granger Collection, New York; **676** © Colin Paterson/PhotoDisc: Green/Getty Images; **677** *top* © Bettmann/Corbis; *center* © 2002 Margaretta Mitchell; *bottom* © Fred Viebahn/Rita Dove; **681** *Ice Cream Dessert* (1959), Andy Warhol. Photo © Andy Warhol Foundation/Corbis © 2007 Andy Warhol Foundation for the Visual Arts/Artists Rights Society (ARS), New York; **684** © Kevin Fleming/Corbis; **685** *top* © Bettmann/Corbis; *center* © Touhig Sion/Corbis Sygma; *bottom* © Christopher Felver/ Corbis; **689** *Flower* (1964), Andy Warhol. Screenprint printed on white paper, 23″ x 23″. © Art Resource, New York © 2007 Andy Warhol Foundation for the Visual Arts/Artists Rights Society (ARS), New York; **690** *top* J. P. Beato III/The Battalion © Texas Agricultural and Military University; *bottom* AP/Wide World Photos; **692** AP/Wide World Photos; **693** *top* © Nancy E. Crampton; *bottom* © Wojda/Free/Corbis Sygma; **694–695** © Franco Vogt/Corbis; **698** left, *Municipal Bonds* (2004), Byron Spicer. Mixed media, 45″ x 45″. © Hespe Gallery; right © Franco Vogt/Corbis; **699** © Bob Daemmrich/PhotoEdit; **700** *top*

The New York Times Company; *bottom* © Spencer Platt/Getty Images; **702** Leslloyd F. Alleyne Jr./Journal Inquirer/AP/Wide World Photos; **703** *top* © Christopher Felver/Corbis; *bottom* Photo taken by Colin Beltz and used courtesy of the Red Wing Republican Eagle; *center* © Sam Falk/New York Times Company/Getty Images; **705** From *Wings* by Christopher Myers. © 2000 by Christopher Myers. Reprinted by permission of Scholastic, Inc.; **707, 709** Photo by Sharon Hoogstraten; **711** © Corbis; **714** © Royalty-Free/Corbis; **715** © Harry Redl/Time Life Pictures/Getty Images; **718** *Returning to the Trenches* (1914–15), C. R. W. Nevinson. Oil on canvas, 51 cm × 76 cm. © Gift of the Massey Collection of English Painting, 1946/National Gallery of Canada, Ottawa. Courtesy of the Nevinson Estate/Bridgeman Art Library; **720** © Tobbe/zefa; **721** *top* The Granger Collection, New York; *bottom* National Archives; **726–732** © Jason Ernst/Age Fotostock America, Inc.; **733** © Paul Vozdic/Getty Images; **740** © Siede Preis/Photodisc/Getty Images.

UNIT 8

741 *left, Tumbling Flowers* (1954), Hyacinth Manning-Carner. © Hyacinth Manning-Carner/SuperStock; *right* © Brand X Pictures/Getty Images; **742–743** *The Persistence of Memory* (1931), Salvador Dali. Oil on canvas, 9¹/₂″ × 13″. Museum of Modern Art, New York. © 2000 Foundation Gala-Salvador Dali/VEGAP © 2007 Salvador Dali, Gala-Salvador Dali Foundation/Artists Rights Society (ARS), New York; **746** *left* © Carl Van Vechten/Corbis; *left* © Bettmann/Corbis; *right* © Darryl Bush/Getty Images; **750** © Ron Fehling/Masterfile; **751** © 2002 Marilyn Knapp Linn; **764** CinemaPhoto/Corbis; **765** Berko/Time Life Pictures/Getty Images; **770** © akg-images; **771** *top* © MGM/ The Kobal Collection; *center #1* © Universal/The Kobal Collection; *center #2* © Paramount/The Kobal Collection; *bottom* © Paramount /The Kobal Collection; **772** *background* © Joe McDonald /Corbis; *top left, bottom left, The Birds* © 1963 Alfred J. Hitchcock Productions, Inc., courtesy of Universal Studios Licensing LLLP; **773** *left, right* © MGM/The Kobal Collection; **774** © Lluis Real/Age Fotostock America, Inc.; **775** Photo © Steven Hopp; **777** © Tadashi Miwa/Getty Images; *top right* © Sarma Ozols/Getty Images; **778** *bottom left* © ImageState-Pictor/PictureQuest; *center left* Sushi and chopsticks © Anthony Johnson/Getty Images; *center right* © Stone/Getty Images; *bottom right* © Tadashi Miwa/Getty Images; **782** © Tony Anderson/Getty Images; **783** Photo by Barbara Savage Cheresh; **785** © 2003 Aflo Foto Agency; **786** *left* © Tom Lazar/Earth Scenes/Animals Animals; *right* Roy Toft/National Geographic Image Collection; **790** © Susan Meiselas/Magnum Photos; **791** The Granger Collection, New York; **796** © Alamy Images; **797** © Mike Simons/Getty Images; **802** © Pete Stone/Corbis; **803** *top* © Bettmann/Corbis; *bottom* © Hulton Archive/Getty Images; **805** © Bettmann/Corbis; **806–810** The Granger Collection, New York; **812, 818** © Alain Choisnet/Getty Images; **819** © Eric O'Connell/Getty Images; **822** © Carsten Peter/National Geographic Image Collection; **826** © Siede Preis/Photodisc/Getty Images.

UNIT 9

827 *left, Jazz Player III* (1991), Freshman Brown. Collage. © SuperStock; *right* © Frans Lemmens/Iconica Limited/Getty Images; **828** Reprinted with the permission of Random House, Inc., from *The House on Mango Street* book cover by Sandra Cisneros; © Reprinted by permission of Vintage Books, a division of Random House, Inc. Used by permission of Vintage Books, a division of Random House, Inc. Book design by Cathryn S. Aison, hand lettering by Henry Sene Yee; **828–829** © Margo Cohn; **830** © Charles and Josette Lenars/Corbis; **832** © Bettmann/Corbis; **835** © J Sohm/VOA LLC/Panoramic Images; **836** © The Image Bank/Getty Images; **837** © Michael Brennan/Corbis; **839** © Aaron M. Priest Literary Agency, Inc.; **842** Courtesy of the *Limerick Leader,* Limerick, Ireland; **845** © Hulton Archive/Getty Images; **852** © Chris Rainier/Corbis; **853** Photo by Loce Momaday/Courtesy of Royce Carlton, Inc.; **855** © David Muench/Corbis; **857** © Courtney Milne; **863** © The New York Public Library/Art Resource, New York; **874** Photo courtesy Suraiya Nathani; **875** Photo of Judith Ortiz Cofer is reprinted with permission from the publisher Arte Publico Press. © 2005, University of Houston, Houston, Texas; **877, 888** © Bettmann/Corbis; **889** *top* Reprinted with permission of *The Dallas Morning News; bottom* © Bettmann/Corbis; **891** © U.S. News & World Report, L. P. reprinted with permission; **892** © 1963 Bill Mauldin, reprinted with special permission from the Chicago Sun-Times, Inc. 2004; **894** © Ed Kashi/Corbis; **895** © Corbis; **897** © Images.com/Corbis; **902** © Ryan McVay/Getty Images; **903** *top, Portrait of Bashō,* Kameda Bosai. Hanging scroll in ink and color on paper. Gift of an anonymous donor. © New Orleans Museum of Art (80.181); *center* © Bettmann/Corbis; *bottom* © Charlie Gross, **906** © Digital Vision Ltd./SuperStock; **914, 920** © Sam Barricklow/Jupiterimages; **915** © Michelle D. Bridwell/PhotoEdit; **922** © Siede Preis/Photodisc/Getty Images.

UNIT 10

923 *left, The Proposal* (1872), Adolphe-William Bouguereau. Oil on canvas, 64³/₈″ × 44″. Gift of Mrs. Elliott L. Kamen, in memory of her father, Bernard R. Armour, 1960 (60.122). © The Metropolitan Museum of Art, New York/Art Resouce, New York; *right* © ArenaPal/Topham/The Image Works; **924–925** *left to right, A Bridal Couple,* (about 1490). Southern Germany. Oil on wood, 77.5 cm × 51 cm × 7.5 cm. © 2004 The Cleveland Museum of Art; *Francesca da Rimini* (1837), William Dyce. Oil on canvas, 142 cm × 176 cm. National Gallery of Scotland, Edinburgh. © Bridgeman Art Library; The Granger Collection, New York; Clip from *Romeo and Juliet* courtesy of Paramount Pictures; *Romeo and Juliet,* Claire Danes, 1996 © 20th Century Fox/courtesy Everett Collection; **926** The Granger Collection, New York; **927** Illustration by John James/Temple Rogers—Artists' Agents; **928** Much Ado About Nothing poster © Samuel Goldwyn Films, Courtesy Everett Collection; **929** The Granger Collection, New York; **930** © Andrea Pistolesi/Getty Images; **938** © 1993 Jay Ullah/Stern/Black Star; **941** *left* © Dmitrij Matvejev/Anzelika Cholina Dance Theatre, Lithuania; *center left* © ArenaPal/Topham/The Image Works; *center* Chicago Shakespeare Theater's production of Romeo and Juliet toured to 14 communities in the Southeast United States, as part of the National Endowment for the Arts Shakespeare in American Communities initiative. Martin Yurek as Mercutio (left) and Ryan Kitley as Tybalt (right). Photo by: SteveLeonardPhotography.com, courtesy Chicago Shakespeare Theater; *center right* © ArenaPal/Topham/The Image Works; *right* Marian Hinkle as Juliet and Jay Goede as Romeo in The Shakespeare Theatre's 1993–1994 production of *Romeo and Juliet,* directed by Barry Kyle. Photo by Richard Anderson; **943** © Dmitrij Matvejev/Anzelika Cholina Dance Theatre,

Lithuania; **949** *top left* © Robbie Jack/Corbis; *bottom left* ©ArenaPal/Topham /The Image Works, Inc.; *right* Chicago Shakespeare Theater and Second City Theatrical's production of the *Romeo and Juliet Musical, The People vs. Friar Lawrence, The Man Who Killed Romeo and Juliet.* Nicole Parker as Juliet and Keegan-Michael Key as Romeo. Photo by Michael Brosilow, courtesy Chicago Shakespeare Theater; **954** Jean Stapleton as Nurse and Marin Hinkle as Juliet in The Shakespeare Theatre's 1993–1994 production of *Romeo and Juliet,* directed by Barry Kyle. Photo by Richard Anderson; **959** *top* © Elliott Franks/Arena Pal/Topham/The Image Works, Inc.; *right* © ArenaPal/Topham/The Image Works; *bottom left* © Reuters/Corbis; **962** © Robbie Jack/Corbis; **965** Katie Atkinson as Juliet and Brian Weaver as Romeo in Shakespeare & Company's 2004 Spring Tour Production of *Romeo and Juliet.* Directed by Kevin Coleman. Photo by Kevin Sprague; **969** © ArenaPal/Topham/The Image Works; **974** © Chris Bennion Photography; **979** © Don Pierce/University of Victoria Photographic Services; **985** *top left* © Orlando-UCF Shakespeare Festival; *top right* © Royal Shakespeare Company; *bottom* © The University of South Carolina Department of Theatre and Dance, Directed by Dennis Krausnick, Scenery by Kim Jennings, Lighting by Jim Hunter, Costumes by Kenneth Wolfe; **993** Chicago Shakespeare Theater's production of Romeo and Juliet toured to 14 communities in the Southeast United States, as part of the National Endowment for the Arts Shakespeare in American Communities initiative. Martin Yurek as Mercutio (left) and Ryan Kitley as Tybalt (right). Photo by: SteveLeonardPhotography.com, courtesy Chicago Shakespeare Theater; **998** © Royal Shakespeare Company; **1009** *top left* © Scot J. Mann/Atlanta Stage Combat Studio; *top right* © Chris Bennion Photography; *bottom* © 2004 Susana Raab; **1019** © ArenaPal/Topham/The Image Works; **1025** *left* © Gary Wayne Golden; *center* The Seattle Repertory Theatre's 2003 Romeo and Juliet poster © Sedgwick Rd.; *right* © Wieslaw Walkuski; **1029** © Don Pierce/University of Victoria Photographic Services; **1035** Marian Hinkle as Juliet and Jay Goede as Romeo in The Shakespeare Theatre's 1993–1994 production of *Romeo and Juliet,* directed by Barry Kyle. Photo by Richard Anderson; **1039** *top left* © Royal Shakespeare Company; *right* © Clive Barda/ArenaPal/Topham/The Image Works, Inc.; *bottom left* © ArenaPal/Topham/The Image Works, Inc.; **1044** © ArenaPal/Topham/The Image Works, Inc.; **1049** © Bob Daemmrich/The Image Works; **1052, 1053, 1054** *left* Clip from *Romeo and Juliet* courtesy of Paramount Pictures; *bottom* © Image 100/Alamy / Royalty-Free; **1055** *top* © 20th Century Fox/courtesy Everett Collection; *bottom* Stills from *William Shakespeare's Romeo and Juliet,* courtesy of Twentieth Century Fox. All rights reserved; **1056** *left* © Dmitrij Matvejev/Anzelika Cholina Dance Theatre, Lithuania; *2nd from left* © ArenaPal/Topham/The Image Works; *center* Chicago Shakespeare Theater's production of Romeo and Juliet toured to 14 communities in the Southeast United States, as part of the National Endowment for the Arts Shakespeare in American Communities initiative. Martin Yurek as Mercutio (left) and Ryan Kitley as Tybalt (right).Photo by: SteveLeonardPhotography.com, courtesy Chicago Shakespeare Theater; *center right* © ArenaPal/Topham/The Image Works; *right* Marian Hinkle as Juliet and Jay Goede as Romeo in The Shakespeare Theatre's 1993-1994 production of Romeo and Juliet, directed by Barry Kyle. Photo by Richard Anderson; **1057** Courtesy Everett Collection; **1058, 1059, 1060** Clip from *Romeo and Juliet* courtesy of Paramount Pictures; **1062** © Digital Stock Royalty Free; **1063** *Ovid* (1500–1503). Fresco. Post-restoration. Duomo, Orvieto,

Italy. Photo © Scala/Art Resource, New York; **1070, 1076** © Jupiterimages; **1077** *left* © Comstock Images/Getty Images; *right* © Rosie Hardman-Ixer; **1084** © Siede Preis/Photodisc/Getty Images.

UNIT 11

1085 *left, Scylla and Charybdis,* from the *Ulysses Cycle* (1580), Alessandro Allori. Fresco. Banca Toscana (Palazzo Salviati), Florence, Italy. Photo © Erich Lessing/Art Resource, New York; *right* © Corbis; **1086–1087** © Don Mason/Corbis; **1088** *top* © Corbis/Royalty-Free; *bottom, Procession of Trojan Horse into Troy,* G. D. Tiepolo. The Granger Collection, New York; **1089** Detail of a frieze representing a procession of mythological divinities, muses, graces, etc. Oil on plaster. Chateaux de Malmaison et Bois-Preau, Rueil-Malmaison, France. Photo © Gerard Blot/Art Resource, New York; **1090** *left* © 2004 Warner Bros./Photofest; *right, Homer* (about 150 b.c.). Marble sculpture. Museo Nazionale Archeologico. Photo © akg-images; **1091** © GeoNova LLC; **1092** *top, Ulysses Returns Chryseis to Her Father,* Claude Lorrain. Louvre, Paris. Photo © Scala/Art Resource, New York; **1093** *top left* Plaque with the return of Odysseus (about 460–450 b.c.). Classical Greek. Melian. Terracotta, Height 7 $^3/_8$″. The Metropolitan Museum of Art, Fletcher Fund, 1930. (30.11.9) © 1982 The Metropolitan Museum of Art/Art Resource, New York; *bottom left, Ulysses* (1931–1932), Georges Braque. Pastel, 180.5 cm × 73.5 cm. Private Collection. Photo © Visual Arts Library/Art Resource, New York © 2007 Artists Rights Society (ARS), New York/ADAGP, Paris; *top right, Odysseus Slaying the Suitors* (400s b.c.), Penelope Painter. Attic red figure painting on kylix. Height 20 cm. Inv F 2588. Antikensammlung, Staatliche Museen zu Berlin, Berlin. Photo by Juergen Liepe. © Bildarchiv Preussischer Kulturbesitz/Art Resource, New York; *bottom right* Illustration by Innes Fripp in *Tales of the Gods and Heroes* by Sir G.W. Cox. © Edwin Wallace/Mary Evans Picture Library; **1094** *top to bottom* © Araldo de Luca/Corbis; *Odysseus and Polyphemus* (1896), Arnold Bocklin. Tempera on wood, 65.5 cm × 148.5 cm. Private collection. © akg-images; *Ulysses Returns Chryseis to Her Father,* Claude Lorrain. Louvre, Paris. Photo © Scala/Art Resource, New York; Detail of *Tilla Durieux as Circe* (about 1912–1913), Franz von Struck. Oil on paper, 53.5 cm × 46.5 cm. Private collection. Photo © akg-images; **1105** *The Ship of Odysseus,* Francois-Louis Schmeid. From *Homer, the Odessy,* published Paris (1930–1933). Colour lithograph. Private collection, The Stapleton Collection. © 2007 Artists Rights Society (ARS), New York/ADAGP, Paris. © Bridgeman Art Library; **1100** © Liu Jin/AFP/Getty Images; **1105** *The Ship of Odysseus,* Francois-Louis Schmeid. from Homer, the Odessy, published Paris (1930-1933). Colour lithograph. Private collection, The Stapleton Collection. © 2007 Artists Rights Society (ARS), New York/ADAGP, Paris © Bridgeman Art Library; **1111** © Araldo de Luca/Corbis; **1140** AP/Wide World Photos; **1141** *Penelope Embroidering* (1903), Mrs. H. de Rudder. Photo © Mary Evans Picture Library; **1143** *Athene and Telemach,* from *Odyssey II* (1975), Marc Chagall. Lithograph on Arches paper. 16.9″ × 13″. Photograph by George R. Staley. Courtesy the Georgetown Frame Shoppe. © 2007 Artists Rights Society (ARS), New York; **1149** © Bettmann/Corbis; **1154, 1157** Illustrations by N.C. Wyeth from *The Odyssey of Homer,* translated by George Herbert Palmer. © 1929 by N.C. Wyeth. © renewed 1957 by Carolyn Wyeth. Reprinted by permission of Houghton Mifflin Company. All rights

reserved; **1163** Detail of plaque with the return of Odysseus (about 460–450 B.C.). Classical Greek. Melian. Terracotta, Height 7³/₈″. The Metropolitan Museum of Art, Fletcher Fund, 1930. (30.11.9) © 1982 The Metropolitan Museum of Art/Art Resource, New York; **1166** © Lindsay Hebberd/Corbis; **1170, 1176** © Neil Emmerson/ Getty Images; **1177** © Charles Gupton/Corbis; **1184** © Siede Preis/ Photodisc/Getty Images.

UNIT 12

1185 *left* © Zac Macaulay/Getty Images; *right, collage, center left to right* Cover of *Walking Softly in the Wilderness* by John Hart. Cover photo by Art Twomey. Reprinted with the permission of The Sierra Club, San Francisco, California; © Getty Images; Courtesy of the National Audubon Society; *cover background* © Brand X Pictures: Four Seasons; *foreground* © Rich Phalin/istockphoto.com; *bottom book pages, left top to bottom* Jupiterimages Corporation; © Brand X Pictures/PunchStock; © Michael and Patricia Fogden/Minden Pictures/Getty Images; *right, top to bottom* Michael and Patricia Fogden/Minden Pictures/Getty Images; © Altrendo Nature/Altrendo/Getty Images; © Jupiterimages Corporation; **1186–1187** © Digital Vision Ltd./SuperStock; **1188** Ken Chernus/Stone/Getty Images; **1192** © 2005 Infospace, Inc. All rights reserved. Reprinted with permission of Infospace, Inc.; **1193** 2005 County of Sacramento, California; **1195** © Skokie Public Library; **1196** *left* © PhotoDisc Green; *right* © Brian Hagiwara/Brand X Pictures; *background* © 1994 Artbeats; **1197** *top to bottom* Cover from *The Concise Geography Encyclopedia.* © Kingfisher Publications Plc 2005. Reprinted by permission of Kingfisher Publications Plc., an imprint of Houghton Mifflin Company. All rights reserved.; Cover of *The American Heritage Student Dictionary* © Houghton Mifflin Company, all rights reserved; Cover images *inset top* © Larry Brownstein/Getty Images; *inset top right* © Digital Vision/Getty Images; *inset center* © Cartesia/Getty Images; *inset bottom left* © Alan & Sandy Carey/Getty Images; *inset bottom right* © C Squared Studios/Getty Images; © McDougal Littel art; Cover of *Roget's II Thesaurus* © Houghton Mifflin Company. All rights reserved; Cover of *Chambers Reference Atlas* (2005), Edited by Editors of Chambers. © Houghton Mifflin Company, all rights reserved, Cover image © Getty Images; **1198** From *InfoTrac,* by Gale Group, reprinted by permission of The Gale Group; **1199** *top to bottom* © Time Life Pictures/Getty Images; © Wall Street Journal; © American Veterinary Medical Association; **1203** American Veterinary Medical Association; **1204** *left to right* © 1996 PhotoDisc, Inc.; © 2001 PhotoDisc, Inc.; © 1999 PhotoDisc, Inc.; **1205** *top* © The Dallas Morning News. Reprinted with the permission of The Dallas Morning News; *bottom* © Reuters/Corbis; **1209** © PictureNet/Corbis; **1210, 1230** © PictureQuest/Jupiterimages Corporation; **1231** © Image Source/ Alamy Images.

STUDENT RESOURCE BANK

R3 *top* © G.R. Roberts Photo Library; *bottom* Illustration by Gary Hincks; **R6** *top* © Getty Images (Royalty-Free); *bottom* Illustration by SlimFilms; **R7** © Mapping Specialists; **R14** *left, right* © Paul Simcock/ Brand X Pictures/PictureQuest; *center* © Photodisc/Getty Images; **R15** *top left* Galen Rowell/Corbis; *top right* David Muench/Corbis; *bottom*

Illustration by Gary Hincks; **R20** NASA; **R84** © Digital Vision/Getty Images (Royalty-Free); **R92** © Coneyl Jay/Getty Images.

BACK COVER
© Brand X Pictures.